To CHRIS,
From the Ladies of
the Bible Study Group
with all good wishes
June 1981

May the Lord bless and protect you
May the Lord's face radiate with
joy because of you; may He be gracious
to you, show you his favour and
give you His Peace.
Numbers 6 v 24.

THE NEW BIBLE COMMENTARY: REVISED

THE NEW BIBLE COMMENTARY Revised

Edited by

D. GUTHRIE BD, MTH, PHD
Lecturer in New Testament, London Bible College

J. A. MOTYER MA, BD
Principal of Trinity College, Bristol

Consulting Editors

A. M. STIBBS MA
formerly Vice-Principal, Oak Hill Theological College, London

D. J. WISEMAN OBE, MA, D LIT, FBA, FSA
Professor of Assyriology, University of London

INTER-VARSITY PRESS

Inter-Varsity Press
38 *De Montfort Street, Leicester LE*1 7*GP, England*

The New Bible Commentary first published December 1953
Second edition November 1954
Nine impressions 1955–1968
Third edition, completely revised and reset April 1970
Reprinted 1970, 1972, 1973, 1975, 1976, 1977, 1979, 1980

ISBN 0 85110 615 3 (IVP Edition)
  0 85110 821 0 (International Christian Handbooks)

Printed in Great Britain by
BILLING AND SONS LIMITED,
Guildford, London and Worcester

*Inter-Varsity Press is the publishing division of the Universities
and Colleges Christian Fellowship (formerly the Inter-Varsity
Fellowship), a student movement linking Christian Unions in
universities and colleges throughout the British Isles, and a
member movement of the International Fellowship of Evangelical
Students. For information about local and national activities in
Great Britain write to UCCF, 38 De Montfort Street, Leicester
LE1 7GP.*

Preface

The first edition of this commentary, edited by the late Professor F. Davidson with the assistance of the late Rev. A. M. Stibbs and the late Dr E. F. Kevan, was published in 1953. It was an immediate success. A further printing followed by a second edition appeared the following year. Since then it has been reprinted many times both in Great Britain and in the USA. There has been, however, considerable progress in biblical studies in recent years. This led the Publications Committee of the Inter-Varsity Fellowship to decide that the time had come to undertake a full-scale revision of the commentary. Although the demand for the original edition continued as strong as ever, it was clear that there were now many ways in which the book could be improved.

This volume contains twelve General Articles in addition to commentaries on each of the sixty-six books of the Bible. Five of the former and thirty-seven of the commentaries are entirely new contributions. All the other material has been revised, most of it very extensively.

The general aim of the commentary has remained the same—to provide for the serious student of the Bible a new and up-to-date treatment of the text which combines unqualified belief in its divine inspiration, essential historical trustworthiness and positive Christian usefulness with careful scholarship. Restriction on space has meant, of course, that authors had to curtail discussion of some speculative matters regarding dates and questions of authorship. Standard Introductions to the Old and New Testaments, such as those by Professor R. K. Harrison[1] and Dr Donald Guthrie,[2] should be consulted on these points, and also the relevant articles in *The New Bible Dictionary*.[3] It should also be borne in mind that a one-volume commentary cannot be expected to devote the same space even to matters of exegesis as is found in commentaries on single books of the Bible.[4] If the reader, therefore, finds some particular problem verse either given scanty notice or perhaps no notice at all, it is not because the author failed in his duty but because there had to be many a hard choice between priorities.

The most noticeable major alteration in this new edition is the use of the Revised Standard Version text as a basis for the commentary in place of the Authorized Version or King James Version. But thought has been given to the needs of those who will be using it in conjunction either with the Authorized Version or with other translations and many of the major differences between the versions are commented upon. A number of changes in format have also

[1] *Introduction to the Old Testament*, 1969. Wm. B. Eerdmans Publishing Company, Grand Rapids; Inter-Varsity Press, Leicester.

[2] *New Testament Introduction*. Third edition (revised) 1970. Inter-Varsity Press, Leicester; InterVarsity Press, Downers Grove, Illinois.

[3] 1962. Inter-Varsity Press, Leicester; Wm. B. Eerdmans Publishing Company, Grand Rapids.

[4] A number of the contributors to this volume have written or are writing for the Tyndale Commentary series, edited by Professor D. J. Wiseman (Old Testament) and Professor R. V. G. Tasker (New Testament). .

been introduced, all of which, it is hoped, will make the volume easier to use.

The Editors and Publishers are greatly indebted to the many contributors to this volume who have placed their talents, time and experience so whole-heartedly at their service. As will be seen from the list of names, they come from a wide range of church affiliation and are serving in universities, theological colleges and churches in many parts of the world. It is natural that they should differ among themselves in some matters of interpretation. It ought perhaps to be stressed, therefore, that each contributor is responsible only for the article or articles appearing over his name and neither he nor the Editors are to be regarded as necessarily endorsing everything that is written elsewhere in the book.

With the production of the new edition of this commentary the Universities and Colleges Christian Fellowship (formerly called the Inter-Varsity Fellowship) continues its work of providing material designed to promote more thorough Bible study. The study course *Search the Scriptures*[5] covers the whole Bible in approximately three years. *The New Bible Dictionary* in 2,300 articles provides background information on a great variety of biblical subjects, and makes an excellent reference work and useful companion to the present volume. With these and a good reference Bible, the average student will find himself well equipped with the basic Bible study aids he requires.

Considerable help in the preparation of this volume has been received from a wide circle of friends and advisers. It would be invidious to single out one or the other for special thanks, but mention must be made of the careful work in checking both manuscripts and proofs which has been carried out by Miss Mary Gladstone MA and Miss Clare Richards MA of the Publishers' editorial department. The Editors have benefited considerably at every stage from the help which they have given.

The original edition was sent out with the prayer that God would use it by His Spirit to help many to gain from the Scriptures a fresh and increasing understanding of His ways and of His will for men. We echo that prayer, knowing as we do that today it is as important as it has ever been to bring the whole of life to be tested and guided by the authoritative Word of God.

DONALD GUTHRIE
ALEC MOTYER
ALAN M. STIBBS
DONALD J. WISEMAN

[5] Revised 1967. Inter-Varsity Press.

Contents

PART THREE The New Testament

Sketch maps and tables

Contributors

An asterisk placed against the title of an article indicates joint authorship.

James T. H. Adamson, MA, BD, STM, Minister of First United Church (United Church of Canada), Ottawa, Ontario: *Malachi.*

The late **Oswald T. Allis,** DD, PHD, formerly Professor of Old Testament, Westminster Theological Seminary, Philadelphia: *Leviticus.*

Gleason L. Archer Jr, BD, PHD, Professor of Old Testament, Trinity Evangelical Divinity School, Deerfield, Illinois: *Micah.*

John A. Balchin, MA, BD, Minister of First Presbyterian Church, Papakura, New Zealand: *The Song of Solomon.*

Joyce G. Baldwin, BA, BD, Dean of Women, Trinity College, Bristol: *The history of Israel, Ruth, Esther.*

G. R. Beasley-Murray, MA, PHD, DD, James Buchanan Harrison Professor of New Testament Interpretation, Southern Baptist Theological Seminary, Louisville, Kentucky: *The apocryphal and apocalyptic literature*, Ezekiel, The Revelation.*

Hugh J. Blair, MA, PHD, Professor of Old Testament Language and Literature, Reformed Presbyterian Theological Hall, Belfast, and Minister of Ballymoney Church (Reformed Presbyterian Church of Ireland), Co. Antrim: *Joshua.*

G. W. Bromiley, DLITT, DD, Professor of Church History and Historical Theology, Fuller Theological Seminary, Pasadena, California: *The authority of Scripture.*

F. F. Bruce, MA, DD, FBA, Emeritus Rylands Professor of Biblical Criticism and Exegesis, University of Manchester: *The poetry of the Old Testament, The wisdom literature of the Old Testament, The apocryphal and apocalyptic literature*, Between the Testaments, The fourfold Gospel, Judges, The Acts of the Apostles, 1 and 2 Thessalonians.*

John T. Carson, BA, DD, Minister of Trinity Church (Presbyterian Church in Ireland), Bangor, Co. Down: *Zephaniah.*

The late **F. Cawley,** BA, BD, PHD, formerly Principal, Spurgeon's Theological College, London: *Jeremiah*.*

R. Alan Cole, BA, BD, MTH, PHD, Federal Secretary, Church Missionary Society (Australia) and Lecturer in Old Testament Language and Literature, University of Sydney: *Joel.*

A. E. Cundall, BA, BD, Senior Lecturer in Old Testament Studies, London Bible College: *Ezra and Nehemiah.*

The late **Francis Davidson,** MA, DD, formerly Professor of Old Testament and New Testament Language and Literature, United Original Secession Church of Scotland and Principal of the Bible Training Institute, Glasgow: *Romans*.*

H. L. Ellison, BA, BD, formerly Senior Tutor, Moorlands Bible College: *1 and 2 Chronicles.*

Francis Foulkes, BA, BD, MA, MSC, Lecturer in Biblical Studies, St. John's College, Auckland, and Lecturer in Biblical History and Literature, University of Auckland: *Philippians.*

Alexander Fraser, MA, BD, formerly Minister of Cumlodden and Lochfyneside Church (Church of Scotland), Glasgow: *Nahum.*

Donald Guthrie, BD, MTH, PHD, Vice-Principal, London Bible College: *The Pauline Epistles, John, Colossians, Philemon.*

R. K. Harrison, MTH, PHD, DD, Professor of Old Testament, Wycliffe College, University of Toronto: *Deuteronomy*.*

E. S. P. Heavenor, MA, BD, PHD, Minister of St. Michael's Church (Church of Scotland), Crieff: *Job.*

George S. Hendry, MA, DD, Professor of Systematic Theology, Princeton Theological Seminary, Princeton, New Jersey: *Ecclesiastes.*

R. E. Higginson, MA, BD, Vicar of Weeton, Preston, Lancs.: *Zechariah.*

Norman Hillyer, BD, STH, ALCD, formerly Librarian, Tyndale House, Cambridge; Vicar of Hatherleigh, Devonshire: *1 and 2 Corinthians.*

The late **J. B. Hindley,** B ENG, MA, formerly Vicar of Wellington, Shropshire: *Hosea.*

Hywel R. Jones, BA (Wales), MA (Cantab.), Minister of Grove Chapel, Camberwell, London SE5: *Exodus.*

Derek Kidner, MA, ARCM, formerly Warden, Tyndale House, Cambridge: *Isaiah.*

Meredith G. Kline, PHD, THM, Professor of Old Testament, Gordon-Conwell Theology Seminary, S. Hamilton, Mass.: *Genesis.*

William Sanford LaSor, PHD, THD, Professor of Old Testament, Fuller Theological Seminary, Pasadena, California: *1 and 2 Kings.*

Leslie S. M'Caw, MA, formerly Principal, All Nations Bible College: *The Psalms*.*

The late **G. T. Manley,** MA, sometime Fellow of Christ's College, Cambridge, and Vicar of St. Luke's Church, Hampstead, London NW3: *Deuteronomy*.*

I. Howard Marshall, BA, MA, BD, PHD, Professor of New Testament Exegesis, University of Aberdeen: *Luke.*

Ralph P. Martin, MA, PHD, Professor of New Testament, Fuller Theological Seminary, Pasadena, California: *Romans*, Ephesians.*

Samuel J. Mikolaski, MA, BD, DPHIL, Professor of Christian Theology, Regent College, Vancouver, British Columbia: *Galatians.*

A. R. Millard, MA, MPHIL, FSA, Rankin Senior Lecturer in Hebrew and Ancient Semitic Languages, University of Liverpool: *Jeremiah**.

Leon Morris, MSC, MTH, PHD, formerly Principal, Ridley College, Melbourne; Canon of St. Paul's Cathedral, Melbourne: *1, 2 and 3 John.*

J. A. Motyer, MA, BD, Principal, Trinity College, Bristol: *Old Testament theology, The Psalms*, Amos.*

The late **R. E. Nixon,** MA, formerly Principal, St. John's College, Nottingham: *Matthew.*

J. I. Packer, MA, DPHIL, DD, Professor of Systematic Theology, Regent College, Vancouver, British Columbia: *Revelation and inspiration.*

D. F. Payne, BA, MA, Senior Lecturer and Head of Department of Semitic Studies, The Queen's University, Belfast: *1 and 2 Samuel.*

D. W. B. Robinson, MA, Bishop in Parramatta, New South Wales; formerly Head of New Testament Department, Divinity School, University of Sydney: *Obadiah, Jonah.*

J. Ruffle, MA, Keeper of Archaeology, Birmingham City Museum: *Introduction to Proverbs.*

L. E. H. Stephens-Hodge, MA, Vicar of Cullompton, Devon; formerly Tutor at the London College of Divinity: *Lamentations, Habakkuk.*

The late **A. M. Stibbs,** MA, formerly Vice-Principal, Oak Hill Theological College, London: *The Pastoral Epistles, Hebrews.*

The late **C. E. Graham Swift,** MA, formerly Minister of Cape Town Baptist Church: *Mark.*

J. A. Thompson, MA, MSC, BD, B ED, PHD, formerly Reader in Department of Middle Eastern Studies, University of Melbourne: *Numbers.*

A. F. Walls, MA, B LITT, Professor of Religious Studies, University of Aberdeen: *Proverbs*.*

Ronald A. Ward, MA, BD, PHD, Rector of the Stone Church (Anglican Church of Canada) and Rural Dean of Saint John, New Brunswick; Examining Chaplain to the Archbishop of Fredericton: *James.*

J. W. Wenham, MA, BD, formerly Warden, Latimer House, Oxford: *Moses and the Pentateuch.*

David H. Wheaton, MA, BD, Principal, Oak Hill Theological College, London, and Canon of St. Albans Cathedral: *1 and 2 Peter, Jude.*

D. J. Wiseman, OBE, MA, D LIT, FBA, FSA, Professor of Assyriology, University of London: *Haggai.*

The late **Edward J. Young,** BA, THM, PHD, formerly Professor of Old Testament, Westminster Theological Seminary, Philadelphia: *History of the literary criticism of the Pentateuch, Daniel.*

Abbreviations

BIBLICAL BOOKS

Books of the Old Testament

Gn., Ex., Lv., Nu., Dt., Jos., Jdg., Ru., 1, 2 Sa., 1, 2 Ki., 1, 2 Ch., Ezr., Ne., Est., Jb., Ps. (Pss.), Pr., Ec., Ct., Is., Je., La., Ezk., Dn., Ho., Joel, Am., Ob., Jon., Mi., Na., Hab., Zp., Hg., Zc., Mal.

Books of the New Testament

Mt., Mk., Lk., Jn., Acts, Rom., 1, 2 Cor., Gal., Eph., Phil., Col., 1, 2 Thes., 1, 2 Tim., Tit., Phm., Heb., Jas., 1, 2 Pet., 1, 2, 3 Jn., Jude, Rev.

GENERAL ABBREVIATIONS

art.	article (in *NBD, etc.*)
AV	Authorized Version (King James), 1611
cf.	compare
Ecclus.	Ecclesiasticus
ET	English translation
Gk.	Greek
Heb.	Hebrew
Hitt.	Hittite
JB	Jerusalem Bible, 1966
LXX	Septuagint (pre-Christian Greek version of the Old Testament)
mg.	margin
mod.	modern
MS, MSS	manuscript(s)
MT	Massoretic Text
NEB	New English Bible, 1961 and 1970
NT	New Testament
OT	Old Testament
1QIsa	*Scroll of Isaiah* (Qumran text)
1QS	*Rule of the Community* (Qumran text)
q.v.	which see
RSV	Revised Standard Version, 1946 and 1952
RV	Revised Version, 1885
Syr.	Syriac
Targ.	Targum
Vulg.	Vulgate

REFERENCE BOOKS AND JOURNALS

(Editions have been indicated by small superior figures thus: *LOT*[9])

ANET	*Ancient Near Eastern Texts* (ed. J. B. Pritchard), 1950
Ant.	*Antiquities* (Josephus)
Arndt	*Greek-English Lexicon of the New Testament* (W. F. Arndt and F. W. Gingrich), 1957
BA	*Biblical Archaeologist*
BASOR	*Bulletin of the American Schools of Oriental Research*
BJRL	*Bulletin of the John Rylands Library*
CAH	*Cambridge Ancient History*
CB	*Century Bible*
CBC	*Cambridge Bible Commentary*
CBSC	*Cambridge Bible for Schools and Colleges*
CDC	*Cairo Geniza Documents of the Damascus Covenanters*
CGT	*Cambridge Greek Testament*
DOTT	*Documents from Old Testament Times* (ed. D. W. Thomas), 1958
EB	*Expositor's Bible*
EQ	*Evangelical Quarterly*
ExpT	*Expository Times*
HDB	Hastings' *Dictionary of the Bible*, 5 vols., 1898–1904
HNT	*Handbuch zum Neuen Testament*
IB	*Interpreter's Bible*
ICC	*International Critical Commentary*
IDB	*Interpreter's Dictionary of the Bible*
ISBE	*International Standard Bible Encyclopaedia*[2] (ed. J. Orr), 5 vols., 1930
JBL	*Journal of Biblical Literature*
JSS	*Journal of Semitic Studies*
JTS	*Journal of Theological Studies*
JTVI	*Journal of the Transactions of the Victoria Institute*
LOT	*Introduction to the Literature of the Old Testament*[9] (S. R. Driver), 1913
MNTC	*Moffatt New Testament Commentary*
Moffatt	*A New Translation of the Bible* (J. Moffatt), 1935
NBC	*The New Bible Commentary* (ed. F. Davidson *et al.*), 1953
NBD	*The New Bible Dictionary* (ed. J. D. Douglas *et al.*), 1962
NLC	*New London Commentary*
OTMS	*The Old Testament and Modern Study* (ed. H. H. Rowley), 1951
PEQ	*Palestine Exploration Quarterly*
Phillips	*The New Testament in Modern English* (J. B. Phillips), 1958
SJT	*Scottish Journal of Theology*
TBC	*Torch Bible Commentary*
TDNT	*Theological Dictionary of the New Testament* (ed. G. Kittel)
TNTC	*Tyndale New Testament Commentary*
TOTC	*Tyndale Old Testament Commentary*
VT	*Vetus Testamentum*
WC	*Westminster Commentary*

Transliteration

HEBREW

א = '	ד = ḏ	י = y	ס = s	ר = r
בּ = b	ה = h	כ = k	ע = '	שׂ = ś
ב = ḇ	ו = w	ך = ḵ	פ = p	שׁ = š
ג = g	ז = z	ל = l	פּ = p̄	תּ = t
ג = ḡ	ח = ḥ	מ = m	צ = ṣ	ת = t
ד = d	ט = ṭ	נ = n	ק = q	

Long Vowels		Short Vowels	Very Short Vowels
(ה)ָ = â	ָ = ā	ַ = a	ֲ = ᵃ
ֵ = ê	ֶ = ē	ֶ = e	ֱ = ᵉ
ִ = î		ִ = i	ְ = ᵉ (if vocal)
וֹ = ô	ָ = ō	ָ = o	ֳ = ᵒ
וּ = û		ֻ = u	

GREEK

α = a	ι = i	ϱ = r	ῥ = rh
β = b	κ = k	σ, ς = s	' = h
γ = g	λ = l	τ = t	γξ = nx
δ = d	μ = m	υ = y	γγ = ng
ε = e	ν = n	φ = ph	αυ = au
ζ = z	ξ = x	χ = ch	ευ = eu
η = ē	ο = o	ψ = ps	ου = ou
θ = th	π = p	ω = ō	υι = yi

PART ONE

General Articles

The authority of Scripture

THE BIBLICAL WITNESS

Our thinking concerning the authority and inspiration of Holy Scripture must start always from the fact that the Bible itself assumes everywhere that it is a message directly given by God Himself. In this first section it must be our main task to substantiate that fact and to discuss its implications. But one preliminary question must first be answered. When we assert the unique authority of the Bible, is it legitimate to appeal to the Bible's own testimony in support of that assertion? Is it not a most outrageous form of question-begging to make the Bible itself the first and final arbiter in its own case? Are we not guilty of presupposing the very thing which we are asked to substantiate?

The answer to this question is, of course, that we do not turn to the Bible for proof, but for information. Rational arguments may be advanced in favour of the unique authority of Scripture, but in the last analysis we accept that authority by faith. We accept it only in so far as the Bible itself requires it. In other words, it is only as the inspiration and authenticity of the record are a (necessary) part of the revelation that we confess the Bible as the supreme rule of faith and life. If the Bible did not make that claim, we should have no call to believe it. Nor could we have general confidence in the teaching of Scripture. But if the Bible stands before us as the authoritative Word of God, the Word which itself claims authority, then it is as such that we must reckon with it, receiving that Word and the authority of that Word, or resisting it.

Does the Bible make any such assertion of authority? If it does, what does that assertion imply? With regard to the first question, the answer is so vast that our main difficulty is that of compression. In the OT as in the NT the claim to a more than human authority is everywhere implicit, and in many places it finds direct and open expression. It is claimed, e.g., that Moses received from God both the moral law and also more detailed commandments, even extending to arrangements for the Tabernacle. The prophets maintained that they were not speaking their own words, but the message which God Himself had given to them. The Lord Jesus Christ spoke with authority because He was conscious of speaking not merely as the historical Teacher but as the eternal Son. The apostles had no doubt as to the authoritativeness of their pronouncements, whether they were quoting our Lord or developing the Christian message under the guidance of the outpoured Spirit.

It may be objected that in the majority of these cases the claim to authority is made only on behalf of the message delivered and not on behalf of the written record in which that message has been handed down to us. Thus it may well be true that the prophets or Jesus Christ spoke with divine authority, but sometimes we have their words only at second hand. The fact that inspiration is claimed for them does not mean that inspiration is claimed for those who compiled the record of their activity and teaching. If this is so there is no guarantee that what is written in the Bible is a verbatim or accurate account of the message actually delivered.

Against this objection we may set the fact that in the NT especially, and with reference to the OT, definite authority is claimed for the written word of the Bible. This point emerges clearly in many parts of the teaching of our Lord Himself. Thus He answers the tempter with the threefold 'It is written'. On the mount of transfiguration He tells His disciples that it is written of the Son of man that He should suffer many things and be set at naught. To the Jews who searched the Scriptures He gave counsel that 'it is they that bear witness to me'. After the resurrection He interpreted to the disciples in all the Scriptures the things concerning Himself, showing that all things must needs be fulfilled, which were 'written about me in the law of Moses and the prophets and the psalms'. These and similar statements make it quite plain that Jesus Himself accepted the inspiration and authority of the written Word, especially in so far as it gave prophetic witness to His own death and resurrection. It is also clear from verses like Jn. 14:26 and Jn. 16:13 that He expected and promised a similar inspiration in the case of the apostolic testimony yet to be made.

When we come to the apostles we find that their testimony to the divine authority of the Bible is equally clear. In all the Gospels great emphasis is laid upon the inspired foretelling of the work and Person of Christ. The apostle Paul quotes extensively from the OT, and his preaching to his own people is very largely an attempt to prove the Messiahship of Jesus from OT history and prophecy. The statement in 2 Tim. 3:16 sums up the whole attitude of Paul. Whatever translation we adopt it is plain from v. 15 that the apostle has the OT in mind and that he thinks of it as peculiarly inspired by God. The other apostolic writers quote just as frequently from the OT, and in 2 Peter open testimony is borne to the inspiration of the Bible in a way very similar to that in 2 Timothy. In 2 Pet. 1:21 the word of prophecy is traced back to its final author in God the Holy Spirit: 'Because no prophecy ever came by the impulse of man, but men moved by the Holy Spirit spoke from God.' Again, in 2 Pet. 3:16 there seems to be a further allusion to the written Bible as an authoritative word which must be approached with reverence and humility. The latter verse is particularly interesting in that it couples together the Epistles of Paul and the other scriptures, a fairly plain hint that the apostolic authors were conscious of adding to and completing the authoritative Canon of the OT.

Surveying the evidence, we may allow that the passages that treat directly of the inspiration of Scripture are few in number, and that there is no particular assertion of the status or authority of every individual book. On the other hand, we may note that, with the exception of Ezra, Nehemiah, Esther, Ecclesiastes, Song of Solomon, Obadiah, Nahum and Zephaniah, all the books of the OT are directly quoted in the NT; and when we take into account the attitude of the NT to such quotations there can be little doubt that the 'Thus says the Lord' of the prophets was taken to apply to the records of prophetic activity as well as to oral words delivered on this or that specific occasion. The written word was treated as the inspired and authoritative form in which the content of divine revelation had been expressed and handed down.

When we ask concerning the implications of this witness, several important points emerge. First, it may be noted that no specific theory of inspiration is introduced. From the two texts, Jn. 14:26 and 2 Pet. 1:21, it seems that there is a twofold activity: that of the human author on the one hand, and that of the inspiring and controlling Spirit on the other. Certainly there is no doubt as to the final initiative and supremacy of the Spirit. But there is also no suggestion of the obliteration of the personality and individuality of the human author. Again, we may notice that inspiration is seen particularly in the insight of the OT writers into the future activity of God. The prophet was a forth-teller, no doubt; but the ultimate test of his prophecy was the correctness of his insight into the divinely-directed future, and that necessarily meant foretelling. Even in the OT itself the prophet who foretold incorrectly was discredited, and in the NT the main value of the OT is the prophetic witness to Jesus Christ. If it is true that that witness supports the Messianic claim of Jesus, it is also true that the Messianic work of Jesus vindicates the prophetic claim of the OT. A very large proportion of the OT citations are concerned with various forms of that prophetic witness.

A third point is that the historical setting of the OT is everywhere accepted as authentic. Our Lord, for instance, does not question the connection of Moses with the Law, or the Davidic authorship of Ps. 110. The apostles accept all the main events of OT history from Adam and the Fall (1 Tim. 2:13, 14) to the crossing of the Red Sea (1 Cor. 10:1), the Balaam incidents (2 Pet. 2:16), the fall of Jericho (Heb. 11:30), the deliverances under the judges (Heb. 11:32) and the miracles of Elijah (Jas. 5:17). In face of this clear testimony the suggestion has been made that our Lord and the apostles simply shared the common assumptions of their age and made use of the historical happenings only in illustration of their theology. It certainly cannot be denied, however, that, in the NT, belief in the authority of the OT does involve an acceptance of its historical as well as its religious or doctrinal truth. It is worth remembering, too, that if that acceptance means acceptance of the supernatural control and intervention of almighty God, nowhere do we have a clearer or more decisive instance of such intervention and control than in the central facts of the Christian gospel, the life and death and resurrection of Jesus Christ.

Attention is sometimes drawn to the apparent freedom, even arbitrariness, of the NT in its citation of the OT. On the one hand, a common use is made of the LXX Greek, and at times this involves quite extensive divergences from the Massoretic Hebrew. On the other, OT verses are often referred prophetically to Christ when their original application seems to be entirely different. The deduction is that this freedom suggests a far looser conception of inspiration than that traditionally associated with the Bible and its authors. But the following points must be remembered. With regard to the LXX, it is quite possible that in many cases the Greek translation gives a more faithful and coherent account of the original than the MT. Again, the main aim in a translation is to convey the true sense rather than to provide word-for-word equivalents. In view of the inevitable differences in linguistic structure and provenance, this means that a freer rendering is often more truly accurate than a literal. In the LXX the NT authors had a carefully-weighed and long-standing translation with which many of their readers were already familiar. A further point is that, in some cases, the Holy Spirit may have used the LXX to bring out new aspects of divine truth, or to make a more forceful application. Where necessary, of course, importance could be attached even to the minuter details of the original text (cf. Gal. 3:16).

The problem of the prophetic testimonies is no less serious, for here the whole meaning and application seems to have changed. Indeed, it is suggested that the verses have either consciously or unconsciously been misapplied in the search for detailed proofs from prophecy of the Messiahship of Christ. At a first glance, the suggestion looks reasonable enough, for in their original context many of the verses do not seem to have even the slightest Messianic reference. But although it is a collection of writings, the Bible is a single book, and that means that there is a larger as well as an immediate context. Ultimately, all the history of Israel is concentrated and fulfilled in that of the only true

Israelite, and throughout that history the same patterns of divine activity may be observed. Behind the seemingly artificial reference to Rachel in Mt. 2, *e.g.*, there stands a constantly-recurring movement of aggression, death and exile. Taken merely as proof texts, the citations might not be convincing, but in the wider context of the divine purpose and activity they introduce us to types and patterns of which the history of Jesus Christ is the true fulfilment.

We must be careful, of course, not to read into the self-attestation of Scripture more than is actually there. With regard to authorships and dates, *e.g.*, tradition has often been vocal where the Bible itself is silent. The extent of the biblical silence is sometimes rather surprising. We know little about the compilation of the historical books of the OT. We are not told the exact date and circumstances of some prophetic writings (*e.g.* Malachi). We do not know who wrote many of the Psalms or the book of Job. We are not told that Hebrews was written by Paul. The text itself does not tell us that Luke wrote the Third Gospel and Acts, or that the apostle John wrote the Fourth Gospel, although the case for Luke and John rests on sound and legitimate inference. It is as well sometimes to remember that there is this line between a direct biblical testimony and even the reliable evidence of tradition. Otherwise we may easily identify the authority of Scripture with that of historical statements which are outside the scope of Scripture itself.

When all this is said, however, it must be said too that the Bible does lay serious claim to divine origin, status and authority. It states clearly that its message is of God. It traces back its authority through the human writings to the Holy Spirit. It accepts the supernatural both in prophetic utterances and in historical events. It makes no artificial distinction between the inward content of the Word of God and its outward form. By its self-authentication as God's Word written, the Bible challenges us directly either to faith or to unbelief. In our approach to the Bible other considerations may obtrude, but the basic challenge certainly cannot be ignored.

THE REFORMED DOCTRINE

It was upon the foundation of the self-witness of the Bible that the Reformers built their doctrine of Holy Scripture. They adopted this procedure because first and foremost their theology was a theology of faith, a revealed theology. Their starting-point was, therefore, the response of faith to the challenge of the biblical message. They accepted that message on its own terms, and in loyalty to it they tried to understand the Bible as the Bible understood itself. As we have already seen, the Reformed method is regarded as both illegitimate and futile by those who think that theology should be constructed upon purely rational foundations. But the Reformers themselves were theologians of faith, making use of reason only in response and obedience to the

divine revelation. This meant that they were theologians who were pledged in faith to receive the testimony of the Word of God written, even in matters concerning its own nature and being.

The Reformers believed, then, that the Bible was given by God, and that it was inspired both in content and also in form. They did not take any radical step when they propounded this view. The mediaeval church had held a similar view. But they did take the step. Everywhere in their writings we find evidence of a whole-hearted acceptance of the inspiration and authority of the Bible. This is so in spite of the free comments which have led some modern scholars to regard Luther and Calvin as early critics, or at any rate as men who distinguished between the living content of Scripture and the detailed wording, in contrast to their supposedly more legalistic successors. In fact, however, both Luther and Calvin extolled the authority of the letter too. Their remarks on the minor problems should not blind us to the fact that for them Scripture was the divinely-authoritative record upon which all true theology must be founded. The special attitude of Luther to James is linked with his doubts as to its authentic canonicity, so that it does not affect his general understanding.

The Bible was inspired and authoritative, but it was also sole-sufficient in matters of faith and conduct. It would be an exaggeration to say that the Reformers set up the Bible as the only authority in the church. But it is no exaggeration to say that they regarded the Bible as the supreme authority from which all other authorities derived and to which they were all subject. Because it was itself from God, the Bible contained everything necessary both to salvation and to the Christian life. Nothing was to be believed or taught in the church unless it had the sanction either of the plain text of Scripture or of clear inferences from it. The Calvinists extended the direct rule of Scripture even to the details of church order and worship, and the Lutherans and Anglicans all ascribed a negative authority to the Bible in these spheres—*i.e.* they would not permit anything which was excluded by Scripture or repugnant to it.

The emphasis upon the supremacy and sole-sufficiency of the Bible was clearly designed to destroy the mediaeval assertion of an authority of tradition and of the church side by side and on an equality with that of Holy Scripture. A further step in the same direction was the insistence that the Bible must be understood only in its plain and literal sense and not according to the fourfold scheme of mediaeval exegesis. This did not mean that a symbolical or metaphorical sense could not be accorded to what was plainly symbol or metaphor. What it did mean was that a more than literal sense must not be introduced into the ordinary statements of Scripture except in cases where the Bible itself expressly sanctions it—*e.g.* in the understanding of the Red Sea crossing as a type of baptism, or the reference of the OT priesthood to Christ. Parallel types might be drawn for the purpose of spiritual edification, but they were not to be regarded as authoritative for Christian belief or conduct. Should difficulties of interpretation arise they were to be resolved by the comparison of scripture with scripture, the more luminous and straightforward passages being used to illuminate the more difficult and obscure. These exegetical rules were important for two reasons: they cleared away much of the confusion inevitably caused by the mediaeval scheme, thus making possible the erection of a genuine biblical theology; and they destroyed the authority of the official interpreters of Scripture who alone could manipulate successfully the complicated fourfold technique.

The Reformers accepted all parts of canonical Scripture as inspired and authoritative, although they did not accord an equal degree of importance and relevance to every part. The insistence that all canonical Scripture is inspired was directed against some of the Anabaptist groups who could not agree to the full inspiration of the OT. The Reformers saw clearly that the OT is a most important part of the divine witness to Jesus Christ and to saving truth. They argued that the moral teaching of the OT is eternally valid as an expression of God's will for His people. The theological principles underlying God's dealings with Israel are also the same as those underlying His dealings with Christians and the Christian church, thus providing further illustration and confirmation of divine truth. The OT and the NT belong together, the one as preparation, the other as fulfilment.

All parts of the Bible are inspired and authoritative, the Reformers taught, but not all parts are of equal importance. The Mosaic legislation in Leviticus had not the same spiritual or theological value as the Gospel of John, or even the Decalogue. In this respect the Bible is in some sense analogous to the church as the body of Christ. All the members constitute the body and are necessary to it. But although all the members are necessary they are not all of equal importance. Some members are more used than others, and some may be regarded as vital: without them the body would perish altogether. So it is with the Bible. We cannot mutilate the Bible without loss, but some parts are more dispensable than others. If the evangelical message is given, it is possible to be a Christian with only a fragment of Scripture; to be a full-grown Christian it is necessary to have the whole counsel of God.

A certain difficulty arises when the attempt is made to discriminate between the more and less relevant and important passages, for purely subjective considerations threaten to control and perhaps distort our judgment in this matter. Zwingli and Luther both gave helpful rules which are not so very different: the importance and relevance of a passage depend upon the measure in which it serves, first, to promote the glory of God and, second, to reveal and exalt the Lord Jesus Christ. It is because some parts of the Bible do this more directly and plainly than others that they are to be regarded as the more important passages of Scripture. But in the last resort all Scripture is in some way directed towards this twofold end.

The Reformers emphasized the importance of the letter of the Bible, but not at the expense of the sovereignty of the Holy Spirit in His use and application of the Bible message. In the thought of the Reformers the Holy Spirit was not merely the Author of Scripture; He also determined the application of Scripture to its twofold end, and gave to the believer an inward persuasion of the authority of its message as revealed truth. On the first of these further points it need only be added that, while the meaning of the Bible is plain, for an inward apprehension something more is needed than the ordinary rational intelligence. For genuine understanding there is required the illumination of the Holy Spirit which is for the individual the necessary complement of God's outward revelation.

Some modern theologians have seized upon this illumination as true inspiration according to the Reformed conception: *i.e.* the Bible is inspired only in so far as the Holy Spirit uses this or that passage to accomplish an inward enlightenment in the individual Christian. In the Reformers themselves, however, there seem to be few traces of the equation of the individual enlightenment with inspiration as such. The Bible is an inspired record of the divine self-revelation whether this or that individual receives its witness or not. The revelation and the recording of it in written form are both objective acts. Illumination by the Holy Spirit is the subjective complement of these acts within the individual and for the salvation of the individual. As it is God the Holy Spirit who gave the objective record, so it is God the Holy Spirit who effects the subjective illumination. The message and the application of the message are both of God.

The fact that there is that inward enlightenment is the final guarantee of the authenticity of the record, whether in its general teaching or in its self-attestation. Although the Reformers accepted the Bible in faith, they were not unaware of the rational problems involved. The problems were perhaps not so acute then as they are today, but they were sufficiently acute to call for some general answer. The Reformers could advance many reasons in favour of their acceptance of the Bible. They could point, as Calvin did, to those characteristics and qualities which mark it off as an inspired record: its literary quality, its antiquity, its combination of depth and simplicity, its preservation and historical power, its accuracy in the foretelling of the future. In the last analysis, however, the real reason for belief is the inward knowledge of the truth of Scripture which is necessarily present when the Holy Spirit applies that truth to the soul. To the self-attestation of the Bible there is added the inward testimony of the Holy Spirit. But the argument is a rational argument only for the believer. In other words, the truth of the Bible's claim cannot be made a matter simply of intellectual and academic debate. As a fundamental axiom it must be known by experience. It must be known from within. It must be known by faith. Like the Bible itself, this knowledge is given by the Holy Spirit.

With their emphasis on the Lordship of the Holy Spirit the Reformers safeguarded themselves against dead literalism and scholastic rationalism in their understanding of Holy Scripture. They yielded to none in their loyalty to the given form of the Bible. They had a high view both of the Bible itself and also of its inspiration. They believed that the Bible itself is inspired truth. They believed that it is the Word written, a Word given and applied by the Holy Spirit. They taught that the Word must always be respected and received and obeyed. Yet they remembered always that God is the Lord of Scripture and that it is His voice which must be heard if the Bible is to do its work. The Bible is not just an academic textbook of divine truth, the Euclid of the Christian faith. The text is indeed given by God, but it is always in the hands of God and always applied by God. The Bible must be respected and received and obeyed not because it is a fixed and static letter, but because under the Holy Spirit that letter is the living Word of the living God both to the individual and to the church.

MODERN TRENDS

The Roman Catholic view

There are three broad schools of thinking which today challenge what we believe to be the orthodox, scriptural, apostolic and Reformed position in relation to the authority and inspiration of Holy Scripture. First, and not least formidable, is the official Roman Catholic teaching. In one sense this is not a modern view, since the Roman position was fixed at the Council of Trent (1545–63), and for all the ferment in Roman Catholicism it has not yet been altered. In another sense, however, it is very modern, for the related issues are the basic issues of this and every age. The way in which they are settled, both inside and outside Roman Catholicism, might well be the most important single factor in shaping the future course of theology.

In respect of Scripture as the rule of faith, the Roman Catholic seems to adopt a position very much like the orthodox one. For him, the Word of God is an absolute rule. It displaces all private interpretations. It is inspired immediately by God. It is completely trustworthy, not only from the point of view of history, but also from that of doctrine. The value of textual studies is not questioned, since original texts correct errors in copying, give right readings, light up obscurities, and give force to the expressions used. The

Roman Catholic church does not approve of destructive rational or historical criticism, though hand in hand with the new concentration on biblical studies greater freedom has recently been shown in this regard.

Thus far there could be no great quarrel with Roman Catholicism, but now three further questions arise. The first is: What is Scripture? The Roman answer is that Scripture consists of the Old and New Testaments, including the OT Apocrypha. Thus writings which cannot be included in the list of inspired and authoritative books have the same weight in doctrinal discussion as the truly canonical books. Moreover, on the plea that Jerome had access to old and purer texts, and that his work has the sanction of centuries of use, the Vulgate is accorded the rank of a fully-authoritative text. This means that doctrines may be grounded on the Latin text even where it obviously does not render the original correctly.

The second question is: Who is to interpret Scripture? The Roman answer is that Scripture is too obscure to be self-interpreting, and that there is need for a further authority to decide which is the right sense. In the OT the Law was interpreted by Moses and the priests. Today the interpretation of the Bible is in the hands of the church, speaking through *ex cathedra* pronouncements of the pope, the decisions of general councils and statements of the teaching office, together with the expositions of the Early Fathers. Truly, the Bible is the basic authority, but side by side with that basic authority there is the interpretative authority, to which all Christians must bow. The recent surge of biblical study has greatly modified this rule in practice, but the basic principle is still valid: the official Bible officially interpreted is the only legitimate norm, and the papacy is the ultimate interpretative authority.

There is a third question: Does the Bible as a rule of faith suffice, or is there a further and necessary rule side by side with and supplementing the Bible? The Roman answer is that the Bible is not enough. Before the written Word there was an oral tradition, and side by side with the written Word there is today a tradition (both of teaching and custom) derived directly from the apostles, and of equal rank with the Bible. Authoritative tradition consists of teachings universally accepted (*e.g.* the virginity of Mary), and customs practised by Roman Catholics (*e.g.* infant baptism), those manifestly ancient, although not demonstrably apostolic (*e.g.* the Lenten fast), those held by most doctors and not disputed by others (*e.g.* baptismal rites, or the cult of images), and those which are held by apostolic churches, of which Rome is the only one at the present time (*e.g.* the doctrine of the Immaculate Conception). In effect, this means that the appeal to Scripture is set aside in whole areas of life and thought, and, though some modern Roman Catholics, such as Küng, are prepared to argue that Scripture is primary, there is unfortunately no strong evidence that this view has been generally accepted by their communion.

The devastating effects of Roman teaching upon the Bible's authority are clear enough, both in theory and even more so in experience. It must not be forgotten, however, that genuine questions are posed which require precise and accurate handling if this erroneous understanding of biblical authority is to be met and avoided.

There is first the question of Canon and text. Why must the canonical books be given one authority, the Apocrypha another? What is the pure text, and to what extent, if any, can renderings be said to be inspired, or even to what extent can we rely on any text as being fully inspired?

There is, second, the doctrinal question: How is the doctrine of the Holy Spirit in Scripture interpretation to be correctly stated, so as to avoid dangers of ecclesiastical monopoly on the one side, and of fanatical individualism on the other? In what sense are the Scriptures of public interpretation? How far are the expositions of others, the Fathers, or the Reformers—men who manifestly worked with insight and prayer—to be taken into account in our own reading of the Bible?

Third, there are questions of order. To what extent is tradition permissible, if not in matters of faith, at any rate in those of order? Must church life be modelled exclusively upon the detailed practice of Scripture, in such a way that what is not in the Bible is necessarily excluded, or has the church the power to maintain ceremonies and traditions so long as they are in accordance with scriptural principles, and of value for Christian life?

All these questions demand full treatment and answer if a true doctrine of the Bible is to be maintained. Nor should it be forgotten that the error itself might have something to teach us in our answers, e.g. the danger of exalting one translation (Vulgate, or AV) into the infallible Word, or the undoubted worth of previous expositions, not of course as infallible authorities, but as useful guides. On the other hand, the primary task is undoubtedly the positive one of presenting the biblical doctrine of the authority of Scripture as the basis of all genuine theology.

Liberal Protestantism

A second unorthodox teaching is that of liberal Protestantism. This is a modern movement in every sense, for, though there are historical parallels, its development has been largely during the post-Reformation period, and it has provided a view of the Bible which, allowing for varieties of presentation, is still that of many Protestant theologians, ministers and laymen. Rome weakens the authority of the Bible, not by denying its divine origin and unique position, but by adding to it other authorities which rob it of its power. Historical liberalism knows nothing of these subtle methods of peaceful penetration. It attacks the Bible frontally, denying the absoluteness or divine nature of its authority, willing to grant it authority—a limited and relative authority—only on the human level.

A full analysis of this complex liberal movement, in which so many different forms of thought coalesced, is unfortunately quite impossible in this context. All that can be done is to outline the various thought-forms and to indicate the points at which they come into conflict with the orthodox doctrine. Five main movements combined, generally speaking, to produce this modern view of the Bible: 1. Rationalism, which at its best, as with the German Neology, sought to reduce revealed Christianity to the level of a religion of reason, and at its worst, as with Voltaire, sought to laugh Christianity out of court as contrary to reason. 2. Empiricism, or Historicism, which had as its main aim the study of Christianity and all its phenomena along the strict lines of historical observation. 3. Poeticism, which, as with Herder and many of the early critics, approached the Bible as a primitive poetry-book, in which religious truths—partly emotional, partly rational—are set out in aesthetic forms. 4. Emotional Pietism, the special and most important contribution of Schleiermacher, by which the doctrines of Christianity (including that of Holy Scripture) are reinterpreted in terms, not now of reason, or history, or poetry, but of emotional religious experience. 5. Philosophical Idealism, which, in its final form in Hegel, gave a new rational interpretation upon a different philosophical basis: a basis which has as its starting-point the individual thinking ego.

It is not to be supposed, of course, that there are not opposing tendencies in these movements, or that all of them are necessarily present, or present in equal proportions, in every liberal theologian; but generally speaking—and making full allowance for the many points of divergence —these are the movements which together constitute the liberal and humanistic challenge to the orthodox doctrine of Bible authority.

In what does that challenge consist? It consists first in the rejection of a transcendent Deity and of supernatural acts of God. This means that the Bible has to be explained as reason, or history, or poetry, or religion, but not as the Word of God. The Bible is reduced to the level of a human book, outstanding perhaps of its kind, but not above all other books. The Bible has to be studied comparatively, with other books of religion, poetry, history, or rational truth. It is inspired, but only in the same way as all other books are inspired, i.e. by the God immanent in all things. It is liable to error, because it is human, and all things human are equally liable to error. Thus the Bible ceases to be studied as a divine message, a Word of salvation; instead it comes to be studied as a product of the human spirit. In its investigation, questions of authorship, date, circumstances, style and development of thought replace the first and fundamental question, the question as to the content of the revelation of the Creator-Lord and Saviour.

The challenge of liberal Humanism to the orthodox view of the Bible consists also in the comprehension of the Bible within a world-scheme of human progress, although this scheme is in actual fact quite contrary to the teaching of the Bible itself. It is not our present concern to discuss the wider and deeper aspects of the doctrine of progress, important as these are. Our concern is to notice that, according to this doctrine, the thought of the Bible, the history which it records and the culture which it re-presents, are all approached from the human standpoint and forced into the universal human-istic scheme.

At two points this has serious consequences. First, it means that the sequence of the Bible history, as the Bible gives it, has to be rejected, because unfortunately it does not fit the evolu-tionary interpretation. The facts have to be sifted from the so-called additions of religious fancy and worked up into a new scheme. Second, it means that the message of the Bible has similarly to be treated and amended in order that a neat progression of religious thought may be observed. Even if it is granted that in the teaching of Jesus Christ the highest point of all religious thinking is reached, this teaching is still part of the development of the religious instincts and faculties of the race, and the Bible has no superior authority as such, only the authority of the highest human achievement in religion thus far. It will be seen that this is of a piece with the primary rejection of a transcendent God and a transcendent Word of God.

The challenge of liberal Humanism consists again in the individualistic subjectivism which it opposes to the objectivism of the orthodox doctrine of the Word of God. Outward authority is cast off and is replaced by the inward authority of the individual thought or experience. Reason here, emotion there, usurps the place of God. The thought or experience is valid and valuable, not because it accords with an external standard of divine truth, but because it is individual, a single manifestation of the divine spirit immanent in and working through all things. The thoughts and feelings of the great biblical figures have of course the same validity and value, possibly even the highest value, but only as similar manifesta-tions of the same spirit. This means not only that the basic authority of the Bible is rejected, not only that all religion is approached compar-atively and judged relatively, but that every individual becomes a law unto himself in religious matters. God is dethroned, humanity reigns, and in practice humanity means little more than individual man, the thinking or feeling self.

Some specific instances of OT and NT criticism might serve as illustrations. In the OT the first and most persistent theme was that Moses could not have been the author of the Pentateuch or the founder (under God) of the institutions and practices recorded therein. Instead, a theory of gradual literary and religious development was propounded which, instituted by Eichhorn, finally took shape in the Graf-Wellhausen hypothesis of the later 19th century. The heart of this view is that OT religion comes by evolution from below rather than by revela-tion from above. The documents are analysed, dissected, regrouped and redated (J, E, D and P in the Pentateuch) to provide the historical sequence of evidence for this view. More recently the documentary hypothesis has had to be considerably modified, but it has been replaced by similar concepts. The *Sitz im Leben* or Form-Criticism school (*cf.* Gunkel) attempts a thoroughgoing historical explanation of every passage of the OT by relating it to its known or conjectured historical setting. The Scandinavian school (*e.g.* Mowinckel), while prepared for an earlier dating of many passages, *e.g.* in the Psalms, attaches great significance to the back-ground of myth and ritual. A principle of comparative religion is thus invoked to account for the specific development of religion and religious literature in Israel. The modern move-ment of lexical study and biblical theology is on the whole healthier, for its basic concern is to present rather than to explain. Even here, how-ever, it might be presupposed that, *e.g.*, the doctrine of the living, self-revealing God is only a Hebrew concept. Documentary and historical reshuffling can also be adopted as the basis of presentation. Thus quite unwittingly the present-ation is controlled by beliefs alien to those which are in fact presented, with serious effects upon the alleged and intended objectivity.

In the NT field the triadic, Hegelian concept of historical development, which regarded conflict as the mark of authenticity and harmony as the sign of a post-apostolic age, produced the wild excesses of the Tübingen school, so that only a few Epistles remained to Paul. Strauss's *Life of Jesus*, with its attempt to sift the genuinely biographical material from legendary accretions, brought a first wave of demythologizing. Not unrelated was the Jesus of History school, which might lead on the one side to Harnack's reduc-tion of the gospel to divine fatherhood and human brotherhood, and on the other side to Reitzenstein's derivation of Paul's Christology, not from revelation, but from Hellenistic myth and mystery. Schweitzer made an important contribution early in the 20th century with his appreciation of the eschatological character of Jesus' teaching, though he himself, regarding it as mistaken, substituted a not very biblical mysticism, while others, such as Dodd, evaded the issue by putting all the emphasis on realized eschatology. The impasse reached in Synoptic source-criticism combined with other factors to produce the form-critical theory that the Gospels are made up of oral traditions which evolved in the church according to set patterns and on the basis of widely-varying authenticity. An even more developed historical scepticism reappears in Bultmann's demythologizing, which presupposes a mythological form for an essentially existential *kērygma*. Linguistic statistics might seem to bring back a refreshing objectivity on questions of authorship. Unfortunately, however, the use of computers is no safeguard against controlling presuppositions, at least in the NT field. Nor can findings based on implicit rejection of biblical authority be expected to prove anything about this authority either one way or the other. The ultimate problem lies, not in the data, but in the positive or negative response to the self-understanding which is in its way a primary datum.

This, then, is the liberal Protestant challenge to the authority of Holy Scripture. Apart from the detailed work which it necessitates in biblical theology and religion, and in relation to the individual writings, it also raises fundamental issues on which careful thought, definition and statement are demanded. The whole question of an absolute and authoritative revelation has to be considered; the question of that revelation in its relation to history, to Israel, to Jesus Christ, to the Bible itself as a literary product; the question of that revelation in its relation to the world religions, or to so-called natural religion. Again, there is the question of the inspiration of the Bible; the question of that inspiration in its relation to the ordinary poetic inspiration of which literature speaks; the question of the special working of the Holy Spirit of God in its relation to the general working in those activities which can be considered as products of common grace.

These matters have been dealt with in the past, but the new challenge carries with it a call, not for the abandonment of the old doctrine, not for its amendment, but for a new, careful and solidly-grounded statement of it. In one respect, too, it may be asked whether there is not something to be learned from liberal Protestantism even though its presuppositions are unhesitatingly rejected. Has it not pressed the Reformed doctrine of liberal exegesis further and attempted a more thorough relating of the Bible's message to the historical circumstances and even the literary form? The Bible is first of all God's book, as Jesus Christ is first of all Son of God; but it is a human book too, God's book in the world, as Jesus is the Son of man, the Word made flesh. Naturally, no-one who truly accepts the Bible's authority as the Word of God will wish to study the historical setting at the expense of the revealed message, but may he not wish to investigate the historical setting as the means to a better understanding of that message? Can there not be a true and reverent criticism—in the constructive and not the destructive sense— even when hostile and rationalistic criticism is uncompromisingly opposed?

Neo-orthodoxy

A third unorthodox teaching, which has grown up in recent years, largely as a reaction against contemporary Humanism, is that associated with the theology of Karl Barth, or at any rate with the development which that theology has undergone at the hands of many of his looser disciples. It is not easy to make definite pronouncements with regard to this movement, for Barth himself in his definitive *Church Dogmatics* both disowns much of his dialectical stage and also differs plainly from what has commonly come to be called Neo-orthodoxy. Indeed, his discussion of the precise question of the authority of Scripture brings him very close to biblical and Reformed teaching. Hence the wisest course will be to take a broad view of the neo-orthodox movement and to discuss the tendencies within it which are obvious deviations from the orthodox doctrine of Holy Scripture.

These deviations fall into two distinct classes, the one relating to the form of scriptural revelation, the Bible as a book, the other to the content of scriptural revelation, the Bible as the Word of God. As concerns the form, Neo-orthodoxy is at pains to emphasize that the Bible is, outwardly considered, one human book among others. This means that the principle of errancy is accepted. If some theologians, such as Barth, hesitate to list specific errors, others, such as Bultmann, regard the whole scientific and historical side of Scripture as unreliable. God is not the author of Scripture in the sense that He bears responsibility for its detailed words and phrases or backs its information. The Bible is truth in so far as God works through it in self-revelation. It is not truth, however, in the sense that all its statements are true. If God works only through the Bible, as some among the Neo-orthodox allow, it is by the sovereign choice of God, not because there is anything different about the Bible itself. If God uses a fallible book as the agent of revealing grace, this is no contradiction; it is the putting of divine treasure in earthen vessels, the mystery of divine grace, which forces us, as Bultmann puts it, to believe even though we cannot see. Lawful mystery is thus replaced by sheer irrationality, for while it is no doubt a mystery that eternal truth is revealed in temporal events and presented in human words, it is sheer unreason to say that this truth is revealed in and through that which is erroneous.

The second deviation relates to the content of scriptural revelation, the Bible as Word of God. The essential point of Neo-orthodoxy is that the Bible becomes God's Word as the Holy Spirit illumines and applies it to the individual soul. Inspiration is thus identified with what the Reformers call illumination. The authority of the Bible is the authority, not of the abiding text, but of the living voice of Scripture in the here and now of a given situation. Revelation in or through the Bible is revelation as the act of God, God's present revealing of Himself, not the given objective reality of what God has already said and done. It is along these lines that Barth makes an important distinction between revelation or inspiration as an active present on the one side and revealedness or inspiredness as a past passive on the other side. The former is endorsed as the genuine biblical and Reformed view, whereas the latter is rejected. It is interesting that Barth, as distinct from the majority of the Neo-orthodox, displays an awareness that the objective historical reality of the Bible's testimony must be given its due and proper weight. Nevertheless, he does not withdraw the fundamental distinction.

Now within the limits that there can be no objective Word of God without also the application to individual souls, there is truth in this distinction, but beyond those limits it leads in a dangerous direction. Pressed too far it means that the Bible can be authoritative, not as an outward word, but only as the Bible in the individual ego, as an inward experience. Thus, even with insistence upon the fact that Christianity rests upon unique historical events, even with stress upon the transcendence of God, in the last analysis we may easily be left with a faith which depends upon a subjective experience, and with the substantial autonomy of the individual ego. It is only a step from the anthropocentricity of Schleiermacher to the existentialism of Bultmann which is the complement of his demythologizing.

The questions raised by this theology are, of course, the central questions of all thinking upon the authority of Holy Scripture. They bring us to the very heart of the problem. Neo-orthodoxy has at least performed a service by showing that the categories of a dead (as opposed to a living) orthodoxy simply will not do. An abstract objectivism, or a mechanical conception of revelation, is as far from the truth on the one side as is a pure subjectivism or a naturalistic view of revelation on the other. Thus the ultimate problem is that of the relationship of revelation to history on the one side and to the individual believer on the other. Ought we to think that the Bible is trustworthy merely because we can demonstrate its historical accuracy? Ought we to think it authoritative merely because we have come to know the truth of its message through the Holy Spirit, and irrespective of its historical reliability? Ought we not to seek the authority of the Bible in the balanced relationship of the history (the objective Word) and the preaching (the Word applied subjectively by the Holy Ghost)—the history as that which is preached, the preaching as the application of this history?

A COMPARISON WITH THE INCARNATION

It may be suggested in closing that a true doctrine of history and revelation in the Bible will be formulated only when the problem is studied in the light of the similar problem of the incarnation. Christ, the Word revealed, is both God and man, the eternal Son historically incarnate, two natures, one Person. Neither if one denies the deity nor if one ignores the humanity is the true Christ perceived and believed. The man Jesus, very man, is known, confessed and obeyed as the Lord Christ, very God. As there is no incongruity in the Person, for He was conceived of the Holy Spirit, so there is no irrationality in the confession, for it is made in and by the Holy Spirit. This Man has the authority of the Lord.

Similarly Holy Scripture, the Word written, which bears witness to Christ, is both divine revelation and human record, the divine message historically written, of twofold origin, yet one book. To ignore either the divine or the human authorship is to miss the true reality of the Bible and the full profit of its teaching and direction. As there is no incompatibility between the revelation and the human writing, for it is inspired of God, so there is no schizophrenia in reading and believing it as the divine Word, for it is illuminated and authenticated by the Spirit. This book has the authority of the divine Word and testimony.

The parallel must not be pressed too far. For Jesus Christ is Himself God, the Creator, Lord, Revealer and Reconciler, whereas Holy Scripture, even though what is read therein may be read with full persuasion of its authenticity and truth, is still the creature and instrument of God. Nevertheless, the incarnational analogy, properly apprehended and developed as such, may well be the best guide to an understanding which is fully biblical and orthodox and which safeguards the authority and integrity of Scripture both as message and also as history.

G. W. BROMILEY

Revelation and inspiration

Christian theology as taught in the Bible is an organic unit, and should be studied as such. No part of it is properly understood except in relation to the whole. No single doctrine is mastered till one knows its place in the system. Our aim in this article is to formulate the view of revelation and inspiration which the Bible teaches and which underlies this Commentary. Accordingly, our first task must be to indicate the relation in which these topics stand to the rest of Christian truth. The doctrine of biblical inspiration, as we shall see, is a part of the general doctrine of revelation, which in its turn derives from, and must be constructed in terms of, the fundamental doctrines of creation and redemption. In the following exposition we shall try to exhibit these connections, and so to gain a fully biblical understanding of the subjects in question.

REVELATION

The English word 'revelation' may be taken either actively or passively. In the former sense it means that activity of God whereby He makes Himself known to men; in the latter, the knowledge thus imparted. The biblical idea of revelation must be elicited by means of a broad induction of evidence, of which the briefest outline must here suffice.

The Old Testament

The OT constantly affirms that Israel's existence and history as a nation, and her religion as a church, were wholly the result of divine revelation. God had revealed Himself in covenant to Abraham, as *his* God, and had pledged Himself to continue in covenant with Abraham's seed (Gn. 17). Accordingly, He had brought them out of captivity into the promised land, and made them a nation to serve Him (Ex. 6:2–8; 19:3–6; Ps. 105:43–45). He had given them His 'law' (*tôrâ*; lit. 'instruction'), and taught them how to worship Him. Throughout their history He raised up a succession of spokesmen to declare to them 'the word of the Lord'. Again and again at decisive moments He demonstrated His own complete control of circumstances by foretelling what He would do for them before the event (*cf.* Is. 48:3–7).

Israel was very conscious of the uniqueness of her relationship to God (Ps. 147:19, 20). True religion was, to her, precisely the knowledge of Yahweh, and presupposed Yahweh's self-disclosure in covenant. Lacking this, the Gentile world had fallen into idolatry. The revealed religion of Israel threw into relief the essential blasphemy of all other religion whatsoever. Hence, when God revealed Himself to other nations, with whom He had not entered into covenant, it was exclusively in judgment upon them for their sins (Ex. 7:5; Ezk. 25:11, 17; 28:22–24).

The OT verdict upon OT revelation was that it was not a complete whole, but preparatory for something greater. The prophets looked forward to a day when God would reveal Himself by mightier works than ever yet: He would raise up the Messiah, gather His scattered people and establish His kingdom among them. Heaven and earth would be made new (Is. 65:17–25); Israelite religion would be transformed (Je. 31:31–34); and all nations would see and acknowledge the glory of God in Israel as never before (Is. 60:1–14; Ezk. 36:23). On this forward-looking note the OT closes (Mal. 4).

The New Testament

The NT writers were convinced that the meaning of Jewish history and of the OT was to be found in Christ: that, in other words, the course of events in Israel from the very beginning and the composition of the OT over the centuries had been completely controlled by God with the incarnation in view. The implications of this claim led naturally to the fundamental theological idea in terms of which they expounded the subject of revelation. The idea is this: God, the sovereign Creator, who within His world 'accomplishes all things according to the counsel of his will' (Eph. 1:11), foresaw the ruin of the race through sin, determined to glorify Himself by saving a church, and appointed His Son to effect its salvation by His mediatorial ministry. World history has been to date, and will be to the end, nothing more nor less than God's execution of the plan which He then formed in order to compass His goal. After the Son had been raised, exalted and enthroned in His Messianic kingdom, He sent the Holy Spirit into the world in order both to complete the disclosure, which He had Himself commenced while on earth, of His Father's purposes for the church, and also to bring His people, through faith in Himself, into the possession and enjoyment of the salvation He won for them. The revelation of God's plan was duly completed by the Spirit, who made it known in full to the apostles; its performance will be completed by Christ at His 'appearing' (*parousia*), when the church will be made perfect.

This, in barest outline, is the dogmatic framework which underlies the NT teaching about revelation. It is most fully stated in Paul's Epistles (*cf.* Rom. 8:28–39; Eph. 1:3–14, *etc.*) and John's Gospel (*cf.* 6:37–45; 10:14–18, 27–29; 16:7–15; 17), but is more or less explicit everywhere. The main passages relating to revelation fall into three classes:

Passages concerning Christ's disclosure of God. The Son is the perfect image of the Father (2 Cor. 4:4; Col. 1:15; Heb. 1:3) and so is in Himself a perfect revelation of the Father to those who have eyes to see (Jn. 1:18; 14:7–11). All God's 'fullness' dwelt in the incarnate Son (Col. 1:19; 2:9). Those who understand the full significance of His life and death thereby understand the whole eternal purpose ('wisdom') of God for the church's salvation (Col. 2:2, 3; 1 Cor. 1:24 and 2:7–10; see also next section). None can apprehend any part of Christ's revelation of His Father without supernatural spiritual enlightenment (Jn. 3:3–12; 6:44, 45; Mt. 16:17; Gal. 1:16).

Passages concerning God's disclosure of His plan. God's comprehensive scheme for the salvation of His elect out of every nation, Jew and Gentile alike, was the 'mystery', the divine 'wisdom', which God conceived before creation but concealed until the apostolic age. Now it was revealed, and the full meaning of Israel's election and history and of the OT revelation for the first time became clear. All the time God's goal had been, not the salvation of one of the world's many nations, but the creation of a new nation, the members of which were to be drawn from every nation and to receive their spiritual nationality, not by natural, but by spiritual birth (*cf.* 1 Pet. 2:9, 10). The destiny of the regenerate was to be glorified, as their Head ('the first fruits' of the new race, 1 Cor. 15:20, 23) had been already; and His very presence in heaven, 'the *man* in the glory', was a pledge to them that they would some day share that glory with Him. Paul deals with the revelation of this mystery in several important passages which should be carefully studied (Eph. 1:8–12; 3:3–11; 1 Cor. 2:7–10; Rom. 16:25, 26; *cf.* 11:25–36; 2 Tim. 1:9–11). The source of this revelation is God; the mediator of it is Christ (Gal. 1:12; *cf.* Rev. 1:1); the agent in its communication is the Spirit (1 Cor. 2:10–12; 2 Cor. 3:15–18; *cf.* 4:6; Eph. 3:5). In order that it might be conveyed to the church intact, the Spirit inspired the words of apostolic testimony (1 Cor. 2:13), as He had inspired the words of Christ (Jn. 3:34; *cf.* 12:48–50). He caused the apostles to embody the revelation given to them in a 'standard of teaching', the 'pattern of the sound words' (Gk. *typos*, a 'pattern', 'standard'; see Rom. 6:17; *cf.* 2 Tim. 1:13). This is 'the sound doctrine' (1 Tim. 1:10; *cf.* 6:3; 2 Tim. 4:3; Tit. 1:9; 2:1), the apostolic 'tradition' (2 Thes. 2:15; 3:6), the test and norm for the faith and life of the churches.

Passages concerning God's performance of His plan. As was said, God discloses His purposes by what He does as well as in what He says; and any action which marks a further stage in His plan of redemptive history may be called 'revelation'. The NT knows two such acts of revelation yet to come: the appearing of antichrist (2 Thes. 2:3, 6, 8) and the *parousia* of Jesus (1 Cor. 1:7; 2 Thes. 1:7–10; 1 Pet. 1:7, 13). The latter concludes history and ushers in the day of judgment. Christ will then reveal by executive action God's eternal intentions with respect to the impenitent and the saints, wrath for the one and glory for the other (Rom. 2:5–10; 8:18; *cf.* 1 Pet. 1:5).

Such, in brief, is the biblical material from which the theological doctrine of revelation must be constructed. To this task we now turn.

The original revelation

The doctrine of revelation is grounded upon the fact that God made man in His own image, to know, love, worship, serve and so glorify Him. We saw that man's religion, if it is to be true, must be grounded on God's revelation; and God accordingly revealed Himself to Adam as fully as was necessary for Adam to live in fellowship with Him. Adam knew God, then, first through His works of creation. The world on which he looked out bore eloquent testimony to the power and wisdom of its Maker. The created order, though since involved in Adam's ruin (Gn. 3:18; Rom. 8:19–22), still proclaims God's glory (Ps. 19:1f.; Rom. 1:19, 20); much more must it have done so before. Adam knew God, too, by his knowledge of himself; as God's noblest creature, he was a part of God's revelation of His glory, as well as being its recipient. Again, God's works of providence brought him knowledge of his Maker's goodness. If, despite the chaos that has entered the world through sin, the course of events still bears this testimony (Acts 14:17), doubtless it did so far more clearly to Adam when he knew only the garden, the animals God had brought him to rule, and the wife He had made for him (Gn. 2:18–24). Finally, the testimony of God's works was supplemented by verbal revelation (how conveyed we do not know) as and when necessary (Gn. 2:16, 17).

Much of this is necessarily obscure to us. The knowledge of God that Adam enjoyed in Eden before the Fall is as far beyond our comprehension as is the knowledge of God which the church will enjoy in heaven after the resurrection. But the permanent characteristics of God's self-revealing activity are already here made plain, and it is worth our while to pause and note them.

The purpose of revelation. God makes Himself known to man so that man may attain the end of his creation, which is to know, love and worship Him. The transcendent Creator is inaccessible to His creatures until He discloses Himself, and man's knowledge of God, where it exists, is correlative to and consequent on God's prior self-revelation. Adam in Eden needed revelation if he was to live in fellowship with God.

The means of revelation. Revelation is God's personal self-disclosure to His rational creatures. The relationship which it initiates is compared in Scripture to that of husband and wife, father and son, friend and friend (*cf.* Je. 3; Ho. 11:1; Is. 41:8; Mt. 7:11; Jn. 15:15; Eph. 5:25–27). Such a relationship could not be created apart from personal address by God to man. God must open His mind; He must speak. Action out of the context of conversation, movement divorced from explanation, is a very limited medium for making oneself known to another. It was not enough for Adam to see God in His works; he needed to hear His word, to receive verbal or propositional revelation.

Of course, there is more to self-revelation than merely communicating information about oneself, just as there is more to faith than a mere 'notional' acquaintance with truths. In human relationships, personal attitudes, by their very nature, cannot be expressed in propositional form. Their existence can be indicated, and their nature to some extent suggested, by speech, but they can be expressed, and so fully manifested, only by action. So, when God reveals His love to men, the depths of meaning contained in the words in which He avows it to them become clear only in the light of their experience of what He does for them. God's personal attitudes towards men, therefore, require works as well as words for their revelation. But this does not affect our present contention, which is, simply, that without words such revelation could scarcely take place at all.

The effectiveness of revelation. An unfathomable mystery underlies the claim that the transcendent, infinite Creator makes His thoughts known to finite man. But we may not imagine that God is somehow hampered or thwarted in His self-revealing action by the limitations of man's mind. That man's knowledge of God on earth is now, and was before the Fall, imperfect, dim and inadequate to its object in very many ways, is not to be denied. But God made man's mind; and He made it as He did in order that man might be able to apprehend Him in a manner perfectly adequate for the ends of His self-disclosure—*i.e.* for the development of the religious relationship which was man's destiny. He made Adam's mind such that Adam could not but apprehend as much of God as was disclosed to him. And when God reveals Himself to sinful man, He restores to him his lost ability to recognize God's Word for what it is and receive it as such. The activity of trust which results from the exercise of this faculty is in Scripture termed faith; and in Heb. 11:3 the faculty itself is so denoted. It appears correct to say that, in this sense, Adam in Eden had faith, and that it is no more than a restoration to man of what he lost at the Fall when the Spirit implants the faculty of faith in those to whom God intends to make Himself known.

When man fell, he jeopardized his status and corrupted his nature. God therefore adapted His self-disclosing activity to the new situation, integrating it into the redemptive process which He had at once initiated in order to remedy sin's effects. But the three features of revelation noted above remained, and remain, constant.

God revealed as Redeemer

Through sin, man lost his ability to apprehend creation's witness to its God. The meaning and message of the book remained the same, but he could no longer read it; the heavens proclaimed God's glory into deaf ears. 'They did not see fit ('disdained', Moff.) to acknowledge God' (Rom. 1:28). Man had lost his natural inclination to love and serve his Creator; the idea of a life so spent was profoundly distasteful to him (Rom. 8:7). There remained in his heart an indelible sense of God, *i.e.* an awareness that there was something or someone greater than himself whom he should worship and serve, but he refused to let it lead him back to his Maker; for he was now under the sway of unbelief, which the Bible depicts as a positive, devilish thing, a passionate energy of blind denial, a resolute repudiation of the true God (*cf.* Rom. 1:21–32; Eph. 2:2, 3; 4:17–19).

In this situation, the insufficiency of God's self-revelation in creation and providence is manifest. God still shows Himself in His works (Rom. 1:19, 20); but men shut their eyes, and 'by their wickedness suppress the truth' (Rom. 1:18). Thus the continuance of the original revelation leads none to the knowledge of God and serves only to leave the world without excuse for its ignorance of Him. And, even supposing that fallen man succeeded in reading 'the book of the creatures' aright, what he read could only drive him to despair. For this *general revelation* (as it is best called) brings knowledge of a God who hates and punishes man's disobedience and ingratitude (Rom. 1:18), and says not a word about redeeming love. The good news that the God who is merciless to sin is at the same time merciful to sinners is made known only by *special revelation*, which centres upon Jesus Christ; and to this we now turn.

Since the Fall, the Creator has been making Himself known as Redeemer upon the stage of human history, working out the eternal purpose which, as we saw, constitutes the 'mystery' which the apostles declared. The whole plan hinged upon the earthly ministry of the incarnate Son. In the fact of Christ all the types, shadows and prophecies of the OT found their meaning, so that by it Israel's Scriptures were fulfilled (*cf.* Mt. 5:17; Lk. 24:27; Jn. 5:39; Acts 13:26–33; Heb. 7–10). Again, upon this ministry all subsequent redemptive activity is grounded. When He ascended, Christ entered upon the exercise of His heavenly ministry, whereby He conveys to His people by His Spirit the benefits which He secured for them while on earth, and this ministry will not be completed until He perfects His church at His return. And only when the whole church is made perfect, possessing and exhibiting in all its fullness the glory of God (Rev. 21:11), and appearing with its glorified Saviour in a new-created universe (Rev. 21:1-22:5), will God's resources and intentions in redemption be fully manifested, and His purpose of perfect self-display be finally accomplished. Meanwhile, every act of grace brings it one stage nearer completion. The new creation, therefore, no less than the old, God's works of special grace as well as those of common providence, are works of revelation, every one of which declares the glory of God.

Verbal revelation

In the redemptive process by which the church is saved, verbal revelation has an indispensable place. First of all, it was an integral element in the series of acts by which redemption was wrought out. Without verbal revelation, Abraham would never have entered Canaan, nor Moses led Israel from Egypt, nor Jesus' life been preserved in infancy (cf. Gn. 12:1–5; Ex. 3:1 – 6:13; Mt. 2:13–15). Secondly, verbal revelation has always been necessary as a ground for faith. Its importance from this point of view is seen when we consider the soteriological significance of faith. Not merely is faith, as an activity, the instrument whereby a sinner lays hold of Christ and so obtains all promised benefits, but also, as a faculty, faith is, as we saw, the organ of that knowledge of and fellowship with God from which man fell and to which redemption restores him.

Now, the object which brings this faculty into exercise is God's Word, as such (cf. 1 Thes. 2:13). Faith 'hears His voice' and responds to His Word of promise in trust and obedience. Without a word from God, faith cannot be (Rom. 10:17). The reason for this is clear. Without an explanatory word, God's redemptive action could not even be recognized for what it was. The creature, as we saw, cannot know the Creator's mind till He speaks. The case of the incarnation shows that the clearest revelation of God is nevertheless the most opaque to man. Christ, the personal Word of God, expressed and effected His Father's redemptive purpose completely. In Him, God fully manifested Himself in redemptive action; and, for that very reason, the fact of Christ utterly transcended man's powers of interpretation. 'It may be doubted', wrote B. B. Warfield, 'whether even the supreme revelation of God in Jesus Christ could have been known as such in the absence of preparatory, accompanying and succeeding explanatory revelation in words.' Even that is an understatement. How could man ever have learned the utterly paradoxical and eternally mysterious truth, that Jesus was God incarnate and put away the world's sins by dying on a cross, without being told? Accordingly, in order to make possible faith in Christ, God gave the world a verbal explanation of the fact of Christ. This was the gospel, the apostolic kērygma, which announces God's gift of the living Word and promises

eternal life to those who receive Him. It thus appears that the giving of propositional revelations concerning God's redemptive action in history is no mere adjunct or appendage to that action, but is itself part of it, as essential a link in the chain as the events with which those revelations are concerned. For God's redemptive programme includes the conveyance as well as the procuring of salvation, and is not complete until sinners have been restored to faith and knowledge of God through the gospel.

In form and substance, the gospel promise has been one and the same throughout redemptive history, from the time of Adam and Abraham to the present day, namely, a covenant on God's part to be the God of the one to whom He speaks and to safeguard and reward him, both in this life and the next, if he will trust and obey. Saving faith, therefore, has been the same thing from Abel's time onwards (Heb. 11:4). In content, however, the promise grew richer as time went on; for, within the framework of His covenant pledge, God gradually disclosed both the particular blessings which it included and also the objective ground—His own redemptive action—upon which it was based. This revelatory process continued intermittently for centuries. It was thus progressive: not in the sense that each new revelation antiquated the last, but rather in the sense that from time to time God underlined and amplified what He had taught already and added to it further intimations of what He intended to do until He had completed the pattern of truth which was to be fulfilled in Christ. Then, at the appointed time, He sent His Son to achieve redemption and crowned the revelatory process with the unveiling of the gospel and the 'mystery'. From first to last, the progress of revelation had been closely interlocked with the unfolding of God's plan of redemptive history; and the interpretation of the fact of Christ, itself the complete disclosure in action of the Creator as Redeemer, completed it.

The means by which verbal revelation was given were many and varied. Sometimes an abnormal quality of experience was the vehicle of its reception. This was the case with visions, dreams, and prophetic inspiration, which seems to have ranged on occasion from the slow crystallizing of prolonged meditations at one extreme to the hurricane rapture of complete ecstasy at the other. Sometimes, again, God conveyed truth through His chosen organs of revelation merely by His divine concursus—by operating, that is, in and with them in the exercise of their own natural powers and so leading them to His truth through the normal processes of their own thought—historical research, exegesis of canonical Scripture, meditation and prayer, logical and theological reasoning. Much of the Wisdom literature, the OT historical books and all the NT writings save the Apocalypse appear to have resulted from revelation of this sort. Limitations of space preclude any discussion of these modes of revelation. But it is important to notice before we pass on that there is in Scripture no indication of any difference in the purity and reliability of revelations mediated through these various kinds of experience. All organs of revelation, however limited they may appear in themselves, become in the hands of the sovereign God completely effective to the end for which He employs them.

Biblical revelation

In order to ensure the safe preservation of what He had revealed, God 'inscripturated' it. The book which He thereby produced contains, not all the verbal revelations ever given (*cf., e.g.*, the reference in 2 Ch. 9:29 to prophetic books which have not survived), but those which were relevant for the book's designed purpose; which was, not merely to provide a ground for personal faith and guidance for individual Christian living, but also to enable the world-wide church in every age to understand itself, to interpret its history, to reform and purify its life continually, and to rebuff all assaults made upon it, whether from within, by sin and heresy, or from without, by persecution and rival ideologies. All the problems that ever faced or will face the church are in principle covered and solved in this book. For the Christian Bible, though a very human book, recording much sin and error, reflecting in many places the weaknesses and limitations of its authors, is yet—and this is the fundamental truth about it—a divine product, whose *auctor primarius* is God.

The proof of this divine authorship of the Bible (*i.e.* the proper ground of faith in it) may here be indicated. It is twofold:

The testimony of Christ (the external proof). This proof comprises two propositions. First, Christ's authority demands the acceptance of the OT as divinely inspired. His witness concerning its character is unambiguous and emphatic. To Him, it was not a miscellany but a unity, 'scripture' (singular: Jn. 10:35), whose authority was permanent and absolute because of its divine origin (*cf.* Mt. 5:17–20; Lk. 16:17; Mt. 19:4–6). Arguments from Scripture, therefore, possessed for Him clinching force (Mt. 22:32, 41ff.; Jn. 10:34, 35, *etc.*). The emphatic 'it is written' was final, and settled matters. His whole ministry was one great testimony to His acceptance of the divine authority of the OT; for He preached and healed and died in obedience to what He found written (*cf.* Mt. 8:16, 17; 26:24, 54; Lk. 4:18–21; 18:31–33; 22:37). He, the teacher to whom the Christian church professes subjection, was Himself in everything subject to His Father's word in the OT Scriptures. The apostolic writers everywhere echo this witness (*cf.* 2 Tim. 3:16; 2 Pet. 1:20, 21, the phrase 'oracles of God' in Rom. 3:2, and the quotation of OT passages, spoken in their context by men, as words of God, or of the Holy Ghost, *e.g.* Mt. 19:4, 5; Acts 4:25, 26; 13:34, 35; Heb. 1:6ff.; 3:7).

Second, Christ's authority demands the accept-ance of the NT as possessing the same character as the OT. Jesus taught His disciples to read the OT Christologically, as a prophetic revelation of the things concerning Himself (Lk. 24:24, 25, 44, 45; Jn. 5:39, 46). The apostles did so (*cf.* Acts 3:18, 24; 1 Pet. 1:10–12), claiming that it was written primarily for the guidance and benefit of Christian believers (*cf.* Rom. 4:23, 24; 15:4; 1 Cor. 9:10; 10:11; 2 Tim. 3:16), and that it could not be understood at all by those who would not read it in the light of Christ (2 Cor. 3:14–16).

Now, seeing that God had inscripturated His earlier, prophetic revelations so that they might be permanently accessible in an uncorrupted form for the benefit, not merely of old Israel, but of the church universal, it would have been an unaccountable departure from a way of working so well established, and so patently wise and desirable, had He done nothing similar when His crowning revelation was given to the world. The NT, therefore, was only to be expected. Against the background of this presumption, certain facts acquire unmistakable significance. i. Christ promised the Spirit to the apostles so that they might remember and understand what He had taught them already (Jn. 14:25, 26) and receive the further revelations concerning Himself which they could not as yet 'bear' (Jn. 16:12–14). So equipped, they were to be His authoritative witnesses and interpreters to the whole church, in all ages and all parts of the world (Jn. 17:20; *cf.* Mt. 28:19). How, we may ask, could Christ have envisaged this, unless He intended them to write their testimony? ii. The apostles claim that, in virtue of their possession of the Spirit, they teach and write the pure truth of God. They are verbally inspired (1 Cor. 2:13); and a genuinely 'spiritual' man recognizes this fact (1 Cor. 14:37; *cf.* Gal. 1:8; 2 Thes. 3:6, 14). These are unqualified affirmations; and there is no question but that by making them the apostles claimed, and intended to claim, an authority for their own sermons and letters no less absolute than that which they attributed to the OT. iii. Paul quotes Deuteronomy and Luke together, and Peter refers to Paul's Epistles as part of the Canon of Scripture (1 Tim. 5:18; 2 Pet. 3:16). iv. Centuries of Christian exegesis have demonstrated that, theologically, the two Testaments together form an organic unit, each complementing the other in a harmonious testimony to Christ, each bringing to light more and more of the contents and meaning of the other in an endlessly fruitful dialectic of fore-shadowing and fulfilment.

We conclude, that, in the light of Christ's evident intention that His apostles should write their testimony and His promise to equip them for the task, the claims they made for themselves and each other, and the quality of what they produced, lead us irresistibly to acknowledge the NT as the expected and needed completion of the OT.

The testimony of the Spirit (the internal

16

proof). We saw that it is by the use of the faculty of faith that we discern God's Word for what it is. Faith sees the real nature of that at which it looks. This has been the church's experience down the ages. Since it is the Spirit who implants faith and works in believers their acts of faith, the presence of this conviction is termed the Spirit's witness. (See further pp. 6f.)

The Bible, then, is the revealed Word of God, in the sense that in its pages God speaks His mind—all His mind—concerning His purpose for His people. To call the Bible a record of, or a witness to, a revelation made in history is insufficient. The Bible is all this, and more. It is not merely a report of what God said; it is what He says, here and now. It is itself a link in the chain of God's redemptive action. Its contents, heard or read, are the means whereby, on the grounds of the historical ministry of Christ which it records and explains, and through the regenerating action of the Spirit who works in and with the Word, sinners come to know the Father and the Son. It is not the Word of God in the sense that every separate sentence, including the words of evil men, expresses His mind or reflects His will. 'God's Word written' is the Bible as a whole, or, more accurately, the theology of the Bible, that organic unity which our fathers so happily and suggestively termed 'the body of divinity'. Here is the image of God's mind, the transcript of His thoughts, the declaration of His grace, the verbal embodiment of all the treasures of wisdom and knowledge that are hid in His Son. And here faith rests.

INSPIRATION

The meaning of inspiration

Inspiration is not itself a biblical word. It is usually, and most conveniently, defined as a supernatural influence of God's Spirit upon the biblical authors which ensured that what they wrote was precisely what God intended them to write for the communication of His truth, and hence could be truly termed 'inspired', Gk. *theopneustos*, lit. 'breathed out by God' (2 Tim. 3:16). We have already dealt with this subject in constructive statement (see p. 16), and confine ourselves here to the correction of some misconceptions.

The 'inspiration' which secured the infallible communication of revealed truth is something distinct from the 'inspiration' of the creative artist, which does not. The two things should not therefore be confused. Nor does inspiration always imply an abnormal state of mind in the writer, *e.g.* a trance-state, a vision, or the hearing of a voice; nor does it imply the obliteration of his personality. God in His providence prepared the human vehicles of inspiration for their task, and caused them in many, perhaps most, cases to perform it through the normal exercise of the powers He had given them. Many states of mind, as we saw, were compatible with inspiration. There is no reason to think that the authors were always aware that they were being inspired in the sense defined, *i.e.* that they were writing canonical Scripture. Nor is there any ground for asserting that an inspired document could not in God's providence have been compiled from sources by an ordinary process of historical composition, or passed through various editions and recensions before reaching its final form. All that is claimed is that the finished product is *theopneustos*, precisely what God intended for the communication of saving truth.

Since truth is communicated through words, and verbal inaccuracy misrepresents meaning, inspiration must be verbal in the nature of the case. And if the words of Scripture are 'God-breathed', it is almost blasphemy to deny that it is free from error in that which it is intended to teach and infallible in the guidance it gives. Inerrancy and infallibility cannot be proved (nor, let us note, disproved) by argument. Both are articles of faith; corollaries of the confession, which Christ's teaching demands and the Spirit's testimony evokes, that canonical Scripture was breathed out by the God who cannot lie. He who denies them thereby shows that he rejects the witness of Christ, the apostles and the historic Christian church concerning the nature of 'God's Word written', and either does not possess or has not understood the *testimonium Spiritus Sancti internum*.

The problems of inspiration

No Christian doctrine is free from problems; and that for a very good reason. God has put forward His truth as an object for faith, and the proper ground of faith is God's own authoritative testimony. Now, acceptance on grounds of another's authority and acceptance on grounds of rational demonstration are two distinct things. Man's original sin was a lust after self-sufficient knowledge, a craving to shake off all external authority and work things out for himself (*cf.* Gn. 3:5, 6); and God deliberately presents saving truth to sinners in such a way that their acceptance of it involves an act of intellectual repentance, whereby they humble themselves and submit once more to be taught by Him. Thus they renounce their calamitous search after a self-made wisdom (*cf.* Rom. 1:22; 1 Cor. 1:19–25) in order to regain the kind of knowledge for which they were made, that which comes from taking their Creator's word. So as to make this renunciation clear-cut, God has ensured that no single article of faith should be demonstrable as, say, a geometrical theorem is, nor free from unsolved mystery. Man must be content to know by faith, and to know, in this world at any rate, in part. We must not, therefore, expect to find the doctrine of biblical inspiration free from difficulties, any more than are the doctrines of the Trinity, incarnation, or atonement. Nor must we expect to be able to solve all its problems in this world. Nor must we wonder that Christians easily fall into heresy over this doctrine, as over others. It is worth while, however, briefly to indicate the right attitude for faith to adopt in face of some prevalent errors concerning it.

First, the doctrine is sometimes diluted by those who profess to be its friends. It is said that the Bible is the product of inspiration in some sense, but not of verbal inspiration. God revealed truth to the writers, but it was inevitable that, being sinful, fallible men, they should distort it in the course of reporting it. We must expect, therefore, to find error in Scripture. This, however, as we saw, was not the view of Christ and the apostles. It appears to be a mistaken inference from the admitted fact that not all the biblical books are on the same level of spiritual profundity and doctrinal finality; but it amounts to a flat denial that God in His sovereign providence could do what it was evidently desirable that He should do, and so prepare and control the human instruments through whom He caused Scripture to be written that they put down exactly what He intended, no more and no less. In other words, the Bible, on this view, is neither what God intended it should be, nor what Christ thought and taught that it was. Such a position is plainly intolerable.

Secondly, the doctrine is sometimes rejected on the grounds of the internal characteristics of the Bible. Such objections, however, invariably prove on examination to be grounded upon an *a priori*, man-made idea of what a verbally inspired Bible ought to be like, and the very act of bringing them forward as valid grounds for doubting what God says about His book is itself a sign of continued intellectual impenitence, unconscious, perhaps, but no less real for that. The believing method of approach is, rather, to start by accepting God's testimony that the Bible is verbally inspired and then to examine the internal characteristics of Scripture in order to find out what this verbally-inspired Bible is in fact like. The most cursory inspection shows that inspiration has completely accommodated itself to the thought-forms, literary methods, stylistic conventions and characteristic vocabulary of the writers. These are the media through which the inspired truth-content is conveyed, and unless we take pains to acquire a sympathetic understanding of them we shall be in danger of misinterpreting what God has said in terms of them, and thus manufacturing errors where none exist. We must be guided in biblical study by the principle—which is a certainty of faith—that Scripture nowhere misrepresents the truths it was inspired to teach and that every biblical fact has been recorded in the way best adapted for the communication of what the church is meant to learn from it. What that is, however, can be determined in each case only by examining the passage in the context of Scripture as a whole. This is a principle of fundamental importance for biblical interpretation. We must not lose sight of it through controversial preoccupations, nor allow our confidence in its truth to be shaken by difficulties which may confront us when we try to apply it.

One example of its application may be given here. It has sometimes been asserted that the occasional appearance in the OT of sub-Christian attitudes, actions and theological reflections is itself a refutation of the doctrine of an inspired Scripture. But this objection reveals a misunderstanding of the nature of the Bible. We stressed earlier that the Bible is not an aggregate of isolated texts, but an organism, no part of which can be rightly interpreted except in terms of its place and function in the whole. Now, God has included in His Word much exemplary material; and some of the examples He has recorded are bad examples. All is for our learning; but we must learn from different parts of Scripture in different ways. We learn from records of theological and practical error, not by supposing that, because they are included in Scripture, the words and deeds in question must have met with divine approval, but by detecting the mistakes in the light of Bible doctrine and taking warning. Principles of biblical theology must interpret, as they are in their turn illustrated by, facts of biblical history and biography. Scripture must interpret scripture. Once it is grasped that the Bible is an organic unity, that the Word of God is its doctrine as a whole, and that each passage must be understood in the light of, even as it throws light upon, the truth as it is in Jesus, the grounds for this kind of objection vanish.

Lack of space forbids any further development of these principles here. We would conclude by reiterating our fundamental contention, that faith's attitude to the doctrine of biblical inspiration, as to all other doctrines, is one of acceptance on God's testimony. Nothing, therefore, will shake faith's certainty here, for nothing can shake the testimony on which it rests. When faced by difficulties in and objections to the doctrine as he understands it, the believer will infer that the cause is his own failure to comprehend God's testimony rather than God's failure to make the truth plain, and will accordingly be driven back to a closer re-thinking of the matter in the light of a closer study of the biblical evidence. This is how all doctrinal advance has been made throughout the history of the church. And this is how a truer and fuller understanding of the doctrine of Holy Scripture as the inspired, and therefore infallible and inerrant, Word of God, can be reached in our own day.

J. I. PACKER

The history of Israel

The history of Israel is not merely of academic interest: it is of vital importance because God chose to reveal Himself in the down-to-earth experience of a people. He proved Himself to be a God of action who acted in history so that His purposes in choosing Israel might be fulfilled. That is why the history books of the OT were called by the Jews the 'Former Prophets': the history revealed God's ways; when read in that light it will become full of meaning.

The patriarchs. Gn. 11:27 – 50:26

The nation descended from Abraham, Isaac and Jacob, with whom the history begins. This assertion would be questioned by many scholars, who think that later theological insights have so moulded Israel's early traditions that they cannot be read as straightforward history, and yet it can be supported by external evidence from a mass of material unearthed from the Ancient Near East. While the OT remains our only source of information about the patriarchs, the world in which they lived in the first half of the 2nd millennium BC has been documented in an astonishing way. From tablets found at Mari and Nuzi we know that individuals in Semitic tribes bore names such as we find in the patriarchal narratives; customs recorded in Genesis are referred to there; journeys made by the patriarchs were along routes now known to have been highways of commerce at that period; conditions in Transjordan and Palestine known from contemporary sources agree with the picture given in the biblical narrative. Such correspondences plainly support the historicity of the patriarchal narratives, for conditions changed during the 14th century BC, when a period of political upheavals began, and were never again reproduced.

Abraham's original home was Ur of the Chaldees, a city already ancient in his day. He migrated to Haran in northern Mesopotamia but subsequently moved into Canaan, where Isaac, Jacob and Jacob's twelve sons continued to live as semi-nomads. Jealousy of Joseph, the favourite son of his father, caused his elder brothers to sell him into slavery, and thus he arrived in Egypt, eventually to be exalted to the highest rank under the pharaoh, who most probably belonged to the Asiatic Hyksos dynasty which controlled Egypt c. 1710–1570 BC. God's providence in using Joseph to organize the food supplies in Egypt, and so to save his family from starvation, is clearly demonstrated. Once settled in Goshen (in the E Delta) Israel's descendants

stayed there long after the famine had ended; their prosperity and fecundity made them a considerable proportion of the population, so that a 'king . . . who did not know Joseph' feared them and subjected them to slavery, till they longed and prayed to escape. The building operations described at the beginning of the book of Exodus are generally identified with those of Sethos I (1302–1290) and Rameses II (1290–1224), who re-established Egypt's capital in the NE Delta after a gap of more than 250 years.

Moses and the Exodus. Ex. 2:1 – 15:21

The account of the infancy and providential training of Moses is well known. His name (Heb. *Mōšeh*) means 'one who draws forth' (Ex. 2:10). The Egyptian name, found in compounds such as Tuthmosis, means 'child', and would be the obvious sound-equivalent. There is ample evidence that Semites permeated every stratum of Egyptian society in the New Kingdom, and that Moses would not have been the only foreigner being trained at court for a responsible post in the government. His rash murder of an Egyptian occasioned his flight eastwards to the Sinai peninsula, where he found a home with the Midianite Jethro/Reuel, and spent his days sheep-minding under the desert conditions to which he was later to return with the Israelites.

Only the insistent call of the God of his fathers at the burning bush could move Moses to return to Egypt to deliver Israel from the iron grip of the pharaoh. Disastrous plagues that ruined the economy and proved the impotence of Egypt's gods, the Nile, the frog, the sun, hardened the pharaoh's opposition until the death of the first-born forced him to yield. The whole sequence of events, beginning with the plagues and ending with the path across the Red Sea (most probably one of the modern Bitter Lakes), demonstrated unmistakably the intervention of God to redeem His people from slavery. Its full significance was made plain at Sinai: God had brought them out of Egypt to make them His own, and Moses acted as mediator in establishing the covenant between God and the people, who undertook to keep all God's will revealed in His law (Ex. 19:1–8; 24:1–11). Redeemed from slavery they were now to inherit a land of their own where they could live according to the religious and social pattern laid down for them.

That the Exodus is a historical event is no longer doubted. It is improbable that a background of slavery would be invented; prophets and psalmists refer constantly to the deliverance from Egypt and to the covenant made at Sinai, for their own message is based upon these events and the law then given. Most scholars agree that the Exodus took place in the 13th century BC because conditions in Egypt at that period best agree with the information given in the biblical accounts. According to a monument inscribed by Pharaoh Merenptah in 1220 BC, Israel was already in Canaan by that date. The Exodus is therefore dated c. 1280, and the entry into Canaan c. 1240, though it is not yet possible to reconcile every detail with these dates. For this reason some still hold a 15th-century date, while others would prefer one slightly later than 1280. For a fuller discussion see the Introduction to Exodus.

The conquest and occupation of Canaan. Joshua, Judges, 1 Sa. 1–7

Moses' leadership continued throughout the desert wanderings until his death on Mt. Nebo, within sight of the promised land. His successor, Joshua, had already been commissioned to take the Israelites across the river Jordan, to conquer and exterminate the inhabitants of the land, and to settle the tribes in their inheritance. According to the writer of Joshua events again proved the power of their covenant God working on their behalf: the Jordan in flood was dammed upstream, so enabling an easy crossing by the fords of Jericho (Jos. 3:1 – 4:24); the city of Jericho fell without a battle (Jos. 5:13 – 6:27); victory in the nearby hill country at Bethel-Ai, followed by Joshua's decisive defeat of first the southern and then the northern coalitions, forced the whole population to admit his supremacy (Jos. 7:1 – 12:24). Yet he did not leave an occupying army behind him. Throughout the campaigns his headquarters were at Gilgal in the Jordan valley, where the territory was divided between the tribes, each of which had to fight its own battles in occupying and possessing its land. This fact explains some apparent contradictions within Joshua-Judges. Some cities, defeated and destroyed once, would be rebuilt and repopulated, only to be taken again. Jabin king of Hazor was killed by Joshua (Jos. 11:1, 10), but was evidently succeeded by an heir of the same name (Jdg. 4:2). Jerusalem had a chequered career: cf. Jos. 15:63 with Jdg. 1:8, 21.

This general picture is confirmed by archaeological excavations. The sites of Bethel and Lachish show evidence of destruction in the latter half of the 13th century BC, while at Hazor the lower city was destroyed then, never to be inhabited again. The site of Ai is not certain, and nothing significant remains of the Jericho of Joshua's day. The massive walls, once thought to have belonged to the city Joshua destroyed, are now known to date from the Early Bronze Age, over 1,000 years earlier.

Some scholars assert that the presentation of the history given in Joshua is an over-simplification: that much of the Israel of the judges' period had not descended from those who experienced the Exodus, that the arrangement into twelve tribes was a later artificial imposition on the facts, and that the conquest of the land was a complex process, undertaken not as a united effort, but by individual tribes at different periods. A fuller discussion of these views is given in the commentary on Joshua and Judges.

Occupation was undoubtedly a slow process. Canaanites remaining in the land harassed the new settlers, especially in the north where Jabin 'king of Canaan' had iron-plated chariots. Sisera, his captain, pitched camp in the upper Kishon valley. Deborah and Barak attacked with an army drawn from five of the tribes, and from their vantage-point on Mt. Tabor routed the enemy, helped evidently by a providential storm that turned the little stream into a mighty river, and the valley into a quagmire in which chariots became a liability. Sisera's defeat marked the end of Canaanite domination (Jdg. 4–5).

There were also invasions. All the near neighbours tried to take advantage of the unsettled conditions. Judges tells in some detail about four invasions in order to recount the story of God's provision. Moab was driven out of the Jericho region by the cunning of Ehud (Jdg. 3:12–30). When for seven successive years bedouin had helped themselves to the harvest in the valley of Jezreel and on the coastal plain, Gideon, with a handful of men on Mt. Moreh, terrified them in the night so that they fled in panic, never to return (Jdg. 6–7). Jephthah's victory was over intruding Ammonites east of the Jordan (Jdg. 11), while Samson was meant to protect Dan's territory from the Philistines (Jdg. 13–16). These men were typical charismatic leaders or 'judges', with whom God's Spirit 'clothed himself' (Jdg. 6:34, RV mg.) to rescue His people in spite of their apostasy. The scanty records also suggest that there was continuous leadership at times by men who are also called 'judges', but of whom, apart from Jephthah, little is known save their names (Jdg. 10:1–5; 12:7–15).

The last five chapters of the book reveal disgracefully low moral standards and irregular religious practices, although the annual festival at Shiloh (Jdg. 21:19) and the mention of burnt-offerings and peace-offerings at Bethel (Jdg. 21:2–4) suggest some order. If Gideon's father had a Canaanite shrine and others protested at its destruction, we can infer that worship of fertility-gods was widespread at that period. Such apostasy accounted for continual defeat and oppression. The popular opinion, however, seems to have been that the continuous rule of a king would enable the country to avoid periods of decline. Thus, after his victory, Gideon was invited to rule (Jdg. 8:22), but he upheld the theocratic ideal and refused. Abimelech's limited and self-appointed kingship (Jdg. 9) need not be considered, but the demand for a king was to recur, and the refrain, 'In those days there was no king in Israel', implies that a king would have insisted on moral order and social justice. In the circumstances 'every man did what was right in his own eyes' (Jdg. 17:6; 21:25).

Eli's lead as priest-judge at Shiloh (1 Sa. 1–4) is referred to incidentally as background to the story of Samuel. Such improvement as there was during his time was rapidly counteracted by the unscrupulous and immoral behaviour of his sons. When they took the ark of the covenant into battle against the Philistines, hoping that its presence would ensure victory, not only was Israel defeated, but they themselves were killed and the ark captured; Eli died, and the God of Israel appeared to be impotent. Excavation of the site of Shiloh suggests that the primitive temple was violently destroyed c. 1050 BC, maybe on the occasion of this battle (cf. Je. 7:14; 26:6).

Samuel, the great prophet-judge, recalled Israel to loyalty to the Lord at Mizpah (1 Sa. 7:5–14); he enabled them not only to defeat and subdue the Philistines when they attacked unexpectedly, but also to recover lost territory. Apart from the fact that he lived at Ramah and judged Israel all his life, visiting Bethel, Gilgal and Mizpah annually (1 Sa. 7:15–17), little detail concerning his ministry is given till his old age, when the demand for a king was renewed.

Establishment of the monarchy: the reign of Saul. 1 Sa. 8:1 – 31:13

A people ambitious for national prestige could not tolerate the uncertainty over succession involved in the theocratic tradition. Differences of opinion about kingship, reflected in the text of 1 Sa. 8–12, are usually attributed to conflation of sources, but Samuel makes no secret of the fact that he prefers the charismatic tradition, of which he is a representative, though God has led him to anoint a king. The two view-points may, therefore, reflect Samuel's own conflict in accepting the innovation.

The reign of Saul vindicated Samuel's judgment. His valiant defence of Jabesh-gilead (1 Sa. 11:1–13), and his generous attitude to those who had opposed him promised well, but in the face of a Philistine army (1 Sa. 13) he presumed to take upon himself the offering of sacrifices in preparation for the battle, and so incurred the condemnation of Samuel as he did once more when, having been victorious over the Amalekites, he failed to carry out the extermination policy commanded by God before the battle (1 Sa. 15). He may have resented Samuel's authority over him, but whatever his motive he was rejected by God, his son was not to succeed him, and Samuel was sent secretly to anoint David in his stead (1 Sa. 16). Indecision, even schizophrenic behaviour, marked the last years of his reign, and he met his end on Mt. Gilboa at the hand of the Philistines, whom he had allowed to penetrate far into his territory (1 Sa. 31). What remained of his army was reassembled E of the Jordan under his captain, Abner, and, Jonathan having been killed, Ishbosheth his brother became king in Gilead.

Meanwhile David was king in Hebron over the tribe of Judah; skirmishes and intrigues during the next 2 years brought about the downfall, first of Ish-bosheth and then of Abner, so that eventually the northern tribes were prepared to acknowledge the leadership of David, and anointed him their king in Hebron (2 Sa. 2:1 – 5:3).

The reign of David. 2 Sa. 5:4 – 1 Ki. 2:11; 1 Ch. 11:1 – 29:30

Once he had control of all the tribes, David could begin to take the initiative. The first incident recorded is his seizing of Jerusalem by a ruse from the Jebusite inhabitants, and his establishment of the city as his capital, thus bridging what had been a gap between Judah and the northern tribes. Such consolidation was against the interests of the Philistines, who launched an attack in the valley of Rephaim, to the W of the city. David defeated them so decisively that they never again seriously menaced Israel (2 Sa. 5:17–25). Though David was not permitted to build the Temple (1 Sa. 7) he appointed the site and prepared the materials (1 Ch. 22; 28:11 – 29:9). The presence of the ark of the covenant within the city (2 Sa. 6) ensured the future of Jerusalem as the focal point of Israel's worship, while the renewed fortifications, the building of the royal palace (2 Sa. 5:11, 12), and the presence of the king and court provided a capital of which Israel could be proud.

Successful military exploits enabled David, with the help of his professional troops, to occupy the land 'from Dan to Beersheba'; Canaanite strongholds such as Dor (RSV 'Naphath-dor'), Megiddo, Taanach and Bethshean evidently came to terms with Israel (1 Ki. 4:11, 12); other traditional enemies were subjugated (2 Sa. 8:1–15), thanks partly to the weakness of the great powers. Thus David's empire extended from the Egyptian border and the Gulf of Aqabah to the northern Euphrates, and tribute from Moab, Edom, Ammon, and Aramaean states to the NE enriched the treasury.

Though outwardly prosperous, David was to experience strife and division in his own family. The question of the succession was complicated by his preference for Solomon, son of Bathsheba, the unlawful wife of his later years (2 Sa. 11). It is not surprising that his older sons Absalom and Adonijah tried to usurp the throne (2 Sa. 15–18; 1 Ki. 1:5–7). Flight, exile, disloyalty and attempted revolt among the northern tribes marked the last years of a brilliant reign but, in spite of all, David evidently commanded the allegiance of the majority of Israelites, and none of the near neighbours was as yet prepared to challenge the kingdom in war, even though there had been good opportunities to do so.

The reign of David, despite all its shortcomings, was the most ideal that Israel ever knew. Under him the kingdom was united;

the empire was extensive; Jerusalem was established and promised to have a great future; the people had a mind to help make it great by building the Temple. David's best legacy to his successor was the unfinished task that gave purpose and drive to the early years of Solomon's reign. No less important was David's personal example, for he was 'a man after God's own heart'. Naturally gifted with powers of leadership, a warm outgoing disposition, courage, and a fine physique, David would have commanded respect in any community, but the Bible does not commend a man for his natural gifts. It is rather in his failures that the greatness of the man is seen. Where but in Israel would a king publicly admit to faults in his private life? David twice accepted the rebuke of a prophet (2 Sa. 12:1–15; 25:10–17), and through repentance experienced the wonder of forgiveness, while at the same time taking his punishment. He genuinely desired God's glory and appreciated the meaning of worship, as is evident from the psalms attributed to him; moreover he knew God in experience as his Rock and Shield and Deliverer, not only in victory, but even in defeat. Repentance, faith and worship had made him great.

The reign of Solomon. 1 Ki. 2:12 – 11:43; 2 Ch. 1–9

From the beginning it was clear that Solomon was not of the calibre of his father. A sense of insecurity drove him to liquidate his personal enemies, whereas David had been steadfast in waiting for God to vindicate him and so confirm his kingship. Once established on the throne he concentrated on the main tasks of his reign: consolidation of the empire, building projects, and organization of the administration. For all this the needed wisdom was promised. Expansion of trade brought unprecedented prosperity to Israel; widened horizons introduced foreign cultures, especially through the many marriage-alliances of the king; building operations demanded skilled workmen from Tyre, while the merchant navy based at Ezion-geber was dependent on Tyrian sailors to operate it (1 Ki. 9:26–28). Trade in horses and chariots involved regular journeys to Egypt, Syria, and countries of Asia Minor (1 Ki. 10:28, 29). Such cosmopolitanism may well have given rise in Israel to a renewed interest in wisdom literature. Solomon would have been well placed to collect and exchange the wise sayings attributed to him (1 Ki. 4:29–34). The mention of secretaries and a recorder (1 Ki. 4:3) suggests official records, and in the opinion of many, this was a time of literary renaissance, based on Israel's own background and historic tradition.

The story of 1 Kings concentrates on the wonder of the Temple buildings, with their carved cedarwood overlaid with gold, but points out that, whereas 7 years were spent on the Temple, 13 were needed to complete the royal palaces (6:38 – 7:1). Such projects involved vast labour forces, raised by conscription. Taxation was an added burden, made necessary by the size of the royal household and the increased number of officials. Moreover taxation in kind necessitated store-cities, which also had to be constructed and fortified. Little wonder that as time went on discontent increased. A wealthy king and court indulging their own pleasure at the expense of the poor was quite contrary to the traditions of Israel. Foreign gods were being worshipped by the king in blatant disregard for the law. Signs of decline were observable in the empire, for Edom and Damascus were ready for revolt, while at home Jeroboam had taken advantage of a responsible office to plan rebellion (1 Ki. 11). Solomon's death precipitated a crisis which resulted in the division of the kingdom (1 Ki. 12).

The young Rehoboam had not sensed the discontent of the people; in his immaturity he decided to assert his authority by threatening oppressive measures, and thereby lost all ten northern tribes. Jeroboam, back from exile in Egypt, was ready to step in as their leader, and became the first king of an apostate kingdom, which survived little more than 200 years.

The northern kingdom (Israel) c. 931–722 BC. 1 Ki. 12 – 2 Ki. 17

The history of the northern kingdom may be divided into four periods:

1. c. 931–880 BC. Egyptian raids early in Jeroboam's reign ceased owing to weakness at home. Throughout these years there was hostility between Israel and Judah. Jeroboam set up shrines in Bethel and Dan in order to consolidate his kingdom by preventing pilgrimages to Jerusalem, but no northern capital became permanent. The two reigns of Jeroboam (1 Ki. 12:25 – 14:20) and Baasha (1 Ki. 15:16–21; 15:33 – 16:7) each lasted about 20 years, only to be followed by a change of dynasty, the second leading on to civil war, from which Omri eventually emerged as leader (1 Ki. 16:8–22).

2. c. 880–841 BC. The dynasty of Omri was noted for cessation of hostilities between Israel and Judah, and for the establishment of the new city of Samaria as the capital (1 Ki. 16:23–28). Phoenician builders helped to plan the spacious palace where king and court could live in luxury. Alliance with Tyre was strengthened by the marriage of Omri's son Ahab to Jezebel, a Phoenician princess (1 Ki. 16:31). Israel gained international prestige and importance, for even Assyria was aware of Omri, as Shalmaneser's 'Black Obelisk' proves. Alliance between Israel and Judah made possible at least a temporary subjugation of Moab (2 Ki. 1:1) and Edom (2 Ki. 3:4ff.). Political and commercial success may well have been urged as an argument in favour of sensual Canaanite worship. Certainly Yahweh-worship was banned during Ahab's reign, while official status was given to the cult of Melkart of Tyre, until Elijah publicly demon-

strated on Mt. Carmel the unique power of Yahweh, the living God (1 Ki. 18). Even then the battle with Jezebel was not over. Tyrian influence in social morality is seen in the episode concerning Naboth's vineyard, as a result of which Elijah pronounced the violent destruction of Omri's dynasty (1 Ki. 21).

Throughout the 9th century the Syrian state of Damascus harassed Israel's NE border, except for the short period culminating in the battle of Qarqar in 853 when Israel and Syria joined forces to defeat Assyria. It was in a battle against Syria for possession of Ramoth-gilead that Ahab lost his life (1 Ki. 22:1–40). Syrian pressure continued during the reigns of his sons Ahaziah and Jehoram and it was from Ramoth-gilead that Jehu was commissioned to exterminate the house of Omri (2 Ki. 9:1–3).

3. 841–752 BC. The dynasty of Jehu was the longest Israel knew. Jehu's revolt (2 Ki. 9:4 – 10:28) was instigated by the prophets, supported by the Rechabites and the army, and probably welcomed by the common people. His purge rid the land of Jehoram, Ahaziah of Judah, and Jezebel, of seventy direct descendants of Ahab in Samaria and of forty-two relatives of Ahaziah. He went on to wipe out a temple full of Baal-worshippers. Though he seemed to be a champion of the right, Jehu had no genuine concern that Yahweh should be honoured in his kingdom. The extermination of so many able-bodied men left Israel weak, and no match for Damascus, who annexed her territory E of Jordan (2 Ki. 10:32, 33) and even penetrated to the plain of Jezreel, occupying fertile areas to the W and southwards along the coast (2 Ki. 12:17). Recovery was made possible only because Damascus was invaded by the greater power Assyria in 803 BC. Thus Jeroboam II (2 Ki. 14:23–29), the fourth and greatest king of the dynasty, was able to regain lost territories, and restore the boundaries of Israel. He achieved unprecedented prosperity, enriching court, landowners and traders, but the common people, far from sharing the nation's wealth, were further impoverished. Such disregard for the Mosaic traditions, coupled though it was with punctilious religious observance, called forth the censure of Amos and Hosea. Social evils were an outward manifestation of the deep estrangement from Yahweh. There was still time for a change of heart, but war and captivity were the burden of the prophets' message. If Assyria had drawn the enemy from Israel's gates it was only a limited respite. Moreover Jehu's dynasty was insecure. Jeroboam's successor Zechariah was assassinated (2 Ki. 15:8–12).

4. The last 30 years 752–722 BC. 2 Ki. 15:13–31; 17. After only one month Shallum the usurper met his death at the hand of Menahem, who reigned 10 years. By paying tribute to Assyria he temporarily averted occupation. His son Pekahiah reigned 2 years, only to be assassinated in the palace by Pekah, son of Remaliah,

who adopted an anti-Assyrian policy and tried to force Judah into coalition with Israel. Partly in response to an appeal from Judah (2 Ki. 16:5–8), Assyria invaded northern Israel, capturing several towns and taking prisoners. Hoshea slew Pekah and became the last king of the northern kingdom. When he refused tribute to Assyria, Samaria was besieged for 3 years, captured, and the population deported. The message of Amos and Hosea had been vindicated.

The southern kingdom (Judah) c. 931–587 BC. **1 Ki. 12:21 – 2 Ki. 25:21; 2 Ch. 11:1 – 36:21**

Judah had the initial advantage of an established capital and a splendid Temple with an authorized cultus, upheld by a divinely-appointed line of kings. The southern kingdom, which was stripped of its treasures in Rehoboam's reign by Egypt (1 Ki. 14:21–31), was less prosperous, less accessible, and less attractive to would-be conquerors than Israel.

The third king, Asa (1 Ki. 15:9–24), was a reformer, who aimed at purifying worship. Politically he sought help from Syria against the northern kingdom, but during Jehoshaphat's reign that followed, alliance with Israel involved Judah in fighting her one-time allies. Though Jehoshaphat (1 Ki. 22:41–50) was a just and able ruler his son's marriage to Athaliah introduced the baneful influence of the northern kingdom (2 Ki. 8:18). At the time of Jehu's revolt, when David's line was threatened with extinction, one child was saved from Queen Athaliah's knife to perpetuate the dynasty. Jehoiada, supported by the army and the common people, succeeded in enthroning the young Joash and putting Athaliah to death (2 Ki. 11). The new reign began with repairs to the Temple and religious reforms, but this good start was not maintained. When Hazael of Syria threatened to attack Jerusalem he was bribed with Temple treasures to withdraw. Joash was assassinated in the palace c. 796 BC (2 Ki. 12).

During the 8th century the outstanding king was Uzziah, whose father Amaziah was also murdered (2 Ki. 14:17–20). Uzziah (2 Ki. 15:1–7; 2 Ch. 26), also called Azariah, strengthened the kingdom by subduing neighbouring peoples, building up his armies, and fortifying Jerusalem and other cities. In his time Judah experienced a prosperity unknown since Solomon's death. It was in the last year of his 52-year reign that Isaiah had a vision of the Holy One of Israel, and was called into His service (Is. 6). Together with Micah he was to have a message for Judah during the critical period of Assyria's encroachment, which began with the reign of Tiglath-pileser III in 745. When Israel and Syria made a coalition to oppose Assyria and threatened to force Judah to join (734), Ahaz refused Isaiah's advice (Is. 7) and appealed to Assyria for help, thus involving Judah in paying tribute. Assyrian forces were already in the W. In 732 Damascus fell and the N of Israel was annexed. Only 10 years afterwards, of the three kingdoms Judah alone survived. In spite of Assyria's victories plots were made by Egypt (*e.g.* Is. 30:1–7) and Ashdod (Is. 20) to rebel. Isaiah advised neutrality, but Judah was implicated, especially after 705. The result was a crushing Assyrian invasion, widespread destruction, and the survival only by a miracle of besieged Jerusalem, when King Hezekiah (715–686) responded to the preaching of Micah and Isaiah. So crucial was this event that it has been recorded three times: 2 Ki. 18:13 – 19:37; 2 Ch. 32:1–23; Is. 36–37. The state was spared for a further 100 years.

The reign of Manasseh (2 Ki. 21:1–18) reversed all that had been accomplished through Hezekiah. Assyrian ways, especially in religion, became the fashion, and any prophetic protests ended in bloodshed. Only after his death and that of his son was effective reformation attempted, in the reign of Josiah (639–609) (2 Ki. 22:1 – 23:30). The decline of Assyria enabled him to begin to reject foreign cults in his 8th and 12th years, spurred on by the haunting imagery of the prophet Zephaniah. In 626 Jeremiah responded to God's call to prophesy, and in 621 the discovery of the book of the law in the Temple gave further impetus towards reform. In spite of all the outward improvements Jeremiah could give no encouragement that judgment on Jerusalem would be averted again. Doom was inevitable. This unpopular message involved him in suffering and imprisonment. The prophet Habakkuk questioned the revelation he received that Yahweh would use Babylon to punish His people. Popular opinion was that the Temple was inviolable, and that its presence ensured the safety of Jerusalem, but Jeremiah in Jerusalem and Ezekiel in Babylon prophesied the downfall of both city and Temple.

Babylonian armies first marched through the land claiming allegiance in 605 BC (2 Ki. 24:1); Judah's disloyalty caused Nebuchadrezzar to seize Jerusalem in 597, when king Jehoiachin and leading citizens were taken as prisoners to Babylon (2 Ki. 24:8–17). The final sack of the city in 587, and the further deportations, brought Judah's national history to an end (2 Ki. 25). Its former territory became part of the province of Samaria after the murder of the governor Gedaliah, and the flight of Johanan and his company to Egypt. The fact that Edom supported the enemy, and later appropriated Judah's territory, completed Judah's humiliation, as the prophecy of Obadiah makes plain.

Exile and return. 2 Ch. 36:20–26; Ezr. 1–6

Both Jeremiah and Ezekiel had prepared the nation for complete collapse, and had insisted that any hope for the future must be centred in the exiles in Babylon (Je. 24; 29; Ezk. 11). Ezekiel continued his ministry, at least until 571 BC (Ezk. 29:17), but with a new message once the predicted fall of the city and its destruction had taken place (Ezk. 33:21). Then he could promise a new covenant, national resurrection, a new Jerusalem.

Prediction began to be worked out in history through Cyrus, king of Anshan, who rapidly established himself as the conqueror of the Near East; Babylon fell to him in 539 BC. As it was his policy to restore exiled peoples to their own lands and encourage them in their traditional worship, the Jews had their opportunity to return to Jerusalem. The opening chapters of Ezra describe how a nucleus did so, and laid the foundation of the new Temple without delay, but then discouragement, and opposition from the settled population of the province, with whom they refused to co-operate, brought the work to a standstill until 520, when the prophets Haggai and Zechariah, by rebuke and encouragement, caused a new start to be made. By 516 the new Temple was complete.

The prophecy of Malachi and the records concerning Ezra and Nehemiah (Ezr. 7–10; Nehemiah) shed some light on the rest of the Persian period. Opposition continued, and the little community lacked the leadership it needed. Thus it was that Ezra, the expert in the holy books, and Nehemiah, the personal courtier of the Persian king, perceived that they had a mission in Jerusalem. Nehemiah travelled there in 445 BC. By his astute handling of opposition, and realistic planning for the building of the city walls, he accomplished that task in 52 days (Ne. 6:15). After a gap of nearly 150 years Jerusalem was again a walled city. Its population was increased, and it became a more worthy capital of the little province of Judah. Legislation was passed by Nehemiah the governor to ensure the continuation of Temple worship, but it was Ezra who centred attention on the law of Moses and made its strict observance the responsibility of every Jew. There was no immediate hope of political freedom, nor of setting up a king, but law-keeping was within their power, and this became the steadfast aim of loyal Jews, in whatever country they lived. For a discussion of the date of Ezra's arrival in Jerusalem and of the relationship between him and Nehemiah, see the commentary on Ezra-Nehemiah.

The historical records of the OT go no further, but prophetic interpretation had established once and for all certain basic lessons to be drawn from them. First of all, the Lord was close at hand, fully aware of injustice, corruption and inhumanity in Israel's social and political life. If He was at the same time 'out there', afar off, filling heaven and earth, that only showed how impossible it was for a man to escape the judgment of His all-seeing eye. A man's routine choices in day-to-day living were of utmost importance, for they revealed his priorities. What the Lord demanded was clear: impartial law-courts, honest trade in the markets, just wages, generosity to the poor and defenceless, as well as sincere and loyal worship. Secondly, Israel was not the victim of some blind fate, but was responsible for the disasters that overtook her. Isaiah had made this plain: 'If you are willing and obedient you shall eat the good of the land; but if you refuse and rebel, you shall be devoured by the sword' (1:19, 20). That God meant what He said had been proved in Hezekiah's time, for when he obeyed and humbled himself to take the prophet's advice Jerusalem was spared. Thirdly, human responsibility did not conflict with the truth that God was in control of the affairs of men and nations. He was Lord of history, as well as creator of the universe. He could take the kings of Babylon or Persia and make them the unwitting tools of His purpose. It followed that Israel's dis-

obedience could not thwart God's purposes. If her kings were faithless, He would provide a Davidic ruler who would fulfil all His will. If the terms of the old covenant had been broken, the Lord would make a new covenant, forgive Israel's sin and cause her to keep His laws. Far-reaching promises remained unfulfilled when prophecy ceased; centuries passed, yet the faithful in Israel never lost their conviction that, when the time was right, the Lord of history would break in and fulfil all He had promised. The world owes a teleological view of history to OT revelation.

J. G. BALDWIN

Old Testament theology

From the outset the OT offers itself to the reader as the story and description of a relationship: the relationship between God and the world. This relationship is, of course, asymmetrical. God is ever the transcendent One, and His rights and powers over the world do not imply reciprocal rights for the world over God.

Certainly it is this notion of relationship which dominates OT thinking, so that even if we consider the central revelation concerning the divine nature itself, that God is holy, this holiness is not considered in the abstract, nor even to any extent in or for itself, but rather as it impinges upon the world and man. Vriezen is surely right when he notes that 'the characteristic difference between the Old Testament teaching concerning God and the conception of God among the other oriental peoples is the absolute transcendence of God's Being' and when he immediately adds the qualification, 'a transcendence which nevertheless does not detract in any way from the communion between God and man' (*An Outline of Old Testament Theology*, 1958, p. 148).

Within the present brief compass, any treatment of OT theology is necessarily very selective, and much must be omitted. We must content ourselves with examining this truth as it appears in three interlocking circles of OT thought.

CREATION

The first and fundamental way in which the OT displays the relationship of the transcendent God with the world is the doctrine of creation. In starting here we do not in the least dissociate OT theology from either the history or the religion of Israel. To be sure, like every other doctrine, the doctrine of God the Creator was specially relevant to certain periods of Israel's life: it figures largely, for example, in the teaching of Isaiah (*cf*. 40:12–14, 25, 26; 42:5; 44:24; 45:18, *etc*.). But the time is long past when there is any justification for a late date for the origin of the doctrine of creation, whether inside Israel (*cf*. Vriezen, *op. cit*., p. 184; Albright, *From Stone Age to Christianity*, 1957, p. 260) or outside (*cf*. G. von Rad, *The Problem of the Hexateuch and other Essays*, 1966, ch. VI, 'The Theological Problem of the Old Testament Doctrine of Creation' (1936), esp. p. 142). The OT starts by stressing a truth which Israel always held, the truth of God the Creator, and thus it gives to all its teaching that world-wide perspective which reaches its climax and becomes

effective in the Person and work of the Lord Jesus Christ.

The absolute Creator

Monotheism is basic and essential to Gn. 1. It belongs to the very fabric of the material and could certainly never have been achieved by some process of purging a polytheistic original of its offensive elements (*cf*. Y. Kaufmann, *The Religion of Israel*, 1961, p. 68; see further on the intrinsic monotheism of Israel's faith, *e.g*. M. H. Segal, *The Pentateuch, Its composition and its authorship*, 1967, pp. 125ff.). This monotheism is displayed, negatively, by the absence of reference to any other god, especially at those places where surrounding paganism would have insisted upon the introduction of this or that god to perform this or that individual function. Thus, for example, fertility of plants (Gn. 1:11) is not something achieved by the direct intervention of Baal, the supposed god of fertility, but is a natural capacity created into vegetable life by the Creator God. Again, the phrase 'without form and void' (Gn. 1:2) contains none of the features associated with the Babylonian Tiamat, the chaos-monster, the implacable foe of the creator, nor indeed any of the functions which the Greeks associated with the idea of Chaos. The Hebrew words *tōhû wabōhû* do not signify 'the contrary of creation' (*pace* E. Jacob, *Theology of the Old Testament*, 1958, p. 144), nor do they admit von Rad's submission that 'it is hardly possible to conceive the idea of a created chaos, for what is created is not chaotic' (*Old Testament Theology*, Vol. 1, 1962, p. 144). In Je. 4:23 (*cf*. Is. 40:17, where *tōhû* is translated *emptiness*) the phrase clearly means a world reduced to its bare material substrate, a world from which order, purposeful existence and value have been withdrawn. Thus the *tōhû wabōhû* of Gn. 1:2 does not contain the vestige of or even suggest any opposing divine being, but is (as indeed the order of the narrative implies) the opening move in the Creator's work, the creation of the material to which He subsequently gives order, form and life.

This continuing creative activity is attributed to the word of God (Gn. 1:3; *cf*. Pss. 33:6, 9; 148:5), which instances both the effortless ease with which the mammoth task was accomplished and also the immediate relationship between God and His world, leaving no room for the intrusion of any supposed god. Creation by the word of God finds its verbal co-ordinate in *bārā*, 'to create'. By an apparently conscious narrowing of its contemporary use outside Israel (*cf.* G. von Rad, *Genesis*, 1961, p. 47), the OT restricted this verb to divine creative activity, so that in its active use God is always its subject, and in its passive use His agency is presumed. It describes the sort of act which because of its greatness (*e.g.* Is. 45:8), or newness (*e.g.* Je. 31:22), or transcendence of man's capacity (*e.g.* Is. 4:5) requires the divine Agent. It is hardly correct to say that by etymology the verb expresses 'creation *ex nihilo*', but undoubtedly its usage (*e.g.* Gn. 1:1) involves this idea. On the other hand, each instance of the verb must be examined in its own right to decide whether the newness created by God is that of an absolutely new beginning or of giving a new turn or dimension to what was already there in embryo or in preliminary form (*e.g.* Is. 65:18; *cf.* commentary on Gn. 1:1, 20-23; *NBD*, art. 'Creation').

The creation of man

The supreme example of divine creative activity is man. Of the six instances of *bārā* in the creation narrative one describes the absolute origination of all things (Gn. 1:1), one is used compendiously to summarize the whole divine work (2:3), one marks the introduction of animal life (1:21) and the remaining three are concentrated on the creation of man in the divine image. This, quite apart from the careful structure of Gn. 1 in which verses 26, 27 are a clear and intended climax, displays man as the crown of creation.

From this we must insist that man is not the result of the operation of blind, self-originating and perpetuating forces. He is distinctively the work of God, whether we ultimately find this distinctiveness in an absolute act of creation whereby *de novo* man in the image of God entered the stage of earth, or whether the distinctiveness was the donation of the divine image as the crown of a divinely-superintended process of growth and development.

At all events, the emphasis in the creative act rests on the novelty that now for the first time the divine image is seen in a creature. The words used, *image* (*selem*) and *likeness* (*demûth*), have an undoubted reference to outward form (*e.g.* 1 Sa. 6:5; 2 Ki. 16:10), and we must not resist the implication that while God is Spirit (Is. 31:3) and outward appearance does not belong to His essence, yet there is an outward appearance which is suitable to the invisible glory of God (*e.g,* Nu. 12:8) and in this likeness man was created. This affords a basis for the dignity which Scripture ever accords to the human body.

Ringgren, however, is undoubtedly to be heard when he reminds us (*Israelite Reltgion*, 1966, pp. 124f.) that Ancient Near Eastern rulers 'set up images and statues of themselves in places where they exercised or claimed to exercise authority. The images represented the ruler himself as symbols of his presence and authority'. This rightly focuses attention on the fact that it is in man's position, nature and functions that we are to see the image of God: his deputed rule of the world (Gn. 1:28-30), his moral capacity to live under law and promise (Gn. 2:16, 17), his intellectual awareness of his environment (Gn. 2:19), and, throughout, his communion with God. It is possible that the complex oneness of man and woman in marriage is also itself a reflection of the diversified unity of God which the OT reveals (*cf.* G. A. F. Knight, *A Biblical Approach to the Doctrine of the Trinity*, 1953, p. 17).

The nature of man is aptly summed up in the phrases *dust from the ground* and *the breath of life*, these two not remaining as isolated constituents but being blended together into the unity of *a living being* (Gn. 2:7). As aspects of human nature they are, of course, correctly distinguishable and separable for thought. Thus man is 'flesh' (*bāśār*), viewed externally (*e.g.* Ezk. 23:20, RSV *members*), or in his association with other living creatures (*e.g.* Gn. 6:17). He is also, psychologically considered, a 'person' (*nepeš*), *i.e.* an individual centre of conscious life, an *ego* with its distinctive emotions and desires (*e.g.* Jb. 16:4, '*you . . . my place*'; Ex. 23:9, *heart, i.e.* 'feelings'); he possesses 'spirit' (*rûaḥ*), the motive power and energy of the person, which both stimulates him to act (*cf.* Ex. 35:21) and can be used to express the person himself considered as a source of action (*cf.* Dt. 2:30). Moving between these terms, the OT also uses words wherein what we call the physical and the psychological are fused. The 'heart' (*lēḇ*) denotes the person (or *nepeš*) as a centre of thought (*e.g.* Ps. 45:1), conscience (*e.g.* 1 Sa. 24:5) and emotion (*e.g.* Dt. 6:5; *cf.* 'kidneys', *kelayôt*, RSV *heart* in, *e.g.*, Pss. 7:9; 16:7; 73:21); the 'hand' (*yad*) denotes the conative aspects of personality, man as doer (*e.g.* Dt. 2:7, 24; in Dt. 32:36 *yad* is translated 'power'). The significance, however, of this use of 'heart' and 'hand' is that it stresses the unity of human nature: man is body, man is 'soul'—one person. (See further A. R. Johnson, *The Vitality of the Individual in the Thought of Ancient Israel*, 1949.)

God and history

The transcendence and immediacy of the Creator is nowhere more clearly delineated than in the 'world-view' of the OT. The Creator remains in immediate, executive, creatorial control of His world, whether considered as the sphere of human history (*e.g.* Is. 40:21-25) or in its intricate natural processes (*e.g.* Is. 40:26). It is this fact which gives rise to the linear view of time in the Bible: the 'recurring' features of experience are not governed by inner necessity or fate, but are freshly given to man by deliberate divine grace and faithfulness (Gn. 8:22; Je. 33:20, 25). This sovereign control and direction covers all experience, individual (*e.g.* Gn. 45:5-9; 50:20; Is. 54:16, 17), and national (*e.g.* Am. 9:7; Hab. 1:6; 2:16), catering even for the very details of events themselves (*e.g.* Is. 37:26–29; Am. 3:6).

In His world-government God is revealed as wise, powerful and holy (*cf.* Is. 40:12–14, 22–24, 25; Ps. 104, where vv. 1–9 display ordering power, vv. 10–24 wisdom, vv. 25–32 sustaining power, and vv. 33–35 holiness; *cf.* Ps. 93; see on Jb. 38–40). In the matter of theodicy, therefore, as in the concluding chapters of Job, there is no escape from the rigour of biblical theism. Human logic cannot justify its desire to explain experience by supposing that God can err, or fail, or pass false judgment.

Within these attributes of God, displayed in His world-rule, holiness predominates and qualifies all the others. This is, of course, equally true of the whole revelation of God given in Scripture. Seven out of every twelve references to the 'name' of God—*i.e.* His revealed nature—qualify it as 'holy'. Whether the root meaning of 'holy' (*q-d-š*) is 'separation' or 'brightness' (see Vriezen, *op. cit.*, p. 149, for references to literature), the idea is that God is in Himself of such a positive nature that man cannot approach or behold Him. Constantly men are described as in terror of their lives if found in the presence of God (*e.g.* Ex. 33:20; Jdg. 6:22; 13:22), but as H. H. Rowley well remarks, 'what makes him tremble is not the consciousness of his humanity in the presence of divine power, but the consciousness of his sin in the presence of moral purity' (*The Faith of Israel*, 1956, p. 66). The ethical holiness of God, though decisively experienced and revealed in the case of Isaiah (6:3–5), did not originate there but is an unvarying feature of the OT understanding of God (*e.g.* Gn. 3:8, 24; Hab. 1:13).

Man's life on earth is automatically lived out under the scrutiny of this divine holiness, and this is seen in the realms of nature and history. As to the former, what we call the 'forces' of nature reflect the conditions prevailing between man and God, because natural forces derive their energies from God. Thus thorns and thistles follow on the first sin (Gn. 3:17f.). In the same way, the Israelite doctrine of prosperity differed diametrically from that of surrounding paganism. To the Canaanites, prosperity, defined in agricultural terms, depended on the capricious activity of Baal who could be enticed into action only by sympathetic magic. Consequently, Canaanite religion rested upon infamies such as 'sacred' prostitution in which the human act of fertility was designed as a broad hint to the god to function similarly. In Israel, prosperity found its collateral in obedience (*e.g.* Dt. 28; 29; Hg. 1:9–11; 2:15–19; Zc. 6:15). The moral holiness of God which rules the world requires the moral obedience of man. It is in line with this teaching that OT faith must needs assert the prosperity of the godly (Ps. 1), not because this was invariably so in experience but because revealed truth called for such a confidence that God would vindicate and reward His people. Ultimately the doctrine finds its climax in the unparalleled prosperity of the Messianic kingdom (Ho. 2:21–23; Am. 9:13–15), for the whole creation must burgeon with its proper splendour when at last God and man are at one and Eden is more than restored (*e.g.* Is. 11:1–9).

The government of history by a holy God is a topic which raises questions today, because it is clear that the OT appeals to the direct action of God in a way which offends modern modes of thought. The attack by Sennacherib on Jerusalem both raises problems and also offers characteristic biblical solutions. Sennacherib was designed by God to be His tool for punishing sinful Judah (Is. 10:5, 15), being spoken of as if he had no personal volition or responsibility in the matter but was a puppet under sovereign management. Yet, his work accomplished, he is to be punished for his pride in daring to attack Mt. Zion (Is. 10:12–14)! We are not here concerned with other aspects of the story of Sennacherib, as, for example, that the Lord's purpose was not in fact to deliver Jerusalem over to him, but rather to defend the city against him. It is simply that Isaiah's great poem on the Assyrian attack raises in an acute form the problem of the relationship between divine sovereignty and human responsibility. How can Sennacherib be, at one and the same time, the rod in the Lord's hand and also a culpable human aggressor? The solution of the dilemma appears to be this, that there were two reasons for the Assyrian attack. Had Sennacherib been asked, he would have replied in terms of personal pride and an assumed right to govern the earth. That is to say, he came for sinful reasons, meriting the punishment he ultimately received. But there was also a secret reason for his coming: the divine (and, to Sennacherib, undisclosed) will to punish a sinful city. The holy God neither excuses nor implicates Himself in nor originates the sinful motives of men, but He does rule and overrule them.

The Spirit of God

The rather mysterious reference (Gn. 1:2; *cf.* Jb. 33:4; Pss. 33:6; 104:30; Is. 40:7; 42:5) to the Spirit of God at creation, apparently acting as a mediator of the divine will, the executive link between the transcendent God and His world, is filled out by subsequent references to the Spirit as accomplishing exactly this function in the rest of the OT, in which there is a remarkably full doctrine of the Spirit of God. The Spirit originates from God, being 'poured out' (Pr. 1:23; Is. 32:15; 44:3; Ezk. 39: 29; Joel 2:28f.) or 'falling' (Ezk. 11:5) on men. The Spirit 'rests' upon men (Nu. 11:25, 26, 29), or 'clothes himself' with them (Jdg. 6:34; 1 Ch. 12:18; 2 Ch. 24:20), indwelling them for specific tasks. He is actively present (Nu. 24:2; Jdg. 3:10; 11:29; 1 Sa. 19:20, 23; 2 Ch. 15:1; 20:14, in all of which the translation 'came upon' represents the verb *h-y-h*, 'to be actively present'), quickening or impelling (Jdg. 13:25), filling with power (Jdg.

14:6, 19; 15:14; 1 Sa. 10:6; 11:6; 16:13. The verb is *ṣ-l-ḥ*, which may mean 'to penetrate into' (*cf.* Vriezen, *op. cit.*, p. 170) but more likely means 'to be strong'), and inspiring (2 Sa. 23:2; Ne. 9:20). In these references, the activity of the Spirit empowering mighty deeds possibly predominates, but this is by no means the only work accorded to Him. He endows the whole people of God (Is. 32:15; 44:3; 59:21; Ezk. 39:29; Joel 2:28f.), especially the great Messianic figures (Nu. 11:17; 27:18; 1 Sa. 16:13; Is. 11:2; 42:1; 48:16; 61:1). He is the agent in individual regeneration (Ezk. 36:27), and is characteristically associated with the work of the prophets (Nu. 11:29; 1 Sa. 10:6, 10; 2 Sa. 23:2; 1 Ki. 22:24; 1 Ch. 12:18; 2 Ch. 15:1; 20:14; 24:20; Ne. 9:20; Ezk. 11:5; Joel 2:28f.; Zc. 7:12). E. Jacob (*op. cit.*, p. 125) correctly urges that 'it is clear that for all the prophets it is not the spirit but the word which qualifies them for their ministry. . . . But the word presupposes the spirit, the creative breath of life, and for the prophets there was such evidence of this that they thought it unnecessary to state it explicitly.' (*Cf.* A. B. Davidson, *Old Testament Prophecy*, 1904, p. 152.)

By virtue of the recurring title, Spirit of God, it is clear that we must speak of the Spirit as divine, but the evidence requires us to go further to speak of a divine Person. He possesses the divine attributes of holiness (Ps. 51:11; Is. 63:10), goodness (Ne. 9:20; Ps. 143:10) and wisdom (Gn. 41:38f.; Ex. 31:3; Is. 11:2; 40:13; Dn. 4:8, 9, 18; 5:11, 14); where He is present God is present (Ps. 139:7); He is vexed by sin as God is (Is. 63:10; *cf.* Zc. 6:8). 'The Spirit', says G. A. F. Knight, 'receives the personality and the very character of God Himself' (*op. cit.*, pp. 54f.).

REVELATION

It is a short step from the notion of the Spirit of God as the inspirer of the prophets to the general topic of revelation in which, again, we see the basic truth that the transcendent God comes near to men. He comes near to make Himself known, an activity for which Hebrew typically uses reflexive verbs (*e.g.* Gn. 35:7; Ex. 6:3), for the initiative rests with God and 'there is no suggestion anywhere in the Old Testament that the reception of revelation is dependent on any particular predisposition in man, faith or anything else' (L. Koehler, *Old Testament Theology*, 1953, p. 100).

The angel of the Lord

The immediacy of God's approach to man is well seen in the activity of the angel of the Lord (Gn. 16:7ff.; 19; 21:17ff.; 22:11ff.; 31:11ff.; 48:15f.; Ex. 3:2ff.; 14:19–22 (with 13:21 and 14:24); 23:20f.; 32:34; Jdg. 2:1ff.; 6:11ff.; 13:2ff.; Is. 63:8f.; Ezk. 40–48, see 44:2; Ho. 12:4 (*cf.* Gn. 32:24ff.); Zc. 1–6, noting 1:12f. with 3:6–10; Mal. 3:1). The particular point at issue is clearly established by these references, namely that God takes the initiative to draw near to His people in self-revelation and direct communication. It is certainly not inappropriate to note how often the angel is both identified with the Lord (*e.g.* Gn. 22:11, 12) and distinguished from Him (*e.g.* Gn. 22:15, 16). E. Jacob (*op. cit.*, p. 77) speaks of Him as 'the double of Yahweh', and yet the relationship is not one of simple identity (*cf.* J. Pedersen, *Israel III and IV*, 1953, pp. 496f.), for Ex. 33:1–3 says that the angel (in whom, none the less, is the 'name', the full nature of Yahweh, Ex. 23:21) will go with Israel lest, were Yahweh Himself to go, He would consume them for their provocation. The paradox of this divine angel was not solved until the revelation of Him who is both distinct from God and yet identical, who, without diluting the divine holiness yet kept company with sinners and who, without denying God's wrath, is yet the supreme outreaching of God's mercy, Jesus Christ our Lord.

Revelation in nature and history

God is known by His works. His activities in creation can be used to declare His omniscience (*e.g.* Ps. 94:8–11), His greatness (*e.g.* Ps. 95:3–5), His ability to meet with His people both in deliverance (*e.g.* Is. 50:2, 3) and judgment (*e.g.* Am. 4:12, 13). It is questionable, however, whether the mere contemplation of nature would expose these facets of the divine nature or whether Israel's existing knowledge of the Creator has prompted this illustrative use of His works. Certainly Ps. 19:1–6 appears to suggest that there is a knowledge of God preached by His created universe, and that this knowledge is available everywhere, but the passage itself contains a remarkable caveat couched in a paradox: granted that *their words* go out all over the world (v. 4), nevertheless *there is no speech, nor are there words* (v. 3). While Weiser holds the meaning to be that the message of nature is not restricted to any particular language but is heard by each man in his own tongue (*The Psalms*, 1962, 198f.), it is more likely that the emphasis rests on the inarticulate nature of the message (*cf.* A. F. Kirkpatrick, *The Psalms*, 1910, *in loc.*; J. H. Eaton, *Psalms*, 1967, *in loc.*): it is not couched in verbal terms. In nature each man hears what he says to himself. To some the appeal is the beauty of the world; to another there is the abhorrence of its cruelty and violence. Thus arises what William Temple so aptly called 'the hunger of natural religion' (*Nature, Man and God*, 1935, pp. 519f.)—the hunger being that no escape is offered from the self; no sure objective word is heard. It is no wonder, then, that Ps. 19:7ff. moves on to that sure testimony which God has spoken to His people. Nature is an uncertain guide. Man's sin has blighted its face with thorns and thistles; it holds its secrets back from a race in revolt against its God.

Turning to history, much the same is the case. All history is ultimately the work of God (*e.g.* Am. 9:7) but the OT registers no claim for a general revelation of God in history. Indeed, we are even assured that the search for God in His providential works is foredoomed to failure (Ec. 3:11), and experience teaches us that every man reads historical events in the light of his own presuppositions and makes selection among their lessons to suit his own taste.

Comparison of Gn. 15:7 with Ex. 20:2 uncovers a central OT truth concerning the revelation of God. The wording is almost identical: the Lord brought Abram from Ur and Israel from Egypt, yet, in context, the former is no more than a statement of fact whereas the latter is the summary of a revelation of God. In other words, while God is the supreme Agent in all history, chosen tracts or events of history are made the ground of special revelations of God to man by the attaching to them of an authorized interpreter. The fact that God brought Israel out of Egypt would signify nothing to us of the nature of God were it not for the presence and work of Moses as interpreter (*cf.* E. Jacob, *op. cit.*, p. 184; P. K. Jewett, in *Revelation and the Bible*, edited by C. Henry, 1959, p. 48; A. Richardson, *Christian Apologetics*, 1947, pp. 140f.).

The God who speaks

By definition the word which God speaks is dynamic in power and cannot fail to accomplish its purpose. This was illustrated in creation (Gn. 1:3; Ps. 33:6). It is by the same powerful word that God governs nature (Pss. 147:15, 18; 148:8) and leads history to its determined goal (Is. 45:23). This irresistible word (Is. 55:11; *cf.* Gn. 24:50 where *thing* translates *dabar*, 'word') is superintended in its operation by God Himself (1 Sa. 3:19; Je. 1:12) and even partakes of the holiness of God, for to reject His word is to reject Him (1 Sa. 15:23; Is. 63:10). It is not inexact to speak, as Knight does (*op. cit.*, p. 16), of the word of God as an '*alter ego* of God'.

How is this word made available to man to teach him of God? The basic reply has already been stated: the revelation of God is made by means of events to which an authorized interpreter has been attached by God. But what is the relationship of the interpreter to the event? Our general consideration of the possibility of revelation in history has shown us that something more is needed than a mere attempt to be wise after the event.

The classic instance of the coinciding of history and interpretation is the work of Moses and the Exodus. It is quite clear that Moses was made wise before the event, and that the God who speaks precedes the God who acts. Before the divine act of deliverance Moses was already armed with an outline of the course of the events (Ex. 4:22f.), and, as interpretative clues to the coming acts of God, he had already been taught, by intelligible, verbal, propositional communication from God, the great truths of God's holiness (Ex. 3:5), His name (Ex. 3:14), His immutability (Ex. 3:15), His purpose to adopt Israel (Ex. 4:22), and to redeem His people in pursuance of His covenant (Ex. 6:6, 7). While, therefore, it is often asserted by OT specialists (*cf.* N. W. Porteous, 'The Theology of the Old Testament', in Peake's *Commentary on the Bible* (Eds. M. Black and H. H. Rowley), 1963, pp. 152f.) that revelation comes in the course of the sequence wherein the act is followed by the interpretation, this suffers from two grave defects. The first is that it is destructive of all certainty in the knowledge of God, for Moses' interpretation would in this case be merely first in time but could not exercise any other claim to precedence over alternative views of the Exodus. Far more important than this somewhat theoretical defect is its conflict with the only evidence we possess on the subject of divine revelation in the OT, namely, the OT itself. The personal divine confrontation and speech which we noted in studying the angel of the Lord continues to be the basic mode of revelation, except that from Moses onwards God made selection among men of those whom He would send with His word.

The uniform testimony of the prophets agrees with the position outlined in Ex. 4:16; 7:1, 2. The prophet is a person who speaks the very words of God (*cf.* Je. 1:9; 36:2, 4; Ezk. 2:7 – 3:3; see on Am. 1:1). There is mystery but no unreality when the prophets claim their words to be both their own and the Lord's. It is evident that their privilege of being verbally inspired did not devalue their personalities, for greater, more distinct and more colourful persons the world has yet to see. We need to remember that no prophet was ever a divine afterthought. In each case the man had long been prepared and set apart for the task (*cf.* Je. 1:5) so that by being himself he could be God's man for that time and his personality could impart to the word of God exactly those tints which God required (*cf.* B. B. Warfield, *The Inspiration and Authority of the Bible*, 1951, pp. 155f.; *NBD*, art. 'Prophecy, Prophets').

COVENANT

At the centre of the world-view of the OT and at the centre of what God has revealed about Himself lies the doctrine of the covenant. Ps. 103 is typical of this: the universality of vv. 6 and 19 brackets the special concern of God for Israel (vv. 7–18), and the preoccupation of this description of the chosen people is the covenant revelation (with v. 8, *cf.* Ex. 34:6). 'Covenant' is thus the very heart of OT theology, the central essence of what it teaches us about God.

Covenant terminology

The word 'covenant' (*berît*) occurs first in Gn. 6:18, and thereafter it marks the main epochs of God's dealings with His people (*cf.* Gn. 15:18; 17:1f.; Ex. 2:24; 6:5; Dt. 4:13; Is. 54:10; Je. 31:31–34; Ezk. 37:26). There is some dispute as to its precise meaning, and advocates are found for the suggestions that its root is a verb 'to eat', pointing to the communal meal in which an agreement was sealed (*cf.*

Gn. 31:54; also the phrase 'covenant of salt', Nu. 18:19; see G. A. F. Knight, *A Christian Theology of the Old Testament*, 1959, p. 218); or that *bᵉrît* comes from the Assyrian *beritu*, meaning 'bond' or 'fetter'; or, as suggested by M. Noth (*The Laws of the Pentateuch and other Essays*, 1966, p. 112), that an Akkadian preposition *birît*, 'between', developed into a noun 'mediation'. Any or all of these meanings corresponds well with the word as used in the OT. Confining ourselves to the covenant of God, the word signifies the bond of communion with Himself into which God, by sovereign action, brings the chosen people. A covenant among men, between equal parties, was a reciprocal arrangement, possibly even a bargain in which obligations were mutually balanced between the contracting parties. But the divine covenant was not between equals; it was imposed by God, acting, as we shall see, in sovereign grace. This aspect of the covenant has found useful illustration in the suzerainty treaties of the Hittite kings (*cf.* H. H. Guthrie, *God and History in the Old Testament*, 1961, pp. 42ff.; G. von Rad, *Old Testament Theology*, Vol. 1, 1962, pp. 132ff.).

The verbs used in connection with the covenant ought to be noticed. There are three mainly in use, each imparting a distinct significance. The verb *kāraṯ*, 'to cut' (*cf.* Gn. 15:18), is used with reference to the solemn inauguration of a covenant according to the appropriate forms. It points to ceremonies such as Gn. 15:9, 10; Je. 34:18. Another verb, *qûm*, used in its causative formation, and translated 'to establish' (*e.g.* Gn. 6:18) signifies 'to bring into operation', or 'to fulfil (what was promised)'. The third verb, *nāṯan*, 'to place' or 'appoint' (translated 'make', Gn. 9:12; 17:2) points to the bond of the covenant as the abiding mode of relationship between the two parties concerned. It is important to keep these differing significances in mind, not least because in English translations 'make' is common to the first and third of the verbs, but to distinguish them enables us to see correctly, for example, that Gn. 17 is not a new departure but an elaboration of the relationship formally inaugurated in Gn. 15 (*cf.* M. H. Segal, *The Pentateuch, Its composition and its authorship*, 1967, p. 33).

God in the covenant

The delineation of God throughout the dealings with Noah, Abraham and Moses is very consistent. The idea of the divine holiness is not specified by name until Ex. 3:5, after which it dominates the Mosaic revelation: the whole story of the Exodus is contained between the fires of 3:2 and 19:18, which in each case (3:5; 19:20–24) are explained to mean the unapproachable holiness of God. But the same view of God is clearly implied in Gn. 6–9. The judgment of the Flood arises out of the provocation offered to the divine nature by universal sinfulness (Gn. 6:5–7), and even in the rather unclouded story of Abraham the darker shades are not absent (*e.g.* Gn. 15:12–14, 16), even though the total biblical emphasis on sin, repentance and judgment is missing in the patriarchal stories.

The partner of God's holiness is ever His law, His holy requirement among men. Just as the holiness of God becomes more clearly defined as the covenant process matures from Noah to Moses, so does the place and nature of law. The obligations laid on Noah are related only in general to his covenantal position (Gn. 9:1–7); in the case of Abraham, the obligation, vague as it is, lies clearly within the covenant (Gn. 17:1, 2). For Moses and Israel, the giving of the law of God, itemized and enforced, is the goal of the whole historical movement which began in Egypt (*e.g.* Ex. 3:12) and provides the substance of the covenant (*e.g.* Dt. 4:13).

Alongside these elements in the covenant-revelation of God lies His grace. This is first seen, and specifically mentioned, in the election of Noah to be the covenant-man (Gn. 6:8). The usage of the phrase '(Noah) found favour' (*cf.* Gn. 19:19; 47:25, where 'may it please' translates the phrase 'let us find grace in the sight of') can best be understood by reversing it, 'favour found (Noah)'. It always implies that something happens contrary to desert, something which originates in the graciousness of the giver and not in the merits or efforts of the recipient. Thus the whole covenant process is an outflow of divine grace, whereby, in the context of a deserved judgment, a man, and through him his descendants, was elected to mercy.

In the story of the Exodus, the same grace is at work to deliver the enslaved people. Of the three main features which reveal the grace of God to Israel, it must suffice here to mention two, and reserve for a moment the third. It is in the Exodus narrative that the verb 'to redeem' (*gā'al*, Ex. 6:6; *cf.* Is. 43:3) is used for the first time in its distinctive sense (L. Morris, *The Apostolic Preaching of the Cross*, 1955, pp. 9ff.), and it is in connection with this act of redemption, coupled as it is with the insistence on the divine holiness, that the meaning of the divine name, Yahweh, is first declared.

The significance of *Yahweh* (Ex. 3:13–15) as a verbal formation continues to be the subject of dispute (*cf.* J. A. Motyer, *The Revelation of the Divine Name*, 1959, esp. pp. 24ff.). Assuming its association with the verb *h-y-h*, 'to be', it is important to remember that this signifies not so much 'existence' as 'active reality'. Even granting, therefore, that the obscurity of the Name may in part be deliberate, indicating the hidden depths of the divine nature as yet undisclosed (*cf.* B. W. Anderson, *The Living World of the Old Testament*, 1958, p. 34), yet, as to what it does reveal, there is nothing substantial to choose between W. F. Albright's preference for 'I bring to pass what I bring to pass' (*i.e.* 'I do what I choose'; see *op. cit.*, pp. 15f.), and that of most others (*e.g.* B. W. Anderson, *op. cit.*, p. 34; U. E. Simon, *A Theology of Salvation*, 1953, p. 89), 'I will be what I will be' (*i.e.* 'I will be actively present as I choose'). In each case the

Name is, as it were, a bracket in which certain truths will be set according as God confirms His word in coming events. In a word, the Exodus revelation of Yahweh, the covenant revelation, can be summarized by saying that He is the God who saves His people and judges His enemies: the God of holy redemption.

Sin and sacrifice

The third manifestation of divine grace to Israel, and one which is deeply rooted in the holiness of God and therefore stamped with the hall-mark of Exodus theology, was the fixing of the sacrificial system in its classical form. Sacrifice had, of course, been known from the earliest times, and, in particular, was associated with the epochs of the covenant. In the case of Noah, the offering of sacrifice is one of the features of man in covenant with God (Gn. 8:20–22); with Abram, sacrifice is made central to the inauguration of the covenant (Gn. 15:9, 10, 18) but its significance is not explained. At the Exodus we see why sacrifice is central to the covenant and exactly what it means.

It was the Passover which effected the deliverance of Israel from Egypt. Moses had been forewarned (Ex. 4:21ff.) that the 'plagues' would only increase bondage until the decisive issue of the firstborn was reached. This crisis came when at length Pharaoh broke off negotiations with Moses, and God said 'Yet one plague more' (Ex. 10:28 – 11:3). However, when that final plague came, it was the blood of the Passover lamb which proved decisive, for therein lay Israel's safety through that night of judgment.

The twin ideas of propitiation and substitution lie at the heart of Ex. 12. It is essential to the proper understanding of the meaning of 'blood' in the OT sacrifices (cf. A. M. Stibbs, The Meaning of the word 'Blood' in Scripture, 1954) to note that for some reason the blood beneath which the Israelites sheltered kept them safe from divine judgment (Ex. 12:13, 22, 23). When God looked upon the blood He found no reason to proceed further against those who were in that house.

It is difficult to see how the generally accepted view that 'blood' signifies 'life released' (cf. C. R. North, art. 'Sacrifice' in A. Richardson, A Theological Word-book of the Bible; Vriezen, op. cit., p. 292) can have any bearing on the Passover event. The force of the instructions given for the Passover is that every calculation is to be made so that the lamb, when dead, exactly matches the needs of the people (Ex. 12:3, 4) and that Israel is to enter into the death of the lamb by occupying the night in feeding upon it. The regulation that nothing shall remain underscores their preoccupation with its state of death (Ex. 12:10). The needs of the story, as well as the subsequent derivative legislation, are alone met by the assumption that the blood smeared on the door-posts proclaimed the death of the lamb, and if this is the case, then its death is necessarily an act of substitution, whereby the lamb, exactly assessed to match the people (Ex. 12:4), took the place of God's firstborn, Israel (Ex. 4:22), who thus survived the night wherein Pharaoh's firstborn perished. (See further J. A. Motyer, 'Priestly Sacrifices in the Old Testament' in J. I. Packer, Eucharistic Sacrifice, 1962.)

The Passover story says nothing more than that the blood delivered Israel from divine judgment. In the subsequent Mosaic legislation it became clear that the need to be thus delivered arose from man's state as sinner, and that without blood-shedding there was no remission. The once-for-all deliverance effected by the Passover sacrifice was prolonged for the enjoyment of the individual Israelite in fellowship with God by the continual blood-shedding associated with the burnt-offering, the peace-offering and the sin-offering. The whole rationale of this sacrificial system is crystallized in Lv. 17:11. In this key verse it is too readily assumed that because the life of the flesh is in the blood then the shedding of blood means the release of the life. But to hold this is to snatch a phrase out of its context. The shedding of blood must meet the requirements of the twice-repeated idea of 'making atonement' and, as L. Morris has shown decisively (op. cit.), this involves the idea of 'paying a price', an idea which is met only if the shedding of the blood terminates the life which it once fostered in the flesh of the animal. Again, the shedding of the blood must match the phrase 'I have given it to you'. Surely it is one of the strangest interpretations of the meaning of sacrifice to say that life is released as a gift to God (North, art. cit.) when the key explanatory verse insists that it is God's gift to man! Again it must be asked, does not this require the notion of the divinely provided substitute (cf. Gn. 22:7, 8, 13)? It is not out of place to note that the constant feature of sacrifices, the laying-on of the offerer's hand, is only satisfactorily explained as the designation of a substitute offering (Lv. 1:4; 3:2; 4:4; cf. 16:21).

The covenant Mediator

The OT is supremely the book of expectation. From the start, people are shown as living under hope of a promised deliverer (Gn. 4:1; 5:29; cf. NBD, art. 'Messiah'). This promise narrowed and clarified in the course of history. The promise was first concentrated in the seed of Abraham (Gn. 22:18, where RSV descendants translates 'seed', a word which may very well mean a single descendant, e.g. Gn. 4:25 where another child translates the same form of the same word). Then, later, the promise was associated with the royal house of David (e.g. 2 Sa. 7; Pss. 2; 72; etc.). Meantime, Moses himself linked the promise with the notion of a coming Prophet (Dt. 18:18f.; cf. NBD, art. 'Prophecy'). Thus, from many main angles of Israelite life, a 'Messianic' expectation came into focus (cf. H. L. Ellison, The Centrality of the Messianic Idea for the Old Testament, 1953). In particular, the expectation was given a covenant context in the hope of the perfect King (Is. 9:1–7; 11:1ff.; 55:3), the perfect Priest with the perfect Sacrifice (Is. 52:13 – 53:12; 54:10), the perfect Deliverer (Is. 59:16–21; 63:1–6), the perfect Lawgiver (Je. 31:31–34), and the perfect Mediator-Prince (Ezk. 45; 46; cf. 37:25–27).

It is at this point that OT theology comes full circle, for it is in the covenant-Messiah that the note of universality inherent in the doctrine of God the Creator finds its ultimate expression: in Him the call goes to the Gentile also (Is. 42:1–4; 49:6). In Him also that ground-truth, the transcendent God who meets with men, finds absolute expression, for the OT has this as its climax, a divine Messiah (cf. B. B. Warfield, *Biblical and Theological Studies*, IV, 'The Divine Messiah in the Old Testament', 1952; *NBD*, art. 'Messiah'), the God-man of Ps. 45:6, 7 (RV, not RSV), addressed as God, and yet acknowledging God, the 'arm of the Lord' (Is. 53:1; cf. Ex. 6:6), God Himself come down to effect salvation for the world.

J. A. MOTYER

History of the literary criticism of the Pentateuch

From the earliest Christian centuries hostile criticism of the Bible, and not least of the Pentateuch, has made its appearance (see E. J. Young, *An Introduction to the Old Testament*, 1958, pp. 108–117). It was, however, in the post-Reformation period that rationalistic criticism began to make its most distinctive appearance, and in the interests of space we must confine our attention to this. It may be seen, *e.g.*, in the work of Masius (d. 1573), a Roman Catholic lawyer, who held that Ezra may have made certain interpolations in the books of Moses. Likewise the Spanish Jesuit, Benedict Pereira (*c.* 1535–1610), held that there were considerable later additions made to the Pentateuch.

Benedict Spinoza (1632–77) denied the Mosaic authorship of the Pentateuch, attributing it on the whole to a later compiler, probably Ezra. Certain parts, however, he did attribute to Moses. Quite possibly we should attribute the actual beginnings of the documentary hypothesis to Hans Witter (1711), who held that there were two parallel accounts of the creation which were to be distinguished by their usage of the divine names.

It is with Jean Astruc (1753) that the origins of the documentary hypothesis are usually associated. Astruc held that Moses had before him written documents which he employed in the composition of Genesis. These old memoirs contained the history of Moses' ancestors from the very creation of the world. According to their contents Moses divided these documents into pieces and then assembled them, one after another, thus forming the present book of Genesis. It will be noted that Astruc did not deny that Moses was the Pentateuch's author.

What led Astruc to do this was the presence of supposedly duplicate accounts of the same incidents, the different use of the divine names and the non-chronological order of certain events. Astruc placed in a column which he labelled A those passages in which the divine name Elohim (French, *le Dieu*) was employed and in another column B those which used the name Jehovah, or, more properly, Yahweh (*l'Eternel*). It was necessary, however, to postulate the presence of fragments of twelve documents in all before Astruc was satisfied with his accomplishment.

Astruc's work in itself apparently had little influence. Eichhorn asserted his independence of Astruc but performed essentially the same task, carrying it out far more thoroughly. He is probably the first to designate the two 'sources' by the initials J and E, standing for Jehovah (Yahweh) and Elohim. (Yahweh is the covenant name of God, and Elohim is the ordinary Hebrew word for God.) At first Eichhorn held that Moses himself had pieced together the sources, but later he maintained that they were put together by an unknown redactor.

In 1798 Karl David Ilgen made the suggestion, which was to have later influence, that there were two Elohists and one Yahwist. What was of particular significance was the fact that he assigned to his second Elohist passages in Gn. 1–11 which Astruc had regarded as belonging to the Yahwist. In other words, what formerly had been thought to belong to J was now seen to be more closely related to E, and thus it was becoming apparent that in themselves the divine names were not a sufficient criterion for the partition of Genesis into diverse documents. This work of Ilgen laid the foundation for the later writings of Hupfeld.

The view that there were two basic documents in Genesis was commonly known as the two document theory. De Wette carried the investigation further, however, by bringing Deuteronomy into the picture. In 1805 in his doctoral dissertation De Wette maintained that Deuteronomy was composed during the reign of Josiah (622 BC) and argued that, inasmuch as it is presupposed in the other Pentateuchal books, they must be later. Thus, there were actually three documents, labelled J, E and D (and according to Ilgen, E²).

Not all scholars held to this position and there were various modifications which may briefly be mentioned. Several men held to what has been termed a 'fragmentary hypothesis', which essentially held that the Pentateuch consisted of a mass of fragments, pieced together by a later redactor. In opposition to this some men maintained that there was really only one basic document, and that this basic document had been supplemented with excerpts from another. The basic document was generally held to be E and the supplements were made from the J document. Not all advocates of this hypothesis, however, were in agreement upon this particular point. This view did not maintain the field very long. It was pointed out that the J passages which were inserted into E might very well contain allusions to the E passages, but why should the E passages, supposedly the basic document, contain any reflections upon material in the inserted J passages?

The modified documentary hypothesis

Precisely 100 years after Astruc produced his

34

volume, the documentary hypothesis underwent a serious modification. Hints as to this modification were already present in the work of Ilgen. It remained for Hermann Hupfeld, however, to give the modification its impetus. Hupfeld took up the idea advanced already by Ilgen that the E document was not continuous, but consisted of two documents, one of which was closer to J than to the remainder of E. Thus, according to Hupfeld, there was a first Elohist and a second Elohist. In addition there was also the Yahwist document and Deuteronomy, and the order which Hupfeld assigned was E¹, E², J and D. In time the first Elohist became known as the priestly document because of its interest in priestly matters, which were quite arbitrarily seen as including genealogies, itineraries and even Gn. 1 which evidences no priestly associations whatsoever. Thus the four documents came to be labelled, P, J, E, D. Deuteronomy was considered to be latest of all.

There are certain difficulties in this partition which should be noted. Hupfeld's second E begins at Gn. 20, whereas the first E practically concludes at that point. Thus it would seem that one document had been broken into two. Furthermore, the second E apparently presupposes parts of the first E. The content of the first E is largely genealogical and statistical and such material is not the property of any one particular writer. Inasmuch as the documentary hypothesis involves so much difficulty, Hupfeld found it necessary to make rather full use of a redactor.

Hupfeld's work was a landmark in the history of OT negative criticism, and before proceeding to trace the development of such criticism further, we may point out a few of the difficulties which the documentary hypothesis creates. There are positive claims made in the Bible that the Law is from Moses. In the Pentateuch itself there are express statements to the effect that Moses did write what God had commanded him (cf. Ex. 17:14; 24:4–8; 34:27; Nu. 33:1, 2; Dt. 31:9), but even more telling is the observation that almost everything in Exodus to Deuteronomy at least makes an implicit claim to stem directly from Moses. The Mosaic claim belongs to the fabric of these books (see the introductions to the commentaries on these Pentateuchal books). Furthermore there is a unity in the Pentateuch which the documentary hypothesis does not satisfactorily explain. If the first five books of the Bible were put together in the manner which this hypothesis demands, it is difficult, if not impossible, to understand how the result could be the unity which the Pentateuch actually does exhibit. Such a manner of putting books together is unnatural; no other great work of literature (to say nothing of the question of the Bible's inspiration) was produced in the manner which this view demands.

The divine names clearly are not suitable nor sufficient criteria for partitioning the biblical books into documents in the manner presupposed by this view. Even Astruc had difficulty along this line. In at least five chapters of Genesis the Deity is not mentioned at all, and yet these chapters are divided among J, P (E¹) and E². Obviously criteria other than the divine names must be employed. In seventeen chapters of Genesis and in Exodus 1 and 2 the name Yahweh does not occur and yet it is asserted that portions of 'J' are found in each of these chapters. Likewise there are fifteen chapters in which the word Elohim is not to be found. It would appear then that the names are not adequately distributed throughout Genesis to form the basis for division or partition into documents. The distribution is most pronounced in Gn. 1 – 3 where the combined form Yahweh Elohim appears 20 times. Sometimes it is possible to explain these variations on theological grounds, but this is not always the case.

In Ex. 3, to take but one example, there would seem to be good warrant for assuming that the names are used on the basis of their theological significance. This becomes increasingly evident, when we consider what the purpose of the chapter is, namely to show that the Elohim whom the fathers had known is the Yahweh who will enter into covenant with His people. Hence, although the chapter begins with the use of Elohim, it soon introduces the term Yahweh. In v. 4, a stumbling-block for critical analysis, both names are used, for the transition between Elohim and Yahweh is not yet complete.

In v. 6 Yahweh introduces Himself, and not until the conclusion of His speech in v. 10 do we again meet the term Elohim (v. 11). The One to whom Moses speaks is Elohim, but in the speech of God to Moses, God designates Himself as Yahweh (e.g. vv. 15, 16, 18), for it is as the covenant God of redemption that He will send Moses to lead the Israelites from Egypt. Thus theological considerations may very well often form the reason why a particular designation of God is employed.

It should furthermore be noted that the designation Yahweh occurs in passages which are often attributed to P, and Elohim in those which are assigned to J. Too often, a redactor must be brought in to explain phenomena which conflict with the documentary analysis. (See further E. Nielsen, Oral Tradition, 1954, pp. 93ff.) Ex. 3:4 serves as a good example. Here, we read, 'When Yahweh saw that he turned aside to see, Elohim called to him out of the bush.' In thus piecing together different fragments of the various documents, the redactor tears in sunder what was originally a unified narrative. To take but one example: Gn. 1 (attributed to P) speaks of everything as very good. Gn. 5 (also attributed to P) stresses the great reign of death over mankind, broken only by the case of Enoch. What caused the change from 'very good' to 'and he died' in ch. 5? No explanation is found in the so-called P fragments. The explanation is given in what the 'critics' attribute to JE, namely chs. 2 and 3. Did the original P, then, have any explanation of the change, *i.e.* of the Fall of man? If it did, why did the redactor or compiler omit it?

Furthermore, this redactor (or redactors, or schools, or call them what one will) was often guilty of gross carelessness. The principal example is the placing together of Gn. 1 and 2, which we are told constitute two different accounts of creation, with differing outlooks. If this were the case, one may wonder why the redactors bungled so badly. Why place side by side two conflicting creation narratives? If the redactors did that, they can hardly have been men of greatness, and yet these bunglers produced the Pentateuch. Here is a psychological phenomenon which has not yet been explained by adherents of the documentary analysis. Actually, of course, there are not two accounts of creation in Genesis; ch. 1 is a creation account, but ch. 2 describes the preparation of the Garden of Eden for man. (See further, the commentary on Genesis, *in loc.*)

Another of the reasons alleged in favour of multiple authorship of the Pentateuch is, as we have seen, the existence of duplicate accounts of the same event, it being rightly thought unreasonable that a single author would do this. Thus we are told, *e.g.*, that in Genesis there are two accounts of the expulsion of Hagar (16:4ff. and 21:9ff.). The former belongs to the J document, and the latter to E; they have been editorially harmonized by the invention of an angel who sent Hagar back after the first expulsion. Again, there are two accounts of the naming of Beer-sheba (21:31; 26:31ff.), and no less than three accounts of deceitful action in passing off a wife as a sister (12:10ff.; 20:1ff.; 26:6ff.).

From the point of view of the documentary theory the problem arises that 'duplications do not always occur in *different* documents—as, in theory, they ought to do—but in no inconsiderable number of cases fall within the limits of the same document. Thus E has a second visit to Bethel as well as P (Gn. 35:6, 7); J has two denials of wives (Gn. 12 and 26). . . . This suggests that even were the similarity of incidents as clear as is alleged, it would not necessarily prove different authorship' (J. Orr, *The Problem of the Old Testament*, 1908, pp. 236f.).

The matter can, of course, be settled only by detailed examination of the passages, and in the cases of the concealment of the wives' real status this shows how unnecessary the theory is. In the first place, Gn. 20:13 relates that we are here dealing with a general policy. If we take this statement seriously there is no inherent improbability in the similarity of the stories. But in fact the similarity is not great. *E.g.*, Pharaoh acts with the peremptory authority of a great ruler (12:19–21), hustling Abram from Egypt, but Abimelech, a petty chieftain, comes to Abraham as to an equal, inviting him to settle in the land where he pleases (20:15); whereas Abraham goes to Gerar in the course of his wanderings, Isaac goes because of famine (20:1; 26:1); whereas Sarah is taken into Abimelech's household, Rebekah is not (20:2; 26:8); whereas Abraham was invited to remain, Isaac is asked to go (20:15; 26:16), but not, as in the case of Abram in Egypt, because of the deception he had practised, but because 'you are much mightier than we' (26:16). In other respects also the individual colouring of each story could be brought out so as to show that the overlapping is virtually confined to the single common fact that each is concerned with the attempt to pass a wife off as a sister, a practice which is said to have been, in Abraham's case, a general policy.

Each case of alleged duplication must be subjected to this sort of detailed examination, and, as in the present case, it can confidently be asserted that nothing will be found giving substantial ground for supposing this sort of multiplication of sources for the Pentateuch.

The development hypothesis

One thing can truthfully be asserted concerning the study of the documentary hypothesis: it was kaleidoscopic. As early as 1834 Eduard Reuss had suggested that the basic Elohistic document (*i.e.* P), instead of being the earliest, was really the latest. It was some time, however, before this idea began to take hold. Karl Heinrich Graf had studied the legislation of the Pentateuch and from this study came to the conclusion that the priestly document was in reality the latest. Julius Wellhausen in *Die Komposition des Hexateuchs* (1876–77) brought this position to dominance. His style of writing was clear and convincing, and he is really the man to whom the development hypothesis owes its existence.

The development hypothesis is built upon the documentary hypothesis and is, as its name suggests, a hypothesis to the effect that the religious institutions of Israel underwent a development from earliest beginnings until they attained their final form. Wellhausen began by asking whether the Law was the starting-point for the history of ancient Israel or for the later Judaism. A number of OT books, he held, did come from the period of the Exile; may it not have been that the Law also came from this period? Wellhausen tells of his early experiences in reading the OT and how he found it difficult to believe that the Law was earlier than the prophets.

We may perhaps best understand the nature of Wellhausen's development hypothesis if we consider one important aspect thereof, namely the question of the place of worship. In the NT, said Wellhausen, both Jews and Samaritans recognized that there was to be only one central place of worship. They differed as to where this was but agreed in acknowledging that there should be only one central place for worship. This belief, however, had not always been held in Israel but came into being only during a long process of time. Before the building of the Temple, there is no trace of any sanctuary which could claim exclusive legitimacy for worship. Instead there appears to have been a multiplicity of sanctuaries and this was probably a heritage from the Canaanites. When the Israelites entered Palestine, Wellhausen tells us, they took over many of the high places and sacred sanctuaries.

From the fact that, after the battle of Michmash, Saul erected an altar, we can see that altars might be built at any place whatsoever (*cf.* 1 Sa. 14:33ff.). The growth of the Solomonic Temple tended to bring about the idea of centralization of worship, as did the decrease of family sacrifices. Actually, said Wellhausen, the books of Kings give a false picture of the situation, for the land was considered to belong to Yahweh, and hence any spot was suitable for worship. With the fall of Samaria, however, a change began to appear. Amos and Hosea had declared that some of the former sanctuaries were an abomination to the Lord. Their zeal, however, was directed not so much against the sanctuaries themselves as against the cultic practices that were carried on there. When Samaria fell, Judah had a clear field, and Jerusalem soon became recognized as the legitimate centre of worship. Samaria had fallen, but Sennacherib could not take Jerusalem, and so this city gained in prestige and importance.

There are, asserts Wellhausen, three stages in the Law which correspond to the stages of history just outlined. In Ex. 20:24–26 a multiplicity of altars is assumed as a matter of course. Worship could occur wherever one wished. The patriarchs are pictured (although Wellhausen of course denied the historicity of the patriarchal period) as worshipping not at one central altar, but where they willed. In this period what was important was the theophany in and for itself; its occurrence might be at any particular place.

As the book of the covenant (*i.e.* Ex. 20:23 – 23:33) and the so-called document J represent the first period of Israel's history, so Deuteronomy represents the second. In Deuteronomy alone do we find an insistence upon restriction of worship to the one chosen place; here only does the demand make itself so felt in its aggressive novelty and dominate the whole tendency of the law-maker. Deuteronomy uses old material but shapes it to agree with this fundamental purpose. The writer now permits what formerly had been forbidden, and prohibits what previously had been allowed. Deuteronomy therefore was an outgrowth of the conditions of the times and must be assigned to the day of Josiah. The book, or at least a part of it, was written at this time for the purpose of bringing about a centralization of worship. It therefore was not the work of Moses, but really a forgery, for it purported to be words which God spoke to Moses, and throughout it gives the impression of having been delivered to those who have not yet entered the land of promise.

With respect to the 'priestly code', Wellhausen points out that, like Deuteronomy, it also claims a centrality of sacrifice. Whereas in Deuteronomy, however, this unity of the cult is commanded, in the 'priestly code' it is presupposed, and is regarded as a matter of course. Thus, there is a contrast between Deuteronomy and the 'priestly code'. The one is the centre of movement and conflict; the other proceeds as though everything has been settled for a long time. Deuteronomy gives the idea; the 'priestly code' gives the idea as history. It cannot think of religion without one sanctuary; it cannot imagine Israel without it, and in this light it has rewritten Israel's earlier history. Thus, to take but one example, the Tabernacle was really patterned after the Temple, and not *vice versa*. Coupled with this idea of development of the place of worship was also a development in the nature of sacrifice, of the sacred festivals, the priests and the Levites, the idea of God, *etc.* Here, undergirding all, was the theory of evolution, which Darwin had popularized.

The response to Wellhausen

That the position of Wellhausen held the field for a long time cannot be denied. The development hypothesis which Wellhausen presented has finally gone by the board, but not the underlying documentary hypothesis, which today is as widely held (in one form or another) as ever. Two factors led to the downfall of the development hypothesis. In the first place the inherent weaknesses of Wellhausen's position were soon pointed out, and secondly, the discoveries of archaeology showed that Wellhausen could not possibly be right. Other factors also have doubtless entered into the picture, but these two in particular led to the demise of the development hypothesis.

Almost immediately scholars began to indicate the logical fallacies of which the noted German had been guilty. It did not necessarily follow, to take but one example, that a law had not existed because people paid no attention to it. Men such as W. L. Baxter, William Henry Green, Geerhardus Vos, Wilhelm Möller and later Oswald T. Allis have given searching analyses of the development hypothesis and have cogently presented its weaknesses. In particular the hypothesis is so thoroughly unscriptural that it cannot be accepted by anyone who has a high regard for what Scripture teaches concerning the date and authorship of its own documents.

Even during Wellhausen's lifetime, archaeology began to speak with a powerful voice. Finally, with the discovery of the Nuzi tablets (1925) it became clear that the background of the patriarchs, given in the book of Genesis, far from being unreliable, was remarkably accurate. The light which archaeology has brought to bear upon this question seems constantly to be increasing, so that it is becoming increasingly uncommon for scholars to agree with Wellhausen's estimate of the historical value of Genesis. It has also become apparent that much of the material found in the so-called 'priestly code' is very ancient. In many other respects also, archaeology has spoken with compelling voice. Wellhausen's books today offer little more than antiquarian interest, a strange fact when one considers the dogmatism that accompanied his presentation.

The school of form-criticism

With the study of archaeology there also came to light new information about the cultures of the ancient world. Ancient religions were studied and compared with the Scriptures. Hermann Gunkel wrote a book which in some respects contained within it the seeds of overthrow for the development hypothesis. Gunkel's purpose was to show how the material of Genesis was taken over from other cultures and adapted to Israelitish needs, and also to point out what value it finally received in Israel. It is in this process of transformation (*Umbildung*) that, according to Gunkel, the characteristic of Israelitish religion appears. What is peculiar to Israelitish religion is the belief that God has revealed Himself in the history of Israel.

Hence Gn. 1 is not a free construction of the composers, for old traditions stand behind the priestly writing. The narratives or sagas of Genesis were the stories which the ancient Israelites told, stories which from generation to generation had been handed down until they finally took on a crystallized form. In the beginning these sagas had no particular relation one to another but as time went on they came to be attached to some favourite figure such as Abraham. Only at a later time did they become collected into larger units, namely the documents which were known as J, E, *etc.*, and these were finally pieced together. The actual unit of investigation, however, according to Gunkel, is the individual saga or narrative, and the investigator's task is to determine the original form and as far as possible the historical situation that gave rise to the individual unit. Actually, such a procedure would destroy the unity of the supposed documents in which the units are now found.

The literary history of Israel, taught Gunkel, was really the history of the types. Every old literary type had originally its life-situation that called it into existence at a particular place. To discover the type, we must ask questions such as, Who speaks? Who listens? What voice determines the situation? What action is attempted? We must also study the history of the collection of the individual units.

Gunkel's work was carried out by others, notably Hugo Gressmann, who applied the same methods of study to the book of Exodus. In fact the entire OT was subjected to this particular approach in a series of four volumes known as *The Writings of the Old Testament* (*Die Schriften des Alten Testaments*, 1911). This approach to the OT became very influential and undergirds almost all 'critical' study of the present day.

In the approach of form-criticism there are certain considerations that must be taken into account. In itself there can be nothing objectionable in seeking to determine the form in which Scripture appears. We must distinguish, to take the most common examples, between prose and poetry. It may also be that there were certain types of writing in which the authors of Scripture engaged. This method, as it is commonly employed, however, is extremely subjective. It seeks to discover the original unit, and in so doing is willing to pare away anything which it regards as a secondary or later accretion. At this point, the subjectivism enters. Who is to say what is original and what is later? That the procedure is indeed subjective appears when one considers how diverse are the studies that have been made by various individual form-critics. Particularly is this true in connection with the study of the prophetical books. Men do not agree, and the disagreements are serious. Furthermore, once the supposed original unit has been obtained, certain questions arise which really cannot be answered. What was the life-situation that gave rise to the unit? Usually we do not know, for the unit itself often says little or nothing about such matters. Unconsciously critics are influenced by the context of Scripture which they have cast away in their study. Furthermore, it is then often impossible to determine who the speaker was. It is, therefore, understandable that the late Ivan Engnell maintained that it was not possible to reach the very words (the *ipsissima verba*) of the prophets. Form-criticism, as it is often practised, leads to scepticism.

Certain recent developments

Not all scholars followed in the stream of Wellhausen and Gunkel. Some went their own way. In 1908 B. D. Eerdmans approached the question of the Pentateuchal problem in a manner quite different from that espoused by the majority of scholars. He found four differing stages of development, proceeding from the polytheistic to the monotheistic. The discovery of Deuteronomy brought about a monotheistic rewriting of earlier material, and further expansions came after the Exile.

In 1912 Rudolf Smend asserted that there were two Yahwists who paralleled one another side by side. In addition he held to the unity of the E document, but thought that D and P were the subject of many additions. In 1922 Otto Eissfeldt took up this theory, designating Smend's J[1] as L (for 'lay source'). Eissfeldt's argumentation is based primarily upon the presence of supposed duplicate accounts.

Deuteronomy became the subject of much research, some holding that it came from northern Israel and others dating it after the Exile or at least at the time of the Exile. In 1925 Möller wrote in defence of the Mosaic authorship of Deuteronomy, pointing out cogently that the book often reflects upon the first four books of the Law. In 1963 Meredith G. Kline sought to show that the book was composed in the general style of the suzerainty treaties of the Hittites. Inasmuch as the book contains a historical prologue, which, he argues, characterized the early treaties, it must be early, consonant with Mosaic date and authorship.

Gradually a time of disintegration began to set in. With the discoveries of archaeology many fixed notions had to be abandoned, and men were writing on specialized problems.

A leading representative of the so-called 'Leipzig School' (*i.e.* the school of OT studies founded by the late Albrecht Alt) is Martin Noth. Noth presented a particular variety of the documentary hypothesis, but his most significant work is probably his view of the early history of Israel.

Noth regards the Pentateuch as the product of a long process of growth which was influenced by various interests and tendencies. Traditions, originally oral, were written down and only later were collected into a large literary work. The so-called documents J and E, according to Noth, had a common basis. Noth distinguishes a Tetrateuch (the first four books of the Pentateuch) from the Deuteronomic work of which Deuteronomy forms the basis, the remaining books of the complex being Joshua, Judges, 1 and 2 Samuel and 1 and 2 Kings. Thus there are actually two great complexes of traditions represented in the Pentateuch and historical books (the 'Former Prophets') of the OT. Noth's presentation is very detailed and he deals with the history of the various themes found in the documents with great thoroughness.

In addition to the many arguments that can be advanced against the documentary analysis generally is the fact that Deuteronomy reflects upon, and gives the appearance of being based upon, the previous books of the Pentateuch, in particular upon the fact of the Exodus. This fact of the Exodus is the foundation of the history that follows. Why is it treated so basically in the book of Exodus, being described as though by a contemporary, whereas in Deuteronomy and subsequent books it appears as something that has happened in the past?

Noth is perhaps best known for his treatment of the early history of Israel. Heinrich Ewald (d. 1875) had maintained that in the description and enumeration of the tribes the number twelve was basic. Noth held that in early Israel there had been a sacral covenant or confederation of the twelve tribes after the nature of the amphictyonies of the Greek city-states. The heart of this amphictyony, which supposedly arose during the time of the judges, was the cult, situated at a central sanctuary. The laws were the ordinances of this religious arrangement.

Several considerations, however, make it very questionable whether Noth's interpretation of early Israelitish history is correct. In the first place the situation in Greece and Italy was quite different from what it was in Israel. In Greece the amphictyony served to protect and to unite already existing small city-states. The Philistine confederacy seems to have been closer to this arrangement. The Israelites, however, were tribes which had entered Palestine from the desert. They were not city-states.

Jos. 24, to which appeal is made for the establishment of the unity of the tribes, rather presupposes this unity as already in existence. Again, although the OT has words for many details of religious worship, there is no Hebrew word to denote an amphictyony. Nor does the OT mention any arrangement which might legitimately be designated an amphictyony. During the period of the judges the tribes were not united, as Noth's theory assumes, but were divided. When, under Samuel, they asked for a king, their request was political and not religious. Hence there actually is no evidence to support Noth's thesis.

The study of traditions

Of particular significance is the work of Gerhard von Rad, who takes his starting-point with Dt. 26:5b–11. This passage he regards as a cultic credo. What is of significance, he says, is the fact that there is no mention whatever of the events at Sinai. From this, and also from the consideration that he thinks this same phenomenon is present in other passages (*e.g.* Ex. 15; Ps. 136), he concludes that the Sinai traditions were originally separate from those of the Exodus and the conquest. Von Rad does not necessarily deny the historicity of the patriarchs as individuals, but holds that they held to the form of worship known as 'The God of the Fathers', each patriarch worshipping his own god. Not all of the tribes were in Egypt, but only the Rachel tribes.

These Rachel tribes entered the land of promise and there formed a loose association (amphictyony) with the Leah tribes which were already in the land. What united them was their common faith in their god Yahweh. Over the course of years, priests of the Yahweh congregations taught the people.

The Yahwistic editor, somewhere along the line, united the Sinai traditions with those of the Exodus and the conquest. Much of Israel's religious thought thus came to her through the Canaanites, although originally it may have gone back to the Babylonians. Von Rad's thesis is quite radical. It may be pointed out that in covenant documents the place of ratification of the covenant is often not mentioned, and hence, in the Deuteronomy passage one would not necessarily expect any mention of Sinai by name. Furthermore, his view proves too much. The Deuteronomy passage omits everything between the Exodus and the entrance into Palestine. If therefore the Sinai traditions are not a part of the original, neither is much else.

Conclusion

To trace the development of various approaches

to the Pentateuch is interesting and instructive. When, however, the student departs from the direct claims of the Bible itself, he finds that he is involved in serious difficulty. None of the theories mentioned really does justice to the facts of Scripture. It is only when the claims of the Bible (including its claim that, in the ultimate and most real sense, God is its Author) are taken at face value that one can do justice to Scripture. What the future will bring forth, one cannot know. Nevertheless, the Word of our God will stand for ever; theories come and theories go, but the Scriptures will continue to bless mankind, for they are the Word of the eternal God.

EDWARD J. YOUNG

Moses and the Pentateuch

The Christian who tries to take the guidance of Christ in his understanding of the OT is not bound by tradition when it comes to such matters as authorship. Indeed he is warned not to put the traditions of men on a level with the Word of God (Mk. 7:13). He is, however, bound by everything that is specifically taught in the OT, since: 'To Christ the Old Testament was true, authoritative, inspired. To Him the God of the Old Testament was the living God, and the teaching of the Old Testament was the teaching of the living God. To Him, what Scripture said, God said' (see the author's *Our Lord's View of the Old Testament*, 1964, p. 40).

It may seem at first sight that a historian who approaches the Bible with the belief that its statements are true must be already so prejudiced that his conclusions can be of no value, for the true scholar, it is said, should be a man with an 'open' mind. Yet this plausible reasoning conceals a fallacy. For obviously no-one is fit for scholarly research unless his mind is already filled with many facts and many ideas, just as no-one is fit for scientific research unless he already has a good grasp of the facts and principles of his branch of science. A man's fitness for fruitful research depends upon his understanding of the basic principles of his subject. It is no help to a physicist to have an 'open' mind about the carefully-established laws of physics. A firm grasp of the known is the key to the exploration of the unknown. This does not mean that some laws may not be capable of more precise determination or of more satisfactory formulation; this is part of the function of research. But any scholar must build on the known, if he is to advance into the unknown.

The belief that Jesus is a dependable Teacher comes from the inner witness of God Himself, which causes the Christian to believe his Lord's claim: 'Heaven and earth will pass away, but my words will not pass away' (Mk. 13:31). 'Every one . . . who hears these words of mine and does them will be like a wise man who built his house upon the rock' (Mt. 7:24). He is thus predisposed to accept Christ's view of the OT. He believes that this will be the key to its understanding. And he is not disappointed.

The dominant theory of Pentateuchal criticism combines two strands, the documentary and the development theories, both of which are based on the supposition of large-scale internal contradictions in the OT. This theory has come under heavy fire (see 'History of the Literary Criticism of the Pentateuch', above, pp. 34ff.). Many of the supposed contradictions are obviously not contra-dictions, and all are fairly contestable. The door is wide open for those who believe that the contents of the OT, when rightly understood, form a harmonious and organic unity. If this belief is correct—if, in other words, it is a soundly grounded principle of theological science—there will be no need to fudge the answers. The established principle will help, not hinder, the finding of answers to the unsolved difficulties. The principle should engender great patience and great honesty when dealing with an intractable problem, and a preparedness to leave it unsolved, if no satisfactory solution can be discovered—for there is plainly no disgrace in admitting one's lack of omniscience, and quite certainly the truth of God can never be promoted by dishonest argument. Christ therefore bids us approach our problem holding fast to the truth of Scripture, but with minds completely open to all possibilities which do not conflict with the inspired utterances of the Spirit.

When we attempt to define with greater precision the biblical doctrine of Scripture (which we stated in general terms in our opening paragraph) we observe two points. First, the purpose of all God-breathed Scripture is 'for teaching, for reproof, for correction, and for training in righteousness, that the man of God may be complete, equipped for every good work' (2 Tim. 3:16). That is to say, the historical details of the Bible are not important for their own sake, but only for the part they play in making known God's ways to men. Thus it is that obscurities in the Bible have never been a bar to a man's understanding of the ways of God, provided he has been willing to know the truth. The central teaching of the Bible has always remained clear, even for those with a bad text and a bad translation. Small divergences in text and occasional divergences of meaning in the translations were of course well known in NT times, but they rightly caused no doubts as to the trustworthiness of the revelation contained in them.

Second, the description of Scripture as 'God-breathed' suggests that the proper basis for detailed, scholarly discussion is the Scriptures as they were originally given. The moment of 'inspiration' was the moment of utterance, when God 'breathed' the Word which was committed to writing. This means two things: first, that the best text is that closest to the original. (It is the textual critic's task to try to determine which of the small variants are most likely to have been original.) Second, that the text in the original language is to be preferred to that in the

41

translations. A translation, ancient or modern, may of course be useful in bringing out some particular aspect of the original, and a modern expositor (like the writers of the NT) may quote from a translation without in any way impugning the ultimate authority of the original.

This then gives us three principles on which to approach the subject of the authorship of the Pentateuch. 1. We are not bound by tradition. 2. We are bound by the text of Scripture as originally given, in so far as this may be determined. 3. We are aware of a measure of corruption in the transmission of the text, which does not vitiate the revelation of the Pentateuch, but which must be taken into account when evaluating the evidence for authorship in detail.

The Pentateuch, when considered as a whole or as five distinct books, is in fact anonymous. Certain passages are said to have been originally written by Moses (Ex. 17:14; 24:4; 34:28; Nu. 33:2; Dt. 31:9, 22, 24), but nowhere is it said that Moses was the author of a complete book. We are not therefore bound by the ancient Jewish tradition, either in its more extreme form (espoused even by Josephus and Philo) which said that Moses wrote the whole Pentateuch, including a (prophetic) account of his own death and of the events immediately following; or in its more moderate form (mentioned in the Talmud) which said that Moses wrote everything except the concluding section of Deuteronomy, which was written by Joshua.

There seem in fact to be other post-Mosaic elements in the Pentateuch besides its ending. In this respect Deuteronomy stands somewhat apart from the other books. In Genesis–Numbers there is remarkably little that can be claimed with any assurance as even probably post-Mosaic, and less that can be regarded as demonstrably post-Mosaic; but there is enough to show that the traditional Jewish solution is somewhat too simple. In Gn. 14:14 there is mention of the city of Dan, which got its name from the Danites who later conquered it (Jos. 19:47; Jdg. 18:29). In Gn. 36:31ff. we are given a list of Edomite kings 'who reigned in the land of Edom, before any king reigned over the Israelites'. Ex. 16:35: 'The people of Israel ate the manna forty years, till they came to a habitable land; they ate the manna, till they came to the border of the land of Canaan' could have been added to the account of the early journeyings by Moses just before his death, but it looks more like an editorial comment. Then there is the noteworthy saying: 'The man Moses was very meek, more than all men that were on the face of the earth' (Nu. 12:3). It could be argued that this was the unself-conscious remark of a man of supreme humility, but to most people it looks like the remark of an editor. Probably the same could be said of Ex. 11:3: 'The man Moses was very great in the land of Egypt.'

The problem of the very large numbers poses a further question, but this concerns transmission of the text, rather than authorship. I have dealt with this matter at length in *Tyndale Bulletin*, 18, 1967, pp. 19ff., 'Large Numbers in the Old Testament'. I have there argued that figures in the tribal censuses in Nu. 1 and 26 are made up by the erroneous adding together of the number of *'allûpîm* (fully-armed soldiers) and the number of *mē'ôt* (fighting units of roughly a hundred men). The former, wrongly vocalized as *'ªlāpîm* (thousands), were added to the latter (which for the various tribes ranged between twelve and twenty-seven 'hundreds', *i.e.* one *'elep* two *mē'ôt* and two *'ªlāpîm* seven *mē'ôt*), to give the present numbers. On this reckoning the Israelite fighting force would have numbered about 18,000 and the whole migration about 72,000. The census lists and a number of other numerical problems all presuppose a stage where the figures presented considerable difficulty to readers and where deliberate attempts were made to restore them to order. But such attempts at correction, though made long after the time of Moses, in no way point to a post-Mosaic original.

Some entirely committed conservatives like G. C. Aalders (*A Short Introduction to the Pentateuch*, 1949, p. 107) think that they can identify other post-Mosaic passages, such as Nu. 21:14f.; 32:34ff. These could be post-Mosaic, but they are too uncertain to have any evidential value in determining the date of authorship. At most their late date could be regarded as a reasonable possibility once a post-Mosaic date for the compilation of the book had been established on other grounds.

It is clear from this that there is not enough demonstrably late material in Genesis–Numbers to demand post-Mosaic authorship. With documents which were both national records and the *tôrâ* for religious instruction, it is only to be expected that in the course of 1,000 years there might be the modernizing of an archaic name, the bringing up to date of a genealogical list, the slipping in of an explanatory comment or the attempt to clear up textual obscurities. Aalders argued from Gn. 36:31 that the final revision of the Pentateuch must be dated in the monarchy, and from the evidence of the use of the Pentateuch in Jdg. 1–16 (which must be dated before the capture of Jerusalem; see Jdg. 1:21), not later than the seventh year of King David's reign. He is cautious as to how great a part was played by Moses and how great a part by later contributors, but he seems to incline to the view that the latter had an inspired and creative role, and that their additions were more than just interpretative glosses. But in fairness it needs to be recognized how few in fact are the demonstrably post-Mosaic elements, and how unwise it would be to build a weighty historical argument upon them.

When we turn to Deuteronomy, however, the case is somewhat different. There the claim is explicitly made that the bulk of the material was put into writing by Moses. 'When Moses had finished writing the words of this law in a book, to the very end' (31:24), he committed it to the care of the Levites, who were to keep it beside the ark of the covenant. His instructions, couched in 'I' and 'we' language, retain their original hortatory form. But in Deuteronomy, as we have it now, there is unquestionably post-Mosaic editing, notably in the concluding chapters and presumably in the introduction (1:1–5) and in some of the explanatory notes and remarks (2:10–12, 20–23; 3:9, 11; 4:45–49). It is indeed attractive to suppose that all (or almost all) of the passages where Moses is referred to in the third person are by an independent narrator, though there is nothing unusual about an author writing of himself in the third person. The narrator writes as one who actually observed the events he records and there is nothing said by him which need have been written long after Moses' death. Yet, in spite of the Talmudic tradition, he could hardly have been Joshua, since Joshua would probably not have described himself as 'full of the spirit of wisdom' (34:9).

If we are to do justice to the explicit statements of the OT, there are two main options open to us. We can place the writing up of the Mosaic and pre-Mosaic materials in the early monarchy. Apart from the numerical difficulties we can accept the Pentateuch virtually as it stands, without the intrusion of any glosses, as an anonymous work written in the days of Saul or David. Alternatively, we can regard Genesis–Numbers as the work of Moses which has undergone a tiny handful of minor modifications during the course of its transmission, and Deuteronomy as his farewell discourses, committed to writing by Moses himself, but written up by a narrator somewhat later, during the time of Joshua's leadership.

I should wish to argue for the latter, on the ground that Mosaic authorship best explains both its superlative qualities and its apparent deficiencies. No sense can be made of the history of the world unless Moses is recognized, not only as a historical figure, but as one of the greatest figures of all time. It can be safely said that the appearance in the world of the ethical monotheism of Judaism represents the most far-reaching influence in the whole history of mankind. Out of Judaism arose Christianity and Islam, and (indirectly) science and (pervertedly) Communism. This, the greatest effect in the life of man, demands a great cause. It demands a genius. It demands that we see Moses as perhaps the supreme genius of all time.

It is true that the other historical books of the Bible are great literature and that we have no certain knowledge of their authorship, but the Pentateuch—and Genesis in particular—is unique. With artless simplicity the foundation of the whole Judaeo-Christian biblical tradition is laid. As F. D. Kidner says: 'If its chief architect was not Moses, it was evidently a man of comparable stature' (*Genesis*, TOTC, 1967, p. 16). But where is a man of *comparable* stature to be found? Moses not only had immense natural gifts, but he was the one 'whom the Lord knew face to face' (Dt. 34:10). Living on the borderland between the sophisticated culture of Egypt and the profound simplicity of the Israelite faith, he had opportunities granted to no other man. In the furnace of affliction in Egypt, he meditated deeply on the medley of traditions which were current, either in literary or in oral form, among the Israelite people. He was able to sort true from false and relevant from irrelevant till there formed in his mind a crystal-clear picture of the one, true, living God, who had chosen Israel as His covenant people. Genesis represents the essence of Mosaic religion and the foundation of the religion of the whole Bible.

Mosaic authorship explains not only its content, but its style. In a thoughtful article, 'The Glosses in the Book of Genesis and the J E Theory' (*Exp T*, 67, 1956, p. 333), M. S. Seale tells how, in the course of translating Genesis into colloquial Arabic, he was struck by the frequent use of synonyms and glosses. Why? 'Out of sheer necessity. He is writing for a people and a nation plus a mixed multitude (Ex. 12:38 and Nu. 11:4); but the peoples are themselves a great mixture: they are of bedouin origin, Aramaean domicile, Egyptian upbringing, and Canaanite connections. Glosses and explanations, plus an extensive use of words taken from Arabic, Akkadian, Aramaic and Egyptian, are for such people an absolute necessity.'

Genesis is a unity, summarizing the divine revelation prior to the time of Moses. Leviticus, being essentially a handbook for the priests, is a unity. Deuteronomy, the Second Law, is also a unity. Exodus and Numbers, however, do not look like the work of a tidy-minded editor. They are made up of a somewhat heterogeneous collection of laws and history and do not betray the same obvious unity of conception. It is easier to see them as the virtually unedited memoirs of Moses, which later generations did not feel at liberty to tamper with, than to see them as a careful composition of the monarchy period. It is best to suppose that all the documents were committed to the care of the high priest, along with the Deuteronomic law, which was to be read to the assembled Israelites every 7 years (Dt. 31:9ff.). Perhaps, as G. T. Manley suggested (*The Book of the Law*, 1957, p. 162), it was the high priest Eleazar himself who prepared Deuteronomy for public reading. The discourses of Moses could not be read in the first person without explanation, and it would be very natural for the elderly leader in preparing his script to add his own comments and reminiscences. (How naturally would the strange parenthesis in Dt. 10:6–9 be accounted for.)

But these details are trivia. The towering figure of Moses is the key to the history and to the literature.

J. W. WENHAM

43

The poetry of the Old Testament

The poetry of the Bible is not restricted to those books which we usually distinguish as 'the poetical books'—Job, Psalms, the Song of Solomon and Lamentations, with the versified wisdom of Proverbs and Ecclesiastes. A great part of the books of the Prophets consists of prophetical oracles in poetic form; and here and there throughout the historical narrative we come upon longer or shorter passages of poetry. These are sometimes said to be derived from collections of poetry such as the 'Book of the Wars of Yahweh' (Nu. 21:14) or the 'Book of Jashar' (Jos. 10:13; 2 Sa. 1:18; 1 Ki. 8:12f., LXX). Some writers have gone further, like Eduard Sievers, who in his *Metrische Studien* (1901–7) traced the elements of an earlier poetical form beneath the prose narratives of such books as Genesis and Samuel (in a manner comparable to the attempt of some classical scholars to detect the elements of Saturnian metre beneath the earlier books of Livy's *Roman History*). But the results of such a study are too disputable to be included in this brief survey.

The NT, too, has a greater poetical element than is often realized. The five canticles of Luke's nativity narrative are well known, but the prologue of John is probably also based on a Christian hymn. The researches in particular of John Jebb, Bishop of Limerick (*Sacred Literature*, 1820), and C. F. Burney (*The Poetry of our Lord*, 1925) have shown how many of the sayings of Jesus were cast in the established forms of Hebrew poetry. Not only did this ensure their being easily memorized, but, 'since Jesus appeared to His contemporaries as a prophet, and prophets were accustomed to give oracles in verse, it is credible that we have here something approaching His *ipsissima verba*' (C. H. Dodd, *History and the Gospel*, 1938, pp. 89f.).

The NT Epistles, too, seem to contain some fragments of poetry: early Christian canticles probably underlie the Christological passages in Phil. 2:6ff. and Col. 1:15ff., the quotation *Awake, O sleeper . . .* in Eph. 5:14 (from a primitive baptismal hymn?) and the summary of the *mystery of our religion* in 1 Tim. 3:16, to mention no more. Then the last book of the NT is full of canticles, but there is no space here to discuss 'the metrics of Revelation—a fascinating subject which must be left to future investigators' (C. C. Torrey, *Documents of the Primitive Church*, 1941, p. 212).

Poetical forms

The two distinctive features of biblical poetry are rhythm of thought and rhythm of sound.

Rhythm of sound we are familiar with in most European poetry, where it commonly appears in a regular pattern of accented and unaccented syllables in the line or group of lines, and also in the form of rhyme. In the poetry of biblical Hebrew, rhythm of sound depends almost entirely on the regular pattern of accented syllables. It is undecided whether the number of unaccented syllables in the line played any significant part in early Hebrew poetry (as it did in some other early Semitic poetry), and if so, what. 'The crucial question of Hebrew metrics is the problem of the *number of permissible unstressed syllables*' (A. Bentzen, *Introduction to the Old Testament*, i, 1948, p. 121). The sense of satisfaction, however, which our poetry affords by means of rhyme is largely produced in Hebrew poetry by another kind of rhythm altogether—what we have called rhythm of thought or sense. This sense-rhythm is usually known as parallelism, and it appears in early Egyptian, Mesopotamian and Canaanite poetry as well as in Hebrew poetry.

The credit for determining the characteristics of Hebrew poetry belongs largely to two Englishmen—Robert Lowth, Professor of Poetry at Oxford and later Bishop of London, whose epochal *Academic Lectures on the Sacred Poetry of the Hebrews* were published in Latin in 1753, and a later Oxford scholar, George Buchanan Gray, Professor of Hebrew in Mansfield College, whose work on *The Forms of Hebrew Poetry* appeared in 1905. More recently H. Kosmala has emphasized the importance of the sequence and balance of sense-units rather than stressed syllables for the rhythm and structure of Hebrew poetry ('Form and Structure in Ancient Hebrew Poetry', *VT*, XIV, 1964, pp. 423ff.).

Hebrew parallelism takes various forms, which can best be explained by means of actual examples. We have, first, complete parallelism, where a line or distich consists of two 'stichoi', each of which exactly balances the other. Such a distich is

> *Israel does-not know,*
> *My-people does-not understand* (Is. 1:3),

where *Israel* balances *my people* and *does not know* balances *does not understand*. Because the two 'stichoi' are exactly synonymous with each other, each saying the same thing in different words, this form of parallelism is also known as identical parallelism. S. Gevirtz (*Patterns in the Early Poetry of Israel*, 1963) has shown how the Ugaritic and Hebrew poets had at their disposal a substantial corpus of conventionally-fixed pairs of words (comparable in a way to the permanent epithets of the Greek epic) on which they drew freely for purposes of parallelism.

Another form of complete parallelism is known as antithetic parallelism, because the one 'stichos' gives the obverse of the other. A good example is found in Pr. 15:20:

> *A-wise son makes-a-glad father*
> *but-a-foolish man despises his-mother.*

Yet another kind of parallelism is that known as 'emblematic' parallelism, where one 'stichos' makes a statement in literal terms and the other repeats it in figurative terms. This can be done in various ways; a good example is Ps. 103:13:

> *As-a-father pities his-children,*
> *So-Yahweh pities those-who-fear-him.*

Here there are three accented syllables in each 'stichos'. It is apposite here to remark that much of the genius of Hebrew poetry lies in its employment of vivid and concrete similes or metaphors which (like parables, but more briefly) convey truth to the hearer pungently and effectively.

Occasionally the parallelism may be more elaborate, and take an introverted or chiastic form. Ps. 30:8–10 is commonly cited as an example of this:

> *To-thee, Yahweh, I-cry; and-to-Yahweh I-make-supplication.*
> *What-profit (is there) in-my-blood if-I-go-down to-the-Pit?*
> *Will-the-dust praise-thee? will-it-tell-of thy-faithfulness?*
> *Hear, Yahweh, and-be-gracious-to-me; Yahweh, be a-helper to-me.*

Here 'stichos' 1 is paralleled by 'stichos' 4, and 'stichos' 2 by 'stichos' 3, the accentual pattern being 5 : 4 : 4 : 5. A similar but not identical chiasmus appears in the sayings of Jesus, *e.g.* in Mt. 7:6:

> Do not give dogs what is holy;
>> And do not throw your pearls before swine,
>> Lest they (the swine) *trample them under foot*
> And they (the dogs) *turn to attack you.*

Thus far we have quoted examples of complete parallelism, where each unit of thought in one 'stichos' has its counterpart in the other 'stichos', and the parallel 'stichoi' have the same number of accented syllables. But we have also to reckon with incomplete parallelism, where, *e.g.*, one of the units of thought in the former 'stichos' has no counterpart in the latter 'stichos'. Take, *e.g.*, Ps. 1:5:

> *Therefore-the-wicked will-not-stand in-the-judgment,*
> *Nor-sinners in-the-congregation of-the-righteous.*

The verb 'will not stand' in the former 'stichos' has no counterpart in the second 'stichos'. But the number of accented syllables is kept even by the fact that 'judgment' (with one accented

syllable) in 'stichos' 1 is balanced by 'congregation of the righteous' (with two accented syllables) in 'stichos' 2. Similarly in Is. 1:3a:

> *The-ox knows its-owner,*
> *And-the-ass its-master's crib*

there is nothing in 'stichos' 2 corresponding to 'knows' in 'stichos' 1, but compensation is made by having two accented syllables, 'its-master's crib', in the second as against one, 'its-owner', in the first. This phenomenon, called by Gray 'incomplete parallelism with compensation', is quite common in biblical poetry. Occasionally the parallelism is so incomplete that we are left with nothing but compensation, and then we have what Lowth called 'synthetic parallelism', but Gray, less ineptly, 'formal parallelism'. It is, in fact, not parallelism at all; there is only sound-rhythm and no thought-rhythm. An example is Ps. 27:6a:

> *And-now my-head shall-be-lifted-up*
> *Above my-enemies round-about-me.*

There we have three accented syllables in each 'stichos', but no parallelism of sense at all.

At other times when the parallelism is incomplete there is no compensation, and thus we get 'stichoi' of unequal length, which can be arranged in regular patterns. One such pattern corresponds roughly to our common metre, where we have alternating 'stichoi' of four and three beats. A good example of this 4 : 3 pattern in the OT is Jeremiah's description of Chaos-come-again (4:23–26):

> *I-looked-on the-earth, and-lo waste-and-void,*
> *And-the-heavens, and-not their-light;*
> *I-looked-on the-mountains, and-lo they-were-quaking,*
> *And-all the-hills moved-to-and-fro.*
> *I-looked and-lo there-was-no man,*
> *And-all-birds of-the-air had-fled;*
> *I-looked and-lo the-fruitful-land a-desert,*
> *And-all-its-cities laid-in-ruins before-Yahweh.*

But a much commoner form of 'incomplete parallelism without compensation' is the 3 : 2 pattern. This pattern has been called the *qînâ* or 'dirge' metre, ever since Karl Budde first identified it in the book of Lamentations. Compare La. 3:1:

> *I-am-the-man who-has-seen affliction*
> *Under-the-rod of-his-wrath.*

It is by no means confined to this kind of poetry, however; it may serve as the vehicle of joyful trust, as in Ps. 27:1:

> *Yahweh is-my-light and-my-salvation;*
> *Whom shall-I-fear?*
> *Yahweh is-the-stronghold of-my-life;*
> *Of-whom shall-I-be-afraid?*

And C. F. Burney (*The Poetry of our Lord*, pp. 137ff.) has traced it in several of the sayings of Jesus in the Gospels.

One form of parallelism which we have not

mentioned yet is what is called step-parallelism or climactic parallelism; it is found 'where one member (or part of a member) in one line is repeated in the second, and made the starting-point for a fresh step' (T. H. Robinson, *The Poetry of the Old Testament*, 1947, p. 23). A good example is found in the opening 'stichoi' of Ps. 29, with the step-effect produced by the repeated 'Ascribe to Yahweh'; another is provided by Ps. 92:9—

> *For-lo, thy-enemies, Yahweh,*
> *For-lo, thy-enemies shall-perish;*
> *All-evildoers shall-be-scattered—*

which is of special interest because it shows so close a similarity in form to a passage from the Baal epic discovered among the Ras Shamra tablets (C. H. Gordon, *Ugaritic Handbook*, Text 68, lines 8f.):

> *Lo thy-enemies O-Baal,*
> *Lo thy-enemies thou-shalt-slay,*
> *Lo thou-shalt-destroy thy-foes.*

W. F. Albright refers to this parallel in *The Archaeology of Palestine*, 1960, p. 232. On the same page he quotes a tristich from the Aqhat or Dan'el epic which in language rather than form reminds one of Ps. 21:4:

> *Ask-thou life Aqhat my-boy,*
> *Ask-thou life and-I'll-give-it-thee,*
> *Life-immortal and-I'll-grant-it-thee.*

The passage from Ps. 92:9 is noteworthy not only as an example of step-parallelism but also because the pattern takes the form of a tristich and not a distich. The rhythmical scheme is 3 : 3 : 3. Another tristich pattern occurs in Ps. 24:7–10:

> *Lift-up, O-gates, your-heads,*
> *And-lift-up, O-doors of-eternity,*
> *And-shall-enter the-king of-glory . . .*

Here we have a set of four tristichs, forming two short strophes.

The presence of strophes in biblical poetry has been much discussed, and certainly a strophic arrangement can be detected here and there. A repeated refrain is good evidence for a strophic arrangement. Such a refrain we get in Pss. 42 and 43 (originally one psalm), showing that the strophes end respectively at vv. 5 and 11 of Ps. 42 and v. 5 of Ps. 43. Another example is the oracle in Is. 9:8 – 10:4 (with Is. 5:25ff.), with its refrain: 'For all this his anger is not turned away and his hand is stretched out still.' Further examples of strophic arrangement have been recognized in the sayings of Jesus.

Strophic arrangement is also involved in the acrostic schemes sometimes found in biblical poetry; thus in a purely formal way Ps. 119 inevitably consists of twenty-two strophes of eight 'distichs' each.

Non-biblical parallels

We have already quoted parallels between certain poetical passages from the OT and passages from the Canaanite poems discovered at Ras Shamra. The decipherment and study of the Ras Shamra documents (which are dated *c.* 1400 BC) have thrown a great deal of light on the circumstances of early Semitic poetry. For one thing, these documents have completely falsified Gunkel's theory that the longer poetical passages in the Bible are relatively late, since (as he thought) a ballad period of considerable duration came first. The Baal epic discovered at Ras Shamra, *e.g.*, had not less than 5,000 lines. That the Song of Deborah (Jdg. 5) is practically simultaneous with the incidents it celebrates (*c.* 1150 BC) has been generally agreed, but one can trace a tendency now, under the impact of the Ras Shamra evidence, to agree that other poems to which the Bible ascribes an early date do in fact belong to the period in which the Bible places them. Albright argues, *e.g.*, that in their original forms such poems as the Song of Miriam in Ex. 15 and the oracles of Balaam in Nu. 23–24 may well have been composed in the 13th century BC. (*The Archaeology of Palestine*, 1960, pp. 232f.; 'The Oracles of Balaam', *JBL*, LXIII, 1944, pp. 207ff.).

Among other contacts between biblical and non-biblical poetry we should note in particular the numerous resemblances between Ps. 104 and the Egyptian king Akhnaton's *Hymn to Aton* (*c.* 1377–1360 BC). But alongside all these and other resemblances we must mark the divergences; the stamp of Israel's covenant-monotheism imparts a basic religious uniqueness to all the poetry (as to all the prose) of the OT.

Text and exegesis

Attempts are commonly made to emend the text of poetical parts of the OT to make them conform to some metrical scheme. In view of the wide variation of metrical arrangements which present themselves to us, however, this is a criterion for establishing the text which should be used with great caution. As it is, one scholar's emendations based on this principle rarely win the approval of other scholars. It may be conceded that where we have an almost complete alphabetic acrostic we can be reasonably sure that it was originally complete, but that in itself does not guarantee that any particular emendation aimed at restoring the complete acrostic is the right one. As for restoring the original text by regard to the number of accented syllables in the 'stichoi' of a poetical passage, we have given an example above of this procedure, in the citation from Je. 4:23–26. The closing words of the passage as we have it in the received text ('before his fierce anger') were omitted from our citation, as they could not be accommodated to the 4 : 3 metre and were therefore treated for the moment as a prose expansion. But there is no assurance that the passage did in fact originally conform entirely to the 4 : 3 pattern.

On the other hand, a recognition of the basic forms of biblical poetry, particularly the forms of parallelism, makes an important contribution to accurate interpretation. It will prevent us, for example, from thinking that an author is making two separate statements when he is actually saying the same thing twice.

But what we should emphasize above everything else is that the study of these poetical forms, whatever its limitations may be, and into whatever other fields it may lead us, is primarily important because of such help as it can give us in understanding the text of Scripture better. 'After all', as T. H. Robinson reminds us in his study of this subject (*The Poetry of the Old Testament*, p. 46), 'it is sound exegesis which should be the final aim of all other branches of Biblical study'—and therefore of this branch too.

F. F. BRUCE

47

The wisdom literature of the Old Testament

The canonical wisdom literature of the OT consists of the books of Job, Proverbs and Ecclesiastes, together with a number of Psalms, e.g. Pss. 4; 10; 14; 19; 37; 49; 73; 90; 112 and the 'Prayer of Habakkuk' (Hab. 3). In the Apocrypha, wisdom literature is represented chiefly by the book of Ecclesiasticus (*The Wisdom of Jesus ben-Sira*, written in Hebrew c. 180 BC and translated into Greek by the author's grandson in 132 BC) and the book of Wisdom (probably written by an Alexandrian Jew early in the 1st century BC or AD). The book of Baruch (especially 3:9 – 4:4, where wisdom is identified with the law) and 4 Maccabees (which presents the Maccabean martyrdoms as examples of the triumph of right reason over human passsions) have also their contribution to make to the wisdom literature of the Apocrypha. In the NT the Epistle of James might well be classified as a 'wisdom book'.

The practical wisdom of the ancients takes the form first of popular proverbs (Heb. *māšāl*, plural *mešālîm*) which express in pithy terms certain observed regularities, whether in the external world of nature or in human behaviour ('A red sky at night is the shepherd's delight'; 'There are none so deaf as those who will not hear', and the like). A more developed form is the riddle or parable. The riddle of Samson (Jdg. 14:12ff.), the fables of Jotham (Jdg. 9:7ff.) and Jehoash (2 Ki. 14:9) and the parables of Nathan (2 Sa. 12:1–4) and the wise woman of Tekoa (2 Sa. 14:4–7) come to mind as well-known examples; the parable, of course, reaches its perfection in the Gospels.

A further stage is reached when men begin to reflect upon the phenomena of nature and life, and come to realize that the popular generalizations are very often inadequate to cover all the facts. Problems like the suffering of the righteous and the meaning of life engage men's thoughts and are grappled with in such works as Job, Ecclesiastes and the Problem Psalms.

True wisdom (Heb. *ḥokmâ*) to the Hebrew thinkers was not simply intellectual speculation. It was practical in the best sense: it had a very real moral and religious content. 'The fear of Yahweh is the beginning of wisdom'; the truly wise man (Heb. *ḥākām*) is he who views all life in a spirit of reverence towards God. Contrari-wise the fool (Heb. *nābāl*) is the man devoid of moral and religious sensibilities; when he says in his heart, 'There is no God', he is not being a 'free-thinker' but behaving as if there were no God.

The wisdom literature of the OT is not some-thing by itself. It is rather the expression of a moral and intellectual movement dating very early in the history of Hebrew religion and paralleled outside Israel. The wisdom books tell the story of earnest seekers after truth, who wrestled with problems both old and new. In the quest after reality we are indebted to thinkers of all races. The OT bears ample witness to the pursuit of wisdom by Israel's neighbours. Thus in 1 Ki. 4:30f. Solomon's wisdom is said to have 'surpassed the wisdom of all the people of the east, and all the wisdom of Egypt. For he was wiser than all other men, wiser than Ethan the Ezrahite, and Heman, Calcol, and Darda, the sons of Mahol'. In Ob. 8 we have Yahweh's warning, 'Will I not on that day . . . destroy the wise men out of Edom, and understanding out of Mount Esau?', with which may be compared Je. 49:7: 'Is wisdom no more in Teman? Has counsel perished from the prudent? Has their wisdom vanished?'

There is nothing surprising in finding the observed generalizations of everyday experience repeated in the proverbial lore of many nations. 'Even a fool who keeps silent is considered wise; when he closes his lips, he is deemed intelligent' (Pr. 17:28). That is something which most people have observed, and we do not think of borrowing in either direction when we find the same proverb in Sanskrit literature in this form: 'Even a fool, covered with fine clothes, is fair in the assembly up to a point; yea a fool is fair so long as he utters no word.'

But it is not simply in these generalizations that we can trace similarities to biblical wisdom. We might profitably consider the significance of the fact that it is only in its wisdom literature that the Hebrew Bible canonizes the utterances of non-Israelites. Job and his friends are given an Edomite setting in birth and residence; and to the Israelite wisdom of Proverbs are appended collections of sayings by sages of Massa in N Arabia (Pr. 30:1 – 31:9).

Egypt, Mesopotamia and (at a later period) Greece provide us with further parallels. In Egypt, e.g., we have Imhotep—priest, physician and architect—famed as the author of proverbs as early as the opening years of the IIIrd Dynasty (c. 2700 BC), while two or three centuries later the maxims of Ptahhotep constitute, as J. H. Breasted put it, 'the earliest formulation of right conduct to be found in any literature' (*The Dawn of Conscience*, 1935, p. 129). The downfall of the Old Kingdom (c. 2200 BC) inspired other sages with a more pessimistic view of life, as they reflected on the vanity of material fortune;

48

but one of these, Ipuwer, looks beyond the present evils to the advent of a righteous king who will bring rest to men as a shepherd to his sheep and who is described in terms not unlike those of Ps. 72 and some other Messianic passages of the OT (*cf.* E. J. Young, *My Servants the Prophets*, 1952, pp. 200ff.).

The closest approximation that Egypt shows to biblical wisdom literature, however, is in the sayings of Amenemope, a wise man of the XXIst Dynasty (*c.* 1150–930 BC). Amenemope was more or less contemporary with Solomon, and his *Wisdom* presents some remarkable parallels to the book of Proverbs, especially to Pr. 22:17 – 23:12. In one place, indeed, Amenemope's *Wisdom* has been thought to illuminate the text of the biblical book, namely in Pr. 22:20, where the Hebrew word *š-l-šwm* may be vocalized not *šālišîm* ('excellent things', so AV and RV following *Qᵉrē*) nor *šilšôm* ('heretofore', so RV mg. following *Kᵉṯîḇ*), but *šᵉlôšîm* ('thirty', so RSV). Amenemope's *Wisdom* consists of thirty sections, and in one place it refers to them in the words: 'Consider these thirty chapters.' The verse in Proverbs is therefore held to be a parallel ('Have I not written for you thirty sayings of admonition and knowledge?'). But the amended vocalization is not certain, and in any case there are other ways of accounting for the undoubtedly striking parallels than by the supposition of direct borrowing either way.

To some of the other forms of wisdom literature in the Bible we find parallels more readily offered by Mesopotamia. The problem of the righteous sufferer, which finds classic expression in the book of Job, was treated in several Mesopotamian works, but notably in the composition called *Ludlul bel nemeqi* ('I will praise the lord of wisdom'). It describes the case of a man whose fortunes were very similar to Job's, although the treatment is much inferior to that of the Hebrew book. The pessimistic strain in Ecclesiastes, again, seems to echo passages from the *Gilgamesh Epic* and from the *Dialogue of Pessimism* in which a Babylonian master and his slave conclude that no values exist—in short, that all is vanity.

Such pessimism is not restricted to any one age or country; and some of the most striking parallels to Ecclesiastes are to be found in the writings of Greek thinkers like Theognis (*c.* 500 BC). Many of these parallels have been collected by H. Ranston in *Ecclesiastes and the Early Greek Wisdom Literature*, 1925, but here again we should not be too hasty in assuming that the very considerable similarity in thought and expression implies direct literary dependence. Like causes produce like effects all over the world. Wisdom lore, whether written or unwritten, is not only the fruit of experience but presupposes that experience is not illusory, but that it provides valid evidence enabling us to reach certain conclusions about human life and the world in general.

'The Wisdom Literature of both Egypt and Mesopotamia', wrote Sir Frederic Kenyon, 'goes back to much earlier periods than the corresponding Hebrew books. The Hebrew writers were engaging in a kind of literature common to Eastern countries, and were no doubt influenced by the productions current in the countries to east and west of them; but their writings are not direct copies. They are original compositions in the same vein, and in their best portions, such as the praise of Wisdom as the mouthpiece of God, they reach a higher plane of thought and of emotional expression than their neighbours and predecessors' (*The Reading of the Bible*, 1944, p. 52).

In spite of numerous similarities, the Hebrew wisdom literature bears unmistakable features which distinguish it from the wisdom literature of other nations. These distinctive features are the product of the unique revelatory character of Hebrew religion, with its emphasis on one living and true God. Wisdom in the biblical literature is divine wisdom; in the deepest things of human need the clearest and surest light comes from the nation to which God chose to make Himself known. The 'words of the wise' which correspond to the *Wisdom* of Amenemope are spoken or recorded in order 'that your trust may be in the Lord' (Pr. 22:19). OT wisdom, in fact, is closely related to other manifestations of Israel's covenant faith.

The OT knows a narrative form of wisdom literature (*cf.* Ec. 9:13–16) exemplified particularly in the motif of the loyal son of Israel who, banished from home through no fault of his own, succeeds by wisdom in attaining high honour in a foreign land in face of malice and envy. This motif appears as early as the story of Joseph, 'a man ... in whom is the Spirit of God' (Gn. 41:38), and is specially common in the exilic and post-exilic age, as in the records of Daniel, in whom were found 'light and understanding and wisdom, like the wisdom of the gods' (Dn. 5:11), of Mordecai, whose careful forethought procured his advancement to be next in rank to Xerxes and who 'sought the welfare of his people and spoke peace to all his people' (Est. 10:3), and (outside the Hebrew Bible) of Tobit and Ahiqar. Daniel, in fact, belongs almost as much to wisdom literature as to apocalyptic; the close association between wisdom and apocalyptic which it displays (*cf.* 12:10, 'those who are wise shall understand') persists for long; *cf.* Rev. 13:18, where the decoding of the number of the beast 'calls for wisdom'.

The Hebrew wisdom movement was closely associated with Solomon, who became the royal patron of the school, and whose name continued to be attached to wisdom literature well into the Christian era (*cf.* the 2nd-century AD *Odes of Solomon*). 'Historical probability combines with trustworthy tradition in ascribing to the period of Solomon's reign a remarkable development of the national character. This was manifested in the various departments of commerce, art and literature, in all that we call civilization; and whatever the extent of Solomon's extant writings, over and above those Proverbs which "the men of Hezekiah, king of Judah", copied out, it is clear that it is from his time that the strain of teaching known by the specific name of "Wisdom" takes its rise and derives much of its character' (W. T. Davison, *The Wisdom-Literature of the Old Testament*, 1894, pp. 12f.). Thus Solomon may be called the father of Hebrew wisdom *literature*, although, as it has been said, there was no lack of non-literary Hebrew wisdom before his time.

The establishment of the united monarchy marked the beginning of an age of cultural 'enlightenment' in Israel. There were wise men at David's court, notably Ahithophel, whose counsel was 'as if one consulted the oracle of God' (2 Sa. 16:23), and Nathan, whose official designation is 'Nathan the prophet' but who admonishes David in the parabolic fashion of the sage (2 Sa. 12:1ff.). The *genre* of the 'court chronicle' at the courts of David and Solomon attained a distinction (2 Sa. 9–20) never to be surpassed in Hebrew literature. Solomon himself, over and above his practical shrewdness, is credited with a comprehensive knowledge of natural history and with the authorship of many wise sayings and songs; his reputation for 'wisdom' excited the curiosity of distant rulers and sages (1 Ki. 3:16ff.; 4:29ff.; 10:1ff.).

In addition to royal wisdom, there was a vigorous tradition of popular or 'clan' wisdom in Israel, reflections of which may be recognized here and there throughout the OT (*cf.* the proverbial reputation of the wisdom of the city of Abel, 2 Sa. 20:18), and especially in the prophets. The influence of such traditional wisdom in Amos has been pointed out by H. W. Wolff (*Amos' geistige Heimat*, 1964); Hosea, Isaiah, Jeremiah and Habakkuk provide further examples (*cf.* D. A. Hubbard, 'The Wisdom Movement and Israel's Covenant Faith', *Tyndale Bulletin*, 17, 1966, pp. 3ff.).

That the sage stood alongside the prophet and priest in popular estimation as a mediator of divine truth is suggested by the language of Jeremiah's enemies in Je. 18:18: 'the law shall not perish from the priest, nor counsel from the wise, nor the word from the prophet.' The wise men (Heb. *ḥᵃkāmîm*) transmitted their 'wisdom' from generation to generation; they had their schools, disciples, doctrines and collections of sayings (*cf.* Pr. 1:6; 24:23; Ec. 9:17; 12:11f.). But, while priest, sage and prophet had each his own function and method of communication, we should not erect impenetrable barriers between the three categories as though there could be no overlapping between them.

The practical relevance of wisdom for daily life is set forth in the various collections brought together in the book of Proverbs. God, it is insisted, is a righteous God; His world is a moral world, marked by temporal reward for righteousness and temporal retribution for wickedness or folly. The more poignant and intractable

problems of life lie beyond the horizon of Proverbs. 'Proverbs seems to say, "Here are the rules for life; try them and find that they will work". Job and Ecclesiastes say, "We did, and they don't".' (D. A. Hubbard, *art. cit.*, p. 6).

The book of Job presents the climax of a long process of grappling with these pressing problems. Earlier products of this process are the Problem Psalms. Two types are discernible in these poems and are quite characteristic of the whole school. There is the calmer philosophical type (Pss. 14; 19; 90) which contemplates the godless world made by a good God, the glory of the cosmos and the conscience and the mystery of mortal yet immortal man. Here the soul of man stands naked in the presence of the great and grim realities of life. Again, there is the type where the sage wrestles with doubt, his pulse agitated by fear (Pss. 10; 37; 49; 73). As the psalmist considers the boastful wicked, he cries out in distress: 'Why dost thou stand afar off, O Lord? Why dost thou hide thyself in times of trouble?' The prosperity of the evil-doers and the adversity of the righteous are recurring themes in the *ḥokmâ* literature. Nor are the problems left suspended in mid air. A good way is travelled towards solution. Ps. 37 answers, 'The prosperity of the wicked does not last.' Ps. 49 declares, 'Death brings the evildoer to condign punishment.' Ps. 73 concludes more positively that 'true prosperity belongs alone to the godly'.

The book of Job propounds two crucial questions: 1. Will a man serve God for God's sake alone? (*i.e.* is there such a thing as purely disinterested goodness?) and 2. Why should an innocent man suffer? The traditional answer to the second question is first given by Job's three friends, that sin and suffering are invariably wedded together. The divine principle of the moral government of the universe is retribution. Sin and suffering are without exception cause and effect. To repudiate this hard truth, not in its essence but in its inflexible incidence, Elihu is introduced into the argument. He advances with the solution that suffering is not penal but disciplinary, not given to punish but sent to profit. The teaching goes a stage further when Job comes into the divine presence and contents himself that the answer rests with God and all is well.

Qoheleth (Ecclesiastes, perhaps meaning 'the arguer') has the form of a 'royal testament'; it corrects in its doctrine the materialism, fatalism and pessimism of its age. The three ways essayed in its day and all down the generations are exposed in all their futility as answers to the problems of 'how to be happy in the world as it is'—the ways of knowledge, pleasure, and the power of money. The teaching of the book is that there is one way, the way of wisdom—albeit a cautious and unambitious wisdom which is content with the satisfaction of a day's work well done and the enjoyment of plain food and drink when one has thus acquired an appetite for them, together with the pleasures of family life. With these, one should be thankful for small mercies; the world is too full of injustice, the future too uncertain and death too final for a man to set his hopes too high, for all the 'eternity' that has been planted in his heart.

In all their attempts to deal with the most persistent problems of life, the wisdom books do not call in a new world to redress the balance of the old. The examination is restricted almost entirely within the limits of the present earthly life. Only when we come to the relatively late book of Wisdom do we find the doctrine of immortality freely invoked.

The concept of divine wisdom played no small part in preparing the way for the coming of Christ. In the Synoptic Gospels Jesus appears as a 'greater than Solomon' (Mt. 12:42; Lk. 11:31); in them, as also in the Fourth Gospel, He speaks on occasion in the role of wisdom (cf. Mt. 11:28ff. with Ecclus. 51:23–27, which is dependent in its turn on the invitation of wisdom in Pr. 8:4–21). Behind the Logos doctrine of the Johannine prologue we can see the personified wisdom of OT times, portrayed especially in the famous passage in Pr. 8:22ff. where wisdom sits as God's assessor at the creation of the world. In this and other ways the wisdom movement led on to the advent of Him 'whom God made our wisdom'. The wisdom books, when illuminated by the incarnation of Jesus Christ and viewed accordingly in the light of their end, may be accepted as setting the stage for the personal wisdom of God who declares 'I am the way, and the truth, and the life'—the final solution of the problems of man and the world.

(On the subject of this essay see, in addition to works mentioned above, O. S. Rankin, *Israel's Wisdom Literature*, 1936; M. Noth and D. W. Thomas (eds.), *Wisdom in Israel and in the Ancient Near East*, 1955; G. von Rad, *Old Testament Theology*, I, 1962, pp. 418–459; W. Zimmerli, 'The Place and Limit of the Wisdom in the Framework of the OT Theology', *SJT*, XVII, 1964, pp. 146ff.; W. McKane, *Prophets and Wise Men*, 1965; R. N. Whybray, *Wisdom in Proverbs*, 1965; J. L. Mackenzie, 'Reflections on Wisdom', *JBL*, LXXXVI, 1967, pp. 1ff.)

F. F. BRUCE

The apocryphal and apocalyptic literature

THE TERM APOCRYPHA

The noun 'Apocrypha' normally designates those books which are contained in the Latin Vulgate but which are not in the Hebrew OT. Their presence in the Vulgate is due to their inclusion, with the exception of 2 Esdras, in the Greek translation of the OT, the Septuagint (LXX), which was the source of the Latin version of these books. It is commonly asserted that this fact shows that the Greek-speaking Jews of Alexandria gave them full canonicity, and that the primitive church, which took over the Greek Bible, did likewise. The books in question are largely of Palestinian origin and were mainly written in Hebrew or Aramaic; they were popular both in Palestine and in the Dispersion but seem to have been put on a different plane from the canonical Scriptures in all places. C. C. Torrey, accordingly, considers that the best equivalent of the term 'Apocrypha' is the 'outside' books.

Though this is a good equivalent it is not the literal meaning of *apokryphos*. The Greek term means 'hidden' and was applied to books which were kept from the public eye and allowed to be read only by a privileged circle. Far from being an opprobrious term, therefore, it connotes the special value of the books so described. It seems to have been so applied to the works of the Jewish seers who were especially active between the 2nd century BC and the 1st century AD. These writings were issued under the name of ancient heroes and prophets of Israel and were kept hidden until those days; even so, they were not for the public but for those worthy to read them. 2 Esdras 14 relates how Ezra dictated to five scribes ninety-four books, twenty-four of which were the OT writings (the Minor Prophets being considered as one book) and seventy being for 'the wise among your people. For in them is the spring of understanding, the fountain of wisdom, and the river of knowledge' (14:46, 47).

This shows not only that these books were valued 'above' the OT, but that the apocrypha here included much more than those books comprising our collection; they were rather the apocalyptic books of the same order as 2 Esdras itself.

Origen uses the term 'apocrypha' to designate the apocalyptic works, while he regarded our collection of 'apocrypha' as canonical. It was Jerome, in his *Prologus Galeatus* to 1 and 2 Samuel, who first used the term of those books which we commonly call 'apocryphal', *i.e.* those which other early Christian writers called ecclesiastical, or suitable for reading in church.

The truth of the matter appears to be that the apocrypha, in the sense of the outside books, were at first regarded as constituting all sacred books not in the Canon; some were more popular than others, and the more popular ones have come down to us in the Latin Vulgate; but the so-called 'pseudepigrapha' (*i.e.* the books issued under the name of an ancient writer) were also highly valued in many circles and ought not to be regarded as apart from the others. For this reason it would almost seem desirable to let the term 'apocrypha' suffice to cover all the books which are included in the phrase 'Apocrypha and Pseudepigrapha'. Torrey has adopted this procedure in his book *The Apocryphal Literature*, 1945.

THE BOOKS UNDER REVIEW

The following is a brief characterization of the books of the Apocrypha and Pseudepigrapha.

The Apocrypha proper

1 Esdras contains most of the material found in the canonical Ezra, but prefaces it by reproducing 2 Ch. 35:1 – 36:21 and adds the account of Ezra's reading of the law recorded in Ne. 8 (with the omission of Nehemiah's name). It is a variant Greek version of that part of the Chronicler's work which it covers—perhaps preserving the original LXX rendering. It includes the story of the three courtiers, one of whom is said to be Zerubbabel, at the feast of Darius—the original source of the proverb, 'Great is truth, and strongest of all!' (1 Esdras 4:41). *2 Esdras* is a 1st-century AD apocalypse put into the mouth of Ezra, in some respects the most tragic of all apocalypses.

Tobit is a romantic story telling how his piety in burying the untended dead was rewarded in his latter days, and how his son Tobias gained a wife; it was probably written at the end of the 3rd century BC. Hebrew and Aramaic fragments have been found at Qumran. *Judith* is another piece of elevating fiction, narrating how she delivered her city from the Assyrian army; it may have come from the Maccabean age, *c.* 150 BC. *The Additions to the Book of Esther* consist of material which is supplemental to the canonical book, such as prayers and decrees mentioned during the story; they were meant to add a religious element to the book.

The Wisdom of Solomon is often felt to be the loftiest production of the intertestamental period; it is the work of a Greek-speaking Jew of Alexandria, a good example of Jewish wisdom-writing, and it especially dwells on the theme of retribution and the folly of idol-worship. The date of composition has been put variously between 150 BC and AD 40. *Ecclesiasticus*, often called 'The Wisdom of Jesus ben-Sira', is a similar work to the foregoing, but is a Sadducean writing and, despite the years of reflection and experience of the author, is of more slender spirituality than the former work; it was issued *c.* 180 BC in Hebrew, and translated into Greek by the author's grandson *c.* 132 BC.

Baruch, with *The Letter of Jeremiah*, is a composite book, mainly directed against idolatry. The former may have been composed in the 3rd century BC, the latter in the 2nd century BC. Of the additions to Daniel there are three, all later than the original work: *The History of Susanna* tells how the youth Daniel displayed his wisdom in vindicating an innocent woman who had been condemned to death (hence the proverb, 'A Daniel come to judgment'); *The Prayer of Azariah* and *The Song of the Three Young Men* are represented as having been uttered in the fiery furnace; *Bel and the Dragon* are two separate stories, narrating how Daniel discredited the priests of Bel and exploded the idea that the dragon was a god—and the dragon also! *The Prayer of Manasseh* is a prayer of repentance put into the mouth of the king of this name in the Bible, based on 2 Ch. 33:12f., 19, and may have been written in the 2nd century BC.

1 Maccabees is our chief primary account of the struggle of the Jews, led by the sons of Mattathias, against Antiochus Epiphanes and his successors. The author, who probably wrote under John Hyrcanus (135–104 BC), was an excellent historian, as objective as it was possible for a partisan of the Hasmonaeans to be. *2 Maccabees* deals with a section of the period covered by the former book, notably with the exploits of Judas Maccabaeus, and is much more highly coloured than the earlier work. It is written from an early Pharisaic viewpoint, stressing the resurrection hope for the martyrs under Antiochus; it also shows a special interest in the Temple.

The Pseudepigrapha

The Book of Enoch (*1 Enoch*) is the most important apocalypse of this class of writings; it is certainly composite, though whether it comes from one period or is a gradual accumulation of traditions ascribed to Enoch from 200 BC to the mid-1st century AD is still being debated; its most important contribution is its conception of the heavenly Messiah, the Son of man, in the section called the 'Similitudes of Enoch' (*1 Enoch* 37–71). Fragments of all sections of the book but this have been identified in Aramaic among the Qumran texts.

The Book of Jubilees is a rewriting of Genesis, purporting to show that the law was observed from Eden, enjoining a purely solar calendar and dividing history into periods of 'jubilees',

i.e. 49 years (7 weeks of years); it is often dated *c.* 100 BC. Hebrew fragments of the book have been found at Qumran. *The Testaments of the Twelve Patriarchs* perhaps was written at about the same time, and represents the last counsels and prophecies of each of the twelve sons of Jacob as they are about to die. While the Greek text of the *Testaments* represents a Christian recension, earlier recensions of two of the *Testaments* in Aramaic and Hebrew have been found at Qumran.

The Sibylline Oracles are Jewish books imitating the style of the pagan Sibylline oracles in order to propagate Jewish thought among Gentiles; they come from the 2nd century BC and onwards. *The Assumption of Moses* may have appeared during the lifetime of our Lord; it sets out to give a history of the world, under the guise of prophecy, from Moses to the end, which is of course the writer's own time. *The Book of the Secrets of Enoch* (*2 Enoch*) presupposes the former book of Enoch and is thought to have appeared in the mid-1st century AD, although some date it later by several centuries. It gives elaborate descriptions of the seven heavens and anticipates a 1,000-year kingdom of God on earth.

The Syriac Apocalypse of Baruch (*2 Baruch*) is almost certainly dependent on 2 Esdras and is a composite work, purporting to have come from the scribe of Jeremiah. It was written in the latter part of the 1st century AD. *The Greek Apocalypse of Baruch* (*3 Baruch*), while having affinities with the former work, is independent of it and is slightly later in date. *The Psalms of Solomon* are eighteen psalms written in the name of Solomon, but they come from the pen of a Pharisee or someone with a similar outlook. They are in the style of the canonical Psalms and were written in the latter half of the 1st century AD after the Roman conquest of Judea; they condemn the Hasmonaeans and look forward to the coming of the Messiah of David's line.

3 Maccabees tells of an attempt to massacre the Jews in the reign of Ptolemy Philopator (222–205 BC), which ends in the triumphant vindication of the holy people. *4 Maccabees* is a philosophical treatise which uses the stories of Maccabean martyrs to illustrate the writer's thesis of the supremacy of right reason. *The Letter of Aristeas* describes the supposed circumstances of the translating of the Hebrew Scriptures into Greek. *The Martyrdom of Isaiah*, as the title indicates, tells of the sawing of Isaiah in two. Although Charles dates it in the 1st century of our era, there is reason to think that the book from which it comes, *The Ascension of Isaiah*, is as a whole a Christian product of later date, but it perhaps incorporates an earlier narrative of Jewish origin, showing affinities with the Qumran literature.

The Books of Adam and Eve give us a great deal of 'information' about the lives of the ancestors of the race and emanate from the

1st century AD. *Pirqe Aboth*, or 'The Sayings of the Fathers', is a collection of sayings of notable Rabbis, covering the period of the 3rd century BC to the 3rd century AD. *The Story of Ahiqar* is a legend written about the 5th century BC telling of the wisdom of this sage and was popular throughout this period we are considering (*cf.* Tobit 14:10). *The Apocalypse of Abraham* and *The Testament of Abraham* both come from the 1st century AD and are Jewish works with Christian interpolations. *The Lives of the Prophets* shows by its title what it contains; it comes from the same era as the former two books and has been similarly expanded by Christians. *The Testament of Job* has received little attention but is conjectured by some to have been written in the 1st century BC. *The Zadokite Documents*, two early mediaeval Hebrew manuscripts from the synagogue of Old Cairo, incomplete but to some extent complementary, are now known to belong to the literature of the Qumran community; other fragments from the Qumran caves suggest that the work dates from the beginning of the 1st century BC.

The discovery in 1947 and the following years of the (mostly fragmentary) remains of some 500 documents in eleven caves at Qumran, NW of the Dead Sea, has greatly increased the extant body of Jewish literature of the period with which this article deals. These documents appear to have formed part of the library of a separatist community which had its headquarters in that region for the two centuries from *c.* 130 BC to *c.* AD 70. This community, which exhibits some affinities with the Essenes described by writers of the 1st century AD, was characterized by a remnant mentality, eschatological convictions and a bold and creative system of biblical exegesis. By no means all the Qumran texts fall within the apocryphal and apocalyptic categories; in addition to biblical manuscripts and biblical commentaries they include material bearing on the life, beliefs and worship of the community.

Reference has already been made to some works previously known which, thanks to these discoveries, are now accessible in their original languages. In addition, there are portions of a 'Daniel' cycle which never gained admittance either to the canonical or to the deutero-canonical book of Daniel, including the *Prayer of Nabonidus*, an Aramaic text which tells how the last king of Babylon was sore afflicted for 7 years 'in the city of Teman' and, when he confessed his sins, received help from a Jewish exile. The *Genesis Apocryphon*, also in Aramaic, contains imaginative expansions of the patriarchal narratives. Other texts have such titles as *The Sayings of Moses*, *The Psalms of Joshua*, *The Vision of Amram*, *The Book of Mysteries* and (evidently a favourite, to judge from the number of copies) *The Apocalypse of the New Jerusalem*. When all these have been published and studied, they promise to add greatly to our understanding of the background of the NT.

THE TEACHING OF THE APOCRYPHAL LITERATURE

The doctrine of God

There is a tendency in all this literature, increasing as time goes by, to think of God in terms of His transcendence. There is a reluctance to mention the divine name, so that various circumlocutions are used instead. In 1 Maccabees God is not mentioned once directly, but is usually referred to as 'heaven'; *e.g.* 'It is not on the size of the army that victory in battle depends, but strength comes from Heaven' (1 Macc. 3:19). With this we may compare the way in which the Jewish writer Matthew in his Gospel constantly uses the phrase 'the kingdom of heaven' instead of 'kingdom of God' as in the other Gospels. The Rabbis often refer to God as 'the Holy One, blessed be He', as in the following example: 'You are to give just account and reckoning before the King of the kings of the kings, the Holy One, blessed be He' (*Pirqe Aboth* 4:29). For the same reason, the doctrine of angels developed much in this period, to avoid the necessity for God to interfere directly in the affairs of the world. In the OT the Lord is a 'man of war' who fights Israel's battles. In 2 Maccabees it is angels who fight for Israel, and in the Qumran *Rule of War* holy angels are present with the army of the 'sons of light'. In 1 Maccabees the process is still further accentuated in that neither God nor angels fight, but the good generalship of Judas gains the victory; the thought is that it is not fitting that God should actively intervene in matters of this order. Similarly the direct contact that God has with creation in the OT is replaced by multitudinous angels, some of which are appointed to look after the lightning, others after the snow, rain, clouds, darkness, heat, cold, frost, *etc.* On the other hand, the doctrine of demons naturally came into prominence, though here other causes were at work.

With such a view of God, the thought of His sovereignty was prominent. The consummation has not only been foreseen, it has been ordained, even to the precise hour. Individuals share in this process of predestination, but not to the exclusion of their freedom. The author of the *Psalms of Solomon* believed in God's complete sovereignty over man but also said, 'Our works are subjected to our own choice and power to do right or wrong in the works of our hands' (9:7). Similarly God's transcendence did not exclude altogether His relationship with men; increasingly His Fatherhood was recognized. The phrase, 'Your Father, who is in heaven' occurs in *Pirqe Aboth* 5:23. *Cf.* also, 'The Lord will rejoice in His children, and be well pleased in His beloved ones for ever' (*Testament of Levi* 18:13; 4:2; *Sibylline Oracles* 3:702; *3 Maccabees* 6:28; *Pirqe Aboth* 3:19).

The law

The law is eternal and of supreme importance

to man. In *Jubilees* it is said that all the righteous men of old observed the law, as indeed the angels of heaven, so that the work of Moses at Sinai was not to make it known for the first time but to re-promulgate it. It is the sum of the revelation of God. For most Jews, the law (*Torah*) included the oral tradition, which was claimed to have come down from Moses through the prophets and the men of the great synagogue. This tradition, as reduced to writing from *c.* AD 200 onwards, included multitudinous applications of the law to all possible circumstances (the *Mishnah*), together with further explanations of these explications (the *Gemara*), and they both formed the *Talmud*, of which there were two collections, the Jerusalem and the Babylonian. Our Lord's attitude to this mass of tradition is well known, but its observance was the life-blood of most orthodox Jews. Both Rabbis and apocalyptists agreed in teaching that one's only hope of obtaining the life of the world to come lay in obeying its precepts.

Wisdom

The attributes of wisdom as set forth in Pr. 8:22–31 were much thought on in this era, particularly as Greek thought made itself felt in Judaism. There is a long and beautiful description of wisdom in the Wisdom of Solomon (7:22 – 8:1), where it is said to be 'a breath of the power of God, and a pure emanation of the glory of the Almighty . . . For she is a reflection (Gk. *apaugasma*, *cf.* Heb. 1:3) of eternal light, a spotless mirror of the working of God, and an image of his goodness'. Both in the books of Wisdom and Ecclesiasticus there are set forth proverbs of practical wisdom.

At the same time speculation increased in the conception of 'the word of God'. Its activity is startlingly portrayed in Wisdom 18:15, 16: 'Thy all-powerful word leaped from heaven, from the royal throne, into the midst of the land that was doomed, a stern warrior carrying the sharp sword of thy authentic command, and stood and filled all things with death, and touched heaven while standing on the earth.' The reference is to the slaughter of the firstborn in Egypt. In this same book, 9:1, 2, the word is identified with wisdom: 'O God of my fathers . . . who hast made all things by thy word, and by thy wisdom hast formed man. . . .' With this teaching should be compared the view that wisdom and the law are one and the same. This view constantly appears in these books, especially in Ecclesiasticus and *Pirqe Aboth*. *E.g.* Ben-Sira gives a lengthy description of wisdom in Ecclus. 24 and then says, 'All this is the book of the covenant of the Most High God, the law which Moses commanded us . . .' (Ecclus. 24:23). Likewise the law and the word are one, as in *Pirqe Aboth* 3:19, 'Beloved are Israel in that to them was given the instrument by which the world was created . . .' The importance of these developments for the student of the NT is clear; they provide the background against

which the prologue to the Fourth Gospel may be studied. What the Jew claimed for wisdom, the word, the law, John claimed to be fulfilled in Jesus the Word incarnate.

Sin

The origin of sin was much discussed in these times. The answers given to the question varied, but they mostly tended to centre on the Fall. Sometimes it is Eve who is largely to blame (Ecclus. 25:24), sometimes Adam (2 Esdras 7:118), sometimes the devil (Wisdom 2:24) or even the fallen angels (*1 Enoch* 10:7, 8). On the other hand, the author of *2 Baruch* would protest at the view that we may all lay the blame on our forbears: 'Though Adam first sinned and brought untimely death upon all, yet of those who were born from him, each one of them has prepared for his own soul torment to come, and again each one of them has chosen for himself glories to come . . . Adam is therefore not the cause, save only of his own soul, but each of us has been the Adam of his own soul' (*2 Baruch* 54:15, 19). With regard to atonement for sin, the sacrifices are the main means, as in the OT. But works are also efficacious to this end; *cf.* Ecclus. 3:3, 'Whoever honours his father atones for sins', and Tobit 12:9, 'Almsgiving delivers from death, and it will purge away every sin.' Against sentiments of this order Paul vehemently protested. The merits of saints were also pleaded (2 Esdras 8:28, 29) and in one book at least the martyrdom of faithful confessors is also regarded as making satisfaction for sins (*4 Maccabees* 6:28, 29).

Ethics

The chief end of man is to understand and obey the law. As one Rabbi put it, 'If you have practised much Torah, do not take credit for yourself, for you were created to do this' (*Pirqe Aboth* 2:9). In an age when the law was considered to be the sum of the revelation of God, this view was inevitable. Unfortunately, it led to the teaching of salvation by works in a crude fashion, as when Aqiba compared God to a shopkeeper who gives men credit when they keep the law and exacts payment for their debts when they fail (*Pirqe Aboth* 3:20).

Nevertheless, on the whole there is an advance in ethical conceptions in this literature as compared with some phases of the OT. Several times in the *Testaments of the Twelve Patriarchs* the exhortation is given, 'Love the Lord and your neighbour' (*e.g. Testament of Issachar* 5:2), a remarkable anticipation of our Lord's teaching. The same book has lofty teaching concerning forgiveness, as *Testament of Gad* 6:3–7: 'Love one another from the heart; and if a man sins against you, speak peaceably to him, and do not hold guile in your soul; and if he repents and confesses, forgive him. But if he denies it, do not get into a passion with him, lest catching the poison from you he takes to swearing and so you sin doubly. And even if he denies it and yet has a sense of shame when reproved, stop reproving him. For he who denies may repent so as not to wrong you again; yes, he may also honour you and be at peace with you. And if he is shameless and persists in his wrongdoing, even so forgive him from the heart, and leave to God the avenging.'

Such passages as this run so parallel to some of our Lord's instruction that Charles is inclined to consider that He was acquainted with the *Testaments* and used them. It may be so, though we cannot be sure. Moral maxims tend to be no-one's property in an atmosphere where preaching is the bread of life, as it was to the Jew of this time. Moreover, the fact that we have the *Testaments* in a Christian recension leaves open the possibility that the influence, if any, was exerted in the other direction.

Eschatology

It is in this subject where development is most marked in the intertestamental period. Advance is particularly noticeable in the conceptions of personal immortality, the kingdom of God, and the Messiah.

Personal immortality. As far as we can tell, even the earliest Israelites believed in man's survival of death. But it was to a colourless existence that they expected to go, in which one could not hope for fellowship with God. Ps. 88 is instructive in this respect; to the psalmist, the beyond is 'the land of forgetfulness', 'the dark', the place where the dead have no fellowship with God, for 'they are cut off from thy hand'. With such a conception of the afterlife as this, some considered it as all but non-existence: 'Look away from me, that I may know gladness, before I depart and be no more!' (Ps. 39:13).

Clearer understanding was gained on this matter as the saints of God reflected more on their fellowship with God, and related that experience to the certainty of the coming of the kingdom of God. Job thus believes that he will see God's vindication of his innocence after death (Jb. 19:25–27), and the writer of Ps. 139 believed that even Sheol could not exclude God: 'If I make my bed in Sheol, thou art there' (v. 8). So also the writer of Ps. 73 looked forward to God's continuing His fellowship with him by welcoming him to glory after death (vv. 24, 25).

Such teaching is the exception, however, and it was not received by all. Ben-Sira, a Sadducee, wrote, 'Whether life is for ten or a hundred or a thousand years, there is no inquiry about it in Sheol' (Ecclus. 41:4), this statement being a plain denial of retribution by God after death. It was left to the Hasids, the forbears of the Pharisees, to develop the teaching of the more spiritual sons of Israel. There is a remarkable parallel to our Lord's teaching on this matter in *4 Maccabees* 7:18, 19: 'As many as with their whole heart make righteousness their first thought, these alone are able to master the weakness of the flesh, believing that unto God

they do not die, as our patriarchs Abraham and Isaac and Jacob did not die, but that they live unto God.' We have travelled to the opposite pole of Ben-Sira's dictum in the words of the Rabbi who said, 'This world is like a porch before the world to come. Make yourself ready in the porch, that you may enter the banqueting hall' (*Pirqe Aboth* 4:21). Such is the constant viewpoint of the apocalyptists and it is they who made it so widespread in the Judaism of our Lord's day.

The kingdom of God. We may trace three stages of thought on this. In the OT the kingdom is anticipated to be earthly and eternally of the earth. The famous Messianic prophecy of Is. 11:1–9 is typical. The early apocalyptists dwelt much on such passages as these and produced some highly sensuous pictures of that time. *1 Enoch* 10:17f. says that the righteous shall live to a good old age and beget thousands of children; their seed shall produce a thousandfold, every measure of olives shall yield ten presses of oil, *etc.* This is the source of Papias's well-known description of the millennium.

Is. 65:17–22 speaks of a renewed heaven and earth, but it is not clear to what extent this is meant to apply to the moral or physical realms. Certain apocalyptists, however, of the 1st centuries BC and AD put forward the view that the Messianic kingdom, though to be established on earth, is of temporary duration and will give place to an eternal kingdom of the heavens. In *2 Enoch* this is linked with the notion that the history of the world is to last for 7,000 years, the last 1,000 being the millennial kingdom, after which the eternal kingdom will begin a new creation (*2 Enoch* 32:2 – 33:2). To this writer the temporary kingdom is clearly of great importance. But in 2 Esdras it has assumed a decreased significance, owing to the pessimism of the author as to this world; it is limited to 400 years in duration, at the end of which time the Messiah and all living will die (2 Esdras 7:29f.).

In view of the latter development, it is not surprising that some apocalyptists abandoned altogether the idea of a temporary Messianic kingdom, and looked only to the eternal kingdom in the new heavens. Such is the expectation of one line of tradition on which the author of *2 Baruch* drew. He evidently felt this earth to be unworthy of the kingdom of God: 'Whatever is now is nothing, but that which will be is very great. For everything that is corruptible will pass away, and everything that dies will depart, and all the present time will be forgotten, nor will there be any remembrance of the present time, which is defiled with evils' (*2 Baruch* 44:8f.).

Whatever view is taken as to the nature of the kingdom, its coming is usually conceived to be 'catastrophic', as in the dream of Nebuchadrezzar in Dn. 2. In some books, however, we find the thought that the kingdom would come to its fullness only gradually, as in *Jubilees* 33 and

2 Baruch 73–74. In the former work, the kingdom is conceived to come in ever-increasing fullness as the law is more fully studied and obeyed.

Similarly, all the apocalyptists expected the kingdom to appear *soon*; they stand in the end of the days. Yet in several works it is stated that the great day would be hastened still further by repentance. 'On the day on which Israel repents, the kingdom of the enemy will be brought to an end' (*Testament of Dan* 6:4). In the *Assumption of Moses* 1:18, therefore, the last day is called 'the day of repentance in the visitation which the Lord will make in the consummation of the end of the days'.

These different aspects of the kingdom of God could not but affect their adherents' views on immortality. It had long been recognized that since the purpose of God was the establishment of the kingdom, that purpose embraced not merely the generation of the end-time but all the godly. Hence the doctrine of resurrection came into clear focus. In the OT, that doctrine appears in Is. 26:19 and Dn. 12:3. Now, however, modifications arose. If the resurrection anticipated is to a kingdom of earthly bliss, naturally the resurrection body is of the same nature as the present body; so we find in the *Sibylline Oracles* 3:179–192: 'God will fashion again the bones and the ashes of men and will raise up mortals once more as they were before.' Such a resurrection, of course, takes place at the commencement of the kingdom. But when the temporary kingdom is expected, the resurrection is postponed till the end of that kingdom; such is the case in the *Book of the Secrets of Enoch* where God tells Adam that He will take him from the earth 'at my second coming' (32:1), *i.e.* at the end of the 7,000 years of the earth's history. This writer seemed to conceive of the resurrection as being spiritual and not purely material; thus we read, 'The Lord said to Michael, "Go and take Enoch from out his earthly garments, and anoint him with my sweet ointment, and put him into the garments of my glory" ' (22:8). Such writers as the author of the Wisdom of Solomon, who expected no earthly realization of the kingdom, occasionally looked for resurrection to occur immediately on death; the author of Wisdom, indeed, shows the influence of Greek conceptions of immortality—at least for the righteous. This thought, however, does not appear to be native to Palestinian Judaism and it was not generally accepted.

The Messiah. The Messiah is not mentioned in a number of OT prophets (*e.g.* Amos, Zephaniah, Nahum, Habakkuk, Joel, ?Daniel). Similarly, He is absent from several apocryphal books (the four Maccabean books, Judith, Tobit, 1 Baruch, Wisdom, *Assumption of Moses*, *2 Enoch*). Charles accordingly infers: 'It follows that in Jewish prophecy and apocalyptic the Messiah was no organic factor of the kingdom' (R. H. Charles, *Religious Development between the Old and New Testaments*, 1914, pp. 75, 76). Although it is a doubtful assumption that, in all the cases mentioned, the silence of the writers necessarily implies their rejection of the expectation of a Messiah, the statement of Charles is generally valid. The great difference between the eschatology of the OT and the NT is the relative importance of the Messiah; in the NT, eschatology is wholly bound up with the Person and work of Christ.

In those passages of the OT in which the Messiah takes a prominent position in the kingdom, it is to be noticed that normally He begins to play a part after the establishment of the kingdom; He Himself does not found it. Ps. 110:1 sums up the position: 'The Lord says to my lord: "Sit at my right hand, till I make your enemies your footstool." ' Similarly in most of the apocalypses, the Messiah does not commence His activity till the kingdom is founded. One of the most important exceptions is the *Similitudes of Enoch*, to which we shall return presently.

Again, in the apocalypses, the Messiah almost always comes from the seed of David, as in the OT. A puzzling conception meets us, however, in the *Testaments of the Twelve Patriarchs*, where salvation is said to arise from Levi and Judah and not from Judah alone. Most commentators insist that the Messiah in this book is viewed as springing from Levi; that is certainly the case in *Testament of Reuben* 6:7–12. It is equally clear that in *Testament of Judah* 22 and 24 the Messiah is stated to arise from Judah. Moreover, the normal view of the *Testaments* is that salvation is to arise from Levi and Judah, and not from one tribe alone.

The only satisfactory interpretation seems to be that this writer expected two Messiahs and not one. The reason for such a startling view is not simply the heroic achievements of the Maccabean leaders, who were of the tribe of Levi, but because of the importance attached by this writer to the priesthood. Judah is made to say, 'To me the Lord gave the kingdom and to him (Levi) the priesthood, and he set the kingdom beneath the priesthood. . . . As the heaven is higher than the earth, so is the priesthood of God higher than the earthly dominion. . . .' (*Testament of Judah* 21:1f.). The importance of this development, taking place so close to the birth of our Lord, lies in the preparation it must have had among the Jews for the preaching of a Messiah whose great work was atonement.

When the Messiah appears in the singular in the Qumran texts, the Davidic Messiah is meant, but sometimes two Messiahs are mentioned, one priestly and the other lay ('the Messiahs of Aaron and Israel'); the priestly Messiah will be head of state in the new age and the lay Messiah will be subordinate to him, just as the Davidic 'prince' in Ezekiel's new commonwealth is to be subordinate to the priesthood. Along with these two anointed personages the Qumran community expected the prophet like Moses (Dt. 18:15ff.) to arise in the end-time.

Another great deviation from the traditional picture of the Messiah is that given in the *Similitudes of Enoch* (*1 Enoch* 37–71). No longer is the Messiah a merely human figure; He is a transcendent being, pre-existent and exalted above all creatures, and is to be manifested in the last times, not only to rule for God but to establish the kingdom. He is closely associated, if not identified, with the community of the righteous and chosen people of God, and can be individualized in someone who is outstandingly righteous—in *1 Enoch* 71:14 he is individualized in Enoch, who is divinely appointed to pronounce judgment on the ungodly at the last assize.

According to Charles, here for the first time are applied to the coming Deliverer the titles of the Christ, the Righteous One, the Elect One, and the Son of man (see *1 Enoch* 52:4; 38:2; 45:3, 4; 46:1–6, respectively), all of which appear in the NT. Many means were used by God to prepare the way of the Lord and to bring about that 'fullness of time' for the coming of His Son from heaven about which Scripture speaks. In this sense these writings, with their references to the coming Deliverer, were important, for they were part and parcel of the general historical situation which God overruled for His saving purpose.

G. R. BEASLEY-MURRAY

F. F. BRUCE

Between the Testaments

The OT narrative comes to an end with the Persian Empire firmly in control of Western Asia. The last monarch whom it mentions by name is 'Darius the Persian' (Ne. 12:22)— either Darius II (423–404 BC) or Darius III (336–331 BC), the last king of Persia. When we open the NT another world power dominates the Near East and indeed the whole Mediterranean world. Luke connects the birth of Jesus with a decree issued by Caesar Augustus, the first Roman Emperor (27 BC – AD 14), 'that all the world should be enrolled' (Lk. 2:1), and dates the ministry of John the Baptist 'in the fifteenth year of the reign of Tiberius Caesar' (AD 14–37), successor to Augustus (Lk. 3:1). It is by a Roman judge that Jesus is condemned to death and by a Roman form of execution that the death-sentence is carried out; it is by a Roman citizen that the Christian message is carried most vigorously into the Mediterranean area, and the NT ends with the power of Rome threatening to exterminate the church, yet destined to be overcome by it.

Between the last king of Persia and the establishment of the Roman presence in the Near East, this area was dominated by the Graeco-Macedonian régime of Alexander the Great and his successors. There are some apocalyptic allusions to this régime in Daniel and one or two other OT books; but even the apocryphal books tell us little of the Graeco-Macedonian rulers apart from the brief period in the 2nd century BC covered by the books of Maccabees. Yet apart from some acquaintance with the background of this 'intertestamental' period the NT itself cannot be properly understood.

The conquest of the Persian Empire by Alexander the Great (331 BC) brought no constitutional changes either to Samaria or to Judea. These provinces were now administered by Graeco-Macedonian governors in place of the former Persian governors, and tribute had to be paid to the new overlord in place of the old one. The Jewish Dispersion, which had been widespread under the Persian Empire, from Susa to Syene and Sardis (the Sepharad of Ob. 20), now found new centres, especially Alexandria and Cyrene. The influences of Greek culture inevitably began to give evidence of their presence among them. These Hellenistic influences were in some directions good: we may think in particular of the situation among the Greek-speaking Jews of Alexandria which necessitated the translation of the Pentateuch and other OT writings into Greek in the 3rd and 2nd centuries BC, and thus made the knowledge of Israel's God accessible to the Gentile world. On the other hand there was a tendency to imitate features of Hellenistic culture which were inextricably interwoven with paganism and which in other ways as well blurred the distinction between Yahweh's 'peculiar people' and their neighbours. How far a prominent Jewish family could go in unscrupulous assimilation to the unworthier aspects of life under the Hellenistic monarchies is illustrated by Josephus's account of the fortunes of the Tobiads, who enriched themselves as tax-collectors on behalf first of the Ptolemies and then of the Seleucids (*Ant.* xii. 160–222).

Among the dynasties which inherited Alexander's Empire, the two which chiefly affect the history of Israel are those of the Ptolemies in Egypt and of the Seleucids who dominated Syria and the lands beyond the Euphrates. From 323 to 198 BC the Ptolemies' rule extended from Egypt into Asia as far as the Lebanon range and the Phoenician coast, including Judea and Samaria. In 198 BC the Seleucid victory at Panion, near the sources of the Jordan, meant that Judea and Samaria were now tributary to Antioch instead of Alexandria. The defeat which the Seleucid king Antiochus III suffered at the hands of the Romans at Magnesia in 190 BC, and the heavy indemnity which they imposed on him, involved an enormous increase of taxation for his subjects, including the Jews. When his son, Antiochus IV, attempted to redress the situation by imposing his sovereignty over Egypt (in the two campaigns of 169 and 168 BC), the Romans forced him to relinquish these ambitions. Judea, on the SW frontier of his kingdom, now became a region of strategic importance, and he felt that there was grave reason for suspecting the loyalty of his Jewish subjects. On the advice of unwise counsellors, he decided to abolish their distinctive nationhood and religion, and the climax of this policy was the installation of a pagan cult—the worship of Zeus Olympios (punningly altered by the Jews into 'the abomination of desolation')—in the Temple at Jerusalem in December, 167 BC. The Samaritan temple on Gerizim was similarly diverted to the worship of Zeus Xenios.

Many pious Jews endured martyrdom at this time sooner than forswear their religion. Others took up arms against their Seleucid overlord. Among the latter were members of the priestly family of the Hasmonaeans, headed by Mattathias and his five sons. The outstanding son of the five, Judas Maccabaeus, was a born leader of men, who excelled in guerrilla warfare.

His initial successes against the royal forces brought many of his fellow-countrymen under his leadership, including a large number of the pious people in Israel, the *ḥªsîdîm*, who considered that passive resistance was not enough in face of the present threat to their national and religious existence. Larger armies were sent against them by the king, but they too were routed by the unexpected tactics of Judas and his men. It became clear to the king that his policy had misfired, and Judas was invited to send ambassadors to Antioch to discuss conditions of peace. Antiochus had military plans for the reconquest of seceding territories in the eastern part of his kingdom, and it was important to reach a settlement on his Egyptian frontier. The basic Jewish condition was, naturally, the complete abrogation of the ban on Jewish religious practice. This was conceded, and the Jews were free again to practise their ancestral religion. The concession was followed at once by the purification of the Temple from the idolatrous cult which had been installed in it, and its rededication to the age-long worship of the God of Israel. The dedication of the Temple at the end of 164 BC (ever afterwards commemorated in the Festival of Hanukkah; *cf.* Jn. 10:22) was probably not envisaged in the terms of peace, but in itself it might have been accepted as a *fait accompli*.

Judas and his brothers and followers, however, were not content with the regaining of religious liberty. Having won that success by force of arms, they continued their struggle in order to win political independence. The dedication of the Temple was followed by the fortification of the Temple hill, facing the citadel or Akra which was manned by a royal garrison. Judas sent armed bands to Galilee, Transjordan and other regions where there were isolated Jewish communities and brought them back to the safety of those parts of Judea which were controlled by his forces.

Such a succession of hostile acts could not be overlooked by the Seleucid government, and further armies were sent against Judas. Judas fell in battle in the spring of 160 BC, and for a time the cause which he had led seemed lost. But events played into the hands of his successors. In particular, the death of Antiochus IV in 163 BC was followed by a lengthy period of intermittent civil war in the Seleucid Empire, between rival claimants to the throne and their respective partisans. Jonathan, the brother of Judas who took his place as leader of the insurgent party, lay low until times were propitious, and then by diplomatic dealing won rapid and astounding advancement. In 152 BC Alexander Balas, who claimed the Seleucid throne on the doubtful ground that he was the son of Antiochus IV, authorized Jonathan to maintain his own military force in Judea and recognized him as high priest of the Jews, in return for Jonathan's promise to support his cause.

Antiochus IV had begun his intervention in Jewish religious affairs, which ultimately had brought about the Hasmonaean rising, by deposing the legitimate high priest of the house of Zadok, and appointing other high priests at his own discretion, in defiance of ancient custom. Now a Hasmonaean accepted the high priesthood from a man whose title to bestow it was based on his claim to be son and successor to Antiochus IV. So much for the high ideals with which the struggle had begun!

The pious groups who had lent their aid to the Hasmonaeans at a time when it seemed that only by Hasmonaean might could religious freedom be regained, were disposed to be content when that goal was attained, and grew increasingly critical of the Hasmonaeans' dynastic ambitions. But no feature of these ambitions displeased them more than the Hasmonaean assumption of the high priesthood. Some of them refused to recognize any high priesthood other than the Zadokite one, and held aloof from the Temple worship while it was controlled by an illegitimate hierarchy. These went down to the wilderness of Judea and formed the Qumran community (known to us in recent years from the Dead Sea Scrolls); they may be regarded as one among several 'Essene' groups of the period. One branch of the Zadokite family was permitted to found a Jewish temple at Leontopolis in Egypt and function in the high-priestly office there; but a temple outside the land of Israel could not be countenanced by those *ḥªsîdîm* who had any regard for the law.

In 143 BC Jonathan was trapped and put to death by one of the rival claimants for mastery of the Seleucid kingdom, but he was succeeded by his brother Simon, under whom the Jews achieved complete independence from the Gentile yoke. This independence was granted in a rescript from the Seleucid king Demetrius II in May, 142 BC, by which the Jews were released from the obligation to pay tribute. Simon followed up this diplomatic success by subduing the last vestiges of Seleucid ascendancy in Judea, the fortress of Gazara (Gezer) and the citadel in Jerusalem. Demetrius had embarked on an expedition against the Parthians, and could take no action against Simon, even had he so wished. Simon received signal honours from his grateful fellow-Jews for the freedom and peace which he had secured for them. At a meeting of the popular assembly of the Jews in September, 140 BC, it was decreed, in consideration of the patriotic achievements of Simon and his brothers before him, that he should be appointed ethnarch or governor of the nation, commander-in-chief of the army, and hereditary high priest. This triple authority he bequeathed to his descendants and successors.

Simon was assassinated at Jericho in 135 BC by his son-in-law Ptolemy, son of Abubus, who hoped to seize supreme power in Judea. But Simon's son, John Hyrcanus, thwarted the assassin's plans and secured his position as successor to his father.

The Seleucid king Antiochus VII, who had tried to reassert his authority over Judea during Simon's later years, succeeded in imposing tribute on John Hyrcanus for the first few years of his rule. But the death of Antiochus VII in battle with the Parthians in 129 BC brought Seleucid overlordship over Judea to a decisive end.

In the seventh year of John Hyrcanus, then, the independent state of Judea was firmly established, 40 years after Antiochus IV had abolished its old constitution as an autonomous temple-state within the Empire. The devotion of the ḥᵃsîdîm, the military genius of Judas and the statesmanship of Simon, together with increasing division and weakness in the Seleucid government, had won for the Jews more (to all outward appearance) than they had lost at the hands of Antiochus IV. No wonder, then, that the early years of independence under John Hyrcanus were looked back to by later generations as a kind of golden age.

It was in the time of John Hyrcanus that the final breach between the majority of the ḥᵃsîdîm and the Hasmonaean family came about. John was offended by their objections to his tenure of the high priesthood, and broke with them. From this time onward they appear in history as the party of the Pharisees, although it is not certain that they owed that name (Heb. pᵉrûšîm, 'separated ones') to the fact of their withdrawal from their former alliance with the Hasmonaeans, as has frequently been supposed; they owed it rather to their avoidance of association with those who did not share their scrupulous regard for the laws of purification and tithing. They remained in opposition to the régime for 50 years. Those religious leaders who supported the régime and manned the national council appear about the same time with the name Sadducees. In the NT the wealthy chief-priestly families belong to the Sadducean party.

John Hyrcanus profited by the growing weakness of the Seleucid kingdom to extend his own power. One of his earliest actions after the establishment of Jewish independence was to invade Samaritan territory and besiege Samaria, which held out for a year but was then stormed and destroyed. Shechem was also captured and the schismatic Samaritan shrine on Mt. Gerizim, erected towards the end of the Persian Empire, was demolished. The Samaritans appealed to the Seleucid king for help, but the Romans warned him not to interfere. The Hasmonaeans, at an early stage in their struggle, had secured a treaty of alliance with the Romans, who lost no opportunity of weakening and insulting the Seleucids, and this treaty was renewed by John.

To the south of his kingdom John warred against the Idumaeans, conquered them and forced them to accept circumcision and adopt the Jewish religion. He subdued Greek cities in Transjordan and invaded Galilee.

His work in Galilee was continued by his son and successor Aristobulus I (104–103 BC), who forced the subjected Galilaeans to accept Judaism, as his father had done with the Idumaeans.

According to Josephus, Aristobulus assumed the title 'king' instead of that of 'ethnarch' with which his grandfather and (so far as we know) his father had been content, and wore a diadem in token of his royal estate. No doubt he hoped in this way to enjoy greater prestige among his Gentile neighbours, although his coins designate him, in language more congenial to his Jewish subjects, as 'Judah the high priest'.

Aristobulus died after a year's reign and was succeeded by his brother Alexander Jannaeus (103–76 BC), who married his widow Salome Alexandra. A more inappropriate high priest than Jannaeus could hardly be imagined. He did go through the motions of his sacred office on occasions of high ceremony—and did so in a way that deliberately offended the sentiments of many of his most religiously-minded subjects (especially the Pharisees). But the master-ambition of his reign was military conquest. His pursuit of this policy brought him many reverses, but by the end of his reign he had brought under his control practically all the territory that had been Israelite in the great days of the nation's history—at a ruinous cost to all that was of value in his people's spiritual heritage.

Greek cities on the Mediterranean seaboard and in Transjordan were his special targets for attack; one after another he besieged and conquered them, showing by his ruthless vandalism how little he cared for the true values of Hellenistic civilization. He modelled his way of life on that of the cruder Hellenistic princelings of Western Asia. Feeling against him on the part of many of his Jewish subjects reached such a pitch that, when he suffered a disastrous defeat at the hands of a Nabataean force in Transjordan in 94 BC, they revolted against him and even enlisted the aid of the Seleucid king, Demetrius III. But other Jewish subjects of Jannaeus, however much they disliked him, found the spectacle of a Seleucid king being called to help in a revolt against a member of the Hasmonaean family too much for their patriotism; they volunteered to support the cause of their hard-pressed king and enabled him to put down the revolt and send the Seleucid contingents packing. The barbarity of the revenge which Jannaeus took against the leaders of the revolt (who included some outstanding Pharisees) was long remembered with horror.

Jannaeus bequeathed his kingdom to his widow, Salome Alexandra, who ruled it as queen regnant for 9 years. She bestowed the high priesthood on her elder son, Hyrcanus II. In one important respect she reversed the policy of her predecessors; she befriended the Pharisees and paid attention to their counsel throughout her reign.

Her death in 67 BC was followed by civil war

between the supporters of the claims of her two sons, Hyrcanus II and Aristobulus II, to succeed to supreme power in Judea. Aristobulus was a typical Hasmonaean prince, ambitious and aggressive; Hyrcanus was a nonentity, but was easily manipulated by those who supported his claims in their own interests, among whom the dominating personality was the Idumaean Antipater, whose father had been governor of Idumaea under Jannaeus.

The civil strife between the two brothers and their respective partisans was halted by the Romans in 63 BC, in circumstances which brought Judea's short-lived independence under the Hasmonaeans to an end.

In 66 BC the Roman senate and people sent their most brilliant general at that time, Pompey, to bring to a successful conclusion their 20-year-old war with Mithridates, king of Pontus, who had carved out an empire for himself in W Asia from the lands of the decadent Seleucid kingdom and neighbouring states. Pompey was not long in defeating Mithridates (who fled to Crimea and committed suicide there); but having done that he found himself faced with the necessity of reorganizing the political life of W Asia. In 64 BC he annexed Syria as a province of Rome, and was invited by various parties in the Jewish state to intervene in its affairs too and put an end to the civil war between the sons of Jannaeus.

Thanks to Antipater's shrewd appraisal of the situation, the party favouring Hyrcanus showed itself willing to co-operate with Rome, and Jerusalem opened its gates to Pompey in the spring of 63 BC. The Temple, however, which was separately fortified and was held by the partisans of Aristobulus, sustained a siege of three months before it was taken by Pompey's forces.

Judea now became tributary to Rome. She was deprived of the Greek cities which the Hasmonaean kings had conquered and annexed, and the Samaritans were liberated from Jewish control. Hyrcanus was confirmed in the high priesthood and leadership of the nations; but he had to be content with the title of 'ethnarch', for the Romans refused to recognize him as king. Antipater continued to support him, determined to exploit this new turn of events to his own advantage, which (it must be conceded) coincided largely with the advantage of Judea.

Aristobulus and his family endeavoured time after time to foment rebellion against Rome so as to secure power in Judea for themselves. For many years, however, these attempts proved abortive. Successive Roman governors kept a firm grip on Judea and Syria, because these provinces now lay on the eastern frontier of the Roman Empire, beyond which was the rival Empire of Parthia. The strategic importance of this area may be gauged by the number of dominant figures in Roman history who play a part in the history of Judea in these years:

Pompey, who annexed it to the Empire; Crassus, who as governor of Syria in 54–53 BC plundered the Jerusalem Temple and also many Syrian temples while collecting resources for a war against the Parthians, but was defeated and killed by them at Carrhae in 53 BC; Julius Caesar, who became master of the Roman world after defeating Pompey at Pharsalus in Thessaly in 48 BC; Antony, who dominated the eastern provinces of the Empire after he and Octavian had defeated Caesar's assassins and their followers at Philippi in 42 BC; and then Octavian himself, who in 31 BC at Actium defeated Antony and Cleopatra (the last ruler of the Ptolemaic dynasty of Egypt) and thereafter (27 BC) ruled the Roman world alone as the Emperor Augustus. Throughout the vicissitudes of Roman civil and external war Antipater and his family made it their settled policy to support the chief representative of Roman power in the East at any one time, whoever he might be and whichever party in the Roman state he might belong to. Julius Caesar in particular had reason to be grateful for Antipater's support when he was besieged in Alexandria during the winter of 48–47 BC, and conferred special privileges not only on Antipater himself but on the Jews as well.

This confidence which the Romans learned to place in Antipater's family was manifested outstandingly in 40 BC, when the Parthians invaded Syria and Palestine and enabled Antigonus, the last surviving son of Aristobulus II, to regain the Hasmonaean throne and reign as king and high priest of the Jews. Hyrcanus II had his ears cropped to prevent him from ever functioning as high priest again. Antipater was now dead, but an attempt was made to seize and liquidate his family. One son, Phasael, was captured and killed, but Herod, the most gifted of Antipater's sons, escaped to Rome, where the senate nominated him king of Jews, at the instance of Antony and Octavian. It was his task now to recover Judea from Antigonus (who was left in peace by the Roman commander in Syria when the Parthian invaders were driven out) and to rule his kingdom in the interests of the Romans, as their 'friend and ally'. The task was not easy, and its successful completion in 37 BC, with the storming of Jerusalem after a siege of 3 months, secured for Herod a bitter ill-will on the part of his new subjects which no effort of his could remove. Antigonus was sent in chains to Antony, who ordered him to be executed. Herod tried to legitimize his position in Jewish eyes by marrying Mariamne, a Hasmonaean princess, but this marriage brought him more trouble than help.

Herod's position was precarious for the first 6 years of his reign. Although Antony was his friend and patron, Cleopatra longed to incorporate Judea in her kingdom, as her earlier Ptolemaic ancestors had done, and tried to exploit her ascendancy over Antony to this end. The overthow of Antony and Cleopatra in 31 BC, and Herod's confirmation in his kingdom by the conqueror, Octavian, brought him some relief externally, but domestic peace was denied him both in his family circle and in his relations with the Jewish people. Yet he governed Judea with a firm hand, serving the interests of Rome even better than a Roman governor could have done. He put down insurgency ruthlessly, and left as tangible memorials of his reign new cities such as Sebaste (on the site of the ancient Samaria) and Caesarea (a seaport with artificial harbour on the Mediterranean coast) and great buildings, the most illustrious of which was the renovated and enlarged Temple in Jerusalem.

When Herod died in 4 BC, his kingdom was divided between three of his surviving sons. Archelaus governed Judea and Samaria as ethnarch until AD 6; Antipas governed Galilee and Peraea as tetrarch until AD 39; Philip received as a tetrarchy the territory E and NE of the Sea of Galilee which his father had pacified in the emperor's interests, and ruled it until his death in AD 34.

Antipas ('Herod the tetrarch' of the Gospel story) inherited a full share of his father's political acumen, and continued the thankless task of promoting the Roman cause in Galilee and Peraea and the surrounding regions. Archelaus, however, had all his father's brutality without his genius, and soon drove his subjects to the point where they petitioned the Roman emperor to remove him so as to prevent a revolt from breaking out. Archelaus was accordingly deposed and banished, and his ethnarchy was reconstituted as a Roman province of the third grade. In order that its annual yield of tribute to the imperial exchequer might be assessed, the governor of Syria, Quirinius, held a census in Judea and Samaria. This census provoked the rising of Judas the Galilaean (Acts 5:37); while the rising was crushed, its ideals lived on in the party of the Zealots, who insisted that the payment of tribute to Caesar, or to any other pagan ruler, was an act of treason to Israel's God. The Zealots maintained resistance to Rome until the war of AD 66–73, and the destruction of Jerusalem.

After the census, Judea (as the province of Judea and Samaria was called) received a prefect or procurator as governor. This governor was appointed by the emperor, and was subject to the general supervision of the imperial legate of Syria. He was regularly drawn from the equestrian, not the senatorial, order, and had auxiliary, not legionary, troops under his command. The early Roman procurators (until AD 41) exercised the privilege of appointing the high priest of Israel—a privilege which, since the end of the Hasmonaean dynasty, had been exercised by Herod and Archelaus after him. The procurators sold the sacred office to the highest bidder, and its religious prestige was naturally very low. By virtue of his office the high priest presided over the Sanhedrin, or council of elders, which administered the internal affairs of the nation.

The Sanhedrin and the Roman government of Judea both have their parts to play in the Gospel account of the trial of Jesus. The Roman government convicted Him on the capital charge of claiming to be 'king of the Jews', and this was the indictment fixed to His cross, the translation into political terms of His claim, expressed or implied, to be the Messiah. When the high priest, presiding over the inquiry which preceded His appearance before Pilate, asked Him point-blank if He was the Messiah, He replied that henceforth the Son of man would be seen seated at the right hand of the Almighty and coming with the clouds of heaven. In these words He avoided the political implications of a Messiahship conceived in terms of David's royal heritage and indicated that His mission was bound up rather with that of the Son of man, manifested on earth in humiliation and suffering, but vindicated by God as the one through whom His good purpose would find a prosperous fulfilment.

These strands of 'Messianic' hope (if we use that adjective in its widest sense) can be traced back to the Law, the Prophets and the Writings, to the Prophet like Moses of Dt. 18:15, to the coming Prince of Gn. 49:10; Nu. 24:17, and several of the 'royal' psalms (especially Pss. 2 and 110), to the Servant of Yahweh in Is. 42:1 – 53:12 and to the 'one like a son of man' of Dn. 7:13f., to mention no more. How these concepts were variously developed in the inter-testamental period, giving rise to the expectation which greeted Jesus as the one 'of whom Moses in the law and also the prophets wrote' (Jn. 1:45) is brought out in the article on 'The Apocryphal and Apocalyptic Literature' (pp. 57f.).

F. F. BRUCE

The fourfold Gospel

See also the Introductions to the Commentaries on the four Gospels

THE GOSPEL COLLECTION

We are accustomed to call the first books of the NT the Four Gospels. Before the 4th century, however, the whole fourfold collection was usually called 'the Gospel'—the one and only Gospel of Christ—and the four components of the collection were distinguished by the addition of the words 'according to Matthew', 'according to Mark', and so on. Behind the written gospel, recorded by the four Evangelists, was the spoken or oral gospel, the good news or *euangelion* proclaimed by Christ and His disciples. The Christian use of the word *euangelion* and its cognates goes back to the use of the verb *euangelizomai* in the LXX of such passages as Is. 40:9; 52:7; 61:1 (*cf.* Christ's application to Himself of the last scripture in Lk. 4:18).

Irenaeus, bishop of Lyons in Gaul, writing *c.* AD 180, regards the fourfold Gospel as one of the axiomatic facts of the universe. There are four quarters of the world, he says, and four winds, and thus it is natural that the church universal should rest upon four pillars, and these pillars are the four Gospels (*Against Heresies* iii. 11.8).

For Irenaeus to write thus confidently about the number of the Gospels, there must have been by his time general agreement in the churches throughout the world that these four were uniquely authoritative. And such a measure of agreement must have taken some time to materialize. In fact, we can trace a recognition of the fourfold Gospel back from the time of Irenaeus to the beginning of the 2nd century. The 'Muratorian Canon' is evidence of its recognition by the Roman church about the time of Irenaeus, as also is the composition of the anti-Marcionite Prologues to the Gospels a few years earlier. Tatian, an Assyrian Christian, *c.* AD 170, turned the fourfold Gospel into a continuous narrative or 'Harmony of the Gospels', known as the *Diatessaron*, which in a Syriac form remained for nearly 250 years the favourite, if not the official, version of the Gospels in the Assyrian church. (Here and there Tatian amplified the fourfold record by using a fifth source, the *Gospel according to the Hebrews*.)

Tatian was a pupil of Justin Martyr, in whose writings reference is made to 'the memoirs of the apostles'. Justin does not mention Matthew, Mark or Luke by name, nor does he refer to John as an Evangelist, but he fairly certainly makes use of all four Gospels, referring to Mark as Peter's memoirs, and if there are traces of

Gospel material in his words which may come from the pseudonymous Gospels of Peter or Thomas, these traces are remarkably slight compared with the extent of his use of the Four.

About the same time as Justin was writing in Rome, there appeared in Asia Minor a work called *The Epistle of the Apostles*, which is also a witness to the fourfold Gospel.

In 1935 some papyrus fragments were published by the British Museum trustees (*Fragments of an Unknown Gospel and other Early Christian Papyri*, ed. H. I. Bell and T. C. Skeat), which appear to be the remnant of a manual designed to teach people the Gospel stories. Their importance for our present purpose is that they belong to the first half of the 2nd century and were certainly written by someone who had the fourfold Gospel before him and knew it well, for all four Gospels are drawn upon.

Also from the first half of the 2nd century comes the Docetic *Gospel of Peter*, written, according to E. J. Goodspeed, in Asia in the first decade of the 2nd century. This clearly indicates its author's acquaintance with the Synoptic Gospels and very probably also with the Fourth Gospel.

The *Gospel of Truth*, a treatise reflecting the outlook of the Valentinian school of Gnosticism, composed *c.* AD 140–50, possibly by Valentinus himself, shows agreement with the apostolic tradition on the Canon of the NT in general and the fourfold Gospel in particular: it is a meditation on the story told by the Gospels, especially Matthew and John.

In the early decades of the same century Papias, bishop of Phrygian Hierapolis, wrote his *Expositions of the Oracles of the Lord*, in which he referred by name to Mark's Gospel and Matthew's compilation of Logia, drew probably upon the writings of Luke, and, if we may believe the anti-Marcionite *Prologue to the Fourth Gospel*, told how John dictated his Gospel 'while still in the body' in order to give it to the churches. Eusebius, to whose quotations we owe nearly all our knowledge of this lost work of Papias, says nothing of any reference by Papias to John's Gospel, but he does say that Papias used 'testimonies' (proof-texts?) from John's first Epistle; and in view of the close connection between that Epistle and the Fourth Gospel, it is likely that Papias knew that Gospel.

Thus we can trace the existence and recognition of the four Gospels back to the early years of the 2nd century. The fourfold Gospel, as a single collection, dates from shortly after AD 100; in fact, from about the same period as saw the formation of the other great collection in the NT Canon, the Pauline corpus.

THE ORAL GOSPEL

But what of the history of these four Gospels in the 1st century? To examine this we must go back to the days immediately succeeding the great events of AD 30—the passion, resurrection and ascension of our Lord and the following Day of Pentecost. These days witnessed the beginnings of what has been called 'the gospel behind the Gospels'. True, the gospel had been proclaimed even earlier: Jesus and His apostles before His passion had announced 'the good news of the kingdom of God'; but the full significance of this good news could not be apparent until after the great salvation-bringing events had taken place. Jesus and the apostles announced that the kingdom of God had drawn near, as indeed it had in His own Person. But the manner and implications of its drawing near were fully unfolded only in His death and resurrection. 'The kingdom of God is conceived as coming in the events of the life, death, and resurrection of Jesus, and to proclaim these facts, in their proper setting, is to preach the gospel of the kingdom of God' (C. H. Dodd, *The Apostolic Preaching and its Developments*, 1936, pp. 46f.). There still remained the future consummation of the kingdom, associated with the appearance of Jesus as the Son of man 'with power and great glory' to exercise the universal authority and judgment received from His Father; this consummation (to be preceded by the world-wide proclamation of the good news) was but the last of a series of events of which the others were the saving facts just mentioned.

The God of the Bible is the God who reveals Himself in mighty acts; the God of the fathers, who had revealed Himself to Israel in the never-forgotten events of the Exodus and Eisodus, had now revealed Himself in mightier acts, by which a greater redemption had been wrought, in the Person of Christ. This was the burden of the earliest apostolic proclamation of the Christian message and it is to the records of that proclamation that we must turn to learn what the gospel behind the Gospels was.

Some idea of the outline of this proclamation, commonly referred to nowadays by its Greek name *kērygma*, can be gathered (1) from the Pauline and other NT Epistles and (2) from the reports of early Christian preaching in Acts.

The Pauline and other NT Epistles

The Pauline Epistles were written to people already familiar with the *kērygma;* any reference to it in them will therefore be incidental and reminiscent. There are two outstanding references in 1 Corinthians (AD 55). In 1 Cor. 15:3ff. Paul reminds his readers of the message whose proclamation had brought them salvation: 'that Christ died for our sins in accordance with the scriptures, that he was buried, that he was

raised on the third day in accordance with the scriptures, and that he appeared to Cephas, then to the twelve. Then he appeared to more than five hundred brethren at one time, most of whom are still alive, though some have fallen asleep. Then he appeared to James, then to all the apostles . . .' The message thus summarized Paul says that he himself received from others (Gk. *parelabon*) before he handed it on in turn (*paredōka*) to the Corinthians. It is a fair guess in this connection that Paul made good use of the fortnight which he spent with Peter when he went up to Jerusalem to make inquiries of him (*historēsai*) c. AD 35 (Gal. 1:18).

This summary, brief as it is, contains more than a recital of the 'bare events' of a certain person's death, burial, rising again and appearing to a number of people who knew him. These events are interpreted: the person in question was the expected Messiah of the Jews ('Christ'), His death was in some sense endured for the sins of others, and both His death and resurrection were in accordance with the purpose of God revealed in the sacred scriptures of the Jewish people.

The other reference in this Epistle (1 Cor. 11:23ff.) is marked by the same two verbs—*parelabon*, 'I received by tradition' (a tradition going back to the Lord Himself), and *paredōka*, 'I handed on'. In it Paul reminds his readers of a single incident which occurred on the night of the betrayal of 'the Lord Jesus'—His institution of an act of breaking bread and drinking wine in memory of Himself, an act which, Paul says, was to be repeated by Christians, who would thus 'proclaim the Lord's death until he comes'. This last clause suggests that the story was not yet complete; at least one event remained to finish it off.

From incidental references in the same Epistle we learn that the Messiah's death took the form of crucifixion, a fact which proved a stumbling-block to many who heard the Gospel story. From other Epistles of Paul we gather that Jesus was born a Jew and lived under the Jewish law, that He was not only a descendant of Abraham but also a member of the royal house of David, that while His death was the Roman death by crucifixion, yet some responsibility for it rested with Jewish leaders. From 1 Tim. 6:13 we learn that He appeared before Pontius Pilate and 'made the good confession', although, according to 2 Tim. 4:1, He was Himself the divinely-appointed Judge of living and dead. At the time when Paul was writing, Christ was believed to be exalted at God's right hand (an expression going back to Ps. 110:1). As for His being appointed Judge, 'we must all appear before the judgment seat of Christ' (2 Cor. 5:10). This judgment appears to be linked with the future appearance of Christ, an event to be accompanied by the rising of the believing dead and the receiving of immortality by those then living, at the sound of the last trumpet (1 Cor. 15:52f.; *cf.* 1 Thes. 4:16). That Paul's *kērygma* contained some account of this consummation of the divine redemption in the *parousia* of Christ is evident, *e.g.* when he writes to his Thessalonian converts, reminding them of their conversion, as follows: 'You turned to God from idols, to serve a living and true God, and to wait for his Son from heaven, whom he raised from the dead, Jesus who delivers us from the wrath to come' (1 Thes. 1:9f.). This eschatological element is as constant in the NT *kērygma* as it was dominant in the message of the OT prophets.

Paul insisted (1 Cor. 15:11) that the factual basis of his gospel was the same as that preached by the other apostles. It is not surprising, therefore, to find in 1 Peter the same facts presented as the foundation of the *kērygma*: the death and resurrection of Jesus the Messiah, His exaltation to God's right hand, His glory yet to be revealed—all presented as the fulfilment of OT prophecy and as basic for the receiving of salvation. The writer claims to have been a witness of Messiah's sufferings, and elaborates the saving events, especially the demeanour of Christ in His undeserved suffering and death, in such a way as to reproduce the thought, and perhaps in some places the very language, of the primitive apostolic preaching (*cf.* C. H. Dodd, *op. cit.*, pp. 97f.).

A third NT writer, the author of Hebrews, assumes that his readers have a similar knowledge of the same fundamental facts.

In the earliest preaching, then, as reflected in the Pauline and other NT Epistles, we can distinguish the following elements:

a. God has visited and redeemed His people by sending His Son the Messiah, at the time of the fulfilment of His purpose revealed in OT scripture. *b.* Messiah came, as was prophesied, of Israel's race, of Judah's tribe, of David's royal seed, in the Person of Jesus of Nazareth. *c.* As the prophets had foretold, He died for men's sins upon a cross, was buried, and *d.* rose again the third day thereafter, as many eyewitnesses could testify (this note of personal ocular evidence is specially emphasized). *e.* He was exalted to God's right hand, whence *f.* He sent forth His Spirit to those who believed in Him, while *g.* He Himself was later to return to judge all men and consummate His redemptive work. *h.* On the basis of these facts remission of sins and 'the life of the age to come' were offered to all who repented and believed in the good news; and those who believed were baptized into Christ's name and formed into a new community, the Christian church.

Early Christian preaching

An examination of the speeches ascribed to Peter and Paul in the first half of Acts leads to the conclusion that they are not the free invention of the historian, but reliable summaries of the earliest Christian preaching. Of these speeches the most important are those delivered by Peter in Jerusalem on the Day of Pentecost (2:14–36) and in Caesarea in the house of Cornelius (10:34–43) and that delivered by Paul in the synagogue of Pisidian Antioch (13:16–41). Further fragments of the *kērygma* can be traced in 3:13–26; 4:10–12; 5:30–32; 8:32–35. In all these we find the same message as is reflected in the Epistles. The message itself is called the good news; it is announced as the fulfilment of OT prophecy; its subject is Jesus of Nazareth, a descendant of David, whose public life dated from the ministry of His forerunner John the Baptist and whose mission was divinely attested by His works of mercy and power, to which the early preachers bore personal witness. He was betrayed to His enemies, handed over to the Romans by the Jewish rulers, who despite Pilate's desire to release Him insisted on His death, preferring the release of a murderer. He was consequently crucified (a fact referred to more than once in language reminiscent of Dt. 21:23, 'A hanged man is accursed by God'), taken down from the cross and buried, raised by God the third day, the apostles constantly emphasizing their personal witness of His resurrection. By this, they claimed, God declared Him to be Lord and Messiah. Thereafter He ascended into heaven and took His seat at God's right hand, whence He sent forth His Spirit upon His followers; He was to return thence to assume His divinely-given office as judge of the living and the dead; meanwhile the call to those who heard the gospel was to repent, believe, be baptized and receive the remission of sins and the gift of the Holy Spirit.

The Acts and the Epistles tell the same story. The message in its essential outline was the same message every time. Stereotyped religious teaching was the regular practice throughout the world in those days and the gospel formed no exception.

The Markan outline

A similar outline of the *kērygma* has been discerned as the skeleton on which the body of Mark has been constructed. C. H. Dodd's exposition of this thesis ('The framework of the Gospel Narrative', *ExpT*, XLIII, 1931–2, pp. 396ff.), in spite of criticism to which it has been subjected (especially by D. E. Nineham, *Studies in the Gospels . . . in memory of R. H. Lightfoot*, 1955, pp. 223ff.), retains its cogency and is capable indeed of being amplified. Mark begins where the outlines of the *kērygma* begin, with the activity of John the Baptist, and ends with an account of the passion and resurrection of Christ which, as in the other Gospels, receives what might appear from a purely biographical viewpoint to be a disproportionately large amount of space. But this is one prominent feature of the *kērygma* in all the forms in which we can trace it. The passion narrative is generally recognized to have been told in considerable detail as a unity from the earliest days of apostolic preaching.

Mark consists chiefly of *kērygma*, of the message about Jesus. The primitive Christian preaching was concerned more with what Jesus did than with what He said. In fact, Mark gives us a wonderfully accurate idea of that early preaching. The outline which forms its skeleton connects a brief summary of the Baptist's ministry (1:1–13) to the passion narrative (14:1ff.) by links which, when joined together, correspond rather well to the outline reconstructed from other NT passages leading up to the passion narrative. In the actual preaching, the outline would have been expanded by means of illustrative matter, increasingly so as the gospel was proclaimed among people previously unacquainted with the story of Jesus. *E.g.*, such a statement as that Jesus was 'a man attested to you by God with mighty works and wonders and signs which God did through him', or that He 'went about doing good and healing all that were oppressed by the devil' (Acts 2:22; 10:38), would be amplified in practice by instances of healings and of other works performed by Him.

The self-contained sections or *pericopae* which make up the bulk of Mark give us a good idea of the illustrations used in the primitive preaching. Some of these take the form of 'paradigms' (as M. Dibelius called them), examples cited in the early preaching, incidents which lead up to some notable utterance of Jesus, for the sake of which the incidents were remembered and related. These paradigms very often involved a controversial element, and the notable utterance to which they lead up is Jesus' answer to the objections raised against something which He or His disciples did or said. In Mark there are two outstanding groups of these controversial incidents—one of five in 2:1 – 3:6, and one of three in 12:13–34. These two groups probably existed as such in the oral stage before their incorporation into Mark; indeed, from the mention of a combination of Pharisees and Herodians in both 3:6 and 12:13, it has been suggested that they at one time formed one group, which was divided into two in order to be inserted in two different contexts in the Markan outline.

Form-criticism

The study of the 'forms' assumed by the various categories of the gospel tradition, especially in its oral, pre-literary phase, is called Gospel form-criticism. The German word *Formgeschichte* ('form history') suggests, as the English term does not, the study of the history of the tradition as revealed by the development of its 'forms'.

The main classification of the material distinguishes between narratives and sayings, though these two classes overlap, as when a narrative is related for the sake of the pointed utterance to which it leads up (hence sometimes called a 'pronouncement story'). Other outstanding narrative forms are miracle stories (especially those involving healing) and stories about Jesus (*e.g.* the baptism, temptation, transfiguration and resurrection narratives); outstanding 'sayings' forms are wisdom sayings, prophetic and apocalyptic sayings, community rules, 'I' sayings and parables. There are other ways of classifying the Gospel material, but no matter which schemes of classification and cross-classification are followed, a Messianic picture of Jesus is consistently yielded: 'we can find no alternative tradition, excavate as we will in the successive strata of the Gospels' (C. H. Dodd, *History and the Gospel*, 1938, p. 103).

But does this picture reflect the facts of the ministry or the faith of the early church? This question, which is raised insistently by many European form-critics and answered confidently in the latter sense, depends not so much on classification of forms as on two arguments: *a.* that the Gospel tradition in its earliest stages consisted mostly of isolated *pericope* which were joined together by the Evangelists with transitional summaries devoid of historical content (an argument countered by C. H. Dodd's recognition, noted above, of a continuous kerygmatic outline in Mark's transitional summaries); *b.* that the life-setting of each *pericopē* should be sought in the experience and needs of the primitive church. That the preservation of various elements in the tradition and the form in which they were preserved are related to the life-setting in the primitive church need not be questioned, but this does not preclude an original life-setting in the ministry of Jesus. Although the possibility of establishing this original life-setting except in a handful of instances is widely denied, the situation is by no means hopeless; detailed study of the units in the tradition, and especially comparative scrutiny of the parallels in the Synoptic and Johannine records, yield an increasing total of positive results (see C. H. Dodd, *Historic Tradition in the Fourth Gospel*, 1963). There is no need to accept uncritically the argument that the historicity of all Gospel material is suspect which is paralleled in rabbinic tradition or can be accounted for in terms of the church's Easter faith, or the claim that in such cases the burden of proof lies on those who maintain the authenticity of the tradition.

The quest of the life-setting is of value for its help towards an appreciation of the situation in early church worship and witness within which the Gospel tradition was moulded and transmitted, and in so far as form-criticism makes it possible to move back from the setting of the Gospels in the 1st-century church to the original setting of their material in the ministry of Jesus it makes its peculiar contribution to the study of the NT and Christian beginnings.

THE WRITTEN GOSPELS

The four Gospels fall naturally into two groups, the first three on one side and John by itself on the other. The first three are commonly called the Synoptic Gospels, a name apparently given them first by J. J. Griesbach towards the end of the 18th century, because they have so much common material that they can be conveniently arranged in three parallel columns as a 'synopsis', a form in which they may be studied together.

Since Mark's record largely represents the pattern of the early *kērygma* and Peter appears in Acts as the chief preacher of this *kērygma*, we have some degree of confirmation of the tradition received and recorded by Papias, that Mark, having acted as Peter's interpreter, later committed to writing the preaching of Peter. We see, too, how little *practical* difference there is between the 19th-century view which attributed the matter common to all three Synoptists to a common dependence on the primitive oral preaching, and the view now generally held, first set on a firm basis by Lachmann in 1835, that Mark's record (or something very like it) is a major source of the First and Third Gospels, since it incorporated that oral preaching committed to writing. We should expect that the oral preaching was delivered first in Aramaic and then in Greek, as the area of apostolic activity widened; considerable traces of the earlier stage are found in the Aramaisms underlying the Greek of our Gospels.

Even Mark, however, contains some account of the teaching of Jesus as well as of His works, and the other Gospels contain a much higher proportion of His teaching than Mark does. While the doings of Jesus formed the basis of the *kērygma*, His teaching (*didachē*) was not forgotten, but served as the basis for the instruction in righteousness imparted to those who had believed the good news. The NT Epistles consist of teaching rather than preaching, and the ethical instruction which they convey is in strict harmony with the teaching of Jesus recorded in the Gospels. We may compare, *e.g.*, the ethical teaching of Paul in Rom. 12:1 – 15:6 with that of the Sermon on the Mount in Mt. 5–7.

Alongside the oral preaching or *kērygma*, then, there was the oral teaching or *didachē*, and these two both underlie our Gospel records. We may compare Luke's description of his Gospel in Acts 1:1 as the story of 'all that Jesus began to do (*kērygma*) and teach (*didachē*)'. One important corpus of the teaching has been discerned behind those passages common to Matthew and Luke which are not found in Mark. These passages (amounting to something over 200 verses) are usually indicated by the letter Q, and when viewed in isolation, especially in the order in which they appear in Luke, they present a striking measure of homogeneity and continuity, although to suppose that the source must be identical with such reconstructions as some scholars have made by isolating these verses and setting them in order is going beyond what is warranted. The Q passages were probably drawn from a collection of the sayings of Jesus set in a brief narrative framework, first composed in Aramaic and later circulating in more than one Greek version— very probably the compilation of the Lord's oracles which Papias ascribes to Matthew. Its contents have been viewed as comprising

four main groupings, which have been entitled *a*. Jesus and John the Baptist, *b*. Jesus and His disciples, *c*. Jesus and His opponents, *d*. Jesus and the future.

The *kērygma* as recorded by Mark and the *didachē* as recorded in the Q-source are the two chief sources of the Synoptic tradition, but there are others. Chief among these should be reckoned the very valuable sources from which Luke drew much of his special information, conveniently denoted by L. A good part of this may have been derived from the circle of Philip at Caesarea (Acts 21:8). Luke's nativity narratives of the Baptist and Jesus represent what W. Sanday called 'the oldest evangelical fragment, or document, of the New Testament, and in any case the most archaic thing in the whole volume'. They may have been based on the memory of some members of the Jerusalem church which Luke visited in AD 57 (Acts 21:15ff.). A probable view envisages Luke as having amplified his collection of the sayings of Jesus (his Q-source) by means of the oral information which he could acquire at Antioch and Jerusalem and especially Caesarea; to this he added at a later time the information obtainable from Mark, perhaps during the period which found them both together in Paul's entourage in Rome (Col. 4:10, 14).

The eschatological discourse in Mk. 13 (reproduced in Mt. 24 and Lk. 21) perhaps circulated independently in written form—in part if not in whole—a considerable time before its incorporation in the Gospels, even as early as AD 40. Something like it formed the basis of the eschatological instruction which Paul gave at Thessalonica in AD 50 (*cf.* 2 Thes. 2:1–11, and especially v. 5). Probably the first Evangelist also drew independently on part of it for one section (vv. 17–23) of the mission charge in Mt. 10.

The First Gospel also has important material peculiar to itself, including a nativity narrative independent of Luke's, some narrative (especially centring on Peter) which was apparently preserved in 'Nazarene' or Jewish-Christian circles, and a body of teaching (M) on similar lines to that of Q, but with a more pronounced Jewish flavour. If Q represents the teaching tradition of the church of Antioch, M may represent that of the church of Jerusalem.

Luke arranges his sources in alternate blocks, apparently inserting blocks of Markan material into his other material (Q+L) which, as many scholars in this country hold, already existed in the form of 'Proto-Luke', while Matthew conflates his sources, *i.e.* selects portions from them which he shapes into new unities. A consideration of Matthew's arrangement of the sayings of Jesus has commonly led to the conclusion that he rearranged them according to their subject-matter into five great discourse-groups, each dealing with some aspect of the kingdom of heaven: discourse I (Mt. 5–7), the law of the kingdom; discourse II (Mt. 10), the proclamation of the kingdom; discourse III (Mt. 13), the growth of the kingdom; discourse IV (Mt. 18), the fellowship of the kingdom; discourse V (Mt. 24–25), the consummation of the kingdom. (The discourse of Mt. 23 is omitted from this pattern; this should provoke the question whether the fivefold arrangement is not imposed on Matthew rather than inherent in the Gospel itself.)

In the great sermon of Mt. 5–7, *e.g.*, we find not only the substance of the parallel sermon in Lk. 6:20–49, but also many other 'Q' sayings found in other contexts in Luke, as well as some peculiar to Matthew. To be sure, we must not always assume that two fairly similar passages in Matthew and Luke must come from a common source; much that is reckoned to Q may have come to Luke from one of his special sources, especially where there is no real verbal identity with the Matthaean parallel. Even so, the likelihood remains strong that in Matthew the material has been regrouped in the manner indicated; and the narrative-sections (almost all Markan) which precede the various discourse-groups in Matthew have also had their matter rearranged to suit this topical order. Not that Luke also did not depart on occasion from the order of his sources; for instance, he puts our Lord's visit to Nazareth earlier than is chronologically warranted, probably so as to set the programme of His Messianic mission proclaimed in His synagogue sermon there in the forefront of his account of the ministry. Luke's choice and arrangement of his material also indicate that he had a much greater 'biographical' interest in Christ than had the other Evangelists; this is what we might expect in the one Greek among the NT writers.

It should be added that some scholars see no need to postulate a separate sayings-source, since they regard it as sufficient to suppose that Luke derived his Q-material from Matthew. This view raises greater difficulties than it removes; it would then, among other things, be very difficult to explain the principle of Luke's dispersal of this material throughout his work.

When, however, we have discovered (or think we have discovered) the oral or documentary sources of our Gospels, we must not think that we have sufficiently accounted for these Gospels. The questions treated in this article are mere *prolegomena* to the really important studies of the Gospels themselves which follow. Each of our Gospels is an individual work of literature, with an ethos and genius all its own; each emphasizes a particular aspect of the Person of Christ, and all three Synoptists together with the fourth Evangelist combine to present us with the portrait of the Christ whom we know.

The study of the special interests and emphases of the individual Evangelists has received fresh and welcome attention of late; it is commonly known by its German designation *Redaktionsgeschichte* (lit. 'history of redaction') and corrects the imbalance resulting from a one-sided concentration on form-criticism. Matthew—perhaps the spokesman of a school (*cf.* K. Stendahl, *The School of St. Matthew*, 1954)—is well described as a 'scribe . . . trained for the kingdom of heaven . . . who brings out of his treasure what is new and what is old' (Mt. 13:52); he arranges the teaching of Jesus according to subject-matter in discourses which would serve as a manual of instruction for catechists and catechumens in the church. His interest in the church as a community destined to endure from the time of Jesus to the 'consummation of the age' stands out clearly in his record. Mark brings out in a distinctive way the 'Messianic secret': the true nature of Jesus' Person and mission was largely veiled, even from the disciples, during the ministry, and not until His death on the cross is the veil removed—an event symbolized by the rending of the Temple veil and interpreted in the centurion's confession (Mk. 15:38f.). Luke views the ministry of Jesus as a continuation of the mighty works of God narrated in the OT, indeed as the consummation of those mighty works, and yet as something which in turn was to find its own continuation in the apostolic history. The saving act of God, as he saw it, was accomplished at the mid-point of time. John restates the essential gospel story without modifying its essence: here we see the incarnation on earth of the eternal Logos or self-expression of God, active in the new creation as earlier in the old creation; here, in the ministry and supremely in the death of Jesus, the glory of God is revealed for all who have eyes to see.

Only a small part of the sayings and doings of Jesus has been recorded by the four, but what they have recorded has been so selected that we know Him—even as a character in history, to say nothing of His living and abiding presence with His people—better than we know many about whom more details have been handed down to us. This selection forms no small element in that inspiration of the Gospels which helped to fulfil our Lord's promise to His disciples that the coming Spirit would bring to their remembrance the things that He Himself had taught them, and would reveal their significance.

The portrayal of Jesus as Messiah or Son of God pervades all the strata of our Gospel material, even the most primitive of them, no matter how it is classified and cross-divided. Even in the earliest forms of the Gospel tradition Jesus is one who makes total claims on men, who asserts His authority in forgiveness and judgment, and makes obedience to His own teaching the criterion of men's bliss or woe. One famous Q-logion, preserved in Mt. 11:27 and Lk. 10:22, has been called 'an aerolite from the Johannine heaven': 'All things have been delivered to me by my Father; and no one knows who the Son is except the Father, or who the Father is except the Son and any one to whom the Son chooses to reveal him.' This is the line of our Lord's teaching which is elaborated in the Fourth Gospel—and not there only, for traces of it are found in the writings of Paul and in Hebrews, as well as in the early 2nd-century hymn book called the *Odes of Solomon*, in the letters of Ignatius and in the *Sayings of Jesus* discovered among the Greek Oxyrhynchus papyri, and more fully in the Coptic version called the *Gospel of Thomas*. It has been argued with some probability that two of the great Christological passages in the NT (Phil. 2:4ff. and part of the prologue of John) were based on early Christian hymns; at any rate, the aspect of the Person of Christ which they present is no late development in Christian theology, but goes back to His own words. This is the aspect emphasized in the Fourth Gospel, but not at the expense of our Lord's real manhood; indeed, John is at pains to insist on His manhood as against Docetic tendencies. But despite the many differences between this Gospel and the other three, it is as faithful to the basic outline of the primitive *kērygma* as they are; beginning with the baptism of John, all the cardinal facts are here—the anointing of Jesus with the Holy Spirit and power, His mighty works of grace and authority, His ministry both in Galilee and in Jerusalem, His betrayal, arrest, trials before the high priest and Pilate, His crucifixion, burial and resurrection, His ascension, exaltation, and coming to raise the dead and judge the world.

Tradition from the 2nd century onwards has associated the composition of the Fourth Gospel with Ephesus, and recent attempts to find its origin in Alexandria or elsewhere have not been successful. It may be that each of the Gospels was at first associated with some single centre of Christian witness: *e.g.* Mark with Rome, Matthew with Antioch, John with Ephesus. Other Gospels had local and temporary vogue, but these four, because of their intrinsic worth and apostolic authority (direct or indirect), transcended local limitations and speedily became accepted as the fourfold Gospel by the church universal. For each of them coincided in its aim with the mission of the church in the world; the explicit object of the Fourth (Jn. 20:31) is equally applicable to all four: 'these are written that you may believe that Jesus is the Christ, the Son of God, and that believing you may have life in his name.'

F. F. BRUCE

The Pauline Epistles

The importance of the Pauline Epistles within the NT cannot be exaggerated. From a chronological point of view these letters are generally acknowledged to have been written before the Gospels. For this reason the interpretation of the Gospels must in some measure be guided by the interpretation of the Epistles, always bearing in mind nevertheless that the teaching and work of Jesus is the basis for Pauline theology. These factors are important in any approach to Paul and his Epistles.

THE LETTERS IN THE LIFE OF THE CHURCH

Although these letters are known as epistles they differ from the general run of Greek epistles in that they were not designed for a literary audience. At the same time they must be distinguished from private letters in that they are designed for a semi-public purpose. In fact, they create a new category, unparalleled in contemporary literature. Their form is specially adapted to meet the practical and doctrinal needs of the early Christian communities. None of them was produced with a literary purpose, not even such an Epistle as Romans, which is of all the Epistles most like a theological treatise.

Because of their essentially practical purpose these letters throw considerable light upon the Christian churches during the primitive period. They reflect the struggle of Christianity against its pagan environment. They do not conceal that problems of a moral kind arose. Moreover, they make clear that some churches were so mixed in their understanding of Christian truth that it was easy for errors of doctrine to gain support. There was no uniformity among the churches in the matter of organization, and in one church (Corinth) considerable disorderliness seems to have crept in.

The letters must be viewed, therefore, as the work of a Christian missionary who was daily burdened with the care of the churches (*cf.* 2 Cor. 11:28). Some were produced during periods of intense activity, while others belong to times of enforced leisure, as for instance, the captivity Epistles. It cannot be supposed that the earlier Epistles were the result of long reflection. They represent, both in content and style, the spontaneous response of the apostles to situations demanding immediate action and advice. It is for this reason that the Epistles abound in digressions. It can readily be imagined that Paul wrote or dictated most of his letters with a variety of other concerns upon his mind.

At the same time he is deeply conscious that he writes authoritatively. His letters never give the impression of being casual expressions of opinion. To Paul there was no doubt about the way Christian life and thought should develop and it was this conviction that gives such power and vitality to his letters.

THE COLLECTION OF PAUL'S LETTERS

The letters were at first sent to widely distributed centres, but at some period during the early history of the Christian church a collection of the letters was made. It is impossible to reconstruct the precise circumstances in which this occurred. In all probability it happened gradually. Paul himself advised the exchange of his letters among neighbouring churches (Col. 4:16), and it may reasonably be supposed that this practice was soon extended to include churches farther afield. It is certain that not only Paul but some of his closest associates kept in liaison with the Gentile churches. Such men as Timothy, Titus and Tychicus would carry news of Paul's activities from church to church and would awaken a desire to read other Epistles which Paul had produced. But our understanding of this whole process rests largely on conjecture. It is not until the second century that evidence for the actual emergence of an authorized collection of Paul's Epistles is found. This particular collection was also a heretical one, formulated by Marcion about AD 140. It contained all the Pauline Epistles except the Pastoral Epistles. Indeed, Marcion concentrated on Paul's Epistles to the exclusion of other NT books. Even in the Gospels Marcion admitted only a mutilated edition of Luke. Nevertheless, the evidence is valuable because it may be concluded that Marcion would not himself have formed a collection of Paul's Epistles if such a collection had not first existed in orthodox circles. It was the practice of pseudo-Christian leaders to imitate the orthodox literature. Tertullian, in dealing with such teachers' approach to the Scriptures, maintained the principle that truth must necessarily precede error. By about AD 180 the position in the orthodox churches may be ascertained not only from the testimony of such writers as Irenaeus, but also from such a list as the Muratorian Canon. This latter list ascribes to Paul the thirteen letters which claim his authorship in the NT.

At a much earlier date there is evidence of the use of some of the letters in the Apostolic Fathers, which at least implies a collection of some kind.

But it is impossible to be certain of its contents. The same may be said of the reference in 2 Pet. 3:16, where the difficulties in understanding Paul's Epistles are mentioned. The expression 'all his letters', which is there used, is not further defined and it is impossible to be sure what it embraced. But certainly some group of Paul's Epistles were already widely known at that time.

A recent theory has advocated that no collection of Paul's letters was made until about AD 90, but this theory is based on several doubtful assumptions, such as the existence of a period during which Paul suffered neglect, which was only dispelled when Acts was published. But this in turn presupposes a late date for Acts which is open to challenge. It is highly improbable that Paul's Epistles should lie stored in the archives of various churches for a period of 30 years, when so many people owed so much to his influence.

THE GROUPING OF PAUL'S LETTERS

There are thirteen Epistles in the NT which claim to be written by Paul. These fall naturally into four groups. The earliest letters were those to the church at Thessalonica, both of which were written from Corinth during Paul's second missionary journey. He had established the church there soon after arriving in Europe, subsequent to his work at Philippi. His movements during the period between establishing the church and writing the Epistles involved visits to Beroea and Athens.

The next group are sometimes described as the great evangelical Epistles, comprising 1 and 2 Corinthians, Romans and Galatians. The first three of these were certainly written on the third missionary journey and the last most probably was, although some date this as the earliest of all Paul's Epistles (see Introduction to Galatians). It was during his three years at Ephesus that he wrote first to the Corinthians. His stay there was nearly over, as 1 Cor. 16:8 shows. From there he moved to Troas, crossed over to Macedonia and spent three months in Greece. It was while he was in Macedonia that 2 Corinthians was written, after he had met Titus who had just visited Corinth. When Paul arrived in Greece he undoubtedly visited Corinth and it was while he was there that Romans was written. By this time his work in the East was finished and he was turning his face towards Spain. Before setting out for the West he determined to visit Jerusalem to take the collection for the poor Christians in Judea. This action led to his arrest, captivity and subsequent despatch to Rome.

The third group of Epistles, known as the captivity Epistles, are so called because in all of them Paul states himself to be a prisoner. These are Ephesians, Philippians, Colossians and Philemon. It has been traditionally believed that these Epistles were written during the period of Paul's imprisonment in Rome and there is much to be said for this opinion. But an alternative view is that Philippians and possibly the others also were sent from Ephesus. The difficulty with this alternative view is that there is no certain knowledge that Paul was ever imprisoned at Ephesus. At best it is no more than a conjecture, although it may be a true one. It is probably desirable to maintain the close connection between these Epistles, at least in the case of Ephesians, Colossians and Philemon, which are closely linked in content as well as in the historical circumstances of the writer. All four of these Epistles are reflective in tone and this is understandable if Paul is a prisoner. He has contact with various Christian companions, however, from whom he is able to learn details of the needs of the churches. These letters, with the possible exception of Ephesians, were sent as the earlier letters in response to various practical situations—the growth of heresy, the question of fellowship, material and spiritual, the needs of a runaway slave. It is probable, if the Roman theory of the origin of these letters be upheld, that Philippians was written first and then Ephesians, Colossians and Philemon all about the same time.

The fourth group is the Pastoral Epistles, comprising 1 and 2 Timothy and Titus. These three Epistles imply that Paul must have been released after the Roman imprisonment of Acts 28, for in 1 Timothy and Titus Paul is no longer a prisoner. By 2 Timothy, however, he is once more on trial for his life and it is clear that he thinks the end is near. This Epistle has been described as Paul's swan song. All these Epistles are similar in style and content and are well regarded as a separate group. In them are instructions about arrangements within the churches which have been invaluable in dealing with questions of church order. But they are also revealing in some aspects of the personality of Paul. They are a fitting conclusion to the literary labours of the great apostle, especially as they are addressed not to churches but to two of his most trusted co-workers.

THE TEACHING OF THE APOSTLE

In approaching the theology of Paul it must be remembered that our information is culled from a variety of different documents, none of which was designed to present a systematized body of doctrine. The various emphases in each Epistle are mainly dominated by immediate practical needs. This naturally leads to difficulties when attempts are made to discover the structure of Paul's thought. It is important to discern, for instance, what essential features make up the unity of Paul's theological approach. To do this it is necessary first to consider the background of that approach.

Influences upon the apostle

Jewish background. Paul leaves his readers in no doubt about the nature of his Jewish background. He was a Hebrew of the Hebrews (Phil. 3:5), and an adherent of the strictest sect, the Pharisees. This not only exercised a profound effect upon him, but was a matter of no small pride to him. He had been taught by the famous Gamaliel and had progressed further than most of his contemporaries in Judaism (Gal. 1:14).

Difficulties confront any attempt to define the precise nature of 1st-century Judaism as Paul knew it, for much of the available data is drawn from later sources. Rabbinic Judaism undoubtedly had many strong roots in the 1st century, but its more developed forms did not arise until later than the time of Paul. Moreover, within Judaism itself there were Hellenistic influences, particularly outside Judea. Even within Palestine itself tendencies were appearing which showed some syncretism between Jewish thought and Hellenism, as the Dead Sea Scrolls bear witness.

It is impossible to appreciate some of the dominant features of Pauline theology without reference to the tensions which existed in Paul's mind prior to his conversion. Judaism was essentially legalistic in its approach and the apostle's evident frustration under this system becomes clear when he refers to his past experience (cf. Rom. 4–7; Gal. 1–4). He knew justification by works to be impossible because he had experienced its impossibility. Yet Judaism was a quest for righteousness, and no religious system which did not offer an adequate means of attaining this would ever have satisfied the soul of Paul. It was perhaps this more than any other single concept which his Jewish background contributed in the development of Paul's theology.

Another feature of Paul's religious approach was the dominance of OT influence upon him. Although in most cases he uses the LXX version, he is essentially Jewish in his use of the OT Scriptures. In this he contrasts with Philo of Alexandria who allegorizes the history. But Paul sees the revelation of God in the acts of history.

As a Jew Paul was a firm believer in one true God. Moreover he had a convinced view of the holiness of God. In Judaism this led to transcendentalism, but in Paul's Christian theology there is no question of God being remote. He is brought near through Jesus Christ. But there can be no doubt that for his exalted conception of God Paul is mainly indebted to his Jewish heritage.

The notion of salvation which formed so cardinal a feature of Paul's theology was prepared for by Jewish thought and particularly the OT cultus. If the details of the cultus did not occupy much of his attention when he wrote his letters, as for instance it did for the writer to the Hebrews, the basic idea of man's need for a mediator was supported by Judaism. In the latter there developed a variety of mediators, but Paul saw at once that there could be only one.

Hellenistic background. It has already been pointed out that Hellenism had made some inroads upon Judaism, not only in the Diaspora but also in Palestine. Moreover, Paul himself was reared in a Hellenistic environment. Although he apparently spent part of his education in Jerusalem, he was nevertheless a native of Tarsus which had a reputation for its university.

Some scholars have traced evidences of the influence on Paul of Stoic rhetoric, such as the use of various technical terms, play on words, antitheses and the diatribe forms. But if such art forms were used, the content of Paul's thought shows no trace of indebtedness to Stoic philosophy. The Epistles of Paul are no examples of rhetorical exercises. They are rather practical expressions of a living faith.

Some scholars have made much of the possibility of orientalism influencing Paul's thought, especially that form of it which found expression in the mystery religions. So R. Reitzenstein and W. Bousset maintained that Paul's system of thought must be placed against the background of the mystery religions. The idea of a dying and rising god, of redemption through sacramental means, of knowledge as a practical fellowship, are all aspects of mystery religions for which parallels may be found in Paul. But those who belonged to this school of thought were mistaken in assuming that similarities indicate common origin, in failing to stress the fundamental distinctions, and in using evidences drawn from too late a period for Paul's time. Bultmann's theory of Gnostic influences suffers from the same defects.

Conversion experience. The profound effect of Paul's conversion clearly dominated his theology. It was an experience so evidently proceeding from divine revelation that it at once gave the apostle a high view of God and of His purposes for him. Central to this experience was the indisputable fact of the resurrection of Christ. On the Damascus road Paul encountered the risen Christ. There is no doubt that he accepted that encounter as a real event. It was not the product of his imagination. It formed the basis of his Christian assurance. He had had a revelation from God which no man could gainsay. The fact that in Acts Luke three times records Paul's conversion experience shows that others were not unmindful of the crucial place the experience had in the mind of the apostle.

In Pauline thought the resurrection of Christ is the key to the understanding of many major concepts. His view of the Person of Christ is directly determined by this event. In Rom. 1:4 he shows that Jesus was designated Son of God by the resurrection, by which he means that His divine character was then fully manifested. In Rom. 10:9 confession of Jesus as Lord is linked with belief in the resurrection. There can be no doubt that in this confession the early Christians were equating Jesus with God (cf. O. Cullmann, *The Earliest Christian Confes-*

sions, 1949, pp. 58f.), and Paul has no hesitation in embracing the same confession. Furthermore, the Messianic status of Jesus is everywhere assumed by the apostle. Not only is this seen in the preponderance of the name Jesus Christ or Christ Jesus, but also in his basic presuppositions. He would understand Messiah in the Jewish sense of an official figure who would bring deliverance, but his concept of deliverance differed from the Jewish expectation in that it was wholly spiritual.

It was through the resurrection that Christ's work of redemption was vindicated (*cf.* Eph. 1:19ff.; Phil. 2:7ff.). In itself it supplies power to the believer (Gal. 1:1–4; Phil. 3:10). It is the basis of the believer's justification (Rom. 4:25). It is the guarantee of the believer's own resurrection (1 Cor. 15). No further evidence is necessary to demonstrate the overwhelming importance of the resurrection in Paul's theology. He speaks from personal experience of the risen Christ first encountered on the Damascus road.

The major themes

It is impossible in brief compass to do justice to the wide range of Paul's theology. This is not in fact our present intention. Rather it is to introduce the major themes so that the general reader can more readily trace these through the Epistles. Whereas Paul did not set out a systematic account of his theology, it is necessary to grasp something of the pattern behind the separate parts if the significance of the different Epistles is to be appreciated.

Teaching about God. Paul's view of God was deeply influenced by the OT and by consequent Jewish beliefs. It was, too, essentially the same as that found in the teaching of Jesus. His view of God was lofty, but he did not follow the mistake of his Jewish contemporaries in making God remote (transcendentalism). His conception of God was dominated by the idea of grace, by which he understood God's unmerited favour (*cf.* Rom. 1:5; 1 Cor. 15:9, 10). Paul could never get away from the thought that the whole process of salvation was initiated by God and did not depend on man's own efforts. He was deeply aware of the love of God in Christ and never tired of expressing it (*cf.* Eph. 3:18, 19). Yet with this aspect of God's love and mercy Paul believed passionately in the righteousness of God. This concept especially dominates the Epistle to the Romans (*cf.* 1:4, 17; 3:21f.). God is not only holy Himself, but demands that His creatures should be as holy as He is. It is this that for Paul explains men's universal need of the gospel. The sinfulness of all men does not arise from an arbitrary definition or tenet of theology. It is based on man's evident contrast with the nature of God.

Because holiness cannot regard sin as anything other than abhorrent, Paul's concept of God's righteousness is necessarily linked with his view of God's wrath. This comes out most clearly in Rom. 1:17, 18. The notion of wrath must not be watered down. It strongly expresses the divine displeasure with sin, although it is concurrent with God's love for the sinner (Rom. 5:8). It is only against this exalted view of God's character that Paul's doctrine of redemption can be grasped.

Teaching about Christ. It is evident even on a cursory reading of Paul's Epistles that he had a high view of Christ. It is equally evident that he was not much interested in the events of the life of Jesus. What is the explanation of this? It has already been pointed out that Paul's conversion experience had introduced him to the risen Christ. This was an experience independent of any knowledge of the human Jesus. Yet although Paul shows little interest in Jesus' human life, it would not be true to say that it had no relevance for him. He records such features as His human birth, His sinlessness, the institution of the Supper, His poverty and death and resurrection. These incidental references suggest that the apostle assumes more than he states. He was particularly concerned that faith should not be based on sight (*cf.* 2 Cor. 5:16). Yet he shows no consciousness of a dichotomy between the Christ of faith and the historical Jesus.

There are many facets to Paul's view of Christ. The part of Christ in creation is frequently stressed. He not only has created all but sustains all. But whenever the apostle draws attention to creatorship, the idea is always associated with what Christ has done in the sphere of salvation (*cf.* Col. 1:15ff.). At the same time there is no clear distinction between the creative works of God and those of Christ.

The pre-existence of Christ is assumed. 'God sent forth his Son' (Gal. 4:4). The incarnation is seen as a voluntary act of humiliation (2 Cor. 8:9). The clearest statement regarding the pre-existence is found in Phil. 2:6–11, where the voluntary character of Christ's setting aside His heavenly glory is specially brought out. The process of humiliation led to Lordship through suffering.

There are several figures of speech which are used by Paul to describe Christ. He is the last Adam (1 Cor. 15:45), the image of God and the first-born (Col. 1:15), the head of the body (Eph. 4:15; Col. 1:18), to mention a few. The apostle is certain that Christ holds the supreme position in both church and the created order. And yet one of his main themes is that believers can be 'in Christ'. He never ceased to marvel at the condescension of the glorified Christ in His relationship to believers.

Although there are some passages which seem to imply the subordination of Christ to God, there are others which can only mean that He was God. Of the former the most notable are Gal. 4:4; Rom. 8:32; Phil. 2:9; 1 Cor. 15:28. Of the latter, attention should particularly be drawn to Rom. 9:5 and Col. 2:9.

Aspects of the work of Christ. It was part of the primitive *kērygma* which Paul had received from others that Christ died for our sins according to the Scriptures (1 Cor. 15:3). These were the elements of fact and interpretation which formed the basis of early Christian theology. The apostle must have meditated long on the mystery of what Christ has done for man, for he uses a variety of different figures to convey something of the wealth of his reflections on this theme. Only the most important can be mentioned here, but the careful student of the Pauline Epistles will have no difficulty in adding others.

The idea of *propitiation* occurs in Rom. 3:25 in relation to man's sin and it is clear that Paul uses the word in a sacrificial sense. The idea is not, however, the placating of an angry deity. Rather, God Himself provides what is necessary to atone for sin. The apostle makes clear that only through faith can the benefit of this work of Christ be appropriated.

Another familiar Pauline figure is that of *redemption*. This is drawn from the contemporary practice of freeing slaves on payment of a ransom. Paul does not apply the metaphor in any strict commercial sense, but he was deeply conscious that Christ had done something to deliver him from the power of sin (*cf.* Rom. 3:24; Gal. 4:4f.; Eph. 1:7).

The idea of *reconciliation* arises from a consideration of man's alienation from God and this again is a recurring Pauline theme. He refers to our reconciliation to God by Christ's death (Rom. 5:10). He considers his mission is to beseech men to be reconciled to God (2 Cor. 5:18ff.), but he also refers to the cosmic idea of reconciliation. The latter idea comes in Col. 1:20, the reconciling to Himself of all things, whether on earth or in heaven. This opens a conception of reconciliation far broader than the idea of personal harmony.

Closely allied to the theme of reconciliation is that of *adoption* (*cf.* Rom. 8:15; Gal. 4:5, 6). Through Christ, believers become sons of God and by the Spirit cry, 'Abba! Father!' Such a new relationship requires a specific work of God in Christ to make it possible.

Undoubtedly a dominating theme of the apostle's is *justification by faith*, especially in Romans and Galatians. Paul sees no possibility of a man obtaining righteousness except through faith in what Christ has done. Hence any idea that a man may get right with God through his own efforts was unthinkable to him.

Teaching about the Spirit. Paul's doctrine is in full agreement with the references to the Spirit in the teaching of Jesus, especially in the Fourth Gospel. The Spirit's work is closely linked with that of Jesus. The Spirit rests upon Him, is concentrated in Him, is given out by Him and aims to glorify Him. The Spirit is the agency through whom God in Christ communicates with His people (*cf.* Rom. 5:5; 8:16; 15:19; 1 Cor. 2:10f.; Gal. 4:6; Phil. 1:19; 1 Thes. 1:5). It is through the Spirit that we realize our sonship and can cry, 'Abba!

Father!' (Gal. 4:6). Moreover, our bodies have become the temple of the Spirit (1 Cor. 6:19). Paul's most concentrated teaching on the Spirit's activity is in Rom. 8, where the work of the Spirit in the believer is set in contrast to the work of the flesh. The apostle was undoubtedly a man of the Spirit.

Because of the close connection between the Spirit and the Father and the Son in Paul's Epistles it may be said that he adumbrates a doctrine of the Trinity, even if this is not systematically worked out.

Teaching about the church. In these Epistles there are two different ways in which the apostle uses the term *ekklēsia*, sometimes of local churches (*e.g.* 1 Thes. 2:14; 2 Thes. 1:4) and sometimes of the universal church (*cf.* the expression 'the church of God' in the Corinthian Epistles and the idea of Christ as Head of the church in the captivity Epistles).

The apostle uses three main figures of speech to describe the functions and relationships of the church: 1. *The architectural metaphor.* The idea of the church as a building may go back to Jesus' statement about building on the rock (referring to Peter's statement in his confession— Mt. 16:16f.). The foundation is Christ upon which Paul and others have built in their missionary work (1 Cor. 3:10–15). The local Christian community is conceived of as God's temple (1 Cor. 3:16). In Eph. 2:20f., the metaphor is applied more widely to the whole church, of which individuals and communities form parts and of which Christ is the corner-stone. In this Epistle the apostles and prophets are seen to be foundational to the church, no doubt viewed historically.

2. *The metaphor of the human body.* This figure occurs in four of the Epistles and may justly be regarded as particularly characteristic of Paul's thinking about the church. In Rom. 12:5 the emphasis lies on the variety within the unity of the body, the members all possessing different gifts. Very similarly in 1 Cor. 12:14ff., the variations within the whole are brought out, since each member is essential to the well-being of the whole. The Lord's Supper illustrates this essential oneness in the idea of one loaf and one body (1 Cor. 10:17). In Eph. 1:23; 4:12; 5:23, Christ is Head of the body and Saviour of His people. This is a development since the life and existence of the body is dependent on the Head. Apart from Christ the church cannot grow, indeed it cannot even exist. Similar ideas are expressed in Colossians (*cf.* 1:18, 24; 2:19).

3. *The marital relationship.* This imagery is used of a single local community in 1 Cor. 11:3. The same thought is applied to individual Christians in 1 Cor. 6:15ff. But again, in Eph. 5:22ff., the whole church is in mind under the imagery of the bride. The uniting of bride and Bridegroom serves as a remarkable illustration of the union of believers with Christ, which Paul himself recognizes as a mystery.

There are other considerations which show

Paul's approach. His emphasis on the need for love between brethren (*cf.* 1 Thes. 5:15; Gal. 5:14; 6:10; Rom. 12:12–21; Eph. 4:16) is integral to his thought. Moreover, God has given gifts (*charismata*) to the church and these are to be used for the edification of the whole.

Teaching about the future. There can be no doubt that Paul expected the *parousia* (or second coming of Christ). Most of his Epistles speak of this eschatological event. Its imminence, however, is more stressed in the earlier (*e.g.* 1 and 2 Thes.) than the later Epistles. The apostle came to recognize that the possibility of the *parousia* occurring in his lifetime was increasingly remote. But he never lost his sense of the certainty of the event. He does not give much attention to describing future events. He looks forward to being with Christ (Phil. 1:23), but is sufficiently conscious of his present responsibilities to be willing to continue as he is.

In his great discussion on the resurrection of the body in 1 Cor. 15, he shows the centrality of this belief for the Christian faith. If Christ is not risen faith is vain, and since Christ is risen so shall those who are in Christ be raised with a spiritual body. In this Paul departs from the current Greek idea of the immortality of the soul alone. (See 1 Cor. 15:44; 2 Cor. 5:1-3.)

Another of Paul's great eschatological concepts is the judgment seat of Christ, which had a moulding effect upon his ethical ideals. The thought that each would give account of his actions exerted a sobering influence (*cf.* 2 Cor. 5:6–10). He lived as a man ever mindful of his accountability to God.

D. GUTHRIE

PART TWO

The Old Testament

PROHIBITION AND USE

Genesis

INTRODUCTION

TITLE

Like the traditional names for the other Pentateuchal books, the title 'Genesis' is derived from the LXX. The Jews called the first book of the Law *bᵉrēšît*, 'in the beginning', according to the ancient practice of naming books after their opening word(s). 'Genesis' means 'origin', an apt designation for the book which as a whole is the prologue to the OT's history of Israel and which, in the creation record of its own prologue, traces the origins of all human history.

AUTHORSHIP

As part of the broader issue of Pentateuchal criticism the authorship of Genesis is discussed elsewhere in this volume in the General Articles 'Literary Criticism of the Pentateuch' and 'Moses and the Pentateuch'. For those who accept the claims to Mosaic authorship common to the other four books, particular importance attaches to two types of evidence for the Mosaic authorship of Genesis, a book in which explicit claims to such authorship are lacking.

First, there is the interpenetration of Genesis and the rest of the Pentateuch through numerous themes continued from the former into the latter, thus making the last four books dependent upon the first. Random illustrations of some of the varieties of such interrelationship are: the resumption of the genealogical line of Gn. 46 in Ex. 1:1ff. and 6:14ff.; the recalling of the narrative of the twin brothers, Esau and Jacob, and the blessing of Esau (Gn. 25ff.) as the justification of the instructions given to Israel concerning their encounter with Edom (Dt. 2:4ff.; *cf.* Nu. 20:14ff.); and the similarity of the end of Deuteronomy to that of Genesis. The supposition is hardly plausible that the second layer (Ex.–Dt.) was produced independently of and even by an earlier author than the foundational layer (Gn.).

Of special significance, secondly, is the NT's witness to the writing of the whole Law by Moses (see especially Jn. 1:45; 5:46f.). Quotations made by Jesus and His disciples from here and there in the Pentateuch and attributed to Moses indicate that our Lord accepted the then prevalent Jewish view that Moses wrote all five books of the Law. To argue that the inspired NT authors claim Mosaic authorship only for the particular passages they cite as Mosaic (judging also perhaps that no Genesis passages are thus cited) is to assume that they had deliberately engaged in a higher critical investigation leading them to a rejection of the current tradition of the Mosaic authorship of Genesis (and perhaps leading them to a rejection of Mosaic authorship of parts of Ex.–Dt.). Or else it is to assume that knowledge of this higher critical partitioning of the Pentateuch was imparted to the NT authors by special revelation. Neither of these assumptions appears to be acceptable. If that is so, the NT endorses the Jewish tradition of Mosaic authorship of the Pentateuch, not excluding Genesis.

HISTORICITY AND LITERARY PARALLELS

Many are of the opinion that Gn. 12–50 is only to a limited and uncertain extent historical simply because it narrates events which took place long before they were recorded in writing and were known only through accounts received via oral transmission extending over centuries. And Gn. 1–11 is regarded as quite unhistorical, not merely because of the extreme remoteness of the ages described but even more because parallels to the material in Gn. 1–11 are known in the mythological literature of the Ancient Near East. Texts dealing with subjects like the creation of the world and the origin of human cultures, the Deluge, and pre- and post-diluvian dynastic genealogy are known to have existed in pre-Mosaic times, some of them corresponding to Gn. 1–11 even in the general combination and arrangement of these topics.

But it is gratuitous to conclude from the mere existence of parallels to Gn. 1–11 in mythological form that the biblical account must also be non-historical. One can also judge that the events of Gn. 1–11 are historical. That being the case, it would not then be at all surprising if the story concerning them should come to be mythologized in pagan traditions, while being preserved in authentically historical form within the stream of tradition of which Gn. 1–11 is the inspired deposit. To what extent special revelation was involved in the preservation of this historical record, both in its initiation and in subsequent renewal and refashioning (including the Genesis stage), we do not know exactly, but we must reckon with special revelation as a prominent factor in the process, the more so as it is recognized that that course of transmission continued over many thousands of years.

Decisively in favour of the judgment that Gn. 1–11 is not mythological but a genuine record of history is the testimony of the rest of the Bible. The material in these chapters is unquestionably interpreted by inspired writers elsewhere in Scripture as historical in the same sense that they understand Gn. 12–50 or Kings or the Gospels to be historical.

Literary analysis of Gn. 1–11 points to the same conclusion. These chapters cannot be identified as non-historical on the basis of any generally applicable literary criteria. Neither are they distinguishable from Gn. 12–50 by significant differences in their literary character. There is no great divide between Gn. 11 and Gn. 12. In fact, Gn. 11 interlocks with the preceding and following narratives. Through its genealogy of Shem it integrates the history of Abraham and the ensuing genealogical lines (Gn. 12 on into the NT) with the world map of Gn. 10, the oracle of Noah (Gn. 9), and the genealogy of Adam (Gn. 5). The genealogical nature of this link emphasizes that both the preceding and following narratives are concerned with everyday, earthly (even though at the same time redemptive) history.

Gn. 1–50 is history throughout, and when the writing of history is informed by divine inspiration the resultant product is a fully trustworthy historical record, however remote in time the human historian may have been from the events recorded. This position does not permit an easy side-stepping of questions raised by the inevitable comparison of the conclusions of modern research in the various sciences with the historical presentations in the early chapters of Genesis. All we can hope to do here, however, is to draw attention in the commentary to certain features of the narrative style of Genesis, such as the frequently topical rather than chronological arrangement of materials, recognition of which may help us to avoid some of the impasses into which a more wooden traditional exegesis has often led, and may even contribute to the discovery of new possibilities for a fruitful interrelating of special and general revelation. See the commentary also for references to archaeological data illuminative of the historical reliability of the patriarchal narratives.

If Moses, in composing Genesis, was not dependent on the Near Eastern literature that exhibits parallels to Genesis, neither did he ignore it. But it would seem that, where he deliberately develops the biblical account of an event so as to mirror features of the pagan version, it turns out to be for the polemical purpose of exposing and correcting the world's vain wisdom by the light of revealed theology. The elaboration of this is not possible here, but an illustrative case would be the treatment of the Babylonian epic account of creation, known (from its opening words) as *Enuma Elish*. Acquaintance with it is evidenced in the Genesis accounts of creation (ch. 1) and of Babel-building (ch. 11), but in both passages the epic's world-view is repudiated, even ridiculed, and most effectively so at the points of obvious formal correspondence.

LITERARY AND THEOLOGICAL STRUCTURE

The outline of the commentary below follows in its major headings the genealogical sections into which Genesis is formally structured and seeks in its sub-divisions to express the unfolding theological message of the book.

Beyond the prologue (1:1 – 2:3) Genesis is divided into ten sections, each introduced by a superscription embodying the formula '*ēlleh tôlᵉḏôt*, 'these are the generations of' (slightly modified in 5:1). In five cases genealogical data constitute a large part or even the majority of the section (5:1ff.; 10:1ff.; 11:10ff.; 25:12ff.; and 36:1ff.). The placing of the entire Genesis narrative in this genealogical framework is a clear sign that the author intended the account to be understood throughout as a real life history of individual men, begotten and begetting. This genealogical line is resumed in subsequent biblical historiography, the Genesis lists being recapitulated and carried forward until the lineage of Adam has been traced to Jesus, the second Adam (*cf.* especially Lk. 3:23–38).

One of the major disservices of the documentary hypothesis, at least in its classical formulation, was to disrupt the unity of Genesis, and leave as a series of unrelated, overlapping and even contradictory fragments what ought rather to have been seen as the harmonious and coherent development of a single theme. Even though it understood the 'generations-formula' to be editorial sub-divisions inserted by the P-writer, yet it failed to treat them seriously. The following outline, however, and the commentary based on it, seek to show that Genesis possesses a natural unity, and that when it is seen in its unity the major positions of the documentary theorists neither accord with the facts nor are required as explanations.

The particular positioning of the several genealogical lists in Genesis was determined by the book's major thematic concern with the history of God's covenantal relationship to men. This covenant theme is traced in Genesis from the original relationship of God and man, the covenant broken by the Fall, through the redemptive re-establishment of fellowship, which eventually became concentrated in the Abrahamic covenant. At the close of the book we are on the eve of the Mosaic fulfilment of the Abrahamic covenant in the covenant at Sinai and the Israelite theocracy, which itself was the provisional prefiguration of the eternal kingdom of the new covenant. Those eras that did not witness epoch-making developments in covenant history, and especially those genealogical branches that were separated from the continuing covenant community, are covered in the briefer of the ten sections, consisting largely of genealogical data. Also, the separated genealogical lines are regularly surveyed and dismissed first, before the more ample presentation of the history of the elect remnant, the recipients and bearers of the accumulating covenant revelation and the line leading to Israel and the Messiah. The genealogical framework thus provided an altogether fitting structure for the historical treatment of the covenant theme, for God administers His covenant not in atomistically individual terms but to His servants together with their families, even to the thousandth generation of those who love Him.

OUTLINE OF CONTENTS

COMMENTARY

1:1 – 2:3 PROLOGUE

The Genesis prologue presents those historical truths which are the necessary presuppositions for the valid pursuit of human knowledge. Among its normative disclosures are those of the divine act of absolute creation *ex nihilo* and of a specific, terminated creation era within which appeared all the significant variety of earth's hosts. The prologue's literary character, however, limits its use for constructing scientific models, for its language is that of simple observation and a poetic quality, reflected in the strophic structure, permeates its style. Exegesis indicates that the scheme of the creation week itself is a poetic figure and that the several pictures of creation history are set within the six work-day frames not chronologically but topically. In distinguishing simple description and poetic figure from what is definitively conceptual the only ultimate guide, here as always, is comparison with the rest of Scripture.

1:1-13 Creation's kingdoms

1:1-5 Day one. 1 The simple, chiselled, Hebrew style of this prologue favours regarding this verse as an independent declaration. If *the beginning* denotes the entire creation period, the verse could be a summary-heading. Ch. 1 would not then make a specific declaration about the world's absolute origins. Pr. 8:22f. and Jn. 1:1, however, support understanding *the beginning* as the commencement of the seven-day history. *God created* will then describe absolute creation *ex nihilo*. Consistently in the use of this verb (Heb. *bārā'*) the activity is divine, the product extraordinary or wondrously new. On this interpretation, *the heavens and the earth* are viewed in their earliest, not perfected state, yet as a totality, this being the idiomatic force in Hebrew of such contrasted pairs. *Cf.* Ne. 9:6 for the possibility that hosts of angels are in the author's purview. **2** *The earth*, here seen in its deep-and-darkness stage (*cf.* Jb. 38:8ff.), was destined to be man's habitation (Is. 45:18; *cf.* Pr. 8:30f.). In so far as they furthered that purpose, various developments were called *good* (vv. 4, 10, 12, 18, 21, 25, 31). The presence of the Creator-Spirit was the earnest of the transformation of deep-and-darkness into distinct realms (the theme of the first triad of days). **3** *God said*: creative ordering proceeded by mere executive decree (*cf.* Heb. 11:3; Jn. 1:3). **4, 5** The phenomenon of daylight, according to God's purpose as revealed in the names He gave (*cf.* Jb. 38:12ff., 19), was introduced not to eliminate earth's darkness but to alternate with it in the goodly order of *Day* and *Night* (*cf.* Ps. 104:20-23).

1:6-8 Day two. 6 *Firmament* (Heb. *rāqîa'*) designates the sky according to its appearance as a canopy, or vast tent, spread by God about His chambers (*cf.* Ps. 104:2; Pr. 8:27; Is. 40:22). *Let it separate the waters from the waters.* By this separation the atmospheric heaven and the waters on earth were distinguished, a first step in bounding the deep. **7** The waters below required further bounding (*cf.* v. 9). The waters above are the clouds (*cf.* Pr. 8:28, AV) or, poetically, the rain reservoirs in God's 'lofty abode' (Ps. 104:13).

1:9-13 Day three. 9 By a further ordering of the primaeval deep, dry land appeared as another earth-realm (*cf.* Pr. 8:25, 29; Ps. 104:7-9). **10** The realm of waters below (*cf.* vv. 6f.) now had the more precise character of land-bounded waters, or *Seas*. **11, 12** The natural means to support life having been made available

(*cf.* 2:5), the divine Sower scattered the seed of His creative word and the earth at His feet broke forth into green growth. *Each according to its kind.* Establishment of the major lines of differentiation in life forms is attributed to the closed era of the six days (*cf.* vv. 21, 24f.). Plants and trees, the two kinds of vegetation specified, are mentioned again in the work of the sixth day (vv. 29f.), which in the poetic structure of the account matches day three. *Cf.* Ps. 104:13-18.

1:14-31 Creature-kings

1:14-19 Day four. The first triad having delineated major kingdom-spheres, the second triad recapitulates the series (with correspondence between the successive days of each triad), appointing kings over these realms. Thus, day one (beyond v. 1) dealt with the separation of light from the darkness (v. 4), producing the cycle of day and night (v. 5), and the topically parallel day four introduces the creatures God made *to rule over the day and over the night, and to separate the light from the darkness.* Day four supplements by describing the cosmic system through which the results described in day one were achieved. The expressions *let there be* and *God made* are used here, as elsewhere in this passage, for acts of origination. Chronologically, this making of the heavenly luminaries (the work of day four) began in the beginning when God created the heavens and it continued along with the further fashioning of the earth described in the first three day-stanzas. In pagan thought the divine stars control human destiny; in Genesis the luminaries minister to man as servants of God, regulating day and night, supplying *signs* by which man may order his life and labour (*cf.* Ps. 104:19ff.; Jb. 38:7, 31ff.).

1:20-23 Day five. Here appear the fish of the sea and the birds of the air (*cf.* vv. 26, 28, 30), the living creatures that dominate the realms surveyed in the parallel second day. Chronologically, the earliest part of day five's work preceded at least the latest developments depicted under day three. 'Let the waters swarm' (v. 20, RV mg.; *cf.* Ps. 104:25ff.) describes the teeming results, not the method of production. The sheer supernaturalism of the latter is suggested by the formula that follows, *God created*. God's blessing in v. 22 is embodied in the creative command imparting the capacity of reproduction.

1:24-31 Day six. The sixth day contains two works, each concluding with God's recognition of purpose fulfilled (vv. 25, 31; *cf.* vv. 9, 11). Corresponding to the dry land with its vegetation, the distinctively new sphere of the parallel third day, are the land creatures of day six, their dominion claiming earth's produce (see vv. 29, 30). **24** *Let the earth bring forth* (*cf.* v. 12) suggests the possibility that already existing earth material was used as a matrix within which God's act of creation was performed. **26** *Let us make man in our image.* The explanation of the first person plural forms is probably that the Creator speaks as heaven's King accompanied by His heavenly hosts. Where this usage appears elsewhere ministering spirits hover nearby (*cf.* 3:22, 24; 11:7 and 18:21 (*cf.* 18:2; 19:1); Is. 6:8). Men and the celestial spirits alike are personal-religious creatures involved in responsible, historical relationship to God. This divine image is neither losable nor reducible, but its ethical direction is reversible. It assumes its proper form, of course, in conformity to God's holy will. **28** *Fill the earth and subdue it.* The dominion of man, the God-like king, only begins with his natural realm, the dry land of day three, thence to be extended by cultural conquest over all the creation kingdoms of the first triad of days and over all the creature-kings of the second triad (*cf.* Ps. 8:5-8). **30** The subordination of both animal and plant kingdoms to man's royal service having been affirmed, the lesser rule of animals over vegetation is noted. **31a** *Cf.* Pr. 8:30f.

2:1-3 Creator-King

2 *God finished.* This finishing of God's work assigned to day seven is not a further creating, for it is paralleled by God's resting. Both finishing and resting are viewed positively and characterize the seventh day as a distinct state of triumphant consummation for the Creator. This state had a temporal beginning but it has no end (note the absence of the concluding evening–morning formula). Yet it is called a 'day', so advising us that these days of the creation account are meant figuratively. **3** *God blessed the seventh day.* Man's history too was to lead from work begun to work completed and kingship perfected. God extended the promise of entrance into the divine sabbath (*cf.* Heb. 4:1ff.) by stamping the creation pattern of the seven days as a recurring symbolic cycle on man's daily existence. The sabbath day in particular was sanctified to be a constant source of blessing to man as the sign of his eternal hope. Also, by calling the royal image-bearer to follow in his Creator's way (*cf.* Ex. 20:8-11), the sabbath summons man to continual re-consecration of his servant-kingship to the glory of his Creator-King.

2:4 – 4:26 THE GENERATIONS OF HEAVEN AND EARTH

2:4 On *these are the generations*, see the Introduction above. Since the genitive in this formula is uniformly subjective, the reference is not to the origin *of the heavens and the earth* but the sequel thereof, particularly the early history of the earthlings. The first part of this verse, therefore, must be taken not with the preceding but the following account, which is not, then, presented as another version of creation. *When they were created* is literally 'in their being created'. This expression is used like the grammatically equivalent 'in their going forth from Egypt' (Dt. 4:45; 23:4; Jos. 5:4) and 'in your passing over the Jordan' (Dt. 27:4,

12) to denote an era according to its opening and formative event. *Cf.* also Gn. 33:18; 35:9. The reference in 2:4a (*cf.* the parallel in 4b) is evidently to the entire ante-diluvian period spanned in 2:4 – 4:25. *The Lord God* (Heb. *yhwh 'ĕlōhîm*). The combination of the generic *'ĕlōhîm*, 'God', and proper name, *Yahweh*, is found repeatedly in Gn. 2 and 3. *'ĕlōhîm* is used in Gn. 1 for God as Creator; it denotes God as He is known through His revelation in creation and general providence, including man's inward and intuitive knowledge of God. *Yahweh* is used alone beginning with Gn. 4; it is God's personal name describing Him as revealed through His historical–covenantal revelation as the Lord of eschatological purpose and sovereign fulfilment. The transitional combination, 'Yahweh God', in Gn. 2 and 3 serves to identify Yahweh, the covenant Lord, as God, the Creator. Such multiple designations of deity were common in the biblical world.

2:5-25 Man's original beatitude

2:5-8 Man in the garden of God. 5 Follow RV, 'and no plant of the field was yet in the earth'. AV obscures the Hebrew idiom for an emphatic negative. RSV would treat vv. 4b-7 like a long clumsy sentence, making Gn. 2 teach that man was created before vegetation. *For the Lord God had not caused it to rain.* During the creation era, punctuated though it was with acts of super-natural origination, the preservation of life was by natural means. Thus the Creator did not originate plant life before the availability of water, whether through a process of nature or through artificial irrigation devised by man.

6, 7 *A mist went up* (preferably, 'began to go up'). These verses describe the provision of the two things mentioned as missing in v. 5. The uncertain *mist* (Heb. *'ēd*) probably refers to subterranean waters springing up over the ground. *The Lord God formed man.* Man's one-ness with the created world is brought out by the similarity of *'ādām (man)* and *'ădāmâ (ground)*; the first man was of the earth, an earthling (*cf.* 1 Cor. 15:47). Man's first breath was the very *breath of life* which God breathed out; an intimacy of created mode is suggested that is consonant with the nature of man who, though an earthling, stands in image-relationship to God (*cf.* 1:27). The creature thus animated was not previously alive and it was nothing short of man, the image of God, that now by this immediate divine action first became a living being (*cf.* 1 Cor. 15:45). For man's eschatological potential see 1 Cor. 15:46ff. **8** 'Had planted' would be a proper translation. *Eden* could be a Sumero-Akkadian loan-word meaning 'steppe', but appears to be a name here meaning 'delight'. As the garden of God (*cf.* Is. 51:3; Ezk. 28:13; 31:9), the garden was a holy place and man's position there involved priestly vocation. The preparation of the garden is developed in vv. 9-14; the assignment of man in the garden in vv. 15-17.

2:9–14 Source of life. 9 The garden of God, the Source of life, ministered abundantly to man's life, aesthetic and physical. *The tree of life* symbolized the prospect of a glorified life (*cf.* Rev. 2:7) to be attained according to the Lord's law of probation (*cf.* vv. 15–17). *The tree of the knowledge of good and evil,* like the tree of life, was named after the destiny to which it would lead. To know good and evil is to be seasoned in discriminating between opposites. The context indicates the sphere of discrimination, such as physical sensation (*cf.* 2 Sa. 19:35) or, as here, ethical-religious experience (*cf.* 1 Ki. 3:9; Heb. 5:14).

10 The river system which kept the garden well watered (*cf.* Gn. 13:10) perhaps exemplifies the *mist* (*'ēd*) phenomenon (*cf.* 2:6). **11–14** The narrative's concern with real earthly history is apparent in the geographical notes, especially the familiar *Hiddekel* (i.e. 'Tigris') and *Euphrates* (v. 14). *Pishon* ('Gusher') and *Gihon* ('Bubbler') are not known, and this suggests the possibility of vast changes in the terrain between Adam and Moses. Eden's fertility and its surrounding treasures fulfilled the promise of its name (*cf.* on v. 8) and manifested the favour of God.

2:15–17 Law of the Lord. 15 recapitulates v. 8, adding man's commission. Subjugation of the earth (*cf.* 1:28) began with cultivation of the garden. *Keep it* is perhaps a cultic charge, *i.e.* to guard the sanctity of God's dwelling; *cf.* the use of the same verb *šāmar* in 3:24; Ne. 13:22; Zc. 3:7. **16** *Commanded the man.* For true covenant servants the law of the Lord is a delight (*cf.* Ps. 1:2); it gave direction to man's original state of blessedness. **17** The tree of knowledge, as the focus of probation, stood in Adam's path to the tree of life, the sacramental seal of the proffered consummation of blessing. *You shall die.* Though probation's proper purpose was unto life, the law of God's covenant placed Adam, as it did Israel at a later day, before life and good, death and evil (*cf.* Dt. 30:15ff.).

2:18–25 A wife for the man. 18 *It is not good.* Only when man existed male and female could the work of the sixth day be called 'very good' (*cf.* 1:27, 31), for only then could the divinely-ordained cultural programme unfold to its genealogical fullness (*cf.* 1:28a). *A helper.* The woman was made for the man (*cf.* 1 Cor. 11:9), yet not as his slave-girl but his queen. *Fit for him* (Heb. *kᵉnegdô*) suggests primarily correspondence, likeness (*cf.* vv. 20, 23); as man is the image and glory of God, so the woman is the glory of the man (1 Cor. 11:7). **19** Read 'now . . . God had formed'; thus the Hebrew can and should be translated (*cf.* v. 8). **20** *The man gave names.* God's naming activity (1:5, 8, 10), by which He assigns to the creation kingdoms their meaning, was imitated by man in this process of giving the creatures name interpretations. A prophetic function is thus seen to be added to the royal and priestly aspects of man's role in God's kingdom. **21, 22** The *deep sleep* was not so much an anaesthetic for the man as a veil about the woman until she was prepared to be led as a bride to her wedding. Paul understood this record of the woman's origins as straightforward history, observing that 'man was not made from woman, but woman from man' (1 Cor. 11:8). Scripture itself thus provides us with the direction to be followed in our exegetical approach to the narrative materials of this chapter. Following that direction in our exegesis of the account of the origin of man in 2:7 particularly, we find ourselves pointed away from any theoretical reconstruction in which the creative act that produced Adam is attached organically to some prior life process evolving at a sub-human level. **23** *Woman, because she was taken out of Man.* The assonance of *'îš* and *'iššâ* (man and woman) reflects the original name interpretation of the woman as derivative from, and hence of a kind with, the man (*cf.* vv. 18b, 20). **24** *They became one flesh.* In their origins of the one flesh of Adam, and in their separation still male-female correlatives of one kind, they become one flesh in a new sense as God joins them in marriage (*cf.* Mt. 19:4ff.). This verse is a divine directive. **25** *Cf.* 3:7.

3:1–24 The entrance of sin

3:1–7 Transgression of the law. 1 *The serpent.* Unless the entire paradise-Fall account is regarded as an allegory or some other non-historical form, which the rest of Scripture does not support (see the Introduction), there is no suggestion in the context that the serpent is not to be interpreted literally. Indications of literal intent are the comparison with other actual creatures and the terms of the divine judgment (3:14). The serpent was the instrument of Satan, who turned man's God-given probationary opportunity into an avenue of temptation (*cf.* Mt. 13:38f.; Jn. 8:44; Rom. 16:20; 1 Jn. 3:8; Rev. 12:9). *More subtle.* The camouflaged, sinuous movement of the serpent made it symbolically suitable as a medium for the wiles of the devil. **2, 3** By engaging in apologetic discourse with the challenging serpent, the woman accepted Satan's violation of the law of God's kingdom whereby all things visible had been placed under man's rule. She thereby yielded to the usurped authority of Satan. She spoke in God's defence, not, however, as a faithful witness but as an autonomous judge. Though Eve had thus already stumbled, the complete Fall of man was to involve not just the deceiving of the woman but the transgression of the man (v. 6b). **4** *You will not die.* First, Satan had challenged the stipulations of covenant law, God's norm for the present; now he contradicts its sanctions, God's interpretation of the future.

5 *God knows that . . . you will be like God.* With one stroke Satan re-interpreted God as a devil, a liar possessed by jealous pride, and the way of the curse as the way to blessing. Diverting attention from the spiritual direction of man's likeness to God, the tempter reduced the issue to a merely formal, existential matter of ascent along a supposed scale of being towards god-hood. **6** *She took . . . and ate.* In expression of her new anti-faith and her consent to Satan's theology, the woman risked the divine threat. *And she . . . gave. Cf.* 1 Tim. 2:14. From apologete for God to devil's advocate! *And he ate.* By this disobedience of the one man sin entered into the world and death passed upon all men (*cf.* Rom. 5:12ff.). **7** *They knew they were naked.* The similarity of *'ērummîm* ('naked'; *cf. 'arûmmîm,* 2:25) and *'ārûm* ('subtle', 3:1) suggests a word-play: the kind of God-likeness that resulted from following the serpent's counsel was religiously a devil-likeness. The sense of shame attaching to physical naked-ness (*cf.* 2:25) manifested consciousness of inner nakedness, the stripping of the glory of holiness from the soul. *Made themselves aprons.* Sin had side-tracked human inventiveness down a frustratingly remedial road.

3:8–19 Judgment of God. The Lord of the covenant instituted His lawsuit against the unfaithful vassals. It began with interrogation (vv. 8–13), and proceeded at once to a verdict (vv. 14–19). Divine justice could not be denied, but there was the unique wonder of a triumph of mercy through justice (*cf.* v. 15).

8 *God walking.* Theophany in human form was evidently a mode of special revelation from the beginning. *Hid themselves*—as though the guilty could find refuge from God in the sanctuary of God! Their own terror condemned them, for in such an ordeal of confrontation with the divine Judge the heart's reaction reveals the truth and anticipates the verdict (*cf.* Rev. 6:15f.). **10** *Because I was naked.* This was an evasive half-truth. Adam's sense of nakedness was, like his fear, an evil con-sequence of his rebellion. **11, 12** When God cut through this subterfuge, exposing the act of disobedience as the root of evil (*cf.* v. 17), the sinner avoided confession of guilt only by the blasphemous expedient of virtually blaming God for his fall—*the woman whom thou gavest.* **13** The woman seeks to absolve herself from blame by pointing the finger at the subtle serpent. **14** *Cursed are you.* There is no trial for Satan, just the pronouncing of doom. Satan's instru-ment, slithering in the dust, subject to trampling, becomes a symbol of his humiliation and con-demnation. *Above* (lit. 'from') has been under-stood by some to mean 'by being made separate from', but the regular use of this preposition to express the comparison 'more than' is preferable here. **15** *I will put enmity between you and the woman.* The allegiance recently transferred to Satan will be again reversed; God will sovereignly effect a reconciliation with Himself. *Between your seed and her seed.* Beyond the woman, the whole family of the true humanity, becoming her spiritual seed by faith, will stand in continuing conflict with those descendants of fallen Adam who obdurately manifest spiritual sonship to the devil (*cf.* Jn. 8:33, 44). The latter identify with the devil in the battle and so participate

too in his ultimate perdition. *He shall bruise your head, and you shall bruise his heel.* The 'you' still contending in the remote future points past the mere serpent to Satan. This focusing on an individual from one side in connection with the eventual decisive encounter suggests that the *he* too is not the woman's seed collectively but their individual champion. Since this verse elaborates the declaration just made of Satan's doom, the point of the contrast between the wounding of head and heel is that the first is fatal, and the second is not. Clearly, however, the redemptive victory would involve suffering. The special redemptive programme would require as its field a general history of man. Hence the curse of the broken covenant (*cf.* 2:17) announced to the fallen pair as representative of the en-visaged generality of mankind was modified (vv. 16–19) by the principle of common grace. **16** *In pain.* Travail would now characterize man's genealogical development and the re-instituted marriage relationship would be dis-turbed by sinful inclinations towards abuse of its authority structure (*cf.* 4:7 for the idiom). **17, 18** *Cursed is the ground because of you.* The cursing of the ground consisted not in the intro-duction of new features, like thistles, but in God's providential use of the ground, which hitherto had ministered to man's welfare (*cf.* 1:29), as a medium of His judgment-curse against him (*cf.* 8:21; Jb. 31:40; Rom. 8:20ff.). **19** *To dust you shall return.* Because the ground entered into the composition of man (*cf.* 2:7), the curse on the ground became a power unto death working in his very members (*cf.* Nu. 5:16ff.). Death, formerly present in nature in subservience to man, would now terrorize man the covenant-breaker as the wages of his sin.

3:20–24 Hope of restoration. 20 *Eve.* Man's generic designation became his proper name, Adam (*cf.* 3:17; 4:25); but the generic appellation of the woman was replaced by the proper name, *ḥawwâ.* The sound-play on *ḥay,* 'living', reflects Adam's faith as he gave this name to the woman, his reference probably being to her spiritual seed who should trample under foot the prince of death and so wrest life from the curse (*cf.* 3:15; 1 Tim. 2:15; Rom. 16:20). **21** *The Lord . . . clothed them.* This remedy for the obstacle to their approach to God (*cf.* 3:10) symbolized God's purpose to restore men to fellowship with Him. The sinners' shame, as a religious problem, could not be covered by their own efforts (*cf.* 3:7). Implied in God's provision is an act of animal sacrifice; what is explicit, however, is not the sacrificial mode but remedial result. **22** *Like one of us; cf.* above on 1:26. Through the probation-temptation man had come to experience the full dimension of the conflict of good and evil, as celestial creatures had previously known it. *Eat, and live for ever.* Punishment for such unworthy grasping of the sacrament of life would be to grant the coveted exclusion from physical death, and this would, paradoxically, make men's state of death and alienation permanent, since reconciliation could come only by a sacrificial dying (cf. 3:15, 21). **23** Although man's expulsion from the garden mercifully forestalled that possibility, the exile-judgment was of course a manifestation of God's displeasure with fallen man. **24** *The cherubim, and a flaming sword . . . to guard the way.* Protection of the sanctuary (cf. on 2:15) was now assigned to beings who elsewhere too are found as guardians of God's throne (cf. Ex. 25:18ff.; 1 Ki. 6:23ff.; Ezk. 10; 28:14ff.), while man was viewed as a potential intruder. Yet God preserved the sanctuary with its tree of life, so reaffirming the hope of a restoration from exile, even though the way of return led through the death-curse of God's judgment-sword.

4:1–26 Man in exile

4:1–16 Banishment of humanity's firstborn. 1 In Hebrew *qayin* (*Cain*) and *qānîtî* (*I have gotten*) form a pun. For Eve the name was probably related authentically to the explanation. *With the help of the Lord* is better translated 'from the Lord', giving the preposition (*'et*) a meaning well attested elsewhere. Eve's explanation was a believing response to God's earlier revelation concerning both redemptive and common grace (cf. 3:15f.). **2** *Abel* (Heb. *heḇel*, 'breath, vanity'). Was this a posthumous naming (cf. 4:25c) or a reflection of earlier experience of the curse's frustration (cf. 5:29; Ec. 1:2ff.)? From **2b** it is clear that the Scriptures disallow historical reconstructions locating the earliest phase of food production and animal domestication relatively late in man's cultural development. **3** *In the course of time*; possibly upwards of 130 years (cf. 4:25; 5:3). Whether any of the daughters of Adam and Eve (cf. 5:4) were born during this time and already had been given in marriage to one of the brothers is uncertain (cf. 4:17, 25). *Offering.* In both cases the offering is formally one of thankful homage. **4** An expiatory purpose is not explicitly indicated even for Abel's offering; the stress on *firstlings* and *their fat portions* suggests consecration. **5** How God's favour was registered in the case of Abel over against Cain is not stated; see, however, Lv. 9:24; Jdg. 6:21; 1 Ki. 18:38; 1 Ch. 21:26; 2 Ch. 7:1ff.; cf. Ex. 14:24. That acceptance depended on the offerer's spiritual standing is suggested by the reference to the persons along with their gifts (vv. 4b, 5a) and confirmed by Heb. 11:4. **7** *Sin is couching at the door*, or, 'sin is the demon at the door', *rōḇēṣ* ('couching') being rather regarded as the Akkadian word *rābiṣum*, an 'entrance demon', here used not to suggest such a being, but in illustration of temptation's assault on Cain and recalling the serpent of Gn. 3.

8 *Cain said to Abel.* RSV, following the versions, unnecessarily adds to the MT (cf. RSV mg.). *Against his brother.* In jealous reaction to the manifestation of God's favour (v. 4; cf.

3:15), sin exerts its divisive power. Not mere social disorder was involved but radical religious discord, the enmity of the serpent's seed against the seed of the woman. Jesus interpreted Cain's murder of Abel as the first shedding of martyr's blood (Mt. 23:35; Lk. 11:51). **9** *Where is Abel?* Cain's hiding of the evidence of sin exposed sin's continuing love of concealment (cf. 3:8ff.). *I do not know.* Cain was a liar like his father, the devil (cf. 3:4). *Am I my brother's keeper?* By a virtual confession of a sin of omission Cain sought to cover his violent sin of commission. **10** *The voice of your brother's blood.* Martyr blood invokes the vengeance of God as covenant Protector (cf. Mt. 23:35; Heb. 11:4; 12:24; Rev. 6:9ff.). **11** *You are cursed from the ground.* Cf. 3:14, 17. Whether 'from' is here separative or derivative, Cain's judgment actually included both the increased recalcitrance of the soil (**12**; cf. 3:18f.) and separation from Eden, not as an outpost but an outcast. **14** *From thy face I shall be hidden.* The irony of the sentence is that it dooms Cain to what he desired. *Whoever finds me will slay me.* This reference probably includes wild beasts (cf. the related 9:2ff.), but possibly envisages also the peopling of the earth in coming years. **15** *Vengeance shall be taken on him.* The human community had to expand before a special judicial institution was established. *A mark on Cain.* Taking our cue from 9:2ff. again, the 'sign' appointed to Cain may have been the dread of man instilled in beasts (cf. 35:5). **16** *Cain went away from the presence of the Lord.* The race's firstborn, crown prince of the earth, portrays the tragic direction of fallen man: into exile, without God, without hope in the world.

4:17–24 Cainite culture. In Genesis an account of side branches precedes the genealogy of the principal line leading to Israel; so here, Cainites come before Sethites. **17** *His wife.* She would be a daughter of Adam (cf. 5:4), whether born (and even married) before Cain's banishment is uncertain. *A city*; i.e. a settlement protected by structures of some sort from a threatening environment. The rise of cities prepares for the emergence of kingship. *Enoch* means 'consecration'. Here begins the theme of man's passion to establish his own name in the earth. **18** *Father of.* The idiom allows for remote ancestry; very considerable stretches of time must be spanned in this verse. Father–son terminology was even used for the professional relationship of the head of a guild to other members (cf. v. 20). **19** *Two wives.* Lamech's abuse of the creation ordinance of marriage exemplifies the ungodly spirit of Cainite culture. **22** Metal-work in late pre-diluvian times need not surprise us in view of evidence before 6,000 BC (perhaps early post-diluvian) of its use; the iron was probably meteoric. *Tubalcain.* Cain's name was preserved in his royal successors. **23** *I have slain.* The judicial office degenerated into a vengeful tyranny in this heir of the murderous spirit of the dynasty's founder. **24** *Lamech seventy-seven fold.* The divine protection which Cain was glad to receive, Lamech scorned. Cainite culture culminated in defiance of Him to whom it should have been dedicated. **4:25, 26 Cult of Yahweh.** Though the section Gn. 2:4 – 4:26 is largely concerned with sin's entrance and escalation, it closes with a notice of the preservation of a people of God and their worship. **25** Eve, according to her explanation of his name, saw in *Seth* God's restoration of the second covenant generation after its disappearance in Abel's martyrdom and Cain's excommunication. **26** *Call upon the name of the Lord.* There had been individual worship, including external rites (*cf.*, *e.g.*, 4:2ff.). Now the religious worship of the community of faith was organized for their corporate covenantal consecration to the name of Yahweh.

5:1 – 6:8 THE GENERATIONS OF ADAM

The story now doubles back upon itself (*cf.* the recapitulation in the days of Gn. 1) to pick up the line of Adam through Seth, and thus to survey again the period of 'the world that then was', tracing it now to its very close. **1, 2** An introduction (vv. 1b, 2) added to the heading (v. 1a) grounds this section in the prologue-history (*cf.* 1:26ff.), as was the preceding section (cf. 2:4.) *Named them Man.* The generic use of *'ādām* contrasts with Adam as proper name in this context.

5:3–32 Covenant genealogy: Adam to Noah

As **3** shows, the sons listed in a genealogy need not be firstborn (or descended therefrom) and the age figure need not indicate when the subject first became a father. *In his own likeness*; *cf.* v. 1 and 1:27. Man too reproduces according to his kind (*cf.* 1:11f.), the divine image being transmitted in the process, yet as misdirected in man's Fall. **4, 5** *All the days that Adam lived.* Mesopotamian traditions reflect the race's memory of remarkable longevity, especially in pre-diluvian times. Whatever the physiological explanation, a providential purpose was the preservation of mankind, still few in number, young in technology, and obliged to cope with a fractious environment. *And he died.* With this refrain each biographical strophe ends, each except the last (yet *cf.* 9:28) and one other (see v. 24). Only violent death was mentioned in the Cainite section. Gn. 5 records 'natural' death inflicted as God's common curse on all (*cf.* 3:19). **22-24** The expression *walked with God* is unusual (see 6:9; *cf.* Mal. 2:6; Zc. 3:7); the experience evidently involved special revelation received (*cf.* God's walking in 3:8) and proclaimed (Jude 14f.). *He was not, for God took him.* Exempted from death (Heb. 11:5; *cf.* 2 Ki. 2:3, 5, 9ff.), Enoch's bodily translation into 'heaven' was a sign during the long pre-diluvian sway of the curse that

reconciliation with God ultimately includes victory over death. **29** *Shall bring us relief*; the Hebrew verb is in assonance with *Noah*. For *out of* read 'from' (Heb., lit.) *the ground*. In Hebrew the reference to the accursed ground stands last, explaining the burdensome character of human labour. RSV rearranges, suggesting that the ground will somehow be the source of relief. Believers' hope in the world of promise (*cf.* Heb. 11) intensifies their awareness of God's curse on present cultural endeavours; contrast Cainite Lamech (4:23f.). **32** *Shem, Ham, and Japheth.* Shem was the oldest (*cf.* 7:11; 11:10); Ham, the youngest (*cf.* 9:24).

The genealogies of Gn. 5 and 11:10ff. are selective, not complete. The genealogical terms they employ are frequently used for remote descent. Selective genealogies are common in Scripture and elsewhere. Moreover, the symmetrical structure, with partiality for conventional numbers, which often signalizes selective listings, is found in Gn. 5 and 11:10ff. If we follow LXX in 11:10ff., each series contains ten individuals, the tenth in each case having three sons. *Cf.* especially the triple fourteen form of the obviously selective genealogy of Mt. 1, the tenfold scheme of generations in Genesis, and the tenfold selective genealogy of Ru. 4:18–22. The antiquity of the race cannot, then, be determined even approximately from the data of Gn. 5 and 11:10ff. The concern of Gn. 5 is the continuance of the covenant community through the entire pre-diluvian age.

6:1–8 Cult of man

6:1–4 Deified sinners. The theme of titanic kingship is resumed from 4:24, with the royal wives and dynastic exploits. Here the pinnacle of abominations is reached, provoking divine vengeance. **2** *The sons of God* could be translated 'the sons of the gods'. Ancient texts attest to an ideology of divine kingship; human kings were called sons of various gods. This blasphemous cult was a culmination of the Cainite name-lust (*cf.* 4:17). As in v. 1, *daughters of men* are the daughters of men in general. By *such of them as they chose*, polygamy is meant (*cf.* 4:19), as practised in royal harems. **3** *My spirit shall not abide in man for ever.* The verb has also been translated 'act in', 'rule in', 'strive with', 'shield'; *cf.* perhaps Jas. 4:5. The point becomes clear in the contrast: *not for ever . . . but a hundred and twenty years.* Man was sealed unto judgment, waiting at the set limit of divine forbearance. Problematic for the interpretation of the offenders as angels is the concentration of God's judgment against *man* and *flesh.* If Jude 6 does associate angels with this episode, that aspect could be incorporated as a supplementary dimension into the above interpretation. **4** *Nephilim . . . the mighty men.* Giant stature may be involved (*cf.* Nu. 13:33), but political dominance is probably indicated by *the mighty* (*cf.* 10:8ff.). In the courts of the divine kings powerful princes arose, extending their fathers' sway by tyrannical injustice (*cf.* v. 11). V. 4 appears to be inexplicable if vv. 1f. are interpreted as religiously mixed marriages of Sethites and Cainites. For *men of renown* read literally 'men of a name'. This again is the motif of 4:17ff.

6:5–8 Repentant deity. 5 As sinners multiplied (*cf.* v. 1), so did sin. According to God's analysis, human depravity was total. **6** *The Lord was sorry; cf.* AV, 'it repented the Lord'. In the strange cult of man sinners are deified and God does the repenting! It was the unchangeableness of the divine purpose, threatened by the near extinction of the woman's seed, that paradoxically required the change in divine government, an intrusion of radical judgment interrupting the administration of common curse and grace (*cf.* 3:16ff.). **7** *I will blot out* is an adumbration of watery judgment. **8** *Noah found favour*. This section, like the preceding (*cf.* 4:25) concludes on a note of hope.

6:9 – 9:29 THE GENERATIONS OF NOAH

6:9a The heading-formula here applies not to the subject's descendants (for Noah's descendants see 10:1ff. and 11:10ff.), but to the historical developments of his life-time. The extended treatment is indicative of the Flood's epoch-making importance (*cf.* 2 Pet. 3:5ff.). Since the ark-occupants' horizon evidently limits the meaning of the geographical observations (see on 6:13ff.), the narrative does not directly affirm a universal flood; nor does it deny one. Neither a local nor a universal flood involves difficulties insuperable to supernatural intervention, and no view should be rejected solely because it involves such intervention. The relevance of alleged evidence of a catastrophic flood at one time or another is rendered uncertain by our ignorance of the date of the Flood (see comments on Gn. 5 and 11:10ff.). For the same reason deductions drawn from the assumption that all mankind was destroyed are precarious, for we cannot say what portions of the earth were populated at an unknown date. Nevertheless, the Flood stands out in Scripture as the most general judgment between creation–Fall and the final consummation. At the least the Flood severed the central trunk of human history, the ark-remnant excepted, so terminating the old world and justifying the NT's representation of it as universal in its significance and as marking the end of one epoch and the beginning of another in God's programme of redemption.

6:9b – 8:19 Diluvian covenant

6:9b – 7:10 Strategy for salvation. 6:9b Integrity (*tāmîm*, RSV *blameless*) marked Noah's allegiance to the Lord among his contemporaries (*generation*, a different Hebrew word from 'generations' in v. 9a). **13** *God said to Noah*. The time of God's first disclosure concerning the Flood probably marked the start of the 120-year count-down (*cf.* 6:3, 5ff.). If 6:13 dates that early it antedates the birth of Noah's sons (*cf.* 5:32; 7:6) and 6:13–21 then summarizes a series of directives reaching to near the close of the 120 years (*cf.* v. 18b). *With* ('*et*) *the earth* suggests that man's whole world will share in his judgment (*cf.* 6:7, 17). But the point is probably man's removal 'from the earth' as in 6:7; 7:4, 23 (on '*et*, 'from', *cf.* on 4:1). Later (v. 17) the mode of removal is specified as a Flood.

Here, and repeatedly, universal terminology is used to describe the Flood's devastation (*cf.* 6:7, 13, 17; 7:4, 21ff.; 8:21; 9:11, 15). Such terminology is sometimes used, however, in a limited sense (*cf., e.g.,* 41:56f.; Dn. 2:38; 4:22; 5:19). Moreover, the Flood history is manifestly related from the local perspective of the ark-occupants (*cf.* 7:18ff.). On the other hand, the range of nations arising from Noah's sons in the post-diluvian era (*cf.* Gn. 10, especially v. 32; *cf.* 9:19) points to extensive depopulation in parts at least of Asia, Africa, and Europe. This favours a more than local interpretation.

14–16 *Ark* translates *tēbâ*, 'box', found elsewhere only in Ex. 2:3, 5. This 'vessel', about $450 \times 75 \times 45$ feet was designed for steady floating—the course, knots, and destination were completely in the hands of God. Salvation is of the Lord, by faith (*cf.* Heb. 11:7). **18** *My covenant*. Rather than taking this verse as an anticipation of 9:9ff., this covenant should be understood as the relationship within which the Flood-salvation was effected; see on 8:1. Like the new covenant, it was confirmed not by an oath symbolizing judgment (*cf.* Gn. 15:17–21) but by a real passage through an actual divine judgment. **22** *He did all that God commanded*. Noah was mediator of the covenant. By obedience to the covenant law, *i.e.* to construct and enter the ark-kingdom, he became the saviour of the elect remnant. To the rest of his generation, disobedient to the last (*cf.* 1 Pet. 3:20; Mt. 24:37ff.; Lk. 17:26f.), he was a prophetic witness (*cf.* 2 Pet. 2:5).

7:1–10 The period of construction and forewarning completed (6:11–22), a week (v. 4) was allowed for embarkation. Supplementing the stipulation that one pair of each animal-kind enter (6:19f.; 7:2b, 9), *seven pairs* (7:2a, 3) were required for clean animals and birds. According to another view, clean animals were to enter 'by sevens'; against this are the repeated male-female pairing and the absence of specification concerning an odd seventh. The clean-unclean distinction was possibly along the lines of Lv. 11 and Dt. 14, but had reference to sacrifice (*cf.* 8:20) rather than eating (*cf.* 9:3).

7:11–24 Ordeal by water. *The flood* (Heb. *mabbûl*, 6:17; 7:6, 7, 10, 17) denotes the cataclysmic phenomena of the forty-day period (7:14, 17) dated in v. 11. Apparently *mabbûl* is also applied, in extension of the precise usage in the Flood record proper, to the year-long episode (9:11, 15, 28; 10:1, 32; 11:10). Its chief element was torrential rains (vv. 11b, 12), though a surge of terrestrial waters contributed to the inundation (v. 11). By these waters God subjected the old world to the ordeal of His judgment, with its dual verdicts of condemnation and (for the elect remnant) of justification (*cf.* 1 Pet. 3:20). **13** *On the very same day.* The completion of embarkation and the beginning of the deluge synchronized. **16** *The Lord shut him in.* This sealing of the elect unto vindication was also a closing of the door of the kingdom on those outside. The theme shifts from God's protection of Noah's family through the *mabbûl* (vv. 11-16) to the prevailing of the waters (vv. 17-24; *cf.* 8:4). Chronologically the narrative recapitulates, for the forty days of the *mabbûl* are the first forty of the 150 days of prevailing (*cf.* 7:11, 24; 8:4). The prevailing is concerned with the effects of the *mabbûl*, particularly on the ark, on the mountains, and thus on all land life outside the ark. The rising water level, though involved, is not the distinctive feature of the prevailing. **17-19** Each verse begins by stating with increasing intensity that the waters *prevailed*. They lifted the ark from its land moorings, carried it away, and covered the mountains. **20-24** Read v. 20 as in AV: 'Fifteen cubits upward did the waters prevail; and the mountains were covered.' This summarizes vv. 17-19. By rising 15 cubits, the draught of the ark, the waters bore it up. Continuing to rise, they covered all the mountains in sight (*cf.* 8:5), so removing all land refuge. The prevailing continued *a hundred and fifty days*, for although life outside the ark had perished even within the *mabbûl* period, other aspects of the prevailing (viz. the covering of the mountains and floating of the ark) continued longer (*cf.* 8:4).

8:1-19 Vindication in judgment. Again there is chronological recapitulation as the theme becomes the subsiding of the waters (vv. 1-12); for the subsiding began as soon as the forty-day *mabbûl* ended and continued through the last 110 days of prevailing. Then it continued almost another half year (*cf.* vv. 4, 13), being followed by the time of re-emergence (vv. 13-19).

1 *God remembered Noah.* God's faithfulness in fulfilling His covenant promise is characteristically expressed as a remembering of His covenant (*cf.*, *e.g.*, 9:15f.; Ex. 2:24; 6:5; Lk. 1:72) or the individual(s) to whom He made covenant promises (*cf.*, *e.g.*, 19:29; Ex. 32:13). *God made a wind blow*; *cf.* 1:2; Ex. 14:21. **3-5** *Came to rest* shows that a favourable verdict was rendered at the end of the ordeal. From this verb, *nûaḥ*, the name Noah may derive. *Ararat* was a land near Lake Van in Armenia, strategically central for post-diluvian emigration. The ark landed on the highest mountain within the view of its occupants, not necessarily the highest in Ararat. The computation in v. 3b and the date in v. 4a coincide. Hence, the statement that *the waters had abated* means they were

lacking (*ḥāsar*, lit.) the 15 cubits necessary to prevail over (*i.e.* to float) the ark at its location. This lack resulted from a previous process of receding (v. 3a) that began when the *mabbûl* phenomena terminated (v. 2; *cf.* 7:11f., 17). According to 7:24, the date of the ark's grounding marked the end of the waters' prevailing. Therefore, the prevailing of the waters over the mountains (*cf.* 7:19ff.) must also have ended by then. The situation was probably that the peak of the mountain on which the ark landed had become visible above the waters even before the grounding (and will then have served as the gauge of the recession recorded in v. 3a), but the other mountains within the range of vision were not seen until later (v. 5). The complete subsiding, however, involved further this emergence of the surrounding mountains and later still the re-appearance of all the land observable from the now uncovered ark (v. 13). Evidently the limited perspective from the ark's opening (*cf.* 6:16) before the covering was removed, plus the contours of the terrain around the ark, prevented a view down onto the lower slopes and valleys.

6-12 The successive reconnoitring missions of the raven and dove(s) were well calculated to keep Noah informed on the progressive recession at these lower, unobservable elevations. **13** About a month after these bird episodes the Noahic exodus began. Like the Mosaic it was related to a beginning of months (*cf.* Ex. 12:2). *Noah removed the covering.* As he did so the light of God's new day streamed into the darkness of the ark-tomb, the beginning of a veritable resurrection after the passage through the sea of death. From the new vantage-point Noah could see that the waters were removed from even the lower areas. **14-19** More time was allowed for the ground to dry and perhaps for plants to grow. Then, one year and ten days after God had sealed the ark unto judgment (whether lunar or solar year is uncertain), He commanded the survivors to come forth, vindicated, to inherit the new world.

8:20 – 9:17 Post-diluvian covenant

8:20-22 Covenant protectorate. 20 The arkbuilder *built an altar*; so his culture found its true goal in religious dedication *to the Lord.* **21** Noah's sacrifice also expressed propitiation (*cf. the pleasing odour*). From this redemptive work of special grace the blessings of common grace issue (vv. 21b ff.). *The Lord said in his heart.* The turning aside of God's wrath is underscored by repetition of the form (*i.e.* the divine musing) and language of His earlier judicial decree (*cf.* 6:5ff.). *Curse the ground.* The diluvian ground-cursing consisted in using nature to curse man, not in changing nature. *For* (Heb. *kî*). This might be translated 'though'. But this clause probably continues to quote the verdict of 6:5ff.; *i.e.* it explains what is meant by *because of man.* **22** *Shall not cease.* This covenant promise established the earth as a protectorate of heaven—until the final judgment.

9:1-7 Covenant mandate. Divine blessing and command combine as mankind is recommissioned to the kingdom programme assigned him at the beginning. The covenant is at once a revelation of God's law and grace, and in both a sovereign administration of His lordship. **1** *Be fruitful* (*cf.* 8:17). The post-diluvian covenant is one of life. Its stipulations deal with the propagation of life (vv. 1 and 7), life's protection and sanctity (vv. 2 and 5f.), and its sustenance (vv. 3f.; *cf.* 8:22). Implicit in these stipulations is the continuance of the creation ordinances of marriage and labour. **2,3** The dread of man was surely on beasts previously and man's eating of animal flesh may likewise be a renewal of a pre-diluvian appointment. **4** The prohibition of blood had its rationale in blood's sanctity as a symbol in altar sacrifice. **5, 6** That human life might be protected, God ordained the cutting off of every kind of man-slayer. *Of every man's brother.* The murder of man by man is always fratricide. *By man shall his blood be shed.* During Lamech's dynasty human life was in jeopardy as much through the tyranny of the royal judiciary (*cf.* 4:23f.) as through the violence of common criminals. This reaffirmation of the state's power of the sword regulates it by insisting that the punishment does not exceed, but matches the crime. *For God made man in his own image.* This could explain both the enormity of murder and the dignity of man that justified assigning him so grave a judicial responsibility.

9:8-17 Covenant sign. **9** *I establish my covenant.* God's covenants regulate an order of life under His suzerainty. A peculiarity of this one is that it is an interim arrangement without eschatological sanctions. **10, 11** It is a covenant of life but only of earthly life, subservient to God's redemptive covenant of eternal life. Another peculiarity is that it does not revolve around a personal relationship between God and a people, but is *between me and the earth* (v. 13), *i.e.* it embraces the impersonal creatures and the earth itself (as almost every verse reiterates). God's pledge to stabilize the natural order, not devastating the world again before the end-time, dominates the arrangement. **12-17** Agreeably, *the sign of the covenant* is a divine guarantee to man and a reminder to God of His commitments as world-Protector. *My bow* translates *qešeṭ*, the usual meaning of which is the weapon. Thus, the recurring rainbow imposed on the retreating storm by the shining again of the sun is God's battle bow laid aside, a token of grace staying the lightning-shafts of wrath.

9:18-27 Covenant in prophecy

9:18-23 Community divided. **18** *Ham was the father of Canaan.* This anticipatively connects Ham's sin (v. 22) and the curse on Canaan (vv. 25ff.). **19b** *Cf.* 10:1ff. **20** Translated literally this reads, 'Noah, the husbandman, began and planted a vineyard'. RSV here unnecessarily foists a contradiction upon the biblical record (*cf.*, *e.g.*, 4:2). **22** *Ham saw . . . and told.* This act of malicious disrespect, if it did not evidence a present encroachment of the serpent's seed within the remnant family, yet foreboded such. The exposure of nakedness recalls Satan's work (*cf.* Gn. 3); the covering of nakedness (v. 23) recalls the divine clothing of fallen man (3:21) and so bespeaks a spirit devoted to the imitation of God.

9:24-27 Patriarchal curse. **24** *When Noah . . . knew what his youngest son had done.* This introduction relating the pronouncement to the offence shows it is primarily a curse. To the same effect is the repetition of the curse on Canaan in connection with the blessings on Shem and Japheth. This utterance belongs to the series of personal curses which began with the primaeval curse against Satan (3:14) and continued with that against Cain (4:11). Its terms must not be secularized, but must be understood within the sacred history entailed in God's judgment against Satan. **25** *Cursed be Canaan.* In each case the curse (or blessing) does not apply to all the members of the ethnic groups represented by the individual named but rather finds an outstanding fulfilment in the history of the group. Thus, Shem and Japheth are blessed in their descendants just as Ham is cursed in his. The mention of Ham's son, Canaan, simply makes it more obvious in that case and points directly to the fulfilment in view. *A slave of slaves shall he be to his brothers.* The opposition between Canaan and the other two, who are identified with the covenant community, declares his reprobation. The subordination of Canaan signifies the defeat of Satan's seed; the woman's seed would crush their head. There is a pun on Canaan's name; *kāna'* is used for subjugation and indeed with reference to Israel's conquest of Canaan, the fulfilment of Noah's curse (Dt. 9:3; Jdg. 4:23). **26** Follow RSV mg., 'blessed be the Lord, the God of Shem'. The doxology contains the benediction. The curse on Satan (3:15) implied salvation for God's elect; so the curse on Canaan was the means of blessing to Shem-Israel. Israel possessed its promised kingdom by dispossessing Canaan. *Shem* means 'name'; the blessing was Shem's identification with God's covenant name, Yahweh, as seen particularly in the Abrahamic covenant. **27** *God enlarge* (*yap̄t*) *Japheth* (*yep̄eṯ*). The outstanding development in redemptive history that found Japhethites entering the Abrahamic covenant community was the NT's apostolic mission to the Gentiles.

28, 29 The section on the generations of Noah has the popular envelope form, beginning (6:9a) and closing with genealogical formulae. These verses complete 5:32. The computation perhaps reckons the *mabbûl* strictly, as only the first forty days.

10:1 – 11:9 THE GENERATIONS OF THE SONS OF NOAH

The multiplication of the race was attributable to the creative blessing of God (8:15ff.; 9:1, 7; *cf.* Acts 17:26). Yet this new dispersion (10:1ff.) must also be seen as a curse, a continuation of man's exile-history (*cf.* 3:23f.; 4:16). The affixed Babel episode (11:1ff.) accents that perspective.

10:1–32 Diaspora of the nations

The order is that of seniority except that the chosen Semite line comes last according to the usual pattern, even though they are here traced alongside rather than directly to Israel (11:10ff.). The descendants total a conventional seventy, an indication that exhaustive listing is not the purpose. Apart from obvious exceptions like Nimrod, the 'sons' are collective units, genealogically related to the Noahic branch to which they are assigned. Because of early intermarriages and later community interblending, certain groups could trace their lineage to more than one line. Within the three major divisions subgroupings were distinguishable by the geographical, linguistic, ethnological, and political differences cited in the colophons (vv. 5, 20, 31). **10:2–5 Sons of Japheth.** According to generally-accepted identifications, the Japhethites occupied territory N and NW of the Fertile Crescent. Noah's oracle (9:27) prophesied their enlargement as the prelude to their grand-scale entrance into the covenant. Agreeably, they are here found stretching to the ends of the earth (with v. 5 *cf.* Is. 41:5), to the isles which would receive the summons to the Messianic kingdom (*cf.*, *e.g.*, Ps. 72:10; Is. 49:1ff.). **10:6–20 Sons of Ham.** Their location was in general SW of the Fertile Crescent. **8** Read as in AV, 'he began to be a mighty one'. Nimrod's royal title recalls 6:4. **9** Prowess in hunting man-slaying beasts was an important and, in Mesopotamia, a peculiarly royal skill (*cf.* 9:5). **10** AV reads 'The beginning of his kingdom was Babel, and Erech, and Accad and Calneh, in the land of Shinar'. *Shinar* is Babylonia. 'Calneh' is not mentioned elsewhere; *all of them* (RSV) is obtained by a simple alteration of the vowels of the Hebrew word. **11** *He went into Assyria* (*cf.* Mi. 5:6); AV translates 'went forth Asshur'. Possibly Nimrod's activity at Babel is that described in 11:2ff.; if so, *cf.* 10:11 and 11:8f. **15–18** The Canaanite peoples anticipate the conquest lists of Israel that document the fulfilment of Noah's curse (*cf.* 9:25). **19** Similarly the delineation of Canaanite territory previews Israel's promised possession. Canaan's curse is also in view in the list of doomed cities of the plain (v. 19b). **10:21–31 Sons of Shem. 21** *Father of all the children of Eber.* Noah associated the covenant line with Shem (9:26). This was realized in Abraham, 'the Hebrew' (*i.e.* Eberite); *cf.* 11:10, 16, 26. The Semites occupied the area between the Japhethites and Hamites around the Arabian subcontinent. **25** *Peleg . . . the earth was divided* (*nip̄l°g̱â*). Does the pun refer to the bifurcating of the Eberites into the chosen line through Peleg (*cf.* 11:17ff.) and the Joktan line (10:26ff.), or was Peleg's family involved in the dispersion from Babel (11:1ff.)? **32** is the colophon for the entire chapter. *On the earth* translates *'ereṣ*, a Hebrew word of variable scope, which here denotes the known world of the nations listed.

11:1–9 Dispersion from Babel

1, 2 *The whole earth.* If *'ereṣ* is used as in 10:32, the linguistic observation applies to a situation not long after the Flood and this verse bridges a lengthy interval. If *'ereṣ* refers to *the land* (*'ereṣ*) *of Shinar* the perspective of v. 1 is not universal; *cf.* v. 9. In either case, the migrating group of vv. 2ff. is only a part of mankind. Their pre-Babel migration belonged to the process of dispersion from Ararat already under way (*cf.* Gn. 10) and their own further dispersion from Babel (vv. 8f.) is recorded as a special judgment on their blatant embodiment of the ungodly spirit that again after the Flood characterized human civilization. **4** The *city* once more (*cf.* Gn. 4) becomes the cultural focus of mounting human arrogance. *Tower* (*miḡdōl*) could be a fortress; Dt. 1:28 and 9:1 speak of cities fortified up to heaven. Parallels to the account of the building of Babylon and its temple-tower (*cf.* the Babylonian epic *Enuma Elish*) suggest the *miḡdōl* was a prototype ziggurat or temple-mound, first found in classical form early in the third millennium BC. On the lust for *a name*, *cf.* 4:17, 22ff.; 6:4; 10:9. **5** *The Lord came down to see.* As in Ps. 2 God laughs at the counsel of kings, so here He ridicules and humbles the vanity of the tower-builders, for He must descend (so the anthropomorphism) to catch sight of their proud pinnacle far below. **7** *Let us go down*; *cf.* 1:27; 3:22; 18:2, 21; 19:1. *Confuse their language.* The confusion possibly resulted from a protracted natural process, but probably a supernatural intervention is intended, a strange miracle of confusion to be answered at Pentecost by another divine descent and a miracle of linguistic fusion. The text does not attribute all language differentiation to this event, nor even claim it as the first instance of such after the Flood, nor deny linguistic variations before the Flood. **8** *Scattered them.* What the Babelites thought to avert befell them more disruptively than was elsewhere transpiring naturally. **9** *Babel, because there the Lord confused* (*bālal*). Whatever its original meaning, the name meant 'gate-of-god', according to popular etymology in the Sumerian and Babylonian renderings. The satirical polemic of the Mosaic narrative appears in this Babel-*bālal* pun. Viewed through this interpretative episode, the dispersion movement of Gn. 10 appears as a curse, a centrifugal force separating men and retarding the subjugation of the earth (*cf.* v. 6b). Yet in sin's context this curse proved a blessing for it also retarded the ripening iniquity that accompanied civilization's progress (v. 6) and so it forestalled such judgment as would have interfered with the unfolding of redemption.

11:10-26 THE GENERATIONS OF SHEM

The era from the Flood to the age of Abraham surveyed in the preceding section is here re-capitulated, the topic now being the lineal relation of Shem to Abraham. This was par-tially given in 10:21-25, but here the whole interval is spanned and the fuller genealogical pattern used for the covenant line in 5:1ff., with its additional statistics from the family register, is followed. Omitted, however, are the closing total of each individual's years and the state-ment of death. The evidence of cultural se-quences in the empire centres and elsewhere for thousands of years before Abraham shows that this genealogy, if interpreted as complete, would be too brief for the over-all period of time involved, and so confirms the selective interpretation. Certainly also we ought not to suppose (as would be necessary if the list were complete) that Noah was alive in Abraham's day and that Shem and most of the others listed were alive at Abraham's call. Would Joshua then have been justified in describing Israel's fathers of Abraham's generation solely in terms of Terah's idolatry (Jos. 24:2)? Also problematic for that interpretation would be the progressive reduction of the life span from 600 years to some 200 years in the course of what would be ten contemporary generations within some 300 years. See comments on 5:1ff. for the significance of the symmetrical literary pattern. To obtain a total of ten names in 11:10ff., the name Cainan, found in LXX and Luke's genealogy (Lk. 3:36), must be included after Arpachshad. Gn. 11 affords no basis for dating the Flood, even to the nearest thousand years.

10 *A hundred years old . . . two years after the flood.* Consistency with the data in 5:32 and 7:11 is demonstrable given various combinations of the following possibilities: Shem was born (or even begotten) at the end of Noah's 500th year; the *mabbûl* (*flood*) is meant in its proper sense of the first forty days; the begetting of Arpachshad was in the second year (not neces-sarily at its close) after the *mabbûl*. Some of the names in this genealogy are attested in extra-biblical sources, all pre-Mosaic. It was not uncommon for the names of persons and places to be the same. The names of the follow-ing ancestors of Abraham have been found as place-names in NW Mesopotamia: **18** *Peleg*; **22** *Serug*; **24** *Nahor* (*cf.* v. 26); **26** *Terah*. The place-name Haran (v. 31; Assyr. *ḥarrānu*, 'main road') is not identical with that of Abram's brother *Haran* in v. 26. Evidently the home-land of the Eberites of Peleg's line was in the north.

11:27 – 25:11 THE GENERATIONS OF TERAH

Man's kingship under God had found expres-sion in Noah's kingdom in the ark. Now the kingdom of God is given to Abram to be possessed in God's promises, by faith. The heavenly kingdom was to appear first in pre-Messianic typical form, then in the correspond-ing reality of Messianic fulfilment. The Abra-hamic narrative is concerned throughout with the themes of the kingdom inheritance and the king-dom heir, with emphasis on the former in 11:27 – 15:21 and the latter from ch. 16 on-wards. The appearance of Terah's (not Abram's) name in the 11:27a heading accords with the Genesis framework's concern with the gene-alogical origins of the twelve tribes of Israel, for they stemmed from Terah not only through Abram but through Sarai (20:12) and through Rebekah, Leah, and Rachel of the lineage of Nahor, son of Terah.

11:27 – 15:21 Abram's kingdom inheritance

11:27-32 Terah's migration. 28 *Ur of the Chaldeans.* The usual identification with Baby-lonian Ur is questioned since lower Mesopo-tamia was not called after the Chaldeans until a thousand years after Abraham. The evidence of personal and place-names (*cf.* 11:18ff.) and of social–legal traditions indicates ancestral associations with the north. Gn. 24:1-10 and Jos. 24:2 seem to assign a northern homeland to the Terahites. Hence the old identification of Ur with a northern site has been renewed, with appeal to the ancient 'Haldai' designation of that area to explain 'of the Chaldeans'. From such a location, but not from southern Ur, *Haran* would fall on the route to Canaan (*cf.* v. 31). **30** *Sarai was barren.* The theme of the heir is anticipated from the outset. **31** *Together*, Hebrew *'ittam*, which AV translates 'with them', could also be 'from them', *i.e.* from Nahor's family (*cf.* v. 29).

12:1-9 Abram's summons to Canaan. Judging from Stephen's interpretation (Acts 7:2ff.; *cf.* Gn. 15:7; Ne. 9:7), Abram received God's call while still in Ur. The arrangement at 12:1 is then determined by the topic and not by chrono-logy. Stephen also placed Abram's departure from Haran (v. 4) after Terah's death (11:32). In view of the age data in 11:26, 32 and 12:4, that would mean Abram was born when Terah was 130 and the reason Abram's name is listed first in 11:26 and 27 is not Abram's primogeniture but his importance. The Samaritan Pentateuch obviates this last problem by assigning 145 years to Terah, not 205.

1 *The Lord said.* The Abrahamic covenant was initiated by the word of God—imperative and promissory. It was a suzerainty covenant, establishing the Abrahamic community as a divine protectorate, with both stipulations and guarantees. *Go from your country.* Idolatrous allegiances of the Terahite household (*cf.* Jos.

24:2) must be forsaken and commitment given to the lordship of Yahweh. 2 *A great nation*; *gôy* ('nation') involves territory and people. Abram's faith perceived in this promise the city of God belonging to a better, heavenly country (*cf.* Heb. 11:10ff., 16), a heavenly Jerusalem that is the common destiny of all the woman's chosen seed from Abel to history's last witness to Jesus (*cf.* Heb. 11:4ff., 39f.; 12:22), the city-kingdom of which the Israelite kingdom in Canaan was a provisional foretaste until the Messianic age had come. For *you will be a blessing* read as in RV, 'be thou . . .'. It is a creative benediction, or fiat. The Abrahamic kingdom was a reinstituting of the creation kingdom (*cf.* 35:11), now to be attained through a redemptive process. 3 *By you all the families of the earth will bless themselves.* The NT's interpretative quotation of this, following LXX, indicates that the nations are actually blessed through the Abrahamic covenant (see Acts 3:25; Gal. 3:8). A reflexive translation in this verse is consistent with that, for those who bless themselves by Abram show they are prepared to relate to him in a brotherly fellowship of blessing, and God here promises that such will actually be blessed. The blessing is mediated through Abram and his seed (*cf.* 22:18; 26:4; 28:14), yet is God's blessing. These two aspects meet in the identification of the mediator-seed as Christ (*cf.* Gal. 3:16). *Him who curses you I will curse.* In God's becoming Abram's covenant Lord, the Noahic benediction on Shem was being fulfilled—with its corollary curse on Canaan (*cf.* 9:26).

4 *So Abram went.* Not all that is narrated of Abram's conduct is commendable, but there is a series of exemplary acts of obedience in faith that secured for him the title 'friend of God', *i.e.* one who manifests loyalty to God (*cf.* 2 Ch. 20:7; Is. 41:8; Jas. 2:23). *Lot went with him.* Lot's prominence may be due to the possibility he offered Abram of an heir. The common practice of adoption would readily suggest itself to Abram under the circumstances of Haran and Terah's deaths and Sarai's barrenness (*cf.* 11:28-30). 5 *Canaan.* Though not specifying Canaan as the promised land, God's summons (vv. 1ff.; *cf.* Heb. 11:8) evidently pointed Abram in that direction. 6 *Canaanites were in the land* (*cf.* 13:7). This statement, immediately preceding the designation of Canaan as God's territorial grant to Abram's descendants (v. 7), contrasts the actual situation to the ideal in the promise. 7, 8 *An altar to the Lord.* This altar, built at the site of Yahweh's theophany, expressed Abram's faith that this land was Yahweh's to give. So, too, a second altar was erected further south in the very shadow of Canaanite cities behind and before. 8b *Cf.* 4:26. 9 *Journeyed on.* Such was to be the pilgrim character of the patriarchs' lives in Canaan (*cf.* Heb. 11:9ff.). *Negeb*, literally 'dry', is the indefinite area of the highlands in the south. Archaeological evidence of settlements in the Negeb between the 21st and 19th centuries BC supports biblical chronological data placing the patriarchs' residence there in that same period.

12:10-20 Egyptian sojourn. 10 *Down to Egypt.* Reports of Egyptian border officials show that it had long been customary to grant refuge to Asiatics who came seeking relief from famine (*cf.* 26:1ff.; 43:1ff.). 13 The stratagem of passing off Sarai as *my sister* had been agreed upon when they left Terah's house (*cf.* 20:13). It involved a half-truth, for Sarai was Terah's daughter, though not by Abram's mother (*cf.* 20:12). Possibly there was a further element of truth in the deception. From the area of Abram's origins comes evidence of the legal institution of 'sistership', a status that could be secured by a wife. It afforded special privilege and would constitute superior credentials, as in a foreign court. In a fratriarchal society (*cf.* 24:29 and the prominence of Laban, Rebekah's brother), a woman given in marriage by a brother enjoyed a dual wife-sister status. The stratagem as employed by Abram (and later Isaac) was intended primarily to hide his identity as husband; but the sister status (if such it was) would have meant additional advantages. The patriarch's weakness gave occasion for a manifestation of the Lord's faithfulness as covenant-Protector, cursing those who were inimical to the fulfilment of the covenant-programme and preserving the appointed ancestress of Israel to bear the heir of promise (vv. 17ff.). 16 *He dealt well with Abram.* God's prospering of Abram out of Pharaoh's wealth did not mean approval of his subterfuge; it was a matter of grace. The inclusion of camels among Abram's expanding possessions is not anachronistic. There is clear evidence of domestication of the camel at the beginning of the 2nd millennium BC, even though their common use in caravans dates considerably later. 17 *Great plagues.* The whole pattern of Abraham's experience in Egypt forms a remarkable parallel to Israel's sojourn there.

13:1-18 Territorial grants and claims. 1 Though not mentioned in 12:10-20, Lot had been in Egypt, benefiting from Abram's favoured status (v. 5) and acquiring a taste for luxuriant valleys (*cf.* v. 10, 'like the land of Egypt'). 2 *Very rich . . . in silver, and in gold.* Even before Abram journeyed to Canaan his company and possessions had become substantial at Haran (*cf.* 12:5). The Terahites were perhaps merchants engaged in caravan trade. Was that the purpose of Terah's journeying from Ur and was it the business opportunities found at Haran, the caravan city, that curtailed the journey to Canaan? Abram may well have been trading along the known donkey-caravan routes of the Negeb during his years there. *Cf.* 20:1; 34:10; 42:34. His flocks and herds would be natural adjuncts of his commerce and the military contingent in his company (*cf.* 14:14) would be protection for his caravans. The patriarchs were certainly not desert nomads. The ass was their regular beast of burden. Their home stations were near urban centres but in the more sparsely populated hill country. They were resident aliens in their associations with cities. Isaac's agricultural enterprise (26:12) may represent a transition to a more settled state, but the generally transient mode of life accentuated their pilgrim-stranger position in the land.

5-7 *Could not support both.* Even his wealth tried Abram's faith by reminding him how limited was his liberty in the promised land; *cf.* v. 7b. **8-13** Yet within the scope of his prerogatives Abram displayed the generosity of faith. The way chosen by Lot betrayed impatience to secure the promised bounty of the land (v. 10) without due regard to the covenant's ethical demands (*cf.* v. 13). **14, 15** After Abram's land grant and Lot's claim came Yahweh's grant and Abram's claim. In its definition of the land this revelation was transitional between the vagueness of 12:7 and the precision of 15:17ff. **16** The 'great nation' promise of 12:2 was also elaborated. **17** *Walk through the length and breadth.* Cf. Jos. 24:3. This was probably a symbolic legal rite by which one staked claim to real estate. A walk of faith, indeed! **18** *At Hebron.* Abram settled more permanently here, entering into parity covenants with the local princes (*cf.* 14:13), yet building an altar, his third, in confession of Yahweh as great Overlord of the land and claiming it for Him.

14:1-24 Overlord of Canaan. 1, 2 The precise political situation envisaged in Gn. 14 and the particular kings have not yet been identified. Many of the names, however, are recognized as authentic types for the early second millennium BC. Characteristic of that period, too, were coalitions for political power. The equivalent of the name *Arioch* has been found in the Mari and Nuzi documents. *Chedorlaomer* consists of two elements in a typical Elamite name pattern and means 'servant of (the goddess) Lakamar'. *Tidal* corresponds to Tudhalia, a Hittite royal name. The once-favoured identification of *Amraphel* with Hammurabi is now known to be impossible on linguistic grounds, as well as on the ground that the famous Babylonian king lived centuries after Abram. *Shinar* stands first, perhaps, to give a Babelite ideological colouring to the enterprise of the four kings (*cf.* 11:2ff.). The identity of *Ellasar* is uncertain. *Goiim* (the Hebrew means 'nations') possibly designates a group of cities in Asia Minor federalized under Tidal. *Elam*, to the SE of Babylonia, dominated the coalition. There was a strong Elamite dynasty about 2000 BC. **3** *Valley of Siddim (that is, the Salt Sea).* In the centuries between Abram and Moses the plain to the S of the Lisan had become a shallow extension of the Dead Sea. **4** *In the thirteenth year.* Chedorlaomer's vassal treaty had been imposed shortly before Abram came to Canaan. **5** *Came and subdued.* Expeditions of comparable distance

are attested for Mesopotamian kings even before 2000 BC. The invasion route followed the King's Highway, a caravan route running from the north southwards to the Gulf of Aqabah (by-passing the cities of the plain), and thence NW through the Negeb, circling back on the Valley of Siddim. The Transjordan area (like the Negeb) had extensive permanent settlements from about the 21st to the 19th centuries BC. This condition then abruptly ceased, but not necessarily as an immediate consequence of Chedorlaomer's invasion.

13 *Abram the Hebrew.* Like the other leaders in this context Abram is ethnically identified. He was a descendant of Eber ('*ibrî*, 'Eberite' or 'Hebrew'). Consistently in the OT the usage of '*ibrî* is ethnic. The question arises whether Eberites appear in literature outside the Bible, and specifically whether the Habiru mentioned in texts from all over the Near East during the 2nd millennium are such. The Habiru were apparently professional militarists with perhaps an original ethnic unity. Theoretically, the originally ethnic term '*ibrî* might have acquired a professional significance in connection with a branch of Eberites who became militarists (*i.e.* the Habiru), while the ethnic meaning was preserved in the OT for the Abrahamites. It would then be plausible to interpret the term in the professional (Habiru) sense even in Gn. 14:13. But the whole theory would require substantiation and the phonetic equation involved is highly problematic. Moreover, the section beginning at Gn. 14:13 finds its climax in a benediction-doxology (vv. 19f.) in series with Noah's (*cf.* 9:26), which suggests that Abram is here called *the Hebrew* to relate the Abrahamic fulfilment of Noah's covenant promise to Shem through the genealogical connection (*cf.* 10:21).

14 *Led forth his trained men,* or 'drew (as a sword) his retainers'. Vassal covenants stipulated that the vassal must dispatch forces to protect the overlord's interests at the report of trouble. Yahweh's peculiar territorial claims were impinged upon by Chedorlaomer's claims on Canaan, and therefore Abram acts. **15** *Routed them.* No supernatural assistance is implied. The total size of the confederate force (*cf.* vv. 13, 24) and other factors are not known. **17, 18** *King's Valley.* The location is uncertain but is conjectured to be near Jerusalem (*cf.* 2 Sa. 18:18). Neither is it altogether certain that the Melchizedek episode transpired here. The verb in v. 18 may be pluperfect 'had brought out'. *Melchizedek.* Cf. Ps. 110:4; Heb. 7:1ff. *Salem* is Jerusalem (*cf.* Ps. 76:2). *God Most High* (Heb. '*ēl 'elyôn*); each word is used for a deity in Canaanite texts, but the One on whom Melchizedek called as '*ēl 'elyôn*, confessing Him the Maker of heaven and earth, was identified by Abram as Yahweh, the Creator. It thus appears that during Abram's sojourning in Canaan a settled community of true faith existed under the priesthood of the king of Salem. Melchizedek was greater than Abram, but the Messianic seed of Abram would be a greater than Melchizedek.

19, 20 *Blessed be Abram . . . enemies into your hand.* The blessing of the elect again has as its corollary the cursing of those who would curse them (*cf.* 9:26; 12:2f.). *A tenth.* By this tribute payment Abram testified that, whatever authorities exercised control over Canaan, Yahweh was Overlord over all. **21-24** His oath was probably sworn before Melchizedek. Vassals were customarily allowed to retain the spoil of battles fought for their suzerains, but it was the latter's prerogative to stipulate this in their treaties. The king of Sodom apparently sought to assume that role but Abram rejected the relationship. Vassal treaties prohibited subordination to any other royal benefactors. Rejection of the king of Sodom's proposal was the consistent negative counterpart to Abram's positive oath of allegiance to Yahweh as his covenant Lord.

15:1-21   Yahweh's   covenant   oath. The covenant was ratified first by divine oath (Gn. 15), and afterwards by human oath (Gn. 17). The vassal-oath was characteristic at this time of extra-biblical covenants, but on occasion suzerains would also commit themselves by oath, particularly in connection with land grants (*cf.* vv. 18ff.).

1 *In a vision.* If this 'vision' covers the entire chapter, it apparently included a variety of psychological states from sleep-like trance (vv. 12ff.) to a waking state with supersensory awareness (vv. 5, 10f., 17; *cf.* 2 Ki. 6:17). If the narrative is arranged chronologically, a period of daylight (or a longer period) intervenes between vv. 5 and 12. If it is arranged topically, a plausible reconstruction would involve the following: v. 7 describes the episode's beginning; vv. 1b–4 belong to the trance of vv. 12ff. (note the appropriateness of God's *fear not* (v. 1) to Abram's dread (v. 12)); the waking experience of vv. 5f. belongs with that of vv. 17ff. *Shield* (Heb. *māg̱ēn*); *cf.* Pss. 3:3; 28:7; 33:20. If, by altering the vowels, this word were read as *mōg̱ēn*, the translation would be 'I am giving your reward'. **2–5** *What wilt thou give me?* Fulfilment of the kingdom promise depended on Abram having a dynasty to inherit it. **2b** contains an obscure pun on 'Damascus' but **3** clarifies Abram's plaint. He had followed the Mesopotamian custom, well attested between 2000 and 1500 BC, whereby childless couples adopted an heir (in some cases a former slave). Adoption contracts stipulated that a natural son subsequently born would replace the adopted son as chief heir. That is the legal context of God's reassurance. **6** AV reads, 'he believed in the Lord'. The verb *'āman* here expresses trust in God and therefore confident assent to His revelation of supernatural saving grace. This statement may refer to an actual 'Amen' spoken by Abram, for so vassals responded in covenant ceremonies to the proclamation of the associated rewards and penalties (*cf.* Dt. 27:15–26). **6b** *Cf.* Rom. 4:3, 17ff.; Gal. 3:6ff.

The subject of the heir (vv. 1–6) is treated in subordination to the kingdom promise prominent in the verses that follow. **7** *I am the Lord who brought you from Ur.* This self-identification and reference to God's redemptive initiative corresponds to the standard opening sections of classic treaties, the preamble in which the royal covenant-maker proclaimed his style and title, followed by the historical prologue in which he recounted his mighty acts (*cf.* Ex. 20:2). **10** *Cut them in two.* The oath ritual for which Abram prepared was customary in treaty ratifications. From it derived various idioms for making a covenant, like the Hebrew 'cut a covenant' (so v. 18, lit.). The curse conditionally invoked in the oath was symbolized by this slaying and sundering of animals, signifying 'so may it be done to him who breaks this covenant' (*cf.* 1 Sa. 11:7). **11** The *birds of prey* portrayed the final act in the curse symbolism; *cf.* Je. 34:17–20. **12** *A deep sleep*; *cf.* 2:21. *Great darkness.* In this dread setting came the forewarning of Egyptian bondage.

The length of the sojourn in Egypt is stated in a round number (with v. 13 *cf.* Ex. 12:40) and as four 'generations', or better, 'lifetimes' (v. 16), calculated at about a century each (less than the patriarchs' own life spans). V. 15 shows that these four centuries did not include the 215 years spent by Abram, Isaac, and Jacob in Canaan, for the sojourn was to be experienced by Abram's descendants after his own death. **14** *I will bring judgment.* Long postponement would terminate in fulfilment of God's kingdom promises (*cf.* 12:3) at the provisional OT level through mighty acts of redemptive judgment (*cf.* Acts 7:17). The blessing of the Abrahamites would be accomplished through the cursing of the Egyptians and Amorites who cursed them (*cf.* 12:3). **16** *The iniquity of the Amorites*; *cf.* Lv. 18:24ff.; 20:22ff.; 1 Ki. 14:24. God's times (*cf.* Dn. 2:21) are not arbitrary, nor is His forbearance for ever (*cf.* 2 Pet. 3:9f.). **17** *Smoking fire pot and a flaming torch.* The theophany utilizes, as often elsewhere, the elements of fire and smoke to indicate God's presence; *cf.* especially Ex. 3:2ff.; 13:21f.; 19:18. By passing alone between the pieces God swore fidelity to His covenant promises, and took upon Himself all the curses symbolized by the carcasses. **18** *The Lord made a covenant*— such was the meaning of the strange ritual. *From the river of Egypt to the great river. Cf.* 1 Ki. 4:21. Several non-biblical treaties have geographical sections like this, listing the cities and defining the boundaries confirmed to the vassal. The land belongs to Abram's seed only within the terms of the covenant and thus only in *the* seed of Abram, Christ, in whom the land-promise is transfigured into its cosmic antitype (*cf.* Rom. 4:13) and the heirs of Abraham become the universal covenant community of the NT, there being neither Jew nor Greek in Christ.

16:1 – 22:19 Abraham's dynastic heir

16:1-15 Ishmael, son of the bondwoman. 1 The theme of the heir is reintroduced from the aspect of the natural obstacles challenging faith (*cf.* 11:30). In the ten years since the departure from Haran (see v. 16; *cf.* 12:4) the promise had been reiterated, but Sarai continued barren and alternate hopes focusing on Lot and Eliezer had been frustrated. **2** Sarai's suggestion that Abram take Hagar as a concubine was in keeping with the practice of that day as attested in legal code and marriage contract. The latter sometimes stipulated that a barren wife must acquire a slave-woman for her husband. Sometimes a wife received a personal maid as a marriage gift (*cf.* 29:29; 30:3); all legal rights over this maid's child belonged to the wife. **4** Laws governing this type of arrangement provided for precisely the contingency described in this verse by permitting the wife to reduce the maid to her former status but prohibiting her sale. **5** 'My injustice upon you' is the literal translation of the Hebrew. Sarai appealed to Abram to enforce her legal rights. It was his responsibility to redress the wrong that was 'upon' him. **6** Hagar wins our sympathy but she was legally in the wrong.

7 *Angel of the Lord. Cf.* 21:17ff.; 22:11, 15; 24:7, 40; 31:11ff.; 48:16. Not form but function was primary in this mode of revelation, the theophany being usually of human appearance, but not always so (*cf., e.g.,* Ex. 3:2). As the term *mal'ak*, 'messenger', itself suggests, the distinctive idea is that of being sent on a mission. This angel is sent by the Lord and even prays to the Lord (*cf.* Zc. 1:12f.), yet speaks as God and is otherwise identified as the Lord. Thereby intimations were afforded of personal distinctions within God, and, in particular, of the coming of the Son as One sent of the Father to fulfil the covenant (*cf.* Mal. 3:1). (See further the section on 'Theophany' in the Introduction to Exodus, p. 116—Ed.) *Shur* was perhaps the Egyptian frontier wall; in any case, Hagar fled towards her homeland (*cf.* 12:15f.). **8** *Cf.* 3:9; 4:9. **10** *Cf.* 13:16; 15:5. The universal blessing to come through Abram, though primarily redemptive, involved also the benefits of God's common grace, universally bestowed. Hagar's innumerable descendants (*cf.* 25:12ff.) would live in the guarantees of the post-diluvian covenant (*cf.* 8:20ff.) but not in the eternal order pledged to Abram's promised seed (*cf.* 17:18ff.). **11** Such annunciations are common in Canaanite epics of the 2nd millennium BC. *Ishmael* means 'God hears', *i.e.* He had heard the fugitive's cry. **12** The *wild ass*, a favourite creature in desert hunts, illustrated the proud nomad independence of the Ishmaelites. **13** The RSV rendering of Hagar's explanation of the name *God of seeing* is excessively free, but it is probably correct in centring the idea not on God's seeing her but her seeing God, and that without fatal consequence. **14** In line with this, *Beer-lahai-roi* would mean 'well of seeing-alive'. **15** *Hagar bore Abram a son.* On this son Abram's hope would now naturally be set, but this last resort to natural means to bring God's promise to pass will end in disappointment. In this matter of the crucial first heir, the redemptive covenant must be seen as realizable only through the supernaturalism of divine intervention.

17:1 – 18:15 Covenant ratification. 17:1 *Ninety-nine*; *cf.* 16:16; 17:17, 25. The thought of an heir by Sarai was now a laughing matter (*cf.* 17:17; 18:12). *The Lord appeared*; *cf.* v. 22; 12:7; 18:1. *I am God Almighty.* Suzerainty treaties thus began with the titles of the great king (*cf.* 15:7). The etymology of *šadday* is still uncertain but 'Almighty' conveys its evident sense; *cf.* 28:3; 35:11; 43:14; 48:3; Ex. 6:3; Ezk. 10:5. *Be blameless; i.e.* genuinely and unreservedly committed to God's service (*cf.* 6:9). **5** *Abraham*, a lengthened form of Abram ('the father is exalted'), is explained, by a sound-play, as *father of a multitude* (Heb. *ab-ḥamôn*) *of nations*. The name's prophetic meaning should not be sought in the Abrahamic nations like the Ishmaelites and Edomites, for the same promise is made to Sarai (v. 16), but rather in the hosts of all nations who become Abraham's children by sharing his covenant faith (*cf.* Gal. 3:29). **6** *Kings.* The promised line was royal. From it, as to the flesh, came Christ, following His OT precursors, the kings of Israel. **7** *An everlasting covenant.* The covenant had a provisional phase, but in Abraham's Messianic seed (*cf.* Gal. 3:16) and His kingdom it stands for ever. **8** *I will be their God.* Yahweh creates a people and identifies Himself with them as their Lord.

9 *You shall keep my covenant.* The covenant is law as well as gospel (*cf.* 12:1; 17:1; 22:2). **10** *Circumcised.* The practice of circumcision found earlier among other peoples was adopted to serve as the sign of incorporation into the Abrahamic covenant. Its continuing significance is learned from the function it performed at its institution. Covenants were ratified by oaths, the oath-curses being dramatized in symbolic rites (*cf.* 15:9ff.). A characteristic curse was that of cutting off the vassal to destruction and cutting off his name and seed. Accompanying this was a knife rite. So circumcision was the knife rite by which the Abrahamic covenant was cut. **14** shows that it symbolized the curse of excision from the covenant community. More precisely, the circumcision of the male organ of generation symbolized the cutting off of descendants. Yet as the sign of an oath acknowledging God's lordship, circumcision also signified consecration (*cf.* Rom. 4:11). Ancient vassal covenants included with the vassal king his kingdom and descendants. Similarly, the Lord administered His covenant to Abraham not simply as an individual believer-confessor but as the head of a community, in this case a family household, including children and slaves (vv. 12f., 23ff.), and that through ongoing generations (vv. 9, 12).

15 *Sarah* is a variant of Sarai, 'princess', but strangely the meaning of the change is not intimated. Curiously, however, the names of both Abram and Sarai are changed by adding the same sound, 'ah-ah', as though God were laughing with the parents-to-be! Combining a pun with His promise He put laughter into their very names: the union of aged Abraham and Sarah will produce Laughter-Isaac (lit. 'he laughs'). **17** *Then Abraham . . . laughed.* The humour of it all did not escape him but, as his next request showed, his laughing was not yet in the free abandon of full faith. **18** *That Ishmael might live.* In covenantal terminology, the aspirant to a vassal throne was made to 'live' if the great king established him on the throne, particularly when he had been 'killed', *i.e.* rejected in his claims by rivals. Abram, staggered by God's great joke, would settle for Ishmael as the kingdom heir. **20** *Father of twelve princes.* God *heard* Abraham. Ishmael would receive dynastic status as patriarch over an amphictyonic league, though not over the twelve-tribe kingdom of God. **21** *My covenant with Isaac.* Legally, a natural son, even though born after the son of a slave-wife, became chief heir.

As to occasion, 18:1–15 is connected with 18:16ff. but in theme it is related to ch. 17. The promise of the heir is confirmed in the form found there (*cf.* 17:21 and 18:10, 14); the covenant ceremonies are evidently supplemented; and the laughter motif is continued and culminated in a remarkable word of God (18:14). **18:1** The Lord's new appearance was soon after the last. The approaching supernatural birth was heralded by repeated angelic visitations. *Mamre*; *cf.* 13:18; 14:13. **2** The expression *behold, three men* suggests sudden appearance. One of the three was the angel of the Lord (*cf.* vv. 13, 17; 16:7ff.). **3** Read as in AV, 'My Lord'. The Hebrew *'aḏōnāy*, reserved for reference to the divine Lord, is rejected by RSV in favour of *'aḏōnî*, a general polite form of address. But Abraham might be expected to recognize the angel of the Lord after only a brief interval. Does not such recognition explain his addressing this angel? Also the mention of Yahweh in v. 13 were otherwise too abrupt. **5–8** The meal may well have been the confirmation of the covenant relationship (*cf.* Ex. 24:9–11). Appropriately, then, it is followed by the word of confirmation.

10 *At the tent door behind him.* The Hebrew may also be translated: 'And she was behind it (*i.e.* the door)'. **12** In either case Sarah's thoughts were secret and her laughter (again the effect of the impossible annunciation) concealed within herself. As Jesus' disclosure of Nathanael's private doubts was evidence of greater things to be performed by Him, the Mediator of angelic visitation (Jn. 1:45–51), so Yahweh's manifestation of divine knowledge in the

exposure of Sarah's inner incredulity was a sign that He who came with angel ministrants would perform the greater miracle of bringing life from Sarah's dead womb. **14** *Is anything too hard for the Lord?* His infinite wisdom makes the laughable believable. **15** On Sarah's faith in spite of this fearfully foolish reaction, see Heb. 11:11.

18:16 – 19:38 Lot's separated line. 18:16 A second stage of the heavenly mission (*cf.* 18:1ff.) began with the departure of Yahweh's two angel servants (recapitulated in v. 22), or better, with God's consultation with them (vv. 17–19) and His declaration to Abraham (vv. 20f.). **17** *Shall I hide from Abraham.* As God's friend (*cf.* on 12:4) Abraham might hear the secret counsel of His covenant (*cf.* Ps. 25:14). **19** *Bring . . . what he has promised him.* Abraham was singled out not that the Abrahamites should for ever enjoy greatness as an élite religious enclave, but that they might be the instrument for universalizing the fear of Yahweh with its attendant blessings (*cf.* v. 18b; 12:3b). *Righteousness and justice* as well as power and blessing characterize God's kingdom. **20, 21** The slight variation between *zeʿāqâ* and *ṣeʿāqâ*, both translated *outcry*, is brought out by the difference between 'outrage' and 'outcry'. The outcry is either the offence clamouring for punishment (*cf.* 4:10) or the plea of the oppressed seeking judicial protection. The legal proceedings began with a special investigation (*cf.* 11:7). The facts were fully known to the Judge and His verdict a foreknown conclusion (*cf.* 19:13) but the openness of the situation as described in v. 21 suggests that the Sodomites were receiving a final opportunity to repent. **22ff.** God's tentative statement also created an opportunity for Abraham to engage in intercession.

25 *Shall not the Judge of all the earth do right?* Abraham's long faith-struggle with the disparity between historical reality and God's promises had led him to this solid conviction as a foundation for dealing with the problem of divine providence. Abraham was not pleading for individual rather than corporate judicial treatment in God's government of the world. Rather, he understood God's decree against Sodom as an in-breaking of ultimate covenant judgment (*cf.* Lk. 17:28f.; 2 Pet. 2:6), and such judgment must cut through the ambiguities of general historical associations, so that the community of the righteous is not destroyed with its wicked fellow-citizens. In the case of Sodom, the only way Abraham saw to avoid violating the radical justice required in such judgment was to turn God from His announced purpose. Hence Abraham sought to save Lot (*cf.* 19:29) by pleading that Sodom be spared. God answered that, if necessary, He would withhold His judgment in order to protect a righteous remnant; but the sequel shows it was not necessary. When God deems iniquity ripe for final judgment, He does not spare; but He does deliver His covenant people out of the judgment, whether they be fifty or ten or a smaller family (like Noah's or Lot's).

19:1 *In the evening.* Yahweh's messengers appeared at Sodom miraculously soon (*cf.* 18:22), commissioned to gather in the elect before the descent of doom (*cf.* Mt. 24:31; Mk. 13:27). **2,3** Lot, though lacking in Abraham's spiritual strength, was a righteous man, at odds with his ungodly environment (*cf.* 2 Pet. 2:7f.). On v. 2b, *cf.* Lk. 24:28f. **4** Outside Lot's family there was not one righteous in any quarter of the city; it was worse than Abraham had dared to suggest (*cf.* 18:32). **5** *That we may know them*; *cf.* Jdg. 19:22; Rom. 1:27. **8** The warp given to Lot's spiritual and moral perspective by his unhappy choice of Sodom had distorted his judgment, producing vacillation and shockingly confused compromise. **9** The Sodomites' perverse violence confirmed the 'outcry against Sodom' (18:20). **11** *Blindness* (*cf.* 2 Ki. 6:18) was not so much loss of sight as a sudden striking of the tormentors with a severe disorientation that frustrated their purpose. **12** *Have you any one else here?* The offer of deliverance in terms of family relatedness to Lot is the same as in the case of Noah at the Flood. **13** *Cf.* 18:21. **14** *Who were to marry his daughters.* The language also allows that the marriages had already taken place and that Lot, therefore, had daughters living with their husbands in addition to the two daughters with him. *Jesting.* Again we have the word *ṣāḥaq* and the idea of laughable divine announcements. *Cf.* Lk. 17:28f. **16** *The Lord being merciful.* The remnant's imperfections did not thwart the purpose of grace. **22, 23** *Zoar.* The name (*ṣô'ar*) is related to Lot's designation of it as a trifle (*miṣ'ar*). This city was evidently located to the S of the area destroyed. All these cities were situated in what is now the shallow southern extension of the Dead Sea. **24** *Brimstone and fire.* Deposits of sulphur (brimstone) and asphalt (*cf.* 'bitumen pits', 14:10) are found in the coastal area of the Dead Sea. It has been speculated that the ignition of natural gases by lightning, possibly in association with an earthquake disturbance in this rift valley, started the conflagration with its rain of sulphurous fire and the pall of asphalt smoke (v. 28). The destruction would nevertheless be supernatural, for the timing and extent of the fiery havoc were precisely ordered to fulfil the announced word of God and the discriminatory purpose of His judgment. **25** *All the valley* (*cf.* vv. 28f.). Admah and Zeboiim, as well as Sodom and Gomorrah, were overthrown (Dt. 29:23; Je. 49:18; 50:40; Ho. 11:8; *cf.* Is. 1:9f.; 13:19; Ezk. 16:46ff.). **26** *A pillar of salt*; *cf.* Lk. 17:32. The salt mass known as Gebel Usdum on the SW shore of the Dead Sea attests to the presence of the agent of encrustation. Archaeological light on the episode is afforded by the site Bab ed-Dra a few miles E of the plain cities and evidently a place of pilgrimage for their citizenry. Use of this site ceased in the 21st century BC. **28** *Cf.* 13:10.

29 *Cf.* 2 Pet. 2:9 and comments on 18:23ff. As warrior-prince Abraham had saved Lot earlier (Gn. 14); now he does so as prophetic covenant-mediator (*cf.* 8:1; 20:7). **30** Fear (perhaps of future seismic episodes) drove Lot into the mountain caves. **31–38** trace the separated line of Lot through his two Sodom-tainted daughters to the Moabites and Ammonites, who increasingly became objects of denunciation by Israel's prophets. Separation from Abraham was separation from the future of the covenant kingdom.

20:1–18 Protection of the royal family. The charming divine comedy of Isaac's birth links the laughter of the annunciation (Gn. 17ff.) with the joy of fulfilment (21:1ff.) by a smiling disclosure of Sarah's rejuvenation (the prelude to her conception of Isaac), intimated through the ludicrous episode of Abimelech's passion to include the ninety-year old damsel in his harem and sagacious old Abraham's bemused floundering in difficulties supposedly left behind in long-departed youth (vv. 5, 11ff.).

1 *From there*; *cf.* 18:1, 33. Some interpret *between Kadesh and Shur* as the caravan route Abraham plied as a merchant while his alien residency was in Gerar. **2** *My sister. Cf.* on 12:13ff. *Abimelech.* This Gerar dynasty was Philistine (*cf.* 21:32, 34; 26:1). The Philistines of the patriarchal age had settled into a Semitic way of life. Their relationship to the patriarchs in political covenant (21:22ff.; 26:26ff.) contrasts with the Israelite–Philistine hostility in the period of the judges. *Cf.* 10:13f.; Am. 9:7. Abimelech was apparently a worshipper of the true God (*cf.* vv. 3ff.). **3** *A dead man. Cf.* Is. 38:1. Abimelech, as well as his wife and harem, was victim of the sudden affliction (*cf.* vv. 7, 17). **4, 5** *An innocent people.* Abimelech raised a question similar to Abraham's (*cf.* 18: 23ff.), but in self-defence. He could plead an innocence of ignorance as to Sarah's married status, but he was nevertheless guiltily responsible for abuse of the marriage ordinance through his harem (*cf.* 4:19ff.; 6:1ff.). **6b, 7** See Ps. 105:15. *A prophet.* As mediator of God's covenant, Abraham received and communicated God's will and in this relationship had peculiar access for intercession (*cf.* Jb. 42:8). *You shall surely die*; *cf.* 2:17; 3:4. Abimelech's act threatened Abraham's promised dynasty and God's threat to Abimelech extended to his dynastic family (*cf.* on 17:18; Ps. 105:13f.). **9–13** Abraham's embarrassment before Abimelech and a certain similarity discernible between his treatment of Sarah and Lot's offer of his daughters remind us that the divine favour on Abraham too was of grace. **16** *Vindication*; lit. 'covering of eyes', *i.e.* a means of diverting attention from an offence. By his lavish gifts Abimelech would have Sarah forget her experience in his court. If v. 16d explains v. 16c, the point is that, in spite of indignity suffered, Sarah's honour was by the royal gift restored in the eyes of others.

21:1–34 Isaac, heir of the covenant. 1 *Cf.*

98

17:21; 18:10, 14. **3** *Cf.* 17:19. **4** By circumcising Isaac, Abraham consecrated to Yahweh the people of promise. **5** *Cf.* 17:17. **6, 7** *God has made laughter*. Sarah voiced her magnificat (*cf.* Ps. 113:9). She repeated the pun on 'Isaac' (*cf.* 17:17-19), mindful of the astounded laughter others would add to that of the parents. She anticipated that this congratulatory laughter would also be derisive, with herself the butt of the joke (*cf.* Ezk. 23:32). **8** The weaning feast would be in Isaac's second or third year. **9** Follow AV. The word *ṣāḥaq*, 'mocking', is used again with the overtones of vv. 6b, 7. Ishmael was making a laughing-stock of the royal family on the occasion that highlighted the absurdity Sarah had herself described (*cf.* v. 7). Paul interpreted this as a persecution of the son of promise (Gal. 4:28f.).

10 On Hagar's household status, see on 16:2ff. According to the law codes, Ishmael was entitled to an inheritance share, but Sarah was determined that Isaac should be sole heir. That could be legally achieved, for there was legal tradition stipulating that a son by a slave woman could forgo his inheritance claim in exchange for freedom. *Cast out*. Sarah would compel them to go free! **11-13** Abraham, though reluctant because of natural affection for Ishmael (*cf.* 17:18), acceded when so instructed by the Lord. **14-16** *The child*. Ishmael at his expulsion was about sixteen (*cf.* 16:16; 21:5). Hagar evidently sought for a while to support the fainting youth but his weight proved too much and she was forced to free herself. **17-19** *God heard* is a play on 'Ishmael' (*cf.* 16:11). By supernatural intervention Hagar was directed to life-saving water. This forestalled failure of God's promises concerning Ishmael made earlier (see 16:12; 17:20; 21:13). **20, 21** Ishmael's marriage to an Egyptian and his nomad rovings in the Sinai peninsula underscore the separation of the Ishmaelites from the Abrahamic covenant.

22-24 *At that time*. The Beer-sheba covenant is loosely related to the context; possibly it preceded even Isaac's birth. Pursuant to Abimelech's invitation (20:15), Abraham had settled on what was apparently the border of his jurisdiction. Abimelech, politically and militarily superior, was nevertheless impressed by the divine protection under which Abraham operated and proposed the formal establishment of brotherly relationship. *Phicol* is a Semitic name, meaning 'word of all (*i.e.* the gods)'. **25, 26** Abraham saw in Abimelech's friendly overtures an opportunity to broach the subject of a water source he had prepared but which was then, unknown to Abimelech, seized by his servants. **27-31** The parity covenant was ratified as usual by both parties taking the oath. Other regular features were the use of animals for the covenant cutting and the presence of witnesses. God Himself was *the* Witness. As a special witness to Abimelech that he had agreed to the special provision acknowledging Abraham's

right to the well, Abraham gave him seven ewe lambs. **32** The name *Beer-sheba* reflects three features of the covenant. *Be'ēr* means 'well'; *šeba'*, 'seven'; and *nišba'*, 'swear'. **33** The *tamarisk* Abraham planted was probably regarded as another witness. *Everlasting God*. From God's revelation of His covenant as 'everlasting' (17:7f., 13, 19) Abraham learned to worship and trust Him as the immovable foundation of his hope (*cf.* 12:8; 13:4).

22:1-19 Death and resurrection of the heir. 1 *God tested Abraham*. The whole pilgrim way was a continual test, but this was a special test of focal significance (*cf.* v. 12).

2 *Offer him*. Abraham must go beyond circumcision's partial and symbolic cutting off. By an ultimate consecration of Isaac to God in death-judgment he must demonstrate the truth of his oath of allegiance. The demand laid on Isaac's life reaffirmed God's verdict on man as sinner and so proclaimed the need for deliverance; but it also seemed to cut off the possibility of that deliverance. For the death of the divinely designated seed of promise would terminate the programme of salvation and empty the promise of meaning. Abraham's faith overcame the conflict between obedience and hope by accounting Yahweh able to raise up the sacrificed one (*cf.* Heb. 11:17-19). *Moriah; cf.* 2 Ch. 3:1, where it is identified with Solomon's Temple site at Jerusalem. **8** *God will provide* does not imply foreknowledge of the outcome, for then there were no trial of faith. **13** *Behold a ram*. In the combination of God's Self-maledictory oath of Gn. 15 (see on 15:17) and this divinely-provided substitute, the vicarious curse-bearing of God's own unspared Son was prefigured (*cf.* Rom. 8:32). **14** *The Lord will provide* (*yhwh yireh*) refers to the event of v. 13 in the language of v. 8. *It shall be provided*, or '(Yahweh) is seen', *i.e.* Yahweh appears in order to provide. From the perspective of Isaac's succession rights as vassal king under the Suzerain Yahweh, his virtual death and resurrection (*cf.* Heb. 11:19) was a deposition and restoration. Interestingly, the figure of death and resurrection is used in ancient treaties to describe just this sort of thing. See on 17:18. **16** *I have sworn, says the Lord. Cf.* 24:7; Ex. 32:13. The remarkable combination of *says the Lord* (*ne'um yhwh*) with the divine oath reappears in Ps. 110:1 and 4, an oracle that also concerns royal appointment, here of God's Son, through whom the Gn. 22:15-18 oracle is fulfilled. *Because you have done this. Cf.* v. 18. It was not that by his obedience Abraham merited this blessing. God's rewards are as much acts of His grace as is His original choice of the recipients. Yet by virtue of the special guarantees God was pleased to affix to Abraham's supreme triumph of faith, it stood in a causal relation to the fulfilment of the Abrahamic covenant (*cf.* 26:3, 5, 24; Ps. 105:42). We are thus taught that Abraham's seed of Old and New Testaments inherit the world via the righteousness of faith (*cf.* Rom. 4). **17** *Possess the gate of their enemies. Cf.* 14:20.

22:20 – 25:11 Royal succession

22:20–24 Nahor's collateral line. Developments in the family of Abraham's northern kinsmen are presented not in formal genealogy but as news received and acted on (*cf.* 24:4ff.). Terah's son, *Nahor*, had married a daughter of Haran (*cf.* 11:27, 29). His grand-daughter *Rebekah* (*cf.* 24:15) and great grand-daughters Leah and Rachel became ancestral mothers of God's people Israel. Twelve sons of Nahor are mentioned but an amphictyonic league does not seem implied. The omission of Laban (*cf.* 24:29) centres attention on Rebekah and this focus on the Israelite ancestresses continues in Gn. 23 and 24.

23:1–20 Sepulchre for the royal family. 2–4 The reference to *Canaan* prepares for the thought thrust upon Abraham by the exigencies of Sarah's burial—he was still *a sojourner* in the promised land, not lord, not even a small property owner. He might have followed whatever burial procedure was allowed for aliens, but in the face of his family's dying without receiving the promises (Heb. 11:13) he desired to express his faith in their ultimate reception of the inheritance beyond death (*cf.* Heb. 11:19). A family sepulchre would not be a legal claim to the possession of Canaan, but it would be a prophetic sign. His request *give me property* does not mean give without payment. Abraham, though only a resident alien, was requesting the right to acquire property in perpetuity. Similarly, Ephron did not offer a free gift (v. 11). **5** These pre-patriarchal *Hittites*, one of the early complex of peoples in Canaan (*cf.* 10:15; 15:20; Dt. 7:1; Jdg. 3:5), were Semitized. If not related to the earlier Hattian people of Anatolia, these Hittites of S Palestine possibly represented a commercial penetration preceding the broader Hittite movement into Anatolia resulting in their Empire there in the mid-second millennium BC. **6** *A mighty prince* is literally 'a prince of God'. That the Abrahamic community was God's protectorate was commonly known (*cf.* 21:22); moreover, this community was sizeable and its leader very wealthy (*cf.* 24:1, 34). **9** *Cave of Machpelah.* According to provisions found in the Hittite law code and apparently more generally followed, a landholder continued to be responsible for the dues on a recognized unit of property unless he disposed of it in its entirety. Abraham would avoid transfer of these obligations to himself by purchasing only the cave *at the end of his* (Ephron's) *field*, while Ephron insisted on selling the entire unit—field and cave—as the conclusion repeatedly notes (vv. 17, 19, 20; *cf.* 49:29ff.). Thus, in becoming a property owner in Canaan, Abraham had to acknowledge more publicly than ever the currently more ultimate proprietorship over this land enjoyed by the

Canaanite authorities, rendering to them now his land dues.

24:1–67 A queen for Abraham's co-regent. 1 Sarah's death and Abraham's own advanced years (*cf.* 17:17; 23:1; 25:20) suggested the timeliness of a final disposition, securing to Isaac the covenant blessings of land and descendants. **2** *Under my thigh* is an allusion to the genital organ. This oath gesture probably had reference to the malediction symbolized by circumcision. The charge given the servant contains the last recorded words of Abraham; this also points to its testamentary nature. **3** *Not . . . from the daughters of the Canaanites.* The inheritance of Canaan must come to Abraham's descendants, not as a natural development through intermarriage with the Canaanites, but as a supernatural gift through divine judgment on the Canaanites. In fact, intermarriage would frustrate the promised kingdom programme, for the Abrahamites, thus compromised and corrupted, would fall under judgment with the Canaanites. **6–8** *Not take my son back.* God had issued the summons to Canaan and there the covenant patriarchs must exercise their faith-reign unless God Himself ordained otherwise. Scripture's last quotation of Abraham is fittingly a word of faith in the Lord's faithfulness to His promises. **10** *City of Nahor; i.e.* Haran (*cf.* 29:4 and above on 11:26ff.). **14** The proposing of a sign to discover the elect mother of Israel belongs to an era of special revelation (*cf.* v. 7).

15ff. God's answer (vv. 15–25) surpassed the prayer (vv. 12–14), evoking doxology (vv. 26f.). With v. 15, *cf.* 22:20ff. Though the servant was not yet informed that Rebekah was of Abraham's kindred (vv. 23f.; *cf.* vv. 4, 38) she had fulfilled the prayer-sign, and his gifts (v. 21) marked a preliminary recognition of her as the appointed bride. Laban's prominence (v. 29; *cf.* v. 53; 25:20) and Bethuel's secondary role (*cf.* vv. 15, 24, 50) reflect a fratriarchal arrangement in which the jurisdiction over the brothers and sisters is given to one brother. **50, 51** Rebekah's family was impressed, like the Hebron Hittites and Abimelech, with the divine protectorate enjoyed by Abraham, and could not oppose this mission, even had the marriage not been so obviously favourable. **58** *I will go.* The sister's consent to a proposed marriage in a fratriarchal situation is attested in a marriage record from Nuzi. **60** The family's farewell blessing was formally similar to the blessing already promised to the Abrahamites by God (*cf.* 22:17). **62–67** The account of the conclusion of the mission, prospered by the Lord, concentrates on Isaac to the exclusion of Abraham and specifically depicts Rebekah as Sarah's successor (v. 67, AV). Isaac is thus portrayed as already patriarchal co-regent. Agreeably, the steward over all Abraham's household calls Isaac *my master* (v. 65; *cf.* v. 36).

25:1–11 Isaac's succession. The interest of this closing narrative of Abraham's life is on the clearing of Isaac's exclusive claim to covenant inheritance (vv. 1–6) and his succession as covenant patriarch (vv. 7–11).

1 The marriage with *Keturah* may have occurred during Sarah's lifetime, chronological sequence yielding again to topical arrangement. Since within three years of Sarah's death Abraham was reckoning seriously with the possibility that his own death was nigh (*cf.* 24:1ff.), the relationship described in vv. 1–6 is improbable after Sarah's death. Also, Keturah is called a 'concubine' (1 Ch. 1:32; *cf.* v. 6). **2–4** The Keturah tribes are traceable to NW Arabia; *cf.* above on 17:5. **6** *Sons of his concubines;* perhaps the plural is abstract, *i.e.* 'concubinage'. *He sent them away.* This dismissal may have occurred at Ishmael's expulsion or, more probably, when Isaac became co-patriarch with Abraham (v. 5, *cf.* above on 24:62–67). **8** *Cf.* 15:15; Heb. 11:13. *Was gathered to his people.* This is the sequel to death; it is not a reference to burial (*cf.* vv. 9f.; 35:29; 49:33 and 50:13). **11** *God blessed Isaac.* According to promise (17:21) the son born in Abraham's hundredth year was confirmed over the covenant inheritance in the hundredth year after Abraham entered the land.

25:12–18 THE GENERATIONS OF ISHMAEL

Ishmael had been the subject of particular divine promises made to Hagar (16:10ff.) and Abraham (17:20; 21:13). The fulfilment in Ishmael's descendants is noted before the history of the Abrahamic kingdom proceeds. In this control of mankind outside the line of promise it is again manifested that Yahweh, Lord of the Abrahamic covenant, is God of all the earth, directing all history by His sovereign providence. **16** *By their villages and by their encampments.* The more settled and the wandering Ishmaelites are thus distinguished. *Twelve princes.* This suggests a sacred-political confederation (*cf.* 17:20). **18** Their nomadic sphere was far-flung across the NW Arabian wilderness and was threateningly hostile (*cf.* 16:12), not least to the Israelites (Jdg. 6:33ff.; especially Jdg. 8:24; *cf.* Jdg. 7:12 with Gn. 25:18b; Ps. 83:6).

25:19 – 35:29 THE GENERATIONS OF ISAAC

25:19a This heading is joined to the subsequent narrative in the same way as the 11:27 heading. Also, just as the 'generations of Terah' centred at once on Abraham, so the 'generations of Isaac' focus upon Jacob. Isaac occupies a more significant position than Terah, however, who stood merely at the genealogical source, the notice of his death coming early in the section (11:32). Isaac, heir of Abraham, dwelling prosperously in Canaan afforded a picture of covenant fulfilment. Moreover, he stands as patriarchal head over the whole history of this era, the record of his death closing this section (35:29).

25:19b – 28:9 Isaac's inheritance and heir

25:19b–34 Election of Jacob. 20 *Aramean of Paddan-aram.* The line leading to Israel, though directly traced to Shem through Arpachshad rather than Aram, had become associated with Aramaeans (*cf.* Dt. 26:5). **21** The barrenness of Isaac's wife and most of the other recorded features of Isaac's life are similar to experiences of Abraham and served the same disciplinary purposes of faith. **22** *Went to inquire.* Rebekah, as perhaps Isaac too, had recourse to a sanctified place, probably one of the patriarchal altars, in her distressed calling on God. Why, she wondered, had God healed her barrenness, if the issue of her conception would be unhappy, as the inner struggle made her fear it would. **23** *The elder shall serve the younger.* Cf. 9:25–27. By divine pre-appointment a place in the Abraham–Isaac succession was conferred on the younger of the struggling twins. Prenatal appointment of the son of a particular bride to the official position of firstborn, in preference to sons by another wife and irrespective of actual primogeniture, is attested in the Ancient Near East. See Rom. 9:10–12. **25** *Red* (*'admônî*) anticipates the later play on Esau's other name, Edom (*cf.* v. 30). *Hairy* (*śē'ār*) is the basis of the name-pun, Esau (*'ēśāw*); *cf.* also Seir (*śē'îr*). **26** *Heel* (*'āqēb*) is used to explain *Jacob* (*ya'aqōb*), found also in contemporary extra-biblical sources and meaning 'he (God) protects'.

29–34 The divine oracle, confirmed by this birth-omen, began to be fulfilled in Esau's sale of his birthright to Jacob. The birthright regularly conveyed a double inheritance share. In this family the entire 'blessing of Abraham' (28:4), the covenant patriarchate, was involved. From Nuzi comes evidence of the transfer of a prospective inheritance share of real property from one brother to another in exchange for a few sheep. Perhaps it was only the double share that Jacob could thus secure by barter; for later both brothers sought Isaac's testamentary blessing, evidently to secure family headship and a generally prosperous prospect (Gn. 27). **34** *Cf.* Heb. 12:16. Esau's name *Edom* identifies him with his profane preference for the red stuff (*'ādōm*) in the pot. It could only have been in spite of Jacob's unworthy behaviour that he was the object of God's elective love (*cf.* Mal. 1:2f.).

26:1–33 Isaac under the Lord's protectorate. These episodes follow Abraham's death (see vv. 1, 15, 18) but the earlier of them possibly preceded the birthright exchange (*cf.* 25:29ff.). Their position between the two supplanting episodes suggests their purpose is to portray the inheritance Jacob coveted. **2–4** The prohibition, turning Isaac from trust in the arm of Egypt, compelled him to look alone unto the special providence of God, who confirmed to him the Abrahamic covenant (*cf.* v. 12). Here was the lesson needed by grasping young Jacob, too! **5** *Cf.* above on 22:16. **6–11** *Cf.* above on 12:13ff. and 20:1ff. Since *Abimelech* was evidently a Philistine dynastic title (*cf.* 1 Sa. 21:11 and the heading of Ps. 34), this need not be the individual Abraham encountered in Gerar decades before. He is of similar character, however, and the advanced age he would have reached would explain why Rebekah's jeopardy is related to the Gerarites, not to a royal harem. Abimelech's chance discovery of Isaac 'sporting' (v. 8; AV translation of *mᵉṣaḥēq*, the name-pun again) with Rebekah speaks anew of sovereign divine protection. **12–16** God's special oversight in the face of famine and Philistine harassment (see vv. 14, 15) resulted in such agricultural success and general prosperity that the pilgrim aliens overshadowed the native city-state (v. 16).

18–22 *Cf.* 21:25ff. The encampments at 'Contention' (*Esek*) and 'Enmity' (*Sitnah*) led to the spacious, fruitful peace of 'Room' (*Rehoboth*). **23** Again at *Beer-sheba*, where Abraham had dug a well and resided, Isaac's servants found new water sources (*cf.* vv. 25, 32). **24, 25** Here God renewed the covenant guarantees, prompting Isaac's special cultic acknowledgment of his Lord (*cf.* 21:33). **26** Concerning *Phicol* (*cf.* 21:22) the same possibilities of identity exist as for Abimelech (see above on v. 8). **27–31** The Abimelech–Isaac covenant renewed the Abimelech–Abraham covenant (*cf.* especially 21:23). Out of the mouths of the Philistines God brought a witness that His promise concerning Isaac in Philistine country (*cf.* v. 3) had been fulfilled. Having registered his complaint, Isaac suffered his visitors to gloss diplomatically over the border incidents and consented to the parity treaty, ratified by a covenant meal and a mutual oath. **33** *Shibah* is, like 'Shebah', a form of the number seven; thus Isaac confirmed the name given by Abraham. There is also in the context a word play on the oath-taking (*nišba*) of v. 31 (*cf.* v. 32, *that same day*). Thus out of the reluctant earth and disgruntled men the Lord had wrested for Isaac an earnest of paradise.

26:34 – 28:9 Isaac's testamentary blessings. Bracketing the account of Esau's loss of the firstborn's blessing are records of his marriage alliances outside the line of promise (26:34f. and 28:6–9). His first marriage possibly preceded some Isaac episodes which are described in Gn. 26.

27:2 *Behold I am old.* This was legal terminology for introducing final testaments. Isaac was 137 years old and lived forty years longer (*cf.* 35:28). Isaac's purpose to give Esau the blessing (vv. 1–4) and Rebekah's scheme to divert it to Jacob (vv. 5–17) stemmed from the spirit of favouritism (*cf.* 25:28).

20 *The Lord . . . granted me success.* The deceiver, vainly taking God's name, spoke more

truth than he realized. **23** *So he blessed him* is the outcome; **24–29** supply the details. Rebekah's comprehensive deceit was directed to all Isaac's remaining senses, except hearing; but touch, taste and smell silenced his ears. Isaac's poetic blessing (vv. 27b–29) does not adhere to previous promise terminology. It is as though the ambiguity of the situation prevented a more forthright formulation. Yet the covenant blessing was encompassed in the headship over Isaac's household (*cf.* above on 25:23); other features included were the paradise land, nationhood with dominion and mediatorship of divine judgment. Cf. Heb. 11:20. **33** *Yes, and he shall be blessed.* Legal evidence from Nuzi shows that oral wills delivered by a dying father and cited in court were of decisive validity. They had an oath character (*cf.* v. 7, 'before the Lord'). Isaac was stunned by the recognition that in spite of his own purpose to the contrary the prenatal oracle (*cf.* 25:23) had been made effective through the inspired testament he had uttered in irreversible legal form. **34ff.** *Cf.* Heb. 12:17. **36** *Supplanted*; from Hebrew *'āqab*, 'take by the heel'. Distraught Esau saw the event as a repetition of the birthright exchange, a fulfilment of the birth-omen, and an explanation of Jacob's name (*cf.* 25:26; Je. 9:4; Ho. 12:3). **39, 40** *Away from the fatness.* The preposition (*min*) means either 'of' (as in Jacob's blessing, v. 28) or 'away from'; the latter is required here by the context and by Edomite history (*cf.* too Mal. 1:3). Edom's mountains discouraged cultivation; their inhabitants were driven from the ploughshare to the sword (*cf.* 25:27). Israel dominated Edom, especially from the monarchy onward (*cf.* Nu. 24:18; 2 Sa. 8:14), but Edom was periodically successful in independence efforts.

41ff. The sins of all concerned in the business of the blessing began at once to take their toll. To deliver Jacob from Esau's vengeance (v. 41), Rebekah, expert at scheming, was obliged to deliver her favourite over to her similarly talented brother Laban (vv. 43ff.), and apparently died before it was propitious to recall Jacob (v. 45; *cf.* 49:31). **46** Her shrewd approaches to both Jacob and Isaac (*cf.* 26:34f.), appealing to their concern for her happiness, ironically led them to bring upon her precisely the evils from which they sought to spare her.

28:1ff. See on 24:3. **4** *Blessing of Abraham.* The atmosphere had sufficiently cleared by the time of this farewell confirmation of the testamentary blessing for Isaac to identify Jacob's blessing forthrightly as that which God bestowed in the Abrahamic covenant. The mission to secure a wife prompted an emphasis on the blessing of numerous progeny. The language echoes Gn. 17 especially, including the divine designation, *'ēl šadday* (see on 17:1). On 4b, *cf., e.g.,* 17:8a; 26:3 and contrast 27:28. **5** summarily anticipates 10ff. before this section on Isaac's patriarchal activities closes. **6–9** Esau's choice of an Ishmaelite wife (*cf.* 26:34f.; 36:3) showed regard for Isaac, yet underscored his separation from the Abrahamic inheritance.

28:10 – 35:29 Jacob's Syrian sojourn and return

28:10–22 God's covenant with Jacob. This era forms a circle from the ratification of God's covenant protectorship over Jacob at Bethel back to Bethel and the confirmation of that covenant (35:1–15). **10** *Left Beersheba . . . toward Haran*; *cf.* 26:23; 28:5. Jacob's actual enjoyment of the patriarchal office was long postponed. In his flight from Canaan, patriarchal history reverted to its beginnings among the idolatrous Terahites, necessitating a new summons to Canaan. So Jacob was rebuked for his supplanting tactics. **12** *Ladder*; better 'ramp' or 'staircase', like those on the artificial temple mounds or ziggurats leading from the god's dwelling at the top to men below. The Hebrew suggests that the ramp extended both towards earth and heaven, rather than that it was supported, like the Babel structure, upon the cursed earth. It anticipated the heavenly city that descends from above (*cf.* v. 17; Rev. 21:2, 10). *Angels of God*; *cf.* 11:7; 18:2; Ho. 12:4f. They ascended with the results of their earthly reconnaissance (*cf.* Zc. 1:11) and descended to execute God's will. **13, 14** 'Beside him' (see RSV mg.; Heb. *'ālāyw*) is better than *above it* (*i.e.* the staircase); *cf.* 35:13. The angel of the Lord stood there, sent by God, yet Himself God, revealed and present to Jacob; *cf.* Jn. 1:51. God's covenant disclosure contained the standard treaty features of preamble with identifying title and, in His Self-identification as God of Abraham and Isaac, a virtual historical prologue recalling His mercies to the patriarchal dynasty (v. 13b). The full-orbed covenant inheritance, already conveyed through Isaac's inspired blessing, was now directly confirmed by the Lord (vv. 13c, 14). **15** *Wherever you go*. The divine protectorate over Jacob extended, as did Yahweh's power, beyond the special domain of Canaan. The promise of guardianship during Jacob's sojourn, with guarantee of return, was the Lord's explanation of the dream symbolism. **19** *Bethel*, 'house of God' (*cf.* v. 17), the name Jacob gave to the revelation site, was extended afterwards to the nearby city of Luz (*cf.* Jos. 16:2; 18:13), already called Bethel, by way of anticipation, in Gn. 12:8 and 13:3. **20** *Vow.* Jacob ratified the covenant with a vow of allegiance pledging his tributary tithe. Cf. vv. 14, 20, 22. **21** The last clause is (contrary to RSV) part of Jacob's account of what God would do for him; Jacob's own promise begins in v. 22. **22** *Pillar . . . God's house.* Cf. v. 18. There is evidence outside the Bible also of pillars associated with covenants being called 'house of God'. See also 35:7, 15. This proved to be Jacob's Damascus road vision of the Lord. It turned the circumcised son of the covenant from seeking salvation by works to securing it through a faith-struggle that led to a new name.

29:1 – 30:24 Origins of the tribal fathers.
29:1–12 The circumstances of the origins of the twelve tribes advertise the purely gracious character of Israel's election. The special superintendence promised at Bethel led Jacob directly to the bride-to-be, Rachel (v. 6). Attraction to Rachel and eagerness to commend himself somehow to Laban (for he lacked the lavish credentials of the steward who came for Rebekah) inspired Jacob to impressive feats of gallantry (vv. 9f.) in defiance of local custom (vv. 3, 8). **13** The potential of service in such a man brought Laban running again (*cf.* 24:29ff.) **14** *You are my bone and my flesh*. This expression found in ancient adoption forms is one of the details suggesting that Laban adopted Jacob. At Jacob's arrival, sons of Laban are not mentioned; a daughter was tending the sheep. See further below on 30:25ff.; 31:1ff., 14ff., 19ff. **15** Whatever Jacob's technical status was, as exploited by Laban it became an oppressive servitude. Under pretence of generosity Laban modified the family relationship, in which an uncalculating generosity might be expected of him, by reducing Jacob to a hired labourer's condition. **18** Aware of Jacob's love for Rachel, Laban would forestall the request that she be given in marriage, as daughters sometimes were to adopted sons. He greedily anticipated the generous bridal present that love would offer. **21ff.** Worse still, in crude disdain of holy ordinance, human dignity, and all natural feeling he contrived to double his bargain, making love pay its extravagant price twice. The Nuzi tablets (including texts dealing with adoption) attest the wedding gift of a handmaid to a daughter (*cf.* vv. 24, 29). **31** *Rachel was barren*. After Leah's wedding week but before the second seven years of his service, Jacob received Rachel as a second wife. **32–35** To Leah, the unloved bride of deception, the first of the tribal fathers were born amid family tensions and disharmony. *Reuben*; *cf.* ra'ā . . . be'onyī, '(the Lord) has looked upon my affliction'. *Simeon*; *cf.* šāma', '(the Lord) has heard'. *Levi*; *cf.* yillāweh, '(my husband) will be joined'. *Judah*; *cf.* 'ôdeh, 'I will praise'. From two of these sons of Leah arose the royal-Messianic and priestly tribes in Israel.

30:2 *Am I in the place of God?* Some budding sense of dependence on the covenant Lord emerges in Jacob's exasperated retort. **3** On concubinage as a customary practice in cases of a wife's barrenness, see above on 16:2. *Upon my knees*. Placing the infant on the knees (normally of the father, though here of the adoptive mother) signified acknowledgment. **6** *Dan*; *cf.* dānanni, '(God) has judged me', *i.e.* intervened as her defender. **8** *Naphtali*; *cf.* naptūlēy 'elōhīm niptaltī, lit. 'wrestlings of God I have wrestled'. The periods covered by 29:32–35 and 30:1–8 probably overlapped. The chronological relation of 30:9–13 (which, of course, follows 29:32–35) to 30:1–8 is uncertain. **9** So intense was the sisters' struggle for supremacy that Leah, though four times a mother, matched Rachel's strategy of concubinage. **11** *Gad*; *cf. bāḡāḏ*, 'with fortune'. **13** *Asher*; *cf. bᵉ'ošrî*, 'with my happiness' and *'iššᵉrûnî*, 'they will call me happy'.

14ff. *Mandrakes*, known as an aphrodisiac, were Rachel's next strategem to overcome her barrenness, but proved ineffectual; in fact, her plan became the occasion of increasing her rival's advantage. **17** *God hearkened to Leah.* Again the record stresses the true source of life's blessing. **18** *Issachar*; *cf. śᵉḵārî*, 'my hire' and *śāḵôr śᵉḵartîḵā* (v. 16), 'I have hired you'. **20** *Zebulun*; *cf. zēḇeḏ*, 'gift' and *yizbᵉlēnî*, from a root of uncertain meaning. **21** *Cf.* 37:35; 46:7. **22** *God hearkened to her.* Rachel eventually sought the blessing aright. **24** *Joseph*; *cf. 'āsap̄*, '(God) has removed' (v. 23) and *yôsēp̄*, 'may (the Lord) add' (v. 24). Chronologically, vv. 14–20 overlap part of vv. 10–13 and vv. 22–24 precede v. 21 and probably overlap vv. 19f.

30:25–43 Despoiling the oppressor. 25 When the fourteen years of bride payments were completed (*cf.* 31:41), Joseph's birth coinciding with this, Jacob desired to return to Canaan where his inheritance through Isaac awaited him. By now, natural sons had been born to Laban (*cf.* 31:1), replacing Jacob as chief heirs (*cf.* above on 15:4 and 29:14ff.), and Jacob's prospects of counter-balancing his deteriorated inheritance share by negotiating a favourable new contract with wily Laban were dim. **26** *Let me go.* Laban's permission was necessary for Jacob to leave with the family for which he had paid by his service. It resembled the case of a departing slave (*cf.* Ex. 21:2ff.). One explanation is that the service contracts were operating in subordination to an adoption relationship that made Jacob's independent proprietorship contingent on Laban's death (*cf.* 31:43). **27–33** At Laban's insistence Jacob suggested an arrangement for continued service. His wages would be the sports appearing among Laban's flocks. **34–36** Since these were relatively rare Laban readily agreed, immediately instituting measures that reduced further the odds of any dark, spotted lambs appearing among the normally white sheep or any kids with white markings among the normally dark goats. **37–43** Jacob's counter-measures accorded with the theory of prenatal conditioning by visual impressions. These verses condense six years' history (*cf.* 31:41) during which Laban repeatedly imposed changing stipulations (31:7f.) in a vain attempt to stem the tide of Jacob's wealth, mounting at his expense (vv. 42f.). The success of Jacob's strategy was attributable to the special providential favour of the God of Bethel (*cf.* 31:9ff.).

31:1–55 Exodus. Jacob's labours of the first fourteen years increased Laban's estate (*cf.* 30:27, 30), but their effect now was to diminish the inheritance of Laban's natural sons (vv. 1f.). Jacob's determination to leave, however, was

not merely his reaction to his rivals' increasing hostility but his response to God's special directions (v. 3; *cf.* v. 13). His appeal to his wives (vv. 3ff.) referred apparently to an earlier dream revelation (vv. 10–12) and a more recent divine command (v. 13; *cf.* v. 3), though the two are not distinctly distinguished. Rachel and Leah accepted Jacob's explanation of his enrichment as the blessing of God (vv. 5, 7, 9, 11f., 16) and honoured his divine commissioning (v. 16), perhaps the more easily because of the congruence of God's command with plots that had crossed their own minds. For Laban had shown no disposition to bestow on them any part of the bridal price (*i.e.* the wealth that accrued to him through Jacob's services) as was normally done in that area (v. 14f.). Accordingly, they reckoned that what God was now taking from their father and giving to their husband was no more than their own (v. 16). It was Laban's own precaution (*cf.* 30:36; 31:19) that provided Jacob with his opportunity to lead his whole household away stealthily (vv. 17ff.).

19 *Household gods.* Rachel probably stole these 'teraphim' (RV) when Jacob sent for her (*cf.* v. 4), anticipating his plan. Since adoption tablets stipulated that the chief heir should receive the father's gods, possession of them conveyed some legal advantage in respect of inheritance. Adoption texts also stipulate that the gods belonged to real sons born subsequent to the adoption. In the contemptuous treatment given these figurines by the fugitives (*cf.* especially v. 34) Laban's gods were judged with him. **23** Laban's pursuit covered about 300 miles. Jacob's company had ten days to cover somewhat less than that, for he would have stationed his flocks strategically for departure. **24** The night before Laban overtook Jacob, God intervened decisively (*cf.* vv. 29, 42), warning the pursuer from pressing his enforceable legal claims against Jacob in any way whatsoever (*cf. either good or bad*). The Lord's role was thus that of Kinsman-Protector securing release for the virtual slave (*cf.* the 6 years, 31:41; Dt. 15:12). **32–35** The extreme penalty proposed and Laban's agitation show the great legal importance of the teraphim. Laban's futile attempt to prove his accusation created an excellent opportunity for the defence and Jacob pressed the advantage with a passionate statement of the moral case in his favour (vv. 36–42). **39** *I bore the loss.* According to Hammurabi's laws, a shepherd who presented the remnants as evidence was not liable for the losses Jacob describes. **42** *Empty-handed.* Laban would have dismissed Jacob, not with festive music (*cf.* v. 27), but with less consideration than was due to a slave (*cf.* Dt. 15:13f.). Jacob's self-vindication became a confession of his avenging God. **43–54** *All . . . is mine.* Laban stated the legal fact (*cf.* above on 30:26), but afraid to defy God's warning abandoned his case and under pretence of paternal magnanimity suggested a mutual non-aggression pact (vv. 44ff.). God was the real covenant Witness (vv. 49f., 53); the pillar and cairn (vv. 45–52), named by each of the apparently bilingual participants in his native tongue (vv. 47f.), were symbolic witnesses. Each man bound himself by oath (v. 52f.), Laban identifying Nahor's and Abraham's God in a Terahite syncretism (v. 53a; cf. 12:1), but Jacob invoking God by a name related distinctly to the Abrahamic covenant. The covenant meal (vv. 46, 54) sealed the arrangement. The stipulation against taking other wives (v. 50) is also found in extra-biblical marriage contracts. The invoking of divine oversight (v. 49) arose from mutual suspicion and sought protection not for the other but for themselves from the other's malice.

32:1 – 33:17 Victory in Transjordan. 32:1 Cf. 28:12ff. **2** The two armies referred to by the name Mahanaim (see also RSV mg.) are possibly the angels and Jacob's company. If 32:11ff. (Heb., 2f.) belongs chronologically within the course of events described in vv. 3ff., the two armies might be the angels and Esau's force (cf. 2 Ki. 6:15ff.). The site of Mahanaim might then closely adjoin Penuel. **3** On Esau as a threat, cf. 27:41ff. Esau had been establishing himself in Seir (cf. 36:6ff.). **6–8** The advance mission's report to Jacob was ominous enough to prompt immediate defensive tactics of a kind common to caravans. **9–12** Jacob's prayer with its self-effacement and reliance on God for the fulfilment of previous promises evidences the inner work of transformation that inevitably accompanies the election of grace. *This Jordan.* (Heb. Yardēn) may here have its generic meaning, 'river'. *Two companies* is a further play on 'Mahanaim'. **13–21** Improving on the preliminary arrangements (cf. vv. 7f.), Jacob sent ahead a generous present of cattle selected in proper proportions for breeding. **22** He then immediately forded the Jabbok. This verse is an opening summary, the details following in vv. 23ff. **23** Actually Jacob himself, after sending his family across, was to remain the night where he was (cf. v. 13). **24** Before entering the land of inheritance, he must undergo an experience that sealed him as a man of faith and pointed him by a mysterious sign to the ultimate source of saving blessings. *A man.* It was the captain of the Lord's hosts (cf. vv. 1f. and Jos. 5:13f.; Ho. 12:3). *Wrestled* (Heb. wayyē'ābēq) puns on Jabbok. In the Near East law cases were sometimes settled by an ordeal or test (cf. Nu. 5:11–31). One mode of this was combat by wrestling. The encounter reveals the fundamental character of the quest for God's kingdom as a struggle by fallen men for justification. In this ordeal the outward course of the wrestling was a reflex of the concurrent spiritual encounter. **25, 26** *He did not prevail against Jacob.* The divine Adversary was also the electing-saving Lord who strengthened Jacob with grace to wrestle on against Himself lest he be overcome and condemned! So by per-

sistence in believing supplication Jacob emerged from the ordeal with a blessing (cf. Ho. 12:4). *He touched* (Heb. nāga' b-) may signify 'smote' (cf. vv. 31f.). The justification was achieved through suffering. Since the thigh was regarded as the seat of the reproductive powers, the smiting of Jacob's thigh was a sign of the smiting of that descendant of Jacob who should be smitten of God (Is. 53:4) and by His sufferings and overcoming justify Jacob and all God's elect (Is. 53:11). The angel's desire to depart before daylight expressed God's concern lest Jacob perish through beholding His face unobscured by the darkness (cf. 16:13; Ex. 33:20; Jdg. 6:22f.; 13:22). With reference to this Jacob named the site *Peniel*, 'the face of God' (v. 30). **28** *Israel.* This name is found also in the Ugaritic texts. The divine element ('ēl, 'God') would normally be subject, i.e. 'God strives' (cf. RSV mg.) but a different sense is assigned here (i.e. 'He strives with God'). Jacob had prevailed over Esau; now, over God (cf. Ho. 12:3). **29, 30** In his new name, Israel, Jacob's query was already answered (cf. too Jdg. 13:17f.), as his response shows.

33:3 Sevenfold bowing was a widely attested form of homage, fit for a king. **4–9** By the blessing of Him in whose hand is even the heart of kings (cf. 31:34; Pr. 21:1) the dreaded meeting proved a reconciling reunion. Ignoring the servants' explanations (cf. 32:17ff.), Esau yet acknowledged Jacob's offer, so as to decline it (v. 9). **10, 11** Jacob urged him to accept, because Esau's acceptance of so substantial a gift would give formal expression to his acquiescence in Jacob's possession of the disputed inheritance, and would serve as a deterrent to any future rekindling of hostility. *Like seeing the face of God.* Jacob recognized through Esau's reconciled countenance that the God of Peniel was making His face shine upon him. **12–16** Hence he felt no need for the armed protection Esau offered; besides, he was unwilling to incur obligation to Esau. **17** Jacob continued in the Transjordan area for a possibly prolonged period; close to a decade must have elapsed between departure from Syria and the Shechem episode (cf. 34:1).

33:18 – 34:31 Entry into Canaan. 33:18 *On his way from Paddan-aram* (cf. 35:9). A long period is thus characterized by its opening act; cf. 'in their going forth from Egypt' (Dt. 4:45; 23:4; Jos. 5:4). *Safely*, or 'in peace'; not as an invader but according to agreement (cf. v. 19; 34:21). **19** For the faith involved in Jacob's purchase, see above on Abraham's purchase of Machpelah (Gn. 23). **20** Recognizing his return as fulfilment of covenant promise (cf. 28:15), Jacob erected an altar near Shechem, as had Abram on his arrival (12:7). Cf. Jos. 8:30. *El-Elohe-Israel.* Using his new name, Israel, Jacob confessed that El (cf. Isaac's use of this divine designation in blessing Jacob, 28:3) was his God (cf. 28:21).

34:1 *Dinah* must have been some 14 years old, but cannot have been more; she was born after Leah's four sons (cf. 30:21), and Joseph, who was about a year older than Dinah, was only seventeen at the later occasion recorded in 37:2. **2** *Hivite*; cf. 10:17. **5** The fratriarchal practices of Laban's household re-emerge when Jacob defers to Dinah's brothers (no doubt to Leah's sons particularly) in the handling of her abduction (vv. 5, 7, 13ff.). **7** *In Israel*. The author saw the nation budding in the expanding community of Jacob's household. **10** The privileges Hamor offered were the same as those which figure in directives regulating the activities of Hittite merchants in foreign lands. **13** *Deceitfully*. Though it was the brothers' duty to secure Dinah's release (cf. v. 26b), resort to the stratagems of war was not justifiable. **14–17** Reprehensible also was their demeaning of the covenant sign of circumcision. **20–24** Hamor's successfully diplomatic camouflage, persuading the Shechemite council to approve its own doom, viewed the proposed arrangements as a confederation whose level of prosperity would exceed that of the Shechemites by themselves (v. 23). **25–31** The vengeance exacted by Jacob's sons was a ruthless aggression in violation of the law of exact retribution for the crime, mercilessly multiplying the very offence (cf. vv. 27b, 31). Jacob's reproof of the two instigators of the atrocity stressed the folly of imperilling their own households (v. 30), but how thoroughly he reprobated their deed appears in the curse he uttered in his final testament (cf. 49:5–7).

35:1–15 Covenant renewal. 1 In the crisis precipitated by the Shechem massacre (34:25ff.) Jacob's divine Protector intervened with directions and defence (cf. v. 5). He summoned Jacob back to Bethel, the site of His original covenant revelation to him, for the fulfilment of his vow (cf. 28:20ff.; 31:13). **2** *Jacob said*. Jacob's authority over his own covenant household continued even though the fratriarchal approach had been accommodated (cf. on 34:5). *Put away the foreign gods*. Exclusive devotion to the Suzerain was the covenant's first stipulation. Cf. 31:19. *Purify*. On the process of ritual sanctification, cf. Ex. 19:10. **4** *Rings*. These would be amulets with idolatrous significance. *Near Shechem*. At a later covenant renewal here, Joshua similarly demanded the removal of foreign gods, recalling the idolatry of Israel's ancestral household beyond Euphrates (Jos. 24:1ff., 23). **5** The *terror from God*, gripping Israel's foes with irrational paralysis or panic, was the work of the angel of the Lord, going before them (cf. Ex. 23:23, 27; Gn. 32:1ff.). **7** The altar, *El-bethel*, witnessed to the Lord's sovereign faithfulness. **8** Cf. 24:59. **9** The renewal of the covenant in vv. 9ff. made appropriate Jacob's renewal of the name of the site (v. 15; cf. 28:19). On the theophany (cf. v. 13), cf. 28:12ff. **10–12** God summarized His previous revelations to Jacob: the name-blessing, Israel, and the promise of royal nationhood in Abraham's land (cf. 17:1b, 4ff.; 28:13f.). The

traditional elements of treaty-making are found here in God's words: His title, the stipulations and sanctions, the historical prologue (cf. the dominant motif: from Bethel to Bethel). *Be fruitful and multiply*. Incorporation of the creation mandate (cf. 1:28) in place of the usual promise of descendants indicates that the Abrahamic covenant was in continuation of the original, broadly human programme of the creation covenant. **14** The stone *pillar* was the customary covenant witness (cf. Jos. 24:26f.).

35:16–29 Dynastic succession. This closing section of 'the generations of Isaac' is concerned with matters affecting the family leadership, immediately and in the future. The account of Benjamin's birth (vv. 16ff.) rounds out the record of the twelve tribal leaders' origins. The twelve are then listed according to their mothers (vv. 23ff.) and thus according to legal rather than chronological priorities. A notice is inserted of Reuben's offence (v. 22) by which he forfeited the birthright (cf. v. 23; 49:4). Isaac's death (v. 29) meant Jacob's succession as covenant patriarch. **17b** Cf. 30:24. **19** *On the way to Ephrath*. En route between the sojourn at Bethel and more prolonged sojourn near Bethlehem (vv. 21f.) Rachel died in childbirth and was buried. According to 1 Sa. 10:2 (cf. Je. 31:15) the place was possibly near, even north, of Jerusalem. **27** *At Mamre*. Since his return from Paddan-aram and before locating in the Hebron area (cf. 37:14), Jacob may well have visited Isaac there. **28** Isaac lived some twelve years after this reunion. **29** His burial found his twin sons at peace.

36:1 – 37:1 THE GENERATIONS OF ESAU

Before the history of the central line of Jacob proceeds, a brief survey of Esau's branch line is made. It displays the carrying forward of God's revealed purpose concerning Esau (cf. 25:23) and of Isaac's inspired blessing on him (cf. 27:39f.). Jacob's sons were listed individually in summary of their origins in Paddan-aram (35:23–26) and later are listed again as en route to Egypt with their nearer descendants who headed major divisions in Israel (see 46:8ff.; cf. Nu. 26:5ff.). Similarly, Esau's sons born in Canaan are listed (36:2–5), then again as relocated in Seir with their sons who were significant for national divisions (36:9–14), as is explained in the repetition of their names in the Edomite chieftain (Heb. '*allûp̄*, also interpreted as 'clan') list (36:15–19).

The formula (36:1), which divides Genesis from 2:4 onwards into ten parts, marks the subdivision beginning at 36:9, which relates the Edomite phase of Esau's history. The explanation of Esau's departure (36:7) perhaps implies that Esau's presence in Seir at the time of Jacob's returning from Paddan-aram (cf. 32:3) was only preparatory to a later move there by his entire clan. With the shift of focus from the family of Esau to the nation of Edom, it was in order to consider the line of the Horite Seir (36:20-30), whom the Lord dispossessed before Esau (*cf.* Dt. 2:12, 22) and with whom Esau's descendants intermarried (*cf.* 36:2 and 24, 12 and 22). Remarkably, while the explicit promise of king and kingdom made to favoured Jacob (35:11; *cf.* 17:6; Nu. 24:7; Dt. 17:14ff.) was still unfulfilled, kingship emerged in Edom, the land of scarcely-blessed Esau (36:31). There is no need, therefore, to suggest that this reference to kings in Israel could have been made only after the establishment of the monarchy, and that this verse must be a much later insertion. Its reference is to the divine promise of kings, as indicated. The list of Edomite kings (36:32-39) indicates an elective, not dynastic, office, the importance of the chiefs appearing in the additional list arranged with special attention on geographical and administrative divisions (36:40-43). The inclusion of the transitional 37:1 within the Esau-Edom section (contrast 25:11) underscores the rejected and separated character of this Esau history.

37:2 - 50:26 THE GENERATIONS OF JACOB

This last genealogical division of Genesis covers the period of Jacob's patriarchal authority (37:2a), begun upon his return to Isaac in Canaan as a co-regency with his ageing father. Joseph is prominent in the narrative as he follows his special vocation as preserver of the covenant family, exercising authority over them by virtue of his eminence in Egypt. He represented a new type of leadership in Israel—one by special divine selection and charismatic endowment, Joseph's particular gift being wisdom. Nevertheless, he remained subordinate to Jacob within the covenant structure. In the broader history, this era was introductory to the great redemptive act of deliverance under Moses. Under divine compulsion Jacob led the covenant community out of the land of promise to sojourn in what would become a house of bondage. This development fulfilled God's ominous word to Abraham (15:13), but stood under the promise of restoration after 400 years (15:14, 16).

37:2 - 45:28 Jacob's kingdom-heirs

The spiritual transformation previously wrought in the elect individual, Jacob, is now multiplied. The whole family of Jacob is refashioned into an OT church-community of faith, united in filial and brotherly love under Israel, the servant of the Lord.

37:2-36 A house divided. 2 Early indications of Joseph's future pre-eminence made him the object of jealous hatred, especially, it seems, among the four sons of the handmaids, who ranked lowest (*cf.* 30:3-13; 33:2). Their sullen resentment led to slothful service, dutifully reported by the favourite. **3** *Son of his old age.* Except for Benjamin, all the sons were born during Jacob's second term of service, but

Joseph was the son born to the beloved Rachel after her long barrenness. The brothers discerned in the special *robe*, whether ornamented, vari-coloured, or long-sleeved, Jacob's intention to honour Joseph with the birthright forfeited by Reuben (*cf.* 35:22; 1 Ch. 5:1f.). **5-8** In Joseph's doubled dream they sensed a divine predestinating disclosure. Professional dream interpretation is attested in much Ancient Near Eastern literature, including reference works listing dream symbols and meanings. **9-11** The second dream extended Joseph's dominion beyond his brothers to the parental heads of the household. Jacob took offence, not knowing that Joseph's dominion over him would operate within the context of the family's enforced stay in Egypt, and would not involve a usurpation of his patriarchal authority.

12ff. The pastoral activity in the Shechem area without harassment from the outraged Canaanites (*cf.* 34:30) spoke of God's continuing providential protection. **18ff.** The murder in the hearts of the brothers could not plead righteous indignation as an excuse this time (*cf.* 34:31) but only conceal itself with a cruel lie (vv. 31f.). Reuben's countersuggestion (vv. 21f.) was accepted only because it seemed still to entail eventual death for Joseph in the deep cistern. The plea for mercy proved ineffectual (*cf.* 42:21) until baited with the lure of extra profit (vv. 26f.) beyond Joseph's double inheritance share, lust for which was the root of all this evil. Judah's plan unwittingly thwarted Reuben's (vv. 22, 29f.) but did save Joseph from death.

28 The members of the Ishmaelite (vv. 25, 27, 28b) caravan who bought Joseph are called *Midianites*; those who sold him in Egypt, Medanites (v. 36, Heb.). Midian and Medan were two sons of Abraham by Keturah (*cf.* 25:2), but probably no distinction is intended in Gn. 37. The sellers are called Ishmaelites in 39:1. In Jdg. 8:24 also, certain 'Midianites' are identified as 'Ishmaelites'. The racial significance of 'Ishmaelite' possibly yields to a secondary meaning like 'traders'. This identity of Midian and Medan, and the use of Ishmaelite as a descriptive title covering both, removes the often-asserted need to divide this narrative between the putative sources in order to explain its alleged contradictions. Afar off, the approaching caravan was identified as that of 'traders' (v. 25), but when they *passed by* they were discovered to be Midianite. The return to the title 'traders' (v. 28b) serves to underline the callousness of the brothers' treatment of Joseph. In v. 28 the subject of *drew Joseph up . . .* is Joseph's brothers (*cf.* 45:4f.). *Twenty shekels*; *cf.* Ex. 21:32; Lv. 27:5.

31-36 The rankling robe (*cf.* vv. 3f.) became legal evidence to confirm the transfer of Joseph's inheritance to his rivals (*cf.* Ex. 22:13 and above on 31:39). Jacob, deceiver in his youth, was cruelly deceived (v. 33), but the Lord he now feared was already so overruling (v. 36) that the very son whose death Jacob mourned (vv. 34f.)

would yet mourn his death with all Egypt's honour (*cf.* 50:1ff.).

38:1–30 Alien alliances. 1 *From his brothers.* Judah's separation further illustrates the disunity of Jacob's community (*cf.* ch. 37). This must have occurred soon after Joseph's sale, for within the time from then to Jacob's descent into Egypt, slightly more than two decades, Judah married, had sons, and they also married. Ch. 38 spans the period to 42:1. *Went down.* Judah descended from Hebron in the mountains to the Philistine hill country. The move was downward by covenant standards too, for its outcome was fraternizing with the Canaanite Hirah and marriage to the Canaanite Shua (v. 2). *Cf.* above on 24:3ff. **7** *The Lord slew him.* In the sudden death of his firstborn, Judah was confronted with the rapid degeneration that had resulted from his intimate Canaanite alliances (*cf.* Gn. 19). **8** *Offspring for your brother.* Such levirate marriage was practised widely (*cf.* Hittite and Middle Assyrian law codes) and was later regulated for Israel by Moses (Dt. 25:5ff.). The firstborn of the new marriage was reckoned as heir of the deceased brother, continuing his name. Onan coveted the firstborn's portion for his own name. **9, 10** In his despicable refusal to perform his fraternal obligation and in God's judgment Judah received a monitory reminder of the brothers' sin against Joseph. **11** Yet he too conspired against Tamar's right and Er's name.

12ff. Tamar was eventually undeceived and schemed to obtain satisfaction from Judah, now a widower. This had legal precedent, for in some areas the deceased's father could take the widow. **18** *Signet*; a cylinder seal worn on a cord about the neck, a personal signature. *Staff;* these sometimes figured as symbols in concluding transactions. **21** *Harlot.* This term $q^e \underline{d}\bar{e}\check{s}\hat{a}$, 'cult prostitute, votary', used in reference to Tamar, reflects the abysmal corruption of Canaanite culture to which the covenant family was exposed particularly by moves like Judah's. In the Canaanite fertility cult men and women were set apart for sexual immorality as for a holy function (as the root meaning of $q^e \underline{d}\bar{e}\check{s}\hat{a}$ signifies). **24** *Burned.* Though in sending Tamar back to her father's house (v. 11) Judah designed to be rid of her, he now asserted his patriarchal jurisdiction, seeing a way to be free of her and appear righteous at the same time. According to the later Mosaic legislation, burning, the severest penalty, was prescribed for certain extreme cases (*cf.* Lv. 20:14; 21:9), and stoning was the penalty for a case like Tamar's, as betrothed to Shelah (*cf.* Dt. 22:20ff.). **26** *More righteous than I.* Both had practised deception, but she to secure her legal rights and he to circumvent his legal-paternal obligations. **29** *Perez*; an ancestor of David's dynasty (*cf.* Ru. 4:18ff.; 1 Ch. 2:3–15; Mt. 1:3).

39:1 – 41:57 Preservation of the preserver. Going back some 20 years to the time of 37:36, the narrative at 39:1 turns to the providential developments in Joseph's career that were preparing for Jacob's household a way out of the increasingly dangerous conditions depicted in chs. 37 and 38.

39:1 *Potiphar*; probably an abbreviated form of the Egyptian name Potiphera (*cf.* 41:45), 'whom the sun-god has given'. *Captain of the guard*; or 'chief steward' (*cf.* on 39:21). Slave lists from this period attest to the presence of many Asiatics on Egyptian estates, most of them war-captives but many, like Joseph, obtained through commercial importation. *Pharaoh*, being unnamed, has been variously identified as belonging to the Middle Kingdom (XIIth Dynasty 1991–1786 BC), the XIIIth (Egyptian) Dynasty, or the Hyksos era (*c.* 1720–1550 BC), not to mention the radical later chronology. **2** *The Lord was with Joseph* (and vv. 21, 23); *cf.* Ps. 105:17. **3** *Cf.* 30:27. **4** Joseph's title as *overseer of his house* reflects a common Egyptian title. Extrabiblical evidence for Semitic slaves in Egypt shows that some attained positions of domestic trust.

9 *How . . . can I . . . sin against God?* Joseph's persisting integrity exemplified the spiritual power of divine grace operative through the covenant. The world's influence might invade the chosen community (*cf.* Gn. 38) but a holy witness to God's name would also be carried from Israel into the nations. **12** *His garment* (and vv. 15, 18). For the second time a coat of Joseph is made to lie about him (*cf.* 37:31ff.). **14** *A Hebrew* (and v. 17); *cf.* above on 14:13. Gn. 39 – Ex. 10 forms one of three clusters in the OT where 'Hebrew' appears. Though a simple equation of Hebrews and Israelites sometimes seems in view (*cf.* Ex. 5:1–3), 'Hebrews' possibly denotes a broader group of Eberites in this section. Its derogatory flavour on Egyptian lips reflects Egyptian bias against Asiatics. **20** *Into the prison*; *cf.* Ps. 105:18. Death was the expected penalty for the crime charged. **21–23** The divine favour that secured the milder penalty continued in the prison, bringing to Joseph the esteem of Potiphar's (*cf.* 40:3 and 39:1) assistant there.

40:2 *Chief butler*, better 'cupbearer', corresponds to the title of an Egyptian officer, a confidant and adviser of Pharaoh. *Chief baker*, as an attendant on Pharaoh, was another high official. **4** *Charged Joseph with them.* Joseph's trust was over administrative affairs in the prison; superiority over the high-ranking prisoners was not implied (*cf.* 41:12). **5** *Each dream with its own meaning. Cf.* above on 37:5ff. The dream data were derived from the dreamer's familiar function and concern but were so shaped by God as to be prophetic. **8** *Interpretations belong to God. Cf.* 41:16, 25ff. The Egyptian officials were dismayed by their lack of access to their favourite dream interpreters but the Hebrew slave rejected such professionals as charlatans. **13** *Lift up your head.* Joseph used a key expression capable of opposite meanings to describe first the cupbearer's pardon and restoration to honour (*cf.* 2 Ki. 25:27, RV; RSV, 'graciously freed'), then the decapitation of the baker (v. 19).

The narrator accents the device by using the phrase in a third sense, *i.e.* 'to give attention to (the pending cases)', in his account of the fulfilment (v. 20). **14** So confident was Joseph of his divine gift of interpretation that he requested a return of kindness from the cupbearer. **15** *Stolen out of the land.* Basing his claim to pardon on his actual guiltlessness, Joseph correctly described his brothers' deed in stripping him of his rights, freedom, and inheritance for their own enrichment, as a theft. **19** *Birds will eat the flesh.* The impaling and devouring of the corpse was an extreme aggravation of the penalty and disgrace (*cf.* Dt. 21:22), particularly for an Egyptian courtier, for whom mummification and a splendid sepulchre were of paramount concern.

41:1 *Pharaoh dreamed.* The providential series of dreams concludes: the middle pair (40:5ff.) proved the means for involving Joseph in the third pair (*cf.* 41:9ff.) and this last pair served to fulfil the first pair (37:5ff.). The doubling of the dreams signified the certainty of the divine purpose revealed (41:32). **2–7** For supplementary details see vv. 17–24. The repetition of long sections is part of the Ancient Near Eastern story-telling art. **8** *All its wise men.* The accessibility of Pharaoh's experts only compounded his frustration (*cf.* on 40:8). **9** *I remember my faults,* or 'remissness' (abstract plural); *cf.* 40:14, 23f. **14** *Called Joseph.* The de-Semitizing of Joseph's appearance began in deference to Egyptian custom and particularly court etiquette. Monument paintings of Egyptians depict clean-shaven faces and white linen dress. **16** *It is not in me.* Joseph engaged in this virtual wisdom contest forthrightly in the name of his God (*cf.* vv. 25, 28, 32; Dn. 2:27–30).

29–32 *Seven years of famine* would follow seven bumper crop years leaving no trace of their reserves (v. 31). The seven-year famine is known not only as a motif in ancient epics but as a reality in Egyptian historical records. **33–41** Joseph's prompt proposing of provident measures (vv. 33ff.) so heightened the impression made on Pharaoh's court that they were persuaded of his supernatural insight (v. 38; *cf.* Dn. 5:11ff.) and acknowledged him the man for the position he proposed (vv. 39ff.; *cf.* Ps. 105:21f.). Since Joseph was set as chief steward over Pharaoh's 'house' (v. 4), in command over *all the land of Egypt* (v. 41), directly responsible and subordinate only to Pharaoh (v. 40), his office may well have been that of grand vizier. Other Asiatics are known to have achieved similar eminence in Egypt's government in the 2nd millennium BC. **42** Joseph's investiture, with robes of honour and wide golden collar, was traditionally Egyptian. **43** *Second chariot;* or, chariot of the second-in-command. **45** *Zaphenath-paneah* is still of uncertain meaning. *Asenath* is a type of name attested in the early second millennium. *On,* or Heliopolis, was cultic centre of Re, the sun-god. *Potiphera; cf.* on 39:1. Joseph's entrance into the court with his change of name (*cf.* Dn. 1:7) and marriage to a priest's daughter completed his outward Egyptianization. His bold confession of the God of Israel would prevent his cultural adjustments being misunderstood as a religious capitulation.

46a *Cf.* 37:2. **50–52** Joseph's explanations of the names of *Manasseh* and *Ephraim* continued his witness to his God, with thanksgiving. He had forgotten the house of Jacob (v. 51) only in the sense that the hardship brought on him by his brothers was a thing of the past by virtue of the remarkable turn of providence. **53–57** The progressive fulfilment of Pharaoh's prophetic dreams set the stage for the final act in the fulfilment of Joseph's own dreams.

42:1 – 45:28 Remnant and reconciliation. 41:57 – 42:5 *Cf.* above on 12:10. For the chronology see 45:6. In the common emergency the whole family acted together under Jacob's authority. Benjamin now occupied the favourite's position, a circumstance on which Joseph's imminent testing of the ten would pivot.

42:6ff. *Bowed themselves before him.* Unawares they fulfilled the dreams they had gone to desperate lengths to defeat (*cf.* 37:5ff.; 42:9). Their failure to recognize Joseph is explained by his thorough Egyptianization, the incredible circumstances of the encounter, and Joseph's studious concealment of his identity. Evidently foreign grain distributions fell under Joseph's immediate supervision. Subsequent re-telling of the conversation of vv. 7ff. (see 43:7 and 44:19f.) indicates that Joseph elicited the family history (vv. 11ff.) by further questioning not recorded here. **15** *You shall be tested.* The real question was, of course, not whether they were spies, but whether they had had a change of heart. **17–20** *He put them . . . in prison,* then, showing leniency, released them in the name of his fear of God (*cf.* 20:11) to stir their consciences with the memory of how they enslaved without pity that brother they described as 'no more' (v. 13). *Cf.* vv. 21f. **21–26** *He took Simeon* (v. 24), the second oldest, as hostage after discovering the innocence of Reuben, the oldest (vv. 22f.). The subtle correspondence between the treatment each brother received and his responsibility in the selling of Joseph (*cf.* too 43:33) intensified their guilty sense of a divine vengeance stalking them (v. 21). Perhaps too they wondered whether this uncanny Egyptian practised arts of divination (*cf.* 44:5, 15). Joseph put them in that old situation again of appearing before Jacob without one brother (*cf.* vv. 33f., 36).

27 *As one of them opened his sack.* According to this and v. 35, only one of them chanced to open his sack with the money at the lodging-place, the others discovering theirs at home. The abbreviated version of the homeward trip as reported to the steward in 43:21 telescopes the initial and later discoveries of the money bundles. Actually the whole picture is simplified, for to meet the needs of Jacob's clan and justify the trip by ten men, more than ten sacks of grain must have been brought back. **28** *What is this that God has done?* Joseph's strategy was working. Already under suspicion, they felt they could never clear themselves of the inevitable charge of theft. **29–36** It appears that they withheld this crushing fact from Jacob until the multiple discovery in his presence let the cat out of the bag (v. 35). **37** Reuben as eldest assumed responsibility, displaying again admirable qualities (*cf.* 37:21ff.; 42:22). **38** But Jacob, perhaps remembering Reuben's earlier offence (*cf.* 35:22), refused his offer of surety. Such was Jacob's partiality towards Benjamin that he repressed concern to deliver Simeon rather than part with Benjamin under ominous circumstances.

43:1–8 But the preservation of the lives of all in the midst of continuing famine demanded the perilous trip—with Benjamin. **9, 10** *I will be surety for him.* It was Judah who prevailed with Jacob, assuming full responsibility for Benjamin's safety under pain of the loss of Jacob's blessing and thus of disinheritance. By the transforming grace that produced the Jacob–Israel change a new spirit of solidarity and self-sacrifice had arisen in the house divided. **11–15** Sadly resigned (*cf.* v. 14b) to the second journey, Jacob made practical, propitiatory arrangements (*cf.* 32:13ff.), committing the matter to God, almighty in His providential government (v. 14).

16–34 Observing Benjamin's presence, Joseph put his now long-meditated plan into operation (16ff.) **23** *The God of your fathers.* The steward had been taken into Joseph's confidence and perhaps even accepted the faith of Joseph. His explanation explained far more than the brothers' immediate puzzle (vv. 21f.) and at a more profound level than they were thinking; but they were too nervously distracted to hear his broad hint. Indeed, they were so wary of the steward's unpredictable master that his very hospitality alarmed them (v. 18). At the dinner they failed to leap to the one logical explanation of his behaviour, with his concern for Jacob (v. 27), affectionate favouritism for Benjamin (vv. 29f., 34), and exact knowledge of the interlocking sequence of births of these sons of four mothers (v. 33). The Egyptians' eating scruples (v. 32) derived from ideas of ritual purity. The brothers' lack of resentment towards the highly preferred Benjamin (v. 34) suggested a heart-conversion but Joseph had a more positive, ultimate test prepared (44:1ff.).

44:1 *Each man's money.* The purpose of this feature, not subsequently mentioned again, was probably to enflame the brothers' smouldering sense that God was mysteriously dealing with them for their great sin, summoning to repentance (*cf.* 42:28; 43:23). It would also lend plausibility to a punishment based on communal responsibility, so making Joseph's insistence on isolating Benjamin for punishment more arresting. **2** *The silver cup* served to separate Benjamin as peculiarly guilty, while the sacred character attributed to it (*cf.* vv. 5, 15) made its theft a crime worthy of death (*cf.* 31:32). **4** *A short distance.* Apprehension of a thief in the act, or virtually so (as when his hot scent was followed and the loot discovered in his possession), resulted legally in peremptory and extreme punishment (*cf.* 31:22ff.; Jdg. 18:22ff.). The search of the overtaken suspect was regarded as a veritable ordeal, its outcome incontestable (*cf.* 31:36ff.). **5** *By this that he divines.* Divination by water was a widespread ancient practice. Joseph's alleged divining by the cup was certainly part of the contrived situation he fabricated with his steward's assistance. **9** The penalty the brothers pronounced before the search was that customary for the alleged crime (*cf.* vv. 2 and 4). **11–13** The search ordeal with its exposure of the money bundles (*cf.* on v. 1), the astounding correspondence of its sequence to the brothers' ages (*cf.* 43:33), and the shattering exposure of Benjamin, had the desired effect. **14–17** However innocent they may have known themselves to be in the present inexplicable instance, they were convinced that God was judging their ancient guilt (v. 16; *cf.* 42:21f.). Joseph's theatrical claim (v. 15) increased their alertness to the supernatural and prompted the confession voiced by Judah as group spokesman (*cf.* vv. 14, 16; 43:3ff.). Then Joseph increased the pressure by insisting that the ten return to Jacob—without Benjamin—in peace (v. 17)!

33 *Let your servant remain instead of the lad.* More than this Joseph could not hope for. God had so changed his brothers' hearts that Judah's plea and self-offer carries away our thoughts involuntarily to the Servant born of his tribe who offered Himself for the transgression of His people.

45:3, 4 Stunned silence followed the Egyptian's *I am Joseph* and in spite of all assurances (vv. 4ff.) a persistent uneasiness remained for many years (*cf.* 50:15). **5** *God sent me.* Though stressing the sovereign providence in absolute terms (*cf.* 'not you . . . but God', v. 8a), Joseph's intent was not to deny his brothers' guilty responsibility (his whole strategy had aimed at stirring their consciences). But now that a godly sorrow gripped them, Joseph would turn them from remorseful backward looks to thankful appropriation of the future God's mercy had provided (vv. 8b ff.). **6** *Neither ploughing nor harvest*; the two words express a compound idea, 'no yield from tilling'. **7** *A remnant.* God had been preserving a remnant people to bear His revelation from the Fall in Eden through the desolation of the Flood, and out of the idolatry that overwhelmed the nations. Joseph properly traced that Messianic strand in Israel's history in his own day. **8** *Father to Pharaoh* is the equivalent of a title held by Egyptian viziers. **10** *Goshen* was an Egyptian region (*cf.* 47:6, 27) in the E Delta area (*cf.* 47:11) and thus not far from the court at Memphis (whether in XIIth or XIIIth Dynasty, or in the Hyksos era). Yet as a place highly suitable for the cattle (47:4–6) disdained by Egyptians (*cf.* 46:34) it afforded relative seclusion. **11** It thus had advantages for the immediate emergency, since Joseph could conveniently provide for Israel there, and for the long-term sojourn that would ensue, for the isolation would make possible the preservation of Israel's distinctive convenant-culture under conditions favourable to their unity and growth. **17, 18** Pharaoh changed the form of Joseph's orders to Israel's household (cf. vv. 9ff.) into a personal invitation from himself. Joseph's specific intention of locating the family in Goshen he had kept private with his brothers, adroitly securing Pharaoh's consent to that only when the time came (cf. 46:31ff.). **19** *Wagons*; probably large two-wheeled carts such as are pictured in Egyptian scenes. **22** *Five* (or 'several') *festal garments*. Joseph no longer need have qualms about sending off Benjamin in his own old position among the sons of Jacob – not even with a favourite's robe! **24** His concern was only with the possibility of recriminations among the ten as they returned to Jacob and the dreaded necessity of confessing to him their great sin. **26, 27** Easily persuaded of Joseph's death, Jacob was a doubter concerning his 'resurrection', only persuaded by the evidence of his senses. **28** *I will go*. So spoke the man Israel, and Israel the nation was destined to emerge in a land not theirs, their return to Canaan requiring God's mighty acts in Exodus and conquest that stamped on Israel's possession of the kingdom the character of a sovereign grant from a divine Saviour.

46:1 – 47:27 Israel's descent into Egypt

46:1–27 Pilgrim house of Israel. Jacob discerned through the remarkable course of events, divinely disclosed beforehand in Joseph's dreams and afterwards prophetically interpreted by him (cf. 45:5ff.), that God had sent a man ahead and now purposed for Israel's household to go down to Egypt (cf. Ps. 105:17, 23). Cf. above on 24:8. **1a** Consideration of God's warning to Abraham of a sojourn in a foreign land (15:13ff.) would make the departure from Canaan a challenge to the depths of Jacob's faith in the covenant's future. **1b** He responded with renewal of commitment to Beer-sheba, patriarchal altar site on the borders of the land (cf. 21:33; 26:23–25). **2–4** Here also Jacob received the last in the series of special revelations that marked his pilgrim life, much like the first in its circumstances and reassurances (cf. 28:12–15). The Lord dispelled any lingering uncertainty concerning Jacob's duty (v. 3b); in Egypt itself the promises would begin to be fulfilled (v. 3c; cf. 12:2; Ps. 105:24). *Bring you up again*. As the last clause in v. 4 indicates, Jacob would have the joy of reunion with Joseph but would die in Egypt (cf. 45:28; 46:30). God's promise of restoration was meant, therefore, for Israel become a nation (cf. v. 3c; 15:14, 16). **8ff.** *These are the names of the descendants of Israel, who came into Egypt.* Like the section on the generations of Esau (cf. 36:1ff.), that on the generations of Jacob (37:2ff.) distinguishes

two geographical phases—in Canaan and removed from Canaan, the latter marked here by a new genealogical list supplementing that of 35:23ff. (cf. 36:9ff.). The epochal import of the emigration to Egypt for the history of Israel and the promises (cf. Dt. 10:22) called for a formal catalogue at this point. Stylistically the conventions of such lists are followed (cf. above on Gn. 5), particularly selectivity to achieve conventional totals, in this case seventy (v. 27; cf. Gn. 10; Ex. 1:5; 24: 9). As comparison with the later list in Nu. 26 shows, the selection was designed primarily to include besides the tribal heads the founders of the fathers' houses in Israel, the major tribal sub-divisions. *Jacob and his sons* (v. 8). This shows that Jacob is included in the seventy, as does the notation in vv. 26f., apparently meaning that without Jacob, Joseph, and his two sons the total is sixty-six. Hence Jacob is to be counted among the thirty-three in the Leah category (v. 15). So also is Dinah (cf. *daughters*, v. 15), Er and Onan being omitted (v. 12). Category descriptions in such lists refer to the general situation rather than dwell on the particular circumstances of each individual. Cf. 35:26b, where Benjamin is an exception. Note also here v. 18, where the 'sons' of Zilpah include Serah (v. 17). Similarly, the whole company is described as coming into Egypt (vv. 8, 26)—not necessarily with Jacob, hence Joseph is no problem—but chronological limitations prove that some of the descendants (besides Ephraim and Manasseh) were born in Egypt. Judah's son Perez (cf. 38:29) surely did not have the sons Hezron and Hamul (v. 12) before the departure; neither did Benjamin, not yet twenty-five, already have ten descendants including grandsons (v. 21; cf. Nu. 26:38ff.). Further, on Reuben's four *sons* (v. 9), cf. 42:37. Stephen (see Acts 7:14) follows a literary tradition (cf. LXX) which includes five additional descendants. The actual size of the clan with the wives and daughters, servants and their households (cf. 30:34) would be several or even many times seventy.

46:28 – 47:27 Israel, blessed and blessing. As Pharaoh opened the door of blessing to Israel (47:6), blessing was returned upon his house through the pronouncement of Jacob (47:7, 10) and Joseph's continuing wise administration (47:13ff.). Cf. 12:3. Later, a reversal of Egyptian policy towards Israel would bring God's judgments upon them.

46:28 *Sent Judah before him.* Judah's role as trusted negotiator had been established (cf. 43:3ff.; 44:18ff.). His mission was to arrange details of the rendezvous in Goshen. **29** *He presented himself*, lit. 'showed himself'. For this appearance of Jacob's son from the dead in the glory of Egypt, an expression is used hitherto reserved in the narrative for theophany (cf. 37:9f.). **31–34** Joseph's programme for Jacob's household was calculated to protect them from Egypt's pagan influences. But he skilfully effected this without offence to the Egyptians by arranging for Pharaoh to act to separate the Israelites out of regard for Egyptian prejudice (v. 34b). **47:1, 2** In both Joseph's preparatory audience with Pharaoh (v. 1; *cf.* 46:31f.) and that of his brothers (v. 2; *cf.* 46:33f.), their occupation as shepherds and their present location in the pastures of Goshen were so stressed as virtually to put the desired decision in Pharaoh's mouth (*cf.* vv. 5f., 11f.). **6** Pharaoh's favour extended to the appointment of capable Israelites to officialdom.

9 *The years of my sojourning.* Jacob's assessment of his life is not a complaint (*cf.* 48:16a) but a soberly accurate account. In common with Abraham and Isaac he was a stranger in Canaan, his life orientated to a future city of God (*cf.* Heb. 11:13ff.); but his alien residency in Canaan was even more troubled and his life-span (as he correctly anticipated, *cf.* v. 28) briefer than theirs (v. 9b). Moreover, he must die as a sojourner outside the promised land. **11** *Land of Rameses*; Goshen is thus given, by anticipation, its later name. **13** *The land of Canaan.* Joseph's wisdom brought blessing to the promised land, while contributing to the Egyptian overlordship there. **14ff.** The economic measures instituted by Joseph were viewed by the Egyptians themselves as a favour, indeed, as their salvation (*cf.* v. 25) in the desperate famine emergency (vv. 13, 20). **18** *The following* (lit. 'second') *year.* The last of the seven famine years predicted had apparently passed, for Joseph now contemplates sowing and taxable harvests (*cf.* vv. 23ff.). **20** *The land became Pharaoh's* in fact, as it had been previously in theory. Egyptian evidence shows that the situation described here, including the priestly exemptions recorded in vv. 22, 26, existed by the New Empire period. **21** 'Removed them to cities' (AV), *i.e.* for more efficient distribution—but why at this late stage? Perhaps translate, 'from the cities', *i.e.* where they had come to be near the granaries and in order now to sow their fields again (*cf.* v. 23). RSV's *made slaves of them* follows LXX tradition and suits the context before (v. 20) and after (vv. 23, 25). **27** *Multiplied exceedingly*; *cf.* above on 46:3.

47:28 – 50:26 Israel's hope of restoration

Dying in faith (*cf.* Heb. 11:13ff.), Jacob prophetically made testamentary disposition first concerning Joseph's family (ch. 48; *cf.* Heb. 11:21), then concerning all his sons (ch. 49). Further, he charged Joseph in his capacity as Egyptian lord (47:29ff.) and all the brothers as obedient sons of the covenant (49:29ff.) to bury him in the promised land. And Joseph, dying in faith, spoke of the Exodus of the Israelites (50:24ff.; *cf.* Heb. 11:22).

47:28 – 48:22 Joseph's commission and double inheritance. 47:29 *The time drew near*; *cf.* on 27:2. On the gesture accompanying the oath (vv. 29, 31a), *cf.* on 24:2. **30** 'I will lie with my fathers' (AV). This should not be equated with burial (so

RSV) but understood as an aspect of Jacob's dying, which was to be followed by the transporting of his body into Canaan and finally burial there. Jacob's insistence on burial at Machpelah expressed his attachment by faith to the Abrahamic covenant and his trust in God's promises of the kingdom to be established in Canaan (*cf.* on Gn. 23). **31** Appropriately, therefore, he worshipped (v. 31b). The 'staff' (LXX, for Heb. *maṭṭeh*, instead of *bed*, *miṭṭâ*) would be an identifying link with Canaan (*cf.* 32:10). For the legal testamentary character of the patriarchs' dying blessings (chs. 48 and 49), *cf.* on 27:33.

48:1 The relationship of 47:29ff. to 48:1ff. is uncertain. *After this* need not refer to the immediately preceding charge. In fact, Heb. 11:21b appends 47:31b to the ch. 48 episode (unless Heb. 11:21 refers to 48:12b). Joseph's *two sons* were about twenty years old. **3, 4** Jacob recognized the source of the blessings he was about to communicate in God and traced their content to the revelation at Bethel (*cf.* 28:13ff.; 35:10ff.). **5** *Shall be mine.* This was a declaration of intent to adopt the two grandsons, thus elevating them both to the status of tribal heads and thereby giving Joseph, according to his dreams (37:5ff.), the position of firstborn with a double representation among the tribes of Israel (1 Ch. 5:1f.; *cf.* Dt. 21:15ff.). **6** Joseph's additional sons would be subsumed under the tribes of Ephraim and Manasseh. **7** The allusion to Rachel and her burial was prompted by the honouring of her son Joseph. Her sepulchre would be apart from Jacob's in ancestral Machpelah (*cf.* 47:30; 49:29ff.) but her name would be honourably remembered in Joseph's double inheritance.

8ff. The actual adoption is connected with the testamentary blessing of the two grandsons. **12** *From his* (*i.e.* Jacob's) *knees*; perhaps the legal rite formalizing adoption is implied. **14** *Crossing his hands.* Repeatedly the last became first (both Jacob and Joseph were examples), attesting that the covenant blessings are not secured by the course of nature but as sovereign gifts of God. **15, 16** *He blessed Joseph*; the sons who were being blessed now stood in Joseph's place among the tribal fathers. *The angel who has redeemed me.* Jacob knew the covenant as a living reality (v. 15) in which the Lord approached him in the sacramental visibility of the angel, assuming the role of nearest kinsman (as the verb 'redeemed' implies) to deliver Jacob from every threat to his life and liberty (see on 16:7). *Bless the lads.* Jacob blessed in that he effectively invoked God's blessing. **19, 20** *Younger brother shall be greater.* Both Ephraim and Manasseh entered tribally into the inheritance which God gave to His people (v. 16b), yet Ephraim attained greater prominence in Israel's history. **21** Jacob's hope of restoration would not be realized in Joseph's lifetime, and hence the prophecy would be repeated when Joseph was dying (*cf.* 50:24). **22** *Mountain slope.* Jacob punned on *šᵉkem*, 'shoulder', the name of

112

the city of Shechem. For near it they had a possession (cf. 33:19f.) which was a pledge of the future conquest of Canaan here prophesied. *I took*; the tense is prophetic perfect, *i.e.* the past tense is used, as often in Hebrew, to express the certainty with which a future event would happen. Jacob and Joseph here represent their descendants. Joseph was buried at Shechem (Jos. 24:32; cf. Jn. 4:5). 'One . . . above thy brethren' (RV); as privilege of the firstborn. Cf. Jos. 17:14ff.

49:1-33 Jacob's prophetic testament. *Cf.* Dt. 33:1ff. These death-bed (v. 33) blessings (v. 28) of the original twelve were testamentary and prophetic. 1 'In the latter days' (RV). This testamentary vision looked beyond the Mosaic Exodus and restoration to the Messianic (see on vv. 10ff.). At the same time the general tribal characterizations here given received historical embodiment during the OT phase of God's kingdom. Leah's six sons are treated first (vv. 3-15), then the four sons of the handmaids (vv. 16-21), and Rachel's two last (vv. 22-27). The pre-eminence of the Judah and Joseph tribes in Israelite history is prophetically matched here by the prominence of their blessings. Reuben, Simeon, and Levi are included as tribes belonging to the future covenant nation and to that extent are blessed. Yet it is the shadow cast by their crimes over their blessing that receives all the notice (vv. 3-7), thereby providing a dark foil against which Judah's glory bursts forth (vv. 8ff.). 3, 4 *Cf.* 35:22; 37:3; 48:5; 1 Ch. 5:1f. 5, 6 *Cf.* 34:25ff. 7 *I will divide them*; this was a destiny opposite to the sentiment of Levi's name (cf. 29:34). Levi's cities were distributed among other tribes. For the later change of this curse into blessing see Dt. 33:8ff. 8, 9 *Shall praise you*; Hebrew *yôdûka*, a pun on *yᵉhûdâ*, Judah. *Bow down before you.* The charismatic leadership over Israel assigned to Joseph in his generation would take royal form (cf. v. 10) in Judah, in the dynasty of David, who by his military prowess and political sagacity triumphed over Israel's enemies on every side (vv. 8b, 9).

10 *The sceptre shall not depart.* The royal dignity of Judah attained in David was made permanent by the Davidic covenant (cf. 2 Sa. 7:16), fully realized in the Kingship of Jesus Christ. 'Until Shiloh come' (AV). The Hebrew text here contains the word *šylh*. The versions, however, apparently reflect a reading *šlh*. If we follow the lead given by the versions, we read the word as *šellôh*, equivalent in Hebrew to *'ašer lô*, meaning 'that (which) to him'. One possibility then is to understand it to mean 'that which belongs to him (*i.e.* Judah)': Judah will continue to be the royal house until all that is rightfully his comes to him; or again (as RSV) 'he to whom it (*i.e.* the sceptre or kingship) belongs'. Ezekiel evidently treats the passage in this latter way (Ezk. 21:27; in the Hebrew Bible 21:32; cf. Ezk. 19), apparently in a Messianic sense; his treatment of *š(y)lh* could involve free

punning. If the MT *šîlôh* is followed (as in AV), then the traditional understanding of it as a Messianic title meaning something like 'the establisher of peace' (cf. 1 Ch. 22:9), will deserve the preference over the interpretation of Shiloh as the Ephraimite city (*e.g.* 1 Sa. 1:3). In Christ, Lion of the tribe of Judah (Rev. 5:5; cf. Gn. 49:9) and Prince of peace (Is. 9:6), the turning-point was reached in the Davidic dynasty, not terminating it but introducing its final and complete expression. To Christ is *the obedience of the peoples, i.e.* of the nations universally (cf., *e.g.*, Ps. 72:8-11; Is. 11:10), and only His reign produces the peace of ultimate and eternal paradise (vv. 11f.; cf., *e.g.*, Ps. 72:15f.; Is. 11:6ff.). If the Hebrew consonantal text *šylh* is differently divided, one possibility is *šay lôh*, 'tribute-payment to him', the last two clauses of v. 10 then being parallel. Again it would be to Judah's Messianic Descendant that this international acknowledgment comes.

13 *At the shore* (Heb. *lᵉḥôp̄*). Is this another instance of the preposition's meaning 'from' ('apart from the shore'), for Zebulun's later tribal allocation was not maritime? 16 *Dan shall judge* (*yādîn*). Many of Jacob's blessings involve such Hebrew word-plays. 18 *I wait for thy salvation, O Lord.* This irrepressible 'Come quickly' may have been inspired by Jacob's apprehension of the trials to be faced or by his longing for the kingdom to be inherited. 22ff. Upon Joseph, separated to pre-eminence among his brethren (v. 26), Jacob pronounced blessings in peace (vv. 22, 25b) and war (vv. 23f.), tracing them all to God, whom he identified repeatedly as his own (cf. 'of Jacob', 'of Israel', 'of your father', vv. 24f.). MT in v. 26 reads: 'have prevailed above the blessings of my progenitors (*hôray*) unto ('*ad*) the utmost bound (*ta'āwaṯ*) of the everlasting hills' (AV). RSV prefers *harᵉrê* '*ad, eternal mountains*, and *bounties* for *ta'āwaṯ*; cf. Dt. 33:15; Hab. 3:6. 29 *He charged them.* The twelve as a group of equals were entrusted with the mission of faith already assigned to Joseph (cf. 47:29ff.). 33 *Was gathered to his people*; cf. 47:30.

50:1-26 Covenant guardianship. The era of the patriarchs was over and the covenant community and witness came under the guardianship of Joseph as the prototype of a new, charismatic leadership in Israel, one that would resume with Moses and culminate in Christ. 2 *Embalmed Israel.* The associated religious beliefs, particularly the Egyptian idea of immortality, were not adopted with the Egyptian art of mummification. It was rather utilized in the interests of Jacob's postponed burial in Canaan, itself a testimony to Israel's own distinctive hope. 4ff. Diplomatic considerations, or possibly disqualification from appearance in the royal court by reason of his mourning, explain Joseph's indirect approach to Pharaoh. 5 *I hewed out*; Jacob had prepared a place for his burial in the cave Abraham purchased (cf.

49:30; 50:13). **7-9** The exodus of Jacob according to Joseph's request amid the honour of Egypt was a pledge of Israel's later departure with Egypt's treasures, following Moses' negotiations with Pharaoh. **10** Similarly the entrance of Jacob into Canaan from across the Jordan in vv. 10ff. witnessed to and found its counterpart in Israel's conquest of the land under Joshua. **11** *Abel-mizraim*, 'meadow (or watercourse) of the Egyptians' puns on '*ēḇel*, 'mourning'. Possibly the Egyptian escort remained here while Jacob's sons completed the mission that registered before the eyes of the Canaanites Israel's continuing claims in their land. **18** *Fell down before him*. Again Joseph's dreams were strikingly fulfilled and the reconciliation of Israel's house confirmed (v. 21). **19, 20** *Cf.* above on 45:5ff. **22** *A hundred and ten years* (and v. 26) was esteemed by Egyptians the ideal life-span. **24, 25** *His brothers*; Joseph's kinsmen in general may be meant. *God will visit you*. Joseph emulated Jacob's dying faith, confessing the covenant God and hope by prophetic word (v. 24; *cf.* 48:21; ch. 49) and commission (v. 25; *cf.* 47:29ff.; 49:29ff.). **26** On v. 26b, *cf.* on v. 2 and see Ex. 13:19; Jos. 24:32. *So Joseph died*, but Israel in Egypt continued under the covenant guardianship of the God of Abraham, Isaac, and Jacob unto the day of redemption.

MEREDITH G. KLINE

Exodus

INTRODUCTION

TITLE AND AUTHORSHIP

The Greek translation of the OT (the LXX) bestowed the title Exodus (Gk. *exodos*, 'a going out') on this book; in the Hebrew Bible it is named after its opening words, viz. 'and these are the names'. Moses has been denoted as its author by Hebrew tradition (Ecclus. 45:5), by the Lord Jesus Christ (Mk. 1:44) and by His disciples (Jn. 1:45). Besides this we have the testimony of the book itself in 17:14, and this is nowhere explicitly contradicted. For further examination of the subject, see the article on 'Moses and the Pentateuch' (p. 41), which gives the position adopted here.

THEME AND PURPOSE

The key verses to the understanding of the book are 19:3–6, and from them two main subjects arise: the judgment of the oppressors and the deliverance of the oppressed (19:4), and the constitution of the delivered as the people of God and their characteristics (19:5). The main body of the book deals with these two themes and is divisible on this basis: *e.g.* 1:8 – 19:2 deals with judgment and deliverance, and 19:7 – 40:38 deals with the new society thus brought into being. In addition, there are two link sections which, together with the above, serve to give consistency and harmony to the book. These are 1:1–7 which shows how the Israelites came to be in Egypt and which paves the way for 1:8 – 19:2, and 19:3–6 which shows how they came to be at Sinai and prepares the reader for 19:7 – 40:38.

The main events recorded in this book are related to these two locations, Egypt and Sinai, and they are the two foci of the book, the latter being viewed as the goal of the former. The intervening wandering in the wilderness is viewed as the consequence of the deliverance and the necessary prelude to the constitution of the Israelites as the people of God. The emerging outline is simple and clear. 1:1 – 19:2—how the Israelites came to be in Egypt and how they came from there to Sinai; 19:3 – 40:38—how they consequently became, and were to manifest themselves as, a distinct nation.

The title given to the book by the Greek version, as we noted above, embodies its central and inescapable theme, that of God's deliverance of slaves in bondage that they might become a people for His own possession, service and glory. This is the central act recorded in the book, but attention is given also to certain of the resultant privileges and responsibilities; this theme is concluded in Leviticus. All this foreshadows a greater exodus (deliverance) to come through the Lord Jesus Christ's death, and the emergence of those who were 'no people' as the people of God. The covenant He sealed by His blood creates the church; this the OT adumbrates and in it the OT believers participate.

THE DATE AND ROUTE OF THE EXODUS

The most helpful treatment of this subject is to be found in K. A. Kitchen's book *Ancient Orient and Old Testament*, 1966, pp. 57–75. Reference may also be made to the relevant section in the article 'Chronology of the Old Testament' in *NBD*.

Although there is no attestation of Israel's presence in Egypt in Egyptian records, there is no ground for denying or querying the biblical statement that *twelve* sons of Jacob went to Egypt (Ex. 1:1–5) and that their descendants came up from there (Ex. 24:4).

There is considerable debate, however, as to the date of the Exodus, and two main schemes of dating are advanced for the Exodus–conquest period. Neither is without some supporting internal evidence, but as yet neither is wholly free from objection. We shall list the more important data below and then tender a view for the purpose of this commentary, but the reader is referred also to the above-mentioned works, and in addition to the following: C. de Wit, *The Date and Route of the Exodus*, 1960, and M. F. Unger, *Archaeology and the Old Testament*, 1965. There are two suggested dates for the Exodus. The first is *c.* 1440 BC and the second *c.* 1290 BC.

Exodus *c.* 1440 BC (according to Prof. M. F. Unger)

1. 1 Ki. 6:1. The fourth year of Solomon's reign would be *c.* 961 BC and therefore the Exodus would be *c.* 1441 BC and the entry to Egypt *c.* 1870 BC, in accord with Ex. 12:40, 41. If this scheme is not accepted, then the Exodus-monarchy period has to be telescoped as a consequence. 2. Thutmosis III (1482–1450 BC) was a conqueror and renowned builder and is suited as the pharaoh of the oppression, and Amenhotep II as the pharaoh of the Exodus. 3. Events in Palestine, as they are reconstructed from archaeological finds, *e.g.* the mention of the invading Habiru in the Amarna letters and the fall of Jericho, confirm that the entry took place *c.* 1400 BC.

This view comes to grief in connection with Ex. 1:11, however, at the above point, and is a little naïve as regards the methods of OT chronology, assuming as it does that one has simply to add up the numbers given in the Bible in order to arrive at firm dates, whereas it is more likely that in many cases figures given represent a formal reckoning of so many years to a generation, rather than the exact passing of that number of calendar years.

Exodus c. 1290 BC (according to K. A. Kitchen)

1. For the building of the store-cities, Ex. 1:11 gives a date at the *end* of the oppression. Ra'amses was founded by Sethos I but built by Rameses II who acceded in 1304 or 1290 BC. 2. The stele which records Merenptah's victory over the Libyans c. 1220 BC mentions that Israel was subdued along with other peoples in Syria-Palestine. Thus Israel was in Palestine by c. 1220 BC. The 40 years' wandering in the wilderness is not a mere cipher, and so we have 1290 to 1260 for the Exodus and 1250 to 1220 for the invasion. 3. The presence of strong kingdoms in Edom and Moab was impossible before 1300 BC. 4. Excavations at sites in Palestine show that the invasion began in the second half of the 13th century. The evidence at Jericho needs careful scrutiny because during the time it was in ruins whole levels of the city were washed away, but Lachish, Bethel and Hazor fell about this time. The collapse of Ai defies dating, however. 5. The Habiru are not to be identified with the invading Israelites because they were a diverse people, native Canaanites, and are attested from the 18th to the 12th centuries. 6. As regards 1 Ki. 6:1 and the 480 years mentioned there, addition of the separate time-references in the Exodus—1 Kings corpus gives 553 years plus three unknown amounts. In connection with this the methods of Ancient Near Eastern historical writing need to be recalled, because here narratives are not synchronized with others by a system of cross-references but listed as successive rather than contemporaneous.

Such is the relatively indecisive state of the dating of the Exodus. It is the later date that we shall adopt for the purpose of this commentary. The route taken, with the tentative locations of the stopping-places mentioned, appears on the map below (p. 123). Reference should also be made to K. A. Kitchen's article 'Wilderness of Wandering' in *NBD*.

THEME STUDIES

The Self-disclosure of God: miracle and theophany

God manifests Himself by acts in the realm of human history (Ex. 6:7) but also by acts in the realm of nature, for He is Creator and Lord of all. He is always greater than nature and reveals Himself through it, but is never to be confounded with it. The OT witnesses to the order of nature (Gn. 8:22; Ps. 104:19, *etc.*) because of the character of the Creator who is wise, perfect and stable, but it also places on record the fact that God can throw nature into an upheaval (controlled by Him) in order to reveal His majesty, power and holiness. This is miracle, and it is seen in Exodus in the nature-miracles of the plagues, the Red Sea, the water from rock, the manna and quails, the pillars of cloud and of fire, and Sinai engulfed in a cloud and yet aflame.

Where these phenomena admit of a natural explanation, they are accorded a measure of acceptance by an age that still does not like to acknowledge supernatural incursions by God into His universe. But where no such explanation is forthcoming, this acceptance is completely wanting, particularly in connection with the truths revealed by God, or the messages uttered from Sinai in spoken and written words. Such phenomena are described as factual occurrences, invested with a significance intended by God, and interpreted by revelation to and through Moses, and ought to be accepted as such. The Creator is not only at liberty to transcend laws He has made for the universe, but also has the ability to do so, both in speech and action.

The angel of the Lord. He is of particular interest and point here. The ministry of angels was, until Moses, the distinctive means of divine revelation to the elect, but ceased to be so from the time of the Mosaic revelation, for these truths and institutions made angelic visitations less necessary. This is theophany. The following references and facts are to be studied in connection with the angel of the Lord, who is a 'man' and no winged creature. 1. Gn. 16:7ff. In v. 11 the Lord is spoken of in the third person, but in v. 13 the angel is spoken of as God. 2. Gn. 18. Among the three men who appeared to Abraham, one is distinguished as the Lord (vv. 20, 26) from the two others who are called 'angels' and are said (19:13) to be sent by the Lord. 3. Gn. 22:11ff. The angel of the Lord calls from heaven as if he were God Himself, and Abraham obeys as he would obey God. Yet in v. 16 the angel is distinguished from the Lord and obeys Him by giving the message. 4. Gn. 24:40. The angel is distinguished from the Lord once more, and does His bidding in leading. 5. Gn. 48:15, 16. Here there is complete identification between the angel and the Lord. 6. Ex. 3:2. The angel is identified with the Lord. 7. Ex. 13:21 compared with 14:19 seems to view the designations as being interchangeable. Yet *cf.* Nu. 20:16. 8. In Ex. 33:20 the two are distinguished, but this chapter is of special importance for it is because the Israelites cannot suffer God's own presence, following their apostasy, that the angel is sent. God can dwell with sinners through the angel without consuming them (33:3), but the angel cannot be trifled with or he will judge, being the manifestation of the holiness of God. Yet in 33:14 God's presence goes with them in the form of an angel; *cf.* Is. 63:9. Here is God accommodating Himself to sinners without diminishing His divinity. 9. Jos. 5:14. The prince of the Lord's army is distinct from the Lord, but then identifies himself with the angel who appeared to Moses (v. 15), and is identified with the Lord in 6:2.

From these factors it appears that the angel of the Lord was at times identified with the Lord Himself, and that the whole divine nature was present in him. The angel of the Lord is a form of the Lord's Self-manifestation. There are, however, other references where the angel is distinct from the Lord. This stresses that even in the OT there is some diversity within God, the one Subject, and it adumbrates the appearing of His eternal Son. 'It is now easy and inevitable to see in the Angel of the Lord the clearest Old Testament foreshadowing of the Second Person of the Trinity. Where else in Scripture is there One Who is identical with the Lord and yet distinct; Who, without abandoning His deity, yet kept company with sinners; Who walked as a man among men; and Who, without denying the wrath of God, yet represents the supreme outreach of mercy?' (J. A. Motyer, *Introducing the Old Testament*, 1960, p. 11). See further the General Article, 'Old Testament Theology', p. 29.

The glory of God. This is an important theme in the book and it appears in relation to the deliverance and wandering in the wilderness, the ratification of the covenant and the Tabernacle. The comment that follows here will bear a relation to all these contexts.

It could be concluded that a discussion on this theme should be related to a discussion on the being and attributes of God. In the OT, however, 'glory' is the visible and supernatural manifestation of the supreme and incomparable majesty of God. The Hebrew word for 'glory' (*kāḇôḏ*) means 'weight' or 'substance', and comes to mean the honour stemming from the manifestation of the sum total of God's attributes, and also from the awe which such a revelation inspires in those who behold it; *cf.* Ps. 96:5–9.

The face of God. The 'presence' of God is His 'face'; *cf.* Ex. 33:20. 'My face' and 'me' are interchangeable and so 'the face' stands for God's own presence. To see God as He is is possible only through a Self-disclosure which, though true and reliable, is not exhaustive. The presence of God was never a mere sense of the numinous, but always the presence of a known, personal and distinctive Deity.

The Name of God. Ex. 6:3 is important for the criticism of the Pentateuch (see the introductory article 'History of the Literary Criticism of the Pentateuch'; also J. A. Motyer, *The Revelation of the Divine Name*, 1959).

In Ex. 3:14, 'I AM WHO I AM' represents only one possible translation of the divine Name, for the verb could equally mean 'I was' or 'I will be'. It is used in this last sense in 3:12. It is undoubtedly correct to acknowledge that the Name is deliberately mysterious, preserving 'much of His nature hidden from curious and presumptuous enquiry' (J. C. Connell, *NBC*, 1953, *in loc.*). The Name, therefore, reflects the truth that God can be known only as He chooses to reveal Himself, and this, indeed, leads us to the central value of the otherwise enigmatic title which He chose. The verb used means 'to be an active, present reality'. Thus, for example, in the familiar phrase 'the word of the Lord came to . . .' (*e.g.* 2 Sa. 7:4) this same verb occurs, being customarily given in English translation 'came', but really expressing the felt and active presence of the word. In exactly the same way, the God of Israel declares that His presence and power will be made known to His people in the events of the Exodus. It is not simply that He will engineer these events, but that they will constitute a visible declaration of His name; *i.e.* His character will be revealed in and by them.

It does not matter, therefore, whether we accept the translation 'I am' or 'I will be', or the other possible variant, advocated by Albright (*From Stone Age to Christianity*, 1957, pp. 15, 16), 'I bring to pass'. The meaning is the same: the events reveal the Person. It must be remembered, however, that Moses was not sent to these events as a mere observer, gleaning what he could by watching, but as an instructed and prepared interpreter. The essence of the revelation of God was given verbally, especially in the doctrines of holiness (*e.g.* Ex. 3:5) and redemption (*e.g.* Ex. 6:6, 7), and it is this primary propositional revelation (*i.e.* revelation by means of intelligible words and propositions, revealed truth) which enabled Moses to interpret the Exodus correctly and which gives his interpretation of the events the same divine authority as the events themselves in revealing God. Through Moses and the Exodus, therefore, the divine Name received its classical OT definition: 'Yahweh your God brought you out of the land of Egypt' (Ex. 20:2). When we recall that this redemption necessarily involved judgment upon Egypt, the full revelation can be stated in summary form: Yahweh (in RSV, 'the LORD') is the God who saves His people and judges His enemies (see on Am. 3:2, and see further J. A. Motyer, *The Revelation of the Divine Name*, pp. 21–24).

In Ex. 6:2, 3 the Name as such was not unknown but the significance was; *cf.* Je. 16:21 for an exact parallel. The Name is the Person active and revealed, and the use of the future tense involved can be summed up by saying that a changeless God would ever meet the need of His people; the Name is dynamic rather than abstract. In Exodus the unfolding of the character of the Person thus named is in connection with His activity described in 6:4–9; *cf.* 33:19.

Covenant

Consult J. A. Thompson, *The Ancient Near Eastern Treaties and the Old Testament*, 1964 and J. Murray's article 'Covenant' in *NBD*. See also the General Article, 'Old Testament Theology', pp. 30ff., above.

The Hebrew word *bᵉrît* ('covenant') has two possible etymological derivations. One is *bārâ* ('to eat'), referring to the cultic meal which usually accompanied covenant-making ceremonies; *cf.* Gn. 26:30. The phrase *kāraṭ bᵉrîṭ* ('to make—lit. cut—a treaty') lends credence to this by pointing to the cutting (slaying) of animals for the covenant feast. The other one is to derive the noun from an Assyrian root, *beritu*, meaning 'bond' or 'fetter'. Vriezen (*An Outline of Old Testament Theology*, 1960, p. 141) translates it as 'a bond of communion' and so preserves both possible derivations.

Covenant types and patterns in the Ancient Near Eastern world. The idea of covenant was widespread in the Ancient Near East, and the OT contains a variety of covenants: *personal, e.g.* David and Jonathan, 1 Sa. 18:1–5; 20:1–16; *parity, e.g.* Abraham and Abimelech, Gn. 20:28ff. (tribes or descendants were involved here); *suzerainty, e.g.* God and Israel at Sinai, Ex. 19ff. It is this latter form in which we are interested because of the very close connection between this Ancient Near Eastern literary form and the actual pattern of the Sinai covenant. This pattern, used in Hittite suzerainty (or vassal) treaties, came to serve as the perfect literary vehicle for the expression of God's relationship with Israel. This pattern idea of covenant was in vogue from 1500 to 700 BC and was not a late development of Israel's religion under the insight and influence of the 8th-century prophets (as Wellhausen thought), but was the very source of it. The typical Hittite suzerainty covenant was set out as follows, and a pattern of this kind appears in Ex. 19:3–8; 20:1–17, and also in Deuteronomy and in Joshua.

1. Preamble: the names, titles and attributes of the great king are set out. 2. Historical prologue: the past relations of the parties are described, with emphasis on the benevolence of the king to the vassal; *cf.* Ex. 19:4. 3. Stipulations: obligations imposed on the vassal are here set out in detail; *cf.* Ex. 20:1–10. 4. Deposition of the covenant document: to be read annually to the people; *cf.* Ex. 24. 5. List of gods, both of the king and of the vassal, who acted as witnesses. 6. List of curses and blessings; *cf.* Dt. 27.

The significance of 'covenant'. In the OT it is not true to say that a covenant was merely a legal bond, although it was expressed in the language of current jurisprudence. What is more important is the prior election by God, and His deliverance, of those with whom such a bond is made. This combination of privilege and obligation leads us to the central significance of the covenant idea, which is the relationship between God and Israel. This relationship is not an agreement, nor a compact arrived at by discussion among equals. It is 'a sovereign administration of grace' (J. Murray) which results in communion between Israel and God. The covenant is sovereignly administered, and obligation ensues on the part of Israel.

The covenants and the Sinai covenant. In Gn. 9:9–17 the covenant with Noah is clearly established in love and forbearance by God with Noah as the fount of the new race to people the purged world. God plans, reveals, confirms ('my bow') and keeps this covenant irrespective of man's response.

In Gn. 15, in the covenant with Abraham the promises made are centred on salvation, and are particularistic (in excluding Ishmael and in not being to all flesh). The promises and blessings are such that by their very nature they demand consecration in the recipient.

The Sinai covenant is made with Israel in confirmation of the covenant with Abraham (Ex. 2:24; 3:16). It is not legalistic for it was made with a chosen, redeemed and already adopted people (Ex. 2:25; 4:22; 6:6–8). It is a spiritual relationship which occupies the central place here; *cf.* Ex. 6:7.

Seeing that the covenant cemented a relationship, the demands of God's holiness must be brought to bear upon the people by way of regulating the communion and conditioning the enjoyment of its blessings. 19:5, 6 and 24:7, 8 ought not to be understood in such a way as to cause the making of the covenant to depend on the promise of obedience forthcoming. The covenant is made; what is conditioned on obedience is the enjoyment of its blessings. Thus holiness (Lv. 19:2) is to be the result of the covenant relationship and hence arises the OT conception of law and ritual.

Law

Law, or Torah (Heb. *tôrâ*; *cf.* the article 'Law' in *NBD*), means a teaching or a decision given for a particular case, and in its extended significance stands for the whole body of rules governing man's relations with God and with other men. Since all the OT legislative codes are found in the Pentateuch, it is itself referred to as 'the Law' or *tôrâ*.

The great variety which exists within the law can be sampled by comparing together the 'codes', *i.e.* those sections of the Pentateuch which because of either their literary style or their distinctive content have suggested that they originated as individual statements of Israelite law. For example, there is the Decalogue (Ex. 20:2–17) with its high moral tone and its categorical (or apodictic) commands; there is the so-called 'book of the covenant' (Ex. 20:22 – 23:33), exemplifying Israelite casuistic or case-law, laws covering specific situations and couched in the form 'If . . . then . . .'; the Deuteronomic code (in its essence, Dt. 12–26; *cf.* G. T. Manley, *The Book of the Law*, 1957), while it covers many of the topics found in other codes, nevertheless has a marked literary style and flavour; or there is the law of holiness (Lv. 17–26) which so clearly influenced Ezekiel and the post-exilic situation but which, of course, need not itself be post-exilic in origin.

All these codes or types of law live against a background of jurisprudence extending far into pre-Mosaic history, and there is nothing in either their content or their extended form which requires a post-Mosaic date. Hittite treaties, Hammurabi's law code and the whole range of Sumerian law make it needless, on grounds of anachronism, to query the Mosaic origin of OT law. Equally, specific difficulties alleged against Mosaic authorship are often not impossible of solution. The ongoing work of scholarly research has left far behind the suggestion that the Decalogue expresses a morality too advanced for the Mosaic age and it is now commonplace for Moses to be acknowledged as the source of the 'ten words' (e.g. H. H. Rowley, 'Moses and the Decalogue', in *Men of God*, 1963, pp. 1–36; and for a fuller survey of opinion J. J. Stamm and M. E. Andrew, *The Ten Commandments in Recent Research*, 1967). The existence of slightly differing versions of the Decalogue in Exodus and Deuteronomy (5:6–21) is most easily explained on the presupposition of Deuteronomy itself, that Moses in his farewell speeches reviewed the words which God had spoken through him but in direct address took the liberty of small variation and adaptation.

Of more direct consequence for the book of Exodus is the argument that since the laws often envisage a settled community, frequently of an agricultural character (e.g. Ex. 20:22–26; 23:10, 14–17), they must stem from and reflect the actual existence of such a community. But the testimony of Exodus itself, and indeed more explicitly of Deuteronomy (e.g. Ex. 23:23–33; Dt. 6:1), is that these laws were given prospectively. Though spoken by divine inspiration in the desert they look towards the settled community which Moses envisaged throughout. Being well acquainted with the needs and forms of settled life he could without difficulty legislate for it. Thus the tribal federation seen in the assembly of Jos. 24 could well give a focus and reaffirmation to these laws, but is not required as their point of origin.

What are the distinctive features of Israelite law? (See W. Eichrodt, *The Theology of the Old Testament*, Vol. 1, 1961.) First, the entire law is ascribed to God. Not only the cultic law but also the civil law is invested with the authority of God, and any breach of it is open revolt against God. Thus the law is lifted above the world of human arbitrariness and relativism. It might be objected that in the Code of Hammurabi the authority of Shamash is invoked at the beginning and the end. The main body of the material, however, is linked with Hammurabi, the human lawgiver, the deputy of Shamash. In the Pentateuch the law is laid down by God, and to Him the human mediator is subservient. This law (see on 20:1ff.)

covers the whole of the national and individual life, investing it with high spiritual significance. The striking and unique feature is the conjoining of moral precepts with religious commands.

Secondly, the law exhibits a higher view of human life, and a consequent abolition of gross brutality in punishment of the guilty. 'One crime—one punishment' is a unique feature of Israelite justice. Penalties could not be multiplied arbitrarily as in Assyria, nor was bodily mutilation practised to the same degree; it was, in fact, specifically curtailed (21:24). This is evidence of a feeling for humanity, but also of an insistence on equity. This latter part is important, for in Hittite law (c. 1250 BC) there is a relaxation of the old severe code, but at the expense of justice and morality; murder, e.g., is no longer punishable by death. In Israel, penalties are relaxed only when the nature of the crime demands it, and thus absolute standards are not undermined.

Thirdly, there is but one law for all. It is undeniable that the laws of Hammurabi, e.g., are weighted in favour of the ruling classes, but in the OT one is struck by the legal safeguards proposed for the defenceless, e.g. widows and orphans (Ex. 22:22), strangers (Heb. *gerim*, 'refugees', folk seeking political asylum, 23:9), debtors (21:1ff.) and slaves (23:12). In this matter also it is the divine origin of the law which gives rise to these humanitarian precepts. Israel is to reflect in conduct what God has done for them and what He is in Himself (22:21; 23:9; Dt. 10:17–20).

The Tabernacle: the environs, appearance, furnishings and significance

The Tabernacle occupied the centre of the camp (Nu. 1:50) and was surrounded on the sides by the tents of the Levites (Nu. 1:53), while Moses and the priests encamped in front of it (Nu. 3:38). Thus it appeared that God who was in the midst of His people was yet apart from them by reason of His holiness. The Tabernacle faced east (Ex. 27:13) and was enclosed by curtains of fine twined linen, hanging from pillars of brass with connecting silver rods. It was at one end of a court also enclosed by curtains; the entrance to this was at the centre of the eastern end and was marked by a hanging curtain (27:16) supported on four pillars of brass.

Passing behind the entrance curtain, then, the worshipper found himself in the court. Before him, and between him and the Tabernacle, was the bronze altar of sacrifice (27:1–8) signifying that all who entered were defiled by sin and could approach God only by way of sacrifice or shed blood (Lv. 17:11). This altar was tended by the priests. The worshipper might slay his offering, but the priest had to perform the sacrifice (Lv. 1–7). Within this sacred enclosure the sacrificial meal (peace-offering) was to be eaten. Near the altar stood the laver for the use of the priests who carried out the sacrifices (Ex. 30:17–21).

119

Directly behind the altar of sacrifice stood the Tabernacle, which only the priests were permitted to enter. Its dimensions were 10×30 cubits, and in all probability the entrance was at the exact centre of the court. The Tabernacle consisted of two parts. There was a wooden structure (Heb. *miškān* or 'dwelling') which took the form of three sides of a rectangle, at the front of which, instead of a fourth gilded board, was a curtain screen called the outer veil (Ex. 26:36f.). Beyond this veil there was a second which divided the interior into two rooms, the Holy Place and the Holy of Holies (26:31–33). This veil had cherubim embroidered on it to symbolize the immediate presence of God. The Holy of Holies was apparently a perfect cube of 10 cubits.

The *miškān* had no roof but coverings which were spread laterally over the top, sides and rear. The inner covering was exactly like the veil which separated the Holy Place from the Holy of Holies. Above this covering there was one of goats' hair, then one of rams' skins dyed red, and above it another of seal or porpoise skins. The entire front of the dwelling was concealed, and only the priests were permitted to pass behind to the Tabernacle in performance of their duties. When they did so, they found themselves in the Holy Place (26:33). It was lighted by the golden lampstand which had seven lamps (25:31–40) and which stood to the left; these lamps were to be fed with pure olive oil, and they were tended by the priests (Lv. 24:1–4). It burned from evening until morning (Ex. 27:20; *cf.* on Lv. 24:1–4) and not during the day. Its principal significance was undoubtedly symbolic, displaying Israel's 'relation to God as the possessor and reflector of the holy light that was in Him' (Fairbairn).

The table for the bread of the Presence (25:23–30; in older translations 'the shewbread') was on the right-hand side, and on it were twelve cakes of unleavened bread and cups probably containing wine or oil (v. 29). They were an offering and memorial of the daily food of the people which was returned to God as it came from Him. The loaves were changed every sabbath and, having been consecrated, were eaten by the priests in the Holy Place (Lv. 24:5–9). The placing of frankincense on the loaves connects the table with the altar of incense, and stresses the idea of an offering.

The altar of incense was the most important furnishing of the Holy Place, indicated by the fact that it stood before the veil which separated the Holy of Holies from the Holy Place. On it, morning and evening, the priest (Ex. 30:7ff.) placed a pot of incense, and the fire, kindled by God Himself, was never to be allowed to go out (Lv. 6:13). The incense symbolized the prayers of God's people.

The Holy of Holies was separated only by this veil, behind which none might pass save the high priest, and he only on one day in the entire year, the Day of Atonement (Lv. 16). In the Holy of Holies was only the ark of the covenant, containing the Ten Commandments. Above the ark was the mercy seat which was of pure gold and overshadowed by the cherubim. The ark was the throne of God, and there He spoke. The Holy of Holies was in complete darkness as far as natural light was concerned. It was filled with the brightness of the Shekinah, the light of God's presence. This light was seen in the pillar of cloud and of fire, which abode on the Tabernacle while Israel rested in their tents and which, when it was moved, guided the people on their journey (Nu. 10:34). This cloud, which represented the presence of the Lord and which had the appearance of fire by night (40:38), sent out fire to kindle the sacred, undying fire on the altar (Lv. 6:12, 13; 9:24), and also to punish the wicked and disobedient.

The whole pattern of the Tabernacle was designed to emphasize the fact that God dwelt amid but apart from His people. He is invisible and spiritual, exalted and unapproachable in holiness; His people are sinful and cannot enter His holy presence. His blessings had to be mediated by a priesthood through sacrifices, and could be received only by those who brought and offered blood sacrifices. All this has obvious relationships with the NT.

OUTLINE OF CONTENTS

COMMENTARY

1:1 – 4:31 THE STAGE IS SET

1:1–7 A historical review

This condensed recapitulation of Gn. 46:8–27 serves as link material between these two books. This list concentrates on the immediate descendants of Jacob and includes twelve sons, his daughter Dinah, fifty-one grandsons, his grand-daughter Serah and four great-grandsons, besides himself. To this number must be added the 'household', *i.e.* the wives and servants of each son and grandson—totalling more than seventy! In the genealogy, the sons of the legitimate wives are placed first and then those of the concubines.

5 The number 'seventy-five' in Acts 7:14 and in LXX of Gn. 46:27, compared with the *seventy* here, has been variously explained: by supposing that (*a*) though only seventy went down with Jacob, Joseph called for seventy-five, not knowing that three wives of Jacob and two sons of Judah had died; or that (*b*) Stephen, in addition to the sixty-six mentioned in Gn. 46:26, reckoned the twelve wives of Jacob's sons, omitting Judah's who was dead, and Joseph's who was in Egypt, as well as Joseph himself, for the same reason; or lastly (*c*) that in Gn. 46:20 the LXX adds the sons of Ephraim and Manasseh from the

genealogy in 1 Ch. 7:14–21 while the Hebrew list omits them because they were not born until afterwards. In one of these three ways the variation of the LXX from the Hebrew may be readily accounted for. Stephen's adherence to the former is explicable on the basis that he quoted from the most current version without correction on a matter so small, and not that he was out to correct the Hebrew text.

7 The rapid increase and influence of the Israelite people was in accord with the covenantal promise in Gn. 17:2 and *the land* would be the territory of Goshen rather than the whole of Egypt.

1:8–22 The beginnings of the oppression

8 There is no compelling reason to regard this *new king* as the inaugurator of a new dynasty (as in the view which dates the Exodus in the 15th century) but simply as denoting a king who began a new policy toward the Israelites. In accord with the 13th-century dating of the Exodus (see Introduction, 'The Date and Route of the Exodus'), this would be Sethos I (1302–1290 BC) who was neither acquainted with Joseph, nor even aware of his services to Egypt, and thus cared little for Joseph's descendants. Sethos I was renowned for his building programme, and this accords with the measure taken in v. 11.

9, 10 The growth of the Israelite population posed an acute problem for Pharaoh in that, as they occupied border territory, their defection to the enemy in the event of an invasion would be a decisive factor in the fortunes, or even collapse, of the Egyptian Empire. **11–22** The Egyptians were unwilling to dismiss them, however, and to miss a chance of turning their presence to profit; Sethos I devised a plan to meet both needs. He sought to consolidate the area with two store-cities, which were towns housing arms and supplies for defence and attack, and also by controlling the increase in the Israelite population by forced labour and child slaughter. This latter move was thwarted through the covenant care of God and the bold defiance of the Hebrew midwives. These obeyed His will and they were blessed with families themselves (not 'houses' as in AV). This is the first presage of the triumph of God over Pharaoh, and it is from this initial victory that the great deliverer comes.

2:1 – 4:31 The first stages in God's purpose of judging and saving

2:1–22 The instrument of the deliverance. 1–9 This is a stylized account of the birth and upbringing of Moses; it is therefore understandable that the names of the parents are omitted and that no reference is made to Aaron, who presumably was born before the edict of Pharaoh. The dark environmental background to Moses' birth serves to emphasize the sovereign activity of God. This male child was not only successfully concealed and then spared by Pharaoh's daughter herself as she was moved to compassion by his cries, but was even formally returned to his own mother to be weaned, for which she was paid. After that he was to be adopted by the royal princess—the daughter of Israel's oppressor. Thus Moses came to be learned in Egyptian lore (*cf.* Acts 7:22), and the faith of his parents was vindicated (*cf.* Heb. 11:23).

10 His name (see 'Moses' in *NBD*) reflects his double ancestry as the adopted son of Pharaoh's daughter and the actual son (as the princess herself acknowledged) of Hebrews. The Egyptian *mǎšě* (*ms*, 'child') represents the first thought of the adoptive mother, and this was hebraicized as *mōšeh*, from the verbal root *mǎšâ* meaning 'to draw out'. The actual form *mōšeh* is an active participle, 'one who draws out'. It may be that Pharaoh's daughter was persuaded to this form by reference to herself who became a mother by 'drawing out' the 'child', or that the form was the implied prayer of the actual mother, 'May the Lord draw out His people.'

11–14 Moses soon identifies himself with the oppressed rather than the oppressors (*cf.* Heb. 7:24ff.). By slaying the Egyptian he renounced his adoptive state, but his concern is not immediately obvious to his people. This act reveals that Moses as yet is not ready for the task, for it is by meek obedience to God (*cf.* Nu. 12:3; Jas. 1:20) and not unrighteous wrath, and by God's power, not his, that his people were to be delivered. This discipline in trust and obedience was to take 40 years.

15–17 Moses flees for safety, a fugitive from the law, and seeks refuge with the Midianites, a semi-nomadic people who were descended from Abraham by Keturah (*cf.* Gn. 25:1). The territory intended here was probably in the SE of the Sinai peninsula. Moses rests at a well, the centre of social life in the Ancient Near East. Here again he acts in defence of the downtrodden, suggestive of the fact that God is already secretly preparing him in character and temperament for his life's work of rescuing slaves. **16** *Priest of Midian*. Priestly offices were undertaken by heads of tribes or families. **18–22** *Reuel* ('Ragual' in AV Nu. 10:29 is the Gk. equivalent), or Jethro (see on Nu. 10:29ff.), becomes Moses' father-in-law in return for services rendered, and in time comes to worship the same true God as Moses; *cf.* ch. 18. Moses' son's name is composed of *gēr* ('stranger') and *šām* ('there').

2:23–25 The need for deliverance and its source. In accord with the dating scheme adopted, the Pharaoh whose death is mentioned here would be Sethos I (see on 1:8), who was succeeded by Rameses II (1290–1224 BC). The clear teaching of this brief but important passage is that God hears His people's cry and sees their need in tender compassion, but not as a helpless, saddened spectator. He is one who in sovereign love and power acts on the need He sees and the cry He hears, because He has taken a covenant oath upon Himself in respect of these people. God had begun to prepare a deliverer before His people had cried for deliverance, however, and with the death of Pharaoh the time arrived for the deliverer to return to Egypt. Thus plainly is the Lord of history a God of grace, and the God of grace is the Lord of history.

3:1 – 4:17 The call of Moses and his task described, with divine assurances of ultimate success. Mt. Horeb, or Mt. Sinai (the former usually denotes the mountain range and the latter the particular peak in question), has been identified in ancient tradition with Gebel Musa, located at the tip of the Sinai peninsula. This fits in with the tentatively plotted path of the Israelites in their wanderings (consult the map). Here, far from Egypt, the deliverer is finally prepared by God by being humbled in spirit (3:1–6), admitted into God's purposes (3:7–10) and assured of God's presence and power (3:11 – 4:17). Moses calls this 'the mountain of God' after his experiences there.

1–6 Moses' humbling before the presence of God. This is brought about by a Self-revelation of God as He is. The 'burning bush' is not in any way a symbol of Israel. God is living (the burning bush was not consumed and therefore the flame was self-maintaining), and holy (fire or flame was an emblem of the purity that constitutes a threat to sinners; *cf.* Gn. 3:24). This is not only a revelation of God Himself, but also a mirroring of what God was to become in the life of Moses, and of what was to be the source and mainspring of his ministry: not an inquisitiveness into the supernatural (v. 3), nor a mere compassionate defence of the down-trodden (2:11), but a concern for the glory of God in His covenant people. *The angel of the Lord*; see the note in the Introduction, p. 116.

7–10 Moses' initiation into the purposes of God. God's purpose is to prove that He knows the condition of His people and cares for them by manifestly condescending to their cry and need, and by bringing them from harsh bondage to possess a land at present occupied by others. Moses is told this, and is appointed as one chosen and sent to lead the people out of bondage. From poverty they were to enter a land of plenty and a land of some expanse; *cf.* Dt. 6:3. Thus the first movement of God towards Moses is to outline in words what He proposes to do. God does not simply act and then leave men to puzzle out the interpretation of what He has done. He starts by making Moses wise before the event, so that the activity of God, when it comes, confirms the word already spoken (*cf.* v. 12).

3:11 – 4:17 Moses is assured of the power of

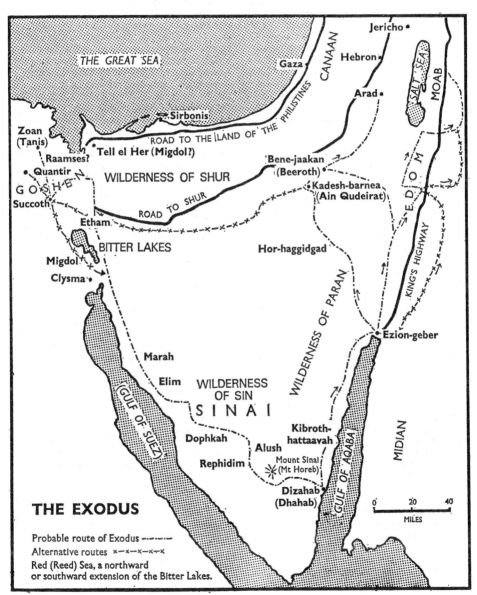

THE EXODUS

Probable route of Exodus ·—·—·—·
Alternative routes ×—×—×—×—×
Red (Reed) Sea, a northward or southward extension of the Bitter Lakes.

God. His old impulsive nature has been humbled and now his reluctance before the magnitude of the task is brought to light, and is overcome by suitable assurances. Four objections are advanced by Moses and each is answered by God. **11, 12** First, there is the problem of complete unfitness for the task described. This is met by a promise of constant accompaniment and thus complete provision, with added assurance that the liberated slaves (for the deliverance would come to pass) would join him in worship on the very mount on which he stood. The sign, in that it lacked a present fulfilment, was a further incentive to faith in the promises of God.

13–22 Second, Moses raises the obstacle of the people's ignorance of the character of God and hints that thereby they will not believe the message he brings. Moses is not here asking for the bare name of God which has not been made known to them, but rather for the inner significance of a name already known (*cf.* 3:6). *I am who I am*. The answer given to him amounts to this (see the Introduction on 'The Self-disclosure of God' for fuller details), that God will prove Himself to be ever dependable and sufficiently resourceful to meet every need of the people, and in this case will both outmatch Pharaoh in a contest of might, and also deliver and enrich His people. **18, 19** It might be concluded that this request amounts to an untruth and to an attempt to provide a way of escape under a religious pretext. About this, two things should be said. First of all, the animals used in sacrifice by the Hebrews would have been a source of offence to the Egyptians (*cf.* 8:26); secondly, this simple request was aimed to reveal Pharaoh's true character and so ultimately to magnify the power of Israel's God over so obdurate a foe. **21, 22** After the Egyptians have felt the power of God's hand they will be glad to be rid of their slaves and their profit-making labour, to such an extent that they will give their riches in response to a mere request (*cf.* 12:35, 36).

4:1–9 Third, though thus assured that God will reveal His name (character) in irresistible might and grace, Moses is still hesitant on the ground that he is unsure that the Hebrews will accredit his call and receive him as God's servant. Power to perform three confirming wonders is given to him to meet this contingency. The point about the nature of these wonders is that they will have weight with the Hebrews in their environment of Egyptian magic (*cf.* 7:8f.) and make no demands on their faith as in the case of Moses on the mount (*cf.* 3:12). It is foolish to judge them by modern standards.

10–17 Fourth, every argument of Moses is adequately answered, but he is reduced again to his inner sense of inability, and in particular he mentions his lack of eloquence. Confrontation by God and converse with Him have not altered matters in this respect. Moses is then made aware that he is pleading impotence before the Omnipotent who bestows and increases faculties and gifts as He wills, and he is promised that he will learn to speak by speaking what he is taught by God. Moses is unbelieving in this respect, and arouses God's holy displeasure by asking for a substitute to be sent. A helper is given to meet this need, namely Aaron who will be the mouthpiece (prophet) of Moses. But this is a double-edged provision (see ch. 32). Divine truth is to be made known to Moses, and to be declared by Aaron. **15, 16** perfectly exhibit the nature of revelation, that it is a verbal disclosure both of what God wishes to teach to the unknowing, and also of inspiration and communication, that this is sovereignly superintended by God so that what He chooses to reveal may be infallibly communicated.

4:18–31 The response of Moses and his reception by the people. 18–20 Moses prepares to return to Egypt with Jethro's approval and at God's command, now that the time has come, with a view to doing God's bidding, but he is forewarned again that immediate success will not be forthcoming. Even so he is commanded to confront Pharaoh with God's sovereign reality and His claim that His enslaved people should be freed in order to serve Him, and to add a warning of the consequences that will attend a refusal in the face of the continuing performance of the signs. **21** foreshadows the response of Pharaoh to this call (*cf.* 7:13, *etc.*) and God's response to this by way of judicial hardening (*cf.* 9:12; Rom. 1:24). **23** The contest is for the respective 'firstborn' (a relation of special endearment and honour). Both may survive, but both will not die. God will see to this. His own 'firstborn', the whole nation of Israel, will be delivered.

24 God is no respecter of persons, however, and 'special' servants must obey as well as perform their special task. Moses is to be punished by God for neglecting to circumcise his son. Gn. 17:14 was seriously intended, and now God rises up to enforce His requirements. **25, 26** Zipporah perceives the cause of Moses' affliction, and takes it upon herself to do what Moses should have done. She circumcises the boy and associates Moses with the act by touching him with the blood from the circumcision wound. *A bridegroom of blood*. To think of this remark as upbraiding is more than likely a by-product of the unfortunate AV translation. Her words are more probably of relief and gratitude that her marriage, threatened with termination in the death of Moses, is thus renewed. He has become her bridegroom once again thanks to the blood of the circumcision. The force of this little incident in the story of redemption cannot be exaggerated. Deeply ingrained now in Moses' heart is the truth that it is the wrath of God (not of Pharaoh) from which man needs protection, and that God has Himself supplied sufficient protective covering in His covenant of grace and its ordinances. It is this truth which is seen in its perfection on

Passover night and in connection with the blood of the lamb.

27 Moses and Aaron meet at Horeb and Aaron becomes Moses' mouthpiece (prophet). **29–31** They are then received by the Israelites with their elders, and the stage is set for the ensuing conflict. Whose son is to die? Whose son is to be delivered? *Cf.* v. 23.

Notes. **The hardening of Pharaoh's heart.** Pharaoh's heart was already filled with blind pride and self-will when Moses appeared to him on the first occasion (5:1ff.; *cf.* 1:9, 10, 16; 3:19). His heart was hard already and for this he was responsible. God might have softened his heart and disposed him to allow the Israelites to depart, but He chose to act otherwise (9:16; *cf.* Rom. 9:17), and, by an outpouring of His just wrath, to bring to naught Pharaoh's inveterate and increasing opposition, and to judge him for it. This also applied to his subjects on the same ground (14:17). God is at perfect liberty to use His words and works to soften hearts, as in the case of Moses (3:6), or so to ordain it (Rom. 9:18) that they should be the means of throwing into marked relief the natural and deep-seated antipathy of others, as in the case of Pharaoh (5:1–10; 7:10–13, 22, 23, *etc.*). Pharaoh hardens his heart, *i.e.* resists God, when given a command or a temporary alleviation of chastisement (*e.g.* 9:34, 35). This is no chance happening, however, and it is itself the outworking of the wrath of God who 'gives men up' to the dominating power of their own innate desires as a present judgment on their sin (Rom. 1:24, 26, 28).

This is what is meant by the seemingly bold statements that the Lord hardened Pharaoh's heart. It does not mean that God bestows perversity to Pharaoh's heart by a direct internal act, as He bestows His grace, nor that He does something to Pharaoh against Pharaoh's will, but that what Pharaoh wants to be, viz. an opposer of God, God ordains that he shall be. Conversely, Pharaoh wants to be this, not because God ordains it, but because he so desires.

Circumcision. This was not unknown in the Ancient Near Eastern world, but what must be noted is the special significance attached to it in Israel. The distinctive feature about its observance in Israel is that it was performed in infancy, and as such it could not be a rite for initiation into manhood, nor a pre-marital rite. Gn. 17 shows it to be a spiritual sign, and only secondly a national sign. Primarily it was a seal of the covenant movement of God to man, in connection with which man responded to God in obedience. That it was principally a covenant seal is attested by the circumcising of the male infants to whom God could pledge His blessings within the covenant (*cf.* Gn. 17:7) but who could not at that stage respond in covenant obedience. Even in the OT, the rite was to symbolize the 'circumcising of the heart' (Dt. 30:6) by God's outworking of His gracious covenant within the household unit (Gn. 17:7).

5:1 – 15:21 JUDGMENTS AND DELIVERANCE

5:1 – 11:10 Preliminary judgments on Egypt

5:1 – 7:13 The first round of interviews. 5:1–5 The first interview with Pharaoh reveals him to be unmoved either by God's authority or by human compassion. **6–14** As a result the bondage is intensified instead of liberty being granted. **15–21** Likewise, the Hebrews are unbelieving in their complaining. Their lot was easier before the alleged deliverer came! **22, 23** Moses needs reassurance and turns to God (*cf.* 1 Sa. 8:21), as he does on similar occasions later. **6:1–9** The assurance he is graciously given is reminiscent of the original terms of his call. The Name was not unknown to the patriarchs, but the full significance of God's character thus designated was to be revealed to these afflicted and embittered slaves by a powerful, compassionate deliverance with positively enriching consequences. All this was in accord with the covenant made with their fathers. But it all falls on deaf ears and crushed spirits. See Introduction for notes on 'the Name of God' and 'covenant'.

10–13 Moses is being made bolder in the work he is called to do but is still prone to decide what God can or cannot do with him. Seeing that he is unsuccessful with his own people, how can he impress Pharaoh? Moses ought to know that eloquence cannot deliver, for what is needed is a 'heavenly charge' or command that emboldens and makes all other service or work impossible (*cf.* Acts 4:20). **12** Just such a heavenly charge is God's reply to Moses' confession of *uncircumcised lips*. He acknowledges that his powers of speech are no more than those which belong to the natural man, but that the lips needed for this mammoth task need the touch of divine grace and a gift of speech from God Himself. Thus, though he transfers the idea of circumcision from its primary setting, he retains the essential idea of an act of God marking and making a man His own.

14–25 The genealogy is inserted to pinpoint the lineage of Moses and Aaron, and data are omitted on a principle of conscious selection for this purpose. It is not, however, a needless intrusion. Like many of the genealogies in Scripture, its purpose is to show the steadily-unfolding plan of God. All through the Egyptian bondage, God was quietly and unobtrusively at work so that when the moment of deliverance came His instruments of deliverance were there to meet it. **26, 27** Consequently we read that *these are the Aaron and Moses, i.e.* the men thus born according to the faithfulness of God. But they go to their work, not as the descendants of the great ones of the past, but armed freshly with the word of God. **28–30** Lest this point should be missed, it is somewhat emphasized here. The reply to man's native inability (uncircumcision) is the gift of the very words of God.

7:1 sees the resumption of the narrative broken off at 6:13 and the scheme of God's immediate purpose is disclosed. **2–6** Pharaoh is again to be challenged in God's name, though his obduracy will increase in spite of the plagues that God will bring upon the land and the people. Mere plagues will not deliver, however, but another act of a special nature will, and Egypt will thus be convinced of the supremacy and Lordship of God alone. **8–13** In working within history, God condescends to people in their environment. The incident related here is evidence of this. But it is also evidence that God goes beyond the bounds of current custom or practice and so manifests His sovereignty. Snakes could be temporarily immobilized to correspond to rods and hence the imitation of the Egyptian magicians, but Aaron's serpent returning to a rod demonstrates the omnipotence of God. But still Pharaoh would not bow. See also the article 'Magic and Sorcery' in *NBD*.

7:14 – 11:10 The first nine plagues. The relevant article in *NBD* should be consulted. These plagues fulfil the promise in 3:19, 20 and are intended to reveal the superior power of Israel's God over the gods of the Egyptians. The nine plagues manifest natural phenomena which occur in the Nile valley, and the miraculous element in them is to be found in their timing, intensity and distribution. It has been shown that these occurrences can be connected with an unusually high inundation of the Nile from July or August to the following March. 'The excessive inundation may have brought with it microcosms known as *flagellates* which would redden the river and also cause conditions that would kill the fish. Decomposing fish floating inshore would drive the frogs ashore, having also infected them with *Bacillus anthracis*. The third plague would be mosquitoes, and the fourth a fly, *Stomoxys calcitrans*, both encouraged to breed freely in the conditions produced by the high inundation. The cattle disease of the fifth plague would be anthrax contracted from the dead frogs, and the 'blains' on man and beast (sixth plague) a skin anthrax from the *Stomoxys* fly of the fourth plague. Hail and thunderstorms in February would destroy flax and barley, but leave the wheat and spelt for the locusts whose swarming would be favoured by the same Abyssinian rains which had ultimately caused the high inundation. The thick darkness would be the masses of fine dust, *Roterde* (from mud deposited by the inundation) caught up by the *khamsin* wind in March' (K. A. Kitchen, *Ancient Orient and Old Testament*, 1966, pp. 157f.). The crucial point here is that it is the Nile, an object of worship in Egypt, which is turned into an instrument of judgment and havoc (*cf.* 12:12). God is in control even of His foes and can exalt Himself over them by means of natural disorders.

7:14–24 In the case of the first plague the sign is announced beforehand so that Pharaoh may realize why this is taking place, and the warning given is no idle threat. **22** The magicians may have obtained clear water, as in v. 24, to try to explain the occurrence in a different way. Black magic was rife in Egypt and counterfeits were far from being impossible! In connection with the magicians see 2 Tim. 3:8, a characteristic of the 'last days', *i.e.* the interval of time between the two comings of the Lord Jesus Christ.

7:25 – 8:15 The sign of the second plague is announced beforehand with the same purpose in mind, and when it takes place it is counterfeited. But only God can remove the frogs, and does so in response to prayer uttered on the basis of a show of penitence from Pharaoh. Temporary afflictions do not change the heart, however, and the profession of the lips can be unreliable.

8:16–19 The third plague is sent without any warning as a direct response to Pharaoh's duplicity, and for this reason the magicians cannot counterfeit it. The devil is bound when God wishes to manifest Himself conspicuously, as in this case. The confession of the magicians is evidence of this.

8:20–32 The fourth plague demonstrates the purposeful and discriminating activity of God which is behind all the plagues, in that the Hebrews were clearly exempted from this one. **24** The fly mentioned here would destroy property. **25** Again a superficial response is offered and the Israelites are permitted to sacrifice *within the land*. This is refused and while complete permission is given it is withdrawn as soon as the flies are removed by God in answer to Moses' prayer.

9:1–12 Again a division is made between the Egyptians and the Hebrews in the inflicting of the fifth plague (vv. 1–7). But as Pharaoh continues his stubborn resistance, the sixth plague (vv. 8–12) is sent without warning, and not only are the magicians unable to counterfeit it, but they are victims themselves. Now judicial hardness is set to work, and Pharaoh is given up to his own wicked heart.

9:13–35 Before inflicting the seventh plague, special explanations are given. **20** The Egyptians who believe the Lord's word are not to be smitten; **25** they save themselves and their cattle. Pharaoh is now to be the object of the manifestation of the justice and might of God against sin, and he is ripening for the final judgment. **27, 34, 35** reveal that he cannot repent in spite of what he knows. In all this, the Hebrews are unscathed.

10:1–20 The plague of locusts is now threatened. Pharaoh's servants have responded like their master (*cf.* 9:34) and so are to become monumental lessons to succeeding generations. **2** *Made sport*; better 'acted ruthlessly' or 'severely' (*cf.* 1 Sa. 31:4). It can have the bad meaning of immoral wantonness (*cf.* Jdg. 19:25), but here it pinpoints the sovereign power of the Lord before which the Egyptian Pharaoh and his servants are as mere playthings. It does not, of course, ascribe wantonness or thoughtless cruelty to God. **7** shows that some of Pharaoh's servants are not as hardened as their master; **10** but the bitter irony of Pharaoh is unabated. **16, 17** The locusts produce a temporary change and this is judged in the succeeding plague.

10:21-29 The ninth plague, darkness, is of special significance. Rē', the sun-god, was one of the chief deities of Egypt, and yet the Hebrews alone have light in their dwellings. Still Pharaoh is obdurate, and Moses will not take less than total liberty. To banish Moses is to say a final farewell to hope and peace.

11:1-10 The warning of the final plague is given but the time of its occurrence is not specified. **7** Sudden, overwhelming grief will be the portion of many families, but the Hebrews will be safe. **10** The significance of this must not be missed. It acts as a conclusion to the first section of the narrative of judgments and deliverance. A terminus has been reached. The acts of God, in which there is no redemption, but only sterner enslavement through the hardening of Pharaoh's heart, are over. The narrative as it were draws a line under them. They are distinct and separate from the work of redemption to which the Lord now proceeds.

12:1 – 14:31 The final judgment on Egypt and the ending of the bondage culminating at the Red Sea

The Jews' civil year began in the autumn, following the harvest, but here (12:1) is the institution of an ecclesiastical year beginning in the spring, and commemorating the deliverance.

The final judgment on Egypt was one of God's outpoured wrath, and the provision of the Passover sacrifice served to make an even more conspicuous division between the Egyptians and the Israelites, providing the latter with a means of peace in a day of wrath, and liberty from bondage issuing in pilgrimage. This, according to the NT, is a clear type of the death of the Lord Jesus Christ, of Christian salvation, and of the walk of faith that follows. Therefore the Passover sacrifice was to protect the Israelites, and to provide them with the deliverance which the earlier plagues could not procure.

12:1-28 The Passover. The characteristics of the sacrifice and God-given regulations for the use of its blood and body are full of meaning. The lamb or kid was to be a yearling, a male (costlier than the female) and without any physical blemish—perfect. Its death (blood) was to be a substitutionary atoning token to God for the Hebrew families. The roasting by fire of the whole and its complete consumption by eating or burning marked the complete consecration of the sacrifice to a holy purpose, and the partaking of it with holy awe and repentance (unleavened bread and bitter herbs, v. 8) indicated that what was thus offered to God was accepted by Him and in turn made the means of liberty and life to His people.

The blood is what God looked for (v. 13) and what provided safety (v. 23) for those who sheltered beneath it (v. 22). They were truly safe—against them 'not a dog shall growl' (11:7) on a night when death stalks abroad (12:12), because the death of the Passover sacrifice is the substitute for the 'first-born son', the nation (4:22, 23). The Feast of the Passover was to be observed perpetually because it enshrined this truth (12:26, 27) and in this sense it would be a memorial, to man and not to God. The Feast of Unleavened Bread marked the decisive suddenness of the deliverance (v. 39) and the dedication and redemption of the first-born proclaimed the fact that all Israel was God's ransomed firstborn, lest they forgot (13:2).

5, 6 *In the evening*; literally 'between the two evenings', *i.e.* either between the sun's decline and sunset, or between sunset and nightfall. According to Josephus, the *lamb* (it was invariably a lamb rather than a kid) was killed between the ninth and eleventh hour, *i.e.* three to five o'clock (*cf.* Mt. 27:45-50). **11** This applies only to this celebration but the point is of permanent relevance: the redeemed are committed to pilgrimage. **13** All was not given automatically to the Hebrews—commands had to be kept, promises received with trust and blood sprinkled before safety could be theirs. **15-20** This festival was to precede future observances of the Passover, and to be marked by an absence of leaven and a cessation from toil—spiritual, holy rest is to follow deliverance. **22** *Hyssop*; the shape of this plant was admirable for the purpose designated, and thus it came to be a symbol of purification (*cf.* Ps. 51:7). **24** This was a family ritual and the children were to look upon this past event as their past (*cf.* Pss. 44:1-3; 66:6).

12:29-51 The killing of the firstborn and the ending of the bondage. 31 *Cf.* 10:26. The arrogance of Pharaoh (10:28) contrasts strikingly with this belated acquiescence in what Moses there required. Truly 'all flesh is grass. . . . The grass withers . . . when the breath of the Lord blows upon it.' This plague fulfilled the terms of the original warning to Pharaoh (*cf.* 4:23). **32** The dismissal of the Hebrews is out of personal concern—*bless me also*. **36** The Egyptians give all that they are asked for, just to see the Hebrews departing, as the Lord had told them (*cf.* 3:20-22).

37 *Six hundred thousand.* This is a round figure doing service for the figure given in Nu. 1:46, and includes only adult males. **38** The *mixed multitude* included Egyptians by intermarriage, and other Semites who had entered Egypt. They were not to be dismissed, but neither was their presence to lead the Hebrews into any compromise, nor to result in the blurring or distorting of the distinctive covenantal elements of Hebrew faith, religion and life. On the contrary, every 'stranger' (v. 48) could participate in all the spiritual benefits the Hebrews enjoyed, provided that each one was circumcised, *i.e.* 'came near to the Lord'. (For the numbers of departing Hebrews, reference should be made to the relevant part of the article 'Wilderness of Wandering' in *NBD*.) **40, 41** This figure corresponds to the more general date in Gn. 15:13. This period of time began with the entry of Jacob into Egypt (Gn. 46:6, 7) and ends with the day of deliverance 430 years later.

13:1–16 The setting apart of the firstborn. 2 This is a command which calls for dedication of that which has been delivered, and while it would literally refer to the firstborn of man and beast, it is intended to symbolize and apply to the call to the whole nation (the firstborn) which has been redeemed (*cf.* Rom. 12:1). Sanctification follows, made possible by initial redemption. This vivid reminder within each family circle would be needed (Dt. 6:3–15). **8–10** Hebrew religion neither groped after the unknown, nor was incarcerated in formal ritual; the heart that remembered with joy and gratitude the saving act of the known God was the prime necessity in worship. This still remains true in the additional ritual of Leviticus. **9** The Egyptians had words written on strips of cloth which they wore as amulets. A similar custom came to be practised by Jews later when at prayer. Phylacteries (see *NBD*) bound on the head and the left hand contained handwritten copies of Ex. 13:1–10; 13:11–16; Dt. 6:4–9; 11:13–21. This became the custom in intertestamental times but here, and in v. 16, is pure metaphor, which stands as a further witness to the essential inwardness of true religion in the OT.

13 This command definitely prohibits infant sacrifice and is an expansion of v. 2; 22:29 is to be interpreted in agreement with it. The ass is taken as a representative of unclean animals, valuable as a beast of burden, and was to be redeemed or destroyed. These are the alternatives—dedication or destruction.

13:17–22 The beginning of the journey. 17 The direct route to Canaan was *the way of the land of the Philistines* (consult the map on p. 123). **18** These were a strong, warlike people and the Hebrews were unprepared for such a contingency in spite of their thoughts otherwise. But it was God's purpose to reveal Himself as the only warrior in the overthrow of Egypt and the invincible helper in the battle with Amalek. Easy escape was the prelude to the demanding discipline of trust and obedience. The apparently roundabout route was dictated by God's knowledge of the fickleness of the people whom He would bring safely home, and by His desire to guard them from trials which would prove too much for their faith (*cf.* 1 Cor. 10:13). This is one of the explanations of puzzling acts of God with His people.

19 The prediction of Joseph came true (*cf.* Gn. 50:25), and he who died in faith was carried to the homeland towards which he had looked (*cf.* Heb. 11:22). **21** These visible symbols of

God's presence were their constant guide and accompaniment (*cf.* Nu. 10:33–36; Ex. 33:14, 15). See note on 'theophany' in the Introduction.

14:1–31 The 'Red Sea' crossing. This was at the same time ultimate judgment and irreversible deliverance and it brought the people to a national self-consciousness that was truly religious. It was so outstanding that it was never forgotten as a fact, though the demands of the covenant on which it was based often were. It was regarded as the conclusive proof of God's love and the just basis of His claim to their devotion (Je. 2:6; Ho. 12:13). Consult the map for the route to the crossing-place; it appears that this occurred at the Sea of Reeds ('Red Sea' is a mistranslation), near modern Qantarah.

2 The locations cannot be identified with certainty, but it appears that the Hebrews were led by visible emblems of God's presence into a cul-de-sac. They were hemmed in by the Bitter Lakes and a mountain range, with impassable water before them, and an intractable foe behind them. **3** Hence the taunt of the Egyptians is to some purpose; **11** and the rebellion of the Hebrews is the symptom of their faithless panic. In this situation, prior (vv. 1–4) and additional revelation (vv. 15, 16) emboldens Moses, convincing him that, contrary to appearances, the situation is entirely under God's control, having been brought about by Him that He may display, and Israel may see, *the salvation of the Lord.* The whole situation was to be overturned: the foes were not to be seen again, God would be glorified in judgment of sinners; the freed slaves were to fear pursuit no more, God would be glorified in deliverance of the hopeless and helpless.

19, 20 The people are defended by the Lord, and the cloud covers the Egyptians with darkness, but gives light to the Hebrews (RSV mg.; *cf.* 24:16, 17). See also the note on 'theophany' in the Introduction. The power is God's alone, but it is exercised through His appointed servant. The crossing is miraculous in the sense that God uses a natural agent (a strong east wind) with positively supernatural results (dividing the waters). **25** The acknowledgment of the Egyptians is the partial fulfilment of vv. 17, 18; the reaction of those who remained in Egypt would also come into the situation. The Hebrews, on the other hand, believe, fear (v. 24) and rejoice (15:1).

15:1–21 The song of the redeemed

The song of Moses is a poetical version of the prosaic account in the previous chapter, and this ought to be remembered in its interpretation. Moses' paean of praise is ascribed to the sovereign Lord (vv. 1–3) for what He has done against the arrogant Egyptians (vv. 4–12), and for what He will yet do against the inhabitants of Canaan (vv. 13–18). The evidence of God's irresistible and gracious power just given, forming the first part of His covenant promise (vv.

3, 16), is sufficient warrant for praising Him in anticipation for what remains to be done (vv. 13, 17). All this attests God's uniqueness and transcendence (v. 11). This one act of deliverance has revealed the very eternal depth of His character (cf. Introduction), but He was also the God who revealed Himself to this nation's forefathers (v. 2). This one act has revealed His power against His foes and love for His people; this is the foundation of His endless reign (v. 18; cf. Ps. 66:5–7). God purposes not only to deliver His people but to dwell with them (v. 13) and to be the object of their worship (v. 17) and the source of their blessing (v. 13). Cf. Rev. 15 and note the context and the theme of this endless song.

20, 21 Miriam, the prophetess, takes up the same theme and leads the women in praise and a solemn but spontaneous dance of joy.

15:22 – 19:2 FROM THE RED SEA TO SINAI

15:22 – 17:16 At Marah, Elim, the wilderness of Sin and Rephidim

This is a record of sinful complaints. At Marah, the cry is 'What shall we drink?'; in the wilderness of Sin they say, 'What shall we eat?' In spite of the suitable provisions which were miraculously provided in both cases and the gift of further water at Rephidim, they still ask, 'Is the Lord among us or not?' Such is the recalcitrance of this people, which increases in frequency and consequent seriousness after the covenant-making at Sinai (see the historical narratives of the book of Numbers). On account of this a whole generation dies in the wilderness.

The action of God's providence as shown in the miracle at Marah will be repeated in the characters of His people if they obey God's law (15:26). This test of obedience is implemented in the wilderness of Sin (see map) by the supernatural provision of manna. The people are thus without excuse should they forsake their Deliverer who provides for them and does not leave them to die in the wilderness (16:4). This manna has no known parallel and its daily continuance, sabbaths excepted, until they ate of the fruit of the land of Canaan (16:35; cf. Jos. 5:12) is nothing short of miraculous. The Lord tests Israel by this, but also manifests Himself to Israel by means of it. Some is to be kept as a memorial of how Israel was sustained in the wilderness (16:33). The sabbath is not new; it was a creation ordinance (Gn. 2:1–3), and is here introduced as a means of rest and benefit, commanded and provided for the people. God will provide for man on this day without his toiling for his food.

The testing and striving at Massah and Meribah does not go unpunished, though water is miraculously provided, for a foe comes against Israel. Amalek (cf. Gn. 36:12, 16) is overcome not by picked warriors and persistent combat, but by supplication and intercession. The curse and judgment that falls upon Amalek is by way of retribution for the abominations they had in common with the Canaanites and for their action against Israel (Dt. 25:17–19; 1 Sa. 15).

For the locations of Marah, Elim and Rephidim, see on Nu. 33:7–15.

15:22–27 At Marah and Elim. 22 In the wilderness of Shur (see map) the Israelites come to Marah after some 30 to 40 miles traversed, and here the Exodus motif is repeated, namely that realized dependence upon and crying to God precedes the solution He gives. This is a walk 'by faith, not by sight', and even those delivered depend on God for survival as much as they had to depend upon Him for deliverance. **25** That there might be a tree with natural properties for sweetening brackish water is not impossible, and if one takes this view the miracle would consist in the use of natural elements to a supernatural effect. The fact that God used a tree, planted long since and now grown to maturity, makes this incident an example of anticipatory providence. He had begun to prepare for their need long before the need arose. How out of place their complaints! Prayer was the only requirement. **27** The rest and refreshment of Elim with water in abundance was another evidence of God's care, but this was soon forgotten (see below, 17:1–16) at Rephidim.

16:1–36 In the wilderness of Sin. 2, 3 The people now prefer food to liberty, and even to life itself. What they petulantly require will be a further means of testing their faith, obedience and satisfaction with God alone. **4, 5** They are to use the *bread from heaven* in accord with His law and to keep none except on the sixth day. But in this they disobey (vv. 20, 28). **8** Their sin is not made light of; its constant repetition is being noted and is ripening for judgment (vv. 20, 27, 28).

13 The common quail migrated across the Red Sea in large numbers at this time and, faint after a long journey, could be caught with ease. The miraculous element consists in the time of their arrival. This was not a staple diet but a luxury; they came as a fulfilment of God's promises in v. 12 and give additional evidence that it was the Lord who brought them out from Egypt and that their murmuring was against Him, and not His servants (cf. v. 8). In addition, the quails could be a punishment when sought by those who despised the manna (Nu. 11:4–7, 31–35). **14** Each morning after the dew there was found on the ground a *fine, flake-like thing* like hoar-frost with a honey taste, which could be ground and used in cooking and baking. Several partial parallels to this are known to exist in the Sinai peninsula, *e.g.* honeydew-producing insects leaving sweet, light-coloured drops on tamarisk twigs. There is no complete parallel, however, and the *mān* known to the Israelites remains wholly in the realm of the supernatural. God suffered them to be hungry so that by providing manna He could teach them that 'man does not live by bread alone, but . . . by everything that proceeds out of the mouth of the Lord' (Dt. 8:3; *cf.* Dt. 8:16; Jn. 6:25–29; Rev. 2:17). The fact that it bred worms every day except the sabbath was to prove that trust for each day's needs and obedience regarding the sabbath would be rewarded.

18 *Omer* occurs only in this chapter. The word means a small bowl which according to v. 36 contained approximately 4 pints. **33, 34** This is an anticipation of the erection of the Tabernacle. The jar of manna was placed with the tables of the law in the ark.

17:1–16 At Rephidim. 1 *Cf.* Nu. 33:1–49 for a summary account of the journeys. **4** Moses is being victimized by open rebellion and so turns to the Lord. **6** *Horeb* here stands for some peak other than Sinai in the same mountain range. The miracle is further evidence of God's condescending care, but also of His remonstrating with such an obdurate people in spite of their religious protestations. **8** *Amalek*. The Amalekites were a branch of the Edomite race, descendants of Esau (Gn. 36:12, 16). They were a nomadic people and were especially hostile to Israel (*cf.* Dt. 25:17, 18). **10** Hur was the grandfather of the craftsman Bezalel (1 Ch. 2:19, 20). He shared the government with Aaron when Moses went up to Sinai. **11–13** This posture of prayer denotes supplication, but in that it was Moses who prayed, mediation is included. **16** *A hand upon the banner of the Lord!* The Hebrew literally rendered would be as in RV mg., 'a hand is lifted up upon (against) the throne of the Lord!' This was Amalek's sin, and the God who does not give His glory to another smote him.

18:1–27 The visit and counsel of Jethro

This visit affected for all time the constitutional history of Israel, for here is the separation (not divorce) of the legislative and judicial functions of the community. What had been happening was that cases requiring a legal decision had been brought to Moses to be settled. He would adjudicate, and his decisions (case-law) would become 'the statutes of God'. He does not give the settled code in detail but in principle (*cf.* Ex. 20:1–17), and here he is represented as pronouncing on cases as they arose. The decisions thus given, especially in difficult cases (v. 26), would form precedents for future cases (*cf.* 21:1). Collections of such laws are in 20:23 – 23:33. See further the notes in Introduction on 'law' in connection with ch. 20.

2–9 Moses' father-in-law, impressed by what he has heard of the deliverance, visits him and brings Moses' wife, Zipporah, and his sons. **10** Jethro is moved to praise God for all that He has done and proceeds to counsel Moses as to how he may lighten the burden of ruling the people. **11** Jethro the Midianite, though a descendant of Abraham, is not a pure monotheist, though he may be confessing more than

the supremacy of the Lord over all other gods. **12** The sacrifice he offers is due to his position as head of a tribe and is of the 'sin-offering' kind, for sacrifice was not unknown before Sinai; *cf.* Gn. 4:4.

15, 16 Moses' answer is important for two reasons. Firstly, it shows that the people want a decision from God and that Moses can give it to them in connection with the immediate dispute, and secondly, that he can also impart moral statutes. **19–22** Jethro's answer does not abolish Moses' prime office, but makes provision for others to deal with minor cases. These men were to fear God rather than man, and were not to take bribes. **23, 24** This arrangement is submitted to Moses and not forced upon him, and the whole is submitted to God for approval.

Note. The 'Kenite hypothesis'. The origin of Yahweh-worship in Israel is traced by some to the influence of the Kenite clan, and of Jethro in particular. Holding that no knowledge of Yahweh existed in Israel prior to Moses, they urge that, while residing with Jethro, he learned of the storm-god of the Kenites, whose seat was on Mt. Sinai, and then introduced this deity to the Hebrews. Support for this is derived from the fact that Moses was living among the Kenites when Yahweh appeared to him at Sinai. The theory, of course, is maintained against the express testimony that the God of Sinai is none other than the God of the Hebrew patriarchs. The alleged summoning of Yahweh from Sinai by Deborah in her song (Jdg. 5:4) is interpreted in a grossly literalistic manner and in complete violation of the fact that Yahweh is with Israel in Canaan. In Nu. 10:29 Hobab the Kenite is invited to come with the Hebrews that they might do him good, and not *vice versa*. In Ex. 18 Jethro is the learner and not the teacher and his sacrifice (v. 12) follows his faith, testified in v. 11, which in turn follows on the report he heard of the deliverance wrought (v. 1). He is a convert.

There are, therefore, no real grounds for positing this hypothesis. See further 'Kenites' in *NBD*.

19:1, 2 At Sinai

The Israelites reached Sinai in the third month after they left Egypt, and they stayed there for nearly a year (Nu. 10:11). *The wilderness of Sinai* would be the open land before the mountain. On Sinai the cloud rested (*cf.* v. 9). The goal had been reached.

19:3 – 24:18 THE ESTABLISHING OF THE COVENANT

19:3–6 The purpose of God declared

3 In accordance with 3:12, Moses ascends the mount. **4** That the people have arrived thus far is entirely attributable to the power and care of God (*cf.* Dt. 32:10–12; Rev. 12:14), and is in accord with His covenant purpose for them (see Introduction). This purpose is stated here as follows: that they should be a unique people, chosen, prized and blessed in that they should be separated to God's will, each enjoying access to Him, and each employed in His worship and service. This is to be actualized in obedience to His law, and it is this purpose which must be declared to the people. To this purpose the Israelites were to feel the inner constraint by the memory of past and present mercies (*cf.* Rom. 12:1).

5 *My own possession* (Heb. *segullâ*, 'a special possession'); the truth of divine election underlies this. (*Cf.* Dt. 7:6. In Mal. 3:17 this term is referred to the faithful Israelites of the ideal future, and in 1 Pet. 2:9 and Tit. 2:14 it is referred to the church.) The justice of this election is based on God's right to do what He wills and to choose whom He wills, for all belong to Him by right of creation. **6** This is what Israelites (God's people) are to be in contradistinction to all others, viz. a kingdom whose citizens are all priests, each having the right of access, worship and devotion to God. In Is. 61:6 the Israelites of the ideal future are thus described, and the fulfilment in the church is seen in 1 Pet. 2:5–9. A *holy nation* is one separated from other nations and devoted to God. This privilege was also a duty and again is referred to the ideal Israel of the future (Is. 62:12) and to the church (1 Pet. 2:9).

19:7–25 The formal acceptance, by the people and their preparation to hear the Lord's voice

The people take an oath of allegiance and submission to the Lord's purpose as to their lawful ruler and sovereign. The terms of the covenant call for the acceptance of the people, although the terms cannot be altered in any way, and once accepted they become legally binding. Having submitted themselves, the people are now to see the manifestation of the Lord's presence and to hear His voice, that they may be deeply affected by His majesty, the awesomeness of the bond to be made and the truth of what Moses will communicate to them as the Lord's demands.

In this way the biblical relationship of law and grace is given its abiding definition. Specifically in 3:12, but by implication throughout chs. 3 to 9, it is taught that Sinai is not a chance stopping-place on the journey to Canaan, but the very goal of the Exodus pilgrimage in its first stage. By the will of God His people, redeemed by the blood of the lamb (*cf.* 12:13), come not only under His general guidance (*cf.* 13:21, 22) and are separated from the world (*cf.* 14:27–31), but come also under His detailed requirements for their daily life and worship (*cf.* 20:1 – 24:8). The law of God, therefore, is not a ladder whereby the unsaved gain heaven, but a pattern of life whereby the saved display their sonship (*cf.* Dt. 14:1, 2) and their status as the redeemed (*cf.* Ex. 20:2).

The preparation to hear the Lord's voice involved them in a symbolic act of cleansing by washing their garments and in abstinence from sexual intercourse (v. 15). This latter demand is noteworthy in the light of facts from other contemporary Ancient Near Eastern religions in which sensuous orgies were incorporated into the ritual performed. Israel's religion was 'different', having a supernatural origin. The call of the trumpet is the prelude to the royal proclamation, and the accompanying supernatural manifestations with the natural elements in upheaval on Sinai are to impress the Israelites, to curb their sinful and persistent curiosity (*cf.* Ex. 3:3) and to reveal a holy yet gracious God.

9 God intends to accredit His messenger before His people. **12** *Bounds*; the mountain was fenced, for it became God's seat and even sanctified people were not to touch the mountain, on pain of immediate death by stones or arrows. **16** See the note on 'theophany' in the Introduction. **19** Here is an external voice to Moses, and not the processes of inner conscience and internal reflection on his part. The theophany is not a poetic accessory. This is important for our understanding of the fact of revelation. 'God spoke . . . to our fathers' (Heb. 1:1).

20:1 – 23:19 Laws to apply the demands of the covenant

20:1–20 The Ten Commandments. See introductory notes on 'covenant' and 'law'. The fact that the Decalogue was uttered by the voice of God Himself without any intermediary is a witness to its authority and enduring validity. This is further emphasized by the fact that the commandments were twice written by God and on stone tablets (31:18; 32:15, 16; 34:1, 28; *cf.* Dt. 10:4). The first pair were shattered by Moses to symbolize the effect of Israel's apostasy (32:19); the second pair were placed in the ark (25:16; *cf.* Dt. 10:5).

This law was intended to be the means whereby the demands of the theocratic covenant were made known and applied to the people. The principles of 20:2–17 are expanded in 20:22 – 23:33, and this is used to ratify the covenant in ch. 24. These principles embrace the whole order of life in its Godward and manward relationships, and comprise in summary form the whole law of God. The preponderantly negative form of the commands is God's protest against sin in the midst of His redeemed people, but is also a pointer to the triumph of grace in that this protest becomes the rule of life and not the instrument of death. The singular form of address, 'you' (AV 'thou'), while standing collectively for Israel, more particularly refers to each Israelite.

2 This is the equivalent to the historical prologue of a Hittite suzerainty treaty (see note on 'covenant' in the Introduction). This is not a commandment, but the basis on which they all rest, namely that God is personal and sovereign in His gracious dealings with His people who love and obey Him (v. 6). **3** This is the first command against polytheism, and by implication God's right to exclusive adoration and obedience is asserted. *Before me*; 'in my sight', *i.e.* where Israel lived and worshipped. **4** This is the fundamental tenet of the faith of Israel; *cf.* Dt. 6:4. This second command is directed against image-worship, and it is general in scope, including attempted representations of God or of any idols of creatures. Such things debase the Creator and the creature who worships them. At Sinai no form or similitude was seen: only a voice was heard. **5, 6** The command of the previous verse is here developed. God will not allow what is His just due in terms of reverence and obedience to be given to anything else. God's honour is tied in with the people's worshipful service. This is a manifestation of God's inflexible, righteous character. God does not punish the children for their fathers' sins except when they perpetuate them and when the sins committed involve certain social and physical consequences. The important thing is that those punished thus are those who 'hate' God. His mercy transcends His wrath, and His blessing upon those who love and obey Him reaches a thousand generations.

7 To take the name of God *in vain* is to use it with any idle, frivolous, blasphemous or insincere intent. This does not prohibit solemn or legal oaths, but it does forbid false swearing (*cf.* Lv. 19:12). To *hold guiltless* is to leave unpunished. **8–11** *Remember*; this is no new command. It goes back to Gn. 2:1–3. This could have been forgotten by the Israelites while in Egypt, and there are no references to it in patriarchal times. It was to be observed perpetually. Six days' labour entitled a man to one day's rest, but this day was the memorial of God's good work of creation for the benefit of man and as such offered an eminently suitable occasion for worship. It was made for man. It was either a weariness (*cf.* Am. 8:5) or a delight (*cf.* Is. 58:13). **12** This is our first duty manward, and the family unit is the foundation of social order and peace. The observance of it reveals a well-ruled character, and augurs well for the future security of individual and nation. God's blessing rests upon the observance of this to the effect described.

13 This refers to unauthorized killing, *i.e.* murder. This law is amplified with reference to accidental, and therefore excusable (21:13; Nu. 35) and justifiable (Ex. 22:2), homicide. Capital punishment is authorized killing (Gn. 9:6) and so is 'lawful' war (Dt. 20). **14** The purity of the married state is another foundation of social life and is to be maintained on pain of punishment (Lv. 20:10). **15** The right to own private property is to be respected, and the penalties for theft are given (Ex. 21:16; 22:1). **16** This prohibits false witness, particularly in a court of law (23:1), but not only there; defamation of character is forbidden. The penalties are given in Dt. 19:16–21. **17** Man's inward state, his thoughts and desires, are not hidden from God

and come under His law. This lies at the root of the five commandments that precede. **18f.** Love is the motive for keeping this law, but fear is also spiritually healthy lest love be debased.

20:21-26 The general form of worship. 22 We begin with the code (book) of the covenant (20:22 – 23:33; see note on 'law' in the Introduction) and the links between this body of law and the Decalogue we shall note as we proceed. **23** The first and second commandments are re-echoed, giving specific directions to enable the Israelites to worship God acceptably. **24** The altar of earth or unhewn stone was to emphasize the simplicity of true worship, and the access to God given to every Israelite. Steps up to the altar would involve the worshipper in immodest exposure of nakedness as he ascended in his ordinary dress (*cf.* 28:40–43). These altars were to be erected at places where God would reveal Himself, and where He would bless yet again.

Note. Ex. 20:24–26 and Dt. 12. It is maintained that this Exodus law, which allegedly grants unrestricted liberty in worship, must come from an earlier date than that prescribing worship at a single central sanctuary, with which it obviously disagrees. This alleged conflict is based on a mistaken exegesis of the Exodus passage, for in it there is neither the unrestricted liberty of worship, nor the unlimited number of sanctuaries which are claimed. To begin with, this law must be firmly connected with the preceding history; by 'the places where I record my name' are meant the plain of Moreh (Gn. 12:6), Mt. Moriah (Gn. 22:2), Beersheba (Gn. 26:23), Bethel (Gn. 35:1) and Rephidim (Ex. 17:8, 15). This description does not refer to places of worship co-existing simultaneously, but as denoted successively in the Self-disclosure of God in Exodus. This explains and legitimizes the instances of Gideon (Jdg. 6:25, 26), Manoah (Jdg. 13:16), David (2 Sa. 24:18), Solomon (1 Ki. 3:4, 5) and Elijah (1 Ki. 18:31ff.). There is nothing here which conflicts with Deuteronomy, for though Dt. 12 gives the general rule of worship at the central sanctuary, Dt. 27 gives directions for the building of an altar on Mt. Ebal precisely in the manner of Ex. 20:25.

21:1 – 23:13 Civil judgments. These were given as verdicts in cases that arose, and they became established precedents for the future; *cf.* Ex. 18:13ff.

21:2–11 gives the law of slavery relating to Hebrew slaves (the case of foreign slaves is dealt with in Lv. 25:44–46). A person could be sold into slavery by his parents, or he could be sold for theft (22:1) or insolvency (*cf.* Am. 2:6), or he might be obliged to sell himself (*cf.* Lv. 25:39). Also, he might be born a slave. **2, 3** In Israelite law the slave was not a mere chattel: he had rights, and could leave free in the seventh, or sabbatical, year in the state in which he entered bond-service, as single or married. This was the basis of the labour system. **4** If the slave married and reared a family while a slave, they remained the property of his master, presumably for a period of 6 years. **5** Provision was made for life service also, and the pierced ear was the mark of a devoted life-long servant. **6** To *bring . . . to God*; to perform this ceremony as in the presence of God before the judges, at the door-post of the home in which the slave served. **7** The rights of the female slave were jealously guarded, though liberty was not given to her after a 6-year period of service. **8** She could not be sold to a non-Israelite, and if her master was displeased with her before taking her as his concubine her liberty could be bought. **9** If she was for his son then she became a daughter. **10** If another concubine was taken by the master, she was to be provided for. **11** If this was not forthcoming, liberty was to be given her.

21:12-17 The law relating to capital offences. For unpremeditated homicide the penalty was modified and cities of refuge were appointed later (*cf.* Dt. 19:1-13). **14** The horns of the altar were falsely regarded as offering protection (*cf.* 1 Ki. 1:50; 2:28ff.). This was a pagan practice and there is no divinely-given authorization for it in the OT. Cities of refuge were provided for those guilty of unpremeditated homicide, but for the murderer there was no shelter from the execution of the divine law. **15-17** Smiting or cursing a parent (*cf.* Ex. 20:12) and kidnapping were also capital offences.

21:18-36 The law relating to physical injuries as caused by humans (vv. 18-27), animals or sheer neglect (vv. 28-36). **18-27** In decreeing penalties, note that consideration was taken of the status and sex of the sufferer, the character of the injury and the consequences arising from it. **20, 21** The life of a slave was thought less of than that of a free man, though the slave was no mere chattel. **22** The loss of a child was to be compensated at the regulation of arbitrators, but if the woman died then the law of capital murder applied. **25** The law of exact retribution as stated here was commuted to a money fine even in Mosaic times (*cf.* Nu. 35:31) and not applied if a slave was injured, for the slave was given liberty; he could not be injured at will. **28-36** Animals also were slain for violating the sanctity of human life, and though the owner was not held responsible in the first instance, if he had been warned then he suffered death along with his animal. If the relatives of the dead man were willing to accept a money compensation, however, the owner escaped death. A master was to be compensated for the loss of a slave by such means. The patent justice of vv. 33-36 is worth noting.

22:1-15 Various laws relating to restitution of goods. **1-4** The law relating to theft of oxen or sheep and to burglary. When the stolen animals were slaughtered or sold, restitution was higher in the case of the more useful ox. If it had not been sold or killed, the animal appropriated was to be returned and a double sum repaid. A thief could be sold into slavery for his theft, or justly killed if he burgled at night. By daylight he could be recognized and

apprehended and so he could not then justly be killed. **5, 6** The law respecting compensation for damage either by cattle or by fire. **7-13** The law relating to compensation for loss or damage in the case of deposited material. The judges, acting on God's guidance, were to decide whether the material or money had been misappropriated. **11** Solemn swearing was to be believed. **14, 15** Hired animals were the borrower's responsibility except when they were in the presence of the owner.

22:16 – 23:13 Various moral laws. **22:16, 17** The unbetrothed daughter was part of her father's property, and her value would be diminished by the loss of her virginity. Compensation had to be paid and the man had to marry her. Should the father refuse, the marriage price was still to be paid. **18** Consult the article 'Magic and Sorcery' in *NBD*. Sorcerers were utterly opposed to the whole religion and faith of Israel, and were to be destroyed. **19** Such debasement of man needed to be judged drastically and purged away. **20** The ban (Heb. *ḥērem*) referred to by the words *utterly destroyed* was the handing over to God, by extermination, of what could not be allowed to remain in His sight as it was so offensive (*cf.*, *e.g.*, Jos. 6:17-19). **23, 24** God's judgment is just retribution. **25ff.** The poor were not to be at the mercy of the rich, and no essential article was to be kept as a pledge, such as a *mantle* which served as a cloak by day and a blanket by night. **28** Reverence is to be shown to God, and to those whom He has set in authority. **29-31** These laws are to symbolize the consecration of the nation to God.

23:1-3 Evidence in a court of law is to be true and to show no partiality (*cf.* 20:16). It must not be swayed by a majority decision, nor by pity. **4, 5** Even an enemy's beast is to be preserved. **6ff.** The justice given must reflect God's justice, for He will not remain inactive. **9** Have pity on strangers, for you once were like them (*cf.* Mt. 7:12; Eph. 4:32). **10-13** The seventh year and the seventh day are to be honoured; the immediate reason is philanthropic and economic, but the command in v. 13 shows that the provident goodness of God is behind this too.

23:14-19 Ceremonial legislation. **14-17** The three annual festivals are dealt with at greater length in Lv. 23 and Dt. 16. The fact that they appear here in brief statement form is testimony that an experience of deliverance and reception of covenant were at the heart of Israelite religion. Consult the *NBD* article 'Feasts'. The feasts began with that of Unleavened Bread in which a hasty and effective deliverance was gratefully remembered, and in this a thank-offering was brought to the sanctuary. Then the goodness of the Provider was remembered at harvest time, and at ingathering. These commands were tokens that the wandering Israelites would one day be in Canaan according to God's promise. All able-bodied males were to participate as representatives of their families. The women were not obliged to come owing to other duties at home, but were not forbidden (*cf.* 1 Sa. 1:18). **18** This refers to the Passover, and the *fat* is the choice part of the sacrifice which was to be consumed by fire. **19** The *first fruits* are to be offered to God, for He gave them. The heathen practice referred to in 19b was a vain attempt to increase fertility and productivity by magical arts.

23:20–33 Summary of the principles of God's future dealings

If Israel is obedient to God's voice, then He will lead her, bring her in, destroy her foes, settle her in the land, expand her territory and influence. This purpose is one of the main themes of Deuteronomy and Joshua.

20 *An angel*; see the note on 'theophany' in the Introduction. To rebel against him is to rebel against God, and this will not be pardoned. **24** *Pillars*; idolatrous stones carved with some heathenish symbol. **25b, 26** These are the blessings that would fall upon Israel, and God's activity outworks the sum total of the blessings of the covenant. **28** *Hornets*; this is a metaphorical description of God's activity. **31** Israel will extend from the SE coast of the Mediterranean Sea to the Euphrates. **32, 33** To allow their foes to settle with them will not only be an enticement to sin but a route to destruction. *Cf.* the book of Judges.

24:1–18 The ratification of the covenant

Moses is still on the mount; having received all the laws and recounted them to the people, he returns at God's bidding with the people's submission and their divinely-chosen representatives, who have together sealed the covenant by sacrifice. Then Moses is called on by God to wait upon Him for the engraved laws on tablets of stone.

1 *Nadab and Abihu* are the two sons of Aaron; they and the seventy elders constitute the representatives and witnesses of the people. The people are to remain at the foot of Sinai; the representatives are to ascend part of the way, but Moses goes up to the clouded, fiery summit. **3, 4** He recounts and records the laws of the Lord, and to them and their Author they submit in a legal and formal, yet gracious and blessed, covenant. An altar is built surrounded by twelve pillars symbolizing the twelve tribes, and the covenant is ratified by blood sacrifice. Covenants were ratified in various ways; by eating salt together (Nu. 18:19), by partaking together of a sacrificial meal (Gn. 31:54; *cf.* v. 11), or by passing between the divided pieces of a slaughtered sacrifice (Gn. 15:10, 17; Je. 34:18f.), but especially by the use of blood. **5–8** Here God and the people are joined together by the sacrificial blood cast against the altar (representing God), and sprinkled on the people. The significance of blood is that of atoning death; see on the Passover which is the key to the whole sacrificial system of Israel. The blood is first sprinkled on the altar, for the primary need is always propitiation, the quieting of the wrath of God. When the people have committed themselves to a life of obedience, the blood is then sprinkled upon them, for it is in the context of their attempt to walk the way of holiness that God's people become aware of their need of the atoning blood. *Cf.* 1 Jn. 1:7 – 2:2. The burnt-offering is described in Lv. 1 and symbolizes the entire submission of the offerer to God in confession and consecration. The peace-offering emphasizes the same truth but includes the added feature of a feast of communion between God and man through sacrifice. **9–11** The elders eat the flesh of the peace-offerings and behold the inner brightness of what was, from without, the darkened cloud. They see the glory of God in the theophany (see Introduction) and, far from being consumed, feast in His presence in the glory of surpassing beauty. **12** Moses and the elders have probably returned to the people before this call summons Moses to the summit to receive the law. **13, 14** His servant Joshua accompanies him, but only so far, and he delegates his judicial authority to Aaron and Hur.

25:1 – 31:18 THE INSTITUTIONS OF THE COVENANT—THE TABERNACLE AND THE PRIESTHOOD

25:1 – 27:21 Free-will offerings for the ark, the bread of the Presence, golden lampstand and the Tabernacle, with the pattern for their construction

God is enthroned and manifested at Sinai, but Israel is not to stay at Sinai for ever. She must press on to Canaan, and God will go with her, and as she moves on He will dwell in the midst of His people.

25:8, 9 The sanctuary. This sanctuary and its furniture are to be constructed according to a divinely-given blueprint, but by the free-will offering of the people. Moses is given the pattern and to him the materials must be given. The Israelites came out of Egypt with spoil (12:36) and Amalek's conquest (v. 17) would have enriched them further. The sanctuary (Heb. *miqdāš*) is a holy place, but the Tabernacle (*miškān*) in v. 9 is a dwelling-place. The Tabernacle expresses certain truths, and it is safer to speak of it as a 'type' only in connection with those uses and things which actually symbolized something to the Israelites, and to which the NT explicitly attaches a symbolical meaning. We are on safe ground when we emphasize the significance of the names by which the Tabernacle was clearly known to the Israelites. It was a 'dwelling' to represent God's co-dwelling with His people; a 'tent of meeting' to express the truth that God does meet His people and reveal Himself to them; and it was a 'tent of the testimony' to remind the Israelite that within it, in the ark, was the law that was to regulate his life. We shall note the significance of other items as we proceed.

25:10–22 The ark of the covenant and the mercy seat. 10–17 The *ark* was a chest or coffer, the main purpose of which was to hold the two tables of the law, but in it were also stored the jar of manna (*cf.* 16:33, 34), and Aaron's rod. It was sited in the Holy of Holies, and became the symbol of God's presence. Such arks were common in Israel's environment, but this one was unique in that it housed the law and not an image; God is spiritual and holy. It was overlaid with pure gold, whereas its appurtenances were made of gold in which there was some measure of alloy. **17** The *mercy seat* was a rectangular plate on top of the ark of similar dimensions ($4 \times 2\frac{1}{2}$ ft). The word for this (Heb. *kappōreṭ*) means 'to cover' but in the form used here it means to 'make atonement'. (See L. Morris, *The Apostolic Preaching of The Cross*, 1955.) It was not merely a covering lid, but a sacred object in itself. It was a single slab of solid gold. **18–20** It was overshadowed by two *cherubim* (winged creatures, representing celestial beings), which were to protect the mercy seat, the ark and its contents; their outstretched wings were to provide a throne for the invisible but present God. **22** At the place where sin is propitiated God was to be found and mercy bestowed.

25:23–40 The table and the lampstand. 23–30 The *table of acacia wood.* This was the same wood as was used for the ark. It measured $3 \times 1\frac{1}{2}$ ft and was 27 inches high. **30** The *bread of the Presence* (AV 'shewbread') consisted of twelve baked cakes, set out in two rows (*cf.* Lv. 24:6). Frankincense was placed on each row, and they were offered to the Lord by fire (Lv. 24:7). The significance of the bread is not plainly revealed, but it is probably a recognition that God is man's provider and sustainer, and it is man's duty to acknowledge this in worship. There is no suggestion that it is food for the deity.

31–40 *The lampstand* (AV 'candlestick'; see plate XIVa in *NBD*) was of pure gold, and consisted of three branches ending in flower-shaped lampholders on each side of the main stem which also supported a lampholder. Again the significance of this is not made plain, but it is obviously connected with light-bearing and witness through worship.

26:1 – 27:21 The Tabernacle. There is much repetition involved in the description of the Tabernacle and its furniture, and this evidences the importance with which it was regarded. First, the pattern shown to Moses is described (chs. 25–31), then the execution of the work is recorded (chs. 35–39), a concluding summary is added (39:33–43), and finally an account of its erection is given (40:1–33). We shall not comment on this each time it occurs. For a general description of the Tabernacle the reader is referred to the relevant article in *NBD* and to plate XIVa in the same book. See also the note in the Introduction.

26:31 The inner sanctuary was to be marked off by a single *veil* (curtain) embroidered with cherubim, the symbol of the divine Presence, and in this only the ark and mercy seat were housed. **27:1–8** The altar for the burnt-offering was to be made in accord with 20:21–26 and was presumably a hollow box filled with earth. The ornamental horns (v. 2) were regarded as its most sacred part, and it was to those that the sacrificial blood was applied, and to which criminals held in vain hope of refuge (*cf.* on 21:12–17). **9–21** give details of the court of the Tabernacle and the burning light. The court enclosed the Tabernacle, and within the court the altar and the laver were placed. The entrance was at the eastern end of the court, furthest from the Holy of Holies, and thus God was still distinct from, though He dwelt with, His people. The burning light, supplied by the people and tended by the priests, symbolized God's presence and the consequent realization of this on the part of the people.

28:1 – 29:46 The institution of the priesthood and the service of consecration

With the law given, the Tabernacle planned and the requirements for its use in worship outlined, the necessity arose for a priesthood to officiate in these matters and to bless and guide the people. The high priest and every other priest acted as intermediaries between the people and God for such purposes. This is made evident in the description of the garments of the priests, and particularly by the fact that the names of the tribes were to be engraved on the shoulder-pieces of the ephod, and on the stones of the breastplate of judgment (28:29, 30). Aaron was selected for this purpose because he was Moses' mouthpiece. The ministry of the high priest adumbrated that of the Lord Jesus Christ (Heb. 7:1 – 10:39).

28:6 *Ephod*; a short linen garment of the same material as the veil of the Tabernacle, joined at the shoulder, and the two open sides bound together by an embroidered girdle. **12** *Cf.* Is. 49:16. **31** The *robe* was the garment beneath the ephod. **35** The sound of the bells was an announcement of the continuation of the ministry of intercession. *Lest he die*; holy things are to be handled with due reverence and obedience. **37, 38** The *turban* (AV 'mitre') was itself crowned by the plate of gold which proclaimed *Holy to the Lord*. The remembrance of God's holiness was the chief characteristic of the Israelites' worship. Aaron was to secure God's acceptance of the people.

29:1–46 The service of consecration. The priesthood itself was not free from sin, and therefore there could be no consecration without atoning blood. As the priests were to serve before God in matters so essential for the people, all this had to be done according to God's requirements. It is significant of God's grace that He reveals and makes provision for the things He demands. The consecration of Aaron and his sons to the priesthood was completed

135

by the following items: washing for purification (v. 4), investiture to office (vv. 5–9), putting on the official robes, anointing, sacrificing for atonement and consecration (vv. 10–21), and filling their hands to authorize them to sacrifice (vv. 22–28).

1 The *bull* was for the sin-offering (*cf.* vv. 10–14). *Two rams.* One was for a burnt-offering (*cf.* vv. 15–18), and the other was for consecration (*cf.* vv. 19–22). **10** The laying on of hands symbolizes the fact that this is no mere donation of the animal to God, but that the worshipper is intimately involved and represented in what happens to the victim which is his substitute (*cf.* Lv. 16:21). **12** The manipulation of sacrificial blood (see on the Passover) is important. Here it is smeared on the altar to symbolize its Godward significance, *i.e.* that it satisfies the justice of a holy God upon the sinner by providing proof of life laid down in death, and so meets the need of the sinner in the sight of God. **13** The best and choicest parts of the sacrifice are burned to symbolize Godward devotion to the uttermost. **14** When a sin-offering was offered for priests or for the whole community including the priest, the flesh was burnt (*cf.* Lv. 4:15, 21). This ram was to be offered as a burnt-offering (*cf.* Lv. 1) of utter submissive devotion to God. **19, 20** This was essentially a peace-offering (*cf.* Lv. 3), the special characteristic of which was that the flesh of the sacrifice was eaten by the worshippers (vv. 32–34). **20–25** This sacrifice is modified to suit the occasion. **20** The touching with blood of the organs of hearing, handling and walking is to represent the need for the priest to be cleansed in all these functions. **24** The priests are hereby authorized to present their first sacrifice by offering the most sacred parts of the animal to God. **25** Moses is to burn these on the altar. **26–28** Part of the ram of consecration is returned to Aaron and the priests as their perquisite. In this meal, signifying God's acceptance of all that has been done and the bestowal of His favour, the consecration of the priests is complete. **33** To make *atonement* is to satisfy the just demands of God upon the sinner by way of substitution, so that the sinner does not have to suffer himself. **35** This whole ceremony was to be repeated for seven days. **37** The altar was to be consecrated likewise, and to be most holy. **42** The call to continued devotion was to be symbolized by the daily burnt-offering. At the *tent of meeting* God would dwell with them. All is made holy not by any intrinsic 'material' worth, but by the spiritual presence of God, visibly displayed. **45, 46** This is an epitome of the covenant purpose and blessing.

30:1 – 31:11 The pattern and workmen for other data regarding the Tabernacle

30:1-10 The *altar to burn incense* stood before the veil which curtained off the Holy of Holies. It was closely associated with the ark and the Holy of Holies but was outside the veil as the priest officiated at it daily. **9** The altar was for incense only, and for incense prepared in the prescribed manner (*cf.* vv. 34 ff.; Nu. 3:4, 'unholy fire'). **11-16** Money for the service of the Tabernacle. This was no mere levy or tax. It was not only the means of providing for the worship of the Tabernacle, but rather the reminder that the whole populace was preserved by the mercy of God and that their sinful souls were forfeit to Him. The sum was so small that all could pay, and it thus became an act of worship; but also it was so small that it was a token of the fact that no sum of money could redeem the soul. In addition it reminded the rich and poor that all were in the same need before God, dependent on Him for redemption. Ex. 38:25–28 shows the use to which this money was put: it was for the very foundations of the Tabernacle. **17-21** The *laver* was for the priests to wash their hands and feet in before they offered sacrifice. *Lest they die*: this serving had to be done by cleansed servants (*cf.* on 28:35). **22-33** The *anointing oil* signified the bestowal of the Holy Spirit for special purposes. It was to be specially compounded and was not to be used for general purposes. All that was related to the worship in the Tabernacle was consecrated by it, and as such, if properly used, would be a means of grace and blessing to worshippers. **34-38** Similar care was to be taken with the holy incense.

31:1-11 The craftsmen to be employed. For such work not only skilled but spiritual men were needed, marked out by God for this work. In the OT the Holy Spirit was active in, among other things, endowing the agents of God's rule (*cf.* Jdg. 6:34; 1 Sa. 10:10).

31:12-18 The sign of the sabbath and the tables of the law

The sabbath was a distinguishing feature between Israel and the other nations. It marked Israel's faithfulness, and her observance of it was an instrument in God's hand for her sanctification. This is why the prophets took sabbath-keeping as a test of the true religious condition of their contemporaries (*cf.* Je. 17:19–27; Ezk. 20:12–24). **18** The promise of 24:12 is fulfilled, and the Ten Commandments are divinely recorded, as well as being divinely given.

32:1 – 34:35 THE COVENANT BROKEN AND RENEWED

It is striking that the very book which records and exults in God's glorious deliverances and provisions does not hide the grave sinfulness of the people thus dealt with. Their murmurings at the Red Sea, at Marah, in the wilderness of Sin and at Rephidim evidence their frailty. But at Sinai they entered into covenant with God, and had accepted the law, pledging their obedience to all of it. Their rebellion therefore is more serious than murmuring complaint – it is open apostasy.

32:1–10 The apostasy of the golden calf

Their only complaint is Moses' failure to re-appear, although they had sent him to the mount to hearken to their God on their behalf. Scarcely six weeks have passed before the people thus blessed are clamouring, at the very foot of Sinai, for a replica of the gods they saw worshipped in Egypt. Moses, not God, is referred to as the one who brought them out of Egypt. Aaron gives way (*cf.* Pr. 25:26) and idolatry and polytheism follow at the foot of the mount from which the commandments were given. **4** The *calf* that Aaron makes is a throwback to life in Egypt. There living animals were regarded as sacred, and gods were represented as having animal heads and even animal bodies as well. Hence the cult of the bull, Apis, later called Serapis.

5, 6 Aaron adds to the people's sin by building an altar and holding a feast to God who is to be worshipped under the guise of this calf. In Egypt they had lapsed into idolatry (*cf.* Lv. 17:7; Jos. 24:14; Ezk. 20:8), and now an air of sanctity is given by the high priest to their identification of Yahweh with these monster-gods. The outcome of such worship was not true holiness but the *play*, or orgiastic dance, which characterized pagan religions (*cf.* 1 Cor. 10:6ff.). **7–10** *Your people*; seeing what they have done, God cannot refer to them as His in any real sense of the truth. They have turned aside quickly, and speedily would God avenge His name and justly pour out His wrath upon them. Even though the emergency has arisen, God's purpose will not be overthrown. Just as God began with Noah after the judgment of the Flood, so will He begin with Moses.

32:11 – 33:23 Interceding and purging

Moses is instantly moved to intercede. None of God's servants has ever sat idly back and failed to seek a stay of judgment or to urge the people to repent. *Cf.*, *e.g.*, Gn. 18:22ff.; Am. 7:1–3. This does not mean that they contend with God against His justice, but they cry, 'In wrath remember mercy' (Hab. 3:2).

32:11–14 Moses' prayer. 11 He refers to *thy* people, and the basis of his intercession and the ground of his hope is the honour of God (*cf.* Je. 14:8, 9, 19–22; Dn. 9:17ff.). He uses three arguments in prayer, on his settled conviction that God is a 'jealous' God. God's jealousy is His zeal for His own glory in His people, on account of which He will neither break His promises nor fail to execute His threats. Moses reminds God of what He has done; **12** of what His foes will say if He exterminates His people now; **13** that He has given promises to the forbears of these people which must be kept. **14** *Repented*; God does not need to repent as men do, for He does not err, nor is He baffled or overcome. But when He is said (by an anthro-pomorphic description) to repent, He changes not His purposes, but a course of events previously threatened, because the altered conduct of His people no longer calls forth what He had originally promised. It is a change in His dealings with people, not a change in His character or His purposes.

32:15–29 The people are punished. Though wrath may not be outpoured, sin is not excused or overlooked. Moses meets Joshua (*cf.* 24:13) and they return to camp together, with the tablets of the law. The law is shattered by Moses to illustrate to the people the meaning of their apostasy. His anger is not a fit of temper but the upsurge of righteous indignation. God will feed Israel, but Israel is made to feed upon the work of her own hands by way of judgment, and so it is with God's judgment of false religion in every age. When people must drink water fouled by their own religious leaders, God will judge them (*cf.* Ezk. 34:12ff.). Aaron's self-excusing is pathetic, as indeed is every attempt to exonerate oneself from sin. The people are blamed, but the calf allegedly made itself! Aaron should have stood against them. The people must be purged, and those who are on the Lord's side must do this. **16** *The work of God* is divinely revealed and recorded, and therefore possesses His authority, abiding reliability and truth. **21** Moses discerns that the people were the source of this evil, but he does not underestimate the responsibility of Aaron in giving way to them and of bringing guilt upon them by not opposing their wicked desires. **24** Aaron's excuses reveal his weakness before both the people and Moses. **25, 26** When restraints are removed, not only do the people suffer, but God's honour is corrupted, and consequently the people must be purged. **27** The Levites take up Moses' call and execute those who have worshipped the idol calf. **29** For this, they are rewarded with the priesthood. *Cf.* Nu. 25:10–13.

32:30 – 33:23 Moses again intercedes and is shown God's glory. 32:30 – 33:11 In his initial intercession, such is Moses' love for the people that he offers his own life as the means whereby their pardon and peace may be secured, but God does not accept such sacrifice for oneself or for another (*cf.* Ps. 49:7). Moses' prayer is no formal petition, but the yearning of a burdened spirit. *Cf.* Rom. 9:2, 3.

32:32 *Blot me . . . out.* This expression is borrowed from the practice of keeping registers of citizens. Ps. 69:28 and Is. 4:3 refer to those who persevere in faithfulness and are preserved in a time of judgment. **33, 34** God has mercy on the people, but will punish individuals within this mercy. The nation, however, is to be led by an angel, and not the unmediated presence of God (see note on 'theophany' in the Introduction). **33:1–3** God remains faithful and the promise made with their fathers is to be kept, but He cannot walk with such people without consuming them, and so an angel is sent instead. **4–6** The people show spontaneous signs of penitence, and submit to God's demand. This is a new departure. Repentance brings an immediate response from God. **7-10** This reference shows how the worship of God was carried out during the interval between the time of the Exodus, or Sinai, and the completion and dedication of the Tabernacle. Moses *used to take* (*i.e.* before the apostasy) . . . *the tent of meeting*, which later gave its name to the Tabernacle, outside the camp to commune with God, who though with His people was yet apart from them. There Moses was given communion with God to a degree shared by no other; others worshipped at their *tent door*. **11** *Face to face*. This expression is clearly to be understood in terms of the words that follow, *as a man speaks to his friend*. That is unrestricted communion in which nothing is withheld and nothing cloaked (*cf.* Nu. 12:8; Dt. 34:10).

33:12-23 The tempo of intercession is now increased. Moses has asked and now he is seeking (v. 13), then knocking (vv. 15, 18). God has promised to be with these people and to bring them into the promised land, but their sin, though it has not negated this promise (*cf.* v. 2), has restricted God's grace and favour (*cf.* v. 3). It is this attenuation of God's favour that urges Moses to pray not merely for a physical entry, but for the presence of God in glory amid the people. He does not want the land of promise without God (v. 14), and the land of promise is nothing to the people without the same Presence (v. 16). It is God's presence which bestows obvious favour and assurance on His people, and marks them out as His own, for His glory. Therefore Moses concludes on the basis of the covenant: God must come with us. Such praying is answered. God will accompany Moses and the people, and the rest of Canaan will be given to them (v. 14). Such an answer emboldens Moses to request even more, for he is now convinced that God's favour does rest upon him and that the people have been in principle restored to full covenant favour. He prays for a sight of God's glory (see Introduction for note on 'the glory of God'). He is yearning for a special disclosure of God—not physical sight, for he knows that no *man* can see God and live, but for a spiritual perception of who God is and what He will be and do for him and his people. God reveals Himself by His Name, and yet He will redeclare this to Moses by making all His 'goodness', *i.e.* comeliness or beauty, pass before him. Moses is to hear old truths but with a new splendour. A veil will momentarily be drawn back, and God will pass by.

17 To find *favour* in God's sight is not to earn it but to have it bestowed upon one, because God 'knows' us in His election and calling (*cf.* Ex. 3). **19** See the Introduction for the note on 'the Name of God'. This verse absolutely excludes all notion of earning or meriting the divine mercy. God is merciful to whom He will and not to all, in the sense mentioned here. Rom. 9:15, which teaches salvation

by grace alone, bestowed in accord with sovereign election, expounds the true meaning of this verse. **23** Moses is to see the afterglow which is a reliable indication of what the full splendour is to be.

34:1-35 The covenant renewed

This promised vision of the covenant God is the basis of the renewal of the covenant which has been broken by idolatry. The covenant is renewed through the repromulgation of the law of the covenant. It is again written by God but Moses is to prepare the tablets on this occasion. There is no contradiction between vv. 1, 27 and 28. The situation is that in v. 27 Moses is commanded to write the contents of the preceding verses, 'these words'; in v. 28 God is the subject of the last verb and not Moses. The contents of this chapter are a selected abbreviation of the 'book of the covenant', with additional features of promise and warning justified by Israel's apostasy and the Canaanite situation with which she will soon be confronted.

3 The mountain is to be sacrosanct, for God will be present there. **6, 7** Luther called these verses 'the sermon on the Name'. Though inexhaustible in love, mercy and forgiveness for thousands upon whom He sets His love, He is just and righteous and though His anger is not impetuous it is real and the guilty will not be excused. **8** Moses' response of hasty obeisance is an inward recognition of the Lord. **9** Moses as mediator is penitent in supplication. **10** God reaccepts the people and promises them further wonders of deliverance in connection with their entry into and occupation of the land. **11** These laws are set out by way of commandments for Israel's future. Their foes will be driven out but Israel is to beware (*cf.* 23:24, 25, 32, 33). **12** Those in covenant with the one living God cannot align themselves with pagan beliefs or religious practices; they must exterminate them. The people of God must be pure. See the book of Judges for the record of the outworking of this warning. **13** *Pillars* and *Asherim*. The former were of stone and were identified with the deity, usually male; the latter were of wood and were devoted to the same purpose. **14-16** Religious syncretism was and is an offence to the holy and jealous God. Intermarriage with Canaanites was a constant source of woe among Israelites and their kings. **18-26** A repetition of 13:13, 14; 23:12, 15-19. See the comments in these places. **21** *In ploughing time and in harvest*. An additional warning of the temptation which would arise in an agricultural community. **24** This is an additional feature, with obvious reference to the time when they would be in Canaan. God would defend the land when the males were engaged in His worship. **29-35** *Cf.* 2 Cor. 3:7-18. Moses removed his veil when he spoke with God, or with the people in His name, but veiled his face in ordinary daily life.

35:1 – 40:38 THE CONSTRUCTION AND ERECTION OF THE TABERNACLE

These chapters narrate the execution of the commands given to Moses in chs. 25–31 and do so in the main by a verbatim repetition. See these chapters for details of the work involved.

35:1 – 39:43 The people offer willingly and the work is carried out according to pattern

35:1-3 Before any work is commenced the law of the sabbath is reiterated, for God's work must also be done in accord with His law. This corresponds to 31:12-17 in its position and content. *Kindle no fire.* This law is implied in 16:23. **4, 5** Gifts are acceptable to the Lord only when they are given gladly from the heart. This emphasis is repeated in vv. 21, 22, 29; *cf.* 25:2; 36:2; 1 Ch. 29:9; 2 Cor. 9:7. **10ff.** All were to offer, but the actual work was open only to those with God-given ability and desire. God makes use of the people's different artistic abilities (see especially vv. 25, 26, 30; 36:1). **36:2-7** This was no spasmodic giving; there was a superabundance of what was necessary, and the people had to be stopped.

36:8 – 39:43 The work is carried out. **38:8** The *mirrors* were made of polished bronze, and were used for sacred purposes because of the self-denial of the devoted women. **39:43** Moses supervised all the work, checked that it had been carried out according to divine plan and then blessed the people.

40:1-38 The Tabernacle is set up and the glory of the Lord comes down

1-33 The constituent parts and furnishings had been made, and now needed to be put together and the Tabernacle erected. Divine instructions were disclosed as to how and in what order this was to be done. In this, emphasis was placed on the anointing (consecrating) and washing and investiture of the priests (cleansing for officiating). See Introduction for the note on 'the Tabernacle: the environs, appearance, furnishings and significance'.

34-38 The cloud, the visible evidence of God's favour, now rested on the Tabernacle, the centre of Israel's life, as the place of worship and the source of law. God fills the Tabernacle, and while even Moses cannot enter, yet there is symbolized God's own presence, so that His people may have recourse to, pardon from, and communion with Him in accord with the appointed means. God is with His people, whom He redeemed from the hand of the enemy.

CONCLUSION

The purpose of God in electing and delivering these people is at last achieved, and it is that God might dwell with those whom He has brought to Himself by substitutionary blood and saving power. He tabernacles with those who, as a consequence of His grace to them, submit themselves to Him with grateful love, to live unto Him and His glory in accord with His law. Worship and obedience flow from renewed hearts, and the cloud of God's glory confirms and reveals God's favour towards and delight in them.

All that characterized their bondage which was so oppressive has been swept away. Their old foes they would never see again (14:13). Their servitude of toil, tears, affliction and woe had become a memory not attaching to bondage but to deliverance, and a cause for endless rejoicing (15:1-18). Their deliverer was King over all and for ever, and yet He dwelt with them, and they with Him.

A new estate and condition had come into being in which God glorified Himself by hearing, answering and blessing His people. Being set free and called to be God's own 'treasured possession' they confess joyfully and unitedly that they are His subjects: 'All the words which the Lord has spoken we will do' (24:3, 7). His service and presence is their blessing.

Are not these the essential lineaments of the 'exodus' our Lord accomplished at Jerusalem by His death (*cf.* Lk. 9:31)? Did He not come in order that 'we, being delivered from the hand of our enemies, might serve him without fear, in holiness and righteousness before him all the days of our life' (Lk. 1:74, 75)? Sin, guilt, condemnation, eternal woe and Satan's power are all brought to an end by the power of the blood of the substitutionary sacrifice of the Son of God, who bestows newness of life to those whom He delivers, and in whom He dwells by His Spirit.

But as yet we are not free from our foes and ills. The song of Moses (Ex. 15) will be joined by a song to the Lamb-King (Rev. 15:3) who governs, keeps and leads His quickened and obedient people to heaven. There all the former things attaching to our earthly, mortal, sinful bondage are done away. 'Death shall be no more, neither shall there be mourning nor crying nor pain any more, for the former things have passed away' (Rev. 21:4). In the heavenly, eternal Tabernacle we 'shall see his face', and shall 'reign for ever and ever' (Rev. 22:4, 5).

HYWEL R. JONES

Leviticus

INTRODUCTION

TITLE AND CHARACTER

Leviticus is the third of the five books which compose the 'law' of Moses. It contains ten of the fifty-four pericopes or sections into which the Pentateuch was divided for the annual reading of the Law in the synagogue. The later Jews called it *Wayyiqrā* ('and called'), using the initial phrase of the first verse. The name Leviticus is derived from the Greek (LXX) version. It is appropriate in a general way, since the priests were, of course, Levites in the sense of being members of the tribe of Levi. But it is inexact and to that extent misleading.

The book is especially intended for the priests. Aaron and his sons are mentioned many times in it. The Levites are mentioned only in one short passage (25:32f.). But while the book is a manual for the priests, it is to be noted that many of the laws are introduced by the phrase, 'Speak to the children of Israel'. Obviously this is because these laws, many of which required the services and mediation of the priest, concerned the people directly and vitally and formed an important part of that law which it was to be the special responsibility of the priests to teach the people (Dt. 31:9; 33:10; Ne. 8). Leviticus is in no sense an esoteric book. The people were entitled and expected to know exactly what was required of them, and of their priests, in that service of the sanctuary which so deeply concerned every true Israelite.

BACKGROUND

The place and time at which these laws were first given is carefully defined as during the sojourn at Mt. Sinai (7:38; 25:1; 26:46; 27:34), which lasted until 'the second year, in the second month, on the twentieth day of the month' (Nu. 10:11). The statement of 1:1 presupposes the erection of the Tabernacle which has just been described in Ex. 40. The mention of the eighth day (9:1) must refer to the day following the seven days of consecration of Aaron and his sons (8:33), which are apparently to be counted from the setting up of the Tabernacle on the first day of the first month (Ex. 40:2). The sin of Nadab and Abihu followed at once (Lv. 10:1, 2). The words 'and he did as the Lord commanded Moses' (16:34, AV), which are added to the ritual of the Day of Atonement, are important because they add to the record of the law itself the record of its first observance, which took place nearly five months after Israel left Sinai. The mention of the ark in connection with the ritual for this day is a further evidence of the early date of

Leviticus, since the ark, which is mentioned many times in the Pentateuch and in the historical books of the OT, disappeared at the time of the Babylonian captivity, as was foretold in Je. 3:16. There was no ark in the second Temple to which period some commentators assign Leviticus. Note also Lv. 23:44 which states that 'Moses declared to the people of Israel the appointed feasts of the Lord'. Finally, it is to be noted that the deliverance from Egypt is represented as an actual personal experience (cf. 11:45 and 18:3 with 26:45) and the possession of the land is represented as still future (14:34; 19:23; 23:10; 25:2). Such facts as these should be noted carefully by the reader of Leviticus, since they serve to show that the exilic or post-exilic date for the book which is asserted or assumed by many scholars (recently, e.g., by Bright, Eichrodt, Noth, Snaith) is not in accord with the express statements of Scripture itself.

AUTHORSHIP

Nothing is said in this book as to the writing down of the laws which it contains. But the fact that these laws were given through Moses is stated again and again. The phrase 'and the Lord said to Moses' occurs about 30 times. Twenty of the twenty-seven chapters begin in this way. Aaron's name is occasionally joined with that of Moses (11:1; 14:33; 15:1); but he is directly addressed only once (10:8). In view of the statements which occur in Exodus, Numbers and Deuteronomy regarding the writing down of the commandments given to Moses (e.g. Ex. 24:4, 7), we are entitled to assume that these instructions, which so vitally concerned the welfare of God's people, and many of which are so precise and even minute in their requirements as clearly to require careful recording, were committed to writing either by Moses himself or at his command and under his supervision.

(For notes on the problems raised by the documentary theories of the compilation of the Pentateuch see the General Articles, 'The History of the Literary Criticism of the Pentateuch' (p. 34) and 'Moses and the Pentateuch' (p. 41) —Ed.)

SOURCE

Leviticus consists almost entirely of laws uttered by God Himself. God spoke to Moses 'from the tent of meeting' (1:1; cf. Nu. 7:89), or on the Mount (Ex. 25:1), or 'at the door of the tent' (Nu. 12:5). Consequently these laws have a high and heavenly character which sets them apart from laws of man's devising. This is emphasized by the express command: 'You shall not do as they do in the land of Egypt, where you dwelt, and you shall not do as they do in the land of Canaan, to which I am bringing you. You shall not walk in their statutes. You shall do my ordinances and keep my statutes and walk in them. I am the Lord your God' (Lv. 18:3, 4).

This comprehensive statement is followed by many examples of heathen practices which the Israelites are to shun and which are stigmatized as 'abominations' (18:26ff.). The Sinai religion was monotheistic, spiritual and ethical. The cults of the neighbouring peoples were polytheistic, idolatrous and often highly immoral. The worship of goddesses as well as gods introduced an element of sensuality into their rites (orgies and religious prostitution), as illustrated by the sin of Shittim (Nu. 25) which corrupted the people instead of elevating them, and were contrary to the spirit and the letter of the law of Moses (cf. Ex. 19:15; 20:26). As in the case of many ethnic cults today, a man could be better than his religion. Molech-worship (Lv. 20:1-5) was one of the heathen practices particularly denounced.

In view of the emphasis which is placed today by many scholars on comparative religion with a view to exhibiting the similarities between the religion of Israel and the ethnic cults, and even to derive it from them, it is important to keep in mind that the consistent emphasis throughout the Bible, and nowhere more evident than in Leviticus, is on *difference*. The religion of Israel is unique and distinctive. The resemblances are of minor importance and may even be misleading if the fundamental differences are not kept carefully in mind. *Cf.*, *e.g.*, the bread of the Presence (AV 'shewbread') (pp. 163f.).

PURPOSE AND APPLICATION

The immediate purpose of this book is to set forth those laws and principles by which Israel is to live as the people of God. Their God is a holy God; they are to be a holy people. 'You shall be holy; for I the Lord your God am holy' is its emphatic demand. His sanctuary is in their midst; and when they worship there they stand 'before the Lord', a phrase which occurs about 60 times in this book. This means separation from uncleanness and sin, and since they are sinful and prone to sin, it necessitates atonement for sin and purification from it and from all uncleanness. Hence the law of sacrifice is placed impressively at the beginning. See the note on the significance of the sacrificial ritual at the end of the section on pp. 147f.

The laws of Leviticus are very varied. They are both general and specific; they are both ceremonial and moral; they are severe and also merciful. They separate Israel from the nations and set her apart for the service of the God who has made this people His own by delivering them from Egyptian bondage. In so far as these laws are purely ceremonial, they are temporary and binding only during the Mosaic dispensation to which they belong. They had immediate reference to Israel as a nation which was to be governed in every aspect of its national and individual life by the law of Moses. In this strictly historical sense this book has great interest for the Christian reader. It tells him how God dealt with Israel as a people 'under age' and in need of training and preparation. Furthermore, in the case of many of these laws, *e.g.* the dietary laws, hygienic principles may be involved which have perpetual value and significance. To eat pork, *e.g.*, may be wholesome under certain conditions and unwholesome under others. For the NT application and interpretation see 1 Cor. 10:31; Rom. 14:20. In so far as these laws are moral, they are of perpetual obligation; and since the Christian is, like the Jew, prone to evil and constantly tempted to break the law of God as set forth in the Decalogue, they demand of him, as of the Israelite of old, perfect obedience to the moral law of God. See on Dt. 4:8. The insistent demand of Leviticus that Israel be holy because the God of Israel is holy is confirmed and strengthened in the NT (1 Pet. 1:15).

The book is particularly notable in that it brings together in blended harmony two elements which are regarded by many as quite distinct and even as incompatible. On the one hand, Leviticus is the most thoroughly legalistic of all the books of the OT. It seeks to govern either by broad principle or specific precept the whole of the life of the people of God. Its demands may be summed up in the words of the apostle 'whether you eat or drink, or whatever you do, do all to the glory of God' (1 Cor. 10:31). Its insistent challenge and persistent demand is, 'You shall be holy; for I the Lord your God am holy.' On the other hand, there is no book in the OT which more clearly sets forth the redemption which is in Christ than does Leviticus. It faces the question of Job, 'How can a man be just with God?', and answers it in such words as the following: 'He shall bring his offering . . . .' 'And he shall lay his hand on its head . . . .' 'And he shall confess the sin he has committed . . . .' 'And he shall slay it . . . .' 'And the priest shall sprinkle the blood . . . .' 'And he shall make atonement for him, and it shall be forgiven him.'

This is the NT gospel for sinners stated in OT terms and enshrined in the ritual of sacrifice; and it finds its fullest expression in the ritual of the Day of Atonement. 'For the like of the great day of atonement we look in vain in any other people. If every sacrifice pointed to Christ, this most luminously of all. What the fifty-third of Isaiah is to Messianic prophecy, that, we may truly say, is the sixteenth of Leviticus to the whole system of Mosaic types, the most consummate flower of the Messianic symbolism' (S. H. Kellogg). To understand Calvary, and to see it in its tragic glory, we must view it with all the light of sacred story centred upon it. With Isaiah, the 'evangelical' prophet of the old dispensation, and with the writer of the Epistle to the Hebrews, we must turn to Leviticus and read of the great Day of Atonement, and of the explanation which is given of it there: 'For the life of the flesh is in the blood: and I have given it to you upon the altar to make an atonement for your souls: for it is the blood that maketh an atonement for the soul' (Lv. 17:11, AV). Thus we shall see the great drama of redemption unfolding before our eyes and, in the light of the type, begin to understand the Antitype.

OUTLINE OF CONTENTS

COMMENTARY

1:1 – 7:38 THE SACRIFICES

It is significant of its great importance that this manual of sacrifice, as we may call it, is placed first, that the laws regarding the sacrifices precede even the ordination of the priests who are to perform them. Similarly in Numbers the census of the tribes is placed before the celebration of the Passover which is stated to have preceded it in time (Nu. 1:1; 9:1).

1 This code is introduced impressively. The opening word 'and' (AV, RV) connects it directly with Ex. 40:34f. *Called* is a much stronger expression than *spoke*. It suggests a peremptory summons (*cf.* Ex. 24:16; Nu. 12:5) and an important communication (*cf.* Ex. 3:4). It is used of the proclaiming of the feasts (23:2, 4, 21, 37) and of the announcing of the Day of Atonement (25:10). *Called . . . and spoke*, instead of the usual *spoke*, increases the emphasis. *From the tent of meeting* is a better rendering than AV 'tabernacle of the congregation'. See on Ex. 25:9. RV and RSV use 'tabernacle' for the *miškān*, the structure formed of the gilded boards and covered by the linen covering embroidered with the cherubim (*cf.* Ex. 26:7), and 'tent' ('*ōhel*) for the tent composed of curtains which covered it or for the structure as a whole (*cf.* Ex. 40:19, 34). AV, by rendering '*ōhel* both as 'tent' and as 'tabernacle', occasions confusion. The statement indicates definitely that the Tabernacle had already been erected and thus connects Leviticus with what immediately precedes in Exodus.

Before considering this section in detail, it will be well to note carefully several points with regard to it. First, the sacrifices are discussed twice and from different viewpoints: *a.* 1:2 – 6:7, the Lord's portion of the sacrifices, *b.* 6:8 – 7:36, the portion of the priest and of the offerer. Then the five kinds of offering (burnt, cereal, sin, guilt, peace) are discussed independently, without regard to any possible connection between them. In the third place, the description and inventory given here is not complete but is supplemented by other statements, both those previously made and others to follow (*e.g.* no mention is made of the drink-offering or of the bread of the Presence). Fourthly, the order of description varies here between the two viewpoints given above and is not the order of performance. (For a note on the significance of the sacrifices, see pp. 147f.)

1:2 – 6:7 The Lord's portion of the sacrifices

2 *Speak to the people of Israel.* These laws concern all the people. It is as important for the layman to understand his duties as for the priest to perform his correctly. *Brings an offering* (RV 'offereth an oblation'). The Hebrew word *qorbān* (*cf.* Mk. 7:11) is used of gifts as well as of sacrifices (*e.g.* Nu. 7:11). These offerings are now more precisely defined. *Cattle* would include such unclean animals as horses, asses and camels. *Cf.* Ex. 9:3, where Pharaoh's 'live stock' is stated to consist of horses, asses, camels, herds and flocks. *Herd* means the bovines, while *flock* includes sheep and goats. Only these domestic animals and certain birds could be offered in sacrifice.

1:3-17 The burnt-offering. (See also under 6:8-13.) **3** *Burnt offering.* So called because all the flesh was consumed on the altar. Hence it is occasionally called the whole burnt-offering (Dt. 33:10; Ps. 51:19). *Cf.* also Lv. 6:22f. The Hebrew word for 'burnt-offering' ('*ōlâ*) means 'that which goes up', either because all the offering ascended as a 'pleasing odour' to God (v. 17), or because the entire animal, and not simply part of it, was offered (went up) on the altar. This sacrifice is mentioned first, apparently, as being the most conspicuous, even if not the most important. Note that the great bronze (AV 'brasen') altar is called 'the altar of burnt offering' (Ex. 30:28; 31:9; Lv. 4:7, 10, 18). *Cf.* also the direction in 4:24, 33 'where they kill the burnt offering'. It is also noteworthy that the 'continual offering' (*tāmîd*) was a burnt-offering (Ex. 29:42; Nu. 28-29).

That the burnt-offering might be a voluntary offering is indicated by the contrast between 1:2; 2:2 and 4:2; 5:15. But this is not taught in 1:3, where *that he may be accepted* is a better rendering than AV 'of his own voluntary will'. The animal must be a male without blemish. This was also the case with the guilt-offering (*cf.* 5:15). **4-9** The ritual is carefully described. The offerer brings his animal to the door of the tent of meeting, places or presses his hand on its head, makes confession over it (16:21; *cf.* Dt. 26:13ff.), slays it *before the Lord*, flays it, divides it 'into his pieces' (AV), *i.e.* according to its joints (*cf.* Ex. 12:46; Nu. 9:12; Jn. 19:36), and washes the inwards and the legs. The priest collects the blood and sprinkles it round about upon the altar, and burns all the flesh on it. Note the emphatic phrase, *Aaron's sons the priests* (1:5, 8, 11; 2:2; 3:2). The rite of sacrifice is distinctly a priestly function. Neither priest nor offerer partakes of any part of the sacrifice. But the hide goes to the officiating priest (7:8).

In this sacrifice, in contrast with the sin- and trespass-offerings, the stress seems to be on the complete consecration and dedication of the offerer. This is made especially clear in Rom. 12:1, where the words 'your bodies' and 'a living sacrifice' indicate clearly that Paul had the burnt-offering in mind. But the words *it shall be accepted for him to make atonement* and the sprinkling of the blood around the altar make it quite clear that dedication must be preceded by confession and expiation (*cf*. 17:11). *To make atonement* is literally 'to cover over'. It implies the covering over of sin as something upon which the God of Israel who is holy cannot look (Hab. 1:13; *cf*. Pss. 51:1, 9; 103:12; Is. 43:25; 44:22; Mi. 7:19; also Heb. 10:1–4). Sin must be covered over with atoning blood. It is used both with reference to persons (as here, *cf*. 4:20) and to things (*e.g*. the altar, Ex. 29:36).

It is a *burnt offering, an offering by fire, a pleasing odour to the Lord*. Fire-offering is a term which is applied to all those sacrifices, any part of which was burned on the altar. *Pleasing odour* is used of most of them and probably applies to all. The words are an anthropomorphism which is not to be taken literally; it should be regarded as a human way of describing the satisfaction which the Lord takes in the offerings of His people. This applies also to the words 'bread of God' (food) which are used of the sacrifices as a whole (21:6, 8, 17, 22f.), and also of the peace-offerings (3:11, 16). Some take these statements literally and insist that they indicate a crude and primitive conception of the meaning of sacrifice. But such a view is forbidden by the larger context. The ignorant and carnal may have held this low view. But the fact that at this very time, when these laws were being given, Israel was being fed with manna at the hand of God, should have convinced them that the God who fed them did not need to be fed by them, but that it was His good pleasure to receive back from His children a portion of the good things which He had given them, as a sign of the recognition on their part that it was He who sustained their lives and gave them every blessing. Ps. 50 belongs to a much later date, but it expresses clearly and emphatically the Mosaic conception of the meaning of sacrifice.

10–13 The requirements in the case of the sacrifice of a sheep or a goat are the same as in that of the bull. The place of sacrifice is to be the north side of the altar. This is mentioned only here, but it applies to all of the sacrifices except the peace-offering. **14–17** When the offering consists of a bird, the ritual is much simpler, but follows the same general pattern. Birds were offered, either as the required and regular sacrifice (*cf*. 12:6) or as a substitute for the normal sacrifice, permitted and accepted because of the poverty of the offerer (*cf*. 5:7–10).

2:1–16 The cereal-offering. (See also under 6:14–18.) **1** Like the burnt-offering this oblation is described as voluntary: *When any one* ('soul' or 'person', as often in Leviticus) *brings a cereal offering*. It is here described independently but usually accompanied the animal sacrifices (*cf*. Nu. 15:1–16). The main ingredient was fine flour. Consequently *cereal offering* is preferable to AV 'meat offering'. The flour is usually mixed with oil (7:10; *cf*. 5:11) and may have oil poured on it (vv. 6, 15); *frankincense* is placed on it. It may be either uncooked or cooked. **2** The priest takes a *handful* to burn on the altar, which handful must contain all the frankincense. This portion is called the *memorial* (Heb. *'azkārâ*), probably because the frankincense (*lebônâ*), being one of the four elements in the holy incense (Ex. 30:34) which was offered on the golden altar twice daily by the priest for all the people at the hour of prayer, was intended to serve the same purpose in the case of the individual worshipper and bring him into remembrance before God. *Cf*. the headings of Pss. 38 and 70, which indicate that they were to be recited at the time of the offering of this memorial.

3 The smallest cereal-offering, one-tenth of an ephah (6:20), was more than 3 quarts. Since a 'handful', which was the amount to be burnt on the altar as a fire-offering, would be a relatively small part of it, it is stated here that the remainder is *most holy* and is to be the portion of the priests. This means that the priest's portion was to be eaten only by male members of his family and in a holy place, *i.e*. within the court of the Tabernacle (6:16; *cf*. 10:12f.). This was also the rule for the sin-offering (6:25–29), and the guilt-offering (7:16), and the bread of the Presence (24:9). It did not apply to the burnt-offering for the obvious reason that that offering was wholly consumed on the altar. On the other hand, the peace-offering was *holy*. The entire family of the priest might eat of this portion, and most of the sacrifice became the portion of the offerer and was to be eaten by him, his family and his needy friends or dependents (Dt. 12:11–18). It must be eaten in a *clean* place, but not necessarily within the court of the Tabernacle.

11–16 Salt is to be used with all the sacrifices. Salt stands for permanence, for incorruption. Hence the expression, *the salt of the covenant with your God* (*cf*. Nu. 18:19; 2 Ch. 13:5). *Leaven* and *honey* may not be used with the fire-offerings; they may not be placed on the altar. But both may be offered as *first fruits* (*cf*. Ex. 23:16f.; 34:22f.; Lv. 23:17f.). This seems intended to guard against the inference that leaven and honey were unclean in themselves. Ex. 12:39 states definitely that the reason for eating un-leavened bread when Israel went out of Egypt was that they went forth in haste and had no time to leaven it. The meal, the oil and the wine of the drink-offerings (which is not mentioned here, but frequently or usually accompanied the meal-offerings), were the three most important elements in the daily food of the people, frequently summarized in the phrase, 'grain, and wine, and oil' (*e.g.* Dt. 12:17). Consequently the cereal-offering and the oil which went with it and the accompanying drink-offering constituted an oblation of the daily food of the people. In offering it they recognized that they received their daily food from God. Oil, in view of its use in connection with the anointing of the priests and in the golden lampstand, symbolized also the gracious presence of the Holy Spirit in illumination and sanctification.

3:1-17 The peace-offering. (See also under 7:11-34.) **1** *If a man's offering is. . . .* Like the burnt-offering, the peace-offering may be voluntary. The animal may be *male or female,* and must be *without blemish.* Like all the other fire-offerings, it differs from the burnt-offerings in this respect that only part is burnt on the altar. This portion is carefully described. **3, 4** It consists of the *fat* which is upon the internal organs, together with the *kidneys* and the *appendage of the liver.* **9** In the case of the sheep, the *fat tail* is included. This was regarded as a luxury, and might weigh, in the case of the adult animals, 10-15 lb. or even more. These details are repeated in the case of the sin-offering (4:8f., 19, 26-35) and also apply to the guilt-offering (7:3f.).

16 The reason is that it is *food offered by fire for a pleasing odour. All fat is the Lord's.* **17** The solemn injunction is added that the prohibition of eating the fat or the blood is to be perpetually observed. *A perpetual statute throughout your generations* is an expression which occurs 17 times in Leviticus. Dt. 12:15f., 21-24, however, makes no mention of the fat but only of the blood. Nevertheless, it is not to be regarded as modifying this perpetual statute. The cases are quite distinct. The killing and eating described in Deuteronomy is not a peace-offering. It is not made at the altar, but within 'any of your towns' (Dt. 12:15). The blood is poured out on the ground and covered with earth. Finally, the 'unclean' (Dt. 12:15, 22) may eat of it as well as the 'clean', a permission which proves conclusively that Dt. 12 is not dealing with the peace-offering at all (*cf.* Lv. 7:20f.). Since the term 'peace-offering' apparently implies that the worshipper is in a state of reconciliation with God (otherwise he would not be permitted to eat of the flesh of his offering), it is to be noted that the laying on of hands is stressed (vv. 2, 8, 13) as well as the manipulation of the blood. All the fire-offerings were expiatory. The failure to provide for the substitution of a bird in the case of a poor man is noticeable. The reason is probably that since the rite was a sacred meal which the offerer was expected to share with his family and friends, especially the poor and needy, a bird would not be adequate for the purpose; and the poor man, who could not afford a sheep or goat, might and should be invited to partake of the peace-offerings presented by his well-to-do friends and neighbours.

4:1 – 5:13 The sin-offering. (See also under 6:24-30.) **4:2, 3** *If any one sins . . . then let him offer* (*cf.* 5:15). The sin- and guilt-offerings are obligatory as atonement for specific sins. The sins are sins of ignorance or error. The man has sinned unwittingly and has done something which the Lord has commanded not to be done (*cf.* vv. 13, 22, 27). The list of such sins given in 5:1-4 indicates that more than mere ignorance is involved. Such uncleanness as is described, *e.g.,* in 11:24-28 (*cf.* 17:15f.) is removed simply by washing and abstaining from acts of worship (which involve presence at the Tabernacle) until sunset. But if a man has contracted such uncleanness without being aware of it (and 'it is hidden from him', 5:2) and has consequently failed to comply with the law of purification (11:27f.), then he has sinned and is *guilty. When he comes to know it,* then he must offer a sin-offering. Here the sin is clearly one of ignorance. But on the other hand, failure to come forward to testify to a crime when witnesses are publicly summoned may be due to any one of several reasons, as may also the case of the rash oath. These may be sins of infirmity or weakness, without being sins of defiance (the 'high hand') for which there is no remission.

In ch. 4 the sin-offering is considered with special reference to the status of the one whose sin is to be expiated: the anointed priest (*i.e.* the high priest, 8:12) (vv. 3-12); the whole congregation (vv. 13-21); a ruler (vv. 22-26); one of the common people (vv. 27-35). Guilt varies according to rank. **3** The anointed priest occupies a position of great importance. He is one of the people, but he represents all the people. Hence his sin brings guilt upon all of them. **5-7** Since he ministers in holy things and by virtue of his office is permitted to enter the Holy Place, his sin has profaned the Holy Place and atonement must be made in the Holy Place. Blood must be brought into the Holy Place and sprinkled toward the veil and placed on the horns of the gold altar. **13-21** The same ritual is to be performed when all the congregation sins, apparently because Israel, ideally considered, is a 'kingdom of priests' (Ex. 19:6), and the Lord dwells in her midst. In this case the laying on of hands must be performed by the elders as representing the people. In the case of the lay individual, whether *a ruler* (v. 22) or *one of the common people* (v. 27; RV mg. 'people of the land'), the blood is not brought into the Holy Place, but applied to the horns of the altar of burnt sacrifice and poured out beside it. The ruler offers a male goat, the common man a goat or a ewe-lamb. In all cases the fat is burnt on the altar as in the case of the peace-offerings (vv. 10, 31). But with regard to the rest of the sacrifice an important distinction is to be observed. In the case of the animals whose blood has been brought into the Holy Place, the rest of the flesh is to be burned *outside the camp,* in a clean place where the ashes of the sacrifices are poured out (v. 12). The principle involved is that the one for whom the sin-offering is presented must not partake of any of it (*cf.* 6:24–30). The priest may not do this when making atonement for his own sin, nor when he makes atonement for the whole congregation of which he is a member. *Cf.* Heb. 13:10–13.

5:1–6 specifies, as we have seen, certain sins as requiring a sin-offering: failure to come forward to testify when summoned, unclean-ness through contact with the carcase of an unclean animal or with the uncleanness of a human being, or taking a rash oath. All of these being joined together by *or* may be regarded as forming a protasis, the apodosis of which begins with v. 5. They are treated as sins of ignorance (see 4:13; 5:2, 3, 4). So when he realizes his guilt, or it is brought to his attention, he is to *confess* it and *bring his guilt offering . . . for the sin . . . for a sin offering.* This rendering seems to identify the sin- and the guilt-offerings; and AV in its chapter summary treats 5:1–13 as relating to the guilt-offering. There is obviously a close connection between them. For the words 'and is guilty' ('*āšēm*) come from the same root as 'guilt-offering' ('*āšām*), and are used in 4:13, 22, 27 of sins which require a sin-offering, and in 5:17; 6:4 of those which require a guilt-offering. But since the difference seems to lie in the fact that the guilt-offering requires and must be preceded by restitution, and since restitution is not mentioned until 5:14f., it seems best to regard the description of the guilt-offering as beginning with 5:14. It is true, of course, that the mention of the guilt-offering already in 5:6 is somewhat confusing, if this special form of sin-offering is not discussed as such until 5:14f. But this may be intended to indicate the close connection between the two. The RV mg. rendering 'for his guilt' instead of *his guilt offering* is doubtful, to say the least.

7 Since the sin-offering is obligatory in such cases as have been stated, due allowance may be made in the case of the poor who cannot afford a costly offering. Instead of the lamb the offerer may present *two turtledoves or two young pigeons.* One is to be offered as a sin-offering; the other as a burnt-offering. Since in the case of the sin-offering all the flesh except the fat became the portion of the priest (6:26), the explanation is probably correct, that because of the difficulty or impossibility of removing the fat in the case of the bird, the flesh of the one bird was wholly consumed on the altar as representing the Lord's portion of the sin-offering (but called a burnt-offering, because it was wholly consumed on the altar) and the other given to the priest as representing his portion of the sin-offering. This would account for the requirement that two birds be presented.

11 In the case of the extremely poor a further concession is made: a cereal-offering may be substituted for the animal sacrifice. Being a sin-offering it differed from the usual cereal-offering in an important respect: it was offered without oil and without frankincense. **12** Furthermore the handful which was offered as a memorial

was burnt on the altar *upon the offerings by fire to the Lord.* This clearly gave it the value of a bloody sacrifice, by virtue of its being mingled with the fire-offerings which were on the altar. Hence it could be called *a sin offering*, and in offering it the priest made atonement for sin. In this way, what appears to be an exception to the principle that 'without the shedding of blood is no forgiveness of sins' (Heb. 9:22) really ceases to be an exception but rather serves to illustrate the principle of vicarious substitution which it is the main object of the ritual of sacrifice to illustrate and enforce.

5:14 – 6:7 The guilt-offering. (See also under 7:1–10.) The distinctive feature of the guilt-offering is, as we have seen, that it is made in the case of a sin which requires restitution, and restitution must precede the performing of the sacrifice. Two cases are specified.

5:15, 16 The first is the withholding of *the holy things of the Lord, i.e.* of such tithes, offerings, firstlings, *etc.* as belonged to God and must either be presented to the priest or redeemed. **17** The second case had to do with acts *which the Lord has commanded not to be done.* Since the same phrase is used here as in 4:2, 13, 22, 27, the difference must consist in the fact that the trespass requires restitution.

6:1–7 The next section deals with acts which involve injustice or injury to one's fellow-men. In all these cases the property withheld is to be restored with the addition of one-fifth of its value, a fine which both served to reimburse the rightful owner and to punish the guilty party. *Cf.* Nu. 5:6–8. The offering in every case is a *ram* (*cf.* 19:21f.), also called a 'male lamb' (14:12), 'a male lamb a year old' (Nu. 6:12). The trespass-offering formed part of the ritual for the cleansing of the leper (Lv. 14:12) and of the Nazirite (Nu. 6:12).

6:8 – 7:38 The portion of the priest and of the offerer

Up to this point, except in the case of the cereal-offering (2:10; *cf.* 5:13), attention has been focused on the Godward side of the sacrifices: the manipulation of the blood and the portions to be consumed upon the altar or burned outside the camp. A series of laws is now given which deal particularly with the portion of priest and offerer. This subject is introduced by the words *Command Aaron and his sons* (v. 9) and each topic commences with the words *this is the law of* (vv. 9, 14, 25, *etc.*). Each of the laws already discussed is now dealt with from this angle.

6:8–13 The burnt-offering. (See also under 1:3–17.) Since the entire animal is consumed on the altar, there are only two matters of importance: the disposal of the ashes and the tending of the altar-fire. This fire is never to be allowed to go out. It is the sacred fire kindled on the altar by God Himself. Furthermore the burnt-offering is to burn continually upon the altar as the token of Israel's consecration to

God. The statement that the burnt-offering shall burn during the night indicates that this law has the continual burnt-offering (Ex. 29:38–42) primarily in view.

6:14–18 The cereal-offering. (See also under 2:1–16.) **15** With the exception of the *memorial*, the entire offering goes to the officiating priest. **16** Like the sin- and guilt-offerings, it is most holy and must be eaten in *a holy place*, *i.e.* within the courts of the Tabernacle (*cf.* v. 26). **18** Follow AV, 'shall be holy'. *Cf.* 6:27, RSV. This apparently means that those who by virtue of their office are entitled to eat of the sacrifice are to remember that they may do so only if ceremonially clean. What applies to the laity (7:20) would be even more essential in the case of the priest and his sons. The eating of the priest's portion of the cereal-, sin- and guilt-offerings was restricted to males (6:18, 29; *cf.* 7:6; Nu. 18:8–10).

6:19–23 To the law of the cereal-offering of the people there is added a brief statement regarding the continual cereal-offering for the priests. It is to be offered by the anointed priest (Aaron or his successor in office) perpetually, morning and evening. It would seem to be a kind of priestly counterpart of the perpetual burnt-offering. Since it is offered for the priests, no part of it can be eaten by them; it is to be wholly burnt.

6:24–30 The sin-offering. (See also under 4:1 – 5:13.) In the case of this sacrifice, all the flesh except the fat became the portion of the officiating priest: **26** *the priest who offers it for sin shall eat it.* The holiness of this portion is particularly stressed. It is most holy and everything that touches it must be or becomes holy. This applies even to the vessel in which it is cooked. **27** Here, where the reference is to things, *whatever* is the preferable rendering, although RSV mg. gives 'whoever'. *Shall be holy, i.e.* be treated as holy and therefore withdrawn from common use. **28** It must be thoroughly washed or, if made of earthenware, be broken. **29** Every male of the priests may eat of the sin-offering. **30** But again it is pointed out that this is not permissible when the offering is made for the priest himself.

7:1–10 The guilt-offering. (See also under 5:14 – 6:7.) Since nothing has been said in the earlier passage about the Lord's portion in this sacrifice, the law as already stated for the peace-offering (3:3f.) and for the sin-offering (4:8–10), instead of simply being appealed to, as, *e.g.*, in 4:26, is repeated in detail (7:2–5). It is then stated that the portion of the priest is the same in this offering as in the case of the sin-offering. Everything except the Lord's portion goes to the priest. The cereal-offerings referred to in this connection are the cereal-offerings which accompanied the animal sacrifices just mentioned.

7:11–34 The peace-offering. (See also under 3:1–17.) The peace-offering is the only one of the sacrifices (burnt, sin, guilt, peace) of which the offerer is permitted to partake. Consequently, the Lord's portion, the priest's portion and the

offerer's portion are carefully distinguished. The Lord's portion is the fat, which is burned on the altar (vv. 22–25). The priest's portion (vv. 30–34) consists of the 'breast' and the 'thigh' (whether fore-leg or hind-leg is meant is not certain). The manipulation, waving and offering (AV 'heaving'), apparently signified that the offerer gave these portions to God through His priest, whose portion they thus became. All the rest of the flesh becomes the portion of the offerer, but with certain restrictions. **15, 16** If the offering is a vow or a free-will offering, any remainder may be eaten on the second day. But if it is *for thanksgiving*, it can be eaten only on the day of sacrifice. What is not eaten is to be burnt. One object of this requirement was clearly to encourage a generous and hospitable spirit, the inviting of friends or neighbours, especially the poor and needy, to share in this joyful occasion (Dt. 12:12).

With the sacrifice the offerer is to present cakes of several different kinds. **12** Some are made with or mingled with oil and are unleavened. **13** But he is also to offer *cakes of leavened bread.* **14** The words *from each offering* indicate that the priest is to receive both leavened and unleavened cakes as his portion, together with the manipulated offerings, which are his. Since the daily food of the people included leavened bread, this would indicate the hallowing and offering of a portion of their daily food to God in the person of His priest. But leavened bread could not of course be placed on the altar. It should be noted that these cakes are not a cereal-offering (*minḥâ*). No incense is placed on them and no portion is burnt on the altar. They simply accompany the peace-offering and are partaken of by both priest and people. The priest's portion is called an *offering*. It is particularly stressed that the waved and offered portions belonged to the priests by a perpetual statute. They are called the 'anointing-portion' (v. 35, RV) of the priests because these portions were assigned to them on the day of their consecration to the priesthood. While the peace-offering is holy, it is not 'most holy' (*cf.* 7:6). This is indicated by the fact that it is to be slain in the court (3:2), and can be partaken of by the offerer and by any 'clean' person. The idea which is most prominent in connection with this sacrifice is that of joyous communion with God, and of fellowship with one another in this act of worship.

7:35–38 The divine origin of the laws recalled. *This is the portion. . . . This is the law.* This elaborate treatment of the sacrifices is summed up in verses which draw attention to the fact that they are the divine perpetual provision for Aaron and his sons, and which stress the nature of their origin as being commanded by the Lord at Sinai.

The significance of the ritual

As we study these sacrifices we are impressed with the clearness with which they point forward to and have their fulfilment in the redemptive work of Christ. In the holy supper, the Christian remembers the death of Christ as his sin- and guilt-offering, a sacrifice made once for all at Calvary and in which he can neither participate nor share. He has communion with Christ as his Passover and peace-offering, as he partakes of the sacred symbols of His broken body and shed blood, even drinking of the cup, because the wine of the sacrament symbolizes the blood which was shed to atone for sin and which has become the source and fountain of life for every believer (Jn. 6:53). He dedicates himself anew to His service by presenting his own body a living sacrifice (the burnt-offering) to his Lord. And he looks forward to the coming forth of his great High Priest, from the heavenly Temple into which He has entered, to complete and crown His glorious redemption by receiving unto Himself His redeemed ones who are keeping the feast until He comes. See also the note on the NT interpretation of the Day of Atonement (pp. 156f.).

In view of the practical universality of some form of sacrifice among ancient peoples, the question has naturally been often discussed as to a possible connection between the Mosaic cultus and the practices of the neighbouring peoples. That there should be certain resemblances is only to be expected. But these should be estimated in the light of such considerations as the following.

The Pentateuch represents the Mosaic ritual as a direct revelation from God: 'the Lord said to Moses'. It repeatedly warns the people against adopting the customs and practices of the Egyptians or of the Canaanites. Its antecedents, where they exist, are to be found in the practices of the ancestors of Israel, going back to the earliest times. There are differences which are so thoroughgoing that they far outweigh any surface resemblances. These differences are both negative and positive. On the negative side we may note that there is no connection with divination or augury; no religious frenzy, self-mutilations, or sacred prostitution, sensual and orgiastic fertility rites being utterly forbidden; no human sacrifices; no sacrifices for the dead; no appeal to *quid pro quo* motive. On this last point we may note further that the amount of the offering was immaterial. The law 'prescribes for the whole year not quite 1,300 animals as public sacrifices, or on the average three or four daily'. Hecatombs were of no avail (Mi. 6:7).

On the positive side the most important differences are the emphasis on the ethical— the sinfulness of sin and the necessity of atonement; the necessity of a right attitude on the part of the offerer, with the stress on repentance and loyal obedience to the law of God; the unique sacredness of the blood as representing the life of the animal accepted in substitution for the offerer as the propitiation for his sins. All these considerations taken together show that, whatever the resemblances, the Mosaic

ritual breathes a quite different spirit from that of the cults of other nations, and is essentially unique.

8:1 - 10:20 THE CONSECRATION OF AARON AND HIS SONS

This narrative stands in close relation to that in Ex. 28, 29. We have seen that in Exodus the construction of the Tabernacle is dealt with three times. Chs. 25-30 deal mainly with its construction and furnishing but include instructions regarding the vestments of the priests and their consecration (chs. 28, 29); chs. 35-39 deal with the execution of the instructions regarding the Tabernacle, and ch. 40 with its erection and its acceptance by God. We might have expected that the account of the consecration of the priests would follow immediately, as the natural sequel of the dedication of the Tabernacle, and form a part of Exodus. But since the chief function of the priests is to offer sacrifice and also because the offering of sacrifice on their behalf formed an indispensable part of their own consecration, the manual of sacrifice given in Lv. 1-7 is very properly made to precede this important section.

8:1-36 Aaron and his sons consecrated by Moses

2 The abruptness of the language, *Take Aaron and his sons with him, and the garments, and the anointing oil, and the bull . . . and the two rams, and the basket of unleavened bread* carries us back directly to Ex. 29:1-3 where all these things are enumerated. Hence the use of the definite article. That this rite is to be regarded as the conclusion of the consecration of the Tabernacle and a continuation of Ex. 29-40 is also indicated by the frequency of the phrase *as the Lord commanded Moses* or its equivalent (15 times) which runs like a refrain through those chapters. The unique position of Moses (*cf.* Ex. 28, 29), who was over the whole house of God as a servant (Nu. 12:7; Heb. 3:2, 5), is made clear. Thus Moses offers Aaron's sin-offering (8:14-17); and the wave breast of the offering of consecration, which would normally have been the portion of the officiating priest, becomes Moses' portion (v. 28; *cf.* Ex. 29:26).

3 The ritual of consecration to the priesthood and investiture with office was elaborate and impressive; and it was performed in the presence of all the congregation at the door of the tent of meeting. **5** Note the solemn introduction: *This is the thing which the Lord has commanded to be done.* **6-9** Aaron and his sons were first washed with water, and Aaron was then arrayed in his holy garments (*cf.* Ex. 28). **10-11** Then Moses anointed the Tabernacle, the altar and all its vessels, including the laver. **12** After that he poured oil on Aaron's head (*cf.* Ps. 133:2). The purpose was sanctification and consecration. **13** Having clothed Aaron's sons, **14-17** he proceeded to offer a sin-offering, **18-21** a burnt-offering, and **22-29** a consecration-offering. The latter is the only one not mentioned in the manual. The Hebrew term is *millu'îm*, literally 'fillings', because 'to fill the hand(s)' is the technical term for investing with office. **31** It resembled the peace-offering in that the ones for whom it was offered were permitted to partake of the flesh. But in this case the special portion of the priest, the waved breast and offered (AV 'heaved') thigh, could not be eaten by Aaron and his sons, because the offering was made on their behalf by Moses. So the former was assigned to Moses as his portion (v. 29), since he acted as priest, and the latter was burned on the altar (vv. 25, 28).

Aaron and his sons laid their hands upon the head of the sacrificial animal in the case of all of these offerings as a sign that they were offered on their behalf. But it is significant that the blood of the sin-offering was used to cleanse and sanctify the altar at which the priests were to minister. The placing of the blood of consecration on ear, thumb and toe (vv. 23, 24), the sprinkling of oil mingled with sacrificial blood on Aaron and his sons (v. 30) and the pouring of oil on Aaron's head (v. 12), symbolized the consecration and sanctification in varying degree to holy office and use. **33, 34** Aaron and his sons were not to go out from the door of the tent of meeting during the seven days of their consecrating, and the same sacrifices were to be repeated on each of the seven days. Consequently an exception was made to the rule regarding the eating of the peace-offerings which could be eaten on the day after they were offered (7:15–18). These were to be eaten the same day. During these seven days Moses performed the same sacrifices on each day, and Aaron and his sons remained in the court of the Tabernacle.

9:1–24 Aaron takes up his office

1 *On the eighth day, i.e.* the day which marked the end of their consecration, *Moses called Aaron and his sons. Called* suggests the solemnity of the occasion. Every act performed by Aaron is commanded by Moses. **5** The whole congregation is brought together to stand *before the Lord* so that the Lord may appear to them and manifest His glory (vv. 4, 6, 23f.) as a sign of His approval and ratification of everything that has been done (*cf.* Ex. 40:34f.).

7 The sacrifices which Aaron performed for himself and his sons and for the people—Aaron and his sons were Israelites first of all—were a sin-offering and a burnt-offering (vv. 2, 8, 12). Those which he performed for the people were a sin-, a burnt-, a cereal- and a peace-offering (vv. 3, 4). Since the ritual has already been described, detailed discussion is not needed. It is to be noted, however, that the order followed here is apparently the regular, and we may say the logical, order for the offerings—sin-, burnt- peace-offering. Thus the three basic ideas are emphasized: first, atonement for sin, then dedication and consecration of life, and finally communion with God in the eucharistic meal. In Lv. 14:10–20 the order of the offerings of the cleansed leper is guilt-offering (vv. 12–18), sin-offering (v. 19), burnt-offering and cereal-offering (v. 20). *Cf.* 14:21–32 where the same order is prescribed. This would indicate that the offering which involved restitution, if offered, came first of all, preceding even the sin-offering.

22 After all the sacrifices had been offered, Aaron blessed the people. He did this while still standing by the altar. The blessing was probably the formula of blessing given in Nu. 6:22f. **23** Then Moses and Aaron *went into the tent of meeting.* The reason for this is not stated. But it is proper to infer that at this time Moses placed Aaron in charge of the Holy Place, the lampstand, the table of the bread of the Presence and the altar of incense, and instructed him as to his duties, all of which Moses had performed from the day of setting up the Tabernacle (Ex. 40). Then they came forth and both blessed the people. And the glory of the Lord was manifested, as on the day of the setting up of the Tabernacle. **24** The fire which burnt up the sacrifices was the sacred fire which was not to be allowed to go out. The word *shouted* implies joy and rejoicing. But the joy was mingled with awe, for they *fell on their* faces in worship before the Lord.

10:1–20 Sacrilege and its consequences

In this historical section, the account of the consecration of Aaron and his four sons is followed at once by the record of the sacrilege which led to the tragic death of the two oldest who had beheld the glory of the Lord in the Mount (Ex. 24:1). **15** That this event followed immediately and is to be regarded as the sequel of the ceremony of consecration is indicated by the reference to the *goat of the sin-offering.* This must be the offering referred to already in 9:3,15.

17, 18 Its blood had not been carried into the Holy Place as was done with Aaron's own sin-offering. It was the sin-offering for the people and the flesh was the priests' portion. Consequently its flesh should have been eaten by the priests in the Holy Place. The reason given is very significant: *It . . . has been given to you that you may bear* (RV mg. 'take away') *the iniquity of the congregation, to make atonement for them before the Lord. Cf.* Ex. 28:12, 29, 30, 38. The function of the priests was one of mediation. This seems to mean that the priests by eating the sin-offering exhibited God's gracious acceptance of the sacrifice just as, by permitting the offerer to partake of his peace-offering, He indicated His acceptance of both gift and giver. Instead it had been burnt (whether on the altar or outside the camp is not stated). This may mean either that the surviving sons of Aaron could not eat of their portion under such terrible circumstances, or that they did not dare to do so because they felt themselves to be involved in, or contaminated by, the sin of their brethren, since all four were priests. They had therefore burnt the carcase of the goat which was the people's oblation, even as they had been required to burn the flesh of their own sin-offering, outside the camp (9:11).

That they erred in this is made clear by vv. 17f. 20 indicates that whether Aaron's scruples were primarily those of a father or those of a priest, the reason or excuse which he gave for the conduct of his surviving sons, and which apparently reflected his own attitude, was regarded by Moses as satisfactory. Mercy joined with judgment!

1 The exact nature of the sin of Nadab and Abihu is not fully explained. Note the words, *Now Nadab and Abihu . . . took*. Nothing has been said in chs. 8 and 9 about the offering of incense. They are represented as acting entirely on their own initiative and not at the command of Moses. *Offered unholy fire* (*cf*. Ex. 30:9); apparently fire not taken from the bronze altar. Both of them did it. The offering of incense on the golden altar was the duty of the high priest (Ex. 30:9) or of *one* of the priests (Lk. 1:9). For them to take precedence over their father in the first performance of this solemn function was an act of presumption. For the two of them to undertake it at the same time suggests rivalry and jealousy. Their act may also have been presumptuous because the time for offering incense (morning or evening) had not arrived. These and still other elements may have entered into this act of sacrilege. The occasion was so solemn and the ritual had been performed with such care, everything being done 'as the Lord commanded', that such impulsive and arbitrary departure from it as Nadab and Abihu were guilty of must have been highly presumptuous and sacrilegious.

8–11 Significant in this connection is the special revelation and prohibition which is made directly to Aaron and not through Moses. It is at least possible, though by no means certain, that we are to infer from the introduction at this point of this law prohibiting the use of wine or strong drink by the ministering priest (*cf*. Ezk. 44:21) that Nadab and Abihu acted as they did because they were under the influence of liquor. Whatever the explanation, the incident is a solemn warning against every sin of presumption, self-assertion and levity.

In view of the definite statements which are made in the manual regarding the portions of the animal and vegetable offerings which are to be given to the priest, it is rather remarkable that there is no corresponding statement about the drink-offering. It would be natural to infer that a portion of the drink-offering was poured out on or beside the altar and that the rest would be assigned to the priest as his portion to be drunk with his meat and his bread after his service at the altar was completed. The analogy of the Passover (*cf*. Mt. 26:29) would favour this. But according to Jewish tradition all the drink-offering was poured out; either on the altar of burnt sacrifice (Ex. 30:9 might imply this), or at the foot of the altar (Ecclus. 50:15), or perhaps part on the altar and the rest at its base. **10, 11** The reason for this perpetual rule is that the priests may be able to *distinguish between the holy and the common, and between the unclean and the clean, i.e.* observe carefully all the ritual and ceremonial requirements of the law, and that they may teach the people of Israel all the statutes of the law. See Dt. 17:11; 24:8; 33:10; *cf*. Mi. 3:11.

This whole tragic incident may properly be regarded as intended to impress on Israel, both priests and people, the holiness of their God and to warn them against any presumption or laxity in performance of the law of sacrifice which is so carefully stated in chs. 1–7. It also taught the important and needed lesson that no man is indispensable to God. Four priests were indeed very few to perform the service of a sanctuary which was to be the centre of worship for several million persons. Yet God put away half of their number at the very outset for disobedience. God is able of the 'stones to raise up children to Abraham'.

This terribly impressive event concludes what has been called 'the law of the sanctuary' and we pass on now to consider 'the law of daily life'.

11:1 – 15:33 LAWS REGARDING UNCLEANNESS

'Unclean' (defiled) is the conspicuous word in this group of chapters. It occurs more than 100 times. Almost equally noteworthy is the rare occurrence of the word 'sin' (evil, wickedness). This indicates that here the emphasis is on the ceremonial rather than on the ethical. Yet it does not follow that uncleanness is a matter of minor importance. Failure to do what God has commanded is sin, whether the act be ceremonial or moral. Unclean is the antithesis of holy. Everything which is inconsistent with God's holiness may be described as uncleanness. It may be purely ceremonial, as the touching of a dead body, or it may be crimes which are so shocking to the moral sense that it is a shame even to speak of them (18:20–25). In most cases the uncleanness is quite temporary, lasting only 'until the evening' (11:25), and in certain cases requires the washing of the garments or of the person in water. But it may cover a considerable period of time and require the presenting of a sin-offering. Ceremonial purity was indispensable for a holy people. The uncleannesses that are dealt with are of several kinds.

11:1–47 Uncleanness due to animals

This subject is discussed under two aspects, living animals as food and contact with dead animals.

11:1–23 The question considered from the standpoint of diet. *Cf.* on Dt. 14:1–21. These verses prescribe the flesh which may or may not be eaten. Four classes are distinguished:

2–8 Quadrupeds. Only those animals which divide the hoof completely and which chew the cud may be eaten. This rule is precisely stated and then four examples of animals which do not meet the requirements are given: *camel, rock* *badger, hare* and *swine*. The *hare* is not a ruminant, nor is the *rock badger* (AV 'coney', which is generally identified with the rock badger, *Hyrax Syriacus*). Both are rodents. But the fact that their jaws are constantly in motion gives the appearance of chewing the cud. This indicates clearly that the description is not intended to be strictly scientific, but simple and practical. The clean animals are not named here (*cf.* Gn. 7:2), but Dt. 14:4, in listing them, adds to the three domestic animals (ox, sheep and goat) seven of the wild animals which are also members of the ruminant family (the *Pecora*, according to present-day classification). For the average Israelite this restricted the meat diet largely to those domestic animals which were used in sacrifice.

9–12 Sea food. Only fish which have both fins and scales may be eaten. This rules out eels, shell-fish, lobster, crab, oyster, frog, *etc.*

13–19 Birds. This is stated entirely from the negative side. *And these you shall have in abomination among the birds* introduces a list of twenty, including several species. Dt. 14:11 states positively, but briefly, 'you may eat all clean birds' without naming them, and then gives a list almost identical with the one given here. The clean birds would include doves, pigeons, sparrows. No mention is made of eating eggs (*cf.* Dt. 22:6f.). Many of the prohibited birds are birds of prey. Birds which fed on carrion, like the kite and vulture, would be especially obnoxious.

20–23 Insects. These are defined as *all winged insects that go upon all fours*. The phrase 'that go upon all fours' (lit. 'upon four legs') must mean 'those which walk or crawl like a quadruped', since six legs are characteristic of the great class of *Insecta*. All are banned with the notable exception of four classes of the locust family which are distinguished by their long jumping legs. If the RSV rendering of v. 23 is followed then the phrase *which have four feet* cannot mean the same as v. 21 *that go on all fours, i.e.* it must be taken as referring to insects which do not have the large jumping legs. By inserting the word *other* in v. 23 AV and RSV assume the two phrases to be more or less synonymous. This is probably the correct meaning. The fact that a sweeping statement is made after a definite exception to it has been already given should not confuse the careful reader.

11:24–42 The question considered from the standpoint of physical contact. The words 'carcase' (11 times) and 'when they are dead' (twice) indicate that the reference is to dead animals. The AV renders v. 26 by 'the carcases of every beast' taking the position that contact with a living animal, such as the camel or the ass, which were unlawful for eating, did not render one ceremonially unclean. This became an issue between Pharisees and Sadducees in later times, the latter holding that contact even with the living animal produced uncleanness.

29–38 enlarge upon vv. 20–23, which have

merely stated the general prohibition and the important exceptions in the case of winged creeping things. **29, 30** Here eight kinds of *swarming things* are particularly specified as abominable. Yet, as has been indicated, the emphasis seems to be on the contamination produced by their carcases. They are clearly unclean as food. **31** But also their dead bodies render unclean; *whoever touches them when they are dead. . . .* **35–37** The defilement extends to *any part of their carcase.* **41** The prohibition of the eating of the flesh of *swarming things* is sweeping and comprehensive. The law regarding uncleanness through contact with the carcases of any creeping thing may perhaps be regarded as singling out these eight animals for special mention because contact with their carcases was especially likely to take place. It is to be noted that in this chapter the rare word *abomination* (*šeqeṣ*) is used of the eating of sea animals (vv. 10–12), birds (v. 13), winged creeping things (vv. 20, 23), and creeping things (vv. 41, 43). This confirms the conclusion that vv. 24–38 refer to uncleanness occasioned by contact with dead animals, and that v. 41 resumes the discussion of dietary laws.

11:43–47 The people of God must be holy. This law regarding man's relation to the animal kingdom over which he has been given dominion is followed by a most impressive sanction. **44, 45** *For I am the Lord your God; consecrate yourselves therefore, and be holy, for I am holy. . . . For I am the Lord who brought you up out of the land of Egypt, to be your God; you shall therefore be holy, for I am holy* (*cf.* 1 Pet. 1:15–17). The necessity of holiness was first stressed in connection with the eating of those portions of the sacrifices which were for the priests and the people, and also in connection with the entire ritual of the consecration of Aaron and his sons. Now in this section the same command is most impressively applied to the daily life of the entire people. *Cf.* 19:2; 20:7, 8, 26; 21:6–8, 15, 23; 22:9, 16, 32 where the same or similar sanctions occur.

46, 47 This section then concludes with a summary, the closing words of which are important: *to make a distinction between the unclean and the clean and between the living creature that may be eaten and the living creature that may not be eaten. Cf.* 20:25, 26. The first part of this summary seems to refer to uncleanness through contact with that which is unclean, especially that which is rendered unclean by the fact of death, and the second part to those living things which are proper for food and those which are prohibited.

12:1–8 Uncleanness due to childbirth

The command to be fruitful is given in Gn. 1:28 and renewed to Noah after the Flood (Gn. 9:1). We are expressly told that it was obeyed by the post-diluvian ancestors of Abram (11:11, 13, *etc.*). The consistent attitude of the OT may be summarized in the words of Pss. 127:3; 128:3f.

Fruitfulness was a sign of divine favour; barrenness was regarded as a reproach (Gn. 30:23). Consequently, the laws given here and elsewhere regarding the marital relationship and parenthood are both impressive and significant. The only adequate explanation of the seeming anomaly presented by the command to be fruitful, the joy attending the realization of parenthood, and the uncleanness which is associated with it and which finds its most pronounced expression in the prolonged purification required of the mother after she has performed the high function of womanhood, must be found in the fact of the Fall and the curse pronounced on woman immediately after it. Pain and suffering were to be the accompaniment of motherhood (Gn. 3:16). Regarding Adam we read: 'When Adam had lived a hundred and thirty years, he became the father of a son in his own likeness after his image' (Gn. 5:3). When this took place Adam was a fallen and sinful being. He was under the curse pronounced by God, 'in the day that you eat of it you shall die' (Gn. 2:17). So of Adam, and of all but one (Enoch) of his descendants mentioned in Gn. 5, the last word spoken is 'and he died'.

From this it follows that, although the birth of a child is a joyous event, it is also a solemn one. For the birth of the child will inevitably be followed ultimately by its death, and by eternal death unless the child is made an heir of life through the redemption which is in Christ. It is in this sense that we must understand David's words, 'Behold, I was brought forth in iniquity and in sin did my mother conceive me' (Ps. 51:5). David is not here reflecting upon the virtue of his own mother; she may have been a paragon among women. He is thinking of that inherited taint, that original sin, which she had transmitted to him and which was the root cause of the grievous sin against womanhood of which he is so painfully conscious at the time of composing the Psalm. Consequently, according to the law, everything connected with parenthood is treated as unclean, and especially as rendering the person unfit for the performance of religious duties. In fact the strictness with which anything which suggests the sexual and sensual is banned from the worship of God (Ex. 19:15; 20:26; Lv. 15:16–18) is one of the most noteworthy characteristics of the religion of Israel and distinguishes it most sharply from the religions of the neighbouring peoples who worshipped gods who were male and female and even made orgiastic (fertility) rites a prominent feature in the worship of these gods.

2–4 In the case of the birth of *a male child*, the uncleanness of the mother as far as the home is concerned lasts until *the eighth day*, when the rite of circumcision is to be performed on her son (*cf.* Gn. 21:4). Then *for thirty-three days* she is still to be unclean as far as public religious duties are concerned. **5** In the case of the birth of *a female child* both periods are doubled. No reason is assigned. Since this is described as a

period of uncleanness, the explanation is probably to be sought in connection with the considerations mentioned above. It does not seem probable that the reason is purely physical or biological. **6–8** At the termination of this period of forty or eighty days she is to bring a yearling lamb for a burnt-offering and a fowl for a sin-offering, or two fowls, if she cannot afford a lamb. *Cf.* Lk. 2:24. The specifying of the age of the lamb is exceptional (Ex. 12:5; 29:38; Lv. 9:3; 14:10, *etc.*), and is usually stated in the case of sacrifices for the feast days. The concluding words are impressive: *and the priest shall make atonement for her, and she shall be clean.*

For the Christian of today this ancient law has special significance. Christians should realize that marriage ought not to be contracted lightly, that they should marry 'in the Lord' (1 Cor. 7:39) in order that they may claim the promises and blessings of the covenant for their children (1 Cor. 7:14). They may not like to be told that their children are sinful and unclean. But they need to remember that this is so. The view is widely held today that children are born good, that they should be allowed to develop naturally, that self-expression should be encouraged, and discipline and restraint reduced to the minimum. Christian parents who realize the truth set forth here will pray earnestly that the children who have been born in sin may be 'born again', may be regenerated by the Holy Spirit. They pray that they as parents may be enabled to train up their children in the nurture and admonition of the Lord. Guidance, restraint, discipline and religious instruction are quite as essential as self-expression, in most cases far more essential.

13:1 – 14:57 Uncleanness due to leprosy

As in the case of the two subjects last discussed, it is important to remember that leprosy is dealt with solely from the standpoint of the uncleanness which it occasions. It is most frequently called in AV, RV 'the plague' (lit. 'stroke') or 'the plague of leprosy' (*e.g.* 13:2, 3; RSV *a leprous disease*). The man who has it, or is suspected of having it, is *unclean*, so unclean that he must be *shut up* (mentioned 8 times), apparently outside the camp (14:3), while his case is being decided. Then, if the verdict is unfavourable, he must be removed from the camp until he is healed (13:45f.). The possibility of recovery is thus plainly included in the decree of banishment. But it is to be noted that, while elaborate rules are laid down for the recognition of leprosy and for distinguishing true leprosy from other diseases with which it might easily be confused, nothing is said about the treatment of the disease. This has led some to the conclusion that it was incurable, and even that it was not an ordinary disease, but a visitation from God. The cases of Miriam (Nu. 12:10–15), Gehazi (2 Ki. 5:27) and Uzziah (2 Ch. 26:19–23) are appealed to as proof of this. But were such the case it would seem as if the nature of the affliction and the cause of it would have been so plain that the elaborate rules for detecting it might have been dispensed with. Apparently we must distinguish between what we may call ordinary cases and such extraordinary cases as the ones just mentioned.

It is interesting to note that leprosy is not included in the diseases which the Lord threatens as a punishment for apostasy, regarding which it is said 'of which you cannot be healed' (Dt. 28:27, 35). The language of 14:2f., *This shall be the law of the leper for the day of his cleansing* and *if the leprous disease is healed in the leper*, seems to make it quite plain that leprosy was not incurable. Otherwise we would have to hold that *leper* here is to be understood to mean 'the man under suspicion of being a leper', or else that the elaborate ritual for the cleansing of the leper could be performed only in such a case as Miriam's when the hand of God was plainly manifested both in the smiting and the healing.

13:1–46 How leprosy is to be recognized. Detailed discussions of the rules laid down for the detection of the disease cannot be entered into here. It is clear that it was hard to distinguish from a number of other diseases which were common among the Israelites. None of the more frightful symptoms of what we know as leprosy is mentioned here. It may be that the disease differed somewhat from the leprosy of NT times and from the leprosy which became such a scourge in Europe in the Middle Ages. But it is to be remembered that these laws have to do with the detection of the disease in its early stages and also that Aaron's words in pleading with Moses on behalf of Miriam describe with terrible clearness the real nature of the disease and its terrible results: 'Let her not be as one dead, of whom the flesh is half consumed when he comes out of his mother's womb' (Nu. 12:12). And Moses' prayer that God will heal does not necessarily mean that direct supernatural intervention was the only hope for the leper.

13:47–59 Leprosy in garments. A closely related subject is now dealt with in this section. Leprosy in a garment is discussed in connection with leprosy of the body, apparently because it was an immediate concern of the people. Significant is the regard which is shown for the property rights of the people. The destruction of an entire garment might mean serious hardship, especially to the poor (Dt. 24:10–13). So only the corrupted part is to be destroyed (v. 56). *Malignant leprosy* (vv. 51f.; 14:44); the AV word 'fretting' seems to be used here in the sense of 'gnaw', *i.e.* make holes, to describe an infection that is not superficial but penetrating. The Hebrew word occurs only in these passages and in Ezk. 28:24, where the reference to briars and thorns favours such a meaning. The LXX and Vulgate render by 'persistent'. Some have thought that the reference is to a form of mildew in the case of the garments, and to a form of dry rot in the case of the houses.

14:1–32 Cleansing and restoring the leper. The ritual for the cleansing of the leper is given in detail and is quite elaborate. In some respects it resembles the consecration of the priests (chs. 7–9) and the ritual for the Day of Atonement. It covers a period of seven days, with special rites on the first and eighth. **2–9** Cleansing is specially stressed and this involves shaving of the hair (*cf.* Nu. 8:7). *Hyssop* is used as at the Passover (14:4ff.; *cf.* Ex. 12:22), together with *cedarwood* and *scarlet stuff* which are also used in making the water of purification (Nu. 19). **7** The releasing of one of the birds *into the open field* suggests the sending away of the scapegoat (Lv. 16:21f.). But there may be no connection.

8 The ritual of the first day restores the leper to the camp but not to his home and the intimacies which were associated with it. Note that it was not sacrificial. The blood was not brought to the altar. The rite was one of purification. **10ff.** On the eighth day the cleansed man is to offer three lambs in sacrifice: a male lamb for a guilt-offering, a ewe for a sin-offering, a male lamb for a burnt-offering. In the case of the poor, birds may be substituted for lambs as sin- and burnt-offerings. But apparently, as indicated by v. 21, the guilt-offering must be a ram. The ritual of the oil (vv. 15–18, 26–29) is particularly detailed and impressive. It is to be placed on the right ear, thumb and toe of the leper, on which the blood of the guilt-offering has already been placed, and to be sprinkled with the finger of the priest seven times before the Lord. Then the rest of the handful is to be poured out on his head (*cf.* 8:23f.). This apparently represents the consecration of the restored leper to the service of his covenant God. It suggests an analogy between the admission (in this case, the re-admission) of an unclean person (a Gentile) into the congregation of Israel, God's holy people, and the consecration of an Israelite to the special and peculiarly holy function of a priestly mediator between Israel and their God. Since the leper had for a time been debarred from the community and service of the sanctuary, which involved payment of tithes and offering of sacrifices, a guilt-offering is required to atone for his failure in these respects.

The order of the offering of the sacrifices is guilt-, sin-, burnt-offering. The fact that the offering for these three sacrifices is three tenth parts of fine flour justifies the conclusion that a cereal-offering was to be offered with each of the three sacrifices, since one-tenth was the regular cereal-offering with a lamb (Nu. 29:4; Ex. 29:40).

Although the leper is constantly described as 'unclean' and not as a sinner, despite the fact that the 'stroke' of leprosy may, as in the case of Miriam, be the punishment for grievous sin, it seems proper to see in the fact that leprosy is dealt with so elaborately an indication that this particularly loathsome and intractable disease is to be regarded as a type of that indwelling sin in which all the afflictions and ills of mankind have their cause and origin. If death is the curse pronounced by God upon sin, and contact with death is defiling, then disease which undermines health and is a stepping-stone to death carries with it a certain defilement whether it be infectious in the medical sense or not. We cannot affirm with certainty that the mention of hyssop in Ps. 51 ('Purge me with hyssop, and I shall be clean') contains an allusion to the cleansing of the leper and justifies the inference that David is thinking of himself as a moral leper. But it seems not improbable.

14:33–57 Leprous houses in the land of Canaan. The leprosy of a house is dealt with separately because it concerns the future. 34 *When you come into the land of Canaan. Cf.* 19:23; 23:10; 25:2, which also refer to this future time. Israel was at the moment dwelling in tents; and the leprosy of stone houses was a matter which did not yet concern them. The words *and I put a leprous disease in a house* are decidedly arresting. They suggest, and have been taken to imply, a special supernatural plague visited upon a house because of the sin of its builder (like leprosy in an individual). But it is to be remembered that the Bible frequently ignores secondary causes and agencies. We note here the same regard for property as in the case of the garment. The destruction is to be restricted as much as possible. It is also to be noted that the ritual for the cleansing of the house is the same as that prescribed for the first stage in the cleansing of the leper, that which restored him to the congregation of Israel.

15:1–33 Uncleanness due to issues

Since this chapter deals with matters of sex, it stands in close relation with ch. 12 and must be interpreted on the same general principles. The conditions which are dealt with are both normal and abnormal. But in either case they are treated as defiling. In the case of the former, the uncleanness usually lasts only until sunset and is removed by washing with water. In the latter case, the uncleanness continues for seven days after normal health has been restored. Then the man or the woman shall bring to the priest an offering consisting of two birds, one of which shall be offered as a sin-offering, the other as a burnt-offering (vv. 14f., 29f.; *cf.* 5:7–10). In both cases it is said that the priest shall *make atonement* by means of the sacrifices. Whatever the nature of the uncleanness, every person who comes in contact with the unclean person or thing shall bathe, wash his clothes and be unclean until the evening.

The law of Moses refers elsewhere to a number of diseases besides those dealt with here (*cf.* 26:16, 25; Dt. 28:22, 27f., 35). It is perhaps significant that it does not refer to them here in dealing with the subject of uncleanness. Abnormalities and deformities are dealt with in 21:16ff.; Dt. 23:1. *Thus you shall keep the people of Israel separate* refers primarily to the uncleannesses mentioned in ch. 15, as is indicated by the summary which follows (vv. 32f.). But it is

applicable to all the defilements mentioned in chs. 11–15.

16:1–34 THE DAY OF ATONEMENT

The Day of Atonement (23:27f.; 25:9) is the most important of all the holy ordinances with which the book of Leviticus is concerned, for it was the day on which atonement was made for *all* the sins of *all* the congregation of Israel (see vv. 16f., 21f., 30, 33f.). In this respect it stands apart from all other private and public ordinances connected with the worship of Israel. It is also signalized by the fact that it is the only day in the year for which fasting is required: *you shall afflict yourselves* (vv. 29, 31; 23: 27, 32; Nu. 29:7). This phrase might also be rendered 'humble yourselves'. Arrogant self-sufficiency and self-will were characteristic of Israel from the beginning (*cf.* Dt. 8:2, 3, 16 where the same verb is used), and it was met with constant reproof and chastening. Fasting would be the outward expression of their sorrow and repentance. In this regard the Day of Atonement stands in marked contrast to the annual feasts which were times of rejoicing, especially the Feast of Tabernacles (23:40; *cf.* Dt. 12:7, 12; 16:11, 14).

In view of this, its position in the book may properly be regarded as significant. The fact that the full description of its ritual is given here instead of in Lv. 23 which describes all the feasts, or in Nu. 28, 29, which prescribe the special offerings for each of them, seems to be intended to emphasize both its importance and its uniqueness. It stands by itself among all the public ordinances prescribed for Israel. On the other hand, like many of the other ordinances, it is given a definite occasion or historical setting, the death of Nadab and Abihu for sacrilege (v. 1). In fact some scholars regard the words *after the death of the two sons of Aaron* as implying so close a connection between this chapter and ch. 10 that they are inclined to regard chs. 11–15 as an insertion. Were this the case, it is difficult to understand why this insertion should consist only of these chapters and not include chs. 17–22 especially since it is in them that the moral element predominates over the ceremonial.

The chapter has both a backward and a forward reference. The one concerns especially Aaron and the priests (*cf.* Nu. 4:17f.) and is to warn them against sacrilege and the frightful danger which attends it. The other is the application to the people. The grace of God in providing an all-sufficient atonement for sins of ignorance and frailty is set forth before the more heinous transgressions are described. The sins for which there is no forgiveness, which are to be punished by excision or death (see especially ch. 20), stand out in all their moral hideousness in the light of the seven times repeated 'all' of this chapter. The implication is clear that such sins as those for which there is no forgiveness (sins of presumption, AV of the 'high hand') prove the perpetrator to be no true Israelite at all, but a moral leper unworthy of the covenanted mercies of the God of Abraham and Moses. The tendency in rabbinical Judaism has been to make this atonement all-inclusive. But such an interpretation is clearly excluded by the fact that the entire generation of wrath perished for disobedience in the wilderness (cf. Heb. 10:28). Whatever the explanation, the position of this chapter is certainly a significant one.

16:1-10 Aaron's preparation

2 *Tell Aaron your brother*. Cf. Ex. 28:1ff. It seems clear that the choice of Aaron for this high office was primarily due to his relationship to Moses (Ex. 4:14) as was his choice to be Moses' 'prophet'. It was Moses' intercession which saved Aaron after the sin of the golden calf (Dt. 9:20). The Bible both recognizes (Gn. 21:13) and ignores human relationships (Ex. 32:27). Since Aaron and his sons have been mentioned already about 60 times in Leviticus, the words *Aaron your brother* may suggest the loving care with which Moses is to impress this law upon him, *lest he die*. But cf. Ex. 28:1-4. It is this fact which made the attitude of Aaron and Miriam described in Nu. 12:1f. such a personal grief to Moses as well as so serious a challenge to the unique position assigned him by God Himself. *The holy place* means the Holy of Holies as is indicated by the words *within the veil* (cf. vv. 3, 16, 17, 20, 27). Every one of the sacrifices described or ordered in chs. 1-15 is included in this prohibition. Most of the ritual of sacrifices was conducted in the court. **3-5** Only exceptionally was the blood of the sacrifices brought into the Holy Place. Now the one occasion on which it may be brought 'within the veil' and into the Holy of Holies is dealt with in careful detail. When he does this, Aaron is to wash himself and then put on linen garments (the symbol of purity) instead of the usual ornate apparel distinctive of the high priest. The sacrifices he is to offer are of two kinds: for himself and his sons, *a young bull for a sin offering and a ram for a burnt offering*; for the people, *two male goats for a sin offering, and one ram for a burnt-offering*.

6-10 give a brief and partial summary of the procedure as regards the sin-offerings. The bull and the goats are both presented before the Lord and the lot is cast over the two goats.

16:11-14 The sin-offering for the priests

These verses describe the ritual for Aaron's bull which is presented before the Lord. **11** *And shall make atonement for himself and for his house* apparently refers to the laying on of hands, either by himself alone as representing also his sons, or by his sons also. **12** He is to fill the entire censer (lit. 'the fullness of the censer') with coals from the altar of burnt-offering and to take two handfuls (lit. 'the fullness of his (two) hands') of incense. **13** There is to be a great cloud of incense sufficient to cover the

mercy seat *lest he die*. The blood is to be sprinkled with his finger upon the front of the mercy seat and before it, seven times.

16:15-19 The people's sin-offering

The ritual for the goat which is the sin-offering of the people is now described. Apparently the cloud of incense in the Holy of Holies suffices for both sin-offerings; and the blood is to be similarly manipulated. The reason for this is stated with great care. **16** Aaron is to *make atonement for the holy place, because of the uncleannesses of the children of Israel, and because of their transgressions, all their sins*. For their sins have defiled it. **20** Note that this cleansing is to include the entire tent of meeting and the altar of burnt-offering.

16:20-22 The scapegoat

20 *The live goat* has already been referred to in vv. 8-10. The AV rendering 'scapegoat' and the RV and RSV rendering *Azazel* in vv. 8 and 10 represent the principal interpretations of the meaning of this remarkable ritual. The former rendering is an ancient one, being supported by the LXX and the Vulgate. It is based on the assumption that the word ʿᵃzāʾzēl comes from a root ʿāzal meaning 'to remove' (such a reduplicated form would be rare, but not without analogy). The chief argument in its favour is that it is scriptural and appropriate. The thought of removal of guilt is closely related to that of atonement for sin. Ps. 103:12, 'As far as the east is from the west, so far does he remove our transgressions from us', perfectly expresses this idea. That this is the meaning is indicated by the emphasis which is placed on the words *sent away* or *let . . . go* (vv. 10, 21, 22), *wilderness* (vv. 10, 21, 22) and *solitary land* (v. 22; AV 'not inhabited'). The rendering 'Azazel' takes the word as a proper name. In its favour is the fact that 'for Azazel' (v. 10) seems to stand in contrast with 'for the Lord' (v. 9). But if it is the name of a well-known demon of the desert or a name of Satan, it is strange that it should occur only here in the entire Bible. And if the reference is to a demon whom Israel feared, who exerted a powerful influence upon them and needed to be appeased, it is hard to understand why emphasis should be placed on the remoteness of the abode of this menacing being, a remoteness which might increase as Israel journeyed to Palestine. Sin is not a remote but an ever-present factor in the life of man (Gn. 4:7). Furthermore the idea of atonement for sin as involving a ransom or sin-offering to Satan, or to an unknown demon of the desert (and still more the idea of the goat bearing to the demon the tidings that atonement for sin has been made), would involve the recognition of a hostile demonic power. This is expressly forbidden in 17:7. Certainly in a ritual which represented the holiest and most sacred rite of OT religion we should not expect to meet anything which was suggestive of demonism or polytheism. (See article 'Azazel' in *The International Standard Bible Encyclopaedia*.)

16:23–28 The offerings completed

After Aaron has performed those duties which require him to enter the Holy of Holies, he is to lay aside his linen garments, bathe, and then put on the regular garb of the high priest, which is so fully described elsewhere, and which is stated to be 'for glory and for beauty' (Ex. 28:2). Then he is to come forth from the Holy Place and complete the ritual in the outer court, the offering of his burnt-offering and that for the people, also to burn the fat of the sin-offering since it is only the manipulation of the blood which has thus far been described. This is to be done in the usual manner.

16:29–34 Some further instructions

29 This special day is to be a *statute . . . for ever*. **34** The rite is to be observed *once in the year* on the tenth day of the seventh month, and it is to be comprehensive, for the sanctuary and the priests who minister there and for the children of Israel, *because of all their sins*. In v. 29, for the first time in Leviticus, the stranger (*gēr*) is mentioned. (See on Dt. 1:16.) While he has no part in this national rite, he is to conform to its requirements (*cf*. Ex. 12:19, 48f.). The Decalogue and the book of the covenant both recognize and provide for the presence of these 'strangers' in Israel. In view of the privileges which they enjoy they must conform to many of Israel's laws and customs (*cf*. 17:8, 10, 12, 13, 15).

34 Note that we are told that 'he did as the Lord commanded Moses' (AV; RSV mistranslates the Hebrew here: *cf*. 24:23 where the construction is the same). This must mean, as stated above, that the national apostasy at Kadesh did not take place until after the first observance of the Day of Atonement. That it could not have been observed subsequent to the apostasy and during the years of wandering is indicated by three facts. First, exclusion from the land was the punishment for refusal to take possession of it. This penalty was paid in full by the generation which transgressed: it was not remitted. Secondly, circumcision was not practised during the years of wandering (Jos. 5:1–9), although it was the indispensable sign and seal of the covenant (Gn. 17:9–14). Thirdly, Am. 5:25f. indicates that Israel fell away into idolatry during this period (*cf*. Acts 7:42f.).

In view of the singular importance which attaches to this day—the later Jews have called it 'the Day'—it is remarkable that no express reference to its observance is to be found anywhere in the OT (Is. 58:3 is too general to appeal to). This is hard to account for, especially since mention of it would seem to be natural and appropriate in connection with the events described in 1 Ki. 8:2, 65f.; Ezr. 3:1–6; Ne. 8, all of which were important events which took place in the seventh month at about the time of the Day of Atonement. It is to be noted, however, that the OT mentions only four Passovers (those of Joshua, Hezekiah, Josiah, Ezra) in treating of a period of about 1,000 years; also that from the time of the renewal of the covenant by Joshua no mention is made of the covenant rite of circumcision, except by implication (*e.g.* the Philistines are described as uncircumcised), or in a figurative sense (Je. 6:10; 9:26). The argument from silence, the inference that failure to mention a rite means that it had not yet been introduced, proves too much. It would place the date of the institution of this rite after the time of Ezra and Nehemiah. Furthermore it is to be noted that the sacrifices of this day are the only ones which are directly connected with the ark. The blood of the sin-offerings for Aaron and the people was to be sprinkled on or toward the mercy seat. The Hebrew word for 'mercy seat' is *kappōreṯ* ('covering' or 'expiation'). It was pre-eminently the place of atonement. Hence the name, *yôm kippûr* (Day of Atonement). Yet Jeremiah definitely foretells the time when the ark will be forgotten (3:16); and we know that after the Babylonian captivity the ark was not brought back with the other sacred vessels. There was no ark in Zerubbabel's Temple nor in that of Herod. Consequently this connection with the ark points to an early date for the introduction of this rite.

It is particularly to be stressed that while, as we have seen, the OT is practically silent with regard to the post-Mosaic celebration of this all-important rite, the writer of the Epistle to the Hebrews represents it as that rite of the Mosaic covenant which most clearly sets forth the atoning work of Christ; both by way of resemblance and of contrast (Heb. 9, 10). The high priest alone could enter the Holy of Holies. He did this 'once a year' (9:7), and he offered sacrifices for himself and for the people, and then he came forth from the sanctuary. The Lord Jesus entered 'once' (9:12, 26; 10:12–14) into the heavenly sanctuary offering once for all His own blood, not for Himself, but only for the sins of others and, having purchased an eternal redemption by His blood, He will come again from the heavenly sanctuary to bless His saints whom He has redeemed. See also the notes on the significance of the sacrificial ritual at the end of the first section (pp. 147f.) and the Introduction (pp. 141f.).

Since the destruction of the Temple (by Nebuchadrezzar and again by Titus) and the loss of the ark made it quite impossible to carry out fully the ritual of sacrifice, which is the aspect particularly stressed both in this chapter in Leviticus and also in Hebrews, later Jews have been forced to regard 'afflicting themselves' (Lv. 16:29, 31), understood to mean repentance, restitution, good works, and suffering, as the only 'atonement' which God requires of the Jew for all his sins. Thus the words, 'without shedding of blood is no remission (Heb. 9:22, AV), which epitomize the meaning of the OT ritual of sacrifice—a ritual which, according to the law, finds its supreme illustration in the Day of Atonement and, according to the gospel, finds its fulfilment in the cross—become a dead letter to the modern Jew, as they do to the Unitarian, because the cross, of which the mercy seat of the ark is the type, is a stumbling-block and a mystery to him.

17:1–16 THE PLACE OF SACRIFICE AND THE SANCTITY OF BLOOD

It has been customary in critical circles for many years to treat chs. 17–26 as a distinct section and to call it 'the holiness code'. To do this destroys the close connection which clearly exists between chs. 16 and 17 and also between ch. 17 and the manual of sacrifice in chs. 1–7. Whatever may be said of chs. 18–26, ch. 17 belongs to what precedes. It may properly be regarded as supplementary, but a climactic supplement or conclusion to the first part of Leviticus.

Since the Day of Atonement exhibits in a superlative degree the significance of sacrifice in the life of the covenant people, and points out the unique sacredness of the blood in that on this one day the sacrificial blood is brought into the Holiest Place and sprinkled on the ark of the covenant itself, to obtain the remission of all the sins of all the people, it is appropriate that in this next chapter the two aspects of sacrifice which specially concern all the people should be particularly emphasized.

The introductory formula is specially impressive. Notice that it is all-inclusive as well as being very emphatic. **2** *This is the thing which the Lord has commanded* (*cf.* 8:5; 9:6). **3–7** *If any man of the house of Israel*. The universal application of the law now to be declared is specially emphasized (*cf.* vv. 8, 10, 13). *Kills*; the same word as occurs in 1:5, where it is used of the slaughtering of the animal which has been brought for sacrifice. The reference here is to the domestic animals which were regularly used for that purpose. They are to be brought to the door of the Tabernacle and offered as peace-offerings. This served both to gratify the desire of the people to eat flesh and also established the proprietary right of God, more particularly in those animals which were so often offered to Him in sacrifice. It had two further aims: to prevent eating blood (vv. 10ff.) and also to prevent the sacrificing of these animals *in the open field*, which is at once defined as offering them to 'he-goats' (RV) or *satyrs*, an act which was not only idolatry (19:4; 26:1, 30) but was accompanied by orgiastic rites (v. 7). *Cf.* Ex. 34:15f.; Lv. 20:5f. This indicates that such idolatrous practices were common among the Israelites at the time of the Exodus, having been learned by them in Egypt. The worship of Pan flourished, as we know, in ancient Greece and Rome. Consequently this law was not primarily a requirement that the Israelites sacrifice these animals to the Lord as peace-offerings instead of simply devouring them anywhere

they pleased, but rather that they offer them to the Lord instead of sacrificing them to the 'satyrs'. It is the substitution of an act of true worship for one of idolatry and licence. And it shows plainly how deeply the sojourn in Egypt had influenced the life of Israel. *This shall be a statute for ever*. In its negative aspect, the prohibition of eating with the blood and of idolatrous practices, this statute was irrevocable under the Mosaic dispensation. On its positive side it was later modified by Moses to accord with the changed conditions which would result from settlement in the land (Dt. 12:20–24), changes which affected the letter without changing the spirit of the law. The difference between Leviticus and Deuteronomy here shows clearly that the former preceded the latter and not *vice versa*.

8, 9 refer more particularly to a 'killing' which is intended to be an act of worship. This is indicated by the specific reference to burnt-offering in addition to sacrifice (*i.e.* of peace-offerings; see v. 5), since no part of the burnt-offering was used as food.

10 *I . . . will cut him off*. Usually the passive is used (see vv. 4, 9, 14 and 7:20, 21, 27). Here, as in 20:3, 5, 6, the stronger form is used. This has been understood to mean that the cutting off is to be an act of God. The sacredness of the blood is taught very early. Although in other respects unlimited, the permission given to Noah regarding the eating of flesh was qualified by the words, 'Only you shall not eat flesh with its life, that is, its blood' (Gn. 9:4). Here the fact is repeated three times that the life of the animal is in the blood (vv. 11, 14); and it is to be regarded as sacred because God has made it the means of expiation for sin by requiring that it be presented upon His altar. **13** Consequently, even in the case of animals not suited for sacrifice, the blood must be treated reverently. It must be poured out upon the ground and covered with dust (*cf.* on Dt. 12:16). **15, 16** make a further exception. If a man eats flesh with the blood ignorantly, not realizing the way in which the animal had died (this must be the meaning), he shall bathe himself and be unclean until the evening.

It is noteworthy that while for the modern Jews the ritual of sacrifice has lost all meaning, they still adhere strictly to the requirement concerning eating with the blood. Blood is still sacred for them as the symbol of life and the sacredness of life, but not for the reason so emphatically stated in the OT—its connection with atonement for sin. A strict Jew will eat only *kosher* meat, *i.e.* meat 'rightly' and 'properly' prepared.

18:1 – 20:27 SINS AGAINST THE MORAL LAW

18:1–30 Prohibited degrees and sensuality

1–5 The introduction is very impressive. The Lord's people are to keep His commandments.

Their standards are not to be determined by the practices of Egypt where they were in bondage or of Canaan which they are to possess. The statutes and ordinances of their God are to be their sole standard of conduct; and the reward of obedience is life (*cf*. Dt. 30:15–20). **2** The sanction is: *I am the Lord your God.* That the 'abominations' about to be described were practised in Egypt, and even among other cultured nations of antiquity, is a well-known fact. Modern marriage laws are largely based on the limitations stated in this chapter. But they have not seldom been made more strict than the law requires.

6–18 6 The general principle involved is stated: *None of you shall approach any one near of kin to him* (lit. 'the flesh of his flesh'). Consanguinity or affinity is referred to repeatedly (vv. 12, 13, 14, 15, 16, 17; *cf*. 20:19); and it is stressed by such expressions as *which is the nakedness of your mother, it is your father's nakedness, for their nakedness is your own nakedness.* **18** That this phrase 'uncover the nakedness of' refers to actual marriage is made especially clear by the words *while her sister is yet alive.* Illicit intercourse would come under the general heading of adultery or harlotry and be condemned as such (Dt. 22:13–30). On the other hand the use of such an expression, instead of the usual phrase 'to take a wife', is probably intended to stress the fact that such unions as are condemned here and in ch. 20 cannot be true marriage, and that they are due to passion rather than natural and holy affection. No other reason is given for these prohibitions, however, except the fact of kinship. This may imply that the intimacies which result from near kinship or affinity are such as to render marriage unnatural or improper. But it also seems to be well established as a fact of experience that marriages between near relations are likely either to be barren or to result in unhealthy offspring. The prohibition which has occasioned the most discussion and controversy is marriage with the deceased wife's sister, and it is only comparatively recently that it has been made legal in England. Yet the meaning of the law seems to be clear. The words *as a rival*, AV 'to vex her', 'to be a secondary wife' (all three are possible renderings), taken in connection with the words *while . . . yet alive*, indicate that such a marriage is not barred on grounds of affinity; it is lawful, but only after the death of the wife. This is intended to prevent a man from divorcing his wife in order to marry her sister, a temptation which might easily result from the intimacies of family life. It is to be noted that only in one case is a moral judgment passed on these practices which are prohibited (v. 17).

19 apparently refers to the contracting and consummating of marriage. *Cf*. 20:18 and 15:24. **20–23** deal with particularly heinous sins. Adultery violates the sanctity of the home. It involves the breaking of two of the Ten Commandments (Ex. 20:14, 17). It undermines the foundations of human society. *You shall not give any of your children to devote them by fire to Molech*; better 'pass through the fire', as AV. Plainly this prohibition refers to the abhorrent practice of infant sacrifice and that this awful sin is the sin of the parent (*cf*. 20:2–5). For an Israelite to do this is to *profane* the name of his God. Other monstrous and unnatural sins are particularly denounced. They are *abomination* and *perversion*. Yet most, if not all, of them were widely practised among the cultured peoples of antiquity.

24–30 form a concluding summary. These things are heathen practices which Israel is particularly to avoid. The promise to dispossess the Canaanites is coupled with the solemn warning to Israel of similar treatment in case of similar conduct. The sequence of tenses is difficult. AV 'which I cast out' translates a participle and is better rendered *which I am casting* (or, 'going to cast') *out*. It refers to the (imminent) future. AV and RV render most of the verbs in vv. 25, 27 in the present tense. But the sequence of tenses would favour making them refer to the past as RSV, especially in view of their rendering of the last verb in v. 28, 'as it spued out (RV 'vomited out', as RSV) the nations (RV 'nation', as RSV) that were before you'. It is to be noted, therefore, that this verb is ambiguous. If accented on the penult, it is the perfect tense (AV, RV, RSV, LXX, Vulg., Syr.). If accented on the ultima (the Massoretes), it is a participle, and may, like the participle in v. 24, refer to the future. The former rendering seems definitely preferable. Unless the use of the past tense is regarded as proleptic, which is unlikely, we must then face the fact that past and premonitory judgments are here referred to.

We have very little information on this subject. The fact that ten nations occupied the land in the days of Abraham (Gn. 15:19ff.) may mean that it had been a bone of contention for centuries; and that these nations lived peaceably together seems highly improbable. Situated at the bridgehead between Asia and Africa, the land was singularly exposed to the ravages of invading armies. The words 'the iniquity of the Amorites is not yet complete' (Gn. 15:16) suggest that there may have been severe visitations of judgment in the past. Famine, pestilence, the sword, and evil beasts (Lv. 26; *cf*. Ezk. 14:21) may have already taken a heavy toll. There may be more truth in the evil report of the spies than we might be inclined to suppose: 'a land that devours its inhabitants' (Nu. 13:32). 'Devour' and 'vomit out' suggest disorders that would decimate the inhabitants of the land and drive many of them into exile. But however severe these former judgments may have been, and they must have been sufficiently severe and also recent to be referred to here, they are only a foretaste, so to speak, of the judgment which is about to fall on the Canaanites, and which surely will be visited on Israel also if she follows their example. Those who regard the command to exterminate the Canaanites as 'cruel' should consider carefully the reason which is given for it. The impressive sanction *I am the Lord* (*your God*) appears in vv. 2, 4, 5, 21, 30.

19:1–37 A collection of sundry laws

These laws are so various that it is difficult to classify them. **2** They are introduced by the solemn exhortation *You shall be holy*; *for I the Lord your God am holy*, and fifteen times the words *I am the Lord* (*your God*) are repeated in its thirty-seven verses. They are both ceremonial and ethical, and the latter belong to both of the tables of the Decalogue. Thus **3, 4**, are covered by the fifth, fourth, and second commandments of the Decalogue. Reverence (AV 'fear') for parents, keeping of the sabbath, shunning of idolatry are placed first as particularly important. That 'fear' is sometimes used in the sense of 'revere' or 'reverence' is made clear by v. 30 where 'fear my sanctuary' appears as *reverence* in AV and RV. *Cf.* Dt. 6 where 'love the Lord' (v. 5) is preceded (v. 2) and followed (v. 13) by 'fear the Lord', and see on Dt. 9:19. 'Love' to God is not demanded in Leviticus and love to man only in 19:18, 34. But it is to be remembered that it is referred to in the Decalogue (Ex. 20:6) and quite frequently in Deuteronomy.

5–8 concerns the eating of the flesh of peace-offerings (*cf.* 7:15–18). **9, 10** The law regarding gleanings comes under the general summary of the second table of the Decalogue, which enjoins love of one's neighbour (*cf.* 23:22; Dt. 24:19–22). **11, 12** rest upon the eighth and third commandments. **13, 14** are closely related to the eighth commandment and the principle of humanity underlying it. **15, 16** are an exposition of the ninth commandment. **17, 18** stand in close relation to the tenth commandment and conclude with those words which represent the summary of the second table, *you shall love your neighbour as yourself.* 'Neighbour' seems here to refer to the fellow-Israelite. Note the words *sons of your own people* which immediately precede. Its use in Ex. 3:22 of the Egyptians does not prove a wider range for its ordinary use, since the conditions in Egypt were abnormal and Israel in Canaan was to be a separated people. But the broader meaning is indicated, or the meaning is broadened, by v. 34, where the law of love is extended to include the non-Israelite *stranger* (*gēr*). This fact is beautifully illustrated by Jesus' choice of the Samaritan to determine the meaning and scope of the word 'neighbour' (Lk. 10:29ff.). See Dt. 10:18 and *cf.* note on Lv. 25:35–55. In the case of vv. 19–37 which begin and conclude with an exhortation to obedience, it almost seems as if an element of contrast had been intentionally introduced to emphasize the fact that every department and phase of life is covered by the ordinances of God. **19** Thus the law of purity is to apply to the breeding of cattle, the sowing of seed and the texture of garments, and also to the planting of fruit-trees (vv. 23–25). *Cf.* Dt. 22:9–11. **20–22** But in between them is

placed the law governing the guilt with a bond-woman. As regards the first of these prohibitions, since the word 'cattle' is broader than 'herd' and 'flock' and includes both clean and unclean animals, this law must be regarded as prohibiting the breeding of mules. Consequently, mules in the OT, first mentioned in David's time, are properly to be regarded as a foreign importation (*cf.* 1 Ki. 10:25). **26–28** may all be classed as heathen practices to be condemned as such. The same is true of v. 31. **29** Similarly the sin of prostitution is probably mentioned here for the same reason, as being a heathen practice. **30** On the other hand, this verse, enjoining reverence for the sabbath and the sanctuary, while referring back to v. 3 would seem to connect naturally with v. 32. **33, 34** The law of the stranger forms the counterpart of vv. 17, 18, expanding the scope of the law already given. **35, 36** further apply the eighth commandment; and the chapter concludes with the oft-repeated reminder *I am the Lord your God, who brought you out of the land of Egypt* (*cf.* 11:45; 22:33; Dt. 5:15, *etc.*).

20:1–27 Sundry laws regarding very heinous offences

2 AV 'again' (RV 'moreover') is simply 'and' in Hebrew and joins this chapter closely with the preceding. Molech-worship has already been briefly denounced (18:21). But here, as in the rest of the chapter, severe penalties are pronounced on those who are guilty of some of the offences already described. Molech was the god of the Ammonites (1 Ki. 11:7). The name contains the same consonants as the word 'king' (Heb. *meleḵ*) apparently combined with the vowels of the word meaning 'shame' (*bōšeṯ*), to change the word from an honourable title to one of dishonour. It is always written with the article 'the Molech', as if an appelative. This form of idolatry was particularly repulsive because it involved human sacrifice, the offering of children or infants, to the idol. The exact nature of this horrible rite is not certainly known. It has been interpreted as an act of purgation which did not involve death; as a sacrifice which resembled animal sacrifices in this respect, that the victim was first slain and its body then burned as an offering to the idol (Ezk. 16:20f. hardly justifies this interpretation); as a sacrifice in which the victims were actually burned alive. That human sacrifice is meant seems to be clearly taught in Ps. 106:38; Je. 7:31; 19:4f.; Ezk. 23:37–39; Mi. 6:7. And it is quite possible that the Phoenician practice of placing living infants in the arms of the idol to perish in the flames burning within it is what is meant, which would account for the severity with which it is denounced. Dt. 12:31 implies that this awful practice was not confined to the worship of a single god, but was a prominent feature of Canaanite worship in general. This grievous sin is to be punished by stoning. **3** Note the words *defiling my sanctuary and profaning my holy*

159

name which indicate that this act was not merely horrible in itself but a gratuitous and intentional defiance of the exclusive right of Yahweh, as the covenant God of Israel, to the worship of His people, and one which the Lord would not permit to go unpunished. **5** If the people ignore or condone it, He will not do so, but will cut off the man and those who participate with him.

6 The means by which Israel's neighbours sought to ascertain and if possible control the future are next condemned (*cf.* 19:31) and the penalty of excision is pronounced. *Cf.* v. 27 which orders the death of the medium, and see Ex. 22:18. The words *playing the harlot* apparently connect this sin closely with that of vv. 2–5. In Dt. 18:9–14 both are included among the means of ascertaining the future.

7, 8 contain a solemn exhortation to holiness (*cf.* 18:1–5; 19:1, 2) and to the keeping of the commandments of God, which has both a backward and a forward reference. That **9–21** deal with some of the most heinous of the sins already mentioned in chs. 18, 19 is indicated by comparing v. 9 with 19:3. Cursing of father or mother is a grievous violation of the fifth commandment. Adultery, incest, unnatural vice, bestiality are to be most severely punished. The fact that the phrase *uncover the nakedness*, which occurs frequently in ch. 18, also appears seven times in this chapter and nowhere else in the Pentateuch, indicates the close connection between these two passages. The penalties are variously described: *shall be put to death* (vv. 10, 12, 13, 15), *stone him with stones* (vv. 2, 27; *cf.* 24:14ff.), *burned with fire* (v. 14; *cf.* 21:9), *cut off* (vv. 5, 17, 18), *bear iniquity* (vv. 17, 19), *bear their sin, they shall die childless* (v. 20), *they shall be childless* (v. 21). Note also the words used to describe these crimes: *committed incest* (v. 12), *committed an abomination* (v. 13), *wickedness* (v. 14), *impurity* (v. 21).

22–26 remind the Israelites that the enormities just described are those of the people whose land they are to possess. It has 'vomited out' (*cf.* 18:25) its inhabitants for their abominations, and Israel will suffer the same fate if she practises them (*cf.* 18:28). Yet the land is their inheritance and it is a goodly land (Ex. 3:8, 17). The Lord has *separated* them. Note the fourfold use of this word in RV vv. 24–26. This section indicates quite clearly that a principal aim of the dietary laws of ch. 11 was to make and promote a definite separation between Israel and the Canaanites. Since eating and drinking were an important part of the daily life of the people, and since vv. 22–26 serve as a kind of conclusion to this great body of laws, ceremonial and moral, which the people are to observe, a reference back to ch. 11 with which it begins is entirely appropriate. *That you should be mine.* Here the whole aim of the law is briefly summarized. The Lord's people must keep His law if they are to be truly His.

27 is simply the further application of v. 6. The mediums who lead the people astray are to be punished by stoning (*cf.* v. 2; 24:14). By returning again to this subject, the heinousness of this sin (*cf.* Dt. 18:9–14) is particularly stressed. It is a sin of idolatry, and Israel must shun idolatry in every form.

21:1 – 22:33 INSTRUCTIONS FOR THE PRIESTS

21:1-9 The priests must be holy

If the people are to separate themselves from everything evil, how much more so the priests! They are not to defile themselves (21:1, 3, 4), nor to profane the name of their God (v. 6); they are to be holy to Him (v. 6, 7) and must be treated as such (v. 8). The reasons given are their high rank—a priest *is a husband among his people* (v. 4)—and *they offer the offerings by fire to the Lord*, the *bread of their God* (v. 6), a statement which makes it clear that the offering of sacrifice was their chief function. *The bread* (food) *of their God* is a phrase used frequently in this chapter (vv. 6, 8, 17, 21, 22; *cf.* 22:25, also 3:11, 16).

The particular matter first dealt with is defilement by contact with the dead. This they must avoid, except in the case of their next of kin. Death being the penalty of sin, contact with it was defiling. The failure to mention the wife when mother, father, son, daughter, and sister are specified must mean that the wife's position is unique. She is not *his nearest of kin* (v. 2) but 'one flesh' with him (Gn. 2:24); to mention her would be superfluous. The command to abstain from pagan practices (*cf.* Lv. 19:27f.; Dt. 14:1) applies to priest and people alike. A priest must obviously be exemplary in all his conduct. He will of course marry. But he must marry a virtuous woman and one who has not been divorced. Again the reason is repeated: he ministers in holy things (vv. 7, 8). For the daughter of a priest to become a harlot is especially heinous and to be most severely punished.

21:10-15 Special rules for the high priest

In view of the unique holiness of the high priest, the rules against defilement are more rigid than in the case of the ordinary priest. This is because the consecration of his God is upon him. The holy oil has been poured on his head and he wears the holy garments. He may not exhibit the usual tokens of grief and may not defile himself with any dead body, the exceptions made for the ordinary priest being definitely withdrawn. **12** The direction that he is not to leave the sanctuary probably means not to leave it in order to do honour to the dead, not that he was always to stay in the courts of the Tabernacle. **13** A further restriction is that he must marry a virgin of his own people. His wife must be a daughter of Israel. **15** *That he may not profane his children, i.e.* render them and himself unfit for holy office and for sharing in holy things, by an unworthy marriage such as that described in v. 14a.

21:16–24 The effect of physical deformity

Just as the animals offered in sacrifice must be without blemish, so must the priests be who offer them. But those who are debarred from serving at the altar are to be permitted to eat of the holy things which are the priest's portion. Mention is made of abnormalities both of deficiency and of excess, *e.g.* six fingers instead of five. Castration came under this head, and eunuchs were barred from the congregation (Dt. 23:1; *cf.* Is. 56:3ff.).

22:1–16 Defilement disqualifies the priest from touching holy things

While the priests are set apart to be holy ministers of the sanctuary, it is to be observed that they are liable to the same uncleannesses as are the laity. In addition to such abnormalities as have been mentioned above, a priest may become a leper, he may have an issue, or he may have come in contact with that which is unclean. This uncleanness makes him a source of pollution as long as it lasts and he must not touch any consecrated or holy thing lest he defile it. The principles laid down here have already been stated elsewhere. *Cf.* Heb. 5:2; 7:28. **10, 11** A distinction is drawn between the family of the priest and his slaves on the one hand and a sojourner or hireling. While the latter belong to the household of the priest, this does not entitle them to eat of the holy things. But a childless widow who returns to her father's house becomes once more a member of his family. A man who eats of the holy thing without being aware that he is doing so must replace it and as in the case of the guilt-offering he is to add one-fifth to it.

22:17–33 Rules for the offering of sacrifices

18, 19 They must be *without blemish*, a law which concerns both priests and people even including the strangers. See on Ex. 12:5. This is essential *to be accepted* (*cf.* on 1:3). **23** The only exception is the free-will offering. **24** refers to the gelding of animals. RV interprets this verse to mean that gelding was absolutely prohibited: 'Neither shall ye do this in your land.' This was the view of Josephus (*Ant.* iv. 8.40). AV and RSV understand it to apply only to animals intended for sacrifice (*cf.* RV mg.). **27** The requirement that the animal be *seven days with its mother* apparently means that not until then was it to be regarded as having an independent existence (*cf.* the law regarding circumcision, Gn. 17:12). **28** The law forbidding the slaying of the mother and her young on the same day suggests the thrice-repeated prohibition of the seething of a kid in its mother's milk (Ex. 23:19; 34:26; Dt. 14:21). Apparently both were designed to impress upon the Israelite the fact that the strong tie which binds the members of the human family together has its counterpart in the affection which the lower animals show toward their young, protecting them even at the cost of life,

and so to prohibit wanton cruelty. Such acts might be required by, and pleasing to, a Chemosh or Molech, but not to the God of Israel. See also note on Dt. 14:21. **29, 30** stipulate that a sacrifice of thanksgiving must be eaten the same day. See 7:15. All of these commandments have the sanction, *I am the Lord.* To break them is to *profane* His holy name. By their very diversity they make it clear that the law of the Lord is to govern the life of Israel, priest and people, in all its aspects and in every detail.

23:1–44 THE HOLY CONVOCATIONS

1, 2 In this chapter we are given a list of those meetings (Heb. *mô'ēd*; the same word is used as in the phrase 'tent of meeting'), or 'appointed feasts' which were to be proclaimed as *holy convocations*. This word *mô'ēd* is rendered '*feast*' in AV, as is also another word, *hag*. RV renders the former by 'set feast' with margin 'appointed season', the other by 'feast', with a view to distinguishing them. The emphasis in the case of the former word is apparently on the time. Hence a literal rendering of v. 4 would be: 'These are the meetings (appointed seasons) of the Lord, even holy convocations, which you shall proclaim in their appointed seasons.' The joyousness of most of these occasions is indicated by the fact that the word *feasts* (*hag*) is also used of them. They are called *convocations* because the people were called together by the blowing of the silver trumpets (Nu. 10:1–10).

23:3 The sabbath

God's resting on the seventh day is referred to in Gn. 2:3 and there are various indications of the keeping of a seven-day week (Gn. 29:27) and of the sacredness of the number seven (*e.g.* Nu. 23:1). But it is in connection with the giving of the manna that the sacredness of this day as a day of rest for Israel is first made clear (Ex. 16:5, 22–30). The giving of a double portion on the sixth day freed Israel from all necessity to work on that day; and God's resting on the seventh day from the providing of the manna was a reminder of His resting on that day from the work of creation. The same words, though not the same phrase, are used to describe it here as in Ex. 16: It is a *sabbath of solemn rest* (*šabbāt šabbātôn*). Here, as in Ex. 20:9 and Dt. 5:13, the command to work on the six days is coupled with the command to rest on the seventh. A man who works on weekdays is entitled to the rest of the Lord's day. The resting on this day is much more complete than in the case of the other set feasts which prohibit only *laborious work* (see vv. 7, 8, 21, 25, 35, 36), which apparently prohibits only the carrying on of one's ordinary business or the performance of manual labour, but not the preparation of food. Consequently, while the sabbath is a holy convocation, it differs from the other set feasts in this most important respect. It also differs in the fact that it is observed weekly while they are annual. In this we have also a definite indication that the regular, frequently occurring, weekly sabbath was intended to be a holier day than any of the set feasts. Yet in the history of the church there has been a strong tendency, as there is today, to stress the importance of special occasions and to minimize that of the Lord's day, the first day of the week which is the only holy day expressly sanctioned in the NT. See on Dt. 5:12ff.

23:4-8 The Passover and the Feast of Unleavened Bread

Since the sabbath differs from all other set feasts in several important respects it is separated from them by v. 4 which serves the place of a heading to introduce the annual feasts. See Ex. 23:14-17; Dt. 16. 5 First among the annual feasts is the Passover. No description is given since it has been fully described already in the account of its institution. See Ex. 12 and notes there. 6-8 The same is true of the Feast of Unleavened Bread which is so closely connected with it. Nu. 28:16-25 goes into much more detail with regard to the ritual for this feast.

23:9-14 The offering of firstfruits

This is the third of four laws (cf. 14:34; 19:23; 25:2) which apply to the future occupancy of the land. 10 The sheaf ('ōmer) of the first fruits (cf. Dt. 24:19; Ru. 2:7, 15) is to be presented as a 'wave-offering' (9:21; 14:12, 24). Since the same word is used of a dry measure (Ex. 16:16ff.), defined as the tenth part of an ephah (Ex. 16:36), the view is held that the sheaf must contain enough grain (barley, since barley ripens two or three weeks before wheat) to produce an omer of fine flour for a cereal-offering. 11 In the phrase the morrow after the sabbath, 'sabbath' has two possible meanings: it may refer to the regular weekly sabbath, which has just been mentioned, or to the Passover as the day of holy convocation, which was followed by the week of Unleavened Bread. The Pharisees took the one view, the Sadducees the other. 12 This offering of the sheaf was to be accompanied by a burnt-offering, with cereal- and drink-offerings. On this occasion the size of the cereal-offering is double the usual.

Here the drink-offering is mentioned for the first time in Leviticus. It has already been referred to in Ex. 29:38-42 in the law regarding the continual burnt-offering. Why there is no reference to it in Lv. 1-7 which deals particularly with the sacrifices is not clear. The fact that it is mentioned so frequently in connection with the offerings for the set feasts might suggest that it was not, or need not be, offered on ordinary occasions or in the case of private offerings. But Nu. 6:17 and 15:1-12 indicate that such an inference is unwarranted. It was apparently never an independent offering under the law, but accompanied the cereal-offering. This may be the reason why it is not mentioned in chs. 1-7. A further reason may be that it was not to be

offered until Israel entered the land (23:10). But this reason did not apply to the continual burnt-offering, which is not mentioned in Leviticus but has already been described in Ex. 29:38-42.

The offering of the firstfruits symbolized the consecration of the entire harvest to God: and not until it was offered were the people permitted to partake of it (v. 14). This law has a definitely typical significance and is referred to in the NT. It is used of the Gentile Christians (Rom. 8:23), of the ancestors of the Jews (Rom. 11:16), of individual Christians (Rom. 16:5) and of Christ as the firstfruits from the grave (1 Cor. 15:20, 23). See also 1 Cor. 16:15; Jas. 1:18; Rev. 14:4.

23:15-22 The Feast of Weeks

The fact that this feast is not introduced by the words 'The Lord said to Moses' has led to the inference that Pentecost (šābu'ōṯ) is a continuation or complement of the Passover. In the Talmud it is called 'aṣārtâ (cf. 23:36 where this word is used of the eighth day of the Feast of Tabernacles and rendered 'a holy convocation'). Seven weeks are to be counted from the sabbath (see above) on which the wave-offering of the firstfruits was made. 17 Then a new cereal-offering in the form of two wave loaves is to be offered. They are to be of fine flour, baked with leaven and are described as the first fruits to the Lord. Since the daily bread of the Israelites was leavened, this naturally implies the consecration of the daily food of the people to God. The offerings consist of burnt-, sin- and peace-offerings. Since this marked the end of the harvest of wheat, it is appropriate that the law regarding gleaning should be repeated here (see 19:9). See on Dt. 16:9-12.

23:23-44 The feasts of the seventh month

In view of the sacredness of the number seven, it is natural that the seventh month should be made distinctive. It has three special occasions: the Feast of Trumpets, the Day of Atonement, the Feast of Tabernacles.

23:24, 25 The Feast of Trumpets. This is briefly described. The blowing of trumpets on the first day of the month directed special attention to this important season of the year, the completion of the agricultural season. It was to be marked by two of the great events of the year. It is described as a day of solemn rest, a memorial of blowing of trumpets, and as a holy convocation. According to Jewish tradition the trumpet used on this occasion was not the silver trumpet of Nu. 10:2-10, but the šōp̄ār, the ram's horn (yōbēl) which was used on specially solemn occasions, notably to proclaim the year of jubilee (cf. also Jos. 6.). No servile work is to be done; and sacrifice is to be offered. This remembrance-blowing may be understood in two senses: God reminding the people of their duty to prepare themselves for the solemnities which this month has in store for them: and the people reminding God of His covenant and of His goodness to their fathers and to them. The word 'trumpet' does not occur in Hebrew. The word *t^erû'â* may denote either 'shouting' of people, or trumpet-'blast'. Perhaps both were included. This day, the first of Tishri, is called by the Jews *rōš haššānâ*, the beginning of the year. It is the beginning of the civil year, new year's day.

23:26–32 The Day of Atonement. This festival, which has been so fully described in ch. 16 as regards the duties of Aaron, the sacrifices to be performed and the way in which they are to be performed, is described here entirely from the standpoint of the duties of the people. It is to be *a sabbath of solemn rest* (v. 32; Heb. *šabbāṭ šabbāṭôn*). No work of any kind is to be done and fasting is to be observed; they are to afflict their souls. Disobedience will be most severely punished. *Cf.* Nu. 29:7–11, which deals especially with the offerings.

23:33–44 The Feast of Tabernacles. This resembles the Passover and the Feast of Unleavened Bread in several important respects. Both are primarily historical feasts, the one recalling the Exodus, the deliverance from Egypt and the circumstances of their flight, the other recalling the long sojourn in the wilderness. Both are of considerable length, extending over eight days. Both are closely connected with the daily life and happiness of the people, the one standing at the beginning, the other at the close of the agricultural year. A marked difference is that in the latter feast there is no prohibition of the use of leaven. Nu. 29:12–38 describes this feast in greater detail, listing the special offerings for each day. The total is remarkable. The burnt-offering consists of bulls, rams and lambs. The number of rams (two) and of lambs (fourteen) remains the same for each of the seven days, while the number of bulls begins with thirteen and is reduced gradually to seven, making a total of seventy bulls, or an average of ten a day. On the eighth day the offering is one bull, one ram and seven lambs. On each of the eight days there is a sin-offering consisting of one goat. It is carefully pointed out that each separate burnt-offering is to have its cereal-offering and its drink-offering. It is rather remarkable that the number of the bulls is decreased from day to day instead of increased.

The set feasts which have just been described are summed up in words very similar to v. 4. Then a further law is given with regard to the Feast of Tabernacles. The people are to live in booths for seven days that their generations may know that the Lord *made the people of Israel dwell in booths* (v. 43) when He brought them out of the land of Egypt. And the people are to *rejoice before the Lord* (v. 40). Thus the fasting of the Day of Atonement as a sign of sorrow for sins is speedily followed by the joy of this festival. It is remarkable that it is called *the feast of booths* (v. 34; AV 'tabernacles', Heb. *sukkôṭ; cf.* vv. 42, 43), since elsewhere in the Pentateuch, except for Gn. 33:17, the word

'booth' nowhere occurs, the Israelites being said to have dwelt in tents. The thought which is stressed is of course the frail and temporary character of the dwellings of the people during the wilderness sojourn. Thus Jerusalem is likened by Isaiah to a cottage (booth) in a vineyard (Is. 1:8), so frail and poverty-stricken has the abode of the daughter of Zion become. It should hardly be necessary to point out that the word 'tabernacles' has nothing at all in common with the word 'Tabernacle' as used of the sanctuary of the Lord. The words are entirely distinct. *Cf.* the references to this feast in 2 Ch. 8:13; Ezr. 3:4; Ne. 8:13–18; Zc. 14:16–19.

While these feasts were seasonal and suited to an agricultural people, the emphasis placed on historical events is clearly for the purpose of keeping alive in the minds of the people the great deliverance from Egypt in its most important aspects.

24:1–23 THE HOLY OIL, THE BREAD OF THE PRESENCE, THE SIN OF BLASPHEMY

24:1–4 The oil for the lampstand

Olive oil was used for illumination, for anointing, and in cooking as an article of food. All three were assigned a function in the service of the Tabernacle. Here only the first is referred to. The oil for the lamps of the golden lampstand was to be pure, beaten oil (Ex. 27:20). The oil for anointing was spiced (Ex. 25:6; 35:8). Oil was one of the free-will offerings of the people at the time of the construction of the Tabernacle and apparently was to continue to be so. The tending of the lamps is here assigned to Aaron, but in Ex. 27:21 his sons are included with him as qualified to perform this important duty. 3 *From evening to morning . . . continually* indicates that the lights burned throughout the night. 1 Sa. 3:3 would seem to mean that the lamps were given only sufficient oil to last until the morning. *Cf.* the distinction made in Ex. 30:7f. between trimming (lit. 'making good') the lamps in the morning and lighting (lit. 'causing them to ascend') in the evening. If this is the correct view, we may assume that the lamps were lighted in the evening with fire from the altar of burnt sacrifice. According to others, continually means that the lamps burned both day and night.

24:5–9 The bread of the Presence

In Ex. 25:23–30 the description of the table of the bread of the Presence is given. But the bread itself is simply mentioned. Here the details of the service are described. Each loaf is to consist of two-tenths of an ephah (about 6 quarts), probably prepared with oil like the cereal-offering, though this is not stated. 6 They are to be placed *in two rows*, or 'arrangements' (hence the Hebrew expression 'bread of arrangement' for the bread of the Presence in Chronicles (*e.g.* 2 Ch. 2:4) and Nehemiah (Ne. 10:33)), which probably means in two piles of six cakes each. Beside (probably better than AV 'upon') each pile, frankincense was placed, either in a bowl or a spoon. As in the case of the cereal-offering, it was not baked with the cakes; but according to later tradition it was burned on the altar of burnt sacrifice, together with the offerings of oil and wine, at the end of the seven days when the bread was taken from *before the Lord* and eaten by the priests. *Cf.* Ex. 25:30; 35:13; 39:36. A possible reason for the placing of these two laws in between chs. 23 and 25, which seem to belong together, may be to direct attention to the important fact that permanent and un-varying rituals such as these are entirely independent of, and not affected by, the annual feasts and special days which have just been described.

This rite may suggest the lavish offerings of food which the Egyptians and Babylonians were accustomed to make to their gods. In Erech, *e.g.*, 243 loaves were baked daily to supply the various temples of the city. The god Anu received thirty of them; and they were served in two morning and two evening meals. The object was to feed the god as human beings were fed. The fact that they were actually used to feed the priests who offered them was a hidden mystery, as is made strikingly evident by the apocryphal story of Bel and the Dragon. The bread of the Presence in Israel was quite different. The loaves represented the twelve tribes of Israel. After seven days the twelve were replaced by others and were then eaten by the priests and their families. This was required and it served to show that the rite was a symbolic one. Like the jar of manna (Ex. 16:33) which was to be kept as a perpetual memorial, the bread of the Presence was a daily confession by Israel and reminder to Israel that all her temporal blessings came from God. The idea of feeding the deity was an utterly pagan idea which was contrary to the teachings of both the Law and the Prophets, according to which it was Israel's God who supplied all the needs of His people. *Cf.*, *e.g.*, Ex. 16–17; Nu. 11; Ho. 2:8; Ps. 50:9–14, which has its echo in Paul's address on Mars Hill (Acts 17:25).

24:10–23 The sin of blasphemy and crimes of violence

The brief historical episode recorded in vv. 10–16 may have occurred between the revelations which precede and follow it. *Cf.* Dt. 4:41–49 and Nu. 15:32–36 for similar examples. The half-Israelite referred to probably belonged to the 'mixed multitude' of Ex. 12:38. **10** *Went out* (or 'came out') *among the people of Israel* hardly suggests that he was not living in the camp, but rather that he went abroad in the camp, engaged in a brawl with an Israelite, and became profane in his abuse of his opponent. When he is brought to trial, his mother's name and connections are briefly mentioned, probably because he owed

his presence in the camp entirely to her. His father may have been dead; at any rate his name is not given. It is the principle, not the person, that concerns us. This was an obvious and flagrant breach of the third commandment. But that commandment did not assess the penalty, except that the guilty one would not be held 'guiltless' by God. **12** The problem was further complicated by the irregular status of the culprit. Hence he was put *in custody, till the will of the Lord should be declared to them.*

22 The answer (*cf.* Nu. 7:89) deals especially with the actual situation; but it also establishes the principle that no distinction is to be made between Israelite and non-Israelite in such matters. It is to be noted that blasphemy is here grouped with crimes of a violent nature such as murder, unlawful wounding, *etc.* This may indicate simply the enormity of this sin of the lips. It may also suggest that the strife of which the act of blasphemy formed the most serious part was a very violent one and threatened the life or limb of his opponent (*cf.* Ex. 21:22; Dt. 25:11). At least it is clear that these laws, which have already been given in Exodus (see 21:12, 23–36), are repeated here primarily for the purpose of making the law regarding blasphemy and other serious offences apply to the sojourner and stranger just as much as to the native-born Israelite.

With regard to this *lex talionis*, three things are to be noted. First, it was intended to be a law of exact justice, not of revenge. Secondly, it was not private vengeance, but public justice. Thirdly, by excluding murder from the crimes for which ransom is permissible (Nu. 35:31f.) it makes it probable that compensation for injuries was often or usually allowed to take the form of a fine. The claim that 'there is in Jewish history no instance of the law of retaliation ever having been carried out literally—eye for an eye, tooth for a tooth' may or may not be justified, although such mutilating of the body was contrary to the spirit of the Mosaic law. Yet for centuries in Christian lands, torture and mutilation was the customary punishment for crime, and often, contrary to both the spirit and the letter of the Mosaic law, it was utterly out of proportion to the offence. This incident serves to remind us of the grievousness of the sin of profanity, which is one of the great evils of today.

25:1–55 THE SABBATICAL YEAR AND THE YEAR OF JUBILEE

25:1–7 The sabbatical year

The principle of a regularly recurring day of rest has been dealt with in ch. 23 in connection with the annual feasts, and in a way which strongly emphasized the septadic principle. This principle is now carried still further, to the establishing of the sabbatical year and of the jubilee. In the law of the sabbath rest, the principle is applied to all human beings, whether free or bond, and also to the cattle (Ex. 20:10), to the ox, the ass, or any cattle, as beasts of burden (Dt. 5:14), as well as to the sojourner. Here it is extended to the land. 4 Every seventh year the land is to have *a sabbath of solemn rest* (*šabbāṯ šabbāṯôn*) from sowing and reaping. The land is to be left untilled and that which grows of itself, called in v. 6 *the sabbath of the land* (*i.e.* what the sabbath of the land produces of itself), is to be food for all alike, for the owner and the servant, for the sojourner and the cattle. It is not the product of human industry and it is to be free to all. Furthermore, the promise is given that the yield of the sixth year, being ordered and blessed by God, will be sufficient (vv. 18–22) for this period of rest. It is the law of the manna on a larger scale (Ex. 16:22). This at least suggests that the sabbath increase (vv. 6, 7), unlike the gleanings of the ordinary year which were assigned to the widow and orphan, will suffice for the actual needs of everyone (*cf.* Ex. 16:17f.). According to Dt. 31:10 this year is not to be spent in idleness, but to be used for the teaching and training of Israel in the law of God.

25:8–55 The jubilee

25:8–22 Rules for its observance. 8 The fiftieth year is carefully defined as the one following seven sabbatical years. **9** It is introduced by 'sending abroad' throughout the land the *loud trumpet* on the Day of Atonement of the fiftieth year. The trumpet (Heb. *šôp̄ār*) used was the horn (*qeren*) of the ram (*cf.* Jos. 6:4f.) and consequently, by abbreviation, *yôḇēl* (ram), from which the term 'jubilee' is derived, becomes synonymous with trumpet. *Cf.* Ex. 19:13, 19, where both words are used. This trumpet blast, which introduces the jubilee, is like the trumpet sound which prepared and summoned Israel to become the covenant people of their God. The same law regarding sowing and reaping applies to this year as to the sabbatical years which preceded it; and since it began in the autumn it seems clear that the sabbatical years did the same. **10, 13** It is a year of liberty, a year of return to possessions and to family. **14–17** This return to normality, as we may call it, is to be on a strictly equitable basis. Buying and selling are to be carried on with due regard to the approaching year of jubilee. **20** *And if you say, 'What shall we eat in the seventh year?'* This seems to imply that the hypothetical objectors have the sabbatical year only in mind. But the answer includes the larger problem as well, the case when the sabbatical year is followed by the jubilee. **21, 22** This is indicated by the mention of *three years* and of the *eighth* and *ninth* years. The answering of the greater difficulty includes, of course, the solution of the lesser.

25:23–34 The law of redemption. 23 The principle involved in the law of redemption is that the land belongs not to any man but to God. They are not owners but *strangers and sojourners*, tenants by courtesy of the land which God has given to them. They are tenants at will, the will

of God. See Ex. 22:21 and on Dt. 10:19. **25–28** The reclaiming of land may be done by a kinsman, by the man himself, or it will take place automatically in the year of jubilee. **29** But this does not apply to *a dwelling house in a walled city*, which can be redeemed only within a year of its sale, apparently because this has no direct connection with the land and its cultivation. **31** On the other hand, houses in villages are covered by the provision probably because farmers and shepherds dwell in them. The Levites and their possessions come within a special class.

25:35–55 Treatment of the poor brother and of non-Israelites. 35 is difficult. *As a stranger* (RV 'sojourner') and AV 'though . . a sojourner' are both possible renderings. RSV and RV seem better because the laws given here make a clear distinction between Israelite and Gentile. Note the *if your brother* (vv. 25, 35, 39, 47) and *your brethren the people of Israel* (v. 46). Loving the stranger (see 19:34 and Dt. 10:18) does not mean that no distinction is to be made between him and the brother Israelite. Rather the status of the Israelite is shown to be completely different. Loans made to him must be without interest. On this question of usury see on Ex. 22:25; on Dt. 23:19. If he sells himself, he is to be treated as a hired servant and not as a slave; he is to be treated with leniency and is to go free at the jubilee should this come before the termination of his six years of service (Ex. 21:2–4; Dt. 15:12f.). **44–46** The law of release does not apply to the non-Israelites; they may be treated as slaves incapable of redemption. The principles of redemption are then extended to the case of a man who sells himself to a sojourner or stranger who, as indicated above, is required to obey the requirements of the law, or at least not to transgress them. **47–54** The Israelite in such a position may be redeemed or simply go out at the jubilee, and he must not be rigorously treated. **55** The reason for this difference is that the Israelites are the Lord's servants and He has freed them from bondage to men, notably the bondage of Egypt.

26:1–46 BLESSINGS AND CURSINGS

The immense importance which attaches to the keeping of the law, which has just been set before the people and the priests in such detail, is summed up by Moses in Dt. 30:15, in the words 'See, I have set before you this day life and good, death and evil'. *Cf.* Lv. 18:5. No reference is made to the solemn rite which is to be observed at Shechem (see Dt. 11:26–29; 27:4ff.; Jos. 8:30–35). But here, as on that solemn occasion, the issue and the choice are placed before Israel with the utmost plainness, all the more impressive in this case because the Lord, while speaking of course through Moses, addresses the people in the first person (note the frequently recurring 'I') and without any introductory phrase. *Cf.* Dt. 27, 28 where Moses speaks in the name of the

Lord. **1, 2** Idolatry in any form is to be shunned, the sabbath is to be kept, and the sanctuary of the Lord is to be reverenced. These three matters are first singled out for special emphasis because of their importance and also because of all that is involved and implied in their observance.

26:3–13 Blessings as a reward of obedience

These blessings are only as it were an amplification of the promise given in Ex. 19:5f. They give an idyllic picture, such as Isaiah delights to paint, of the prosperity and peace which is the reward of obedience to God. The Lord will give rain and the earth will yield its bounty. The harvest and the ingathering will be so abundant that it will require months instead of days to gather it. And with plenty there shall be peace. Neither man nor beast will be able to injure them or stand before them. **9** The Lord *will have regard* (lit. 'turn') to them. **11** He will set His Tabernacle among them and will not abhor them. This last striking statement seems like an anticlimax, but is not. For Israel is a sinful people which deserves to be abhorred, and would be, were it not for the love and grace of their God. **12** *And I will walk among you.* We are reminded of Gn. 3:8. The land of Canaan will be like the garden of Eden, because the God of Eden will dwell there with His people. The Lord who will do all this is the One who delivered them from Egypt, the greatest proof of His love and almighty power. Again and again in the OT it is referred to as evidence of this love and of the fact that Israel belongs to God and owes Him allegiance. See, *e.g.*, Jos. 24:17.

26:14–45 The chastisements for disobedience

26:14–33 The evils described. It is significant that the evils which are threatened are described much more fully than the blessings that are promised. Man being what he is, sinful and prone to evil, fear is, in many if not most cases, a stronger stimulant to the will than love. **14** *But if you will not hearken to me.* A sharp contrast is suggested by the one 'if' of obedience (v. 3) and the many 'ifs' or 'if nots' of disobedience (vv. 14, 15, 18, 21, 23, 27). The Hebrew verb translated 'hearken' has three main renderings in English: 'hear', 'hearken' and 'obey'. The old saying 'to hear is to obey' is especially applicable to Hebrew. Here obeying (hearing) is contrasted with despising, abhorring and disobeying which amount to breaking the covenant. Note especially the word *contrary* (used 7 times), which suggests Am. 3:3. The thought of reciprocity is stressed throughout. God will deal with Israel exactly as she deserves.

The evils which are threatened are in the main four: pestilence (vv. 16, 25), famine (v. 19), wild beasts (v. 22), and the sword as typifying war and the desolations which will result from it (vv. 25–39). The contrast with the rewards of obedience is made very glaring. *Cf.* vv. 7, 8 with vv. 17, 36–38. Four times the word *sevenfold* is used (vv. 18, 21, 24, 28). This rendering is better than

AV 'seven times' since it is apparently the intensity rather than the duration that is referred to. It should not be connected with the prophetic 'times' of Daniel. But both Jeremiah and Ezekiel seem to have this chapter clearly in mind. Jeremiah speaks of four kinds of punishments (15:3f.). *Cf.* Ezk. 14:12–21. Both of these prophets refer especially to the sword. Dispersion is also definitely threatened here. Israel will be scattered *among the nations.*

26:34–39 The climax of desolation. 34 *Then the land shall enjoy its sabbaths* while Israel is in exile. *Cf.* 2 Ch. 36:21 where the same expression occurs with reference to the Babylonian captivity. This works out the inference that during the centuries between the conquest and the captivity exactly seventy sabbatical years (corresponding to the length of the captivity) had not been observed. But it does indicate that this Mosaic law requiring sabbath rest had been grievously abused and had been largely neglected. Isaiah, Jeremiah and Ezekiel reprove Israel for failure to keep the sabbath (*cf.*, *e.g.*, Je. 17:19–27). But they make no mention of the sabbatical year. Nor does Jeremiah represent the seventy years as a sabbath for the land (see Je. 25:8–11; 27:6–8; 29:10). **36, 37** The *sword* is described in v. 25 as executing the *vengeance for the covenant*, a terrible phrase which suggests 'the wrath of the lamb' (Rev. 6:16).

26:40–45 The result: confession and forgiveness. 40 Follow the RV, 'and they shall confess'. **41** The 'if' does not come till v. 41b, *if then their uncircumcised heart is humbled.* When punishment has finally resulted in confession, if the people who have been scattered among the nations humble themselves, knowing that it is God who has brought them into their evil state, and *make amends for their iniquity* (v. 42) then the Lord will remember His covenant with their fathers. The implication is that He will restore them to the land promised to their fathers, since its possession was an important element in the covenant promise. But it is noteworthy that this is here left to inference, quite different from Dt. 30:1–5, where return to the land is definitely promised on condition of repentance. **46** concludes this group of laws with the emphatic declaration that they were delivered to Israel through Moses at Sinai (*cf.* 7:38).

27:1–34 VOWS AND TITHES

The subject of vows and free-will offerings has been mentioned several times in this book in dealing with the subject of sacrifices (see 7:16; 22:18–23; 23:38). Here 'devoted' or 'sanctified' oblations (Heb. *qorbān*), which could not be offered in sacrifice, are discussed separately. The votive offerings here referred to consist of persons, animals, houses, fields. It is to be observed that in most cases no actual change in ownership takes place. The emphatic word is *valuation*, AV 'estimation', which occurs about twenty times. We have already met it in connection with the guilt-offering, which required the addition of one-fifth to the estimated value of the property which must be restored (5:15f.). Here it is used of the value to be assigned to a person or to property.

2-8 In the case of persons, the estimation varies according to sex and age. It apparently contemplates the possibility of a man's vowing (to give) himself or some person of his household to the Lord. The valuation varies between 50 shekels and 3 shekels. That it is expected that the person will be *redeemed* in money is made clear by v. 8. Thus, if a man valued at 50 shekels were not able to pay the full amount, the priest was to suit the estimate to the ability of the maker of the vow to make good his vow or pledge.

9-13 In the case of animals a distinction is made between clean beasts which could be used in sacrifice and unclean beasts. The former became the property of the Lord and could not be redeemed by the owner. The law was interpreted to mean that the priests might sell such animals to those who wished to offer a sacrifice, but not to the original owner. In the case of an unclean beast, the original owner might redeem it by paying a fifth more than the valuation.

14, 15 In the case of a house the same principle applied. If the owner wished to redeem it he must pay an additional one-fifth.

16-25 The case of the field was much more complicated, since it involved the question of the jubilee. But the owner could redeem it by adding one-fifth. The estimate was to be in terms of the sowing of the field, which was a relatively simple way of determining its value in an agricultural community. If he failed to redeem the field, which was his inheritance, or if he sold it (surreptitiously) after having devoted it, then he lost all claim to it when the year of jubilee came round. The field became the property of the priests. The value of a field which a man had purchased was to be reckoned in terms of the nearness of the jubilee, since it then returned to its original owner. Here (v. 25) and three times elsewhere in the Pentateuch (Ex. 30:13; Nu. 3:47; 18:16) it is stated that the shekel of the sanctuary contains 20 gerahs.

26, 27 Firstlings belonged to the Lord (*cf.* Ex. 13:2, 12; Dt. 15:19-23), so could not be dedicated. But the firstlings of unclean animals could be redeemed by paying the extra one-fifth. If not redeemed they could be sold (see Ex. 13:13).

28, 29 *Devoted* or 'banned' persons or things are an exception to the law regarding redemption. They cannot be redeemed and a banned person must be put to death. This must refer to the solemn and terrible ban (Heb. *ḥērem*) which was placed, *e.g.*, on Amalek, on Jericho and on Achan, and not to the vows and acts of 'sanctifying' mentioned earlier in the chapter. See on Dt. 2:34. The placing of such a ban upon nation or individual was certainly not within the right of any private person, but must have been of the nature of an official sentence pronounced by God through Moses, or through the duly constituted leaders. *Cf.* Jos. 6:17-19.

30-33 deal with the question of tithes. Onetenth of the increase of the fields, of the trees, of the herd or flock is holy to the Lord. A man may redeem part of it by paying the usual one-fifth additional. But this exception does not apply to animals. On the tithes *cf.* Dt. 12 and 14. The apparent discrepancy between Leviticus and Deuteronomy was harmonized by the Rabbis by distinguishing three different tithes: the first, the second, and the third or 'poor' tithe.

34 The closing statement is briefer and less definite than that of 26:46. It may be regarded, therefore, as referring primarily to ch. 27 and not to the entire book. But however understood, this concluding statement is in accord with the total impression given by Leviticus, *i.e.* that it consists of laws given to Moses for Israel at Sinai.

OSWALD T. ALLIS

Numbers

INTRODUCTION

TITLE

The title 'Numbers' is an English translation of the Latin *Numeri*, itself a translation of the Greek (LXX) *Arithmoi*. It was so named because of the considerable attention to numbers throughout the book, but especially in the early chapters and in ch. 26. The Hebrew title, *bᵉmiḏbār*, literally 'in the wilderness' (1:1), is a truer indication of the contents of the book, which traces the journey of Israel from Egypt to the plains of Moab.

AUTHORSHIP

Traditionally Numbers is one of the five books of Moses, and there is, in fact, a great deal about Moses in the book. He is the central character throughout, and it is repeatedly stated that the laws and regulations which it contains were given through the agency of Moses and Aaron (1:1; 3:44; 6:1; 8:1, *et passim*). The impression is certainly given that these laws and regulations go back to the time of the wandering in the wilderness (*e.g.* 9:1; 15:1f.; 15:32ff.), and that many of the incidents took place there too (*e.g.* 13:1f.; 20:1; 22:1, *etc.*). Although there is no formal statement in the book that Moses actually wrote it, 33:2 refers to his having kept a list of stopping places on the journey from Egypt, and, of course, the fact that Moses did write is referred to elsewhere in the Pentateuch (*e.g.* Dt. 31:9). (For further examination of the question of authorship, in which the basic Mosaic character of the material in the Pentateuch as a whole is stressed, see the General Article, 'Moses and the Pentateuch', pp. 41ff.).

The present writer believes, however, that to ascribe the book to Moses *in its present form* is to overlook several important facts. For example, throughout the book Moses is referred to in the third person, the typical style of a narrator (*e.g.* 1:1; 2:1; 3:1, 11, 14, *et passim*). Again, to ascribe every utterance of the book to Moses directly makes him the author of his own commendation as the meekest of men (12:3), which would hardly be the best evidence for the reality of the claim! Further, if it is claimed that Moses is the author not only of Numbers but of the whole Pentateuch, differences in details between the different books relating to sacrifices, festivals, *etc.* call for some explanation.

How then are we to decide the question of authorship? There is considerable agreement today between scholars of widely differing schools that Numbers, in common with the rest of the Pentateuch, received its present shape,

and at least some of its present material, at some time later than that of Moses himself. While not all are agreed how much goes back to Moses himself or at least to his times, it is argued by many that a distinction must be made between the time of origin of the basic laws and narratives and the time when the book received its final form. There is no insuperable difficulty in holding that these laws and the narrative which accompanies them originated in their essential form in the days of Moses. How they were transmitted until they were committed to writing, whether orally or partly in written form, it is not possible to say. Perhaps the major features of the book were committed to writing in the early days of the monarchy, but the date of the final composition is quite unknown.

SOURCES AND THEIR TREATMENT

Clearly the final editor(s) must have drawn on source material, whether oral or written. Some of this material is demonstrably ancient. For example, there are several ancient poems (*e.g.* 21:14ff.), important items of ancient geography (*e.g.* 22:5), and pieces of historical information which are consistent with the known events of the 13th century BC, and which find supporting evidence in archaeological data. All these point to an early origin for at least some of the sources. These as well as the other material available to the editor(s) were gathered and arranged so as to make certain theological issues clear (the normal method of the men who wrote much of the OT).

Naturally some questions arise. Where speeches are reported, *e.g.*, are the actual words of the speaker recorded or merely a summary, or is it a free rendering (*cf.* the problem of the words of Jesus in the Gospels)? Again, in references to ancient institutions and ceremonies, is it possible that the account in Numbers as we now have it is a description of what these became in later centuries—the same in spirit and in essence, but different in detail? Certainty about such questions is not always possible, but it cannot be ruled out that some such modifications may have taken place in the course of transmission and in the light of experience.

The so-called classical documentary hypothesis, which has held sway in OT studies for over a century now, provided a very neat, if somewhat artificial, analysis of Numbers into its various sources. On this theory Numbers was divided between the P (Priestly) source and the JE (Jahwist – Elohist) sources as follows: chs. 1:1 – 10:10; 15; 18–19; 28–31, and smaller portions of other chapters are assigned to P, while chs. 22:2 – 24:25 completely, and portions of 10:11 – 12:16; 13; 14; 16; 17; 20–21; 25–27; 32–36, are assigned to JE. It is now recognized that the scheme was much too artificial. It is quite impossible to define 'documents' P and JE with sufficient accuracy to make the analysis into these sources beyond question. Nevertheless, on this basis, Numbers was conceived as an early historical epic (JE), interwoven with later legislation and a priestly reinterpretation of the significance of the facts recorded (P) which would enable Israel to understand more clearly her divine origin, call and destiny. Such a view, despite its artificial character, has something to commend it provided that a considerable degree of flexibility is allowed in defining the nature of P and JE. If the JE material is regarded as a collection of ancient epic material, and if the P material is regarded as a collection of legal and cultic material, likewise of considerable age, indeed ultimately Mosaic in origin, then the theory is not very different from the view proposed in this commentary. The final editor undertook the task of welding all his material together into its present shape so as to suit his purpose. This view should not be thought of as implying that the final picture was so wide of the mark and so distorted from the original story that it bore little or no resemblance to what actually took place. Rather those who hold it believe that the editor, with authentic material at his disposal, arranged this so as to preserve in its broad outline the true course of events, and to represent the essence of ancient institutions and rituals, even though a degree of idealization may have taken place so that they appeared in the final work in the form they came to have after the experiences of the intervening centuries.

SOME SPECIAL PROBLEMS

The question of numbers

In the book of Numbers a special usage of the terms 'thousand' (Heb. *'elep̄*) and 'hundred' (Heb. *mē'â*) is encountered in the census lists of chs. 1–4 and 26, and in the account of the Midianite war in ch. 31. The census lists represent an ancient tradition of tribal quotas of men available for war, so that the terms in question signify military units of some kind (*cf.* 1 Sa. 8:12; 22:7; 2 Sa. 18:1, *etc.*). The exact numerical value of the terms is unknown. Alternatively, by vocalizing the consonants *'-l-p* to read *'allup̄* we have the meaning 'leader' or 'captain'. Elsewhere again the term *'elep̄* denotes 'family' or 'tent-group' (*e.g.* Jdg. 6:15; 1 Sa. 10:19; Mi. 5:2). Assuming that the terms in Nu. 1–4; 26 and 31 are military in nature and that the lists are ancient and authentic, it is possible that a later compiler of ancient source material misunderstood the true meaning of the terms and, assuming them to be numbers, simply added them up and arrived at the total 603,550 in 1:46. Or

alternatively the term *'allup̄*, 'captain', may have been confused with *'elep̄*, 'thousand', so that, *e.g.*, in 1:39 the 62,700 men of Dan may have read originally '60 captains, 2,700 men', or even '60 captains, 27 *mē'ôt*'. The problem is thus complex and a variety of mathematical solutions has been offered (*e.g.* R. E. D. Clark, *JTVI*, 1955; G. E. Mendenhall, *JBL*, 1958, LXXVII, Part I; J. W. Wenham, *Tyndale Bulletin*, 18, 1967).

Laws relating to sacrifices, festivals, vows, etc.

A comparison of Numbers with other books which refer to sacrifices, festivals, vows, *etc.*, *e.g.* Exodus, Leviticus, Deuteronomy, Ezekiel, shows that there are differences in detail between the prescriptions in the various books (see Commentary). In some cases it is, of course, possible to harmonize the evidence, and in others it might fairly be said that we simply lack the clues which were anciently available to make the story coherent. Another explanation is that, although these institutions had a basic form already in the days of Moses, and although they preserved the spirit and the essential elements of the early forms, there were modifications at various times during the centuries of use, and that the form set out in Numbers represents the usage at the time of the final compilation of the source materials. The words of W. F. Albright (*The Biblical Period*, 1963, p. 19) in reference to the so-called 'priestly code' are apposite: 'How much of this ritual goes back to Moses himself it would be idle to conjecture in the present state of our knowledge; the spirit and much of the detail may be considered as ante-dating the Conquest of Canaan— in other words, as going back to Mosaic origins.'

The general historicity of Numbers

There are few today who would deny that at least some genuine historical events lie behind the book of Numbers. Some, like Martin Noth, would argue that particular events had reference only to particular groups of people, but that when the many tribal elements were eventually welded together in Canaan to form Israel, their different tribal traditions, each of which may have had a basis in history, were streamlined to give a connected narrative with an 'all Israel orientation'. Such a view would allow that the group which was present at Sinai was not necessarily the same group that made the journey around Transjordan after a stay at Kadesh in order to enter Canaan from the east.

It is here proposed that the present literary shape is not secondary and artificial but that it results from the simple fact that the original events took place in the same sequence, or approximately so. There may be uncertainty about the identification of place-names, or about the exact itinerary, or about the exact numbers of people, or even about the exact nature of some of the events which seem to have been recorded in symbolic form (*e.g.* ch. 31). Perhaps also the sequence of events does not follow in exact chronological order so as to satisfy the canons of modern historical criticism. Perhaps, again, the description of the sacrifices, festivals, *etc.* represents a later developed form. But despite all these possibilities, most of which are inherent in ancient literary methods, it is here argued that the narrative is based on contemporary evidence and is essentially true to the original facts. Archaeological evidence, although it does not establish this view, is not inconsistent with it.

By comparison with modern critical history writing, Numbers is seen to be of a different order, for it sets out to make clear the divine significance of events. Exact details of how and when events took place are often omitted and the exact nature of events is sometimes difficult to reconstruct. But the significance of the event is plainly declared. For the people of Israel this was more important. Of what profit was it to know the exact details of an event if the meaning of the event was not understood?

The ancient poems

The poems of Balaam in chs. 23, 24 have a number of unusual features. Their content and style are homogeneous and point to a period between the middle of the 13th and the end of the 12th century BC as the time of composition. Ancient poetic devices, ways of spelling and orthography may be discerned in the Hebrew text. The geographical and historical background to the poems is consistent with the period of the Sea Peoples of the early 12th century BC (see Commentary). Other poems in 21:14, 15 and 21:17, 18, 27–30 seem to have been taken from ancient sources like the *Book of the Wars of Yahweh* or the repertoire of ancient ballad singers (21:27).

Religious value

Like every other OT book, Numbers was a vehicle for conveying God's truth to the people. While the book as we have it today represents the work of an editor and compiler of ancient materials who selected and arranged his materials so as to set forth important religious truths, we ought not to conclude that these truths were unknown before the editor gave expression to them. Israel's faith was an ancient one and was woven into her very life. At its basis was the belief that Yahweh the God of Israel was a personal, living God who stood in a peculiar relation to the people whom He had chosen. The book of Numbers expounds several important aspects of the being and activity of Yahweh the God of Israel.

Yahweh's presence in Israel. He who brought Israel from Egypt and made a covenant with them at Sinai was in their midst always, caring for them and guiding them. This is illustrated by the cloud ever present among them (9:15–23); by the explicit declaration, 'I the Lord dwell in the midst of the people of Israel' (35:34); by His response to the physical needs of Israel on many occasions (*e.g.* 11:31f.; 20:2–13), despite

their grumbling; by His deliverance of His people from their enemies, enabling them finally to occupy their lands (*e.g.* 21:1–3, 21–35; 31:1–54, *etc.*); and by His protection even from the sinister intentions of Balak, king of Moab (chs. 22–24).

Yahweh's discipline of Israel. Yahweh used the wilderness experiences for the discipline, training and nurture of His people. They were chastened for acts of rebellion either against Himself or against the leaders He had chosen for Israel, for grumbling, for acts of apostasy, and for presumptuous acts. Divine judgment fell on the people as a whole (11:1–3; 21:6; 25:1–5, 6–13), upon the tribal chiefs (14:36f.), upon the Levites (ch. 16), upon Miriam (12:10) and upon Moses and Aaron (20:12f.). Thereby Israel learned that Yahweh alone was Sovereign and that no act of rebellion and no attempt to share allegiance with another god would pass unjudged. It was, however, the discipline and chastisement of love.

Yahweh's purposes. Since Yahweh was the Lord of history, His promises to the patriarchs to give them a land and descendants would be fulfilled. These were part of His purpose both for His people and for the world. Having chosen Israel and taken them into a covenant relationship, He would never repudiate His people but would remain faithful to His covenant. Hence neither Israel's unfaithfulness, nor the attacks of the nations on Israel as she journeyed, nor the devices of a diviner could hinder the unfolding of Yahweh's purposes. He would have His people enter the land of Canaan despite every opposition.

Yahweh's holiness. Narratives and laws in Numbers combine to demonstrate that Yahweh is holy. He will not tolerate any attempt on Israel's part to share her allegiance to Him with another deity (25:1–18). Despite His holiness, however, He could be approached with proper reverence, with due regard for proper procedures, and when men had put away every uncleanness. The sanctuary, the system of priests and Levites, the sacrifices, the feasts and the various ritual observances all served both to preserve Yahweh's holiness and also to stress His sovereignty, which extended even to the details of Israel's common life and daily worship. There was always the possibility of having one's sins 'covered', for Yahweh was both the Judge and the One who abounded in steadfast love and forgiveness (14:18, 19).

These significant truths about the nature and the activity of Yahweh should have taught Israel that Yahweh required her allegiance, her loyalty, faithfulness to His covenant, confident trust in His promises, a proper acknowledgment of His sovereignty and holiness, dependence on Him in the hour of need and danger. Moreover, He required each individual Israelite to respect the life, the family and the property of his fellow-Israelite, to show concern for his less fortunate brother, to demonstrate a willingness to co-operate with his brother in significant ventures of national importance, and to reject any inclination to turn his brother aside from loyalty to Yahweh by persuading him to worship another god.

Clearly, such a noble picture of the ways of God with His people is significant for the modern believer. God is unchanging in His ways and His people are the subject of His loving concern in every age. He who draws them into the new covenant made with Him in the Lord Jesus Christ will care for them, guide them and deliver them no less carefully than He did in the case of Israel. His kindly discipline will be felt at times for He is ever a loving Father who chastens His children. He remains the Lord of history and His promises concerning the ultimate outcome of His purposes remain. The

company of believers in the 20th century AD is caught up in His purposes too and no power in heaven or on earth can finally hinder the fulfilment of His purposes. He still requires utter loyalty from His people (Rom. 12:1). He has made a way of approach to Himself through His Son, the Lord Jesus (Heb. 7–10) in whom all the intention of the old covenant sacrificial system was fulfilled. Moreover, in the daily life of every single believer today He expects conduct which is consistent both with their high status as members of the covenant family, and with their profession about their life in Christ. In brief, all that we have stated above in reference to the religious value of Numbers for the ancient people of Israel may with equal relevance be claimed for the Christian.

OUTLINE OF CONTENTS

COMMENTARY

1:1 – 10:10 THE PREPARATION FOR THE JOURNEY FROM SINAI TO CANAAN

The biblical narrative dealing with events at Sinai begins at Ex. 19 and continues on into Nu. 10. It then moves to the story of the onward journey to the promised land. The preparations for that journey are given in the first ten chapters of Numbers.

1:1–54 The first census

1:1–3 God commands the census to be taken. 1 The Hebrew name for the book, *bemiḏbār* (lit. *in the wilderness*), is the fourth word in the Hebrew of v.1. LXX gave the book a descriptive title which, translated into Latin, lies at the basis of the English name. (See Introduction.) God's command to take a census came on the *first day of the second month* after Israel had left Egypt. It was in the wilderness of Sinai, the exact site of which is unknown. Traditionally Sinai is Gebel Mûsa, although it may have been Gebel Serbâl some 20 miles to the north-west, or even a mountain in the region of Kadesh. Fittingly, God spoke with Moses in the *tent of meeting.* **2, 3** The *census* concerned the males from 20 years old and upward in the whole congregation of Israel. The purpose was to determine military potential; so the use of the terms 'thousand' (Heb. *'elep̄*) and 'hundred' (Heb. *mē'â*) should be understood in a military sense (*cf.* on 11:21, 22; and see Introduction).

1:4–16 The census officials. 4 Moses was to choose a man from each tribe who was the head of his fathers' house. These men are called 'leader' (Heb. *nāśî'*) elsewhere (*cf.* 2:3–31; 7; 10:14–28), and were important figures in tribal life. **5–15** A list of the men chosen is now given. Apart from the Judahite names *Nahshon* and *Amminadab* (v. 7), none of these is known outside Numbers (*cf.* Ex. 6:23; Ru. 4:18–21). Most of the names are, however, theophoric, *i.e.* they contain the name of God, 'El' or 'Shaddai'. Other names contain the element *'āḇ* ('father'), *'am* ('kinsman'), *'aḥ* ('brother'), *e.g. Abidan* (v. 11; Heb. *'aḇîḏān*, 'the divine father has judged'), in the manner of the West Semitic sentence-names common during the period 2000 to 1000 BC but which went out of use later. **16** *Clans* (AV 'thousands') here translates Hebrew *'elep̄*, elsewhere in this passage a military unit (*cf.* on vv. 2, 3). That it can thus be used to denote a sub-clan also shows the versatility of the word and its tendency to depart from a merely numerical meaning.

1:17–46 The details of the census. 17–19 Moses and Aaron, assisted by the twelve leaders, proceeded to carry out the census. **20–46** The numbers given here at the beginning of the journey should be compared with those in ch. 26 for the end of the journey. In the following list the two are given, with the later number in brackets: Reuben, 46,500 (43,730); Simeon,

59,300 (22,200); Gad, 45,650 (40,500); Judah, 74,600 (76,500); Issachar, 54,400 (64,300); Zebulun, 57,400 (60,500); Ephraim, 40,500 (32,500); Manasseh, 32,200 (52,700); Benjamin, 35,400 (45,600); Dan, 62,700 (64,400); Asher, 41,500 (53,400); Naphtali, 53,400 (45,400). The order of this list differs somewhat from that in Gn. 29–30. The sons of Leah and Rachel are in the order of their birth but the sons of Bilhah, viz. Dan and Naphtali, and the sons of Zilpah, viz. Gad and Asher, are out of order. Further, while Simeon decreased greatly over the years, Manasseh increased greatly. The total number of the tribes that later comprised Israel outnumber the later Judah tribes by five or six to one. The numbers in any case create special problems of interpretation (see Introduction).

1:47–54 The duties of the Levites. 47–49 The Levites were not numbered by their ancestral tribe (*cf.* 3:21–39) since they were not required for military service. **50, 51** The task of the Levites was to care for the Tabernacle of the testimony and all its furnishings, to take it down, to carry it, to set it up and to *tend* it. This last verb (Heb. *šāraṯ*) is used for all kinds of noble service, but particularly of service associated with Israel's worship of Yahweh (*cf.* Ex. 28:35; Dt. 10:8; 17:12, *etc.*). The *tabernacle of the testimony* was so designated because it housed two stone tables on which were written the Ten Commandments (*cf.* Ex. 31:18; 40:20). The word 'testimony' could be translated 'covenant stipulations'. Unauthorized persons were forbidden to approach the sanctuary on pain of death. **52–54** Whereas the non-Levites pitched their tents around their own standard, the Levites pitched around the central sanctuary, thus protecting it and obviating any desecration of it which might incur the wrath of Yahweh (*cf.* 16:46; 1 Sa. 6:19, 20).

2:1–34 Position of the tribes in the camp and on the march

Some commentators have regarded this chapter as an idealization of what Israel actually did in the wilderness and have proposed that the chapter was influenced by Ezk. 48. That biblical writers used artificial literary devices at times need not be denied. Nor were they always as concerned with spatial and chronological precision as we are today (the temptations of Jesus, *e.g.*, have a different order in Matthew and Luke).

But even if it be granted that the arrangement of the tribes is here idealized we ought not to conclude that there was no plan at all either for the march or for the encampment. Presumably there was a need for some orderly procedures, which is the essence of what is here depicted. The tent of meeting stood as the central feature of the whole arrangement whether Israel was in an encampment or on the march and symbolized the divine presence in Israel's midst at all times. It was no longer outside the camp (cf. Ex. 33:7f.) but in the very centre.

2:1-31 The order of the camps. 1, 2 Each tribal group was to camp beside the *standard* of the leader of its group of tribes. In addition the *ensigns* of the various ancestral houses were displayed. There were four tribal leaders, Judah, Reuben, Ephraim and Dan, and presumably twelve ancestral houses. Jewish tradition ascribes a lion to Judah, a human head to Reuben, an ox to Ephraim, and an eagle to Dan. Just how close the various encampments were to the central sanctuary is not clear. The Hebrew expression *facing* (Heb. *minneḡeḏ*, literally 'away from', 'opposite') can also mean 'at a distance' (cf. Dt. 32:52, where it is translated 'before you'). Certainly in Jos. 3:4 the distance between the ark and the people was 2,000 cubits, *i.e.* about 1,000 yards. **3-9** The tribes were deployed in four groups. On the east side under Nahshon the leader of Judah were Judah, Issachar and Zebulun. **10-16** On the south side were the tribes Reuben, Simeon and Gad under the leadership of Elizur of Reuben. **17** The tent of meeting followed Reuben. Some difficulty is encountered with this verse. Comparison with 10:17-21 shows a different order of march: in 2:17 the three families of the Levites followed Reuben; in 10:17 the sons of Gershon and the sons of Merari who carried the Tabernacle went ahead of Reuben while the third Levitical family, the Kohathites, followed Reuben (cf. 10:17-21). This would seem to be a more natural order, as it allows time to elapse for the erection of the Tabernacle before the sacred objects, carried by the Kohathites, arrived. Evidently the expression *in the midst of the camps* ought not to be interpreted too literally. In fact the Levi tribes were both preceded by and followed by other tribes and so were 'in the midst'. **18-24** On the west side were Ephraim, Manasseh and Benjamin under the leadership of Elishama of Ephraim. **25-31** On the north side were Dan, Asher and Naphtali under the standard of Ahiezer of Dan. The leaders in each case were those who assisted in the census.

2:32-34 General summary. The grand total of fighting men given in 1:44-46 is here repeated. The number of Levites is given in 3:39 since no reference has yet been made to the census of the Levites.

3:1 – 4:49 The census and duties of the Levites

The Levites were not counted with the secular tribes and so were the subject of a special census (vv. 14-51). They were distinct from the priests of the sanctuary (vv. 1-4) and were their servants (vv. 5-13). A study of the Levites throughout the whole period of Israel's history shows that their status varied from time to time. Originally they were simply one of the secular tribes. Levi, a son of Leah (Gn. 29:34) gave rise to a family which was originally a non-priestly tribe (Gn. 34; 49:5-7). The Levitical ancestry of Moses is

affirmed (cf. Ex. 2:1; 6:19f.; Nu. 26:59; 1 Ch. 6:1-3). In later times, however, as the number grew quite beyond the needs of the sanctuary at Jerusalem, there were many Levites who never came to Jerusalem. In practice only one group of the whole Levitical family functioned as priests. Yet theoretically all the tribe of Levi were priests (cf. Dt. 18:1, 'the Levitical priests, that is, all the tribe of Levi'). The later distinction made in Ezekiel confirmed what had been a *de facto* distinction much earlier (cf. Ezk. 44:6-31).

3:1-4 The descendants of Aaron. 1 These verses hark back to Ex. 6:23 and Lv. 10:1f. where the sons of Aaron are given. The expression *generations* (Heb. *tôlᵉḏōṯ*), common in Genesis (cf. Gn. 5:1; 6:9, *etc.*) where it provides the framework for the whole narrative, can sometimes be translated 'story', and so this verse could be translated: 'This is the story of Aaron and Moses at the time when Yahweh spoke with Moses on Mount Sinai.' **2, 3** Aaron's four sons are named, all of them *anointed* to act as priests. The term 'ordain' means literally 'fill the hand', *i.e.* 'entrust to the hands of'. Quite apart from any divine institution it would be altogether reasonable and in keeping with ancient custom for Moses, the promulgator of Yahwism, to give a leading role to his own tribe and family in the organization and protection of this new religious constitution given by Yahweh to His people (cf. Ex. 29:7-9; 40:15). **4** Nadab and Abihu, sons of Aaron, died without heirs when they introduced unauthorized fire into the sanctuary (cf. Lv. 10:1, 2), so that only Eleazar and Ithamar of Aaron's sons lived to function as priests *in the lifetime of Aaron their father*. Eleazar, as the elder son, took precedence but both branches were still serving in David's time (cf. 1 Ch. 24:1-4).

3:5-10 The Levites as servants of the priests. 5, 6a The Levites were first 'brought near', probably to Yahweh (cf. 8:16) and then set before Aaron. **6b-10** It was the duty and privilege of the whole tribe of Levi to serve the Lord. But there was a division of tasks within the tribe. Aaron and his sons attended to the priesthood and the rest of the tribe were at their service performing duties in the Tabernacle for the priests and for the whole congregation. Only Aaron and his descendants, Eleazar or Ithamar, Zadok or Abiathar, were authorized to perform priestly duties. Unauthorized priests were in danger of death.

3:11-13 The significance of the Levites. The Levites were representatives for the firstborn (cf. Ex. 22:29, 30; 34:19, 20). Instead of taking the firstborn for His service, Yahweh substituted the tribe of Levi (cf. Nu. 3:40-51). **3:14-39 The census of the Levites. 14-16** The census of the Levites proceeded as Yahweh commanded. It was a census of every male from a month old and upward (cf. 1:3). **17** The division of the Levites into three, *Gershon and Kohath and Merari* agrees with 26:57 and Ex.

6:16–19. **18–20** Gershon is further divided into two sub-groups, Kohath into four, and Merari into two. *Cf.* the division of the Levites into five families, Libni, Hebron, Mahli, Mushi, and Korah in 26:58. **21–26** The Gershonites, who numbered 7,500, camped west of the sanctuary under the leadership of Eliasaph. They had charge of all the coverings, curtains, cords, of the Tabernacle, the tent and the court (*cf.* 4:24–28). On the march they followed Reuben (*cf.* 10:17). **27–32** The Kohathites numbered 8,300, following the LXX. (The total of v. 39 requires a reduction of 300 in one of the tribes and the proposal to read the letters *š-l-š* meaning 'three' in place of *š-š* meaning 'six' is generally accepted.) This group encamped on the south side of the Tabernacle under the leadership of Elizaphan. They had the responsibility of the most sacred objects of the Tabernacle furniture, *the ark, the table, the lampstand, the altars, the vessels . . . and the screen* separating the Holy Place from the Holy of Holies. All these items were too holy to be transported in wagons but were carried (*cf.* 4:14, 15; 7:9). **33–37** The Merarites under the leadership of Zuriel camped on the north side of the Tabernacle and numbered 6,200. They had charge of *the frames . . ., the bars, the pillars, the bases . . . pegs and cords* (*cf.* 4:29–33). **38** Moses and Aaron and his sons occupied the fourth side of the square surrounding the sanctuary on the east. Their responsibility was *the rites within the sanctuary*, whatever had to be done for the people of Israel. **39** The total number of Levites from a month old and upward was 22,000.

3:40–51 The census of the firstborn in Israel. 40–43 A census of all the firstborn males in Israel from a month old and upward was taken. The count was 22,273. The Levites numbered 22,000. The difference of 273 required some compensation if Yahweh were to take the Levites *instead of all the first-born among the people of Israel.* **44–51** Compensation was achieved by the payment of five shekels of silver for each of the 273 Israelites not matched by a Levite, the shekel being *reckoned by the shekel of the sanctuary.* While this latter expression may reflect more settled times and show the hand of the editor, presumably even in Moses' day there was some official weight for the transaction of daily business. The silver so collected, referred to as *redemption money*, was given to Aaron and his sons. The term 'redemption' derives from the root *p-d-y* and can be translated 'ransom', a term from commercial law referring to money paid to liberate persons or things which have fallen into the possession of another. The number of firstborn, viz. 22,273, seems small in comparison with 1:46 where the males over twenty numbered 603,550. It is not clear on what basis the numbering was done, unless it was that the reference is to the firstborn of those in Egypt whose lives were spared and for whom the Levites were taken as a substitute (*cf.* v. 13). In any case the number in 1:46 is uncertain in view of the term 'thousand' (see Introduction).

4:1–49 The Levites: their numbers and duties. It is impossible to say how far the picture here represents the exact ancient practice, but there were cult objects in Moses' day and modern study suggests that the picture here is, at least in broad outline, a reflection of ancient practice.

1–20 The Kohathites. 1–3 The Kohathites whose duties were concerned with the furniture of the sanctuary are placed first (*cf.* 3:21–32 where the Gershonites are first). The present census is not concerned with the question of equating Levites with the firstborn (*cf.* 3:40–51) but with males from 30 to 50 years of age *who can enter the service, to do the work in the tent of meeting.* These age limits varied over the years (*cf.* 8:23–26; 1 Ch. 23:24, 27; 2 Ch. 31:17; Ezr. 3:8). The term *service* (Heb. *ṣābā'*) is used of military service in 1:3 ('go forth to war') but elsewhere in the OT also for the trials of the Exile (*cf.* Is. 40:2 'warfare', but see RSV mg.), or for toil and trouble (*cf.* Jb. 7:1 'hard service'). The comparison with military service suggests that the Levites were as carefully organized for the service of Yahweh as the militia for battle (*cf.* 1 Tim. 1:18). **4** The sphere of service for the Kohathites was *the most holy things*, which seems to refer to the Holy of Holies (*cf.* Ex. 26:33). **5, 6** When the camp was struck, Aaron and his sons dismantled and packed the sacred objects of the sanctuary so that the Kohathites might not see them or touch them. The curtain or *veil of the screen* which hung before the Holy of Holies was used to cover the ark. Then a second covering of *goatskin* (or perhaps dolphin skin) and a third covering, *a cloth . . . of blue* (or bluish purple), were placed over the ark for protection from the elements and from prying eyes. The bluish-purple outer covering marked out the ark for all to see. Finally the poles, normally removed only for packing and unpacking, were placed in position (*cf.* Ex. 25:15). **7, 8** *The table of the bread of the Presence* was covered by a similar bluish-purple cloth and the *plates* ('deep-dishes', 'basins', Heb. *qᵉʿārâ; cf.* Nu. 7:13), the *dishes*, small incense vessels (lit. 'hands'), the *bowls*, and the *flagons* used in the Tabernacle rituals were placed on it. A *cloth of scarlet* was spread over all these and finally *a covering of goatskin* (or dolphin skin) before the carrying poles were inserted. **9, 10** The seven-branched *lampstand* with its accompanying utensils, *lamps, snuffers,* (ash)*trays* (or incense receptacles; Heb. *maḥtâ*) and oil-vessels were all wrapped in the animal skin and laid on their *carrying frame* which was perhaps a pole or a flat board. **11** The *golden altar* (*cf.* Ex. 30:1, 3; and for its use Lv. 4:7) which stood before the inner veil was covered with a bluish-purple cloth and animal skin and its carrying poles were attached. **12** The vessels used in the *sanctuary* were also wrapped in bluish-purple cloth and animal skin. **13, 14** The ashes were removed from the large altar (*cf.* Ex. 27:1f.) and it was covered with a reddish-purple cloth. Finally the various utensils used at the altar were placed on it, the whole was covered and the carrying poles inserted. *Firepans* (Heb. *maḥtâ*), *cf*. v. 9; *forks*, perhaps three-pronged flesh-hooks (*cf*. 1 Sa. 2:13); *basins* were used for throwing blood against the corners of the altar. **15** When Aaron and his sons had covered all these sacred items they were committed to the Kohathites for carrying. **16** Eleazar, in addition to general responsibilities over the leaders of the Levites (*cf*. 3:32), had the charge of the oil for the light, the incense, and the regular cereal-offering, as well as the general care of the Tabernacle. **17–20** The work of the Kohathites was thus closely associated with that of the priests. Yet they were never to see or touch the vessels of the Holy of Holies. The expression *even for a moment* is a vivid one, literally 'as a swallowing', *i.e*. the time taken to swallow one's spittle.

21–28 The Gershonites. This group was responsible for the less holy furniture of the Tabernacle, the curtains, screens, ropes for the whole structure, the tent and its court (*cf*. Ex. 26:1–14). Wagons were provided to carry these burdens (*cf*. Nu. 7:7). The Gershonites were under the care of Ithamar, the younger of Aaron's surviving sons who was himself a Kohathite (*cf*. Ex. 6:16, 18, 20, 23). According to these verses Eleazar, son of Aaron, had more significant responsibilities than did Ithamar, suggesting that the Zadokite Levites as they were later known (*cf*. 1 Ch. 24:3, 6) had precedence over the Ithamar Levites.

29–33 The Merarites. The lowliest tasks of all, the care and transport of the frames and accessories (*cf*. Ex. 26:15–30) were committed to the descendants of Merari over whom Ithamar stood as overseer. They too were provided with wagons (*cf*. Nu. 7:8).

34–49 The census numbers for the Levites. **34–48** The numbers of males eligible for the service of the Tabernacle were Kohathites: 2,750, Gershonites: 2,630, and Merarites: 3,200, a total of 8,580. **49** is difficult to translate. One proposal is: 'It was on the command of Yahweh under the direction of Moses that they numbered them each one according to his task and according to what he had to carry. Thus they were numbered according as Yahweh commanded Moses.'

5:1 – 6:27 Regulations for the Nazirite and miscellaneous laws

5:1–31 Miscellaneous laws and regulations. Not all the laws in this section appear to have specific reference to a camp, although vv. 1–4 suit such an environment. The rest are of more general application and would apply wherever problems of human relationships arose.

1–4 The exclusion of the ritually unclean from the camp. The presence of the Tabernacle and the ark symbolized the presence of Yahweh in the camp which thus became a holy area from which every unclean thing was to be excluded including lepers (*cf*. Lv. 13; 14), men and women

suffering from a discharge (*cf*. Lv. 15), or individuals who had touched a dead body (Heb. *nepeš*, 'spirit', used as widely as English uses the word 'person'; *cf*. Nu. 19:11f.). The seclusion of women in the camp at the time of menstruation was practised in the east until recent times.

5–10 Breach of trust and restitution of stolen property. **5, 6** This law is an extension of the law in Lv. 6:1–7. When someone caused harm or loss to his fellow Israelite it was tantamount to an offence against Yahweh. **7** Such men incurred guilt and were bound to confess their wrong and to make restitution (Heb. *'āšām*) equal to 20 per cent of the value of the damage or loss. The term *'āšām* is used in the OT both for the so-called 'guilt-offering' (*cf*. Lv. 6), and for the compensation payable. **8** Where there was no living relative or kinsman (Heb. *gō'ēl*) to whom restitution could be made, the compensation was given to the priest along with the ram of atonement to cover the man's evil deed. **9, 10** The priests received other offerings also. *Offering* (Heb. *terûmâ*, used, *e.g*., in Lv. 7:14, AV 'heave-offering') signifies the reserved portions lifted off from the sin-offering.

11–31 The law of jealousy. This law concerns the case of a man's wife who is found to be pregnant and the husband suspects he is not the father.

11, 12 When a man suspected his wife of unfaithfulness, provision was made for a strange trial by ordeal. The accusation is that the wife *goes astray* (Heb. *śāṭâ*, *i.e*. commits marital unfaithfulness) and *acts unfaithfully* (Heb. *mā'al*; *cf*. its use in Jos. 7:1, 'to break faith') towards her husband. **13** Sexual misconduct is clearly intended, for the verse reads literally 'a man lies with her with the emission of seed'. The act was without her husband's knowledge and without witnesses. **14, 15** Whether the husband had grounds for suspicion or not, once a jealous spirit possessed him he took his wife to the priest, bringing as a sacrificial gift on her behalf a tenth of an ephah of barley meal without oil or frankincense. The absence of these latter items suggests a sin-offering (*cf*. Lv. 5:11). The offering was called a *cereal offering of jealousy*, which brought the wrongdoing to mind. **16–18** The priest then set the woman *before the Lord*, *i.e*. at the entrance to the sanctuary, with her hair loosed (*cf*. Lv. 13:45) and the cereal-offering in her hands. Meantime he had taken *holy water*, presumably from the bronze laver, in an earthen vessel into which he had put dust from the floor of the Tabernacle. Then, holding *the water of bitterness that brings the curse* in his hand he required the woman to take an oath. The exact meaning of *bitterness* (Heb. *mārîm*) is not clear. It has been derived from roots meaning 'bitter', 'test', 'pass by'. Since the context is one of trial by ordeal we might translate 'waters of testing'. The expression *that brings the curse* is a single word in Hebrew and is probably a participle derived from the root '-*r*-*r*, 'curse' or 'cast a spell'. The water was regarded as a means of producing the result of

vv. 21, 22, 27. **19–22** After the warning of vv. 19, 20 the priest made the woman take *the oath of the curse*, i.e. to declare the truth of the matter on pain of suffering the consequences if she spoke falsely. The consequences were expressed in severe terms. 'May the Lord make you a curse (*an execration*, Heb. '*ālâ*) and an imprecation (*an oath*, Heb. *š^eḇû'â*) among your people when the Lord causes your thigh to sag (*fall away*) and your belly to distend (*your body swell*); may this water that induces (*brings*) the curse enter your belly (*body*) causing the belly to distend (*make your body swell*) and the thigh to sag (*your thigh fall away*).' To this the woman was required to reply 'Amen, Amen'. Jewish tradition in the Mishnah Ṣoṭah argued that the sin started with the thigh and finished with the womb so that both were to suffer judgment.

23, 24 The final act of the ritual was to write the curses on a document, wipe them off into the water of bitterness, and make the woman drink the mixture. **25, 26** Then the cereal-offering of jealousy was taken from the woman, waved before the Lord, and brought to the altar where a handful of it was burned as a token portion. **27** Unfortunately it is not clear in the narrative precisely how the guilt or innocence of the woman was decided. Presumably the guilty woman suffered some ill effects, bitter pain, swelling of the body, the sagging of the thigh (was all this a picture of a miscarriage?), and subsequent reproach among her people as an adulteress. **28** The innocent woman, however, gave birth to the child and to others thereafter. It is probably quite unnecessary to see in the several references to the woman drinking (vv. 24, 26, 27) separate occasions of drinking. Ancient Hebrew writers did not follow western methods of expressing themselves, and v. 24 could be an anticipation of later verses. Only after the oath had been sworn and the offering presented did the woman drink. **29–31** The closing words of the chapter indicate that this law applied only to the case of an adulterous woman. Men in ancient Israel could marry more than one wife and have concubines too. Only in the case of another man's wife could he commit adultery.

Such trials by ordeal were common in the ancient world in cases of infidelity. The ceremony recorded here is notable for its leniency in comparison with the fierce ordeals prescribed in pagan circles, and also for the fact that it was more likely to result in a verdict of innocence whereas the others were certainly weighted in the direction of guilt. Strange as the whole circumstance and ritual may seem to us, it compares so favourably with non-Israelite practice that it may be taken as evidence of that generally considerate attitude of the law of Moses towards women.

6:1–21 Regulations for the Nazirite. The institution of the Nazirite vow could be observed by both men and women. It was designed to provide for the setting apart of a person by means of a vow in order to undertake some special service for Yahweh. The rules first define the character of the vow (vv. 1–8); then the procedure to be followed should the vow be broken (vv. 9–12); and finally, the special ceremonies to be observed once the vow was fulfilled (vv. 13–21).

1–8 The Nazirite vow. 1, 2 The Nazirite vow was one of a number of special vows that an Israelite might take (*cf*. Lv. 22:21; 27:2). The term, *nāzîr*, in Hebrew derives from the root *n-z-r*, 'to vow', its special significance being 'to withhold from wonted use'. It is a passive participle meaning 'one who has made a vow'. The same root occurs in the verb *separate himself*. **3, 4** The Nazirite was bound to abstain from alcohol or anything that might ferment and produce alcohol, such as wine, strong drink, grape juice, grapes fresh or dried. The terms translated *seeds* (Heb. *ḥarṣannîm*) and *skins* (Heb. *zāg*) are of uncertain meaning. **5** The hair and beard were to remain uncut during the period of the vow and the person was to remain holy or set apart. *Cf*. Samson, Jdg. 16:17, 22. *Locks*. The noun (Heb. *pera'*) derives from the same root as is used in 5:18 to describe a woman's hair loose and flowing (*cf*. Jdg. 5:2 where 'the leaders took the lead' might probably be translated 'the flowing locks were loosed', a reference to a Nazirite vow undertaken for the purposes of a holy war against Sisera). **6–8** The Nazirite was forbidden to touch a dead body—even in the case of close relatives—because the mark of his Nazirite state (*separation*) was on his head.

9–12 Procedure following a broken vow. 9 If a Nazirite touched a dead body unwittingly or accidentally, as when a man died suddenly beside him, his vow must begin all over again. His consecrated head was to be shaved and he undertook seven days of purification, after which his head was shaved again. **10–12** On the eighth day the least expensive form of offering, *two turtle doves or two young pigeons*, were brought to the priest at the door of the tent of meeting, one for a *burnt offering* and one for a *sin offering* because his sin was unwitting. Thus covered he began anew his period of separation and offered a guilt-offering, possibly to compensate for his delay in fulfilling his vow.

13–21 Procedures following the fulfilment of the vow. 13a The Nazirite vow was not a permanent vow but was terminable. There were proper procedures to be observed and a variety of offerings to present. *Cf*. the offerings of the eighth day for the consecration of a priest (Lv. 9:1–22). **13b–17** The Nazirite was brought (or came, the text is obscure) to the door of the tent of meeting to offer a gift to Yahweh consisting of an unblemished male lamb in its first year for a *burnt offering*, an unblemished ewe lamb in its first year for a *sin offering*, and an unblemished ram as a *peace offering* along with the prescribed cereal-offerings and drink-offerings to be offered by the priest. **18** The Nazirite shaved his consecrated head at the door of the tent of meeting and burned the hair in *the* *fire . . . under the sacrifice of the peace offering.* The Lord's portion in this case was the fat, the kidneys and the liver (*cf.* Lv. 3:9–11). The hair belonged with these items as things that were holy (set apart) to Yahweh. Hair was especially significant not only in Israel, but in many other lands, perhaps because its rapid growth symbolized the divine strength that was given to men (*cf.* Samson, Jdg. 13–16). **19, 20** Presumably the officiating priest took the normal portions of the ram of the peace-offering, *i.e.* the thigh, while the priests took the breast as in Lv. 3:6–11; 7:28–34; 10:14, 15. In the Nazirite ceremony the priests received symbolically from the hand of the released Nazirite the shoulder of the ram after it had been boiled, and one of the wafers. These he waved before the Lord and then took them as his own holy portion together with the breast and the thigh. Since the peace-offering was normally one in which the offerer himself shared (*cf.* Lv. 7:11–21) it would seem that the conclusion of the Nazirite vow was celebrated with a family sacrificial meal and the drinking of wine. **21** The offerings prescribed were the minimum but it was open for the Nazirite to offer *what else he can afford.* The only proviso was that he must discharge the vow he promised.

6:22–27 The priestly benediction. 22, 23 Here is one of Israel's most beautiful benedictions expressed in three pairs of invocations addressed to Yahweh, Israel's God. **24** First, Yahweh is invited positively to *bless* the people (with crops, herds, flocks, good seasons, offspring, *etc.*), and negatively to *keep* them (from all evil, bad harvests, enemies, barren flocks and herds, childlessness). **25** Secondly, Yahweh is invited to turn towards His people in pleasurable acceptance of them (*cf.* Ps. 31:16) and to bestow His favour on them. **26** Thirdly, He is invited to *lift up his countenance* towards His people in recognition and approval and to give them *peace, i.e.* to grant them totality of well-being, wholeness and completeness in every way. **27** In the act of blessing the people the priest put the divine *name* on Israel, *i.e.* he declared that they belonged to God since His name connoted His person, and he who has God's name upon him is assured of God's blessing.

7:1 – 8:26 The offerings of the leaders and miscellaneous laws and regulations

7:1–89 The offerings of the leaders of the tribes. This chapter, perhaps the longest in the OT, is a monotonous repetition of one formula repeated twelve times with a change only in the name of the leader and the tribe. Such repetition emphasizes the very great generosity of the leaders as an example for future generations. The gifts provided for the equipment and transport of the Tabernacle and its furniture. The offerings of each leader were a silver plate weighing 130 shekels, a silver basin of 70 shekels, both full of fine flour mixed with oil for a cereal-offering, a golden dish of 10 shekels full of incense, one young bull, one ram, one male lamb a year old for a burnt-offering, one male goat for a sin-offering, and for the sacrifice of peace-offerings two oxen, five rams, five male goats, and five male lambs a year old. The gifts were brought 'on the day when Moses had finished setting up the tabernacle, and had anointed and consecrated it with all its furnishings, and had anointed the altar with its utensils' (v. 1). The Tabernacle had been set up on the first day of the first month in the second year after the Exodus (*cf.* Ex. 40:17). On the first day of the second month the census was ordered (*cf.* 1:1, 2). The events of ch. 7 must precede those of ch. 1; the order is not chronological. Possibly the information in this chapter was placed here because of references to the wagons and transport.

1–10 The wagons and the oxen. **2** The *leaders* are those of ch. 2 arranged in the same order. **3** They brought *six covered wagons,* one for every two leaders, and twelve oxen, one for each leader. The other gifts were brought on successive days, gold and silver vessels, and the various offerings for the dedication of the sanctuary and for the first offerings. The exact nature of the wagons (Heb. *ṣāḇ,* Akkad. *ṣumbu*) is not clear. In some traditions (Sifra and Targum Onkelos) these were covered wagons, in others (Symmachus) they were wagons for military service. In Is. 66:20 the word is translated 'litters'. The translation of the Jewish Publication Society of America is 'draught carts'. **4–8** The wagons and oxen were accepted by Moses and given to the Levites, two to the Gershonites, and four to the Merarites. **9** The Kohathites did not receive wagons since they had to carry the holiest of the Tabernacle furnishings on their shoulders. The expression *holy things* is singular in the Hebrew text and refers collectively to the sanctuary and all that was in it. **10** The term *dedication* (Heb. *ḥanukkâ*) became popular in later times in Israel.

11–88 The gifts for the dedication of the altar. The rest of the chapter is devoted to a detailed listing of the gifts of the leaders according to a standard formula. Several types of offering are mentioned: cereal-offering, burnt-offering, sin-offering, peace-offerings. Incidentally, the sin-offering is not listed among the offerings at the dedication of the later sanctuaries, the first Temple (*cf.* 1 Ki. 8:64), or the second Temple (*cf.* 1 Macc. 4:53, 56). In the list of vessels the silver plates (Heb. *qeʿārâ*) were deep dishes weighing 130 shekels (*c.* 52 oz.), the silver basins or bowls (Heb. *mizrāq*) were used for tossing the blood on the altar and weighed 70 shekels (28 oz.), and the golden dishes (Heb. *kaḇ*) were small vessels shaped like the palm of the hand and weighed ten shekels (*c.* 4 oz.). The grand total of all the offerings is carefully listed at the conclusion of the individual lists.

89 Moses in the tent of meeting. The concluding verse of the chapter makes the simple declaration that Yahweh spoke with Moses from between the two golden cherubim which rested on the mercy seat when Moses went into the tent of meeting (*cf.* Ex. 25:18–22; 37:7–9).

8:1–26 Miscellaneous laws and regulations. 1–4 The lighting of the lamps. **1–3** Instructions for the making of the lamps occur in Ex. 25:31–40; 37:17–24. The instruction here concerns the setting up of the lamps by Aaron (*cf.* Ex. 30:8; Lv. 24:2f.). His sons shared the responsibility (*cf.* Ex. 27:21). The lamps were to shed their light towards the front of the lampstand across to the table on the north side (*cf.* Ex. 40:22–25). **4** The lampstand was made of *hammered* (or beaten) . . . *gold* and was evidently beaten out both towards its base and towards its flower-shaped oil cups *according to the pattern which the Lord had shown Moses* (*cf.* Ex. 25:9, 40). It is idle to conjecture the exact manner in which Moses discovered the will of Yahweh in this matter.

5–22 The purification and presentation of the Levites to Yahweh. **5–7** There was an elaborate ritual for the purification of the Levites. **6** *Cleanse.* The verb is *ṭihar*; *cf.* the stronger verb *qiddēš*, 'to consecrate', used of the priests in Ex. 28:41; Lv. 8:12. First, *water of expiation* was sprinkled on them (*cf.* complete washing of priests, Lv. 8:6); then all the hair was shaved from their bodies and their clothes were washed (*cf.* new clothes of the priests, Lv. 8:13). **8, 9** Being thus cleansed they brought *a young bull and its cereal offering* as a burnt-offering, and *another young bull for a sin offering*. Moses presented the Levites at the tent of meeting where *the whole congregation of the people of Israel* was assembled to lay their hands on the Levites. **10** The laying on of the hands must have been done in some representative way, *e.g.* by the laying of the hands of the twelve tribal leaders upon representative Levites. **11** Similarly Aaron's offering the Levites before the Lord as a wave-offering was symbolic. As such they were allotted to the priests for the service of Yahweh. **12** Thus set apart, the Levites laid their hands on the animals they had brought and Aaron offered these as an *atonement* (covering). These verses are of considerable value as evidence for the meaning of the laying on of hands. In v. 10, the Levites are designated by this rite to act as substitutes for the nation, and, by equality of reasoning, the animals are thus appointed to substitute for the Levites. The same substitutionary significance of the rite is found in Lv. 16:21. **13** This verse does not suggest a second wave-offering but is merely repetitive, as so often in Hebrew. **14, 15** Thereafter the Levites were ready to commence their duties. **16, 17** Once again the representative character of the Levites is affirmed. They were a substitute for the firstborn of Israel (*cf.* 3:11–13) and they were wholly given to Yahweh (*cf.* 3:9). There is a backward reference here to the firstborn of Egypt which may indicate that the original comparison was made with the firstborn of Israel who were delivered in Egypt (see on 3:40–51). **18, 19** The Levites were to act as a

cover or screen between the people and the Holy Place so that none of the common people might approach the sanctuary and risk sudden divine judgment (*cf.* 1:53). *Atonement* here takes its original sense of 'cover'. **20–22** The instructions were carried out according to the divine command. *Purified themselves*, literally 'to de-sin oneself', *i.e.* remove the defilement of sin.

23–26 Age limits for Levites. **23, 24** The lower age limit here is twenty-five (*cf.* thirty in 4:3, and twenty in 1 Ch. 23:24, 27, *etc.*). Evidently the age limit varied from time to time. The compiler of ancient records simply recorded the variant practices. **25, 26** Although the Levites retired from normal duties at fifty they could give voluntary service and assist their younger brethren.

9:1–14 The supplementary Passover

9:1–8 A new problem for Moses. 1–3 Normally the Passover was observed at the appointed time on the fourteenth day of the first month (Nisan) according to the statutes and ordinances laid down (*cf.* Ex. 12:24–27; Dt. 16:1–8). It was held *in the evening* (lit. 'between the two evenings', *cf.* Lv. 23:5). **4, 5** The story is here set immediately after the setting up of the Tabernacle and a month before the census was taken at Sinai. **6–8** When some of the people were prevented from observing the Passover because of defilement through touching a corpse they sought advice about their own observance of the feast. It was a new problem and required divine guidance which Moses sought.

9:9–14 The solution. 9, 10 After consulting Yahweh Moses made known generous provisions both for the ritually unclean and for absent Israelites. **11, 12** The Passover was still to be observed but it could be postponed until the fourteenth day of the second month. It is assumed that the absentee would return so that the exile is not in view. The law was thus neither rigid nor automatic as to time, although observance of the feast was obligatory. The regulations in other respects were the same (*cf.* Ex. 12:8, 46). **13** This supplementary provision was not intended to encourage carelessness or abuse, however. All who were eligible and were at home and ritually clean were bound to keep the feast at the appointed time. Any man who absented himself was regarded as *cut off* from the people. Such a man was to *bear his sin*, *i.e.* to suffer the consequences of his sin. It is not clear what the expression 'cut off' denoted, whether excommunication or death, or whether the execution was to be human or divine. But in a close-knit covenant community neglect to commemorate with gratitude the great historic event which gave the nation birth was a heinous offence, and even ostracism and excommunication was 'death' of a kind. **14** *Stranger*, a resident alien or temporary sojourner (for whatever reason, *cf.* Gn. 15:13; Ex. 2:22; Dt. 10:19) who dwelt in Israel, shared its life and was subject to its laws (*cf.* Ex. 12:43–49). His sharing in the Passover feast did, of course, demonstrate Yahweh's concern for all under-privileged people, the fatherless, the widow and the resident alien alike (*cf*. Dt. 10:18).

9:15 – 10:10 The fiery cloud and the silver trumpets

9:15-23 The fiery cloud was both a symbol of the divine presence and a guide to the Israelites as they travelled (*cf*. Ex. 13:21, 22; 40:34-38). As they were about to leave Sinai the divine leadership was re-emphasized.

15, 16 *Tent of the testimony* (in the Pentateuch only here and in 17:7, 8; 18:2) is an alternative name for 'tent of meeting'. Whatever the nature of the cloud (and it is well-nigh useless to attempt an explanation, although some feasible ones have been offered), its brightness declared God's majesty and its darkness shrouded His glory (*cf*. 1 Ki. 8:12). The cloud was conceived as descending on the Tabernacle in order to show that Yahweh had taken up His abode there. (This was spoken of as the 'Shekinah' in later Jewish thought.) The cloud covered the Tabernacle *by day* (the phrase is lacking in the Hebrew but occurs in the main ancient versions; *cf*. RSV mg.), and *by night* it glowed. **17, 18** The movement of the cloud gave warning that the time had come to move camp. **19-23** The period during which the cloud remained over the camp varied from one day to *a longer time* (Heb. *yāmîm*, *i.e.* a year; *cf*. Lv. 25:29; Jdg. 17:10, *etc*.). The whole narrative, despite our uncertainty about the nature of the phenomenon, provides striking evidence of Israel's conviction that it was God who had led them by His providential care. They made camp, broke camp, and performed the service of God *at the command of the Lord*, literally 'at the mouth of Yahweh'.

10:1-10 The silver trumpets. 1, 2 So that Moses might have effective communication with the people and the leaders, either to summon them or to warn them that they were to break camp, two *silver trumpets* (Heb. *ḥaṣōṣᵉrâ*) were made of beaten silver. To judge from later representations on Jewish coins and on the arch of Titus in the Roman forum, these were long straight metal tubes with flaring ends, perhaps 3-4 feet long. They were distinct from the rams' horns (Heb. *šôpār*) or a second type of trumpet (Heb. *yôḇēl*). **3, 4** It is presumed that the trumpets sounded a different note. When one long blast on the two trumpets was blown *all the congregation* gathered *at the entrance of the tent of meeting*. If a long blast was blown on one trumpet only the leaders assembled. **5** A special kind of blast, an *alarm*, gave warning to the Judah camps on the east side to move. **6, 7** When the alarm was blown the second time the camps of Reuben on the south side were to move. LXX includes reference to similar alarms warning the Ephraim camps on the west and the Dan camps on the north. This alarm was evidently distinguishable from the trumpet blast which summoned the assembly and which was not an alarm. According to later tradition (Mishna Rosh Hashanah, 4:9)

the alarm was a succession of short blasts and was distinct from the sustained blast. **8** It was the priests who blew the trumpets, thus symbolizing the divine control over the camp. **9** Two further uses of the trumpets envisage the more settled conditions in the land. In time of war, when Israel faced her adversaries, an alarm was sounded to bring the needs of Israel to Yahweh's remembrance and to ensure victory. **10** Then again, at joyous religious celebrations, at regular festivals, and at new moons, trumpets were to be blown over the burnt-offerings and peace-offerings to bring Israel to Yahweh's remembrance. The phrases *that you may be remembered before the Lord* and *serve you for remembrance before your God* do not imply that Yahweh had forgotten His people but rather that Israel would not presume upon Yahweh even though He might declare *I am the Lord your God*.

10:11 – 12:16 THE JOURNEY FROM SINAI TO PARAN

Eleven months after arriving at Sinai (*cf*. Ex. 19:1) the Israelites broke camp and moved on. The story of what happened in the wilderness between Sinai and Kadesh is now recounted.

10:11-36 The departure from Sinai

10:11-28 The Israelites break camp. 11-13 In the second year after leaving Egypt in the second month the cloud moved on. Israel had been at Sinai just under one year. The journey led by stages to the wilderness of Paran, the traditional home of Ishmael (*cf*. Gn. 21:21). The exact location is not known. It was west of the Arabah, south of the Negeb (*cf*. Nu. 13:17) and between Midian and Sinai (*cf*. 1 Ki. 11:18) and is sometimes identified with the desert of Et-tîh in the north-centre of the Sinai peninsula. **14-16** The three camps of Judah under Nahshon—Judah, Issachar and Zebulun—went first. **17-21** When the Tabernacle had been dismantled the Gershonites and Merarites followed Judah with the three camps of Reuben under Elizur—Reuben, Simeon and Gad—following behind them. The order differs from that in ch. 2, but, clearly, no contradiction is involved, for the Kohathites carrying the sanctuary (*holy things*, Heb. *miqdāš*) remained in the centre of the advance, and it was a matter of practical convenience that the Gershonites and Merarites should proceed in advance so that the Tabernacle might be set up in a new resting-place ready for the arrival of its sacred furniture. **22-28** Then came the three camps of Ephraim under Ammihud—Ephraim, Manasseh and Benjamin—and in the rear the three camps of Dan under Ahiezer—Dan, Asher and Naphtali.

10:29-32 Hobab plans to return home. Four separate problems, of varying complexity, centre on these verses. The first is that here Hobab is described as a Midianite, whereas in Jdg. 4:11 he is said to be a Kenite. It is possible that we have here simply an indication of the overlapping of the ancient tribes. Jdg. 8:22–24, *e.g.*, speaks of Midianites who were Ishmaelites, and 1 Ch. 2:55 mentions Rechabite Kenites. The second problem is that here and in Ex. 2:18, Moses' father-in-law is named Reuel, but his name is given as Jethro in Ex. 3:1; 4:18; 18:1, 2. This problem is finally insoluble because we do not have the evidence which would lead to a solution. The double tradition of the name is most easily understood on the supposition that he possessed both names (*cf.* Jacob–Israel), though this does not explain why sometimes one was used and sometimes the other. (See *NBD*, art. 'Jethro'.) The third problem concerns the identity of the *Hobab* mentioned in this passage. Some commentators (*e.g.* A. E. Cundall, *TOTC Judges*, 1968, p. 56) identify Hobab with Jethro and regard Reuel as a remote ancestor. Those who identify Jethro with Reuel usually understand Hobab to be Moses' brother-in-law, a relationship which is made clear by alternative translation of the verses concerned (see Jdg. 4:11, RV). In the present passage we would suggest that the words *Moses' father-in-law*, or 'whose son-in-law Moses was', be understood to refer to *Reuel the Midianite*. Likewise in Jdg. 4:11 we ought to understand that the purpose of the verse is to tell us precisely to what branch of the Kenites Heber belonged, and that in fact the verse identifies the Kenites in question by two defining clauses: first that they were Hobab's branch of the clan, and secondly (as in Jdg. 1:16) that they were 'in-laws' of Moses. All these verses would then support the contention that Hobab was in fact Moses' brother-in-law. The fourth problem is whether Hobab consented to go with Moses or not. In the light of the subsequent presence of Kenites (Jdg. 1:16, *etc.*) with Israel, it is likely that Hobab acceded to Moses' request.

31 *You know how we are to encamp.* Some translators have proposed rendering this 'you know how to lead us' (reading *hanḥōṭēnû* for *ḥᵃnōṭēnû*), arguing that it makes a better parallel to *serve as eyes for us*. But clearly Moses wanted to provide a scouting service which in a hostile country would be needed just as much when they were in camp as when the people were on the move.

10:33–36 The ark and the people set out. 33, 34 The first stage of the journey from *the mount of the Lord* (the mountain where the law was given, Sinai) took three days. An alternative name for Sinai is Mount of God (*cf.* Ex. 3:1; 4:27; 18:5; 24:13, *etc.*) or Horeb. An apparent difficulty in this passage is that it appears that the ark preceded the Israelite column, whereas in vv. 13–28 and 2:17 the Tabernacle and its furniture, which might be presumed to include the ark, were set in the midst of the advancing Israelites. The present verse corrects our misapprehension and completes the picture: the ark preceded the advancing host to symbolize divine leadership on the journey (*cf.* Dt. 9:3; Jos. 3:3ff.).

Nothing in v. 21 or in 2:17 would necessarily preclude this. The remainder of the sacred vessels followed the camp of Reuben. The central issue, that Yahweh guided His people on their journey, is quite clear. **35, 36** Two ancient ritual formulae close the chapter. They seem to be snatches from ancient poems which hold the motif of the holy war strongly. When the ark went forth to battle men cried,

> 'Arise, O Yahweh! Let thy enemies
> be scattered;
> Let them that hate thee flee before thee.'

Cf. Pss. 68:1; 132:8. When the ark returned from battle men sang,

> 'Return, O Yahweh,
> To the countless hosts of Israel.'

The meaning is probably that after the victory Yahweh is invited to return to the midst of His people and to abide there. It is possible that Ps. 24 is a song of celebration when the ark returned after a victorious battle. *Cf.* also 1 Sa. 4:1–10.

11:1 – 12:16 Incidents between Sinai and Kadesh

The journey through the wilderness to Kadesh was marked by grumbling and acts of unfaithfulness in which Israel displayed deep ingratitude to God for His past mercies and well-nigh rejected the leadership of Moses. Chs. 11 and 12 deal with several motifs interwoven with one another, the flight of the quails, the manna, and the appointment of the seventy elders. The chapters provide an interesting illustration of the way Hebrew writers could hold several motifs together in one narrative.

11:1–3 Complaints at Taberah. 1 The people complained of their *misfortunes*. The verb complain (Heb. *'ānan*) occurs only here and in La. 3:39. The Akkadian cognate means 'sigh'. No doubt they suffered real deprivations. But in the midst of their complaining some calamity befell them described as *the fire of the Lord*. No explanation is given. In any case Israel understood a great many natural phenomena as acts of God, which, of course, they are. One could think of a number of possibilities among people living under a scorching desert sun. Some destruction was done in the outlying parts of the camp. The people called on Moses to plead with Yahweh and the trouble passed. The place was called *Taberah*, literally 'burning' (Heb. root b-'-r, 'burn'). The place cannot be identified with certainty.

11:4–9 Complaints about the manna. 4–6 The writer here blames the *rabble* for inciting the Israelites. These were probably the 'mixed multitude' of Ex. 12:38, the 'riff-raff', as the word has been translated. They had *a strong craving* for flesh and recalled the food they once enjoyed in Egypt, fish, cucumbers, leeks, onions, garlic, which contrasted with the plain food of the desert with its staple diet of manna. **7–9** An editorial note explains the reference to manna, what it was, how it was collected and prepared for eating. It was, no doubt, a divine provision, but none the less it may have been a natural substance. The *Tamarix gallica mannifera*, or *ṭarfa* tree, exudes a sweet, sticky, dark yellow substance by night which falls to the ground in small globules like the coriander seed, about the size of a peppercorn. As the day advances these melt in the sun. The season in the western Sinai peninsula begins at the end of May and continues into June and July, the time when the Israelites were in the desert (*cf.* 10:11). It resembles the resinous gum bdellium. The people asked 'What is it?' (Heb. *man hû*), hence the name *man*, or manna (*cf.* Ex. 16:15). It was collected early and ground up with simple hand-mills or mortars similar to those still used in the east. (See further on Ex. 16:1ff.)

11:10-15 Moses expostulates with God. 10, 11 The story of vv. 4-6 is now resumed. The complaint about food was only one of the many problems that confronted Moses and he expostulated with God. *Why hast thou dealt ill with thy servant?* His complaint, which was a lengthy one, gives a good picture of an overwrought leader for whom the sole responsibility for the people was too great a burden. **12** The pronouns *I* are emphatic. It was not Moses but God who brought this people to birth. But Moses had all the responsibility of them. **13-15** With a pathetic appeal to God the overwrought Moses confessed that the burden was too heavy for him to bear. If he must continue to carry the people, he requested, like others after him, that he might die (*cf.* Je. 20:14-18).

11:16-24a The divine response. 16, 17 Yahweh's reply was to instruct Moses to choose out seventy experienced *elders* and *officers* and take them to the door of the tent of meeting where he would meet them and endow them with a share of the spirit which Moses possessed. Clearly Moses' endowment was greater than theirs so that they were to be subordinate. The officers, as distinct from the elders, were originally scribes but acted as subordinate officials alongside the elders (*cf.* Ex. 4:29; 5:14. Clearly here the elders are the acknowledged leaders and the officers hold intermediate executive positions). **18** God, having remedied Moses' personal complaint, now dealt with the people. He promised them flesh, but since the meal they were about to eat was regarded as, in some sense, a sacred meal they were required to *consecrate* themselves, *i.e.* to make themselves ritually clean. **19, 20** The provision of flesh would be abundant but it would also be a judgment, for the people would eat gluttonously for a whole month until the flesh became *loathsome* and came out at their nostrils, a vivid metaphor of surfeiting. The fulfilment of their desire became their judgment. **21, 22** Moses, puzzled by the greatness of the promise, asked where such an abundance of flesh might come from for 600 'thousands' (military units) of fighting men, from flocks or herds, or from the sea. **23** Yahweh merely asked whether Moses imagined that His hand was

shortened (*cf.* Is. 50:2; 59:1, *etc.*). The sequel comes in vv. 31-35 after the story of the elders has been concluded.

11:24b-30 The appointment of elders. 24b Following the instructions given to him, Moses gathered seventy elders. **25** Yahweh came down as at Sinai (*cf.* Ex. 19:9, 18) in a special visitation and bestowed some of the *spirit* (Heb. *rûaḥ*), or supra-human power which Moses possessed, upon the elders. It ought not to be concluded that the spirit was something physical or material. Up to that time Moses alone had had the divine enablement for the task of administration. If others joined him, clearly they must share in the same 'spirit'. But we ought not to press the idea of dividing up what Moses had among others, but rather that through him as mediator there was granted to others something of what God had given him. When the spirit rested upon these men *they prophesied.* The same verb is used elsewhere of some kind of ecstatic behaviour (*cf.* 1 Sa. 10:11; 19:20, 23; 1 Ch. 25:1-3; 2 Ki. 3:15). The experience in the case of these elders was only temporary and marked their entrance into their sacred office; *they did so no more* but returned with Moses to the camp. Intense emotional response resulting in physical reactions are not unknown even today on the occasion of a man's induction to a noble office. **26** That the bestowal of the spirit was not dependent on the elders being in the same place at the same time is clear from the fact that two men, Eldad and Medad, who had been selected among the seventy but had not left the camp, were also endowed with the spirit and prophesied in the camp. **27, 28** Even Joshua misunderstood when a young man reported that Eldad and Medad were prophesying in the camp and urged Moses to forbid them. **29, 30** Moses rebuked Joshua for becoming excited (the word *jealous*, Heb. *qānā'*, denotes 'become excited either with zeal or jealousy'). *Would that all the Lord's people were prophets, that the Lord would put his spirit upon them!* was Moses' reply, for he recognized that the spirit enabling him was not his own, and therefore not motivated by any thought of self-glory, but the divine Spirit. (See further the General Article, 'Old Testament Theology' on the Person and work of the Holy Spirit in the OT.) The principle here enunciated by Moses is applicable to every age. Would that today all the Lord's people were prophets, *i.e.* spokesmen for God, and that the Lord would put His Spirit upon them.

11:31-35 The quails and God's judgment. 31 The outcome of the people's demand for flesh is now described. The Lord sent a wind which brought quails from the sea, probably the Gulf of Aqabah. This is a natural phenomenon and still today the quails migrate in the spring (March, April) from Africa and return in the autumn (September). They travel up the Red Sea and cross the Sinai Peninsula towards Palestine and often fall exhausted to be picked up by local inhabitants for eating or for sale.

In the present narrative the quails were distributed over a total width of two days' journey. *And about two cubits.* A very old interpretation understands this to refer to the flight of the birds about 3 feet above ground, so that they were easily caught in nets. It may be, of course, that we ought to understand *let them fall* in a more literal sense and that the quails came in such abundance that they covered the ground to a depth of 3 feet. Either way it is a miracle of divine timing and of divine abundance. 32 For two days and the intervening night the people collected the birds. The smallest catch was *ten homers*, over 100 bushels, surely an indication of gluttony. The Hebrew text occasions some difficulty. It appears to read, *they spread them out for themselves all around the camp.* The verb 'spread out' (Heb. *šāṭaḥ*) occurs in some MSS with the second and third consonants of the root transposed to give the verb *šāḥaṭ*, 'slaughter'. If this reading is accepted there is an easy transition to the next verse. 33 The birds freshly slaughtered were gluttonously devoured. The *plague* that broke out may have been some violent stomach upset. 34 Evidently numbers died, for the place was called *Kibroth-hattaavah* (lit. 'graves of craving'). The place cannot be identified with certainty. One possibility is Ruweis el-Ebeirig a few miles north-east of the traditional Sinai. 35 The next stopping-place was *Hazeroth*, possibly 'Ain Khudra a little further on.

12:1–16 The uniqueness of Moses. The heart of the present chapter is the challenge of Aaron and Miriam to the privileged position and uniqueness of Moses.

1, 2 Ostensibly Miriam and Aaron complained that Moses had married a Cushite woman. The verb, however, is third person feminine singular, suggesting that originally it was Miriam alone who spoke. Later, Miriam alone was punished (v. 10). The ostensible ground of the complaint appears to be that Moses married a foreign woman: the reference may even be to Zipporah, who was, of course, a Midianitess (Ex. 2:15), for Midian and Cushan are linked, *e.g.* in Hab. 3:7. But the real challenge was, *Has the Lord indeed spoken only through Moses? Has he not spoken through us also?* Miriam did have certain gifts. She is called a prophetess in Ex. 15:20 and is linked with Moses and Aaron in Mi. 6:4. **3** Whatever gifts and functions Miriam and Aaron might have had, however, Moses was unique. He was *very meek, i.e.* a humble man who was more concerned to be the servant of Yahweh than to advance his own status. **4, 5** God was concerned to vindicate His servant and summoned him and Miriam and Aaron to the tent of meeting, where He called Miriam and Aaron apart and declared His mind. **6–8** The utterance of God is given in poetic form in the standard 3:3 metre of Hebrew epic poetry. There are some textual difficulties. One possible solution is as follows:

'Hear my words: If there is a prophet among
     you
I the Lord make myself known to him in a
     vision: I speak with him in a dream;
Not so with my servant Moses: He is trusted
     throughout my house.
With him I speak mouth to mouth: plainly,
     and not in riddles: And he beholds the form
     of the Lord.
Why then do you not shrink: from speaking
     against my servant Moses?'

In substance God was saying that His communication with Moses was in the immediacy of personal contact, but with others by way of dreams and in riddles. The recognition of this unique status should have kept Miriam and Aaron from every jealous complaint. **9, 10** Divine judgment fell on Miriam and she became *leprous, as white as snow.* Her complaint was not, however, true leprosy, but a milder skin complaint (*cf.* v. 12; Lv. 13:10ff.). **11, 12** Aaron at once acknowledged Moses' supremacy saying, *Oh, my lord, do not punish us because we have done foolishly and have sinned*, or alternatively, 'Do not account to us the sin which we have committed in our folly' (Jewish Translation). **13** Moses, fearing that Miriam might become a true leper, asked the Lord to deliver her. **14, 15** Miriam was spared the full judgment of leprosy but had to suffer public shame by being excluded from the camp seven days. The argument is that even in a family dispute which resulted in the father administering such a strong rebuke (*cf.* Dt. 25:9; Is. 50:6) a seven-day period of shame would follow; how much more when God's authority is flouted! Nevertheless, the divine displeasure was tempered with restoring grace. The mercy of God towards sinful men in every age is a continuing wonder. He may chastise His children as a loving father, but even His judgment is tempered with mercy, as many a believer in this 20th century has discovered. **16** The next stage of the journey took the people to the wilderness of Paran.

13:1 – 20:13 THE SOJOURN AT KADESH IN THE WILDERNESS

The period which the Israelites spent around Kadesh was important and probably allowed time for consolidation after the experience at Sinai. It lasted a whole generation (14:34). Details are few. The period began in fear and lack of faith following the return of a reconnaissance party from the land of Canaan and it ended with a plan to enter Canaan from the east rather than from the south.

13:1–33 The mission and report of the reconnaissance party

13:1–17a The selection of the spies. 1–3 The reconnaissance party comprised a representative leader from each of the twelve tribes. **4–16** Apart from Joshua (*Hoshea*), son of Nun of the tribe of Ephraim, and *Caleb*, son of Jephunneh of the tribe of Judah, these men are not otherwise known, although several of the names are known simply as names. As usual, the names had meanings (see *IB*, Vol. II, pp. 204, 205).

13:17b–20 The commission of the spies. The task of the spies was defined. Information was required from both the Negeb (south country) and the mountain regions about the nature of the land, the strength and number of the people and the character of the cities, whether open encampments or walled towns. Moses encouraged the party and asked them to bring back samples of the fruit of the land. It was *the season of the first ripe grapes*, the end of July.

13:21–24 The reconnaissance in Canaan. 21 The reconnaissance extended from Zin in the south to Rehob in the north (probably Bethrehob, 2 Sa. 10:6, near Laish-Dan, Jdg. 18:27–29). *Near the entrance of Hamath* may be the name of a place, Lebo-Hamath, in the Beqa' Valley between the Lebanon and Anti-Lebanon ranges. **22** The investigation began in the Negeb and extended to Hebron in its first phase. Hebron was known to the patriarchs under another name (*cf.* Gn. 23:2; 35:27) and Abraham, Isaac, Jacob, Sarah, Rebekah and Leah were buried in the region. The town was founded 7 years before Zoan (Tanis or Avaris), the capital of the Hyksos rulers in Egypt (*c.* 1720–1570 BC). Descendants of a former mighty warrior Anak lived in Hebron. **23, 24** On their return the spies gathered grapes, pomegranates and figs in the *Valley of Eshcol* (lit. 'cluster').

13:25–33 The return and report of the spies. 25, 26 Forty days later the spies reported to Moses and Aaron and all the people at Kadesh and displayed the fruit they had brought. **27–29** Three features of the report are significant in the light of modern archaeological discovery. First, the reference to *milk and honey* is a traditional description of a fruitful land. The Egyptian Tale of Sinuhe (*c.* 2000 BC) uses this expression of the area north of Galilee. Secondly, the reference to fortified cities is factual. Numerous walled cities, 5 to 15 or 20 acres in size, were scattered over the land, *e.g.* Jericho, about 7 acres. Thirdly, the population was indeed a mixed one. Written records show the presence of Amorites, Hittites, Canaanites, Indo-Europeans, *etc.* The *Amorites*, who had come to Palestine in great numbers before 2000 BC, are known to have been in the mountains both E and W of the Jordan. The *Hittites* were offshoots of the powerful Hittite Empire in Asia Minor. The *Canaanites* inhabited the fertile areas of the Jordan Valley and the coastlands. The *Amalekites* were nomads. Other groups were probably ancient indigenous people. **30** Caleb and Joshua advised the immediate occupation of the land as being within the competence of the people. **31–33** The majority report betrayed fear and lack of faith and discouraged the people with a terrifying account of *a land that devours its inhabitants* and of the presence of giants and Nephilim, sons of the legendary Anak before whom Israel would be as grasshoppers. How typical of God's people in every age! Fear and lack of faith have often been the cause of stagnation and lack of advance towards victory, resulting in final defeat. The man of faith is assured of victory because, finally, the victory is the Lord's.

14:1–45 The reaction of the people and the judgment of God

14:1–10a The complaints and rebellion of the people. 1–3 The first reaction of the people was to cry aloud and to weep while they murmured against Moses and Aaron, declaring that it would have been better to remain in Egypt than to die by the sword in the wilderness and surrender their wives and children as spoil. **4** In an attitude of rebellion the people determined to choose a leader to take them back to Egypt. **5** Moses and Aaron prostrated themselves in earnest pleading before the people. **6–10a** Caleb and Joshua *rent their clothes* and assured the people that the land was *an exceedingly good land* and that if the Lord were pleased to do so He would lead them there. Only they must not rebel against Him, nor fear the people of the land whom they would destroy with Yahweh's help. The only response of the people was to threaten to stone those who pleaded with them.

14:10b–19 The intercession of Moses. 10b–12 The glory of the Lord was presently displayed at the tent of meeting, and the Lord accused Israel of unbelief despite all the *signs* He had *wrought among them*. The signs were the miracles and wonders performed in Egypt. God now proposed to strike the people with *pestilence* and to disinherit them. In their place He would make of Moses *a nation greater and mightier than they*. **13–16** Moses' plea with God on behalf of the people is a moving one. Were the Egyptians to hear that God proposed to disinherit the people they would inform the inhabitants of the land who at present believed that Yahweh was in the midst of this people where He was to be seen *face to face* and whom He overshadowed by the pillar of cloud and the pillar of fire. If He were to destroy them the nations who knew His *fame* (reputation) would conclude that He lacked the power to bring His people into the land, with the result that He would be disgraced. **17–19** Moses now urged Yahweh to show His power and to display His character as One who was *slow to anger, and abounding in steadfast love, forgiving iniquity and transgression, but will by no means clear the guilty, visiting the iniquity of fathers upon children, upon the third and upon the fourth generation*. This formula, repeated from Ex. 34:6, 7, occurs in whole or in part in an almost liturgical fashion in several places in the OT (*cf.* Joel 2:13; Jon. 4:2). *Steadfast love* (Heb. *ḥeseḏ*) is a peculiarly significant word expressing the qualities of loyalty, faithfulness and steadfastness which are to be found in One who is true to His covenant and to His obligations. It occurs about 250 times in the OT with strong overtones of the loyalty and the commitment to one another of the parties to a covenant. Moses' plea was a strong appeal to God's gracious nature for He had *forgiven this people, from Egypt even until now.*

14:20–25 The divine answer. 20–23 God's answer was to pardon the people. He would not wipe them out in their entirety. But none of the rebels or doubters who had seen His glory or witnessed His acts of deliverance in Egypt and in the wilderness, and who had tested Him and disobeyed Him over and over again (lit. *these ten times*), would enter the land of promise. This declaration was made on oath: *As I live, and as all the earth shall be filled with the glory of the Lord, none of these men . . . shall see the land.* **24** Caleb, however, who was controlled by *a different spirit* and had followed the Lord fully, would enter the land of promise and his descendants would possess it. **25** The final word from Yahweh was that Israel was to turn back southwards. The way north was cut off by the Amalekites and Canaanites who dwelt in the fertile valleys.

14:26–38 The death of a faithless generation. 26, 27 The complaints or murmurings of the Israelites referred to in previous chapters reached a climax with the outburst of 14:1–10. Three times in v. 27 their murmuring is mentioned. Now God declares His mind. **28–33** With an oath—*As I live*—God declared that all those above twenty who had murmured would perish in the wilderness, except Joshua and Caleb. The children for whose future the murmurers feared (*cf.* v. 3) would enter the land, albeit after a period of being *shepherds in the wilderness.* The verb *swore* in v. 30 is literally 'lift up the hand', a common gesture in oath-taking in many lands. **34, 35** According to the number of days the spies spent in reconnaissance, *forty*, would be the number of years spent in the wilderness. The number is probably a symbolic one denoting a generation. In a bold metaphor God expresses His *displeasure* (lit. 'alienation, enmity'). God had spoken; His word would come to pass. **36, 37** The passage seems to imply a sudden *plague* or calamity which carried off the offenders, although this is not certain. Their death may have occurred over a period of time. **38** Joshua and Caleb were spared according to the promise.

14:39–45 The presumption of the people and their defeat. 39, 40 Further evidence of Israel's rebellious attitude is now seen in their refusal to accept the command to turn back into the wilderness. Despite their fearful attitude when they first received the report of the spies, they now determined to press on with the conquest, seeking to cover that first offence with a glib confession, *We have sinned.* **41–43** Moses declared that the people were *transgressing the command of the Lord* and would not succeed but would fall before the Amalekites and Canaanites. In such a campaign, which was no holy war, the Lord would not be with them. **44, 45** The people *presumed* (lit. 'were headstrong, reckless') and were severely defeated and chased as far as Hormah, possibly Tell el-Mishash, 10 miles E of Beersheba. The name *Hormah*, derived from the root *ḥ-r-m*, means 'complete destruction'. The victory over the Canaanites was delayed for 'many days' (Dt. 1:46) or alternatively 'forty years' or a 'generation'. (See further on Nu. 21:3.)

15:1–41 Miscellaneous laws and regulations

Five sets of regulations have been grouped here by the editor(s). They were to apply to Israel, 'when you come into the land you are to inhabit'. Even if, in their present form, they represent the work of an editor, it ought not to be concluded that Moses was silent about what Israel should do under more settled circumstances.

15:1–16 The prescribed cereal- and drink-offerings. 1, 2 This legislation does not apply to the wilderness period, although it is not unlikely that similar provisions, albeit perhaps not so complex or so prescribed, were in force in the wilderness, *e.g.* the giving of a cereal-offering of some kind. **3–5** When an offering was made from the herd or flock a cereal-offering was to be associated with it. The term *offering by fire* is applied to any offering that was burned, whether completely like the whole burnt-offering, or partly burned like the peace-offering (*cf.* Lv. 3:3–5). When such sacrifices were offered either to fulfil a vow, or as a free-will offering, or as a regular appointed feast, a cereal-offering of flour mixed with oil, and wine for a drink-offering, were to accompany the sacrifice. For a lamb the quantity was one tenth of an ephah of fine flour, one fourth of a hin of oil and a fourth of a hin of wine. The ephah was a little under 5 gallons and the hin about 6½ pints. **6, 7** The prescriptions for a ram were two-tenths of an ephah of flour, a third of a hin of oil and a third of a hin of wine. **8, 9** The prescriptions for a bull were three-tenths of an ephah of flour, a half a hin of oil, and a half a hin of wine. The quantities increased with the size of the animal. *Cf.* Ezk. 46:4–15 where there is no drink-offering. *Pleasing odour* (vv. 3, 7, 10) is a metaphor in which God is pictured as taking pleasure in the smoke of the offerings which rose heavenwards. The way in which the drink-offering was used is not defined, but it was probably poured over the offering to provide a pleasing odour (*cf.* v. 7).

11–16 These regulations were to apply both to the *native* Israelite and to the *stranger*, the resident alien. Three different words are used in these verses to describe the legal provisions which governed Israel: *law* (*tôrâ*, v. 16), *ordinance* (*mišpāṭ*, v. 16) and *statute* (*ḥuqqâ*, v. 15). *Law* (lit. 'teaching') indicates that this material came by revelation, direct from the divine Teacher; *statute* (from the verb 'to engrave') indicates its abiding, unchangeable nature; and *ordinance* is the particular application of the divine will to specific topics and situations.

15:17-21 The offering of coarse grain. A portion of the first *coarse meal* was taken from the threshing-floor and made into a *cake. Offering.* The AV term 'heave offering' refers to the 'lifting up' or removal of a portion for Yahweh. The offering of the first of the grain symbolized the fact that all the grain had come from God and was His by right. The law was probably intended to mean that from each new batch of barley meal a token portion was extracted for the use of the priests.

15:22-31 The sin-offering for unknown sins. 22–26 Two classes of unwitting sin are in view here. The first is that of the community. *Cf.* Lv. 4 and 5 where two other classes are added. The ritual here is much simpler than that in Leviticus. Here, the congregation was required to offer one young bull for a burnt-offering, and one male goat for a sin-offering, together with the appropriate cereal- and drink-offering. *The priest shall make an atonement for all the congregation of the people of Israel.* Both they and the resident alien were then forgiven. 27–29 In the case of an individual who committed sin unwittingly the sin-offering was a female goat a year old. The same law applied to native Israelites or resident aliens. 30, 31 By contrast the man who acted *with a high hand, i.e.* wantonly or deliberately, whether Israelite or resident alien, was to be cut off from Israel and to bear the consequences of his iniquity. What this judgment implied is not clear (see on 9:13). On these categories of sin, *cf.* the General Article, 'Old Testament Theology'; and for the significance of these ancient cultic ceremonies for the modern man, read the section 'Religious value' in the Introduction, p. 170. See also comments on chs. 28, 29.

15:32-36 The sabbath breaker. 32, 33 An example of sinning with a high hand is now given. A man was found *gathering sticks on the sabbath day.* He was brought to Moses and Aaron and the whole congregation for judgment. 34, 35 The case was adjourned until Yahweh had *made plain what should be done to him.* The penalty was death by stoning (*cf.* Ex. 31:14f.; 35:2). 36 The fact that the whole congregation was to be involved in the stoning meant that the responsibility was distributed over everyone. The sentence was carried out *outside the camp.* Whether the law was applied in this exact fashion as a regular thing in Israel is doubtful.

15:37-41 The wearing of tassels. 37, 38 The people were commanded to make *tassels* (AV 'fringes') on the *corners* of their garments. The terms are variously interpreted. Possibly the fringe was continuous around all four edges of the garment. The threads of the fringe were twisted together in groups to form a fringe of tassels. At each corner there was to be a cord of blue. 39–41 The function of the tassels was to remind the people to obey the commandments of Yahweh and not to follow their own will.

Obedience was the mark of a holy people. Some of the phrases in vv. 40 and 41 are reminiscent of Ex. 20:1f.; Lv. 19:36; 22:33; 26:13, *etc.* The recollection of the saving acts of Yahweh was a strong motive for obedience. The same motif appears in the secular treaties of Moses' time.

16:1-50 The rebellion of Korah and of Dathan and Abiram

The two struggles depicted here were, no doubt, typical of many such. One of these was a revolt led by Korah the Levite and the other was a revolt led by laymen Dathan and Abiram. In each case the rebels were challenged to put the matter to the test and in each case the authority of Moses and Aaron was upheld. The stories are interwoven in the present narrative and some difficulty is experienced in following the details of each. As in the books of Kings, the writer keeps both stories under consideration. There is no reason to deny that the two revolts occurred simultaneously.

16:1-11 The names of the rebels and the rebellion of Korah. 1 The names of the rebels and the genealogy are given. 2, 3 It would appear that with these verses the narrative turns to the rebellion of Korah. *Took men.* The Hebrew text is uncertain. The verb 'take' appears alone and the word 'men' is lacking. An alternative suggestion is that the root is not *l-q-ḥ*, 'take', but *w-q-ḥ*, 'act insolently'. In that case v. 2a simply states that the rebels listed acted insolently. Then the narrative begins, *They rose up before Moses, with a number of the people of Israel, two hundred and fifty leaders of the congregation.* These *well-known men* challenged Moses and Aaron: *You have gone too far!* It was a protest against the setting apart of the family of Aaron for the duties and privileges of the priesthood. 4–7 Moses prostrated himself in entreaty to God, for the offence was grievous. Then he bade Korah to prepare for a test. The mention of Korah here indicates that the passage is concerned with the rebellious Korahite group. The next day Korah and his group were to appear before the Lord with censers in which there was fire and incense and God would show who was holy (set apart), they or Aaron. Then Moses turned back their accusation against them, *You have gone too far!* 8–11 Moses then reminded the Levites of the privileged position they occupied. They had been set apart from all Israel for the service of the Tabernacle, no small thing. Would they seek the priesthood also? Their revolt was against Yahweh, for who was Aaron that they should murmur against him? It is clear that the rebelling group is a group of Levites. Either the 'leaders' of v. 2 were Levites, or supporting leaders who are neglected in the subsequent events (but *cf.* vv. 16, 17).

16:12-15 The rebellion of Dathan and Abiram. 12 The rebelling laymen are introduced. They were Reubenites. Moses summoned them before him but they refused to come. 13, 14 The nature of their rebellion is revealed in their reply to

Moses. They held the view that Moses should have been content to lead the people out of Egypt. Why should he now act as a *prince*? In any case he had not led them to the promised land of milk and honey nor given them an inheritance of fields and vineyards. All that was a blind for his ambition. The Hebrew idiom *put out the eyes* is equivalent to 'throw dust in the eyes'. **15** Moses in anger asked the Lord not to receive their offerings. For his part his whole attitude had been one of the highest integrity, for he had never defrauded any man (*cf.* 1 Sa. 12:3).

16:16–24 The testing of Korah. 16, 17 The command given to Korah (vv. 6, 7) is repeated. It seems that the 250 men of v. 2 were Levites. In addition to this group Aaron would appear before the Lord with his censer. **18, 19** The challenge was accepted and next day the Levites appeared as commanded with the whole congregation. *And the glory of the Lord appeared.* **20, 21** Moses and Aaron were bidden to stand apart from the assembled company lest they were consumed with them. **22–24** Moses and Aaron, realizing the impending judgment, fell down and called on God, *the God of the spirits of all flesh* (*cf.* 27:16), *i.e.* the God who sustains the physical life of all creatures. Their plea was, 'When one man sins will You be wrathful with the whole community?' But the Lord commanded Moses to urge the people to withdraw from the dwellings of Korah, Dathan and Abiram. The two stories seem to overlap at this point and some commentators have asked whether the phrase in v. 24, *dwelling of Korah . . .*, might not have read originally 'the Tabernacle of Yahweh' since the noun *miškān* ('dwelling') is not normally used for the dwelling of individuals but commonly for the Tabernacle. Comparison with v. 32 indicates that Korah was included in the judgment of Dathan and Abiram. Perhaps the literary expression is a device for indicating that all the rebels were caught up finally in the divine judgment.

16:25–34 The testing of Dathan and Abiram. 25 The trial of Dathan and Abiram is next described. The elders of Israel were present. **26, 27a** Once again the people were urged to stand apart from the tents of the rebels lest they were swept away. **27a**, along with vv. 24 and 32, constitutes a special problem since these verses appear to be generalized statements in which the rebels of both groups are mentioned together. The present section is concerned with Dathan and Abiram. **27b–30** Dathan and Abiram appeared with their families at the door of their tents as Moses drew near. Moses declared the nature of the test. If the men were innocent no calamity would befall them but they would die a natural death in due course. But if the Lord did something spectacular (*creates something new*, lit. 'creates a creation') by opening up the ground and swallowing them and their families, it would be proof that they were guilty. It was a grim reminder of the doctrine of family solidarity. The doctrine, which has its positive value,

expresses the view that a man's evil deeds may sometimes involve his family in judgment. **31–34** When Moses had finished speaking the ground opened and swallowed up the offenders and their families and goods. The people fled in terror lest the judgment should touch them also.

16:35–50 The judgment of Korah and the aftermath. 35 Resuming the story of the Korahite revolt from vv. 16–24 the narrator tells us that *fire came forth from the Lord, and consumed the two hundred and fifty men offering the incense.* **36–40** A question arose as to what should be done with the censers which had been used illegally. Their fire was to be scattered so that no-one might use this 'holy' fire since, even if it was used illegally, it had entered the sanctuary and so belonged to the Lord. The censers likewise were holy and could not be used for secular purposes. They were to be beaten into *plates* to cover the altar and to remain as a warning and a reminder of what would happen to others who followed Korah's example. Only priests might approach the sanctuary to offer incense before Yahweh. **41** The troubles were not yet over, for the next day the people blamed Moses and Aaron for the death of Korah's group. **42** In a hostile demonstration the people gathered at the tent of meeting. **43–45** When Moses and Aaron appeared, the Lord bade them withdraw from the people so that He might consume them in a moment. They both fell prostrate in intercession. **46–50** Moses commanded Aaron to run to the sanctuary to bring his censer which carried the legitimate fire and incense, so that he might provide an *atonement* (covering) for the people against the judgment (*plague*) that had broken out. The plague was stopped as Aaron *stood between the dead and the living*, a beautiful picture of a greater Aaron whose coming lay over 1,000 years in the future. Even so 14,700 people died (whatever the terms 'thousand' and 'hundred' mean here).

17:1–13 The story of Aaron's rod

The final demonstration of the privileged status of the Levites is now described. But whereas in ch. 16 negative proofs were offered in which contenders against the Levites were rejected and destroyed, the Levites are here approved by a positive test and are exalted over the other tribes.

1–5 Moses was directed to take a rod for each tribe (*fathers' house*, ancestral family) and to write the tribal name on it. Aaron's name was written on the rod of Levi. The rods were then placed in the tent of meeting before the ark of testimony. God would cause one of the rods to sprout and thus make clear for all time the question of privilege and authority and put an end to murmuring. **6, 7** The rods were gathered as commanded and placed before the Lord. **8, 9** Next day, Aaron's rod, *i.e.* the rod of Levi, had sprouted and produced blossoms and almonds whereas the other rods were as before. Israel acknowledged the evidence. **10, 11** The rod of Aaron was returned to the sanctuary *to* *be kept as a sign for the rebels.* **12, 13** The chapter closes with an acknowledgment by the people that death awaited all who approached the Tabernacle, except, of course, those authorized to do so, viz. the Levites.

18:1 – 19:22 Dues and duties of priests and Levites and regulations for purification

In logical sequence the editor(s) has arranged the material so as to have the duties and privileges of the tribe of Levi set out following the events of ch. 17. The Aaronites were thereby established in their priestly position and the Levites in their special sphere of service. Now the dues of the people to the priests and Levites, and of the Levites to the priests can be defined.

18:1–7 The duties of the Levites. 1 In order to avoid further disasters resulting from the approach of unauthorized persons to the sanctuary, the tribe of Levi was to have the responsibility. Aaron and his sons were to *bear iniquity in connection with the sanctuary,* as well as in connection with the priesthood, *i.e.* they were to take all the risks and undertake the penalty of approaching God in the sanctuary. **2–5** It was the task of the rest of the tribe of Levi to minister to Aaron while he and his sons officiated in the sanctuary. The Levites were not, however, to come near the altar or the holy vessels, under pain of death. **6, 7** *I give your priesthood as a gift* (lit. 'a service of a gift') means that the service was a gift or privilege granted by God Himself. The Levites were a gift to the priests from the Lord.

18:8–20 Revenue due to the priests from the people. 8 The maintenance of the priests came from the wide range of offerings and included whatever was kept back of the offerings made to God, *all the consecrated things of the people.* These were to be the portion of Aaron and his sons in perpetuity. **9, 10** In addition, whatever was not consumed on the altar fire (*reserved from the fire*), every offering, every cereal-offering, every sin-offering, every compensatory (guilt-) offering, all described as *most holy things* because they were never to leave the sanctuary, were to be eaten by the priests alone. **11–13** Further, every wave-offering, *i.e.* every portion 'lifted away' from an offering, was theirs. These included the firstfruits, the best of the oil, the wine, and the grain and were to be used for the support of the families of the priests who might eat them provided they were ritually clean. **14** All the devoted things, *i.e.* items banned from common use such as booty taken in war (*cf.* Jos. 6:17, 19), or things given as an offering, belonged to the priests (*cf.* Lv. 27:21). **15a** The firstlings provided another source of support. **15b, 16** Firstlings of man and unclean beasts had to be redeemed (Heb. root *p-d-h,* 'to get by payment what was not originally one's own'). A standard redemption price (Heb. *pedûyîm*) of 5 shekels was payable (*cf.* Lv. 27:6) for children or beasts a month old. **17, 18** The firstborn of clean beasts, oxen, sheep and goats,

could not be redeemed but were *holy, i.e.* they belonged to the Lord. These were slain, their blood sprinkled on the altar, their fat burned for a pleasing odour to God, and their flesh given to the priests in the same way as the breast and right thigh of other offerings (*cf.* Lv. 7:29–34). **19, 20** *All the holy offerings* were given to the priests as a perpetual due under a *covenant of salt, i.e.* a covenant which was never to be broken (*cf.* Lv. 2:13). This provision was made because the tribe of Levi had no inheritance among the people.

18:21–24 Revenues due to the Levites from the people. 21 The Levites were supported by the tithes of the people in return for their service at the tent of meeting. The nature of the tithe varied from time to time (*cf.* Dt. 14:22, 23; Lv. 27:30–33; 2 Ch. 31:6). **22, 23** In a sense, the people were under an obligation to the Levites who took upon themselves the risk of approaching the holy things and bore *their iniquity, i.e.* they accepted responsibility for the people and took the risk on their behalf (*cf.* v. 1). **24** Like the priests, the Levites had no inheritance but were supported by the tithes.

18:25–32 Revenues due to the priests from the Levites. 25–28 The Levites were required to pass on to the priests, as Yahweh's representatives, a tithe of the tithes which they received as an offering. This was to be regarded as the equivalent of the original tithe which was taken from the new grain on the threshing-floor or the new wine in the wine-press. **29** The Levites were to give *the hallowed part* of all the gifts to the Lord, which was really a contribution to the priests. It was to be the *best* (lit. 'fatness') of the gifts. **30, 31** The other nine-tenths of the tithe belonged to the Levites and was available to be eaten in any place by the families of the Levites. It was their due for service in the tent of meeting. **32** But these holy gifts were available to the Levites only after they had taken off the portion for the priests. Otherwise the Levites would have been just as guilty as would the ordinary citizen who ate any of his harvest before he had given a tithe to the Levites. They were forbidden to *profane* ('make common') the holy things on pain of death. But once they had presented the tithe of the tithes to the priests they need not *bear . . . sin by reason of it, i.e.* they were free from the evil consequences that attended the touching of holy things.

19:1–10 The ritual of the red heifer. Contact with dead bodies brought defilement and needed to be ritually cleansed. This was achieved by the ritual of the red heifer.

1, 2 When a man touched a dead body he was required to bring a *red heifer without defect.* The word really has the positive meaning 'perfect' or 'whole'. It is strengthened by the negative *no blemish.* Absolute perfection is thus demanded. It is never to have borne a *yoke: i.e.* it is to be wholly yielded to the Lord's sole service. *Red* is required, possibly as a reminder that blood alone can remove sin. **3** The heifer was presented to Eleazar, Aaron's son, and was then slain outside the camp. **4, 5** Some of her blood was sprinkled by Eleazar seven times toward the front of the tent of meeting and the corpse was burned under the supervision of Eleazar who cast into the fire *cedar wood and hyssop and scarlet stuff*. Each of these had a symbolic meaning (*cf.* Lv. 14 for the ritual for cleansing a leper). **7, 8** The ritual left both the priest and the man who burned the heifer unclean. Each was required to *wash his clothes* (the verb used in Ps. 51:2, 7; Je. 2:22, *etc.*, of cleansing from sin), and to *bathe* (Heb. 'pour water over') their bodies but remained unclean until evening. **9, 10** The ashes of the heifer were gathered by a ritually clean man and deposited in a clean place outside the camp to be used for preparing *water for impurity*, *i.e.* water for the removal of ritual uncleanness. *For the removal of sin* (lit. 'it is a sin-offering') indicates that the red heifer, although not a sin-offering in the technical sense (*cf.* Lv. 4), served to remove sin (*cf.* v. 17 where it is called a *burnt sin offering*).

19:11–13 General rules for cleansing. 11, 12 Anyone who touched a corpse was unclean for seven days. He was required to cleanse himself (lit. 'un-sin himself') with the purifying water on the third and on the seventh day. The seven-day period emphasized the seriousness of the matter. **13** By neglecting to cleanse himself ('de-sin' or 'un-sin' himself) a man defiled the Tabernacle of the Lord and was to be cut off from Israel. *Water . . . . . thrown upon him* suggests a more violent action than sprinkling (*cf.* Lv. 1:5, 11; 3:2, *etc.* The word means 'dash').

19:14–22 Special rules for cleansing. 14 Special applications of the general rule are now discussed. First, everyone who entered the tent of a dead man was unclean. **15** Open vessels without a cover were unclean. **16** There was a variety of occasions when one might touch a corpse in the open field. Some are listed. For this reason tombs and graves were painted white in later times (*cf.* Mt. 23:27; Acts 23:3). **17–19** In all cases a clean person dipped a hyssop branch into the cleansing water made from running water to which some ashes of the burnt sin-offering had been added, and sprinkled the unclean man and all his property on the third and on the seventh day. Then on the seventh day the man would be cleansed (lit. 'de-sinned'). He could wash his clothes and bathe himself and be clean at evening. **20** Men who ignored this ritual were to be cut off from the assembly as those who defiled the sanctuary. **21** Finally, the man who sprinkled the cleansing water, or anyone who touched the water, was to be unclean till evening—the shortest time that ritual uncleanness could last. **22** Whatever the unclean person touched was unclean, and those who touched such objects were likewise unclean till evening.

20:1–13 Final events at Kadesh

20:1 Miriam's death. 1 The people arrived at Kadesh in the wilderness of Zin in the first month. No year is given but it was subsequent to the second year after the Exodus when the Israelites first arrived in Kadesh, and probably subsequent to their turning back along the road to the Red Sea after they rejected the advice of Joshua and Caleb to enter the land (*cf.* 14:25). Possibly Kadesh remained a centre during the long years of wandering. Miriam may have died at almost any time during their stay around Kadesh.

20:2-13 The waters of Meribah. 2–5 Once again there was a shortage of water (*cf.* Ex. 17:1–7) and once again the people contended with Moses as they craved for the abundance of Egypt (*cf.* Nu. 11:4–6) saying that it were better to die with their brethren (*cf.* 16:35, 49; 17:12f.). **6–9** Once again Moses and Aaron pleaded with the Lord to spare them, and once again the Lord commanded Moses to take his rod and to bring water from a rock. This rod appears several times in the story of Moses (*cf.* Ex. 7:20; 14:16, *etc.*). **10–13** The narrative is tantalizing at this point. Moses and Aaron were refused entry to the promised land but the exact nature of their offence is not clear. Many suggestions have been made, *e.g.* that Moses struck the rock twice, thus betraying anger; or that Moses made arrogant personal claims: *Shall we bring forth water for you out of this rock?*; or, following Ps. 106:32, 33, that the people provoked Moses to speak rash words; or that Moses and Aaron failed to lead the people after the report of the spies (*cf.* Dt. 1:37; 3:26; 4:21). But the record merely gives the Lord's words as: *Because you did not believe in me, to sanctify me in the eyes of the people of Israel*. It was an occasion when the Lord *showed himself holy among them* (Heb. *qiddēš*, a play on Kadesh; *cf.* Meribah, a play on *rîb*, 'to strive'). In some way Moses and Aaron offended Yahweh.

20:14 – 22:1 THE JOURNEY FROM KADESH TO THE PLAINS OF MOAB

Israel, frustrated in her attempt to enter the promised land from the south, determined after years of delay to gain entry from the east. The story of their journey to the plains of Moab is told in several places (*cf.* Dt. 2:1–15; Jdg. 11:17, 18).

20:14–21 Israel and Edom

14 Moses sent messengers to the king of Edom. His reference to Israel as *your brother Israel* recalled ancient tribal links between Jacob and Esau, now become Israel and Edom (*cf.* Gn. 25:20–34). **15, 16** Moses then recounted the *adversity* (AV 'travail') of Israel in Egypt as well as Yahweh's deliverance of His people through His agent (lit. 'angel' or 'messenger'; *cf.* Ex. 23:20). **17, 18** Hoping for some kindly response, Moses sought permission to traverse *the King's Highway*, promising not to turn aside like common invaders. This ancient road, little more than a track for caravans then, is marked today by ancient sites strung out along the Roman road and the modern road as well. Archaeological work has been undertaken at some of these and all have been surveyed. Despite Moses' pleas Edom refused passage. **19, 20** Further argument was ruled out when Edom made a hostile demonstration against Israel. A similar experience with Moab is reported in Jdg. 11:17, 18. We know today that both these kingdoms were ringed with fortresses the remains of which have been identified by archaeologists.

20:22 – 22:1 The death of Aaron and the defeat of opposing kingdoms

20:22–29 The death of Aaron. 22 Leaving Kadesh, Israel journeyed to *Mount Hor* on the borders of Edom. The traditional Gebel Nabi' Hārûn near Petra is too far east and Gebel Maḍurah near Kadesh seems more likely. **23–28** On arrival at Mt. Hor Moses took Aaron and Eleazar his son to the mountain top where the high priestly garments of Aaron were removed from him and placed on Eleazar who was henceforth to be high priest. It was the hour of Aaron's death. **29** The people mourned for *thirty days*, the normal period of mourning (*cf.* Dt. 34:8, mourning for Moses).

21:1–3 Conflict with the king of Arad. 1 The Canaanite king of Arad in the Negeb area, hearing of the movement of Israel in the region of *Atharim* (possibly Tamar or Hazazon-tamar in the Arabah a few miles south of the Dead Sea), attacked them and took captives. *Arad* was an important site in biblical history (*cf.* 33:40; Jos. 12:14; Jdg. 1:16). There is a Tell Arad in the same general area at present under excavation but it is thought that this represents another town and that the Arad of the present narrative is Tell Malḥata some 7 miles southwest. **2, 3** Israel sought the Lord's help, and true to her promise that she would destroy completely (Heb. verb derived from *ḥērem*, 'ban') Arad and its villages if the Lord gave her the victory, she *utterly destroyed them*, calling the place *Hormah* (root *ḥērem*). It was a simple and unrefined application of the principle that all that opposed the will of God was under His judgment. The principle was correct. Its setting and application were within the context of the holy war (*cf.* on 31:1–54), and belong to the doctrine that Israel's God is the Lord of history, a holy God, hating sin, brooking no opposition and working out His moral purposes. The armies of Israel were mobilized in the interests of these purposes on more occasions than one. The practice of the holy war has, of course, no place whatever in Christian thought or action, though its principles remain true for our personal and corporate resistance to sin and to sinfulness. The place-name, *Hormah*, occurs more than once in the accounts of the wanderings and the conquest (especially Nu. 14:45; Dt. 1:44; Jdg. 1:17), and has sometimes been thought to indicate duplicate accounts of the same event and even to involve contradiction. It is simpler, however,

to understand the name in Nu. 14:45 and Dt. 1:44 as Israel's private and painful recollection of the major military and spiritual catastrophe of the Mosaic period, and to treat Nu. 21:3 as an editorial note inserted later, referring to the victory recorded in Jdg. 1:17 by which the old name, Hormah, became significant of the victory God gives His people and became attached to the city formerly called Zephath.

21:4–9 The bronze serpent. This incident became significant in later centuries for Jews and Christians alike (*cf.* Wisdom 16:5–7; Jn. 3:14).

4 Leaving Mt. Hor, Israel travelled south *by the way to the Red Sea* (lit. 'Sea of Reeds', Heb. *yam sûp̄*) to skirt the western border of Edom. How far south they went on this road is not clear. On the way *the people became impatient.* **5, 6** They complained about the food, the water, and *this worthless food, i.e.* the manna. The AV 'light bread' takes the Heb. *q⁽ᵉ⁾lōlēl* to mean 'light' rather than 'worthless'. *Fiery serpents.* Divine judgment came in the form of desert snakes with a venomous, burning bite (hence they are called in Heb. *s⁽ᵉ⁾rāp̄îm*, fiery ones). Many people died. **7** The people confessed, *We have sinned, for we have spoken against the Lord and against you.* **8, 9** In answer to Moses' prayer God revealed that he should make a bronze (AV 'brass' is not strictly correct) representation of a serpent and set it on a post, commanding the people to look upon it and live. Thus was Israel taught that only in God was there deliverance. The simple invitation to look and live (*cf.* Is. 45:22) was a test of faith. Poisonous snakes could be rendered harmless only by the mercy of God.

21:10–20 The journey from Mt. Hor to the plains of Moab. 10–13 Identification of the sites is not certain. *Oboth* (lit. 'water skins') may be 'Ain el-Weiba, 15 miles south of the Dead Sea, west of Punon (mod. Feinan). *Iye-abarim* (lit. 'ruins of Abarim') is possibly Maḥay, bordering on Moab to the east (*the sunrise*). Such an itinerary would suggest a road leading east to the Arabah after a short southerly journey from Kadesh, then north along the Arabah skirting the western boundary of Edom to the Wadi Zered, thence east along the Zered valley, turning north around Moab's eastern boundary until the Wadi *Arnon* (mod. Wadi el-Mûjib) was crossed, the boundary between Moab and the Amorites. This itinerary would agree with that in Jdg. 11:16–18. **14, 15** A brief extract from *the Book of the Wars of the Lord*, an ancient collection of war songs, is quoted here because of its reference to valleys which ran into the Arnon. The text is difficult. The AV follows the Vulgate. **16–18** At Beer, unidentified, the people found water and sang another ancient song of which Israel must have had many. **19, 20** Finally, passing by places of uncertain identification (although *Bamoth* is possibly Khirbet el-Quweiqiyeh), Israel reached the valley in the region of Moab, at the peak of *Pisgah*, overlooking Jeshimon (Heb. *y⁽ᵉ⁾šîmôn*, lit. 'the wasteland' or *desert*). Pisgah was one of the high ranges of the Moabite plateau jutting out towards the Dead Sea with a fine view of Canaan to the west. The highest point of the range is Mt. Nebo.

21:21 – 22:1 The defeat of the Amorite kings. Fortresses surrounding the kingdoms of Edom, Moab, and of the Amorites made it impossible for Israel to reach the land of Canaan. They were frustrated by Edom and Moab but penetrated the line of fortresses of the Amorite kingdoms.

21-32 Sihon. When Moses sought passage for Israel through Sihon's territory in terms similar to those he spoke to Edom (*cf.* 20:14-21), Sihon not only refused but came out to attack Israel at *Jahaz*, possibly the modern Khirbet Umm el-Idhâm about 5 miles north of Dibon. **24** It gave Israel the opportunity to meet one of these kings in battle, overcome him, and penetrate his line of fortresses. Before long Israel had occupied Sihon's territory between the Arnon and Jabbok gorges and eastward to *Jazer* which stood at the western boundary of the Ammonites. It has been identified with Khirbet Jazzir near modern es-Salṭ, 12 miles south of the river Jabbok. **25, 26** Heshbon, Sihon's capital, was taken as well as the neighbouring towns in the area which formerly belonged to Moab but had been taken by the Amorites. The reference to *cities* in these areas is important in determining the date of the Exodus. There had been very few urban settlements in Transjordan for many centuries before about 1350-1300 BC. Hence the Exodus must have taken place at a date when Israel would find towns in this area. **27-30** An ancient ballad, formerly sung by the Amorites themselves to commemorate their victory over the Moabites, is here quoted to point up the change in the fortunes of Heshbon. The last section has suffered in transmission and is variously translated. The Jewish translation of v. 30 reads,

> 'Their dominion is at an end, from Heshbon to Dibon,
> And from Nashim to Nophah which is hard by Medeba.'

33-35 Og. The defeat of the Amorite kingdom north of the Jabbok followed soon after. Proceeding up the caravan route to Bashan, Israel met Og and defeated him at Edrei, possibly the modern Der'ā 40 miles east of the Jordan. Og was slain and all his family. Thus Israel gained a foothold in Transjordan where she maintained a vital interest throughout the days of the kings and was often engaged in defensive wars to maintain her hold on the area.

22:1 The encampment opposite Jericho. *The plains of Moab beyond Jordan at Jericho* constituted something of a terminus, the last stopping-place before Israel crossed the Jordan. The area probably comprised the flat plain east of Jordan opposite Jericho (*cf.* Jos. 4:13; 5:10), a well-wooded and well-watered area north of the Dead Sea. A number of incidents took place here, the subject-matter of the next major section of Numbers.

22:2 – 32:42 EVENTS ON THE PLAINS OF MOAB

22:2 – 24:25 Balak and Balaam

In the following three chapters which contain some of the oldest poetry in the Bible, the story is told of how Balak, king of Moab, fearful of the advancing Israelites, hired a diviner from the land of Amaw both to divine and to curse (22:2-14). Reluctant to come (22:15-35), Balaam eventually arrived (22:36-40) and delivered four oracles (22:41 – 24:25) all of which depicted Israel as a nation that would prosper. Balak finally dismissed Balaam.

22:2-14 Balak's fear of Israel and the first invitation to Balaam. 2-4 The fearful Balak (lit. 'destroyer'), learning of the defeat of the Amorites, shared his misgivings with the elders of Midian. **5** He decided to send messengers to bring Balaam the diviner from *Pethor* (possibly the Pitru of Assyrian inscriptions) near the Euphrates (*the River*) in the *land of Amaw*. (AV 'his people' is incorrect. The land has now been identified in cuneiform documents.) The messengers told Balaam of the arrival of a people from Egypt and of Balak's intention to attack them. **6** Balaam was invited to come and *curse* this people (or 'cast a spell', the original meaning of the root). He was thought to have the power to bless or bind by a spell. **7, 8** The elders of Moab and Midian took the *fees for divination* with them, an essential part of the arrangement (*cf.* 1 Sa. 9:7f.). **9-14** However, a divine restraint was on Balaam as he became aware that this people was destined for blessing and he replied: *The Lord has refused to let me go with you.*

22:15-21 Balak's second invitation. 15-17 Balak, anxious for Balaam's help, sent a second, larger embassy with many honoured leaders (princes) and the promise of great honour. **18** Unmoved by these promises Balaam insisted that he could only do as Yahweh commanded. **19, 20** That night, perhaps in a dream, God made known to him that he was to go with the ambassadors of Moab and Midian. Such an apparent change in the divine purpose is not unknown elsewhere in the OT (*cf.* Je. 18:1-11). A change in the conditions could alter the divine purpose. That God should forbid Balaam to go (v. 12), then permit him (v. 20), then be angry with him for going (v. 22) may merely indicate that while it was not God's will for Balaam to curse Israel, He might nevertheless permit his going in order to demonstrate to Balaam the strength of divine restraints he did not understand, and to Balak the peculiar character of this people he feared. Even so, Balaam received one further warning of the divine displeasure at the whole incident. The words (v. 19) *what more*, however, are probably intended to underline the fatal flaw in Balaam's character. In the long run (*cf.* 2 Pet. 2:15; Jude 11) covetousness was his ruination (*cf.* Nu. 25:1ff.; 31:8; Rev. 2:14). If he really meant the high-sounding words of v. 18, then v. 19 is a *non sequitur*, for the Lord has already spoken. It is on this point that the story revolves. In v. 20 we see the fearful power of the human heart apparently to bend God to its own will, while feigning to concede the essence of what God wants (*only what I bid you, that shall you do*). The same principle is voiced in Ps. 106:15. 21 In the morning Balaam went off with the princes of Moab.

22:22–35 Balaam and his ass. 22–27 Balaam set out with his *two servants*, identified in the Palestinian Targum as Jannes and Jambres (*cf.* 2 Tim. 3:8). On the way the ass stubbornly halted and turned into a field. The *angel of the Lord*, some manifestation of God Himself (see Introduction to Exodus), confronted him *as his adversary* (Heb. *śāṭān*; *cf.* Jb. 1:6–9; Zc. 3:1). Balaam beat his ass (as commonly in the east) and it entered a narrow path between walls (probably low stone walls) with vineyards on either side. The appearance remained and the beast clung to one wall catching Balaam's foot. Again the diviner beat the animal. It rushed into a narrow space where it could not turn and finally crouched down beneath Balaam only to be beaten again. 28–30 At this point Balaam heard the ass complaining about his ill-treatment of a faithful servant. Although such a phenomenon is outside normal experience men have sometimes sensed that God's creatures spoke to them. 31–34 Then Balaam saw the angel of the Lord and understood the behaviour of the ass. It was one more warning to a man whose way was *perverse* (the Heb. text is obscure here). Balaam confessed *I have sinned, for I did not know that thou didst stand in the road against me.* He offered to return home. 35 But a divine purpose could yet be fulfilled and the Lord permitted him to go with the princes of Balak, but to speak under His constraint.

22:36–40 The meeting between Balak and Balaam. 36–39 The two men met on the frontier of Moab at the city of Moab (or Ar of Moab, *cf.* 21:28) and went to Kiriath-huzoth (lit. 'city of streets'). On the way Balaam declared that he would speak only what God gave him, a true view of prophecy. 40 Balak sacrificed oxen and sheep and sent the flesh to Balaam and his companions (called *princes*).

22:41 – 24:25 Balaam's oracles. In the course of the next few days Balaam uttered four oracles. The Hebrew of these, which are poetic in form, is of a very ancient kind, indicating that in their present form they are as old as the 10th century BC so that their original form could be older still.

22:41 – 23:12 The first oracle. 22:41 Balak first took Balaam up to Bamoth-baal (lit. 'high places of Baal') to view *the nearest of the people* (Heb. *qāṣeh*, 'extremity', could be either the near or the far extremity). 23:1–3 Balaam commanded Balak to build seven altars and provide seven bulls and seven rams (seven evidently being the approved number in such exercises). Then they

offered on each altar a bull and a ram. Balaam bid Balak wait while he went away to a bare height to receive his oracle. 4–6 God met him and gave him His word which he then declared to Balak and his officials. 7, 8 The oracle declared that Balak had called Balaam from the land of Qedem (*eastern mountain*), *i.e.* Aram, to curse Israel. But this was not possible since God had not cursed this people. 9, 10 Looking down from the top of the mountain he saw Israel below as a group not to be reckoned among the nations and asked, *Who can count the dust of Jacob, or number the fourth part of Israel?* Fourth part is really parallel to 'dust' and the Heb. *rōḇaʿ* should be derived from the root *r-b-ʿ*, 'dust'. Balaam concluded, *Let me die the death of the righteous, and let my end be like his!* perhaps a kind of oath declaring that he was ready to die if his words were untrue. 11, 12 The oracle did not please Balak but Balaam declared he could speak only what Yahweh gave him.

23:13–26 The second oracle. 13, 14 Thinking that the result might be different if Balaam saw only a part of Israel, Balak *took him to the field of Zophim, to the top of Pisgah.* 15–17 The same ritual was performed and again Balaam went off to receive an oracle. 18–20 Another oracle was given in poetic form in a 3:3 metre which declared that God was not a man that He should lie or change His mind. It was His intention to bless His people. 21 Again, Balaam could discern no misfortune for this people since Yahweh was with them and a royal shout of triumph was among them. 22 God had brought this people from Egypt. *Horns* symbolizes strength (*cf.* Dt. 33:17; Zc. 1:18, 19). The strength is either the Lord's (see RV), or Israel's (RSV). 23 No divination and no enchantment could therefore succeed against them. 24 Here was a people that would act as a lion or a lioness, the double description, male and female, stressing the totality or completeness of mastery possessed by Israel. 24, 26 In anger Balak commanded Balaam neither to curse nor to bless.

23:27 – 24:9 The third oracle. 27, 28 Balak tried yet a third vantage-point, the top of Peor overlooking the desert. (There was a Beth-jeshimoth below the hills in the plains of Moab; *cf.* 33:49.) Balaam was still looking to the west. 29, 30 The same ritual was repeated. 24:1 But this time Balaam abandoned omens and simply looked down on Israel. 3 Then God's spirit came upon him and he declared his third oracle (Heb. *neʾûm*, a special term for 'a divine utterance', used here three times). 4 The names El (*God*) and Shaddai (*Almighty*), ancient names for God, appear in this verse. Balaam received the vision of God as he lay prostrate before God with his eyes *uncovered*, freed from all blurring hindrances. 5–9 All he could see was Israel's fair tents stretching like valleys (or perhaps palm trees) and gardens beside a river, or like noble aloe or cedar trees. Prosperity and an abundant population would be his lot while his dominion would be stronger than that of Agag (the first king to be destroyed by Israel; *cf.* 1 Sa. 15:32f.). El had delivered him from Egypt and was his strength so that he would overthrow nations as a lion devours prey. Balaam's final words to Israel were, *Blessed be every one who blesses you, and cursed be every one who curses you.*

24:10–25 The fourth oracle. **10** Balak's anger was aroused and he struck his hands together in contempt (*cf.* Jb. 27:23; Lam. 2:15). Hired to curse Israel, Balaam had blessed them three times. Balak ordered Balaam to return at once to his home. **11** Balak had promised to honour Balaam but Yahweh the God of Israel had prevented this. **12, 13** Balaam recalled that originally he had told Balak's messengers that he could speak only the word of Yahweh (*cf.* 22:18). **14** As he departed for his homeland he made a final pronouncement in which he referred to Israel, Amalek, the Kenites and perhaps others. **15, 16** After introductory words he declared that he had received a vision from the Almighty (Shaddai). **17, 18** He saw Israel in the future (*not now . . . not nigh*) when the stars of Jacob would arise and the tribes of Israel would crush Moab. The usual translation, *A star shall come forth out of Jacob, and a sceptre shall rise out of Israel,* has given rise to many Messianic speculations and even the men of the Dead Sea Scrolls community regarded this passage as Messianic. There is, however, some reason, in view of the archaic nature of these poems, to read the plurals 'stars' and 'tribes' and to take v. 17 as having reference rather to Israel's political progress in coming days. *The sons of Sheth* are probably the ancient inhabitants of Moab known as the 'Shutu people' in early Egyptian documents. **18** Edom too would be dispossessed and her capital Seir overthrown. **19** Thus would Israel hold dominion over those who had opposed her passage along the King's Highway, Edom and Moab. **20** Amalek too, an ancient nation, would perish. **21** The Kenite, secure in his mountain fastness, would likewise waste away. (There is a play on words here; *Kenite,* Heb. *qēnî,* is related to *qēn, nest.*) **21, 22** The closing verses of this oracle are difficult and very different translations are proposed. W. F. Albright proposes for vv. 21 and 22:

'Thy abode, O Smith (Kenite), is perennial:
    And thy nest is set in the cliffs,
And yet they shall become fuel, Thy dwellers,
    even as I look.'

This rendering removes the reference to Asshur and enables us to keep the passage in its ancient setting. **23, 24** are also difficult. Albright, albeit with some emendations, translates:

'The isles shall be gathered from the north,
    and ships from the furthest sea,
And while I gaze they pass over—So he also
    shall perish for ever!'

It is not entirely clear which people are referred to in these verses but it is not unthinkable that vv. 23 and 24 refer to the invasion of the Sea Peoples along the Mediterranean coastlands in the 12th century BC. Contemporary Egyptian texts refer to 'foreigners of the north', from 'isles in the midst of the sea', making plundering incursions 'from their isles'. Broadly, however this fourth and last oracle proclaimed the overthrow of every enemy of the emergent nation visible on the plains below Moab's heights. **25** Little wonder that Balak dismissed so unprofitable a diviner. The two men parted and went their separate ways.

25:1–18 Apostasy at Peor

In the events of the previous three chapters Israel played no part. But two cases of immoral conduct with non-Israelite women which led to involvement in the worship of foreign gods are now described.

25:1–5 Immorality with Moabite women. 1–3 *While Israel dwelt in Shittim the people began to play the harlot with the daughters of Moab* (i.e. Moabite women). The act was both physical and religious (*cf.* Rev. 2:14). *Shittim* (lit. 'acacia tree'), probably Tell Kefrein, was the last stopping-place before crossing the Jordan (*cf.* Jos. 2:1; 3:1). Israel was invited to share in religious festivals of the local Baal at Peor and probably of Chemosh, the god of Moab. **4** Moses was commanded to punish the leaders publicly (lit. 'in the face of the sun'). The mode of punishment is not clear and a variety of translations for the Hebrew verb have been offered—'impale', 'expose', 'hang', 'cast down' (based on Arabic root). The latter method is known elsewhere in the OT (*e.g.* 2 Ch. 25:8–12; *cf.* Lk. 4:29). Possibly the men were slain and then cast over a cliff to lie unburied, exposed to the sun. Only thus could judgment on the whole people be averted. **5** It was *the judges of Israel* who undertook the execution.

25:6–18 Immorality with Midianite women. 6–9 In the second incident the people came weeping to the tent of meeting because of a plague that had broken out. An Israelite man had brought home a Midianite wife. Phinehas, son of Eleazar the high priest, followed the couple to their tent and slew them, halting the plague but not before *twenty-four thousand* (Heb. *'elep,* exact sense not clear; see on 1:2, 3, *etc.*) had died. **10–13** For his zeal (*jealousy*), God made a *covenant of peace* with Eleazar. A vowel change in *šālôm,* 'peace', would yield *šillum,* 'reward' (*cf.,* however, Mal. 2:5), and the sense may be that the promise of *perpetual priesthood* to Eleazar and his descendants was the reward of his zeal. The later Zadokites traced their descent to Eleazar through Phinehas (*cf.* 1 Ch. 24:3). On that day Phinehas made an *atonement* or 'covering' for the people. **14, 15** The Israelite offender was Zimri, a Simeonite, and the Midianite woman was Cozbi (lit. 'deceiver'), the daughter of a Midianite chieftain. **16–18** Thereafter Israel was to harass the Midianites who are here blamed for both incidents in which Israel was beguiled.

26:1–65 The second census

Now that the journey was virtually over a new census was necessary, both in order to assess the military strength of Israel for invasion, and also for the purpose of allotting the territory of Canaan. The first census was taken by Moses and Aaron (ch. 1). Now, after a generation, Moses and Eleazar take a second census. There are some differences between the two.

26:1–4 Moses and Eleazar instructed to take a second census. 1–4 After the plague of ch. 25 Moses and Eleazar were instructed to take a second census (*cf.* 1:1). As previously, the men of twenty years and upward, *i.e.* the men of military age, were to be numbered. The opening words of v. 4 are lacking in Hebrew. The sentence begins *from twenty years old and upward*, suggesting the omission of some words from the text.

26:5–51 The census of the secular tribes. Comparison with the first census shows that the total number of adult males had decreased by 1,820. Seven tribes increased and five decreased in number. The order of the tribes is different. Here Reuben, Simeon and Gad are mentioned first and Judah, Issachar and Zebulun second, whereas the order is reversed in ch. 1. In the next block of names Manasseh precedes Ephraim (vv. 28, 35; *cf.* 1:32, 34).

5–11 The subdivisions of Reuben are the same as those set out in Gn. 46:9 and the numbers are 2,770 less than in Nu. 1:21. The editor has here inserted comments on Dathan and Abiram who were destroyed along with Korah (ch. 16). The comment in v. 11 agrees with the fact that there were Korahites in post-exilic times (*cf.* 1 Ch. 26:1–19). Evidently only some of the Korahites were involved in the incident of ch. 16. **12–14** The Simeonites were reduced by 37,100 (*cf.* 1:23). The subdivision of the tribe follows Gn. 46:10. **15–18** The tribe of Gad had 5,150 fewer males and some of the names of the sub-tribes vary slightly from those in Gn. 46:16. **19–22** Judah gained 1,900 (*cf.* 1:26). **23–25** Issachar gained 9,900 (*cf.* 1:29). **26, 27** Zebulun gained 3,100 (*cf.* 1:31). **28–37** The total Joseph family gained 2,500 although Ephraim lost 8,000 (37; *cf.* 1:33). **38–41** Benjamin increased by 10,200 (41; *cf.* 1:37). **42, 43** Dan increased by 1,700. **44–47** Asher increased by 11,900 (47; *cf.* 1:41). **48–50** Naphtali decreased by 8,000 (50; *cf.* 1:43). **51** The same problem arises here as in ch. 1 since the significance of the terms *thousand* and *hundred* is not clear, excepting that they denoted military units. Misunderstanding of the exact meaning of these terms and the assumption that they were simple numbers led the final editor to the mathematical calculation of v. 51 (*cf.* 1:46).

26:52–56 Two principles of land allotment. Two principles are enunciated: **52–54** first, that division of the land was to be made according to the number of people in the tribe; **55, 56** and secondly, the land was to be allocated by lot. These two principles might

seem to be in conflict. Some commentators have suggested that the general locality was decided by lot while the exact limits of each tribal area was decided according to the size of the tribes. Another possibility is that even before the conquest the size and location of each inheritance area was decided. Inside that broad area the family units were to be decided by lot.

26:57–62 The census of the Levites. 57 As previously (*cf.* 1:47; 3:14–43) the Levites were numbered separately. **58** The method of describing the Levites is different. The three main families are Gershon, Kohath and Merari, but in place of eight subdivisions (*cf.* 3:17–20), only five are given here—Libni, Hebron, Mahli Mushi and Korah. Four of these occur in 3:18–20 but Korah is new (*cf.* ch. 16; 26:11). **59** The descent of Aaron, Moses and Miriam through Amram and Kohath to Levi is traced. **60, 61** The sons of Aaron are given as Nadab and Abihu (see ch. 16), Eleazar and Ithamar.

26:63–65 An important observation on the census. The editor notes that only Caleb and Joshua are common to this census and the first census (*cf.* 14:30). The old Israel needed to be remade before the people could enter the land of promise.

27:1–11 The daughters of Zelophehad

In general, women in the Ancient Near East were not able to inherit property. The 'firstborn' of a man had special privileges (*cf.* Dt. 21:15–17) even if he was born of a secondary wife. If a man died without a son, levirate marriage was the rule, *i.e.* the dead man's brother was required to take his wife and raise up a son to him (*cf.* Dt. 25:5–10). The present arrangement permitted daughters to inherit.

1–4 When a certain Zelophehad, a man of Manasseh, died without a son, his five daughters came to Moses and Eleazar and the leaders to plead that although their father had died, he was not one of the rebels associated with Korah (*cf.* ch. 16), but his death was due to his sharing in the general sin of all who came out of Egypt. Why then should he lose his inheritance because he had no son? Should not the inheritance pass to his daughters? **5–7** *Moses brought their case before the Lord* and was directed to *cause the inheritance of their father to pass to them.* **8–11** A new law was enunciated. If a man died without a son the daughter could inherit; failing a daughter, the inheritance passed to his brother; failing a brother, the next of kin became the heir. The procedure seems to have been an alternative for levirate marriage. In either case the property was retained in the family. Some commentators interpret this incident as a symbolic way of expressing the claim of Manasseh to areas on the west of Jordan, *i.e. an inheritance among their father's brethren.* Be that as it may, the law is differently presented in 36:1–9 where it is modified so as to prevent the transfer of the inheritance should a woman marry.

27:12–23 Joshua appointed as Moses' successor

12–14 In view of Moses' impending death the Lord called him to go to the *mountain of Abarim* (defined as Mt. Nebo in Dt. 32:49, lit. 'the mountains of the other side'). Here he would see the land he was forbidden to enter because of his rebellion (*cf.* 20:12) and then he would be gathered to his people like his brother Aaron. **15–17** Moses called upon Yahweh *the God of the spirits of all flesh* (*cf.* 16:22), *i.e.* the God who gives physical life to all living creatures, to appoint a successor who would *go out* and *come in* before Israel (*cf.* Jos. 14:11; 1 Sa. 18:13, 16; 1 Ki. 3:7, *etc.*) lest the people be leaderless, *as sheep which have no shepherd.* **18–20** Moses was commanded to take Joshua, a man in whom *the spirit* dwelt, and lay his hand upon him in the presence of Eleazar and the people. This was not to endow him with the spirit which he already had, but visibly to mark him out as leader. He would be given his *commission* (lit. 'commanded') and invested with some of Moses' *authority* (Heb. *hôḏ*, 'honour', 'prestige'). **21** Thereafter he would seek the divine will through the *Urim* (the sacred lot) and exercise authority over the people. **22, 23** In the subsequent ceremony Eleazar played little part, although thereafter he would be God's spokesman to interpret God's will to Joshua.

28:1 – 30:16 Regulations for public worship and vows

These chapters, which give an elaborate and carefully-defined list of instructions concerning the offerings to be made in Israel, have sometimes been regarded as very late. But it is impossible to decide exactly how detailed the regulations were in Moses' day apart from this and similar passages (*cf.* Lv. 23). Even granting that the final editor brought ancient material up to date, it seems precarious to assign these chapters completely to the post-exilic period (the P document). There is great wisdom in the proposal of W. F. Albright (see Introduction, p. 169) that the spirit and much of the detail of the so-called 'priestly code' (of which much of Numbers forms a part) may be considered as ante-dating the conquest of Canaan, *i.e.* as going back to Mosaic origins.

The modern reader will sometimes ask whether such detailed prescriptions as are set out in these chapters are relevant to this modern age, since the prescriptions do not apply in the worship of the Christian church today. Clearly, the prescriptions for worship in one age do not necessarily apply in another and modifications are constantly being made to old forms of worship. What one needs to do in these cases is to recognize behind each expression of worship the great principles. These remain and find newer expressions in the course of time. The ancient Tabernacle and its rituals and feasts gave testimony to the belief that God was in the midst of His people, that He could be approached, and

that with Him in the midst the people ought to order their lives in accordance with the fact that God the holy One dwelt among them. The whole system demonstrated to Israel, and to men of all ages, that sinful men may approach God through a consecrated mediatorial priesthood, that constant cleansing for sins was possible, that constant guidance for life was available and that great saving acts of God in centuries past could be remembered by noble festivals and feasts such as Passover and the Feast of Tabernacles.

With the coming of the Lord Jesus Christ the necessity for all the temporary forms, shadows of the true (*cf.* Heb. 10:1), was past. He was at once the sacrifice for all sins and the High Priest who offered the sacrifice. By His Spirit He guides His people today. His saving work wrought at the cross may be remembered each time men gather at the Lord's table 'to proclaim the Lord's death until he comes'. Yet the 'shadows' and 'symbols' of the OT system, if understood as pictures of the true, have much to teach the modern Christian and they should be studied for the light they give on the great underlying principles of God's ways with men.

28:1, 2 Introduction. God instructed Moses to tell the people to present God's offering, the food (or meat) for His fire-offerings, and His pleasing odour, each in their proper season. *Offering* is here collective, covering every offering that was burned and turned into smoke which could ascend heavenwards to God.

28:3–8 The daily offerings. 3–6 The fire-offering that constituted the regular offering was basic to the whole sacrificial system since it continued day after day (*cf.* Ex. 29:38–42; Lv. 6:19–23). The details varied from time to time (*cf.* 2 Ki. 16:15; Ezk. 46:13–15). Here the offering is one male lamb in the morning and one male lamb in the evening (lit. 'between the evenings'), along with a tenth of an ephah of fine flour for a cereal-offering mixed with a fourth of a hin of oil. The whole was burned as a fire-offering to Yahweh. **7** Accompanying each lamb was a drink-offering of a fourth of a hin to be poured out in the *holy place*, evidently the courtyard where the great altar stood. The drink-offering is here called *an offering of strong drink* but possibly the phrase denotes merely a drink-offering, since the word (Heb. *šēḵār*) may be a technical word related to the Akkadian *šikaru*. Elsewhere the term denotes an intoxicating drink. **8** The term *minḥâ*, here translated *cereal offering*, seems to include both the animal and the grain offerings, since the evening offering of a lamb is compared with the morning offering (*cf.* 1 Ki. 18:29).

28:9, 10 The sabbath offering. 9 On the sabbath two male lambs a year old, each with its grain, oil, and drink-offering were offered. **10** These were in addition to the regular offerings, so that on the sabbath the offerings were doubled (*cf.* Ezk. 46:4, 5).

28:11–15 The offerings for the new month. 11 At the beginning of each new month the burnt-offering was considerable—two young bulls, one ram, seven male lambs a year old as a burnt-offering. **12–14** The prescribed grain and drink-offering appropriate to each was also offered (*cf.* Ezk. 45:21, 22). **15** In addition a male goat was offered for a *sin offering*.

28:16–25 Offerings for the Feast of Unleavened Bread. 16 On the fourteenth day of the first month the Passover was kept. No offerings are mentioned, since offerings as such belong to the sanctuary and the Passover was a home festival (*cf.* Lv. 23:5–8). **17** On the fifteenth day the Feast of Unleavened Bread began and continued for seven days. These two feasts were originally different but were later joined together, as here. The unleavened bread was eaten for seven days. **18** The first and seventh days were days of *holy convocation* on which *no laborious work* was done (*cf.* v. 25). **19–21** Each day a considerable offering was made to Yahweh—two young bulls, a ram, seven male yearling lambs, all without blemish and each with its appropriate cereal-offering (*cf.* Ezk. 45:23, 24). **22** A male goat for a sin-offering was also offered each day. **23–25** All these were additional to the regular daily burnt-offering.

28:26–31 Offerings for the Feast of Weeks. This was a one-day feast, the details of which varied from time to time both as to the length of the feast and as to the animals offered (*cf.* Ex. 23:16; 34:22; Dt. 16:10, 11). The festival is called the Feast of Harvest in Ex. 23:16, and the Feast of Weeks in Ex. 34:22. The offerings are the same as for the feasts of New Moon and Unleavened Bread. The feast is not mentioned in Ezekiel.

26 *On the day of the first fruits, i.e.* the day when Israel brought the firstfruits of the ground to the Lord, an offering was made (*minḥâ*, see on v. 8) and a day of holy convocation was observed when no laborious work was done. **27–29** The burnt-offering, which was a pleasing odour to God, consisted of two young bulls, one ram, seven male lambs a year old with their cereal-offering and oil. **30** A male goat was also offered *to make atonement* for Israel. **31** All these were additional to the regular daily offering.

29:1–6 Offerings for the Feast of the Seventh Month, the Feast of Trumpets. 1 On the first day of the seventh month there was another day of holy convocation in which all work ceased. The day was a day of trumpet blowing. **2–5** *A burnt offering, a pleasing odour to the Lord* was offered comprising one young bull, one ram, seven male lambs a year old, each with the appropriate cereal-offering and oil, and a male goat for a sin-offering (*cf.* Lv. 23:23–25). **6** These offerings were additional to the offerings made normally at new moon, and the regular daily offerings (*cf.* 28:11–15). This day is not mentioned in Ezekiel.

29:7–11 Offerings for the Day of Atonement, the tenth day of the seventh month. 7 This was another day of holy convocation. But on this day the people were to *afflict* themselves, *i.e.* fast and refrain from all work. The day came to be known as the Day of Atonement (Heb. *yôm kippûr, cf.* Lv. 23:26–32). **8–10** The offering was a burnt-offering, consisting of a young bull, a ram, seven male yearling lambs, all of them without blemish and all accompanied by the appropriate cereal-offering and oil. **11** On the same day a male goat was offered for a sin-offering, *besides the sin offering of atonement* (Heb. *ḥaṭṭā'ṭ hakkippurîm*), which consisted of a bullock (*cf.* Ex. 29:36; 30:10; Lv. 16:11), and the regular daily offering.

29:12–38 The offerings for the Feast of Booths. 12 The offerings on this occasion were the most numerous of the whole year. The feast began on the fifteenth day of the seventh month with a holy convocation and continued for seven more days. *Cf.* Lv. 23:33–36, 39–43. **13–16** On the first of the eight days of festival the maximum number of beasts was offered, *thirteen young bulls, two rams, fourteen male lambs a year old,* all without blemish, each accompanied by its cereal-offering and oil. In addition one male goat for a sin-offering, as well as the regular daily offering with its cereal- and drink-offering were offered. **17–34** On each succeeding day one less bull was offered until the seventh day, but the rest of the offerings remained the same. **35** On the eighth day there was *a solemn assembly* (Heb. *'aṣereṭ*), or 'closing day'. **36–38** The offerings for the day were one bull, one ram, seven male lambs a year old, all without blemish, along with their cereal- and drink-offerings, as well as one male goat for a sin-offering, besides the regular daily offering. These offerings agree with those of the first and tenth days of the seventh month (vv. 1, 7). In Ex. 23:16; 34:22 no duration is given for the celebration of this feast. Dt. 16:13–15 appears to specify seven days only, but should probably be understood in the same sense as Ezk. 45:25 where we may well understand the regulation to mean the fifteenth day and the seven subsequent days, a total of eight in all, as in the present passage.

29:39, 40 General offerings. The chapter concludes with an important observation. The offerings referred to here are statutory and prescribed (*appointed feasts*). But there were also private *votive offerings, freewill offerings, burnt offerings, cereal offerings, drink offerings,* and *peace offerings.*

30:1–16 The law of vows, particularly women's vows. After a brief statement about the obligations of men in the matter of vows the major part of this chapter (vv. 3–16) is devoted to vows made by women.

1, 2 The vow of a man. Men in Israel were unconditionally bound by a vow of any kind. Two kinds of vows are referred to here, the *vow to the Lord,* a term with wide connotation, and an oath to bind oneself by a *pledge* (Heb. *'issar,* from the root '-s-r, 'to bind'). The second of these vows seems to have reference to secular obligations, while the first is concerned with religious obligations. But the usage may have been a little more flexible. Vows are discussed elsewhere in the OT, in Nu. 6:2ff.; Lv. 5:4, 5; 27:1ff.; Dt. 23:21–23; Pss. 22:25; 50:14, *etc.* A complete section of the Jewish Mishnah is devoted to vows, the Nedarim. But more comprehensively a man was bound to do *all that proceeds out of his mouth.*

3–5 The vow of an unmarried daughter. 3 A young woman *in her youth,* and in her father's care (*while within her father's house*), could only undertake a vow or pledge with her father's approval. **4** If her father learned of the vow and did not repudiate it, the vow stood. **5** If the father disapproved the day he heard of it, the vow was invalid. The Lord would forgive her failure to fulfil her obligation because of her father's intervention.

6–15 The vows of married women. There are three cases: the betrothed woman who made a vow unknown to her father but discovered by her husband after marriage (vv. 6–8), the widow or divorced woman (v. 9), the married woman (vv. 10–15).

6–8 Where a woman is given in marriage *while under her vows or any thoughtless utterance of her lips,* the husband may repudiate these on the day he hears of them. If he learns of the obligations and does not repudiate them, they stand. No penalty attaches to the woman where her husband repudiates her vows. **9** The widow or divorced woman is completely responsible for every vow or pledge she takes. **10–15** If a woman enters into a vow or pledge when in her husband's house, the husband may make them null and void on the day he hears of them. In that case no penalty attaches to the woman for breaking her vow or pledge. But if the husband does not object, the woman is responsible to fulfil her vow or pledge. If the husband some time later seeks to make the vow or pledge null and void *he shall bear the iniquity, i.e.* he is held responsible for his wife's undertakings.

16 The law of vows summarized. The last verse is a simple summary of the law of vows in the two broad areas of a man and his wife, and a father and his daughter.

31:1–54 The holy war against Midian

The holy war featured prominently in the early history of Israel. In theory, since Yahweh is the Lord of history, He will work out His purposes despite opposition and will overthrow every opponent. Israel's task was to co-operate with Him. He was leader of Israel's armies and would assure them of victory, although not every war was a holy war. After the battle, captives and booty belonged to Yahweh and were either 'devoted' entirely to Him and destroyed, or preserved at His will in whole or in part. The present story concerns a campaign against Midian, or rather a part of Midian, since despite vv. 8–17 the Midianites remained a powerful group long after the days of Moses; *cf., e.g.,* Jdg. 6–8. The passage gives a good picture of how the holy war was to be conducted, how

warriors who participated were to be purified, and how the spoil was to be divided. The great numbers of people and animals are evidently symbolic rather than strictly mathematical.

31:1–6 The call-up. 1–3 Moses as Israel's leader was instructed to avenge Israel on the Midianites because of the incident of Peor (*cf.* ch. 25). **4** Each tribe had to provide one unit of men (Heb. *'elep̄*; the translation *thousand* is incorrect). **5, 6** Twelve 'thousands' armed for war were selected and placed under the leadership of Phinehas (*cf.* 1 Ch. 9:20) who took with him *the vessels of the sanctuary,* possibly the ark (*cf.* Nu. 10:35f.; 14:44; 1 Sa. 4:4; 2 Ch. 5:5), and *the trumpets for the alarm* (*t^erû'â*). See on 10:3ff. The word for 'alarm' probably refers to a number of short trumpet blasts.

31:7–12 The defeat of Midian. 7, 8 As in other holy wars, males were to be slain. Among these were five Midianite *kings,* called elsewhere 'elders' (22:4) or 'leaders' (Jos. 13:21). Balaam, the central figure of chs. 22–24, who evidently had eventually joined the Midianites, was also slain. **9–12** Women and children were taken captive, flocks, herds, and property were taken as booty, *cities* (permanent settlements) and *encampments* (nomad settlements) were burned, and the spoil was brought to Moses, Eleazar, and the people.

31:13–18 The destruction of the Midianites. 13–16 Moses met the returning army and at once expressed displeasure that the officers had spared the women who had caused Israel to sin at Peor (*cf.* 25:16–18). **14** provides a good example of the use of 'thousand' and 'hundred' as a military unit. **17, 18** The army was commanded to kill all male children as well as these offending women. The young virgins were to be taken by the warriors. The incident must have been a local one since Midianites are well known in later centuries.

31:19–24 The purification of the warriors. 19, 20 Contact with dead bodies in the war made the warriors and their captives unclean. Purification according to the ritual of ch. 19 was necessary. Those who were unclean had to remain outside the camp for seven days. On the third and seventh day they had to purify themselves (lit. 'de-sin') as well as their garments, *etc.* **21–24** A further ritual of purification by fire was required. *Everything that can stand the fire,* evidently all the metal objects, had to be first passed through the fire and then purified (lit. 'de-sinned') with *the water of impurity* (*cf.* 19:1–22). Objects that could not stand the fire had to be washed with the water. Finally, on the seventh day the men washed their clothes and returned to the camp.

31:25–54 The distribution of the spoil. 25–27 The spoil was divided equally between those who went to war and those who remained at home, a good illustration of tribal solidarity (*cf.* 1 Sa. 30:24, 25). **28** Yahweh received a tribute of *one out of five hundred* (one-fifth of 1 %) of the persons and animals. **29** This was taken and given to

Eleazar as *an offering to the Lord.* **30, 31** The Levites received *one drawn out of every fifty* (2%) of the people's portion of persons and animals. **32** *The booty remaining of the spoil that the men of war took* is then listed. The exact definition of *the booty remaining* is not clear but presumably it covered what was left after the removal of the sheep and cattle eaten during the campaign, and the personal booty taken by the soldiers from the slain consisting of the items listed in v. 50. **33–47** The numbers appear to be excessive and are probably symbolic in some way, although, to be sure, the arithmetic is carefully worked out, *e.g.*, v. 38. That 12,000 Israelites (v. 5) could overthrow a people among whom there were 32,000 virgins (v. 35) and bring back 800,000 animals without the loss of a single life (vv. 48, 49) suggests that we are dealing with a numerical scheme that is not normal. **48** The military usage of the terms 'thousand' and 'hundred' is clear in this verse. **49, 50** In gratitude for God's signal blessing the men brought the Lord's offering to the sanctuary *to make an atonement* (Heb. verb *kipper*, 'cover') before the Lord. Perhaps the verb had the connotation suggested by the noun *kōper*, 'ransom' (*cf.* Ex. 30:12). **51–54** The value of gold in the offering was 16,750 shekels, *i.e.* 6,700 oz. calculating at two-fifths of an ounce per shekel, an enormous quantity. Again, the number may be symbolic. This offering was taken to the tent of meeting by Moses and Eleazar as a *memorial*, a reminder to Israel of a remarkable incident in which they experienced the help and deliverance of Yahweh.

32:1–42 Settlement of two and a half tribes in Transjordan

The tribes of Reuben, Gad and half Manasseh were the first to be allotted their portion, but lest their withdrawal should discourage the rest Moses required them to help their brethren before they could actually exploit their land in Transjordan.

32:1–5 The request of Reuben and Gad. 1, 2 The area requested by Reuben and Gad was *the land of Jazer and the land of Gilead, i.e.* the area between the Arnon and the Jabbok rivers. It was a good place for animals. **3–5** Nine towns in the region are listed. Several can be identified. *Ataroth* is probably Khirbet ʿAṭṭarûs 8 miles north-west of Dibon; *Dibon* is modern Diban 4 miles north of the Arnon; *Nimrah* is in the vicinity of Tell Nimrin, well to the north; *Heshbon* is modern Ḥesbān, the capital of Sihon; *Elealah* is the modern el-ʿAl north-east of Heshbon; *Beon* may be Beth-baal-meon, the modern Maʿîn 10 miles south-south-west of Heshbon. *Sebam* and *Nebo* cannot be identified. It is of interest that the Moabite stone found at Dibon in 1868, dating to the middle of the 9th century BC, states that the men of Gad dwelt in Ataroth from of old (line 10). This monument refers to several of these names.

32:6–15 Moses' indignation. 6, 7 This proposal of Reuben and Gad angered Moses because it could possibly *discourage the heart of the people of Israel from going over into the land which the Lord has given them.* **8–13** Moses recalled the story of the spies when the ten discouraged the people who then turned back (*cf.* 13:31–33) with the result that only Caleb and Joshua would enter the land. **14, 15** The present action was reminiscent of that former one and a new *brood of sinful men* had arisen to provoke the Lord.

32:16–19 The promise of Reuben and Gad. 16 Clearly some protection was needed for the women and children of Reuben and Gad. The men would build *sheepfolds* (lit. 'walls for sheep'), and *cities*, probably fortified, for their families. **17–19** Then they would go armed with their fellows till they too had possessed an inheritance on the west side of Jordan. *Cf.* Jos. 1:12–18.

32:20–33 Moses' conditions. 20–22 The promise is now stated formally. Only after the Lord had driven out the enemies on the west side of Jordan were Reuben and Gad *free of obligation to the Lord.* **23** If they failed they would have sinned against the Lord: *your sin will find you out, i.e.* judgment would inevitably befall them. **24–27** Reuben and Gad formally accepted the conditions. **28–32** A public occasion is depicted in which Joshua and Eleazar and the tribal leaders were informed and in which the men of Reuben and Gad declared their intention to help their brethren on oath. **33** The area assigned to Reuben and Gad was that formerly occupied by Sihon and Og the Amorite kings (*cf.* 21:21–35). At this point in the narrative the half-tribe of Manasseh is joined with Reuben and Gad. See vv. 39–42.

32:34–38 Cities built by Reuben and Gad. 34–36 Some of these cities were mentioned in v. 3, viz. Dibon, Ataroth, and Beth-nimrah. Among the others *Aroer* is the modern ʿArâʿir, a fine site overlooking Wadi Arnon at present being excavated; *Jogbehah* is possibly Jubeihât 5 miles north of Amman; *Beth-haran* is south of *Beth-nimrah* on the eastern edge of the Jordan valley. **37, 38** The cities built by Reuben are mentioned in v. 3 except *Kiriathaim*, the modern Khirbet el-Qureiyât 3 miles north-west of Dibon, mentioned also on the Moabite stone.

32:39–42 The conquest of Gilead by clans from the tribe of Manasseh. 39 The explanation of the inclusion of the half-tribe of Manasseh among those who occupied Transjordan is now given. Three of the clans of Manasseh, Machir, Jair and Nobah, occupied this area which was the original territory of Manasseh. Later they had a share to the west of Jordan (*cf.* Jos. 17:14–18). **40–42** The distribution of the area between the three clans is shown here. It was the area formerly occupied by Og (*cf.* 21:31–35).

33:1 – 36:13 MISCELLANEOUS APPENDICES

The book of Numbers concludes with a number of appendices—an itinerary of the journey from

Egypt to the plains of Moab (ch. 33), tribal boundaries (ch. 34), cities of refuge (ch. 35), and a concluding chapter on the inheritance of women (ch. 36).

33:1–56 The itinerary from Egypt to the plains of Moab reviewed

The whole journey from Egypt to the plains of Moab is now reviewed. Eleven stages are noted between Rameses and Sinai (vv. 1–15), twenty from Sinai to Ezion-geber (vv. 16–35), one to the wilderness of Sin, *i.e.* Kadesh (v. 36), and nine to the plains of Moab (vv. 37–49). Few of these can be identified today, and some of the notable places like Massah-Meribah and Taberah are not listed here. Probably the actual number of stopping-places was far more than those listed here. (See map in Exodus, p. 123.)

33:1–4 Introduction. 1, 2 Moses is recorded as having kept a log book of the various *stages* (Heb. *massaʿ*, lit. 'a plucking up', *i.e.* the striking of the camp). The stages are described in terms of the starting-point. **3, 4** *Rameses* (*cf.* Ex. 1:11), the ancient Tanis, is probably modern Qanṭîr. Israel set out *triumphantly* (lit. 'with a raised hand') while the Egyptians were recovering from the tragic events of Passover night.

33:5–15 From Rameses to Sinai. 5, 6 The next stopping-place was *Succoth*, probably Tell el Maskhûṭah, and thence they went to *Etham* which some identify with an ancient fortress between the two Bitter Lakes (Egyptian *ḥtm*, 'fortress'). **7–15** The itinerary to Sinai thereafter follows Ex. 12:37 – 19:2. One proposal is that the way led west of the Bitter Lakes, crossed the shallow waters south of the Great Bitter Lake and followed the western arm of the Red Sea south for *three days' journey* (*cf.* Ex. 3:18; 15:22) to *Marah*, which on the view that Sinai lay in the peninsula may be ʿAin Ḥawâra, some 25 miles down the Gulf of Suez. Then *Elim* may be the oasis of Wadi Gharandel, *Dophkah* may be Serâbît el-Khâdim, and *Alush*, Wadi el-ʿEshsh. *Rephidim* was probably Wadi Refâyid (*cf.* Ex. 17:1; 19:2).

33:16–36 In the wilderness. 16 Twenty camping-places are noted from Sinai to Ezion-geber. *Kibroth-hattaavah* is possibly Ruweis el-Ebeirig a few miles north-east of Mt. Sinai. **17–34** The next twelve places cannot be identified. *Moseroth, Bene-jaakan, Hor-haggidgad* and *Jotbathah* occur in Dt. 10:6, 7 (where Moserah is Moserath and Gudgodah is Hor-haggidgad). **35, 36** *Ezion-geber* is at the head of the Gulf of Aqabah, probably the modern Tell el-Kheleifeh which has been excavated. It is some 50 miles from here to Kadesh.

33:37–49 From Kadesh to Moab. 37–39 Many years elapsed before Israel left Kadesh to travel on. At Mt. Hor Aaron died aged 123 years (*cf.* 20:22–29). **40** Only passing reference is made to conflict with Arad (*cf.* 21:1). **41–49** The itinerary then follows chs. 20, 21. *Punon* is possibly modern Fenian, a place where copper mines were worked. *Iye-abarim* along the Wadi Zered is possibly modern Maḥay (*cf.* 21:10–12). *Dibon-gad* is

mentioned on the Moabite stone as Mesha's capital. *Almon-diblathaim* may be the Beth-diblathaim of Je. 48:22. Finally *Beth-jeshimoth* is possibly Tell el-ʿAzeimeh and *Abel-shittim*, Tell Kefrein, both in the Jordan Valley opposite Jericho, marking the last camping place on the plains of Moab before crossing the Jordan.

33:50–56 Final instructions before crossing the Jordan. 50, 51 Instructions about the treatment of the people west of Jordan follow. **52** Israel must drive out the Canaanites, *etc.* and destroy their cult objects, *figured stones* (*i.e.* carved statues in stone), molten images, and high places. **53, 54** The land of the dispossessed inhabitants was to be distributed by lot. **55, 56** By way of warning Israel was told that if the inhabitants were not driven out they would remain as *pricks in your eyes and thorns in your sides.* If Israel failed in this task, Yahweh would do to them what they thought to do to the inhabitants of Canaan.

34:1–29 The ideal boundaries of Israel

While Israel remained on the plains of Moab any boundaries on the west of Jordan could only be theoretical. Even after they crossed the river many years of warfare lay ahead. Indeed, only in the days of David and Solomon did Israel's boundaries ever approximate to the ideal. Yet the ideal remained through the centuries (*cf.* Jos. 15–19; Ezk. 47:13–23, *etc.*).

34:1–15 The boundaries fixed. 1, 2 The land of Canaan is defined as *the land of Canaan in its full extent.* **3–5** On the south the line ran from the southern end of the *Salt Sea* (Dead Sea), south-west along the border of Edom via the *ascent of Akrabbim* ('scorpions'; mod. Naqb eṣ-Safâ), across the wilderness of Zin to Kadesh-barnea its most southerly point, then north-west through the unidentified Hazar-addar and Azmon to the *Brook of Egypt* (Wadi el-ʿArîsh) and thence to the Mediterranean Sea. It may be remarked that this identification of the Brook of Egypt is not undisputed. See *NBD*, 'Egypt, River of', for fuller discussion. **6** The western boundary was the Great Sea (Mediterranean), although except for a brief occupation in Hezekiah's day (*cf.* 2 Ki. 18:8) this area was never in Israel's hands. **7–9** The northern boundary ran east from an unidentified point on the Mediterranean Sea to an unidentified Mt. Hor (clearly not the one of 20:22), and thence probably north-east to the *entrance of Hamath* (probably Lebo-hamath, at the head of the Orontes). The other places cannot be identified unless *Hazar-enan* (lit. 'enclosure of the spring') is Banias, although some identify it with Qarya-tein, the last oasis before Palmyra. **10–12a** The eastern boundary is identifiable once it touches the *shoulder* (ridge) *of the sea of Chinnereth* (lit. 'harp-shaped'; *i.e.* the Sea of Galilee). Thence it followed the Jordan to the Dead Sea. **12b, 13** *This shall be your land with its boundaries all round* refers merely to the area west of the Jordan since the area to the east has already been described. It was to be divided by lot among the nine and a half tribes. **14, 15** The area in Transjordan, *eastward, toward the sunrise*, was already occupied by two and a half tribes. The phrase *beyond the Jordan . . . eastward* might well be thought to betray the hand of one who wrote, later, on the west of the river. This is not, however, necessarily the case. The word translated *beyond* (Heb. *'ēber*) probably really means 'in the region of', and consequently is often found with associated words like 'eastward' or 'westward' (*e.g.* Dt. 4:41; 11:30) so as to fix its precise reference. In references like Jos. 9:1 and 1 Ki. 4:24 (where RSV actually translates it 'west') it is used to refer to the west bank by a writer living on the west of the river. The expression in the present passage is therefore simply equivalent to 'on the east side of Jordan' and permits no conclusion to be drawn as to the location of the writer. (See further G. T. Manley, *The Book of the Law*, 1957, p. 49.)

34:16–29 The allotment officers. 16–18 The allocation of the land was committed to Eleazar, Joshua, and one *leader* from each tribe. **19–29** The leaders are named in order from south to north. At the time Dan was still in the south so that the time is prior to Jdg. 18. Only Caleb is known among the leaders. The names, however, provide interesting insight into Israel's name system, *e.g. Shemuel*, 'name of God'; *Elidad*, 'God has loved'; *Hanniel*, 'favour of God'; *Elizaphan*, 'my God protects'; *Paltiel*, 'God is my deliverance'; *Pedahel*, 'God has redeemed', *etc.*

35:1–34 The Levitical cities

35:1–8 The cities and pasture lands of the Levites. 1–3 The Levites, no longer a secular tribe, had no possession in the land. Since they could not all be occupied at the central sanctuary at one time they were allotted forty-eight cities in the areas of the secular tribes. In addition *pasture lands* were set apart around the cities for their flocks and herds. **4, 5** It is difficult to form a clear idea of the disposition of the pasture lands. They were to *reach from the wall of the city outward a thousand cubits all round, i.e.* 500 yards. Further, Israel was to measure outside the city 2,000 cubits (1,000 yards) on each side of the city. Many ingenious solutions have been offered, but one of the simplest is that on each side of the city there was an area, 500 yards outward from the city wall and 1,000 yards long, for the Levites. The rest of the land, if any, was for the people. But it is safest to treat the picture as symbolic. *Cf.* Ezk. 48:8–14 where the priests and Levites were allotted strips of territory across the middle of the land. **6–8** Of the forty-eight cities, six were reserved as cities of refuge (see vv. 9–15). The manner of allocation is described in Jos. 21. Whether the Levites owned these pasture lands personally is not clear. Some passages in the OT suggest that at times priests and Levites bought, sold, and owned land (*cf.* Lv. 25:32–34; Je. 32:7–12). The forty-eight cities

were to be taken from the secular tribes according to the principle that the larger tribes gave more than the smaller ones (*cf.* 26:54; 33:54).

35:9–15 The cities of refuge. 9–12 According to ancient Semitic law, when one man killed another, whether deliberately or accidentally, the blood of the dead man was avenged by a kinsman according to the law: 'Whoever sheds the blood of man, by man shall his blood be shed' (Gn. 9:6). In this simple form the law was indiscriminate since there was a difference between accidental homicide and wilful murder. Among some peoples refuge from the avenger (Heb. *gō'ēl*) could be found at a sanctuary. In Israel six cities were set apart where a killer might shelter till he came before the congregation for judgment. **13–15** Three cities were situated beyond Jordan and three in Canaan. They were available to the people of Israel, to the resident alien, and to the temporary resident alike (*cf.* Dt. 4:41–43; Jos. 20:7, 8).

35:16–34 The definition of manslaughter and murder. 16–18 When one man struck another with a lethal weapon such as an iron instrument, a stone, or a wooden implement, murder might be suspected. **19** In such cases the avenger was at liberty to seek the killer's life. **20, 21** Again, previous hatred, or deliberate lying in wait, or enmity pointed to murder and the avenger was at liberty to slay the killer. **22–25** But there were many cases of accidental homicide where no harm was intended. In such cases the congregation declared the man's innocence and rescued him from the avenger and allowed him to live in one of the cities of refuge *until the death of the high priest*. **26–28** But if the man ventured beyond the bounds of the city and was caught by the avenger he might be slain. **29** Certain legal details are now given. **30** More than one witness to a murder was required. **31, 32** The payment of a ransom (Heb. *kōper*) for the life of a murderer, or even for his safe return to his home in the case of accidental murder, was forbidden. **33** Killing of any kind was serious and proper penalties were required, for when a man's blood was shed Yahweh's land was polluted and could be purged only by the blood of the killer. **34** Israel was to avoid defiling the land at all costs. Evidently with the anointing of a new high priest the various cleansing and sanctifying rituals associated with his anointing freed the land where Yahweh dwelt among His people from the defilement caused even by accidental death.

36:1–13 The daughters of Zelophehad and the inheritance of women

When the question of the inheritance of the daughters of Zelophehad was first discussed (*cf.* 27:1–11) it was decreed that where a man had no sons his daughters might inherit their father's property. But a further question arose in the case of such heiresses as subsequently married.

1–4 The heads of some of the families of Manasseh expressed concern that the marriage of girls who inherited their father's property might remove to another tribe what had been allotted to Manasseh. **5-9** Moses sought the will of Yahweh and commanded that women should marry within the tribe of their father, thus preserving the total inheritance of a tribe for that tribe. **10-12** The daughters of Zelophehad subsequently married men of Manasseh. But the provision seems to have been a very special one since inheritance in Israel was normally through the male line. For this very reason levirate marriage was instituted (*cf.* Dt. 25:5-10). **13** The closing verse of Numbers is a subscription to the body of laws covered in the closing chapters, either chs. 22-36 or chs. 27-36 (*cf.* the closing verse of Leviticus).

J A. THOMPSON

Deuteronomy

INTRODUCTION

TITLE

Among the Jews the fifth book of the law was known by the name *'ēlleh hadd^eḇārîm* ('these are the words') or by the shorter form *d^eḇārîm* ('words'), taken from Dt. 1:1. An alternative title, *mišneh hattôrâ* ('copy of this law'), was derived from Dt. 17:18, and this was sometimes shortened to *mišneh*. The English title was taken from the LXX Greek phrase *to deuteronomion touto* ('this second lawgiving') in Dt. 17:18, following the Vulgate rendering of *deuteronomium*. The idea of a 'second' or 'repeated' lawgiving is unfortunate, since the expression in Dt. 17:18 should be rendered 'a copy of this law'.

The LXX title was apparently given to the work because Deuteronomy consisted mostly of a recapitulation of enactments contained in the book of Exodus and sections of Leviticus and Numbers. However, the book was not simply a repetition of earlier material, but followed a specific treaty-pattern in its elaboration of the principles and responsibilities of the people of God as they stood in covenant with Him. It constituted a promulgation in untechnical language of the implications of the spiritual relationship established at Sinai, and had as its concern the assembled congregation of Israel rather than an exclusive group such as the priestly house of Aaron, whose needs were amply met in the more technical sections of Exodus and Leviticus. When Levitical priests were mentioned in Deuteronomy it was essentially from a lay standpoint. As a result, they were upheld as ministers and teachers of the law, who by their very position in the religious community claimed the loyalty and support of the people.

BACKGROUND

Deuteronomy contains the addresses delivered by Moses in the closing months of his life to the Israelites as they were assembled in the plains of Moab. The book perpetuates the traditions preserved in Exodus to the effect that Moses habitually recorded events, statutes and other material, and makes claim to be substantially the work of the great Hebrew lawgiver himself. The time and place of the discourses are specified carefully (1:1–5; 3:29; 4:46; 29:1), and need to be kept firmly in mind in attempting to establish the proper background of the book.

At the time the speeches were given, the Israelites were encamped in the plains of Moab. The area was a rather distinctive section of Moabite territory, whose core comprised the plateau E of the Dead Sea between the Wadis Arnon and Zared, but which for considerable periods of Moabite history extended well to the N of the Wadi Arnon. The plains of Moab consisted of a well watered, productive area along the River Jordan, stretching from the Dead Sea N to the Wadi Nimrin for a distance of some 8 miles. The Moabites appear to have occupied this territory at an early period in their history, since it was already known by the name found in the OT when the Amorite king Sihon drove the Moabites S to the Wadi Arnon.

For a generation the covenant people had been disciplined by life in the Sinai peninsula. Although they had spent some of that time at Kadesh-barnea, in the region of 'Ain Qudeis and 'Ain Qudeirat, they had been forged by the circumstances of their life into a homogeneous spiritual unit and made ready by divine grace for the occupation of the promised land. Now, as they paused in the lush pastures of the plains of Moab and looked W towards Jericho and the plain of the Jordan, their long-cherished objective was at last within reach. Territorial gains had already been made in the region E of the Jordan, and were being consolidated by the tribes of Reuben, Gad and the half-tribe of Manasseh. Now the remaining Israelites were at a critical point in their history, and though their general morale was high they were about to confront strong temptations and severe trials under the guidance of a new leader who as yet had to prove himself as a warrior and an administrator.

At this time Moses, who had been forewarned of his death, called the people together and in his addresses he reminded them of the mighty acts of God wrought on their behalf. Having regard to the future conquest of Canaan he outlined the divinely ordained constitution of the new theocracy which was to be established in the promised land. He encouraged the Israelites to faith and obedience, warned against the perils of idolatry and apostasy, foretold punishment for a nation which forsook the high ideals of the Sinai covenant, and at the same time promised blessings from God if Israel was faithful to her divine commission.

He repeated the 'ten words', first given 'from the midst of the fire', and expounded their significance. He then recapitulated laws received on various occasions, some of the enactments being of considerable antiquity and dating back in all probability to the patriarchal period; some revealed during the stay in the region of Horeb, and others being the result of divine revelation on differing occasions. The collection was cast into a treaty structure, and adapted in such a way as to provide guidance for Israel in the promised land. The laws are most aptly summarized in the words 'You shall love the Lord your God with all your heart, and with all your soul, and with all your strength, and with all your mind; and your neighbour as yourself', cited in Lk. 10:27 from Dt. 6:5, with the addition by Christ of the words, 'Do this, and you will live' (Lk. 10:28). The importance of Deuteronomy for Christ and the primitive Christian church can be judged from the fact that the NT contains over 80 citations from or references to this book, and these ought to be studied carefully if its meaning for the Christian is to be understood and its message received.

AUTHORSHIP AND DATE

Ancient Hebrew and Samaritan tradition was unanimous in attributing the authorship of Deuteronomy to Moses, and this is confirmed by Ne. 8:1. Whereas the Hebrew text made no specific claims concerning the transcription of Leviticus and Numbers, it stated distinctly that Deuteronomy was to be regarded substantially as the work of Moses. In Dt. 1:5 he was said to have 'explained' the law and subsequently to have written it in a book which was placed beside the ark of the covenant and delivered to the Levites for safe keeping (Dt. 31:9, 26). The reference to 'this law' (Dt. 17:18), a copy of which was to be made and given to future kings of the nation, was apparently to the particular enactment concerning the king and not to Deuteronomy as a whole. However, such a mention presupposes either that the people knew that Moses was recording his speeches day by day, or that he actually had the text of his address in front of him as he was delivering it. Further indications of an early date for the written form of much of Deuteronomy can be seen in the passages in Joshua which presuppose it. These are far too numerous and too closely integrated with surrounding material to enable them to be regarded as later insertions with any plausibility, and this points once more to an early date for Deuteronomy.

Liberal scholarship in the 18th and 19th centuries AD was virtually unanimous in rejecting any assertion of Mosaic authorship for the work, and assigned it with entirely unwarranted confidence to the activities of an unknown prophet who compiled it somewhat before 621 BC, the date of Josiah's reformation (2 Ki. 22;23). It was thought to have been written with the aim of promoting such reforms as were undertaken at that time, not the least of which was the centralization of cultic worship in Jerusalem. Wellhausen suggested that, to further his aims, the author concealed his work in the Temple fabric and permitted it to be 'discovered' when renovations to the building were being undertaken. This supposed relationship between the work of the 'Deuteronomist' and the reform movement under Josiah has long been central to the liberal view of Pentateuchal origins, since other documents were generally dated in relationship to Deuteronomy.

Some scholars went even further in that they favoured a post-exilic date for Deuteronomy, theorizing that the scroll recovered from the Temple fabric was the 'Holiness Code' (Lv. 17–26), and assigned the book to between 520 and 400 BC, the latter date being postulated by the Uppsala school. Certain 19th-century critics, however, dated Deuteronomy in either the reign of Hezekiah or that of Manasseh, while one or two writers regarded Samuel as the author. From a different standpoint von Rad held that Deuteronomy arose in circles of 'country Levites' who had access to the sacred literary traditions of the Israelites, and who were intensely concerned with the movement for national and military rehabilitation after the events of 701 BC, when the Assyrians had invaded Judah (*Studies in Deuteronomy*, 1953, pp. 60ff.). This view represented an interesting departure from that of classic German liberalism generally.

A more realistic solution to the problems of authorship and date has been provided recently by studies in the similarity between the Sinai covenant and the suzerainty or vassal type of international treaty current in the Near East from the 3rd millennium BC. Normal secular treaty documents contained the following elements: *a.* a preamble, identifying the author and giving his attributes; *b.* the historical prologue, usually stressing the suzerain's benevolence; *c.* the treaty stipulations, in both general and more specific terms; *d.* the divine witnesses and guarantors of the treaty; *e.* the blessings or curses which would occur according as the covenant was kept or violated. Provisions for a periodic public reading of the treaty provisions by the vassal were also generally included in such agreements.

This Near Eastern treaty pattern is applicable to several OT passages, including those recording the Sinai covenant (Ex. 19:3–8; 20:1–17), but it is particularly evident in the structure of Deuteronomy when the latter is viewed as a single literary unit. Following the above outline, Deuteronomy can be related to the treaty-formulation in these particular respects: *a.* preamble (1:1–5); *b.* historical prologue (1:6–4:49); *c.* stipulations (5:1–26:19); *d.* curses and blessings (27:1–30:20); succession arrangements and public reading (31:1–34:5). These remarkable parallels in form would indicate clearly that the book of Deuteronomy was compiled deliberately as a covenant-renewal document in the best traditions of the 2nd millennium BC.

The question of a date in the Mosaic age is important, since such international treaties occurred as late as the time of Esarhaddon (681–669 BC), and the suzerainty-treaty form as such does not therefore of necessity require a 2nd-millennium BC date for Deuteronomy. However, there appear to be certain decisive differences between 2nd- and 1st-millennium BC covenants, the most important being that the historical prologue was completely absent from treaties formulated after the end of the 2nd millennium BC. Form-critical studies of this kind recognize not merely the antiquity of isolated elements in Deuteronomy, but the early age of the Deuteronomic treaty in its entirety, and set it firmly against the background of the Mosaic age.

The critical view of Deuteronomy as a 'pious fraud' must now be abandoned, if only because there is no archaeological evidence whatever for documentary or literary fabrications in the 2nd millennium BC. The assertion that the central-ization of worship in Jerusalem was one of the prime reasons for the compiling of Deuteronomy must be viewed with grave suspicion also. The book lays no stress on the claim of Jerusalem to be the sole place of worship, and contains no legislation to that effect. The real emphasis of Dt. 12 is not on the contrast between many altars of God and one, but between the pagan Canaanite altars and the place where God's name was to be revered.

As von Rad correctly observed, the command in Dt. 27:1-8 to erect an altar on Mt. Ebal and inscribe the law upon prepared stones raised a serious obstacle to the liberal theory of cultic centralization in Jerusalem (*Studies in Deuter-onomy*, 1953, p. 68; see also G. T. Manley, *The Book of the Law*, 1957, pp. 20, 132, 134f.). The primitive character of the enactment in Dt. 27:1-8 is shown by the absence of words such as *ba'al* ('Baal') and *bāmôṯ* ('high places'), as well as by the indefinite nature of the topography. Clearly the Jebusite city of Jerusalem is the least likely claimant to such a responsible title as the sole place of Israelite worship. It should be noted that Jerusalem as a proper name does not occur in the Pentateuch, though found in the 14th-century BC Tell el-Amarna letters. The assump-tion that the 'Salem' of Gn. 14:18 is an abbrev-iated form of Jerusalem is gratuitous, since the reference is more probably to a site in the Jordan Valley S of Scythopolis, and may have been the Salim of Jn. 3:23. While Deuteronomy prescribed a central site, Mt. Ebal, for Israelite national and spiritual aspirations, it did not require the cultus as such to be centralized there. It is not without significance that the Samaritans, an ancient Jewish sect, have revered the Ebal-Gerizim area as the location where God chose to put His name, and they are undoubtedly right in their belief that the altar erected 'near' Mt. Gerizim is the only one built to the specifications of Moses.

The foregoing comments indicate that there are strong arguments for the essential Mosaicity of Deuteronomy. The freshness of the narrative gives the reader a sense of participation with the author in the crossing of the Wadi Zered (2:13), of halting at the wilderness of Kedemoth (2:26), turning on the road to Bashan, and halting at last in the valley over against Beth-peor (3:29). An abundance of rather incidental geographical details in the book points to a familiarity with the background of 2nd-millennium BC Moabite history and topography. The reminiscences of Moses often intrude with unexpected suddenness into his discourses (9:22), and even into the delivery of the laws themselves (24:9), reminding the reader of his private thoughts, emotions and prayers.

The character of Moses as revealed in the earlier books is also apparent in Deuteronomy. His ardent spirit (Ex. 2:12, 13) reveals itself in outbursts of fiery indignation (Dt. 9:21ff.) and emotional appeal (10:12-22). The effect of his early education (Acts 7:22) is shown in his skill as a leader, organizer and writer. This towering Israelite legislator confronted and surmounted difficulties during the wilderness period which would have defeated a lesser man. Though not a demagogue, he was able to communicate the will of God to his fellows with great effectiveness, and his prose and poetry are abiding monuments to his literary and spiritual genius. As the devoted 'servant of the Lord' (Dt. 34:5) the name of his God was continually on his lips, and his marshal-ling of personal spiritual resources in times of crisis marked him out as the greatest of all Hebrew leaders. The picture of Moses thus presented in Deuteronomy is completely con-sistent with what is found in the historical sections of Exodus and Numbers, and furnishes for the reader a realistic image of a mortal man as contrasted with the highly idealized depictions of later Judaism.

Ever since the Mosaic authorship of Deute-ronomy was questioned on the ground that Moses could not have written the section re-cording his own death, the matter of post-Mosaic additions to Deuteronomy has been an important consideration. Whatever the nature of the book which Moses compiled, it most probably did not contain chs. 32-34, these doubtless being added shortly after Moses died so as to complete the narrative content. Joshua may have written the account of Moses' death, as Jewish tradition has maintained, or the con-cluding verses of the book could have been the work of Eleazar, but the actual facts of the situation are unknown.

Phrases such as 'beyond the Jordan' (*'ēber hayyardēn*) have been taken as indications of post-Mosaic authorship. Since the reference is generally to the E region of Gilead, Reuben and Gad, the standpoint of the author is assumed to have been that of a resident in Canaan, and as such would preclude Mosaic authorship. How-ever, the expression also refers to the territory W of Jordan as well (3:20, 25; 11:30), so that in effect the phrase simply means 'Transjordania', a usage which was non-specific and went back to patriarchal times. Explanatory glosses such as the phrase 'as at this day' (*kayyom hazzeh*) in 2:30 present no difficulties either, since in anti-quity, and particularly in Egypt, it was the practice for scribes to make regular revisions of earlier literary material and amend the text by such devices as more modern place-names, explanatory glosses and the like. The simplest and most probable account of the authorship of Deuteronomy is that Moses formulated the legislation himself according to previous treaty-patterns, adding the material from ch. 27 to ch. 31 at a later period. Of the remaining sections, the song (32:1–43) and blessing (33:1–29) would doubtless be delivered orally before being committed to writing.

DATE

The general background of the book is that of the last days of Moses, and there can be no doubt that it is in essential harmony with a date in the later part of the 2nd millennium BC. The more complex Israelite social organization of the settlement in Canaan was anticipated and legislated for, but it was clearly not yet a reality at the time of writing, for the topographical and geographical setting of Deuteronomy is a Transjordanian one. Of particular importance for the date is the treaty-pattern of the book, including a historical prologue, which was commonly found in later 2nd-millennium BC covenants but was consistently omitted in 1st-millennium BC suzerainty treaties. Other elements such as the final benediction have greater affinities with the patriarchal period than with the time of Josiah or the post-exilic era. The legislation of chs. 13 and 20 was applicable to the conquest period, and would have been anachronistic had it been written during the monarchy. All historical references are to events which occurred prior to the conquest, and the author betrays no knowledge of such notable occurrences as the division of the kingdom during the monarchy period, or even of earlier events such as the Philistine oppression as depicted in Judges. Archaeological excavations at the sites of Ai, Bethel, Lachish, Debir and Hazor have furnished positive evidence for their destruction in the second half of the 13th century BC, following the pattern of conquest depicted in Joshua. This accords with a date of about 1280 BC for the Exodus from Egypt. If the bulk of Deuteronomy is to be dated firmly within the lifetime of Moses, as the evidence indicates, the entire work was most probably in its final form during the next generation or two.

TEACHING

The dominant theme of Deuteronomy is a covenantal one, and in this respect the book is akin to Exodus and Joshua. The moral and religious implications of the Sinai agreement were expressed in a non-technical manner, as befitted the understanding of a people whose responsibility it was to comprehend clearly their obligations in the light of such a covenant. Characteristic of Deuteronomy is its monotheistic outlook, which, while establishing the supremacy of the God of Israel, was careful to recognize the dangers presented by the deities of pagan nations. The might of God formed the assured ground for the establishing of a covenant which, when viewed by Israel in the light of 2nd-millennium BC suzerainty treaties, was clear and definite in its implications. Thus Deuteronomy is concerned primarily with the over-all concept of the covenant relationship, in the realization that the future destiny of Israel as the people of God lay in a punctilious observance of the stipulations to which by common consent the Hebrews had become party.

In his hortatory discourses Moses promised Israel that the selfsame power which had wrought a miracle of deliverance at the time of the Exodus, and which had sustained the people through a generation of wilderness wanderings, would continue to undergird them in the promised land provided that the conditions attaching to the covenant agreement were honoured by the Israelites. To this end Deuteronomy contains positive assurances that God will be with His people continually, alike in prosperity and adversity, and will fight for them in battle as He did at the time of the Exodus from Egypt. The Israelites must never forget, in their newly-won freedom, that they were once in bondage in Egypt (5:15), and that it was divine power which rescued them from that hopeless situation (4:21). They must revere their God with their whole being (4:29; 5:10) because He had first loved them (4:37), and since they had promised allegiance to Him they must have no contact whatever with false gods worshipped by pagan peoples (7:24; 11:16).

Because the Sinai covenant disclosed God as a holy and moral being, any people bound to Him by solemn agreement must of necessity also manifest His ethical characteristics in their way of life. Thus the Israelites were required to be one people knowing the divine precepts (5:1), and above all must be a holy nation to the Lord (7:6; 14:2, 21). The profound humanitarian spirit which illumines the Pentateuch generally is evident in the stipulation that, because the Israelites are brothers, they must care for those who are less fortunate than themselves, including the alien, the orphan and the widow (10:18).

The prophetic character of Deuteronomy has long been recognized by liberal and conservative scholars alike, and consistent with this standpoint are the attitudes of optimism, faith and trust in the divine power which the author manifests. The positive, futuristic outlook of the book can be well illustrated by reference to the two most frequently occurring phrases in Deuteronomy, namely 'go in and possess', which is found 35 times, and 'the land which the Lord your God gives you', which occurs 34 times. In accordance with His promise to their ancestors God has provided a good land for the Israelites (1:25), that they might possess it for an inheritance (4:21). Promises of blessing are an important feature of Deuteronomy, and these (7:13) will be implemented when God gives His people respite from their enemies (3:20). Provided that the Israelites honour the covenant stipulations (5:1) they will enjoy prosperity (2:7; 4:40), will be blessed with a productive land (6:11; 12:15), and will lead long and fruitful lives (4:26).

But just as there are promises of blessing in Deuteronomy, so there are warnings against apostasy. The Israelites are told explicitly that 'curses' will overtake them if they disobey the commands of God (28:15), and they will be decimated by such scourges of the ancient world as 'fever, inflammation . . . drought, and with blasting, and with mildew' (28:22). All their highest aspirations will be confounded (28:29), foreign nations will oppress them (28:31ff.), and they will become 'a byword, among all the peoples' (28:37). If they persist in disobedience, these 'curses' will pursue them until they are completely destroyed (28:45). All 'sins' are condemned (15:9), particularly idolatry, which is an 'abomination' (7:25). So serious was the whole question of national sin that rulers were instructed to be rigorous in their punishment of major offences against covenant spirituality (13:8), so that the people might be deterred from iniquitous behaviour (13:5, 11). A central place of God's choosing (12:5, 11) would be established as a focal point for national aspirations, and there the Israelites would honour the name of God and worship before Him (12:7). However, they could not expect automatic and unvaried blessings just because they were in covenant relationship with God. Only as the stipulations were observed and the Sinai agreement was honoured in spirit would God prosper the fortunes of His people.

OUTLINE OF CONTENTS

COMMENTARY

1:1-5 INTRODUCTION

1 *The words that Moses spoke.* Moses as an individual is mentioned 99 times in the NT, and all such references throw light on this book. This is the first of several statements to the effect that the pronouncements were first made in oral (4:45; 29:2; 31:30; 32:44) and subsequently in written (17:18; 31:9) form. The Ten Commandments provide a parallel (5:22; 9:10). The discourses were spoken during the last few months of the aged Hebrew leader's life. *All Israel*: a phrase characteristic of Deuteronomy. The trials, hardships and errors of the nation during the wilderness period had served to purify it and weld it into an integrated spiritual force ready to confront the tasks lying ahead in Canaan. The expression *all Israel* recurs in 11:6; 18:6; 21:21; 27:9; 31:11; 34:12. *Beyond the* (AV 'on this side') *Jordan.* This phrase occurs 18 times in Deuteronomy and Joshua. The former contains much geographical detail, particularly in the opening and closing chapters, and always views Palestine from the outside. Because the topography of Deuteronomy is usually general rather than specific, the phrase means nothing more than 'Transjordania'. It refers 12 times to the eastern, and 6 times to the western side of the Jordan, and AV varies the translation accordingly. The reference is sometimes made more specific by the addition of a qualifying phrase. Its use in Nu. 32:19; Jos. 12:1, 7; 1 Sa. 14:4 for each side alternately indicates that the expression in itself affords no conclusive evidence of the standpoint of the particular writer. *The wilderness* (Heb. *miḏbār*, 'pasturage', 'steppe-land', 'wilderness'). A term applicable to any uninhabited tract of land, whether fertile or barren. *The Arabah* (AV 'the plain'). When used with the definite article it applies generally to the rift valley extending from the Sea of Tiberias to the Gulf of Aqabah (*cf.* Dt. 3:17; 2:8). The plural term 'Araboth' usually described certain waste areas within the Arabah, especially near Jericho and in the wilderness of Moab. *Suph* (AV 'Red Sea'). Either a place-name (so RV, RSV) of uncertain location, or a shortened form of *yam sûp*, which AV understood as referring to the Gulf of Aqabah. However, *yam sûp* is more correctly translated 'Reed Sea' than Red Sea. The relation between Suph and the Suph(ah) of Nu. 21:14 (RV, RSV) is uncertain. *Tophel.* This and the following sites correspond roughly with those in Nu. 33:18-20, which are on the route from Horeb to Kadesh-barnea. Perhaps some of the 'words' were first spoken in these areas.

2 *Eleven days' journey.* From the traditional site of Sinai to Dahab on the E coast of Sinai, up the coast and across to Kadesh-barnea ('Ain Qudeirat and vicinity) has recently been shown to take 11 days. *Horeb* (lit. 'dried up', 'desolate'; *cf.* Je. 44:2). An alternative OT name for Sinai, perhaps referring to the general area rather

than the mount of God itself (Ex. 3:1). *Kadesh-barnea* was an important station during the wilderness wanderings to which the Hebrews apparently returned periodically. It was the first terminus of the journey of Israel from Sinai, from which the spies were dispatched to Canaan and to which they returned (Nu. 12:16; 13:26). While the designation *Kadesh* ('holy') was applied to several biblical sites, Kadesh-barnea is best located in the region of 'Ain Qudeis and 'Ain Qudeirat, some 50 miles SW of Beersheba. **4, 5** *In the land of Moab.* The fertile uplands of Moab provided the background for the addresses of Moses as recorded in Deuteronomy, not long before the actual entrance into Canaan. The first stage of conquest had been completed with the defeat of the Transjordanian kings Sihon and Og (Nu. 21:33-35; *cf.* Dt. 3:1-11), and the settlement of Reuben, Gad and the half-tribe of Manasseh (Nu. 32:1-33). *Explain* (AV 'declare'; lit. 'to engrave', 'to explain' and so 'to expound'). It recurs only in 27:8 and Hab. 2:2 with reference to writing. *This law.* Tôrâ, uniformly translated 'law', is probably derived from the Hebrew verb *hôrâ*, 'to direct', 'to teach', and so can be rendered 'instruction'. The scope is thus much wider than that of the English term 'law', since it embraces 'commandments, statutes and ordinances' (4:1, 2) as well as the whole range of divine revelation. Here *tôrâ* refers to the discourses which follow, and in Deuteronomy generally to the whole or part of Moses' teaching. *Tôrâ* was used of the instruction given by fathers, or the sages who addressed their pupils as 'son' (Pr. 3:1; 6:23; 7:2; 13:14), or by mothers (Pr. 1:8; 6:20; 31:26). *Tôrâ* is never used to describe ordinary direct communication between God and man, but of divinely revealed material through human intermediaries. In Deuteronomy the word occurred in the singular only, thus indicating an organized or integrated collection of material. In time the term *tôrâ* became the Hebrew name for the Pentateuch (Ezr. 7:6; Mt. 12:5), or for the entire OT (Jn. 10:34; 15:25). The rhythmical stress-patterns of Dt. 27:15-26 might imply that poetic form was being employed as an adjunct to learning and memory. In the NT the following uses of the corresponding Greek term *nomos* should be noted: the OT (Jn. 10:34); the Pentateuch (Lk. 24:44); the OT dispensation as a preparation for Christ's coming (Mt. 11:13); the moral law (Lk. 10:26); the Jewish administrative and ceremonial law or 'law of ordinances' (Eph. 2:15) which are not binding upon Christian people.

1:6 – 4:43 THE FIRST DISCOURSE

1:6 – 3:29 Historical prologue

In the 2nd-millennium BC Near Eastern suzerainty or vassal treaties the historical prologue surveyed in retrospect the previous relations between the two contracting parties, and pointed out that past benefactions by the suzerain formed the basis for the vassal's gratitude and future obedience.

1:6–18 Appointment of captains. Moses' first discourse (1:6 – 4:43) commences with a long retrospect of the events narrated in Nu. 10–32, for which the prospect of possessing 'the land' served as a climax. **7** *In the hill country and in the lowland, and in the Negeb.* Broadly speaking, Palestine can be divided into five distinct regions consisting of the coastal plains, the central hilllands, the rift valley, the plateaus of Transjordania, and the desert areas. West of the Jordan, the 'vale' or Shephelah is a low hill-tract situated between the coastal plain and the central high ranges ('the hills'), the latter running N from Hebron and rising up to about 2,000 feet above sea-level, while the AV 'south' (Heb. *negeḇ*; lit. 'the dry') was an undefined region beginning to the S of the Gaza-Beersheba road and ultimately merging with the Sinai peninsula highlands. *Amorites . . . Canaanites.* In the 3rd-millennium BC Sumerian and Akkadian sources the Amorites were uncivilized desert nomads, who moved into Babylonia in strength *c.* 2000 BC and established dynasties there. Amorite settlers occupied the Lebanon region after 1900 BC, while others went further S and E into Transjordan. In the OT the Amorites were regarded as part of the Palestinian hill-country population (Nu. 13:29; Jos. 5:1; 11:3), but in a wider sense the term 'Amorite' was similar in usage to 'Canaanite'. Israel had to conquer 'Canaan' (Nu. 13:17–21), *i.e.* Palestine, and ultimately overcome all the people in the land of the Amorites (Jos. 24:15, 18). The Canaanites and Amorites were well settled in Syria by 2000 BC, and Canaanite culture reached its height under the Phoenicians, being revealed in modern times by excavations and discoveries at Ras Shamra (Ugarit). Properly speaking, the term 'Canaanite' describes the NW Semitic people and culture of W Syria and Palestine prior to the 12th century BC. **8** *The Lord swore to your fathers.* The promise to the fathers, confirmed by an oath (Gn. 22:16), is again referred to in 1:35; 4:31; 6:10, 18, 23; 7:8, 12; 8:1, 18; 9:5; 10:11; 11:9, 21; 13:17; 19:8; 26:3, 15; 28:11; 29:13; 30:20; 31:7, 20, 21, 23; 34:4. An inspired NT commentary can be read in Heb. 6:13–20. Moses constantly reminded the people that God's love for them was not the result of any intrinsic merit (Dt. 7:7; 9:4), but proceeded from divine grace alone (*cf.* Eph. 2:8) and God's promise to the patriarchs. The elements of that promise, namely the seed, the land and the widespread blessing, are all repeated here.

9 *I am not able alone to bear.* Here and in **12** Moses conceded his inability to handle the situation by himself, and **13** chose to delegate his authority. *Your heads.* Rulers, whose appointment was urged by Jethro (Ex. 18:19) and doubtless sanctioned by God, were now finding a place in the permanent legislation (Dt. 16:18). **15** *Officers* (Heb. *šōṭerîm*). In Egypt (Ex. 5:6)

such persons were scribes or organizing officers who worked under the foremen to keep count of the quota of bricks. In the rescued Hebrew society their function was to serve captains (*commanders*) and others as subordinates, no longer as slaves but as free men working for justice and victory (16:18; 20:5, 8, 9; 29:10; 31:28). **16** *Judges.* Their appointment and duties are further defined in 16:18; 17:9; 19:17, 18; 21:2; 25:1. They dispensed justice, punished the offender and vindicated the righteous, insisting upon scrupulous fairness and impartial justice (v. 17; 16:19, 20). *The alien* (AV 'stranger'; Heb. *gēr*, 'sojourner'). A settler among another people, as distinct from the foreigner, the length of stay of the latter being temporary only. In the tribal organization of Israel four units can be distinguished, namely the nation, the tribe, the clan, and the household or family (Jos. 7:16ff.). An alien could be adopted into the clan, although the *zārîm* of Is. 1:7; Je. 5:19; 51:51; Ezk. 7:21; 28:7, 10; Ob. 11 were virtually the same as enemies. The *gēr* had many privileges in Israel, and was required to be treated with love and respect (Ex. 22:21; Dt. 10:19; 24:19–21). The humanitarianism of the Mosaic law is one of its most notable civil elements as contrasted with the Babylonian Code of Hammurabi. Solicitude for all whose position might leave them open to exploitation and oppression is a marked feature of Deuteronomy.

1:19–46 Mission of the spies. 19 *Great and terrible wilderness.* See on 1:1. The barren and desolate nature of the terrain to the N of Sinai has impressed travellers for many centuries with its dreary and forbidding aspect. The rugged mountain peaks seem as though they had been burnt with fire, and the earth is covered with a layer of stones and sharp black flints. Yet there exist several oases with wells or springs, and there are a few upland plains at the feet of some of the eminences in the granite ridges of the Sinai region. These plains sustain a surprising degree of vegetation after the winter rainy season, and doubtless helped to support the Israelite flocks and herds during the wanderings. Five areas of the Sinai peninsula, namely Shur, Etham, Sin, Paran and Zin, are described in this connection as 'wilderness'. **21** *Go up, take possession.* This is a characteristic phrase relating to the Hebrew entry into the promised land. Israel's enemies will not be able to resist her (7:2). It is always necessary for God to encourage His people to 'possess' all that He has so graciously promised them. The Hebrew word *yāraš* means 'to subdue', 'take possession of', 'dispossess', and generally relates to land or property. Thus Israel would acquire claim to Canaan by casting out or supplanting its previous occupants, whether by conquest or inheritance. *Yāraš* occurs no fewer than 52 times in Deuteronomy, being found even in the legal sections (*e.g.* 19:2, 14; 23:20), and indicates that the whole complex of thought underlying its usage belongs essentially to the conquest period. *Dismayed* (AV 'discouraged').

The fear of the Lord should cast out the fear of man (3:2, 22; 20:3, 4; 31:6, 8; Jos. 1:9). **22** *You came near.* Although the younger members of the audience had been born after the spies were sent out, Moses nevertheless identified them with their elders who had been present in their youth. **24** *Eshcol.* A wadi situated a few miles N of Hebron and famed for its fertility, of which its grapes were characteristic (Nu. 13:23, 24; 32:9). **25** *A good land.* This factor is emphasized repeatedly by Moses (3:25; 4:21, 22; 6:18; 8:7, 10; 9:6; 11:17), along with the concept that it is a divine gift. Besides constituting a convincing demonstration of God's grace, these emphases furnish proper grounds for the respect of ancient boundaries (19:14) and for the sanctity of the soil (21:23). They are connected with promises of victory (27:2, 3), with blessing (15:4) and with warnings of judgment (28:52). The Hebrew word *nāṭan,* translated here and in some 60 other places as *gives,* is rendered 'set before' in 1:8, 21; 4:8.

28 *Fortified up to heaven.* Many walled cities of the Middle and Late Bronze Ages (1950–1200 BC) have been excavated in Palestine. Hyksos cities have been uncovered at Tell Beit Mirsim, Tell es-Sulṭân and Hazor, being characterized by large fortifications of beaten earth with a sloping revetment and a surrounding moat. *The sons of the Anakim.* The descendants of an eponymous ancestor Anak, whose original home may have been Hebron. Their gigantic stature was proverbial (Dt. 9:2), and they were thought to be descendants of the Nephilim. The high walls and the Anakim have their counterpart in the Christian life (Eph. 6:12). **29** *Do not be in dread.* Discouragement led **32** to the sin of unbelief, despite indications to the contrary, and so to inevitable judgment (*cf.* v. 34). With true historical insight Moses seeks to bring home to the rising generations the lessons of the past. **31** *As a man bears his son.* A beautiful simile, depicting a father carrying his young son when he is too weak or too tired to walk (*cf.* Ho. 11:1–3). Perhaps Paul had this in mind in Acts 13:18 (see RV mg. *Cf.* Ex. 19:4; Dt. 32:11, 12).

34 *The Lord . . . was angered.* The wrath of God is referred to in both OT and NT (see, *e.g.,* Ps. 78:31; Jn. 3:36; Rom. 1:18), and all attempts to explain it away merely violate the integrity of the text. Divine wrath is one attribute of a God who 'maintains his rights' (Ex. 20:5, 'a jealous God'). **35** As exhibited here the punishment was one way of dealing with the rebellious spirit which would have brought early ruin to the nation. To avert this the task of conquest was assigned to the younger generation now addressed. **36** *Caleb* (lit. 'dog', *i.e.* 'slave of'). One of the spies sent by Moses to reconnoitre Canaan, and the subsequent conqueror of Hebron. He was particularly commended as God's 'servant' (Nu. 14:24). Moses is now concerned with two of his own contemporaries, namely Caleb and Joshua, who were faithful. The story of Caleb (Nu. 13; 14; Jos. 14:6–14; 15:13–19; Jdg. 1:12–15)

is full of inspiration to all who have committed themselves wholly to the Lord. **37** *Angry with me also on your account.* Moses was never able to recall his own exclusion from the promised land without being reminded of the seriousness of disobedience. The whole concept of the covenant demanded complete obedience and surrender on the part of Israel to the revealed will of God. His own punishment for disobedience was an indication of the way in which the Israelites themselves would be excluded from future divine blessings if they were not completely surrendered in purpose and deed to the will of God. This latter attitude is an important element of the spirituality of the new covenant also. It is improper to argue from the expression 'on your account' to the conclusion that Moses thought of himself as dying outside the land as a substitute-offering for the people of Israel. The role of Moses was that of a leader, prophet and mediator of the divine revelation, and nowhere in the Pentateuch is there the slightest suggestion that he was ever to become a sacrificial victim, willingly or otherwise, for the failings of his people. The only atonement required for sin under the Sinai covenant was that which was provided for in the sacrificial legislation of the Torah. Although Moses had incurred God's anger by disobeying His command, it had taken place as a consequence of the people's action. The leader has always to share in the responsibility for failure on the part of his flock, however occasioned. Divine displeasure was recorded because it led up to the mention of Joshua as the successor of Moses. **38** *Encourage him* (lit. 'make him strong'). Exhortations or admonitions to 'be strong' are frequent in Scripture. Here Moses sets an example in encouragement. *Inherit.* This word, *nāḥal,* is also applied to the land. Its common meaning is seen in 12:12; 21:16, but its most frequent use is in connection with the divine gift of the land of Canaan. See 3:28; 4:21, 38; 12:9, 10; 15:4; 19:3, 14; 20:16; 21:23; 24:4; 25:19; 26:1; 29:8; 31:7. **39** *No knowledge of good or evil.* This technical construction, known as *merismus,* employs the opposite components of a situation to designate the totality of the situation itself, and is Sumerian in origin. Thus the entire sphere of 'morality' is in view here.

41 *We . . . we . . .* Abrupt emotional changes are typically Semitic. However, the enthusiasm of the Israelites for battle constituted no real atonement for earlier sin. **44** *Amorites.* In Nu. 14:43 they were called 'Canaanites', which was the wider use of 'Amorite'. See on 1:7. *Hormah.* A city of Simeon in the S of Judah near Ziklag (Jos. 15:30; 19:4), forming the limit of Canaanite pursuit through Seir towards Kadesh-barnea (Nu. 14:45). **46** *Many days.* While much of the wilderness sojourn was spent at Kadesh, part of it occurred in the neighbouring wastelands.

2:1–8 On the borders of Edom. 1 *Mount Seir.* After the repulse at Kadesh the Hebrews turned back towards the Reed Sea and skirted Mt. Seir, the Edomite mountain range, of which Seir is the typical summit. The mountains rise to the S and E of the Dead Sea, and in early times accommodated a Horite population until the descendants of Esau took over the territory (Gn. 14:6; 36:20). **3** *Northward*. By this time the Israelites had made their way along the SW border of Edom, and would then proceed along the SE border. **4** *Your brethren the sons of Esau.* The request from Kadesh seeking a passage through Edom along the King's Highway was refused (Nu. 20:14–21), but from Dt. 2:28, 29 it would appear that some Edomites were quite willing to sell food to the Israelites. Although the Edomites and Israelites were far from being kindly disposed to one another, the bitter enmity of a later period (Je. 49:7–22; Ob. 8ff.) was not yet in evidence. **5** *Do not contend* (AV 'meddle'). The Hebrews were forbidden to engage in battle with the Edomites. The friendliness shown also to Moab (Dt. 2:9) and Ammon (Dt. 2:19) as 'brethren' is characteristic of the patriarchal and Mosaic eras, and attests to the contemporary nature of the narrative. *To Esau.* As sovereign over the nations, God determines their boundaries. Though David fought against the descendants of Esau and subjugated them (2 Sa. 8:14), he did not dispossess them. **8** *Elath.* Most probably to be identified with Ezion-geber at the N end of the Gulf of Aqabah, and developed by Solomon as an ore refinery about 960 BC.

2:9–15 The approach to Moab. 9 *Ar*. The capital of Moab, situated on the frontier in the Wadi Arnon, but whose precise location is uncertain. Aspects of the early history of the city were known to the Israelites from the Book of the Wars of the Lord (Nu. 21:15) and from popular proverbs (Nu. 21:28). **10** *The Emim*. The 'dreaded ones' of Gn. 14:5, the early inhabitants of Moab conquered by Chedorlaomer. **11** They were considered to belong to the peoples known as the *Rephaim* (*cf.* Gn. 15:20), a name unknown in an ethnic sense outside the OT. At the time of the conquest of Canaan the Rephaim were probably spread over a wide area, and apparently known by different local names. In Moab they were called Emim, while in Ammon, where they preceded the later Zamzummim (Dt. 2:20, 21). They were evidently people of great stature. **12** *The Horites*. The ancient inhabitants of Edom defeated by Chedorlaomer (Gn. 14:6), said to be descended from Seir the Horite (Gn. 36:20), and distinct as an ethnic group from the Rephaim. They were driven out by the sons of Esau, and probably joined other Horite groups in central Palestine (*cf.* Gn. 34:2). The non-Semitic Hurrians, known in the OT as Horites, formed part of the indigenous population of Alalakh (Syria) in the 18th century BC. **13** *The brook Zered*. A mountain-torrent (*naḥal*) or wadi crossed by the Israelites on their journey to Moab. In Nu. 21:12 it is mentioned as a camping-ground, which accords with the instructions here to *rise up*. These wadis are a distinctive feature of Transjordania, though the identifica-

tion of the Wadi Zered is uncertain. Probably it is the modern Wadi el-Ḥesa, which runs into the Dead Sea from the SE. **14** *Thirty-eight years*. The 40 years in the wilderness (2:7; 8:2, 4; 29:5) include also the first year from the crossing of the *yam sûp* to the departure from Sinai and the final year spent in conquering the eastern territories.

2:16–37 Victory over the Amorite kings. 18, 19 *Moab ... Ammon*. The Moabites and Ammonites, the descendants of Lot by an incestuous relationship (Gn. 19:37, 38), are to be treated as 'brethren', in contrast with the Amorites, an alien race sunk in idolatry (see on 2:5). **20** *Rephaim*. See on 2:11. These formidable pre-Israelite inhabitants of Palestine had settled in some strength in Ammon before the later Ammonites dispossessed them, and were known as *Zamzummim*. **21** *Anakim*. Descendants of an ancestor named Anak. This group also formed part of the pre-Israelite population of Palestine. Their huge stature and formidable appearance became proverbial, being taken as a standard of comparison to stress the size of the other peoples (Dt. 2:10; see on 1:28). They were met with principally in the highland country (*cf.* Jos. 11:21). **23** *The Avvim* (AV 'Avims') were an aboriginal Canaanite people, the Avites of Jos. 13:3; 2 Ki. 17:31, who lived near Gaza and were destroyed by the Caphtorim. *Gaza*, marking the southern limit of Canaan, was an important Philistine seaport, being mentioned often in Assyrian annals from the 8th century BC onwards. *Caphtorim*, probably to be identified with the *kap-ta-ra* mentioned in a 2nd-millennium BC school text from Assur, was the land from which the Philistines came, most probably Crete. This primitive unglossed terminology points to an early date for the passage. **25** *This day I will begin*. We learn from Nu. 21:4 that the Israelites were greatly discouraged, so that these new words of encouragement were timely. A fresh step forward was to be taken, and the Lord prepared the way before them. See v. 31 and *cf.* 11:25.

26 *Wilderness of Kedemoth*. The desert area around Kedemoth, probably the modern Qasr ez-Za'feran, about 7 miles NE of Dibon. *Cf.* Jos. 13:18. *Words of peace*. The messengers carried proposals for a peaceful passage through the land, along with guarantees of payment for provisions purchased (*cf.* Nu. 21:21, 22). **27** *Only by the road* (Heb. *badderek badderek*). The specified road and no other is to be followed. (*Cf.* Nu. 21:22, 'by the King's Highway'.) **29** *The Moabites who live in Ar*. With the inhabitants of Seir, these Moabites were an exception to the general unfriendliness of the Transjordanians. (See on 2:9.) **30** *The Lord ... hardened his spirit*. What in Nu. 21:23 is attributed to Sihon's unfriendliness is here seen as part of the divine purpose. The OT steadily refuses to see any inconsistency between human freedom and divine sovereignty. God is never spoken of as hardening the heart of a good man. The word *spirit* is used here in the sense of 'will', where the attitude of the individual becomes more and more resolutely opposed to the divine purpose. (*Cf.* Ex. 7:3, *etc.*) Because the ancient Hebrews ascribed all causality to God as the author of all created things, it was both natural and proper for them to see the response of Sihon in the light of the larger activity of God. 31 *I have begun to give . . .; begin to take possession . . . occupy.* See on 1:21. Hebrew *yāraš* here means both 'possess' and 'inherit'. Now that God has prepared the way, it is the responsibility of the Israelites to enter in by faith and possess the promised inheritance.

34 *Utterly destroyed* (Heb. 'treated as *ḥērem*'). The *ḥērem* was a ban of extermination, used in Deuteronomy in connection with persons (*e.g.* 20:17, 18) or objects (*e.g.* 7:26) dedicated to the worship of false gods. At a time when war was a sacred act, the ban, though ruthless in some respects, made chaotic looting impossible by devoting the spoils to the god of the victors, and by giving the enemy an opportunity to surrender their city without a struggle. For the Hebrews, persons and objects associated with pagan cultic rites were to be regarded with abhorrence, as sin should always be, as corrupt and corrupting, and as fit for nothing but complete destruction lest the 'ban' should subsequently fall upon those who had spared them. 36 *Aroer.* A Transjordanian city, mod. 'Ara'ir, on the N bank of the Arnon (Wadi Mojib), about 14 miles E of the Dead Sea. It was the southern limit both of the Amorite kingdom of Sihon and the tribal holdings of Reuben. 37 *Cities of the hill country.* The district surrounding the sources of the Jabbok near Amman, inhabited by the Ammonites and lying E of the tableland of 3:10. The description is such as a traveller would give who had first-hand information about the territory.

3:1-17 The conquest of Bashan. 1 *Bashan.* The fertile region E of Jordan and N of Gilead, separated from the latter by the river Yarmuk. The word *Bashan* means 'fertile'. (*Cf.* 32:14.) *Edrei.* An important stronghold in the Amorite kingdom of Og, overlooking the uplands between Gilead and Hermon, and identified with mod. Der'a. 2 *Do not fear him.* However formidable the opposition may appear, the true believer is commanded to go forward in faith, knowing that the issue is decided not by might, nor by power, but by the divine Spirit (Zc. 4:6). 4 *Argob.* A district of Transjordan containing 60 strongly fortified cities and some unwalled towns. Its exact location is uncertain, but in Dt. 3:14 its westward extent was given as the border of the small kingdoms of Geshur and Maacah. 9 *Hermon . . . Sirion . . . Senir.* Sirion ('glittering') was the Canaanite name for Mt. Hermon, known to the Amorites as *Senir*. Hermon is the southern peak of the Anti-Lebanon range, and Senir (AV 'Shenir') was probably a separate part of the ridge, though the name may have been applied loosely to the whole of the snow-capped range. 10 *Cities of the tableland* (AV 'plain'). The word

mîšôr is generally used for an elevated plateau, as distinct from the '*arāḇâ* or lowland plain. In this case the plateau of Moab is meant. *Salecah*, or Salcah, a city in the extreme E of Bashan which came within the territory occupied by Gad (1 Ch. 5:11). 11 *A bedstead of iron.* This rendering is dubious. The Aramaic form signifies a 'coffin', hence the view that in reality it was a black basalt sarcophagus, the Hebrew for which, however, is '*arôn*. Perhaps the reference to the bed of Og was intended to indicate his huge size. The relic appears to have fallen into the hands of the Ammonites, and was kept in Rabbah, located 25 miles NE of the Dead Sea. *Common cubit* (Heb. 'cubit of a man'). A linear measure of about 18 inches.

12 *Reubenites.* Occupants of territory E of Jordan, where the grazing was suitable for a pastoral tribe. 13 *Manasseh.* Six of the seven families comprising the tribe of Manasseh occupied land in Gilead, the rugged hill country bounded on the west by the Jordan, on the north by the Yarmuk, and on the south by the valley of Heshbon. After the settlement in Canaan Joshua allowed eastern Manasseh to return to the conquered territory of Heshbon and Bashan. 14 *Geshurites . . . Maacathites.* Inhabitants respectively of Geshur, a small Syrian city to the NE of Bashan (Jos. 12:5; 13:2, 11), and Maacah, a small state SE of Mt. Hermon under Aramaean control. *Havvoth-jair* (Heb. 'the tent-villages of Jair'). Probably situated in the hill country between Mt. Gilead and the Yarmuk. Each tent-village was probably the homestead of a clan. 17 *Chinnereth.* The city (*cf.* Jos. 11:2) named after Gennesareth, the Sea of Galilee (*cf.* Nu. 34:11). *The Salt Sea, i.e.* the Dead Sea. *The slopes of Pisgah.* Wherever 'pisgah' occurs in the Hebrew it is accompanied by the definite article (*happisgâ*), showing that it is not meant to designate a single location, but is a common noun. The word thus describes any ridge crowning a hill or mountain, and which from a distance presents an irregular outline. Such ridges occur commonly in Transjordan, and in this case perhaps the southern slopes of Jebel Osha, overlooking the Dead Sea, are intended to be understood (see on 3:27).

3:18-29 Joshua appointed leader. 18 *I commanded you.* Moses addresses himself to the tribes of Reuben, Gad and the half-tribe of Manasseh. See Nu. 32:20-24. 20 *Until the Lord gives rest. Rest* is one of the foremost of blessings promised in the 'land', and is one of the privileges of God's people (Heb. 4:9). The word includes freedom from oppression by one's enemies, and peace of spirit, as well as the usual meanings, and is given its highest expression in Christ (Mt. 11:28). *Beyond the Jordan.* Unlike the expression in 1:1, the W side of the river is referred to here. 21 *I commanded Joshua.* The outline of the relationship between Moses and Joshua will repay study. Joshua is first seen as an army officer (Ex. 17:9), then as Moses' minister (Ex. 24:13) and devoted adherent (Nu.

11:28). Moses' love for Joshua appears in Dt. 1:38; 31:3; Nu. 27:18-23. This particular command is not mentioned in Nu. 32, since it is not relevant to the situation therein related.

23 *I besought the Lord.* The thought of his own exclusion arises in Moses' mind, and he recalls his prayer. His request was that he might go over and might see, the first part of which was forbidden and the second allowed. Other prayers of Moses are recalled in Dt. 9:20, 26. For the Israelites he sought and obtained pardon; for himself, the Lord's own presence and a vision of His glory. He also taught the people to pray (21:8; 26:5, 13). **24** *What god is there . . .?* A rhetorical question which had no bearing on any belief in the real existence of false gods. There can be no doubt about the genuine monotheism of Moses at this point. He is making clear his conviction of the supreme power of God as the one and only true deity, yet at the same time bearing in mind the fact that the worship of other gods is a possibility. The latter had certainly been demonstrated during the sojourn in Egypt, and on at least one notable occasion in the wilderness (Ex. 32:1ff.), showing that even the covenant people of God could be seduced to the worship of alien deities which were in fact nonentities. *Cf.* Dt. 5:7. **25** *Let me go over.* To W Palestine, not as leader but as a humble member of the community to whom the divine decree would still apply. **27** *Pisgah.* See on 3:17. This crest was carefully described in Dt. 34:1 as 'Mount Nebo, to the top of (the) Pisgah, which is opposite Jericho', and was most probably Jebel Osha. From this vantage-point can be seen snow-capped Hermon to the N, the Dead Sea, the Negeb, and other areas of W Palestine. **29** *Beth-peor* (lit. 'The house (temple) of Peor'). Here the people had committed grave sin (Nu. 25; Ps. 106:28-30), and nearby Moses was buried (Dt. 34:6). This verse concludes the historical review in the first discourse which began at 1:6.

4:1-40 A call to obedience

4:1-8 The purpose and value of the law. 1 *O Israel, give heed.* Moses now claims the attention of the people as he begins to expound the law of the Lord. The call to 'take heed', 'take to heart', and the need for implicit obedience to God's commands are frequently repeated. See, *e.g.*, 4:39, 40; 8:20; 9:23; 13:4, 18; 15:5; 26:14, 17; 27:10; 28:1, 2, 15, 45, 62; 30:2, 8, 10, 20. *Statutes.* The word *ḥuqqîm* comes from a root meaning 'to engrave', and so refers to permanent rules of conduct prescribed by authority and recorded for the guidance of the individual or society. *Ordinances* (AV 'judgments'). Judicial decisions arrived at by authority or ancient custom which serve as future precedents for the guidance of judges in certain specified cases. The words 'statutes and ordinances' usually occur in this order in Deuteronomy to indicate the importance of unquestioning obedience to the divine will. The casuistic or 'case

law' of Ex. 21:1 - 22:17, doubtless intended for judges, provides an example of the ordinance or *mišpāṭ*. The word is also used of the decisive acts of God, judging the wicked and vindicating the innocent. Hence 'statutes and ordinances' together cover all the laws and precepts. The two terms are again mentioned, sometimes in conjunction with 'commandments' in 4:5, 8, 14, 45; 5:1, 31; 6:1, 20; 7:11; 8:11; 11:1, 32; 12:1; 26:16, 17. 'Statutes' occurs alone in 4:6; 6:24; 16:12, and with 'commandments' in 4:40; 6:17; 10:13; 27:10; 28:15, 45; 30:10. *That you may live.* Every word of God is the 'bread of life' (8:3), and His words point the way to eternal life (Mt. 4:4; 19:17; Jn. 6:63). **2** *You shall not add.* Ancient suzerainty treaties frequently contained some such prohibition as this. Here the command creates a sharp distinction between the word of God and the word of man, a distinction also stressed by Christ (Mt. 5:17-19; 15:6). When the oracles of God were completed, a further warning of the same kind was added (Rev. 22:18, 19). This does not mean that no modifications could be made to the Mosaic enactments as circumstances required, but that no fundamental change of ethos should be entertained. *Commandments.* The term *miṣwâ* can be applied to any kind of command, whether temporary or permanent, general or particular. In 4:13 and 10:4 *dābār* ('word') rather than *miṣwâ* ('commandment') is used. **3** *Your eyes have seen.* Moses frequently appeals to the experience of his hearers in an attempt to gain their sympathies, reminding them of what they had seen (1:19; 3:21; 7:19; 11:7; 29:2, 3), heard (4:12; 5:23) and known (7:15). *Baal-peor.* The heathen deity worshipped in Peor (*cf.* 3:29) with abhorrent cultic rites (*cf.* Nu. 25:1, 2). Baal was the head of the Canaanite pantheon, and was worshipped under different names in varying localities. Canaanite worship was highly sensuous, immoral and depraved. (*Cf.* Ho. 9:10.)

5 *That you should do them in the land.* Much of the Mosaic law has an ethical timelessness about it which demands the observance of the Christian. For Israel, the law was a guide to the nature of God and the responsibilities of the covenant relationship as well as a means of organizing social life in the promised land. The legislation mentioned would be put into operation on a proper basis at a future time, namely when the wandering Israelites had crossed over into Canaan and occupied it. As such it has a prospective nature, and should not be taken to presuppose the developed social conditions normally occurring in a settled community. The ceremonial and judicial regulations of the Israelites served until the fuller revelation in Christ, so that these were merely transitory in nature and binding upon the Jews only, not the early Christians. *Cf.* Mt. 8:4; Lk. 11:42; Gal. 4:9; 5:1-6; Heb. 9:9, 10. **7** *A god so near to it.* This great privilege was the secret of the uniqueness of Hebrew religion, no intermediary being required to enable the worshipper to approach

God in prayer. **8** *All this law.* These words presumably refer to the bulk of Deuteronomy. What significance has the Mosaic law for the Christian reader? While the law exhibits some transitory elements not binding upon Christians, it also contains eternal principles of justice, holiness and truth, enshrined in the Decalogue and underlying all the legislation. These are binding upon all generations of Jews and Christians alike. Such laws are quoted as commandments in the NT with the words 'for it is written'. See Mt. 4:10; 5:17; Rom. 13:9; 1 Pet. 1:16. Again, as part of the inspired Scripture, the whole book is written for our learning (Rom. 15:4), and is 'profitable' (2 Tim. 3:16). Finally, the NT states explicitly that Moses wrote of Christ (Jn. 5:46). Jesus quoted Deuteronomy frequently, using it especially at His temptation (*cf.* Mt. 4:4 and Dt. 8:3; Mt. 4:7 and Dt. 6:16; Mt. 4:10 and Dt. 6:13).

4:9-24 The covenant of the Lord. 9 *Take heed, and keep your soul.* (*Cf.* 1 Tim. 4:16.) Moses was addressing a generation whose responsibility it was to transmit the revelation to future Israelites, hence the repeated emphasis upon 'teaching'. *Soul* means 'self' here, indicating that survival depended upon recollection of and loyalty to the Sinai covenant. *Lest you forget.* The basic principle to be borne in mind is the spirituality of God and His abhorrence of idolatry and apostasy. The duty of remembrance is stressed both positively and negatively (see 5:15; 7:18; 8:2, 18; 9:7; 15:15; 16:3, 12; 24:9, 18, 22; 25:17; 32:7 and 4:23, 31; 6:12; 8:11, 14, 19; 9:7; 25:19). This is supplemented by the command to teach and write, thus laying the foundation for a body of Holy Scripture. **10** *At Horeb.* Deuteronomy is full of Mosaic reminiscences. They fall into four groups relating, first, to Egypt and the journey to Sinai; second, to the giving of the law at Sinai; third, to the journey from Horeb to Kadesh; and finally, to the events of the last two years. Those of the second group occupy much of chs. 5, 6, 9 and 10, referring to the covenant, the Ten Commandments, the apostasy of the golden calf, the giving of the second tablets and the separation of the tribe of Levi. *Learn to fear.* Repeated in 14:23; 17:19; 31:13. *Cf.* 6:24; 8:6; 10:12; 28:58. Reverence towards God is as important in the worshipper as the sense of dutiful love. Both are emphasized as elements in the covenant relationship between God and His people. **11** *In darkness. Cf.* Ex. 19:18; 20:21; Ps. 97:2. The God who dwells in unapproachable light (1 Tim. 6:16) is hidden by darkness from the eyes of sinful men. **12** *Out of the midst of the fire.* This phrase occurs 10 times (4:12, 15, 33, 36; 5:4, 22, 24, 26; 9:10; 10:4. *Cf.* 32:22), showing the deep impression made on Moses, to whom God first revealed Himself in the burning bush and then in the fires of Sinai. Fire symbolizes the majesty of God and the mighty elemental forces under His control (Ps. 104:4), as well as the essential holiness of God (*cf.* Dt. 4:24). Christ will appear in the midst of fire at

His second coming (2 Thes. 1:7, 8). **13** *His covenant.* This is the first of 27 recurrences in Deuteronomy of this important theme. The word *bᵉrîṯ* was used of a contractual agreement based upon conditions (*cf.* Gn. 21:32), and also of a binding relationship between God and man. Contracts of various forms were a prominent feature of Ancient Near Eastern life, and were ratified in various ways. Here the reference is to God's act of pure grace in taking Israel into a specified spiritual relationship at Sinai. The fact of ratification (Ex. 24:1-8) made the compact binding upon both parties, and it comprised the 'ten words of the covenant' (Ex. 34:28; *cf.* Dt. 9:9) together with the 'statutes and ordinances' which the Israelites promised to obey in the light of the covenant. Thus the 'promise' preceded the 'law' (Gal. 3:15ff.). *He wrote them.* An explicit statement twice repeated (5:22; 10:4) of the divine origin of the covenant commandments. *Two tables of stone.* Near Eastern suzerainty treaties were generally made in duplicate form, one copy of which was deposited with the vassal for periodic reference. The Sinai 'law' is thus properly a suzerainty treaty rather than a legal code as such, and is in accord with the ancient international treaties of the type used to formalize the relationship of a suzerain and a vassal. In covenant-renewal documents, of which Deuteronomy is a good biblical example, it was customary in the Ancient Near East for modification of the stipulations, particularly modernization, to be carried out. This fact explains the various differences between the Ex. 20 and Dt. 5 forms of the Decalogue. Thus Dt. 5:21 adds 'his field' because the imminent occupation of Canaan made land-ownership a matter of immediate relevance.

15 *Take good heed.* The fact that Israel saw no physical indications of deity was no warrant for formulating a material representation of God. The warning against idolatry was timely in view of pagan practices. **16** *A graven image.* Pottery figurines of pagan deities, many of them goddesses exhibiting crude and exaggerated sexual characteristics, have been unearthed from numerous sites in Canaan. The licentious rites of the Baal votaries stood in stark contrast to the moral purity demanded by the Mosaic law. **17, 18** *The likeness of any beast . . . .* A warning against totemistic worship. The Egyptian deity Anubis had the head of a jackal, while Thoth had the head of a hawk. **19** *Sun . . . moon . . . host of heaven.* Temples dedicated to the moon existed at Ur and Harran in the days of Abraham. The sun was worshipped at On (Heliopolis) in Egypt (Gn. 41:45), while astral worship was common in the Ancient Near East. **20** *Iron furnace.* One whose fire was strong enough to melt iron ore. *His own possession. Cf.* 9:26. A doubly inalienable relationship which Israel could not renounce any more than God could. **24** *A devouring fire*, consuming whatever arouses divine indignation. The fire which purifies precious metals also burns up whatever is worthless or corrupt, so that fire is symbolic of God's holiness and righteous judgment. *Cf.* Heb. 12:29. *Jealous.* Probably the best translation of *qannā'* here is 'one who maintains his rights', since God's zeal for holiness and equity demands such practical expression.

4:25-40 An appeal for fidelity. 26 *Heaven and earth.* The silent witnesses of all our vows and our general behaviour, outlasting all human vicissitudes (*cf.* 30:19; 31:28). The emphasis of the *merismus* here is that it constitutes an appeal to all creation. *Live long.* Length of life was one of the blessings often associated with obedience (5:16, 33; 6:2; 11:9; 17:20; 22:7; 25:15; 30:18, 20; 32:47. *Cf.* Ps. 21:4). **27** *Scatter.* If the Israelites prove unfaithful they will be disinherited (Nu. 14:12) and exiled from their promised territory. Yet if they repent they will, of God's mercy, be gathered in again from remote places (30:1-5; *cf.* Mt. 24:31). **28** *Serve gods.* . . . Bondage to pagan nations will humiliate the apostate servants of the living God by compelling them to revere inanimate objects fabricated by human beings. **29** *All your heart . . . soul.* The words are repeated (6:5; 10:12; 11:13; 13:3; 26:16; 30:2, 6, 10) so as to show the unreserved nature of the consecration which God expects from His servants. The *heart* is the 'will' or seat of emotional and purposive response, while the *soul* is the 'self' or personality. **30** *Obey his voice.* This injunction appears again in 8:20; 9:23; 13:4, 18; 15:5; 26:14, 17; 27:10; 28:1, 2, 15, 45, 62; 30:2, 8, 10, 20, and stresses an important part of the covenant stipulations. **31** *Merciful* (Heb. *raḥûm*). The word denotes 'compassion', and is so rendered in 13:17; 30:3. The devouring fire of the perversely wicked is the merciful and gracious God of the penitent sinner. *The covenant.* The basis of Israel's selection as the chosen of God. **32** *The days that are past.* An appeal to history to justify the divine claims, an attitude which is typically Mosaic. Moses refers particularly to the signs accompanying the Exodus, and the repeated allusions to Egypt are explicable only if he was the real author of the book. See 1:2, 7, 30; 4:20, 34, 37, 45, 46; 5:6, 15; 6:12, 21, 22; 7:8, 15, 18; 8:14; 9:7, 12, 26; 17:16; 20:1; 23:4; 24:9, 18, 22; 25:17; 26:5, 8; 28:27, 60, 68; 29:2, 16, 25; 34:11. To the miracle of the Exodus are added memories of God's mercies in the way to Mt. Sinai, the manna (8:3, 16), and the water from the rock (6:16; 8:15; 9:22; 33:8). **34** *Trials* (AV 'temptations', RV mg. 'evidences'). Such as the testing of Pharaoh's character or the proving of Israel. *By a mighty hand and an outstretched arm.* See also 5:15; 7:19; 11:2; 26:8. An expression symbolizing divine intervention in history. **37** The Heb. *'āhab,* used of the electing love of God, corresponds to the Greek *agapē* of the NT. Such love is a spontaneous expression of grace, bestowed apart from any merit in its object (9:6). This appeal, based on God's love manifested to the patriarchs, is reiterated in 7:7, 8, 13; 10:15; 23:5. Moses can find no other ground than this for God's sovereign choice of

Israel. Grace and election are thus linked at an early stage (*cf.* Rom. 8:28; 11:28, 29). Through Israel and the elect remnant God manifested Himself fully in Christ in the fullness of time (Gal. 4:4). Moses pleads with Israel to reciprocate God's love, another persistent theme of Deuteronomy. See 5:10; 6:5; 7:9; 10:12; 11:1, 13, 22; 13:3; 19:9; 30:6, 16, 20. **39, 40** *This day.* As Moses' life draws to a close he expresses himself with even greater urgency. See 6:6; 7:11; 8:1, 11. *That it may go well.* This theme recurs in 5:16, 33; 6:3, 18; 12:25, 28; 22:7. It is one of the results of obedience and, as with other material blessings, it emerges from the love which unites God with His people.

4:41-43 Transjordanian cities of refuge appointed

41 *Three cities.* These places of asylum were mentioned principally in Nu. 35:9-34 and Jos. 20:1-9, and were now located by Moses in the conquered territory. In Israel the responsibility for punishing a murderer rested upon the nearest male relative (*gō'ēl*). The unintentional murderer could find asylum in one of these three Levitical cities, thus preventing the extension of a blood feud. Dt. 19:1-13 also provided for three cities on the W side of the Jordan. Ancient Near Eastern peoples generally furnished absolute security for fugitives in the form of certain shrines or sacred precincts. The cities W of Jordan flourished during the united monarchy, so there is no reason to regard the Transjordanian cities of refuge as either unhistorical or non-Mosaic in provenance.

4:44 – 26:19 THE SECOND DISCOURSE

4:44-49 The covenant stipulations: historical prologue

This section, which in Ancient Near Eastern vassal treaties outlined the historical relations between the contracting parties, defined carefully the locale and time of the second discourse and prepared the way for the stipulations mentioned in 4:45 and presented in detail later on (12:1 – 26:19). The latter were given in full view of Beth-peor (46; see on 3:29), which added emphasis to their warnings. **45** *Testimonies* (Heb. *'ēdôt*) here means an 'exhortation' or 'reminder' of the covenant implications. In Ex. 25:21, 22 the Decalogue itself is described as the 'testimony', witnessing as it does to the basic elements of the covenant. **48** *Sirion* (AV 'Sion'). See on 3:9. The Canaanite name for Mt. Hermon, found here, 3:9 and Ps. 29:6 only. **49** *Pisgah.* See on 3:17.

5:1 – 11:32 BASIC COMMANDMENTS

5:1 – 6:25 Posterity to be instructed in the Horeb revelation

5:1-21 The Decalogue. The Ten Commandments constituted the essence of the law and the basis of God's covenant with Israel. They summarized the religious and social obligations of the Israelites, and constituted the revealed foundation for the new stipulations about to be promulgated. The Decalogue is binding upon the conduct of all believers, for when Christ instructed the young ruler to keep the commandments if he desired to 'enter life' (Mt. 19:17), He constituted them as in fact a rule of life. When He spoke of them as 'the commandment of God' as contrasted with human traditions (Mt. 15:3), He recognized their binding force. Only divine grace can enable men to keep them; yet it is for this very purpose that grace is given. Law and grace are thus bound together. **1** *Hear, O Israel.* Repeated in 4:1; 6:3, 4; 9:1; 20:3 and 27:9 to mark the beginning of a new appeal for obedience on the part of Israel. *The statutes and the ordinances.* See on 4:1. These detailed commandments follow in chs. 12–26, after chs. 5–11, which deal with the Decalogue and the exhortations based on them. *Be careful* (AV 'keep', RV 'observe'). A characteristic phrase repeated in 5:32; 6:3, 25; 7:11; 8:1; 11:22, 32; 12:1, 32; 15:5; 17:10; 19:9; 24:8; 28:1, 15, 58; 31:12; 32:46. Knowledge is a prerequisite to performance.

3 *This covenant.* The responsibility and privilege of the covenant is recalled by reference to the actual place, and the Hebrew idiom emphasizes that it was made 'not only with our fathers, but also with us'. **4** *Spoke.* One of the most important scriptural emphases is that God is One who communicates His revelation in intelligible words. **5** *He said.* What follows is practically a verbatim repetition of the Decalogue in Ex. 20:1–17. As a suzerainty treaty this latter can be analysed as follows: preamble (20:2a); historical prologue (20:2b); general commandments (20:3); specific stipulations (20:4a, 5a, 7a, 8, 12a, 13–17); curses (20:5b, 7b); blessings (20:6, 12b). The difference in Deuteronomy seems to be that, being part of an exhortation addressed to a new generation, Moses does not hesitate to amplify or even change the wording of the Exodus version slightly for better emphasis. Thus the narrative is more rhetorical and homiletical than its Exodus counterpart.

6 *I am*, or 'I the Lord am your God'. The assertion of that eternal power which governs human destiny prefaces the demands made by God upon man. *Cf.* Ex. 3:14 and Jn. 14:6. The covenant name (Ex. 6:2, 3) brings God into direct suzerainty relationship with His chosen people. This selfsame personal relationship between God and man in Jesus Christ is the basis of the Christian experience. The assertion of divine existence is followed by the recollection of God's saving power. **7** *Before*, or 'besides'. If 'before' means 'to my face', the Israelites are forbidden to provoke God by means of unreal idols. The meaning 'besides' contains a demand for absolute and sole worship of the God of Sinai. The stringent rules against worshipping false gods (13:1–18), the insistence upon the purity of worship (16:1–22) and the observance of the covenant (29:1–29) all illumine this first great commandment.

8 *Graven image.* A prohibition of the worship of the true God under an improper or false form. The deity cannot be venerated under an image such as that of the golden calf, a sin which Moses may well have had in mind in varying the text from its Exodus counterpart. God can be known truly only as He has revealed Himself, first, in words, and secondly, through the incarnate Christ. **9** *Jealous.* See on 4:24. God asserts His rights in the covenant relationship. *The iniquity of the fathers.* That the consequences of this are indeed visited upon the offspring is a fact of experience, **10** as is the validity of God's promise to show *steadfast love.* This latter term (*ḥeseḏ*) is untranslatable, but is here associated with covenanted mercies, as in Hosea. AV renders it by 'mercy', but this does not begin to exhaust the meaning of the word. Its etymological origin is uncertain, but it is always closely connected with the two concepts of covenant and faithfulness. It thus implies 'unfailing love grounded in a covenant', and is used both of God's attitude towards His people and of the response He desires from them (*cf.* 1 Jn. 4:11, 19), the latter occurring especially in Hosea.

11 *In vain.* The Hebrew *lašāw'* can mean 'for vanity' or 'for falsehood'. The Hebrews are forbidden to swear false oaths by the name of their God. In Hebrew thought *the name* is closely identified with the person who bears it with respect to his character (*cf.* Mt. 1:21) and authority. God's name is holy (Ps. 111:9; Lk. 1:49), glorious and fearful (Dt. 28:58), and its richness is revealed by Moses (Dt. 32:3), the prophets (Ps. 99:3; Is. 63:12, 14) and the Saviour Jesus (Jn. 17:6, 26). To keep this commandment we need divine grace, and therefore the Christian prays 'hallowed be thy name'.

12 *Observe the sabbath day* (Heb. *šāmôr*; in Ex. 20:8 it is *zāḵôr*, 'remember'). Moses used a stronger term here because he was exhorting the people to observe God's commands. This commandment provides for rest from labour by setting aside a definite time for divine service. It is a foreshadowing of the eternal sabbath rest (Heb. 4:9). To the nation of Israel it also constituted a token of their redemption from bondage and their entrance upon a new life of liberty. It was thus prophetic of the day of resurrection (Rom. 4:25), and so became 'the first day of the week' and 'the Lord's day' of John's vision (Rev. 1:10). There is no fundamental contradiction between the commandment here and its counterpart in Ex. 20:8–11. In the latter the sabbath belongs to the Lord as His special day, having been blessed and set apart for worship and rest. In Dt. 5:12, the people are commanded to observe the sabbath in the manner already commanded in Exodus, and the fact that the sabbath belongs to the Lord is once more mentioned. **14** The humanitarian emphasis of this verse is an additional reason for sabbath observance. There is no need to devise complicated explanations of the origin of such amplifications of the original commandment. They are exactly such as would arise naturally in the mind of a fluent speaker, especially in the light of years of experience of trying to guide his people in the proper observation and the extent of meaning of the fourth commandment. **15** *Remember.* This comment is a reminder that servitude in Egypt was uninterrupted by any form of sabbath. By observing a weekly rest in the promised land their labours would be differentiated from slavery.

16 *Honour your father and your mother.* This injunction deals with one of the closest of human relationships. To his parents the individual owes his very existence, and for this alone they demand due honour. Long life is promised as an incentive to obedience (*cf.* Eph. 6:2). Honour to parents is limited by the honour due to God, who is supreme. Both allegiances are perfectly combined in Christ (Mt. 10:37; 19:29; Lk. 2:49, 51; Jn. 19:26, 27).

17 *You shall not kill.* This commandment declares the sanctity of the life of those made in the divine image. All life proceeds from God, and must be treated with reverence (*cf.* Gn. 9:4–6). The life of animals meant for food can be taken with impunity, and where justice requires it, the life of murderers also. For the latter, God empowers judges and magistrates (see Dt. 17:2–7; 19:12; Rom. 13:4). The guilt of murder is incurred when man, for his own wicked ends, takes his brother's life which the Creator had bestowed for His own glory. Then his brother's blood cries out from the ground for justice (Gn. 4:10; *cf.* Dt. 21:1–9).

18 *Neither . . . commit adultery.* This injunction establishes the rule of a holy married life, and accounts for the detailed regulations for moral purity, the number and strictness of which testify to its importance (21:10–17; 22:1 – 23:18; 24:1–5; 25:11, 12). God instituted marriage (Gn. 1:28; 2:24; Mt. 19:4–6) and used it to signify His love to Israel (Ho. 2:14–20) and the union between Christ and His church (Mt. 9:15; Eph. 5:32). Adultery is used as a symbol of Hebrew unfaithfulness (Dt. 31:16) and of Christian apostasy (Jas. 4:4).

19 *Neither . . . steal.* As with his existence and his powers, so man's possessions are a divine gift (see Dt. 8:17; 1 Cor. 4:7). Man is therefore responsible to God for his attitude to material things, and improper or illegal acquisition of them, such as by stealing, is a sin.

20 *Neither . . . bear false witness* (Heb. 'vain'). See on 5:11. This embraces all forms of slander, defamation and misrepresentation, and deals with wrong inflicted orally as contrasted with the three previous injunctions dealing with the results of actual deeds. The Christian, like his Master, must bear witness to the truth (Jn. 18:37) as it is in Jesus (Eph. 4:21).

21 *Neither . . . covet.* This commandment is different from all others in that it relates to the state of the heart rather than to outward conduct. Therefore only God can see when it is broken. Negatively it precludes unlawful desire for others' possessions; positively it inculcates contentment

and faith (Heb. 13:5, 6). The slight variation from Ex. 20:17 might suggest the period prior to the settlement in Canaan. Coveting might well have been far less of a temptation during the period of Israel's wanderings than would be the case following their entrance into the promised land, when the property or possessions of a neighbour might perhaps become an object of desire under conditions of sedentary life. (See also on 4:13.)

5:22–33 The commandments delivered. An exhortation to obedience recalls the circumstances under which the law was originally given. **22** *No more.* See on 4:2 and *cf.* Rev. 22:18. **24** *His glory.* See Ex. 33:18. **27** *Hear.* The people heard the thunder but Moses heard the words (*cf.* Jn. 12:29; Acts 9:7). Moses is here the mediator between God and the people (see Gal. 3:19), and so is a type of Christ. **29** *Always.* The Sinai experience was all too soon to be followed by the apostasy of the golden calf.

6:1–9 Exhortation to remember. Moses proceeds to instruct the people in the commandments as they in turn are to teach their children. The instruction will be partly written (Dt. 6:9) and partly oral. **2** *You and your son.* The frequent shift from the singular to the plural, *i.e.* from the individual to the nation, would be appropriate in a spoken address. **3** *Milk and honey.* Repeated in 11:9; 26:9, 15; 27:3; 31:20. **4** *Hear, O Israel.* See on 5:1. Moses proceeds to declare God's uniqueness and Israel's response in undivided loyalty. This verse begins the celebrated Hebrew *Shema*, consisting of Dt. 6:4–9; 11:13–21 and Nu. 15:37–41, which is recited in the liturgy twice daily by pious Jews. Christ added the phrase 'with all your mind', and described vv. 4 and 5 as 'the first and great commandment' (Mt. 22:37, 38; Mk. 12:29, 30; Lk. 10:27). *One Lord.* This phrase has several renderings (see RSV mg.). The meaning seems to be that God is 'the only God', so that participation in the covenant precludes the recognition of any other deity. **8** *You shall bind them.* Jews of a later age interpreted this literally by enclosing written portions of the law in small cases called phylacteries, and binding them on their hands and foreheads. (*Cf.* Mt. 23:5.) **9** *You shall write.* Writing is one of the most ancient of human arts. In the time of Moses there were several languages used for purposes of communication, in which scribes were required to be proficient. Writing would have formed part of Moses' general education in Egypt (*cf.* Acts 7:22).

6:10–19 Lessons from the past. From this section Christ quoted two verses at His temptation. In citing v. 13 He replaced (according to the Greek text of Mt. 4:10) the word *fear* by 'worship' in response to Satan's challenge. **12** *Take heed.* The dangers of forgetting their dependence on God's goodness are brought home to the Hebrews. **14** *Other gods.* Repeated in 7:4; 13:6, 13; 17:3; 28:36, 64; 29:26; 30:17; 31:20. For purposes of clarity the current phraseology concerning 'other gods' is used, but without endorsing their reality. They are 'the work of men's hands' (4:28). **16** *Massah* means 'testing' or 'proving' (see Ex. 17:7; Dt. 9:22). Man is forbidden to test God by questioning His power or protection. (See also Mt. 4:7; Lk. 4:12.)

6:20–25 Future generations are to be taught. 20 *What is the meaning . . . ?* The story of the deliverance from Egypt, acted out as a drama, will recall for subsequent generations God's power and grace. **23** *He brought us out.* Moses links divine grace in redemption with the way of life set before Israel. (*Cf.* Rom. 4:25.) **24** *For our good.* The prescribed statutes and ordinances are uniformly conducive to a clean, just and holy life. (*Cf.* 10:13.) **25** *Righteousness.* This is a key word in the OT, and should be studied as background for such NT passages as Rom. 3:21–26 and Phil. 3:6–9. Hebrew *ṣedeq* ('righteousness') involves normality; whatever is straight and upright; justice, both human and divine, and moral righteousness. Here, keeping God's commands will be accounted as meritorious.

7:1 – 11:32 Exhortations to fidelity and obedience

7:1–11 Israel's call to complete separation. 1 *Clears away.* For the nations mentioned here see Gn. 10:15–18; 15:19–21; Ex. 3:8, 17; 13:5. They were to be dispossessed before Israel could claim her promised abode. The *Hittites* mentioned here were probably the descendants of early migrants from Asia Minor, and were equivalent to native Canaanites. **2** *Utterly destroy*; *i.e.* consider them as *ḥērem*, and as such exterminate them. See on 2:34. **5** *Pillars . . . Asherim.* In Canaanite religion the pillar was identified with male deity, especially Baal, and as such was forbidden to Israel. Remains of Canaanite pillars have been found at Gezer, Byblos, Hazor and Ras Shamra. *Asherim* appear to have been some kind of wooden images. In AV the word 'Asherah' is consistently translated 'grove'. **6** *A people holy.* (*Cf.* Ex. 19:5, 6.) Owing to their divine calling Israel could not afford to be contaminated by corrupt cultic forms. *For his own possession* (AV 'special', RV 'peculiar'). The word *seḡullâ* originally applied to ownership of property, and here to Israel as God's very own possession. (*Cf.* 14:2; 26:18; Tit. 2:14; 1 Pet. 2:9.) **8** *Redeemed.* Repeated in 9:26; 13:5; 15:15; 21:8; 24:18. The verb *pāḏâ* means 'to ransom', 'to redeem'. In ancient Israel both property and life could be redeemed by making the appropriate payment. In the NT, human redemption is achieved solely by the sacrificial death of Christ. (*Cf.* Mk. 10:45; Lk. 1:68; 1 Pet. 1:18, 19.) **9** *Covenant and steadfast love.* See on 4:13 and 5:10. *Ḥeseḏ* is frequently associated with the covenant (7:12), and is also used for the graciousness existing between friends as well as for divine mercy.

7:12–26 Blessings and encouragements. Having now explained God's purpose in choosing Israel, Moses promises blessings if the Hebrews keep His laws, and exhorts them to faith and courage. **13** *Love.* While the love is unconditional, the blessings are dependent upon obedience. *Grain.* National prosperity and health will be matched by an ample supply of the principal agricultural products of Canaan. **15** *The evil diseases of Egypt.* Another illustration from Egyptian life springs to mind. The Egyptian climate was far from healthy, and an ancient writer, Pliny, described the land as 'the mother of worst diseases'. **20** *Hornets.* Whether or not the use of *ṣir'â* is metaphorical, this particular wasp could inflict a sting which under certain conditions would prove fatal. **24** *Make their name perish.* This emphasis is repeated in 9:14; 12:3; 25:19 (*cf.* Rev. 3:5). The name of false gods should be obliterated from memory, but that of the Lord should remain at His sanctuary and with His people. **25** *Abomination.* Mentioned again, mainly in connection with idolatry or impurity, in 12:31; 13:14; 14:3; 17:1, 4; 18:12; 22:5; 23:18; 24:4; 25:16; 27:15; 32:16. **26** *Accursed* (Heb. *ḥērem*, 'devoted'). The 'ban' was classified under three headings: the war ban, the justice ban and the private ban, representing three different degrees of severity. See on 2:34.

8:1–20 Promises and exhortations. 1 *The land.* The wilderness experience had been intended to teach Israel trust in and reliance upon the divine promises and power. Now that the nation was about to occupy fertile Canaan, it was even more important to remember past guidance and provision. **2** *These forty years.* Moses' reminiscences include the experience in Egypt, the journey to Sinai and the giving of the law (9:7 – 10:11), and the final journey to Kadesh (1:1 – 2:14). With these were given accounts of such discouraging lapses as the leprosy of Miriam (Nu. 12:10; Dt. 24:9), the judgment upon Dathan and Abiram (Nu. 16:27; Dt. 11:6), and the incident at Meribah (Nu. 20:10–13; Dt. 1:37; 32:51). The way in which these incidents were described, and their correspondence with actual events most likely to impress Moses himself, furnish striking evidence of authenticity. **3** *By bread alone.* Spiritual as well as physical forces sustain human existence, as was recognized by Christ at His temptation (Mt. 4:4; Lk. 4:4). To deny the existence and reality of spiritual factors is to separate oneself from a fundamentally important area of reality. **4** *Your clothing.* A vivid way of demonstrating the sustaining power of God during the wilderness wanderings. **5** *Disciplines his son.* For the Semites, such conduct was intended to inculcate reformation and righteousness in the offspring. (*Cf.* Heb. 12:5–11; Dt. 1:31; 32:6.) **7** *A good land.* See on 1:25. The physical contrast between the arid wastes of the Sinai region and the rich areas of Palestine have impressed travellers for many centuries. These verses detail the most important physical aspects of the terrain to show its richness in natural resources. **9** *Iron . . . copper. Iron* was abundant in the Wadi Arabah region, and also near Mt. Carmel and Mt. Hermon. *Copper* (AV 'brass') ores were widespread in Sinai, Midian and Syria. The fact that both copper and iron could be mined near Ezion-geber was a literal fulfilment of this verse. **15** *Flinty rock*. On two occasions water was brought out of the rock, once in Horeb (Ex. 17:6) and again at Kadesh (Nu. 20:8), and the word for 'rock' is different in each case. In Ex. 17:6, as here, it is *ṣûr*, used in Dt. 32:4, 13, 15, 18, 30, 31 metaphorically of God as the believer's source of strength. In Nu. 20:8, *selaʿ*, sometimes used to describe a crag or a fortress of stone, was employed. The phenomenon of water issuing from rock testifies to the water-retaining properties of Sinai limestone. **17** *My power*. Wealth comes from God's gift of the land by the use of time, ability and energy, which are also divine endowments.

9:1–29 The people reminded of their sins and shortcomings. Israelite victories over the inhabitants of Canaan are not due to intrinsic merit, but to the iniquity of the indigenous peoples, whom God has planned to root out and replace by a faithful Israel, bidden to 'possess' the land. **2** *Anakim*. See on 2:28. **5** *The wickedness of these nations*. From excavations at Ras Shamra (Ugarit) and elsewhere in Canaan it is now known that the native religion of the land was one of the most depraved, sensuous and corrupt of its kind in the Ancient Near East. *That he may confirm the word*. In establishing Israel in Canaan God is honouring His promise to the patriarchs. While the calling of Israel is unconditional and irrevocable, coming as it does from God's love (*cf.* Rom. 11:29), the blessings are contingent upon obedience. The promise is to Abraham's 'seed', namely Christ (Gal. 3:16) and to all who are 'in Him'. The blessings of the gospel demand obedience from Christ's followers also. **6** *Stubborn* (AV 'stiffnecked'). The figure is probably taken from a stubborn ox which refuses to submit to the yoke. Moses proceeds to substantiate his allegation. **10** *The assembly*. Any group or its representatives, intending organized communal action. In the LXX, Hebrew *qāhāl* is translated *ekklēsia* or 'church' (*cf.* Acts 7:38). Both terms imply a collection and an election. As Israel was called out of Egypt, so the Christian church is called by God out of the world. **15** *I turned*. In this historical review Moses condenses the narrative and does not follow the strict chronology of Ex. 32. **18** *I lay prostrate*. Better, 'I prostrated myself'. Here again the narrative is condensed and rearranged. **19** *Afraid*. Hebrew *yāḡar*, a rare word for 'to fear', is used in this verse with reference to a premonition concerning future events. **20** *I prayed for Aaron*. Only Moses could have made this statement. Because of his special position in the community Aaron had to bear much of the responsibility for what had happened. **21** *The calf*. The destruction of that which had occasioned the sin must precede the removal of the guilt. *The dust of it*. A further condensation of the golden calf incident in Ex. 32. **22** *Massah*. See on 6:16. The provocation of Rephidim, where the name Massah first arose, occurred before the Israelites reached Mt. Sinai,

the others taking place subsequently. The three names are descriptive of the events. **23** *Did not believe*. Unbelief was the cardinal sin in the old dispensation as well as the new (1:32. *Cf.* Jn. 16:9; Heb. 3:1 – 4:10).

10:1–11 The ark and the Levites. These verses conclude the retrospect of the events at Horeb. Moses allows his thoughts to travel from his repeated intercession back to the Decalogue and the tablets deposited in the ark of the covenant, still in their midst; to the death of Aaron, to Eleazar and to the Levites, who were most probably standing nearby as he spoke. **3** *I made an ark*. It was actually made by Bezalel (*cf.* Ex. 25:10–22; 35:30–34). Gold-covered wooden receptacles or portable shrines were used in the Ancient Near East in pre-Mosaic times. The ark of the covenant was unique as the repository of the stone tablets, the documents bearing the covenant stipulations. **6** *From Beeroth*. . . . Vv. 6–9 are probably a gloss added by Moses when he wrote down the discourse. In Nu. 33:31–33 the stations are named in a different order and with some change of designation, but since the presence of water (*Beeroth* means 'wells') is mentioned in connection with two of them, they may have been visited more than once. *Eleazar*. The office of high priest was thus perpetuated, and the choice of Eleazar suggests that Aaron's sin had been forgiven. **8** *At that time*; *i.e.* of the sin of the golden calf and its sequel. *Set apart*. One of the twelve tribes, the Levites, was specially chosen for service in the sanctuary, one of their duties being to carry the ark. *To stand*. To minister to God in the offering of sacrifice, a duty reserved for the priests alone (Nu. 3:10).

10:12–22 What God requires of His people. A final review of the reasons for, and the consequences of, obedience to the Lord. *Cf.* Dt. 6:5; Mt. 22:37, and the answer given by Micah to the question asked in v. 12 (Mi. 6:8). For Moses, reverential worship of God is fundamental to all religious expression. **15** Though God created the cosmos, He and He alone chose Israel *above all peoples*. Their response should be a degree of submission and love because of His firm promises. *Cf.* Rom. 2:29. **17** The lofty monotheism of this verse is typical of Deuteronomy. **18** *Fatherless . . . sojourner*. *Cf.* 14:29; 16:11, 14; 24:17, 19, 20, 21; 26:12, 13; 27:19. Pronounced social and humanitarian concerns are an important feature of the Mosaic legislation. The *sojourner* could not claim the protection of either family or clan, nor had he any inheritance in the land. Yet he was requested to keep the sabbath (5:14) and the national feasts (16:11, 14; *cf.* Acts 2:10), and was included in the covenant (Dt. 29:11, 12). He thus belonged to the Israelite fraternity, and was an object of special responsibility (*cf.* Mt. 25:35; Acts 14:27; Eph. 2:19). **19** *Love the sojourner*. This demand for Israel to love the alien is without parallel in Ancient Near Eastern legislation. While the Israelites were commanded to honour and fear their parents and to listen to the prophetic message, they were commanded also to enter into a relationship of affection with the sojourner as a reminder of God's love during the Egyptian captivity.

11:1–25 Motives to love and obedience. Personal experience of God's mighty acts should lead to love and submission. **1** *Charge.* Occurs only here in Deuteronomy, and means that which is to be guarded or observed in relation to God. In other Pentateuchal books the word is used frequently of the charge of the Tabernacle (*e.g.* Lv. 8:35). **2** *His outstretched arm.* See 4:34; Ex. 6:6. A graphic description of God's protecting care. **3** *Signs . . . deeds.* God reveals Himself by mighty acts as well as by words. (*Cf.* Mt. 11:4; Jn. 2:11.) The miracle of the Exodus is mentioned in Acts 7:36; Heb. 11:27–29. **6** *Dathan and Abiram.* God's miracles of judgment are also object-lessons. The omission of Korah here was probably a concession to the feelings of the Levites (10:8), among whom were some surviving Korahites. (*Cf.* Ps. 106:17.) **10** *The land of Egypt.* Irrigation was a permanent problem in ancient Egypt, consuming much time and labour. Egyptian fields had to be watered artificially, like a vegetable garden, and not naturally by rain. In Canaan, fertilization took place during the autumn rains, which fell providentially at the time of sowing, and the crops were helped towards maturity by the spring rains, ready for harvesting in May and June. *With your feet.* The reference is to a water-wheel and pump worked by the feet. **11** *Hills and valleys.* Hence, terrain with a larger rainfall than flat land. **18** *Lay up.* Moses again appeals to the will of the people, for with this the Lord must be sought (4:29), loved (6:5), and served (10:12). The will must be 'circumcised' (10:16), since wicked thoughts arise there (9:4; 15:9; *cf.* Mt. 15:18). *Frontlets.* See on 6:8. **19** *Teach them.* While Moses did not address the children directly, he imposed upon their parents the duty of seeing that they were instructed in the law. **20** *Doorposts . . . gates.* In the houses of orthodox Jews even today there can be seen on the exterior doorpost a *mezzuzah* (lit. 'doorpost'), a small receptacle containing a copy of Dt. 6:4–9, in compliance with the ancient custom. **21** *Heavens . . . earth*; *i.e.* as long as the cosmos endures. **24** *The western sea* (AV 'uttermost', RV 'hinder'). The Near Eastern peoples 'oriented' themselves by facing E, so that the S was on their right hand. The *western sea* is thus the Mediterranean.

11:26–32 A blessing and a curse. These seven verses sum up the second discourse, and at the same time form an introduction to the detailed commandments. There is a strict impartiality to the justice of God (Ezk. 18:25–29; 33:17–20), and the entire future of the nation depends on the right choice being made. **28** *Other gods.* See on 6:14. These are unfamiliar, though equally alien, deities. **29** *Gerizim . . . Ebal.* The two most prominent hills in the natural centre of Palestine, used to represent symbolically the blessing and the curse. These are cherished locations in

Samaritan traditions. **30** *Gilgal.* The word means a 'circle' or 'cairn' of stones, and was used to designate several localities. One such 'gilgal' has been found near Shechem. *Oak* (mg. 'terebinths'). See Gn. 12:6.

12:1 – 26:19 DETAILED COMMANDMENTS

12:1 – 16:22 Statutes governing worship and a holy life

12:1–14 Idolatry to be destroyed. The specific stipulations of this section have their counterpart in Near Eastern international treaties, consisting of the obligations to be imposed upon and accepted by the vassal, including a prohibition against any foreign alliances. Here Moses lays down the regulations for the religious, civil, social and domestic life in Canaan, and adds encouragements and warnings. **1** *In the land.* The immediate entry of Israel into Canaan governs all that follows (*cf.* 12:10; 26:1). When Israel is settled in the land, sacrifices will be offered only at a specific location to be chosen by God. **2** *Surely destroy.* Better, 'completely destroy'. The land must be cleansed from all idolatry so that it can be holy to the Lord (*cf.* Lv. 11:44, 45). This duty is implicit in the first two commandments of the Decalogue. *Hills.* Worship at these places was accompanied by depraved rites. The *places* are designated by a general term (Heb. *meqômôṯ*), and are not the *bāmôṯ* ('high places') or local shrines. (*Cf.* 1 Ki. 15:14.) The fact that *bāmôṯ* does not occur in Dt. 12–26 is enough to dispose of the theory that the chief object of the legislation was to prohibit the use of 'high places'. **3** *Pillars.* See on 7:5. **5** *The place,* forming a rallying-point for the Israelites wherever they resided, without stipulating that the cultus should be centralized there. God designated various places periodically where offerings could be brought. In Dt. 27:5 an altar was ordered to be built on Mt. Ebal. Thereafter Shiloh was for some centuries the place of God's choice, but during the early settlement period Shechem was a recognized shrine (Jos. 8:30ff.; 24:1ff.). There is no suggestion that Jerusalem, which at that time was a Jebusite stronghold, should form the centre around which the Israelites could rally, or that it was the place of God's choosing. The location of the central sanctuary in Jerusalem was strictly a product of the early monarchy. (*Cf.* 2 Sa. 7:1ff.) The prophet Gad ordered David to build an altar on the threshing-floor of Araunah in Jerusalem (2 Sa. 24:18). Other instances occur in Jdg. 6:26; 13:6–20; 1 Ki. 18:32. *Make his habitation* (Heb. *lešiḵnô*). Expressing the same thought of the divine presence as the term *Shekinah*. **6** *Burnt offerings.* Regulations for these had already been given in Lv. 1–7. *Tithes.* See 14:22ff.; Lv. 27:30–33. The offering of tithes and firstlings was obligatory, the others voluntary. *The offering that you present* (AV 'heave offerings of your hand'). The Hebrew *terûmâ* means 'a contribution for sacred uses', probably so called because it was taken from a larger portion. (*Cf.* Lv. 7:14, 32; Nu. 15:17-21.) The law of *the firstlings is* given in Dt. 15:19-23. **7** *You shall eat.* Chs. 12, 14 and 15 deal mainly with the food of the people eaten in various ways. The word *you* could refer either to the Levitical priests or to those persons bringing the sacrifices. The sanctuary, where the offering of the sacrifices occurred, was also a centre for the trial of difficult cases (17:8, 10). Thus the Tabernacle had already become a unifying centre of national worship. *You shall rejoice.* See 12:12, 18; 14:26; 16:11, 14; 26:11; 27:7. (*Cf.* Jn. 15:11; Phil. 3:1; 4:4.) Joy is an essential element of the Christian religion, and is a spiritual blessing distinguishable from happiness. **8** *Whatever is right.* The disruption of life caused by the Transjordanian campaigns had made orderly worship difficult. This verse may have been intended to prohibit the use of private altars for sacrifice. **11** *Make his name dwell there.* See 12:21; 14:23, 24; 16:2, 6, 11; 26:2. The Tabernacle was erected that God might be represented as dwelling in the midst of His people (Ex. 25:8; Jn. 1:14; Rev. 21:3). **12** *The Levite . . . within your towns.* As a tribe the Levites had no territorial holdings, but were to be scattered among the tribes, with certain cities and their environs about to be assigned to them (*cf.* Nu. 35:1-8). In the meantime, as a sojourner, the Levite was to be the object of special care (see 12:18, 19; 14:27).

12:15-32 The killing of animals for food and sacrifice. Meat was not a prominent part of the diet of most Israelites, being consumed mainly by the upper classes. Meat was eaten by all on occasions of sacrifice and feasting, and these verses require such celebrations to take place at the central point of assembly. The principles enunciated stress the sacredness of all life as the direct gift of God, and a distinction is made between 'holy things' (v. 26) to be offered in sacrifice or dedicated to a religious purpose, and that which is simply killed for food (vv. 15, 20, 21), the latter also being God's provision. **15** *Gazelle . . . hart.* Not being domestic animals they were not acceptable as sacrificial offerings, though 'clean' in other respects. These species of game were apparently plentiful at the time; subsequently, and in the city, they were regarded as a delicacy (1 Ki. 4:23). **16** *The blood.* See Lv. 17:11. Blood, as the vital element and symbol of life, is treated with great reverence in the OT (*cf.* Gn. 9:4-6), especially in connection with covenant and sacrifice, a noteworthy foreshadowing of Christ's atonement (see Lv. 16; Heb. 9:12-14; 1 Pet. 1:18, 19; 1 Jn. 1:7). **25** *Do what is right.* See 13:18; 21:9; and for the contrast see 4:25; 9:18; 17:2; 31:29. **27** *The blood of your sacrifices.* See on 12:16. **30** *How did these nations serve . . .?* The Hebrews were forbidden to enquire as to how the inhabitants of Canaan worshipped their deities, for if an alien cultic form influenced Hebrew devotions, a debauched and apostate practice would soon follow. **32** *You shall not add.* See on 4:2.

13:1-18 Enticements to idolatry. Moses warns against the dangers of religious seduction by false prophets, confused visionaries and base men. If the injunctions appear severe, it should be remembered that the purging of the land involved also the removal of any Israelites who were enticed into sin by Canaanite immorality. The NT is equally severe (see 2 Thes. 2:8; Rev. 14:9-11). **1** The false *prophet* is an all too familiar OT figure, and is seen in the NT as a minister of Satan, seducing to evil (Mt. 24:24; Rev. 19:20). It is important to note that the divine revelation through Moses was of a normative nature. The true prophet reflects the spirituality and ethos of the God who delivered the Israelites from Egypt with power, and all subsequent prophecy was to be judged as to its truth or falsity in the light of this definitive standard. *A wonder, i.e.* a portent, pointing to a future happening. **3** *Testing you.* That the prediction may be fulfilled is no necessary proof of validity, for the real test is of a different nature. **5** *Purge the evil.* These stringent measures were necessary during the Mosaic period, and are in full accord with the character of the contemporary situation. See also 17:7, 12; 19:13, 19; 21:9, 21; 22:22, 24; 24:7. **6** *Your brother.* Incitements to apostasy may be present even in the family circle. (*Cf.* Mt. 10:36.) **9** *Your hand . . . first,* in inflicting capital punishment. (*Cf.* 17:7.) In these extreme circumstances the convicting witness had to bear the initial responsibility of the act, regardless of his feelings. **11** *All Israel shall hear, and fear.* See 17:13; 19:20; 21:21; 31:12, 13. Punishment is to be administered publicly as a deterrent. **13** *Base fellows* (AV 'children of Belial'). A scriptural term for habitual criminals. *Have gone out,* with the set purpose of religious seduction. **14** *Make search.* A further important principle of justice is here enunciated, namely that the fullest investigation should precede punishment. Much of British common law can be traced to the Mosaic enactments. **17** *Devoted.* (*Cf.* Jos. 7:10-26.) The punishment of idolaters and apostates must not be a thing of material gain for Israel.

14:1-21 Clean and unclean meats. 1 Moses repeats (see Lv. 11) the rules of bodily health applicable to *the sons of the Lord.* They are no longer obligatory for the Christian, though they still enshrine important precepts of hygiene and preventive medicine. As such they deserve more than passing attention. *Cut yourselves.* As sons of God they must not deface His image (1 Cor. 3:17), as the heathen did in their cultic rites (1 Ki. 18:28). So on 7:6. **2** *A people holy.* See on 7:6. **4** *The animals you may eat.* Clean species desirable for food (see Lv. 11:2-8). Domestic animals precede those of the chase. **5** *Ibex,* better 'antelope', and *antelope,* better 'wild ox'. **7** *Hare . . . rock badger.* These appear to chew the cud but do not do so actually. In any case they do not conform to the principle laid down in v. 6. **8** *Swine.* The pig is the intermediate host of several parasitic organisms, and even under the best of modern culinary conditions its flesh can transmit these unwholesome infestations which under some circumstances can cause death. **9** *Fins and scales.* See Lv. 11:9–12. There is an implied prohibition against those edible crustacea which feed upon garbage and putrefying matter. **12–18** The birds mentioned in these verses feed on carrion, and are also prohibited. **20** *All clean winged things.* Cf. Lv. 11:21, 22, where, as here, the reference is to edible locusts. **21** *Dies of itself.* Such meat is unsuitable for human consumption because of the toxins already present in it. The sale of meat from fallen animals is prohibited in most civilized countries. *Boil a kid.* Cf. Ex. 23:19; 34:26. This unnatural custom was practised superstitiously by the Canaanites, perhaps to promote fecundity.

14:22–29 Tithes. When Moses spoke these words the principle of tithing was already well accepted in Israel. Tithes were first given as a token of gratitude (Gn. 14:20) or devotion (Gn. 28:22). Man's wealth is a divine gift, and is held in trust for God (Dt. 8:18; Mt. 25:14). To mark the sacredness of the whole, a definite proportion is to be set aside and dedicated at the sanctuary. This is the so-called 'second tithe', as contrasted with that tithe of the produce given to maintain the Levites (see Nu. 18:26–28). **22** *All the yield,* including the 'grain', 'wine' and 'oil' of v. 23, with the tithe being computed separately on each year's produce. **23** *Learn to fear, i.e.* be filled with a sense of dependence upon God. **25** *Turn it into money.* Those who lived too far from the centrally appointed sanctuary could change their tithe into money and purchase whatever they needed for the festival of rejoicing. **28** *All the tithe.* This was due in the third and sixth years of the sabbatical period instead of the second tithe. In those years what would have been the second tithe was kept at home for the poor to eat.

15:1–18 The Lord's release. Every seventh year was to see the remission of all debts by divine command. **2** *Not exact it, i.e.* not press his neighbour for payment. The year of release for debtors and bondservants (v. 12) alike was probably the one in which rest was also decreed for the land (see Ex. 23:10, 11; Lv. 25:2, 3). The statute points to a future agricultural situation where each family would have its own holdings. The remission of the loan was absolute, thereby becoming a gift. **3** *Foreigner* (Heb. *nokrî*) as distinct from the *gēr* of 10:19. The foreigner was a trader, mainly Egyptian, and would be well able to pay. **4** *There will be no poor.* This would occur only if the condition of obedience in v. 5 was fulfilled. **7** *Heart . . . hand.* Charity should proceed from man's heart, as it does with God. *Poor brother.* Even today the Jew still feels a sense of responsibility in this matter. **9** *Your eye be hostile.* Thus refusing to assist him on the ground that the loan will not be refunded. **12** *Sold.* The release is extended to bondservant and bondmaid alike, thus enlarging the provisions of Ex. 21:1–6. A person could 'sell himself' into bondage and thus be devoid of resources. **14**

Liberally. At the time of emancipation the master was required to furnish proper equipment to enable the servant to begin a new life, and this is a further indication of the humanitarian spirit of the Mosaic legislation. **15** *Redeemed.* See on 7:8. **17** *Bondwoman.* A servant rather than a concubine.

15:19–23 Firstlings. Follows 14:22–29 logically, and enunciates the principle that all firstborn creatures should be dedicated to God, since all life is His gift. **20** The offering must not be delayed beyond a *year.* **21** As with other sacrifices it must be without *blemish.* In the light of Lv. 27:26 and Nu. 18:17, 18, it would be obvious to the audience as to who had to eat the firstling.

16:1–17 Three pilgrimage feasts. See Ex. 23:14; 34:18; Lv. 23:4; Nu. 28:16. These were to be celebrated at the chosen place of assembly, and commemorated an historical event of national importance as well as marking the three seasons of the agricultural year. **1** *Abib.* Hebrew 'of the fresh ears of corn', the later Nisan. **2, 3** The *passover* feast was closely related to that of *unleavened bread.* For the former, a lamb was prescribed (Ex. 12:21) to be sacrificed in the evening; for the latter, a ram and bullocks from the *herd* (Nu. 28:19) were offered the following day. *Remember.* An important emphasis in Deuteronomy. The NT counterpart of the Passover is also a feast of remembrance (Lk. 22:19), to be celebrated with a putting-away of malicious and wicked 'leaven' (1 Cor. 5:7, 8). **8** *A solemn assembly.* On the seventh day of the Passover festival. This important feast was designed to help the Hebrews review their spiritual values and rededicate themselves to God's service. **10** *The feast of weeks* or 'seven weeks'. It is the 'feast of harvest' (Ex. 23:16) and the 'day of the first fruits' (Nu. 28:26). *A freewill offering.* Whereas the Passover offering was prescribed, that of the Feast of Weeks was left to the discretion of the worshipper. Since 50 days elapsed between the offering of the barley sheaf at the beginning of the Passover and the celebration of the Feast of Weeks, the latter became known as Pentecost (see LXX, Lv. 23:16). In NT times it was made significant for the Christian by the outpouring of the Holy Spirit (Acts 2:14–18). **13** *The feast of booths.* See Lv. 23:42. In Ex. 23:16; 34:22 it is called the 'feast of ingathering'. The 'feast of tabernacles' (AV) marked the end of the agricultural year after the harvesting of barley (v. 9) and wheat (v. 13), and after vintage (v. 13). It reminded Israel that her life rested upon divine redemption which ultimately involved forgiveness of sin (2 Ch. 30:22), and thus separated the feast from pagan harvest festivals.

16:18–20 Administration of justice. 18 *Judges and officers.* See on 1:15 and 1:16. Moses provides here for an ordered civil government by defining the status of officers in the Hebrew commonwealth. **19** *Partiality.* Cf. 1:17; 10:17; Acts 10:34; Jas. 2:9.

16:21, 22 Prohibition of heathen symbols. The

authenticity of Deuteronomy is attested by the fact that only Canaanite cultic forms are legislated against, not those of surrounding countries from a later period. **21** *Asherah.* See on 7:5. **22** *Pillar.* A stone with sacred significance (Gn. 28:18), a witness to an agreement (Gn. 31:52), an obelisk (Is. 19:19), or, as here, a carved representation or symbol of a pagan deity.

17:1 – 26:15 Laws relating to specific domestic, moral and religious situations

17:1 The perfect offering. *Blemish.* See Ex. 12:5; Lv. 22:17–33. Sacrificing less than the best to God is a profanation of His service (*cf.* Mal. 1:8; Heb. 9:14).

17:2–13 Civil ordinances. 2 *Man or woman.* The eradication of idolatry was the duty of all who encountered it. **6** *Two witnesses*, of unquestioned veracity and unanimous opinion. No torture was to be applied in order to extract a confession, and the severe penalty was to be imposed only on the basis of irrefutable evidence. (*Cf.* Mt. 18:6; Jn. 8:17; 2 Cor. 13:1; Heb. 10:28.) **7** *The evil.* LXX reads 'evil man'. (*Cf.* Mt. 6:13, RV.) Hebrew thought tends to identify sin concretely with the sinner. **9** *You shall consult them.* The sanctuary court was intended to try those cases deemed too hard for local courts, and *the judge* would be the senior presiding officer at the sanctuary. **12** *Presumptuously.* Strict adherence to court decisions was essential for the well-being of the theocracy.

17:14–20 Law of the kingdom. The selection, duties and qualifications of a king are considered here, where the king replaces the supreme judge. Monarchy is permitted rather than appointed, and the ruler must himself be subject to the law. This section warns in advance against the dangers implicit in Ancient Near Eastern kingship. Because these were familiar to intelligent observers in the 2nd millennium BC, it is not necessary to suppose that this passage was written in retrospect long after the time of Moses, to recall the perils which the rule of Solomon had brought into Israelite life. **15** *Will choose.* A native Israelite will be selected by God (*cf.* 1 Sa. 10:24). Foreign rule would conflict with the covenant ideal. **16** *Multiply horses.* The king must not aspire to military greatness but must foster the objectives of the covenant. The warning was necessary at a time when Egypt had become proficient in the use of chariots and horses as military weapons, following Hyksos and Canaanite traditions. **17** *Turn away.* To idolatry, as did Solomon (*cf.* 1 Ki. 11:4, 5). **18** *A copy of this law, i.e.* of the enactment relating to the king and his duties. The phrase was incorrectly understood by the LXX to refer to all of the fifth book of Moses, hence the name Deuteronomy or 'second law' was given to it. *Levitical priests*, the custodians of the law (see 31:26). **20** *He and his children.* Hereditary or dynastic rule is entertained as a possibility here.

18:1–8 Revenues of priests and Levites. 1

Levitical priests. A special class, indicated by the fact that different portions are assigned to priests in 18:3–5 and to Levites in 18:6–8. Whereas some priests taught the law (31:9–13), the Levites had actual custody of the book (31:25, 26), which was kept near the ark of the covenant. **3** *The priests' due.* Further portions unmentioned in Numbers, consisting of parts of animals slaughtered for ordinary consumption. **8** *Patrimony.* Either proceeds from the sale of his estate (Lv. 25:33) or fees due to him.

18:9–14 Witchcraft. This section comprises stern admonitions against any indulgence in sorcery. **10** *Burns his son.* The worship of Moloch was notorious for human sacrifice. *Divination.* A general term covering the magical practices which follow. **11** *Necromancer.* Cf. 1 Sa. 28:7. **13** *Blameless.* Whole-hearted in the service of God.

18:15–22 The future prophet. In a Messianic section Moses announced a successor in his office as prophet. Peter (Acts 3:22) and Stephen (Acts 7:37) afterwards recognized the fulfilment of his words. Cf. Jn. 5:46; Heb. 3:2–6. Traditional Jewish exegesis thinks of a prophet arising in each generation, but this is untrue historically. **15** *Like me.* The expression specifically means 'like me at Horeb, mediating a fresh and normative revelation of God'. Moses was a type of Christ both in his life and office. Like Jesus his life was spared in infancy, he renounced a royal court to share in the conditions of life of his brethren, and he became a captain of salvation to Israel. He was faithful (Heb. 3:2), full of compassion and love (Nu. 27:17; Mt. 9:36), a powerful intercessor for his people (Dt. 9:18; Heb. 7:25) speaking with God face to face and reflecting the divine glory (2 Cor. 3:7). Like Christ he was a mighty prophet in word and deed (*cf.* Lk. 24:19), a revealer of God's will and purpose (Dt. 6:1; Rev. 1:1); a mediator of the covenant (Dt. 29:1; Heb. 8:6, 7) and a leader of the people (*cf.* Is. 55:4). **21** *How may we know . . . ?* True prophets can be distinguished from false. They must be God's prophets (Dt. 13:1–3), their word must be fulfilled (1 Ki. 22:28; Je. 28:9), and they will honour the written law (Is. 8:20). False prophets will continue to the end of the age (Mt. 24:11; 1 Jn. 4:1–3; Rev. 19:20).

19:1–13 Cities of refuge. See on 4:41. Having already separated three cities in Transjordan, Moses now provides for three more sanctuaries on the western side (*cf.* Nu. 35:14), and gives instructions concerning them. The rules regarding homicide, like some other laws in Deuteronomy, deal with customs still more ancient, confirming some and amending others. The legislation has elements in common with several Near Eastern codes, but the Mosaic law places a higher value on human life (*cf.* on 5:17), and sets a more elevated standard of love to God and to one's neighbour. **3** *The roads.* The Talmud says that the way was marked by signposts bearing the words 'To the City of Refuge'. **6** *The avenger.*

The nearest relative of the deceased (Nu. 35:12). Blood-revenge, still prevalent among Arab tribes, was thus curtailed. **9** *Three other cities.* To be added if Israel ultimately possessed all the land promised to Abraham (Gn. 15:18). No late author would have invented such a provision. **10** *Upon you.* If no cities of refuge existed, blood-guilt would rest upon the land. *Cf.* 21:1–9. **12** *Elders.* In a patriarchal society the senior members of the families, clans and tribes occupied a superior position, and formed a local authority for transacting judicial and other business (see 21:20; 27:1; 29:10; 31:28).

19:14 The landmark. These could be either of ancient native origin or those established by the Israelites themselves (see 27:17). Removal of such signs, once established, was equivalent to theft.

19:15–21 The law of witness. See on 5:20 and 17:6. Whereas in Jewish law intention to commit a crime was not a punishable offence, it was the opposite in the case of conspiring witnesses, whose very intention constituted the essence of their crime. In Jn. 5:31–46, Christ cites three witnesses to His own claims, and two witnesses testify to Him in Rev. 11. *Cf.* 2 Cor. 13:1. **17** *The priests.* It was their duty to search out the truth in judgment. In a later age their descendants sought false testimony against Jesus (Mt. 26:59–68). **21** *Eye for eye.* This *lex talionis*, or law of equal retaliation, occurred also in the Semitic Code of Hammurabi, whereas among the Hittites it was restitution which was emphasized. The rule is used here in connection with the punishment of a false witness. The words of Mt. 5:38–42 apply to personal conduct.

20:1–20 Laws of warfare. Even in wartime certain humanitarian principles apply. The reasonableness and mercy of these provisions stand in sharp contrast to the brutality of the later Assyrians. **1** *You shall not be afraid.* God's people need this encouragement constantly (1:29). The deliverance from Egypt, a constant inspiration to Moses, is used here to inculcate courage; elsewhere for complete dedication (4:20), for sabbath observance (5:15), for reverential fear (6:12), humility (8:14), penitence (9:7), kindness to strangers (10:19), obedience (11:2, 3), mercy to the poor (24:18, 22), and thanksgiving (26:5, 8). **2** *The priest.* In rabbinical times this special representative was designated as 'the priest anointed for the war'. **5–8** The exemptions here were of a compassionate nature. Nothing ought to distract from the objective of that victory which is the Lord's. (*Cf.* Lk. 14:18–20.) **6** *Enjoyed its fruit.* Only in the fifth year was the fruit of a tree permitted to be eaten (see Lv. 19:23–25). **10** *Terms of peace.* War was waged only as a last resort. There are two principles in operation here: God's proclamation of peace and goodwill on the one hand, and the inevitable judgment of evil on the other. These undergird both the covenant and the gospel. (*Cf.* Mt. 10:12, 13.) **17** *Utterly destroy.* See on 2:34. (*Cf.* Jos. 11:12–15.) The command in this extreme form is found only here. (*Cf.* Rev. 21:27.) **20**

Not trees for food. Fruit-bearing trees were to be spared because of the life-principle within them, and for future use. This would act as a control over erosion of the soil.

21:1–9 Undetected homicide. 3 *Slain man.* One murdered in open country by an unidentified assailant (*cf.* v. 1). The elders and judges of the nearest settled community had to make atonement according to a specific prescription. **4** *Shall break.* The sacrifice was to take place in rough valley terrain where a flowing stream would remove the heifer's blood. Atonement and cleansing go together here, and point to Calvary (Heb. 9:13, 14). **8** *Forgive.* Spoken by the priests, imply'ng that the local inhabitants had failed to make the roads safe for travellers. **9** *Purge.* Were the murderer to be discovered subsequently, he would suffer the extreme penalty of the law.

21:10–21 Domestic ordinances. The law for marriage with a captive woman displayed a remarkable respect for feminine individuality. **12** *Shave her head.* A common eastern rite of renunciation and purification. **13** *A full month.* To allow her to grieve properly and to accustom her to her new surroundings. The humanitarian tone of this legislation is unique in the ancient world. **14** *No delight.* If the captive becomes repulsive to her husband she is to be divorced, not reduced to the level of a bondwoman. **15** *Disliked.* A relative term only, expressing preference. *Cf.* Gn. 29:31; Mal. 1:2, 3. **16** *First-born.* This right was already ancient (Gn. 27:1, *etc.*) and is attested by archaeological discoveries from the patriarchal period. **18** *Stubborn.* To their children, parents are ideally God's representatives, hence obstinate rebellion is akin to repudiation of divine grace. Here the parents have an equality of function and responsibility, as in the fifth commandment. **19** *Elders.* The father is not despotic, and so both parents must bring the charge before the leaders appointed to arbitrate *at the gate*, the oriental forum.

21:22, 23 The curse of the tree. While stoning was the approved means of execution, hanging was imposed as an additional disgrace after death. According to Jewish tradition this regulation was never actually carried out, but remained on the statute-book as the strongest possible warning against disobedience to parents and the resultant entrance upon a life of crime. *Cf.* Gal. 3:13; Jn. 19:31.

22:1–30 Rules of charity and purity. The miscellaneous character of the precepts in vv. 1–12 has perplexed those who regard these chapters as a legal code, but it is natural enough in a spoken discourse. The first three verses recapitulate Ex. 23:4, 5, but with wider implications. **2** *Restore.* Failure to do so is theft. **5** *Shall not wear.* In a society where male and female dress was similar, proper sexual differentiation was an important protection against perversion, immodesty and immorality. **6** *Nest.* The sanctity of the parental relationship is stressed here, with the female bird being a surrogate for a mother. In view of the necessity for maintaining a 'balance of nature', this is a wise and humane provision. **8** *Parapet*. Necessary on the flat roof of an oriental house to prevent anyone on the roof from falling off. **9** *Two kinds*. Since God has made obvious distinctions in nature, it is unwise for man to obliterate them. The 'kinds' are of a mutually exclusive nature. **10** *Ox . . . ass*. It is cruel to yoke the weaker animal to the stronger. God's loving care extends to the whole of His creation (*cf*. Mt. 10:29). **11** *Mingled*. Static electricity in the mixture will cause discomfort to the wearer. **12** *Tassels*. A distinctive sign to the Israelites and others that they were the Lord's people. *Cf*. Nu. 15:37–41; Lk. 8:44. **13** *Spurns her*. He who falsely accuses his bride of unchaste behaviour prior to marrying him shall be fined and prohibited from divorcing her. The mere satisfaction of physical passion is a totally inadequate basis for marriage. **18** *Whip him*. According to the Talmud this comprised 'forty stripes save one'. **21** *Folly* (Heb. *nᵉbālâ*). A euphemism for grave sin. **23** *Betrothed*. Betrothal was considered in the orient as equally binding with marriage, hence a betrothed woman was styled 'wife' (Mt. 1:20). **30** *Uncover*. Enforcing the prohibitions against certain degrees of sexual relationship in Lv. 18:6–13.

23:1–8 Membership in the congregation. Israelite community life has overtones of that found in the primitive Christian church, including its holiness and catholicity, its exclusiveness and inclusiveness, and its nature as the earthly representative and particular possession of the Lord. **1** *Crushed*. The exclusion of emasculated persons was a protest against heathen cultic practices, and forestalled their introduction in Israel. **2** *Bastard*. The offspring of an adulterous or incestuous relationship or marriage. **3** *Ammonite . . . Moabite*. The masculine forms indicate that males were meant. Female proselytes could marry male Israelites, however, as with Ruth. **4** *Balaam*. This is a convenient place for Moses to summarize his reminiscences concerning the recent past. These include the unfriendly actions of Edom and Ammon (2:1–14), the victories over Sihon and Og (2:30 – 3:11; 29:7, 8; 31:4), the settlement of the two and a half tribes (3:12–22), the references to his own sin at Kadesh (1:37; 4:21; 31:2; 32:51; 34:4), the people's sin at Beth-peor (4:3), the plague of fiery serpents (8:15), and Balaam's exploits (Nu. 22:4 – 24:25).

23:9–25 Various social rules. **12** *Outside the camp*. Cleanliness in the camp is ordered both for health and for personal purity, consonant with the Lord's presence in their midst. **15** *Escaped*. A fugitive, non-Israelite slave seeking an asylum in Canaan from a harsh master. **17** *Cult prostitute*. One of the degrading aspects of Canaanite religion, involving both male and female prostitutes. **18** *Dog*. The Hebrew term for a sodomite. **19** *Lend upon interest*. Loans to foreigners were usually of a commercial nature,

and thus an interest charge could be levied without objection. When the loan was from a rich man to his poor neighbour, the imposition of interest violated the law of brotherly love. *Cf*. Ex. 22:25; Lv. 25:36. **21** *A vow*. See Nu. 30:2ff.; Dt. 12:6, 26. **25** *Standing grain*. The fields in Palestine were open to the passer-by, and the yield was so plentiful that he could take whatever he wished. *Cf*. Mk. 2:23, 24, where the sabbath was violated by the action of rubbing the ears, an act which for the Pharisees was a form of threshing, and thus of manual work.

24:1–4 The bill of divorce. *Cf*. Mt. 5:31; 19:7. This is not a law instituting or regulating divorce, but a regulation concerning this ancient Semitic custom. A man must have a definite grievance, and a formal document must be issued. **1** *Some indecency*. The expression is vague, and no precise meaning is agreed for it. The later rabbinic school of Shammai allowed divorce only if the wife was guilty of unchastity, whereas that of Hillel thought of indecency in the broadest sense, implying that a wife could also be divorced for reasons other than unchastity. **3** *Bill* (lit. 'a writing of cutting off'). While the marriage bond was holy and inviolable, it could be terminated under certain conditions. Christ's teaching interprets this law correctly and sets it in right relationship to the primitive law.

24:5–22 Humane regulations. **5** *Newly married*. Public responsibilities are not to be imposed upon a bridegroom for one year. **6** *In pledge*. Removing one of the millstones would make the other useless, and so deprive the family of daily bread. The spirit of this legislation is reflected in Mt. 6:32; Lk. 12:30. **7** *Stealing*. For the Semites, man-stealing was the occasion for a blood feud. The Code of Hammurabi made it a capital offence. **8** *Leprosy*. The laws concerning *ṣāraʿat*, a generic term, are found in Lv. 13 and 14. **9** *Miriam*. Every wilderness experience was to be regarded as a lesson illustrating God's will and purpose for His people. *Cf*. 25:17. **14** *Not oppress*. The most advanced modern social legislation cannot surpass the concerned humanitarian approach of these chapters. **15** *On the day*. The poor labourer must not be exploited. *Cf*. Lv. 19:13. **16** *The fathers*. *Cf*. Ezk. 18:4, 20.

25:1–19 Rules of justice, mercy and purity. **1** *Condemning*. Corporal punishment was not to be used to extract a confession, and was to be applied only after the suspect was found guilty. **3** *Forty stripes*. Even in punishment the dignity of the individual is to be respected. Justice is to be tempered with mercy, and chastisement must be distinguished from humiliation. The Jews kept the letter (2 Cor. 11:24) but not the spirit of this law. **4** *Muzzle*. *Cf*. Pr. 12:10. The claims of the lower aspects of creation upon human sympathies are typical of the Scriptures. While God cares for the oxen (1 Cor. 9:9), He cares more for human beings. **5** *Her husband's brother*. This custom, known as levirate marriage, goes back to patriarchal times (Gn. 38:8), and is here modified in certain particulars. It averted the calamity of the family name becoming extinct. *Cf.* Mk. 12:18–27. **9** *Pull his sandal.* To signify the transfer of property. See Ru. 4:7, 8. *Spit in his face.* Showing contempt for the person who refused to exercise the levirate (the Latin word *levir* means 'husband's brother') principle. **19** *Blot out.* Justice involves the punishment of the wicked as well as the care of the needy, and in this case it required the obliteration of the most savage and inhuman of the Canaanite peoples.

26:1–15 Firstfruits and tithes. See on 14:22. The forms for the presentation of firstfruits and tithes constitute a beautiful model of prayer and praise. The ceremony was to be an occasion of thanksgiving to God for His great mercies. **3** *The priest.* The high priest or his deputy. *Declare,* *i.e.* solemnly proclaim. **4** *The basket.* Its contents would demonstrate that Israel now possessed the land in accordance with the divine promise (Gn. 28:13). The firstfruits contain the promise of the harvest, which God will provide in due time. **5** *Aramean* (AV 'Syrian'). **5–10** This beautiful prayer is a brief epitome of Hebrew history, recalling the mighty deeds of God. The formula is strikingly Mosaic in style and content, referring to the *hard bondage*, the cry for deliverance, and the redeeming *outstretched arm*. **12** *Finished paying.* The festal character and generous method of distribution show that the 'second tithe' for the poor is intended here. *Cf.* 14:28. **13** *Removed.* It has not been retained secretly for personal use (*cf.* Acts 5:2), but all that is due to God has been paid. *Cf.* Mal. 3:10.

26:16–19 Concluding exhortation

This closing section reminds the Israelites of their obligations and privileges in the covenant relationship. **16** *This day.* Implementation of the pledges requires implicit obedience on the part of Israel. *Cf.* Heb. 4:7. **17** *Declared.* Perhaps a legal term, connected with the imposition of covenantal obligations, and possibly associated with some otherwise unrecorded token of assent by the people. **19** *Above all nations.* The signal reward of a loyal and obedient Israel. *Cf.* 28:10.

27:1 – 31:8 THE THIRD DISCOURSE

27:1–10 The law inscribed and obedience commanded

With the completion of chs. 5–26, the narrative form is resumed. Moses now gives a threefold directive about 'this law' just delivered, that it may be all the more deeply impressed upon the people. **1** *The elders,* who would be responsible for carrying out the injunctions after Moses had died (Jos. 8:33). **2** *Large stones.* Many such inscribed stelae have been found in the Near East, as with the Code of Hammurabi, the Merneptah stele, and others. *Plaster.* A coating of lime or cement, following Egyptian custom. **3** *Shall write.* Ancient inscriptions vary in length, of course, the one on the rockface at Behistun being about three times as long as Deuteronomy.

All the words. The phrase suggests that a written document was either in existence or was in process of preparation, from which a copy could be made on the stones. The inscription might have contained the contents of the Second Discourse, or an abstract of it. **4** *Ebal.* The valley, flanked by the twin slopes of Ebal and Gerizim, formed a natural amphitheatre eminently suitable for the occasion. See on 11:29. **5** *No iron tool.* See Ex. 20:25. Prohibiting iron tools would avoid all attempts at making graven images. **6** *Unhewn* (Heb. 'whole', from the same root as 'peace'). The expiation of sin results in peace and the renewal of the personality. **8** *The stones;* *i.e.* those of v. 4, not the rough stones of the altar. The laws were to be inscribed *very plainly,* presumably in large, clear script so that the words of the law could be read and understood easily. This provision presupposed a moderate degree of literacy amongst the Israelites. Many examples of ancient scripts have been recovered from Canaan, particularly from the Amarna age and somewhat later. **9, 10** *This day.* The obligations of fulfilling the divine commandments are now imposed, to be followed by the consequences of obedience and disobedience.

27:11–26 Curses

This particular element was an important part of Near Eastern international treaties, since it reminded the vassal of his fate were he to repudiate the stipulations in any way. **12** *These shall stand.* The tribes chosen for blessing were all descended from Leah or Rachel. Jewish interpreters regard this ceremony as antiphonal in nature, **14** with the Levitical priests speaking the curse and **15ff.** the people responding in assent with *Amen,* 'so be it', a solemn affirmation to a preceding statement. *Cursed.* The inevitable result of divine holiness as applied to a particular mode of behaviour. The curses are twelve in number, corresponding to the twelve tribes. The second, fifth and sixth commandments are quoted; the remaining curses relate to serious breaches of honesty or purity. **24** *In secret.* Presumably by calumny. The sins are all such as might be committed privately, hence all the people are called upon to repudiate them openly. **26** *Confirm.* A comprehensive summary, making the law binding on each individual Israelite. Thus the people bind themselves under a curse (*cf.* Acts 23:12) to keep the whole law. *Cf.* Ne. 10:29; Gal. 3:10. Christ took this curse upon Himself (Gal. 3:13), thus setting the believer free.

28:1–14 Blessings

As with the curses, this section was also prominent in suzerainty treaties of the 2nd and 1st millennia BC. It generally came towards the end of the document, and enumerated the benefits accruing to the vassal if the covenant was kept. Pagan deities were normally adduced as witnesses to this end among the Ancient Near Eastern peoples. **1** *Obey.* Blessing for Israel was always contingent upon obedience. On the lips of Moses these utterances were warnings given in mercy, which, if they had been heeded, would have saved the Hebrew people from great misery. 3ff. *Blessed*. The benedictions are pronounced on the nation, the family and the individual, and cover Israel's life in city and field, offspring, crops, cattle, produce and daily bread. 9 *Establish you*. 'Raise up' (*cf*. Mk. 5:41), as in Dt. 18:15, 18, denoting the establishing of something new and abiding. 10 *Called by the name of the Lord*. See on 5:11. Thus the Israelites are His people, living under His protection (Pr. 18:10). The name of Yahweh was placed upon the sanctuary (Dt. 12:5), and in that name the Israelites were to swear (6:13), to bless (10:8) and to prophesy (18:19). It is abundantly clear from this section that the Israelites entered the land of Canaan armed with a defence against the fertility cults which were in existence there. God had promised to meet all the material and spiritual needs of His people under the forthcoming conditions of sedentary life, and in consequence it was unnecessary for them to follow the practices of Canaanite cult-worship in order to experience prosperity. This passage indicates that the God of Sinai was in fact a genuine fertility deity, but of a vastly different order from that of the cultic impostors of Canaan. For the Israelites, moral obedience to the covenant deity would constitute the guarantee of fertility and productivity.

28:15–68 Solemn curses

These represent the immediate counterpart of the foregoing blessings, indicating that God's laws have both an obverse and a reverse side. 15 *Will not obey*. Complete surrender to the will of God is always a necessary prerequisite to blessing. Unwillingness to obey the divine precepts can only result in disaster. 21 *Pestilence*. Any epidemic outbreak. 22 *Smite you*, with five plagues on human beings and two on the crops. 24 *Powder*. The sandstorms caused by the sirocco. 27 *Boils of Egypt* (AV 'botch'). A staphylococcal infection. 31 *Before your eyes*. While you are completely unable to prevent it. 36 *Bring you*. A startling prediction of the Exile. *Cf*. 2 Ki. 24:12–16. 50 *Stern countenance*; *i.e.* having no regard for compassion or humane treatment. 52 *Shall besiege*. The gruesome scenes here predicted (vv. 52–57) were accomplished in the sieges of Samaria (2 Ki. 6:28) and Jerusalem (La. 2:19–22). 58 *Awful name*; *i.e.* of awe-inspiring character. The following names of God in Deuteronomy should be noted: 'the living God' (5:26); 'the Lord, the God of your fathers' (6:3); the 'God of gods and Lord of lords' (10:17; *cf*. Rev. 19:16); 'the Rock . . . a God of faithfulness' (32:4); 'the Most High' (32:8); 'the eternal God' (33:27). Most commonly He is called 'the Lord your God'. 64 *Will scatter*. These prophetic words have been fulfilled several times in Jewish history from 722 BC onwards, and not least in the present century. 68 *In ships*. At the destruction of Jerusalem the Romans consigned many

Jews into slavery, transporting a large number to Egypt by ship. The irony of captivity in Egypt had once again overtaken them (*cf*. Ho. 8:13).

29:1 – 31:8 Stipulations

29:1–29 Renewal of the covenant. The argument of earlier discourses is summarized in the form of stipulations, the covenant theme being prominent throughout. 1 *The covenant*. The original agreement made at Sinai was quickly broken. Now, at the end of his life, Moses calls for a new commitment of the people. The curses of the law can be offset by the blessings of obedience in the promised land. 4 *A mind to understand*. They did not possess sufficient spiritual insight to appreciate properly the mercies of God. In attributing such incapabilities to God, the Hebrew lawgiver is merely following OT traditions generally in relating everything to Him as the ultimate source or ground of existence. 5 *Led you*. God is here the speaker. *Cf*. 8:2–4. These words are quoted in Am. 2:10. 6 The desert discipline was the pathway to the knowledge of the Lord, which is the highest good. 10 *All of you*. The covenant of grace is all-embracing, from heads and elders (see on 19:12) to 11 little children and the menial slaves. *Cf*. Acts 2:21. 12 *Enter into . . . covenant*. See Gn. 17:7, 8. 16 *The nations*. A reference to their contacts with Edom, Ammon and Moab. 17 *Idols* (lit. 'inanimate blocks'). Moses, like other OT authors, invariably spoke of idols with scorn and derision. It is important to notice that, seen through Israelite eyes, the deities of pagan nations were always inanimate things. This view stood in stark contrast to that held by the devotees of such gods (*cf*. 1 Ki. 18:26ff.), who superstitiously attributed many exaggerated functions to them. For Moses, the deadness of the pagan deities only served to enhance the monotheistic faith associated with the Sinai covenant. 18 *Beware*. An ellipsis, the full form of which should read, 'I adjure you to enter into this oath and covenant, lest there be . . .' 19 *The sweeping away of moist and dry alike* (AV 'to add drunkenness to thirst', RV 'to destroy the moist with the dry'). Evidently a proverb, denoting an all-embracing form of destruction. 21 *Written*. Another of the many references in Deuteronomy to literary activity amongst the Hebrews of the Mosaic age. The curses are not only a warning but a testimony to the sure judgment of God upon those who despise His Word (*cf*. Heb. 10:29). 23 *Admah . . . Zeboiim*. Two of the cities of the plain, whose destruction became a synonym for divine judgment. Their association with Gaza (Gn. 10:19) suggests an original location at the S end of the Dead Sea. *Cf*. Ho. 11:8. 26 *Not allotted*. Another reminder that contact with pagan deities was absolutely prohibited to the Hebrews. 29 *Secret things*. Certain matters of eternal significance belong to God alone, while others are revealed to men. The law has been given for the obedience of Israel, and if the kingdom is sought in this way, everything else needful will be added (*cf.* Mt. 6:33). The verse can be better translated, 'The secret things belong to the Lord our God as well as the revealed things; for us and for our children it is requisite to carry out always all the words of this law.'

30:1–14 The power of repentance. Knowing the sinfulness of human nature and its inevitable consequences, Moses calls for repentance. This is closely associated with the covenant ideal, for the title *the Lord your God* occurs no fewer than twelve times in vv. 1–10. Moses stresses the nearness of the divine word, and the simplicity of faith. 3 *Restore your fortunes* (AV 'turn thy captivity'). *Cf.* Ne. 1:9, where vv. 2 and 3 are quoted. *Gather you.* In announcing the second advent, Christ united this with other prophecies and promises of the old dispensation (Mk. 13:26, 27). 4 *Fetch you.* The return from Babylon was made possible by the decree of Cyrus in 538 BC, and began under Zerubbabel. Zechariah (2:6, 7) prophesied a further influx. 6 *Circumcise.* God will transform the wills of His repentant people, bringing them once again into line with the covenant ideals. Circumcision was the outward token of membership in the covenant nation of Israel, and in the Christian church it was replaced by baptism. 10 *Written.* Not the 'secret things' (29:29), but the revelation of God. Moses refers to the latter as *the voice of the Lord your God* (*cf.* v. 8), thereby attesting to its inspiration and authority. We can therefore speak of this book confidently as the Word of God. 11 *This day.* This note of immediacy occurs more than 60 times in Deuteronomy. *Cf.* Heb. 4:7. *Not too hard* (AV 'not hidden'). Vv. 11–14 should be compared carefully with Rom. 10:5–8, where Paul expounds them of Jesus Christ, the incarnate Word. Moses stated that the word did not remain inaccessible in heaven, but was given to men in simple speech which they could understand. 13 *Beyond the sea.* As the word was not above them, so it was not beyond the horizon over the W sea. Paul varies the metaphor slightly to suit his purposes, but the general meaning is the same. 14 *Very near you.* The appeal to the will and intelligence (*heart*) is a marked feature of Deuteronomy, the word occurring some 34 times. It is the 'heart' that matters (Mt. 15:18), and when that is obedient to God in surrender, the blessings of His grace follow. (See on 4:29.)

30:15–20 The choice between life and death. 18 *Over the Jordan.* As the end approaches, Moses refers more frequently to the crossing of the river, an act in which he would not participate (see 31:2, 13; 32:47). 19 *Heaven and earth.* The unchanging cosmos, which outlasts human vicissitudes. *Cf.* 4:26. *Choose life.* One of the most precious spiritual blessings results from free human choice. 20 *To Abraham.* See on 1:8.

31:1–8 Transfer of leadership. 2 *No longer able.* At an advanced age Moses announced the approaching end of his leadership, placing the Israelites in the care of Joshua (v. 3) and his

teaching office in the hands of the priests (v. 9). 3 *Joshua.* Having long since been made leader of the army (Ex. 17:9) and recently invested with a degree of Moses' own authority (Nu. 27:18–23), Joshua is now to receive his commission directly from the Lord (*cf.* vv. 14, 23). **6, 7** *Be strong.* Moses first exhorts the people, and then Joshua. See Jos. 1:6, 9, and *cf.* Eph. 6:10. 8 *Goes before you.* God will lead His people as in earlier days, so Joshua must be confident of success.

31:9–30 DEPOSITION OF THE LAW

31:9–13, 24–26 Deposit of text

In Ancient Near Eastern suzerainty treaties there was invariably a clause which required that the treaty document should be in the deposit of the vassal, and should be read publicly at intervals to remind the vassal of his obligations. Here Moses, having committed the law to the care of the Levites, enjoins that it shall be read periodically to the assembled people. 9 *Moses wrote.* These words, and the phrase 'Moses wrote this song' in v. 22, are the only explicit statements in this book as to what Moses himself wrote (*cf.* Nu. 33:2). The phrases, 'these are the words' (1:1; 29:1), 'this is the law' (4:44), 'this is the blessing' (33:1), may be the work of a compiler who was attempting to arrange the source material, but there can be no certainty about this. While it may also be very difficult to decide precisely which words Moses did or did not write with his own hand, there can be absolutely no question whatever as to the essentially contemporary nature of the record, and thus of the basic Mosaicity of Deuteronomy. *This law.* All indications are that Moses intended in his own lifetime to make a record of divine law which should be permanent. *Cf.* the contrast between 'his writings' and 'my words' in Jn. 5:47.

24 *The very end.* The first command to Moses to write occurs in Ex. 17:14, and this is the last reference to his activity in this field. From early times Jewish tradition has included the whole Pentateuch in the 'book of the law'. 25 *Levites.* See on 18:1. 26 *Put it.* The whole law-code, containing the Sinai covenant and the covenant in the plains of Moab (29:1), was deposited beside the sacred ark, inside which were the tablets containing the foundation principles of the Sinai covenant.

31:14, 15 Joshua commissioned

14 *The tent of meeting* (AV 'tabernacle of the congregation'; Heb. *'ōhel mô'ēḏ*). Used in Ex. 33:7 of a structure based on the pattern of a simple desert shrine which antedated the Tabernacle proper and was pitched outside the encampment with Joshua as its sole attendant (Ex. 33:11). The word *miškān* was commonly used for the Tabernacle as such. 15 *Appeared.* The cloudy pillar which had accompanied them through their wanderings (Ex. 33:9) now reappears as God speaks 'face to face' with Moses for the last time.

31:16-23, 27-30 Witnesses to the covenant

In secular international treaties the invocation of deities as witnesses to the treaty was an important element in the process of ratification. Here God commands that His witness to Himself shall be attested by means of a song which would perpetuate the covenant concepts and serve as a continuing witness. **16** *Where they go.* The people among whom the Hebrews were to live would beguile them by means of immoral pagan cultic practices. **19** *Write this song.* The verb is in the plural, since both Moses and Joshua were to write it (*cf.* 32:44). *A witness.* God has two witnesses to the covenant, *i.e.* the written law and the song. **21** *I know the purposes.* God's foreknowledge encompasses the evil tendencies of human nature. *Cf.* Gn. 6:5; Jn. 2:25. **22** *The same day.* In the Ancient Near East, anything of importance was committed to writing within a short period of its occurrence. This is an explicit claim to Mosaic authorship of the song. **29** *In the days to come. Cf.* Gn. 49:1; Nu. 24:14. Such apostasy became widespread in the judges' period (*cf.* Jdg. 2:11-16; 3:7). A similar prediction for the Christian church was made by Paul in 2 Tim. 3:1. **30** *Finished.* The commencement and ending of the writing, first of the book (v. 24) and then of the song (v. 30), are noted carefully.

32:1-43 MOSES' SONG AS A WITNESS TO THE COVENANT

At the crossing of the *yam sûp*, Moses sang to the Lord (Ex. 15:1), and he ended his ministry to God with another hymn of joy within sight of the promised land. Both compositions anticipate the glorious future consequent upon the wilderness experience. The theme of this song is the name of the Lord, His loving care for people, His righteousness and His mercy. These are contrasted with the ingratitude and faithlessness of Israel, and the nature of divine justice is emphasized throughout. **2** *Gentle rain*, needed by young grass for its steady growth. **3** *I will proclaim.* The revelation of the name and attributes of God to Moses at the time of his call (Ex. 3:13-15) fully accounts for his concern and enthusiasm for *the name.* **4** *The Rock.* This word is repeated in vv. 13, 15, 18, 30, 31, 37. Here it denotes God's eternal strength and stability as a refuge for frail men. *A God of faithfulness.* True to His own word and promise. *Iniquity.* Better, 'injustice'. **5** *Blemish.* The text presents some problems, and could read, '. . . . who are not His sons, but a disgrace'. The meaning seems to be that the iniquity of Israel is no necessary reflection upon the nature and quality of divine goodness. **6** *Your father.* While all men are God's creatures in a general sense, only the redeemed are true children of God (Jn. 1:12). **8** *The peoples.* The song recalls the teaching of Gn. 10 and 11. In Gn. 10, all nations were included in the covenant of grace, and their boundaries were assigned to them. In ch. 11, however, they were

'separated' as the result of pride. This dilemma was resolved when Israel was chosen to be the means of God's blessing to the world. *Cf.* Rom. 11:25; Eph. 2:11-18. **10** *Found him.* This and subsequent verses depict the tenderness of divine love for Israel. *The apple of his eye, i.e.* the pupil of the eye, upon which sight so greatly depends. **11** *An eagle.* A reference to the traditional solicitude of this bird for its young. The parent eagle, in teaching her young to fly, protects them and encourages them to imitate her own movements. Thus the calling, training and protection of Israel are all depicted in this figure of speech. **13** *Honey out of the rock.* Not the alcoholic drink known popularly amongst the ancients as 'honey', but the natural product of the bees. The countless fissures and crevices of the dry limestone rocks supported many small flowering plants well suited to the needs of bees. **15** *Jeshurun.* A poetical title honouring Israel, rendered 'beloved' in the LXX. **16** *Strange gods.* In view of Israel's calling to be a witness to Jehovah and His holy ways, her separation from idolatry was of vital importance. **17** *Sacrificed to demons. Cf.* Ps. 106:37; 1 Cor. 10:20. *New gods.* Upstart deities imported from pagan nations. **21** *Stirred me to jealousy.* Quoted in Rom. 10:19. The divine 'jealousy', like the divine 'provocation', always has as its aim to recall God's people to their Creator and Lord. *No god.* Lit. 'with a no-god . . . with a no-people'. The thought is repeated in Ho. 1:9. **31** *Our Rock . . . our enemies.* In vv. 28-33 Moses speaks in his own person and longs for Israel to consider and understand God's dealings with them. Their enemies are instruments which He uses to accomplish His purposes (*cf.* Is. 10:5). Constant victory is God's will for His people, and though He may be constrained to deliver them into the power of their enemies, He can also rescue and restore them. **32** *The vine of Sodom.* The heathen are compared to a vine whose stock comes from *Sodom* and *Gomorrah,* cities synonymous in antiquity with gross wickedness. **35** *Vengeance is mine.* Quoted in Rom. 12:19; Heb. 10:30. **39** *I, even I.* The song reaches a climax in its assertion of the absolute sovereignty of God. **40** *I lift up my hand,* betokening a solemn declaration (*cf.* Rev. 10:5). **43** *Praise his people.* This verse is quoted verbatim from the LXX in Rom. 15:10. The song, like the Apocalypse, uses the imagery of the battlefield to picture the awesomeness of divine judgment, but having done this it calls on the Gentiles to rejoice with His restored and pardoned people.

32:44 – 33:29 FINAL CHARGE AND FAREWELL

32:44-47 Last exhortation of Moses

44 *This song.* The antiquity of this composition is being recognized increasingly by modern scholarship. *Joshua* (AV, RV 'Hoshea', Heb. *Hôšēa',* 'salvation'). The original name of Joshua, which was changed by Moses (Nu. 13:8, 16). The occurrence of his original name in the Hebrew suggests that it was still the name by which he was commonly known. **46** *Lay to heart*. The duty of forthcoming generations to keep the covenant is again stressed. **47** This is no empty responsibility, but one of the greatest importance for the future welfare of the nation.

32:48–52 Moses warned of his impending death

The special notice of time (v. 48) and place (vv. 49–51) suggests a contemporary narrative. **49** *The Abarim*. The plural of a word meaning 'across' or 'beyond', referring to the mountainous range in NW Moab overlooking the N end of the Dead Sea. *Cf.* Nu. 21:11; 27:12. *Nebo*. The summit of the range known as Abarim; according to local Muslim tradition it can be identified with Jebel Osha. **51** *Meribath-kadesh*. There is a play on the root of *kadesh*, which means 'holy', and is reproduced in the word for *revere* (AV 'sanctify'). Moses is prepared to bear his share of the responsibility for the act of apostasy (Nu. 20:10–13; 27:14), even to the very end.

33:1–29 Final blessing

1 *His death. Cf.* Gn. 25:8; 49:33. The wording may imply that the verse was an editorial addition, perhaps written at the death of Moses or shortly thereafter, to introduce the content of the benediction. Archaeological discoveries in Mesopotamia have shown the authentic nature of the patriarchal blessings found in Genesis. While the Mosaic benediction is a prophetical utterance of prayer and praise, it follows the tradition of Jacob's blessing (Gn. 49:1–27) in declaring poetically the favour of God as bestowed upon each individual tribe. The omission of Simeon here may be deliberate (perhaps in an attempt to maintain the number of the tribes at twelve; but see on v. 6), but this is not a serious matter, since the Simeonites were gradually absorbed into the tribe of Judah. Whereas the song (ch. 32) is an admonition, the benediction foreshadows a bright and prosperous future for Israel. *The man of God. Cf.* Jos. 14:6; Ps. 90 (title). The title was occasionally applied to the prophets (*e.g.* 1 Sa. 9:6). Here it means '*the godly man*'. **2** *Shone forth*. The giving of the law is likened to the fiery glow of an eastern sunrise, dispelling the darkness with its bright beams. *Holy ones*. Better, 'from the holy myriads'. The LXX reads 'angels' for 'holy ones'. *Cf.* Ps. 68:17; Acts 7:53. The rendering *flaming fire* is uncertain, and AV 'fiery law' gives a better sense. **3** *They followed*. The meaning of this word is uncertain. AV has 'sat down'. Perhaps the reference is to pupils seated at the feet of the teacher, ready to receive instruction. **4** *Moses*. Perhaps this phrase is an explanatory insertion, of the kind possibly represented by v. 1. *Possession*. Better, 'heritage'. **5** *The Lord became king*. A conjectural emendation of the Hebrew text. Better, 'there was a king over Jeshurun'. In this way God's kingdom of Israel has its true beginning, *Jeshurun* being a poetic name for the Israelites (see on 32:15; *cf.* Is. 44:2).

6 *Reuben*. In the order of the tribes the children of Leah and Rachel have precedence, followed by those of their handmaidens. There is a reference to the diminished number of this tribe through the rebellion of Dathan and Abiram (Nu. 16:1–30). Codex A of the LXX makes this verse read, 'Let Reuben live and not die, and Simeon, may he be many in number.'

7 *Judah*. It has been suggested that this verse may have come originally immediately after v. 10, and had become displaced in transmission. Aside from the fact that this would be rather unusual in a poetic composition of this kind, such a situation would imply that v. 11 also belonged to the blessing of Judah.

8 *Levi*. Moses' own tribe, hence the benediction is full and detailed. *Thummim . . . Urim*. These seem to have been objects kept in the high priest's breastplate (Ex. 28:30; Lv. 8:8), which was a pouch fastened to the ephod. By them the priest could declare God's will both to leader (Nu. 27:21) and to people (Dt. 33:8, 10). They were not mentioned after the early monarchy, and prophecy seemed to make them unnecessary. Once prophecy ceased, their use was revived (*cf.* Ezr. 2:63; Ne. 7:65). From the nature of questions in 1 Sa. 23:9–12, it would appear that consulting the Urim and Thummim was a form of casting lots. This might well be the case if *Urim* was derived from *'ārar*, 'to curse' (*i.e.* a negative reply) and *Thummim* from *tāmam*, 'to be perfect' (*i.e.* a positive response), but the facts of the matter are rather uncertain. **9** *Of his father and mother*. Family interests must not be allowed to sway the priest in the discharge of his religious duties (*cf.* Ex. 32:27–29). *Observed thy word*. The priests and Levites were charged with the preservation of the law and the instruction of the people (31:9). **11** *Bless . . . his substance*. See on v. 7. *The loins*. The locale of physical strength.

12 *Benjamin*. The meaning of this verse may be that Jehovah, like a shepherd, carried a favoured animal on His *shoulders* (*cf.* Lk. 15:5). Since this latter word was used in Jos. 15:8 to denote the side of the hill on which the Jebusite stronghold of Jerusalem was situated, it may here be an allusion to the fact that the permanent shrine of Israel was to be in Benjamite territory.

13 *Joseph*. The promise of 'choicest fruits' was fulfilled each spring in the fruit-laden valleys of Ephraim and Manasseh. **16** *The favour of him that dwelt in the bush*. The reference is to the burning bush of Ex. 3:2. *Prince among his brothers*. The idea of pre-eminence is strongly marked here. **17** *Horns of a wild ox* (AV 'unicorns'). A species of buffalo (*rᵉ'ēm*) now extinct, and used as a synonym of enormous strength (Jb. 39:9–11).

18 *Zebulun* is assured of success in his commercial dealings (*going out*). *Issachar* is promised prosperity in domestic and agricultural pursuits (*in your tents*). **20** *Gad*. Swiftness and strength were needed for this tribe of mountain-dwellers who lived in

Transjordan in the former Amorite territory of Sihon. **21** *A commander's portion* (AV 'a portion of the lawgiver', RV mg. 'a ruler's portion'). Presumably a choice area of land worthy of a martial leader. *He came*, namely to the help of the western tribes in the battle for Canaan (Nu. 32:31, 32).

22 *Dan*. In Gn. 49:17 Dan was compared with a serpent for subtlety. Here he is spoken of as a young agile *lion*, and both images describe aptly the adventurous spirit characterizing the tribe of Dan. The land of *Bashan* was well known in antiquity for the size and strength of its cattle (Dt. 32:14).

23 *Naphtali*. To this tribe was assigned the beautiful and fertile land W and S of the Sea of Galilee.

24 *Asher*. The territory of Asher was famous for its olives, which grew in great profusion. **25** *Your bars*. Although Asher's territory was in the N, it would be given strong protection from its political enemies. *As your days, so shall your strength be*. This beautiful promise has brought comfort and blessing to every succeeding generation of believers (*cf.* Mt. 28:20).

26 *None like God, O Jeshurun*. The AV rendering, 'none like unto the God of Jeshurun', is to be preferred here, for God is being praised in His position as the God of Israel. He is above, beneath, before and around His people. The concept of a God *who rides through the heavens* is found in Ugaritic poetry also. **27** *The eternal God*. We too partake of eternal life as we find our permanent abode in Him. *Underneath are the everlasting arms*. Another promise of distinctive beauty, indicating the inexhaustible resources of God for the believer. **28** *Dwelt in safety . . . alone*. Once again the Hebrew people are reminded of their pastoral ideal of 'every man under his vine and under his fig tree' (Mi. 4:4; Zc. 3:10). **29** *Your enemies shall come fawning* (AV 'shall be found liars', AV mg. 'shall be subdued', RV 'shall submit themselves', RV mg. 'yield feigned obedience'). The general allusion seems to be to the insincere homage given by the vanquished to the victor. The final note is one of victory through the protective *shield* and conquering *sword* of the Lord. *High places*. The rendering 'backs' suits the context better. With these lofty sentiments Moses took formal leave of the Israelites, whose interests and aspirations he had nurtured for so long. Had the nation continued in this spirit of promise, its history and its influence in the world would have been very different.

34:1–8 DEATH OF MOSES

1 *Moses went up*. The writer records Moses' last act of obedience as he goes up to the appointed place on a rocky height (32:49). All but two of his own generation had passed away, and his mission was now accomplished. But before he dies, his prayer to see the land is granted. There is great beauty and pathos in this verse.

Moses next appears in sacred history on another mountain, again speaking 'face to face' with his Lord (Mk. 9:2–4). *Pisgah*. The word denotes any jagged ridge, and would describe aptly the mountain's highest peak, Jebel Osha, as seen from beneath (see on 32:49). **1–3** *All the land*. The view seen from Jebel Osha on a clear day agrees exactly with this description in every detail, from snow-capped Hermon, Galilee, the Mount of Olives, Bethlehem, to the Dead Sea and beyond. **5** *The servant of the Lord. Cf.* Heb. 3:5. Moses was in many respects a model servant, in death as well as in life. *Died there*. God was true to His promise that Moses would never cross into the land of Canaan. **6** *He buried him in the valley*. In some depression on the mountain range close to the summit, according to Muslim tradition. As is the case with so many other important personages in Scripture, the actual location of the burial-place is unknown. The personality of the human servant is consistently effaced in order that the glory might be given to God (*cf.* Jn. 3:30). **7** *A hundred and twenty*. In Ancient Egypt the epitaph 'he died aged one hundred and ten' was the highest accolade which could be bestowed upon an individual of outstanding character and practical ability, whatever his precise chronological age at the time of death (*cf.* Gn. 50:26; Jos. 24:29; Jdg. 2:8). By these standards Moses had led an unusually rich, productive and beneficial life. **8** *Thirty days*. The same period of mourning as had been appointed for Aaron (Nu. 20:29).

34:9–12 CONCLUSION

This section is obviously post-Mosaic, and was probably the work of either Eleazar or Joshua himself. There seems little doubt that it was a proper part of Deuteronomy within a generation or two after the death of Moses at the very latest. **9** *Full of the spirit of wisdom. Cf.* Ex. 28:3. The Holy Spirit, who spoke by the prophets, was present in both Moses and Joshua. *Moses had laid his hands upon him. Cf.* Gn. 48:14; Nu. 27:18; Acts 13:3. Blessing, commissioning and the conferring of spiritual gifts were all symbolized by the imposition of hands. **10** *There has not arisen a prophet since*. Whatever prophets may have arisen before this phrase was written, none was equal to Moses in the ways specified, nor were there any afterwards until the coming of the One whom Moses foretold (18:15). As a prophet Moses led the people (Ho. 12:13), delivered to them the revelation committed to him (Dt. 29:29) and pointed them to their future Messiah (18:15). *Face to face*. See Ex. 33:11. **12** *For all the mighty power*. Not only in word did God work through Moses, but in deeds which were never to be forgotten. The signs and wonders wrought in Egypt constituted an important element in the larger stream of redemptive history for the most significant of all acts of deliverance accomplished by Christ on Calvary.

G. T. MANLEY   R. K. HARRISON

Joshua

INTRODUCTION

It has been said that the history of the world is the history of its great men. To be applied to history as a whole, that statement would require considerable qualification, but it can be set down as an accurate description of the kind of history to be found in the book of Joshua, which, quite literally, is Joshua's book. It begins with his divine call and commission, and it ends with the record of his death. It is his leadership under God that binds the story of Israel's conquest of Canaan into a coherent whole.

THE MAN AND HIS TASK

Many things marked Joshua out for leadership. He was of the house of Joseph, which commanded most authority at this stage in the history of Israel; his grandfather, Elishama, had led the tribe of Ephraim through the wilderness and possibly had had the care of the embalmed body of his great ancestor, Joseph, carried up for interment in the promised land. His contact with Egyptian civilization and culture—for he was born in Egypt and had taken part in the Exodus (Nu. 32:11f.)—also fitted him, as it had fitted Moses, for the task of forging his people into a nation. It is significant in this connection that one of his last appeals in his final message to the people reminded them how their fathers had served other gods in Egypt (Jos. 24:14). As Moses' personal attendant and colleague in closest contact with him in the leadership of the people, Joshua had been naturally marked out as his successor, and he must have learned much from his master and from his own experience during the years of wandering in the wilderness. As Moses' companion at Sinai (Ex. 24:13), and as superintendent of the tent of meeting (Ex. 33:11), his leadership had already been manifested and acknowledged.

His faith and courage had been amply revealed in the minority report submitted by Caleb and himself in favour of an invasion of Canaan from Kadesh, in contrast to the timid report of the other ten spies: 'If the Lord delights in us, he will bring us into this land and give it to us' (Nu. 14:8).

He had also already shown his prowess as a military commander in leading the forces of Israel which repelled the attack of the Amalekites at Rephidim, when they fell upon the rear of the Hebrew host, which was encumbered with women, children and baggage (Dt. 25:18). He won a decisive victory, and his generalship was the human channel through which came the answer to the prayers of Moses on the mountain-top (Ex. 17:8ff.). This was the man, so highly qualified by nature, by training and by experience, whom God raised up to lead the Hebrew tribes into Canaan. But his supreme qualification lay in the fact that all his gifts, training and experience were fused into a dynamic force by the touch of God. It was at the call of God that all his potentialities were called forth, and that call brought to the leadership of Israel a man assured of his divine commission; it summoned to the task a soldier who had put on the whole armour of God.

AUTHORSHIP AND AUTHENTICITY

Any consideration of the composition of the book of Joshua must take into account its position in the Hebrew Canon. From one point of view it looks back: the promise made to Abraham finds fulfilment in the conquest of Canaan, and Joshua marks the climax of all the history which has gone before. This viewpoint is reflected in the traditional criticism which sees Joshua as a continuation of the Pentateuch, and links the six books together as a Hexateuch. According to this view, the same basic sources, J, E, D, P, are found in Joshua as in the Pentateuch, with J, E and D found in chs. 1–12, and P in the latter half of the book, dealing with the delineation of the tribes. This traditional critical view has been modified in several directions, perhaps most significantly in a tendency to explain the alleged conflict between sources not by a long chronological evolution—this has been discredited by archaeology—but by the existence of various circles of oral tradition in different places and with different spheres of interest. E. J. Young (*An Introduction to the Old Testament*, 1958) gives compelling reasons for rejecting the concept of a Hexateuch: one of the most important of these is the clear distinction drawn in Hebrew tradition between the Pentateuch and the Early Prophets, at the head of which stands Joshua.

From a second point of view Joshua looks forward: the conquest marks not an end but a beginning, the beginning of the history of Israel in her national homeland. This viewpoint is reflected in the theory which sees the book as part of a great historical literary unit stretching from the time of Moses to the Babylonian Exile. Martin Noth, followed to a large extent by John Bright in *IB* and by many modern scholars, represents this assessment of the forward-looking nature of Joshua and maintains that not only Joshua but also Deuteronomy must be separated from the Pentateuch and the sources which have been identified in it, and linked with Judges – 2 Kings. Noth holds that this history, reflecting the prophetic insistence that continued national well-being depends on implicit obedience to the commands of God, was the work of a compiler who put together a mass of material from various sources. Among these was the Deuteronomic code (Dt. 4:44 – 30:20): this was the theological basis of the whole history, and, accordingly, the compiler has been called the Deuteronomic historian, D. Noth finds much material in Joshua that on his reckoning is pre-D, and is not JE. Jos. 1–12, *e.g.*, consisted of a series of aetiological legends, *i.e.* legends which grew up to explain the origin of some landmark or custom, and a few hero-legends. This aetiological method has been justifiably criticized when it is unsupported by any external evidence. (See J. Bright, *Early Israel in Recent History Writing*, 1956.)

Noth's view has proved to be a healthy reaction against the traditional criticism. Particularly valuable is his insistence that chs. 13–21 are not P, the product of a post-exilic priestly idealization of the land allocation as it should have been. But his basic assumptions are no more acceptable than those of earlier criticism. While there was certainly editing of the sources used in the compilation of Joshua—one of these sources, the Book of Jashar, is named in Jos. 10:13—there is no evidence that the sources of this section of the OT have, as Noth supposes, been freely worked over by a Deuteronomic editor, who has recast the material to reflect the theological standpoint of the prophets. Further, like earlier criticism, his view takes no account of the traditional division of the Hebrew Bible and the distinction between the Law and the Early Prophets. Again, he seems to ignore the basic form of Deuteronomy, whose structure shows a remarkable resemblance to the literary pattern of the Ancient Near Eastern treaties and covenants of the mid-second millennium BC. This unmistakable resemblance confirms the early date of Deuteronomy, as against Noth's dating in the 6th century BC. (For the covenant pattern, see Jos. 8:30–35 and chs. 23, 24.)

Jewish tradition has consistently ascribed the bulk of the book of Joshua to Joshua himself, though the author is nowhere identified in the Bible. Some facts which suggest a date for the composition of the book nearly contemporary with Joshua are the following. *a.* The author was apparently an eyewitness of some of the events described. *E.g.*, the text of 5:1, as in AV, reads 'until we were passed over'. This may not be decisive, since some MSS, the Massoretic editors and the versions read, as RSV, 'until they had passed over'. But there does not seem to be the same textual doubt in 5:6, which reads 'which the Lord had sworn to their fathers to give us'. The pronoun 'your' in 15:4 suggests autobiographical writing. *b.* The frequent use of the phrase 'to this day' and the context in which it

occurs suggest an early date. Note 6:25, which suggests that Rahab was still alive, though the phrase may refer to her descendants rather than to her personally. But undoubtedly 15:63 points to a pre-Davidic date (*cf.* 2 Sa. 5:6f.), and 16:10 to a pre-Solomonic date (*cf.* 1 Ki. 9:16), though it can be argued that the language used would have been inappropriate before the monarchy had been established. *c.* There are internal evidences of an early date: references to 'Great Sidon' (Jos. 11:8; 19:28) alongside 'Tyre' and to the Phoenicians as 'Sidonians' (13:4–6) suggest a date earlier than the 12th century BC, when Tyre became the foremost Phoenician city; the use of a stone or a cairn of stones, like the stones commemorating the crossing of the Jordan, the cairn over Achan's body, and those at the graves of the kings of Ai and other towns, to mark outstanding events suggests an early period in Israel's history; the Philistines have obviously not yet become a major menace to the Israelites, as they did after 1200 BC, according to Egyptian records; in 11:22 it is the Anakim, not the Philistines, who inhabit cities that later were Philistine—Gaza, Gath and Ashdod; and the list of the inhabitants of the land in 12:8 does not include the Philistines.

There are, however, other references which suggest a date later than the time of Joshua, the most obvious being the reference to his death in 24:29, 30. There are also references to events which did not occur until after Joshua's death: *e.g.*, the conquest of Hebron by Caleb (15:13, 14; *cf.* Jdg. 1:10, 20). It can be argued, however, that the phrase 'after the death of Joshua', in Jdg. 1:1, refers only to part of the chapter, vv. 1–9, 16–19, that the rest of the chapter is undated, and that, consequently, 1:10–15, 20 could belong to the time of Joshua. (See K. A. Kitchen, *Ancient Orient and Old Testament*, 1966, p. 66.) Similarly, while the capture of Debir by Othniel appears to be subsequent to the southern campaign of Joshua (Jos. 15:15–19; *cf.* Jdg. 1:11–15), it may be argued, as by Kitchen (*ibid.*), that 'Debir was smitten twice by the Hebrews; once during Joshua's flying campaign, and a second time by Caleb and the Judahites beginning a permanent settlement'.

The migration of the Danites to Laish, described in detail in Jdg. 17, 18, is summarized in Jos. 19:47, where Leshem stands instead of Laish. If this was due to pressure by the Philistines, as is generally supposed, it might be taken as indicating a later date for at least this part of Joshua, when the Philistines had become a threat to Israel. But the reference to Jonathan in Jdg. 18:30 as the grandson of Moses suggests that it may not have been so much later than Joshua's time after all.

On all the evidence, therefore, it seems that while nothing really definite can be said about the authorship and date of the book, there is considerable support for the view that the sources from which it is derived were contemporary with the events described, and that the book took its form at an early date. It is significant that recent writers are much more willing than were writers of an earlier day to accept the historical value of the materials to be found in Joshua. Archaeological research has done much to confirm the authenticity of the history that we have here. Excavations have established conclusively that several important cities of Canaan were destroyed in the latter half of the 13th century BC, the probable period of the Israelite conquest. The excavations at Bethel (mod. Beitin), Lachish (mod. Tell ed-Duweir), Eglon (mod. Tell el-Hesi?), Debir (mod. Tell Beit Mirsim), Hazor (mod. Tell el-Qedah) have provided evidence of violent conflagrations at this time. Heavy layers of ash tell something of the completeness of the devastation, and the location of the towns excavated, in the centre, the south and the north of the land, confirms the biblical account of Joshua's campaigns as striking fiercely in those areas. Further, archaeology's assessment of the age and historical significance of the lists of cities and boundaries in Jos. 13–21 would put their date very much earlier than writers of the Wellhausen school were prepared to do. W. F. Albright, *e.g.* (*Archaeology of Palestine*, 1949, p. 229), writes, 'A good case in point is the list of Levitic cities in Josh. xxi and 1 Chron. vi, which Wellhausen, followed by most subsequent critics, considered an artificial product of some post-exilic scribe's imagination. Careful examination of this list in the light of all known archaeological facts makes it quite certain that the list is much more ancient.' Basing his argument on the ground that not one of the cities in Jos. 21 was founded after 950 BC, Albright writes, 'A date between about 975 and about 950 BC may thus be fixed for the extant form of the list, which seems to have had a prehistory going back to the Conquest' (*op. cit.*, p. 230). G. E. Wright confirms Albright's view, and is prepared to go further. 'In my opinion', he writes in an essay on 'Present State of Biblical Archaeology' in *The Study of the Bible Today and Tomorrow* (1947), 'the same can be held for the list of tribal cities and perhaps even for the boundaries in Jos. xv–xix. . . . If this is the case, then there is no reason whatsoever to ascribe these lists in Joshua to the priestly writers of the post-Exilic period.' It is clear that recent archaeological study is not prepared to accept these lists as an idealization produced by a post-exilic writer. It must be emphasized, however, that the truth of the Bible is not dependent on the confirmation of archaeological research. As Donald J. Wiseman has written (*Revelation and the Bible*, 1959, p. 316), 'Ultimately the truth or "confirmation" of the Old Testament rests in God and does not depend on the human science of archaeology, valuable though it is.'

THE DATE OF ISRAEL'S CONQUEST

It is now widely accepted that the Exodus took place *c.* 1280 BC, and that the conquest of

Canaan was therefore *c.* 1240 BC, though it should be recognized that there is some difficulty in fitting all the data supplied by the biblical records and by archaeological research into a precise chronology.

Biblical data to be taken into account include the following. *a.* In Gn. 15:13 it was predicted to Abraham that his descendants should be sojourners in an alien land for 400 years. Similarly, Ex. 12:40 gives the time that Israel dwelt in Egypt as 430 years. The date of the patriarchs, however, can be no more than conjectural, though recent study of the patriarchal era in its context suggests *c.* 1700 BC as a likely date for Israel's going down into Egypt. This would give a date in the 13th century or thereabouts for the Exodus. *b.* In Jdg. 11:26 Jephthah speaks of Israel's dwelling in Transjordan for 300 years before his time. Jephthah's date, too, must be conjectural, though, coming late in the period of the judges, it has been set *c.* 1100 BC. This would give a date *c.* 1400 BC for the conquest. *c.* 1 Ki. 6:1 states specifically that the fourth year of Solomon's reign was the 480th year after the people of Israel came out of the land of Egypt. Since the fourth year of Solomon's reign was *c.* 960 BC, this gives a date of *c.* 1440 BC for the Exodus and *c.* 1400 for the conquest.

There are, however, other biblical figures which appear to give a period considerably less than the 480 years of 1 Ki. 6:1. A comparison of Nu. 1:7 and Ru. 4:20ff. suggests that Nahshon, who belonged to the period of the Exodus, was separated from Solomon by only six generations. It is probable that here we have an incomplete genealogy: this is borne out by the fact that 1 Ch. 6:3–8, 50–52 gives ten generations between Aaron and Zadok, who was high priest in Solomon's reign. But even ten generations could not span the period in 1 Ki. 6:1. Again, Gn. 36:31ff. gives a list of eight kings who reigned over Edom before the time of Saul, and one of these was reigning in the time of Moses (Nu. 20:14). The reigns of at most eight kings could not conceivably stretch to 480 years. Further, in the story of the migration of the Danites in Jdg. 18, Micah's priest, Jonathan, is described as the grandson of Moses, according to the true reading (RSV as against AV). If, as is generally supposed, the Danite migration was due to pressure by the Philistines, who were not aggressively active until about 1200 BC, this gives an approximate date for Moses again in the 13th century, and suggests that the period from Moses to Solomon could not have been more than about 300 years.

The biblical data seem to suggest two possible dates for the conquest—a date in the 15th century BC (supported by 1 Ki. 6:1 and possibly by Jephthah's 300 years) and a date in the 13th century (supported in the main by the other passages cited). It is partly on these grounds that H. H. Rowley (*From Joseph to Joshua*, 1950) makes a synthesis of both possibilities and argues for two entries into Canaan—one in the

Amarna age and one at the time of Joshua. Involved in this theory is the supposition that some tribes were already in Palestine before the time of Joshua, and possibly some were never in Egypt at all. But the biblical evidence is entirely opposed to this view: there is nowhere in the Bible any explicit evidence of more than one Exodus or for any tribes not having been in Egypt. All the explicit evidence points the other way, and the book of Joshua adds its weight to the evidence that all of Jacob's sons entered Egypt and that all their descendants, the twelve tribes, shared in the Exodus and the conquest. The twelve stones of the memorials at the Jordan, and the allocation of the land among twelve tribes are eloquent testimony that it was a united people, composed of all the twelve tribes, who took possession of the land. K. A. Kitchen (*op. cit.*, pp. 70f.) has shown conclusively that the evidence adduced from extra-biblical sources for Rowley's view is quite illusory, and that the placing of Simeon and Levi's attack on Shechem in the Amarna age is similarly contrary to fact. The chronological problems of the conquest cannot be solved by Rowley's synthesis.

Before attempting a synthesis of the biblical data, it may be helpful to summarize the archaeological evidence. This suggests for the most part that the conquest should be dated in the 13th century BC. The following findings are relevant. *a.* Ex. 1:8–11 records that the people of Israel were forced to labour in the building of Pithom and Ra'amses. The city of Ra'amses was rebuilt under the pharaohs Sethos I (*c.* 1302–1290 BC) and Rameses II (*c.* 1290–1224 BC), after whom it was named. The Exodus, therefore, is best dated after the accession of Rameses II. *b.* A stele of victory set up by Merenptah *c.* 1220 BC indicates that the Israelites were already in Palestine, though possibly not yet as a settled community. This would give a date for the conquest some years before 1220 BC. *c.* Nelson Glueck's explorations in Transjordan suggest that the Israelites could not have left Egypt before 1300 BC, since Nu. 20, 21 indicate that they encountered Edom and Moab in the wilderness, and neither of these two kingdoms was established before that time. *d.* Excavations have dated the destruction of Canaanite cities, *e.g.* Lachish, Debir, Bethel, Hazor, in the second half of the 13th century. Excavations at Jericho, which might have been expected to yield decisive information on the conquest, have proved inconclusive. John Garstang's work at Jericho had convinced him that Jericho fell *c.* 1400 BC, but more recent work by Kathleen Kenyon suggests that he was mistaken, and that the destruction which he associated with Joshua occurred several centuries earlier. Identification of the Hebrews with the Habiru of the Amarna letters, which had been taken to support an early date for the conquest, has been similarly discounted by more recent study.

It seems, therefore, that the present assessment of the archaeological data takes it as supporting a 13th-century date. The problem remaining is how to reconcile 1 Ki. 6:1 and the date derived from Jephthah with this, and, more urgently—for archaeology is neither inspired nor infallible—with the other biblical data referred to above, relating to the number of generations between the time of the Exodus and the reign of Solomon and between Moses and the migration of the Danites in Jdg. 18. Jephthah's 300 years, as suggested by K. A. Kitchen (*op. cit.*, pp. 74f.), 'could . . . be an aggregate of partly concurrent periods', and, in any case, the dating of Jephthah *c.* 1100 is largely conjectural (see further *TOTC Judges*, 1968, pp. 28–34). 1 Ki. 6:1 provides a more difficult problem. There are the faintest grounds for suspecting the text in this passage: some MSS of the LXX read 'four hundred and forty years'. This does not help in the computing of the dates, but it lends some credibility to the suggestion that at some stage 'four hundred and eighty years' was written for 'twelve generations'. There is evidence that 40 years came to be a conventional way of thinking of a generation: Israel spent 40 years in the wilderness until the generation that had left Egypt had died. If, then, the 480 years of 1 Ki. 6:1 can be taken as representing twelve generations, and if a generation (from the birth of father to the birth of son) can be taken more accurately as about 25 years, we are left with a period of 300 years for the interval between the conquest and Solomon, and arrive at a date for the conquest in the 13th century.

THE MORAL PROBLEM IN ISRAEL'S WARFARE

The indiscriminate extermination of the Canaanites recorded in the book of Joshua has proved a stumbling-block to many who accept the divine inspiration of the scriptural record. Can we believe that God really commanded the Israelites utterly to destroy the inhabitants of the land? If He did, is such a revelation of His character consistent with the revelation of the Father that Christ has given us?

Modern criticism has two ways of cutting the Gordian knot. Some maintain that the accounts of the extermination of the Canaanites were written long after the events which they profess to describe, and that they give an ideal picture of what later ages considered should have happened if the worship of Yahweh was to be kept pure. In other words, the atrocities described never really happened. Others assert that the revelation of God that we have in the early religious history of Israel is His revelation of Himself limited by the capacity of those who had to receive it, and that the conception of His commanding the destruction of the Canaanites represents a very primitive stage of religious development.

In our consideration of the authorship and authenticity of Joshua we have already given reasons for dismissing the former of these two explanations; the latter now demands some attention. The theory holds that the Israelites of this period mistakenly thought of Yahweh as their tribal God, who naturally commanded the destruction of His people's enemies. Later revelation (*e.g.* the book of Jonah) was to show that God had purposes of love and mercy for nations outside the commonwealth of Israel, and so the earlier revelation was transcended. But this theory, however inviting it may seem, does not really give a satisfying explanation of the problem. It is true that the knowledge of God had to grow more and more as His people were able to bear it, and that the OT at best could give but a partial revelation of Him; but we cannot believe that a later revelation should flatly contradict an earlier one. God may reveal Himself progressively, but He must reveal Himself consistently if we are to accept His revelation of Himself at all.

Can we then find an explanation which does honour both to the inspiration of the record and to the God whom it reveals? It is necessary at the outset to get a clear idea of what was involved in the devotion of the Canaanite cities to destruction. To take Jericho as an example, the city, its inhabitants and all that it contained were 'devoted' or 'put to the ban' (Heb. *ḥērem*; 6:17 'devoted to the Lord for destruction'; 6:18 'devoted to destruction'; 7:1 'devoted things'). This meant, as G. A. Cooke describes it, that 'anything which might endanger the religious life of the community was put out of harm's way by being prohibited to human use; to secure this effectively it must be utterly destroyed' ('Joshua', *CBSC*). It seems therefore that the ban had a religious and a prophylactic function: it was a religious service, and it was a protection for the religious life of Israel. It is along these two lines that a solution of our problem must be sought.

First, then, the destruction of the Canaanites was, as the record again and again proclaims it to be, a religious service. The people of Israel were the instrument by which God exercised judgment on the gross wickedness of the people of the land. Just as He had destroyed Sodom and Gomorrah for the same kind of unspeakable corruption, without the instrumentality of human hands, so He used the Israelites to punish and root out the cancerous depravity of the Canaanites. If there be a moral government of the world at all, such a dread possibility of judgment and divine surgery, however executed, cannot be excluded. Gn. 15:16 indicates that the Israelite invasion was, in fact, exactly timed to serve the moral purposes of God. Incidentally, it is noteworthy that the ban, being a religious service, imposed a moral restraint against the looting and excesses which were the normal, more terrible accompaniments of the warfare of the times. This was no lust for booty or for blood; it was a divine duty which must be performed.

The second function of the ban was prophylactic. If the religion of the Hebrews was to be kept pure and untainted, all possibility of infection by the abominations of the heathen must be removed. The means of removing the dread infection was a drastic one, but, in view of the revelation that the Hebrews were to transmit to the world, who will say that it was unjustified? It is significant that where there was failure in Israel's high task, the reason is seen in their failure to carry out the divine command of extermination. And so, for the sake of God's moral government of the world, for the sake of Israel, and for the sake of the message that Israel was to bring to the world, it was necessary that an evil nation should be utterly destroyed.

THE RELIGIOUS TEACHING OF THE BOOK

The criterion of the religious value of any book is, what does it tell us about God? What truth of God does it reveal? The book of Joshua throws light upon three aspects of God's relationship to man:

God's faithfulness

Long years before, the promise had been given that the people of Israel would possess the promised land (*e.g.* Gn. 15:7, 18–21; 26:2–5; 28:13, 14). It had seemed that that divine purpose had been thwarted by man's sin and disobedience; but God's plan could not finally be defeated, and this book gives the story of fulfilment in the conquest of Canaan. (See 11:23; 21:43–45; 23:14.)

God's holiness

This is seen in His judgment upon the original inhabitants of the land. The iniquity of the Amorites at last was full, and Israel became the instrument of His punishment (see 6:17; 10:40; 11:20; 23:3; *cf.* Lv. 18:24, 25). But God's holiness is seen no less in His insistence that His instrument of judgment must be holy. Again and again it is stressed that this is a holy war, and that Israel will succeed in the task committed to her only as every evil thing is put away from her (see 3:5; 7:11–13; 23:12, 13, 16; 24:19, 20).

God's salvation

The name Joshua means 'Yahweh is salvation', and the book of Joshua illustrates a most important aspect of the salvation which God gives. Exodus sees God's salvation basically as deliverance from bondage: Joshua goes on to teach that God's salvation involves victory and possession and rest (see 21:43, 44). The conquest of Canaan and Israel's possession of the land show God's acting on behalf of His people to fulfil His promise of a salvation that goes far beyond liberation from bondage.

The name Joshua is the Hebrew form of Jesus, the name that is above every name. Is it any wonder that Christian devotion has seen in Joshua a 'type' of Christ, and in this book a picture of the life of victory and possession that is ours in Him? Crossing the Jordan has often been thought of as symbolical of death; but it is much more helpful, and truer to the facts, to think of it as symbolizing the entrance into the life of fullness of blessing to which the Captain of the Lord's host brings us. Salvation for the Christian includes victory and possession and rest. 'Therefore, while the promise of entering his rest remains, let us fear lest any of you be judged to have failed to reach it' (Heb. 4:1).

OUTLINE OF CONTENTS

COMMENTARY

1:1–9 JOSHUA'S COMMISSION

Joshua is divinely called to the task which he is to undertake as Moses' successor. Cf. Dt. 34:9.

1:1, 2 The continuity of the task

These opening verses bring Joshua on to the stage, and are a necessary prologue to the story of the conquest. In spite of the death of Moses, the work must go on: the continuity of the nation, of its task and of God's promises to it, is not broken by the change of leadership.

1 *Moses' minister.* Joshua's position as Moses' chief assistant is underlined here. The Hebrew word for 'minister', *mᵉšārēṭ*, refers to official rather than menial service, and since it normally refers in the OT to Temple service, there is possibly a reference here to special religious service (*cf.* Ex. 33:11); Joshua's function from the very beginning was a religious one.

1:3–9 Promise and command

There is a promise to the people of the land

which God is in process of giving to them (vv. 3, 4); and a promise to Joshua of divine authority, divine presence and divine faithfulness (v. 5). Then are given God's commands (vv. 6–9); this is always the biblical order: first the promise, then the command. Be strong, be courageous, be obedient to the law of God, and success will inevitably follow, for the cause is God's.

4 *All the land of the Hittites* refers not to the whole Hittite Empire, but to the part of it which lay between the Euphrates and the Mediterranean, *i.e.* N Syria. **5** *I will not fail you*; literally 'I will not drop you'. *Cf.* 10:6, where it is translated 'do not relax your hand'. **7, 8** *The law which Moses my servant commanded you . . . This book of the law* is the book referred to in Dt. 31:24, 26. *Cf.* Dt. 31:9, 11. This law must be the subject of constant mediation. *Cf.* Dt. 5:29–33; 6:4–9; Ps. 1:2, 3. **9** *Have I not commanded you?* The campaign upon which Joshua and the people are entering is unmistakably divine. Joshua is no bandit, no aggressor; he is simply a servant carrying out the commands of his superior. *Cf*. Dt. 31:1–8.

1:10 – 5:12 THE ENTRY INTO CANAAN

This section includes the mobilization of all the tribes, the sending out of the spies, the preparations for the crossing of the Jordan, the crossing and its commemoration, and the first encampment in the promised land.

1:10–18 Mobilization

1:10, 11 A disciplined people. The army which awaited the order to advance into Canaan was well organized and disciplined, a much more effective fighting force than the undisciplined mob which had come out of Egypt. **10** *The officers of the people.* The Hebrew literally reads 'those who write or record', originally the tally clerks in Egypt who kept the count of the bricks (Ex. 5:6), eventually becoming, as here, subordinate leaders of the people. **11** *Within three days.* It seems that the spies had already been sent out, though the account of their mission is not recorded until later; the record does not follow the chronological order of events. It may be, however, that 'three days' is a conventional expression for 'soon', without specifying an exact date (*cf*. 2:16).

1:12–18 A united people. At this supremely critical moment the tribes were happily a vital unity, and the Reubenites, the Gadites and the half-tribe of Manasseh, whose inheritance had already been allotted to them on the east of the Jordan (*cf*. Nu. 32), responded with alacrity to the reminder that they were committed to marching with their brethren against the western land. It was this unity with its definitely religious basis that made Israel a force to be reckoned with. **14** *Beyond the Jordan.* Literally 'across the Jordan', the side referred to being left to the understanding of the reader, though frequently it is defined more particularly, as in v. 15 'toward the sunrise', or in 5:1 'to the west'. The use of the phrase in 12:1, 7 and elsewhere for each side alternately shows that it gives no evidence for the geographical location of the writer. *Armed*; either 'in companies' from a word suggesting 'divided into five parts', or, as in Ex. 13:18, 'equipped for battle'. 'In battle array' might combine both senses. **16–18** The army's willingness to submit to Joshua's leadership is clearly related to his spiritual fitness for it. **17** *Only may the Lord your God be with you, as he was with Moses!* In early Israel the right to leadership was always related to possession of God's Spirit. *Cf*. 1 Sa. 10:6; 11:6.

2:1–24 The mission of the spies

The spies were sent to view the land and, particularly, to report on the strategically important city of Jericho which stood at the entrance of the mountain passes into the interior.

The conquest was to be achieved by three crushing campaigns—against the centre, described in chs. 7–9, the south, ch. 10 and the north, ch. 11. The crossing of the Jordan, therefore, and the capture of Jericho, were the key to the whole campaign.

2:1 The spies sent out. Shittim has been identified by Nelson Glueck with Tell el-Hamman, in the foothills of the eastern edge of the Jordan valley. It was the site of the Israelites' last camp before advancing into Canaan. *Cf*. Nu. 33:49. This location, at some distance from the Jordan, supports the supposition (*cf*. 1:11) that the spies had been sent out from there before the Israelites moved to the edge of Jordan.

1 *Secretly*; literally 'silently'. Joshua's intention was probably concealed from the Israelites as well as from the Canaanites, lest an unfavourable report should again dishearten the people. *A harlot whose name was Rahab.* Attempts have often been made since the time of Josephus to represent Rahab merely as an innkeeper, but the Hebrew word used, the LXX translation and the NT references (Heb. 11:31; Jas. 2:25) confirm the accuracy of the ordinary translation.

2:2–7 The spies suspected and concealed. 2, 3 The uneasy suspicions of the king of Jericho confirm the panic in the city reported to the spies by Rahab (see vv. 9–11). *The king of Jericho* was no more than the ruler of a tiny city-state; these were characteristic of Canaan at this time, and their independence and lack of unity, except in a few cases when some of them combined to meet Israelite pressure, were contributory factors to Israel's success. **4, 5** We have here a very imperfect morality. The NT commends Rahab, not for her falsehood, but for her faith. **2:8–21 Rahab's faith and loyalty. 9–11** Into her dark and tragic life had come some faint glimmering of the truth that here in Israel there was a God above all the gods she had ever known. Stories of His great deeds and the success in war of His people had reached the city. *Cf*. Dt. 2:25; 7:23; 11:25. She was prepared to trust herself to the power and mercy of this supreme God, and it was that faith which saved her. **12** *Dealt kindly . . . deal kindly.* The Hebrew word is *ḥesed*, applied generally to God's covenant love for His people, but also in relationships on the human level to the same kind of steadfast loyalty. *Cf*. 2 Sa. 10:2. **17** *Guiltless*; rather 'free from the oath'; *cf*. Gn. 24:8. **18, 19** Rahab's faith, immature though it may have been, was the saving of herself and her family, for she received from the spies the promise that when the city fell the house with the *scarlet cord* hanging from the window would be spared. Some identify this scarlet thread with the cord with which she let the spies down (v. 15), but the words are different.

2:22–24 The spies return and report. At Rahab's suggestion, the spies hid themselves for three days. The hills around Jericho are full of caves, and so would have given them ample cover.

They then returned to Joshua, probably by swimming the Jordan, with their report of the utter despondency and alarm of the Canaanites. **24** *Fainthearted;* the same word as 'melt away' in v. 9.

3:1-13 Preparations for a holy war

The people were given two reminders that this was a holy war on which they were entering —the leadership of the ark of the covenant (vv. 3, 4) and the necessity for consecrating themselves for the task (v. 5). The people were to be led across the Jordan by the ark, borne by the priests of the tribe of Levi. The ark served two purposes in the life and worship of the people of Israel: it was an outward symbol of the presence of God with His people, and it served as a receptacle for the two tablets of the Decalogue (*cf.* Ex. 25:12). Both these purposes were of great significance now at this vital point in Israel's history; the people had to be sure of the divine leadership, and they had to be sure of direction for the untrodden way that lay before them. (V. 11 may be translated, 'Behold, the ark of the covenant. The Lord of all the earth is passing over before you into Jordan.') The ark was the sign that God was going before His people, to lead them against their enemies.

4 The ark was further the symbol of the instruction that they would need for future guidance. This seems to be the significance of the distance between the people and the ark: not so much their necessary separateness from the holy God, as that they must stand back so as to view how wonderfully, miraculously and clearly God will lead them. **5** The cleansing of the people. *Sanctify yourselves*; this was necessary because God was about to work miraculously among them, giving evidence of His presence with Joshua no less than with Moses. The whole situation created an atmosphere of supernatural power waiting to be exercised; this is to be God's doing, not Israel's.

9-13 In Scripture, word and miracle go hand in hand, the former predicting and explaining, the latter confirming. So it was that God made Moses and all the prophets wise before the event, proving by fulfilment that the word they spoke was not theirs but His. And so here Joshua outlines and explains the coming events. The fulfilment then gives divine authentication of Joshua's leadership. **11** See note above.

3:14 – 4:18 The crossing of the Jordan

Commentators have suggested that two differing accounts of the crossing have been combined in this passage. Certainly if we read 4:5 as it is usually translated it gives the impression that the crossing had not yet been started, whereas we gather from 3:16, 17 and 4:1 that the people had already completed it. But 4:5 can be translated, 'Pass over to where the ark of the Lord your God is in the midst of Jordan.' With this reading it is possible to reconstruct the history without finding any breaks or discrepancies in the

narrative. Those who have attempted to solve the intricacies of this narrative by appeal to differing accounts woven together have overlooked the fact that the story told here is intrinsically complex. The historian was faced with the task of relating three distinct and overlapping events: the story of the priests and the ark (3:14-17; 4:11-18), the story of the people crossing Jordan, and the story of the memorial stones, both those taken from the river (4:4-8) and those set up in the river (4:9). Thus when both at 3:17 and 4:10 he makes reference to the people crossing over, it is to show in the first case that the priests remained motionless throughout the crossing, and that the incident of the memorial stones took place while the crossing was still in progress. Identical features of narrative art are found in ch. 10 where the incidents of the overthrow of the confederate forces, the miracle of the 'sun standing still' and the flight of the kings have to be dovetailed into one vivid record. The sequence of events is then seen to be as follows:

3:14-17 The twelve tribes pass over Jordan. 15

The priests bearing the ark took up their stand on the brink of Jordan, which was brim-full at this time of the year, swollen by melting snows. **16** As they advanced to mid-channel the bed of the river was dried up before them; the stream was checked in its course *far off, at Adam, the city that is beside Zarethan.* This has been placed 16 miles up the river from Jericho, and it seems probable that a stretch of 20 or 30 miles of the river bed was left dry. An interesting parallel to the event recorded in this chapter has been found in the pages of an Arabic historian, describing how in AD 1266 near Tell ed-Dâmiyeh, which many experts have identified with Adam, the bed of the river was left dry for ten hours in consequence of a landslide. Other parallels have been quoted: in 1927 an earthquake caused the west bank to collapse near the location of Adam, and the Jordan was dammed up for more than twenty-one hours. These events may indicate a 'natural' explanation of what happened centuries earlier, but to accept that explanation does not detract in any way from the supernatural intervention which opened the way to Israel just at the moment when they needed to cross. The priests standing in the dry bed of the river as the whole nation passed over were the sign that this was the doing of the Lord.

4:1-9 The crossing commemorated. When the people had crossed, Joshua took the twelve men whom he had already chosen (*cf.* 3:12), and commanded them to go back to where the priests were standing with the ark, and to take out of the river twelve stones which were afterwards set up as a memorial at Gilgal. Joshua then set up twelve other stones in the midst of the Jordan where the feet of the priests stood. **2-5** The two sets of twelve stones, *according to the number of the tribes of the people of Israel,* bore eloquent testimony to the fact that all twelve tribes were in the wilderness together and that all entered Canaan at the same time.

4:10–18 The crossing completed. The priests stood in their places until the memorial stones had been arranged for and all the people had hastened across. Then they crossed last of all and the river returned to its spate of full flood. **12–14** A note is inserted to stress the fact that the eastern tribes marched with their brethren across the Jordan, and to draw attention to the event as a fulfilment of the promise given to Joshua in 3:7. **15** This verse should be understood and translated as resuming the main thread of the narrative after the parenthetic vv. 12–14. 'So then, the Lord said to Joshua . . .', or even, 'For the Lord had said to Joshua . . .'

4:19 – 5:12 Encampment at Gilgal

4:19, 20 *They encamped in Gilgal.* Here the stones taken out of the Jordan were set up as a memorial, and here the camp of Israel was based for the campaign. The name Gilgal means 'circle' or 'rolling', from Hebrew *gālal*, 'to roll', and there may well have been a circle of stones already there. Jdg. 3:19, if it is the same Gilgal referred to there, speaks of 'sculptured stones near Gilgal'. But the name was now applied by Joshua to the rolling away of the reproach of Egypt when Israel renewed their acceptance of God's covenant in the renewed rite of circumcision; *cf.* 5:9.

4:21–24 The continuity of God's acts. Future generations were to be reminded that the God of their fathers was their God, the living God, the God who is constantly acting to redeem His people. **23, 24** *The Lord your God dried up the waters of the Jordan for you . . . as the Lord your God did to the Red Sea . . . for us . . .* This is an interesting substantiation of the testimony of the Pentateuch that a whole generation had perished in the wilderness leaving only Joshua and Caleb as survivors. Joshua was therefore one of a diminishing company who at this stage could say 'us' in connection with crossing the Red Sea.

5:1 Effect of the miraculous crossing. This note of the effect of the miracle on the surrounding nations (*cf.* 2:9–11) presupposes the passage of a length of time during which the news reached them. It is inserted here as an immediate fulfilment of the purpose of the miracle as given in 4:24 and to explain how it was now possible to engage undisturbed in the religious ceremonies of vv. 2–12. *Amorites . . . Canaanites.* From early times Palestine was known as the land of the Canaanites; the Amorites penetrated into Canaan from the north, and settled in the hilly district on both sides of the Jordan. *There was no longer any spirit in them.* This terror secured a breathing-space for Israel and gave opportunity for the renewal of the rite of circumcision.

5:2–12 A people restored to the covenant relationship. 2 *Circumcise the people of Israel again.* For nearly 40 years the rite of circumcision had been neglected, not because there had been lack of opportunity, but because the nation was under judgment (*cf.* Nu. 14:34). If the people had been circumcised during the years of wandering it would have seemed that all was well, and that the covenant had never been suspended. But now they are back to the old relationship again, and they can once more bear in their bodies the seal of the covenant. *Flint knives.* At this time, in the 13th century BC, bronze tools had largely replaced stone implements, and iron was soon to replace bronze, but in this religious observance of long standing the use of ancient materials and methods persisted. *The second time* means not that they had been circumcised already, but that they were returning to their former condition as a circumcised nation in covenant with God. **6** It was not the vicissitudes of the journey that caused the suspension of the rite of circumcision, but the gross disobedience of the generation which consequently perished in the wilderness. **9** *The reproach of Egypt* suggests that the years of wandering had given the Egyptians reason for taunting the Israelites with being forsaken by their God; the renewal of the miracle of the Red Sea at the Jordan (*cf.* 4:23) made it clear that they were Yahweh's people once again.

10 Since the people were now back on covenant ground, the next step was to keep the Passover. According to Ex. 12:43–49 no uncircumcised male could eat the Passover, but now all the men of Israel were qualified for the sacred feast of commemoration of deliverance. Involved in their remembrance of past deliverance was surely the confidence that God would once again give them the victory over the forces that threatened them. **11, 12** The people now took the first step of entering on their inheritance by eating the produce of the land which was theirs by covenant. The writer records the stopping of the divine provision of manna (*cf.* Ex. 16:35) now that it was no longer needed.

5:13 – 12:24 THE CONQUEST OF CANAAN

5:13–15 The divine Commander

As a prologue to the advance we have this most significant account of Joshua's encounter with 'a man . . . with his drawn sword in his hand'. This must have been a time of special anxiety and suspense for Joshua. The Jordan was crossed; there could be no going back now. The burden of leadership lay heavily upon his shoulders. But at the very moment when he was 'by Jericho' (v. 13), literally 'in Jericho', *i.e.* in the region of Jericho, anxiously reconnoitring the strong city which lay in Israel's path, there appeared to him the representative of Yahweh, who called himself 'commander of the army of the Lord' (v. 14). There can be no doubt that this was God Himself as seen in human form: ignoring the artificial break made by the beginning of a new chapter, it is correct to see 6:2 as following on from 5:15 in a continuous narrative, with 6:1 as a parenthesis. The visitant of 5:13 becomes 'the Lord' of 6:2. *Cf.* 'the angel of the

Lord' frequently identified with God, *e.g.* in Gn. 16:7-11, compared with 16:13. This was none other than the pre-existent Son of God Himself. (See Introduction to Exodus, pp. 116f. and also 'Old Testament Theology', p. 29.)

13 *Are you for us, or for our adversaries?* Joshua had been thinking of the conflict as being between two sets of opposing forces, Israelite and Canaanite, and he was anxious to know if this armed warrior was to be his ally in the struggle. The answer was to the effect that he was not an ally, but a commander to whose leadership and control Joshua himself must submit. Thus he is reminded again that this is a holy war in which his position is that of a servant from whom obedience (v. 14) and reverence (v. 15) are due. **14** The position of *I* in the verse is emphatic: 'No, for I am commander of the army of the Lord. Now I have come.' The ultimate responsibility is borne not on the shoulders of a human leader but by God Himself. *The army of the Lord* includes the heavenly hosts, the forces of nature (*cf.* 10:11) and the army of Israel.

The story of the conquest which follows shows the divine Commander guiding and influencing and controlling human strategy. It may help to make the history more intelligible if we glance at the broad outline of that strategy. There were three stages in the conquest. The first consisted in the capture of Jericho and Ai (chs. 6–8), which opened up the passes into the interior of the country. A wedge was thus driven between the northern and southern sections of the country and the second and third stages in the campaign were the defeat of the southern confederacy (chs. 9, 10) and the northern confederacy (ch. 11) in turn.

6:1 – 8:35 The first stage in the campaign: Jericho and Ai

6:1-27 The capture of Jericho. Archaeological confirmation for the destruction of Jericho by Joshua is not nearly so conclusive as for other cities destroyed at this time. John Garstang, excavating in 1929–1936, thought he had discovered the walls which had fallen down in Joshua's day; but Kathleen Kenyon, excavating from 1952 to 1958, concluded that practically nothing of the city of Joshua's time was found by Garstang, and that most of the objects uncovered by him should have been dated much earlier, probably 300 years before Joshua's conquest. There is some evidence from the pottery recovered that a settlement did exist at Jericho in the 13th century BC, but remains from that period are very meagre. There have to be taken into account the thoroughness of Joshua's destruction of the city and the erosion of five centuries' exposure of the city until it was rebuilt in Ahab's reign (1 Ki. 16:34; 869 BC). 'The net result . . . is that a 13th-century Israelite conquest of Jericho cannot be formally proven on the present archaeological evidence, but neither is it precluded thereby' (K. A. Kitchen,

art., 'Chronology of the Old Testament', *NBD*). And, as Kitchen says in his article on 'Jericho' (*ibid.*), 'The narrative of Jos. iii–viii within which the fall of Jericho is recounted is known to reflect faithfully conditions in, and topography of, the area.' The fact is that the capture of Jericho was the key to Joshua's whole campaign, and the biblical record must be accepted as authentic.

1-5 Divine commands for the attack. **1** *Jericho was shut up from within and without*; the Hebrew, as in AV mg. reads, 'did shut up and was shut up'. *Cf.* Paul in 2 Cor. 7:5, 'fighting without and fear within'! **4** Note the significance of the number *seven*—seven priests, seven trumpets, seven days, seven circuits of the walls on the seventh day—as indicating perfection, completeness, consummation. *Trumpets of rams' horns*; better as in RV mg., 'jubile trumpets'. The Hebrew, *yôḇēl*, is found outside the references to the year of jubilee (see Lv. 25:8ff.) only here and in Ex. 19:13, where there is a similar religious significance. This suggests that the trumpets carried by the priests had a ceremonial rather than a martial reference. This was a religious, not a military, undertaking.

6-27 The destruction of the city and the deliverance of Rahab. The angel of Yahweh had given explicit instructions for Jericho's capture, and these were carried out to the letter. Seven priests, bearing seven trumpets blown continually, and followed by the ark of the covenant, marched in solemn procession around the city for seven days, preceded and followed by the silent army. Each night they returned to the camp at Gilgal. On the seventh day the city was compassed seven times and then, amid the blast of the trumpets and the great shout of the people, 'the wall fell down flat' (Heb. 'in its place, where it stood'), 'so that they went up into the city, every man straight before him, and they took the city' (v. 20). Even if a secondary cause of the event, such as an earthquake, could be given, it cannot explain its miraculous occurrence just at the critical moment of Israel's advance. 'By faith the walls of Jericho fell down after they had been encircled for seven days' (Heb. 11:30). Certainly the narrative neither gives ground for, nor leaves room for, such anti-supernaturalist and minimizing views as that the marchers served to distract the attention of the watchers from Israelite sappers at work undermining the walls! (*Cf.* C. G. Howie, *The Old Testament Story*, 1967, p. 35.)

8 The constant blowing of the ceremonial trumpets served not only to remind the Israelites of the spiritual nature of their conflict but also to strike terror into the hearts of their adversaries; the awesome sound, persisting day after day, must have suggested supernatural power. **9** The position of the ark in the midst of the armed men of Israel is significant: God is in the midst of His people, and together they encompass the city. *Cf.* at the Jordan (3:4), where the ark was separated. Does this make a distinction between a miracle in which the people had a share, however passive, and one in which they had none?

17–21 Jericho was *devoted to the Lord for destruction* (Heb. *ḥērem*), *i.e.* its inhabitants and all that it contained were put under a special ban, which prohibited all contact between them and the people of Israel. In the case of the inhabitant (v. 21) and all other living things, this meant their destruction. It was both God's judgment on the sin of Jericho (*cf.* Gn. 15:16), and a safeguard of the purity of Israel from contamination. (Contrast Nu. 25, and see Introduction, pp. 233f.) For *lest when you have devoted them*, read 'lest you covet . . .' as suggested by LXX (Heb. *taḥmᵉdû*, for *taḥᵃrimû*). *Cf.* 7:21, 'I coveted them and took them'.

22, 23, 25 *Cf.* v. 17. In accordance with the covenant made with Rahab, she and her family were saved. Here we see the principle of the ban in reverse, the principle of saving faith and saving identification with the people of God (*cf.* on 7:24–26). They were set *outside the camp of Israel* because they were Gentiles and ceremonially unclean, but they were ultimately identified with the people of Israel. How well, then, does Rahab become an exemplar of true faith (Heb. 11:31; Jas. 2:25)! *Cf.* Eph. 3:6. **24** In the case of the wealth of Jericho, since any contact with a 'devoted' thing involved implication in its contagion and fate (*cf.* Jos. 7:1ff.), the treasures were taken for the Lord's house. **26, 27** The putting of Jericho to the ban included the pronouncing of a curse on anyone who should afterwards rebuild it as a fortified city. In the time of Ahab, 500 years later, this anathema was disregarded by Hiel the Bethelite at the cost of the lives of his two sons; *cf.* 1 Ki. 16:34. But a more immediate violation of the ban had much more disastrous consequences for Israel, when they went up against Ai.

7:1–26 Reverse at Ai and Achan's sin. Archaeological investigation into the site of Ai presents a very real difficulty. 'The peculiar problem of the conquest of Ai is more difficult for the modern exegete than it was for the children of Israel' (Burrows, *What Mean These Stones?* 1941, p. 272). The excavation of the site usually identified with Ai, Et-Tell, has shown that it was unoccupied from *c.* 2400 BC to 1200 BC, and lay in ruins all that time (hence presumably its name, Heb. *hā'ay*, 'the ruin'). On this evidence it was The Ruin before Joshua attacked it at all.

Four main explanations of the discrepancy between the biblical account and the findings of archaeology have been suggested. *a.* Later Israelites attributed the ruins of 2400 BC to Joshua, who was a legendary destroyer of Canaanite cities. This explanation is quite unacceptable, since it denies the historicity of the biblical account. *b.* The view of L. H. Vincent suggests that the inhabitants of Bethel, the neighbouring city, had established a military outpost at Ai to check the advance of the army of Israel against their own town: this outpost, set on the old ruins, was of such modest propor-

tions and of such a temporary nature that it has left no 13th-century remains to betray its existence to the excavator. This view fails to explain the existence of a king of Ai (Jos. 8:29; 12:9). *c.* W. F. Albright suggests that the story of the fall of Ai is really the story of the capture of Bethel, and that the tradition represented by the account in Jos. 8 referred originally to Bethel. Support for this view is lent by the fact that there is no account of the capture of Bethel in the book of Joshua, though archaeologists have established that it suffered destruction at the same time as the neighbouring Canaanite cities, and Jos. 12:16 lists it among the cities and kings defeated. The difficulty is that the text of Jos. 8 makes a distinction between Bethel and Ai (*e.g.* v. 17). Whether this was a clear-cut distinction is perhaps open to question. It is significant that in Ezr. 2:28 and Ne. 7:32 Bethel and Ai are taken together, suggesting some kind of integration between them, and this may reflect an earlier assimilation of some kind. It is also noteworthy that the exact location or extent of Bethel seems in a little doubt: for the most part it is identified with Luz (Gn. 28:19; 35:6; Jos. 18:13); but in 16:1, 2 it is clearly distinguished from it: might it be that there was a clearly-defined Bethel, and a less clearly-defined Bethel-Ai? And that what we have in Jos. 8 is Bethel-Ai, or, perhaps better here, Ai–Bethel? It is significant that the successful attack on Ai involved precautions against a counter-attack from Bethel (8:12ff.), and that 8:17 specifically links the two cities together (*cf.* 12:9). This is largely speculation, however, and it is perhaps safest (*d*) to question the archaeological evidence: the identification of Ai with Et-Tell may be wrong. It has been suggested, *e.g.*, by K. A. Kitchen (*Ancient Orient*, p. 63) that Et-Tell may be Beth-Aven. Other evidence may yet be forthcoming of the Ai of Joshua's day.

Whatever are the problems of the location of Ai, for Israel it marked the next obvious objective in their path. Situated on sharply rising ground to the west of Jericho, it was strategically located on the eastern edge of the central ridge, commanding the main route from Gilgal into the interior.

1–12 Reverse at Ai and its cause. The high hopes of the invaders received an unexpected setback. **1** anticipates by giving the reason for this reverse, and then the history proceeds. *Broke faith;* this was essentially a breach of the covenant. **2–5** On the advice of the spies which Joshua had sent forward to make a reconnaissance, only part of the army was sent to attack the city, though it is made clear later that this was not the cause of the repulse. It may have been that Israel's rash self-confidence was part of the outworking of the transgression of the ban. The garrison of Ai sallied out, and the Hebrews were driven in retreat down the steep descent towards *Shebarim*, or 'the stone quarries', leaving thirty-six of their number dead. **5** *The* *hearts of the people melted*: the expression used of their enemies in 2:11. The cause was not merely the defeat and the loss of fighting men, but a terrible misgiving that Yahweh's help had been withdrawn from them. **7** The chief element in Joshua's dejection was the thought that the defeat would mean renewed hope for the Canaanites and the dishonour of God's name.

10 God turns the thoughts of Joshua from the defeat and its implications to its moral cause and to the need for action. **11** The Lord advances from the general to the particular in framing the indictment, and the emphasis is heightened in the Hebrew by the repetition of the phrase 'and also' before each item of the charge. The sin of one member of the community was held to be that of the whole people. Israel was now a nation, and the sin of the individual was the sin of the nation until the nation repudiated it and expiation was made.

13-26 The transgressor identified, his sin acknowledged and punished. **13** *Sanctify yourselves*. Just as the breach of faith (v. 1) was specifically an act of disloyalty within the covenant, so Israel must assemble as the holy, or sanctified covenant people (*cf.* Ex. 19:10, 11) when the Lord comes among them as Judge. **14** The word translated *brought near* (*cf.* vv. 16ff.) has often a similar religious significance. **16-18** By the sacred lot, solemnly taken, Achan was identified as the one who had broken the ban. **19** *Give glory to the Lord God of Israel* by confessing the sin and confirming the accuracy of the divine identification of the sinner. **20, 21** Achan made confession that he had taken gold and silver and one *beautiful mantle from Shinar* and had hidden them beneath his tent, from which they were now fetched and poured out (rather than 'laid', v. 23) as an offering to the Lord. **24-26** Achan in touching 'devoted' objects had become contaminated, and therefore himself 'devoted' because he had wilfully identified himself with that which was under God's curse. Contrast the opposite experience of Rahab (2:3-6, 8-11, 21; 6:17, 25; *cf.* Mt. 1:5). The final scene in the valley of Achor (lit. 'troubling') saw the execution of the sentence when Achan was stoned to death and he and all that he had were burned with fire. Did Achan's family share in his destruction? It is difficult to be certain. **25** The plural *them* may refer only to his possessions, and 22:20 is not conclusive on the question since it can refer just as naturally to the thirty-six who died because of his sin. The law of Dt. 24:16 clearly prohibits the putting to death of an offender's relatives, unless, of course, their knowledge of his sin involved them in his guilt. Possibly, sharing his tent, they could not fail to be aware of his crime. By Achan's death the act of sacrilege was expiated, God's burning anger was turned away (*cf.* vv. 1, 26), and the scene of the tragedy, the valley of Achor, became a door of hope as the people set their faces once more to the advance.

8:1-29 Capture of Ai. 1, 2 Renewed encourage-ment. Now that the situation had been restored, God encouraged Joshua to go forward. *All the fighting men*; not because all were needed to gain the victory, but so that the morale of all might be restored. **2** It is noteworthy that this time all the spoil and the cattle were to be given to the Israelites; Achan might have waited for his booty.

3-22 Strategy of attack. Joshua made use of an ambush to take and destroy the city. The text provides two problems here, for there seems to be a discrepancy between vv. 3-9, which speak of 30,000 men being set in ambush on the west side of the city, and v. 12, which gives the number in the same position as 5,000. Numbers are notoriously subject to copyists' errors, and it may be that such a mistake has been made here, and that 5,000 should be read in both places. Another possible explanation is that 30,000 originally referred to the whole fighting force employed. But a much more satisfactory explanation is that there were two ambushes, one to deal with Ai and the other with a possible threat from Bethel. **17** tells that the men of Bethel—a city two miles from Ai, but hidden by intervening heights, and linked in some way politically with Ai (*cf.* 12:9)—joined in the pursuit after Israel; and it seems reasonable to assume that Joshua would make preparations to guard against such an attack from Bethel. (Though the men of Bethel were defeated at this time and their king slain, *cf.* 12:16, it is uncertain whether the city was actually occupied or destroyed. Its capture is recorded in Jdg. 1:22-26. Chronologically this may have preceded the death of Joshua, in spite of the reference to this event in Jdg. 1:1, for these verses precede the second mention of Joshua's death in Jdg. 2:8.) A second problem arises from the number of fighting men said to be involved in the first ambush: *thirty thousand* (v. 3) seems an impossibly large contingent for such a purpose. R. E. D. Clark ('The Large Numbers of the Old Testament', *JTVI*, 87, 1955, pp. 82ff.) has put forward the entirely plausible suggestion that the text should read 'thirty captains'. The Hebrew word *'elep̄*, translated 'thousand', can also be translated 'captain'. With this translation, what we have here is a carefully-selected commando unit of thirty men, *mighty men of valour*, chosen for the critical and dangerous task. (See also J. W. Wenham, 'Large Numbers of the Old Testament', *Tyndale Bulletin*, 18, 1967, especially pp. 24-26, 41.) Their assignment was to enter the city and set it on fire after its defenders had sallied forth to chase Joshua and his men. Joshua's strategy therefore involved three groups—a small commando unit to enter Ai, 5,000 men to deal primarily with the men of Bethel, and the main army, led by Joshua himself, to decoy the men of Ai out of the city. Wenham, however, suggests that the 5,000 of v. 12 is a textual corruption of the 30,000 of v. 3, and thus that only two groups were involved.

13 RSV translation adapts the Hebrew to read

Joshua spent that night, instead of 'Joshua went that night' (Heb. *wayyālen* for *wayyēlek*); some commentators go further, and by the addition of one Hebrew consonant emend the last word of v. 9 to read, as in v. 13, *in the valley*. Neither emendation is necessary, and both serve only to support the contention that we have here two parallel accounts of the same incident. Vv. 3–9 describe the setting in motion of Joshua's plans: the first night the small unit of thirty men is sent off to its position, while Joshua remains with the rest of the people; next day (v. 10) Joshua and the people march the sixteen miles or so to the neighbourhood of Ai; that night (vv. 12, 13) the ambush (v. 13 'rear guard') of 5,000 men is set between Ai and Bethel, while Joshua and the main body of the army take up their positions in the lower ground in front of Ai. **18, 19** *The javelin*, Joshua's weapon, probably gave the signal to the men lying in ambush by reflecting the sun from its flat blade.

22–29 Victory and aftermath. The strategy proved entirely successful: the city was occupied and set on fire; the inhabitants, attacked in front and from the rear, were put to the sword. **28, 29** Ai was utterly destroyed, and became like its name, *a heap of ruins*; its king was slain and his body hanged on a tree until sunset (*cf.* Dt. 21:23) and then buried beneath a great heap of stones, a standing memorial to another milestone in Israel's advance.

8:30–35 Renewal of the covenant at Shechem. In a religious act of the utmost significance Joshua now reminded the Israelites of the true nature of their conquest. The goal of the pilgrimage was the mountains appointed by Moses for this solemn ceremony of covenant renewal (Dt. 11:29), but it is very likely that the ceremonies centred upon Shechem, which lay in the valley between the mountains and which was hallowed by association with the patriarchs. Shechem was the scene of a subsequent covenant ceremony (Jos. 24), but it is needless to say as some do (*e.g.* G. W. Anderson, 'Joshua', in *Peake's Commentary on the Bible*, 1962, *in loc.*), that these are duplicate accounts of the same incident. It is eminently reasonable that both at the entrance upon life in Canaan, and again when he sensed that his leadership was ending, Joshua should face the people with the inescapable challenge to covenant obedience. In accordance with the express command of Moses, he called them to renew their covenant allegiance to Yahweh and to hear the conditions on which they were to retain possession of the land. See on Dt. 11:29, 30; 27:1–26.

Several points call for comment. *a*. It is surprising that we are told nothing about the capture of Shechem, an ancient walled town. Yet the people have a service of dedication just outside its gates, here and again at the end of Joshua's life (*cf.* 24:1ff.). There are two possible explanations. One is that the book of Joshua does not profess to give an exhaustive account of the conquest of Canaan: the omission of any account of the capture of Shechem may have no significance. Another explanation is that the people of Shechem were not hostile to the Israelites. Gn. 34 describes how the city came into the hands of Jacob; the Amarna letters reveal that *c*. 1380 BC Labayu, the prince of Shechem, was in league with the Habiru, who may have had some link with the Hebrews. It is possible that Jacob had passed control of Shechem to a related group of Semitic peoples, who had some faith in Israel's God, and that when Israel entered Canaan they found in the inhabitants of Shechem a people who had some kinship with them. H. L. Ellison (*Joshua–2 Samuel*, Bible Study Books, Number 2, Scripture Union, 1967, p. 9) suggests that this would explain the language of Jdg. 9, where the citizens of Shechem are Israelites, but feel themselves superior to Israel.

It is significant, however, that they seem to have had a very imperfect and syncretistic form of faith in Yahweh, which seemed to allow them to worship one of the Canaanite Baals. See Jdg. 8:33; 9:4 for references to Baal-berith as the god of Shechem. There is, however, no direct evidence in the biblical record for any such linkup with Hebrews already in Canaan, though the assumption is not impossible. And there is certainly biblical evidence strongly opposed to the view of many modern scholars that it was at Shechem that tribes which had never been in Egypt or at Sinai joined those who had come out of Egypt in a complete amphictyony, or sacred union, of twelve tribes now brought together under the leadership of Joshua (*cf.* 4:1ff.).

b. The difficulty of a march through enemy territory to Shechem presents no real problem, for the country between was very sparsely populated, probably because of inadequate water supplies. Furthermore, there is ample testimony to the terror caused by the invasion, and the consequent paralysis of local opposition (*e.g.* 5:1; 9:24).

c. For the nature of the covenant here renewed and ratified, and its close resemblance to the suzerainty covenants of the late second millennium BC, see on Jos. 24, where details of a similar national covenant are given more fully. One feature here not explicitly referred to in Jos. 24 was the solemn ceremony involved (vv. 30, 31).

31ff. An altar of undressed stones was erected on Mt. Ebal, and solemn sacrifices were offered. A copy of the law of Moses was written upon plastered stones and read aloud to the vast multitude, and public proclamation was made of its blessings and cursings. Six tribes on Gerizim said 'Amen' to the blessings and six on Ebal said 'Amen' to the curses. 'History can furnish few scenes so impressive in moral grandeur as that of a nation thus solemnly embracing God's law as the rule of its life and the condition of its prosperity' (Fairweather, *From the Exodus to the Monarchy*). **33** *Sojourner as well as homeborn* included peoples like the Kenites who had joined with Israel in the wilderness, individuals like Rahab and her family, and, later, the Gibeonites.

9:1 - 10:43 The second stage: the campaign in the south

Israel's successes against Jericho and Ai had two contrasting consequences. On the one hand, opposition hardened and became more highly organized (9:1, 2; 10:1–43); on the other, some of the inhabitants of the land were prepared to make terms with the invaders (9:3–27).

9:1-27 Compromise with the Gibeonites. 1–3 The central part of the country was thrown wide open to the invaders by the defection of the Gibeonite cities: Gibeon, Chephirah, Beeroth and Kiriath-jearim; *cf.* v. 17. They are called 'Hivites' (*cf.* v. 7) though possibly this should read, as in LXX, 'Horites' (*cf.* Gn. 36:2, 21). **4, 5** By pretending that they were ambassadors from a far country and therefore constituted no mere threat to Israel's advance, their representatives induced the Israelites to form an alliance with them and to guarantee that their lives would be spared. *Made ready provisions.* This alters the Hebrew word by one consonant, making it conform to v. 12, but it is perhaps better to translate the unusual Hebrew verb in the original, as RV, 'made as if they had been ambassadors', or 'disguised themselves'. Their *worn-out* clothes, *patched sandals*, and obviously old provisions convinced the leaders of Israel that they had indeed come from a far country. **9, 10** The deception was strengthened by the pretence that they had apparently heard only of the exploits of Israel beyond Jordan and knew nothing of Jericho and Ai. **14, 15** A treaty was concluded before the deception was discovered: the men of Israel *partook of their provisions*, thereby pledging themselves to friendship; they *did not ask direction from the Lord*, but made a covenant-treaty with them. This may have been a full vassal treaty of the pattern of the time (see on Jos. 24); it certainly included, as events showed, protection against the vassals' enemies.

16-21 The deception discovered. The discovery of the fraud was made when Israel came to the cities of the Gibeonites; but the agreement was sacred and could not be annulled, despite the protests of some of the people. Justice was done by reducing the Gibeonites to the position of slaves of the sanctuary. **21** *Drawers of water.* Excavations have shown that the Gibeonites were experienced in drawing water; this is evident from a great pool in the heart of the city of Gibeon with an interior circular staircase leading down to the source of the water 80 ft. below.

22-27 A curse that became a blessing. 23 *Now therefore you are cursed.* They were doomed to perpetual slavery yet the curse that came upon them was a blessing. 'Blessed are those who dwell in thy house' (Ps. 84:4). **27** That was the curse that fell on the Gibeonites—to be attached for ever to the congregation and to the altar of the Lord, *in the place which he should choose.*

Such is the grace of God. It was for the Gibeonites that He wrought the miracle of the battle of Beth-horon (*cf.* 10:7–15), and it was among them afterwards that He pitched His tent (*cf.* 2 Ch. 1:3); and in still later days, when priests and Levites failed, He made them take their places. Since Joshua *made them . . . hewers of wood* (Heb. *nāṭan*, lit. 'gave'), they came to be known as *nᵉthînîm*, or 'given ones', 'temple servants', Ezr. 2:43; 8:20.

The defection of the Gibeonites at this stage helped Joshua to drive a wedge still further into the central part of Canaan: this, and the possibility that he might use the resources of the great city Gibeon to intensify his attack against the whole land, explains the urgency with which the five kings of the Amorites now moved against Gibeon.

10:1-43 Defeat of the southern confederacy. 1–6 The confederacy united against Gibeon. The news of the treaty between Israel and the Gibeonites was the signal for war. Five kings of the Amorites resolved not only to punish their former allies for their treachery, but to crush Joshua at a point where defeat would be fatal to his plans. The confederacy was led by Adoni-zedek, king of Jerusalem (*cf.* Melchizedek in Gn. 14:18), which had for long been a city of great influence; the other members were kings of Hebron, Jarmuth, Lachish and Eglon. Their united forces laid siege to Gibeon, whose inhabitants urgently appealed for help, under the terms of their treaty with Israel. **6** *Do not relax your hand*, literally 'do not drop your hand'; *cf.* 1:5. *All the kings of the Amorites that dwell in the hill country*; not an exaggeration, for these five kings did represent all of this area.

7ff. Victory and the miracle of the sun's standing still. **8** Joshua, encouraged by a reminder of his original commission (*cf.* 1:5), made a forced march by night from Gilgal, and fell upon the allied force at Gibeon. **10, 11** *The Lord threw them into a panic*, and they broke and fled, past Upper and Lower Beth-horon, which were linked by a pass, *the ascent of Beth-horon*, running from the central hill country, where Gibeon lay, to the more rolling hill country bordering the coastal plain, where three of the allied cities, Libnah, Eglon and Lachish, were located. But they were not destined to escape, for the Lord intervened once again to help His people, and a great storm of hailstones killed multitudes of them and completed the rout.

12-15 There follows a quotation taken from the Book of Jashar, which seems to have been a collection of songs in praise of the heroes of Israel. It records Joshua's prayer: *Sun, stand thou still at Gibeon, and thou Moon in the valley of Aijalon* and asserts that in answer *the sun stood still, and the moon stayed, until the nation took vengeance on their enemies.* Two questions are raised by the passage. Where does the quotation begin and end? And how are we to explain the miracle here recorded? The quotation evidently begins at v. 12, and since Joshua did not return to Gilgal until after the utter defeat of the enemy—his return is narrated in v. 43—we must take it that the quotation goes on until the end of v. 15. The alternative is to follow the LXX reading, which omits v. 15; since it is identical with v. 43, and since vv. 14 and 42 have identical endings, it is possible that a copyist inserted it in error. In that case, vv. 13b and 14 can be taken as a prose repetition of the poetry of vv. 12b and 13.

A second question is, Did the sun stand still? One suggested explanation of the episode is that the narrator has taken what was merely a highly figurative poetical description of God's intervention on behalf of Israel as historical fact. But there is no reason to reject a more literal interpretation, though this passage has often been the butt of scientific scorn, much of which, it seems possible, may be based on a misunderstanding. It has usually been assumed that Joshua prayed for the day to be prolonged. But is it not possible that what Joshua needed even more, since, as is expressly stated in v. 9, came upon the camp of the enemy by night, was that the darkness should continue and the night be prolonged for his surprise attack? That it was early morning when he made his request is evident from the position of the moon in the valley of Aijalon (to the west) and the position of the sun over Gibeon (to the east) (v. 12). The answer to his prayer came in a hailstorm which had the effect of prolonging the darkness. An investigation of the exact meaning of the Hebrew words used confirms this interpretation. The word translated *stand still* (Heb. *dôm*) means literally 'be silent' and frequently has the sense 'cease' or 'leave off' (*cf.* Ps. 35:15; La. 2:18). Similarly the word translated *stayed* (Heb. '*amad*), *stood still* in v. 13b, has the sense of 'cease' (*cf.* 2 Ki. 4:6; Jon. 1:15). The basic meaning of the word translated 'go down' (Heb. *bô'*) in the phrase *did not hasten to go down* is 'come', or 'go'. It is true that throughout the OT this word, when applied to the sun, normally means 'set', or 'go down', *e.g.* in Gn. 15:12, 17; 28:11; Ex. 17:12; 22:26; Jos. 8:29; 10:27, *etc.*, and that the Hebrew words normally applied to sunrise are *yāṣā*, to go forth, or *zaraḥ*, to arise. But there is one instance, again significantly in a verse that is set in poetical form, where the verb *bô'*, 'to come', is parallel to *zaraḥ*, 'to arise': Is. 60:1, 'Arise, shine; for your light is come, and the glory of the Lord has risen upon you.' 'Light' here admittedly is not the same as 'sun', but in Jb. 31:26 the word translated 'sun' is the word used here for 'light' (Heb. '*ôr*). It is possible to argue, therefore, that the word *bô'* in a poetical setting, as here in Joshua, can apply to the coming of the light and the rising of the sun. The phrase *for about a whole day* can better be translated as 'when day is done' (Heb. *keyôm tāmîm*; *cf.* K. A. Kitchen, *op. cit.*, p. 64). So 13b can be translated, 'The sun ceased shining in the midst of the sky, and did not hasten to come, (so that it was) as when day is done.' And so in the darkness of the storm the defeat of the enemy was complete. It should be noted that one is not disparaging the miraculous nature of the occurrence by suggesting that there was a less spectacular divine intervention than is postulated by the more customary interpretation, which takes it that the day was lengthened. It was still God who lengthened the night by a miraculous intervention on behalf of His people.

16–27 Death of the five kings. **16** The five kings had taken refuge in a cave at Makkedah, but the pursuers did not halt to deal with them. **22, 23** Afterwards, they were brought out; **24** when the captains of the Israelites had put their feet upon the necks of their prisoners to symbolize complete subjection, they were slain, their bodies hanged on trees until the evening and then entombed in the cave where they had fled for shelter. There are no grounds whatever for describing this, as Noth does, as an aetiological tale composed for the purpose of explaining the cave with its mouth blocked by great stones and the five notable trees. It is much more credible that the memorial was derived from the history of events that happened than that the history was fabricated to explain the memorial. John Bright (*A History of Israel*, 1960, p. 119) urges that the evidence for the factuality of this narrative is 'really very impressive', noting in particular that Debir (v. 38), and Lachish (v. 31) 'are known to have been destroyed in the latter part of the thirteenth century' and that 'the succeeding occupation is typical of early Israel'.

28–39 Completion of the southern campaign. The victory at Beth-horon inaugurated a campaign, which may have lasted for a considerable time, and the whole of the southern part of Canaan was finally brought under Israel's control. Joshua's strategy at this time seems to have consisted of a series of swift, devastating attacks against key Canaanite cities, to crush their inhabitants but not necessarily to occupy the cities themselves. As Yehezkel Kaufmann puts it, Joshua's campaigns were 'wars of destruction and extermination, not of occupation by immediate settlement' (*Biblical Account of the Conquest of Palestine*, 1953, p. 86).

40–43 Summary of the conquest. The area conquered is first defined according to its natural geographical divisions: **40** *the whole land, i.e. the hill country and the Negeb and the lowland and the slopes. The hill country* consists of the Judean highlands; *the Negeb* (Heb. *negeb*, 'the dry') of the semi-arid steppes that stretch away to the desert in the south; *the lowland* ('the Shephelah') of the foothills between the coastal plain and the central highlands; and *the slopes*, probably the territory sloping eastward to the Dead Sea (*cf.* 12:8). Some scholars (*e.g.* O. Eissfeldt, *CAH* II, revised edition, 1965, ch. 34, 'The Hebrew Kingdom', pp. 4ff.) have discounted the accuracy of the summary given in these verses, contrasting it with the more gradual conquest suggested by Jdg. 1. But archaeological investigation has confirmed that the cities of this area, *e.g.* Lachish, Eglon, Debir, suffered violent and complete destruction about this time, 1250–1200 BC. There is, therefore, no ground for doubting that Joshua did launch a series of devastating attacks on key Canaanite strongholds, that these attacks demoralized the Canaanites and gave the Israelites a firm foothold, though the land was not entirely subdued at this time; later passages (*e.g.* 11:13; 13:2–13; 15:63) show clearly that much remained to be done. *He left none remaining, but utterly destroyed all that breathed* has to be qualified as in v. 20: 'the remnant which remained of them had entered into the fortified cities'; the only survivors were those who managed to make their escape. *As the Lord God of Israel commanded*; *cf.* Dt. 20:16. **41** The record then defines the limits of the conquest *from Kadesh-barnea to Gaza, and all the country of Goshen, as far as Gibeon.* Goshen has not been definitely identified but obviously refers to an area in the south of Canaan. **42** The summary of the conquest makes it quite clear that this was the Lord's doing: *the Lord God of Israel fought for Israel.* Archaeological research has shown how strongly fortified the Canaanite cities were, and how advanced was their civilization; Israel's victory was nothing short of miraculous.

11:1–23 The third stage: the campaign in the north

11:1–15 Defeat of the northern confederacy. Joshua's successful campaign in the south aroused the alarm of the northern Canaanitish kings. Led by Jabin, king of Hazor (lit. 'the fortress'), they formed a huge confederacy against Israel. This included Jabin's nearest neighbours, but the call to arms was not confined to them; it included the kings in the hill country of the north and in the Arabah south of Chinneroth, an area northwest of the lake of Galilee, and also the remnants of the defeated armies of the south, Canaanites, Amorites, *etc.*

4 The strength of the confederacy depended not only on massive numbers; they had a strong force of *horses and chariots*. **5** They mustered at *the waters of Merom*, lying between Lake Huleh and Lake Tiberias, 10 miles west of Jordan, with copious springs flowing southward into the Sea of Galilee. **6** Joshua's understandable fear was answered by the assurance of the divine presence and of complete victory. He was commanded to burn the chariots and hamstring the horses of the enemy, so that they could not be used afterwards by the Canaanites or by the victorious Israelites, who might thus be tempted to put their trust in horses. A sudden attack, probably after a swift forced march, once again struck panic into the hearts of the Canaanites. **8** As promised, *the Lord gave them into the hand of Israel*, who smote them and pursued them in headlong flight.

10 *Joshua turned back* from the pursuit and destroyed the great city of Hazor. Excavations, made particularly by Y. Yadin since 1955, have shown that in the time of Joshua the site covered almost 200 acres, and was probably occupied by about 40,000 inhabitants. The city consisted of an upper city—the older part, dating back to the third millennium BC, and occupying about 25 acres—and a lower city to the north, added in the early part of the second millennium BC, and occupying about 150 acres. This latter area is so large that Garstang thought that it was only an enclosure for horses and chariots, but later investigation has shown that the area contained a well-built city. Yadin found conclusive evidence that Hazor was destroyed about the middle of the 13th century BC, and attributed this destruction to Joshua. Of special interest are the remains of Canaanite temples and objects of worship, which reveal that the religion of Hazor involved the worship of the sun-god in association with a bull. **13, 14** The utter destruction of Hazor was exceptional, perhaps because of its size and importance; other cities *that stood on mounds* (Heb. *têl*) were not destroyed. Perhaps now that the Israelites were established in the land these were no longer a danger, but rather an advantage to settlers. **15** Once again obedience to the commands of the Lord is seen to be the secret of success (*cf.* 1:8): as *the Lord had commanded Moses his servant, so Moses commanded Joshua, and so Joshua did.*

11:16–23 Summary of the conquest. The battles of Beth-horon and Merom and their aftermath were decisive, and the power of the Canaanites to resist the invaders was shattered. All organized resistance was broken down. **21** A special note is made of the defeat of the Anakim, perhaps because it had been they who had terrified the spies of Israel so disastrously over forty years before (Nu. 13:33). **23** *The land had rest from war* in the sense that no more pitched battles were required. But the completion of the campaign took 'a long time' (v. 18), and even at the end of Joshua's life there remained 'very much land to be possessed' (13:1). To deal with the parts of the country still unsubdued was now to be the responsibility of the individual tribes.

12:1–24 List of conquered Canaanite kings

This list may be regarded as an appendix to the history of the wars of Joshua, concluding the story of the conquest before going on to the division of the land. **1–6** deal with the conquests *beyond the Jordan toward the sunrising*, *i.e.* on the eastern side of the Jordan: these were gained under Moses. **7–24** The remainder of the chapter lists Joshua's successes in Canaan *on the west side of the Jordan.* It is remarkable that such a small country should contain so many kings; these had merely local authority, over city-states. The multiplicity of divisions was one factor that made the task of the Israelites easier than it might otherwise have been, though it should be noted that in face of an external threat the kings tended to combine their forces, as at Beth-horon in the south and Merom in the north. **23** *Goiim in Galilee* follows the LXX, and is probably correct. AV 'king of the nations of Gilgal' is unintelligible.

Probably Harosheth-ha-goiim (Jdg. 4:2) is meant.

13:1 – 22:34 THE DIVISION OF THE LAND

When we come to this section of the book of Joshua, with its detailed lists of boundaries and cities, one has a certain sympathy with Calvin when he wrote, 'I would not be very exact in delineating the site of places, and in discussing names, partly because I admit that I am not well acquainted with topographical or chorographic science, and partly because great labour would produce little fruit to the reader.' And yet it must not be forgotten that accurate and detailed descriptions of the boundaries and cities of the tribes were vital for the tribes themselves, for these were the title-deeds of their inheritance.

Considerable discussion has centred around the probable dates of the lists which we find here. Many modern scholars believe that these lists were of varied origins, that they were drawn up at various times and revised some time between the 11th and 7th centuries BC. Earlier criticism had attributed them to P, and had seen in them a post-exilic priestly writer's view of what the extent and distribution of Israel's inheritance should have been. But more recent criticism would date them much earlier. The list of cities, it is claimed, is grouped according to the later administrative districts of Judah, but scholars disagree about when this division into administrative districts was made. Alt's view is that the list of cities in Jos. 15 is based on a list of the twelve provinces of Josiah's kingdom. W. F. Albright maintains that Jos. 21 is a list of Levitical cities of David and Solomon's time, on the ground that no town in the list was founded after 950 BC. John Bright considers that these lists were probably set down in the reign of David but that they reflect premonarchical conditions. H. L. Ellison (*op. cit.*, p. 15) suggests that 15:20–62 'is an appendix put in by a later editor giving the organization of Judah under the monarchy after the time of Solomon .... He divided the land into twelve portions, normally near the old divisions (1 Kings 4:7–19). . . . When the kingdom was split under Rehoboam, Judah was divided into twelve administrative districts to emphasize its claims to remain the true Israel.' The RSV paragraphing of Jos. 15 underlines this twelvefold partition.

Points which must be taken into consideration in a discussion of the dating of these lists are as follows. *a.* There certainly was detailed administrative organization in David's time (*cf.* 1 Ch. 23–27). It has been pointed out, however, by Albright (*Archaeology and the Religion of Israel*, 1953, p. 120), that David's administration organized in part on Egyptian models: his division of functions between recorder and secretary (*cf.* 2 Sa. 8:16, 17, and his council of thirty (*cf.* 1 Ch. 27:6) are said to be derived from Egyptian official institutions. This might suggest that not only the officialdom but the civic organization of David's time had its roots in an earlier day nearer to the period of direct Egyptian influence on Israel. *b.* Since many of the Levitical cities, *e.g.* Gezer, Ibleam, Taanach, were not Israelite at all before David's time, it has been suggested that the actual allocation of these cities should be ascribed to him. It should be noted, however, that the lists in Joshua do not refer exclusively to towns which were then, or ever, in Israel's actual possession: this was an ideal allocation of the land as it might have been if Israel had been faithful and diligent in driving out the original inhabitants. (*Cf.* the Philistine towns listed in 15:45–47.) *c.* Some of the towns are given names which they formerly had, *e.g.* Baalah, later Kiriath-jearim (15:9), Kiriath-arba, later Hebron (15:54); the use of Debir, formerly Kiriath-sepher (15:15) suggests later editorial revision. *d.* John Rea in *The Wycliffe Bible Commentary* asserts that 'this method of delineating borders—proceeding in order by topographical landmarks, from town to mountain to town to river, *etc.*—is almost exactly paralleled at this same period in history in the agreement defining boundaries accorded by the Hittite king Suppiluliuma to Niqmadu of Uragit, ruler of a vassal city-state on the Syrian coast (Claude Schaeffer, *Le Palais Royal d'Ugarit*, IV, 10–18)'. This confirms the possibility of such detailed and accurate lists in Joshua's day. *e.* In 925 BC Shishak invaded Palestine and subdued Judah; a campaign list of his, discovered at Karnak, names many Palestinian towns. It is significant, however, that few of the names listed by him in the Negeb and neighbouring areas are found in the Joshua passages, whereas many of them appear as personal or clan names in the later genealogical lists of 1 Ch. 2 and 4. This suggests, as John Rea (*op. cit.*) points out, that 'the lists of towns in Joshua belong to a time *before* the descendants of Judah and Simeon began to occupy the Negeb and to give their names to new settlements that were in existence by the time of Shishak'. *f.* The possibility of copyists' errors in lists of unfamiliar names may explain some discrepancies, *e.g.* Jos. 15:32, where the total is given as 'twenty-nine cities', though thirty-six are listed.

On the evidence available it is difficult to come to any conclusion regarding the dating of the lists as we have them in these chapters, but it seems certain that, whatever later editing of them may have been done, their basic form dates back to the conquest. There is no reason to discount the care and accuracy with which the representatives of the tribes (*cf.* 18:4–9) did their work when they surveyed the land and recorded their findings. A similar land survey for the whole land might well lie behind the lists which we have in these chapters. And it can be argued that David (or Solomon or Josiah or Jehoshaphat) for the purposes of administration made use of much older physical divisions of the land.

Who made the allocation? 13:7 suggests that it was Joshua; 14:1 that it was Eleazar the priest and the heads of families; 14:5 that it was the people as a whole. These, however, are not mutually exclusive. The ultimate responsibility was Joshua's; lots, no doubt, were cast by Eleazar, assisted by the heads of families; and the people as a whole accepted the allocation that was made.

13:1 – 19:51 Allocations to the tribes

The necessarily detailed account of the settlement of the tribes given in these chapters may make it difficult to see the wood for the trees, and so it may be helpful to indicate in advance the broad outline of the allocation.

Reuben, Gad and the half-tribe of Manasseh already had their territory allotted to them on the east of Jordan; cf. Nu. 32:1–42. Their settlement is described in Jos. 13. Of the territory which was already in possession on the west of Jordan the main division was between the tribes of Judah and Joseph; the allotment made to the other tribes depended on this fundamental division. The tribe of Judah were given their possession in the south, the territory of the five kings (ch. 15); with them were associated Caleb (14:1–15; 15:13–19) and, in the later division of the land, the tribe of Simeon (19:1–9) because 'the portion of the tribe of Judah was too large for them' (19:9). The powerful house of Joseph, *i.e.* the tribes of Manasseh and Ephraim, received the rich inheritance of central Canaan (chs. 16, 17). They were handicapped, however, by the row of fortresses, Bethshean, Ibleam, Dor, Taanach and Megiddo (17:11, 12; cf. 16:10), which barred the road to the north, and complained of the inadequacy of their possession (17:14). Joshua challenged them to clear the forested areas of their mountain territory, and assured them that they should hew down its powerful inhabitants and finally dispossess the Canaanites, 'though they have chariots of iron, and though they are strong' (17:15–18). Joshua chose Timnath-serah for his own inheritance (19:49, 50).

Between these two powerful sections of the nation, Judah and Joseph, territory was later assigned to Benjamin (18:11–28), and, nearer the sea coast, to Dan (19:40–48); but the tribe of Dan had difficulty in maintaining themselves against the inhabitants of the coastal plain (cf. Jdg. 1:34, 35), and later migrated to the far north (Jdg. 18). The remaining tribes, Zebulun, Issachar, Asher and Naphtali, which, like Simeon, Benjamin and Dan, had not had their portion allotted to them in the first division of the land, were later established in the northern part of the country. See 19:10–39.

13:1–7 Command to divide the land. 1 Though there still remained *very much land to be possessed*, Joshua's age and growing frailty demanded that an allotment of the land, by anticipation if not by complete conquest, should be made. **3** may be an editorial note to explain that what

PALESTINE DIVIDED AMONG
THE TWELVE TRIBES

was later the territory of the Philistines belonged in Joshua's day to the Canaanites. The lands still unconquered are listed roughly from south to north. *The Shihor* may be the lowest reaches of the easternmost branch of the Nile, or, possibly, the Wadi el-Arish, which flows into the Mediterranean about 90 miles east of Egypt and 50 miles west of Gaza. (See K. A. Kitchen, 'Egypt, River of', *NBD*.) **6** The command was given for a division of the whole land between the nine and a half tribes, since God's intervention made final victory assured.

13:8–33 Territory of the two and a half tribes. Reuben, Gad and the half-tribe of Manasseh had already been allotted their portion in eastern Palestine, and the boundaries of each of these tribes were now fixed, Reuben being placed in the south, Gad in the centre and Manasseh in the north. *Cf.* Nu. 32 and Dt. 3:12–17. **14** *To the tribe of Levi alone Moses gave no inheritance.* Moses had left instructions for the allocating of cities to the Levites (*cf.* Nu. 18:20–24; 35:1–8), but they were to have no tribal area. The appointing of their cities is dealt with later in ch. 21.

14:1 – 15:63 Territory of Caleb and Judah. 14:1–5 describes the method by which the allocation of the whole land of Canaan was made, and repeats the explanation of the separate treatment given to the two and a half tribes and the tribe of Levi in ch. 21. **6–15** Caleb now sought the fulfilment of the promise made to him in Dt. 1:36 (cf. Nu. 14:24, 30), and at his own request was given the strong city of Hebron for his inheritance out of the possession of Judah.

15:1–19 (cf. Jdg. 1:10–15, 20) describes how he claimed and enlarged this inheritance by conquest, aided by the valour of his kinsman Othniel who became his son-in-law. Harmonization of this passage with the account of Joshua's attack on Debir in 10:38, 39 is best achieved by the assumption that a second assault was necessary some time later than the lightning attack made by Joshua. Vv. 2–12 give the south, east, north, and west boundaries of the territory of Judah; 20–62 list the cities of Judah, comprising twelve districts in four geographical areas: **21** in the Negeb, *the extreme South*; **33** the Shephelah, *the lowland*; **48** *the hill country*; **61** *the wilderness*. According to the LXX a group of towns has dropped out after v. 59. If these are inserted, vv. 45–47 should be taken as one paragraph, thus still giving twelve districts. **63** indicates the failure of the tribe of Judah to dispossess the Jebusites of Jerusalem.

16:1 – 17:18 Territory of Ephraim and Manasseh. The territory of Ephraim and the remainder of the half-tribe of Manasseh in Canaan was, as we have seen, the central part of the country. Ephraim had the rich district north and south of Shechem (the southern portion), and Manasseh the northern part, fringed by the Canaanite fortresses that guarded the fertile plain of Esdraelon. Their inability to penetrate beyond these was a cause of complaint (17:14), but Joshua in effect told them that if they were the great people they claimed to be they could extend their territory by clearance and conquest. But the Israelite infantry were understandably afraid of the horses and iron-plated chariots of the Canaanite armies, which were most effective instruments of war on congenial terrain. **17:3–6** The daughters of Zelophehad claimed and received the possession promised to them by Moses under the stipulations for families without sons; cf. Nu. 27:1–11; 36:1–12. **11** *The third is Naphath*; probably an editorial note explaining that the third city on the list, Dor, is the Dor of Naphath-dor and not En-dor in the plain of Esdraelon.

18:1 – 19:51 Territory of the seven tribes. 18:1 It seems that the previous division of the land was carried out in Gilgal; but now the whole congregation removed to Shiloh, the earliest of the Hebrew sanctuaries, and set up the Tabernacle there (cf. 1 Sa. 1:3; Je. 7:12). **2–9** For the seven tribes who were still without defined inheritance a survey of the land was made by a commission of twenty-one members, three from each tribe. **5** stresses that the further allocation of the land must be made with due regard to the positions already occupied by Judah and Joseph. **10** The whole remaining territory was then divided up into seven portions for which lots were cast in Shiloh. **11–28** Benjamin's inheritance was allotted between that of Judah

and Ephraim; **19:1–9** Simeon's was taken out of the possession of Judah, which had proved too large for them. Simeon was ultimately absorbed into Judah in literal fulfilment of the curse pronounced on Simeon and Levi (cf. Gn. 49:7). **10–39** The northern part of the country was allotted to Zebulun, Issachar, Asher and Naphtali. Issachar was settled on the northern border of Manasseh, separated from it by the line of Canaanite fortresses already mentioned. Zebulun had the area immediately north of Issachar, comprising the inland plain which was traversed by the most useful trade route of antiquity, the 'Way of the Sea', and extending to the sea coast. Asher and Naphtali divided the territory still farther north, Asher's possession lying along the coast and stretching to the great commercial city of Tyre, and Naphtali's to the east of it. **40–48** Dan's allotment was a small territory compressed into the narrow space between the north-western hills of Judah and the sea. **47** indicates that this territory was too small for them; and this is supplemented by Jdg. 1:34, which tells that the Amorites (the Philistines) forced them into the hills. The majority of the tribe accordingly migrated later to the far north and settled in Leshem (Laish); a full account of the migration is given in Jdg. 18, q.v. **49–51** After all the land had been allocated, Joshua chose his own inheritance in Timnath-serah in the territory of Ephraim.

20:1 – 21:45 Cities of refuge and cities of the Levites appointed

20:1–9 Cities of refuge appointed. According to the directions given in the law of Moses (Nu. 35:9–34; Dt. 19:1–10), the six cities of refuge were set apart and 'designated' (v. 9) for the asylum of those who had committed unintentional homicide. **1–6** The main points of the Mosaic regulations are summarized from Nu. 35:9–34; Dt. 19:1–10. **4, 5** Added to the Mosaic regulations is a note on the special responsibility of the elders of the city. **6** The regulations, *until he has stood before the congregation for judgment* and *until the death of him who is high priest at the time*, are to be interpreted, as is clearly seen from Nu. 35:24, 25, as meaning that the manslayer was to stay in the city of refuge until he had been taken back to his own city to be tried by the congregation: if proved guilty of murder, he would be handed over to the avenger of blood, but if proved innocent of intent to kill, he would be taken back to the city of refuge, there to remain until the death of the existing high priest. The death of the high priest, as the only regular national official at the time, marked the end of a definite period.

In Dt. 4:41–43 Moses set apart three cities east of Jordan. In Dt. 19:1–10 he ordered three more to be set apart when Israel took possession of the land, and provided for a third group of three if these should prove to be necessary, which they never did. **7–9** The six cities are now set apart and designated, three on each side of the Jordan, located strategically in the north, in the centre and in the south. Kedesh was in northern Galilee, Shechem in central Palestine, and Kiriath-arba (Hebron) in the hill country of Judah. On the other side of Jordan, the exact location of Bezer is unknown, though, being in the territory of Reuben, it must have been northeast of the Dead Sea; Ramoth in Gilead is in the territory of Gad in the centre; and Golan in Bashan is farther north.

21:1–45 Cities of the Levites appointed. When all the tribes had received their inheritance, the Levites claimed the cities which had been promised to them by Moses (*cf.* Nu. 35:1–8). As the representatives of the Hebrew faith and the ministers of its worship, it was necessary that they should be dispersed throughout the whole nation, and also that they should maintain their distinct position. To achieve both these purposes, they were given forty-eight cities out of all the tribes, along with the circle of pasture land around each of them. It may be that this pasture land, as distinct from agricultural land, was to be a reminder of the simple life which Israel had lived in the wilderness, and a constant recall to the simple religion with which that life was linked. Certainly the Levites were to be the custodians of the nation's spiritual life.

4–42 Levi's three sons gave their names to the three great branches of the Levites, the Kohathites, the Gershonites and the Merarites. The Kohathites were subdivided into the priests (Aaron's sons) and those who did not fill the priestly office. The Levitical cities were therefore divided among these four sections of the Levites. The Levites were not the exclusive possessors and inhabitants of the cities which were allocated to them. Debir, *e.g.*, was the possession of Othniel, a non-Levite (*cf.* 15:15–19), though here (v. 15), it is listed as a Levitical city. The regulation meant that the Levites were given adequate room within the Levitical cities, and the right to the pasture lands around them.

43–45 This concludes the allocation of territory and cities, and the section ends with a passage extolling the faithfulness of God. *Not one of all the good promises which the Lord had made to the house of Israel had failed; all came to pass.*

22:1–34 Return of the eastern tribes and setting up of the altar of witness

The final incident of the settlement was the dismissal of the eastern tribes to their own inheritance on the other side of Jordan.

22:1–9 Farewell to the two and a half tribes. Having commended them warmly for their loyalty, Joshua sent them off with a solemn warning not to let their isolation make them forget their allegiance to Yahweh. **9** *Their own land of which they had possessed themselves by command of the Lord through Moses* seems to be an adequate answer to the frequently-expressed criticism of the two and a half tribes

for taking their inheritance on the nearer side of Jordan.

22:10, 11 Erection of a memorial altar. Deeply conscious of the barrier presented by the Jordan, and anxious to denote their unity with the main body of Israel, the eastern tribes built a massive altar on the bank of the Jordan. It seems clear that the altar was built on the western side of Jordan; the phrase *on the side that belongs to the people of Israel* in the report that came to the assembly of the people betrays the very attitude that the two and a half tribes feared, for it virtually disowned the tribes on the other side. It is significant that the two and a half tribes chose an altar as the symbol of their unity with the other tribes of Israel, recognizing that the basis of their unity was their common worship and their common faith. Modern study of the constitution of Israel has increasingly recognized this: until the time of the monarchy, the tribes of Israel were to a considerable extent independent units, but held together by their common loyalty to Yahweh, their covenant God. This spiritual unity found expression in worship at a common sanctuary. On this account, Israel's tribal constitution has come to be known as an amphictyony, the name given by the Greeks to similar units grouped around a central shrine. (See John Bright, *A History of Israel*, 1960, pp. 142ff.) In a sense, the altar at the Jordan was a symbol of the reality of the amphictyony.

22:12–20 Israel's protest against possible partition. The innocent act of the two and a half tribes was misconstrued by the western tribes as an attempt to set up a second altar of sacrifice, contrary to the Mosaic law (*cf.* Lv. 17:8, 9), and a deputation was sent from Shiloh, the site of the Tabernacle, the centre of Israel's worship, to investigate the alleged treachery of their brethren. Headed by Phinehas, who was noted for his zeal for the Lord and his opposition to pagan practices (*cf.* Nu. 25:6–18), the deputation reminded the eastern tribes of the disasters to the whole community that had followed previous acts of apostasy at Peor and Ai, and magnanimously suggested that if the land to the east of Jordan was *unclean*, in the sense of not being hallowed by the evident presence of Yahweh, the eastern tribes could take their possession in the west (v. 19).

22:21–29 Defence of the eastern tribes. The eastern tribes made their defence in the most solemn terms, swearing by the three names of their God (El, Elohim, Yahweh), twice repeated, *the Mighty One, God, the Lord*, that the altar which they had built was nothing more than a permanent monument to their kinship with the tribes across the river. Their action was motivated by a real fear lest their children should fail to realize their connection with the commonwealth of Israel.

22:30–34 Happy ending. Even a zealot for pure religion like Phinehas was satisfied. The explanation of the eastern tribes was promptly accepted and a happy reconciliation ensued: the altar itself became a perpetual witness of the episode.

23:1 – 24:33 JOSHUA'S LAST DAYS

The book of Joshua begins with his call to leadership; it ends with his farewell addresses and the account of his death. It has been suggested that chs. 23 and 24 are two accounts of the same event, since both addresses cover much of the same ground; but it seems best to consider ch. 23 as Joshua's informal address to the leaders of the people and ch. 24 as a formal, public renewal of the covenant.

23:1–16 First address

In ancient Israel and indeed among ancient nations in general, the parting words of national leaders and heads of families were very highly regarded (*cf.* Gn. 49; Dt. 32, 33), and Joshua's farewell address to the leaders of the people must have made a very deep impression. **2** It seems best to read *Joshua summoned all Israel, i.e. their elders and heads, their judges and officers.*

3–16 The address can be summarized under two main headings. The first is God's part (vv. 3, 5, 9, 10, 13–16). This consists of (*a*) what He has done (vv. 3, 4, 9, 10, 14). Joshua reminds his hearers of what they themselves have seen: how God has fought for them, given them an inheritance, driven out their enemies, enabling them to be victorious against impossible odds (v. 10 is a generalization, 'one of you can put a thousand to flight') and proving utterly faithful to His promises (v. 14). *b.* What He will do (vv. 5, 13, 15, 16). God's continuing help for Israel and Israel's continuing success are promised (v. 5). Vv. 13, 15, 16 indicate that this is contingent on Israel's faithfulness to the covenant. Apostasy would mean the turning of all the good they had known to terrible evil. The second main heading is man's part. Israel's responsibility included four things: obedience to God's law (v. 6), separation from the idolatrous nations of Canaan (v. 7; in v. 12 intermarriage is specifically forbidden), loyalty (v. 8) and, including everything else, love (v. 11).

24:1–28 Second address and renewal of the covenant

One of the most important landmarks in recent study of the Old Testament was the publication of George Mendenhall's 'Law and Covenant in Israel and the Ancient Near East' (*BA*, 17, 1954; reprinted separately, 1955). In this study he pointed out striking parallels in form between the covenant at Sinai and the formal treaties drawn up between the great king and his vassal states within the Hittite Empire in the period *c.* 1450–1200 BC. These suzerainty covenants followed a regular pattern; a preamble, in which the author of the covenant is identified; a historical prologue, in 'I—thou' form, describing past benevolent acts performed by the great king for the benefit of his vassal;

stipulations, general and particular, indicating the obligations imposed upon and accepted by the vassal, including no dealings with the great king's enemies, good relationships with other vassals and active support for the king as required; a provision for the depositing of a copy of the covenant in the vassal's sanctuary and for its periodic public reading; a list of deities invoked as witnesses of the covenant; and blessings and curses as sanctions of the covenant.

It is quite clear that what we have in Jos. 24:1–28 is a renewal of the Sinaitic covenant, brought up to date, and that it follows closely the pattern of the classic suzerainty covenant. One of the features of that type of covenant was the necessity for its renewal from time to time. And that is exactly what we have at Shechem, where Joshua called the people of Israel together to confirm their covenant relationship with their God (*cf.* Dt. 31:9–13). The exposition of the chapter may usefully follow the divisions of the classic mid-second millennium BC covenant form.

2a Preamble: the Author of the covenant is identified as *the Lord, the God of Israel.* **2b–13** Historical prologue or retrospect: here Yahweh Himself recapitulates His past beneficence to His people: the call of Abraham (vv. 2–4) and the deliverance from Egypt (vv. 5–7) were evidences of his special relationship to His people. In their own experience, the defeat of the Amorites (v. 8) and the frustration of Balaam's evil designs (vv. 9, 10), the crossing of the Jordan and the capture of Jericho (v. 11), and the defeat of the nations of Canaan, brought the history of Yahweh's mighty acts on their behalf right up to date (vv. 12, 13). **12** *The hornet*; Garstang argued very persuasively for identifying this with Egyptian forces which had devastated the land before Israel moved in. The cogency of his argument depended to a large extent on his dating of the conquest, which is now generally rejected: in any case, there is no evidence that the Egyptian forces ever pillaged the territory of Og and Bashan, *the two kings of the Amorites.* It is most unlikely that a literal plague of hornets is referred to, and perhaps the best clue to the meaning of the vivid figure used is found in the parallel passage in Dt. 7:20–23: 'The Lord your God will send hornets among them. . . . The Lord your God will give them over to you, and throw them into great confusion, until they are destroyed.' Panic and wild confusion, like that caused by an invasion of hornets, were God's advance secret weapon, by the help of which Israel would conquer. What is stressed is that the victory was gained not by force of arms but by God's miraculous intervention, *not by your sword or by your bow* (*cf.* Ps. 44:1–3).

14, 15 The stipulations: the basic stipulation is exclusive loyalty; *put away the gods which your fathers served beyond the River, and in Egypt.* Joshua was wise enough to indicate that there were alternatives: *whether the gods your fathers* *served in the region beyond the River, i.e.* in Ur of the Chaldees, *or the gods of the Amorites in whose land you dwell.* These latter were to prove a constant temptation in Israel's later history. There were alternatives, but Joshua indicated his irrevocable choice: *as for me and my house, we will serve the Lord.*

16-18 gives the people's all too glib and ready acceptance of the stipulations of the covenant. It is significant that their response in vv. 17, 18 is based on their acceptance of the truth of the claims made by their divine Benefactor in vv. 5-12. They were virtually saying 'yes' to what God had said to them. Joshua therefore bound them in a renewed covenant in the most solemn way possible. **19, 20** Joshua reminds them that it was no slight thing which they were binding themselves to do: *you cannot serve the Lord.* He declared that Yahweh is a holy and jealous God and is therefore not to be worshipped or served lightly. When he solemnly asserted, *He will not forgive your transgressions or your sins.* he was not laying down a general rule regarding forgiveness (which is always promised to the repentant sinner), but was referring to the particular sin of blatant denial of God, as v. 20 clearly shows: *if you forsake the Lord and serve foreign gods. . . .* (*Cf.* Nu. 15:30, which also declares that there is no forgiveness for sin *with a high hand.*) There seems to be a parallel in this passage in Joshua to the teaching on the unpardonable sin of Mt. 12:31, 32, where there is no forgiveness for those who blatantly ascribe to the evil one (Baal-zebub or Be-elzebub) the deeds done by the mighty power of God. Joshua warned the people that to ascribe to the Baals of Canaan the power which belonged to Yahweh alone was a sin which, persisted in, could not be forgiven. **21** The people met Joshua's challenge and warning with the confident assertion, *Nay; but we will serve the Lord.* **22** The witnesses: there could be no appeal to pagan gods as witnesses, as in the Hittite treaties, but the people themselves are named as witnesses of the covenant. **23** Were there *foreign gods* among them? The Hebrew word translated *among you* can be translated 'within you'; the seeds of possible idolatry were in their hearts.

26 Depositing of the covenant: *Joshua wrote these words in the book of the law of God,* no doubt to be deposited, as in Dt. 31:26, 'by the side of the ark of the covenant'. **27** A great stone set up under the famous oak of Shechem was declared to be a witness to the people's solemn declaration. It is of interest to note that a great limestone pillar has been recovered by archaeologists excavating the site of Shechem. The normal blessings and cursings attached to such covenants are not explicitly inserted, as they are in Dt. 28, but they are implied in the warnings of this verse and of vv. 19, 20. *Cf.* the previous renewal of the covenant at Shechem in Jos. 8:30-35.

So the last public act of Joshua was to lead his people in a great act of covenant renewal.

24:29-33 Joshua's death and burial

Joshua died at a good old age, and the greatest tribute to his life was paid when the sacred historian wrote, *And Israel served the Lord all the days of Joshua, and all the days of the elders who outlived Joshua.*

The book closes with the account of the burying of the body of Joseph, carried through all the wanderings of the wilderness and at last laid to rest in the promised land, in the sacred ground of Shechem. It may be, as many commentators have maintained, that his burial took place long before the death of Joshua. But surely it was inspired editing which placed the account of it here, symbolizing at the close the message of the whole book of Joshua, the faithfulness of God.

HUGH J. BLAIR

Judges

INTRODUCTION

The book of Judges (Heb. *šōpᵉṭîm*) is so called from the successive figures who are depicted in it as raised up by Yahweh to deliver the tribes of Israel from their enemies and to 'judge' them— *i.e.* not necessarily to rule them, but to execute the judgment of God on their behalf. The word *šōpᵉṭîm* is cognate with the Phoenician word by which, according to Roman writers, the chief magistrates of Carthage were known 1,000 years later (*suffetes*). In the Samaritan records the judges are called 'kings'. In the Hebrew Bible Judges is the second book of the 'Former Prophets', following Joshua and preceding Samuel and Kings.

HISTORICAL BACKGROUND

Judges deals with the first two or three centuries following the entry of the tribes of Israel into Canaan under Joshua (*c.* 1250–1200 BC). This period coincides with the beginning of the Iron Age in the Middle East. The Iron Age was inaugurated when an effective and economic process for smelting iron was devised. Iron is much commoner than copper and tin, the constituents of the metal which gave its name to the preceding Bronze Age, but not so easy to work.

To be sure, we have isolated examples of some wrought-iron implements several centuries earlier, frequently of meteoric iron; but not until the metal could be produced in bulk did its use begin to affect the course of civilization. When such a process was devised, the consequences were radical and far-reaching, for agriculture and industry as well as for warfare. The first place where it was devised was apparently in the district of Kizzuwatna, in eastern Asia Minor, in the territory of the Hittite Empire, *c.* 1400 BC. The Hebrew word for 'iron', *barzel*, is borrowed from Hittite *barzillu*. The kings of the Hittites and of the neighbouring Mitanni Empire adopted a policy of secrecy over the production, and controlled the output and export of iron. The Mitanni kings sent presents of iron objects to the Pharaohs, until Mitanni was conquered by the Hittites *c.* 1370 BC. Presents of this kind were cautiously rationed; when one monarch (perhaps a king of Assyria) wrote to ask the Hittite king Hattusilis III for a supply of iron *c.* 1260 BC, his royal 'brother' put him off on various pretexts and sent him only one dagger. Such a policy of secrecy, however, was no more successful in antiquity than today; and by *c.* 1200 BC the Bronze Age in the Middle East, with its great civilizations, passes out in the crashing of empires, and the Iron Age dawns amid barbaric invasions.

In the OT the advent of the Iron Age is reflected in the iron bedstead (or was it a basalt sarcophagus?) of Og king of Bashan, a museum-piece for later ages (Dt. 3:11); in the iron chariots of the Canaanites (Jos. 17:16), including Sisera's 900 chariots of iron (Jdg. 4:3); and in the Philistine retention of the monopoly of iron-working to the disadvantage of the Israelites (1 Sa. 13:19–22).

The Israelite entry into Canaan and settlement in the land was contemporary with a great movement of peoples in the Middle East (probably itself the result of large-scale 'folk-wanderings' in the Eurasian steppe-lands), which involved the downfall of the Minoan, Hittite and Mycenaean Empires. Canaan found itself the centre of a great movement of invading bands, both from the land and from the sea. Its connection with Egypt was close under the Asiatic Hyksos Dynasties (*c.* 1720–1580 BC); and the kings of the XVIIIth Dynasty (1580–1319), who expelled the Hyksos rulers, added Canaan to the Egyptian Empire. But towards the end of that Dynasty we find the cities of E Canaan attacked by people called the Ḫabiru, a name given to semi-nomadic groups whom we meet all over W Asia from the 18th to the 13th century BC. The word 'Ḫabiru' may be identical with 'Hebrews', the name of the group to which the Israelites belonged, though these Ḫabiru are probably not to be identified with the Israelites led by Joshua. The diplomatic correspondence of the reign of Akhnaton (1377–1360 BC), recorded on the tablets uncovered at Tell el-Amarna in 1887, contains despairing pleas from provincial governors in Canaan for help against the Ḫabiru— help which never came. (See F. F. Bruce, 'Tell el-Amarna', in *Archaeology and OT Study*, ed. D. W. Thomas, 1967.)

In the earlier years of the XIXth Dynasty (1319–1200) an attempt was made by the Egyptian kings to reconquer Canaan, in the course of which they came into conflict with the Hittite Empire N of Palestine. After the indecisive battle of Kadesh on the Upper Orontes in 1297, the two emperors struck a treaty (*c.* 1280) and agreed on the delimitation of their realms— wisely, because both had cause to look anxiously over their shoulders at menaces from fresh quarters. The Hittite king was threatened by the Assyrians on the E, while from the W the Aḥḥiyawa (Achaeans?) pressed him hard, themselves pushed by the force of folk-migrations farther inside Europe; as for Egypt, its coasts began to be attacked by raiders from the sea. These were repulsed by Merenptah (*c.* 1230 BC), as was also a second raiding coalition in the reign of Rameses III (*c.* 1194); but, unable to gain a footing in Egypt, some of them settled on the Canaanite coast. Of these the most notable were the Philistines, who speedily established and maintained their hegemony over great areas of Canaan until the reign of David (1010–970). It was they who gave to the country its name of Palestine, abridged from Greek *Syria Palaistinē, i.e.* 'Philistine Syria'.

ERA OF THE JUDGES

In this historical setting we must place the Israelites' entry into Canaan and the era of the judges. The events of Judges may be dated between 1250 and 1050 BC.

J. Garstang, who placed the entry into Canaan *c.* 1400 BC, in conformity with his dating of the destruction of Jericho, worked out in his book *Joshua-Judges* (1931) a system of coincidences of the chronology of Egypt and Israel in the period of the judges, by which he made it appear that the successive periods of 'rest' in Judges corresponded with those periods in which the Egyptian influence was dominant in Palestine. The periods of oppression then coincided with the years in which the Egyptian power was weaker and the peoples in and around Canaan could act with greater freedom. There are, however, grave difficulties in the way of dating the invasion of Canaan so early as Garstang does. It was not, apparently, until the 13th century BC that the Transjordanian kingdoms were founded, and they existed as kingdoms towards the end of the wilderness wanderings. Again, Garstang's scheme assumes all the judges to have been consecutive, whereas internal evidence indicates that some of them at least arose simultaneously in separate parts of the land.

Above all, Garstang's correlation of the archaeological date of the site of Jericho with the biblical record must be radically revised in the light of the expeditions led by K. M. Kenyon (1952–58). Of the last Late Bronze Age town (Joshua's Jericho) practically nothing remains, because of erosion; Garstang's identification of one of the lines of town walls as belonging to Joshua's Jericho proved to be mistaken. Archaeological evidence for dating Joshua's capture of Jericho is therefore lacking, but the Israelite destruction of other Canaanite strongholds is best dated archaeologically towards the end of the 13th century BC.

AUTHOR'S APPROACH TO HISTORY

The title 'Father of History' is traditionally, and with reason, accorded to Herodotus, the Greek historian, who wrote in the second half of the 5th century BC. His predecessors were mere annalists or chroniclers; but a historian must be something more. He must see the underlying operation of cause and effect; he will have a philosophy of history by which he can present the course of events as the expression of basic principles. In this respect Herodotus had predecessors in the historians of Israel. To them history was the story of God's dealing with His people and the other nations; they penetrated beneath the surface to find the root cause of events in the ways of God. The historians from Joshua to 2 Kings display the 'Deuteronomic' philosophy of history, so called because it finds clearest expression in Deuteronomy. The cause of prosperity is found in obedience to the will of God, and especially in avoidance of the native Baalism of Canaan, with its demoralizing fertility cults; adversity is the sure sequel to departure from this strait path. This attitude is plain in the framework of Judges. The people's lapsing from the worship of Yahweh and their serving of other gods is regularly followed by foreign oppression; then they cry to Yahweh in their affliction and He raises up a deliverer for them.

This picture of the history of the period is no pious fiction. When the tribes maintained their loyalty to Yahweh and the Sinaitic covenant, symbolized by the ark, they were united and strong; when they lapsed into Baalism their bond of union was lost and they were divided and weak. The times of deliverance were therefore generally accompanied by a return to the faith which they had learnt in the wilderness, in the strength of which, nomads as they were, they were able to overthrow the more highly civilized nations of Canaan.

DATE AND COMPOSITION

As for the date of the book in its present form, we have a few indications: the words 'as long as the house of God was at Shiloh' (18:31) imply a time later than the destruction of Shiloh in the days of Samuel; the repeated words 'In those days there was no king in Israel' (17:6; 18:1, *etc.*) suggest a date under the monarchy; the reference in 18:30, 'until the day of the captivity of the land', probably indicates the Assyrian captivity in the 8th century BC, *i.e.* the carrying away of the population of Galilee by Tiglath-pileser III in 732.

The author's 'philosophy of history' may suggest a date after Josiah's reformation (621 BC), which was based on the recovery of the Deuteronomic law-code. Indeed, the whole corpus of the 'Former Prophets' is widely regarded today as one continuous historical work, covering the period from the settlement in Canaan onwards, composed under the influence of Josiah's Deuteronomic reformation (with an appendix carrying the story on to the middle of the Babylonian exile, 562 BC). This view (propounded especially by M. Noth) has much more to be said in its favour than that of G. Hölscher and O. Eissfeldt which regards the 'Former Prophets' as being based on continuations of the main Pentateuchal sources. E.

Robertson, in *The Old Testament Problem* (1950, pp. 159ff.), finds internal evidence that Judges belongs to a time when the rivalry between Jews and Samaritans was keen. Jdg. 1:21, indeed, more naturally indicates a date earlier than David's capture of Jerusalem (*c.* 1003 BC), and Jdg. 1:29 must be earlier than the acquisition of Gezer by Solomon (*c.* 950). But such evidences of earlier date simply show that the component parts of Judges are mostly older than the finished book as it has come down to us. For the author had at his disposal much ancient material, the oldest being the Song of Deborah (5:2–31a), contemporary with the event it celebrates. Most of his materials he has arranged so as to bring out his philosophy of history. The main part of the book—the tale of repeated falling into idolatry, foreign oppression and deliverance—is put in a framework built up on a recurring form of this nature: 'And the children of Israel did evil in the sight of the Lord, and the Lord sold them into the hand of A, king of B, who oppressed them x years. And they cried to the Lord, and he raised up a deliverer for them, C the son of D, and he prevailed against A, king of B, and delivered Israel, and the land had rest y years (or: and he judged Israel y years).'

Into such a framework as this are fitted the oppressions of Cushan-rishathaim, Eglon, Jabin, Midian, Ammon, and the Philistines, with the corresponding deliverances wrought respectively by Othniel, Ehud, Deborah and Barak, Gideon, Jephthah and Samson. This main part of Judges (3–16), from which the book receives its name, contains also the incident of Shamgar (3:31), the story of Abimelech (9:1–57), and brief notes on the five minor judges, Tola and Jair, and Ibzan, Elon and Abdon (10:1–5; 12:8–15). Perhaps the author envisaged a total of twelve judges (comprising both major and minor); *cf.* the estimate in 1 Ki. 6:1 of the period from the Exodus to the foundation of Solomon's Temple as 480 years, *i.e.* twelve generations.

All this is preceded by an introductory section which includes *a.* a summary of the conquest of the land (1:1 – 2:10), drawn from one or more early sources, some parts of which are incorporated also in the narrative of Joshua, and *b.* a statement of the author's philosophy of history, explaining why so many of the Canaanite and other non-Israelite inhabitants were left in the land (2:11 – 3:4).

The book draws to a conclusion with two unattached narratives, chronologically referring to the earlier part of the period of the judges, which have not been incorporated into the author's framework: *a.* the northward migration of the tribe of Dan and the establishment of their sanctuary (17;18) and *b.* the war against Benjamin (19–21). Both of these narratives illustrate the unsettled conditions of a time when 'there was no king in Israel: every man did what was right in his own eyes'.

IMPORTANCE OF THE AGE OF THE JUDGES

The tribes of Israel in this period constituted an amphictyonic league—an expression borrowed from Greek history, denoting an association of cities or other groups sharing a common sanctuary and linked by their obligations to it. The common sanctuary shared by the tribes of Israel was that which housed the ark of the covenant, the palladium of the sacred bond which united them in the worship of Yahweh. Before the settlement in Canaan the ark was housed in a movable tent-shrine. After the settlement, Shiloh was chosen as the site for the ark and its shrine (*cf.* Jos. 18:1; Jdg. 18:31; 21:12ff.; 1 Sa. 1:3), although other sites appear to have been used from time to time, such as Gilgal (Jdg. 2:1), Mizpah (Jdg. 20:1) and Bethel (Jdg. 20:18); *cf.* 2 Sa. 7:6 where, as late as the reign of David, Yahweh says, 'I have not dwelt in a house since the day I brought up the people of Israel from Egypt to this day, but I have been moving about in a tent for my dwelling.'

This inter-tribal sanctuary, staffed by a priesthood which traced its lineage back to Aaron (Jdg. 20:28), was Israel's one cohesive institution before the establishment of the monarchy. Its unifying influence could operate only when the tribes' sense of covenant loyalty was strong. It survived the various vicissitudes recorded in Judges, but when it was destroyed by the Philistines and the ark was captured by them (1 Sa. 4; Je. 7:12ff.; 26:6, 9), only the personality and achievement of Samuel, and his inauguration of the monarchy, saved Israel's national identity.

The period of the judges, then—'Israel's iron age', as it has been called (in a spiritual, not economic, sense)—was a period of adaptation to the conditions of life in Canaan, a period of struggle for national survival. If we were restricted to the book of Judges, the struggle might appear foredoomed to defeat; how defeat was turned into victory is told in the sequel, in the books of Samuel.

Religiously, it is presented as a period during which the nation was being fashioned by its God in the furnace of affliction to be His chosen instrument for the furtherance of His purpose in the world. Unedifying as the details of many of the individual episodes may be thought, together they portray the God of Israel's unceasing faithfulness to His covenant with His people, in spite of their recurrent unfaithfulness, as He deals with them in mercy and judgment, showing them what is practically involved for them in being His people and having Him as their God.

Later generations looked back to the period of the judges as one during which God acted signally for the defence of His people. Thus Samuel, in his farewell address to Israel, reminds them how God delivered them from Egypt under Moses and Aaron 'and made them dwell in this place'. 'But', he goes on, 'they forgot the Lord their God; and he sold them into the hand of Sisera, commander of the army of Jabin king of Hazor, and into the hand of the Philistines, and into the hand of the king of Moab; and they fought against them. And they cried to the Lord, and said, "We have sinned, because we have forsaken the Lord, and have served the Baals and the Ashtaroth; but now deliver us out of the hand of our enemies, and we will serve thee." And the Lord sent Jerubbaal and Barak, and Jephthah, . . . and delivered you out of the hand of your enemies on every side; and you dwelt in safety' (1 Sa. 12:8–11). Other incidents in the period of the judges are referred to in 2 Sa. 11:21; Is. 9:4; 10:26. But the most outstanding tribute to the men of this period is paid in Heb. 11:32ff., where 'Gideon, Barak, Samson, Jephthah' are named among those who 'through faith conquered kingdoms, enforced justice, received promises, . . . escaped the edge of the sword, won strength out of weakness, became mighty in war, put foreign armies to flight'.

OUTLINE OF CONTENTS

COMMENTARY

1:1 – 2:5 PARTIAL CONQUEST OF CANAAN BY ISRAEL

1:1–21 Conquest of south Canaan

1 *After the death of Joshua.* This is best regarded as an editorial note; the death of Joshua appears in its chronological setting at 2:8. Jdg. 1 is a collection of miscellaneous fragments: vv. 2–21, the conquest of S Canaan by Judah and affiliated groups; vv. 22–26, the capture of Bethel by the Joseph tribes; vv. 27–36, a list of cities from which the central and northern tribes could not drive out their Canaanite inhabitants. On the relation between these fragments and the narrative of Joshua see G. E. Wright, 'The Literary and Historical Problem of Joshua x and Judges i', *Journal of Near Eastern Studies*, 5, 1946, pp. 105–114 (with critique by H. H. Rowley, *From Joseph to Joshua*, 1950, pp. 100f.). *Who shall go up first for us?* Nu. 21:1–3 records an Israelite invasion from the south earlier than that from the east; *cf.* Jdg. 1:16, 17. **3** *And Judah said to Simeon his brother.* A tribe or nation is often spoken of in terms of its ancestor; this is obviously so here, but it is also found in places where it is not so obvious. Simeon ceased at an early date to be a separate tribe and was incorporated with Judah. **4** *Then Judah went up.* Part of this territory had been inhabited by Judah and his family before the descent into Egypt (Gn. 38). *The Canaanites and the Perizzites.* The Perizzites are obscure, but may have been an indigenous people of different race from the Canaanites. **5** *They came upon Adoni-bezek at Bezek.* This Bezek was presumably in the S of Canaan, but is otherwise unknown. The name of its king means 'lord of Bezek'. **6** *Cut off his thumbs and his great toes.* Probably to degrade him by mutilation, and not

merely to disable him from the use of weapons. **7** *They brought him to Jerusalem.* The earliest city, on the hill Ophel, S of the Temple area, is shown by archaeological evidence to go back to *c.* 3000 BC. Jerusalem is mentioned in Egyptian texts *c.* 1900 BC, and is perhaps the Salem of Gn. 14:18. The Canaanite city was a mixed Hittite–Amorite foundation (Ezk. 16:3). It was one of the chief Canaanite city-states in the Amarna age (*c.* 1400–1360 BC).

8 *And the men of Judah fought against Jerusalem, and took it.* The book of Joshua records the killing of the king of Jerusalem (Jos. 10:22ff.; 12:10), but not the capture of his city. Proponents of the earlier chronology connect the present incident with the Ḥabiru threat to Jerusalem under its king Abdi-ḥiba in the reign of Akhnaton (*c.* 1370 BC); but the details of the two situations do not match. If Jerusalem here is the Jebusite capital, its capture can have been only an isolated incident in the conquest, followed immediately by its recapture by the Jebusites (*cf.* 1:21). But R. P. S. Hubbard ('The Topography of Ancient Jerusalem', *PEQ*, 98, 1966, p. 137) suggests that the Jerusalem captured by the Hebrews under Joshua was not the Jebusite capital on Ophel but a settlement on the SW hill. **10** *Now the name of Hebron was formerly Kiriath-arba.* Kiriath-arba means 'city of four', *i.e.* tetrapolis or fourfold city, pointing to an early 'confederacy', which is the meaning of the name Hebron. According to Nu. 13:22 Hebron was built 7 years before Tanis (Zoan) in Egypt. This probably refers to the Hyksos fortification of Tanis (Avaris), which dates the foundation of Hebron *c.* 1725 BC. Jdg. 1:10–15 is parallel to Jos. 15:14–19, where the capture of Hebron as well as of Debir is ascribed to Caleb. *And they defeated Sheshai and Ahiman* *and Talmai.* These are named as 'children of Anak' (meaning perhaps 'the long-necked people') in the narrative of the spies in Nu. 13:22. *Cf.* Jdg. 1:20.

11 *From there they went against the inhabitants of Debir.* The capture of Debir was easy after Hebron was taken. Its former name *Kiriath-sepher* (or Kiriath-sopher) means 'city of books' (or 'city of scribes'). The site (mod. Tell Beit Mirsim) has been excavated; the Late Bronze Age city is found to have been burnt *c.* 1230 BC, and thereupon rebuilt with thinner walls, a smaller population and a lower culture. **13** *Othniel the son of Kenaz, Caleb's younger brother, took it.* The 'sons of Kenaz' (Kenizzites), along with such other nomads as the Kenites (v. 16) and the Jerahmeelites, were fused with the tribe of Judah.

16 *The descendants of the Kenite, Moses' father-in-law.* RV renders 'Moses' brother in law', regarding the Kenite in question as Hobab *(cf.* 4:11). Hebrew *ḥōṭēn* (lit. 'circumciser'?) means *father-in-law*, but if vocalized *ḥāṭān* it might mean 'brother in law' (RV). But the normal meaning of *ḥāṭān* is 'son-in-law' or 'bride-groom' (*cf.* Ex. 4:25, 26), because at one time he was apparently circumcised by the father-in-law on the eve of marriage. Hence the translation should read 'whose son-in-law Moses was'. (See also on Nu. 10:29-32.) The Kenites (from Heb. *qain*, 'smith') were a nomad people, evidently travelling tinkers, inhabiting the Negeb and Arabah, neighbours of the Amalekites. *The city of palms;* *i.e.* date-palms. This expression usually denotes Jericho (*cf.* 3:13); but the reference here may be to Tamar ('palm'), 85 miles S of Arad. *Which lies in the Negeb near Arad.* *Cf.* the defeat of the king of Arad in Nu. 21:1-3. The Canaanite city of *Arad* is identified by Y. Aharoni with Tell el-Milḥ. **17** *So the name of the city was called Hormah,* *i.e.* 'devotion', in the sense of complete destruction. See Nu. 21:3 for another account, and *cf.* also Nu. 14:45; Dt. 1:44. Aharoni identifies Hormah with Tell el-Meshash, near Tell el-Milḥ; both sites have abundant water supplies quite near and were occupied in the Middle and Late Bronze Age periods. **18** *Judah also took Gaza . . . Ashkelon . . . and Ekron.* These cities, with Ashdod and Gath, were shortly afterwards (early in the 12th century) occupied by the Philistines. **19** *He took possession of the hill country.* The Canaanites continued to maintain their centres of civilization on the lower ground which their iron chariots enabled them to control. Their knowledge of the working of iron, which the Israelites did not acquire till two centuries later, was derived from the Hittites and Mitanni (see Introduction). **20** *And Hebron was given to Caleb.* *Cf.* Jos. 15:13. **21** *But the people of Benjamin did not drive out the Jebusites who dwelt in Jerusalem.* *Cf.* Jos. 15:63 where Judah is named instead of Benjamin. *Cf.* also Jos. 18:28. Jerusalem lay on the tribal border of Judah and Benjamin. The Jebusites were probably an Amorite group who settled on an earlier Hittite foundation in Jerusalem. *The Jebusites have dwelt with the people of Benjamin in Jerusalem to this day.* This suggests a date for this part of Judges earlier than *c.* 1003 BC, when David took the city, although the mixed Hittite–Amorite population continued to live there after that time; *cf.* Araunah the Jebusite (2 Sa. 24:16) whose name has been thought to be an Indo-European Hittite word for 'nobleman', or 'freeman' (*arawanis*).

1:22-26 Capture of Bethel

22 *The house of Joseph also went up against Bethel.* We turn now from southern to central Canaan. Bethel means 'the house of God' (*cf.* Gn. 12:8; 13:3, 4; 28:19; 31:13, *etc.*); the name suggests an ancient sanctuary. Excavations on the site (mod. Beitin) show that the Late Bronze Age city was attacked and burnt in the latter part of the 13th century BC. Here its capture is the first and most notable exploit of the house of Joseph. **26** *And the man went to the land of the Hittites,* *i.e.* into N Syria, beyond the upper Orontes, the boundary between the Hittite and Egyptian Empires. This may indicate that the man was himself a member of the immigrant Hittite population which had settled in the hill country of Judah. The new city of *Luz* which the man founded is unknown, though the place-name Lazi in the Alalaḫ tablets may be connected with it.

1:27-36 Cities which Israel could not take

27 *Manasseh did not drive out . . . Beth-shean . . . Taanach . . . Dor . . . Ibleam . . . Megiddo.* Vv. 27 and 28 are parallel to Jos. 17:11, 12. The cities named formed a line of Canaanite strongpoints across the plain of Esdraelon from E to W, separating the Joseph tribes in central Canaan from the northern tribes. *Beth-shean* was occupied by Egyptian garrisons until the reign of Rameses III (1198-1167 BC). *Taanach*, mod. Tell Ta'annek, *c.* 5 miles SE of Megiddo. Its 12th-century occupation ended *c.* 1125 BC in a violent destruction (*cf.* 5:19); see P. W. Lapp, 'Taanach by the Waters of Megiddo', *The Biblical Archaeologist*, 30, 1967, pp. 2ff. Early in the 12th century *Dor* was occupied by the Tjeker, one of the wandering sea-peoples. *Ibleam*, mod. Khirbet Bil'ameh, *c.* 10 miles SE of Megiddo. *Megiddo* was under Egyptian control during the first half of that century; it was destroyed about the same time as Taanach (*cf.* P. W. Lapp, *loc. cit.*, p. 9).

29 *And Ephraim did not drive out the Canaanites who dwelt in Gezer.* This is parallel to Jos. 16:10. *Gezer*, in the SW of the territory of Ephraim, did not pass under Israelite control until *c.* 950 BC (*cf.* 1 Ki. 9:16). It was conquered by Egypt during the XVIIIth Dynasty and again during the XIXth, according to Merenptah's claim (*c.* 1230 BC). It occupied a strategic position on the road from the coastal plain to Jerusalem *via* the valley of Aijalon.

31 *Asher did not drive out . . . Acco, or . . . Sidon.* It was only along the Phoenician coast that the Canaanites maintained their independence, which they did until the 6th century BC. *Acco* (NT Ptolemais) was used as a port though it had no properly protected harbour. *Sidon* in the time of the judges was more prominent than its sister-city Tyre, which gained the ascendancy by the time of David. *Cf.* Jos. 19:28f. Sidon had been subject to Egypt under the XIXth Dynasty but defected under its ruler Zimri-ada in the Amarna age. It was raided by the Philistines *c.* 1150 BC, and its inhabitants fled to Tyre. **33** *Naphtali did not drive out . . . Beth-shemesh, or . . . Beth-anath.* These were two sanctuaries, the former dedicated to the worship of the sun-god, and identified by J. Garstang with Kedesh–Naphtali of 4:6; the latter dedicated to the worship of Anath, the Canaanite goddess of fertility who appears in the Ras Shamra tablets as the consort of Baal. **34** *The Amorites pressed the Danites into the hill country.* This pressure soon caused the Danites to migrate northwards (see ch. 18). The *Amorites* (*i.e.* 'westerners'—from the Akkadian viewpoint) were Semitic invaders from the Arabian desert who arrived in the Fertile Crescent *c.* 2000 BC. By 1750 they ruled the main cities from Syria to Babylon. **35** The Amorite cities formed a barrier between the Joseph tribes and Judah. **36** Their eastern border is given as *the ascent of Akrabbim* (*i.e.* 'scorpions') in SE Judah near the S of the Dead Sea, the district in which lay the Amorite Hazazon-tamar of Gn. 14:7.

2:1–5 The angel of the Lord at Bochim

1 *Now the angel of the Lord went up from Gilgal to Bochim.* The angel of Yahweh is the expression widely used in the OT to denote Yahweh Himself in His manifestation to men. *Cf.* Jdg. 6:11–24; 13:3–21. *Gilgal* (the name implies the presence of a circle, probably of standing stones) lies between the Jordan and Jericho, possibly on the site of mod. Khirbet el-Mefjir, 1½ miles NE of Jericho. For *Bochim* the original text seems to have had 'Bethel', a reading which is preserved in LXX. This may point to an early movement of the ark and its tent-shrine from Gilgal (Jos. 4:18f.) to Bethel (Jdg. 20:26f.). **2** *You shall make no covenant with the inhabitants of this land.* The words quoted in vv. 2, 3, are part of the terms of Yahweh's covenant with Israel (*cf.* Ex. 23:33; 34:12–16; Nu. 33:55; Dt. 7:2, 5, 16; 12:3). **5** *They called the name of that place Bochim, i.e.* 'weepers'. Some have seen a connection with the 'oak of weeping' below Bethel (Gn. 35:8).

2:6 – 3:6 WHY SOME GENTILE NATIONS WERE LEFT IN THE LAND

2:6–10 The death of Joshua and the elders

6 *When Joshua dismissed the people.* Cf. Jos. 24:28–31 for a parallel to vv. 6–9, with some variation in the sequence of sentences. **10** *And*

there arose another generation after them, who did not know the Lord. Here begins the actual sequel to Joshua. For the language of this verse *cf.* Ex. 1:8.

2:11–13 The idolatry of the Israelites

11 *And the people of Israel did what was evil in the sight of the Lord and served the Baals, i.e.* the local varieties of the chief fertility-god of Canaan (see v. 13). **13** *They forsook the Lord, and served the Baals and the Ashtaroth.* Baal ('lord') was a familiar name for the storm-god Hadad, son of El in the Canaanite mythology. He personified the rain and fertility-forces of nature, and his cult, calculated to ensure the fertilization of the ground by regular rainfall, was marked by the 'sacred marriage' and orgiastic rites operating as a form of sympathetic magic. *Ashtaroth* is the plural of Ashtoreth or Ashtart (Gk. *Astarte*), the deity of the planet Venus, and in Palestine the consort of Baal. (In N Syria, his consort was Anath: see on 1:33.) There was a tendency to turn to Baal-worship in peace-time, as it was thought to ensure good harvests, but the pressure of invasion and war made Israel mindful of the God of their fathers who had led them to victory against all their foes.

2:14–19 Summary of the period of the judges

14 *They could no longer withstand their enemies.* In those periods when they exchanged the invigorating worship of Yahweh for the enervating Baal-worship, the sense of Israelite unity was lost because of the weakening of the covenant-bond which, in binding them to Yahweh, bound them also to each other; they thus presented a divided front to their assailants. **17** *They played the harlot after other gods.* Idolatry is regularly represented as spiritual adultery, as the covenant relation between Yahweh and Israel is conceived of in terms of a marriage.

2:20 – 3:6 The leaving of some nations to prove Israel

21 *I will not henceforth drive out before them any of the nations that Joshua left when he died.* Three reasons are given for Yahweh's allowing the Canaanites to remain in the land alongside Israel: to punish Israel for religious apostasy (2:3, 20, 21); to test Israel's fidelity to Yahweh (2:22; 3:4); to provide Israel with experience in warfare (3:2). Dt. 7:20–24 adds a fourth reason: to prevent the land from becoming a wilderness. **22** *That by them I may test Israel.* What we should express by a clause of result is here (as commonly in Hebrew) expressed by a clause of purpose. **3:1** *That is, all . . . who had no experience of any war in Canaan, i.e.* the generations following that which took part in the invasion and conquest. Here and in v. 2 the slowness of the conquest is represented as providential, to teach succeeding generations the art of war. *Cf.* Ex.

23:29, 30; Dt. 7:22. **3** *The five lords of the Philistines, i.e.* the rulers of the five chief city-states, Ashdod, Ashkelon, Ekron, Gaza and Gath. The word translated *lord* (Heb. *seren*) is not Semitic, but apparently a native Philistine word, taken by them from their Anatolian home. It appears to be cognate with the (pre-Hellenic) Greek *koiranos* or *tyrannos*; *cf.* hieroglyphic Hittite *tarwana*. The *Philistines* seem to have come from Caria in Asia Minor. The Philistine guards of the palace in Jerusalem are called 'Carites' (Heb. *Kārîm*) in 2 Sa. 20:23, RV mg.; 2 Ki. 11:4, 19. The other name, Cherethites, by which they are sometimes called (1 Sa. 30:14; 2 Sa. 8:18), indicates a connection with Crete in the course of their migration southwards (*cf.* Am. 9:7, where God brings up the Philistines from Caphtor, *i.e.* Crete). About 1190 BC they settled in Palestine in territory previously occupied by the Avvim (*cf.* Dt. 2:23). They later expanded N and E, conquering most of Palestine (see Jdg. 13:1). They are depicted on the monuments wearing helmets crowned with feathers, a head-dress which the ancients considered typically Carian. Their armour, as described in 1 Sa. 17:5–7, is reminiscent of that of the Homeric warriors. *And all the Canaanites.* Those mentioned in 1:27–33. *And the Sidonians, i.e.* the Phoenicians, so called because at this time their chief town was Sidon (see on 1:31). *And the Hivites who dwelt on Mount Lebanon.* These have not been identified with absolute certainty. The attempt by A. E. Cowley and A. H. Sayce to equate them with the Achaeans (comparing Heb. *Ḥiwwî* with Hitt. *Aḥḥiyawa*) has not commended itself. They are generally identified with the Horites; either they were a branch of the Horites, or else 'Hivite' wherever it occurs should be amended to 'Horite'. LXX reads 'Hittites' here. The Horites (or Hurrians) invaded northern Mesopotamia and Syria from the eastern highlands; by the 18th century BC they already formed part of the indigenous population in and around Alalaḥ (N Syria). About 1550 BC they established the kingdom of Mitanni in Upper Mesopotamia. Many of the patriarchal customs appear to be of Horite origin. In the 15th and 14th centuries they spread so rapidly in Canaan that one of the Egyptian words for Canaan is *Ḫuru*. In Joshua's day they occupied four cities NW of Jerusalem —the Gibeonite confederacy (Jos. 9:7, 17). *From Mount Baal-hermon as far as the entrance of Hamath.* Mt. Baal-hermon (later Mt. Hermon) is the more easterly range parallel to Lebanon, running SW from Damascus. For *the entrance of Hamath* read 'Labo of Hamath', identified with mod. Lebweh, 14 miles NNE of Baalbek. **4** *They were for the testing of Israel.* See on 2:22. **6** *And they took their daughters to themselves for wives* . . . This procedure was a breach of the early injunction laid down in the covenant of Ex. 34:10–16 (repeated in Dt. 7:1–5).

3:7–11 OPPRESSION UNDER CUSHAN-RISHATHAIM AND DELIVERANCE BY OTHNIEL

7 *And the people of Israel did what was evil in the sight of the Lord.* This section gives us the full formulation of the repeated pattern in which the main episodes of Judges are set, with the bare minimum of detail added: the name of the oppressor, the duration of the oppression, the name of the deliverer, and the length of the ensuing period of 'rest'. *And serving the Baals and the Asheroth,* the male and female vegetation-deities respectively. *Asheroth* is a rare plural of Asherah, a Canaanite goddess who is named in the Ras Shamra tablets as the consort of the supreme god El. Asherah is regularly mistranslated 'grove' in AV, an error which goes back to LXX. Elsewhere the female counterparts of the Baalim are the Ashtaroth (*cf.* 2:13), and Ashtaroth may be the original reading here too (so two Heb. MSS and the Vulg.), the more so as the normal plural of Asherah is Asherim. *Cf.* 6:25. **8** *Cushan-rishathaim king of Mesopotamia* (Heb. *Aram-naharaim*). Egyptian records mention a district called *Qsnrm* (Kushan-rom, 'high Cushan') in the land of Naharen, in N Syria. M. G. Kline suggests that Cushan-rishathaim was a Ḥabiru chief from this area, and that his overthrow by Othniel explains the disappearance of the Ḥabiru as a power to be reckoned with in W Asia (*The Ḥa-BI-ru—Kin or Foe of Israel?*, 1957). But it is strange that a monarch from the north should have been repelled by a hero of S Judah. Possibly a southern invader is intended, *Cushan rosh Teman* ('Cushan chief of Teman'), in which case *Aram* should be emended to *Edom,* as so often elsewhere in the OT. His name has been vocalized in Hebrew so as to give the sense 'Cushan of double-dyed wickedness'. **9** *Othniel the son of Kenaz, Caleb's younger brother, i.e.* the conqueror of Kiriath-sepher and son-in-law of Caleb (*cf.* 1:13). **10** *The Spirit of the Lord came upon him.* Similar language is used in Judges of Gideon (6:34), Jephthah (11:29) and Samson (13:25; 14:6, 19; 15:14); and in 1 Samuel of Saul (10:10; 11:6) and David (16:13). These leaders have therefore been called 'charismatic', since they owed their position to the special power which resulted from an outpouring of the divine grace.

3:12–30 OPPRESSION UNDER EGLON KING OF MOAB AND DELIVERANCE BY EHUD

3:12–14 Oppression under Eglon

12 *And the Lord strengthened Eglon the king of Moab against Israel.* The land of Moab lay E of the Dead Sea, having the Arnon as its northern boundary and the Zered as its southern. Eglon invaded Canaan by the same route as that which the Israelites had followed, crossing the Jordan and occupying the region of Jericho. It was natural, therefore, that his chief opponent,

Ehud, should have been a Benjaminite (v. 15). According to N. Glueck, the kingdom of Moab, like the other Transjordanian kingdoms (Bashan, Heshbon, Ammon, Edom), was founded in the 13th century BC, their inhabitants having previously been nomadic. The Moabite capital was Kir-hareseth. 13 *The Ammonites and the Amalekites*. Ammon, the people most closely related to the Moabites, lived to the NE of them. The Amalekites were nomads (kinsmen of the Edomites) who were centred for long to the S of Canaan. They harassed Israel considerably during the wilderness journey. *The city of palms*, i.e. Jericho (cf. 1:16). There is no question of the rebuilding of Jericho, which lay derelict from its destruction under Joshua until the 9th century (1 Ki. 16:34); what is indicated is a temporary occupation of the oasis at 'Ain es-Sultan.

3:15–30 Deliverance under Ehud the Benjaminite

15 *The Lord raised up for them a deliverer, Ehud, the son of Gera, the Benjaminite, a left-handed man*. The last word is in Hebrew 'iṭṭēr yaḏ yᵉmînô (lit. 'bound of his right hand'). Cf. the same phrase in 20:16, also with reference to Benjaminites. LXX and Vulg. render 'ambidextrous'. *The people of Israel sent tribute by him to Eglon*. Probably to Jericho, to judge by the reference to Gilgal in v. 19. 19 *The sculptured stones near Gilgal*. Hebrew pᵉsîlîm means lit. 'graven (images)' or 'carvings'—perhaps figures carved on the standing stones from which Gilgal received its name (see on 2:1). *Silence*. Hebrew hōs, an onomatopoeic word, like English 'Hush'.

20 *As he was sitting alone in his cool roof chamber* (lit. 'in his upper-chamber of coolness'), a room built on the flat roof, well aired by large windows (cf. the window through which Ahaziah fell in 2 Ki. 1:2). 22, 23 *And the dirt came out* (RV 'And it came out behind'). Better 'and he went out into the porch'. This clause in the Hebrew is so like the following one, *Then Ehud went out into the vestibule*, that they may well be two conflated variant readings of one and the same clause; but there is some doubt of the proper meaning of the two rare words translated 'porch' and 'vestibule'. 24 *He is only relieving himself* (lit. 'surely he is covering his feet'); cf. 1 Sa. 24:3. 25 *They took the key and opened them*. The key was a flat piece of wood furnished with pins corresponding to holes in a hollow bolt. The bolt was on the inside, shot into a socket in the doorpost and fastened by pins which fell into the holes in the bolt from an upright piece of wood (the lock) attached to the inside of the door. To unlock the door one put one's hand in by a hole in the door (cf. Ct. 5:4) and raised the pins in the bolt by means of the corresponding pins in the key. 27 *He sounded the trumpet in the hill country of Ephraim*, which lay N of the territory of Benjamin, and had probably also been invaded by Eglon.

3:31 EXPLOITS OF SHAMGAR BEN ANATH

31 *Shamgar* does not seem to have been an Israelite; the name (Hurrian šimiqari) is repeatedly attested in Nuzian texts. The words *son of Anath* may mean that he was a native of Beth-anath—probably in the south (cf. Jos. 15:59) rather than in Galilee (see on 1:33)—or some other place where Anath had a sanctuary. But even if he was a Canaanite, his attack on the Philistines *delivered Israel*. J. Garstang identified him with Ben Anath, a Syrian sea-captain, son-in-law of Rameses II (c. 1260 BC). In that case, the Philistines whom he attacked must have been an earlier vanguard of the main body which settled on the Palestinian coast fifty years later. (As for the *oxgoad*, Sir C. Marston suggested that that was the name of his ship!) But the identification is highly improbable for chronological and other reasons. Some LXX and other recensions repeat this verse at the end of Jdg. 16 in a more 'Philistine' context; but its present position is more chronologically apposite. That Shamgar was a man of considerable fame is evident from the way in which he is recalled in the Song of Deborah (Jdg. 5:6).

4:1–24 OPPRESSION UNDER JABIN KING OF CANAAN AND DELIVERANCE BY DEBORAH AND BARAK

4:1–3 Oppression under Jabin and Sisera

2 *And the Lord sold them into the hand of Jabin king of Canaan, who reigned in Hazor*. Hitherto the oppressors have come from the E and SE and overrun parts of southern and central Canaan; now we have a northern menace. Hazor (mod. Tell el-Qedah) lies some 4 miles SW of Lake Huleh and was the capital of a Canaanite kingdom which dominated its neighbours; cf. Jos. 11:10 ('Hazor . . . was the head of all those kingdoms'). Its site was identified by Garstang in 1927. It occupied a key position—a large protected camp-enclosure (ḥāṣôr) dating back to Hyksos times—and was connected with Sidon by a permanent road. The site was excavated in 1955–58 by the Israel Exploration Fund under Y. Yadin. The main tell (c. 25 acres) was occupied in the 3rd millennium BC; the large lower area to the north (c. 150 acres) was enclosed and occupied in the early 2nd millennium (probably by the Hyksos); the enlarged city could have accommodated nearly 40,000 inhabitants. The lower city was never reoccupied after its destruction in the 13th century BC—probably under Joshua (cf. Jos. 11:1ff.; v. 13 makes it plain that Joshua also destroyed the settlement on the tell, but that was reoccupied). The Jabin king of Hazor of Jos. 11 led a coalition which was defeated by Joshua at the Water of Merom, which flows into the Sea of Galilee from the NW; the Canaanite army of Jdg. 4 and 5 was defeated in the Kishon valley further W. It is commonly held that Jdg. 4 combines a

victory over Jabin of Hazor by Zebulun and Naphtali with a victory over Sisera of Harosheth by a wider combination of tribes, celebrated in Jdg. 5. The Canaanites here are those mentioned in 1:27, 33 as dwelling among the Manassites and Naphtalites. *The commander of his army was Sisera.* Sisera is a non-Semitic (possibly Illyrian) name. *Harosheth-ha-goiim, i.e.* 'Harosheth of the nations', perhaps El-Haritiyeh, SE of Haifa, or rather the neighbouring Tell el-'Amr (so Albright); another suggestion is Tell el-Harbaj, overlooking the right bank of the Kishon. 3 *For he had nine hundred chariots of iron.* This force of armed vehicles made Sisera invincible until a situation arose in which, instead of being a source of strength, they became a hindrance. The mustering of the united tribes of Israel against him under Barak coincided with a storm in which the Kishon, normally a dry river-bed, rapidly became a raging torrent in which the chariotry was engulfed.

4:4–16 The battle of Kishon

5 *She used to sit under the palm of Deborah.* This should not be confused with the oak under which an earlier Deborah was buried 'below Bethel' (Gn. 35:8). The name Deborah means 'bee'. *And the people of Israel came up to her for judgment.* She was thus a *šōp̄eṭeṯ* in the normal and non-military sense, but the charismatic element was present in her too, as she was a prophetess. 6 *Barak.* The name means 'lightning'; *cf.* Carthaginian Barca. *Kedesh in Naphtali.* A sanctuary identified by Garstang with Bethshemesh of 1:33. *Mount Tabor.* At the meeting-place of the tribal territories of Issachar, Zebulun and Naphtali. 7 *The river Kishon.* A wadi which quickly becomes an impetuous torrent in time of rain; it runs NW through the valley of Jezreel into the Mediterranean on the N side of Mt. Carmel. 11 *Heber the Kenite . . . had separated from the Kenites.* See on 1:16. Here we have a Kenite family separating itself from the main body in the S and coming as far N as the valley of Jezreel to live. If the Kenites still plied their trade as tinkers (denoted by the word *qayin* from which their name is derived), they were probably more mobile than other ethnic groups and neutral in the latter's quarrels. 15 *And the Lord routed Sisera and all his chariots.* The manner of the discomfiture is made plain in the older, poetical version of 5:20–22. A sudden and terrific rainstorm filled the wadi, making it impassable and bogging the chariots. The situation was repeated when Napoleon defeated the Turkish army at the Battle of Mount Tabor on 16 April, AD 1799.

4:17–24 The death of Sisera

18 *She covered him with a rug.* Properly 'with a fly-net' (Heb. *sᵉmīḵāh*). 19 *She opened a skin of milk, i.e.* curds (*cf.* 5:25), the modern 'lebben', which has a markedly soporific effect. 21 *Jael the wife of Heber took a tent peg.* For a more vivid description of his death see 5:26f. The

mallet and tent-peg, for pitching the tent, were ready to her hand, as pitching the tent was a woman's work. *As he was lying fast asleep from weariness. So he died.* The RSV (following AV) is better than RV ('for he was in a deep sleep; so he swooned and died'); it depends, to be sure, on a change in the vocalization (*wᵉyā'ēp̄* for *wayya'ap̄*), but 'he swooned' is not what we should naturally say of a man through whose temples a tent-peg had been driven. 24 *Until they destroyed Jabin king of Canaan.* The prose narrative is continued in 5:31b. The poetical version of Sisera's defeat intervenes.

5:1–31a THE SONG OF DEBORAH AND BARAK

1 *Then sang Deborah and Barak.* This song takes its place alongside other poetical records of episodes in the conquest of Canaan. It may have been preserved, like these, in some such collection as the Book of Jashar (*cf.* Jos. 10:13) or the Book of the Wars of Yahweh (*cf.* Nu. 21:14). These records are practically contemporary with the events they celebrate, and the Song of Deborah is the longest and most important of them. It is the oldest element in Judges, as is evident from its archaic language, some of which was unintelligible as early as the LXX translation of Judges. Attempts have been made by drastic emendation to restore the original form of the song, but few of these have been widely accepted. The song may be divided thus: vv. 2, 3: exordium of praise; 4, 5: invocation of Yahweh; 6–8: the desolation under the oppressors; 9–18: the mustering of the tribes; 19–23: the battle of Kishon; 24–27: the death of Sisera; 28–30: the mother of Sisera awaits his coming; 31a: epilogue.

2 *That the leaders took the lead . . .* The call to join battle in the spirit of their covenant unity went through the northern and central tribes; it was for the various communities, under their leaders, to decide whether to respond or not. The majority on this occasion responded. 4, 5 *Lord, when thou didst go forth from Seir.* The picture is of Yahweh in the midst of the storm-cloud coming to His people's defence from the region where He had first revealed Himself to them, by *the region of Edom* into Canaan. *Cf.* Dt. 33:2; Ps. 68:7ff.; Hab. 3:3ff. *Yon Sinai.* Heb. *zeh sînai*, here and in Ps. 68:8 probably a title of Yahweh, 'the One of Sinai'. 6 *In the days of Shamgar, son of Anath, in the days of Jael.* See on 3:31. We naturally think of Jael as the wife of Heber the Kenite, celebrated in 5:24, but it is strange to find her coupled with Shamgar in this way, and the allusion here may be to someone of an earlier generation, no longer known. 7 *Until you arose, Deborah, arose as a mother in Israel.* The old Hebrew *qamtî* may be second singular feminine as well as first singular, and possibly Deborah is here apostrophised as in v. 12, hence the RSV rendering as against the repeated 'I arose' of AV and RV. From the phrase

a mother in Israel, which is used of a city in 2 Sa. 20:19, it has been inferred that the town of Daberath (Jos. 21:28; 1 Ch. 6:72), mod. Dabûri-yeh, at the W foot of Tabor, was originally meant, but this is quite improbable. **8** *When new gods were chosen, then war was in the gates.* A significant sequence: see on 2:14. *Was shield or spear to be seen among forty thousand in Israel?* This reflects the unarmed state of the Israelites during their twenty years' oppression; *cf.* their disarmament under the Philistines in 1 Sa. 13:19ff. Notice the estimate of the contemporary Israelite manpower; *thousand* (Heb. *'elep̄*) may denote a military division considerably less than a numerical thousand (see on 6:15 and 20:2). **10** *You who ride on tawny asses.* A mark of nobility; *cf.* 10:4; 12:14. **11** *There they repeat the triumphs of the Lord.* His *triumphs* (lit. 'His righteous acts' or 'righteousnesses') are those by which He intervenes for His people to give them salvation and victory. The co-operation of the northern and central tribes was due not only to the pressure of a common foe but also to a common memory of the covenant with Yahweh, which revived at such a time. The song regards all the tribes as worshippers of Yahweh. The word *repeat* or 'chant' (*y°ṯannû*) is an Aramaism, the presence of which in Hebrew of so early a date is noteworthy (*cf.* 11:40). The actual sense is 'sing responsively', and the reference is to the songs of victory sung by the maidens at the wells in the following times of peace. (The same verb probably occurs in Ps. 8:1, 'Thou whose glory above the heavens is chanted'.)

14 *From Ephraim they set out thither into the valley.* This rendering follows the A-text of LXX, which presupposes '*ēmeq* ('valley') for '*°mālēq*; the Hebrew text is represented by RV 'Out of Ephraim came down they whose root is in Amalek'. Some of the Amalekite nomads from the S had, like Heber the Kenite (4:11), left their home and invaded central Canaan (*cf.* 3:13; 6:3f., 33; 12:15). *Following you, Benjamin.* This is probably the battle-cry of the tribe of Benjamin, to be rendered 'After you, Benjamin!' or 'Forward, Benjamin!' (*cf.* Ho. 5:8, RV mg., AV). *From Machir.* Usually E Manasseh; here, perhaps, E and W Manasseh combined. *Those who bear the marshal's staff.* Read with RV mg. 'the staff of the writer' (Heb. *šēḇeṭ sōp̄ēr*). The staff was probably the scribe's wand of office. Reference at this date (*c.* 1125 BC) to a writer is no more surprising than the mention of 'the city of books' in 1:11. Writing, and alphabetic writing at that, had been practised for some centuries along the Syrian coast, from the primitive alphabet of Serabit in the Sinai peninsula (an early form of the original North Semitic alphabet from which the Phoenician and other Semitic alphabets were derived), to the cuneiform alphabet of Ras Shamra (an adaptation of the same North Semitic alphabet). Quantities of papyrus were exported from Egypt to Phoenicia *c.* 1100 BC. *Cf.* Jdg. 8:14. **17** *Gilead stayed beyond the Jordan.* This refers to the tribesmen of Gad who, like their Reubenite neighbours (v. 16), did not take part in the struggle. *And Dan, why did he abide with the ships?* Garstang suggests that the reference is to the later, northern home of the Danites and that the ships were on Lake Huleh; but it is more natural to think of their earlier home on the W coast of Canaan, and even if their northern migration had already taken place (*cf.* 18:1ff.), some of them certainly remained behind (*cf.* 13:2). *Asher sat still at the coast of the sea.* The territory of Asher was soon encroached upon by the Phoenicians.

19 *At Taanach, by the waters of Megiddo*, i.e. by the torrent of Kishon. For *Taanach* and *Megiddo* see on 1:27; both cities were destroyed *c.* 1125 BC, probably as a sequel to the victory celebrated in this song. **20** *From heaven fought the stars, from their courses they fought against Sisera.* The reference is to the cloud-burst which flooded Kishon and swept away Sisera's chariotry; for the language *cf.* that of the poetical fragment of Jos. 10:12ff. **23** *Meroz* has been (very tentatively) identified with Khirbet Marus, between Hazor and Kedesh in Naphtali. Meroz apparently played false to some special obligation resting upon it. (The A-text of LXX reads *Mazōr*, which resembles mod. el-Mazār in the valley of Jezreel.)

24 *Most blessed of women be Jael.* The feminine hand has been discerned in the space allotted in the song to Jael's exploit, as also in the vivid depicting of Sisera's mother (vv. 28ff.). **25** *She brought him curds* (Heb. *ḥem'āh*); see on 4:19. **26** *She put her hand to the tent peg.* This was her left hand, as LXX and other versions say. It is not necessary to conclude that in the parallelism of this verse *hand* must be synonymous with *right hand* and *tent peg* with *workmen's mallet*: Burney aptly compares Pr. 3:16. *She crushed his head.* The verb (Heb. *ḥālap̄*) is used of piercing in Jb. 20:24.

28 *The mother of Sisera gazed through the lattice.* The closing scene of the song is unforgettably vivid and moving. The network of crossed laths which covered the window-opening (the *lattice*) may have been decorated outside in the Egyptian manner. **29** *Nay, she gives answer to herself,* as if to convince herself that all was well; but RV mg., 'Yet she repeateth her words unto herself', may be right; in spite of the ladies' reassuring confidence, her forebodings will not be stilled. **30** *A maiden or two for every man.* The word for *maiden* (Heb. *raḥam*) is found on Mesha's Moabite Stone (*c.* 850 BC) in the same rather contemptuous sense (like Eng. 'wench'). *Dyed stuffs embroidered.* The Hebrews excelled in the art of dyeing, as is evident from the description of the wilderness tent of meeting and the priestly robes. They may have acquired the art from the Egyptians. Excavation reveals that wool dyeing was a leading industry in Debir and Benjamite Mizpah. *For my neck as spoil* (lit. 'on the necks of the spoil', as RV). The changing of one vowel-point gives the more probable reading followed by RSV. **31a** *So perish* *all thine enemies, O Lord!* The epilogue of the song, invoking a malison on Yahweh's enemies and blessing on His friends, is markedly parallel to Ps. 68:1–3; *cf.* also the war-chant which accompanied the ark's advance (Nu. 10:35).

5:31b – 8:32 OPPRESSION UNDER MIDIAN AND DELIVERANCE BY GIDEON

5:31b – 6:6 The Midianite oppression

31b *And the land had rest for forty years.* This is actually the conclusion of the prose narrative of Jabin's overthrow, following on from 4:24. **6:2** *And the hand of Midian prevailed over Israel.* The Midianites were nomads from the desert who for the first time were using domesticated camels on a large scale. This made long-distance raids easy. They probably came from their home round the head of the Gulf of Aqabah (*cf.* Ex. 2:15ff.) N through Transjordan, by the same route as that previously taken by the Israelites, crossing the Jordan and invading central Canaan, penetrating as far W as Gaza (v. 4). It may have been on their way through Transjordan, in the land of Moab, that they met the defeat at the hands of Hadad I, king of Edom, mentioned in Gn. 36:35. *The people of Israel made for themselves the dens which are in the mountains,* an explanation of the rock-dwellings in the hill country of Ephraim and Judah. 3 *The Amalekites and the people of the East.* These had attached themselves to the Midianites. For the *Amalekites* see on 3:13; they seem to have made a habit of joining invasions of Canaan from Transjordan. *The people of the East* (Heb. *benê qeḏem*) is a general description of the nomads in the Syrian desert. *Cf.* Gn. 29:1, where however, the expression is used of the pastoral people of Upper Mesopotamia. *Cf.* the Egyptian tale of Sinuhe who *c.* 1900 BC found refuge with an Amorite chieftain who lived a semi-nomadic life in the country of Qedem. 5 *Like locusts for number.* The simile is apt, for it suggests their destructiveness as well as their multitude.

6:7–10 The prophet

8 *The Lord sent a prophet to the people of Israel.* The message of the prophet is not unlike that of the angel at Bochim. The words in the latter half of v. 8 are reminiscent of the preamble to the Ten Commandments (Ex. 20:2). 9 *I delivered you from the hand of the Egyptians.* Some have seen here a reference to encounters with the Egyptians in Canaan, but this is not necessarily implied; the Exodus satisfies the reference. 10 *I said to you.* The following words summarize once more the injunctions of Ex. 34:10–16; Dt. 7:1ff. *Cf.* Jdg. 3:5, 6.

6:11–24 The angel of the Lord visits Gideon

11 *The angel of the Lord.* See on 2:1. *Under the oak at Ophrah.* For this kind of oak or 'terebinth' (Heb. *'ēlāh*), a sacred tree, *cf.* Gn. 13:18; 14:13; 18:1; 35:8; Ho. 4:13. Ophrah is not certainly known; one suggested site is Et-taiyibeh, 8

miles NW of Beth-shan. *Joash the Abiezrite.* Abiezer was a sub-tribe of Manasseh, belonging to the western division of that tribe (*cf.* 5:14). *His son Gideon was beating out wheat in the wine press.* Probably with a staff or rod, a method sometimes used for small quantities of grain (*cf.* Ru. 2:17). 13 *Where are all his wonderful deeds which our fathers recounted to us?* For the language as well as the general sentiment, *cf.* Ps. 44:1ff. 14 *And the Lord turned to him.* This alternation between Yahweh's angel and Yahweh Himself is common in such theophanic narratives. 15 *My clan,* 'my *'elep̄*' (as in Mi. 5:2); the same word as is usually translated 'thousand', though it may not always have this strict numerical sense (see on 5:8 and 20:2). 18 *My present.* Hebrew *minḥāh* is an unusual term for a meal, but natural if an offering to a divine being is intended. 20 *Put them on this rock, and pour the broth over them.* The surface of the rock served as an improvised altar. The broth may have been poured as a libation into one of the cup-shaped rock-hollows which are found in Palestine and England alike. 21 *The angel of the Lord vanished from his sight.* For the whole theophany, as for its closing scene, *cf.* Jdg. 13:3–21. 22 *Alas, O Lord God!* For the fear of death and divine reassurance *cf.* Jdg. 13:22f. *Cf.* also Ex. 33:20, 'man shall not see me and live'. 24 *The Lord is peace.* Heb. *Yahweh šālôm,* the name being here connected with the words *Peace be to you* (Heb. *šālôm leḵā*) of v. 23.

6:25–32 Gideon overthrows the altar of Baal

25 *Take your father's bull, the second bull seven years old.* The evidence of the versions indicates *šāmēn,* 'fat' (*cf.* Lk. 15:23), instead of *šēnî,* 'second', as the original text here and in vv. 26, 28. The animal was probably reserved for sacrifice. *Pull down the altar of Baal . . ., and cut down the Asherah that is beside it.* For *Baal* and *Asherah* see on 2:13 and 3:7. We are here confronted by a situation in which Yahwism and Baalism have been syncretized, Yahweh being perhaps regarded as one of the Baalim. Joash has a name containing Yahweh ('Yahweh has given'), but he erects an altar to Baal and an image (or sacred pole) of Asherah, and calls his son Jerubbaal ('May Baal give increase') which, as a result of the present iconoclasm, is given the new significance 'Let Baal contend' (see on v. 32). **26** *On the top of the stronghold here, with stones laid in due order.* On the altar thus erected, in accordance with the directions of Ex. 20:25, was piled the wood of the Asherah which Gideon cut down, and on that the bullock was laid and consumed. **31** *Shall be put to death by morning.* It was perhaps evening before the demolition of Baal's altar was brought home to Gideon. Joash evidently held considerable authority in the community; probably he knew his neighbours well enough to realize that, if he gave a decisive lead, they would follow. *Let him contend for himself.* For the irony, *cf.* 11:24; also 1 Ki. 18:27. **32** *He was called Jerubbaal.* The name acquires a new sense, as the equivalent of 'Let Baal contend' (Heb. *yāreḇ Ba'al*). In 2 Sa. 11:21 it appears as Jerubbesheth, in accordance with the convention of replacing Baal by *bešeṯ, bōšeṯ,* 'shame' (as in Ishbosheth, Mephibosheth, *etc.*).

6:33–35 Gideon gathers an army

33 *Crossing the Jordan they encamped in the Valley of Jezreel.* It was probably at this time that the Midianites killed Gideon's brothers at Tabor (8:18). **34** *But the Spirit of the Lord took possession of Gideon* (lit. 'clothed himself with Gideon'). An expression repeated in 1 Ch. 12:18; 2 Ch. 24:20. It denotes complete possession; Gideon becomes the garment of the Spirit and thus enters the succession of Israel's charismatic leaders. **35** *And they went up to meet them.* Practically all northern Israel is indicated; the omission of Ephraim, the most powerful of the central tribes, is noteworthy in view of the sequel.

6:36–40 Gideon's fleece

39 *Let me speak but this once.* For the language *cf.* Gn. 18:32. Gideon may have reflected after the former sign that, as the rocky threshing-floor would in any case dry more quickly than the fleece, it was not really a 'sign'; the reverse result would be truly remarkable.

7:1–8 The reduction of Gideon's army

1 *The spring of Harod, i.e.* the spring of trembling, possibly referring to v. 3, *Whoever is fearful and trembling* (Heb. *ḥārēḏ*). It may be identified with 'Ain Jalud, which springs from the foot of Mt. Gilboa (probably the 'fountain' of 1 Sa. 29:1). *The hill of Moreh* ('the oracle-giver') may be Jebel Neḇi Daḥi to the N of Gilboa, across the valley of Jezreel. **3** *'Let him return home.' And Gideon tested them.* This last clause is based on a conjectural emendation. The Hebrew text is rendered in RV: 'Let him return and depart from mount Gilead.' The only Gilead known to us is in N Transjordan. Was there another Gilead in Naphtali? C. F. Burney reads 'Galud' ('coward'?) here; *cf.* mod. 'Ain Jalud. Another suggestion is to emend to 'Gilboa'. **4** *I will test them for you there.* The nature of the test is not quite clear in the MT; to lap with one's tongue like a dog (v. 5) cannot be done by putting one's hand to one's mouth (v. 6). Kneeling to drink and lapping might 'seem to amount to criminal carelessness in presence of the enemy' (Burney); the 300 who conveyed water from the spring to their mouths in their cupped hands would be able to keep a wary eye open for sudden attack. But we should bear in mind the possibility that the test was quite arbitrary: God might thus make trial of Gideon's unquestioning obedience and show him His power to use as His instruments any whom He pleased.

7:9–14 Gideon in the camp of Midian

12 *Like locusts . . . as the sand.* Cf. 6:5. The numerical analogies are typical oriental hyperbole. **13** *A man was telling a dream to his comrade.*

Dreams were treated as of high importance; it is clear throughout the OT that a dream has an interpretation, though that cannot always be discovered. *A cake of barley bread, i.e.* a 'scone' or 'bannock'. Barley was the commonest cereal in Palestine and barley bread was the staple food of the poorer people.

7:15–25 Gideon's victory

16 *He divided the three hundred men into three companies.* The threefold division of forces appears elsewhere in the OT; *cf.* 1 Sa. 11:11; 2 Sa. 18:2. The surprise attack by night is also illustrated in 1 Sa. 11:11. Here the sudden appearance of the lights at close quarters, the sound of the trumpets, and the war-cry from 300 throats, 'For the Lord and for Gideon', struck panic into the Midianites. The *trumpets* were horns of cattle or of rams (Heb. *šôp̄ārôṯ*). The pitchers (*empty jars*) served the double purpose of guarding the torches from the wind and hiding the light until the critical moment. **19** *The beginning of the middle watch.* Implying a division into three watches, of about four hours each. The time therefore was about 10 p.m. **22** *As far as Beth-shittah.* The places mentioned cannot be certainly identified, but it is obvious that the Midianites fled towards Jordan, and crossed it (*cf.* v. 24) at points where their retreat could best be cut off by men of Ephraim. **23** For the tribes named *cf.* 6:35. **25** *Oreb and Zeeb.* Meaning 'raven' and 'wolf' respectively. 'The slaughter of Midian at the rock of Oreb' is remembered in Is. 10:26; *cf.* also the reference to 'the day of Midian' in Is. 9:4, alluding to this same rout. The sites of the *rock of Oreb* and the *wine press of Zeeb* are unknown. *And they brought the heads of Oreb and Zeeb to Gideon beyond the Jordan, i.e.* in Transjordan, where he had gone in pursuit of the Midianite kings Zebah and Zalmunna (8:4).

8:1–3 The Ephraimites' complaint

1 *What is this that you have done to us . . . ?* The Ephraimites seem to have thought that the failure to enlist their aid at the outset was calculated to deprive them of the honour of a share in the victory; perhaps also they did not like the idea of a strong 'northern bloc' from which they were excluded. Gideon, however, speaks them fair and appeases their resentment. His treatment of them is in striking contrast to Jephthah's later on (12:1ff.).

8:4–21 Pursuit and capture of Zebah and Zalmunna

4 *Faint yet pursuing.* Possibly we should read with some of the versions 'faint and famished'. **5** *The men of Succoth.* This place (meaning 'booths') lay in Transjordan, N of the Jabbok. *Zebah and Zalmunna, the kings of Midian,* vocalized so as to mean 'sacrifice' and 'shelter withheld'. **7** *I will flail your flesh,* perhaps by laying them on a carpet of thorns and threshing them as corn is threshed. **8** *Penuel.* Some 5 miles E of Succoth (*cf.* Gn. 32:30f.), probably to be identified with the more easterly of the two mounds called Tulul edh-Dhahab. **9** *I will break down this tower.* The tower of Penuel was an Amorite fortification of *c.* 1700 BC (the same period as the Tower of Shechem, 9:6, 46ff.); it was rebuilt by Jeroboam I (1 Ki. 12:25). The site was strongly fortified, commanding the entrance into the Jordan valley from the Jabbok gorge. **10** *Now Zebah and Zalmunna were in Karkor.* The place is not known, but must have been near *Nobah and Jogbehah* (v. 11). The name of *Jogbehah* is preserved in mod. Jubeihât, 6 miles NW of Amman. The site of *Nobah* is identified with a 'tell' near Safut. **11** *For the army was off its guard; cf.* 18:7, 27. **12** *Threw all the army into a panic* (Heb. *heḥᵉrîḏ*). Burney (unnecessarily) emends to *heḥᵉrîm* ('devoted' or 'destroyed utterly'); so Josephus (*Ant.* v. 228), 'he destroyed all the enemy'. **13** *By the ascent of Heres. Heres* is a rare word for 'sun', hence AV 'before the sun was up'. The words may be a scribal doublet of the last clause of v. 12. **14** *He wrote down for him the officials and elders of Succoth.* The AV translation ' "described" ' has obscured to the English reader an important biblical item on the early diffusion of the alphabet' (J. A. Montgomery). It was the invention of alphabetic writing (see on 5:14) that enabled ordinary people to read and write. The older ideographic and syllabic scripts were by their very nature the preserve of a specialized class. The youth possibly *wrote down* a list of the chief men of Succoth on a piece of pottery. **16** *And with them taught the men of Succoth,* as though the verb had its usual sense 'caused to know' (hiph'il of *yāḏaʿ*); but D. W. Thomas points out an alternative meaning of this root: 'made quiet or submissive' (*cf.* Jdg. 16:9; 1 Sa. 14:12). **18** *Where are the men whom you slew at Tabor?* See on 6:33. **19** *As the Lord lives,* or 'by the life of Yahweh'; the form of oath implies belief in Yahweh as 'the living God'. **21** *For as the man is, so is his strength.* It would be an honour to die by the hand of a warrior like Gideon, who besides might be trusted to kill them at one blow, and not bungle the business as the boy might. *The crescents that were on the necks of their camels.* These 'little moons' (LXX) were probably threaded on necklaces and worn as amulets. They may indicate that these bedouin were moon-worshippers.

8:22–32 Gideon's rule over Israel

22 *You and your son and your grandson.* It is a hereditary monarchy that Gideon is invited to set up. **23** What is ostensibly Gideon's refusal might be an oblique acceptance (*cf.* Gn. 23:6, 11, 15); whichever his own attitude was, his son Abimelech attempted to perpetuate his father's ascendancy (9:1–6). *The Lord will rule over you.* For the idea of God as Israel's sole king *cf.* 1 Sa. 10:19. **24** *Because they were Ishmaelites.* Possibly trading nomads. This is a striking parallel to the interchange of the terms 'Midianites' and 'Ishmaelites' in the story of the sale of Joseph

(Gn. 37:25ff.; 39:1). Both Ishmael and Midian are recorded as sons of Abraham. **26** *One thousand seven hundred shekels of gold.* About 42 lb avoirdupois. **27** *And Gideon made an ephod.* Possibly here and in 17:5 *ephod* means something different from the priestly vestment called by that name; in any case, an ephod of gold would scarcely be meant for wearing. Whatever it was, it was apparently used for divination. **31** *His concubine who was in Shechem also bore him a son.* The chief difference between his other *seventy sons* (v. 30) and Abimelech was probably that their descent was reckoned through the male line, and his through the female. They would belong to their father's clan of Abiezer, he to his mother's Shechemite family; *i.e.* he was the son of a *ṣadîqa* marriage (see on 14:2).

8:33 – 9:57 THE STORY OF ABIMELECH

33 *As soon as Gideon died.* In 8:33–35 the author gives an ethical summary of the following narrative. *Baal-berith.* See on 9:4 and 46. **9:1** *Now Abimelech the son of Jerubbaal went to Shechem to his mother's kinsmen.* If Gideon himself declined a hereditary monarchy, some of his family had other ideas; *cf.* v. 2 where Abimelech appears to envisage the possibility of the sons who belonged to the Abiezer clan exercising a condominium over that part of the country. Abimelech, however, who retained his mother's Shechemite citizenship, forestalled any possible attempt by his Abiezrite brothers by killing them; and he established a kingdom with its centre at Shechem. *Shechem* (mod. Balâtah) was first settled in the 4th millennium BC; the earliest inhabitants have left nothing but pottery comparable to the 'Neolithic B' pottery found at Jericho (although this was the Chalcolithic Age in N Syria and Mesopotamia). It was occupied continuously throughout the Middle and Late Bronze Age. At Shechem Abram built his first altar after arriving in Canaan (Gn. 12:6, 7). It was seized by the sons of Jacob before the descent into Egypt (Gn. 34:25ff.; *cf.* Gn. 48:22). In the Tell el-Amarna correspondence (*c.* 1370 BC) Shechem is allied with the Ḥabiru. Although there is no record of its being captured by Joshua, it figures as a religious centre after the conquest. The Israelites under Joshua possibly found it occupied by their kinsmen, and it entered the Israelite covenant-league as a separate city-state. Shechem appears in Jos. 20:7; 21:21 as a Levitical city and city of refuge; the blessings and cursings were recited on the hills Ebal and Gerizim which overlook it (Jos. 8:30–35); there Joshua gathered all Israel before his death (Jos. 24:1), and there Joseph's bones were buried (Jos. 24:32). The name of the place means 'shoulder', from its position on the saddle between Ebal and Gerizim. It is 'the natural capital of Canaan' (A. T. Olmstead), 'the uncrowned queen of Palestine' (A. Alt). Its importance continued to be observed by the Samaritans, who made it their holy city; it is at the adjacent Greek foundation of Neapolis (mod. Nablus) that the Samaritan community survives to this day. (See G. E. Wright, *Shechem: The Biography of a Biblical City*, 1965.) **4** *The house of Baal-berith.* The divine name (Baal or 'lord' of the covenant) refers to the confederacy in which Shechem was associated with her neighbours (*cf.* v. 46). The 'house' or temple is identified with G. E. Wright's 'Temple 2b', first located by E. Sellin in 1926, which was completely destroyed at the end of the Late Bronze Age. **5** *Upon one stone.* A mass public execution is implied. **6** *Beth-millo, i.e.,* 'house of the fortress', probably the same as the Tower of Shechem in v. 46. (*Millo* is a fortress set upon a 'filling'; *cf.* 2 Sa. 5:9; 1 Ki. 9:15, 24; 11:27.) *All Beth-millo* in that case would be one group of *all the citizens of Shechem. And made Abimelech king, by the oak of the pillar at Shechem.* The oak or terebinth was no doubt a sacred tree (that of Gn. 12:6; 35:4?) associated with a standing-stone (that of Jos. 24:26?). The standing-stone was probably the large pillar (*maṣṣēḇāh*) which stood in the Temple court (two smaller ones stood on either side of the door). The kingdom of Abimelech was not an extensive one; it hardly extended beyond W Manasseh. **7** *On the top of Mount Gerizim.* The sacred mountain of the Samaritans (*cf.* Jn. 4:20f.) lay SW of the city. *Cried aloud.* By standing on one of the cliffs overhanging Shechem Jotham would make himself heard by the citizens. **8** *The trees once went forth to anoint a king over them.* For this type of fable *cf.* that of King Joash in 2 Ki. 14:9. The fable reflects a poor opinion of the value of kingship. The *bramble* (v. 15; 'briar'), which is good for nothing else, has the necessary leisure to become king of the trees, but it cannot afford them shelter, and is more likely to catch fire and involve them all in its ruin. Trees which perform some useful service (as Gideon had done) have no time to become king. This contempt for monarchy may well reflect an early date. The fable is cast in rhythmical form. **10** *The fig tree.* The commonest fruit-tree of Palestine. **13** *My wine which cheers gods and men.* It cheered gods by being offered to them in libations. **18** *Abimelech, the son of his maidservant.* Jotham uses a word meaning 'slave-concubine', deliberately ascribing to her a status inferior to her real one, as implied in 8:31. **21** *Went to Beer and dwelt there. Beer* simply means 'well' and the name is therefore widespread; this one may be El-Bireh, between Shechem and Jerusalem.

23 *The men of Shechem dealt treacherously with Abimelech.* They broke their agreement with him by revolting against him and reverted 'to their Bronze Age, city-state pattern of government' (G. E. Wright). **25** *And they robbed all who passed by them along that way.* Thus depriving Abimelech of the dues which he exacted from merchants passing through his realm. **26** *Gaal the son of Ebed.* He offers himself as leader to the native Shechemites against Abimelech

and his governor Zebul. **27** *And they went out into the field.* The time of grape-harvest is meant, when the grapes were gathered and trodden in the wine-vats—the Shechemite counterpart to the Israelite Feast of Ingathering or Tabernacles. The ensuing merry-making was chosen as an occasion for throwing off their allegiance to Abimelech. **28** *Did not* (better 'Should not') *the son of Jerubbaal and Zebul his officer serve the men of Hamor the father of Shechem?* In spite of the massacre of Gn. 34:25f., the Shechemites still maintain the connection with *Hamor*, the ancestor of their clan. Hamor means 'ass'; Albright points out that the sacrifice of an ass was an essential feature of a treaty among the Amorites in the 18th century BC, and compares the evidence of a Shechemite federal treaty in the name Baal-berith. **31** *And he sent messengers to Abimelech at Arumah.* It appears that Abimelech did not live in Shechem, but in Arumah (v. 41, sometimes identified with El 'Ormeh, between Shechem and Shiloh), and set Zebul over Shechem as his lieutenant-governor: this may partly account for the Shechemites' hostility to him. **34** *Laid wait against Shechem in four companies.* So the contingent in the city under Zebul was literally a 'fifth column'. **37** *Look, men are coming down from the centre of the land.* The *centre* (or 'navel') *of the land* is the round summit of Gerizim, regarded as the central eminence of the hill country of central Canaan. The *Diviners' Oak* or terebinth may be the 'oak' (terebinth) of Moreh' (Gn. 12:6).

42 *The men went out into the fields,* where they were attacked and slaughtered by two of Abimelech's detachments, approaching from two directions, while the third detachment breached the city gate. **45** *He razed the city and sowed it with salt.* The destruction of Late Bronze Age Shechem is archaeologically attested late in the 12th century BC. The sowing *with salt* was a symbolic sentence of infertility as a punishment for the city's breach of covenant with Abimelech. It was rebuilt by Jeroboam I as his first capital after the disruption of the monarchy (1 Ki. 12:25). **46** *The Tower of Shechem.* This was probably the Beth-millo of v. 6. The narrative of vv. 46–49 might be a sequel to what precedes, or an incident in it; archaeological evidence favours the latter alternative. The tower or temple-fortress was situated on the acropolis of the city. What the people of the tower *heard* was probably Abimelech's breaching of the city gate and entrance into the SE quarter of the city. *The stronghold of the house of El-berith* was probably part of the Tower of Shechem or Beth-millo. El as a divine title is found widely distributed over Palestine at an early date. The supreme god bears this name in the Ras Shamra tablets and in the Phoenician historian Sanchuniathon. We gather that at Shechem it was El who was invoked as patron of the federal union, and who thus came to be called El-berith ('God of the covenant') or, as in v. 4, Baal-berith ('Lord of the covenant'). **48** *Mount Zalmon.* Its name means 'shaded', perhaps because of the woods which covered its slopes (*cf.* the Transjordanian Zalmon of Ps. 68:14). The present Zalmon cannot be certainly identified; it may have been a peak of Gerizim, or perhaps Jebel el-Kebir. **50** *Then Abimelech went to Thebez.* Mod. Ṭûbâs, *c.* 10 miles NE of Nablus, on the road to Beth-shan. This town, a dependency of Shechem, had joined in the revolt against Abimelech. **51** *There was a strong tower within the city*, which served as a place of refuge like that in Shechem. **53** *A certain woman threw an upper millstone.* Lit. 'a stone of riding' (Heb. *pelaḥ rekeḇ*). *Cf.* 2 Sa. 11:21, where an allusion is made to this incident as a warning against going too near the wall of a besieged fort or city. **54** *Draw your sword and kill me.* *Cf.* Saul's request to his armour-bearer to prevent the Philistines from taking him alive (1 Sa. 31:4). **55** *The men of Israel.* The rebels were native Shechemites; the Israelite population perhaps supported Abimelech because of his relation to Gideon. **56** *Thus God requited the crime of Abimelech.* The author of Judges draws a moral after his fashion.

10:1–5 TOLA AND JAIR: MINOR JUDGES

1 *There arose to deliver Israel Tola the son of Puah, son of Dodo, a man of Issachar.* *Tola* was a tribal name; a son of Issachar is named Tola in Gn. 46:13, *etc.* *Dodo* ('beloved') is perhaps the same name as David. These minor judges (Tola and Jair in this chapter and Ibzan, Elon and Abdon in ch. 12) have no mighty deeds recorded of them, such as are told of the great judges. Their function may have been more purely judicial: Albright describes them as 'intertribal arbitrators'. We may compare Samuel, who later in the 11th century went in circuit from place to place judging Israel (1 Sa. 7:15–17). E. Robertson, less convincingly, calls them 'military leaders holding office at a time when no military activity was called for', and hazards the suggestion that they were appointed by the high priest of the time, a suggestion supported (for what it is worth) by Samaritan tradition. **3** *Jair the Gileadite.* Gilead in the tribal genealogies is the son of Machir, who was Manasseh's son by an Aramaean concubine. Jair is the same name as NT Jairus. **4** *And he had thirty sons.* That these should ride on ass-colts is intended as a mark of distinction; *cf.* what is said of Abdon's sons and grandsons in 12:14. *Called Havvoth-jair, i.e.* the tent-villages of Jair. In Nu. 32:41; Dt. 3:14 and 1 Ch. 2:23 Havvoth-jair is associated with Jair the grandson of Judah's grandson Hezron who married a daughter of Machir. **5** *And was buried in Kamon.* Probably Qamm in Gilead.

10:6 – 12:7 OPPRESSION UNDER AMMON AND DELIVERANCE BY JEPHTHAH

10:6–18 The Ammonite oppression

7 *He sold them into the hand of the Philistines and*

into the hand of the Ammonites. The *Philistines* invaded the Israelite territory W of Jordan from the coastal plain where they had settled over a century before, while the *Ammonites* overran the Israelite territory in Transjordan. The Ammonite menace is dealt with first, as that was quickly crushed—for the present, at any rate—but we find a recrudescence of the Ammonite threat some decades later, at the beginning of Saul's reign (1 Sa. 11:1ff.). The Ammonites, like their Moabite kinsmen and other Transjordanian neighbours, appear to have organized themselves as a kingdom in the 13th century BC. In their present invasion of Israelite territory they were apparently accompanied by the Moabites (see on 11:15 and 24), as Eglon had been by the Ammonites (3:13). **11** *And the Lord said to the people of Israel.* Probably by the mouth of a prophet, as in 6:8ff. *Did I not deliver you from the Egyptians and from the Amorites, from the Ammonites and from the Philistines?* References respectively to the Exodus, the overthrow of Sihon (see on 11:13ff.), and the deliverance under Ehud (3:13) and Shamgar (3:31). **12** *The Sidonians also, and the Amalekites, and the Maonites, oppressed you.* There is no other reference to a Sidonian oppression; for Amalek *cf.* 3:13; 6:3. For *Maonites* LXX has 'Midianites'; the name may be associated with mod. Ma'an near Petra (*cf.* 1 Ch. 4:41; 2 Ch. 20:1; 26:7). **16** *He became indignant . . .* Lit. 'short', *i.e.* impatient.

17 *And the people of Israel came together, and they encamped in Mizpah.* Mizpah ('watchtower') may be identical with the Mizpah where Jacob and Laban piled the 'cairn of witness' (Gn. 31:46ff.), and also with Ramath-Mizpeh or Ramoth-Gilead (Dt. 4:43; Jos. 13:26; 1 Ki. 4:13), *c.* 40 miles N of Amman.

11:1–11 Jephthah chosen as captain

1 *Jephthah.* Hebrew *yiptāḥ*, probably shortened from *yiptaḥ-'Ēl*, 'God opens (*sc.* the womb)' which is cited as a proper name in Sabean. *The son of a harlot.* Therefore, like Abimelech, he was half-Canaanite, and not acknowledged as a member of his father's clan. **3** *The land of Tob.* Probably to the N of the kingdom of Ammon, on the E of Transjordanian Manasseh. *Worthless fellows collected round Jephthah.* These 'empty men' were probably 'broken men', such as later gathered to David in the cave of Adullam, men for various reasons severed from their clans or other communities. *And went raiding with him.* Jephthah, in other words, was a brigand chief. **6** *Come and be our leader.* Hebrew *qāṣîn*, cognate with Arab *qadi*, one who gives a legal decision; LXX renders *archēgos*, applied to Christ four times in the NT. **11** *And Jephthah spoke all his words before the Lord at Mizpah.* A solemn compact was made at this sanctuary between Jephthah and the elders of Gilead, they confirming with an oath their undertaking to make him their ruler, and he similarly swearing a sort of 'coronation oath'.

11:12-28 Jephthah's protest to the king of Ammon

13 *Because Israel . . . took away my land.* The reference, as we gather from Jephthah's reply, is to the territory of Sihon, which (according to Nu. 21:26-30) Sihon had taken from the Moabites. From this and the mention of Chemosh in v. 24 it is commonly inferred that vv. 12-28 originally concerned a dispute with the Moabites, in which case *or the land of the Ammonites* (v. 15) would be an editorial addition. But if we take the text as it stands, it is plain that both Moab and Ammon were engaged in this dispute with Israel. *From the Arnon to the Jabbok and to the Jordan.* The southern, northern and western boundaries respectively of Sihon's kingdom, which was bounded on the east by Ammon. Sihon may well have carved out his kingdom at the expense of Ammon as well as of Moab. **15** *Israel did not take away the land of Moab or the land of the Ammonites.* Indicating (as has been said) a Moabite-Ammonite association at this time. **16** *Went through the wilderness to the Red Sea, i.e.* the *yam sûp* ('sea of reeds'), here (as in Nu. 33:10f.) the Gulf of Aqabah. No mention is made here of the events at Sinai, as they were irrelevant for Jephthah's purpose. *And came to Kadesh, i.e.* Kadesh-barnea, to the S of the Negeb, on the border of the kingdom of Edom. **17** *Israel then sent messengers to the king of Edom.* Cf. Nu. 20:14-21. *And they sent also to the king of Moab.* This is not recorded in the Pentateuch. The Israelites accepted the unfavourable answer given by their kinsfolk the Edomites and Moabites, but took violent action against the Amorite Sihon when he did the same. **18** *The wilderness, i.e.* of Zin. *And went around the land of Edom and the land of Moab, i.e.* passing S and E of Edom and E of Moab, instead of following the 'king's high way' which ran from S to N through these kingdoms and the kingdoms of Sihon and Og. Cf. Nu. 21:4, 13. Strong fortresses barred the way on the frontiers of the kingdoms of Edom and of Moab. It must have been spring when Israel journeyed E of those territories, for only then could enough water and grazing have been found. *The Arnon was the boundary of Moab.* On the N, dividing it from Sihon's kingdom, and later from the territory of Reuben.
19 *Israel then sent messengers to Sihon.* Cf. Nu. 21:21ff. *Heshbon.* Mod. Hesbān, 16 miles E of Jordan and 24 miles N of Arnon. **20** *Jahaz.* This place (not yet identified) is mentioned on the Moabite Stone as an outpost of the king of Israel against Moab, and later taken by Mesha and added to Dibon, which was 4 miles N of Arnon. **22** *From the Arnon to the Jabbok.* In the division of the land the northern part of this territory went to Gad and the southern to Reuben. **24** *Will you not possess what Chemosh your god gives you to possess?* Chemosh was the god of the Moabites, the Ammonite deity being Milcom (1 Ki. 11:5). Jephthah's language does not necessarily mean that he himself regarded

Chemosh and Yahweh as national deities on an equal footing, though it would not be surprising if a half-Canaanite like Jephthah did take this attitude. Mesha, on the Moabite Stone, ascribes his defeats and victories to the anger and favour of Chemosh. Jephthah argues that the two deities had shown their will—Yahweh by giving Israel victory over Sihon, and Chemosh by not enabling Moab to resist Sihon's earlier encroachments. In either case the divine will must be accepted as a *fait accompli*. The very fact that Yahweh had done more for Israel than Chemosh had been able to do for Moab proved the superior power of Yahweh. Certainly the author of Judges (and possibly even Jephthah himself) did not believe in the independent existence of Chemosh, but for the sake of the argument ironically took Chemosh at his worshippers' valuation and showed that, even so, he was not much of a god (*cf.* 6:31). The appeal to this passage as a 'parade example' against Israelite monotheism is inept: 'the objectivity of the approach *ad hominem* is entirely characteristic of Hebrew thought and literature before the Exile' (W. F. Albright, *From the Stone Age to Christianity*, 1946, p. 220). **25** *Are you any better than Balak . . . ?* The fact that the king of Moab at the time of the overthrow of Sihon made no attempt to reclaim the land won by Israel from Sihon, even if it had previously been Moabite territory, is a strong argument against the present claim. **26** *Aroer.* The southernmost 'city' of Sihon's kingdom, on the N bank of the Arnon. *Three hundred years.* An inclusive number indicating that they were now in the 3rd century since the events referred to; the actual interval may have been about 150 years.

11:29-40 Jephthah's victory and vow

29 *Then the Spirit of the Lord came upon Jephthah,* who thus enters the list of the charismatic leaders. *And he passed through Gilead and Manasseh.* Probably W as well as E Manasseh, to raise his army. *And passed on to Mizpah of Gilead* (reading Heb. *'el* for *'et*), where the Israelite camp was (10:17), from which *he passed on to the Ammonites.* **30** *And Jephthah made a vow to the Lord.* It is customary to cite the similar story told by Servius (Latin commentator on Virgil) about Idomeneus, king of Crete, who was caught in a storm while returning home from the Trojan War, and vowed to sacrifice to the gods in return for his safety whatever should first meet him on his arrival home. This proved to be his son. **33** *And he smote them from Aroer to the neighbourhood of Minnith . . . and as far as Abel-keramim, i.e.* 'the plain of vineyards'. Aroer is on the north bank of the Arnon, 4 miles SW of Dibon. The other two places, presumably in the same general area, are unidentified.
34 *And behold, his daughter came out to meet him.* The simple and moving narrative-style of this passage illustrates Hebrew story-telling at its best. It has sometimes been inferred from vv. 38-40 that Jephthah commuted his daugh-

ter's fate from burnt-offering to perpetual virginity, but this is hardly warranted by the narrative. The plain and restrained statement that he *did with her according to his vow* (v. 39) is best taken as implying her actual sacrifice. Although human sacrifice was strictly forbidden to Israelites, we need not be surprised at a man of Jephthah's half-Canaanite antecedents following Canaanite usage in this matter. The author of Judges does not approve of his action; he may well have regarded it as a symptom of the state of affairs at a time when 'every man did what was right in his own eyes' (*cf.* 17:6; 21:25). The closest biblical parallel is Mesha's sacrifice of his eldest son (2 Ki. 3:27). *Cf.* also the sacrifice of Iphigenia and Polyxena in Greek legend. The nobility of character shown by Jephthah's daughter has made her one of the world's great heroines; *cf.* stanzas 45–62 of Tennyson's 'Dream of Fair Women'. 37 *Bewail my virginity.* Dean Stanley compared Sophocles's picture of the Theban maiden Antigone bewailing her virginity before going to her living death as the price of obeying the call of sisterly duty. 40 *The daughters of Israel went year by year to lament the daughter of Jephthah.* The verb rendered *lament*, or rather 'celebrate' (RV) or 'chant', is the same as that rendered 'repeat' in Jdg. 5:11. The custom seems to have been a diversion to this particular purpose of a vegetation festival after the fashion of the annual wailing for Tammuz. Epiphanius says that in his day (4th century AD) Jephthah's daughter was honoured at Shechem by the Greek name *Korē* ('Maiden') —the name by which Persephone was honoured.

12:1–7 Jephthah's strife with Ephraim

1 *The men of Ephraim were called to arms.* This tribe now expresses resentment against Jephthah, as previously against Gideon. Probably they aimed at establishing their hegemony among the tribes; otherwise, as the Ammonites had crossed Jordan and attacked some of the western tribes, including Ephraim (10:9), it is strange that Ephraim did not accept Jephthah's invitation to join his forces against Ammon (v. 2). 4 *Then Jephthah gathered all the men of Gilead and fought with Ephraim.* Evidently Ephraim had crossed Jordan and invaded Gilead, to pursue their quarrel with Jephthah. The Ephraimite taunt, *You are fugitives of Ephraim, you Gileadites,* implied that these Transjordanians were deserters from the Joseph tribes. 5 *And the Gileadites took the fords of the Jordan against the Ephraimites.* The invaders of Transjordan, worsted, were making their way home again, when they found their retreat thus cut off by the Transjordanians. The linguistic test that followed shows that in the Ephraimite dialect, as in Amorite and Arabic, *s* took the place of *sh*. The word *Shibboleth* (*šibbōleṭ*) means 'a stream in flood'. Similarly, in the border wars between Scotland and England, a Northumbrian intruder in Scotland was immediately detected by his speech when he responded to the

invitation to pronounce the word 'tree', and was summarily dealt with. 7 *Was buried in his city in Gilead* or 'in his city, Mizpeh of Gilead', a reading supported by some MSS of LXX.

12:8–15 IBZAN, ELON, ABDON: MINOR JUDGES

On the role of these minor judges see on 10:1. 14 *Who rode on seventy asses.* See on 10:4. 15 *In the land of Ephraim, in the hill country of the Amalekites. Cf.* 5:14 for Amalekites in central Canaan.

13:1 – 16:31 OPPRESSION UNDER THE PHILISTINES AND EXPLOITS OF SAMSON

13:1–25 Annunciation and birth of Samson

1 *And the Lord gave them into the hand of the Philistines for forty years.* Having dealt with the Ammonite invasion, the author now turns to the other invaders mentioned in 10:7. These *forty years* lasted at least until the second battle of Ebenezer (1 Sa. 7:10ff.), if not until the reign of Saul. At the end of Saul's reign (*c.* 1010 BC) we find that the Philistines have penetrated as far inland as Beth-shan (1 Sa. 31:10). 2 *There was a certain man of Zorah, of the tribe of the Danites. Zorah* (mod. Ṣarʿa) lay on the boundary of the old Danite territory and that of Judah. The northward migration of the Danites (18:1ff.) had probably taken place by now; if so, a remnant must have remained in the old territory. *And his wife was barren and had no children.* The birth of the coming child was thus marked by such divine interposition as attended the births of Isaac, Samuel and John the Baptist; and was announced by an angel, as were the first and third of these. 3 *The angel of the Lord appeared to the woman.* As before, *the angel of the Lord* is Yahweh in manifestation; *cf.* Gn. 16:7, 13; Jdg. 2:1; 6:11, 12. 5 *The boy shall be a Nazirite to God from birth.* Therefore his mother, too, must observe some at least of the Nazirite precautions for the time being, especially those pertaining to food and drink (vv. 4, 14). On the Nazirite vow see Nu. 6:2ff. It might be undertaken for a stipulated period (*cf.* Acts 18:18; 21:23ff.) or, as here, for life. The word itself (Heb. *nāzîr*, hence 'Nazirite' is the preferable spelling) is a passive participle meaning 'consecrated' or 'dedicated'. The Nazirite abstention from strong drink is implied in Am. 2:12. *And he shall begin to deliver Israel from the hand of the Philistines.* This may mean 'he will be the first to save . . .'; the work was continued by Samuel, Saul and Jonathan, and completed by David.

15 *Let us detain you, and prepare a kid for you.* The narrative at this point becomes remarkably similar to 6:18ff., though there are differences, *e.g.* in the angel's response to the offer of a meal. 17 *What is your name . . . ? Cf.* Gn. 32:29. 18 *Why do you ask my name, seeing it is wonderful?*

For the angel's unwillingness to reveal his name, *cf.* Gn. 32:29. Hebrew *pelî'*, rendered *wonderful* (AV 'secret'), is found again in Ps. 139:6, in the feminine *peli'āh*. *Cf.* the noun *pele'* (from which this adjective is derived), rendered 'Wonderful' in Is. 9:6. **19** *So Manoah took the kid with the cereal offering.* Hebrew *minḥāh* (see on 6:18) is here used of something additional to the burnt-offering, hence in the sense 'cereal offering' as in the vegetable oblation of Lv. 2:1ff. *And offered it upon the rock to the Lord.* 'To this day, the rock-stepped altar, covered with cup holes, is sprinkled with the blood of animals sacrificed by it' (A. T. Olmstead). *To him who works wonders* (Heb. *maplî'*) shows how the divine visitor lived up to his 'wonderful' name. **20** *The flame went up toward heaven from the altar. Cf.* 6:21. **22** *We shall surely die. Cf.* 6:22f., with comment. *For we have seen God.* Lit. 'for it is a god that we have seen'. **23** *If the Lord had meant to kill us.* The woman's common sense prevails over her husband's numinous terror.

24 *And the woman bore a son, and called his name Samson* (Heb. *šimšôn*, derived from *šemeš*, 'sun'; *cf.* the neighbouring place-name Beth-shemesh). This name has been thought to fit in well with the view that the story of Samson, like the 'labours' of Gilgamesh and Heracles, is in origin a sun-myth. The arguments for this view are very slender, although it has been elaborated by several scholars. There is much more to be said for Burney's statement that the Samson narratives 'possess unique value as illustrating the village-life of the time, and the relations between Israelites and Philistines living in the border-country'. Twelve 'labours of Samson' have been reckoned: i. slaying the lion; ii. killing the Philistines at Ashkelon; iii. sending the foxes among the corn; iv. the slaughter near Etam; v. bursting the cords of the men of Judah; vi. the massacre with the jawbone; vii. carrying off the gates of Gaza; viii. quenching his thirst in Lehi; ix. breaking the seven bowstrings; x. bursting the new ropes; xi. tearing away the loom and web; xii. pulling down the pillars. This enumeration, however, does not lie on the surface, and other ways of counting the episodes are possible. It is unlikely that the quenching of his thirst in Lehi should be reckoned a 'labour'. In any case, we are not dealing with mythology here. (The Semitic kinship with *šemeš* is nevertheless more probable than the suggested derivation of his name from Hurrian *Šapš*.) **25** *And the Spirit of the Lord began to stir him.* Thus Samson too becomes a charismatic hero. His 'judging' does not seem to have had a judicial character, but to have consisted in the exploits by which he became his people's champion against the enemy. *Mahaneh-dan.* See 18:12 for the origin of the name ('Camp of Dan') and the location of the place. *Between Zorah and Eshtaol.* Eshtaol, in the lowlands of Judah, is frequently identified with Eshwa', 1½ miles NE of Zorah. The name (from Heb. *šā'al*, 'ask') may indicate the site of an ancient oracle.

14:1-20 The wedding of Samson

1 *Samson went down to Timnah,* which, like Zorah and Eshtaol, lay on the boundary between Judah and Dan (*cf.* Jos. 15:10; 19:43), but at this time seems to have been occupied by Philistines (mod. Khirbet-Tibneh, 3 miles SW of Beth-shemesh). **2** *Now get her for me as my wife.* The fathers of the prospective bridal pair arranged the details of an ordinary wedding, including the fixing of the bride-price. In the event, however, it seems that it was not the ordinary type of marriage that was concluded, in which case the bride would have come to live with Samson, but the *ṣadîqa* union (*cf.* 8:31) in which the bride remained with her own family, being visited by her husband from time to time, and any children would belong to their mother's family. **3** *The uncircumcised Philistines.* So the Philistines are distinctively called, for the other peoples whom the Israelites knew at this period, the Egyptians, Canaanites, *etc.*, practised circumcision like the Israelites themselves. *Get her for me.* This time the pronoun *her* is emphatic; in answer to his parents' suggestion that he would do better to marry an Israelite wife, he says 'Get her and no other'. **5** *A young lion roared against him.* In OT times the lion was common in Palestine, especially in the 'jungle' of Jordan, but also in other parts of the country. **6** *He tore the lion asunder as one tears a kid.* The rushing of the divine power upon Samson enables him to act with strength above the ordinary (*cf.* v. 19; 15:14). The rending of the lion is paralleled in ancient art, where mighty figures (*e.g.* Enkidu, the comrade of Gilgamesh) are depicted rending a lion down the middle by tearing its hind legs apart. *And he had nothing in his hand.* So Heracles strangled the Nemean lion with his hands. Josephus, possibly under the influence of the Heracles story, says that Samson strangled the lion. **8** *There was a swarm of bees in the body of the lion, and honey.* The carcase was by now thoroughly dry. Herodotus has a comparable story of a swarm of bees and a honeycomb found in the skull of Onesilos. We should not see here an allusion to the ancient belief, attested by Virgil, that bees were generated in putrefying carcases; this belief may have arisen from observation of the drone-fly in such an environment, but would not explain the presence of the honey. **9** *He scraped it out into his hands.* This was a violation of the Nazirite code, which forbad contact with a corpse (Nu. 6:6), and may explain why he did not tell his parents that he had taken the honey out of the dead lion.

10 *Samson made a feast there.* The fact that the feast was held at the bride's home and that the bridegroom's companions were Philistines suggests that the marriage was of the second type referred to above (see on v. 2). The writer explains it as an ancient custom, implying that at the time of writing it had become obsolete. **11** *When the people saw him.* We may perhaps read 'because they feared him' (*keyir'ātām* for *kîr'ôṯām*). *Thirty companions.* The 'sons of the bride-chamber' of Mk. 2:19 (RV). They may originally have been intended as a bodyguard for the bridegroom, but on this occasion they seem to have served as bodyguard for the others present against the bridegroom. **12** *Thirty linen garments and thirty festal garments.* The *linen garments* were large rectangular sheets which might be worn by day and slept in at night; the *festal garments,* as the phrase indicates, were suits for festive occasions. **14** *Out of the eater . . .* In Hebrew the riddle takes the form of a rhythmical couplet, the two lines having three beats each.

15 *On the fourth day.* The LXX and Syriac versions have *fourth day,* which agrees with the *three days* of v. 14; but the Hebrew text has 'seventh day' (so AV, RV). Even with the reading *fourth day* there is still a discrepancy with **17** *the seven days;* where exactly the corruption lies is not easy to determine now. **18** *Before the sun went down.* Or perhaps 'before he entered the bridal chamber'. *What is sweeter than honey . . .?* Again a rhythmical couplet, this time with two beats to the line. Samson's retort, *If you had not ploughed with my heifer . . .,* is a couplet of three beats to the line with rhyme as well as rhythm. Burney translates it well: 'If ye had not plowed with this heifer of mine, Ye would not have found out this riddle of mine.' **19** *And he went down to Ashkelon,* 23 miles away, on the coast, one of the cities of the Philistine pentapolis (*cf.* 1:18). *In hot anger he went back to his father's house,* without entering the bridal chamber. **20** *His companion, who had been his best man. Cf.* 'the friend of the bridegroom' in Jn. 3:29.

15:1 – 16:3 Other exploits of Samson

15:1 *At the time of wheat harvest.* This varied in Palestine according to the locality and climate, but fell about May (*cf.* the festival of Pentecost). Wheat was sown in November or December. *Samson went to visit his wife with a kid,* to appease her for his insult in leaving her so abruptly at the time of the wedding. But to take away the disgrace in which she was involved by Samson's desertion, her father had already given her in marriage to Samson's 'best man'. **2** He now offers Samson instead *her younger sister. Cf.* 1 Sa. 18:19ff., and for a less close parallel Gn. 29:23ff. **3** *This time I shall be blameless . . .* Render, with RV mg., 'This time shall I be quits with the Philistines'. **4** *So Samson went and caught three hundred foxes.* This is the proper meaning of Hebrew *šûʿāl,* but it is often supposed that 'jackals' are meant here, as jackals are gregarious and easily caught, whereas the fox is solitary and more elusive. But foxes are probably intended all the same. The use to which Samson put them is very similar to the custom at the Roman feast of Ceres (the corn-goddess), when foxes with burning torches attached to their brushes were hunted in the circus. **6** *Burned her and her father with fire.* Several MSS and versions read 'burnt her and her father's house'. *Cf.* the

threat in 14:15. **8** *He smote them hip and thigh.* Lit. 'leg upon thigh'; probably a wrestling term, like English 'cross-buttock'. The action is illustrated in Babylonian cylinder-seals where Gilgamesh is represented as using this device in wrestling. *He went down and stayed in the cleft of the rock of Etam.* Of proposed identifications of this 'cleft', that above the Wadi Isma'in, 2½ miles ESE of Zorah, is most probable.

9 *Made a raid on Lehi.* The place (meaning 'cheek', 'jawbone') may have been so called from the appearance of its crags, and can be identified with mod. Khirbet es-Siyyaj ('the ruin of Siyyaj'), where Siyyaj seems to be a loanword from Greek *siagōn* ('jawbone'), which is the rendering of Lehi found in Josephus and some Greek versions of the OT. *Do you not know that the Philistines are rulers over us?* The people of Judah are obviously well content with the Philistine domination, and resent the disturbance caused by Samson's feud with them. **15** *And he found a fresh jawbone of an ass.* Lit. 'a moist jawbone'; an old one would have been too brittle. J. G. Duncan mentions the possibility that jawbones fitted with three or four flint knives may have served as primitive weapons. **16** *With the jawbone of an ass . . .* Samson's exultant shout takes the form of a couplet with four beats to the line. For *heaps upon heaps* read perhaps 'I have heaped them in heaps'. It is not easy to reproduce in English the play on words in Hebrew between 'ass' and 'heap' (both *ḥᵃmôr*). Moffatt partly substitutes rhyme for word-play: 'With the jawbone of an ass I have piled them in a mass! With the jawbone of an ass I have assailed assailants!' This, however, loses sight of the *thousand men.* **17** *He threw away the jawbone out of his hand; and that place was called Ramath-lehi,* i.e. 'the height of Lehi'; but there is a word-play with *rāmāh* ('throw'), as if the name meant 'the throwing of the jawbone' (though *rāmāh* is not the word rendered 'he cast away'). **19** *And God split open the hollow place that is at Lehi.* Hebrew *maḵtēš,* rendered *hollow place,* is lit. 'mortar'; it was evidently a rock-depression containing a spring, the origin of which is thus accounted for. The misleading AV rendering ('God clave an hollow place that was in the jaw') is due to the fact that the Hebrew word for *jaw* (*leḥî*) is the same as that of the place; but the rendering is the more absurd because the narrator refers to the spring as existing in Lehi in his day. *En-hakkore.* Lit. 'spring of the caller' (this is the name of the partridge in biblical Hebrew, because of its distinctive call-note). **20** *And he judged Israel in the days of the Philistines twenty years,* c. 1070–1050 BC. There is no indication that in his case the word implies a judicial or military office; and the exploits are confined to the SW, especially the Philistine border.

16:1 *Samson went to Gaza.* Gaza was the most southerly city of the Philistine pentapolis. It was much older than the Philistine settlement; it is mentioned in the Tell el-Amarna tablets (14th century BC), and was temporarily captured by Judah (Jdg. 1:18) before its occupation by the Philistines. It is fanciful to see in this narrative support for the sun-myth interpretation of the Samson saga, as some do, by drawing an analogy with the sun coming forth as a bridegroom from his chamber and rejoicing as a giant to run his course (cf. Ps. 19:5). 2 *And lay in wait for him all night at the gate of the city. They kept quiet all night.* Kittel emends the first *all night* to 'all day'; the sense being that the men of Gaza watched the gates by day, but relaxed their vigilance at night, because the gates were closed then. 3 But thus they played into Samson's hands, for he rose by night and went out, lifting the barred gates with their posts and carrying them away on his shoulders, *to the top of the hill that is before Hebron, i.e.* on the E side of Hebron, where no doubt they were pointed out by later generations. Hebron (see 1:20) is some 38 miles E of Gaza.

16:4–31 Last exploits of Samson

4 *He loved a woman in the valley of Sorek, whose name was Delilah.* This place seems to have been the Wadi es-Sarar. A ruin N of the wadi, *c.* 2 miles from Zorah, still bears the name Surik. It is not clear whether *Delilah* was an Israelite or a Philistine, though the narrative suggests the latter. Her name is Semitic (meaning 'devotee'; possibly her full name included the name of the deity whose devotee she was). It recurs in the Greek text of 1 Ch. 4:19 in the genealogy of the tribe of Judah. But Semitic names are found among the Philistines not unnaturally, since the Philistine immigrants brought few women with them and must have intermarried with the people of Canaan. 5 *The lords of the Philistines.* See on 3:3. *Eleven hundred pieces of silver, i.e.* 1,100 shekels, nearly 30 lb weight. No convincing reason has been offered for the figure 1,100 rather than, say, the round number 1,000. *Cf.* 17:2. 7 *If they bind me with seven fresh bowstrings,* made of twisted gut. 9 *The Philistines are upon you, Samson.* We are to understand that they were in readiness in case Samson had told the truth; when his strength is proved they remain hid and he thinks that she is playing with him. *So the secret of his strength was not known,* or rather, 'his strength was not brought low'.

11 *If they bind me with new ropes. Cf.* his binding by the Judeans in 15:13. 13, 14 *If you weave the seven locks of my head with the web.* Delilah, we may understand, having the sleeping Samson's head in her lap (as in v. 19), weaves his hair into the warp and beats it up into the web *with the pin,* a flat piece of wood, so that his hair actually becomes part of the woven material. The loom would be the primitive type with two upright posts fixed in the ground, the one holding the yarn-beam and the other the cloth-beam. When Samson wakes up, he goes off, loom and all fixed to his hair, dragging the upright posts out of the ground.

19 *And had him shave off the seven locks of his head. Cf.* the Greek story of how Minos took Megara when the golden lock of Nisos its king was shorn. 20 *I will go out as at other times, and shake myself free.* This may imply that he was already bound as well as shaved. 21 *And he ground at the mill in the prison.* Lit. 'he was (continually) grinding', probably at a hand-mill with saddle-quern. It is doubtful if the large mill, which was normally turned by an ass, such as is called a *mylos onikos* in Mt. 18:6, was known as early as this. 22 *The hair of his head began to grow again,* implying a concurrent return of his strength.

23 *Dagon their god.* Dagon (cf. Heb. *dāḡān,* 'grain') was a Semitic corn-deity, a temple of whom has been found at the Amorite city of Mari on the Euphrates (18th century BC). He was introduced by the Amorites into Syria, and his name appears on the tablets of Ras Shamra, where also he had a temple. The Philistines evidently took over his cult. 24 *Our god has given our enemy into our hand . . .* Their chant of triumph is a rhymed quatrain with two beats to the line. 25 *Call Samson, that he may make sport for us.* Presumably he was to perform 'strong man acts'. *They made him stand between the pillars.* The character of the building is illustrated by discoveries at Gezer and Gaza. The roof was supported by wooden pillars set on stone bases. It was flat, consisting of logs of wood stretching from one wall to beams supported by the pillars and from these beams to other beams or to the opposite wall. The temple at Gezer had a forecourt leading into a paved inner chamber, separated from it by four circular stones, on which the wooden pillars stood. Samson probably stood between the two central pillars, if there were more than two. The Philistine lords and ladies were in the inner chamber; the crowd watched from the roof. 27 *Samson made sport,* in the forecourt, and then asked the boy to lead him to the central pillars to rest against them. Then, putting an arm round each, and bending forward so as to force them out of the perpendicular, he brought the roof down. The weight of people on the roof may have made the feat all the easier. 28 *That I may be avenged upon the Philistines for one of my two eyes.* A grim jest; another possibility is 'one vengeance for both my eyes'. 31 *His brothers and his family came down.* Manoah was evidently dead by this time, despite Milton's effective introduction of him in *Samson Agonistes.*

17:1 – 18:31 MICAH'S PRIEST AND THE DANITE MIGRATION

17:1–13 Micah's priest

2 *The eleven hundred pieces of silver.* See on 16:5. *About which you uttered a curse.* Or simply 'took an oath' (*i.e.* to dedicate the sum to religious purposes), which would involve a curse upon anyone who violated it. When Micah acknow-

ledged that he had taken the money and restored it to the purpose to which his mother had dedicated it, she neutralized the curse by invoking a blessing on him. **4** *His mother took two hundred pieces of silver.* Perhaps, like Ananias and Sapphira, keeping back part of the sum originally dedicated. The *graven image* will have been one carved out of wood and overlaid with silver; the *molten image* would be entirely of silver. There are, however, indications in the text that only one image is meant; *and it was* (not 'they were', as in AV) *in the house of Micah.* We are not told what form the image(s) took, but that of a young bull is not unlikely. **5** *And the man Micah had a shrine,* lit. 'a house of god(s)', attached to his dwelling, to which people would come to ascertain the divine will. *And he made an ephod and teraphim.* For the divining *ephod, cf.* 8:27. *Teraphim* were probably images of household goᵈs, also used for divination (*cf.* Gn. 31:19; 1 Sa. 19:13). *Installed one of his sons, who became his priest.* The term *installed* or 'consecrated' (Heb. *millē' yāḏ*) means lit. 'filled his hand', *i.e.* with portions of a sacrifice (*cf.* Ex. 28:41, *etc.*). There were priests other than those of the family of Levi, who are distinguished as 'the Levitical priests' (as in Dt. 18:1). But it appears from this narrative that a member of the tribe of Levi was preferred when he was available. When the national worship was centralized at the Temple in Jerusalem under the monarchy, only the Aaronic priesthood was recognized. **6** Hence the explanatory remark of a writer who lived under very different conditions and was recording events of an earlier age: *In those days there was no king in Israel; every man did what was right in his own eyes.*

7 *There was a young man of Bethlehem in Judah, of the family of Judah, who was a Levite.* As he was Moses' grandson (18:30), he was a Levite by birth. Yet he is reckoned a member of the clan of Judah. The Levites, having no tribal territory of their own, depended on other tribes' hospitality (*cf.* 19:1), which explains why this one lived in Bethlehem and is reckoned in Judah. The Levites had a close connection with the southern tribes, especially with Judah. *And he sojourned there.* Hebrew *gēr šām,* which is identical with the name of the Levite's father (18:30); the original text here may have been 'and he was Jonathan the son of Gershom'. **10, 11** *Be to me a father and a priest.* For *father* used as a term of honour *cf.* Gn. 45:8; 2 Ki. 6:21; 13:14. In v. 11 exactly the opposite relationship is figuratively employed: *the young man became to him like one of his sons.* But there Micah's care of him is implied. *Ten pieces of silver a year.* About 4 oz. avoirdupois. **13** *Because I have a Levite as priest.* Quite obviously a Levite was regarded as possessing special priestly qualifications. Among the Minaeans of Arabia the cognate words *lawi'u* and its feminine *lawi'atu* appear with the sense 'person pledged for a vow or debt' (*cf.* Samuel).

18:1–31 The Danite migration

1 *The tribe of the Danites was seeking for itself an inheritance to dwell in.* According to 1:34 it was the Amorites (themselves no doubt pressed by the Philistines) who exercised pressure on the Danites. The story of their migration is summarized in Jos. 19:47, where Laish is called Leshem. **2** *From Zorah and from Eshtaol.* See on 13:25. **3** *They recognized the voice of the young Levite.* This suggests that they knew him before, when he lived in Bethlehem, the connection between the tribes of Judah and Dan being fairly close. Or they may simply have recognized by his voice that he came from their neighbourhood. **5** *Inquire of God, we pray thee.* This was the evident object of Micah's 'house of gods' (17:5, AV). (The retention of *thee* from AV and RV must be an accidental oversight in RSV.) **7** *Came to Laish.* Mod. Tell el-Qadi (Arab. *qadi,* 'judge'; *cf.* Heb. *Dan*), at one of the sources of Jordan. It is called Lus(i) in Egyptian texts of *c.* 1850–1825 BC. *Had no dealings with any one.* Perhaps we should read with some MSS of the Greek and Syrian versions, 'had no dealings with Syria' (*'ᵃrām* instead of *'āḏām*). The district was isolated from Phoenicia by the Lebanon range and from Syria by Hermon and the Anti-Lebanon range. The account of the Laishites shows that it was not enough in ancient, any more than in modern, times for a people to live in quietness and neutrality if they wished to be secure against aggression. In this case it gave the Danites all the more reason to expropriate them, **10** especially as their land had *no lack of any thing that is in the earth.*

11 *Six hundred men.* The fewness of the men of war is a measure of the weakness of this tribe. **12** *Encamped at Kiriath-jearim.* A city of Judah, 8 miles W of Jerusalem, on the Benjaminite border. *On this account that place is called Mahaneh-dan, i.e.* 'Camp of Dan'; *cf.* 13:25. **16** *Stood by the entrance of the gate,* presumably leading into the courtyard of Micah's house. **19** *Put your hand upon your mouth.* For the idiom (denoting silence) *cf.* Jb. 21:5; 29:9; 40:4; Pr. 30:32; Mi. 7:16. *Be to us a father and a priest. Cf.* 17:10. **24** *My gods which I made.* We may trace here some irony on the writer's part similar to that expressed at greater length in Is. 44:9ff. **28** *It was in the valley which belongs to Beth-rehob.* The valley is El-Biqā', between Lebanon and Hermon. *Beth-rehob,* not the Rehob of 1:31, is unknown. **29** *They named the city Dan.* It became the northernmost point of the land of the twelve tribes: *cf.* the phrase 'from Dan to Beer-sheba'.

30 *Jonathan the son of Gershom, son of Moses, and his sons were priests to the tribe of the Danites.* For *Gershom, cf.* Ex. 2:22. The Massoretes, jealous for the reputation of Moses, inserted a suspended 'N' between the 'M' and the 'S', as though the name were Manasseh, not wishing to disguise the true sense, but implying that this idolatrous priest behaved in a way befitting a descendant of Manasseh—either the wicked king of that name (2 Ki. 21:1ff.; 2 Ch. 33:1ff.) or (more probably) the renegade Zadokite who founded the schismatic priesthood of the Gerizim sanctuary (Josephus, *Ant*. xi. 302ff.)—rather than of Moses. But the Rabbis knew and admitted that Moses was meant. If no generation is omitted in this man's genealogy, the Danite migration must have taken place at an early point in the early period of the judges. Probably some Danites remained behind in the southern territory (*cf.* 5:17; 13:2). The presence at Dan of a priesthood descended from Moses would give the place high prestige, which explains why Jeroboam I chose it as one of the two national shrines for the northern kingdom. Jeroboam's bull-calf at Dan may well have been the 'descendant' of Micah's graven image, which probably enough had the same form. It served as the visible pedestal for the invisible presence of the deity. *Until the day of the captivity of the land*, *i.e.* probably the captivity of the Galilaean population under Tiglath-pileser III in 733–732 BC (2 Ki. 15:29), which would put an effective end to the priesthood and cult at Dan. Houbigant, however (following a conjectural interpretation by D. Qimḥi), emended *the captivity of the land* to 'the captivity of the ark' (reading *hāʾārôn* for *hāʾāreṣ*), taking the phrase as a duplicate of 'as long as the house of God was at Shiloh' (v. 31). But the effect of the Philistine victory at Aphek was hardly felt so far N as Dan. **31** The introduction of the note *as long as the house of God was at Shiloh* may have been intended to indicate that the Dan cult was of comparable antiquity to that of Shiloh. *Shiloh* is mod. Seilun, *c*. 19 miles N of Jerusalem and 12 miles S of Shechem. There the 'tent of meeting' was set up soon after the entry into Canaan, to serve as the central sanctuary for the amphictyonic league of the tribes of Israel (Jos. 18:1; *cf.* also Jos. 21:2; Jdg. 21:12, 19ff.). But the house of God at Shiloh in the early chapters of 1 Samuel was a more stable structure than simply a tent. The destruction of Shiloh is not mentioned in 1 Samuel, but we can infer that it was destroyed by the Philistines after the battle of Aphek (1 Sa. 4:10), and this is borne out by Je. 7:12ff.; 26:6, 9; Ps. 78:60ff. Danish excavations in 1926 and 1928 showed that there was an extensive settlement at Shiloh in the 12th and early 11th centuries BC until its destruction *c*. 1050 BC.

19:1 – 21:25 THE WAR AGAINST BENJAMIN

19:1-30 The outrage at Gibeah

1 *A certain Levite was sojourning in the remote parts of the hill country of Ephraim*. Either on the western or eastern flanks of the Ephraim highlands. *Who took to himself a concubine from Bethlehem in Judah*. Like the Levite of chs. 17 and 18, this Levite had connections both with the Ephraim highlands and with Bethlehem in Judah. **2** *And his concubine became angry with*

him. So several versions in place of Hebrew text, 'played the harlot against him'. **3** *To speak kindly to her*. Lit. 'to speak to her heart' (as in Is. 40:2). **8** *Tarry until the day declines*. AV 'and they tarried until afternoon', though it depends on an emendation, is preferable, as the father-in-law in v. 9 gives the day's declining as a reason for their staying another night. **9** *The day has waned toward evening*. Lit. 'the encamping of day', *i.e.* the time to pitch camp for the night. Nomadic idioms survived even when the Israelites had become a settled population. *Cf.* 2 Sa. 20:1; 1 Ki. 12:16. **10** *And arrived opposite Jebus* (*that is, Jerusalem*). The city was still in the hands of the Jebusites. **12** For this reason the Levite refused to spend the night there, though in fact it could not have treated him less hospitably than Gibeah, a *city of . . . the people of Israel*. Jebus appears as a name for Jerusalem only here and in 1 Ch. 11:4, 5, and is probably derived from the name of the Amorite group (Jebusites) who settled there. See on 1:21. **13** *At Gibeah*. Mod. Tell el-Ful, 4 miles N of Jerusalem. It was a town of Benjamin, later known as 'Gibeah of Saul', because it was the home and capital of Saul (1 Sa. 11:4). Excavations at Tell el-Ful have shown that the first fortress of Gibeah was founded soon after the conquest and destroyed in the 12th century BC; the second fortress, that of Saul, has also been uncovered. *Or at Ramah*. Further N than Gibeah, on the way to Bethel. *Cf.* 4:5.

16 *An old man . . . from the hill country of Ephraim*. As the Levite himself was; but it adds point to the story that the one man in Gibeah to offer hospitality to the strangers was not a Benjaminite. **18** *I am going to my home*. So LXX, rightly, for 'the house of the Lord' (MT, AV); the pronominal suffix meaning 'my' has been misread as an abbreviation for Yahweh. **22** *Base fellows*. The Hebrew word is vocalized so as to mean 'worthless' (Heb. *bᵉlî*, 'without', and *yaʿal*, 'worth'). 'Sons of Belial' (AV, RV) are then 'lewd fellows of the baser sort' (*cf.* Acts 17:5, AV). Other suggestions are that Belial means either 'the world of the dead' (a natural sense in 2 Sa. 22:5; Ps. 18:4; see RV mg.), lit. 'the place from which there is no coming up', or 'lord of night', or 'place of swallowing up'. In post-biblical Jewish writings Belial (Gk. *Beliar*) is the name of a person, the antichrist or incarnation of wickedness (*cf.* 2 Cor. 6:15). The unpleasant narrative of these verses (22–24) is strikingly similar to the tale of Sodom (Gn. 19:4–8). **23** *Do not do this vile thing*. The laws of hospitality here, as in Gn. 19, obviously took precedence over considerations of chivalry towards the female sex. **29** *He took a knife . . .* This dismemberment and distribution of a body as a call to national action is paralleled in 1 Sa. 11:7; there, however, a yoke of oxen is so used and the distribution is accompanied by a threat to do the same to the oxen of anyone who will not join against the enemy. The *twelve pieces* into which the woman's body was divided no doubt correspond to the number of the tribes of Israel. The practice plainly imposed a solemn obligation on those to whom the grisly tokens were sent, calling on all to act in the spirit of the national covenant. **30** *From the day that the people of Israel came up out of the land of Egypt.* The Exodus, marking the birth of the nation, provided a starting-point from which events might be reckoned (*cf.* 1 Ki. 6:1). The outrage at Gibeah stood out as a monument of wickedness for centuries to come (*cf.* Ho. 9:9; 10:9).

20:1–48 The destruction of Gibeah

1 *The congregation assembled as one man.* The Levite's summons had been effective; here all the tribes are gathered together—from N, S, and Transjordan—and they meet *in Mizpah,* 5 miles NW of Jerusalem (not the Transjordanian Mizpah of 10:17, although the meaning 'watchtower' is the same). **2** *Four hundred thousand men on foot that drew the sword.* This figure is in keeping with the Pentateuchal censuses, but the word rendered 'thousand' here as there (Heb. '*elep̄*) may denote a much smaller unit, 'practically, perhaps exactly, equivalent to the subdivision of the tribe which was technically known as a father's house; *cf.* Jdg. 6:15' (*Westminster Bible Dictionary*). See on 5:8. **6** *For they have committed abomination and wantonness in Israel.* The same word (Heb. *nᵉḇālāh*) as is translated 'vile thing' in 19:23, 24; for the whole phrase *cf.* Gn. 34:7; Dt. 22:21; Jos. 7:15; 2 Sa. 13:12f. **13** *Put away evil from Israel. Cf.* for the phrase Dt. 17:12. This dissociation of the community from wickedness committed within it is the basis of social punishment. **15** *Twenty-six thousand.* Most of the versions read '25,000', which accords better with the later statements in vv. 35 and 47. Benjamin was small in proportion to the other tribes; it numbered one-seventeenth of the whole. **16** *Seven hundred picked men.* If this figure has been repeated from v. 15 by dittography, as Vulg. suggests, then the men of Gibeah are the 700 skilful slingers. *Left-handed.* LXX and Vulg. 'ambidextrous'; see on 3:15, and *cf.* 1 Ch. 12:2. *And not miss.* The Hebrew verb is *ḥāṭā',* commonly used in the moral sense of 'sin'. **18** *Went up to Bethel.* This ancient sanctuary continued to be used as a religious centre throughout the northern monarchy. Here AV, following Vulg., renders 'the house of God', meaning Shiloh, from the mention of Phinehas and the ark in vv. 27, 28. But the ark did not always stay in the same place. **26** *Burnt offerings and peace offerings, i.e.* piacular sacrifices to expiate the cause of their defeat, followed by a communion sacrifice and feast. **28** *Phinehas the son of Eleazar, son of Aaron, ministered before it in those days.* This incident therefore belongs to the same generation as the migration of the Danites (*cf.* 18:30). *Phinehas* (Heb. *pínḥās*) is a word of Egyptian origin, meaning 'the Nubian' or 'the child of dark complexion' (*cf.* Nu. 25:1–13). Israelites with Egyptian names (*cf.* Moses) are found in

the tribe of Levi. **29** *So Israel set men in ambush round about Gibeah.* The tactics are similar to those used against Ai (Jos. 8:12ff.). **31** *One of which goes up to Bethel and the other to Gibeah.* For *Gibeah* here we probably ought to read Gibeon—mod. El-jib, *c.* 6 miles NW of Jerusalem and 4 miles from Gibeah. **33** *Baal-tamar.* On the border of Judah and Benjamin. The name means 'lord of the palm' and the place may have been called after a Canaanite deity of that name. **35** *The men of Israel destroyed twenty-five thousand one hundred men of Benjamin that day.* Leaving as survivors only the 600 of v. 47; the original total being 25,700 (see on v. 15). See also comment on *thousand* in v. 2. The statement here is an anticipatory summary of the narrative of vv. 36–46. **38** *The appointed signal.* The word for 'signal', found also in Je. 6:1 and in the Lachish letters, means a torch-beacon. *Cf.* Jos. 8:20f. **40** *The whole of the city went up in smoke to heaven.* The destruction of Gibeah at this period is confirmed by excavations carried out by American archaeologists in 1922–23. **43** *Trod them down from Nohah. Cf.* 1 Ch. 8:2. *Opposite Gibeah.* Or Geba, on the direct route from Gibeah to Rimmon. Geba is *c.* 6 miles NNE of Jerusalem, and **47** *the rock of Rimmon* is about as far again in the same direction. The name survives in the mod. village Rammun. It is a detached limestone eminence, cut off by ravines on N, W and S, and containing caverns in which the fugitives could live.

21:1–25 Reconciliation

2, 4 *And the people came to Bethel . . . and built there an altar.* A strange action, as 20:26 makes it clear that there was an altar there already. It has been suggested (*e.g.* by Burney) that the original reference here was to the building of an altar at Mizpah. **5** *They had taken a great oath.* Lit. 'the great oath had been': the reference may be to some peculiarly solemn form of oath. **8** *No one had come to the camp from Jabesh-gilead.* This is believed to have stood on the site of mod. Tell Abu Kharaz, 9 miles SE of Beth-shan on the E of Jordan, on the N bank of the Wadi el-Yabis. **10** *Twelve thousand of their bravest men.* For *thousand* see on 20:2. **11** *This is what you shall do. Cf.* the policy adopted at Moses' instance with regard to the Midianite women (Nu. 31:15ff.). **12** *And they found among the inhabitants of Jabesh-gilead four hundred young virgins.* To the marriage of these girls with the Benjaminite survivors may be due the close relationship of later days between Jabesh-gilead and the tribe of Benjamin (especially in the time of King Saul, a Benjaminite); *cf.* in particular Saul's action in defence of the Jabeshites against the Ammonites (1 Sa. 11), and the Jabeshites' rescue of Saul's body from the walls of Beth-shan (1 Sa. 31:11ff.). And in view of Saul's connection with Gibeah, was there some early tie which deterred the Jabeshites from joining the war of vengeance against that town? By the time of the incident of 1 Sa. 11 (*c.* 1025 BC), Jabesh was again quite populous. *They brought them to the camp at Shiloh,* which served as an inter-tribal centre (*cf.* 18:31; 21:19ff.).

19 *So they said.* Presumably to the Benjaminites, at least to the 200 who were still unprovided with wives. Hence the particularity with which the location of the feast is described. *Behold, there is the yearly feast of the Lord at Shiloh.* This feast (Heb. *ḥag̱*, lit. 'pilgrimage') was a local variety of the Feast of Tabernacles, here more particularly to celebrate the ingathering of the year's vintage (*cf.* 9:27). This may have been the feast which Elkanah and his family attended annually at Shiloh (1 Sa. 1:3ff.). The dancing of the maidens formed part of the 'harvest home' celebrations. **21** *Seize each man his wife.* A reversion to the practice of marriage by capture. The rape of the Sabines in Roman legend is a well-known parallel. **22** *Grant them graciously to us.* They adduce two reasons for the acquiescence of the men of Shiloh: they had not seized the maidens as an act of war; and they had thus delivered the Shilonites from the guilt of voluntarily handing over their daughters, which would have been a breach of the oath sworn at Mizpah (v. 1). **25** *In those days . . .* Quoted from 17:6; *cf.* also 18:1; 19:1; an appropriate note on which to end this narrative in particular, and the book of Judges in general.

F. F. BRUCE

Ruth

INTRODUCTION

It is not difficult to account for the wide appeal of this little book. From a literary standpoint alone it has outstanding merit: symmetry of form, convincing characterization, restraint, dignity, and a gently repetitive style which accords well with the speech of peasant people. The story moves smoothly from tragedy in Moab to a happy ending in Bethlehem without the slightest trace of moralizing, yet the characters are wholly praiseworthy, and selfless loyalty is rewarded.

NATURE AND AUTHOR

This short story with its pastoral setting may easily be sentimentalized by the modern reader. The 20th-century urban dweller has not had to experience the toil and weariness of harvesting by hand under a blazing sun, and he may take too sophisticated a view of the marriage of Ruth and Boaz, which was the culmination of consistent faithfulness and family loyalty. On the other hand, in an attempt to see the book in its Near-Eastern setting, some scholars have suggested that it had its origins in mythology, Babylonian or Egyptian, or in a cult-myth of ancient Bethlehem, though there is no convincing evidence for such theories. More widely accepted is the view that it is a historical novel. Evidence educed by R. H. Pfeiffer (*Introduction to the Old Testament*, 1952, p. 718) in favour of fiction and against historicity includes the following points: unpleasant features have been eliminated from the barbaric picture of the times given in Judges; the characters of Ruth, Naomi and Boaz are idealized; the names of some of the characters so fit their role in the story that the author must have coined them. For a note on the last point see the commentary on 1:2–4. The whole atmosphere of the book of Ruth is indeed different from that of Judges but it would be difficult to prove that it was less true to life. To be fair to the author it is obvious that account must be taken of his intentions as revealed in the text.

The opening formula, which is reproduced in the AV and RV as 'and it came to pass', is the accepted introduction to historical narrative (*cf.* AV Jos. 1:1; Jdg. 1:1), while the last verses link Ruth and Boaz with King David. No further evidence is needed to prove that the writer intended his book to be taken as historical, though it deals with an ordinary family and not with the exploits of the great. It is a true story beautifully related, through which the deep faith and spiritual insight of the unknown author are revealed.

PURPOSE

If his purpose was to tell a good story the author certainly achieved his aim, but he also had a keen interest in David, of whom no childhood story is given in the history, and, having access to this material, wanted at least to tell something of his ancestry. About the middle of the last century the view was promulgated in Germany and Holland that the book of Ruth was written as a protest against the rigorous measures of Ezra and Nehemiah in their attempt to combat mixed marriages. While it is true that the book would discourage Jewish exclusivism in favour of a missionary attitude to the surrounding nations, it is doubtful whether the author wrote with this as his conscious purpose. Propagandists make their points less subtly. The whole episode impressed the writer as an unforgettable example of God's providential care for those who put their trust in Him, irrespective of their race, and therefore he delighted to record the story with all the artistry of which he was capable.

DATE

Though the events are set in the time of the Judges, the necessity of explaining the shoe ceremony in 4:7 indicates that some time elapsed before they were recorded. In Dt. 25 the loosing of the shoe, the spitting and the pronouncement of the curse implied that the unwilling kinsman was blameworthy, whereas in Ru. 4 the handing over of the shoe seems only to symbolize the renunciation of a right. Its weakened significance in Ruth suggests that Deuteronomy is earlier. Certainly the nearer kinsman had not reckoned with the obligation of marrying Ruth, so it may well be that, although the custom of levirate marriage was remembered, it was already falling into disuse. Within as little as a generation or two the shoe ceremony might well have required explanation.

Scholars who hold that the book was a protest against the policy of Ezra and Nehemiah are committed to a post-exilic date in the 5th or 4th century BC. Others favour a post-exilic date for different reasons, such as the place of the book in the Hebrew Canon (see below), linguistic considerations, or a late date for Deuteronomy which pushes Ruth into the post-exilic period. An assessment of the date of the Hebrew has to take into account two undisputed factors: (1) the Hebrew is classical; (2) there are Aramaisms in the text. Scholars differ widely in the conclusions they draw from these facts. Some use the presence of Aramaisms to support a post-exilic dating, while others point out that in the time of Hezekiah the leaders in Jerusalem were well able to understand Aramaic (2 Ki. 18:26), that from the time of David there had been close links between Syrian Aram and Israel which might be expected to result in linguistic borrowing, and that in any case some so-called Aramaisms have proved to be early West-Semitic terms, which would be part of the ancestry of both languages. Nothing in the language, therefore, points specifically to a post-exilic date. On the contrary the general Hebrew style is markedly different from that of books known to be post-exilic, and S. R. Driver says it 'stands on a level with the best parts of Samuel' (*LOT*, p. 454). It may be argued that the writer adopted an archaic style in keeping with the period of which he was writing, but it seems more likely that he lived in the pre-exilic period, perhaps 100 years or so after the time of Ruth. Some have suggested the reign of Solomon, a period of literary production in Israel, as a likely date.

PLACE IN THE CANON

In our English Bibles the book of Ruth follows Judges, as it does in the LXX and Vulgate translations. In printed Hebrew Bibles, however, Ruth appears in the last section to be accepted as canonical, the Writings, where it is the second of the five scrolls which were used liturgically in the synagogue by the 6th century AD. Ruth was read at Pentecost. The Babylonian Talmud, which is older than the 6th century, began the Writings with Ruth, followed by Psalms. Other lists put Ruth as the first of the five scrolls because it belonged first chronologically. Evidently the book was first placed among the Writings and was later transferred to the place where it belongs historically, between Judges and Samuel.

THEOLOGY

Names of God

Each of the main characters bears testimony to a deep faith in the Lord, 'Yahweh', whose name occurs eighteen times in four short chapters. 'As the Lord lives' (3:13) underlines the conviction that He is near at hand, intimately aware of every individual life, and, though He disciplines through famine and bereavement, He turns barrenness into fertility, graciously recompenses those who trust Him, and is the source of all true blessing. The name Yahweh had been revealed supremely at the Exodus, when God delivered the Israelites from slavery, brought them to Sinai and entered into covenant with them; to use the name was to recall His gracious deliverance and the security of His covenant promise. In 1:16 and 2:12 the context requires the general name for God, 'Elohim'. The only other divine name which occurs, '(El) Shaddai', comes to Naomi's lips when, weary from her journey, she meets her one-time neighbours and nostalgically recalls her early married life in Bethlehem (1:20, 21). By avoiding the intimate

name and using the more distant one Naomi was conveying her feeling of estrangement. Had not promised blessings been withheld from her? J. A. Motyer (*The Revelation of the Divine Name*, 1959, pp. 28, 29) has shown from the contexts in which this name occurs in Genesis that it underlined human powerlessness and spoke of the God who could transform situations of human helplessness. Naomi was painfully aware of her weakness and need. Though her faith was dim her use of the name 'Almighty' was a reminder of His power to do great things, and He did not fail her.

Redemption

The twenty occurrences of the verb 'to redeem' (Heb. *gā'al*) in so short a book are a reminder that the word was in common use in Israel. It belonged to the realm of family law: each member of the family had obligations to protect the other, and none should be lonely or destitute. The near relative who bought back family property (Lv. 25:25), or secured the freedom of an enslaved brother (Lv. 25:47-55), or avenged a murder (Nu. 35; Dt. 19:6), was known as the *gō'ēl*. The book of Ruth extends his duties to providing an heir for a relative who has died childless. The law of levirate marriage, outlined in Dt. 25:5-10, envisaged several brothers and their families sharing one home. If one brother died without having a son, the next brother was to take the widow and provide an heir for his dead brother. In the case of Ruth, who had no brothers-in-law, a more distant relative was expected to marry her. When the OT asserted that Yahweh was Israel's *Gō'ēl* it underlined His covenant promise, by which Israel became His own possession (Ex. 19:5). He dwelt among His people (Ex. 25:8) and was their divine Kinsman, ready to deliver and protect them. The special contribution of this book to the subject is to make clear that the *gō'ēl* alone possessed the right to redeem, and yet was under no obligation to do so. The willing, generous response of Boaz was, in a very small way, a foreshadowing of the great *Gō'ēl*, who was to descend from him.

Kindness

The Hebrew word *ḥesed*, which occurs in 1:8, 2:20 and 3:10, is much richer in meaning than its English counterpart 'kindness' would suggest. Supremely it is the characteristic of God Himself: 'the Lord deal kindly with you' (1:8), '... the Lord, whose kindness has not forsaken the living or the dead!' (2:20). It is a word closely related to the covenant because it is in the covenant that the gracious approach of God to sinful human beings is most clearly seen. The song rejoicing in the deliverance from Egypt proclaims, 'Thou hast led in thy steadfast love (*ḥesed*) the people whom thou hast redeemed' (Ex. 15:13). Deuteronomy shows the link very clearly: 'the Lord your God is God, the faithful God who keeps covenant and steadfast love . . .' (7:9). It is a word which includes the warmth of God's fellowship as well as the security of His faithfulness.

It follows that those who have experienced the Lord's *ḥeseḏ* should be transformed by it, and so show this quality of love to others. Both Naomi and Boaz do so, but it is Ruth the Moabitess who is said to have shown *ḥeseḏ* (3:10), where Boaz has particularly in mind moral uprightness, as well as selfless love and loyalty (2:11). Where such love and faithfulness is demonstrated in personal relationships the Lord is at work. In Ruth's case the moment of moral choice in

showing *ḥeseḏ* to Naomi was the moment of her conversion, when she made Naomi's God her God, though no doubt the conviction had long been forming within her that Yahweh was the living God, whom she desired above all else. We are probably right in conjecturing that the lives of the Israelites with whom she had been so closely related had drawn her towards Him. This book, like the Psalms, shows us how joyous and satisfying Israel's religion was, and how attractive it became to others when God's people reflected His faithful love to them in their dealings with one another.

OUTLINE OF CONTENTS

COMMENTARY

1:1–22 RETURN TO BETHLEHEM

1:1–5 Famine and bereavement

1 *The days when the judges ruled* are described in all their lawlessness in the book of Judges, but no precise information is given here to enable us to co-ordinate the two books. Perhaps it was during one of the periods when 'the land had rest forty years' (Jdg. 3:11; 5:31) that famine struck Bethlehem, whose name meant ironically 'house of bread'. *Bethlehem in Judah* distinguished the place from the northern Bethlehem (Jos. 19:15). The book of Judges bears independent testimony to the fact that moral standards in Bethlehem compared favourably with those in other places, notably Gibeah (Jdg. 19). Mention of the birth-place of David would capture the special interest of Jewish readers from the very beginning. When famine struck, one man of initiative took his family on a 50-mile journey to the eastern side of the Dead Sea valley to *the country of Moab*. The Hebrew word means literally 'field', but, as much of Moab is steep rocky hills, it probably refers to the fertile plateau, 2,000–3,000 ft high, south of the river Arnon. From the hills south of Bethlehem it would have been possible to see this plateau on the horizon to the south-east, across the Dead Sea.

2 The name *Elimelech*, meaning 'Melek is God' or 'God is king', occurs in the Amarna letters of the 14th century BC in the form *Milkilu* (*DOTT*, pp. 39–41), and is therefore ancient. Moreover, names compounded with *melek* are confined to the pre-exilic period. *Naomi* means 'my pleasant one' and is probably derived from a feminine form of *naaman*, an adjective used in the Ras Shamra texts of *c.* 1400 BC, and therefore ancient also. The suggested meanings of *Mahlon*, 'weakly' and *Chilion*, 'pining', are merely conjectural, but even if these meanings were accepted their appropriateness would not prove that the names were coined by the author. *Ephrathites*; Ephrath, the ancient name for Bethlehem (Gn. 35:19), persisted in the adjectival form. **4** Though many guesses have been made, the meaning of the names *Orpah* and *Ruth* is not known. They are Moabite and not Hebrew in form. Thus the names are entirely in keeping with the story. Ruth was the wife of Mahlon, as we know from 4:10. The marriage of the sons took place during their 10 years in Moab, where they had settled down. **5** Elimelech's death (v. 3), followed later by the death of Mahlon and Chilion, could have been the occasion for censure upon them for settling in an idolatrous land, but the author is content to state the facts as they concerned Naomi. The stress is on the anguish of her bereavement, especially as she was left without either means of livelihood or hope for the future.

1:6-18 Departure from Moab

6, 7 This interesting example of news reaching other lands of what was going on in Israel, shows how other nations observed Yahweh's dealings with His people and had opportunity to believe in Him. Naomi, reminded of the goodness of the Lord, longed once more for home, and for a share in His blessing. Orpah and Ruth set out with her, intending to go with her to Bethlehem, though they were under no obligation to do so. They seem to have been genuinely fond of their mother-in-law, and were reluctant to allow her to return alone. **8, 9** Naomi for her part thought only for their future; she wanted each of them to feel free to return to her mother's house, where they would find security in a second marriage. They had shown kindness to their husbands and to Naomi, and now she prayed that the Lord would show His kindness to them by blessing their future homes. For a note on the word 'kindness' see Introduction, 'Kindness'. **11-13** In reply to their protestations Naomi argued that in their case the law of levirate marriage (*cf.* Introduction, 'Redemption') could not possibly apply. She had no more sons and was unlikely to have any. Seeing therefore no likelihood of marriage for them in Judah, her sympathy went out to them, especially as their suffering was a result of the Lord's dealings with her. **14** Orpah found the argument persuasive and returned home. **15** Naomi did not blame her; in fact she urged Ruth to do the same, to go back to her own people and to Chemosh, the national god of Moab. **16, 17** It now became clear that Ruth no longer wished to serve Chemosh, but was determined to give her allegiance to the God of Israel, whom she had come to know through the life and witness of her husband and Naomi. The words recorded in vv. 16, 17 are the epitome of utter loyalty and selfless devotion. No ulterior motive influenced her decision. She identified herself with Naomi, and even bound herself by an oath to stand by her to death. The oath, *May the Lord do so to me and more also . . .* occurs elsewhere only in the books of Samuel and Kings.

1:19-22 Arrival in Bethlehem

19 All superfluous detail is omitted. As though silhouetted together against the skyline *the two of them went on*. Their arrival caused a stir of interest and excitement, especially amongst the women. Their question may suggest that they hardly recognized her because she was so changed, or that they were surprised and overjoyed to see her again. **20** Naomi quickly cut short any rejoicing by revealing the depth of her despair in a play on her name. Far from being one in whom the Lord delighted, she renamed herself *Mara*, 'bitter', in view of the trouble she had been through. For a note on the significance

of *the Almighty* (Shaddai), see Introduction, 'Names of God'. When Naomi accused the Almighty of dealing hardly with her she was forgetful of the gracious power of the God she was complaining of; she had a wrong picture of both her God and her past. **21** Though she says she *went away full*, the famine had been a disaster at the time, and now in her 'emptiness' she had the opportunity to prove that the Lord could fill her need. *The Lord has afflicted me.* This RSV translation is an emended version of the Hebrew, following the LXX, Syriac and the Vulgate. The Massoretic text means 'the Lord hath testified against me', as in AV and RV, *i.e.* her sufferings are a sign of God's disapproval. The emendation both changes the construction by omitting the preposition and alters the form of the verb. **22** The story-teller recapitulates and repeats the refrain *they came to Bethlehem*, but he prepares us for the next episode by adding *at the beginning of barley harvest*, which was in April. An inscription known as the Gezer Calendar, dating from the time of Saul or David, divides the year according to the farmer's activities, and mentions 'Month of barley harvest' (*DOTT*, p. 201). Had the author been writing centuries later, he could easily have introduced an anachronism.

2:1-23 GOD'S GRACIOUS PROVISION

1 At this point the narrator skilfully introduces the fact that a relative of Elimelech was still living in Bethlehem, but the Hebrew avoids the term *gō'ēl*, which would have anticipated too much. Naomi knew of him but determined not to make use of him. By mentioning the fact in advance the author was able to show how wonderfully God over-ruled. *Boaz*, whose name probably meant 'in him is strength', was *a man of wealth*. The idea behind the Hebrew word is that he was gifted in every way. Perhaps Elimelech had once been described in similar terms. **2** Ruth, who knew nothing about Boaz, proposed to take advantage of the ancient law permitting the needy to glean in the fields at harvest time (*cf.* Lv. 19:9; 23:22; Dt. 24:19), so sparing Naomi the toil and humiliation such work involved. **3** Not knowing the place, she would follow other women to the harvest fields, where men would be cutting the grain with a sickle, women would be binding the sheaves, and anything left over would be the property of the gleaners. The author could see the hand of God at work in leading her to *the part of the field belonging to Boaz*. It is a surprise to read that wealthy Boaz owned only part of the field, but in the absence of hedges cultivable land was divided into strips, marked by boundary stones; one such strip is meant. **4, 5** The work was already in progress before Boaz arrived, for he had a servant in charge. *The Lord be with you*, words familiar from their liturgical use, are found only here in this precise form. The Lord was known and acknowledged in everyday work. *Whose maiden is this?* is a reminder that every woman belonged to someone in a tribal society; Boaz took a personal interest in those who worked on his land, and he did not recognize Ruth. **7** As a foreigner Ruth could not assume that she had a right to glean, but had been careful to ask permission. The second half of the verse has been translated from the LXX and Vulgate, as the RSV margin shows. The Hebrew, followed by the AV and RV, does not make easy sense. The Jerusalem Bible emends to, 'So she came and has been on her feet from morning till now.' Maybe she was resting when Boaz arrived, and the foreman wanted to vouch for her diligence.

8-10 Approving this testimonial, Boaz addressed himself to Ruth, urging her to remain in his fields, and promising her special protection. Evidently she could not assume that she would be respected, nor had she any right to the precious water, which had to be brought from the well, and was often in short supply. Contrary to custom, it is the young men here who draw the water. The generosity of Boaz overwhelmed Ruth. **11, 12** He explains that he had heard about her kindness to Naomi and that he wanted her to experience the reward which only the God of Israel could give. She had so recently come to trust Him, and Boaz wanted to encourage her faith. His lovely metaphor *the God of Israel, under whose wings you have come to take refuge* is taken up frequently in the Psalms, and by Jesus in Mt. 23:37. When a mother bird spreads her wings over her young to protect them with her life, the preying enemy cannot even see them. How much more concerned the Lord is to defend all those who take refuge in Him! **13** *You are most gracious to me* is more literally 'let me find grace', a turn of speech that expresses thanks by anticipating further favour.

14 The meal of bread and *wine, i.e.* vinegar mixed with oil, was supplemented with *parched grain*, in this case barley, roasted over a fire. Ruth sat with the reapers and was given her own portion of harvest fare, from which she kept back a share for Naomi. The RV 'she left thereof' gives better sense than the RSV. Her intention to share her food with Naomi may have prompted Boaz to tell the young men deliberately to increase the amount she could glean. **17, 18** The gleaner would not usually have much to show for a long day's work in the hot sun, but Ruth threshed out *about an ephah of barley.* The ephah was about the same as an English bushel, and a bushel of barley weighs about 50 pounds. In addition she brought to Naomi the parched corn she had saved. **19** *Where have you worked?* If this is the meaning of the second question it adds nothing to the first. Strictly the Hebrew conjunction means 'whither' and not 'where', and Prof. D. Winton Thomas has argued that the Hebrew verb '*āsāh* used here means 'to turn' rather than 'to make' in this context (*The Bible Translator*, Oct. 1966, Vol. 17, No. 4). According to his translation, 'and

whither didst thou turn?', Naomi is making her question more specific. **20** Naomi's delighted exclamation conveys her wonder at the Lord's over-ruling in leading Ruth to the field of Boaz. When she explains that he is one of their *nearest kin* she uses the word *gōʾēl*; already she foresees that the Lord may be permitting her to make some approach to him. **21-23** Ruth availed herself of the protection of Boaz until both barley and wheat harvests had ended. After this there would be no means of livelihood.

3:1-18 A CLAIM TO KINSHIP

1-6 Marriage was arranged by parents, and it was fitting that Naomi should take the initiative in providing a home and security for Ruth. The harvest had been gathered, and now winnowing of the barley was in progress. Naomi had laid her plans carefully, and had checked that Boaz would be spending the night at the threshing-floor, protecting his grain. Having washed and anointed herself with aromatic oils, Ruth was to put on her *best clothes*, or, more likely, her big outer garment, which would both provide warmth in the chill of the night, and enable her to remain incognito until the strategic moment came. Naomi's instructions are explicit; behind them may lie some accepted custom. The text emphasizes that Ruth did all she was told to do, and so makes it clear that Ruth was in no sense to be blamed for her intrusion into the threshing-floor; indeed it may have taken some courage on her part to obey her mother-in-law. After the traditional feasting at the end of the day of harvesting, Boaz might be expected to retire in good humour, and sleep soundly. By removing the cloak that acted as a blanket from the feet of Boaz, she would ensure that he would eventually wake up and notice her at his feet. She would then be able to put before him in privacy the claim she wished to make.

7-9 Nothing interfered with the out-working of the plan. The vivid detail *he went to lie down at the end of the heap of grain* is striking. The author must often have seen farmers protecting their harvest in this way. When Boaz suddenly awoke to find a woman there, his first concern was to identify her. Did he guess that Naomi might attempt to claim the rights of kinship? When Ruth asked him to spread his cloak over her she was speaking symbolically of marriage. The same figure of speech is found in Ezk. 16:8b. **10** Boaz not only put the best possible construction on Ruth's action, but went so far as to invoke a blessing upon her for all her acts of kindness. He implies that it would have been more natural for her to have married one of the young reapers than to make this appeal to him, for he probably belonged to her father-in-law's generation. Ruth's circumspect behaviour in the harvest fields, where friendships may often have been formed, had not escaped the notice of Boaz, nor of the community generally. **11-13** This fact enabled Boaz to comply with her request provided that a nearer kinsman relinquished his right to act as her *gō'ēl*. Boaz was legally bound to put the case to the nearer relative before he could take the responsibility on himself. If Naomi knew of the existence of this other relative, she must have decided that she would prefer Ruth to be under the protection of Boaz. **14** As soon as it began to dawn Boaz deemed that she should return home, in the safety of daylight, but unobserved by prying eyes. He wished to give no occasion for gossip. **15** The *mantle* may have been a corner of her large cloak or a headdress. The Hebrew word occurs elsewhere only in Is. 3:22. The *six measures of barley* were a tangible assurance of goodwill as well as a generous gift to Naomi. Though the type of measure is not specified, no doubt she was given as much as she could conveniently carry. **16** Naomi's question is translated literally in the AV, 'Who art thou, my daughter?', but the sense of the idiom is given in the RSV, *How did you fare?* **18** Ruth now had to stay patiently at home until the affair was settled. The dénouement is awaited with all the suspense of a drama.

4:1-17 THE KINSMAN-REDEEMER

The last scene is the open square at the city gate, where legal matters were decided and the business of the town transacted. **1, 2** Boaz lost no time in fulfilling his promise, but made his way to the gate as the most likely place to find his relative first thing in the morning, when business was beginning. Though this man remains anonymous in our story, Boaz would have hailed him by name. Clearly Boaz is a man with authority in the community, for he takes command of the situation, and the elders put themselves at his disposal as witnesses. This is a confirmation that he was no longer a young man. **3, 4** For the first time we learn that Naomi had land which she was offering for sale. So far as we know a widow had no right of inheritance, but she would be acting on behalf of her sons. By selling the field to the *gō'ēl* it would be kept in the family, and she would realize a little capital on it. The RSV retains from the AV the archaic *parcel of land* instead of adopting the more usual *portion*. Boaz puts the option clearly, stating that if the nearer relative does not redeem it he will, but the reply comes, *I will redeem it.* **5, 6** Only now is the crucial subject broached. Elimelech had a right to an heir; Ruth his daughter-in-law was still living, and the man who bought the field had the duty of raising an heir for the dead. If a son was born the field would revert to him, and so the *gō'ēl* would have impaired his own inheritance because his sons would not inherit what he had bought. Moreover he would have another family to keep. In the light of this refusal the generosity of Boaz becomes the more apparent. Many of the laws of the OT involved willingness for material loss, and revealed maturity of faith in those who obeyed. **7-10** The elders heard the next-of-kin pass on

to Boaz the right of redemption, but to complete the transaction the symbolic ceremony of handing over the sandal had to be performed (*cf.* Introduction, 'Date'). The sandal symbolized possession (*cf.* Jos. 1:3), and so the witnesses testified that Boaz was the legal heir of Elimelech, and therefore of Mahlon and Chilion. Ruth's first male child should be known as 'son of Elimelech', thus perpetuating *the name of the dead.* **11** Others besides the official witnesses had by this time gathered at the city gate to affirm the legality of the transaction, and to add their blessing to that of the elders. The blessing implies that more than one child was hoped for. Rachel and Leah, together with their handmaids, had borne Jacob twelve sons; Boaz would be rewarded if Ruth bore him many sons to add to his prestige and prosperity. **12** At first sight mention of the unsavoury story of Judah and Tamar (Gn. 38) seems a little out of place, but the author had two good reasons for introducing it. Firstly, it referred to levirate marriage, but, whereas Tamar had been tacitly refused, Boaz had honoured the obligation. Secondly, there was a special local interest. Perez, who was born to Tamar as a result of her strategem, was an ancestor of Boaz (v. 18), and doubtless of many others in the Bethlehem district, for the genealogies mention only three sons of Judah, from whom the whole tribe descended.

13, 14 The birth of a son to Ruth is attributed directly to the Lord's blessing, but the one congratulated is Naomi, because she is no longer desolate, but has a 'son' through whom Elimelech's name will be carried on. **15** The new-born child will give her a new lease of life, and be a comfort to her in her old age. Though a tribute is paid to Ruth, it is Naomi who is the central figure. **16, 17** By taking the baby on her knee Naomi was symbolizing the fact that she was adopting him, and the words of the neighbours reveal that they so interpreted her action. There is a difficulty in v. 17 which would be removed if *gave him a name* could be deleted, as in the Peshitto version, so that it read, 'The women of the neighbourhood said, "A son has been born to Naomi." They named him Obed.' As it stands there is no connection between the introductory words 'gave him a name' and the exclamation that follows. An early scribe may have inserted the verb twice by mistake. *Obed* is a short form of the name Obadiah, meaning 'servant of the Lord', a worthy name for the grandfather of great King David, mention of whom brings the story to its climax. 1 Sa. 22:3, 4 tells of David's visit to Moab; he may even have known Ruth. Some commentators think that the original story ended here.

4:18-22 CONCLUSION

The concluding genealogy, tracing the connection between Perez and David, may have come from the same source as 1 Ch. 2:4-15. The main reason for thinking that it was added later is that Elimelech's name does not occur, in spite of the insistence in the story that the first-born son should continue his family. Instead Obed is called son of Boaz. *Hezron* is named in the list of those who went down into Egypt with Jacob (Gn. 46:12). From Ex. 6:23 we know that *Amminadab* and *Nashon* were contemporary with Moses, but as only one generation separates Nashon from Boaz, the genealogy must be abbreviated. *Salmon* is another form of the name 'Salma' in 1 Ch. 2:11, but in v. 51, where Salma is called 'father of Bethlehem', another man, a descendant of Caleb, is meant.

Whether or not the genealogy was part of the original book, it makes a fitting ending to the story, by linking Ruth with the wider Bible history. The writer wanted us to know that future destinies were in the balance when Ruth made her apparently private decision to stand by Naomi and worship the God of Israel. More hung in the balance than even he could know, for this is not the last mention of her in the Bible. As the ancestress of David, Ruth had the honour to be among the forebears of Jesus Christ (Mt. 1:5).

J. G. BALDWIN

1 and 2 Samuel

INTRODUCTION

In the Hebrew text the two books of Samuel formed one only. The present division is inconvenient, for it breaks up the story of David and the account of Saul's disaster on Gilboa. The authors of the Septuagint (LXX) took the books of Samuel and Kings as a complete history of the kingdom, and divided it into four sections called 'Books of the Kingdoms' (or 'Reigns'). The Latin Bible in due course altered this to 'Books of the Kings'; so that the books of Samuel were called the first and second 'Books of the Kings' respectively.

Since the 16th century, most Hebrew Bibles have followed the arrangement of dividing the original book of Samuel in two, and have called the parts the first and second books of Samuel. Most English versions adopt the same practice, but in the AV these books have, as sub-title, the first and second 'Book of the Kings', and 1 and 2 Kings have, as sub-title, third and fourth 'Book of the Kings', respectively.

DATE AND AUTHORSHIP

The name of Samuel is very appropriately used as a title for 1 and 2 Samuel, since he is the central figure of the first chapters, and also the man who anointed both Saul and David, the chief characters of the remainder of the two books. The title does not imply that he wrote the books; he could not possibly have done so, for his death is recorded as early as 1 Sa. 25:1. He may well have been the author of one of the source documents used by the final author; 1 Ch. 29:29 shows that Samuel was a writer. (On the sources, see Appendix 1.)

There can be no doubt that early and reliable sources were available to the author, but he himself cannot have lived (or, at least, written) before the death of Solomon, since the divided monarchy is alluded to in 1 Sa. 27:6, in terms which suggest that more than one king had succeeded Solomon. The earliest possible date for the whole work would thus be the end of the 10th century BC. The quality of the Hebrew and the absence of Aramaisms point to the early date of the sources, rather than to the early date of the completed work; it is generally agreed that the author provided a minimum of editorial addition and comment. Almost certainly the books of Samuel as we know them were formulated as part of a bigger historical work, namely Joshua–Judges–Samuel–Kings; if so, the final editing cannot have taken place before the Exile, since the books of Kings carry the story down to that era (6th century BC). But it seems likely that a first edition, so to speak, probably substantially the same as the final work, was written long before the Exile: 1 Sa. 27:6 must have been penned before the monarchy ended, but it is clearly an editorial comment, not drawn from a source document.

PURPOSE

The purpose of the books of Samuel, like the question of authorship, cannot be considered in isolation from the other historical books, Joshua, Judges and Kings. Israel's history, from the triumphant conquest of Canaan to the ignominious departure into Exile, is presented in terms of God's relationship with that nation, and in particular with its leaders. The function of the books of Samuel is to direct attention to the beginning of the monarchy, with all its high hopes and potentialities.

In the popular view, we may fairly assume that David will have been recalled with pride and nostalgia, Saul probably with rather mixed feelings, while Samuel was possibly remembered as a great prophet but a poor national leader, who had been unable to achieve much against the Philistines. The historical facts were given by the writer of 1 and 2 Samuel, not just to enlarge his public's acquaintance with its own history, but to put those facts in their proper religious perspective. Thus readers past and present learn why a change of national constitution came about, and why Saul failed to achieve true greatness; while from the history of David lessons are taught about the qualities, the character and the behaviour demanded from the man who aspires to lead the people of God, as also about the way God will deal with such a man, in one circumstance after another. For this reason, the Bathsheba episode is not shrugged off as the minor peccadillo of an otherwise great and good king, but shown to be the turning-point in his reign.

Through the narratives it is also revealed how God is ever present, in one way and another, with His people. While Israel suffered from time to time, often owing to the failure of her leaders, God was yet always providing 'some better thing' for them. And in this way the books of Samuel pointed forward, as they looked back, and provided inspiration for the dark days under a Manasseh or a Nebuchadrezzar.

DUPLICATE ACCOUNTS

A feature of the books of Samuel to which

repeated attention has been drawn is the occurrence of a number of 'duplicate accounts', or, in other words, pairs of very similar narratives. The most obvious example is the pair of stories about David's sparing Saul's life (1 Sa. 24; 26), but it is by no means the only 'duplicate'. Twice the fall of Eli's house is foretold (1 Sa. 2:31–36; 3:11–14); twice Yahweh's rejection of Saul is announced (1 Sa. 13; 15); twice David is introduced to Saul's court (1 Sa. 16:17–22; 17:55 – 18:5); twice he flees to Achish king of Gath (1 Sa. 21; 27). Two or even three duplicate accounts have been found in the story of Saul's becoming king (1 Sa. 8–12); but that complex of events constitutes a special case, which is best treated separately (see Appendix 2).

There is rarely any historical difficulty in such twin narratives; if David spared Saul's life once, he may just as easily have done so twice. Some readers may feel that would be too great a coincidence; but it is clearly not impossible. The most difficult historical problem arises over the question of David's being introduced to Saul; for Saul's conversation with Abner recorded in 1 Sa. 17:55–58 does seem to imply that the young warrior was unknown to the king, in spite of David's earlier service as a royal musician and armour-bearer (1 Sa. 16:21–23). However, the difficulty is not insuperable (see commentary in loc.).

But the real answer is surely to be found in the purpose of the writer. Even if in each case one of the pair of 'duplicates' came from a separate source from its twin (which is very doubtful), the compiler and author must have used both quite deliberately. In effect, the repetition of similar incidents serves to give emphasis to certain points the writer wishes to make. In this fashion the author has stressed and underscored the fact that it was no accident that Eli's house was rejected, nor that Saul and his succession was put aside by God; it was no mere chance that brought David to Saul's court; nor was it a mere passing whim of David's that saved Saul's life. The divine hand and purpose in history are thus unmistakably shown to the reader.

Moreover, there is often a sequence in the paired episodes. This is particularly true of the accounts of David's arrival at court and of his flight to Gath (see commentary in loc.). Again, when the writer uses remarkably similar language in the second of a duplicate pair, we may be sure he is deliberately reminding the reader of the former incident; this applies especially to the twofold mention of the sneering proverb about Saul's 'prophetic' powers (1 Sa. 10:12; 19:24). Finally, the 'difficulty' is sometimes occasioned by the very art of the writer. He is no doubt giving only part of the conversation between Saul and Abner, following David's victory over Goliath, in 1 Sa. 17:55–58; but the purpose of what is recorded is to emphasize the minor and virtually unknown capacity in which David had served Saul in the past, in contrast

with the position of eminence and prominence which he is now to occupy at the same court. (In this connection, it is to be observed that much of the direct speech in the Bible may well be abbreviation or paraphrase of the original statements or conversations.)

In short, to view two similar stories as mere duplicates of each other, divergent at that, is to lose much of the point and effect of the narrative.

THE TEXT

It is unfortunate that the Hebrew text, as we have it in the Massoretic Text, of the books of Samuel has been relatively poorly preserved. There are a few occasions where something has been lost altogether (cf. 1 Sa. 13:1), and quite a number where the MT offers poor sense, if any. As it happens, the LXX translation provides better sense in the majority of these instances, and it is almost inevitable that scholars should have made considerable use of the LXX to elucidate the Hebrew. Footnotes in the RSV will give some idea of the number of times that such procedure has been thought necessary; the Jerusalem Bible (JB) makes considerably greater use still of the LXX.

In general, it is not considered wise to emend the Hebrew text too readily on the basis of the LXX; one cannot often be sure what precise Hebrew text the LXX translators had in front of them (their Vorlage), especially since they were prepared to introduce considerable changes in wording and meaning if they felt it proper to do so. Even where the books of Samuel are concerned, therefore, too heavy a dependence on the LXX is to be discouraged. However, the value of the LXX for these books has been enhanced by the discovery among the Dead Sea Scrolls of some fragmentary MSS of Samuel which show marked Septuagintal affinities. This find suggests that the LXX Vorlage of Samuel was a different recension of the books from that which was the basis of the MT. Nevertheless, caution remains necessary, and decisions between variant readings will still have to be made on the basis of the scientific criteria used in textual criticism; sometimes the MT will be right, at other times the LXX.

The particular textual problems surrounding 1 Sa. 17; 18 are discussed separately, in Appendix 4.

In view of the number of uncertainties of text and translation, it is impossible in a brief commentary to treat each one in detail. The RSV has therefore been followed without comment (RSV mg. often draws attention to the uncertainties, in any case), except where there seem particularly strong reasons for either elaborating or disagreeing.

CHRONOLOGY

The dates of Samuel, Saul and David cannot be ascertained with precision, and different scholars hold rather different opinions on some points (notably the length of Saul's reign; see on 1 Sa. 13:1). Samuel's period of office may be tentatively assigned to the years 1075–1035 BC, the battle of Aphek having occurred not earlier than 1050. Saul's reign overlapped with Samuel's career, and its beginning may be roughly dated at 1045. With a little more certainty the death of Saul can be assigned to *c.* 1010, and the reign of David *c.* 1010–970.

FURTHER READING

Attention is often drawn in the commentary to the works of two recent writers, namely H. W. Hertzberg (*I & II Samuel: a Commentary*, 1964) and W. McKane (*I & II Samuel: Introduction and Commentary*, 1963). For detailed notes these should be referred to; and the standard Introductions to the Old Testament and Bible Dictionaries will yield full bibliographies. To view the reigns of Saul and David in historical setting, readers should consult the relevant sections in J. Bright, *History of Israel*, 1960, or M. Noth, *History of Israel²*, 1960.

A good Bible atlas is indispensable for a proper understanding of a number of passages in the books of Samuel. L. H. Grollenberg, *Atlas of the Bible*, 1965, or G. E. Wright and F. V. Filson, *Westminster Historical Atlas to the Bible*, 1953, may be recommended. On archaeological data relevant to the period, J. A. Thompson, *The Bible and Archaeology*, 1962, ch. 6.

OUTLINE OF CONTENTS

(In this analysis the two books are treated as a whole)

COMMENTARY

1 Sa. 1:1 – 7:14 SAMUEL'S EARLY YEARS

The historical situation presupposed at the start of the narrative of the books of Samuel is that of the end of the period of the judges; 1 Samuel is the sequel to the book of Judges. There are two recurring themes in the books of Samuel: the problem of the leadership of God's people, Israel; and the presence of God in their midst. The former motif means that the history of Israel is presented in terms of the lives of three outstanding individuals—Samuel, Saul and David—while the second motif involves frequent mention of shrine and ark. The two themes come together when the Lord is said to be 'with' one leader or another.

1:1 – 3:21 Samuel and Eli

The first section of 1 Samuel, accordingly, brings before us two successive spiritual leaders, Eli and Samuel; and the scene is the principal sanctuary of the Israelites during the period of the judges, Shiloh (cf. Jdg. 18:31). It was destroyed by the Philistines c. 1050 BC.

1:1-8 Elkanah and his two wives. Attention is first drawn to Samuel's parents, Elkanah and Hannah, a God-fearing couple who regularly visited Shiloh to worship. Yet Hannah was far from happy, due not only to her own barrenness but also to the unkind conduct of Elkanah's other wife. Polygamy was tolerated under the law of Moses (Dt. 21:15-17), but it was not the original divine intention (cf. Mt. 19:3-8), and could cause great misery. Barrenness was accounted a great disgrace for a Hebrew woman. **1** *Ramathaim-zophim* is a longer form of the usual Ramah (cf. v. 19); the second part of the name links it with *Zuph* (mentioned later in the verse), an ancestor of Elkanah descended from Levi via Kohath, according to 1 Ch. 6:22-38. Thus *Ephraimite* must refer to geographical location, not ancestry. **4, 5** The *portions* were of meat, part of a sacrificial meal. Hannah received *only one*, since she had no mouths but her own to feed, if RSV is correct; but a 'worthy' or 'double' portion (see AV, RV) is not impossible—the Hebrew text, though obscure, at least suggests it, and such an act by Elkanah would partly explain Peninnah's conduct.

1:9-18 Hannah's prayer and its answer. Hannah made a special plea to God for a son, which involved a vow that he should be dedicated to God from his earliest years. The passage makes clear that Samuel was the special provision of God, not of course only for Hannah, but for Israel as a whole; this was no natural birth. **9** *Eli the priest was sitting* where he could be consulted, while his sons saw to ritual tasks (see v. 3). **11** Samuel was to be a Nazirite, in fact. The regulations for Nazirites are given in Nu. 6, although there it is clear that the Nazirite

vow was normally of temporary duration. (See *NBD*, art. 'Nazarite'.)

1:19-28 Samuel's birth and dedication to God. God's miraculous gift of a son, followed by the boy's total dedication to God, is epitomized in the phrases 'asked . . . of the Lord' (v. 20) and 'lent to the Lord' (v. 28). (In Heb. one verb, *šā'al*, provides both meanings.) There is irony here, and concealed theological significance, for the fact is (as any Hebrew reader would have known at once) that Saul's name, not Samuel's, means 'asked'. Samuel, in fact, was all that Saul was not.

20 The name *Samuel* means something like 'his name is God', or 'a godly name'; W. J. Martin has suggested that, in naming him, Hannah uttered some such sentence as 'I asked for him a godly name' (see *NBD*, art. 'Samuel'). **21** *The yearly sacrifice.* Evidently Elkanah's pilgrimage was an annual event (in spite of the injunction of Ex. 23:17). Most modern commentators hold that it was the Feast of Tabernacles. **2:1-10 The song of Hannah.** Hannah's song is denied to her by most commentators, chiefly because of the specific reference to a king (v. 10). The song is not irrelevant to the situation, however: Israel had its adversaries, and God's agent in deliverance would be His anointed. We may therefore think of Hannah as specially inspired to see that Samuel's career would lead to Israel's salvation from the Philistine threat. On the other hand, v. 1 stands apart (see RSV), and is perhaps the only sentence attributed directly to Hannah (similarly, in Jn. 3, it is difficult to decide precisely what is direct speech). The narrator may have inserted at this point a well-known psalm (from the Feast of Tabernacles liturgy, conceivably), which he saw as particularly appropriate to the situation in Hannah's time. The song is comparable in many ways with the Magnificat (Lk. 1:46-55). 'The psalm puts the birth, and hence the life, of Samuel in the context of the all-powerful saving acts of God' (Hertzberg). **5** *The barren has borne seven* provides an adequate link with Hannah's personal situation; it is not to be taken literally, of course. **6** *Sheol*; i.e. the abode of the dead. **10** *Anointed* (in Heb. the word from which 'Messiah' is ultimately derived) is a common expression in the books of Samuel, with their constant theme of God's chosen leader.

2:11-26 The sanctuary at Shiloh. A contrast emerges between the serene godliness of the boy Samuel and the corrupt practices of Eli's sons; Eli seems to have been a helpless onlooker. **11** *Elkanah went home*, presumably taking the rest of his family with him. **13** *The custom* was plainly a bad one; the following verses indicate that Hophni and Phinehas took from the offerer what belonged to his own sacrificial feast; and they insulted God by demanding their portion before His was burnt on the altar (see Lv. 3:3–5; 7:29–34). **18, 19** The *ephod* was a priestly robe; the *little robe* was for more general use. **20** *Loan . . . lent* (or as RSV mg.) again picks up the theme of Samuel's name (*cf.* 1:20). **21** does more than tell us family news; it shows the blessing deriving from Samuel's office. **25** *Who can intercede . . . ? I.e.* there was no machinery for arbitrating between priests and God. The purposes of God for Eli's sons are here revealed in advance of the punishment meted out to them (4:11); but their disobedience was of their own volition. Yet 'the punishment of sin may consist in the sinner's loss of his freewill' (Eichrodt).

2:27–36 A prophecy about the priesthood. The prophecy is comprehensive, predicting not merely the death of Eli's sons, but also Samuel's succession to Eli himself, and the rise of the line of Zadok. The passage teaches that historical vicissitudes are both morally conditioned and very much under divine control. As with Hannah's song, we may choose to think that the original oracle has been amplified by the inspired writer to show in greater detail God's plans for the priestly leadership of His people; but it is an impossible task to set the limits of divine revelation to the prophets.

There are a number of textual obscurities in this passage.

31 Fulfilled in the Nob massacre (ch. 22). **35** makes explicit the proper harmony between priest and king, respectively cultic and political leaders of Israel. **36** predicts the menial tasks that await Eli's posterity.

3:1–21 The Lord appears to Samuel. In fulfilment of the prophecy of ch. 2, Eli begins to retire into the background, Samuel coming into prominence (*cf.* how the Gospels depict John the Baptist from the time of the baptism of Christ).

1 *The word of the Lord was rare.* This is both an introduction to the narrative that follows and a statement of Israel's sorry plight. Probably we are to assume that the faults of Eli's family had occasioned the rarity of the divine voice. **3** *The lamp of God* was not the seven-branched candlestick, as that was never allowed to go out (Lv. 24:2). Samuel was lying near *the ark* for the purpose of receiving any word from God, yet **7** he had never before experienced any such revelation; hence his first reactions to the voice of God.

10–14 rehearse, but in different words, the prophecy received by Eli (2:27–36). **10** *As at other times*: not to Samuel, but to his predecessors in attendance beside the ark. **19** Samuel shows predictive powers. **20** *A prophet.* As a priest, Samuel could function only at Shiloh, but as prophet his importance reached *from Dan to Beer-sheba, i.e.* as far as the most northerly and most southerly sanctuary-cities of Israel. He is thus depicted as a national figure and no longer a child (*cf.* 4:1).

4:1 – 7:14 War with the Philistines

The writer's attention now turns to the Philistine threat (last treated in Jdg. 13–16). But the presence of God is still the underlying theme; this section might be sub-titled 'the adventures of the ark' (L. H. Brockington).

4:1–10 Israel suffers defeat. The mention of *Aphek*, which lay due W of Shiloh, on the edge of the coastal plain, shows that the Philistines were making inroads into the hill country, having fully mastered the plain. The Israelites therefore mustered and endeavoured now to drive them out of the hills, but were routed.

1 The first part of the verse belongs in ch. 3, and appears there in several ancient versions. *Ebenezer* was later to be the scene of an Israelite victory (see on 7:12). **3, 4** The Israelites were making a fetish of *the ark*, for while they recognized that God was responsible for their defeat, they considered that the physical presence of the ark must inevitably bring victory. The ark was viewed as His throne; and since He was *the Lord of hosts* (lit. 'armies', but the hosts of heaven rather than of Israel), His presence would win the day for Israel. **5** The *shout* acclaimed the presence of God (*cf.* Ps. 47:5). **6–8** The Philistines were polytheists, and assumed that the Israelites were. **8** The Philistines apparently had a confused knowledge of Israel's previous history. **9** shows how far the Philistine aggression had gone.

4:11–22 The fall of Eli's house. The second, and much heavier, defeat led to the fulfilment of the prophecies of chs. 2, 3. Scripture does not dwell on the misery suffered in consequence by Israel, nor does it recount the subsequent sacking of Shiloh by the Philistines. Our knowledge of the latter disaster comes from archaeological excavations at Shiloh (together with hints in Je. 7:12; 26:6). It is the loss of the ark which is the real disaster in the narrator's eyes (see vv. 18–22).

18 Only here are we told that Eli was a judge, as well as a priest. The brief editorial note links the story with the book of Judges, and places it in the on-going scheme of history. **21** *Ichabod.* The second part to the name signifies 'glory', but the initial *I* is of uncertain meaning—'there is not', 'where is?', or 'alas for'. **22** *Departed*; lit. 'gone into exile'. Ps. 78:60f. briefly recalls the disasters of this chapter.

5:1–12 The ark in Philistine hands. We now follow the ark to the temple of Dagon in Ashdod. Dagon was a corn deity, whose cult extended from S Palestine to Mesopotamia; there was another temple to him at Ugarit, and the Ras Shamra tablets call Baal 'son of Dagon' (see *IDB*, art. 'Dagon'). But Dagon had neither defeated Israel nor captured the ark, which remained the property of Yahweh. His presence was by no means confined to the ark, but neither did He abandon it. If Israel had suffered defeat, He emerged victorious.

1 *Ashdod* was one of the five major Philistine

cities, which are all listed in 6:17. Samson had destroyed the Dagon temple in Gaza (Jdg. 16). **4, 5** *Threshold*. Possibly the pedestal (podium) of the idol is meant. Zp. 1:9 is reminiscent of the custom here related. The threshold became taboo because it had been in direct contact with the idol. **6** *Tumours*. The mention of mice in 6:4f. (and also in this verse, in LXX) suggests bubonic plague, an epidemic spread by rodents, of which swollen lymph-glands in the groin are characteristic. **8** *The lords of the Philistines* were the rulers of the five cities, which were independent but capable of very efficient collective action. **11** *Deathly panic*; 'fatal' may be the sense, *i.e.* that the panic caused fatalities over and above the victims of the epidemic.

6:1–12 The return of the ark. The ark came back to Israelite soil without the slightest effort by the men of Israel to retrieve it and in spite of the Philistine resort to pagan soothsayers (probably the sense of 'priests', v. 2) and diviners. Thus the overruling hand of God is evident.

2 *To its place* (JB 'to where it belongs'). The Philistines may not even have known it had come from Shiloh. There is in effect a double question here—where shall we send it, and how? **3, 4** The *guilt offering* will not have been on the levitical pattern; the Philistines practised a form of sympathetic magic, patently. The number *five* here, and the mention of all five cities in v. 17, indicate that the plague had affected all of Philistia, not merely the three cities mentioned in ch. 5. **5** *Your mice that ravage the land.* Probably it was the depletion of food-stocks by the mice that concerned the Philistines, who can scarcely have understood that bubonic plague was carried by rodents. **5, 6** The diviners' suggestions were plainly in the nature of an experiment. They found themselves with no precedent to follow, but they relied on their knowledge (such as it was) of Egypt's plague experiences when in contact with the Israelites. **7** *Milch cows* would not normally be used to pull carts, and would therefore not be inclined to follow any particular route. Moreover, they, like the *new cart*, would never have served to carry anything profane. In other words, the Philistines observed every conceivable taboo. **9** *Beth-shemesh* was just in Israelite territory, a few miles SE of Ekron. Originally allotted to Dan ('Ir-shemesh', Jos. 19:41), it was later a Levitical city within the tribal holding of Judah (Jos. 21:16). **10–12** The cows might well have headed *home* to their *calves*, but instead they made straight for *Beth-shemesh*.

6:13–20 The ark at Beth-shemesh. In spite of the understandable Israelite joy to see the ark returned—a real boost to Israelite morale—events soon made it clear that the ark was not to be trifled with. Symbol of the divine presence, it was holy and therefore dangerous (a common concept in the ancient world); W. McKane has suggested that the distinctive concept expressed here is that the ark was equally dangerous to Israelite laymen (as opposed to the priesthood)

as it was to the Philistines. (*Cf.* 2 Sa. 6:1–11.) All was well while the Levites (v. 15) handled it, but casual curiosity was punished (v. 19). God's presence among His people commands both reverent awe and also joy in His salvation.

14 *Joshua* was a common name in Israel; this Joshua was a local land-owner. The *great stone* was a natural landmark, utilized as an altar on this occasion, and it served for many years to remind Israel of the ark's history (see v. 18). **15** *The Levites*: one of the few references to Levites in Samuel and Kings. The frequently-made assertion that such a detail is unhistorical (deriving from the practices of a later date) is less compelling when one notes the very casual introduction of the Levites in this passage, whereas in 2 Sa. 6 there is no specific mention of them; one would have expected an editor rewriting such passages in the light of his own day to have mentioned Levites without fail in 2 Sa. 6, wherever else he omitted to do so. **16** *The Philistines* are satisfied; the ark has returned home and been received with due ceremonial. **18** *The golden mice* were five in number (see v. 4); the *villages* will have been reckoned with the *cities* for purposes of enumeration. *This day*; *i.e.* the date of the final composition of the book. **19** The men who died were guilty of breaking the law of Nu. 4:20. There were *seventy* who died; the additional 50,000 (*cf.* AV, RSV mg.) of most Hebrew MSS is difficult to account for, and a totally impossible figure.

6:21 – 7:2 The ark at Kiriath-jearim. Kiriath-jearim lay some 9 miles NE of Beth-shemesh, in the direction of Shiloh. The fact that Shiloh now lay in ruins explains both why the ark did not return to it and why Israel lamented. J. Bright and others have maintained that the Philistines, though glad to get rid of the ark, nevertheless would not let it out of their general supervision. This may be so; but on the other hand, they did not hinder its removal from Beth-shemesh, and later on Saul did nothing even when victorious to move it from Kiriath-jearim.

7:1 *Abinadab* and *Eleazar* are not otherwise known. **2** *Twenty years*. This period scarcely suffices to bring us to the events in David's reign recorded in 2 Sa. 6 (but see on 13:1). It may therefore relate to the national repentance of vv. 3, 4. *Lamented* is a doubtful word in the Hebrew, and perhaps Hertzberg is right to emend the text, producing the rendering 'departed from the Lord (to serve idols)', which neatly introduces v. 3.

7:3–14 Victory under Samuel's leadership. The ark rests now for twenty years, but the God of the ark is by no means inactive; He reveals Himself through Samuel, who now reappears, no longer as priest at Shiloh, but primarily as political leader. His advice to Israel makes it clear that idolatry was rife and that the Philistines had followed up their victory at Aphek (ch. 4). As a prelude to success in battle, turning from idolatry was essential; this theme is frequent in the book of Judges (see, *e.g.*, Jdg. 2).

3, 4 *Ashtaroth* is the plural of Ashtoreth, a fertility goddess widely revered in the ancient Fertile Crescent, and frequently associated with Baal in the OT. The plural (of this word, and of Baal in v. 4) refers to the local manifestations of these deities. Baal was native to Canaan, but the implication here is that he was to be viewed as a foreign deity so far as Israel was concerned. **5** *Mizpah* lay approximately half-way between Jerusalem and Shiloh, though its exact site is disputed. It was an important city at various periods, and another sanctuary-city (where Samuel exercised judicial functions, v. 16). **6** *Drew water . . .*: not evidenced elsewhere, but, with fasting, it was no doubt a symbol of repentance. **9** Samuel acts as a priest, but at a different sanctuary, and indeed in a way that is unique in the OT; the sacrifice had atoning significance, at any rate. **10, 11** The Israelite victory can be attributed only to Yahweh; in any case, Israel had not the weapons to fight the well-armed Philistines (*cf.* 13:19–22). They could and did pursue, however. **12** Although the sites cannot be precisely identified, it is possible that the earlier Philistine victory (4:1f.) occurred near a different *Ebenezer*. If so, Samuel deliberately gave the name, in view of its meaning, to the new battle-site. **13, 14** Fidelity to Yahweh thus brings its military and political reward. The victory was only temporary and far from conclusive, and this is implicit here (the latter part of v. 13 shows that warfare was continuous). Samuel could accomplish no military masterstroke, and the Philistines established some garrisons in the Israelite hills before his death. But before we dismiss the picture here presented as idealized and unrealistic, we must remember that the narrator and his first readers were well aware that Saul was the first Israelite leader to achieve major successes against the Philistines. The writer carefully states, however, that he is describing the whole of Samuel's lifetime, not just the part of it that preceded Saul's becoming king; he is in fact tacitly placing Samuel above Saul, despite the latter's royal title, in the hierarchy of Israel. **14** *From Ekron to Gath*; *i.e.* the border territories. *The Amorites* were the non-Israelite inhabitants of Canaan, who often felt more kinship with the Philistines (who shared their religion, for instance); their peacefulness now is a sign of the Israelite success.

7:15 – 15:35 SAMUEL AND SAUL

This section portrays Samuel throughout as the divinely-appointed leader in Israel, even while it introduces us to the enigmatic figure of Saul, Israel's first king. If Saul was in different ways markedly inferior both to Samuel and David, nevertheless the institution of the monarchy was a significant milestone in the history of Israel, and it is not surprising that several chapters are devoted to the theme. For a study of the literary and historical problems of these chapters, see Appendix 2.

7:15 – 12:25 Saul becomes king

7:15 – 8:3 Samuel's position in Israel. Samuel, like Eli before him (4:18), was a judge in Israel, both in the special sense common in the book of Judges, *i.e.* a leader and deliverer raised up by God, and also in the sense more familiar to English readers. His life as a dispenser of justice revolved round a number of sanctuaries (vv. 16, 17). (On the function of such sanctuaries, see A. E. Cundall, 'Sanctuaries in pre-exilic Israel', *Vox Evangelica*, IV, 1965, pp. 4–27.) But despite his own high qualities, his sons gave rise to popular discontent.

7:16 Legal decisions were customarily given at sanctuaries. Since the ark of the covenant contained the Ten Commandments, one may reasonably infer that laws were referable at all the Israelite sanctuaries. **8:1** *Judges* in the juridical sense only. **2** *Beer-sheba* lies at the southern extremity of Palestine, and its mention draws attention to the extent of Samuel's influence. Josephus (*Ant.* vi.3.2) places one son at Bethel instead. **3** *Cf.* 2:12. The frequent unsuitability of human succession is a recurring theme of the OT historical books, from Gideon to the descendants of David.

8:4–9 The popular plea for a king. We can well understand the elders' demand, from a political point of view. Stability was what Israel lacked, as the vicissitudes depicted in Judges show. The tribal elders connected this with the lack of stable leadership. Philistine pressure, of course, lay behind their demand. But from the religious aspect, the demand (however sensible and far-sighted a move politically) was tantamout to rejecting Yahweh from being king. It must not be supposed that a human king would in some way take God's place, or place Him at a distance from His people. The judges, including Samuel, had been leaders who had demanded allegiance from the Israelites, with full divine approval. The chief difference between judge and king was simply that of continuity; kings establish dynasties. The theological point here is that judges had been individually appointed by Yahweh, at times of His choosing; Israel's defeats had been caused by their own sins, not by political incompetence by the judges. But instead of learning this lesson from their past national history, and showing repentance and trust in Yahweh as a result, the elders considered that a stable leadership would prevent the ups and downs of the past; this decision amounted to an attempt to bypass God, and in effect rejected His future leadership and power of choice, despite the willingness of the elders to allow Him (through Samuel) to select for them the first king.

5 *Like all the nations.* Many of Israel's neighbours had long-established monarchies; the desire to ape foreign peoples was in itself a sign of apostasy. **6** The demand was no compliment to Samuel. **7** The portrayal of God as *king* over His people is a common feature of OT and NT; but see especially Jdg. 8:22f. **8** The rejection of

Yahweh is no more than the culmination of past apostasy. **9** If the elders are interested solely in political expediency, then the political implications of their request are to be put to them fairly and squarely.

8:10–22 Samuel's advice rejected. Samuel's speech paints no rosy picture of the side-effects of the inauguration of the monarchy: forced labour and conscription, heavy taxes, and finally sheer despotic tyranny. But once Israel has so chosen, there is no turning back. It has often been maintained that Solomon is the prototype of the description in these verses; but recently-discovered evidence (from Alalakh and Ugarit) makes it plain that 'the nations round about' long before Samuel's time had bitter experience of the cost of the privilege of having a monarchy. (See K. A. Kitchen, *Ancient Orient and Old Testament*, 1966, pp. 158f.) Naturally, however, the historian stressed those characteristics which his readers would recognize only too clearly; but to make the description relevant is not to make it unhistorical.

16 *Cattle.* There seems no strong reason to prefer this reading to the Hebrew 'young men' (*cf.* AV, RSV mg.). **18** *Cf.* 1 Ki. 12:4. **20** The elders again express their desire to be like other nations. Here they make it explicit that it is the immediate military problem that chiefly concerns them. **22** We are not to suppose that God's hand was forced. The situation did indeed need desperate measures, and the divine plan all along was to choose His anointed in His own good time. Dt. 17:14–20 gives the pattern for a king who would obtain divine approval.

9:1–14 Saul comes to Ramah. The scene shifts, with skilful dramatic effect, to the man who was soon to become Israel's first king. Saul's lack of personal ambition is emphasized by the narrative: he was merely looking for lost donkeys, with no thought in his head of political greatness; he did not even recognize Samuel when he met him (vv. 18,19)! Nevertheless, he came from a family of substance and his own personal appearance was kingly enough.

1 Perhaps '*a man* of Gibeah *of Benjamin*' was the original reading; although neither the Hebrew MSS nor the ancient versions give the place-name, its inclusion has been favoured by many commentators. *A man of wealth* represents a Hebrew phrase often referring to valour (*cf.* AV 'a mighty man of power'); here wealth is certainly intended, but possibly valour too. **3–5** The route cannot be traced in full detail, but it was no straight road. The denouement took place in Ramah, Samuel's home-town, as the mention of *the land of Zuph* indicates (*cf.* 1:1). The name Ramah has probably been deliberately avoided, because the narrator, a very skilful raconteur, does not wish to give the game away too soon that a meeting with Samuel is imminent; similarly the name Samuel is avoided until v. 14. **6–8** The literary artistry continues: Saul is in Samuel's very home-town, and the great prophet-judge is looking for a king; yet Saul is virtually

ignorant of Samuel, and is advised by a mere servant to seek him out, with a trivial request about donkeys! Saul even puts difficulties in the way; it is the unnamed servant who resolves them. It is quite improper, and totally ignores the writer's art and skill, to argue (as older commentators often did) from these verses that Samuel was an obscure village seer; it is perfectly credible that a young rustic like Saul should not have known Samuel or much about him, and it is the whole purpose of the narrative to depict Saul as an innocent abroad, not to demote Samuel. **6** The final clause must mean that Saul and his servant want to know about the goal of their journey; here again there is effective dramatic irony, for their imagined goal was a few donkeys, their real but quite unforeseen goal a throne and a kingdom. **9** See Appendix 3. **11–13** are entirely consonant with earlier statements about Samuel—he is neither merely 'local' nor only a 'seer'—but the narrator still as it were disguises him from the reader. *The high place* was the shrine itself.

9:15–25 Samuel entertains Saul. At last the future is disclosed: Saul is to be king and to defeat Israel's enemies. The divine purpose stands revealed: Yahweh has no interest in the rebellious elders' wish to ape other nations (8:20), but He will respond to the ordinary people's cry of distress for relief from the Philistines.

16 relates back to 7:3f. The word *prince* (Heb. *nāgîd*) is not the usual word for king, but in the context the use of the verb *anoint* makes it clear that kingship is meant. The word may mean 'designated', but M. Noth's view that its significance is 'king-designate' is not well supported by OT usage. M. Buber (cited by Hertzberg) has suggested, attractively, that the noun picks up the verb 'to tell' (Heb. *n-g-d*) used in verses 6, 8, 18, 19. **17** Similarly *saw* (Heb. *rā'āh*) picks up Samuel's function as a 'seer' (*rō'eh*). *Rule* is an unusual verb (lit. 'keep in check') and may imply the considerable powers of a king over his subjects (*cf.* 8:11–17). **18** Note once again the skilful narration: God has spoken, Samuel knows everything, but Saul is still ignorant even of Samuel's identity! **20** *I.e.* Saul can in future have as many donkeys as he likes, and anything else besides. *All that is desirable in Israel* (lit. 'the desire of Israel') may mean the kingship specifically. **21** Saul replies with becoming modesty, if with exaggerated humility; his family was by no means poor or uninfluential, although Benjamin was admittedly a small tribe. **22–24** find Saul treated with signal honour at the feast, but still without any explanation from Samuel. **24** *The upper portion* is obscure (*cf.* RSV mg.): lit. 'the-upon-it'. 'The sirloin' is a possibility (on the basis of Ugaritic parallels). At any rate, Saul was provided with a very large portion (*cf.* on 1:4, 5).

9:26 – 10:8 The private anointing of Saul. The first anointing of Saul, on the outskirts of Ramah, was a purely private affair; not even

Saul's servant was permitted to witness it. In the same way David was privately anointed in the first place (1 Sa. 16). The nation had yet to 'choose' Saul by other means.

10:1 Anointing marked out a man set apart by God for kingly office. It was also the means by which kingly powers were granted. From this time on—even after his rejection—Saul was irrevocably the anointed of Yahweh (*cf.* 24:6). The *kiss* was no doubt part of the ritual. **2** *Rachel's tomb* is near Ramah, N of Jerusalem, here and in Je. 31:15. Traditionally the tomb is located near Bethlehem, S of Jerusalem, but all that Gn. 35:16, 19 indicates is that Rachel was somewhere between Bethel (N of Ramah) and Bethlehem when she died; to this Mt. 2:16ff. adds nothing. **3** The provisions were for sacrificial observance at the Bethel shrine. **4** A providential supply: *cf.* 9:7. **5** *Gibeath-elohim* (usually abbreviated to Gibeah, as in v. 10) was Saul's home, and lay half-way between Ramah and Jerusalem. The *garrison* reveals the extent of Philistine dominance. *A band of prophets*: evidently ecstatics, who acted in concert; these two characteristics may have distinguished them from the seers of the time (see Appendix 3). **6** *The spirit of the Lord* . . . ; *i.e.* Saul will be true successor to the judges, who were all thus directed by God's Spirit. **7** The three signs together free Saul from trivial concerns, indicate the goodwill of his future subjects, and assure him of his own fitness to rule Israel. **8** *Gilgal* is to be Saul's ultimate destination, and his place of failure (13:7–14); the text does not make it clear when he was to go there, but Samuel must obviously have discussed this with him; only the gist of the conversation is given by the narrator. Saul had already visited Gilgal before the events of ch. 13, according to 11:14f. The best solution to the problem seems to be that Samuel was referring to the mustering there for battle, whenever that might take place.

10:9–16 The signs fulfilled. Here again the narrative is abbreviated, and the fulfilment of the first two signs predicted by Samuel is taken for granted. The most important fact is related, that Samuel's choice of Saul as king had clear divine approval.

9 *God gave him another heart*, transforming him into a great leader and warrior. **11, 12** What should have been a hint to Saul's acquaintances of his imminent leadership aroused only surprise and unfavourable comment. The twin proverbs were plainly discourteous to Saul: what was he, a respectable local citizen, doing in the presence of these roaming madmen of unknown and dubious antecedents? (Hertzberg aptly cites Acts 2:13ff. as a comparable insult to Spirit-filled men.) These verses suggest something of the initial opposition to Saul. The proverb is repeated in 19:24 (on which see comment). **13** *High place*. LXX has 'Gibeah', more appropriately, in view of the family conversation that follows. **14–16** The story of the lost donkeys (begun in 9:3) is rounded off. It is not explained

why Saul's uncle, rather than his father, questioned him about his dealings with Samuel. The brief narrative here is also concerned to show that Saul's kingship is still a secret, even from his own kin.

10:17–27 The public anointing of Saul. The nation as a whole now enters the picture again, as in ch. 8; vv. 18, 19 repeat the gist of Samuel's words recorded in that chapter. Mizpah is the stage for the next scene.

19 *Thousands*. The word in context scarcely seems to bear a numerical connotation, and JB, with more probability, renders it 'clans' (as indeed RSV does in Nu. 1:16). The twofold use of the Hebrew word (*'elep̄*) may explain some of the large numbers of the OT. **20, 21** *Cf.* Jos. 7:16ff. Saul hides himself away; the theme of the hidden king is maintained to the last. **22** *They inquired again of the Lord* implies that the preceding casting of lots was a religious, not a secular, ceremony and probably involved the use of Urim and Thummim. *Cf.* 14:41f.; see also *NBD*, art. 'Urim and Thummim'. **23–25** bring together the earlier themes, (a) that Saul was God's choice as leader, (b) that kingship as such was not an unalloyed blessing for Israel; the latter aspect is implicit in v. 25. The *book* may have been drawn from Deuteronomy, or at least incorporated Dt. 17:14–20. It was most probably the new constitution, since monarchy was an innovation in Israel. The document was preserved in the sanctuary at Mizpah. **27** *Worthless fellows*. While the doubts of some Israelites were only natural (kingship was a newfangled idea; and what qualifications did Saul have, in any case?), to refuse Saul allegiance was to defy the choice of God.

11:1–15 The Ammonite incident. The narrator switches suddenly to a new topic without divulging his purpose, which is to show how it came about that the initial opposition to Saul was won over, and how the king proved himself. It is clear from vv. 3, 4 that Saul had not yet asserted his authority.

1 Both *Jabesh-gilead* and the *Ammonite* people were located E of the Jordan. The distance between them itself shows the weakness of Israel; the Ammonites must have dominated Transjordan. *The men of Jabesh* were seeking a definition of their rights under the lordship of *Nahash*. **3** This old-world request reads oddly in our days of total warfare. Till relatively recent times, warfare was conducted according to a strict etiquette. **6, 7** Saul's experience of *the spirit of God* and his action in sending *messengers* made him another 'judge'; but his threat was regal enough, and perhaps for the first time since the conquest of Canaan, all the tribes obeyed the summons. The mention of *Samuel* is significant. **8** *Bezek* was W of the Jordan, but probably too far north for Philistine interference. The numbers seem too high (though in correct proportions); since LXX presents even greater numbers, the text must have suffered early corruption in transmission. **10** *We will give ourselves up to you.*

AV 'We will come out unto you' is more literal, and in fact better. This message must have been to the Ammonites, and while it was intended to mislead them, the verb is often used for going out to do battle, the real intention of the men of Jabesh. 12–15 tell us of a new ceremony, a natural sequel to the events of the previous chapter. *Saul and all the men of Israel rejoiced greatly*: a prelude to ch. 12, for Samuel had more sober thoughts.

12:1–15 Samuel's final address to Israel. 'Samuel's Farewell', as this passage is widely known, is really more of a defence of his administrative leadership, which he is now relinquishing to Saul; he is not yet laying down his priestly functions. In context, the locale must be Gilgal (11:15); but the passage is widely held to be connected with Mizpah, since the tenor of it is hostile to the monarchy, and it therefore links up with 10:20–24. (On this whole question, see Appendix 2.) The 'established legal formula' (McKane) of vv. 3 and 5, it is argued, makes the passage late (and so unhistorical). But such a view is by no means unavoidable, for such a set formula (if indeed it was: evidence is lacking) could well have figured in the new constitution (*cf.* 10:25). At the same time, since we have in this chapter direct speech, we may view the narrator as partly responsible for the actual wording (see on 2:1–10); he was after all using Samuel's address as a sermon to his own generation. But in view of Saul's later rejection, and the fact that Judah remembered him with little pleasure, or approval, it is noteworthy that the hostility expressed in this passage is towards monarchy as such, not to Saul himself. Historically, it is entirely plausible that Samuel should have resented Israel's partial rejection of him.

1–5 In effect, Samuel declares that he has kept the covenantal stipulations; on this topic, see J. Muilenburg, 'The form and structure of the covenantal formulations', *VT*, 9, 1959, pp. 360–364. **2** *My sons*. Their venality (8:3) is not under consideration; their mention is to illustrate Samuel's age and length of service to Israel. **6–12** Such historical retrospects were commonly part of covenant procedures in the Ancient Near East (and *cf.* Jos. 24); they laid a basis for the ensuing stipulations. Samuel's whole speech fits such a pattern and situation, as the whole nation (some for the first time) now adopts its new constitution, under which its primary obligations were to Yahweh, and only in the second place to the monarch. **11** All these judges appear in the book of Judges, except for *Samuel*, whose name reads oddly on his own lips; an attractive alternative found in some ancient versions is 'Samson'. **14, 15** Samuel makes plain to Israel that monarchy in itself will not save them from the ups and downs of the past (see on 8:7f.).

12:16–25 The conclusion of the ceremony. A sign from heaven ratified the renewal of the covenant, and confirmed the truth of Samuel's words. It also served to give the prophet an important function under the new constitution; it was the king, not the prophet, who was in danger of being swept away.

17, 18 *Thunder* recalled the covenant institution at Sinai (*cf.* Ex. 19:16); *rain*, virtually unknown in Palestine at this time of year, was a miraculous sign. **19** Note that there is no suggestion that the clock can be put back; Saul is in any case God's own choice as king. **21** *Vain things*; *i.e.* idols. **23** This statement opened the way for Samuel's successors in the prophetic office. It shows Samuel, too, as mediator of the covenant.

13:1 – 14:52 War with the Philistines

It was largely the Philistine threat which had brought Saul to the throne; it was to be his life's work now to combat their aggression. These two chapters recount his major victories over this powerful enemy.

13:1–7 The Israelites muster for battle. There are a number of difficulties in this chapter, which are discussed in some detail by McKane and Hertzberg. An initial problem is that of date: how soon after Saul's coronation did these battles take place? The strong probability is that they occurred early in his reign; the Philistines would scarcely have allowed him to reign long over Israel unmolested. Moreover, the link between this passage (note v. 8) and 10:8 makes it unlikely that any long period intervened. The difficulty is that Saul now has an adult son (Jonathan, v. 2), whereas he himself was a 'young man' (9:2) when he became king. However, early marriage was customary among the Hebrews, and Saul could have been in his middle thirties and still had a son able to bear arms.

1 Clearly the original numerals have been lost in transmission. Acts 13:21 says that Saul reigned for forty years, probably a round number. This figure is much more likely, in view of the age of Ish-bosheth at Saul's death (*cf.* 2 Sa. 2:10), than the mere two years allowed him by M. Noth (*History of Israel*, p. 176). **2, 3** *Gibeah* and *Geba* are unfortunately very similar names, and the sites lay reasonably near each other; some confusion between them is possible in this passage. Geba lay to the N of Gibeah, just S of Michmash (v. 5), where the battle was to take place. **4** *Gilgal* lay further E, near the Jordan, and so provided a safer mustering-place. *The garrison*. The word could equally mean 'prefect', and is so translated by Hertzberg. **5** *Thirty thousand*: 'three thousand', read by Lucian's recension of the LXX, and by the Syriac, seems more credible. *Beth-aven* seems to be another name for either Bethel (*cf.* Ho. 4:15) or Ai. **6, 7** Israel's fears and cowardice explain the impatience Saul was now to exhibit.

13:8–15 Saul's first breach with Samuel. In disobeying Samuel's explicit instructions (10:8), Saul's real excuse was that sacrifice had to be offered to ensure success in battle. His men were already deserting, and to omit such an important act would have been disastrous to morale.

8, 9 *The time appointed by Samuel.* The passage can scarcely mean, as Hertzberg claims, that Saul in fact obeyed Samuel's instructions to the letter. Presumably Saul waited right up till the seventh day, but could not bring himself to wait until it was over. **13, 14** Samuel's rebuke denied Saul a dynastic succession; and David—though not by name—is for the first time brought before the reader. **15** According to the LXX, it was Saul, not Samuel, who made for Gibeah (Geba?). *Six hundred men.* Saul's forces had dwindled away to a fraction (*cf.* v. 2); Samuel's displeasure may well have caused further desertions.

13:16–23 The Philistine movements. The Israelite soldiers were not only much depleted but also inadequately armed (vv. 19–22). Hence the Philistines felt confident enough to dissipate their own forces to some extent by sending out raiding-parties.

19 The Philistines had a virtual monopoly of iron. **21** *A pim* was a weight (estimated at $\frac{1}{4}$ oz). The Philistines naturally charged a high price for sharpening potential weapons. **23** *The pass of Michmash.* On the topography of the battle see especially S. R. Driver, *Notes on the Hebrew text and the topography of the Books of Samuel, in loc.*

14:1–15 Jonathan's exploit. An act of outstanding, even foolhardy, courage on the part of Jonathan brought a resounding and unexpected victory. But two signs demonstrated that it was God who gave the victory.

2 *Gibeah.* See the commentaries for discussion of the geographical difficulty. **3** prepares the way for v. 18; it also relates back to 4:19–22. *Ahijah* is the 'Ahimelech' of ch. 22. The *ephod* was a priestly vestment; see on v. 18. **4, 5** A narrow point of *the pass* hid Jonathan from both the opposing armies. **6** *Uncircumcised.* Such the Philistines were, unlike most of Israel's neighbours, but the term is in effect more religious than physical. This was indeed a holy war, as the rest of the verse emphasizes. **10** Hence Jonathan can confidently expect a sign from God. **11** Presumably the Philistines thought that the two lone individuals were deserting to them. **13** The precise details are not clear, but evidently the Philistines came to grief through utter surprise. The final part of **14** is difficult and perhaps corrupt; the intention seems to be to indicate the site of the skirmish. **15** The fall of the outpost guarding the pass has immense repercussions; observe that the raiding parties (*cf.* 13:17) were too scared to rejoin the main army. An *earthquake* adds to the Philistine *panic*: a sure sign of God's favour to Jonathan.

14:16–23 The resulting battle. The main Israelite force, under Saul's direct command, now took an interest, and routed the Philistine army.

16 *Gibeah.* As in v. 2, Geba may be intended (*cf.* JB). **18** *The ark* had been at Kiriath-jearim

when last mentioned (7:2), but there is no reason why it should not have been brought, temporarily, to the battle-field (as in ch. 4). However, many commentators (and JB) prefer to accept the LXX reading 'ephod', perhaps rightly, in view of vv. 3 and 41. **19** In any case, Ahijah was about to consult the oracle of God, the Urim and Thummim, in accordance with Saul's wishes, when the latter abruptly changed his mind; there was no time to spare, battle must be joined. **20–22** At the sight of Saul victorious, deserters change sides again and fugitives return to the fray. **23** *Beth-aven.* Cf. 13:5. Lucian's reading 'Beth-horon' (*cf.* 13:18) is preferred by some commentators (R. de Vaux, together with JB, among modern writers). In either case, the Philistines were driven well to the west, and out of the hills. Aijalon (v. 31) is very near Beth-horon, and its mention supports that reading.

14:24–35 Two unfortunate incidents. Saul's oath may have been intended to make some reparation for his failure to wait for a priestly oracle (*cf.* vv. 18, 19). Jonathan's ignorance of the oath may well have been due to his absence from Saul's army during his exploit. The curse pronounced by Saul was well criticized by Jonathan (vv. 29, 30), for it not only weakened the Israelite pursuers but also occasioned breaches of cultic regulations, the soldiers being too weary and hungry to give them a thought.

25, 26 *The forest.* Since the Hebrew word can also mean 'honeycomb', it is possible that the statement here means that the people came upon honeycombs on the ground in the open country; *cf.* JB. **32, 33** For the regulations, see Lv. 17:10–14; Dt. 12:23. **34** Saul attempted by sacrifice to atone for the ritual breach. **35** Probably the *altar* was long known as Saul's altar, as Hertzberg suggests.

14:36–46 Consequences of Jonathan's error. Even in the account of the battle, the progressive estrangement between Saul and his God is evident. Saul's chief fault, in these early days of his reign, seems to have been impulsive and ill-considered action. The passage is intriguing: it shows an insecure king outvoted by his troops and it leaves unanswered the question as to the rectitude of the actions of Saul, Jonathan, and the people.

Assuming that RSV and most commentators (as against AV) are right to follow the LXX at v. 41, we find this passage the most instructive in the OT about the *Urim* and *Thummim*, the mysterious priestly oracle. It would seem that it consisted of some form of casting lots, and the answer could be one of two possibilities, 'Yes' or 'No'; it could also yield a neutral answer, evidently, and that is why Saul got no answer that day (v. 37). Ex. 28:30 tells us that the Urim and Thummim were carried in the breastpiece of the ephod or priestly robe. See *NBD*, art. 'Urim and Thummim'.

39 shows the folly of such rash oaths, with the dramatic irony that Saul even mentioned his son by name. The story is reminiscent of

Jephthah's vow (Jdg. 11:30–40). **45** *He has wrought with God.* The soldiers cannot credit that God could both achieve victory through Jonathan and pronounce judgment on him. The *vox populi* prevailed, though it is not explained how Jonathan was *ransomed*; it was presumably by sacrifice of some kind (*cf.* v. 34). **46** marks the end of this first battle.

14:47–52 Outline of Saul's reign. During his reign, Saul achieved victories over enemies on all sides. Apart from the Philistines (the major foe), most of the hostile peoples were located E of the Jordan.

47 *The Ammonites*: *cf.* ch. 11. *Zobah*, an Aramaean kingdom, lay N of Damascus. **48** *The Amalekites* (to the S of Israel) are mentioned separately, since the next chapter is concerned with Saul's defeat of them. **49** *Ishvi* is better known as Ish-bosheth, a derogatory form of his name ('man of shame'). *Jonathan, Malchishua,* and another son not here named, died at Gilboa (31:2). **50** Saul's cousin *Abner* played a big part in Ish-bosheth's career too. **52** Saul gradually accumulated a standing army, a necessary innovation in Israel.

15:1–35 The defeat of Amalek

The Amalekite war is recounted in detail, because it led to the final breach between Saul and Samuel. The Amalekites were an ancient foe of Israel (*cf.* Ex. 17:8–16); they were hence under the divine curse (Dt. 25:17–19). The story now related undoubtedly presents a serious moral problem to the modern reader, although none will dispute that Amalek deserved signal punishment. It is their 'utter destruction' (v. 3) that is the difficulty. However, the very phrase, in Hebrew, means 'to devote to Yahweh'; *i.e.* their deaths were regarded not as an execution but as being in some sense sacrificial. Secondly, in a world much less individualistic than ours, there was little conception of singling out the guilty parties; misdeeds brought guilt on the whole community. From a historical standpoint, moreover, Saul's failure to deal more vigorously with the Amalekites left them free to harass S Judah for a further generation.

15:1–9 The attack on Amalek. That Saul must be obedient is stressed at the start of the narrative. His failure to do so was not prompted by any humanitarian motives. It is even possible that his disobedience was deliberate; as king, he may have determined to show himself independent of Samuel's authority. It is harder to interpret 13:8–12 in this way, however. **4** *Telaim* (probably the Telem of Jos. 15:24) can tentatively be located a few miles S of Beersheba. *Judah* naturally sent troops, in view of her proximity to Amalekite territory. The numbers in this verse seem too great; early textual corruption may be the reason. **5** *City*: more of a fortified village, in modern terms; the Amalekites were nomadic. **6** *The Kenites,* also nomads at an earlier period, had always been well-disposed towards the Israelites (*cf.*

Nu. 10:29–32; Jdg. 1:16). **8, 9** Saul began to obey Samuel's command, but then changed his mind, perhaps again on impulse.

15:10–31 Samuel's intervention and Saul's rejection. Immutability is the theme of this passage (especially v. 29). In the previous chapter, Saul's oath had come to nothing, perhaps through no fault of his own; now he is fully to blame (despite his efforts to lay the blame elsewhere) for breaking his word to Yahweh, and punishment is inescapable: God does not act on impulse.

11 *Repent* here signifies grief, and a change of attitude; not a change of mind, as in v. 29. 'God is not slavishly bound by his own decisions' (Hertzberg). **12** *Carmel*: a place in S Judah (Jos. 15:55), not the mountain range of 1 Ki. 18. **13** Saul is confident (as in 13:11) that he has obeyed. **15** Ignoring the matter of Agag, Saul maintains that the animals are intended for *sacrifice*. But worshippers normally had a part in sacrifices, which had been expressly forbidden as regards these particular animals. **22** sums up the consistent prophetic approach to sacrifice and the cultic worship: *cf.* Am. 5:21–24. **23** Samuel announces the divine rejection of Saul; previously he had been denied a dynasty (13:13, 14), now his own office is spurned by Samuel in the name of Yahweh. **24, 25** Saul seeks to gain forgiveness, but perhaps with little sincerity, and certainly with a fresh attempt to allocate the blame elsewhere. Moreover, it looks as if he is specially interested in maintaining appearances, though it is possible that his words were motivated by genuine piety. **27, 28** The name *Saul* is supplied by RSV (contrast AV); the natural, and perhaps preferable (so McKane, at least), understanding of the verse is that it was Samuel himself who tore his robe. At any rate, Samuel swiftly interprets the action as a symbol of God's purposes. Note the fresh allusion to David. **29** *The Glory of Israel* is a unique term for Yahweh; the Hebrew word (*nēṣaḥ*) emphasizes the eternal nature of Yahweh, which is appropriate in this context of His immutability. **30** Again Saul pleads for Samuel's support, at least in outward appearance. His position owed much to Samuel's past support, after all.

15:32–35 Samuel's departure. This section of the book ends with the final parting of the ways. Saul remains the man in power, but no longer as the man of God's choice. Samuel, the earlier leader, now departs to anoint Saul's successor, and then quietly steps out of the picture.

32 *Cheerfully*, which offers reasonable sense (especially if his remark implies that he still thinks his life has been spared), is an unlikely interpretation of the Hebrew. An emendation, 'tottering', commends itself to Hertzberg. The JB has 'reluctantly', and then follows the LXX, making Agag say 'truly, death is a bitter thing'. **33** Despite Samuel's words, the execution was a ritual one, in fulfilment of the 'devotion' of Amalek to Yahweh, and not politically motivated. Nevertheless, justice is seen to be done.

35 Note that Samuel could not view Saul's failure with detachment.

16:1 – 31:13 SAUL AND DAVID

The remainder of Saul's reign is the story of his relationship with David, so far as the first book of Samuel is concerned. Saul has been rejected by the God of Israel, and Samuel is an old man; but God's man of the future is already on the scene, in the person of the youthful David. God has not left His people leaderless. The rest of 1 Samuel shows how God equipped David for his future career, watched over him through every danger, and exhibited him to the nation as the man of God's favour.

16:1 – 17:58 David reaches the royal court

David's proper place was at the royal court, but he would scarcely be welcome there as successor-designate to Saul. These two chapters describe how his own abilities brought him to Saul's side.

16:1–13 The anointing of David. This narrative is not unlike that of 9:1 – 10:1; in both cases Samuel anointed, privately, an unsuspecting young man to kingly office. Both were equally attractive individuals. The narrator thus demonstrates that David was in no respect Saul's inferior. Note the continuing narrative skill: not until the last moment is David's name revealed, although clues to his identity appear in vv. 1 and 11.

1, 2 Samuel appears as a human enough figure, both sorrowful over Saul's fall from grace and fearful of his power. *Sacrifice* at Bethlehem may well have been routine for Samuel, even though it is not listed in 7:16f. A major city of Judah, it lay 5 miles S of Jerusalem. *If Saul hears it, he will kill me*. We are given here the first hint of the suspicious and vindictive side of Saul's character. The route from Ramah to Bethlehem passed through Saul's capital, Gibeah. **4, 5** *Peaceably*. J. Skinner rendered the question (which may have had cultic or political reference), 'Is this an auspicious visit?' **6** *Eliab*: called Elihu in 1 Ch. 27:18. **7** A clear allusion to the rejected Saul (9:2); *i.e.* David is to be solely God's choice, whereas Saul had been to some extent a popular choice. **9** *Shammah*: various forms of the name are found (*cf.* 2 Sa. 13:3; 21:21; 1 Ch. 20:7). **10** 1 Ch. 2:14, 15 names three other brothers, then David as the seventh. One brother remains unnamed in the OT. **11** *We will not sit down* (to the sacrificial meal): other renderings are possible, all of cultic reference. **13** *In the midst*. Hertzberg translates 'from the midst', thus making the anointing secret from David's brothers. *David* is now at last named, and recognized as being in the true line of succession to the judges and Saul, in view of the activity of God's *Spirit* in him.

16:14–23 David enters the royal service. As David receives the Spirit of God, so Saul loses it progressively, with concomitant loss of mental powers. One can well understand Saul's experi-

ence in psychological terms. His position was undermined by Samuel's defection, and his anxieties were not unnatural, especially since the Philistines never ceased their hostility. His earlier prophetic trances may have gradually led to emotional breakdown. But, ironically, it is Saul's very disturbance of mind that leads to David's coming to the court.

14 Saul's mental disturbance is envisaged as a punishment from God. **18** *A man of war*. Although David had not yet fully relinquished his pastoral duties, he already had some military experience, and had shown ability as a soldier. **21** Hence he was made an armour-bearer, not merely a court musician. **21, 22** may perhaps refer to a time after David had killed Goliath. The OT historians not infrequently pursue a theme to its ultimate consequences, then return to fill in the details. *Saul loved him*. Quite possibly Saul's liking was not very personal; simply admiration of his looks and his music.

On the textual and historical difficulties of chs. 17; 18, see Appendix 4.

17:1–11 The Philistine challenge. A Philistine army moved into the hills of W Judah, and Saul sent his own army to meet them. But instead of joining battle, the enemy decided on a fight between champions; such a practice was not uncommon in ancient warfare.

4 *Goliath*. His name is mentioned only here and in v. 23 (and *cf.* 21:9). De Vaux and Hertzberg view the name as a later insertion, in view of 2 Sa. 21:19 (see commentary *in loc.* and Appendix 5); such a possibility cannot be completely ruled out. His *height* was about ten feet. **5–7** The thoroughness of his protection, as much as the size and weight of the armour and weapons, is emphasized. **11** Even *Saul* shies away from such a challenge, as well he might.

17:12–30 David visits the Israelite army. It is now revealed that David was not at this particular time acting as Saul's armour-bearer (note v. 15). His arrival on the battle-scene was therefore due to divine overruling; the narrator does not need to make this fact explicit.

12 *Ephrathite*; *i.e.* from Ephratah, a district evidently adjoining Bethlehem (*cf.* Mi. 5:2). **13** As in 16:6–9, only *the three eldest sons of Jesse* are named. **25** prepares the way for David's advancement. JB renders the final clause 'and grant his father's House the freedom of Israel'. **26** David injects the first theological note into the narrative. **28–30** Eliab's reaction sounds like jealousy, and is reminiscent of the opposition to Joseph from his elder brothers.

17:31–40 Saul interviews David. Saul's approach to the issue of the day is purely military; David's reply, and his refusal of Saul's armour, underline the miraculous nature of the preservation of his life in dangers past and present. Note that there is no hint in the interview that Saul is unacquainted with David (see Appendix 4).

38, 39 Full *armour* was reserved for the very few in Israel (*cf.* 13:19, 22). **40** It is true that the picture of David here (as in vv. 34ff.) is pastoral, rather than of a trained armour-bearer. This fact may be due either to the chronology (see on 16:21), or simply to the narrator's intention to heighten the contrast between the unarmed, inexperienced stripling and the mighty giant warrior. The victory cannot but be God-given (note v. 47).

17:41–49 David kills Goliath. The discussion between David and his giant adversary will strike the modern reader as improbable, but this will again have been part of the etiquette of ancient battle.

45 Once again, David stresses that he is acting as champion not so much for Israel as for God Himself (*cf.* vv. 26, 36). In other words, the Philistines are throwing scorn on Yahweh, ultimately, not just on the Israelite army. **47** *The Lord saves* is the key-note not only of this story, but of the whole Bible. Modern scholars frequently term the history contained in the Scriptures as 'salvation-history' (in German, *Heilsgeschichte*).

17:50–58 The results of David's victory. The narrator is less interested in the Israelite rout of the Philistines than in the story of David's advancement. Previously he had come to the royal court in a minor capacity; now he was to come in his own right, as a man whom Saul could scarcely turn away. There is thus a dramatic sequence of events in chs. 16; 17 which is lost sight of when scholars find 'two divergent traditions' (see Introduction).

51–53 *Gath and Ekron* were the two nearest of the five Philistine cities. **54** This verse presents problems, since Jerusalem was not yet in Israelite hands: it fell to David himself when he had become king (2 Sa. 5); and since David had come straight from Bethlehem, to what does *his tent* refer? Moreover, we read later of Goliath's sword being at Nob (21:9). C. F. Keil, long ago, maintained that David left the giant's head in the Israelite part of Jerusalem (*cf.* Jdg. 1:8), outside the Jebusite fortress, and that by the *tent* David's home is meant. More recently, Hertzberg has suggested that the giant's skull was at a later date taken to Jerusalem and displayed there (it could even explain the NT name Golgotha); and by a slight emendation he makes *his tent* 'the tent of Yahweh', *i.e.* the sanctuary at Nob. It appears that Nob was very near Jerusalem (see on 21:1), and conceivably was later viewed as virtually part of the city. **55–58** is a passage (omitted by LXX^B) that certainly seems to imply Saul's ignorance of David's family, though not necessarily of himself. A. M. Renwick (in the first edition of this Commentary) suggested that chronologically 16:22 follows ch. 17, an explanation that would readily solve the dilemma. But the emphasis in the general context is that David is now to become more than a minor court functionary. Ch. 18 shows him taking a place in the royal family (*cf.* 17:25) and Saul's interest now in David's antecedents is quite natural. He was under the various obligations named in 17:25.

18:1 – 20:42 David and Jonathan

It is interesting that David's stay at Saul's court is told almost entirely in terms of his relationship with Jonathan. Theirs was indeed a matchless and proverbial friendship; but the narrator had a purpose in recounting it so fully. Apart from his interest in the whole question of succession, he is at pains to show that the very man whom David displaced in succession to the throne was his best friend. In other words, the descent of Saul itself acknowledged the legitimacy of David's rule.

18:1–9 David's honour and success. Jonathan's admiration and respect for David were as immediate as they were genuine. Everyone, in fact, hurried to acclaim David—everyone, that is, except Saul.

2 does not of course mean that visits to Bethlehem were forbidden to David; it is simply a mark of David's advancement that he becomes a permanent officer at court (*cf.* v. 5). **4** The outward marks of the *covenant* (v. 3), no doubt. Clothing possessed something of the wearer's personality, so that each man gave himself to the other, in effect. **5** *Was successful*: the verb denotes skill as well as success. **6–8** mark the start of Saul's jealousy. Observe also the dramatic irony at the end of v. 8. On the face of it, the singers seem to have been tactless, to say the least; yet probably this was a fixed parallelism, implying only David's equality with Saul—the Hebrew word translated *ten thousands* is rarely precise, and 'myriads' gives a better idea of the singers' meaning. But Saul's prematurely suspicious frame of mind is indicated by the fact that he chose to take the word in its precise sense. **9** *Eyed*: either 'kept his eyes on' (McKane) or 'turned a jealous eye on' (JB).

18:10–30 Saul's attempts on David's life. Saul's fears are intelligible, for his own position was largely based on prestige (or so he felt), and now David's reputation was beginning to outweigh his own. Had David been unscrupulously ambitious, indeed, Saul's fears would have been far from groundless. However, his early efforts to remove David misfired; the final scheme recounted in this chapter served only to increase David's fame and bring him right into the royal family! These events proved, as even Saul had to recognize, that 'the Lord was with David' (v. 28).

10 *Raved*: like an ecstatic prophet (*cf.* AV 'prophesied'). **11** *Twice* may refer forward to 19:9, 10. But the verb *cast* is rendered 'raised' in some versions—the difference is very slight in Hebrew—and this reading is quite possible (hence JB 'brandished') and would suggest a mere momentary impulse. **13, 16** *He went out and came in*. Note the technical term for military activity. **17** Saul's promise (only to be broken) was in fulfilment of 17:25. **18, 23** express typically oriental courteous humility. Nevertheless, it is clear that David had no money for a bride-price.

19:1–10 Jonathan's intervention fails. Jonathan's friendship now revealed itself in action, as he pleaded with his father.

1 Saul's jealousy now goes beyond reason; he is prepared to suborn murder. **2, 3** seem a trifle obscure; the drift of Jonathan's advice was that David would be able to see at a glance if Saul angrily refused Jonathan's pleas, and then be able to escape without delay; whereas if Saul was prepared to listen to reason, David could be called at once and put in the picture (as in fact happened). The *secret place* must have been somewhere where David could see but not overhear. **8–10** Fresh military successes by David arouse Saul's enmity once more, and history repeats itself (*cf.* 18:10, 11); this time the text is quite definite that Saul threw the spear, and that the impulse was no momentary whim.

19:11–24 David's flight. David's life is now saved by his wife Michal, Saul's daughter. Thus in this chapter two of Saul's children, one after the other, help to preserve the man who is to supplant their father as king.

13 *An image.* W. F. Albright understands the Hebrew word (*tᵉrāpîm*) to mean 'old rags' here. Elsewhere, however, the word refers to household deities. Acceptance of such household gods was a very old custom (*cf.* Gn. 31:19, 30–35), and despite the prohibitions in the law of Moses, they were never fully eradicated before the Exile (*cf.* 2 Ki. 23:24). While Michal's love for David is emphasized, lies and idolatry patently marked her character, and some see this portrait as a tacit reproof of her father. **18** *Naioth* was some part of *Ramah* where **20** a school of prophets resided. Samuel headed this prophetic group. Evidently great prophets such as Samuel and Elijah (*cf.* 2 Ki. 2) saw the potentialities of the roaming bands (such as we met in ch. 10), and channelled their energies to good use. It may be that such schools transmitted much of the OT literature. **20–23** The spirit of prophecy is, as it were, infectious; Saul's messengers and even the king himself are forced to succumb to the power of the Spirit of God in this abode of the prophets, and they 'prophesy' despite themselves. **22** *Secu* is unknown and perhaps incorrect; LXX is quite different (see JB). **24** Saul lost all control of himself (*cf.* 18:10) and the sneering proverb of 10:10ff. was again levelled at him. This is not a duplicate (and hence conflicting) account of the origin of this taunt, but deliberate repetition to show how such characteristics mark Saul's whole career. 'Going too far' was his consistent failing.

20:1–11 David consults Jonathan. Many commentators feel that this story comes oddly after ch. 19, and must come from a distinct source. Certainly after the events of ch. 19 David can have been in no real doubt as to Saul's intentions; but this chapter does not in fact suggest that he had—rather to the contrary (v. 3). It was Jonathan who could not believe it of his father (v. 2). The point of the story is that David is still a court member and would be acting very

improperly if he absented himself at the festival time (v. 5); so he consults with Jonathan, to try to get him to elicit from Saul a guarantee of David's safety (*cf.* v. 21). Saul's hostility might, after all, have passed for the moment, and David had no wish to offend him beyond recall by quitting the court without permission. Hence the plea regarding a festival at Bethlehem (v. 6); but even so in the upshot Saul was the more bitter against David.

5 *Let me go.* David had to ask permission, which presumably Jonathan was authorized to grant. The *new moon* was specially celebrated; *cf.* Nu. 10:10; 28:11–15. **7** *Determined*: a firm decision as opposed to a momentary impulse. **11** In going to *the field*, the two friends wished to plan the ploy of vv. 19ff., rather than to escape eavesdroppers.

20:12–23 David and Jonathan renew their covenant. In the course of laying plans and pledging loyalty, Jonathan takes friendship a step further: he recognizes explicitly that David will one day be king, and exhibits not the least jealousy or resentment.

14 *The loyal love* (Heb. *ḥeseḏ*) *of the Lord*; *i.e.* 'loving constancy such as Yahweh himself both desires and demonstrates' (Eichrodt). L. H. Brockington comments, 'Love and loyalty are the very essence of any relationship based on a personal covenant; in Hebrew these two aspects are bound together in the single word *ḥeseḏ*' (Peake's *Commentary*, 1962 edition, p. 327). **19** *When the matter was in hand* represents an obscure phrase (lit. 'on the day of the action (affair)'). The allusion may be to 19:2, otherwise to some unrecorded event. **23** *Between you and me* is a covenantal phrase, several times repeated in Gn. 31:44–54.

20:24–34 Jonathan divines Saul's intentions. Jonathan had previously pleaded for David with his father, and Michal had tricked the king; now for the first time Saul is openly challenged. Jonathan's covenant with David outweighed filial respect.

26, 27 *Not clean*; *i.e.* ritually impure due to something unforeseen, and so ineligible to take part in the sacrificial meal. *Cf.* Lv. 15:16; Dt. 23:10. But such impurity lasted only till nightfall, so on the following day it became clear to Saul that David's absence could not thus be explained. **30** *Saul's anger* expressed itself in the most offensive language. **31** Saul ignores the threat David posed to himself, and instead endeavours to arouse Jonathan to his own danger. **33** *Cast.* JB 'brandished' is almost certainly the correct rendering here. See on 18:11. **34** *Disgraced*: by publicly declaring David to be a traitor.

20:35–42 David and Jonathan part. Having been accused of disloyalty to the crown, Jonathan might have been spied on, and the reason for the ploy with the arrows becomes clear. As the two friends part, their covenant bond is again stressed. **38** Jonathan's words may have been intended to prevent the servant lad from exploring too diligently. But probably they contain a *double* *entendre*, and were equally meant for David's ears. **40** Jonathan may have feared that the youth might have been set to spy on him. **41** Note David's sign of respect for the crown prince; so too he later viewed Saul's person as sacrosanct (24:6; 26:9). **42** *Jonathan went into the city*. There is no suggestion that he should have accompanied David into exile. He was duty bound to stay beside his father.

21:1 – 26:25 David as a fugitive

David was now to enter on a long period as a fugitive, pursued implacably by Saul.

21:1–15 David at Nob and at Gath. This chapter illustrates the extremities to which David was driven; he visits the central shrine (since Shiloh's destruction), but dare not seek its sanctuary, and then pays a first visit to the Philistine city of Gath. At both places he finds himself compelled to lie and deceive. His behaviour at Nob in particular left much to be desired, but the narrator neither reproves nor commends him, since that is not the point; the writer's purpose is to show how far David was driven in order to remain alive.

1 *Nob* (if the same as that of Is. 10:32) was very near Jerusalem; Mt. Scopus is a tentative location for it. *Ahimelech* (see on 14:3) was the priest in charge, and Eli's grandson. In visiting him, David continued to demonstrate (as in 19:18) his good relations with cultic personnel, although on this occasion disaster was to result, for which David later expressed regret (22:22). **4, 6** *Holy bread, bread of the Presence* (AV 'shewbread'): *cf.* Ex. 25:30. **5** *Vessels* is euphemistic: we may translate 'bodies'. **6** *Cf.* Mk. 2:23–28. **7** *Detained*: *i.e.* Doeg was ritually unclean that day, and waiting to perform some religious obligation the next day. *The chief of Saul's herdsmen*: perhaps read 'the mightiest of Saul's runners' (McKane). **9, 10** See on 17:54. As Hertzberg points out, there is a touch of humour here, in that David should enter Philistine territory wearing Goliath's sword! **11** *The king of the land* is a rather premature designation; the Philistine populace apparently drew a false conclusion from the singers' words (*cf.* 18:7). **12–15** make it plain that we have here no duplicate nor anticipation of ch. 27. As yet the Philistines were unaware of the breach between Saul and David: naturally enough, since it was not even known yet at Nob.

22:1–5 David's continued wanderings. While David remained on the move, we now see him beginning to organize his affairs, so far as was possible.

1 *Adullam* was a city in the W Judean hills not so far from the Philistine border. *The cave* was presumably nearby. Modern Khirbet 'id al-ma is probably the site, with its many capacious caves. A slight alteration will give 'stronghold' for 'cave', perhaps rightly. **2** David was to weld this motley band into an effective military unit. **3, 4** *Moab*. As the book of Ruth tells us, David had Moabite blood in his veins.

By his action now he saved his parents from Saul's vindictiveness. **5** *Gad* (whose mention shows that David was not without prophetic support) advises him to return to *Judah*. The *forest of Hereth* has been located a few miles E of Adullam.

22:6–23 The massacre at Nob. Saul's suspicions and vengeful nature were no longer directed solely at David. His own men felt the whiplash of his tongue, while the innocent priests of Nob were slaughtered.

6 *Discovered* reads a little oddly; a minor emendation gives 'had joined up'. *Saul was sitting . . .* : *cf.* Jdg. 4:5. **7** *Benjaminites*. Evidently Saul's immediate court was drawn from his own tribe only. **8** *To lie in wait*. Saul claims that David is no fugitive, but a revolutionary. His accusations against Jonathan were not followed up; Hertzberg suggests that Doeg's statement took the blame off Jonathan. **14, 15** Ahimelech's self-defence constitutes a noble defence of David, too. **20–23** While David does not emerge blameless for this tragedy, yet in him we see regret, and it is clear that Abiathar knew whom to trust and support. The writer is not seeking to whitewash David, rather to indicate how events turned to his profit. Abiathar's support may be judged to have been valuable; he carried the ephod, with which David could repeatedly enquire of Yahweh: one such occasion follows at once, in 23:2. With Zadok, Abiathar later officiated at David's Jerusalem shrine (*cf.* 2 Sa. 15:24).

23:1–14 David at Keilah. Not only was David subject to divine protection during this period (v. 14), he was also prompted by God to give real service to Israel (and in particular to his native Judah).

1 *Keilah*: a city of Judah a little S of Adullam. **3** *I.e.* why invite the anger of a second enemy? The argument of David's men was plausible enough. **6** explains the means (the Urim and Thummim: see on 14:41) by which David was able to *inquire of the Lord* (vv. 2, 4). **12, 13** The men of Keilah dared not shield David, in view of the fate of the priests of Nob. His willingness to save them from any reprisals on Saul's part will have given them a second reason for gratitude to him. **14** quietly underlines the insecurity of David's position; *Ziph* lay considerably farther south, in still less fertile country. Throughout this chapter David is seen moving steadily southwards, and deeper into wilderness terrain.

23:15–18 Jonathan visits David. There is dramatic irony here: Saul and his troops could not locate David (v. 14), but Jonathan had no difficulty in finding his friend. This was their last meeting; David (and the reader) received fresh assurance of the final outcome of the desperate situation.

17 *I shall be next to you*. This statement of Jonathan's intention of supporting David indicates that he had no premonition of his own fate. **18** The two men renew their covenant (*cf.* 18:3).

23:19-28 The Ziphite betrayal of David. Jonathan's assurances were well timed, immediately preceding David's most dangerous situation yet. It is evident how dependent he was on goodwill from his fellow Judeans.

22, 23 David had naturally acquainted himself with the terrain of the Judean hills. **24** *The Arabah* is the rift valley through which flows the Jordan and where lies the Dead Sea; it continues S to the Gulf of Aqabah. **27, 28** The unwitting human agents of David's deliverance are the Philistines! One can readily see that Saul's irrational determination to kill David played right into the Philistine hands.

23:29 – 24:7 The incident at En-gedi. Here David's dangerous situation is highlighted, and also his lofty view of the status of royalty. One can see an apologetic element in ch. 24: David never exhibited any animosity towards Saul, who in his rational moments went so far as to acknowledge David's right to the throne. A faction supporting the house of Saul may have had a long existence after Saul's death. (See also on ch. 26, where a similar incident is recorded.)

23:29 *En-gedi*, on the shores of the Dead Sea, has fresh water flowing through it, but lies in a very barren region. **24:4, 5** To touch Saul's clothing was tantamount to touching his person; see on 18:4. This concept explains David's immediate remorse.

24:8-22 David and Saul confer. The climax of the chapter is v. 20, which once again emphasizes that David will inevitably come to the throne, a position of inviolability (*cf.* v. 6). **8** describes a daring and courageous act, for David was heavily outnumbered (contrast 22:2 with 24:2). *David bowed . . . :* note David's courtesy and humility (*cf.* v. 14). **15** David places himself in God's hands rather than in Saul's. **17** again has a hint of the apologetic about it; David's 'overthrow' of Saul's dynasty may well have raised doubts about the legitimacy of his reign. **22** *David swore this*: an oath fulfilled in 2 Sa. 9 (though see 2 Sa. 21:1-14). *The stronghold* is probably Adullam again; *cf.* 22:1. Wisely, David placed little reliance on Saul's change of heart proving permanent.

25:1 Death of Samuel. This verse stands in isolation, and is presumably chronologically placed; *cf.* 28:3, where the ensuing narrative is linked with the fact of Samuel's death. Also, there may well be theological point in the death of Samuel so soon after Saul had at last acknowledged that David would be his successor (24:20). *Paran*: JB and virtually all commentators follow the LXX reading, 'Maon' (*cf.* v. 2); Paran lay far to the SW.

25:2-13 Nabal's rebuff. While Nabal's behaviour towards David will not have been typical, this story well illustrates the difficulties David's band faced in none-too-fertile country, and makes it plain that local land-owners must have viewed him with mixed feelings, if not outright hostility. Hospitality to a group of six hundred men is a costly business.

2 *Carmel* of Judah, near *Maon*. **3** *Nabal*. There is deliberate irony in the description of him, for his very name means 'obstinate fool' (*cf.* v. 25). *Calebite*. This area, S of Hebron, was Calebite, but Hertzberg suggests a further irony here, since the name 'Caleb' means 'dog' (*cf.* 24:14). **4** Sheep-shearing was a festival time (*cf.* v. 8), an occasion for festivity and goodwill. **7, 8** David had been a good friend to Judah in defeating the Philistines at Keilah (23:1-5), but it is only hospitality, not reward, that he claims. **13** shows that David's men were increasing in number; *cf.* 22:2.

25:14-44 David and Abigail. From the factual point of view, the narrative relates how David became a property-owner in Judah, and tells us of the beginnings of the royal harem. Theologically, vv. 28-31 are the most significant.

14-17 Nabal's own men confirm David's claim (v. 7). Evidently Nabal was refusing to carry out accepted custom on either political or personal grounds. **26, 31** Abigail's counsel to avoid vindictiveness was wise (as David acknowledged, v. 33), and David followed it to the end of his career. These two verses also contain dramatic irony, since in fact Nabal is going to die and Abigail to become David's wife. **29** *Life . . . shall be bound in the bundle of the living* is a striking metaphor, to denote the watchful care God takes over David's life (*cf.* Mt. 6:25-34). **30** *Prince*: see on 9:16. **37, 38** Nabal's fate could be interpreted as a stroke. **43** *Jezreel* was nearby (*cf.* Jos. 15:55, 56), and like Carmel must be distinguished from the better-known northerly place-name. **44** recalls the reader to the situation (of Saul's unremitting hostility); the verse relates back to 19:11-17, forward to 2 Sa. 3.

26:1-16 David spares Saul's life again. Many commentators view this chapter as a divergent account of the incident related in ch. 24. However, the details are as different as the theme is alike; and the wealth of geographical description in both chapters suggests accurate knowledge of events, which in turn supports the historicity of both accounts. The first two verses are reminiscent of the earlier story, and this feature must be deliberate; possibly the author wished to convey that the event he is about to recount had actually occurred before the incident related in ch. 25.

2 *Three thousand chosen men*: *cf.* 24:2. **3-5** This time, however, it would appear that not all of them were present in Saul's *encampment*. **6** *Zeruiah*: David's sister (1 Ch. 2:16). *Abishai*: *cf.* 2 Sa. 23:18. **9** reiterates 24:6; **10** but this time David knows more of the future. His prediction came true (ch. 31). **12** *A deep sleep*. The same Hebrew word appears in Gn. 2:21. **13** David shows caution he had not exhibited on the earlier occasion (24:8). **16** *You deserve to die* contains a hint of Abner's fate in store (2 Sa. 3).

26:17-25 David and Saul confer again. As in 24:9-22, David protests that he is innocent of treason, and Saul temporarily comes to his senses, for the second time. In spite of the similarities, there is a new note struck here, anticipating the next chapter. Saul's unrelenting pursuit of David will drive him out of 'the heritage of the Lord' (v. 19), and Saul is cursed for it in advance.

18, 19 The cause of the quarrel, David says, can only be himself, Yahweh, or a third party; since the first two are innocent, the third party (tactfully anonymous) must shoulder the blame. **19** There were no sanctuaries to Yahweh outside Israelite territory, so to worship at all in Philistia would mean idolatry. Worship was much more tied to sanctuaries than was the NT worship (*cf.* Jn. 4:20–24). It is unnecessary to infer from this verse that David thought Yahweh to be 'operative' only in Israel; such a view is ruled out by 30:7, 8. **20** RSV mg. shows how in its transmission this verse became assimilated to 24:14. **21** Saul's invitation to David was no doubt genuine, but his emotions were so unstable that David would have been a fool to agree. **25** In the event, both parties separated once more. It is again impressed on the reader that David's future is certain, and that Saul knows it.

27:1 – 30:31 David in Philistine territory

Events now moved inexorably to their climax in the battle of Gilboa (ch. 31). These chapters are unusual in that the reader learns a good deal about the Philistine manoeuvres, but relatively little about the Israelite preparations for battle. The reason is that the narrative follows David, who spent this period among the Philistines, subordinate to them.

27:1 – 28:2 David as a Philistine vassal. Despite his earlier experience (*cf.* 21:10–15) David returned to Gath; he felt he had no choice. This time he was welcomed, no doubt because of the 600 men he commanded, and he was established as a Philistine vassal at Ziklag. Here his native wit enabled him to deceive his overlord, by attacking mutual enemies of Israel and Philistia while pretending to have raided his own people. The butchery and deceit here practised by David are indicative of the desperate situation in which he found himself.

6 *Ziklag* lay well south, only 12 miles N of Beer-sheba. Once a Simeonite city (*cf.* Jos. 19:5), it had been appropriated by the Philistines; as noted here, it was afterwards crown property in Judah (see also Introduction). **8** The *Geshurites*, *Girzites* and *Amalekites* were nomadic desert tribes who frequently raided the neighbouring settled populations. Saul, too, had attacked the Amalekites (ch. 15). **10** *The Negeb* is the sparsely-populated area lying between the more fertile hills of Judah to the north and the desert to the south. It is very dry, as its name in Hebrew testifies. Three specific districts of it are here mentioned. **12** Had David really attacked *his people Israel*, Achish's words would have been completely true. **28:1, 2** David was in a quandary, but could only comply. There is

dramatic irony in Achish of Gath designating David and his men as his bodyguard, for not many years later Gittites were to provide David's bodyguard.

28:3–25 Saul consults a medium. The narrator's attention returns to Saul, who is shown to be at the end of his tether; only a medium can counsel and sustain him. His problem was that the Philistine armies were resorting to a new strategy; hitherto they had fought in the hills, where their more sophisticated weapons gave them little advantage, and where the Israelites were on familiar terrain. But now they marched into the plain of Jezreel, keeping to level ground, and threatened to cut off Saul from the northern group of tribes.

3 *Cf.* 25:1. *Mediums . . . wizards.* Necromancy was consistently attacked by OT laws and by the leaders of Israel, but it was evidently too popular to be totally eradicated. See Lv. 19:31; Dt. 18:9–14; 2 Ki. 21:6. **6** *Urim*: see on 14:41. **7, 8** *Endor* is situated N of Shunem, where the Philistine army lay, and Saul's journey from the Gilboa hills (S of the plain of Jezreel) was no doubt difficult and dangerous; that he embarked on it at all is a mark of his desperation. **12** It is not clear how it came about that the woman suddenly recognized Saul. A few LXX MSS read 'Saul' instead of *Samuel*, perhaps rightly; but Hertzberg attractively conjectures an emendation, 'When the woman *heard the name* Samuel . . .' **13** *A god*; *i.e.* a supernatural figure. **14, 15** The narrative strongly suggests that this really was Samuel, and not a mere apparition or hallucination. The foreknowledge and uncompromising statements attributed to him in the verses that follow also stamp him as being genuinely Samuel. **16–18** The denunciation of Saul pronounced in 15:26, 28 is still operative. **19** Saul learns his fate, in no uncertain terms, and **20, 21** he is brought to his lowest ebb.

29:1–11 David is sent back to Ziklag. One wonders if David had any thought of trying to sabotage the Philistine battle-plans; be that as it may, he was spared the necessity by the very natural suspicions of the Philistine leaders. Patently Achish had been completely fooled by David's words and actions.

1 *Aphek*. Unless this was some local town, to be distinguished from that of 4:1, we must conclude that the episode related in this chapter took place prior to the Philistine encampment at Shunem (28:4), since Aphek lay much farther south. *Jezreel* is at the foot of the Gilboa range. **2** *Lords*: a special term for the rulers of the five Philistine cities, of whom Achish was one. **5** *Cf.* 18:7; 21:11. The Philistines evidently knew this song at their expense only too well. **9** *As an angel of God* may have been a common saying; *cf.* 2 Sa. 14:20; 19:27. **11** *I.e.* the Philistines advanced on the Israelite army (*cf.* v. 1) to do battle.

30:1–31 David defeats the Amalekites. David's return to Ziklag proved opportune: indeed, he was only just in time. So the actions of the Philistine rulers in dismissing him enabled him not only to avoid fighting against fellow-Israelites, but also to retrieve the families of himself and his men and to earn fresh gratitude from the people of Judah (vv. 26–31). Note, too, the literary skill with which the narrator leaves the reader in suspense as regards the outcome of the battle of Gilboa; once again (as in ch. 28) he breaks off that major story to interpose a separate incident.

1 *The Negeb*: see on 27:10. **2** The Amalekites were planning to sell their captives as slaves. **7, 8** *Cf.* 22:20; 23:6, 9ff. Nomadic raiders are not easy to locate. **14** *The Cherethites* were kin to the Philistines. **16** shows that Ziklag had not been the only city to suffer from the Amalekite raid. **21–25** A quarrel among his men leads to David's first legal enactment. **31** *All the places where David and his men had roamed.* David thus repaid hospitality, and no doubt won over any potential Nabals (*cf.* ch. 25).

31:1–13 Defeat and death of Saul and Jonathan

31:1–7 The battle of Gilboa. Worsted in battle, the Israelite troops tried to escape into the safety of the hills, but many of them, including Saul and Jonathan, were overtaken by the pursuing Philistines.

1 *Now the Philistines fought* runs on from 29:11. **2** See on 14:49. *Abinadab* also appears in 1 Ch. 8:33. **4** *Saul* killed himself; an Amalekite told David a different story (2 Sa. 1:10; see commentary *in loc.*). **7** *The valley*: better, 'plain', *i.e.* of Jezreel. Israel is here reckoned as threefold: N of Jezreel, E of the river Jordan, and the main territory (S of the plain). The Philistines were able to enter each part of this territory, though their influence in Transjordan was limited, in fact.

31:8–13 The rescue of Saul's body. The first book of Samuel ends on a fitting note. Saul's first royal act had been to rescue Jabesh-gilead (ch. 11); its citizens now repaid him, posthumously.

9 RSV mg. may be preferable to the text. **10** *Ashtaroth* is the plural of Ashtoreth, which is probably the original reading here. She was the pan-Semitic goddess of war (and especially of fertility), known in Mesopotamia as Ishtar, to the Greeks as Astarte. Her *temple* is not here located; Ashkelon has been suggested. *Beth-shan*: a major city, E of the plain of Jezreel, near the Jordan. **12** *Burnt* is probably correct, although 'anointed with spices' has been put forward as the appropriate rendering here (*e.g.* Hertzberg). Burial was the Hebrew custom, but the fate of the bodies till this juncture may have been thought to require special treatment. Care was taken not to burn the bones, at any rate.

2 Sa. 1:1 – 8:18 THE EARLY YEARS OF DAVID'S REIGN

The time was ripe for David to succeed Saul to the throne of Israel; the king rejected by God was dead. But difficulties and obstacles still lay before David. Nevertheless, his rise to power

continued to be marked by clear signs of the divine hand, and R. A. Carlson has characterized this period of David's life as 'David under the blessing', in contrast with his later years (see Carlson, *David: the Chosen King, passim*).

1:1–27 David's reaction to the news of Saul's death

The fall of Saul and his house was pre-ordained, and in one sense was but a necessary stage in David's rise to power; but on the other hand it was a tragedy for Israel, and David's reactions were consistent with his conception of the sanctity of the person of the Lord's anointed (*cf.* 1 Sa. 24:6; 26:11). David's regrets were undoubtedly genuine.

1:1–16 The Amalekite messenger. The messenger's story is basically the same as that of 1 Sa. 31, but with some differences, principally the claim that he had given Saul the *coup de grâce*, whereas in 1 Sa. 31:4 Saul's death was suicide. The stories are not irreconcilable; v. 9 is most naturally interpreted as implying that Saul was already wounded, and it is certainly possible that his own sword-wound (31:4) did not immediately have fatal effect. However, it may be best to view the Amalekite's tale as either exaggerated or partly untrue (with R. H. Pfeiffer, Hertzberg). Conceivably David's words in v. 16 contain a hint that he was not entirely convinced by the story; and see on 4:10. There can be no doubt that the Chronicler believed 1 Sa. 31, which he reproduced in 1 Ch. 10; he pays no attention to 2 Sa. 1.

2 *The third day.* It would have taken a messenger this long to travel the 100 miles from Gilboa to Ziklag. It is significant that the Amalekite reported to David, not to Saul's surviving son, Ish-bosheth; he viewed David now as king (*did obeisance*). **6** *By chance.* If the man was not one of Saul's retinue, he may have been looting the corpses. The Philistines did not discover Saul's body till the day after the battle (1 Sa. 31:8). **13** *A sojourner*; *i.e.* a foreigner now resident in Israel.

1:17–27 David's elegy. The beauty of the lament, its sincerity, and the correctness of its ascription to David are all widely recognized. The elegy may have been called 'the Song of the Bow', which would help to explain the problem of the Hebrew text of v. 18 (*cf.* RSV mg.).

18 Evidently *the Book of Jashar* was one source used by the author of the books of Samuel. *Cf.* Jos. 10:13. **21** *Upsurging of the deep* represents an emendation of the Hebrew; but, despite the parallel of sorts with *dew or rain*, it is not very convincing. 'Treacherous fields' (JB) follows a preferable emendation. **23** *They were not divided.* Some commentators have seen a certain pious hypocrisy in this remark, but it is after all true that Jonathan never left his father's side, in spite of their very different feelings towards David. **24** indicates how successful Saul had been against the Philistines. **27** *The weapons of war* is a metaphorical description of Saul and Jonathan.

2:1 – 4:12 David and Ish-bosheth

It is not surprising that Saul's surviving son, Ish-bosheth, should have attempted to succeed to the throne. It may seem surprising that the victorious Philistines should have permitted David to become king of Judah; but it is highly probable that he continued for the moment as their vassal. They were, after all, in alliance with several petty kings of Canaanite cities; and it would have served them well had David permanently divided the Israelites into two mutually hostile camps.

2:1–11 The rival kings. The willingness of the tribe of Judah to make David king and to break away from the northern tribes was by no means a foregone conclusion; hence David's fresh consultation of the sacred oracle. His message to Jabesh-gilead was a shrewd political move; Jabesh lay well N of Ish-bosheth's capital Mahanaim (v. 8). But we do not know how they responded.

1 *Hebron*: a major city of Judah, well S of David's native Bethlehem. **2** *Cf*. 1 Sa. 25:42f. **4** *Cf*. 1 Sa. 31:11ff. **7** A tacit invitation. **8** There is no doubt who had the real power. *Mahanaim* lay E of the Jordan: since the battle of Gilboa, the Philistines will have made an Israelite capital W of the river an impossibility. **9** *The Ashurites*: the Hebrew word normally refers to the Assyrians, a clear impossibility in this context. The Hebrew text has probably resulted from a scribal confusion of two names, the men of Geshur (an Aramaean state, N of Gilead) and the men of Asher. The Targum reads 'men of Asher', probably correctly, while the Syriac and Vulgate have Geshurites. Ish-bosheth's control over '*all Israel*' must have been very much on paper, for 1 Sa. 31:7 has given the *de facto* situation. **10, 11** *Two years*: Hertzberg would prefer to read 'seven years', to conform with David's reign over Judah in Hebron. But probably v. 11 telescopes David's early reign; no doubt he reigned over Judah in Hebron two years, over all Israel in Hebron a further five and a half years, and then moved his capital to Jerusalem.

2:12–32 The battle of Gibeon. Of the 'long war' (3:1) between David and Ish-bosheth only this incident is related. The purpose of the narrative is to show how the blood-feud began which led to Abner's death. The battle seems to have commenced as a representative combat (like that of 1 Sa. 17), although the word 'play' (v. 14) is puzzling. Hertzberg took it that a mock duel somehow went wrong and led to disaster.

12 *Gibeon* was an important city of Benjamin, not far N of David's territory. **14** *Play*: the verb normally refers to general sporting behaviour. If it means here to hold serious combat (so JB), then the death of all 24 contestants made the representative battle inconclusive, and a general battle therefore followed. **18** *Zeruiah*: David's sister (*cf*. 1 Ch. 2:16). **23** *Butt*. The Hebrew noun is of uncertain meaning, but it appears possible

that Abner did not intend to kill Asahel, merely to deter him. **24** Note the misprint 'Gideon' (for 'Gibeon') in some editions of the RSV. **25** Apparently Abner received reinforcements from the locality. **29** *The Arabah*: the Jordan valley, in this context. *The whole forenoon*: the Hebrew is obscure, and 'through a ravine' may be correct. (AV, RV 'Bithron', as a proper name, is still a possibility.)

3:1–5 David's family. The mention at this point of David's family provides a contrast with the insecurity of Ish-bosheth's position. Since becoming king, David had evidently married four additional wives, among them a princess of Geshur (Maacah, v. 3). This marriage probably cemented an alliance which helped to isolate Ish-bosheth, since Geshur was an Aramaean state lying to the N of Gilead.

2 *At Hebron*: *i.e.* before David moved his capital to Jerusalem, where other sons were born to him (*cf*. 5:13–16). *Ahinoam*: *cf*. 1 Sa. 25:43. **3** *Chileab*: the name is suspect, in view of LXX variations and 1 Ch. 3:1 ('Daniel'). *Abigail*: *cf*. 1 Sa. 25:42.

3:6–11 The rift between Ish-bosheth and Abner. To approach the royal concubines was tantamount to claiming the throne (*cf*. 16:20ff.), and without doubt Abner's action was treasonable. One wonders whether he really wished to supplant Ish-bosheth, or whether he merely wanted an excuse to desert to David's camp.

8 *Am I a dog's head of Judah*? *i.e.* a contemptible traitor. The phrase 'of Judah' does not appear in the LXX, and is perhaps to be omitted, since Ish-bosheth had not accused him of supporting David. **9** Abner now, like Saul and Jonathan at an earlier date, acknowledges explicitly that David is God's chosen king.

3:12–21 Abner defects to David. David refused any underhand negotiations with Abner; he may even have expected a refusal to return Michal to him. She was Saul's daughter, and as such would greatly strengthen David's claim to Saul's throne; the fact that Ish-bosheth meekly complied is significant.

14 *Cf*. 1 Sa. 18:20–27. **15, 16** *Cf*. 1 Sa. 25:44 ('Palti' is merely a shorter form of the name). One can sympathize with *Paltiel*, but the blame must be laid on Saul rather than David. **17–19** indicate that Ish-bosheth's cause was already lost, before his death. Even his own tribe, *Benjamin*, were ready to make David their king. **21** *In peace*; *i.e.* with no suspicion of his fate.

3:22–39 The assassination of Abner. Joab's hostility to Abner was natural enough, on account of the blood-feud between them, and secondly because Abner, with all his military experience, might well have replaced him as David's commander-in-chief. Whether he really believed in his accusations of treachery and espionage (v. 25) is hard to say. It is astonishing that David made no reply, but he can scarcely have tacitly supported Joab's subsequent actions, for the murder of Abner was an embarrassment to him.

28 David knew that divine retribution was inevitable. **29** *Who holds a spindle*: 'fit only for women's work' (L. H. Brockington), effeminate. **30** Evidently *Abishai* had some hand in the murder (*cf.* v. 39). **36** Clearly David succeeded in dissociating himself from complicity in the murder. **39** An unusual confession of weakness on David's part.

4:1–12 The assassination of Ish-bosheth. The death of Abner further demoralized Ish-bosheth's realm, and it fell apart, the murder of Ish-bosheth himself completing the process.

2, 3 *Be-eroth* is linked with Gibeon in Jos. 9:17, and its inhabitants may well have suffered along with the Gibeonites (*cf.* 21:1) at Saul's hands. This would well explain a basic hostility to Saul and his family in Be-erothites like *Baanah* and *Rechab* here. **4** Though it interrupts the narrative, this verse is not irrelevant, since it brings into the picture the nearest kin to Saul apart from Ish-bosheth, and lays a foundation for ch. 9. **6** RSV here follows the LXX, which provides better sense than the Hebrew (*cf.* AV). **7** *The Arabah*: *cf.* 2:29. **10** David recalls the events narrated in ch. 1; it may be noteworthy that he says nothing of the Amalekite's claim to have killed Saul. **12** contrasts honourable and dishonourable burial.

5:1–25 David defeats the Philistines

David's last rival had now fallen, but he had still to make himself king of the whole nation, and to defeat the Philistines. He wasted no time in either respect.

5:1–5 David becomes king of all Israel. There was no thought in anyone's mind that Mephibosheth, Saul's grandson, should reign; the situation demanded a warrior, not a cripple (4:4). **2** Two motives impelled the northern tribesmen to turn to David: his past reputation in battle, and the fact of Yahweh's promises to him. *Shepherd* was a term applied frequently to kings; see especially Ezk. 34. *Prince*: see on 1 Sa. 10:1. **3** The view put forward by A. Alt that the north and south were united in the person of the king, and not constitutionally, is widely held today. **5** summarizes David's reign, and leads on naturally to the story of Jerusalem's capture.

5:6–16 Jerusalem captured and made the capital. Jerusalem was already a very ancient city; at the time of the Israelite conquest of Canaan the Jebusites held on to it (Jdg. 1:21), though apparently the men of Judah conquered it, or part of it, at one time (see on Jdg. 1:8). It now lay in a Canaanite enclave, which tended to isolate Judah from Benjamin and Ephraim, and its capture was an important step in the consolidation of David's kingdom. **6** The Jebusites considered their fortress impregnable. **7** On the place-names, see *NBD*, art. 'Jerusalem'. **8** This verse in Hebrew in any case requires some emendation, and the word for *water shaft* is of uncertain meaning. Various other translations of it have been offered (*e.g.*

'(scaling) hook', by W. F. Albright); the LXX reads 'dagger'; and the parallel passage in 1 Ch. 11:6 has no mention of the word. However, it is quite likely that Joab (see 1 Ch. 11:6) was able to penetrate the city's defences by means of a weak point in the system of water-supply. Hertzberg has suggested, attractively, that due to his exploit the spring En-rogel (on the E of the city) was originally named 'Joab's Well', later corrupted to 'Job's Well' (as it is known today). *The house* here quite possibly means the Temple (*cf.* JB). **9** *The Millo*: part of the city's defences, to which Solomon was to pay special attention (1 Ki. 9:15). **11, 12** 'It becomes clear that David now draws foreign attention upon himself. He finds respect and recognition' (Hertzberg). The Lebanon region was noted for its building materials and skills. Observe that the exaltation of David is not for his own sake but for his people's: a democratic concept of kingship unusual in the ancient world. **13–16** continues the list of 3:2–5. *Eliada* appears as 'Beeliada' in 1 Ch. 14:7. Note how far down the list *Solomon* comes.

5:17–25 Philistine attacks repulsed. Once the whole of Israel was united behind David, the Philistines could view him no longer as an ally or vassal. Chronologically, the battles now recounted may well have preceded David's capture of Jerusalem.

17, 18 *The stronghold*: probably Adullam is meant (*cf.* 23:13, 14 and 1 Sa. 22:1), although *the valley of Rephaim* was quite near Jerusalem. The Philistine strategy was to isolate Judah from the northern Israelite tribes. **20** *Baal-perazim*, in view of the meaning of the name, was no doubt so called after the battle. The 'break-through' suggests a frontal assault, contrasting with the different tactics employed by David in the second battle (v. 23). **21** The Philistines had brought *idols* on to the battle-field, hoping to ensure victory (*cf.* 1 Sa. 4:3, 4). David later had them burnt (*cf.* 1 Ch. 14:12). **22** The Philistines saw no reason to change their strategy or tactics; **23–25** David, on the other hand, altered his tactics most successfully. **25** *From Geba to Gezer*; *i.e.* the Philistines were driven out of the hill country.

6:1 – 7:29 David, the ark, and the house of God

Saul had never shown any interest in the ark of the covenant, and he had offended both the prophets and the priests. David, the king of God's choice, reversed Saul's acts and policies completely, and emerged with yet greater promises of divine blessing.

6:1–23 The ark brought to Jerusalem. A more elaborate account is given in 1 Ch. 13 and 15. David thus transformed Jerusalem into the central sanctuary, as well as capital and royal city. This act inevitably brought the king into close contact with the cultus and the priesthood. **2** *Baale-judah*: called Kiriath-jearim in 1 Sa. 7:1. See on 1 Sa. 4:4. **3** *A new cart*: *cf.* 1 Sa. 6:7. *Sons* (a more general term in Hebrew than in

English) probably means here 'grandsons', in view of the lapse of time and the omission of Eleazar's name (*cf.* 1 Sa. 7:1). 6 *Nacon* is an unlikely name; the 'Chidon' of 1 Ch. 13:9 seems preferable. 7 RSV follows 1 Ch. 13:10, since the Hebrew is here obscure; but 'for this crime' (JB) is a possible rendering. The punishment of Uzzah has often been objected to as excessive, especially as his intention was good; but the majesty of the Holy One was symbolized by the ark. It was necessary to teach the Israelites the infinite holiness of God, sometimes by 'terrible acts'. See Nu. 4:15. 10, 11 *Obed-edom the Gittite*: his name means 'worshipper of Edom' (*i.e.* a deity called Edom, in all probability); it is ironical that a Philistine and an idolater should become host to the ark, and be blessed! 12–15 A number of modern commentators hold that we have here a description of the annual re-enthronement of Yahweh, at a new year festival (the Feast of Tabernacles). Evidence for this is remarkably tenuous, and K. A. Kitchen has commented that 'it is ludicrous to force specific historical occasions like 2 Sa. 6 . . . into a New Year mould'. (See his *Ancient Orient and Old Testament*, pp. 102–106, and literature there cited.) 14 An *ephod* was a priestly garment, much shorter than the usual outer garment (*cf.* v. 20). 15 *Shouting*: a ritual cry; *cf.* Ps. 47:5. 19 *Portion of meat* is a guess; 'raisin cake' (JB) or the like is preferred by several commentators. 20 Michal's reaction may have resulted from her father's notoriety as a consequence of his actions at Naioth in Ramah (1 Sa. 19:24). 22, 23 may imply that David withdrew from her, but we cannot be sure.

7:1–17 Nathan's prophecy. This passage is in many ways the most important of the books of Samuel. David's noble wish to build a 'house' for his God was set aside, and instead God promised him a 'house' (*i.e.* a dynasty); God is no man's debtor. But more than that, the dynasty was to be 'for ever' (v. 16); this was the basis of the Messianic hope, fulfilled in the NT. Through David's house, too, God would provide salvation for Israel (vv. 10, 11). For a brief account of critical discussions of this chapter, see *OTMS*, p. 101 (and literature there cited). 1 The narrator here jumps, chronologically (further battles are mentioned in ch. 8), in order to conclude the story of the ark and the sanctuary. 2 *Nathan*, a worthy successor to Samuel, is here first mentioned. 6 *Dwelling*: the Hebrew word implies a place of temporary residence— in the Pentateuch, it is used of the Tabernacle. The structure at Shiloh had been in one sense a 'permanent' building, but it had suffered destruction. In the NT, *cf.* Jn. 4:21; Acts 7:48,49; 17:24. 7 God still moves at the head of His people. 8–13 Only when Israel achieves stability (under Solomon) will God permit Himself a permanent dwelling. 13 is elaborated in 1 Ch. 22:7–10. 14 *I.e.* unworthy kings will not affect the stability of the dynasty. The first part of this verse indicates a special relationship between God and

the Davidic king (*cf.* Ps. 2:7). 15 *My steadfast love* represents a Hebrew word (*ḥeseḏ*) bearing covenantal associations; *cf.* Is. 55:3.

7:18–29 David's prayer. David humbly accepts the unsolicited promise from God. It is interesting that he connected the divine promises to him with the earlier promises to the nation which he ruled; thus the 'Davidic covenant' and the Sinaitic covenant are linked together. The passage 'opens up perspectives which extend far beyond the history of Israel' (Hertzberg).

18 *King David went in*; *i.e.* into the temporary shrine for the ark. 19 There is a textual problem here (*cf.* RSV mg.), as elsewhere in this prayer. 23, 24 *Cf.* Ex. 19:3–6.

8:1–18 Further victories of David

8:1–14 Various campaigns. The divine promises of ch. 7 are exhibited to the reader as finding partial fulfilment immediately, although chronologically many of the campaigns here summarized took place before Nathan's prophecy (*cf.* 7:1). On the campaigns in Transjordan, see Bright, *History of Israel*, pp. 181f.

1 *Metheg-ammah* should mean 'bridle (? control) of the metropolis', and probably refers to Gath, a key Philistine city (*cf.* 1 Ch. 18:1). But a variety of interpretations is possible. 2 The violence to *Moab* suggests treachery on their part, in view of the earlier friendly relations (*cf.* 1 Sa. 22:3, 4). 3 *Zobah* was a small Aramaean kingdom near Damascus; 5 hence their kinsmen came to their aid. 6 The final clause, though theological, may reflect something of the surprise which David's victories caused. 8 Rather different forms of the place-names appear in 1 Ch. 18:8. 9 *Hamath*: another Aramaean state, lying over 100 miles N of Damascus. 12 *Edom*: the Hebrew reads 'Aram' (= Syria), probably rightly (*cf.* AV). 13 *Edomites*: here too the Hebrew refers to Syrians, but RSV is right to emend. The two place-names are scarcely distinguishable when the Hebrew script is written without the vowels (as it was for many centuries).

8:15–18 David's officials. David's territorial acquisitions will have necessitated a good deal of organization and administration, and this brief list of royal officials comes very appropriately at this point; 20:23–26 gives a later list. The passage also serves to introduce the chapters that follow, where attention centres on the royal court, instead of the battle-field.

15 *Justice and equity*; *i.e.* David himself was directly responsible for the judicial administration, a fact which later played into the hands of Absalom (*cf.* 15:3). 17 presents some textual problems and uncertainties. Presumably we should reverse the names *Ahimelech* and *Abiathar*, for a start (*cf.* 1 Sa. 22:20). According to biblical genealogies, both *Zadok* and *Abiathar* were descendants of an *Ahitub* (not necessarily the same man): *cf.* 1 Ch. 6:8; 1 Sa. 22:9. It has been widely conjectured, however, that Zadok was not even a Levite; he may in that case have been priest in Jerusalem to 'God Most High'

(Gn. 14:18) before David's capture of the city (as H. H. Rowley suggested). But an equally attractive possibility, which accepts the biblical genealogies, is that Saul had made Zadok high priest after the Nob slaughter. It seems considerably more likely that David should have tried to placate the followers of Saul, by uniting Saul's high priest with his own, than that he should have accepted the pre-Israelite (?Jebusite) priest of Jerusalem. One might add that since David himself seems to have become in some sense a priest-king, 'after the order of Melchizedek' (Ps. 110:4), there will scarcely have been any place in the hierarchy for an existing Jerusalem priest. 18 *The Cherethites and the Pelethites* were groups of 'sea-peoples' akin to (or part of) the Philistines. Indeed, the second name may well mean simply 'Philistines', to which it is very similar, by word-play to yield assonance with the first name. *David's sons were priests* is an interesting statement; Keil, with an eye on the different wording of 1 Ch. 18:17, rendered the Hebrew word, normally meaning 'priests', as 'confidants'. However, if as king in Jerusalem David did inherit some priestly functions from Melchizedek, he may well have delegated them, in whole or part, to his sons.

9:1 – 20:26 KING DAVID AND HIS COURT

This long section presents a scarcely-edited court history of David, which may well have come from a single literary source (see Appendix 1). The chapters do not recount a series of unconnected episodes, however; there is a clear theme, which might be entitled 'the man of God's choice'. In ch. 9 we find David showing covenant-kindness to the grandson of his enemy Saul; then, by contrast, we see him betraying and murdering a man loyal to him (ch. 11). David thus departed from the will of God. Yet this series of events led to the birth of Solomon, the man chosen by God to succeed David. The rest of the section shows how other sons of David by their misdeeds punished their father for his sins, and yet were prevented, by divine overruling, from wresting the throne from either David or Solomon. 'The narrative of the Succession' is therefore a title for 2 Sa. 9–20 (with 1 Ki. 1; 2) favoured by many modern writers.

9:1–13 David and Mephibosheth

This chapter provides a contrast with David's actions recounted in ch. 11; and it also lays a basis for the parts played by Mephibosheth and Ziba in the revolt of Absalom (16:1–4; 19:24–30). **9:1–8 Mephibosheth is summoned.** The fears of Mephibosheth are readily explained when we consider that in the ancient world kings were accustomed to exterminate all members of a previous dynasty. It is also probable that the events recorded in 21:7–9 had already occurred. Hertzberg has pointed out, moreover, that David's opening remark, to suspicious ears, will have

sounded remarkably like Herod's in Mt. 2:8. 1 *For Jonathan's sake*; *i.e.* David plans to fulfil his covenant with Jonathan (1 Sa. 20:42). 3 *Cf.* 4:4. 4 *Machir* was a rich land-owner (*cf.* 17:27–29). *Lo-debar*, though not identified, lay in N Gilead, not far from Jabesh, whose citizens had befriended Saul (1 Sa. 31:11ff.). 6 *Mephibosheth* is a later form of an original 'Merib-baal' (*cf.* 1 Ch. 8:34). 7 *The land of Saul*; *i.e.* his personal estates in Benjamin.

9:9–13 Mephibosheth at court. Mephibosheth was not only permitted life and property, he was given an honoured place at court; in this generosity David went beyond what his covenant with Jonathan had required—it was, in fact, 'the kindness of God' (v. 3). 10 appears a trifle self-contradictory. H. P. Smith explained it by commenting, 'Presence at court would rather increase than diminish his expenditure.' 12 *Mica*: through him Saul's line continued for no few generations (1 Ch. 9:41–44).

10:1 – 12:31 Warfare with Ammon and its consequences

The Ammonite war was the background to David's affair with Bathsheba and its sequel; the campaign not only gave David the opportunity for his adultery but also provided the means by which he encompassed the death of her soldier-husband, Uriah.

10:1–19 The defeat of Ammon and its allies. David was friendly disposed to Hanun because of some kindness received from his father, Nahash: perhaps when a refugee in the neighbouring country of Moab (1 Sa. 22:3, 4). Saul had attacked Nahash (1 Sa. 11), so it was not unnatural that the latter should afterwards befriend David when Saul was pursuing him. The warfare which now broke out between David and Hanun is interesting, since it led to one of the few conquests of David of which we know the causes. While Hanun provoked David to declare war, yet one can appreciate something of the suspicion with which neighbouring rulers must have viewed the powerful king of Israel. 5 *Jericho* lay on the road between Ammon and Jerusalem, and was a frontier city before David's conquest of Ammon. 6 It was natural for the Ammonites to look for allies in the Aramaean kingdoms to the north; *cf.* 8:3–12. 16–18 relate briefly a campaign very reminiscent of that recorded in 8:3ff. Since ch. 8 presents a summary of David's victories, we may well have here the same campaign under consideration, now set in its appropriate chronological and historical context. The only difficulty is that the numbers are different; but this is not conclusive evidence, since a comparison of this passage with 1 Ch. 19:16–19 suggests textual corruption.

11:1–13 David's relations with Bathsheba and Uriah. V. 1 provides the link between the campaign, E of the Jordan, and David's adultery with Bathsheba, in Jerusalem; the story of the campaign is resumed in 12:26. 1 *The time when kings go forth*: dramatic irony, since this is precisely what David did not do! *Rabbah*: Rabbath-ammon (modern Amman) was the Ammonite capital. **2** David's initial action was natural enough, but it is not really clear whether Bathsheba's was quite innocent of coquetry. Conceivably a sheer coincidence started the disastrous chain of events; at any rate, Bathsheba is nowhere treated as a guilty party. **3** Both *Eliam* and *Uriah* figured among David's outstanding warriors (*cf.* 23:34, 39). Though a *Hittite*, Uriah must have worshipped Yahweh, for his name means 'Yahweh is my light'. **4** Such an act would have been natural enough for many monarchs of the ancient world; Israel's views of the rights of the king were very different (*cf.* 1 Ki. 21:5–7, 19). **8** *Wash your feet*: an idiom of the time, put into clearer words in v. 11. **11** *Booths*. McKane suggests that the reference is to the Feast of Tabernacles rather than to ordinary soldiers' tents. Some time must have elapsed since the spring (v. 1), certainly, so possibly by now six months had passed. Evidently there was a prohibition of marital relations at such a time, at any rate. **13** Despite his drunken state, Uriah did not lapse; it is not impossible that a rumour of his wife's adultery had reached him.

11:14–27 The death of Uriah. David knew that Joab of all people would not object to becoming party to murder! Joab, indeed, took it upon himself to improve on David's scheme, and by doing so brought about the death of several good soldiers besides Uriah. David's plan would have caused only Uriah's death, but would have been too obvious.

20, 21 are a trifle odd, constituting a detailed anticipation of David's possible response to the news; even so, it is unnecessary to follow Hertzberg in rearranging the verses (with some LXX support) to put the words on David's lips. David was, after all, expecting to learn of the death of a single individual. *Abimelech*: see Jdg. 9:53. *Jerubbesheth* is a variation of the name 'Jerubbaal', *i.e.* Gideon (*cf.* Jdg. 7:1). **27** David exhibited indecent haste, which suggests that the mourning was a mere formality; of course, Bathsheba's pregnancy will have dictated expedition.

12:1–14 Nathan's denunciation. The deed had been done which was to change David's whole life, but some months passed (11:27) before any consequence followed. Nathan's previous prophetic message to David had been one of unlimited divine blessing (7:8–16), and it is evident that David had not the least suspicion that Nathan's visit to him now foreboded any ill for him. Nathan's parable was doubly clever: not only did it invite him to condemn himself (unawares), it also appealed to him as head of the judiciary (*cf.* 8:15). **1** David was not the only man in Israel who received direct guidance from God. **5, 6** The *fourfold* restoration was in accordance with the law (Ex. 22:1); the additional death penalty reveals the extent of David's anger at the un-

named wrongdoer. **8** *Your master's wives.* Nowhere else is it stated that David took over Saul's concubines, but such was common practice for an aspirant or claimant to the throne (*cf.* 3:7; 16:22). The point of this verse is that David already possessed a considerable harem, and his adultery was therefore the more inexcusable. **9** *The sword of the Ammonites.* Nathan's words are now contemptuous: David had sunk so low as to get his enemies to do his murderous work for him. **10–12** The punishment will fit the crime. The predictions were fulfilled in the violent deaths of Amnon and Absalom in David's own lifetime, not to mention the later bloodshed (like Athaliah's purge, 2 Ki. 11:1), and in Absalom's public appropriation of the royal concubines (16:22). **13** David's contrition was immediate and genuine (*cf.* Ps. 51, noting the title). He never called Nathan his enemy, as Ahab did Elijah (1 Ki. 21:20). Equally immediate was the pronouncement of forgiveness, for David should have died, by law and by his own verdict. It is to be noted that God's pardon and punishment are not necessarily mutually exclusive. **14** *Utterly scorned the Lord.* RSV mg. gives the literal sense of the Hebrew (which could be rendered as in AV); we have here a reverential circumlocution.

12:15–25 The child's death and the birth of Solomon. Nathan's final pronouncement was the first to find fulfilment: the child of the adulterous union must die. Here the sins of the father were certainly visited on the child. David's reactions to the boy's sickness and death led him to fly in the face of conventions of the time, and no doubt his courtiers were shocked as well as puzzled. Some commentators share their puzzlement, but David's reasoning seems perfectly intelligible.

23 *I shall go to him.* It is the inevitability and immutability of death that is the point; David is not here concerned with questions of the afterlife. **24** *Solomon*: the name may well be connected with the name of the city, Jerusalem; possibly Solomon was the eldest son to be born there, of a wife of David as opposed to a concubine (*cf.* 5:13, 14). **25** The second name, *Jedidiah*, 'beloved of the Lord', was a sign to David that this son would not die; whether or not David knew it at the time, it also marked out this boy as his successor to the throne.

12:26–31 The capture of the Ammonite capital. The campaign against Ammon had occasioned David's adultery and all that had resulted from it; the story of the warfare, interrupted at 11:1, is now brought to a conclusion. V. 26 is a summary of the rest of the paragraph.

27 *The city of waters* refers not to the whole city of Rabbah, but to the covered passage linking the city with its water-supply (comparable with the Siloam tunnel of Jerusalem at a later date). **30** *Their king* (Heb. *malkām*) was evidently understood by LXX as the name of the Ammonite deity Milcom (*cf.* Zp. 1:5). This may indeed be the correct interpretation of the word, and it is accepted by JB, for instance; but on the whole 'their king' seems preferable, despite the very considerable (but not impossible) weight of his *crown*. **31** Hard *labour* is the understanding of this verse favoured in RSV and most modern commentaries. The torture view (*cf.* AV) is, however, possible: a cruel fate indeed. The nature of the items listed supports the former interpretation, but a slight textual alteration is required (*he'ĕḇíḏ*, 'made . . . toil', for *he'ĕḇír*, 'made . . . pass'). The use of conquered peoples in forced labour was common and natural.

13:1 – 18:33 David and his eldest sons

The central figure of the next few chapters is Absalom, David's third son (*cf.* 3:2, 3); Amnon, the eldest son, was murdered by him, and it seems likely that the second son must have died young, since he does not figure at all in the succession narratives. At any rate, by murdering Amnon, Absalom was free to make his own bid for the crown.

13:1–22 Amnon outrages his half-sister. We continue to trace the unhappy fortunes of David, brought about by his own misconduct with Bathsheba. It is noteworthy that the whole episode of Absalom's rebellion began with the same sins of which David had been guilty: sexual immorality leading to murder. **1** *Tamar* was the half-sister of *Amnon* and full sister of *Absalom*. **2** *Impossible*: prohibited by Lv. 18:11; Dt. 27:22; but Tamar suggested (v. 13) that a dispensation could be arranged (Abraham had married his half-sister, after all). But in the context the impossibility seems to have been a practical one, *i.e.* she was too carefully secluded. In any case, Amnon was bent on seduction, not marriage. **3** *Shimeah*: see on 1 Sa. 16:9. **6–11** The pains taken by Amnon make it plain that his action was no whim of the moment. **12** Tamar's reply would suggest that Israel's standards of morality were higher than those of surrounding peoples; Amnon's misconduct would leave a permanent social stigma upon her. This fact further explains her comment in v. 16. **18** *A long robe with sleeves* (AV 'a garment of divers colours'): see on Gn. 37:3. **19** Tamar's actions were those of a widow mourning for her husband. **21** David's anger led him to do nothing; some ancient versions append a statement that his inaction was due to his love for Amnon (*cf.* JB). **22** Absalom too did nothing, but with very different feelings and intentions.

13:23–39 Amnon's death and Absalom's flight. Absalom revealed himself no less skilful than his father had been in procuring a man's death (*cf.* ch. 11). At least it may be said for Absalom that his hatred of Amnon was not devoid of justification. **23** *Baal-hazor*. There are two possible sites, one 12 miles, the other only 4 miles, from Jerusalem. *Sheepshearers*: *cf.* 1 Sa. 25:4 (see commentary *in loc.*). **29–33** The uproar and confusion led to exaggerated rumours; *Jonadab* showed his 'craftiness' (v. 3) by divining the real situation

and advising David of it. **34** *But Absalom fled* This statement interrupts the narrative at this point, whereas it is appropriate in v. 37; however, almost certainly the clause should be read as the final statement of Jonadab's speech: 'Amnon alone is dead, and Absalom has fled.' *Cf.* JB. **37** *Absalom fled* to his mother's family (*cf.* 3:3) in *Geshur*, NE of David's realm. **39** is a difficult verse; the sense must be that David gradually became resigned to Amnon's death and anxious to see Absalom again.

14:1–20 The woman from Tekoa. Joab's intervention may well have been motivated by a desire to put both parties, David and Absalom, in his debt. The skilful plan he devised made play of the fact that David was the man to whom law-suits were brought (*cf.* 8:15); Nathan had also cleverly taken advantage of this fact (12:1–6). **2** *Tekoa* lay 6 miles S of Bethlehem. **5–7** The problem posed by the woman was a realistic one, which would still ring true among bedouin today. The point (both in the story and its application) is that there are those only too ready to take over the heritage. **8–11** The woman, about to be dismissed, pleads for an immediate decision, and gets one. **9** *The guilt*: since any decision is bound to conflict with a sacred family duty. **11** The *avenger of blood* was the nearest kinsman to the dead man; his duties are outlined in Nu. 35; Dt. 19. **13** David could not fail to recognize Absalom in this statement. **14** *We must all die . . . ; i.e.* life is all too short. Possibly the woman was also thinking of Amnon's death ('he had to die some time'). *But God will not take away . . .*: here RSV accepts a slight emendation dating back to Ewald, and the sense is that God, in all His great mercy, will not punish the merciful man. In the Hebrew text as it stands, it is God who *devises means* (*cf.* AV); this reading is perfectly intelligible, inviting David to act as God Himself does, in mercy. David himself knew what it was to be an outcast, and had lived to see his life spared and to enjoy a triumphant home-coming. The LXX is different again; *cf.* JB. **17** David's abilities as a judge were God-given and God-like; Absalom's later complaint (15:4) was not levelled at David's lack of ability but at his lack of time to attend to his forensic duties. **18–20** David immediately revealed his skill and discernment in recognizing Joab's hand.

14:21–33 Absalom's return. If it was Joab who engineered Absalom's return to Israelite soil, it was the latter himself who contrived his readmission to the royal court. This he did in a very arrogant fashion. It is apparent in this passage that neither father nor son was a man to forgive and forget.

26 sets the stage for the mode of Absalom's death (*cf.* 18:9, 14). The weight is computed as about 3½ or 4 lb. *By the king's weight*: the royal weight was a recognized standard (among others) in both Babylonia and Israel. **27** *Three sons*. 18:18 suggests that they must have predeceased their father. **33** The implication is that Absalom was now (but not hitherto) recognized by David as the crown prince. He was the eldest surviving son (if we may assume that Chileab, *cf.* 3:3, had died).

15:1–12 Absalom's conspiracy. Absalom could be patient and methodical. As he had waited two years before assassinating Amnon (13:23), so now he spent four years (v. 6) quietly laying plans for revolt. He used his personal charm to good effect, and he played upon the injustices which clearly were felt in the kingdom. He also displayed a clever technique of combining pomp and ceremony (v. 1) with the common touch (v. 5).

2, 6 *Israel* may refer to the northern tribes as opposed to Judah, as Hertzberg maintains. But if Absalom tried to play upon regional jealousies, it is remarkable that he raised the standard of revolt at Hebron, ex-capital of Judah (v. 10). On the whole, it seems preferable to take *Israel* in its wider sense. **8** One imagines David must have wondered why Absalom had been so slow to fulfil his *vow*. **11** implies that Absalom had scarcely any following in the capital itself. **12** We are not told why *Ahithophel* was prepared to join the conspiracy. Since he was Bathsheba's grandfather (*cf.* 11:3; 23:34), one would not have expected this of him, unless it was because he felt that David had tarnished his grand-daughter's reputation.

15:13–37 David's flight. David was taken unawares, but even so he was quick to assess the strategic situation; his years as a fugitive from Saul had given him valuable experience. He knew the best escape-route, and took it: he needed time, more than anything else. He spared his capital from attack (just as the Turkish and German forces did for Jerusalem in 1917, Hertzberg has observed). With him went his bodyguard, but not the ark. The ark had often accompanied Israelite troops into battle, and to many of David's men it could have seemed ill-omened to abandon it now. But David saw the matter differently, and had both a theological and a practical reason (vv. 25–28) for returning the ark to its shrine. **16** *The king left ten concubines*: they were taken over by Absalom (16:21, 22). **17, 18** *The last house*; *i.e.* on the road E out of Jerusalem, near the Kidron valley (*cf.* v. 23). Here David reviewed his forces. For the *Cherethites* and *Pelethites*, see on 8:18. **19–22** *Ittai* reacted much as Ruth did to Naomi (*cf.* Ru. 1:15ff.). David's calm acceptance of the situation, to the extent of calling Absalom 'king', is remarkable. **20** *Stead-fast love* (Heb. *ḥeseḏ*) is a covenantal term, and its use to a non-Israelite here is noteworthy. **24** RSV has rearranged the verse (contrast AV), to bring the name of *Abiathar* to the fore. The phrase *and Abiathar came up* in the Hebrew text stands near the end of the verse, and could be translated 'and Abiathar offered up' (viz. 'sacrifices'). It seems best to follow the Hebrew in this way; Abiathar was the senior man of the two, but fell into disgrace at Solomon's

accession (see especially 1 Ki. 2:35). If Abiathar was offering sacrifices at the shrine, inside the city, it would explain why Zadok is mentioned first and separately here, and why Abiathar's name is missing in v. 27 (*cf.* RSV mg.). (But if so, the phrase 'and Abiathar' in v. 29 would have to be viewed as a scribal addition, and deleted.) **30–37** The defection of *Ahithophel* was a bitter blow, but immediately God provided a counter-balance in the person of *Hushai* and David was able to form a sort of spy-ring to counteract the sagacity of Ahithophel. **37** reveals that David got away, and *Hushai* returned to *the city*, just in the nick of time.

16:1–14 Ziba and Shimei. This chapter cleverly presents two pairs of contrasts, as the king and the usurper encounter differing reactions to the new situation. As for Ziba, there can be no doubt that in bringing David provisions he had his eye on his own advantage, though it is of interest that he must have anticipated David's ultimate victory over Absalom. Shimei's violent hostility was due to his kinship with Saul; in view of his actions, David will have been the more ready to believe ill of Mephibosheth, who was even more closely related to Saul.

1 *Ziba*: *cf.* ch. 9. **3** Mephibosheth later denied Ziba's story (19:27). It is indeed difficult to suppose that Mephibosheth could have seen any advantage for himself in the situation, though he might well have decided to wait and see. **8** *A man of blood*. Shimei was no doubt thinking of Abner and Ish-bosheth, and probably too the progeny of Saul whose deaths are recounted in 21:7ff. **9** *Abishai*: Joab's brother (*cf.* 2:18; 18:2). **10** *What have I to do with you?* *i.e.* 'our attitudes are totally different'. **12** David felt that his present disasters were more than he deserved. The Hebrew text's 'iniquity' (RSV mg.) makes this even more explicit ('my iniquity' would mean 'the iniquity done to me'). **14** *The Jordan* (read by Lucian) has probably dropped out of the Hebrew text by accident. After a barren route, on which they were constantly harassed by Shimei, the waters of the river will have been more than acceptable.

16:15–23 Hushai and Ahithophel. Absalom similarly meets a contrast, in a false friend and a true; but in this case the difference is not self-evident, and Absalom is deceived. Hushai, naturally suspect, cleverly ingratiated himself; the (deliberate) flaw in his logic was to suggest that Absalom had been in any sense 'chosen' (v. 18).

19 *So I will serve you*; *i.e.* Absalom was crown prince, so would be king one day in any event; his claim to the throne was therefore legitimate, if premature. **21** *Ahithophel* advised a course of action, in an act of kingly prerogative (*cf.* 3:6), which would remove all possibility of a late reconciliation between David and his son. **22** The public deed was the greatest possible insult to David.

17:1–14 Ahithophel's plans thwarted. Ahithophel's sagacity was highly prized by both

David and Absalom (16:23), and his reputation was well deserved. He now proffered a second piece of brilliant advice to Absalom; speed of action was extremely important, and it was quite true that David's death was the only thing Absalom needed to achieve, for then his claim to the throne would be beyond dispute and David's supporters would flock to his standard, like a bride returning home after a casual tiff. Hushai's advice sounded equally plausible, designed though it was to buy time for David. It is interesting to observe the mechanics of his success in persuading Absalom: they were *a.* eloquence, *b.* the appeal to do things on a grandiose scale, *c.* flattery. The flattery consisted in the suggestion that Absalom should lead in person, whereas Ahithophel had planned to take command himself; thus Hushai's counsel contained a veiled disparagement of Ahithophel. **14** Hushai's success was above all due to God's overruling, for Absalom was not God's choice for king. Absalom was free to choose which plan he wished; but God can act within 'acts of personal freedom' (Eichrodt).

17:15–29 Events preceding the battle. While this passage is concerned with a variety of events which led up to the battle, it also reveals how things went David's way; he received intelligence of Absalom's movements, and adequate provisioning, while Absalom lost his best adviser and the most skilled general in Israel (v. 25). **16** Hushai was apparently not completely sure that Absalom would after all follow his advice rather than Ahithophel's. **17** *En-rogel* (later called 'Job's Well') lay in the valley SE of Jerusalem. **18** *A well*: perhaps a dry cistern in which two lads could easily hide, and the existence of which could readily be concealed. **23** *Ahithophel* already knew the outcome, if Absalom did not; his perception never deserted him. **24** Some time must have elapsed, for David has by now organized his forces, and moved well N to Ish-bosheth's former capital (*cf.* 2:8). *Absalom* too had had time to muster a large army, with which he now marched into Transjordan (keeping S of David's forces). **25** *Nahash* must be a scribal error for 'Jesse', David's father, which is read by Lucian (and *cf.* 1 Ch. 2:16, 17); the erroneous name derives from v. 27. *Amasa* was cousin both of Joab and Absalom. **27** *Shobi* was doubtless David's deputy in Ammon; his father *Nahash* had been its king (*cf.* 10:1). It is clear that Absalom had few supporters E of the Jordan, since both Shobi and *Machir* (formerly a friend of Saul's family, *cf.* 9:4) might well have been hostile to David. **28, 29** The provisions include neither perishables nor luxuries.

18:1–18 Absalom's defeat and death. When battle was finally joined, David's seasoned troops made good use of difficult, rocky and wooded terrain. The statement that 'the forest devoured more people that day than the sword' (v. 8) is well illustrated by the fate of Absalom himself. David appears in this story to have lost some of

his native shrewdness, for he failed to appreciate fully that the death of either Absalom or himself would settle the issue, and render further strife pointless.

5 *Deal gently . . .* : a statement which combines both confidence and weakness. **13** The soldier knew well Joab's ruthlessness; and he probably remembered the fate of the assassins of Ish-bosheth (4:12). The reading 'at the risk of my life' (RSV mg.) would make his point more explicit. **14, 15** *Heart* may not be literal, in view of the statement that *ten young men* actually despatched Absalom; Joab's act may have been symbolical rather than deadly. The same Hebrew word is used a second time in v. 14 to signify the 'midst' (AV) of *the oak*. **16** Absalom's death means the end of the revolt, so Joab wisely brings the pursuit to a close. **18** It may be conjectured that Absalom had erected this monument upon the death of his three sons (*cf.* 14:27). The pillar will have been near Jerusalem, though it is certainly not the present-day structure named after him, in the Kidron valley.

18:19–33 David hears the news. Joab preferred to send a slave as a messenger, rather than Ahima-az, in case David reacted violently to the news of Absalom's death. Moreover, a dark-skinned Cushite (= Ethiopian) will have been a messenger of ill omen. This passage is superb literature, intensely dramatic, and so patently derives from an eyewitness that some have deduced that Ahima-az was the author (and thus probably the author of chs. 9–20 as a whole). **19** *Tidings*: the Hebrew word carries the implication of good news; *Ahima-az* was full of the victory, and unaware of the possibility that David might consider his news as tragic. **25** '*If he is alone . . .*'; *i.e.* a group of men running would indicate a rout. **27** It is not altogether clear why David should be so sure that Ahima-az must have *good tidings*. Hertzberg suggests that David would interpret a band of people as a rout, one man as the messenger of victory; McKane retorts that one man might as easily be a messenger requesting urgent reinforcements; this may be true enough, but we cannot expect David to have been too coldly analytical at such a critical moment. It seems simpler, nevertheless, to suppose that David knew Joab would send a messenger of ill omen, such as the Cushite, if the news were bad. **29** *Ahima-az* was prevaricating; Joab had told him explicitly that Absalom was dead (v. 20). **33** David's lamentation is deeply pathetic, the sincerity of it beyond any doubt. To such a pass had his own sins brought him (*cf.* 12:10).

19:1 – 20:26 David's return and Sheba's revolt

With the death of Absalom, further intrigues for the succession to David's throne seem to have ceased until the very end of his reign, when the struggle between Adonijah and Solomon took place (*cf.* 1 Ki. 1; 2). But Absalom's revolt produced its aftermath of disunity among the tribes of Israel, from which yet another revolt broke out. Ever since David's adultery with Bathsheba, trouble and unhappiness marked his reign.

19:1–15 Preparations for David's return. David's unrestrained grief could have led to political disaster, and Joab's brutal plain speaking was justified—and successful. Vv. 9–15 reveal not only the basic distrust between Judah and the northern tribes, but also the fact that David had lost much of the support of his own tribe. It may be that in trying to keep on good terms with the northern tribes, David had put himself at a distance from Judah.

9, 10 *At strife* (JB 'quarrelling'): this phrase makes it clear that the argument that follows was not everybody's opinion: *cf.* v. 40. *The Philistines* had been thrust back, and no doubt some Israelites would willingly have returned to the pre-monarchic constitution, or else perhaps sought a new king. **11** *Zadok and Abiathar* were the king's intimates, and he could trust them implicitly (*cf.* 15:35f.). **13** *Amasa* had been Absalom's military commander (17:25). In making him his own commander, David no doubt hoped to win over those adherents of Absalom who feared reprisals. At the same time, there can be no doubt that David took pleasure in dismissing *Joab* from his post; he never forgave Joab (*cf.* 1 Ki. 2:5f.). McKane maintains that the move was very foolish, since it punished loyalty and rewarded sedition, and will have given nobody any faith in David's powers of judgment. This seems true enough; events soon reversed David's decision, and the narrator may be hinting that David's old shrewdness was deserting him, in his bitter distress at his son's death. **15** David returns in state; no slinking home for him (contrast v. 3).

19:16–39 David is welcomed back. This passage is the dramatic reversal of 16:1–14. There we read how David encountered reviling and apparent disloyalty on his road E from Jerusalem; now as he returns triumphantly to the capital he is greeted very differently.

16 *Shimei*: *cf.* 16:5–8, 13. As a *Benjaminite*, he was well placed to make contact with David at the earliest possible moment, since Gilgal and the ford (v. 15) were in Benjaminite territory. **17** The same holds true for *Ziba*; *cf.* 16:1–4. **18** *They crossed the ford*: note the RSV mg., meaningless as it stands, but very probably the Hebrew word for 'ford' could also mean 'ferry' (as S. R. Driver first suggested). JB says that Ziba and his men 'worked manfully ferrying the king's family across'. **21, 22** *Abishai* still felt murderous towards *Shimei*, but David's peaceable attitude was unchanged (*cf.* 16:9–12). **23** The *oath* protected him only so long as David lived; *cf.* 1 Ki. 2:8f., 36–46. **24** *Mephibosheth* this time put in an appearance (contrast 16:1ff.); he had exhibited the conventional signs of mourning ever since David's departure from the court. (Note that *son* in Hebrew can also do duty for 'grandson'.) **26** It is clear from v. 24 that Mephibosheth

was not completely immobilized by his lameness, but presumably he had been too late to get away from Jerusalem before Absalom's arrival there, in consequence of Ziba's deceit. Speed had been essential (see on 15:37). **27** *Like the angel of God*: so too had the woman of Tekoa described David's powers of judgment (14:17). If Mephibosheth was totally innocent (as he probably was, though the narrator never makes a judgment), we may feel that David's verdict (v. 29) was scarcely fair to him. However, Ziba had given David unambiguous and practical support at a critical juncture. **28** *You set your servant . . .*; *i.e.* David had already shown him unwarranted mercy and generosity. **29, 30** David's verdict is reminiscent of the proverbial judgment of Solomon, and Mephibosheth's response is not unlike the harlot's reply to Solomon (*cf.* 1 Ki. 3:25f.); but apparently David did not thereupon change his decision, as Solomon did. **31** *Barzillai*: *cf.* 17:27ff. **37** Presumably *Chimham* was his son.

19:40 – 20:3 Faction and revolt. The whole chapter so far has mentioned virtually nothing that would have marred the joy and triumph of David's return to power. But v. 40 immediately brings home to us the truth of the situation: only half of the northern Israelites had as yet decided to renew their support of David. It now appears that David's appeal to the men of his own tribe (vv. 11–14), and their response (v. 15), had caused no little offence to the rest of the nation, and bitter quarrelling broke out. Sheba was not slow to take advantage of this unhappy situation.

41 *David's men*: his personal troops. **42** *The king is near of kin to us*: this fact was indeed the whole source of the trouble, and such a reply was calculated only to increase jealousy and resentment. **43** *Ten shares*. Obviously Judah is the eleventh tribe, but who is the twelfth? After the disruption of the monarchy following Solomon's death, it was of course Benjamin; but McKane holds that it was probably Simeon in this context; its territory lay due S of Judah. The difficulty about taking Benjamin as the tribe here coupled with Judah is that the rebel, Sheba, was a Benjaminite. However, Ziba and Shimei and their Benjaminite followers (*cf.* vv. 16f.) were probably very prominent in the procession, and the other tribal representatives might readily have bracketed Benjamin with Judah. Undoubtedly the first readers of 2 Samuel would automatically have assumed that Benjamin was meant. The final sentence of the chapter suggests that *the men of Judah* got the better of the argument, but only annoyed the northerners the more thereby. At any rate, it was in this situation that Sheba saw his opportunity.

20:1 *Sheba*, as *a Benjaminite*, may have tried to pose as the true successor to Saul. **2** *All the men of Israel*: the very ease with which Sheba's revolt was quelled makes it clear that this rebellion was anything but unanimous. This phrase must therefore mean merely the dissident elements of all the tribes. **3** is a footnote to the

Absalom episode (*cf.* 15:16; 16:22). Nobody in future must have sexual relations with *the ten concubines*. In a sense they were indeed *in widowhood*.

20:4–13 Joab and Amasa. Amasa's military record is not one to inspire confidence; as Absalom's commander, he had suffered a very heavy defeat, and now his slowness to carry out David's orders could have resulted in fresh disaster. Again it was the highly-trained royal bodyguard ('your lord's servants', v. 6) on whom David had to rely. David's continuing grudge against Joab is evident from the fact that Joab's brother Abishai was appointed to command the king's troops. But Joab nevertheless seized the opportunity to retrieve his lost position—even if it meant assassinating his own cousin.

6 *Cause us trouble*: the Targum (followed by RSV) has probably correctly interpreted a Hebrew idiom (*cf.* RSV mg.). **8** *Amasa came to meet them* must suggest that he was hurrying to catch them up, since he had been S, to Judah (v. 5), whereas Gibeon lay N of Jerusalem. *It fell out*; *i.e.* into Joab's hand, not on to the ground, **10** since Amasa failed to see it. *Joab and Abishai*: apparently Abishai had by now relinquished command to his brother. **11, 12** Joab posted a man to prevent Amasa's troops from dispersing (*cf.* v. 22).

20:14–22 The end of the revolt. It is soon evident what small support Sheba could command: Joab's speedy pursuit probably discouraged many who might otherwise have joined the rebel army. As it was, Sheba was finally pinned down in a city at the extreme north of Israel (very near Dan), with only his own clan, the Bichrites, fighting for him. In the event, the death of Sheba himself terminated the revolt.

18 *Let them but ask counsel at Abel*: the proverb is textually uncertain and somewhat obscure; it looks as if Abel of Beth-maacah had a long-standing reputation for sagacity and peaceful settlement of disputes. The LXX reading is to different effect, and is utilized by JB: 'Let them ask in Abel and in Dan if all is over with what Israel's faithful ones have laid down.' Equally obscure, this statement would make the two neighbouring cities true guardians of Israel's traditions. **21** *The hill country of Ephraim*: the N section of the mountainous range lying between the coastal plain and the Jordan valley; Sheba's tribe was Benjamin (*cf.* v. 1), which lay in this hilly area. **22** *Joab returned to Jerusalem to the king*, unconcerned by his earlier deposition and by the new murder he had committed. David could do no other than restore him to his earlier command (v. 23), but he did not forget or forgive. Possibly Joab extracted an oath from David as Shimei had done (19:23); only in his will did David attack either man (*cf.* 1 Ki. 2:5f., 8f.).

20:23–26 David's officers. The return of Joab to the capital, knowing that he was again commander-in-chief, leads on naturally to a list of David's officials in the later part of his reign. An earlier list appears in 8:15–18; naturally some names have changed over the years. See comment on the earlier passage.

24 *Adoram* (= Adoniram) continued in his unpopular office right through Solomon's reign, and was stoned to death at the beginning of Rehoboam's (1 Ki. 12:18). **25** *Sheva*: the name, possibly of Egyptian origin (see McKane, *in loc.*), appears in a variety of forms (in the versions, and at other points in the Hebrew text), and may just refer to the 'Seraiah' of 8:17. **26** *Ira the Jairite* is possibly the same man who appears in 23:38; if so, 'Ithrite' may be the preferable description of him, and this could make him a Levite, if 'Ithrite' means 'man of Jattir' (as the Syriac Peshitta suggests): *cf.* Jos. 21:14. If correct, *Jairite* links *Ira* with Gilead (*cf.* Nu. 32:40f.). In any case, the mention of Ira as *David's priest* is poignant, silently underlining the fact that no longer were 'David's sons' (8:18) in this favoured position. So this long section of 2 Samuel ends with the unspoken recognition that David had lost much that was near and dear to him, in consequence of his sins of adultery and murder.

21:1 – 24:25 DAVID'S REIGN: PROBLEMS AND PROSPECTS

These final four chapters are often referred to as an appendix to 2 Samuel; they offer a variety of material, drawn from widely different periods of David's life, and they interrupt the story of the succession struggles (resumed in 1 Ki. 1). There is nevertheless more unity of theme, and deliberate purpose on the part of writer, than is at first apparent. *a.* These chapters widen the scope of the problems David had to face, and describe famine, warfare and plague. *b.* They show how God provided guidance and loyal supporters for David in all these difficulties. *c.* They show how it was his very experience of the vicissitudes of life, and of the goodness of God, that made him 'the sweet psalmist of Israel'. *d.* Both in the psalms and the closing narrative, future perspectives are opened; the focus of the Bible historians is always the present and the future.

The six sections contained in these four chapters are arranged chiastically: natural disaster, military exploits, poem, poem, military exploits, natural disaster.

21:1–22 Famine and warfare

Hitherto David's troubles, as recorded in 2 Samuel, were largely those caused by intrigues in his own family, and revolts stemming from them. Other problems are now highlighted; the story of the famine also illustrates the legacy of ill-will from Saul's reign which David had to tackle.

21:1–14 The execution of Saul's family. Most commentators place this episode early in David's reign, and prior to his honouring Mephibosheth at court (see comment on ch. 9); possibly, however, v. 7 would suggest otherwise. Saul's attack on the Gibeonites had been in defiance of Joshua's covenant with them (Jos. 9:15), obtained by trickery though it was. National bloodguilt interfered with the course of nature, and famine ensued. The view of H. Cazelles (*PEQ*, 87, 1955, pp. 165–175) that this passage describes a fertility rite after the Canaanite manner is well answered by McKane, *ad loc.*

1 It is possible that David consulted the oracle at Gibeon (*cf.* 1 Ki. 3:4; 2 Ch. 1:3). **2** *Saul had sought to slay them* . . . : in trying to consolidate his kingdom, Saul's desire to outroot Canaanite enclaves was perfectly intelligible. We do not know, however, precisely how and when this episode occurred. **3** Only if the Gibeonites would pronounce a blessing would the curse they had previously uttered be rendered void; *cf.* Jdg. 17:2. **6** Some ritual form of execution is intended; the exact manner of it is not clear in the Hebrew (*hang* is therefore too specific). **8** *Merab*: *cf.* 1 Sa. 18:19. The name 'Michal', read by most of the Hebrew mss, is clearly wrong (*cf.* 6:23); probably an early scribe inserted the better-known name by error. **10** A period of up to six months, for summer rain is rare after the barley harvest (April or early May). However, the rain itself signalled the end of the drought which had occasioned the famine (v. 1), and was a sign of divine favour. **12–14** *Cf.* 1 Sa. 31:10–13. The sign of the rain, heralding the end of the famine, gave David freedom to honour the memory of Saul and Jonathan (and of the seven men recently executed too, if the LXX of v. 14 may be followed). By this deed David no doubt had a further motive, namely to avoid giving the impression that he had had these men executed out of a desire for revenge on Saul. **14** *Zela* is unknown as a proper name, and it could perhaps be a noun denoting a tomb-chamber; if so, the tomb was presumably at Gibeah, Saul's family home. *God heeded supplications for the land*; *i.e.* the rain in due course produced renewed fertility and food.

21:15–22 Incidents from the Philistine wars. The first episode here recounted marked the close of David's active military career, which thus ended as it had begun, in battle with a giant Philistine warrior. All four of the Philistines listed here were huge men, and we may see God's hand in the skill and courage given to the Israelites who overcame them. David was dependent on divine protection and on loyal human support.

15, 16 *And David grew weary*: this is the reading of the Hebrew, and it makes good sense; but the text of both verses is suspect. **17** *Abishai*: David's nephew, Joab's brother (*cf.* 2:18). The final sentence lays emphasis on 'the key position of the king in the community' (McKane); McKane considers the metaphor to be drawn from the Tabernacle ritual (*cf.* Ex. 27:20); *cf.* 1 Ki. 11:36. **19** *Elhanan . . . slew Goliath*: this statement appears plainly at variance with 1 Sa. 17. Various explanations and emendations are

possible, such as that adopted by the AV. The problem is discussed fully in Appendix 5.

22:1 – 23:7 Two psalms of David

It is impossible to prove (or disprove) the Davidic authorship of these two sacred poems, but it is noteworthy that Hertzberg allows the traditional authorship of both. The first of them is identical (but for minor variations) with Ps. 18, and A. Weiser too, in his commentary on Psalms (*in loc.*), agrees that at least it was composed in the period of David. The two psalms together are reminiscent of the Song and the Blessing of Moses (Dt. 32; 33).

22:1–15 A song of David. For detailed notes on this psalm, see the commentary on Ps. 18. Its relevance at this point is clear; *cf.* especially vv. 1 and 51. 'A fitting epilogue to David's story' (L. H. Brockington), the poem looks both back and forward, reflecting on the victories God had already made possible and the promises He had offered for the future. The emphasis on moral behaviour in vv. 21–25 will have constituted a sermon worth heeding to David's descendants on the throne of Judah.

23:1–7 David's last words. It has been suggested that these were David's last words as an inspired author; and this may be so. There is, however, something of the nature of a last will and testament about these verses, comparable with Dt. 33. (More prosaic testamentary dispositions of David are given in 1 Ki. 2.) There are a number of difficulties of text and translation in the psalm.

1 *The sweet psalmist f Israel*: the reading of RSV mg. is possible (one could recall 1 Sa. 18:7), but the traditional rendering is to be preferred. Some scholars deny this psalm to David on the uncertain grounds that he would scarcely have described himself so. In any case, it is possible that the psalm proper begins at v. 3. **4** The comparison of justice in a king with the fruitfulness of *rain* and *sun* is skilful and effective; ch. 21 has shown the sad effects of lack of rainfall. *Sprout*: 'sparkle' (JB) is better, and gives more vivid imagery. **6, 7** *Godless men* . . . ; *i.e.* dangerous men require very careful handling, but there are nevertheless ways of dealing with them and destroying them.

23:8–39 David's mighty men

The remainder of the chapter consists of a catalogue of David's warriors (who enabled him to become king, according to 1 Ch. 11:10), with a brief account of a few of their valorous exploits. It is explicitly stated more than once that God Himself was responsible for their achievements.

23:8–23 Exploits of David's outstanding warriors. Evidently there were two 'orders of chivalry' among David's soldiers, the Three and the Thirty, the former group being the more notable. The similarity of the numbers 'three' and 'thirty' in Hebrew has given rise to textual errors and confusion here and there (as RSV mg. reveals); and some of the names appear in variant form in 1 Ch. 11. The historical context of vv. 8–17 is that of the Philistine wars.

13 *Three of the thirty*: to be distinguished from 'the Three'. Their names are not given; Hertzberg's suggestion that they were the three sons of Zeruiah—Joab, Abishai and Asahel—is improbable, largely because Joab's name does not stand in the list of the Thirty (vv. 24–39); presumably, as commander-in-chief, he stood outside and above the two groups. *Adullam . . . the valley of Rephaim*: these names indicate that this episode took place during the fighting described in 5:17–25. **16** *He poured it out to the Lord*; *i.e.* as a drink-offering. **18** *Beside the three*: since the Hebrew would more naturally mean 'among the three', it seems likely that the numeral should be altered, giving 'among the thirty' (so JB); *cf.* v. 23. **20** *Ariels of Moab*: the word 'ariel' should mean 'lion of God'; if so, then either Moabite lions of exceptional size or else Moabite warriors (*cf.* AV, JB), referred to metaphorically as lions, must be intended. Other possibilities exist. **23** *Cf.* 8:18.

23:24–39 'The Thirty'. There are two numerical problems here, arising from the fact that the chapter appears to list more than 30 warriors, but less than 37 (*cf.* v. 39). The first problem is the more easily explained: it would seem that 'the Thirty' was replenished from time to time, as one man was killed (*e.g.* Asahel) and another was employed elsewhere (like Benaiah). A group of constant size like this may have been formed on an Egyptian pattern (*cf.* J. Bright, *History of Israel*, p. 186). Additional names therefore appear; several more again are listed in 1 Ch. 11:41–47. As for the 'thirty-seven in all', the question is complicated by textual problems in the passage. As the list stands (in RSV), there are 31 individuals listed in vv. 24–39, to whom Abishai (v. 19) and Benaiah (v. 23) should be added; if the 'sons of Jashen' (v. 32) numbered 4, then we have a final count of 37. But probably Jashen himself, not his sons, stood in the original text, *cf.* JB; and 'Jonathan, Shammah' (vv. 32f.) should probably read 'Jonathan the son of Shammah'. Accepting these two alterations to the RSV list, we now have precisely 31 names in vv. 24–39; to reach 37, we may add the names of 'the Three' (vv. 8–12), Abishai and Benaiah, and then assume that the commander, Joab, completes the list (he is in fact named incidentally in v. 37).

24 *Asahel* died very early in David's reign (*cf.* 2:23), which suggests that 'the Thirty' were first organized while David was in Ziklag. **25** *Elika*: the omission of his name in the LXX and in 1 Ch. 11 must be accidental. **39** Hertzberg considers it intentional and significant that the last name is that of *Uriah*, who was to be betrayed by the very man he supported so nobly.

24:1–25 Census and plague

Despite its problems for the modern reader, this chapter neatly rounds off the books of Samuel and the story of David's reign. David had pre-

viously encountered warfare, revolt and famine; now pestilence brings fresh distress to Israel and the king. But God overruled in the whole matter, from beginning to end; the result was the acquisition of the very site on which was to stand Solomon's Temple, the majestic symbol of God's presence in the midst of His people. Thus the book ends on a note of deliverance and blessing, pointing forward into the indefinite future. Hertzberg, comparing the chapter with the Flood story of Genesis, comments: 'new blessing comes as a consequence of punishment and destruction.'

24:1–14 The census and its consequences. To the modern reader it is far from clear why it was sinful to hold a census; and if it was, it disturbs him afresh that God Himself should have prompted the sinful act. It must be allowed, first of all, that God's anger against Israel (v. 1) will not have been due to some arbitrary whim. God's reasons for action are not always revealed, but conceivably (as C. F. Keil suggested) the sin of rebellion (against David) was being punished. The sin in holding a census, it is generally held, was one of arrogance; it was God's prerogative to multiply the nation and to number it. Even Joab knew it to be a false move.

1 *Again*: the allusion is to the famine of ch. 21. *The Lord . . . incited David*. This writer recognizes the overruling hand of God, whereas the later historian was more interested in the mode of the incitement, namely Satanic tempting (*cf.* 1 Ch. 21:1). **2** *From Dan to Beer-sheba*; *i.e.* the census is to be a complete one. Indeed, it went beyond the traditional confines of Israel (*cf.* vv. 5–7). The purpose of the census will have been the reorganization of the tax, military service, and forced labour systems. **5** The areas named here lay in Transjordan. **6** *Kadesh* is more likely to be Kadesh-naphtali, in N Israel, than the old Hittite capital, Kadesh on the Orontes, far beyond the boundaries of Israel. In any case, the mention of *Kadesh in the land of the Hittites* is derived from Lucian, and we cannot be sure that it was the original reading. (See 'Kadesh (on the Orontes)' in C. F. Pfeiffer (ed.), *The Biblical World*, 1967.) The Hebrew has 'Tahtim-hodshi' (*cf.* AV), a name otherwise unknown. **7** *All the cities of the Hivites and Canaanites* lay on the coastal plain, between *Tyre* and Philistia. **9** The numbers seem astonishingly large, though the number credited to Israel is even greater in 1 Ch. 21:5. There is probably some basis for the figures, but early textual corruption cannot be ruled out. **10** It is not stated what led David to feel remorse; 1 Ch. 21:7, however, tells us that Israel began to suffer before David's change of heart. **11** *David's seer*: see Appendix 3. **13** The first two choices had already afflicted David and his kingdom (precisely three years of famine, *cf.* 21:1). The choices grow in severity, but by way of compensation diminish in duration.

24:15–25 The pestilence and its consequences. Even in punishment, the mercy of God was to be seen, and an altar was built at the place where the angel was observed to stay his hand. This site, hitherto a threshing-floor just N of David's capital, was the scene where God's presence was remembered, in all its terror and mercy, and here, very appropriately, Solomon's Temple was presently erected (cf. 1 Ch. 22:1; 2 Ch. 3:1). It may seem strange that no mention of the Temple is made in this passage, but it must be remembered that the earliest readers of 2 Samuel will have known perfectly well that Araunah's threshing-floor was the site of the Temple.

15 *The appointed time* refers to the time of the evening sacrifice on the same day. *From Dan to Beer-sheba*; *i.e.* throughout the whole territory where the census had been conducted (cf. v. 2). **16** *The angel*: the agent of God in both punishment and deliverance. *Araunah* appears to have been a Hittite name (*a-raw-wan-ni*, 'aristocrat'),

unfamiliar in form to the Israelites, and so gradually pronounced in a more Hebraic fashion; hence the 'Ornan' of Chronicles. He may have been the previous ruler of Jerusalem (cf. C. H. Gordon, *Ugaritic Manual*, p. 234). **17** David's prayer, though it does him credit, was in fact too late; divine mercy was already at work. The fact that David was unaware of God's decision is insufficient to warrant finding a divergent account in vv. 17, 21, and 25; the narrator is clear that both the early cessation of the plague and the purchase of the threshing-floor were intended by God. **22–24** Araunah's offer and David's refusal of the gift are both reminiscent of Gn. 23:11ff. **25** The deliverance of Jerusalem is the note on which 2 Samuel ends; the kingdom and the Temple site remain intact and in God's hands, ready to be handed on to David's descendants.

Appendix 1
THE SOURCES OF THE BOOKS OF SAMUEL

There can be no doubt at all that the writer of the books of Samuel made use of some earlier documents, though it is impossible to know how many. No single individual lived right through the eras of Samuel, Saul and David; and statements incorporating the phrase 'to this day' (*e.g.* 1 Sa. 27:6) suggest a further lapse of time before the author's own date. Attempts have therefore been made to isolate the sources from which the author took his material; and a number of quite different schemes have resulted.

The simplest scheme is probably that associated with the name of K. Budde, and which is conveniently outlined, as adapted by Pfeiffer, in R. H. Pfeiffer, *Introduction to the Old Testament*. This is a two-document hypothesis; one source is labelled 'early', the other 'late', and Budde himself maintained that these sources were identical with those which had been found in the Pentateuch and known respectively as J and E. This precise link with the Pentateuch is denied by many scholars, however, and so this hypothesis about 1 and 2 Samuel does not necessarily stand or fall with the Wellhausenian documentary analysis of the Pentateuch.

While some attention is paid by scholars holding the two-document hypothesis to questions of language and style, the general approach is rather one of subjective historical criticism: the material in Samuel is first sorted into pairs of 'duplicate' or 'divergent' accounts, historical judgment is then passed on each incident, and finally the more 'reliable' material is credited to the 'early' source, the less reliable to the later conjectural document. Even where material is not duplicated, it can be assigned to one source or the other on the basis of its credibility. To quote Pfeiffer, 'In contrast with the lucid and objective presentation of historical events and

personalities which characterizes the early source, the late source . . . is clouded with legends and distorted by theories' (p. 362). On such a basis, then, David's arrival at Saul's court as a harpist is early, whereas his victory over Goliath and arrival at court as a warrior is late (and unhistorical); David's sparing Saul's life in the Ziph wilderness is early, the similar incident at En-gedi is late; and so forth.

A number of modifications of the two-document view have been propounded: notably O. Eissfeldt's argument that in the books of Samuel, as in the Pentateuch, a 'Lay' source (L) must be found, in addition to J and E. It should be added that most scholars, including Budde, attribute a certain amount of material to a much later hand, often presumed to be that of the final redactor or the 'Deuteronomist' himself.

Various objections might be raised to the two-document hypothesis. It seems incredible, for one thing, that two documents should have existed of remarkably similar content, the one almost wholly reliable, the other almost totally worthless historically: and why, if they did exist, any writer should have thought it worth while to conflate them is past comprehension. It is clear, moreover, that if it can be shown that many of the 'duplicate' accounts are in fact of equal credibility, and are not mutually exclusive, the two-source hypothesis loses its whole basis. The so-called duplicates are of several quite different types, and to assess their historical value as Budde and his predecessors did is a drastic oversimplification.

A more complex documentary hypothesis was put forward over 60 years ago by A. R. S. Kennedy in his *Century Bible* commentary. His approach was much more reasonable, and continues to find favour, especially with British scholars (*e.g.* G. W. Anderson, in *A Critical Introduction to the Old Testament*; H. H. Rowley, in *The Growth of the Old Testament*). Kennedy found five distinct source documents: a history of Samuel's early years, a history of the ark of the covenant, a history of the monarchy favourable to it, a history of the monarchy hostile to it, and a court history of David. There is much to be said for the accuracy of this analysis; the most doubtful point is whether there really were two documents treating the institution of the monarchy in such different ways. If there were (and most scholars are convinced on the point), it may at least be averred that it is unnecessary to view the hostile account as late and unreliable (see Appendix 2). Kennedy also found material not deriving from any of these sources, such as that drawn from unwritten traditions.

Modifications of this hypothesis too are to be found, notably that of A. Weiser, who posits only four 'original independent fundamental literary units' (*Introduction to the Old Testament*, p. 162). But he lays much greater stress on traditions, and the gradual gathering of them, than Kennedy did.

One source used by the writer of the books of Samuel is named in 2 Sa. 1:18, 'the Book of Jashar'. Its contents (perhaps consisting entirely of poetry) can only be guessed at, however, so this reference will not help us greatly in the attempt to find sources. Otherwise, it is certain that biographical material must have been available to the author: the court history of David, perhaps composed by Ahima-az (see on 2 Sa. 18:19–33), certainly figured among such documents. 1 Ch. 29:29 makes reference to records written by (or associated with?) Samuel, Nathan and Gad, and these three documents alone could well have covered the whole period under discussion in the books of Samuel. The story of David's years as a fugitive might have been written by Abiathar. In addition to documents, no doubt some unwritten traditions were available to the final author, but what use he made of them is impossible to tell.

The author was not a mere compiler, and at times he must have paraphrased or expanded what he found in his sources; references to his own day, and an explanatory verse like 1 Sa. 9:9, render this fact beyond dispute. Most commentators believe that 2 Sa. 7, in particular, was considerably expanded by the author; we might make a comparison with Jn. 3, where it is very difficult to distinguish our Lord's words from those of the Evangelist. High literary skill is evident many times over in the books of Samuel. These various facts explain a certain literary heterogeneity within 1 and 2 Samuel, and also make it impossible to arrive at a completely satisfactory source analysis of these books.

Appendix 2
THE INSTITUTION OF THE MONARCHY

It is generally held among scholars that the section of 1 Samuel recounting the institution of the monarchy derives from two, if not three, different documentary sources. The one account (appearing in 1 Sa. 8; 10:17–27; 12) is bitterly hostile to the monarchy, whereas the other (in 1 Sa. 9; 10:1–16; and continuing in ch. 13) recounts the story objectively, even favourably, with no hint of disapproval. Ch. 11 is often held to come from a third source, but to have been interwoven with the second strand; and for practical purposes it needs no separate treatment.

It appears to be the difference in tone from one passage to another which proves to be the most cogent argument for this division. But other conflicting elements in the narrative are often mentioned as additional proof. In one strand, Samuel is a minor local seer, in the other a great national figure; in one strand, Saul is chosen king by lot in a tribal assembly, in the other he is privately anointed by Samuel. And no fewer than three place-names are associated with Saul's becoming king: Ramah (9:5, by implication), Mizpah (10:17) and Gilgal (11:15).

Once it has been decided that two divergent accounts have been conflated in 1 Sa. 8–12, the question arises which story is correct and original. The answer has usually been that the strand hostile to the monarchy is the unhistorical one. 'We have in this document', wrote A. R. S. Kennedy, 'the bitter reflections of a member of the Deuteronomic school, who regarded the defections and excesses of the monarchy as largely responsible for the sins of the people, and the consequent destruction of the state' (in his *Century Bible* commentary, p. 18). For Kennedy and many other scholars, the idea of a theocracy was late—exilic or postexilic; and therefore passages in 1 Samuel in any way critical of the monarchy were dismissed as idealistic and quite unhistorical.

Among some recent scholars, however, there has been a tendency to view the 'hostile' passages as considerably earlier and more reliable than was thought by Kennedy, for instance. As J. Bright has insisted, a step as drastic as the institution of the monarchy undoubtedly 'evoked opposition from the beginning' (*History of Israel*, p. 167). The idea of Yahweh as 'king' of Israel was a very old one (*cf.* Ex. 15:18), and opposition to human royalty had been expressed by Gideon (Jdg. 8:23)—unless that passage too be viewed as late and unhistorical (as is often done). Besides, the very fact that Israel existed so long without a monarchy, in a world where kings were the norm, reveals that there must have been some basic inhibitions against such an institution. Moreover, the faults and excesses of human rulers were no secret in Israel's world (see on 1 Sa. 8:11–17).

Once it is allowed that the material in the 'hostile' strand can be equally early, it becomes not only possible but indeed necessary to try to account for the differences between the two strands. In the first place, it is nothing short of a mistake to argue that Samuel is a minor local visionary of no political importance in 1 Sa. 9 (see commentary); as Bright says, 'That he (Samuel) took a leading role in the proceedings is witnessed by all the strands of the narrative' (*ibid*).

At first glance, it appears a more serious problem that there should have been no fewer than three 'coronation' ceremonies, at three different places; but this again is not really so improbable as it may seem. To begin with, the sequence is entirely plausible. Samuel chooses and anoints his man privately, in the first place. He then calls together a national assembly, and presides over a 'tribal election', where, however, the casting of lots was a religious ceremony, and in which Samuel was perfectly sure that the divine guidance would give the same answer as to him privately. That some should stand aloof is not surprising; and it took some effective military action on Saul's part to bring all Israel behind him. It is eminently reasonable that Samuel should now arrange a fresh ceremony,

as it were of ratification, after Saul's triumph over Ammon. The three centres, Ramah, Mizpah and Gilgal, were moreover three of the four sanctuary-cities where Samuel had special responsibilities (*cf.* 1 Sa. 7:16).

It is often forgotten, in this connection, that David too was made king on three separate occasions: privately in Bethlehem (1 Sa. 16:13), over Judah at Hebron (2 Sa. 2:4), and over all Israel at Hebron (2 Sa. 5:3). Passing over Solomon's reign, we may further observe that his successor Rehoboam had to go to Shechem to be made king (1 Ki. 12:1), and it is beyond doubt that he had already been anointed king in his capital, Jerusalem.

The important issue is the historical one, and if the historical problems can be resolved, then it is of little consequence whether the material of 1 Sa. 8–12 derives from one source or a number. It must freely be admitted that the writer of the books of Samuel drew on a variety of sources (see Appendix 1). Even so, it is not fully established that there are two distinct strands discernible in these particular chapters. It may be observed that the 'hostile' passages never once express hostility to Saul himself (despite his later rejection), but only to rebellious elders, who were sternly advised of the dangers inherent in a monarchy. Secondly, the differing standpoint of different sections of the narrative often seems to be due to the literary skill of the writer; on this point, see especially the commentary on 1 Sa. 9.

Appendix 3
'SEER AND PROPHET' (1 Sa. 9:9)

1 Sa. 9:9 is an explanatory editorial addition, a sort of footnote. The word 'seer' was evidently the word in the literary source here utilized by the compiler and author of the books of Samuel; and, moreover, the word was very appropriate in this passage, because Samuel is being portrayed as fulfilling that particular function ('seeing' where the lost donkeys were). However, it is also clear that later readers might in some way misunderstand the term, and so the biblical writer explained it for his own generation, as a word formerly equivalent to the word 'prophet'. Up to this point in the narrative, the wider term 'man of God' had been used for Samuel; while it was not a phrase, being much less precise, which would create any misconceptions, it would not have been adequate in 9:9, since the author wished to lay a foundation for the subsequent use of the word 'seer' (vv. 11, 18ff.).

One is free to imagine that the word 'seer' had something of an unfortunate connotation by the 8th century BC, if Mi. 3:7 yields a clue. The real

point of distinction may be that the seer was a man who worked on his own (as opposed to prophets, who moved in small communal groups, *cf.* 1 Sa. 10:5) in Samuel's era, but was one of a professional group at a later date. Alternatively, the term may have become restricted, by the time of Micah, to those who practised divination of a pagan kind ('seeing' fate in the stars or in animals' livers, *etc.*): astronomy, hepatoscopy, and other similar practices. Divination of this type was sternly denounced in Dt. 18:9–14; it is clear that it must have been common among the Canaanites.

Whatever the case, it may be said that the 'seer' had an important local role in the time of Saul; and that the term is not in the least derogatory either to Samuel or to David's seer, Gad (2 Sa. 24:11).

See discussions by B. D. Napier in *IDB* (art. 'Prophet, Prophetism') and by J. A. Motyer in *NBD* (art. 'Prophecy, Prophets').

Appendix 4
PROBLEMS OF 1 SAMUEL 17;18

A very important MS of the LXX, namely Codex Vaticanus (LXX[B]), is remarkably shorter than is the Hebrew text in 1 Sa. 17; 18. Such material as it contains it shares with the longer narrative, but it does not have two large sections of these chapters, namely 17:12–31 and 17:55 – 18:5. (Other lesser omissions are 17:41, 50; 18:10, 11, 17–19, 30; with parts of some other verses.) Thus Codex Vaticanus says nothing of Jesse's sending David with provisions for his brothers at the battle-front; nor of David's response to Goliath's challenge, and how he was brought to Saul; nor of Saul's enquiry about David's father's identity; nor of David's subsequent appointment in Saul's army; nor of Saul's first attempt, with a spear, on David's life.

The intriguing fact about these omissions is that despite them LXX[B] presents a perfectly intelligible and coherent story in itself; thus the question inevitably arises, which version is original, the longer or the shorter? The shorter narrative, it must be admitted, raises fewer problems than the longer one. Since nothing is said of Jesse's sending David from Bethlehem, nor about David's being brought before Saul, the impression is given in LXX[B] that David was at Saul's side throughout; this fits in well with 16:21ff. Moreover, the shorter version conveys no suggestion that David and/or his father were unknown to Saul; this fits in well with 16:17–21. Thirdly, another 'duplicate account' is done away with, since only one story of Saul's throwing a spear at David is recounted (19:9f.).

Older scholars (such as A. R. S. Kennedy) were inclined to view the shorter version, contained in LXX[B], as original, since it presented fewer difficulties. A basic canon of textual criticism, however, is that the more 'difficult' reading is the more likely to be original, and a modern scholar (McKane) states bluntly that he finds 'no adequate grounds for departing from MT' (*i.e.* the longer, Hebrew, text). Since the discovery of the Dead Sea Scrolls, it has been observed that a Hebrew recension of the books of Samuel akin to the LXX translation evidently existed in the last century or two BC, and it is

often held that there will have been more than one recension of the Hebrew text available to the LXX translators. Such a possibility only throws the problem back a stage, however; the original compiler or author of 1 Samuel must have written down one version or the other, and it is still a fair question to ask which was the original.

It remains a possibility that the shorter account originated as an abbreviation of the narrative, omitting passages which were not absolutely essential to it, and which were in essence duplicated elsewhere. That is not necessarily to say that the abbreviator felt the 'difficulties' of modern critics—although he may well have done —but simply that since it was stated elsewhere in 1 Samuel that David came to Saul's notice and his court, entered his service as his armour-bearer, and was later nearly killed by Saul's spear, these details needed no repetition. But it is in fact a mark of this biblical author's technique to emphasize certain facts by recounting two similar incidents; and this fact alone supports the originality of the longer text.

One significant omission of LXX[B] may serve to show the probability that its shorter narrative is an abbreviation. It omits the passage about Saul's promising his elder daughter Merab to David and then marrying her to another man (18:17ff.). There is no difficulty about this passage (even if a few scholars, such as H. P. Smith in the *ICC* series, have found one, an ancient author or translator would scarcely have done so), but nevertheless it is a story very similar to that of Michal, who did in fact marry David but was later forcibly married to another man. The recounting of two such stories is characteristic of the original author; the omission of one of them looks like a characteristic of the man responsible for the shorter version of 1 Sa. 17 and 18.

For attempted solutions of the historical problems, see the commentary; and on the whole question of 'duplicate accounts', see the Introduction to the books of Samuel.

Appendix 5
THE ELHANAN PROBLEM (2 Sa. 21:19)

The statement of 2 Sa. 21:19 (as it stands in the Hebrew text, and in the RSV) that Elhanan killed Goliath is apparently in flat contradiction with 1 Sa. 17, where we read the well-known story of David's victory over Goliath. The verse in 2 Sa.

21 must also be set against its parallel in 1 Ch. 20:5; such a comparison indicates clearly that some textual corruption has taken place in the transmission of the verse in either Samuel or Chronicles or both.

It may be helpful to set out in English and Hebrew (in transliteration) the relevant parts of both texts:

2 Sa. 21:19   ... and Elhanan the son of Jaare-oregim, the Bethlehemite, slew Goliath ...

1 Ch. 20:5   ... and Elhanan the son of Jair slew Lahmi the brother of Goliath ...

2 Sa. 21:19   *wayyak 'elḥānān ben ya'rê 'ōrᵉḡîm bēṭ hallaḥmî 'ēṭ golyāṭ*

1 Ch. 20:5   *wayyak 'elḥānān ben yā'îr 'eṭ laḥmî 'ăḥî golyāṭ*

It is universally agreed that the second part of Elhanan's father's name, as it appears in 2 Samuel, is to be deleted as a scribal error (of dittography); it means 'weavers', and appears again in its rightful place at the end of the same verse. The name of Elhanan's father, then, was either *ya'rê* or *yā'îr*; of the two, the latter is much preferable, and is found elsewhere as a proper name (*e.g.* Nu. 32:41). The form *ya'rê* is most unlikely as a proper name; but a reasonably slight change would transform the word into *yišay*, *i.e.* Jesse.

The 'Bethlehemite' of Samuel would seem more probable than the 'Lahmi' of Chronicles. But it is not easy (on purely textual and linguistic grounds) to decide between the simple 'Goliath' of Samuel and the 'brother of Goliath' of Chronicles. It has often been argued, however, that the relatively unknown Elhanan in fact killed Goliath, that the writer of 1 Samuel 17 transferred the deed to his hero David, and that the Chronicler deliberately interpolated the word 'brother' in 1 Ch. 20:5 in order to harmonize the variant accounts. However, in view of the certain textual corruption in 2 Sa. 21:19, and the fact that the Hebrew word for 'brother' is so very similar to the reading of Samuel, such an assertion is by no means unavoidable. Three other possibilities exist:

1. That Elhanan killed Goliath, and that David killed an unnamed Philistine giant. The name 'Goliath' could be a late scribal addition in 1 Sa. 17 in both its occurrences (and also in 1 Sa. 21:9).

2. That David killed Goliath, and that Elhanan killed his brother. In this case, the Chronicles text may be viewed as correct in all respects, although it would make no difference if 'Bethlehemite' were preferred to 'Lahmi'.

3. That Elhanan and David were different names for the same person, just as Solomon bore another name, Jedidiah (*cf.* 2 Sa. 12:24f.), which appears only in this one verse in the Bible. In that case, the name of the father must of course be corrected to 'Jesse'. Slight support for this view may be drawn from the statement of 2 Sa. 21:22 that 'these four ... fell by the hand of David and by the hand of his servants', since David had no personal hand in killing any one of the four Philistines here listed unless he was in fact Elhanan.

In view of the textual problems, it is at any rate a precarious argument to insist that 2 Sa. 21:19 contradicts 1 Sa. 17.

D. F. PAYNE

1 and 2 Kings

INTRODUCTION

The book of Kings—for it is one book, and not two—is a sequel to the book of Samuel. Indeed, in LXX, where the division into two books is first found, Kings is entitled 'Of the Kingdoms, 3' and 'Of the Kingdoms, 4', with the two divisions of Samuel being the first and second books of the Kingdoms. In the English Bible, 1 and 2 Kings are considered to be 'history', but in the Hebrew Bible Kings is the fourth of the Former Prophets (Joshua, Judges and Samuel being the first three). The relative position of the books in the two Canons, however, is the same, and the term 'history' in the English Canon must be thought of as 'holy history' or 'prophetic history' (*i.e.* history seen through the prophet's eyes). 1 and 2 Kings tell the history of the people of Yahweh—the prophetic history, let us keep in mind—from the last days of David (possibly *c.* 970 BC) to the closing days of Jehoiachin in the Exile, at a time somewhat after 562 BC but prior to the return from Exile in 538 BC.

AUTHOR

The author of the work is not named in Scripture. Jewish tradition (Mishna *Baba Bathra* 15a) attributes Kings to Jeremiah. Since Jeremiah was contemporary with Josiah and the remaining kings of Judah down to the fall of Jerusalem, this would be a very attractive theory. Further, it would account for the otherwise inexplicable absence of Jeremiah in the book of Kings (the Jeremiah of 2 Ki. 23:31; 24:18, father of Hamutal, obviously was not the prophet, who was not married, Je. 16:1). However, Jeremiah was taken to Egypt by the pro-Egypt party (Je. 43:6, 7), whereas the ending of 2 Kings shows remarkable familiarity with the events in Babylon. We therefore conclude that Kings was written by an unidentified prophet in Babylon probably *c.* 550 BC.

To speak of an 'author' is perhaps a bit misleading, for the work indicates a number of sources that were obviously written by other authors. Further, there is an extended portion (2 Ki. 19:9 – 20:19) that is very closely related with a portion of Isaiah (37:9 – 39:8), some parts with exact verbal agreement, and there are portions closely paralleling Jeremiah and Chronicles. Moreover, there are clear stylistic differences (as, *e.g.*, in the Elijah and Elisha cycles) that suggest other sources which have not been named. But there seems to be no compelling reason to fragment the work into L, J, E, the Davidic court narrative, the Elijah cycle, the Elisha cycle, the Ahab source, the Isaiah source,

prophetic sources for stories of Ahijah, Shemaiah *et al.*, the pre-Deuteronomic editor, and finally the Deuteronomic author, as various scholars have done. Rather, we may assume that there were various accounts, both oral and written, including some rather stilted court records and some fine prophetic messages, that were used by the creative mind of the author under the influence of the Holy Spirit.

THE DEUTERONOMIST

The relationship between the religious point of view of Kings and that of Deuteronomy is obvious. The basic problem to be solved is whether the book of Deuteronomy was the product of the closing period of Judah, written to establish the single sanctuary at Jerusalem, as is commonly held by a great many scholars today, or whether the book of Deuteronomy, essentially from Moses' time and recovered in the days of Josiah, was responsible for the 'Deuteronomic' reforms and, indeed, for the 'Deuteronomist' himself. If Deuteronomy was the product of the Josianic period, or of any period from the fall of Samaria to the fall of Jerusalem, and if it was written to establish the primacy of the Jerusalem sanctuary, then we are forced to explain not only the complete absence of the name Jerusalem from the book of Deuteronomy, but also the detailed knowledge of the wilderness period, the wilderness *Sitz-im-Leben*, and the Deuteronomic point of view of Joshua, Judges and Samuel. The trend of scholarship, of course, has been to attribute all of these to the Deuteronomist.

It is our conviction, and that will be evident in the commentary, that Deuteronomy is essentially Mosaic (with later additions and probably considerable editing), that the influence of Deuteronomy continued, in greater or lesser degree, at least to the time of Solomon (hence its influence on David and Solomon in planning and completing the Jerusalem sanctuary), and that the Deuteronomic reforms of Josiah as well as the Deuteronomic viewpoint of the author of Kings resulted from the finding of Deuteronomy in the Temple in the days of Josiah.

PURPOSE

It seems clear that the author was trying to convey a message, not merely to write history. The message is Deuteronomic, as a reading of Dt. 7 or 9 or 11 (particularly 11:26–28), or many other portions will clearly indicate. The purpose, in a word, is to show that Israel—the total nation —as the people of Yahweh is expected to keep the law of Yahweh, particularly the purity of worship of Yahweh, and that there is blessing in so doing, and punishment for failure to keep His law.

Since the king stands in the place of the nation, the author has chosen to proclaim his message principally by telling the story of the kings. It is noteworthy that each king's reign is judged not on political grounds but on religious grounds alone: he 'did what was evil in the sight of Yahweh', or 'he did what was right in the eyes of Yahweh'. Perhaps the most striking example of this is Omri of Israel, by political measure one of the greatest of the kings of Israel, who is dismissed with eight verses and summarized in the statement, 'Omri did what was evil in the sight of Yahweh, and did more evil than all who were before him.'

METHOD

The author uses the chronological method to tell his story. Since there are two simultaneous lines of kings through much of the period (from the division of the kingdom to the fall of Samaria), he interweaves them, almost without exception telling the complete story of one king's reign, and then going back to pick up the story of his contemporary or contemporaries in the other kingdom. An exception to this method is found in the case of Ahab, where the story is broken by a large portion of the 'Elijah cycle'. Another exception is the reign of Jehoram (Joram) of Israel, which is interwoven with the Elisha story. Further complicating this situation is the fact that the name of the 'king of Israel' in the Elisha cycle is regularly omitted. A third exception is the account of Jehoash of Israel which is interrupted by the closing events of the Elisha story and by the introduction of the reign of Amaziah of Judah.

For the kings of Israel the author usually gives an introductory statement consisting of a. the date of accession, synchronizing it with the king of Judah; b. the name of the capital where he reigned; c. the length of the king's reign; and d. a brief summary of his character (see 1 Ki. 15:33f.). For the kings of Judah, the introductory statement consists of a. the date of accession, synchronizing it with the king of Israel (omitted after the fall of the northern kingdom); b. age at accession; c. name of the queen-mother (except for Jehoram and Ahaz); and d. summary of the king's relation to the law and comparison with 'David his father' (see 1 Ki. 15:1–5). Two are given unqualified approval (Hezekiah and Josiah), six modified approval (Asa, Jehoshaphat, Jehoash, Amaziah, Uzziah, Jotham), and ten are severely criticized. For the kings of Israel and the kings of Judah alike, the author uses summary formulae consisting of a. reference to the Book of the Chronicles of the Kings of Israel or Judah as appropriate; b. the king's

death and place of burial; and c. the name of the successor (see 1 Ki. 15:7, 8). (The formula is omitted in the cases of kings who were deposed or assassinated.) The *Book of the Chronicles of the Kings of Israel* is mentioned 17 times, and the *Book of the Chronicles of the Kings of Judah* is mentioned 15 times. These are not to be confused with the biblical books of Chronicles.

CHRONOLOGY

Since the lengths of the reigns of the kings are given, it should be a simple matter to total these figures and get a check. Unfortunately this does not work. Rehoboam of Judah and Jeroboam of Israel became kings at the same time, and Ahaziah of Judah and Joram of Israel died at the same time, but the total of the years in Judah is 95 and in Israel 98. Again, Athaliah of Judah and Jehu of Israel began to reign at the same time, while the fall of Samaria (Israel) is given as occurring in the 6th year of Hezekiah of Judah. The total for the northern kingdom during this period is 143 years, and for Judah 165 years. Obviously there are problems to be solved. If we introduce extra-biblical material, such as the dates of Egyptian pharaohs or Assyrian kings, we find the problems further complicated.

Part of the difficulty lies in the system of counting the length of a reign, for in some cases the accession year was not counted and the count begins with the next New Year, while in other cases the accession year was counted—and this is not indicated in the text. Further, there are a number of co-regencies, or periods during which the successor reigned simultaneously with the incumbent, and in some cases the length of a king's reign includes the years he ruled as co-regent— again the text does not indicate this, although the synchronism sometimes makes it obvious. When these difficulties are worked out, there remain a few problems that have not been solved, such as the 12/13-year discrepancy in the time of Jotham–Ahaz–Hezekiah of Judah and Pekah–Hoshea of Israel (Thiele's 'Pattern Twelve-thirteen'). *NBD* approaches this problem as a continuation of the system of co-regencies.

Biblical data will give us relative and synchronistic dating only. Astronomical observations and Assyrian *limmu*-lists, along with other data, enable us to attach calendar dates to certain events. The battle of Qarqar is thus firmly dated at 853 BC, and accordingly the death of Ahab of Israel. Likewise the accession of Jehu is firmly dated at 841 BC. A Babylonian tablet enables us to set the exact date of the capture of Jerusalem, 15/16 March 597 BC. From the fixed dates we work backward and forward, using the biblical data, to establish all other dates from the death of Solomon to the fall of Jerusalem in 587/6.

TEXT

A comparison of the MT with LXX and Vulg. will

show that the text of Kings has been subject to some editorial alteration and dislocation. The text of LXX is often shorter, and the Lucianic recension of the Greek would appear to be more reliable in places. The Qumran text of Kings, although fragmentary, indicates that there was a Hebrew text that stood closer to LXX than does MT. This is further evidence that we must not blindly follow the present Hebrew text (= MT), but rather should make careful critical use of all existing evidence in order to try to get back to the original Hebrew text.

BIBLIOGRAPHY

C. F. Burney, *Notes on the Hebrew Text of the Book of Kings*, 1903.

John Gray, *I & II Kings. A Commentary*, 1963.

C. F. Keil, *The Books of the Kings* (*Biblical Commentary on the Old Testament*, ed. C. F. Keil and F. Delitzsch), tr. by J. Martin, 1950.

James A. Montgomery, *A Critical and Exegetical Commentary on the Book of Kings* (*ICC*), ed. H. S. Gehman, 1951.

J. Skinner, *I and II Kings* (*CB*), 1904.

Norman H. Snaith, *The First and Second Books of Kings* (*IB*), 1954.

CHRONOLOGY OF 1 and 2 KINGS

JUDAH		ISRAEL		OTHER	
931–913	Rehoboam	931–910	Jeroboam I	945–924	Sheshonq I
913–910	Abijam			915–900	Tabrimmon
910–870	Asa	910–909	Nadab		
		909–886	Baasha	900–860	Ben-hadad I (?)
				898–866	Ethbaal I
		886–885	Elah		
		885	Zimri	(898–843	Ben-hadad I) (?)
		885–880	Tibni	(860–843	Ben-hadad II) (?)
*873–848	Jehoshaphat	§885–874	Omri		
		874–853	Ahab	859–824	Shalmaneser III
*853–841	Jehoram	853–852	Ahaziah	853	Battle of Qarqar
841	Ahaziah	852–841	Jehoram	843–796	Hazael
841–835	Athaliah	841–814	Jehu		
835–796	Joash	814–796	Jehoahaz		
796–767	Amaziah	*798–782	Jehoash	796–770	Ben-hadad III/II
*790–740	Azariah (Uzziah)	*793–753	Jeroboam II		
		753	Zechariah	750–732	Rezin
		752	Shallum	747–727	Tiglath-pileser III
		752–742	Menahem		
		741–740	Pekahiah		
*†751–732	Jotham	§752–732	Pekah	732	Fall of Damascus
†735–716	Ahaz	731–722	Hoshea	727–722	Shalmaneser V
*728–687	Hezekiah	722	Fall of Samaria	722–705	Sargon II
*696–642	Manasseh			705–681	Sennacherib
				690–664	Tarhaqa
642–640	Amon			669–627	Ashurbanipal
639–609	Josiah			626–605	Nabopolassar
				612	Fall of Nineveh
609	Jehoahaz			610–595	Neco II
608–597	Jehoiakim			605–562	Nebuchadrezzar II
597	Jehoiachin			595–589	Psammetichus II
597	Capture of Jerusalem				
597–586	Zedekiah				
586	Destruction of Jerusalem			589–570	Apries (Hophra)
562	Jehoiachin released			562–560	Amēl-Marduk

* overlapping date indicates co-regency
§ overlapping date indicates claim to throne
† Jotham's 16-year reign ended in 735

RECONSTRUCTION OF CHRONOLOGY
OF THE KINGS OF JUDAH

(Data given in Scripture are shown in bold type; dates estimated on the basis of reasonable limits shown in italic)

King	Year of Birth	Father (with age of father)	Year Co-regent (with age)	Year King (with age)	Years Reigned	Ended Reign (with age)
Rehoboam	*971*			931 **(41)**	**17**	913 *(58)*
Abijam	*950*	Rehoboam *(21)*		913 *(37)*	**3**	910 *(40)*
Asa	*929*	Abijam *(21)*		910 *(18)*	**41**	870 *(59)*
Jehoshaphat	908	Asa (21)	873 **(35)**	870 (38)	**25**	848 (60)
Jehoram	886	Jehoshaphat (22)	853 **(32)**	848 (37)	**8**	841 (45)
Ahaziah	864	Jehoram (22)		841 **(22)**	**1**	841 (23)
[Athaliah]				841	**7**	835
Joash	843	Ahaziah (21)		835 **(7)**	**40**	796 (47)
Amaziah	821	Joash (22)		796 **(25)**	**29**	767 (54)
Azariah (Uzziah)	808	Amaziah (13)	790 **(16)**	767 (31)	**52**	740 (68)
Jotham	776	Azariah (32)	751 **(25)**	740 (35)	**16**	735 (41)
					20*	732 (44)
Ahaz	755	Jotham (21)	735 **(20)**	732 (23)	**16**	716 (39)
Hezekiah	741	Ahaz (14)	728 **(13)**	716 **(25)**	**29**	687 (54)
Manasseh	709	Hezekiah (32)	696 **(12)**	687 **(21)**	**55**	642 (67)
Amon	664	Manasseh (45)		642 **(22)**	**2**	640 (24)
Josiah	648	Amon (16)		639 **(8)**	**31**	609 (39)
Jehoahaz	632	Josiah (16)		609 **(23)**	⅓	609 (23)
Jehoiakim	633	Josiah (15)		608 **(25)**	**11**	597 (36)
Jehoiachin	615	Jehoiakim (18)		597 **(18)**	⅓	597 (18)
Zedekiah	618	Josiah (30)		597 **(21)**	**11**	586 (32)

* The 20th year of Jotham is mentioned, but his reign is 16 years.

OUTLINE OF CONTENTS

(In this analysis the two books are treated as a whole)

COMMENTARY

1:1 – 2:46 THE LAST DAYS OF DAVID AND THE ACCESSION OF SOLOMON

1:1–53 The struggle for succession

This seems to be a continuation of 2 Sa. 20:22, but after an interval of some years. We are not necessarily to suppose that these events took place in a short time just prior to David's death. **1:1–4 David's old age. 3** *Shunammite*, a person from Shunem (*cf.* 2 Ki. 4:8), a village in the plain of Jezreel (probably mod. Solem), not far from Nazareth. **4** *The king knew her not* in a marital relationship; there is no reason to assume that this was a test of the king's virility to determine whether he was any longer fit to be king. She was brought in as a nurse, but the request of Adonijah (2:17) and Solomon's reaction (2:23) suggest that Abishag was considered to be David's concubine.

1:5–10 Adonijah is proclaimed king. Adonijah, David's oldest living son (*cf.* 2 Sa. 3:2–4), is accepted as the heir by Joab and Abiathar and decides to take the throne. **5** *Horsemen*, perhaps 'horses'; mounted cavalry did not come into Israel until later. **6** *Displeased*: LXX 'punished' may make better sense. RSV changes AV 'bare him' to passive, *was born*, an inferior emendation. AV also adds 'his mother', necessary for the sense. **8** *Shimei, and Rei*: possibly 'Shimei the friend' following Josephus, since each of the other persons in the verse has a descriptive title. **9** *Sacrificed.* The word means 'to slaughter', usually for sacrificial purposes. *En-rogel* is the present Bir 'Ayyub near the village of Silwan. **10** *He did not invite . . .* : failure to invite Nathan and Benaiah, and particularly Solomon, may indicate that Adonijah was planning to exterminate them, since if he had invited them to a meal he would have been committed to preserve their lives.

1:11–14 Nathan's plot on behalf of Solomon. 11 *Has become king* does not accurately portray the situation; Adonijah had started the process, but he had not yet been crowned king. **12** Nathan's advice indicates clearly that Adonijah would have put both Solomon and his mother Bathsheba to death. **13** The words are in polite address. **14** *Confirm*; lit. 'I shall fill out your words'. There is no record that David made such a promise to Bathsheba, but there is no reason to suppose that Nathan has fabricated this from nothing.

1:15–21 Bathsheba before David. 15 An indication of the type of service Abishag was rendering to David is perhaps given by the fact that she was not dismissed from the room when Bathsheba entered. **16** *What do you desire?* Lit. 'What is with you?' **18** *Adonijah is king*: *cf.* v. 11, and note v. 20. **21** *Offenders*; lit. 'those who have missed the mark'; it often means 'sinners'. There can be little doubt that Adonijah, once he assumed the throne, would find some sufficient reason to put Solomon and Bathsheba to death.

1:22–27 Nathan before David. 24 Nathan refers to Adonijah's plot as though it were the result of David's promise. The criticism is not that David had no right to do this, but that he had brought reproach upon Nathan, Zadok and Benaiah. **25** *Joab the commander of the army*, based on LXX, probably the correct reading (*cf.* AV).

1:28–31 David vows to make Solomon king. 31 *May my lord King David live for ever!* The customary greeting to an oriental king.

1:32–37 David acts. He does not plan for the preliminary steps alone, but for the actual anointing and crowning of Solomon as king. This will, of course, anticipate Adonijah's coronation and put Adonijah in the position of having to overthrow the king if he wishes to press his claim. **33** *Gihon*: the present 'Ain Umm ed-Daraj in the upper part of the Kidron valley, the waters of which were later carried by Hezekiah's tunnel to the pool of Siloam (2 Ch. 32:30). Mounting Solomon on David's *own mule* probably symbolized the kingly claim.

1:38–40 Solomon is anointed as king. 38 *Cherethites . . . Pelethites*, probably Cretans and Philistines, the use of foreign mercenaries being one means of circumventing plots to assassinate the king (see also on 2 Sa. 8:18). **39** *The horn of oil*: a specific horn of olive oil used for anointing the king. *Tent*: the portable covering where the ark was kept, not necessarily the Tabernacle constructed in the wilderness several centuries earlier. **40** *Playing on pipes*: LXX 'danced with dances', which may be more reasonable. *The earth was split by their noise*: a figure of speech not to be pressed literally.

1:41–48 Adonijah is outmanoeuvred and his plot collapses. 41 *The city*; rather 'the citadel', or walled fortress of the city. **42** *A worthy man*. The term suggests a man of wealth, not one living on the king. **47** *Congratulate* (AV 'bless'); this was not merely a human congratulation but an invocation of divine blessing. **48** *One of my offspring*, based on LXX. The beginning of a dynasty was a new experience for Israel. Saul and David were 'charismatic' rulers. This is the first time a king's son has ascended the throne of Israel.

1:49–53 Solomon spares Adonijah. 50 Taking *hold of the horns of the altar* was to stay the hand of the avenger (*cf.* Ex. 21:14). **51** The altar was perhaps near the tent (v. 39). **52** *If . . . a worthy man*: Montgomery translates, 'If he behaves like a gentleman.' Solomon recognizes that Adonijah has taken refuge at the horns of the altar and therefore spares his life, but at the same time he obligates Adonijah to refrain from any further attempt upon the throne. **53** *Go to your house*: possibly house-arrest; at any rate it is retirement from public life.

2:1–12 David's final, twofold charge and death

2:1–4 The charge concerning Solomon. This may have occupied a number of years (*cf.* 1 Ch. 22:6 – 29:25). The passage has been described as 'Deuteronomic' and inserted by a later editor, but the king was responsible to know and to transmit the material in Deuteronomy (Dt. 17:18f.; *cf.* Jos. 1:1–9). See Introduction.

2:5–9 The charge concerning David's enemies. It has been suggested that these are not David's instructions, but decisions made by Solomon and ascribed to David. For the murder of Abner, *cf.* 2 Sa. 3:27 and for Amasa, 2 Sa. 20:8–10. Joab had murdered the two generals in a time of peace. Keil suggests that in each case David was unable to punish Joab, and therefore transmitted to Solomon the responsibility. **5** *My loins, my feet*: cf. RSV mg., Heb. 'his'. **6** *Wisdom*: here, practical intelligence, knowledge of the facts and discrimination in the use of them. *In peace*: Gray renders 'unscathed'. **7** *Deal loyally* (Heb. *ḥeseḏ*): action required by the terms of a covenant. *With such loyalty they met me* (Heb. 'thus they approached me'). Cf. 2 Sa. 17:27ff.; 19:32ff. **8** For the *curse of Shimei*, cf. 2 Sa. 16:5ff.; 19:16ff. The curse was thought to be still powerful and therefore had to be turned away. Cursing a ruler was a capital offence (Ex. 22:28).

2:10–12 David's death. 10 *Slept with his fathers*: a euphemism for 'died'. *The city of David*; i.e. Mt. Zion (cf. Acts 2:29). On the length of David's reign, generally dated 1010–971 BC, cf. 2 Sa. 5:4f. **12** This is an inclusive statement of what follows, more fully expanded in 1 Ch. 29:23–25. According to one Greek MS Solomon was 12 years old at the time of his accession; according to Josephus (*Ant.* viii.7.8) he was 14. Rehoboam was born about the time Solomon became king (14:21).

2:13–46 Solomon's purge

2:13–27 Adonijah asks for Abishag. Adonijah goes to Bathsheba and asks her to get Solomon to give him David's nurse Abishag. Solomon understands the request to be a claim on the throne (see on 2 Sa. 3:6–11), for according to the custom of the day, the appropriation of the royal harem was the right of the new king (cf. 2 Sa. 16:21f.). He therefore orders the execution of Adonijah. **15** Adonijah felt he had a legitimate claim to the throne. **19** The queen mother is seated at the right hand of the king, the place of honour and authority. **22** *On his side are Abiathar . . . and Joab*: RSV follows the versions. Abiathar was banished, since as a priest he was sacrosanct. **26** *Anathoth* (mod. Anata), about 3 miles NE of Jerusalem (cf. Je. 1:1).

2:28–35 The death of Joab. Apparently thinking not of the murders, but that he had supported Adonijah, Joab flees to the place of refuge. However, there is no sanctuary for a murderer, which Solomon judged Joab to be. **34** *Buried in his own house*: possibly buried under the floor of the house, although the land around it would also be called 'house'. *Wilderness*: 'steppe', low-quality grazing land in E Judea, usually too stony for cultivation. **35** *Benaiah* is given Joab's place and *Zadok* is made priest. The Qumran community of the Dead Sea Scrolls claimed to be the true descendants of Zadok. The priesthood was supposed to be hereditary and not subject to political appointment; Solomon, therefore, has introduced a principle of grave consequence.

2:36–46 Shimei's palace-arrest and death. Shimei, while not crossing the Kidron, violates the command not to go out of Jerusalem to any place whatever (v. 36). Solomon uses this as a reason to carry out David's command (1 Ki. 2:9; contrast 2 Sa. 19:23). **39** *Gath*: Gray identi-

fies it as Libnah, 30 miles SW of Jerusalem. **45** *King Solomon shall be blessed*: the direct action to invalidate the curse of 2 Sa. 16 (cf. J. Gray, art. 'Blessing and Curse', *HDB*, rev. 1963, pp. 109f.). **46** The second part of the verse summarizes the preceding chapter, but is taken by some to be the introduction to the next section.

3:1 – 11:43 THE REIGN OF SOLOMON

Solomon's reign can be evaluated politically and spiritually. Politically, it is splendid. Spiritually, it deteriorates into idolatry. For some strange reason, Christian literature has idealized Solomon so that he hardly resembles the scriptural portrait.

3:1 – 4:34 Solomon's wisdom and splendour

3:1 Solomon's marriage-alliance. This section would seem to be without chronological intent. *He took Pharaoh's daughter*; i.e. 'he married'. The identity of this Pharaoh is not known; it probably was not Shishak (14:25) but one of the kings of the weak XXIst Dynasty. The marriage was obviously a political arrangement and according to 9:16 the dowry was Gezer (possibly to be amended to read Gerar). In LXX v. 1 is joined with 9:16, and both are placed after 4:34 (MT 5:14).

3:2–4 Worship at the high places. The 'high place' was a shrine in use in Canaan before the Israelites came into the land. Later the high places were used by the Israelites, often with opposition from the prophets. It is not necessary to suppose that v. 2 is an apology on the part of a later editor, who was excusing the people since there was no House of Yahweh in Jerusalem; it is entirely possible to assume that the author here at the beginning of the story is pointing out some of the weaknesses of Solomon's reign. On the other hand, we must recognize that the Lord always dealt with His people in the situation in which they were at the time, seeking to lead them on to something better. God was willing to meet the king in the great high place at Gibeon (v. 5), even though in another few generations the high places would become abominable; but then so would the sacrificial acts performed in accordance with the letter of the law of Moses but in violation of its spirit. **4** According to 2 Ch. 1:1–13 the sacrifice at Gibeon was an inaugural religious ceremony in lieu of the coronation (cf. 1 Ki. 1:39; 1 Ch. 29:22). Zadok was apparently priest of Gibeon (1 Ch. 16:39) and there may have been an Aaronite priesthood there from the time of Joshua (Jos. 9). This would explain why the Tabernacle and the brazen altar (2 Ch. 1:3, 5) were brought there, probably from Shiloh. Keil says the high places were consecrated to the worship of Yahweh and were essentially different from the high places of the Canaanites, which were consecrated to Baal, but this would be difficult to prove. *Gibeon* (mod. El-Jib), located 6 miles NW of Jerusalem. *Solomon used to offer*.

The Hebrew imperfect could mean that this was a regular act of Solomon, or it could indicate the total of Solomon's offerings on all of the occasions when he went to Gibeon. *A thousand burnt offerings*: not necessarily to be taken as a mathematical count, but possibly a figure of speech meaning a very large or very important offering.

3:5–15 Solomon's dream and Yahweh's reply. 6 *Steadfast love* (Heb. *ḥeseḏ*, 'covenant love'). Both David and God had kept the covenant. **7** *A little child*. Not to be taken literally (as in the tradition that Solomon was only 12 or 14); it is an oriental figure of speech expressing humility: *cf.* the words following. *I do not know how to go out or come in*. A figure of speech indicating lack of experience in his new office (*cf.* Nu. 27:17). **9** *Mind* (AV 'heart'): the Hebrew word for 'heart' is perhaps closer to our word for 'mind'. It includes the emotions and the will and judgment to discern between good and evil. **11** *Life*: Hebrew *nepeš* is usually translated 'soul', but is closer to 'person' or 'life'. *Understanding to discern what is right*: lit. 'discernment to hear judgment' (Heb. *mišpāṭ*), which has the meaning not only of 'decision', but also the divine principles on which the decision is made. **15** If the ark had not yet been brought to Jerusalem, this verse has to be accepted as a later addition; or if this verse is to be taken at face value, it would indicate that the entire paragraph is in the nature of a summary before the story of Solomon is told in detail and includes the later period of his life after the ark had been taken to Jerusalem. The account in Chronicles omits this portion.

3:16–28 The two harlots and Solomon's decision. The wisdom which God had given Solomon is now described in a typical case. It is wisdom in the practical sense, but is nevertheless ascribed to God (v. 28). **16** Note the right of access on the part of common members of the kingdom to the king's presence. **22** This verse shows, as does the entire story, intimate details of the argument before the king. **26** *Heart* (AV 'bowels', Heb. could mean 'womb'). According to Hebrew psychology strong emotional feelings were located in the abdominal area. In our popular psychology we locate them in the heart. **28** *Render justice* (AV 'do judgment'). Again Heb. *mišpāṭ* is used, here specifically of the decision which resulted from the application of divinely-given wisdom.

4:1–6 Solomon's organizational ability. 2 *High officials*: better than AV 'princes'. **3** *Secretaries* (AV 'scribes'): in other references there is only one scribe or secretary. Montgomery translates 'Azariah the son of Zadok the priest (was) over the year, and Ahijah the son of Shisha, the secretary', reading *Elihoreph* as 'over the year'. But *ḥōrep̄* regularly means 'autumn', and nowhere in Hebrew means 'year'. The suggestion, however, is worthy of serious consideration. **4** *Abiathar*, a reading very much suspect, since Abiathar had been demoted from the priesthood at the outset of Solomon's reign (2:35). **5** *Priest*

and king's friend: probably better 'Zabud, son of Nathan, a priest, was the king's friend', a title used in the Tell el-Amarna letters of a regular petty-official, the duties of which we do not know. Hushai was 'the king's friend' in David's time (2 Sa. 15:37). However, Keil takes 'priest' to be equivalent to 'friend of the king', or 'privy councillor'. *Nathan*, probably the son of David mentioned in 2 Sa. 5:14, not the prophet. **6** *In charge of the palace*: AV 'over the household' is closer to the Hebrew. *Forced labour* (AV 'tribute'): the Hebrew word indicates the corvée which, strictly speaking, was forced labour. *Adoniram*; see on 2 Sa. 20:24 and *cf.* 1 Ki. 12:18.

4:7–19 Solomon's administrative districts. These districts probably followed the old tribal boundaries, and the officials are of high rank, two of them sons-in-law of Solomon (vv. 11, 15). **7** *Officers*: Heb. 'those appointed'. **8ff.** *Ben-hur, Ben-deker, Ben-hesed, etc.* AV is correct in treating these as patronymics, *the son of Hur, the son of Deker, etc.*, the proper names having been lost. Montgomery suggests that the original copy in the royal archives had the names in tabular form and that the edge of the document was damaged, which would account for the fact that in several cases the name is missing and only *the son of* remains. **16** *Bealoth* (AV 'in Aloth'), possibly 'Maaloth', with LXX. **19** *Of Judah*: not in the Hebrew text, but certainly correct.

4:20–28 Solomon's wisdom summarized. The author, in no apparent order, shows that Solomon's wisdom exceeds all known human wisdom. In LXX the order of verses is different. **21** (The beginning of ch. 5 in MT.) According to this verse, the extent of Solomon's kingdom was as great as the promise made to Abraham (*cf.* Gn. 13:14–17; 15:18); but Solomon lost control of Edom (11:22, LXX), and Rezon of Syria took over Damascus (11:24f.). **24** *The region west of the Euphrates* (AV 'on this side the river', Heb. simply 'in all the trans-river (trans-Euphrates) area'). It is not necessary to assume that the author lived E of the Euphrates to use such an expression; it was the standard term for the region, just as Transjordan was for a long period of time. According to Gray, the term *Trans-Euphrates* came into use first in the Assyrian records in the middle of the 7th century, which is three centuries later than this record. *Tiphsah*, later Thapsacus, an important crossing of the Euphrates river (mod. Qal'at Dibs). **25** *Every man under his vine and under his fig tree*: the idyllic conditions which the common man desired. *From Dan to Beer-sheba*: the traditional limits of Palestine (*cf.* Jdg. 20:1; 1 Sa. 3:20). **26** *Stalls of horses*: the meaning is indicated in 2 Ch. 32:28 and supported now by Akkadian, Aramaic, and Arabic cognates. *Horsemen* generally refers to mounted cavalry, only coming into use in Assyria at this time. Possibly the term was more general at this earlier date. Solomon's trust in horses is hinted at here. We know from other passages that he went in for horse trading. **27** The estimate has been made that 4,000–5,000 persons were cared for at Solomon's court. **28** *Swift steeds* (AV 'dromedaries'): RSV is clearly to be preferred.

4:29–34 Solomon's wisdom. Some scholars find evidence that this section is late, although possibly preserving an early tradition. But the type of wisdom ascribed to Solomon is nature-wisdom, and is of the kind found in Mesopotamia and Egypt at least a century before Solomon, and possibly as much as 2,000 years before Solomon (*cf.* Ptahhotep). **29** *Largeness of mind* (AV 'largeness of heart', CB 'breadth of mind'). The statement probably refers to Solomon's broad interests. **30** *The people of the east* (lit. 'the sons of the east'), a term generally applied to the Arabian and Edomite tribes SE of Palestine, the traditional home of wisdom (*cf.* Jb. 1:3). The word translated *east*, however, can also mean 'former time'. **31** *Ethan . . . Heman, Calcol, and Darda*: persons no longer known to us, but obviously connected with some tradition of wisdom. **32** *Proverbs*; *i.e.* figures of speech setting forth a truth in the form of simile or metaphor. Many of Solomon's proverbs have been preserved in the book of Proverbs. His songs have probably not been preserved, although some of them may be found in the Song of Solomon. **33** The reference to *trees, beasts, birds, reptiles*, and *fish* probably indicates the use of them in connection with his proverbs (see Pr. 30:25f. and *cf.* Jdg. 9:8–15).

5:1 – 7:51 The erection of the Temple

Cf. 2 Ch. 2:1 – 5:1; Josephus, *Ant.* viii.2.6–9. Solomon accomplishes what David dreamt about: to build a house for Yahweh. He draws on the skill and craft of the Tyrians (Phoenicians), the slave-labour of conquered peoples, and enforced labour of Israelites. He mortgages part of his kingdom. At last, he has a splendid Temple—and probably an even more splendid palace. But was it right? We assume that it was; yet God has been able to get along without a temple since AD 70, and even while it was standing Jesus indicated that it was unnecessary for true worship (Jn. 4:21–24). Moreover, it became a tempting attraction for foreign plunderers. But when we have admitted this much, we must add that God was pleased to use it, as He used the sacrificial system, until the 'better things' had come. This passage contains a number of unusual technical words as well as a number of textual corruptions, and should be studied in the light of a good, detailed commentary and dictionary articles on the Temple and its furnishings.

5:1–12 Solomon gets Hiram of Tyre to help. *Cf.* 2 Ch. 2:1–16. **1** 5:15 in MT. *Hiram*: short form of 'Ahiram'. In Chronicles the form 'Huram' is found. *Tyre*: an important city-state on the coast in the north of Palestine that was coming into supremacy over the other Phoenician city-states. *Hiram always loved David* (AV 'ever a lover of David'); 'friend' would be a better translation (*cf.* Est. 5:10; Ps. 38:11; Je.

20:4; *etc.*). **3** With this reason given why David did not build the Temple, *cf.* 2 Sa. 7:12ff. and 1 Ch. 22:8ff.; 28:2ff. **4** *Adversary* (Heb. *śāṭān*): originally a common noun which later became the name for 'the Adversary' (*cf.* Nu. 22:22; 1 Sa. 29:4; *etc.*). **6** *Sidonians*: probably broader than 'the people of Sidon', and meaning those of the Phoenician city-states in general. **9** *Rafts*. The place where they were to be broken up is identified in 2 Ch. 2:16 as Jaffa, but the excavations of Maisler (Mazar) at Tell Qasileh at the mouth of the Yarkon river just N of Jaffa indicate that that may have been the place. **11** *Cors of wheat*: the 'cor' was a little less than 6 bushels. *Twenty thousand cors of beaten oil*: LXX reads 'twenty cors'. As a liquid measure the cor was something more than 50 gallons (US), or 48 gallons (British). *Beaten oil* is oil crushed with a pestle in a mortar, as distinguished from that which was crushed by a heavy roller in a press. **12** *Treaty* (AV 'league', Heb. 'covenant'): a solemn religious ritual.

5:13–18 The corvée in Israel. *Cf.* 1 Ki. 9:15, 20ff.; 2 Ch. 2:2, 17f.). The corvée, or levy of forced labour, was a type of taxation in the ancient world and had been begun in Israel by David (2 Sa. 20:24). It would seem that Solomon made the Canaanites permanent slave-labourers (*cf.* 9:20f.), whereas the Israelites were required to give 4 months out of the year in work (5:13f.; 2 Sa. 24:9). It is unnecessary to attempt to make Solomon a humanitarian. **14** *In relays* makes more sense than 'by courses' (AV); the Hebrew word suggests 'replacement'. **16** *Three thousand three hundred chief officers* indicates a ratio of about one officer to 15 men; 9:23 suggests 550 officers. **17** *With dressed stones, i.e.* stones cut so as to fit with each other in the building, so-called 'margin-drafted masonry', a feature of the Phoenician stone-masons' work. **18** *The men of Gebal* (AV 'the stonesquarers'): the Hebrew is quite difficult; it seems to read 'the Gebalites, the people of Byblos', but the Greek translator did not understand it this way.

6:1–10 The building of the Temple. *Cf.* 2 Ch. 3:1–14; Josephus, *Ant.* viii.3.1–3. The Temple was not intended to house a congregation, neither was it a private chapel for the king. It was built to house the ark and to symbolize the presence of Yahweh. Many scholars have worked over the details, and there are still many points of disagreement and uncertainty. In addition, there are many differences between LXX and MT.

1 *Four hundred and eightieth year*. This would put the Exodus about 1447 BC, which is not in keeping with other evidence, either biblical or extra-biblical. There are indications that this verse may be a late gloss in the text. It is inserted two verses earlier in LXX, and reads '440' instead of '480'. A different word for *month* is used from that found in the rest of the chapter, and *the month of Ziv* was *the second month* of the later Babylonian calendar, but the eighth month of the pre-exilic calendar. LXX omits *in the month of Ziv*. **2** The height and breadth of the Temple are exactly twice those of the Tabernacle. *Cubit*, normally 6 handbreadths, or 18 inches. According to 2 Ch. 3:3, these were the larger cubits of 7 handbreadths or about 21 inches. (See *NBD*, art. 'Weights and Measures', II. *b* and *e*.) In either event, the Temple was not a large building, being 90 ft to 100 ft long and 30 ft to 35 ft wide, interior dimensions. 3 *The vestibule in front of the nave* (AV 'porch before the temple'): it is difficult to determine exactly what is meant. *The nave of the house* (Heb. 'the temple of the house'): possibly 'the main hall of the house'. 4 *Windows with recessed frames* (AV 'windows of narrow lights'): Gray reads 'windows of close lattice-work'. 5 *A structure against the wall of the house* (AV 'chambers'): Gray suggests a platform around the nave and storeys. 6 The three storeys, each of which is wider than the one below it, suggest some kind of buttressing of the outer walls, with the use of the space above the stages or levels of the buttress. The total amount of rebatement of the wall is 3 cubits (*c.* 4½ ft), which may suggest the thickness of the wall at the bottom. 8 *The lowest story* (Heb. and AV 'middle story'); RSV is based on LXX and Targ. *South side*: the word for 'south' literally means 'right' (*cf.* AV), and the direction would be determined by the way a person is standing. *By stairs* (AV 'with winding stairs'): the Hebrew word is not found elsewhere in the OT; LXX and Vulg. 'spiral staircase'. A spiral staircase was found in an 18th-century palace excavated by Woolley at Tell Atchana. In later Hebrew the word means 'trapdoors'. 10 RSV adds *each story*, which makes better sense than 'the entire house was five cubits high'.

6:11-13 Yahweh's word concerning the Temple. Yahweh is more concerned with Solomon's 'walk'—his way of living—than with the details of the Temple. This section is not found in Chronicles. Some scholars think that it is a late insertion in Kings, too late to find a place in LXX.

6:14-22 The interior of the Temple. The passage is difficult, with repetition and little continuity. Montgomery thinks that there are two threads of the story. 15 *From the floor of the house to the rafters of the ceiling* follows LXX. 16 *Twenty cubits of the rear of the house* (AV 'on the sides of the house'); Gray, however, reads 'the innermost part of the shrine'. Again, *from the floor to the rafters* follows LXX. AV 'even for the oracle' is based on a misunderstanding of Hebrew *dᵉḇîr*, 'sanctuary, Holy of Holies'. 17 *The nave in front of the inner sanctuary*. The word usually translated 'temple' seems to mean here, as in v. 3, the interior portion in front of the Holy of Holies. 18 *In the form of gourds* (AV 'with knops', Gray 'relief work'). This verse is omitted in LXX. 19 *The inner sanctuary*: see v. 16. *The innermost part of the house*; AV 'the house within' is better. 20 seems to belong with v. 17. The Hebrew makes little sense and RSV *the inner sanctuary*, based on Vulg., seems more likely. Since the Holy of Holies was a cube (30 ft each way), the assumption is often made that its floor was raised above

the level of the floor of the main room before it. There is no statement to this effect, however. The height of the nave according to v. 2 was 30 cubits (45 ft). The last part of the verse contains two words that cannot be precisely defined; it may possibly mean 'he gilded it' [the holy place] with pure gold and 'he gilded an altar of cedar'; 21 similarly, 'Solomon gilded the inside of the house with pure gold'. The gilding could have been with liquid gold, but this is not proven. *Chains of gold*: the meaning is uncertain; Gray suggests 'the screen'. 22 is either repetitious, or perhaps a summary. The Hebrew reads literally, 'he gilded with gold until completion all the house, and all the altar which belongs to the Holy Place he gilded with gold'.

6:23-28 The cherubim. These cherubim are not to be confused with the cherubim of the mercy seat (Ex. 25:18-20). According to 2 Ch. 3:10-13 the cherubim were at the rear wall facing toward the curtain. Gray suggests that they may have stood diagonally at the inner corners facing out; but *cf.* v. 27. 23 It seems that v. 26 should be placed between the first and second parts of this verse. 26 The cherubim were 10 cubits (15 ft) high—in other words, half the height of the Holy of Holies—and the outstretched wings of the two cherubim spread from wall to wall and touched at the centre.

6:29-36 The interior walls, floor and entrance. 29 *In the inner and outer rooms*: the meaning is not certain. The Hebrew seems to say 'from the inside to the out', which would be more in agreement with AV 'within and without'. *Open flowers*: omitted in LXX; if it belongs here, the suggestion has been made that it might refer to garlands of flowers. 30 *The floor of the house*. Objection has been taken to the statement that the floor was covered with gold, but however unlikely it may seem, the Hebrew says clearly 'the floor of the house he gilded with gold within and without'. The latter part of the verse is even more difficult. RSV avoids the problem by reading *in the inner and outer rooms*. 31 The entrance to the Holy of Holies was fitted with *doors of olivewood*, lit. 'one of oil'. The second part of the sentence is incomprehensible: *the lintel and the doorposts formed a pentagon* (AV 'were a fifth part of the wall', MT 'a fifth'). It would appear that there was a curtain (2 Ch. 3:14) and the chains or screen (v. 21) as well as the door panels. 33 *The entrance to the nave*, or the room in front of the sanctuary, likewise was made of olivewood. *In the form of a square*: lit. 'from a fourth'. *The two leaves of the one door were folding*: the word means 'rolling', possibly on hinges, but more likely on some support that rolled on the floor to keep the doors from warping. If so, we are probably not to think of two folding-doors of two panels each, but of two large doors with two smaller doors inserted in them, or even two pairs of doors, an outer and an inner. 35 The doors likewise were gilded *with gold evenly applied*, whatever this may mean. The word translated *evenly applied* basically means 'made straight or even'. The suggestion has been made that the gold was inlaid, in other words, made even with the surface of the carved wood. Hezekiah cut off the gold to pay tribute to Sennacherib (2 Ki. 18:16). 36 *Three courses of hewn stone and one course of cedar beams*: probably to be understood, as Montgomery suggests, as the use of timbered masonry, which is used throughout the Middle East as protection against earthquake, the wooden beams serving to tie together the courses of masonry and to allow a bit of flexibility in the walls.

6:37 – 7:1 Summary of the time in building. 37 *Month*: the older word is used here, as it is the first time in v. 38. The second time a later word is used. Some scholars therefore feel that there has been an addition to v. 38. **38** *In all its parts, and according to all its specifications*: lit. 'in all its words and all its sentences', a graphic figure of speech. **7:1** *House*: probably referring to the entire complex of buildings to be described, occupying 13 years of building.

7:2–12 The House of the Forest of Lebanon and the other buildings. This section is not in 2 Chronicles. We must think of a large complex of buildings. To the N was the Temple and its court; S of the Temple, the royal palace and its court; behind it, the House of Pharaoh's daughter. S of the palace was the Hall of Pillars and the throne room, and farther S the House of the Forest of Lebanon. The whole area was enclosed within a great court surrounded by a wall of hewn stones and cedar beams.

2 *The House of the Forest of Lebanon* was obviously larger than the Temple (150 ft × 75 ft × 45 ft compared with 90 ft × 30 ft × 45 ft). *It was built upon three rows of cedar pillars* (Heb. 'four'); RSV follows LXX. **3** *Above the chambers that were upon the forty-five pillars*: it is not clear whether the Hebrew says 'forty-five pillars' or 'forty-five chambers'. **4** suggests that there may have been three rows of chambers. *Window frames*: possibly latticed, *cf.* 6:4. **5** *Windows* (Heb. 'posts'): possibly 'lintel'. **6** *The Hall of Pillars.* It is not clear just what is implied here; one suggestion is a vestibule portico. *Canopy* (AV 'thick beam'): possibly a cornice or some projection. **7** *From floor to rafters*: Heb. 'from floor to floor' makes little sense; AV reads 'from one side of the floor to the other'. The Hall apparently served for administering justice to those who came to the king in person. **8** *His own house*: mentioned only in passing. *In the other court back of the hall*: perhaps a parenthesis; Gray reads 'and his own house, where he was to dwell, the second court, was within the portico'. The *hall for Pharaoh's daughter* is mentioned but not further described. **9** *Stones . . . sawed with saws*: Palestinian limestone when first quarried is quite soft and hardens with exposure. *From the court of the house of the Lord* is reconstructed on the basis of v. 12; Heb. 'from the outside' makes little sense. **10** *Stones of eight and ten cubits*, probably referring to the length, 12 ft to 15 ft. Such huge stones are found

from Herodian times in Jerusalem; I have also seen them at Taht-i-Suleiman, N of Pasargade, Iran. It is interesting that Solomon's name is connected with them, although they obviously were in a construction of a much later date. **12** *Cf.* 6:36.

7:13–47 The work of Hiram. *Cf.* 2 Ki. 25:13ff.; 2 Ch. 4:11–18. We do no wrong if we admit that the Israelites were not skilled craftsmen. To get the workmanship he wants Solomon engages Hiram of Tyre (not the king, but a craftsman of the same name).

7:13, 14 The description of Hiram. 13 *Hiram*: in 2 Ch. 2:12, 13 and 4:16 he is called 'Huram-abi', the son of a Tyrian father and Israelite mother. **14** *Of the tribe of Naphtali*: 2 Ch. 2:14 says 'Dan', which was just beside Naphtali. *Wisdom, understanding, and skill*: the last word is literally 'knowledge', but all three have a practical connotation applying to the craft of Hiram. *Bronze* (AV 'brass'): Heb. can mean either 'copper' or 'bronze', but brass had not yet been invented.

7:15–22 The bronze pillars. 15 RSV has drawn on LXX and Je. 52:21; Heb. 'he fashioned two columns of copper, eighteen cubits the height of the one column and a line of twelve cubits going around the second column'. AV is closer to the Hebrew but has still taken liberties in translating. The meaning is clear enough: each column was 27 ft high, 18 ft in circumference (about 6 ft in diameter), and the thickness of the metal was 3 in., the centre being hollow. The columns would be quite thick for their height, and would not have the gracefulness of Greek columns. In 2 Ch. 3:15 they are described as 35 cubits high, which seems clearly to be erroneous. The casting of them was an art in itself, possibly the 'lost wax' method (see LaSor, *Daily Life in Bible Times*, 1966, p. 96). The columns seem to have been free-standing, serving as ornamentation rather than support. The use of free-standing columns in front of the Temple is attested in coins which were found at Sidon and on the sculpture which tells that the pillars before the Baal temple at Tyre held a fire which glowed at night. It has been suggested that the pillars in front of Solomon's Temple may have contained a sacred fire reminding the Israelites of the pillar of cloud by day and the pillar of fire by night of the wilderness period; but all suggestions are largely speculative. **16** *Molten bronze*: 'cast bronze' would be clearer. The capital was 5 cubits (7½ ft) high, making the column and capital approximately 34½ ft, which would seem to be higher than the Temple itself. We are not told, however, the thickness of the Temple's roof. **17** *Two nets of chequer work* is based on LXX; the Hebrew is problematical. *A net for the one capital, and a net for the other capital* is based on LXX: Heb. 'seven for one and seven for the other' differs by only one letter. **18** *Pomegranates*: Heb. 'pillars'. *Top of the pillar*: Heb. 'the top of the pomegranates'; it seems obvious that these two words have been transposed in the Hebrew text.

AV has followed the Hebrew. **19** *The pillars in the vestibule*: these have not been mentioned previously, and some scholars believe the verse was added as an afterthought. In LXX, vv. 19, 20 follow 21, and 22 is missing. **20** AV makes practically no sense, and RSV has considerable rewording; Heb. 'and capitals on the two columns also above in connection with the belly (or bulbous part) which was beyond (or opposite) the chequer work; and the pomegranates two hundred rows about upon the second crown (capital)'. Some reconstruction is obviously required to make this clear and meaningful. **21** *Jachin*: 'he establishes'; *Boaz*: 'in him is strength'. Numerous suggestions have been made concerning these names, but there seems to be no compelling reason for refusing to take them in their simple form. **22** *Lily-work*. This may have been suggested by v. 19, or that in turn may have been drawn from this statement.

7:23–26 The bronze sea. *Cf.* 2 Ch. 4:2–6. **23** *Molten sea*: the only place in the OT where the word 'sea' is used in a figurative sense. 15 ft in diameter and 7½ ft high, it was cast of copper or bronze. The circumference is only approximate; LXX reads '33 cubits', which is mathematically more inaccurate than the Hebrew. The shape of the sea is not given, but its contents may help us estimate it. **24** *Gourds* (AV 'knots'): probably some kind of open bud. *Thirty cubits* (Heb. 'ten', AV 'ten in a cubit'): but the peculiar Hebrew construction (used in chs. 6, 7) probably means 'by the cubit'. **26** *A handbreadth*: approximately 3 in., a sixth of a cubit. *Two thousand baths*: the size of the 'bath' is not certain, but it is generally taken to be about 4⅞ gallons, which would make the capacity just under 10,000 gallons. LXX transposes vv. 25 and 26.

7:27–37 The ten stands. **27** *Ten stands of bronze* is better than AV 'ten bases of brass'. *Four cubits*: each stand was about 6 ft square and 4½ ft high. Each of these stands had four wheels of about 27 in. in diameter (to judge from v. 32). For an illustration of the laver in bronze with wheels, see *NBD*, p. 1244, Fig. 205. This passage is full of highly technical details, and it seems to have been written by one who knew the craft well, but the explanation of each of these points is no longer clear. The movable lavers were for the distribution of water for purification (2 Ch. 4:6), and for cleaning the altar and the court.

7:38, 39 The ten lavers. The actual lavers are here described: each held 40 baths, or about 192 gallons—which is about three-quarters of a ton of water. Adding the weight of the bronze we can readily see that these lavers were not portable. If the lavers were semi-circular, 6 ft in diameter, fitting in the crown, on top of the stand which was already 4½ ft high, this would mean the stand and laver combination was about 7½ ft high. The height of the cast bronze sea, as well as the height of the lavers, was too great for anyone simply to walk up and use the water in them. We must therefore assume that there was some system, possibly a siphon, to get the water for use.

7:40–44 The pots, shovels, basins. *The pots* (AV 'lavers'): the Hebrew means 'lavers', except in 1 Sa. 2:14 where it refers to a cooking cauldron. LXX and Vulg., as well as 2 Ch. 4:11, indicate that the word used here originally was a cooking-pot.

7:45–47 The place of casting. **45** *Burnished bronze*: metal that has been scoured or polished to make it shine. **46** Recent excavations at Deir-'Allā, N of the river Jabbok (generally identified as Succoth), show that it was a centre of metallurgy; deposits of metal slag, furnaces, and part of a crucible with copper still in it have been found. The whole region extending N for several miles was a centre of metallurgy in the period of the Hebrew monarchy, probably because the clay was of the proper kind to make moulds and because the people through the generations had built up expertise in metallurgy. Charcoal could be made from the scrub oak growing in nearby Transjordan. The prevalent N wind down the Jordan valley would provide the proper draught for achieving the necessary temperature. The copper ore would have been brought from the hills E and W of the Arabah, in the S part of the Jordan rift.

7:48–50 The golden vessels. *Cf.* 2 Ch. 4:19 – 5:1. There is a noticeable contrast between the detail of the preceding section and the lack of detail in this. Other passages, such as 2 Ki. 12:13; 25:14ff.; Je. 52:18ff., do not indicate a quantity of gold such as is described here; nor are these vessels mentioned in the account of the gold furnishings in 1 Ki. 6:20ff. Hence many scholars are inclined to question whether this portion belongs with the original description. **48** *The golden altar*: not mentioned in 1 Ki. 6:20, unless the one made of cedar wood was covered with gold. It seems more likely that this was the altar of incense. *The bread of the Presence* (AV 'shewbread'): *i.e.* bread that was placed before the Lord. **49** *Lamp-stands*: 'candelabra' might be more accurate. 2 Ch. 4:20 does not specify ten of these. **50** *Cups* (AV 'bowls'): either translation is possible. *Dishes for incense* is more meaningful than AV 'censers'. *Sockets* (AV 'hinges'); it seems unlikely that the door-sockets in the floor and lintel would be of gold, hence some other part of the door may be intended. The word used here does not occur elsewhere in the OT.

7:51 David's offering. Apparently David had begun consecrating gold, silver and vessels for the 'house' he wanted to build for Yahweh (*cf.* 2 Sa. 8:11).

8:1–66 The dedication of the Temple

Cf. 2 Ch. 5:2 – 7:22; Josephus, *Ant.* viii.4. This portion is the heart of the first part of 1 Kings. A number of scholars see a great amount of scholarly editing here, but see remarks in Introduction.

8:1–11 Bringing the ark into the Temple. This passage is in much shorter form in LXX. When the ark is in the Temple, the Temple is filled with the cloud, the visible evidence of the glory of Yahweh. **2** *The month Ethanim*: the seventh month of the calendar which began with the spring equinox; later it was called Tishri, which came around the autumn equinox, or in the latter half of September. The principal feast was the Feast of Ingathering, or Tabernacles. According to 1 Ki. 6:38 the building of the Temple had been completed in the 8th month, *i.e.* 11 months earlier. Many scholars feel that the dedication was delayed so that it might come at the time of the New Year. (According to the calendar still in use, the beginning of the year fell on the first day of Tishri.) Some scholars hold that this was the occasion of the great festival marking the Kingship of Yahweh, but if this was indeed such an outstanding festival for the Israelites Scripture is remarkably silent about it. **6** *The inner sanctuary of the house*: here identified as the Holy of Holies, or the Most Holy Place; *cf.* 6:16. **8** *The ends of the poles were seen from the holy place*: this suggests possibly that the ark was placed crossways (N–S) within the holiest place, and that the veil before it was at a slight distance inside of the opening so that the staves could be seen on each side extending beyond the area obscured by the veil. **9** *There was nothing in the ark except the two tables of stone*: according to Heb. 9:4 the ark also contained Aaron's rod and a pot of manna. Some scholars think that Hebrews contains the tradition of a later time when these other items were present. This however is not the only solution to the difficulty, but it is best to admit that we do not know the precise answer. **10** *A cloud filled the house*: the presence of the Lord is symbolized visually as in the days of the Exodus (Ex. 14:19, 20) and the Tabernacle (Ex. 33:9). It would not seem that this cloud remained perpetually, for it is not mentioned again until Ezekiel in a vision saw the glory of God departing from the Temple (Ezk. 9:3; 10:4; 11:23).

8:12–21 Solomon's address to the people. *Cf.* 2 Ch. 6:1–11. This is generally called 'Deuteronomic', meaning after the time of Josiah (621 BC). In any view, Deuteronomy was influential in the religious life of the nation. It is as reasonable in our opinion to suppose that Moses was the originator of this spiritual resource as it is to suppose that some unnamed prophet in the 7th century was responsible for it. We see no compelling reason to reject the traditional view that David and Solomon, as well as other kings, were strongly influenced by the Mosaic traditions, whether these were in the present written form at that time or not. The 'address' is based partly on historical fact and partly on theological thought to show that the house was not necessary for the existence of Yahweh in Israel, but was His way of symbolizing for all to see the truth of His actual presence. The original dedication, according to LXX, was a song taken from the Book of Jashar. **12** *Hath set the sun in the heavens*: taken from LXX; according to Gray LXX is clearly a literal translation from the Hebrew original. **13** *An exalted house*: some would take the original word here to mean 'prince' and read it 'a royal house'.

8:22–53 Solomon's prayer of dedication. *Cf.* 2 Ch. 6:12–42. This is more than a prayer of dedication; it includes a prayer for the royal family, for the true significance of the Temple, and for national problems, such as defeat, drought and other calamities. There is also a prayer for the proselyte who comes to the faith of Israel from the outside, for the time of war, for captivity, and a conclusion. **22** *Stood*: Solomon is described as standing in prayer. Art from the Ancient Near East always indicates inferior standing and the superior seated. Thus kings are represented as standing before the sitting deity. *Altar* is mentioned here for the first time in the description of the Temple in Kings. See on 2 Ch. 4:1. **23** *Steadfast love* (AV 'mercy', Heb. *ḥeseḏ*): a very important word which means the situation that exists as a result of a covenant that has been made, and the obligations of the parties to that covenant. 'Covenant love' is a very good translation; 'grace' or 'mercy' would be acceptable only if the term is being applied to the members of the covenant. **25** Here the covenant with David is clearly in view. **8:27–30 To hear this prayer and all prayers. 27** The concept of divine omnipresence is considered by some to be a later addition, but the idea had to start sometime and somewhere. **8:31, 32 To condemn the guilty and vindicate the righteous. 32** *Righteousness*: in the sense of conformity with the accepted custom. **8:33–40 For the people in time of national calamity. 33** National calamities are regarded as the result of sin, certainly the prophetic concept. **37** *Blight*: blasting, the drying out of plants as the result of the hot wind from E or S. *Mildew:* the result of too much moisture in the spring. *Locust or caterpillar*: the various kinds of locusts are a continual plague to farmers in the Middle East. **8:41–43 For the foreigner in the land. 41** *Foreigner* (AV 'stranger', Heb. *noḵrî*): strictly those who are not Israelites who had come to worship Yahweh; the alien living in Israel was called *gēr*. **42** *Great name, . . . mighty hand, . . . outstretched arm*: obviously reminiscent of the deliverance from Egypt and Sinai (Dt. 4:34; etc.). **8:44, 45 For the people in war.** This portion and the following are generally said to be exilic additions, but certainly the history of the Ancient Middle East is a history of continuous warfare— and Solomon was enough of a realist to know that. **8:46–53 For return from captivity.** Again, an 'exilic addition'. But Hammurabi's law Code, among other documents that are much earlier than Solomon, speaks of redeeming captives and returning them to their own land. There is nothing in these verses so specifically exilic that we must date them in the Exile. **47** *We have sinned, and have acted perversely and wickedly.* Here are three Hebrew words for 'sin': the first, *ḥāṭā*, 'a failure, a missing of the mark'; the second, *'āwā*, 'iniquity', or 'the result of deliberate action'; the third, *rāšā*, 'not conforming to what is true, straying from the accepted norm'. In v. 50 yet another word is used, *pešā*, 'rebellion, revolt against God or His law'. **51** Here we see clearly the concept of *ḥeseḏ*, covenant love: even though these people have rebelled, Solomon presents them to God as *thy people, and thy heritage, which thou didst bring out of Egypt*, the people with whom God had entered into covenant by His grace. Therefore He was obligated to deal with them according to that gracious covenant. The NT equivalent is 'while we were yet helpless, at the right time Christ died for the ungodly'. **53** *Thou didst separate them from among all the peoples of the earth, to be thy heritage*: the election of the people of God, a theme which runs throughout the Bible and apart from which biblical theology is impossible. There is no reason whatever to say that here it means ritual separation.

8:54–61 The blessing. See on 2 Ch. 7:1 and *cf.* Josephus, *Ant.* viii.4.2, 3. Solomon blesses the assembly of Israel and calls on them to be wholly true to Yahweh. **54** *Where he had knelt.* We may assume that Solomon has fallen to his knees in the course of the intercessory prayer. At the beginning he was standing (v. 22). **59** *As each day requires* is better than AV 'as the matter shall require'; *cf.* 'Our daily bread' in the Lord's Prayer. **60** The purpose of election is clearly stated: *That all the peoples of the earth may know that the Lord is God* (*cf.* Gn. 12:3; 22:18).

8:62–64 The dedicatory sacrifice. *Cf.* 2 Ch. 7:4–10; Josephus, *Ant.* viii.4.4, 5. **63** Gray says, 'The numbers may be near the truth, though of course round numbers.' This was the beginning of the daily sacrifice which was offered for the sins of the nation as long as the Temple stood. It is replaced by the intercession of Christ which He makes daily for His people (Heb. 7:25).

8:65, 66 The feast. The seven-day feast was apparently held simultaneously throughout the kingdom, much as Passover is held today. **65** It was possibly the Feast of Tabernacles, often called *the feast*. *Entrance of Hamath*: at the S entrance to the valley between the Lebanon ranges, 100 miles N of Galilee, generally understood to be the Beqa' in what is now S Lebanon. *Brook of Egypt*: probably Wadi el-'arish in Sinai. *Seven days*: from LXX (Heb. 'seven days and seven days'); **66** indicates that LXX is correct.

9:1–28 Solomon's apogee

The description of Solomon is continued (*cf.* 3:1 – 4:34). The order is somewhat unstructured, and the story following of the visit of the queen of Sheba seems to interrupt the story of Solomon's commercial ventures.

9:1–9 Yahweh again appears to Solomon. *Cf.* 2 Ch. 7:11–22. The first appearance (3:3–14) was for Solomon; the second appearance is for Solomon's dynasty. The Davidic covenant is ever in view, and the kings will be known as 'David's sons', never as 'Solomon's sons'. **1** *All that Solomon desired to build*: AV 'all Solomon's desire' is, strictly speaking, closer to the Hebrew. The word *ḥešeq* is a strong word of physical attachment, affection, or love, and here would

seem to refer to Solomon's love for the Lord. **3** *I have consecrated.* The separation between the 'holy' and the 'profane' is meaningless when man-made, and has true significance only when God Himself declares a place or a person 'holy'. **4, 5** *If you will walk before me*: the covenant is in sight again; but it is always considered the covenant with *David*, the throne is always looked upon as David's throne, and the king as David's son. **8** RSV and AV fail to translate the Hebrew, which says 'this house shall be high'. Scholars feel that Old Latin and Syriac indicate a better reading; therefore RSV translates *will become a heap of ruins*. (For textual discussion, see Gray, *I and II Kings*, 1963, pp. 220, 222.)

9:10–14 Dealings with Hiram of Tyre. *Cf.* 2 Ch. 8:1, 2; Josephus, *Ant.* viii.6.4. This passage has caused much difficulty, particularly in the light of the parallel in Chronicles. **11** *Twenty cities*: Solomon gave these to Hiram probably because he had used up the available wealth of the country, hence needed a loan (*cf.* v. 14). *Galilee* (Heb. 'circuit', region') probably was merely part of a longer name, such as 'Galilee of the Gentiles'. Other areas also are called Galilee. **13** *The land of Cabul*: possibly a village 8 miles from Acre and 5 miles NW of the site of Jotapata, which agrees with the statement in Josephus, *Ant.* viii.5.3. A popular etymology has been suggested meaning 'like nothing', but this once-accepted explanation is now questioned. According to 2 Ch. 8:2 Hiram gave the land to Solomon, interpreted by some to mean that Hiram was displeased with it and returned it. **14** *Talent*: a unit of weight equalling 3,000 shekels, later 3,600 shekels. If the shekel was 0·4 oz the talent of gold would be worth $42,000 at $35 per ounce, and the whole sum about $5,000,000 (or about £2,000,000). There are other ways of figuring this which yield different results.

9:15–23 Details of the corvée. *Cf.* 2 Ch. 8:3–10; Josephus, *Ant.* viii.6.4. Read 1 Ki. 5:13–18. The non-Israelites were pressed into slave labour; the part the Israelites were forced to take is problematical: *cf.* v. 22. **15** *Account* is better than AV 'reason'. *Forced labour* (AV 'levy'): the corvée. *Millo*: probably part of the defence work for Jerusalem (*cf.* 11:27); the root of the word means 'fill'. *Hazor*: excavation shows that it was one of the most significant fortresses in N Galilee. *Megiddo*: also one of the most important fortifications, this one controlling a pass between the plains of Jezreel (Esdraelon) and Sharon. At both sites the fortifications are well built. **16** *Pharaoh*: not identified; one suggestion is Psusennis (JB). *Gezer*: scholars are inclined to read this as 'Gerar' (see on 3:1). **17** *Lower Beth-horon* controls one of the approaches to Jerusalem. **18** *Baalath*: identified by Josephus with Baalath in Dan (Jos. 19:44), SW of Beth-horon (Jos. 15:11). *Tamar in the wilderness*: MT 'Tadmor', and so 2 Ch. 8:4, which would be Palmyra in the Syrian desert; however this is not otherwise indicated in the OT. If we associate Baalath with Tamar in the S, then it may be one of the

Baalaths E of Beer-sheba (cf. Jos. 15:24–29). Tamar was one of the SE limits of the land (Ezk. 47:19; 48:28), possibly Hazazon–Tamar (Gn. 14:7) or the city of palms (Jdg. 1:16). The list follows geographical order if we take Baalath to be the one near Beth-horon and Tamar to be in the S. *In the land of Judah*: 'Judah' is added by RSV. **19** *In Lebanon*: some scholars feel these words have been inserted on the basis of 2 Ch. 8:6. **22** *But of the people of Israel Solomon made no slaves*: but *cf.* 5:13 and 11:28. Likewise the implication that they were the soldiers, the officials, *etc.*, must be harmonized with the presence of foreign mercenaries that were the backbone of David's army. *His captains* (Heb. *šālîš*, 'third-man'); *i.e.* third in the chariot besides the warrior and the charioteer, ultimately a man quite close to the king (2 Ki. 7:2, 17, 19).

9:24 Pharaoh's daughter's house and the Millo. *But Pharaoh's daughter . . .*: possibly we should read 'then' or 'only then', *cf.* 3:1–4. *Millo*: *cf.* v. 15.

9:25 Solomon's offerings. In view of the daily sacrifices, it is possible that we are to understand that Solomon himself served as priest on these three occasions. *Three times a year*: possibly the Feast of Unleavened Bread, the Feast of Weeks (seven weeks later), and the Feast of Tabernacles (in the autumn). *The altar*: *cf.* 8:22.

9:26–28 The Red Sea fleet. *Cf.* 2 Ch. 8:17, 18; Josephus, *Ant.* viii.6.4. **26** *King Solomon built*: we assume that Phoenician shipbuilders actually constructed these ships (*cf.* v. 27). **28** *Ophir*: the location is not clearly identified. Possibilities are S Arabia, the coast of the Red Sea known as Punt, the ruins of Zimbabwe in E Africa, or possibly India. S Arabia is perhaps the favourite choice of scholars. *Four hundred and twenty talents*: by the method used in 9:14 this would be more than $17 million or £7,000,000 (LXX '120', and 2 Ch. 8:18 '450').

10:1–29 The visit of the queen of Sheba

Cf. 2 Ch. 9:1–9, 12; Josephus, *Ant.* viii.6.5f. Scholars now agree that the visit was probably historical. The Sabaean kingdom flourished from about 900 to 450 BC. A number of queens of the 8th and 7th centuries are listed in Assyrian inscriptions. It is not certain whether *Sheba* refers to the kingdom in the S part of the Arabian Peninsula or to some of its outposts in the N part of Arabia. A reasonable cause for the visit of the queen can be found in Solomon's control of the head of the Gulf of Aqabah (hence of the route that would cross from Arabia to Egypt) and in the sea trade that he had inaugurated, which would seriously threaten the caravan trade that had made the S Arabian kingdoms great. The excuse for her visit, of course, would be her desire to see the famous king.

10:1–5 The queen and her retinue. 1 *Hard questions*: probably riddles or tests of practical sagacity. **4** *Wisdom*: practical wisdom, administrative sagacity. **5** *His burnt offerings which he offered* (AV 'his ascent by which he went up'); the verse is difficult. Some scholars believe that this is a reference to the great royal processional. At any rate it was the climax of all of the other splendid things that she witnessed. *There was no more spirit in her*: Montgomery suggests 'she was left breathless'.

10:6–10 Her words and gifts to Solomon. 7 *Your wisdom and prosperity surpass the report*: lit. 'you have added wisdom and goodness to the fame that I heard'. **8** *Happy are your wives* (RSV, LXX, Syr.) seems to be the much more likely reading, particularly coming from a woman; *cf.* MT and AV 'happy are thy men'. **9** is an echo of the Davidic covenant, and is almost Messianic in its statement (*cf.* Pss. 2; 110; Is. 9:6, 7; 11:1–5). **10** *A hundred and twenty talents*: *cf.* 9:14. *Spices*: S Arabia is famous for these.

10:11, 12 The wealth brought by the fleet. *Cf.* 2 Ch. 9:10,11; Josephus, *Ant.* viii.7.1. This seems to break into the story of the visit of the queen of Sheba (in the parallel in Chronicles, exactly the same thing is found). **11** *Almug wood*, elsewhere in the OT 'algum' (*cf.* 2 Ch. 2:8): sandalwood is often suggested; other suggestions are pine, amber, and red coral. **12** It was made into supporting beams, lyres and harps. *Supports*: 'steps' is probably meant. In Chronicles it is terraces (AV).

10:13 Solomon's gifts to the queen. According to ancient tradition, the queen also took back with her a child begotten by Solomon from whom the emperor of Ethiopia traces his direct lineage, but of this Scripture knows nothing, recording only that he gave (lit., see RV mg.) 'according to the hand of king Solomon', *i.e.* in a way commensurate with the resources of such a king.

10:14–25 Solomon's great wealth. *Cf.* 2 Ch. 9:13–24; Josephus, *Ant.* viii. 7.2, 3. **14** *Six hundred and sixty-six talents of gold*: about $28 million or over £11,000,000 (*cf.* 9:14). Most commentators consider this to be incredibly high, and it does not include the revenue specified in v. 15. **15** *Traders*: LXX reads 'taxes of the merchants', which seems to be most likely, and requires only a very minor emendation of a Hebrew word. Taxation on goods passing through the country or through the trade-routes controlled by the country was always a large item. Pliny said that wares from India when they reached Rome were 100 times the original cost. The Aramaeans or Syrians in these states became strong and powerful because they dominated the desert trade-routes. *Kings of Arabia*: MT 'kings of mixed people' is probably to be emended with several versions and 2 Ch. 9:14. **16** *Shields of beaten gold*: the gold was either made into shields, or the shields were covered or inlaid with gold; in either case it was a sort of a royal treasury. *Six hundred shekels of gold* (MT omits 'shekels'): about 15 lb., or about $8,400 or £3,500 (*cf.* 2 Ch. 9:15, 16). **17** *Shields*: small shields, probably circular. *Three minas*: a mina was 60 shekels, about 24 oz;

a shield weighed about 5 lb. and was worth about $2,500 or £1,000. **18** *Ivory throne*: probably made of wood with large ivory inlays; the gold was either inlaid in the ivory, or *overlaid* on the rest of the wood. **19** *At the back of the throne was a calf's head*: based on LXX with a change of vowels in the Hebrew word (AV 'the top of the throne was round behind'). For 'calf's head' 2 Ch. 9:18 has 'footstool', but this word differs only in one letter from a word meaning 'lamb'. Originally, therefore, both texts may have referred to the lamb or calf decoration. **22** *Ships of Tarshish*: usually identified with Tartessos, a Phoenician settlement in Spain. However, the suggestion has been made that this word is formed on the root *ršš*, 'to refine', and means something like 'metal refinery' (Albright), thus these would be ships that are connected with refineries and mines. At any rate the term indicates a type of ship and not its destination. There is no reason to suppose that the ships went through the Red Sea and circumnavigated Africa to reach Spain. (See *NBD*, art. 'Tarshish'.) *Ivory*: lit. 'elephant's tooth'. *Apes, and peacocks*: the suggestion that this should be translated 'apes and baboons' has merit. Josephus reads 'ivory, Ethiopians, and apes' (*Ant*. viii.7.2) which suggests that the Heb. was *sukkiyyîm*, 'negroes', rather than *tukiyyîm*, 'apes', but this has no support in the versions.

10:26–29 Solomon's commercial ventures. *Cf.* 2 Ch. 1:16; 9:25–28; Josephus, *Ant*. viii.7.3, 4. Solomon dealt in the import and export of horses and chariots, but the exact details are not clear. We assume that he served as a 'middleman'. **26** The figures are not incredible. *Horsemen*: probably to be read 'horses'. **28** *Egypt*: many scholars take this to refer to Musri, later Cappadocia, N of the Taurus mountains. *Kue* (AV 'linen yarn'): there seems to be no doubt that a place often mentioned in Assyrian records and elsewhere is intended, approximately the same as Cilicia, S of the Taurus mountains. Wood for the building of chariots also would be found on the slopes of the Taurus mountains, which makes the story self-consistent. **29** *Egypt*: again probably Musri; if so, Egypt is not mentioned here at all, but the account is limited to Syria and the Hittite territory. The end of v. 29 is rather meaningless in AV; Montgomery suggests 'making export through their agency', and Gray 'the kings of the Hittites and the kings of the Aramaeans got them by exports through them'.

11:1–43 Solomon's decline

Cf. Josephus, *Ant*. viii.7.5–8. This portion is omitted in Chronicles, which, according to some scholars, is due to the unwillingness of the Chronicler to tell anything unfavourable about the kings of Judah. LXX seems to be more objective than MT, but possibly this is due to editorial work.

11:1–8 Solomon's foreign wives and his idolatry. Many of Solomon's marriages were doubtless marriage-alliances, a type of foreign diplomacy practised in antiquity, and Solomon was obliged to honour the religious convictions of his wives and to provide for their various kinds of worship. **2** Foreign marriages seem to be the point of criticism rather than having many wives. **3** *Seven hundred . . . three hundred*: cf. Ct. 6:8, 'sixty queens and eighty concubines, and maidens without number'; many scholars think the figures in 1 Kings are hyperbole. David had 15 wives (1 Ch. 3:1ff.), Jeroboam had 18 wives and 60 concubines (2 Ch. 11:21), Abijah had 14 wives (2 Ch. 13:21). On the other hand, Chosroes II had between 3,000 and 12,000 concubines, and Sultan Mulay Ismail is reported to have had 2,000 wives and 800 concubines. **4** *Wholly true to the Lord*: Heb. probably 'at one with', or 'at peace with the Lord'. **5** *Ashtoreth*: deliberately misvocalized from 'Ashtart' on the basis of the word *bōšeṭ*, 'shame'. The Canaanite fertility goddess was Ashtart (Gk. Astarte). *Milcom* and *Chemosh* (v. 7) were the national gods of the Ammonites and Moabites, and we may assume that Ashtart was the female counterpart. *Goddess*: in OT there is no word for 'goddess'; MT says 'the god of the Sidonians'. **7** *The abomination of Moab*; LXX 'the god of Moab'; likewise, the god of the Ammonites. *The mountain east of Jerusalem*: the Mount of Olives; in 2 Ki. 23:13, 'the mount of corruption'; in 2 Ch. 28:3 this is located in the valley of Hinnom, which is S of Jerusalem.

11:9–13 Yahweh's judgment on Solomon. Again the covenant with David is brought into view. The kingdom is to be torn away from Solomon, **12** but not in his lifetime, **13** nor entirely. The Davidic dynasty and city will both continue. *One tribe*: the tribe of Judah, possibly absorbing Simeon; the OT always refers to ten tribes in the northern kingdom and one in the southern kingdom. Although Ahijah tore the cloak into twelve strips of which ten were to be for the northern kingdom, only one was to remain for the Davidic throne (see 11:32).

11:14–22 The revolt of Hadad of Edom. This is a summary statement not necessarily in chronological order. The revolt of Hadad occurred early in Solomon's reign (*cf.* v. 21). This passage has numerous difficulties, as the study of LXX will quickly show. **14** *Adversary*: Heb. *śāṭān*, which later becomes the name of the principal adversary (see on 5:4). On the use of Satan as a proper name, *cf.* 1 Ch. 21:1. *Hadad the Edomite*: Syria ('Aram') in v. 25 seems to be a mistake due to a miswritten letter. Some scholars find two sources, but *ICC*, following Kittel and Stade, rejects such source-analysis. For this name of an Edomite king, see Gn. 36:31–39. **15** There is no mention of this anywhere else in the OT. *Every male in Edom*: as usual with this type of expression this is hyperbole and not to be pressed literally, as the next verses indicate. In this passage the name is sometimes spelt 'Hadad' and sometimes 'Adad'; this is no reason for considering the original to be two different accounts of two different persons. **17** *A little child*: Heb. more like 'a young boy', or 'a little youth'. **18** *Midian*: if this was E of the Gulf of Aqabah it occasions a minor difficulty. We should work with the possibility that Midian was E of the head of the Gulf of Aqabah; in other words, E of Ezion-geber. *Paran*: sometimes identified with Wadi Feiran near Mt. Sinai (see Glueck in *BASOR*, 71, 1938, p. 7). **19** *Tahpenes*: believed to be an Egyptian title meaning 'the wife of the king', in which case 'the queen' is an attempted translation or explanation. *Queen*: Heb. 'lady'.

11:23–25 The revolt of Rezon of Damascus. Not only was the S part of the land stripped away by Hadad's revolt; the Aramaean region dominated by Damascus also rebelled. Solomon's kingdom is being whittled away. **23** *Rezon*: the rise of Rezon followed the defeat of Zobah (2 Sa. 8:3). **24** He became the head of a group of bandits, succeeded in capturing Damascus, and was a source of irritation and opposition during Solomon's reign. **25** *Syria*: 'Aram' is to be emended to 'Edom'. This verse would be a summary for both of the preceding accounts.

11:26–40 Jeroboam ben Nebat and Ahijah. There are numerous textual problems. Moreover, in order to account for the events that follow, we must assume that Jeroboam was involved in a serious plot that forced him to flee the country and at the same time gained him considerable reputation with the northern tribes, so that later they would turn to him for leadership. This may have been an attempt on his part to gain advantage for the northern tribes through the position that he occupied. **26** *Son of Nebat*: Nebat was deceased; Jeroboam's mother is described as *a widow*. *Zeruah* means 'leper'; names such as this were sometimes given to ward off evil spirits. **27** introduces the reason for the revolt as well as the time, which was after the building of the Millo, therefore 20 years or more after the beginning of Solomon's reign. **28** *Very able* (AV 'a mighty man of valour'): both miss the point. He was a man of property, doubtless inherited, and therefore had obligations to the crown. He was also energetic, or *industrious*; hence Solomon put him in charge of the public burdens (RSV *forced labour*, but not the corvée). *The house of Joseph*: this may refer to Ephraim and Manasseh rather than all of the northern tribes; Nebat was an Ephraimite. According to LXX, Jeroboam built a city in the hill country of Ephraim, raised a force of 300 chariots, fortified the city, and aspired to the kingdom. This would certainly fit the statement in v. 26. JB, however, translates: 'Solomon was building the Millo . . .; noticing how the young man set about his work, (he) put him in charge of all the forced labour of the House of Joseph.' **29** *Ahijah the Shilonite*: he was from Shiloh, where the ark had been (*cf.* 1 Sa. 4:3, 4). LXX adds 'he turned aside from the road'. **30** *Tore it into twelve pieces*: see on vv. 9–13. Gray thinks that Simeon remained with the northern tribes, indicated by a pilgrimage from the north to Beer-sheba (Am. 5:5) and by other shrines in

Simeon (Am. 7:9), and that Benjamin adhered to Judah. Most of Benjamin, however, was in Israel. **32** *One tribe*: LXX and Vulg. read 'two', but this is obviously an attempt to make the total come out to twelve. The rule of 'the more difficult reading' supports MT at this point. **34** *Ruler*: AV 'prince' is better. Montgomery thinks that this is a limitation on the authority of Solomon who had already been the glorious king. Other scholars emend the text to agree with LXX 'I will forbear with him.' **37** *King over Israel*: 'Israel' is used here with reference to the northern tribes, since one tribe is to remain in the Davidic line at Jerusalem (v. 36). **38** *If you will hearken*: note the conditional covenant with Jeroboam. *Will build you a sure house*: but this was to be as discipline for the house of David, and not a replacement for it. **39** *But not for ever*: it was to be limited; the Davidic covenant was not. **40** *Jeroboam arose, and fled*: as a result of the attempted coup. *Shishak*: the first historical name that can be identified in the Bible. He is generally identified with Sheshonq I, founder of the Libyan XXIInd Dynasty, 945–924 BC.

11:41–43 The death of Solomon. The formula is introduced that will regularly be used of each of the kings. **41** *The book of the acts of Solomon*: otherwise unknown. It seems to stand in the series of official records later called by the general name 'the Book of the Chronicles of the Kings of Israel (or Judah)'. **42** *Forty years*: possibly a round number, but certainly not far from the actual length of reign. Solomon's reign is dated *c.* 970–931 BC. **43** *Rehoboam*: the form of this name comes from Greek rather than from Hebrew, hence the theory that 'Jeroboam' was a name deliberately made on the form of 'Rehoboam' carries no weight.

12:1 – 14:31 THE DIVISION OF THE KINGDOM

This period of history can be divided into three parts: *a.* from Jeroboam to Omri in the north and from Rehoboam to Asa in the south, a time of mutual hostility; *b.* under Ahab, Ahaziah, and Joram in Israel, and Jehoshaphat, Joram, and Ahaziah in Judah, a time of friendship due to a marriage-alliance; *c.* from Jehu of Israel and Joash of Judah to the fall of Samaria in Israel, a time of hostility.

12:1–24 Rehoboam succeeds Solomon

Cf. 2 Ch. 10; Josephus, *Ant.* viii.8.1–3. The text here is somewhat difficult and it offers a number of problems. It would seem that v. 2 should be read before v. 1, in agreement with the material in LXX, Vulg., and 2 Ch. 10:2. The plan throughout this section is to carry the story through the reign of one king to his death, and then return and pick up the story of his contemporary kings in the other kingdom (see Introduction).

12:1–5 Rehoboam seeks coronation by northern tribes. The purpose of going to Shechem was to be recognized as king by the northern tribes.

This deep-seated division of the kingdom is found in the days of Saul, who was chosen by lot from a northern tribe (1 Sa. 10:21) and, it would seem, chosen by both Israel and Judah at Gilgal (1 Sa. 11:15; *cf.* 11:8). Likewise David was chosen king of Judah (2 Sa. 2:4) and only after 7½ years did he become the leader of Israel (2 Sa. 5:3ff.). It would be unthinkable for Rehoboam to have been made king of Judah at Shechem, which subsequently became the first capital of the north (1 Ki. 12:25). Rehoboam was about 41 when he was crowned (*cf.* 1 Ki. 14:21). **2** *Jeroboam returned from Egypt* (RSV, LXX, Vulg., 2 Ch. 10:2), but MT, AV 'Jeroboam dwelt in Egypt'. **3** *Jeroboam*: the sentence makes better sense if this name is omitted. *All the assembly of Israel*: the northern tribes. Rehoboam would surely have been crowned at Jerusalem. **4** *Yoke*: used elsewhere concerning the subjugation of a foreign nation; the burden of taxation and enforced labour had been far more serious than we usually recognize. Rehoboam could still have held the north, probably, with wisdom such as the elders had given him.

12:6–11 Rehoboam accepts advice of young men rather than seeking the wisdom of the elders. 8 *The young men who had grown up with him*: men about his own age, around 40. The word translated 'young men' literally means 'children': probably a derogatory statement. **10** *My little finger*: LXX, Vulg. and Syriac, a good paraphrase; MT and 2 Ch. 10:10 'my littleness'. **11** *Scorpions*: a whip with barbed points.

12:12–15 Rehoboam's reply to the northern tribes. The reply is anything but diplomatic. It is difficult to understand his logic in this plan of action. At any rate, it fails utterly. **12** *Jeroboam*: some scholars would delete the name Jeroboam with LXX; Gray puts this verse between 13 and 14. **15** The religious interpretation of the event is added: *the Lord* makes use of such events to accomplish His will. Modern historians reject such attempts to probe into the divine mind—but this is the essence of faith.

12:16–20 The revolt of the northern tribes. Israel, feeling shut out of Rehoboam's planned government, withdraws. We get some idea of the extent of democracy that was present in the 'monarchy' of Israel. **16** *To your tents*: an idiom meaning 'Let's go home!'; the northern tribes are here withdrawing from the house of David (*cf.* 2 Sa. 20:1). **17**, which is not in LXX, is difficult to understand. It may refer to Israelites who had preferred to move into Judah, or possibly— perhaps even more probably—Israelites of Benjamin who were therefore northerners but who lived in and around Jerusalem. **18** *Adoram*: probably the Adoniram of 1 Ki. 4:6 and 5:14 who had been in charge of forced labour and was therefore the worst possible representative that Rehoboam could have sent. **19** *Has been in rebellion*: a good illustration of the primary meaning of the word which is often used for 'sin' in the sense of rebellion against the known will of God (*cf.* Am. 1). *To this day*: this was written

before the destruction of the northern kingdom, *i.e.* before 722 BC. **20** *Made him king over all Israel*: Jeroboam, it would seem, had just returned from Egypt and was called to the assembly and made king. There must have been sufficient antecedent events to account for such action. If vv. 3 and 12 are correct in MT, then Jeroboam was already in on the events at Shechem, but that makes v. 20 meaningless. *The tribe of Judah only*: LXX adds 'and Benjamin', but this would require reconstructing the last clause for the singular 'tribe', and the word 'only' would be out of place. The inclusion of Benjamin in v. 21 may indicate that Judah used force on the neighbour to the north, or the word may have been a later addition.

12:21–24 Rehoboam's plan for war averted. *Cf.* 2 Ch. 11:1–4. This paragraph will have to be understood against other clear-cut statements. According to these verses Rehoboam is going to attempt to force the northern tribes back into his kingdom by war, and the prophet Shemaiah talks him out of it. But according to 1 Ki. 14:30, there was continuous warfare between the north and the south through all of his reign. **21** *A hundred and eighty thousand chosen warriors*: this figure seems far too high and the emendation '18,000' has been suggested. LXX has '120,000', which would still be too high. **22** *Shemaiah*: appears only here and in 2 Ch. 11:1–4; 12:5–8, 15. **24** LXX has a long passage after this verse with no counterpart in MT, but with many statements that are parallel to other passages in MT.

12:25–33 Jeroboam consolidates the northern tribes

12:25 Jeroboam builds Shechem. He locates the first capital of the northern kingdom in a strategic place, geographically and religiously. Its religious ties, however, were not only with the patriarchs but also with the Canaanites, who had a cult shrine there before Abraham came to the place. *Built*: so MT; but actually he rebuilt it and fortified it to make it his capital. *Shechem*: just E of the modern town of Nablus, between Mt. Ebal and Mt. Gerizim. *Ephraim*: the whole region was known as 'Ephraim', although strictly Shechem was in the boundary of Manasseh. *Penuel*: in Transjordan at the ford of the Jabbok. This may have been an attempt to keep the Transjordan areas from Rehoboam, or it may have been connected with the invasion of Sheshonq (Shishak) who mentions Penuel on the inscription telling of this campaign, but there is no OT record of this.

12:26–28 Jeroboam's plan against Jerusalem. The motivation seems to have been political rather than religious. Jeroboam was not willing to give the people occasion to come under the influence of the Jerusalem kings. **28** *Two calves of gold*: Albright has argued that these were not representations of Yahweh but simply the pedestals upon which the invisible Yahweh stood, thus corresponding to the winged cherubim in Solomon's Temple. However, v. 28 seems to have a polytheistic view. The Hebrew word translated *your gods* could be translated in the singular as it is elsewhere, but the verb here is also plural. Some scholars take this statement to be the original and Ex. 32:4, 8 as a later account which changed the plural to singular. But the Exodus passage also has plural verbs. Albright's position therefore is not to be hastily rejected.

12:29–33 The golden calves in Bethel and Dan. Again we see strategy in Jeroboam's plan. In effect, he has 'sacralized' the borders of the country, and at the same time planted one shrine on the pilgrim's road to Jerusalem. **29** *Bethel*: 11 miles N of Jerusalem in Ephraim, on the main road of pilgrims going to Jerusalem. *Dan*, in the extreme N, at one of the sources of the Jordan river where there was already a Canaanite shrine. **30** RSV follows LXX; MT is translated in AV and is less meaningful. **31** *High places*: Jeroboam is also charged with establishing worship on high places and appointing priests who were not from the Levites. *All the people* (AV 'the lowest of the people'): more accurately 'the mass' or 'the whole range of the people'. **32** *Eighth month*: possibly Jeroboam also changed the date of the Feast of Ingathering from the seventh month. Some scholars, however, feel that Jeroboam was not the innovator, but that the religious innovations were made in Jerusalem (see the pertinent remarks of Montgomery in *ICC*, p. 256). Gray thinks the festival is the New Year's festival. He assumes that Rehoboam became king of Judah at the New Year's festival at Jerusalem and a day or two later appeared at Shechem for the same purpose, and that Jeroboam established the same festival a month later for his own coronation. But the OT says far less about the New Year's festival than the scholars do!

13:1–32 Jeroboam consecrates priests (*cf.* 12:31)

13:1–10 The man of God rejects Jeroboam· This is sometimes looked upon as a midrash from a later period inserted at this point. On the other hand the introduction of the miraculous fits the biblical pattern whereby the miraculous is part of a significant event at the beginning of a new period. **1** *A man of God*: the title used in this story for the prophet from Judea, whereas 'prophet' is used for the northern prophet. *By the word of the Lord*: lit. 'in the word of the Lord', the 'word' possibly being the compelling power. **2** *Josiah by name*: predictive prophecy in the OT is generally by principle and not by specific detail; only Josiah and Cyrus are mentioned by name. Therefore many scholars, including some staunch conservatives, insist that the names are later additions. Keil, seeking to get around this problem, suggests that the meaning of the name, 'he whom Yahweh supports', was the prophecy, and this was fulfilled afterwards in the name. His argument is less convincing when we apply it to the name Cyrus.

13:11–32 The old prophet in Bethel and the man of God. This is a difficult passage, and there is

much disagreement among commentators. The 'prophet' who gives the 'man of God' a false message is later used by Yahweh to declare His word. The man of God is killed by a lion because he listened to the lying message of the prophet. **11** *Sons*: Hebrew is singular here, but plural in the following verse. **12** *His sons showed him the way*: MT 'his sons saw'; LXX and Vulg. suggest the reading found in RSV. **18** *A prophet*: the prophet includes the man of God in the prophetic title. *But he lied to him*: some feel this is a later addition to the story. Keil does not agree; on the other hand he refuses to look upon the old prophet as a false prophet. The prophet used sinful means and the false pretence that he had been directed by an angel in order to have a closer relation to the man of God in Judah. The story however centres on the man of God and his disobedience. Gray suggests that the local prophet sought to enhance his own prestige. **20** *Table*: at that period tables were found only in the houses of the very rich, or the royalty. Here it would probably be a leather mat spread on the ground. **21** *Thus says the Lord*: if we are to assume that the prophet was a false or lying prophet, then God has broken through to use him even as He did Balaam. **22** *Your body shall not come to the tomb*: meaning that he would die a violent death away from home and not be buried in the grave of his fathers. **23** *Prophet*: the only place in the story where this word is used with reference to the man of God except in the prophet's words (v. 18). The suggestion has been made that a prophet might be a false prophet, but a man of God is always a man of God. **24** *Lion*: lions of a small breed were known in the Middle East and did not become extinct until about the 12th century AD. **29** *Brought it back to the city*: RSV is based on LXX; MT 'he came to the city of the old prophet' makes sense but is awkward; AV mistranslates. **32** seems to have been added later when Samaria was the capital and the cities were known as *cities of Samaria*.

13:33 – 14:20 Conclusion of Jeroboam's reign

This resumes the story interrupted at 12:31.

13:33, 34 Jeroboam consecrates priests. 34 *Sin*: 'to miss the mark'; possibly 'failure' would be better here, but since it definitely involved Jeroboam's relationship to God 'sin' can be used.

14:1–18 The death of Jeroboam's son. Lacking in LXX, but fragments are found in the extra passage in LXX 12:24*a-n*. Abijah is seriously ill, and Jeroboam sends his wife to inquire from Ahijah the prophet whether the boy will live. The prophet foretells not only the death of the son, but also the end of Jeroboam's dynasty. **3** *Some cakes* (AV 'cracknels'): possibly cakes with seeds sprinkled on the top. **5** The punctuation at end of verse in RSV is better than in AV. **9** *Provoking me to anger*: an emotion often ascribed to God in the Bible, which modern scholars attempt to explain away. By way of reply Snaith (*IB*) says, 'This modern idea with its tendency toward deism does not do justice to the biblical idea of a definite and personal opposition to sin which is evident everywhere on the part of God.' **10** *Every male*: Hebrew literally translated in AV. *Both bond and free*: in Hebrew two words which are not precisely clear, but the general sense is conveyed better by RSV than by AV. *Will utterly consume the house*: RSV again carries the meaning better than AV. The prophecy foretells the end of the dynasty of Jeroboam which was fulfilled in the death of his son Nadab. The details of the prophecy indicate that there will be a violent overthrow of the dynasty. **14** *And henceforth*: the end of the verse is difficult. Keil supports AV. RSV, following a suggestion by Kittel, makes sense but has no MS or version support. **15** *The Euphrates*: lit. 'the river', but generally used of the Euphrates. Some scholars therefore assume that this was added to the text after the fall of Samaria. *Asherim*: wooden poles at a Canaanite shrine, not 'groves' (AV). **17** *Tirzah*: the first mention of this place, which became the capital of northern Israel in the time of Baasha (1 Ki. 15:21).

14:19, 20 Summary of the reign of Jeroboam I. For the stylized formula concerning the rest of his acts and reference to the Book of the Chronicles of the Kings of Israel, *etc.*, see Introduction. Jeroboam's reign can be dated c. 931–910 BC.

14:21–31 Conclusion of Rehoboam's reign over Judah

Normally the author tells the story of a king from beginning to end, and then picks up his contemporaries in the opposite kingdom. Here, the story of Rehoboam, begun in 12:1–24, is interrupted by the story of Jeroboam, which also is interrupted. Rehoboam's reign can be dated c. 931–913 BC.

14:21–24 Judah's evil practices. *Cf.* 2 Ch. 11:5 – 12:16; Josephus, *Ant.* viii.10. **21** For the formula that will be used for each of the kings of Judah, see Introduction. **22** *Judah*: LXX 'Rehoboam', but 'like king like people'. **23** *High places . . . pillars . . . Asherim*: elements of Canaanite religion. **24** *Male cult prostitutes*: AV 'sodomites' misses the point. Heb. q^e*dāšîm* 'ones set apart' includes men and women set apart for religious cult prostitution. This is also the word for 'holy', meaning 'set apart (for Yahweh's service)'.

14:25–28 Shishak's invasion of Judah. *Cf.* 11:40. Shishak used the division into two kingdoms as an opportunity to move into the land. His inscription in Karnak lists about 150 places that he 'captured'—in most cases this word probably means that he took tribute from them. The tribute that he took from Rehoboam is mentioned in v. 26. Albright proposes 940–920 BC for Shishak's reign.

14:29–31 Summary of the reign of Rehoboam. 30 *War*: probably a state of cold war, with the building of border fortifications but without open warfare. **31** *Abijam*: the versions read 'Abijah'.

15:1 – 16:28 THE WARS BETWEEN ISRAEL AND JUDAH

This is a period of warfare between the two kingdoms, and then it degenerates into a series of civil wars in the northern kingdom. Five kings of Israel (and a sixth contender) are included, while in Judah there are only the brief reign of Abijam and the long reign of Asa.

15:1–8 Abijam of Judah

Cf. 2 Ch. 13; Josephus, *Ant.* viii.11.2, 3. Abijam is 'tolerated' for David's sake. This theme we shall find often, until there seem to be only two persons in view: David, and David's ideal son who is never realized until Jesus is born. **1** *In the eighteenth year of King Jeroboam*: the first of the synchronisms; every king is dated in similar fashion (see Introduction). Abijam's reign can be dated c. 913–910 BC. **2** *Abishalom*: usually identified with Absalom the son of David; hence Maacah was David's granddaughter. In 2 Ch. 13:2 she is called 'Micaiah the daughter of Uriel'. If we assume that 'Micaiah' is a mistaken reading for 'Maacah', then we may suppose that Tamar the daughter of Absalom married Uriel (so Josephus, *Ant.* viii.10.1). **3** *True*: Heb. šālēm, basically 'wholeness' or 'integrity' and then 'peace'. We might translate 'his heart was not at peace with the Lord his God' (*cf.* 11:4). **4** Notice again the reference to the Davidic covenant. **6** *Rehoboam*: *cf.* v. 7. V. 6 makes no sense in this account of Abijam. LXX omits the verse. **7** *Book of the Chronicles of the Kings of Judah*: this is not the canonical book of Chronicles, since the biblical book also quotes this book on the war between Jeroboam and Abijah (*cf.* 2 Ch. 13:3–20); see Introduction.

15:9–24 Asa of Judah

Cf. 2 Ch. 14–16; Josephus, *Ant.* viii.12. Asa is a reformer, removing the cult prostitutes and idols. He is also responsible for the introduction of a foreign alliance, bribing the king of Damascus to attack Israel which in turn causes Israel to take the pressure off Judah. It is possible that there had been a previous agreement between Judah and Syria, but Israel had moved her S boundary closer to Jerusalem.

15:9–15 Asa's reforms. Judah, as well as Israel, assimilated Canaanite cult practices, and had done so since the days of Solomon, at least. Probably there was a popular level of worship that was always inclined to accept such idolatries. Asa attempts to remove these from Judah. His reign can be dated c. 910–870 BC. **10** *Maacah*: Asa's mother's name is the same as that of Abijam's mother, hence some have supposed that he was Abijam's brother. Others suggest that Maacah was Asa's grandmother, the queen mother (v. 13). Asa instituted sweeping religious reforms including the removal of the queen mother. **13** *Abominable image* (lit. 'shocking', or 'frightful'); Vulg. takes this as a phallic symbol, but there is no other support for this view. *Queen mother* (Heb. 'lady'). The word for 'queen' is used of the queen of Sheba, of Queen Esther, Queen Vashti, and twice in the plural (Ct. 6:8, 9); it is never used of the individual queens of Israel and Judah. *Kidron*: the valley between Jerusalem and the Mount of Olives. **14** *The high places*: Keil labours to show that these were not devoted to idols but were unlawful altars to Yahweh. In the prophets, however, we find the people carrying on idolatrous practices at the high places, so there is little point in trying to explain them away. Canaanite sin and idolatry pervaded all levels of the Israelite people except those few stalwart kings and prophets whom the Lord used for His purposes. *Wholly true*: see on 15:3.

15:16–22 War with Baasha of Israel. *Cf.* 2 Ch. 15:19 – 16:10. This is really a continuation of the war that had been started by Rehoboam against Jeroboam. It was often a 'cold war', but certainly at times it was more than that. Possibly Abijam had previously pushed north (2 Ch. 13:19), in which case Baasha is now regaining lost territory. He builds a fortress just N of Jerusalem, after persuading Ben-hadad of Damascus to break his treaty with Baasha and invade the northern part of Israel. This is the first time we meet the Aramaean city-states, which will play an important part in the history of Israel. Foreign allegiance will become the bane of kings as reflected in the prophets (*cf.* Is. 7:4–9; 8:6–8, *etc.*). **17** *Ramah*: about 4 miles N of Jerusalem. **18** *Ben-hadad*: Hadad was the chief god of the Aramaean pantheon, the Storm god, or Thunderer. *Tabrimmon*: Ramman or Rimmon is another name of the same god, and the compound name Hadad–Rimmon is also found (Zc. 12:11). *Hezion*: the suggestion that this should read 'Rezon' (11:23, 24) seems to be no longer valid (*cf.* Albright in *BASOR*, 87, 1942, pp. 23ff.). **20** *Ijon, Dan, . . .*: the places mentioned are all in the extreme north of Israel, principally in the upper Jordan valley. **21** *Tirzah*: several miles NE of Shechem, identified as Tell Fara', and apparently established as the capital by Baasha (v. 33). **22** *Proclamation*: an extraordinary levy or corvée in order to destroy the fortifications at Ramah and build others for King Asa at Geba. *Geba*: some believe this is Gibeah, but the name Geba (one of the forms of the word meaning 'hill') can be applied to a number of sites.

15:23, 24 Summary of the reign of Asa. 23 *Diseased in his feet*: some have supposed this was dropsy. **24** *David his father*: the use of 'father' and 'son' in connection with the name of David is to be noted.

15:25–32 Nadab of Israel

Cf. Josephus, *Ant.* viii.11.4. Nadab is noteworthy for destroying the house of Jeroboam. **25** Nadab actually reigned less than *two years*, as a comparison of vv. 25 and 33 will show. His reign may be dated *c.* 910–909 BC. According to one system of reckoning, if a king started to

reign before the New Year and continued to reign into the new year, he reigned 'two years'.

15:27–30 Baasha's conspiracy. 27 *Baasha the son of Ahijah*: Ahijah is described as from the house of Issachar, distinguishing him from Ahijah the Shilonite (v. 29). *Gibbethon*: a Philistine city E of Ekron in the original territory of Dan; Nadab was strong enough to attempt to extend his borders westward. **29** *He killed all the house of Jeroboam*: the end of the first northern dynasty fulfils Ahijah's prophecy (14:10). **32** *War between Asa and Baasha*: *cf.* 14:30; 15:7, 16.

15:33 – 16:7 Baasha of Israel

Cf. Josephus, *Ant.* viii.12.3, 4. Asa and Baasha both had long and nearly simultaneous reigns, Asa's being about 14 years longer. Hence, most of the details of Baasha's reign have already been told in the account of Asa.

15:33, 34 Introductory statement. See Introduction for format. **33** *In the third year*: see on v. 25. The reign of Baasha may be dated *c.* 909–886 BC.

16:1–4 Yahweh's word to Jehu concerning Baasha. Jehu ben Hanani was an obscure prophet, cited as author of a history incorporated in 'the Book of the Kings of Israel' (2 Ch. 20:34) in the days of Jehoshaphat of Judah (2 Ch. 19:2), which would have been more than 50 years after the present oracle. His prophecy is remarkably like that which Ahijah uttered against Jeroboam (14:7–11), but this in itself is not sufficient reason to reject either account.

16:5–7 Summary of Baasha's reign. 7 seems superfluous; some scholars hold that vv. 2–4 are an editorial rewrite of the prophecy against Jeroboam and assume that v. 7 is the only original statement on the subject.

16:8–14 Elah of Israel

The record of Elah is interrupted by the account of Zimri's conspiracy. **8** *Two years*: the son of Baasha reigned less than two years, since he came to the throne in the 26th year of Asa (v. 8), and died in the 27th year of Asa (v. 10). The reign of Elah may be dated *c.* 886–885 BC. **9** *Drinking himself drunk*: it seems that Elah's reign was in trouble from the first. **10** *Zimri*, whose father's name is not even mentioned, was commander of half of the chariotry; this suggests a division in the military. **11** *He did not leave him a single male of his kinsmen*: according to Snaith (*IB*), this was to make it impossible for any male relative to act as the *gō'ēl*. **12, 13** This is taken as fulfilment of Jehu's prophecy against the house of Baasha.

16:15–20 Zimri of Israel

The state of affairs in Israel was very bad, and there were factions among the people as well as rivals for the throne, Zimri, Tibni and Omri being named. **15** *Zimri reigned seven days*: Israel was again engaged in war against Gibbethon (*cf.* 15:27) and when news came that Zimri had killed the king, troops in the field made Omri, the commander in the army, king over Israel. But there was also Tibni (v. 21). **17** *They besieged Tirzah*: Zimri had seized the capital and Omri marched against it at once. **18** *He went into the citadel . . . and burned the king's house over him*: Zimri must have recognized at once that he did not have power to take control, so he died by his own hand after 'reigning' 7 days. His reign was probably in 884 BC.

16:21-28 Omri of Israel

Omri was perhaps the most important of all the kings of Israel, from the standpoint of secular history: this should give us some idea of the viewpoint of 'holy history'. Omri's capital, Samaria, gave its name to the country for ever after. Omri is the only Israelite king named in the Mesha Inscription, which records afflictions by his sons, but names only Omri. Jehu the usurper was known to the Assyrians as 'the son of Omri' (see on 2 Ki. 9:2). A century after Omri's dynasty had fallen, some Assyrian inscriptions still referred to his land as 'the house of Omri'.

16:21, 22 The struggle with Tibni for the throne. *Cf.* Josephus, *Ant.* viii.12.5. The statement that *all Israel made Omri king* (v. 16), as is so often the case with statements including the word 'all', must be read in the light of other passages. **21** makes it clear that the people of Israel were not entirely behind Omri, half of them followed Tibni and wanted to make him king. **22** gives no indication of the time, and we might suppose that the struggle between the followers of Omri and the followers of Tibni was brief. Zimri, who reigned only 7 days, came to the throne in the 27th year of Asa (*c.* 884; v. 15) and Omri did not come to the throne until the 31st year of Asa (*c.* 880; v. 23). This suggests that there were 4 years of civil war. One MS of LXX states that 'Zimri reigned 7 years', but this does not fit the other chronology, nor does it fit the description in v. 17, which indicates a very quick end to Zimri's coup.

16:23, 24 The founding of Samaria. Omri moved the capital of Israel to Samaria, a hill about 8 miles NW of Shechem, rising about 300 ft above the surrounding plain. Excavations have uncovered the walls of his palace. **23** *Reigned for twelve years*: this must include the years of civil war, *six years . . . in Tirzah* (of which only two were truly regnal).

16:25-28 Summary of Omri's reign. Omri's reign may be dated *c.* 880–874 BC. **25** *Did more evil than all who were before him*: this is Scripture's measure of Omri. **26** Religiously, he was worse than Jeroboam, and other than the fact that he founded the capital at Samaria, that is about all that is told of him. The revolt of Mesha, king of Moab, is recorded in 2 Ki. 3:4ff., but there is nothing about the oppression of Moab by Omri and his sons, which lasted 40 years according to the Mesha Inscription. Micah refers to 'the statutes of Omri' (Mi. 6:16), suggesting that he must have had some kind of legal

reform, but we know nothing further about them.

1 Ki. 16:29 – 2 Ki. 1:18 AHAB AND ELIJAH

The story of Ahab is broken up by the interweaving of the story of Elijah, and only concludes at 22:40. In some ways the conflict between Ahab and Jezebel on the one hand and Elijah on the other is the crucial hour for Yahwism. The king and queen would wipe it from the face of the earth; only Elijah is able to stem the tide.

16:29-34 Ahab of Israel

Cf. Josephus, *Ant.* viii.12.1 – 13.1. Ahab was guilty of two great sins: he walked in the sins of Jeroboam, and he married Jezebel the daughter of Ethbaal the king of Sidon and a very zealous promoter of Baal worship (v. 31). Their daughter Athaliah for a period usurped the throne of Judah. According to Josephus (*Contra Apion* i.18.8), the granddaughter of Ethbaal was Dido, who founded Carthage. Ethbaal is identified by Josephus as a priest of Astarte.

29 *The thirty-eighth year of Asa*: Ahab is the seventh king of Israel since Asa came to the throne of Judah. Ahab's reign can be dated *c.* 874–853 BC. **34** *Hiel of Bethel*: LXX 'Ahiel', probably the full form of the name. The meaning of this verse is much debated; according to the Targum, Hiel sacrificed his oldest son when he built the place and his younger son when he set up the doors. Some scholars look upon these as 'foundation sacrifices'; others reject this idea rather strenuously. It is possible that some simple tragedy happened to these two sons, but since there was a curse on the rebuilding of Jericho (Jos. 6:26) the deaths would be considered as the result of this curse. The formulaic conclusion of the record of the king's reign is not found until 22:39, 40. Most of the intervening chapters are given over to accounts of the prophet Elijah.

17:1 – 19:21 Introduction of the Elijah cycle

The term 'Elijah cycle' has no particular critical significance; it simply is a convenient way to refer to the portion of Kings that tells of Elijah the prophet. Elijah, who is to the prophets as Moses is to the law, is presented to us without introduction other than that he is called 'Elijah the Tishbite'. Yet it is obvious that there must have been quite a history of his activities before the event in 17:1. Ahab called him the 'troubler of Israel' (18:17). Obadiah, the household steward of Ahab, refers to the fact that they had sought out Elijah everywhere (18:10). The reputation of mysterious disappearances is hinted at in 18:12. Certainly there had to be an anterior reputation for Elijah to create such an effect upon Ahab, particularly for Ahab to take seriously the prophecy of drought in 17:1. It would seem that Elijah was connected in some way with the schools of the prophets which we find in Bethel, Jericho and Gilgal (2 Ki. 2:3–5; 4:38). One measure of his stature is to be found in the fact that he was the man raised up by God at the time that Baal worship threatened the very existence of the worship of Yahweh in Israel. His place in the NT also underscores his importance. The forerunner of the Christ was to come in the spirit and power of Elijah (Lk. 1:17). Moses and Elijah, as representatives of the law and the prophets, stood with Jesus on the Mount of Transfiguration (Mt. 17:3; Lk. 9:31). The description of the works of the two olive trees in Rev. 11:4ff. clearly relates them to Moses, who had the power to turn water into blood and to smite the earth with all kinds of plagues, and Elijah, who had the power to shut heaven that it rained not in the days of his prophecy. Skinner says of Elijah, 'He is to be ranked as the greatest religious personality that had been raised up since Moses' (*CB*, p. 222).

17:1–7 Elijah and the ravens. Miracles in the OT are not commonplace, and therefore they are not simply the product of the imagination. They occurred only at those extremely important periods of history when the very power of God was needed in order to maintain His people and their testimony: *e.g.*, to deliver them from the bondage of Egypt, or to give them the land of Canaan, or to preserve the true faith in the presence of the efforts of Jezebel to destroy the knowledge of Yahweh.

1 *Tishbe*: based on LXX. The Hebrew consonants could be vocalized this way, but MT 'of the settlers' is followed by AV. *Gilead*: according to tradition Elijah came from Tishbe in Naphtali (Tobit 1:2) and settled in Gilead in Transjordan. If this tradition is true—it is almost unanimously rejected today—it is remarkable that in the days of Jesus those who searched the scriptures said 'out of Galilee arises no prophet'. *Neither dew nor rain*: Josephus (*Ant.* viii.13.2) records that according to Menander there was a full year's drought in the time of Ethbaal, father of Jezebel. **3** *The brook Cherith*: traditionally identified with Wadi Qelt near Jericho; but the following words indicate that it was in Transjordan. **4** *Ravens*: some scholars have attempted to read this as 'Arabians' (which has the same consonants as the Heb. word for 'ravens'), but the tendency today is to leave the story as it is and accept it as the faith of Israel, even if not the faith of modern rationalists. Gray accepts the reading 'Arabs', feeling it fits the context better since the second part of the story is in Phoenicia.

17:8–16 Elijah and the widow of Zarephath. Elijah is sent by Yahweh to Zarephath near Sidon, where he is fed by a widow. The request of Elijah that the widow take her last bit of meal and oil and give it to him for food is not an act of selfishness on Elijah's part, but a test of the woman's faith. To judge from her oath in v. 12 it would seem that she was a worshipper of Yahweh, even though a Gentile. **9** *Sidon*: one of the chief cities of Phoenicia, located on the coast N of Galilee, in what today is Lebanon. Elijah was keeping out of the territory of Ahab. *Zarephath*:

identified with the modern Sarafand, some 8 or 9 miles S of Sidon on the Mediterranean coast. **12** *Jar* is certainly to be preferred to AV 'barrel'. **14** The miracle followed, in that the meal (flour) and oil never ran out for the 'many days' of the drought. Gray suggests that the generosity of the widow touched the conscience of her better-provided neighbours. Christ refers to this event in Lk. 4:25f.

17:17–24 Elijah raises the widow's son. 17 *No breath left in him*: it has been questioned whether the son was dead or merely near to death. He appeared to be dead to his mother (v. 18), and to Elijah (v. 20). The expression 'no breath left' in Hebrew would imply death. Modern medical ability to restore life after complete heart-stoppage makes us slow to give a positive answer, but we are dealing with a situation long before modern medical knowledge. **18** *What have you against me*: the Hebrew expression would appear to be the same as that used by Jesus to Mary at Cana (Jn. 2:4). The widow felt that the presence of the man of God had brought to light some sin of hers which was the reason for the death of her son. **19** *Upper chamber*: probably a room on the roof with an outside stairway. Gray says, 'Removal of the invalid was a matter of simple hygiene.' **21** *He stretched himself upon the child three times*. We miss the point if we feel that this manipulation of the son by Elijah was a means of resuscitating him; at the same time we recognize that the same technique is mentioned in two other cases (2 Ki. 4:34f.; Acts 20:10). The exact significance we do not understand. **22** *The soul*. We must be careful not to attempt to build a doctrine on this passage such as the idea that the soul leaves the body at death or the soul returns to the body at resuscitation. While this idea may be true, the Hebrew word means 'life' rather than 'soul'; the concept of the soul is not clearly found in the OT. **24** This is a remarkable statement of faith on the part of the woman, but we ask ourselves whether its value ended there. There is no indication that she spread this faith to her own people, and since she was not in Israel she could not convey it to the Israelites. The telling of the story by Elijah himself might lack conviction in the absence of witnesses. So perhaps its greatest value was in strengthening the faith of Elijah, who several times appears to need such spiritual help. *The word of the Lord in your mouth is truth*: better 'the word of the Lord is really in your mouth' (Moff.).

18:1–19 Elijah is sent to Ahab. 1 *In the third year*: according to the customary way of counting time this could have been at the end of two years; the NT, however, indicates a drought of 3½ years (Lk. 4:25; Jas. 5:17). It is possible that Keil is right in referring v. 1 to the period of time that Elijah was with the widow at Zarephath, to which would be added the length of time he was in the wadi Cherith. **3** *Obadiah*: not the prophet by that name, but the steward of Ahab's household (see on 1 Ki. 4:6), described as a God-fearing man who had protected the prophets of

Yahweh when Jezebel was seeking to exterminate them. **4** *Prophets of the Lord*, possibly the 'sons of the prophets' or the 'school of prophets'; but we should be slow to accept many of the fantastic suggestions made about such men. They have little place in the OT and therefore little place in OT religion (*cf.* 1 Sa. 10:5–13; 2 Ki. 2:3–5). *Cave*: Montgomery says the word is generic and translates 'cave region'. Mt. Carmel abounds in caves, over 2,000 having been counted. **5** *The horses*: Shalmaneser III refers to 2,000 horses furnished by Ahab at the time of the Syrian coalition. We therefore can imagine the strain put on the resources of the land in time of famine.

7 *Obadiah recognized him.* There is no indication that they had met before and some have supposed that it was Elijah's dress or appearance that identified him. However, Obadiah's question seems to have been, 'Is it really you?' which would suggest a previous meeting. **9** Montgomery takes this as only a generous excuse: Obadiah was thinking of the prophet's safety. **12** *Spirit*: the Hebrew word can mean 'wind' or 'spirit'. We should be slow to insist that it means spiritual levitation. If Obadiah had in mind a strong wind he still thought of it as coming from the Lord; hence the miraculous element is still present. **13** *Jezebel killed the prophets*: obviously there were originally more than the 100 that Obadiah had saved. **15** *The Lord of hosts*: the first occurrence of this name in Kings. Various meanings have been suggested for 'hosts': the armies of heaven (planets, stars, *etc.*), the armies of angels, natural forces, the armies of Israel, or the limitless resources of the divine nature. Gray says the reference is undoubtedly to the armies of Israel, for the first occurrence is in the account of the Philistine wars (1 Sa. 17:45, which, he holds, was written before 1 Sa. 1:3). To Gray the title expresses the intimate link between the Lord and His people. The genitive *of hosts* is, however, strictly impossible as a translation of the Hebrew, which really requires either that *Lord* and *hosts* are nouns in apposition to each other, thus signifying that the Lord possesses in Himself every possible potency, or else that the expression is abbreviated from *Lord* (God of) *hosts*, with one of the above meanings. (See *NBD*, p. 480a, sect. *h*.)

17 *You troubler of Israel*: *cf.* Jos. 6:18; 7:24f. **18** Elijah throws the words back in Ahab's teeth. *You have forsaken the commandments of the Lord*: LXX omits 'the commandments', making this much stronger, 'You have forsaken Yahweh.' *The Baals* (AV 'Baalim', the Heb. plural of Baal). The local Baals were shrines, or manifestations of one Baal, and older works that spoke about 'many Baals' are now discredited. Baal was the principal god of the Canaanite religion, a nature-religion that used ritual prostitution as a kind of sympathetic magic to achieve the fertility of the ground. Heb. *ba'al* means 'master', or 'husband'; *be'ûlāh* applied to the land of Canaan was 'the land that was married'. In Canaanite

eyes, Baal both owned and fertilized the land. Beulah, however, came to have a more glorious meaning (*cf.* Is. 62:4; see *NBD*, art. 'Beulah'). Carmel was one of the heights on which were located places of worship to Baal, and in choosing this Elijah moved into Baal's own home territory for the contest. **19** *All Israel*: obviously hyperbole. There would doubtless have been representatives from each of the tribes; but it is nothing short of folly to suppose that everyone left their homes and climbed Mt. Carmel for this event. *Mount Carmel*: a prominent mountain ridge rising to an elevation of about 1,800 ft and jutting into the Mediterranean just below the Bay of Haifa. There is a Carmelite monastery dedicated to Elijah and a grotto at the western end, but this cannot be the location of Elijah's miracle. Probably the ruins of El-Muḥraqa, which is one of the highest points of Mt. Carmel, and toward its SE end, is the location. *Prophets of Baal*: lit. 'the Baal', always used with a definite article in Hebrew, although this has not been preserved in English translation. *Four hundred prophets of Asherah.* Some scholars believe that this is an intrusion into the text, since they are not part of the account later. Keil suggests that they found a way of evading the command and simply did not show up. LXX interpolates this in v. 22, probably to harmonize it with v. 19. Since the sign of the definite direct object is lacking from the second clause it is tempting to suppose the text originally read 'the 450 prophets of Baal even 450 prophets of Asherah who eat at Jezebel's table'; the word 'fifty' is lacking in the second part of the sentence. Since Asherah was Baal's consort, as is clear from Ugaritic materials, this would not be an impossible statement.

18:20–40 Elijah and the prophets of Baal on Carmel. The contest with the prophets of Baal on Mt. Carmel is one of the most dramatic stories in the OT. Historically, we could say that it saved Yahweh-worship in Israel. In view of the subsequent marriage-alliance between Israel and Judah, we might even extend this to say that the knowledge of the Lord in both Israel and Judah could have been wiped out for ever if the Lord had not raised up Elijah at this moment. The contest was not to demonstrate which of two gods was greater, but to demonstrate which was the true God and the other no god at all.

20 *Ahab sent to all the people*: indicating the awe that he must have had for Elijah. **21** *How long will you go limping with two different opinions?* This was possibly a popular expression of the day, lost to us now. It seems to be literally, 'Till when are you hopping at two forks?' The sin of the people had been not in rejecting the worship of Yahweh, but in trying to combine it with the worship of Baal. Such syncretism is always considered to be broad-minded, whereas the other is narrow-minded. But Yahweh of Israel left no room for other gods. Elijah makes this clear: *If Yahweh is God, follow him; but if*

Baal, then follow him. **26** *From morning until noon.* The scene seems to be rather calm up to this point, but there is no answer, and the prophets of Baal carry on their ritual around the altar. **27** This is rather strong language. Montgomery says, 'Elijah's satire in a nutshell is the raciest comment ever made on pagan mythology.' *For he is a god*: this is irony; if he is a god, he should be able to hear. *Gone aside*: a euphemism, 'He has left the room'. *He is on a journey*: Rashi takes this to mean 'to the privy'. For a nature god, these gross references to the natural are quite to the point, but it is better to retain 'journey' in the plain sense as a joke at a so-called god who was now here now there. **29** *The time of the offering of the oblation*: probably about 3 p.m. The prophets of Baal put on a frenzied ritual between noon and that time, but there was still no answer.

30 *He repaired the altar of Yahweh that had been thrown down.* Keil supposes that there had been an altar built by the worshippers of Yahweh on Carmel, but the author of Kings seems elsewhere to be opposed to altars on high places; and if indeed Elijah has moved into Baal's own territory here, then we must rethink this whole matter. In LXX, vv. 31, 32a are in the middle of v. 30. V. 32a and v. 30b seem to be mutually incompatible. The ritual that follows has no efficacy in itself. Possibly Elijah is mimicking the prophets of Baal. Certainly he is making it obvious that if Yahweh is to answer it must be a genuine miracle and not a false miracle. **32** *Two measures of seed*: about 5 gallons. If this refers to the capacity of the trench it is hardly enough. If it refers to the amount of ground that that amount of seed would sow, as older commentators suggested, it seems to be far too much. We are content to admit ignorance at this point. **33, 34** Obviously 12 jars of water were enough to soak the wood, wet the ground around the altar, and fill the trench.

36 *At the time of the offering of the oblation*: see on v. 29. It is possible that Elijah was already constructing the altar to Yahweh during the closing, frenzied part of the ritual of the Baal prophets. The subsequent events require sufficient time left in the day to slaughter the prophets of Baal, to go back to the top of Carmel and look for the cloud, and to rush down to the foot of the mountain and race about 17 miles to Ahab's summer capital at Jezreel. *God of Abraham, Isaac, and Israel*: it is interesting that Elijah used 'Israel' instead of 'Jacob', possibly implying a rebuke to the northern kingdom for considering itself to be Israel. **37** Elijah's prayer is in line with his original challenge, that they may know that Yahweh is the true God. *Turned their hearts back*: a debated statement, some believing that it means God restored their hearts to the original faith; others that He was the original one to turn their hearts away or harden them because of their own sins. This is not the place to solve this problem. **38** *Then the fire of the Lord fell*: the effect on the people, of course,

was profound (v. 39). Saint Yves suggests that there was some pyrophoric preparation used in building the altar that reacted when water was poured on it to ignite the fire. A more common suggestion is that the response came by lightning. Gray says, 'We believe that what actually happened was that the clouds appeared and massed as a result of Elijah's prayer in vv. 36, 37, 42ff.; then the lightning, which ignited his sacrifice.' As Rowley points out, the sky was cloudless. He goes on to point out that no man could produce lightning at will from a cloudless sky or from any sky; no man can direct the fall of lightning to any object he wishes. The suggestion that Elijah poured naphtha, which he obtained from a nearby source, on the altar and that he used a magnifying lens to focus the sun's rays and ignite the fire, is clearly ridiculous, and is only the frenzied attempt to hold on to the Bible without having the faith to believe it. Rowley well says, 'That something remarkable happened is overwhelmingly sure. . . . If the story we are examining today is dismissed as a fabrication, then either the whole story of the reign of Ahab as well as the story of Elijah must be dismissed or the defeat of the prophets of Baal is left without explanation' ('Elijah on Mt. Carmel', *BJRL*, 43, 1961, pp. 269ff.). **40** *And killed them.* The slaughter of the prophets of Baal had possibly two significant meanings: it was retribution for Jezebel's attempt to slaughter the prophets of Yahweh; at the same time it was the fulfilment of the law which pronounced death on false prophets (Dt. 7:2f.; 13:13ff.).

18:41–46 Yahweh sends rain to end the drought. Having demonstrated conclusively that Yahweh and not Baal is God, Elijah is now ready to call upon God for the rain. Until this first effect is demonstrated there would of course remain the possibility that Baal was responsible for the rain. **43** Sending his servant to the top of Mt. Carmel *seven times* was probably not intended as a ritual, but simply a detail of the story. **44** *Go up*: this expression is difficult to understand. Possibly it is a figure of speech, recognizing the higher position of a king. Elijah's faith that the small cloud would develop into a great rainstorm is obvious in his words to Ahab. **46** *Ran before Ahab.* It has been suggested that this was the act of a loyal servant, the 'outrunner' (*cf.* 1 Ki. 1:5), and the public testimony that he was indeed the king's true servant, seeking not to oppose the king but to win the king to worship Yahweh. On the question of whether it would be possible to run that distance (about 17 miles), Paul W. Harrison reports that Arab runners in the desert can cover 100 miles in less than two days. The biblical text makes it clear that Elijah was able to do this because *the hand of the Lord* was on him; in other words, he was granted supernatural power and stamina.

19:1–3 Jezebel and Elijah. Immediately following his triumph over the prophets of Baal Elijah seems to fall into deep depression. Jezebel's threat on his life can hardly be the entire

cause. **3** *Then he was afraid* follows LXX and
Syr.; MT, with different vowels, reads 'when he
saw' (so AV). Keil, refusing to admit that Elijah
was afraid, reads 'when he saw how it was, he
went for his life'. Keil takes this as not to save
his life but to care for his soul. Both of these
seem to avoid the obvious meaning that Elijah
was just plain afraid. *Beer-sheba*: the S limit of
Judah, where Elijah left his servant, possibly
because he did not expect to return.
    19:4–8 Elijah flees to Horeb. Utterly despon-
dent, it would seem, Elijah asks Yahweh to end
his life. **4** *A broom tree*: common to the wadis
in the desert, sometimes growing to a height of
10 ft. *It is enough*: Keil supposes that Elijah was
already of great age, but this is without textual
warrant. **5** *An angel*: omitted in LXX, but without reason in the light of v. 7. **6** The meal seems
to have been miraculous not only in its source
but also in its sustaining power, for Elijah went
on for 40 days and 40 nights. **7** *The angel of the
Lord*: possibly the second Person of the Godhead
is intended, as in the theophanies in Genesis
(Gn. 16:7). However, the article may simply
refer to the angel previously mentioned, and
Keil apparently so takes it. **8** *Horeb*: traditionally
another name for Sinai. Some scholars find two
separate traditions and two separate places
intended. The distance from Beer-sheba to Horeb
is only 200 to 300 miles, depending on the route,
and should not require 40 days. The figure may
be symbolic, or it may be that Elijah was making
no sustained march to Horeb.
    19:9–18 The still small voice. 9 *A cave*: lit.
'the cave'. Since the story is reminiscent of
Moses' experience at Sinai, it is possible that this
means the identical 'hole in the rock' where
Yahweh appeared to Moses (Ex. 33:21ff.). *What
are you doing here, Elijah?* Is this a rebuke, or
is Yahweh simply giving Elijah an occasion to
express his feeling? If the latter, **10** his reply is
one of despair, or possibly even a rebuke that
Yahweh has allowed such things to happen.
These verses occasion some difficulty and it has
been suggested that the first part of v. 11 does
not belong here, or possibly even that vv. 9a–11a
should be omitted. If the first part of v. 11 is
omitted, then we assume that Elijah was standing
in the cave while the following events took place,
and this is what v. 13 suggests. **11** The appearance
of Yahweh is in part a reply to the unvoiced
criticism of Elijah. The wind, the earthquake
and the fire were modes that Yahweh used on
occasion; certainly this was according to Elijah's
nature, but on this occasion the Lord was not
in them. **12** *A still small voice*: this expression is
beautiful and has become classical. The Hebrew
is even more picturesque: 'the sound of gentle
quietness', or even 'gentle silence'. **13** Elijah of
course covered his face at the presence of the
Lord. Gray notes that although the significance
of the still, small voice has been taken to be the
revelation that the violent measures taken at
Carmel were not the methods of Yahweh, the
commission to anoint Hazael and Jehu to execute

the purpose of Yahweh by violent means does
not support this interpretation. Yahweh's word
is stern, designed to overthrow kingdoms. **13b, 14**
are a repetition of vv. 9b, 10, but this is probably
intentional. **15** *The wilderness of Damascus*: the
Syrian desert. Elijah's implied rebuke of Yahweh's inactivity is answered by the still, small
voice and the events it foretells, specifically vv. 16,
17. God is slow to anger, but He does not contain
His wrath for ever. **15, 16** *Anoint Hazael . . . Jehu
. . . Elisha*. It has often been pointed out that
these details were not carried out literally.
Elijah did not anoint either Hazael or Jehu;
these commands were carried out by Elisha and
then only figuratively in the case of Hazael, and
by secondary command in the case of Jehu (2 Ki.
9:1), nor did Elijah literally anoint Elisha. The
term 'anoint' implies a call for a special purpose,
whether there is an actual ceremony of anointing
or not. It is unnecessary either to put the Horeb
experience at the end of Elijah's life or to claim
that the actual commission was a 'pious fiction'
in order to justify the high-handed methods of
Elisha. **17** *Him who escapes . . . shall Elisha slay*:
again, the statement is not to be taken literally
(*cf.* 2 Ki. 2:24). **18** *I will leave*: RSV is definitely
to be preferred to AV 'I have left'. This was a
statement concerning the future; after the punishments of v. 17 there would still be a remnant in
Israel.
    19:19–21 Elijah casts his mantle over Elisha.
Elisha understood the act to mean that he was
to follow Elijah. The response of Elijah probably
is meant to indicate that the call is not from the
prophet but from Yahweh. Elisha is identified
only as 'the son of Shaphat'. The place is not
indicated. **19** *Ploughing with twelve yoke of oxen
before him, and he was with the twelfth*: probably
to be understood to mean that his workmen were
ploughing with the other eleven yoke (*cf.* Lk.
14:19). *Cast his mantle upon him*: instead of
anointing him, Elijah performed this symbolic
act, **20** the meaning of which must have been
understood immediately by Elisha in the light
of his reply. **21** Elisha served a farewell dinner
and then became Elijah's servant. *And ministered
to him*: *cf.* Ex. 24:13, where Joshua is called the
minister (AV) or servant (RSV) of Moses. Elisha
does not appear again until 2 Ki. 2:1.

20:1–43 Ahab's wars with Syria

Cf. Josephus, *Ant.* viii.14. We leave the Elijah
cycle for a while and resume the story of Ahab.
If this chapter is in chronological order we
assume that Yahweh is manifesting His grace
to Ahab for the sake of Israel. The dating of this
chapter is a problem. The battle of Qarqar
occurred in 853 BC; at that time Ahab was allied
with Damascus and nine other Aramaean city-
kingdoms against Shalmaneser III of Assyria.
According to Shalmaneser's inscription (D. D.
Luckenbill, *Ancient Records of Assyria and
Babylonia*, 1927, I, §610f.) Ahab had 2,000
chariots and 10,000 infantry; the total forces of
the allies were 3,940 chariots, 1,900 horsemen,

1,000 camels, 62,900 infantry. Ahab was fatally wounded fighting against the king of Damascus at Ramoth-gilead *c.* 852 BC. It would seem that the victories over Ben-hadad of Syria were several years earlier and that the treaty with Ben-hadad (20:34) was a step toward a coalition against the Assyrians. After the battle of Qarqar we assume that Israel and Damascus were again at war.

20:1-6 The demand of Ben-hadad. It is not clear just what is implied in this paragraph, but possibly the first statement is a declaration that Ahab is considered to be a vassal of Ben-hadad, and the second a demand for delivery of the persons and the wealth. **1** *Ben-hadad:* that this Ben-hadad is the same as the one who warred against Baasha (15:18ff.) is possible but unlikely. 'Ben-hadad' may of course have been a common title of the king who was a 'son of Hadad', their national god. *King of Syria:* the Syrians (or Aramaeans) never formed a great kingdom, but were a coalition of city-kingdoms, or city-states. Ben-hadad formed an alliance with 32 of these kings, a figure which is not unreasonable, as an inscription from Zinjirli, with a reference to 30 kings, shows. **3** *Your silver and your gold . . . are mine:* this might have been taken as *de facto* recognition **4** to which Ahab agreed, but **5, 6** were almost insulting and indicated unconditional surrender. **6** *Nevertheless I will send my servants:* possibly to be translated 'for if I have to send my servants tomorrow . . .'.

20:7-12 Ahab's reply. 7 *The elders of the land:* probably older men (heads of families) from all the tribal regions. *I did not refuse him;* perhaps 'should I not refuse him?' **10** *The gods do so to me, and more also:* a solemn vow; Ben-hadad vowed to level Samaria to the ground. **11** *Let not him that girds . . . :* Ahab's reply is proverbial; in Hebrew it consists of just four words. **12** *In the booths:* instead of tents, shelters were made of branches and leaves. *Take your positions:* lit. 'set', which is probably to be translated 'Attack!' *And they took their positions:* lit. 'and they set', *i.e.* they attacked.

20:13-21 Yahweh routs the Syrians. 13 *A prophet:* otherwise unidentified. The plan of battle he suggests to Ahab is to send out 232 servants of the governors of the districts at noon when Ben-hadad and his kings are drinking in their booths; and then when Ben-hadad's men come out, to send against them 7,000 trained soldiers (*cf.* v. 19). In the confusion the Aramaean kings flee, but their horses and chariots are captured. **15** *All the people of Israel, seven thousand:* of course the figure does not fit the statement. LXX suggests 'all the men of substance'. Otherwise we must understand 'all' to mean a representation of all tribes. **21** *Captured:* so LXX; MT 'smote'. Possibly the horses were used to further the rout of the Aramaeans.

20:22-30a The Syrians attack again and Yahweh smites them. 22 *In the spring:* Heb. 'the return (or cycle) of the year', which is generally taken as the spring equinox (see 2 Sa. 11:1).

Snaith (*IB*) states that the kings of the Near East went to war in the autumn, after the harvest was in. This is questionable, for the rainy season followed shortly afterwards, and conducting a war in the rainy season was all but impossible. According to Gray, late spring and summer was the regular season for military expeditions. **23** *Their gods are gods of the hills:* Ben-hadad was convinced by his advisers that the Israelites had won because their God was a hill-god and they had fought on their own ground. **26** *In the spring:* see on v. 22. *Aphek:* at least five places are known by this name. This was probably a site in the plain of Esdraelon, but it may have been in the N part of the plain of Sharon, or possibly E of the Sea of Galilee commanding the pass on the road from Damascus, which would imply that the Israelites had taken back the region in Transjordan. Gray prefers el-Fiq, E of Lake Tiberias. **29** *A hundred thousand foot soldiers:* this figure seems hyperbolic. Notice that the combined forces of eleven kingdoms against Shalmaneser III totalled only 62,900 infantry. **30** *The wall fell upon twenty-seven thousand men:* again the figure raises questions. One suggestion is that the destruction of the city wall opened the way for the death of the soldiers who had fled into the city.

20:30b-34 Ahab spares Ben-hadad. Doubtless from fear of the power of Assyria, Ahab is only too willing to spare Ben-hadad, and at the slightest sign of leniency Ben-hadad's servants press the petition. **34** *My father . . . your father:* these terms need not be taken literally; they are often used of more remote ancestors. There is no record of any warfare with Omri, the father of Ahab. Specific towns in upper Galilee were taken from Israel in the time of Baasha (15:20), who might be said to be Ahab's 'father' in the sense of his predecessor. On the other hand, the reference to *bazaars* (not 'streets', as in AV) in Samaria would mean that this concession had been made in the days of Omri, since he established Samaria.

20:35-43 A prophet rebukes Ahab for sparing Ben-hadad. 35 *The sons of the prophets:* disciples of the prophets, appearing in the Bible in the time of Elijah and Elisha, but also mentioned by Amos (see on 18:4). **38** *Bandage over his eyes: i.e.* on his forehead. (AV 'ashes on his face' is to be rejected.) **40** *So shall your judgment be: cf.* Nathan and David (2 Sa. 12:1-7). The method was designed to bring the verdict from Ahab himself, which was immediately forthcoming. **42** *Your life . . . for his life.* It is folly to praise the lenient policy of Ahab and to condemn the harsh policy of the prophets; God was concerned with protecting His people Israel. Ben-hadad had already caused enough destruction and death to Israel. Ahab had denied trust in Yahweh by entering into foreign alliances. Ben-hadad had been delivered into Ahab's hand that he might punish him once and for all, and Ahab had failed to do that. The result would be untold suffering for the people.

21:1-29 Ahab and Naboth's vineyard

In LXX ch. 21 follows 19, then come 20 and 22.

21:1-4 Ahab's request and Naboth's refusal. 1 *Naboth*: no further identification except that he had a vineyard adjoining the summer palace of Ahab in Jezreel. **2** *Give me your vineyard*: Ahab's request may seem reasonable, offering to exchange or buy Naboth's property. **3** Naboth's refusal, however, is not only reasonable but religious. According to the Mosaic law, he had responsibility to his family, both past and future (Lv. 25:23-28; Nu. 36:7ff.). Similar rules of inheritance are found in other law codes of the Ancient Middle East. Gray points out that to have accepted Ahab's proposal would have relegated the family of Naboth to the status of royal dependants.

21:5-10 Jezebel's wicked plot against Naboth. 8 The fiction of communal justice is noteworthy. Ahab was personally influential, and the persons in the story had long been accustomed to follow the lead of Ahab. **10** *Base fellows*: lit. 'sons of Belial'. The meaning of the Hebrew word is not fully clear; it may be composed of the words for 'without' and 'profit'. *Cursed*: Heb. 'blessed', a euphemism, because it was considered blasphemy even to mention the cursing of God; wherever the expression comes up in Scripture or in Jewish religious writing, the word 'bless' is used instead of 'curse'. *The king*: cursing the king was a capital offence (Ex. 22:28). *Stone him to death*: cf. Lv. 24:16. For the requirement of two witnesses, cf. Dt. 17:6; 19:15. It is amazing how Jezebel is careful to follow Deuteronomic law—and if this is later 'Deuteronomic' redaction, then the story falls apart.

21:11-14 Naboth's death. 11-13 are repetitious; LXX abbreviates. According to 2 Ki. 9:26 Naboth's sons were put to death at the same time, perhaps to forestall any problems of inheritance. The legal basis probably was that sons would have been implicated in a plot against the king. However the text does not tell us this.

21:15, 16 Ahab possesses Naboth's vineyard. 15 *Jezebel said*: it is obvious that she was dominating each step of the plot.

21:17-26 Elijah's prophecy to Ahab. We return to some of the stories in the Elijah cycle at this point. **19** *In the place where dogs licked up the blood of Naboth . . .* : the prediction is not fulfilled literally, one of many instances in Scripture, showing that we must accommodate our view of prophecy to the inductive data of Scripture itself. Complete fulfilment does not necessarily involve literal fulfilment. (*Cf.* 2 Ki. 9:26.) **20b-26** include passages similar to 14:10f.; 16:3, 13. **20** *You have sold yourself to do what is evil*: a graphic way of expressing his choices in life. **21** *I will . . . cut off from Ahab*: a prophecy of the end of the dynasty. *Every male*: AV translates literally. *In Israel*: LXX omits. **22** refers to two previous dynasties, those of *Jeroboam* and *Baasha*. **23** *Cf.* 2 Ki. 9:36. **25, 26** sound like an editorial observation, the preceding portion

having been drawn from an oral or written source.

21:27-29 Ahab's repentance. The repentance, while shallow, was apparently genuine, judging from the word of the Lord; therefore the evil prophecy was to be delayed to the day of his son.

22:1-40 Ahab's final Syrian war

Cf. 2 Ch. 18; Josephus, *Ant.* viii.15.3-6.

22:1-4 Alliance with Jehoshaphat of Judah. Jehoshaphat of Judah is obviously a vassal of Ahab of Israel, which may have been one of the reasons for the marriage-alliance between the two families. **3** *Ramoth-gilead belongs to us*: Ramoth-gilead had apparently not been handed back to Israel after the treaty of Aphek (20:34; *cf.* 2 Ki. 8:28). **4** *I am as you are, my people . . .* : Jehoshaphat agreed to participate in the campaign in words that sound like submission. The three years of peace between Syria and Israel (v. 1) may have been the period during which alliances were being made preparatory to the battle of Qarqar. Now that the Assyrian menace has withdrawn into the background, Ahab feels it is time to take back Ramoth-gilead, an important city because it was on or near the eastern caravan route, sometimes identified with the modern city of es-Salt. Glueck identifies it with Tell-Rāmith, 4½ miles SE of er-Ramtha; Gray suggests Ḥuṣn-'Ajlûn, SE of Irbid. On the marriage-alliance, *cf.* 2 Ch. 18:1; 2 Ki. 8:18.

22:5-12 Advice from the prophets. There are true prophets and false prophets, and there is only one difference between them: the true prophet speaks what Yahweh tells him to speak; the false prophet speaks what he is paid to say, what he thinks he should say, or in some cases what he is Satanically inspired to say. **5** *Inquire first for the word of the Lord*: Jehoshaphat wishes to know the will of the Lord before joining battle. *The prophets . . . about four hundred men*: obviously prophets of Yahweh and not of Baal, yet they were subsidized by the king and therefore said what he wanted to hear; they told him to go to war. **7** *Is there not another prophet*: Jehoshaphat doubts their prophecy, whereupon Ahab refers to Micaiah ben Imlah. Gray points out that Jehoshaphat regarded a prophet as an instrument of the revelation of God's will to the community, not as an agent of the throne to influence God. **10** *At the threshing floor*: Gray translates 'public place'. The scene is sketched at the city gate where the two kings are sitting in their robes and on their thrones. 'The threshing floor' may have been the ancient name of the open space by the gate, but there is really no reason why a threshing-floor could not have been near the city gate. **11** *Horns of iron*: a prophet named Zedekiah graphically symbolizes the victory over the Syrians (*cf.* Zc. 1:18-21).

22:13-28 The prophecy of Micaiah. 15 *Go up and triumph*. His first answer is in the words that the king wants to hear; but the king immediately recognizes that this is false, whereupon he gives the true prophecy: Ahab would be killed and his army scattered. **20** *Who will entice Ahab*: the recognition of the true prophets and false prophets has always given difficulty. The explanation that Micaiah gives—*a spirit from the Lord . . . a lying spirit*—fails to satisfy many modern minds, but it is consistent with other passages of Scripture (*cf.* Jb. 1, 2; Zc. 3:1, 2). Basically it attributes the message of the false prophets to a lying spirit which ultimately comes from the Lord. This follows logically from monotheism and can be softened only to a degree by introducing the concept of the Satan, who is himself in the power of Yahweh even though he may instigate the false prophet. In this scene, as in others, the responsibility of the human being for his choice is not removed. Ahab has both the message of the lying prophets and the message of the prophet of Yahweh, and he fatally makes his decision to go against Ramoth-gilead. **24** *How did the Spirit of the Lord go from me to speak to you?* In other words, by what authority does Micaiah give a prophecy different from that of the other prophets? **26** *Take him back to Amon . . .* : possibly for safe custody; however see the following note. **27** *In peace*: victorious; Ahab chooses to believe the other prophets. **28** Micaiah's reply offers a test of false prophets.

22:29–36 The battle of Ramoth-gilead. 30 *Your robes* (LXX 'my robes'): to avoid the fulfilment of Micaiah's prophecy Ahab attempts to disguise himself by putting on Jehoshaphat's robes, and according to LXX, he has Jehoshaphat put on his, possibly to divert the prophecy to Jehoshaphat, or possibly (as Gray suggests) so his army would see what they took to be their king leading them. **31** *Thirty-two captains*: the number is not mentioned in Chronicles, and may be a scribal addition from 20:1. *Only with the king of Israel*: the king of Syria apparently is concerned not with the destruction of the Israelite army, but with the death of the king. This may have been strategic in view of the continuing Assyrian menace. **32** *It is surely the king of Israel*: Jehoshaphat is nearly seized through mistaken identity. **34** *Between the scale armour and the breastplate*: a chance shot strikes the king of Israel and, though he bravely remains in the chariot through the battle, in the evening he dies and the disheartened army returns home.

22:37–40 Summary of Ahab's reign. The better works of Ahab, 'the ivory house which he built, and all the cities that he built', are only hinted at. He was exceedingly evil (*cf.* 21:25, 26). **37** *The king died*: probably late in 853 BC. The battle of Qarqar took place in July or August of 853, according to Shalmaneser's record, and Ahab was involved there. Since Assyrian dates are controlled by the record of a solar eclipse (15 June 763 BC), this is a 'firm' date. **38** *The dogs licked up his blood*: partial fulfilment of Elijah's prophecy (*cf.* 21:21ff.). He was buried in Samaria, however; Naboth died in Jezreel. *The harlots washed themselves in it* follows the Hebrew; AV and some versions read 'they washed his armour'. Neither statement makes very much

sense in the context. **39** *The ivory house*. Excavation of this palace brought to light many ivory carvings that were inlaid in the furniture and possibly in the walls also.

1 Ki. 22:41 – 2 Ki. 1:18 Conclusion of the Elijah cycle
Cf. 2 Ch. 20:31–34. When the original one-volume work was divided, '2 Kings' should have been indicated either at this point or at v. 51 (see Introduction).

22:41–50 Jehoshaphat of Judah. *Cf.* 2 Ch. 17–20; Josephus, *Ant.* ix.1–3. Most of the details of the reign of Jehoshaphat have already been told. Here are added: the unsuccessful attempt to open up the trade-route from Ezion-geber, and Jehoshaphat's refusal to enter into a trade-alliance with Ahaziah. Jehoshaphat is mentioned again in 2 Ki. 3:4ff. **41** *Jehoshaphat*: Abijam and Jehoshaphat are the only kings of Judah so far to have names compounded with the Yah-(Jeho-)/-yah (-ja or -jah) element (for Yahweh). Hereafter, except for Ahaz, Manasseh and Amon, all the kings of Judah will have such Yahwistic names. Ahaz may, however, be an abbreviation of Jeho-ahaz. *In the fourth year of Ahab*. There is a problem of chronology here, with a discrepancy of about 4 years; one solution is to assume a co-regency beginning in Asa's 39th year (*cf.* 2 Ch. 16:12), *c.* 873 BC, and to count Jehoshaphat's 25-year reign from that time. (For discussion, see E. R. Thiele, *The Mysterious Numbers of the Hebrew Kings*, 1951, p. 65.) The reign of Jehoshaphat may be dated *c.* 870–848 BC. **43** *He walked in all the way of Asa*. In the summary, Jehoshaphat is praised for his manner of life, for making peace with Israel, and for getting rid of the remains of cult prostitution: he is criticized for not removing the high places. **48** *Ships of Tarshish*: see on 10:22.

22:51–53 Ahaziah of Israel. *Cf.* 2 Ch. 20:35 – 21:1; Josephus, *Ant.* ix.2. **51** *He reigned two years.* He began to reign in the 17th year of Jehoshaphat, and his successor began to reign in the 18th year (2 Ki. 3:1), hence one actual year is counted as two regnal years. The reign of Ahaziah may be dated *c.* 853–852 BC. **52** *He did what was evil.* Ahaziah is summarized in the worst possible way: he acted in the manner of Ahab, of Jezebel, and of Jeroboam; **53** he served Baal.

2 Ki. 1:1–4 Ahaziah's injury and Elijah's mission. 1 *Moab rebelled*: *cf.* 3:4–27. The Mesha Inscription would put it in the 2nd year of Ahaziah. **2** *The lattice*: the details are not fully clear; probably there was a room built on the roof with a latticed window, partly for privacy and partly to keep out the strong light and to allow ventilation. *Baal-zebub*: lit. 'the fly-god', as LXX translates. From Ugaritic documents we conclude that his name was Baalzebul ('prince Baal' or 'Baal the prince'), similar to the form found in the NT. There was apparently a temple or centre of worship at Ekron, the Philistine city about 15 miles S of Joppa (Jos. 13:3). **3** *The angel of the*

Lord said to Elijah: God sent Elijah to protest against this religious syncretism, and to foretell the death of Ahaziah.

1:5–8 Elijah's prophecy. 6 *Is it because there is no God in Israel.* We fail to understand the religion of the OT if we do not understand the 'jealousy' of Yahweh. **8** *A garment of haircloth*: lit. 'a lord of hair', probably meaning that he owned a garment made of sheepskin, goatskin, or possibly camel-skin (*cf.* 1 Ki. 19:13; Zc. 13:4; Mt. 3:4). The king recognized Elijah from the description.

1:9–16 The captains and their fifties. Commentators find difficulty with this portion, for the action is not in keeping with the rest of the Elijah cycle. JB thinks it is an addition, traceable to the disciples of Elisha. Montgomery speaks of 'the preposterousness of the miraculous element' and its 'inhumanity with the destruction of the innocent fifties'. Keil points out that the demand was insolent, and he adds that the first two groups must have been guilty of some crime which they had to expiate with their death. This sounds like special pleading. We can agree with Keil that the double miracle was designed to show the authority which belonged to the prophet as the representative of God, but we can scarcely measure the morality of the act by NT standards. **13** *The captain of a third fifty*: the third captain saved his life and the life of his men by his entreaty, and then Elijah was instructed to go down with him.

1:17, 18 Summary of Ahaziah's reign. The conclusion of the account and the naming of his successor does not follow the standard formula (see Introduction). Moreover the chronology of 1:17, unless it follows a different system, is incompatible with the other references. In 3:1, Jehoram became king of Israel in the 18th year of Jehoshaphat who reigned 25 years (1 Ki. 22:42). This puts the accession of Jehoram from six to nine years earlier than the date in 1:17 (see on 22:42). Thiele suggests that Jehoram became co-regent in 3:1. **17** *His brother*: based on LXX and Syr. Hebrew does not include the word; but note the statement that Ahaziah had no son, and 3:1 where Jehoram is called 'the son of Ahab'.

2:1 – 10:36 THE ELISHA CYCLE

In this section are a number of stories about Elisha, including several miracles. Elisha's first miracle is the healing of the waters of the spring at Jericho, described in *IB* as 'the first of a series of wonder tales which are associated with the story of Elisha. They are unique in the O.T.'. We must frankly admit that the type of miracle generally performed by Elisha differs from other biblical miracles. In fact some of these miracles violate the first canon proposed to differentiate between true and spurious miracles, namely that there is a moral or ethical purpose in the true miracle, whereas the spurious miracle has no purpose other than to cause amazement. Once we

have admitted this for the Elisha miracles, we are free to defend almost all of the remaining miracles in the Bible according to the canon of moral purpose. It remains therefore for us to discover a new purpose behind the miracles of Elisha.

2:1–25 Elijah is taken up and Elisha succeeds him

2:1–8 Elijah and Elisha go to the Jordan. 1 *Gilgal*: obviously not the one in the Jordan valley near Jericho, but another near Bethel, for they *went down* to Bethel (v. 2). Šanda supposes that it was near Baal-shalishah (4:42), either at Khirbet Sarisiyeh (14 miles N of Lydda) or Kefr Thulth (16 miles N of Lydda), and suggests that Gilgal was Jiljiliyeh, 6 miles W of Kefr Thulth. The story implies that the Lord has made known something of His plan not only to Elijah but also to Elisha and to the sons of the prophets (vv. 3, 5). **2** *Tarry here*: Elijah seems to want to face the experience alone; Elisha refuses to leave him. **3** *The sons of the prophets*: the word 'son' is used in the OT to mean *a.* a direct descendant, *b.* a distant descendant, and *c.* an apprentice in a guild. Obviously it is this last meaning that is used for the sons of the prophets, who were men who had attached themselves or were called to a prophet for training. By itself, the term would be capable of use for both true and false prophets. **5** *At Jericho*: there were sons of prophets in Bethel and in Jericho that we know of, and at least fifty of them (v. 7). **8** *The water was parted*: *cf.* Ex. 14:21.

2:9–12a Elisha's request and Elijah's departure. We are not specifically told that Elijah did not die, and his appearance with Moses on the Mount of Transfiguration certainly carries no such implication, since Moses according to Scripture had died and his body had been taken by the Lord (Dt. 34:6) or his angel (Jude 9). **9** *Let me inherit a double share of your spirit*: RSV hints at the correct meaning. False ideas have persisted: *a.* that Elisha had twice the gifts of the Spirit that Elijah had, which obviously is false in the light of Scripture (however, many who advocate this have done so in the name of Scripture); *b.* that Elisha received two-thirds of the portion of the Spirit that Elijah had. The figure—indeed the very expression—is taken from Dt. 21:17 where the double portion is the portion of the firstborn, or the heir. Elisha is asking to be recognized as the firstborn or heir of Elijah in relation to the other sons of the prophets. Elijah recognizes that this is not his to give, but that God can give it if He will. **11** *A chariot of fire and horses of fire*: note that it is not stated that Elijah was taken up in the chariot of fire. The chariot of fire separated Elijah and Elisha, and *Elijah went up by a whirlwind.* Not everyone was able to see the fiery chariot (*cf.* 6:17). Joash saw it on the occasion of Elisha's death (13:14). **12** *The chariots of Israel and its horsemen!* A cryptic statement, probably meaning that Elijah was of more value to Israel than all its horses and chariots.

**2:12b–18 The spirit of Elijah rests on Elisha.
12** *Rent them in two pieces*, expressing grief. **14** *And struck the water* has no basis in either the Hebrew or the versions. Lucian and some MSS of Vulg. add 'and it was not divided'. English translations cover the fact that the phrase 'and he smote the waters' appears twice in this verse, by translating the second time to make it a dependent clause. The insertion of 'and they were not divided' after the first gives occasion for the question, 'Where is Yahweh, the God of Elijah, even He?' MT by its accents divides the verse differently, 'Even he, and he smote . . . ,' which makes little sense. **16** *Let them go, and seek your master*; the prophets who had followed saw Elisha with the mantle of Elijah, but how much more they had seen is not included. We are not told that they had seen the chariot of fire, or Elijah going up in the whirlwind. We are not even told that they had seen Elisha part the waters of the Jordan with Elijah's mantle. We can assume that Elisha told them something of what had happened, but obviously they did not fully believe the account and sent 50 men to search the mountains for him. After 3 days they reported that he had completely disappeared.

2:19–22 The curing of the spring at Jericho.
This first miracle of Elisha's is among the 'least objectionable' of his miracles, for in this case the spring which was the source of life to the city had gone bad and, according to a popular view (superstitious or otherwise), its water was causing miscarriages. **19** *The land is unfruitful*, 'land' meaning the inhabitants, people and animals, although the verb used here refers only to human beings. **21** *Threw salt in it*. We do wrong to suppose that the salt corrected the cause, for Yahweh did it.

2:23–25 The disrespectful boys and the bears.
This miracle presents more of a moral problem. It has been pointed out that Elisha was a prophet and no-one has a right to make fun of the Lord's prophets. But when this has been said, we must admit that there still is a far different spirit here than that of one who, when He was reviled, did not revile in return (1 Pet. 2:23). **23** *Small boys*: these were not 'little children' (AV). The Hebrew is 'youth' and is used also of older servants; 'little' may refer to character rather than age or size. *You baldhead*: Elisha probably had his head covered (which is a necessity in the Middle East because of the strength of the sun), and since he lived 50 years after this (13:14) it is unlikely that he was bald at this time. The term therefore was one of reproach.

3:1–27 The war with Moab

With this we should read the Moabite account in the Mesha Inscription (Moabite Stone).

3:1–3 Jehoram of Israel. The story of Jehoram needs the additional material of ch. 9 from which it has been separated by the material of the Elisha cycle. He removed the pillar of Baal but otherwise followed the sin of Jeroboam. His mother, Jezebel, was living throughout his whole reign (see 9:30). Jehu also destroyed a pillar of Baal (10:26), which raises the question whether there were two, and Jehoram destroyed only one. **2** *The pillar of Baal*: Gray points out that the Zenjirli Stele of Panammu has both an inscription and a relief of the god Hadad, likewise the stele by Ben-hadad to Baal-melqart has a low relief of the god. He suggests that this may be a similar stele with a carved image of Baal.

3:4–8 Rebellion of the king of Moab against Israel. 4 *Sheep breeder*. The word used here is found elsewhere in OT only in Am. 1. In a Ugaritic text a person appears as chief of the priests, chief of the sheepmasters or shepherds; hence the term is looked upon as an official office, but this can hardly be the case in Amos. Gray translates 'hepatoscopist' (a liver-reader), on the basis of UH 62, 54ff. *Annually*, based on the Targum. *A hundred thousand lambs, and the wool of a hundred thousand rams*: the payment seems to be rather high. LXX infers that it was a one-time payment, as indemnity. **8** *The way of the wilderness of Edom* would apparently mean by Wadi Ḥesi. This should have water in it throughout the year; but they found no water (v. 9).

3:9–12 The coalition of Israel, Judah, and Edom.
Jehoram of Israel and Jehoshaphat of Judah are joined by the king of Edom. After a long march, Jehoshaphat asks for a prophet of Yahweh. Elisha is near by. We are not told whether he had been sent there by the Lord or whether he had accompanied the armies; Gray thinks they must have made a detour around to the head of the Wadi Ḥesi far to the east, since it took a week, and since the morning sun was on the water (v. 22). **11** *Who poured water on the hands of Elijah*: he ministered as the servant of Elijah.

3:13–20 Elisha prophesies deliverance. 13 *What have I to do with you?* Elisha's remark to Jehoram is rather trenchant, and the king's reply seems to be equally sarcastic, blaming their present predicament on the Lord. **15** *Bring me a minstrel*. For Jehoshaphat's sake Elisha agrees to seek the will of Yahweh, which he does by calling for the minstrel to play. Possibly we are to assume that Elisha had a minstrel with him for this purpose. It is too much, however, to assume that all prophets used music to induce some kind of ecstasy, for our only other indication of this is 1 Sa. 10:5ff. and this is not the same. **16** *I will make* (AV 'make'): MT has an infinitive which can serve as an imperative; but it also can serve as translated in RSV, which seems more likely in the context. *Full of pools*. Some interpreters have supposed that a storm in the mountains of Edom during the night brought water down into these pools. Others assume that the soldiers were ordered to dig and in this way they provided a place for ground water to gather. But everyone would have known about ground water; hence Gray thinks it was a flash-flood (*cf.* v. 20). **19** *Every fortified city*: Glueck discovered over 60 fortified settlements of the Iron Age in Moab.

Fell every good tree: in war this was banned (Dt. 20:19f.).

3:21–27 Partial victory over Moab. 21 *Able to put on armour*: instead of ages, descriptions are used; a boy fit for military service is called 'one wearing a girdle', as distinct from one running around with a loose shirt. *Frontier*, the S boundary. **22** *Red as blood*: from the red soil, or from the colour of the sunrise. **24** is somewhat difficult, but rsv seems to have the general sense. **25** *Kir-haresheth* is identified with Kerak, the southernmost fortress of Moab. *Conquered*, referring to Kir-haresheth, in the light of v. 26 is probably a poorer translation than av 'smote it'. **26** *When the king of Moab saw that the battle was going against him*, he sacrificed his eldest son upon the wall, probably at Kir-haresheth, as a burnt-offering to Chemosh, the god of Moab. *The king of Edom*. One suggestion is that the king of Moab felt that his best chance to disrupt the coalition was to seek to get the king of Edom on his side. Other scholars, however, feel that this is a textual error for king of Aram: in other words the king of Moab was seeking to get an embassy through to get the help of the king of Aram. This hardly seems likely, but in any event it failed. The reading 'Aram' is actually found in the Old Latin text. **27** *There came great wrath*: the tide of battle suddenly turns and the Israelite coalition withdraws. Some scholars take the statement to mean that the sacrifice performed by the king of Moab was efficient and that Chemosh turned his anger against Israel—a highly unlikely suggestion. It is of course possible that the Israelites believed that the sacrifice to Chemosh was efficacious in his own land. The popular beliefs of the Israelites were often at variance with the revealed truth, or the views of the prophets.

4:1 – 8:15 Stories of Elisha

Cf. also ch. 9. This section includes a group of stories about Elisha, each story giving an account of some miraculous deed. These stories do not seem to be in chronological order.

4:1–7 Elisha and the widow's jar of oil. The widow of one of the sons of the prophets, identified in the Targum as the wife of Obadiah (1 Ki. 18:4), is faced with a debt and the creditor is going to take her two sons as slaves. When she appeals to Elisha for help he tells her to borrow vessels and fill them with oil from the small jar that she had. Snaith in *IB* makes the fine statement that 'the quantity of the oil was limited only by her faith in collecting empty vessels'. She sells the oil and uses the money to pay off the debt and to support her and her sons. Josephus adds (*Ant.* ix.4.2) that the money had been borrowed by Obadiah in order to feed the prophets. For the law on seizing the sons as slaves, see Ex. 21:7; Lv. 25:39; Am. 2:6; 8:6; *etc.* **2** *Jar*: an unusual word; it may refer to a very small vessel normally used for unguents.

4:8–37 Elisha and the Shunammite woman. (See also 8:1–6.) Shunem was a village a few

miles N of Jezreel. **10** *Lamp*: not a 'candlestick' (av), or a 'lampstand', but an ordinary pottery saucer-lamp with a pinched nozzle. **16** *When the time comes round*: av 'according to the time of life' is probably better. Montgomery suggests 'according to the time of pregnancy'. It is quite similar to Gn. 18:10, 14. **21** *Shut the door*: to retain the *nepeš* or life-essence. **23** *New moon . . . sabbath*: these were already observed in Israel, but there is no support for the theory that on such days the people went to the prophet's house for religious service or instruction. *It will be well*: Heb. *šālôm*, which could simply be 'goodbye', terminating the discussion. The journey from Shunem to Carmel is about 25 miles. We assume that the servant was to walk beside the ass continually urging it on. **25** Elisha *saw her coming* and sent Gehazi to greet her, but obviously he had not been told her problem. **27** *The Lord . . . has not told me*. This does not imply that it was an unusual situation. We have no basis in Scripture to assume that prophets were omniscient; the Lord revealed to them only what He wanted them to know. **28** She rebukes him, pointing out that she had not asked for the son nor for the sorrow that followed. **31** *No sound or sign of life*: the child was really dead, which was not so clearly stated in the case of Elijah and the son of the widow at Zarephath (see on 1 Ki. 17:17). **35** *He stretched himself upon him; the child sneezed seven times*. In LXX 'the prophet stretched himself seven times upon the child', and there is no reference to sneezing. There are overtones of similarity between this miracle and the miracle that Elijah performed on the son of the widow at Zarephath (1 Ki. 17:17–24), but there are no other miracles in the OT having the slightest similarity to these.

4:38–41 Elisha and the poisoned pottage. As in the case of salt in the spring at Jericho (2:19–22), we are not to suppose that the meal in itself was effective. It was merely a prophetic act, and the miracle came from God. **38** *A famine*: probably that of 8:1. *Sitting before him*. It is sometimes assumed that they were there for instruction; a noun *yeshiva* from the verb 'to sit' later comes to mean 'school' (*Ben Sira* 51:29).

4:42–44 Elisha and the twenty loaves. There is no indication that this immediately follows the preceding miracle. As a matter of fact, it is likely that there is no famine at this time. We may assume that the men who were fed were members of Elisha's school of prophets. The offering of firstfruits should be made to the priests, but this does not prove that there were then no priests in Israel; we know that there were. It may be a private protest against the prophets of the crown at Samaria and a recognition that the true representative of God was Elisha. **42** *Baal-shalishah*, sometimes identified with a place about 14 miles N of Lydda in the Sharon plain (*cf.* 1 Sa. 9:4). If the 100 represent the school of prophets, we may notice that the figure 50 occurs in 2:7, 16, 17 and there were 100 prophets hidden by 50s in 1 Ki. 18:4. This is hardly enough to assume that such a school was formed normally of 50 or 100 prophets.

5:1–19a Elisha and Naaman the leper. At this time Israel seems to be a vassal of Syria—which may put it toward the end of the life of Elisha. The king's name is not given; it appears as Benhadad in 8:7. Likewise the name of the king of Israel is not given. 1 *The Lord had given victory to Syria* is in line with the views expressed in Am. 1. *Leper* is used for a number of different types of disease in the OT, but rarely if ever refers to Hansen's disease, commonly called 'leprosy'. 3 *Prophet*: Elisha here is not called 'man of God'. The verb *cure* means 'to heal', or 'cleanse'; used only here (3 times) in the OT. Gray suggests the Akkadian cognate *asapu*, 'to practise exorcism'. 5 *Ten talents of silver*: 30,000 shekels (about 12,000 oz; see on 1 Ki. 9:14). *Six thousand shekels of gold*: Heb. omits 'shekel'; AV adds 'pieces', but coinage had not yet been invented. A gift of 2,400 oz of gold would be lavish; together with the silver and 10 changes of garments, it is very much so.

11 Naaman was expecting some kind of a ritual of exorcism that would include calling on the name of Yahweh and waving the hand. 12 *Abana and Pharpar*: commonly identified with the Barada which flows through the centre of Damascus, and the Awaj, which flows farther S in the oasis of Damascus. 15 *Present*: Heb. lit. 'blessing', as in AV, but at least 6 times in the OT it means 'present' (*cf*. Gn. 33:11). 16 *I will receive none*. Elisha refused a gift. In a world of false prophets and wonder-workers, the true prophet of Yahweh could not afford to give the impression that he was living off his office, that he was prophesying for a morsel of bread or anything else. Neither could he give any indication that he was responsible for the ability to heal; this was the work of the Lord. 17 *Earth*: Naaman wanted to take soil from the holy land back to his home so he could continue to worship Yahweh. 18 He had one reservation, however; it would be necessary for him to accompany his king into the house of Rimmon (or Hadad), the god of Damascus, and whenever he did so he wanted to be pardoned by Yahweh. *Leaning on my arm*: a figure of speech indicating that he was the servant who was closest to the king. 19 Elisha's answer is non-committal, but it has given scholars all sorts of problems in former generations, and even led to establishing an artificial difference between true worship of the false god and joining in the ritual act without any faith in the act.

5:19b–27 Elisha and Gehazi. 21 *He alighted*: lit. 'he fell', but the Hebrew word means 'to get down suddenly' (Gn. 24:64; Am. 3:5), so we can translate 'he got down quickly'. 22 *A talent of silver*: 3,000 shekels (1,200 oz), no small amount. Naaman doubled this amount, putting the silver in two bags for two servants to carry. We assume that they had beasts of burden to haul such a weight of silver. 24 *The hill*: AV 'the tower', lit. 'theophel', but certainly not the one in Jerusalem.

We assume that it was a part of the city where Elisha lived. LXX and Vulg. take it as 'evening darkness', misreading the Hebrew word. 25 *Where have you been?* 'I didn't go anywhere.' A very human touch in the story. 26 is somewhat difficult. Literally it is 'Did not my heart go with you when the man got down from his chariot to meet you? Is it a time to accept silver and to accept clothing, *etc.*?' Why the other items are added here is not clear. Targ., attempting to figure out the problem, inserted the words 'And thou hast thought in thy heart to buy olive orchards . . .'. 27 The severity of the punishment can be explained at least in part by the very serious negative effect the act of Gehazi would have on Naaman, resulting in the lowering of the reputation of the office of the true prophet of Yahweh.

6:1–7 The floating axe-head. This story seems to assume that we understand that the sons of the prophets lived in a common building (*cf*. 4:38). The place is often identified with Gilgal on the erroneous assumption that Gilgal is the one near Jericho, but see on 2:1. Possibly it was the school at Jericho. 4 *Trees*, such as willow, tamarisk, acacia and pine, used for light and not heavy timber (Gray). 5 *Axe*: lit. 'iron', but obviously an axe. *It was borrowed*: Heb. 'it was asked', or 'begged', suggesting that the sons of the prophets did not have funds to purchase such things. Keil says, 'The object of the miracle was similar to that of the stater in the fish's mouth (Mt. 17:27).'

6:8–23 The Syrian army captured. 8 *Shall be my camp*: probably meaning 'Let us make an ambush'. 9 *Are going down there*: probably to be translated 'have hidden themselves'. Montgomery rejects this suggestion, however, suggesting that the word may mean something like a military descent. 10 RSV attempts to get at the meaning by inserting *he used to warn him*. It indicates a close relationship between Elisha and the king of Israel. 12 It is assumed by some scholars that the reputation of Elisha's ministry to Naaman had gone before him; but the chronological sequence is certainly not clear. Gray thinks the very closeness between Hazael and Elisha might account for the allegation. 13 *Dothan*, about 10 miles N of Samaria and a very strategic location with a view of the roads N–S and E–W. 14 The size of the army is not indicated, but we get the impression that the king of Syria felt that the capture of Elisha would be difficult. 15 *The servant of the man of God*: Montgomery reads 'at dawn the man of God' but the rest of the verse is meaningless unless there was a servant who was filled with fear and whose eyes were opened to see the chariots of fire. 16 One of the great statements from Elisha's ministry. 19 *This is not the way*: the verse causes problems to those who feel that a man of God can under no circumstances speak a lie. However, we have to accept the statement in Scripture as it is. 21 *My father*: a rather unusual term of address by the king of Israel to Elisha. It would seem to belong to a different period from the next episode. See v. 31; *cf.* 8:9 and 13:14. **22** has caused much difficulty, and at least one version inserts the word 'not': 'Would you slay those whom you have not taken captive?' This is not found in other versions. The difficulty however is unresolved. JB says, 'Unless an anathema had been pronounced by Yahweh, and apart from individual cases, it was not Israelite custom to kill prisoners of war, *cf.* 1 Ki. 20:31.' Elisha pleads for them and they are feasted and then sent away. The result is probably indicated intentionally in the closing words, *The Syrians came no more on raids into the land of Israel.*

6:24–31 The siege of Samaria. It is not possible to date this event precisely. If this is the Ben-hadad who was assassinated in 844 BC the incident would fall in the reign of Jehoram. One thing is certain: there is no close connection in time between vv. 23 and 24. **24** *Afterward*: obviously not the event in v. 23. *Ben-hadad*: according to JB, Ben-hadad III of Damascus. Gray thinks it could only have been Ben-hadad III the son of Hazael. **25** *An ass's head.* The ass was unclean and therefore could not be eaten; but conditions had become unbearable. *Eighty shekels*: LXX '50 shekels', but even 50 shekels is almost $30.00 (over £12). *The fourth part of a kab*: 'kab' is not used elsewhere and there is no certainty of the quantity. Rabbinic sources indicate 2 quarts (see *IDB*, vol. 4, p. 835a). See, however, *NBD*, p. 1323. *Dove's dung*: it is suggested that this was the popular name of some weed. *Five shekels*: perhaps $3.00 (over £1). **26, 27** *Help, . . . O king!* The king's answer indicates the extremity of the situation. *If the Lord will not help you*: Montgomery prefers 'Not so! Yahweh save thee!' **28** In compassion the king asks the woman what her particular problem is. **29** The cannibalism described seems incredible to us, but all the details here can be paralleled from other historical writings. *Cf.* Dt. 28:56f.; La. 2:20; 4:10; Ezk. 5:10. Josephus cites cannibalism in the siege of Jerusalem (*Wars* vi.3.4), and likewise it appears in Ashurbanipal's siege of Babylon (D. D. Luckenbill, *Ancient Records of Assyria and Babylonia*, 2, §794). **30** The king was wearing *sackcloth* beneath his clothing, in secret but probably sincere penitence. **31** A bit difficult, but RSV certainly has the sense of it. We are not told the background or why the king blamed Elisha. We assume that Elisha had urged him to withstand the siege of the Syrians, promising deliverance. On the other hand the famine might have been the result of the 7-year drought which Elisha had prophesied (see 8:1).

6:32 – 7:2 Elisha's prophecy. 32 *This murderer* (Heb. 'son of a murderer'): AV translates literally, but the Hebrew idiom simply means that he belongs to the class of murderers. It is not necessary to apply this to Jehoram, son of Ahab. There may be some confusion in these verses because of the similarity of the Hebrew words for 'king' and 'messenger'. *The king*: Heb. 'he'.

33 *The king*: Heb. 'messenger'. V. 33 is difficult and does not seem to fit the king's purposes expressed in v. 31. It would make sense, however, if we assume that Elisha had previously told the king not to yield to Syria, but to withstand the siege and the Lord would deliver them. **7:1** *Measure*: a *seah*, a third of an *ephah*, about a bushel. **2** *Captain* (Heb. 'third man'; see on 1 Ki. 9:22): the king's aide *on whose hand the king leaned.*

7:3–15 The flight of the Syrians. 4 is quite complicated, but RSV has the meaning. **5** *At twilight*: in the evening (see v. 12). **6** *The sound of chariots.* The explanation of the flight of the Syrians is given. Gray thinks it was a 'rumour' rather than a *sound.* How this miracle was performed we are not told. *The kings of the Hittites,* the Syro-Hittites. *The kings of Egypt*: better 'Musri', for nowhere in Scripture or outside does the expression *the kings of Egypt* occur. Musri was Cappadocia, and neighbour to the Syro-Hittites (see on 1 Ki. 10:28f.). The Musri are known to have been in alliance with Damascus against Assyria in 853, 849, and 846 BC. However, it is unlikely these events are earlier than 842. Mention of Ben-hadad indicates a date after 797 BC, when Ben-hadad III came to the throne. **9** *Punishment*: Heb. 'evil', or its consequences; hence RSV is correct. The lepers were sure that if they did not let everyone in on the good news they would suffer some kind of punishment. **10** The report was incredible, and **12** the king suspected a plot. **13** *One of his servants* suggests that he risk *five horses*, which would be little risk since they would perish of starvation anyway. This is a very complex verse, but the meaning seems to be clear. **14** *Two mounted men*: there is no contradiction, since the mention of five was merely a suggestion.

7:16–20 The people of Samaria plunder the Syrian camp. 16 *A measure of fine meal. IB* makes this $1.50 a bushel; barley half that price. **18–20** are quite repetitious. Some scholars reject the portion as a doublet; others accept it as a moralizing summary of the writer. The captain, who had doubted Elisha's prophecy, does not live to see its fulfilment.

8:1–6 Sequel to the story of the Shunammite woman. This seems to be a continuation of the story in 4:8–37. Obviously the dates of the two parts of the story have to be placed on each side of the 7-year famine period, and the end of that period has to be placed prior to the healing of Naaman, at which time Gehazi became a leper (5:27). On the rights of possession, *cf.* Ex. 21:2; 23:10f. **3** *Appeal to the king*: lit. 'cry to the king', as in AV, the verb being a legal term; *cf.* Akkadian *ragâmu*, 'to cry out, make a claim'.

8:7–15 Elisha and Hazael of Syria. This incident is probably to be dated before that in 6:27 – 7:20, since the Ben-hadad of that episode was the son of Hazael. The passage obviously has several difficulties. The event took place between 846 and 842 BC, for in the Bull Inscription of 846 BC Shalmaneser III records victory over Ben-hadad, and in his Obelisk Inscription, 842

BC, he records a victory over Hazael in Damascus. In an undated inscription he says that Hazael, son of a nobody, seized the throne. This would have been during the reign of Jehoram of Judah and at most 3 years before Jehu seized the throne of Israel. We may possibly assume that Elisha had been sent to Damascus to anoint Hazael, since this had been part of the commission given to Elijah at Horeb (1 Ki. 19:15), which Elijah must certainly have transmitted to Elisha. We might suppose that the event is later than the healing of Naaman, which would account for Elisha's reputation at the court in Damascus. **9** *All kinds of goods . . . , forty camel loads.* Commentators have questioned this vast amount of material. It was customary to take a gift (*cf.* 1 Sa. 9:7; 1 Ki. 14:3; Ex. 23:15). **10** *Say to him, You shall certainly recover.* MT reads 'Say, you shall not recover', but in the light of the versions and 18 Heb. MSS, the reading 'to him' seems to be original, and the change to *not* (which involves but one letter in Hebrew and no change in pronunciation) seems an attempt of a later scribe to get rid of an embarrassing lie on the part of the man of God. This can be rationalized by supposing that the king would have recovered if he had not been smothered to death. The second problem that has bothered interpreters is the involvement of Elisha in the murder of the king. Did he put the idea in the mind of Hazael? V. 13 may suggest this. **11** also has difficulties. Who *fixed his gaze*, and *stared* at whom? Generally it is taken to mean that Elisha gazed at Hazael, and the suggestion has been made that he went into a trance at this point and received a vision of the horrors that Hazael would commit as king. Josephus, the Lucianic Greek version and a few modern scholars make the subject 'Hazael', because a new subject is introduced in the latter part of the verse, *and the man of God wept.* **12** The details seem to have originated in a vision which the Lord gave to Elisha. *Cf.* 2 Ki. 10:32f.; Am. 1:3–5. Then again, 2 Ki. 13:3–7; Ho. 10:14; 13:16 cast light on the prophecy. **13** *Who is but a dog*: a common cliché of humility, found in several documents of the Ancient Middle East. **15** *Coverlet*: a Hebrew word otherwise unknown. Gray suggests a 'net', woven of rough goat-hair and used as a tent cloth, a mosquito net, or, if soaked, an air conditioner. He thinks the point is that someone would come to take the netting away, wet it again, and hang it up, and they would notice that the king had died—supposedly (Gray doesn't say) an accidental death. This plays fast and loose with the text. The subject is not mentioned. JB adds, perhaps facetiously, 'Presumably this was how Hazael murdered Ben-hadad, not how Ben-hadad committed suicide.'

8:16–24 Jehoram of Judah

Cf. 2 Ch. 21:1–20 (much fuller); Josephus, *Ant.* ix.5. **16** *In the fifth year*: see 8:25 and 1 Ki. 22:42, 51; 2 Ki. 3:1. Jehoshaphat must have

been co-regent with Asa, and the reigns of Ahaziah and Jehoram of Israel must be reckoned from the time when he was sole king. The reign of Joram of Judah may be dated *c.* 848–841 BC, with co-regency from *c.* 853. *Joram,* a shortened form of Jehoram. The two kings therefore had the same name, and the northern king is normally called 'Joram'. MT adds 'Jehoshaphat was king of Judah' after *king of Israel*, but this is omitted in LXX, some Heb. MSS, and RSV. **17** *Eight years*: the figure varies in the versions, apparently in an attempt to work out the chronology. **18** *Daughter of Ahab*: in v. 26 Athaliah is named as granddaughter of Omri. **19** *His sons*: MT 'before him', but many Heb. MSS and the major versions support RSV. **21** *Zair*, sometimes identified with Zoar of Gn. 13:10. Gray suggests it might be Zior of Jos. 15:54, 5 miles NE of Hebron. **22** *Then Libnah revolted*: nothing else is known about this revolt, and the site has not been positively identified.

8:25–29 Ahaziah of Judah

Cf. 2 Ch. 22:1–6; Josephus, *Ant.* ix.5. His reign is very brief, and can be dated in 841 BC. The author breaks into the record of Ahaziah to tell of Jehu king of Israel, and we read of Ahaziah's death in 9:27–29.

9:1 – 10:36 Jehu's revolution

9:1–10 The anointing of Jehu. Elisha sends one of his disciples to Ramoth-gilead to anoint Jehu. Joram had taken Jehu there to make war with Hazael (8:28), but Joram was wounded and returned to Jezreel and Ahaziah of Judah had gone to pay a visit to Joram. The anointing is carried out in secret, but as soon as Jehu's fellow-officers learn of it they proclaim him king. The secret anointing was similar to that of Saul and David (1 Sa. 10:1; 16:13). **2** *Jehu* was also the name of a prophet (1 Ki. 16:1). *Nimshi*: *cf.* v. 20 and 1 Ki. 19:16; he is otherwise unknown. In Assyrian inscriptions Jehu is called 'son of Omri', but obviously 'son of Omri' is used in a very loose sense. The Black Obelisk of Shalmaneser III recording the paying of tribute by Jehu, datable in 841 BC, is one of the fixed points in working out the chronology of the kings of the OT. Jehu's dynasty will be the longest in the history of Israel, but the name of Omri will continue to be used in foreign inscriptions. (For the Black Obelisk Inscription, see *ANET*, p. 281.) **3** *Anoint*: the verb in Hebrew is from the same root as the word for 'Messiah', which means 'the anointed'. **4** *The young man, the prophet*: MT repeats 'the young man' before *the prophet.* **5** *In council.* The suggestion has been made that Jehu and his commanders may have been hatching up a plot to overthrow the government. **7–10a** *Cf.* 1 Ki. 17–19; 21:23; 14:10ff.

9:11–13 Jehu proclaimed king. 11 *This mad fellow.* It has been suggested that this word was regularly used for the prophets because of their ecstatic behaviour. Gray has a very good comment including the words 'certainly what impresses us is the sanity rather than the abnormality of these great figures . . . in our opinion, the truth is that ecstasy was indeed a characteristic of Hebrew poetry but that this varied in degree from the wild and often pointless behaviour and utterance of the "sons of the prophets" ' (p. 488). **12** *That is not true*: in Hebrew just one word, bluntly, 'lie'. They knew something important had happened and that Jehu was simply trying to stall, and they were not disappointed with the true report. **13** *Bare steps*: the meaning of the Hebrew word is not known, and many suggestions have been made, 'the landing at the top of the steps' being the most satisfactory guess. (*Cf.* Mt. 21:7.)

9:14–20 Jehu hastens to Jezreel. Jehu acts at once to keep the news from getting back to Jezreel ahead of him, for this would give the king a chance to mount resistance. **14, 15** repeat what was said in 8:28, 29 and sound like a scribal insertion at this point. Some scholars propose reading 'Jehu' for Joram in v. 14b which then would say that when Joram returned to Jezreel he left a guard at Ramoth-gilead under the command of Jehu. **17** *He spied the company of Jehu* (LXX 'he saw a dust cloud'), and at once sent a horseman to discover what it was. This was repeated when the first did not return, and by the time the second one had reached them the guard was able to discern Jehu's driving. **19** *What have you to do with peace?* Heb. idiom, 'What do you and peace have in common?' **20** *Furiously*: lit. 'madly', from the same root as 'mad fellow' in v. 11; Targ. and Josephus read 'quietly', but this does not fit the rest of the story.

9:21–26 Jehu, the reformer, slays Joram of Israel. 22 *Harlotries, sorceries*: these words are obviously used figuratively; yet the religious practices of Baal worship make the figures all too appropriate. **23** Joram sees that he is about to be assassinated and tries to flee and warn Ahaziah; Jehu is too fast for them.

9:27–29 The death of Ahaziah of Judah. 27 *Beth-haggan*: the proper name is better than AV 'the garden house'; it is generally identified with En-Gannim, modern Jenin, 7 miles S of Jezreel, and 1 mile N of *Ibleam*, mentioned later in the verse. *And they shot him*: RSV follows Syr. and Vulg., which makes good sense. **28** *Cf.* 2 Ch. 22:9, which seems likely to be a midrash. **29** *Eleventh*: cf. 8:25 'twelfth'; we assume that the reign was less than a year. The verse is out of place according to the usual scheme.

9:30–37 The death of Jezebel in fulfilment of Elijah's prophecies. 30 *She painted her eyes*: lit. 'put her eyes in antimony' or 'kohl'; it seems she wanted to die in all her beauty. **31** The height of sarcasm; better rendered, 'How are you, you Zimri, murderer of your master?' This refers to Zimri who wiped out the house of Baasha (1 Ki. 16:9–15), but who reigned only 7 days. **34** Gray sees here a typical Semitic communal meal serving to bind Jehu in the community, but there is no hint of this in the text. It seems rather that he was allowing occasion for fulfilment of the word of Elijah, **36** to which he refers. *Cf.* 1 Ki. 21:23.

10:1–11 The purge of Ahab's house. Jehu undertakes the destruction of every male in the royal line, to forestall a blood feud and to protect his own dynasty. His approach is clever. He subtly challenges them to put the successor on the throne, which they wisely refuse to do and bow before him, offering to meet his terms. His terms are the heads of the king's descendants, which they send. **1** *Seventy sons*. The figure may be symbolic, and the word 'son' does not necessarily mean direct sons (*cf.* Ex. 1:5). *Letters*, meaning 'a letter'. *Rulers of the city*: MT reads 'Jezreel'; RSV follows LXX and Vulg. We suggest that the actual letter might have begun with the words 'To the elder princes of Jezreel and to the guardians of [the line] of Ahab speak:' and then continued with v. 2. This is the standard opening of a letter, and it makes clear that Jehu is directing his remarks to the former line of Ahab which had been located at Jezreel. *Saying*: perhaps the equivalent of 'speak' found in documents of the period. **5** *He who was over the palace, and he who was over the city*: titles of offices. *Guardians*: the word that is used of Mordecai with reference to Esther; no doubt some of the house of Ahab were minors. **9** *You are innocent*. Probably a word of assurance that the blood-bath is over, or that no further revenge will be allowed. **11** suggests that Jehu wiped out not only the immediate male descendants, but all of the noblemen, close friends, and priests. For *great men*, or 'noblemen', however, Lucian reads 'all his kindred'.

10:12–14 The massacre of Ahaziah's kinsmen. Because Jezebel's daughter had married the king of Judah, the house of Ahaziah is also an abomination to Jehu, so he orders their death. **12** *Beth-Eked*: Eusebius identified it as Baitqad, about 3 miles NE of Jenin. Gray suggests that the place may have been a market centre. **13** It is not clear how the kinsmen of Ahaziah had failed to hear of the assassinations. **14** *Forty-two*: some scholars feel that this number has some kind of symbolism; if so, this figure is a round number (*cf.* 2:24).

10:15–28 The massacre of the Baal worshippers. 15 *Jehonadab the son of Rechab*: the Rechabites, who insisted on living in the old ways of their fathers, dwelling in tents, and having nothing to do with Canaanite customs, are mentioned only here and in Je. 35. For the genealogy of Rechab, cf. 1 Ch. 2:55; 4:11ff. Jehonadab was the 'father' or leader of the sect (Je. 35:6). According to Josephus (*Ant.* ix.6.6) Jehu and Jehonadab were friends of long standing. Jehu wants to know if Jehonadab is in agreement with his policy. He is. *Is your heart true . . .?* from LXX; Heb. 'Is it right with your heart as my heart is with your heart?' for which Montgomery suggests, 'Do we see straight and alike?' *Jehu said* is omitted in Hebrew but found in LXX and obviously necessary for the sense. **16** *He had him ride*: Heb. 'they'; LXX and versions read 'he' which is obviously correct. **18** Jehu may have been using a play on words: Heb. *'āḇaḏ*, 'served'; *'āḇaḏ*, 'destroyed'. To a person not paying close attention, the words would sound alike. Both words are used in the last sentence in v. 19. **19** *All his worshippers.* We may assume that in spite of Jehu's intent, some will slip through to worship Baal another day. *Sacrifice*: the Heb. word means both 'to sacrifice' and 'to slaughter'. *With cunning*: 'by subtlety'. **20** *Sanctify*: Syr. and Targ. read 'call'. The expression 'sanctify an assembly', however, is regularly used. *Solemn assembly*: an unusual Hebrew word, possibly a closing festival (Lv. 23:36; Dt. 16:8), in which case there would be a double meaning here. **22** *Wardrobe*: apparently special garments were used for the Baal service. **24** *He went in*, as LXX; Heb. 'they'. **25** *The inner room of the house of Baal*: Hebrew seems to say 'city of the house of Baal', which makes no sense; but the same or a similar Hebrew word is now known to mean 'altar' or 'inmost shrine', according to Ugaritic evidence. **26** *The pillar . . . in the house of Baal*: Heb. 'pillars'; but *burned it* supports the singular. The word usually refers to a stone image, possibly carved in low relief, but obviously this could not be burnt, so we must either assume a wooden pillar or emend the word *burned* to 'broke', which would fit v. 27. **27** *To this day*: i.e. to the time of the writing of this account.

10:29–31 The word of Yahweh to Jehu. In spite of his anti-Baal reforms, Jehu does not attempt to clean up the idolatry of Jeroboam, nor does he strive to walk in the law of the Lord. For his reform measures God promises him a dynasty that will last until the fourth generation.

10:32–36 Summary of Jehu's reign. 32 The weakness of Assyria made it possible for Hazael to take over all of the territory E of the Jordan, which was held until Adad-nirari III conquered Damascus in 805 BC. Thus Yahweh began to cut off parts of Jehu's kingdom. **33** *Aroer*: modern Araʿir just N of the Wadi Mujib (Arnon) about 10 miles E of the Dead Sea. **36** The reign of Jehu may be dated 841–814 BC.

11:1 – 17:41 FROM JEHU'S REVOLT TO THE FALL OF THE NORTHERN KINGDOM

This is a hectic period for Israel, including Elisha's last message, war with Amaziah of Judah, a time of conspiracy and overthrow of rulers, the paying of heavy tribute to Assyria, and finally the siege and capture of the northern kingdom by Assyria. During the same period, Judah has her problems, beginning with the usurpation of the throne by Athaliah the daughter of Jezebel, and including both the reforms of Jehoash and the idolatries of Ahaz. But most of all, it is a period of increasing dependence upon foreign alliance, rather than trust in Yahweh. At this time, Yahweh sends His servants the prophets, notably Isaiah and Micah to Judah, and Amos and Hosea to Israel.

11:1–20 Athaliah of Judah

Cf. 2 Ch. 22:10–23; Josephus, *Ant.* ix.7. The reign of Athaliah may be dated 841–835 BC.

11:1-3 Athaliah usurps the throne, but Joash is placed in safe custody. 2 *Jehosheba, the daughter of King Joram*, according to 2 Ch. 22:11, was the wife of Jehoiada the high priest. *About to be slain*, a paraphrase; Heb. participle simply means 'being slain'. *And his nurse*: critics suggest that this is a gloss from Chronicles. *Bedchamber*: according to Josephus (*Ant.* ix.7.1), a room where mattresses and couches were stored. **3** *In the house of the Lord*: probably the priests' quarters, since Joash remained with the priest's wife.

11:4–16 The overthrow of Athaliah and crowning of Joash. 4 *Jehoiada*: see on v. 2. *Captains of the Carites*: probably the 'Cherethites' in 2 Sa. 20:23; in 2 Ch. 23:1–21 the Levites take the place of the Carites. **5–7** The passage is obscure; some scholars omit v. 6. In any event the *coup* was planned for the sabbath and if Skinner is correct, this was because two companies of the guard were in the Temple on the sabbath and only one company in the king's house. In any event, it seems that they immediately placed the young Joash under heavy guard and proclaimed him king. **12** *Testimony*: some scholars emend to read 'bracelets' (*cf.* 2 Sa. 1:10), but the word *testimony* is supported by all versions and according to Gray was the feature of the coronation ritual associated with the covenant of David, and signified the king's obligations in the covenant.

11:17–20 The covenant of the people. The Davidic dynasty had been broken temporarily by the reign of Athaliah. It is therefore appropriate that the covenant should be proclaimed once more. **18** *Mattan*: perhaps the full name was Mattan-Baal, 'the gift of Baal'; *cf.* Mattaniah, 'the gift of Yahweh'.

11:21 – 12:21 Jehoash (Joash) of Judah

Cf. 2 Ch. 24:1–14; Josephus, *Ant.* ix.8.2–4. Joash is a faithful king, but unable to accomplish reforms.

11:21 – 12:3 Introductory statement. Joash is only 7 when he comes to the throne, hence his reign is unusually long. **21** *Jehoash*: the longer form of the name, normally 'Joash'. In the Hebrew text this is 12:1. **1** *Forty years*: according to Gray this includes the 6 years' reign of Athaliah; however, Thiele is able to work out his chronology without this feature. The reign of Joash may be dated 835–796 BC. **2** *All his days*; in AV and the ancient versions this is taken to be modified by the following clause, which limits the faithfulness of Joash to the days during which he received instruction from Jehoiada. This would be in line with the statement in 2 Ch. 24:2.

12:4–16 Repairs to the Temple. There may be a hint of mishandling of money. At any rate Joash felt it necessary to undertake the refurbishing of the Temple, but after 23 years nothing has been done; therefore he takes firmer measures. We find it hard to praise him for waiting so long. The 'Joash chest', which has become the model for collections in some Christian churches, was originally designed to forestall the dishonesty of the priests, the money being counted by the king's secretary and the high priest. The men to whom they gave the money to pay the workmen were considered to be more honest than the priests who had been by-passed. **4** *Each man is assessed*: this follows LXX and seems to be a reasonable explanation of the Hebrew word used. It seems clear that there were two kinds of money involved—the tax and the voluntary offering. **5, 7** *Acquaintances*: a technical term which occurs in Ugaritic texts along with priests, temple prostitutes, and silver casters. The suggestion has been made that they were 'assessors', possibly to help the priests fix the costs or value of sacrificial animals and other offerings. Montgomery suggests a class of Temple tellers, similar to the money-changers of Mt. 21:12. There is no date given for this plan to repair the Temple. It might have been not many years before the 23rd year (v. 6), but this seems unlikely.

9 *Beside the altar.* This probably should be emended with Codex A of LXX to read 'pillar', which would put it by the door where the guardians of the threshold would have custody of it. The suggestion has been made that the breach between the king and Jehoiada the priest (2 Ch. 24:6–14) may have occurred at this time. Gray supposes that Jehoiada was old and incapable and there was neglect of the Temple, and Joash used this step as a means of freeing himself and his nation from priestly domination. The first step was to get rid of the assessors, or tellers, in the Temple; the second step was to relieve the priests of their responsibility; and the third step was to assert royal authority in the Temple by putting a royal fiscal officer alongside the chief priest in handling the funds. **10, 11** *Money*: coinage was not yet in existence. Metal was weighed out, and as early as the 9th century standard weights of metal were stamped with the mark of private tradesmen guaranteeing the purity and the weight—which was the first step toward coinage. It is possible that the assessor had the responsibility of evaluating metal that was brought to the Temple, and this became one of the functions of the king's secretary and the high priest when they *counted and tied up in bags the money*. The words used in the Hebrew here literally mean 'fashioned and counted', the first word possibly meaning 'to smelt into ingots' (*cf.* Je. 18:11; Zc. 11:13). In the light of this discussion we can see how money-changers had become a necessary part of the Temple. **13** These items had disappeared from the Temple in the looting and the various attempts to buy off foreign powers. Possibly this was another restriction on the priests to prevent them from manufacturing such items.

12:17, 18 Joash buys off Hazael of Syria. 17 *Against Gath.* To reach this point Hazael and the

Syrian army had to come through much of Judah, probably with the consent, willing or otherwise, of Israel. Jerusalem was in serious danger and Joash bought time at the expense of the treasuries of the Temple and the palace.

12:19–21 Summary of Joash's reign. The perilous state of affairs is indicated by the fact that Joash's servants conspired to put him to death. According to 2 Ch. 24:25, 26, the assassination was in revenge for Joash's part in the death of Zechariah, son of Jehoiada. **20** *The house of Millo*: *cf.* Jdg. 9:6; Gray suggests the quarters of the garrison, or barracks.

13:1–9 Jehoahaz of Israel

This is a dark period in the history of the northern kingdom. The king did evil and the Lord gave the country into the hand of Hazael king of Syria and his son Ben-hadad. In response to the appeal of Jehoahaz, Yahweh gave some relief in the days of Ben-hadad. **1** *In the twenty-third year of Joash*. The reign of Jehoahaz may be dated *c.* 814–796 BC. **7** *An army of more than fifty horsemen and ten chariots and ten thousand footmen*: *cf.* the size of Ahab's army according to the Assyrian record: 2,000 chariots and 10,000 footmen.

13:10–13 Jehoash of Israel

Cf. Josephus, *Ant.* ix.8.6, 7. Jehoash is also called Joash, which adds to the confusion with Jehoash (Joash) of Judah. His 16-year reign, which is dismissed with the evaluation in v. 11, may be dated 798–*c.* 782 BC. **10** *Thirty-seventh year*: according to 13:1 and 14:1 it should be the 39th year, hence we assume a co-regency of 2 years, 798–796 BC. **12** *Cf.* 14:11.

13:14–25 Closing events of the Elisha cycle

Elisha draws near to the close of a long ministry that extended over more than 60 years and six kings of Israel. His age is not told, but estimated to be between 80 and 90. His final prophecy is in symbolic action, and serves to rebuke the lack of faith of Joash of Israel.

13:14–19 Elisha's last message to Jehoash of Israel. 14 The words of Joash to him are reminiscent of Elisha's words to Elijah at the time of his translation. **16** *Draw the bow*: *cf.* Joshua stretching out the spear (Jos. 8:18). Some scholars believe this is sympathetic magic, but there is no indication of this in Scripture. It and the striking of the ground seem to be purely symbolic.

13:20, 21 Elisha's death. His bones are instrumental in yet one more miracle. The place is not identified. Since the Moabites regularly invaded the region it may have been Jericho. **20** *The spring of the year*: lit. 'the coming in of the year'; Snaith thinks it was autumn.

13:22–25 Victories over Syria. The symbolic prophecies of Elisha are fulfilled. About the time that Ben-hadad became king, Syria is turned back and Israel is given relief. Some scholars feel this was partly due to the fact that the Assyrian king Adad-nirari III subjected Damascus in 805, but this date does not fit the biblical chronology, nor does it supply a basis for altering the biblical chronology.

14:1-22 Amaziah of Judah

Cf. 2 Ch. 25; Josephus, *Ant.* ix.9. Amaziah is a strong king, putting to death the murderers of his father, defeating the Edomites possibly while trying to extend his kingdom to the Gulf of Aqabah (*cf.* v. 22), and attempting war with Jehoash of Israel. In this last phase he is defeated and Jerusalem is looted. The people revolt against Amaziah, pursue him to Lachish, and put him to death.

14:1-7 Introductory statement. Amaziah is a 'good' king, but he does not remove the high places. He avenges his father's death. He defeats the Edomites and takes Sela. **2** *He reigned twenty-nine years*: some scholars would reduce this figure to 9 years, but this would not agree with v. 17 which states he lived 15 years beyond Jehoash of Israel. Thiele assumes a co-regency with Azariah beginning in Amaziah's 6th year, which would be a 24-year co-regency, unusually long, but then so is Azariah's 52-year reign. The reign of Amaziah may be dated *c.* 796-767 BC, but possibly from 791 Azariah was co-regent. *Cf.* 14:21. *Jehoaddin*: so Q and versions; MT 'Jehoya-din'. **5** *He killed his servants*: he put to death those who had been responsible for the assassination of his father, but **6** *he did not put to death the children*: *cf.* Dt. 24:16. **7** *Valley of Salt*: the plain S of the Dead Sea. *Sela* is often identified with Petra (Jdg. 1:36: Is. 16:1); but here that would seem to be miles out of the way. According to Gray, Jdg. 1:36 locates Sela in the Arabah S of the Dead Sea, near the Ascent of Scorpions. That would fit the present text. Gray supposes that when the Aramaeans penetrated as far as Gath this gave the Edomites occasion to take over some Judean territory. The independence of Edom at this time is found in the Assyrian Inscriptions and also reflected in Am. 1:11, 12.

14:8-14 War with Jehoash of Israel. 9 The parable of the thistle and the cedar is almost an insult thrown at Amaziah by Jehoash. Amaziah is not frightened, so they engage in battle at Beth-shemesh with disastrous results. **10** *Be content with your glory*: this gets the meaning very well; the Hebrew is contemptuous: 'Be glorified and stay home!' **11** *Beth-shemesh*, W of Jerusalem; hence Jehoash was marching from the coastal region. With the temporary collapse of Syria, Israel must have taken over the territory adjacent to the Philistines. According to 2 Ch. 25:6ff., Amaziah had Israelites in his army but sent them back before invading Edom, creating bad blood between the two nations. **13** *Four hundred cubits*, about 600 ft. *Ephraim Gate*: generally taken to be in the N wall. *Corner Gate*: some place at the NE (or NW?) angle. The destruction of the wall could not have been very great, since Ahaziah repaired it and refortified it rather easily (2 Ch. 26:9). **14** *Hostages*: the only mention of hostages in the OT; possibly an effort to enforce peace.

14:15, 16 Summary of the reign of Jehoash of Israel. This is an unusual arrangement, for generally the author tells the story of one king to the end of his reign. Jehoash of Israel was introduced in 13:10, and Amaziah of Judah in 14:1. Their summaries are now given in the same order. See Introduction.

14:17-22 Summary of the reign of Amaziah of Judah. See note on previous section. **17** *Fifteen years*: this figure is rejected or altered by many scholars (*cf.* on 14:2). **19** *Conspiracy*: we are not told who was responsible and the reason for it. It is reasonable to assume that it was a reaction against his going to war with Israel. *Lachish*, identified with Tell ed-Duweir, *c.* 25 miles SW of Jerusalem. **21** *All the people*. Perhaps the conspiracy was an intrigue of just a small group, possibly some of the military. *Azariah*, also called 'Uzziah'. *IB* suggests that 'Uzziah' arose by the accidental omission of a letter from Hebrew 'Azariah', but we would have to assume that this had happened not only in Kings but also in Chronicles, Isaiah, Hosea, Amos and Zechariah. It is much better to assume that one form was the throne name and the other a personal name. *Sixteen years old.* There are serious chronological difficulties here. By reading the verse as past perfect, 'The people had taken Azariah when he was sixteen and made him king' (either as co-regent, or possibly even as a rival king of Amaziah), we avoid the difficulty, and at the same time can account for the position of this statement at this point in the text. *Cf.* 14:2. **22** *Elath*: the modern town of Aqabah at the NE corner of the Gulf of Aqabah, opposite the Israeli town which bears the name Elath today.

14:23-29 Jeroboam ben Joash (Jeroboam II) of Israel

Cf. Josephus, *Ant.* ix.10.1, 2. According to some scholars, Jeroboam II was the most successful of all the kings of Israel. The prosperity of the land in his days is reflected in Amos, Hosea and Is. 28. In reconstructing the chronology of the period, we conclude that he became co-regent *c.* 793 for a period of about 12 years before assuming the sole reign of the northern kingdom. **23** *The fifteenth year of Amaziah*: this must mark the beginning of the sole reign, while *forty-one years* would seem to include a co-regency of 12 years. The reign of Jeroboam II may be dated *c.* 782-753 with a co-regency from *c.* 793 BC. **25** *The entrance of Hamath*: see on 1 Ki. 8:65. *The Sea of the Arabah*: either the Dead Sea or the Gulf of Aqabah. *Jonah the son of Amittai, the prophet*: *cf.* Jon. 1:1. *Gath-hepher*: a town in Zebulun (Jos. 19:13). **26** *None left, bond or free*: see on 1 Ki. 14:10. **27** *He saved them by the hand of Jeroboam*: God used Jeroboam, in spite of what is said about him in v. 24. **28** Some scholars feel this should be reworded, possibly 'his might in war with Damascus, and how he turned away the wrath of Yahweh from Israel'. As the verse stands it is not clear.

15:1–7 Azariah (Uzziah) of Judah

Cf. 2 Ch. 26 (with a long addition); Josephus, *Ant.* ix.10.3, 4. Little is recorded of Azariah's reign except the fact that he was smitten with leprosy (*cf.* 2 Ch. 26:16–21). Jotham was acting king or co-regent for about 13 years. **1** *Azariah.* Montgomery assumes that Azariah was the throne name, Uzziah an adopted name. Much confusion has resulted from the appearance of the name 'Azriau of Yaudi' in the annals of Tiglath-pileser for the year 738 (D. D. Luckenbill, *Ancient Records of Assyria and Babylonia,* 1, §770, *etc.*). It is inconceivable that a king of Judah could have connections that far north at such a weak period of his history. It is equally difficult to believe that two kings of the same name could be occupying different territories of the same name, or very similar names; yet the solution offered by a number of scholars is that Azriau was king of the northern kingdom of Yaudi, later known as Sam'al in N Syria, modern Turkey. This is not the place to enter into a discussion of this very complex problem. We note that Montgomery in *ICC* subscribes to the northern Yaudi view. Thiele opts for the identification of Azriau of Yaudi with Azariah of Judah and gives some bibliography on the discussion (*Mysterious Numbers of the Hebrew Kings,* p. 78). **2** *Sixteen . . . fifty-two*: Azariah became co-regent at the age of 16, in the year 790. His accession *in the twenty-seventh year of Jeroboam* (v. 1), which would be 767, was when he became sole king. The *twenty-seventh year* includes the years of Jeroboam's co-regency; it was the 15th year of his sole reign. The reign of Azariah may be dated 767–740 BC, with co-regency from *c.* 790.

15:8–31 Internal collapse in Israel

The story at this point becomes almost chaotic, and there is every indication that Israel has almost collapsed as a nation. The instability of the time is seen in the fact that four kings occupied the throne and two kings were murdered in the years 753–752. Jeroboam II died, Zechariah was assassinated after a reign of 6 months, Shallum was assassinated after a reign of one month, Menahem seized the throne, and about the same time Pekah began to count the years of his reign, suggesting some incapacity or lack of authority on the part of Menahem. It seems highly probable that the chronological difficulties (*e.g.* Pekah's 20-year reign) are to be solved by assuming that rival kings claimed the throne during the same period.

15:8–12 Zechariah of Israel and Shallum's conspiracy. *Cf.* Josephus, *Ant.* ix.11.1. This is the end of the dynasty of Jehu; *cf.* the prophecy of 10:30. **8** *Thirty-eighth year of Azariah,* counting the co-regency, gives the date for the reign of Zechariah 753 BC. He reigned 6 months. **10** *At Ibleam*: by a slight change in the consonants, agreeing with the Lucianic Greek; Heb. 'before the people', which makes little sense. This emendation, which has no other support in the

ancient versions, appeals to scholars because it was near Ibleam that Jehu had murdered the princes of the house of Judah when he usurped the throne of Israel (*cf.* 10:14); but this is not necessarily a good reason for accepting it.

15:13–15 Shallum of Israel. 13 *Thirty-ninth year of Uzziah: cf.* 15:8; the date for Shallum's reign is *c.* 752 BC. **14** *The son of Jabesh*: many scholars prefer to read this as 'a man of Yasib', a place not far from Tappuah, an emendation in v. 16 (where see note). In the Assyrian record Shallum is called 'son of nobody', which means he was a usurper.

15:16–22 Menahem of Israel. After a brief period of civil war, during which Menahem cruelly destroys the region around Tiphsah, he seizes the throne and reigns nominally for 10 years. Part of this time at least, he is able to maintain his reign by paying tribute to the Assyrian king Tiglath-pileser. **16** *Tappuah,* based on Lucian (Heb. 'Tiphsah'); scholars rejected this reading since Tiphsah was on the Euphrates —but this was on the surface ludicrous since there are other places by the same name, one of which at least (6 miles SW of Shechem) would fit the general description. We assume that the supporters of Shallum were hiding out there, or that Shallum had come from that region. Tappuah, on the other hand, was on the border between Manasseh and Ephraim near Yasib (Jos. 17:7); *cf.* on v. 14. **17** *The thirty-ninth year of Azariah,* from the beginning of his co-regency in 790, therefore 752. Thiele believes he has established it precisely in the month of Nisan 752 (*Mysterious Numbers of the Hebrew Kings,* p. 74). The reign of Menahem can be dated 752–742 BC. **19** *Pul the king of Assyria*; because of an unfortunate mistranslation of 1 Ch. 5:26, Pul and Tiglath-pileser (there spelt 'Tilgath-pilneser') were looked upon as two different persons, in spite of the fact that the verb is singular (see on 1 Ch. 5:26). The name 'Pul' occurs in the Babylonian king list, apparently the name which Tiglath-pileser took when he became king of Babylon in 729. In Ptolemy's chronology, this name is represented as *Poros,* an understandable pronunciation due to the inability of the Egyptian to pronounce the L-sound. *A thousand talents of silver*: 3 million shekels. **20** *Fifty shekels from each man* would indicate 60,000 taxable persons. Since these are called 'men of wealth', it gives us a sidelight on the size of the upper class denounced by the 8th-century prophets, Amos, Hosea and Isaiah. The tax was not great, about $25 (£10) from each.

15:23–26 Pekahiah of Israel. Little is recorded of this king. He reigns 2 years, does evil, and is assassinated in a plot led by his captain Pekah. **23** *Fiftieth year of Azariah: cf.* 15:8; the reign of Pekahiah can be dated 741–740 BC. **25** Hebrew adds the names 'Argob' and 'Arieh', generally taken to be personal names; Jerome understood them to be place-names. RSV has removed them, suggesting that they belong to the places listed in v. 29.

15:27-31 Pekah of Israel. Little is told of Pekah, other than the significant fact that during his reign the king of Assyria takes large portions of Galilee and Transjordan from the northern kingdom and carries a large number of the inhabitants into captivity. There are serious problems of chronology, and some scholars reduce his reign to 2 years. But it seems unlikely that he could have gained such importance as, *e.g.*, that reflected in Is. 7 in such a short reign. Moreover several synchronisms in the OT are based on Pekah's reign, and it becomes difficult to explain these if he reigned only 2 years. Since Pekah was a usurper, we cannot fall back on a hypothetical co-regency. Yet he claims a reign of 20 years. Thiele makes the interesting suggestion that by counting his reign from the death of Shallum, Pekah may have hoped to blot out the dynasty of Menahem from the record (*Mysterious Numbers of the Hebrew Kings*, p. 115). **27** *The fifty-second year of Azariah*; *cf.* 15:8; the reign of Pekah can be dated 739–732 BC, with a reign as pretender from *c.* 751 BC. **29** *He carried the people captive*: the first mention of any captivity in the history of Israel (*cf.* Is. 9:1). The conspiracy of Pekah with Rezin of Damascus is described in Is. 7. The Assyrian invasions in 734 and 732 were probably the result of the appeal of Ahaz of Judah. **30** The conspiracy of Hoshea and the assassination of Pekah occurred in 732. Tiglath-pileser tells that he carried off the people of the land of *Bit-Ḫumria* ('the house of Omri') and their king *Paqaḫa* ('Pekah'), and placed *Ausi* ('Hoshea') over them as king. Whether Tiglath-pileser put Hoshea on the throne or whether it was a popular revolt, Hoshea became a tributary to the Assyrian king. *Twentieth year of Jotham*: it seems impossible to synchronize this with the statement that he reigned 16 years (v. 33; 2 Ch. 27:1, 8), unless we accept a period after his reign officially ended. Ahaz most certainly was king in 734–732 (Is. 7:1–17; 8:1–8), and Hoshea did not begin to reign until *c.* 732 BC. This would be the only example of a king's reign being counted as ended before his death or capture.

15:32-38 Jotham of Judah

Cf. 2 Ch. 27; Josephus, *Ant.* ix.11.2. Jotham, the son of Uzziah, or Azariah, came to the throne at the age of 25. In his days the Syro-Ephraimite coalition attempted an invasion of Judah. Chronicles tells of Jotham's extensive building operations and success over Ammon, which may have triggered the Syro-Ephraimite offensive. The chronological points present difficulty. If Jotham came to the throne in the 2nd year of Pekah, and reigned 16 years (v. 32), we find a problem in v. 30 which says that Pekah was slain in the 20th year of Jotham. It appears that Jotham not only had 12 years of co-regency with his father Azariah (Uzziah), but also that Ahaz became co-regent during the last 4 years of Jotham's reign. On this basis Jotham's sole reign is reduced to 4 actual years. The dates are 740–735

BC, with a co-regency from 751 BC. For the background of Jotham's reign, read Is. 2–5.

16:1-20 Ahaz of Judah

Cf. 2 Ch. 28:1–4; Josephus, *Ant.* ix.12.

16:1-4 Introductory statement. Ahaz introduces abominable idolatries into Judah. **1** *The seventeenth year of Pekah*: see on 15:27–31; this would be *c.* 735. *Ahaz*, a short form of Jehoahaz (in Tiglath-pileser's inscription '*Yauhazi*'). The dates of the reign of Ahaz are *c.* 732–716, with co-regency from 735 BC. **2** *Twenty years old*: according to one scholar this would make him 11 when his son Hezekiah was born; according to another scholar he was only one when Hezekiah was born! LXX and Syriac of 2 Ch. 28:1 read 'twenty-five' instead of 20. Thiele, by assuming co-regencies, arrives at the age of 14 or 15 for Ahaz when Hezekiah was born (*op. cit.*, p. 19); this figure is not incredible. If Ahaz became co-regent in 735, Jotham would have been only 41, since he was 25 in 751 (15:33). We assume that Jotham was in weak health, and his death in 732 at the age of 43 would tend to confirm this (see on 15:27–31). **3** *He even burned his son as an offering* (lit. 'made him to pass through the fire'), not as a ritual but as an actual burnt-offering, or holocaust (so Josephus), perhaps occasioned by some crisis. According to Jeremiah it took place in the valley of Hinnom at a place named Tophet, which means 'burning'.

16:5, 6 The alliance of Rezin of Syria and Pekah of Israel. These kings attempt to force Ahaz to join them in a revolt against Assyria, or so it would seem from the way the story develops. **5** *Rezin*: according to Assyrian texts *Rasôn*, or *Raṣûn*. They actually besieged Jerusalem; read Is. 7 in the light of this fact; read also 2 Ch. 26. According to 2 Ch. 28:6–15, Ahaz had heavy casualties, but the coalition of kings was unable to get him to go into battle with them. He secured his water supply (Is. 7:3), and then called for help from Tiglath-pileser. **6** RSV emends to omit the name 'Rezin', and to change 'Aram' to *Edom* the first two times it occurs; the third time, Heb. actually has 'Edomites'. These emendations almost certainly are right. It is highly unlikely that Rezin, who was having trouble with Assyria on the N, could have been engaged with Edom or the city of *Elath* in the far S. In Hebrew writing the change is a matter of a 'tittle'. AV has emended *Edomites* in the last case to 'Syrians', but Elath never belonged to Syria. *Men of Judah*, lit. 'Jews', the first use of the term for the subjects of the kingdom of Judah.

16:7-9 Ahaz appeals to Tiglath-pileser and thereby becomes a vassal. 7 The actual words of submission are included here: *I am your servant and your son.* Tiglath-pileser records the tribute of Jehoahaz of Judah (D. D. Luckenbill, *Ancient Records of Assyria and Babylonia*, 1, §800f.): this is the first mention of Judah in Assyrian inscriptions. **9** *Kir*: location not known; Gray takes it as a common noun, 'city'. (*Cf.* Am. 9:7.) The word is lacking in LXX.

16:10–18 Ahaz builds a new altar. Tiglath-pileser is subjugating Damascus and Ahaz goes there, probably to pay tribute. An altar catches his fancy, and he decides to have one like it built in Jerusalem. The altar was Assyrian and Ahaz was doing honour to the gods of Assyria (*cf.* Olmstead, *History of Palestine and Syria*, p. 452). **10** According to the inscription from Zenjirli, Panammuwa the father of Bar-Rekkab died in a camp of Tiglath-pileser, probably at *Damascus*, for the body was brought home from there. The date of the visit to Damascus was probably in 732. **13** The elements of Temple sacrifice are mentioned: the holocaust or whole *burnt offering*, the *cereal offering*, the *drink offering* or libation, and the *peace offerings* (see LaSor, *Daily Life in Bible Times*, pp. 67–69). The wine-offering or burnt-offering is mentioned in 2 Ki. 3:20; and the evening-offering or cereal-offering in 1 Ki. 18:29. **14, 15** According to Syr., Targ., and LXX, it would seem that Ahaz sacrificed his offering on the old altar and used the new altar for the purpose of oracles (*to inquire by*; *cf.* 1 Ki. 8:22, 54). 'For getting oracles' (so Calvin) would imply the introduction of the Babylonian custom of seeking omens in the sacrifice. **17, 18** Ahaz was breaking up the metal furniture, using the metal to pay tribute (*cf.* 1 Ki. 7:23ff.). **18** *The covered way for the sabbath* (LXX 'the foundation of the seat'): possibly 'the covering of the seat' was the original reading (*IB*). *The palace*: LXX and AV 'the house', probably the house of the Lord.

16:19, 20 Summary of the reign of Ahaz of Judah. From this time on, with the exception of two or three rebellions, Judah is a vassal state of Assyria—a fact usually overlooked by Bible students.

17:1–41 The end of the northern kingdom

In some ways, this is the heart of 2 Kings, completing the stage of history that was begun when Yahweh declared the division of Solomon's kingdom through Ahijah the prophet and by the agency of Jeroboam ben Nebat. The northern kingdom was to serve as an example to the house of David—although Judah learnt little from the experience of Israel, and had to go through the same judgment of destruction and exile. The author has set forth the divine viewpoint in 17:7–23.

17:1–6 Hoshea, the last king of Israel. *Cf.* 1 Ch. 5:26; Josephus, *Ant.* ix.14. Hoshea ascends the throne and reigns until the fall of Samaria. He is vassal of Assyria (in fact, Tiglath-pileser claims to have put him on the throne), but after a few years Hoshea withholds his tribute to Assyria and makes overtures to the king of Egypt. As a result Shalmaneser, who had come to the throne of Assyria, lays siege to Samaria and after 3 years captures the city and exiles the people. **1** *Twelfth year of Ahaz*: this is one of the dates that according to the thesis of Thiele has been shifted by 12 years; it was the 4th year of the co-regency or the first year of the reign of Ahaz,

or 732. The reign of Hoshea can be dated 731–722 BC. **3** *Shalmaneser*: Shalmaneser V, who came to the throne in 727/6. Some scholars assume that Shalmaneser made two campaigns, the first to receive tribute and the second to punish Samaria; there is no record of this in the only one of Shalmaneser's annals which survives. *Became his vassal*: probably 'had become his vassal'; *cf.* 15:30. **4** *So, king of Egypt.* There are numerous difficulties here. No such king is known, and the word for 'Egypt' in Hebrew is capable of at least two other meanings. *So* has been identified with the Pharaohs Shabaka, the first king, and Shabataka, the second king, of the XXVth Dynasty. Sargon mentions Sibu, a 'Tartan' or general of Egypt whom he defeated at Raphia in 720. Therefore we should probably read 'Sewe'. We can assume that because of internal pressure Hoshea was forced to turn to Egypt for help against Assyria. Shalmaneser promptly moved in to punish him. If the action in v. 4 is identified with that of Sargon in 720, it of course is slightly out of place here chronologically. We consider the problem too difficult to solve with the existing information.

5 *Invaded*: no doubt Shalmaneser's invasion of 724, and the *three years* would be inclusive of the fall of Samaria in 722. This date is fairly well established. The ability of the city to withstand siege for that period of time is a tribute to the engineering skill of Omri and Ahab. Sargon II, who succeeded Shalmaneser V in 722, records for his first year that he besieged and took Samaria, carried away 27,290 inhabitants and other plunder, and settled people from other lands there. (Sargon is mentioned in Is. 20:1, but he is not mentioned here.) The biblical text would indicate on first reading that Shalmaneser actually conquered Samaria. The opinion of scholars is divided at this point; Olmstead is convinced that Shalmaneser actually conquered the city while Sargon took credit for it; Thiele suggests that Sargon may have been the general in charge of the siege when Samaria fell and therefore took credit for it. The relationship of Sargon to Shalmaneser is a debated point. According to one inscription he claims that he was the son of Tiglath-pileser and therefore a brother or half-brother of Shalmaneser, but there is no further confirmation of this. It is entirely possible that he was a usurper. The absence of records from Shalmaneser makes it impossible to discuss this point further.

6 *Carried the Israelites away.* It was standard procedure in the days of the Assyrians and the Babylonians to remove all who might be responsible for any kind of rebellion or treachery to other areas. In the case of the Assyrians, the plan was to put them in small groups so that they would lose their identity and mingle with the local populations. On the other hand the Babylonians transferred their captives to settlements where they could maintain their identity. *Halah*, possibly *Ḥalaḫḫu*, E of Haran, if a place-name (as AV); but LXX takes it to be a river, in which case it might be the Balikh river. *Habor*, taken to be a place in AV and a river in RSV, the Khabur. *Gozan* is a river further unidentified. *The cities of the Medes*: further identification impossible; some would read 'the mountains of the Medes'. One of Sargon's triumphs was the conquest of Media. We must remember that Galilee and Transjordan had already been taken into captivity by Tiglath-pileser III, therefore the number of exiles listed in Sargon's inscription represents only the people of Samaria and the surrounding region.

17:7–18 The reason for the fall of Samaria. The theological explanation of the historical event is set forth in considerable detail, hence we know more about the theology than the history of this critical period. **10, 11** *Pillars* and *Asherim* . . . *high places*: see on 1 Ki. 14:15; 18:17ff.; 2 Ki. 10:15–28. **16** *Molten images* were introduced by Ahaz; **17** likewise the *divination and sorcery*.

17:19–23 Summary of Israel's iniquity. As 'the way of David' is the ideal of Judah, so 'the sins which Jeroboam did' expresses the history of the northern kingdom. **19** *Judah*: often in the prophets Israel serves as a warning to Judah. **23** *Until this day*: evidence of a later point of view, but I see no reason to make this paragraph 'post-exilic'.

17:24–41 The origin of the Samaritans. 24 After the northern kingdom was conquered and many of its people taken into exile, the Assyrian king imported peoples from other places. *Cuthah, Avva,* and *Sepharvaim* are considered to be in Syria near *Hamath* on the Orontes. **25, 26** The appearance of *lions* (*cf.* 1 Ki. 13:24) was considered by the king of Assyria to have resulted from the ignorance of the god of the land by these people who had been imported; and therefore priests were brought. **27** *One of the priests*: Gray suggests 'some' or 'chosen ones of the priests'. **30** *Succoth-benoth*: many interpretations have been suggested; none is very convincing. *Nergal* was the god of Kutu. *Ashima*, possibly a goddess of the Assyrians, but some would read 'Asherah'. **31** *Nibhaz* and *Tartak* are unknown. *Adrammelech*: some would read 'Adad-melekh', and the following word 'Anu-melekh', Adad and Anu being ancient gods of Babylonia. *The gods of Sepharvaim*: again none of the many suggestions seems compelling. All of these religious practices are used as lessons to the people of the Lord who will read this account.

18:1 – 21:26 JUDAH AND THE ASSYRIAN EMPIRE

This period covers about 100 years, and coincides with the gradual decline of the Assyrian Empire from its zenith to mediocrity. This is the final phase of the history of Judah and is told in much detail, although the detail frequently is religious and not simply historical.

18:1–12 Hezekiah of Judah

Cf. 2 Ch. 29–32, an almost exact duplicate in Is. 36–39; Josephus, *Ant.* ix.13 – x.2. Hezekiah is

listed as one of the greatest of all the kings of Judah, who gave himself to religious reform. His reign was contemporary with that of Shalmaneser, Sargon II and Sennacherib. Historians complain that we have more information about Hezekiah's boils than we have about the political situation. For the first time a canonical prophet (Isaiah) takes an active part in state politics.

18:1–8 Introductory statement. The religious estimate of this reign is entirely good, comparable only to that of Josiah. **1** *Third year of Hoshea*: this is one of the data that are out by 12 years (Thiele). Kitchen (in *NBD*) rejects Thiele's theory and says that co-regencies will account for the differences; but this would mean that Hezekiah became co-regent in 728 at the age of 13, when Ahaz was only 26 and had reigned only 6 years. Gray supposes that Hezekiah was adopted as heir-apparent in 729 at the age of 10 (by my calculation, 13). **4** The suggestion has been made that this portion was taken from the reforms of Josiah. It is true that there are many parallels but, as Gray points out, there is no good reason to deny Hezekiah the credit of the reformation described here. It certainly fits in with the period of Isaiah as well as the reforms of Josiah fit in with the period of Jeremiah. On *the bronze serpent, cf.* Nu. 21:9. **8** *From watchtower to fortified city*: this is a merism to indicate all types of Philistine holdings.

18:9–12 The fall of Samaria. Except for chronological data, this paragraph repeats in condensed form what is told in 17:3–8.

18:13 – 19:37 Jerusalem besieged by Sennacherib

Cf. Is. 36:1 – 39:8. The story is told at great length, but the military and political details are hardly mentioned.

18:13–16 Hezekiah pays tribute. 13 *Fourteenth year of King Hezekiah*, another element in the problem of chronology. Sennacherib came to the throne in 705 and his third expedition is dated positively at 701. If the 6th year of Hezekiah was 722 (the fall of Samaria, 2 Ki. 18:10), then the 14th year could not have been 701. Any attempt to change the figures, such as to read 'twenty-fourth' instead of *fourteenth*, involves the ages of Hezekiah and Ahaz, and several different scripture references. We conclude that Hezekiah became king in his own right in 716/15 and reigned until 687 BC. Sennacherib tells of this invasion (*cf. ANET*, pp. 287f.). He claims to have laid siege to 46 walled cities and many villages, to have taken 200,150 people, and to have shut up Hezekiah in Jerusalem 'as a bird in a cage'. His figure, '30 talents of gold, 800 talents of silver, plus many other items', is in close agreement with the statement of vv. 14–16. Possibly the 300 *talents of silver* of v. 14 was in minted form, whereas the '800 talents of silver' in Sennacherib's record included the silver mentioned in v. 15. The value of the gold and silver in v. 14 by one calculation is about $1,750,000 (£730,000); according to another estimate, $5,650,000 (about £2,350,000).

18:17-37 The taunts of the Rabshakeh. *Cf.* 2 Ch. 32:9-19; Is. 36:2-22. **17** *Tartan*: Akkadian for 'second in command', the commander-in-chief of the army (*cf.* Is. 20:1). *The Rabsaris*: a high military official (*cf.* Je. 39:3). *The Rabshakeh*: probably a high civil official. These are treated as proper names in AV. *The conduit of the upper pool*: site not positively identified; possibly a conduit to bring water from the Virgin's pool to the pool of Siloam (*cf.* Is. 7:3). **18** *Eliakim*: *cf.* Is. 22:20. For the offices, see on 1 Ki. 4:2, 3. According to Is. 22:15ff., *Shebnah* is 'over the household' and is denounced, and *Eliakim* is to replace him. Some scholars consider the two Shebnahs as different persons. **23** Rabshakeh taunts them with a wager, and **25** also with the boast that he has come at the command of Yahweh. We need not assume that this was true, or even if it was true that Rabshakeh knew it. **26** *Aramaic language*: the language in general use in diplomatic and commercial circles, but obviously not understood by the common people of Judah at this time. We assume that the Rabshakeh was speaking Hebrew through an interpreter. **27** His reply to Eliakim is insulting and **28** his appeal to the people over the heads of their leaders in *the language of Judah* (or Hebrew) is an indication of his boldness. **31, 32** indicate that the conditions of exile will not be difficult if the people go meekly. **34** *Hamath, etc.*: Syrian cities which had been taken over by Sennacherib (*cf.* 17:24). Lucian and Old Latin insert 'Where are the gods of Samaria?'

19:1-7 Isaiah's counsel. At last the king turns to Isaiah, who has steadfastly opposed alliance with Egypt (Is. 30:1-7, 15; 31:1-9). **2** *The prophet Isaiah*: the first appearance of the canonical prophet in the historical books of the OT. **4** *The remnant that is left*: *cf.* the name of Isaiah's son (Is. 7:3).

19:8-19 The message from Rabshakeh. 9 *Tirhakah* poses a problem of date, since his reign is dated 688-670 BC. Some have supposed a second invasion by Sennacherib at that later date. Others assume that Tirhakah was acting as general (he is not called 'Pharaoh') for his uncle Shabataka, but this raises the objection that Tirhakah was much too young to have been the general in 701. In our text it seems that the rumour of the approach of the Egyptians caused Sennacherib to rush back to Assyria, but according to record the Assyrian king defeated Pharaoh and his allies at the battle of Eltekah in 701. Scholars assume that it was news of an impending revolt in Babylon that caused Sennacherib to leave the west and return to his homeland. **12** *Gozan*: perhaps Tell Ḥalaf (Gray), the name of a river in 17:6. *Haran*: a chief trading city of NW Mesopotamia on the Balikh river. *Rezeph*: one of several places with this name; this one is on the road from Haran to Palmyra. *Eden*: the Aramaean state Bit-adinni near Haran. *Telassar*: site unknown; Gray suggests Til-Bashir. **13** *Sepharvaim*: see on 17:24. *Hena*: site unknown.

19:20-34 The prophecy of Isaiah. *Cf.* Is. 37:21-35. **21-28** are sometimes described as a 'taunt song' in *qinah* metre. **22** *The Holy One of Israel*, a common expression throughout Isaiah (see Introduction to Isaiah). **23** *Densest forest*: AV 'the forest of his Carmel'; to treat *karmillo* as a proper name here makes little sense (*cf.* 2 Ch. 26:10, AV and RSV). **24** *All the streams of Egypt*: AV 'all the rivers of besieged places'. *Egypt* is not in the Hebrew; on the other hand this word for 'river' generally means 'Nile' in the OT. MT reads 'I will dry up', LXX and Vulg. translate in the past tense; but Sennacherib actually never invaded Egypt, and the future tense makes better sense. **25** *Cf.* Is. 10:5-11. **28** *My hook in your nose.* Esarhaddon's relief at Zenjirli shows Tirhakah of Egypt and Baalu of Tyre each with a ring in his nose and the cords in the hand of the conqueror. *Cf.* 2 Ch. 33:11. **29** Isaiah predicts the deliverance of the land, with at most the loss of harvest for 2 years. This is a prophecy in prose. **30** *Cf.* the doctrine of the *remnant*, set forth by Isaiah in Is. 10:20-22, although the same word does not appear here. For the miraculous deliverance, *cf.* Is. 30:15; 31:1-5. **32** This does not agree with Sennacherib's inscription of his campaign of 701 BC, where he mentions a rampart, and may support the view that the oracle refers to a later campaign. In his cylinder inscription Sennacherib does not claim to have attacked Jerusalem.

19:35-37 The deliverance from Sennacherib. *Cf.* Is. 37:36-38; 2 Ch. 32:21-23. **35** *That night*: in Hebrew indefinite 'on such a night', omitted in Isaiah and Chronicles. *A hundred and eighty-five thousand*: there is no evidence outside the Bible of such tremendous loss; in Chronicles it is much more moderate. Herodotus (ii.141) tells of the tradition that the army of Sennacherib was routed in the vicinity of Pelusium in a single night, when mice infested the camp and ate the quivers, bow-strings, and leather shield handles. Some have suggested that this may refer to the same situation, although the location does not fit; a pestilence such as bubonic plague may have been behind both stories. In any event Sennacherib did not take Jerusalem at this time. **37** *Nisroch*: otherwise not known; scholars suggest the god Nusku, worshipped at Nippur; others suggest Marduk. *Adrammelech and Sharezer.* According to Eusebius, Sennacherib was killed by his son, Ardumuzanus or Adramelus (these may not be the same person), and was succeeded by Nergilus who was killed by the Adramelus just mentioned. Nergilus could be Nergal-sharezer, which could be the *Sharezer* here. The Assyrian records do not give the names of the assassins but simply state that Sennacherib perished by the hand of one of his sons. The assassination took place in 682 BC.

20:1-21 Conclusion of Hezekiah's reign

20:1-11 Hezekiah's illness. *Cf.* Is. 38-39; 2 Ch. 32:24-26. **1** *Set your house in order*: *cf.* 2 Sa.

17:23. **6** *Fifteen years*: calculated from Hezekiah's death in *c.* 687, this could mean that the illness occurred in 701, which would be the year of Sennacherib's siege (*cf.* v. 1, 'in those days'). There is an objection to this date, on the grounds that Merodach-baladan (v. 12) was king of Babylonia 721–710 and again in 702 for a few months, at which time he was hardly in a position to send an embassy anywhere. But Merodach-baladan started to regain his throne in 705, at the death of Sargon, and during the next few years he was trying to cultivate as many allies as possible. We should probably date Hezekiah's illness prior to the siege of Jerusalem, perhaps between 705 and 702, and not take the prophecy of 15 years as a means of establishing the date of the illness. **7** Some scholars have suggested that the illness could not have been very serious if a poultice of *figs*, commonly used for opening boils, was sufficient to heal him. This ignores, however, the divine element which lies behind the story, even if not mentioned specifically in this verse. *That he may recover*: RSV translates as a purpose clause, which makes sense in the context; AV reads it as simple past tense, 'he recovered' (*cf.* Is. 38:4–22). **9** *Ten steps*: AV 'degrees'; we need not suppose a sundial; the construction of steps can be arranged so that the shadow cast by the sun gives an approximation of the time. A recent suggestion, based on the word in the Dead Sea Isaiah scroll, proposes a shrine for astral worship on some rooftop, and an eclipse of the sun as the sign. But this would not account for the details of the story nor for the psychological effect on Hezekiah described in the text. Whether the sun was actually moved backward, or some refraction of its rays caused its shadow to move backward, is a discussion based on attempts to find more than the biblical text actually says. **11** *The sun*, based on Syriac (*cf.* Is. 38:8); Hebrew lacks 'sun'.

20:12–15 The embassy from Merodach-baladan. *Cf.* Is. 39:1–8; 2 Ch. 32:31. **12** *Merodach-baladan*: MT 'Berodach', an obvious mistake arising from the similarity of *B* and *M* in the older script. Josephus says the aim of the embassy was to secure Hezekiah as an ally (*Ant.* x.2.2). **13** Snaith points out that there is something to be said for the date 702, for Hezekiah actually did revolt. *Hezekiah welcomed them* (Heb. 'listened to them'): a difference of one letter in Hebrew would read 'Hezekiah rejoiced', or 'was glad', which agrees with LXX, Vulg., Syr., and Is. 39:2.

20:16–19 Isaiah rebukes Hezekiah. 17 Some scholars put this prophecy at a later period, doubtless following the widely-held principle that there can be no predictive prophecy. This principle, however, fails to explain the psychological effect which the prophets had on their contemporaries. Entirely apart from the fact that God could reveal these things to Isaiah, there is really nothing in these verses that had not already been the experience of many smaller nations that had been carried into captivity by

the Assyrians. If someone objects that it is Babylon that is mentioned, it may be replied that Babylon is already challenging Assyrian rule, and it was a Babylonian embassy that caused Hezekiah to commit this folly. **19** *Peace and security in my days*: in the spirit of the sorry words from Munich in 1939.

20:20, 21 Summary of Hezekiah's reign. 20 *The pool and the conduit*: probably a reference to 'Hezekiah's Tunnel' discovered nearly 100 years ago; the Siloam Inscription describes the completion of the tunnel. Is. 22:9ff. may indicate that the Siloam tunnel was built after 701.

21:1–18 Manasseh of Judah

Cf. 2 Ch. 33:1–20; Josephus, *Ant.* x.3.1 – 4.1. Manasseh reigned longer than any other king in Judah, coming to the throne as co-regent in 696, becoming sole ruler in 687/6, and ruling until 642. He is described as the worst of all the kings, and the sins of Manasseh are given as the reason for the judgment on Judah (24:3). The peak of Assyrian prosperity in the west came during his reign. In 671 Esarhaddon invaded Egypt, and for the next 20 years at least, Assyrian troops continually moved back and forth on the coastal route to Egypt—which provided peace and security for Judah, but also meant that Judah was vassal to Assyria. Manasseh's name occurs in several Assyrian inscriptions, but the account in Kings deals mostly with his religious apostasy.

21:1–10 The abominations of Manasseh. 2 *The abominable practices of the nations*: these are described in the following verses. **3** *High places*: see on 1 Ki. 3:2. Manasseh is the only king of Judah likened to Ahab of Israel. *The host of heaven*: Manasseh reintroduced astral worship. **6** *Burned his son*: part of the worship of Melek (Molech), *cf.* 16:3. It was practised in the valley of Hinnom (2 Ch. 28:3; Je. 32:35). *Soothsaying . . . augury . . . mediums . . . wizards*: ancient practices that possibly had never completely died out, but Manasseh gave them the support of the throne. It makes little sense to claim that Deuteronomy was written to offset the abominable practices of this period, when so many of these can be traced back before the time of Moses. **7** *Asherah*: see 1 Ki. 15:13. **7–15** According to some scholars these verses are the work of a later editor, *c.* 550 BC, who had to account for the fact that Jerusalem was destroyed and the kingdom brought to an end. But this ignores the reason why Jerusalem was destroyed. According to the consistent biblical picture, prophets undoubtedly living and prophesying before the date of the destruction were already saying such things, and Jerusalem refused to listen.

21:11–16 Yahweh's word to Manasseh. Idolatry and wickedness did not begin with Manasseh in Judah. To suppose that the 'editor' had any such notion is to infer that there was no sin at Sinai, no disobedience against Yahweh in the days of the judges, no idolatry in Solomon, and no prophetic voice in the land crying out against idolatry prior to 550 BC. Manasseh is the culmination of all rebellion against Yahweh; he represents the antithesis of David, an 'Antidavid' whose purpose is to destroy the Davidic covenant. It is significant that there is no prophetic voice during the reign of Manasseh. **13** *Measuring line . . . plummet*: see Am. 7:8. **16** Josephus (*Ant.* x.3.1) says that Manasseh slew some every day. According to tradition he slew Isaiah the prophet, sawing him asunder (*cf.* Heb. 11:37).

21:17, 18 Summary of Manasseh's reign. Nothing further is added, except that he was buried *in the garden of his house*; we are not told why this deviation from the usual interment.

21:19–26 Amon of Judah

Cf. 2 Ch. 33:21–25. Amon reigned only 2 years, and followed in his father's footsteps. There is no indication that Amon was made co-regent with Manasseh—a notable fact, considering the age of Manasseh and his long reign. **19** *Jotbah*, about 20 miles N of Ezion-geber (Nu. 33:33). **23** Amon was assassinated at the age of 24 by his *servants*, but **24** *the people* avenged his death by killing the conspirators and made Josiah, his son, king.

22:1 – 23:30 THE REFORMS OF JOSIAH
22:1–20 The book of the law

22:1, 2 Introductory statement of Josiah's reign. *Cf.* 2 Ch. 34:1 – 35:27. Josiah is an ideal king in many ways, and in the book of Kings, he and his great-grandfather Hezekiah are the only kings receiving unqualified approval. The reign of Josiah is approximately contemporary with the prophet Jeremiah, yet strangely there is no mention of Jeremiah in Kings and only a passing reference to Josiah in Jeremiah's prophecy. Ashurbanipal of Assyria was a weak king, and Josiah could pursue a course of independent action. **1** *Eight years old*: the grammar suggests a higher number. His sons Jehoiakim (23:36) and Jehoahaz (23:31) were 25 and 23 when he was about 39, which would make him a father at 14 or 15—but this is not impossible. If he was hidden for 7 years, the figure *eight* is in order. Moreover, if we were to read 'eighteen', it would mean that Amon was only 7 when Josiah was born. The death of Josiah may be accurately dated by the Babylonian Chronicle at 609; therefore he became king in 639.

22:3–7 The repairs to the Temple. Snaith (*IB*) supposes that Josiah could not begin repairs until after the death of Ashurbanipal, and then the Scythian invasion further held up the plan. **3** *Eighteenth year*: 621 BC, 5 years after the death of Ashurbanipal. According to 2 Ch. 34:3, Josiah's reform in Jerusalem began in the 12th year of his reign, which would be 628. **4** The procedure is the same as followed by Jehoash (12:9–15).

22:8–13 The discovery of the book of the law. The details of the story sound like the result of

many tellings, an indication of the great importance of the event. **8** *The book of the law*: this has become a primary item of critical study. The earliest critical view was that it was the 'D'-document, probably Dt. 12–26, which had been recently written, and was 'found' to give it prestige. Scholars have modified this view in so many different ways that little remains of the original theory. On the other hand the conservative view, that it was the entire Pentateuch, does not commend itself if for no other reason than the tremendous size of the scroll of the Pentateuch. **8, 10** The book of the law was read publicly twice in a part of the same day. Since the reforms were so closely related to the material in Deuteronomy, there can be little doubt that the book of the law was either Deuteronomy, or a substantial portion of it.

22:14–20 The prophecy of Huldah. Scholars are inclined to accept this as an accurate record, for it is extraordinary to have a woman speak for Yahweh. Both Jeremiah and Zephaniah were active; an artificial writing of the account would almost certainly have made use of one of these prophets (*cf.* 2 Ch. 34:20–28). **15** *The man*. Snaith notes that the king is but a man: 'This needs to be remembered in the face of all attempts to show that among the Hebrews the king was regarded as divine.' **16–20** The prophecy of the destruction of the Temple and the carrying of the inhabitants into exile, according to some scholars, was written by the later editor. But in the light of the experience of so many other nations, and particularly of the northern kingdom, there is no reason for even a rationalist to have to date this passage after the fact.

23:1–30 Josiah's religious reforms and subsequent death

Cf. 2 Ch. 34:29–32.

23:1–3 The making of the covenant. In some ways, the religion of the OT is the covenant between Yahweh and His people. It is above all fitting to re-establish this relationship in a time of religious revival. **3** *The pillar*: *cf.* 11:14. *Joined in*: AV 'stood to' represents the Hebrew, and probably describes the actual ritual of standing within the covenant symbols.

23:4–20 The destruction of the cult places and objects. *Cf.* 2 Ch. 34:3, 4, 7, 33. **4** *Priests of the second order*: perhaps it should be 'the second priest' (*cf.* 25:18 and Je. 52:24). *Fields of the Kidron*: Lucian has 'lime kilns of Kidron'. **5** *Priests*: the word used here always refers to priests of a foreign religion (Ho. 10:5; Zp. 1:4; perhaps Ho. 4:4). *Constellations*: the Hebrew word occurs only here in the OT, but is used commonly in rabbinical Hebrew for the signs of the zodiac and the planets; it seems to be part of astral worship. **6** *The brook Kidron*, later called the 'Valley of Jehoshaphat', the scene of the final resurrection and judgment of the world. *Cf.* the end of the verse with Ex. 32:20. **7** *Cult prostitutes*: probably including both sexes, although the word is masculine (*cf.* Dt. 23:17).

Hangings (Heb. 'houses') is a Jewish traditional interpretation, and finds support in an Arabic word having the same consonants. **8** *The high places of the gates*: the same consonants would read 'the high places of the satyrs', or 'goat demons' (see Lv. 17:7; 2 Ch. 11:15). **9** is difficult to interpret; it suggests that these priests were admitted to the sacred meal but were not allowed to sacrifice. **10** *Topheth*, probably 'fireplace', referring to *the valley of the sons of Hinnom* where children were burnt as sacrifices (*cf.* Dt. 12:31; Je. 7:31). The valley of Hinnom was located on the S side of Jerusalem, and came to be known as Gehenna (see on 16:3). **11** *Precincts*: meaning unknown; probably some kind of structure W of the Temple (1 Ch. 26:18). Some scholars take the word to be Persian and therefore date this portion very late, but a Babylonian etymology has been suggested. (*Cf.* Montgomery, *ICC*, p. 540.) *Chariots of the sun*: part of the symbol of the solar deity, hence solar worship, or the worship of the sun god, is intended here. **13** *The mount of corruption*: see on 1 Ki. 11:7. Scholars believe that the word *corruption* has been repointed from the word for 'anointing oil', and that this refers to the Mount of Olives, E of the brook Kidron. **15** *He pulled down and he broke in pieces*, based on LXX; Heb. 'he burned the high place' makes little sense. **18** *The prophet who came out of Samaria*: see 1 Ki. 13; but the passage is difficult.

23:21-23 The celebration of the Passover. This was the climax of the reformation, and followed the description in Dt. 16:1-8. According to some scholars, this was the first Passover ever held in Jerusalem, hence new regulations were needed. Neither this passage nor 18:4 makes mention of the Passover of Hezekiah (2 Ch. 30). The Passover, like all religious ritual, certainly shows signs of development historically. At the same time it seems impossible to separate it from the Exodus, since it is so deeply woven into the cultus as well as the faith of the people of the OT.

23:24-27 Further reforms and the Lord's word. Josiah presses the reform throughout Judah in order to establish the words of the law. There seems to be little point in supposing that the author/editor could not understand why this did not turn away Yahweh's anger and therefore added vv. 26, 27. The great 8th-century prophets had spoken, and Jeremiah and Zephaniah were even then speaking: if we remove from their prophecies all warnings that are like these verses, there would be little left! **24** *Teraphim*: household images (*cf.* 1 Sa. 19:13-16; Gn. 31:32, 34). **25** Expressed in the words of the *Shema* (Dt. 6:5), which was obviously already liturgical.

23:28-30 Summary of Josiah's reign. *Cf.* 2 Ch. 35:20-27. The great reform suddenly collapses, when Josiah marches his army to Megiddo to oppose Pharaoh Neco and is killed. The city of Nineveh had fallen in 612 BC through a two-pronged attack by the Medes and the Babylonians. We do not know the reason why Neco was

marching; possibly he wanted to support the tottering Assyrian kingdom, or more likely he wanted to take Syria for himself. Likewise the reason why Josiah decided to march to Megiddo is not given. He may still have been under some obligation to Assyria, although this seems unlikely and certainly is not mentioned; or he may have been moving to extend his own authority (*cf.* 2 Ch. 35:20-24). The suggestion that Josiah went out at the invitation or demand of Neco is flatly contradicted by the account in Chronicles. **29** *Neco*: Neco II of Egypt, 610-595 BC. AV Neco 'went up against the king of Assyria', following the logical meaning of the Hebrew, seems to make no sense and RSV is better, *Neco went up to the king of Assyria*. The confusion of *'el* 'to' and *'al* 'against' is quite common in the OT. **30** *Dead*: the Hebrew could mean 'dying', which agrees with the account in Chronicles, but the construction of the Hebrew sentence would be a bit strange. *Megiddo*: from Heb. *har me giddôn*, 'Mount Megiddo' is derived from Greek 'Armageddon' (*cf.* Rev. 16:16). Notice that *the people made Jehoahaz king* to succeed Josiah.

To suggest that with the death of Josiah the whole 'Deuteronomic structure, which the first editor had erected, fell to the ground' (Snaith, *IB*) is to speak of a structure which the critics have erected. The so-called first editor would never have written the book if his hopes had collapsed—or was he supposed to have been writing as the events occurred?

23:31 – 25:30 THE LAST DAYS OF JUDAH

From the death of Josiah to the destruction of Jerusalem is but a short span, and the events pass at an ever-quickening pace. In 22 years there will be 4 kings, and 3 invasions of Jerusalem.

23:31-35 Jehoahaz of Judah

Cf. 2 Ch. 36:1-4. Manasseh was Hezekiah's son, and Jehoahaz had Josiah for a father: in each case, the son of the reformer was 'evil'. We must ask ourselves, Why? Hezekiah forgot to ask the Lord before he opened his treasury to the Babylonians, and Josiah forgot to ask whether he should go to Megiddo—is there any connection? **31** Jehoahaz was not the oldest son of Josiah (see v. 36). Apparently the people felt he would be a better king. *Jehoahaz* was his throne-name; his private name was 'Shallum' (Je. 22:10ff.; 1 Ch. 3:15). *Reigned three months*: confirmed by the Babylonian Chronicle which states that Neco's campaign in 609 lasted from Tammuz (June/July) to Elul (August/September) (D. J. Wiseman, *Chronicles of Chaldaean Kings*, pp. 62f.). **32** *He did what was evil*, but he did not have much opportunity. Gray suggests that he turned to Egypt for aid, but this does not fit the events in vv. 33, 34. More likely he opposed turning to Egypt for support and Neco put him in bonds, laid the land under tribute, and made Eliakim king in his place. **33** *Riblah*: an important city about 20 miles S of Hama, in the Beqa' near Qadesh on the Orontes. *A hundred talents of silver*: about $240,000 (or £100,000) at today's price. *A talent of gold* at the official rate is about $42,500 (£17,500). 34 *Eliakim* was the older son of Josiah; *Jehoiakim* was probably his throne-name. Jehoahaz was taken to Egypt and died there. 35 In contrast to the tribute in the days of Manasseh which was imposed upon the wealthy, this tribute, very much smaller, was imposed upon the entire country, suggesting that the country was very poor.

23:36 – 24:7 Jehoiakim of Judah

Cf. 2 Ch. 36:5–8; Je. 22:18, 19; 26:20–23; 36:1–26; 1 Esdras 1:32–36; Josephus, *Ant.* x.5.2. (Josephus contains a long extract from Berossos, our primary authority for this portion of Nebuchadrezzar's empire.) Jehoiakim reigns for 11 years, part of the time as a vassal to Nebuchadrezzar. After 3 years, Jehoiakim revolts, which is possibly to be taken in connection with Neco's march northward (according to Je. 46:2 in the 4th year of Jehoiakim). This was the occasion for Nebuchadrezzar to destroy Neco and extend his authority to the border of Egypt. It was probably at this time that a number of the royal family and nobility were taken to Babylonia (Dn. 1:1–6; but *cf.* Je. 52:28). There are difficulties to be resolved. According to Josephus, in his 8th year Jehoiakim refused to pay tribute and Nebuchadrezzar sent a punitive expedition; this would agree with the Babylonian Chronicle which records an encounter with Egypt in Palestine in that year.

23:36, 37 Introductory statement. *Jehoiakim* (Eliakim, v. 34) is put on the throne by Neco, forced to pay tribute to the Pharaoh, and he *did what was evil in the sight of the Lord*, which is not further described. Jehoiakim's influence in Egypt is suggested by Je. 26:21–23. His reign may be dated 608–597 BC.

24:1–4 Nebuchadrezzar's reign. This great king of Babylon reigned 605–562 BC. His name is regularly given as Nebuchadrezzar in Jeremiah, which is nearer the Babylonian *Nabu-kudurri-uṣur.* 1 *Jehoiakim became his servant three years*: 603–601, if we accept Josephus' figure, but it is also possible that Nebuchadrezzar as the commander of the Babylonian army immediately moved toward Jerusalem after Neco had withdrawn to Egypt in 608, in which case Jehoiakim's revolt would be in 605. In that year Nebuchadrezzar was on a campaign in the west and had to return home to receive the throne on his father's death. 2 The picture would fit a time when Babylon was preoccupied elsewhere and the border tribes were making the most of the occasion. *The prophets*: Jeremiah and Uriah (Je. 26:20ff.). For background see Je. 7:16–18; Ezk. 8:5–18.

24:5–7 Summary of Jehoiakim's reign. 6 *Slept with his fathers* indicates a peaceful death, but according to 2 Ch. 36:6 Nebuchadrezzar 'bound him in fetters to take him to Babylon', and Jeremiah (22:19) says he was to have 'the burial of an ass' (*i.e.* none). One suggestion is that Jehoiakim revolted again and when Nebuchadrezzar attempted to take him to Babylon, he was wounded and died and his body was cast away. 7 Babylon was at last in control of the west.

24:8–17 Jehoiachin of Judah

Cf. 2 Ch. 36:9, 10; Je. 29:2; 1 Esdras 1:41–44; Josephus, *Ant.* x.6.3 and x.7.1. The young king reigned only 3 months, during which Jerusalem was in siege. According to the Chronicle of Nebuchadrezzar the siege extended from Chislev (December) to Adar (March) 598/597. For an evaluation of him see Ezk. 17:12–24. 8 *Jehoiachin*: his throne-name; his real name was Jeconiah (1 Ch. 3:16) or in brief Coniah (Je. 22:24). 12 *The eighth year of his reign*: the first time the scripture writer has used foreign dating; Nebuchadrezzar's 8th year would be 597 BC; Je. 52:28 'seventh year' is based on a different system of calendration. According to a Babylonian tablet, the capture of Jerusalem is dated to 15/16 March (2 Adar) 597. 13 *Cf.* Je. 27:19f. *All*: the word is frequently used figuratively in Scripture (*cf.* 25:15). From Dn. 5:2; Ezr. 1:7–11 we assume that only the vessels that were too large to be carried away were cut up. The others were taken to the temple of Marduk in Babylon. The story of Jehoiachin is continued in 25:27–30. It is obvious that he was considered to be the legal or true king of Judah. 13, 14 Some scholars claim that this refers to the destruction of Jerusalem of 586. However, the figures in vv. 14, 16 do not agree with those in Je. 52:28–30, as Snaith points out (in *IB*). 15 *Cf.* Je. 27:20. 16 *Cf.* Je. 52:28ff.; some scholars prefer Jeremiah's figures.

24:18 – 25:7 Zedekiah of Judah

Cf. 2 Ch. 36:11–21; Je. 39:1–10; 40:7 – 41:18; 52. The struggles between the pro-Egyptian and the pro-Babylonian parties in Judah are reflected in Jeremiah; Zedekiah apparently falls in with the pro-Egyptian party. When Psamtik II came to the throne of Egypt in 593 BC he stirred up trouble in the western provinces of the Babylonian Empire. With his successor Apries (Hophra), who came to the throne in 588, this unrest apparently breaks out as rebellion, doubtless involving Zedekiah. 18 *Zedekiah*, whose name was Mattaniah (v. 17), was full brother of Jehoahaz and uncle of Jehoiachin, as Je. 52:1 and LXX of 2 Ch. 36:10 indicate; the Heb. of 2 Ch. 36:10 therefore has to be reinterpreted. 20 The writer has skipped over the intervening years of Zedekiah's reign and does not tell us the reason for the revolt. Since there was a revolt under Hophra (Je. 44:30) in 588, it seems logical to tie Zedekiah's revolt in with this.

25:1 The date is given according to the Babylonian calendar. The siege began toward the end of December; hence the year had begun in March. Why it took 19 months to capture Jerusalem is not clear. In the light of Je. 37:5 we may assume there was some diversion of the

Babylonian forces, probably including Hophra's rebellion. The revolt broke out in 588, the 9th year of Zedekiah (25:1). **2** *The eleventh year* would be 586 and **3** *the fourth month*, Tammuz (June/July). **4** *The king . . . fled*: from LXX; lacking in Hebrew. Cf. Je. 39:4; 52:7. *The Arabah*: here the Jordan depression or the steppe land E of Jerusalem. Zedekiah apparently escaped from the SE corner of the city and made his way toward Jericho through the desert. **6** He was captured near Jericho and taken to the Babylonian king at Riblah (*cf.* 23:33). **7** His punishment is recorded here, but his death is probably recorded in Ezk. 12:12ff.

25:8–30 The destruction of Jerusalem and the Exile

Cf. 2 Ch. 36:14–21; Je. 52:12–30. The Babylonians burnt the entire city, Temple, palace and houses, deported the population, leaving only the farm workers. This was a deliberate punishment and destruction of the city. According to Albright the virtual depopulation of Judea has been confirmed by archaeological research (*Archaeology of Palestine*, pp. 140ff.; *Recent Discoveries in Bible Lands*, ch. 17).

25:8–21 The destruction of Jerusalem. 8 *The nineteenth year*, 586, and *the seventh day* of *the fifth month*, July/August. Lucian and Syr. read '9th day', which agrees with the Jewish tradition that on the 9th of Ab the Temple was destroyed, as was the Temple by Titus in AD 70. Jeremiah records captivities in the 7th year (52:28), in the 18th year (52:29), and in the 23rd year of Nebuchadrezzar (52:30). Wiseman and Albright prefer 587; Thiele and others, 586. **16, 17** *Cf.* Je. 52:20–23. There is no reference to the bronze bulls (*cf.* 2 Ki. 16:17). **18–21** The men who had been responsible for the revolt were put to death by Nebuchadrezzar at Riblah.

25:22–26 Gedaliah is made governor of the land of Judah. According to Josephus (*Ant.* x.9.1f.), Gedaliah was gentle and generous, but put his trust in men who were unworthy of it—which ultimately led to his assassination. **23** *In the open*

country: *cf.* Je. 40:7; these words are not in the Hebrew text. *Mizpah*, the seat of local government now that Jerusalem has been wiped out (*cf.* 1 Ki. 15:22), identified with Tell en-Nasbeh, about 9 miles N of Jerusalem, one of the few undisturbed sites at this time, according to archaeological discovery. It is interesting to note that *Gedaliah's* father supported Jeremiah's position against the pro-Egyptian party (Je. 26:24). A clay stamp seal found at Lachish from this period has the reading 'belonging to Gedaliah who is over the house', almost certainly this Gedaliah. *Ishmael*: nothing further is known about him. *Seraiah*, the grandson of Hilkiah the priest (1 Ch. 5:39, 40, MT). **25** It seems that Gedaliah and all those representing Babylonian authority were assassinated, and **26** the assassins and those who supported them fled to Egypt. *Egypt*: there was a considerable settlement of Jews in the Delta (*cf.* Is. 19:18, 19 and Josephus, *Ant.* xiii.3.1). Somewhat later we find Jews settled at Elephantine in Upper Egypt.

25:27–30 Jehoiachin is freed from prison. 27 The chronology is still counted with reference to Jehoiachin and this is synchronized with the year that *Evil-merodach* became king of Babylon. The new king, whose name should be pointed to read 'Amēl-Marduk', reigned from 562 to 560 BC. *Graciously freed*: Heb. 'lifted up the head' (*cf.* Gn. 40:13). **29** *Dined regularly at the king's table*: *cf.* 2 Sa. 9:7; 19:33; 1 Ki. 2:7. Cuneiform tablets from the period 594–569 BC refer to provisions supplied to Jehoiachin (in Babylonian *Yaukin*) together with his five sons. It is obvious from the date of these tablets that Nebuchadrezzar had treated Jehoiachin with the respect due to a king, and the action of Amēl-Marduk was the liberalizing of that policy. The Jews in Babylonia reckoned the years by those of Jehoiachin's captivity (*cf.* Ezk. 1:2), an indication of their faith that the Davidic covenant was still in effect and the line of David was still in Yahweh's care.

WILLIAM SANFORD LA SOR

1 and 2 Chronicles

INTRODUCTION

ITS POSITION IN THE CANON

The English versions follow the LXX and Vulg. in placing Chronicles immediately after Kings, but in the Hebrew Bible Chronicles is the last book of the OT. It will have occupied that position as early as the time of Christ (see on 2 Ch. 24:20f.). In Hebrew it is one book (though the printed Hebrew Bibles have followed the Christian tradition); the division into two goes back to the LXX.

TITLE AND DATE

Our name, Chronicles, is derived from a suggestion by Jerome. It is a fair rendering of the Hebrew title *diḇrê hayyāmîm*, *i.e.* 'The events of days' or 'Annals'; but it does not fairly express the nature or purpose of Chronicles. (See below under 'Purpose'.) The name used in Roman Catholic translations, Paralipomena, goes back to LXX via Vulg. It means 'things omitted' (from Kings), not a very suitable name.

An obvious *terminus a quo* for the date is given by 2 Ch. 36:22, *i.e.* 537 BC. The evidence, however, seems conclusive that Chronicles and Ezra-Nehemiah were originally one book. This would bring the date down to after 430 BC. The list of the descendants of Zerubbabel (1 Ch. 3:19–24) to the sixth generation suggests a date not earlier than 400–340 BC (but see note on this passage). Ne. 12:10f., 22f. brings the list of high priests down to Jaddua, who lived about 332 BC. Rudolph (*Esra und Nehemia*, 1949) maintains, as is intrinsically quite possible, that these are later scribal additions, and dates the book shortly after 400 BC. Albright (*JBL*, 1921, pp. 104–124) from other premises reaches a similar date. In any case dates later than 300 BC may be ruled out as improbable. The weakness of the arguments for a late date may be judged from Pfeiffer, *Introduction to the Old Testament*, pp. 811f.

AUTHOR

The facts just given make it very difficult to accept the Jewish ascription of authorship to Ezra, as does also the fragmentary description of Ezra's activity. But it seems that the tradition has been misunderstood, and that it is only the genealogies (1 Ch. 1–9) that are attributed to him (see *Jewish Enc.*, *in loc.*). If so, Delitzsch's view that Ezra was the compiler of much of the material used by the Chronicler may well be right, or even Welch's (*Schweich Lectures*, 1939) that the bulk of the book is pre-exilic. In either case the Chronicler will remain unknown to us by name.

PURPOSE

A chronicle differs from a history in that it is a record of passing events without any clear principle of selection in what is included and what omitted. The 'Chronicler' is obviously writing history, for there is a very clear principle both in his additions to Samuel and Kings and in his omissions. His additions concern mainly the Temple and its services and such incidents as exalted the religious side of the state in contrast to the civil. Obviously he is concerned mainly with Israel as a religious community. His omissions show that he is concerned with the development of two divine institutions, the Temple and the Davidic line of kings. Hence only the death of Saul is mentioned; his reign, David's sin, Absalom's rebellion, Adonijah's attempted usurpation are all omitted. The history of the northern kingdom, which was in rebellion against both of God's institutions, is mentioned only where it touches the fortunes of Judah.

That is why Chronicles is said to represent the priestly standpoint; it is concerned with the working out of what God has ordained and not, as Samuel and Kings, with the prophetic standpoint of how God dealt with His people and so revealed Himself.

The reasons for the writing of Chronicles are not far to seek. The post-exilic community had to understand how it had come into existence, that it was a true continuation of the pre-exilic kingdom (hence the genealogies), and what was the role of God's gift, the Temple and its services, that had been entrusted to them. The omission of so many familiar scenes from Samuel and Kings underlined that, though those that had returned from exile were few in number, God had always been eliminating from the history of His people that which was in rebellion against Him.

In an age when there is an ever-growing tendency to abandon the old revelation of God in the Scriptures, Chronicles has its lesson of encouragement and warning for us.

SOURCES

It is clear that the main source of Chronicles is Samuel and Kings. In addition reference is made to a number of other sources, twenty in all, *e.g.* 1 Ch. 5:17; 9:1; 23:27; 27:24; 29:29; 2 Ch. 9:29; 12:15; 13:22; 24:27; 26:22; 27:7; 33:19; 35:25, *et alia*. While there is no need to doubt that these sources existed (for their interpretation see *ICC*), it does not follow that the Chronicler must have made direct use of them, for he may have been using one or more works based on them.

369

It is improbable, though not impossible, that all these sources should have survived the Exile. He normally follows Samuel and Kings very closely, though he is prepared to make alterations at times; there is no reason for supposing that he has not followed his other sources equally closely, though there is evidence that he felt free to recast their language.

HISTORICAL VALUE

It is clear that Chronicles read by itself would give an unbalanced view of Israelite history; but it is equally clear that its author presupposed a knowledge of Samuel and Kings on the part of his readers so that criticism on this ground has no validity. More difficult is the large number of discrepancies between Chronicles and Samuel and Kings, some real, some imaginary. This is probably the reason why, in the Talmud, we find its historical accuracy queried, though not its canonicity.

In modern times the truth of all sections not found in Samuel and Kings has been queried (they have even been regarded as inventions of the Chronicler). But in the few cases where archaeology can pass an opinion it has tended to be favourable, and today the criticisms of scholars are normally much more cautious. There is no reason to doubt the essential accuracy of the Chronicler and his sources. Some of the discrepancies may be due to textual corruption

in his sources, and in places the text of Chronicles has been poorly transmitted.

One of the main problems in Chronicles is bound up with the numbers contained in it. Many are impossibly large, some disagree with Samuel and Kings, others are incompatible with the discoveries of archaeology. Yet there are other numbers that will not make sense of the usual suggestion that we are dealing with plain exaggeration, e.g. the 300 chariots in 2 Ch. 14:9 contrasted with the million footmen. The most obvious solution is that we are dealing with textual corruption either in the sources or in the transmission of Chronicles. A study of the variants in the genealogies will show how much of this there has been. There is, however, another aspect to be considered. Numbers from a thousand upwards were used not merely as round figures, but also hyperbolically (cf. HDB, III, p. 564; ISBE, p. 2159). So in a number of cases mentioned in the commentary probably only a large, or very large, number is meant. There is a discussion of the large numbers in the OT by R. E. D. Clark in JTVI, Vol. 87, 1955, pp. 82ff. and by J. W. Wenham in Tyndale Bulletin, No. 18, 1967, pp. 19ff. In this difficult area of biblical interpretation all conclusions are, of course, necessarily tentative.

For the chronology of the period covered by 1 and 2 Chronicles see Introduction to 1 and 2 Kings.

OUTLINE OF CONTENTS

1 CHRONICLES

2 CHRONICLES

10:1 – 36:23   The kings of Judah

10:1 – 12:16	Rehoboam
13:1–22	Abijah
14:1 – 16:14	Asa
17:1 – 20:37	Jehoshaphat
21:1 – 22:9	Jehoram and Ahaziah
22:10 – 24:27	Joash
25:1 – 26:2	Amaziah
26:3–23	Uzziah
27:1–9	Jotham
28:1–27	Ahaz
29:1 – 32:33	Hezekiah
33:1–20	Manasseh
33:21–25	Amon
34:1 – 35:27	Josiah
36:1–23	Downfall and restoration

COMMENTARY

1:1 – 9:44 GENEALOGIES

The purpose of the genealogies is one with the main purpose of Chronicles. It is plain that the Davidic line and the descendants of Levi are the chief interest (note the pointed omission of the house of Eli, which did not serve the Jerusalem Temple in a high-priestly capacity; cf. 1 Ch. 24:3). Next in importance are the two tribes especially connected with the monarchy, Judah and Benjamin. The passing mention of so many in the genealogies shows that their later omission is deliberate; they were not serving God's purposes. On the other hand the mention of many of no importance is the guarantee that none of God's people are forgotten.

Many of the names are taken from other canonical books; the sources of the others are generally not given, but the fragmentary nature of many of them is the best evidence that the Chronicler had portions of old records before him. In many cases, as elsewhere in Chronicles, there are variants in spelling compared with the same names in other canonical books. An * is placed against the form usually considered correct; where no * occurs we cannot be sure which is the original form. It will be seen that generally, but not always, it is the form in Chronicles that is inferior. For this the copiers of Chronicles are often responsible, not the author.

1:1 – 2:2 Genealogies from Genesis

The extremely condensed form of much of this section shows that a knowledge of Genesis was assumed.

1:1–4 The antediluvian patriarchs. See Gn. 5:3–32. Note the omission of the line of Cain in full conformity with the principles of Chronicles.

1:5–23 The genealogy of the nations. See Gn. 10:2–29. 6 *Diphath*; *'Riphath' (Gn. 10:3). 7 *Rodanim*; 'Dodanim' (Gn. 10:4). 17 Note that *Uz, etc.* were the sons of Aram. *Meshech*; *'Mash' (Gn. 10:23). 22 *Ebal*; 'Obal' (Gn. 10:28).

1:24–27 The descent of Abraham. See Gn. 11:10–26.

1:28–33 The descendants of Abraham through Ishmael and Keturah. See Gn. 25:12–16 and 1–4.

1:34 The descendants of Abraham through Sarah. Note that the Chronicler always uses *Israel*, not Jacob, consistently with his general outlook.

1:35–54 The descendants of Esau. See Gn. 36:10–14, 20–43. 36 *Zephi*; *'Zepho' (Gn. 36:11). In Gn. 36:12 *Timna* is the concubine of Eliphaz and the mother of Amalek. 39 *Homam*; 'Hemam' (Gn. 36:22). 40 *Alian*; 'Alvan' (Gn. 36:23). *Shephi*; 'Shepho' (Gn. 36:23). 41 *Hamran*; 'Hemdan' (Gn. 36:26). 42 *Jaakan*; 'Akan' (Gn. 36:27). 50 *Hadad*; 'Hadar' (Gn. 36:39). *Pai*; 'Pau' (Gn. 36:39). 51 *Aliah*; *'Alvah' (Gn. 36:40).

2:1, 2 The sons of Israel. See Gn. 35:22–26. The only explanation for the unusual position of Dan is that it was dropped by a scribe, placed in the margin and entered the text in its present position.

2:3 – 4:23 Genealogies of Judah

It seems impossible now to unravel these genealogies with any certainty; the difficulties are due in part to the incomplete and sometimes even fragmentary nature of the genealogies and in part to the possible duplication of names. Textual corruptions and the fact that we are sometimes dealing with names of places rather than of persons further complicate matters.

2:3–9 Some descendants of Judah. 3 Some descendants of *Shelah* will be found in 1 Ch. 4:21; 9:5; Ne. 11:5. They are not dealt with here because the Chronicler wishes to reach the royal house as soon as possible. *Bath-shua*, i.e. the daughter of Shua. Cf. Gn. 38:2. 5 *Hezron and Hamul*. See Gn. 46:12. The list of Hezron's descendants commences in v. 9. It must not be assumed that Hamul was childless. Cf. Nu. 26:21. 6 *Zimri*; *'Zabdi' (Jos. 7:1). It is quite probable that *Ethan, Heman, Calcol* and *Dara* are to be identified with the Ethan the Ezrahite (*i.e.* descendant of Zerah), Heman, Calcol and Darda of 1 Ki. 4:31, in which case Mahol will be an intermediate link between them and Zerah. **7** *Carmi* was son of Zabdi (Zimri). *Achar*; 'Achan' (Jos. 7:1). The form in Chronicles is probably deliberate (*cf.* Jos. 7:26). Achan was Carmi's grandson; this and the failure to mention the link between Carmi and Zimri presuppose a knowledge of Joshua in the reader. **8** RSV is not justified in changing 'the sons of Ethan' to *Ethan's son*; the remainder have been omitted for the sake of brevity.

9 The interpretation of the genealogies of Judah as a whole will depend in large measure on the interpretation of this verse. *Chelubai, i.e.* *Caleb (cf.* v. 18; there is no justification for the spelling *ch*), is identified by most scholars with Caleb the Kenezite (see 1 Ch. 4:15; Jos. 14:6), a non-Israelite incorporated into the tribe of Judah (Nu. 13:6). To do so is automatically to deny the authenticity of a considerable portion of these genealogies and to make a considerable part of Judah non-Israelite. It is much easier to assume two individuals, this Caleb antedating the hero of the conquest by several centuries. The mention of *Achsah* (v. 49; *cf.* Jos. 15:17; Jdg. 1:13) does not necessarily invalidate this view. The later Caleb's daughter must have been born after his incorporation into the tribe of Judah, and he may well have chosen the name deliberately. *Jerahmeel.* His descendants are mentioned in 1 Sa. 27:10; 30:29. They are usually taken to be a non-Israelite clan that later coalesced with Judah. This would again destroy the historicity of the genealogy. It is much simpler to suppose that the descendants of Jerahmeel, who in any case were settled in the south of Judea, retained their nomadic habits longer, and so in the days of David were reckoned separately from the rest of Judah.

2:10–17 The ancestry of David. See Ru. 4:18–22. **11** *Salma.* So Ru. 4:20 (Heb.); 'Salmon' in Ru. 4:21; Mt. 1:5. Jesse had eight sons (1 Sa. 16:10, 11); only seven are mentioned here. 1 Ch. 27:18 mentions a son Elihu, but this is almost certainly a variant of Eliab. The missing son probably died young. **16** *Abigail.* According to 2 Sa. 17:25 she was the daughter of Nahash, in which case she was David's half-sister, or step-sister. **17** *Jether the Ishmaelite*; 'Ithra the Israelite' (2 Sa. 17:25, Heb.).

2:18–24 The descendants of Caleb. See also on 2:42–55. **18** The context does not suggest that Caleb had two wives. Either Jerioth was another name of Azubah, or there is a textual corruption. Rudolph is probably correct with the emendation 'And Caleb the son of Hezron begat by his wife Azubah Jerioth, and her sons were . . .', Jerioth being a daughter. **20** *Bezalel*; see Ex. 31:2. **21** *Afterward Hezron, i.e.* after v. 9. **23** *But Geshur and Aram . . .* The time of the loss of these cities is nowhere indicated, but it was probably before the reign of Ahab. **24** RSV rightly follows LXX and Vulg. This was probably

before the Mosaic lawgiving, which forbade such a marriage.

2:25–41 The descendants of Jerahmeel. Nothing is known of any of those mentioned here. **31** There is an apparent contradiction with v. 34. *Ahlai* may be a grandson by some daughter other than that mentioned in v. 34.

2:42–55 Further descendants of Caleb. See also on 2:18–24. This is probably a supplementary genealogy to that in 2:18–24. There are few points of contact between them. **42** RSV is probably incorrect in following LXX with *Mareshah his firstborn.* Rudolph is probably correct in rendering 'Mesha his first-born, who was the father of Ziph, and his second son Mareshah, the father of Hebron'. It should be noticed that a number of names in these verses are names of towns. It is not always possible to interpret these remarks with certainty. Sometimes it means that a man had given his name to a town. *E.g.,* **50** in a case like *Shobal the father of Kiriath-jearim* it is clear that Shobal had founded or re-founded Kiriath-jearim, not that he had a son of that name. **55** is a statement that the Recha-bites were originally a Kenite family (*cf.* 2 Ki. 10:15; Je. 35) who were incorporated into Judah.

3:1–9 The sons of David. With the list of David's sons *cf.* 2 Sa. 3:2–5; 5:14–16. **1** *Daniel*; 'Chileab' (2 Sa. 3:3) = 'all the father', obviously a pet name. **5** *Shimea*; *'Shammua'* (1 Ch. 14:4; 2 Sa. 5:14). *Bath-shua*; *'Bathsheba'* (in 2 Samuel and 1 Kings). Her father's name *Ammiel* is possibly only a variant of 'Eliam' (2 Sa. 11:3). Are we to understand that Shammua (Shimea), Shobab, Nathan were also her sons? If so Solomon stands last as the most important. It is more probable that the three younger are not named. **6** *Elishama, Eliphelet*; *'Elishua, Elpelet'* (1 Ch. 14:5; *cf.* 2 Sa. 5:15). In both these cases the second rendering is obviously the correct one, otherwise there would be two pairs of brothers with the same name. See v. 8. **8** *Eliada.* So 2 Sa. 5:15; *'Beeliada'* in 1 Ch. 14:7. See on 1 Ch. 8:33.

3:10–16 From Solomon to the captivity. 10 *Abijah*; so elsewhere in Chronicles; in 1 Kings 'Abijam'. **12** *Azariah*; so generally in 2 Kings; but elsewhere in Chronicles, in 2 Ki. 15:13, 32, 34, and the prophets, 'Uzziah'. **15** *Johanan*, not otherwise known. **16** *Zedekiah his son.* This is not the Zedekiah who was Jeconiah's uncle (mentioned already in v. 15), who followed him on the throne.

3:17–24 The house of David from the captivity. It should be noted that neither of the NT genea-logies of our Lord makes any use of these names, except **17** *Shealtiel* and **19** *Zerubbabel.* According to Ezr. 3:2; Hg. 1:1; Mt. 1:12; Lk. 3:27 Zerubbabel was the son, which may mean grandson, of Shealtiel. The natural inference of vv. 17–19 is that he was his nephew. An old Jewish explanation interprets v. 18 as listing the sons of Shealtiel. Another explanation would be that he was grandson of both Shealtiel and Pedaiah. **18** *Shenazzar*, quite likely the Shesh-bazzar of Ezr. 1:8, where see note.

This section, so important for the dating of Chronicles, cannot be interpreted with any certainty. The difficulty is the connection between the two halves of v. 21. The usual interpretation is that vv. 21b–24 mention various other branches of the Davidic house, whose connection with Zerubbabel is unspecified, and of only one of which have we further details. On the basis of this Young (*Introduction to the Old Testament*, 1953) argues that we have only two generations from Zerubbabel given us, and therefore there is no obstacle to Ezra's authorship. There is weight in the argument, but it cannot be accepted as it stands, for, even if Shecaniah was not a contemporary of Hananiah, he can hardly be from an earlier generation than that of Zerubbabel, and we have four generations reckoned from him. Also we cannot reject out of hand the reading of the LXX, Vulg. and Syr.: 'And the son of Hananiah was Pelatiah and Jeshiah his son, and Arnan his son, and Obadiah his son, and Shechaniah his son.' If this reading is correct, we have eleven generations from Zerubbabel.

4:1–23 Fragmentary genealogies of Judah. This chapter is a collection of fragments which have little or no connection one with another or with the lists in ch. 2. **1** *Carmi*. A comparison with 2:9, 19, 50 will show that it should be Caleb. **9, 10** *Jabez* (lit. 'he giveth pain') has special attention given him because his ·faith was triumphant over his name, which was regarded as possessing almost magic power. **13** *Othniel* and **15** *Caleb*. These verses must be interpreted in the light of Jos. 15:17. They confirm the impression created by Jos. 14:6 that Caleb was a non-Israelite adopted into the tribe of Judah, for his genealogy does not link up anywhere. **21** *The sons of Shelah*; see on 2:3. **22** *And returned to Lehem, i.e.* Beth-lehem. Though unconnected with it, it is an interesting reminder of Ruth. We have no indication how *Joash and Saraph* came to occupy positions of high authority (*ruled* is too strong) in Moab. **23** *Potters*. Archaeology has shown that the potter's craft was hereditary.

4:24 – 5:26 Genealogies of Simeon, Reuben, Gad and Manasseh

4:24–43 The descendants of Simeon. 24 *Cf.* Gn. 46:10; Ex. 6:15; Nu. 26:12–14. There are a number of minor variations in the form of the names and it is difficult to determine which are correct. **28–33** *Cf.* Jos. 19:2–8. **31** *Until David reigned*. This points out that at this time one town (Ziklag, 1 Sa. 27:6), and possibly more, became the possession of Judah. **39–43** describe some of the conquests of Simeon and clearly show that the division into ten tribes and one in the time of Rehoboam (1 Ki. 11:30) must not be interpreted too literally. Simeon neither separated from nor lost his identity in Judah. **39** *Gedor*. Site unknown; perhaps we should read 'Gerar' with LXX. **43** *And they destroyed the remnant of the Amalekites*. In the light of 1 Sa.

14:48; 15:3; 2 Sa. 8:12 some time in the reign of David or Solomon is probably meant. We know nothing further of this Simeonite kingdom in Mt. Seir, though Is. 21:11, 12 may refer to it. *To this day* refers presumably to the time when this source of Chronicles was written.

5:1–10 The descendants of Reuben. 3 *Cf.* Gn. 46:8, 9; Ex. 6:14; Nu. 26:5–9. Chronicles does not give all the names mentioned in Numbers, nor does it indicate how **4** *Joel* is to be linked with Reuben. **6** *Tilgath-pilneser*; **'Tiglath-pile-ser'* (2 Ki. 15:29). **9** *He also dwelt to the east.* Part of the reason for this expansion into the steppe country E of Gilead seems to have been Moabite pressure on their original territory. **10** *Hagrites*; AV 'Hagarites' suggests a connection with Hagar which may not be justified. It is quite likely that this war is the same as that mentioned in vv. 18–22.

5:11–17 The descendants of Gad. There is no obvious reason why the details in Nu. 26:15–18 have been omitted. **17** *Jeroboam king of Israel.* Obviously Jeroboam II; see 2 Ki. 14:23.

5:18–22 The war with the Hagrites. See on v. 10. This section, together with 4:34–43, should warn us against assuming that the Bible history is necessarily complete. There may be many other gaps in Samuel and Kings which Chronicles has not filled. This was a major victory leading to an important addition of territory.

5:23–26 The descendants of Manasseh (eastern half-tribe). Earlier details are omitted to avoid overlapping with 7:14–19. **25, 26** *Cf.* 2 Ki. 15:29 and note that this captivity of the Transjordan tribes is not mentioned in 2 Chronicles. **26** *Pul and Tilgath-pilneser* (see on v. 6) are the same man, Pul being his personal name which he retained as king of Babylon and Tiglath-pileser his throne-name as king of Assyria (see *DOTT*, pp. 57, 83). See on 2 Ki. 15:19.

6:1–81 Genealogies of Levi

It should be borne in mind that the information of this chapter is repeated and extended in 1 Ch. 23–26.

6:1–15 The high-priestly line *Cf.* also vv. 49–53. The list is obviously incomplete; not only does it deliberately omit the names of the Shilonite high priests, the house of Eli, but also Jehoiada (2 Ch. 22:11), Urijah (2 Ki. 16:11) and Azariah (2 Ch. 26:20). The motive for the omissions is unknown.

6:16–48 The Levitical genealogies. First we have three genealogical trees beginning at vv. 20, 22 and 29 respectively. Then we have the genealogies of *Heman* (33–38), *Asaph* (39–43) and *Ethan* (44–47) in reverse. That of Heman is the same as that beginning in v. 22, and that of Asaph may perhaps be linked with that in v. 20; no plausible connection can be made between the other two. A comparison of vv. 22–28 with vv. 33–38 will reveal big variants. **16, 20, 43** *Gershom*; 'Gershon' in 6:1 (AV) and always in the Pentateuch. **28** *Samuel. Cf.* v. 33. This is the prophet Samuel. *Cf.* 1 Sa. 1:1; 8:2. It shows that the description 'Ephrathite' (AV) in 1 Sa. 1:1 must be interpreted in the same way as the phrase 'of the family of Judah' in Jdg. 17:7 (where see note), and that he was a Levite, though it could not be inferred from 1 Samuel (see on 1 Sa. 1:1). Were this invention, we could confidently expect him to have been linked with the Aaronic priesthood.

Advocates of the Merenptah and Rameses II dates of the Exodus, c. 1225 or c. 1290 (see Introduction to Exodus, p. 116 and to Judges, p. 252), point out that from Aaron to Zadok (3–8, 50–53), Korah to Heman (22–28, 33–37) and Mahli to Ethan (44–47) are in each case eleven names, and from Shimei to Asaph (39–42) are twelve. They argue that this cannot be a coincidence and that this number of generations comfortably spans two centuries, but could hardly span the four centuries demanded by the 15th-century date for the Exodus. The argument must be treated with respect, for it shows that, if the genealogies have been shortened, there must have been some principle at work in the choice of the number to be mentioned. On the other hand it must not be overlooked that the argument demands a shortening of the list in vv. 33–35, and ignores the lists beginning with vv. 20 and 29, as well as the direct line of Korah to Shaul (v. 24). These are all too short, and if they have had names omitted we can have no certainty that this has not been done with the others.

6:49–53 The descendants of Aaron. Cf. vv. 4–8 and see on 6:1–15.

6:54–81 The Levitical cities. For this section see Jos. 21:1–42. Chronicles shows some rearrangement and abridgement. There are numerous variations in the names, due mostly to copyists' carelessness. **61** The text is corrupt. For the meaning see Jos. 21:5.

7:1–40 Genealogies of Issachar, Zebulun (?), Dan (?), Naphtali, Manasseh, Ephraim and Asher

7:1–5 The descendants of Issachar. 1 Cf. Gn. 46:13; Nu. 26:23–25. Puah; 'Puvah' in Genesis and Numbers. *Jashub.* So in Nu. 26:24, but 'Iob' in Gn. 46:13.

7:6–11 The descendants of Zebulun (?). If these verses are taken as a genealogy of Benjamin, it seems impossible to reconcile them with ch. 8, nor is it possible to explain why two genealogies should be given. No genealogy of Zebulun is given, and since this is the place where it might be expected from the geographical point of view, it is very widely, and possibly correctly, held that we have here a genealogy of Zebulun obscured by scribal errors, but Rudolph does not agree. See *ICC* or *Cam. Bible* for details.

7:12 The descendants of Dan (?). In precisely the same way as in the preceding verses a genealogy of Dan is generally found here, and with more probability, but if so the text has been seriously mutilated; for details see above.

7:13 The descendants of Naphtali. See Gn. 46:24f.; Nu. 26:48f.

7:14–19 The descendants of Manasseh. Cf. 1 Ch. 5:23f. The information is fragmentary and not easy to interpret. A number of the names in Nu. 26:28–34 are not reproduced. **15** *Zelophehad.* See Nu. 26:33; 27:1–11. **16** *Maachah the wife of Machir.* In v. 15 she seems to be his sister, but there are signs of textual mutilation here.

7:20–27 The descendants of Ephraim. For the first four names in the list see Nu. 26:35–37, although the spelling varies. Of the remainder it seems impossible to say whether they were sons or descendants of Ephraim—the non-mention in Nu. 26 is inconclusive (cf. *Beriah* in v. 23). So we cannot say whether **21** *Ezer* and *Elead* are his sons. **22** *Their father* is inconclusive, as the word is used loosely in Hebrew of any ancestor. The cattle-lifting raid (v. 21) must have been made from Egypt. **24** presents problems that cannot be answered. Not only have we no other information about *Uzzen-sheerah*, but its site has never been identified. The whole verse suggests connections of the Israelites with Canaan during their sojourn in Egypt (so also v. 21), which have left no trace in the Pentateuch, but which may point the way towards a solution of some of the problems connected with the conquest. **25–27** Joshua's genealogy is given. Until *Ammihud* the names are unknown from the Pentateuch. It is worth noting that there are more names in it than in any comparable genealogy. The refusal to give more details about the Joseph tribes must be deliberate and links up with the consistent ignoring of the northern kingdom throughout the book as a rebel against the God-appointed Davidic kingship and Aaronic priesthood.

7:28, 29 The territory of the sons of Joseph. Not a complete list of towns, but an indication of the borders by the mention of the main border towns. Such a mention, unique in the genealogical lists, for there is no real comparison with the mention of the Levitical cities (6:54–81), is probably intended to indicate that all later attempts of the Joseph tribes to obtain wider rule, e.g. Abimelech (Jdg. 9), the Ephraimite attack on Jephthah (Jdg. 12), and Jeroboam the son of Nebat (1 Ki. 11:26) were usurpation.

7:30–40 The descendants of Asher. 30, 31 Cf. Gn. 46:17; Nu. 26:44–46. The only new name is *Birzaith*, which is generally taken to be the name of a town. **32–39** The names are all otherwise unknown. **34** *Shemer* and **35** *Helem* are almost certainly the same as **32** *Shomer* and *Hotham*; probably Shemer and Hotham are the correct forms. **39** *Ulla* is probably miswritten for one of the names in the previous verse. **40** The figure given links neither with the census figures in Numbers nor yet with 1 Ch. 12:36. With our fragmentary knowledge we cannot fix the period to which the number refers.

8:1–40; 9:35–44 Genealogies of Benjamin

The very full details about Benjamin as contrasted with most of the other tribes should not be put down to the availability of greater information, but should be regarded as a tribute to Benjamin's loyalty to the Davidic line. The parallel list in 7:6–12 has been regarded as a corrupted genealogy of Zebulun and Dan; see comments *in loc*. In any case it cannot be harmonized with this chapter.

8:1–5 The immediate descendants of Benjamin. *Cf*. Gn. 46:21; Nu. 26:38–40. The divergences between these three passages are very great, and no convincing harmonization has been offered. **1** *Bela his first-born*; 'Bela' and 'Becher' (Gn. 46:21). Nu. 26:38 omits 'Becher'. In Hebrew 'Becher' and 'firstborn' have the same consonants. **3** *Abihud*. Otherwise unmentioned; in the light of v. 6 it is probably to be read '(Gera) the father of Ehud'; *cf*. v. 6.

8:6–28 The descendants of Ehud. This is probably the best way to treat these verses. For Ehud *cf*. Jdg. 3:15, although the identification is not certain. **6–8** are as obscure in Hebrew as in English and serious textual corruption probably exists. Various attempts at emendation have been made but they are probably of little serious value. All the names in this section are otherwise unknown to us. **8** No indication is given as to what took *Shaharaim* to Moab. **12** *Who* (*i.e*. Elpaal) *built Ono and Lod*. We are unable to date the incident. **13** *Who put to flight . . .* Again the incident cannot be dated. **28** *These dwelt in Jerusalem*. It is generally assumed that this is a reference to the post-exilic city and the inference is then drawn that the bulk of the names given are of post-exilic Benjaminites. This must be considered a most hazardous assumption, the more so as none of the names are found in 9:1–17 (*cf*. Ne. 11:1–19), which specifically deals with the post-exilic community in Jerusalem. As virtually the whole of Jerusalem lay within the tribal area of Benjamin, we may expect there to have been a large Benjaminite population in the period of the monarchy. *Cf*. v. 32.

8:29–40 The house of Saul. *Cf*. 9:35–44. These parallel passages are virtually identical, but where there are textual variations the latter is normally the better preserved. The RSV has in two obvious cases corrected one from the other, and as this is indicated in the margin attention is not here drawn to the fact. For other variations see AV mg., RV mg. **30** *Baal*. Read with 9:36 and LXX, 'Baal, Ner'. **31** *Zecher*. In 9:37 'Zechariah, and Mikloth'. **32** *These also*. Probably refers to Mikloth and Shimeah (or Shimeam), in which case the verse as a whole would refer to a Benjaminite settlement in Jerusalem after its capture by David (*cf*. v. 28). **33** Reference to 1 Sa. 9:1 will show that Chronicles omits a large section of Saul's genealogy, once again showing that the gaps in Chronicles are often deliberate. A comparison of 1 Sa. 9:1 with 1 Sa. 14:51 will show that Kish and Ner were brothers. Hence scholars may be correct in proposing here: 'And Ner begat Abner; and Kish begat Saul', though there is no support from MSS or versions. The Hebrew seems

incompatible with 1 Sa. 9:1, but this could be corrected to read 'Kish, the son of Ner, the son of Abiel'. *Abinadab*. So 1 Sa. 31:2, but omitted, probably by scribal accident, in 1 Sa. 14:49. AV mg., RV mg. are wrong in equating him with Ishvi. *Esh-baal*. In 1 Sa. 14:49 'Ishvi' (RV); everywhere else Ishbosheth. As Ishbosheth means 'man of shame', it needs no argument to show that this could not have been his name. Baal is not a proper name but a title—'Master'. In the period of the judges and under Canaanite influence it was applied by many to Yahweh. The custom seems to have been prevalent in the family of Saul. *Cf*. 'Baal' (v. 30) and 'Merib-baal' (v. 34). Late scribes found the custom so abhorrent that they put in the place of Baal *bosheth*, 'shame' (so Ishbosheth, Mephibosheth for Merib-baal, Jerubbesheth for *Jerubbaal), or El, 'God' (so Eliada, 2 Sa. 5:16; 1 Ch. 3:8, for Beeliada, 1 Ch. 14:7), or Jah (so Ishvi for Esh-baal). The various consonantal and especially vowel changes involved are only a matter of euphony. **34** *Merib-baal*. Though the English versions hide the fact, the second occurrence in 9:40 is spelt 'Meribaal'. Either spelling gives a good meaning in Hebrew. In 2 Samuel it is spelt 'Mephibosheth'; see above on v. 33.

39, 40 do not occur in the parallel passage, as all that was necessary there was to show that Saul's line continued. It is quite likely that we have his genealogy carried down to the Exile.

9:1–34 Post-exilic family heads resident in Jerusalem

9:1–16 The family heads. See Ne. 11:1–19, where a similar list is given. There are considerable variations, but only one outstanding case will be mentioned. Both Nehemiah and Chronicles show signs of copyists' carelessness. It should be noted that no effort is made to link the names of this chapter with the detailed genealogies of the preceding chapters. The former give the framework in which the history of the divine ordinances unrolls; the latter stress that the post-exilic community was a legitimate sequel of what had gone before.

1a seems rather to be a summary of the preceding chapters than an introduction to the section which follows. **1b** *The Book of the Kings of Israel*. AV 'the book of the kings of Israel and Judah' follows LXX, Vulg., Targ. If we accept this, we must assume that 'and Judah' has dropped through haplography. **2** is almost incomprehensible as it stands. It can be best understood as a compression of Ne. 11:1, 3. *First* is probably to be taken in the sense of 'principal'. *Israel* has the meaning here of non-Levites. *Temple servants* (Heb. *nethinim*). *Cf*. Ezr. 2:43; Ne. 11:3. Probably non-Israelite Temple slaves descended from the Gibeonites. *Cf*. Jos. 9:27. **3** *Ephraim, and Manasseh*. Though no details are given they are probably specially mentioned as an answer to the Samaritan claim to be the true representatives of these tribes. 2 Ch. 11:16; 15:9; 30:11, 18; 34:9 stress that a considerable number

of northerners had joined Judah at various times.
5 *Shilonites*; *i.e.* Shelanites (Nu. 26:20), descendants of Shelah. *Cf.* 1 Ch. 2:3; 4:21. **11** *The chief officer of the house of God.* The meaning is not clear. It probably does not mean high priest, unless it refers to Ahitub. *Cf.* 2 Ch. 35:8. **14** *Merari*; 'Bunni' (Ne. 11:15).

9:17–34 The gate-keepers and their duties. There are a number of difficulties here, due probably to over-compression of the original record. The organization of the gate-keepers is dealt with also in 1 Ch. 26:1–19. The reason for the section here is not so much any special importance of the names mentioned as a stress that the post-exilic community was primarily a religious community.

17 *Gatekeepers.* Many think that a contrast with v. 14 is intended by the Chronicler and that the gate-keepers were not Levites. This is improbable; *cf.* ch. 26 and see on 9:26. **18b–21** stress the importance of the gate-keepers. They exercised their office already in the wilderness. Just as they had guarded the tent erected by David, so they had the Tabernacle. *Hitherto*; *i.e.* up to the time of the Chronicler; no change is implied. **20** *The Lord was with him.* Render 'May the Lord be with him!' Such phrases were very common in post-exilic Judaism when speaking of the illustrious dead. **21** *The tent of meeting.* Not, as the context would suggest, the Tabernacle, but the tent that housed the ark in David's time. *Zechariah. Cf.* 26:2, 14. **22** *David and Samuel the seer.* The simple explanation would seem to be that, while the institution of gate-keeper went back to the time of Moses (v. 19), the ornate Temple to be built by Solomon demanded a great development of the service. The same was true of the Levitical singers. It is not clear what Samuel's role was; it is, however, reasonable to suppose that he may have prepared David from time to time for his coming responsibilities as king, or even have left written advice. Otherwise David's initiative in this sphere of organization is not easy to understand. **24–26** The general setting supports Rudolph's emendation: 'The four head gatekeepers were entrusted with the gates on the four sides . . . for the four chief gatekeepers were on duty continually. They were Levites.' The most natural interpretation of the last clause is that the lower order of gate-keepers were not Levites, but the general tenor of the passage does not suggest this, nor was this the case in NT times. It seems safer to assume that compression has led to lack of clarity.

28 *Some of them.* This could refer to the gate-keepers; but since the verses that follow cannot possibly do so, it is better to assume that here we have the beginning of a very compressed outline of some of the principal servile duties of the Levites and even priests (v. 30). **33, 34** read like the heading or conclusion of lists that have been omitted.

9:35–44 The genealogy of the house of Saul

See above, on 8:29–40. From one point of view it might have been better to detach these verses from the genealogies and to have counted them as the beginning of the Book of David. They serve to link the story with the past as recorded in 1 Samuel.

10:1 – 29:30 THE REIGN OF DAVID

10:1–14 The death of Saul

See commentary on 1 Sa. 31:1–13. Apart from vv. 13 and 14, which give the reasons for Saul's fate, the two passages are virtually identical, the differences calling for no comment. In this, the sole longer reference to Saul's life, we learn something of the Chronicler's interpretation of history. As Saul had been appointed king by God, he could not be passed over in silence; but as he had later been rejected, an account of his death—the final proof of his rejection—was sufficient. David had been God's king from the time of his anointing by Samuel; the period of his rejection by men, however, is passed over in silence as being contrary to the will of God. But see on 12:1–22. The Chronicler is silent regarding the short reign of Esh-baal (Ishbosheth) for the same reason.

11:1 – 12:40 David is made king

The Chronicler normally follows the order of Samuel, but his omissions make the by no means clear chronology of the earlier book still more obscure. For information on these points see the relevant comments on 2 Samuel.

11:1–9 David, anointed king, captures Jerusalem. See 2 Sa. 5:1–10. **4** *That is Jebus. Cf.* Jdg. 19:10. The name Jerusalem in the form 'Urusalim' is as old as the Amarna tablets, *c.* 1390 BC, and a similar form is found in the Egyptian Execration Texts from the 19th and 18th centuries. *Cf.* Gn. 14:18. But the Jebusites, whose centre the city was, may well have used the name Jebus. **6** *Joab . . . became chief.* This information is peculiar to Chronicles and is in no contradiction with 2 Sa. 2:13. The commander-in-chief of the king of Judah would not automatically have become commander-in-chief of the king of all Israel. **8** *Joab repaired the rest of the city.* Again the information is peculiar to Chronicles, but the variants in some Heb. MSS, LXX and Syr. suggest that the text may be faulty.

11:10–47 David's mighty men. For vv. 10–41a see 2 Sa. 23:8–39. Owing to the natural link of this section with ch. 12, the list of David's mighty men has been put at the beginning of his reign; this must not be taken to imply that the incidents recounted took place before David became king. **10** is peculiar to Chronicles. Its meaning must not be pressed too far. The majority, but probably not all, of the mighty men were with David in exile. **12, 13** Clearly as a result of a scribal error several lines have dropped out between these verses. *Cf.* 2 Sa.

23:9b, 10. **41b–47** are a continuation of the list peculiar to Chronicles. The names do not occur elsewhere. We can hardly doubt that the author of Samuel deliberately ended the list with Uriah the Hittite in order to underline the heinousness of David's sin. **42** *And thirty with him*; in its setting obviously a scribal corruption. Moffatt may be correct in rendering 'captain of a Reubenite company of thirty'.

12:1–22 David's adherents in exile. This section is peculiar to Chronicles. With one possible exception the names are otherwise unknown. This is sufficient to show that the list is no mere invention by the Chronicler, who would surely have introduced the names of great men of the time, if he had composed it himself.

1–7 give a list of Benjaminites (v. 2) who supported David. They are mentioned first because their action was the more remarkable, when we consider that Saul belonged to their tribe. A comparison of v. 1 with vv. 8, 16 shows that they were not the first to join David in point of time. **4** *Ishmaiah of Gibeon*. His name is not in ch. 11. It may be that the list of mighty men is not complete as the Chronicler's additions (11:41b–47) suggest; or simply that Ishmaiah was worthy not merely to be a member of the thirty, but to be over them, or possibly a member of a third thirty. **6** *The Korahites*. Probably not Levites. Korah was a son of Kohath, and the Kohathite cities were not in Benjamin.

8 *From the Gadites*. The Spirit moves as it pleases Him; no indication is given of the motives that drove these men from across the Jordan to join David while he was still a fugitive in the wilderness of Judea. Their action was the more remarkable, as it exposed their relations to Saul's vengeance, which they would be powerless to hinder. The fact that they 'separated themselves unto David' (AV, RV) suggests that they could not even reckon on the sympathy of their fellow-tribesmen. *At the stronghold. Cf.* v. 16. Probably the cave of Adullam is meant, but it cannot be affirmed with certainty. **10** *Jeremiah. Cf.* v. 13. In Hebrew the names are spelt differently. **15** *Cf.* Jos. 3:15. The Jordan flows through a flood plain as much as 150 ft below the level of the main Jordan valley and from 200 yards to a mile wide. It is the *ga'on ha-Yarden*, the jungle or pride of Jordan (mistranslated in AV 'the swelling'). In spring it is filled from side to side with rapidly-flowing water. Not only did this handful of men cross this natural obstacle, but they routed those on both sides who, in the interests of Saul, tried to stop their march. **16** *The men of Benjamin and Judah*. Though those from Judah probably predominated, the Benjaminites are mentioned first for the reason mentioned under vv. 1–7. David's suspicion reflects exactly the conditions of 1 Sa. 23. **18** *Then the Spirit came upon Amasai* (lit. 'Then the Spirit clothed himself with Amasai'). So Jdg. 6:34; 2 Ch. 24:20. Amasai, who was *chief of the thirty*, is unknown from the list of the mighty

men. Some conjecture that Abishai is meant; others Amasa. See 2 Sa. 17:25; 19:13.

19 *Some of the men of Manasseh*. For the background see 1 Sa. 29; 30. **20** David had to pass through the territory of Manasseh as he returned to Ziklag. The action of these Manassites was not as meritorious as that of the others already mentioned, for by this time Saul's fate was clear. **22** *A great army*. There was evidently a continual increase of David's strength during the time he was king in Hebron. *Cf.* 2 Sa. 3:1. *Like an army of God* refers to size, not quality; it is a common Hebrew idiom.

12:23–40 The forces that came to Hebron to make David king. This account, which is peculiar to Chronicles, gives every impression of having been derived from the old official account of David's recognition and coronation, which may well have been hardly legible in parts. Note that we are not given the size of the contingent from Issachar, and there is a diversity in the size of the contingents which is hard to explain if we assume the correct transmission of the numbers. **27** There is no reason to assume that *Jehoiada* was the father of Benaiah (11:22, *etc.*, but see on 27:5); nor is it stated that he was high priest. **28** Presumably *Zadok* is David's high priest of the same name. **32** *Men who had understanding of the times. Cf.* 2 Sa. 20:14–22, especially v. 18. Abel of Beth-maachah was in Issachar.

13:1 – 17:27 David and the ark

This section represents 2 Sa. 6:11 – 7:29 with considerable additions of a religious nature. In order to enhance the importance of David's dealings with the ark, the Chronicler has presumably put the first attempt to bring it to Jerusalem out of its proper chronological position as shown in 2 Samuel.

13:1–14 The first attempt to bring the ark to Jerusalem. Except for vv. 1–4 see 2 Sa. 6 and comments there. **1** *David consulted*. The Chronicler is obviously making more of the occasion than the writer of Samuel, but the consultation described in vv. 1–4 is clearly implied by 2 Sa. 6:1. The ark was the symbol of the unity of the tribes of Israel based on a common worship of Yahweh. For it to be brought to Jerusalem meant that the city would be the religious as well as the political centre of Israel. David wanted popular and unanimous approval for this. **2** *Our brethren who remain*; *i.e.* those who had not come to the consultation. *The cities that have pasture lands. Cf.* Nu. 35:1–5.

5 *So David assembled all Israel*. In spite of appearances there is no contradiction between this and 2 Sa. 6:1. All Israel was present in its chosen representatives. Virtually all passages referring to the gathering of all Israel are to be interpreted thus. *Shihor* is in Is. 23:3; Je. 2:18 the Nile, but in Jos. 13:3 it is, as here, the Brook of Egypt, the Wadi el-Arish (Nu. 34:5; Jos. 15:4, *etc.*). *The entrance of Hamath*. This is in Hebrew *Lebo-hamath*, which today is generally identified with Lebweh, a town near the source of the Orontes (see also on 1 Ki. 8:65). 6 *Baalah*; *i.e.* the Kiriath-baal of Jos. 15:60, a Gibeonite city. The name was evidently changed to Kiriath-jearim to avoid the hated name of Baal. 9 **Chidon*; 'Nacon' (2 Sa. 6:6).

14:1–17 Early events in David's reign. See 2 Sa. 5:11–25 and comments there. 4–7 See on 1 Ch. 3:5–8. 12 *And they were burned*. Chronicles deliberately avoids the possible ambiguity of 2 Sa. 5:21. For the burning *cf*. Dt. 7:5, 25. 16 **Gibeon*. 2 Sa. 5:25 has 'Geba', but LXX has 'Gibeon'.

15:1–24 Preparations for the second attempt to bring up the ark. This section is peculiar to Chronicles. 2 Sa. 6:12 (1 Ch. 13:14) tells how David hears of the blessing on the house of Obed-edom. This shows him that Yahweh had no objection to the removal of the ark, and this leads him to the true reason for the death of Uzzah.

1 *David built houses for himself*. There is no contradiction between this and 13:14; 14:1 took place long before the first attempt to bring the ark to Jerusalem. *A tent*. Not the Tabernacle, which was in Gibeon (1 Ch. 16:39; 2 Ch. 1:3). We are not told how the Tabernacle came to be moved there—but note that Gibeon was a neighbour of the less important Kiriath-jearim—nor why it was not moved to Jerusalem as well. It may be that David already had the project of a Temple in his mind, and so it suited him to respect the inevitable protests of the Gibeonites. Equally it may have been disintegrating through old age. 2 *No one but the Levites may carry the ark of God*. The reason why a new cart was used in the first instance (1 Ch. 13:7) is quite clearly because God had tolerated that method for the return of the ark from the Philistine country (1 Sa. 6:7). They had not learnt that God's exceptions do not put aside the express revelation of His will. David now recognized the mistake.

4ff. It is very striking that the names of the Levites do not link up with the Levitical lists in chs. 23–26. Had these lists been a mere invention of the Chronicler, as is so often suggested, he would surely have tried to link them up for the sake of verisimilitude. 12 *Sanctify yourselves*. This refers to outward, ritual holiness. It involved washing (Ex. 19:10, 14), the avoidance of defilement (Lv. 11:44) and refraining from sexual intercourse (Ex. 19:15). It is not sufficient to be holy; there should be the outward appearance as well. 18 *Their brethren of the second order*. ICC and *Cam. Bible* propose 'their brethren twelve'. RSV rightly omits the scribal error 'Ben' found in AV, RV. 21 *Azaziah* is omitted in 16:5. *Obed-edom*. The name appears frequently in 1 Chronicles and it is not certain whether more than one individual is intended. It is simplest to assume that there was only one of this name. The ark was lodged in his house. It is usually assumed that 'Gittite' (1 Ch. 13:13) must mean from Gath; but it is incomprehensible that the ark should have been left with a Philistine, nor would he

have been willing to take the risk on himself. In addition Gath (lit. 'winepress') appears in its dual form Gittaim as a place in the vicinity of Kiriath-jearim (2 Sa. 4:3; Ne. 11:33) as well as in a number of compound place-names. See on 2 Sa. 6:10, 11. Quite naturally, as the result of the divine favour, he was appointed one of the special guardians of the ark (v. 24). As he served well, he and his sons were appointed door-keepers for the Temple to be built by Solomon. *Cf*. 1 Ch. 26:14, 15. On the day of the bringing up of the ark to Jerusalem Obed-edom and his companion Jeiel (v. 18) acted exceptionally as singers (v. 21), and so Berechiah and Elkanah were made temporary guardians of the ark (v. 23). This seems the simplest interpretation. ICC and *Cam. Bible* propose far-reaching textual reconstructions, which seem unnecessary. Obed-edom is a good example of the results of faithfully using unexpected opportunities of service. 20, 21 *According to Alamoth . . . the Sheminith*. *Cf*. the titles of Pss. 46; 6 and 12. 24 *Jehiah*. Probably the Jeiel of v. 18.

15:25 – 16:3 The ark brought to Jerusalem. See 2 Sa. 6:12–19. 26 *Seven bulls and seven rams*. This is the sacrifice of the elders and captains; David's sacrifice was an ox and a fatling (2 Sa. 6:13).

16:4–7 The ministry before the ark. The smaller number of names compared with the lists given in ch. 15 is accounted for by the ministry in the Tabernacle at Gibeon. See v. 39. 5 It is probable that the mention of *Obed-edom* and *Jeiel* and the second mention of *Asaph* are to be referred to a scribal error. See on 15:24 and *cf*. 16:38. See also on 15:21.

16:8–36 The psalm of praise. It should be noted that the RV, RSV do not state that David was responsible for this psalm. It is actually composed from three psalms: Ps. 105:1–15 (vv. 8–22); Ps. 96:1–13 (vv. 23–33); and Ps. 106:1, 47, 48 (vv. 34–36). For a commentary the relevant passages should be referred to. There are a number of minor variants, some deliberate, some accidental. In the latter case the text of Psalms gives the better reading.

None of the three psalms used is Davidic and all are later, possibly even post-exilic. *Cf*. v. 35; Ps. 106:47. The Chronicler evidently found no psalm in his authority and so put together a suitable piece. By drawing from the Psalms and choosing anonymous ones he did not imply Davidic or contemporary authorship. 36b is the doxology of Book IV of the Psalms but here it is a statement of fact, not a call to worship. It is the only doxology to take this form, so it has evidently been taken from Chronicles.

16:37–43 The service in Jerusalem and Gibeon. This section is really a continuation of vv. 4–7, beginning with a summary of them. 38 *Obed-edom and his sixty-eight brethren*. RSV follows LXX and Vulg. More probable is 'Obed-edom and Jehiah' (*cf*. 15:24), or possibly 'Obed-edom and Hosah', in each case with 'and their sixty-eight brethren'. 39 *Zadok the priest*. We are obviously to infer that Abiathar, the senior in age, was in Jerusalem with the ark. It may well be that Zadok already was the priest of the Gibeon sanctuary. The presence of the Tabernacle implied the ministry of a priest of the highest rank. **42** *The sons of Jeduthun. Cf.* v. 38. This seems to refer to the sons of Obed-edom.

17:1–27 David's wish to build a Temple; God's answer; David's thanksgiving. See on 2 Sa. 7:1–29. The variations are minor. **5** *But I have gone from tent to tent . . .* 2 Sa. 7:6 gives the correct reading: 'I have been moving about in a tent for my dwelling.' **6** **Judges;* 'tribes' (2 Sa. 7:7). **17** *And hast shown me future generations.* See on 2 Sa. 7:19. It would seem that the text of both Samuel and Chronicles is faulty; there is no really satisfactory emendation.

18:1 – 20:8 David's wars

18:1–13 A summary of the wars. See 2 Sa. 8:1–14. **1** *Gath and its villages.* This is probably the correct interpretation of 2 Sa. 8:1. **4** *A thousand chariots, seven thousand horsemen.* The LXX of 2 Sa. 8:4 agrees with Chronicles. **8** **Tibhath* and *Cun;* 'Betah' and 'Berothai' (2 Sa. 8:8). The sites of these towns are uncertain, but they are probably in the Anti-Lebanon. **9** **Tou.* So also the LXX in 2 Sa. 8:9. **10** *Hadoram;* 'Joram' (2 Sa. 8:10). **12** The victory evidently involved a number of contingents acting to some extent individually, for in 2 Sa. 8:13 the credit is given to David, and in Ps. 60 (title) to Joab. In any case the subject in v. 13 must be David.

18:14–17 David's officers. See 2 Sa. 8:15–18. **16** *Ahimelech the son of Abiathar.* RSV has followed the LXX, Vulg., and 2 Sa. 8:17, regarding 'Abimelech' (AV) as a scribal error. See 1 Sa. 22:20; and on 1 Ch. 24:3. It is generally assumed that we should read both here and 2 Sa. 8:17 'Abiathar the son of Ahimelech', but Abiathar may already have been in semi-retirement through age, letting his son replace him. **Shavsha;* 'Shisha' (1 Ki. 4:3), 'Seraiah' (2 Sa. 8:17), 'Sheva' (2 Sa. 20:25). The variants in spelling are probably due to his having been a foreigner; *cf.* 'Uriah the Hittite', 'Ittai the Gittite'. **17** *David's sons were the chief officials. . . .* A deliberate, but correct, alteration of 2 Sa. 8:18, 'were priests'. By the time of the Chronicler the term 'priest' had become too technical to be used as it could be in Samuel. The original concept of a priest was that of an attendant on the god.

19:1 – 20:3 War with the Ammonites. See 2 Sa. 10:1 – 11:1; 12:26–31. **6** *A thousand talents of silver.* An immense sum, for Amaziah could hire 100,000 men for a hundred talents (2 Ch. 25:6). As the mention of Mesopotamia is in anticipation of v. 16, it is probable that this is the total sum spent on foreign mercenaries during the war. *Mesopotamia;* Heb. *'aram-naharayim,* the area immediately across the Euphrates and very much smaller than that included under the name Mesopotamia today, or perhaps rather the ancient Naharin, or N Syria. **7** *Thirty-two thousand chariots.* This is an impossible number.

Shalmaneser III claims that the coalition he defeated at Qarqar put 3,940 chariots in the field against him (*cf. DOTT,* p. 47). A comparison with 2 Sa. 10:6 will show that we have the sum of two bodies of footmen; the chariots are not mentioned there. **18** *Seven thousand chariots.* 2 Sa. 10:18 has 'seven hundred chariots', the more possible reading. **Forty thousand foot soldiers.* In 2 Sa. 10:18 'forty thousand horsemen'. **20:1** *David remained at Jerusalem.* At this point the account in 2 Samuel inserts the story of Bathsheba and the death of Uriah, *etc.* (2 Sa. 11:2 – 12:25). The Chronicler's omission of the story is not to whitewash David; he wants to give the divine pattern, not the aberrations from it. No blame is attached to him. There were affairs of state that demanded his attention. **3** *And sent them to labour,* reading *wayyāśem* for *wayyāśar.* Extreme servitude rather than massacre is indicated.

20:4–8 The death of Philistine champions. See 2 Sa. 21:18–22. **4** *Gezer;* 'Gob' (2 Sa. 21:18). *Sippai;* 'Saph' (2 Sa. 21:18). **5** *And Elhanan the son of Jair slew Lahmi the brother of Goliath the Gittite.* 2 Sa. 21:19 reads: 'And Elhanan the son of Jaare-oregim, the Bethlehemite, slew Goliath the Gittite.' It is axiomatic with the extreme critic that 2 Samuel is correct and as a result the story in 1 Sa. 17 is merely a worthless tradition. The reading of this verse is then dismissed as an attempt on the part of the Chronicler to get rid of a discrepancy. For a detailed discussion see on 2 Sa. 21:19 and Appendix 5 to Samuel. There is no adequate reason for not accepting the statement of Chronicles.

21:1 – 22:19 The preparations for the Temple

Except for ch. 21 this section is peculiar to Chronicles. Even ch. 21 has a different setting, for here it is not told as a story in itself but simply as an account of how the site of the future Temple came to be bought. The question of where these chapters are to be placed in David's life is discussed in the comment on 22:2.

21:1–27 The census and the plague. See 2 Sa. 24. **1** *Satan.* In 2 Samuel David's act is attributed to God's moving; here to Satan's. But the difference is only apparent. Popular Christian ideas of Satan, in so far as they are derived from the NT at all, are the result of that unsound exegesis which forgets that the foundations of all NT conceptions are in the OT. In the OT Satan, however evil, is an angel of God, a minister of God, a being who has only as much power as God entrusts to him. *Cf.* Jb. 1 and 2; Zc. 3:5. So Satan here is only the minister of God's purposes. **5** It does not look as though the divergence between the numbers given here and those found in 2 Sa. 24:9 is due to textual corruptions. No entirely satisfactory explanation has been given (but see on 2 Sa. 24:9). **7** *God was displeased.* This verse is not represented in Samuel and must be looked on as anticipating the development of the story. There can be no question of the plague coming on

Israel until after David's choice (vv. 13, 14). Moreover Samuel is quite clear that it was David's conscience, not the divine punishment, that made David recognize his sin. **12** *Three years of famine.* In 2 Sa. 24:13 the Hebrew has 'seven'. The Chronicles reading, with which the LXX of 2 Samuel agrees, is to be preferred. **15** *Ornan the Jebusite*; 'Araunah the Jebusite' (2 Sa. 24:16). The difference in the consonantal text is small, and the variations probably go back to its being a foreign name. *Cf.* on 18:16. **20** *His four sons . . . hid themselves*; *i.e.* to avoid seeing the angel. *Cf.* vv. 15, 16. *Now Ornan was threshing wheat.* Obviously this was before the angel came; Ornan would then have hidden himself with his sons. Jewish tradition pictures him as hiding in the cave which undoubtedly existed under the rock over which the Holy of Holies was later placed, and which can still be seen under the Dome of the Rock (the Mosque of Omar). **25** *Cf.* 2 Sa. 24:24. It is generally recognized by all who are not out to discover discrepancies that there is no contradiction here. 2 Samuel gives the price of the rocky threshing-floor, Chronicles of the whole area (*the site*). The surroundings will have been bought somewhat later (and, since there was no plague to be stopped, at a much stiffer price); but it is characteristic of the Chronicler that he fuses the two events.

21:28 – 22:1 The choice of the Temple site. The syntax of this section is difficult. Vv. 29 and 30 should be printed in brackets; 22:1 follows straight on from 21:28. **28** *He made his sacrifices there* would be much better rendered 'when' or 'after he had sacrificed there'. This has been interpreted to mean that from this time on there were sacrifices on this site; but neither the Hebrew nor the context supports this.

22:2–5 David's preparations for building the Temple. While this and the following sections are not dated, a consideration of the evidence in 1 Kings clarifies the position. The only rational interpretation of Adonijah's attempt to make himself king (1 Ki. 1:5) is that he hoped to face his father with a *fait accompli* made possible because David had never publicly designated his successor. *Cf.* on 1 Ki. 1:5, 11. After 22:17 this could hardly be the case. So we are forced to look on chs. 22–29 as covering a limited period of time, from 22:6 onwards being after Solomon's anointing as king (1 Ki. 1:39). The apparent break at 23:1 is due to the use of a new source, not any lapse of time (see note *in loc.*).

It is often claimed that Chronicles is irreconcilable with 1 Kings. But 1 Ki. 2:1 in itself implies an interval between Solomon's anointing and his father's death. It is no unusual thing for a crisis to call out unrealized reserves of vigour in an old man. Most chronological outlines find it hard to allow Solomon a full 40 years' reign, and so strongly suggest a period of co-regency with his father (see also on 22:17). It is quite typical of Chronicles that while it ignores 1 Ki. 1 it reveals knowledge of it by 29:22.

2 *Aliens.* This is an accurate but possibly misleading translation. The Hebrew *gēr* is a tolerated sojourner. These remnants of the old inhabitants had not accepted the worship of Yahweh and therefore their presence in the land was not of right but of tolerance. David's treatment of them here is an anticipation of Solomon's policy (see on 1 Ki. 5:13–18; 2 Ch. 2:17f.; 8:7f.). If the treatment seems harsh, and it was, it must not be forgotten that those living in a land were expected to worship the god of the land. At the time conditions in this type of work were so hard that it was not considered suited to freemen.

22:6–19 David's charge to Solomon and the princes. 8 *You have shed much blood.* This is not mentioned in the prophetic message recorded in ch. 17, nor does Solomon repeat it in 1 Ki. 5:3. The truth will have come to David as he pondered on God's refusal to allow him to build the Temple. Very frequently God does not explain His refusals but allows them to be interpreted afterwards through prayer and the Word. **9** *I will give him peace from all his enemies.* As so often, although no condition is expressed, one is implied. *Cf.* 1 Ki. 11:14ff. There is no suggestion that Solomon stood higher morally than David, and still less that David's wars were not justified. Even then men felt that warfare was a contradiction of the divine order. David was paying for the sins of his predecessors. Had Israel been faithful in the conquest of the land, they would not have experienced the dark period of the judges, and David would have ruled over a people too strong to be lightly attacked, as was Solomon's fortunate position. **12** *Only, may the Lord grant you discretion and understanding.* Was it his father's prayer that prompted Solomon's request? See 2 Ch. 1:8ff. **13** *Cf.* God's charge to Joshua in Jos. 1:7ff. **14** *With great pains.* This is an attractive but uncertain translation of a difficult Hebrew phrase. *Cf.* other translations. RSV is supported by Rudolph. The numbers in this verse, if taken literally, would make David a much richer king than Solomon, which is contrary to the whole tenor of Scripture. It is better to treat them as equivalents of large, very large, enormous. **15** *Craftsmen without number.* This is to be understood as 'more than enough'; they would have been numbered for the purposes of pay and rations.

17 *The leaders of Israel.* This translates the Hebrew *śar*, usually rendered 'princes'. These were not principally or even primarily members of the royal family, but the tribal leaders and the civil and military officials (and so elsewhere in the OT). In other words, this passage implies Solomon as co-regent or at least king-designate. See on vv. 2–5 above.

23:1 – 26:32 Organization and duties of the Levites

23:1, 2 The last acts of David. No long interval need be read into the text between this section and the preceding one. The language implies merely a new section, probably based on a different source. These verses are a summary telling how David made Solomon king (*cf.* 28:1 – 29:25); he gathered the leaders of Israel (*cf.* 27:1–34), with the priests (*cf.* 24:1–19) and the Levites (23:3–32; 24:20 – 26:32). As so often in Chronicles when it comes to detail the order is reversed, except for some supplementary details about the Levites.

23:3–23 The twenty-four orders of Levites. 3 *Thirty years and upward.* See on 23:24. Though not expressly stated it may be inferred that they were under 50 (*cf.* Nu. 4:3). **4** Attempts to regard the figures here as absurdly high overlook the fact that the Levites were divided into 24 courses. 1,000 overseers on duty at one time, considering the scale of the work, is not unreasonable; the same applies to the other groups. *Officers and judges. Cf.* Dt. 17:9; 2 Ch. 19:8, 11. **6** The number of Levitical orders corresponded to the 24 orders of priests. This passage (vv. 6–23) is largely paralleled by the obviously fragmentary section 24:20–31. The minor variants in names call for no mention. What is more important is that only 22 orders can be counted, or 23, if, as seems probable, *Eleazar* (v. 22) is reckoned as the head of one through his daughters. We cannot say where the name may have dropped out. It may be in v. 9, where *Shimei* reveals some textual corruption (*cf.* v. 10), or in v. 16, where only one of Gershom's sons is mentioned. **7** *Ladan*; 'Libni' (1 Ch. 6:17). Many think that Ladan may have been a descendant of Libni.

23:24–27 The age of Temple service. It is impossible to interpret this section with certainty, but its general meaning is clear. David, as he considered the future, saw that the ornate ritual of the Temple would need more Levites, but that their actual service would be easier. He therefore ordered that once the Temple was completed the age at which service should begin should be lowered from 30 to 20. It is not clear whether a second census was taken or not. See on 24:1–19.

The importance of this section is that it shows that a command in the law could be changed by lawful authority without any reference to an alleged Mosaic tradition. Why then, if modern criticism is right about the growth of the Pentateuch, should all the later laws have been attributed to Moses?

23:28–32 An outline of the duties of the Levites. These regulations were necessary, as many of the Levites had been carrying out priestly duties at the smaller and less regular sanctuaries. *Cf.* 2 Ki. 23:8f. and especially Jdg. 17:7–13; 18:30. **30** There were a great many technical ritual acts involved in the bringing of sacrifice, and in these the Levites helped. By NT times the proportion of priests to Levites had so increased that the latter had been to a large extent ousted from this service.

24:1–19 The priestly courses. During the period of declension under the judges there was plenty of work for the descendants of Aaron at the many local sanctuaries; but now that Jerusalem was to become the central sanctuary, they were too many. The position would, in any case, have been created by the natural growth in population. They were divided up into 24 courses, which meant a fortnight's priestly duty a year, besides being on call at the great festivals, when in any case they should be in Jerusalem. As in the Jewish calendar the year has 13 months on an average of about 2 years in 5, the period of service would gradually move round the year. In NT times the service was for 2 separate weeks in the year and the great festivals (see Edersheim, *The Temple*, for this and other details of the NT period), and it may well have been so from the first. **3** *Ahimelech of the sons of Ithamar. Cf.* v. 6, 'Ahimelech the son of Abiathar', and see on 18:16. It would seem that the family tree was Ahitub, Ahimelech (1 Sa. 22:9), Abiathar (1 Sa. 23:6), Ahimelech. It is easy to see how confusion could have arisen. Here the text will be correct. Abiathar was too old by this time to be troubled with administrative details. **4** The smaller number of descendants of Ithamar can easily be explained by the misfortunes of the house of Eli, especially the massacre of the priests of Nob (see 1 Sa. 22:11ff.). **5** *Officers of the sanctuary and officers of God.* The two phrases should probably be regarded as synonymous. The whole verse probably means that except for the number of courses no distinction in honour was made between the two families. **6** *The scribe Shemaiah ... a Levite.* The stress is not so much on his being a Levite, but that he was not the royal scribe. *One father's house being chosen for Eleazar and one chosen for Ithamar.* The order of service was decided by lot, the choice for the first 16 courses being alternately from Eleazar and Ithamar. Some of the priestly names which follow seem to occur in Nehemiah. See on Ne. 12:1 in *Cam. Bible.* **10** *Hakkoz. Cf.* Ezr. 2:61; Ne. 3:4, 21.

24:20–31 Levitical families. *Cf.* 23:6–23. This section is obviously fragmentary, the Gershonites being omitted without obvious reason. In vv. 26 and 27 there seems to be textual corruption. We have no other evidence for Jaaziah as a son of Merari; he was probably a later descendant. **26** *Beno* is not a proper name; it is literally 'his son'. In v. 26 it has probably entered by dittography from v. 27, where it may well be an error for Bani.

25:1–31 The families and courses of the singers. 1 *The chiefs of the service.* Obviously the Temple service is meant. *Who should prophesy.* While there is probably a reference to 1 Sa. 10:5, it seems clear that these chosen singers are being given an honour higher than that of the ordinary Levite. It may be that many Christians do not rank music high enough in the service of God. **2–4** The names listed here are found again with certain minor variations in vv. 9–31. **4** *Hananiah. . . .* Some think that these last nine names are improbable as names. Taking the consonantal text and occasionally dividing the words otherwise the following sense is obtained:

*Be gracious unto me, O Jah, be gracious unto
me!*
Thou art my God whom I magnify and exalt.
O my help when in trouble, I say,
Give an abundance of visions.

It is thought that this feature cannot be accidental
and therefore one of the few reasonable explanations is that some early scribe saw the possibility
of reading this petition in the names of Heman's
sons and altered them slightly for his purpose.
5 Note that *Heman* is called a seer. *And three
daughters*. This may imply that they too took part
in the Temple worship. *Cf.* Ps. 68:25. **8** *Teacher*.
Better rendered 'the skilful' as in v. 7 (RV),
though RSV interpretation may well be correct.
It is simpler to omit the last clause with LXX.
The 288 were the skilful ones, the remainder
(making a total of 4,000; see 23:5) were the
scholars. Both classes were divided into 24
courses to match those of the priests and
Levites.

**26:1–19 The courses and stations of the door-
keepers.** *Cf.* 9:17–27. It is not clear how the gate-
keepers' duties were divided up. While 24 names
seem to be mentioned in vv. 1–11, there is no
suggestion that there were 24 courses. **13** Lots
were cast for the place, not time of service. Vv.
8, 9, 11 may suggest that there were 93 chief
door-keepers; but this may be an incorrect
inference, as 9:22 says 212. These would be the
chiefs of the 4,000 (23:5). Vv. 17, 18 give a total
of 24 (chief?) door-keepers on duty at a time.
16 *For Shuppim*. Omit; it is a case of dittography
from the previous verse. There is no such name
in the genealogy, and LXX does not know it.
Shallecheth and **18** *the parbar*. Neither can be
identified with certainty.

26:20–32 Various Levitical officers. 20 *And of
the Levites, Ahijah had charge*. Read with LXX,
'And the Levites their brethren were over.' The
alteration required is very small. Two treasuries
are here mentioned; that of *the house of God*
under the descendants of Ladan, and that of
the dedicated gifts under the descendants of
Amram. **21** *Jehieli*; *'Jehiel' (23:8). **22** *The sons
of Jehieli*. Probably to be deleted. *Zetham* and
Joel were brothers of Jehiel (see 23:8). **27** *The
house of the Lord*. This need not mean the Temple.
The earlier dedications were probably for the
repair of the Tabernacle, and the upkeep of the
tent in Jerusalem. *Cf.* 15:1. **29** *Outside duties*. *Cf.*
Ne. 11:16. It is quite probable that they were
collectors of Temple dues and royal taxes (*cf.* v.
30). There is no obvious reason why there should
be only **30** *one thousand seven hundred men* for
W Palestine, while there were **32** *two thousand
seven hundred* for Transjordan. This is one of the
many indications that, while the numbers in
Chronicles are often hard to understand, they
are not inventions.

27:1–34 The civil leaders of the nation

27:1–15 The army courses. *ICC* and *Cam.
Bible* assume that we have here the number of
the royal bodyguard, which at 24,000 a month

would be excessive. But this is not said. In any
case the impression clearly created by 2 Samuel
is that the royal bodyguard consisted mainly of
foreign mercenaries, the Cherethites and the
Pelethites (2 Sa. 8:18; 20:23; 1 Ki. 1:38). If we
picture them as scattered over the kingdom, the
number is reasonable. It should be noticed that
v. 7, with its reference to Asahel, implies that
this division was of long standing, though
perhaps in a less developed form. Asahel was
killed when David was still king in Hebron
(2 Sa. 2:19ff.). Though the forms of the names
vary slightly in places, all the 12 chiefs seem to
come from the list of David's mighty men. **5**
Benaiah, the son of Jehoiada, the priest. This
could be the Jehoiada of 12:27. Since, however,
there is no other suggestion that Benaiah was a
priest, we may well be dealing with a scribal
error based on an association of ideas with 2 Sa.
8:18. Benaiah acted as emergency executioner
(1 Ki. 2:25, 29, 34, 46), a post we can hardly
associate with a priest.

27:16–24 The tribal officers. These were appointed at the time of the census (see vv. 23, 24).
We have 13 names. Zadok probably represents
the whole people. The two halves of the tribe of
Manasseh are reckoned separately. Gad and
Asher are omitted, possibly by a defect of transmission. It is not likely to have been to preserve
the number 12, as that had already been broken
by the introduction of Zadok. **18** *Elihu*. Presumably 'Eliab' (1 Sa. 16:6; 1 Ch. 2:13). **23** *Below
twenty years of age*. The omission of those under
20 conforms to the wilderness pattern (Nu. 1:3);
it is implied by 2 Sa. 24:9; 1 Ch. 21:5.

27:25–31 Various royal officers. These are the
chief stewards of David's landed property. Note
that **30** *Obil* and *Jaziz* are foreigners.

27:32–34 The king's counsellors. This list is
of a rather different nature from that of David's
officers (see 18:14–17; *cf.* also a later list, 2 Sa.
20:23–26), though some names are common to
both; if so, they are found here in their capacity
of counsellors. Like the previous list it has no
particular connection with its setting at the end
of David's reign. One at any rate had been dead
for some time. **32** *Jonathan, David's uncle*. Not
otherwise mentioned. On the basis of 20:7 many
would render 'David's nephew'. While the
Hebrew allows this, it seems unnecessary and
on the grounds of age unlikely. *Jehiel*. Evidently
the tutor of the king's sons. **33** *Hushai . . . the
king's friend*. *Cf.* 2 Sa. 15:32, *etc.* 'The king's
friend' is an official title, probably borrowed
from Egypt; hence the AV 'companion' is to be
rejected as misleading. *Ahithophel*. See 2 Sa.
15:31, *etc.* **34** *Jehoiada the son of Benaiah*;
though otherwise unknown, there seems no
reason for reversing it and reading 'Benaiah the
son of Jehoiada'. For reasons of age it can
hardly refer to the well-known Benaiah's son.
Abiathar. Presumably the priest of that name.

28:1 – 29:30 Solomon made king

There is every probability that, after a hurried

anointing like that described in 1 Ki. 1:39, the new king would as soon as possible be introduced in a solemn assembly to the representative leaders of the people for their confirmation of what had been done. 'Made Solomon . . . king the second time' (29:22) shows that the Chronicler knew of Adonijah's attempt and its result. The proper interpretation of 23:1, 2 (see comment *in loc.*) rules out the possibility that the first time is the one mentioned in 23:1. He is silent about Adonijah in conformity with his purpose of omitting, so far as possible, deviations from the divine pattern.

28:1–10 Solomon presented to the national assembly. 1 *With the palace officials.* Though the Hebrew word is sometimes used more generally, it is not likely to be the case here. AV mg. and RV mg. correctly render 'with the eunuchs'. This is the first mention of this abomination at the Israelite court: but *cf.* 1 Sa. 8:15, RV mg. The corruption of power had acted quickly. **2** *Then King David rose to his feet.* In normal circumstances, as many archaeological discoveries suggest, David would have spoken seated, the more so because of his age. His standing emphasizes the religious nature of the occasion. David, the chosen of Yahweh (v. 4), presents to the people the new chosen of Yahweh (v. 5), who has been chosen for the special purpose of building the Temple (v. 6). Though there is no direct affirmation of God's choice of Solomon in Samuel and Kings, yet 2 Sa. 12:24, 25 may hint at it. **5** *To sit upon the throne of the kingdom of the Lord over Israel.* Cf. 29:23, 'the throne of the Lord'. The king was Yahweh's deputy. **10** *Take heed now.* This charge is continued in v. 20.

28:11–19 The plans of the Temple. Our interpretation of the passage will depend on our interpretation of *plan* (v. 11). Ex. 25:40 clearly suggests an original seen by Moses, which he was later to describe to those carrying out the work. As Ex. 25 seems to lie behind this section, it is probable that David described to Solomon the vision that he had had by inspiration. (See v. 19, *from the hand of the Lord*, and *cf.* mg., which is probably correct.) If this is right, then *the writing* in v. 19 is the account in Exodus of the Tabernacle, the necessary modifications of which to suit the Temple David was caused to understand by inspiration. This is the more likely, as there has never been any satisfactory typical interpretation given to those details of the Temple where it varied from the Tabernacle; note Hebrews is concerned with the latter, not the former. The Bible never suggests a heavenly prototype of the Temple as it does of the Tabernacle. **18** *His plan for the golden chariot of the cherubim.* Better, as in RV, 'the chariot, even the cherubim'. The cherubim were thought of as forming God's chariot. *Cf.* Ps. 18:10 and especially Ezk. 1.

28:20, 21 Concluding encouragement for Solomon. The thought resumes from v. 10. The LXX shows us that a section has accidentally been dropped at the end of v. 20. It reads, 'Now behold the pattern of the porch (of the temple) and of the houses thereof, and of the treasuries thereof, and of the upper rooms thereof, and of the inner chambers thereof, and of the house of the mercy-seat, even the pattern of the house of the Lord.'

29:1–9 David's appeal for liberality and the response. David announced a huge gift from his own private fortune for the building of the Temple over and above the sum mentioned in 22:14, and used this as the ground of an appeal to the generosity of the assembly. The motive is less likely to have been the need for further gifts than the wish to make as many as possible have a share in the building of the new Temple. It seems impossible to accept the figures both of David's and the people's gifts as they stand. How enormous they are cannot so easily be judged by turning them into modern currency as by comparing them with the tribute that Sennacherib was able to wring out of Hezekiah (2 Ki. 18:14) or Tiglath-pileser from Menahem (2 Ki. 15:19). Some idea of the quantities can be obtained from the Moffatt translation. **1** *The palace* (Aram. *bîrâ*); this late word is used only three times of the Temple. But *hêḵāl*, the word normally translated Temple, also has as its root meaning palace or great house. **5** *Consecrating himself* (lit. 'filling his hand'). This is a technical term of inducting a person into the priestly office (*cf.* Ex. 28:41, *etc.*); but here it is used metaphorically with the approximate sense 'who will offer willingly like one consecrating himself to the priesthood?' (*ICC*).

7 *Ten thousand darics.* The daric was a Persian gold coin (an obvious anachronism indicating the date of Chronicles) worth about a guinea. The difference between the very large number of talents and the small amount in darics may be because the latter refers to minted coins (the talent is a weight). As, at present, we have no evidence for minted coins earlier than the 7th century BC, we cannot disprove the suggestion that this may be a complete anachronism due to a misunderstanding of his source by the Chronicler.

29:10–19 David's closing prayer of thanksgiving. One of the finest prayers in the OT. **13** *We thank thee, our God, and praise thy glorious name.* The Hebrew expresses continual action. Moffatt renders well, 'Hence, O our God, we ever thank thee and praise thy glorious name.' **15** *We are strangers before thee.* The thought is not that we are strangers to God. The picture is of the notoriously insecure position of the stranger; but as they dwell before, *i.e.* in the sight of, God, they are secure. *There is no abiding.* Better, as in RV mg., 'there is no hope', *i.e.* apart from God. **17** shows that the merit of the gifts for the Temple lay not in their amount but in that they had been given willingly. David trusts that God, who knows men's hearts, will see the same willingness in the others as has been already seen in him.

29:20–25 The close of the assembly: Solomon

made king. 20 *And worshipped the Lord, and did obeisance to the king.* The word normally translated 'worship' in the OT means to prostrate oneself. Hence, as here, it can be used equally for God and the king; RSV has felt compelled to translate the one word twice in two different ways. 22 *King the second time.* See note at the beginning of this section. *And Zadok as priest.* We do not know enough of the customs at the time to be dogmatic, but a literal interpretation seems to be hazardous. Zadok is always presented to us as joint high priest, so any such consecration (or reconsecration) seems to be excluded. There is no evidence for the reconsecration of the high priest at the accession of a new king. It is easiest to regard this as the Chronicler's hint at the deposition of Abiathar, known to his readers from 1 Ki. 2:26. 23 *The throne of the Lord.* See on 28:5. 24 *And also all the sons of King David, pledged their allegiance.* An indirect reference to Adonijah (1 Ki. 1:53). 25 *Such royal majesty as had not been on any king before him in Israel.* Translated thus, the comparison is limited to David and Saul. It is likely that we should take the Hebrew to mean 'such royal majesty which was not on any king more than on him in Israel'. This would refer to Solomon's successors as well.

29:26–30 A summary of David's reign. 27 See 1 Ki. 2:11. 29 *Samuel the seer* (Heb. *rō'eh*), . . . *Gad the seer* (Heb. *ḥōzeh*). See on 1 Sa. 9:9 and Appendix 3 to Samuel. The former term, used of Samuel in 1 Sa. 9:9, 11, suggests something akin to clairvoyance; the latter suggests the seeing of dreams or visions. 30 *The circumstances that came upon him; i.e.* his vicissitudes. *Upon all the kingdoms of the countries.* Obviously only those countries with which David had contacts are intended.

2 Ch. 1:1 – 9:31 THE REIGN OF SOLOMON

The Chronicler gives us very little information that is not in Kings, though a few of his additions are of importance. Some of his omissions, like Adonijah's attempt on the throne and Solomon's apostasy and its results, are in conformity with his general purpose; we get the impression that the majority of them are merely to save space. The most remarkable feature is the manner in which, instead of closely following Kings, he has repeatedly rewritten, expanded and contracted it.

1:1–17 Solomon confirmed in the kingdom by God

1:1–13 Solomon's initiatory sacrifice and vision at Gibeon. 1–6 The bulk is peculiar to Chronicles. Obviously such an initiatory sacrifice would be carried out with great pomp. 7–13 are an abridgement of 1 Ki. 3:5–15 (where see commentary). 3 *The tent of meeting of God.* The non-mention of the Tabernacle by Kings may imply that it was no longer in use but had been honourably lodged in the Gibeon sanctuary. That would explain why David had not brought it to Jerusalem to house the ark.

1:14–17 Solomon's wealth. See 1 Ki. 10:26–29, with which it is virtually verbally identical, and *cf.* 2 Ch. 9:13–28. Such a heaping up of bullion was bound to have an inflationary effect, which would affect the farmers worst of all.

2:1 – 5:1 The building of the Temple

For this section see 1 Ki. 5:1 – 7:51. The Chronicler omits the details of Solomon's other buildings (1 Ki. 7:1–12) and also some of the details of the Temple itself.

2:1–16 Solomon and Hiram. See 1 Ki. 5:1–12. The Chronicler has a considerably expanded form of the correspondence. Since vv. 7, 13f. bear the stamp of authenticity (*cf.* 1 Ki. 7:1), it is likely that we have a condensed version in Kings. 2 is a doublet of 2:18 (*q.v.*). 3 *Huram the king of Tyre.* Except in 1 Ch. 14:1, where it is found in the mg. of the Hebrew, Chronicles always uses this form instead of *Hiram, found in Samuel and Kings, which in turn is short for Ahiram. 7 *A man skilled to work in gold . . . trained also in engraving.* Archaeology has fully borne out Israel's backwardness in the arts at this time. 8 *Cypress, and algum timber*; for the former see 1 Ki. 5:8; for the latter see on 1 Ki. 10:11f., and the parallel of 2 Ch. 9:10f. The latter have probably been accidentally introduced here, though in our ignorance of the exact kind of timber intended we cannot be sure. 10 For the quantities of food listed see on 1 Ki. 5:11.

11–16 The authenticity of Hiram's answer has been objected to on the ground of the religious language he uses. In a polytheistic society politeness to a neighbour's god cost nothing. 13 *Huram-abi.* See on 1 Ki. 7:13, 14. There are no grounds on which we can choose between Huram and Hiram; the name of the king is no guide. Some claim his name was Huram-abi (or abiv), which is possible, but more likely it should be: 'Huram, my (his) trusted counsellor.'

2:17, 18 The preparation of a labour pool. See also vv. 1, 2 and see on 1 Ki. 5:13–18.

3:1–4 The construction of the Temple. See on 1 Ki. 6:1–10. In Chronicles the account is strangely truncated. 1 *Mount Moriah*; *cf.* Gn. 22:2; the only place where Mt. Zion or the Temple mount is so called. Note that in Genesis Moriah is the name of a district, not of a hill. 4 *Its height was a hundred and twenty cubits*; if the porch was like an Egyptian pylon, the height is possible; if it was a portico, as seems more likely, for the general style seems to have followed a Phoenician pattern, we must omit the 100 as an accidental corruption.

3:5–14 The interior of the house. See on 1 Ki. 6:14–36. Again the description is greatly abbreviated, but a few details are added. 5 *The nave*; *i.e.* 'the holy place'. *Cypress.* On the basis of 1 Ki. 6:15 we must interpret this of the floor and possibly of the ceiling, the material of which is not mentioned in Kings. *Chains*; a word used only of ornamental chains, the links here being of flowers; *cf.* 1 Ki. 6:18, 29. *ICC* renders 'garlands'. 6 *Parvaim*; perhaps in Arabia, but not identified. **8** *Six hundred talents*; on the most likely calculation nearly 65,000 lb., a seemingly impossible figure (*cf.* on 1 Ch. 29:1–9). **9** *Upper chambers*; *cf.* 1 Ch. 28:11. It is not clear what is referred to. **14** *The veil*; not mentioned in Kings, even as Chronicles does not mention the doors.

3:15–17 The bronze pillars. See on 1 Ki. 7: 15–22. **16** *He made chains like a necklace.* The textual emendation adopted by RSV is small and almost certainly correct.

4:1 The bronze altar. Not in Kings; its non-mention cannot be explained with certainty, for it assumes its existence (1 Ki. 8:22, 64). One might assume that it had dropped from the text by a scribal error, were it not that it is not mentioned in the summary in 1 Ki. 8:41–43; 2 Ch. 4:11–16 (!) either. Perhaps the easiest explanation is that the bronze altar was brought from Gibeon (1:5), but it was then found to be too small (7:7) and so was later replaced by a much larger one (*cf.* 4:1 with Ex. 27:1). Chronicles, summarizing as it does, mentions the later altar in the general description, while Kings, dealing with what was made for the dedication, does not mention it. This is contradicted by 7:7, but this could be a later mistaken scribal addition. Would an altar surface of 90 sq. ft really have been too small?

4:2–6, 10 The sea and the lavers. See on 1 Ki. 7:23–37. The difficult description of the stands for the lavers in Kings is omitted. **5** *Three thousand baths*; 1 Ki. 7:26 has 'two thousand'; see commentary *in loc.*

4:7 The lampstands. *Cf.* 4:20f. Note that *he* refers to Solomon, not to Huram. There is no suggestion that the gold articles were made by the latter.

4:8 The tables. *Cf.* 4:19 and 1 Ki. 7:48.

4:9 The courts. See on 1 Ki. 7:2–12.

4:11–18 A summary of Huram's work. Virtually identical with 1 Ki. 7:40–47 (*q.v.*).

4:19 – 5:1 The golden vessels. Virtually identical with 1 Ki. 7:48–50 (*q.v.*). **19** *The tables for the bread of the Presence.* 1 Ki. 7:48 has, obviously correctly, only one table. The other nine had value only as ornaments. The increased number of tables and lamps was demanded mainly by the quadrupling of the floor-space of the Holy Place.

5:2 – 7:22 The dedication of the Temple

This section is virtually identical with the corresponding section in 1 Ki. 8:1 – 9:9, the few additions giving mainly liturgical information.

5:2–14 The moving of the ark. See on 1 Ki. 8:1–11. **4, 5** *The Levites took up the ark . . . the priests and the Levites brought them up.* Chronicles alters 'priests' (1 Ki. 8:3) to *Levites* (v. 4), and the Hebrew omits *and* between priests and Levites (v. 5). RSV has followed the versions and some 24 Hebrew MSS. One must ask, however, whether this is not one of the cases where the more difficult reading should have been followed. The Chronicler may simply have been following the common phrase in Dt. 18:1, *etc.*

It is very far from clear from the Pentateuch whether priests or Levites had to carry the ark. It may well be that the latter carried it up to the Temple site and then the former took over. In any case it is clear that the distinction between the descendants of Aaron and the other members of the tribe of Levi was not so strictly enforced at this time. **5** *The tent of meeting.* If we possessed only Chronicles we should naturally interpret this in the light of 1:3. From 1 Ki. 8:4 it is more natural to interpret it of the tent erected in Jerusalem by David to house the ark, for Kings does not otherwise mention the old Tabernacle.

11b–13a are an addition by Chronicles stressing the pomp of the occasion; obviously all available priests and Levites were on duty, not merely the weekly course (*cf.* 1 Ch. 24). The blowing of the trumpets was specifically a priestly duty (Nu. 10:8).

6:1 – 7:3 The actual dedication. See 1 Ki. 8:12–61, from which this account differs only very slightly. **13** *A bronze platform.* This information is omitted by Kings. **40–42** take the place of 1 Ki. 8:50b–53. As they are in no way alternatives, it is likely that the concluding verses in Kings have dropped out by a scribal error in Chronicles. On the other hand Kings may well have deliberately omitted the conclusion here. **7:1–3** is not in Kings. **1** For *fire came down from heaven cf.* Lv. 9:24; 1 Ch. 21:26; 1 Ki. 18:24, 38. The remainder is an enlargement of 5:13b, 14. Chronicles omits Solomon's blessing of the people (1 Ki. 8:54–61), perhaps in disapproval of the king's taking priestly functions on himself. There was always a strong temptation to the king to arrogate priestly functions to himself in imitation of his heathen neighbours (*cf.* 1 Sa. 13:8–14; 2 Ch. 26:16–20).

7:4–10 The sacrifices and feast. See 1 Ki. 8:62–66. **7** *The bronze altar.* See on 4:1. **9, 10** *On the eighth day . . . On the twenty-third day.* This is difficult to reconcile with 1 Ki. 8:65f., where the picture seems to be of a 7-day dedication festival (8th to 14th Tishri), followed by the Feast of Tabernacles (15th to 21st Tishri), followed by the dismissal of the people next day. Chronicles, finding in its additional sources that the people had been dismissed on 23rd Tishri, rightly understood that there had been an extra day. Kings reckons a 7-day dedication feast with the Day of Atonement (10th Tishri) in the middle, *i.e.* 8th to 15th Tishri, followed by Tabernacles a day late, *i.e.* 16th to 22nd Tishri. Chronicles reckons the dedication feast as including the Day of Atonement, *i.e.* 8th to 14th Tishri, followed by Tabernacles (15th to 21st Tishri), plus the eighth day closing festival (Lv. 23:36). So it is a question of how the festivities were broken up, and perhaps no clear line of demarcation was drawn, as there will have been little or no distinction between the two halves.

7:11–22 God's answer to Solomon. See 1 Ki. 9:1–9. There are only minor verbal differences except for vv. 13–16, which are merely an expansion of what is implicit in 1 Ki. 9:3.

8:1 – 9:31 Solomon's glory

See 1 Ki. 9:10 – 10:29; 11:41–43. The differences between Kings and Chronicles are for the most part insignificant. 1 Ki. 9:11–16 are omitted, while 2 Ch. 8:13–16 have no parallel in Kings.

8:1, 2 Solomon's transactions with Hiram. See 1 Ki. 9:10–14. It is often alleged that Chronicles here contradicts Kings. It is more likely that the Chronicler disapproved of Solomon's transactions with Hiram, and therefore mentions only the final incident in them, which, however, is not mentioned in Kings (see commentary *in loc.*). It could be that from the first these cities were intended to serve as a pledge for ultimate payment.

8:3–11 Solomon's levy and city building. See 1 Ki. 9:15–24. **3** The campaign against *Hamath* is peculiar to Chronicles. Hamath had voluntarily become tributary to David (2 Sa. 8:9ff.) and probably took advantage of his death to try to regain independence. This, the only campaign waged by Solomon, was probably very brief. **4** *Tadmor in the wilderness* was interpreted by all the versions as Palmyra, about half-way between Damascus and the Euphrates. Tadmor existed already in the time of Tiglath-pileser I of Assyria, *c.* 1100 BC, so it may have been in Solomon's possession. Since, however, in 1 Ki. 9:18 the true reading is certainly Tamar (see commentary *in loc.*), the mention of Hamath may have misled some scribe. *The store-cities which he built in Hamath* may have been to cover the northern approaches of Israel (*cf.* on 1 Ki. 8:65). **10** The discrepancy of *two hundred and fifty* with the 550 of Kings hardly calls for comment; the number will not have remained constant throughout the reign. In fact if we add the figures in 1 Ki. 5:16 and 9:23 we get the same total as when we add 2 Ch. 2:18 and 8:10. **11** The statement about *Pharaoh's daughter* is hard to understand. *My wife shall not live . . .* is misleading, for it suggests that the objection was that she was a foreigner; in fact we should render 'no wife of mine shall dwell . . .' (*Cam. Bible*, Moff.). It is no longer possible to reconstruct the circumstances.

8:12–16 Solomon's worship. It would seem from v. 16 that this section originally wound up the description of the building of the Temple. All modern commentators agree that the LXX should be followed, at least in part, in v. 16, as does RSV.

8:17, 18 Solomon's Red Sea trade. See 1 Ki. 9:26–28. **17** *Then Solomon went* need no more be taken literally than the parallel in Kings 'And king Solomon made a navy'. **18** *Huram sent him . . . ships.* It is absurd to read into this that ships were transported overland. There is such shortage of timber round the Gulf of Aqabah that it would have to be brought from Phoenicia, and it was probably to a large degree shaped in advance. It is true that they would possibly

have been sent via the Nile and the canal linking the Nile and the Red Sea, but this is not suggested by the text.

9:1–12 The visit of the queen of Sheba. Almost verbally identical with 1 Ki. 10:1–13 (*q.v.*).

9:13–28 The trade and riches of Solomon. See 1 Ki. 10:14–29. To 1 Ki. 10:26–29 we really have a doublet in 2 Chronicles, viz. 1:14–17 and 9:25–28. **16** For the weight of the *three hundred shields* see on 1 Ki. 10:17. **18** *A footstool of gold* is merely a corruption of the text of 1 Ki. 10:19 (see commentary *in loc.*). **21** *The king's ships went to Tarshish.* The Chronicler knew only of traffic based on Ezion-geber (8:17; 9:10) and since v. 21 is obviously the same as 1 Ki. 10:22, we are dealing with a careless scribal error. The ships may have gone as far as India but they did not circumnavigate Africa to reach the Mediterranean where Tarshish was (Jon. 1:3). Nor are the products brought back Mediterranean products. The same error has slipped into 20:36, 37. It is true that there was more than one Tarshish, for it was a generic name for a port where copper ore was loaded. So there could have been a port on the Indian ocean with this name, but we have no record of it, nor is there any mention of a suitable cargo from it.

9:29–31 Summary of Solomon's reign. See 1 Ki. 11:41–43. The Chronicler omits the story of Solomon's idolatry and troubles, even as he does that of David's sin and its results, and just for the same reason. He is concerned with the monarchy as an institution rather than with the personal failings of those that sat on the throne; see Introduction, p. 369.

10:1 – 36:23 THE KINGS OF JUDAH

10:1 – 12:16 Rehoboam

Chronicles brings us a number of interesting points, some of importance, which are not mentioned by Kings.

10:1–19 The disruption. See 1 Ki. 12:1–19. Note the deliberate omission of 1 Ki. 12:20. Not even the making of Jeroboam king is to be mentioned. For the Chronicler the northern kingdom is from the first apostate, which, of course, in the truest sense it was.

11:1–4 Civil war averted. See 1 Ki. 12:21–24. **3** Note the insertion *and to all Israel in Judah and Benjamin.* The Chronicler constantly insists that there were always elements of the northern tribes that remained loyal to the Davidic king. This is too readily overlooked when we are dealing with certain modern theories.

11:5–12 The organization of Judah. Not in Kings. As soon as Jeroboam could organize the north it was bound to be stronger than Judah both in its population and natural resources. Jeroboam was an ambitious man not likely to be content with what God had given him, and so Rehoboam did his best to strengthen his diminished kingdom. **6** *He built;* i.e. he refortified. This may have been after Shishak's invasion, for all the towns are in the south. On the other hand he must have known that Shishak would support Jeroboam (1 Ki. 11:40), so it may be that his best efforts were inadequate.

11:13–17 Immigration from Israel. *Cf.* 1 Ki. 12:31; 13:33. **14** The mention not merely of *Jeroboam* but also of *his sons*, *i.e.* his successors, shows that while the major part of the immigration of priests and Levites took place at once, yet it continued over a period, the turn of phrase in Hebrew in v. 13 being consistent with this. *Cast them out.* We may be sure Jeroboam would have been glad to keep them, but by his insistence on a Canaanized version of Yahweh worship he had made it impossible for those who were loyal to remain. We may be sure some will have put their pocket before their conscience and stayed. **15** *Satyrs* (Heb. *śāʿîr*) are the demons or *jinn* believed to inhabit desert and waste places; they were looked on as hairy, or of animal shape; hence RV 'he-goats' (*cf.* Lv. 17:7 and Robertson Smith, *The Religion of the Semites*, p. 120). The return to nature worship meant a return to old superstitions. *The calves which he had made*; important as showing that Chronicles takes a knowledge of Kings for granted. **16, 17** The natural interpretation is that some of those who disobeyed Jeroboam's ban then came to Jerusalem to worship and made their permanent home there; *cf.* 15:9.

11:18–23 The royal family. 18 Rehoboam's chief wife was *Mahalath*, whose parents were *Jerimoth*, an otherwise unnamed son of David, and *Abihail*, a niece of David's. **20** But his favourite wife was *Maachah*, or Michaiah (13:2), the grand-daughter of *Absalom* (*cf.* v. 20 with 13:2). **23** *And procured wives for them.* He was following Solomon's policy of trying to strengthen the throne by suitable marriages both for himself (v. 21) and his sons.

12:1 Rehoboam's idolatry. See 1 Ki. 14:21, 22. It is not clear why we have no details, for they are clearly implied in 14:2, 3. *All Israel* means in Chronicles the southern kingdom.

12:2–12 Shishak's invasion. *Cf.* 1 Ki. 14:25–28. We have Shishak's own account of the invasion recorded on the outside wall of the temple of Karnak. This and other archaeological evidence (see *ANET*, pp. 242f., 263f.) shows that Israel was engulfed as well as Judah, even Ezion-geber being probably destroyed, and that Egyptian overlordship must have lasted some years. It is probable that no resistance was offered. **3** *Sukkiim*; unidentified. **7** *Some deliverance*; better 'deliverance within a little while' (RV mg.); the Egyptians could not keep up their effort for long. **8** *That they may know my service*; that it is better than serving others. **12** *Conditions were good in Judah.* It is far from certain that this is better than 'and moreover in Judah there were good things found' (RV). It is clear that while the north gladly accepted the Canaanized distortion of Yahweh worship patronized by Jeroboam, it did not really get a grip of Judah till the reigns of Ahaz and Manasseh.

12:13–16 Summary of his reign. *Cf.* 1 Ki.

14:29–31. **15** *Iddo the seer.* As the mg. suggests, there seems to be a textual corruption here.

13:1–22 Abijah

Cf. 1 Ki. 15:1–8. **1** No satisfactory explanation of the difference between the forms *Abijah* in Chronicles and Abijam in Kings has been given; so we cannot decide which was his real name. **2** For his *mother* see on 11:20. **3** The size of the armies should be compared with the census figures (2 Sa. 24:9; 1 Ch. 21:5). This was an all-out effort at conquest. **4** *Mount Zemaraim*; *cf.* Jos. 18:22. **5** *A covenant of salt* was unbreakable (Nu. 18:19). Abijah was far from practising what he preached (1 Ki. 15:3); but what was settled religious policy in the north was still only an aberration in Judah. **6, 7** His picture of the disruption is rather fanciful, for Rehoboam was 41 when he came to the throne (12:13). **12** Abijah claims it is a holy war. **15** *God defeated.* There would seem to have been some form of supernatural intervention. **17** We must take the *five hundred thousand picked men* as no more than 'a very large number', for the only result of the victory was the capture of a few border towns which Asa soon lost (see on 1 Ki. 15:16–22).

14:1 – 16:14 Asa

14:1–5; 15:16–18 Asa's reformation. See 1 Ki. 15:9–15. There is no reason for thinking that Asa's reformation was really in two stages. The impression arises from the way the material from Kings has been joined to other sources. Maachah's *image* (15:16) must have been disposed of right away.

1 If we put together 1 Ki. 15:28 and 16, it becomes clear that the *ten years* is only a round figure. **3–5** only make explicit what is implicit in 1 Ki. 15:12. **3** *He took away the foreign altars and the high places.* It is alleged that this is a deliberate contradiction of 1 Ki. 15:14 (see commentary *in loc.*). The self-consistency of Chronicles is then vindicated by suggesting that 2 Ch. 15:17 is either a later addition from Kings or that *Israel* there means the northern kingdom. The more reasonable explanation is that *foreign* should be construed with *high places* as well as *altars*; he removed these high places that could make no legitimate claim to existence.

14:6–8 Asa's defensive measures. Not in Kings, but *cf.* 1 Ki. 15:23.

14:9–15 Asa's victory over Zerah. Not in Kings. **9** Zerah is generally, but with little linguistic justification, identified with Pharaoh Osorkon I or II and there is a little archaeological evidence to favour an invasion by the latter. But he is called *ha-kushi*, 'the Cushite' (RSV *the Ethiopian*). Cush is either Ethiopia, *i.e.* the Sudan, or part of Arabia (Gn. 10:7; 2 Ch. 21:16, *q.v.*). Since the XXIInd Dynasty of Egypt was not Ethiopian, though they may have controlled part of the Sudan, it is quite possible that it was an Arabian invasion, but with Egyptian backing (*cf.* 16:8, 'Libyans'). Note the nature of the booty

(v. 15) which would suit an Arab invasion. The *three hundred chariots* is proof enough that the numbers are not invented; therefore *a million* probably means no more than an exceedingly large number. **13, 14** *Gerar* and the neighbouring cities were Philistine; they had probably aided Zerah. **15** *The tents of those who had cattle.* A possible emendation; 'cattle owners' is probably better.

15:1–15 Azariah's exhortation and its results. Not in Kings. The main thought of the passage is clear enough. **1** Azariah explained the victory **2** by saying 'The Eternal was on your side, because you were on his side' (Moff.) and so **7** encouraged them to carry through the reformation which till that time had been carried on only at the official level. **10** This was sealed at a great popular gathering at the Feast of Weeks. **3–6** It is these verses that create a difficulty. They seem to describe the position under the judges, and are apparently a commentary on the last section of v. 2. But whether they are Azariah's words or a comment by the Chronicler is not clear. **10** *The fifteenth year* compared with 14:1 shows that no complete chronology of Asa's reign is being attempted; see too on 15:19. **9** *Those from Ephraim, Manasseh, and Simeon who were sojourning with them.* They may have migrated to Judah, especially in the troubled time when Baasha wiped out the house of Jeroboam (1 Ki. 15:27–29); but why Simeon? There is no evidence for their living elsewhere than in the south, and they were always part of Judah. Indeed they had so become part of Judah that their separate existence is no longer mentioned in 1 Ki. 11:36; 12:20. The tribal portion of Simeon (Jos. 19:1–9) could not have been attached to the northern kingdom. Either it implies that until now their hearts had been with the north, or more likely it is an unintelligent correction of an early scribal error.

15:16–18. See above, with 14:1–5.

15:19 – 16:6 Asa's war with Baasha. See 1 Ki. 15:16–22. The figures in 15:19; 16:1 are impossible, for Baasha died in the 26th year of Asa. It has been suggested that the original reading was '. . . unto the five and thirtieth year (*i.e.* of the kingdom), that is, in the fifteenth year of the reign of Asa . . . in the six and thirtieth year, that is, in the sixteenth year of Asa', and it is supported by Thiele, *The Mysterious Numbers of the Hebrew Kings*,[2] pp. 57–60, but it remains more plausible than convincing.

16:7–10 Hanani's rebuke of Asa. Not in Kings. **7** Hanani tells Asa that if he had trusted he would have defeated the combined armies of Baasha and the Syrians, though the Lucianic Greek suggests that we should read 'the army of the king of Israel'. **10** Asa's reply was to *put him in the stocks*. The stocks, which could have been nicknamed 'Little Ease', were even more an instrument of torture than their much later English counterpart. When he *inflicted cruelties* (better 'tortured', Moff.) *upon some of the people*, it may have been for showing sympathy with

Hanani. This is the first recorded instance of the ill-treatment of a prophet.

16:11–14 Summary of Asa's reign. *Cf.* 1 Ki. 15:23, 24. **12** If, as is probable, the *physicians* were foreigners, the condemnation is easily understandable, as their cures will have had more of magic than of medicine about them. **14** *They made a very great fire in his honour*; they did not cremate him, but burned spices (*cf.* Je. 34:5); the worthy funeral for a worthy king is being stressed.

17:1 – 20:37 Jehoshaphat

17:1–6 The character of his reign. 3 *In the earlier ways of his father.* RSV is correct in following some Hebrew MSS and LXX in omitting David (*cf.* chs. 14 and 15 with 16). **6** *He took the high places . . . out of Judah*; *cf.* on 20:33 and on 14:3. The lack of detail about Jehoshaphat's reformation shows it was no more than the rectifying of slackness since Asa's reformation (*cf.* on 19:4).

17:7–9 Regular teaching of the law. Arguments about the ability or otherwise of people to read at a given time are often far from reality. The cost of a scroll of the law would have been beyond the means of all but the richest in the time of Jehoshaphat. The priests should have known it by heart, but that could not be taken for granted in a time of religious slackness.

17:10–19 Jehoshaphat's greatness. 11 *The Arabs.* If Zerah was an Arab (see on 14:9), this may have been a result of Asa's victory. **14–18** The numbers of Jehoshaphat's army are among those in Chronicles that we can no longer explain. See Introduction, p. 370. They are far too high when compared with those available to Ahab and with the probably inflated figures given by Shalmaneser III in his account of the battle of Qarqar (see *DOTT*, p. 47; *ANET*, pp. 278f.), and indeed with the evidence of archaeology generally. If we divide each figure by ten, we reach a total 112,000 of trained soldiers, not militia, which would have been within the powers of Judah at the height of its prosperity and comparable to the half-million militia in the time of David (2 Sa. 24:9).

18:1–34 Jehoshaphat's alliance with Ahab. See 1 Ki. 22:1–38. Except for vv. 1, 2 and the details following Ahab's death (1 Ki. 22:36–38), which have no bearing on Jehoshaphat, the parallels are almost identical. The main changes are intended to put Jehoshaphat more in the centre of the picture. **1** *He made a marriage alliance with Ahab*; see 2 Ki. 8:18, 26; *cf.* on 1 Ki. 3:1.

19:1–3 Jehoshaphat's alliance rebuked. 1 *In safety* (lit. 'in peace'); *cf.* 18:26, 27. **2** *Jehu the son of Hanani.* In 1 Ki. 16:1 Jehu the son of Hanani pronounces the doom of Baasha; in 2 Ch. 16:7 Hanani the seer rebukes Asa. This Jehu is probably the grandson of the Jehu in 1 Ki. 16:1. It was not rare for names to alternate like this in some families. *Because of this, wrath has gone out against you*; fulfilled in the invasion of 20:1.

19:4–11 Administration of law. 4 *Jehoshaphat dwelt at Jerusalem*; *i.e.* he paid no more visits to

Israel. *And brought them back to the Lord*; purity of religion could be bought only at the price of eternal vigilance.

A closer study of the Mosaic legislation will show that it is incomplete, though the Pharisees, by ingenious exposition, were able to make it cover all life; this becomes particularly obvious when it is compared with an ancient code like that of Hammurabi. In other words it did not entirely replace the existing tribal law, but showed how it had to be modified and developed. That meant that side by side there had been, from the first, civil (Ex. 18:25, 26) and religious (*cf.* Ex. 21:6; 22:8, 9, RV) judges. This is clearly legislated for in Dt. 16:18; 17:8–12. **5** In his reform Jehoshaphat appointed civil *judges* throughout the land, probably because the old system, based on family headship, had broken down. **8** In Jerusalem there was a mixed court of appeal: *to give judgment for the Lord, i.e.* cases covered by the law of Moses; *to decide disputed cases, i.e.* civil cases. **11** There were two chief judges, *Amariah the chief priest* (1 Ch. 6:11), and *Zebadiah* representing the king. Increasingly the king was withdrawing from the actual administration of justice to a position where he could see that it was being administered.

20:1–4 An invasion by Moabites and their allies. This invasion must have been earlier than the campaign in 2 Ki. 3, which may have been a sequel to it. **1** *Some of the Meunites.* The Meunim are mentioned in 1 Ch. 4:41; 2 Ch. 26:7. They were, if not Edomites, resident in Edom, and are (in vv. 10, 22) connected with Mt. Seir. The reason why the name Edom is not mentioned is that Edom at this time was under Judah (*cf.* 1 Ki. 22:47; 2 Ki. 3:9). These were some of the inhabitants who linked up with the invaders as they passed through their territory. **2** *From Edom.* Hebrew has 'from Syria'; this confusion between '*dm* amd '*rm* is frequent. To cross *the sea, i.e.* the Dead Sea, they had passed round its southern end through Edom. In any case the water at that time probably stretched only as far south as Masada. **3** *Jehoshaphat feared*, for he knew this was the expression of the divine wrath (19:2).

20:5–19 Jehoshaphat's prayer and the divine answer. 5 *The new court*; see on 1 Ki. 7:2–12. Evidently changes had been made since Solomon's time of which we are not told. **17** The reason for the particular form of victory promised is that Yahweh had brought the invaders as a punishment. Since they had achieved their purpose Yahweh would remove them Himself. This is the more striking because of Jehoshaphat's own strength.

20:20–30 The deliverance. 21 Jehoshaphat's trust is seen in the singing of praise before the fulfilment of the promise. *In holy array*; here, as elsewhere (1 Ch. 16:29; Pss. 29:2; 96:9; 110:3), this replaces AV 'the beauty of holiness'. A possible translation would be 'in holy attire'. **22** *The Lord set an ambush.* Action by Jehoshaphat is excluded. It could refer to action by the in-

habitants of the overrun area, but far more likely by supernatural agents, otherwise unspecified. *They were routed*; explained by v. 23. **24** *The watchtower*; better 'the outlook point' (*Cam. Bible, ICC*). **26** *Beracah; i.e.* blessing. The name is preserved near Tekoa to this day.

20:31–37 Summary of Jehoshaphat's reign. See 1 Ki. 22:41–50. **33** *The high places . . . were not taken away. Cf.* 17:6; we have the same type of contradiction as between 14:3 and 15:17 (*q.v.*). The simple fact was that nothing short of the drastic steps taken by Josiah could abolish them, if the people resisted the royal policy. The high place (Heb. *bāmâ*) did not have to be on a hill, though it often was; *bāmâ* implies no more than the platform on which the cult objects were placed; there was no need for a building, and the whole could be quite insignificant. Until Josiah desecrated the sites (34:5), destruction meant little, for it was the site rather than the cult objects that was holy. **35–37** It is not clear why Chronicles should single out the section about Jehoshaphat's fleet as it does. *To Tarshish*; they were ships of Tarshish to go to Ophir; see on 9:21.

21:1 – 22:9 Jehoram and Ahaziah

21:1–10 Jehoram's reign. See 2 Ki. 8:16–22. Except for vv. 2–4 this is identical with the passage in Kings (*q.v.*). **4** There is no reason suggested for Jehoram's act. The fact that it was not confined to his brothers, but he *slew . . . also some of the princes of Israel* (Moff. renders correctly 'of the nobility in Israel'—Israel being, as usually in Chronicles, the southern kingdom), suggests that he was removing opponents to his intended religious policy.

21:11–20 Jehoram's apostasy and its results. Not in Kings. **11** Since in 23:17 (2 Ki. 11:18) only one temple of Baal is mentioned, it is probable that Jehoram deliberately prepared for the introduction of Baal worship by fostering a debased form of Yahweh worship. Note that his son's name, Ahaziah (22:1), is compounded with Yah. **12–15** The difficulty about Elijah's letter is that Elijah was indubitably dead by this time (*cf.* 2 Ki. 3:11, in the reign of Jehoshaphat). We may only suppose that it was written before his translation so that, when Athaliah tried to carry out her mother's policy in Judah, she should be faced by the memory of her mother's great opponent. **16** *The Arabs, who are near the Ethiopians*; see on 14:9. **17** *All the possessions they found that belonged to the king's house.* There is no suggestion that they captured Jerusalem; *cf.* 22:1. *Except Jehoahaz, his youngest son.* This is no contradiction with 22:1. Jehoahaz = Yah + ahaz, Ahaziah = ahaz + Yah; both mean 'Yahweh has grasped'. **19** *His people made no fire in his honour*; see on 16:14.

22:1–9 Ahaziah. See 2 Ki. 8:25–29. Vv. 7–9 have no close parallel in Kings. **1** *Cf.* 21:16, 17. *The inhabitants of Jerusalem.* It may be that the country people were so opposed to the policy of the court that they would have been willing to transfer the crown to some other branch of the Davidic family. **2** *Forty-two years old*; an obvious scribal error; *cf.* 21:20; 2 Ki. 8:26. **2–6** See on 2 Ki. 8:25–29. **6** *He returned to be healed*; obviously Jehoram.

7 presupposes a knowledge of 2 Ki. 9:1–28, but **9** is irreconcilable with 2 Ki. 9:27, 28 and **8** with 2 Ki. 10:12–14, if we are to assume that Chronicles means to put their death before Ahaziah's. It is likely that we have to do here with a case of major textual disorder. What we may not do is to ascribe a deliberate contradiction to the Chronicler, for, as is his custom, he has already by v. 7 referred the interested reader to Kings for further details. **9** *The house of Ahaziah had no one able to rule the kingdom.* The slaughter of 21:17; 22:8 had removed everyone able to stand up to Athaliah.

22:10 – 24:27 Joash

22:10–12 Athaliah as queen. See 2 Ki. 11:1–3.

23:1–15 The plot against Athaliah. See 2 Ki. 11:4–16.

23:16–21 The covenant. See 2 Ki. 11:17–20.

24:1–14 The repair of the Temple. See 2 Ki. 11:21 – 12:16.

24:15–22 The apostasy of Joash. Not in Kings, though hinted at. It is very strange that some scholars doubt the authenticity of this section. Why should the Chronicler so wantonly blacken the reputation of a king like Joash? The merciful silence of Kings is more easily understood in the light of this passage.

The overthrow of Athaliah and the reforms that followed it were largely the work of the country people (the 'people of the land'). **17** *Now after the death of Jehoiada the princes of Judah came*; better 'the nobles of Judah' (Moff.). **18** The inheritors of the old court tradition came and won him back to the old ways. **20** *Zechariah the son of Jehoiada . . . stood above the people.* The present vast, almost level, Temple area was built by Herod. At that time the altar was considerably higher than the court with the worshippers. **21** *They conspired against him*; probably some trumped-up charge as in the case of Naboth (1 Ki. 21:8–13). *They stoned him . . . in the court of the house of the Lord*; *cf.* Mt. 23:35; Lk. 11:51. Our Lord's reference to Zechariah shows that in His time Chronicles stood in the Hebrew Canon, where it now does, as the last book. Zechariah is mentioned as the last martyr to be named. *In the court of the house of the Lord*; 'between the sanctuary and the altar' (Mt. 23:35). Rabbinic tradition made this murder one of the chief reasons for the destruction of Solomon's Temple. Certainly Judah never fully recovered spiritually from Joash's apostasy.

24:23–27 Punishment for apostasy and death of Joash. See 2 Ki. 12:17–21. **27** *In the Commentary on the Book of the Kings*; *cf.* 13:22. It is not clear what authority is intended by this name.

25:1 – 26:2 Amaziah

25:1–4 Amaziah's accession. See 2 Ki. 14:1–6.

25:5–13 The victory over Edom. *Cf.* 2 Ki. 14:7. **5** The result of Amaziah's census was to show a considerable fall since the days of Asa (14:8). **6** *He hired also a hundred thousand mighty men of valour from Israel.* In the light of 2 Ki. 13:7 it is clear that once again we are dealing with round figures to express a large number. **7** *Israel, with all these Ephraimites.* This explanation of the term Israel is given because it is normally used of the southern kingdom in Chronicles. **8** The LXX suggests that this verse is corrupt. As it stands, it tells Amaziah that, do what he may, he will be defeated. *ICC* and Moff. may be correct in making a small insertion and rendering 'Go by yourself, strike your own blow, be brave in battle; God will not let you fall before the foe' (Moff.). RSV follows the LXX. **11** *The Valley of Salt*; *cf.* 2 Sa. 8:13; probably the extension of the rift valley south of the Dead Sea. In any case the Dead Sea did not extend so far south at that time (*cf.* on 20:2). The usual identification of Sela (2 Ki. 14:7) with Petra is far from certain, especially as there is no trace of Joktheel (2 Ki. 14:7), the later name of Sela, linked with Petra. **12** Why *ten thousand* captives were massacred is not said; but see Am. 1:11, which is not much later in time. It is probable that Amaziah's victory gave him the control only of the route down to Elath (26:2; *cf.* 2 Ki. 8:22; 14:22). The mercenaries had marched home in anger (v. 10). **13** When they reached *Samaria* they heard that Amaziah was away in Edom, so they raided Judah. This is the only reasonable meaning that can be given to the Hebrew. Rudolph may be correct in seeing a textual corruption; he suggests 'Migron' (*cf.* Is. 10:28) for *Samaria*.

25:14–16 Amaziah's idolatry. Not in Kings; but note the hint in 2 Ki. 14:3. The Bible is never concerned with a man's justification for his actions, but with his actions. Amaziah's rather contemptuous dismissal of the prophetic warning (v. 16) shows that he regarded the whole incident otherwise. He held the debased view of Yahweh by which He was the supreme god, but yet one god among others. His victory over Edom was proof of Yahweh's victory over the gods of Edom (about whom we have no information). Yet they were gods in spite of their defeat, so **14** he brought their images to Jerusalem to deprive the Edomites of their help. Even captive gods deserve respect, so he *worshipped them, making offerings to them*. Did the magnitude of the unexpected victory even make him think that the Edomite gods had changed sides? But that did not mean for Amaziah a rejection of Yahweh. For the prophets Yahweh stood alone, and so the placing of other gods beside or even under Him meant rejecting Him.

25:17–24 Amaziah's encounter with Joash. See 2 Ki. 14:8–14 with which it is virtually identical. **17** *Then Amaziah . . . took counsel*; better 'let himself be counselled' (Moff.); this was the divine misleading (*cf.* 18:18–22).

25:25 – 26:2 Summary of Amaziah's reign. See 2 Ki. 14:17–22 with which it is virtually identical.

26:3–23 Uzziah

26:3–5 Introduction to reign. See 2 Ki. 15:1–4. The relation of the names Uzziah and Azariah is not clear; the former means 'Yahweh is my strength', the latter 'Yahweh has helped'.

26:6–15 The wars and greatness of Uzziah. 7 For the *Meunites*, see on 20:1. **9** Not sufficient is known of pre-exilic Jerusalem to interpret this verse with certainty. **10** The *towers* were for the protection of the cattle. *The Shephelah*, the low hills between Judea and the Philistine plain. *In the plain*; 'in the tableland' (RV mg.), probably of Transjordan (*cf.* v. 8).

26:16–23 Uzziah's sin and its punishment. *Cf.* 2 Ki. 15:5–7. Uzziah's wish to perform priestly functions was, in fact, his giving way to the constant temptation of the kings to look on themselves as 'divine kings'; see 1 Ki. 12:27. He was smitten with leprosy rather than another disease, because leprosy was considered a token of special divine judgment.

27:1–9 Jotham

See 2 Ki. 15:32–38. **3** *Ophel*; part of the old Jebusite city, perhaps the citadel, which became 'the city of David', remaining an important part of Jerusalem (*cf. NBD*, p. 618a).

28:1–27 Ahaz

28:1–4 Ahaz' apostasy. See 2 Ki. 16:1–4. **3** *Burned his sons*. The parallel has the more probable 'his son' (2 Ki. 16:3).

28:5–15, 17–19 The Syro-Ephraimite attack. See 2 Ki. 16:5, 6. We have here in addition the information about the Edomites and Philistines (vv. 17, 18) and about Israel's treatment of the prisoners they had taken (vv. 6–15). It would seem that there was a change of heart in some in the north, when it was already too late; *cf.* 2 Ki. 17:2. **15** *The city of palm trees*; *cf.* Jdg. 1:16; 3:13.

28:16, 20–27 The appeal to Assyria and its result. See 2 Ki. 16:7–16. **16** *To the king of Assyria*; RSV and the versions are probably correct in reading the singular. **20** *Tilgath-pilneser*; *i.e.* Tiglath-pileser (*cf.* 1 Ch. 5:6, 26; 2 Ki. 15:19). *And afflicted him*; doubtless by the amount of tribute demanded. **23** *He sacrificed to the gods of Damascus which had defeated him.* Vv. 22, 23 are really parenthetic and refer to the time of the Syrian attack; this has no connection with 2 Ki. 16:10 (*q.v.*). **24** *Ahaz . . . cut in pieces the vessels of the house of God.* This probably refers to the incident of 2 Ki. 16:17 with perhaps other items as well; 29:18, 19 show that there had been no widespread destruction of the Temple vessels. *Ahaz . . . shut up the doors of the house of the Lord.* As is clear from Kings, Ahaz continued to worship Yahweh after his fashion, and 2 Ki. 16:12–16 clearly indicates the continued use of the Temple courts. Ahaz may have considered the imageless sanctuary unsuited for his worship. This is supported by the continued use of the Temple in the worse apostasy of Manasseh.

29:1 – 32:33 Hezekiah

Over half the information in Chronicles is peculiar to it, and where it is paralleled by 2 Kings and Is. 36–39 the information has been largely abbreviated and rewritten.

29:1, 2 Hezekiah's reign. See 2 Ki. 18:1–3.

29:3–19 The cleansing of the Temple. Not in Kings. **3** He *opened the doors of the house of the Lord*; see on 28:24. **4** *The square on the east*; *cf.* Ezr. 10:9. **5** *The filth*; the accumulated dirt of years of neglect. **7** *They also shut the doors of the vestibule*; see on 28:24. *They . . . have not burned incense or offered burnt offerings*; this is superficially in direct contradiction to 2 Ki. 16:15. Just as the prophets refused to regard the Canaanized worship of Yahweh as anything but Baal worship, so Hezekiah refused to look on the sacrifices offered on an Assyrian altar as offered to Yahweh; for him they were sacrifices to the Assyrian gods. **8** *The wrath of the Lord*; see the disasters of ch. 28. **10** *To make a covenant with the Lord*; *cf.* 15:12; 23:16; 34:31. The motive was good, but the power to keep the covenant lacking. **12–14** The record of names of the Levites confirms what we know from other sources (*e.g.* Pr. 25:1), that the time of Hezekiah was a time of literary activity leaving considerable records to the future. **16** *To the brook Kidron*; *cf.* 15:16; 30:14. **19** *Which King Ahaz discarded*; *cf.* on 28:24.

29:20–36 The renewal of Temple worship. Not in Kings. **21–24** The opening service was one of atonement in which seven he-goats were brought as a sin-offering, and seven bullocks, rams and lambs as a burnt-offering. A careful study will show that the sin-offering was always accompanied by a burnt-offering. The choice of seven animals may be due to the associations of the number, or because the people were divided into seven categories; three are mentioned in v. 21—*kingdom* means the royal house, *sanctuary* the priests and Levites. **25, 26** The mention of the music is probably due to Ahaz having changed the Temple music along with his other ritual rearrangements. There will have been musical accompaniment to the burnt-offering from at least the time of *David* (*cf.* 1 Ch. 23:5; 25:1), and probably earlier. **27** *The song to the Lord*; it is now virtually universally recognized that the vast majority of the psalms were written for use in the Temple on various occasions; **30** makes it clear what was sung. *The princes*; here probably the chief priests (*cf.* on 1 Ch. 25:1). **32, 33** The comparatively small number of offerings under the circumstances shows how greatly Judah had suffered under Ahaz. Normally (Lv. 1:5, 6) the killing and flaying of the burnt-offering was the worshipper's duty; **34** the exception here may be due to their being congregational (v. 32) rather than personal offerings. *The priests were too few.* Urijah, the high priest (2 Ki. 16:10ff.), had done nothing to oppose Ahaz, but had cooperated. He probably drew in many of the other priests, while most of the Levites may have stood aloof (*were more upright in heart*).

30:1–12 The invitation to keep the Passover. Not in Kings. **1** The choice of the *passover*, **2** even though it would have to be kept in the *second month* (*cf.* Nu. 9:10, 11), was deliberate. The chief feast of the Canaanized Yahweh worship was Tabernacles (*cf.* 1 Ki. 12:32), the great nature New Year feast, but Passover was the New Year feast of the supernatural Yahweh who ruled history. Since the destruction of Samaria occurred in 723 BC, but Hezekiah did not come to the throne till 716 BC, *Ephraim and Manasseh* (v. 1) refer to those not carried into captivity (see 2 Ki. 17:6). As Hezekiah was tributary to Assyria, the new settlers will have had no objection. **10** That Hezekiah's messengers went only as far as *Zebulun* suggests that in the far north of Galilee the Israelite elements had already disappeared.

30:13–27 The celebration of the Passover. Not in Kings. **14** Even as the priests had cleansed the Temple, so the people now cleansed the city. *Into the Kidron valley*; *cf.* 15:16; 29:16. **15** The zeal of the people shamed the backward priests and Levites so that they sanctified themselves in time. **17** The burden on them was heavier than usual, for the Levites had to kill the lambs instead of the worshippers doing it, **18** for many of them were ritually unclean. In many cases the uncleanness needed 7 days for removal, and the pilgrims had not reached Jerusalem in time to carry out the regulations. **20** *The Lord . . . healed the people*; *i.e.* forgave them (*cf.* Ps. 41:4; Je. 3:22; Ho. 14:4). **23** The Feast of Unleavened Bread was doubled in length; *cf.* on 7:9, 10. This was felt to be a rededication of the Temple. **24** The mention of the offerings is because they were mostly peace-offerings, which were mainly eaten by the worshippers. **26** *There had been nothing like this in Jerusalem.* It was not the Passover celebration that was unique, but the **great joy.**

31:1 Destruction of idolatrous shrines. *Cf.* 2 Ki. 18:4. **1** *Pillars . . . Asherim*; see on 1 Ki. 14:23, and *NBD*, art. 'Asherah'. It being a purely popular demonstration, the representatives of Assyria in the province of Samaria had no grounds of objection.

31:2–21 The organization of the priests and Levites and their support. Not in Kings. **2** Hezekiah regulated the priestly and Levitical courses, **3** the official contribution to the sacrifices and **4** the tithes. **5–10** These were brought in with great generosity. **6** *The dedicated things.* The RSV rightly treats the Hebrew (see mg.) as impossible, but probably oversimplifies. The text has been damaged by haplography and should read '. . . and the tithe of the produce of the field, which had been consecrated . . .'. **7** Owing to the rainless Palestinian summer they could be piled in heaps in the open. This long unpractised generosity made it necessary to organize, or reorganize, the control of the tithes. This involved the making of a register of those entitled to receive them.

32:1–8 Preparations for Sennacherib's invasion. There are only minor contacts with Kings, but *cf.* on 2 Ki. 18:13–16. **3, 4** *Cf.* on 2 Ki. 20:20. **5** *The Millo*; *cf.* 1 Ki. 9:15. *Weapons*; more likely 'missiles' (Moff.). **7, 8** *With us . . .*; perhaps a recollection of Isaiah's Immanuel ('God with us') prophecy (Is. 7:14).

32:9–23 Sennacherib's threats. This is a summary of 2 Ki. 18:17 – 19:37 (*q.v.*). Note that 2 Ki. 19:9–13 is introduced parenthetically in v. 17; v. 18 continues v. 16. **20** The prayer of *Hezekiah* is given in 2 Ki. 19:15–19; the prayer of *Isaiah* is not mentioned in Kings. It is characteristic of the Chronicler that with the evil kings he goes into details with their defeats, but only hints at the extent of the troubles of the good kings. The very way in which he weaves in 2 Kings into his narrative shows that he knew his readers were familiar with it.

32:24–33 Summary of Hezekiah's reign. 24 See 2 Ki. 20:1–11. **25, 26, 31** See 2 Ki. 20:12–19. **30** See 2 Ki. 20:20. **27** *Cf.* 2 Ki. 20:13. **33** *In the ascent of the tombs of the sons of David.* The rendering, though possible, is improbable. 'A preferential place among the tombs' seems to be the sense (*cf.* AV).

33:1–20 Manasseh

Cf. 2 Ki. 21:1–18. **1–10** See 2 Ki. 21:1–15; Chronicles omits the details of God's message. **3** The plurals *Baals, Asherahs*, where Kings has the singular, should not be stressed. **6** *Sons*; *cf.* on 28:3. Such sacrifices were very rare. *In the valley of the son of Hinnom*; *cf.* Je. 7:31. Chronicles, which stresses the religious side, omits the murders (2 Ki. 21:16). **11** Late in his reign (648–647 BC) there was a rebellion against Ashurbanipal in favour of his brother, viceroy in Babylon. Whether Manasseh was involved or only suspected, he was taken *with hooks* (lit. 'with thorns') and *bound with fetters . . . to Babylon*. For the custom see on 2 Ki. 19:28. Ashurbanipal was probably in Babylon because of the rebellion just suppressed. It was some time before he could turn to the west, so Manasseh was taken very late in his reign to Babylon and his reign after his return must have been very brief. This explains why his repentance and reformation (vv. 12, 13, 15–17) are not mentioned in Kings and why they left no lasting impression. It should be noted, too, that Chronicles does not mention the removal of the altars of the host of heaven. Having once accepted these signs of Assyrian rule, he would not have dared to reject them now. This explanation, however, leaves many questions unanswered. It seems clear that he had time only to make a beginning, and that Amon immediately restored all the idolatry. **14** cannot be interpreted with certainty in our lack of closer knowledge of pre-exilic Jerusalem. **18** *His prayer to his God . . . .* **19** *And his prayer.* The Prayer of Manasseh in the Apocrypha has no claim to be regarded as authentic.

33:21-25 Amon

There are only minor variants from 2 Ki. 21:19–26 (*q.v.*). No motivation for the assassination is given. Amon may have been the vicious son of a bad father, or it may have been out of disgust for his following of a discredited policy.

34:1 – 35:27 Josiah

34:1, 2 Introduction. *Cf.* 2 Ki. 22:1, 2.

34:3–7, 33 The reformation. Superficially at least, the Chronicler is further from Kings in his account of Josiah's reformation than elsewhere in his book. This is partially due to the peculiarities of Kings. This section in it was almost certainly written by an eyewitness for eyewitnesses. He, therefore, felt himself free so to present the facts as to lay the main stress on what he considered the really important details. The Chronicler wished to take over 2 Ki. 22:3 – 23:3 as intact as possible, and so he amalgamated the details of clearing out the rubbish of the past in this section without caring for chronological order.

3 *Eighth year . . . twelfth year . . .* **8** *eighteenth year.* The main reason for the gradual introduction of the reformation was that it was political as well as religious. In Josiah's 8th year (632 BC) Ashurbanipal, the last great king of Assyria, had just died. Failure to worship the Assyrian gods, and even more the removal of their symbols and altars from the Temple, would be regarded as a sign of rebellion. Josiah and his advisers evidently decided that they must act slowly to find out the repercussions. Josiah was 16 in the 8th year of his reign and probably came of age then. **4, 5** It should be obvious that these verses preceded the rebuilding of the Temple, at least in part, while **6, 7** followed it (*cf.* 2 Ki. 23:15–20). **4** *And strewed it over the graves . . .* **5** *burned the bones of the priests on their altars.* The former profaned the 'holy' dust of the cult objects and images, the latter profaned the altars and the 'holy' ground on which they stood. **6** *In their ruins.* This makes no sense. The cities have long since been rebuilt. The most likely meaning is 'in their places', *i.e.* it was both altars and the sanctuary sites that were profaned. **7** *Then he returned to Jerusalem.* A clear sign that he is borrowing from 2 Ki. 23:20.

34:8–14 The repair of the Temple. See on 2 Ki. 22:3–7. **9** The mention of *Manasseh and Ephraim and from all the remnant of Israel* is probably to those from the northern tribes who had settled in the south (11:16; 15:9), rather than to those left in the north, for, unlike Hezekiah's reign (30:11), there is no special mention of people from the north at Josiah's Passover.

34:15–19 The finding of the book of the law. See on 2 Ki. 22:8–13.

34:20–28 Huldah's message. See on 2 Ki. 22:14–20. **20** *Abdon the son of Micah*; 2 Ki. 22:12 correctly 'Achbor the son of Michaiah'. **22** *The son of Tokhath, son of Hasrah*; 2 Ki. 22:14 correctly 'the son of Tikvah, son of Harhas'.

34:29–32 The covenant. See on 2 Ki. 23:1–3. The omission of the prophets in v. 30 is deliberate; see 2 Ki. 22:14.

34:33. See above, with 34:3–7.

35:1–19 Josiah's Passover. *Cf.* 2 Ki. 23:21–23. For the significance of the keeping of the Passover see on 30:1, 2. **3** *Put the holy ark in the house . . .* ; presumably it had been removed for the period of repairs. There is, however, much to be said for Rudolph's small amendment, which makes the passage read, 'From the time that they placed the holy ark in the house which Solomon . . . built, you have had nothing to carry on your shoulders, so now serve the Lord your God and his people Israel.' **4** *Following the directions of David . . .*; see 1 Ch. 23:26. *And the directions of Solomon*; *cf.* 8:14. **6** *Kill the passover*; *cf.* 30:17, but since the same reason did not hold good, it is likely we should not stress the phrase. **7, 8** *Bulls.* These were for peace-offerings during the Feast of Unleavened Bread; *cf.* on 30:24. **11–13** It would seem that the actual Passover sacrifices and the later sacrifices of the week have for brevity been amalgamated. **18** *No passover like it had been kept . . .*; *cf.* 30:26. Passover had been overshadowed by Tabernacles celebrated as the New Year feast.

35:20–25 Josiah's death. See on 2 Ki. 23:29, 30a. **25** *Jeremiah also uttered a lament for Josiah*; this has not been preserved. Obviously it has no relation to the book of Lamentations.

35:26, 27 Summary of Josiah's reign. See on 2 Ki. 23:24–28.

36:1-23 Downfall and restoration

36:1–4 Jehoahaz. See on 2 Ki. 23:30b–35. **3** *Laid upon the land*; *i.e.* 'fined the country' (Moff.); the tribute was heavier than it would otherwise have been as a punishment.

36:5–8 Jehoiakim. See on 2 Ki. 23:36 – 24:7. We should presumably look on v. 7 as anticipatory of v. 10, though it may refer to the incident of Dn. 1:2. It was due to Jehoiakim's sins and rebellion that Jerusalem was taken and the Temple ransacked.

36:9, 10 Jehoiachin. See on 2 Ki. 24:8–17.

36:11–13 Zedekiah. See on 2 Ki. 24:18 – 25:7. **10** *His brother Zedekiah.* Read with the versions 'Zedekiah, his father's brother'. With the legitimate king in exile, and the Temple ransacked, the Chronicler has no reason for describing the last agony of Jerusalem. **13** The last generation in the city is well typified by its perjured king.

36:14–21 The destruction of Jerusalem. Chronicles gives merely a general summary showing how the destruction of the city was the inevitable result of its sin. **20** *To him and to his sons*; *i.e.* his successors, Evil-merodach (2 Ki. 25:27), Neriglissar and Nabonidus, the last two being usurpers. **21** *Until the land had enjoyed its sabbaths.* The implication is that the sabbatical year was not observed under the monarchy (*cf.* Lv. 25:1–7; 26:34, 35). *Seventy years.* Judah was subject to Babylon from the battle of Carchemish (605 BC,

Dn. 1:1) till the fall of Babylon (538 BC), *i.e.* 67 years, 70 being a round number.

36:22, 23 Restoration. These verses are identical with the opening verses of Ezra; see Introduction to Ezra. That Ezra and Chronicles were originally one book is shown by the last verse's ending in the middle of a sentence.

H. L. ELLISON

Ezra and Nehemiah

INTRODUCTION

THE RELATIONSHIP OF THE BOOKS

The two books of Ezra and Nehemiah were originally one, being attached to the book of Chronicles to form a composite historical work for the period from Adam to Nehemiah. A comparison of 2 Ch. 36:22f. with Ezr. 1:1ff. indicates this continuity, while a similarity of style and interests (the Temple and its cultus, statistics and genealogies, *etc.*) in Chronicles and Ezra suggests a unity of authorship. Ezra and Nehemiah cover a period of history not dealt with in the books of Kings (unlike Chronicles, which, in measure, is a duplication of history) and so were detached from Chronicles and given a more prominent place in the third section (the Writings or Hagiographa) of the Hebrew Canon.

COMPARISON WITH 1 ESDRAS

There are two distinct Greek translations of Ezra–Nehemiah: the LXX (Esdras B), which follows the Hebrew text, and 1 Esdras (Esdras A, usually called the Greek Ezra). The latter, written in elegant Greek, contains the last two chapters of 2 Chronicles, the whole of Ezra and concludes with Ne. 7:73b – 8:12. It probably reflects a better Hebrew text than the Massoretic text but the translation is very free and its historical and chronological details are unreliable, and so the biblical Ezra is to be preferred. The Jewish historian Josephus bases his work upon 1 Esdras.

The confusion which sometimes arises over the different titles used to distinguish between the various texts may be resolved by the following table:

English	LXX	Vulgate
Ezra/Nehemiah	= Esdras B	= 1 & 2 Esdras
1 Esdras	= Esdras A	= 3 Esdras
(Apocrypha)		

HISTORICAL BACKGROUND

The Babylonian Empire was finally overthrown by the Medes and Persians when Babylon fell in 539 BC. Cyrus, the Persian king, was an enlightened character who reversed the repressive policies of the Assyrians and Babylonians. He showed restraint towards those he conquered and consideration towards those who had been forcibly removed from their countries under the previous administration, encouraging them to return to their homelands. Whenever possible he allowed the subject peoples local autonomy and in particular he posed as the champion of the indigenous religions. A contemporary inscription, the Cyrus Cylinder, records, '. . . the gods who live within them (*i.e.* the cities) I returned to their places . . . All of their inhabitants I collected and restored to their dwelling-places.' It was under this policy that a number of Jews, under the leadership of a prince of the Davidic line, were allowed to return to Jerusalem in 538 BC.

The books of Haggai and Zechariah provide considerable supplementary detail, whilst the book of Malachi (which cannot be accurately dated) probably throws light on the general situation before the arrival in Jerusalem of Ezra and Nehemiah. Contemporary documents include the Cyrus Cylinder, noted above, and the Elephantine Papyri. The latter, written in Aramaic, preserve some correspondence of a Jewish military colony in Upper Egypt in the 5th century BC. Bagoas the Persian governor of Judea, Johanan the high priest (*cf.* Ezr. 10:6; Ne. 12:22) and Sanballat the governor of Samaria (Ne. 2:19, *etc.*) and his sons, are mentioned in these documents.

The Persian kings involved in this period are:

559–530	Cyrus
530–522	Cambyses
522–486	Darius I (Hystaspes)
486–465	Xerxes I (Ahasuerus)
465–424	Artaxerxes I (Longimanus)
424–423	Xerxes II
423–404	Darius II (Nothus)
404–358	Artaxerxes II (Mnemon)

THE RELATIONSHIP OF EZRA AND NEHEMIAH

Controversy still rages around this problem, which is undoubtedly the greatest unsolved difficulty of the two books. Arguments, both for and against the various views, are notoriously inconclusive. The salient points may be summarized as follows.

The date of Nehemiah's return

This is the fixed point of the discussion. Nehemiah was at Jerusalem from the twentieth year of Artaxerxes I (Ne. 2:1) to the thirty-second year (Ne. 13:6), *i.e.* 445–433 BC. He returned to Jerusalem for a second term after an absence of unspecified duration at the Persian court (Ne. 13:6). One of the Elephantine Papyri, dated 407 BC, which refers to Johanan, presumably Jonathan, the grandson of Eliashib, Nehemiah's contemporary (Ne. 3:1; 12:10f., 22) and to Delaiah and Shelemiah, sons of Sanballat, Nehemiah's enemy, precludes a date for Nehemiah in the reign of Artaxerxes II.

The date of Ezra's return

Amongst a multitude of hypotheses three main possibilities emerge.

1. That Ezra arrived in Jerusalem in 458 BC. This is the traditional view, which identifies the king noted in Ezr. 7:7f. as Artaxerxes I. This would mean that Ezra preceded Nehemiah, which accords with the biblical order. One weak point in favour is that Ezr. 8:36 makes no mention of a governor in Jerusalem, which, some allege, suggests that Ezra arrived before Nehemiah's appointment. Against this, Nehemiah himself refers to 'former governors' (Ne. 5:15).

There are several objections to this view. Many of these are inconclusive, and it must be borne in mind that even the cumulative effect of a large number of such arguments falls short of proof. In the list which follows, a.–h. are considered to be weak and i.–l. must be treated seriously.

a. A 'wall' is mentioned in Ezr. 9:9 (AV, RV, RSV mg.) which is held to refer to Nehemiah's wall. But the reference could be figurative, as suggested by the RSV 'protection'. There is considerable evidence (Ezr. 4:12, 23; Ne. 1:3) of an abortive attempt to build a wall in Jerusalem just before Nehemiah's arrival. If this was under Ezra's direction, such an overstepping of his authority would have put him in disfavour with the Persian officials, and prevented him from carrying out his specifically religious functions. But since the events in Ezr. 9, 10 appear to take place soon after Ezra's arrival in Jerusalem, there was a gap of about 10 years before this abortive attempt was made, increasing the probability that the reference in Ezr. 9:9 is figurative.

b. Ezra was surrounded by multitudes in Jerusalem (Ezr. 10:1), whereas Nehemiah found the city sparsely populated (Ne. 7:4) and had to institute a policy of repopulation (Ne. 11:1). But Ezr. 10:1 specifically notes that the crowd was drawn from the outlying areas.

c. Four treasurers were appointed by Nehemiah (Ne. 13:13), an arrangement which was still operative when Ezra arrived (Ezr. 8:33). But a tradition of appointments of this kind easily establishes itself, and Nehemiah, in a time of disorder, may simply have appointed four honest men as replacements.

d. It is held that Ezra's unprotected journey, during the early and disturbed period of Artaxerxes I, is unlikely. But the point of Ezr. 8:21ff. is that there was grave danger, which involved an unusual sense of dependence upon God.

e. Nehemiah arrived at a ruined city, whereas Ezra does not indicate any insecurity. But since Nehemiah's commission was specifically connected with the wall and the defence of Jerusalem, a concentration of interest on this aspect is only to be expected.

f. Nehemiah was forced to deal with economic irregularities (e.g. Ne. 5:1–13). Why did Ezra allow these to continue if he was on the scene earlier? This is an argument from silence. In any case, abuses can arise very quickly, as happened during Nehemiah's relatively brief absence from the capital (Ne. 13:6–31).

g. It is held that Nehemiah's reforms were somewhat impromptu, whereas Ezra's were based on the law. Yet the latter apparently failed, if he arrived first. This objection overlooks the differences in position and personality between the two men. Nehemiah appears as the more vigorous, dynamic character. Moreover, he wielded the civic authority, whereas Ezra's appeal was moral and spiritual. The problem of mixed marriages was clearly a recurring one, being dealt with by Ezra (Ezr. 9, 10), by Ezra and Nehemiah together (Ne. 9:2; 10:30) and by Nehemiah independently (Ne. 13:23–29). Even allowing that Ezra failed, in measure, before Nehemiah's arrival, this would not invalidate the position which he held in later Jewish tradition. An Ezra may well need the support of a Nehemiah before he can fulfil his potential.

h. Ne. 12:26 lists Ezra after Nehemiah, and Ne. 12:47 omits any reference to Ezra between Zerubbabel and Nehemiah. The reason for this may simply be the priority given to the civic authorities.

i. Few, if any, of those who returned with Ezra appear in the list of those who built Nehemiah's wall (Ne. 3). But Ne. 3 mentions only the chief builders, who are likely to have been long-standing residents in Jerusalem.

j. Nehemiah was the contemporary of Eliashib the high priest (Ne. 13:28). Ezra was the contemporary of Jehohanan (Ezr. 10:6; cf. Ne. 12:22), the grandson of Eliashib. Therefore Nehemiah must have preceded Ezra. This is a weighty point, although Ezr. 10:6 gives no indication that Jehohanan was high priest at that time.

k. The mission of Ezra was concerned with the promulgation of the law (Ezr. 7:12), yet, if the traditional view be accepted, the law was not read in public, apparently for the first time, until c. 444 BC (Ne. 8:1–8), a delay of c. 13 years. This remains a major problem. The silence is explicable if Ezra exceeded his mandate by his building operations, and fell into disfavour with the Persian authorities. It must be admitted, however, that there is no actual evidence to connect Ezra with the unauthorized attempt to build the wall (Ezr. 4:7–23). Nor is there a scrap of evidence to suggest what Ezra was doing, on the traditional dating, between 458 and 444 BC. 1 Esdras attaches Ne. 7:73b – 8:12 to the Ezra narrative, which would allow for an earlier dating of the law-reading ceremony, but this demands the elimination of Nehemiah's name (Ne. 8:9) as a gloss.

l. When Nehemiah made his census, he utilized the list of those who returned with Zerubbabel (Ne. 7:6–72) but is silent concerning those who returned with Ezra (Ezr. 8:1–14).

2. That Ezra arrived in Jerusalem in 398 BC. This view identifies the king of Ezr. 7:7f. as Artaxerxes II. In favour of this view is the fact that it eliminates any suggestion of failure in Ezra's ministry; indeed, it allows it to be decisive. Moreover, it accounts for the embarrassing fact that Nehemiah and Ezra appear to ignore each other's contributions, which would be unusual if they were contemporaries. Another point urged in its favour is that it is unlikely that the Persian authorities would countenance two sponsored Jewish officials at the same time. This, however, is indecisive, since the spheres of authority of Ezra and Nehemiah were quite distinct. Another point urged in its favour is that the historical situation at this time, when Egypt had just been lost to the Persian Empire, would encourage the Persians to treat Judea liberally, in the hope of gaining its loyalty. The appointment of Ezra, with a free hand to promote the Jewish religion based upon the law, would serve such a purpose.

There are, however, two main objections to this view:

a. The so-called Passover Papyrus of the Elephantine texts, dated 419 BC, indicates that the religious affairs of the Jews of the Dispersion were already being regulated through Jerusalem on the authority of the Persian king. This was the province of Ezra, and his appointment, as Ezr. 7:25f. suggests, was the initial one of this kind. Ezra therefore must have been in Jerusalem before 419 BC and a date in the reign of Artaxerxes II is invalidated.

b. The view involves several textual emendations. Nehemiah's name has to be eliminated in Ne. 8:9 (this has the support of 1 Esdras) and Ezra has to be omitted from Ne. 12:36 and possibly 12:26. Ezra and Nehemiah could not both have been associated with the events of Ne. 9, 10. A good working rule is that the greater the textual surgery involved, the greater the improbability of a theory.

3. That Ezra arrived *c.* 428 BC. This involves a slight emendation, in which the date for Ezra (Ezr. 7:7f.) becomes 'the thirty-seventh year' of Artaxerxes I. This means that Ezra's return would be soon after the commencement of Nehemiah's second term of office. It is surmised that Nehemiah, realizing his own limitations, may even have arranged for Ezra and a company of priests and Levites to return to Jerusalem. This view satisfies the tradition that the two men were contemporaries and allows Ezra's work to complement and complete that of Nehemiah. John Bright is one of many who champion this view strongly and maintains that it solves the problem '. . . in a manner which is, I believe, both plausible and faithful to the evidence' (*A History of Israel*, 1960, p. 386). The outstanding difficulty is the unanimity of all the versions concerning the date in Ezr. 7:7, 8.

The complexity of this problem is obvious, and the reasons supporting the various views often appear ingenious rather than convincing. Certain difficulties attach to the traditional view but nevertheless it remains the most convincing, although dogmatism is ruled out. It involves no textual surgery or emendations and connects reasonably with the strong evidence for a fresh influx of settlers in Jerusalem and a major attempt to rebuild its walls just prior to Nehemiah's return. Clearly, a great deal was hoped for from this. If this was not under Ezra's leadership it is not easy to account for. If it was the abortive conception of Ezra, designed to bring stability into Jerusalem and thus make religious reform possible, then the difficulties attaching to the earlier part of his career are explicable. The traditional view, therefore, is retained as the best working hypothesis.

THE RELIABILITY OF THE CHRONICLER

One of the assumptions often underlying the rejection of the traditional view is that the Chronicler, through ignorance, has confused the order of Ezra and Nehemiah. The peculiar difficulties attaching to the Chronicler are admitted (see the introductory article to 1 and 2 Chronicles) but this particular suggestion must be resisted. The autobiographical Nehemiah memories are distinct in style and content from the books of Chronicles and Ezra. The present order of Ezra and Nehemiah probably results from the fact that the Chronicler himself added the Nehemiah memoirs to his own work, with no attempt at chronological integration.

There is evidence to suggest that the Chronicler was, in fact, a near contemporary of Ezra and Nehemiah. The Davidic line, in the post-exilic period, is extended to a maximum of six generations; some believe it to be no more than four (1 Ch. 3:15–24). Allowing *c.* 25 years for a generation, the last-mentioned of the line must be dated soon after 400 BC. Similarly the last-mentioned high priest is Jaddua (presumably the great-grandson of Eliashib, Ne. 12:22), who probably commenced his high priesthood in the early decades of the 4th century BC. Such use of genealogies is admittedly tenuous, since names could be added to complete a list, but at least it provides some evidence for dating purposes. In any case the Chronicler was so close to Ezra and Nehemiah, even allowing a date as late as *c.* 350 BC, that a major chronological blunder is unlikely. Indeed, the view that Ezra himself was the Chronicler is maintained by W. F. Albright and other leading scholars (W. F. Albright, *The Biblical Period from Abraham to Ezra*, 1963, p. 95).

SOURCES

As well as the personal memoirs of Ezra and Nehemiah we may note the following: Ezr. 1:1 – 4:7; 6:19–22 is probably a free composition of the Chronicler, utilizing various sources, including possibly the books of Haggai and Zechariah. Ezr. 4:8 – 6:18; 7:12–26 is in Aramaic (the diplomatic language of the period) and contains official correspondence with the Persian authorities, with connecting sections. There are many lists, genealogies, inventories, *etc.*, some of which are integral parts of the Ezra or Nehemiah memoirs. These include Ezr. 1:9–11a; 2:1–70; 7:1–5; 8:1–14; Ne. 3:1–32; 7:1–73; 11:3–36.

EZRA AND JUDAISM

As a result of the Babylonian attack of 588/587 BC, the Davidic line and the kingdom as such virtually came to an end and the Temple was destroyed. The Jews in exile, under the leadership of Ezekiel, reflected on this tragedy and construed it as the chastisement of God for their apostasy. Clearly a new focal point of unity was required unless they were simply to disappear as a nation. This was found in their allegiance to the law, the Mosaic covenant and its attendant symbols of sabbath observance and circumci-

sion. After the return from the Exile, the rebuilt Temple provided a rallying point for the small theocratic community, but the years from 520 BC, when the Temple was dedicated, were years of mediocrity. It was Ezra, building upon the foundation of Nehemiah's political achievements, who gave a new sense of impetus to his people. The law-book which he expounded (Ne. 8:1–8) was certainly not new in content and not necessarily new in form. But Ezra initiated a new era in which the Pentateuch was not simply a book of laws but a manual of instruction covering every detail of life, developed by a technique of exposition which assumed both oral and literary forms. Ezra became the 'father of Judaism' and this way of life, which centred upon an unswerving allegiance to the Torah, not only moulded Jewish life from that point on, but enabled it to survive the searching historical crises of the succeeding centuries. Ezra must not be blamed for the unlovely features of later Judaism. The fact is that his policies saved Judea from oblivion in a particular historical situation.

Ezra

OUTLINE OF CONTENTS

COMMENTARY

1:1 – 2:70 THE RETURN FROM EXILE

1:1–4 The decree of Cyrus

The authenticity of this decree need not be doubted. When Cyrus conquered Babylon in 539 BC one of his first acts was to allow the communities which had been deported by the Babylonians to return home. Exception has been taken to the wording of this decree, which seems to suggest that Cyrus was a worshipper of Yahweh. In fact, this is paralleled in the Cyrus Cylinder where he ascribes his victories to Marduk, whilst in a text discovered at Ur it is Sin, the moon-god, who grants him victory. It was the policy of Cyrus to conciliate the indige-

nous religions of his vast empire. The Hebrew form of the decree appears to be the official, heraldic proclamation to the Jews (*cf.* 6:1–5).

1 *The first year of Cyrus*; *i.e.*, the year in which he conquered Babylon. He had been king of Persia since 559 BC. *By the mouth of Jeremiah*; Cyrus was the instrument through which Yahweh fulfilled His word (*cf.* Je. 25:11f.; 29:10). **2** *He has charged me*; *cf.* Is. 44:28; 45:13. **4** A connection with the Exodus (*cf.* Je. 16:14, 15) appears in this enrichment of the returning exiles by their neighbours (*cf.* Ex. 12:35f.).

1:5–11 The response to the decree

6 *All that was freely offered*; this indicates the

offerings designated for the Temple (*cf.* v. 4b). **7** *The vessels of the house of the Lord*; Nebuchadrezzar had plundered the Temple in 597 BC and again in 587 BC 2 (*cf.* Ki. 24:13; 25:13ff.). It was standard practice for a conqueror to place the gods of the vanquished in his own sanctuary (*cf.*, *e.g.*, 1 Sa. 5:2). Since the Jewish faith was imageless, the Temple vessels served as a substitute. The enlightened Cyrus permitted the return of the captured gods and, in this case, the Temple treasures. **8** A problem attaches to the identity of Shesh-bazzar. Some believe that he is to be identified with Zerubbabel. Others distinguish Shesh-bazzar as the uncle or great-uncle of Zerubbabel (*cf.* 1 Ch. 3:17ff., assuming that Shenazzar is the same as Shesh-bazzar). Possibly Shesh-bazzar died soon after the return. A third view regards Shesh-bazzar as the officially-appointed leader and Zerubbabel as the popular, but unofficial leader. (See on Ezr. 5:14–16.) **9–11** RSV follows 1 Esdras. The Hebrew text is faulty, since the total number of items is actually 5,469 and not 5,400 as the Hebrew states (see RSV mg.). In Hebrew, numbers were written in words in the earlier period; later on letters were used to express them, while in popular Aramaic a sign notation was employed. Understandably, then, numbers were peculiarly susceptible to copyists' errors in transmission. The journey from Babylon to Jerusalem would take approximately 4 months (*cf.* Ezr. 7:8, 9).

2:1–67 The register of the returned exiles

The same list, with some variations in names and numbers, appears in Ne. 7:6–73 and 1 Esdras 5:4–46. It is not easy to account for the discrepancies. A. Weiser explains the inclusion of the same list twice by the fact that it already stood in the two sources used by the Chronicler, although he observes that the literary connection is looser in Ne. 7 (*Introduction to the Old Testament*, 1961, p. 322). Others have suggested that later scribes were less meticulous in their copying of the books of the Writings, the third section of the Hebrew Canon. Allied to this there is the possibility that the list of those who returned in 538 BC was modified and expanded to include others who returned subsequently, and even some who, though they had never been in exile, were fully in sympathy with the returned exiles. Seven groups may be distinguished:

2a The leaders. *Zerubbabel* was either the son of Shealtiel (*cf.* Ezr. 3:2; Ne. 12:1; Hg. 1:1), or of Pedaiah, brother of Shealtiel (*cf.* 1 Ch. 3:19). Possibly it was a case of levirate marriage (*cf.* Dt. 25:5f.). *Jeshua*, or Joshua, the first high priest after the Exile, was the grandson of Seraiah, the last high priest before the Exile (*cf.* 2 Ki. 25:18). *Nehemiah* was not the famous wall-builder. The corresponding lists in Nehemiah and 1 Esdras include twelve names; one appears to have dropped out here, for considerable importance was attached to the number of the tribes (*cf.* Ezr. 6:17; 8:35). **2b–35** *The men of the*

people of Israel. The family groups are identified either by the names of their ancestors or the names of their towns. **36–39** *The priests*. The relatively high proportion of priests amongst those who returned was doubtless due to the prospect of a new Temple, with its opportunities of service. **40–42** *The Levites*. Only 341 Levites returned, in contrast to 4,289 priests! Their inferior status in the post-exilic period probably made them reluctant to return. At a later date Ezra encountered the same tendency (Ezr. 8:15). **43–54** *The temple servants* (AV 'Nethinims'). This group is mentioned only by the Chronicler (*cf.* 1 Ch. 9:2; Ezr. 8:20). The name comes from the root of the Hebrew verb 'to give'. A plausible theory, supported by the considerable number of foreign names, is that they were prisoners of war allocated to the Temple for the more mundane tasks (*cf.* the Gibeonites, Jos. 9:27). They were certainly inferior to the Levites. **55–57** *The sons of Solomon's servants* (*cf.* Ne. 11:3). The names in this group are mostly foreign but no plausible explanation of its origin has been advanced. They were probably another group of Temple-labourers. **59–63** Those of uncertain genealogy. Genealogies were of great importance in ancient Israel. A man who had no knowledge of his tribe or clan was under a serious disability, and was specially excluded from the priesthood (v. 62). **61** *Barzillai*; *cf.* 2 Sa. 17:27; 19:32–39; 1 Ki. 2:7. **63** *The governor* (AV 'the Tirshatha'); a Persian title, 'the One to Be Feared', which approximates to 'His Excellency'. It was used of Nehemiah (*cf.* 8:9; 10:1) but here it refers to either Shesh-bazzar or Zerubbabel. *Urim and Thummim* (*cf.* Ex. 28:30; Nu. 27:21; 1 Sa. 14:41f.; 28:6). These were kept in the breastplate of the high priest and were used to ascertain the divine will. Most likely they were marked, flat stones which could be interpreted by the various combinations of the markings. (See *NBD*, art. 'Urim and Thummim'.) There is no evidence of their actual use in the later period of the monarchy or in the post-exilic period.

64–67 The final statistics. The same total (42,360) is given in Nehemiah and 1 Esdras but in none of the three do the constituent parts add up to this, indicating errors in interpreting numbers or in transmission (see the introductory note on this chapter). It is interesting to observe that no attempt at harmonization has been made. The list of possessions shows that the Jews had accumulated considerable wealth in exile (but *cf.* 1:4). **65** *Singers*; these were secular entertainers, in contradistinction to the Levitical singers (v. 41). **66** *Horses . . . mules* were the more sophisticated beasts of burden.

2:68–70 Arrival in Jerusalem

68 *The house of the Lord*. Although the Temple was in ruins, the site continued to be used in the exilic period (*cf.* Je. 41:5). **69** The differences from the Nehemiah account (Ne. 7:70–72) are capable of explanation. The Ezra version is a condensed account in which the offerings of the governor, clan chiefs and the people have been grouped together and a cash estimate of 20,000 gold darics added in lieu of the 50 basins (*cf.* Ne. 7:70). The precise totals for the silver minas and priests' garments in the Nehemiah version are here represented by round figures. One textual emendation is assumed in the harmonization of the two accounts: it is that the unlikely figure of 530 priests' garments of Ne. 7:70 should read as 500 silver minas and 30 priests' garments.

3:1 – 4:5 THE WORK OF RESTORATION BEGUN

3:1–6 The re-establishment of worship

The first recorded act after the return of the Jews to their homeland was the presentation of their free-will offering (*cf.* 2:68). The Feast of Booths (*i.e.* Tabernacles; v. 4), occurring on the 'seventh month' (v. 1), was presumably the first of the three great national feasts after their settlement in their towns, when the people were required to be present at the central sanctuary (*cf.* Lv. 23:33–36). The great ceremony of Ne. 7:73b – 8:12 took place at the same time of the year. The Feast of Tabernacles, which commemorated the wilderness wanderings, would now also serve as a reminder of the return from the Exile. A comparison with 3:8 makes it clear that this was the seventh month of the first year after their return.

2 Jeshua takes precedence here over Zerubbabel in view of the religious nature of the occasion (*cf.* 3:8; 5:2; Hg. 1:1, *etc.*). **3** In honouring the Lord through the erection of the altar on its proper site the people sought to ensure His protection against the *peoples of the lands, i.e.* the mixed population which was consistently hostile to any attempt to restore Jerusalem's fortunes (*cf.* on 4:1, 4). **5** *The new moon* marked the first day of the month and was a holy day. Nu. 28:11–15 lists the offerings for this occasion. Some scholars, on the basis of Isaiah's condemnation (Is. 1:13f.) believe that it was not of Mosaic origin, but the prophets' objection was to the abuse of the cultus, not the cultic practices themselves. **6** The revival of the cult preceded the erection of the Temple.

3:7–13 The laying of the foundations of the Temple

One can readily understand the deep, emotional stresses which such an occasion would produce. A comparison with Je. 33:10, 11 reveals their consciousness of the part they were playing in the fulfilment of prophecy. The tragedy of the national humiliation and the apparent futility of their endeavours would be felt acutely and would conflict with the spontaneous expressions of joy (vv. 12f.).

7 Notice the obvious attempt to follow the pattern of the building of the first Temple (*cf.* 1 Ki. 5:7–12). **8** The Levites acted as building superintendents. The minimum age before entering full Levitical service was reduced from 25 years (*cf.* Nu. 8:24) to 20 years in David's reign (*cf.* 1 Ch. 23:24), presumably to increase the number available. **9** *Jeshua* was the Levite of 2:40. **10** A comparison with 5:1f. and the book of Haggai shows that little was achieved until 520 BC, apart from the actual laying of the foundations. **11** *They sang responsively.* The singing was antiphonal, with either two choirs, or a choir and a priest-soloist. This is a feature of many psalms. The words preserved in our text would be the chorus (*cf.* 1 Ch. 16:34; 2 Ch. 5:13; 7:3; Ps. 136). *Steadfast love* (Heb. *ḥeseḏ*) has particular reference to love and loyalty within the covenant relationship.

4:1–5 Opposition in the reign of Cyrus

The opposition hinted at in 3:3 becomes explicit here.

1 *The adversaries,* or 'the people of the land' as v. 4. The significance of the latter phrase varies considerably in the biblical period. Originally it indicated an influential group, possibly the principal land-owners (*cf.* 2 Ki. 23:30). Haggai appears to apply it to the returned exiles (Hg. 2:4) whereas his contemporary, Zechariah (*c.* 520 BC) uses it of those who had not gone into exile (Zc. 7:1–5). By the Chronicler's time (*c.* 400 BC) it refers to the hybrid population, later known as the Samaritans, descended from groups settled in the area by the Assyrians (*cf.* 2 Ki. 17:24–41). Since Jerusalem was within the province of Samaria at this time there would be mutual resentment based upon long-standing rivalry. **2** *Esar-haddon* (681–669 BC) was following the Assyrian practice in this deportation. Such a policy effectively stifled any nationalistic spirit. It would also result in a syncretistic religion, which Hezekiah and Josiah's reformations had been unable to purify (*cf.* 2 Ki. 23:19; 2 Ch. 30:1–10; 34:6f.). **3** The refusal by Zerubbabel and Joshua constitutes a claim that the newly-restored Jerusalem community was the true Israel. Such an exclusive attitude has been widely criticized, but it is difficult to see how the Jewish faith could have survived apart from the drawing of such sharp distinctions. **4** The fear noted here is exemplified in Zc. 8:10. Haggai shows that selfishness, apathy and procrastination also contributed to the poor morale of the Jews. **5** A comparison with v. 24 shows that the story is resumed at that point.

4:6–23 FURTHER OPPOSITION TO BUILDING PROJECTS

This section interrupts the chronological sequence, but it has been included here because it also deals with opposition to Jewish building projects.

4:6 Opposition in the reign of Xerxes (486–465 BC)

Since the Temple was completed in 515 BC this must refer to more general opposition during the reign of Xerxes (the biblical Ahasuerus). *The beginning of his reign; i.e.* his accession year. The opponents of the Jews were not wasting any time before exerting pressure on the king.

4:7–23 Opposition in the reign of Artaxerxes I (465–424 BC)

4:8 – 6:18 which contains mostly official correspondence linked by short, narrative sections, is written in Aramaic, the *lingua franca* of the Empire. The objection in this period was to an attempt to rebuild the wall of Jerusalem (vv. 12, 16). Notice the subtle threefold appeal: the king would suffer financially (v. 13), his honour would be impaired (v. 14) and his Empire would be diminished (v. 16).

8 *Rehum* and *Shimshai* may have constituted a permanent royal commission investigating affairs in the provinces. **9** The imposing list adds authority to the letter. **10** *Osnappar* is the Aramaic equivalent of Ashurbanipal (669–630 BC). *Beyond the River.* The capitals indicate that this was the official designation of the fifth Persian satrapy, which included all Palestine and Syria. **12** This verse is highly important evidence for a migration of Jews in the reign of Artaxerxes. If the traditional dating of Ezra's return (*c.* 458 BC) be accepted, the verse could well indicate the group which returned with him. The cessation of the building, which was unauthorized, may have been that reported to Nehemiah (Ne. 1:1ff.). Ezra may have realized that no effective reform could be achieved without the security of a wall, but he had no commission for this, hence the appeal to Nehemiah. Apart from this reconstruction, there is no historically-attested connection for this group. **14** *We eat the salt*; *i.e.* 'we are in the king's service'. Covenants were often ratified with salt (*cf., e.g.*, 2 Ch. 13:5). **15** *The records of your fathers.* This would include the Assyrians and Babylonians, to whom the Persians regarded themselves as lawful successors. **19** Evidence may have been discovered of rebellions in Judah in 701, 601 and 587 BC, amongst others (*cf.* 2 Ki. 18:7, 13; 24:1, 20). **21** The decision was, in fact, later revoked by the same king (*cf.* Ne. 2). **23** No time was lost and no energy spared in enforcing the king's decree (*cf.* again Ne. 1:3).

4:24 – 6:22 THE TEMPLE COMPLETED

4:24 – 5:2 A ministry of encouragement

The date is now 520 BC (*cf.* Hg. 1:1; Zc. 1:1). The contemporary records of Haggai and Zechariah throw light upon this period, and the former, in particular, shows how the people needed to be stimulated after 16 years of discouragement. Similarly, after so much official opposition, the Jewish leaders would need a great deal of encouragement to sponsor further rebuilding. They received this in full measure from the two prophets.

5:3–17 The challenge to the Jewish rebuilding programme

Tattenai, who is mentioned in a contemporary business document as 'the governor of Trans-

Euphratia', appears to have dealt fairly with the Jews, which contrasts with the unmasked hostility of ch. 4. The vigorous nature of the rebuilding project is apparent (v. 8) but there is no hint that it extended beyond the Temple. This militates against the view that it was part of a nationalistic movement, encouraged by the internal dissensions within the Persian Empire after the death of Cambyses in 522 BC.

8 *Huge stones*; literally 'stones of rolling', *i.e.* so large that they had to be moved on rollers. **12** The destruction of 587 BC is viewed in a theological perspective, in contrast with the attitude of 4:15. **14–16** The inference is that *Shesh-bazzar* had died by this time. If, as was suggested in the Introduction, he was the Persian-appointed leader, it would account for the fact that in this official communication he is tactfully mentioned as laying the foundation of the Temple, whereas Zerubbabel, possibly the popular leader, is given prominence in the domestic account (*cf.* 3:8–11). Understandably, the Jews did not wish to weaken their case by admitting their neglect over a period of 16 years. **17** The decree was not discovered at Babylon, but such was the efficiency of the Persian organization that it was found at Ecbatana (6:2). Tattenai enquires whether the king wishes to ratify the decree, if it be found.

6:1–12 Darius encourages the work of rebuilding

Darius was clearly following, and even extending, the policy inaugurated by Cyrus of encouraging the native religions of his subjects. The care and diligence displayed in this matter reflects creditably upon the Persian administration. The record which was found at Ecbatana was not a formal decree (*cf.* 1:1–4) but a memorandum containing brief details of the building specifications. Since Cyrus had promised governmental aid this was a necessary formality! In the Elephantine Papyri there is a brief memorandum concerning the rebuilding of the temple there.

2 *Ecbatana* was a pleasantly-situated fortress which was used as a summer residence by the Persian kings. **3** *Its height shall be sixty cubits.* Since this is double the height of Solomon's Temple (*cf.* 1 Ki. 6:2) it is reasonable to assume that it relates to the length of the projected building, which is not otherwise indicated, and that the height has dropped out. **6–12** The original decree of Cyrus is now reinforced by a strongly-worded one from Darius, who probably had Jewish advisers to ensure that the wording was appropriate. There is no direct evidence of lavish official support in Haggai or Zechariah. This is hardly surprising, since all Haggai's prophecies, and most of Zechariah's, were directed at getting the work on the Temple restarted, in the second year of Darius (*cf.* Hg. 1:1; Zc. 1:1, *etc.*). The decree of Darius did not come until the work was well advanced (6:8).

6:13–18 The consecration of the Temple

The 'credits' for the rebuilding operation included

Darius, Tattenai and the Jewish elders. But greater prominence attaches to the ministry of Haggai and Zechariah, and especially to God as the ultimate Initiator. The Temple was completed on 12 March 515 BC, a little over 70 years after its destruction. The dedication ceremony has parallels with its prototype in Solomon's reign (*cf.* 1 Ki. 8), although on a less lavish scale, indicating a smaller and poorer community. **14** *Artaxerxes*; the mention of this king is anachronistic. He was possibly included here because he, at a later date, contributed to the beautifying of the Temple (*cf.* 7:21–28).

6:19–22 The celebration of the Passover

The Passover, observed after many of the outstanding events in Israelite history (*e.g.* Nu. 9:5; Jos. 5:10; 2 Ki. 23:21ff.; 2 Ch. 30), followed one month after the dedication of the Temple. Passover marked the beginning of the year in the Mosaic legislation (*cf.* Ex. 12:2), but due to the influence of the Canaanite (autumn–autumn) calendar it was the Tabernacles feast-complex which commenced the year during the period of the monarchy. In the post-exilic period, Passover assumed its rightful place, doubtless influenced by the spring–spring calendar of Babylonia. **21** Two groups are indicated; the returned exiles, and those who had not been in captivity but were prepared to make a clean break with the idolatrous practices of the Samaritans, *etc.* The returned exiles were not completely isolationist, but their objection to the Samaritans was based on religious grounds which were not insurmountable. **22** *Had turned the heart of the king of Assyria.* Notice how the Chronicler traces God's influence upon heathen emperors (*e.g.* 1:1; 7:27). The reference to the king of Assyria is an obvious scribal error, although Darius, of course, reigned over the territory formerly held by the Assyrians.

7:1 – 8:36 EZRA'S RETURN TO JERUSALEM

7:1–28 Artaxerxes appoints and sponsors Ezra

If the traditional date for Ezra's return (458 BC, see discussion in the Introduction) is accepted, then almost 60 years divide chs. 6 and 7. This period, apart from the brief reference in 4:6, is one of complete obscurity, only illumined by the possibility that the book of Malachi dates from *c.* 465 BC. What happened to Zerubbabel is conjectural. Most likely his death, and that of Joshua the high priest, brought an end to the high hopes that centred upon them (*cf.* Hg. 2:20–23; Zc. 6:9–14). Until Ezra and Nehemiah returned to Jerusalem and brought order and stability into its life, the life of the despised community of the Jews followed a very mediocre course.

7:1–5 Ezra's genealogy. This is obviously selective, its intention being to trace back Ezra's line to Aaron himself. A comparison with other data (*e.g.* 1 Ch. 6:3–15) helps us to fill in the gaps.

Son of is frequently equivalent to 'descendant of'.

7:6–10 Ezra's journey to Jerusalem. In the pre-exilic period a scribe was no more than a secretary (*cf.*, *e.g.*, 2 Sa. 8:17; 1 Ch. 27:32), but after the Exile, when prophecy declined and the authority of the law became paramount, the office of scribe increased in importance. The best summary of the duties of a scribe is found in v. 10. He was both the preserver and the interpreter of the law. **7** *The seventh year of Artaxerxes.* For a full discussion on the identity of this king and possible emendations of the year, see the Introduction. The 4-month journey from Babylonia would be about 900 miles.

7:11–26 The letter of Artaxerxes. Doubt has been cast upon the authenticity of this letter because of its markedly Jewish tone and the extremely generous support which is promised. The former objection may be answered by assuming that Ezra himself, in his official position as 'Secretary of State for Jewish Religious Affairs' (such is the implication of v. 12) drew up the letter. The latter objection is weakened by the undoubted generosity of other Persian kings; such a price was a small one to pay for peace and stability in part of the Empire. The scope of Ezra's ministry included the entire area of the fifth Persian satrapy (see on 4:10) and allowed him the right to appoint magistrates over all Jewish communities. This would include the Samaritans and explains their attitude to Ezra, whom they styled 'Ezra the accursed'. The purpose was to secure conformity to recognized Jewish practice. In the light of this, it is unlikely that 'the book of the law' (see on Ne. 8:1 where this matter is further discussed), with which Ezra was associated, was a new creation, or there would be the risk of upsetting the Jerusalem (and other) communities, thereby promoting discord rather than concord. Considerable incentives to return were given to the priests, *etc.* (v. 24). **25, 26** The implementation of these provisions, if taken literally, must have involved Ezra in a great deal of travelling over an extended period. This may account for the relative silence of the years between 458 and 445 BC.

7:27, 28 The commencement of Ezra's memoirs. The abrupt change to the first person reveals the autobiographical nature of the account. These verses and the remainder of the book are in Hebrew. The character of Ezra, though not as clearly delineated as Nehemiah's, is revealed in the outburst of praise to God. His exultation over the beautifying of the Temple reveals the heart of a priest. His natural timidity, revealed here and in 8:21ff., was overcome by the consciousness that *the hand of the Lord my God was upon me.*

8:1–14 The list of those who returned with Ezra

There are slight differences between this list and its counterpart in 1 Esdras 8:28–40. Here the total is 1,496, while in 1 Esdras it is 1,690.

13 *Those who came later* translates one Hebrew word, 'last'. It may indicate, as the RSV infers, that other, smaller groups followed Ezra's company.

8:15–23 Preparations for departure

For a possible reason for the poor Levitical response see on 2:40ff. Such a situation would greatly inconvenience the programme which Ezra was to implement, and hence his urgent appeal for reinforcements. Before the party set off, a fast was held at the assembly point. The background of this is more than just the natural hazards of a long journey; it was a time of great unrest, particularly in the western half of the Persian Empire. Clearly Ezra considered an escort to be necessary, but since this betokened lack of faith in the Lord the alternative was to rest implicitly upon Him. Nehemiah, who was not travelling with a large company, had no qualms about accepting an escort (*cf.* Ne. 2:9).

15 *Ahava* (*cf.* v. 21); the site of both the river and the town are unknown. **17** *The place Casiphia* is also unidentified. The concentration of cultic personnel may indicate that there was a Jewish temple there, as at Elephantine. The word for 'place' is used of the Temple itself in 9:8.

8:24–30 The custody of the Temple treasures

The value of these gifts was well over a million pounds but this is by no means inconceivable in view of the immense wealth of the Persian Empire.

24 (*Cf.* vv. 18, 19, 30.) There were twelve priests and twelve Levites.

8:31–36 The journey to Jerusalem

31 A comparison with 7:9 shows that all the preliminary preparations, including the fast, were completed in 12 days. **32** Nehemiah took a similar rest period (*cf.* Ne. 2:11), necessary after such an arduous journey. **36** *The king's satraps.* There was normally only one satrap in the province Beyond the River, with several subordinate governors. Possibly the terms were used somewhat loosely. The non-reference to a governor in Jerusalem is not determinative in view of Ne. 5:14ff.

9:1 – 10:44 THE PROBLEM OF MIXED MARRIAGES

9:1–5 The magnitude of the problem

Ezra had been in Jerusalem about 4½ months (*cf.* 8:31; 10:9) when the officials brought to his notice the problem of mixed marriages. The offenders were probably those who had returned with Zerubbabel; many of them had established families (*cf.* 10:44), which rules out those who returned with Ezra. 10:18–43 lists 111 guilty men. The law of Deuteronomy (*e.g.* Dt. 7:1–5) warns of the pernicious effects of mixed marriages, and the history of Israel from the period of the judges onwards exemplifies this (*e.g.* Jdg. 3:5f.). Hence the firm line taken by Ezra. The same

stand was taken by Nehemiah (Ne. 13:23–28) and Malachi (Mal. 2:11, 13ff.) which suggests that this was a recurring problem, possibly due to a preponderance of men amongst those who returned.

3 It was customary to show grief by rending garments and by shaving the hair (*cf.* Jb. 1:20; Ezk. 7:18). Ezra's extreme measures betoken the intensity of his concern. Notice that his appeal was moral and religious, with no appeal to his official status or power. Reformation can never be achieved by force.

9:6–15 Ezra's vicarious intercession

Ezra's prayer and confession should be compared with Ne. 9:6–38 and Dn. 9:4–19. He does not stand apart from his people and coldly condemn them. Rather, although personally guiltless, he fully identifies himself with them in their guilt and need, an example to all would-be intercessors. The danger was that God's judgment would again fall upon His people, as it had in the events leading up to the Exile, but without the promise of a remnant to provide for a new beginning (vv. 8, 14). But apart from this element of divine chastisement, there is no doubt that had the practice of intermarriage been continued and extended, then the Jews would speedily have lost their national identity. Similarly, the NT warns against marriage with unbelievers (*cf.* 2 Cor. 6:14).

8 *A secure hold*, literally 'a nail' or 'tent-pin'. The reference is a figurative one; just as a tent-peg secures the whole tent, so those who returned from exile to rebuild the Temple and re-establish its cultus were the support of the whole nation. **9** *Protection* (lit. 'a wall'); it is doubtful if any attempt at rebuilding the wall (as in 4:7–23) had been undertaken so soon after Ezra's return. Therefore the reference is best understood figuratively, as in the RSV.

10:1–44 The situation remedied

The vivid detail of this chapter suggests that it once formed part of Ezra's memoirs. Possibly the Chronicler adapted it, changing the account to the third person and possibly shortening it, *e.g.* in the foreshortened speech of v. 10f.

10:1–5 The impact of Ezra's prayer. 1 It is unwarranted to suggest, as does Batten in the *ICC*, that Ezra's prayer 'was evidently intended to produce an effect upon the audience rather than upon God, perhaps like many other public prayers'. Nevertheless, the effect of such evident concern was dramatic. It prompted the people to take a certain initiative themselves which would guarantee greater success than a reformation forced upon them. **2** Their spokesman, Shecaniah, does not appear in the list of offenders. **3** A covenant was the most binding form of self-committal (*cf.* 2 Ch. 15:12–15).

10:6–17 Procedure for dealing with the situation. The sense of urgency which activated the Jews is shown in their prompt assembly at a most unpropitious time from the point of view of the weather. All but an insignificant minority, whose view was nonetheless noted (v. 15), were in favour of reform, and a committee of investigation seemed the most propitious way of dealing with an evidently large-scale problem. **6** There is no suggestion that either Jehohanan or Eliashib was high priest at this time. According to Josephus, who follows the traditional dating, Joiakim, the father of Eliashib, was the high priest when Ezra arrived in Jerusalem. Both his son Eliashib and his great-grandson Jehohanan could have had private rooms in the Temple precincts. **9** *The ninth month*; *i.e.* December, when the *heavy rain* could be bitterly cold. **14** The local officials, accompanying the offenders, would ensure accuracy of detail. **16, 17** The committee took

three months to complete its investigations. **10:18–44 The list of guilty men.** The RSV lists 111 men (17 priests, 10 Levites, 84 men of Israel), an emendation of v. 38 reducing by two the 113 of the AV. The length of time in the investigation may suggest that other cases were considered in which divorce proceedings were not considered necessary. The unhappiness caused by these broken homes must be set not only against the initial transgression involved in the contracting of the marriages, but also against the ultimate blessing to the whole world that could only come through a purified community. The offence had to be dealt with sternly, and sentiment was not allowed to influence the profound principles involved.

Nehemiah

OUTLINE OF CONTENTS

COMMENTARY

1:1 – 2:11 NEHEMIAH RETURNS TO JERUSALEM

1:1–3 The appeal to Nehemiah

This was undoubtedly an effort to secure the support of Nehemiah, an important official with access to the Persian king. An attempt to rebuild the wall in Jerusalem, which cannot be other than that noted in Ezr. 4:7–23, had ended disastrously and the Jews desperately needed a friend in high places.

1 *The words of Nehemiah*. This introduces the 'Nehemiah memoirs', one of the outstanding autobiographical masterpieces of the ancient world. *The month Chislev* was the ninth month. *The twentieth year*; archaeological evidence makes it certain that this was in the reign of Artaxerxes I (see the discussion on the date of Nehemiah's return in the Introduction). But there is a copyist's error either here or in 2:1, where the date is Nisan, the first mon h. Probably 1:1 should be emended to 'the nineteenth year'. *Susa* was the winter capital of the Persian kings. **2** *Hanani*; *cf.* 7:2.

1:4–11 The response of Nehemiah

Nehemiah was probably in close touch with the

Jerusalem community and he may have known of the attempt to rebuild its wall. But there was a grave personal risk involved if he championed the cause of a distressed Jerusalem, since his master had accepted the estimate of Jerusalem as a rebellious and seditious city, and ordered an end to the illegal building operations (*cf.* Ezr. 4:17–22). Any request to Artaxerxes would involve asking him to rescind a decree made no more than a few years before. Like Ezra (Ezr. 9:6–15) and Daniel (Dn. 9:4–19), Nehemiah shows his complete identification with his people, accepting the rightness of God's judgments (v. 8) but recalling also the graciousness of the divine promises (vv. 5, 9). Nehemiah knew the law and quoted from such passages as Lv. 26:33 and Dt. 30:1–5. If the suggested emendation to the year (v. 1) be accepted, then this period of waiting upon God and seeking the propitious moment lasted 4 months.

11 *Cupbearer*. This was a position of complete trust. Nehemiah would not be the only cupbearer, but it would give him access to the king. His main duty was to taste the wine in the presence of the king to ensure that it was not poisoned. Most officials in this position were eunuchs, and since there is no indication that

Nehemiah was married it is unlikely that he was an exception.

2:1-8 Nehemiah seizes his opportunity

The sense of high drama is preserved in the narrative. Such was the absolute power of a monarch of this period that to appear sad in his presence could cause dismissal or death. Sadness, after all, might suggest the dissatisfaction of a plotter. In this sharp crisis Nehemiah retained his composure and had the courage to mention, in general terms, the cause of his distress. Artaxerxes was discriminating enough to realize that there was a question underlying Nehemiah's observation. To Nehemiah this was the crucial moment. The extended prayers of the previous 4 months were now followed by the shortest of 'holy telegrams'. The prayer life of Nehemiah is itself an absorbing study (*cf.* 1:4–11; 2:4; 4:4f., 9; 5:19; 6:9, 14; 13:14, 22, 29, 31). A comparison with 5:14 shows that Nehemiah's appointment as governor of Jerusalem was made about this time. This involved the separation of Judea from Samaria. There is evidence that shortly before this incident there was a revolt by Megabyzos, satrap of Beyond the River, and the creation of an independent Judea, with a governor loyal to the king, may have seemed a wise measure to Artaxerxes.

1 *Nisan*. For a discussion on the date see on 1:1. **6** *I set him a time*. Nehemiah actually returned after 12 years (*cf.* 13:6) but this was probably extended from an earlier agreed period. **7f.** Nehemiah had obviously given careful thought to what would be required, a characteristic feature of the man.

2:9-11 Nehemiah arrives in Jerusalem

No time-reference is supplied. Sanballat and Tobiah, who would learn of Nehemiah's plans through the official correspondence, immediately assumed their role of chief opponents. This would be primarily political, since Samaria would no longer control Judea. Sanballat is mentioned in an Elephantine Papyrus, dated 408 BC, as governor of Samaria. The names of his sons, Delaiah and Shelemiah, suggest that he worshipped Yahweh. Possibly he was born in Beth-horon, in Ephraim. Tobiah probably governed the area east of Judea. He was either subordinate to Sanballat, or hand in glove with him (*cf.* 4:1–3; 6:12, 14).

2:12 – 3:32 THE BUILDING OF THE WALL COMMENCED

2:12–16 Nehemiah's preliminary survey

Nehemiah's capacity for detailed planning (*cf.* vv. 7f.) is again in evidence. His secret reconnaissance would acquaint him with the actual situation and thus enable him to deal with any opposition through an 'it-can't-be-done' attitude. The city walls at this period were probably limited to the north-eastern and south-eastern hills. **13** The *Valley Gate*, Nehemiah's starting-point, was probably on the south wall, in the south-west corner of the city. The *Dung Gate* was *c.* 500 yards (*cf.* 3:13) to the east. **14** If the *King's Pool* was the Pool of Siloam, then the *Fountain Gate* was on the eastern wall; **15** and the *valley* was the Kidron. Nehemiah then retraced his steps, making no attempt at a complete circuit. Recent archaeological excavation reveals that the area he covered was, in fact, the critical one, where the destruction of walls and buildings on a very steep slope had caused a completely chaotic state of affairs. It is now known that Nehemiah made no attempt to follow the existing line of the wall in this area but built his wall upon the ridge of the south-eastern hill (Ophel), *i.e.* above the area of acute destruction.

2:17–20 Nehemiah encourages the people to build

Nehemiah could now speak with personal experience. But no doubt the greatest factor in his appeal to the people was his remarkable testimony to the way in which God had controlled matters to that point. The shadow of opposition was not long in coming, however; clearly Sanballat had his informants in Jerusalem. Nehemiah confronts this with a strong faith in the living God.

19 *Geshem*; John Bright describes him as 'known from inscriptions as a powerful chieftain of Qedar (Dedan) in north-western Arabia. Under nominal Persian control, he governed the province of Arabia, which at this time included both Edom and Southern Judah. Nehemiah had enemies on all sides' (*op. cit.*, p. 366). *Are you rebelling* . . . This was sheer bluff on Sanballat's part, but such a policy of intimidation, with the events noted in Ezr. 4:23 still painfully fresh in Jewish minds, had every prospect of success. **20** *You have no portion or right or memorial in Jerusalem*. This forthright declaration of particularism was precipitated by the unswerving animosity of Sanballat and his friends.

3:1–32 The list of builders

It is not certain that Nehemiah was the author of this section. More likely the list was preserved in the Temple and subsequently incorporated by the Chronicler. Only the leaders of the 42 sections are named. The name of Ezra is not mentioned and there is uncertainty whether any of those who returned with him can be positively identified. This is not decisive evidence that Ezra and his party returned after Nehemiah. Those mentioned would be, in the main, well-established citizens of Jerusalem. If Ezra was in Jerusalem at this time, he, like Nehemiah who is also unmentioned, would probably be in an official supervisory capacity. The description commences with the Sheep Gate, at the eastern end of the north wall and proceeds in an anti-clockwise direction. All classes participated in the project, including priests (v. 1), goldsmiths and perfumers (v. 8), rulers and the womenfolk (v. 12), Levites (v. 17) and merchants (v. 32).

1 The high priest and a priestly group with him gave a good lead to the people. **5** *The Tekoites* were the inhabitants of Tekoah, about 10 miles south of Jerusalem. Their rulers were either in sympathy with Sanballat or afraid of reprisals if they openly identified themselves with Nehemiah. Their territory was on the fringes of civilization, adjacent to the area controlled by Geshem (*cf.* 2:19). The jarring note which this verse introduces is compensated for by the mention in v. 27 of the extra portion which the Tekoites built. Other groups also accepted a second allocation (*e.g.* vv. 11, 19–21, 24, 30). Evidence of an incomplete list is provided by the fact that the first allocation of some of these is not recorded (*e.g.* v. 11). **10** *Opposite his house* (*cf.* v. 30b). Nehemiah seems to have followed a policy of assigning men to their own local section of the wall, where they would have a personal interest in the security provided by a well-constructed section (*cf.* 4:14).

4:1 – 7:4 THE WALL COMPLETED IN SPITE OF OPPOSITION

4:1–6 Opposition by ridicule

This was the first of a series of attempts to thwart the rebuilding operations. Although Samaria, Judea, *etc.*, were within the Persian Empire, local rivalries were not precluded. But there was a limit to these, and Sanballat was probably influenced by the knowledge of the favour which the king had shown to Nehemiah. Ridicule, far from being an innocuous weapon, often succeeds in discouraging an enterprise where more direct methods fail. **2** *Will they finish up in a day?* A sarcastic question inspired by the prodigious activity of the Jews. *And burned ones at that.* The effect of fire is to crack and so weaken the slabs of stone. The accusation here and in v. 3 is that this was a jerry-built structure. **4f.** The imprecatory prayers of the OT, inconsistent with Christian standards, were within the context of the covenant relationship with Yahweh, whose honour was involved in this attack on His people. **6** *For the people had a mind to work.* This, together with Nehemiah's dynamic leadership, made for the success of the project.

4:7–23 Opposition by the threat of armed intervention

Jerusalem was now completely surrounded by hostile factions: Samaria to the north, Ammon on the east, Geshem and his Arabs to the south and Ashdod, a former Philistine city now the centre of another Persian administration unit, to the west. A direct confrontation was out of the question, since Artaxerxes had authorized the building, and so a policy of infiltration and terrorist activity was planned. Nehemiah countered this by careful planning, based on sound psychology; the people would resist tenaciously when their own families were in jeopardy (*cf.* 7:3). There seems to have been a period of acute

danger when work was completely suspended (vv. 13ff.). After this, the building was resumed in an atmosphere of instant readiness for defence. **9** Notice this OT counterpart to 'Praise the Lord and keep your powder dry'. Reliance upon God is not incompatible with the taking of sensible precautions. **10** A supplementary discouragement was the very immensity of the task. Archaeology witnesses to the thoroughness of the Babylonian destruction of 587 BC. **11, 12** The whispering attack was particularly effective amongst the Jews who lived in outlying areas and to whom Sanballat and his associates had readier access. **14** *Remember the Lord*; Nehemiah frequently recalls the people to their basic trust in Yahweh (*cf.* vv. 9, 20). **22** This measure strengthened the reserves of manpower in the capital, but would make the provincial cities more vulnerable. The attitude of the nobles of Tekoa (*cf.* 3:5) may have been influenced by this consideration. **23** *The men of the guard*; a contingent of Persian soldiers is probably indicated, although the main escort party (*cf.* 2:9) had probably returned by this time. *Each kept his weapon in his hand*, Hebrew 'each one his weapon the water'. The precise meaning is not clear, but the inference is that complete preparedness was maintained, whether when washing (as AV delightfully suggests), or during any other activity.

5:1–19 Nehemiah's social and economic measures

Since Nehemiah is unlikely to have called *a great assembly* (v. 7) in the middle of an urgent reconstruction scheme, and since v. 14 is clearly retrospective, it is usually held that these events took place after the rebuilding of the wall. It is just possible that the economic pressures caused by the building programme, in which most normal income would be suspended, brought the underlying abuses of vv. 1–5 into such prominence that Nehemiah was forced to give urgent attention to them.

5:1–13 Social injustices remedied. Three classes were involved: the landless, who were desperately short of food (v. 2); landowners who, because of a severe famine, had been compelled to mortgage their properties (v. 3); those forced to borrow money at exhorbitant rates to meet the Persian taxation upon property (v. 4). The lament of v. 5 is probably a composite one, reflecting the condition of all three groups. Slavery within Israel was permitted, within well-defined limits (*cf., e.g.,* Ex. 21:2–11; Lv. 25:39–43; Dt. 15:12–18), but interest was not to be charged on loans to poor fellow-Israelites (*cf.* Ex. 22:25; Lv. 25:35ff.; Dt. 23:19f.). Nehemiah's relief measures included the return of all alienated property and the cessation of future payment of interest, thus allowing those who had borrowed money to pay off the capital sum in due course. **8** The Jewish nobles, taking advantage of Nehemiah, had sold their fellows to foreign masters, knowing that Nehemiah's policy was to buy them back. **9** Notice the appeal to the national conscience and testimony to other nations. **10** Nehemiah admits that he has been forced into the policies he now wishes to outlaw. One assumes that his interest charges were more reasonable than those of others. **11** *The hundredth of money, etc.*, probably relates to the monthly interest rate. **13** *I also shook out my lap.* A gesture symbolizing complete rejection.

5:14–19 Nehemiah's unselfish government. In a completely guileless manner Nehemiah catalogues his praiseworthy achievements as governor, against a background of the exhorbitant demands normally made by a man in his position. **14f.** Normally the people would be taxed for the support of the governor's establishment. *The former governors who were before me.* Not a reference to Shesh-bazzar or Zerubbabel but to those immediately preceding Nehemiah, either the governor of Samaria or a subordinate official at Jerusalem. **16** Nehemiah and his servants had taken their full share in the rebuilding programme. **17f.** He extended generous, but not ostentatious, hospitality (*cf.* the provision made for Solomon's household, 1 Ki. 4:22f.). **19** (*Cf.* 13:14, 22, 31) Nehemiah's memoirs may have been a votive offering presented to the Lord in the Temple.

6:1–14 Further opposition to the rebuilding of the wall

6:1–4 Opposition by intrigue. The progress on the wall having advanced so swiftly that the danger of armed attack was considerably lessened, Sanballat and his accomplices now attacked the leader himself. Their aim was to lure him away from his supporters in Jerusalem, to make his assassination easier, or to facilitate an attack upon Jerusalem in his absence. **2** *Ono* was 'neutrally' situated between the provinces of Ashdod and Samaria, but it was 19 miles from Jerusalem.

6:5–9 Opposition by blackmail. The earlier expedient having failed on four occasions, a fifth attempt was made to intimidate Nehemiah. An open letter was one that could, and therefore would, be read by anyone who handled it, thus broadcasting the innuendo. It was written upon a fragment of pottery, leather or papyrus. Two points lent weight to this attack: Geshem was an important official whose word would carry weight with the Persian authorities; and the insinuation concerning Nehemiah's pretensions to the throne might have a ring of plausibility to a Persia very sensitive to any suggestion of rebellion, especially in the light of past events in this area. Nehemiah refused to bow to this pressure, giving the answer of complete integrity and seeking added strength from the Lord.

6:10–14 An attempt to discredit Nehemiah. Since Tobiah is twice mentioned first (vv. 12, 14) it is assumed that, with his known contacts in Judah (vv. 17ff.), he took the lead in this plan. **10** *Shemaiah*, a prophet (v. 12), is unknown apart from this passage. The inference is that he claimed to have a special revelation for Nehe-

miah concerning a plot on his life. His suggestion to Nehemiah that they might meet a second time in the Holy Place of the Temple, from which all but the priests were specifically excluded on pain of death (*cf.* Nu. 18:7), would give Nehemiah a bad reputation and alienate the priests, if acted upon. Less likely is the view that Shemaiah was inviting Nehemiah to seek sanctuary in the Temple. *Shut up* can hardly mean that he was ceremonially unclean, since this would debar him from the Temple. Possibly it refers to a state of prophetic ecstasy. **14** False prophecy seems united in opposition to Nehemiah, as it was to his counterparts in pre-exilic Jerusalem.

6:15–19 The wall completed

The task was completed in an unbelievably short period, although doubtless a certain 'touching up' was done later. The fact of divine assistance, implied throughout the narrative, was evident even to their adversaries.

15 *Elul* was the sixth month, *i.e.* August–September. From the point of view of agriculture the building operations were well timed, coming between the main cereal-harvest and the vintage-harvest. **18f.** *The daughter of Meshullam.* Meshullam was one of the leading wall-builders (*cf.* 3:4, 30). Nehemiah faced a well-organized fifth column amongst his own leading citizens but there is no suggestion that he took any reprisals against its members.

7:1–4 Safety precautions in Jerusalem

The practically-minded Nehemiah did not rest on the security afforded by the newly-constructed wall, but took steps to see that an adequate guard, under loyal supervision, was established. Later on he was to deal with the problem of a sparsely-populated Jerusalem (*cf.* 11:1f.).

1 All three classes mentioned could be Temple personnel. The problem of available and dependable men for guard duties must have been considerable. **2** *Hanani and Hannaniah.* The name, in its shorter or longer form, was a common one (*cf.* 3:8). The need for trustworthy leadership is emphasized by 6:18f. **3** *Each opposite his own house.* Another instance of a wise understanding of human nature (*cf.* on 3:10; 4:14).

7:5 – 13:3 OTHER EVENTS DURING NEHEMIAH'S FIRST TERM OF OFFICE

7:5–73a The register of those who returned with Zerubbabel

This list, which was probably stored in the Temple archives, was probably the basis of Nehemiah's repopulation measures (*cf.* 11:1f.). It is made quite clear that it is not Nehemiah's own census-list (vv. 5f.). The list is practically identical with that of Ezr. 2, where see notes.

7:73b – 8:18 The great law-reading ceremony

7:73b – 8:8 The law read and expounded. In 1 Esdras the account of Ezra's reading of the law follows Ezr. 10 and the name of Nehemiah is missing (*cf.* Ne. 8:9). It is questionable whether such a ceremony as this could have been arranged before Nehemiah brought security to the city, and order out of the heaps of rubble. The chapter, then, is best located in its present position, although it may be the Chronicler's paraphrase of what was originally a part of the Ezra memoirs. It is instructive to note that the initiative (8:1) appears to come from the people, although the readiness with which Ezra and his company were able to comply suggests that it was a contrived initiative. It appears that this was the first time that the law had been read or expounded (*cf.* v. 12b) in this way, since the reaction caught the leaders by surprise (v. 9).

8:1 *The book of the law of Moses.* It has been commonly supposed that this was the priestly code, brought by Ezra from Babylon, and which subsequently became the framework of the completed Pentateuch. Such a view labours under the grave disability that the Samaritans, who hated Ezra and could not conceivably have received anything from him, accepted the completed Pentateuch. It is plausible to suggest therefore that the Pentateuch had been completed long before this, that it was this which was read by Ezra, and that the reaction of the people was due to their ignorance of its provisions. **4** The number of Ezra's assistants varies in the versions. **5f.** The reverent attention to the Torah, and the attitude of standing during its reading, were to become characteristic of later synagogual Judaism. **8** *They read . . . clearly.* This could refer (with RSV mg.) to an extempore translation; possibly some of the people understood only Aramaic, not Hebrew (*cf.* 13:24).

8:9–12 The reaction of the people. There are similarities to the response of Josiah when the lost 'book of the law' was read to him (*cf.* 2 Ki. 22:8–13). It needed considerable effort on the part of the leaders (probably Ezra is the speaker in v. 10) to convince the people that the day was one of rejoicing. **9** The name of Nehemiah is absent from 1 Esdras, which also misreads 'the governor' for a proper noun 'Attharates'. Some would therefore advocate omitting Nehemiah's name as a later gloss. Possibly the omission in 1 Esdras was deliberate, since the writer was concerned solely with Ezra, not Nehemiah.

8:13–18 The celebration of the Feast of Booths (Tabernacles). The essential character of this festival was thanksgiving (*cf.* Dt. 16:13ff.; compare the detail of Lv. 23:33–43). It was known in Solomon's time (*cf.* 1 Ki. 8:2) and by Hosea in the northern kingdom (*cf.* Ho. 12:9); it was observed in the preceding century by Zerubbabel and his company (*cf.* Ezr. 3:4). Yet its detailed provisions were unknown even amongst the religious leaders (v. 13f.)! The answer probably lies in the fact that the character of Tabernacles changed fundamentally under Canaanite influence, during the monarchic period, becoming the feast associated with the Davidic covenant (*cf.* 2 Sa. 7) and losing some-

thing of its connection with the wilderness period, in Judah at any rate. The reading of the law was one of the prescribed features of Tabernacles (*cf.* Dt. 31:9–13). No mention is made of the Day of Atonement, held on the tenth day of the seventh month, just before the Feast of Tabernacles (fifteenth to the twenty-second day of the month). The Chronicler must have known of the existence of this feast and could have included it in his account had it been kept at this particular time.

9:1–37 The great national confession

A majority of scholars accept that this chapter originally followed Ezr. 10, which would allow for a three-week interval between the two events (Ne. 9:1; *cf.* Ezr. 10:17). This arrangement makes good sense, since both occasions were connected with the fact of separation from non-Israelites (Ne. 9:2). Such plausibility does not eliminate the possibility of a connection with Ne. 8–10, wherein the conviction of sin, caused by the reading of the law and temporarily suppressed by the leaders as inconsistent with a joyous occasion (8:9–12), is now allowed to find its natural expression two days after the conclusion of the Feast of Booths. In this new ceremony three hours of reading the law were followed by three hours of confession and worship (9:3).

Ezra's prayer (vv. 5–38) opens with an acknowledgment of God's majesty and then continues with a recital of the major turning-points of Israel's history. The first of these is the call of Abraham (vv. 7f.), which was virtually the beginning of history for the Hebrews. The next turning-point is the Exodus and the giving of the law (vv. 9–14). In the wilderness period God's gracious mercy contrasted with the waywardness of His people (vv. 15–23). God's favour was again shown in the conquest of Canaan (vv. 24f.) but Israel continued to be rebellious, in spite of the warnings of the prophets and the deliverances wrought by the judges (vv. 26, 27, 30). God had chastised His people through other nations, yet with forbearance and purpose (vv. 30f.) and this had at last produced the humility and repentance and absolute trust that was an essential element in the covenant between Him and Israel.

4f. No convincing explanation has been given of the differences between the names in vv. 4 and 5. **14** *Thou didst make known . . . thy holy sabbath.* The command concerning the sabbath is in the ethical Decalogue (Ex. 20:8ff.), the book of the covenant (Ex. 23:12) and the ritual Decalogue (Ex. 34:21), suggesting that it was a foundational element in Israelite religion. It was made a covenant sign at the time of the Exodus.

9:38 – 10:27 The leaders who participated in the covenant

10:1 The signatories occur in the reverse order of 9:38. *Nehemiah the governor.* If these events be connected with Ezr. 10 (see introductory note to Ne. 9:1–37), then Nehemiah's name must be removed as a gloss if the traditional view concerning Ezra's return, or the view that he returned in 398 BC, be held. *Zedekiah*; otherwise unknown, but his position, between the governor and the priests, suggests that he was a person of consequence. **2–8** Most of these names recur in 12:1–7. As only four priestly families arrived with Zerubbabel (*cf.* Ezr. 2:36–39), others may have developed from them or arrived subsequently. **9–13** All but four of the Levites are mentioned in 8:7; 9:4, 5; 12:8. **14–27** Variations in the list of the leading secular families when compared with Ezr. 2 may be due to such variable factors as movements, subdivisions or even the extinction of families.

10:28–39 Provisions of the covenant

The stipulations of the covenant included the forbidding of mixed marriages (v. 30), details of sabbath-observance and the sabbatical year (v. 31) and the provision of an adequate income for the maintenance of the cultus (vv. 32–39). An obvious connection between these and the reforms initiated by Nehemiah during his second term of office (13:10–31) has led some scholars to suppose that this covenant was part of Nehemiah's policy to eradicate such anomalies. More likely is the view that his anger on that occasion was vented against those very abuses which the people had solemnly covenanted to rectify only about 12 years before.

30 This was a recurring problem in this period (*cf.* Ezr. 9, 10; Ne. 13:23–27). **31** The law does not specifically exclude sabbath trading but this was clearly understood (*cf.*, *e.g.*, Je. 17:21, 22; Am. 8:5). For the law of the sabbatical year see Lv. 25:2–7; Dt. 15:1ff. These provisions, which would have alleviated the recent distress in Jerusalem and district (*cf.* Ne. 5:1–4) were apparently not observed at any stage in Israel's history prior to this point, largely through the pressures of vested interests (*cf.* 2 Ch. 36:21, where the 70-year exile is viewed as punishment for this non-observance of this custom during 70 sabbatical years, *i.e.* 490 years). **32** *The third part of a shekel* was less than the recognized amount (*cf.* Ex. 30:13; Mt. 17:24), probably owing to the impoverished economic situation. **34** *The wood-offering*; this stipulation is a natural development from the command to keep the altar fire continually burning (*cf.* Lv. 6:12f.) **37** The tithes of cattle are not mentioned here (*cf.* Lv. 27:32) although the firstborn are mentioned in v. 36 (*cf.* Nu. 18:15–18). Possibly there was a shortage of cattle at this time of poverty which made some relaxation of the law desirable.

11:1 – 12:26 Lists of inhabitants

11:1–24 Citizens of Jerusalem. The list of vv. 3–19, with minor variations, corresponds with that in 1 Ch. 9:2–17, and probably relates to those already resident in Jerusalem. It includes the rulers (vv. 3–9), priests (vv. 10–14), Levites (vv. 15–18) and gatekeepers (v. 19). These were augmented by a compulsory 10 p.c. levy drawn from surrounding areas and an unspecified

number of volunteers (v. 2). **20–24** Amongst some general notes concerning the oversight of the Temple personnel there are two items of peculiar interest: v. 23 an imperial provision was made for certain classes; v. 24 a representative of the Jewish people was in attendance at the Persian court. The likelihood of these arrangements is increased by documentary evidence of the nature of Persian rule, particularly the interest shown in religious affairs.

11:25–36 Villages occupied by the Jews. The verses list towns and villages in the former territories of Judah (vv. 25–30) and Benjamin (vv. 31–36). No reason can be given for the non-mention of important settlements mentioned elsewhere in Ezra and Nehemiah, *e.g.* Tekoah (Ne. 3:5), Beth-zur (3:16), Bethlehem (7:26). Kiriath-jearim (7:29), Jericho (7:36), *etc.* **25** *Kiriath-arba*; the old name of Hebron (*cf.* Jos. 14:15). **30** *From Beer-sheba to the valley of Hinnom*, *i.e.* from the southern to the northern boundaries of Judah.

12:1–9 Priests and Levites who returned with Zerubbabel. The Chronicler has grouped together several lists in 12:1–26. The interpretation of these is most difficult. The four priestly families of Ezr. 2, with the exception of Passhur, are mentioned here. The extra names probably relate to their descendants in Nehemiah's day, the building of the Temple and the development of the cultus calling for extra, specialist family groups.

12:10f. The genealogy of post-exilic high priests. This is a continuation of the list of 1 Ch. 6:3–15. *Eliashib* was the contemporary of Nehemiah (*cf.* 3:1). *Jonathan*, or Johanan (*cf.* 12·22), or Jehonanan (*cf.* Ezr. 10:6), is mentioned in texts from Elephantine dated 411 and 408 BC.

12:12–21 A list of priests in the time of Joiakim; *cf.* v. 10.

12:22–26 A list of the Levites in the time of Joiakim and subsequently. A number of sources are indicated by the three time-references (vv. 22, 26), although only one is nominated (v. 23). The completion of these lists appears to be after the lifetimes of Nehemiah and Ezra (v. 26).

12:27–43 The walls dedicated

The Nehemiah memoirs are again resumed, possibly amplified by the Chronicler in vv. 27–30. No reference to time is indicated but some scholars infer from 2 Macc. 1:18 that the date was the twenty-fifth of the ninth month, *i.e.* three months after the completion of the walls. If the traditional dating of Ezra's return (viz. 458 BC) be rejected, then either his name must be removed from v. 36, or else the dedication ceremony must be put impossibly late.

12:27–30 Levitical reinforcements. These would be necessary to cope with the extra demands on the cultic personnel (*cf.* v. 43). The purification (v. 30) was presumably by the application of sacrificial blood.

12:31–43 The procession around the walls. The two companies appear to have started from a point on the south wall, possibly at the Valley Gate. The first processed in an anti-clockwise direction and the second in a clockwise direction, the meeting-point being in the Temple area. Each was led by a choir (vv. 31, 38). Hoshaiah (v. 32), who is otherwise unknown, seems to have occupied a position in the first company corresponding to Nehemiah's in the second, Ezra being given a special place with the first priestly contingent. Numerous sacrifices were offered on an occasion of great rejoicing (cf. the multiplied references to joy in v. 43).

12:44–47 The care of the Temple personnel

This section derives from the Chronicler, who had a peculiar interest in the Temple cultus and its officials. In particular he stresses the part played by David in the planning of the cultus of the first Temple. Nehemiah, with Zerubbabel, is singled out for praise in view of his support of the Temple staff (cf. 13:10–14).

47 The Levites paid the tithe of the tithe to the priests (cf. 10:38; Nu. 18:25–32).

13:1–3 The heathen excluded from the congregation

The connection of this section is obscure. The opening words imply that it was the same occasion as 12:44 but the more obvious connection is with the following incident, i.e. the clash between Nehemiah and Tobiah the Ammonite (13:4–9; cf. 2:19). It provides yet another illustration of the perennial problem of the relationship between the Jews and their heathen neighbours.

1 It was found written. The reference is to Dt. 23:3–6 (cf. Nu. 22–24). More liberal treatment was afforded the Edomites and Egyptians (cf. Dt. 23:7f.) but the post-exilic situation appears to have demanded a more stringent application of the law.

13:4–31 NEHEMIAH'S SECOND TERM OF OFFICE

13:4–9 The scandal concerning Tobiah the Ammonite

This incident had its genesis during Nehemiah's temporary absence from the Persian court, in accordance with his agreement (cf. 2:6). The kind of problem which Nehemiah faced is well illustrated here. There was an obvious liaison between the officials in Jerusalem and the leaders of the surrounding provinces, but an alliance between the high priest (cf. 3:1; 13:28) and Tobiah, one of Nehemiah's principal enemies and a leading opponent of the attempt to rebuild the wall, beggars the imagination (cf. v. 28). Nehemiah's vigorous action not only removed the offence, but it allowed the chambers to be used for their rightful function.

4 Now before this. This is not an accurate time-reference, as it may relate to an incident in Nehemiah's memoirs which has been omitted. The chambers of the house of our God. The construction of the Temple provided for a great deal of subsidiary accommodation, which was used by the cultic officials for cultic purposes (cf. 1 Ki. 6:5; Ezr. 8:29; 10:6; Ezk. 40:6f.). 6 The thirty-second year of Artaxerxes king of Babylon, i.e. 433 BC. Babylon was the administrative centre of the Empire and one of the residences of the Persian kings.

13:10–14 Provision for the Levites

The legislation of 10:35–39 is presupposed. Neglect of the Levites inevitably affected the standard of religious life in the Temple. Eliashib the high priest was obviously blameworthy (vv. 4f.) and must have been a party to the dishonest practices which Nehemiah sought to rectify by the appointment of four reliable treasurers (v. 13).

10 Each to his field. According to Dt. 18:1 the priests and Levites were not allowed to own land, a stipulation which was not obeyed in the post-exilic period.

13:15–22 The law of the sabbath enforced

Two classes of offenders are apparent: the Jews themselves, while not actually selling on the sabbath, were preparing or transporting their wares (v. 15); Phoenician traders were actually trading on the sabbath (v. 16). Possibly the nobles had a responsibility to police this kind of conduct (vv. 17f.). Nehemiah took preventative action and threatened more direct measures to those who failed to take the hint or even attempted to break the blockade by setting up their stalls outside the city (vv. 19ff.). The operation, superintended in its earlier stages by his own servants, who had the greater authority, then reverted to the control of the Levitical gatekeepers (cf. 7:1).

13:23–29 The question of mixed marriages again

If the traditional dating for Ezra be accepted then he had dealt with this same problem almost 30 years before (cf. Ezr. 8, 9), whilst incidents and legislation during Nehemiah's first period in Jerusalem (e.g. Ne. 9:2; 10:28ff.) show that it continued to be a thorny issue. Now, during Nehemiah's absence, it had arisen again, doubtless encouraged by an example within the high priestly family (v. 28). The ecumenicity of our present generation must not blind us to the danger of the extinction of the Jewish religion which this practice presented. In a historical situation men like Nehemiah built a wall of separation about the Jews which enabled them to fulfil God's universalistic purposes. Once more Nehemiah displayed characteristic vigour (vv. 25, 28); if he was a eunuch (see on 1:11) he displayed none of the effeminateness characteristic of this group. Josephus (Antiquities xi.7.8) uses an incident which has similarities with v. 28 to explain the complete rupture between the Jews and the Samaritans, culminating in the building of the rival Samaritan temple on Mt. Gerizim. His dating is at fault, however, for he sets the incident almost a century late, in the early years of Alexander, although he is probably correct in dating the Samaritan temple at this time.

25 Presumably, as well as guarding against future violations, he made the offenders put away their foreign wives.

13:30, 31 Finale

Nehemiah's achievements were considerable. The building of the wall, together with his other economic, social and religious measures, set the Jerusalem community, which had been in a desperate plight for almost a century, on a secure foundation. With Ezra's great contribution centring upon the law, the two men made it possible for Judaism to survive in the succeeding centuries. Had the liberal opposition party, led by the high priest Eliashib, succeeded in blunting their sharply-defined policy, it is difficult to conceive how the Jewish faith could have survived.

A. E. CUNDALL

Esther

INTRODUCTION

The story of Esther is set, not in Palestine, nor even in Babylon, but farther east still in a capital of the Persian Empire, throughout which Jews of the post-exilic period were scattered. Cyrus the empire-builder, well known for his liberal attitude to conquered peoples, allowed Jews to return to Jerusalem after he had conquered Babylon in 539 BC. Darius, the Persian king mentioned in Haggai and Zechariah, organized the administration of his huge empire during his reign (522–486). Ahasuerus, the Persian monarch of Esther, was his successor.

The narrative tells of the grand vizier Haman, who, as a result of a private grudge against one Jew, plotted the extinction of all Jews living within the Persian Empire. Such was the extent of the Empire that virtually the whole race would have been wiped out. In such a crisis providential intervention was to be expected, and it came through Esther, the Jewish girl who had been chosen queen by the monarch. In an unforeseeable way circumstances so fell out that Haman became the victim of his own plot, the Jews were delivered, their enemies were liquidated, and a Jew was appointed to the position of greatest influence next to the king. This miraculous reversal of affairs was celebrated throughout the Persian Empire, and is still celebrated annually by Jews in every part of the world at the festival known as Purim. The scroll of Esther is read each year as part of the celebrations, the congregation joining in at suitable places to express their approval or disapproval, as the case may be, so that the story is better known than any other part of the OT to the ordinary Jew. Moreover, whenever persecution has been the experience of Jews throughout the centuries, this book has fostered the assurance of ultimate deliverance and survival, and kept alive nationalistic hopes; hence its great popularity among them.

TEXT AND PLACE IN THE CANON

One result of this popularity is that there are more MS copies of Esther than of any other book of the OT. Another is that rabbinic comment on the book abounds from early in the Christian era. This has been preserved in the Talmud and is still revered by Jewish scholars. Early translations of the book contain a variety of readings different from the Hebrew, so raising problems concerning the original text. The LXX is particularly important in this respect because it was probably translated as early as the 2nd century BC, and yet contains over 100 verses that are not in the Hebrew. These additions can be read in the Apocrypha, where they have been separated from their original place in the story, and put together as *Additions to the Book of Esther*. At the end of a very detailed consideration of all the early texts and versions L. B. Paton concludes that the Massoretic text, on which our English versions are based, 'unquestionably represents the purest form of the text that has come down to us, and it must be taken as the basis for all critical discussion of the book' (*ICC, Esther*, p. 47). The LXX additions probably arose as an attempt to improve on the original book by introducing a more obviously religious emphasis.

The book as we have it almost certainly comes from one author, for though some have thought that the last section, 9:20 – 10:3, is a later addition to the original, their arguments have not been entirely persuasive. The alleged change in vocabulary and style is accounted for by the change from narrative to directions for the observance of Purim. Moreover, it is not quite true that mention of Purim is confined to this section, for it is anticipated in 3:7, and indeed the story seems to be told with the express purpose of commending observance of the festival. Such unity of purpose presupposes one author.

Of the five scrolls in the third section of the Hebrew Canon Esther is generally the last, because Purim is the last festival of the Jewish year. In our English Bibles it comes after Ezra and Nehemiah, books with which it shares a Persian background.

THE ORIGIN OF PURIM

The derivation of the word *pûrîm* puzzled earlier commentators, who connected it with the Hebrew word *pûrā* meaning 'wine-press', and thought that the festival might have originated from a Greek cask-opening feast. Another suggestion was that the wine-press spoke of the wrath of God, revealed in action when Judas Maccabaeus won his victory over Nicanor on the 13th Adar 161 BC. Against this is the fact that the day of the month is wrong, and there is early evidence that the two festivals were quite distinct (2 Macc. 15:36). Other scholars tried to find a Persian or Babylonian feast from which Purim might have originated, but no suggestion commanded wide support. It is now well known that *pûrîm* is a plural word deriving from the Assyrian *pûru*, which occurs in texts of widely differing periods in the sense of 'lot'. The information given by the writer in 3:7 has proved correct, and no better explanation of the origin of Purim has been put forward than the one he has given.

HISTORICITY

During the last 200 years there has been almost unanimous agreement among commentators that the book is not to be read as sober history. Some have contended that it is pure fiction; others have seen in the names of the principal characters reminiscences of Marduk and Ishtar, deities of Babylon, in rivalry with Humman and Mashti, gods of Elam, and on these grounds have postulated that pagan mythology lies behind the story; another recent view is that it is a historicized wisdom tale. The most popular current opinion takes account of the accuracy of the local colour in the story, and designates it a historical novel, thus acknowledging much of the evidence for historicity, but judging the plot itself to be imaginary.

The days of Ahasuerus are so far removed from our time that it is easy for objections to the historicity of the story of Esther to be based on a subjective assessment of its credibility rather than on knowledge of Persian affairs during the 5th century BC. We are fortunate to have independent information from five main sources:

1. *The Histories* of the Greek historian Herodotus, which are readily available in English in a paperback edition. Writing during the second half of the 5th century BC after travelling extensively, Herodotus traced the events which brought Persia into conflict with Greece. Chs. 7–9 deal with the period to which our book belongs. They reveal the king, who was called Xerxes in Greek, to have been capricious, sensual, cruel and despotic, and while it is true that he was not the only Persian king to demonstrate the characteristics, Herodotus corroborates the picture of Xerxes given us in Esther. Other parallels between the two books are pointed out in the course of the commentary.

2. An inscription of Xerxes found at Persepolis and translated in *ANET* (p. 316) enables us to read his own testimony: 'I am Xerxes, the great king, the only king, the king of all countries which speak all kinds of languages, the king of this big and far-reaching earth. . .' There follows a list of the nations he ruled.

3. Excavations at Shushan by French archaeologists have unearthed a text in which Darius relates how he built his palace, using materials from every part of the Empire. Xerxes completed what his father had begun. The whole palace complex, surrounded by a high mud-brick wall, was to the west of the city, between it and the river Choaspes, which provided water for the royal 'paradise' or garden round the throne room. The entrance to the palace, known as the king's gate, was to the east, and inside the gate, to the right, was the treasury, but straight ahead were three courtyards surrounded by living quarters, and on the right of the innermost was the harem. Three large halls still had to be traversed before the throne room was reached. It was an Apadana, or hall of pillars, 65 ft in height and approached by wide stairways, all of which would have been guarded. The impression intended by the designer would have been one of spacious coolness, and, for the monarch, remote dignity. Besides the palace and the residential area Darius built a citadel, and all were enclosed in the great outer wall and surrounded by a moat.

4. A cuneiform tablet from Borsippa, near Babylon, mentions Marduka as a high official at the court of Susa during the early years of the reign of Xerxes, under Uštannu, satrap of Babylonia and 'Beyond the River'. Marduka was an accountant or a privy councillor. This Marduka has been identified with Mordecai, who, if this suggestion be accepted, would have been an official of some importance before his appearance in Esther. His connection with the king's gate would have been an official one, and it is thought that he may have had the trusted position of gate-keeper.

5. In a collection of tablets from the reigns of Artaxerxes I and Darius II more than a hundred Jewish names occur in connection with important positions in the realm. We know that Nehemiah was cup-bearer to King Artaxerxes I (Ne. 1:11), but we can now add that several Jews were even governors of administrative districts. This would not have been true in the time of Darius I, and so a change must have come about some time between his reign and that of Artaxerxes, that is, in the time of Xerxes. S. H. Horn (*Biblical Research*, IX, 1964) suggests that the influence of Mordecai could have accounted for it (10:3).

All this information strongly supports the historicity of Esther. The author knew as much as we do, and perhaps even a little more, concerning the king, the city, and the situation about which he was writing. His book begins with the traditional Hebrew formula used in history writing, he names a source of information by which his statements may be verified (10:2), and he refers to people and customs as though he knew Persian court life from the inside. One unsolved problem concerns the name of Xerxes' queen. According to Herodotus she was Amestris, the daughter of a Persian general, and she was already married to Xerxes by the time events recorded in Esther began. How this information is to be reconciled with our story we do not yet know, but the difficulty is not insurmountable in a polygamous society, especially when the volatile character of the king is taken into account. Other points relevant to historicity are dealt with in the course of the commentary. They are mainly arguments from silence or questions concerning the probability of the story.

AUTHORSHIP AND DATE

We do not know who wrote the book, and the suggestion that Mordecai was the author is based on a misunderstanding of 9:20. All the same the writer is likely to have been a Jew, for his nationalism permeates the story, and his knowledge of Persian words and customs suggests that he lived in that land, before the Persian Empire fell to Greece. Only so can the author's accurate knowledge of Persian ways be accounted for. Nevertheless there are those who would attribute it to the Greek period, and specifically to the 2nd century, on the grounds that it breathes the nationalistic feeling of the Maccabean era or the fierce patriotism of the time of John Hyrcanus. It is true that the earliest mention of the feast of Purim is in 2 Macc. 15:36, and that Josephus is the first to quote the book, but the absence of evidence does nothing to prove that the book had not been in existence earlier.

PURPOSE AND SIGNIFICANCE

There can be no doubt that the author's purpose was to record the amazing deliverance of the Jewish people under Xerxes, and to see that the memory of it was kept alive through later generations by the observance of the annual Purim festival. Even to the present day the miracle of Jewish identity, preserved amid the multitude of other cultures, is an undeniable fact of history, as is the miracle of Jewish survival, notwithstanding all the attempts that have been made through persecutions, pogroms and concentration camps to prevent it. God has not cast off His ancient people, but continues to deal graciously with them because He keeps His promise for ever. Yet Esther is part of the Christian as well as the Jewish Canon of Scripture, and rightly so. The promises of God are the heritage of all believers, and therefore that providence which protected His people in Persian times still operates on behalf of His church, guarding and sustaining it in all its dangers, obvious or subtle. More than that, the book asserts the rule of the sovereign providence of God in all the affairs of men, whether they like it or not.

TEACHING

1. The book shows the worthlessness of superstition as a guide to life. Haman never even lived to see his 'lucky' day, for God, and not some impersonal fate, controls the destinies of men. 2. There was no question of the Jews deserving God's favour; no-one ever has deserved it, and Mordecai and Esther were no better than most; moreover, in seeking to run all their enemies to the death they were positively blameworthy. 3. The book reveals the sovereignty of God at work in a particular situation, accomplishing His purposes, but without in any way overriding the 'free' decisions and actions of the people involved. To be sure the king was sleepless, and so had the annals read to him just at the right time, but Haman was pursuing his own evil intent in getting up betimes, and it was exactly that evil intent which, by God's will, hastened his destruction. Mordecai made prudent use of his privileged position 'in the gate', while Esther for her part had to resolve to do what was right and carry her resolve into action. God's outworking of His purpose did not eliminate human responsibility for moral decision and moral action, and yet if Esther had failed He would not have been thwarted, for relief and deliverance would have risen for the Jews 'from another quarter' (4:14). Even the fact that God is not mentioned in the book makes it all the more clear that He rules sovereignly all the time, and not only in response to human request. He turns human evil to fulfil His just purposes, but without Himself being tainted with the sin. On the other hand, when human wills are put at His disposal, then the blessing received is commensurate with the bounty of His sovereignty.

OUTLINE OF CONTENTS

COMMENTARY

1:1–22 THE PERSIAN KING DETHRONES HIS QUEEN

1:1–9 A display of royal splendour

1 *Ahasuerus* represents the Hebrew transliteration of the Persian name Khshayarsha, better known to us in the Greek form Xerxes. He succeeded his father Darius and reigned 486–465/4 BC. His correct identity is assured by the author's note on the extent of his empire, *from India*, i.e. the area drained by the Indus river, a territory added to Persia's domains by Darius, *to Ethiopia* or Cush, now the North Sudan, conquered by Cambyses, king of Persia 530–522. *One hundred and twenty-seven provinces.* Herodotus (iii. 89) says Darius 'set up twenty provincial governorships, called satrapies', but these were taxation areas, whereas the biblical writers use a different word, and refer to racial units. **2** The Hebrew verb suggests 'when King Ahasuerus came to take up his throne in Susa', but why in the third year of his reign? Presumably he had previously ruled from one of the other royal residences, at Ecbatana or Babylon. *Susa* is the Greek and Shushan the Hebrew form of the Persian Shushin or Shushim. This city, the ancient capital of Elam, had been rebuilt by Darius, and seems to have been Xerxes' winter residence. In summer it was unbearably hot. **3–5** We are to understand that the *banquet*, mentioned in v. 3, but referred to in more detail in v. 5, lasted *seven days*. It was the culmination of a six months' exhibition of the king's resources, to which delegates had flocked from all over the empire: officials, courtiers, the army of Persia and Media (RSV has inserted the word *chiefs*), nobles and provincial governors. The Persians are known to have held huge feasts, a whole city sometimes partaking at once. The purpose of the gathering may well have been to plan Xerxes' Greek campaign of 482 BC (Herodotus vii. 8). That done, all the assembled company present in Susa was feasted with wine for seven days in the spacious courtyard of the palace, overlooking the royal gardens. **6, 7** The writer skilfully conjures up the splendour of the scene, with its cool white and blue muslin curtains, marble pillars, gold and silver couches and multi-coloured mosaic floor. Each goblet was of unique design, and the supply of wine was unlimited, so wealthy was the king. **8** There appears to be a contradiction here, but it may be that the first two clauses should be combined as in the LXX to read, 'and the drinking was according to no prescribed law', i.e. the servants were to satisfy each individual guest's desire. **9** We know from the book itself that custom did not prevent wives from dining with their husbands. The large numbers probably made necessary a separate feast for the women guests.

1:10–22 Queen Vashti defies her husband

10 No hint is given as to the reason for Vashti's defiance, but it is of no importance for the story. **12** The king's dignity was publicly affronted by her refusal, and some strong measures to enforce his authority were certain to be taken. **13** Wise men were regularly in attendance on an oriental monarch to give advice, but *wise men who knew the times* specifies astrologers, and the second part of the verse lays stress on their ability in matters of justice. **14, 15** That seven were specially selected to serve in the immediate presence of the king is noted by Herodotus and referred to in Ezr. 7:14. It was their duty to advise the king in all matters. The names given are Persian. **16–18** Memucan voiced the opinion of the council of seven. Not only the king's honour but male supremacy generally was at stake, therefore strong sanctions must be applied to prevent anarchy. **19, 20** If Vashti were deposed by an irrevocable edict and replaced, such a danger would be averted. Though no extra-biblical reference to the irrevocability of the laws of the Medes and Persians has come to light, such a doctrine is in keeping with their pride, which would be injured by an admission that their laws could be improved. **21, 22** That the king should send out the decree in all the many languages of his vast empire is generally thought to be an exaggeration. Aramaic was widely understood and was used for state business from Egypt to India. There is, however, plenty of evidence that Xerxes delighted in the number of different peoples who composed his realm (*cf.* Introduction, 'Historicity', 2) and, with representatives of many of them in his court, translations could have been made. All the same there is something a little ludicrous about this decree that a husband was to take charge in his own household, for this was the rule in an oriental home; that his language was to be spoken in the home, would presumably apply in the case of a mixed marriage. The law was not even enforceable.

2:1–18 THE CHOICE OF A NEW QUEEN

1 *After these things* suggests a lapse of time, and since v. 16 tells us that it was the seventh year of Ahasuerus before Esther went into the king's presence, it is likely that the Greek war intervened before the king gave a thought to Vashti. **2–4** Lest he should reinstate her the courtiers suggested that he should choose a new queen from among the most beautiful girls of his realm. Little imagination is needed to appreciate the horror caused by the round-up of these girls, whose fate it was to be carried away from their homes to be secluded for life as the king's concubines. What a liability to be beautiful! **5–7** It is in this connection that we first meet Mordecai and his cousin Esther, who lived in Susa. *A Jew.* Though the word derived from 'Judah', it was used from the time of the Exile to designate any Israelite. The well-known names

415

Shimei (*cf.* 2 Sa. 16) and *Kish* (*cf.* 1 Sa. 9:1) could refer either to immediate ancestors of Mordecai or, more probably, to the famous Benjamites of the early monarchy, in which case the relative pronoun *who* in v. 6 must refer to Mordecai. Yet if he had been carried away captive in 597 BC it is not likely that he would be taking part in affairs in the year 480. This verse is often cited as an example of the writer's historical inaccuracy, but he may well have been using an elliptical expression, meaning, 'whose family was carried away . . .'. Mordecai showed practical piety in bringing up the orphan girl, but, living in the citadel, he would have had difficulty in hiding her from the king's officers who had to supply the harem. *Hadassah* is Esther's Hebrew name and means 'myrtle'. The name 'Esther' most probably derives from the Persian word for star, though some connect it with the Babylonian goddess Ishtar.

9 From the beginning Esther became a favourite with Hegai, the eunuch in charge of the harem; she accepted without question the beauty preparations and the food provided, unlike Daniel who protested against breaking the food laws. **10** To protest was impossible for her if she was to obey Mordecai's instruction, given most likely for her benefit, so that her chances were not prejudiced by her race. Some commentators, however, suggest that Mordecai was ambitious, and hoped for promotion through her. Still another view is that the writer inserted this note simply because the plot required it. **11** Mordecai could not enter the harem, but he had his own way of discovering each day that all was well with Esther. **12–14** Though these girls had every luxury, and could choose any adornment to enhance their beauty, they returned from the king's presence to the house of the concubines, mere chattels, awaiting the king's pleasure, if indeed he ever remembered them again. It is understandable that Mordecai should have wanted to make life as bearable as possible for his adopted daughter. **15–18** Esther made no extravagant demands when her turn came to meet the king during the month Tebeth (Dec/Jan) 479 BC. During the Exile the Jews adopted the Babylonian names for the months of the year. The king's delight in Esther was immediate. She was crowned queen, and the glad occasion was marked by a special feast, by the proclamation of an amnesty, and by the distribution of royal gifts. *Remission of taxes* is an interpretation. The Hebrew word means 'release' (AV), and, as well as remission of taxes, could imply a holiday (RSV mg.), a release of prisoners, or a release from military service.

2:19–23 THE KING'S LIFE IS SPARED

19 No fully satisfying explanation of the statement that *the virgins were gathered together the second time* has been put forward. If a queen had been found, why should further virgins be required? It seems reasonable to assume that girls from a distance might arrive late, and likely that a man such as Xerxes would not be satisfied without further concubines. The incident is mentioned to indicate when it was that the plot against the king was discovered. Mordecai evidently had ample opportunity as he went about his business *at the king's gate*, to know what was going on in the palace. **20** Though queen, Esther continued to obey Mordecai as if he were her own father. (Is there not an indirect reference to the fifth commandment here?) If Mordecai had been ambitious it would have been in his interests not to remain incognito but to allow Esther to seek promotion for her nearest relative. As it was, circumstances ultimately brought about the honour that he might have engineered for himself. **21–23** By some chance Mordecai became aware of a plot devised by two eunuchs of the royal bodyguard to put the king to death. It was as a result of such a plot that Xerxes finally lost his life, but on this earlier occasion Mordecai secretly passed the news to Esther, who reported it in Mordecai's name. Not only were the conspirators hanged, but the incident was written up in the *Book of the Chronicles*, the court diary, which was kept *in the presence of the king*.

3:1–15 HAMAN'S EDICT

1 *After these things* calls attention to another lapse of time. V. 7 mentions Xerxes' twelfth year, so Haman was promoted at some time between the seventh and twelfth years of his reign. *The Agagite* was understood by Josephus to mean that Haman was descended from the Agag of 1 Sa. 15. On this ground Josephus, and many other commentators, assumed that Haman was an Amalekite and therefore a traditional enemy of the Jews. In this case Mordecai was continuing the ancient enmity between the house of Kish and the Amalekites, and his victory would be seen as the outworking of the curse against them (*cf.* Dt. 25:17–19). Though this is possible the significance of the word 'Agagite' is by no means sure. Agag was not the name of an individual but the title of the Amalekite king; it seems hardly likely that a tribal name should derive from a title. Whatever his lineage Haman was promoted to the rank of grand vizier, maybe unexpectedly, and maybe from an unimportant position, for **2** particularly points out that the king had had to command all court officials to bow before him. Reluctance on the part of the courtiers to do so is implied. It is puzzling to know why Mordecai refused obeisance; Israelite subjects were expected to prostrate themselves before their king (*cf.*, *e.g.*, 2 Sa. 18:28) and before other leaders (*cf.* 2 Sa. 18:21). **4–6** The only explanation offered is that Mordecai claimed exemption on the ground that he was a Jew. Probably the inference is justified that Haman was demanding not mere allegiance but worship, and Mordecai would not break the first commandment. The LXX additions to the book (13:14) take this view by putting into the mouth of Mordecai a prayer in which he says that he would not bow down to any but the Lord. If fear of idolatry lay behind the refusal to bow down then no Jew would bow down, and Haman's decision to take vengeance on the whole people becomes understandable. Similar acts of revenge involving wholesale slaughter are recorded by Herodotus (i. 106; iii. 79). Jews in Judea had already experienced antagonism against them because they insisted on keeping themselves separate (*cf.* Ezr. 4; Ne. 4, 6). In Esther, however, anti-semitism proper makes its appearance with Haman's express intention of wiping out the Jewish race. It might well seem incredible that one man's injured pride should lead to such an irrational conclusion if it were not that history has produced an equally irrational attack on the Jews in the 20th century.

7 It was *in the first month* of the year that Passover commemorated the deliverance from Egypt; ironically in the same month Haman began to plot destruction. The Persians, like all Near Eastern people, were very superstitious (*cf.* Ezk. 21:18–23); Haman was no exception, hence the casting of lots to ascertain the most propitious time for carrying out his designs. *Day after day* . . . The probable meaning is that lots were cast first of all for the day of the month and then for the month of the year. *Pur*, a non-Hebrew word, has now been found in Assyrian texts with the sense of casting a lot (*cf.* Introduction, 'The Origin of Purim'). **8** Haman carefully avoided naming the Jews when he accused them to the king of having their own law, which was true, and of disregarding the law of the land, which was not true, except in the one detail that concerned his status. They had been taught to seek the peace of the city of their exile (*cf.* Je. 29:7) and had done so. This subtle blend of truth and error provided a plausible case for ridding the land of such a stubborn and potentially dangerous element in the population. **9** Financial interests added a further incentive. It is not clear where this huge sum of money (the equivalent of at least £3,000,000) was to come from. V. 13 implies that those who carry out the massacre will keep the plunder, and they would no doubt help themselves to a share of it; even so land belonging to those who suffered the death penalty normally became crown property in the Near East (*cf.* 1 Ki. 21:15). Haman would be expected to make some profit himself and still have funds to pay into the king's treasury. It is not impossible, however, that Haman was already very wealthy (*cf.* Herodotus i. 192 for an idea of the wealth of the Persian governor in Babylon) and could promise the money from his own capital. **10** Xerxes had not even the interest to enquire the name of the people who were to die, but was content to take a rest from responsibility, and leave the country's affairs in the hands of his grand vizier. Once in possession of the king's ring there was no limit to Haman's

power, for worked into the ring was the official seal, the ancient equivalent of a signature. With it he could pass any decree he liked in the name of the king. **11** Whatever Haman did with the people or the money the king would approve of it.

12, 13 Without delay the edict was drawn up, copied, translated, sealed and sent to all parts of the empire by means of the postal system inaugurated by Cyrus (Herodotus v. 14; viii. 98). The decree would reach even distant parts of the empire with months to spare before the thirteenth day of Adar. Those who treat the book as fiction regard this date as the author's delaying device; those who take the book as history see the outworking of Pr. 16:33. God had controlled the disposing of the lot, and superstitious Haman would not dare to disregard it. **15** The incident closes with a brilliant dramatic contrast: on the one hand the nonchalant king and courtier with their wine; on the other the people of the city, apprehensive at the publication of so arbitrary an edict.

4:1 – 5:14 AN ALLY AT COURT

1–3 Mordecai and Jews everywhere publicly displayed the traditional signs of mourning: they had no 'house of the Lord' to visit as Hezekiah had done in a time of national emergency (*cf.* 2 Ki. 19:1), but they would resort to prayer just the same, as they fasted and wailed and daubed themselves with ashes. **4, 5** Everyone except the unfortunate women closeted in the harem understood the mourning, but the queen had to find out its meaning through Hathach, the eunuch who attended her. **7** Mordecai, who could reveal not only his own experiences but the sum mentioned between Haman and the king, was well informed. **8** Hathach returned with a copy of the decree which he was to explain to Esther, perhaps because she could not read Persian, and with the challenge to her to use her influence with the king.

11 Court ceremonial protected the king against unwanted intruders, but this particular detail is unattested outside this book. Esther's concern for her own safety has been commented upon, but it is very human, and a mark of the genuineness of the story. As the queen of a polygamous and capricious monarch, who had not given a thought to her for a month past, she might receive even less sympathy than a stranger could expect. What reason had she to think that she would be able, simply by stating her case, to reverse a decree of favoured Haman? **13, 14** Mordecai's argument is brutal in its clarity. Death awaited her whether she approached the king or not, therefore she had nothing to lose. If she failed then help would come from somewhere else, for Mordecai was convinced that the Jewish nation would somehow be saved from extinction, but she could be the chosen instrument for this very crisis. God's name is not mentioned, but Esther is being encouraged to see that there was a divinely ordered pattern in her life, and that this was her moment of destiny. **16, 17** Though Esther accepted the challenge, her reply reveals her deep sense of inadequacy. The plea for support in a three-day fast indicates her dependence on divine help, for prayer would be the purpose of this emergency measure. *If I perish, I perish.* Esther made her resolve with great courage, but without any conviction that she would succeed. A way forward was evidently made clear to her during the days of fasting.

5:1 Esther took her courage in both hands and, wearing her regalia, approached the king as he sat in state in his audience chamber. For a representation from Susa of Darius seated on his throne, and holding his sceptre, see art. 'Darius', *NBD.* **2, 3** The golden sceptre extended to her indicated that she might approach, and the invitation could not have been more reassuring. **4, 5** Nevertheless Esther moved with caution. A private dinner party would prepare the way. **6–8** Even after that Esther's intuition told her that her strategic moment had not yet come. Though she cannot have foreseen it, her second invitation played an essential part in bringing about her opportunity. **9–12** Haman was overwhelmed with a sense of his own importance at being the only guest at the royal table. That this was to happen a second time was the climax of his boast to his circle of friends. **13, 14** The memory of Mordecai's defiance was the only barrier to his complete satisfaction; in this Haman is true to type, for it is the lesser men who exaggerate slights, while the great can afford to overlook them. The excessive height of the gallows, 83 ft or approximately the height of the city walls, need not be an exaggeration, especially as it was Haman's purpose to make a spectacle of Mordecai's downfall. Haman is confident that the king will pass the death sentence at his request.

6:1–14 AN UNEXPECTED DEVELOPMENT

While Jewish commentators see God at work in the events recorded in this chapter, most others judge that such a series of coincidences is more characteristic of fiction than of real life. The reader will decide in the light of other apparent coincidences, both in Scripture and in present-day experience, whether or not the events recorded are improbable.

1 In his sleeplessness the king ordered his servants to read to him from the royal diary, mentioned in 2:23. The Hebrew indicates that they kept on reading, evidently all through the night. **2, 3** Eventually they came to the record of Mordecai's service in saving the king's life. **4, 5** A reward was due, and the king, requiring some suitable suggestions, invited the early arrival at court to make them. **7–9** Haman, who was preoccupied with his own evil scheme, jumped to the conclusion that any special honour must be meant for him, and made the most

extravagant proposal he could think of. Everyone would think the king himself was coming, for all the outward trappings of royalty were to be used. The practice of setting crown-like headdresses on horses is attested by Assyrian reliefs. **10, 11** The king had no idea of the irony of the situation in which he was placing his favourite. He alone was ignorant of the feud between Mordecai and Haman, and of the fact that Haman's decree was directed against the Jews, and therefore included Mordecai; the mortification of Haman as he proclaimed his enemy to be the man whom the king delighted to honour, would not escape the people of Susa. **12** Mordecai was not given any permanent change of status, but returned to his usual place in the king's gate. Haman, however, returned home, utterly humiliated, as the act of covering his head indicates. **13** Those who had so recently encouraged him to take vengeance now sensed a change of fortune and superstitiously recalled that no-one ultimately prospered who plotted against the Jews. **14** Guests were usually fetched and escorted to oriental feasts. This time Haman arrived 'in haste' and was altogether at a disadvantage.

7:1–10 ESTHER'S REQUEST

1–3 Within 24 hours the whole situation had so changed that, when the king again invited Esther to state her petition, she was able boldly to make it, requesting first her own life and then that of her people. The Jew is still very aware of his personal involvement in the destiny of his people. Esther's request has been incorporated into two Jewish liturgies. **4** *We are sold* refers to Haman's bribe. They were being sold for annihilation and not merely for slavery; so much is clear, but the last clause is obscure. The word translated *affliction* elsewhere in the book always means 'enemy'. The AV is consistent in keeping this meaning here, and the sense of the AV is, 'although the enemy cannot compensate for all that the king will lose in tribute when they have been killed'. This is not satisfactory because it does not explain why Esther would have held her tongue, and this the context demands. The RSV is not satisfactory because it fails to keep the grammatical connection between the clauses, and does not make the sense any clearer. This is an ancient difficulty, for the early versions do not provide any help, and so far no satisfactory solution has been proposed. **5, 6** Not until Esther names Haman does the king link Esther's plea with Haman's plot. **7** The king shows a very usual reaction to stress in getting up and striding out of the room, and Haman takes advantage of the momentary absence of the king to plead for the queen's mercy. **8** He is still prostrate before the reclining queen, probably clasping her feet as a suppliant (*cf.* 2 Ki. 4:27), when the furious king returns, ready to put the worst possible interpretation on Haman's posture. *As the words left the mouth of the king.* The AV keeps the singular 'word' as in the Hebrew. This could be translated 'judgment' and imply that the king immediately pronounced his verdict, after which courtiers covered the criminal's face. **9** Harbona, one of the inner circle of seven in 1:10, added yet another offence to Haman's account when he pointed out the gallows which had been intended to end the life of Mordecai, the king's favourite. Many commentators suggest that Esther should have interceded for Haman, or at least corrected the king's false inference, but this is to underestimate the tension created by the king's fierce outburst, which would have precluded any interruption. **10** The author found satisfaction in this outworking of justice, which well illustrates Ps. 9:16b, 'The wicked are snared in the work of their own hands.'

8:1–17 A NEW GRAND VIZIER AND A NEW EDICT

1 In accordance with the law already referred to (see on 3:9), the property of Haman was confiscated by the king, who bestowed it upon Esther. She had by now disclosed to the king her relationship with Mordecai, and accordingly he became one of the privileged few with access to the king's presence. **2** Once promoted to be grand vizier by the gift of the royal signet ring, and to be manager of Esther's estate, he came into all the prestige and authority that Haman had known. **3** Though so much had been accomplished, Haman's edict was still in force, hence Esther's request that it should be annulled. **4** This time the king extends his golden sceptre to indicate that she should rise and stand before him. **5, 6** Her concern is for the Jews of the provinces, though all were still due to perish, including Mordecai and herself. **7** The king indicates that he is favourably inclined towards the Jews. **8** He cannot annul the previous edict which has gone out in his name, but a second can counteract it.

9 This second edict is accordingly drawn up and sent to all who received Haman's document and also, in Hebrew, to Jews of every province. **10** The RSV translates the difficult vocabulary of this verse better than the AV. The swiftest steeds will deliver the new edict. **11, 12** It is instructive to compare the new edict with that of 3:13; the exact treatment intended for the Jews is to be meted out to their enemies. Since the old edict remains in force the Jews can defend themselves only by anticipating the attack on the day appointed. **15–17** The appearance of Mordecai in his state robes and crown of office coincided with the publication of the pro-Jewish edict to produce a great ovation from the population of Susa; whereas Haman's decree had caused perplexity, that of Mordecai resulted in gladness, particularly for Jews, first in Susa, and then in every place as the news arrived. Such a providential outworking of events in favour of the Jews convinced many of the power of their God, and caused them to become proselytes.

9:1–32 THE ORIGIN AND OBSERVANCE OF PURIM

The purpose of the writer in relating these events is fulfilled in this chapter, which explains how matters turned out on the 13th of Adar.

1 The emphasis is on the amazing reversal of all that had been intended by the enemies of the Jews, for the animosity of one man had spread to his supporters everywhere. **2–5** The Jews made their attack on all their enemies with extraordinary success. The rulers, torn between two contradictory edicts, favoured the one published by the current régime, especially in view of Mordecai's popularity. **6–10** With such support the Jews were able to wipe out their enemies, including 500 in Susa, together with the ten sons of Haman, whose names are traditionally printed in perpendicular type in Hebrew texts, a device which draws attention to them, as though to gloat over them. The Jews' studious refusal to take any spoil, even though they had the right to do so (*cf.* 8:11) is carefully noted here and in vv. 15, 16. At least they had no mercenary motives. **11–15** The report on the day's events in Susa prompted the king to enquire whether the queen had any further petition to make. Though we have no means of knowing the exact situation, in the light of such facts as we have Esther was extremely vindictive in asking for a further day's slaughter in Susa. To respond to the grace of God by hatred to men was particularly despicable. The purpose of hanging the dead bodies of Haman's sons would be to let all Susa know their fate. **16–19** It is possible to translate the verbs of v. 16 by the pluperfect, and this makes better sense. The author wants to arrive at his main point, which is to explain that, whereas in the provinces the 14th day of Adar was a holiday, in Susa, owing to the two days of bloodshed, the holiday was celebrated on the 15th. Modern Jews hold their festal meal towards the evening of the 14th, just a month before Passover. The practice of exchanging gifts of food on days of rejoicing is mentioned again in Ne. 8:10, 12.

20–22 The providential turn of events in favour of the Jews was so remarkable that the occasion deserved to be commemorated by an annual celebration. By order of Mordecai, who first wrote some account of the deliverance to be remembered, both the 14th and 15th days of Adar were to be annual feast days, and an occasion for remembering the poor. **23–28** The Jews accepted the institution of the festival, agreeing that it should be perpetuated through every generation of Jews, and celebrated by Jews and proselytes in every part of the world. Vv. 24, 25 may be a quotation from Mordecai's letter, following from the second clause of v. 23. The story is much abbreviated, and there is an ambiguity at the beginning of v. 25, where the name 'Esther' has been inserted in the AV and RSV as the subject of the verb, because the Hebrew verb has the feminine ending. The RV translates, 'when *the matter* came before the king', and the LXX makes the verb refer to Haman, who had just been mentioned. It is strange that the author should refer to Esther without repeating her name, for it had not appeared in the text since v. 13, but to add 'Esther' does avoid emending the Hebrew. The particular detail emphasized in this summary is that Haman cast *Pur*; the word recurs in v. 26, with its Hebrew plural ending, *Purim*, the name by which the festival has always been known. **29–32** A second letter, issued by Esther and Mordecai together, was sent out to endorse the original edict. *Words of peace and truth* would be the greeting with which oriental letters began, and the purpose of this second message was to add the name of the queen to that of Mordecai, so strengthening the authority behind the decree. V. 31 mentions for the first time fasting in connection with Purim; when this was to be observed is not specified, but the 13th of Adar, Haman's 'propitious' day, would be the obvious choice. Jews still keep this day as Esther's fast before the Purim celebrations proper, which, besides the reading of the roll of Esther in its traditional chant, accompanied by the blessings and hymns, include the festive meal and jollifications. In v. 32 the RSV rightly interprets the Hebrew idiom, *it was recorded in writing*. No particular book is meant.

10:1-3 CONCLUSION

The author brings his work to a close with a brief historical note, in which he refers the reader to a source of further information; he may himself have been referring to this document when he began the chapter, intending to tell more about the reign of King Xerxes, but he contented himself with drawing attention to the story of Mordecai recorded there. The final note about Mordecai, commending his wholly good influence, is couched in thoroughly biblical terms. The prophet Zechariah says of Jerusalem's coming king, 'He shall command peace to the nations' (Zc. 9:10), and no ruler could do more than speak *peace to all his people*, even if there is a hint that Mordecai specially sought the welfare of the Jews.

J. G. BALDWIN

Job

INTRODUCTION

AUTHORSHIP

The author is unknown. Various suggestions have been made: Job, Elihu, Moses, Solomon, Isaiah, Hezekiah, Baruch the friend of Jeremiah, *etc*. None can be established. All that can be said with certainty is that he was a loyal Jew who refused, however, to be shackled by every detail of the popular creed, in particular its remorseless bracketing of suffering and sin.

DATE AND BACKGROUND

Uncertainty also shrouds the question of date. There are no direct references to historical events which might assist in the dating of the book.

A distinction has to be drawn between the age of the historical background to the book which we find in the prologue (chs. 1–2) and epilogue (42:7–16) and the rest of the book. The former is clearly pre-exilic. The atmosphere is patriarchal. Wealth is reckoned in cattle and Job appears as his own priest (1:5). There is a reference to Job in Ezekiel (14:14). The historical basis would be preserved by tradition from generation to generation, until it was incorporated into the book of Job with the addition of the poetic form in which we find the dialogue.

Some have maintained that the tradition was maintained orally; others have favoured Duhm's theory that prologue and epilogue are fragments of a popular book (*Volksbuch*) where the story of Job appeared. A. B. Davidson argues cogently that the reflective atmosphere of the book and the knowledge of distant lands in it exclude a date earlier than the age of Solomon. He maintains that probabilities favour the age of the captivity of Judah (597 BC). The suggested dates vary between 600 and 400 BC. The question of date is not really important. Oesterley and Robinson say with truth: 'There are few poems in all literature whose date and historical background are of less importance than they are in the book of Job.... It is a universal poem, and that is one of the features which give it its value and interest for us today.'

There are interesting points of contact with other books in Scripture. *Cf*. Jb. 3 with Je. 20:14–18 and Jb. 15:35 with Is. 59:4. There are striking similarities between the figure of Job and the Servant of the Lord in Isaiah. *Cf*. Is. 50:6; 53:3 with Jb. 16:10; 30:9ff. See also Ps. 8:4 (Jb. 7:17); 1 Cor. 3:19 (Jb. 5:13); Jas. 5:11.

TEXT AND LITERARY STYLE

The Hebrew text has given much difficulty to scholars. The authors of the original LXX found the text so difficult that almost a quarter of the book was missing. There are passages which defy translation as they stand in the early Hebrew text known as the Massoretic. Many unique words were used which led some to imagine that the book was originally written in Arabic or in Edomite and then translated into Hebrew. It is sounder to hold with W. A. Irwin that we are dealing with a Hebrew dialect different from that found usually in the OT.

In the opinion of William Neil the best translation of Job is that of James Moffatt. In spite of occasional arbitrariness, Moffatt worked with the sensible assumption that, whatever happened to the text in the course of the years, it originally made sense.

Job includes both poetry and prose. The prologue and epilogue are in prose, while the main part is made up of three cycles of dialogue in poetry.

Job has clear affinities with Hebrew wisdom literature but the genius of the book defies exact classification. It has a worthy place beside the great tragedies of history from Greek to modern times. There are many unforgettable passages.

CONTENTS AND VALUE

The setting of the story is 'the land of Uz', about whose precise location there is some uncertainty. The slight biblical evidence which we have points to the region east of the southern Lebanons.

Four friends of Job, Eliphaz, Bildad, Zophar and Elihu, represent all that orthodox theology could say about the significance of the calamities which had devastated Job's happiness and stability. With the possible exception of Elihu, their contribution was seriously restricted by an inexorable interpretation of suffering in terms of personal sinfulness. If they had merely set out to establish human solidarity in sinfulness, they would have obtained Job's immediate assent, for nowhere does he claim to be a perfect man: but when they first hinted, and then directly affirmed, that Job's suffering was the inevitable harvest of seeds of sin sown when the eye of God alone was upon him, Job vehemently and consistently denied the accuracy of their judgment.

The book of Job is a universal book because it speaks to a universal need—the agony of the human heart when wracked by 'the heart-ache and the thousand natural shocks that flesh is heir to'. The testimony of a woman dying of cancer, that the book of Job spoke to her need as no other book in the Bible, is sufficient evidence. Great Christians and great poets have added their voices to the testimony of great sufferers, in appreciation and admiration of the truths the book conveys, sometimes through the medium of the most magnificent poetry. Luther held that Job is 'magnificent and sublime as no other book of Scripture'; Tennyson spoke of it as 'the greatest poem of ancient or modern times'.

What, then, has the book to say to the universal need?

It is a striking reminder of the inadequacy of human horizons for a proper understanding of the problem of suffering. All the human figures in the drama speak in total ignorance of Satan's allegations against Job's piety, reported in the prologue, and of the resultant divine permission to prove his point, if he can. Against the background of the prologue Job's sufferings appear, not as damning evidence of the divine judgment upon him, as his friends had sought to establish, but as proof of the divine confidence in him. We must avoid the *naïveté* of using language which might seem to indicate that an omniscient God needed such a demonstration of His servant's integrity, to silence, as it were, some tiny doubt in His mind: but we are entitled to find here a suggestion of the truth that now we can only 'see in a mirror dimly'. Job and the others were trying to fit together the pieces of a puzzle without having all the pieces within their grasp. Consequently the book of Job is an eloquent commentary on the inadequacy of the human mind to reduce the complexity of the problem of suffering to some consistent pattern. It is a book where silent men accomplish more than speaking men. *Cf.* 2:13; 13:5.

But while the author would certainly have recommended humility in any contemplation of the fact of suffering, he would not have advocated despair. He believes in a God who has the answer to human need. The appearance of men to counsel Job leads to controversy, disillusionment and despair; the appearance of God leads to submission, faith and courage. The word of man is unable to penetrate the darkness of Job's mind; the Word of God brings abiding light. The God of the theophany does not answer any of the burning questions that are debated so hotly in the course of the book; but He answers the need of Job's heart. He does not explain any phase of the battle; but He makes Job more than conqueror in it. (See detailed note at the beginning of ch. 40.)

Like the other books of the OT Job is forward-looking to Christ. Questions are raised, great sobs of agony are heard, which Jesus alone can answer. The book takes its place in the testimony of the ages that there is a blank in the human heart which Jesus alone can fill.

OUTLINE OF CONTENTS

COMMENTARY

1:1 – 2:13 PROLOGUE

1:1–5 A good man in a sinning universe

1 His character appears in a remarkable light as *blameless and upright*. *Blameless* does not imply sinless perfection, which is never claimed for Job. Rather it encourages us to think of Job as a moral all-rounder, a man of balanced, full-orbed character. Spurgeon could have said of Job, as he said of Gladstone: 'We believe in no man's infallibility, but it is restful to be sure of one man's integrity.' His moral and spiritual stability moved in the setting of a secure universe. **2** The gift of children, **3** extensive material possessions and **4** domestic unity and rejoicing all contributed to his happiness. The words of Ps. 1:3 could be applied without qualification.

5 His moral maturity was explained by his profound reverence for God. The profundity of his spirituality is seen in the account of his domestic piety. Spiritually ambitious for himself, he was no less so for his family. His regular sacrifices provided against the bare possibility that his children had sinned against God. *In their hearts* reveals impressively that Job's spirituality did not skim on the surface; it was aware of the necessity of praying 'Create in me a clean heart, O God' (Ps. 51:10).

1:6–12 The sky begins to darken

6 We are introduced to a dramatic heavenly council attended by *the sons of God*, *i.e.* the angels, including Satan. We are not to look for any 'full-dress' doctrine of Satan as depicted in orthodox theology. He does not appear as a fallen angel but has regular access to heaven (1:6; 2:1). The name *Satan* is preceded by the definite article; *cf.* Moff. 'the Adversary'. Professor N. H. Snaith summarizes his role by saying: 'He is God's Inspector-of-man on earth and man's adversary in heaven.' He is an agent of God whose duty is to give the closest attention to human virtue and vice. He appears as the supreme cynic of the heavenly court. **8** God's affectionate praise of His servant (*cf.* Ps. 149:4) calls forth the ugly question, **9** *Does Job fear God for nought?* **10** The material possessions hedging in his life, according to Satan, are a sufficient explanation of his piety. **11** Remove the hedge, and the piety will disappear. The charge is that material prosperity is not an accretion to Job's faith but the root cause. The removal of the root would mean the withering of the bloom.

12 The challenge is accepted by God, but the theatre of investigation must not extend beyond Job's possessions to his person. The stage is set for the drama of which the book of Job is the discussion.

1:13–22 The storm breaks

Four staggering blows fill Job's world with pain. **15** The Arabs (Moff., for *Sabeans*), **16** the lightning, **17** the Chaldeans and **18, 19** a whirlwind sweeping over the desert deprive him of flocks and servants and, most agonizing of all, of his family. But with all the waters of affliction going over him he could still say in the words of Bunyan's Hopeful in the river of death: 'I feel the bottom and it is good.' So the lie was given to the adversary's insinuation. The loss of possessions had not entailed the loss of faith. **20** Grief might change his appearance; it could not cheat him of the consolations of faith. He faced affliction in the attitude of the worshipper. **21** In that attitude he found strength to give us one of the most beautiful expressions of submission to the will of God in the fragrant story of faith. In the darkest hour of his life he could bless God. *Naked I came from my mother's womb*. The general idea has a parallel in 1 Tim. 6:7. Just as we bring no material adornment with us into the world, so we cannot take anything with us when we leave the world. The precise meaning is more difficult. Perhaps *mother's womb* is a reference to the womb of Mother Earth, an interpretation followed by Ewald and others. *Cf.* Gn. 3:19. **22** *Or charge God with wrong. Wrong* conveys the idea of 'tastelessness, insipidity, and so, want of moral discernment' (Strahan). *Cf.* our colloquial condemnation of an action as 'in bad taste'.

2:1–8 The storm sweeps on

A second heavenly council ushers in an extension in the adversary's theatre of investigation. **3** He will not admit that he has been mistaken about Job's *integrity*. The Lord claims that Job has come through the furnace of affliction as pure gold. **4, 5** The adversary complains that the trial has not been radical enough. He accuses Job of callousness. So far calamity has affected only the lives of others. His own skin has been untouched. Let his own person be involved and there will be no more 'holding fast his integrity'. *Skin for skin!* was probably a common proverb. Skins were in common use for business transactions. The charge is that Job was willing to give up the skins of others—cattle, servants and children—provided that his own skin was safe. **6** The adversary is given an opportunity to prove his point. Job's person is no longer shielded. **7** The identification of diseases bearing ancient names is by no means a simple matter. The *sores* may indicate a painful form of leprosy. All that can be said with certainty is that Job suffered from a distressing skin eruption. Nothing more aggravating and depressing can be imagined. **8** *The ashes* is a reference to the local refuse-heap outside the walls of the town. There the dung and other rubbish was burnt at regular intervals. It was the happy hunting-ground for dogs on the prowl for carcases which often were tossed there, and for the local urchins who were always eager to root about among things unwanted by others. There, in this place of discarded things, sat the man who once had been 'the greatest of all the people of the east' (1:3).

2:9–13 Reactions to the storm

2:9, 10 Job's wife. 9 The loss of family, of possessions, and now last of all, her husband's health, leaves her faith in ruins. She recommends that Job should *curse God*, even if death is the outcome of his blasphemy. Death is preferable

to his present hapless lot. **10** Job sees another support for his faith taken from him. He can no longer count on her spiritual support in the stern battle his faith is fighting. Resolutely he sets aside her suggestion. It is worthy only of impious (so Moff., RV mg., for *foolish*) folk. He bows before the sovereign hand of God whether it bestows or takes away, whether it caresses or strikes. He could have prayed 'Thy will be done' with a depth of meaning that it does not always possess in so-called Christian prayer.

2:11–13 Job's friends. Job's friends have not always received the credit due to them. A 'Job's comforter' has come to be a very doubtful distinction. **11** In fairness to these men let us remember that when a multitude of fair-weather friends mysteriously disappeared, their friendship staunchly faced the storm. They had once rejoiced with a rejoicing Job; they were no less ready to weep with a weeping Job. **12** The sight of Job's disfigured countenance filled them with profound anguish. **13** For *seven days* they sat in silent sympathy with the sufferer—surely clear evidence of the sterling worth of their friendship. The ministry of silence helped Job much more than the ministry of words (*cf.* 13:5). There is a warning here for those who seek to comfort sorrowing hearts.

3:1 – 14:22 FIRST CYCLE OF SPEECHES

3:1–26 Wretched life! Blessed death!

We hear a cry of anguish from a soul quivering with agony. In this and in other speeches we must not submit every statement to microscopic examination, assuming that every word has been thoroughly weighed before utterance and is an exact expression of Job's deepest thoughts. Job was soon to complain that his friends were training their verbal armoury upon the speeches of a desperate man, which he himself readily acknowledged were as wind (*cf.* 6:26). As this hurricane sweeps before us, we must marvel, not at every twist it takes, but at the agony of spirit behind it.

3:1–12 Job curses his birthday. 4 *May God above not seek it.* God is thought of as summoning forth the successive days. *Cf.* Is. 40:26, where He summons the stars. May the day which summoned Job to wretchedness never be called forth again! **5** *Let the blackness of the day terrify it.* The reference is to eclipses. **6** *Let it not rejoice among the days of the year.* May it be blotted out from the calendar, from the joyful company of the days! **7** A proud joyful voice had once welcomed his coming into the world (*cf.* Jn. 16:21). May such a voice never be heard again on that night! **8** *Let those curse it who curse the day*, i.e. the sorcerers, thought of as having the power to make a day unlucky. *Leviathan.* Some see here a reference to the dragon of popular mythology who, by twisting himself round the sun, could cause eclipses; others, to the monster whom God vanquished at creation. In ch. 41 Leviathan is the crocodile.

3:13–26 Life's fitful fever. 13 The troubles of life are contrasted with the placid sleep of death. The more Job dwells on the fact of death the more he finds himself fascinated by it. He thinks of his company in the dormitory of death: **14, 15** distinguished men; **16** still-born children; **17** *the wicked* whose passions no longer shake themselves (*cf.* Is. 57:20) or other people; *the weary* who at last have found a place of rest; **18** slaves who no longer hear the taskmaster's strident shout; **19** *the small and the great*, once severed by the world's standards, now lying side by side.

St. Francis of Assisi could address death as 'Thou, most kind and gentle death'. Job could have used exactly the same language but for different reasons. For St. Francis, death was a creature of his God and King whom he could summon to praise the Creator like other creatures—a signpost lit with the radiance of immortality pointing to a heavenly home where a Father's love had planned many glad surprises. For Job, it was an escape from life, an anaesthetic which would make his soul forget the 'slings and arrows of outrageous fortune'. **20** The *light* of life appears as a doubtful privilege. It only shows up the hapless lot of the miserable and the embittered. **21** In Job we have a man in whose eyes death is no longer the prince of terrors to be shunned, but a prize to be sought with the avidity of a man digging for treasure. **23** The *light* can only mock the man who has lost the way in life, who has the feeling that *God has hedged* him in at every turn. Strahan comments pertinently: 'Light without liberty is a poor boon.' The most brilliant light can only mock a man in a dungeon, or a bird in a cage. In sharp contrast to this mood, see Ps. 118:5. **24** *For my sighing comes as my bread.* Moff. probably has the sense: 'Sighs are my daily bread.'

4:1 – 5:27 Eliphaz speaks

4:1–11 He offers advice. Job has broken the silence. Eliphaz now offers words of help, of healing and of warning. **2** He hopes that by so doing he will not offend his friend; but he is in the grip of the inner constraint of truth. His duty to his friend, to his own convictions, and to his God forces him to speak. **3–5** His first appeal to Job is to one who has been a distinguished member of the 'ministry of encouragement' in the past. He had been quick to help all who were treading the *via dolorosa*. Now that he was on that way himself, let him apply the comfort he had offered to others. **6** Let him turn to the consolations of religion and to the testimony of a clear conscience.

7–11 The lesson of Job's fine record of service to those in need has been underlined. Eliphaz now gives expression to the thoughts set in motion by Job's cry of anguish. Job had revealed a passionate longing for death. Let him remember that sudden, unnatural death is the portion, not of the righteous, but of the wicked. *Cf.* 5:26.

4:12 – 5:7 Job's criticisms answered. Eliphaz replies to Job's implied criticism of God's treatment of him. How can frail, imperfect mortal man venture to raise critical eyes to his Maker? **12–16** He bolsters his argument by impressively narrating a vision which he had once experienced. **17** The mysterious voice had clearly demonstrated the absurdity of mortal man expecting to be *righteous before God.* **18** When complete trustworthiness and service without error cannot be claimed by God's heavenly servants, **19** how dare any man, with his fleeting life, with his only partially successful quest after wisdom, imply by his demeanour that he has a right to make that claim? *Before the moth* means 'sooner than the moth' or 'like the moth' (LXX, RV mg.). **21** *Tent-cord.* Their death is compared to the collapse of a tent by plucking up the tent-cord.

5:1 Job's appeal against God can find no support among the angels. The case of morally and spiritually senseless people who are fretful under God's chastening rod (*cf.* 5:17) ought to be a solemn warning against making any such appeal. **2** *Jealousy.* 'Indignation' (RV mg.) makes excellent sense. **3** Such impatience merely paves the way for further calamities, a truth Eliphaz deduces from his observations of life. **4** *The gate* of the town was the place where eastern justice was administered. **5** *Out of the thorns* may refer to the raids of nomads bursting through the thorn hedges about the fields. **6, 7** Trouble does not germinate itself, says Eliphaz; it springs from man's evil heart, as inevitably as sparks fly up from a fire.

5:8–27 Job urged to appeal to God. 8–16 Eliphaz extols the power, kindness and justice of God. **17** Accept, he says, *the chastening* of such a God, sent presumably to correct some flaw in the character, and all will yet be well. **18** The Almighty hurts to heal. Bear the hurt, and the healing will extend to every conceivable trouble; **19–27** it will ensure prosperity for field, flock and home alike, a prosperity for ripe old age to enjoy. A man in harmony with God is in harmony with nature too. **19** *Six . . . seven.* The numerals have the force of 'in every conceivable case'.

There is much to admire in Eliphaz. First, he is the most sympathetic of Job's friends. He does not probe Job's soul with clumsy fingers. His wounds are not the wounds of a foe, but the faithful wounds of a friend. Second, he comes, not as a man puffed up with human philosophy, but as a man with a real experience of God. He feels God has spoken to him about suffering; that is why he must speak to Job. His words again and again have a ring about them which we find echoed in other scriptures. With 5:13 *cf.* 1 Cor. 3:19 (the only clear case of quotation of the book of Job in the NT). With 5:17 *cf.* Ps. 94:12; Pr. 3:11; Heb. 12:5, 6.

But while Eliphaz is the most sympathetic of Job's physicians, he is still a physician who fails. There is no acknowledgment of the extraordinary submission to God Job has already shown (*e.g.*, in 1:21 and 2:10). There is no clear word of sympathy in all his words. Strahan refers to him as 'a theologian chilled by his creed'. He resembles a commander urging soldiers who have been exhausted by struggling against fearful odds to still more resolute endeavour, without a word in praise of what has already been accomplished.

Again, his ready assumption that Job's suffering must be the reaping of his own sinfulness ill-equipped him to be a true comforter. He was not wrong to claim that he had a divine explanation of the facts of human suffering. Experience abundantly testifies that in countless ways man brings trouble upon himself by his sinfulness. Eliphaz was a mouthpiece of divine revelation there; but when he went on to assume that he had a divine commentary upon all the facts of human suffering and that he had correctly diagnosed Job's case, it was the word of man, not the Word of God. He has not stood where we have stood, witnessing the clash between God and the accuser in the heavenly places, where issues of which Job and Eliphaz are ignorant are being decided. He has not learnt the salutary humility of Paul's confession of the limitations of human knowledge: 'now we see in a mirror dimly'. How often a man must find a place for that confession in his religious thinking, and not least of all with regard to the problem of suffering!

6:1 – 7:21 Job answers Eliphaz

6:1–13 A cry for fair play. Eliphaz obviously views with disapproval Job's impatience under suffering, and the latter accuses him of looking only at one side of the balance. **2, 3** Eliphaz censures the weight of the impatience: but if only he were to look at the affliction side, he would find the load there immeasurably heavier. **4, 5** Job feels like a man into whose body the almighty Archer is sending poisoned arrows. He cannot help their poison going right through him; he cannot help wild, delirious words. Is due allowance being made for that? There is reason for his cry of agony. His is not a case of 'much ado about nothing'. **6, 7** He has lost his taste for life, which he compares to 'insipid food and saltless' (Moff.). *The slime of the purslane.* *Cf.* AV, RV, Moff. 'the white of an egg'. **8–10** For death, on the other hand, he has an eager taste. The prospect of death is his only comfort. The fearlessness of Job's attitude to death is emphasized. His mind runs to meet the thought of death, even death through a gateway of unsparing pain. He has nothing to fear from death, nor from the God whose commands he has never denied. **11–13** Life has made too heavy demands upon his strength and patience. He can fight no further battles for he is no superman, with the strength of stones and with flesh of brass. Natural resources are exhausted.

6:14–30 A rebuke to his friends. A man who is sinking under affliction ought to be able to count on the sympathy of his friends. **14** It is impossible to be sure of the meaning of this verse. *Cf.* AV 'To him that is afflicted pity should be shewed from his friend; but he forsaketh the fear of the Almighty'; RV '. . . . even to him that forsaketh the fear of the Almighty'; Moff. 'Friends should be kind to a despairing man, or he will give up faith in the Almighty'. Job has been denied human pity. **15, 16** In a striking figure he compares his friends to brooks. We have a picture of them, bound by snow and ice in the cold weather and thawing with the return of warmer weather, until at length they dry up altogether. **18–20** We are next given a glimpse of Arabian caravans hurrying towards the brooks, only to be disappointed. They swing away into the desert to their doom. **21** A reason for the friends becoming broken cisterns whose waters have failed is suggested: the fear roused by a contemplation of Job's calamities has chilled their sympathy. They are afraid that to take Job's side would mean standing on the other side from the God who has it within His power to bring similar trials upon them.

To the end of the chapter there is a contrast between what Job expected from his friends and what he actually received from them. **22–24** He had not requested aid, but he had hoped for genuine sympathy and for forthright dealing. Instead, there had been insinuations against his integrity. **25–27** His friends had made the mistake of dealing with the wild, whirling speeches of a desperate man as if every word was cool and calculated. **28** He is ready to stand by his integrity, to look the whole world in the face with clear conscience and steady eye. **29** *Turn* has the sense 'change your ground; look for some other interpretation of my suffering'. **30** Job asks, 'Is my moral taste perverted? Cannot I differentiate between good and evil?'

7:1–10 The hardness and brevity of human life. In a series of striking figures Job pictures life as a hard struggle. **1, 2** It is like a distasteful period of service laid upon a hired servant, whose only consolations are the cool shadows of the evening, in which the day's work is forgotten, and the wages which he receives at the end of the day. **3, 4** Job can think of no sweeter rest, and no more valuable wages, than death. Is it any wonder when life holds sleepless nights and loathsome disease? **5** *Worms* means that his sores breed maggots. **6–10** He proceeds to dwell on the brevity of life. Life is a swiftly moving shuttle; wind; an insubstantial, fading cloud, moving towards the grave—the realm from which there is no return to familiar scenes.

7:11–21 A remonstrance with God. 11 Impelled by the weight of human misery and by his own suffering, he utters a bitter complaint. **12** The divine treatment of him might almost seem to imply that he was like the sea, to be kept under restraint, or a cruel monster endangering the order of the universe. **13–16** What accounts for this unremitting superintendence of him, which has scared the wits out of him and made him detest life? **15** *My bones*. Job has been reduced to a skeleton. **17, 18** The atmosphere is strikingly different from that of Ps. 8:4, where the question arresting the attention is, 'How can a majestic, powerful God stoop so low that He notices and plans for insignificant man?' Here the question is rather, 'If God is so great, why can't He leave man alone?' **19** *Till I swallow down my spittle* is an expression still in use among the Arabs, meaning 'for a single moment'. **20** *Watcher of men*. Moff. 'thou Spy upon mankind'. Why must this great God be so restlessly on the prowl? Here Job seems to think of God as an irate inspector, whose visits are always followed by unhappiness, for He is certain to find fault. What can the little sin of a little man mean to the mighty God? Can He not find it in His heart to forgive? **21** Soon a divine approach in forgiveness will be too late, for the sleep of death will have overtaken him. In these verses we find a mistaken view of sin. It argues: 'I don't see that my sin can make very much difference to God. It is not asking much of a mighty God to forgive the little sins of little men.' There is a thoroughly modern ring about such words. Compare the puzzled question of a dying farmer following upon the vicar's call to him to repent: 'What harm have I ever done Him?' He would have united with Job in wondering how his sin could disturb Almighty God. Gladstone was on safer ground when he held that the tiniest sin that settled on his soul gave God as much pain as the speck of grit blown into his own eye. If Job could have listened to Calvary's commentary upon sin that is 'sinful beyond measure' (Rom. 7:13) his language would have been different. It is because God is so great, not in spite of it, that He has taken such drastically sacrificial action to deal with what people term so lightly the 'little sins of little men'.

8:1–22 Bildad speaks

8:1–7 A rebuke. This friend calls upon Job to bow before traditional wisdom. **2** First he rebukes Job for his 'wild and whirling words' (Moff.) which have involved a criticism of God's dealings with him and with humanity as a whole. **3** Bildad stands forth as the champion of the justice of God. **4** Goodness and evil alike reap the harvest they have sown. Job's children had sown evil; God sent them an evil harvest. **5** Let Job sow goodness; let him adopt the attitude of a humble suppliant; **6** let him be *pure and upright*, **7** and the harvest he will reap will defy comparison with anything in his past experience.

8:8–19 Tradition. 8–10 Listen to the voice of the past which has the last word to speak about the issues we are discussing. Behind this section is the assumption that 'they are short-lived ignorant moderns, not wise and happy antediluvians' (Strahan). Pearl after pearl of that ancient wisdom is offered for Job's examination and instruction. The perils of the ungodly man appear in striking figures. Bildad does not expressly say 'Thou art the man'; but he is certainly keeping

his mind open to the possibility of unrighteousness in Job. **11, 12** The picture is of the waters of the river receding from the papyrus and the reed-grass growing on the fringes. The healthy vegetation then withers and dies, sooner than any herb. **13** The hope of the ungodly man does not save him (*cf.* Rom. 8:24); it damns him, for his hope is not in God but in himself. **14** It is as insubstantial as a spider's web. **15** The household which he has always looked upon as solid and lasting will suddenly crumble beneath him. **16–18** He is a plant with the evidences of healthy life upon it, which suffers sudden destruction. The picture in v. 17 is of a plant with its roots snaking their way through the stones of the stone heap, going deep down into the earth. **19** *The joy of his way* is difficult. If this reading is followed, Bildad must either be speaking ironically or he is describing what has been a joyous way of life. The LXX reads 'This is the end of the godless' (*cf.* Moff. 'So ends a godless man').

8:20–22 Destiny. Is Job a man of integrity? If so, eventually he must find himself in a world of rejoicing. Calamity rounds off the life of the ungodly alone. We find two grave deficiencies in Bildad which make his words worse than useless from Job's standpoint. First, he was tragically lacking in the sympathy for which Job craved. His assumption that the sudden death of Job's family was the divine punishment for their sinfulness was a sword thrust into an agonized heart. Job knew that it was untrue. In the second place, he was totally hidebound by tradition. He was so busily engaged in looking into the past that he quite failed to realize that Job was feeling out for a richer and more intelligent experience of God than anything he himself had known. He assumed that the whole of the divine Word had been spoken; he would have been hostile to the thought that a clearer, more dynamic word was yet to be spoken through prophets, saints and apostles, and uniquely through One who was the Word come down from heaven.

9:1 – 10:22 Job answers Bildad

9:1–16 How can a man be just before God? The theme of the whole of this chapter is the impossibility of obtaining justice from God. Job does not attempt a detailed answer. He fastens rather on a general principle accepted by all the friends and expounded by Eliphaz in 4:17—the impossibility of mortal man appearing just before God. **2** Job accepts the truth of the principle, but goes on to deny that there can be a grain of comfort in it. **3** What is the point in attempting to establish one's innocence before a God of infinite wisdom, who can ask a thousand unanswerable questions? **4–10** He is a God of infinite power too, shaking heaven and earth, heaping up marvels beyond human ken. Plead one's case before such a God? How futile! **11** When God transfers His attention from nature to man, His power sweeps on just as arbitrarily.

12 When He pounces on His prey who can challenge His action? **13, 14** When even the stoutest rebels at length have to capitulate before the naked power of God, how can he, Job, or anyone else, hope to stem its onward rush by mere words, no matter how carefully marshalled they may be? The *helpers of Rahab*. The reference may be to a current myth which spoke of the overthrow of an assault on heaven made by the sea monster Rahab and her confederates. **15** Even stainless innocence, Job goes on, would be struck dumb before Him, and would only break the menacing silence at length to blurt out a plea for pity. **16** Even if God had answered Job's call that God and he should meet in some judgment-court, he is sceptical about receiving a fair hearing.

9:17–24 A complaint against God. A terrible picture of God follows: **17** a God storming and striking without cause; **18** not giving him a moment's breathing-space; **19** relying not on justice but on might; **22** destroying good and evil men indiscriminately; **23** laughing at the tortures of the innocent; **24** allowing the earth to be the happy hunting-ground of the wicked, covering the faces of judges so that they do not see aright. How can he expect a fair hearing from such a God? **20, 21** Job is tortured by the fear that he would be so upset and bewildered that he would confess a guilt that did not belong to him in reality. *I am blameless.* Squarely he takes his stand on his integrity. He cannot relinquish that even if he dies for it. Connect this with **22** *It is all one.* Probably the sense is: 'It is all one whether I live or die. Life has become obnoxious.'

9:25–35 The brevity of life. **25, 26** Job turns from the wounds of the world to consider his own sorrows and the fleeting nature of life. **27** When more optimistic feelings struggle towards the surface, **28, 29** they are driven down again by the knowledge that God is determined to hold him guilty. He may as well give up the unequal struggle. **30, 31** Job is up against a God who intends to duck in filth a man genuinely craving for purity of soul. **32, 33** 'Oh that I were dealing with man and not God!' cries Job; 'for then I would be on ground where I could feel at home. But it is not so, nor is there an umpire to ensure fair play for God and me'. **34, 35** The chapter closes with Job turning sadly from what might have been to the stern reality he knows— the terrifying divine rod smiting him. If only God would take away, he would be able to speak out fearlessly in affirmation of his innocence, for he has a clear conscience.

In the remarkable yearning for the God of the mysterious, terrifying beyond to reveal Himself in the fabric of understandable human experience, one is reminded forcibly of the words of Browning's *Saul*: ''Tis my flesh that I seek in the Godhead.' In this cry for an umpire between God and man we see a prophetic reaching out for the 'one mediator between God and men, the man Christ Jesus' (1 Tim. 2:5). There was no finally satisfactory answer to Job short of the incarnation. The passage is strongly forward-looking to Bethlehem.

10:1–7 An appeal to God. 1, 2 With no umpire to help him, Job is forced to appeal directly to God, in an attempt to solve the mystery of the divine antagonism to him. Every suggestion his distraught imagination can concoct is now expressed, no matter how extraordinary. **3** Is the divine oppression of him a paying concern? **4** Can it be explained by divine short-sightedness, which means that God cannot see clearly what He is doing in His dealings with men? **5, 6** Or can it be that, like man, God knows that His span of life is limited? Therefore He must punish what He suspects to be sinfulness before there has been time to examine the case thoroughly. **7** Even while expressing these suggestions Job knows their emptiness. He cannot get past the conviction that God must know him to be a man of integrity.

10:8–22 The depths of despair. 8, 9 There follows an appeal to the divine Potter who has lavished such painstaking care upon His handiwork. **10–12** Both in the antenatal period and the years which followed Job can see many signal evidences of divine preservation. What was the goal before the divine mind in such dealings with him? **13ff.** In the answer which follows we see Job touching depths of doubt and despair blacker than anything found elsewhere in the book. The Potter has concentrated on making the vessel especially beautiful so that, in the hour when He decides to mar it, the contrast between past and present may be all the more striking. 'All the while this was thy dark design!' (Moff.). **14** Job feels that he is dealing with a God who is swift to note even trivial sins. **15** His imagination quails at the prospect of what would happen if he were really guilty. Righteousness makes no difference. He still has to hang his head, cowed before a God **16** who, like a fierce lion, delights in hunting him with relentless assiduity. **17** *Fresh hosts.* The thought is that host after host of the afflictions which are God's witnesses against his integrity lurk about him. **18–22** There are two pathetic cries in these verses: 'Would that my one and only cradle had been the grave!' and 'Cannot I have a brief breathing-space before the perpetual night of death?'

11:1–20 Zophar speaks

11:1–6 Job is rebuked. 1, 2 Zophar bluntly reproves Job for his prodigality in empty words. **3** He cannot expect men who know better to stand by in silence. **4** Job's words have implied a claim to straight thinking and straight living. **5, 6** If only God would speak, he would find both claims utterly shattered. His puny human wisdom would wilt before the vast sweep of the divine wisdom; and he would discover that, in actual fact, God was recompensing his sinfulness very lightly.

11:7–12 God's wisdom magnified. 7–9 The meaning of this powerful and memorable passage is well brought out in Moffatt: 'Can you discover the deep things of God? can you reach the Almighty's range of wisdom? Higher it is than heaven—how can you match it? deeper than death—how can you measure it? Its scope is vaster than the earth, and wider than the sea.' **10, 11** It is this wisdom which passes its verdict upon vain man, and such a verdict must be infallible. **12** Let Job submit to the breaking-in process which the divine wisdom wants to carry through, and there is hope that genuine understanding will be the final outcome, even though, like other men, he has the stubborn stupidity of *a wild ass's colt*. The meaning is that Zophar sees no more hope for stupid people than for a wild ass to be born human. Stupidity can be lost only in the vast sea of divine revelation.

11:13–20 A call to repentance. 13, 14 Zophar now calls on Job to put away all known sin and portrays the glittering rewards of repentance. **15** One result will be the ability to look the world in the face fearlessly and unashamedly. *Cf.* 10:15. **16, 17** It will lead also to forgetfulness of the misery of the past, whose darkness will be swallowed up in the brilliant light of the present; **18, 19** and to security and hope (*cf.* 7:6). **20** But if there is no repentance, the only hope left for Job will be to breathe his last.

Zophar is the narrow dogmatist *par excellence.* We find in him two flaws characteristic of his type. In the first place he is too confident in his religious standpoint. We find no traces of a humble 'I do not know'. He is right in maintaining that he is in touch with truth (see, *e.g.,* 11:7–11, which speaks of the peerless, transcendent wisdom of God). He is wrong in thinking that he has all the truth. He understands not a whit more than Job about the reason for Job's sufferings. Second, he is lacking in humility. He is swift to call Job to go down on his knees at the recollection of the limitations of human knowledge. Yet, as he talks down to Job, he forgets that the mind scrutinizing his sufferings is limited too. Unknown to himself, his deductions from Job's misery have a far greater stamp of the wild ass's colt (11:12) on them than the most agonized cries of the sufferer.

12:1 – 14:22 Job answers his friends

12:1–12 He resents their assumed omniscience. Up to the present Job has given only scant attention to the sentiments of his friends. **2–4** Now he brings to bear his powers of sarcasm and logic upon their facile assumption that they have a right to talk down to him. **5** How easy for them to mouth their glib commonplaces in their still secure and comfortable world! **6** If he had been a successful robber and not a religious man, his position perhaps would have commanded greater respect. *Their god in their hand.* The only god these robbers worship is their own power, as symbolized by the sword in their strong hand. **7–9** Job now states his familiarity with everything that they have said about the wisdom and power of God. Even the beasts of the field are not

ignorant of that. The voice of nature is one and undivided in that respect. **10** He is also aware that all life is in the hand of God. The question perturbing his mind, which his friends will not face, concerns the use to which God puts His power. What kind of character controls the operation of the power? **11** He is not prepared to swallow down, unexamined and undigested, the opinions of others, no matter how ancient, if they do not commend themselves to his moral and spiritual palate. **12** Moffatt is probably right in translating: 'Wisdom, you argue, lies with aged men . . . ?' *Cf.* 8:8–10.

12:13–25 A description of divine power. Job pictures God's power sweeping on indiscriminately and irresistibly, devastating the earth in natural calamities, shattering the influence of the wise, the mighty, the respected, bringing them to power only in order to grind them down again, saddling the people with leaders whose idea of the direction they are taking is no clearer than that of one groping in the dark, or of an intoxicated man. We look in vain for any principle integrating the divine actions which he describes, and feel that we are meant to conclude that for Job in this hour there was none. **18** *The bonds of kings* are the bonds by which they control the people. **22** The exact force of this verse is elusive. Perhaps there is a reference to God's exact knowledge of the most deeply concealed secrets of the heart. *Cf.* Is. 29:15.

13:1–12 He rejects their counsel. Again Job turns from his friends, scathingly and impatiently. They whitewash with lies and are futile physicians of the soul, seeking to justify the ways of God by maxims of ashes and defences of clay. He accuses them of being, not genuine allies of God, but cringing sycophants, using twisted arguments to bolster a cause they support out of a wholesome respect for their own skin. We may compare them with a man supporting the cause of a bully, not because he is interested in the rights and wrongs of the cause, but because he is afraid of the man's strong right arm. The friends have made much of God's omniscient gaze upon Job. Are they remembering that the very same gaze is upon the motives for their championship of God? How will they fare when they stand at the bar of the majesty and the omniscience of God? **9–11** A striking hint is given that sincere opposition to God may fare better than insincere support of Him.

13:13–28 He appeals to God. 13 Conscious that further appeals to his friends are useless, Job turns to God. **14–18** He is aware that such an appeal is a risky affair, but he cannot prevent himself defending his case. **19** Recklessly he calls for a successful challenger of his innocence. If such a person could be found, he would not have one further word to say.

15 In the understanding of the section the interpretation of this verse is both crucial and difficult. RSV *I have no hope* wrecks many a good sermon following AV 'Though he slay me, yet will I trust in him'! This RSV rendering adopts an alternative Hebrew reading *lō'* (not) for *lô* (for him), which gives the translation '. . . I will not wait' or 'I have no hope'. Similarly RV mg. reads 'Behold, he will slay me; I wait for him' (*i.e.* to strike). W. A. Irwin argues against the excision of hope from v. 15 and recommends the translation, 'Though he may slay me, I will not delay; but I will argue my ways to his face.' The following points must be remembered in support of this position: *a.* Blank hopelessness does not seem to fit in with v. 16, with its assertion that the verdict will go favourably for Job and that it is only godless people who have reason to be afraid in God's presence. *b.* It is perfectly possible to say that in v. 15 there is an anticipation of the fine insights of 14:13–17. *c.* The thought of vv. 9–11, that God is opposed to the dishonesty of the friends, suggests a just God who will not disappoint the hopes of those who put their trust in Him. Perhaps the sermons on the basis of the AV of v. 15 can stand after all!

20, 21 Job proceeds to appeal for a fair hearing from God. This would mean the removal of the heavy hand now upon him and of the numbing, frightening sense of the divine majesty. **22** If these conditions are granted, he will be equally happy in the role of plaintiff or defendant. **23–26** As it is, he is ignorant of the charge against him. He asks for a clear statement of the reason for the divine hostility, which has issued in such a harsh sentence. Can it be that God is making him smart for the unthinking irresponsibilities of youth? **27** Whatever the reason, there is no denying the reality of the situation: the drastic restrictions God has imposed upon him. And yet, what is the target of the divine enmity? **28** Just a humble creature, tossed about by life, with the mark of corruption upon him.

14:1–22 The yearning for an after-life. 1–6 It is strange, says Job, that divine justice should fasten on a creature like man. His existence is fleeting, troublous, and involved in the universal sinfulness of humanity. Why then must a single individual, who is no heinous sinner, incur such a weight of divine displeasure? Cannot God grant the creature of a day a brief breathing-space from trouble? **7–12** The fate of things is contrasted with the fate of persons, to the advantage of the former. A felled tree may sprout again, but death writes an inexorable 'nevermore' on man's life. **13–15** The gloom of the picture penetrates Job's spirit so profoundly that there is a dramatic revulsion from it. His soul soars up in quest for the light of a worth-while hereafter. At present he feels the rod of the God of wrath across his shoulders. Presumably he must bear it while the present life lasts. But after that? He gives expression to the lovely dream of the God of grace granting him asylum, first in *Sheol*, the abode of the dead, and then calling him back to an existence in which He, the Creator, would yearn over the work of His hands. If I could believe that, says Job, 'I could endure my weary post until relief arrived' (14b,

Moff.). They are the words of a man who cannot let go his faith in the God whose present dealings are a blank mystery to him; a man raising questions which Jesus alone can answer. *Cf.* Jn. 11:25; 2 Tim. 1:10, *etc.* **16, 17** The glory of the dream fades in the recollection of the grim facts of the present. The God of grace retires to the background, and Job imagines a God who, miser-like, keeps constant check on every sin; **18, 19** a God who pulverizes the mightiest works of nature and dashes the hopes of man. **20** Death is the supreme trump card of man's divine Antagonist. **21** It makes man unable to rejoice in the rejoicings of the children he leaves behind, or to weep with them in their perplexities. **22** It does not even mean the cessation of his own pain. This may refer to the terrible idea that the soul in Sheol had sympathy for the decomposing body, feeling the touch of corruption upon it.

15:1 – 21:34 SECOND CYCLE OF SPEECHES

15:1–35 Second speech of Eliphaz

Eliphaz has been cut to the quick on finding Job treading under foot the pearls of wisdom let drop by his friends. It seems that their attempts to make Job bow in humble submission before the all-wise and all-powerful God have been unsuccessful. Perhaps he will be warned in time by a commentary upon the divine judgment descending upon the wicked. This is the spearhead of the friends' attack in the second cycle of speeches. It seems that the consolations of God (v. 11) of which they have been the mouthpiece have been too small for Job. Perhaps the terrors of God will bring him to his senses.

As we listen to Eliphaz we feel that his pride has been wounded as well as his religious convictions.

15:1–16 Job's attitude criticized. 1–6 Eliphaz accuses Job of being a windbag and irreligious at heart. His assumption of integrity and his criticism of God have been a crafty defence mechanism. **7, 8** He accuses Job of being self-important. He talks like some primeval man, existing from the beginning of things, like a member of God's secret council, like a man with a monopoly of wisdom. **9–13** How preposterous to reject the testimony of age and experience! **14–16** His talk throughout has tragically ignored the uncleanness of man who greedily gulps down iniquity as a thirsty man drinks water. If only he would raise his eyes to the God before whom the very angels and the heavens are stained!

15:17–35 The fate of the wicked. Eliphaz takes up Job's statement in 12:6. **17–19** He calls to his aid the words of the wise, reaching back to the good old days when there were no foreign influences to corrupt morality and religion. **20** Job had claimed that wicked men enjoy security. Monstrously untrue! Such security as they have is dogged by constant pain; **21** it is haunted by the dread of coming calamity, the first threatening murmurs of which their ears are for ever catching. **22–24** And when at last the dreaded darkness descends, all hope must be surrendered. For them, now, only violence, hunger, trouble and anguish. **25, 26** In their hour of fleeting security they may make their proud assaults upon the Almighty, as if their stout shields could keep them safe; **27** they may play the role of successful, bloated sensualists; **28** they may be guilty of the impiety of rebuilding ruined cities which have borne the curse of God. **29, 30** But the final darkness of the day of doom is gathering, which will blot out their prosperity. **31–35** Their fate is the fate of a plant, withering and dying prematurely.

16:1 – 17:16 Job answers Eliphaz

16:1–5 He spurns such empty comfort. 2, 3 *Windy words.* Eliphaz has accused Job of being a windbag rebel against God (*cf.* 15:2–6). Job hurls back the accusation that his friends are windbag comforters. **4, 5** If he were comforter instead of sufferer, there would be genuine substance in the comfort he would offer.

16:6–17 His desperate condition described. The woefulness of his impasse is drawn in poignant fashion. **6** Speech and silence alike are powerless to ease his misery. **7, 8** His gaunt frame is proof positive that the grip of his divine Antagonist is upon him. **9** In his afflictions he feels that God is straddling him like a wild beast, looking down on its powerless prey with flashing eyes. **10, 11** The hostility of God is echoed in the hostility of men, 'the pack of petty foes that howl at the heels of his greater enemy' (A. B. Davidson). **12, 13** At the end of v. 12 the figure changes: God appears as an archer, sending a stream of arrows into his vitals. **14** Yet another change of figure: God is now a warrior, repeatedly breaching the walls of the stronghold of his soul. **15–17** These divine assaults have condemned him to habitual mourning and humiliation; and yet the target of these assaults has been an innocent man.

16:18–21 His faith again triumphs. Once again Job rises from the profoundest depths to the greatest heights. He has been unable to let go his innocence in face of the insinuations of his friends. Now we find he cannot let go his God in face of his ugliest doubts and fears. **18** When an unjust death lays in the dust his innocent life, the voice of his innocent blood will rise to highest heaven. *Cf.* Gn. 4:10. **19** And there in heaven he suddenly catches sight of a divine Champion, a divine Sympathizer, who will be prepared to vouch for his integrity. **20, 21** Tearfully he appeals to the heavenly Witness to support his cause in the teeth of the insinuations of his friends, and of the shattering blows of the God who is responsible for his earthly afflictions. This passionate longing for a heavenly Witness on his side strikingly points forward to the Christian thought of 'an advocate with the Father, Jesus Christ the righteous' (1 Jn. 2:1). Here faith is reaching out for a 'God for us'.

Again, Jesus alone can answer Job. *Cf.* Heb. 9:24.

16:22 – 17:16 The brevity and sorrow of life. 16:22 – 17:2 The appeal gains force when he remembers that the years are rolling him forward inexorably towards the grave. Away with the mocking hopes of a bright tomorrow outlined by his friends, when the misery of today will be forgotten! Away with all hopes offered by men! **3–5** Only God can undertake suretyship for him. **6ff.** The misery of Job's present lot is described. He has become the butt of moralizing and insult. **8, 9** Righteous men may well be astonished at such suffering for such a man, though it cannot break their inflexible determination to pursue the way of righteousness whatever the price. Scholars have differed widely about these two verses. Some have maintained that the sentiments sound strange on Job's lips, and have suggested that they have strayed to their present place from a speech of one of the friends. This conjecture seems unnecessary. Delitzsch speaks of the passage as 'a rocket which shoots above the tragic darkness of the book lighting it up suddenly although only for a short time'. In a similar strain A. B. Davidson describes it as 'perhaps the most surprising and lofty in the book'. **10–12** The gloom deepens as the chapter proceeds. Again the hope of the friends that Job's night would be changed to day are swept aside. **13–16** His only hope is in the grave for which he has almost family affection.

18:1–21 Bildad's second speech

Bildad has nothing new to say and certainly nothing that can have any significance for Job. A portrayal of the doom of the wicked can speak only to a man with a guilty conscience.

18:1–4 Introduction. These verses introduce his main theme and reveal how keenly he resents Job's attitude to the attempts of his friends to be helpful. **2** Bildad accuses Job of hunting for far-fetched arguments which are mere words without any real content. **3** Job is treating them like unintelligent cattle. **4** He has accused an angry God of tearing him (*cf.* 16:9), while in reality he is tearing himself. His attitude virtually demands that the whole earth, with its moral order, should be turned upside down to substantiate his criticism of God and his championship of himself.

18:5–21 The fate of the wicked. 13 *The firstborn of death.* Moff. 'deadly disease'. The general sense is: 'Death's most loyal henchman will be his foe.' **15** *Brimstone is scattered.* Strahan comments: 'It was the custom to spread salt over places which had come under a ban; and brimstone, suggestive of the cities of the plain, may have been used to symbolize a deeper curse.'

19:1–29 Job answers Bildad

R. S. Franks speaks of this chapter as the 'watershed of the book'. From the most tragic sense of dereliction, Job rises to the most triumphant affirmation of faith.

431

19:1-22 His humiliation at God's hand described. Anger gives way to sorrow as he addresses the friends. **2-4** Even if he has sinned, his sin cannot harm them. *Ten times* means 'often' (*cf.* Gn. 31:7). **5-12** He complains that God is bent on humiliating him. Not content with prostrating him through this personal antagonism, God has enlisted a perfect host of co-operators. **13-20** Job's relatives, intimate friends, servants, and his very wife, all turn from him with loathing and he is thus robbed of the affection of those who mean most to him. **21** Quite broken down by the realization of his lonely state, Job pathetically appeals to his friends for pity. The tragic relationship between Job and his friends appears in a clear light. Surely, says Job, the realization that the hand of God is afflicting him ought to move them to pity. Yet it was for that very reason that they could not pity him. Their inflexible creed would not allow them to do so. They had to choose between their friend and their faith. **22** demonstrates as strikingly as any verse in Scripture the extent of our debt to the Lord Jesus Christ as regards our view of God. In our Christian era, our complaint against men must often be that they are not godlike enough (*cf.* Lk. 6:35, 36; Eph. 4:32). But Job's complaint against his friends was that they were too godlike. In their attitude to his suffering, which was gradually becoming more unsympathetic, he imagined he saw a reflection of the attitude of God who seemed so callous about the weight of sorrow with which He was crushing him down to despair.

19:23-29 Faith again triumphs. He looks into the future to find the hope, denied him by the present, blazing forth again. **23, 24** If only his case could be recorded in a book, on a leaden tablet, or in an inscription graven on the face of a rock! Surely generations to come would react more favourably to it than does his own. But, dramatically and impressively, we see that this man cannot for long rest content with the thought of a future 'well done' from the lips of humanity. His sense of alienation from man is infinitely less serious than his sense of alienation from God. There we have the key to the agony of heart which we see in the book.

25-27 Suddenly we have a wonderful vision of a *Redeemer* or 'Vindicator' (RSV mg.) appearing to champion his cause, to allow him to hear the 'not guilty' for which he craved, and to give him a vision of God. In general it must be said that no Christian can read vv. 25-27 without finding the passage a mirror of the One who 'always lives to make intercession' (Heb. 7:25), who has 'brought life and immortality to light through the gospel' (2 Tim. 1:10). But 'we must not turn Job into a modern Christian' (Wood). He was unaware of the priceless jewels encased in his words. 'He was like an aeolian harp across which the wind sweeps making music', says G. C. Morgan.

Wood treats vv. 25-27 as a vision corresponding to that of Eliphaz (4:12-21). While this is not impossible the evidence seems to be lacking. The Hebrew text of the passage is extremely difficult, making dogmatism about every interpretation out of place. *Redeemer* (Heb. *gō'ēl*) is rendered 'One to champion me' (Moff.). Strahan summarizes the role of the *gō'ēl* by saying, 'The *gō'ēl* was the nearest blood-relation on whom civil law imposed the duty of redeeming the property or person of his kinsman, and criminal law that of avenging his kinsman's blood if it was unjustly shed.' Is the Redeemer man or God? In recent commentaries Irwin (1962) and Wood (1966) have favoured the former view. Irwin finds the clue to his nature and function in the Ras Shamra literature which refers to 'the messenger of the gods who was instrumental in the release of the dead god of life'. This is purely conjectural. It is surely sounder to expound *gō'ēl* against the background of Job's thought in other passages. He has called upon God as his Judge (13:15-18); as his Witness (16:19); as an Advocate to plead his cause (16:21). It is difficult to see, then, why some scholars find it impossible to hold that Job viewed God as his *gō'ēl*. The same epithet is applied to God in Ps. 19:14 and in many passages in Isaiah (*e.g.* 41:14; 44:6; 47:4; 60:16; 63:4, 9). The truth is, however, that we have insufficient evidence to state precisely Job's conception of the person of the *gō'ēl*. The stress is certainly on the role of the *gō'ēl*: to vindicate him in the eyes of men and to effect reconciliation with God. *At last.* Heb. *'aharon* can mean 'last' or 'later'. The passage does not tie down the vindication of Job's innocence to some distant resurrection day; it merely points to a coming vindication. Various translations are possible for *upon the earth*; *e.g.*, 'on the dust' or 'on my grave'. *Cf.* 7:21; 17:16.

26 *Without my flesh* may also be rendered 'from my flesh' (RSV mg.). This may mean that Job was expecting to be a spectator at his vindication from the vantage-point of a body of flesh, or that he looked forward to being present at the scene as a disembodied spirit. We cannot be certain of the meaning. **27** *On my side*, or 'for myself' (RSV mg.). *Cf.* Luther's great remark that the whole of religion lies in the personal pronouns. No hearsay opinion of God for Job! *And not another.* RV mg. has the interesting alternative 'not as a stranger' (*cf.* Moff. 'estranged no longer'). This suggests the beautiful thought that Job was eagerly anticipating the time when the God of the present, who so often appeared as a 'mystery God', as a Stranger with slumbering depths of puzzling hostility to him, would appear in His true character as a Friend who would be quick to reverse the adverse opinion the present life was writing across him. The thought of the coming vindication overwhelms him. **28, 29** The chapter closes with a note of warning. Job's Vindicator will punish those who have arrayed themselves against him, assuming that they have diagnosed the real cause of his affliction.

20:1–29 Zophar's second speech

Zophar's text is the brevity of the wicked man's prosperity, and the inevitability of doom—a text equally cruel and irrelevant for Job's case. The text is expounded with power, heat and impetuosity. **2** The whole of his speech must be interpreted in the light of his remark, *My thoughts answer me, because of my haste within me.* Haste can be responsible for an incorrect view of man (*cf.* Ps. 116:11, AV, RV); and no less for an incorrect or partial view of God. 'His haste explains his theology,' says Strahan. 'Had he taken time to observe and reflect, he would have said, "Some sufferers are saints"; had he taken still more time, he might even have added, "And some are saviours".' Suffering Job appears in a false light as sinning Job. The false light on man results from a distorted vision of God. There is nothing in Zophar's words to suggest that God is anything more than an impatient judge, as impatient as Zophar himself. 'When the zealot makes his own opinions and sentiments the standard of divinity, there is a magnified Zophar on the throne of the universe' (Strahan). **26** *A fire not blown upon*; *i.e.*, a fire for whose blazing there is no natural explanation. *Cf.* 1:16.

21:1–34 Job answers Zophar

21:1–6 Introduction. Zophar's words sting Job into giving a more detailed answer to the theme of the friends than anything that has yet appeared in the second cycle of the dialogue. **2, 3** He appeals for a fair hearing. That is the only consolation he wants from them. **4** His task is difficult enough without lack of co-operation from man, for his complaint is directed against the God of heaven. **5, 6** The very thought of pursuing it fills him with dread, but honesty compels him to face the tremendous facts his own observations are thrusting in upon him.

21:7–22 The prosperity of the wicked. Job flatly contradicts Zophar's dogmatic picture of the wicked (*cf.* 20:4, 5, 11, *etc.*). **7–12** In bold colours he paints their enduring prosperity in home, family, field and flock. **13** At the end of the day they pass away without a struggle. **14, 15** All this in spite of the flat defiance their manner of life has thrown in the face of God. **16** *Is not their prosperity in their hand?* cf. Moff. 'Are they not masters of their fortunes?' **17–19** It is no reply to say, as the friends might be inclined to say in defence of their position, that the children of the wicked will feel the weight of the divine displeasure. That would imply that the wicked would get off scot-free. They cannot feel the weal or woe of their children after them. **22** Suddenly Job accuses the friends of presumption in their cut-and-dried theories about divine government. They are virtually teaching God how He ought to govern, instead of facing the facts as they are. **21:23–34 The facts as Job sees them. 23–26** One man dies in effortless prosperity; another in abject misery. **27–31** Who has a right to assume that virtue explains the former and vice the latter? That is theory and not fact, theory that is wrecked on fact as can be borne out by the testimony of those who have a broad knowledge of men and affairs and who can point to specific cases where wickedness seems to pay. **34** In view of that, what comfort can he expect to find in his friends' sweeping generalities, which are based on cases which suit their argument and which conveniently ignore those which do not? **32, 33** describe how an honourable burial is given to the wicked man. His grave is carefully guarded; his success inspires widespread imitation. In v. 33 those who *go before* and *after* are members of the funeral procession.

22:1 – 31:40 THIRD CYCLE OF SPEECHES

22:1–30 Third speech of Eliphaz

22:1–5 The reason for suffering. Eliphaz proceeds to demonstrate that there must be some reason for human afflictions. The key cannot be found in God, since human morality cannot affect His almighty power. The explanation must be sought, therefore, in man. Is Job being punished for piety? Inconceivable! Then he must be paying for his wickedness. **3** To Eliphaz the answer to the question he poses is undoubtedly negative. It would be clearly positive to the writers of such passages as Je. 31:20; Ho. 11:8; Mt. 23:37; *etc.* In his estimation, the aloof God in the icy altitudes of His remote heaven could not be concerned in His own person about human virtue or vice. See on 7:20. He could not have said, 'God so loved the world . . .'; he could only have said, 'God has so legislated for the world . . .' He had no cross on Calvary to inform him of the love and agony on God's heart as He surveys sinning men and women, and of His gladness when they allow themselves to be set in the right relationship to Him. He knew nothing of the miracles in which Christianity glories— 'the election of man, from nonentity, to be the beloved of God, and therefore (in some sense) the needed and desired of God, who but for that act needs and desires nothing, since He eternally has, and is, all goodness' (C. S. Lewis).

22:6–20 Job is openly accused. Now that Eliphaz has ventured out into the open with what has previously been only hinted by him, he proceeds with specific charges against Job. **6–9** He fathers on him the typical outrages of an oriental tyrant. It is implied that he has been practising a 'Jekyll and Hyde' existence. **10, 11** This sinfulness has been responsible for Job's present calamities. **12** Instead of giving to the exalted Lord of highest heaven the respect that is His due, **13, 14** he has wrongfully assumed that His remoteness guarantees the slackness of His supervision of human affairs. **15** As a result he has trodden the way of the godless, **16** and at the end of that way is doom. **19, 20** The moral conscience of the righteous man approves the judgment of God. **15** is linked closely with vv. 12–14. Moffatt renders: 'Is that the line you choose, the line that evil men took long ago?' **17, 18** Many scholars treat these verses as an insertion. They strongly remind us of the words of Job in 21:7–16 (see especially vv. 14 and 16). **18a** sounds especially strange on the lips of Eliphaz and **19** certainly follows v. 16 much more smoothly than it does v. 18.

22:21–30 An invitation to return to God. The mild spirit of Eliphaz breaks through the fire-and-brimstone preaching, in a passage full of beauty and spiritual truth, when it is lifted out of its narrow application to Job and interpreted generally. **21** Man finds authentic *peace*, not in his sins, but through the forgiveness of them; **22** through acceptance of the truth revealed by God; **23** through a humble return to God and **24, 25** through a new judgment of values whereby the preciousness of the divine treasure eclipses all else. **26** Such peace will bring with it joy, **27** communion with God, **28–30** triumph and usefulness to others. Vv. 24 and 25 are interesting in that they reveal a beautiful distinction between religious and material values. **30** The reading is uncertain. The LXX, Syriac OT, Vulgate and RV all accept the Hebrew 'him that is not innocent'. RV has: 'He shall deliver even him that is not innocent: yea, he shall be delivered through the cleanness of thine hands.' RSV surely makes the better sense.

23:1 – 24:25 Job answers Eliphaz

23:1–17 Job's heart laid bare. He is no rebel against God; he does not complain for the sheer joy of complaining. **2** He has made a real effort to restrain his cries of protest, but his misery has wrung them out of him. *His hand.* The LXX and Syriac OT have 'my hand'. This would give the translation, 'My hand is heavy upon my groaning', *i.e.* 'I am attempting to control it'. **3–7** If he does rebel, it is against what seems to be God's arbitrary wrath. Thus he expresses a passionate longing to find the God of grace. Such a God would deal intelligibly with him, meting out justice to his cause and not numbing him by a parade of sheer power. The wistful cry of these verses from a man seeking to find God can be answered only by Jesus, in whom God takes the initiative to find man. (*Cf.* Jn. 14:9.) **8–12** The frustration of his longing to find God is expressed. The most untiring efforts to bring about the meeting for which he yearns are fruitless, although God has the means of knowing the integrity of his heart of hearts. **10** *He knows the way that I take.* Literally, as in RV mg. 'the way that is with me'. Moffatt translates 'how I live'. In the words *When he has tried me, I shall come forth as gold* we are probably not to detect a reference to the gold which comes through the refining fires of suffering; nor is there an arrogant claim on the part of Job that his nature is gold all the way through. Rather he is contradicting the insinuations of his friends. They maintained that Job was being punished

for secret dross in his nature, which he had successfully screened from men. In his sufferings, according to them, God was tearing the screen aside.

13–17 The longing to find God is somewhat clouded over. Job finds himself wearily toiling up the hill of predestination 'with its icy altitudes' (W. M. Macgregor). His sufferings have been determined by an iron decree. **15** W. A. Irwin criticizes the translation *I am terrified*, pointing out that essentially the same word is rendered by 'overwhelm' in 22:10. He translates: 'Therefore I am overwhelmed because of him, and I fear him.' **17** The exact force of this verse is elusive. A. B. Davidson (following one MS) translates: 'For I am not dismayed because of the darkness, nor because of myself whom thick darkness covereth.' If this translation is adopted, the verse means that Job's most baffling problem was not the external darkness of calamity about him, nor the darkness that had invaded his own person, but rather his sense of the arbitrariness of the divine action.

24:1–25 The providence of God. Job puts the problem in a world setting. Various classes of wrongdoers are mentioned. Why does God not intervene? **1** Note the Moffatt rendering: 'Why has not the Almighty sessions of set justice? Why do his followers never see him intervening?' **5–8** These verses describe aborigines, driven into the wilderness by the oppression of a stronger race. **6** *Fodder* is coarse food more suitable for animals than for human beings. **10, 11** Wretched labourers are depicted, working for an inadequate wage, hungry and thirsty in the midst of plenty. **13–17** depict the nefarious doings of **14** the murderer, **15** the adulterer and **16** the robber. **17** *Friends with the terrors of deep darkness.* Apparently there is a contrast between the attitude of respectable people and that of the night-birds. The former dread the darkness with its unknown terrors; the latter 'love darkness rather than light, because their deeds are evil' (*cf.* Jn. 3:19). Their familiarity with the darkness had bred contempt. If they know fear, it is during the day, perhaps because of the knowledge that justice will then find it easier to catch up with them. **18** *Upon the face of the waters.* Perhaps the picture is of a twig, hurried along on the surface of a swiftly moving flood (*cf.* Ho. 10:7).

The chapter is difficult because it is not easy to distinguish between Job's sentiments and those of his friends. **18** *You say* follows the insertion of the RV mg. **22, 23** should probably be ascribed to Job. If **24** is his, we are to look for the force of it, not in *a little while* but rather in 'as all other' (following the LXX). In defiance of the sentiments of his friends Job maintained that there was nothing abnormal about the death of the wicked.

25:1–6 Bildad's third speech

The shortness of the speech has caused considerable comment. There are two main views: *a.*

'We deal with a tattered manuscript' (Irwin). This is either a fragment of Bildad's speech or 'a collection of platitudes thrown together to supply the lack of Bildad's speech'. *b.* We are meant to conclude that Job has run his friends' arguments into the ground. Dogmatism has nothing new to say. This short speech is not a case of *multum in parvo*, but an indication that the ideas of the friends are all but exhausted.

2, 3 Taking the speech as it stands, Bildad strives to bring Job to his knees before the might of God. **4–6** When the mightiest heavenly bodies must tremble before Him, subdued and convicted, how can insignificant and corrupt man hope to look up, unafraid of what the light may disclose? *Cf.* 4:17ff. and 15:14ff. There is point in the speech, but in the sense intended by Bildad it cannot help Job. The latter never claims that there is no darkness in him, but only that there is not the darkness suspected by his friends.

26:1–14 Job answers Bildad

Job demonstrates that he understands what Bildad has said about the might of God. His controversy with him and with the others cannot be explained by failure to stand where they have stood in appreciation of the omnipotence of God; it must rather be explained by his honesty in facing certain puzzling facts of experience which they have either overlooked or suppressed. A. B. Davidson has the chapter heading: 'Job rivals Bildad in magnifying the greatness of God.'

2–4 embody the most pointed sarcasm. Such words of wisdom as have been offered Job bear the stamp of the inspiration of some great person! **5, 6** speak of the divine power operative in the underworld. *The shades.* The Hebrew word is *rᵉpā'îm.* Two usages of it should be noted. It refers to pre-Israelitish people (*e.g.* Gn. 14:5; 15:20). It can also refer to the dead (*e.g.* Ps. 88:10). Schwally maintained that 'it was applied by the Israelites to people who were dead and gone, and of whom they knew little'. Probably it is better to translate, 'The shades beneath the waters tremble, their inhabitants (*i.e.* of the waters) also.' *Abaddon* is a synonym for *Sheol.* There are two other occurrences of the word in Job (28:22; 31:12) and seven in the whole Bible.

In **7–13** Job shows that heaven and earth and sea have the same testimony with regard to the power of God. How mighty must be the God of an ordered universe! **9** *The moon.* It is probably better to read with RSV mg. 'his throne'. God's 'throne' is covered with clouds. **13** *Serpent.* See on 3:8. **14** rounds off the chapter in a most impressive way. Moffatt translates: 'And all this is the mere fringe of his force, the faintest whisper we can hear of him! Who knows then the full thunder of his power?' The idea is that when you have fully described your most exact impressions of the power of God, there is always infinitely more that could be said.

27:1 – 31:40 Job replies to his friends

It has been suggested that at this stage in the book we are to imagine a pause. Job waits in vain for Zophar to speak; but the friends have shot their bolt. On this hypothesis there now follow two general replies to the friends, introduced by the same words, *Job again took up his discourse* (27:1; 29:1).

27:1–6 Job reaffirms his innocence. Job again repudiates the charges insinuated or directly affirmed by his friends. **2** His affirmation is introduced by what Strahan calls 'the most extraordinary form of oath in the Scriptures'. He swears by a God *who has taken away* his *right.* It is a remarkable picture of a man whose faith is abiding with him in the storm, who still can call 'my God' the God he is tempted to imagine is forsaking him. **5, 6** He cannot doubt the reality of almighty God, or the fact of His government of the world; it is the mode of His government, and in particular its application to himself, which puzzles him. The present vexations cannot be explained by his sinfulness.

27:7–23 The end of the wicked. This passage presents a number of difficulties. The connection between Job's affirmation of innocence and this picture of the end of the wicked is hard to fathom. The friends had maintained that sinfulness was the clue to Job's adversity, and had accordingly denied his innocence. That denial was the logical outcome of their creed. And now, without a trace of warning, Job appears as a perfervid believer in that creed. In the second place the passage flatly contradicts what Job has already said about the prosperity of the wicked. *Cf.* 21:22ff.; 24:1ff., and note the contrast between 27:14 and 21:11. We have no parallel to these verses in Job's speeches in any other part of the book. On the other hand, the passage would sound perfectly in place on the lips of the friends. There are two alternatives: *a.* We may argue that Job is modifying his previous sentiments. 'He strengthened all the arguments of his friends' is G. C. Morgan's comment on the passage. According to one interpretation, in ch. 26 we found him rivalling Bildad in magnifying the greatness of God while retaining a larger creed than his. Perhaps in this passage the author meant us to think of Job as sympathetic with the general truth of his friends' sentiments, but unwilling to accept the arbitrariness and the narrowness of their application of them. *b.* On the other hand, many scholars hold that there has been a dislocation in the book at this point and they attribute this section to Zophar, which would mean that all the friends speak three times.

11 *Concerning the hand of God.* The words have a somewhat strange ring. He is undertaking to teach people whose previous speeches have revealed that they are past masters in the lesson. **18** *Like a booth* refers to the flimsy construction erected by the nightwatchman in a vineyard. **23** The clapping of hands is a token of indignation (see, *e.g.*, Nu. 24:10).

435

28:1–28 God's gift of wisdom. The chapter consists of a fine poem on wisdom which is meant to teach that wisdom is completely beyond the reach of man unless the quest is carried through in the setting of *the fear of the Lord.* Many scholars doubt whether the chapter can be attributed to the original drama and they treat it as a later addition. In the first place, the connection between chs. 27 and 28 is elusive. Second, this placid acquiescence in the superior heights of the divine wisdom contrasts strangely with many of Job's statements before and after this stage in the book. Elsewhere Job appears as 'a chained eagle, who spreads his wings and dashes himself against the bars of his cage; he would soar unto God's place and pluck the mystery out of the darkness' (A. B. Davidson). See, *e.g.*, 23:3; 31:35ff. One must, however, bear in mind that it is unreasonable to expect level-headed consistency in a sufferer. We have seen striking inconsistencies in Job's view of God. God has appeared sometimes as foe, sometimes as friend. The pendulum may also have swung in respect of Job's thoughts on human understanding of the ways of God. Whatever our view of the place of ch. 28 in the book, there can be no doubt about its value. We are brought face to face with the truth that true wisdom means faith in God and renunciation of evil; it is the reverence which acknowledges that there are more things in heaven and in earth than are dreamt of in human philosophy; it is the obedience to the will of God, however mysterious, which brings the seeker for truth much further than intellectual speculation (*cf.* Jn. 7:17). Wood says finely: 'One effect of this chapter is to slow down the movement of the previous arguments between Job and his friends. It is like the gentle application of the foot-brake in a motor-car with a view to reducing speed . . . It provides a pause in the journey and gives the traveller an opportunity to look back and see how far he has come and how far he has still to go'. In ch. 28 the 'traveller' looks back upon the futility of the wisdom of the friends with their relentless equating of suffering and sin. He also looks forward to the only possible answer in the Word of God conveyed in the Yahweh speeches. Chs. 29–31 restate the problem to which the Word of God alone has the solution.

1–14 In these verses we have a picture of man's successful and unresting activity in worrying out of the earth its treasures of precious ores and stones. **3, 4** The miner is seen groping his way through the darkness, carrying through complicated underground operations. *They swing to and fro.* The passage is obscure. RSV seems to imply descent into a deep shaft by a 'swinging' basket. Irwin points out that this is anachronistic. The Hebrew word behind 'shafts' is literally 'stream-beds'. Irwin interprets the 'swinging' of the devious turnings of the tunnels in regions where human feet do not tread. **9, 10** describe the miner cutting through the rocks. **5** is meant as a contrast between the quiet growth of the corn above ground and the miner's forceful tactics underground.

7, 8, 12–14 The narrative speaks of a quest which must baffle the most careful ingenuity of man or beast: the quest for wisdom. **12** Earth cannot work out an answer to the question, *Where shall wisdom be found?* The words of this verse may well have circulated among thoughtful men in Israel as a riddle. **15–22** Wisdom cannot be obtained in any human market. All living things and the dark forces of the underworld are alike impotent to answer the question asked in v. 12 and again in v. 20. The most they can do is allude to a vague rumour about wisdom which they have heard.

23–27 The only One who can answer the question is indicated. The God who can restrain the mighty forces of the universe, the God of creation, has an exact mastery of the hidden things of wisdom. **28** If man would travel profitably towards an apprehension of that wisdom, of which God is, and can be, the only possessor, he must be godfearing and moral.

29:1–25 Job's memory of a golden past. This is one of the most effective chapters in the book. The sources of Job's happiness are portrayed with consummate skill.

2–4 First, he was a God-preserved man. We have the pathos of the whole book in *In the days when God watched over me.* At the heart of his past happiness was the conviction that God was watching over him. His present misery is explained by the feeling that God is no longer watching—or, if watching, with unreasonably critical eyes. **5** Second, Job was a domestically happy man. In the reference to his *children* we hear the 'sob of a great agony' (G. C. Morgan). **6** Third, he was a prosperous man. *The rock poured out for me streams of oil* does not refer to a prosperity emerging even from unlikely quarters, as we might imagine. The olive tree thrives in a rocky soil, and oil presses are hewn out in the rock. **7–10, 21–25** In the fourth place, he was a universally respected man. When he took his seat as a city councillor it was noted with respect by all classes of the community. His opinion was waited upon with respect, and when it had been expressed there was nothing more to say. His speech was like refreshing rain for drooping spirits. His very smile was a tonic for the irresolute.

11–17 These verses explain the 'well done' invariably written by men across Job's name. The man who was 'watched over' by God was scrupulous in watching over the interests of the needy. **16** Even perfect strangers could depend on his thorough championing of their cause. **14** In all these social activities, righteousness was his garment and justice his turban. The idea is almost that justice incarnated itself in Job. *Cf.* Jdg. 6:34, which can be rendered 'But the Spirit of the Lord clothed itself with Gideon'. **12–20** Job's anticipations for the future at that time, so rudely shattered by the calamities described in the first two chapters of the book, are here portrayed. He expected an unbroken prolongation of the 'golden' days. 19 speaks of a prosperity in touch with unfailing springs; 20 of manly strength symbolized by the bow.

30:1–31 The contempt into which he has been brought. The grey *now* stands in bleak contrast to the golden 'then'. The misery of the present approaches from every quarter. **1–15** First it comes from without. He is insulted by men, even by the 'underdog' class, which in the old days he had been quick to befriend (*cf.* 29:11–17). **4–8** The miserable lot of the men who now reviled Job is depicted. They are grateful to scrape a miserable livelihood from the roots of the ground and to make their bed in rocky barren places, when respectable men harshly refuse them a place to lay their head. Such is the lot of people with an unknown and unloved name. **9–15** Now Job himself is a target for the skits and the crude contempt of such people. **11** speaks of unrestrained humiliation at the hands of God. RV mg. yields the good sense of God loosening Job's 'bowstring'. *Cf.* 29:20. **12** The *rabble* distressing Job appears as a host beleaguering a city, **13** making escape impossible, **14** and then pouring in when the wall has been breached.

16–18, 30 Second, misery approaches from within. He describes the tormenting burning pains of his disease. **18** is difficult. *With violence it seizes my garment* may not be right. LXX has 'my garment is disfigured'. AV 'By the great force of my disease is my garment changed' gives the picture of his garment hanging loosely on his shrunken frame. **18b**, on the other hand, seems to imply a tight-fitting garment. Peake suggests that the reference is to certain abnormally swollen parts of his otherwise emaciated body.

19–23 Third, misery approaches from above. He is dealing with a God who has cast him into a miry pit (*cf.* Ps. 40:2), and now is cruelly indifferent to his cry for help. God's tempest of trouble is inexorably sweeping him forward to the grey portals of the house of death. **24** The Hebrew is obscure. Dillmann translates 'Howbeit, doth not a sinking man stretch forth his hand?', giving the excellent sense that a drowning man will grasp at a straw. Job felt himself sinking in a storm he imagined a cruelly callous God had sent. Yet again and again the cry rose in his heart, 'Lord, save me'. It was the hand of faith reaching out for a Saviour he could not yet firmly trust. **25, 26** Underlying these verses we hear the note: 'If only God had dealt with me as generously as I have dealt with others, how different my present position would be!' **27** describes his feelings in ferment, while **28** and **31** portray the sorrow that has taken the place of the gladness of old. **29** speaks of his ostracism from the civilized community. **28** *Blackened* is a reference to black mourning garments. **30** *Black*, through disease, is a different word.

31:1–40 Job's final protestation of innocence. This chapter gives a very remarkable insight into the character of the man. His ideas are not easy-going and unambitious, but exacting and inward. 'He judges himself by an almost evangelical standard of excellence,' says Strahan. Duhm speaks of the chapter as the high-water mark of the OT ethic. We shall note several striking correspondences with NT teaching. Job makes six main claims for his former way of life.

a. **1–12** He was untainted by immorality. **1, 7, 9** His external conduct had been pure, but no purer than his secret thoughts (*cf.* Mt. 5:8, 28). Adultery appears in a terrible light. **2, 3** First, it deserves the punishment of God. The purity of Job's action had emerged from a background of the 'fear of the Lord, that is wisdom' (28:28). **11** Second, it deserves the punishment of man, for it is an offence, not only against God, but against society. **10** *Grind for another* refers to the lowliest form of bondage, that of a slave-woman at the mill (*cf.* Ex. 11:5). **12** Third, it is *a fire* that has in it the threat of indiscriminate destruction—of a man's health, home, happiness (*cf.* Pr. 6:27, 28).

5–8 paint on a canvas wider than that of sensualism. Here Job denies vanity and deceit of any kind. **5** Strahan effectively speaks of *falsehood* (AV 'vanity') as 'masked nothingness'. **6** Job is not afraid of the scales of God's justice, if only they are fair. **7** If his claim to integrity is unsound, **8** he will gladly forfeit the produce of his work in the field.

b. **13–23, 31, 32** He was untainted by thoughtlessness. **13–15** His servants always received fair play from him, for he remembered that there was a God in heaven to whom he was answerable—the Creator of both master and servant (*cf.* Eph. 6:9). **15** surely stands out as a gem because of its remarkable social consciousness (*cf.* Pr. 14:31; 22:2). **16–20** Nor was it possible for his household to complain of frugal catering any more than they could complain of injustice. But his kindness was not confined within the walls of his own household; it went out to seek and to save the needy, the poor, the widows and the fatherless. Exploitation and oppression of the weak were foreign to his nature, **21** though he could easily have used his influence to twist the justice offered by the courts. Rather he had been a help of the helpless. **17** is particularly striking. His full stomach had never made him indifferent to the empty stomachs of others. No Lazarus was allowed to lie at his gate, unnoticed and unhelped (*cf.* Lk. 16:20). **31, 32** He was 'given to hospitality' (Rom. 12:13, AV), when he could not have the faintest chance of return (*cf.* Lk. 14:12–14).

c. **24, 25** He was untainted by what G. B. Shaw called the 'Gospel of Getting on'. He made friends by means of 'the unrighteous mammon' (*cf.* Lk. 16:9), but his attitude to his riches never ran the risk of the warning: 'You cannot serve God and mammon' (*cf.* Mt. 6:19–21, 24).

d. **26–28** He was untainted by secret hankering after idols. **27** speaks of the throwing of the kiss of adoration to the heavenly bodies.

e. **29, 30** He was untainted by bitterness towards his enemies. In such a passage Job is travelling in the direction of our Lord's words in Mt. 5:44.

f. **33, 34** He was untainted by insincerity. 'His true eyes had never practised how to cloak offences with a cunning brow', because he dreaded popular disapproval, and more especially the disapproval of the great families.

35–37 The recollection of his past way of life causes Job to break into an almost reckless 'not guilty' cry, with which he challenges high heaven. Note especially v. 35. The appearance of the indictment would not confuse or humiliate him. He would carry it triumphantly, joyfully and openly (v. 36); and with princely, confident step enter the presence of the Adversary he had found so elusive, ready to give Him an exact account of his daily walk (v. 37).

In this chapter Job has so far claimed that neither the voice of man nor the voice of God can convict and confuse him. He is guiltless of such charges as his friends have sought to fasten on him. **38–40** He goes further and says in effect: 'Even if my land had a voice, no more could it condemn me.'

32:1 – 37:24 THE ELIHU SECTION

For the following reasons many scholars maintain that the Elihu section is an interpolation by another hand: *a.* There is no mention of Elihu in prologue or epilogue. *b.* There are linguistic and stylistic differences from the rest of the book. *c.* The Elihu speeches, it is maintained, add nothing to what has gone before.

On the other hand, Budde, Cornill, Kamphausen, Wildeboer, Sellin, Bauer and Peters have argued for the originality of the speeches. It seems highly unlikely that a later interpolator, writing with a knowledge of the activities of the Satan mentioned in the prologue, should ignore the prologue altogether.

Characteristics of the Elihu speeches are a profound atmosphere of reverence for God; a view of sin deeper than that which appears elsewhere in the speeches of the other friends; the appearance of God as a Teacher (35:11; 36:22), intent on leading man through the discipline of suffering to a wiser way of life. Budde maintains that the supreme function of the speeches is to expose Job's most potentially dangerous characteristic—spiritual pride (33:17; 35:12; 36:22). The curative value of suffering has no doubt appeared in other speeches, but not with the same emphasis.

32:1–22 The reason for Elihu's intervention

Throughout this chapter there is a clear ring of 'necessity is laid upon me' (*cf.* 1 Cor. 9:16). The failure of the friends to answer Job's doubts and fears had forced him into the controversy. As he had listened, a twofold anger had burned in his breast—against Job, because of the confident eyes he was raising unflickeringly towards

heaven, and against the friends for their failure to refute Job. We are surely meant to remember that it is an angry young man who is speaking. **2–5** There are four references to his anger in these verses. Such a recollection will blunt the charge of boastfulness frequently made against Elihu. Hahn, *e.g.*, dismisses him as 'a most conceited and arrogant young man'. (For his boastfulness see especially vv. 14, 17, 18.) But anger may readily sweep a man beyond the strict frontiers of balanced humility. Also we must remember that it is an oriental man who is speaking and his words are meant for oriental ears. In such a setting the boastfulness, so clearly detected by Western ears, would assume almost a commonplace character. Cox looks upon his introduction as 'little more than a string of scholastic formulae, sentences which were the current form of debate'. Wood is surely right in his verdict: 'The much maligned Elihu deserves to be better treated than is customary.'

6–16 Elihu points out the reason for his silence up to the present stage in the debate: a young man's natural respect for grey hairs had sealed his lips. But a still more authoritative respect had broken the seal: **8** his respect for the revelation of God which could come to young men as to old. Men who are 'great' in age are not always 'great' in their appreciation of spiritual wisdom. Silence now could only mean greater respect for the person of man than for his God. Elihu was not built on such lines (see vv. 21, 22). Old men had failed to pierce Job's defence. Let them not conclude that it must be impregnable in the face of every human attack. Let them not say: 'We found him too clever for us! It must be God, not man, who puts him down!' (v. 13, Moff.). Job has not yet had to reckon with Elihu's distinctive assault upon his positions.

17–22 graphically depict a man in the grip of the constraint of what he felt to be the truth of God. *Cf.* 1 Cor. 9:16. He was bursting to speak. Only speech could relieve the inner tension.

33:1–33 Elihu denounces Job's attitude to his sufferings

1–7 In the opening verses of this chapter Elihu maintains that he is utterly sincere, **3** speaking directly from his heart, **4, 6** and also that he is on exactly the same plane as Job in creaturely dependence upon God. Job had complained that the spectacle of the divine might numbed and terrified him (*cf.* 9:34; 13:21), making it impossible for him to do himself justice before God, either in thought or in word. **7** No such complaint could have relevance in the verbal warfare to which Elihu was challenging him. Job's present assailant was a man like himself.

8–13 Elihu rebukes Job for maintaining his integrity and for charging God with hostility to him. Such a charge against the great God, whose greatness immeasurably transcends the power or wisdom of man, is totally unfounded. And yet Job seemed to assume that such a God would be prepared to assume the role of a disputant like some party in a petty human squabble! But while God will not speak as a disputant, He will speak (as the mighty God that He is) in ministries of mercy. Yet Job has denied that very fact. **13** *My words*. RSV refers to such passages as 9:16 and 19:7. LXX has the reading 'his words'. A. B. Davidson renders v. 13: 'Why dost thou contend against Him that He giveth not account of any of His matters?'

14–30 Elihu refers to the various ways through which a patient God seeks to give an account of Himself in human affairs. First, **15, 16** He speaks through dreams and visions, through which He would leave the seal of His instruction upon human minds, and **17** reclaim men from evil purposes **18** which must issue in death and destruction without His intervention. Second, **19** He speaks through pain (*cf.* Heb. 12:6). **20** Suffering may deprive a man of his appetite and **21** of his firm, healthy flesh; **22** it may bring him to the very jaws of death, where the destroying angels await him; but it may give God His chance with the soul. **23** speaks of the intervention of *an angel* of mercy to cheat the destroying angels of their prey by interpreting to the sufferer the meaning of the chastening rod and the correct reaction to it. *One of the thousand* presents the idea that God has an indefinite number of ministers of mercy under His command. **24–30** speak of the results which follow a right response to the approach which a gracious God makes to the sufferer. First, **25** his body regains its health. Second, **26** health of soul is restored, with the joy which is its inevitable fruit. *He accepts.* Man is given back his righteous standing with God. Third, **27, 28** joy of soul issues in joyful witness to others concerning God's dealings with the soul.

31–33 Elihu now challenges Job to speak if he has anything worth saying. 'I fain would see you cleared' (v. 32b, Moff.), he says. But if he cannot speak words of wisdom, let him listen to him.

34:1–9 Job's complaints summarized

Silence follows Elihu's challenge to Job, so his denunciation of Job's sentiments continues. **2** He appeals first for the ear of all intelligent listeners. **3, 4** Let there be discrimination between words of truth and words of error. In which of these categories must Job's words be placed? Elihu condenses Job's speeches into two complaints: **5, 6** the first is that God has wronged an innocent man, inflicting a wound on him quite capriciously. **7** Such words, says Elihu, only go to show up Job as a man with a unique and insatiable thirst for scorning, **8** a man of faulty opinions, which surely must be a significant commentary upon the faulty company he has been keeping. **9** In the second place Job has complained that 'it is no use for man to be the friend of God' (Moff.).

34:10–33 Job's first complaint refuted

10–12 Job has complained of unrighteousness in

God's dealings with him. With all the conviction of his pious nature Elihu affirms that God is just, and that He has placed man in a moral universe. Man reaps what he sows, whether the sowing is of evil or goodness. He supports his affirmation by various considerations.

First, absolute authority belongs to God and to God alone. **13** The control of the universe has not been foisted on Him by some other power. That might entail indifferent or self-regarding government. Self-regard on the part of God would shatter the fabric of the universe in an instant. **14, 15** Man is utterly dependent upon the 'breath' of God (*cf.* Gn. 2:7). In v. 14a AV mg. has the interesting translation, 'If he set his heart upon himself.' If human life is maintained by the breath of God, where is there a motive for injustice in God?

He argues in the second place **17** that the very continuance of the rule of God implies justice in that rule. **18** The charge of injustice is a serious enough one to make against earthly monarchs, for justice wielded in an unjust way has the seeds of ruin in it (*cf.* Mt. 12:25); **19** but how can such a charge be made against the Creator of all men, whether princes or paupers, who shows partiality to neither prince nor pauper, but cares for all alike? Again, where is there a motive for injustice?

Up to the present stage in the chapter Elihu has been moving on somewhat theoretical ground. **20–28** He now turns to more practical considerations. God's omniscience guarantees His justice. People and princes alike feel the weight of God's might. **23** *A time.* The verse is to be understood against the background of Job's appeal to God for 'sessions of set justice' (24:1, Moff.). Divine knowledge of human ways and judgment upon them are simultaneous.

29 Elihu moves from a general contemplation of God's working in history towards Job's case. Is there a ring of 'Thou art the man' about *a man*? The argument of the verse seems to be: whether nations or individuals are passing through days of quiet enjoyment of God's presence, or days when they lose sight of His face in the midst of trials, they must take the way of uncomplaining submission to His will. **30** His justice is fairly administered for the good of men. **31, 32** Elihu then asks Job 'if any man who uses the language of penitence will presume to dictate to God the chastisement he should receive' (Strahan). **33** Elihu emphatically dissociates himself from Job.

34–37 Elihu then calls for the verdict of thinking men with regard to Job's rebellious words. For Elihu, Job's rebellion is more terrible than his trials. Until he surrenders that rebellion, for his own good the trials must continue. **37** *He claps his hands.* See on 27:23.

35:1–16 Job's second complaint refuted

Job had argued that righteousness brings no advantage to the righteous man—no more than if he had been a flagrant sinner (*cf.* 21:15; 34:9).

5–7 Elihu's reply is that human virtue or vice cannot bring any advantage to the transcendent God. **8** It is other men, and not God, who have reason to be concerned about human conduct. For the error in Elihu's argument, see on 7:20 and 22:3.

Elihu proceeds to demolish certain considerations which might seem to support Job's contention that no advantage is attached to righteous conduct. **9, 12** There is the problem of unanswered prayer. **13** Elihu believes that when prayer is unanswered it is *empty*. It is a case of 'You ask and do not receive, because you ask wrongly' (Jas. 4:3). A deep religious note is missing from the prayer. **11** It is a cry of pain, which does not raise man any higher than the level of the beasts. The divine Teacher has loftier altitudes of trust in store for man (*cf.* 36:22). **10** *The night* is, of course, the night of suffering. God can teach the teachable, even through suffering.

The thought of God as a Teacher, intent on steering man through a rough and thorny maze of pain to a deeper experience of Himself, gives us an important distinction between Elihu and the friends. For them, God appears more characteristically as a Sovereign or Judge.

14, 15 The translation is problematical. A. B. Davidson makes good sense in the rendering, 'Yea when thou sayest, Thou seest Him not, the cause is before Him; therefore wait thou for Him.' Similarly Moff.: 'Hush! only wait for him.' In v. 15 Elihu says that God is quite lenient in His treatment of those whose approach to Him is shallow. This leads some people to take advantage of Him. **16** If Job continues to multiply *words without knowledge* he will fall into this danger.

36:1 – 37:24 The mighty works of God

Attention!—to a man of 'unerring insight' (v. 4, Moff.) into the ways of God with man in general and with Job in particular. **3** *From afar* means that his argument is going to range widely through the realm of truth.

5–7 Behold a mighty and gracious God! His providence is trustworthy, adamantly opposing the wicked, vigilantly superintending the righteous. **8–10** Even when they are cramped and constrained by affliction, the divine Teacher is intent on leading them through to a large place (*cf.* v. 16) where they acknowledge and renounce the transgression that had involved them in affliction. **11–15** Obedience to the Teacher leads to happiness; disobedience, to ruin. **13** *Anger* refers to their smouldering resentment against God. *They do not cry* means 'they do not pray', with the content of trust in their prayers which is pleasing to God (*cf.* 35:10). **17–25** The action of a mighty and gracious God, which has been generally enunciated, is now applied to Job's particular case. **18** *The greatness of the ransom* is evidently a reference to the severity of the afflictions through which he

is passing. Nothing else can win for him that larger trust in God to which he is being called through his afflictions. His own strength certainly cannot do it. **20** The force of the word *night* is elusive. Cox sees a reference to Job's loathing of life; Davidson, a synonym for judgment. *Cf.* Job's frequently expressed desire to meet God in judgment. **21** is logically difficult. The first part expresses a warning against turning to iniquity; the second states that this has been done already. *The Complete Bible* renders the second part: 'Because for this you were tried by suffering.' RSV can, however, yield excellent sense, in the warning against persisting in the way of rebellion which Job has already chosen in preference to walking the way of affliction with meekness. **22, 23** There will be a change if only he will behold the God of sovereign might, the mighty Teacher who is answerable to no-one. **24, 25** Down on our knees before such a God! That is the place for man.

36:26 – 37:24 In a passage full of literary beauty and spiritual significance Elihu takes up again his theme of the greatness of God. He calls the phenomena of nature to witness to the might of God.

a. **27, 28** The formation of the rain drops.

b. **36:29 – 37:5** The thunderstorm. **30** is difficult. A. B. Davidson translates, 'Behold, He spreadeth His light around Him, and covereth Him over with the deeps of the sea.' He interprets *sea* as referring either to the 'masses of water in the thunder clouds which enshroud the Almighty', or to 'the sea on earth . . . as it were drawn up from its bottom in cloud and vapour to form the pavilion of the Lord'. **31** speaks of the thunderstorm both as a minister of God's judgment and of His mercy (accompanied as it is by fructifying rain).

c. **6–10** The snow and ice. He describes the paralysing effect of the rigours of winter upon human work and upon the animals. The helplessness of man before the severity of the weather is meant to serve as a timeless reminder that he is creature and not Creator.

d. **11–13** The clouds. These move in accordance with the divine command on ministries of discipline or mercy to man or land. **12** *They* refers to the individual lightning flashes.

14 The weight of testimony of *the wondrous works of God* to the God operative in them is now applied to Job's case. It ought to pull him up in his tracks in the way of rebellion along which he had been hurrying; it ought to make him a reverent listener to the Word of the Lord spoken through such impressive testimony to the might of God. **15–18** Only One is *perfect in knowledge* of the ways of the Lord in nature. Man must confess the imperfection of his knowledge when confronted by the phenomena of nature.

19 Human understanding of the ways of the Lord with man is similarly conditioned by the limitations of the human mind. Such limitations make it impossible, in the first place, for man to address God aright (*cf.* Rom. 8:26). **20** By presumptuous speech a man is running the risk of destruction. **21** Second, a man cannot appear with confidence before a God whose majesty must completely blind him. **22** How much more must the light of God's majesty dazzle him! *Golden splendour* is literally 'gold': the reference is evidently to the splendour of the light which results when the north wind sweeps away the clouds. **23** Third, these limitations mean that man cannot understand God aright. See Moffatt's moving translation: 'The Almighty is beyond our minds. Supreme in power and rich in justice, he violates no right.' **24** In view of such human limitations, man's proper role is to lean, not on his own intelligence (the force of *wise in their own conceit*), but on God in reverential fear.

38:1 – 41:34 THE LORD ANSWERS JOB

38:1-3 Job is called to account

The silence of heaven in face of Job's challenging cries is broken. **2** has been applied by some commentators to Job; by others to Elihu. *Counsel* implies that in His dealings with Job God was not acting in a haphazard way, but according to consistent, intelligent design. All the speeches up to the present stage in the book, both by Job and the four friends, had sent shadows across that truth. **3** An interesting word is used for *man*: *geḇer*. 'It denotes man, not in frailty but in his strength, man as a combatant' (Strahan). Repeatedly Job had used language (*e.g.* 31:35-37; 13:22) which seemed to suggest that in him God would find a worthy combatant. Ironically God takes him at his own valuation. But it is not long before the frail creature bows in abject confession of need before a fresh revelation of the mighty Creator (see 42:6). The combatant becomes a worshipper.

38:4-38 The marvels of the inanimate world

38:4-11 Earth and sea. Was Job a partner with God in creation, initiated in all its mysteries? **7** poetically speaks of stars and angels alike joining in the paean of praise on creation's morning. **8-11** magnificently depict the sea bursting forth from the womb, with clouds and darkness as its swaddling clothes, not as a rebel, but as a creature of God, called forth by God, controlled by God.

38:12-15 The dawn. Job is reminded of his fleeting life in contrast to the antiquity of the world and God's eternal being. The effect of the dawn on the wicked, who 'love darkness rather than light', is then described. **13** The dawn shakes them out of their treasured refuge. **14** portrays the effect of the dawn on the earth. *Dyed.* This emendation is unnecessary as the Hebrew makes good sense as it stands. RV is better: 'It is changed as clay under the seal; and all things stand forth as a garment.' Detail, beauty, and colour appear. 'It' in v. 13a is the dawn, but in 13b the earth.

38:16-21 Job's ignorance of hidden things. Job

is asked if he has roamed at large through the deep springs that supply the sea, and through the mysteries of the underworld. **18** Does he know the extent of the earth's surface? **19, 20** Is he versed in knowledge about the home of light and darkness? Can he conduct them to their proper spheres and then bring them home again? **21** Could there be a better example of irony than that found in this verse?

38:22-30 Natural phenomena. Even common things like snow and hail, the artillery of heaven, wind, rain, lightning, frost and ice, are mysteries too great for Job. **24** The distribution of the light may be a reference to the diffusion of light over the earth. **26, 27** are noteworthy. Let not proud man imagine that he is the sole object of the divine providence. God not only sends His rain 'on the just and on the unjust' (Mt. 5:45); He remembers also the dreary, uninhabited regions of the world. The inference is that providence is a much more involved affair than Job had imagined. **28** *A father* refers to a human father; *i.e.*, is the rain Job's offspring?

38:31-38 The universe. Does Job control the constellations and the heavens? **31** *The chains of the Pleiades* (RV 'the cluster of the Pleiades'). The precise meaning of the verse is elusive. Cox interprets it: 'Canst thou bring back the gracious fruitful warmth of spring, and release the frozen earth from winter's sterile bands?' **32** There are various identifications of *the Mazzaroth*—the Zodiac or part of it, the Morning or Evening Star, or the constellations (Heb. *mazzālôṯ*) of 2 Ki. 23:5. **33b** refers to the popular belief that the heavenly bodies exercised an influence over the affairs of men. **36** The meaning of the Hebrew is uncertain. AV 'Who hath put wisdom in the inward parts? or who hath given understanding to the heart?' is surely wrong. This would break the continuity of the portrayal of the marvels of the inanimate world by a sudden reference to man. Moffatt translates: 'Who taught the feathery clouds, or trained the meteors?' **38** describes the soil caked by the sun.

38:39 – 39:30 The marvels of the animal kingdom

38:39 – 39:4 Job's ignorance of their ways. A contrast between man and God is implied in these verses. Man is disposed to kill the *lion*, certainly not to assist in finding food for him or for the cubs. God, on the other hand, cares for him and for the cubs. Let Job, who had accused God of savagery in dealing with him, remember God's attitude even to savage beasts. RV and Moffatt have 'lioness' for 'lion'. Lk. 12:24 is the NT answer to the question in v. 41.

39:5-12 The wild ass and the wild ox. The first reference, to *the wild ass*, is to an animal very different from the domestic ass—fleet of foot, graceful, wandering in herds over vast stretches of country. The emphasis is on its freedom. It is as high-spirited as if it had been suddenly released from captivity. This is not a work of man. The emphasis in the reference to *the wild ox* is on the animal's strength and unreliability. Can Job use this creature for agricultural purposes as men use the tame ox? Only One can control him, the God who created him.

39:13–18 The ostrich. 13 *The pinions and plumage of love* is a reference to the proverbial cruelty of the ostrich (*cf.* La. 4:3). The discussion of the ostrich is based on the popular belief that she neglects her young. There have been various explanations of this belief. *a.* The bird sometimes wanders away from her eggs during the daytime and loses her way back. *b.* 'Apparently some eggs are laid outside the nest, and either by accident or design, those eggs are used for food for the newly-hatched chicks. The broken pieces of egg-shell seem to have given rise to the view that the ostrich neglects her young' (Wood). Of the modern ostrich the *Encyclopaedia Britannica* writes: 'The parents display great solicitude for their young.' **16** *She has no fear* means that she does not care if her labour in laying eggs goes all for nothing. **17** is suggestive; her proverbial foolishness is ascribed to an act of God. Man does not know the reason for the act of God; he cannot, for he does not possess the Creator's wisdom which ranges the universe. **18** is a reference to the great speed of the ostrich when running.

39:19–25 The horse. 19 *Strength.* RV has 'quivering mane'; AV 'thunder' may be right here. This is the normal Hebrew word for thunder with the qualification that it is usually masculine, not feminine as here. Perhaps the author is comparing the arched neck of the war-horse to the bow in the sky in stormy weather. **20** *Locust. Cf.* Rev. 9:7.

39:26–30 The hawk and the eagle. *Toward the south* refers to the southward migration of the bird when the cold weather comes. The description of the eagle's powers and habits is particularly vivid. Job is further shown his human frailty by being reminded that he has no say in such matters.

40:1 – 41:34 The mighty power of God

40:1–5 Job's self-esteem shattered. We are now moving towards the human response to the divine word, introduced by the question given in v. 2. Ironically God had taken Job at his own evaluation as a combatant (see on 38:3). Has Job, the combatant, any answer to offer after listening to the impressive commentary upon the wonders of nature, animate and inanimate, which the God of nature had graciously granted him? But the revelation of heaven has made the defiant combatant a humble worshipper. **3–5** Here we have a classic illustration (*cf.* 42:1–6) of the results which must always follow when the silence of heaven is broken, when the almighty God appears with a fresh revelation of Himself, to which man listens in that posture of faith without which 'it is impossible to please him'. At such times the speech of earth is stilled; Job could have bitten out his tongue for some of the hot words of complaint which he had poured out. At such times man sees himself in his true

light: *I am of small account.* It is not a confession of sin, although there is no doubt that Job would have immediately acknowledged the sinfulness of some of his words and attitudes. It is rather a confession of insignificance. As he looked away from himself to the God he was seeing in a more impressive way than ever before, he saw himself in a new perspective.

Some commentators are unimpressed by Job's reaction. They seem to regret the spectacle of Job in retreat, 'cowed' and 'bludgeoned' by this too-overwhelming revelation. Clearly they prefer the earlier Job who had been 'Honest to God' in downright rebellion. Irwin writes: 'His complete surrender and humiliation has provoked comment by students of the Prometheus drama that the tortured Hebrew is a figure far inferior to the Greek god who could not be broken with thirty thousand years of acute agony.' It is felt that the unconditional surrender of Job places a strain on our credulity. Disappointment is also expressed that Job's searching questions are simply under the carpet.

'Retreat' is surely the wrong word to use. In Job's reply we are rather in touch with an advance to a more adequate view of God, and to at least something of what Paul called the 'secret and hidden wisdom of God' (1 Cor. 2:7). Man is not in a position to comprehend every aspect of the meaning of the human situation. Job came to the realization that what had been, and still was, a puzzle to him was no puzzle to God.

At this stage of the book it would be a greater tax on our credulity if Job were portrayed carrying on his one-man war with God. In his eagerness to prove his integrity he had travelled dangerously towards imagining that he could attain to equality with God. He deserved the divine irony in such a word as 'Deck yourself with majesty and dignity; clothe yourself with glory and splendour' (40:10). To have persisted in his attitude would have pushed him right over the brink of the sin behind all other sins, to which the serpent lured Adam and Eve in the glittering dream 'You will be like God, knowing good and evil' (Gn. 3:5). But the Satanic whisper cannot survive the divine Word. That Word brought a transformation which the word of man had been totally unable to achieve. From chs. 3 to 37 we have one long commentary on the inadequacy of the word of man, and the wisdom of man, to explain the mystery of suffering. Eliphaz, Bildad, Zophar and Elihu had all poured out words, without speaking a single word which brought conviction or comfort to Job. Job's replies had also failed to interpret the mystery; they had also darkened God's 'counsel by words without knowledge' (38:2). The Word of God came and the strife of words was over. It did not come through a carefully reasoned argument, dealing a deathblow to Job's intellectual difficulties by its inexorable logic; it did not come through a cut-and-dried explanation of the strands of suffering in Job's experience. There is silence on such issues; silence about the question of retribution, which had bulked so large in speech after speech; silence about the disciplinary aspect of suffering. The Word came through a fresh vision of God—of the mighty, majestic God behind the marvels of animate and inanimate nature, painstakingly attentive to the unexpected and the insignificant (see especially 38:26, 27, 39; 39:30), towering above human might and wisdom.

The Word in the vision convinced Job that he could trust such a God. It brought home to his heart the realization that providence was a much more involved and painstaking affair than he had imagined it to be. He had been like a man living in a stuffy room, whose closed windows had been shutting out God's clean, sweet air, and whose drawn blinds had been excluding God's sunshine. With the appearance of God, the windows had been thrown open and the blinds had gone up. God did not answer the problems of his mind, but He did answer Job; He healed the wound of his heart and brought quiet resignation flooding back into his heart. This was not a man who was 'cowed' or 'bludgeoned', but a man who was convinced that all was well with the world because the everlasting arms could not fail. And yet Job had never heard that most impressive divine Word, which has given mankind the clearest vision of God, and the most indisputable evidence that God can and must be trusted—the Word of the cross. The vision of the God of nature made Job a worshipper. How much more can the vision of the God of Calvary bring the sufferer to his knees, 'lost in wonder, love, and praise'!

40:6–14 God's power in the moral order. The irony that has been running through the divine speech is strongly reflected in these verses. G. C. Morgan sees in the passage 'satire as gentle as the kiss of a mother when she laughs at a child'. **8** asks if Job is prepared to hold on to his own innocence, at the price of rejecting the justice of God. **9** The thought now swings from the natural order of the universe (chs. 38–39) to the moral order. Has Job the mighty arm and the commanding voice of God? **10** If so, let him take God's glorious garments; **11–13** let him mount the throne of the universe, to send the thunderbolts of his anger speeding against the proud and the wicked. **14** Then, and only then, can he pass an intelligent judgment upon the divine ordering of things and earn the divine 'well done'. *Acknowledge* (RV 'praise'). Strahan points out that the Hebrew word used here (*yāḏâ*) is 'ordinarily used by a worshipper who is lauding or giving thanks to God'. Here the Creator lauds the creature!

40:15–24 Behemoth. In 40:15 – 41:34 we have a description of two monsters, *Behemoth*—usually identified as the hippopotamus—and *Leviathan*—usually identified as the crocodile. The atmosphere of the passage is that of chs. 38 and 39 rather than of 40:6–14. Its force in the argument proceeds on some such lines as: Can

Job assume sway over the material order as represented by these formidable creatures? It is a much more formidable undertaking to stand forth as a combatant against their Creator (41:9–11). By this turn in the argument the Lord closes the last possible escape route by which Job might have tried to make sense of his predicament. The adversities of life can be brought within a framework of logical explanation if one is able to say that God is not wise enough always to make our circumstances match what we may deserve, or if, though wise, He is thought to be nevertheless unjust in His nature, or finally, if, though He is both wise and just, yet He lacks the power to put His wisdom and justice into effect. In His speeches to Job, the Lord opened on the theme of loving, detailed, provident wisdom (38:1 – 39:30); the second theme (40:1–14) is God's power in the moral order, His ability to abase the proud and to tread down the wicked (40:11, 12). Thus His moral justice is asserted. The marvels of physical strength, Behemoth and Leviathan, are intended to point to the awesome power of God. To men, these giants represent untamable strength, but yet they must submit if their Creator *bring near his sword* (v. 19). How powerful then is God! Along the line of this threefold argument, God brings Job to his final position of repentance and faith. He cannot argue his way out of his difficulty by denying the wisdom, justice or power of God, but he can, after he has seen just how wise, just and powerful God is, rest humbly and trustfully upon Him. **19** Cf. RV. **24** *Can one take him with hooks* adopts a reconstruction of text. AV 'He taketh it with his eyes' and RV 'Shall any take him when he is on the watch . . .?' follow the Hebrew 'in his eyes'.

41:1–34 Leviathan. The formidable qualities of the crocodile are emphasized in vv. 1–9. Ironical questions run through the passage. **1, 7** Can Job look upon the crocodile as a suitable object on which to demonstrate his fishing ability? **4** as a domestic servant? **5** as a plaything? **8** might be paraphrased to mean: 'Meddle with him in any of these ways, and you will rue the day.' **6** RV translates: 'Shall the bands of fishermen make traffic of him?' **9** *The hope of a man*: i.e. of getting the better of him. **10, 11** If a creature is too formidable to assail, what then must be said about the Creator of all things? Cf. Rom. 11:35. God is indebted to no man. Man has given him nothing; He has given man everything. So it is preposterous for man to imagine that he can stand on an equal footing with God. Yet some of Job's reckless challenges to God had almost implied that he could.

12–34 A description of the crocodile is given here. **13** *Double coat of mail*. RV follows the LXX in translating 'double bridle', i.e. his jaws. **18–21** describe his steaming breath, luminous in the sunshine. **22** *Terror dances before him* is a graphic description of the terrified movements of other creatures when the crocodile appears. **25** *Crashing* is possibly the sound of the wash caused by the movements of his body in the waters.

42:1-6 JOB'S RESPONSE TO THE DIVINE WORD

Cf. 40:1-5 and see commentary *in loc.* The one who had been a combatant against God is now seen as a worshipper, humbly confessing his sinfulness, and entering into an experience of the divine forgiveness. The unveiling of God's glory led to an unprecedented experience of the divine forgiveness. *Cf.* Rom. 3:23. Associated with this new experience of sin is, first, an unprecedented confidence in God's providence. 2 *All things* certainly include the fulfilment of a beneficent divine purpose in Job's suffering. *Cf.* Rom. 8:28. Job the rebel had no confidence that no divine purpose could be *thwarted*; Job the humble penitent possessed it in rich measure.

Second, Job now completely renounces the force of human words and human reason. 3 '*Who is this that hides counsel without knowledge?*' is an echo of 38:2. His words, his wisdom, in which he had prided himself, had merely cast a clumsy screen across the consistent pattern running through God's dealings with him. 4 We have a further echo of God's words here. *Cf.* 38:3; 40:7. Answer a challenge like that, with his puny human mind, unable to grapple with the range of the divine wisdom? Impossible! Job the rebel would have had a different answer to give.

Third, 5 Job can rejoice in a fully personal religious experience. In comparison with the radiant personal faith the vision had brought to him, his earlier religious experience had been a matter of hearsay and not of personal experience.

42:7-17 EPILOGUE

The text now passes from poetry to prose, the style of writing used for the prologue. The conclusion opens with the condemnation of the three friends, Eliphaz, Bildad and Zophar. The omission of Elihu from public censure is significant and may have bearing upon his repudiation of the traditional theology that suffering necessarily implies sin and is always in proportion to its gravity. The three friends are charged with not speaking *of me what is right* (vv. 7, 8). Their view of the divine character was erroneous, especially in the case of God's rule upon earth and His dealing with men. Job, on the other hand, is commended. This, of course, does not mean that everything he had said was right. The narrative continues to portray the integrity of Job. The patriarch freely forgives the hurt that false words had given and even makes intercession for the three pseudo-comforters. God upholds Job publicly as a righteous man.

42:7-10 Job's spiritual blessings

The passage provides a beautiful picture of the spiritual and material tokens of this divine approval, of which the spiritual tokens are of supreme significance. 7, 8 Note first that God refers to Job as *my servant* four times in these two verses. One is reminded of the suffering Servant of Isaiah 53. (*Cf.* 1:8.) Then God commends Job for his sincere quest for truth, and censures the friends for their opposition to that quest. The large sacrifice mentioned in v. 8 is surely meant to indicate how much they were out of favour with God. We remember, of course, and are meant to remember passages in the friends' speeches, redolent with beauty and spiritual truth, while not infrequently Job had gone perilously near error, rebellion and blasphemy: but, as McFadyen has pointedly said, 'Job was right in his intellectual temper, in the drift, the impulse, the sheer intrepid honesty of his thought . . . . Out of all the welter of the discussion, Job stands as the champion of intellectual and religious freedom with the seal of the God of truth stamped upon his disfigured brow.' The passage is a striking warning that 'intrepid honesty' in facing the facts of existence —no matter how disturbing and unfamiliar—is much more pleasing to God than timid clinging to familiar and comfortable ideas in the teeth of the evidence. 9, 10 Finally, God honours Job's prayers for his friends. Job enters the company of the great interceders—Abraham, praying for Abimelech, and Moses for Pharaoh. The costly sacrifice was not enough: prayer was necessary. Is this a hint that orthodox ritual was insufficient to deal with human sin? (*Cf.* Ps. 51:16, 17.)

42:11-17 Job's material blessings

In passing from the spiritual tokens of God's approval to the material, it is striking to note 10 that it was when Job was praying for others that his material prosperity was restored. It was when his attention was focused on the spiritual interests of others that all other things were added to him (*cf.* Mt. 6:33). These verses speak 11 of the restoration of friendship; 12 of property; 13-17 and of family. This OT drama fittingly ends with the words *And Job died, an old man, and full of days. Cf.* Gn. 25:8; 35:29. As a sort of commentary upon the great passage of resurrection hope (19:25-27) the LXX adds 'and it is written that he will rise again with those whom the Lord raises up'.

Anyone who is familiar with modern commentaries on Job will be aware that many scholars do not believe that the epilogue is in fact a fitting conclusion to the book. Crucial reasons advanced are:

a. It is a 'sad concession to a low view of providential dealings' (Cheyne), to portray these material tokens of the divine approval.

b. The epilogue is open to the charge of falsity. Life often does not have a fairy-tale ending. The epilogue therefore is open to the very charge which Job levelled against his friends, *i.e.* that their theories did not fit the facts of human experience.

c. It is difficult to accept 42:7, 8 as a true description of the dialogue. It is claimed that a rebuke to Job is implied in the divine speeches, and that they echo what the friends had reiterated again and again, and what Job had decisively rejected.

Such considerations led scholars like Peake, Sellin, Duhm and Franks to hold that the author adapted an earlier book of Job and put in a dialogue of his own in place of the original speeches. Irwin claims that the author of the dialogue was 'too penetrating and too honest ever to have offended his readers with these superficialities' (*i.e.* of the epilogue). He postulates 'one more ancient writer who was stirred by the greatness of the Dialogue'.

There is an adequate answer to all the above difficulties.

a. The unfairness of Cheyne's criticism appears from various considerations. At a time when there was no clear picture of a life after death, how could the fact that righteousness is woven into the very texture of reality, and must ultimately bear the stamp of God's vindication, be demonstrated, unless on the canvas of this present life? There is no inconsistency in this since the aim of the book has not been to deny that there is a connection between righteousness and material prosperity, but only that the connection is invariable. We should also remember that Job's material prosperity has been shattered as a test of Satan's insinuations about the sincerity of Job's piety. The march of events has given the lie to Satan. Justice now demands some restitution.

b. How can the charge of falsity be laid at the door of the epilogue? This would only be valid if its message was: 'This is what happened to Job in the end and it will happen to everyone else in exactly the same way.' Nowhere is there a shred of evidence that the author dwelt in a fairy-tale world. On the contrary we have every right to hold that he was no less penetrating and observant than the author of the Psalms which reflects so clearly the problem of the prosperity of the wicked. There is no real evidence that in a moment of weakness he allowed an old ending to an old story to stand, although it really did not square with his own convictions, or that the ending is the work of a less resolute mind.

c. There is no insuperable difficulty in looking upon 42:7, 8 as a true description of the dialogue provided that it is remembered that the crux of the argument of the friends was that Job was being punished because he was a sinner in a sense that was not true of them. This was not the case and, of course, is not implied in the divine answer. Conviction of sin came, but it came through the vision of God, not through the views of the friends. Job came to realize that his sin was self-sufficiency: but this is the sin of every mortal man—including Job's friends. Their distinctive error was that they equated their own religious orthodoxy with the mind of God.

For these reasons it is possible to maintain a common authorship of prologue, dialogue and epilogue. The epilogue leaves us with a note of hope, not with a mechanical answer to the problem of suffering. All servants of God may not be treated as this great servant was, but all can rest assured that, however paradoxical life may appear to be, God has the whole world, and every human life, in His hands. The paradoxes of Job point forward to Calvary. William Neil finished his commentary on Job with the words: 'We have reached the heart of the message of Job when we can say: "Nothing in my hand I bring, simply to thy Cross I cling" or echo Paul's words in Romans 8:35–39.'

E. S. P. HEAVENOR

The Psalms

INTRODUCTION

The use of the Psalms in centuries of Christian worship is sufficient evidence to show that, without discounting the problems involved, there is no part of the OT in which the Christian finds himself more easily and more completely at home. We readily see here the same God who has now been fully disclosed to us in Christ; we see men of the same flesh and blood as ourselves, wrestling with, and finding God sufficient for, situations which are in principle the same as ours. We are deeply challenged and frequently rebuked by recognizing that their love for God, their joy in knowing Him, and their willingness to suffer for their faith far outstrip ours, notwithstanding that to us God has shown His love 'in that while we were yet sinners Christ died for us' (Rom. 5:8). Indeed, just as we soon learn in the NT that the era of grace is not without law, so pre-eminently in the Psalms we learn that the era of the law was not without grace. Joy and peace in believing, as well as the tribulations by which we must enter the kingdom, have ever been the experience of the Israel of God.

AUTHORSHIP AND COMPILATION

The OT is full of poetry and song. In this way Moses celebrated the Exodus (Ex. 15), and Deborah and Barak marked the defeat of Sisera (Jdg. 5). Ordinary folk like Hannah (1 Sa. 2), David (e.g. 2 Sa. 1:17ff.) and Hezekiah (Is. 38:9ff.) among the kings, and many of the prophets (e.g. Is. 37:21ff.; Hab. 3) marked their most significant experiences in song. It is no surprise, therefore, that out of such a religion there should emerge this anthology of its psalmody. But very difficult questions nevertheless remain: from what sources and by what steps did the Psalter come into its present form?

The superscriptions

At first sight the origin of the Psalms seems to be no problem at all. For the most part they are furnished with superscriptions or 'titles', and the majority of these contain a personal name which could conceivably be that of the author. 'David' features in seventy-three superscriptions (e.g. 3; 4; 5), the 'sons of Korah' in eleven (e.g. 44–49), 'Asaph' in twelve (e.g. 73–83; cf. other individual names in 88; 89; 90).

In assessing the value and meaning of these superscriptions, it no longer constitutes any problem that the ascription of a psalm to David involves us in supposing a very early date of composition. Psalm-study has long since left behind the curious fashion of insisting that the bulk of the Psalter originated in Maccabean times, and, for reasons which we shall presently explore, it is now quite commonplace to find the monarchy presupposed as the era of psalm-composition, and to find David reinstated as the 'sweet singer of Israel'. There is every reason to place reliance in traditions like that preserved in 1 Ch. 16, that David was the organizing spirit behind the schools of Temple-singers. But on the wider question of the date of the Psalms in general, we may note the opinion of Kaufmann that 'there is no psalm whose plain sense (as distinct from the midrashic romancing of modern exegetes) requires a dating later than the exilic Psalm 137' (E. Kaufmann, *The Religion of Israel*, 1961, p. 311).

Weiser appears willing to extend the possibility of early dating equally to the superscriptions. He writes: 'The term $l^e d\bar{a}w\bar{i}d$ ('to David') in the titles of individual Psalms is . . . of an earlier date than the collection of "Davidic Psalms" which is hinted at in Ps. 72.20 . . . and can probably be traced back to a custom practised already in pre-exilic times by collectors of psalms at the Temple' (A. Weiser, *The Psalms*, 1962, p. 96). If this is the case, the way lies open for a more balanced assessment of the evidence of the LXX on the titles, for it has often been urged that there are so many Septuagintal variations from the Massoretic text that we are bound to conclude that we are dealing with a very unreliable textual tradition. Stated thus broadly, this is very far from the truth. The tendency of the LXX is to confirm the Massoretic text of the titles, and then, in not a few cases, to add something further. This does not, however, invalidate the Hebrew tradition: it confirms it. And if a considerable lapse of time occurred between the Hebrew titles and the LXX, such additional material is by no means unforeseeable.

Even so, however, the superscriptions do not solve the question of authorship. What does the preposition 'to' mean in the expression 'to David' ($l^e d\bar{a}w\bar{i}d$)? While it can imply authorship, as Hab. 3:1 shows, more literally it means 'belonging to'. In the case of psalms rooted in stated personal experiences (e.g. 3), it is easiest to understand 'belonging to' as a statement of authorship, for there is no good reason for disputing the accuracy of these historical allocations. But where a psalm 'belongs to the sons of Korah' is it not easier to understand that this was part of their recognized repertoire and to be found in the 'hymn-book' which they had compiled for their own use? Or again, ᵗhe superscription of Ps. 102 is clearly intended to suggest on what sort of occasion the psalm can most suitably be used, just as modern hymn-books divide hymns into convenient categories. Weiser (*op. cit.*, p. 96) takes this further with the suggestion that *lᵉdāwîd*, similarly, means 'for the use of the David (*i.e.* the Davidic king)'— a psalm to be recited by the king as he carried out his royal function in public worship. This last suggestion belongs, of course, with Weiser's total view of the Psalms and of the part played by the king in the Temple cult, but at the moment it serves to show that no simple solution offers itself as to the meaning of the superscriptions.

The ascription *lamᵉnaṣṣēaḥ*, found fifty-five times (*e.g.* 4–6) and now usually though still tentatively understood as 'to the precentor' or 'choirmaster', suggests that at some point a 'master of the Temple music' made a collection out of existing sources. Apart from Pss. 66; 67, this ascription is always coupled with some personal ascription, 'to David' or 'to Asaph', *etc.*, which shows that the 'choirmaster' was careful to acknowledge copyright. But none of his superscriptions contains the name of more than one individual, and if such names only point to 'collections' and not to 'authors' it is rather too much of a coincidence that no psalm should have been found to 'belong', for example, both to 'David' and also to 'Asaph'. This reason-ing would lead us to suppose that, in the case of Ps. 88, the choirmaster, on taking the psalm into his collection, intended his superscription to mean: 'This psalm was first included in the Korahite collection, and was composed by Heman the Ezrahite.'

Editorial work

Even when we grant that the bulk of Pss. 3–41; 51–72 once formed an independent 'Davidic' collection, and that other such collections are still visible in the Psalter (*e.g.* the 'Songs of Ascent', Pss. 120–134; or the 'Hallelujah' psalms, 111–113; 116–118; 135; 136; 146–150), and that collectors like 'the choirmaster' were at work, we are still very far from being able to explain how the Psalter reached its present arrangement and size.

Several facts combine to indicate that it grew by stages. First, Pss. 14 and 53 are identical, save that the former uses the personal name, *Yahweh*, for the God of Israel, and the latter uses the noun *'ĕlōhîm* (meaning 'God') through-out. Coupled with this is the observation that the usage of *Yahweh* predominates throughout Pss. 3–41, and that of *'ĕlōhîm* throughout 42–83. It is unreasonable to suppose that the same editor included one psalm twice in his anthology, and consequently we must assume two editors, one of whom worked in a situation which tended to avoid using the divine name. A similar editorial situation must be assumed in connection with the identity of Ps. 70 with 40:13–17, and 108 with 57:7–11 and 60:5–12. Second, as we noted above, 72:20 must have originated as an editorial note marking the complete edition (as far as was

known) of the psalms of David. Third, a glance at the numbers of the 'Hallelujah' psalms above shows that they are not gathered into one section, but are spread through the latter part of the Psalter. This suggests a piecemeal process of growth rather than a consistent editorial policy carried out in one act of compilation. The fourth indication of the growth of the Psalter and the absence of a single, over-all editorial policy is provided by the musical and liturgical directions (*e.g.* the word 'Selah'). These are not spread evenly through the Psalms: 'Selah' occurs sixty-seven times in Pss. 1–89 but only four times subsequently.

The 'Five Books'

By whatever hands and under whatever pres-sures it was shaped, we have 150 psalms arranged into five 'books', probably with the deliberate intention of matching the five books of the Law with five of praise. The division between the books is marked by an editorially appended doxology (41:13; 72:18, 19; 89:52; 106:48). There is no doxology at the end of the Psalter, possibly because Ps. 150 in itself offers a shout of praise which aptly concludes both the fifth book and the whole collection.

THE INTERPRETATION OF THE PSALMS

The Psalms offer to the Bible student an out-standing opportunity for practising the analytical approach to Scripture. The reader should come to each psalm on the assumption that here is a self-contained unit of writing, that it has a single theme, and that it develops its theme in a clear, concise way. This is, of course, a generalization: it does not seem to apply, for example, to Ps. 119. The psalm under study should be read and re-read until its theme has been discovered, and until by the same process it is gradually becoming clear how the thought moves from one section to another. Special attention should be paid to connecting words like 'because' and 'therefore' which link the sub-sections together. By this process the modern reader can come to see in what circumstance the ancient writer composed this meditation, what pressures were heaviest upon him, and what consolations and reassurances he found in God. It is by finding out what the psalm meant to the author that we find what it may now mean to us.

Historical situations

One help which the Psalms themselves sometimes give to the reader is the association of some individual psalm with a stated historical situa-tion (Ps. 3 and thirteen others). The present mood of OT study is unsympathetic towards these suggestions of origin, and would agree with G. W. Anderson in saying that 'the poetry of devotion is related to recurring situations in congregational worship and in the life of the believer, rather than to specific incidents in history' (*A Critical Introduction to the Old Testament*, 1959, p. 174). But many of these psalms have a warmth and urgency which is more readily explained in another way, namely that a recent personal experience has been not so much described as expressed in terms of the general truths which it embodied. Helmer Ringgren writes thus of the 'laments' in the Psalter, that they are not the 'life history of the individual' but express his distress in typical and universal terms, for 'their purpose is not to describe an event but to assign it to familiar categories'. He urges that 'this classification helps the individual to understand his suffering and to show him the way to obtain aid' (*Israelite Religion*, 1966, p. 181). As we shall see, *e.g.* in Ps. 51 with its extremely detailed dating, this is exactly what has happened, and in fact to take the historical heading seriously explains several otherwise inexplicable points in the psalm. It is, in fact, usually possible at least to say this, that if a man of deep spirituality generalized on the specified experience, this could well have been his exposition of the matter.

The work of Hermann Gunkel

The progress of psalm-study in this century has been based on the attempt to place each psalm accurately in the situation which gave it birth (*Sitz im Leben*), and the most influential writer has been Gunkel, whose classification of the psalms laid the foundation on which others have built. Gunkel, working between 1900 and 1926, turned specialist attention away from the often profitless task of trying to determine the date of origin of a psalm to the more satisfying task of probing its content and discovering its central idea. 'Gunkel', says A. R. Johnson ('The Psalms' in *The Old Testament and Modern Study*, ed. H. H. Rowley, 1951, p. 165), 'sought as a first step to classify the psalms according to their types and then, only secondarily and on the basis of this, to deal with the question of authorship and date.' This procedure is surely correct, and in Gunkel's hands was marked by much perception and common sense. A fuller discussion of Gunkel may be found in Johnson's essay: here we can do no more than sketch out the main categories which he distinguished, and which were five in number: 1. *Hymns*, *i.e.* psalms dwelling on the greatness and attributes of God, His acts in creation and history. Ringgren aptly sums up these psalms as 'descriptive praise' (*op. cit.*, p. 179). They include Pss. 8; 19; 29; 68; 100; 103; 105; *etc.* 2. *Communal laments*, used by the assembled congregation in times of national threat. Pss. 44 and 74 are typical. 3. *Royal psalms* (*e.g.* 2; 18; 20; 45; 72) were supposed by Gunkel to have been used by the reigning Davidic monarch as part of his royal ritual in the public worship of the Temple. Gunkel tried to find a specific historic occasion for each and, *e.g.*, assigned Ps. 132 to a celebration of the anniversary of the founding of the Davidic dynasty. 4. *Individual laments*

formed for Gunkel the largest single group (*e.g.* 3; 5; 6; 7; 22; 42–43; 51; 88) and gave expression to individual grief, but in the setting of the assembled congregation. He noted a great similarity of structure in these psalms, and pondered specially the frequent note of assurance or certainty of being heard by God which they contain. Of this two explanations were thought possible: either that in the course of his lament the sufferer received inner assurance from God (*e.g.* 6:8–10), or that into his lament there was injected a word from God spoken by one of the Temple personnel (*e.g.* 55:22; *cf.* 2 Ch. 20:4–13, 14–17). Gunkel insisted on the individualism of these psalms, as against the view that they gave merely personalized meditations on party strife within post-exilic Judaism. 5. *Individual songs of thanksgiving.* Very often the individual laments vowed thanksgiving to God in the event of deliverance (*e.g.* 54:6). Gunkel recognized the public fulfilment of such vows in a separate group of psalms, including 18; 30; 32; 34; 116; 118.

The Psalms and the cult

Throughout Gunkel's work there is the conviction that the Psalms belong in the setting of the public worship, or cult, of Ancient Israel. Very often the Psalms themselves reveal their cultic orientation: they delight in God's house (84:10); they see the entrance to God's presence as provided by the 'holy hill', the 'tabernacle' and the 'altar' (43:3, 4); they include cultic directions (118:27, see commentary); they see inward piety as necessarily expressed in outward religious acts (116:13, 14, 17, 18). It is difficult to see how it could ever have been held that the Psalms were opposed to the practice of animal sacrifice. This was never, in fact, a well-founded theory. The verses to which it appealed (*e.g.* Ps. 50:13, 14) could support the case only if their context (50:5) were ignored (see further on Ps. 51). It is now recognized that, far from being anti-cultic, the Psalms are rooted in the cult, and, like the rest of the OT, insist that sacrifice as an outward act is useless unless it accurately reflects the inner state of the worshipper's heart: they must be 'sacrifices of righteousness' (4:5, AV; RSV 'right sacrifices'), sacrifices proceeding from a right disposition.

The ancient annotations included in the titles of the Psalms reinforce this cultic relationship, probably indicating in what way the various psalms were best suited for public use: among these words are 'psalm' (*mizmôr*, Ps. 3 and fifty-five others), and 'song' (*šîr*, Ps. 30 and thirteen others), though the difference between these is not clear; 'prayer' (Ps. 17 and four others), 'praise' (Ps. 145) and 'for instruction' (Ps. 60) are self-explanatory; three words are of doubtful meaning: 'Shiggaion' (Ps. 7; *cf.* Hab. 3:1) probably means 'dirge'; 'Miktam' (Pss. 16; 56–60) is hesitatingly associated by some with 'gold'—'a Golden Psalm', perhaps expressive of the estimation in which it was held; but by others, with more probability, with a verb meaning 'to cover', and hence associated by them with 'covering' or expiating sin. The psalms in question would be used in the rite of the sin-offering. All the psalms thus described are, however, concerned with protection from worldly foes, and this may be the sense in which they are 'psalms of covering'; 'Maskil' (Ps. 32 and twelve others) is certainly related to a verb meaning 'to have insight', and may mean 'a didactic poem'. Another group of descriptive words seems to have reference to the musical ordering of worship: 'for the flutes' (Ps. 5), 'with stringed instruments' (Ps. 4); 'Sheminith' (Ps. 6 and twelve others) may mean a particular 'eight-stringed' instrument, or eight-part arrangement; 'Gittith' (Pss. 8; 81; 84) may be related to the word for 'wine-press' and therefore point to the use of some joyful music such as was associated with the ingathering. A word which remains totally unexplained is yet the most frequent of all, 'Selah' (*e.g.* Ps. 3:2, 4, 8; seventy-one times in all). It seems to be a technical term, but whether it bears on the music, the voice(s) of the speaker(s), or the response of the worshippers remains unsettled. It may be related to a verb meaning 'to build up', hence 'raising of voice', crescendo of music, transposition to higher tone; or to a word meaning 'pause', hence 'musical interlude' or 'period of meditation'; or it may be an acrostic of three letters 's-l-h', meaning either 'change of voices' or 'repeat'. Finally, many psalms seem to include in their titles a suggestion of what tune should be used (9; 22; 45; 46; 53; 56; 57; 60; 80; 88).

All these things have been pointing to the cultic setting of the Psalms, but it has really only been under the impulse of Gunkel that detailed exploration has taken place. One distinctive line of enquiry is associated with the name of Mowinckel, who, while agreeing that the significance of the Psalms is to be sought by means of their setting in the cult, has urged in particular that the focal point of this setting is Yahweh's enthronement as universal King, depicted in an annual Temple-ceremony. Mowinckel insists that the opening words of Pss. 93; 97 and 99 (*cf.* 96:10) must be translated 'Yahweh has become King', and that they constitute the joyful cultic shout at the annual feast. By similarity of content with these psalms, he finds the same cultic setting suitable for 46; 48; 76; 87; 120–134 and many others (for fuller study see Johnson's essay mentioned above, and also his book *Sacral Kingship in Ancient Israel*, 1955).

There is, of course, no mention of such a festival in the historical books of the OT, but it is known that, in his anxiety to detach the ten tribes from their old affiliation to Yahweh and to the house of David, Jeroboam proposed to centralize religion at a northern shrine and to do so by means of 'a feast on the fifteenth day of the eighth month like the feast that was in Judah' (1 Ki. 12:26–33), and that in this feast he, as king, played a leading part. This suggests the existence of a Judahite feast whose emphasis was on God and king, and conceivably it could have been the Feast of Tabernacles, held annually exactly a month earlier than Jeroboam's imitation. In the admittedly much later reference in Zc. 14:16ff. Tabernacles is firmly linked with kingship and prosperity.

It is doubtful if thought on this subject would have proceeded even thus far were it not for the discovery of a 'New Year Festival' in Babylonian religion, which (it is often claimed) provided a pattern for identical celebrations throughout the Fertile Crescent. The chief Babylonian god, Marduk, was proclaimed as creator-king and to him was ascribed the pre-creation victory over the forces of chaos (figured by 'the deep') and present victory over all other gods (*cf.* Pss. 93; 95:3–5). The combat leading to this victory was dramatically represented, the reigning king portraying the victorious god. But the king also played a part in his own position as mediator between the god and the people. In this he was first ritually humiliated (*cf.* Ps. 89) until all hope of a revival of his rule was gone, but at the very eleventh hour he was delivered by divine intervention (*cf.* Pss. 46; 48), the opposing forces were routed, stability was restored, and prosperity guaranteed for another year. In Babylon, the fertility which promised prosperity was promoted also by the so-called 'sacred marriage' in which the king united himself with a chosen girl, and some have held that even this aspect was taken into Israel and is reflected in Ps. 45 and in the Song of Songs. But, apart from this, Ps. 46:8 with its invitation 'Come, behold', and Ps. 48:9, translated 'We have depicted', are said to point to Temple dramas associated with the New Year Festival.

The few references in the Psalms just given poorly represent the wealth of material which these theorists have combed from the Psalter, and must be viewed simply as typical. It should also be stressed that not all would allow that features such as the 'sacred marriage' were adopted in Judah: Israel's distinctive religious position would not permit wholesale taking over of pagan rites, and in particular a fundamental difference opened up between Babylon and Israel in that the former only required the exact performance of the ritual in order to secure divine favour, whereas in Israel the requirement was throughout righteousness, and the New Year Festival, if it existed, was more in the nature of an annual national act of consecration.

But theory remains theory and the strength of the opposition may be gauged by noting that both de Vaux (*Ancient Israel, Its Life and Institutions*, 1961, pp. 504ff.) and Martin Noth (*The Laws of the Pentateuch and other Essays*, 1966, pp. 145–178) have ranged themselves against it, the latter insisting, for example, that the existence of a common pattern of festival is extremely doubtful, that monarchy was a 'late-starter' in Israel and contained an element of election by the people which made it different in kind from the so-called 'divine king-ship' of the Ancient Near East, and that there is no necessity to suppose a ritual of the divine king if the person were not there.

Another line of enquiry into the Psalms, arising from Gunkel's fundamental studies, is associated with the names of Weiser (see A. Weiser, *The Psalms*, 1962) and von Rad (*cf.* Ringgren, *op. cit.*, pp. 191–197). The psalms which centre on the divine Kingship, or which presuppose the person of the human king, and, indeed, the majority of the rest of the Psalter, were composed for the celebration of the Feast of Tabernacles which was pre-eminently a 'covenant' feast, and whose regular celebration was commanded in the Law (Dt. 31:10). Such celebrations are reflected, so it is held, in Jos. 24 and Dt. 26. The constituents of this festival were typically Israelite: some representation of the coming of God to be with His people (*e.g.* Ps. 50:2, 3), even though we do not know how such a theo-phany would be portrayed. Ps. 50 suggests that it was by means of light; Is. 6:4 by smoke; Ex. 19:16 by trumpets. Second, the great histori-cal acts of Yahweh were rehearsed (*cf.* Ps. 136), His will for His people was proclaimed (*cf.* Ex. 20) and to Him was ascribed Kingship over all creation. It is suggested that Ps. 8 accompanied some sort of dramatic representation of the work of creation in which the Davidic king played the role of the first man, representing all man-kind.

Once again we remain in the realm of theory, except that here we are dealing with a known Israelite festival involving distinctively Yahwistic concepts. But proof remains impossible. Much value, however, has accrued to psalm-study by these investigations, and in particular a new appreciation of the place and importance of the king, and a new and vigorous sense of continuing Messianic expectation centred upon his person (see *NBD*, art. 'Messiah').

LEADING IDEAS OF THE PSALMS

It is impossible to offer more a than bare sum-mary of the rich field of teaching constituted by the Psalms, but under each topic representative psalms will be mentioned in the hope that re-ference to them will open up the subject for the reader.

One of the most remarkable features of the Psalms is that, though personal testimony is their chief mode of expression and the first personal pronoun abounds, yet the clearest impression left is not of man but of God. In this respect the Psalms are the OT in miniature. They assert that God is the Creator (8; 104), but this is no abstract concept merely of how the world began: it is the ground of His present, active and powerful rule over all things as King (29; 96–99). The righteousness of His rule is often noted (11; 75), but in the great rhapsody of divine Kingship (145) we see that righteous-ness is plaited into a threefold cord with great-ness and graciousness (*cf.* 146). The goodness of God (34) is inseparable from His holiness (103), and finds its obverse in the clear truth·of His wrath (38). Another pair of matching truths is the universalism of God's rule (67) and the particularism of His choice of Israel (87), and these are linked by the figure of the Messianic King to whom, in His capacity as Davidic and priestly (110) ruler of Israel there is promised a world-wide sway (2; 72).

Both to His people as a whole (80) and to the individual (23) God is the Shepherd. While this provides a basis for the absolute confidence which looked to God alone for deliverance (16; 25; 31), recognizing His attentiveness to the needs of His own (3; 27; 57; 90; 91), it also gave rise to the problems of divine providence, the frequent adversities of God's people, individual (10; 12; 37; 73; 77; 88) and collective (44; 74; 80). It is in the light of this fact—that God's people have ever experienced suffering and enmity (54; 55; 56)—that we must understand the apparently automatic linking of righteous-ness and prosperity in Ps. 1. This is not a testi-mony of invariable experience but a credal statement: 'Since our God is good, and there is no other God, then it must be well for the righteous.'

The experience of adversity and enmity pro-duced the fierce denunciation of their foes which has caused such offence especially to sensitive Christian ears. It is customary simply to allude to such passages as proper subjects of condemnation, evidences of the distance which separates the revelation of Christ even from the best of earlier men. And, indeed, can the Christian have any fellowship with the desire for the sudden destruction of foes (35:8), their death (55:15), the breaking of their teeth (58:6), the destitution (109:10) and massacre (137:9) of their children?

It is, however, unconvincing merely to write these passages off as 'Old Testament morality', because, first, similar praying and even rejoicing is found in the NT (Gal. 1:8, 9; Rev. 6:10; 18:20; 19:1–6); second, equally with the NT, the OT teaches the duty of love (*e.g.* Lv. 19:17, 18), God's hatred of violence (Ps. 5:6), and the propriety of returning evil with good (Pss. 7:5; 35:12–14); third, the psalms in which the imprecations are found in almost every case contain sentiments which ought to be the envy of the Christian: in Ps. 71, *e.g.*, as against the 'offending' v. 13, note the experience of God claimed in vv. 2–7, the worship of v. 19, and the desire to testify in vv. 8, 15, 16, 18.

Turning to a more positive assessment, it must be clearly grasped that all the offending passages are prayers. There is no indication that adversaries were personally rebuffed by either word or deed. The persecuted men flew to God, and even though they certainly expressed them-selves with vigour, fundamentally they assert their contentment to leave all to God, a course of action which Christians are commanded to follow (Rom. 12:19ff.). This trust in divine action is based on the revealed truth of the righteous judgment of God (see Ps. 7, where the imprecation of v. 6 rests on the theology of vv. 11–13). J. R. W. Stott aptly comments: 'I do not find it hard to imagine situations in which holy men of God do and should both cry to God for vengeance and assert their own righteousness. Since God is going to judge the impenitent, a truly godly person will desire him to do so, and that without any feelings of personal animosity' (*The Canticles and Selected Psalms*, 1966, pp. 11, 12, 154).

In summary, the motives behind these imprecations were three in number: first, the moral passion of a holy man (*e.g.* 139:21, 22). Stott confesses that 'I myself would find it hard to echo these sentiments. The reason for this is not, however, that they are beneath me, but that they are beyond me. . . . I cannot attain to desires for divine judgment without vindictiveness nor to assertions of my own righteousness without pride' (*loc. cit.*). Second, they were moved by a zeal for the clearing of God's good name (*e.g.* 9:16–20; 83:16, 17), and third, by a determination to be realistic. Is it right to pray that God will avenge His persecuted people? If it is—as assuredly it must be—then the precise petitions of Ps. 137:7-9 are often involved, even if in our polite way we prefer to leave them unsaid. In the same way, we would readily pray Ps. 143:11, but hesitate over its realistic corollary, v. 12; likewise, we happily pray for the second coming without stopping to think that we are actually praying for the events of 2 Thes. 1:8. Possibly, therefore, our sense of offence at the imprecations arises not so much from Christian sensitivity as from our general inexperience of persecution and our failure to make common cause with Christians under the lash. 'The victory of God', says Hubert Richards, 'cannot be had without the crushing of evil. It is an absurd sentimentality to want the one without the other' (*The Psalms in Latin and English*, 1964, p. viii).

But there was more to the psalmists' facing of the facts of life than imprecatory praying. When they affirmed the 'creed' of Ps. 1, they were in fact holding fast to four great truths. First, they would have admitted that because God looks for righteousness (4; 5; 15; 24; 50) and opposes the ungodly (52), they, acknowledging their own sinfulness (51), must expect life to contain an admixture of adversity. Second, the oft-remembered goodness of God to Israel (78; 81; 114) bred a confidence that He would never utterly forsake His people—a confidence which proved well founded, as the many testimonies, individual (18; 40; 116) and national (46; 47; 48), show. Third, they asserted that the privilege and wealth of having the Lord for their God outweighed any transitory, earthly tribulation. The Psalms abound in this sort of joy (9; 100; 136; 150); they speak of a loving longing for God (63), satisfaction in His presence (123; 131), desire for His house (42; 43; 84), the goodness of His revelation (19), delight in His law (40; 119), and the wonder of forgiveness (32; 51). Out of personal travail, one psalmist spoke for all: 'My flesh and my heart fail, but God is the strength of my heart and my portion for ever' (73:26).

Fourth, the psalmists asserted the blessed hope of a life with God hereafter in glory (see on Pss. 6; 16; 17; 30; 49; 73; 88; 115). This has been and remains a matter of dispute among OT students, but it seems broadly true to say that the further we move from the era when a supposed evolution of religious thought was taken as the arbiter of OT beliefs, the more we approach what Robert Martin-Achard so well described as 'the discovery of the imperishable blessedness of the man who lives in God' (*From Death to Life*, 1960, p. 165). This, above all, is the conviction of the psalmists as they faced life and death, and it is the conviction which a study of their writings will, please God, impart to us also.

COMMENTARY

BOOK ONE. PSALMS 1–41

PSALM 1. LIFE'S ALTERNATIVES

This psalm well serves as an introduction to the whole collection, for it deals with a theme close to the heart of the psalmists: the alternative characters of men, displayed in alternative modes of conduct, and issuing in alternative destinies. It is closely associated with Ps. 2 which deals with the same themes on a national level. The psalm is not, however, to be understood as promising unvarying prosperity to the godly man at all times. The OT knows life too well to do that, and, for instance, it is interesting to note

that the opening psalms of Book 2 (Pss. 42–44) show us the godly man and the godly nation in extreme adversity (*cf.* Pss. 73; 74). Ps. 1 is a sort of 'creed'. Just as we say 'I believe in God the Father Almighty', and yet sometimes pass through experiences which seem to suggest that He is neither our Father nor Almighty, so also Ps. 1 is an assertion of the blessedness of the righteous man and the faith that God will see him through, as indeed v. 6 insists.

1 The psalm begins by showing the distinctive public life of the righteous. The verbs (*walks . . . stands . . . sits*) indicate not sinless perfection but the resolute cast of the man's mind: he has determined to differ from the principles (*counsel*) which govern the life of the wicked, to make no common cause (*stands*) with those whose lives 'miss God's mark' (*sinners*), to shun the fellowship (*sits*) of the avowed enemies of God (*scoffers*; *cf.* Pr. 21:24). **2** This resolute will is rooted in his secret life of *delight* in what the Lord teaches (*law*), and of continuing meditation on it. Thus we are taught that the resolute will which governs the outer life is rooted in emotions captivated by God's truth, and a mind constantly fed upon His teaching. **3** could open with the words 'And consequently': such a secret life as v. 2 describes yields a distinctive harvest. Drawing vitality from the law of God as from a river, it is fruitful, evergreen and prosperous. It may not necessarily be what the world would call prosperity. **4, 5** By contrast, *the wicked* are as worthless as *chaff*, possess no stability, are helpless before divine *judgment*, and have no share in the fellowship of God's people. **6** The ultimate significance of these alternative modes of life and thought is found in the attitude of *the Lord*. It is He who *knows the way of the righteous*; *i.e.* He watches over and approves of their whole character and conduct (*cf.* 2 Tim. 2:19), guaranteeing for them a destiny in diametrical contrast to that of the wicked (*cf.* Jn. 3:16; Rom. 6:23).

PSALM 2. PLOT AND COUNTERPLOT

This is rightly regarded as a Messianic psalm. It was probably based upon a historical occasion such as that recorded in 2 Sa. 5:3 or the coronation of one of the Davidic kings. Another aspect of the situation is outlined in Ps. 83:5ff. But the distinction of Ps. 2 lies in its discernment of the cosmic crisis behind a national event.

The poem represents the whole world organized against the Lord in deliberate opposition to His rule, and points the contrast between the agitation and futility of rebellious peoples and the equanimity and immutable purposes of God.

1–4 The sovereign God

1 The question is rhetorical not analytical; for any revolt against God is regarded as baseless. The collective power of *nations* and *peoples* can only *plot in vain*. **2, 3** Just as the NT sees the Christian as opposed by the ungodly world (*cf.* Jn. 15:19) and its rulers (*cf.* Eph. 6:12), so here the OT sees God's universal purpose for His anointed (*cf.* Ps. 72:8–11) under attack from the world and its rulers. Historically the object of their attack was the *anointed* of the Lord, viz. David (*cf.* 1 Sa. 24:6); prophetically it was the Messiah (*cf.* Acts 4:25–27). **4** But as the One who *sits in the heavens* and as *Lord* (Heb. '*adōnāy*, 'sovereign'), God's position and power give Him such confidence in the face of opposition as to make it laughably pathetic.

5, 6 The appointed king

5 *Then* has peculiar force: it signifies the termination of the age of man's apparent freedom and the establishment in the earth of the divine purpose. So sure is this appointed climax that God does not hesitate to allow centuries to the rebellious nations so that all their plans may mature, all their objections to His rule may be voiced and every resistance attempted. In this He is governed by His own merciful desire to save (2 Pet. 3:8, 9), and by His absolute justice which judges none before his own deeds have made him ripe for judgment (Gn. 15:16). Then, in the fullness of time, He intervenes with *wrath* (lit. 'blowing nostril') and *fury* (lit. 'burning anger') and **6** utters His emphatic word (*cf.* Rom. 1:18; 2 Thes. 2:8–13), *I have set my king on Zion, my holy hill* (*cf.* Heb. 1:2, 3). Emphasizing the divine purpose (lit. 'as for me, I have set . . .'), the psalm points to the person and the place: God's king in God's city, the destined world-ruler.

7–9 His charter of kingship

It is imagined that the rebellious nations, gathered in tumultuous revolt upon the earth, have been momentarily quelled by the divine declaration which echoes from heaven. In the silence which is supposed to follow, David himself addresses the assembled kings and peoples. If, as some hold, this psalm reflects a ritual enacted at the time of a coronation or annually on its anniversary, how dramatic this would all be! First of all he asserts his kingship to be authorized by the Lord on the grounds of relationship (v. 7), endowment (v. 8) and vocation, *i.e.* the power to overcome (v. 9).

7 The phrase *You are my son* can be paralleled in Ps. 89:26, 27, and the words *today I have begotten you* may be understood historically as referring to the day of David's enthronement, indicative of his adoption as God's son (*cf.* 2 Sa. 7:14), and truly fulfilled in Jesus Christ. Acts 13:33 and Rom. 1:4 declare that He was acclaimed 'Son' by the very fact of the resurrection. Heb. 1:5 and 5:5 quote the phrase as associated with the incarnation and priesthood of Christ. **8** Similarly the promised gift of the peoples and realms of this world came to be a Messianic expectation and has long been understood of Christ. **9** Rev. 2:27 quotes this verse in connection with 'the end', *i.e.* the coming of Christ in glory and power. *Cf.* also Rev. 19:15.

10–12 The moment of decision

In the second part of David's address he reverts to the reality of the situation described in vv. 1–3. That peril has not passed; the crisis is not yet resolved; the elasticity of the divine *Then* (v. 5) has not yet snapped; the issue may still be moulded by men. **10** Hence the appeal to the *kings* and *rulers of the earth*. **11, 12** The alternatives of wrath or refuge, perishing or blessing lie before them.

PSALM 3. PRAYER CHANGES THINGS

Pss. 3 and 4 are related as being prayers of the morning and evening, in each case following a period of great danger and rich protection. The occasion indicated by the title is completely suitable to the content of the psalm. **1** The king's distress of heart arose from the magnitude of the rebellion (*cf.* 2 Sa. 15:13) and **2** from the prevalent feeling that not even God could help David now. But note that trouble drives David to God in prayer, not from Him in disbelief (*cf.* 1 Sa. 30:6). **3–8**, which express his reaction, are a sublime expression of unquenchable trust in God.

1–4 Despondency at nightfall

The sombre developments of the day are summed up in an evening prayer and left with the Lord in confidence that He has heard and heeded. **3** In his danger, the Lord is his *shield*; in his humiliation, He is his *glory*, *i.e.* having God he has everything, even if he is bereft of all else (2 Cor. 4:7–11), and He may be trusted, the One who shall vindicate David against his enemies and detractors, to lift up his head. **4** All this confidence rests upon experience of answered prayer (the verbs represent unvaried custom), and upon revelation of the nature of God as He has shown Himself on *his holy hill*, whether this refers to Sinai or Zion. It was this knowledge of the Lord which enabled him to sleep (v. 5).

5, 6 Vigorous faith at morning

The Lord sustains me. The freshness of body and serenity of faith with which the writer awoke the next morning were due to an implicit assurance of divine mercy and preservation. This not only rid ominous circumstances of any power to intimidate but initiated a claim to actual triumph over them.

7, 8 A call to God

But one night of safety has not dispelled the danger, and prayer remains David's resource. **7** The latter part of this verse could be a reference to past deliverances (*cf.* RV), in which case former mercies act as present encouragements. But in RSV David recalls the changeless faithfulness of God, and then **8** looks to Him as the sole bestower of *deliverance* or salvation, and the sole source of His people's blessedness.

PSALM 4. AN EVENING PRAYER

V. 8 shows that this is an evening prayer, which we may well associate with the same period of danger indicated in the title of Ps. 3.

1, 2 Appeal

1 At night as much as in the morning the Lord is David's resource, to whom he appeals on the ground of personal relationship and changelessly holy character as (lit.) 'my righteous God'.

Equally he is encouraged by God's former deliverances, giving him *room* to move when he had been enclosed in distress (*e.g.* 1 Sa. 23:26–29), and by God's *gracious* disposition towards him. **2** While David waits in prayer before God he makes a meditative appeal to his opponents whom he imagines to be gathered before him. In the turmoil that followed the rebels' initial failure to organize promptly the capture of the fleeing king, through Absalom's mistake in not following Ahithophel's advice (see 2 Sa. 17:1ff.), there was opportunity to have second thoughts about supporting Absalom. David metaphorically appeals to them, charging them with dishonouring the royal dignity he has received from God and recalling the proud misrepresentations of the facts which had led them to join the rebellion (*e.g.* 2 Sa. 15:1–6).

3, 4 Warning

David reinforces his appeal by a warning reminder of his special place in God's providential ordering of affairs. **3** He makes no reference to his position as the Lord's anointed but simply to his *godly* character. Being innocent of their charges he confidently trusts the Lord to intervene for him (*cf.* Ps. 66:18). **4** As ever, human anger trembles on the brink of sin (*cf.* Eph. 4:26; Jas. 1:20) and before continuing in their opposition they would do well to listen to the voice of conscience speaking in their *hearts*.

5 Admonition

Right sacrifices, indicative of a heart desirous of being at peace with God, offer the way of restoration, and in calling his opponents to take this course David summons them from their baseless reliance on Absalom to *trust in the Lord*.

6–8 Testimony

The way of trust is a blessed one. **6** He recalls that in contrast to the *many* opponents of 3:1 there are *many* looking to God alone for alleviation, and resting as they do this on His unchanged character as shown in the Aaronic blessing (*cf.* Nu. 6:26), for when the Lord looks with radiant face upon His people then their fortunes change and they are blessed indeed. **7** In support of this, he also confesses joyfully that in his own case a desperate plight had been transformed by an inward sense of divine grace, which far surpassed the material blessings of food brought by the aged Barzillai (*cf.* 2 Sa. 17:27–30). **8** *Alone.* The Hebrew word may mean either that God alone gives him protection or that God makes him to dwell in safety even when alone (*cf.* RV mg.).

PSALM 5. A MORNING PRAYER

This is a companion to the previous psalm: the circumstances are similar but v. 3 marks it as a morning prayer.

1–3 The invocation

The urgency of his need once more drives him to prayer. **2** The titles of *my King and my God* imply a relationship between David and the Lord which enables him to claim the aid of supreme power and righteousness. **3** *In the morning.* As the first act of the day he (lit.) 'sets (it) in order' and the reference may be either to an ordered statement of his needs in prayer (*cf.* RV) or to a duly presented sacrifice. Then in complete trust he will *watch* in expectation of the Lord's response.

4–8 God's way with the wicked

This expectant confidence is based on the character of God which is so unlike that of the men who oppose him, and is so highly esteemed in his own heart. **4, 5a** Three negative statements, followed **5b, 6** by three positives show the inflexible opposition of God to the wicked, in particular to people of *boastful* self-importance, liars, and those of ruthless and dishonest conduct to others. The speaker then emphasizes in two respects his own differing characteristics. **7** In reverential awe he worships in God's house (*cf.* Ps. 27:4). **8** In his trouble, his ambition is for God to guide him. Not only does he need to know the right; he needs to have removed all those obstacles which would hinder him from walking in God's way. *Make thy way straight*; *i.e.* 'make thy pathway unimpeded'.

9–12 God's way with the righteous

This part of the psalm deals with the same elements as the previous section, *i.e.* the wicked and the godly, but the orientation and emphasis are quite different. Vv. 4–6 consider the wicked as in the sight of God; vv. 9, 10 describe them as they are in life. Vv. 7, 8 form a humble confession of trust in God; vv. 11, 12 speak of jubilant confidence in God's blessing. The prayer has become more precise and faith has become much more assured. **9** Sins of speech are once more singled out for special condemnation (*cf.* vv. 5, 6), and **10** are seen as leading directly, and by the providence of God, to destruction. This principle of sin bringing its own inevitable results is frequently expressed in the Psalter. *Cf.* Ps. 28:4 and see Gal. 6:7, 8.

PSALM 6. A PRAYER OF ANGUISH

This psalm further stresses the same message as the preceding three: that the proper reaction to trouble is to pray. But a new factor enters the discussion here: the possibility that human hostility is the outward expression of divine disapproval, and it is specifically against this that the psalmist now prays, for the troubled man must always search his conscience for sins which provoke God, and supplicate for mercy and restoration.

1–7 Opposition countered by prayer

While clearly still oppressed by human foes (vv. 7, 10), the psalmist's primary fear is that God has become his enemy, and this absorbs all his attention in his prayer. The prayer rests upon three grounds: first, **2, 3** he pleads his present need. The anguish is so severe that both his *bones*, his bodily frame, and *soul*, his inner resources of mind and spirit, are on the verge of breakdown. Of them both he says that they are *troubled* (lit. 'terrified'). His condition is one of the utmost terror, felt both physically and nervously. For this condition, his tranquillizing agent is prayer. Second, **2** he pleads the nature of God, whose broad characteristic towards the troubled is to be *gracious*, and **4** whose particular attitude towards His own people is one of *steadfast love*. His prayer is an effective antidote to his trouble because it leads him to repose on such a God as this. Third, **5** he pleads the fact of his eternal destiny. This verse does not describe the invariable lot of the dead in OT thought. It is speaking exclusively of one sort of death, the death presupposed by the opening verse, death under the wrath of God. Should one die with God as his unreconciled enemy, what hope could he possess? Against such a fate the psalmist pleads (*cf.* Pss. 30:3, 9; 88:5). **6, 7** Such hopelessness results in bitter sorrow.

8–10 Prayer issues in assurance

These verses are best interpreted as an anticipated experience of what is most desired. It may be coloured by memories of former occasions, but this is primarily an intuitive sense of a fulfilment which is yet in the future. **8, 9** The intervention of God is a direct response to his sorrow and supplication and will invert all their values and utterly and unexpectedly throw them into confusion (*cf.* Pss. 35:4–8; 83:13–17; 2 Thes. 2:4–10; 2 Pet. 3:3–10). **10** is a more sober but equally confident expectation of that fulfilment; his opponents will be disgraced by the obvious contradiction of their expectations. In place of his own terror (v. 3) they will be *sorely troubled* ('terrified'). 'If God is for us, who is against us?' (Rom. 8:31).

PSALM 7. AN APPEAL FOR JUDGMENT

This is another prayer for divine protection against ruthlessness and calumny. *Cush* (see title) is not named in the chronicles of the time. The Talmud identifies him with Saul; he may have been one of Saul's fanatical fellow-tribesmen, like Shimei (2 Sa. 16:5). It is generally assumed that the poem belongs to the period of Saul's persecution of David. See introduction to Ps. 52.

1–10 An appeal to God

1, 2 The situation is one of flight from cruel

enemies, of which one is particularly to be feared because his malevolence seems as violent as that of an angry *lion*. **3–5** reveal a conviction of personal innocence almost as vehement as that of Job when he closed the debate with his friends (Jb. 31). Evidently those who sought David's life accused him also of dishonour, *i.e.* of attempting to seek vengeance on the anointed Saul. The words of v. 4b recall the incident of 1 Sa. 24:1–12. **6, 7** Prayer, however, is still the sole resort of the godly man. In the face of base calumny, he does not answer back, but submits his case to the judgment of God (*cf.* 1 Pet. 2:23). The psalmist links his own vindication with a vision of the trial of all humanity before the high court of heaven (*cf.* Is. 43:9). The Judge of all the earth (Gn. 18:25) necessarily does right, and very often individual acts of divine judgment are associated with God's universal office as Judge in order to affirm their correctness and finality (Is. 3:13–15). **8** So here it is as though the court of heaven were already constituted and the universal trial begun. The psalmist first appeals to God for a favourable judgment upon himself on the grounds of his own *integrity*. **9** He then asks for a true judgment on the wicked, those who seek his destruction, on the ground that, in such an ultimate and true assessment of life, all evil *doing* must be disclosed as engendering its own condemnation. Righteousness is seen here as no mere outward conformity. *Minds and hearts*, thoughts and emotions come under divine scrutiny, and **10** none may look to God as his protective *shield* except the inwardly *upright*.

11–17 The divine judgment

11 That God *has indignation every day* reveals that it is part of His unchanging nature to be hostile to all that offends His righteousness. **12, 13** This reaction is depicted in the imagery of irresistible aggression—the sharpened sword, taut bow, deadly weapons and fiery darts—encountered by the sinner who obstinately advances to his doom because he will not turn to the central fact of God's grace and mercy. **14–16** The whole career of wickedness is then described in its beginning, its action and its end (*cf.* Jas. 1:15). **14** The evil man of his own nature gives birth to falsity and error; **15** his work fails in its design and becomes a snare to himself (*cf.* Ps. 9:16); **16** his plans and methods ultimately cause his ruin (*cf.* 1 Sa. 25:39; also Mt. 21:33–41; 25:24–28). **17** All these thoughts evoke in the psalmist a profound conviction of God's worthiness of praise, not only for His innate *righteousness* but because of His sure response to this appeal for judgment, whose name is *Yahweh, the Most High*.

PSALM 8. MANKIND, A PARADOX

Unlike the supplicatory psalms which immedi-ately precede and follow, this poem is meditative and lyrical. The first and last phrases are identical and form a frame for profound ideas concerning God's essential being and His works on earth.

1, 2 The universal majesty of God

1a *O Lord, our Lord*. Lit. 'O Yahweh, our Sovereign'. Speaking as an Israelite who knows his God as Yahweh, the psalmist acknowledges that none other than He is the universal sovereign ruler. It is from this truth that the assurance of faith springs: I am in the care of Him whose hand controls all and whose will as sovereign none can gainsay. **1b, 2** is both difficult to translate and to understand. RSV and RV give the most likely alternatives. RV suggests that the majestic glory of God, seen stamped upon the heavens, is equally seen when He takes the insignificant babes of the earth and uses them to confound the ungodly. Maybe the psalmist was present when the simple faith of a child silenced an arrogant opponent! RSV rather enquires how the invisible *glory* of a God who is *above the heavens* is to be seen and known. The answer is found in two acts of God: first, when children grasp and rejoice in the simple truths of God, His glory is truly seen; secondly, when the moral law which sets a *bulwark* against unrestrained sinfulness is contemplated, God's glory is seen. The mention of the restraining of *the avenger* (*cf.* Nu. 35:14–28) supports this latter view.

3–9 The inscrutable ways of God

A sense of paradox is being developed in the psalm, and this is now elaborated with respect to man's existence. **3** Meditation upon the varied work of creation in the skies (*cf.* Jb. 36:22 – 37:12) and in the heavenly bodies (*cf.* Ps. 19:1–6; Jb. 9:7–10; 38:31–33) brings a conviction of man's frailty and insignificance. **4** *Man . . . son of man*. The Hebrew words denote man's lowly origin and human frailty. Why should God remember any man and, indeed, never leave him alone (*cf.* Ps. 144:3; also 33:13–19 and Ex. 3:15, 16)? Reason and observation can offer no answer to this question. It can be met only by divine revelation, one which discloses a concept of man that seems wholly incompatible with man's own inferences. The essential purpose of creation as revealed of old discloses a threefold peculiarity which lifts man from the negligible to a position of amazing eminence. **5** He has been created by God as 'but little lower than God' Himself. This image of God imparted to man is accompanied by certain attributes, *glory and honour*, which mark out man as superior to all other creatures. **6–8** Moreover, the world and its forms of life have been placed under man's authority (Gn. 1:26–28). **9** This consciousness of a high calling and destiny evokes in the psalmist the ultimate and exuberant praise of the final verse.

It must be noted that the NT amplifies this psalm and also interprets it with reference to Christ. Heb. 2:5–9 first quotes the LXX version (where *'elōhîm* is translated *angelous*) and then bases its argument upon a full and literal exegesis of v. 6b. The statement *Thou hast put all things under his feet* is taken to be a prophetical allusion to Jesus. In a similar way 1 Cor. 15:27 also interprets this same verse of Christ, in whom is fully seen the dominion which God intended man to have and which, in Christ, all the redeemed will ultimately share.

PSALM 9. THE BASIS OF PRAISE

This is the first of the so-called acrostic or alphabetical psalms, making use of the successive letters of the Hebrew alphabet to commence the opening word of its verses. In this case the acrostic is not complete as only the first eleven letters, with one omitted, are used. The acrostic may be continued (though still imperfectly) in Ps. 10, and it is possible that the editor who associated Ps. 10 with Ps. 9 because of the suitability of its content imposed this somewhat artificial appearance of unity to bind them together. Ps. 9 (see especially vv. 3, 5, 6) could well have originated in a situation such as is described in 2 Sa. 5:17-25. It possesses a very coherent structure, such as is frequently exemplified in the Psalms. In vv. 1-10 the psalmist testifies of his thanksgiving to God, and in vv. 11-18 invites the whole company to join in praise. Within these sections we then have, first, the explanation why praise is thus offered (4, 5; 12-14), namely because of God's acts of deliverance; secondly, the situation which resulted from those acts (6; 15); and finally the abiding truths exemplified in God's acts, the nature of His universal rule (7-10; 16-18). The psalm then aptly concludes with a desire for His world rule to be established forthwith (19, 20).

1, 2 *Wonderful* is a word the OT reserves for things, people (*cf.* Is. 9:6), or deeds which are miraculous or supernatural. David here discerns the hand of God in his deliverance and cannot but testify. **3, 4** The historic cause of his elation and thanksgiving is, first, victory in battle, whereby God has vindicated David's kingship. Truth and righteousness have been demonstrated as being with David's cause. **5, 6** Secondly, he rejoices in the destruction of his enemies, who have ceased to exist as dangerous foes. **7, 8** The abiding truths which he sees to be exemplified in these experiences are, first, the perpetuity of God's righteous rule; the themes of God's inexhaustible being and essential justice are used to bind together the spheres of His celestial enthronement in power and His terrestrial administration of ceaseless vigilance. **9, 10** Secondly, he praises God for the infallibility of His gracious care; all men who acknowledge and obey the Lord (*those who know thy name*) can fully rely upon His protective care when they are harassed and oppressed.

11, 12 The historical basis of the psalmist's praise is particularly his own, but the religious basis can know no such restrictions; hence he calls upon the whole company who have heard his testimony to give world-wide publicity to the acts of the God who is known *in Zion* (*cf.* Ps. 96:3, 7-10). Such corporate recognition of God's sovereignty could not be evoked in the same way as the psalmist's, but it could be induced by the realization among men that the eye of God is inescapable (*cf.* Ps. 33:13-15). All bloodshed caused by human motives is repugnant to God (Gn. 9:5; *cf.* Lk. 11:50, 51; Rev. 6:10) and His intervention is to be expected.

13, 14 are a typical 'cry of the afflicted' (v. 12) to which God hearkens and upon which He acts. Peril has thrust him to *the gates of death*, *i.e.* to the very edge of life (*cf.* Ps. 107:18, 19); but his hope in God is that he will come again to the gates of Jerusalem where he will testify to divine deliverance. **15, 16** are a statement of the psalmist's own faith, expressing the general truths reaped from individual experience. Disaster to the wicked, whether actual or anticipated, usually assumed to be the operation of 'natural retribution' (*cf.* Ps. 7:15, 16), is an aspect of divine irony wherein God's essential righteousness is inexorably displayed (*cf.* Gal. 6:7, 8; 2 Cor. 5:10). **17** Those men who wickedly ignore God or rebel against the principles of godliness must surely die. *Sheol* is the place of the dead. **18** On the other hand *the needy* and *the poor* are just as surely the objects of God's special care. Contrast vv. 5b and 6. The frequent reference in the Psalter to 'poor and needy' does not necessarily imply material destitution; the phrase is applied to all who have been reduced to utter dependence upon God (*cf.* Mt. 5:3).

As though to compensate for the activity of evil-doers, there is always the possibility of the intervention of God. **19, 20** The confident trust in the Lord which marked the opening verse is now focused in a petition that He should assert His power, judge the peoples of the earth (*cf.* Ps. 7:6-9), and so awe the arrogant by a demonstration of His majesty that every man shall have to confess his own human weakness and ephemeral nature (*cf.* Jas. 4:14).

PSALM 10. A PRAYER IN A TIME OF SOCIAL DISORDER

Apart from the acrostic relationship of Pss. 9, 10 (see introduction to Ps. 9), they are also linked in theme and phrasing. In particular, vv. 1-11 are well seen as an expansion of the brief prayer with which Ps. 9 concludes.

The theme is a familiar one in all periods of church history, and not least today: the apparent impunity with which ruthless men go their self-seeking way, regardless of God or man, allowing neither morality nor humanity to set limits to their methods or objectives. No thoughtful person who has faced either organized crime or the impersonal Juggernaut of vested commercial interests will have escaped the feeling of helplessness which the psalmist here shows. But he is in fact by no means helpless, for he believes in a living, reigning, merciful and just God to whom the ultimate victory belongs.

1–11 Why is God silent when wickedness abounds?

Evil men and their deeds could never prosper if divine righteousness immediately checked their wickedness. But, on the other hand, wickedness could never bring its own condemnation unless wrongdoing found some expression. **1, 2** The psalmist's perplexity has arisen because God continues to seem indifferent long after injustice among His people has become flagrant, frequent and full-grown (*cf.* such Pss. as 22; 35; 37; 38; 73).

3–11 give a detailed description of the ways of the wicked. They are characterized, first of all, by self-sufficiency based on worldly success. **3** *The wicked boasts*; *i.e.* sings praise to himself, thus making his own desire into his God (*cf.* Hab. 1:15, 16). **4** Note Ps. 14:1 and Jb. 21:14, 15. It is not that evil man denies the existence of God (atheism was virtually unknown among Jews at this time), but **5, 6** he ridicules the notion that God is concerned how men behave. The absence of immediate punishment upon wrongdoers is always a strong argument for a sinner whose values are located wholly within this world, so that even death has little menace for him (see Job's vehemence about this in Jb. 21:17). **7** There is also an inner falsity which springs from his evil desires. Guiltiness is added to blindness, and this is incurred first through speech and then **8** in secret deeds against the innocent and helpless. **9** These cruel practices are described again, **10** the deceitfulness is restated and **11** the primary falsity of his speech is again expressed.

12–18 An appeal to God to intervene

Apart from v. 1 the theme of the first part of the psalm has been 'the wicked', to whom there were a score of references; in the second part the theme is *the Lord* and He is mentioned a dozen times. The direction of thought is changed from details of wicked practices to characteristics of God's rule. These are wholly at variance with the notions of evil men whose inward assurance about God's indifference is altogether untrue. **14** The afflictions of His people are not only observed but become occasions of divine action. **15** The psalm thus becomes an appeal to God that He would intervene and eliminate wickedness. **16** The psalmist finally comes to rest on the ever-comforting and secure truth that *the Lord is king for ever and ever*. But there are two sides to this truth. On the one hand *the nations*, which here means (as in 2:1) organized opposition to God, whether explicit or implicit, must disappear. There is no future for ungodliness in any form. **17** On the other hand, there is the truth of an equally inevitable comfort for the godly oppressed whom the Lord first hears, then strengthens with inner resources in *their*

heart so that they may endure, and **18** finally delivers, for the ultimate impossibility is that *man who is of the earth*, mere earthly, creaturely man (*cf.* Ps. 9:20; Is. 2:22) should have the last word.

PSALM 11. A SONG OF STEADFASTNESS

The theme of serene Godward trust even in face of peril is the same as characterized Ps. 10:16–18. This poem may reflect David's attitude at the time when friends advised him to flee from the brooding envy of Saul even before the third and most serious attempt on his life (see 1 Sa. 18:11; 19:10); but the psalm belongs to all occasions when evil powers threaten the security and well-being of God's people. The vision of the enthroned God is the great stabilizing factor of life. The psalm opens with an affirmation of faith (v. 1a). This is then debated: the argument of the opposition (vv. 1b–3); the reply of faith (vv. 4–6). The psalm concludes (v. 7) by giving the verdict to the original affirmation.

1–3 The warning by prudence

The advice *Flee like a bird . . . what can the righteous do?* may have been given to David by friends, or it may represent the voice of expediency in David's own heart. 1 Sa. 27:1 shows how common and persuasive the voice of worldly prudence is—and how deceptive, as the subsequent history of David among the Philistines proves. **2** The power of the opposition and their capacity for surprise attack *in the dark* unite to undermine the position of faith. **3** The argument is strengthened by an appeal to general considerations: 'Wherever the foundations of society are undermined, what have good and righteous men ever done to prevent its collapse?' (see RV mg.). Prudence dictates the abandonment of the sinking ship.

4–7 The watching by God

Over against the danger of current events and the apparent ineffectiveness of innocency (v. 2c) and goodness (v. 3b) there is the supreme and vigilant holiness of God. He whose habitation is heaven, and whose authority is enthroned over all, is nevertheless ceaselessly scrutinizing the behaviour of all men (*cf.* Pss. 33:13–18; 94:9). **4** We watch, as it were, God's face—the *eyes* which miss nothing, the narrowing of the *eyelids* as He assesses the character and conduct of men. **5** Then we watch His providential ordering of life whereby *the righteous and the wicked* alike are tested and proved (*cf.* Jas. 1:12; 1 Pet. 1:6, 7), for the Lord does nothing without enquiry and examination (*cf.* Gn. 18:20, 21). He responds in no uncertain manner to what He sees: to the godly He extends His protective presence; **6** upon the wicked, whose deeds are repugnant to Him, He sends the disasters of natural calamity (*cf.* Gn. 19:24; Ps. 18:7–14).

7 Faced with these two differing aspects of life, the psalmist has no hesitation in adopting the latter and committing himself to the ever-watchful Lord who loves those who seek His righteousness. In utter contrast to unsettled days and the uncertainty of life, the heart that steadfastly trusts the Lord shall have, after being tested, peace in His presence. *Cf.* 1 Pet. 5:10; Rev. 7:14–17.

PSALM 12. UNTRUTH VERSUS TRUTH

Although this psalm belongs to the large group of laments over the success of evil-doers (*e.g.* Pss. 7; 10; 17; 25; 37), its theme is more specialized than some. The activity of the wicked is primarily felt by the innocent and godly as being in the realm of speech, *i.e.* the falsification and perversion of the divine gift of language. Hence the intervention of the Lord must be not only in deeds but in words. The poem sets the effective purity of God's word over against the specious claims of vain lips, and adds yet further testimony to the serious view the Bible takes of sins of speech.

1, 8 The social trend

The first and final verses outline the contemporary corruption of society, with worthless and base men in positions of influence and power, so that wickedness is openly approved and upright men of godly faith are being squeezed out of public life.

2–4 The specious tongue

Communication amongst men is riddled with falsity, flattery, duplicity, and vanity of speech (*cf.* Jas. 3:5–10). The acme of human pride is when men forge language into such a powerful weapon that deceitful propaganda seems invincible.

5, 6 The sublime truth

Although the vain and vile may disdain the poor man who cries to God, their contempt is as groundless as their pride. The truth is that God is quite aware of the oppression of the faithful and at the right moment He will intervene to bring them security. 6 *Silver refined in a furnace.* This imagery of a crucible, from which the fully-refined silver is poured down into moulds set in the earth, is an apt illustration of the purity, value and applicability to worldly needs of the divine word, swiftly revealed and lastingly preserved. Elsewhere in the OT the process of refining is almost always applied to the children of God, who are purged in the furnace of affliction. *Cf.* Ezk. 22:17–22; Mal. 3:3.

7 The sure trust

The word of God which has been acclaimed so fervently (v. 6) is now appropriated by the trusting heart. Because God is kind (v. 5) and His word true, He can be fully relied upon to safeguard the godly even when *on every side* around him, and *exalted* over him, he can see nothing but *the wicked* and their *vileness*.

PSALM 13. DESPONDENCY CHANGED TO CONFIDENCE

Continuing the lament for the degeneration of society, Ps. 13 is a personal and poignant cry. Its initial mood is one of tedious frustration and strained patience; but the very act of appealing to God stimulates the psalmist's hope so that the final mood is one of joyous appreciation of God's work and purpose in his life. Prayer is not only the proper reaction of the godly to trouble, it is also his medicine against depression in the face of it.

1, 2 A need

The words *How long . . . for ever?* are a question wherein hope and despair pursue each other in closed circle (*cf.* Pss. 74:10; 79:5). The four aspects of sorrow are: a sense of being forsaken by a God who has forgotten him; the hopelessness of one who cannot get through to a God who continually hides Himself away; ceaseless inner hurt and grief; and defeat at the hands of vaunting foes. These are not unconnected experiences, for to be out of touch with God brings the personality to the point of breakdown and leaves us at the mercy of foes, human and spiritual. We may note at once that in the course of the psalm the psalmist found relief of his essential need in experiencing again joy and satisfaction in God.

3, 4 An appeal

Despairing need gives way to prayer in which each necessity in turn is laid before God. Even when God appears to have forsaken him, the psalmist's faith holds firm. Believing intercession is the antidote to overwhelming grief and defeat. 3a First, in respect of the averted face of God, he pleads *Consider* (lit. 'look') *and answer*, and the depth of his faith is revealed in his continuing grasp of the personal relationship expressed in the words *my God.* 3b Second, he reveals the nature of his confessed inner grief, the fear lest he should die uncomforted by any sense of God's favour. 4 Third, he prays against continuing humiliation before his foes.

5, 6 An assurance

To envisage that from which his soul is utterly averse is to rebound by faith into the experience of satisfaction. The sober reflections and strong appeals of vv. 1–4 give place to the fundamental attitude and disposition of his heart. *But I; i.e.* 'as for me, I do trust in Thee'. *My heart shall rejoice . . . I will sing.* His despondency is changed to confidence as his faith lays hold on four characteristics of the Lord: His steadfast love, His delivering intervention, His readiness to give that which truly delights men, and His abounding goodness to the very man who had been restless. This irrepressible hope, always clarified and crystallized by prayer, is one of the constant features of the Psalter (*cf.* also 1 Cor. 15:19; Heb. 6:18, 19).

PSALM 14. OUTLINE OF A CORRUPT SOCIETY

This description of degenerate and unrighteous men primarily refers to humanity as a whole and not merely to a period of extreme moral decay in Israel. This is endorsed by the use of the first three verses in Rom. 3:10–12. The psalm was rewritten in later years and reappears as Ps. 53. The poem adopts alternately the viewpoint of earth and heaven.

1 The iniquity of men

Fool, or 'vile person' (1 Sa. 25:25); *i.e.* a man wholly indifferent to the moral standards of the law, and who daily adopts as his own principle the belief that deity cares nothing about the differences between men's behaviour. Out of this practical atheism proceeds an evil influence upon men, for *they are corrupt*, or 'spread corruption', a life abhorrent to God—the constant meaning of *abominable*—and a total absence of moral worth.

2–4 God's inquiry and verdict

The question of ultimate standards of moral conduct is ceaselessly raised by the Lord. **2** He is meticulously concerned about men's deeds, and notes any who *act wisely*; *i.e.* any man who governs his life according to divine wisdom. **3** The diagnosis given here cannot be supplied by the godless man, for he has repudiated objective goodness, righteousness and truth. Indeed this is the first characteristic of such men; everyone has *gone astray* from right living and become tainted in his nature (*cf.* Jb. 15:16). Hence, without exception, all are workers of evil; *there is none that does good*. **4a** might be rendered 'Shall the workers of iniquity not know?'; *i.e.* these things will not remain hidden from those who pillage God's people as casually *as they eat bread*. Doubtless the standard example is Ex. 5:10–19.

5, 6 Fear comes upon the wicked

The psalmist pictures himself watching as the evil-doers come to the place and moment of truth envisaged in v. 4, as, *e.g.*, the formerly enslaved Israel watched the Egyptians fight in vain against the Red Sea (Ex. 14:24, 25). Yet always God is with the righteous and the cloudy-fiery pillar at the Red Sea indicates what this divine presence can mean (Ex. 14:19, 20). **6** Furthermore, no machinations or counter-attacks of the wicked can deprive the *poor*, here meaning those who are downtrodden by the world, from finding *refuge* in the Lord.

7 A prayer for divine blessing

It is all very well, however, to recall thrilling experiences of the past, but what about now? The psalmist faces the present by looking to God to *restore the fortunes of his people*.

PSALM 15. THE QUALIFICATION FOR FELLOWSHIP WITH GOD

This brief poem sets out the ideals which the psalmist believed God would expect in His guests. The blameless character is assessed by personal and social conduct only; *i.e.* the standard is purely ethical. A description in similar terms is found in Ps. 24:3–5 and in Is. 33:14b–16.

1, 5b The theme set

These verses set the theme of the poem, viz. the godly man's highest aspiration. **1** On the one hand it is to have freedom of access to the presence of God—typified by His *tent* (the traditional emblem of His presence and by His *holy hill* or Mt. Zion (the historical symbol of His effective rule amid the vicissitudes of national policies). **5b** On the other hand, it is to have security and also steadiness or consistency of character and conduct, whatever the circumstances, so that, as a righteous man, he *shall never be moved*, *i.e.* he will enjoy safety and display stability.

2, 3 Personal conduct

2 On the positive side he is blameless in manner of life (*cf.* Gn. 6:9; 17:1), actively upholding *right* dealing in all transactions, wholly free from duplicity because his heart is set upon *truth*. **3** Negatively he is one *who does not slander*, *i.e.* go about as a tell-tale, unkind and discourteous in speech. He is careful to avoid mere gossip (*cf.* 1 Tim. 5:13), never taking advantage of a fellow-man, careful not to distress his friends by foolish and tactless talk about things they have done and since regretted.

4, 5a Social conduct

4 Again the positive traits in the ideal character are first given. In that there are two paths in life, he is careful to estimate people by their moral standards rather than by other factors. He discounts *a reprobate*, a man who, for whatever reason, merits being despised, and respects any man who honours and fears the Lord. The negative side is next stressed. Should he have undertaken a duty, or sworn a bond, which later proves to be irksome and costly, he does not evade his responsibility, for the spoken word of a vow is a sacred thing (*cf.* Jos. 9:19); **5a** in relation to material wealth, he rejects the typically grasping practices of usury (*cf.* Lv. 25:36, 37; Pr. 28:8). Open-handed generosity is more the mark of the children of God (*cf.* Mt. 10:8). He will have nothing to do with the corruption of justice by bribes, least of all if the inducement seems to injure an innocent party.

PSALM 16. THE WAY OF FAITH

The psalm is ascribed to David (*cf.* Acts 2:25; 13:35, 36), and contains a number of expressions which would suit well the period of David's life when he was an outlaw. It falls into three divisions.

1–4 The marks of the believer

These are four in number: **1** God is the object of his trust in the sense that he *takes refuge* in Him; **2** to him Yahweh is his sovereign *Lord* and utterly sufficient, so that apart from Him he desires no good thing; **3** he acknowledges the worth and delights in the fellowship of *the saints* (lit. the 'holy ones'), the people set apart for God's possession and in whom His holy character is seen (*cf.* 2 Thes. 1:10); **4** he shuns all false worship (*cf.* Jos. 23:7; 1 Jn. 5:21).

5–8 The present blessings of the believer

These are a satisfied heart (vv. 5, 6); counsel and correction (v. 7); and security (v. 8). **5** The literal rendering is 'Yahweh is the portion of my share and of my cup'. The mention of *cup* suggests that the first word refers to a portion of food. The meaning then becomes 'Yahweh is all that I need to satisfy hunger and thirst'. *My lot* could be an abbreviation for 'the land that has become mine by casting lots' (*cf.* Nu. 26:56), but equally a different thought could be introduced: 'You are in control of my destiny.' In this case, v. 5 teaches the sufficiency of the Lord for present (5a) and future (5b) alike. **6** *The lines*; *i.e.* the portion of land measured out to him by line. *Cf.* Ps. 78:55; Am. 7:17. **7** *My heart* (lit. 'kidneys'; used figuratively of the seat of the emotions and the conscience; *cf.* Ps. 73:21, 22), which *in the night* watches kept with God *instructs* him, involving both correction and direction. **8** presents a beautiful picture of the psalmist hidden behind God, who stands between him and his foe, yet also as a friend at his *right hand*.

9–11 The prospects of the believer

These are preservation from death (vv. 9, 10); the path of life made known to him (v. 11a); joy in God's presence (v. 11b). David is thinking of his future prospects in this world; but his words shine with deeper meaning. **9** The gladness is explained by the fact **10** that the Lord will not (lit.) 'abandon my soul for Sheol to possess', which signifies that dreaded death under divine wrath and rejection (see on Ps. 6:5). **11** By contrast to this, the *path of life* is revealed, and in context this is most naturally seen as the 'path which leads to life' and terminates *in thy presence* in *fullness of joy*. This was true for David as for every other believer before and since, be-

cause in its deepest and fullest sense it is true of Christ (Acts 2:25–28; 13:35).

PSALM 17. A RIGHTEOUS MAN'S PRAYER FOR VINDICATION

Three psalms are entitled 'A Prayer of David' (17; 86 and 142), but this is the most spontaneous of them. It may well express his fervent cry in the desperate situation at Maon (1 Sa. 23:26), especially as David was very confident of his integrity at that time (1 Sa. 24:11). The intensity and urgency of his prayer is conveyed not only in the general impression of anxiety but also in the three facets of his appeal.

1–5 His desire to be heard

1, 2 Such words as *hear, attend, give ear, let thy eyes see* give shape and force both to the shrill cry (Heb. *rinna*, a loud cry) from his heart, and to the strong conviction of his own righteousness. These are thrown into greater prominence, first by an implicit comparison with the prayer of *lips . . . of deceit*, and secondly by his clear sense of innocence, shown in his willingness to be scrutinized by *thy eyes* which *see the right* of the matter. **3–5** This second element in his appeal, viz. his integrity, is more fully stated. This conviction is supported and asserted first by reference to God's testing of his inmost soul as though by an exhaustive examination, yet without disclosing anything false. Secondly, he declares that in his dealings with men he has always watched and carefully heeded the word of the Lord (*cf.* Ps. 119:11), in consequence of which he has never strayed from nor stumbled in the path indicated by God.

6–12 His prayer for protection

The note of passionate appeal is reintroduced in such words as *I call, thou wilt answer me, incline, hear, show*, and there is again an indirect allusion to his opponents (v. 7c). The new note, as compared with the peremptoriness of vv. 1, 2, is that of worship and trust. **7** Note the phrase *Wondrously show thy steadfast love*, where the adverb points to God's supernatural power and the adjective and noun point to His unchanging grace, and the concept of God as a *refuge* for the trusting heart. The object of his prayer, *i.e.* his need of protection from his attackers, is specified more exactly in vv. 8–12. **8** First there is his own desire to be tenderly cared for, as though he were immensely precious to God, who would as instinctively and immediately protect him as a man reacts to any threat to *the apple* (pupil) *of the eye*, or as lovingly welcome and hide him as a mother-bird spreads her feathers over her chick (*cf.* Dt. 32:10, 11). **9** This desire is quickened in him because he is surrounded by *deadly enemies*, *i.e.* men whose aim is his death.

Then his enemies' character is portrayed in various aspects. **10** *They close their hearts to pity* and utter threats, confident of their power. **11**

And, because they have surrounded David and his friends, they already see the psalmist's company cast to the ground as captives. **12** One (or each) of the attacking men is like an enraged *lion* (*cf.* Ps. 7:2; 1 Pet. 5:8), and the thought of his stealthy power introduces the final phase of the prayer.

13–15 His plea to be vindicated

This abrupt and repeated call to God is the natural reaction to the analogy of a lurking lion ready to spring upon him at any moment. **13** The psalmist calls upon his protector to intervene and to *confront* his enemy, so making him to cower down. Nothing but a decisive act of God, coming as an armed man with *sword* and **14** mighty power (*hand*) will suffice for this emergency.

The contrast is now developed between the essential characters of the wicked and the godly. The psalmist's foes are *men . . . of the world*; *i.e.* men whose sphere of activity and range of thought are wholly in the physical realm (*cf.* 1 Jn. 2:15–17). The grim but yet spiritual realism of the Psalter appears at this point. The psalmist recognizes first that he cannot pray against his foes without calling into operation that law of divine providence which punishes the wicked by satiating their wicked desires, and beyond that there is the fact of heredity, as expressed in Ex. 20:5. This is realistic praying, and it is found in the Word of God in order to warn us to look at the implications of what we pray for, and to be sure that in all our prayers our conscience is as clear as that of the psalmist, and our ambitions as holy. **15** His ambition is not to own earthly wealth, but to enjoy unbroken fellowship with God. His supreme desire is to experience the *form* of God (*cf.* Nu. 12:8). This, of course, includes the notion of an unclouded vision of God when the cloud of enmity is past, but the context suggests that the psalmist is contrasting himself with those (v. 14) who have no hope beyond this world. He speaks of awaking to the eternal vision of God (*cf.* Is. 26:19; Dn. 12:2; Phil. 3:21; 1 Jn. 3:2; Rev. 22:4).

PSALM 18. DAVID'S VICTORY SONG

This appears to be a version of 2 Sa. 22, slightly revised to make it suitable for general use. The title indicates the circumstances of this jubilant thanksgiving. His deliverance from *all his enemies* (see title) would suggest the period after 2 Sa. 8, when his life was crowned by almost unbroken successes. The words *the servant of the Lord* in the title are not found in 2 Sa. 22. The phrase is a highly honourable one and, apart from two references to Joshua, is almost always applied to Moses, or used prophetically of the Messiah.

1–3 Introduction

1 The forceful and unusual first word is very striking: *rāham* means to *love* very tenderly, as with a mother's love. **2** God is called a *rock* both by the precedent of Moses (Dt. 32:4, 18, 30, 31, 37), the history of Israel (Ex. 17), and David's own experience (1 Sa. 23:25, 28). The seven graphic titles ascribed to God in this verse are all expressive of impregnability and reflect the dominance of this thought during the years when he was hunted by Saul.

4–19 Dire peril and divine deliverance

4, 5 His feelings at this time are likened to those of a drowning man swirled round in strong floodwaters, or of a wild beast in a net. **6** There was none who could help except the Lord, so to Him David cried out in his distress. The verb is in the present tense, as if the event was still vividly before him. **7–15** God came to his aid. The divine coming is described in the most vigorous and awesome manner; the spiritual fact is translated into a disturbance of nature so profound that it might almost seem as though creation was being undone. The divine advent is seen as associated with smoke and blackness and the voice of words, as when the law was given at Sinai. It is also marked by brilliant radiance and lightning as in the swift illumination of the revelation of grace (*cf.* Heb. 12:18–24). Note that there is no similitude of God Himself in all this tumult (*cf.* Dt. 4:11, 12). The contrast of God as intangible and yet mighty, as inscrutable yet inescapable, lies behind the imagery, and yet the parallelism with the imagery of Sinai (Ex. 19) calls to mind that the God who came to save David did so by virtue of His long-ago revealed character as the Saviour of His people (Ex. 6:6, 7). The imagery is terror-striking, but the revelation is of saving grace.

16–19 This act of God was intensely personal, and in this account of the psalmist's deliverance the background of the natural world fades away. Even his powerful foes are mentioned only indirectly, for the experience was so intimately his own. Hence the repetition of *He . . . me . . .* and the culminating marvel that the Lord delivered him out of all his troubles *because he delighted in me*. **16** There is a suggestive parallel here with the rescue of the child Moses from forces which threatened to crush him. The verb *drew out* is found only here and in Ex. 2:10. The whole passage has many parallels also with the divine intervention described in the book of Job (*cf.* Jb. 36:29 – 38:1).

20–27 The ground of God's intervention

This section is an expansion of the thought that God delights in the psalmist. There are two aspects: David's character and work (vv. 20–23) and God's way (vv. 24–27). The intervention of God on his behalf is the reward of his godly living. This protective care is not claimed as of right, but the fact of it is asserted in the simplicity of a heart that feels unembarrassed even in the searching holiness of the court of heaven. David's righteousness is not limited to his relations with Saul; it has been upheld in every phase of his life which he claims to be upright, honourable, merciful, single-hearted and pure. **23** *I kept myself from guilt* (lit. 'my iniquity'); *i.e.* 'I have been so careful to be a man of God that I have not done anything which could be called "my iniquity"', *i.e.* something which had become, as it were, a part of me' (*cf.* 1 Ki. 14:8; Acts 23:1). The principle underlying this section is that God reinforces the character which men choose to acquire, behaving toward them as they behave to Him (*cf.* 1 Sa. 2:30; Rom. 1:28).

28–45 The high calling of God

David's two declarations of personal righteousness, and of the divine principle whereby God deals with men in accordance with their character, are plainly endorsed by the preceding account of his deliverance. That is only one instance; but they can be supported also by the whole course of David's life. The psalm now deals with these larger aspects of David's life.

28, 29 The dynamic of David's life is *the Lord my God*, whose indwelling light and vigour both maintain the burning glow of personal existence and give incentive and power whereby difficulties are overcome. *Cf.* 1 Sa. 30:8, where the word 'band' is in Hebrew the same as *troop* here. *Leap over a wall.* A reference, perhaps, to the incident of 2 Sa. 5:6–10. **30, 31** God is worthy of all honour and adoration, not merely because of the blessings He bestows but because of His essential qualities—absolutely *true* in all He says and *perfect* in all He does. Therefore He cannot protect those who are antagonistic to Him, but to those who trust Him, He is utterly trustworthy. Beside Him there is none other (*cf.* Is. 45:5, 6). **32–36** David has been carefully trained by God. This preparation has been physical; health, strength and agility have been provided to bring David's way to completion. It has also been instructional—skill in the use of warlike methods and arms had been gained—and moral: the Lord had freely given His own equipment for resistance, His sustenance in danger, and His *gentleness* (v. 35 mg.); *i.e.* His understanding patience or, more literally, meekness, during all the long years since He so graciously raised a shepherd lad to a throne of power (*cf.* Ps. 23:5, 6). **37, 38** David eagerly accepts the purpose of this training. In fullest confidence that God has efficiently and adequately prepared him for this task, he undertakes the subjugation of his foes. **39** It is God who works in him. The conquest of his foes is really the Lord's doing. **40** God had made his enemies *turn their backs* in retreat; thereupon he cut them off. **41, 42** It was inevitable therefore that any prayer by such rebellious foes would be unheeded by God; consequently David was able to crush their opposition.

43–45 The climax of his supremacy is now described. Not only had all civil insurrection been put down (*cf.* 2 Sa. 3:1), but God had made David the head of many nations (*cf.* 2 Sa. 8);

and even those peoples with whom there had been no previous contact would acknowledge his sovereignty as soon as they heard of him. There is some historical support for this in 2 Sa. 10:18, 19, but there is also a prophetical aspect. *Cf.* Is. 52:15 and Ps. 2:8.

46–50 Conclusion

The pre-eminent inference from these reflections is the living reality of God to whom David is inexpressibly grateful. **47** The phrase *gave me vengeance* implies no vindictiveness; it is a declaration that God and not man had vindicated the rightness of a cause. **49** The psalm concludes with a promise by David that he will utilize his dominion over many peoples to spread abroad the praise of his God, a concept which Paul adjusts to the reign of David's Lord (Rom. 15:9), in whom salvation and loving-kindness are fully exhibited. **50** Finally, David names himself in connection with the permanent alliance with God which was ultimately fulfilled in the eternal kingdom of the Son of David. *Cf.* 2 Sa. 7:12–16; Lk. 1:32, 33.

PSALM 19. THE TWO WITNESSES TO GOD

Apart from the concluding prayer, the psalm obviously falls into two parts, vv. 1–6 and 7–13. Each part deals with a source from which man may acquire knowledge of God, first by inference from the visible cosmos, and secondly by instruction through the Torah, or law. These are respectively the material and the moral realms. Without the physical light of the sun and the spiritual light of the divine commandments, all life would fail.

1–6 The physical glory of the universe

1–4a The glory of the firmament. The wonder of the sky is a constant stimulus to praise in the book of Psalms (*cf.* 29; 93; 104). The emphasis here is upon objective testimony rather than subjective interpretations. **1** The heavens ceaselessly declare the glory of God; *the firmament*, or extended expanse of the sky, reveals Him by being His workmanship; **2** each day speaks to the following day, and each night makes Him known. **3, 4** While they themselves are silent and inarticulate, their testimony is heard everywhere. *Cf.* Rom. 1:19, 20.

4b–6 The special glory of the sun. Far from worshipping the sun, the psalmist regards it as an agent of God who has set up a tent in the vast heavens for the sun's continual use. Certainly the wide range of the sun's light and heat is a reflection of God's universal power and knowledge. This thought leads to a meditation upon the inward light afforded by the law, or Torah.

7–13 The perfect glory of the Torah

7–10 The moral effect of the law. Whereas the

visible creation bears witness to God's ever-lasting power and divinity, the revelation of Himself is given to the children of Israel in the Torah. This distinction is observed in the replace-ment of *God* (vv. 1–6) by *the Lord* (*i.e.* Yahweh) (vv. 7–14). Six aspects of the inward work of the Lord are described. **7** The Torah is *perfect*, or inerrant (*cf.* Jas. 1:25), bringing strength and comfort to men. *The testimony, i.e.* the word which testifies to God's character and will (pre-eminently the Decalogue), transforms the *simple, i.e.* the open-minded person who is otherwise liable to be swayed by whoever happens to be speaking (*cf.* 2 Tim. 3:15). **8** *The precepts of the Lord* are definite rules, the keeping of which gives a clear conscience. *The com-mandment* is a divine imperative which shines as a guiding light to men who seek the way of life (*cf.* Acts 26:18; Heb. 11:13). **9** *The fear of the Lord*, which it is the law's aim to inculcate, brings freedom from debasing practices (*cf.* Ps. 106:35–40). His *ordinances* governing social life and practice are absolutely true and righteous. **10** All these qualities make the inward revela-tions of the Lord more desirable than wealth and more pleasurable than honey. The whole passage is elaborately extended in Ps. 119.

11–13 The personal desire for a life free from sin. Just as the first part of the poem focused thought upon the sun, so the second half con-centrates on a man's life. Meditation upon the revealed will of Yahweh turns into prayer for absolute cleansing from hidden defects in character and conduct. The law is esteemed as a major factor in living a true life, but it holds no guarantee of purity outside personal conviction. What of inadvertent and unwitting acts of sin and error? 'The Lord Himself must thoroughly cleanse my life and also prevent me from proud and impulsive sins which swiftly become habitual and turn me into an enemy of God.' This attitude of mind is labelled *great transgression* (*cf.* 1 Jn. 3:19–21).

14 Concluding prayer

This last verse echoes the dual themes of the poem: the outward word and inward meditation of the psalmist, and the objective reality and manward activity of the Lord.

PSALM 20. PRAYER FOR THE KING BEFORE BATTLE

This and the following psalm form a pair, describing the people's intercession and thanks-giving before and after a battle in which they were led by the king. Weiser (see Introduction) finds difficulty in accepting this and suggests that here we have an example of a psalm used in celebrating or commemorating the king's coronation, and seeking his prosperity during the coming year. The use of the personal pro-nouns, 'you', 'I', and 'we', indicate the three sections in the psalm.

1–5 Intercession by the people

It is uncertain whether the scene of the prayer is the sanctuary in Zion or the vicinity of the battlefield. **1** God's *name* means 'all that God has revealed about His character'. The prayer is for that fullness of protection which God's revealed nature would lead us to expect. The primary emphasis of this section is on the initial word, *the Lord*: He is requested to *answer, protect, send . . . help, give . . . support, remember, regard*. The Lord *grant . . . and fulfil* all the king's plans, so that his people may shout for joy and wave their banners in triumph. But the triumph will be the Lord's. All the victories of God's people are from Him and arise out of His gracious acceptance of a perfect sacrifice. **3** *Regard with favour your burnt sacrifices* suggests an actual service before the altar (*cf.* 1 Sa. 7:9); but the comprehensive *all your offerings*, **4** *all your plans*, **5** *all your petitions* may indicate a retrospective view inclusive of all previous acts of worship.

6 Assurance for the king

It is not clear whether the king, or possibly a prophet present at the liturgy (*cf.* 2 Ch. 20:14ff.), is speaking; in either case the note of confidence is intended for the Lord's *anointed* one, whom the Lord will answer from heaven by mighty acts of salvation.

7–9 Final confession, anticipation and prayer of the people

7 The allusion to enemies who trust in speedier and more powerful armies is timeless. A general principle is being enunciated, not a reference to any specific foes. The power of and appeal to *the name of the Lord* is vividly illustrated in 1 Sa. 17:45. **8** This trustful committal of their cause to the Lord fills them with such expecta-tion of success as to warrant the use of the perfect tense, as though the conflict were over, but **9** the reality and tension of the moment leads the assembled warriors to plead for *victory*. In the Bible assurance never breeds complacency, but rather offers ground for urgent prayer and calling upon God to save.

PSALM 21. THANKSGIVING FOR THE KING AFTER BATTLE

The connection with the previous psalm is neatly summarized by comparing 20:4 with 21:2. But the difficulty of associating them as prayer before and thanksgiving after battle appears in that the defeat still seems to be future (21:8ff.). Weiser, who notes this problem, again associates the psalm with some royal festival: 'a fragment of the ritual of the coronation of the king'. This would provide a positive foundation for the ele-ment of Messianic expectation rightly found here, for the Davidic kingship was consciously ack-nowledged from early times as a figure of the true.

1–7 An acknowledgment of the Lord's goodness to the king

The main thought of exuberant praise is focused upon the present moment. **3** *A crown of fine gold*. There may be an echo here of the Ammonite crown (*cf.* 1 Ch. 20:2), but there is also the actual Davidic crown bestowed by divine favour, and all its prophetic overtones. **5** Divine *glory* . . . *splendour and majesty* are bestowed upon him (*cf.* Ps. 8:5) and **6** he is made to be blessed and to be a blessing for ever as he rejoices exceedingly in the presence of the Lord. These Messianic ideas are often incorporated in the NT (*e.g.* Heb. 1:8, 9; 2:9; Rev. 5:12–14). **7** Finally the reason why the king has been so divinely blessed is his attitude of trust in the Lord. The title *Most High* belongs to Melchizedek's God (Gn. 14:18) whom Abram identified with Yahweh (Gn. 14:22). The special worship of Yahweh as 'God Most High', widely evidenced in the Psalms (*e.g.* 9:2; 46:4; 47:2; 92:1), was probably popularized by David's capture of Jerusalem, Melchizedek's city, and may have become expressive of that aspect of the divine nature most closely associated with the function of the royal-priest. As a title it signifies supreme dignity, unhampered power and universal sway.

8–13 The king's power extolled

The change of theme is marked by the alteration from 'thou' (the Lord) and 'he' (the king) of the previous verses to 'you' (the king) and 'the Lord' in this section. This is a forceful address to the king by his subjects who exalt his supremacy over all enemies. **9** The destruction of enemies by the majesty of the king's presence is a Messianic idea (*cf.* Mal. 3:1, 2; Mt. 21:40, 41; 2 Thes. 1:7–9).

13 The last verse is spoken by king and people to the Lord. They pray for the continued expression of the divine power and glory. So shall their boundless praise be sustained.

PSALM 22. SALVATION IN EXTREMITY

To Christians this psalm is inseparably associated with the crucifixion, not only because the opening words were quoted by the Lord, but because the first part of the poem seems to describe His bodily condition and emotional experience. Yet the first meaning of the poem must be sought in the days of its composition, although the Spirit of God undoubtedly constrained the psalmist so to frame his expression that it acquired a significance beyond the range of his own life (see Acts 2:30, 31a). What that experience was cannot be precisely stated: it could well be founded on some dark period of David's ever-painful and sometimes despairing outlaw days; to some it is the voice of the Davidic king speaking in the annual royal liturgy, sensing his helplessness in the face of surrounding foes, his utter dependence on God, and in the end rejoicing in confident assurance of divine aid. Either way, its prophetic Messianism is well founded.

1–21 Suffering and prayer

1–11 Despair and two appeals to precedent. 1, 2 The poignant words indicate the perplexity of spirit which has been induced by the severe affliction and the apparent heedlessness of his God. He still trusts in God, but finds intolerable the suspense of waiting for evidence that God has not turned from him. Three comfortless thoughts possess his mind: his suffering (*groaning* . . . *cry* . . . *no rest*), his ceaseless supplication (*words* . . . *by day* . . . *by night*), and the utter silence of God (*forsaken* . . . *far* . . . *not answer*). The order of the thoughts in the psalm indicates that the last is uppermost in his mind. Here is the problem of 'the silence of God'. **3–5** In the absence of any response from God the sufferer is cast back upon his former beliefs, foremost among them being the concept of God as just and righteous. This belief is strengthened by the long precedent of Israel's praises for deliverance in earlier years. God had not failed to help those who *trusted* Him in previous generations. **6–8** Why should the speaker be an exception and his trustfulness be turned into a reproach? As soon as his thought touches upon himself he becomes engrossed with his affliction. He is despised as *a worm*, not recognized as one with human rights, or features (*cf.* Is. 52:14). For the laughter of ridicule, the lips opened in the language of abuse, and the excited turning of heads in the animated conversation of a crowd, see Lk. 23:35; Mt. 27:39, 43. For the action of trustfulness *cf.* Ps. 37:5.

9, 10 The thought of dependence upon one who delighted in him reminds the psalmist of the days when, as a baby, he was dependent upon his mother. But the very fact of his birth is sure evidence of divine intervention in human life, and a habit of reliance upon God was implanted in him with his own life and his mother's milk. **11** This section ends with a plea for the realization of God's presence even as He has been nigh in the years since his infancy, because now there is no-one to help and *trouble is near* (*cf.* Jb. 3:24–26).

12–21 Intense anguish in the immediate distress. The mood changes here from the humiliation of misunderstood relationships (God does not heed his need, and men do not respect his person) to the pain of a tormented body. In the intensity of this anguish there is no reminiscence comparable with vv. 4 and 9, and the awful loneliness of soul implied in v. 1 is replaced by the unforgettable impression of a multitude of savage faces which enclose him like a ring of snarling dogs. The telling of such an experience is sharpened by a series of graphic metaphors. **12, 13** He likens his tormentors to fierce animals ready to devour him. **14, 15** His physical weakness and complete helplessness are vividly portrayed. **16** Then a note of evaluation enters.

The crowd consists of *evildoers*, who are *dogs*, *i.e.* worthless people (*cf.* 2 Sa. 16:9). But the personal anguish quickly reasserts its dominance, for the mass of howling beasts have begun to bite and gnaw at his feet and hands; **17** while burning eyes already mark out the portions of his body which teeth will soon devour. **18** Next, the scuffle of attacking beasts is replaced by the allocation of his clothing amongst his enemies. **19–21** Yet is his reliance upon God unblemished by disbelief: indeed, in the uttermost extremity of his soul, the bond with his Lord stands out the clearer in a strong cry for the aid of His presence. **21** The RV should be consulted for another view of this verse (*cf.* RSV mg.), namely that what begins as a sentence of final appeal ends as a cry of immeasurable relief. God has broken His silence.

The details of Calvary are all so clearly here; mockery (v. 8), shame (vv. 13, 17), the pain of crucifixion (vv. 14–16)—for even if 'pierced' (v. 16) is an uncertain translation (*cf.* mg.), the agony to hands and feet is specifically mentioned —and the parting of garments (v. 18). All this took place by the agency of those who neither knew the Scriptures nor had any interest in fulfilling them, and provides dramatic and unanswerable evidence of the divine inspiration of the Bible and of the faithfulness of God to His Word.

Furthermore, the incidental revelation of the Lord Jesus Himself should not be overlooked, and in particular of His sinlessness. There is no note of confession in the psalm; the intense suffering does not seem even to raise the possibility of some sin lurking in the background, and throughout the suffering described here the sufferer remains utterly sinless in his relation to God (vv. 1–11, 19–21), to his persecutors (vv. 6, 7, 12, 13, 16–18) and to himself (vv. 6, 10, 14, 15 are notable for the absence of self-pity). *Cf.* 1 Pet. 2:22–24.

22–31 Assurance and testimony

The remainder of the psalm consists of praise and thanksgiving to God for His faithfulness and glory. The theme is *thy name* (v. 22), which is simplified in v. 24 to mean the Lord's compassion, honour and gracious attentiveness. But the sphere wherein His praise is to be heard has two parts, one immediate and local, *i.e. the congregation* or assembly of those who are his brethren by blood and by faith, the other more comprehensive in time and place.

22–26 Praise among his brethren. 22–24 Those descendants of Israel who reverence God are urged to bow before the Lord because of His greatness and magnanimity as disclosed in His actions. **25** Because all his praise is stimulated by God's salvation which has come to him, David invites other humble and godly men to join with him in the votive meal he has vowed to give to his Deliverer (*cf.* Lv. 7:16), and **26** in the imaginative anticipation of their presence he pronounces a benediction on his guests: *May your hearts live for ever!*

27–31 Praise by all mankind. The sense of having experienced the reality of God's essential goodwill toward the trustful heart prompts the psalmist to call upon all peoples. **27** He can foresee no other outcome than that the nature of God should be known and revered throughout the earth. **28** Is He not the supreme sovereign? (*Cf.* Je. 16:19; Zc. 14:9; Rev. 11:15.) **29** Even *the proud* will partake in His worship (*cf.* Is. 49:7; Phil. 2:10): indeed every mortal man shall render homage to the immortal Lord (*cf.* Is. 25:6; Rev. 19:9; 22:17). **30** An endless *posterity* shall serve Him and the story of His great deed of deliverance shall be the permanent heritage of every generation (*cf.* Lk. 1:48–50). **31** Each shall come into being and shall declare the Lord's effective righteousness (*cf.* Is. 59:21).

No experience of suffering and of divine deliverance other than our Lord's experience of the cross and resurrection has had such a universal result. It is, indeed, impossible to imagine that any man of the ancient world, whether David or another, could in fact have seriously considered that his individual experience of God would have world-wide and time-long repercussions. The psalm therefore cries out to be seen as predictive prophecy, and is best satisfied by supposing that David consciously wrote in this hyperbolic fashion, being inspired by God to speak of his greater Son.

PSALM 23. SHEPHERD AND HOST

This poem owes much of its charm to the skilful blending of contrasted imagery which covers the major aspects of human life, viz. outdoors (vv. 1, 2) and indoors (v. 6b); peace (v. 2) and peril (v. 4b); the possibility of evil (v. 4b) and the prospect of good (v. 5); times of invigoration of soul (v. 3a) and times of ominous gloom (v. 4a); the experience of following (vv. 1, 2) and a life of stable security (v. 6b). Nevertheless, all the literary facets of this lyrical gem are focused upon the Lord whose tender care, ceaseless vigilance and perpetual presence impart to life all its colour and satisfaction. Indeed the sevenfold activity of the Lord described in vv. 2–5 (He makes, He leads, He restores, He guides, Thou art with me, Thou preparest a table, Thou anointest my head) is framed within the name of *the Lord* (the first and final words of the poem).

The dominant concept is that of God as guide and protector through the vicissitudes of life. The suggestive imagery of a shepherd as applied to the Lord goes back to the days of patriarchal pastoralism (*cf.* Gn. 48:15) and it has been constantly enriched ever since (*cf.* Ps. 78:52–54; Is. 40:11; Ezk. 34:1–23; Jn. 10:1–18). A second concept is introduced in v. 5—that of the Lord as a host of boundless benevolence. This imagery of man as a surprised guest at a sumptuous feast provided by God is likewise an integral part of the whole biblical panorama from the symbolism of Joseph the provider of food (Gn. 43:34) to the miracle of the feeding of five thousand (Mt. 14:19) and the parables of the great supper (Lk. 14:15–24) and the marriage feast of the Bridegroom (Mt. 22:1–14; Rev. 19:9).

1–4 Pilgrimage

David is completely dependent on the Lord as a sheep on its shepherd. The two aspects are serenity, as of lying down in green pastures and by restful waters, with a suggestion of physical well-being; and safety, as of a protected journey along right paths, with a suggestion of personal calm and mental ease because anxiety is impossible when His strong care is evident. The theme is weighted in the direction of innocent carefreeness, and a bond with the shepherd of inexplicable affection.

Life's two great problems, the one largely unrecognized, the other all too pressing, are contained in these verses. 1–3a The first is the problem of pleasure, for it should never be far from the believing mind to query: How can a holy God deal so lovingly with a sinner like me? 4 The second is the problem of suffering, the question raised by the onset of life's adversities. 3b takes the solution as far as the Bible permits us to go. Life is directed by the Shepherd along *paths of righteousness*, paths which are right in His eyes, and all He does is suitable to His *name*, i.e. utterly in harmony with His revealed nature.

5, 6 Hospitality

These verses stress David's careful discernment of the Lord's munificence as the perfect host. The two aspects are fullness—the provision for his needs and enjoyment is complete in every sense, it is unhampered by any human antagonists; and finality—the rich relationship with the Lord is unlimited, and the privilege is fully personal. Contrast the use of *thou* with the use of *he* in the earlier part.

PSALM 24. AN ANTHEM FOR THE INVESTITURE OF JERUSALEM

The great occasion in David's life when he brought the ark of the Lord from the house of Obed-edom to the recently captured city of the Jebusites was joyfully celebrated by several chants and psalms (2 Sa. 6; 1 Ch. 15:16–23). This psalm may well have been composed for this occasion, or possibly for one of its anniversaries. The psalm was greater than the occasion, and has generally been interpreted as prophetic of Christ's ascension after victory over death and sin (see v. 8 and *cf.* Col. 2:15; Heb. 2:14, 15) and of His ultimate sovereignty over all (see v. 10 and *cf.* Rev. 5:11–14; 17:14).

1–6 Approaching the hill of Yahweh

This processional hymn has two themes. 1, 2 The first is the divine sovereignty over the material

(v. 1a) and human (v. 1b) world, a sovereignty arising from His position as Creator (v. 2). If David had been pondering the vicissitudes by which both the ark of God and he himself had been brought to this day (1 Sa. 5; 6; 30:1–6; *etc.*) he would well have marvelled at a sovereign providence.

3–6 The second theme is the righteousness required of men if they are to be blessed of God. Imperceptibly the theme of the divine sovereignty has given way to that of divine holiness. Possibly he recalled 1 Sa. 6:20; certainly the events of 2 Sa. 6:6, 7 would be fresh in his mind. How can a man have that holiness without which none can see God (Heb. 12:14)? 4 A comprehensive holiness of *hands* (outward) and *heart* (inward), an unblemished loyalty towards God and towards men (*cf.* Ps. 15:4). 5 offers the explanation of a life acceptable to God: only then may a man stand before Him, when He has bestowed a *blessing* in terms of 'righteousness' (as *vindication* should be translated; *cf.* AV, RV). David discovered that through the offering of sacrifices (2 Sa. 6:13) he could stand with safety, and even with joy (2 Sa. 6:14), before the holy God of the ark. This doctrine of imputed righteousness came to its fullness in the sacrifice of the Lord Jesus and our standing before God through Him (*e.g.* Phil. 3:9). Such a blessing can come only from *the God of his salvation*. But how may this blessing be ours? 6 replies that it belongs to those who *seek him* who is Jacob's God, the God who transforms the twister into the prince (Gn. 32:28). The word *generation* is of disputed meaning, but probably signifies a company of people with a common characteristic, in this case of having received the greatest blessing, as did Jacob, by asking for it.

7–10 Entering the gateway of Zion

The procession is halted awhile before the city's closed gates and the demand for entrance, *i.e.* submission, is formally made in the name of *the King of glory*. 7, 9 The command to *lift up*, or extend, the gates and archways implies, as Weiser says, that 'doors built by the hands of men are not adequate to admit the mighty God'. 8 In reply to the ceremonial challenge of the sentries the name of the incoming king (*cf.* 2 Sa. 6:2b) is declared to be *the Lord, mighty in battle*. David had recently captured the Jebusite stronghold and won many other battles. This designation alone was insufficient to warrant the opening of the gates, and 9 the call to provide access to the city is repeated. 10 The Lord's presence and pre-eminence in Zion is based on grounds other than His intervention in Israel's historic battles. The Lord is king of all in His own right, possessing powers and qualities which transcend earth and time. The King of glory is *the Lord of hosts* (*cf.* 1 Ki. 22:19), the Lord who possesses every potentiality and power, and who alone has the right to be called Yahweh, the Omnipotent.

PSALM 25. A PERSONAL PRAYER

This is another acrostic psalm. It expresses the alternation of fervent petition and sober meditation which often characterizes the soul's waiting upon the Lord. There are three main moods in the prayer, but they are closely bound together.

1–7 A plea for guidance

This is a prayer in itself, but its themes are dealt with more fully in the following verses; *e.g.* with the prayer for vindication from his enemies (vv. 2, 3), *cf.* vv. 19–21; with the expression of his need for instruction and guidance by the Lord (vv. 4, 5), *cf.* vv. 8–10 and 12; his penitence (vv. 6, 7) is brought out again in v. 11; and his avowal of trust in God (v. 1) is repeated in v. 15.

The situation is a familiar one in the Psalms. **1, 2** Trouble, in the shape of treacherous enemies, urges the psalmist to trustful prayer. We see again into the mind of these men of old: prayer was their sole weapon against the foes, to whom they neither answered back nor acted vengefully. His prayer is, first, heartfelt: this is expressed by the word *lift up my soul*, for the soul is the centre of the whole being, and here he raises it above earthly interests so that it may focus upon God alone; secondly, trustful, and thirdly, **3** expectant, as he associates himself with those who *wait for thee*, a phrase which is full of expectancy of divine action.

4, 5 Faith, however, if it does not display obedience, is false to itself and to its object. Consequently there follows the plea for guidance in all the truth of God on the ground of a sincere and a full allegiance to Him (*cf.* Ex. 33:13; Ps. 86:11; Jn. 14:15). But, as ever, obedience, while it shows the reality of faith, does not in itself purchase the goodwill of God. **6, 7** Therefore, having given this pledge of the reality of the faith from which his prayer proceeds, the psalmist now turns to expose the ground on which faith rests, the mercy, love, forgiveness and goodness of God.

8–15 The goodness of the Lord

8 In a common manner of OT meditation, the final thought of one passage is made the theme of the following section. The *goodness* of God (*cf.* v. 7) is reiterated here, and a conclusion drawn from it. Because He is absolutely good and true, *therefore* He is sure to offer help to sinful men uncertain of the right way of life. This conclusion is not, of course, logical. In fact it is contrary to logic that a God who is *upright*, 'straight' in all His ways, should have any contact with *sinners*. That He does so illuminates the gracious, forbearing quality of His perfect nature. Behind the word *sinners* lies the idea of 'going astray' or 'missing the road', and **9** they are further defined as *humble*, the word being repeated so as to emphasize what sort of sinners may expect divine aid: those who are 'lowly' before Him, and **10** who are committed to a life of obedience. **11–15** This intimacy of the Lord with sinners is

developed and successively the promises are made of forgiveness, guidance, security, friendship and deliverance, arising respectively from an attitude of confession, reverence and reliance.

16–22 A prayer for deliverance

The metaphor of being trapped in a net has reminded the psalmist of his present predicament, and this evokes a passionate supplication for deliverance. **16–18** He is particularly oppressed, for his troubles have isolated him from all friends and his heart is swamped with anxieties, so he cries for deliverance, attentive care and forgiveness. **19–21** Nor are these fears and troubles subjective; his enemies are as implacable and violent as they are numerous, hence the appeal for protection and vindication.

22 *Redeem Israel, O God.* Just as in vv. 1–3 personal petition broadened to include all in the same situation, so here the private grief takes into its purview the national grief. True prayer can never be selfish or exclusive. The whole church is the responsibility of the individual member.

PSALM 26. THE WAY OF THE WORSHIPPER

This psalm expresses the uneasiness of any devout soul when immersed in a godless society. J. H. Eaton (*Torch Commentary*, 1967) suggests that parallels with such 'royal' psalms as 18 (esp. vv. 20f.); 28; 101 suggest that the speaker here is the Davidic king, hard pressed by some national crisis.

1, 2 His approach to God

The outspoken request for the Lord to *vindicate, prove, try* and *test* him implies a tension which is expressed in the contrasts of the following verses. He does not claim a sinless life but asserts a sincere and consistent endeavour to walk uprightly (*cf.* Ps. 139:23, 24).

3–10 His determination to avoid wicked men

3–5 He describes, on the one hand, the truth and loving-kindness of the Lord and, on the other, the vanity, duplicity and wickedness of certain men. The former he cherishes, the latter he shuns and hates. **3** suggests a deliberate modelling of human life upon the character of God (*cf.* 1 Jn. 4:11).

6–8 His own choice is now described. He will take his place among those who surround God's altar, and in preparation for the act of dedication he will cleanse himself from defilement (*cf.* Ps. 73:13; Ex. 30:17–21). The metaphor of walking (v. 3) is replaced by the more intimate one of entering the house of the Lord. His declaration that he will avoid ungodly men (v. 4) is changed into a song of grateful testimony. The hatred of evil gatherings (v. 5) is replaced by the love of the dwelling-place where he meets the glory of God.

9, 10 He brings his spiritual ambitions to the bar of divine judgment. The prayer is very compressed, but implies: 'Grant me such godly separation from *sinners* (going astray from God), from ruthlessness towards others (*bloodthirsty* acts of inhumanity) and underhand means of securing my own ends (*evil devices* and *bribes*), that at the day of judgment I will not be swept away with such by the wrath of God.'

11, 12 His dedication and assurance

The outcome of the prayer of faith is that **11a** he commits himself to be the sort of person he has asked God to make him, **11b** albeit in constant reliance on a gracious Redeemer; but also his prayer issues in **12a** security and **12b** testimony.

PSALM 27. AN ANTHEM OF DELIVERANCE

The difference between the first and second halves of this psalm is very obvious, and the change after v. 6 from exuberant praise to earnest petition may appear to be an inversion of mood. But it is sound spiritual practice to strengthen oneself in God, before launching on supplication. In this way we pray to a God whom we see clearly, and we finally share with the psalmist that assurance which comes from committing even our gravest crisis into the hand of a known and loved God.

1–3 Whole-hearted trust

A hymn of irrepressible gaiety wherein the threats and needs of life are abundantly met by the Lord. **1** There is a triple parallelism. The Lord is my *light*, my *salvation* and my *stronghold*. **2, 3** Although I am faced with adversaries, multitudes, and the risk of war, my foes stumble in the darkness from which I am freed by His light; the massing of armies cannot affect my experience of heart-peace through His salvation, and the threat of widespread conflict has no power to capture my stronghold.

4–6 A supreme desire

A sublime expression of the constancy of a devout heart. The psalmist is determined to seek the abiding security and joy of God's presence. **4** His desire is to dwell with the Lord, to behold His *beauty* and to *inquire in*, better 'to look with delight upon', *his temple*. This is the longing for the intimate and felt presence of God, sought through the appointed means of Temple sacrifices (*cf.* v. 6b). **5** Thus he will be secure, God sheltering him above and giving him *a rock* beneath. **6** No enemy can penetrate to the man who thus tarries in the place of sacrifice (*cf.* Heb. 2:14, 15).

7–12 A prayer for deliverance from danger

Following the division in rsv, the prayer displays the three essentials of true intercession. **7–9a** It rests upon the invitation of God, **9b, 10** casts

the whole burden upon God alone, permitting no human help, and **11, 12** while seeking the specific request of deliverance it seeks primarily to know and do God's will.

13, 14 The unfailing Lord

These words mark a return to the present moment. They are a testimony and a strong exhortation to steadfast endurance. This conclusion of the anthem emphasizes human frailty, but stresses the fact of divine intervention, the utter certainty of the Lord's sufficiency, and the patience of faith which waits with confidence. *Cf.* Pss. 62:1, 5; 123:1, 2; Is. 40:31.

PSALM 28. A PLEA FOR RETRIBUTION

This psalm was first spoken in some time of peril at the hands of evil men. As often in psalms of intercession, it contains an abrupt note of confident praise (vv. 6–8) indicative of the element of assurance inseparable from the prayer of faith. Both parts of the poem have a personal and a corporate section.

1–5 A cry for help

1 The expressed fear that God might be *deaf* and *silent* does not arise from any lapse of faith, but rather indicates that self-deprecating reverence which is our only proper attitude towards God, and also our recognition that His and our sense of timing may not coincide, and it may be His will to act as if deaf and to lead us into a period of trial (*cf.* Ps. 23:4). The burden of his prayer is separation of himself from the wicked and their ultimate reward. **3** He beseeches His Lord not to drag him away with all the crowd of guilty men; **4** but he pleads even more vehemently for a just recompense to be given to such evil-doers, not vindictively but in demonstration of righteousness. **5** The wicked are without excuse. They deliberately ignore or deny the proofs of the living God, seen in His works (*cf.* Is. 5:12, 18, 19; Rom. 1:18–20).

6–9 Thanksgiving for God's response

This fulfilment of the prayer of v. 2 is not evoked by a sudden surge of remembered deliverances, but by the realization of an immediate response by the Lord. **8, 9** The experience of a divine blessing brings such relief and joy that the psalmist craves a like enrichment for all his people. Are not his subjects the Lord's people? To them He furnishes both the *strength* of a fortress and the tenderness of a *shepherd* (*cf.* Is. 40:11). **8** is more dramatic than rsv (following an emended text) allows. Eaton renders it: 'The Lord—(all) strength is his! he is the stronghold of salvations (intensive plural) for his anointed.'

PSALM 29. THE THUNDER OF GOD

This song of a thunderstorm is heard within the

auditorium of heaven, and the angels are summoned to join in the praise and worship of Yahweh. Vv. 3–9, the core of the poem, describe the passage of a storm from the waters of the western sea across the forested hills of N Palestine, to the waste places of Kadesh in the uttermost borders of Edom (Nu. 20:16). This event is depicted not as a demonstration of natural power, but as a symphony of praise to the Creator.

The descriptive part of the poem falls into three equal stanzas which correspond with the formation, onset and passage of the storm, but the subordination of natural phenomena to spiritual forces is constantly emphasized.

3, 4 The approach of the storm

This is presented by the suggestive repetitions as though of distant mutterings. **3** *Upon the waters*; *i.e.* either the sea or the swollen flood-waters of the coastal hills where rain is already falling. The general impression is one of sultry foreboding, the activity is concealed, power is leashed, the sense of colossal energy speaks of the glory, **4** power and majesty of God.

5–7 Its onset

The word *powerful* (v. 4) announces a new phase, a scene of increasing action as the branches of great trees are tossed about and then torn away by violent gusts which leave the trunks gaunt and shattered. This climax of the storm is vividly described so as to convey the impression of reckless power—like the action of a bull-calf or a young wild-ox skipping about in mad exuberance. *Sirion* is probably Mt. Hermon which appears to join the peaks of Lebanon in a mad dance as the storm swirls about it.

8, 9 The storm passes away

The storm passes over to the distant east-land. With so many trees uprooted the remaining foliage of the forested hills is now insufficient to conceal the splintered limbs and fallen trunks. The impression that is left is one of breathlessness, as though the whole temple of nature echoed with a whispered 'Glory' to the Lord who had but to speak and it would be done, who uttered His voice and the earth melted (*cf.* Ps. 46:6).

These three scenes, suggestive of boisterous energy, depicted in rain-fed torrents, dishevelled forests, and winds dancing into the distance, are set fast within a framework of wholly different quality. **1** The *glory and strength* of the Lord are not fully disclosed in nature's wild power but in the impressive dignity of the high court of heaven, where the angelic 'sons of the mighty' (RV) bow in holy adoration. Indeed the focus of all action and thought is the Lord Himself eternally enthroned, and unwaveringly bestowing upon His people not merely the gift of strength but the blessing of *peace* (vv. 10, 11). The poem skilfully fuses the natural and the

spiritual, but with clear emphasis on the latter aspect. The first word *ascribe* is a call to worship and the last word *peace* implies His will to bless. Divine power prompts one and provides the other, but the created world cannot provide more than an elemental, though fearfully impressive, index to them.

PSALM 30. MOURNING INTO DANCING

The allusion in the title to *the dedication of the temple* might refer to the decision about Ornan's threshing-floor (1 Ch. 21:18–27), and the terrible experience of imminent death which is mentioned in the psalm would be the pestilence which approached Jerusalem (1 Ch. 21:7, 13ff.). Alternatively, it may refer to David's palace which he was prevented from occupying at first because of the great Philistine invasion which reached Bethlehem (2 Sa. 5:11, 18, 22; *cf.* 23:13–17). A third possibility is that the phrase may have been added to the title when the psalm was used at the dedication of the second Temple, in which case the poem in its origin is a personal record of deliverance from some severe distress; but the community, gathered to celebrate the dedication, use his personal expressions as describing their former communal distress and present communal joys. Either of the Davidic associations, however, and especially the second, gives an easier approach to the distinct individualism of the psalm.

1–5 What God hath wrought

1–3 A summary of past experience is presented, the central theme being God's action in bringing David up from the dim depths of the well of the dead into which he had fallen and into which others had sunk beyond recall. This deliverance had disappointed his enemies, who had thought his plight to be beyond the power or likelihood of divine intervention (*cf.* Ps. 3:2). **4, 5** are an expression of gratitude in which personal experience is seen as illustrating a general principle of God's dealings with men, setting a limit to the darkness and ever giving the assurance of approaching dawn and hope.

6–10 The psalmist's plight

He now contrasts the apparent security afforded by prosperity with the appalling silence of death, and recalls a critical period of his past life. **6** It seemed as though the Lord had made him as strong and sure as the mountains. **7** Then illness or sudden peril reminded him that his well-being was God's blessing. *Dismayed* is a strong word in Hebrew implying shattering terror. **8** Appalled by his previous boastfulness, he now called upon the Lord, **9** asking what advantage God would gain by his death, because once he has entered the grave he will no longer be able to praise Him. As in Ps. 6:5 (see commentary *in loc.*), the psalmist does not speak here of death in general—as though OT man entertained no hope beyond the grave—but of a death in which God hides His face in displeasure. For such a death there is indeed no hope beyond.

11, 12 A memorable resolve

The indisputable fact of God's response, whereby his grief was turned to joy (*cf.* Je. 31:13), merits unceasing thanksgiving.

PSALM 31. TRIAL AND TRUST

This psalm has the familiar motif of 'the distress of the innocent'. It was frequently in the mind of Jeremiah. The phrase *terror on every side* (v. 13) occurs in Je. 6:25; 20:3; 46:5; 49:29 and indeed part of v. 13 is actually quoted in Je. 20:10. The simile of *a broken vessel* (v. 12) was a favourite phrase of Jeremiah (*cf.* 18:4; 19:10, 11; 22:28).

1–8 Outline of an effective faith

1–3 The Lord's honour, ability, holiness, graciousness and faithfulness, as known to the trusting soul, are the background to the psalmist's request to Him to demonstrate His nature in his immediate circumstances. The intercession, though urgent, is also filled with peace because of the unreserved confidence in the Lord so ardently expressed in the opening words. **3, 4** *For thy name's sake.* The thought is that, because of the Lord's character or name, He will lead, guide and deliver.

5 Faith toward God is the committal of life to Him (*cf.* Lk. 23:46). **6** The act and confession of so doing strengthens trust and accentuates the difference between truth and falsity (*cf.* Jon. 2:8). **7, 8** The cycle of adoration, expectation and committal is closed by thanksgiving for deliverance. In this respect faith discounts time's delay and lays hold upon things not seen as yet.

9–24 Details of a profound experience

First of all the psalmist deals with his plight. He makes an appeal to the Lord for mercy on the ground of extreme distress (vv. 9–13), and then seeks justification by an act of divine deliverance (vv. 14–18). **9** His distress is poignantly described as affecting his soul and his body. **10** His misery arises from anxiety and uncertainty; **11** his life is withered by the misgivings and cold suspicion of his acquaintances; his enemies have shaken the loyalty even of his friends (*cf.* 1 Sa. 22:22). **12** He feels like a useless broken vessel; his life has become so different from what it once was that his former self is like a man who is dead and forgotten. **14, 15** Nevertheless his trust is rooted in God and all his life is in His care (*cf.* v. 5). **16** He therefore pleads for the evident favour and approval of God, *i.e.* for the radiant joy and peace of His presence. **17b** This would also shame his adversaries and dispel all mists of suspicion about him. Indeed, those who are the source of such calumny and plottings should be imprisoned in the silence of Sheol.

Second, the psalmist deals with the goodness of God. **19, 20** The past experiences of all godly men show that the Lord is especially concerned for their welfare. The resources of His goodness are available for them, and the security of His presence ensures their immunity from the effects of slander and dissension. *Cf.* Ps. 27:5, 6. **21, 22** But his own immediate experience also shows the Lord's goodness; for when he was beleaguered by evil and impulsively said he was beyond God's power to save, yet the Lord heard and answered. **23** An exhortation to all godly people to trust Him implicitly and fully through the future days naturally follows, for once more personal experience has but enshrined a general truth. *His saints* are those of whom the double relationships of 1 Jn. 4:11 are true; their demeanour in all circumstances is that of *faithful* acceptance of and continuance in God's will. **24** Such can well be inwardly encouraged by the psalmist's testimony to maintain their attitude of patient and confident waiting for the Lord.

PSALM 32. THE JOY OF FORGIVENESS

This psalm deals with the blessedness which is known when sin is forgiven and gives insight into the psychological and religious implications of sin and its removal.

1–5 The joy of forgiveness

These verses describe the great satisfaction and joyous freedom of the soul whose sin has been covered, cancelled and cleansed by the wholly righteous Lord. **1, 2** The fact of sin and forgiveness is stated in four ways, and repeated in v. 5 with an emphatic climax. Inserted in this comprehensive statement of a soul's transformation is an account (vv. 3, 4) of the deep conflict which accompanied the previous sense of guilt. **3** The initial impulse to stifle guilt by silence simply thrust it into the subconscious, but it seeped out in symptoms of physical distress—deep-seated pain and involuntary groans. **4** Sleep brought no cessation from such profound disharmony, and its very persistence was an indication of the inescapable hand of God's righteousness. Obstinate persistence in such repression steadily reduced his vigour, like the withering of a tree in a prolonged drought.

5 The turning-point was when he decided to confess to God, who at once both freely forgave and completely dealt with his problem. The clear teaching of these verses, therefore, is that by simple confession sin in all its aspects—the outward act (signified by the word *sin*), rebellious disobedience (*transgressions*), and the inward corruption (*iniquity*)—is completely forgiven, and covered so as to remain no longer an issue between God and man.

6–11 The basis of confident prayer

6 David's personal experience of God's forgiveness (vv. 1, 2) is made the basis of a call for confident prayer by any godly person provided that the plea is offered while the Lord may yet be approached (see mg.). **6b, 7** The implication is that by repentance one comes into a new sphere of divine protection amid the storms of life (*cf.* Lk. 13:3, 5).

8, 9 are the counterpart of vv. 3 and 4. David's guilty silence is replaced by the divine word of sympathetic guidance. **8** The lonely isolation of the impenitent sinner is replaced by mutual understanding: *I will counsel you with my eye upon you* implies that ideal bond between teacher and pupil, between father and son. **9** In contrast to the sensitive response of the teachable heart is the stubborn will, which refuses to draw near to God and must be disciplined by judgment. These thoughts of instruction in godliness and of free confession should be compared with Ps. 51:13–15.

10, 11 speak first of the alternatives which were in mind in v. 5. Sin brings either punishment or mercy; the difference arises from confession to the Lord. His *steadfast love* is such that all who can claim to be righteous (through acceptance of His forgiveness) have a source of pure delight which springs from a guileless heart. Peace is inseparable from purity.

PSALM 33. AN ANTHEM OF WORSHIP

This poem, which has no title, picks up part of the concluding sentence of the previous psalm, but, unlike it, is not a personal record of experience. It is a corporate expression of praise and worship marked by balance of thought and symmetrical structure.

The introduction (vv. 1–3) and the conclusion (vv. 20–22) are clearly distinguished from the main body of the poem. **1–3** describe the enthusiastic singing of a choir accompanied by music. **20–22** describe the fervent faith of the worshippers who are surrounded by the protection and mercy of the Lord. The symmetry and sequence of these ideas are significant. The anthem of praise becomes the prayer of faith. The change is also from the externals of worship to the inward experiences of trust and hope.

In the body of the psalm are two sections, vv. 4–12 and vv. 13–19, the first of which deals with God the Ruler, and the second with God the Judge.

4–12 The all-ruling word of the Lord

Verses 4–11 are made up of four groups, each of four phrases. **4, 5** First the stress is on the fidelity of God to His word. It is *upright*, and this quality is reflected in what God does, what He loves, and in the evidence provided by the created world. Throughout all, He is faithful and steadfast to what He has spoken. *The earth* introduces the next concept: **6, 7** the power of the word of God revealed in the work of creation (*cf.* Gn. 1:3) and in the subjugation even of such turbulent elements as the seas. The question now arises: what response is due to such a God?

8 answers that men should *fear* and *stand in awe* (better, 'go in dread') of Him, **9** because of His irresistible word. **10, 11** contrast the helplessness of the words of men and the certain fulfilment of the words of the Lord. Finally, **12** expresses the blessedness of being linked to this God of effectual rule over the world.

13–19 The all-searching eye of the Lord

The preceding section has implied the following question: granted the blessedness of possessing and being possessed by this great God, how are we to know that we are in this place of blessing? Who are His people? **13** God's choice is not restricted: it is made from *all the sons of men*. This thought leads to the next theme, that of divine comprehensiveness. **14** God looks from heaven to earth and scans every living being. In vv. 13, 14 two Hebrew words for 'look' are used. **15** Moreover, He looks not only upon the outward appearance; He discerns the thoughts and intentions of the hearts which He Himself has fashioned. *Cf.* Ps. 139:1–5; Heb. 4:12, 13.

At this point a striking feature occurs. From v. 4 each new concept has been introduced by a remark in the preceding statement; but **16** brings forward a theme which has no precedent in the poem, that of human impotence. While there has not been the slightest hint of imperfection or peril in all the wide survey of space and time, we are now to infer that the divine scrutiny of mankind has disclosed so prevalent a defect that the need for salvation is unquestionably accepted by all. Certainly there is no earthly power to deliver; neither rank, numbers, personal prowess, **17** nor natural forces (symbolized by the *horse*) can effect redemption. If salvation is to be obtained, God must intervene. **18, 19** Hence, as a final theme the election of the godly is firmly declared. This is not a repetition of the concept of divine sovereignty in vv. 12, 13, but a statement of the basis of true life. There is nothing arbitrary or capricious about it; it is a righteous principle available to all. The fundamental principle is simply that of the Lord's faithfulness; all who honour Him and rest or hope in His mercy and goodness, He will undertake to deliver from death and to sustain in every exigency of life. This inescapable law of faith is the personal counterpart of that immutable lot of the good and the true which was the closing thought of the first half of the poem.

PSALM 34. TESTIMONY

This is an acrostic poem, as is Ps. 25. The title associates the hymn with David's escape from Gath to Adullam (1 Sa. 21:10 – 22:1). See introduction to Ps. 52. *Abimelech* was very possibly the title of the king of Gath, in the same way as 'Pharaoh' was used in Egypt, and 'Agag' among the Amalekites (*cf.* Gn. 20:2; 26:1). In 1 Samuel his name is given as Achish.

The spirit of exuberant confidence in the Lord is of more importance than any logical structure in the poem. Many of its phrases have become an essential part of the vocabulary of devotional worship.

1, 2 Introduction

1 David has reached the point of spiritual certainty where he feels able to say that his praise of God is independent and irrespective of circumstances. **2** It is the product of his *soul*, the very centre of his being, and he desires that it may bring alleviation to those whom life has *afflicted*, or trodden down.

3–8 Personal testimony

The exhortations to *magnify the Lord* (v. 3) and *taste and see that the Lord is good* (v. 8) are a framework for an unforgettable experience. **4** 'I enquired of the Lord, and He answered me.' **5** Indeed, all who look unto Him become radiant-faced, and can never be abashed. **6** The will to help the downtrodden (v. 2) arises from the fact that it was when *poor* himself—the same word—that he *cried*, was *heard*, and was *saved* with full salvation. **7** Out of his people's past, he knows how to interpret his experience: the divine Deliverer, *the angel of the Lord*, intervened to save (*cf.* Gn. 16:7–13; 48:16; Ex. 14:19; Jdg. 6:11–24; *cf.* Jos. 5:13–15).

9–18 General exhortation

9 The personal appeal of v. 3 is here enlarged and generalized. *Cf.* also vv. 6, 7 with vv. 17, 18. Two themes are then elaborated. **10** First, the concept of deliverance from all fears is doubly illustrated by the imagery of young lions going hungry, because even powerful beasts in their prime have less security of life than those who turn to God for sustenance and enjoy His abundant provision. **15** Second, the simile in v. 5 of looking unto the Lord, with its suggestion of reflected radiance (*cf.* 2 Cor. 3:18), is reversed, and it is the eyes of the Lord which are upon the righteous (*cf.* Ps. 32:8) and **16** by His face the wicked shall be abashed.

11–14 Inserted within this general development of the psalm is a sub-section distinguished from the context by its didactic tone. **11** David here teaches his followers what it means to fear the Lord (*cf.* v. 9). **12** The ideal life, the life which is marked by the joyfulness of the Lord's continual benevolence, has three characteristics: **13** strict avoidance of all falsity of speech (*cf.* Mt. 5:37); **14** an uncompromising activity in doing good; perseverance in the quest for peace with men (*cf.* Rom. 14:19; Heb. 12:14). That David and his men acted thus is attested in 1 Sa. 25:14–16. These essential rules for godly living are quoted verbatim in 1 Pet. 3:10–12, and are implicit in such synopses of Christian ethics as that given in Col. 3:8–17.

19–22 Conclusion

This is a summary statement of the two trends and issues of human life. On one hand there is the pursuit of righteousness and godliness which, for all its incidental affliction, is inseparably bound up with the goodness and power of the Lord who maintains the believer's inward strength. On the other hand there is the choice of wickedness and its inevitable doom; by its very antagonism to the good, the practice of evil will entail the ruin of its guilty adherents. Finally, there is an echo of the initial testimony in vv. 1 and 2, and an emphatic assertion that it is impossible for those who trust in the Lord to share in the condemnation of the guilty. (*Cf.* Rom. 8:1, 33, 34.) **20** *He keeps all his bones.* A vivid figure for complete preservation. It was literally fulfilled in the experience of Christ (Jn. 19:36).

PSALM 35. A LITANY

This strong cry of distress could well date from the period when David was being hunted by Saul. It may be regarded as an elaboration of 1 Sa. 24:15. At such a time David's mind would be extremely agitated because of his enemies at Saul's court, the king's instability of character, the awful scope of human ingratitude and hatred, and the elusive details of God's purposes which in themselves were plain and yet contradictory (*cf.* 1 Sa. 24:6, 20). This prayer for judgment on his foes was no expression of secret malice against Saul, for had he not spared his life? It is a plea for the visible demonstration of essential righteousness.

The psalm has three sections, each of which ends with the expectation of thanksgiving for deliverance.

1–10 Prayer for a vigorous deliverance from violence

1–3 are a call to the Lord to help, expressed in the terms of the battlefield. **4–8** are an intimation of what should be done to those who are seeking his hurt (*cf.* Ps. 1:4; Je. 23:12). **9, 10** anticipate the time when fervent praise will be offered to God because of His gracious deliverance. **1** *Contend.* The Hebrew word is often used of disputes at law, but here the court of judgment is the field of battle. *Cf.* vv. 11 and 23.

11–18 Argument for immediate deliverance from injustice

The situation is one in which false witnesses bring fantastic charges against the psalmist. **12** *They requite me evil for good.* His grief is the greater because those who accuse him are ones whom he has befriended. The contrast is presented in some detail. **13, 14** describe his solicitude for others; when they were ill or distressed he sympathized with them so deeply that he virtually identified himself with them (*cf.* Jb. 2:12). He could not have done more even for his next of kin. *I prayed.* Better, as in RSV mg., 'My prayer turned back'. The meaning is that his prayer, though seemingly fruitless, shall return in blessing to himself. **15, 16** When the situation is reversed how differently they act. They do not wait for him to be in great need; he had but to stumble and they gloat over it and initiate a campaign of slander and calumny so that their words rend and stab. **17, 18** This argument closes with an appeal similar to those in Pss. 13:1, 2; 22:19-21.

19–28 Appeal for a statement of acquittal

The situation is now presented as a moral issue; *i.e.* the appeal to the Lord is made solely on the grounds of His *righteousness* (v. 24). **20** The conflict is not now one of weapons but of words; the wrongful imputation of evil against those who are law-abiding (*who are quiet in the land*) can do great mischief unless truth is made known. **21** The inwardness of the issue is seen in that the appeal is not for a stopping of mouths but **25** a silencing of their heart's intention. **23** Hence the urgent appeal to the Lord who is addressed as *my God and my Lord*. Note the Hebrew names here, *'ĕlōhîm* and *'ªdōn* (*cf.* Jn. 20:28), expressive of One who possesses the fullness of divine attributes and the omnipotence of divine power and sovereignty. Such an appeal is possible only because the psalmist has a clear conscience and because his request that those who rejoice at his difficulties should be disgraced (*cf.* v. 4) springs from his deep aversion to the evil desires and practices of such men. **27, 28** His own desire is for the widest experience of God's goodness, hence the concluding intercession that the joyous testimonies of godly men may be incapable of denial by those who were formerly sceptical. *Wink the eye* (v. 19) and *open wide their mouths* (21) are gestures of exultant malice and contempt.

PSALM 36. THE GOODNESS OF GOD

The central theme of this psalm is the loving-kindness of God (vv. 5, 7, 10). In sharp contrast is the picture of a wicked man (vv. 1–4). The psalm ends with a prayer for deliverance, and the assurance through faith of the overthrow of the wicked (vv. 10–12).

1–4 The limitations of evil

1a Transgression is imagined as speaking within the heart of a wicked man who regards it as an oracle (lit. 'The wicked man has an oracle of rebellion in his heart'). In other words, sin leads the sinner to project his evil concepts on to the seat of moral authority, whence God has been dispossessed. **1b** This spirit of rebellion against God assures the sinner that he need have no *fear*; *i.e.* he need not dread any consequences of his conduct. This self-deception of the wicked is due to his deliberate blindness toward God: he shuts himself within himself and, by listening to the smooth words of his own oracle, persuades himself that he is immune from ultimate disgrace

and dereliction. **2** This psychological diagnosis should be read in the light of Mk. 7:21–23 (*cf.* Dt. 29:19). The rejection of the true God inevitably entails the erection of a false god endowed to the full with the deceitful propensities of the rebellious heart.

After thus sketching the philosophy of the self-deceiving sinner, the actual process of his life is described. **3** As often, sins of speech head the list; next the abandonment of moral standards. **4** When he lies resting he does not meditate upon God but is engrossed in base and wicked schemes. His whole life is shaped and set into the pattern of the 'not good' (*cf.* Is. 28:15) and thus he neither recognizes nor rightly reacts to evil.

5–9 The greatness of God

Language is not able adequately to express the attributes of God. Their greatness is of a quality other than size and surpasses any mental concept of it. But language is all we have to convey our apprehension of truth, so the psalmist uses material height and depth to illustrate spiritual dimensions (*cf.* Eph. 3:18), and draws pictures of living needs such as parental protection and thirst's satisfaction to symbolize the rich realities of divine-human fellowship.

5 The *steadfast love* and *faithfulness* of God are as limitless as the heavens and the endless perspectives of the clouds. **6** His *righteousness* and *judgments*, signifying respectively His principles and practices, are as immovable and unfathomable as the mountains and the ocean (*cf.* Rom. 11:33). There is not a man or beast in all the earth that is uncared for by the Lord. **7** His benevolent vigilance is unspeakably *precious* (*cf.* Ps. 139:17). **8** His resources overshadow all people and, like the Garden of Eden, there is no dearth nor drought for the soul which commits itself to Him (the word *delights* is from the same root as Eden). **9** Only by outflow from Him is *life* itself enjoyed, and only by His illumination do we possess the light of truth (*cf.* Jn. 1:9).

10–12 A prayer for continued blessing

10 Whereas the wicked man is unaware of the glories of the divine nature, the godly man has been given some knowledge; hence the only consistent course for the psalmist is to ask the Lord for a continuance of His *steadfast love*, so that **11** he may neither be trodden down by insolent feet nor driven out by impious hands. **12** In faith he foresees the ultimate downfall of the ungodly.

PSALM 37. A MEDITATION UPON THE PROSPERITY OF THE WICKED

This poem is built upon an acrostic of the Hebrew alphabet and consists of a series of thoughts characteristic of OT wisdom literature. *E.g., cf.* v. 1 with Pr. 24:19; v. 5 with Pr. 16:3; v. 16 with Pr. 16:8; v. 23 with Pr. 16:9. There are some resemblances also to statements in the book of Job. *Cf.* v. 6 with Jb. 11:17; v. 10 with Jb. 7:10; v. 19 with Jb. 5:20. The psalmist was certainly troubled by the prosperity and power of wicked men, but he believed this to be only a temporary reversal of true values. The poem should be read alongside Ps. 73, where the issue is seen (v. 17) from a spiritual and not a material standpoint.

The poem has no obvious structure apart from its main thread of confidence in God's future work; this links the various statements together and is particularly symbolized in the repeated words *shall possess the land* (vv. 9, 11, 22, 29, 34).

1–8 Definition of the right attitude to life's problem

Facing the problem of life's inequalities, the initial emphasis is negative (*fret not, be not envious*), but the principal stress is on the positive actions of *trust, take delight in, commit, be still, wait*, all in connection with the sufficiency and goodness of the Lord. 1 Vv. 7b, 8 repeat the exhortations of this verse. 2 On the negative side there is the use of a metaphor so apt that it is frequently used both in the OT and in the NT (*e.g.* Pss. 90:6; 103:15; Is. 40:6–8; Jas. 1:10, 11). 3–5 On the positive side there is the clear concept of a definite transaction between the Lord and the trusting soul. See, *e.g.*, v. 5 (lit. 'Roll your way upon the Lord'); *cf.* Ps. 55:22; 1 Pet. 5:7. This attitude must be maintained by the doing of good (v. 3). 6 On His part there will be the sure vindication of faith, as certain as the noon-day sun, and 4 also He will bestow upon the soul that delights in Him the fulfilment of his desires, *i.e.* Himself. 8 The reminder to *refrain* from angry annoyance at injustice is repeated by James (Jas. 1:26; 3:9); it is far better to be silent and to banish all fretfulness by an un-swerving reliance upon God. *Cf.* Ps. 62:1, 5.

9–22 The psalmist's underlying belief analysed

9, with its *for* and *but*, sets out the basis for the right attitude to the moral anomalies of life. After a little while the wicked shall disappear and the godly shall live undisturbed. 10, 11 Each aspect is expanded (*cf.* Mt. 5:5) and 12–14 the theme thus introduced is further elaborated. The wicked plot, gnash with the teeth, draw out the sword and bend their bow in order to cast down and slay the righteous who *walk uprightly*. 15 But their own weapons shall be their destruction. 16 In contrast, righteous men are altogether different and their worth is measured by moral values, not by material well-being, 17 and by God's estimate of them, displayed by His supporting grace. 18, 19 The meditation now turns to the upright who are further described. Their outstanding characteristic is a security which is not rooted in the circumstances of everyday life, so that when misfortune comes upon them they are not abashed, and in scarcity are still contented (*cf.* Phil. 4:11–13). 20 In contrast, the wicked have no enduring security, no more so than the finest pastures which, for all their brave show, are as insubstantial as smoke (*cf.* Mt. 6:30).

23–33 Belief and testimony

The psalmist's thought now turns to the essential factor in life—the sovereign good pleasure of the Lord. 23, 24 He makes safe and sure the way that a righteous man takes, and even if that man should trip over he is not left prostrate (*cf.* Lk. 10:33–35; Jude 24). This is no fanciful notion but a fact of experience. 25 does not mean that a good man is never destitute (*cf.* 1 Sa. 21:3; 25:8), but that he is never forsaken by the Lord and ultimately, in *his children*, conditions become improved. 27 At all times the only right principle is to keep on doing good (*cf.* Ps. 34:14), because equity in dealing with men and loyalty toward God are always approved by the Lord and fostered by His co-operation. 28, 29 The psalmist's meditation is now turning from the theme of the Lord's providential care to the actual experiences of *his saints*. Not only do they possess this enduring quality but 30 their speech is marked by pleasant reflections upon the law and truth: *the mouth* is the primary evidence of character (*cf.* Ps. 36:3). 31 His life is genuine, for his heart is occupied with God's will. 32, 33 Even though evil men plot against the righteous and accuse him before corrupt judges, nevertheless the Lord will not fail to intervene sooner or later.

34–40 Concluding counsel

34 Set your heart upon the Lord and keep your life on His path; then eventually the downfall of the wicked will be witnessed. This is not a matter for personal gratification; it is demanded by the moral bases of life. 35, 36 The psalmist here adds his second testimony to the effect that he himself had known a wicked man acting as a terrible tyrant and flourishing like a leafy tree in its own native soil; yet he was suddenly cut down and removed from the scene as though he had never existed. 38 All transgressors are bound to be destroyed: there is no possible future for any wicked man. 37 But let everyone take note of what happens to a man who is upright and godly; there is indeed a future for him, and for his posterity.

39, 40 are a confession of faith in the character, power and absolute trustworthiness of the Lord.

PSALM 38. CONTRITION WHEN HARASSED WITHIN AND WITHOUT

This prayer for divine aid was prompted by great physical and moral distress. The descriptive details in vv. 1–8 may be metaphorical (*cf.* Is. 1:5, 6), and this leads Eaton to suggest that it 'may rather have been a psalm in the Temple repertory which could have been used on behalf of any grievously sick person'; but the pronounced element of personal experience in these verses suggests some serious disease. But whatever its point of origin, the title indicates its use in association with 'the memorial offering', designed prayerfully to seek God's intervention in some desperate need.

1-11 The disquiet of sin

1 His experience leads him to infer that the Lord's present attitude to him is one of wrath and displeasure. **2** His agencies are as sharp piercing arrows and strong pressing hand. **3** Ultimately *sin* is the cause of all his distress. **4** These *iniquities* are described first as a suffocating flood (*cf.* Jon. 2:3-5; Ps. 42:7), then as a burden crushing the life out of him (*cf.* Gn. 4:13). The swift change of metaphor accentuates the restless and distraught spirit of a sinner convicted of guilt. **5-7** Beginning with festering wounds, the consequences of his sinful folly are graphically described: a pain-racked body, bent and bowed like that of a mourner; his whole frame fevered and diseased. The description then gradually turns from outward symptoms of the flesh to evidences of an inner malady which is well known to God. **8, 9** There is a general sense of numbness and incapacity, the inarticulate groaning of an aching heart and a troubled conscience. **10** Such a moral malady finds expression in a throbbing heart, a loss of zest in life, dullness of vision, and **11** a suspicion on the part of friends and even of kinsmen which causes them to hold aloof from him, as if he were a leper.

12-17 The decision to turn to God

This thought of other men provides a link for a theme of certainty. **12** He knows that those who have sought his life are now, during his distress, actively plotting and scheming against him. **13, 14** Moreover, because of his sense of guilt, he must behave as though unaware of their slanders, for he cannot plead innocence in a matter of greater moment. *Rebukes*: RV mg. suitably suggests 'arguments'. **15** The external pressure of his enemies clarifies the psalmist's real attitude of heart; his trust is rooted in the Lord. Not only so, he must leave it to the Lord to speak in reply to his adversaries, and **16** so implicit is his trust that he does not even sketch out the nature of the reply, saving only that the Lord vindicates him against their triumphant mockery. **17** For himself, he has reached the end of his tether. There is one step more to penitence.

18-22 The confession of sin

18 He admits his sin, and recognizes that it is this which is the root cause of his sorrow and care. **19** Nevertheless his enemies are still active and numerous and are apparently unaffected by his change of heart. **20** Indeed they are quite ready to repay any graciousness on his part with ingratitude. *I follow after good*; *i.e.* in his behaviour towards them. **21, 22** The prayer concludes with an urgent call to the Lord not

to forsake him nor to be slow to intervene. Faith has not yet risen to the triumphant certainty of Ps. 6:8, 9, but it is implicit in the final words, *O Lord, my salvation!*

PSALM 39. FACING DEATH

The superscription *to Jeduthun* refers to a notable leader of the Temple choir (*cf.* 1 Ch. 16:41, 42; 25:1-6). He is also named in the titles of Pss. 62 and 77.

The psalmist tells of his unavailing effort to keep his trouble to himself (vv. 1-3). He then records the words of a prayer centring on the brevity of life and the seriousness of sin (vv. 4-11), and ends (vv. 12, 13) with a plea for divine mercy.

Two main interpretations have been offered. According to one (see Weiser), the trouble which overcame the psalmist's reticence is not recorded here. His concern in the psalm is the fact that in speaking he broke faith with God and dishonoured Him in the presence of *the wicked* (v. 1). Vv. 4-11 are his plea for forgiveness and to be strengthened against repeating this offence. He asks for a due regard for the shortness of life so that, living as a man about to die, he will be circumspect in all his doings. The final two verses plead for divine aid for the remainder of his pitifully short life.

The other interpretation, offered here (*cf.* Eaton and most commentators), takes vv. 4-11 as the outburst which he longed to avoid but could not contain. Commentators, of course, vary in their understanding of what was in the psalmist's mind, and why he so fervently wished to keep these thoughts to himself.

1-3 Suppression

1 The decision to exercise a strict watch over all that he says and to refrain from complaint about his own distress was motivated by a fear of giving *the wicked* ground for attacking the honour of God. *Cf.* the companion fear expressed in 73:15. **2, 3** This suppression of his feelings, however, simply caused a psychological explosion; he could no longer restrain himself.

4-11 Outburst

The theme of his cry is the brevity and frailty of man's life. **4** In this context, his great fear, the ground of his overpowering anxiety, was of sudden death which came without forewarning upon one who had not been made aware that his *end* was upon him and that *the measure of my days* had run its course. **5a** Against such a death he would have no defence, for it expressed what God had predetermined as his life span, a pathetic *few handbreadths* of time and a veritable *nothing* compared with the eternities of God Himself. **5b, 6** But if he is defenceless because of the irresistible will of God, he is doubly defenceless because of his own human nature. Man is of innate fragility, and even in matters of worldly business and the apportionment of his own resources he cannot pierce into the future so as to make it suit his wishes. How then can he armour himself against death itself?

7 Yet all is by no means lost. There is hope in God expressed in relation to three great realities of life. **8a** First, there is hope of forgiveness. The psalmist reveals a cardinal factor in his fear of sudden death, that of dying unforgiven. Herein also we may surmise why he kept his fears from *the wicked* (v. 1). They would scoff at a man whose religion and faith did not give him security in the face of death, but would take no account of the moral factor of the deadliness of unforgiven sin. Hence they would scorn a God who failed His servants at the last. **8b** Secondly, hope in God touches the matter of vindication from scorners. They would not understand how the regenerate soul senses the divine abhorrence of sin, but they would have their mouths stopped if they saw him triumphing where they expected his downfall. **9–11** Thirdly, there is hope residing in the divine purpose for human life. **9** should be restored to a past tense (*cf.* RV). The psalmist's former silence was due to a reverent acceptance of God's will. Now because God is One in whom he has *hope* (*cf.* v. 7), **10** he looks for a divine decision to lift his burden, **11a** in merciful recognition that, however just the punishment, **11b** it deprives man of his dearest, though fragile, possession, life itself.

12, 13 Prayer

This is the counterpart of vv. 1–3. The dominance of the subjective *I said, I will, I was, etc.* disappears before the objective reference to the Lord whose ear, and word, and benevolence are desired because therein is true life. **12** The plea is based on the kindly mercy of God to whom *tears* constitute a prayer, and who will be as attentive to the *passing guest*, the alien refugee, as He instructed His people to be (*cf.* Dt. 10:18, 19). **13** *Look away from me*; *i.e.* 'turn away thy look of wrath' (*cf.* v. 10). The psalmist beseeches his Lord to attend to his need and yet asks to be spared any further scrutiny of God's critical eye.

PSALM 40. A LITURGY OF A FULL HEART

It may quite well be that the contrasting moods reflected in this poem were occasioned by the circumstances related at the end of the first book of Samuel. The lament over the destruction of Ziklag (1 Sa. 30:4–6), the swift defeat of Amalek (1 Sa. 30:16–20), and the news of the Philistine victory at Gilboa and of the death of Saul with all its implications for David, occurred within three or four days (2 Sa. 1:1). This poem, therefore, may be the expression of his release from a perilous exile wherein had been great gain in Godward trust (vv. 1–3), of his readiness to undertake the expected call to be leader of the people (v. 7) and of dedication to that work

(v. 8), of his recognition that not all his foes had fallen on Gilboa (vv. 14–16), and that many of his deeds in the period of Saul's animosity must now come home with painful consequences (v. 12) if the exile became king. The poem certainly expresses his consciousness of utter dependence on the Lord (vv. 13, 17) as well as his delight in Him (vv. 1–5) and eager service of Him (vv. 6–10). Even though this connection with David's history is, of course, hypothetical, it does show how a psalm of such diversity can yet be a unity arising out of the manifold variety of experience. There is no need therefore to follow those commentators who find it necessary to suppose that several psalms were gratuitously joined together.

The elements of royal dedication which this psalm contains (vv. 6–8) aptly became prophetic of the royal and priestly Messiah (Heb. 10:5–10), while the elements of confession (v. 12) serve to show how short His human prototypes fell of His matchless perfection.

1–5 Thanksgiving

1–3 The past experience. 1 David's patient waiting upon the Lord is noted, not in order to dwell on its duration, but in view of what happened. The Lord's ear was alert to his prayer. **2** God has brought him out of the place of insecurity, and put him firmly on the *rock* of His sufficiency (*cf.* Ps. 18:31–33). He made plain the way of his going (*cf.* Ps. 37:23), and **3** gave him a new song so that many others should hear, reverence and trust.

4, 5 The new song. 4 This rhapsody in two movements first glorifies the way of faith, in which there is *a.* a deliberate choice and action by the man who *makes the Lord his trust*; *b.* a recognition that there is no ground for confidence in *the proud*, men whose promises are hollow; and *c.* a complete rejection of any other supernatural aid as erroneous and *false*, or lying. **5** Next, glory is ascribed to the *Lord my God*, the object of his faith, whose *wondrous* (*i.e.* supernaturally marvellous) *deeds* are a reflection of His inner *thoughts* towards us. He is indeed beyond compare and mercies already experienced are but a fraction of what is still kept in store (*cf.* 1 Cor. 2:9).

6–10 Dedication

6–8 The supreme offering. Supreme among the plans of God which have been disclosed to the ear of the psalmist is that whereby worship is consummated not in the ritual of the blood of beasts as such, but in the willing surrender of the worshipper's life for continual obedience to the will of God. The four offerings here mentioned are detailed in Lv. 1–4. But while they had a rightful place in divine worship centred in the altar, they were not the sole or primary requirement laid upon the worshipper (*cf.* Dt. 10:12f.). Offerings in isolation from the moral and spiritual response of repentance and dedicated obedience were recognized as 'vain' (Is. 1:13). But the

OT never supposed that offerings were a dispensable element in religion, or that all worship could be offered solely through moral response to God. What appear here as alternatives are to be understood as comparatives in order of priority (cf. 1 Sa. 15:22; Ho. 6:6). This passage is interpreted in Heb. 10:5–10 as being spoken by Jesus Christ and fulfilled in Him.

6 *An open ear* (lit., as RSV mg., 'ears thou hast dug for me'). This is a unique expression in the Bible and for its meaning appeal can be made either to the custom of piercing the ear (consecration to perpetual service, Ex. 21:6; Dt. 15:17) or to the idiom of opening the ear, signifying the imparting of a revelation from God (*e.g.* Is. 50:5). The common denominator of these two ideas is obedience and it is most likely that this is what the phrase is intended to stress: God the Creator has hollowed out man's ears, giving him the faculty of hearing in order that he might learn and then obey the divine will.

9, 10 The public testimony. God's work of *deliverance* has been proclaimed before men; it has not been kept for his own secret delight. The faithfulness, mercy and truth of the Lord have been preached before crowds of men, His salvation has been advertised. The movement from v 8 to v. 9 is significant. The reality of a man's testimony about the state of his heart is seen in his willingness to share the good news of God with others. If private religion does not become public it ceases to be true.

11–17 Supplication

11–13 For salvation of soul. The emphasis from the first word is on the Lord. 'Do Thou, on Thy part, not withhold Thy compassions from me, even as I have not withheld (restrained) my lips. Let Thy loving-kindness and truth, which I have not concealed from men, continually be my protection, because a multitude of evils have coiled around me and the consequences of past sins have blurred my vision just when I need to see clearly.' Hence the petition of v. 13.

14–17 For deliverance from danger. 14, 15 This request seeks the overthrow of David's foes by a recoiling upon themselves of all their schemes and slanders against him. **16** This appeal is linked with a desire for blessing upon all who can join from the heart in his song of praise (see v. 3). **17** What if he is *poor and needy*; *i.e.* downtrodden and helpless? The Lord will certainly take thought for him (see v. 5) and free him from all difficulties, however tenacious and troublesome (see v. 2). The poem's whole expression of praise, its reliance upon God's promise and its plea for help are caught up and crystallized in the words of this last verse. None other but the Lord can help; none other is sought for help. May He then *not tarry*.

PSALM 41. ABUSE AND ASSURANCE

The charge against 'my bosom friend' (v. 9) links this poem with Ps. 55:13, 14, 20, 21. If the psalm is to be associated with a particular episode in David's life, it must belong to the treachery of Ahithophel (2 Sa. 15:12, 31), though there is no reference there to David's being, or having been, ill. The main point in the psalm, however, seems to be some notable sickness, during which treachery on the part of once trusted friends became evident. The Lord Jesus Christ used the psalm to speak of His own experience (Jn. 13:18), and in the wonderful variety of Scripture it enshrines the not-uncommon experience of human disloyalty, and speaks for the comfort of those who suffer at the hands of friends.

1–3 A statement of principle

1 While the psalmist includes himself in the category of those who are *poor*, *i.e.* downcast, he is making a general statement valid in all similar cases. Happy is that man who considers how best he may aid the needy. *In the day of trouble* the Lord will be his helper. **2** The wicked hopes of his enemies will be confounded by actual events. **3** Should such a man become seriously ill, he will experience divine support, even to the extent that the Lord becomes his nurse and 'changes all his bed' in his sickness (RSV mg., correctly, for v. 3b).

4–9 David's bitter experience

A specific case, his own, is now cited wherein the principle of benevolence has not been reciprocated. **5** At a time when, because of illness, his enemies were openly desiring and forecasting his death, then those from whom he expected kindness and sympathy returned him deceitfulness and antagonism. **6** Some of those who visited him in his sickness were obviously pleased to find him laid low, and lied when they expressed a desire for his speedy recovery. **7** Their true thoughts were spread abroad outside the sick chamber so that his secret enemies were emboldened to plot against him and **8** circulated rumours of some incurable disease, brought on by evil doing, which would prevent his ever leaving his bed. **9** Bitterest of all was the behaviour of *my bosom friend* (lit. 'the man of my peace'), bound together in a covenant of loyalty (cf. 1 Sa. 18:3), expressed and cemented in the sacred grace of hospitality. The extent of his spiteful animosity is expressed as a spurning of the prostrate sufferer with his heel.

10–12 A sure confidence in the Lord

In spite of the bitter disappointment caused by his trusted companion David's reliance upon God is unimpaired. **10** He not only prays for restoration to health so that he might carry out his duty of just requital as the royal judge, but he affirms a threefold testimony to the Lord: *a.* **11** as the God who reveals His good pleasure in vindicating His own; *b.* **12a** as the God who does not allow virtue (*integrity*) to go unrewarded; and *c.* **12b** as the God who brings sinners (*cf.* v. 4) into a permanent intimacy with Himself.

13 Doxology

The last verse is a doxology added by a compiler

to mark the end of the first of the five books of Psalms (*cf.* Pss. 72:18, 19; 89:52; 106:48). See Introduction, on 'The Five Books'.

BOOK TWO. PSALMS 42–72

PSALMS 42 AND 43. THE LONGING FOR GOD'S SANCTUARY

These two psalms probably constitute one poem: in several Hebrew MSS they are joined together; Ps. 43 is the only poem in the second book to lack a superscription; the theme in both is that of deep grief caused by exclusion from the sanctuary of the Lord; Ps. 43:5 is virtually identical with Ps. 42:5 and 11, providing a refrain which divides the poem into three stanzas.

42:1–5 Yearning and regret

1 The imagery of a timid fallow-deer audibly panting because of extreme thirst vividly expresses the intense and searing sense of want experienced by the psalmist (*cf.* Pss. 63:1; 84:2). **2** His craving to draw near to *the living God*, who is the fountain of living water (*cf.* Je. 2:13), is inseparable from the remembered habit of going up to the sanctuary. But the repetition of *'ĕlōhîm* (*God*) shows that the yearning is for communion with God Himself. **3** The strength of his intense love and longing for God is shown by his constant *tears* over the scepticism of his companions. **4** This atmosphere of unbelief has enhanced his memories of how he used to lead the throng of pilgrims *in procession to the house of God* (*cf.* 2 Sa. 6:15–19). **5** This moody retrospect is suddenly challenged by an upwelling of irrepressible faith and the psalmist calls upon his mournful soul not only to trust in God but actively to hope for His deliverance.

42:6–11 Dejection and hope

6 The second stanza picks out of the refrain the words *cast down*. It is significant of his honesty with God, and also of the tender nature of the God to whom he speaks, that having rightly assured himself that a downcast spirit is unnecessary (v. 5), he at once confesses that he is living on a lower level than his faith would require. The psalmist now reveals to us that he is in the far north, where snow-capped *Hermon* looks down on the head waters of the *Jordan*. How he came to be there he does not disclose, but the deep sadness of his poem suggests that he was one of the many strings of captives led off by invading kings. **7** The thunder of the waterfalls as Hermon's snow melted seemed to answer to the depth of his own sorrows, but at the same time faith reasserted itself: if he found himself storm-tossed, the waves were God's waves. He was still kept by a sovereign Hand. **8** is not easy to connect with v. 7. Owing to the flexibility of meaning of the Hebrew tenses, we may translate it present (as RSV), in which case

he testifies to the comfort he derives from his confessed sense of God's overruling; or we may translate as future (*cf.* RV), in which case the psalmist states his assurance that God will enable him to triumph in the midst of the storms; or the verbs could be past continuous ('used to'), leading into the sad query of v. 9, with its associated complaint of a pain that is physical in its intensity (v. 10), as he faces his taunting adversaries. **9** Nevertheless, not for nothing did he call God his *rock*—One unchangeable in faithful strength, a sure refuge (Ps. 94:22), abundant in overflowing grace (Ex. 17:5, 6)— and the prayer of sadness **11** turns into the exhortation of faith.

43:1–5 Confidence in God

In the third stanza of the complete poem the human elements of distress and despondency are replaced by a realization of God's faithfulness and power. The mood of plaintive regret in the first stanza and of fitful perplexity in the second is changed in the third to one of confidence and trust. **1** The baffling circumstances are still present. Hence his plea for vindication against men who are unkind, deceitful and unjust, and his request for heartfelt assurance in the matter of divine care. **2** God is his supreme resource, why then does He seem to have rejected him? Why must the psalmist go about by himself as solitary as a mourner? Nevertheless, these needs are referred to God precisely because his desire and hope and faith are in Him. **3** Whatever gloom may shade his soul, God Himself is unchangeable *light*; moreover, His *truth* must prevail over all misleading tendencies. Consequently God will surely remove the existing barriers both within and without which hinder him from going up to Mt. Zion. **4** But his desire is not for the place, except in so far as it houses *the altar of God*, which affords access, through the blood of its sacrifices, to God in whom alone is all his satisfaction (lit. 'the God of the joy of my exultation'). **5** This anticipation of unhindered fellowship with God, who is the delight and source of all his joy, introduces the final refrain, unchanged in words but possibly transformed in tone. Faith's rebuke to dejection (42:5) and faith's exhortation in bewilderment (42:11) become faith's triumphant declaration of certainty (43:5).

PSALM 44. THE BEWILDERMENT OF A GODLY PEOPLE

This psalm is the first of several national poems in the Psalter. See, *e.g.*, Pss. 83; 106. In each case the underlying motive is an intense desire to know God's ways and specially to see how His actions in human history can be justified. The usual view regarded national distress or disaster as the direct result of the people's wrongdoing. God responded to their national life by rewards and punishments, giving victory and prosperity at a time of godliness, and sending defeat and dearth when sinful practices dominated the nation. See, *e.g.*, Jdg. 2:16–23; Ps. 106.

Ps. 44 is outstanding because it faces the problem of the sufferings of *godly* people (see vv. 17–22). 'Israel', as Eaton well says, 'is facing the fact that fidelity to God leads to the Cross.'

1–8 Material blessings enjoyed in the days of old

This review of the past first rehearses certain events (vv. 1–3) and then repeats the expression of faith (vv. 4–8) which accompanied and grew out of those events. Foremost in the nation's previous experience was the unique acquisition of the land of Canaan. In references to this event the emphasis was usually placed upon their deliverance from Egypt (*e.g.* Ps. 78:42–53); but here the settlement in Canaan is selected as a historical monument of divine activity not only because it was so amazingly accomplished (*cf.* Dt. 4:35–38) but because it was so obviously the antithesis of their present experience (see v. 11b).

1–3 There could be no mistaking God's aid *in the days of old*: weapons alone were no guarantee of success (*cf.* Pss. 20:7; 33:12, 16). **4–6** Their Lord was a 'man of war' (Ex. 15:3; note also Is. 59:16, 17); that was why they had power to crush all opposition. **7, 8** These memories of triumph are rooted in a God who is still the same, and in whose people's hearts the same triumphant boast throbs as of old. The present tenses of vv. 4–8 thus prepare for the unforeseeable and inexplicable contrast of the following verses.

9–16 The profound dishonour of the present condition

9 The word *Yet* introduces tremendous contradiction. Their King and God has cast off His people and repudiated His connection with them, or so it would appear (*cf.* Pss. 43:2; 89:38). Their armies have gone to battle and the Lord has held back. **10** They are perplexed and at a loss, their enemies despoil them at their pleasure, and **11** the people of the Lord are as helpless as sheep. **12** It looks as though God has given them away, or sold them virtually for nothing. **13, 14** Certainly He has gained no prestige for Himself among the nations. **15, 16** In short, the people of God are humiliated and utterly crestfallen because of the inescapable mockery of men who blaspheme and say 'the promises of the Lord your God are obviously worthless'. Their experience is, in fact, the national counterpart of 42:3, 10.

17–22 The unmerited nature of this experience

17, 18 The sting of all this arises from a lack of any sense of guilt on their part. If they had fallen

away from God (*cf.* Ps. 16) or been disobedient to the covenant (*cf.* Dt. 28:15ff.), then their plight would be understandable. But the national conscience is clear, and yet **19** their country is devastated so that it looks like the dreary haunts of jackals (*cf.* Is. 34:13). **20, 21** There is here a sincere conviction that the trend of national life and policy was without fault before God; and after all, He should know if this was falsely said. **22** Indeed it would appear that the attack upon their national existence can be explained only as being *for thy sake, i.e.* either 'for some inscrutable reason which makes sense only to God' (*cf.* Ps. 23:3b), or 'because we are Thy people and are hated for it' (*cf.* 1 Jn. 3:13). This insight into the discipline of godliness is taken as axiomatic in the NT (*cf.* Mt. 5:11; Jn. 15:20, 25; Acts 14:22; Rom. 8:36; 2 Tim. 3:12).

23–26 The urgent need of divine aid

The pressure of circumstances makes itself felt above any consolation afforded by the great truth just expressed (v. 22), and **23, 24** voices its plight in the daring pictures of God, as asleep, in hiding and forgetful, by which the call for help is made. How outspoken God allows us to be! **25** And with what patience He allows us to plead our necessities as the basis on which prayer is made, **26** though, as ever, the resting-place of faith is, finally, His *steadfast love*.

PSALM 45. A ROYAL WEDDING SONG

This song of a royal marriage was almost certainly prompted by the ceremony of a Hebrew king marrying a foreign princess. The identity of the king is uncertain, for his warlike activities (vv. 3, 5) hardly befit Solomon (*cf.* 1 Ki. 3:1), and his devout character (vv. 6, 7) is not in keeping with Ahab—at least, not after his marriage with Jezebel (1 Ki. 16:31).

The song was included in the Psalter because it illustrated an idea which is frequently used in Scripture, viz. that the human marriage relationship is an echo, or at least an allegory, of the covenant relationship between God and His people. This same basic idea is carried over into the NT where the church is described as the Bride of Christ (see 2 Cor. 11:2; Eph. 5:31, 32; *cf.* Mt. 22:2ff.; 25:1ff.; Rev. 19:6–9).

1 Introduction

The author describes his irrepressible desire to speak of something particularly fine and good, his feelings of appreciative delight on behalf of the king are literally 'bubbling over' and he senses that the eloquence of his pen will be in keeping with so glorious a theme.

2–9 In praise of the royal bridegroom

The description of the king opens with an intimate insight into his personal relationship with God (v. 2), which is no quiescent pietism but issues in active campaigning for truth and right

(vv. 3–5). In explanation of the victory which has been accorded to the king, it is stated that his devotion to righteousness has been rewarded by a divine act of exaltation (vv. 6, 7), which has left him without equal. His exalted status is finally displayed by reference to the fragrance and joy of his circumstances (v. 8), and the fact that the ladies of his entourage are royal in their own right (v. 9), eloquent of the prestige in which neighbouring states hold him. It is no wonder that this eulogy of the Davidic king was seen to be prophetic of Him who alone merits its full meaning (Heb. 1:8, 9).

2 The king's *lips* give the primary evidence of what he is, and such is the impression created by hearing him (*cf.* Jn. 6:68; 7:46) that the psalmist says *therefore, i.e.* 'by this we see that' behind it lies an eternal blessing of divine grace. **4, 5** The spread of Messiah's kingdom is often seen in the OT in terms of conquest (Ps. 110:5–7; Is. 11:12–16), but, as here, the emphasis is not on territorial expansion but on the warfare of the *truth.* **6, 7** The translation *your divine throne* (which is possible but not the most intrinsically likely) expresses the notion that the Davidic king is God's vicegerent, ruling in His name (1 Ch. 28:5; 29:23). We should, however, rather read 'Your throne, O God' (*cf.* RV), allowing the verse to partake of that tension which belongs to the OT view of the Messiah whereby there is a clear suggestion of divinity, while at the same time God can be called *your God* in speaking to Him (*cf.* Is. 9:6, 7; and see *NBD*, art. 'Messiah').

10–17 In praise of the bride

10, 11 The change of subject is intimated by an appeal to the bride. She is exhorted to a loyalty to her husband which supersedes all former loyalties, and is given the reassuring hint that this will be no arduous task because of the ardent devotion which he will bestow on her. **12, 13** Furthermore, to her will come an ingathering of suppliant pagan nations, bringing their resources. The poem speaks of her waiting within the palace, resplendently dressed in her bridal array, **14, 15** whence she will be led to the king *in many-coloured robes,* accompanied by her bridesmaids and with joyful music. The exactness of the portraiture of Christ and the church, coupled with the incorporation of the Gentiles, could hardly be improved.

16, 17 The remaining words about the future are addressed to the king, as is implied in v. 17. There will be an abundant offspring, royal as their father is royal. But the lasting praise of the ongoing *generations* and the ingathered *peoples* will be his alone.

PSALM 46. A SAFE STRONGHOLD IS OUR GOD

This is the first of a group of three poems which have a common theme. God is extolled and adored because He has brought His people through a great crisis which had threatened to become a national calamity.

Two interpretations are suggested. The older view associated the deliverance with the invasion of Sennacherib (2 Ki. 18; 19). The newer view links the psalm with the suggested annual Temple ritual in which the Davidic king was shown in all his human helplessness to be at the mercy of the powers of earth, until the Lord intervened to save him and destroy his foes. Such a dramatized ritual would serve to keep fresh the nature of kingship in Israel. Since both interpretations are hypothetical, the psalm offers an excellent field in which to try out their respective merits.

1–3 Firm anchorage in God while all else is insecure

The emphasis here is on external change. Metaphorically the opposing kings are seen as cosmic forces of destruction threatening the whole fabric of the ordered world of creation. But against all this, says the psalmist, 'God is ours (or, on our side), a refuge and strength, proving Himself an abundant help in troubles of every sort.'

4–7 Joyful assurance in the impregnable city of God

The emphasis here is on internal resources, especially upon the security which ensures serenity even though outward powers rage and threaten. **4** The source of this inward strength is pictured as a stream of quiet content (Ps. 23:2; Is. 33:21; 58:11), as the river of Paradise (Gn. 2:10), symbolic of God's living presence as the following verses depict it. The Hebrew, however, is abrupt, and the word *river* may be meant to point back to the foaming waters of v. 3: no matter what rage and fury is evident in the world, all is so controlled by the sovereign God that it becomes a fair stream for the benefit of His city and people. **5–7** Either of the foregoing interpretations lead well into these verses, stressing as they do the presence of God with His own, and the immediate effective control of God over the whole earth.

8–11 A call to consider the works of the Lord

8 The inference from the crisis must be plain to all peoples. Surely no nation could doubt that the Lord had done astonishing deeds. The rout of the enemy—whether a historical, political foe or a cosmic and spiritual one—was beyond dispute. Yet, greater than the event was the divine power which moulded it, and in the cessation of this campaign the psalmist catches a glimpse of the future inauguration of undisturbed peace, **9** when all implements of warfare will be destroyed (*cf.* Is. 2:4; 9:5). **10** The moral of the psalm is plain: because the Lord is God, let all men cease their efforts to usurp His sovereignty. **11** Note that the refrain in vv. 7 and 11 is threefold: *the Lord of hosts* is His title of divine power, *the God of Jacob* is His title of a covenant relationship, and God *is with us* is His name Immanuel (*cf.* Rom. 8:31).

PSALM 47. OUR GOD IS THE EXALTED KING

This festive hymn elaborates the words 'I am exalted in the earth' which occur at the end of the previous psalm. The main concept is that God, having come down from heaven in power and great might to deliver His people, is now returning to His throne. Such an assumption of dignity and power calls for public acclamation, not only on the part of His people Israel, but also by all the nations (cf. Ps. 66:1–7).

The poem, therefore, has two themes closely interwoven. 1 The first is a call to the peoples of the earth, regarded as assembled to acclaim Yahweh as King, to clap hands and shout, 5 to blow upon the horns and trumpets, 6 to sing psalms of praise, indeed to sing them incessantly and 7 with understanding (see mg.).

The second theme is a description of the majesty of God, who is the cause of their rejoicing. There are three phases. 2, 3 First, the Lord who controls the affairs of men is our King. The Most High inspires us with awe and none in all the earth can withstand Him. 4 He it is who chooses Canaan for our inheritance and we are proud of this token of His love toward us. 8 Secondly, the ascended Lord is our King. Indeed, in this aspect too He is the King of all the earth (cf. Je. 10:6–8; 1 Tim. 1:17; 6:15, 16); and as He has demonstrated His rule in the nature of recent events, He now openly resumes His seat of supreme and holy power. 9 Thirdly, the enthroned Lord is the supreme Sovereign. Because He is thus exalted, there must ultimately be a gathering together of all peoples, represented by their princes, as His people. Abraham will be the father of a multitude of nations and the heir of the world (cf. Rom. 4:16; Gal. 3:7, 14, 29). To God belong all the *shields* of office; *i.e.* all rightful authority wielded by kings and governors. Thus He is exalted beyond all (cf. 1 Cor. 15:24–28).

PSALM 48. REJOICE, FOR THE LORD IS IN MOUNT ZION

The first poem in this group celebrated the nation's deliverance from peril; the second extolled the power and majesty of Him who wrought their salvation; this third poem describes the glory of the city which God has so marvellously preserved. The Hebrew word translated 'greatly' in v. 1 is found also in 46:1 ('very') and 47:9 ('highly'). It is one of the incidental links between these psalms. God greatly helps, is greatly to be exalted, and is greatly to be praised.

1–3 The city of God extolled

Just as the Lord is highly to be praised because He is King of all the earth (47:6, 7), so is His *city* worthy of all honour. Jerusalem was regarded as incomparable in situation (cf. Ps. 50:2; La.

2:15). Heathen nations situated the mountain of the gods in *the far north* (cf. Is. 14:13f.). By thus placing *Zion* in *the far north*, the psalmist subtly claims sole and ruling deity for his God.

4–8 Attackers dismayed and repulsed

4 Even though a league of kings assembled together to besiege the city, 5 yet when they saw its strength they lost heart, became confused, and turned away in panic. 6 The sudden onset of their terror is symbolized by the vivid picture of labour in childbirth, 7 and the greatness of the divine power which induced it by reference to the mighty forces of the wind against which even *the ships of Tarshish*, the greatest of the ancient ships, were helpless.

8 The people's praise is evoked by their witness of God's power. Even as they had heard of God's mighty acts in their fathers' days, so had they seen His hand in Jerusalem's recent history, or, as some hold (Weiser, Eaton, Johnson), in the festival ritual dramatized in the Temple. This seemed to guarantee the city's preservation for ever. Such words were in later years too readily stripped of their spiritual significance. They became the foundation of the fanaticism of the city's religious leaders when Nebuchadrezzar's army besieged it. The real citadel was the heart that trusted in God (cf. Je. 1:18f.).

9–14 A meditation of God's loving-kindness

Since the threat of destruction was removed, the beloved city has been viewed with fresh delight. But behind this affection for Jerusalem there is a deep love for the Lord of the city. When the inhabitants enter into the Temple they know that the loving-kindness of the Lord is more to be contemplated than are the outward forms, such as the number of the city's battlemented towers. Upon such a God, upon Him and none other, they will rely.

9 could be translated 'we have portrayed', with reference to the Temple drama. 11 *The daughters of Judah* are the neighbouring and dependent townships delivered in the deliverance of the capital city. 12 The invitation to *number* ('count') *her towers* looks back to the frightful threat to which the city had been exposed and from which it has come entirely unscathed. 14 *Our guide for ever* arises from one emendation of the Hebrew, but a much lesser change gives 'unto (or 'against', or 'beyond') death', and is to be preferred (cf. RV).

PSALM 49. DEATH DISCLOSES A MAN'S TRUE WORTH

This psalm belongs to the class of 'wisdom' writings, not so much because of literary style, which is in a standard poetical form, but because of its content. It tackles the sort of problem beloved of the authors of Job and Proverbs, namely what is the attitude of the godly man to life's inequalities.

1–4 Introduction

The opening verses are introductory, and have typical 'wisdom' emphases: a universal appeal (vv. 1, 2), the offer of a practical solution to the problem to be proposed (vv. 3, 4).

3 The words *wisdom* and *understanding* are both plural in the Hebrew, signifying the promise of wisdom in full and plenty. There will be no superficiality in the handling of the problem, but a complete solution. **4** The source of this teaching is claimed to be revelation: *I will incline my ear*, *i.e.* to hear God's answer.

5, 6 The problem

Whether recording an actual experience or imaginatively placing himself in a typical situation, the psalmist faces the fears of a man against whom blatant materialists of considerable resources have set themselves. While the interrogative form of these verses suggests that such fears are groundless, the question itself is of great practical importance (*cf.* Jas. 2:6, 7) and the purpose of the psalmist is to provide us with such truths as will steer us safely through such a storm.

7–12 The answer: Part 1

There is a limit to the power of money. **7–9** Such trust in wealth as v. 6 indicated will take a man far in this world, but it cannot buy God off when death comes. *Ransom* and *price* are the stock words of the doctrine of redemption in both Testaments. Note carefully therefore how they involve here the payment of a substitutionary price. **10** All alike die, **11** and the eternal habitation of the grave is the reply to those who sought to perpetuate themselves by giving their names to great estates. **12** In respect of the mere fact of death, man and beast are precisely equal. *In his pomp*, probably 'in spite of his dignity', referring to the many glories of humanity above the beasts. Thus death the leveller gives perspective to life's inequalities, but only a partial answer to life's problems. For seeing that *the wise* also die (v. 10), it is cold comfort indeed to say to one oppressed by opulent neighbours that all will one day be solved by the equality of the grave.

13–15 The answer: Part 2

The real wisdom of the psalmist is to pierce beyond death and to show that the equality in which men come to the grave leads to vividly contrasting eternal destinies. **13, 14** The Hebrew text is difficult. RSV and RV represent the main lines of approach, which make it clear that while details are obscure the main thrust of the verses is unequivocal. On the one hand are the men whose *foolish confidence* was exposed in v. 6. Like the rich man of the parable, they had their good things in *their portion* here on earth (*cf.* Lk. 16:25a), but beyond the grave they are helpless as *sheep*, destined for *Sheol*, the abode of

the dead, committed to the care of a *shepherd* named *Death*, arriving at this destination without any intermediate state or second chance, knowing from henceforth only a greatly diminished existence in a very undesirable home. **15** On the other hand there is the emphatic *But*. In contrast to man's inability to find his own ransom price (*cf.* vv. 7, 8), God provides the ransom price which destroys Sheol's power to retain the soul, and takes the ransomed one to Himself. The verb *receive* almost has the status of a technical term for God's taking of a person to Himself in glory (*cf.* Gn. 5:24; 2 Ki. 2:9; Ps. 73:24). Thus the psalm, taken in its straightforward sense, teaches that the inequalities of life can finally be faced in the light of the blissful redemption which God provides for His own and the contrasting fate of those who preferred alternative objects of faith. Here, as Weiser says, 'is the hope of faith that reaches beyond death and in doing so overcomes death spiritually'.

16–20 The practical lesson

The knowledge of the doom of the ungodly in Sheol removes all lustre from his wealth in this world. **17** The *glory* here is outdone **19** by the darkness there. **20** RSV has made this verse identical with v. 12 by removing the words translated in RV 'and understandeth not'. If for all his dignity man does not understand the eternal issues of life and the way of salvation, then indeed what is his dignity worth (Mt. 16:26a)?

PSALM 50. MAN IMPEACHED AT HEAVEN'S COURT

1–6 Introduction

1 The impressive opening phrase, *The Mighty One, God the Lord* ('*ēl 'ĕlōhîm Yahweh*), is intended to evoke the solemnity and awe proper to the psalm's theme of a Great Assize. The threefold name represents God as the Almighty One, God in the fullness of His Deity, and God as the eternal and gracious One who has made a covenant with His people (*cf.* Jos. 22:22). This God has uttered His voice and summoned all earth's inhabitants to attend His tribunal, to witness the judgment of His people. **2** The summons emanates from Zion and is accompanied by the light of His truth (*cf.* Ps. 80:3; 2 Cor. 4:6; 1 Jn. 1:5). **3** First His word is heard, then His light is seen, and now the poet sees as in a vision the coming of God Himself, whose approach is described in terms of lightning and tempest. **4** *The heavens* and *the earth* are summoned to appear at the Assize as witnesses, for they have been the witnesses of all that has transpired (*cf.* Jos. 24:27). **5** God now calls for the party who is to be arraigned, the people with whom He had *a covenant*, renewed on their part by each succeeding generation, and ratified from the first *by sacrifice* (Ex. 24:3–8). **6** The proceedings open with a testimony by one of the witnesses to the *righteousness* of the divine judge.

7–15 God speaks to His people

7 His word to Israel is one of admonition. He speaks to them as their own God. **8** His accusation is not that they have been guilty of negligence in the ritual of sacrifices; that duty has been regularly performed. **9–13** His charge concerns their motives. They have offered their beasts to Him as though He had immediate need of them and must therefore feel grateful for their generosity. God declares the absurdity of such a view of worship; all man's possessions, all nature in fact, belong to Him. He would be less likely to ask them for food than the ocean would be to ask its fishes for water. As if God needed meat like a man! **14** True worship does not consist in the offering up of the dead flesh of beasts, but in the personal response of thanksgiving (couched in the appropriate sacrifice) and dedicated faithfulness with God (*cf.* Ec. 5:4, 5), **15** coupled with a confident casting of oneself upon God leading to the experience of His help, with consequent praise.

16–23 God speaks to the wicked

16, 17 This stern denunciation is directed against those who speak of God's laws but do not keep them (*cf.* Mt. 7:21–23), *i.e.* men who resent moral discipline and repudiate God's commandments; **18** men who delight in the fellowship of thieves, condone sexual licence, **19** tolerate in themselves an uncontrolled, foul and lying tongue, **20** and even betray those to whom they are bound in blood-brotherhood. **21** God's patience they regard as weakness, and His forbearance, which would give them opportunity to repent, is construed as indifference or even acquiescence. Their casual assumption that God must be as lawless, fraudulent and faithless as themselves will be utterly demolished. Their every deed will be brought before them and its consequences upon their own selves will be shown. **22** *You who forget God. Cf.* Je. 13:25; Ezk. 22:12. The poem concludes with a terrible warning to such godless people (*cf.* Jude 15) and also **23** with the offer of salvation to those who relate their lives Godward in gratitude and obedience. The whole of this section serves as a basis for Rom. 1:18–32; 3:21–25.

PSALM 51. A PENITENT'S PRAYER

The explicit statement in the title associates this psalm with 2 Sa. 12:1–13. As an expression of a heart overwhelmed by shame, humbled and broken by guiltiness, and yet saved from despair through penitential faith in the mercy of God, this poem is unsurpassed.

1–8 Conviction of sin

It is necessary to remember that, immediately David made confession of his sin, Nathan declared the forgiveness of the Lord. David is aware, therefore, of the wonder and immediacy of mercy and of an exceeding great and precious promise of pardon for a very great wrong (2 Sa. 12:13); but he cannot rest in this until full and heartfelt confession has been made, and this is the function of the poem. David's conviction of sin is dominated by four themes.

A sense of personal accountability. Note the frequency of *my iniquity, my transgressions, my sin.* There is no evasion of responsibility here on the grounds of chance circumstance or an instinctive urge; no blaming of ignorance, necessity or evil agency; no attempt to make Bathsheba share the guilt of adultery and murder. The wrong which has been done is David's responsibility and he exhausts the OT vocabulary of sin to express it (*cf.* on Ps. 32:5). His depth of conviction is stressed in the words *my sin is ever before me* (v. 3).

A conviction of having turned against God. Irrespective of Bathsheba and Uriah, his action ultimately was against God. *Against thee, thee only, have I sinned* (v. 4). The psalmist now makes unreserved confession of his guilt so that when God pronounces judgment upon the sinner He may be innocent of any insinuation of caprice, harshness or bias.

A plea for complete cleansing from sin. The phrases are massed together in vehemence and fervour. *Blot out* (v. 1); *i.e.* 'wipe off', as writing is erased (Ex. 32:32), or as water from a dish (2 Ki. 21:13). *Wash me thoroughly* (v. 2) is a launderer's word. Sin is seen as deeply ingrained in life's fabric and needing intensive treatment; *i.e.* bleach away the stain. *Cleanse me* (v. 2), as a leper is declared pure by washing (Lv. 14:8, 9), which cancels his religious defilement and restores him to God's fellowship.

A casting of himself upon God who alone can save him. This has been his implied attitude throughout: against God he had sinned, and to God alone he supplicates. But now this truth becomes explicit. In vv. 5, 6, linked by the repeated *Behold,* he confesses the true depth of his sinfulness as being the natural state of man from birth, and acknowledges the immensity of God's standards and requirements, an *inward being* and *secret heart* conformed to His *truth.* Only God can supply the necessary purging (v. 7), and only God can accomplish total restoration of soul and body from the damage of sin (v. 8).

5 It is not the act of conception or the process of birth which is here deemed sinful, but rather that were one to trace David's personal history back to the moment in which his mother travailed to give him birth, and beyond that to the very instant of conception, he was marred by sinfulness. This is the OT's greatest statement of the doctrine of original sin, and it is not pleaded as an excuse but called as a witness to the depth and extent of man's need as a sinner. **7** *Hyssop* was used to apply the blood of sacrifice (Ex. 12:22). The man who in v. 16 confesses that he knows of no sacrifice which God would accept for his sin, here looks to God in the confidence that some such sacrifice is known to Him and that He will apply its saving efficacy.

9–14 Distress, and a longing for holiness

9–11 The additional concept of sin as separation from God is now introduced with its twofold emphasis upon distress at the possibility of being severed from God for ever and deprived of His Holy Spirit, and a craving for moral health, a cleansed record, a new heart and a steadfast spirit (see mg.). He realizes that when any man sins it is not merely an action against God, but it leads the man himself away in the direction of outer darkness and disgrace. That is the selfish misery of hell.

Penitence implies the dispossession of sinful desires, and the psalmist now expands the positive aspect of his experience. 12 He pleads for a restoration of joy toward God of which he had been robbed by sin, and for an unfettered spirit that shall be ever willing to do right. 13 If he is granted these things, he will be so relieved and transformed that other sinners can be convincingly urged likewise to turn in repentance unto such a gracious God. This verse completes the psalmist's prayer. 14 Why then does he reopen the confession and mention the specific sin of *bloodguiltiness*? There is no explanation of this break in the ordered structure of the psalm unless we accept the heading as true: David cannot rest content until he has spread all his sin before God. There is no confession unless there is detailed confession, and we see in v. 14 the agony of remorse over his complicity in killing Uriah (2 Sa. 12:9).

15–19 True worship

The psalm ends by looking forward to acceptable personal praise of God grounded upon repentance (vv. 15–17), and the corporate worship of a community which God has blessed and made secure (vv. 18, 19). 16, 17 These verses do not deny the principle and practice of sacrifice. No sacrifice was prescribed in the law for adultery and murder, and therefore none could be offered. David could only rely on God's wisdom to provide such a sacrifice (see on v. 7) and himself bring that contrite spirit without which all sacrifice for sin is ineffectual. 18, 19 are not best understood as a post-exilic addition making an individual psalm suitable for corporate worship. The sin of a king threatened his whole people (*cf.* 2 Sa. 24). David's adultery and murder are here seen as having undermined *the walls of Jerusalem*. In his own restoration he pleads for the restoration of his people to favour (v. 18a), security (v. 18b), and fellowship with God (v. 19).

PSALM 52. THE DOOM AWAITING A POWERFUL AND WICKED MAN

This is one of eight psalms which are associated by their titles with David's experiences as an exile from Saul. The others are Pss. 7 (concerning Cush); 59 (Saul seeks to kill David); 56 (David goes to the Philistines at Gath); 34 (David at the court of Abimelech); 57 (he flees to the cave of Adullam); 142 (a prayer in the cave); 54 (David is almost betrayed by the people of Ziph). Ps. 52 is one of the earlier poems. It relates to David's flight to the tabernacle at Nob. The help given him by Ahimelech the priest was reported to Saul (1 Sa. 21:1–9; 22:9–23). This psalm is an expression of David's righteous indignation at Doeg's betrayal.

1–3 The mighty man of mischief and his words

The opening words are vehement, sarcastic and contemptuous. Doeg is not worthy of being named. He is a boaster, one who not only does evil but takes pride in it. He spends his life in antagonism to the enduring mercy of God. He is deceitful, slanderous and false, using his tongue as his principal weapon (*cf.* Pss. 7:14–16; 10:3–11). Throughout the psalm, the tongue is offered as primary evidence of character. As a man speaks, so he is. The parallelism of v. 3 is therefore significant: the love of evil displays itself in a lying tongue. Contrast Ps. 34:11–14.

4, 5 His certain undoing

There is an automatic divine reaction which RSV rather conceals by *But God*. Better 'God likewise' (see RV) or 'God on His part'. This doom is vividly expressed as, in turn, demolition, utter removal, uprooting.

6, 7 The comment of the righteous

The obvious retribution meted out to Doeg would fill all righteous men with *fear* and also with satisfaction at the evident vindication of righteousness. There is no need to read any personal vindictiveness, or mood of retaliation, into this; *cf.* Jb. 31:29. Godly men will turn to each other and comment upon the flimsiness of all life which trusts in temporal power and evil purposes. There is a play here on v. 1, as if to say 'Lo, this wreck is the mighty man who made not God his stronghold'.

8, 9 The psalmist's enduring devotion

In contrast to the fate of the wicked, David sees himself as a flourishing leafy olive tree (*cf.* Ps. 1:3). This destruction of the wicked and permanence of the righteous arise from the character of God, in whose *steadfast love* David trusted. *Cf.* Ps. 34:15, 16.

In the context of this trust, three further marks appear in his life: gratitude, because God has intervened for him; testimony to the loveliness of his God's character; and fellowship with the people of God.

PSALM 53. OPPRESSION, PAST AND PRESENT

This is a revised version of Ps. 14, where see

notes. Its two chief differences are, first, the alteration of the name *Yahweh*, which occurred four times in the earlier poem, and the use of *'ĕlōhîm* in each of the seven references to the Deity. Whatever the reasons behind this change it suggests a more universal scope for the poem than was implied in the former covenant-title of Yahweh, which was exclusively for Israel. Second, the fifth verse of Ps. 14 has been completely rewritten, a fact which suggests a phenomenal deliverance of the nation since the composition of the earlier poem. This may have been the collapse of the Ammonite league (2 Ch. 20:22–24), or, more probably, the supernatural panic of the Syrian army (2 Ki. 7:6, 7).

PSALM 54. GOD IS THE UPHOLDER OF MY SOUL

Soon after David had been joined at Keilah by Abiathar, who had escaped Doeg's massacre at Nob (Ps. 52), he heard that Saul was advancing upon the town to besiege it. Although David had rescued the town from the Philistines, he was warned of the unreliability of the inhabitants, so he and his men fled eastwards before Saul arrived (see 1 Sa. 23:5, 6 and 13). They took refuge in the wild and wooded hills south of Hebron, but their presence was betrayed to Saul by men of the adjoining township of Ziph (1 Sa. 23:19). According to the title, this psalm expresses David's reaction to the animosity of the Ziphites.

1–3 A plea for help

The ever-present characteristic of the Psalms is here: in the face of adversity, resort to prayer. Deliverance is sought *by thy name*, *i.e.* on the grounds of the divine character as protector of the oppressed, and also by means of the manifestation of His might. 3 not only describes David's enemies, but also diagnoses them. Towards him they are *insolent* (lit. 'seething'—whether with anger or pride) and *ruthless*, because of their attitude to God.

4, 5 A profession of faith

Unlike his foes, David could point to God as his source of help. Indeed, he had none other. The Lord was supremely the Helper and the Upholder (*cf.* Ps. 3:5; Is. 41:10; Jn. 14:16–18). Hence it is certain that He will take action to counter the wrong done to David.

6, 7 A promise of gratitude

When David shall have been saved by the name of the Lord (v. 1), he will gladly and freely express his gratitude to that name. In the sincerity of his Godward trust he envisages his defeated enemies and tastes even now of that deliverance which 'He' (or *it*, *i.e.* the good name) will bring about (*cf.* Is. 30:27). The past tenses (v. 7) express the confidence that the Lord will be as good as His *name* (*cf.* Ex. 14:30 – 15:2).

PSALM 55. BAFFLED AND BURDENED, BUT UPHELD

This is the expression of a heart which, deeply wounded by the faithlessness of a friend, turns to God in supplication and confidence. The deep hurt which his spirit has sustained is shown in the almost distracted way in which his poem leaps back and forth between faithless men and the faithful God. In the experience of the psalmist another contrast develops: that between the escapist tendencies of the oppressed man (vv. 6–8), and the genuine way of escape afforded by faith (v. 22).

1–8 Serious forebodings and the desire to escape

The way this supplication is framed indicates the craving for certainty. 1 *Hide not thyself*; *cf.* Ps. 27:4. 2, 3 The psalmist desires an open vision and an immediate reply from God, because he is so *distraught*. He cannot keep silent because of the suspense created by his suspicions, which have grown so rapidly as to be crushing and unbearable. Memories of a host of incidents, unheeded at the time, now suggest a network of evil schemes, and a barrage of malevolent plottings seems to be hurled at him. 4, 5 In such a mood he not only envisages the success of his enemies but has a presentiment of death by violent means.

6, 7 The pressure of events has now become so intolerable that the heart makes a desperate move to escape in fantasy. He would change his conditions altogether and become a dove, dwelling in quiet places remote from men, 8 struggling desperately to reach shelter and security amid a sudden storm. The urge to escape from reality is a perversion of a universal desire to be *at rest*. The motif of 'fleeing away' (from duty, discipline, or from God) is very evident in Scripture, and is a basic factor in man's endless restlessness and discontent. No-one yet found that an escape into the wilderness experience brought rest; rather is it found to be the realm of temptation.

9–15 A prayer for the destruction of the wicked

Agitated thoughts now turn in anger especially against one man, formerly almost as close a friend as a man might desire, who was evidently one of the chief antagonists. 9 The psalmist pleads with God to send among these schemers such a confusion of tongues and division of counsel as will make their work as unsuccessful as Babel (*cf.* 2 Sa. 15:34; 17:4; Gn. 11:7). 10, 11 imply sedition and corruption, both among the soldiers guarding the wall and among the shopkeepers in the streets. Some regard *violence* and *strife* (v. 9) as personified, and the pronoun *they* as referring to these forces. So also with *mischief, and trouble . . . ruin . . . oppression and fraud*. That kind of thing he could have borne; 12–14 what incurs his wrath is the treachery of a trusted friend, one of like status as himself, a frequent companion, one with whom the rich exchanges of understanding had been a pleasure, a man with whom he had known unity of heart as they worshipped God. **15** Let that intimacy be matched by the immediacy of divine judgment; let the ground swallow them all (*cf.* Nu. 16:30–33). We cannot rid our reading of this verse of a tone and sense of vindictiveness, but we need to beware of imputing our emotional reactions to others. The judgment of going *down to Sheol alive* is proper to those who rebel against leaders appointed by God. The psalmist, whether David or a Davidic king, looks here, as his clear allusion to the incident of Korah shows, not so much for personal vindication as for a divine sign of approbation upon his office as king.

16–23 Faith towards God

16 Unlike his enemies, David can call on God with assurance. **17** His incessant cries for help will be heard, his predicament resolved, **18** his dire peril (as in battle) remedied notwithstanding the number of his foes. **19** God, who is eternally enthroned as Judge of righteousness, shall come to his aid and humiliate his foes by His answer. **20** The psalmist's thoughts then revert to his false friend who moved in wickedness against those who were at peace with him and tore up the covenant of friendship between them. **21** His heart was actuated by malice, for all the suavity of his speech. His former words, interpreted now by his subsequent action, are like sword thrusts in the heart.

But neither escapism, regret, indignation or bitter disappointment can provide a satisfactory avenue of life amid the profound personal and civic upheaval. **22** The right course of action is declared at last. It consists of unburdening the heart's sickness and care, and placing all in the responsibility of the Lord. **23** This David is resolved to do, and thereby experiences the divine upholding of the heart itself (*cf.* 1 Pet. 5:7). The Lord watches over righteous persons and allows no fatal deflection to be evilly imposed upon their course. On the other hand wicked, false and murderous men shall never finish their days. Compare the experience of Paul in 2 Tim. 4:10, 11 and 17.

PSALM 56. 'IF GOD BE FOR ME, WHO CAN BE AGAINST ME?'

The title refers to David's first sojourn in Gath when he was evidently under some restraint (*cf.* 1 Sa. 21:13; 22:1). Ps. 34 was composed shortly after his escape from the Philistines, but Ps. 56 is expressive of his misgivings while actually in the hands of Achish.

The psalm's two parts are each followed by a refrain (vv. 4, 10 and 11), while vv. 12 and 13 form a brief conclusion.

1–4 Contrast and tension

1, 2 This exists between *God* and frail *men* (the Hebrew word signifies man as mortal); between

One who is *gracious* (AV 'merciful') and many who *all day long oppress* him and *trample upon* him in their pride. **3, 4** This dilemma of soul leads to the paradox *I am afraid . . . without a fear.* The tension is eased not simply by the decision to trust, but by the realization that God's word will not fail.

5–11 The two watchers

David's life is set between **6** the men who watch his steps and **8** the God who counts his tossings. His stability in trouble depends on the choice made between these. **7** His decision is revealed in the plea that God's righteous wrath should overturn the haughty assumptions and pernicious words of the suspicious Philistines in a general judgment upon all ungodly peoples (*cf.* Ps. 7:6–9; Jude 14–16). **8** God knows all about his life of insecurity, and his tears, registered in heaven, are precious in God's sight. **9** Moreover, his prayers are not merely appreciated by God but are efficacious: *This I know, that God is for me* (*cf.* Rom. 8:31). **10, 11** Hence he is doubly sure of God's power and the Lord's faithfulness, and the refrain of v. 4 is amplified and strengthened.

12, 13 Conclusion

12 Finally he foresees, as if already present, a state of deliverance wherein he shall be carrying out his present vows of praise to God for his complete salvation. **13** Deliverance from death and preservation from falling will enable him always to walk before God *in the light of life.*

PSALM 57. NO DESPAIR IN SPITE OF PERIL

As indicated by the title, this psalm was composed soon after David's escape from Gath (see 1 Sa. 22:1) and it resembles the preceding psalm in both theme and style. Both begin with identical words (*cf.* AV), are in two parts each followed by a refrain (vv. 5 and 11), speak of similar perils (56:1, 2; 57:3), and express the same deep trust in God. *Cf.* 2 Cor. 4:7–11.

1–5 His plight and prayer

1 The imagery of a young bird instinctively seeking protection under its mother's wings is used in Pss. 17:8; 36:7; 91:4. Note the repetition of *take refuge.* This is the same mood of escape from calamities as in 55:6–8, but the movement is not away from God, but unto Him. **2** His prayer is directed to *God Most High.* **3** In this instance God will send forth *his steadfast love and his faithfulness* (*cf.* v. 10) and rescue him from his pursuers who would trample him down. This personification of divine attributes is but a striking way of saying that the steadfastly loving and faithful God will Himself come to the rescue. **4** The imminence of his peril is seen in the fact that the psalmist has to sleep in hidden places while those whose hearts are aflame with enmity, and who speak words that are as sharp weapons, are searching in that vicinity. This seems to be the meaning of v. 4. 5 The *glory*, for whose open display the refrain pleads, must in context be the steadfast love and faithfulness of God (*cf.* v. 3b). The same meaning is clear in vv. 10, 11.

6–11 His preservation and praise

6 The imagery of pursuit by wild beasts is replaced by that of men stealthily laying a trap for a hunted animal. The psalmist feels utterly despondent apart from trust in God, but his faith is so irrepressible and buoyant that he suddenly foresees the whole organization of evil recoiling upon his enemies. The wrong they do with the intention of harming the innocent is seen to encompass their own downfall (*cf.* Pss. 7:14–16; 9:15, 16). 7 Now, as often in psalms of supplication, there arises full assurance of heart and a glad spirit of thanksgiving. 8 The call, *Awake, my soul!* is an exhortation to the best and highest in himself, and the familiar instruments of praise are likewise bidden to rouse themselves from the night of their inactivity so that the dawn of the day of deliverance may be heralded with eager anticipation. 9 To balance these private devotions at daybreak there will be a later general thanksgiving among all the peoples. 10 The theme of praise in both cases will be the heaven-sent *steadfast love* and *faithfulness* (*cf.* v. 3b) which bring the realm of God to this earth. 11 Finally and supremely is the pre-eminence of God Himself far above all.

PSALM 58. 'THERE IS A GOD WHO JUDGES'

A passionate denunciation here of corruption masquerading as justice. The leading problem in this psalm is to decide the meaning of the address *you gods* (v. 1). Some doubt surrounds the very word itself, and it may be that RV is correct in its suggestion that human judges cannot do their work 'in silence'. But the translation *you gods* is the more widely supported. It might have reference to the (hypothetical) New Year Festival (see Introduction), one feature of which was the victory of Yahweh over all gods. Some therefore see Him here exercising His prerogative as Judge, rebuking the false gods for their misleading of men, and including in His reproof their human tools (vv. 3–5). Others, more persuasively, urge that it is not impossible that human judges should receive the title 'gods' as an honorific. *Cf.* the interchangeable use of 'before God' and 'before the priests/judges' (Ex. 21:6; 22:8, 9; Dt. 17:8–13) and the coupling of God and the civil rulers in Ex. 22:28; Dt. 19:17, 18. In this case *you gods* means 'you who sit in God's place, exercising judgment'. Their malpractice is exposed in vv. 3–5. On either view, the remainder of the psalm from v. 6 is a plea that God will take the rule of earth into His own hands.

1–5 The indictment

No matter at what point the indictment begins, it soon clearly focuses on the human heart, giving us a clear view of a nature astray from God. 2 The wrong in the heart leads to the violence of the hands. 3 This inner perversion belongs with our humanity as such, infecting the unborn embryo and the new-born child. 4 It is a deadly poison, and 5 it is also intractable, deaf to all appeals or pressures.

6–9 The petition

The conviction of the accused is taken for granted, and the prosecutor pleads for a sentence which shall bring about the complete removal of such rulers from the earth. In a vivid series of pictures, each of which contains its own implied plea, he asks first 6 that they be rendered harmless and 7a vanish completely. 7b, 8a The second pair of pictures asks that they be shown up in their true colours, both in respect of their transiency and frailty, in spite of the bold show that they make, and then in respect of their essential evil. The third pair of pictures asks for their removal, 8b a removal so complete that it will be as if they had never been and 9 as instantaneous as the striking of the kindled flame on the pot.

10, 11 Conclusion

These verses express vehemently the profound satisfaction experienced by *the righteous, i.e.* the redeemed people of God, viewed by Him as righteous (see on Ps. 24:5), when evil is visibly crushed and removed. The language is figurative (*cf.* Rev. 19:13–18), but the aspiration is praise-worthy: that all other men should at last openly acknowledge the worth of righteousness (*cf.* Phil. 2:9–11) and confess the inescapable judgment of God.

PSALM 59. SAFEGUARDED AMIDST NIGHT'S LURKING TERROR

Although married to Saul's daughter, David was dogged by men commissioned by Saul to kill him (1 Sa. 19:1, 9–18). The content of the psalm agrees well with this ascription.

1–5 Invocation of divine aid

1, 2 The progression gives the sense of mounting alarm: those who at heart are *enemies* now *rise up* for action. From such, known to be those *who work evil*, the worst can be expected, 3 for they will stop at nothing, not even the taking of life. 4 David's innocency (which can be examined in the story in Samuel) gives him firm ground to plead for God's vindicating action. 5 God's intervention as Judge is based first on His omnipotent power as *Lord God of hosts*, His covenanted faithfulness to His people as *God of Israel* and His universal office as the One who in righteousness (*cf.* Gn. 18:25) will judge *all the nations*. We may understand this 'universalizing' of David's individual grief if we consider how in moments of private tribulation we groan for the second coming of Christ.

6–10 Description of a dangerous situation

6, 7 Like scavenger-dogs, David's enemies make the most of night's darkness, their inmost thought being that they are thus covered from all scrutiny, human and divine. **8, 9** By contrast with their confident prowling, David is already safe: mark the present tenses. These verses strikingly contrast his enemies' powerlessness against God (*cf.* Pss. 2:4; 37:13) with his own power in God, who gives him *strength* in his own person and the surrounding protection of a *fortress*. **10** It is notable that his confidence of divine empowering is here entirely related to the character of this personally-known God, who comes to meet David in his need clothed *in his steadfast love*.

11–13 A plea for judgment

David's plea to God for a visitation upon his would-be assassins is now shown to be free of vindictiveness. He is concerned for the imparting of a moral lesson to his people (v. 11), the just punishment of sin (v. 12), and a universal revelation of Israel's God (v. 13). **11** He does not ask for their swift destruction; his people would too soon forget that. Rather he asks that these enemies be somehow made a lasting exhibition of how God opposes sinners and judges them. The writing of the story in Scripture has been God's answer to this. **12** Once again the Psalms declare to us the deep seriousness of sins of speech. In David's mind this *sin of their mouths* is more worthy of mention than their subtle attempts to take his life.

14–17 Affirmation and confidence

14, 15 Parallel in content and spirit to vv. 6–10, he sees the desire of his foes go unsatisfied, **16, 17** while in the light of this experience his own joy and confidence in God are intensified.

PSALM 60. A LAMENT FOR DEFEAT

The title associates this psalm with David's war with Aram-naharaim (*i.e.* Mesopotamia) and Aram-Zobah (between Damascus and the Upper Euphrates). *Cf.* 2 Sa. 8:3–6. Apparently, while the war was being waged in the north-east, Edom and Moab invaded from the south. In this sudden crisis David recalled Joab to bring his forces to bear on the new threat. This psalm conveys the sense of national humiliation resulting from a wholly unforeseen military reverse.

1–4 The people lament a national disaster

1 In a typically biblical way, the psalmist regards God as responsible for every happening. Secondary causes, physical, strategical, cultural, *etc.*, were not necessarily held to be significant. Hence this unexpected military reverse had struck a tremendous blow at the people's morale. **2** It was like an earthquake which rends strong buildings. **3** Divine action had led to defeat; both led to demoralization; the nation reeled as a man who has just drunk drugged wine (*cf.* Is. 51:17; Je. 25:15ff.). Their defeat was all the more demoralizing in that they believed themselves to be the people of the Lord, **4** under whose *banner* (*cf.* Ex. 17:15, 16) they would experience security. The heart of their problem and distress was thus that God's promises seemed to go unfulfilled.

5–12 The king seeks confirmation of a promise of victory

5 What is the reaction to an unkept divine promise? Turn the promise into prayer and plead it before God.

6–8 There is first the promise of God about Israel's dominion: the words are attributed to God. The promises themselves, epigrammatically expressed, may be explained as relating to tenure of the promised land, the special significance of the chosen people, and victory over surrounding foes. Thus *Shechem*, *Ephraim* and *Judah* represent the occupation of land west of Jordan, and *Gilead* and *Manasseh* the eastern occupation; Ephraim and Judah are the main constituent members of the people of God, and bear the marks of the *helmet* for strength, and the *sceptre* for rule; the surrounding countries are designated for subordinate roles, servile to God's people: *Moab* for bathing the feet, *Edom*, the lackey to whom the sandals are thrown, and *Philistia*, to provide the topic for a victory song.

9, 10 The promises have been quoted; now they will be pleaded. Man cannot fulfil the promises of God; if God does not keep them, they fall to the ground. **11** Nor can man even help if God withholds His help. All therefore depends on God, and all is summed up in the single plea, *O grant us help*. But it is the plea of faith. **12** notes that where human aid avails nothing, God can lead His people to victory, and the psalm concludes with a confident forecast of the victory He will win for His people.

PSALM 61. A PRAYER OF A DISTRAUGHT KING

There must have been many moments in the life of David—as of any other king or leader, then or now—when in the loneliness of his office he felt himself at the end of his tether (vv. 1, 2a), urgently needed a new sense of security (vv. 2b, 3), longed to get away from it all (vv. 4, 5), and found his resource in prayer and his true joy in his relationship with God (vv. 6, 7).

1, 2a This is an impassioned plea from a heart burdened by a sense of distance from God, to whom he must cry *from the end of the earth*, and of personal feebleness. **2b** He craves for a realization of security unattainable by his own efforts, *i.e.* to be led 'to a rock that is too high for me' (cf. RV mg.), i.e. to which of himself he cannot attain. But what is this unattainable rock? 3 Nothing other than God Himself. 4 pleads for the hospitality extended to a guest or a refugee, and the motherly love of a bird, fluffing out her wings to house her young. Just as v. 3 supported the plea by appealing to God's nature, so now 5 recalls God's past acts. It probably looks back to the king's coronation day on which he made *vows* to God, and on which God gave him charge over 'the inheritance of the Lord' (cf. 1 Sa. 10:1; 2 Sa. 21:3; 1 Ki. 8:51). Will not the Lord who gave the responsibility give also the grace to bear it? 6 Being devoid of personal strength (cf. v. 2a), he can only continue if God *prolong* his kingship. 7 But mere prolongation in office is not enough: his desire is to live in God's favour and guarded by His emissaries (see on Ps. 57:3). 8 Those who truly pray know that the companion of intercession is dedication. Past vows (v. 5) are not enough.

PSALM 62. GOD ALONE IS MY REFUGE

This is a song of trust wherein the psalmist cannot find words sufficiently strong and significant to describe the absolute security and unalterable strength of God who is accessible to him (cf. Ps. 18:1, 2). Its two parts both deal with the action and reaction between godless and godly men; and are introduced by similar words (cf. vv. 1, 2 and 5, 6).

1–4 The two forces at work in David's life

1 On the one hand God is to David the sole basis and crown of life. God only is real, and in silence his soul waits unreservedly upon Him. It is not only that *from* God *comes my salvation*, but that 2 God is . . . *my salvation*. This relationship is the kingpost of his immediate existence, and though as mortal man he may be slightly displaced by external pressure (cf. 2 Cor. 4:8, 9), he knows that he will not be dislodged. 3 On the other hand men are doing their utmost to wreck his life: he describes them as rushing upon him with menaces and blows; they think he is about to crumple like a collapsing wall or a rickety fence. 4 Their sole concern is to *thrust him down from his eminence* or throne (contrast v. 2), and to that end they have pleasure only in lies and untruths speciously disguised (cf. 2 Sa. 15:2–6).

5–12 The ultimate resolution of the conflict

Observe the contrast between the vision of sense and the vision of faith. To the vision of sense David appears as a wall already about to fall (v. 3), to the eye of faith he is secure in a high tower built upon a rock (vv. 2, 6, 7). To the soul whose trust is wholly in God, time can bring only confirmation of his faith. 5, 6 Hence, in this second portion of the psalm, the fundamental principle of David's life (vv. 1, 2) is reaffirmed more strongly. Cf., e.g., *not be greatly moved*

(v. 2) with *not be shaken* (v. 6). 7 The onslaught of his enemies (cf. v. 3) need not be a cause of anxiety, for his salvation and full regal *honour* rest altogether upon God. 8 Moreover David is confident that his loyal people also will be preserved if they commit their lives unto God. 9 On the other hand, mere men, of whatever social degree, if devoid of faith are devoid of stability (cf. Ps. 39:5, 11; Jas. 1:9–11; 4:14). 10 All reliance upon earthly possessions proves to be disappointing (cf. Pr. 11:28).

The psalm has been consistently forward-looking. It has asked what will be the outcome of life; which man has a future, the man of faith (1, 2, 5–7) or the man of falsehood (3, 4, 9, 10)? 11 A reiterated (and therefore sure, Gn. 41:32) word of God in the psalmist's experience has affirmed three things of God: His *power*, 12 *steadfast love* and exact justice. The outcome of life therefore is in His hands.

PSALM 63. GOD IS MY JOY

According to the title this psalm originated in David's experiences *in the Wilderness of Judah*. The essential value of the poem lies in its expression of continual fellowship with God even though the psalmist is cut off from the outward and visible means of grace, and surrounded by discomforts and perils.

1 Introduction

David's yearning for God was intensified by his keen sense of exclusion from the sanctuary in Jerusalem and his separation from the ark, the symbol of the divine presence (cf. 2 Sa. 15:25, 26). His soul's desire, and his bodily habit of attending worship, were both thwarted by circumstances (cf. Ps. 42:1). The surrounding wilderness of Judah had become a spiritual desert (cf. 2 Sa. 17:29).

2–4 An immutable relationship

2 Some interpret this verse as meaning that in the wilderness David was granted a vision of God no less clear and distinct than that which he had seen in the sanctuary, and causing him in the midst of his despondency to break out in an ecstasy of wonder, 'So I have looked upon thee in the sanctuary, beholding thy power and thy glory.' This would explain the sudden change from sadness to great joy. But the meaning rather is that his longing for communion with God was as strong as in those former days when he had been able to behold God's power and glory in the sanctuary. Where others might be driven by circumstances to cry out for bodily rest and refreshment, David's longings were for God. 3 But, in addition to this, he had lost his throne and kingdom, but he saw that God's *steadfast love* remained and was better than all else.

5–8 A satisfying experience

Humanly speaking David's experiences were of

deprivation and insecurity, but his experience of God is more than compensating. **5, 6** God is his sufficient sustenance, and **7, 8** his shelter. It was in the responsive acts of **6** thinking and meditating and **8** clinging that this spiritual abundance became his.

9–11 A stark contrast

9, 10 Seen in the light of God's favourable goodness to him, David's enemies must surely be destroyed, their souls going to the abode of the dead and their carcases, fallen in battle, will be the prey of jackals (*cf.* 2 Sa. 18:7f.). **11** But David, and, indeed, *all who swear* by God, *i.e.* acknowledge and obey Him, shall rejoice because of God's care and goodness (*cf.* Dt. 10:20).

PSALM 64. PLOT AND PUNISHMENT

A prayer that the schemes and plots of unscrupulous men, who seek to overthrow those who are upright and godly, shall not only be in vain, but shall entail the condemnation of such evil-doers.

1–6 Prayer for protection against plotters

1 The plea is for a deliverance from threatened peril and from the fear or terror of that threat, **2–4** for protection alike from the secret plottings of wicked men and from their open assaults. The condemnation of all looseness or idleness of speech, so frequent in the Scriptures, is here reinforced by an observation of the power of an ill-used tongue to hurt. **3** It is a *sword*, and its words *like arrows*. **5** Behind the tongue, and evidenced by it, lie the *evil purpose* and **6** the *deep mind and heart* of man, here revealed both as deceiving others with his *cunningly conceived plot*, and self-deceived in his supposed immunity from observation and enquiry (*cf.* 2 Tim. 3:13).

7–10 Assurance of divine retribution

The psalmist's faith now overcomes his previous apprehension. That which wicked men desire against the blameless shall prove to be their own undoing. **7** If they shoot arrows against him, God shall shower arrows upon them and wound them; **8** because by words they seek to entrap him, so shall their own tongue trip them up. **9** In such judgment all men shall recognize the work of God and reverence Him. **10** Moreover every godly person shall be glad in the Lord's watchfulness and solicitude for those that are upright in heart, and shall take refuge in Him.

PSALM 65. A SONG OF PRAISE FOR HARVEST

'To have God at *one* point', remarks Weiser, 'means to have him in all his fullness.' In this case, God's goodness in a bountiful harvest provides the thin end of the theological wedge,

and before the psalm is over we have a full-orbed joy in our divine Saviour, Creator, Lord and Provider.

1–4 The forgiving God

1 The *vows* of OT religion were not techniques of putting pressure on God or of driving a bargain with Him. They were a recognition that prayer for His blessings must go hand in hand with consecration, and that thanksgiving can never be merely verbal and must receive concrete expression in lives and goods. Thus *praise* and *vows* are *due* to a bountiful God. **2, 3a** But before there can be any effective approach for purposes of praise, there must be a meeting of the common need of *all flesh* for forgiveness. While the psalmist looks forward to the day when this blessing shall be experienced on a world-wide scale, **3b** he and his people can now enter into the reality of forgiveness, **4** coupled with the blessings of fellowship with God and full spiritual satisfaction. Thus the worshipper becomes a priest, chosen to draw near to God (*cf.* Nu. 16:5), to abide in His courts, and find his highest aspirations satisfied in the good life of His house (*cf.* Ex. 19:6; 1 Pet. 2:9; Rev. 1:6).

5–8 The saving and ruling God

5 From the personal experience of salvation (vv. 3, 4), the psalmist naturally looks back to the great *deeds* of God whereby salvation was accomplished, the Exodus, the Passover and the blood of the lamb. Herein also he discerns a universal *hope*. Only the God who has saved Israel can save the world. **6** This belief is established by an appeal to God's world-wide activity of creation, **7** control of both natural and human forces, and **8** to the fact that it is His ordering of natural phenomena which provides world-wide fear and joy.

9–13 The providing God

The God who saves His people and rules His world has so graciously guided the programme of nature that the praise due to Him is finally presented in a burst of spontaneous and vivid praise for the beauty, richness and comfort afforded by the harvest of fields and flocks. The natural increase is attributed directly to the divine presence and working. (Note the repetition of the word *Thou*.) **9** It is the overflowing *river of God* which gives the former rain to enrich the prepared ground, and the latter rain to swell the grown crops. **12, 13** The whole countryside—upland grazings (*the wilderness*), hillside pastures encircling the cultivated land of the lower slopes, and even the meadows in the valley bottoms—all alike are rich, replete and rejoicing because of the goodness of God (*cf.* Ps. 96:12).

PSALM 66. A SONG OF DELIVERANCE

This psalm was obviously designed for public worship and to celebrate some national deliverance—such an occasion, *e.g.*, as the overthrow of the Assyrian forces under Sennacherib.

1–12 Corporate worship

Note the world outlook of the psalm. **1** Such a call as this, addressed to *all the earth*, implies that the nation's experience of deliverance is of world-wide significance (*cf.* Ps. 47:1, 2). **2** This arises not from the preservation of God's people so much as from the disclosure of God's glorious being—*the glory of his name*—in and through historical events. Hence all peoples are exhorted to proclaim the divine nature in their praises. **3, 4** The sense would be easier if we translated v. 4 'Let all the earth . . .', understanding it as an implied prayer for that universal knowledge of God which provokes universal praise. **5** As a cause and stimulant of such praise all the earth is invited to *come and see what God has done*. **6** Foremost of His deeds hitherto is the deliverance of the children of Israel from Egypt, *i.e.* the dryshod crossing of *the sea. There did we rejoice* (see Ex. 15). It is noteworthy that throughout the Psalter no other historical event is viewed with as much awe and wonder as the Exodus (*cf.* Pss. 18:15–19; 68:7, 8; 74:13–15; 77:16–20; 78:13 and 52, 53; 89:7–10; 106:7–12; 136:10–15). **7** This song now affirms that God is ever the same; His rule is now as wide and His eye as watchful as always; therefore, *let not the rebellious exalt themselves*.

This last clause of v. 7 leads on **8** to a heartfelt hymn of thankfulness for a recent national deliverance which is regarded as being of international importance. **9** This adoration is called forth by the evidence of a present security (*cf.* Ps. 121:3; Jude 24). **10** Associated with their testimony of God's keeping power is a recognition of His moral purposes at work in national history (*cf.* Dt. 8:2–4). **11** To test them God had caused them to lose their freedom like fish in a net. Sore burdens had been laid upon them and **12a** they had known defeat in battle. **12b** But now, the God who appointed the crucible for their testing (*cf.* Mal. 3:2, 3) has brought them to *spacious* liberty.

13–20 Personal worship

This final portion of the song appears to be the testimony of the king, speaking in the person of the community. There are two phases. **13–15** First, he speaks to God on behalf of himself, as representative of the nation. During the previous emergency of threatened calamity he had made certain vows to God which were to be fulfilled when deliverance came. These vows are now being fulfilled, not grudgingly, but in full measure (*cf.* Ec. 5:4, 5; Rom. 12:1). **16–20** Then the king speaks to all godly men on behalf of God to the effect that prayer (*I cried*) mingled with praise (*extolled*) which springs from a pure heart and a good conscience had been and always would be heard and heeded. This basis of effectual prayer, *i.e.* a blameless heart, is a constant element in scriptural teaching (*cf.* Jb.

27:2–9; Is. 1:15–17; 59:1–3; Ezk. 14:2, 3; Jn. 9:31; 1 Jn. 3:21). **20** But beyond all human conditions which lead to answered prayer, there is that without which no words or works of men would avail: the *steadfast love* of God, His unchanging goodwill for His people (Mal. 3:6; Phil. 2:13).

PSALM 67. TO EARTH'S REMOTEST BOUNDS

The Feast of Tabernacles, binding together thanksgiving for God's saving and providing mercies to Israel (*cf.* Dt. 26:1–11) with the universal hope of His bountiful rule over the world (*cf.* Zc. 14:16), provides a good setting for this psalm, occupied as it is with exactly these themes. What God has done for Israel is symbolic of what He will do for the world; national blessings typify universal blessings.

1 is an echo of the priestly benediction in Nu. 6:24–26, and it may well be that this blessing was spoken by the high priest before the assembled people responded in the words of this psalm. **3** and **5** would then be refrains sung from the throats of the multitude with special emphasis, and the same words may have been repeated after v. 7 by the high priest as he concluded this extended benediction (*cf.* the double blessing in Lv. 9:22, 23). The psalm would thus consist of three short motets. **1, 2** Israel is shown as the mirror of God wherein all nations may behold Him. **4** All peoples are regarded as the Israel of God; they are radiantly happy because He judges them (in the sense of 'governs') and fully secure because He governs, or guides, them even as He ruled and led the chosen people through the wilderness. **6** is an acknowledgment of a bounteous harvest. In vv. 6, 7 *has blessed* is past continuous, 'has blessed time and time again'; the continuance of this favour towards Israel would give confidence to the prayer for world-wide reverence. The psalm thus becomes for the church a very apt expression of its missionary aspirations.

PSALM 68. A PROCESSIONAL HYMN

This is one of the most magnificent songs of triumph in the whole of the OT. Its dramatic commentary upon a memorable event, its wide perspective of thought and speech, its spirit of invincible faith in God, and its presentation of the historic past and the envisaged future, combine to make it an outstanding portion of the Psalter.

It was almost certainly written to celebrate the transference of the ark of the Lord from the house of Obed-edom to the new Tabernacle which David had prepared for it on Mt. Zion (*cf.* 2 Sa. 6:2–18) or, possibly, to celebrate an annual memorial of this great procession wherein Yahweh's Kingship would be vividly portrayed and praised. The psalm was constructed around the incident in such a manner as to convey a double teaching. First, the actual journey of the ark from its temporary resting-place to its final abode in Jerusalem is regarded as a dramatic reminiscence of the nation's journeyings from Egypt to Canaan. Secondly, the actual completion of this great historical movement, which was to acquire such profound significance, provides a unique opportunity to present a fundamental theological truth concerning God. The whole action, historical and symbolical, was a tapestry whereon the divine name might be discerned with increasing clarity, *e.g. God* (v. 1; *'ĕlōhîm), his name* (v. 4; *JAH), the Almighty* (v. 14; *'el šadday), the Lord* (v. 16; *Yahweh), the Lord God* (v. 18; *Jah 'ĕlōhîm), the Lord* (v. 19; *'aḏōnāy), God, the Lord* (v. 20; *Yahweh 'aḏōnāy).*

1-18 The procession

1-3 The beginning. The ark is lifted from its resting-place and, because it was the pledge and symbol of God's presence with the people, its movement is a reflection of God's intervention. The scene is an echo of the wilderness experiences as recorded in Nu. 10:35 and Ex. 14:25. **2, 3** aptly recapture the experiences of the Exodus. God's enemies are as helpless before Him as *smoke* before the wind or as *wax . . . before fire,* while, on the other hand, the only part played by God's people is to rejoice in what He has done (Ex. 14:13, 14; 15:1-3).

4-10 The procession sets out. 4 As the ark with the attendant priests, king, and singers moves off along the route, the cry is heard 'Cast up a highway for him who rides through the deserts' (see mg.; *cf.* Is. 40:3; 62:10). The name of this potentate, before whom all obstructions must be removed, is *JAH (cf.* Ex. 15:2). The repetition of the phrase from v. 3, *exult before him,* suggests a further development of thought. The attention is turned from the route of the march to the personal character of God. **5** He is enthroned in heaven, *his holy habitation,* yet He is intimately aware of human needs: He is a father to orphans and the protector of the weak and lonely (*cf.* Ex. 22:22, 23; Jn. 14:18); He cares for the solitary and He delivers the oppressed. **6** He has especially blessed Israel in having brought them out of Egyptian bondage into comparative prosperity; on the other hand, the bodies of rebellious folk who could not enter in because of disbelief were left *in a parched land* (*cf.* Heb. 3:12, 19). **7-10** This brief allusion to the Exodus leads the psalmist to give a brief résumé of that inerasable memory which was now, in a very real sense, being relived.

11-18 The approach to the city. The ark had been sent back from the Philistines in a manner comparable with the release of the children of Israel by the Egyptians; the incident of Uzzah's death had been an echo of the dread and death of Sinai (*cf.* Ex. 19:12; 2 Sa. 6:6, 7). Now that the ark was approaching Jerusalem it was, in one sense, retraversing the route of the invasion and conquest of Canaan. This part of the chant consists at first of a series of disjointed sentences which seem to reproduce the shouts of the crowd. **11** There are the hosts of women that proclaim the tidings (RV; *cf.* Ex. 15:20); contrast the reference to the official singers in v. 25. Some cried one thing, some another; snatches of old war songs (vv. 12, 17), fragments of unpreserved psalms (v. 18), and festive folk songs (v. 13), possibly symbolizing times of prosperity; phrases from traditional forms of tribal challenge and response (vv. 13a, 14; *cf.* Jdg. 5:16a). All these are woven together so as to create a sense of pageantry enriched by memory, even as modern radio and TV documentaries evoke a certain frame of mind by a series of impressions swiftly and successively faded in and out. **13** The spoil, exemplified in the reference to the ornamental *dove,* is received by those who took no part in the fight—an apt recollection that the battle is the Lord's and the fruits are His people's. **14** When God dispersed the hostile kings referred to in this snatch, their flight was reminiscent of snowflakes driven by the wind against the dark wooded slopes of Zalmon (Jdg. 9:46-48). **15** The *mountain of Bashan* was probably the towering, snow-capped Mt. Hermon. **16** Honour, however, lies not in physical majesty but in spiritual dignity, and this the Lord has conferred on Mt. Zion alone.

The procession and its attendant crowd is really a shadow of a greater concourse converging upon the house of God. **17** His hosts are beyond numbers and the divine glory of the sanctuary of Zion is as real as the awe-full theophany upon Sinai. **18** Eventually, as the ark approaches the city gates (*cf.* Ps. 24), the capture of this strong and rebellious city is recalled (2 Sa. 5:6-10), and both events are seized upon as evidences of His irresistible purpose. All around Him bring their gifts. Even those who were rebellious are content that He, *Yah 'ĕlōhîm,* should dwell there.

19-35 The arrival

19-27 The procession ends. 19 As the ark moves on its way, it is not described as an object; it is recognized as a token and symbol of the Lord, the God who is *our salvation.* **20** Hence this fervent adoration of Him to whom *belongs escape from death,* and **21** who wields unquestioned power over all men guilty of defiance no matter how far they may flee in the endeavour to escape Him, **22** whether in distant Bashan, or on the sea-bed. **23**, however gruesome its details, vividly assures God's people that victory will be His gift to them.

24 These thoughts concerning the invisible and irresistible God of righteousness are a fitting prelude to the disappearance of the ark *into the sanctuary.* **25** The priests, singers, minstrels, and the company of girls with timbrels have now passed out of sight, and the whole action of the procession from start to finish is seen to be symbolical of all God's glorious and inscrutable goings through Israel's history. In a sense, Israel has been the procession and the peoples of the earth have been the onlookers. **26, 27** introduce the hymn of praise sung by the concourse. This crowd includes all who have come from *Israel's fountain*, but they are specified under four significant names: from the southern tribes we have *Benjamin*, who provided Israel's first king (1 Sa. 9:1, 2), and royal *Judah*, David's tribe (1 Sa. 16:1; Heb. 7:14); and from the north *Zebulun* and *Naphtali*, possibly chosen because of their zeal in the Lord's cause (Jdg. 5:18).

28–31 The hymn of Israel. This is local and historical, dealing with Jerusalem and Egypt. **28, 29** Because God has been the source of national strength and coherence the people beseech Him, first, to continue to be so; **30** secondly, to rebuke Egypt—*the beasts that dwell among the reeds*—and to constrain *the herd of bulls with the calves, i.e.* the rulers of other peoples around Israel. Thirdly, they pray that God will scatter all potential enemies who would exact *tribute* from Israel and who, with this in mind, *delight in war*. **31** Fourthly, the prayer turns to seek the ever-widening extension of the Lord's rule over the world.

32–35 The hymn of all the earth. 32 The finale of praise swells out to include all earth's kingdoms, for the Lord is high, strong and mighty. **33** He rules the heavens and **34** His power is visible in the skies (*cf.* Ps. 19:1–6): **35** His works performed from His sanctuary in Israel arouse awe throughout the world. Let all men *ascribe* (*i.e.* 'testify') to His mighty power, and proclaim Him blessed because of His faithfulness.

PSALM 69. DESPAIR TRANSFORMED TO PRAISE

This psalm is a companion to Ps. 22; both deal with the theme of undeserved suffering which has been due in large part to a steadfast loyalty to God (*cf.* Pss. 35; 44; 109). The experience implied recalls the suffering of Jeremiah (*cf.* Je. 38:6). Note also the similarities with Lamentations (*e.g., cf.* v. 2 with La. 3:54; v. 12 with La. 3:14; v. 21 with La. 3:15). In vv. 33–36 there are a number of phrases which could be interpreted as references to the Exile and as expressing a longing for restoration.

The psalmist's thoughts move through four phases. His affliction is described, divine help is requested, retribution upon his enemies is desired, and the hope is expressed of deliverance for himself and all others like him. Note the many quotations of this psalm in the NT: *e.g.* v. 4 (Jn. 15:25); v. 9 (Jn. 2:17; Rom. 15:3); vv. 22, 23 (Rom. 11:9, 10); v. 25 (Acts 1:20).

1–12 Despair of himself

There are two parts in this section: the first is factual (vv. 1–6); the second is analytical (vv. 7–12). **1** The psalmist begins with a cry for help,

and then describes himself as a drowning man (*cf.* Jon. 2:5), **2** as one who is bogged in a morass and as one who, crossing a ford, is suddenly swept downstream to deep pools by an unexpected rush of flood-water. **3** Moreover, he is beyond human help, for none has heard his cries, and now he steadily grows weaker. **4** The occasion of this calamity is rooted in the false and unjustified antagonism of his fellows. These have used their power to press upon him claims which are quite unwarranted; they have made him yield up things which he is wrongfully accused of having stolen. **5** This complaint carries no imputation of the psalmist's complete blamelessness: God knows the measure of his guiltiness, for no sins are hidden from Him. **6** Nevertheless he has sought to live an upright life and he foresees despair as taking hold of other godly men who will become discouraged if his urgent need receives no recognition and response from God.

7–12 Having stated the facts of the situation, and **8** adding only the new fact of the unnatural hostility of his own family, the psalmist proceeds to outline the conditions which preceded this perplexing development. Outstanding among these has been his personal allegiance to God. Reproach, separation, misunderstanding, tears, grief, ribaldry, and derision have been his lot simply because, **7** in his zeal for the honour of the God of Israel and **9** for God's house, he has subordinated all personal interests to the welfare and glory of that name. **8** People of all ranks of life, his brothers, **12** the civic elders as well as the dissolute, have scoffed at God and at him.

13–21 Dependence upon God

Nevertheless, and in this lies the anomaly of true faith, the psalmist's trust in God is unshaken. Shame has no power to weaken constancy (*cf.* Heb. 10:32ff.; 12:2), and all reproach would vanish if God so answered as to demonstrate the truth of His promised salvation. **13** The emphasis on *as for me* and *thy faithful help* (lit. 'the faithfulness of thy salvation'; *cf.* RV) is intended to echo the opening words of the psalm, *Save me, O God*, and serves to direct attention to the deliberate parallel between this portion of the psalm and the preceding one. **14** reflects v. 2; the earlier statement of an experience is changed into a prayer for a transforming action. The whole imagery of flood, mire and deep pool (vv. 1–3) is altered from its original sense of extremity and finality to that of a temporary and remediable situation. **15** Let God intervene and old values, meanings and possibilities, even *the pit*, will be done away; all will become new. **16** There is here an intentional contrast with v. 4. Both speak of that which is beyond counting, viz. *the hairs of my head* and *thy abundant mercy*, but whereas the former is a metaphor for those *who hate me*, the latter is descriptive of Him whose *steadfast love is good*. **17** The antithesis is continued in the thought of a *servant* before the face of his righteous master, and the memory of mighty ones who seek his dismissal from life (v. 4b). Such men had wrongfully exacted from him that which was his own (v. 4c), **18** but God is now besought to *redeem* and *set* him *free* (lit. 'ransom', 'pay the price for'); *i.e.* let God reclaim His own possession (the psalmist's soul) and thus undo the work of unrighteousness. **19** The shame and reproach of v. 7 also reappear here. The prayer ends at this point, but the parallel between the two portions of the psalm continues. **20** accentuates the existing plight out of which prayer has been offered and not yet answered. The agony becomes intensified: those who were expected to show compassion and comfort toward him, because of a special bond of understanding with them, prove to be as disappointing and suspicious as his own kinsfolk (v. 8; *cf.* Mt. 26:37ff.). **21** Formerly he had fasted (v. 10), but now his enemies give him *poison for food*.

22–28 Denunciation of his foes

The sense of human injustice, cruelty and dishonour which has been expressed in the preceding verses releases the indignation which hitherto the psalmist has curbed. His denunciation of those who have maltreated him is developed in terms of God's turning upon themselves the consequences which their conduct has effected upon others, such as himself. For example, as they had offered poisonous food (v. 21), **22** let their own feasts be a snare to them. In that they had brought darkness and weakness to him (vv. 2, 3), **23** let them discover what it feels like to have no outlook and no power (trembling loins). They had been zealous in their opposition to him (v. 4); **24** let them experience another's hot indignation pursuing them. They had caused him to be outcast by his family (v. 8); **25** let them become homeless vagrants. They had noticed God's chastening of the psalmist (vv. 10, 11), **26** and had eagerly attacked him as well; **27** let them find out what it is not only to have double sins, but double punishment too. They had sought to deprive him of God's blessing (v. 20); **28** so let them be debarred from the bliss of righteousness and let their name be erased from the register of godly men (*cf.* Ex. 32:32; Is. 4:3; Phil. 4:3; Rev. 20:12, 15; 21:27). The fact that we cannot conceive of ourselves praying this prayer without an emotion of self-seeking vindictiveness ought not to be allowed to colour our view of the psalmist. If he is to pray at all for the open vindication of righteousness and to take his prayer beyond the point of platitudinous generality, it must be something like this, for sin, in the biblical view, has a 'boomerang' quality, and the principle of precise equity is part of the divine nature.

29–36 Dedication to the Lord

29a should be translated 'But as for me' (emphatic as in v. 13), 'who am afflicted . . .'. The psalmist's full reliance upon God brings about the prophetic realization of the Lord's transforming intervention. **30** This stirs him to utmost praise and dedication, *I will praise the name of God with a song*; **31** a form of worship which is more acceptable to God than any sacrifice of *an ox or a bull*. **32, 33** The psalmist feels that the most amazing fact of experience is not distress, frustration, conflict, misunderstanding, retribution, or even death; it is that *the Lord hears the needy*. That truth is cause enough for heaven and earth, the sea and all that therein is to praise the Lord. **35, 36** In this joyous assurance the future can be contemplated with hope; Zion shall yet be redeemed, the desolate cities of Judah rebuilt, and the heirs of the righteous shall dwell there and prosper.

PSALM 70. AN URGENT PRAYER FOR DELIVERANCE

These five verses are the end portion of Ps. 40 (vv. 13 to 17) which has been detached for separate use in the Temple services (see title). A few words have been changed here and there, and the name for God, *Yahweh*, has sometimes been altered to *'elōhîm*.

It has a number of points of agreement with Ps. 69. Both open with a note of urgency, both invoke judgment on the opponents of righteousness (*cf.* 70:2, 3 with 69:23–27), and both appeal to God on the ground of personal necessity (70:5a; 69:29a). Moreover, the psalm of which this was formerly a part, Ps. 40, has also much in common with Ps. 69; both begin with allusions to mire and darkness, and to the action of divine rescue. The difference is that in the former case the experience of deliverance has occurred so that the parched mouth (69:3) has been filled with a new song (40:3; *cf.* 69:30). The experience which this snatch of verses depicts is all too common, even in Christian experience, and it is good to have it isolated in this succinct way. When we are thus tested we may know that our situation is by no means unique (1 Cor. 10:13), and we may see clearly what is our resource and our best line of action.

PSALM 71. THE CONFIDENCE OF A MATURE FAITH

This psalm is the prayer of an old man (vv. 9, 18), and there is a mellowness and serenity about it which is characteristic of a long life spent in reliance upon God (*cf.* vv. 5, 17).

There is a marked parallel between vv. 1–9 and vv. 10–18. The rest of the psalm has a different structure but also falls into two groups corresponding to the previous section.

1–9 Intimate communion with God

The quiet dignity and confidence of these verses are unmistakable. **2** The plea for divine aid is introduced in a gentle phrase and **3** is interwoven with an appreciation that God has always safe-guarded him. The principal feature of this section is the spirit of adoration toward the Lord: each of the first 8 verses speaks of Him with faith and gratitude: **1** *In thee, O Lord*; **2** *thy righteousness*; **3** *thou art my rock*; **4** *my God*; **5** *thou art my hope*; **6** *thou art he*; **7** *thou art my strong refuge*; **8** *thy praise and . . . glory*. The whole passage prepares the way for the personal petition of v. 9. **7** *A portent to many*. The general significance of *portent* is 'something which clearly shows that God is at work'. In the course of his long life the psalmist has become something of an exemplar to the people of God. Consequently how he reacts to trouble now, and how God deals with him, will be seen as a revelation of what God is like and can do.

10–18a Resolution in spite of distress

These verses are really another version of the previous prayer, but they have a wider and a more forward vision. (Contrast, *e.g.*, vv. 6 and 18.) **10** The writer turns to consider his enemies; **13** judgment is desired, **14** hope is an inspiration, **15, 16** praise is foreseen and **18** work is anticipated. **11** His enemies believe that the Lord has forsaken him and are about to attack him. **12** That is why the prayer of vv. 2 and 3 is urgently repeated in the words *O God, be not far from me*. **14** The earlier confession of hope is reiterated. **17** The anticipation of ceaseless praise concerning the *glory* of God (v. 8) is now reinforced by a lifetime of divine tutelage. **18** Finally, the plaintive cry of v. 9 is transformed; the former prospect of failing strength becomes indefinitely deferred until a full life's work has been accomplished.

18b–21 Hope in God

The mood of these verses is comparable with that of vv. 1–10. **19, 20** Not only is there a very real awareness of God's former acts of compassion, but there is a kinship of thought. For example, it was the loftiness of God's holiness which prompted the prayer, *Incline thy ear* (v. 2). Again, the notion of re-birth out of *the depths of the earth*, *i.e.* deliverance from the gates of death, is an extension of the thought of physical birth (v. 6): both are regarded as works of God. But essentially these verses show us that in the Bible old age is a purposeful thing. The man who (v. 18a) longed to be preserved until he had done all that God required of him, now looks forward to receiving all that God has to give him: revival and **21** new personal advances in his experience of God. *Cf.* the longing soul of Moses in his old age (Dt. 3:23–25).

22–24 Praise and adoration

In this last portion the emphasis is placed upon the future, as in vv. 14–18 (the pronoun 'I' is stressed in both v. 14 and v. 22). But in place of enemies and plots are the instruments of praise, the harp and the lyre. He is confident of the answer to the prayer expressed in v. 12 and there-fore extols the *faithfulness* of his God. He had previously looked forward hopefully to declaring *thy deeds of salvation all the day* (v. 15); now he grasps the certainty of so doing, for the rescue of his soul is cause enough for talking *all the day long*. Finally, the spirit of worship is enhanced by the title *Holy One of Israel* (*cf.* Pss. 78:41; 89:18), for it is His holiness above all else which is the inspiration of joyful praise.

PSALM 72. THE IDEAL FOUNDER OF A RIGHTEOUS DYNASTY

The kingly rule which is the theme of the poem is certainly described idealistically, a common feature of the royal psalms, and the basis of their Messianic interpretation. From the earliest days of David's reign brilliant hopes were centred in the monarchy (2 Sa. 7), and in the psalms we see their central features spelt out in detail (see *NBD*, art. 'Messiah'). The heart of this psalm's delineation of ideal kingship is that 'in the role of the KING was focussed the funda-mental requirement: a justice which brings new life to the unfortunate and destroys oppression' (Eaton). Prophetically the psalm looks through and beyond the individual Davidic king for whom it was first sung, reminding him of his high calling, and 'attains a vision of Christ', seeing that 'in him the helpless find the powerful redeemer, and by his fulfilment of royal righte-ousness he will bring healing to all Creation, till none shall hurt or destroy in all God's holy kingdom (Isa. 11.1–9)' (Eaton).

1–7 The king's administration of his own nation

1 The primary characteristic of his rule is *righteousness* and *justice*, the balance of meaning of these words being that the former stresses character and moral principle, the latter ad-ministration and moral practice. Three main truths are brought forward. First, that this king, unlike the oriental despot, is no autocrat but is subject to God's requirements. Hence the prayer is that he may possess *thy* righteousness, a righteousness possessed by, coming from and acceptable to God. **2, 4** Secondly, out of his righteous relationship with God flows a likeness to God in his dealing with his people, his concern for the *poor* and his opposition to the *oppressor*. **3, 6** Thirdly, as ever in OT faith (*cf.* Dt. 28), the fruit of righteousness will be natural fertility and **7** that full-orbed well-being of individual and society, in character and conduct, manward and Godward, which the Bible calls *peace*. The righteous king will be a second Adam, reigning in God's Eden (*cf.* Is. 11:5–9; Am. 9:11–15).

8–14 The king's sovereignty in the eyes of all men

8 So righteous a ruler will inevitably be acknow-ledged outside his own nation, and the extension of his power will include all the earth. The normal bounds of the promised land were the river Euphrates on the east, and the Mediterranean Sea on the west. These are here surpassed (*cf.* Zc. 9:10). **9** *Those who dwell in the wilderness* (see mg.); *i.e.* the nomadic tribes. **10, 11** Foreign states as far afield as *Tarshish* (S Spain), the Mediterranean *isles*, *Sheba* (S Arabia), and *Seba* (Ethiopia), shall honour him with gifts (*cf.* 1 Ki. 10:25). These wide dominions will not be acquired through personal ambition, or desire for imperial fame, but through the intrinsic merit of an ideally righteous administration. **12–14** elaborate the thoughts of vv. 2–4 (*cf.* Jb. 29:11–16). Not only has he sympathy with the helpless (*poor*) and destitute (*needy*), but he esteems each man's life (*blood*) precious and worthy of redemption from evil powers.

15–17 The king's perpetual benevolence and glory

The thrilling prospect of such a king causes the psalm to end in a climax of deeply-felt petitions to God for him. **15** These touch on the honour in which he is to be held, **16** the prosperity of his dominions, **17** and the duration and extent of his kingdom. **15** We could translate 'May

prayer be made *to* him'. This would in the first instance refer to the stream of suppliants, whom a king of this character would rightly attract, but it would also accommodate the thought of the deity of the Messianic King on which the OT quietly insists. **16** The prayer is for unusual fertility: a land cultivated and productive even to the mountain tops, and corn-stalks as sturdy and productive as the cedars of Lebanon! **17** In reference to the Davidic king, the enduring *name* would have a dynastic significance, but once more it is an easy transition to the divine Messiah who lives and reigns for ever (*cf.* Lk. 1:32, 33) and who alone is the universal source of blessing for which prayer is here made (*cf.* Eph. 1:3).

18–20 Doxology

See on Ps. 41:13. These final three verses are, of course, editorial material marking the end of the second book of Psalms, but never was a doxology more appropriately placed than vv. 18 and 19 at the conclusion of Ps. 72!

BOOK THREE. PSALMS 73–89

PSALM 73. THE MYSTERY OF PROSPEROUS WICKEDNESS

Ps. 73 deals with the same theme as Ps. 37 (*cf.* Pss. 49; 94). The problem is that of an apparent inversion of morality and success; in the life of this world evil men prosper while godly men are often in serious distress and need. The emphasis here, however, is not on the temporary nature of the prosperity of the wicked. It may, and often does, persist through life (see v. 4; *cf.* Jb. 21:7–13), although ultimately there must be condemnation. The essential truth for a righteous man was that it is well with him really, *i.e.* the true test of one's well-being consists not in the power and riches of this world, but in personal relationship with God. The discovery of this truth is treated retrospectively.

1–3 Previous doubting recalled

1 *Truly God is good.* This positive statement indicates the absence of doubt in the psalmist's mind now. **2** Nevertheless there had been a time when he had almost turned aside from the path of Godward trust, he had almost staggered through the sudden pull of unbelief (*cf.* Rom. 4:20) and **3** had gone so far as to feel *envious* at the success of those who spoke boastfully and were obviously enjoying more worldly success than he, notwithstanding their *wicked* character and life.

4–12 The facts stated objectively

The characteristics of ungodly men are described first outwardly (conditions and conduct, vv. 4–7), and then inwardly (speech and motive, vv. 8, 9). **4** reads literally 'their dying has no pangs', which RSV has gratuitously changed.

The psalmist is thus not contemplating the temporary well-being of the ungodly (*cf.* Ps. 37:35, 36), but a life-long prosperity ending in peaceful and painless death. This state of affairs is reflected in their conduct. **6** They behave insolently and unscrupulously as regularly as they wear their rich clothing. **7** Their gaze is intent on self-gain and the thoughts and imaginations of their hearts are become utterly vain. **8, 9** It is only to be expected that such behaviour should indicate an exaggerated self-opinion, and their mouths are, as ever, a true index of their hearts. Nothing in either *the heavens* or *the earth* is above or beyond their criticism.

There are other elements in the situation, which increase the sense of mystery that God should tolerate it. **10–12** People are led astray and blasphemy is promoted. Indeed, in v. 10, the Hebrew reads 'his people'; *i.e.* those who had been called out from the ungodly life of the nations and made into a people for God's own possession are being tempted to return to evil and corrupt practices.

13–17 The problem described subjectively

The psalmist himself was tempted to doubt the necessity of a strict integrity of heart and conscience. **13, 14** His adherence to the high moral code of the law seemed vain so far as tangible advantage was concerned; indeed his endeavour to live a godly life brought him no evidences of divine approval, but only a daily chastening. **15** Had he voiced his doubts in public, he would have been a traitor to God's children, encouraging them to doubt. See how the godly man controls his tongue, thinks before he airs his problems, and gives pride of place to the spiritual well-being of others. **16** The more he pondered over the meaning of this inversion of values the more *wearisome* it became. **17** At last he *went into the sanctuary of God* and meditated upon the ultimate state of the wicked. There he discovered a new outlook; he perceived that life had baffled him because he had not looked at it in the light of the final issue.

18–25 The nature of his readjustment is recalled

18–20 The psalmist sees clearly now that the wicked cannot flout God and escape. The question arises, however, when will this overthrow take place? Was the psalmist reiterating a traditional doctrine of inevitable retribution in this world? If so, then he was by no means as clear-sighted as his psalm would suggest, for this would be a pathetically insufficient answer. By far the majority of those who live in proud godlessness pass without evident punishment. Here, then, is the importance of retaining in v. 4 the Hebrew text with its reference to painless death. The psalmist was in fact facing the full rigour of the problem. He saw men go into death unscathed; but he saw that, on awaking, their situation was quite different, one of insecurity, ruin, destruction and terror. Indeed they awake (*cf.* on Ps. 17:15) and see what a *dream* they have lived in, and before the judgment of an awakening God (*cf.* Ps. 44:23–26) all their so-called solid worldly achievement is no more than a *phantom*.

21–25 Very different is the psalmist's awareness of his own life with God. **21, 22** He owns that his period of bitterness made him utterly devoid of insight into the things of God, **23, 24** but now he is alive to the reality of his spiritual wealth: his peace with God, whereby he is *continually with thee*; his security, for *thou dost hold my right hand* (*cf.* Is. 41:10); his sense of God's plan, or *counsel*, guiding his life; and *afterward thou wilt receive* (*cf.* on Ps. 49:15) *me to glory* (*cf.* Lk. 23:43; Acts 7:55, 56). **25** It is not only *upon earth* but also *in heaven* that God and fellowship with God constitute the sufficient and superior wealth of the man of faith.

26–28 The relevance of his belief to the immediate circumstances

26a The readjustment of values, previously described, had to withstand everything which pressed upon the powers of mind and body, bringing them into distress or weariness. This would include the shadow of old age and approaching death. **26b** Nevertheless the knowledge he had gained of God's eternal and blessed fellowship had matured also and the psalmist was able confidently and fervently to state the ends of the whole matter, viz. **27** those who withdraw from God's way would be inevitably destroyed, **28** but, for himself, the proximity of God was the source and cause of all his well-being. The general statement of v. 1 has become a personal confession and a testimony.

Note the contrast between *far from thee* and *near God*.

PSALM 74. A LAMENT FOR THE DESTRUCTION OF THE SANCTUARY

This is one of several poignant lamentations which found utterance at the destruction of Jerusalem and the beginning of exile in Babylon (*cf.* Lamentations and Ps. 79). The tragedy was not merely that the centre of religious life, the Temple, had been destroyed: that which cut the cord of hope and overwhelmed the nation with moral dismay was the inference that God had forsaken them. Where was God's faithfulness to the covenant? As one year followed another, the long duration of the captivity (vv. 1, 3, 10, 19, 22, 23) lent credence to the thought of divine rejection and urgency to prayer.

1–11 The appeal

Disappointment is mingled with bewilderment as the psalmist voices the cry of the people in an insistent 'Why?' to God (vv. 1 and 11). Into the midst of this challenging inquiry is inserted a less emotional statement of their distress (vv. 3–9).

1 The sense of the sovereignty of God over the world is strong in these verses: He has been the Agent; His anger has been manifested in the activities of the enemy. **2** The anomaly is that God's hot anger is directed against those who are His own flock (the 'Shepherd of Israel' is a metaphor much used in the Asaphic psalms), against His own purchase, and the tribe of His own inheritance (*cf.* Ex. 15:16, 17). His wrath is directed even against *Mount Zion*, His own habitation (*cf.* Ps. 68:16). In other words, the people's distress and disgrace were a dilemma because God seemed to be ruining His own work and breaking His own word. **3** Let Him come swiftly (*direct thy steps*) and inspect the appalling ruins of His city and the defilement of His sanctuary.

4 There follows a more or less factual statement of what He would see, but details are given only of the sanctuary. *Thy foes* have made tumult in the place of quiet. Military ensigns have taken the place of divine symbols, **5, 6** and wanton damage has been caused to the beauty and form of the building (*cf.* 1 Ki. 6:29) so that it looks like the derelict waste of splintered and futile stumps that mark a felled forest. **7, 8** Finally the place had been burnt (2 Ki. 25:9, 10; Is. 64:11); and, furthermore, as the enemies' intention had been utter havoc, not only the Temple but the religious life of the people had been destroyed. It is doubtful if the translation *meeting places* can be sustained, as the word elsewhere means the time or occasion of meeting, or the people assembled, but never the place. We may catch the sense of the Hebrew with 'They said in their heart: "The entire race!"' as with fire they put a stop to the festivals of God in the land'. **9** The result was that not a vestige or outward sign of their religious life remained and there was not even a prophetic hint as to how long this would continue (*cf.* La. 2:9).

10 The concluding phrase of this descriptive section, *how long*, is a resumption of the appeal to God in vv. 1 and 2. Profound as the disaster was, the psalmist could not believe it to be permanent. It was unthinkable that the name of the Lord should be left permanently in disrepute. **11** Judgment must surely fall upon their opponents, although for a mysterious interval God's chastening hand was withheld (*cf.* Ex. 15:6).

12–23 The hope

That fervent appeal to God implied a hope which was not wishful merely but reasonable. They were appealing to a God whose character they knew of old; of His power there could be no doubt at all. This conviction is borne out by the emphatic *Thou* of vv. 13–17. The indisputable facts of the Exodus are recapitulated; **13** the division of the Red Sea, the destruction of the Egyptian army (symbolized by the *dragons* of v. 13b; *cf.* Ezk. 29:3), **14** the utter disgrace of the Egyptian power (symbolized by *Leviathan*, usually taken to mean the crocodile), the dishonour to the Egyptian carcases washed up as a prey to robbers and as food for the beasts of the desert. **15** God had wrought this: He also had brought water out of the cleft rock (Ex. 17:1–7) and dried up the perennial Jordan (Jos. 3). **16** Indeed, day and night, the very light and sun, were His. **17** All the physical features (*the bounds*) of earth, all seasonal phenomena, were originated solely by Him.

The appeal and hope is now based, not on grounds of earthly circumstance, but on divine faithfulness. **18** Let Him consider that His name has been blasphemed by a base or foolish people (*cf.* Dt. 32:21). Where then is His honour? **19** His poor family are harassed and defenceless as a dove among wild beasts. Where then is His compassion? **20** The *covenant* whereby He pledged Himself to them seems to be ignored. The land has gone dark because of His disfavour and violence abounds. Where then is His faithfulness? **21** Let not the burdened souls which cry to Him turn back from Him in shame and confusion because of His apparent indifference. Where then would be His mercy and what source of divine praise would remain in earth? **22, 23** Oh that God would act in His own interests—so far as His name on earth is concerned! Let Him remember how vile persons abuse His name and continually cause their clamour to 'ascend' before Him.

PSALM 75. 'GOD IS THE JUDGE'

Unlike the preceding psalm, this poem does not question the goodness of God but rather exults in His sovereignty and righteousness. There is a

background of calamity (v. 8) and a sense of recent relief from serious peril. In this respect the psalm is akin to Pss. 46–48 and probably belongs to the same period (see Is. 36 and 37). The LXX associates it with the Assyrian invasion. If this is correct, it explains why the north remains unspecified for help in v. 6, for it was the direction of the enemy advance. Also the intervention of God at a time He decides (v. 2) admirably suits the Assyrian crisis.

In the following suggested analysis, we may imagine a prophet stepping forward in the assembly with a word from God (vv. 2, 3; *cf.* 2 Ch. 20:4–19). The suggestion that vv. 4–10 were spoken by the king rests upon the content of the verses, only suitable to a royal speaker, and comparison with the royal oath of consecration, Ps. 101.

1 The voice of the people: thanksgiving

The expression of thanks, doubled for intensity, is occasioned by an experience of the *name* of God coming *near* (see mg.; *cf.* Is. 30:27), *i.e.* God Himself acting in the fullness of His revealed character, and doing *wondrous* (or supernaturally marvellous) *deeds* such as He alone could do.

2, 3 The voice of God: sovereignty

If we cast ourselves into the Assyrian crisis we will get the feel of this word of God. Jerusalem was humbled to the dust, and at the very 'eleventh hour', as men reckon things, God acted. But there is no crisis with God. **2** He does not act because things have come to a desperate pass, but because the time appointed for action has come. **3** To the human view the earth is tottering to its doom, but its stability is neither secured by men, nor upset by them. The world and its inhabitants are kept in place by God.

4–10 The voice of the king: dedication

4, 5 The downfall of the arrogant Assyrian (*cf.* Is. 37:23–25) is an object-lesson to all *the boastful*, to all who *lift up* the *horn*, *i.e.* vaunt their own powers. The king is determined to match the acts of the divine King in his own rule, and we might translate his opening word as a response: 'I have determined to say . . .' The reason for speaking out admonishingly to boasters now follows: **6, 7** promotion is not self-achieved, but is the gift of God, **8** and is based on moral factors. For the picture of the Lord's *cup*, *cf.* Ps. 60:3; Is. 51:17; Je. 25:15; Ezk. 23:32–34; note also the cup of joy and salvation, Pss. 16:5; 116:13. **9, 10** As the king sings out in praise to God, he resolves to match this aspect of the divine ways of government also. He too will cut off the wicked and promote the righteous (see mg.).

PSALM 76. A SONG OF DELIVERANCE

The same circumstances which lay behind Ps. 75

form the background of this poem also: it celebrates a victory in which Yahweh has signally revealed Himself. Where Ps. 75 culminated in the dedication of the earthly king, Ps. 76 culminates in certain conclusions about the nature of the divine Kingship.

1–3 Self-revelation: fact and place

1 'Self-revealed' is the first Hebrew word in this psalm and it announces its subject-matter. *Israel* signifies, not the northern kingdom, but the chosen people of God. In the setting of this people, and specifically in the land of *Judah*, God has so made Himself *known* (the verb is reflexive) that His people testify with new enthusiasm that *his name is great*: they see the greatness of His revealed nature. **3** The occasion of the self-revelation was a great victory. Some interpreters see here a historical deliverance of the city, *e.g.* from Sennacherib (2 Ki. 19:32–35; *cf.* on Pss. 46–48); others hold that thinking about the royal city, the Lord's anointed king and the divine King Himself had always included the idea of the opposition of the evil world, and that this was dramatically represented in the ritual of the Temple—the assault of the kings and their overthrow. There is, of course, no need to make these views strict alternatives. Both may well have been true: historical deliverances confirmed the faith regularly expressed in the ritual that the Lord is the Defender of His people.

4–9 Self-revelation: content and response

Compared with vv. 1–3 and 10–12, these verses are a personal address to God. The self-revealing acts of the Lord have become the basis of personal knowledge and personal faith. The phrases alternate between some truth about God and some description of His supremacy: **4** His glorious majesty, **5** supremacy over all the strength of man, whether of heart (courage) or hand, **6a** His powerful word of *rebuke*, **6b** His supremacy over man's weapons, **7a** His awesomeness, **7b** His supremacy over every imaginable foe, **8a** His heavenly authority, **8b, 9** His supremacy over the whole earth in the interests of justice and mercy.

10–12 Self-revelation: conclusions

10 First, the victory has revealed the almightiness of divine providence by which even man's anger is turned to serve God's purposes. **11** Secondly, the only proper response to such a God is integrity, devotion and reverence. **12** Thirdly, the past victory is seen as the pledge and foretaste of His ultimate world-wide conquest.

PSALM 77. THE HISTORICAL BASIS OF HOPE

While there is no objection in principle to hearing in this psalm the voice of communal distress, expressed in individual terms—a view almost unanimous among the older commentators—or the voice of an individual interceding on behalf of afflicted Israel, as recent commentators suggest, the exceedingly personal terms of the psalm are best explained if we assume an individual sufferer seeking comfort in God and finding help in meditating on God's well-remembered acts of redemption for His people. The psalm says nothing of peril, pursuit, hardship, disease, or suchlike difficulties. The root cause of the distress which afflicts the psalmist may be the continued absence of any sign of divine compassion (vv. 7–9), but it is more helpful to picture the psalmist as one whose spirit is overwhelmed—for whatever cause. How well, in this case, he speaks to all who are depressed and prescribes the tonic of remembrance.

1–9 His despondency

2 The extremity of soul is forcefully presented in this imagery of a sick and restless person calling in vain at night for someone to minister comfort. **3** Actually the misery of soul arises from meditation about God, **4** nor is respite easily found in sleep, for God seems to keep his eyes wide open. **5** But this turns out to be a merciful withholding of sleep, for as he ponders over *the days of old*, **6–9** he encourages himself to think that the favour, love, promises and grace of God are changeless. He expresses this in six questions, each expecting the answer 'No'.

10–20 God's acts remembered

10 is specially difficult to translate. RSV should be understood as an act of submission: assured by his own questions that there is no ultimate change in God, he accepts it as his divinely allocated grief that God's hand toward him has changed from favour to distress. Alternatively, we may translate: 'This is my plea, years of the right hand . . .', *i.e.* a prayer of faith, arising from the affirmation of divine changelessness and seeking a restoration of His favour; or again, 'This explains my sickness, years of the right hand . . .'—the all-gracious God has decreed a period of suffering. Whichever is correct, the psalmist ministers a tonic to himself by recalling, first (vv. 11–15), that no human power can withstand God, and that His power is characteristically power to *redeem* His people; and secondly (vv. 16–20), that no natural forces or circumstances can withstand God, and that He uses them rather for the protection and care of His people.

15 *Jacob and Joseph* are mentioned as being the 'founding fathers' of the people who came out of Egypt, but possibly also as being outstanding examples of God's providential care: Jacob and his sons were preserved from famine by Joseph who had been raised from prison and oblivion to rule Egypt, and then the descendants of both were miraculously preserved against Pharaoh's murderous intentions. All this enhances the concept of redemption: it is entirely the work of God who magnifies both His power and His mercy by selecting those who have no power in themselves to help themselves. In mentioning *Joseph*, the psalmist might also have found help in considering the individuality of redemption. **16** The opening of a path through the Red Sea. **17, 18** A poetic development of the divine mastery of the forces of nature in overthrowing the Egyptians in the sea. **19** *Thy footprints were unseen*; probably a reference to the returning waters which obliterated from sight, but not from memory, the path taken by the cloudy-fiery pillar. **20** The contrasting providences of God: one minute the crashing of the storm, the next shepherds with their flock. So He superintends the welfare of His people.

PSALM 78. GOD'S HAND IN HISTORY

Along with Pss. 105; 106 and 136, this is one of the four great national hymns in the Psalter. In each case the dominant theme is the experience of Israel's deliverance from Egypt. The purpose of the psalm is so to rehearse the early story of the nation that future generations might be warned against a repetition of past failures (see vv. 1–11; *cf.* 1 Cor. 10:1–11). Writing some time after the leadership of the nation had passed from the Ephraimite house of Saul to the Judahite house of David (vv. 67–70), the psalmist believes himself to possess the exact clue to past misfortunes and reverses. With great artistry, he refrains from 'applying the moral', but stops abruptly at David's accession and wise rule, leaving the new ruling family to draw its own conclusions.

1–8 Introduction

1 The psalmist calls for attention, **2** promising *a parable*, *i.e.* an instructive discourse, not a mere story but a story with a meaning, and *dark sayings*, or 'riddles', clearly implying that it is their solution which he intends to offer. **3** The material of his discourse is traditional, **4** and he intends to be a faithful steward in passing it to the next generation. **5–8** explain more of the background: God intended this passing on of teaching from one generation to the next (vv. 5, 6) for the express purpose of learning from the mistakes of the past and in particular— here comes the key-idea of the psalm—that they should be warned of the danger of forgetfulness (vv. 7, 8).

9–39 The first exposition of the acts of God

The psalmist is keenly interested to know what went wrong with the monarchy of Saul, and why it was replaced by that of David (*cf.* vv. 67–70). He starts therefore with the wholesale defeat of Saul's well-equipped standing army on Mt. Gilboa (1 Sa. 31). **9** Why such a defeat, when the human prospects of victory were so bright? **10a** The reply is that defeat springs from

disobedience, **10b** rebellion, **11** and forgetfulness. If only they had remembered the acts of God! We are now given a review of the acts of God—with particular reference to His wonders shown in the realm of nature—and of constant rebellion on Israel's part. His acts were redemption (vv. 12–14), provision (vv. 15, 16), judgment (vv. 17–33) and mercy (vv. 34–39). **12** *Zoan* was an ancient capital of Egypt, here used as a poetic parallel for Egypt. **13** *Cf.* Ex. 14:21, 22. **14** *Cf.* Ex. 13:21, 22. **15** *Cf.* Ex. 17. **18, 19** To *test* God is not the same as simply asking for signs (*e.g.* Jdg. 6:36–40), but rather to challenge Him to do what one believes Him to be unable to do. These verses, therefore, are a key passage explaining what such a sinful 'test' is. **22** This is the heart of the sinful 'test', *they had no faith.*

23–31 *Cf.* Ex. 16; Nu. 11. Calvin well remarks on this passage: 'That which his favour . . . would have led him to refuse, he now granted them in his wrath. This is an example well worthy of our attention, that we may not complain if our desires are crossed by . . . God when they break forth beyond bounds. God then truly hears us when, instead of yielding to our foolish inclinations, he regulates his beneficence . . . to our welfare; even as in lavishing upon the wicked more than is good for them . . . he loads them with a deadly burden.' The food was not sought in a spirit of faith to satisfy legitimate need, but in a spirit of doubt to indulge immoderate appetite. To such God replies by granting in wrath exactly what they asked, but to their destruction. **32, 33** Probably a reference to the refusal to enter Canaan (*cf.* Dt. 1:26–46; Nu. 14:1–35) and the following utter pointlessness of the 40 wandering years.

40–72 The second exposition of the acts of God

Tracing the course of divine providence from Egypt (v. 43) to Canaan (v. 54), these verses dwell specially on God's acts in the realm of history, how He dealt with opposing peoples for His own people's sake. At the head of the section, and introducing it, vv. 40–42 take a final explanatory glance back to the preceding exposition of God's acts. Everything God did had been met by disobedience and rebellion, but now we are told of one common denominator of all their ill-dealings with Him: **40, 41** behind the rebelling, grieving, testing and provoking, **42** *they did not keep in mind* . . . (lit. 'they did not remember')—the central folly and sin of forgetfulness.

From this follows the second exposition of God's acts, and it takes the same sequence as the first: His acts were redemption (vv. 43–53), provision (vv. 54, 55), judgment (vv. 56–64) and mercy (vv. 65–72). **43–51** *Cf.* Ex. 7–12. **51** *Ham* was the son of Noah from whom the Egyptians were descended (*cf.* Gn. 10:6). **60** *Shiloh* was the great sanctuary which was finally presided over by Eli (1 Sa. 1–4). We do not read of its destruction but presume that it fell in the same Philistine onslaught which captured the ark. The fall of Shiloh made a deep impression and became an object-lesson in God's dealings with His people (*cf*. Je. 7:1–14). It stands in history as proof that mere religion is not enough for God. If the religious act does not match the state of the heart it is meaningless, and if the heart does not flow through the act into a changed life it is hypocrisy. **65** Very daring comparisons, but how vividly the OT sees God's concern for His people: this is the divine 'jealousy' (*cf*. Is. 42:13, 14). **67** The whole story of Saul's monarchy is summed up by the one word *rejected*. Saul did not achieve any lasting benefit for Israel, and the psalmist leads us dramatically to that event which set the course of history for the next 400 years, the choice of David. **69** *He built his sanctuary* is most easily explained if the psalm was composed after the building of Solomon's Temple. But since the psalmist does not mention the division of the kingdom (1 Ki. 12:1–20)— a fact which would have greatly assisted his argument—we may suggest that when, in Solomon's reign, evidence began to accumulate that old errors were being repeated, he stated his view of the inner workings of the history of the past.

The supreme intention of this dramatic presentation is to show the peculiar responsibility of the Davidic king. God has intervened, not merely to free the nation from their adversaries, Pharaoh (v. 42) and the Philistines (v. 66), but to select Judah to be His people, Zion to be His habitation, and **70–72** David to be His servant who would feed (*be the shepherd of*) His people (*cf*. 2 Sa. 3:18; 5:2). But if the acts of God in redemption, provision, judgment and mercy are not pondered and kept in mind, then again forgetfulness will breed rebellion, and rebellion will issue in defeat. This is the implication of the psalm's abrupt ending, and its abiding lesson for us.

PSALM 79. JERUSALEM MADE A HEAP OF RUINS

This is a companion psalm to Ps. 74. It expresses the plight (vv. 1–4), prayers (vv. 5–12) and promise (v. 13) of God's people in a day of calamity, the Babylonian Exile. Its plea for divine redress and restoration is based on three grounds: first, the agony and distress of His *saints* (v. 2); secondly, the compassionate nature of God (v. 8); thirdly, the ignominy and dishonour which other nations will attach to God's name if He leaves desolate those who are His *servants* and representatives (v. 10). These three aspects of the prayer are interwoven throughout the psalm but they are stressed in turn in its three sections.

1–4 Ruin and massacre

1 *Cf*. Ps. 74:2, 7; also note the fulfilment of Micah's prophecy (3:12) quoted in Je. 26:18.

2, 3 The corpse-strewn battlefield round about Jerusalem was so awful and ominous a memory that it became symbolic of the ultimate judgment of men (*cf*. Ezk. 39:1–20; Rev. 11:8, 9; 19:17, 18). **4** The derision of neighbouring peoples, like Edom, Moab and Philistia, was a continual source of irritation to the afflicted people of God (*e.g*. Ezk. 25:2, 12 and 15; Ob. 12).

5–9 Wrath and mercy

The events of history were considered to be the direct acts of God Himself in accordance with His moral providence, and, of course, the prophets had been clear that He, as righteous Judge, was the real agent in the overthrow of Jerusalem (*cf*. Ezk. 8). But would God never cease to be angry with His chosen ones? A twofold appeal follows: **6, 7** first, an appeal to the divine jealousy. Surely God will not stand idly by while the heathen lay violent hands on His people. **8, 9** Secondly, an appeal to the divine forgiveness. The utter absence of merit on man's part is brought into relation to God's utter readiness to forgive. Sin is seen as inherited from the past, the cause of present need, and offensive to God.

10–13 Revenge and majesty

The final plea of the psalmist goes right outside all personal feelings of distress or vengeance. The intervention of God is sought for His own honour and glory. **10** In the first place there should be no cause whatever for the heathen to scoff at God because of Israel's misery and dereliction. Compare the arguments of Moses about the Egyptian reactions to an exodus that failed (Ex. 32:12; Nu. 14:13–17). **12** Then, in the course of this demonstration of divine faithfulness, power and justice, let the derisive neighbouring states (*cf*. v. 4) experience the derision of the Lord (*cf*. Ps. 2:4), for in reproaching Israel they have really scorned Him. **13** The psalm concludes on the note of dedication, not in a spirit of bargaining with God but because true supplication must be linked with consecration: the vow is of thanksgiving to God and testimony to men.

PSALM 80. AN ELEGY FOR ISRAEL

This psalm is wholly concerned with the northern kingdom of Israel, depicted by the names Joseph, Ephraim, Benjamin and Manasseh— these latter three being reckoned as the 'camp of Ephraim' in the marching order of the people (Nu. 2:17–24). Though Benjamin was often linked with Judah, it was essentially a northern tribe. For example, Saul, the Benjaminite, was an Ephraimite monarch. Either we have here a prayer of devout Israelites referring to the fall of Samaria (722 BC), or else a prayer of the whole exiled community after 586 BC composed by someone with close affiliations with the old northern kingdom.

1–3 Petition

1 The Lord is addressed as the *Shepherd of Israel*. That view of the Exodus which saw in it a flock movement under a divine Shepherd is common to several psalms (*e.g.* 78:52). The Shepherd is, however, the divine King Himself, enthroned between the cherubim of the ark. It seems a great while since any light from God cheered His people (vv. 3, 7, 19). Hence the prayer that He will *shine* (or 'flash') *forth* from the Holy Place for their comfort. Thus Christians, in experiences of life's darkness, look to the light of the second coming (Rom. 13:12; 2 Thes. 1:7f.; Tit. 2:13). **3** The prayer relies wholly on what God can do: He only can *restore* His people (lit. 'cause us to turn' back to Him); He only can welcome them back with shining face, significant of His pleasure in them. Out of this double 'turning'—of us to Him, and Him to us—comes the assurance that we are *saved*.

4–7 The basis of the prayer

We learn here again the gracious truth that as God's people we can come to Him simply pleading our own need: such is His grace and our privilege. **5, 6** These verses are a reminder of the sorrow and the scorn into which God has led them. We may note that there is no loss of faith in Him in spite of their experiences. This is what He has justly done. **4** But the sorest need is now present: that when they seek His answer even their prayers seem to anger Him. Their sense of the divine alienation from them is very great. **7** Hence the added urgency of the renewed petition (*cf.* v. 3), with its appeal now to the *God of hosts*, God the omnipotent.

8–16 The allegory of the vine

At this point, the psalmist breaks off in order to introduce the allegory of the vine which is often used as an emblem of Israel (*cf.* Ho. 10:1; Is. 5:1–7; Ezk. 15:1–6; also Lk. 20:9ff.; Jn. 15:1ff.). **8, 9** The transplanting of a vine slip from Egypt (*cf.* Gn. 49:22) was possible only because of God's special intervention (*cf.* Ps. 44:3). **10, 11** Once planted, the vine flourished so as to spread, during the empires of David and Solomon, over the mountains of Judea as far as the cedar forests of Lebanon, the Mediterranean coast, and the Euphrates river (*cf.* Dt. 11:24). **12, 13** Now all the vineyard is derelict: the gardener has abandoned it and consequently it has been invaded by the Gentiles—symbolized by wild beasts. The threat of Is. 5:5–7 has come true. **14** This leads to the cry of penitence and need. **15, 16** The whole anomaly of careful planting and utter rejection, the assiduous cultivation of the *stock*, or vineyard, and then the outcome of fire instead of fruit, is summed up in these last verses.

17–19 The plea for divine action

Throughout the psalm God has been reminded of the special and beloved place Israel occupies in His plan: they are His flock (v. 1), His people (v. 4), and His vine (v. 8). **17** Now comes the tenderest title of all. When Benjamin was born (Gn. 35:18) at the cost of his mother's life, she, her mind full of her fatal travail, aptly named him Ben-oni, 'son of my sorrow'; but his father, loving the child for the sake of the beloved Rachel, refused the name, calling him rather Benjamin, 'son of (my) right hand'. So is Israel, by grace, to the Lord. **18** And if only God will replace His hand upon the direction of their affairs, Israel will thus become the 'ideal Israel'. **19** Longing for this blessing is expressed in the fullest form of the refrain.

Note the changes in the divine name: *O God* (v. 3); *O God of hosts* (v. 7); *O Lord God of hosts* (v. 19): 'O Yahweh, God the omnipotent', a comprehensive appeal to covenanted grace and supernatural power.

PSALM 81. A HYMN AND HOMILY AT HARVEST-TIME

This psalm is best associated with the Feast of Tabernacles, though some link it with the Passover, on the ground of the reference to Egypt in v. 5. All the great feasts of Israel were, however, based on the Exodus, and Tabernacles associates well with this psalm in that it regularly placed God's law before the people (Dt. 31:9ff.; *cf.* vv. 8–10) and was the feast of the ingathering (Ex. 23:16; 34:22; *cf.* vv. 10, 16).

1–5 The summons

The Feast of Tabernacles began in the middle of the 7th month, *i.e.* at full moon (v. 3b). **4** This festival was a *statute for Israel*, **5** having been instituted by divine *decree*, but better 'for a testimony' (RV), *i.e.* to bear witness to the goodness of the God who *went out over*, *i.e.* imposed His rule upon (*cf.* Gn. 41:45) Egypt at the Exodus. Some (Eaton, *etc.*) hold that at this point in the ceremony of Tabernacles a prophet stepped forward in the assembly to declare the word of God (*cf.* 2 Ch. 20:14), announcing his inspiration in the words *I hear a voice . . .* It is hard, however, to think that a prophet would speak of the Lord as *a voice I had not known*. It is better to understand a reference back to Israel's situation in Egypt when Moses came bearing a message from the God of their fathers now revealed in new terms (*cf.* Ex. 6:2, 3) (so Delitzsch, Kirkpatrick, *ICC*).

6–16 The message

6–10 His work of deliverance. 6 Israel's burden of slave labour and tedious toil in Egypt was suddenly removed. **7** They had called upon God and He came down to deliver (Ex. 6:5ff.). The thick darkness of the thunder cloud (*the secret place of thunder*; *cf.* Ex. 14:20) refers to His immediate presence with them in the 'pillar of cloud'. The allusion to *the waters of Meribah* (meaning 'strife'; *cf.* Ex. 17:7) may be suggestive of the custom at the Feast of Tabernacles of fetching water from Siloam (*cf.* Jn. 7:37) in remembrance of the miraculous provision of water in the wilderness. Whereas the psalm says *I tested you*, Ex. 17:2 says that the people 'put the Lord to the proof'. In other words, life's adversities are deliberately planned divine tests (*cf.* Dt. 8:2–5) to which we respond either in the faith which accepts and trusts or in the doubt which questions and rebels (*cf.* Ps. 95:8, 9; 1 Cor. 10:9ff.; Jas. 1:2-4, 12).

This action of God was inseparable from His commandments to them. **9, 10** Only the first commandment is named here (*cf.* Ex. 20:2–7), for this embodied their essential and distinctive characteristic (*cf.* Dt.6:4, 5; see also Mk. 12:28ff.). But just as blessing preceded the call to obedience (vv. 6, 7), so blessing is promised as its outcome (v. 10b).

11–16 Their waywardness of desire. The keen edge of this reproach lay in the rejection of God by those towards whom He had been especially kind, patient and active. **11** Their wilfulness temporarily frustrated His purpose; **12** in consequence they were left to *their stubborn hearts,* and allowed to walk in *their own counsels* —instead of in His ways.

13 Nevertheless, the repetition of the divine aside (*cf.* v. 8b) suggests a willingness on His part to bless Israel. **14, 15** But the blessings of victory and provision (v. 16) await the response of heartfelt obedience (v. 13). **16** To this the people are called by the promise of even greater blessings than their fathers enjoyed—not water, but *honey from the rock*—for the grace of God is neither exhausted nor limited by even the best of the past.

PSALM 82. UNJUST JUDGES IMPEACHED BY GOD

1 See Ps. 58:1 for a discussion of the meaning of *the gods* mentioned here. The same considerations apply and the same conclusion holds that here the Lord, the supreme Judge, gives judgment in the High Court against earth's corrupt judiciaries.

2–7 constitute the charge and condemnation of those who had exercised judicial authority in a false and unjust manner, *i.e.* having respect of persons (see Lv. 19:15; Jas. 2:1–9), and ignoring necessitous cases. **5** Each of the three sentences contains a testimony: first, about the accused, their lack of moral discernment; secondly, about the helpless, their continuance in unrelieved trouble; thirdly, about society, its fundamental insecurity when justice is mal-administered. **6** Therefore God (*I* is emphatic), who caused these men to be appointed to the office of judges so that they became *sons of the Most High,* **7** pronounces sentence. Their failure entails a death like any descendant of Adam, and a disgrace comparable with the condemnation of many princes in former times.

8 In the final verse the psalmist calls upon God Himself to control all nations and administer true judgment.

PSALM 83. PRAYER, THE REACTION IN CRISIS

No such widespread alliance of adjacent states as is described in vv. 6–8 is mentioned in the OT. The nearest approach to such a situation was the coalition against Jehoshaphat (see 2 Ch. 20:1–12). It may be that, in presenting this urgent plea for help, the writer is stating in a more vivid way the basic spiritual situation displayed in Ps. 2: secular opposition to the kingdom of God.

1–4 The peril

1 The serious nature of the threat is reflected in the impetuous words *O God, do not keep silence*; lit. 'O God, let there be no rest to thee.' **2** This urgent plea is reinforced by the description of the aggressors as *thy enemies* and *those who hate thee.* **3** Secret conferences have been held and plans prepared *against thy people.* The promises of God are an added basis of prayer as *thy protected ones* recalls their coverage by His covenant (*cf.* Pss. 27:5; 31:21). **4** Finally, the imperative need of action by God is implicit in the disclosure of the plot utterly to wipe out Israel and remove from earth the memory of God's chosen people.

5–8 The confederacy described

The forces massed against Israel had two characteristics. **5** They acted with complete unanimity; they had made an alliance against God Himself. **6, 7** Those concerned were mostly the semi-nomadic peoples whose petty kingdoms stretched along the east side of the Jordan valley, *i.e. Edom, Moab, Ammon,* with the *Hagrites* and *Ishmaelites* who lived still farther east (*cf.* 1 Ch. 5:10) and also the people of *Gebal* (south of Edom). In addition, there were the forces of the western seaboard, Philistia and Tyre. **8** And in the background was the might of *Assyria* which had already lent an arm of help to *the children of Lot, i.e.* to Moab and Ammon (Gn. 19:36–38).

9–12 An appeal to history

Ominous situations had occurred previously in Israel's history and astonishing deliverances had been experienced through the unmistakable intervention of God. Two of the most noteworthy were the attack by Sisera (Jdg. 4; 5) and the invasion of the Midianites (Jdg. 6–8). In both cases the Israelites were not merely outnumbered, but also outclassed in aggressive equipment. Nevertheless both perils were amazingly overcome; the menace was swiftly and entirely removed and at very little loss to the Israelites. Compare Isaiah's comment on the second event (Is. 9:4; 10:26).

13–18 The plea for help

13–15 The recollection of previous deliverances

gives passion and eloquence to the cry for immediate help, expressed in three pictures of total vanquishment by divine intervention. **16-18** The supreme aim of this prayer is the glory of God, and the psalmist pleads for an unforgettable experience of humiliation for the opponents of God so that they and all men everywhere might acknowledge *that thou alone, whose name is the Lord, art the Most High over all the earth.*

PSALM 84. REJOICING IN THE SANCTUARY

This is a companion to Ps. 42 (also a Korahite psalm), but whereas that was a lament because of exile from the house of his God, this is a song of joy in the dwelling-places of the Lord of hosts.

1-4 The joy of the house of the Lord

We may well picture a pilgrim newly arrived, exclaiming in rapture over the long-anticipated beauty of the Lord's house. His first reaction is to its loveliness (vv. 1, 2); his second, to its safety (vv. 3, 4). **2** *Longs . . . faints . . . sing for joy.* The tenses of the Hebrew are not reflected here. Possibly, the perfects 'have longed . . . fainted' look back to the breathless anticipation with which he looked forward to his pilgrimage, and the present 'sing for joy' reflects the outburst of fulfilled longing. His *soul* is his innermost being; his *heart and flesh* represent the totality of his being, inward and outward. **3** Seeing even tiny birds making themselves at home, he realizes the safety of God's house, and for himself associates this with the Lord's provision of *thy altars*, the places of sacrifice for sin, reconciliation and communion with God.

5-8 The joy of the pilgrimage

From the vantage-point of his present blessedness in God's house (v. 4), he looks back to the joy that attended his way. **5** Blessing attends those who draw their strength from God and are utterly devoted to pilgrimage. **6** Certainly they will meet dry, desolate places on their journey, places like *the valley of Baca*, but he makes light of its trouble and treats it as if it were a spring of water, and to such joyful faith the Lord responds with His refreshing rains. **7** The pilgrimage is crowned by the meeting with God Himself and **8** fellowship in prayer.

9-12 The joy of the Lord

The prayer for the king is unexpected but is explained by the following verses. If the psalmist is to be preserved in his enjoyment of spiritual privileges, then he must pray for national stability. **9** In this direct sense his communion with God depends on the continuing favour of the Lord to His *anointed* king, who is a *shield* to his people. **10-12** The climax of the psalm lies in these concluding verses: it is not the house that is his delight so much as its Occupant, loved for His nature as *sun and shield*, His bounteous gifts and the simplicity of the way of faith.

PSALM 85. A PRAYER FOR REVIVAL

Written at a time when God's people were enduring some set-back of communal fortunes, this psalm reflects the three dominant thoughts of the godly men who faced the labour and toil of reconstruction.

1-3 God's goodness recalled

Three actions of God are described, viz. their territorial restoration, national forgiveness, and reconciliation to God. This provides a basis for the spirit of prayer and optimism which pervades the psalm. God's past mercies fortify His people for present distress and assure them of future glory.

4-7 Present distress

These verses expose the nature of their trouble: a sense of alienation from God. The past mercies are not being experienced in the present time. **4, 5** Therefore they pray, first that God will be reconciled to them in the putting away of His indignation; **6** secondly that they may be revived so as to rejoice in Him; **7** and thirdly that they may experience fulfilment of the covenant-promises of His steadfast love and their own salvation.

8-13 Promise

8 In this verse the psalmist speaks to himself in tones of hopefulness. He is sure about God; He will *speak peace to his people.* But that is conditional (according to the reading in the text) upon sincerity, or (as the mg. reads, following the Hebrew) upon consistent loyalty. **9-13** represent his perception of the word which the Lord speaks. **9** The blessing of *salvation* will soon be experienced by *those who fear him,* and they will know the reality of God in all His *glory* (*cf.* Is. 60:1ff.) dwelling in their midst (Zc. 2:4, 5, 11). **10** When this salvation comes it will be seen first to involve absolute harmony of the divine attributes: He shows *steadfast love* to sinners without abandoning *faithfulness* to His own holy nature; His *righteousness* of character is not at loggerheads with His gift of *peace* to men (1 Jn. 1:9; Rom. 3:23–26). **11** Secondly, salvation issues in harmony between man and God, and people will live in fidelity under the eye of a righteous God. **12** Thirdly, as ever, the day of salvation is the restoration of Eden: nature itself burgeons with new life. All this is no idle fancy. **13** It is surely grounded in the *righteousness* of God, His absolute adherence to His pledged word and His declared purposes. This *righteousness,* personified as a herald, goes before Him as He draws near with salvation for His people.

PSALM 86. O TURN UNTO ME!

This psalm, something of a mosaic of quotations and reminiscences of other psalms, is an expression of a devout soul seeking the assuring fellowship and strengthening grace of the Lord. The petition for aid against certain foes (v. 14) does not necessarily root the poem in a particular historical situation. A striking feature of the psalm is that each petition is accompanied by a reason why the prayer should be granted.

1–7 Supplication

This is an expectant and humble cry for an experience of God's favour which shall reinvigorate the psalmist's soul and provide confidence respecting the future outlook. This plea is based on a stated relationship with God: **1** he belongs to the *poor* and *needy*, often, as here, synonyms for God's 'dependants'; **2** he is one of the *godly*, the covenant-people, and also a believer. **5** It is also based on the divine nature: *good and forgiving, abounding in steadfast love*. For possible sources of these phrases see, *e.g.*, Pss. 70:5a; 72:2b; 25:20a; Is. 26:3; 25:1; Ex. 34:6; Ps. 55:1.

8–11 Adoration

8–10 This expression of the ground of the psalmist's faith in the Lord comprehends His creative power and ultimate purpose, His essential goodness and continuous activity, His sovereignty over all and His accessibility to man. **11** This estimate of God leads to the desire to become like Him in mind and manner, *i.e.* to be integrated in a life inseparable from Him (*cf.* Je. 32:39). Compare possible sources in, *e.g.*, Ex. 15:11; Dt. 3:24; Pss. 22:27–29; 77:14; 83:18; 25:4; 27:11.

12, 13 Thanksgiving

A climax of praise and worship is reached wherein the godly soul experiences a unity of being which is a partial participation in eternal glory: it is the affirmation of a God-centred life. The basis of this is a former experience of divine deliverance from uttermost desolation.

14–17 Petition

14 Finally, mention is made of certain immediate circumstances of peril. **15** But the confession of faith toward God is repeated (see v. 5). **16, 17** The intensity of the whole prayer is then summarized in the passionate words *Turn to me . . . Show me a sign of thy favour. Cf.* Pss. 25:16; 69:16. The phrase *son of thy handmaid* implies a relationship akin to that of a slave born into his master's household and therefore having a double claim upon his master's protection. With v. 17b *cf.* Ps. 35:4. The words *thou, Lord* in the concluding phrase are emphatic.

PSALM 87. ZION, THE MOTHER OF ALL MEN

This brief psalm is essentially prophetic (*cf.* Is. 2:2; 44:5; 66:23; Zc. 2:11). The vision of Zion as the metropolis of the world-wide kingdom of God is not to be interpreted geographically,

but spiritually (*cf.* Heb. 11:10). The dominant thought is that of a universal and glad acceptance of God as Lord and King, in which allegiance all sources of international friction are removed. *Cf.* Gal. 3:8; 4:26; Heb. 12:22ff.; Rev. 7:9; 15:4.

1–3 Zion exalted by the choice of God

1 The city which God has founded is beloved by Him. **2** The whole city, represented poetically by its *gates*, is pre-eminent above all other dwelling-places. **3** This fact is proved by the *glorious things* which God has spoken about His city (*e.g.* Is. 2:2–4; 4:2–6; 28:16).

4–6 Zion exalted by the ingathering of the Gentiles

The words *This one was born there* (or, *in her*) occur in three separate sentences attributed to God, and contain the basic concept of the whole poem. *This one and that one* refers to the nations such as Rahab (Egypt; *cf.* Is. 51:9; Ps. 89:10); Babylon, from whose great power the children of Israel had been rescued; Philistia, Tyre, both typical of Israel's age-long enemies; and Ethiopia, representative of the remote peoples of the earth. The words *was born there* imply the identity of these Gentile nations with Israel; they receive similar privileges of citizenship (*cf.* Eph. 2:19). Indeed in the spiritual Zion each and every nation, 'this man and that man', shall claim incorporation on the ground of a rebirth, and the Most High Himself shall make it so. When He draws up the roll of the peoples in His city there will be no aliens (*cf.* Ps. 47:9; Am. 9:11, 12; Eph. 3:6; Rev. 7:9, 10).

7 Zion exalted by the testimony of the redeemed

This reconstruction of the basis of society inaugurates a period of great jubilation. Whether folk sing or dance, whatever they may say or do, the theme and ground of their life is *All my springs are in you*. These words summarize the thought that the new life of the redeemed finds its perpetual inspiration and vigour in the experience of dwelling in the city of God.

PSALM 88. A CRY OF AFFLICTION

This lament is unique in the Psalter because of its gloom and unrelieved misery, devoid even of hope. Contrast the conclusions of Pss. 22 and 31 with vv. 15–18. It seems to be a personal elegy by someone who, like Job, was strained between an undeviating trust in God as the sole source of his salvation, and an intensely bewildering experience which appeared to negate the foundation of all such trust. The divisions of the psalm are marked by those verses in which the psalmist recalls how patiently he has prayed to God: vv. 1, 9b, 13.

1–9a Patient faith in the face of calamity

The psalmist's faith is shown by the fact that throughout this troubled psalm he appears as a man of prayer. **1** Here his patience in believing intercession is noted by the words *day . . . night.* **3–5** The situation which prompts this tireless prayer is, in general, that his troubled life is about to terminate in death, a death in which he sees no light of hope, for he feels himself to be dying without a single gleam of divine favour (*cf.* Pss. 6:4; 30:9). **6–9a** But, in particular, he complains of the wrath of God, the alienation of friends and his bitter personal distress.

9b–12 Patient faith in the face of crisis

9b Notwithstanding such travail he does not cease to pray or falter in faith. *Every day* his voice and his posture appeal to God. **10–12** The urgency of his cry is provoked by the finality of death. It is not, of course, that the OT saw all death in these terms, but that, like the NT, it saw the awful possibility of dying under divine wrath, and in that case going beyond the point where God might be expected to intervene in supernatural *wonders*, or where there would be cause to *praise* Him. Not even the covenant *love* and *faithfulness* of God can avail for those who have died under His wrath; they live in *darkness*, aware only of His dread *forgetfulness*. Consequently, this section is full of the sense of crisis; if God is to act on his behalf, it must be now, at once, for all too soon it will be too late. **11** *Abaddon*, meaning 'destruction', was another name for the abode of the dead. See Jb. 26:6; 31:12; Pr. 15:11.

3–18 Patient faith in the face of perplexity

13 But again, though distress has reached critical proportions, faith greets each new day with prayer, in spite of the fact that he is utterly perplexed by God's purposes as seen in his life. **14, 15** Divine wrath, which he cannot explain, has been his long-standing lot, and **16, 17** now the wrath which he has long experienced rises like a flood to swamp and destroy. **18** Not only so, but it is God who has alienated human sympathy from the sufferer so that, literally, 'my friends are darkness', *i.e.* there is nothing to be seen but darkness and hopelessness where he might reasonably and rightly expect light and relief (*cf.* Jb. 6:14–20). Aptly, but dreadfully, the last word of the psalm is *darkness*, and yet therein lies its wonder—the wonder of triumphant faith, that a man should see no light at all but yet go on supplicating in fervent, trustful, ceaseless prayer (*cf.* Is. 50:10). Truly the OT saint can be our master and teacher!

PSALM 89. GOD'S SURE COVENANT AND ISRAEL'S DISTRESS

The last psalm in the third book of the Psalter may be regarded as a companion to the first one, Ps. 73. Both deal with certain questions which confront a godly man in this earthly existence. On the one hand there is the problem of the prosperity of the wicked (Ps. 73), and on the other there is the mystery of how God is faithful to His word when events seem to show His abhorrence of it (Ps. 89). The particular promises which are here called in question by the tide of events are those which God made to David and his dynasty. The psalm stems from some dark days in the experience of one of the Davidic kings, or else, as some hold, it belongs to the annual liturgical drama in which the king's utter dependence upon the Lord was portrayed in his first being humbled to the dust and then receiving an eleventh-hour deliverance by divine intervention. Out of the darkness of either (or both) historical or liturgical despair this wonderful psalm proceeded.

The question which the psalm poses is this: what is to be done when the promises of God are denied by the facts of experience? It answers: turn the promises into prayers and plead them before God.

1–4 Introduction

1, 2 The speaker is the psalmist. He intends to sing, first, of the Lord's *steadfast love, i.e.* of His loving-kindnesses to the children of Israel, and especially to the house of David. Secondly, of His *faithfulness, i.e.* His consistent adherence to His promises and covenants. These two attributes of God are mentioned again in v. 2 together with the same qualities of perpetuity and permanence. They also form the foundation and scaffolding of the psalmist's subsequent worship (see vv. 5, 8, 14, 24, 33, 49). This initial affirmation is an expression of faith, the greatness of which must be measured against the sombre conditions referred to at the close of the psalm. **3, 4** This attitude of faith arises from God's own declaration in former times (*cf.* 2 Sa. 7:8–16), which is quoted as the origin of the psalmist's belief.

5–37 God's majesty and covenant

5–18 The divine attributes extolled. These verses are an expansion of vv. 1 and 2. **5** In place of the psalmist's voice (v. 1), there is the angelic host which extols the ageless wonder of God's ways with men. **6–8** The purpose of these verses is to declare the heavenly uniqueness of the Lord, and therefore to give reason for believing that His promises are sure. Since none of the *heavenly beings*, whether of His immediate *council* (*cf.* 1 Ki. 22:19, 20) or of the general throng *round about him*, can match or resist Him, then surely His *faithfulness* is linked with supreme might and His promise must stand. **9** From this verse the emphasis is upon God's power in the earth rather than in the heavens. He rules the raging sea; **10** He crushed the power of Rahab (*i.e.* Egypt, as in Ps. 87:4), and has scattered all other foes. **11** He possesses heaven and earth. **12** Indeed the whole earth, from one end to the other (*the north and the south*), is His and the most noticeable features of Palestine, Mts. *Tabor and Hermon*, are testimonies and monuments to His greatness. **13** Events have repeatedly shown His mighty arm and strong hand, **14** and furthermore, in earth as in heaven, the divine power is inseparable from the divine righteousness. Once again the implied question arises: are not His promises secure?

As a consequence of this, Israel, chosen by God who is so great, must be exceptionally blessed. They will surely enjoy the victory, and will see how central their king is to the Lord's purposes. **15** *The festal shout* could well be the cry at the Feast of Tabernacles acknowledging the Lord as King. **17** *Our horn is exalted.* The horn symbolizes strength, and its exaltation implies triumphant strength. **18** The *shield* describes the king in his covenanted obligations as the protector of his people.

19–37 The explicitness of the Davidic covenant. These verses expand the truth of v. 18 by showing the place given by God to David and the subsequent blessings David enjoyed. In the development of the psalm so far they come naturally as the logical outcome of being chosen by the all-powerful and all-gracious God, but they are preparing us for the shock of contradiction which the next section is to bring. First, David is described, in himself (v. 19b), in relation to others (v. 19c), in relation to God (v. 20), and secondly, his prosperity is indicated (vv. 21–37). Throughout, the emphasis is on the Lord as the source of each aspect of David's success. The Lord recalls His vow to overthrow David's foes (vv. 21–23), extend his dominions (vv. 24, 25), exalt his sovereignty (vv. 26, 27), and establish his kingdom for ever (vv. 28–37). **19** *Of old* refers back to 2 Sa. 7. **20** *Cf.* 1 Sa. 16:1–13. **25** *The sea* is the Mediterranean; *the rivers* may be a plural of majesty for the 'great' river Euphrates, or it may signify 'all' rivers: the universal dominion of the Davidic king (*cf.* Ps. 2:8; Is. 9:7). **27** *First-born* refers to his adoption as God's son (Ps. 2:7). **30–37** The faithlessness of men does not overthrow the faithfulness of God. His covenant with David was moral in that it did not offer him a 'blank cheque' but contained stated moral requirements and responses of obedience to God (2 Sa. 7:14), but the divine oath vowed a perpetual dynasty. Herein lies the whole dilemma of the psalm.

38–51 The psalmist protests that God has now spurned the covenant

The emphatic *But now* initiates the forceful contrast which is provided by the following verses. The protest has two aspects which reflect the two themes of the preceding part of the psalm. First, the honour and power of God and His goodness to Israel (vv. 5–18) are reversed in the evidences of the destruction He has wrought, the inversion of His promises, and the disgrace and shame brought to Israel (vv. 38–45). Secondly, the explicit and solemn covenant with David (vv. 20–37) is reversed in the inexplicable and seemingly capricious abandonment of the undertaking (vv. 46–51).

38–45 A deliberate parallel. The pattern of the words 'thou hast done so and so' is a deliberate parallel with the similar structure of vv. 9–14. **38** The raging sea is replaced by wrath toward the king, **39** the humiliation of 'Rahab' is surpassed by the degradation of the throne (the crown defiled). **40, 41** The creation of the world, its bounds and its mountains, is matched with the destruction of the kingdom, its frontiers and citadels. **42** The might of the divine arm had exalted righteousness and judgment and made glad the people (vv. 13–15), whereas now it is *the right hand of his foes* which is exalted and it is the enemies who rejoice. **43** He who had been the glory of their strength (v. 17) now fought only in pretence, for His weapons were reversed and harmless, **44, 45** and their throne was covered with shame.

46–51 A deliberate contrast. 46, 47 The first thought, life's weakness and brevity, is the opposite of the strength and permanence of David in vv. 22–29. **48** It seems that God has made men for a mere nothing; all must die and that comparatively quickly. Unless God reaffirms the covenant speedily the Davidic dynasty, the trusting psalmist and all men will come together to the grave and deliverance will be too late.

49–51 The second and final thought, Where are the Lord's faithfulness and mercies?, needs no repetition; but it is the counterpart of His perpetual presence and guidance which were implicit in vv. 30–35. In conclusion the psalmist reverts to his opening words, first concerning the oath sworn to David (*cf.* v. 3), and secondly concerning the song of praise he intended to sing (v. 1). We must not miss what he is actually doing. As he thus epitomizes the promises of God he makes them into prayers. This is equivalent to saying that the last word will not be with the adverse events of history but with the God whose faithfulness now seems called in question but which will yet be triumphantly vindicated.

52 Doxology

See on Ps. 41:13.

BOOK FOUR. PSALMS 90–106

PSALM 90. RECONCILIATION, THE BASIS OF LIFE

Commentators profess either agnosticism or complete disbelief in the ascription of this psalm to Moses. They give, however, no reasons for their hesitation, and there is in fact no good reason for doubting Mosaic authorship. Delitzsch and Calvin are among those who accept the ascription. The core of the poem (vv. 7–12) appears to have as a definite historical background the latter months of the 38 years' wandering in the wilderness when the generation which was adult on leaving Egypt was rapidly dying off (see Nu. 14:21–23), and this sense of Israel's mortality, accentuated by the judgment on their stubborn unbelief, provides an excellent point of origin for the contents of the psalm.

1–6 The eternal Creator and our ephemeral life

1 Since the days of Abraham the people of God had had no abiding place, but it could be truly said that the Lord had always shown Himself to be their perpetual place of rest (Dt. 33:27). The psalm thus opens with the relationship of peace with God: not that He dwells with us (the presence of God) but that we dwell with Him, the privilege of a reconciled people. Against this basic truth the psalm considers the pitiful brevity of human life and the reality of the wrath of God. How could these things be faced and borne if the basic issue of reconciliation were not settled?

The Eternal is now contrasted with the transient. **2** God outlasts even the most enduring things in man's experience, the very fabric of the earth, **3** whereas man himself returns, by virtue of the divine edict upon fallen humanity (Gn. 3:19), to the dust in death. **4** God outlasts and shames into insignificance even the longest time-measurements known to man, **5, 6** while man can offer no resistance to the flood which sweeps him away, is as insubstantial as a *dream*, and for all his fine show perishes as quickly as *grass*.

7–11 Life's sorrows and God's holiness

The security of v. 1, moving through the reference to sin and the Fall in v. 3, is brought into contrast with the dread fact of divine wrath, the opposite of peace and reconciliation. **7** It is this wrath which brings death, **8** and that not just as a physical fact but as a judgment upon our spiritual state. **9, 10** It is this wrath which mars life and makes even extension of days by no means an unmixed blessing. **11** Yet, even so, men neither appreciate nor realize to the full what the wrath of God means. 'And in regard to the fear due to thee, (who considers the power of) thy wrath?' The point is that, though the wrath of God is the leading factor to be considered in a sinful world, people neither take note of it nor regulate their lives in respect of it.

12–17 Prayer for peace with God

Human life is set between two points: the wrath of God, which makes life transient, and peace with God which gives it stability and permanency. The concluding prayer asks for the latter experience. **12** It starts by asking for a change of attitude: first, on man's part, that, taught by God, he may learn wisdom in his brief life; **13** and secondly, on God's part, that He might turn from His just wrath to tender pity, for salvation always ultimately rests upon God's being satisfied to forgive sinners. **14, 15** The prayer next asks for a change in experience: permanent joy and the end of the wrath. **16** And finally it requests a change of prospects: the prolongation of the nation, under divine favour, to succeeding generations, **17** and present security coupled with conscious experience of divine benevolence. Note how the prayer exactly matches the stated needs: the need of knowledge (v. 11) and the prayer for it (v. 12); the experience of wrath (vv. 7–10) and the prayer for salvation (vv. 13–15); the fact of transience (vv. 2–6) and the prayer for continuance (vv. 16, 17). To read all this in the light of Dt. 2:14–17 is to see the exact aptness of the psalm to the Mosaic situation, but its truth runs on to the wonder of the peace with God, the deliverance from wrath, and the eternal security that are ours in Christ.

PSALM 91. THE SECURITY OF FAITH

The vocabulary of protection and deliverance is ransacked to make this the Psalter's central utterance on the security of the believer. Two voices address an unnamed person assuring him of his safety in God: the first voice speaks to him as 'you' (vv. 1–13), and the second voice is that of the Lord (vv. 14–16). It may be that Eaton is correct in thinking that 'a Temple minister speaks to the king (*cf.* 21.8–12) and concludes by citing an oracle for him (vv. 14–16)'. But since this interpretation is not compelled by the contents of the psalm, its message applies directly to every believer. It ought to be noted that RSV achieves this division of the psalm into two voices by altering the Hebrew text slightly in vv. 2 (from 'I will say . . .') and 9 (see mg.). RV is a very faithful rendering of the Hebrew which gives us the concurring testimony of three voices on the theme of security, as follows: v. 1 announces the theme; in v. 2 the psalmist gives a personal testimony; in vv. 3, 4 another voice testifies about the Lord; in vv. 5–8 (note the change to 'you') the Lord testifies to the psalmist. This pattern is then repeated again: v. 9a, the psalmist; vv. 9b–13, the second voice; and vv. 14–16, the Lord.

1–8 The grounds of security

1 Our security rests, first, on the nature of God. He is *the Most High*, the all-ruling God (Gn. 14:19); He is *the Almighty* (Heb. *šadday*), the God who intervenes in saving power when man's strength is quite gone (Gn. 17:1; 28:3; 48:3; 49:25); He is both *shelter*, offering protection (*cf.* Is. 4:6), and *shadow*, offering refreshment (*cf.* Is. 32:2); He offers not only a dwelling-place, but, as the verb *abides* indicates, makes Himself our Host and makes us His protected guests (*cf.* Gn. 19:2), safe because it is His duty to keep us safe. **2** Our security is grounded, secondly, on personal faith. Whether we follow the Hebrew 'I will say' or RSV *He . . . will say*, this verse is testimony of the God *in whom I trust*, and, in trusting, I find in Him both *refuge* and *fortress*, One who gives both safety to those who trust and safety from the danger which threatens.

3, 4 The third ground of safety is God's faithfulness. **3** matches the word *fortress*, safety from, and **4** matches *refuge*, safety for. The security offered covers the *snare* (things visible), the *pestilence* (things invisible), the *fowler* (things human). The doubling of the words *pinions . . . wings* (the security the animal world knows), *shield . . . buckler* (the security man devises) denotes completeness. Central to it all is God's *faithfulness*.

5–8 The fourth security is that of character, the righteousness implied by the contrasting fate of the wicked. **5, 6** This security touches all times, *night . . . day*; all circumstances, *darkness . . . noonday*; all dangers, the *arrow* of the human foe, the unseen foe of *pestilence*, and possibly the demonic foe, *destruction* (so the Hebrew may be understood); **7** all catastrophes, even the gravest which might bring death to a *thousand* or even *ten thousand*. None of these expressions, of course, must be understood as saying that the believer will be untouched by worldly calamities. They are to be understood in the light of Ps. 73, that the believer always possesses a wealth and security in God unknown to the world.

9–16 The blessings of security

9 The opening phrase sets the course of the second section of the psalm, as it describes what follows for the one who has made the Lord his refuge. **10–12** The first blessing is that of God's guidance: the angels of God opening out life's pathway (*cf.* Gn. 32:1, 2; 48:16; Ex. 33:2; Acts 12:6–11). **13** The next blessing is victory, the doubly mentioned *lion* representing every opposition of strength, and the doubly mentioned *serpent* every opposing subtlety (Gn. 3:1). **14–16** But the third blessing receives the most attention, the blessing of fellowship with God. On man's side this fellowship is expressed in *love*, knowledge of God's *name* (*i.e.* intimate awareness and joy in the revealed nature of God), resort to God in prayer; on God's side it is expressed, as the words signify, in the deliverance which makes a way of escape (*cf.* 1 Cor. 10:13), the protection which lifts him high above the danger (*cf.* Ps. 27:5), the constant watchfulness which hears and heeds the cry of need, the presence of God known especially when the need is greatest (*cf.* Ps. 23:4), the intervention of God coming in power to the *rescue*, the bestowal of honour in God's sight, a life spent in true self-fulfilment and satisfaction, and beyond all, the full enjoyment of eternal *salvation*.

PSALM 92. A SABBATH HYMN

The association of this psalm with the sabbath is probably due to its spirit of joyful praise and its outlook upon a world cleansed of sinners and evil-doers. In this latter sense, the psalm may be anticipatory of the eternal sabbath rest for the children of God which in its fullness is yet to come (*cf.* Heb. 4:9ff.).

1–3 Introduction

The praise and worship of God is not merely approved by Him as good but is a most pleasant activity for men (*cf.* Ps. 147:1). **1** Thanksgiving focuses upon the *name* (revealed nature) of God as the redeeming Yahweh and the sovereign *Most High* (*cf.* Gn. 14:19, 20, 22) and **2** upon the *steadfast love* and *faithfulness* which are His constant attitudes towards us. The practice of having morning and evening periods of prayer and praise is often mentioned in the Psalter. See, *e.g.*, Pss. 5:3; 42:8; 55:17; 63:6.

4–9 God's works and His judgment on the wicked

God's activity is seen both in His works of creation and in His rule over the affairs of men. It is the latter which the psalmist has most in mind and is most evocative of his praise. **4** *I sing for joy*, or 'exult', because the designs and purposes of God are actually and continuously being disclosed in history (*cf.* Pss. 33:11; 40:5; 139:17). **5** We are thinking His thoughts after Him but usually find them too *deep* for us to grasp (*cf.* Is. 55:8ff.; Rom. 11:33).

6, 7 Men who are dominated by sensuality or by moral perversity cannot discern this providential government in the world nor understand why the wicked flourish as the spring grass. The psalmist not only declares the destruction of the wicked, but implies that their short-lived prosperity is an intentional lesson to the godly (*cf.* Ps. 73:17ff.). **8** This is because the Lord is exalted in judgment (*cf.* Ps. 29:10) and **9** all opposition to Him or His people shall be thoroughly disrupted.

10–15 Personal blessings and God's goodness to the righteous

Adoration of God frequently arises from a realization that we are not merely observers of God's mercy and judgments, but are ourselves caught up into the pattern of His holy beneficence (*cf.* 2 Pet. 1:2–4; Eph. 2:19ff.). **10** This consciousness of being a partaker with God is often expressed by the psalmists in the metaphors of an upraised *horn* belonging to a source of great power (Nu. 23:22; Pss. 29:6; 89:17) and of an inverted horn out of which flowed the anointing *oil*, symbol of identification and incorporation (*cf.* 1 Sa. 16:13; Ps. 45:7). **11** As he feels almost a partner with God, the psalmist knows that he will see and hear of the downfall of all those who oppose the servants of the Lord. He feels that he is inseparable from the triumphant activity of God.

12 The contrast now reaches its climax. It has been suggested in the antithesis of vv. 6 and 11, and is expanded in the imagery of the tall, erect and ever-green *palm tree* which is so superior to the grass underfoot (v. 7). The cedars of Lebanon were noted for their size and excellence (*cf.* Is. 2:13). **13** The imagery of such great trees growing luxuriantly in the house of the Lord has been found previously in Ps. 52:8. **14** The basic idea is that of permanence and nourishment. **15** But behind it lies the thought of acceptance and eternal security with God which leads on to that fruitfulness in which is seen at work the combination of strength and refreshment in the divine *rock* (*cf.* Ex. 17:5, 6; 1 Cor. 10:4).

PSALM 93. THE LORD'S ETERNAL SOVEREIGNTY

If Jerusalem enjoyed an annual festival in which the Lord was specially worshipped as Creator-King (see Introduction), how suitable this psalm would be for use at it! But suitability does not constitute proof, and the psalm rather bears witness to the richness of the doctrine of God the Creator in the OT. In the structure of the psalm we note that vv. 1, 3, 4 describe situations, while vv. 2 and 5 record testimonies. It is as God's people dwell on the basic truths about Him that they are drawn out in devotion and dedication.

1, 2 The Lord in relation to the world

The thought moves through three consecutive points. **1a** First, there is the reigning God, majestic and mighty; **1b** secondly, there is the stable world, and the conclusion is invited, though not explicitly stated, that the stability of the created order depends on the *strength* of its ruling God; **2** thirdly, the people of God, knowing Him personally and therefore able to speak to Him as *thou*, ascribe strength and stability where it belongs and to whom it belongs. They throw in their lot with the unseen power of God known by faith, for it is 'by faith' that 'we understand that the world was created by the word of God, so that what is seen was made out of things which do not appear' (Heb. 11:3), and that what is seen is also maintained by what does not 'appear', the everlasting God.

3–5 The world in relation to the Lord

The order of the first two of the foregoing three thoughts is here reversed so that first we look at the world, then at God, and finally we hear again the testimony of God's people. **3** *The floods* typify the restless fretfulness of the world against the Lord (*cf.* Ps. 46:3, 6; Lk. 21:25, 26), but **4** they can avail nothing against the Lord who in power is *mightier* and in exaltation is lifted up *on high.* Thus in OT thought God the Creator is both world Sustainer, as in the first section of the psalm (*cf.* Ps. 24:1; Is. 40:25, 26), and world Ruler, as here. **5** The reaction of the people of God, again addressing Him directly, is heard. Since their God rules over all, they acknowledge that He rules them also. His *decrees*, that which He has testified to be what He requires of them, are *sure*, *i.e.* to be relied upon as correctly stating

His will and correctly outlining His rules for them; and His basic requirement of those admitted to the fellowship of His *house* is *holiness*, a requirement He will never relax but which will stand *for evermore.*

PSALM 94. AN APPEAL AGAINST THE DELAY OF GOD'S JUDGMENT

The theme of this psalm is the age-old problem of reconciling what happens in the world with the goodness and power of God. Primarily this psalm expresses the immediate reaction of the natural man to the affirmation of faith in Ps. 93. It is the challenge of harsh realism to the confidence of heartfelt trust, a reminder of the anomaly of man's devilry within the moral order established by God. Apart from the invocation in the two opening verses the psalm falls into three parts, each introduced by an inquiry or protest.

1, 2 Introduction

The appeal has no sense of malice about it, but is simply a cry for recompense (*cf.* Je. 51:56c), that all worldly pride may be terminated and all ungodly deeds recoil upon the perpetrators (*cf.* Jb. 4:8; Ho. 8:7a; Gal. 6:7ff.). This process would inevitably accompany the manifestation of divine truth, hence the appeal *shine forth.* The prayer for recompense rests upon a facet of the character of God.

3–15 How long shall the wicked triumph?

3 The query concerns the present period of time; it does not imply any suspicion of divine impotence. The inquiry is elaborated in three respects:

4–7 Facts. 4 The wicked are described as pouring forth a stream of arrogant and boastful words which spring from self-esteem. **5** They are not only pompous ranters but they also *crush* that remnant of devout souls who form the Lord's people and heritage. **6** The appeal to the divine nature implied in the cry for recompense is strengthened by noting that these oppressors vent their spleen on those helpless ones dearest to the Lord (*cf.* Dt. 10:18; Pss. 68:5; 146:9). **7** In doing this, they act as if it were possible to escape the divine Observer, adding folly to their crimes.

8–11 Principles. 8 The lack of discernment (v. 7) is not on God's part but theirs (*cf.* Jn. 9:39ff.). Three principles are declared.

9 First, the Creator must be greater than His creatures; *i.e.* He who made doors of access to the human mind must have the power and right of entry.

10 Secondly, the moral ruler of great historic movements must exercise His holy authority over every man, *i.e.* if the ordinary nations are trained and instructed in right and wrong (*cf.* Rom. 1:18ff.) and are held responsible for their misdeeds (Rom. 1:32), how much more shall He

Himself, teacher of the knowledge of righteousness, be righteous in His rebukes?

11 Thirdly, the Lord knows fully the nature of human thoughts (*cf.* Ps. 139:1-4; Jn. 2:24, 25) and recognizes that *they*, both the thinkers and their thoughts, are as insubstantial as *breath* (*cf.* Pss. 39:5, 6; 62:9).

12-15 Beliefs. After the historical and philosophical, there is the religious aspect. This is a development of the central thought in the previous paragraph (see v. 10). **12** Blessed is he whom God teaches by imposing a discipline upon him (*cf.* Ps. 119:71; Heb. 12:5-9) and instructing him in the law of the Lord, *i.e.* in the nature and meaning of the divine self-revelation. **13** That man is given peace of heart and mind; he is at rest inwardly, even in times of adversity, which will continue until the full and final judgment of the wicked is effected. **14** That ultimate action is inevitable, and equally sure is the faithfulness of the Lord to His chosen people. **15** Judgment will become righteous (contrast vv. 5, 6) and the upright shall follow the way of godliness without hindrance.

16-19 Who shall champion me against evil?

The belief in an ultimate vindication of the moral order provides a poor defence against immediate and unscrupulous injustice. **16** The query is the natural response of the godly man who is oppressed. The answer is implied 'The Lord is my defender', and this is affirmed in detail in the following three verses which correspond to the three aspects previously outlined. **17** The physical threat of being driven to an unjust death, the silence of the grave (see vv. 5, 6), has been averted solely by the providence of the Lord. **18** The psychological peril of slipping from the path of sober-minded trust in God because of the difficulties of going on has been prevented only by the effectual and sustaining mercy of the Lord (*cf.* v. 8; Ps. 145:14; Jude 24). **19** The spiritual danger of lapsing into the intense solitariness of unbelief has never developed because, whenever anxious *cares* surged round his inmost soul, the *consolations* of the Lord ensured real heart-peace (*cf.* v. 14; Ps. 27:5).

20-23 But are the wicked to claim God as their ally?

The satisfactory testimony of the godly soul, to the effect that the Lord fully sustains him in periods of adversity and oppression, did not touch the external situation which is the root of the whole problem. **20** What, then, is God's relationship to the wicked? Is there any divine approval behind the fact that the wicked are in the places of authority and use legal statutes to make wrong appear right?

The psalmist offers no solution to this point but simply reiterates the three major aspects of the matter. **21** He first declares the existence or fact of injustice, as in vv. 4-7. **22** Secondly, he testifies to the Lord's care and protection in his own case, replacing the abstract principles of

vv. 8-11 by personal experience. **23** Thirdly, he affirms his belief in the power and righteousness of God and in the ultimate retribution upon the wicked, as in vv. 12-15. His answer is practical, not theoretical. In the time of trouble the godly man has God and hope, and that is sufficient.

GENERAL INTRODUCTION TO PSALMS 95-100

These six liturgical psalms have a common theme—the joyous adoration of Yahweh as the supreme Ruler of His creation as well as the covenant God of Israel. Although written separately, they have been fitted together into an elaborate choral work centred on the fact that 'the Lord reigns'. The basic structure is the usual Hebraic alternation of parallel themes and it is almost certain that each of these psalms was sung antiphonally. Similar groups of psalms arranged for choral services of praise occur in 113-118 and 146-150.

The anthem begins (Ps. 95) with the knowledge of God imparted exclusively to Israel in connection with the acts of deliverance in Egypt and at the Red Sea. A larger view develops in Ps. 96; Israel is unnamed and the call to worship is addressed to all nations and creatures. Israel's covenant of Ps. 95, 'He is our God and we are His people', is replaced by the natural and general elements in which God is known as Creator of the heavens and Source of all righteousness and truth.

These two aspects of deity are amplified in Ps. 97, where He is described, first as the supreme One before whom creation is ever on the verge of dissolution, and then as the faithful One whose goodness and holiness are always being disclosed to all people through Zion. This great privilege granted to Israel evokes a jubilant song of praise (Ps. 98), not so much on the grounds of Israel's monopoly, but because of the marvel that the divine revelation of salvation should be made known to the ends of the earth.

Nevertheless, although all creation is under an obligation to praise the Lord, He has chosen Zion as the centre and focus of His self-revelation. Consequently Ps. 99 is the most particular of the whole group—the cherubim in Zion's sanctuary, the divine purpose in the history of Jacob, God's personal response to such leaders as Moses, Aaron and Samuel, and His patient mercy in dealing with a wayward nation. Finally, in Ps. 100 the appeal for universal adoration of the Lord is fused, both with Israel's position as His peculiar people, and with the enduring quality of the Lord's mercy and goodness.

This is the most concentrated song of the divine universal enthronement in the OT. The fact that it bears clear marks of liturgical arrangement and use underlines the celebrating of the Lord's Kingship in Temple festivals, and to that extent underlines the possibility of an annual 'Enthronement' Festival. But once again the abiding value is to enter into the riches of OT teaching on God the Creator King.

PSALM 95. PRAISE THE CREATOR'S POWER AND PATIENCE

This great threefold call (vv. 1, 6, 7a) insists that the nature of our response in worship is determined by the nature of God as revealed.

1–5 A God of kingly power

1, 2 Praise and thanksgiving proceed from the fact that God has saved us, **3** and in doing so has shown Himself to be the supreme God and world Ruler. There is only one *God*, but men do find and follow other objects of worship, and in this sense there are other *gods*. On such an occasion as the Exodus, the Lord revealed His supreme power. **4, 5** The facts of creation reveal the power of the Creator (*cf.* Is. 50:3), but also His sole Deity, for in pagan thought the *depths* were ascribed to Molech, the *heights* to Baal, and the *sea* to Tiamat.

6, 7a A God of special grace

Worship in the prostrate posture of utter dedication arises from contemplating His special care of His own people: bringing them into being, as their Maker, superintending the course of their history as Shepherd, and placing His Shepherd's hand of love on each individual.

7b–11 A God of holy wrath

7b Obedience is His due who so signally showed His wrath against the disobedient. **8** This doubting, rebelling state of the *heart* needs continually to be watched, **9** for it led the wilderness-generation to doubt God's ability (Ex. 17:1–7), to forget the evidence of His work (*cf.* Is. 5:12, 18, 19), and **10, 11** to forfeit the promised land (Nu. 14:21–23; Dt. 1:34–39).

PSALM 96. THE UNIVERSAL KING

This psalm shows the extent to which a missionary universalism had entered OT thought. *All the earth* (v. 1) and all *peoples* (v. 7) are summoned into the church. **1–3** In the first movement of the thought the emphasis is that this universal message centres upon the *name* or character of God as revealed to Israel, and the supernatural *marvellous works* He has done for them.

4–6 The second movement exposes the unreality of other *gods* (*cf.* Is. 2:8, 18, 20; 40:19ff.; 41:21–24; 44:12ff.). On the other hand the glory and power of Yahweh are said to be evident in the heavens. See, *e.g.*, Pss. 19:1–6; 33:6; 104:1–3. The attributes of God are represented in v. 6 as His regalia (*cf.* Pss. 93:1; 104:1); His *strength and beauty* were symbolized in the ark of the covenant combining as it did moral

purity (the Ten Commandments) and pardoning grace (the mercy seat).

7–9 The third movement summons all peoples to homage, praise, offering, prayer, opening full membership of God's people to them through the sacrificial offerings.

10 The fourth movement repeats the theme of Ps. 93:1. Men must realize that the Lord is King and that only in Him does the world become stabilized. This cry of acclamation that the Lord is become King echoes against the background of His creation of the world out of chaos.

11–13 The two final stanzas of the psalm seem to be Messianic anticipations. The effect of His coming will be seen in the realm of creation (*cf.* Is. 44:23ff.; 55:12; also Ps. 24:1), and in the realm of government. *To judge* is not (in the OT) necessarily to condemn, but to rule over and to decide about. When the Lord thus rules, the world will for the first time have an utterly righteous government, and be blessed in the knowledge of the truth.

PSALM 97. KING OF ALL, KING OF ZION

Continuing the concluding thought of Ps. 96, the joy of the coming reign of God is called for in the light of His present reign. First, therefore, *the earth* with its far-flung *coastlands* (v. 1; AV 'isles'), and secondly, *Zion* (v. 8) are urged to *rejoice* and *be glad*. This double summons, with its repeated verbs, gives the division of the psalm.

1–7 The nature of God's sovereign rule

1–3 His rule is marked first by morality, for while much about God remains hidden, as with *clouds and thick darkness* He conceals His blazing glory, He has revealed the principles of *righteousness* and the decisions and acts of *justice* on which His government rests. *Righteousness* is holiness in action (*cf.* Is. 5:16b), and *justice* is righteousness applied to specific cases. God's moral nature is not passive, but is a *fire* of holiness (*cf.* Ex. 19:16–18). **4–6** Secondly, it is marked by universality whereby His world-wide, intense power is made known by means of general revelation (*cf.* Ps. 19:1–6). **7** Thirdly, He is to be adored as the only God.

8–12 The response of God's chosen people

Those facets of the divine rule—the morality, and universal rule of the only God—which will one day be clear to all are at present known to and must govern the response of the chosen people. **8, 9** Thus *Zion*, with all its dependent *daughter* villages throughout *Judah*, is summoned to rejoice in the known reality of the *judgments*, or active rule, of the only God, **10, 11** to model their lives on His known moral requirements, **12** and to adore Him as the sole object of their religious devotion.

PSALM 98. TO EARTH'S REMOTEST BOUNDS

This psalm is obviously suited to the Feast of Tabernacles, the paramount feast of Kingship (*cf.* Zc. 14:16f.). Rooted in the Exodus-events (Lv. 23:42ff.), Israel could recall annually their divine salvation, accomplished before the eyes of the heathen. In the light of the Abrahamic promise (Gn. 12:3) God's saving acts were all implicitly world-wide, and this is the theme of Ps. 98: the saving acts of God for Israel, in which the Gentiles also are saved. Hence there is a summons to rejoice: to God's people (vv. 1–3), who ever find something new as they contemplate His salvation and are stirred to new songs of praise; to the whole earth (vv. 4–6), to hail the Lord's universal Kingship; and to all nature (vv. 7–9)—even to His traditional foes, *the floods* (*cf.* Ps. 93:3)—to greet Him as He comes to rule.

1 *Marvellous* has the connotation of miraculous, supernatural. The *hand* and *arm* signify the personal acts of God: He, by Himself, accomplished the victory. **2** *Vindication* is the word basically translated 'righteousness', and signifies His fidelity to His own nature and to His declared purposes in saving His people. **9** *To judge* means to take up active executive control—in the present case, to right all wrongs, redress all imbalances, and to show Himself publicly to be the sovereign King, which has been His incognito status all the while.

PSALM 99. THE THRICE HOLY GOD

This psalm continues the themes which mark the whole group of psalms dealing with the Lord's Kingship: His enthronement and reign (v. 1), His universal sway centred at Zion (v. 2), His love of righteousness (v. 4), His historical revelation of Himself (v. 7). But more than the others it stresses the holiness of the divine King (vv. 3, 5, 9), marking the divisions of the psalm by this as a refrain.

1–3 The Holy King of the world

1 opens and **2** ends with a reference to *the peoples*, and thus the tone of the section is set. While the Lord's Kingship is centred in Zion and it is pre-eminently there that He is known as *great*, yet all must *tremble* and even the very *earth quake* (*cf.* Is. 6:4) before this *holy* God. *Enthroned upon the cherubim*. The golden figures bowed over the ark (Ex. 25:18–22) were thought of as the 'pedestal' of the invisible throne of God. *Cf.* Isaiah's vision of the enthroned God whose flowing robes filled the Temple (Is. 6:1f.).

4, 5 The Holy King of Israel

4 The only people mentioned here is *Jacob*, and the topic is the nature of the Lord's reign among His own. The Hebrew of v. 4 needs no correction, but reads (*cf.* RSV mg.) 'and the king's strength loves justice'. The 'king' referred to is

the Lord, and to say that His 'strength loves justice' means that He delights to use His royal power in doing right. This has been shown to His people in three ways: **4b** first, in His establishing them as a society based on *equity*, a reference to the just and equitable law which He gave to them; **4c** secondly, in His continuing to insist upon and enforce rules of *justice* and standards of *righteousness*, *e.g.* by acts of wrath and punishment against their rebellions (Jdg. 2:11–23) and by the prophets' denunciations (1 Ki. 21:17–24); **5** and thirdly, by providing a way for them to *worship* in His very presence, made welcome before His holiness. *His footstool* must, of course, be the ark itself. The Lord is enthroned above, and His feet rest on the very foundation of all, the place where the holy law of God is satisfied by the sprinkled blood of atonement upon the mercy seat.

6–9 The Holy King of the individual

Names are named in this section: *Moses, Aaron, Samuel*, and some commentators find in them the assertion of the principle of the mediator, the one through whom God's people come to God. The section, however, seems to dwell on God's dealings with them rather than through them to others, and therefore to stress what the Kingship of God means when it is applied to individual lives. It means, **6** first, the privilege of answered prayer; **7** secondly, the obligation of obedience to revelation; **8** and thirdly, submissiveness to the merciful discipline of God.

PSALM 100. ONE GOD, ONE BLESSED PEOPLE

The theme of the Lord's Kingship reaches its climax in this invitation to all the world (vv. 1, 2, 4) to enter into the blessedness which Israel already possesses (vv. 3, 5) of owning and being owned by such a God (*cf.* Eph. 3:6).

1–3 The Lord is God

1, 2 stress the *gladness* of access and worship, and **3** lays the foundation for this joy in the divine Lord Himself as made known in Israel's experience. His threefold claim to possess His people is registered: first, because of creation, for He *made us*; secondly, because of election, for *we are his people* (*cf.* Eph. 1:11, 18); thirdly, because of providence, for as Shepherd He presides over and guides *the sheep of his pasture* (*cf.* Ps. 95:7).

4, 5 The Lord is good

4 The summons to worshipful *thanksgiving* arises **5** from contemplation of the character of the Lord as good, and especially in that His *steadfast love* for us, and His reliable *faithfulness* towards us, are not dependent on anything in us, nor are they divine whims for a moment, but (as the emphasis in the Hebrew makes doubly clear) they are the abiding attitudes and activities of this good God at all times (*for ever*) and *to all* succeeding *generations*.

PSALM 101. THE DAVIDIC IDEAL

Though some commentators see in this psalm a reflection of the ritual 'humiliation' of the king in the course of the 'annual royal festival (see Introduction), and interpret it as his plea for divine intervention based on the righteousness of his reign hitherto, it is simpler to hear in the psalm the coronation oath of the Davidic king, pledging him to those distinctive ideals which marked the monarchy in Judah. The plea, *Oh when wilt thou come to me?* may be an echo of 2 Sa. 6:9, in which case the psalm belongs to David's very early reign, and could well have originated as his dedicatory vow on the occasion of the coming of the ark to Jerusalem. The Christian mind, of course, runs forward to find here the perfect rule of the true Davidic King, the Lord Jesus Christ.

1–4 Personal standards

Vowing to reproduce in his own reign the characteristics of the Kingship of the Lord (v. 1; *cf.* Pss. 99:4; 100:5), he commits himself to that *blameless* holiness 'without which no one will see the Lord' (v. 2a; Heb. 12:14). This comprehensive blamelessness concerns his private life at home (v. 2c), his desires, both of the eyes (v. 3a) and also in making moral judgments (v. 3b), his determined separation from any sin which might *cleave* (v. 3c; Heb. 12:1), and the inmost thoughts which might knowingly dwell on evil (v. 4). 1 *Loyalty* is the word which, when used of the Lord's attitude to us, is translated 'steadfast love' (*e.g.* Ps. 100:5). 2 *Blameless* is rather the positive idea, 'perfect' (Gn. 17:1; Ex. 12:5). *Integrity* belongs to the same word-group as 'blameless'; both express the notion of 'wholeness', such as admits no base alloy in either the outward life or the inner heart. 4 *Perverseness* is rather 'pervertedness', that which is crooked or twisted off course.

5–7 Household standards

Vv. 6 and 7 emphasize that we are here dealing with the court, those who dwell with the king and minister to him. He here pledges the holiness of both home and business, for the king's palace is also his office. 5 The sly traitor and the proud man are out of court, 6 but the trustworthy man and the man of open integrity are in office. 7 The underhand and the liar are excluded. Sins of speech, of heart and of life have no place before the king.

8 Public standards

This is the tell-tale verse which indicates that the whole psalm belongs to the king, for here is exposed the power of the royal sword to purge society (*cf.* Rom. 13:1–7). Such surgical purging of society is his daily task, laid on him as a

religious necessity as king of the Lord's city. It belongs in perfection to the royal Lord and Lamb (2 Thes. 1:8–10; Rev. 21:22–27).

PSALM 102. A PRAYER OF THE AFFLICTED

An anonymous sufferer brings his grief to God; but the comfort he receives is not that of direct relief, but it comes as he contemplates the changelessness of God in His dealings with His people as a whole (vv. 12–22), and the eternal purpose of God which includes in it such grief as he now endures but which will never let His people go (vv. 23–28).

1–11 A cry of suffering and despair

1, 2 After this invocation he proceeds to describe his present sources of grief: **3** the transience of life, **4, 5** ill-health, **6** loneliness, **7** sleeplessness, **8** opposition and division, **9** sorrow, and **10** the burden of divine anger and apparent desertion.

12–22 The unchanging and compassionate Lord

The contrast between man's nature and vicissitudes and God's nature and unchangeableness is introduced with an emphatic *But thou* (v. 12). This part of the psalm is in three stanzas, each of which has Zion for its central thought.

12–14 The time to restore Zion has come. 12 The changelessness of the Lord is expressed in His eternal throne and His enduring character, or *name* (*cf.* Ex. 3:15). **13** Because of this He will come in compassion to Zion, and there could be no more needful time for His *pity* than now. **14** Yet, though the Lord acts out of His own changelessness, it is thus that He shows respect for the desires of His servants. He is not indifferent to what they so deeply feel.

15–17 The effect of the restoration on mankind. 15, 16 All men will revere the glory of the Lord as revealed in Zion's renewal; **17** but once more the Lord's motive is not simply His own glory, but to respond to the prayers of His *destitute* ones.

18–22 The divine nature of the deliverance. 18 It will be recorded for all time, not just that the Lord delivered Zion, **19, 20** but specifically that He heard *the groans of the prisoners*. In all these three sub-sections, therefore, the changelessness of God has focused on this one point: He hears and answers the prayer of the troubled. In this way we see how the meditation on the Lord's ways with Zion meets the needs of the individual praying sufferer.

23–28 Man's weakness and God's strength

The two opening themes of the psalm are now brought together: man's frailty (vv. 1–11) and God's changelessness (vv. 12–22). But the purpose is to show that the relationship between them is not merely one of contrast. Man's changing fortunes (vv. 23, 24), like the wear and tear of the natural world (vv. 25, 26), are due to the active will of the changeless God. Is the psalmist broken down? It is God who has done it (v. 23). Does nature alter? It is God who changes its face (v. 26). Because our changeful lot is thus embraced by changeless and sovereign mercy, the psalmist can end on the note of confidence (vv. 27, 28). God will not forget His servants, and their descendants, of whom the psalmist is himself one, will be established and secure (*cf.* Dt. 10:15). **24** The psalmist excites the divine pity by noting the pathetic brevity of our span compared with His eternity (*cf.* Ps. 89:47); but, more than this, his prayer is an active expression of his belief in the divine sovereignty: he reposes his frailty in God.

PSALM 103. IN PRAISE OF THE GOD OF ALL GRACE

The psalm is an expression of praise evoked firstly by the psalmist's own experience (note the singular pronouns in vv. 1–5). But it is tremendously strengthened by the evidences of the Lord's amazing compassion and mercy toward men in general: His forgiveness and solicitude for such insignificant creatures as men must lead to universal adoration.

1–5 The individual response

1 Blessing God combines the bowing of the knee in reverence for *his holy name*, **2** and opening the heart in adoring gratitude for *all his benefits*. Upon this task the psalmist focuses his essential self, or *soul*, and unites all his individual faculties. **3–5** The enumerated benefits are all spiritual, for it is here that we see the characteristic goodness of the Lord: He cancels sin's debt by forgiveness, counters the *diseases*, or weaknesses with which sin has infected our being, reverses the rewards of sin, exchanging *the Pit* for the crown, and the death which sin brings for constantly renewed life. **3** *Diseases* signifies here not bodily but spiritual disorder, as, *e.g.*, in Ps. 107:17, 20. **4** *Redeems* describes the action of the 'next of kin' voluntarily shouldering the responsibilities of the helpless, as, *e.g.*, Boaz accepted Ruth (Ru. 4:4, 9, 10). So the Lord makes common cause with us in our sin.

6–19 The testimony of the redeemed people

The opening and closing verses of this section stress the universality of the Lord's benevolence (v. 6) and rule (v. 19), but within this world-wide compass, the intervening verses cite the experience of Israel as typical of the Lord's tender care for the oppresssed. **7** To them, through Moses, the truth about God was *made known*, **8, 9** and this is stated first in the form in which Moses received it (Ex. 34:6, 7). But next, the theology of the Exodus-revelation comes alive in experience in the first person plural testimony of vv. 10–14: **10** far from dealing with us on the basis of our merits, **11** He has made us know *his steadfast love*, as different in its greatness

from anything else we have ever experienced as heaven is high above the earth; **12** secondly, He has finally and completely dealt with our sin; **13, 14** and thirdly, He has bestowed a fatherly pity called forth by consideration of our weakness. **15, 16** Association of ideas links v. 15 with v. 14 and, by contrast with man's native frailty, **17, 18** we learn of his eternal security in the Lord. Throughout these verses the hallmark of the people whom the Lord blesses is stressed: *those who fear him* (vv. 11, 13, 17), which is interpreted finally as the obedient ones (v. 18) within the covenant.

10, 12 The whole vocabulary of sin is in these verses: *sins* are outward acts of wrongdoing; *iniquities* are the inner corruptions of the fallen nature; *transgressions* are wilful rebellions against the known will of God. **13** *Pities*. The noun of the same family means 'a womb', translated in 1 Ki. 3:26 as 'her heart yearned': thus our Father loves us with a mother's love. **17** *From everlasting to everlasting*: not simply in its own nature but *upon, i.e.* in its application to, *those who fear him*, and hence speaking of their eternal security (*cf.* Eph. 1:5, 6).

20–22 The universal summons

Calling upon all created beings and things, and at the last coming back to the personal *soul* with which he started, the psalmist summons forth universal reverential adoration or blessing for such a God of grace.

PSALM 104. IN PRAISE OF THE GOD OF ALL CREATION

This is one of the Scripture's outstanding descriptions of the glory of the natural world; it ranks with Jb. 38 and 39. See also Pss. 8 and 29. The psalm may be regarded as a poetical commentary upon the first chapter of Genesis.

1–23 Description

This survey of the external realm of life covers five aspects, viz. the majesty and power of the Lord God (vv. 1–4); the creation of the major terrestrial features of sea and land (vv. 5–9); the inauguration of a comprehensive water-supply for the maintenance of life (vv. 10–13); the provision of food (especially for man) and of the natural means for secure habitation for men and beasts (vv. 14–18); finally, the institution of the daily and seasonal rhythm of life and work (vv. 19–23). Note the range of thought, from the immensity and versatility of the Lord (vv. 1ff.) to the tiring routine of a day in a man's life (v. 23); from the vast labour and purpose of the earth's creation (vv. 5ff.) to the effortless song of a bird on a tree top (v. 12). Similarly the thirst of wild asses (v. 11) is matched by the hunger of young lions (v. 21); the awesome expanse of the deep waters which clothe much of the earth (vv. 6ff.) is contrasted with the restful greenery of meadows and olive groves

(vv. 14ff.); the timid and elusive goats of the high hills (v. 18) are as well known as the beasts of the forest which creep stealthily in the shadows of evening (v. 20).

In particular these verses declare that all creation is subject to the Creator (vv. 1–9), whereby we see His greatness, and that all creation is ordered by the Creator (vv. 10–23), and blended together so as to provide for the requirements of His manifold creatures. Thus the material universe is subject to the needs of animals and man (vv. 10–18), and the animals and man are in turn subject to the seasonal regulations of the universe (vv. 19–23).

2 As light both reveals and also dazzles, so God both shows Himself and hides Himself (cf. Jn. 1:18). Very aptly, then, is *light* His robe. **3** From the observer's point of view the vaulted heavens rest on earth, and we suppose the psalmist to have been here gazing out over the sea to where the heavens of God's dwelling met the waters. *Clouds . . . wind*: all the natural agencies are active only at His bidding. **5–9** are a poetic fantasy on Gn. 1:6–10; **7** God's *rebuke* is His authoritative command, and *the thunder* is the voice of Him who speaks and it is done (Gn. 1:3, 6, 9, 11, *etc.*; Ps. 33:6).

24–30 Meditation

The psalmist turns now to meditation on the fact that this varied and mighty world is utterly dependent upon its Creator. **24** He exclaims first at the multiplicity and variety of God's *works*, then at the magnitude and richness of the divine *wisdom* that brought into being these creatures. **25** He is particularly impressed by the greatness of the sea. It extends so far and contains so much that moves; in it are countless living creatures, on it move ships and animals, all enhancing the sense of wonder we should have toward God's works. **26** *Leviathan* was the mythical sea-monster (cf. Jb. 41:1ff.), symbolic of the mighty power reposing in created life yet utterly subject to the Creator. **27, 28** All creatures are dependent on God for food, **29** for their experiences of distress, for the duration of their lives (cf. Jb. 12:9, 10; 34:14, 15) and **30** for the renewal of their kind in the following generation. All have been created by the Spirit of God who continuously renews earth's natural life from year to year. In the OT as in the NT the *Spirit* is the Lord and life-giver, seen here in His distinctive creative work.

31–35 Supplication

The satisfaction which the world finds by God's providential ordering gives rise to the question whether God is equally satisfied with His world. **31** The psalmist prays that He may be, **32** and at the same time recognizes that He is of power to make all things conform to His will. **33** Consequently he pledges himself to worship this great God and **34** prays for acceptance. **35** But the other side of the truth must be faced with equal realism. The Creator is the Holy One, and ultimately there is no place for sin in His world· The prayer that He might look with pleasure on His creation requires the prayer that all who offend be removed.

PSALM 105. PRAISE TO GOD FOR THE FULFILMENT OF HIS PROMISE

This is the second of four great songs of Israel's history (cf. also Pss. 78; 106; 136). It deals with Yahweh's covenant with Abraham concerning the land of Canaan and rehearses the events which led to its occupation by the children of Jacob. The emphasis throughout this survey is upon the mercy and faithfulness of the Lord as declared in *all his wonderful works* (v. 2; cf. v. 5). Note the constant repetition of 'he'. The pronouns 'he' and 'his' referring to the Lord occur more than 40 times in vv. 5–45.

This detailed rehearsal 'of what he has done', especially in the deliverance from Egypt, concludes with a very generalized and brief statement about the invasion and possession of the promised land. The purpose of this historical survey is primarily to demonstrate the Lord's faithfulness to His covenant, concluded with Abraham (v. 9), reaffirmed in the Exodus (vv. 26ff.) and brought to an interim climax in the gift of the land, the prize reserved for His *chosen ones* (v. 43). This great covenant, as the psalm shows, is all of God and all of grace. No word is spoken about man, either of his sin or of his response to God. It is in this setting that we come to the final verse and the requirement of obedience (v. 45). Here, as Rodd remarks, 'is the true basis of biblical ethics—to keep His statutes . . . not because of fear of punishment, but out of gratitude for God's great goodness. "We love, because He first loved us" (1 Jn. 4:19).'

1–6 The call to worship

1 Ch. 16:8ff. associates the opening verses with David's bringing of the ark into Jerusalem, and doubtless the psalm owes its final form to its regular use at the great annual festivals while the Temple stood. **1, 2** Thanksgiving and testimony, joy, **4** fellowship with God and **5** remembrance are the characteristic privileges of God's people as their attention is focused on the Lord Himself, known by name (vv. 1, 3), on His works—*wonderful*, in that they demand a supernatural origin, *miracles*, in that they cause men to marvel—and on *the judgments he uttered*, the verbal revelation which explained what He was doing. **6** These privileges are theirs because they are God's *chosen ones*, and the purpose of the psalm is to illustrate the reality of this truth, returning to it again in conclusion (v. 43).

7–15 God's covenant with the patriarchs

7 Is it too incredible that God chose a single people for Himself? Nevertheless it is the truth, for though He has shown Himself to be ruler of *all the earth*, yet He is *our God*, **8** and the history of God's people shows that *he is mindful of his covenant.* **9** It began with *Abraham* (Gn. 15:18; 17:1–14) and was reaffirmed as a *sworn promise* to *Isaac* (Gn. 26:2–5), **10** and to *Jacob* (Gn. 28:13–15). **11, 12** That such a promise could be meaningful was contrary to all natural expectation, **13** and indeed contrary to the experience of the patriarchs, **14** yet the Lord proved that He stood by His choice of them by many protective interventions (*cf.* Gn. 12:17; 20:6ff.; 31:24, 42; 48:15, 16). **15** Thus they were shown to be His *anointed ones, i.e.* the recipients of His special favour (*cf.* Gn. 26:27–29), and His *prophets* holding the privilege of direct access to Him (*cf.* Gn. 18:23–33; 20:7).

16–24 Joseph and the settlement in Egypt

God is faithful also to the darker side of His promises (Gn. 15:13), and here we see Him at work to bring His people into Egypt, yet carefully preparing for their welfare there. **16–19** Natural and personal catastrophes are to be accepted from the will of God, who is thus working out *what he had said*, and it is the part of the man of God to accept the discipline and testing which the Lord thus imposes. **20–22** But the ultimate purpose is glorious. God, in whose hand is even the heart of kings, brought Joseph from the prison to the throne in one triumphant movement. **23, 24** At this point, the stage was set for Jacob's entry into Egypt and his initial prosperity there.

25–38 Moses and the deliverance from Egypt

The ways of God are not to be understood at the moment of their being accomplished, but only in such a retrospect as this psalm gives us. **25** The inscrutability of the divine plans is seen in that it was God who *turned their hearts* to persecute Israel. Yet though the Egyptians were instruments in His hand, they were responsible and culpable for their treatment of Israel, for their hatred was their own response of envy and self-interest to this favoured people (Ex. 1:9–14). **26** Against this enmity God had His plans laid and His servants appointed. **27ff.** The sequence of the plagues here is not the same as in Exodus. In this great psalm of the acts of God, the psalmist sacrifices chronology to put first **28** the plague wherein the Egyptians were first forced to assent to the Lord's claims (Ex. 10:24), then, omitting the fifth and sixth plagues altogether, he groups the remaining six plagues around three ideas: **29, 30** the destruction of Egypt's glory in the pollution of the Nile and the defiling of the royal palaces; **31–35** the humbling of Egypt's pride as the granary of the world (*cf.* Gn. 41:57) in the spoiling of its crops; **36** and the blighting of Egypt's hope for the future in the death of the firstborn. **37, 38** But in all this Israel was a separated people (*cf.* Ex. 8:22; 9:4; 11:7), and their distinctiveness was seen in that they left Egypt rich, whereas it was spoiled; vigorous, whereas it was worn out; and

dreaded where once they had been despised as slaves.

39–41 God's care in the wilderness

Three typical miracles of providence are chosen to illustrate further that they were a separate and chosen people. **39a** The protecting *cloud* contrasts with the destructive covering of the locusts (vv. 34, 35; *cf.* Ex. 10:15); **39b** the *light* contrasts with the darkness (v. 28); **40** the provision of food contrasts with the destruction of food (v. 35) and **41** of water with the judgment upon the Nile (v. 29). Egypt typifies the folly of a merely worldly confidence; Israel is miraculously nourished by divine grace.

42–45 The reasons for this wondrous work

42, 43 Behind all God's dealing with Israel lay His faithfulness to His promises. The great family principle which lies at the heart of the divine covenant (Gn. 17:7, 12) meant that, in the chosen Abraham, his descendants, Israel, were also God's *chosen ones* and this description is now filled out with meaning in the light of the age-long history of divine protection and provision which has been surveyed. **44** But chief among the evidences of divine faithfulness was the possession of the promised land, the great seal upon the promises of God. **45** But just as, on the one hand, God's dealings with Israel looked back to His unexplained choice of Abraham, so, on the other hand, it finds its reason in the responsive life of obedience to which it looks forward. Past blessings constitute an inescapable obligation.

PSALM 106. A SAGA OF SINS AND SALVATION

The same history, which in Ps. 105 was reviewed in order to display the grace of God, is here laid under consideration to show the unworthiness of the chosen people. In the former psalm we saw God's faithfulness in the blessings of the covenant; here we see His faithfulness in its punishments. National hymns which deal with national sins are exceptional, and the composition and preservation of Pss. 78 and 106 can be attributed only to an unquestionable hope and an irrepressible faith in the covenanting God. V. 47 does not require the Babylonian captivity as its setting. There could have been no occasion from the entrance into Canaan onwards when some Israelites were not held in alien slavery and when the nation as a whole was not conscious of surrounding paganism. Pss. 105 and 106 reflect the continuing faith of Israel within the covenant and the liturgical expression of this faith in the Temple festivals.

1–6 Introduction

The body of the poem (vv. 7–46) contains four major movements. These are historical in character but they are not handled in strictly chronological order; the psalmist's main aim was to portray the process of spiritual degeneration in a privileged community. The incidents are grouped into the sequence: the Exodus from Egypt (vv. 7–12); episodes in the wilderness wanderings (vv. 13–23); the defaults when twice they approached Canaan (vv 24–31); and the corruption which followed their settlement (vv. 32–46). This section includes an echo of earlier obstinacy (vv. 32, 33) and an allusion to later instability (v. 43). The introductory words of praise and prayer, expressive of the psalmist's delighting in God, declaring His works, doing His will, desiring His blessing both for himself and for the nation, contrast sharply with the confession of sin in v. 6 and show the reality of the forgiveness of sins and of reconciliation with God.

7–12 The Exodus from Egypt

The psalmist's purpose is to display a double truth: that where grace abounded sin abounded, and where sin abounded grace abounded. Hot on the heels of divine redeeming grace, shown at the Exodus, came immediate resentment at the Red Sea (cf. Ex. 14:11, 12), but God did not cease from His saving grace and, delivering them yet again, caused them to trust and praise.

13–23 In the wilderness

13 How fickle the people were in contrast with the changeless grace of God! Three instances are given of craving for personal satisfaction: in the realm of appetite (vv. 14, 15), political equality within the nation (vv. 16–18), and religious licence (vv. 19–23). 14, 15 The desperate craving for meat at Kibroth-hattaavah was a notable crisis in their journeyings (see Nu. 11:4–34). 16–18 The rebellion against Moses and Aaron arose out of a claim of equality amongst all the congregation (see Nu. 16). 19, 20 The making of the bull calf was particularly offensive to the Lord because it was done at His holy mount of *Horeb* (see Dt. 9:8) and because the Israelites ascribed to this image the wondrous works of the Lord (see Ex. 32:4). Note the persistence of this heresy (1 Ki. 12:28b).

23 For Moses' intercession, see Ex. 32:11–14, 31, 32; Dt. 9:18, 19; cf. Rom. 9:1–3.

24–31 Further rebellion

This third section of the main part of the psalm links together the two blunders of the people when they were within sight of the promised land. 24 On the first occasion, at Kadesh-barnea, *they despised the pleasant land, having no faith in his promise* (cf. Nu. 13:32; 14:41). 28 Some years later, when encamped by Jordan at Shittim (Jos. 2:1; Nu. 25:1ff.), *they attached themselves to the Baal of Peor* with licentious idolatry. This was a serious default from the obligations of the covenant; for it arose not from their inexperienced bewilderment (v. 7) or their concern for their welfare (vv. 15–20), but from an inward rottenness, the recurrent malady of unbelief. 30 Hence the plague which was stayed only by the action of Phinehas (cf. Nu. 25:7, 8).

32–46 Corruption in the promised land

These verses describe how the people *mingled with the nations and learned to do as they did* (v. 35). 36–39 This was a deliberate breaking of the covenant with Yahweh and swiftly led to horrible idolatrous practices (cf. Lv. 20:2–5; 1 Ki. 11:7; 2 Ki. 16:3; Ezk. 16:20ff.; 20:23–30). 40 In consequence of this *the anger of the Lord* was aroused and 41–46 the people were oppressed and humiliated—but not without a continuance of His pity (cf. Jdg. 2:11–23).

47 A concluding prayer

The prayer, addressed to 'Yahweh our God', is based upon God's covenant relationship and arises out of the recollection of His unchanging loving-kindness (vv. 44–46). In some measure its four phrases are related to the preceding errors. *Save us* (cf. vv. 41, 42), *gather us* (cf. v. 35), *give thanks* (contrast vv. 25 and 32), and *glory in thy praise* (cf. v. 12 and contrast vv. 23a, 26).

48 Doxology

See on Ps. 41:13   See also on 1 Ch. 16:36b.

BOOK FIVE. PSALMS 107–150

PSALM 107. THE SONG OF
THE REDEEMED

It is frequently held that Ps. 107 must belong to the post-exilic period, since vv. 2, 3 are most easily explained as referring to the regathered community at worship in the second Temple. This is, however, by no means a necessary interpretation, and it may well be that we find here the pre-exilic community viewing themselves as in principle gathered from the world and all its dangers (cf. Weiser). The psalm is grounded on those truths about God and His relation to Israel which are associated character-

istically with the Exodus: note specially the link between vv. 1, 43 and Ex. 34:5–7, and the emphasis on the Lord as Redeemer and Israel as the redeemed (v. 2; cf. Ex. 6:6, 7). The linked theme of judgment and mercy in vv. 33–43 also owes its origin to the Exodus, where the mercy the Lord showed to His people was in the context of His judgment of His foes.

It is illuminating to see the psalm as a meditation on the nation's history as seen in the light of the revelation of God at the Exodus. God has rescued them from the wilderness experiences which beset their forefathers of patriarchal and Mosaic times (vv. 4ff.), the perils of their own sin (vv. 10ff.), the adversity of circumstances typified by the hostile waters (vv. 23ff.). But from whatever part of national history the psalmist drew his inspiration, he distilled from these experiences their essential elements and transformed them into symbols of much wider applicability, four 'figures of the true' which still reappear over and over again in the history of God's people and in the personal experiences of His children.

The psalm falls into six sections: an introduction (1–3); four matching pictures of redemption (4–32): each stanza opens (4, 5; 10–12; 17, 18; 23–27) by describing a period of former peril from which, in answer to prayer (6, 13, 19, 28), they were delivered by divine intervention, and closes with a reasoned exhortation to praise (8, 15, 21, 31); and a summary (33–43) 'which generalizes the testimony and teaching already given' (Eaton).

1–3 The goodness of the Redeemer

Thanks to the Lord is prompted by the awareness that *he is good*. His goodness is demonstrated in His enduring *steadfast love* (v. 1). This, in turn, has been made known in His work of redemption, specified as deliverance from *trouble* (v. 2), and ingathering from the world (v. 3). **1** The translation *steadfast love* (Heb. *ḥesed*) excellently includes the two ideas of absolute faithfulness and warm affection: the two sides of the Lord's regard for His covenant people (*e.g.* Ex. 2:24; Dt. 7:7, 8; Is. 49:14–16). **2** Both noun and verb *redeemed* express Heb. *gā'al*, the basic idea being that of the 'next of kin' to whom belongs the right to intervene and rescue his afflicted relative (*cf.* Ru. 3:9–13; 4:3–10, and commentary *in loc.*). Clearly the relationship was one of right rather than obligation, and as between God and His people it is entirely gracious that He should so relate Himself to us and bear our misfortunes. In its biblical image *gā'al* always contains the associated idea of 'paying a (redemption) price' (*cf.* L. Morris, *The Apostolic Preaching of the Cross*,[3] 1965, pp. 19ff.). **2, 3** The ideas of redemption from *trouble* and from *lands* (or the unwelcome attentions of other people) continue through the psalm.

4–32 Facets of redemption

Much of life's affliction comes before us in the four stanzas of this section: pilgrimage (4–9), imprisonment (10–16), the soul sickness that heralds death (17–22) and the violent storm (23–32). Behind these may lie some meditation on the wandering Abraham, the blind Isaac (Gn. 27:1), the many sorrows of Jacob (*e.g.* Gn. 37:34ff.), but it is best to see them as typifying that element of 'tribulation' out of which God has ever redeemed His people (*cf.* Rev. 7:14).

4–9 Redemption from personal insufficiency. Man's search for fellowship and fulfilment is examined here. **4** He is shown as looking for a *city to dwell in*, a place of community and security. But at Babel God cursed man's effort to make himself secure by means of an entrenched, defended society structure (Gn. 11:4, 8), and in consequence man has never been able to be the architect of his own salvation by measures of social security, or even to find the perfect *city to dwell in*. **5** Not only so, but there is individual failure to find full personal satisfaction, and each remains in some degree *hungry and thirsty*. **6** All this is solved by prayer which, because it is set in *trouble*, recognizes personal insufficiency. *Distress* is anything which makes life 'narrow' or 'cramped'. Contrast the liberty of the children of God (Ps. 4:1; Rom. 8:21; Gal. 5:1). **7–9** By divine responsive action God's provision is immediate and exact. In contrast to their wandering (v. 4), His way is *straight*, and leads to the fellowship and fulfilment they could not achieve for themselves. **8** *Wonderful* expresses 'supernatural', 'miraculous'. Man can find self-fulfilment only by the steadfast love of God working a miracle.

10–22 Redemption from sin. The cause of distress is now rebellion *against the words of God* (v. 11), and *sinful ways* (involving a different word meaning 'rebellion') and *iniquities* (v. 17). **10–16** This idea, common to the two stanzas, is shown first in the setting of bondage. **10** This is bondage of the mind, symbolized by *darkness* (Rom. 1:21; Eph. 4:18), of the bodily capacities (*irons*), and **12** of the *heart*, the effective centre of personality. **11** *Rebelled* (Heb. *mārāh*) expresses the rebellion which chafes against the word of God. *Spurned* means 'to reject with contempt', the sin in question being exposed in all its presumptuousness by the entitling of God as *the Most High* (*cf.* Gn. 14:19, 20). **12** Just as (vv. 4, 5) man cannot be his own saviour, neither can he find any other man to save him. **14, 16** But no bondage proves too hard for the Lord who can *shatter* even *bronze* and *iron*.

17–22 Secondly, rebellion is shown to issue in sickness. **17** Bodily sickness is, of course, in view, for it is the experience of *some* to be visited clearly and directly in this way, but (see RV, which attempts to translate without emendation of the Hebrew) we ought rather to find reference to that sickness unto death which is the wages of sin (Rom. 6:23). *Some were sick* (Heb. 'fools'; see mg. and *cf.* RV). Added to the ill-fruits of sin is the folly of the sinner (*cf.* 1 Tim. 2:14a; Heb. 3:13). *Suffered affliction* is a reflexive verb, possibly signifying 'bring affliction on themselves'. **20** The *word* of God is the key factor. Just as disobedience to the word (v. 11) ushered in the life and fruits of sin, so the word is God's messenger and instrument (Ps. 147:15) for their salvation (*cf.* Eph. 1:13; Jas. 1:18). **22** Only in connection with redemption from sin does the psalm enjoin *sacrifices* (*cf.* Heb. 9:22; 10:18).

The two stanzas therefore define sin as disobedience (vv. 11, 17), and show its temporal (v. 10), personal (v. 12) and eternal (v. 18) results.

23–32 Redemption in life's adversities. In the course of life's ordinary and necessary activities

(v. 23), the people of God encounter ferocious storms. God is both their author (v. 25) and their finisher (v. 29), and the cry of the utterly needy (v. 28) is sufficient for deliverance. As well as being a great psalm of redemption, this is a great psalm of prayer. **24** What we would thoughtlessly call the disasters of life are in fact the *wondrous* (supernaturally accomplished) *works* of the Lord, **25** to be accepted as His will and **31** subsequently the subjects of thanksgiving (*wonderful works* is the same word). **30** The blessing of a guaranteed outcome to life; *cf.* Ps. 73:24.

33–43 The steadfast love of the Lord

The purpose of these two remaining stanzas is to reduce the illustrative material of the psalm to a statement of principle: that the Lord is both steadfast and loving to His redeemed. Two categories of people appear in these verses: on the one hand there are the wicked *inhabitants* (v. 34) and the oppressive *princes* (vv. 39, 40), both justly punished for their sins. On the other hand, there are *the hungry* (v. 36; *cf.* v. 5) and *the needy* (v. 41) who are both inexplicably blessed, provided for and exalted. What is this but to say that the love of the Lord is utter love? The punishment is merited, but as regards the other group, they are loved for no other reason than that the Lord loves them (*cf.* Dt. 7:7, 8).

Equally, His love is steadfast. Once given it is not withdrawn. These verses seem broadly based on the history of Israel from Egypt onwards: **33, 34** the devastation of Egypt and the drying up of the Red Sea; **35** provision in the wilderness (*cf.* Ex. 17:6); **36–38** the occupation of Canaan (*cf.* Dt. 8:7–17); **39–41** the ups and downs of life in the land. It is this last that is significant. On the basis of vv. 33, 34, we must say that v. 39 presupposes wickedness in the people of God (*cf.* Jdg. 2:11–19; 3:7, 8; *etc.*), but the Lord does not abandon them utterly or finally: He intervenes yet again, and yet again raises them up. **42** Consideration of these things will gladden *the upright*, those who are right with God and before men, convict the wicked, and **43** above all establish the great truth of *the steadfast love of the Lord*.

PSALM 108. ANTHEM OF VICTORY

This psalm is composed of two earlier fragments, viz. Pss. 57:7–11 and 60:5–12. Evidently they were joined together for use in Temple worship. Whoever compiled this psalm selected only those portions which expressed confidence in the Lord. For details consult the notes on the original psalms, but observe the effect created by the juxtaposition of these two fragments. Together they offer a striking instance of true biblical faith. Human steadfastness (v. 1) rests upon divine steadfastness (v. 4; note the connecting *for*). Divine steadfastness is expressed in

great promises (vv. 7–9) which give confidence in coming victories (vv. 10–13).

PSALM 109. RIGHTEOUS INDIGNATION

This is by far the most outspoken of the imprecatory psalms (see Introduction). Its three major sections are a plea for divine help because of a false and unjustified attack upon the psalmist (vv. 1–5), a comprehensive curse invoked upon one man who has clothed himself with cursing (vv. 6–20; *cf.* v. 18), and a prayer for divine protection and for judgment upon adversaries (vv. 21–31). Such vehement imprecations as are found in vv. 6–20 are not easily assigned to one who trusted in the Lord (vv. 21–31) and sought His blessing above all else (vv. 26, 28). There are two approaches to the difficulty. In view of the plain distinction that vv. 6–19 speak only of *him, his* and *he*, while the psalm elsewhere speaks of *they* and *them* who are opposed to *I* and *me*, some (*e.g.* Weiser) have urged that this passage is a quotation of curses directed against, not spoken by, the one who prays (v. 7b). This view finds some further support in that vv. 1–3 declare that *they* have beset the psalmist with words of hate. Yet there has been no just occasion for this attack (v. 3b). The psalmist has given love and received hatred; he has encountered evil in return for good (v. 5). Nor is there anything in the poem to suggest a sudden reversal of this righteous attitude.

Against this view there are four objections. First, that there exists a righteous indignation against evil (*cf.* Mt. 23:13ff.) which is an echo of divine wrath. This psalm is unique only in its detail, not in the nature of its utterances.

Secondly, the imprecatory words in vv. 6–19 are in part a prayer that the Lord should remember His own word (Ex. 20:5b) and visit the iniquities of the parents upon their children (vv. 14, 15). In part, also, they are an appeal, so often heard in the Psalter, to the universal law of retribution (see vv. 17–19 and *cf.* Gal. 6:7). There is, in fact, no essential difference between vv. 19 and 29; if a man deliberately surrounds himself with cursings, he must, inevitably, be the first to feel the backlash of his own malevolence. It must be remembered that 'God deems it just to repay with affliction those who afflict you' (2 Thes. 1:6; *cf.* Jude 15).

A third objection is that Peter in Acts 1:20 not only includes Pss. 69 and 109 within the authorship of David, but attributes the two 'curses' he selects to the inspiration of the Holy Spirit, and asserts that they were prophetically uttered 'concerning Judas' (Acts 1:16). Peter obviously identifies the psalmist with Jesus and sees in Judas the enemy who has returned hatred for love. It is inevitable, therefore, that he should fall into condemnation, and vv. 6–19 point to that.

Fourthly, it must be noted that v. 20 expresses the wish that vv. 6–19 may come upon his foes, and, even if only by this clear implication, he makes them his own.

1–5 A prayer for help

The psalm opens on the note of prayer which it maintains throughout. The purpose of the psalmist is not to initiate vengeful action but to place the whole matter in the hands of Him to whom vengeance belongs (*cf.* Lv. 19:18; Dt. 32:35; Rom. 12:19). Before considering the imprecations we are allowed to feel the provocations. Wickedness, deceit, lies, hatred (vv. 1–3) have been the psalmist's portion, not only *without cause* but in base return for love, prayer and good (vv. 4, 5).

1 *God of my praise* expresses both the fact that he is accustomed to praise God and the fact that God is worthy to be praised. In such a context as the present, it is an indication of the psalmist's spiritual stature that the note of praise is the first to be sounded (in the Heb. taking precedence over the request *Be not silent*). **3** *Attack*; lit. 'make war on'. **4** *Accuse*; Heb. root *śāṭān*, whence Satan. *I make prayer*; lit. 'and I prayer': the juxtaposition of pronoun and noun indicating that the psalmist was 'all prayerful concern' for his foes.

6–20 A prayer for justice

6–15 concentrate upon the ill-desert that should attend the man who has thus acted towards the psalmist, whether we think the singular *him* (vv. 6ff.) to be the ringleader and chief instigator or to be in effect distributive, signifying 'each'. Nothing can diminish the terrible content of this prayer, yet based as it is on the principles of exact retributive justice which Scripture reveals, and addressed to the God from whom those principles derive, it does no more in fact than spell out in detail what we would more readily hide under some such pious formula as 'Thy will be done'. The prayer touches the man himself (vv. 6, 7), the involvement of the future with his present sins (vv. 8–13) and his own involvement with the inherited past (vv. 14, 15).

6, 7 Three opponents: beside him *an accuser* (Heb. *śāṭān*) as *wicked* as himself; before him a judge to pronounce him *guilty*; and above him a God who sees his *prayer* as a tainted thing of *sin*—for there is no mercy for the merciless (Mt. 18:35; Jas. 2:13). **9** *Cf.* the principle enunciated in Ex. 20:5, and illustrated in Jos. 7:24, 25; Am. 7:17. This is not contradicted by Ezk. 18:1f., where the teaching is that the grievous entail of the past does not bind the penitent and consecrated individual. **14** The *iniquity* of former generations is not an excuse for his conduct but an aggravation of his guiltiness (*cf.* Ps. 51:5). This is the individual counterpart of the principle applied nationally in Lk. 11:50, 51.

16–19 explore the grounds on which such a dire sentence might be passed on the wicked man. His basic lack of good will showed first in complete absence of pity for the needy (v. 16a), next in active hostility towards them (v.

16b); he went on to indulge his propensity for malevolence (v. 17), and finally adopted it as the deliberate policy and mark of his life (vv. 18, 19). **16** *Poor and needy* represent those without natural or social resources for their own defence, who easily become 'downtrodden' (as the former word suggests) and are inevitably 'compliant' (as the latter suggests) to more powerful interests. **17** All sin has a 'boomerang' quality: the prayer here takes note of the fact (*cf.* Ps. 37:14, 15). **18** Clothing often has a symbolic force, representing both the character and the capacity of a person (*cf.* Is. 11:5; 59:17; 61:10).

21–31 A prayer for protection

The foregoing anathema describes what God would do to the wicked if they reaped what they had sown. But the psalmist pleads for his own treatment on another basis. **21** *Deal on my behalf* (not as I deserve but) *for thy name's sake* and *because* (of) *thy steadfast love*, an appeal to the character and kindness of God made all the more acute **22–25** because of personal helplessness. **26** introduces the final prayer for divine help. This is uttered in full confidence (as in Pss. 22:22ff.; 35:27ff.; 69:30ff.) because, unlike his opponent, his Lord is characterized by *steadfast love* (*cf.* v. 16). **27** The prayer asks for some unmistakable act of God, **28** whereby God will show that for Him there is a difference between the righteous and the wicked and **29** which will issue in their dishonour: their 'reaping of shame' will be as plain to all as is their outer clothing. **30, 31** The psalmist finally anticipates his action of public praise to the Lord, because, unlike the circumstances of vv. 1, 2, where the adversaries prosecuted him, the Lord is at his right hand as an advocate to protect him and deliver him from his antagonists.

PSALM 110. KING AND PRIEST FOR EVER

The Davidic authorship, divine inspiration and Messianic meaning of this psalm are clearly maintained in the NT (*e.g.* Mt. 22:43–45; Mk. 12:36; Lk. 20:42) and given a Christological interpretation (see Acts 2:34, 35; 1 Cor. 15:25; Heb. 1:13; 5:6; 7:17, 21; 10:12, 13). The exaltation of Christ to 'sit at the right hand of God' is frequently referred to elsewhere (*e.g.* Mt. 26:64; Heb. 1:3; 8:1; 12:2; 1 Pet. 3:22). This does not mean, of course, that it had no contemporary significance. Like all the royal psalms, while it had fulfilment only in the Messiah, it was a pattern held up before the reigning Davidic king to remind him of the ideal which he was expected to embody. Some modern interpreters suggest that this psalm even contains an outline of the ceremony of enthronemment of the king in Jerusalem (*e.g.* L. Dürr, in A. Bentzen, *King and Messiah*, 1955, pp. 22, 23).

The structure of the psalm is interesting. Its two main sections are each introduced by a divine utterance (vv. 1, 4), and the contents of each section are parallel to each other, so that the whole is self-interpreting and complete. Its theme is the royal priest, appointed to be king (1) and universal priest (4), ruling by divine agency both over his own people (2) and his foes (5), enjoying consecrated obedience (3a) and the world-wide extension of his sway (6), continually refreshed with new life (3b) and timely renewal (7).

1–3 The authority of the priestly king

1 *The Lord says* is a very forceful expression, 'Oracle of Yahweh', its solemnity underscoring the importance of the inauguration of David's Lord (*cf.* Mt. 22:45) to the place of highest authority at Yahweh's *right hand* (*cf.* Heb. 1:3, 4). **2** Centred in Zion (*cf.* Heb. 12:22), and destined to expand by the agency of the Lord, His rule is now *in the midst of your foes*—*i.e.* in contrast to the actively spreading rule of vv. 5, 6, the king is here seen with his own people, who are characterized (v. 3a) by glad acquiescent enlistment in royal service. **3** *Upon the holy mountains* gives poor sense: in the light of the promise of foes overthrown (v. 1), and expanding dominion (v. 2) and a gladly volunteering people, it is an anticlimax to find that nothing more is afoot than a march on (presumably) the hills around Zion. The alternative rendering 'in holy array' (RSV mg.; *cf.* 1 Ch. 16:29) gives the view of a priestly people, consecrated and clad for holy service. The king with his attendant priests (vv. 1–3) thus balances the priest with his attendant soldiers (vv. 4–7). *The womb of the morning* is a picturesque way of suggesting where the dew originates. It may also (*cf.* Is. 14:12) be using the language of an ancient mythology to suggest supernatural, heavenly origin for the king. *Your youth.* Does this mean 'the young (men of the people)' whose youthful freshness will be as dew to the king, or 'your youth(ful prime)', in which case *the dew* is God's fresh life ever preserving the king in 'the power of an indestructible life' (Heb. 7:16)? The latter accords well with the foregoing reference to *the womb of the morning*, with the dew as life-giving (Is. 26:19; Ho. 14:5), and as coming secretly (2 Sa. 17:12).

4–7 The power of the royal priest

The positions are now reversed. Yahweh stands at His royal priest's *right hand* (v. 5), lending His power. Authority of position (v. 1) is thus balanced by power of accomplishment (v. 5) issuing in world-wide conquest (v. 6)—a task in which the zeal of the royal priest will allow him to do no more than snatch quick refreshment from the opportune stream (v. 7), an earthly resource contrasting with and matching the heavenly life of v. 3b. **4** *Melchizedek* (Gn. 14:18) possessed a Gentile priesthood which was also acknowledged by Abram and was therefore in principle world-wide. Priest of 'God Most High, maker of heaven and earth', he also possessed in principle world-

wide sway as vice-gerent of his God. Very likely a Melchizedek type of priesthood survived in Jerusalem and was ultimately taken into the line of David, to become a different type of priesthood from that of Aaron and to represent more fully the royal priesthood of Messiah (*cf.* Heb. 7). **6** The military metaphor continues but the picture is that of establishing a universal and unchallenged sway (*cf.* Ps. 72:8–11; Is. 9:7). The OT describes in the terms nearest to hand (*cf.* Is. 11:14–16) what the NT portrays as the universal mission of the church, a warfare (Eph. 6:10f.; 2 Tim. 2:3f.) in the interests of 'another king, Jesus' (Acts 17:7). *Shatter chiefs* (lit. 'shatter (the) head'); *cf.* Gn. 3:15. **7** *Lift up his head; i.e.* in token of lordship and conquest.

PSALM 111. THE WORK OF THE LORD

Pss. 111, 112 are a pair: both consist of ten verses and each poem contains twenty-two phrases which are arranged as an acrostic, the phrases successively commencing with the letters of the Hebrew alphabet. Almost every phrase consists of just three Hebrew words, and in both poems the last two verses contain three phrases and not two as is the case in the other verses. The two psalms deal with twin themes. Ps. 111 is in praise of the Lord; Ps. 112 is a panegyric of the godly man.

The references to the assembled congregation (v. 1), the works of the Lord (vv. 2, 3, 4, 6, 7) and the covenant (vv. 5, 9) suggest that the psalm was designed for use at Passover or Tabernacles in the pre-exilic community. (*Cf.* Weiser; contrast Kirkpatrick.)

1 The psalm opens with the worshipper's declared intention of giving thanks. *Company* stresses the element of 'fellowship' (*cf.* Ps. 25:14), *congregation* the element of 'assembly'. *Upright*, while not etymologically belonging to the 'righteousness' family of words, contains the like ideas of being right with God and right before men, as here (*cf.* v. 8). **2** The psalm proceeds to ground this thanksgiving on what is known of the Lord and His works, noting **2a** their greatness, **2b** how they delight His people, **3** what they declare of God, and **4** how He has required remembrance to be kept of them (*caused . . . to be remembered* means 'appointed a remembrance (feast)'; *cf.* Ex. 12:24–27; Lv. 23:42, 43). The content of the remembrance now follows in neatly rounded form. **4b** Reference to God's character (*cf.* Ex. 34:6) opens and closes the sequence (*cf.* v. 9c); **5** next His covenant with its associated blessings of provision (*cf.* Ex. 16:4, 12) and redemption (*cf.* v. 9a, b); **6–8** finally, and most suitably if the people were engaged in a ceremony of renewing the covenant (*cf.* Dt. 31:9–13), the gifts of the land and the law, *i.e.* a place to live and a manner of life. **9** *Redemption* (Heb. *pᵉḏûṯ*) stresses the price paid (*cf.* Ex. 13:13; Nu. 3:46–48). *Terrible*; 'to be reverenced, or feared'. **10** God is revealed in grace (v. 4), law (v. 7) and holiness (v. 9); so, here, in reverse order, the response is awesome fear (10a), obedience (10b) and praise (10c).

PSALM 112. THE WAY OF A GOOD MAN

The theme of the concluding verse of Ps. 111 is developed, and a description is given of the life of a God-fearing man who is made in the likeness of his God. **1** The proposition is that fear of the Lord and obedience bring blessedness, complete well-being. The facets of a life of well-being are, **2, 3** first, prosperity, seen in influential (2a) and upright (2b) descendants, earthly sufficiency (3a) and personal character (3b); **4, 5** secondly, generosity, translating v. 4 with reference to the 'blessed man', 'he rises up as light . . . for the upright (*i.e.* he is a source of comfort, *etc.*, to his fellow-believers), being gracious, merciful, and righteous' (see RSV mg.). He is thus like God (Ps. 111:4). Generosity marks all his dealings (5a), in the setting of true discernment (*justice*, 5b). **6–8** The third facet of well-being is stability, in adversity (7a) and in character (7b, 8). **9, 10** The psalm concludes with a contrast clinching the argument: the godly man is generous, enduring and exalted; the wicked man is grudging, evanescent and disappointed.

GENERAL INTRODUCTION TO PSALMS 113-118

These psalms have been linked in Jewish liturgies with the feasts of Passover and Tabernacles. In the Jewish home, at Passover, Pss. 113, 114 are sung before the meal and Pss. 115–118 after (*cf.* Mt. 26:30; Mk. 14:26). The title 'Egyptian Hallel' is sometimes given to this collection because of the exceptionally fine poem of the Exodus (Ps. 114), and also in contradistinction to the title 'The Great Hallel' (Pss. 120–136).

PSALM 113. THE UNIQUE LORD

Ps. 113, 114 are well paired. The former states a truth, the latter records the supreme example of that truth. We will grasp Ps. 113 best if we suppose that it is written to answer the question, What is distinctive about the God of Israel? The psalm replies in three ways, rising to the climax of the third.

1–3 His praise

1 While those who serve the Lord and know His nature as revealed in His *name* may well encourage each other to praise Him, **2, 3** He is worthy of praise also for all time and from every place. *Blessed . . . praised.* The form of each verb suggests 'worthy to be . . .'. To 'praise' is to acknowledge with joy what God is;

to 'bless' has the added suggestion of kneeling in worship.

4–6 His exaltation

The 'highness' of the Lord links these verses: **4a** not even the collective might of all humanity, **4b** nor the physical marvel of the lofty heavens can overtop Him. **6** Indeed, He must 'make Himself low' (*cf.* AV, RV; lit. 'who acts in lowliness to see . . .') if He is even to bring the heavens within His vision!

7–9 His compassion

But the true uniqueness of the Lord is not His meriting of universal, endless praise, nor the sheer fact of His transcendence, but **7** that He draws near to the needy to deliver them, **8** to transform their state and **9** to satisfy their longings. *Cf.* 1 Sa. 2:1–8; Pss. 103:4; 105:17–22; Is. 49:19–21.

PSALM 114. THE UNIQUE EVENT

The truth of Ps. 113 now receives its crowning illustration, wherein the Lord is seen to be supreme over the nations (v. 1), identified with the outcast (v. 2), sovereign over the natural order (vv. 3–7), and preserver of the needy (v. 8)—the Exodus from Egypt. Note the absence in this psalm of the effective cause, 'the name of the Lord', which is so conspicuous a phrase in the preceding and following psalms. The omission makes the introduction of 'the Lord' (v. 7) remarkably impressive.

1, 2 Redemption and indwelling

The Lord's redemptive work is not just a beginning, an act of deliverance. It is a total work accomplishing total transformation, catering for every need. In its poetical exemplification of this the psalm opens by asserting that **1** when the Lord redeems, **2** He also indwells. This is the same as to say that He redeems because He loves: His is no impersonal concern for the social amelioration of Israel. He desires this people for Himself, and fulfils the desire by coming to live among them. On the other side, from Israel's point of view, redemption involves **1** separation from the world and **2** separation unto the Lord. *Judah . . . Israel.* The people of God are here described in the light of their main later components, and in the light of the fact that the Lord's *sanctuary* was on Mt. Zion in *Judah*.

3, 4 Creation and completion

That Israel's Redeemer is the world's Creator was shown by the natural marvels attendant upon the Exodus: **3** the dividing of the Red Sea (Ex. 14:21ff.) and of Jordan (Jos. 3:14–16); **4** the marvels at Sinai (Ex. 19:16–18). But the miracle at Jordan also underlines the truth that the Lord brings in to the promised land those whom He brought out of Egypt: He begins, He also completes, and the assurance that He can do so is the supremacy of His power as Creator, whereby no power can resist Him or barrier stand in His way.

5–8 Compassion and provision

5, 6 The questions hurry us forward to the climax: **7** this earth-shaking work (vv. 3, 4), performed by *the Lord* in person, was wrought for one as weak, unimpressive, often even despicable a person as *Jacob*! Behind the work of redemption is the attitude of compassion towards the needy and the sinful. **8** But compassion did more than prompt the action. It prompted those works of provision whereby the pilgrims were sustained on the way (*cf.* Ex. 17:1ff.; Ps. 107: 35).

PSALM 115. NOT TO US, O LORD

This psalm gives an insight into one aspect of Israelite worship: the responsive participation of leader and congregation. This seems a reasonable deduction from the arrangement of vv. 9–11 where we can readily hear a single voice pronouncing the first half of each verse, the second half being a congregational response. Vv. 14, 15 sound like two halves of the congregation responding to each other.

There is, of course, no need to follow the older commentators in requiring a post-exilic date. Those who 'fear the Lord' (vv. 11, 13) are not necessarily Gentile proselytes, and even if the phrase had that technical meaning, there were proselytes at every period of Israel's life. But Ps. 22:23 indicates that the God-fearers in question are the people of Israel. It is altogether simpler to see here the congregation assembled for worship at one of the great festivals in monarchic days.

The opening verses, with their appeal to the glory due to the Lord's name (*cf.* Jos. 7:9; Dn. 9:18, 19; *cf.* Nu. 14:15, 16; Is. 48:11), may suggest that the psalm was designed to focus attention and trust upon God in a time of national emergency, but it is more probable that a festival purposing to recall the mercies of God in Exodus times would equally prompt the remembrance of national shortcomings and issue in this confession that Israel can base no plea on personal deserving but only on the name and nature of God.

1–8 Honouring God

Whether facing some great crisis, or simply looking forward into another year from the vantage-point of an annual festival, Israel emphatically puts God first:
1, 2 Jealous and loving. They are concerned to say before anything else 'Hallowed be thy name', and it is their belief that God is equally concerned. He is jealous for His own glory (*cf.* Ex. 20:5; 34:14; Dt. 4:23, 24; Is. 42:8). But if God were to act solely for His own glory, how could sinful Israel be spared? Therefore the

plea is also to His *steadfast love* and *faithfulness,* expressive of His covenanted attitude towards Israel.

3–8 Alive and sovereign. 3 Were Israel to reply to the taunting question (v. 2; *cf.* Ps. 42:3, 10) it would be that God is in heaven, sovereignly free to accomplish His will, a truth pointed up by a responsive taunt (*cf.* Is. 44:6–20) on the deadness of idols: as to **4a** their material, **4b** origin, **5–7** lifelessness and **8** influence. It is characteristic of the OT's monotheism to see all other gods in this light, for, of course, no idolatrous people thought of its god as dead matter!

9–18 Trusting God

True honour for God passes over into living faith as its first evidence.
9–11 Reliance is the first element in trust. God is able both to support (*help*) and protect (*shield*) those who trust Him. Such simple reliance is to mark every member of God's people: **9** merely to belong to *Israel* is not enough; **10** nor to have a professional status; **11** nor a reputation for religion: all alike must come in personal reliance on Him.
12, 13 Assurance next marks God's people: assurance concerning His attentiveness and His benevolence: He *has been mindful*, He *will bless*, and in this none is overlooked. Not only are the three categories repeated from vv. 9–11, but there is the added reassurance, *both small and great*.
14, 15 Prayer follows as an essential component in genuine trust, for trust is the attitude which seeks God alone for help and sees in Him an utter sufficiency for His people's present (*you*) and future (*your children*) needs. This trustful attitude, expressed in prayer, is grounded on the almightiness of God, exemplified in His creation of *heaven and earth*.
16–18 Dedication is the coping-stone on the edifice of trust. It is confident self-committal. The three verses are in an observable sequence of thought: **16** God, who possesses all things, has allocated this earth as the sphere of human activity. **17** Time is not unlimited: all too soon death comes to silence the voice of earthly praise. **18** Consequently, worshipful adoration and joy in the Lord, starting *from this time* and continuing ceaselessly, should characterize His people. The final *praise the Lord* is the firstfruit of this dedicated spirit.
17 Too often this verse is made the substance of a supposed OT view of death, bringing it into conflict with the evidence, *e.g.*, of Pss. 16:9–11; 17:15; 49:15; 73:23, 24. Reference to Pss. 6:5 and 88:4f. is misplaced, since they are specifically concerned with the awful possibility of death under God's wrath. The present verse is to be understood in the same sense as Cowper's words, 'When this poor lisping, stammering tongue lies silent in the grave'. Then the earthly praise will be over: gone for ever the opportunity to praise the Lord in the circumstances of this life. Of this alone v. 17 speaks, and does not

warrant or invite further deductions concerning the state of the dead.

PSALM 116. THE PATTERN OF DEDICATION

This is a peculiarly personal song. Amid the surrounding psalms of corporate worship, it records the voice of the worshipping individual. We find him, in the presence of the assembled congregation, testifying of a divine deliverance personally experienced, and preparing to offer a sacrifice of thanksgiving (v. 17). Maybe this psalm evidences another feature of the liturgy of the sacrifices: the personal confession of the individual, appropriate to the sacrifice which he is offering.

1–9 I love

Each of the three sections of this psalm is an amalgam of recollection and dedication. In this first part, he recollects how God heard and answered prayer in a time of great need, and he records how, as a result, he loves the Lord (v. 1), will ever continue to pray (v. 2), and will live henceforth for God (v. 9).

1, 2 *Heard . . . inclined.* The second verb adds the thought that hearing prayer is an attitude deliberately adopted by the Lord. **3** Without being told the nature of his trouble, we learn of its severity: it seemed likely to end in *death. Sheol* is the place-name of the abode of the dead. **4** *Name.* He laid hold in prayer on all that God had revealed of Himself. **5** *Gracious . . . merciful. Cf.* Ex. 34:6, 7. The Lord proved true to His name. **6** *Simple.* The word describes the 'young and inexperienced', consequently lacking true guiding principles for life. The thought is that the Lord preserved one who was helpless to preserve himself. **9** *I walk.* The wholesale deliverances noted in v. 8 would be better suited by the dedicatory 'I will walk' (AV, RV). *Cf.* Gn. 17:1.

10–14 I will lift up

V. 10 in RSV sounds a self-congratulatory note which accords ill with the rest of the psalm, and especially fails to prepare for the key verses 12, 13. Possibly we should translate, 'I believed: though I kept saying. . . . It was I who said in consternation . . .' Here the stress lies on the poor quality of the faith which has so signally failed to measure up to the tests of life. But to this poor faith, the Lord replied with *bounty* (v. 12), and realizing how much he yet needs, he resolves to take the proffered salvation (v. 13a), persevere in prayer (v. 13b) and launch out in public commitment (v. 14). **11** Possibly in his time of stress he had looked to men for help, and finding none, fell into a panic, believer though he was. **13** *Cup. Cf.* Ps. 16:5, the cup is one's personal 'lot'; Ps. 75:8, the cup is the portion allotted by the Lord. For the psalmist He has bountifully decreed (full)

salvation (plural of amplification), and he gratefully takes it up.

15–19 I will offer

How is the personal desire to be in a loving relation to God (v. 1) and to experience His saving benefits (v. 13) brought to fruition? This section shares with the previous ones two features of dedication: commitment to pray (v. 17b; *cf.* vv. 2, 13) and to public devotion (v. 18; *cf.* vv. 9, 14). But it adds a new leading feature: love (v. 1) and receptivity (v. 13a) are fulfilled in the offering of sacrifice (v. 17). Only thus is God truly met in fellowship and is the dedicated life solemnized. Behind this supreme moment lies thankful recollection and testimony: the death of God's people does not happen lightly, but is a thing prized and guarded by Him (v. 15). The psalmist's recollection of how near he came to death (*cf.* vv. 3, 8) and yet was drawn back, confirms to him that he is under divine lordship (v. 16a, b) and that his lord's decree was for his liberation from the bondage of trouble (v. 16c). Consequently, dedication must be the order of the day, solemnized in the approved manner, bathed in prayer (v. 17) and sealed by public witness (vv. 18, 19).

17 Thank-offerings were peace-offerings (Lv. 7:11–15), and therefore contained the elements of the fellowship meal (Lv. 7:15) signifying peace with God and men, atonement (Lv. 3:2) as the ground of peace, and consecration (Lv. 3:5).

PSALM 117. ALL NATIONS

This doxology is akin to Ps. 100. Its comprehensiveness offsets the individual prayer of Ps. 116. **1** *All nations*; *i.e.* all Gentiles (note Rom. 15:11). **2** *Great . . . toward us.* The acts of God for Israel (*us*) are of world significance. The chosen people exemplify what God desires on a universal scale, and the salvation He works for them is the salvation of the world.

PSALM 118. HIS STEADFAST LOVE ENDURES FOR EVER

This hymn, expressive of high spiritual elation, is a processional song for varied voices. The occasion cannot be positively determined. Former commentators thought of dedication feasts as in Ezr. 6:15f.; Ne. 8; 1 Macc. 4:54ff.; 2 Macc. 10:1ff. But evidence for any post-exilic date has never been strong. Jewish sources, Targum and Talmud, say that the psalm was used for antiphonal singing in the liturgy and connect it with the Feast of Tabernacles. In line with this, recent exposition associates the psalm with the postulated autumn festival of enthronement in which the Davidic king, symbolically put in jeopardy by his foes, is delivered by the Lord and restored to kingship. The psalm was sung in the triumphal procession, culminating in sacrifice: vv. 1–18, on the way to the Lord's house; vv. 19, 20 at the entrance; vv. 21–25 as the procession moved on to the altar; v. 26, the priestly greeting; and vv. 27–29, the worship accompanying the sacrifice.

1–4 Invocation

The psalm commences and concludes with a phrase that had evidently become a liturgical formula. *Cf.* 1 Ch. 16:34; 2 Ch. 5:13; Ezr. 3:11; Ps. 136. **2–4** For the triple call to praise see Ps. 115:9–11.

5–19 The approach to the Lord's house

The king, as Melchizedek priest (*cf.* Ps. 110:1), leads his people in joyful worship. Behind him and them lies the threat from hostile worldly power (*cf.* vv. 10–12), sometimes actualized in foes such as Sennacherib (2 Ki. 19) but ever-present. *Cf.* on Pss. 46–48, esp. 48:4–8. Whether in symbol as part of the autumn celebration of Tabernacles, or in grim reality, the threat has been dispersed and faith in the Lord vindicated. It is likely that the voice of the royal leader is heard in vv. 5–7, the congregational response in vv. 8, 9; vv. 10–12 are antiphonal, the people responding in the repeated words; possibly we hear the same corporate voice replying to the king in vv. 14, 15b, 16b, and the king's great affirmation at the Temple gate in vv. 17–19.

5 Historically exemplified in 2 Ki. 19:1–3, 15–19. If those commentators are correct who, on the basis of psalms like this, suppose an annual royal festival, there was a symbolic humiliation of the king, instancing the truth that his throne did not depend on force of arms and that, militarily speaking, worldly forces were ever stronger. But the prayer of faith prevailed: David's throne rested on divine promises. **17, 18** The royal psalms are full of the terminology found here: the threat of *death* (*cf.* Pss. 22:15; 48:14 'our guide even unto death', *cf.* RV), **19** the consequent life of *righteousness* (*cf.* Ps. 24:5, RV).

20–26 From the gate to the altar

Possibly the priests, guardians of the Temple, now meet the procession, laying down the condition (v. 20) that none but the *righteous* can enter (*cf.* Pss. 15:1ff.; 24:3–6). The king replies in testimony that God has saved him in answer to prayer (v. 21), thus declaring him to be in the right with God. The popular response (vv. 22–24) rejoices in God's choice of His king and in His bestowing on His people such a day of gladness. Now the priests turn and lead the procession on as they voice prayer and benediction (vv. 25, 26). **20** *Righteous* basically ever means to be 'in the right with God'. **21** Thus the Lord's saving of the king from his foes shows who is accepted before Him and who is not. **22** Isaiah (28:16) uses identical terminology about God's promises to David: it was the error of Hezekiah at that time to seek military security rather than the security of trusting the promises. In standing by

His promises, God chooses the stone which the worldly-wise rejected. *Cf.* Dn. 2:34, 35, 44, 45; Zc. 3:9; 4:7. *Stone* was obviously in common use as a symbol of the Davidic monarchy and a Messianic term. **25** *Save us* has been anglicized as 'Hosanna' (*cf.* Mt. 21:9); it expressed the Messianic longing of the people.

27–29 Sacrifice and praise

The priests now command the initiation of the sacrifice, presumably one of thanksgiving (v. 27). The king first (v. 28), and then the whole congregation (v. 29) voice a testimony of thanksgiving (*cf.* Introduction to Ps. 116) to the Lord as the sacrifice is offered.

27 *Light* is another key idea of the royal psalms. The Lord has brought His king out of death's darkness with light and liberty (*cf.* Pss. 18:28; 97:11). *Bind.* This is a correct literal translation of the verb, but it has a more suitable extended meaning. In activities which involve binding, girding on, harnessing, *etc.*, it also means 'to make ready' or 'to initiate (some activity)': thus 'to make ready' a chariot (Gn. 46:29; 1 Ki. 18:44), 'to initiate' battle (1 Ki. 20:14). The custom at Tabernacles of weaving branches, whether to carry in procession or for making booths, justifies the verb here. Hence: 'Initiate, or prepare the festival with (woven) branches, (and come) up to the horns of the altar.'

PSALM 119. LOVE FOR THE LORD AND HIS LAW

This is an elaborate, ingenious and passionate meditation upon the law of the Lord. 'Law' in the OT should not be confused with Pharisaic legalism. The Hebrew word is *tôrâ*, meaning 'teaching'. It stands for the will of God revealed to Israel. It is the loving instruction of a parent (Pr. 4:1, 2).

The psalm has an acrostic pattern: each of the twenty-two letters of the Hebrew alphabet is made the initial letter of eight verses in the successive sections. The major feature, however, is the repetition of eight synonyms of the will of God: *law* (*tôrâ*), 'teaching', notes that God has made His truth known by personal verbal communication, just as a teacher or parent would; this is also expressed by *word* (*dābār*, or 'imrâ). *Testimonies* ('ēḏôṯ) stresses the content: God has testified of Himself and His requirements. These latter come to man as *statutes* (ḥuqqîm, root ḥ-q-q, to engrave) or unchangeable rules; *judgments* or *ordinances* (mišpāṭîm), decisions which God has made; *precepts* (piqqûḏîm) authoritatively imposed; *commandments* (miṣwôṯ) expecting obedience; all issuing in a *way* (derek), habitual modes of life and thought. (*Cf.* Ps. 19:7ff.) One or other of these terms occurs in every verse of the psalm, except v. 122; but they have no obvious methodical sequence from stanza to stanza. We may reasonably assume, however, that within each stanza the poet was governed by more than the bare consideration of the initial letter of the sayings he selected. There must at the least be a general suitability of one thought to another.

1–8 The way of the Lord is good

Wholesome benefits follow from devotion to God's law: a good life (1), freedom from deviation (3), no cause for shame (6), inner integrity (7). But the Lord looks for deliberate conformity to His will (1), single-mindedness (2), obedience (4), study (6).

3 *Wrong*: that which deviates, a mistake, a misuse, or a perversion.

9–16 The remedy for sin

Defilement (9), inconsistency (10), actual sin (11), all yield to the pure influence of God's word. Hence the need, and the psalmist's determination to be watchful (9), devoted (10), committing the word to memory (11), looking to God for understanding (12), sharing the truth with others (13), subjecting his emotions to the love of God's word (14, 16), giving it concentrated attention (15).

17–24 A light for dark days

When life seems precarious (17) and earthly days seem far from home (19), and authorities are condemnatory and suspicious (22, 23), God's word gives purpose to life (17) and makes it bearable (19). But without divine aid there is no comprehension (18), without obedience no blessing (21, 22). How, then, we should long for God's law (20), delight in and submit to it (24).

18 *Wondrous*; *cf.* Ps. 107:8. **19** *Sojourner*: resident alien. On God's action in relation to His word in vv. 18, 19, *cf.* Lk. 24:32, 45.

25–32 Faithful God, Divine Teacher

God is faithful to His word (25, 28) and to those who love His word (26, 30, 31), but His word can be understood only if He teaches it (26, 27, 29, 32). The word is a source of revival (25), comfort (28), direction (29) when, under God as teacher, the pupil is earnest (27), deliberate (30), persistent (31) and resolved (32).

30 *The way of faithfulness*: the trustworthy rule of life, *i.e.* God's law.

33–40 Single-mindedness

The whole law throughout a whole life (33), the whole heart (34), which delights in it (35) and utterly rejects alternative paths (36, 37)—this is the single-mindedness of one who fears God (38), fears His displeasure (39; *cf.* v. 21) and longs for His blessing (40).

33 *End*: either of the requirements of God, or of his own life. **36** *Gain*. The word is used of self-advancement at any price, exclusive appreciation of the world's wealth. By contrast, it is the *testimonies* which express and possess true value in this life.

41–48 Complete and equipped

Here is a man who is right with God (41), enjoying personal fulfilment (45), and ministering to others (42, 43, 46): the man of God (2 Tim. 3:17) abiding in the word of God (2 Tim. 3:10–16).

41 *Cf.* Eph. 1:13. **44, 45** The element of perseverance; *cf.* Pr. 2:4. **48** *I revere* (lit. 'lift up my hands unto'): the attitude of prayer (*cf.* Ps. 28:2), significant of the reverence felt for God's word.

49–56 Solace and strength

Comfort in trouble (50a), vitality to meet opposition without deviating (50b–52), emotions anchored to true moral values (53), uplifting thoughts when otherwise depression might strike home (54, 55). No blessing surpasses that of knowing and obeying God's precepts (56).

51 *Godless*: translated 'insolent' in v. 21; the idea is 'seething with self-importance'. *Utterly deride*: this verb supplies the noun 'scoffer' (*cf.* Ps. 1:1), the person who feels there is simply nothing to be said on the other side. In 1:1, he is the man who dismisses with contempt the thought of God. Here he equally dismisses the godly man, who is nevertheless maintained by the vitalizing power of God's word. **52** *From of old*: the thought is either that God's word has stood the test of time, or that history abounds in examples of the overthrow of godless scoffers. **53** *Cf.* v. 136. **54** *Pilgrimage*: 'sojourning', residence as alien or refugee; *cf.* v. 19. **56** *That*, or 'because' (AV, RV).

57–64 The Lord is my portion

We cannot have God without His word. Such is the lesson of this section. The man who wants God (57), whole-heartedly desires God's favour and grace (58), seeks His presence (62), associates with those who reverence Him (63) and sees His steadfast love evidenced everywhere (64) must at the same time choose and cultivate the word of God. It is impossible to abide in Him unless His words abide in us (Jn. 15:7).

57 *My portion*; *cf.* Jos. 13:32, 33; 18:7. **58** *Favour* (lit. 'face'); *cf.* Nu. 6:24–26; 2 Sa. 14:24; 2 Cor. 4:6. **61** *Cords*: the snares and pressures introduced by others to make him deviate.

65–72 God's good discipline

God does good (65), teaches good (66), is good (68) and purposes good (71). Of necessity He sometimes must bless us with affliction, but this is both according to what His word leads us to expect (65; *cf.* Jb. 2:9; Ps. 94:12; Pr. 3:11, 12; Heb. 12:5ff.), and designed to attach us the more devotedly to His word (67, 71). The particular affliction appears to have been a smear of lies (69), but it only succeeded in driving him into more whole-hearted devotion to the word (69), a clear-eyed discernment (70), and a supreme valuing of the law of God (72).

66 *Judgment*: a word meaning 'taste', *i.e.* discernment.

73–80 A faithful Creator

In this section, which could well act as a scriptural comment on 1 Pet. 4:19, the verses correspond to each other: 73 to 80, 74 to 79, and so on. Four topics emerge. First, the way of life (73, 80): since God is the Creator, how needful for the creature to understand His commandments (73), with an unmixed devotion, for only in this way will life be lived successfully (80). Secondly, the secret of influence: the Creator looks for mutual helpfulness among those who fear Him (74, 79): the life grounded on the word gladdens (74) and instructs them (79). Thirdly, the meaning of suffering (75, 78): the Lord makes no errors (75a), nor does He act out of character (75b) in afflicting—not even if He uses *the godless* (78, *i.e.* the insolent proud) as His instruments and allows His servants to be wrongfully treated. True godliness is shown in holding on to the word (78b). Fourthly, the assurance of comfort (76, 77): God's mercies can be relied upon, for two reasons: His word promises them (76), and the troubled soul delights in His law (77).

81–88 Lord, how long?

Often the godless seem to have it all their own way (85, 87), and the silence of God baffles His saints. However, even when they ask with perplexity why the promises have not been kept (82, 84), yet their only comfort is those very promises themselves (81, 83, 86, 87), for they are *sure* (86), having originated from His *mouth* (88).

83 *Wineskin in the smoke*; *i.e.* black, shrivelled, past being of further use. **84** The shortness of life is often the basis of appeal (*cf.* Pss. 88:3; 89:47).

89–96 God's word, immutable, inexhaustible

The psalmist views three areas: heaven (89), the long sweep of human history (90) and the created order (90b, 91): all alike bear witness to the unchangeable character of God's word. *All* alike are His *servants, i.e.* they obey His will expressed in His word (91b). This changeless word must therefore be the most secure basis for life in all its aspects (92–96).

96 *Perfection* is an otherwise unused word. It may mean that all that man counts perfect has, in the end, its limitations, but God's commandment is inexhaustible. It could mean 'completeness', contrasting the finite universe (however large) with the infinite extent of God's word.

97–104 Here is wisdom

A man taught by God's law is wiser than opponents (98), would-be teachers (99), the proverbially wise elders (100), the enticements of sin (101). The explanation is that in His word God is the teacher (102), and the result is love (97), desire (103) and sound moral judgment (104).

98 *Thy commandment* . . .: lit. 'Thou—that is, thy commandments . . .'. No distinction can be made between God and what He says. **101** The element of moral discipline in obedience.

105–112 A pragmatic argument

In the foregoing section, the divine origin of the word (98, 102) constrained the psalmist to value it. Now it is its practical usefulness as a guide (105) which makes him solemnly determined (106, 111, 112) to hold to it, in trouble (107), joy (108), peril (109), hostility (110).

105 *Feet . . . path* possibly suggest 'for the next step as well as for the more remote destination'. **111** *Cf.* on v. 57.

113–120 Loving God's law

Nothing opens a window into the OT view of the law of God more than the verb 'love' (113; *cf.* v. 97). To the OT saint, God's law was not the burdensome legal imposition of Pharisaism as the NT reveals it. It was liberating (v. 45), delightsome (v. 103), a joy (v. 111). This love was all-absorbing, utterly excluding the double-mind (113), but to maintain such an attitude requires decisiveness: a seeking of God and an abhorrence of evil (114, 115); it also requires divine strengthening (116, 117), and a recognition that God cannot bless where His word is deserted (118), so that it is necessary deliberately to adopt (119, *therefore*) the contrary attitude. Finally, love is not stunted but rather is fostered by the reverence and holy *fear* due to God and His judgments (120).

114 The sufficiency of God: a true *hiding place* secures from danger; a *shield* protects in danger. **116** *My hope*; *i.e.* of seeing God's promises fulfilled (*cf.* v. 114). **118** *Cunning* here describes the alternative authority espoused when the word of God has been rejected; *cf.* 2 Tim. 4:4. **120** Identical attitudes towards God and His word.

121–128 Grounds of appeal

The psalmist pleads for divine action, first on the ground of his own loyal service (121, 122): his circumstances are due to his obedience, surely God will stand by him (*cf.* Is. 50:5–8); secondly, on the ground of God's pledged word (123); thirdly, of His steadfast love (124); fourthly, of his position as servant (*cf.* Is. 41:9b, 10); fifthly, of the urgent circumstances of the day (126). These are grounds which every believer may plead in prayer. The psalmist's certainty of divine response is indicated by his decisive actions to be pleasing to God (127, 128).

129–136 How God blesses His word

Vv. 129–131 are statements about God's word and the psalmist's response to it: in itself it is *wonderful* (129), *i.e.* a marvel beyond man's power to accomplish; in its effect, it illuminates (130). These features prompt obedience (129b) and spiritual hunger (131). Vv. 132–135 are prayers: God's word is effective only if God uses it for blessing, but when He does, then it tells of His steadfast love (132, see note below), it gives victory to the obedient (133), desire to obey it is a proper ground of appeal for other divine blessings (134), to learn God's statutes is to see

His face (135). Consideration of these benefits provokes tears that any should disobey such a precious and potent thing (136).

132 *As is thy wont*: lit. 'according to the judgment with respect to those who love . . .'. 'Judgment' signifies the revelation of God's mind on some point: in this case, His graciousness to those who love Him.

137-144 God's other Self

The worth of God's word constantly excites the psalmist's devotion to it: so here (139, 140, 141, 143). The peculiar worth of the word as stated in this section is that it mirrors God (137a, 144a), particularly being associated with His *faithfulness*, or 'trustworthiness' (138), and also being described as *tried*, meaning 'purified from all dross' (140), and *true* (142) or veracious.

145-152 The two resources

Vv. 145-147 recall a period of intense prayer, whole-hearted (145), directed to God (146), at cost to self (147), and we must suppose that some crisis was thus combated. Vv. 149-152 speak of a crisis of foes drawing near (150), but the psalmist's resource is that the Lord also is near (151).

Between these sections is a memorable statement of devoted study of God's word (148) which links the other references to the word throughout the verses. Why is he so devoted in meditation? Because effective prayer requires resolute obedience (145, 146), and springs from a grasp of promises (147); and the Lord's nearness is granted to one who can testify (151) with conviction (152) to the truth of His commandments.

153-160 Give me life

Experience of life's afflictions comes to the fore throughout Ps. 119, and especially in this section. Like all the psalmists, when trouble comes he runs to God in prayer, not from Him in rebellion. Three times (154, 156, 159) he prays *Give me life*, appealing in turn to God's *promise*, the will of God; God's *justice* (AV, RV 'judgments'), God's decisions, the mind of God; and God's *steadfast love*, the heart of God. Since God will act only according to His word, none can expect to enter into blessing but those who love and obey it (153, 155, 157); but all who honour it may rest confident that God will keep it (160).

160 *Sum*: God's word in its entirety.

161-168 Honour where it is due

In four areas of life, God's word has pride of place: worldly honour (161), ambition (162), religion (163, see note below), and the use of time (164). This bears a fourfold fruit: peace of conscience (165a), consistent living (165b), assurance of salvation (166), and fearlessness under the scrutiny of God (167, 168).

163 *Falsehood* often refers to false gods, and *abhor* is almost a technical term for the Lord's disgust at pagan religious practices.

169-176 The paradox of blessing

The psalmist chooses to end his great meditation on the word of God by noting again that while for every spiritual blessing we are utterly dependent on God (the prayers of 169-172, reading 171, 172 as in RV, 'Let. . . .'), we can none the less, and must, put ourselves in the way of blessing by obedience to God's word (173-176). Consequently, biblically based prayer and biblically directed obedience are the marks of the godly man, seen in his mind (169), mouth (171, 172), will (173b), emotions (174) and conscience (176).

GENERAL INTRODUCTION TO PSALMS 120-134: THE 'SONGS OF ASCENTS'

These fifteen psalms are each entitled 'A Song of ascents' (AV 'degrees'). The significance of the phrase is uncertain. Different explanations have been suggested. For example, a somewhat vague Jewish tradition says there was a liturgy associated with the fifteen steps between two of the Temple courts and compares the number of the steps to that of the psalms. The LXX title is 'A Song of the steps'. Another suggestion is that they are a collection of songs which the exiles sang on returning to Jerusalem from Babylon. *Cf.* Ezr. 7:9 where the same word 'ascent' is used of the journey from Babylon to Jerusalem. A third explanation is that the phrase denotes the literary style of several of the poems, viz. that the thought progresses by well-marked stages (*e.g.* Ps. 123).

Not wholly satisfactory, but on balance the best suggestion is that these psalms were used by worshippers going up to Zion for the three great festivals of the Jewish year. Even though only one (Ps. 122) is obviously in keeping with the spirit of such pilgrimages, others (*e.g.* Ps. 121) can be easily applied to pilgrim situations.

Whatever the precise meaning of the superscription, one thing is evident; this collection of psalms constitutes a distinctive group, and is, in itself, a miniature Psalter. It can be divided into five groups each consisting of three psalms. The first two groups deal with external pressures on the godly soul, expectant trust in the intervention of God, and the realization of the tremendous stability, power, and righteousness in Him; and the choice of Zion as the hinge on which turn the Lord's purposes for men. The third group has more in common with the Wisdom literature; the viewpoint is much more general, outward and philosophical; there is no mention of divine mercy, redemption or forgiveness, nor of prayer, the services in the sanctuary, nor the house of David; the emphasis on home and family life is peculiar to this group. The fourth group is intensely personal and devotional; the theme is the discipline of patience. The last group is dominated by the concepts of divine choice;

the covenant, the community, and the sanctuary; there is a very real sense of the inheritance of the historic past.

PSALM 120. DELIVER ME

This prayer for relief was prompted by a pervasive atmosphere of untruth and deceit; it is the cry of a man who is spiritually exiled, and summarizes the patience, suffering, and cruel dilemma of the church in a hostile world. Of such slander campaigns the Scriptures give clear examples (Ezr. 4:1ff.; Ne. 4:1ff.), and there must be few believers who cannot identify themselves with the situation of this psalm.

The psalmist records his prayer (vv. 1, 2), anticipates divine retributive action (vv. 3, 4), and laments his uncongenial circumstances (vv. 5–7).

2 The strength of the psalmist's opposition to misuse of the tongue is remarkable. *Cf.* Pss. 5:9; 10:7; 12:2–4; 36:1–4; 52:2–4; 64:1–4. **3** *Be given*: a legitimate translation of the Hebrew 'will he give', but possibly the literal rendering should be retained: the psalmist looks for divine retributive action. *What more* recalls the oath formula (*cf.* 1 Sa. 3:17, *etc.*). Possibly the psalmist had even been involved in legal proceedings in which falsehood had been spoken even under oath by his opponents. He looks therefore for the 'more also' of just retribution. **4** *Cf.* Pss. 7:11–13; 64:2, 3. The *warrior* is the Lord. In return for the arrows of evil words come the arrows of divine judgment. *Broom*: a hard wood giving fierce heat: fire is characteristically the wrath of God against sin (*cf.* Pss. 18:12–14; 140:10). **5** *Meshech . . . Kedar*. Since the former lived between the Black and Caspian Seas, and the latter were Arabian nomads, we have here a metaphor for uncongenial surroundings and not a factual statement of the psalmist's home. **6, 7** The people of God in an alien world are marked by desire for peace, and a form of speech contrasting with that of their neighbours.

PSALM 121. GOD MY HELPER

This song implies a situation of uncertainty, but any possibility of danger is offset by unquestioning trust in the Lord. Its application to the perils of pilgrimage is obvious, and on the whole this sort of setting makes best sense of the psalm.

1, 2 The God of creation

1 The psalmist may *lift up* his *eyes* to the hill of Zion, the goal of pilgrimage and the mount of God (*cf.* Pss. 3:4; 20:2; 134:3), anticipating from Zion's hill and Zion's God all necessary aid; or he may be fearing the perils of a mountain journey, and be looking with apprehension for sudden attack in lonely ravines or passes. **2** Either way, the God of creation, God the almighty is his help.

3, 4 The God of history

His confident answer (v. 2) gives him a testimony to share with others. The God of Israel is no Baal (1 Ki. 18:27), but one who throughout a long history has ever preserved His people. **4** The duplication of words, *neither slumber nor sleep*, is as ever an expression of certainty (*cf.* Gn. 41:32).

5, 6 The God of the individual

The Keeper of Israel (v. 4) is *your keeper*, shading from *sun* and *moon* alike, *i.e.* from all adversaries at all times, day and night.

7, 8 The God of eternity

Not only all adversaries (v. 6), but *all evil*, every sort of trouble, and in all activities of life, and for all time.

PSALM 122. THE JOYS AND DUTIES OF THE CITY OF GOD

At the end of his stay in Jerusalem, a pilgrim reviews his sense of privilege at having been in the city, meditates on what Jerusalem means and calls for prayer.

1, 2 Jerusalem, the source of joy

Anticipation (v. 1) has been succeeded by actualization (v. 2), and the pilgrim's mood is one of unfeigned joy and privilege. *Cf.* 1 Cor. 2:9; Heb. 12:22–24; Rev. 7:9–17.

3–5 Jerusalem, the place of fellowship

The very appearance of Jerusalem, a compact, integrated city (v. 3), suggests visually what is realized there in terms of people: unity, fellowship (v. 4). *The tribes* find in it a common focus and meeting. This unity finds expression in thanksgiving (v. 4c) for God's self-revelation, and finds its centre in the throne and rule of David (v. 5).

3 *Bound*: verb 'to be joined', of diversity united (Ex. 28:7; 39:4), of 'common humanity' (Ec. 9:4). **5** *Thrones*: possibly a plural of majesty, the 'great throne' of David and his dynasty.

6–9 Jerusalem, the object of prayer

The unity of God's people finds expression now in prayer. **6, 7** indicate the terms of the prayer; **8, 9** its motives, love of the brethren, love of God's house, the peace of atonement by sacrifice.

PSALM 123. SOVEREIGN GRACE

None of the psalmists sat in the seat of the scornful (Ps. 1:1), but in many of their prayers they showed themselves very conscious of the society of proud and arrogant men (*e.g.* Pss. 17:10, 11; 22:6–8; 35:19–26; 44:13–16; 69:4–12; 102:3–10). This then is another prayerful exposure of such a situation as gave rise to Ps. 120. Whereas there the theme is one of sad expectation of God's judgment on the defamers, here the theme is the glad certainty of mercy for the defamed. Personal experience of a sovereign God (v. 1) issues in the repose of faith (v. 2): with expectant *eyes* fixed on the single source of power and supply (*hand*), trustfully leaving the decision to Him (*till*). But He is moved by His people's needs. They can plead on the basis of personal need (*for we . . .* , v. 3b).

PSALM 124. THE GRACIOUS SOVEREIGN

This psalm is a series of tableaux depicting rescue from danger. Vv. 1–5 give utterance to the nation's consciousness that the deliverance was Yahweh's doing; vv. 6–8 express their thanksgiving and confidence in Him.

Four deadly dangers are instanced to reveal the magnitude of the threat and the greatness of the deliverance: **3** earthquake (*cf.* Nu. 16:30–32), **4, 5** flood, **6** beast of prey and **7** trap. The completeness of deliverance is shown not by escape alone, but that *the snare is broken*, the danger itself is destroyed. **8** While they adore the sovereign Creator as their Helper, they recognize that the relationship is all of grace: *the name of the Lord*, Yahweh, the Saviour of Israel.

PSALM 125. ABIDING SECURITY

A deep conviction of security and of the unchanging power and faithfulness of the Lord finds expression in this song. The psalm was written in Jerusalem during some period of restlessness and tediousness. Evidently this had overcome many of the faint-hearted amongst the community so that they had turned aside to do as other workers of iniquity, and would be led forth to the like judgment. The psalm falls into two parts: an expression of confidence in God (vv. 1–3) and a prayer and warning (vv. 4, 5). **1** The people of God are defined by their attitude of simple *trust in the Lord*. This trust brings them stability comparable to that of Mt. Zion, **2** and security such as the encircling mountains give to the city. The Lord, who is the object of their trust, is also the means of their security, both present and eternal. **3** This truth is borne out by the emphatic assertion that the sceptre of unrighteous rule shall not rest permanently over the promised land lest, if it did, a general failing of faith should occur among the righteous. The Lord sovereignly controls the trials of His people (*cf.* 1 Cor. 10:13). The Lord in whom they trust and are secure is the Lord of history.

4, 5 He is also the Lord of righteousness and none dares suppose his security in God to free him from the discipline of moral choice and inner goodness. Thus, as always in Scripture, God's sovereignty sets man in a position of moral accountability (*cf.* Ps. 119:91, 94; Is. 10:5, 6, 12).

PSALM 126. SOWING AND REAPING

The gladness of this psalm is unmistakable. Yet there is also a sense of tearfulness, as if the unexpected blessing (v. 1) ought not to have issued in depression (v. 5). The message of the psalm is that there is no simple solution on earth for the problems of the people of God, no single act of God which will bring them into unbroken joy, rid them of trials and temptations, or establish them in perfection this side of heaven. Joy over supreme divine blessings (vv. 1–3) is immediately followed by the onset of new problems, new adversities calling for new acts of God (v. 4), and the task of His people is ever to persevere in faithful continuance in well-doing (vv. 5, 6).

Understandably, commentators have associated this psalm with the period of the return from exile, when God's mighty deliverance was followed by the depression and disappointment so clearly depicted by Haggai (1:5–11) and the local opposition recorded in Ezr. 4. But the psalm suits that period only because it deals in general principles illustrated over and over in the historical books. Weiser allowably makes the verbs of vv. 1, 2 present tense expressive of general truth: blessings bring joy, but the people of God must learn that holiness is perfected by the testings of life (Jas. 1:2–4), and in the will of God there is no other way forward.

1–3 Laughter

Deliverances are always wholly the acts of the Lord. **1** That the people of God should seem to themselves to have been dreaming signifies both their wonderment and also that they did not themselves contribute to the deliverance. **2** Even the heathen recognize only the Lord as the Agent, **3** and this is the consequent testimony of His people, who contributed nothing but gained all.

4–6 Tears

4 But soon the people face the fact that they are as needy and dependent as ever: a new situation finds them in an identical need; yet again their fortunes need restoring. Only a miracle of divine power will suffice: *watercourses in the Negeb!* 'Rivers in the sun-scorched desert in the south, an impossible thought indeed!' (Weiser). But not with God! **5, 6** His word now reassures His people. The similarity of theme in these two verses suggests that v. 5 (*cf.* AV, RV) should be an affirmation, not a prayer. It is not that their efforts contribute to blessing, any more than the farmer can make the seed grow. But if he is not obedient to God's natural laws—even when the task is wearisome unto tears—there will be no harvest. The obedience of His people is the context in which the Lord works miracles of transforming blessing.

PSALM 127. YOUR HEAVENLY FATHER KNOWS

The Bible never places any premium on idleness

or improvidence (*cf.* Ps. 128:2; Pr. 24:30–34), and this psalm neither glorifies slackness nor denigrates effort, but rebukes anxiety. In all, three areas of human endeavour are reviewed: personal prosperity and investment (v. 1a), the building of one's own house; civic or national security (v. 1b); and procreation, the begetting of children (v. 3). Each of these is a fruitful source of the anxiety which the psalmist reproves (v. 2), not in order to take the work out of life, but to take away the worry. His foe is the man whose fretful will to succeed keeps him at his desk from morning to night (v. 2a) and whose meals even become additional committee meetings (v. 2b). Into his thinking the psalmist would inject two truths: the Lord rules, the Lord gives; sovereignty and grace. The outcome of all depends on Him (v. 1) and every needful thing it is His delight to give to His beloved (v. 2). Even children, whose conception and birth has all the appearance of an inevitable cause-and-effect mechanism, are the gifts of the Creator, not the fruitfulness of the procreator (v. 3).

Those commentators may be correct who see this psalm as composed of two originally independent pieces (vv. 1–2, 3–5), but if so the person who united them was of considerable perception. Vv. 3–5 not only add the third area of human activity, thus completing the picture, but supply the perfect illustration of the principle he seeks to inculcate. For while children will not be conceived without parental intercourse, conception and birth—with all the attendant joy (v. 5a) and security (v. 5b) that children bring—are not the result of the intercourse but (in the ultimate analysis) the decision of the Lord.

Hence, the essence of the psalm is thus expressed: *he gives to his beloved sleep* (v. 2c). God's love gift to His beloved is restfulness (the opposite, not of effort, but of restlessness)—to rest in Him in all the ambitions, duties and joys of life.

2 *Sleep.* RV mg. 'in sleep' is a possible but not obvious translation. The meaning, however, remains unaltered. God's will for His children is not fretful care, but rest. *Cf.* Mt. 6:25–34; Lk. 12:16–34. **3** *Cf.* Gn. 20:18; 30:1, 2; Ru. 4:13; 1 Sa. 1:5; Lk. 1:13ff., 24, 25. **5** *Gate:* the centre of communal life, the place where all disputes were settled and business transacted (*e.g.* Ru. 4:1). A large family gave a man a strong position in the ancient community.

PSALM 128. FRUITFUL TOIL

A counterpoise to Ps. 127, this psalm lays down the conditions (vv. 1, 4) for fruitful toil (v. 2a), personal well-being (v. 2b), and a happy home (v. 3), and ends with a prayer for the realization of these blessings (vv. 5, 6).

1 *Fears . . . walks:* just as Jesus, inculcating the principle of non-anxiety, envisaged a person busy in God's affairs (Mt. 6:31–33), so here the repose in God (suggested in Ps. 127:2c) is not one of relaxation but one of mobilization of spiritual energies: reverence issuing in obedience. **2** *Fruit of the labour; i.e.* as distinct from fruitless toil; *cf.* Hg. 1:5, 6, 9; 2:16, 17. The link between obedience and prosperity is unvaried in the OT; *cf.* Dt. 28:1–14 and contrast vv. 15ff. **3** *A fruitful vine:* a happy choice of symbol for a loved wife—like a vine, needing support yet ever giving more than getting in providing joy for her husband (Ps. 104:15a). *Olive shoots:* wine and oil are two symbols of God's unhindered blessing (*cf.* Dt. 8:8; Ho. 2:22). The olive symbolizes vitality and continuance (Ps. 52:8). **4** This repetition of v. 1 is for the purpose of emphasizing that these covetable blessings are properly experienced only in the context of the fear of God. **5, 6** It is not religion as such that brings a man personal and domestic fulfilment. It comes only and specifically from the God who dwells in Zion. Furthermore, no man is an island, and his personal well-being is bound up with *the prosperity of Jerusalem*, the good of God's people.

PSALM 129. THE SUFFERING CHURCH

Ps. 128 might suggest an automatic, experienced link between religion and prosperity. But the well-being of the godly is a position of faith (see on Ps. 1), and this psalm provides another perspective.

1–4 The lessons of history

Hundreds of years in the experience of the people of God are condensed into four verses. Enslavement in Egypt supplies most of the metaphors, but the testimony is of one opponent after another, as the words *from my youth* (*cf.* Ho. 11:1) indicate. Yet the most up-to-date testimony (*now,* v. 1) is of survival. This is due to the righteousness of the Lord, *i.e.* He never deviates from His purposes and promises. *Cf.* Ps. 23:1–4 where both the green pastures and the valley of deep darkness are 'paths of righteousness', right paths appointed by Him.

5–8 The resource of faith

Just as one restoration of their fortunes still leaves God's people needing yet another (Ps. 126:1, 4), so one opponent replaces another, but the resource remains the same: prayer to the righteous Lord who never forsakes His own. Prayer and prayer alone is the reply to opposition. **5** The prayer asks that all opponents may be disappointed of their expectations (*put to shame*), **6** impermanent, **7** fruitless and **8** friendless. The violence of these supplications may well surprise us, but once more the psalmist (see on Ps. 109) is only spelling out details we would prefer to leave vague, and is thereby revealing how far our sanctification falls from the place where we might sinlessly give voice to indignation.

PSALM 130. THE LORD'S THREE COMPANIONS

If this psalm is to be linked with the pilgrim feasts of Israel, its natural association is with the Day of Atonement (Lv. 16). If so, then it is another demonstration of the attitude of the devout individual to public occasions of worship and sacrifice. *Cf.* on Pss. 116; 118.

1–4 Intercession

Attention should be paid in these verses to the forms of address used to God. There are three: first (v.1a), there is LORD, standing for Yahweh, the personal name of Israel's God; the name which holds together mercy and judgment: mercy towards enslaved Israel, holy judgment upon stubborn Egypt (Ex. 20:1). Secondly there is its diminutive, Yah, appearing as LORD (v. 3) and holding the same significance. Finally there is *Lord* (vv. 2, 3b; Heb. *'aḏōnāy*), a name meaning 'sovereign', 'master', pointing to the exalted-ness of God. The psalmist's awareness of exalted holiness makes him realize the *depths* to which sin lowers a man and the problem involved in forgiveness. Yet his awareness of Yahweh the redeemer encourages him to pray.

3 *Iniquities*: the deepest and most inward of the OT words for sin: it represents the corrup-tion of the heart. *Stand*; *cf.* Pss. 1:5; 24:3. Sin's consequences are not only in the realm of con-science (v. 1), but also in the realm of eternity, unfitting a man for God's presence. 4 *Forgiveness*: the first of the Lord's companions (*cf.* v. 7); in Hebrew 'the forgiveness', *i.e.* genuine forgiveness. *Feared*: being aware of the greatness of his sin (vv. 1a, 3), how exceedingly and fearfully great is God who can triumph over it by forgiveness?

5, 6 Expectation

The sinner is impotently helpless in his sin. He can do nothing. Only God can forgive, and for that sovereign act man must wait. 5 It is not, however, a waiting of dull hopelessness or of desperation. The sinner can rest on promises and revealed truths—*in his word I hope*. 6 *Soul*: the personality at centre. We might express the same intensity by saying 'From the bottom of my heart'. *Watchmen*. The idea combines inten-sity of longing with confident expectation.

7, 8 Exhortation

The penitent now has a testimony to share: it is worth while to hope in the Lord! Out of personal experience he calls others to enter into divine for-giveness. 7 The Lord has two more companions with Him (*cf.* v. 4): there is His own *steadfast love*, the love which will never abandon His people, and which is His permanent attitude towards them; there is also *with him . . . plenteous redemption*. Redemption (Heb. *p̄eḏûṯ*) always contains the truth of the 'ransom-price' (*cf.* Ex. 13:13; Nu. 3:46, 47). The steadfast love of the Lord reaches out to sinners by means of a price for sin which satisfies Him. Why does He for-give? Because of *steadfast love*. How does He forgive? Through a *redemption*-price. 8 What does He forgive? *All iniquities* (*cf.* v. 3a).

PSALM 131. SCHOOLED IN HUMILITY

The form of this psalm bears some resemblance to the previous psalm in that it is intensely personal, except in the final verse where Israel is mentioned. In content, it is an eminently suitable companion piece. Humbled by sin and forgiveness, the soul dwells quietly with God.

1 *Lifted up . . . high*: the heart is seen in the eyes (*cf.* Ps. 101:5; Pr. 30:13). *Occupy myself*; *i.e.* my walk and manner of life. 2 *Calmed . . . quieted*. Before weaning, the infant is aware of the mother as the source of food and it frets for the breast. After weaning, it is content to be 'with mother': her presence is enough. So ought it to be between us and God.

PSALM 132. DAVID'S OATH AND THE LORD'S OATH

It is interesting to associate this psalm with the dedication of Solomon's Temple (*cf.* 2 Ch. 6:41f.), or possibly with some anniversary of that event. Suitably to such occasions its form derives from 2 Sa. 7, where David's desire to build a house for the Lord (2 Sa. 7:1–3; Ps. 132:1–10) is transformed into the Lord's promise to build a house for David (2 Sa. 7:11ff.; Ps. 132:11ff.). V. 10 clearly supposes the present rule of the Davidic king, and it may be (*cf.* Eaton) that annually the royal festival contain-ed a re-enactment of the story of the founding of the house, and the depositing there of the ark. This would suitably become the occasion of prayer for the king, and public recollection of the divine oath (v. 11) and the moral foundation (v. 12) on which the monarchy rested. The two halves of the psalm are closely integrated. Note how the prayer (vv. 8–10) is answered in the response (vv. 14–17).

1–10 David's oath

The psalmist requests that the hazards and troubles which David encountered in capturing Jerusalem and bringing thither the ark (*cf.* 2 Sa. 6:8–10; 1 Ch. 21:13, 30) be remembered by the Lord, *i.e.* in blessing to his dynasty.

2 *The Mighty One of Jacob*: this title is found elsewhere only in Gn. 49:24; Is. 49:26; 60:16, always in the context of the prevailing power of the Lord. Suitably, therefore, it would be on David's lips when (contrary to all odds) the Lord had brought him to the throne and subdued all his foes (2 Sa. 7:1). 5 *A dwelling place*: plural in Hebrew, suggesting 'a worthy dwelling'. 6–8 These verses recall in order the sojourn and removal of the ark from Kiriath-jearim (v. 6; 1 Sa. 7:1, 2; 2 Sa. 6:1–3), the call to communal worship at the dedication (v. 7; 2 Sa. 6:17–19;

1 Ki. 8:1–3, 62, 63, 65, 66), and the ceremonial depositing of the ark in its new home (v. 8). **6** *Ephrathah*: possibly an old name for Ephraim, here poetically recalling the shrine at Shiloh. In 1 Sa. 1:1 'Ephraimite' is in Hebrew 'Ephrathite'. Was memory of the ark's whereabouts lost during the twenty years of 1 Sa. 7:2, necessitating first enquiry at Shiloh in Ephraim and the gradual tracing of it to *the fields of Jaar*, *i.e.* Kiriath-jearim? **7** *Footstool*; *i.e.* the ark, above which the Lord was invisibly enthroned (2 Sa. 6:2). **9** *Saints* (Heb. *ḥāsîd*): those who have been the objects of *ḥeseḏ*, the Lord's 'steadfast love'. **10** The very existence of the central shrine with the ark depended on the continued existence of the Davidic throne. Hence the prayer for the king. *Cf.* Ps. 84:9.

11–18 The Lord's oath

God's response to David replaced the king's conception of a permanent, stone building to house the presence of the Lord with a more enduring expression in human flesh (vv. 11, 12) of the Lord's power and steadfast purpose (*cf.* Ps. 89:19–37). Nevertheless, a particular relationship was affirmed between the Lord and a physical locality, *i.e.* Zion; this was *for ever* (vv. 13, 14). Thus there was linked together the Lord's reign over His people, mediated through the anointed king, and His ministry of pardon to them through the priesthood and its sacrifice (*cf.* v. 9a). These are the characteristics of the Lord in Zion: sovereignty, holiness and grace (*cf.* on Ps. 150:1, 2).

11, 12 *Cf.* 2 Sa. 7:12ff. **15** Concern and provision for the *poor* is ever a mark of the Lord and His king (*cf.* Ps. 72:12–14). **16** *Clothe.* Clothing is seen symbolically as expressing character and function. In v. 9a it represents the righteous character of the priests (*cf.* Is. 11:5; Eph. 6:14). In v. 16 it represents their function to dispense salvation in their role as priestly officiants in the sacrifices (*cf.* Is. 59:15–17; 61:10; 63:1, 2). **17** *Horn* symbolizes strength (*cf.* Zc. 1:18, 19); *lamp*, perpetuity (*cf.* 1 Ki. 11:36).

PSALM 133. THE BLESSINGS OF BRETHREN DWELLING IN UNITY

This is a poem about the family unity of God's people. The coming together of the scattered nation at the pilgrim feast would suggest the topic.

The psalmist illustrates the blessings of unity in two ways. **2** First, it is like the special consecrating *oil* of the high priest. Oil has the general significance of joy (*cf.* Pss. 23:5; 104:15) with the related ideas of fragrance (Ct. 1:3) and comfort (Is. 1:6), but the oil of priestly anointing was a sanctifying thing (Ex. 30:22–33). The abundance of the anointing oil (v. 2b, c) suggests how abundantly the Lord blesses and sanctifies His people through their fellowship.

3 In the second place he likens this unity to the refreshing *dew*, heavy as that on high Hermon, and falling also on Zion. The main idea, *dew*, expresses divine refreshment: God's gift of life and fruitfulness (see on Ps. 110:3), but the linking of Hermon (in the northern kingdom) with Zion indicates that God gives His gift to His people when they are in fellowship. The falling of Hermon's dew on Zion would be a miracle, and fellowship is a miracle of divine grace (Eph. 2:11–22) wherein individual blessings are shared with mutual profit. Such fellowship (v. 3b) is something God delights to bless, and is proof of the possession of *life for evermore* (*cf.* 1 Jn. 3:14).

PSALM 134. A PRAYERFUL GREETING AND GRACIOUS RESPONSE

A psalm for the vigil of a night festival (*cf.* Ex. 12:6–8; Is. 30:29). The first two verses are an invitation to worship, extended to those who remain in the Temple throughout the night (*cf.* 1 Ch. 9:33). To *bless the Lord*, to worship Him with thanksgiving and with the bowed knee of adoration, is a fitting work for *servants*. Their privilege is to be in His *house* and presence, and their characteristic occupation is prayer, the lifting up of the hands.

The invitation, spoken by the leader of the worship, meets the congregational response of v. 3. Thus, fellowship is cemented for the night service. The blessing sought is individual (*you* is singular, contrasting with the plural of vv. 1, 2), from Zion's Lord (see on Ps. 132:13, 14), and backed by the Creator's power.

PSALM 135. THE SECURITY OF ELECTION

This glorious hymn of praise has many points of contact with earlier psalms, and there is no doubt that it was composed for festivals of public worship, and was deliberately designed to evoke memories and associations of other songs of praise.

The appointed subject for which the Lord is praised is His choice of Israel to be His people (v. 4). The rest of the psalm expands this theme of election, its nature, reality, and privilege.

1–4 The meaning of election

The invitation to the Lord's servants to praise Him (vv. 1, 2) rests firstly on the revealed nature of the Lord as *good* and *gracious* (v. 3), and then moves on to the particular display of goodness and grace in the choice of Israel (v. 4). **3** *Good* expresses what God is in Himself and is well defined on the one side as His utter moral purity (*cf.* Jas. 1:13); on the other side it is His gracious kindness (*cf.* Jas. 1:17), linked here with *his name*, for the kindly goodness of God to Israel is pre-eminently seen at the Exodus in which also the meaning of His name was made known (Ex. 20:2). **4** *For himself . . . his own possession.* The word *possession* (*cf.* Ex. 19:4–6) signifies the specially treasured and intimately personal property of One who possesses everything. This is the meaning of God's choice of His people (*cf.* 1 Pet. 2:9, 10).

5–14 The reality of election

Five grounds are set forth whereby Israel may be certain that the Lord's choice of them to be His people is a secure reality. **5** His supremacy, whereby His choice cannot be revised by others (*cf.* Jn. 10:28f.); **6** His sovereign independence— therefore His choice was an act of personal will, deliberate and uncompelled (*cf.* Jas. 1:18); **7** His almightiness, whereby, over all the earth, things visible and invisible are at His sole command: He who could do anything He wished, chose Israel; **8–12** His historical acts on the people's behalf, covering deliverance (vv. 8, 9), conquest (vv. 10, 11) and settlement (v. 12)—clear proof of His choice of them as His own; **13, 14** and finally His changelessness, whereby He never alters in Himself or in His attitudes of power and pity towards His people.

15–21 The privilege of election

The predicament of all other nations is exposed by consideration of their gods—**15** their origin, **16, 17** lifelessness and **18** effect. Exclusiveness is part of the essence of the religion of the Bible. To the nations their gods were worshipped as living, but to Israel there was only one living and true God. We must take care to understand 'all gods' (v. 5) in the light of vv. 15–18. The former verse must not be understood to admit their reality as existing but inferior beings. They exist only as supposed and chosen objects of worship. In the same sense, the Christian is warned to keep himself from idols (1 Jn. 5:21).

19–21 How great, then, is the privilege of the people of the only God!

PSALM 136. THE WONDER OF ELECTION

This companion and parallel to Ps. 135 was clearly devised for public worship, the people responding in the recurring refrain. Undoubtedly it tends to be wearisome to us, but it is the purposeful persistence of successive hammer-blows driving home the truth. What, we might ask, is the 'steadfast love' of which we read? How can it 'smite' (v. 10), 'overthrow' (v. 15), slay (v. 18)? Because it is God's active, gracious, saving and providing power towards Israel, the means by which He implements His choice of the people for Himself. This 'steadfast love' is the essence of the goodness of God (v. 1) and the special feature of His supremacy over all claimants to be God (vv. 2, 3); it governs the performance of His *wonders* (v. 4); it fills all His activities in creation (vv. 5–9) and history (vv. 10–22). Yet it is prompted by no merit on the

part of its recipients (vv. 23, 24), and (a mundane but impressive ending) it is concerned to provide daily bread (v. 25). We may search through the whole nature of this exalted *God of heaven*, the God who is free of all earthly limitations and possessor of all heaven's fullness, and find nothing more worthily the object of thankful praise than that *his steadfast love endures for ever* (v. 26).

2 *God of Gods.* Cf. on 135:15ff. He is supreme over all that man may worship, **3** and as *Lord of lords* supreme over all that holds man in bondage. See on 130:2, 'Lord' (*'aḏōnāy*). **4** *Wonders.* Cf. on Ps. 107:8. **5** For creation as evidencing the wisdom of God, *cf.* Is. 40:12–14; Pr. 8:22–31. **6** *Earth upon the waters.* This is not intended to be a comment upon the structure of the universe (the so-called 'three-decker' view) but a realistic poetic observation. Happily, the earth is spread upon the waters! **10–15** In two groups (10–12; 13–15) these verses show the power of God implementing His steadfast love for Israel: each group contains a statement of power (12, 13), of overthrow (10, 15) and of deliverance (11, 14). **12** *Hand . . . arm.* Cf. Ex. 6:1, 6; 13:3; Dt. 4:34; Is. 51:9; 52:10; 53:1. The 'arm of the Lord' stands for the Lord Himself coming to save. **17–22** *Cf.* Dt. 2:26 – 3:13. **23, 24** A succinct picture of helplessness: no resources, many foes. **25** How the very ordinariness and homeliness magnifies the gracious, kindly love of God!

PSALM 137. BITTER MEMORIES, DIRE EXPECTATIONS

The concluding verses of this psalm, which, as Eaton says, 'rank high among the passages in the Old and New Testaments which hurt the conscience', confront us with the problem of imprecatory psalms in a particularly vivid form. Yet it will not do to say (*e.g.* with A. F. Kirkpatrick, *The Psalms*, 1910, *in loc.*) that 'the new law, "Thou shalt love thine enemy", had not yet taken the place of the old maxim, "Thou shalt love thy neighbour and hate thine enemy".' In the first place, this bland command to love and hate belongs not to the OT but to the Jewish traditional law. The OT nowhere commands the hatred of enemies as a principle, though urging it as right in specific cases and for flagrant offences (*e.g.* Dt. 23:3–6) to maintain an attitude of antagonism. Interestingly enough, love of Edomites, the hated foes of Ps. 137:7, is encouraged in Dt. 23:7, 8, though Kirkpatrick fails to take account of this. Secondly, simply to denigrate the imprecations of this psalm as evidence of the untutored conscience of ancient man is to overlook the shining devotion and spirituality of the opening verses.

To a marked degree, therefore, this psalm contains that tension between high, covetable spirituality and strong expressions of animosity which is found throughout the imprecatory psalms (see Introduction). This, in itself, should warn us that no naïve appeal to a supposed lower morality of the OT will solve this problem. Furthermore, the psalmist clearly has not disappeared into the depths of human rage quite as completely as, *e.g.*, Weiser suggests: his spirit of animosity and vengeance exhausts itself in prayer, and there is no suggestion that it ever would, or ever intended to, express itself in deeds. Here also, as in the opening verses, this writer can be a teacher and example for modern man.

It is essential to recall that when the NT quoted another of the imprecatory psalms (69:25), it described it as a scripture 'which the Holy Spirit spoke beforehand by the mouth of David, concerning Judas . . .' (Acts 1:16). That is to say, there is such a thing as the wrath of God (here voiced by the Holy Spirit), there are people who rightly deserve to be the targets of that wrath (Judas or, in Ps. 137, Edom and Babylon), and there are people raised up by God to give expression in words to that wrath (David, the psalmist of Ps. 137, *etc.*). We, whose anger ever trembles on the brink of sinfulness, do well to admit that we could not guiltlessly voice these sentiments. But in doing so we admit, not a greater sanctity nor a more enlightened conscience than the men of old, but a duller moral perception of the eternal significance of right and wrong, a less clear-cut devotion to God and good, and a failure to include in our portrait of the Lord Jesus Christ the NT insistence on 'the wrath of the Lamb' (Rev. 6:16). (*Cf.* W. Alexander, *The Witness of the Psalms to Christ and Christianity*, 1878, pp. 43–58.)

Commentators mostly favour a post-exilic date for this psalm, resting their opinion on the verb tenses in the opening verses, which appear to look back on the Babylonian captivity as past. But one within the period of the captivity could thus look back on a specific incident such as vv. 2, 3 relate, and in general the melancholy beauty of vv. 1–6, which contain no suggestion of Jerusalem revisited or in any way restored, as well as the fresh vigour of the denunciations of vv. 7–9, are better explained as arising from the homesickness and anguish of enslavement. Kaufmann (*The Religion of Israel*, 1960, p. 311) makes this the latest psalm in the Psalter, dating it within the Exile.

1 *Waters.* Israel's captivity in Babylon is often associated with rivers (*cf.* Ezr. 8:15; Ezk. 1:1; Dn. 8:2); the captives may even have been used as slave-labour on irrigation works. But in the present passage it is not their suffering but the mere sight of the Babylonian landscape, so different from that of Zion, that prompts the comparison and leads to tears. **2–4** In the poetical arrangement of the psalm, v. 4 belongs with 5 and 6, but in thought it concludes 2 and 3. Decisive laying up of the musical instruments was the reaction to a request from their captors for Hebrew music, for it exposed the incongruity of *the Lord's song in a foreign land.* **3** *Mirth.* Here we see OT religion through OT eyes: asked for a Temple song, they spontaneously thought

of religious joy. It is well for us to recall that OT religion knew nothing of Pharisaic bondage and burdensomeness. *Cf.* Is. 43:23b.

4 *A foreign land.* There is nothing here of the thought of the Lord being confined to the boundaries of Canaan, but rather that His people, in a foreign land in these circumstances, had the sense of being rejected and cast off by Him. Therefore how could they act as though nothing had happened and all was well? The psalmist knew the seriousness of sin as alienating the Lord and separating His people from Him. **5, 6** Note the strong element of self-imprecation in these verses. The things of God are to have priority in his memories and in his enjoyments. If it is otherwise, then he enters into a curse involving loss of his faculties. If even to this extent, *i.e.* of forgetting Jerusalem or failing to treasure it above all, he sides with the Babylonian and Edomite foes of the sacred city, he does not spare himself the pains he will presently invoke upon them. Thus we see in advance that his wrath is a genuine religious emotion, directed against all ungodliness wherever found, however expressed, and is no mere self-indulgent human vengefulness.

7 *The Edomites* were Israel's ancestral brothers, through Esau, a relationship which Israel had been careful to observe (*cf.* Dt. 2:1–8), but relations between the two nations had been incessantly bitter, culminating in the atrocious Edomite exultation in the fall of Jerusalem (*cf.* Ob. 8–14). **8, 9** These verses should not be taken as a statement of the divine principle of exact retribution, a principle that is safe only in the hands of God, but rather an acknowledgment of the human methods of reprisal. D. R. Jones (on Zc. 14:13, in *Haggai, Zechariah and Malachi*, 1962) uses the words: 'Less a crude piece of Old Testament savagery than the result of empirical realism. This is how things happen in the conflicts of an evil world.' Words could not more exactly introduce the present verses. Here is a man who is so sure of his purity of mind and motive that he can spell out his petition in terms of the actuality of its fulfilment in a hard and cruel world.

PSALM 138. THE ONLY AND TRUSTWORTHY GOD

This is above all things a psalm of confidence in God. The psalmist faces three other existing forces in turn and proclaims in relation to each of them the superior power of the Lord: thus, in relation to other gods (vv. 1–3), the name of the Lord alone is to be praised, and this confidence arises out of the experience of answered prayer (v. 3); in relation to secular authorities (vv. 4–6), he asserts that even they must come to acknowledge the Lord when they learn how the Lord has dealt with him (vv. 4b, 6); and in relation to enemies who threaten him personally (vv. 7, 8), he is confident of his abiding security because of the faithfulness of the Lord to His purposes (v. 8).

What situation best fits a psalm such as this? It is hardly likely that a private individual could think of some purely personal experience as exercising a convincing influence over the kings of the earth. But if the individual were a king himself, such a hope is possible. Were it not for the reference to the Temple (v. 2; assuming, as seems correct, that this means the earthly building which Solomon made) the psalm would fit suitably the career of David (*cf.* 2 Sa. 7:8, 9; 12:7). Of the other kings Hezekiah is, of course, the obvious candidate, for his miraculous deliverance from Sennacherib could clearly give him cause to vaunt over the heathen gods, to sense that a testimony had been at least implicitly made to the kings of the earth, and to feel a new surge of confidence in the power of the Lord. His deliverance was, as a matter of fact, associated with a clear answer to prayer (2 Ki. 19:14ff.). But doubtless there were many occasions on which individual kings were divinely brought to victory and to the renewal of faith.

It may be, however, that some psalmist, at the time of Cyrus' decree (Ezr. 1:1–4), speaks out in the name of the nation (for a similar personification, *cf.* Ps. 129:1–3), celebrating the Lord's overthrow of the gods of Babylon (*cf.* Is. 46:1–7), anticipating the world-wide testimony which the publication of the decree will effect (whether Cyrus was sincere or not is no matter), and expressing buoyant confidence regarding the national future.

1–3 The God who hears

The Lord has dealt with the psalmist in such a way as to capture the devotion of his *whole heart*, and to rule out the possibility of his defecting to worship any of the *gods* (v. 1). Yet it is not so much a matter of what God has done but of what He is, as seen in His deeds; therefore worship is directed towards the *temple*, the place where God had presenced Himself among His people, and His *name*, which summarized all that He had told them of Himself. But in particular He is thankfully adored for *steadfast love* and *faithfulness*, even to an extent which exceeded *everything* previously known (v. 2). The occasion of this revelation was the answering of the psalmist's prayer (v. 3).

1 *The gods*. There is an ambivalence in the OT concerning 'other gods'. It strenuously denies their existence as beings (*cf.* Ps. 115:4–7) but ever recognizes their reality as objects of somebody's worship and their potential to seduce Israel away from the Lord. *Cf.* 1 Jn. 5:20, 21. The psalmist's purpose here is simply to assert the absolute supremacy of the Lord against all such claimants to his worship (*cf.* 1 Cor. 8:5, 6). **2** RSV mg. is to be retained: the Lord's recent *word*, *i.e.* what He replied and then implemented in response to prayer, has outstripped all that the psalmist ever previously knew His *name* to signify.

4–6 The God who acts

Words (v. 4) looks back to the *word* of v. 2: what the Lord replied and then implemented. This act is such as to convince even kings, and to make them rejoice over *the glory of the Lord* as manifested in His *ways*, His characteristic acts (v. 5). And this is His character, to lift up the *lowly* man who has reached rock-bottom, but to alienate Himself from *the haughty* (v. 6).

4 *For*, or 'when'. If the latter translation is accepted, the force is that, should the news of such a God get abroad, it would convince kings, *etc.* **6** *High*; *cf.* Is. 57:15. *The haughty*; *cf.* Is. 2:10–17.

7, 8 The God who purposes

There are two sides to the Lord's love for His own: protection and victory. He preserves them against attack, but also He counter-attacks, dispersing the threat. The psalmist dares to speak of this as habitual divine action (the present tenses of v. 7) because of his assurance of the Lord's inflexible *purpose*, resting as it does on His unchanging *love*. Yet this does not breed in him a mood of complacency, for he ends with a prayer that the Lord will persevere with him until the work is fully finished.

8 *Cf.* the confidence of Phil. 1:6 coupled with the prayer of Phil. 1:9–11.

PSALM 139. NO ESCAPE, NO REGRETS

It is characteristic of the Bible to express its great truths in the context of personal experience. Partly, this is because God is never proposed as a subject for man's intellectual, speculative enquiry (*cf.* Jb. 11:7, 8), but for his devotion, worship and obedience. It is also because the Bible never considers a truth 'known' until it controls the life of the learner. Of all this view of things Ps. 139 is a classic instance. The psalm could be said to teach God's omniscience (vv. 1–6), omnipresence (vv. 7–12), sovereignty (vv. 13–16), and holiness (vv. 17–24), yet in the truest sense nothing could less exactly express the psalmist's mind than these four great abstractions. To the psalmist, omniscience is 'God's complete knowledge of me', omnipresence is that 'God is with me no matter where I am', and so forth. The 'I–Thou' relationship is basic to the poem.

How is this relationship understood? We must reject out of hand any suggestion that the psalmist is a would-be fugitive from God, motivated by an awareness of the danger of his plight as a sinner (*cf.* F. Delitzsch, *Commentary on the Psalms*, 1881; E. J. Young, *Psalm 139*, 1965, both v. 7). Far from being anxious to go where God is not, the psalmist delights in God (v. 17), happily recognizes the permanence of divine companionship (v. 18) and even invites God's scrutiny (vv. 23, 24). This is the psalm, then, not of a man who would escape God if only he could, but of one who knows that he cannot do so and finds no regret, but only joy, in the fact.

Security in God is the central truth of the psalm. God's complete knowledge of him (vv. 1–6) focuses upon God's encirclement and tender care (v. 5); God's omnipresence (vv. 7–12) means that His hand ever guides and holds (v. 10); and God's creative power (vv. 13–16) includes the pre-planning of all his days (v. 16). At all times, in all places and in every circumstance, God is in control and the psalmist is in safety.

We may well ask what prompted him thus to meditate on his happy security. The psalm is a unity. This is evident not simply from the progression of its main sections one from the other (notice the explanatory *for* which opens the new section at v. 13), but also in the matching ideas of the opening and closing verses. The key to the occasion of the psalm (as Eaton clearly notes) is the prayer against enemies (vv. 19, 20). The psalm leads up to this and flows away from it. Under pressure from godless foes, the psalmist meditates upon his joyous security in God (vv. 1–18), prays for their destruction (vv. 19, 20), and finally asserts his own moral disengagement from them and their ways, urging God to search his heart to find that this is so (vv. 21–24).

Two comments may be offered on this. The first is that Ps. 139, besides being one of the greatest of all the Psalms, is also the greatest of the imprecatory psalms. We do not know its date of origin, except to say that the evidence of Aramaisms in the language 'is not firm proof of a post-exilic date' (Eaton), but the situation is clear enough: the onslaught of foes is met by prayer for their destruction. It is interesting to note that some commentators who are forward to charge other imprecatory psalms with low and unschooled moral values hasten to say that here 'the wrathful words . . . need not cause surprise. . . . The psalmist cannot do other than hate them' (W. O. E. Oesterley, *The Psalms*, 1939, p. 557), for the sheer loftiness of the whole psalm peremptorily forbids any other view! As we noted, this feature, in one degree or another, marks all the imprecatory psalms: alongside their imprecations there is some indication of an exalted sense of God, a high value of true religion, a covetable spirituality, and it is this rich theology which prompts and renders inevitable a clear-cut theodicy. In the matter of the judgment due to the wicked the psalmist can no more stand aloof than he can view the divine omnipresence as a mere philosophic abstract unconnected with daily life.

Secondly, to us who also face, in varying measure, daily spiritual harassment from ungodly foes, circumstantial, human or superhuman, this psalmist speaks directly. His message bridges the years to tell us that our resource is restful confidence in God, prayer, and energetic moral commitment.

1–18 Security

1–6 The all-knowing God. God knows him in his own person (v. 1), in his outward actions (v. 2a) and inward thoughts (v. 2b). He knows him at all times, whether as he walks the daily *path* or rests, *lying down*, at night (v. 3a). He knows him in his habitual *ways* and his words (vv. 3b, 4). This intimate, detailed knowledge is seen as part of God's protective, tender care (v. 5), which runs beyond the psalmist's capacity to understand, yet reassures him that he is cared for by a wisdom that is far in excess of his own (v. 6).

2 *Thou* is emphatic. The psalmist knows that he is searched and known in every aspect of his being (v. 1), but the Knower is the personal Lord Himself. This is the 'I–Thou', or better, the 'Thou–I', relationship on which this psalm rests. *Thoughts*, rather in the sense of 'intentions'. Hence, *from afar* means 'long before'. The Lord has 'seen to the heart' of the psalmist's plans even before he himself entertained them. **3** *Acquainted*: 'to be carefully, painstakingly familiar with'. But it may be another verb meaning 'to winnow', 'to sift through and through'. **5** Such knowledge as God possesses of us could be a terrifying thing, but it is here allied to a protective purpose. *Beset*: the verb is often used in the sense 'to besiege', but here, as Oesterley says, it means 'like a rampart round a city "thou dost encircle me".' The strength of this protection is matched by the tenderness of *layest thy hand upon me*; *cf.* Gn. 46:4; 48:14; Jb. 9:33.

7–12 The ever-present God. Another truth about God is that, by His Spirit, He is everywhere present (v. 7), and the absolute reality of this is clarified in a series of contrasts (vv. 8, 9): the world to come (*Sheol*, v. 8), the present world (v. 9); the contrasting dimensions of height (*heaven*, v. 8), depth (*Sheol*, v. 8), and distance (*the uttermost parts*, v. 9). But this omnipresence is the essence of blessedness, for it means that God is present to *lead* and *hold* (v. 10). Furthermore, this divine presence remains the same in all the varied circumstances of life, its *darkness* and *light* (vv. 11, 12).

7 *Thy Spirit*. See the General Article, 'Old Testament Theology', pp. 28f. This verse shows that the OT enjoys the same truth about the Holy Spirit as Jesus expressed in Jn. 14:16–18, the Spirit as the mode of realization of the personal presence of God, involving as it does the divinity and personality of the Spirit Himself. *Presence*: lit. 'face', thus emphasizing that God's personal presence is specifically stressed. **8** *Sheol*: the abode of the dead, the 'paradise' of Lk. 23:43, though in Ps. 6:5 (*q.v.*; *cf.* Introduction to Psalms) it foreshadows the other element in the NT delineation of the world to come (*cf.* Mt. 25:41, 46a). **9** *Wings*. A picture of the swift spreading of morning light over the earth, indicating that not even flight with the speed of light can separate us from God. **10** This key verse tells us how to understand v. 7, *i.e.* not 'that he wishes to escape from God but that escape would be impossible if he wished it'

(Kirkpatrick). **11** *Let only . . .*: RSV unfortunately here suggests that the psalmist desired to be hidden from God. This, of course, would contradict the evidence of v. 10. See RV, 'Surely darkness . . .', *i.e.* expressive of a momentary fear of losing the comfort of God's presence. *Cover* involves a small emendation of the Hebrew, which literally reads 'bruise' (the verb as in Gn. 3:15, hence RV 'overwhelm'). We may have here a play on the idea of darkness, as both a physical circumstance and also a metaphor for the difficulties of life (*cf.* on 23:4). **12** *Darkness is as light with thee*: lit. 'darkness and light are identical', *i.e.* as equally unable to divorce him from the divine presence.

13–16 The all-sovereign God. God is the Creator, superintending both the psychological (*inward parts*, v. 13a) and physical (*knit me*, v. 13b) structure. In this as in all His works He displays *wonderful, i.e.* supernatural, powers, but the implication of this creative work is His intimate knowledge of His creature (vv. 14, 15). The Creator's work, however, covered not only the person concerned (v. 16a), but also the experiences yet in store for that person (v. 16b). Here again is the comfort implicit in the truth: the Creator plans all life; all our experiences are under sovereign control.

13 *Inward parts* (lit. 'kidneys'): used of the seat of emotion and affection, *e.g.* Ps. 73:21; Je. 12:2 (both 'heart' in RSV), and here of the psychological aspect of man. *Knit*, or 'cover', the former representing God's direct activity in the growth of the foetus, the latter His protection of it as it grew; both implying His concern for the physical frame of man. **15** *The depths of the earth* may express no more than that the earth is far below the height of heaven where God is ('the depths, namely, the earth') and yet He knows all about our birth. Or it may be, as Delitzsch urges, that as Adam was formed from the earth, so 'the mother's womb out of which the child of Adam comes forth is the earth out of which it is taken'. **16** *The days that were formed for me.* The Creator does not push out the boat of the individual's life to take its chance on the stream of time. The days were 'formed' (the potter's verb, as in Gn. 2:7) by Him also. Even to this degree does He care for us.

17, 18 Conclusion: the preciousness of security in God. The knowledge of God is precious and inexhaustible, and the presence of God a changeless reality.

17 *Thy thoughts, i.e.* '(these) thoughts of Thee'. **17, 18** *Sum . . . count*: both their collective magnitude and their individual multiplicity. **18** *Awake* refers both to the experience of awaking day after day (*i.e.* the faithful abiding presence of God all through life) and to the great awakening after death (*cf.* Ps. 17:15). *I am still with thee* differs from 'Thou art still with me' in that the latter would express the idea of the presence of God, while the former expresses also the idea of that peace with God whereby we may remain constantly in His presence.

19–24 Commitment

The circumstance revealed in the prayer (vv. 19, 20) was evidently the occasion which moved the psalmist to lay fresh hold on the truth of his security in God. Godless men were upon him, and he would rather that they *depart* (v. 19), yet what moves him is not consideration of his own comfort but detestation of the moral and spiritual values which these men embody (v. 20). The abhorrence voiced in his prayer arises from his unreserved commitment to God whereby he must needs act towards them as they towards God (v. 21), and in his attitude towards them there is nothing but hatred and antipathy (v. 22); no trace or remainder of secret or sneaking admiration for what they are or of envy for the life they live. Yet can anyone have complete self-knowledge? Only God knows all that there is to be known (*cf.* v. 1), therefore let God be the judge of his heart; let God search and expose any remaining wickedness and lead him in the way to eternal life (vv. 23, 24).

19 *Slay the wicked.* Weiser holds that, however justified is the psalmist's outcry against the wicked, he does not here follow the divine course 'which in the end leads to the . . . compassion that Jesus showed on the cross'. But this is to ignore the Jesus of Mt. 25:41, 46a, the Lamb of Rev. 6:15–17, and indeed the whole biblical dimension of the wrath of God. The imprecation here reveals a man who could selflessly and sinlessly rise to the height of the divine hatred of sin. *Men of blood*: guilty of crimes of violence against others. **24** *Everlasting*: contrasting with the impermanence of the wicked (*cf.* Ps. 1:4–6) and partaking of the nature of God (*cf.* Gn. 21:33).

PSALM 140. SLANDER

Pss. 140–143 can be considered as a linked group: they are alike in portraying the reactions of the godly to trouble, each psalm showing a different facet of it (as indicated in the titles in the commentary). Similarities of wording and thought connect them: *cf.* 140:2–4a with 141:2–4a; 140:5 with 141:9, 10a and 142:3b; 140:6 with 142:5 and 143:10; 140:9 with 141:10; 140:13a with 142:7b; 140:13b with 143:10b; 142:3 with 143:4; *etc.* Most noticeably, they are all prayers, revealing that the first reaction to trouble is to take it to the Lord. As to the occasion from which this group sprang, there is no good reason for questioning the assertion made in the psalm-title to Ps. 142.

1–5 A prayer for protection

In structure this psalm consists of two prayers (vv. 1–5, 8–11), each followed by an affirmation (vv. 6, 7, and 12, 13). The first prayer consists of two general pleas for protection (*Deliver . . . preserve*, v. 1; *Guard . . . preserve*, v. 4) followed by statements of the danger which threatens. The description is full, indicating the place which may be given in prayer to sharing all the details of life with God. Thus he exposes the character (vv. 1, 2, 4a), speech (v. 3) and treacherous hostility (vv. 4b, 5) of his opponents, thought, word and deed proceeding in that order. But the particular stress of the psalm is on vicious slander (vv. 3, 9, 11), and on the sly, insidious ways of his foes (4, 5). In these circumstances there is no resource but God.

6, 7 God's care

The psalmist is still at prayer (v. 6b), but the force of the prayer is now to strengthen his own hand by some re-assurance of God's care for him. There are three strands of confidence: his personal relationship with God (v. 6a), his awareness of God's majestic power to save (v. 7a), and his past experiences of divine deliverance (v. 7b).

7 *My Lord*. The printing indicates that this represents the Hebrew *'adōnāy*, meaning 'sovereign Lord'. *My strong deliverer*: lit. 'strength of my salvation', 'my saving strength'; *i.e.* the one whose power to save is available for and directed towards me.

8–11 A prayer for victory

Two views of sin alternate here: first, that it is the object of divine opposition (vv. 8, 10); secondly, that it has a boomerang quality which makes it the cause of its own destruction (vv. 9, 11).

8 In the mystery of divine providence, God sometimes makes use of the wicked as the instruments of His holy punishment of the disobedient (*cf.* Is. 10:5–15 and the General Article, 'Old Testament Theology', pp. 27f.). The psalmist prays that this may not be the case in his present plight. 10 *Pits* are specifically 'flooded areas': thus the verse contains the characteristic divine judgments of fire and flood, indicating a return to the thought of God's opposition to and inevitable judgment upon sin. 11 *Hunt*: his enemies had acted as though he was their prey and they the hunters (*cf.* vv. 4, 5), but their wickedness will yet recoil on them.

12, 13 God's righteousness

The thought of v. 11a is developed. It is contrary to God's righteous ways to allow the wicked to be established, and it is in accordance with His righteousness to uphold the cause of the godly. The present tenses of v. 12 express the general principles of divine providence; the future tenses of v. 13 express the faith of the people of God. 12 *Needy*. The basis of the word is 'to be willing'; hence it came to mean 'pliable', in the bad sense of 'able to be manipulated' or 'pushed round', and 'pliant' in the good sense of 'ready for all Thy perfect will'. Hence 'needy' is often, as here, a word expressive of the socially oppressed but religiously committed man. 13 *In thy presence*: lit. 'with thy face'. The hope of the godly is nothing less than their residence in the very presence of God.

PSALM 141. PROVOCATION

In the stress of trouble, the psalmist senses the danger of being provoked into ill-considered speech (v. 3), into making common cause with the ways and persons of the wicked (v. 4), of refusing the counsels of the righteous (v. 5a, RV), or into a wrong comment upon the overthrow of the wicked when it comes (vv. 5b, 6). The time of trouble can so easily detach us from God and from godliness, and it is against these things respectively (vv. 1, 2 with 8; and vv. 3–7) that he prays.

1–4 Action

The element of urgency in his prayer is noticeable: 1a he looks for *haste* on God's part, 1b for an answer contemporary with his request (*when* has the force of 'while'); 2 he desires God to find in his prayers all the divinely-willed power and acceptability of the appointed offerings. To what end is a prayer of such urgency made? Not for deliverance from trouble but deliverance from sin! His foes were men of unguarded and vicious speech (Ps. 140:3, 11), 3 but he would have God *guard* all that he says. Behind their wicked speech lay their evil heart (Ps. 140:2), 4a but he would have a heart free of inclination to evil. He was aware of their diligent pursuit of devious ways (Ps. 140:4, 5), 4b but such a course is not for him, 4c nor even to be found in the company of such people, however attractive it may appear. The need for godly separation from the words, thoughts, ways and fellowship of the ungodly could not be more fervently stressed. *Incline not*: just as God, for His own holy purposes, may give the wicked liberty to advance their schemes (Ps. 140:8), so also He may punish the godly by allowing the natural evil of their heart to have its way (*cf.* Ps. 78:29–31). The psalmist recognizes that, should his heart cease to be controlled by God for righteousness, then *evil* and *wicked deeds* inevitably follow. *Dainties*: the attractions with which sin adorns itself and with which the ungodly deck their schemes.

5–7 Reaction

The Hebrew (see RSV mg.) of v. 5 is rather better treated in RV. The danger in question appears to be that in a time of stress the advice of the righteous will be arrogantly rejected—specially if the righteous comes with a word of rebuke. He prays that he may take it as a kindness and even as a blessing or anointing which his head gladly receives. In contrast with this reaction of welcome, there is the abiding reaction of enmity which he desires to show against all wickedness (v. 5b). But he also envisages the day when the wicked will be publicly overthrown, and vows that in that day people will hear from him nothing but gracious and kindly words. 5 The Hebrew is abrupt rather than problematical: 'Let the righteous strike me—a kindness! Let (such a one) reprove me—oil for the head—let not my head refuse it!' 6 *True*: lit. 'they shall hear my words, that they are sweet'; *i.e.* hear nothing but pleasant words from me. No words of vindictive triumph, self-gratification, *etc.*, but only what is designed to heal and soothe.

8–10 Refuge

But the wicked have not yet been overthrown, however certain their eventual and utter downfall may be (*cf.* v. 7), and prayer for protection must continue. **8** is the contrast to v. 4: having refused to extricate himself from trouble by the methods and aid of the wicked, he declares that God alone is his refuge: **8a** the sole source from which he expects help and **8b** the sole place in which he seeks shelter. This truth is turned to a prayer for **8c** defence, **9** guidance and **10** retribution.

PSALM 142. LONELINESS

Ps. 141 envisaged the possibility that the righteous might so fail to understand his position that they would come to him with rebukes. The blow has now fallen in a more severe form: he is utterly man-forsaken (v. 4), and faces the problem of isolation. Man-forsaken, but not God-forsaken! The hour of trial is faith's opportunity to lay hold on the faithful God.

1–3 Divine providence

The additional bitterness of his situation appears at once **2** in the words *complaint* and *trouble*, and **3** in the admission of a *faint* spirit. The problem is the same (v. 3b), the subtle hostility of his foes, but before he can state it, a gleam of light appears: *Thou knowest my way* (v. 3a). *Cf.* 'The Lord knows' (Ps. 1:6). This certainly involves the idea of intimate, personal knowledge; it reaches out to include superintendency and possibly even means divine appointment. The snared pathway was as much in His loving, knowledgeable care of His child as the deep darkness of Ps. 23:3b, 4. *Cf.* Dt. 8:14–16.

4, 5 Divine refuge

In contrast to the divine care stands human carelessness. Yet the Lord remains as both his protection (*refuge*) and satisfaction (*portion*). **4** *Refuge*: rather the more negative idea of 'escape'. Among men he can find no way out of his plight. **5** *Refuge*: the positive idea of a place of strength and safety; a different word and idea. *Portion*; *cf.* Nu. 18:20; Jos. 13:33; 18:7; Pss. 16:5; 73:23ff.

6, 7 Divine sufficiency

The two leading thoughts of the psalm are now united: on the one hand the low and dispirited state to which lack of human sympathy, coupled as it was with active hostility from his opponents, has reduced him (vv. 5, 6) and the contrasting thought of divine oversight and faithfulness (vv. 3, 5, 7). His final cry to God is full of assurance. Human strength may be both at an end and overpowered, but God can work deliverance (v. 6), restore freedom of movement (v. 7a) and thankful gladness (v. 7b), and bring back into being the lost fellowship of the righteous (v. 7c).

7 *Prison*: not in the sense of 'gaol', but in the sense of being restricted in movement. *Me* is emphatic, as if to say 'me, of all people—the one they now reject'. *Bountifully*: rather 'completely', meeting every need.

PSALM 143. THE IMMINENT END

This brief series of 'psalms in a time of trouble' now comes to its climax (see introduction to Ps. 140). The psalmist feels that he has reached the limit of endurance: the enemy has metaphorically 'entombed' him (v. 3b)—how suitable to David's experience in 'the cave' (psalm-title, Ps. 142; *cf.* 1 Sa. 23:19ff.)—but now the reality of death seems to draw near (v. 7b); spirit and heart can stand no more buffeting (vv. 4, 7a); God's mercies seem to belong entirely to the past (v. 5), and there is no refreshing sign of His favour in the present (v. 6); there is even the possibility that He too has adopted an attitude of judgment (v. 2). Yet whatever else fails, the spirit of prayer blossoms. The deeper the trouble the more deeply is refuge sought in God. At the same time the wear and tear of prolonged stress is evident in the very form of the psalm. Certainly it is a unity, and in one sense any analysis mars its sustained appeal, but it also has a staccato quality, seen in the eleven petitions in vv. 7–12, in which we enter into the helpless urgency of the flight of this battered soul to his God.

1, 2 Divine forbearance

Each section of this sustained prayer rests on a different ground of appeal. The first of these is the nature of God: the forbearance which looks favourably on the psalmist (v. 1) and which forgoes the divine right of strict judgment (v. 2).

1 *Supplications*: specifically a plea for divine grace. Thus the psalm opens on the note of absence of merit on the part of the intercessor, coupled with the existence of grace for the undeserving in the nature of God. *Faithfulness . . . righteousness*: God's undeviating pursuit of His own declared policies. In this verse, following the line laid down by *supplications*, the reference is to His purposes of grace and salvation for His people. **2** The possibility raised in Pss. 140:8; 141:4 (*q.v.*), that God might be using the psalmist's enemies to bring a merited punishment upon him, is here faced in its basic form. God has every right to assume the mantle of judge, and the psalmist does not deny that he too deserves divine judgment. But if God so acts, then all hope is at an end.

3, 4 Personal exhaustion

The privilege of the people of God is that they may not only plead divine saving grace (v. 1) against the divine right to judge (v. 2) but that, such is the tender relation into which God has brought them with Himself, they can frankly plead on the ground of personal need. The picture here is of chase (v. 3a), capture as the hunter leaps upon the prey (v. 3b), imprisonment (v. 3c), with ensuing hopelessness (v. 4).

5, 6 Spiritual longing

Nevertheless, the truth abides that God 'satisfies him who is thirsty' (Ps. 107:9), and it is this sense of longing for God which now pervades and gives basis to the prayer. It finds expression in remembrance (v. 5) and mute appeal (v. 6). The fact ought to be noticed, for it is characteristic of the psalmists, that in every plight their chief desire was for God rather than for mere release from trouble; *cf*. Pss. 43:3, 4; 63:1–4.

5 *I remember*; *cf*. Pss. 42:4; 63:5–8; 77:5ff. The call to remembrance is impressive in the OT, and is chiefly related to the encouragement drawn from recalling God's deeds of old (*e.g.* Dt. 1:29–33; 7:18; Ne. 4:14) and the consequent motive to obedience (*e.g.* Dt. 5:15; 8:2, 18).

7, 8 Impending finality

Urgency governs the appeal: *Haste . . . fails . . . the Pit . . . morning*. The end of personal strength (v. 7a) yields to the darkness of imminent death (v. 7b). He longs for news of God (v. 8a) and a word from God (v. 8b).

7 *Hide not . . . Pit*. The reference here to death (*the Pit*) is linked with the sense of the loss of divine favour (the hidden *face*). Once more (*cf*. on 6:4, 5; 30:9; 88:10, 11; and see Introduction to Psalms) it is not death as such which appears hopeless, but to die without any light of divine favour. 8 *Morning*: the soon-coming time of light, following the darkness of night (*cf*. Ps. 30:5), therefore metaphorical for hope. *Teach me*. Just as in vv. 5, 6 the longing was for God Himself rather than for the bare end of the trouble, so here the end of the apparent divine aloofness is desired, not because it will automatically dispel the present difficulties, but more because it will make possible a dedicated life of obedience.

9, 10 Personal dedication

The personal and dedicated seeking after God which v. 8 introduced is now elaborated. Deliverance (v. 9a) will give him the opportunity, teaching (v. 10a) will give the knowledge and ability, and guidance by the Spirit (v. 10b) the actual experience of serving God according to His will. The appeal therefore is for the chance to live for God (as contrasted with the possibility of dying in His displeasure, vv. 7, 8), and the basis of the appeal is an exclusive seeking after and devotion to God (vv. 9b, 10a).

10 *Spirit*. See the General Article, 'Old Testament Theology', pp. 28f.

11, 12 Divine righteousness

The psalmist returns to the opening thought of the nature of God. On the ground of His revealed character (*name*, v. 11a), His undeviating pursuit of His holy purposes, especially of salvation towards His people (*righteousness*, v. 11b; *cf*. Is. 45:21–23), and His changeless love to those within His covenant (*steadfast love*, v. 12), the plea is made for preservation (v. 11a; contrast v. 7), the end of trouble (v. 11b) and the complete dispersal of all threat (v. 12). The right of the psalmist so to plead the favour of God comes at the end: the personal helplessness of a *servant* (or 'slave', v. 12b) is linked with the almighty power of the One who is his Lord, and the relationship itself gives him the right to plead for what that Lord alone can do.

11, 12 These verses further illuminate the question of imprecations. We would certainly be happy to pray v. 11, but might shy away from v. 12. This is a failure of realism on our part. There are circumstances (such as David's in respect of the incurable nature of Saul's enmity) where there can be no deliverance without destruction, and to pray for the one is to pray for the other.

PSALM 144. FULL SALVATION

Praise prevails from this psalm onwards to the end of the Psalter. But the present psalm also undoubtedly looks back to the sombre tones of Pss. 140–143, telling us that in God's good time the long desired 'morning' (143:8) dawned, bringing with it a glorying in God which almost defied the resources of language to express (vv. 1, 2), a humbling sense of His condescension (vv. 3, 4), a triumphant re-assurance of His sufficiency for present needs (vv. 5–11) and the prospect of greater blessings yet to come (vv. 12–15). The clear links with Ps. 18 (v. 1b with 18:34; v. 2 with 18:2; v. 2c (RV) with 18:47; v. 5 with 18:9; v. 6 with 18:14; *etc*.) make the psalm (see psalm-title to Ps. 18) eminently suited to the stated occasion of Pss. 140–143 (see psalm-title to Ps. 142). The possible linking of the psalm with the ritual triumph of the Davidic king over his foes in the autumn festival (see Introduction) does not, of course, in any way rule out a basic historical occasion for the composition and therefore the main associations of the psalm.

1–4 Past salvation

The greatness of God (vv. 1, 2) is contrasted with the insignificance (v. 3) and insubstantiality (v. 4) of man. David, secure at last on his throne, ascribes all the glory to God and views with nothing but wonder the fact that he has himself been the recipient of such favours.

1 *Rock* combines the ideas of strength and changelessness (*e.g.* Dt. 32:4; 2 Sa. 22:47–49) with those of refuge (Ps. 31:2, 3) and sustenance (Ex. 17:6; Ps. 95:1, 8). *Trains*. Salvation is all of God; of this the psalm is sure. Yet the enthroned David knows that the God who gave him victory called him to fight. (*Cf*. Eph. 2:4–7; 6:10–17.) 2

Rock. Note RSV mg., and *cf.* RV. The retention of the Hebrew 'my steadfast love' (*i.e.* 'the One who bestows steadfast love on me') aptly sounds the note of the basis of salvation in the love and mercy of God (*cf.* Eph. 2:4). *The peoples under him.* This reading stresses that the whole agency of salvation is God's; the text, as reflected in RV, includes also the idea of David's personal enjoyment of what God alone had done for him. **3, 4** The positive truth of God as the sole Saviour is safeguarded by the negative truth that man can never either deserve or accomplish his own salvation.

5–11 Present sufficiency

David, though enthroned by the wonder of God's acts for him, was yet in need of divine help. What God did in the great deliverance (*cf.* Ps. 18:9) He must continue to do (v. 5), for dangers past (*cf.* Ps. 18:16) are dangers present (v. 7). Yet, having experienced that great past deliverance, his life, though still beset by foes, can never be the same again: it has *a new song* (v. 9).

5 *Bow*; *cf.* Na. 1:3b. God's descent to fight with the foes of His people is pictured as the lowering of storm clouds over the earth. *Touch.* The power of the Creator over the created world (*cf.* Ex. 19:18) is illustrative of His power to save His people (*cf.* Is. 50:2, 3). **7** *Stretch forth thy hand*; *i.e.* the personal activity of God to save (*cf.* Dt. 5:15; Mt. 14:31). *Many waters*: figurative of overwhelming threats (*cf.* Ps. 124:4, 5). *Aliens*: possibly foreign foes, such as in the main were David's concern after his accession, but more likely in a general sense (*cf.* Ps. 142:4 where another form of the same word is translated 'takes notice') of those who hold themselves estranged and aloof in their hostility. **8** *Right hand*: as used in oath-taking (*cf.* Ps. 106:26). They swore fidelity but practised treachery.

12–15 Future expectation

The psalmist looks forward in prayer to the glories awaiting God's people. The key-note is one of certainty. He asks for blessings in family (v. 12), business (vv. 13, 14a) and nation (vv. 14b, c), but he sees these as already secured by the possession of the Lord as God (v. 15).

12 *Youth* points here to young manhood, and the prayer is that, like the *full grown plants,* they may be soundly rooted, and grow without deformity or stunting. *Corner pillars*; *i.e.* both occupying a secure position in the building and at the same time giving stability to the building in which they themselves are secure—the position of the wife and mother in a well-ordered society. *Cut*: or, possibly, 'adorned'. **13** *Cf.* Dt. 28:2–11. **14** *Mischance or failure in bearing.* The reference may be indeed, as RSV, to some disease causing miscarriage among the herds, but we could equally understand the psalmist to turn here to another aspect of the prosperous life: national security. Hence, 'No breach and no offensive and no mourning', the references

being respectively to involvement in a defensive and an offensive war, coupled with the mourning for the dead which accompanies each.

PSALM 145. KNOWING AND PROCLAIMING GOD

The verses of this psalm begin with the successive letters of the Hebrew alphabet. One letter (*nûn*), missing in the Hebrew text, is found (rightly or wrongly, but at any rate quite suitably) in LXX, and appears in RSV as v. 13b (*The Lord is faithful . . . all his deeds*). The reference to the Lord as King (vv. 1, 12, 13), coupled with the mention of abundant harvest (vv. 15, 16), has led Weiser to associate the psalm with the Feast of Tabernacles (*cf.* Zc. 14:16f.), but there is surely no season of rejoicing on which this glorious hymn of praise could not suitably be sung. We enter here into the joyousness of OT religion.

Within an initial (vv. 1, 2) and concluding (v. 21) affirmation of intention to proclaim the Lord, the body of the psalm is a somewhat fugal meditation on three stated aspects of the divine nature: His greatness (v. 3), His graciousness and mercy (v. 8), and His justice or righteousness (v. 17). In the Hebrew these are announced in matching phrases: 'Great is the Lord. . . . Gracious and merciful is the Lord. . . . Just (Righteous) is the Lord', thus providing a broad framework of analysis. But within each subsection the attributes of God are intertwined, for God is One and there is no conflict in the divine nature: thus His greatness includes His goodness and righteousness (v. 7), His graciousness includes His greatness (vv. 11–13), and His righteousness includes His graciousness (v. 17).

1, 2 Introduction: I will bless thy name

The psalmist ascribes the highest place to the God whom he knows for himself as King, but when he contemplates the revealed nature (*name*) of this God he turns rather to adoring and grateful worship (*bless*, v. 1). Eternity will exhaust neither the subject nor the desire for blessing such a God, and in practice this means that *every day* adoring worship will issue in glad shouts of praise (v. 2).

1 *Extol*: lit. 'to ascribe height (to)', as when we sing 'the highest place that heaven affords is His, is His by right'. **2** *Praise*: the verb as in the glad shout, Hallelujah, hence vocal and exuberant praise.

3–7 The Lord is great

All who know God are bound to tell of Him. Though His greatness is unfathomable, yet it is made known (and is therefore the subject of testimony) in His works (vv. 4, 5) and acts (vv. 4, 6) by means of which the Lord has established a (true) report (*fame*, v. 7) of His *goodness* and *righteousness.*

4–7 Note the intertwining of general and

individual responsibility for testimony: *One generation* (4) . . . *I* (5) . . . *Men* (6; lit. 'they', matching *they* in v. 7) . . . *I* (6) . . . *They* (7). **4–6** God's deeds are successively *mighty* (4), *wondrous* (5) and *terrible* (6): the first word stresses their power, the second their supernatural quality, marking them as arising from God and being beyond the scope of man, and the third their ability to inspire awe. **7** *Fame*: the same noun translated 'thus I am to be remembered' in Ex. 3:15; *i.e.* by His deeds God has given a definitive account of Himself.

8–16 The Lord is gracious

The specific divine graciousness to the covenant people (v. 8; *cf.* Ex. 34:6, 7) is accompanied by a universal goodness of God (v. 9), and just as on a universal scale thanks return to Him (v. 10a), so in particular His own people (*saints*, v. 10b) bless Him; and to them belongs the task of testimony (v. 11) to the Lord's kingly power and sway (vv. 12, 13), His faithful promises (v. 13b), and gracious acts of support and supply (vv. 13c–16).

9 *Compassion*: the tender love of a mother; *cf.* on 103:13. **10** *Saints*. This title (Heb. *ḥasîd*) is related to 'steadfast love' (Heb. *ḥeseḏ*), and therefore denotes primarily those who have been the object of the covenant love of the Lord; it then advances to include also the thought of their responsive love towards Him (*cf.* 1 Jn. 4:19) and towards each other within the covenant-family (*cf.* 1 Jn. 4:11).

17–20 The Lord is just

To say that the Lord is just (or righteous) by no means conflicts with saying that He is gracious; rather His justice lives side by side with His kindness (Heb. *ḥasîd*, used here as an attributive, 'possessing and displaying steadfast love'). His righteousness is, in these verses, His discernment of the heart of those who draw near to Him: He knows if they call *in truth* (v. 18), if they *fear* (v. 19) and *love* (v. 20) Him, or if they belong to the *wicked*, the objects of His wrath (v. 20). Yet, though He cannot be deceived, His righteousness is truly the righteousness of grace: the grace which draws *near* (v. 18), responds, *hears, saves* (v. 19) and keeps (v. 20).

21 Conclusion: Let all flesh bless His name

Individual resolve to testify is the fitting response to knowing such a God, but the end of the matter, and by implication through the agency of this testimony, is that *all flesh* will come to know by name and therefore to adore Him.

PSALM 146. INDIVIDUAL PRAISE

The Psalter concludes with five psalms devoted to praise. They contain no word of petition or suggestion of personal need; there is a minimum of historical allusion. All focuses upon God who alone is worthy to be praised. Each psalm

in the group brings to light some particular aspect of the praise which ascends to God, and Ps. 146 strikes the characteristic note of individualism. If 'I' do not praise, then the praise of God is incomplete (*cf.* on 103:19–22).

That which calls forth such fervent individual praise (vv. 1, 2) is the blessedness of trusting in the Lord. In order to clarify this truth, the psalmist first explores what is required in one who is to be trusted (vv. 3, 4). These verses are not to be understood as a cynical command never to trust anyone. The psalm moves at the more fundamental level of the nature of the ultimate object of trust: what, in the long run, is individual life to be founded upon? Man, even princely man (v. 3a), cannot qualify for this position, first because of lack of ability (v. 3b), secondly because of impermanence (v. 4a) and, in consequence, thirdly, because of unreliability (v. 4b). In contrast the Lord has the absolute power of the Creator (vv. 5, 6a); allied to this is His permanent reliability (v. 6b); but, more than all else, that in Him power is wedded to pity (vv. 7–9). His power characteristically operates in the three realms of the social (v. 7), the personal (v. 8a, b) and the moral (vv. 8c, 9). The concluding verse (10) acts as a summary and climax: *the Lord*, the God of grace described in vv. 7–9, *will reign*, *i.e.* will exercise His sovereign power, *for ever*, permanently.

3 *In princes, in a son of man*. A prince, for all his appearance of stability and power (and therefore his seeming worthwhileness as an object of trust) is a mere man. *Son of* is a Hebrew idiom meaning 'in the condition of'. **5** *The God of Jacob*; *cf.* v. 10, *thy God, O Zion*. The distinctive and trustworthy character described in vv. 7–9 belongs to this God exclusively and to no other: the God who is known to Israel and in Zion. This is the exclusivism of the OT. The abstract concept of 'deity' is not enough for a man to trust; nor is any other claimant to the title 'god'. Only one God is worthy of trust and He is to be found only in Jacob and Zion. **9** *Sojourners* were resident aliens, often political refugees and frequently completely dependent on charity and kindness. They are linked therefore with *the widow and the fatherless* as the helpless and potentially neglected and maltreated section of the community. But the Lord equally characteristically chooses them as special objects of His powerful compassion (*cf.* Dt. 10: 18; Ps. 68:5, 6).

PSALM 147. COMMUNAL PRAISE

Developing the theme of the praise that is due to the Lord, this psalm moves from the individual praise of Ps. 146 to the communal praise of God's people, as indicated by the emphasis resting on the chosen city (vv. 2a, 12) and the chosen people (vv. 2b, 19). The exclusivism of the Lord in heaven (Ps. 146) is here matched by the exclusivism of Israel as His only chosen people on earth

(vv. 19, 20). Therefore they are under a special obligation to engage in His praise.

The psalm is in three sections, indicated by the call to praise (vv. 1, 7, 12). Within each section there is a reminder of the tender mercy of the Lord (vv. 2, 3; 9; 13, 14), His authoritative power as Creator (vv. 4, 5; 8; 15–18), and His primary concern with matters of righteousness (vv. 6; 10, 11; 19, 20). The call to praise, therefore, rests on the consideration of His mercy, power and holiness, with special emphasis on the exclusive position of Israel in relation to these divine attributes.

1–6 The Lord's tenderness

Calling attention to the winsome loveliness (the word translated *gracious*, v. 1) of the Lord, the psalm expounds this aspect of God by recalling His concern for the welfare of Jerusalem, for the individual scattered members of His people, and specially for those needing gentle care (vv. 2, 3). This is seen to be an aspect of all the Lord's activities: He is not the God of Israel alone, but the universal Creator whose power is manifested in His detailed care of the stars (v. 4), whereby He shows both might and wisdom (v. 5). On earth, however, moral factors enter the picture, and the Lord is unequivocally for the *downtrodden* and against the *wicked* (v. 6).

2 *Builds up*, in the general sense of making secure or advancing the welfare of. The word does not tie the psalm to any specific occasion (*e.g.* Ne. 6:15). *Outcasts*: a general reference to an event such as the Exodus, as well as, doubtless, to many an individual mercy experienced by members of God's people. **3** *Wounds*: rather 'hurts' or 'pains'; whatever they feel to pain them becomes His concern. **4** The force of the reference to the Creator's power, here and throughout the psalm, is both to keep the universal dimension of the Lord's sway before our eyes, and also to give assurance to God's people: His special regard for them is backed by the power of One who rules all (*cf.* Is. 40:27–31).

7–11 The Lord's delight

This subsection lacks the initial reference to Israel found in the other two (see vv. 2, 3; 13, 14). This is because it is transitional. It designs to show wherein is the Lord's great delight, leading into the final subsection which praises Him for putting Israel in the position, alone among the nations, to give this delight to Him. In the natural world, the Creator shows His concern for His creatures: great natural resources (v. 8a, b) and the immense power of growth (v. 8c) are laid under contribution in order to feed the animal world (v. 9). Yet concerned as He thus is for the physical well-being of His creatures, His greater concern and supreme delight is in those who reverence Him and who rely on the steadfastness of His love (vv. 10, 11).

11 *Steadfast love* is specifically the divine love within the covenant and for the covenant people. The reference therefore prepares the way

for the next section. It raises the question: But who can wait expectantly for His love except those to whom that love has been revealed?

12–20 The Lord's favour

Truly the Lord has blessed Zion with material blessings: security (v. 13a), numbers (v. 13b), well-being (*peace*, v. 14a), provision (v. 14b). But this cannot be all, for physical well-being is not the Lord's chief concern (*cf.* vv. 10, 11). His work as Creator shows Him as ruling the world by His word (v. 15), by which agency He apportions both the hardships (vv. 16, 17) and the alleviations (v. 18) of life. His word, in this sense, is known throughout the world (*cf.* Ps. 19:1–6), but in its precise sense as revelation (v. 19a) and as commandments (v. 19b), that word is known only in Israel (*cf.* Ps. 19:7–14). This nation alone is in a position to give delight (*cf.* v. 11) to the Lord. They have been privileged by the divine choice of them (v. 20a). How well, therefore, they ought to praise Him (v. 20b)!

19 The essential speciality of God's elect is their possession of His word. As the *word* of the Lord, it brings knowledge; as *statutes* and *ordinances* ('specific laws' and 'unchanging precepts') it calls for obedience. The mark, therefore, of God's people is to know and obey Him.

PSALM 148. UNIVERSAL PRAISE

Beyond the praise of the individual (Ps. 146) and of the chosen people (Ps. 147), a praise is due to the Creator from the whole creation. That is the subject of this psalm. *Cf.* Ps. 96:11, 12; Rev. 5:13.

1–6 Celestial praise

The heavenly beings (v. 2), the heavenly bodies (v. 3) and the very constituent parts of the heavens themselves (v. 4) are summoned to praise, on the ground that the Lord is their Creator (v. 5b), Sustainer (v. 6a) and Controller (v. 6b).

2 *Host* here refers to the unnumbered company of beings who are at the Lord's command (*cf.* Ps. 103:20, 21). **4** *Highest heavens* (lit. 'heavens of heavens'): the extension upon extension which modern knowledge has taught us to call space. *Waters above the heavens*: a poetical reference to rain-clouds; *cf.* the similar reference to the wind in Ps. 135:7. **5** *He commanded*. See the General Article, 'Old Testament Theology', pp. 26f.

7–14 Terrestrial praise

Praise must also ascend to the Lord *from the earth* (v. 7a), involving the depths and their creatures (v. 7b), the forces of nature (v. 8), the physical world (v. 9a) with its flora (v. 9b) and fauna (v. 10), and the total human population (vv. 11, 12). The call to praise rests on something that is true in heaven—the sole and supreme exaltation of the Lord (v. 13)—and something that is true upon earth—the establishment there of a people who are His own (v. 14a), who have been made the recipients of His love (v. 14b) and drawn close to Him (v. 14c).

7 *Sea monsters*; *cf.* Gn. 1:21. **8** *Fulfilling his command.* While grammatically this phrase belongs with *stormy wind*, it also indicates generally how the mute creatures, the forces and features of nature do in fact praise the Lord: *i.e.* by being what they are, His subjects occupying the place He has appointed for them and fulfilling the function allotted to them; *cf.* v. 6, where the praise of the heavenly bodies is their subservience to the fixed divine ordinances. **13** *Name.* Implicit here is the idea of special revelation whereby the meaning of the name has been imparted; *cf.* Ex. 3:15; 6:2ff. The question remains how the world's population at large is ever to praise the Lord in terms of a name which has not been revealed to them. The answer is indicated in the next verse. **14** *He has raised* (lit. 'and he has raised'); *i.e.* we are not dealing here with the praise due to Him from Israel, but with an additional reason why the world should praise Him, namely that He has acted to make one people His own people and has therefore established a centre where He may be known (*cf.* Is. 2:2, 3). *Horn*: symbol of strength (*cf.* on Zc. 1:18ff.), figurative here of God's setting of His people as a fixture on earth. *Saints* describes their heavenly relationship, recipients of His love (*cf.* on Ps. 145:10), and this is sealed by saying that they are *near to him*, *i.e.* that the divine love is not bestowed on them as a remote object but is given in the context of an intimate relationship.

PSALM 149. MISSIONARY PRAISE

Ps. 148 ended with an unexplained implication: the world is to praise God because in one of its many nations the Lord has set the knowledge of Himself. The present psalm, expressed in terms of an earthly kingdom of God, sees the chosen people in vigorous action to bring the whole world under the divine sway.

1–4 The people with a song

By means of the *new song* of the redeemed (*cf.* on Ps. 144:9), God's beloved people (v. 1, *faithful*, lit. 'saints'; *cf.* on Ps. 145:10) offer corporate praise. This praise is directed (v. 2) to their *Maker* and *King*, being expressed in bodily, vocal and instrumental fashion (v. 3). The reason is that He continually delights in them (*cf.* on Ps. 147:11), and though they are helpless in themselves He *adorns* them with *victory* (v. 4).

2 *Maker* in the double sense, first that He is Creator, and secondly that, as Redeemer, He has made this people for Himself (*cf.* Ps. 95:6, 7a). *Sons of Zion*: the privilege of membership of the city of God (*cf.* on Ps. 87; also Eph. 2:19). **3** *Making melody*: the word is elsewhere (*e.g.*

Ps. 147:1) translated 'to sing praises'. The reference therefore is to vocal praise with instrumental accompaniment. **4** *Humble*; *i.e.* 'downtrodden' (*cf.* Ps. 147:6). The people of God are usually at the mercy of worldly powers, and their possibility and experience of *victory* (or 'salvation', RV) resides entirely in the Lord.

5–9 The people with a sword

The wording and formation of vv. 5, 6 indicate the beginning of the second section of the psalm here. The reference to the *faithful* ('saints') matches that in v. 1; also there is no verb in the Hebrew of v. 6, which is consequently in apposition to v. 5, indicating another dimension of the praises of the faithful: while they sing with their voices they wield a sword with their hands. In using this sword to take vengeance (v. 7) and to take captive (v. 8), they are carrying out a predetermined judgment and achieving their own glory (v. 9).

6 *Two-edged swords.* The metaphorical meaning of the sword which is found in the NT (*e.g.* Eph. 6:17; Rev. 1:16) belongs to the OT also (*e.g.* Ps. 45:2, 3; Is. 49:2), and the otherwise curious linking of the couch (v. 5) with the sword may mean that the psalmist is being consciously metaphorical here also. The distinctive possession of the Lord's people is His word (see on Ps. 147:19), and with this they go on His warfare to bring the nations into subjection to Him (*cf.* 2 Cor. 10:4–6). This form of thought came more readily to the OT even than to the NT, for the visible kingdom of God was either in reality before their eyes or vivid and dear in memory. It is no wonder, then, that it contributed a whole vocabulary to the notion of the world coming to acknowledge the God of Israel (*cf.* on Ps. 110; Is. 11:14–16; 45:14–25). **7** *Vengeance.* Bearing in mind that the 'day of vengeance' is the darker side of the 'day of salvation' (*cf.* Is. 61:1, 2; 63:1–6; 2 Thes. 1:6–10, noting in v. 10 the idea of God glorified in His saints), we may assume that this psalm emanated from a situation in which the writer was more aware of those features of pagan life which could only expect divine judgment. We ought not to assume that this was his total view of the relation between the people of God and the pagan world, or that he intended consciously to deny what he simply did not wish to mention, namely that along with the inevitable judgment on wickedness went the salvation of those who in all the ends of the earth turned to the God of Israel (*cf.* Is. 42:13–17; 45:22–25). **9** *Judgment written*; *i.e.* in God's predetermined plan of salvation for the world (*cf.* Is. 4:3).

PSALM 150. LET EVERYTHING THAT BREATHES PRAISE THE LORD!

In principle now, as we have followed through the sequence of psalms beginning with Ps. 146, we reach the moment Isaiah foretold when he said, 'To me every knee shall bow, every tongue shall swear' (45:23) and to which the NT church still looks forward, when 'every tongue (shall) confess that Jesus Christ is Lord' (Phil. 2:11). The world has, in vision, been brought into submission to the Lord (Ps. 149:5–9) and the anthem of the redeemed is about to be sung (*cf.* Rev. 5:8–14).

1, 2 Praise commensurate with God

On what grounds is praise here encouraged? First, God is to be praised as He is revealed *in his sanctuary*, the Holy of Holies of the earthly shrine: the God of unapproachable holiness who yet has appointed a sacrifice whereby sins may be forgiven and sinners accepted before Him (*cf.* Lv. 16:13–17; Heb. 9:11–28). Secondly, our eyes rise to *his mighty firmament*, lit. 'the firmament of (in which is seen) His power'. God is to be praised in the role of the Creator, the whole expanse of heaven being the chosen example of His creative power. Thirdly, there is the revelation of God in *his mighty deeds*, which would refer to those demonstrations of powerful acts of mercy and judgment (*e.g.* the Exodus) whereby God has overthrown His foes and saved His people, thus showing that the revelation of holiness and redemption depicted in the sanctuary is no theory but the reality of the divine nature. When, then, the call goes out to *praise him according to* (in a manner commensurate with) *his exceeding greatness* (lit. 'the abundance of His greatness'), it is the greatness of His holiness, His creative power and His redeeming grace which the psalmist has in mind.

1 *Sanctuary.* Some commentators think of the heavenly sanctuary: God's eternal, invisible dwelling. But the thought seems rather to start with the earthly shrine and to end with the contemplation of God in His greatness, as indicated above. **2** *For.* The preposition is the same in the Hebrew as that translated *in* throughout v. 1 (*cf.* RV), and means 'as He is revealed in'.

3–6 Praise commensurate with creation

In 'the uninhibited exuberance of lives devoted to God' (J. R. W. Stott, *The Canticles and Selected Psalms*, 1966, p. 158), every vehicle of praise (vv. 3–5) and every creature capable of praise (v. 6) is summoned to a shout worthy to act as a climax to the joyousness of OT religion, and to be a foretaste of that 'Glory be to the Father, and to the Son, and to the Holy Spirit' which will fill the courts of heaven and last to all eternity.

LESLIE S. M'CAW
J. A. MOTYER

Proverbs

INTRODUCTION

AUTHORSHIP

The general title is 'The Proverbs of Solomon the son of David'. At several points in the book, however, there are rubrics giving the authorship of different sections. Thus sections are ascribed to Solomon at 10:1 and to 'the wise' at 22:17 and 24:23. At 25:1 there is the rubric 'These also are proverbs of Solomon which the men of Hezekiah king of Judah copied'; ch. 30 is headed 'the words of Agur son of Jakeh', and ch. 31 ascribed to 'King Lemuel', or, rather, to his mother.

The Rabbis said, 'Hezekiah and his company wrote Isaiah, Proverbs, the Song of Songs and Ecclesiastes' (*Baba Bathra* 15a)—*i.e.* they edited or published them. As regards Proverbs, this tradition probably has no other basis than the rubric of 25:1.

The accuracy of the ascriptions of authorship made within the text was regarded as highly doubtful in the late 19th and early 20th centuries, but a welcome recent practice of considering the book within the framework of Ancient Near Eastern wisdom has led to the rejection of many of the arguments against Solomonic influence. This kind of study has disposed of such chronological rules-of-thumb as that which claims that short compositions are generally earlier than longer ones. Albright has shown (*Wisdom in Israel and in the Ancient Near East*, eds. M. Noth and D. Winton Thomas, 1955, pp. 1–13) that the closest extra-biblical linguistic and literary analogies to Proverbs are to be found in the Bronze Age. This has resulted in a tendency noted by W. Baumgartner (*Old Testament and Modern Study*, ed. H. H. Rowley, 1951, p. 213) 'to treat seriously the ascription of x. 1 – xxii. 16 and xxv – xxix to Solomon', and has led to more respect for the other attributions which may be considered individually.

Let us consider the several attributions.

1. Solomon

In Proverbs, wisdom is not simply intellectual but involves the whole man; and Solomon at the zenith of his fame is the embodiment of this wisdom. He loved the Lord (1 Ki. 3:3); he prayed for an understanding mind which could distinguish good and evil (1 Ki. 3:9, 12); his wisdom was God-given (1 Ki. 4:29) and accompanied by genuine humility (1 Ki. 3:7). His wisdom was put to the test in practical matters, such as just administration (1 Ki. 3:16–28) and diplomacy (1 Ki. 5:12); it was pre-eminent in the East (1 Ki. 4:30f.; 10:1–13). He composed proverbs and songs (1 Ki. 4:32) and answered hard sayings (1 Ki. 10:1). Much of his lore was drawn from nature (1 Ki. 4:33).

Many of the proverbs in 10:1 – 22:16; 25–29 contain ideas and expressions which may be found elsewhere in the OT and Near Eastern wisdom and it would be ludicrous to claim that Solomon actually conceived each thought, uninfluenced by other writers. He is rather to be seen as a wise and learned man compiling an anthology of wise sayings, his own and others, and leaving on it the imprint of his own personality. In that sense it is his composition.

2. The wise

The nations of the Ancient East had their 'wise men' whose functions extended from state policy to education. (For Egypt, *cf.*, *e.g.*, Gn. 41:8; for Edom, *cf.* Ob. 8.) In Israel, where it was known that 'the fear of the Lord is the beginning of knowledge', 'the wise' had a more important function: in Jeremiah's time they were on a par with priest and prophet as an organ of revelation (Je. 18:18). But, just as the true prophets had to contend with prophets and priests with unworthy motives, so some of 'the wise' compromised their function of declaring the 'counsel of Yahweh' (Is. 29:14; Je. 8:8, 9).

Collections of 'sayings of the wise' occur in 22:17 – 24:22 and 24:23–34. Perhaps chs. 1–9, with their exposition of the aim and content of the 'counsel of the wise' come from a like source. It is virtually impossible to date these collections. Probably they represent the distilled wisdom of many over a considerable period; but much of it is certainly of early date, and Albright's remarks about Bronze Age dating (see above) are relevant to much of them. There is nothing to indicate that the sayings were only of Israelite wise men. Possibly the attribution of the book as a whole to Solomon (1:1) indicates that he compiled these collections in the same way as those mentioned in **1.** above, but drawing more heavily on other sages' wisdom.

3. Hezekiah's men

From 2 Ch. 29:25–30 we learn that Hezekiah took care to restore the Davidic order in the Temple, the Davidic instruments and the psalms of David and Asaph. Perhaps a revival of interest in the 'classic' wisdom of Solomon was another outcome of this reformation, prompted not by mere antiquarianism, but by the desire to explore the wisdom of the greatest of the wise. At any rate 'Hezekiah's men' published the Solomonic collection of Pr. 25–29.

4. Agur the son of Jakeh

We do not know who Agur was, but the ascription of 30:1 can be translated 'the words of Agur son of Jakeh, the oracle' (cf. AV, RV) or 'of Agur son of Jakeh of Massa' (RSV). Massa was an Arab tribe descended from Abraham through Ishmael (Gn. 25:14), and the eastern tribes were famous for their wisdom (1 Ki. 4:30).

5. King Lemuel

The king's mother is given as the source of 31:1–9, but he is likewise unknown, though again he may belong to Massa (see 4. above and the commentary). We need not suppose him to be the author of the magnificent poem on the perfect wife (31:10–31) which forms an appendix to the book.

DATE

The formation of the separate collections into one book may not have been undertaken as one step, and it has already been suggested that much of the compiling and editing may have been undertaken in Solomon's reign. The final form had not been achieved by Hezekiah's reign (25:1) but the text was already established by the time (c. 180 BC) of Ben Sira (Ecclus. 47:17). It probably received its final editing in the period immediately following the return from exile.

FORM AND CONTENT

The word translated 'proverb' (māšāl) comes from a root which seems to mean 'to represent' or 'be like'. Its basic meaning is thus a comparison or a simile, and its germ may be an analogy drawn between the natural and spiritual worlds (cf. 1 Ki. 4:33 and Pr. 10:26). The word is aptly translated 'parable' (AV) or 'allegory' (RSV) in Ezk. 17:2. The word was, however, extended to sayings where no such analogy is evident, and came to designate a short pithy saying or by-word.

But the proverbs in this book are not so much popular sayings as the distillation of the wisdom of teachers who knew the law of God and were applying its principles to the whole of life. The LXX title of the book, *Paroimiai*, which might be rendered *obiter dicta*, gives a good idea of the contents. These are words by the way for wayfaring men who are seeking to tread the way of holiness.

In form the book is similar to the collections of instructions or teachings known from Egypt. The introductory exhortations and the grouping of maxims roughly according to subject indicate that the compiler was following a recognized international literary form. As the modern translations indicate, the work is in poetic form; in many places it is metrically exactly parallel to Ugaritic literature of the 14th/13th century BC.

PROVERBS AND THE WISDOM OF OTHER NATIONS

The many biblical references make it clear that the Hebrews were well aware of the wisdom of Israel's neighbours (1 Ki. 4:30; Je. 49:7; Dn. 1:4; Ezk. 28:3, *etc.*) and the international nature of Solomon's court (1 Ki. 4:34; 10:1–13, 24) provided ample opportunity for the interchange of wisdom. (Wisdom texts survive in quantity from Mesopotamia and Egypt and show an occupation with the same problems that confronted the biblical sages.) It is not surprising therefore that many of the subjects dealt with and attitudes taken find parallels in the extra-biblical texts.

Some superficially close verbal resemblances often disappear under close scrutiny, but have formed the basis for claims that large portions of Proverbs are borrowed from non-Israelite sources. The best-known examples are in the section Pr. 22:17 – 23:11 where, it is often argued, the similarities with the Egyptian *Teaching of Amenemope* are too great to be coincidental. In spite of Baumgartner's claim (*op. cit.*, p. 212) that the 'theory that Amenemope is the original of Pr. xxii. 17 – xxiii. 11 has now been generally accepted', it seems more reasonable to explain the similarities as arising from the same literary and cultural *milieu*. The view that Amenemope borrowed from Proverbs is no longer tenable in view of recent discoveries of manuscripts of the Egyptian text dating from well before Solomon's period.

Notwithstanding the close parallelism of expression there is a world of difference in the underlying philosophy. The texts of Egypt and Mesopotamia are a mixture of morality and opportunism such as one finds in the proverbs of most nations, and wisdom is viewed predominantly as a practical virtue. In Proverbs, the emphasis is on wisdom as a way of life, and the aim of the book is not the achievement of material success but the inculcation of a godly, righteous and sober life.

THE USE OF THE BOOK OF PROVERBS

Principal Wheeler Robinson described OT wisdom as 'the discipline whereby was taught the application of prophetic truth to the individual life in the light of experience' (*Inspiration and Revelation in the Old Testament*, 1946, p. 241). It is this which makes the book perennially relevant. It is a book of discipline: it touches on every department of life and shows God's direct interest in it. Wisdom does not consist in the contemplation of abstract principles governing the universe, but in a relationship with God of reverent knowledge issuing in conduct consonant with such a relationship in concrete situations. The man who refuses this is, frankly, a fool. And wisdom must dominate a man's whole life: not just his devotion, but his attitude to his wife, his children, his work, his business methods, even his table manners. 'For the writers of Proverbs . . . religion means a well-furnished intellect employing the best means to accomplish the highest ends. The feebleness, the shallowness, the narrow, contracted views and aims, are on the other side' (W. T. Davison, *The Wisdom Literature of the Old Testament*, 1900, p. 134).

There is ample evidence that our Lord loved this book. Every now and then we get an echo of its language in His own teaching: for instance in His words about those who seek the chief seats (*cf.* Pr. 25:6, 7), or the parable of the wise and foolish men and their houses (*cf.* Pr. 14:11), or that of the rich fool (*cf.* Pr. 27:1). To Nicodemus He reveals the answer to the question posed by Agur the son of Jakeh (*cf.* Pr. 30:4 with Jn. 3:13). And He reminds those who, like the indiscriminating 'fools' of Proverbs, do not recognize Him or His message that 'wisdom is justified by her children' (Mt. 11:19).

Our Lord, in fact, used in His parables exactly the method of teaching found in Proverbs. The Hebrew *māšāl* is best rendered in Greek as *parabolē*, 'parable', and the same Greek word would translate the Hebrew *ḥîḏâ*, 'dark saying', or 'riddle'. Hence in Mk. 4:11 we see that, to those who do not recognize Him, everything connected with the kingdom appears in the form of riddles or dark sayings which they hear but do not interpret.

Was it from his company with our Lord that Peter derived his fondness for Proverbs? At any rate, his letters show a close acquaintance with the book (*cf.* 1 Pet. 2:17 with Pr. 24:21; 1 Pet. 3:13 with Pr. 16:7; 1 Pet. 4:8 with Pr. 10:12; 1 Pet. 4:18 with Pr. 11:31; 2 Pet. 2:22 with Pr. 26:11). Paul also quotes from and echoes the book (*cf.*, *e.g.*, Rom. 12:20 and Pr. 25:21f.), and when he speaks of 'Christ the power of God and the wisdom of God' (1 Cor. 1:24), the eighth

chapter of Proverbs floods rich meaning into his words. Again, Heb. 12:5f. commands us not to forget 'the exhortation which addresses you as sons', that we 'do not regard lightly the discipline of the Lord'. The quotation is from Pr. 3:11f., and portrays for us the true nature of the book, a study in the paternal discipline of God.

The sayings, like our Lord's parables, need to be pondered to be fully appreciated, and it is probably best to consider each separately, reading only a few at a time. (F. D. Kidner's commentary in the *TOTC* series will be found an excellent companion in this.) 'A number of small pictures crowded together upon the walls of a large gallery are not likely to receive much separate attention from the visitor, especially if he be paying a short visit in a hurry' (Davison, *op. cit.*, p. 126). Conversely, it is important to remember that each saying is part of a whole body of teaching. To take a proverb quite apart from its relationship to the whole and to seek to apply it to any situation may be quite misleading.

TEXTS AND VERSIONS

The Hebrew text of Proverbs is not the easiest of the OT books, but even so does not warrant the drastic treatment it has received from many commentators. Recent philological studies in other Semitic languages (*cf.*, *e.g.*, M. Dahood, *Proverbs and North West Semitic Philology*, 1963) have demonstrated that many proposed emendations are unnecessary. Gerlemann's studies in the LXX (*Oudtestamentische Studien* deel VIII, ed. P. A. H. de Boer, 1950, and *Studies in the Septuagint: III Proverbs*, Lund, 1956) have shown it to be of little help in establishing the text since it has its own distinct literary character.

J. RUFFLE

OUTLINE OF CONTENTS

COMMENTARY

1:1-7 THE BOOK'S TITLE, PURPOSE AND MOTTO

This is the longest title of any OT book. The ascription to Solomon does not mean that he

wrote the whole book (*cf.* 24:23; 30:1; 31:1) but indicates its most illustrious contributor and the greatest figure in the proverbial lore.

1 Vv. 1 and 6 form a single elliptical sentence:

'The proverbs of Solomon . . . written down that you may know. . . .' **2** The reader is invited to learn from the book *wisdom* (the nature of which is explained as the book proceeds) and *instruction*. The latter comprehends the whole concept of spiritual education and discipline (it is translated 'discipline' in 3:11; note its use in Heb. 12:5ff.). **3** To *receive instruction in wise dealing*; better than AV 'of wisdom'. *Righteousness, justice, and equity* are characteristics constantly demanded by the prophets, and are features of the rule of God and His Messiah (see, *e.g.*, Is. 9:7 and 11:4). **4, 5** V. 4 shows that this wisdom is available for the youngest and most inexperienced (*cf.* Is. 35:8), v. 5 that those who have already drawn deep of wisdom's well will yet find abundantly more. *Simple* probably means 'open to every influence'. *Acquire skill* (AV 'attain unto wise counsels') is suggestively translated by the LXX as 'shall acquire a steersman'. This idea is implicit in the Hebrew root. **6** The book is also written to provide a key to all the proverbs of wise men (*cf.* Mk. 4:13). The precise meaning of the word translated in AV 'the interpretation' is uncertain. This translation is possible, but in line with its only other occurrence in the OT, Hab. 2:6, we might translate 'satire', and 'allusion' has also been suggested. RV, RSV, non-committally, have *figure*.

7 forms a sort of motto for the book, and describes its foundation principle. *Beginning* (Heb. *rᵉ'ešît*) implies both starting-point and essence. Without the knowledge and fear of Yahweh, the One true God, the wisdom which affords guidance for the whole of life cannot begin to be acquired. The motto is repeated, slightly differently, at 9:10. *Cf.* also 15:33; Jb. 28:28; Ps. 111:10.

It is worth comparing these verses with Is. 11:1-5, where most of the gifts here set out are shown to be attributes of the Messiah and the outcome of the presence of the Spirit of God.

1:8 – 9:18 THIRTEEN LESSONS ON WISDOM

The address 'my son' begins each lesson except the last, which is given by wisdom herself. A master is addressing his disciple.

1:8-33 The first lesson

1:8-19 Shun evil companions. The disciple is urged to follow the teaching he received from his parents as a child. **8, 9** *Hear*, as often in the OT, means 'obey'. The Hebrew word for 'law' (*tôrâ*) has here its primary sense of *teaching*, as is shown by the parallelism. The content of this teaching is described for us in the book of Deuteronomy; see especially Dt. 4:9; 6:7; 11:19; 32:46.

A lawless state of society is depicted in vv. 10-19. Organized robbery with violence seems to have been endemic in Palestine throughout the biblical period (*cf., e.g.*, Ps. 10:8ff.; Ho. 4:2; 6:8f.), and even in the firmly governed Palestine

of our Lord's day was established enough for Him to base a parable upon it. It is plain from these verses that the desperadoes would not stop at murder to gain their booty. **12** The apparent meaning is a sudden murderous assault; they will pounce upon their victim as avidly as death devours hers. **13-15** But the invitation to an equal share in their ill-gotten gain (v. 14) is to be consistently refused (v. 15). **16**, which is not in the LXX, occurs again at Is. 59:7. **17** The metaphor is difficult. One may follow Oesterley and interpret the *bird* of the instructed disciple: being forewarned, he will avoid the snare of joining such evil company, just as no bird walks into a net that he has watched being laid. But the widely held alternative, that the robbers and such inexperienced youths as follow them, blind to everything but gain, are like birds rushing for seeds scattered on the ground not noticing the trap, is certainly possible. **18, 19** speak of the inevitable fate of those who enrich themselves in this way. When they lie in ambush for others they are, unknown to themselves, compassing their own destruction. *Such are the ways of all . . .; i.e.* 'this is the outcome for everyone . . .'

1:20-33 Wisdom's unheeded appeal. This is the first of the sections in which wisdom is personified. That wisdom which has its origin in the fear of God invites the people at large to learn: but the great mass of mankind refuse to listen, despite the fact that in doing so they bring ruin and distress upon themselves. We are reminded of the manner in which the prophets pleaded with Israel to 'seek Yahweh and live', and met with stubborn lack of understanding. Indeed, there is much in this section that is reminiscent of the teaching of Hosea and Isaiah and Jeremiah.

Vv. 20, 21 describe the manner of wisdom's proclamation. **20** *Wisdom* is either a plural, to express intensity or fullness, or an unusual form of the word. Wisdom is represented as calling out its message in the streets and public thoroughfares (*cf.* RV). The prophets also proclaimed their message in the streets and public places; *cf.* Je. 5:1; Is. 20:2ff. **21** *On the top of the walls*; RSV has followed LXX, probably unnecessarily: the Hebrew text has 'head of bustling' (*sc.* streets); *cf.* AV's 'chief place of concourse'. *The entrance of the city gates* was the place where public and private business was transacted and courts held (*cf.* Ru. 4:1ff.).

Vv. 22, 23 give wisdom's appeal. **22** Three classes who pay no heed are named. *Simple*: the root seems to mean 'open to influence', whether good or bad; in origin the word (*petî*) is morally neutral (*cf.* v. 4). But the people in question refuse the proffered wisdom and thus remain 'simple': so the word comes (as in English) to have an unenviable connotation. *Scoffers* (Heb. *lēṣîm*) are a class we shall meet again. They are wisdom's worst enemies, arrogant, cynical and defiant. *Fools* are represented as hating the knowledge which alone can save them from disaster. There are three words in Proverbs translated 'fool': the *nābāl* (17:7, 21; 30:22; *cf.* 30:32) is boorish, churlish and dull. The *'ewîl* (19 times) is flippant, obstinately careless (10:8; 12:15), without restraint (27:22). Almost as undesirable is the *kesîl* (used here and nearly 50 other places in Proverbs) whom Toy sums up as 'one who is insensible to moral truth and acts without regard to it'. (On all this see Kidner, *TOTC*, pp. 39–42.)

23 may be taken in either of two ways. It is possible that the fools are instructed to turn and face wisdom's reproof, and the *words* which wisdom makes known are contained in vv. 24–33. But it is better, bearing in mind the 'How long?' of v. 22, to take this as a last appeal to the heedless to receive knowledge. *Give heed*; the word is literally 'turn' (*cf.* mg.), an expression often used in the prophets with the sense of 'repent', which is surely the meaning here. The 'spirit of wisdom' is associated with the Messiah (Is. 9:2), and is a privilege of Messiah's people (Eph. 1:17).

Vv. 24–32 describe the general reaction to the appeal and the dire consequences. For calamity will certainly follow such disobedience, and then it will be too late to seek the aid of heavenly wisdom. The wisdom they rejected will laugh in their faces as they have so long laughed at it; the memory of despised knowledge will be bitter to those who are perishing. The search for wisdom induced by the final calamity will be in vain, a note of severe finality which stamps many of our Lord's parables of the kingdom. **29** Note that again *knowledge* and *fear* of God are linked. **32** The simple, exhorted to turn to God (*cf.* v. 23), have turned away from Him, and this will bring about their destruction. *Complacence*; better than AV 'prosperity'. The parable of the rich fool in Lk. 12:16–20 is sufficient commentary here. There is no denial of the fact that the fool may temporarily prosper. **33** holds out the promise of true security for those who do obey wisdom's voice.

2:1-22 The second lesson

2:1-9 The search for wisdom and its reward. This section stresses three things: that wisdom requires diligent search (vv. 1–5), that it is none the less God-given, and not the result of mere human effort (v. 6), and that God watches over and keeps in His will those who receive it (vv. 7–9). The principles involved here are implicit in Solomon's dream in Gibeon (1 Ki. 3:5–15) and are made explicit by Paul in Phil. 2:12, 13. **2, 3** *Heart* has a wider meaning in Hebrew than in English, as it relates to the intellectual and moral faculties as well as to the emotional. The pupil is being exhorted to apply all his powers in the quest for understanding, until he can be said to be shouting out aloud for it. **4** The emphasis is probably less on the fact that silver has to be mined and that the treasure requires intensive search than on the fact that both are immensely valuable. Our Lord takes up and develops this thought, applying it to the

search for the kingdom of heaven (Mt. 13:44). **7** The literal meaning of *stores up* is 'hides away', and *sound wisdom* (Heb. *tûšiyyâ*) may be 'abiding success', *i.e.* the effect of sound wisdom: but note from vv. 9ff. the moral character of this abiding success, and that God hides it away for and not from the righteous. **8** Read with RV 'That he may guard the paths of judgment, And preserve the way of his saints'. In other words, God Himself becomes a shield for His people in order that He may see that what is perfectly right is constantly maintained. *Preserving* means 'watching over': God watches over the path His people take, both to protect them in it and to keep them in the right way. *Saints* represents those who loyally render to Yahweh the love due to Him in the covenant between Him and His people. **9** The virtues named are reflections of His will: see on 1:3.

2:10–22 Some benefits of wisdom. The protection which the possession of wisdom affords is enlarged upon. **11** The *discretion* which is promised contains the idea of purposefulness. Vv. 12–19 mention classes from whose pernicious ways those who have received wisdom may escape. **12** First there is the 'evil man'. The AV rendering suits the context better than the RV, RSV *from the way of evil*; but in either case *cf.* the petition in the Lord's prayer, 'Deliver us from evil' or 'from the evil one'. There are the *men of perverted speech*, literally men who speak things turned upside down, *i.e.* the liars. **13–15** Such men are crooked and perverse. **16** Above all, there is *the loose woman*, against whom many warnings are given in the book. See further on 5:3. **17** Here, at least, the warnings are against the allurements of the adulteress who has known the law of the true God. *Companion* (*cf.* RV, 'friend'); more exact than AV's unwarranted translation 'guide'. But from a passage like Je. 3:1–4 we see clearly that the word was used to designate the marriage partner. Not only does the woman sin against the husband she married in her youth; in doing so she sins against God, to whom, as an Israelite, she is bound in a covenant relationship. It is He who has ordained the marriage covenant, and He who has laid down as part of His covenant, 'You shall not commit adultery' (Ex. 20:14). **18** *Her house* is a steep descent all the way down to *death*, and her victims do not *regain* (or 'attain unto', RV) the ways leading to life which all men desire to reach. 'The process is that wisdom and knowledge, when they become your own way of thinking, and your acquired taste (10), will make the talk and interests of evil men alien to you (12–15). Even *the adventuress* . . . will show up at once as . . . *femme fatale*: who offers a taste of life, and sells you death' (Kidner, p. 62).

20 After this long digression, v. 20 picks up again the thought of v. 11. Not only will God's gift of wisdom protect from these evil ways; it will enable a good and upright manner of life to be followed. **21, 22** *Land*; the primary reference is doubtless to 'the land which the Lord your God gives you' (*cf.* Ex. 20:12; Ps. 37:9-11). But the significance does not stop there, as is shown by our Lord's beatitude, based on Ps. 37:11, 'Blessed are the meek, for they shall inherit the earth.'

3:1–10 The third lesson

The theme is 'trust and obey'. **1, 2** Observance of the teacher's words is urgently enjoined, as a source of long life and peace. The primary reference is to long life on earth, often regarded in the OT as a great good; observance of the fundamentals of right living will enable a man to avoid the worst snares and pitfalls of life. But 'commandments with promise' (*cf.* Eph. 6:2) take a deeper significance as God's revelation unfolds, and our Lord declares that His words are spirit and life (Jn. 6:63). *Teaching*; again from *tôrâ* (*cf.* on 1:8).

This theme is developed in vv. 4–10, and the content of the life-giving teaching referred to in v. 1 is outlined. **3** First *loyalty and faithfulness* must be maintained. This expression means more than appears on the surface. *Loyalty* (AV 'mercy'; Heb. *ḥeseḏ*) is a word which is hard to understand apart from the idea of covenant. It represents covenant-love, and the full range of what that means we see from the 'great commandment' and the one like it (Dt. 6:5; Lv. 19:18; *cf.* Mt. 22:36–40). *Faithfulness* (AV 'truth'; Heb. *'ĕmeṯ*) means 'firmness' and hence 'trustworthiness', 'stability', and eventually what faithfulness demands—reality and truth. So the Lord is 'faithful and true' (Rev. 19:11): the one quality implies the other. *Loyalty and faithfulness* are divine attributes (*cf.* Ps. 25:10, where RSV translates 'loyalty' as 'steadfast love'), and are often linked in the OT. Toy well says they are 'the expression of perfectly good relations between man and man, or between man and God'. The advice to bind these qualities to oneself may be paralleled by the command (Dt. 6:8) to bind on God's covenant commandments, a constant reminder of His requirements. But men require more than to be reminded; and so mercy and truth are to be written upon their hearts, their very minds (*cf.* Je. 31:33). **4** The outcome of this is stated here. *Favour* and *good repute* represent a slight change in the Hebrew, which has 'favour and understanding', but the appropriateness of this combination is not immediately apparent. It may, however, mean that the practice of 'loyalty and faithfulness' will bring about not only divine and human favour, but divine and human recognition as possessing true understanding. We find the great example of this in Lk. 2:52.

In the second place faith is enjoined; faith which includes trust in God (v. 5), acknowledgment of Him in every department of life (v. 6) and reverent awe of Him (v. 7). Relying on one's own human understanding, setting a high value on one's own wisdom (*cf.* Is. 5:21), and living on easy terms with evil are the antithesis of this trusting dependence on Yahweh. **6** *Make*

straight; make plain, clearing obstructions. The word is used in Is. 40:3 of clearing the highway in the desert. The effect of such faith as is described is also physically beneficial. **9, 10** Finally, the pupil is instructed that the reverence due to God involves giving on the part of His worshippers. The *substance* with which he *honours* Yahweh is his wealth, or revenue. He need not fear that this will finally involve him in loss (*cf.* Mal. 3:10–12). The teaching is cast in agricultural terms. The reference to *first fruits* looks back to the law in Dt. 26, where the worshipper annually takes of the firstfruits of his produce and remembers with joy and gratitude God's redemption of Israel and His continuing goodness—the OT harvest festival.

3:11–20 The fourth lesson

The theme of this section is the delights of wisdom, a development of the recurring theme in the third lesson that the teaching brings a rich reward. **11, 12** But first comes a warning that God in His love may bring adversity as well as prosperity upon His children. Bacon's dictum, 'Prosperity is the Blessing of the Old Testament; Adversity is the Blessing of the New; which carrieth the greater Benediction, and the Clearer Revelation of God's favour', must be qualified by such passages as this. The rendering in Heb. 12:6, 'For the Lord disciplines whom he loves, and chastises every son whom he receives', follows the LXX, which has read the same Hebrew consonants with different vowels to obtain the word 'chastises'. (*Cf.* 2 Sa. 7:14.) **13–18** With this warning the teacher expounds the blessings which follow the possession of wisdom. All around him men were engaged in the all-absorbing pursuit of riches and honour. He is therefore at pains to show that heavenly wisdom is a thing infinitely more precious than all those things that men seek after, and, indeed, holds the key to the things most desired by them (v. 17), things which are added as a by-product of the search for wisdom. **14** We may note the germ of yet another of our Lord's parables: that of the pearl of great price (Mt. 13:45, 46). **16** The blessings of the *right hand* rate more highly than the (still desirable) gifts of the *left*: but wisdom gives access to both. **18** As a *tree of life* wisdom is a constantly growing, self-renewing source of life to those that attain her.

19, 20 further show the glory of wisdom and its exalted status before God. It was His guiding principle in creation, and remains so in His government of the universe, whether in epochal cataclysmic events (the reference to the breaking forth of the depths points back to Gn. 7:11) or in the regular moistening of the earth on which life depends. *Dew* may include rain; *cf.* Jb. 36:27f. See further on 8:22–36.

3:21–35 The fifth lesson

We have been watching celestial processes: we are now firmly brought to earth. The same wisdom with which God creates and maintains the universe also has to do with human daily life and personal relations. Sound wisdom and discreet purposefulness (see on 2:7) will be life and health and peace (vv. 21-26).

21 RSV, in order to bring out the meaning more plainly, has reversed the order of the lines (*cf.* AV, where the Hebrew order is retained and where 'them', despite its position, refers, as in RSV, to those who keep sound wisdom). **22** The word translated *soul* (Heb. *nep̄eš*) seems, though this is disputed, to have meant originally 'throat', and thence 'living being', 'person', 'self', 'life'. *And they will be life for your soul* means, then, 'they shall be life to you'. Bearing in mind the parallelism, however, it is possible that *nep̄eš* has here its original sense of 'throat', and is used by synecdoche for the whole body. **23** RV mg. reads, more literally, 'thou shalt not dash thy foot'. **25** The injunction *do not be afraid* when the ruin of the wicked comes may be linked with the numerous passages of hope and encouragement to the righteous with which the prophets mingle their announcements of impending judgment for the nation's sin (see, *e.g.*, Is. 10:24ff.), and with our Lord's words to His people when catastrophe overtakes the world (Lk. 21:28).

27-35 consist of short detached proverbs like those of the central sections of the book, all illustrating the theme already set out in this lesson. James tells us that heavenly wisdom is pure, peaceable, gentle, easily intreated, full of mercy and good fruits, without uncertainty or insincerity, and that it has a diabolical parody whose marks are envy and strife. This is illustrated by the teacher's precepts. **27** The first enjoins prompt payment of debts. The Hebrew reads 'do not withhold good from the owners (*bᵉ'ālîm*) of it'. The LXX may be right in interpreting this of the poor rather than of creditors. 'It would be in harmony with the Hebrew usage to apply the term here to the person who is deserving of your kindness or is in need of it' (Greenstone). **28** The second orders prompt and whole-hearted generosity (*cf.* Jas. 2:16). **29ff.** The others warn against unprovoked attack and violent methods. **31** The *man of violence* may prosper. To the prophets it was only too obvious that he often did. But his unjustly gained wealth is not to be coveted, nor his methods imitated.

32-35 The last group of proverbs brings these injunctions into relation with the fear of the Lord. **32** One way of life is hateful to Yahweh: the other leads to real harmony with Him. *The upright are in his confidence.* Oesterley happily renders 'familiar and confidential intercourse'. **33** On the one way God's curse rests, on the other His blessing (*cf.* Dt. 11:26-28). **34** God rewards with His favour humility, not arrogance (*cf.* the allusions to this verse in Jas. 4:6 and 1 Pet. 5:5). **35** It is the wise, *i.e.* the righteous, just and humble, who eventually receive honour—and that, like a legacy, without conscious effort—not the *fools* (Heb. *kᵉsîlîm*; see on 1:22). The second half of this verse presents difficulties of

translation, but the AV rendering, with its touch of irony, has at least virility and pungency, which most of the suggested emendations do not possess.

4:1-9 The sixth lesson

This section contains a little piece of autobiography. Consumed with desire for the moral and spiritual health of his pupils, the teacher tells of his own father's wise instruction, proved by the experience of his own life, in the effort to impress upon them the urgency of obtaining above all things the 'wisdom from above'.

1 shows the teacher taking up the position of a father to his pupils. *Hear, O sons* is more literal (the word is the same as that which begins all the other lessons), but AV 'children' conveys the idea better. He relates how concerned his own parents were for his welfare. **3** *I was a son with my father*, with the parallelism that follows, implies that the teacher's father took particular care over his son's education. **4-9** Whether the whole of these verses represents the father's words, or whether the teacher is in the later sentences applying them, we cannot tell. Once more, the acquisition of wisdom is seen to provide life (v. 4), protection (v. 6), honour (v. 7) and adornment (v. 9). **7** *The beginning of wisdom is this: Get wisdom.* The AV translation here cannot be warranted, for the Hebrew has only 'the beginning of wisdom is—get wisdom'. This is often abandoned by commentators as unintelligible, but Perowne points out the similarity with the message of 2:1-5, especially if 2:5 is interpreted in the light of 1:7, and the sentence may well be a compression of that message. *Whatever you get*; read with RV 'with all thou hast gotten', and *cf.* Mt. 13:44-46.

4:10-19 The seventh lesson

The theme is 'Abhor that which is evil'. Once more the teacher opens with an urgent injunction to his pupils to be teachable and maintain their grip on the lessons they have learned (vv. 10-13). **10** Once more, the possession of wisdom will confer long life. **11** They have already learned from his teaching in what direction wisdom lies. *Paths of uprightness, i.e.* of moral conduct of life; better than AV 'right paths'. **12** The wisdom which shows itself in such conduct will be a sure guide into true liberty. *Hampered*; a word expressive of the restricted movements of those who leave 'the way of wisdom' and 'the paths of uprightness'. **13** The urgency of gripping this discipline is well illustrated in the accumulation of expressions here. Oesterley renders the last phrase 'because wisdom is all in all to a man'.

14-19 contain warnings to shun the by-paths followed by the wicked (vv. 14, 15), a description of the men who follow them (vv. 16, 17) and vivid, contrasting pictures of what it is like to follow the true road (v. 18) and the by-paths (v. 19). **17** probably refers to the wicked gaining their sustenance by wickedness and violence (*cf.* 20:17), though it may also mean that evil was their food and drink and constant enjoyment (contrast Jn. 4:34). **18** The AV is more literal, but *the light of dawn* conveys the right idea. 'As the sun climbs the heavens, shining brighter and brighter, from the first faint glimmer of dawn till he reaches his meridian height and appears to stay there firm and motionless: so is the path of the righteous. His sun standeth still at last in the heavens, and hasteth not to go down for the whole everlasting day' (Perowne). With this verse *cf.* Is. 2:5.

4:20–27 The eighth lesson

The theme is 'Cleave to that which is good'. Yet another appeal to heed the teacher's life-giving instructions (vv. 20–22) is followed by an appeal to maintain heart (v. 23), speech (v. 24), eyes (v. 25) and feet (vv. 26, 27) in the direction that leads to life.

21 The teacher shows that it is not enough to hear wise instruction: it must be assimilated, pondered, kept at the centre of man's being. *Cf.* Ps. 119:11 and Lk. 2:19. **22** RSV makes the object of both lines singular; AV makes both plural. The Hebrew has a plural and a singular, and might perhaps be rendered, 'They are life to those who find them and health to the flesh of every one of them'. **23** gives the key to this whole series of lessons. Wisdom leads to life, but fundamentally wisdom originates, not in the following out of a collection of wise precepts, but in the heart, the focus of the mind and will and the fountain of action. (For the Hebrew connotation of *heart* see on 2:2.) What backsliding Israel needed was 'a heart to know . . . the Lord' (Je. 24:7). Our Lord's words on this subject which caused such offence (Mt. 15:10–20) draw out the teaching of this verse. For *with all vigilance*, RV mg. 'above all that thou guardest' is preferable. **26** The first phrase is difficult. AV evidently connects the Hebrew with a similar word for scales: it is well to 'weigh up' one's route. RSV *take heed to* assumes a different derivation. RV (and LXX) 'make straight', with its implication of the removal of moral hindrance (*cf.* Heb. 12:13) also fits here, if less happily where the word recurs in Pr. 5:6, 21. The pupil is also bidden to see that his ways are *sure*. The root means 'to make firm'. The road, having been carefully chosen, traced, or cleared of obstacles, is then to be made firm. **27** Thereafter there must be no deviation from it.

5:1–23 The ninth lesson

The theme is wisdom applied to the relations between the sexes. After an opening appeal for close attention (vv. 1, 2) the teacher proceeds to a description of the 'loose woman' and her allurements (vv. 3–6), an injunction to avoid her (vv. 7, 8), a warning of what befalls her victims (vv. 9–14), a call to cherish holy love (vv. 15–19) and a reminder that God is watching continually (vv. 20–23).

3 The *loose* (lit. 'strange') *woman* is a figure who often appears in the book (*cf.* 2:16; 6:24;

7:5; 20:16; 23:27; 27:13 mg.). Broadly speaking, there are four different views of the meaning of the phrase: that it represents Israelite harlots or adulteresses, described as 'strange' because they have no right to the relationship portrayed; that 'strange' has its usual meaning of 'foreign', and Canaanite or Phoenician women are meant (we know that sacred prostitution was practised in Canaanite religion); that the reference is to a foreign cult, perhaps of Astarte the goddess of love, with a strong sexual element, met with in trade relations with neighbouring countries; and that the whole is allegorical and refers to the seductions of Greek philosophy or religion. Of these, the first explanation is the simplest, the most natural, and the one that best meets the statements in 2:17; 7:19f.

4 *End* refers to the consequence of associating with her: she may seem like honey, but those who have dealings with her find the abiding taste is *wormwood*—an insecticide and exceedingly bitter (*cf.* Dt. 29:18; Je. 9:15). *Sheol*; the abode of the dead: we might say 'death'. **6** There are several possible renderings. RSV has cut the knot of a difficult translation, but may give the approximate sense. *She* could equally well be translated 'thou' in both halves of this verse. In the second half, D. Winton Thomas suggests that the word translated *know* in fact comes from a different verb, 'to be quiet'. This would give good sense: 'Her ways are not stable and she is not at rest.'

9–14 describe the conclusion of the Rake's Progress. **9, 10** The picture seems to be of the adulterer, his bodily strength sapped, his worldly goods gone, spending his remaining years as a slave in another's house. *Merciless* is masculine singular. **11–14** More terrible, however, are the pangs of his remorse, which has come too late. *I was at the point of utter ruin* means either 'I have had the narrowest of escapes from the supreme penalty which might have been inflicted for this sin', whether death (*cf.* Lv. 20:10) or otherwise; or 'I have committed the depths of evil even though a member of the holy congregation of Israel'. In this latter interpretation the phrase *assembled congregation* is viewed as a corporate designation for Israel as the people of God, and the fact that the sin was committed in the midst of such a people would constitute an aggravation of it (*cf.* Heb. 12:15). The whole passage is an illustration of 1:26ff. where wisdom is represented as 'laughing' when those who have rejected her realize their error.

From this warning of the evil consequences of sin, the teacher passes to positive instruction on the joy and sacredness of a pure and marital life, in terms similar to those of the Song of Solomon. To the Oriental the love-song is a sacred thing, and there would be nothing indelicate in the terms in which he speaks. **15** urges the learner to delight in his own wife as opposed to 'the loose woman'. **16** If we retain the AV rendering the meaning is that 'purity of married life will diffuse itself abroad like streams from a fountain' (Perowne); but the context is better suited by the RSV, involving a return to the warnings in the last section against promiscuity. **18** The fountain is *blessed* when enjoyed with respect to the laws of God: *the wife of your youth* is 'the wife you married when young', early marriage being customary in OT times.

21–23 again bring all the precepts taught into relation with the covenant of the living God. **21** He watches over every life, whether 'weighing it up' or 'scrutinizing' it (see on 4:26). **22** The rebel rapidly becomes a victim of his own rebellion. **23** The reason is that he has not heeded the divine discipline. In this verse *for lack of discipline* is much to be preferred to AV 'without instruction' (*cf.* Ho. 4:6). Such is the teacher's final deterrent from sin. For the thought of the passage *cf.* Eph. 4:17–19.

6:1–19 The tenth lesson

This lesson is based on the principle enunciated in 5:22. Three examples are taken of the process there described, and a list of seven deadly sins is added.

6:1–5 The surety. In early days Israel's commercial law was straightforward. Borrowing was necessary only for particular emergencies, and so the taking of interest from a fellow-Israelite was strictly forbidden (*e.g.* Lv. 25:36), and if a garment was taken as security for a loan, it was to be returned by nightfall to serve as a blanket (Ex. 22:25–27). With the growth of civilization and foreign trade relations, the practice of suretyship seems to have grown up, a man accepting responsibility for the debts of another. The action of the *Merchant of Venice* revolves, of course, round this or a similar custom. Perhaps further research will throw more light upon what was actually involved. At any rate, in our book it is uniformly condemned. As Kidner remarks, the objections to it come nearer to banishing gambling than to banishing generosity: 'A man's giving should be fully voluntary: its amount (*cf.* 22:27) determined by him (for then its effectiveness can be judged, and competing claims on him assessed), and not wrung from him by events outside his control' (p. 71). It is worth noticing that Proverbs is especially concerned with surety transactions involving strangers (foreign traders?); see, *e.g.*, 6:1; 11:15; 20:16; 27:13.

1 *Given your pledge for a stranger* refers to the act ratifying the transaction. The surety is, like the wicked man of 5:22, trapped by his own folly. In the verses that follow he is urged to make every effort to free himself, importuning, if need be, the one on whose behalf he has made the pledge to release him.

6:6–11 The sluggard. In *The Pilgrim's Progress* Sloth, in company with Simple and Presumption, is seen by Christian asleep by the wayside. By teaching them 'to presume that they should do well at last', Sloth and his companions cause others to follow his example. But when Christiana passes by she sees them 'hanged up in irons a

little way off'. This picture is true to that given in Proverbs. A proverb from nature, such as Solomon made (1 Ki. 4:33), is used to shame the lazy man into action (vv. 6–9), but if he heeds not, his slumber will soon be rudely interrupted (vv. 10, 11) by the stark fact of poverty and need —another example of a fool caught in the toils of his own folly (*cf.* 5:22). **11** *Like a vagabond*; 'highwayman' conveys the right sense.

6:12–19 The 'man of Belial'. A brief but vivid portrait is sketched of what A. D. Power well calls 'The Perfect Bounder' (vv. 12–14). Perverse, deceitful, divisive and vicious, he too will eventually be overthrown as a result of his sin (v. 15).

12 *A worthless person* is literally 'a man of Belial'. 'Belial', meaning 'without profit', is perhaps the only genuine compound word in Hebrew: it is often used in the OT to denote wickedness (*e.g.* Jdg. 19:22), and Paul uses it as a title for Satan (2 Cor. 6:15). **13** *Scrapes with his feet*; AV 'he speaketh with his feet' is a literal translation; RV mg. reads 'shuffleth'. In each case insincerity is implied. *Points*; *cf.* RV 'maketh signs'. Not 'teacheth', as AV.

16–19 The next section also relates to the man of Belial. The seven deadly sins enumerateb as things that God hates are marks of 'the bad lot'. He sins with his eyes (vv. 13, 17), hands (vv. 13, 17), heart (vv. 14, 18) and feet (vv. 13, 18); he is a divider and mischief-maker (vv. 14, 19). We have other 'numerical proverbs' in ch. 30. Perhaps this was originally a didactic form for classroom use, and ran 'What six things does Yahweh hate? . . .'

6:20–35 The eleventh lesson

The theme is the seventh commandment. The exordium treats of the guidance offered by sound teaching (vv. 20–23); and solemn warnings are uttered against the specific sin of adultery (vv. 24–35).

20 *Commandment* and *teaching* (*tôrâ*; *cf.* on 1:8) refer to parental teaching; in v. 23 they seem to refer to the law of the covenant. It was this law, however (*cf.* Dt. 6:6, 7), which was the content of the home teaching of the godly Israelite. The divine law, taught and expounded, provides clear guidance for life. Oesterley makes a distinction between *commandment* as the lamp and the law (*teaching*) as the source of light, and compares the way in which John the Baptist is called a lamp (Jn. 5:35) and Jesus Christ the light (Jn. 1:8f.). At all events God's law is to be inwardly held and outwardly manifested (v. 21), guiding and controlling all activities (v. 22).

24 It is stressed that the law and discipline and correction in the light of it (*cf.* 2 Tim. 3:16) afford protection from the *evil woman*. Here a case might be made out for an allegorical interpretation, and when we remember that the figure of an adulteress is often used in the OT to describe sinful Israel (*cf.* Ho. 2) and that James uses it to describe the worldly Christian (Jas. 4:4, AV), it is clear that the reach of these chapters is far beyond sexual misconduct.

Nevertheless the way in which detail is relentlessly pressed home requires us to believe that the teacher means his words to be taken literally.

25 *Her eyelashes* (or 'eyelids', AV) were probably painted (*cf.* 2 Ki. 9:30). **26** It is not clear whether the teacher distinguishes two types of immoral woman. If this is so, the verse says that a man may be brought to poverty (*cf.* AV 'to a piece of bread') through a prostitute, but runs the risk of his life (by social or legal action) through consorting with an *adulteress* (lit. 'a man's wife'). Probably, however, the same woman is referred to in both parts of the verse. RSV less satisfactorily follows LXX in rendering *For a harlot may be hired for a loaf of bread, but* . . . . **27** *Bosom* means the fold of the garment across the chest. **29** brings us again to the thought of the living God. *Shall not go unpunished*; literally 'shall not be innocent', a state of 'non-innocence' in OT thought inevitably implying punishment. **30** is rather obscure. The simplest explanation is that if a thief who steals to feed himself, though much less despicable than an adulterer, has still to make restitution in full measure (*sevenfold* in v. 31 is probably a general, not an exact term), how much more shall the adulterer pay the penalty? **32ff.** Only in his case is he destroying himself; he can expect condign punishment and public disgrace (v. 33), and will receive no quarter from the wronged husband (v. 34); unlike the thief, he can make no restitution (v. 35).

7:1–27 The twelfth lesson

The theme, like that of the previous lesson, is the peril of adultery. First there is the customary exhortation to observe and ever keep in mind the paternal teaching which is the way of life and is particularly proof against the strange woman (vv. 1–5). The relationships mentioned in v. 4 depict the close personal knowledge of wisdom that the teacher desires in his pupils: *sister* implies family intimacy (*cf.* Mt. 12:50). There follows a passage of superb vividness giving an eyewitness account of how a young man fell a prey to the strange woman (vv. 6–23). This forms the bulk of the lesson, vv. 24–27 pointing the moral.

7 The picture of the victim is skilfully sketched. He is *a man without sense*, a 'simple' man (see on 1:22). This is illustrative of the fact that one who is simple in the negative sense without formed ideas of good and evil is in peril of becoming a fool and a reprobate if he remains uninstructed. **8, 9** We learn that he spent the time from twilight to midnight walking the streets near her house. **10–13** The woman is lustful and restless, *with impudent face* (an excellent translation!) and quite shameless. **14** She introduces a subtle religious pretext. Under the law of the peace-offering (Lv. 7:11ff.), the flesh of the animal had to be eaten by the worshippers on the same day as the sacrifice, or, in the case of a vow, on the following day. The woman, having made her vows to Yahweh, now invites the youth to share in the sacrificial feast. **15** She claims to have looked for him specially to share her table. **16–19** She paints in glowing colours 'the pleasures of sin', and their extraordinary luck in that her husband is away for some time. Actually in the Hebrew she calls him simply 'the man', possibly what Toy calls 'a refined sneer'. **21–23** After some hesitation (implied in v. 21) the youth suddenly capitulates. *All at once* (*i.e.* 'suddenly') is better than AV 'straightway'. The text in vv. 22, 23 is notoriously difficult. RSV has been influenced by LXX, which is rather longer than the Hebrew. Whatever the actual words, the sense is clear: the young man's fate is sudden and drastic.

Having reached this dramatic climax, the teacher closes the lesson with a few solemn sentences. **26** The casualties caused by the evil woman have been innumerable. *A mighty host* (AV 'many strong men') has been slain by her. In other words, 'Let any one who thinks that he stands take heed lest he fall.' It is a strange irony that it was his 'foreign wives' that led to Solomon's own decline from wisdom (1 Ki. 11:1–8).

8:1–36 The thirteenth lesson

The lesson, after a brief introduction by the teacher (vv. 1–3), is given by personified wisdom herself: and with it we reach the high-water mark of the series. In severe contrast with the shuffling, dusk-loving, seductive manner of the woman of the last lesson, wisdom clearly and with dignity and in the most public places pleads with men to receive her and declares the treasures of her reward (vv. 4–21). Wisdom's part in creation is then set forth (vv. 22–31), and she adds her own exhortation to cleave to her in vv. 32–36.

This chapter with its personification of wisdom was interpreted Christologically from the earliest Christian centuries. Certainly Paul (*cf.*, *e.g.*, 1 Cor. 8:6; Col. 1:15–18), the writer to the Hebrews (*cf.* Heb. 1:3) and John (*cf.* Rev. 3:14) see in it terms which have their full meaning only in 'Christ the power of God and the wisdom of God' (1 Cor. 1:24). Theophilus of Antioch, the first Christian writer to use the word 'Trinity' of the Godhead, speaks of 'God, His Word and His Wisdom' (*Ad Autolycum* ii. 15: like other 2nd-century writers he is not clear on the division of functions between Son and Spirit). We may believe that the Fathers were justified in seeing in the personification of wisdom a foreshadowing of that revelation made clearer in the NT of three hypostases in the one God. 'The vivid and august personification falters not on its way, till it presents to us rather than predicts Him, who is "the Wisdom of God", "the Only Begotten of the Father" and "the Son of His Love"; who "became flesh" and "dwelt among us", because from all eternity His delights had been with the sons of men' (Perowne, *CBSC*). Finally we may note that our Lord Himself refers to the personified wisdom of God (Lk. 11:49) in speaking of the prophets and apostles, the mouthpieces of

God's wisdom, who were consistently rejected by God's people.

8:1–21 Wisdom among men. 1–4 In the most conspicuous places wisdom addresses the whole of mankind. **5** Once again we see that discerning shrewdness (*prudence*) is offered to the *simple*, and even hardened *foolish men* (*kᵉsîlîm*; see on 1:22) still have a chance to learn. **6–9** Wisdom's words are true, straightforward and sincere. **10, 11** She offers a rich reward: far richer than the things for which men spend their lives.

Wisdom then explains further what she is. **12** The meaning is that wisdom is demonstrated in actual life by discernment (*prudence*) and possesses the other forms of understanding spoken of in 1:4. **13** Wisdom identifies herself with the *fear of the Lord* (*cf.* 1:7), and God and wisdom hate the same things: wisdom, for all its practical, earthly uses, has no clashes of interest with godliness. **14** Among her other possessions are *counsel* and *strength* (RV 'might'), qualities of kingship which are seen in their fullness in the King Messiah (Is. 9:6; 11:2). **15, 16** This leads naturally to wisdom's part in guiding rulers. Solomon himself asked for wisdom to guide him in his rule (1 Ki. 3:5–12). **17** Wisdom is accessible when sought (*cf.* Lk. 11:9–13). **18–21** Wisdom confers great riches upon those that love her, the greater because they are righteously obtained (vv. 18, 20). That her blessings are more than simply material is shown by the contrasts in v. 19. *Enduring* (AV 'durable') occurs nowhere else in the OT: RV mg. suggests 'ancient'; Koehler (*Lexicon, in loc.*) 'hereditary'.

8:22–36 Wisdom with God. Wisdom speaks now of her part in creation. **22** Since the time of the opening of the Arian controversy in the 4th century this verse has been one of the most discussed passages in the OT. The main point at issue is, what is the meaning of the word *qānâ* translated 'possessed' (Vulg., AV, RV) or *created* (LXX, Targ., RSV). The Arians used the LXX 'the Lord created me' as one of their main proof-texts for their thesis that Christ was a created being. They were confuted on other grounds, but it is highly questionable whether the Hebrew here bears this meaning. The ordinary meaning is 'to get, acquire', as in 1:5, 4:5 and elsewhere. There are other occasions when it could well mean 'create, make' (*e.g.* Gn. 14:19—'maker of heaven and earth' or 'possessor'?; Ex. 15:16—'the people thou hast made' or 'acquired'?) and RSV has so translated it here. But long ago C. F. Burney argued that it meant 'beget', and a parallel in Ugaritic literature often translated 'creatress of the gods' seems to imply parenthood rather than creation. The meanings of possession and parenthood are in fact closely related (see Gn. 4:1, where *qānâ* is again used, and *cf.* the width of meaning of 'got' in archaic English). Whether 'possessed' or more precisely 'begotten', wisdom in Proverbs is inseparable from God, and was with Him from all eternity. **23** *Set up* may refer to God's appointment of wisdom for her task. The word is used in the

sense of consecrate. Originally meaning 'to pour out', it came to mean 'to consecrate by pouring libations'. **24** Wisdom preceded all created things, even the primeval depths (note here and in v. 25 the metaphor of birth; some have argued a royal birth). But that is not all. **30** Wisdom is not only present at, but is the mediatrix of creation. Human craftsmanship is the product of wisdom (Ex. 35:31); so also is the craftsmanship that formed the worlds. 'The versatility of the mind of man is but an image of the versatility of its archetype' (Cheyne, *Job and Solomon*, 1887, p. 118). *Master workman* represents a rare word, and this meaning, though likely, is less than certain. AV has apparently read it with different pointing to give 'nurseling', which certainly makes sense, but fits the whole context rather less effectively. It is not an insuperable objection that Yahweh Himself is presented throughout as the Maker. We may easily and in the same context speak of the owner, the architect and the builder all 'building' the same house. **31** Wisdom rejoiced over the advancing creation, and her joy was complete when it was ready for mankind to live there. A more literal rendering would be 'sporting in the inhabited world of His earth'. With the whole passage *cf.* 3:19, 20.

32–36 In the concluding verses wisdom speaks like a teacher and addresses her audience as *sons*, reminding them again that to love her brings life (v. 35) and to hate her, death (v. 36). 'Sinneth against me' (v. 36, AV); better, as in RSV, *misses me*. The Hebrew word 'to sin' meant originally 'to miss', *i.e.* 'to miss the mark': this original meaning is better here, where the contrast is with *he who finds me*. To miss wisdom is to wrong oneself; to hate her is suicide (v. 36).

9:1–18 Summary of the thirteen lessons

Some of the main topics dealt with in chs. 1–8 are summarized in the form of a picture of wisdom and folly each inviting men to a banquet.

9:1–12 The seven pillars of wisdom. 1 Once more personified, wisdom is now seen as a gracious hostess. There has been much speculation about the *seven pillars*. They have been made to represent things as various as the seven days of creation, the seven liberal arts, the sun and moon and five known planets, and even the first seven chapters of Proverbs (see the list in Toy, *ICC, Proverbs*, p. 185). But they may indicate only the structure of a large and ideally constructed house: Sennacherib's new year festival house, discovered in recent years, has seven pillars.

2, 3 Within her house wisdom has laid a magnificent feast and despatched her maids to call the guests. She goes herself (vv. 3–6) to call whosoever will to her banquet. **4** There is a special place for the uninstructed *simple* and for the ignoramus; **6** they may yet receive life and understanding. 'Forsake the foolish' (AV) (or rather, 'the simple ones', as in v. 4) is the most straightforward translation. Some prefer 'Forsake, ye simple ones'—calling them to a clearcut decision (RSV *leave simpleness* follows LXX). There is an evident connection between this great supper and that described in Lk. 14:16ff.

There follow comments, still by wisdom herself, on the impossibility of making any impression upon the scorners by such an invitation as she was extending to the simple. **7–9** The contrast is not between those invited and those not invited to the banquet, but between the reactions of the scorner and the teachable man to the holy discipline imparted by wisdom. This, too, is an element in our Lord's teaching (*cf.* Mt. 7:6). See also 1:4, 5 and 1:22 and the commentary there. **10**, with its repetition of the motto of the book (1:7), gives the reason for this difference of reaction. Wisdom begins with the fear of God; the cynical scorner can therefore never learn. *The Holy One*; read with RV, RSV (*cf.* AV 'for the holy').

9:13–18 Folly's feast. Folly is also personified —as a harlot. Brazenly she invites the simple to her feast. She makes her invitation as widely known as does wisdom (*cf.* vv. 14, 15 with vv. 3, 4). But whereas wisdom offers a feast indeed and of her own preparation (v. 5), folly offers a paltry meal, stolen, illicit and clandestine (v. 17), and her guests go to their death (v. 18).

13 *A foolish woman*; literally 'a woman of folly'. Perhaps, with RV mg., we should translate simply 'folly'. *Wanton* represents a word of uncertain meaning. *Knows no shame* rests on a slight emendation of the text. Another possibility is 'and is ever restless'.

We may note that the invitations of both wisdom and folly are directed to the simple and ignorant (vv. 4, 16). The wise, though they may still grow in wisdom (vv. 8, 9), and the scoffer (v. 7) need no invitation.

10:1 – 22:16 THE FIRST BOOK OF SOLOMON

The long connected 'lessons' are the prelude to large collections of detached sayings. 'By now the reader is in a position to orientate himself in the thicket of individual sayings . . . and to see in each cool, objective aphorism a miniature and particular outworking of the wisdom and folly whose whole course he has seen spread out before him in Section I' (Kidner, p. 23). The first and much the largest of these collections, estimated to contain 374 proverbs, is attributed directly to Solomon. Whether the collection was made by Solomon himself, by a member of his court, or by a later collector, we have no means of knowing. But the exact figure quoted in 1 Ki. 4:32 suggests that collections may have been made in his lifetime, so that this may be one.

Most of the proverbs are of one type, consisting of two lines, the second pointing a contrast to the first. The arrangement is not quite so haphazard as may at first appear. Often a series of proverbs on the same or a similar subject, or demonstrating the same principle, may be grouped together; or the repetition of a catchword or catchphrase may be the link between proverbs on different subjects. But the proverbs were spoken at different times and there is often no connection between them. It must be stressed that the titles at the heads of sections are only approximate guides to the contents for the sake of convenience.

10:1–32 The rewards of right and wrong living

1 Just as the lessons sometimes begin with an exhortation to follow parental teaching (*e.g.* 1:8; 6:20), the collection opens with a proverb about the response to this teaching. *Foolish* is more than 'stupid'; the son is a k^esîl (see on 1:22). **2** speaks of the reward of uprightness. *Righteousness* is right living. The prophets frequently speak of oppression, cheating and exploitation of the weak as denials of the righteousness God demands in His people. **3** The catchword *righteous* introduces the next proverb dealing with God's supply of the physical needs of His people (*cf.* Mt. 6:11, 33), and His frustration of the evil desires of the wicked.

4, 5 Lest this be taken as an invitation to fecklessness, these verses concern laziness and industry—which affect others as well as oneself. *A slack hand* (lit. 'palm') conveys the idea of the hand hanging loose.

6 *The mouth of the wicked conceals violence*: AV's 'violence covereth the mouth of the wicked' is preferable. From the parallelism we would expect this to refer to the reproaches or blows about the mouth which follow for the wicked as assuredly as blessings on the 'head' of the righteous, but ḥamas (violence) usually refers to wrongful treatment, and it is better to understand it of violent, vicious language enveloping the mouth of the wicked.

7 The effects of righteousness and wickedness continue on earth after death. **9** *Cf.* 2 Tim. 3:9. **10** *He who winks the eye* refers to crafty, insincere conduct. RSV, probably rightly, follows LXX with its excellent antithesis; AV's 'prating fool' seems to have slipped in scribally from v. 8. **11** The righteous man's mouth is a constant source of inspiration, a wayside spring from which wayfarers are refreshed; violent, noxious language covers (so, probably rightly, AV—see on v. 6 above) the wicked man's mouth. We may observe that, as in 6:12f., righteousness and wickedness may be manifest in the heart (v. 8), mouth (vv. 6, 8, 10, 11), feet (v. 9) and eyes (v. 10). **12** A deep saying (*cf.* Jas. 5:20; 1 Pet. 4:8) on love and hatred is linked to v. 10 by the catchword 'covers'. For the meaning of *covers* in this verse, note its opposite in the first line, and that 'covers' is a possible translation of the word normally translated 'bears' in 1 Cor. 13:7.

14 *Lay up*; *i.e.* for the proper occasion. The idea is that while wise men conceal what they know, the fool (an '^ewîl; see on 1:22) is likely to blurt out his stupidity and endanger himself and others in consequence. **15** *Ruin* serves as a catchword. Here it suggests the threat of imminent disaster: in the social revolution of Solomon's time the lot of the poor must have been constant insecurity. When the first half of this saying is repeated, however (18:11; AV is preferable), it is shown that this is not the whole story, and that the rich man's wealth is not in itself a sufficiently strong city. **16** This realistic acknowledgment of the comfort of a good income is immediately followed by a reminder that what really distinguishes between men is how they use their income. Its use and abuse have serious and permanent effects.

18-21 Four proverbs on speech. It is evil both to hide hatred hypocritically, and to manifest it in slander; words are best used sparingly; their value depends on the person uttering them. **21** *Feed* is the word commonly used of a shepherd's care for his flock. The righteous, by virtue of their speech, become pastors; fools die for lack of the wisdom the righteous can impart to others. **22** Yahweh's blessing is unadulterated. (The marginal rendering is dubious.) **24, 25** We return to the former theme of the respective rewards of the righteous and wicked. The latter's life is based on what is temporal and temporary; he dreads the sudden disaster, *the tempest* which removes everything he trusts in. *Cf.* the parable in Mt. 7:24ff.

26 The sluggard reappears, a plague to all who deal with him. We hear a master's judgment on one such wicked and slothful servant in Mt. 25:26. For the converse *cf.* Pr. 25:13. **27-30** Four more proverbs on the fate of the righteous and the wicked. The first three designate life, joy and strength respectively as the blessings of the righteous. **29** While RSV is preferable here, a grammatical alternative would be 'The way of the Lord (*i.e.* the way He deals with men) is a stronghold to the upright'. **30** This takes further the principle expressed in Ex. 20:12 and taken further still by our Lord in Mt. 5:5. **31** *Brings forth*; 'puts forth buds of wisdom' (Moffatt).

11:1-31 Some aspects of wickedness

Dishonest business; pride before a fall; distortions of treacherous men; the riches you cannot take with you; life as an obstacle race; evil desires and their effect; the sudden dissolution of the wicked man's security; destructive speech; the civic effects of righteousness and wickedness; the unwisdom of showing contempt; the talebearer; lack of advice; the menace of suretyship; the gains of good women and bad men; the harvest of our lives; skin-deep beauty; desire and fulfilment; the hidden miseries of moneygrubbing; misdirected search and misplaced trust; losing one's temper; lawlessness and requital.

1 Commercial and business practice is brought into direct relation with the law of God. **2** There is a direct affiliation between wisdom and humility. **3** *The treacherous* (AV 'transgressors') represents a term which frequently stands for those who break or revolt against God's covenant. This in itself makes for distortion (so, literally, *crookedness*). **4** *In the day of wrath*—be it in a sudden disaster, at death, or in the 'day of the Lord' spoken of by the prophets (*cf.* Is. 10:3; Am. 5:18)—it is *righteousness* that delivers, not riches. This is one of many passages in this book which, while limited in its application in its original context, expresses eternal principles and is flooded with fuller meaning for the Christian. **5** A contrast between the respective paths of the *blameless* (connected with the word translated 'integrity' in v. 3), who is able to clear the obstacles from his path as he goes, and the *wicked*, for ever tripping himself up. **6** It is their evil desires which ensnare and overthrow the rebels. **7** *The expectation of the godless comes to naught*; literally 'the expectation of strength perishes': *i.e.* the wicked rich, with their expectation based only on human resources, however powerful in life, find themselves frustrated at death: they cannot even ensure that their children will inherit their prosperity. No book in the Bible is more concerned with eschatology than is the book of Proverbs.

9 *Godless*, or 'apostate', came to mean 'hypocrite' (so AV). Whether by seduction, subversion, or slander, he is destructive, and the best defence is the *knowledge* of a righteous person, who is accordingly not misled. **10, 11** The righteous and the wicked each have their effect on public life. The whole township rejoices at a good man's prosperity and at the fall of the evil. A city is ennobled by the presence within it of men who are blessed of God and overthrown by the *mouth* (*i.e.* in counsel or leadership) of wicked men. (We may recall this principle at work in Gn. 18.) The *city* in mind is a Hebrew walled city (*qiryâ*); the character of the city rulers may be decisive for the whole community. Oesterley points out that these verses belong to a date when Israelite cities were governed by Israelites, *i.e.* before the Exile.

14 This saying about the need for wise guidance in government and the need for taking extensive advice (*cf.* 15:22; 24:6) would have been especially relevant soon after Solomon's death (*cf.* 1 Ki. 12:1-15). **15** 'None ever knew so well that "He who hateth suretyship is sure" as He who having counted the cost became for us "the surety of a better covenant"' (Perowne). **16** A comparison instead of the usual antithesis. A gracious woman wins and keeps renown as surely as violent men seize their booty. **17** *Kind*; the kindness is *ḥesed*, 'covenant love'. The reference is to those covenant obligations which require that a man love his neighbour as himself. In doing so he naturally does good to himself: the cruel man, neglectful of the covenant, does himself damage. **18** The present prosperity of the wicked man is deceptive, since it will not benefit him for ever: the reward of the righteous is certain (*cf.* Gal. 6:7). **19** The Hebrew is very compressed but the sense is not in doubt. The word *kēn* can mean 'as' (so AV) or *steadfast* (RV, RSV).

21 *Be assured*; literally 'hand to hand', apparently a strong asseveration (*cf.* our 'shake on it'). *Those who are righteous*; literally 'the seed of the righteous', *i.e.* righteous people as a whole (*cf.* Jn. 8:39; Gal. 3:7, AV). **24–26** Wealth is not conditional on miserliness, but rather the reverse; and the practice of keeping back food in order to run the price up is reprehensible (*cf.* Am. 8:4–6). **27** Those who seek goodwill find God's favour; those who look for trouble will find more of it than they bargained for. **28** *Wither*; better, 'fall' (*cf.* mg.—RSV has needlessly emended).

30 *Lawlessness*; RSV has followed LXX, and the rendering makes a good antithesis with the first line. *Takes away lives* is certainly a more natural rendering than 'winneth souls' (*cf.* AV—'souls' here will stand for 'persons' or 'lives'). However, the Hebrew text as it stands reads 'a wise man takes (away?) lives', which may mean that by his example he gains the lives of other men, so that his righteousness is a *tree of life* to others as well as himself (Mt. 4:19 could then be an echo of this proverb). **31** Both righteous and wicked will receive their desert on earth. The LXX took this to mean that both will be punished for their sins; *i.e.* if the righteous are to be punished (for even they have sinned), how much more the sinner? It is the LXX rendering which is taken up in 1 Pet. 4:18.

12:1–28 Contrasts in conduct

Differing reactions to discipline; what gives a man roots; the difference wives make; the thoughts, words and fate of the wicked; the differing reputation of differing degrees of sense; on playing the great man; animals know whom it is best to work for; industry and frivolity; the wicked and the righteous; the differing effect of differing people's words; on advice; what to ignore; words good and bad; planning, good and bad; self-betrayal; the outcome of diligence and sloth; anxiety and sympathy; those who help and those who hinder; the reward of the diligent; the two ways.

2 *Condemns* is a legal term; literally 'he will cause to be wicked', *i.e.* God will reckon him as wicked. **4** *A good wife*; the term implies both nobility of character and effectualness in the home: the sketch is filled out in 31:10–31. **5–7** Three contrasts between the righteous and the wicked: in their intentions (so *thoughts*, v. 5); in their words (the righteous do not simply not speak harm, they *deliver* men, v. 6—unless the thought is 'deliver themselves', whereas the plotters tend to trap themselves); and in their ultimate end (v. 7; *cf.* Mt. 7:26). **9** RSV has followed LXX here. AV, RV have used the same consonants with different vowels, to give the meaning that it is better to be of low social status and still have enough to keep a servant than to have a high opinion of oneself and go hungry. The thought is similar: RSV is more direct, and to be preferred, in its expression. **11** The industrious peasant working his own piece of ground triumphs over the trifler who

follows worthless pursuits (RSV) or people (AV, RV). **12** A difficult verse; RSV has emended the text. This reads 'The evil man has desired the net of the wicked but the root of the righteous gives' (AV, RV add 'fruit'), apparently indicating that what bad men desire is delusive, perhaps self-destructive. **14** 'Words can bring in as substantial a return as deeds, for they establish relationships and implant ideas' (Kidner, p. 97). *Cf.* Mt. 12:36; 2 Cor. 5:10. **17–19** Three contrasts in speech. The true witness who declares what is right and the lying evidence; the sharp-tongued whose speech wounds (*cf.* Ps. 106:33) and the helpful, healing conversation of the truly wise; the permanence of true words and the transitoriness of a lie. **20** Not only do the wicked speak lies; their mind (*heart*) is deceitful, a contrast to the joy of those who plan good (the Heb. *šālôm*, 'peace'—*cf.* AV, RV—conveys the idea of general welfare). **21** The wise man must, like the questioner of our own day, have seen apparent exceptions to this principle: he is no Job's comforter. As it was for suffering Paul, it is ultimately an affirmation of faith in a righteous and victorious God: *cf.* Rom. 8:28, 36, 37.

24 The hard worker brings himself responsibility: the lazy man finds himself under the lash in the labour gang. For the background in Solomonic times *cf.* 1 Ki. 9:15ff.; 11:28. **26** The sense is clearly that good men are a help and bad men a hindrance to others on the path of life, but the Hebrew of the first line, which RSV has emended, is obscure. **27** The meaning of some words in this verse is not certain. If LXX and RSV are right in translating *catch* (or if others are right in connecting it with an Arabic root used as a hunting term), the sluggard is too lazy to hunt his food; if AV is right in following Jewish tradition (for which some linguistic support can be adduced), he is too indolent, having so far stirred himself as to hunt, then to cook it. The sluggard wastes what little he accomplishes by not finishing it. The second half of the verse reads literally 'But the substance of a precious man is diligent'. Perhaps AV, RSV are right in transposing *diligent* and *precious*. **28** Again the Hebrew of the second half is obscure. RSV emends. Among other suggestions (needing no major emendation) are 'And the journey of her pathway is no-Death!' or 'But (there is) a way (which is) a path to death' (see Kidner, *in loc.*).

13:1–25 Life and discipline

Wise man and cynic; pure speech; how to be satisfied; telling the truth; riches and poverty; the light that failed; strife the fruit of insolence; easy come, easy go; hope deferred; keeping the commandments; the man of sense; ambassadors good and bad; the uses of criticism; getting one's desire; wisdom and folly are both infectious; due rewards; an education; satisfaction and frustration.

2 The pure speech of a good man will be rewarded (*cf.* 12:14) but the appetite of the treacherous (*i.e.* rebels against God's covenant) is for violence. **3** *Opens wide his lips* suggests a vulgar grin (see Koehler, *Lexicon*, article *pshq*). **4** *Acts shamefully and disgracefully*; or perhaps 'causes to stink and makes ashamed', those who pollute all they touch being contrasted with the righteous who detest falsity. **7** As translated, the antithesis is between miserliness and extravagant display. AV, whose rendering is equally tenable, contrasts true and false riches. A man may be wealthy and not 'rich toward God', or he may be poor and have great treasures (*cf.* Lk. 12:21). We cannot separate this from the thought of Him who though He was rich, yet for our sakes became poor (2 Cor. 8:9) and in whom the verse reaches its height of meaning. **8** There are advantages in wealth and poverty alike. The rich man can use his wealth to get himself out of difficulty; the poor man is less likely to be exposed to such difficulties, or, perhaps, he has 'nothing to lose but his chains'. **9** *Be put out*; perhaps better 'go out', while that of the righteous goes on burning merrily.

12 *Tree of life*; *cf.* 3:18; 11:30, and notes. **13** It is perilous for him who *despises the word* of God—here not necessarily confined to the law of Moses, but certainly including it; *cf.* Is. 30:12. **14** The *teaching* (*tôrâ*, here with its primary sense of 'instruction') of the wise is refreshing and revitalizing. **15** *Faithless*; again the traitors to the covenant are in mind. RSV has followed LXX and other ancient translations in reading *their ruin*; the Hebrew reads 'is perennial'. (AV's 'the way of transgressors is hard', though celebrated, cannot really be sustained.) Another possibility is indicated by G. R. Driver, that the word 'not' has dropped out. The last line would then read: 'The way of the rebels does not last.' **17** *Healing*; or 'security'.

19 'Although there is nothing more sweet than to gain a high and noble desire, fools will not leave their unworthy ways to do that; to do so would be hateful (*an abomination*) to them.' **20** *Will suffer harm.* The Hebrew has a pregnant ambiguity: the companion of fools either 'suffers evil', or 'becomes evil'. **21, 22** 'Proverbs is concerned with the general rule; Job (*e.g.* chapter 21) with the exceptions' (Kidner). **23** On RSV's rendering, the poor man's ground, though potentially fruitful, may be subject to deprivation by injustice. Another possibility is that the latent potentialities may be squandered by lack of judgment (*cf.* AV); the size of one's assets matters less than the discretion applied to their use.

14:1-35 Life in the fear of the Lord

Home building; walking uprightly; the effects of talking; order without adventure; true and false witness; the search for wisdom; profitless company; discerning conduct; ultimate loneliness; permanent residence; the misleading signpost; all our joy is touched with pain; requital; gullibility and discernment; quick temper; the peril of the simpleton; final vindication; neighbours; doing good and evil; labour

and gossip; the ornaments of wisdom and folly; true and false witnesses; the fear of the Lord; prince and people; tranquillity of mind; exploitation of the poor; the glory of a nation; good and wicked servants.

1 *Wisdom*; actually 'wisdom of women' (see RSV mg.), or 'womanly wisdom', doubtless with reference to the family life which may be built or torn down by the wisdom or folly of the wife and mother. *Cf.* the houses of wisdom and folly (both of whom are personified as females) in 9:1ff. **2** Uprightness and perversity ultimately spring from attitudes to God—one of realism, the other of lack of it. **4** RSV has made a slight emendation. AV has 'Where no oxen are, the crib is clean'. The sense would be: 'No oxen, no stable-cleaning—but also no ploughing, and therefore no corn.' Considerable disturbance may be a requisite of growth. **6** The scoffer, however able, fails to find wisdom even when he seeks it, because his cynical arrogance leaves no room for 'the fear of the Lord' (*cf.* 9:10). **9** RSV has emended an obscure first line, which reads literally 'guilt (-offering) mocks at fools'. This might mean that the sacrifices offered by sin mock them by their ineffectiveness (*cf.* Is. 2:11ff.), but seems a curious way to express it. 'Every fool mocks at guilt (-offering?)' is a possible, though not an easy translation (*cf.* AV, RV). AV's 'but among the righteous there is favour' is doubtless right in seeing *favour* as referring to relations among men. The guilt-offering had reference to relations both with God and with other men (*cf.* Lv. 6:1-7). But translation of this difficult verse remains tentative.

10 This beautiful and poignant saying shows that the wisdom teachers were not concerned purely with outward conduct, and illustrates that in this book *heart* can refer to the emotional as well as the intellectual faculties. **17** RSV follows LXX and with the bad-tempered man contrasts the man with *discretion* used in a good sense. The Hebrew text has 'hated' instead of *patient*; one may thus (like AV) take *discretion* in a bad sense—deviousness, which may be a far worse thing than bad temper. **18** This conviction finds its ultimate fulfilment in the events described in Phil. 2:9-11. **25** A witness has it in his power to save or murder life or reputation. In such circumstances, the man who *utters* (literally 'breathes out') *lies* is 'all deceit' (*cf.* RV). **26** *His children*; *i.e.* those of the godly man referred to in the first line.

30 Composure preserves, envy corrodes the person who harbours them. **31** Exploitation of the poor is a direct affront to God. With the whole verse *cf.* Mt. 25:32ff. **32** *Finds refuge*; better 'seeks refuge'. *Through his integrity*: RSV has followed LXX in reading two consonants differently from the present Hebrew, which has 'in his death' (so AV). The godly man thus commits himself to God in his death. AV may be right: though the scope of the teachers of wisdom was normally within this world, an occasional forward glance must not be *a priori* excluded. **33** *Not known*; RSV follows LXX in reading *not*, which is missing in the Hebrew. If the text is not emended, the sense may be that even among fools there is some recognition of the wisdom which is truly at home in the wise man. **34, 35** Proverbs for Solomon's court. The true glory of a nation is in its correspondence with the righteous law of God. 'The study of the things concerning the king is to the thoughtful reader of the Proverbs a study of the things concerning Christ. The ideal elements speak of Him; the actual shortcomings cry out for Him' (R. F. Horton).

15:1–33 On the path of life with a cheerful heart

Gentle answers and hurtful words; responsible speech; God's watch on life; giving words and taking them; laying up treasures; acceptable piety; what God loves and what He hates; on discipline; no hiding place down here; the cynic not as daring as he seems; gladness and sorrow; minds grow by what they feed on; the feast of a cheerful heart; life's desiderata; quick and even tempers; straight roads are easiest roads; father and son; senseless joy; ill-considered plans; a word in season; the upward path; the Lord the widow's friend; on bribery; how far away is God?; the savour of good news; on teachability.

1 *A harsh word*: the Hebrew suggests one that hurts. **2** *Dispenses knowledge*; perhaps better, with AV, 'uses knowledge aright'. The quality, as well as the quantity, of speech is contrasted with the trash blurted out by the fool. **3** *Cf.* 2 Ch. 16:9. **4** Gentle speech is healing, life-giving; twisted speech can crush people (*cf.* Is. 65:14 for the effect of a 'broken spirit'). **8** For God's refusal to be 'bought off' by sacrifice from the basically unrepentant, *cf.* Is. 1:11ff. **11** *Sheol* (the abode of the dead) and *Abaddon* (lit. 'Destruction') are coupled also in 27:20; Jb. 26:6. They are perhaps synonymous, though the latter may refer particularly to the abode of the wicked. They are, like everything on earth, open to God's continual inspection. For the thought, *cf.* Ps. 139, especially v. 8.

19 The sluggard goes for a short cut; as usual, it turns out the hardest way. **25** It is in the nature of *the proud* to devour widows' houses (Lk. 20:47), but God is ever on the side of the exploited: a recurrent biblical theme which in the Magnificat (Lk. 1:46–55) becomes a sort of Marseillaise. **26** *Thoughts*; *i.e.* plans—hateful to God even before their execution.

16:1–33 The Lord's watch on human life

The overlordship of God; arrogance, loyalty and faithfulness; the effects of pleasing God; when a little is better than a lot; the king's place; the business man's place; the king's power; the worth of wisdom; walking on the highway; pride and humility; wisdom's pleasantnesses; the road to death; the commonest incentive; damaging activities; venerable men; self-control; God decides the outcome.

This group of sayings contains several clusters

of proverbs on themes that are similar or related, such as the group on divine sovereignty (vv. 1–4), on the king (vv. 12–15) and on various types of harmful person (vv. 27–30); but sayings on these same themes are found outside the clusters (*cf.*, *e.g.*, vv. 10, 33).

1 A man may make plans, but the execution of them—which becomes concrete in speech (*the answer of the tongue*)—fulfils God's designs. *Cf.* v. 9. **2** A man may be satisfied with himself, but God is the final judge of his behaviour (*cf.* 1 Cor. 4:4). **3** Literally 'Roll your work upon the Lord . . .'. **4** The saying is compressed: there is no sense of an arbitrary predestination of men for the coming evil day. 'The general meaning is that there are ultimately no loose ends in God's world: everything will be put to some use and matched with its proper fate' (Kidner). **6** *Loyalty* (*i.e.* covenant love) *and faithfulness* (see 3:3, 4) are the means of 'atoning for' (lit. 'covering') sin, just as love is stated to be at 10:12. This is not put forward as a formal principle of atonement; it expresses God's basic requirements under the covenant with Israel (*cf.* Mi. 6:6–8; Hab. 2:4) and is closely linked with a deserting of evil ways, caused by reverent awe of God. It also expresses the response to atonement, *i.e.* faithfulness and departure from evil, occasioned by fear of God and grateful love towards Him.

10 *Inspired decisions*; literally 'divination'. The king when he gives a righteous judgment speaks oracularly, like a prophet, and his mouth does not revolt against justice. This prepares us for the portrait of the Messianic King, with His divine judgment (*cf.* Is. 9:7; 11:3, 4). **11** God's stamp is on the standard weights and measures: any unfair practice in trade is in opposition to Him. **12–15** For the OT understanding of kingship see Dt. 17:18–20. How far short of the ideal the actual royal house fell is revealed in history. But the portrait remained, to be drawn more clearly by the prophets and fulfilled in the Kingship of Christ. 'The reckless fury of the Eastern despot . . . is but the abuse of the awful justice of the Archetypal King' (Perowne). **26** This is lifted to a new level by Jn. 6:27. **33** The lot is cast into the lap from the folds of which it is to be shaken out; but it is God who determines what it says. The background is doubtless the sacred lot (*cf.* Jos. 7:14–18; 14:1, 2) but the meaning intended is far wider. God disposes: there is no such thing as chance.

17:1–28 Home, friends and fools

A peaceful home; privileges can be forfeited; the Lord the Refiner; slander and heartlessness; three generations of joy; unbecoming speech; bribery; conciliation and alienation; criticism that sinks in; rebellion, folly, strife, injustice; a friend in need; the surety; twisted mind, crooked tongue; the grief stupidity causes; cheerfulness; setting one's sights aright; crime in court; golden silence.

1 *Feasting with strife*; literally 'strife-offerings', an ironic commentary on substantial 'peace-offerings' consumed amid contention. (For peace-offerings as a family feast *cf.* Dt. 12:11, 12.) **2** Soon after Solomon's death, his own 'servant who dealt wisely', Jeroboam, divided the inheritance with Rehoboam, 'the son who acted shamefully'—and took the lion's share (1 Ki. 12). **3** The drastic tests of human character which God applies are not destructive in their intention: he is purifying *silver* and *gold*; *cf.* 1 Pet. 1:7. **8** *Magic stone*; perhaps an over-translation (*cf.* AV 'precious stone'), but it may well be that the flashing stone in an amulet or talisman is in mind, blinding the briber and the bribed. *Cf.* v. 23.

10 *A cruel messenger* is the messenger (whether human or angelic) of the rebel's doom. Intemperate himself, he is treated in like manner. **14** A quarrel may begin with a slight friction, like a trickle through a tiny hole in a bank. It is wise to leave off before it is aggravated, and a sluice opened. **16** It has been inferred from this that the wise charged a fee for their instruction, but this is not necessary: the picture of the fool turning up with a tuition fee is essentially satirical. Wisdom is an inward thing, and requires not payment but a properly inclined heart. **24** Wisdom is easily accessible to the properly disposed: it is right in front of the man accustomed to straightforward ways. The fool, devious to the end, is looking *on the ends of the earth*—and never seeing wisdom.

18:1–24 Perils and blessings

The selfish individualist; the self-parading fool; fellow-travellers; the wellspring of wisdom; miscarriage of justice; misusing the mouth; the destructive sluggard; the strong tower and the shaky wall; haughtiness, humility and haste; demoralization; the acquisitive mind; giving presents; hearing both sides; disputes and their resolution; the tongue—source of satisfaction and lethal weapon; a good wife; rich and poor; true friendship.

1 RSV, probably rightly, has followed LXX in reading *seeks pretexts*, the same phrase translated 'seeking an occasion' in Jdg. 14:4. (AV is ponderous and obscure here.) **3** Three different words for shame are piled up—the inevitable travelling companions of wickedness. **4** *Deep waters*; *i.e.* hidden. But wisdom comes bubbling out, ever fresh, beyond the risk of stagnation. **10, 11** *The name of the Lord* represents His power and majesty, which affords perfect assurance to the righteous. The wealth of the man of property may indeed be his fortification, but a very insecure one compared with the *strong tower* of the righteous; it is a *high wall* only in his imagination (so RSV mg.; *cf.* AV, RV). **12** *Cf.* 15:33; 16:18.

16 The line between the present (like Jacob's to Esau, Gn. 32:13ff.) and the bribe is sometimes very fine; in any case, Proverbs realistically recognizes the power of the gift (*cf.* 17:8) while uniformly condemning the favouritism and injustice it brings (*cf.* 17:23). **17** The immediate reference is apparently to a legal dispute, but the proverb is of wider application. **18** The conviction that the decision of the lot was of divine decree was probably more effective in ending disputes than endless arguments, often productive only of bitterness. Christians who live in the age of the Holy Spirit may similarly unite when a decision on a disputed course of action has been prayerfully reached (*cf.* Acts 20:14 in context). **19** The text is uncertain. RSV has followed LXX; but AV's 'A brother offended is harder to be won than a strong city' (a paraphrase rather than a translation) may preserve the sense. **20** *Satisfied* in a good sense, or 'sated' in a bad sense. **24** The first line is again obscure and capable of more than one translation. Whether one prefers RSV, or RV's 'He that maketh many friends doeth it to his own destruction', the point of the proverb conveyed in the famous second line remains.

19:1–29 Studies in character

The upright pauper and the worthless rich; deliberation and haste; fuming against God; the power of money; the punishment of false witnesses; enlightened self-interest; position in wrong hands; the wisdom of magnanimity; the possibilities of kingship; domestic miseries and blessings; sloth; keeping the commandments; giving to the helpless is lending to God; over-indulgence; ungovernable temper; future investment; the sovereignty of God; covenant loyalty; the fear of the Lord; forceful rebuke; without natural affection; concentration on truth; depravity; the punishment of fools.

1 *Cf.* 28:6. **2** An 'also' (as in AV, but omitted in RSV) joins this proverb to the preceding. **7** The only three-line proverb in the first book of Solomon. **10** *Luxury*: D. Winton Thomas identifies another root with the same characters, which might yield the translation: 'Administration is inappropriate for a fool . . .'. **12** 'Subordinates may learn tact here, and superiors pleasantness' (Kidner). The proverb is perhaps addressed to the latter, those who have it in their power to bring stress and terror or refreshment and productiveness. *Cf.* the different form in 20:2. **13** *Dripping of rain*; *sc.* through the roof. **14** While a man may inherit his home and wealth from his ancestors, a good wife is God's direct gift. **16** *Cf.* 13:13; Rom. 6:23. **17** It is not sufficient to avoid oppression of the poor: the good man gives active help, and since God identifies Himself with the helpless, such giving turns out in the end to be only a loan—to the Lord. *Cf.* Mt. 25:34ff.

18 *Do not set your heart on his destruction, sc.* by over-indulging and refusing to correct him. **19** An obscure verse: but the sense seems to be that an ungovernable temper is an endless source of trouble to its owner. **22** *Loyalty*; *i.e.* ḥeseḏ, covenant love. *Cf.* Mi. 6:8. **24** The man is so lazy that, having dipped his hand, oriental fashion, in the dish, he cannot be bothered to take it to his mouth. **25** 'When bad men are punished, the morally ignorant are warned'

(Toy). **27** Do not listen to instruction simply to forget it again.

20:1–30 Appearances and realities

Drink; the wrath of the king; avoiding quarrels; no work, no food; insight into character; loyalty professed and real; posthumous blessing; attributes of a good ruler; all have sinned; abominable trade practices; self-revealing activity; the functions of the body, God's handiwork; the value of knowledge; the surety; the after-taste of ill-deserved success; on taking advice; gossip; unnatural behaviour; avenge not yourselves; divine sovereignty; rash vows; the lamp of the Lord; the basis of the throne; age and youth alike have their beauty; effective punishment.

1 *Wine* and *strong drink* are personified as a drunkard, who becomes a blasphemer and *brawler*. **4** *Autumn*; AV, RV have 'by reason of the cold': the meaning is the same on either reading. The sluggard finds it too uncomfortable in the cold season to plough, and then looks in vain for a crop the following year. **5** One aspect of *understanding* is insight into human character. **7** Many boast of their loyalty, but it is desperately hard to find a man who will under all circumstances be absolutely trustworthy. **8** *Winnows*; *i.e.* separates chaff from wheat. *Cf.* v. 5, and Solomon's request in 1 Ki. 3:9. **12** 'Not only the organs of hearing and sight, but their functions are the work of God (*cf.* 16:14). The implication is that what the ear listens to, and what the eye rests upon, should be right and pleasing to God' (Oesterley). **14** The buyer complains that the article is trash, but when he has bought it he boasts to others of the good bargain he has got. **16** *Surety*; see on 6:1. The addressee is the creditor: he should make no advance without security (for the *garment* as security *cf.* Ex. 22:26f.), for a man so reckless is a bad risk. **18** *Cf.* Lk. 14:31. **25** It is possible, on impulse or by imitation, to 'dedicate' more than we really intend. *Cf.* Ec. 5:5. **27** *The spirit of man* marks him off from the beasts. An animal can have a *nepeš* ('soul') but it was into man's nostrils that God breathed the *rûaḥ* ('spirit' or 'breath') of life. That very fact means that even in fallen man God has His *lamp* whereby He searches the inner man (*cf.* 1 Cor. 2:11), bearing witness to Himself by the light of conscience, illuminating the dark corners of the heart. **28** *Loyalty* (*sc.* to the covenant) *and faithfulness* are again marks of the ideal king, and the covenant mercy of God (*righteousness* is the same word translated *loyalty* in the first line) upholds his throne. *Teneo et teneor.* For what such a statement would have meant to Solomon, *cf.* 2 Sa. 7:12ff.

21:1–31 The God who acts

The only Ruler of princes; God weighs the heart; what God really wants; arrogance; diligence; ill-gotten gains; sweeping up the wicked; crooked paths; a nagging wife; ruthlessness; the lessons of discipline; the ruin of the wicked; the agony of Dives; the power of the gift; justice does not

please everybody; luxury leads to poverty; the wise man's treasure and his abilities; self-control; desire and generosity; the abominable piety of the wicked; testimony; bluff; God's sovereignty.

1 The mind of the king—powerful among men as he may seem—is directed by God as firmly as the irrigator cuts and controls the channels. **2** *Cf.* 16:2. **4** *Lamp*; either the standards by which the wicked direct their lives, or the symbol of their prosperity (*cf.* 13:9). **6** *Snare*; RSV has followed LXX; others have read 'seekers of death' (*cf.* AV). Though compressed, the main point is clear enough. **9** 'It is better to dwell in an attic on the roof, than in a double bedroom with a nagging wife' (A. D. Power). *Cf.* 25:24. **12** A verse very difficult to translate. If the text is sound we should perhaps read 'The Righteous One (*i.e.* God; *cf.* Jb. 34:17) observes . . .'. **13** *Cf.* Lk. 16:19–31. **18** *Cf.* Is. 43:3, 4, where Egypt is stated to be the ransom for Israel. 'There is a kind of substitution; a ransom is paid to enable the righteous to escape, and the ransom is the person of the wicked' (R. F. Horton). This makes the picture of the just suffering for the unjust (1 Pet. 3:18) stand out starkly.

21 An OT adumbration of the Lord's 'Seek first his kingdom' (Mt. 6:33). *Righteousness* and *kindness* (*ḥeseḏ*, 'covenant love') are required in God's covenant people (*cf.* Mi. 6:6–8), and those that seek them will have 'all these things' (*life and honour*) as well. **26** *The wicked*; RSV has followed LXX; the Hebrew has simply 'he' (*cf.* AV). But the subject may well be the sluggard of the previous verse; the two should be read together. **28** *A man who hears*; *i.e.* the man who is prepared to listen and understand is the proper contrast to the *false witness*. **29** *Considers*; better, with mg., 'establishes', 'makes sure'. **30, 31** 'Two companion proverbs. . . . Nothing avails against, nothing without, God' (E. H. Plumptre).

22:1–16 Cause and effect in the spiritual realm

Reputation; the common origin of men; prudence; God's rewards; the booby trap; education; the power of the purse; the harvest of injustice; generosity; the author of discord; integrity and charm; the eyes of the Lord; fresh excuses from the sluggard; the adulteress; the economics of oppression.

2 Whatever barriers may exist between men on earth, they have a common origin and a common responsibility to God. **4** This verse, with its close connection between humility, the sense of dependence expressed in piety, and *the fear of the Lord*, sums up several of the main lessons of the book. **7** Just as the rich lord it over the poor, so the borrower, with an equally forced dependence, is under constant obligation to the person from whom he has borrowed. **8** *The rod of his fury will fail*; the time will come when this man will lose his capacity for exercising anger. (For the meaning, *cf.* Is. 10:5.) **14** See 5:1ff. and notes. **16** A dark saying: there seems to be a double condemnation, of exploiting the poor and currying favour with the rich.

22:17 – 24:22 THE BOOK OF THE WISE

See the Introduction, pp. 548 and 549. There is more connection between the sayings in this group than in the previous collection, and many parallels with the sayings of the Egyptian sage Amenemope. It is arguable that, like Amenemope's book, it has thirty paragraphs (see below on 22:20), but the Egyptian work has a more closely-knit order.

22:17–21 The proper function of proverbs

The teacher calls for the attention of the pupil to the sayings he has drawn up for his instruction (v. 17), calls on him to make them part of himself (v. 18) and shows that their aim is to lead to faith in Yahweh (v. 19) and strengthen, to others' benefit, his own grasp of truth (v. 21).

20 *Thirty sayings.* The Hebrew consonantal text has *šlšwm,* which can also be rendered 'three days ago' (hence RV mg., following earlier commentators, 'formerly', which is ingenious but forced); 'things in threefold form' (so LXX and Vulgate—Origen used this rendering to support his threefold approach to exegesis); and, perhaps, 'excellent things' (AV, RV, from a word meaning 'officers', and hence, it is urged, 'pre-eminent', 'excellent'). Amenemope, however, has 'consider these thirty chapters . . .', and it seems simplest to read the text as RSV, and see reference to (approximately) thirty paragraphs in this 'book of the wise'.

22:22 – 23:11 Some things to avoid

Elementary wisdom involves the creation of some fixed aversions. First, exploitation of the poor, whom God Himself protects (22:22, 23); second, the infection of bad temper (vv. 24, 25); third, suretyship (vv. 26, 27—these verses have no Egyptian counterparts); and fourth, violation of boundaries (v. 28; *cf.* Dt. 19:14). A note on the promotion of the conscientious follows (v. 29). Amenemope, who was a civil servant, is equally assured on this point.

The sage's instructions proceed with a passage on table manners (23:1–3) and other warnings about social climbing (vv. 4, 5), and a delightful picture of the miser—the sort of person with whom the social climber may vainly seek to ingratiate himself—at home (vv. 6–8). Conversation with a fool is not recommended (v. 9). Then comes a renewed warning against encroaching on the rights of the (apparently) helpless (vv. 10, 11), for they have a strong Redeemer to act on their behalf.

22:22 *Crush the afflicted at the gate; i.e.* use legal or judicial action against them. (Ordinary justice was dispensed 'at the gate'.) **23** While the preceding verse is parallel to a saying in Amenemope, this corollary has no obvious parallel in the Egyptian. **23:9** *Redeemer*; Hebrew *gōʾēl.* The *gōʾēl* in the OT is the kinsman who

holds or acquires the right and responsibility to avenge blood (Nu. 35:19) and redeem property (Ru. 4:4) and generally to protect the interests of his dead kinsman's family.

23:12–25 What to look for

The appeal to hear instruction is renewed (v. 12) as the next stage of the sage's exposition is unfolded. Discipline, and from an early age, is needed to save a child from (self-) destruction (vv. 13, 14). To see wisdom in his pupil will rejoice his teacher (vv. 15, 16; *cf.* 2 Jn. 4); nor need the man who fears God see anything to envy in those who do not (v. 17): his hopes are set in the future (v. 18). The festive character of the revellers' carousals is illusory (vv. 19–21). The 'first commandment with promise' is then recalled (v. 22): and its happiest fulfilment is in a son who is good and wise (vv. 23–25).

23:26 – 24:2 Snares in the path

The earnest appeal is again renewed (v. 26), as the teacher warns against the prostitute and adventuress, seductive but ruinous (vv. 27, 28); drink, fascinating, debilitating, demoralizing, disabling, addictive (vv. 29–35); and mischievous company, an 'inner ring', to which entrée is nothing to covet (24:1, 2).

26 *Give me your heart; i.e.* attend to me carefully. *Observe;* RV follows some ancient versions in reading 'delight in'. **27** *Deep pit . . . narrow well;* the victim is suddenly trapped, and escape is difficult. **34** *Mast;* the actual word is obscure, but the picture of the nauseated toper could hardly be more vivid.

24:3–22 Studies in wisdom and folly

The acquisition of wisdom and knowledge is compared to the building and furnishing of a house (vv. 3, 4). The relation between wisdom and strength is now sketched out (vv. 5–7; *cf.* 11:14; 20:18). Certain situations show up the fool's incompetence: he cannot speak 'in the gate', the centre for business and legal transactions (v. 7). The calculating schemer and the scoffer who cynically devises folly will be repudiated by public opinion (vv. 8, 9).

Strenuous responsibilities, under which it would be contemptible to surrender, lie at the door of the man who would be wise (v. 10): to stand up for those in danger of death—whether by injustice, oppression by the powerful, or at the hands of a lawless society such as is described in 1:10ff. If this duty is neglected, God, the vindicator of the helpless, will know (vv. 11, 12).

Wisdom has its sweets both now and hereafter (vv. 13, 14): it is not worth the trouble to plunder the righteous, for though he may fall seven times (*sc.* into calamity, not into sin), he always gets up again, while a single disaster is sufficient to overwhelm the wicked (vv. 15, 16). Even so, one must never gloat at the fall of an enemy: in such a case, God's wrath, ever active, may turn from the fallen enemy to those who indulge in such misplaced delight (vv. 17, 18; *cf.* Is. 10:5–11).

After another assurance that the wicked are essentially unenviable (vv. 19, 20), comes a warning of the danger of provoking the wrath of God, or that of the king, His earthly representative (vv. 21, 22).

5 *A wise man is mightier than a strong man.* RSV follows LXX; certainly a sharper utterance than 'A wise man is strong' (lit. 'is in strength'), *cf.* RV. **11** *Stumbling to the slaughter*; G. R. Driver has attractively translated, from another root, 'at the point of slaughter'. **21** Note the use made of this proverb in 1 Pet. 2:17 in context. *And do not disobey either of them*; RSV follows LXX, which makes a better connection with v. 22 (*them both*). But if D. Winton Thomas is correct in rendering the word translated *either of them* by 'those of exalted rank', the Hebrew text may have a very similar force. The normal translation of the Hebrew text, 'do not associate with those who change', is difficult: the verb is intransitive, and can hardly yield the sense 'revolutionaries', and the connection of thought with v. 22 is less clear.

24:23–34 SAYINGS OF THE WISE: ANOTHER COLLECTION

The heading (v. 23a) indicates a new collection of proverbs has begun.

Favouritism in judgment, with its accompanying recognition and justification of wickedness, is abominable: to paint wickedness for what it is wins gratitude (vv. 23b–26). Counting the cost and preparing the materials is a necessary preliminary to any enterprise (v. 27). Baseless accusations and spiteful litigation are alike to be avoided (vv. 28, 29). The picture of the sluggard asleep, his vineyard a wilderness, repeats the words of 6:6–11 with a new and ominous note. **26** *Kisses the lips* seems a little odd in the context. If the word translated *kisses* can bear a sense which it can in post-biblical Hebrew, the rendering could be something like 'He who equips his lips (*sc.* with wisdom) gives a right answer'. **27** The application should not be limited to marriage; early marriage was in any case common among the Hebrews. For the sense *cf.* 1 Ki. 6:7; Lk. 14:28.

25:1 – 29:27 THE SECOND BOOK OF SOLOMON

For the title, see the Introduction, p. 548.

25:2–28 Instructive comparisons

God and the king; contentious litigation and personal relations; fitting speech, fitting speaker; a self-endowed reputation for generosity; quiet importunity; too much sweet stuff; outstaying one's welcome; the broken reed; offensive merriment; doing good to enemies; the analogy of slander; a nagging wife; good news from abroad; on compromise; too much honey; self-control.

2 The ways of God are inscrutable, and this reflects His glory. The king, on the other hand, has a duty to 'get to the bottom of a thing'— that is his glory. **6, 7** *Cf.* Lk. 14:8–11. Note that the last line of v. 7 properly belongs to v. 8, as in RSV. **8–10** *Cf.* Mt. 5:25, 26. **11** *Apples . . . setting*; the precise nature of the fruit and the 'setting' is unknown. 'The whole simile is of uncertain interpretation, but at least its components . . . carry associations of attractiveness, value and craftsmanship' (Kidner). **15** *Cf.* Lk. 18:1–8. **20** *Vinegar on a wound*; RSV follows LXX, probably correctly. Our Hebrew text has 'vinegar on soda'. **21** *Cf.* Mt. 5:44; Rom. 12:20. **27** An obscure verse. RSV has reconstructed the text of the second line eclectically; and AV's 'so for men to search their own glory is not glory' has arbitrarily inserted a negative. D. Winton Thomas, with a slighter emendation than RSV, translates 'and he who despises honour is honoured'.

26:1–12 A book of fools

Honour does not fit fools; the causeless curse; how to handle fools; do you answer a fool?; the danger of employing fools; the fool as pseudo-philosopher; the fool as recidivist; self-esteem the height of folly.

2 The curse that is unjustified never does anyone any harm. This is the only verse in this section which does not explicitly refer to the fool, (*kesîl*; see on 1:22). It is a refutation of the superstition (held by the fools in question?) that the righteous could be hurt by the malicious curse. **4, 5** The apparent contradiction here caused trouble to the Rabbis, who were driven to conclude that 'one refers to the things of the Law and the other to worldly affairs' (*cf. Tractate Shabbath* 30b). It is more likely however that the difference is simply between profitless arguing with a fool at his own level and occasionally, lest he think that he cannot be answered, meeting his prating with wisdom.

8 *Who binds the stone in the sling*; *i.e.* ties it in so that it cannot come out. To promote and give permanence to a fool is just as futile a proceeding. **10** RSV has made the best of a bad job in translating a very obscure, and probably damaged, text. **11** *Cf.* 2 Pet. 2:22. **12** But after all has been said of the fool, he has more hope of redemption than the man who is blinded by self-conceit (*cf.* Rom. 1:22).

26:13–16 A book of sluggards

Excuses for inactivity; the slumbering sluggard; the last point of laziness; the wisdom of the sluggard.

26:17–28 A book of scoundrels

The busybody; the practical joker; the stoker up of fiery quarrels; the purveyor of exquisite whispers; the hypocrite; the liar and flatterer.

23 *Glaze*. This conjectural rendering of RSV (*cf.* AV 'silver dross') is based on a parallel from Ugaritic, and makes good sense. The hypocrite appears smooth, polished, bright: but this conceals an interior of very different appearance. **26, 27** These verses have particular reference to the plausible rogue of the preceding verses.

27:1-27 Remarks on human relations

Boasting of the morrow; self-praise is no praise; the fool's provocation; the ugly dynamic of jealousy; on frankness; possession and desire; the unhappy wanderer; on friendship; the pupil the teacher's testimonial; prudence; the surety; horrid heartiness; the nagging wife; character and intellect developed by human relations; rewards; the mirror of the mind; insatiable desire; the testing nature of praise; the fool inseparable from his folly; the pastoral life.

1 *Cf.* Jas. 4:13–16. **3** *Provocation*; or, with a different sense, 'wrath', as in AV. **5** *Hidden love*; *i.e.* that which does not show itself in administering necessary reproof. **7** A general statement about possessions. To have them does not satisfy; not to have them may cause agonies of envy. **9** *But the soul is torn by trouble*. RSV follows LXX. AV's 'so doth the sweetness of a man's friend by hearty counsel' is more pungent, and fits the first line better; but the Hebrew is obscure. **18** *Cf.* Mt. 25:21. **19** As the water gives a true reflection of a face, so the hearts of men essentially correspond with each other. **20** *Sheol and Abaddon*; see on 15:11. **21** A man's reaction to praise is a severe test of his character; or, perhaps, a man is shown up by the things which he praises. **23–27** The purpose of this short treatise on the pastoral life is no doubt to encourage this industry, the real backbone of Israel's prosperity, and to discourage the corrupting influences of other, superficially more attractive, ways of making money.

28:1-28 Pure religion

Conscience makes cowards—or brave men; national stability; mean oppression; the law as man's protection; only the righteous understand justice; honest poverty; a father's pride and shame; the usurer; abominable piety; the fate of the corrupter; the wealthy man's false confidence; response to triumph; repentance; the happiness of fearing God; unworthy rulers; blood-guilt; the safety of integrity; the fruit of industry; how not to get rich quickly; the corruptible judge; frankness; the unnatural son; trust rather than greed; walking in wisdom; giving and withholding; a people's bane.

2 This saying would be particularly apposite when Hezekiah's men copied it out, for the northern kingdom of Israel had tottered to its ruin after a series of coups and changes of dynasty. **3** *A poor man*; LXX has 'a wicked man', but the text, with its reference to humanity's universal capacity for oppression, makes good sense. The hard-hit landlord or official endeavours to secure his own income in bad times by tightening the screw on those poorer than himself; the result is general starvation. **8** The extortioner and usurer (a forbidden practice in Israel; *cf.* Lv. 25:36f.) will lose his gains to a

more just man. **13** *Cf.* 1 Jn. 1:8f. **17** To be taken alongside 24:11f. **18** *Into a pit*; RSV emends the Hebrew, which has 'in one'. If correct, this may mean 'at one blow, at once' (*cf.* AV, RV).

21 *For a piece of bread*; *i.e.* a man will betray justice for the smallest bribe. **24** Doubtless attempts by children to obtain their parents' property are in mind. Though foreign to the whole spirit of the Mosaic law, there was no specific legislation against it, so a man might say *That is no transgression*. *Cf.* Mk. 7:10–13.

29:1-27 God and society

The sudden end of obduracy; what makes a happy people; a prodigal son; justice the good ruler's hallmark; flattery; the snared path; the rights of the poor; inflammatory scoffers; the blusterer; innocence the target of the violent; self-restraint; encouraging deceit; the common origin of men; justice for the poor; correction; the wicked in authority; revelation a people's guide; hastiness; pride and humility, fear of man, trust in God; favours from rulers, justice from God; what good and bad men abominate.

2 *Rejoice*; RSV has slightly emended the text, which has 'increase'. **3** *Cf.* Lk. 15:13, 30. **6** *Sings and rejoices*; a more forceful parallel is given in one MS, 'runs and rejoices'. **10** RSV has emended the text to avoid the suggestion that 'the upright' seek the life of the blameless. But RV's 'And as for the upright, they (*sc.* the blood-thirsty) seek his life' is tenable. **13** *Cf.* 22:2, and, for the meaning, Ps. 13:3; Mt. 5:45. **15** Solomon might recall that Adonijah had been such a child (1 Ki. 1:5, 6).

18 *Prophecy*; the normal word for the prophetic revelation (*hāzôn*; *cf.* Is. 1:1; Je. 14:14). *Cast off restraint*; the same word is used in Ex. 32:25 and the whole affair of the golden calf is an historical illustration of this verse. *Law*; the revealed will of God (note this is parallel with *prophecy*). The law, the prophets and the wisdom literature meet in this verse. Where the revealed will of God, as expressed in His word, is not kept constantly in view, His people break loose from their allegiance. This is another word which Hezekiah may well have taken to heart. **21** *His heir*. We do not really know the significance of the word so translated (*cf.* mg.), and so the verse is obscure. **23** *Cf.* Mt. 5:3; Lk. 14:11. **24** *The curse*; *i.e.* the judge's adjuration that any who have knowledge of the crime should give evidence.

30:1-33 THE WORDS OF AGUR

30:1-4 The knowledge of God

Agur longs after the knowledge of God and confesses his utter ignorance, shared with the rest of mankind. He has reflected on the immensity of the natural forces, and stood amazed at the One behind them. There may be a touch of sarcasm in the opening words; he was confronted by those who professed to know all about God and His dealings.

1 We do not know who *Agur son of Jakeh* was, or where he flourished. If RSV is right in reading *of Massa*, he was an Ishmaelite; but RV's 'the oracle' is quite tenable. But in any case Agur may have been, like Job and Balaam, a non-Israelite with knowledge of the true God. *Ithiel . . . Ucal.* AV, RSV take these as proper names, doubtless Agur's disciples. But it is possible, by using different vowel points, to gain 'I have wearied myself, O God, and am consumed' (*cf.* RV mg.).

4 Enoch and Elijah ascended; none had been known to return (*cf.* Jn. 3:13). *His son's name*; *i.e.* that of the hypothetical person who has scaled the heights to look on God and precisely measured His creation. Who is he—or (if he lived some time ago) where are the descendants of such a person?

30:5, 6 The word of God

God's revelation must not be mixed with human speculation, which may prove to be utterly wrong. *Cf.* Ps. 18:30.

30:7–9 A prayer

The wise man prays to be preserved from the temptations of riches and poverty alike.

30:10 A detached aphorism

For the fullest application, see Rom. 14:4.

30:11–14 Four studies in arrogance

30:15, 16 Insatiable things

15 *Leech*; a notoriously obscure allusion. If it is the correct translation, the reference may be to blood-sucking creatures, themselves reared on blood, characterized by their insatiability (*they cry* has been supplied by RSV: perhaps *Give, give* are the creatures' names). But the Palestinian haemopis does not attack man.

30:17 The turbulent son

Another detached aphorism. *Cf.* Dt. 21:18–21. The implication is that the corpse will lie unburied for the birds to feed on.

30:18–20 Four wonderful things

The wonder is often supposed to be in their leaving no trace behind them. If this is so, the examples—the serpent particularly—seem curiously chosen. More likely the wonder is 'the easy mastery, by the appropriate agent, of elements as difficult to negotiate as air, rock, sea—and a young woman' (Kidner). **20** *The way of an adulteress* is also wonderful, but a parody of the last. She covers up her sin and calmly says she has done nothing wrong.

30:21–23 Four intolerable things

There are two examples from each sex. **22** *Filled with food*; *i.e.* rich and prosperous.

30:24–28 Four little things and wise

25 The ants do what the sluggard will not do

(*cf.* 6:6). **27** The locusts go in ordered ranks, without jostling one another (*cf.* Joel 2:8).

30:29–31 Four stately things

31 There are some obscurities in this list: the rendering *cock* is based on LXX and other old versions; several other guesses have been made. The *king* in the last example is certain, but *striding before his people* is less so.

30:32, 33 A closing admonition

32 *Put your hand on your mouth*: as a silent admission of blame.

31:1–9 THE SAYINGS OF LEMUEL

See Introduction, p. 549. **1** There is the same ambiguity about *Massa* as in the case of Agur (see on 30:1). King Lemuel provides a short treatise on the duties of kingship, learned from his mother. Is it possible that Lemuel was an Ishmaelite whose mother came from Israel?

2 Lemuel is the son of his mother's *vows* (*i.e.* granted in response to her vows, *cf.* 1 Sa. 1:11). He is urged, and emphatically, to avoid dissipation, either with women or wine (vv. 3, 4), which takes a ruler's mind off his duties, and is thus a cause of injustice (v. 5). Drink is the anodyne of the hopeless—there is no excuse for it in those who are not in this condition (vv. 6, 7). His task is to defend those who cannot speak for themselves (v. 8) and stand out uncompromisingly for justice (v. 9).

31:10–31 APPENDIX: THE PERFECT WIFE

This is a beautiful acrostic poem, the first verse beginning with the first letter of the Hebrew alphabet and each of the remaining twenty-one letters coming in turn. There is no reason to attribute it to Lemuel; it is an anonymous appendix to the whole book, exalting, as Proverbs does elsewhere, the honour and dignity of womanhood, and the importance of a mother's teaching. Here also is a remarkable picture of woman in Israelite society: trusted implicitly by her husband and amply rewarding that trust; hard-working and shrewd, with a liberty of choice and action in a wide range of affairs (v. 16), which she directs to the family good, at the same time remaining generous and kind-hearted (v. 20) and a wise and faithful teacher (v. 26). By contrast the nauseous attractions of 'the loose woman' lose all their glitter. Our book closes with the ringing praise (v. 29) accorded to the perfect wife by the husband and children whose sustenance, comfort, reputation (v. 23) and knowledge of God (v. 26) have all been enhanced by her.

21 *Scarlet*; *i.e.* the best cloth. But the consonants could mean 'double' (thickness; *cf.* AV), which would explain the reference to *snow*. **26** *Kindness* (Heb. *ḥesed*, 'covenant love') is the theme of a good mother's teaching.

A. F. WALLS

Ecclesiastes

INTRODUCTION

STYLE

Ecclesiastes is in many respects an enigmatic book. Disjointed in construction, obscure in vocabulary, and often cryptic in style, it baffles the understanding of the reader. It contains a number of words which are not found in the rest of the OT and whose meaning it is hard to determine with precision. It makes allusion to incidents, customs and sayings which would be easily understood by its original readers but to which we have no clue. It contains apparent inconsistencies which make it difficult to ascertain what the author's own view is. These contrasts have led some to suppose that an original book has been worked over and 'bowdlerized' by several hands. The way in which the writer has put together his material suggests that it was not meant to have any connected sequence of thought running through it. The book may be a collection of fragments or jottings, like Pascal's *Pensées*, with which it has often been compared.

In spite of all its difficulties and obscurities, however, the book exercises a powerful fascination. It is at once apparent to the discerning reader that there is a penetrating observation and criticism of the human scene. The profundity of such of the writer's observations as we can immediately comprehend lures us on to plumb his deeper insights, as once Socrates, delighted with the wisdom of Heraclitus speaking clearly, was led to seek a deeper wisdom in his obscurities.

INTERPRETATION

The crucial problem presented by the book is that of its place within the Canon of Scripture. There were some among the Jews who disputed its right to be included among the sacred books from the beginning, and its presence among them has been a source of bewilderment to many Christians since. Those who think that the prevailing tone of the book is one of disillusionment and despair, tempered only by a modified Epicureanism, must indeed find it hard to see how it can be reckoned among those which are able to make us wise unto salvation through faith which is in Christ Jesus.

Some recent studies of the book, however, have shown this popular understanding of it to be superficial, and have led to a truer appreciation of the peculiar standpoint of the writer. This is probably indicated by his chosen name, Qoheleth (*Qōhelet*) 'the Preacher' (Ecclesiastes is the Greek equivalent of this). The word is connected with *qāhāl*, the public assembly, and it suggests the kind of wisdom delivered by the speaker to those in the outer court, as distinguished from the 'hidden wisdom' which is known only to those who have been admitted to the mystery of God (1 Cor. 2:7). Qoheleth writes from concealed premises, and his book is in reality a major work of apologetic or 'eristic' theology. Its apparent worldliness is dictated by its aim: Qoheleth is addressing the general public whose view is bounded by the horizons of this world; he meets them on their own ground, and proceeds to convict them of its inherent vanity. This is further borne out by his characteristic expression 'under the sun', by which he describes what the NT calls 'the world' (Gk. *kosmos*). His book is in fact a critique of secularism and of secularized religion. For secularism need not be irreligious, and the religion of the Jews tended to be unduly secular and to forget the transcendence of God (5:2). As such, it has an abiding message, and not least for our own time when secularism dominates the minds of men as perhaps never before in history, and religion has gone far to conform and seeks to commend itself as a means of the amelioration of life 'under the sun'. The book of Ecclesiastes discharges an indispensable function within the Canon of Scripture by providing the corrective against all attempts to reduce religion to a mere tool of secularism.

The fatal weakness of secularist utopianism is, as has been said, that it takes insufficient account of the twin facts of evil and death. The eyes of Ecclesiastes are fully open to the vanity and the corruption to which the creation is subject (Rom. 8:20ff.), and the whole book has been aptly described as an exposition of the curse of the Fall (Gn. 3:17–19). The writer sees how these two facts bracket the whole of life under the sun with a negative sign and defy all attempts to force it to yield either sense or satisfaction by itself.

But though the tone of the book is preponderantly negative, it is a mistake to brand Ecclesiastes as a sceptic or an apostle of despair. The melancholy refrain, 'Vanity of vanities, all is vanity', is not his verdict upon life in general, but only upon the misguided human endeavour to treat the created world as an end in itself. He knows all the time that it has a positive significance; how indeed could he take it upon himself to utter such destructive criticism if he did not know? This secret he keeps in the background, except for a hint here and there, because his immediate concern is to dispel all false and illusory hopes which possess the minds of men and of which they must be purged before they can be brought to the hope which is sure and steadfast and which 'enters into the inner shrine behind the curtain' (Heb. 6:19). 'In order that men may be able to find the true happiness, he destroys with merciless blows the false happiness which they continually seek in the world and which yields them only unhappiness' (G. Kuhn, *Erklärung des Buches Koheleth*, 1926). But he knows that the world can yield happiness and enjoyment, as witness his frequent exhortations to seek it (2:24; 3:12, 22; 5:18; 9:7; 11:9), and that we can find in the world a life-work which is worth while (3:12f.; 9:10); otherwise the counsels he offers for life and conduct in this world would be meaningless.

The significance of the world is that it can become a medium for the revelation of God's goodness, wisdom and righteousness. It is only when man treats it as an end in itself, and makes it his chief end to gain the world, that it turns to vanity. But there is a way in which man can accept life under the sun, with its gifts and withdrawals, its apparent irrationalities and injustices, and that is 'from the hand of God' (2:24; 5:18–20). Plainly this is not scepticism or pessimism; it is faith. As it has been expressed by a modern writer, in whom something of the spirit of Ecclesiastes lives again, faith has always protested that 'all things would be absurd if their meaning were exhausted in their function and place in the phenomenal world, if by their essence they did not reach into a world beyond this'; and it has always 'trusted the inward vision, which discerned behind nature a something more divine than nature, *in recessu divinius aliquid*' (W. Macneile Dixon, *The Human Situation*, 1937, pp. 40f.). Ecclesiastes is a sceptic only in so far as he rejects the pretension of human wisdom to elucidate the work of God (3:11; 8:17). He knows that we walk by faith, not by sight; and he

exhibits the necessary humility or reserve of faith in face of the transcendent wisdom of God, of whose eternal providence he is firmly assured (3:14).

The characteristic complexity of his thought with its apparent contradictions or its 'counterpoint' (W. Vischer, *Der Prediger Salomo*, 1926) shows clearly in his utterances on death. On the one hand he speaks of death as the final reduction of life under the sun to nothingness (3:19f.; 9:4–6; 11:8). But to say that he regards death as final extinction is to fail to do justice to another strain in his thought. He repeatedly affirms the certainty of divine judgment (3:17; 11:9; 12:14), and he remains assured, in spite of all the injustices of life under the sun, that 'it will be well with those who fear God' (8:12). His position resembles that of Ps. 49. Like the psalmist he is opposed to any specious immortality erected upon premises derived from life under the sun. The psalmist's verdict, 'Man abideth not in honour: he is like the beasts that perish' (Ps. 49:12, RV), is echoed in Ec. 3:18: 'I said in my heart with regard to the sons of men that God is testing them to show them that they are but beasts.' But over against this the psalmist sets 'the great "But God" ' (Ps. 49:15; *cf.* Eph. 2:4), and in the light of it he modifies his first conclusion: 'Man that is in honour and understandeth not is like the beasts that perish' (Ps. 49:20, RV). The significant phrase in Ecclesiastes, 'they are but beasts', surely indicates that he knew of this understanding which alone gives man pre-eminence above a beast (3:19). At all events, his resolute denial of all human possibilities at least clears the way for the new possibilities of God, and entitles us to speak of Ecclesiastes as standing before the threshold of the resurrection.

OUTLINE OF CONTENTS

As has been pointed out above, the book defies any logical analysis, and therefore no Outline of Contents is presented. The paragraphs, into which the book divides itself, have been indicated by the main headings.

COMMENTARY

1:1–11 Introduction

1:1 The title. *The Preacher.* For the probable meaning of this term see Introduction. The author does not really claim to be Solomon but places his words in Solomon's mouth. We may compare the practice of ascribing written works to famous historical personages which was a familiar literary device in antiquity. It was intended to indicate the type, or genus, of literature to which a work belonged. It was not intended to deceive anyone, and none of its original readers would in fact have been deceived.

1:2 The text of the discourse. *All is vanity.* 'All' for those he addressed, but not for himself; for how could Ecclesiastes pronounce all to be vanity, unless he knew of some validity, some sure ground to which his spirit clung? His object is not to counsel despair, but to refute secularism on its own ground.

1:3–11 Existence a vicious circle. Ecclesiastes goes direct to the heart of the matter without preliminary skirmishing. The world assesses life in terms of profit and loss. But what profit can a man win that he must not finally lose? 'Fool!

This night your soul is required of you; and the things you have prepared, whose will they be?' (Lk. 12:20). The pursuit of wealth stands confuted by man's mortality, as the world itself knows well; for its own poets and philosophers have told it often enough. But men endeavour to screen themselves from the icy wind of mortality by the thought of their posterity and the continuing race. 'Their inward thought is, that their houses shall continue for ever, and their dwelling places to all generations; they call their lands after their own names' (Ps. 49:11, RV). They seek a pseudo-immortality in the fancied perpetuity of their works, or in 'minds made better by their presence', or in 'leaving footprints on the sands of time', or in the idea of 'progress'. But there is nothing to support this in the course of nature, which is circular, as Ecclesiastes points out (vv. 5–7), or in the course of history, which endlessly repeats itself (vv. 9, 10). Progress is ever accompanied by regress. It is only the actors and the scenery that change; the pattern of history remains the same, 'little more than the register of the crimes, follies and misfortunes of mankind'.

1:12 – 2:23 The failure of all attempts to give meaning to existence

1:12–18 The philosophical attempt. Man cannot rest content with a meaningless existence. There is within him an irresistible urge to find rhyme or reason in it; for he is a 'thinking reed' (Pascal). God has implanted in man this unquenchable longing for order and system. Yet it only adds to man's torment; for the jig-saw puzzle of life cannot be completed; some of the parts are missing (v. 15). The attempt to frame a complete philosophic system can be achieved only by doing violence to reality, by making straight 'what is crooked'. The last word of human wisdom, as some of the wisest have realized, is to confess that we know nothing, that the key to the final mystery eludes our grasp. Such is the wisdom of the Tao Te Ching:

> Thirty spokes together make one wheel;
> And they fit into 'nothing' at the centre:
> Herein lies the usefulness of a carriage.
> The clay is moulded to make a pot;
> And the clay fits round 'nothing':
> Herein lies the usefulness of the pot . . .
> Thus it is that, while it must be taken to be advantageous to have something there,
> It must also be taken as useful to have 'nothing' there.

The wisdom which ends in this 'hole at the centre' must needs be vexation of spirit, until it finds 'the wisdom from above' (Jas. 3:17), 'a secret and hidden wisdom of God, which God decreed before the ages for our glorification' (1 Cor. 2:7).

2:1, 2 The sensual attempt. Why bother your head trying to puzzle out the meaning of existence? Have 'a good time', enjoy the pleasures life affords. Listen to Mephistopheles:

> Grau, teurer Freund, ist alle Theorie
> Und grün des Lebens goldner Baum.

But no need to waste words on the madness of this experiment; for it quickly belies its promise.

> Pleasures are like poppies spread,
> You seize the flower, its bloom is shed.

The pleasure-addict cannot escape the 'morning after' and the revulsion of satiety.

2:3–23 The cultural attempt. The failure of the quest for wisdom and the quest for pleasure suggests a compromise, a middle way which avoids one-sided extremes and aims at a rich, varied and balanced life. This is culture. The cultured man is he who lays hold on all the riches of life, pleasure, wisdom and action, and seeks to blend them into one harmonious whole. He soon learns the 'paradox of hedonism' and finds his pleasure, not in sensuality, but in the full exercise of his faculties of mind and will (v. 10). But he cannot finally escape the quiet hour of reflection and self-questioning which comes after the day's labour is done; and then 'the native hue of resolution is sicklied o'er with the pale cast of thought'. Has he attained the true prize of life? Is his reward commensurate with the labour expended? It is certain that wisdom is relatively superior to folly; for the wise man makes a better job of life than the fool. But this relative is cancelled out by the absolute of death, a fact which seriously challenges the worth of wisdom. There is a paradox about wisdom: wisdom means looking forward. While the fool, like the grasshopper, lives for the moment, the wise man, like the ant, dips into the future; he takes his bearings from tomorrow, and endeavours to plot his course accordingly (v. 14). Yet this wisdom is most hazardous; for it is not in our power to foresee, still less to control, the future. 'You do not know what a day may bring forth' (Pr. 27:1). And the wisest plans may be confounded:

> The best laid schemes o' mice an' men
> Gang aft agley.

Note. 12 *What can the man do . . . ?* This would appear to have been a proverbial saying, and its meaning can only be guessed at. It has been suggested that the sentence has been misplaced.

2:24 – 3:15 The wisdom of creation

Is there any way out of the dilemma in which we find ourselves placed as between wisdom and folly? Only by a new wisdom, a wisdom which has a different standpoint and orientation; not the wisdom of this world, nor of the princes of this world (nor, we may add, of the proletariat of this world), but the wisdom of God in a mystery (*cf.* 1 Cor. 2:7). The first axiom of this wisdom is that the creation and its bounty are to be enjoyed. Any wisdom which denies this in the interest of its own man-centred system is presumption. True wisdom proceeds from the given fact of our creatureliness in the midst of creation. Here we are and 'the world is so full of a number of things' to be enjoyed. This is the decree and the gift of God (2:26).

But it is not an easy wisdom; for it must forswear system. A systematic world-view, a *Weltanschauung*, would be possible only if we occupied the centre from which we could survey the whole and see it in its true perspectives. But that is the position of the Creator, not of the creatures. From our creaturely position under the sun we see, as it were, the reverse of the tapestry with many confused lines and loose threads. To seek to unravel it from our standpoint is to become involved in an endless labyrinth. This also is vanity and vexation of spirit.

The beginning of our wisdom is the fear of the Lord (*cf.* Ps. 111:10; Pr. 1:7), and one element of it is the recognition of the divine election in the difference of the times and seasons. Theoretically all times are equal, but this is true only when they are emptied of their contents. We have no experience of empty time. Every time comes to us charged with its own particular challenge and opportunity; and the wisdom of life is to interpret the time (*cf.* Lk. 12:56), the *kairos* (*cf.* Rom. 13:11), the decisive moment (*cf.* Ec. 8:5, 6), the moment on which 'the accent of eternity falls'. 'There is a tide in the affairs of men.'

This incalculable, unrationalizable feature of history and experience is a sore perplexity to man. For man is not merely a creature of time; there is within him that which transcends time; 'Man has Forever'. He seeks to stand back from the time-process and to discern the plan and pattern of the whole. But he is too deeply immersed in it to succeed; the end and the beginning elude him. The tension between Today and Forever in the life of man cannot be completely resolved. Yet man can find Forever in Today by gratefully accepting the gifts of God and doing His commandments.

3:16 – 4:3 The righteousness of God

The moralistic interpretation of life breaks down on the hard fact of human wickedness. The hankering after a moral order is deeply rooted in the heart of man, but it makes him prone to two common delusions. One is the pathetic belief, widely entertained in our time, that order is secured by organization. Even so shrewd an observer as Lenin succumbed to this belief. But the wickedness which makes organization necessary does not stop short at the portals of organization. The egoism which taints individuals taints governments not less, but rather more; for organization magnifies power (4:1), and power is amoral. Then, *quis custodiet ipsos custodes?* (who will take care of the caretakers?). The other attempted solution is the theory of a moral government of history: 'The mills of God grind slowly . . .' This is a more respectable notion, perhaps; yet, in spite of its immense popularity, it yields no real satisfaction to the moral demand. For even if it were true, it

requires for its display a canvas so much larger than the brief span between the cradle and the grave. What comfort is the thought that 'the mills of God grind slowly' to those whose life is altogether ground between the upper and the nether millstones?

> *O dreadful thought if all our sires and we*
> *Are but foundations of a race to be.*

A moral view of life, resolutely pursued, leads to the conclusion that men are beasts. 'Man cannot abide in his pomp, he is like the beasts that perish' (Ps. 49:20). But what about his 'immortality'? 'Who knows whether the spirit of man goes upward?' (Ec. 3:21). What is there in man by himself to suggest that his destiny is so very different from that of the beast? 'That the soul of man is in its own nature Eternall, and a living Creature independent of the body; or that any meer man is Immortall, otherwise than by the Resurrection in the last day (except *Enos* and *Elias*) is a doctrine not apparent in Scripture' (Hobbes, *Leviathan*, xxxviii).

God is the Judge. But the righteousness of God is not subject to our judgment. As the righteousness of God, it belongs to His time, though it may be hidden from ours. He who does not understand this has no choice but to esteem death better than life.

4:4–16 The vanity of life

4:4–6 Of industry, idleness and contentment. What is the motive that inspires human industry and enterprise? It is the desire to do a little more than survive, to outstrip one's rivals, to excel in the competitive struggle. But the attainment of this desire does not yield the satisfaction it promises; for it excites the envy of others, and anxiety lest they should overtake him besets the leader in the race. Without this desire to excel, man would not be man. Yet the irony of it is that it is often the least enterprising, the fool (v. 5), the 'finite clods untroubled by a spark', who obtain the most satisfaction. There must be some happy mean between these extremes.

Note. 5 *Eats his own flesh.* Eats what meat he has without coveting that of others. It is not a reference to the autophagous tendency of idleness, as the English words suggest; this hardly suits the context.

4:7–12 Of solitude and society. Can the motive of profit in human enterprise be balanced by that of benefit to society? Can it be urged that 'unrestricted private enterprise' is conducive to the common good? It is difficult to maintain this when it is observed how strongly the profit motive operates in those who have no society and do not give twopence for it. It is doubtful, indeed, whether one who has no ties of family can have any real feeling for society. On the other hand, where the sense of solidarity is strong, the satisfactions it yields are of a different sort.

4:13–16 Of popularity. Of all the glittering prizes life holds out, surely the vainest is popularity. The promise of youth is always preferred to the petrifaction of age (as witness the studied illusion of perennial youth in contemporary fashion). But youth inevitably becomes age, and then it must endure the pain of seeing the fickle fancy of the mob turn elsewhere.

This passage is highly cryptic, and it is impossible to interpret it with assurance. It seems to contain an allusion to some historical episode with which its contemporary readers would be familiar: a decrepit old monarch succeeded by a brilliant youth who romantically issued from prison amid universal enthusiasm but who rapidly fell into disfavour.

5:1–9 The vanity of worship and service

5:1–7 Wisdom and folly in the worship of God. Surveying the vanity of all things under the sun, Ecclesiastes turns his critical eye upon religion; for secularized man is by no means averse to religion; only, his is a religion which is secularized and humanized. This is the great pitfall of religion, against which warning is given. For there is an inveterate tendency in men to seek to 'make use of God' (*Deo uti*, Luther), to subject God to themselves and their own concerns, to treat Him as an ally, an anodyne or an insurance agency. Characteristic of this man-centred religion is its verbosity; its anxiety to say its say is reflected in a never-ending stream of reports, statements, pronouncements, pamphlets, *etc.* But it loses the ear for the word of God. The word of God is not the echo of our words. It is His own word, His word of judgment and of grace, and before it we must be silent and listen. In our approach to God it is necessary to remember 'the otherness of God', and respect 'the infinite qualitative difference between God and man' (Kierkegaard).

Note. 6 *The messenger*; the priest or minister. *Why should God be angry . . . ?* It is pre-eminently against human infidelity that the wrath of God is revealed.

5:8, 9 Of the civil magistrate. The fear of God is coupled (naturally) with respect for authority in the state. *Cf.* 1 Pet. 2:17. For there is no power but of God: the powers that be are ordained of God. Not that the ruling powers are beyond reproach. On the contrary, there is corruption at every stage of the political hierarchy. Even the highest in the land is not free from sin. Thus the existence of injustice and oppression is not to be marvelled at; for the remedy for this lies not in any human authority. Yet there is a relatively best form of government; and Ecclesiastes expresses his preference for a patriarchal monarchy, where the king is intimately acquainted with the concerns of his (agricultural) subjects—a judgment which is no doubt sound in its emphasis on agriculture and its implied rejection of bureaucracy, but difficult of application to large, industrialized states.

Notes. 8 *Watched by a higher.* The passage is ambiguous, perhaps intentionally. Looking up the ladder of authority we may, according to our vision, see only 'the powers that be', or we may see above them Him who will 'do justice to the fatherless and the oppressed, so that man who is of the earth may strike terror no more' (Ps. 10:18). **9** has been variously translated. The best rendering would seem to be: 'Profitable for a land in general is a king devoted to the tilled field.'

5:10 – 6:12 The vanity of riches and human destiny

5:10 – 6:9 Of wealth and acquisitiveness. The fancied satisfaction of mammonism, which conceives of man's life as consisting in the abundance of the things which he possesses and identifies his state with his estate, is a mirage which continually recedes; for the lust of acquisitiveness, once unleashed, becomes insatiable, and the appetite grows with eating. Capitalism can thrive only on an expanding market, and the circle of supply and demand, however expanded, remains a circle; it cannot be squared. Further, acquisitiveness brings anxiety; for wealth is uncertain (*cf.* 1 Tim. 6:17), the bubble of prosperity bursts, and slump follows boom. Finally, the rich man dies, and what good is all his wealth to him then?

Are we then to commend ascetic renunciation? By no means. The good things of the world are God's gifts to be enjoyed by us with thankfulness and contentment. The key to enjoyment is to substitute grace for grab. 'For everything created by God is good, and nothing is to be rejected if it is received with thanksgiving' (1 Tim. 4:4). Experience shows that the art of enjoyment usually comes readiest to those least cumbered with worldly goods, while those who possess 'all the advantages' may miss it.

Notes. 5:20 *He will not much remember . . .* He who is in correspondence with God, he whose chief end it is to glorify God and enjoy Him, can live in the present and enjoy the gifts of God today, without anxious thoughts for the morrow. *Cf.* Mt. 6:33, 34. **6:3** *And also has no burial.* It has been suggested that this clause has been misplaced and that it belongs to v. 5; it would certainly seem the more likely end of an untimely birth than of one who begot a hundred children, where it is oddly inappropriate.

6:10–12 Of human destiny. The nature and destiny of man are determined by One mightier than him, and he cannot contend with his Maker or add to his stature one cubit. All his endeavours to find enduring substance in this transitory life issue in vanity, and leave him facing the final question.

7:1–14 The wisdom of death

Ecclesiastes sets forth a wisdom of life which takes full account of the great negatives, adversity, sorrow and death. He who would live wisely must lay death to heart and integrate it with his view of life. The wisdom which would see 'life steadily and see it whole' must see death also; it 'exacts a full look at the worst'. The modern flight from death, shown by the avoidance of serious consideration of it in popular thought and even of all mention of it in polite conversation, as if death were a sleeping dog one could pass on tiptoe, is the index of a view of life to which death has no meaning save that of an irrational brute fact which rudely interrupts man's efforts and aspirations. Man's hopes today are bound up with a progressive postponement of death and the dream of its eventual elimination. If Ecclesiastes is able to look death fearlessly in the face, it can only be because he sees it, not as a simple negative, but as a 'horizon', a line marking 'the threshold of metaphysical possibilities' and pointing to a hidden dimension of life. The lessons which he recommends us to gather from the sterner disciplines of experience may be described as a kind of chessboard wisdom: instead of complaining bitterly that the board is all black, or sighing for 'the good old days' when it was all white, this wisdom consists in patient acceptance of its real condition as the ultimate fact which we can know, but which points beyond itself. It is a mistake to suppose that the fatalism of Omar is the only, or the only logical, inference to be drawn from the chessboard character of life.

Note. 11, 12 are difficult to understand in their present context and may have been displaced. Alternative positions suggested for them are after v. 14 and after v. 21.

7:15–29 The excellence and difficulty of wisdom

7:15–22 'Critique of practical reason'. The attempt to reduce the raw material of life to system by means of moral principles breaks on the anomalies of experience. The consistent application of morality plays havoc with life, which will not be forced into this Procrustean bed. There is need of humility and restraint in both the thought and the practice of morality. It must be remembered that all moralities are conditioned by man's finitude and tainted by his sin. We must be careful to avoid moral pride. 'Moral pride is the pretension of finite man that his highly conditioned virtue is the final righteousness and that his very relative moral standards are absolute. Moral pride thus makes virtue the very vehicle of sin' (Niebuhr, *Human Nature*, p. 212).

7:23–28 'Critique of pure reason'. The attempt to reduce the raw material of life to system by means of theoretical ideas breaks down likewise. The most penetrating wisdom cannot reach the final harmony in which the discords of existence are resolved; every attempt comes to grief on the problem of evil, '*das radikal Böse*', in the human heart. Ecclesiastes finds the most obstinate manifestation of evil in the female of the species (v. 26); for him the wisdom of Socrates miscarries on the problem of his wife, Xanthippe.

7:29 The Fall. The conclusion, which is the utmost to which human wisdom can attain, is that man has fallen from the state in which God created him, and through his cleverness has brought about his own undoing. The irresolvable antinomies of life have their focal point in the fact that man is at variance with himself.

8:1–9 The powers that be

The logical inference from the universality of human corruption would be anarchy ('Jack's as good as his master'). But political wisdom is not a logical science, it is a psychological art. It is guided not by what is logically sound and consistent but by what is relatively opportune (v. 5). Thus an authoritarian order of society may be irrational and even evil (v. 9b); nevertheless, loyalty to it is preferable to insurrection. *Cf.* Rom. 13. This is hardly an acceptable doctrine nowadays; yet it is a profound challenge to those who identify change with progress. The idea of reform was no doubt strange to the mind of the writer, who construes criticism of authority as simple insurrection. But his reflections are no less applicable to it. The inability to see the outcome of any proposed change places the *onus probandi* upon those who advocate or instigate it. It is a fact that reforms which are designed to remove one evil often put others in its place; and long-term policies are called in question by the short term of human life. The real problem of life is urgent and cannot be postponed; for the time is limited. 'Now's the day, and now's the hour.' We know not if we shall see tomorrow—and 'what good is it to the primeval horse that one of its descendants wins the Derby?' (K. Heim).

Note. 9 *To his hurt, i.e.* to that of the ruled, not of the ruler.

8:10 The reversal of human judgments

The precise meaning of this very difficult verse cannot now be recovered. About a dozen different interpretations have been proposed. But if we accept the rendering of RV as approximately correct, the thought would seem to be the fallibility of popular judgments either as detected by the writer's own acuter eye or, more probably, as reversed by posterity.

8:11–17 The hidden righteousness of God

The mills of God grind slowly—so slowly that men may easily suppose they do not grind at all. The universe appears indifferent to moral distinctions, and Ecclesiastes is well aware of the difficulties of a too facile acceptance of the Jewish 'philosophy of history' and of attempts to discern divine judgments in the course of events (v. 14). Nevertheless he *knows* of the certainty of judgment, even though it be not manifest in the things that are seen and temporal, and for this cause he faints not and can even laugh at despair (v. 15). Here he shows, more clearly perhaps than anywhere else in the book, that his own soul has an anchor within the veil.

9:1–10 More of the wisdom of death

Life is a course in which all must run together,

all must take the same hurdles and the same hazards, and all come to the same end. There is no anticipation of the judgment, no discrimination in favour of those who 'run the way of God's commandments'; men can turn the race into a wild stampede with apparent impunity. Nevertheless there is a judgment; there are some who are in God's hand, whose works are accepted of Him, and who may devote themselves with a single heart to the task of the moment without anxious thought for the morrow. So long as the race is running there is hope for all, even for those who appear most hopeless; the knowledge that they must die may make the living wise; but for those who have passed the limit hope is gone; for them the day of grace is past, and 'the door is shut' (cf. Mt. 25:10).

9:11–18 Negative corroborations

The wisdom which looks for light beyond the horizon of death receives confirmation from the darkness and confusion of the scene on this side. So, from his scanning of the horizon, Ecclesiastes *saw that under the sun the race is not to the swift, nor the battle to the strong* (v. 11). So true it is that we walk by faith, not by sight. 'Faith is of things which do not appear. And so, that there may be room for faith, it is necessary that all things which are its objects should be hidden. They cannot, however, be more remotely hidden than under their contrary objects, feelings and experiences' (Luther, *De servo arbitrio*). What counts in the world's judgment is wealth and self-advertisement; genuine, unostentatious merit goes unrecognized, unrewarded. This Ecclesiastes describes ironically as the wisdom which he saw under the sun and it seemed great to him (v. 13). *One sinner destroys much good* (v. 18). This clause introduces the next series of reflections.

10:1–7 Of folly and wisdom

Wisdom is excellent, but it is at a disadvantage in comparison with folly, which produces disproportionately large effects. A little leaven of folly can vitiate a whole lump of wisdom, and a single fool can undo the work of many wise men. Further, folly is more immediately evident; it proclaims itself on the street. When folly manifests itself in high places, the course of wisdom is patience and conciliation. Least said is soonest mended. If it be argued that this would justify a policy of appeasement, Ecclesiastes would answer that the wise man is guided by time and judgment (cf. 8:15). There is a time to keep silence, and a time to speak (cf. 3:7). That folly does invade high places is proved by the familiar observation that fools are exalted to honour and dignity in the state, and true worth passes unrecognized.

Note. 6 *The rich*. Ecclesiastes probably means those of hereditary wealth, the aristocracy, as distinguished from the *nouveaux riches*.

10:8–11 Counting the cost

The general import of these gnomic utterances, which may have been current proverbs, would seem to be that no change can be effected without risk, and especially that anyone who interferes with established institutions is liable to get his fingers burned. Before embarking on any such enterprise it is well to count the cost and make sure that one has adequate skill and resources at his command (cf. Lk. 14:28ff.).

10:12–20 Words and deeds

10:12–15 The wise man and the fool. Ecclesiastes here touches on the notorious talkativeness of folly and the capacity for mischief that is inherent in it. Cf. Jas. 3:5, 6.

Note. 15 To know *the way to the city* would appear to have been a proverbial expression for practical wisdom or effective action. The fool can talk plenty, but he is incapable of action.

10:16–19 Slothfulness at court. Ill fares the land when Sybaritism prevails at court.

Note. 17 *The son of free men* (RV 'nobles'). Perhaps a *double entendre*, made possible by the Hebrew idiom which employs the periphrasis 'son of' to form a descriptive adjective: when the king's character and conduct are of a nobility consistent with his birth.

10:20 Reverence due to the king. This warning against seditious talk and 'dangerous thoughts' accords well with Ecclesiastes's attitude of detachment towards politics. It is not a counsel of acquiescence in injustice or oppression but rather a warning against incurring unnecessary risks. Where there is neither the will nor the power to mend matters, mere grumbling and disaffection are foolish.

11:1–6 Directions for charity

If some of the political counsels of the previous chapters have a somewhat conservative, quietistic, 'Lutheran' ring, Ecclesiastes's dialectic now takes a bold, venturesome, 'Calvinistic' turn, as if to show once more that the conduct of life cannot be based on a single principle, but the wise man has regard to 'time and judgment'. In commercial enterprise risks must be taken, and he who will not venture until he has an absolutely safe proposition will wait for ever (v. 4). The future is always unpredictable; accidents will happen to the best regulated businesses; and no-one knows by what 'act of God' (v. 5) the most careful calculations may be upset. The course of wisdom is not to put all our eggs in one basket and not to stake our all on one card but to reduce the risk by dividing it (v. 2).

Note. 1 *Cast your bread upon the waters . . .* It is fairly certain that the primary reference of the words, as Delitzsch has shown, is to the seaborne corn trade. But Ecclesiastes undoubtedly uses this form of commercial adventure to illustrate the course which wisdom suggests in other fields of life, such as the practice of uncalculating charity, to which the words have been commonly understood to refer. *Cf.* Lk. 16:9.

11:7, 8 Respice finem

A wise recognition of the uncertainty of the future makes the present all the more important. The present is the only time at our disposal. Tomorrow is in God's hand: we do not know what it will bring forth. It is on today that 'the accent of eternity' (Heim) lies. Like Christ's 'Do not be anxious about tomorrow', this does not imply disregard of the future. On the contrary, it is made possible only by a true regard for the future, viz. the recognition that the future is God's. The Epicurean philosophy which says *carpe diem*, 'gather ye rosebuds while ye may', contains an element of profound truth, and it is not so very far removed from what Paul says about 'making the most of the time' (Col. 4:5).

11:9 – 12:8 Counsels to youth

11:9, 10 Rejoice. A corollary of Ecclesiastes's emphasis on the present is his counsel to youth to enjoy the season of youth while it is theirs, not to seek to put old heads on young shoulders nor to try to prolong youth beyond its term, but to accept youth with its blessings and opportunities in the sober recognition that youth and age alike are of God's appointment and both are subject to His judgment. *Rejoice . . . the sight of your eyes.* There is nothing in these words to warrant the interpretation that Ecclesiastes is recommending youth to sow *wild* oats; nor can we deduce from them any support for the current idolization of youth, with its ridiculous sartorial illusions. *But know that . . .* 'The great But', in which the wisdom of the Bible is crystallized (Barth). 'All the ways of a man are pure in his own eyes, *but* the Lord weighs the spirit' (Pr. 16:2).

12:1–8 Remember. Man is a creature of time. In the end his creatureliness asserts itself unmistakably in his dissolution. Surely it is elementary wisdom to take account of this ultimate 'horizon' (Heidegger) in any attempt to construe the pattern of existence. Ecclesiastes recommends the frank recognition of our creatureliness even in youth, at the time when it is least apparent and life seems unquenchable. It is only when seen in this perspective that youth can be rightly understood and rightly enjoyed. The 'problem of youth' which bulks so large in our time is in great measure the consequence of a false perspective, a blurring of the horizons, the playing of blind man's buff with death, which is one of the chief follies of the age.

Notes. **1** *Remember also your Creator.* It is to be noted how Ecclesiastes shows his hand here. The prospect of age and death yields him, not *memento mori* (remember you must die), but *memento Creatoris* (remember your Creator). By this he clearly distinguishes himself from all sceptics, cynics and Epicureans, with whom he has often been confused.

2–7 contains a figurative description of the decay and dissolution of life, but the imagery is difficult to interpret in detail. **2** The picture of the approaching storm may be intended to suggest the approach of death in a general way or more particularly the decay of the inner faculties. **3, 4** The imagery is most probably intended to represent the decay of the bodily organs, *the keepers of the house* being the hands, *the strong men* the legs, *the grinders* the teeth, *those that look through the windows* the eyes, *the doors* the ears. The remaining clauses of v. 4 seem all to refer to the decay of the powers of speech and song. *One rises up at the voice of a bird.* If 'one' means 'an old man', this would involve the abrupt insertion of a literal statement in the middle of an elaborate allegory. But apart from that, it is not true that the old rise up at the voice of a bird. The old are less easily roused than the young, especially as they are often deaf (*the doors on the street are shut*)! It is probable that the text is corrupt and the original was to the effect that the voice of the old becomes weak and tends to resemble the treble chirp of a bird.

5 The allegory is abandoned and literal description takes its place: the old are afraid of heights, and they are timid of venturing forth at all. In view of the great and fantastic variety of interpretations that have been suggested for *the almond tree, the grasshopper*, and 'the caper-berry' (RV; *desire*, RSV), it seems best to follow Wetzstein and Hertzberg and take the three clauses literally as descriptions of phenomena of spring and summer: the almond tree blooms, the grasshopper loads itself (with food) and the caper-berry bursts forth—but all these gladdening sights mean nothing to the old man who, after the dissolution of his earthly house (v. 3; *cf.* 2 Cor. 5:1), goes to his long home.

6 The allegory is resumed. The figures of *the silver cord* being snapped and *the golden bowl* broken would seem to refer to the dissolution of soul and body. The life of man is likened first to a golden bowl (containing oil for a lamp) suspended by a silver cord, then to a *pitcher* with which water is drawn from a well. The lamp and the pitcher were both familiar symbols of life in antiquity. **7** *The spirit returns to God who gave it.* Ecclesiastes would seem to have advanced somewhat beyond the position of 3:21, but his words here, while suggestive, are not such as to form the foundation of a hope of immortality. He is viewing the dissolution of body and spirit from the standpoint of 'under the sun', and he simply states that each returns to the source from which it sprang, the body to the dust and the spirit to God (*cf.* Gn. 2:7). As to the final destiny of the spirit after its return to God, it is not his concern to speak of that. **8** *Vanity of vanities . . . .* The author 'has made all earthly things small, and at last remains seated on this dust-heap of *vanitas vanitatum*' (Delitzsch). His argument, like all things under the sun (*cf.* 1:3–11), has come full circle, and he repeats the theorem which he set out to demonstrate (*cf.* 1:2) with an air of finality, as if to say *quod erat demonstrandum*.

12:9-14 Epilogue

The remainder of the book consists of an editorial postscript in the form of a 'commendatory attestation' (Plumptre) of the writer and an attempt to sum up the conclusions of his teaching. Does this come from the same hand as the rest of the book, or was it added by another? The question has been much debated. The change from the first to the third person suggests a change of author, but since the author's name Qoheleth (Ecclesiastes) is a pseudonym in any case, it may indicate only that he now steps forward and makes a brief curtain-speech, as it were, in his own name. We may compare Kierkegaard's editorial notes to his own pseudonymous works. There is no change in the vocabulary and style of the epilogue, which bears a strong resemblance to that of the rest of the book (even in the obscurity of the metaphor in v. 11). It has been questioned whether any writer would speak of himself in terms of vv. 9, 10, which, it is suggested, betray the hand of an admiring follower. But this is to attribute the literary fashions of our day to an age when they were very different. In the ancient world authorship was held of small account, so small indeed that the names of many of the authors of antiquity have been lost. The question men asked of a book was not 'Who wrote it?' but 'What does it say?', and there was no need for an author to make a profession of modesty, since his work was not regarded as a personal achievement or a feat of virtuosity. Even in our own time there have been exceptions to the fashion of literary modesty (which is largely humbug), notably Mr. Bernard Shaw, who sometimes spoke of himself in much more flattering terms than Ecclesiastes, and with less ground.

The most important question is whether vv. 13, 14 are a just summation of the teaching of the book, or, as some allege, a tendentious simplification, made with a view to commending it to orthodox readers. It is certainly difficult to see how any statement of a positive duty for man could be logically deduced from the premise that all things under the sun are vanity. But this is not the logic of Ecclesiastes; for he does not seek the premises of human duty in human theory or of moral values in the 'idea' of God. However much he stresses the difficulties of what man is to believe concerning God, he *knows* (*cf.* 8:12) that these difficulties do not suspend or abrogate the duty God requires of man; and it may be with a view to correcting any rash inference that might be drawn from his theoretical conclusion that he lays his final emphasis on the practical duty of man. The enigma of life may be insoluble by wisdom, but *solvitur ambulando*.

Notes. 11 *The sayings of the wise are like goads.* Though acceptable, they have their sting. The following comparison is typically obscure. The *nails* are usually understood to be tent-pegs, and compared to them are either the great teachers (as RV, 'masters of assemblies') or the great teachings assembled in their works (as RSV, *the collected sayings*); the *one Shepherd* can hardly be other than God, who is the Author and Source of true wisdom. The general idea would seem to be that it is the teachings of the masters, drawn from the fountainhead, which gives stability and strength to life. **12** A final warning is given against intellectualism, directed in the first instance perhaps against the exaggerated pretensions of 'wisdom' in the literature which goes by that name. Ecclesiastes does not despise the intellect (*cf.* 9:17, 18), but he is aware of its limitations (*cf.* 8:17).

13, 14 *The whole duty of man.* This is not the practice of the theory that all is vanity. But Ecclesiastes knows that practice will not wait upon theory or life upon understanding. Theory and practice will remain at variance so long as we are under the sun. The reconciliation, the resolution of the discord awaits the time when faith will give place to sight and every hidden thing will be revealed. So we may say of the last words of Ecclesiastes, *spirant resurrectionem* (they foreshadow the resurrection).

G. S. HENDRY

The Song of Solomon

INTRODUCTION

The book is aptly headed 'The Song of Songs' for it is difficult to find its equal as a piece of writing on human love. It is a song of great beauty and power with delicately chosen imagery from field and garden, animal life and plant life (1:12 – 2:3; 4:12 – 5:1; 6:2, 3, *etc.*). Its dream passages (3:1–5; 5:2–8) have a tender pathos. Its passage on untaken opportunity (5:2–8) has provided the basis for many a sermon on that topic. It is unique in Holy Scripture in that it is the only book that deals solely with human love and this it does incomparably.

AUTHORSHIP

The problems of authorship, purpose and literary type are all inseparably intertwined. The title (1:1) may mean either that the song was written by Solomon or that it is about him. The Hebrew can bear the meaning of both. If the shepherd hypothesis (see below) is adopted the first alternative must be ruled out, for Solomon would hardly write a book that deals him such an ethical blow. Some Jewish tradition (*Baba Bathra* 15a) ascribes the book to Hezekiah. The presence of some later words indicates either a date after Solomon's time or that the book had its final redaction, though not its original composition, in a later period. It may safely be said that neither questions of date nor questions of authorship affect the usefulness and value of the book.

INTERPRETATION

Three related questions are involved here. What is the book's literary category? What is its purpose? How many main characters are involved? For centuries these questions have been debated and, owing to the difficulty of the book, none can afford to be dogmatic in his conclusions.

What then is the nature of the book? Owing to its apparent eroticism the book for centuries has been understood as an allegory of Christ's love for the church. There is, however, no indication that the writing is allegorical and the fanciful, varied and often contradictory results of such a view are not in its favour. The song must be taken literally, *i.e.* as what it appears to be, a song about human love written in the form of a series of dramatic poems with this one unifying theme. The fact that it probably owes its existence in the Canon to an allegorical interpretation is still no basis for the acceptance of such an interpretation. This is not to say that the book may not at times be illustrative of the relation-

ship between Christ and the individual; this view is reflected in the commentary which follows. A further danger of the allegorical interpretation is that readers may be led into an erotic view of his personal relationship with Christ.

This leads on to the purpose of the book. If the nature of the book is an extended dramatic poem or poems on human love, its purpose is to indicate the rightness and value of true love in all its aspects between man and woman. God in His wisdom has included in the Canon of Holy Scripture one whole book on this important matter which, in every generation, suffers tragic abuse. Thus, in its teaching, the Bible attempts to redeem a situation which has become woefully degraded. Even in its detailed description of the human body (4:1–7; 5:10–16; 6:4–10; 7:1–9) we see a reflection of the doctrine of creation that all that God made was 'very good'.

More point is made to this if the 'shepherd hypothesis' be adopted. (See further on this the IVF Bible Study Course *Search the Scriptures.*) This is the view in which the two main lovers are a shepherd and the Shulammite. Between them there is a genuine and pure love. Solomon, however, captures the maiden for his harem and attempts to win her affections through the artificial allures of the palace. He is unsuccessful. While not dogmatically held, this is the view of the text taken in the commentary. For it is felt, among other things, that Solomon is hardly the best example of true, loyal, single-minded love in the light of his 700 wives and 300 concubines and all the dire consequences for the nation that followed in the train of his many love affairs (see 1 Ki. 11). Moreover, Solomon was no shepherd (see Ct. 6:2).

The shepherd hypothesis is also endorsed by the main refrain of the book (2:7; 3:5; 8:4). True love needs no artificial stimuli. Love must not be awakened 'until it please'. See further the commentary on 8:8–12. Pure love successfully resists all the false, sensual allures of this world. The book is a censure on lust, polygamy, infidelity. It encourages a love which is exclusive and absorbing (4:12). It highlights a love which is unquenchable and unpurchasable (8:6f.). It endorses the place of physical love within a legitimate relationship.

For these reasons alone it more than justifies its place in the Canon. Its presence indicates the completeness of Holy Scripture, for God is concerned with every aspect of our living; this is the only book which, as a whole, treats this important subject. Young's comment is apt: 'So long as there is impurity in this world we need, and need badly, the Song of Solomon.'

When this book is used illustratively we are reminded, among other things, of the strength of Christ's love (8:7); His delight to hear the prayer of the church (8:13); the sense of yearning for His presence (8:14); the invitation of Christ to share His company (2:13); the dangers of the failure to respond immediately to His knocking (5:2-8; cf. Rev. 3:20). It may well rebuke us on our lack of passion for God; that our relationship to Him is lukewarm and superficial. If it does this in addition to imparting its clear ethical teaching then our study of it will be amply rewarded.

OUTLINE OF CONTENTS

COMMENTARY

1:1 – 2:7 SOLOMON MEETS THE SHULAMMITE IN HIS PALACE

1:1 The title

See Introduction for questions of authorship. The title indicates the unity of the poem and its superlative nature. As a song on true love this reigns supreme.

1:2–8 The daughters of Jerusalem and the Shulammite

1:2–4 It appears that a number of people speak in this short paragraph. The Shulammite, a young innocent from the country, has been thrust into the king's harem. Clearly she is not at home there and the oversensuous words of the women grate on her sensitive ears. As they see the king approach they long for the touch of his lips on theirs.

2 *O that you* . . . RSV has no textual ground to change 'he' to 'you'. The women are talking to one another about the king. *For your love* . . . It is characteristic of Hebrew that the third person passes easily into the second, and *vice versa*. In any case, perhaps the king is now nearer the harem and another member addresses him. *Your love* might well be translated 'your caresses'; the Hebrew is plural and it fits the context better. *Wine*. An apt description of the intoxicating effect of caressing. **3** *Anointing oils.* Such oils were widely used in the East and were of particular value because of the heat and their pleasing odour. *Your name is oil poured out.* There is a play on words in the Hebrew. 'Oil' is šemen and 'name' šem. While perfume pleases the noses, the name or person pleases the heart. It is commonly recognized that just saying the name of the beloved brings delight. *Maidens*; girls growing to maturity. Cf. Is. 7:14. Probably the women of the harem are referring to themselves here. **4** *Draw me after you* . . . By contrast the Shulammite now speaks. She yearns for her shepherd lover and even though he is absent she calls longingly for him and pleads that he take her away. It is the king who has brought her into his chambers; she has not come willingly. She speaks to her lover as though she were alone with him. True, loyal love is already shining through the lust of the court scene. The last part of the verse gives us the words of the women of the harem. The tone is that of vv. 2 and 3. *Exult* is from the Hebrew root z-k-r, 'to remember' and here it means 'praise', 'celebrate', 'constantly recall'. The love and caresses of the king are a constant topic of conversation in the harem. *Rightly do they love you*. The AV reading, 'the upright love thee', is hardly the meaning of the Hebrew and RSV has rightly translated here. The Hebrew is 'in uprightness' and gives the meaning 'it is not surprising that the harem loves such a king'.

1:5–7 The newcomer to the harem is subject to the contemptuous and perhaps jealous looks of the other women and becomes increasingly self-conscious. She apologizes for her tanned appearance, but it was none of her doing. Her brothers, with no concern for the beauty of her skin, had sent her day after day to work under the relentless sun in the family vineyards. All this was to the neglect of the 'vineyard' of her own complexion. But at least they will recognize that despite her tan she has a beauty equal to any of theirs.

5 *Dark*; not 'black', as AV, but swarthy, tanned, sunburnt. *Comely*; was it not her beauty that had brought her into this miserable situation? *Tents of Kedar*. Kedar is the name of the N Arabian Ishmaelites (cf. Gn. 25:13). The Shulammite likens her skin to their black goat-hair tents. *Curtains of Solomon*. There are parallels of thought here: the 'black tents of Kedar' are parallel to 'I am dark', while 'comely' is parallel to 'curtains of Solomon'. Such curtains were magnificently made and had a beauty all of their own. **6** The Shulammite gives the reason for the colour of her skin. *Swarthy* is a diminutive of the former word. She has not been able to care for her beauty as these pampered, pale-faced women of the palace. *Scorched*; literally 'looked upon'. Poetically, the sun is thought of as having eyes; *cf.* 2 Sa. 12:11. The latter part of the verse gives an indication of her rustic background. *My mother's sons*; a reference to her full brothers. It would seem that her father was dead and this adds even more poignancy to her situation. *My own vineyard*. Some think this is her own lover whom she has lost, but it is more natural to take it as her complexion. **7** *Tell.* The maiden turns from addressing the women of the court and soliloquizes, addressing her absent lover. Could they not make a trysting place at noon? Where is he to be found? *Wanders*; rsv adopts the reading of the Greek, Syriac and Vulgate through a transposition of the Hebrew letters. The idea may be that the Shulammite has no desire to wander up and down looking for the beloved, coming on every other flock but his own. Where will he be at noon so that she can go directly to him? The Hebrew reads 'is veiled', suggesting her feeling of mourning because of her enforced absence from her loved one.

1:8 The daughters of Jerusalem, overhearing her soliloquy, answer her. Their tone is probably ironic as they describe her as *the fairest among women*. Let her go and find him for herself. 'Go back to your shepherd life' is their response to her naïvety. The idea of her wanting to give up royal honours so recently gained seems almost ludicrous to them.

1:9 – 2:7 Solomon talks with the Shulammite

1:9–11 The king, for the first time in the book, gives his attention to the peasant girl, but receives no response.

9 *My love* may be too strong for the Hebrew. It is from the verb 'to associate with', 'to be friends with'. The noun is commonly translated 'friend' or 'companion'. Moffat has 'my dear'. The comparison to an Egyptian mare may fall oddly on our ears. But to Solomon, with his love of horses (particularly Egyptian horses), it was the height of flattery! *Cf.* 1 Ki. 4:26; 10:26; 2 Ch. 9:28. Solomon not only loved them for themselves but also for the considerable money he made in trading them. *Cf.* 1 Ki. 10:28f.; 2 Ch. 1:16f.; 9:25–28.

10 *Your cheeks*. The horse analogy is now dropped, though perhaps there is a transition through the ornamental frills often arrayed on the horse's bridle. *Ornaments*; literally 'rows'. The verb behind this phrase means to 'bore through' and 'string together'. Such a necklace would have several strings, probably of pearls. But her ornaments are nothing compared with what Solomon will give her. Her homely ornaments will be exchanged for plaits of gold and studs of silver. The decorations on Pharaoh's mare will look shoddy compared with what the king will give to his newly acquired bride.

1:12–14 The Shulammite replies to Solomon. **12** Two possible interpretations are, first, that the king, attracted by the heavy scent of the Shulammite, makes his way to her side. Second, that while Solomon was on his couch and absent from the peasant girl she was able to pour forth the fragrance of her love towards her beloved. *Couch*; this word is based on the verb 'to go round' and indicates some kind of semicircular divan, probably a reclining seat, for the king. *Nard*; spikenard, the aromatic ointment used by Mary of Bethany. *Cf.* Mk. 14:3ff. It is a beautiful and apposite symbol of love and, indeed, this is how our Lord uses it. *Cf.* also 2 Cor. 2:14–16. **13, 14** On the second interpretation these verses describe the maiden's feelings towards her shepherd lover. *Bag* describes a small receptacle with crushed myrrh within. *Myrrh*; the *Balsamodendron myrrha* whose liquid produces a strong aroma. *Between my breasts*; memories of her loved one are like the continual aroma from a depository of myrrh so placed on her bosom. Thus the subject is the myrrh and not the lover. *Henna*; a shrub from N India. A paste was made from its leaves and used as a cosmetic by both women and men. It is also aromatic. *Engedi*; the fertile area surrounding the fresh-water springs on the west side of the Dead Sea.

1:15 Solomon continues his flattery. In contrast with v. 16, the adjectives here are feminine and so it is assumed that it is the king who now addresses the Shulammite. Twice beautiful is she, so the repetition indicates. *Dove* suggests tenderness, purity, longing, simplicity. According to some, the dove was the symbol for the goddess of love.

1:16 – 2:1 But the Shulammite is all the time thinking of her shepherd lover. **16, 17** The pronouns and adjectives here are masculine; thus she responds by taking up the turn of phrase used by the king but adding the word *lovely*. Her thoughts again wander to the country. Their couch was no royal mattress but the natural green grass of the field. Cedar tops formed the roof of their house. *Rafters*; the meaning of the Hebrew is uncertain. Its basic meaning is to 'meet' or 'cross', and could well describe the overlapping timber of a ceiling. The general picture remains clear. It is not city and palace which please the Shulammite but forest and field. **2:1** In similar terms she describes herself. *Rose*; many suggestions have been made as to the identity of the plant, but it is certainly not what we understand by rose. The most likely is the *Tulipa sharonensis*, a bulbous plant related to the Syrian mountain tulip. *Lily of the valley*; another bulbous plant of which there are many varieties; perhaps here it is the hyacinth. The use of flower-names in love conversation is not uncommon and is most expressive for attractiveness both of smell and beauty.

2:2 Solomon replies, taking up her imagery. Most certainly she is a lily, and compared with her the other women are but prickly brambles.

2:3-7 The Shulammite replies to this, using similar language. 2, 3 If the Shulammite contrasts with other women as a lily to thorns, likewise the shepherd lover stands out as an apple tree amongst other trees of the wood. *Apple tree*; most likely RSV is correct, though some suggest it is the quince. This, however, is more bitter than the apple and does not fit into the context so easily. *Cf. sweet*. The point of the comparison lies in the refreshment and sweetness of the fruit plus the security that the shade of the apple tree offers. 4 The maiden recalls a meeting she had with her lover. *Banqueting house*; literally 'house of wine'. This would either be a real banqueting house or quite simply a house of love, wine being understood metaphorically. This accords with the second half of the verse. Not only were they together in the house of love but his covering for her was his love also. The idea has led many to think of the protective love of God within the house of God. Wine is one of the symbols of God's sacrificial love for us in Christ. Moreover, it was the blood of the slain lamb that protected the Israelites in Egypt (*cf.* Ex. 12:13, 23).

5 Such love not only protects but sustains and refreshes. Both raisins and apples were used in the fertility feasts of Canaan, but the fruit of procreation is not envisaged here, nor, indeed, anywhere else in the book. *Sick with love* is an evocative expression for the feeling involved in the deep love between man and woman. 6 She continues to express her longing for both support (the left hand under the head) and caress (the embracing right hand). *Embrace*; the Hebrew means primarily 'to enfold' but also 'to caress', to stroke gently with the hand. Such physical desires have the *imprimatur* of God providing that they are in the context of legitimate relationship, as here. 7 These words act as a kind of refrain throughout the poem and this is a key verse in the understanding of true love between man and woman. It is addressed to the other women of the harem, the *daughters of Jerusalem*. *Adjure*; this is the only example in Scripture of adjuring by something other than God. The significance of *gazelles* and *hinds* is not clear but the words come naturally from a lover of the fields where such animals roam freely and beautifully. *Love*; AV quite unnecessarily prefaces with 'my'. The reference is to the false rousing of love as an emotion, not to a lover as a person. Artificial stimulation to love is as much outside the will of God as true physical love is within it. There is a time to embrace and a time not to embrace. So here, as in 3:5 and 8:4, the Shulammite earnestly requests the harem not to resort to false stimulation of love. A true and worthy love should owe nothing to excitement coming from without.

2:8 – 3:5 THE BELOVED'S VISIT AND THE SHULAMMITE'S NIGHT SEARCH

2:8-17 The beloved's visit

2:8, 9 The scene has changed. We move from city palace to country home. The Shulammite is alone and thinks longingly of her beloved. The verses which follow are among the most beautiful not only in this book but in love poetry of any age. Suddenly she hears his voice. We imagine her rushing to the window. *Behold he comes*. And he too is hastened on by the compelling force of his love. He leaps; he bounds. He is sure and fleet of foot like the gazelle or the young stag. In no time he is there peering first through one window and then another until he finds the room where she is. We cannot help understanding the deep feeling of this reunion after separation. This follows the pattern of true love, for love longs to be with the object of that love. How much, too, the Christian should long to see the face of his Lord. Such consummation of the relationship is the great hope of the Christian. And seeing Him we shall be like Him. *Cf.* 1 Jn. 3:2.

2:10-15 Suitably the time is spring, the time of renewal and vitality. Cameron writes, 'After wintry months devoid of fresh life and growth, the stirring vigour of the Syrian spring follows of a sudden upon the early rain. The earth rapidly assumes a mantle of bright green, intermingled with the varied colours of innumerable flowers. The newly clad woodland comes alive with song.' And above the song comes the sweetest note of all, the invitation of the beloved to come away (v. 10). The association of love and spring clearly has a biblical basis! Spring is the time of youth and hope, of joy and love. And does not the Christian long likewise for an eternal spring in his own experience and for a fresh awakening in the church, the bride of Christ? The invitation is pressing and compelling. Twice the beloved urges, 'Arise, my love, my fair one, and come away' (vv. 10, 13). To the Christian whose heart is solely set on Christ there are no problems of the allure of the counterparts of Solomon's court. Paul was a man shut up to one thing because the love of Christ constrained him. *Cf.* 2 Cor. 5:14; Phil. 3:13f. Moses was in a similar tradition. *Cf.* Heb. 11:26. Here is a love that will not let us go, and the true believer does not wish to be let go.

12 The *turtledove* is a migratory bird whose coming indicated the arrival of spring. It is backed by a whole chorus of birds, always a delightful concomitant to the new season. 15 *Foxes*; the meaning and position of this verse are not easy to grasp. Most likely the Shulammite is replying, for she was a keeper of the vineyard (*cf.* 1:6) and this is a vineyard song. She requests that anything which would spoil the vineyard of their lives must be caught and eradicated. Let love be pure and undisturbed. There is no place here for lust, adultery, fornication, cheap sentimental-

ity, or anything else which would spoil true love between man and wife.

2:16, 17 Perhaps the Shulammite senses danger. At any rate she pleads that her lover depart until evening when it would be safer. *Until the day breathes* is an ambiguous phrase, but is more likely to refer to evening (*cf.* RV 'until the day be cool') than morning, as in AV. The shadows flee as the sun sinks. Delitzsch uses this as an illustration of the coming of Christ at the evening of the world's history, when the church as the bride will see the heavenly Bridegroom face to face and welcome Him.

3:1–5 The night search

The Shulammite describes either a dream or a real experience. It is most likely the former, in view of the opening sentence and the fact that her modesty would prevent her running the streets at night. Perhaps the lover had failed to return as she had requested (*cf.* 2:16f.). Sadly she goes to bed and dreams of his absence. In her dream she rises and wanders the streets of the city looking for her lost lover, questioning the watchmen as she goes. She had hardly left them when he is discovered and is clasped to her bosom.

1 *By night*; literally 'by nights'. Moffat has 'night after night'. She may have dreamed this on several occasions. **4** *My mother's house.* Clearly everything was above board if she was prepared to take him there. There need be no deceit in a relationship of pure love. **5** See on 2:7.

3:6 – 5:1 SOLOMON'S PROCESSION AND SONGS

3:6–11 Solomon's approach

The destination of this splendid procession of the king is not clear. It could either be Jerusalem or the northern residence of the Shulammite. In the case of the former the girl is being brought with Solomon to his royal residence. If the shepherd hypothesis is adopted it indicates the king's desire to impress upon the Shulammite his wealth and magnificence in an attempt to overawe her and win her love. This is in vivid contrast to the simple love of the shepherd.

6 *What is that* . . . is a quite permissible translation of the Hebrew and is a question concerning the procession. *Wilderness*; that between Jerusalem and Jericho is a possibility. *Smoke*; from censers of frankincense. **7** *Behold*; as the procession gets nearer it is recognized as the king's. There is a deep sense of drama here. As it comes into view details are noticed. *Sixty mighty men*; Solomon's strong bodyguard. *Cf.* 2 Sa. 23:8. **9** *Palanquin* is a different word in the Hebrew from 'litter' (v. 7) but is a possible translation of a difficult word. *Wood of Lebanon*; cedar and cypress. **10** The magnificence of Solomon's bed is described, and reflects his extravagant court life. The Shulammite prefers the shepherd's shadow (*cf.* 2:3). *Lovingly wrought within*; an extremely difficult phrase. Delitzsch has 'its interior is adorned from love' and is probably as

near as we can get. **11** The specific idea of marriage enters. The court women are summoned to go out to meet the king with his wedding crown, a well-worn adornment, for Solomon had 700 wives (*cf.* 1 Ki. 11:3). *His mother*; the queen mother played a prominent part in coronations and weddings. It may be significant to recall that Solomon's mother was Bathsheba who had an illicit relationship with David.

4:1 – 5:1 Solomon's love song

4:1–7 This exquisite love song is based on the 'wasf', a lyric still used at Syrian weddings today. Its description of the body may not appeal to western ears but nevertheless indicates that man is not only fearfully and wonderfully made but beautifully made too. This is God's handiwork; should it not therefore be admired? God is not only a God of truth but of beauty and such beauty is reflected in aspects of His creation. Moreover, spoken admiration, so long as it is sincere and devoid of flattery, is an important part of love-making and its inclusion here in Holy Scripture elevates it to its rightful level. It is men who have debased it by their lustful desires.

1 First, the eyes are described even though they are partly hidden by the Shulammite's veil. *Doves*; see on 2:14. *Veil*; *cf.* Gn. 24:65. Second, the *hair* which was uncovered is compared to a flock of goats on a mountain side. One imagines these black goats covering the hillside in the same way as the Shulammite's black locks fall gently down from the crown of her head and over her back. **2** Third, the *teeth*, which, because of their smoothness and whiteness, are likened to shorn sheep. *Twins*; upper correspond with lower; they are perfectly regular. **3** Fourth, her *lips* are brilliantly red and, surprisingly for an oriental, thin. Fifth, the *cheeks* remind Solomon of the rounded form and russet tan of the pomegranate. **4** Sixth, the *neck*. The word *arsenal* is the difficult part of this simile. The Hebrew is uncertain. It could mean either 'armoury' from the root meaning 'edges', *i.e.* 'swords'; or 'terraces' or 'trophies' from the root meaning 'to set in a row'. In the latter case the Shulammite's neck is like a tower adorned with trophies. The whole verse indicates regality of bearing. **5** Seventh, the *two breasts* are like twin fawns 'in respect of their equality and youthful freshness' (Delitzsch). **6** is an interruption. As in 2:17, where the same phrase occurs, *until the day breathes* indicates the evening. **7** summarizes: 'you are the perfect model'. The whole passage has been used as an illustration of the fact that Christ sees His church in her final form without spot, wrinkle or blemish. *Cf.* Eph. 5:27.

4:8 – 5:1 is either a continuation of Solomon's love song or, on the basis of the shepherd hypothesis, a song by the shepherd. A third possibility, based on the idea that it is unlikely that the shepherd would be allowed into the court precincts, is that the scene is imaginary, or 'a reminiscence of the dreamy girl'. Certainly there is a different tone to these verses compared with the first half of the chapter.

8 The Hebrew order is important. *With me from Lebanon* implies 'with me and not another' which would support the shepherd theory. The true lover calls upon the maiden to leave the splendour of Solomon's northern court in Lebanon. **9** *You have ravished my heart* is a translation of only one word in the Hebrew, meaning you have 'unheartened me' or 'stolen my heart', a well-used expression of love. One look was enough to overpower the shepherd. *My sister, my bride* is a common term for the lover in ancient love songs, especially Egyptian. The twofold expression indicates an increase of affection. **11** praises the loving words of the betrothed. Her sweet words of tender affection are like milk and honey.

12 *A garden locked*. The exclusiveness of the relationship denoted by this delightful phrase has much to say to our modern situation of infidelity and disloyalty. Marriage must be monogamous in heart as well as in law. With them the gate is barred; no trespassers are allowed. RSV wrongly repeats the phrase in the next line and AV is preferred: 'a spring shut up'. The next phrase, *a fountain sealed*, is in parallel, which confirms the AV reading. Again, it indicates an exclusive relationship; not anyone may taste of her charms. But it also suggests an unceasing inner vitality of love that springs perpetually from within the young girl. **13** *Your shoots*; the expressions of her lovely personality. This phrase is the subject of all that follows in vv. 13-15. She is like a choice garden, beautifully laid out with rich variety of fruit trees, aromatic herbs and shrubs. But she is also the fresh, crystal-clear fountain in the midst of the garden; this thought is an elaboration of v. 12b. *Cf.* Jn. 7:38. *Henna*; see on 1:14. **14** *Nard*; see on 1:12. *Saffron*; The Hebrew word occurs only here in the OT. It is a substance obtained from a crocus plant and used as a condiment. *Calamus*; a spice-giving tree from Ceylon. *Aloes*; an aromatic tree, 120 ft high. Its smell is produced from the burnt wood.

16 is spoken by the maiden and is a passionate invitation to her lover to come and take possession of this garden and to make it fully his own. The invitation to the two winds, the cool north wind and the warm south wind, is given that the fragrant expressions of her personality may be carried abroad to her distant lover. This would entice him into closer communion with her: *eat its choicest fruits*. **5:1** *I come*; the whole verse teems with excitement. The invitation is accepted and the shepherd lover enters the garden and gathers his myrrh, spice, honey and milk. *Eat, O friends* is said either by the shepherd as he invites others to celebrate their love-making, or by a chorus who sympathize with the joy of the happy couple. The joy of the church's union with Christ is celebrated in the bread and wine of the Lord's Supper which speak of a love as strong as death.

5:2 – 6:3 UNTAKEN OPPORTUNITY

5:2-8 The beloved's unexpected visit

This is either a dream similar to that described in 3:1-5, or reality. Either way the verses are packed with vividness, intensity and drama. The bridegroom is first heard knocking at the door, having returned from tending his flock with his hair wet with dew; but strangely the bride at first refuses to open. This is owing either to 'the playful reluctance of love', a kind of teasing, or to sheer 'slumber, sloth and self-indulgence'. The excuses are thin: she has only just completed her preparations for the night and dare not get her feet dirty again merely to open the door. Taking the latter interpretation, it serves as a picture of man's lethargy in response to the insistent knocking of Christ. *Cf.* Rev. 3:20; Lk. 9:57-62. V. 4, however, probably indicates the former interpretation unless there has been a sudden change as she 'came to herself' for as she hears the lover trying the door her heart is pounding with loving excitement. Her dilatoriness is tragically but rightly rewarded. Love must not be played with. On opening the door she discovers he has gone. As before (*cf.* 3:1-5), she rushes out into the night, seeking, searching, asking. But this time the immediate sequence is not so happy for the watchmen brutally cuff and bruise her and snatch off her mantle.

2 *I slept, but my heart was awake* indicates a dream. Was this dream an expression of her subconscious which feared the loss of love? Such dreams are not uncommon. *Dew*; *cf.* Jdg. 6:38. Night dew in Palestine is particularly heavy. **3** *Garment*; that worn next to the skin. **4** *Latch*; literally 'hole'; through this the hand was inserted to unlatch the inside bolt. **6** *My soul failed me when he spoke*. *Cf.* Lk. 24:32. **7** *They beat me*; she must have appeared as a suspicious character, scantily clad with startled face and at such a time of night. Perhaps they had to use force in their attempt to arrest her. Again, such hindrances in dreams where desires are frustrated are not unknown, like the person who is unable to run. **8** Finally, she makes a *cri de coeur* to the women of Jerusalem. *Sick with love*; *cf.* 2:5.

5:9 – 6:3 The Shulammite answers the women's question

5:9-16 The mocking question of the harem (v. 9) affords an opportunity to describe her beloved in the kind of detail characteristic of the book. After a general introduction (v. 10) she describes him from the head down to the legs (vv. 11-15) with a concluding word on his speech (v. 16). To find detailed comparison with Christ at this point does injustice to the text and leads to an erotic appreciation of the Son of God. For a description of our Lord we must turn to passages like Rev. 1:12-16.

10 *Radiant*; Hebrew 'to glow', 'to shine'. It indicates the brightness rather than the paleness of his face. **11** *Gold*; not a reference to colour but nobility of form and carriage. *Wavy* is better than 'bushy' of AV. **12** *Doves*; the comparison lies in the movement of his moist eyes, like the dove which sips at water in the brooks. They look as though they had been bathed in milk, so pure are they and so beautifully set. **13** *His cheeks. . . . . fragrance*; his beard is perfumed. *Lilies*; brilliant red flowers. *Myrrh* refers to the perfume of his breath. **14** *Arms*; better 'hands', as AV. This is a reference to the fingers of the outstretched hands which are like cylinders of gold for their rounded form. *Jewels*; Hebrew *taršîš*, which is a precious stone, probably the chrysalite found in the town of Tarshish, or Tartessus, in Spain: referring to his finger-nails. *Ivory work*; the comparison lies in workmanship rather than colour and describes his beautifully supported body. *Sapphires*; these are part of the previous picture and need not stand for anything in particular. **15** The theme is continued in the description of the legs as *alabaster columns*, a reference again to firmness and strength. The *bases of gold* are the feet. His whole appearance is like the majestic mountain of *Lebanon*, or like the *cedar*, king among trees. *Speech*; literally 'palate' which is considered as the organ of speech. **16** *Altogether desirable*; an exact and delightful summary.

6:1–3 The question of v. 1 is in similar tone to that of 5:9. Mockingly, the women offer to help the Shulammite find her beloved. But she has no need of their help; she knows where he has gone. It was only in her dream (5:2–8) that she had lost him. Distance may separate them but love binds them. He may be in his far-off garden (v. 2) fulfilling his shepherd duties but nothing can break the common bond between them (v. 3). Their mutual love is constant.

2 *Gather lilies*; perhaps he is gathering these for a love posy. The Bridegroom of the church may be 'geographically absent' (*cf.* Jn. 14:2f.; 16:5) but the spiritual union between Him and His bride cannot be impaired (*cf.* Rom. 8:35).

6:4 – 8:14 THE KING FAILS IN HIS PURSUIT OF THE SHULAMMITE: REUNION OF THE LOVERS

6:4 – 8:4 The end of the Shulammite's stay in court

6:4–10 The wooing king enters the scene once more though his description of the maiden takes on a slightly different hue. The purity and constancy of the Shulammite has challenged and rebuked the king and his artificial flatteries. The refrain 'terrible as an army with banners' (vv. 4, 10) is the keynote.

4 *Tirzah* means 'pleasantness', a true reflection of the beauty of this city, which was the capital of the northern kingdom from the time of Jeroboam I (*cf.* 1 Ki. 14:17) to the reign of Omri (*cf.* 1 Ki. 16:23). We see little indication of the date of the poem here. *Terrible as an army with banners*. The last four words translated

one Hebrew word meaning literally 'beflagged things'. We picture troops going forth to battle with their banners unfurled. It speaks of the imposing personality of the Shulammite. But she conquers not by artificial flattery but by constancy and faithfulness. The contrast between true and false love is again in evidence. **5a** Little wonder that Solomon cannot face up to her gaze. **5b–7** more or less repeat 4:1–2.

8 *Sixty queens and eighty concubines*. The king refers to his own harem though considerably underestimates the number. *Cf.* 1 Ki. 11:3 where 1,000 women are at his disposal. The exclusive love of the shepherd stands out in vivid contrast (*cf.* 6:3). **9** Nevertheless, Solomon has to confess that never has he met with one so outstanding as the Shulammite. She is *only one* in contrast to the 60 and 80 of v. 8. *Cf.* 2:2. *Darling . . . flawless*. Her mother shared the verdict of the king. **10** The maidens of the court sing her praise also. *Dawn . . . moon . . . sun*. These 'light' metaphors point to her radiance and purity. She is *blessed* indeed; this is the same word used in the beatitudes. *Cf.* Ps. 1; Mt. 5:3–11.

6:11, 12 The Shulammite reminisces about a previous incident. Consequently, *I went down* might be better translated 'I had gone down'. She may be referring to the story of her capture. Innocently and quite unsuspecting she had gone to inspect her garden when she was whisked away by the king's men. But all depends on the translation of the difficult v. 12. *Fancy* is the word mostly translated 'soul' in the AV but it has a great variety of other meanings. Here, it is probably 'desire' or 'appetite'. *My prince* is an improvement on the AV 'Amminadab', but no-one is sure of the meaning. On the other hand she may be imagining her shepherd lover as a prince among men and in her fantasy she finds herself suddenly transported to a position beside him in his royal chariot.

6:13 It is not clear who is speaking, It sounds an odd request on the lips of the harem after their previous treatment of her. Is it then her own people in the country who long to see her back where she belongs? The fourfold request to return should be noted; it is most intense. V. 13b answers the question of 13a. Her reply indicates that she is unconscious of her beauty. What is there to be seen in her that they should gaze upon her as people gaze on some sort of show or dance. *Two armies*; literally 'Mahanaim': see RSV mg. This is probably the name of a popular dance.

7:1–5 Delitzsch and Harper take the view that the women of the harem are here praising the Shulammite on the beauty of her figure. Are they flattering her so that she will accept the king's approaches? See v. 5. The general direction of the detailed description is from feet to head. *Cf.* previous descriptions in 4:1–7; 5:10–16; 6:4–10. The women describe her either in the dressing room or as she dances. Either way it is to be linked with 6:13a.

1 *How graceful are your feet. Cf.* Is. 52:7.

Queenly maiden indicates her regal bearing. *Rounded thighs* are compared to *jewels* in that both show the mark of a master craftsman. There the similarity ceases. **2** *Your navel*. Some think that this should be translated 'body' but the RSV reading should be kept as it gives more meaning to *rounded bowl*. *Belly*; the comparison with *a heap of wheat* is either that of colour or of plenty. Easterners preferred women of fairly generous proportions. *Lilies* add a touch of beauty. **3** See 4:5. **4** *Ivory tower*; *i.e.* strong and stately. *Pools*; her eyes are clear and sparkling. *Nose . . . Damascus*. The writer seems to indicate that a prominent nose was a feature of beauty though westerners would hardly concur. But fashions in beauty vary from time to time and place to place. On the other hand 'nose' can mean 'face' and so the description may be of a courageous countenance. **5** Mt. *Carmel* was known for its beauty and nobility. *Purple*; black hair sometimes takes on a purple sheen. *Captive*; the idea of a lover being captivated by a woman's locks is not uncommon in love poetry. Harper quotes from the poem 'To Althea from Prison': 'When I lie tangled in her hair, And fettered to her eye.'

7:6–9 Very probably it is the king who speaks at this point, making his last attempt to win over the Shulammite. It is of no avail, however.

6 *Delectable maiden*; literally 'for delights'. The RSV is based on the Syriac reading. Keeping the Hebrew it could be read, as Delitzsch suggests, 'among delights', *i.e.* above all the delights and pleasures of this life. **7** *Palm tree*; *i.e.* tall, slender and graceful. It is a common figure of beauty. *Clusters*; of dates, not grapes as AV. The analogy must not be pressed too literally; it indicates just a general picture of beauty. *Lay hold of*; to secure possession of. The figure then departs from date-clusters to vine-clusters, *i.e.* grapes, which would give a nearer analogy of form. **9** *Your kisses*; literally 'palate', probably indicating speech rather than kisses. The words she whispers intoxicate him like the best wine.

7:10–13 The maiden will have nothing to do with the king's approach. **10** The Christian will echo her reply in time of temptation, when evil does its best to lure him away from his exclusive love for and loyalty to Christ. It is a mutual relationship: we belong to Him and His love is set upon us. We are reminded of the great covenantal formula: 'You shall be my people and I will be your God.' **11** From this verse the girl addresses her true love and invites him to join her as together they make their way into the environment which is characteristically theirs: the fields and the vineyards. By contrast the king's court is like a foreign country to her. **12** *Budded . . . blossoms . . . bloom*; all symbolize the new life of vitality of the spring in their hearts. It is a beautiful picture. The Christian's life should be like an eternal spring in his walk with Christ. *Cf.* Jn. 7:38. **13** *Mandrakes*; literally 'love plants', a stemless perennial of the nightshade family, having emetic, purgative and narco-

tic qualities. Here, only the delightful fragrance is referred to. In the OT it occurs only here and in Gn. 30:14–16. In addition to the new fruit the Shulammite has laid up old fruit in cupboards over the doors that they might enjoy them together. This foresight has a very tender touch and reminds us of the loving foresight of God who has laid up in store such good things for those who love Him; *cf.* Jn. 14:3; 1 Pet. 1:4. These verses strike one of the highest notes of the whole book.

8:1–4 Here the maiden soliloquizes. **1** *Brother*; only a brother having the same mother and a father's brother's son have a right to kiss a maiden among the Bedouin. The girl desires freedom to express her love and for it to be acknowledged publicly. *If I met you outside*. A public display of affection between lovers was condemned, but not so between brother and sister. The Shulammite is saying that if he were her brother then she could kiss him publicly and openly. **2** *House of my mother*; *cf.* 3:4. *Her that conceived me*. This reading is based on the Greek and the Syriac and makes good sense, especially in parallel to the previous line. The Hebrew has 'she (or you) will teach me', *i.e.* teach me how to behave decorously in such a relationship. **3** expresses the desire for intimate embrace though the verse can be translated in the present tense. See on 2:6. **4** repeats the refrain of 2:7 and 3:5, *q.v.*

8:5–14 The lovers are reunited

8:5 The couple approach their home. The question here may be on the lips of the villagers with whom the Shulammite has been brought up. The court and its luxuries and allures are now far away and she is back home in every sense. Her own folk see her arriving, supported by her shepherd lover. As they approach the shepherd tells her how he first made love to her under an apple tree in the garden of the village where she was born.

8:6, 7 Here is a moving description of love by the Shulammite. **6** *Seal*; an ornament worn around the neck so that it would be next to the heart, or a bracelet on the arm. It was a symbol of something intimately dear. So the young shepherd is to own her privately (the *heart*) and publicly (the *arm*). *Love is strong as death*; *i.e.* love is as irresistible as death. Who can resist the power of true love, for its compulsion is all-conquering? This is supremely so with the love of Christ. *Cf.* 2 Cor. 5:14; Eph. 3:19. But let not love be treated falsely for jealousy as its close associate *is cruel as the grave*. Both are all-devouring. Christ has a legitimate jealousy for His bride. *Cf.* Ex. 20:5; 2 Cor. 11:2ff. *A most vehement flame*; literally 'a flame of God'. A divine flame of supernatural power. No human power can put it out. **7** continues the image and brings us the deepest expression used of love in the whole book. Where true love exists, no opposition can destroy it. The waters of sin, death, Sheol, Satan and all the rebellion of mankind could not put out the love of Christ for humanity. But true love is not only unquenchable, it is also unpurchaseable. Solomon had made every effort to buy her love with all the luxuries of the court, but to no avail. The Shulammite speaks from experience.

8:8–10 These verses constitute an unusual paragraph but one which is highly relevant to the whole book, for it deals with the alternatives of a too easy response to love and a resistance to attacks on innocence and womanhood. Such is the theme of the whole book.

8 The Shulammite recalls the attitude of her brothers when she was young, when she was their *little sister* and had *no breasts*. *When she is spoken for* is the time of marriageable age. **9** She can in such a day be either a *wall* resisting the approaches of false love, or a *door* when she allows a man to pass through her defences. In the first case the brothers will reward her with adornment; the *battlement of silver* will be added to the wall she has built. In the second case, if it appears that she will give in too easily they will protect her themselves: *we will enclose her with boards of cedar*. **10** indicates the kind of woman she grew up to be and which has been reflected all the way through the book. When her *breasts were like towers, i.e.* when she was fully mature, her defences were like a solid wall. *Brings peace* means either that Solomon, realizing he cannot conquer her, desists from further amorous

warfare and 'calls it a day'; or that she finds peace in her exclusive relationship with her true lover.

8:11, 12 The train of thought, that love cannot be bought, is continued. Solomon is pictured as a wealthy vineyard-owner—*Baal-hamon* means possessor of wealth—who lets out his vineyard to others in return for which they each pay *a thousand pieces of silver*. By contrast the Shulammite's vineyard (*cf.* 1:6), *i.e.* her own person and love, is not on the market. *Let out* could mean simply 'give'. In that case the 1,000 shekels would be the selling price of the fruit by the recipients of the vineyard. This interpretation is less likely in view of v. 12b. *Keepers of the fruit two hundred.* The pay of those who looked after the vineyard. The true believer will yield to none but Christ; he is crucified to the world and the world to him.

8:13, 14 The book closes with a request from the bridegroom for the bride to speak so that he and his friends may hear her voice. This beautifully phrased request reflects the constant desire of Christ the heavenly Bridegroom to hear the prayers of His people. **14** is her final recorded response. She earnestly requests that he come to her with the speed and agility of a *gazelle* or a *young stag. Mountain of spices* indicates both freedom and extreme delight. *Make haste* anticipates the request of the Bride of the Apocalypse: 'Come, Lord Jesus!' (Rev. 22:20).

J. A. BALCHIN

Isaiah

INTRODUCTION

THE HISTORICAL CONTEXT

Isaiah lived through a pivotal period of his nation's history, the second half of the 8th century BC, which saw the rise of written prophecy in the work of Amos, Hosea, Micah and himself, but also the downfall and disappearance of the greater part of Israel, the ten tribes of the northern kingdom.

In 740 BC the death of King Uzziah (6:1) marked the end of an Indian summer in which both Judah and Israel had enjoyed some 50 years' respite from large-scale aggression. This would soon be only a memory. The rest of the century was to be dominated by predatory Assyrian kings: Tiglath-pileser III (745–727), Shalmaneser V (727–722), Sargon II (722–705) and Sennacherib (705–681). Their ambitions were for empire, not for plunder alone; and in pursuit of it they uprooted and transplanted whole populations, punishing any sign of rebellion with prompt and hideous reprisals.

In 735 Jerusalem felt the shock-wave of their approach, when the armies of Israel and Syria arrived to force King Ahaz into their anti-Assyrian coalition. Isaiah's confrontation of the king (ch. 7) brought to light the real issue of this period, the choice between quiet faith and desperate alliances; and the king's decision to stake all, not on God but on Assyria itself, called forth an implied rejection of him and his kind, and the prophecy of a perfect king, Immanuel, to arise out of the felled stock of the Davidic dynasty.

Israel paid for her rebellion with the loss of her northern regions ('Galilee', 9:1) in c. 734, and of her national existence in 722. For Judah, bordered now by a cosmopolitan Assyrian province (2 Ki. 17:24ff.) in the territory where Israel had always stood, there was every discouragement to patriotic gestures.

But it was a patriot who followed King Ahaz. Hezekiah (for whose chronology see on 2 Ki. 18:1) was a firebrand in whom faith and impatience took turns to kindle the flame. Much of Isaiah's energy was devoted to keeping him out of intrigues against Assyria: see on 14:28–32; 18:1–7; 20:1–6. In the end this struggle came to a head in a bitter conflict between the prophet and a pro-Egypt faction at court, implicit in chs. 28–31. The sequel was Hezekiah's revolt against Assyria (chs. 36, 37), which brought the might of King Sennacherib down upon him in 701 BC, and left the little kingdom of Judah almost prostrate in spite of the miraculous rescue of Jerusalem.

But Isaiah's dealings with Hezekiah were never confined to questions of political prudence, nor to the immediate future; and his last encounter with him pinpoints the difference between these two men of faith. In 39:5–7 Isaiah looks far ahead to the Babylonian captivity, the fruit of the king's disobedience; but the king's only reaction is relief. 'There will be peace and security in my days.' It was an understandable horizon for a monarch; unthinkable for a prophet. So the prophecy goes on to completion in the final section.

The events implied in chs. 40ff. are identified beyond doubt by the name of Cyrus (44:28; 45:1), which carries us at once into the world of the 6th century. This king of Anshan in southern Persia had seized control of the Median Empire by 550 BC and proceeded to conquer Lydia in 547, which comprised most of Asia Minor. This put him in a commanding position against the Babylonian Empire (where the Jews had been captives since before the fall of Jerusalem in 587). This Empire was in any case weak and divided by now, the king, Nabonidus, being absent from the capital (where his son Belshazzar deputized for him) and at odds with the priests. In 539 Cyrus defeated the Babylonian army in the field and his forces entered Babylon without a fight. True to God's prophecy in Is. 44:28 he repatriated the Jews (among other subject peoples) with instructions to rebuild their Temple (Ezr. 1:2–4; 6:2–5). His own inscription, on the 'Cyrus Cylinder' (British Museum), reveals that this was his general policy, in order to enlist the good offices of the gods whom he restored to their sanctuaries (see on 41:25).

A considerable number of Jews returned, but soon fell foul of the 'people of the land' by rejecting their help in rebuilding the Temple (Ezr. 4:3). The whole work came to a halt for nearly 20 years, until Haggai and Zechariah inspired a new attempt in 520, which was completed in 516. Many commentators see this situation, with its human tensions and its preoccupation with Jerusalem and the Temple, as the background presupposed in chs. 56–66. In this commentary, however, the thread that binds the last chapters together is taken to be thematic rather than historical, a preoccupation no longer with Babylon but with the homeland and the mother-city, both as they were in their imperfection and as they pointed beyond themselves to the new heavens and earth, and to the 'Jerusalem above'.

AUTHORSHIP

The traditional view

Until modern times the book of Isaiah was universally regarded as a unity, the product of the 8th-century prophet of this name. A single scroll was used for the whole of it, as we learn not only from Qumran but from Lk. 4:17 (where the chosen reading was from one of the latest chapters), and the same assumption of unity is already evident in Ecclus. 48:22–25, written some 200 years earlier. The NT fully concurs: see, e.g., Jn. 12:37–41; Rom. 9:27–29; 10:20f.

Modern criticism

Apart from a tentative query by the mediaeval Jewish exegete Ibn Ezra, whose remarks elsewhere, however, endorse the traditional view (see R. Margalioth, *The Indivisible Isaiah*, 1964, pp. 11–13) the idea of a multiple authorship of Isaiah has arisen only in the last two centuries. Its simplest, most persuasive form is the ascription of chs. 1–39 to Isaiah, and 40–66 to an anonymous prophet living among the 6th-century exiles in Babylonia. As an appropriate sequel to Isaiah, it was suggested, this work came to be appended to Isaiah's, and, being anonymous, eventually lost its separate identity.

The chief grounds of this view and of its main variants are, first, what S. R. Driver called the 'analogy of prophecy', *i.e.* the fact that prophets usually address their contemporaries (and the people addressed in chs. 40ff. are predominantly the exiles); the second ground is the distinctive style, vocabulary and theological emphasis of chs. 40ff. These will be considered later.

But in fact no scholar holds the theory in this form, for by its own principles it demands to be carried much further. An average analysis will show chs. 1–39, Isaiah's portion of the book, subdivided into a basic collection of 8th-century oracles by the prophet, supplemented by material from later disciples of various periods (*e.g.* chs. 13, 14 from the Babylonian exile in the 6th century; chs. 24–27 from perhaps the end of the Persian régime, in the 4th century). This added material, including many shorter contributions, may amount to some 250 verses of chs. 1–39 (*i.e.* about one-third), and some of the longer units will themselves be analysed as composite, with their own history of growth.

Chs. 40–66 are usually divided into two main parts: Deutero- (*i.e.* Second-) Isaiah (40–55; exilic; say *c.* 545 BC) and Trito- (Third-) Isaiah (56–66; post-exilic; say *c.* 520 BC). The former of these is generally considered a unity, the work of a 'great unknown' disciple of Isaiah; but the latter part (chs. 56–66) is most often thought to come from the second prophet's own followers, of several schools of thought, who interpreted his message to the next generation. Commentators differ over the number of historical situations and of parties (*e.g.* moralist, institutionalist, patriotic, universalist) discoverable here, and consequently in their analysis of Trito-Isaiah;

but at least four sources are commonly isolated in its eleven chapters.

It is important to realize that this suggested galaxy of authors and supplementers is not wholly arbitrary. Once the initial criteria for dividing the book are accepted, they cannot simply be discarded after the first cut; they must be used consistently (with the results we have seen) or not at all. So the attractive simplicity of a supposed two-volume work, by Isaiah and a successor, is chimerical, although the theory is usually pictured in this form. The only viable alternative to a single author is not two authors but something like a dozen.

It is only fair to add that the emphasis of critical scholars has recently been on the unity in this diversity. The supplementers are seen as a school of disciples, steeped in Isaiah's thought, and prophesying in his spirit to new generations. So his teaching, on this view, continued to put out offshoots of new growth for centuries after his death, and his name was appropriately attached to the family of writings fathered by his oracles.

An assessment

In face of the strong tradition of unity of authorship the onus of proof is on those who divide the book. Their chief criteria are not invulnerable.

'*The analogy of prophecy.*' The claim that a prophet stands not only usually but invariably within his own age and addresses his own contemporaries is contradicted by Is. 13:1 – 14:27 (to go no further afield), which is an oracle on Babylon attributed to 'Isaiah the son of Amoz' (13:1). Babylon is here seen not as the Assyrian province that she was in Isaiah's day but as the world power that she became a century later; and Israel is consoled for her long captivity there (14:1–4). The prophecy is in fact a miniature of Is. 40–48, with which it is universally held to be broadly contemporary. Further, there is more than the title-verse to mark it as Isaiah's: the whole passage (as R. Margalioth has shown) abounds in expressions paralleled in Is. 1–39 but in no other prophet. This oracle, signed and, so to speak, fingerprinted, stoutly opposes the criterion by which the many seeming anachronisms in Is. 1–39 and 40–66 are automatically ascribed to a later age.

It is all too possible, in fact, to exaggerate the degree in which chs. 40ff. are exceptional. Not only sizeable units, such as 13:1ff.; 24:1 – 27:13; 34:1 – 35:10, profess to predict or to stand in the midst of far-off events, but many smaller passages do the same (*e.g.* 4:2ff.; 11:1 – 12:6; 19:16–25; 21:1–10; 23:13–18) and are accordingly re-dated by a majority of commentators unless they can be matched to an 8th-century situation. Nor is this a peculiarity of Isaiah: such oracles are found in nearly every prophet, and are similarly criticized. The 'analogy of prophecy' by this time begins to appear a little overworked. One may add, first, that even the supreme anomaly, the naming of Cyrus a century and a half before his time (44:28; 45:1), is not unparalleled (see the predicting of Josiah, at twice this interval, in 1 Ki. 13:2); and secondly, that the power to predict is precisely the proof paraded here that Yahweh alone is God (*cf.* 41:21–23, 26ff.; 44:7, 8, 25ff.; 46:10, 11; 48:3–8; and note that 48:8 blames Israel's deafness, not God's silence, for her ignorance of the new things that were to happen at the end of the exile).

The distinctive style of chs. 40ff. would be a valid argument against Isaiah's authorship only if these chapters were addressed to a comparable situation and audience to those of 1–39. But if they are Isaiah's at all, they are the product of his old age; a message written, not preached; concerned to comfort rather than warn; directed to a future generation with scarcely a glance at the present. These are immense differences. Such prophesying may seem an intrinsic improbability (see above), but one cannot have the objection both ways. For it would be still more extraordinary (granted, for the sake of argument, that Isaiah was the author) if so radical a shift of situation, method and object were to produce no great change of thought and expression.

Certainly one might expect in chs. 1–39, if the whole book is Isaiah's, an occasional foretaste of 40ff., when the latter's themes were momentarily anticipated; and this is so. God's sovereignty in history, a major theme of 40ff., is expressed to Sennacherib in 37:26 (701 BC) in the very tone and terms of the later chapters. 'Have you not heard (*cf.* 40:28) that I determined it (*cf.* 41:4, Heb.) long ago? I planned (*cf.* 46:11, Heb.) from days of old (*cf.* 45:21; 46:10) what now I bring to pass' (*cf.* 46:11; 48:3). There is similar language on this theme in 22:11. On the 'greater exodus', ch. 35 not only matches the finest eloquence of chs. 40ff. (with which it has to be grouped to save the theory of multiple authorship) but also, in almost every verse, uses the special idioms of 1–39. Again, in the visions of ultimate concord, the passages 11:6–9 and 65:25 can scarcely be told apart. These may be comparative rarities, but they are recognizable first-fruits of the later crop.

The *vocabulary* shows a similar pattern. Isaiah's early task of denunciation called for such terms as 'briers and thorns', the 'scourge', the 'storm', the 'remnant'; but the later work of reassurance and vocation emphasized God's initiative to 'create', 'choose' and 'redeem'. His 'purpose' is seen to embrace the distant 'coastlands', the 'ends of the earth' and 'all flesh'; this naturally calls forth the invitation to 'praise', 'rejoice' and 'break forth into singing'. In these chapters the many-sided term 'righteousness' now picks up almost everywhere the colours of salvation (see on 46:12, 13), and even the subsidiary parts of speech reflect the change of subject, for the later chapters abound in those that give warmth and emphasis to an utterance: *e.g.* 'very', 'but now', 'yea', 'behold', 'together',

and the emphatic word for 'not' (Heb. *bal*)—most of which occur indeed in 1–39, but in far fewer places.

Alongside the variations, however, must be put the significant number of terms which are common to both parts of Isaiah but seldom or never encountered elsewhere in the OT. 'The Holy One of Israel' (twelve times in 1–39, thirteen in 40–66) is the best-known example. but several other expressions for God add their smaller testimony: *e.g.* the term *yōṣēr* (one who forms or designs) used with a possessive pronoun (22:11; 29:16; 44:2); 'the high and lofty One' (6:1; 57:15; *cf.* 52:13); 'the Mighty One of Jacob/Israel' (1:24; 49:26; 60:16). There are also rare or unique designations of Israel that occur in both parts, such as 'blind' (29:18; 35:5; 42:16–18), 'deaf' (29:18; 35:5; 42:18; 43:8), 'forsakers of the Lord' (1:28; 65:11), 'ransomed of the Lord' (35:10; 51:11), 'the work of my hands' (29:23; 60:21), the 'planting of the Lord' (5:7; 61:3). (These examples are taken from the fuller list of R. Margalioth, *op. cit.*) It is this large stock of Isaianic expressions that has called forth the theory (for which there is very little supporting evidence) that a circle of disciples perpetuated Isaiah's thought-forms through the centuries. It is simpler to suppose a single mind.

As to the *theology* of Is. 1–39 and 40–66, it should now be clear that these two main parts of the book face different situations and give complementary teaching. But there is more than this. As J. A. Motyer has shown ('The "Servant Songs" in the Unity of Isaiah', *TSF Bulletin*, Spring 1957, pp. 3–7), the prophecies of 1–39 lead up to the prediction of a devastating historical punishment which poses serious theological problems in view of the doctrines and promises set out elsewhere in those chapters. Chs. 40–66 are therefore more than a completion: they are a solution without which 1–39 would end in unresolved discord. And 'if a prophet can be inspired to declare God's truth in the context of history, . . . it is no great demand that he should also be inspired to find the solutions to the theological problems raised by those revelations . . .' (*art. cit.*).

To sum up: the theory of multiple authorship (since dual authorship breaks down into this) creates at least as many difficulties as it appears to settle. (It also raises questions elsewhere in the OT, where pre-exilic prophets appear to use material from this book; but this cannot be pursued here.) It makes Isaiah the author of a torso; it admits a criterion of analysis which leaves few of the prophets the sole authors of their writings; it envisages centuries of creative activity by not only an Isaiah-school but similar groups revering other prophets, whose freedom to expand or adjust their master's work compares strangely with the care, at a not much later date, to transmit it unaltered, and whose very existence is no more than an inference. It also has to account for the unbroken early tradition of Isaiah's unity, and to come to terms with the NT's apparent endorsement of that view.

Certainly it may be argued that the NT is not pronouncing on this question, but quoting without digressing; this is the opinion of many who wholeheartedly accept its authority. None the less it is a more direct exegesis, unless the objections are overwhelming, to take it that 'Isaiah' there means 'Isaiah'; and at every point this hypothesis seems to offer a similar simplicity. The alternatives (of which there are more than

we have mentioned) tend to grow more elaborate the more they are followed through; and this is not a reassuring symptom. Like the Ptolemaic astronomy, postulating more epicycles the more the heavens were explored, the theories of multiplicity tend to cover the facts at an increasing cost in complexity and the disturbance of other parts of Scripture. When this happens, it is usually time to look for a different centre and a tighter, more integrated scheme.

OUTLINE OF CONTENTS

COMMENTARY

1:1-31 A SITUATION OF CRISIS

1:1 The prophet and his period

Isaiah means 'Yahweh (is) salvation', a name well suited to the 'evangelical prophet'. The list of kings indicates that he prophesied for at least 40 years, from about 740 BC, the last year of Uzziah (*cf.* 6:1), until some point after the Jerusalem siege of 701 in the time of *Hezekiah*, whose reign continued to 687/6.

1:2-4 The great accusation

The appeal to *heavens* and *earth* recalls the parting injunction of Moses (*cf.* Dt. 30:19), to which the emphatic *sons* adds a note of personal intensity. In the Lord's direct utterance of vv. 2b, 3 (*I . . . me . . . my*) with the confirming comment of v. 4, we are already at the heart of the crisis: God's family has broken with Him. (V. 3 is still more poignant in the terse original, without the *but*. In v. 4a the sense may well be '(God's) offspring, evildoers!'—the same paradox as in v. 2b.) The title, *the Holy One of Israel*, is almost peculiar to Isaiah, with twelve occurrences in chs. 1–39 and thirteen in 40–66. Elsewhere it is found only twice. It echoes the seraphim's cry (*cf.* 6:3), yet mitigates the remoteness of 'holy' by the fact of God's self-giving to Israel. Ho. 11:9 anticipates the thought.

1:5-9 The devastation of Judah

Whether this is one of Isaiah's later oracles, placed here to open the book on a note of urgency, or whether it is a flash of pre-vision (the 'as' and 'like' of vv. 7d, 8d, rather suggest this, for the prophet seems to be describing what only he can see), either way it highlights certain themes given him at his call. *Cf.* the closed minds of v. 5a with 6:9f.; the devastation of v. 7 with 6:11f.; the sparing of the few in v. 9 with 6:13. Here is the first hint of the 'Remnant' motif, to be prominent as the prophecy develops (see especially 10:20–22).

5, 6 The picture is not of a sick man, but of someone flogged within an inch of his life, yet asking for more. V. 5a makes this point, and the symptoms of 6b are those of inflicted injuries; *sores* should be 'weals', as in 53:5 ('stripes'). **7, 8** The literal reality comes out here: it is the land of Judah trampled under foreign hordes, with only Jerusalem (*Zion*) left standing. It is evidently the aftermath of Sennacherib's invasion, which has its outline in 2 Ki. 18:13, its effects glimpsed in Is. 37:30–32, and its statistics recorded on the Taylor Prism where no fewer than forty-six walled towns are claimed as captured, together with 'innumerable villages' and a fifth of a million people. The *booth* is the field-worker's or watchman's shanty, a forlorn relic of the harvest. **9** So much for glorious Zion—within an ace of being wiped out like Sodom.

1:10–20 Pious corruption and its cleansing

10ff. To be addressed as *Sodom* was virtually charge and sentence in one. As a disaster site, Sodom meant all that Pompeii or Hiroshima have come to signify to us; hence v. 9. For ill repute it stood alone—until Isaiah spoke v. 10. He was supported by Ezekiel (*cf.* Ezk. 16:48) and by our Lord (*cf.* Mt. 11:23), who measured guilt by opportunity. Of all prophetic outbursts at religious unreality (*cf.* 1 Sa. 15:22; Je. 7:21–23; Ho. 6:6; Am. 5:21–24; Mi. 6:6–8) this is the most powerful and sustained. Its vehemence is unsurpassed, even in Amos, and the form and content build up together. First the offerings are rejected, then the offerers (vv. 11, 12); but while God's tone sharpens from distaste to revulsion, the specific accusation is held back to the final lurid phrase of v. 15, when at once the pace quickens with the rain of blows, the imperatives of repentance, in vv. 16, 17, only to throw into relief the measured climax of the passage in the great offer of salvation in vv. 18–20.

God is here repudiating not His ordinances but their abuse by the impenitent, together with the whole notion that piety and perfidy (v. 13c) can ever coexist. The reproach, 'Sons . . . have rebelled against me' (vv. 2ff.), and the charge, 'Your hands are full of blood' (v. 15), are related as organically as the two great commandments (Mt. 22:36–40); therefore repentance must be at once fully practical (vv. 16, 17) and fully personal (vv. 18–20).

18 It is striking that the great offer is introduced, like the great accusation of 2ff., with an echo of the law courts: *let us reason together, i.e.* let us argue our case (*cf.* Jb. 23:7). God must have frank confrontation; but, given this, He can change the unchangeable and delete the indelible (the *scarlet* and *crimson* were not only glaring: they were fast colours); only so can the call, 'Wash yourselves' (v. 16) be anything but a mockery. **19, 20** remind us once more of Dt. 30:15–20 (*cf.* on v. 2, above), which could almost be called the text of the discourse.

1:21–31 God's lament and resolve

1:21–23 Lost purity. 21, 22 As in a funeral dirge ('How are the mighty fallen!', 2 Sa. 1:25; *cf.* the 'How—!' of Is. 14:12; La. 1:1, *etc.*) the theme is vanished glory; even the metaphors for it tail off from the tragic to the trivial (wife . . . silver . . . wine). Only the moral loss is lamented: not David's empire or Solomon's wealth, simply their justice. **23** presents in miniature the same progression from spiritual revolt to social injustice which was traced between vv. 2 and 17.

1:24–26 Refining fire. God takes up His own metaphor from v. 22, to reveal the fiery aspect of love and the merciful aspect of judgment.

It is love, the opposite of indifference, which counts *your dross* as *my foes*; *cf.* 62:1; Rev. 3:19.

1:27–31 Destroying fire. God's line between friend and foe, the *redeemed* and the *destroyed*, runs right through Zion: not between Jew and Gentile but between converts (*those in her who repent, i.e.* who 'turn') and *rebels*. For the latter, the fire is the end, not the beginning. The key to the metaphor of *oaks* and *gardens* (vv. 29, 30) is in v. 31: they stand here for human strength and organization, which one is tempted to trust, *i.e. the strong* man and *his work*, impressive but precarious; *cf.* Am. 2:9. (It is unnecessary to see a reference to idols or fertility rites—*e.g.* the miniature 'gardens of Adonis' whose withering re-enacted the annual death of the god— although these might have suggested the unusual metaphor.) There is a modern ring to the warning that man's very skill can be his undoing, the spark (v. 31) that sets off the conflagration.

2:1 – 4:6 GOD'S JERUSALEM AND MAN'S

2:1 The new heading suggests that these prophecies may have circulated as a unit before their inclusion in the full collection. They alternate sharply between the final glory of Jerusalem and its sordid present.

2:2–5 The city of God

Here, as in the nearly identical Mi. 4:1–5, is seen the true eminence of Zion, that the Lord is in her (*cf.* Ps. 68:15, 16, where higher peaks look on with envy); and this is the only glory of the church. Her role is to draw men (vv. 2c, 3a), not to dragoon them; but their need is of God's uncompromising truth and rule (vv. 3b, 4a; *cf.* 42:4), the firm centre to any perfect circle. The idyllic close to the prophecy (v. 4b, c) cannot be torn away from the opening, or we are left with the bitter caricature of this scene in Joel 3:9, 10. So, both here and in Micah, vision issues in appeal (v. 5), not to dream of a world movement one day, but to respond in the present and on the spot.

Perhaps our Lord had this passage in mind when the first token of the Gentile inflow elicited His prophecy, in Jn. 12:32, of being lifted up (the same verb, in a richer sense, as in the LXX of Is. 2:2b) to draw all men to Himself.

2:6–9 The city of mammon

The flood of superstition (v. 6) alliances (v. 6c), wealth (v. 7a), armaments (v. 7b) and idols (v. 8), making cosmopolitan Judah anything but the light to the nations pictured just above, suggests the days of Jotham or Ahaz, early in Isaiah's career, between the prosperity of Uzziah and the reforms of Hezekiah. Thronged though it is, the land is destitute: it has everything but God (v. 6a).

6 On the reputation of the *Philistines* for soothsaying, *cf.* 1 Sa. 6:2ff.; 2 Ki. 1:2ff. **7** On the materialism shown here see Dt. 17:16, 17. **8** The word for *idols* (Heb. *'elîlîm*) is a favourite term in Isaiah, perhaps because it is identical with the adjective 'worthless' (*cf.* Jb. 13:4). **9** *Man* and *men* are translated 'low and high' in Ps. 49:2, very much as in AV, RV here; but this is to read rather too much into them. They recur, as a way of saying 'everyone', in vv. 11 and 17.

2:10–22 The terror of the Lord

The ominous refrains (vv. 10b, 19b, 21b; 11 and 17) and the immensity of the scene make this a poem of extraordinary power. It consummates Isaiah's opening vision of the Lord 'high and lifted up' (6:1), and provides the final argument against reliance on earthly might, which is a constant theme of his prophecy. The fact that 'the Lord of hosts has a day' (v. 12) gives Isaiah's preaching the same forward thrust as Paul's (*cf.* Acts 17:31)—an element the church tends to lose—and in this passage the reference is clearly to the last day, not some intermediate crisis. The apocalyptic chs. 24–27 will attend to this in closer detail.

The array of high things covers much of what we perennially find impressive in natural resources (vv. 13, 14), constructed defences (v. 15), technical and cultural achievements (v. 16; see below), and above all, in man himself and man-made religion (vv. 17, 18). But the end is more striking still, its scene of frantic haste (like that of Rev. 6:15ff.) throwing into relief the present patience of God, who could reduce us in a moment to ignominious flight and to flinging away what He has so long commanded us to put away (v. 20).

16 *Tarshish* perhaps means a refinery, and ships so named would be those built to carry a cargo of ingots. Or it may stand for Tartessus, in Spain, and for far-ranging vessels (*cf.* 23:6). The rare word for *craft* (AV 'pictures', RV 'imagery') has, it seems, the sense of 'ships', stressing in this instance their beauty, by the accompanying epithet, rather than their size. **22** is absent from LXX, but it has the same important function as v. 5, to translate vision into action. The allusion to *nostrils . . . breath* is to man's slender hold on life; it makes an effective prelude to the next chapter.

3:1–15 Judgment by decay

Here all is as beggarly as in the previous scene it was cosmic and overpowering. It is a study in disintegration, through the pressure of scarcity on a people without ideals. The scarcity, which is desperate, is twofold, of material things (food and water, v. 1; clothing, v. 7) and of leadership (vv. 2ff.). In parts of Judah the prophecy no doubt was beginning to come true by the time the Assyrians had done their pillaging and deporting (see on 1:5–9), but its real fulfilment waited a century to Nebuchadrezzar's removal of the ablest citizens to Babylon (*cf.* 2 Ki. 24:14), leaving behind an utterly weak and irresponsible régime.

2, 3 The list of leading men provides a first-hand glimpse of the society of Isaiah's day, whose respected figures included a liberal sprinkling of charlatans (*diviner . . . magician . . . expert in charms*). **4ff.** But for all the misrule of this company, worse was to come: first in sheer incompetence and resultant anarchy (vv. 4, 5), and finally in a ruin so complete that it would seem irretrievable (vv. 6–8). The *boys* and *babes* of v. 4 are a telling metaphor, like the 'children' and 'women' of v. 12; but the *heap of ruins* (v. 6) may well be meant literally. In spite of the assurance that Jerusalem would not fall to Sennacherib (*e.g.* 37:33ff.) Isaiah saw as plainly as Micah that its final glory (*cf.* 2:2ff.) would have to be preceded by destruction (*e.g.* 22:4f.; 32:14; 39:6; *cf.* Mi. 3:12; 4:1ff.). It was no part of his teaching (though this is often asserted) that God would unconditionally preserve His city.

Paradoxically, the utter defeatism which is predicted in vv. 6 and 7 is traced back in the following verses to the present spirit of bravado. **8, 9** The fine show of free thinking and moral daring described in vv. 8b and 9 not only affronts God Himself, who is the only source of glory (as the striking close of v. 8 makes plain), but leaves one ultimately nothing to believe in. After the sceptic has had his fling, he is left stranded in the wasteland he has helped to produce. So **13–15** pass sentence on Isaiah's swashbuckling contemporaries, who have set the fatal process in motion. Ch. 5 will be more explicit; it will not be more damning.

3:16 – 4:1 Silk to sackcloth

Triviality has never been more mercilessly exposed, or more abruptly overtaken by tragedy. Even the opening parade is jarring as well as absurd, against the ugly background of v. 15 which is its human cost. There is no need for caricature: the twenty-one items of finery (vv. 18–23) make a little kingdom of their own, enough to occupy the whole mind, and utterly vulnerable. The terrible transformation-scene (3:24 – 4:1) has often been enacted, and in vv. 25, 26 the fate of the individuals becomes symbolic of that of the mother-city itself—an image to be used again both of Babylon and Jerusalem (*cf.* 47:1ff.; 52:2).

Although these particular trivialities may seem remote, all generations—and both sexes—have their own solemn absurdities which can be all-absorbing. In the context of these chapters they present us with one more aspect of earthly glory, its emptiness, which must be put to shame before the glory of God. This splendour now breaks through in the following section.

4:2–6 The glory to come

The general tenor of the passage, in its context, is that salvation lies on the far side of judgment. Israel's glory must be that of new growth after destruction, of holiness after a fiery cleansing, and of God's 'Shekinah'—His manifested presence, as in the Exodus days.

593

2 *Branch* is a misleading term for the 'shoot of new growth' which is paralleled by *the fruit of the land*. The point is that Israel must be reborn: from her roots a new crop must spring up when judgment has removed all her present glory and all but a few survivors. It is the renewed community that is in mind at this point; later it will emerge that one Man will be this new growth *par excellence* (*cf.* Je. 23:5; Zc. 3:8; 6:12; and *cf.* similar expressions in Is. 11:1).

3 Notice the individualism: the new Israel will consist of the personally holy and personally saved (*cf.*, with the last phrase, Ex. 32:32; Ezk. 9:4). But **5** depicts them as a community, assembled in a very different spirit from that of 1:13, and overarched by God's glory. This glory will now rest on *the whole site*, since all are holy, not merely on the sanctuary as in the wilderness. The hymn, 'Glorious things of thee are spoken', basing one of its verses on vv. 5 and 6, rightly sees here God's presence 'for a glory and a covering' over and around His church. **6** *Cf.* 25:4, 5.

5:1-30 THE BITTER VINTAGE

A self-contained sequence, this chapter has much in common with its predecessors (for the vineyard metaphor, *cf.* 3:14; for the humbling of the lofty, *cf.* 2:9 with 5:15) and it castigates some of the social sins we have already met. It brings the book's long overture to a strong climax.

5:1-7 The parable

This is a little masterpiece. **1** Its opening, as *a love song*, catches the ear and the imagination; the *vineyard*, like the walled garden and orchard in the Song of Solomon, will surely speak of a bride and her beauty, guarded for the bridegroom. **3, 4** But the listeners are brought up short by the anticlimax and the appeal for their opinion—only to find that like David before Nathan (2 Sa. 12:1-7) they have been assenting to their own impeachment (*cf.* also Mt. 21:40–43). **7** Finally, in the original language, the charge is pressed home by an unforgettable last line, terse as an epigram. Its double word-play defies reproduction, but might be freely rendered: 'Did he find right? Nothing but riot! Did he find decency? Only despair.'

The parable brings home, as nothing else could, the sheer unreason and indefensibility of sin—we find ourselves searching for some cause of the vine's failure, and there is none. Only humans could be as capricious as that.

5:8-23 The six woes

Here 'the wild grapes of Judah' (G. A. Smith's phrase) show themselves in the plainest of terms. The woes follow one another with increasing rapidity, to give a sense of mounting vehemence, as in the *stretto* ending of 1:12-17. They are a sample, not an inventory, related to Isaiah's prevailing theme of human arrogance and its downfall; so they are predominantly the sins of the high and mighty.

The attack has all the bite of personal portraiture. Here are the great, for all to see; they emerge as extortioners (vv. 8–10), playboys (vv. 11, 12; *cf.* vv. 22, 23) and scoffers, whose only predictable values are cash ones (vv. 18–23).

5:8-10 Extortioners. The property law which Naboth defended with his life (*cf.* Lv. 25:23; 1 Ki. 21:3) has become a dead letter, but the craving for empty acres will be ironically fulfilled. **10** The *bath* was a liquid measure equal to the dry *ephah*, of about 8 gallons; the *homer* (not to be confused with the *omer* of Ex. 16:36) was ten times as large (*cf.* Ezk. 45:11). So the harvest was to yield disastrously less than the sowing.

5:11-17 Playboys. Refusal to think, *i.e.* to face God's facts (vv. 12b, 13a), is anathema to the prophets (*cf.* Ho. 4:6; Am. 6:1-7; Je. 8:7), whether it takes the form of mindless religion (*cf.* 1:3, 10ff.), sophistry (*cf.* 5:20, 21), occultism (*cf.* 8:19, 20) or the sodden escapism depicted here. The judgment of these sensualists, like that of the fashion-crazed women of 3:16ff., will be to lose the one thing they have lived for (v. 13b), and to find themselves the object of a more insatiable appetite than their own (v. 14). **14** *Sheol*: see on 14:9, 15; 38:10, 18.

5:18-23 Scoffers. Since Hebrew often uses the same word for a thing and its outcome, v. 18 may mean 'who draw punishment (on themselves) . . ., who draw retribution (on themselves) . . .' (*cf.* Heb. of Gn. 4:13; Zc. 14:19). The next verse tends to confirm this. Alternatively, the metaphor may be intentionally strange, since the scoffer in his perversity is not dragged into sin but tugs eagerly at it, makes sure of it. There are such 'fearless thinkers' in most generations, whether blasphemous (v. 19), perverted (v. 20) or calmly omniscient (v. 21). They cut as fine a figure as the fearless drinkers of v. 22 and the realists of v. 23, who know the value of money.

5:24-30 God's scavengers

24, 25 The repeated *therefore* gives a doubly inevitable note to the judgment, in terms of logical outcome (v. 24) and judicial wrath (v. 25), both of which are always present when God punishes. The hand *stretched out* to strike will be glimpsed again in 9:12, 17, 21; 10:4; so this isolated reference could be a scribal displacement, but is better seen as a shadow of the approaching storm, uniting this chapter of judgment to its successors. **26-30** The army of terrifying precision and ferocity presented in the final verses, machine and wild beast in one, is Assyria's to the life. But this power, the greatest of its day, is at the Lord's beck and call (v. 26)—small comfort to the rebel, for whom this group of chapters ends without a ray of hope.

6:1–13 THE PROPHET'S CALL

Only now do we pause for the inaugural vision, so urgent was the opening call to repentance, and so necessary the detailed scene of these chapters to show what wrung Isaiah's confession from him (v. 5) and what was the context of the decree of hardening (vv. 9, 10). In this vision, the major concerns of the book are discernible: God's inescapable holiness and sole majesty; the glory He has decreed and the clearance it demands; the cleansing of the penitent and the resurgent life that will yet break forth from the stock of Israel.

1 *King Uzziah* died after, not before, Isaiah's call, as 1:1 makes clear. If his death has significance apart from its date, it is that he died a leper, for flouting God's holiness when 'his heart was lifted up' (2 Ch. 26:16, RV; *cf.* Is. 2:17). The themes of *throne, temple,* and 'King' in v. 5, suggest to some writers a festival of divine enthronement (see Introduction to Psalms), but there is no hard evidence for it; their importance in any case lies in showing to whom all human authority must bow.

2 *Seraphim* means 'fiery ones', an epithet suited to the serpents of Nu. 21:6, 8 and Is. 14:29b; 30:6. Here these winged creatures are man-like (*cf. his feet*; 'his hand', v. 6), but the point of the description is to re-emphasize the holiness of God, in whose presence even the dazzling and the sinless are overwhelmed, fit neither to see Him nor be seen (v. 2b), yet swift to serve (v. 2, end) and tireless to praise Him (v. 3). **3** The antiphon, for all its brevity, thunders out (*cf.* v. 4) the nature, name and power of God in its first line (*hosts*, Heb. $s^e \underline{b} \bar{a}$'*ôt*, are the armies, or resources, which He commands in heaven and earth), and in its second line the scope and character of His dominion. *Glory* is the shining-out of what He is, and therefore of His holiness; *the whole earth*, not merely Israel, was made by and for this. The vast implications of it for judgment and salvation are seen in Nu. 14:21ff.; Is. 11:9; 40:5; Hab. 2:14. *Full*. Notice the variants on the theme of fullness in vv. 1, 3, 4.

4, 5 The shaking of foundations, the darkness and the dismay awaken echoes of Sinai (Ex. 19:16–18) and premonitions of judgment: see the NT's comment on all these in Heb. 12:18–29, and note the relevance of Mt. 5:8. It is integral to Isaiah's message that his words will be those of a forgiven man, himself as guilty as those to whom he will offer life or death. **6, 7** It is also characteristic that judgment is prominent in the cleansing: the fiery messenger and burning coal must have presaged at first anything but salvation (*cf.* 1:25f.; 4:4); yet they came from the place of sacrifice and spoke the language of atonement (*forgiven* is from the Heb. verb *k-p-r*, to atone). The *burning coal* symbolizes the total significance of the altar from which it came; that the penalty of sin was paid by a substitute offered in the sinner's place. The symbol, applied to Isaiah's lips, the point at which his need was most pressing, assures him of personal forgiveness.

8, 9 Isaiah's *Here I am! Send me* is doubly remarkable: first for its contrast to his previous despair (v. 5) and to the diffidence of, say, Moses or Jeremiah; and secondly for the fact that this human voice is accepted in the heavenly court. See 1 Ki. 22:19ff. and Rev. 5:1ff. for comparison and contrast. **10–13** The decree of hardening, quoted in full or in part at least six times in the NT (*e.g.* Mt. 13:14f.; Acts 28:26f.), should be read through to its conclusion in vv. 11–13, where the judgment is seen to clear the ground for new growth. Isaiah fulfilled this commission to blind and deafen by proclaiming (not withholding) the truth. God here shares with the prophet the critical significance of his ministry. Sinful Israel has come to the point where one more rejection of the truth will finally confirm them for inevitable judgment. The dilemma of the prophet is that there is no way of saving the sinner but by the very truth whose rejection will condemn him utterly. The one sign of life (*cf.* Jb. 14:7–9; Is. 11:1) is absent from the LXX, which omits v. 13c; but the Dead Sea Isaiah Scroll (1 Q ISa) supports our text, and it is inconceivable that Isaiah's doctrine of the godly remnant should have contradicted his opening commission. So the vision ends with hope: instead of the 'seed of evildoers' (1:4, AV, RV) there will survive *the holy seed*—an expression of infinite promise in the light both of v. 3, concerning holiness, and of the recurrent pledges of the victorious 'seed' in Gn. 3:15; 22:18, *etc.*; Gal. 3:16.

7:1 – 12:6 STORM AND SUN: ASSYRIA AND IMMANUEL

These chapters have been called 'The Book of Immanuel', after the promised child of 7:14; 8:8, whose nature and reign emerge in 9:1–7; 11:1–10, against a background of local menace (7:1ff.) and world-wide dispersion (11:11ff.). The prophecies arise straight out of a contemporary crisis, but they extend to the last days (9:1) and the whole earth (11:9, 10; 12:4, 5).

7:1–17 Isaiah confronts King Ahaz

7:1–9 The call to faith. The date is *c.* 735 BC, and the situation a desperate bid by Israel and Syria to unite their neighbours against the all-conquering Assyria. On Judah's refusal to co-operate, they have arrived in force to replace her king with their own man, Ben-Tabeel (v. 6).

3 Isaiah's intervention, amid the general alarm, is impressive and significant. His son *Shear-jashub* ('A remnant will (re)turn') was a living portent of judgment and salvation (see on 1:27; *cf.* 8:18); the very meeting-place would prove, one day, how fatal was the course the king was set on (*cf.* 36:2); **4** above all, the injunction, *Be quiet, do not fear* was the first of a lifelong series of appeals for trust instead of intrigue (*cf.* v. 9b; 8:12, 13; 28:16; especially 30:15). The appeal was rational enough: Syria and Israel, the *two smouldering stumps*, or 'fag-ends' (Cheyne), would soon be snuffed out. Syria was crushed in 732, while Israel lost her northern territories as early as 734, her national existence in 722, and her racial identity through a series of re-peoplings which continued to at least the reign of Esarhaddon (*cf*. Ezr. 4:2), by the end of which (669) she was indeed 'no longer . . . a people' (v. 8b).

7b–9a The force seems to be that whereas by implication Judah is under the only God, her enemies are inevitably under men—and what men; to name them is enough! **9b**, the call to faith, is the pith of Isaiah's preaching, with a slogan-like play on words, as elusive to the translator as that of 5:7. It might be paraphrased (somewhat after Moffatt): 'Hold God in doubt, you'll not hold out!', or 'Unsure—insecure!'

7:10–17 The sign of Immanuel. 11, 12 To offer any proof that Ahaz cared to name made it clear that the call to faith was (and is) primarily a call to the will (*cf*. Jn. 7:17). To wave the offer aside was to reject God flatly, but Ahaz had already made up his mind. Faith played no part in his religion (*cf*. 2 Ki. 16:3f., 10ff.) or his politics. Behind the smooth scriptural talk (v. 12; *cf*. Dt. 6:16) lay a plan to outwit his enemies by making friends with the biggest of them (*cf*. 2 Ki. 16:7ff.). What kind of friend Assyria would prove, Isaiah made clear in v. 17, reinforced by vv. 18–25.

13ff. Meanwhile God had His own sign, for a wider audience than Ahaz (the *you* in vv. 13, 14 is plural, for David's whole dynasty), and of richer meaning than a show of power. The attendant details partly reassure (v. 16), partly warn (v. 17); the *curds and honey* are enigmatic, as symbols of natural plenty (*cf*. v. 22; Ex. 3:8) yet also of a land depopulated (v. 22b) and untilled (*cf*. 23–25). But the heart of the sign is Immanuel. Who he is remains unsaid; it will emerge in 9:6f.; 11:1ff. Enough, so far, that while the king calls in an army God looks to the birth of a child (*cf*. Gn. 17:19).

How the sign fits the crisis is much debated. As a straight prophecy of Christ (*cf*. Mt. 1:22f.) it may seem too remote to speak to Ahaz; yet the sign was for the threatened *house of David* (vv. 6, 13; see paragraph above), and the very vision of a coming prince was itself a reassurance. *Cf*. 37:30; Ex. 3:12; Rom. 4:11, for signs to confirm faith rather than compel it. See also on 8:1–4, below. But God may have unveiled the distant scene by way of the near. Some suggest that the sign had immediate value in (*a*) the time it indicated (the few years from the conception of a child—any child—now, to his reaching the age of conscious choice: v. 16); or (*b*) the name ('God (is) with us') which a contemporary mother would be moved to give her son—the opposite of Ichabod (*cf*. 1 Sa. 4:21); or (*c*) the rank, if it announced a royal birth, which tends to be a harbinger of hope. (But on any reckoning this child could not be Hezekiah, born some years

before.) These possibilities are not necessarily in conflict with each other, nor with the long-term prediction of Christ.

14 For RSV's term *young woman*, AV and RV have the preferable word 'virgin', supported by LXX as quoted in Mt. 1:23. But the nearest English equivalent is 'girl': it describes a potential bride in Gn. 24:43, and the young Miriam in Ex. 2:8; it presumes rather than states virginity, and is a term outgrown at marriage. Before its NT fulfilment its miraculous implications would pass unnoticed, overshadowed by those of *e.g. a. – c.* above. (For a full discussion, see E. J. Young, *Studies in Isaiah*, 1954, pp. 143–198.) The tenses of *shall conceive and bear* are indeterminate: the Hebrew participles do not distinguish between present and future. **15** *When* should probably be 'until' or 'in order that' (*cf*. AV).

7:18 – 8:22 The choice expounded

7:18–25 Invasion and its aftermath. The two metaphors in vv. 18–20 make the swarms of looting soldiers not only an uncomfortably vivid prospect but clearly a divine scourge, a theme developed in 10:5ff. **20** On the *hired* razor, *cf*. Ezk. 29:18–20. The irony was that Ahaz imagined *he* had hired it. **21–25** The point is the sad spectacle of the promised land reverting to jungle for lack of Israelites, its abundance (v. 22) a rebuke to their sparseness, and its wild state a proof of their decline. (The 'silverlings' of AV, RV (v. 23) are silver coins, denoting the former value of the vines.) It is the kind of reproach that a failing church might receive from inherited glories and commitments which it can no longer sustain.

8:1–4 The sign of Maher-shalal-hash-baz. The sign of Immanuel (7:14ff.), although it concerned ultimate events, did imply a pledge for the immediate future, in that however soon Immanuel were born, the present threat would have passed before he could be even aware of it. But the time of his birth was undisclosed; hence the new sign is given, to deal only with the contemporary scene, and with its darker aspect. *This* child would be of ordinary birth, and by his name, 'Quick-pickings-Easy-prey' (J. B. Phillips), he would be a standing witness (*cf*. 8:18) to God's predictions both about the enemy at the gate (v. 4; *cf*. 7:16) and about Assyria's next victim, Judah itself (*cf*. 7:17). The careful attestation (v. 2) would attract notice and also confirm that the name had preceded the event. (For a later placard see 30:7, 8.)

8:5–8 God's gentle flow, and Assyria's torrent. Since *Shiloah* (*cf*. Jn. 9:7) is another word for 'conduit' (in this case an open aqueduct, not Hezekiah's tunnel, which was still in the future), it was probably the encounter with the king (7:3) that suggested this figure for God's quiet help. By calling in evil to fight evil, Judah would find herself in the path of the very flood she had unleashed; and the land she was jeopardizing was *Immanuel's*. But there is hope as well as menace in the phrase *even to the neck* (v. 8); for Immanuel's sake there is a limit set (*cf.* 10:24ff.).

8:9–15 God our refuge or our ruin. 9, 10 These splendidly defiant verses are the prophet's response to the meaning of Immanuel, *God is with us*; and to the Lord's insistence (*his strong hand upon me*, v. 11) that the people should reshape all their thinking, including their terms for things, and their emotional attitudes (v. 12), round God Himself. **12a** *Conspiracy* may refer to the intimidating coalition of 7:2; alternatively it may mean no more than 'league' or 'alliance', and be the term Ahaz was using for his siding with Assyria (*cf.* E. J. Kissane, *The Book of Isaiah*, 2 vols., 1941, 1943). If the latter, Isaiah is saying 'This is no alliance worth the name'; *i.e.* 'Don't trust Assyria or fear Syria: trust and fear God.' **12b, 13a** are quoted in 1 Pet. 3:14, 15 (which strikingly identify Christ with *the Lord of hosts*); *cf.* the call to a transformed outlook in Rom. 12:2. It is as the most solid of all realities that God is presented here: either all-sufficient or insuperable (vv. 14, 15).

8:16–22 The light withdrawn. The general tenor of the paragraph is that Israel is refusing the light (vv. 19ff.) and thereby losing God's teaching and blessing (vv. 16, 17). All they will have is signs (v. 18); all they can expect is darkness (vv. 20ff.).

But **16–18** are a kernel of immense promise. With the expression *my disciples*, God introduces a new definition of His people and their relation to Him (taken up in 50:4; 54:13, Heb.; *cf.* Jn. 6:45). These are the willing exceptions to 6:9ff.; Isaiah's responsive faith (v. 17) speaks for such, and the little group of v. 18 is seen in Heb. 2:13 as typical of the church gathered round Christ— a model church indeed, teachable, faithful, expectant, conspicuous. On the function of Isaiah's sons as *signs and portents*, see 7:3; 8:1–4. (The speakers in vv. 16 and 17ff. are evidently the Lord (16) and the prophet (17ff.); the imperatives of v. 16 are singular, and there is no individual whom the prophet could be naturally addressing. An attractive alternative to Isaiah as implied recipient of God's message might be Immanuel (*cf.* v. 8c; Heb. 2:13), but Isaiah's sign-bearing sons seem to be in mind in v. 18.)

19–22 The contrast to this godly group is very marked here. With mediums instead of prophets, gibberish instead of teaching, and the dead as guides to the living, it is small wonder that *there is no dawn*. (In v. 20, while RSV has one possibility, RV is perhaps preferable with 'If they speak not according to this word, surely there is no morning (better, no dawn) for them'.) For the prohibition of such practices, see, *e.g.*, Dt. 18:9–12.

9:1–7 The Messianic dawn

1–5 The Hebrew Bible takes v. 1 with the previous chapter, but Mt. 4:15, 16 makes it the opening of our passage. *Zebulun* and *Naphtali* are highly topical here, for they fell to Assyria within months of Isaiah's meeting with Ahaz (see on 7:1–9). So the first part of Israel to suc-

cumb would be the first to see the glory (v. 1b)— a striking prophecy which went unheeded: *cf.* Jn. 1:46; 7:52. The mounting relief and joy in vv. 1–5 as the trappings of war are abolished prepare us to meet the deliverer; but instead of some latter-day Gideon (*cf.* v. 4b) it is the *child* (v. 6) already foretold as Immanuel in 7:14; 8:8. (In v. 3 (2, MT) the Heb. text has 'not' (*lō'*) instead of *its* (*lô*). The two words, identical in sound, are easily exchanged. *Cf.* on 63:9.)

6, 7 Whereas 7:14 concentrates on his birth, and 11:1ff. on his kingdom, 9:6, 7 chiefly emphasizes his person. Other scriptures confirm that the first three titles imply divinity: *e.g. wonderful* regularly means 'supernatural' (*cf.* especially Jdg. 13:18), and it is Yahweh who is 'wonderful in counsel' in Is. 28:29. There have been attempts to reduce *Mighty God* to 'god-like hero' (*cf.* Ezk. 32:21, where, however, the term is plural), but Is. 10:21 uses the identical term alongside 'the Lord, the Holy One of Israel'. *Everlasting Father* has no exact parallel; but the poetic phrase 'everlasting hills' and the divine epithet 'who inhabits eternity' (57:15, Heb.) underline the paradox of so naming a child yet to be born. *Father* signifies the paternal benevolence of the perfect Ruler over a people whom He loves as His children. *Peace* in Hebrew implies prosperity as well as tranquillity, and v. 7 takes up the Hebrew of 'Prince' (in the word *government*) as well as 'peace', adding now the first explicit assurance that the prince will be Davidic (*cf.* 11:1). On the final phrase of v. 7, see Ezk. 36:22; Zc. 8:2.

9:8 – 10:4 The shadow over Samaria

God's hand, poised to strike, was seen in 5:25; the same threat overhangs this passage, punctuating it at 9:12, 17, 21; 10:4. While the northern kingdom is principally in mind (vv. 9, 21), the final passage (10:1–4) might well include Judah, as did 5:24, 25.

9:8–12 Judgment on bravado. To laugh off the facts (v. 10) may put heart into an audience, but it is a refusal to face what the symptoms imply. Nothing can then avert judgment. *The adversaries of Rezin* (v. 11, mg.) would be principally the Assyrians (see on 7:1–9); the pressures of v. 12 may have developed between the Assyrian conquest of Damascus in 732 and Samaria's fall in 722.

9:13–17 Judgment on laxity. Judgment begins with leaders (*cf.* Jas. 3:1) but does not excuse those who follow (v. 17). Among the former it is the prophets who earn God's contempt as well as His censure, compared, as Delitzsch puts it, to 'the tail of a fawning dog'.

9:18–21 Judgment on disunity. Sin, doubly destructive, first reduces society to a jungle, then spreads its fires through it—as our modern strifes still bear witness. But self-inflicted judgment is still *God's* judgment: vv. 19a, 21b.

10:1–4 Judgment on injustice. Not the raw passions of the earlier paragraphs but the legalized wrongs of government (v. 1) make the climax to the series. The haunting questions of v. 3 could undermine the exploits of a lifetime, all of them within the law.

10:5–34 God's axe over Judah

This is an important treatment of God's control of history, in the world at large and among His chosen people. Vv. 9–11 seem to date the oracle after the fall of Samaria (722 BC); but Isaiah's complete prior certainty of this event (*cf.* 8:4) must not be overlooked.

10:5–19 Assyria, God's tool. 5–15 The knowledge that the aggressor is wielded by God puts the question of wicked men's success in its proper context, by showing that it serves the ends of justice when it seems to defy them (vv. 6, 7), and is neither impressive in itself (v. 15) nor ultimately unpunished (v. 12). Its hollowness is self-confessed, incidentally, in the samples of Assyrian thinking: the complacency of vv. 10, 11, the pride of v. 13a, and the thief's mentality of vv. 13b, 14. The strong cities of v. 9 (*cf.* 36:19) mark the enemy's inexorable approach, preserved in the Hebrew word order, from Carchemish on the Euphrates down to nearby Samaria. *Cf.* the more localized, whirlwind advance in vv. 27b–31.

16–19 Of the two metaphors, fever and a forest fire, intertwined in these verses (Heb. has no convention against this), the former has the extra bite, perhaps, of corresponding to the actual means God would use against the Assyrian army (see on 37:36), while the latter reiterates Isaiah's dominant theme of bringing low what is lofty (*cf.* vv. 33f.; 2:12f.).

10:20–23 A remnant converted. Both implications of both terms in the expression 'A remnant will return' (Shear-jashub, *cf.* 7:3) are brought out in this pregnant passage. On the one hand, no more than a sprinkling will survive the approaching judgment or come back from deportation (vv. 22, 23; *cf.* 11:11); on the other hand, *return . . . to the mighty God* (v. 21; *cf.* 9:6) implies conversion. God looks for men who repent; whose trust, unlike that of Ahaz, is in Him rather than in man (vv. 20, 21). Such is the true Israel: it is not the whole mass of Abraham's descendants (see the allusion in v. 22a to Gn. 22:17; *cf.* Rom. 4:16; Gal. 3:7ff.). Paul not only quotes this passage (Rom. 9:27f.) but argues extensively that the 'remnant, chosen by grace' (Rom. 11:5) is a key to God's dealings with Israel and the world.

21 On *the mighty God*, see on 9:6. **22, 23** On the double mention of a *decreed* devastation, note the deliberation with which God acts throughout this chapter: see the poised hand of v. 4 (with 9:12, *etc.*), the impartiality of vv. 12, 25, the concern for simple justice in vv. 2, 22b, and the positive outcome envisaged in vv. 20, 21.

10:24–34 The aggressor halted. This is a double appeal for faith: first by recalling 'His love in time past' (vv. 24–27), secondly by depicting an Assyrian threat suddenly brought to nothing (vv. 28–34). This is pictured as a thrust from the north, covering the last 10 or 20 miles to Jerusa-

lem (but *Rimmon*, v. 27b RSV, is only a conjecture). Since the actual route of Sennacherib's force was to be from Lachish (*cf.* 36:2), southwest of Jerusalem, the aim of the oracle is not, presumably, to inform but to inspire, first conjuring up the most vivid impression of a northern foe swooping on Jerusalem (*cf.* E. J. Young, *in loc.*), then abruptly changing the scene to the toppling of forest giants (vv. 33, 34) —the distinctive judgment metaphor of this prophecy (*cf.* 2:12, 13; 6:13; 10:18, 19). It gives dramatic reinforcement to Isaiah's '*be not afraid*' (v. 24), his watchword throughout the crisis (*cf.* 7:4; 8:12, 13).

11:1 – 12:6 The Messianic kingdom

We return to the theme of Immanuel, and while the fallen fortunes of the royal house (v. 1) reveal the dark side of the sign given to Ahaz (7:13ff.), the rest is bright.

11:1–5 The perfect king. The tree, felled but not finished, makes a telling contrast to the razed forest of Assyria (10:33, 34). In 6:13 the tree-stump was Israel, living on in the Remnant (see also on 4:2); here it is the house of David, and its growing-point is one man.

1–3a *The Spirit* (v. 2), not royal birth alone, fits him for office, like the judges and early kings (*cf.* Jdg. 3:10; 6:34, *etc.*; 1 Sa. 10:10; 16:13), so that he is a Solomon, Gideon and David in one, yet not partially or fitfully endued, but abidingly (v. 2a) and richly. The gifts are threefold rather than sevenfold: *wisdom and understanding* for government (*cf.* 1 Ki. 3:9–12), *counsel and might* for war (*cf.* 9:6; 28:6; 36:5, Heb.), and *knowledge and the fear of the Lord* for spiritual leadership (*cf.* 2 Sa. 23:2). The *delight* (rather than 'quick understanding', AV) of v. 3a carries the implication that the fear of the Lord is fragrant to him.

3b–5 show these powers exercised in turn, making him the guide, guardian and example of his people. It is already emerging in v. 4b that he is supernaturally endowed, and this is clear beyond doubt in the ensuing verses.

11:6–9 Paradise regained. In this idyllic scene the title 'Prince of Peace' (9:6) is perfectly unfolded. Significantly, peace is hard-won: it follows judgment (*cf.* v. 4b) and springs from righteousness (*cf.* v. 5), true to the sequence expounded in 32:17; but its heart is the relationship expressed as *the knowledge of the Lord* (v. 9; *cf.* Je. 31:34). As a picture this is unforgettable, and expresses reconciliation, concord and trust with supreme effectiveness. The reign of Christ already produces this kind of transformation in the sphere of human character, and will ultimately change the whole creation (*cf.* Rom. 8:19ff.). Whether this will be realized literally as depicted here is another matter; it seems better to view this as an earthly expression of the 'new heavens and . . . new earth' (65:17, 25) in which variety will not be enmity, and the weak will be the complement, no longer the prey, of the strong. With v. 9b, *cf.* Hab. 2:14.

11:10–16 The great homecoming. 10, echoed

in v. 12a, bursts the bounds of nationality, while emphasizing that salvation is in only one name under heaven. This king is both *root* and off-spring (*cf.* v. 1) of the royal house: *cf.* Rev. 22:13, 16. Note the voluntary response of the nations in vv. 10, 12a; *cf.* 2:3; 42:4; 51:5, *etc.* At the same time, not all will flock to him, and it is as clear in this passage as elsewhere that those who choose enmity will find, logically enough, destruction (v. 14, *cf.* v. 4). **13, 14** The quenching of *jealousy* (*cf.* 9:20f.) is the human counterpart of vv. 6ff., liberating the combativeness of God's people for its proper use (v. 14; *cf.* Jas. 4:1, 7).

15, 16 The theme of a greater exodus is greatly developed in the later chapters (*e.g.* 35:1ff.; 48:20ff.), and that of *a highway from Assyria* will acquire a richer meaning in 19:23ff.

12:1–6 The song of salvation. After the Exodus allusion (11:16) there are appropriate echoes of the song of Moses: *cf.* v. 2b with Ex. 15:2a, and less exactly, v. 5a with Miriam's response, Ex. 15:21a.

The *anger* that overhung Israel in the refrain of 9:12, 17, *etc.* is at last turned away, and the song celebrates the end of estrangement (v. 1), fear (v. 2) and want (v. 3). It is characteristic of Isaiah that quiet *trust* (v. 2) finds an early place here, and that God's *comfort* is the sequel to captivity (v. 1; *cf.*, *e.g.*, 40:1; 66:13). But God Himself is the true centre of the psalm: God in relation to the singer (vv. 1, 2); God known by His deeds (vv. 4, 5) and His name, *i.e.* His self-proclamation (note the unusual combination *Yah Yahweh*, v. 2, emphasizing the personal name expounded in Ex. 3:14, 15; also Isaiah's special term *the Holy One of Israel*, v. 6); above all, God present in power, *great in your midst* (v. 6).

13:1 – 23:18 MESSAGES FOR THE NATIONS

For all their obscurity of detail, these chapters teach a primary and central truth: that Yahweh's kingdom is the world. This is easy to announce in general terms; to spell it out, as this section does, is to show that this sovereignty is nothing titular, but actual and searching.

The oracles were given at various times (*cf.* 14:28; 20:1); brought together they form a prelude to the world-visions of chs. 24–27, and an interlude between the prediction of the Assyrian crisis in chs. 1–12 and its onset in chs. 28–39.

13:1 – 14:23 Babylon

That *Isaiah the son of Amoz* (13:1; *cf.* 1:1) should prophesy of *Babylon* as the great oppressor, anticipating her role of a hundred years on, has important implications for the authorship of chs. 40–66; see Introduction, p. 589.

13:1–16 The day of the Lord. 2 The poem plunges straight into a battle scene, with the signals and shouts of an attack which turns out to be a wholesale divine judgment (vv. 4, 5).

3 *God's consecrated ones* are His warriors (wars were holy wars: *cf.*, *e.g.*, Joel 3:9, AV mg.) whether they serve Him wittingly or unwittingly. The term is non-moral here, as v. 16, *e.g.*, makes plain.

While *Babylon* is the focal point of the chapter (vv. 1, 19), it stands for something much bigger than itself, since the ambiguous word *earth* (vv. 5, 9), which need mean no more than 'land' (AV, RV), gives place to *world* in v. 11, in a setting of cosmic upheaval such as the NT uses to depict the last days: *cf.* vv. 10, 13 with Mt. 24:29. This is the city of man, not of one nation.

13:17–22 The overthrow of Babylon. 17 *The Medes*, as the major partner in Cyrus's Medo-Persian kingdom, were destined to conquer Babylon under Cyrus in 539 BC. Their military prowess (vv. 17f.), which overthrew the Babylonian Empire, was not needed against the city itself, taken without a struggle; but this was the beginning of the end for Babylon. **19–22** telescope a process which became complete only when Seleucus Nicator abandoned the city in the late 4th century BC, to build his new capital Seleucia, 40 miles away. **21, 22** The creatures of these verses (*cf.* 14:23; 34:11ff.; but 35:7) are not all identifiable, but are evidently repulsive and ceremonially unclean; hence *satyrs*, a kind of demon (*cf.* Lv. 17:7), is a more likely translation in v. 21 than RV mg.'s 'he-goats' (which were clean). The contrast between 'the glory of kingdoms' (v. 19) and this 'haunt of every foul spirit, . . . of every foul and hateful bird' (Rev. 18:2) reappears in the final overthrow of the ungodly world in Rev. 17 and 18—the world whose glory Satan offered to Jesus in Mt. 4:8f.

14:1, 2 The tables turned. Here is the germ of chs. 40ff., and particularly of chs. 56–66 in which the dominance of Israel is a major interest. The starting-point, as in ch. 40, is divine grace, described here in terms of emotion (contrast God's *compassion* (v. 1) with the heartlessness of 13:18) and of volition (*choose*). In this short space two aspects of the Gentiles' future relation to Israel are sketched, showing them as converts or as servants. With the resident aliens of v. 1, integrated into the community, *cf.* 56:3–8. The degrees of service glimpsed in v. 2, ranging from friendly help (2a) to bondage (2b), reappear in, *e.g.*, 66:18–21 and 60:12–14, where see comments.

14:3–23 A taunt for the king of Babylon. 3, 4a God gives the last word on the great conquerors to be spoken by their victims, not their admirers. As to the identity of *the king of Babylon*, it is clearly not the ineffective Nabonidus, the final king (for whom Belshazzar deputized), but the whole dynasty, and the kingdom personified in it. See also on vv. 12ff., below.

The two movements of the taunt-song (vv. 4b–11; 12–21), framed by their prologue and epilogue (vv. 3, 4a; 22, 23), announce their themes at once, in 4b and 12, with the characteristic cry of comparison, 'How . . . !' (see on 1:21). *Cf.* ch. 47.

4b–11 The broken *oppressor* is the first theme: his real epitaph is the unspeakable relief the world feels at his passing (v. 7). God's name for such thrusters is not 'men of destiny' but 'he-goats' (Heb. for the *leaders* of v. 9), a description almost as deflating as the pathetic state to which they are all seen to come. The royal coverlet of v. 11 is the last brutal truth for the hedonist. *Sheol* (v. 9, *etc.*) is the general term for the realm of the dead; it is not the penal hell (*cf.* AV, RV here), for which the NT uses the term Gehenna. The word for *shades* (v. 9) is of uncertain derivation (see article 'Rephaim' in *NBD*); the poetic description here and in, *e.g.*, Ps. 88:10; Is. 26:14, suggests a virtual suspension of existence; but the OT can look beyond this, on occasion, to the resurrection of the body (see on 26:19; 38:18).

12–21 The fallen *Day Star* ('Lucifer', AV) is the second theme: *i.e.* the tyrant's fatal ambition rather than his oppression. This song is often thought to tell of the revolt of Satan (taken with Ezk. 28); but this is a precarious conjecture. The tale of pride and downfall is at most only similar to what is said of Satan in, *e.g.*, Lk. 10:18; 1 Tim. 3:6, and in any case, when Scripture speaks directly of his fall, it refers to the break-up of his régime, not his fall from grace (*cf.* Rev. 12:9ff.).

Some suggest that an existing tale of the morning star, lording it over the rest and falling to earth, may lie behind this poem (there are Canaanite verbal parallels to the personified *Day Star* and *Dawn*, to the title *Most High* and to the picture of a northern *mount of assembly* (v. 13) of the heavenly court); but such a tale, if it existed, has not come to light. The idea of storming heaven, however, was certainly connected with Babylon (*i.e.* Babel, Gn. 11). One of its ironies is the idea that to be *like the Most High* (v. 14) is to be self-exalted, whereas it is to be self-giving (*cf.* Phil. 2:5ff.). The ugliness as well as the brevity of the false glory is powerfully shown in vv. 16–21.

The expression *the depths* (or 'recesses') *of the Pit* (v. 15), matching the hoped-for recesses of the divine mount (v. 13, *cf.* RV), gives an early glimpse of the distinctions within Sheol which become clearer in the NT (*cf.* Lk. 16:26).

14:24–27 Assyria

This briefly reaffirms 10:5–34, on the immediate threat hanging over Judah. **24** God's assertion, *As I have planned* . . . picks up the very word used of Assyria's own plans in 10:7a ('intend'). **25** That the enemy should be broken in his apparent moment of victory, *in my land*, is characteristic of divine strategy (*cf.* Acts 4:27f.). **26, 27** On the *hand* . . . *stretched out*, *cf.* 9:12, *etc.*; 10:13, 15.

14:28–32 Philistia

Vv. 28 and 32 bring this oracle to life. Ahaz the pro-Assyrian is dead; Assyria is in difficulties (v. 29a); now a Philistine mission (v. 32a) arrives in Zion to propose a rebellion—an idea always

after Hezekiah's heart. If this took place in 727, when the Assyrian Tiglath-pileser III died, v. 29a would have added force; but 716/15 is the more likely date (see *NBD*, pp. 217a, 220). It was as sharp a test of obedience for the new king as was that of ch. 7 for Ahaz; and the Philistines were formidable people to offend (*cf.* 2 Ch. 28:18f.) at this time.

God's reply is threefold: first, there is worse yet to come from Assyria (v. 29); secondly, Philistia is a doomed people (vv. 30b, 31); thirdly, true welfare is only in the Lord (vv. 30a, 32). It is the constant message of Isaiah: trust, not intrigue.

15:1 – 16:14 Moab

Intimate knowledge and intense sympathy, ready to alleviate judgment but powerless to avert it, are the special marks of this oracle, which is quoted and expanded in Je. 48. Moab had family ties with Israel (*cf.* Gn. 19:36f.) and particularly with David (*cf.* Ru. 4:17; 1 Sa. 22:3f.), yet it had nothing in common with Israel's faith, and appears in the OT as an evil influence (*cf.*, *e.g.*, Nu. 25) and inveterate enemy (*cf.* 2 Ki. 3:4ff.).

15:1–9 Defeat and flight. 1 The site of *Ar* is unknown; the consonants could be read as 'city', making it another term for *Kir*, *i.e.* Kir-hareseth or -heres (*cf.* 16:7, 11), Moab's chief stronghold (modern Kerak), situated in the south. With Kir fallen, all was lost, but the southward flight to Zoar (v. 5) in Edom suggests that the invasion had swept down from the north, whose cities named here (mostly on the King's Highway, *cf.* Nu. 21:21–30) had looked to Kir for a stand. **5** The anguish of this verse comes through again in 16:7, 9, 11. Sensitivity to the miseries of war (*cf.* Je. 4:19f.) and generosity towards an enemy (*cf.*, *e.g.*, Ex. 23:4f.; Pr. 25:21f.) are not uncommon in the OT, but they are seldom combined as poignantly as here. **7** The refugees clutching their treasures (*cf.* Lk. 12:21) are apparently crossing a frontier; the *Brook of the Willows* may be the Wadi el-Hesy between Moab and Edom. **9** But despite God's compassion, the judgment is from Him, and must increase: *cf.* Mt. 23:37f.

16:1–5 Moab can look to Zion. 1, 2 Moab was advised to 'dwell in the rock' (Heb. *Sela*, *cf.* 2 Ki. 14:7; *i.e.* the Edomite fortress now known as Petra), like a nesting dove (*cf.* Je. 48:28). But here God has stirred the nest (v. 2) to make her seek a better refuge as a vassal of Zion. Lambs were the customary tribute from this sheep-raising country (*cf.* 2 Ki. 3:4). The verb in v. 1 may be either 'send ye' (AV, RV) or *they have sent* (RSV); the former seems preferable.

3–5 can be taken as Moab's plea to Judah (*cf.* RSV's quotation marks), but its Messianic climax makes it more probably God's charge to His people in response to the Moabite deputation (actual or foreseen) of v. 1. Many of Isaiah's oracles arose in this way (*cf.* 14:28ff.; 18:1ff., *etc.*). It is a little classic on the 'caring church', calling it to give its mind (*counsel*), its conscience (*grant* *justice*) and its strength (vv. 3b, 4) to the welfare of these outcasts (whom God seems to name, strikingly, 'my outcasts—Moab' (*cf.* RV)). It is in key with the Messianic régime, glimpsed at the end of this neglected oracle (vv. 4b, 5).

16:6–14 Moab's pride and fall. Moab's fatal ease is captured in the vintage metaphors of Je. 48:11: 'settled on his lees; he has not been emptied from vessel to vessel'. The vine, a mainstay of his prosperity, dominates this oracle as well, with its secondary products (v. 7), exports (v. 8b) and festivities (v. 10), all of them highly vulnerable.

12 has a bitter word-play in the Hebrew of *presents himself . . . wearies himself*, and its memorable final phrase shows the bankruptcy of all pagan religion, very much as our Lord does in Mt. 6:7. **14** *The years of a hireling* mean 'shorter rather than longer', like the grudging timekeeping of an uninterested worker.

17:1–14 Damascus

This is evidently from Isaiah's early days, when Syria and north Israel were hand in glove (see ch. 7), and their kingdoms still intact. Damascus is briefly told its fate, but Israel has the brunt of the rebuke, as well as the indignity of being classed with the heathen, her oracle placed among theirs.

3b, 4, perhaps worded so as to recall the departure of *the glory* in Eli's day (*cf.* 1 Sa. 4:21), give an alarming picture of vanished beauty and, with **5,** methodical depredation. But God's plan to glean a handful of converts, worshipping their *Maker* (v. 7) instead of their manufactures, duly came to pass: see 2 Ch. 30:10f., 25. **10, 11** If this was a tragically wasteful process, these verses show that it was of Israel's choosing, in the double metaphor of the neglected stronghold (v. 10a) and the spoilt harvest (the latter depicts the farmer turning over good land to a fancy crop unsuited to it). **12–14** generalize the assurances given in, *e.g.*, 7:8; 8:4; their most striking parallel is Ps. 46, and their most dramatic illustration (see v. 10) was soon to be provided: *cf.* 37:36.

18:1–7 Ethiopia

1 The word for *Ethiopia* here is Cush, or in our terms the Sudan; but Isaiah includes the region *beyond the rivers* (*i.e.* presumably the Atbara and Blue Nile) which suggests the present Ethiopia. The term for *whirring* (rather than AV's 'shadowing') is not unlike the word 'tsetse', imitating the buzzing of insects. **2** Everything emphasizes that the envoys of this chapter are from the ends of the earth; and the exotic appeal of this fact would be enhanced by their striking appearance (*tall and smooth*—not AV's 'scattered and peeled'!) and formidable reputation (v. 2b)—for Cush had now gained control of Egypt. Yet this deputation, like the rest (see on 14:28ff.), is dismissed with God's *Go*. (AV is again misleading: its insertion of 'saying' in v. 2a changes the speaker and the sense.) **3, 4** God has no need of intrigues: He will bide His time, working as

silently as the seasons (v. 4). The enemy will reach the very *mountains* of Judah (v. 3; *cf.* 14:25), **5, 6** only to be cut down on the verge of victory, like a crop destroyed on the eve of harvest.

7 The final verse seems to look beyond the immediate crisis of Assyrian aggression which had brought the envoys to Jerusalem. Isaiah now sees the travellers in a new light, as the first of many who will come to Zion one day in homage (the Heb., lacking the word *from* in v. 7a, suggests that they will be themselves the homage gift). It is the prospect already seen in 2:3; 11:10; it will be further developed in chs. 60–62; it is expressed exultantly in Pss. 68:31ff.; 87:4.

19:1–25 Egypt

This oracle is a strong expression of the truth that God smites in order to heal (see v. 22). The initial breakdown is followed by a renewal which goes beyond anything promised to a Gentile nation in the OT. Perhaps Egypt is shown here in its two aspects: first, as the worldly power to which Israel was always looking (*cf.* 20:5), but secondly as part of God's world, for which He cares, with a place in His kingdom in which present ranks and races will be quite superseded.

19:1–15 Egypt brought to its knees. 1–4 The metaphor of God's *swift cloud* (v. 1) indicates that poetic imagery will carry the truths of this passage, in which every asset of Egypt is seen to fail. Her spiritual resources are, significantly, the first to crumble: her beliefs, morale (v. 1), unity (v. 2) and worldly wisdom (v. 3). Next will go her freedom (v 4); the *fierce king* could be one of her Ethiopian overlords, *e.g.* Tirhakah in Isaiah's lifetime, or one of her later conquerors, Persian or Greek; it could even be a native tyrant; it is the sequence, from decay to tyranny, that is important rather than an individual's identity. **5ff.** Then God touches her physical lifeline, the Nile, and one by one her industries wither. The final state is one of helpless anarchy (vv. 11–15), all the more mortifying to a nation which had prided itself for 2,000 years on the schooling of its officials. **12** *Cf.* 1 Ki. 4:30. **13** *Zoan* and *Memphis* were the current and the ancient capitals of Egypt; and Zoan (probably Tanis, in the Delta) was remembered as the scene of the great oppression (*cf.* Ps. 78:43). **15** *Cf.* 9:14f.

19:16–25 Egypt converted. The fivefold refrain, *In that day . . .* , is a pointer (as elsewhere, *e.g.* 4:1, 2) to the day of the Lord. Isaiah foresees the conversion of the Gentiles, under the image of that of Israel's most ancient oppressor and seducer (*cf.* 30:2ff.). The process is traced from its beginnings in fear (vv. 16, 17), leading to submission (v. 18) and God-given access (vv. 19ff.: 'altar' and 'sacrifice'), and right on to fellowship (v. 23) and full acceptance (vv. 24f.).

18 If the *five cities* are meant literally, we cannot now identify them. More probably the expression either means 'a few', or else (so Kissane) alludes to the precedent in Jos. 10 where the conquest of five Canaanite cities led on to general victory. *The City of the Sun* would be On, later known as Heliopolis; but the Hebrew spells it here (perhaps punningly) 'city of destruction' (AV, RV). The point, either way, is the spiritual capture of an outstanding stronghold of heathenism. **19** In about 170 BC a temple was built at Leontopolis in Egypt by an ousted high priest, Onias IV, who appealed to v. 19 in justification. But the intention of the verse is, it seems, rather to speak typically: there will be holy ground where all was once profane. With the *pillar, cf.* Jacob's at Bethel, staking the claim to God's own territory (Gn. 28:13, 18).

23–25, reaching out with the other hand to embrace *Assyria* as well—so often coupled with Egypt in the worst of contexts (*cf.* Ho. 7:11; 9:3) —give an unsurpassed vision of the Gentiles' full inclusion in the kingdom. Israel will have only an equal part (a *third*, v. 24; but not third place), and her distinctive titles will be shared out with her cruellest enemies: *my people, cf.* Ho. 2:23; 1 Pet. 2:10; *the work of my hands, cf.* Is. 29:23.

20:1–6 The Ashdod crisis

An inscription by Sargon fills out this picture. The Philistine city of Ashdod had revolted against Assyria, which promptly deposed its king. A new ringleader, Yamani, carried on the struggle, with pledged support from Egypt and Ethiopia, and had also approached Judah. Isaiah's powerful dissuasion turned out to be fully justified: Egypt failed to fight, Ashdod was subjugated, and Yamani, who had fled to Ethiopia, was handed over to the Assyrians' tender mercies.

1–3 The title, *commander in chief*, is *turtanu* in Assyrian; hence AV, RV, 'Tartan'. The year was 711; the revolt had broken out in 713, and Isaiah's slave garb (*naked* would mean clad only in a loincloth) had been adopted then, unexplained, as v. 3 shows. (V. 2 is a parenthesis; see RSV.) The *sackcloth* was perhaps the rough garment distinctive of a prophet: *cf.* Zc. 13:4.

Since Judah was left unpunished by Assyria, it seems that the warning was taken. G. A. Smith points out that this sign language (*cf.* 8:18) brought the message home to the nation, not merely to the court. Isaiah's discomfort and humiliation were the price of his people's safety.

21:1–10 Babylon, 'The wilderness of the sea'

This oracle, like the next, has a strongly visionary quality (in the 'Watchman' metaphor) and a symbolic title. The subject emerges in v. 9 as the fall of Babylon; **1** the phrase *wilderness of the sea* seems to combine two pictures of nature untamed and encroaching, which are more explicit in Je. 51:42, 43. But the same consonants could yield simply 'wildernesses', or possibly (Kissane) 'destroyers'.

2–7 A disjointed, vivid picture builds up of an attack by the Persians (*Elam*) and Medes (v. 2) which will catch the defenders of Babylon unprepared and feasting (v. 5), just as Dn. 5 records

of them. But Isaiah's involvement in the vision is its most striking feature. His great agitation in vv. 3, 4 is akin to Jeremiah's in Je. 4:19ff., even though the fall of this persecuting city, this place of *sighing* (v. 2), is the thing he has *longed for* (v. 4). But these opposite reactions throw incidental light on the writing of the later chapters, in that they are the very feelings of one to whom (as to the exiles) Babylon seemed both prison and home. If Isaiah was indeed to 'speak to the heart' (40:1) of a later generation, as if he were himself one of them, this deep involvement is clearly a prerequisite; it is the inner side of his prophesying. Note, too, his dual consciousness: he stands in some sense apart from his *watchman* self (v. 6), and must report only what he sees and hears (*cf.* Hab. 2:1–3). This objectivity is greatly stressed (vv. 6, 7, 10).

In **8a** (charmingly inconsequent after v. 7, in the standard text; see AV) RSV justifiably follows the Qumran MS. The prophet, just when his vigil appears endless, sees the promised cavalcade, and knows that it spells the end of Babylon. Rev. 18:2 takes up the cry of '*Fallen, fallen*', and treats Babylon as typical of the godless world. **10** The final phrase of the passage, *my threshed and winnowed one*, captures not only the agony, but the purpose, of Israel's long ordeal.

21:11, 12 Dumah

The place-names belong to Edom, but the title *Dumah* (*cf.* Gn. 25:14) may have been chosen for its ominous meaning, 'silence'. The point of the question is 'how long till morning?'—reflecting a time of suffering. The reply is not a platitude but a warning that any respite will be only temporary. *Cf.* Pr. 4:18,19. The three imperatives translated *inquire; come back again*, can be taken at their surface meaning or, more deeply, as the basic divine call: 'Seek, repent, come'. Edom's answer can be gathered from, *e.g.*, 34:5ff. and from Obadiah.

21:13–17 Arabia

13 The early versions read the second *Arabia* as 'evening', which has the same consonants. Possibly there is a *double entendre*: *cf.* v. 11 and the symbolic titles in 21:1; 22:1. The special significance of this oracle lies in its warning to the freest and most inaccessible of tribes that Assyria's long arm will reach even them, at God's command. Those of the far south, Tema and Dedan, will have to succour their more exposed brother-tribe of Kedar. This could mean that the trading caravans will have blundered into war-ravaged parts and returned empty-handed and starving; but Sargon's recorded invasion of Arabia in 715 BC makes it more likely that the fugitives will have been under direct attack. **16f.** *Cf.* 16:14 and comment.

22:1–25 Jerusalem

22:1–14 'The valley of vision'. 1 The symbolic title (*cf.* on 21:1, 11, 13) emphasizes that the prophet's own base, from which he has surveyed the nations, is not exempt from judgment. *Valley*, borrowed from v. 5, may refer to Jerusalem as surrounded by mountains (*cf*. Ps. 125:2), or to some more localized spot (*cf*. Joel 3:12, 14).

2ff. There is a clear contrast between the city's gaiety (vv. 2a, 13) and its grim future. It is not so clear whether the revels are in progress as Isaiah speaks (perhaps after the retreat of Sennacherib, 37:37) or whether we should supply a past verb in v. 2a: 'you who were full . . .', as in the lament of 1:21 (as Kissane suggests). Either way, Isaiah alone sees where this escapism, which is summed up for all time in v. 13b (*cf*. 1 Cor. 15:32), will end.

With characteristic long sight (*cf*. 21:1–10) he foretells the fall of Jerusalem a century away (586), with its famine casualties (v. 2b; *cf*. La. 4:9), its fugitive leaders (v. 3; *cf*. 2 Ki. 25:4f.) and its houses torn down to strengthen the wall (v. 10; *cf*. Je. 33:4). The part played in this by warriors from *Elam* and *Kir* (v. 6) is not mentioned elsewhere; but Kir was in the Assyrian Empire (*cf*. 2 Ki. 16:9), and contingents or mercenaries from these outposts could well have been part of the Assyrian legacy to Nebuchadrezzar.

8–14 For the *house of the forest* as an armoury (v. 8), see 1 Ki. 10:17; for the water supply (vv. 9, 11) *cf*. the preparations by Ahaz and Hezekiah (7:3; 2 Ki. 20:20) in Isaiah's own day. The *two walls* (v. 11) were probably, as J. Gray suggests (on 2 Ki. 25:4), 'the convergence of the walls round the south-eastern hill, with an extension to include both pools'.

Note, in all this, that Jerusalem oscillated between activism (vv. 9–11) and escapism (vv. 12–14); the former was a denial of faith (v. 11b), the latter a denial of repentance. The words of 11b (and of 37:26) are a striking anticipation of chs. 40–66, where God is repeatedly named as (lit.) 'making and shaping' (*who did . . . who planned*), and as doing so from of old. *Cf*. 44:2, 24; 43:7, *etc*. It is another hint of single authorship: see Introduction, pp. 589f.

22:15–25 'This steward, . . . Shebna'. This high official appears again, with Eliakim (*cf*. v. 20), in 36:3ff.; 37:2ff. Possibly he was the leader of the pro-Egypt party (see chs. 30, 31) which scoffed at Isaiah's preaching; but his condemnation here is simply for arrogance and display. Every nuance in God's message to him is scornful, from 'this steward' (v. 15) to 'you shame . . .' (v. 18); it exposes the human craving for recognition and power (and the worldly love of status symbols (tomb and chariots) and the trappings of office, all of them mere husks. A large tomb-lintel of just such an official, describing him as 'over the house' (*cf*. v. 15), has been found and could be Shebna's; but a mortice hole has destroyed the name (see D. J. Wiseman, *Illustrations from Biblical Archaeology*, 1958, pp. 59, 60).

20ff. *Eliakim* stands in strong contrast to Shebna, over whom he seems to have been promoted when they reappear in 36:3ff. Godward he is called *my servant* (v. 20; *cf*. 'this steward',

v. 15); manward, he will be *a father* to his community (v. 21). Yet his downfall (vv. 24, 25) will come from this very paternalism wrongly exercised: *i.e.* from his inability to say 'no' to any 'hanger-on' from his family who claims his patronage. However well intentioned, this is an abuse of his office, and God's firmest pledges are never guarantees to cover this. With the sequence of vv. 23 and 25, *cf*. 1 Sa. 2:30; Je. 22:24; Rev. 2:1, 5.

22 *The key of . . . David* comes in this context of accountability. A key was a substantial object, tucked in the girdle or slung over the shoulder, but the opening words of v. 22, with their echo of 9:6, emphasize the God-given responsibility that went with it, to be used in the king's interests. The 'shutting' and 'opening' mean the power to make decisions which no-one under the king could override. This is the background of the commission to Peter (*cf*. Mt. 16:19) and to the church (*cf*. Mt. 18:18)—with the warning against abuse implied above. Ultimate authority, however, is claimed, in these terms, for Christ Himself (*cf*. Rev. 3:7, 8).

23:1–18 Tyre

Tyre, 'the merchant of the nations' (v. 3), had a longer reach than even Babylon: her traders were known from the Indian Ocean (*cf*. 1 Ki. 10:22) to the English Channel. Rev. 17 and 18 combined the OT oracles on Tyre and Babylon (*cf*. Ezk. 27; Is. 14) for the composite picture of the world as seducer (*cf*. v. 17) and oppressor, over against the city of God.

23:1–14 The repercussions and reasons of her fall. The news is pictured as reaching her ships at Cyprus, her nearest colony (v. 1; see on 2:16 for *Tarshish*), leaving them homeless; as making the sea itself seem childless for lack of her merchantmen (v. 4); as striking dismay into Egypt (v. 5) and as scattering the people of Phoenicia to distant Tarshish (v. 6) or nearby Cyprus (v. 12).

Tyre's colonizing, a development of her trading, is the reference of v. 8; and the obscure v. 10 may picture a distant colony breaking out into anarchy at the parent city's collapse. *Canaan* is used in v. 11 as the name of Tyre and Sidon's home territory, a term which spread to embrace all Palestine; the word *traders* in v. 8, closely related to it, shows how synonymous was the name of her realm with that of business.

The human cause of the overthrow seems in v. 13 to be Chaldaea rather than Assyria, both of which powers subjugated Tyre in part. (Later, the Greeks, and later still the Saracens and the Crusaders, captured and recaptured it.) But the root cause is sought in v. 8 and answered in v. 9: *Who has purposed this . . . ? The Lord of hosts . . .* It is a particular instance of His judgment on *pride* wherever it appears, which is one of the great themes of this book: see on 2:10–22.

23:15–18 Her old appeal renewed. 15 As a fact of history, after each disaster (until the Middle Ages) Tyre recovered after an interval and resumed her trading. The *seventy years* seem to be a round figure to denote a lifetime, like the 'seventy years' of Jewish captivity. But the metaphor of the forgotten harlot (vv. 15–17) makes the renewal at once pathetic and corrupting; we are shown the perennial seductiveness of things material, although the final verse claims them for their proper use. It is the twofold emphasis of Rev. 18:3 and Rev. 21:24.

24:1 – 27:13 GOD'S FINAL VICTORY

After the separate nations (chs. 13–23), now the world as a whole comes into view. These four chapters, often loosely known as the 'Isaiah Apocalypse', show the downfall of supernatural as well as earthly enemies (24:21f.; 27:1), and of death itself (25:8); they contain (26:19) one of the two clear promises in the OT of bodily resurrection. But this wider scene is still viewed from Isaiah's own vantage-point of Jerusalem, with Judah, Moab (25:10ff.) and the great powers of Egypt and Assyria (27:12f.) in the near and middle distance. Overwhelming as the judgments are, the dominant note is of joy, welling up in the songs which frequently break into the prophecy.

24:1–23 Earth and heaven judged

24:1–13 Humanity in chaos. The powerful word-painting is reinforced by repetitions, rhymes and word-plays. **1** The word *twist*, or better 'distort', is a sounder translation than 'turneth . . . upside down' (AV, RV); *cf.* the Jerusalem Bible's vivid term 'buckle'. **5** The reason for the judgment emerges (notice the double 'therefore' of v. 6) in man's flouting of all laws and obligations. Whether the *everlasting covenant* is the divine promise to all living things in Gn. 9:9ff. is not certain beyond all doubt, since the expression in v. 5 could mean simply 'the most permanent of undertakings'; but notice the reference to the Flood in v. 18b. **7ff.** The emphasis on joylessness is a striking comment on what Heb. 11:25 calls 'the fleeting pleasures of sin', and the term *the city of chaos* (Heb. *tōhû*, v. 10; *cf.* Gn. 1:2) is a witness to sin's regressive action, turning God's order back to formlessness. The one ray of hope is the mention of *gleaning* (v. 13), the leaving of a 'few' (v. 6), as in 17:6 and in the explicit 'Remnant' passages, *e.g.* 10:20ff.

24:14–16 Ultimate praise, and present privation. The singing seems to come from the scattered remnant (see on v. 13), which in the light of the gospel can be seen to be God's Gentile as well as Jewish people (*cf.* Jn. 11:52). The expression *in the east* (v. 15) is literally 'in the lights' (hardly 'fires', AV); the translation is supported by the matching phrase *from the west* (v. 14). But this is a foretaste; we are back in the straitened present in v. 16 (*cf.* the same metaphors in 17:4–6).

24:17–23 Cosmic judgment. 17 The first three nouns, strikingly alike in the original, hammer

home the relentlessness of the judgment. **18a** With the unavailing flight, *cf.* Am. 5:19. (**18b** For the background see on v. 5.) **21, 22** *The host of heaven* (lit. 'of the height') would mean in some contexts merely 'the stars' (*cf.* 40:26); but here, as counterparts of *the kings of the earth*, sentenced to be imprisoned and *punished* (*cf.* 2 Pet. 2:4), they are clearly 'the spiritual hosts of wickedness in the heavenly places' (Eph. 6:12). The fullest OT reference to such beings is in Dn. 10:2–21; *cf.* perhaps Ps. 82. In the NT see further, *e.g.*, Rom. 8:38f.; Col. 2:15; Rev. 12:7ff. **23** But the end is sheer glory. If *sun* and *moon* are to lose their lustre, it is only as outshone by light itself, by the Lord reigning in full state. It is essentially the same vision as Rev. 21:22ff.

25:1–12 The great liberation

25:1–5 The end of tyranny. This song breaks out unannounced (unlike those of v. 9; 26:1ff.; 27:2ff.), and by its reiteration of the word 'ruthless' (vv. 3, 4, 5) it voices the special suffering and corresponding gratitude of the weak and hard-pressed. It is an OT Magnificat. **1** Two of the characteristics of God's working ('wonderful things', 'counsels', AV, RV) have already appeared in the names of the promised king (9:6), and will recur in 28:29. On the long maturing of His plans (*of old*), a favourite emphasis in Isaiah, see on 22:11. **2–5** The song accordingly celebrates not only the victory to come (when the enemy's defences will be down, v. 2, his homage received, v. 3, and his clamour silenced, v. 5) but the refuge already to be found in God while evil does its worst (v. 4)—its assault pictured in terms of nature's extremes of driving rain (*storm*) and overpowering heat.

25:6–8 The end of darkness and death. 6 The *feast* introduces a positive note into what is otherwise chiefly an account of ills removed. It has the note of achievement (for a feast is a celebration), of plenty (v. 6b), and of shared delight (note the fourfold *all* in vv. 6–8). Our Lord relished this festive prospect even as He handed a very different cup to His disciples: *cf.* Mt. 26:29.

7 The *covering* or *veil* could be either the mourning (v. 8b) or the blindness (*cf.* 2 Cor. 3:15) of fallen man; both are apposite. **8a** The translation *for ever* is the most straightforward (*cf.*, *e.g.*, 28:28), but the root does also contain the idea of 'victory' (AV; *cf.* 1 Cor. 15:54) or pre-eminence, and is so used in 1 Sa. 15:29 where it appears as 'Glory', and as 'victory' in 1 Ch. 29:11. In either sense, the promise is one of the glories of the OT and the NT. In one verse (*cf.* also Rev. 7:17) the last enemy is gone and the last tear shed.

25:9–12 The end of pride. 9 belongs to the preceding paragraph as well as to this one; but perhaps the conjunction 'for' (v. 10) unites these verses a little more closely. There is a hint of tense expectation, rather than mere passivity, in the verb used for *waited*; *cf.* 26:8; 33:2; 40:31; 49:23b. **10** *Moab*, startlingly local in so universal a scene (*cf.* Edom in 34:5), is introduced as the embodiment of pride (v. 11b; *cf.* 16:6), perhaps especially the pride of little men. The *dung-pit* likewise expresses the indignity as well as the finality of judgment for the proud; *cf.* the sequence in 14:14, 15, 19.

26:1 – 27:1 Triumph after travail

26:1–6 The enduring city. At last our own city comes into view, over against its rival. The latter has a new epithet, 'lofty' (v. 5), to add to those of 24:10 ('chaos'), 25:2 ('fortified'), 25:3 ('cities of ruthless nations'); **1** but our city is *strong*, not with brute force but with the saving activity (1b) of the living God, the 'Rock of ages' (v. 4, AV, RV, mgs.). So our enjoyment of its *walls and bulwarks* depends on our response to Him in truth (v. 2) and trust (vv. 3, 4). **3** The primary stress is on the *mind* (better, the will) *stayed* on God. *Perfect peace* is lit. 'peace, peace', and means positive well-being, not merely lack of strife. *Trusts* is passive here (but active in v. 4), with the sense, 'he is cast upon thee'. **5** Note the levelling of the *lofty*, one of Isaiah's most constant themes from 2:12 onwards.

26:7–18 The long night of waiting. The 'waiting' in this passage is partly for the overthrow of evil by the correction (vv. 9–11) or destruction (vv. 11c, 13ff.) of the wicked, but is fundamentally a longing for God Himself ('for thee . . . for thee', vv. 8, 9). **7** RSV's *level* and *make smooth* are misleading, for the context is anything but easygoing. The verse should run: '. . . is straight; thou dost ponder the path . . .' (*cf.* Pr. 5:6). **8** *Thy memorial name* should be 'thy name and thy memorial', *i.e.* the proclamation of the name, which could be a moving experience in public worship (*cf.* Ps. 34:3; 68:4). The last phrase of v. 13 alludes to this, and scorns the tyrants who have trespassed on the crown rights of Yahweh. **14** That these are earthly overlords, not false gods, is proved by 14a (see on 14:9 for the term *shades*). It is a prediction so certain of fulfilment as to use the past tense (the 'prophetic perfect').

16–18, with their confession of failure and frustration (all too applicable to the Christian church), give another ingredient of this general yearning for better things. There is a similar outburst in the third 'Servant Song', 49:4. Here, as there, God's answer lifts the situation on to a new plane altogether, which is the subject of the next paragraph.

26:19 – 27:1 Resurrection and final judgment. After the prayer of vv. 7–18, the Lord now gives His answer. **19**, though obscure in details, clearly promises bodily resurrection. Its companion statement, Dn. 12:2, adds two further prospects: the resurrection of the unjust, and an eternity of life or shame. Read, with RV, 'my dead bodies' (keeping the Heb. consonants intact, unlike RSV)—for God's servants are still *His* in death, even to their bodies. *Dew of light* (the freshness and promise of dawn; *cf.* Ps. 110:3b) is more probable than 'dew of herbs' (AV, RV), though

either is possible. The last line could be rendered as in RSV, or as in AV, RV, or else, with Kissane, 'thou wilt subdue the land of shades'. On *shades*, see on 14:9.

20 reproduces the same pattern of salvation within judgment as was seen when the Lord shut Noah in the ark, and when Israel in Egypt was directed to take refuge from the destroying angel (Ex. 12:22). **21; 27:1** The judgment is as all-embracing as in 24:21, where 'the host of heaven' corresponds to *Leviathan* here (*cf.* 'the dragon and his angels' in Rev. 12:7ff.). The unusual epithets, *fleeing*, *twisting*, are exactly the terms used of Leviathan (Lotan) in the ancient Canaanite epic of Baal, where the *dragon* and the *sea* are also vanquished. (*Fleeing, i.e.* 'elusive', is a more likely translation than 'prim-aeval' or 'evil', which have been proposed from other roots.) This Canaanite material is reshaped to the divine truth it now conveys—truth which demolishes its pagan structure. Both here and at 51:9f. the context is judgment, not (as in paganism) a supposed struggle in which, before he could proceed to his desired task of creating an ordered world, the creator-god first disposed of the opposition of the gods of disorder.

27:2–13 A people for God

27:2–6 The fruitful vineyard. The loving care (vv. 2ff.) and teeming fruitfulness (v. 6) must both be seen against the setting of ch. 5, the vineyard that failed and was abandoned. Here is the end to which God has been working. **4, 5** These cryptic verses may be understood to mean that God's wrath is no longer against His vineyard, only against the *thorns and briers* (that is, His people's enemies) which overran it in 5:6; and even these antagonists He would rather reconcile than destroy. **6** The *fruit* which will benefit the world is interpreted in 5:7 as justice and righteousness. Note the reminder, as in 37:31, that morally as well as physically, *root* is the precondition of *fruit*.

27:7–11 Fruitful hardship, fruitless power. This section brings out the contrast between the measured hardship which would be the making of Israel (vv. 7–9), and the utter disaster which would break the tyrant (vv. 10, 11).

8 *Measure by measure*: this unique word may mean literally 'by a seah, a seah', *i.e.* carefully meted out, gallon by gallon; or possibly, 'by shooing them away' (*cf.* the next word, which RSV rightly interprets as *by exile*, of which AV makes no sense). In v. 8b, AV's translation cannot be upheld. **9** The renouncing of idolatry is shown as both the condition (*by this*) and the continuing consequence (*the full fruit*) of enjoying God's atonement (*cf.* Pr. 16:6). If exile is a step towards this, it will not be in vain. **10, 11** *The fortified city* is clearly the oppressor's (*cf.* 25:2). Here the description in vv. 10b, 11a is perhaps coloured by the contrasted picture of the well-tended vineyard of vv. 2, 3. With v. 11b, *cf.* 44:18f.; 45:6f.

27:12, 13 Harvest home. The harvest depicted

is that of orchard and vineyard, rather than cornfield, since the gleaning (*one by one*) comes after, not before, the beating, as Kissane points out. *Thresh out* should therefore be 'beat off' (the fruit), as in AV, RV. The two verses show the Lord's final triumph, in terms not of conquest or new creation (as it can be pictured) but simply of persons gathered in and brought home. This is, after all, the heart of the matter (*cf.* Rev. 7:9ff.).

28:1 – 31:9 THE ASSYRIAN CRISIS: GOD'S HELP OR MAN'S?

28:1–29 A challenge to scoffers

Ch. 28, a series of lightning flashes rather than a scene steadily illuminated, challenges the triflers who govern Jerusalem to face the realities of history, of morals and of divine action. Snatches of a fierce altercation seem to be preserved in vv. 7–13 or beyond. The setting is the restless period of intrigue with Egypt which led to Hezekiah's revolt against Assyria and the reprisals of 701 BC described in chs. 36, 37; but the prophecies frequently break out of these narrow confines.

28:1–6 The drunkards of Ephraim. This is clearly an early prophecy, before the fall of Samaria in 721. For its function in this context, see on vv. 7–13, below. **1–4** It catches the outward beauty of that affluent city set on a hill, but sees it as a garland on a drunkard's brow (v. 1b) —a rich metaphor for glory that is incongruous and (v. 4a) quickly fading. The second of these aspects is re-emphasized by the hailstorm threat of v. 2 (a reference to Assyria), to be taken up in v. 17, and by the 'ripe plum' metaphor, as we should put it, of v. 4b. In a single paragraph Isaiah has epitomized the warnings of Amos to this pleasure-loving, drink-sodden city (*cf.* Am. 2:12; 4:1; 6:6). **5, 6** Characteristically, the clouds part for a moment to show the true *diadem* adorning the true Israel, the *remnant* (see on 10:20–23). Notice that *the spirit of justice . . . and strength* (see on 11:2) is *the Lord* Himself, present and active within a man.

28:7–13 The drunkards in office. 7, 8 In the words *these also*, the relevance of the foregoing oracle to its present context becomes clear. The besotted Ephraim had come to grief; now Judah is just such another, from her spiritual leaders downwards. The reeling, vomiting *priest and . . . prophet* are so vividly drawn that this section is thought to preserve an actual encounter between Isaiah and a group of them in conclave.

9–13 In that case vv. 9, 10 may be their taunt (*he . . . he* being Isaiah), and v. 13 his ominous rejoinder, flinging the same words back. The Hebrew of v. 10 is a jingle, almost the equivalent of our derisive 'blah blah', but not quite as meaningless. (For *line, cf.* v. 17a.) *Cf.* J. B. Phillips: 'Are we just weaned. . . . Do we have to learn that The-law-is-the-law-is-the-law, The rule-is-the-rule-is-the-rule . . . ? . . . Yes, with stuttering lips and a foreign tongue will the Lord speak to this people.' *I.e.* make nonsense

of God's sense, and you will get your fill of it from Assyria (v. 11), and your doom from the words that were to save you (vv. 12, 13). The rejected message of v. 12 finds classic expression in 30:15; *cf.* on 7:9b. Paul's quotation of v. 11 in 1 Cor. 14:21 is thus a reminder, true to this context, that unknown tongues are not God's greeting to a believing congregation but His rebuke to an unbelieving one (*cf.* C. Hodge on 1 Corinthians).

28:14–22 The sure foundation and the refuge of lies. 15, 16 As in 8:11–15, but now in a setting of reckless confidence, *covenant* and *cornerstone* are in contrast. The *covenant with death, and with Sheol*, could perhaps allude to an invocation of gods of the underworld, *e.g.* in necromancy (*cf.* 8:19) or in a treaty with Egypt, but is more probably to be understood like the boast in v. 15b of *lies* and *falsehood*; *i.e.* as God's estimate of their hope, put into their mouths. Their version would have been, no doubt, 'Nothing can touch us; our alliances are watertight.' God knew their real enemy, and their professed friends. The *cornerstone* promise, with that of 8:14, is quoted in Rom. 9:33; 1 Pet. 2:6; *cf.* Ps. 118:22. In Is. 8:14 it explicitly signifies the Lord, but here the Lord lays the stone; the two statements meet in Christ, as the NT makes clear. Rom. 9:32, 33 expounds the implications of the faith clause (*cf.* 7:9), *he who believes . . .* (possibly the implied inscription on the stone; *cf.* RSV), and uses LXX's exposition of *will not be in haste, i.e.* 'will not be put to shame'. *Cf.* 49:23b, and by contrast, 30:3, 5. Haste implies anxiety and confusion.

Among the profusion of metaphors, those of storm and flood have appeared in v. 2, to signify the Assyrians; **17** the *line* and *plummet* recall the finality of 30:13f. and of Am. 7:7f.; **20** the scanty *bed* and *covering* say the last word on resources that miserably fail. **21** On *Perazim* and *Gibeon* see 1 Ch. 14:11, 16. God who swept away David's enemies will now sweep away David's kingdom. On such *strange* reversals the next paragraph will have light to shed. Luther, incidentally, found much comfort in reflecting that while judgment is Christ's *strange . . . work*, salvation is His 'proper work'.

28:23–29 The farmer's craft: a parable. The farmer's constant changes and his varieties of treatment, so capricious at first sight yet so expertly appropriate, give the clue to the complex ways of God, who is his teacher (vv. 26, 29). God's strangest work (*cf.* v. 21) is exactly suited, it is implied, to the varied times (v. 24), types (v. 25) and textures (vv. 27, 28) that He handles. **29** Notice the linking of *wonderful* and *counsel*, as in the name of the divine prince of 9:6, and as in 25:1.

29:1–8 A last-minute reprieve for 'Ariel'

1–4 The end of v. 8 identifies *Ariel* as Zion, and in Ezk. 43:15 its meaning is 'altar hearth'; hence Moffatt renders it here (emphasizing Jerusalem's high calling) 'God's own hearth and altar'. The cultic allusion in v. 1b confirms this, but v. 2b gives a grim turn to the metaphor by its hint of a holocaust, just as v. 3a pricks the city's pride in its past (cf. 1a, *where David encamped*).

5–8 The promise of miraculous deliverance had a partial fulfilment in the year 701 (see 37:33–37). But the gathering of 'nations' (vv. 7, 8), the 'siegeworks' (v. 3; cf. 37:33) and the spectacular signs of v. 6, suggest a still greater struggle: cf. Zc. 14:1ff. The nations' disappointment is vividly suggested in vv. 7, 8; there have been already innumerable minor occasions when the world has prematurely licked its lips over the demise of the church.

29:9–24 Israel's inner darkness, deepened and dispelled

29:9–12 A people without vision. 10 The pregnant phrase, *your eyes, the prophets*, shows that Israel is the subject of this oracle, which enlarges on the lessons of Pr. 29:18 and 1 Sa. 3:1ff. **11, 12** A glimpse of such a state, where God's will has become a closed book, is given in Ps. 74:9. The reflexive verbs in v. 9 suggest that the blindness is judicial: self-will has brought its own punishment. Cf. 30:10.

29:13, 14 Religion without reality. 13 Jesus saw this verse as the very image of Pharisaism (Mk. 7:6f.). **14** is its proper outcome, for without depth, cleverness turns in on itself to obscure all that it touches.

29:15, 16 Contempt of the Creator. 15 The mixture of furtiveness and bravado (cf. 30:1) would probably be expressed in unconscious ways, such as the suppression of unwelcome truths (cf. 30:9ff.). Jeremiah (Je. 2:26; 23:23ff.) and Ezekiel (Ezk. 8:12) found the same mishandling of conscience in their day. **16** The unanswerable *potter* illustration is used again in 45:9 and, penitently, in 64:8; Paul takes it up in Rom. 9:20ff.

29:17–21 The great reversal. The absurdity of planning against God (v. 15) will appear when His work is complete, when the best that we know will be transcended (v. 17), and the disabilities and injustices of the present made good (vv. 18–21). **17** The point is indicated in its verbs: *i.e.* the present *Lebanon* (uncultivated, like the wilderness of 32:15) will be *turned into* good land, while the present good land will *be regarded as* mere thicket in comparison with its new fertility.

29:22–24 A people for God's praise. 22 The individual Jacob is meant in 22b: he will no longer (as we should say) turn in his grave at the behaviour of his descendants. **23** The thought of God's people expressing God's holiness (*sanctify my name*), which is a first concern of the Lord's Prayer ('hallowed . . . '), is developed in Ezk. 36:23 and context, and in Eph. 1:4, 6, *etc.*

30:1 – 31:9 Egypt and Assyria in perspective

30:1–5 The shadow of Egypt. The illusory refuge denounced in 28:14–22 is named at last. Ten years earlier, Isaiah had dissuaded Judah

from playing Egypt's game against Assyria (ch. 20); now the mood has hardened, and Judah's envoys are on their way. **4** *His officials* seem to be Pharaoh's, in which case *Hanes* seems implied to be near *Zoan* (which is Tanis, the nearest important town to the Israel border), rather than 50 miles up-Nile as commonly identified. See *NBD* article, 'Hanes', for fuller discussion.

30:6–8 The stay-at-home ally. 6 Isaiah sees the discomforts and dangers of the journey (6a) as typical of the whole enterprise, and the treasures of 6b, so incongruous in the wild Negeb, as a picture of misspent effort and resource. **7** *Rahab*, differently spelt in Hebrew from the familiar name of Jos. 2, is a term for Egypt again in Ps. 87:4 (cf. 89:10). It appears to mean 'arrogant' or 'turbulent', and is associated with 'the dragon' (crocodile?) in Is. 51:9, which is another of Egypt's names in Ezk. 29:3. **7, 8** Moffatt brilliantly renders v. 7c 'Dragon Do-nothing'—a devastating nickname to placard (v. 8) around Jerusalem; as pointed as an earlier slogan had been cryptic (cf. 8:1).

30:9–14 The ill-built structure. Truth and right (v. 10) are shown to be as vital to a community as soundness and accuracy are to a building (v. 13). This is one of the clearest statements of the logic of God's judgments; cf. Ezk. 13:10ff. on (in our terms) papering over the cracks; Am. 7:7ff. on the plumb-line, and Hab. 2:9–11 on the creaking edifice of the tyrant.

30:15–17 The price of unbelief. 15 could be singled out as the distinctive challenge of Isaiah: see on 7:1–9. *Returning* is repentance, turning back to God (cf. 10:21); *rest* and *quietness* are the antithesis of the frantic activism of v. 16 (cf. 28:16); *trust* colours each of these responses with love. **17** The threat sadly reverses the promise of Lv. 26:8; cf. Dt. 32:30.

30:18–26 The good things in store. Egypt and Assyria fade from sight as the glory dawns, depicted first in personal terms (vv. 18–22), then in material (vv. 23–26). **18** Notice the relation between God's waiting and man's (18a, d; cf. 8:17; 64:4), and the boon of His exaltation as Judge (18b, c; contrast 5:15, 16). **20, 21** The intimacy described in vv. 20f. is that of the new covenant (cf. Je. 31:33f.) rather than the final glory, for it does not preclude *adversity* or the possibility of straying, limited though this will be (v. 21). *Teacher* is a plural noun with a singular verb: *i.e.* a plural of God's fullness or majesty, as in RSV; and the word relates to moral instruction or *tôrâ* ('law'). His voice, recalling us, comes from *behind* (v. 21) only when we *turn* aside, not when we follow. **23–26**, in contrast with v. 20a, express in terms of the familiar world the new creation which will utterly transcend it: cf. 60:19ff.; 65:17ff.

30:27–33 The cleansing fire. While these verses survey the immediate situation, naming 'the Assyrians' (v. 31), they further apply to the end-time. **28** One day the godless powers will find themselves caught (like Judah, 8:8) in a rising tide, and drawn by God's *bridle* (like Assyria in 37:29) towards their destruction. **29–32** Yet for us this is liberation (v. 29): every blow of judgment will deserve the sound of *timbrels* (v. 32) like Miriam's (*cf.* Ex. 15:20); **33** but the grave of the oppressors will no longer be the Red Sea, but Topheth (RSV mg.)—*i.e.* the *burning place* of final destruction which the NT calls Gehenna, or hell. Je. 7:31f. tells how this meaning was acquired; the allusion here to *the king* is probably to Molech (RSV mg.; *cf.* 2 Ki. 23:10), which is basically the same word as king.

31:1–5 Some trust in horses . . . 2, 3 The relative power of *flesh* and *spirit*, as seen by Isaiah, quite contradicted his contemporaries' assessment (*cf.* 30:15, 16)—and, for the most part, our own. It is the key to his thinking, and was to be dramatically vindicated (*cf.* the taunt of 36:8f. with the outcome in 37:36ff.). In v. 2, *disaster* rightly interprets the broad term 'evil' (AV, RV; *cf.* 45:7; Am. 3:6). **4, 5** The growling *lion* and the *birds* in flight both depict what is free of man's interference; possibly also (Delitzsch) the formidable and the tender aspects of the Lord as protector (?*cf.* Dt. 32:11).

31:6–9 The rout of Assyria. The supernatural smiting of the Assyrians is recorded in 37:36. **6** But Isaiah is concerned with conversion (*turn*) even more than deliverance; notice his penetrating estimate of the situation (*cf.* 29:15; Ho. 9:9). **7** *Cf.* 2:20; 30:22. **9** With the Assyrians' far from immovable *rock*, *cf.* Dt. 32:31; Is. 26:4. With the Lord's *fire . . . in Zion*, *cf.* its searching implications in 33:14.

32:1 – 35:10 SALVATION AND ITS DARK PRELUDE

32:1–8 A kingdom of true men

This fourth oracle on the coming king (*cf.* 7:14; 9:6f.; 11:1ff.) shows his greatest triumph, in the flowering of his own qualities (given by the Spirit of the Lord, 11:2; *cf.* 32:15) in the character of his subjects, from his office-bearers downwards. (The passage *can* be translated 'If a king reigns in righteousness . . . then . . .', *etc.* But the familiar rendering is both a simpler construction and more relevant to Isaiah's teaching from 7:14 onwards.)

1, 2 After the plural *princes*, the right translation of (lit.) 'a man' (*cf.* AV, RV, v. 2a) is *each*, as in RSV. Here are men in power, using power as God uses it: *cf.* v. 2 with 25:4f.; 26:4. **3, 4** Here too are people using the faculties they have (v. 3; contrast 30:10, 11; 42:20), and finding new abilities (v. 4). **5** Above all, truth has ousted the fictions under which vice takes shelter. With v. 5, *cf.* Lk. 22:25ff., for God recognizes no courtesy titles. **6–8** are not a prediction, but a comment on the terms used in v. 5, rightly expressed in RSV's present tenses.

32:9–20 No smooth path to peace

The pampered ladies of vv. 9ff. (*cf.* 3:16ff.) are only an extreme example of the predominantly escapist society of the time (*cf.* 22:13; 28:15). Note the triple *complacent* in vv. 9–11. **10** If RSV is right in 10a, this oracle dates from about the time of Hezekiah's revolt from Assyria, for which the invasion of 701 was the reprisal. But 10a could equally mean 'for a long period' (*cf.* AV, RV); in any case the disaster of v. 14 and the glory of vv. 15ff. transcend anything that happened in Isaiah's time. The present age since Pentecost (*cf.* v. 15) may be partly in mind in the picture of a people of God emancipated from the earthly Jerusalem (vv. 14, 19).

The basic principle expounded in this poem is that *peace* is not a thing God superimposes on a corrupt society: the ground must be cleared and re-sown with *righteousness*, of which peace is the fruit (vv. 16, 17). For this, the promise of the Spirit (v. 15) is indispensable: it is the secret of the shared gifts of the Messiah described in vv. 1ff., above. On 15b, see on 29:17. Such pictures of a secure and well-watered land (*e.g.* v. 20) express God's 'new things' to come, in terms of things already known.

33:1–24 The longing to be free

This chapter, Psalm-like in its many changes of moods and speakers, seems designed for public use in a national emergency: *cf.* the answering voice of God (vv. 10ff.) with that in Ps. 60:6ff., and the dialogue in vv. 13ff. with Ps. 24:3ff.

33:1–9 The thirst for redress. Denunciation (v. 1), entreaty (vv. 2–4), praise (vv. 5, 6) and lamentation (vv. 7–9) break out in rapid succession. **1** The *destroyer* is left unnamed, for Isaiah is writing (it seems) for other times beside his own, and there will be others whose 'envoys of peace' (v. 7) return rebuffed like Hezekiah's (*cf.* 36:3, 22). **2** *Our arm*, as against 'their arm' (AV, RV), is the reading of a few MSS and versions, but 'their' is better attested—perhaps referring to the army in the field. **8** The deserted *highways* recall (but in different language) the hard times before Deborah (*cf.* Jdg. 5:6), whose victory transformed another desperate situation.

33:10–16 The answering challenge. God's intervention will not be confined to the enemy (vv. 10–12) but will burn out the evil of Zion as well (vv. 13–16). **14** The *devouring fire* is not only His personal intolerance of sin; from another angle it is the sinner's self-immolation (vv. 11f.), brought about by the conjunction of vain pursuits (11a) and aggressive attitudes (11b). On this theme of self-destruction see also 1:31 and, with another metaphor, 30:13.

The heart-searching colloquy in vv. 14ff. recalls those of Pss. 15; 24:3ff. It has been suggested that these are based on ritual admission tests employed at sanctuaries, given an ethical content; it is at least as possible that that of Ps. 24 arose out of the self-questioning of David recorded in 2 Sa. 6:9, and these other examples out of the Psalm. **15** Notice the 'puritanism': the vigorous renunciations recognize the potency of habits, words, thoughts and sense-impressions as the seeds of action. If this verse is negative, it is in order to clarify the meaning of 'pure in heart', in readiness for v. 17.

33:17–24 The bliss of fulfilment. The unforgettable promise of v. 17a, for which the last phrase of v. 15 is indispensable (*cf.* Mt. 5:8; contrast the dismay of Is. 6:5), is the focal point of this passage. Other prospects radiate from it (the spacious countryside, v. 17b, gladdening the eyes after the constriction of siege; and tranquil *Zion* the place of pilgrimage again, v. 20), while memories of tyrants and indignities now past give added zest to the present (vv. 18, 19); but the eye returns to the Lord Himself as source and centre (vv. 21, 22). The authoritative titles, *judge*, 'lawgiver' (AV, RV), *king*, which Judah, like us, was always reluctant to pronounce, are the firm basis of this serenity.

The picture of a city flanked by better defences (v. 21) than Nile or Tigris (*cf.* Na. 3:7, 8)—for they will be waters which no hostile fleet can use—gives rise to a new metaphor in v. 23 for the disarray of the lawless (whether they are Gentiles or 'the sinners in Zion'; *cf.* v. 14). But this is a parenthesis; the passage ends by reaffirming God's enriching, healing and pardoning grace (vv. 23b, 24).

34:1–17 The universal judgment

Just as chs. 24–27 crowned the local oracles with the prospect of final judgment and salvation, so chs. 34 and 35 leave the Assyrian crisis far behind. A further similarity is that amidst these cosmic events, whose majestic description in v. 4 is echoed in Rev. 6:13f., Edom, like Moab in 25:10ff., is singled out over against Zion, whose year of release this is to be (*cf.* v. 8 with 35:4), for a judgment which brings the whole scene suddenly to close quarters. **5–7** The thunderstorm, after encircling the entire horizon, arrives practically overhead in v. 5, and there it remains, for *Edom* symbolizes in Scripture the profane (*cf.* Heb. 12:16) and the persecutor (*cf.* Ob. 10–14), the opposite and adversary of the church. The metaphor in vv. 5–7 is a grim variant of the banquet scene (*cf.* 25:6), dwelling on the butchery behind the sacrificial feast, and using current idiom to show that the whole people, from 'young bloods' and leading citizens (v. 7a) to the least and lowest (v. 4), is doomed. *Cf.* 63:1–6.

8ff. The waste land of vv. 8ff. brings both Sodom and Babylon to mind with the 'brimstone' of vv. 9f. and the haunted ruins of 11ff. (*cf.* 13:19ff.). **11** *Confusion* and *chaos* are the 'without form' and 'void' of Gn. 1:2; they imply here and in Je. 4:23 an undoing of the very work of creation. The mention of *line* and *plummet* gives this demolition a disquieting air of precision, matched only by the care (vv. 16f.) with which the ruins are furnished with appropriate monsters. **14** On the *satyr* see on 13:21, 22ff. The *night hag* is Hebrew 'lilith' (*lîlît*), which could be either some nocturnal creature or a demon; see further under 'Lilith' in *NBD*. It is

worth noting that judgment is pictured, here and elsewhere, as something worse than extinction: the last state is a kind of parody, obscene and (v. 17b) persistent, of the first.

35:1–10 The flowering wilderness

The glory of this chapter is enhanced, if this is possible, by its setting as an oasis between the visionary waste land of ch. 34 and the history of war, sickness and folly in chs. 36–39.

The theme is the coming exodus, a greater than the first. **1, 2** Why the desert should be carpeted with spring flowers (*crocus*, or perhaps narcissus, rightly replaces the traditional 'rose') and shaded with great trees (*the glory of Lebanon*) is a question answered with the news that *the Lord* is to pass this way; **3–6** and His reason for coming emerges in v. 4 (*cf.* v. 10): it is to fetch His people home. Heb. 12:12 treats v. 3 as still relevant to the Christian's hope; and while the healings in the Gospels announce that the new age of vv. 5 and 6 has dawned, the full promise of v. 4b is yet to come (*cf.* 61:2; Lk. 4:19–21; 2 Thes. 1:7ff.).

If God's coming was indirectly portrayed in the opening verses, reflected in the springing wilderness, the upsurge of hope and the miracles of healing (vv. 1–6a), His people's journey home is similarly presented in vv. 6b–10. The desert produces brooks and meadows, the safe highway appears, and finally the singing pilgrims themselves come into view in the last verse, making for Zion.

7, 8 There are some uncertainties of translation and text in these verses. In v. 7a, *burning sand* is similar to the Arabic for 'mirage' (RV mg.), which would make a telling contrast between false and true; but 'mirage' is out of place in 49:10. In v. 7b, the Dead Sea Scroll (1Q Isa) omits one letter (a suffix) from the word which AV translated 'where each lay', to yield the sentence: 'In the jackals' haunt (shall be) a grassy place with reeds and rushes.' In v. 8b, where the text seems to have suffered (*cf.* AV, RV), RSV seeks clarity by omitting four Hebrew words. A simpler expedient, among other suggestions, is to presume the omission of one letter, whose insertion would yield: 'but it shall be for his wayfaring people; and fools shall', *etc.*

So the prophecy reaches a climax which already soars above Isaiah's own times, and anticipates the style and thought of chs. 40–66 (*cf.* the quotation of v. 10 in 51:11) in its lyrical portrayal of the new exodus, the coming of God Himself, the re-peopling of Zion, and the endless joy of the redeemed.

36:1 – 39:8 THE SUPREME TESTS FOR HEZEKIAH

In these four chapters the political situation that has been developing throughout Isaiah's ministry comes to an immense climax, reinforced by two searching tests of the king's faith and integrity, which are to have far-reaching consequences. Apart from Hezekiah's psalm, found only in 38:9–20, these chapters coincide almost word for word with 2 Ki. 18–20, to which the reader is referred for detailed comments.

36:1 – 37:38 The Assyrian onslaught

For details, see on 2 Ki. 18:13 – 19:37. Isaiah omits 2 Ki. 18:14–16 and part of v. 17a.

36:1–22 In ch. 36 we may note, in general, the technique of subversion displayed for all time in the speeches of 36:4–10, 13–20: *i.e.* the tempter's skilful use of truth, barbing his shafts with a few unanswerable facts (*e.g.* the perfidy of Egypt (v. 6) and the failure of the gods (v. 19)), his use of ridicule (v. 8), threats (v. 12b) and cajolery (vv. 16f.); and his perversion of theology—misrepresenting Hezekiah's reforms (v. 7), selecting from Isaiah's preaching (v. 10; *cf.* 10:6, 12), and drawing damaging conclusions from false religions (vv. 18–20). The king's instruction, *Do not answer him* (v. 21), took due account of the fact that the speaker was seeking victory, not truth.

37:1–38 Ch. 37 (see more fully on 2 Ki. 19) is a model of response to intimidation. Hezekiah's steadfastness owed nothing to blind optimism; his *sackcloth* (v. 1) was proof of that. His call for Isaiah's *prayer* (v. 4) showed where his confidence lay, and his metaphor of *birth* (v. 3) proved him a man of vision, whose longings were not for the old order but for the new (note too the evidence of 36:7 for his courageous reforms). His allusion to the *remnant* (v. 4) further suggests attention to Isaiah's preaching (*cf.* 10:20ff.). Upon Sennacherib's renewal of the war of nerves (vv. 9ff.) Hezekiah was again too wise either to dismiss the threat or to succumb to it. His spreading out the letter before the Lord (v. 14) epitomizes the act of prayer, and the candour of his words finely echoes the gesture. As in the Psalms, the situation clarified as he prayed (v. 19), and his motive was raised to the highest level (v. 20).

In Isaiah's successive replies (37:5–7, 21–35) note the absence of personal rancour against those whose policies were now in ruins (*cf.* 28:14ff.; 30:1ff.; on *Eliakim* and *Shebna* (v. 2) see 22:15ff.). In the vivid triumph song of 37:22ff. it was now time to answer Sennacherib's challenge 'On whom do you . . . rely?' (36:5) with the question '*Whom have you mocked?*' (37:23), and to taunt him with not knowing the meaning of his own career (v. 26; note the Isaianic stress on what God *determined . . . long ago*; see on 22:11).

The completed story shows that the very successes which feed human arrogance (in any age) proclaim, when all is known, the sure sovereignty of God.

38:1–21 Hezekiah's illness

For comment on 38:1–8, 21f. see on 2 Ki. 20:1–11.

38:9–20 Hezekiah's lament is similar to the outcries of Job (*cf., e.g.,* Jb. 7), and to various Psalms (*cf., e.g.,* Ps. 88), particularly those that turn to praise. The final words, where the singular gives way to the plural, suggest a public use of the psalm (*cf., e.g.,* Ps. 25:22; 51:18f.).

10 *Sheol* (see also on v. 18 and on 14:9) is pictured here poetically as a city or prison; as a community in v. 18; and as a devouring monster in 5:14. **12** The finality of the *weaver's* action is the point here; in Jb. 7:6 it is swiftness of his shuttle. But swiftness may also be the point of *from day to night*—so short a span.

13–15a There is a Job-like bewilderment in these verses, where Hezekiah's instinctive resort to God as his *security* (*i.e.* surety or guarantor), is checked by the thought that his predicament itself is from Him: *cf.* Jb. 17:3. But if this sharpens the problem, it also begins to resolve it, since a single, perfect will is paramount. See below on vv. 17ff.

15b, 16 are of uncertain meaning, as the different versions indicate. In 15b follow RSV mg. (not text), as in AV, RV; but perhaps the Hebrew verb, with its hint of a procession (*cf.* Ps. 42:4 (MT, 5)), contains the idea 'I will walk with awe'. The reference of *these things* in v. 16a is not clear, and the awkwardness of the Hebrew here suggests a damaged text, on which the ancient versions and the scrolls have no unanimity.

17–20 Here the fact of God's love dawns and clarifies, from the first assurance, *it was for my welfare*, on through the striking phrase, literally, 'thou hast loved my soul from the pit' (RV mg.), to the certainty of forgiveness in v. 17c. The use of *Sheol* as synonymous with *death* is the key to vv. 18 and 19, and to OT usage in general, which concentrates within this set of terms all that is negative in death: a man's severance from the praising congregation; his forfeiting of power and position; his fading into the past; his return to dust. At the same time, it is clear from v. 17 that Hezekiah had envisaged himself as dying without assurance of the forgiveness of sins, and it is in this context that he views life after death as thankless and joyless—as indeed it would be. Meanwhile there are positive aspects expressed in a distinct phraseology: *e.g.* being 'taken' by God (*e.g.* Gn. 5:24; 2 Ki. 2:9; Ps. 49:15), and being 'with' Him (*e.g.* Ps. 73:23; *cf.* Pss. 139:18 and 17:15; and see commentary on Psalms, *in loc.*). *Cf.*, in Is. 26:19, 'live . . . rise . . . awake'. But there is no synthesis as yet. On v. 20, see the opening comments to the chapter.

39:1–8 The envoys from Babylon

For detailed comment, see on 2 Ki. 20:12–19.

The faith of Hezekiah, proof against the heaviest blows, melts at the touch of flattery (notice his delighted account in vv. 3, 4), and the world claims another victim by its friendship. Enough is known of Merodach-baladan to suggest that this enterprising rebel against Assyria had plots to hatch under cover of this visit. But the Bible is silent on this, and Hezekiah is condemned for glorying in wealth and human patronage.

The price of disloyalty is very heavy (vv. 5ff.).

To Hezekiah there was comfort in postponement (v. 8); but not to Isaiah. Evidently he took this burden home with him, and so lived under its weight that when God spoke to him again it was to one who in spirit had already lived long years in Babylon (vv. 6, 7), and could 'speak to the heart' (cf. 40:2) of a generation of exiles yet to be born.

40:1 – 48:22 NIGHT FAR SPENT IN BABYLON

Whatever our view of the relation of chs. 40ff. to their great prelude in 1–39 (see Introduction, p. 589), we emerge in 40:1 in a different world from Hezekiah's, immersed in the situation foretold in 39:5–8, which he was so thankful to escape. Nothing is said of the intervening century and a half; we wake, so to speak, on the far side of the disaster, impatient for the end of captivity. In chs. 40–48 liberation is in the air; there is the persistent promise of a new exodus, with God at its head; there is the approach of a conqueror, eventually disclosed as Cyrus, to break Babylon open; there is also a new theme unfolding, to reveal the glory of the call to be a servant and a light to the nations. All this is expressed with a soaring, exultant eloquence, in a style heard only fitfully hitherto (cf., e.g., 35:1–10; 37:26f.), but now sustained so as to give its distinctive tone to the remaining chapters of the book.

40:1–11 The long-awaited Lord

40:1, 2 The gentle voice. *Comfort* has its familiar meaning here, not its old English sense of 'strengthen'. It is matched by the womanly gentleness of 66:13, and amplified by v. 2, where *speak tenderly* is literally 'speak to the heart', a phrase mostly found in contexts of reassurance or of winning a person back (cf., e.g., Gn. 50:21; Jdg. 19:3; 2 Sa. 19:7; Ho. 2:14). *My people* and *Jerusalem* will often be in evidence in these chapters, separated until the mother-city receives back her children (cf. 54:1ff.).

The expression, *double for all her sins*, can be taken either in the bountiful sense of, e.g., 61:7; Zc. 9:12 (these use another word for 'double') or, with most commentators, in the punitive sense of, e.g., Lv. 26:18, 43; Rev. 18:6. The former would well express the underlying grace of these chapters, but the latter need not be pressed to imply any earning of salvation: only a strong assurance that Jerusalem's sentence is already more than served. It is not impossible, incidentally, that 'double' might mean 'counterpart' or 'equivalent'.

40:3–5 The herald's call. The great processional way (to be lined by all humanity, v. 5) suitably dwarfs the ceremonial routes of heathen festivals. The *wilderness* is doubly significant, both as an example of the barriers that must all yield to the royal progress (cf. v. 4; see ch. 35) and as a reminder of the first Exodus. Ho. 2:14 makes it, in its austerity, a place of repentance and renewal; John the Baptist, with prophetic

symbolism, used the literal wilderness for this very work (cf. Mt. 3:1ff.). But God's coming (cf. Mt. 3:13ff.), and the 'exodus' that He was to accomplish (cf. Lk. 9:31), were to take a wholly unexpected form.

40:6–8 The preacher's word. 6 The brief colloquy in v. 6a introduces the prophet and his responsibility (the RSV reading, *and I said*, retains the Hebrew consonants and is well supported). *All flesh* echoes the impressive 'all flesh' of v. 5, but puts it in perspective in God's overwhelming presence. **8** Without the great ending of v. 8, the passage would have only the wistfulness of, e.g., Jb. 14:1ff.; with it, it reaffirms Isaiah's tireless preaching of faith (cf., e.g., 7:9; 31:3). Its full implications will emerge in 1 Pet. 1:23–25, where *the word*, in its final form as gospel, is no longer the mere contrast to our transience but the cure of it. Cf. 1 Jn. 2:17.

40:9–11 The crier's news. 9 *Herald of good tidings* is a single Hebrew word, of which 'evangelist' is the Greek equivalent (not as a specialized term). It is feminine here, agreeing with *Zion*, and hence Zion is probably the messenger. In 41:27; 52:7 she is the hearer.

40:12–31 God the incomparable

This superb poem rebukes our small ideas and flagging faith, somewhat in the manner of the Lord's challenge to Job (Jb. 38–41), by its presentation of God as Creator (vv. 12–20) and Disposer (vv. 21–26) of a universe dwarfed by His presence. The goal of the passage is v. 31, where human imaginings (v. 18) and doubts (v. 27) give way to the humble expectancy that is urged on us throughout the book (cf. 26:8; see on 7:1–9).

40:12–20 The Creator. Matter (v. 12), mind (vv. 13, 14) and living creatures (vv. 15–17) are all put in their place before their great Originator, seen as He might see them. This is not to empty them of meaning, but to derive their meaning from Him alone (cf. Pr. 8:22ff.; Rom. 11:34). Such a Creator hardly needs our impatient advice or shares our impotence! The view of us through God's eyes makes the man's-eye view of God (vv. 18–20) doubly absurd. The idolater's pathetic efforts are studied at length in 44:9–20; 46:1–7; and the wilfulness that antedates the blindness is exposed in Rom. 1:18–23.

40:21–26 The Disposer. The gigantic similes continue, and should be taken as poetry, not science (with v. 22b, where *curtain* suggests the thinness of gauze, cf. the similes of Ps. 102:26; 104:2). **23f.,** on the transience of potentates, bring the general truth of vv. 6–8 a step nearer to the particular situation of the captives; and **26** draws the true lesson from the majestic progress of the stars: the precision, not the absence, of God's control. The thought is taken further in the final section.

40:27–31 The 'very present help'. 27 The wrong inference from God's transcendence is that He is too great to care; **28** the right one is that He is too great to fail: there is no point at which things 'get on top of' Him. 'He is wise beyond all our thinking' (v. 28d, Knox). But **29–31** make the big transition from power exercised to power imparted, to be experienced through the faith expressed in the word *wait* (v. 31; *cf.* on 25:9). So the final reminder of human frailty (v. 30) is forward-looking: it clears the way for trust and the transcending of natural resources. The phrase, *renew their strength* (v. 31), is literally 'change strength', as one might change into fresh clothes or exchange an old thing for a new. It may be significant that the three final metaphors speak of overcoming one natural impossibility and two natural weaknesses, ending on the note of steady progress.

41:1–29 God and history

41:1–7 God's challenge to the nations. 1 The call for *silence* opens the imaginary proceedings of a court, where God will face the heathen world with a test question. (The call to *renew their strength* looks like an accidental repetition of 40:31, but it may be a warning that the encounter will be formidable.)

2 The point at issue is the alarming progress of the *one from the east*, whom 44:28 will identify as Cyrus. The general consternation proves that the peoples and their gods are taken by surprise. **4** In contrast to their frantic efforts (the details of vv. 7, 8, as of 40:19, 20, indicate that idols, not weapons, are the products in mind) stands the lordly announcement of v. 4. It is the only clear voice in the crisis, and the outcome will vindicate it (*cf.* 44:28; Ezr. 1:2). It sets God's present action in the context of His age-long plan; it is no mere manoeuvre.

(In v. 2, *victory* is literally 'righteousness', which tends in these chapters to have the sense of 'putting right', 'vindication', 'salvation'. But RV's 'whom he calleth in righteousness to his foot' (*cf.* Jdg. 4:10, RV) remains a possible alternative. See also on 46:12, 13.)

41:8–20 God's servant reassured. 8ff. There is sudden warmth in the *but you* . . . and the repeated personal names. The long chain of promises, in the future verbs of vv. 10b–20, is characteristically anchored in the facts of present and past: a pledged relationship (vv. 8, 10a) and an irrevocable choice and call (v. 9). The word *servant* will stamp its own character on the coming chapters, with an increasing emphasis on its implication of self-giving, up to the climax of ch. 53. Here however its only corollary is the Master's protection, which is seen as a many-sided assurance of imparted strength (v. 10), scattered enemies (vv. 11–13), triumph over obstacles (vv. 14–16; *cf.* Mt. 21:21) and inexhaustible provision (vv. 17–20). The divine titles, *the Holy One of Israel* (vv. 14, 16, 20; see on 1:2–4), *your redeemer* (v. 14; *i.e.* your protecting kinsman, *cf.* Lv. 25:25) and *the King of Jacob* (v. 21), set their seal on it.

All this stands against a realistic background of an Israel cowed (*e.g.* vv. 10f.) and puny (*e.g.* v. 14, where, in parallel to *worm*, *men* should

perhaps be translated 'lice'), a fit starting-point for God's grace. **15, 16** A *threshing sledge*, by contrast, was the most solid of objects, being made of heavy boards, flint-studded; it was dragged over the reaped corn to break open the ears, which were then winnowed by tossing them to allow the husks to be blown away (v. 16). The huge scale of the metaphor must have seemed belied by the 'day of small things' that followed the return from Babylon, yet it does not exaggerate the impact of God's people on the world, past and to come.

41:21–29 God's challenge renewed. The tone of vv. 1–7 returns, but now the gods themselves are addressed (*cf.* v. 23). **22–24** The charge of v. 22 is that they cannot even interpret events (*the former things*), let alone predict them (see on vv. 26f.). When their incompetence is added to this (v. 23b), the only conclusion is their unreality (vv. 24, 29)—and the word *abomination* (v. 24) suddenly reveals the taunt as deadly serious. This word is usually reserved for heathen rites or idols (*cf.*, *e.g.*, 44:19); transferred to the worshipper it shows how corrupting is the choice of a lie for one's ultimate allegiance. The point is followed through in Rom. 1:18–32.

Vv. 25ff. cover the ground of vv. 2ff. with some added details. **25** The *north* and east are now mentioned together (*cf.* v. 2), defining more precisely Cyrus's conquests, which overarched the Babylonian Empire from the Persian Gulf to the Caspian and Black Seas. The statement, *he shall call on my name*, must be taken with 45:4; *i.e.* Cyrus would invoke the name of Yahweh (*cf.* Ezr. 1:2f.), yet not as a true convert. This is indirectly supported by his inscriptions, which diplomatically attribute his victories to the gods of the peoples he conquered: *e.g.* to Marduk at Babylon, but to Sin, the moon-god, at Ur.

26f., with their emphasis on prediction, would touch the heathen world on a sensitive spot, since divination was a major preoccupation (*cf.* 47:13), and Croesus of Lydia was to pay dearly for the Delphic oracle's ambiguity over his prospects against Cyrus. (Told that he would destroy a great empire, he joined battle and destroyed his own.) On this challenge to predict events as Yahweh has done, and its bearing on the authorship of these chapters, see Introduction, pp. 589f.

42:1–17 Light for the nations

42:1–9 The first 'Servant Song'. The sudden quietness after the overpowering themes of chs. 40 and 41 has been compared to the still, small voice of 1 Ki. 19:12. Four or five times such a solo passage quietly emerges in these chapters, to portray the Servant as 'the man for others', with an increasing emphasis on suffering in 49:1–13; 50:4–9; and 52:13 – 53:12—followed by the joyful 61:1–4 to enumerate the blessings he distributes.

At the far end of the series he is the one in the place of the many; **1** but here, introduced as *my servant* and *my chosen*, he is closely associated with the 'Israel' of 41:8ff. The enduement with the *Spirit* and the bringing of *justice* (vv. 1, 3, 4), or true religion, however, are features of the Davidic king of 11:1ff.; 32:1ff. (*cf.* the blending of this passage with the kingly Ps. 2:7 at the baptism of Jesus, Mt. 3:17), so that already an individual begins to stand out from the mass of Israel. The close of the chapter (vv. 18ff.) will strongly reinforce this impression.

2–7 The Servant's gentleness, both as unassertiveness (v. 2) and as tenderness to the weak and inadequate (v. 3), is unmarred by any weakness of his own: the words *fail* and *discouraged* (v. 4) pointedly take up the Hebrew terms already used for *dimly burning* and *bruised* (v. 3). The portrait is identified in Mt. 12:15ff., and the glimpse of a waiting world (v. 4c) confirms the character of his mission. *A light to the nations* (v. 6) was one of the earliest designations of Jesus (*cf.* Lk. 2:32) and one of the formative titles of His church (*cf.* Acts 13:47). But while the church was to share in this liberation of the *blind* and the *prisoners* (v. 7; *cf.* 'the lord's servant' portrayed in 2 Tim. 2:24–26), only its Head could be described as God's *covenant*, uniting *the Lord* and *the people* (v. 6; *cf.* 49:8) in His own person (*cf.* Mt. 26:28).

8, 9 tie in this Servant-motif with the themes of chs. 40 and 41 respectively, for Yahweh's jealousy for His true *glory* will chiefly express itself in spreading His light world-wide. This is the coming phase of His design, the *new things* declared *now*, which have been disclosed also in outline 'from the beginning' (41:26f.; *cf.* Gn. 12:1–3, AV, RV).

42:10–12 The world acclaims its Master. Outbursts of singing are a feature of these chapters (*cf.* 44:23; 49:13; 52:9, *etc.*), as of chs. 24–27, and are closely akin to Pss. 93; 95–100, in theme and language: 10 *cf.* v. 10a with Ps. 96:1; 98:1; and v. 10b with Ps. 93:3; 96:11; 98:7. Here not only nature but the nations break out into singing, for joy at the liberation just recounted. 11 Israel's bitter rivals, *Kedar* (*cf.* Ps. 120:5ff.) and the Edomite *Sela*, last heard of in contexts of judgment (21:16f.; 34:5ff.), demonstrate the breadth of this grace. But see the next paragraph.

42:13–17 The Lord declares His zeal. The violent similes, *like a man of war* (v. 13), ... *like a woman in travail* (v. 14), dispose of any idea of grace as a mere softening of God's mood. Rather, His *fury* (v. 13) against evil, and His pent-up zeal to redress it (v. 14; *cf.* Lk. 12:50), supply as much of the motivation as do His tenderness (v. 16a) and constancy (v. 16b) towards its victims. Salvation will only come through judgment, and will not be for the impenitent (v. 17). Cf. 63:1–6, the fiery complement of ch. 53.

42:18 – 48:22 Inconstant servant and unchanging Lord

There is a restless interplay in these chapters between the grace of God and the wilfulness of His people, whose determination to destroy themselves is only outmatched by His tenacity, expressed in classic form in 43:21 (AV): 'This people have I formed for myself; they shall shew forth my praise.'

42:18–25 Blind leaders of the blind. This bitter anticlimax to the portrait of the true servant (vv. 1–9), of the waiting world (vv. 10–12) and of the eager Redeemer (vv. 13–17) is vividly apposite to the church's perennial failure to live up to its calling. In Isaiah's first vision, to see and hear without perception (*cf.* vv. 18–20) was a danger-signal (*cf.* 6:10f.); here it is a crippling disability. The futility of the incompetent messenger (*cf.* 'I saw a great tumult, but I do not know what it was', 2 Sa. 18:29) is Israel's futility, and it is wilful: he is an heir of the covenant (v. 19b; see note below); he has the capacity (v. 20) and the data (v. 21) for the knowledge of God's will; he is still invited to *attend and listen* (v. 23). Even the plight he is now in is designed to teach, not destroy him (v. 25b); but the lesson, so far, is lost on him.

Note. 19 *My dedicated one* is hardly the most probable sense of *mᵉšullām*. RV translates it as 'he that is at peace with me' (*cf.* Ps. 7:4 (5, Heb.)); the passive form suggests 'he that has been brought into peace (friendly relations)'. See also the term 'Jeshurun', 44:2.

43:1–21 Grace abounding. The *but now* (v. 1) is a feature of these chapters, as the love of God, continually rebuffed, continually returns with the initiative. The same Hebrew expression is found at 44:1; 49:5; 52:5; 64:8 (7, Heb.).

1–7 give Israel in eloquent detail the assurance Christ gives to His church, that the gates of Hades will not prevail against it. Fire and water, peoples and distances, can take no toll: *every one* (v. 7) will safely arrive (*cf.* 40:26) whom God calls *mine* (v. 1). Some of the many strands that bind them to Him are enumerated, such as creation, redemption, call (v. 1), love (v. 4), adoption (v. 6) and the honour of His name (v. 7). The unique relationship is emphasized by the bold figure of a human *ransom* (vv. 3, 4; *cf.* v. 14)—*i.e.*, great nations have fallen and will fall to make way for Israel. Pr. 21:18 speaks in similar terms; the other side of the matter is that the nations will gain from Israel far more than they lose (*cf.* 42:1–9), and that her ultimate ransom must be a very different victim (*cf.* 53:8f.).

8–13 face Israel again with her sin against the light (v. 8; *cf.* 42:18ff.); yet she is held to her high calling as *servant* and *chosen* (v. 10), as much for her own instruction (*that you may know ...believe ... and understand*, v. 10) as that of the world. Her very history testified for Yahweh (vv. 10–12); one day the title, *my witnesses*, was to have its full force (*cf.* Acts 1:8), but for the present Israel appears as a passive and reluctant exhibit. The forensic setting is that of 41:1ff., 21ff.; the point at issue is the non-existence of any God but Yahweh, in ages past, present or to come (vv. 10b, 11, 13).

14–21 name *Babylon* for the first time since

39:7, and while the Hebrew of v. 14 has its obscurities, the main thrust of the passage is a clear promise of a greater exodus, in which God's wonders in the desert (vv. 19f.) will outmatch even those of the Red Sea (vv. 16–18). The promise is once again rooted in the covenant: note the terms of relationship in vv. 14, 15, and of election in vv. 20c, 21.

For its real fulfilment we must look beyond the modest homecomings from Babylon of the 6th and 5th centuries, although these are certainly in view, to the exodus which the Son of God accomplished at Jerusalem (Lk. 9:31; cf. 1 Cor. 10:4, 11), which alone justifies the language of this and kindred passages. See also on ch. 35 and on 40:3–5.

43:22–28 Grace despised. 22–26 Israel's devastating response to divine ardour is a yawn of ennui. No rebuff could be worse; yet it gives occasion for a penetrating comparison between religion as a burden (vv. 23b, 24a) and as grateful homage (v. 23a) to the burden-Bearer (vv. 24b, 25; cf. 46:3, 4), who once again offers to prove His case in open court (v. 26: cf. 41:1).

27 *Your first father* is probably Jacob in this context, as the Israelites are being reminded that they have little to boast of, either in their ancestry or in their spiritual leaders (*mediators*). **28** The final thrust is deadly, for *utter destruction* is the Hebrew term *ḥērem*, reserved for such objects of judgment as Jericho or the Amalekites, with whom no compromise was to be endured. It is the strongest term in the language.

44:1–28 The living God and His great design. 1–5, reopening an apparently closed question with a characteristic *but now* (see on 43:1), amazingly reaffirm the ungrateful Israel's calling as *servant* and *chosen* (v. 1, repeated in v. 2), together with the affectionate *Jeshurun* ('upright' (?); cf. Dt. 33:5, but see too 32:15; cf. on Is. 42:19), and go on to promise greater things to come. The outpouring of the Spirit (v. 3) is a glimpse of the new covenant, as in Je. 31:31ff.; Ezk. 36:26f.; Joel 2:28f.; and the confessions of allegiance in v. 5 are a rare foretaste of the Gentile conversions, like those of Ps. 87:4–6 (where however it is God who enrols them). These new *offspring* of Israel will mark the flow of God's living water, just as a line of *willows* marks the course of a river (vv. 3, 4). The book of Acts traces part of this current of life through the *thirsty land.*

6–8 give the very essence of these chapters, with their emphasis on God as Israel's champion (*Redeemer*, v. 6; cf. 41:14), their explicit monotheism (vv. 6b, 8b), their stress on prediction (v. 7b) and their reassuring tone towards a diffident Israel (v. 8).

9–20 preach the same message from the other side, turning the visual appeal of idolatry into an embarrassment, sparing no aspect of it. It is a favourite theme of these chapters: cf. 40:18ff.; 45:20; 46:1–7. All worship of *things*, given by God (v. 9, cf. v. 14) and shaped by man, contains the same absurdity and blasphemy (cf. Rom.

1:25). Man's eventual inability to see this (which is as modern as it is ancient) comes of a prior refusal to face it (vv. 18ff.; cf. Rom. 1:21).

21–28 return to the positive and joyous revelation of the true God. **21** The opening call to *remember* refers probably to the matters to which Israel can already testify (cf. v. 8), as well as to the heathen follies just described; there is a similar call in 46:8. But the Lord's repeated claim to control and predict the course of history is now dramatically renewed by the specific promises of vv. 26–28. The veiled predictions of good news for Jerusalem and of a liberator, in 41:2, 25ff., are suddenly unveiled to reveal *Cyrus* and his edict of rebuilding; a prophecy which duly came to pass (cf. Ezr. 1:1ff.). Such minuteness of detail is paralleled only in 1 Ki. 13:2, where Josiah is named 300 years before his time. **27** The reference to *the deep* is another allusion to the Exodus, a reminder of God's ability to perform these new wonders. **28** The term *my shepherd* implies no more than God's employment of this ruler for His own ends: see 45:4b, and on 41:25.

45:1–25 The God of all the earth. 1–8 put the Lord's control of Cyrus in the setting of His total sovereignty (v. 7), His world-wide self-revelation (v. 6), and His will to vindicate the right (v. 8).

1–3 The term *anointed* is the basis of the title Messiah; but its OT use is general, chiefly for God's anointed kings (cf., e.g., Saul: 1 Sa. 24:6f., etc.). Here it stresses that Cyrus is appointed and equipped for a supreme task to which all his victories will be the prelude. Every phrase of vv. 1b–3a highlights these successes; e.g. the *treasures of darkness* are those that are the most carefully hidden, as being the most precious. (As conqueror of Croesus and of Babylon, Cyrus was to acquire incalculable wealth.) **4** But the act that was the point and climax of his career, the release of Israel (cf. v. 13), was doubtless a minor episode to Cyrus, so faulty are human valuations (cf. 55:8). His acknowledgment of Yahweh (cf. Ezr. 1:2–4), as of other deities, seems to have been superficial (see on 41:25): a recognition of His existence and influence (v. 3b) without a corresponding personal knowledge (v. 4b).

7 *Light and . . . darkness, . . . weal and . . . woe,* are typically Hebraic expressions, as pairs of opposites, for 'all that is' (cf., e.g., Ps. 49:1, 2). *Woe* is literally 'evil', but this Hebrew word is too general a term to suggest that Isaiah is making God the author of wickedness; see rather Jb. 2:10; Am. 3:6; Rom. 11:36. Some have seen here an attack on Zoroastrian dualism, with its rival gods of good and evil; but this verse is equally opposed to polytheism, the target of most of these chapters' invective. There is no clear evidence that Cyrus was a Zoroastrian as were some of his successors.

9–13 turn from Cyrus to a rather querulous Israel (the plural subjects of the verbs of v. 11, and the allusion to Cyrus in the third person (v. 13), indicate this change), with a classic rebuke to the suspicion that God is fumbling His work (*cf.* 29:16). **9** RSV's *no handles* is very weak; follow RV: 'or thy work (say), He hath no hands?' **11** But RSV rightly takes v. 11's imperatives as highly ironical, the equivalent of indignant questions. **12** The object-lesson from the starry skies has been similarly, if more gently, used in 40:26ff.

14–25, foreseeing the great influx of the Gentiles, leap far beyond the liberation. Chs. 60–62 will take up the theme more fully. Here it is expressed first in an address to Israel (vv. 14–19) and then in an appeal to mankind to acknowledge its Lord, as one day it must, and thereby find salvation in company with the nation it once despised (vv. 20–25).

14 Such names as *Egypt, etc.,* and the details of *chains* and homage, depict God's triumph in terms of the contemporary scene, using the vivid colouring of human victories. In the fulfilment, these will be transcended, as vv. 20–25 make plain. The Gentiles of this verse are those that were never yet within Israel's empire; their surrender will be as total as that of prisoners of war, yet in reality it will spring from conviction (vv. 14c–16) and issue in salvation (vv. 22, 24).

15 The expression, *a God who hidest thyself,* may perhaps be a continuation of the converts' confession, acknowledging the invisible God instead of their idols; more probably it is Israel's exclamation at God's inscrutable ways, 'past finding out'. **18, 19** reply that, for all this, He has worked to a great design and has unequivocally revealed Himself. *Chaos* is *tōhû,* as in Gn. 1:2 ('without form'); v. 18b looks on to the end in view at the creation (*cf.* the phrase *to be inhabited*), the transforming of an initial formlessness into a habitable world. So too, a glorious end will be achieved with Israel.

22–25 The concluding verses are remarkable first for their picture of world-wide and heartfelt conversions, and secondly for the bold use the NT was to make of vv. 23, 24, applying them directly to Christ in Phil. 2:10, 11 (and indirectly in Rom. 14:9, 11). *Cf.* the use made of 8:12b, 13a in 1 Pet. 3:14, 15.

46:1–13 The helpless gods of Babylon. It is in keeping with the sharpening focus of the whole scene (*cf.* the explicit references to Cyrus (44:28; 45:1) and to Babylon and its overthrow, 47:1ff.) that particular gods are now specified. **1** *Bel* ('lord'; *cf.* Baal) was a title transferred from the old god Enlil to Babylon's patron deity, Marduk, whose son *Nebo* (Nabu) was the god of learning. Their names appear in, *e.g.,* Belshazzar, Nebuchadrezzar. Both gods were commonly transported in processions, but in this scene they are monstrous refugees, weighing down their struggling pack-animals. The contrast between these *burdens,* on the one hand, with their demands on money and muscles (vv. 6, 7), and on the other hand the lifelong burden-Bearer, Yahweh (vv. 3, 4), brings the series of attacks on idolatry in these chapters to a telling climax.

The theme of prediction, a constant ingredient of these passages (*cf., e.g.,* 41:23), receives its classic statement in v. 10a, and the twin realities of the conqueror's career—as both predatory and predestined—are set side by side in v. 11a (*cf.* 41:2, 25; 44:28; 45:1ff.).

12, 13 *Deliverance* is literally 'righteousness', a word with several layers of meaning. Basically it means what is right, *i.e.* as it should be, in its proper state. So it can include the ideas of rectitude, of justice and of righting what is wrong. In these chapters the last of these senses is predominant, even shading into that of victory (see on 41:2); but the ethical dimension is not lost (*cf., e.g.,* 48:1; 53:11; 58:2), and here it should take precedence in v. 12, as 'righteousness', leaving the secondary sense, *deliverance,* to emerge in v. 13, parallel with *salvation.*

47:1–15 Babylon doomed. This is a dirge, or taunt-song, in the characteristic fall-away rhythm of such poems (it can be felt, in translation, in the succession of a longer and a shorter phrase within v. 2a, and again within v. 2b). *Cf.* 1:21ff.; 14:4ff.

It is Babylon's proper fate: there can be no mercy, for she has shown none (v. 6; *cf.* Jas. 2:13). Yet the description is not without pity. We are watching the triumph of justice, but equally the tragedy of the sinner. Dust, toil; nakedness, shame; silence, darkness (vv. 1–5)—these symbols of damnation have an added bitterness by the glimpse of the arrogant gaiety ('you pampered jade', v. 8, C. R. North) which they quench for ever (vv. 7–11). We can enter into her sinking of heart as the trusted expedients fail (the 'enchantments', 'sorceries' and horoscopes of vv. 12–14), and the old associates drift prudently away (v. 15) like the fair-weather friends that they are.

The records amply confirm, incidentally, Babylon's profusion of magical rites, alluded to in vv. 9b, 12f.; and Ezk. 21:21 vividly depicts a selection of them in use by Nebuchadrezzar.

48:1–22 'Love to the loveless shown.' 1–8 The shift of attention from Babylon back to Israel is far from flattering. Their glib talk of *the Lord* and *the holy city* (vv. 1, 2) accords ill with their persistent idolatry (v. 5); they emerge in fact as hardened hypocrites (vv. 1, 4, 8). It is a darker picture than that of the faithlessness of 40:27 and even the coldness of 43:22, although it was anticipated in the sin against the light implied in 42:18ff. The argument from prophecy, hitherto directed against the heathen (*cf., e.g.,* 41:21ff.), now has to be turned against God's own people, these determined sceptics (vv. 3–8). See Introduction, pp. 589f.

9–22 All this, however, serves only to reveal God's patience for what it is: unmerited (v. 9), constructive (v. 10; see note below), resolute (v. 11). After all His outspokenness He can still affirm both His call (v. 12) and His love (v. 14; *cf.* Dt. 7:7, 8), and give the liberating command, *Go forth* (v. 20). It will re-echo through the coming chapters: *cf.* 49:9; 52:11; 55:12; 62:10.

Yet this is no rhapsody; the high price of self-will is stated and re-stated as nothing less than a farewell to *peace* (vv. 18, 22)—*i.e.*, to all health of soul and society. The sad realism of v. 22 will reappear at 57:21, and the book will end on the still harsher note of 66:24.

Notes. 10 presents problems of translation. RV, RSV assume a small miscopying in v. 10a (the Heb. has 'with' (AV), which could also mean 'at a cost of' or 'in the character of'; this is a single letter, easily confused with *like*). In v. 10b, the Dead Sea Scroll (1 Q Isa) supports RSV's *tried*; but 'chosen' is the normal meaning of the word found in the standard text (*cf.* AV, RV). **16** ends with a startling change of speaker: no longer the Lord, as in vv. 15, 16a, but one *sent* by Him, as the *Spirit* is also sent. It could be the prophet, but it is more meaningful if it anticipates the 'me' of 49:1; 50:4; 61:1; in other words, the Servant in whom Jesus was to see Himself. It is a remarkable glimpse, from afar, of the Trinity.

49:1 – 55:13 THE DAWN OF REDEMPTION

49:1–13 The second 'Servant Song'

The limits of this passage have been variously fixed, usually at vv. 1–6. But each of vv. 5–8 introduces part of God's answering commission to His servant; and v. 8, which echoes 42:6, cannot be shorn of its sequel.

After ch. 42, with its mutually incompatible portraits of 'my servant' (42:1ff., 18ff.), the question of Israel's unfitness has become more and more acute. The coming chapters will resolve the tension, not by this servant's dismissal or improvement, but by the clear emergence of a true Servant whose mission will be first of all to Israel itself.

In this passage this is apparent at once from the Servant's clear conscience. In 49:1ff. he shows no contrition for the sins deplored in 48:1ff., or the blindness of 42:18ff.; only a sense of being trained for God's moment (vv. 1–3; *cf.* 48:16d). The unresponsiveness of Israel is something he has done battle with, not shared (v. 4), and although he is addressed as 'Israel' (v. 3), his mission field is itself 'Israel' (v. 5) before us in the world (v. 6).

This paradox of an Israel sent to Israel is insoluble in OT terms, since no king, prophet or priest is big enough for the title. It is part of the powerful thrust of the OT towards the NT, in which Jesus stands forth as the sole worthy and rightful bearer of the name Israel. Meanwhile the two opposing portraits of ch. 42 have been brought together, with the one bearer of the name Israel entrusted with a converting mission towards the other. Also the theme of conquest through service, broached in 42:1ff., has begun to sound the note of suffering and rejection (4, 7), which will increase in sharpness and significance in the third and fourth 'Songs'.

8 V. 8a is quoted by Paul in 2 Cor. 6:2 as a saying now fulfilled; *cf.* our Lord's use of Is. 61:1, 2a in Lk. 4:18–21. On the expression, *a covenant*

to the people, see on 42:6. **9ff.** The *prisoners* flocking home in vv. 8–13 are visualized as the dispersed of Israel throughout the world, not merely at Babylon (*cf.* v. 12 with v. 22); but the allusion to v. 10 in Rev. 7:17 shows that we may rightly see also the Gentiles leaving their *darkness* for their new homeland (*cf.* 44:5). **12** *Syene*, *i.e.* Aswan, on the Nile (where a Jewish colony existed from the 6th century BC), is an emendation, supported by the Qumran Isaiah Scroll, of the standard text's 'Sinim'. The latter could be China (the Chinese are *Sinai* in Greek), if the Hebrews knew the name as early as this.

49:14–23 Comfort for Jerusalem

14 The deserted ruins of Zion are a feature of these chapters, personified as a woman bereft of husband and children. **15, 16** God's reply here is typical: first, she is not bereft, for He cannot forget her; **19, 20** secondly, she has her best days before her, when her new family will overflow all her bounds. The NT applies such promises not to 'the present Jerusalem' but to 'Jerusalem above' (Gal. 4:25–27; *cf.* Is. 54:1), *i.e.* the universal church in heaven and earth. The ruins of the city were indeed rebuilt in the 6th and 5th centuries, but these prophecies transcend the modest scale of those events. **22, 23** On the abject surrender pictured here, see on 45:14–25. On *those who wait for me*, see on 25:9.

49:24 – 50:3 Comfort for the captives

There is a double misgiving reflected here, over the power and the will of God to save. The former is answered by affirming God's control of history (49:25, 26) and of creation (50:2, 3), and the latter by a comparison between His character and Israel's (50:1)—for there is no fickleness in Him as there is in her, and no pressure on Him from outside (*my creditors*). Her sins alone (v. 1b) account for the breach (*cf.* 59:1, 2); the Lord's attitude is, by implication, that of Ho. 3:1–3, where the erring wife is loved and brought home.

50:4–9 The third 'Servant Song'

After the display of patient gentleness in the first 'Song' (42:1ff.) and the acceptance of frustrating toil in the second (49:4, 7), here the Servant faces the active spite and fury of evil. It is only a step, the reader feels, to the cross. There is no hint now of even the momentary discouragement of 49:4; the Servant has set himself to learn (v. 4) and to give (v. 6), as one dedicated in mind and body. **4** The plurals, *those who are taught*, emphasize that he is accepting the common course of training (*cf.* Heb. 5:8), and the element of reiteration in the phrase *morning by morning* suggests a lifelong attentiveness to God's unfolding will, 'the matter of a day in its day' (*cf.* 1 Ki. 8:59). The consequent authority and aptness of his words are those of the prophet *par excellence*.

So his suffering, while still unexplained

(until ch. 53), is already fruitful, as all suffering can be. 5 Godward, he makes it his offering of obedience; 6 manward, a voluntary, costly gift, not a resented exaction (*I gave . . . ; I hid not . . .*); 7–9 inwardly, he uses his discredit and isolation to clarify his sole trust in God. In Rom. 8:31ff. Paul sings the Christian's variant of this song, for whom Another's righteousness silences the accuser, and for whom God's help (vv. 7a, 9a) is now explicitly declared as love (Rom. 8:35, 37, 39).

50:10, 11 An epilogue to the song

The two verses seize on the words of faith just uttered, to make them the pivot of life or death for the hearer. 10 Commitment to God is clearly allegiance at the same time to His Servant, whose words are binding and his faith normative (*cf.* vv. 7–9). It is a pointer to his identity, as a single individual and a master of disciples. 11 describes either the persecutors (*cf.* v. 6 and, *e.g.*, Ps. 118:12) or, more probably, those who are self-sufficient, in contrast to v. 10. Its last line may be a generalization on the sorrow which is always the end of sin, but it may anticipate the NT teaching on punishment after death. C. R. North renders it, 'You shall die and go to a place of torment.'

51:1–8 More sustenance for faith

Faith, which 'comes from what is heard' (Rom. 10:17), is nourished by the three messages introduced by 'hearken' (v. 1) . . . 'listen' (v. 4) . . . 'hearken' (v. 7). They confirm the call of 50:10 to an unflinching trust, by an appeal first to look back to Israel's humble beginnings, to see what God can do with 'but one' (vv. 1, 2); then to look ahead to the promised consummation both in this world (vv. 4, 5) and in the next (v. 6); finally to look at present humiliations against such a background (vv. 7, 8). The thought of man's mortality, in the light of God's eternity, is echoed from the Servant's words in 50:9. 6 The translation, *like gnats*, as against the weaker expression 'in like manner' (AV, RV), plausibly postulates here a collective singular of the noun used in Ex. 8:16, 17 (12, 13, Heb.).

51:9 – 52:12 Mounting expectancy

Quick repetitions lend urgency to the whole section, which takes its tone from the opening, 'Awake, awake'. Man's appeal draws out an answering assurance and challenge, marked by God's own reiterations: 'I, I am he' (v. 12), 'Rouse yourself, rouse yourself' (v. 17), 'Awake, awake' (52:1), finally 'Depart, depart' (from Babylon), 52:11.

51:9–11 The Exodus surpassed. 9, 10 *Rahab* and *the dragon* and *the sea*, which would suggest to a non-Israelite the chaos-powers confronting the gods at creation (*cf.* on 27:1), are symbols here of the Exodus, as v. 10 makes clear. *Rahab* has already been Egypt's nickname in 30:7 (where see note). On rather similar symbolism for the final judgment, see on 27:1. 11 But

Isaiah's plea for another Exodus stirs his memory of a promise already here, and this verse quotes, almost to the letter, 35:10.

51:12–16 The captive comforted. 12–14 God Himself (*I, I . . .*) is the ground of comfort, both as Maker, in contrast to the transience of mere creatures; 15, 16 and as God of the covenant (*your God . . . my people*), who counts His call of Israel the crowning glory, not the anticlimax, of the startling series, *heavens . . . earth . . . Zion*. Note that *Zion* is a term for the people themselves in the last phrase of v. 16. V. 16a recalls the charge to the Servant in 49:2; and in fact, it is as bearer of God's *words* to the world that Israel has chiefly fulfilled her calling.

51:17–25 The tables turned. The 'you' is not plural but feminine singular throughout this passage, which consistently personifies the mother-city (see on v. 16, above). Of the various metaphors, that of the 'bowl' or 'cup of staggering' destined to change hands (vv. 17, 22) conveys the main message, while the pathos and brutalities of defeat are made vivid by the groping and prostration in vv. 18, 23, and by the simile of the trapped deer (v. 20). The sight of 'every street' (v. 20) littered with the dying was to leave its mark deeply on Lamentations (*cf.*, *e.g.*, La. 2:11, 12, 19, 21).

52:1–10 The good news of peace. 1, 2 God's call, *Awake, awake*, throws back at Israel her own prayer of 51:9, in a retort which is the best answer. *Cf.* a comparable rejoinder by our Lord in Mk. 9:22, 23. 3–5 The main object of these verses is to rid the redemption metaphor of any notion of a commercial transaction. As 50:1 pointed out, Israel's overlords have no claims on her, nor on God: they are His agents (and far from guiltless at that), not His creditors. While 1 Pet. 1:18, 19 will give a fresh nuance to v. 3b, the sovereign salvation of God, for the sake of *my name . . . my name* (vv. 5, 6; *cf.* Ezk. 36:21; Rom. 2:24), is here the sole concern.

7–10, movingly portraying the arrival of the news (*cf.* 2 Sa. 18:19ff.), bring out the three component factors of every such experience: first the messenger, whose lustre is that of his message (and this must be a despatch, as Paul points out in Rom. 10:15, nothing less); secondly the *watchmen*, those who are 'looking for . . . redemption' (Lk. 2:38), otherwise the news will fall on deaf ears; thirdly the event, which is here none other than the Lord in action (vv. 8b–10), seen not from afar, but close to (*eye to eye*, means 'face to face'; *cf.* Je. 32:4). Notice the Psalm-like outburst in vv. 9, 10 (*cf.* Ps. 98:3, 4; see above on 42:10–12).

52:11, 12 The clean break with Babylon. The picture is of a priestly procession, not the unceremonious departure of Ex. 12:33. The homecomings in Ezr. 1:5ff.; 7:7ff. were to have something of this character, and Ezra himself took the promise of divine escort fully to heart (Ezr. 8:22) and was not disappointed. But behind the literal departure from Babylon, Rev. 18:4 sees a greater movement, the withdrawal

of the church from the embrace and judgment of the world, 'lest you take part in her sins, lest you share in her plagues'.

52:13 – 53:12 The fourth 'Servant Song'

From the great homecoming we turn to the solitary figure whose agony was the price of it. We are at the heart of the book, the centre of its whole pattern of sin and righteousness, grace and judgment.

The poem, unusually symmetrical, is in five paragraphs of three verses each. It begins and ends with the Servant's exaltation (first and fifth stanzas); set within this is the story of his rejection in sections two and four, which in turn frame the centrepiece (vv. 4–6) where the atoning significance of the suffering is expounded. God and man, reconciled, share the telling (see the 'my' and 'I' of the outer sections, and the 'we' and 'our' of 53:1–6).

52:13–15 The joy set before him. Here is heaven's endorsement of the brave words of 50:7–9, applying to the Servant terms of exaltation that can characterize God Himself (*cf.* 'high and lifted up', 6:1; 'high and lofty', 57:15; *cf.* also the other term for 'high' in 5:16; 55:9). The 'many' ranged against him will give place to the 'many' convicted and enlightened (vv. 14, 15; note the return of this word, at a deeper level, in 53:11, 12). **15** The translation *startle*, supported by the LXX, makes a good opening to the sequence, roused—silenced—convinced. But 'sprinkle' (AV, RV), which is grammatically suspect but not indefensible (see E. J. Young, *Studies in Isaiah*, 1954, pp. 199ff.), would also suit the context well with its implications of sacrificial cleansing (*cf.* 1 Pet. 1:2) and perhaps of covenant making (*cf.* Ex. 24:6, 8; a different word).

53:1–3 The disdain of men. The gulf between revelation and opinion is very plain, in the contrast between what is *heard* (and so potentially *revealed*; *cf.* v. 1 with Rom. 10:16, 17, 21) and what is naturally attractive (v. 2) or impressive (v. 3). *Cf.* the reaction to the humiliated Jesus in, *e.g.*, Mt. 27:39ff.; Jn. 19:5ff., and to the preaching of the cross (1 Cor. 1:23). *Sorrows* and *grief* (v. 3), which recur in v. 4, are lit. 'pains' and 'illness'—which might suggest to the reader either a sick man or one sick at heart, as in Je. 15:18. But there is another category, that of the physician's voluntary involvement; for he is also a man of pain and sickness in the sense that he gives himself to these things and their relief. This is the sense defined in Mt. 8:17, quoting Is. 53:4.

53:4–6 'O sweet exchange . . .'. This is the central stanza, in every sense. Here the meaning of the Servant's disgrace breaks through, with the inverted word-order of v. 4a to stress the exchange of roles, and the emphatic pronouns *he* and *we* (vv. 4a, 4b) to expose man's misunderstanding: 'Our ills *he* bore, and our pains he carried; yet *we* thought. . . .'

4, 5 The meaning grows in clarity through these verses: the pain he is bearing is ours (v. 4);

it is the punishment of sin (v. 5a); it is the price of salvation (v. 5b). But it remains a paradox, one of God's ways which are higher than ours (55:9), as we are reminded by the startling conjunction of *his stripes* (*i.e.* weals; *cf.* 1:6) and our healing, as cause and effect. **6** is perhaps the most penetrating of all descriptions of sin and atonement, uncovering the fecklessness which is second nature to us, and the self-will which isolates us from God and man alike; but also the divine initiative which transferred our punishment to the one substitute. The metaphor whereby *iniquity* is *laid on him* is clarified by, *e.g.*, Gn. 4:13; Lv. 5:1, 17 (where one pays one's own penalty) and by, *e.g.*, Lv. 10:17; 16:22 (where the liability falls on another). Note the expressions, *all we . . . us all*, which give the verse an identical beginning and end in the Hebrew; grace wholly answering sin.

53:7–9 Wicked hands, willing victim. The victim's silence (contrast the outcry of another 'gentle lamb', Je. 11:19; 12:3) springs from love and faith, as Jesus was to show (1 Pet. 2:23, 24), not from weakness or prudence. C. R. North translates v. 8a: 'After arrest and sentence he was led away'; the whole stanza irresistibly evokes the trial of Jesus and its sequel (see on v. 9).

8 Acts 8:33 supports AV's 'who shall declare (better, 'consider') his generation?' but the Hebrew allows the more oblique translation of RV, RSV. The word used for *generation* mostly denotes 'contemporaries' (*cf.* Ex. 1:6), 'circle' (*cf.* Pr. 30:11, AV; Ps. 24:6) or 'life span' (*cf.* Gn. 15:16); but the sense is perhaps clearest if it can mean 'posterity', as some hold. **9** *Made* is literally 'gave', *i.e.* 'appointed'; the abrupt introduction of *a rich man* was to remain an enigma until the event of Mt. 27:57, 60, and it still embarrasses those to whom detailed prediction is unacceptable. But the ancient versions and the Scrolls confirm the authenticity of *rich*, the latter source indeed correcting a plural found in the LXX, and restoring the singular, as found in our text.

53:10–12 Crowned with glory and honour. In this stanza vindication is complete. The persecutors fade from view, to reveal *the Lord* (emphatic in v. 10; *cf.* Acts 4:28) and the Servant (v. 12, *he poured out his soul*) as the ultimate doers of what has been done. Further, in each verse the Servant's resurrection and triumph are clearly implied, while even more facets of his atonement appear than in vv. 4–6.

10 *An offering for sin* is literally 'a guilt-offering', the sacrifice which spoke of compensation or satisfaction. The Hebrew of this verse can make either 'his soul' (*i.e.* himself) or the Lord ('thou', AV, RV) the offerer of the sacrifice; but v. 12 will leave no doubt of the Servant's self-giving. **11, 12** Other aspects of his saving work are shown in terms of justification (*accounted righteous*), sin-bearing (see on v. 6), identification (*numbered with the transgressors; cf.* Lk. 22:37) and *intercession*, *i.e.* intervention. He is presented as priest and sacrifice, patriarch (v. 10b) and king. Finally, the *many . . . many* in vv. 11, 12 (*cf. great*, v. 12a, the same word), for whom the one suffered, reappear in fulfilment of the opening promise (*cf.* 52:14, 15, 'many . . . many').

54:1–17 The teeming mother-city

This chapter's exuberance, peace and security spring from the dereliction and death just described, which cut across the description of the great home-coming at 52:13. In Christian terms, the Calvary of ch. 53 is followed by the growing church of 54 and the gospel call of 55.

54:1–10 Wife and mother. Paul linked this passage with the story of Sarah and Hagar (*cf.* Gal. 4:27), and saw here the true church, its members born from above (see also on 49:14–23). The promise of world-wide expansion (v. 3; *cf.* 49:19) and the hint of coming strains upon the old structure (v. 2) were to be vividly borne out in the age of the apostles. For the metaphor of the erring wife, see 50:1; here however, with rare sympathy, not the guilt but the pain (v. 6) of the estrangement is put to the fore, with the corollary of the tenderness of reunion (vv. 7, 8)— its permanence seen to be as unconditional and as undeserved (*cf.* 'compassion', v. 10) as the promise of Gn. 9:11, and (we can now add) of Mt. 16:18b.

54:11–17 Gem-built city. The narrow tent of v. 2 and the shattered Jerusalem are equally outshone by this union of beauty and strength, a glowing picture of the church, to be elaborated in Rev. 21:10ff. But its meaning is translated into non-pictorial terms in vv. 13ff., where the 'righteousness' of v. 14 and the impregnability of vv. 15–17 are rooted in the fact of universal personal discipleship (v. 13; *cf.* 8:16; Je. 31:34), which is one of the marks of the new covenant. This is the true strength of God's city, which is promised not immunity from attack but the unanswerable weapon of truth (v. 17; *cf.* Lk. 21:15).

55:1–13 Grace abounding

This call to the needy is unsurpassed for warmth of welcome even in the NT. The chapter builds up twice to a climax, first in vv. 1–5, then, over a still greater range, in vv. 6–13.

55:1–5 Poverty, abundance, mission. 1–3 The fourfold *come* is as wide as human need (note the stress on unsatisfied longing in vv. 1, 2, as in, *e.g.*, Ec. 1:3; Jn. 4:13) and as narrow as a single individual (note the intertwined singulars and plurals in v. 1, more evident in AV, RV). The Bible closes with an echo of it (*cf.* Rev. 22:17), and Jesus made the same identification of *come . . . and eat* with *come to me*, in Jn. 6:35. The paradox of *buy . . . without money* throws into relief the twin facts of sure possession and total dependence which are implied in grace; *cf.* the union of the undoubting and the undeserving in Heb. 4:16.

3–5 raise the invitation to the fully personal

plane, engaging mind and will and drawing the hearers into *covenant*, to share in the world mission of the Messiah. *David* is named only here in chs. 40ff., but this is enough to identify the kingly Messiah of 7:14, *etc.* with the Servant of 42:1, *etc.*, for whom the nations wait. (The suggestion, sometimes made, that the promise given to David in 2 Sa. 7:12–16 is here transferred from king to people, goes ill with the emphasis in v. 3b on its permanence. Rather, David's vision in Ps. 18:43–45, 49, of nations subdued for a witness to the Lord, is enlarged by the prospect of nations converted: *cf.* v. 5 with Zc. 8:20–23; 9:9, 10.)

55:6–13 Sin, pardon, glory. 6–9 If man is hungry and needs satisfying (vv. 1–5), he is also *wicked* and needs salvation. God's calling and seeking (vv. 1ff.) must be matched by those of the sinner. V. 7 is a classic statement of repentance, challenging the mind (*cf.* the NT word for 'repentance') and the will, the habits (*ways*) and the plans (implied in the Heb. for *thoughts*). It is both negative (*forsake*) and positive (*return*, or simply 'turn'), personal (*to the Lord*) and specific (for *mercy*); and its appeal is reinforced by the shortness of the time (v. 6) and the abundance of the promise (v. 7).

10, 11 The declaration of vv. 8, 9 not only looks back to verse 7, but on to vv. 10ff., to shame us out of our small expectations. God's thoughts are farther-reaching and more fertile, as well as higher, than ours. The comparison of His word with *rain and . . . snow* suggests a slow and silent work, transforming the face of the earth in due time. The reference is to His decree (*cf., e.g.,* 44:26; 45:23) rather than His invitation or instruction, which can be refused (48:18f.; *cf.* the similar imagery to that of v. 10 in Heb. 6:4–8).

12, 13 His decree is given in these verses, combining the joys of liberation (v. 12a), of the Lord's own coming (*cf.* v. 12a with 52:12; 12b with Ps. 96:12, 13) and of the healing of the old devastations (*cf.* v. 13a with 7:23–25 and perhaps Gn. 3:18). Notice the living *memorial*, (lit. 'name') and *sign*, unlike those of 'conquering kings', in which the Lord delights.

56:1 – 66:24 THE GLORY AND SHAME OF ZION

Whereas chs. 40–55 surveyed the Babylonian exile, tracing the pattern of redemption largely in terms of the Israelite home-coming, the remaining part of the book fixes our attention on the homeland, which is seen partly in its too-familiar aspect as a place of corruption (56:9 – 59:15a) and devastation (63:7 – 64:12), but shown also as it will appear when God has come to the rescue, to make it 'a crown of beauty', the centre and magnet of the whole earth (chs. 60–62). The final chapters (65, 66), like the prelude (56:1–8), show God's welcome of the outsider and the heathen to His holy mountain and eternal kingdom, but press home the peril of an everlasting exclusion from these glories.

In structure, then, there is a certain symmetry within this group of chapters, somewhat akin to that of the fourth 'Servant Song' (see on 52:13ff.), in that the centrepiece (chs. 60–62, the glorified Zion) is flanked by the twin poems of God's vengeance and salvation (59:15b, ff.; 63:1–6), and these in turn by the scenes of sin and suffering (56:9 – 59:15a; 63:7 – 64:12); while the whole is enfolded by the promise of the ingathering of the outcasts of Israel and the world (56:1–8; 65:1 – 66:24).

56:1–8 A welcome for the outcast

1, 2 After the exhilarating climax to chs. 40–55, these verses present the sober obligations of integrity (v. 1) and unworldliness (v. 2) that are the plain fare of salvation. In v. 1, *righteousness* displays two of its facets by being coupled with both *justice* (*i.e.* fair dealing) and *salvation* (RSV's *deliverance* is lit. 'righteousness' again); for God's righteousness is oriented towards putting things right, not merely towards condemning them as wrong; *cf.* Rom. 3:21–26; see also on 46:12, 13.

3–8 produce a similarly practical translation of the missionary vision of chs. 40–55 into modest terms, in the concern shown for the *eunuch* and the *foreigner*, outsiders in the midst of Israel. The former are shown that the law against them (*cf.* Dt. 23:1) was given in love (to make this cruel mutilation abhorrent in Israel, if nowhere else) and this love now sensitively matches their handicap with something *better* (v. 5), answering their physical exclusion with the words *in . . . and within*, and their lack of a posterity with the word *everlasting*. The *foreigners* are likewise treated according to their attitude, not their birth—a principle already established by God's acceptance, despite Dt. 23:3, of Ruth the convert. But the great words of v. 7b were too big for the Temple's trustees: *cf.* Mt. 21:13; Acts 21:28. With the little-known v. 8, *cf.* Jn. 10:16: one of several indications that our Lord knew these chapters intimately.

The importance of the *sabbath*, reiterated in this passage (vv. 2, 4, 6), emerges most clearly in the two supporting phrases in v. 4b, making this day not an end in itself, but a mark of love for God (*cf.* 58:13) and loyalty to the covenant (*cf.* Ex. 31:13).

56:9 – 59:15a The shame of Zion

56:9–12 Watchmen asleep. See, by contrast, 52:8; 62:6. Our own phrases, dumb dogs, sleeping dogs, greedy dogs, are all, substantially, in vv. 10, 11a, and they characterize the spiritual leaders (*watchmen*; *cf.* Ezk. 3:17), while *shepherds* is an OT term for rulers. The sequence is instructive: spiritually, to have no vision (v. 10a; *cf.* 1 Sa. 3:1) is to have no message (v. 10b) and to drift into escapism (v. 10c) and self-pleasing (v. 11a); meanwhile the civil leadership (vv. 11b, 12) will improve on this example with stronger excess and blither optimism.

57:1–13 Flagrant apostasy. The watchmen have relaxed (56:9–12), and evil has duly flooded in.

The times could well be those of Manasseh, Hezekiah's apostate son, whose persecution of the innocent (2 Ki. 21:16) would accord with v. 1, and whose burning of his own son (2 Ki. 21:6) matches the revival of Molech-worship here (vv. 5b, 9).

2 The *beds* are tombs or biers (*cf.* 2 Ch. 16:14, Heb.); the thought of the verse is akin to Rev. 14:13. **5** The theme of *lust* refers to the sexual fertility rites of Canaanite religion, rampant also in Jeremiah's early days (*cf.* Je. 2:20ff.). (On v. 5b, see the first paragraph, above.) From speaking of literal whoredom it is a natural transition to the figure of Israel as the wife turned prostitute. In **6–13** (where *you* is consistently feminine singular) the metaphors such as *bed*, *symbol* (*i.e.* harlot's trade sign), *perfume*, *etc.*, are intertwined with the actualities, such as *sacrifice* and *idols* in the religious realm, and *envoys* in the political realm. Whether v. 9a refers to religion or politics is uncertain; the Hebrew text has 'the king', which could be either *Molech* (see first paragraph, above) or an earthly ally (*cf.*, *e.g.*, 30:2–5).

There is loving perception in the picture of weary doggedness in v. 10, and of infatuation and coming disillusion in vv. 11–13. The whole passage is a fit companion to Ho. 1–3 and Lk. 13:34f.

57:14–21 Abundant grace. 14 Repetitions, such as *build up, build up* and, later, *peace, peace*, are highly characteristic of chs. 40–66 (*cf.*, *e.g.*, 40:1; 52:1; 65:1); so too is the triumph of grace, which is presented here in many forms. The Exodus theme characterizes grace as strong and resourceful; **15** the conjunction of the *lofty* and the *humble* displays its condescension; **16,** echoing Gn. 6:3, speaks of its forbearance; above all, **17, 18** expound it as a frank resolve to reclaim the undeserving and unpromising, summed up in the memorable first line of v. 18. **19** So the offer of grace is crystallized, to reappear in Eph. 2:17 as the germ of Paul's gospel to the Gentiles. **20, 21** The plight of *the wicked* is consequently seen, more clearly than in 48:22, in terms of the salvation they have refused. Only their choice separates the 'peace, peace' of v. 19 from the *no peace* of v. 21.

58:1–14 Cant and reality. God's trumpet-call (v. 1) to the formalists is related to the previous indictment (57:1–13) much as Rom. 2 is to Rom. 1, and its emphasis is largely that of the Gospels and of James. Negatively (vv. 1–5), note the conjunction of religious punctilio (vv. 2, 5) and social ruthlessness (vv. 3b, 4) which the pious of every generation seem to take in their (or our) stride (*cf.* Mt. 23; Jas. 4:1ff.), but which God finds nauseating (*cf.* 1:15). Positively (vv. 6–14), the redefinition of fasting as social reform (v. 6), loving care (v. 7), and a forgoing of the luxury of 'pointing the finger' (v. 9b), is a foretaste of our Lord's constructive approach to the law.

9 The promise, *Then you shall call . . .*, looks back to the unanswered prayers of v. 3 (*cf.* Jas. 4:3, 8ff.), and its rich development in vv. 9b–12 is an expression of the principle of Mt. 7:2: 'The measure you give will be the measure you get.' **11** The beautiful simile of the *watered garden* reappears in Je. 31:12. The whole series of metaphors in vv. 10–12 repays study. **13, 14** But lest it should seem that philanthropy is all, these verses describe the strictness and the gladness of the sabbath-keeping God desires. If fasting is to be an opportunity to show love to our neighbour, the sabbath should express first of all our love of God (though both the foregoing passage and the sabbath practice of Jesus insist that it must overflow to man). It will mean self-forget-fulness (v. 13a) and the self-discipline of rising above the trivial (v. 13b). But to people of this spirit God can safely give great things (v. 14).

59:1–15a Mutual alienation. This passage is largely the dark counterpart of ch. 58. There is the same problem of unanswered prayer, and a similar reply (vv. 1, 2). But whereas ch. 58 describes true righteousness and its blessings, ch. 59 depicts sin (vv. 3–8) and its obliteration of all values (vv. 9–15): *cf.* v. 10 of each chapter. The end is chaos, with human life (in Hobbes's phrase) 'solitary, poor, nasty, brutish and short'.

2 classically explains God's seeming inactivity as the effect of *separation*; not expounded here in terms of His revulsion (as at 1:15), but as the proper product of sin itself. **3ff.** The spreading anarchy of vv. 3–8 clinches the point; if this is sin, not even society survives it, let alone man's fellowship with God. **5, 6** The *adders' eggs* and *spider's web* speak tellingly of, first, the poisonous influence of evil men, propagated by the very attempts to stamp it out (v. 5b; *cf., e.g.*, the effects of banning obscene art), and secondly the futility of relying on their policies or promises (v. 6), flimsy as gossamer.

7, 8 Paul drew on these verses in Rom. 3:15–17 in building up to his climax concerning our universal guilt. **9**, with its *therefore*, ushers in the progressive consequences of choosing evil. **10** The groping in broad daylight is the judgment that Jesus' contemporaries courted (*cf.* Jn. 3:19) and suffered (*cf.* Jn. 12:35–40). **14** The four personified figures, with *truth* (*i.e.* trustworthiness) lying prostrate—it is always 'the first casualty' in disordered times—may have contributed something to the imagery of Rev. 11:7, 8. **15** Perhaps the most revealing touch is the victimizing of the decent man, the only one out of step. It is a worse breakdown than that of Am. 5:13; *i.e.* not only public justice has warped, but public opinion with it.

59:15b–21 The solitary Rescuer (*cf.* 63:1–6)

Divine action is the only possible bridge between the shame of Zion just described and the glories to follow (see the comment introducing the section 56:1 – 66:24).

16, 17 The Lord's concern is even sharper than our versions suggest. *Wondered* should be 'was appalled', as at 63:5. With this unshared indignation *cf.* Jesus' solitary grief and anger in Lk. 19:41, 45. The armour and clothing in v. 17 reaffirm the point of v. 16b; the Lord has no

external aids in fighting evil: only His pure and intense rejection of it. *Victory* and *salvation* share the same Hebrew root; *righteousness* seems to have both its dynamic, crusading sense and its more static meaning of integrity (*cf.* on 46:12, 13). So God's armour here illuminates Eph. 6:13ff.: it is what He uses, not only what He gives.

This zeal is governed by strict justice: **18** bristles with words of retribution: *repay . . . render* ('repay'); *requital . . . requital* (*cf.* Rom. 12:19); but it clears the way for a kingdom of converts. **19–21** No place of origin will disqualify (v. 19) or qualify (v. 20) a man for membership; the test is spiritual (vv. 19a, 20b; *cf.* Mt. 8:10–12), and the *covenant* is recognizably the new covenant, whose participants will not only 'all know' the Lord (Je. 31:34) but all speak for Him as a nation of prophets: *cf.* Nu. 11:29; Joel 2:28.

60:1 – 62:12 The glory of Zion

These glowing, exultant chapters depict blessings that transcend the old order and even, in places, the Christian era itself; but the language is that of the OT ordinances and of the literal Jerusalem: it will need translating into terms of 'the Jerusalem above' (*cf.* 54:1ff.; Gal. 4:26). Also Rev. 21 draws freely on ch. 60 for its picture of the radiant city from heaven; and the interpretation of that vision (of which more than one view is possible) must affect that of the present prophecy. The view taken here is that the return of dispersed Israelites to Jerusalem is made the model of a far greater movement, the world-wide inflow of converts into the church, and that the vision repeatedly looks beyond this to the end, the state of ultimate glory.

60:1–9 Lodestar of the nations. The *you* and *your* of this chapter are feminine singulars, addressing the mother-city, Zion (see on 49:14–23; 51:17–25; 54:1–10), whose *sons . . . and . . . daughters* (v. 4) are of every nationality, not only of the Israelite dispersion; *cf.* Ps. 87:3–6; Gal. 4:26. So *the nations* (v. 3) and the *coastlands* (v. 9) are more than mere carriers of this homeward traffic: they themselves furnish a large part of it as seekers who *come to* (Zion's) *light* (v. 3) and *wait* expectantly for the Lord (v. 9), homing *like doves* to their loft (v. 8; *their windows*). But see also on vv. 10–16. The *gold and frankincense* (v. 6) remind the Christian reader of the harbingers of this migration in Mt. 2, whose homage then, however, was disputed and whose gifts included the premonitory myrrh (*cf.* Mk. 15:23; Jn. 19:39)—pointers to the struggle that still lay ahead.

On the setting and symbolism of, especially, vv. 6–9 (of which v. 7 is crucial to the understanding of the chapter), see the introductory remarks to the section 60:1 – 62:12, above. The priestly terms of v. 7 preclude a purely literal interpretation of the prophecy, since the NT insists that there can be no return to a worship based on sacrificial *rams . . . altar* and *house*, which were 'but a shadow of the good things to come' (Heb. 10:1; *cf.* Heb. 13:10–16; Jn. 4:21–26). On *Tarshish*, see on 2:16.

60:10–16 The sweets of conquest. The Gentiles of this passage are not converts but subjects, conquered rather than won. Scripture always envisages many such (*cf.*, *e.g.*, Lk. 19:27; Rev. 20:7ff.). In metaphors of victory and its fruits—foreign labour (v. 10), immunity from attack (v. 11a; *cf.* Rev. 21:25f.), exotic tribute (v. 11b), and the like—God promises the triumph of His kingdom and the endless (v. 15) felicity of His people. The apparent imperialism of the passage only expresses the sober truth that to reject God's sway is suicide (v. 12), and that the meek will inherit the earth.

60:17–22 The full blaze of glory. *Gold* instead of *bronze* is a characteristic divine exchange (*cf.* 61:3, 7), in telling contrast to human decline and devaluations (*cf.* the makeshifts in 1 Ki. 14:26–28 and the pathos of La. 4:1ff.). The passage is so packed with these new glories that it can only be portraying the final perfection, where, in a people *all . . . righteous*, no *overseers* or *taskmasters* will be needed but the constraint of right and concord (v. 17b), and no defence but the *salvation* which is inseparable from God (*cf.* 59:17), and the *praise* which is trust made perfect. The living centre of this glory is revealed in the two middle verses, 19, 20, viz. the immediate presence of God. Rev. 21:23; 22:5, confirm that this vision outruns not only the OT but the Christian era, expressing in earthly terms (*cf.*, *e.g.*, v. 22) the new creation of which 65:17ff. will speak again.

61:1–4 The song of the Lord's Anointed. Although the term 'the Servant of the Lord' is absent from this song (as indeed from 50:4–9), it seems artificial to make the 'me' of v. 1 a new speaker. Our Lord saw His mission revealed as clearly in this song as in the others (*cf.* Lk. 4:17–21; 7:22); and we may notice, in this 'Spirit'-endued (*cf.* 11:2; 42:1) and 'anointed' one, a blending of terms that relate to the Servant and the Messianic King.

The joyful task here is a fit sequel to the travail of the earlier songs (see on 42:1), the fruit of which was glimpsed in 53:10ff. Our Lord could quote this passage at the outset of His career because He had already accepted, in His baptism and temptation, the role of suffering Servant, and with it the cross. These are the 'benefits of His passion'; His miracles spoke the same language.

The setting continues to be the captivity, viewed in turn from Babylon (v. 1b) and the ruined Jerusalem (v. 3). To its first hearers the promise would be as literal as the earlier threat of exile (*cf.* 39:6); but as fulfilled by Jesus (*cf.* Lk. 4:21) it inaugurated the blessings proclaimed in the beatitudes and elsewhere to the downtrodden (*afflicted* is translated 'poor' in LXX, using the word found in Lk. 4:18; 6:20; 7:22), and particularly to those who *mourn* (*cf.* perhaps Am. 6:6). *The opening of the prison* was to be spiritual, too, as John the Baptist had to learn

(was his question of Lk. 7:19 provoked by the hopes he had pinned on the 'manifesto' of Lk. 4:18?). Notice the element of slow maturing and patient reconstruction implied in the metaphors of *oaks* and *ruined cities*.

But Jesus' marked omission of the words *the day of vengeance . . .* (*cf.* Lk. 4:19, 20) points on tacitly to a final stage yet to be fulfilled: *cf.* Mt. 25:31ff.; Acts 17:31; 2 Thes. 1:7, 8. In its various contexts, then, the prophecy is seen in the bud, the flower and, by implication, the full fruit. See further on 63:4.

61:5–9 The ample compensation. This passage is sometimes thought to fall below the generous missionary spirit of, *e.g.*, 19:24, 25; 45:22; 66:18–21, as though it relegated the Gentiles to perpetual servility. This is to mistake metaphor for fact. Under the figure of a priestly Israel served by foreigners (vv. 5, 6) and enriched by its former plunderers (vv. 7, 8), the reality is the people of God (whose status is not national: *cf.* 1 Pet. 2:10; Rev. 7:9), vindicated and enjoying their full inheritance as kings and priests (*cf.* 1 Pet. 2:9; Rev. 1:6), while the pride of man is humbled and his power harnessed. On the Gentiles seen as the vanquished, see on 60:10–16; on Gentile converts see on 19:16–24; 60:1–9. 7 With the promised *double portion*, *cf.* possibly 40:2.

61:10, 11 The song of the justified. With this outburst of joy, *cf.* 12:1ff. and the songs in chs. 24–27. Note the two metaphors for righteousness: first as the *robe*, on which the perfect comment is 'the best robe' of Lk. 15:22, festive and wholly undeserved; secondly as *shoots* of plant life, products of *what is sown*, whose inherent vitality issues in growth and form. The former depicts righteousness as conferred from outside (*cf.* Rom. 3:22); the latter as springing from within (*cf.* Rom. 8:10); both make it the gift of God. On its shades of meaning, *cf.* on 46:12, 13.

62:1–5 The bridal beauty of Zion. This is another poem in the series (beginning at 49:14, ending with 66:7ff.) that depicts Zion as a woman yearning for her husband and family. But here the stress is on God's side of the reunion: the energy of His will (v. 1a), the height (v. 1b) and width (v. 2) of His ambition for her; the pride He takes in perfecting her (v. 3), His joy in bringing home the outcast (v. 4a); and the central mystery—that this is not philanthropy but ardent love (vv. 4b, 5b).

1, 2 *Vindication* is literally 'righteousness', which is a preferable translation (*cf.* 61:10, 11), even though the parallel terms *salvation* and *glory* indicate that this is far from a mere legalistic rectitude. **4** Of the four names here, the last two have passed into (and out of) the Christian vocabulary as Hephzibah and Beulah (see RSV mg.), and their occurrence together illustrates the contrast between the biblical faith and the Canaanite cults; for the metaphor of God as Husband is one of fidelity (*cf.* on 50:1) and *delight*, whereas Baal as husband was little more than a source of fertility. **5** Zion's *sons* may disrupt the metaphor to our ears, but are meant to enrich it by the reminder that the godly are as much wedded to as produced by their mother-city, whose restoration is their delight as well as God's.

62:6–12 Hastening the great day. As in 61:1–4, the great home-coming is viewed from both the centre and the circumference: from the waiting Jerusalem (vv. 6–9, 11b, 12) and the farthest corners of the earth (vv. 10, 11a). Each of these provides its picture of the human preparations appropriate to God's decisive moment. **6–8** God first gives certain men a concern for Zion like His own (*cf.* vv. 6b, 7a with 1a), summoning these *watchmen* (*cf.* 56:9ff.) and remembrancers (see on 63:7; *cf.* 2 Sa. 8:16, AV mg.) to importunate prayer (*cf.* Lk. 11:8; 18:7 with the bold figure of vv. 6b, 7a), which He encourages with explicit promises (vv. 7, 8). **10** Secondly He calls on those who are in bondage to claim their liberty, and to give a lead to the distant *peoples* from whom He would bring Zion's citizens home. On the latter's identity, see on 60:1–9. **12** Notice finally the fourfold name of this ransomed community (*cf.* the new name promised in v. 2); a triumphant climax to this group of chapters.

63:1–6 The solitary Avenger

This is the companion piece to 59:15b–21 (*cf.* v. 5 with 59:16). While both treat of judgment and consequent salvation, this poem with its dramatic dialogue (*cf.* Ps. 24:7–10) highlights the 'day of vengeance' (v. 4), a theme which was blended in 61:2 with that of restoration. The two activities are related causally, as victory (with its bloodshed) is to liberation (with its joy and peace); the NT endorses the sequence, developing this poem in Rev. 19:11–16, where Jesus is the warrior. But in both testaments God has first described a refuge from His judgment (*cf.* 53:5).

1, 2 *Edom* and its city *Bozrah* have already typified the impenitent world in 34:6. Now there is a play on the name Edom (*red*) and indirectly on Bozrah, a word similar to 'grape-gatherer'. *Announcing vindication*: read 'speaking in righteousness' (*cf.* AV, RV). As in 45:23; 55:11, it refers to God's unfailing completion of what He announces. Notice *mighty to save*: this is the dominant interest, even in this judgment passage. **3** The phrase, *I have trodden the wine press alone*, may remind the Christian of Calvary, but its meaning (*cf.* Rev. 19:15) is that God alone cares enough and has power enough to carry through the work of judgment.

63:7 – 64:12 The crying needs of Zion

The glories of chs. 60–62 and the vision of decisive action in 63:1–6 stir the prophet to one of the most eloquent intercessions of the Bible, as he surveys the past goodness of God and the present straits of His people.

63:7–14 God's former mercies. 7 Isaiah is

doing the work of a 'remembrancer' (*cf.* 62:6); his resolve, *I will recount*, is literally 'I will bring to remembrance'. **8** In the metaphor of a father's hopes for his children he picks up the opening theme of the book (1:2, 4), and in **9** he draws freely on the book of Exodus; *cf.* in turn Ex. 3:7; 33:14; 19:4. In v. 9a, retain *he was afflicted*, rather than the marginal reading; *cf.* on 9:3. **10–14** The terms are close to those of Ps. 78: *e.g. rebelled and grieved* (*cf.* Ps. 78:40); also the simile of leading animals to pasture in vv. 13, 14 (*cf.* Ps. 78:52, 53, 72). But he uses the terms with a new intensity (*cf.* v. 9a), and with a new emphasis on the *holy Spirit* as the Lord in the midst of His people (vv. 10, 11, 14). In vv. 10–14 the reference is to the post-wilderness rebellions of Israel, for which they were chastised (v. 10) but not cast off. For the sake of His former mercies the Lord still led them on; *cf.* vv. 13b, 14 with Ps. 78:72, where David continues the work of Moses.

63:15 – 64:12 God's forlorn family. The plea, three times over, *Thou art our father* (63:16; 64:8), gives this prayer its special intensity, as the sense of estrangement struggles with that of acceptance.

The symptoms of estrangement are partly outward, with the enemy treading down *thy holy people* (63:18), *thy holy cities* (64:10) and *our holy . . . house* (64:11); but far more serious are the inward symptoms: the spiritual hardness of 63:17, the ravages of sin described in 64:5b, 6 (a brilliant portrayal of its power to imprison, deprave and disintegrate), and a general listlessness (64:7) which makes the condition humanly incurable.

In all this there is seen the judgment of God, who has *withheld* His intervention (63:15b), *harden*ed their hearts (63:17; *cf.* 6:10) and *delivered* them *into the hand of* their *iniquities* (64:7). The last of these phrases makes it clear that God is not to blame for their spiritual plight: it stems from their own dalliance with sin.

On the other side there is a Father's constancy to appeal to (see the opening comment, above); it is more tenacious than man's (*cf.* 63:16 with 49:15; Ps. 27:10), and of longer standing (*of old*, 63:16b); further, it is proved by His mighty interventions *for those who wait for him* (64:4; *cf.* 8:17; 30:18)—and why should these not be renewed (64:1–5a)? (The NT points out how unimaginably they would be transcended: *cf.* 1 Cor. 2:9, 10.) Above all, the Father is appealed to as the Maker (64:8) who knows all and controls all. This submissive trust is a very different spirit from that of 45:9, 10; it makes the prayer, which resolutely began with praise (63:7), a model for all who must cry out of the depths.

But it ends with a question. God's answer will reveal how much or little the prophet's contrition has been echoed by his people.

65:1 – 66:24 The great divide

Far from ending in a general radiance, these chapters unsparingly sharpen the contrast of light and darkness, and strip away all cover of privilege. It is an end as searching as that of Revelation and the parables of judgment, pursuing to the last the implications of Isaiah's inaugural vision (ch. 6).

65:1–16 The owned and the disowned. 1, 2 The Hebrew as it stands agrees with Rom. 10:20, 21 in referring v. 1 to the Gentiles and v. 2 to the Jews. RSV, however, with most modern commentators, applies both verses to the Jews by understanding 'sought' and 'found' as *ready to be sought, etc.* (which goes beyond the known use of the 'tolerative Niphal'; nowhere else does this construction imply a non-event) and by re-vocalizing 'was not called (by)' to *did not call* (on). The latter change is supported by the ancient versions, but not by the Isaiah Scroll. Read the verse therefore as in AV, RV and Rom. 10:20, and see it as God's answer to the complaint of 63:19, rather than a mere echo of 64:7.

The Gentiles, then, are to be brought in, and apostate Judaism rejected (vv. 1–7); but vv. 8–10 reaffirm the promise of a 'remnant' of godly Israelites (see on 10:20–23). God's dividing line clearly runs not between Jew and Gentile as such, but between 'seekers' and 'forsakers' (vv. 10c, 11a), who are respectively blessed and cursed in vv. 13–16.

3–7 With the forbidden rites, *cf.* 57:3–10. The earlier deviations were predominantly licentious; the present ones are provocative, brushing aside God's altars (vv. 3b, 7b; *cf.* Dt. 12:2–7), dabbling in necromancy (v. 4a; *cf.* Dt. 18:11), defiantly eating forbidden flesh (v. 4b; *cf.* 66:17; Dt. 14:3, 8), and claiming a magical 'holiness' from these perversions, potent like a spell (v. 5a, lit., 'for I am holy to you'). For the crowning insult see v. 11.

8 The simile of the good grapes in a poor cluster relates the 'Remnant' theme to that of the spoilt vineyard of ch. 5, using perhaps the opening of a vintage song to make the point, since '*do not destroy*' seems to be a tune-name in the titles of Pss. 57–59. **10** On *the valley of Achor*, with its troubled past and hopeful prospect, see Jos. 7:26; Ho. 2:15. **11, 12** *Fortune* and *Destiny*, Gad and Meni, were worshipped in Syria and elsewhere. Note the word-play in v. 12a: *I will destine you* . . . With the *table* and *cups*, *cf.* 1 Cor. 10:21, 22, where Paul's question, 'Shall we provoke the Lord . . . ?' (*cf.* our v. 3) could indicate that he had this chapter in mind.

13–16 Here the opening rhythm is that of a dirge or taunt-song (*cf.* 14:3ff.), and the sharp contrasts anticipate those of the Gospels: *cf.*, *e.g.*, Mt. 25:31ff.; Lk. 6:20–26; Jn. 3:36. The name, *the God of truth*, in tacit contrast to 'the God of Abraham', *etc.*, probably emphasizes fulfilment, over against promise. *Truth* is literally 'Amen', *i.e.* what is sure and faithful; *cf.* our Lord's expression, 'verily, verily' ('amen, amen'), and His title in Rev. 3:14.

65:17–25 New heavens and earth. The new is portrayed wholly in terms of the old, only without the old sorrows; there is no attempt to describe any other kind of newness. Hence the familiar setting, Jerusalem, and the modest satisfactions, largely the chance to 'enjoy the work of (one's) hands'. This allows the most important things to be prominent in the passage: the healing of old ills (v. 17b); joy (vv. 18, 19); life (v. 20; see below); security (vv. 21–23a); fellowship with God (vv. 23b, 24; contrast *offspring of the blessed* with 'offspring of evildoers', 1:4) and concord among His creatures (v. 25).

The point of *a hundred years old* (v. 20) is that in this new setting a mere century is shamefully brief, so vast is the scale.

This leaves the question open whether the passage promises these blessings literally, or depicts the final state by means of earthly analogies. If the conditions are literal, they will be those of the millennium, as in a straight reading of Rev. 20, where the resurrected saints appear to coexist with people of the present order, before the final judgment. Against this, however, is the sequence whereby the new creation (vv. 17, 18) precedes these blessings here, but follows them in Rev. 21:1. For this reason it seems that we should take this passage as an analogy, and its allusions to *the sinner* (v. 20) and *the serpent* (v. 25) as promises of judgment and victory. The wicked will no longer flourish, or the strong prey on the weak, or the tempter escape his sentence (*cf.* v. 25: with Gn. 3:14, 15), in the perfect world to come. But all this is expressed freely, locally and pictorially, to kindle hope rather than feed curiosity. Notice finally the implication, by the allusion to 11:6–9, that this is brought to pass not by a bare creative fiat, but through the Messianic king.

66:1–5 Worshippers, welcome and unwelcome. This is no protest against rebuilding the Temple, as some have suggested, for God commanded it (Hg. 1:2ff.). Rather, it is a rebuke to ecclesiasticism—the spirit that would build human walls round God (vv. 1, 2a; *cf.* 2 Sa. 7:6, 7; Acts 7:48–50, 54). **2b** Note the distinctly chastened attitude that God expects of us, as in Lk. 18:13, since man is not only small but sinful. See, however, 57:15.

Ecclesiasticism also breeds unreality (v. 3) and intolerance (v. 5). **3** The Hebrew runs literally, 'slaughtering the ox, smiting a man', *etc.*, and could either mean (with most versions) that a merely correct ritual is like senseless slaughter and idolatry (*cf.* 1:13; Je. 7:21, *etc.*), or else that at present it is coexisting with brutality and sacrilege. The intolerance in v. 5 was acted out, almost to the letter, in Jn. 9:24, 34. It is one of the earliest allusions to purely religious persecution and theological hatred, one of the darkest stains of the church.

66:6–17 The last intervention. Although the terms of this section and the next are still those of the OT, with its Temple (v. 6), chariots (v. 20), new moons and sabbaths (v. 23), they clearly concern the end-time. **7–9** stress the utter newness of the event, which mocks the slow processes of history: the *nation . . . brought forth in one moment* is the equivalent of 1 Cor. 15:51, 52: 'we shall all be changed . . . in the twinkling of an eye'. V. 9 gives the triumphant final answer to Hezekiah's message to Isaiah in 37:3.

10–14 The exuberant family scene of these verses, concluding the poems on Zion as wife and mother (see on 49:14–23), is now centred on Zion's children (*cf.* Gal. 4:26). Note that the mother-city is really the secondary, not the primary, source of their wealth and comfort: all is from the Lord, even motherhood (v. 13), although He uses the redeemed community to dispense His gifts. The last two lines of this verse give the 'whence' and 'where' of this help: *I will comfort you; . . . comforted in Jerusalem.* Direct fellowship with God, and full involvement in His church, are held together here. In Jn. 16:22 Jesus gave v. 14a a strongly personal reference.

15, 16 The *fire* and *sword* are the harsh aspect of every divine intervention (*cf.* Mt. 10:34; Lk. 11:49–51), but this is the final one (*cf.* v. 24; 2 Thes. 1:7–10). While it has reference to *all flesh*, the special objects of wrath are the apostates of v. 17 (*cf.* Lv. 11:7, 29; Is. 65:3–7), who have known the light and despised it. **17** The *one in the midst* was perhaps the leader in a magico-religious rite: *cf.* Jaazaniah 'in their midst' in Ezk. 8:11.

66:18–24 The nations gathered in. On a millennialist view, the Lord's coming will be followed by the further evangelizing of the world, the full return of Israel, and the establishment of Jerusalem as the world's capital and centre of pilgrimage. Alternatively one may take this final section to be an epilogue that spans the first and second comings of Christ. V. 18 will then state His purpose for the world, and vv. 19–21 His means of carrying it out: the *sign* set among men (Christ crucified and risen; Mt. 12:38–40?); the *survivors*, or saved remnant, sent to the nations (v. 19); and the gathering of

His people into His *Jerusalem* (v. 20), Gentiles being admitted to full membership with Jews (v. 21). Jerusalem on this view is not the literal city: *cf.* again Gal. 4:25, 26. Vv. 22–24 would describe (still in OT terms) the states of final glory and perdition.

In more detail: in **19** the names represent the distant outposts of Israel's world. *Tarshish* was probably Tartessus in Spain; *Put and Lud* are mentioned with Ethiopia in Je. 46:9; Ezk. 30:5; *Tubal* is located in the far north in Ezk. 39:1, 2; *Javan* is Greece. **20, 21** From earth's remotest parts, then, the dispersed of Israel will be brought to Jerusalem like a homage-offering by the Gentiles. There is a double meaning in this term (Heb. *minḥâ*), which stood for the *cereal offering* in Lv. 2, *etc.*, but also for a vassal's tribute to his overlord. But these Gentiles, too, will be acceptable: not only like *a clean vessel*, fit to convey the Israelites, but as *priests and Levites* themselves. (Grammatically, *some of them* could refer to the returned Israelites, but the anticlimax is improbable.) Paul uses a striking variant of this symbolism in Rom. 15:15, 16.

22 With *the new heavens, etc.*, *cf.* 65:17. **23** *New moon* and *sabbath* have ceased to be binding on the Christian (*cf.* Col. 2:16), and it is implausible to suggest that these 'shadows' will be reinstated. They stand here for their substance, the joyful dedicating of all life to the Creator.

24 *Cf.* Dn. 12:2b; Mk. 9:48. In the synagogue, v. 23 is read again after v. 24, to soften the ending of the prophecy. But it is a true ending. 'It is plain' (to quote G. A. Smith) 'that nothing else can result, if the men on whose ears the great prophecy had fallen, with all its music and all its gospel, . . . did yet continue to prefer their idols, their swine's flesh . . . their sitting in graves, to so evident a God and to so great a grace.'

Seek the Lord while he may be found (55:6).

DEREK KIDNER

Jeremiah

INTRODUCTION

HISTORICAL BACKGROUND

When God called Jeremiah in 627 BC, Assyria had made Judah a subject under tribute. Assyria, however, rapidly weakened when the death of Ashurbanipal (c. 627 BC) precipitated civil strife. The Empire soon crumbled, its capital city, Nineveh, being sacked in 612 BC after a two-year siege. Ashuruballit, the last Assyrian monarch, maintained himself at Harran for two years longer, but potentially succession to Assyrian power lay open to any master-soldier of the day. Necho of Egypt marched his forces along the Mediterranean coast and inland to bolster the Assyrian remnant. On the way he was opposed at Megiddo by Josiah of Judah, whom he defeated and killed (609 BC; 2 Ki. 23:29f.). After the death of Josiah, his people anointed Jehoahaz, his son, as king, but Necho deposed him in favour of Jehoiakim, his brother, who was bound thereby to further Egyptian interests (2 Ki. 23:31ff.). Necho met his master, however, in Nebuchadrezzar, crown-prince of Babylon, who routed his forces at the historic battle of Carchemish (605 BC), and drove him back to his own frontiers, thereby putting an end for the time being to Egyptian ambition to rule the East (cf. 2 Ki. 24:7). Thus it came about that Judah, hitherto subject to Assyria, now passed under the control of Babylon. After Carchemish and his accession to the throne of Babylon, Nebuchadrezzar led his army through Syria and Palestine, subduing Ashkelon (late 604 BC) and unsuccessfully attacked Egypt in 601 BC. Jehoiakim submitted to him in 605–4 BC, but after the Babylonian forces retired in 601 BC turned again to Egypt. Renewed Babylonian activity early in 598 BC cowed Syria and various nomad tribes, and culminated in a large force attacking rebellious Judah. Jerusalem fell, after a siege of two months, in March 597 BC (2 Ki. 23:36ff.). Jehoiakim had died shortly before; Jehoiachin, his son and successor, was carried captive to Babylon with some of his people (2 Ki. 24:8ff.). Zedekiah was given the throne of Judah as a vassal of Babylon, although Jehoiachin, his nephew, was considered king in exile.

Egypt was unable to oppose Babylonian power beyond her own frontiers by force, and instead she sought to weaken through disaffection the bonds imposed by Nebuchadrezzar upon Syria and Palestine. Necho was succeeded in Egypt by Psammetichus II, and presumably it was he who sought to persuade these countries to enter a league with Egypt against Babylon. Zedekiah was one of those approached on this score, and there clearly seems to have been a pro-Egyptian party at court. Hananiah, the prophet, was especially prominent. But Jeremiah set his face steadfastly against the proposal (cf. 2:18, 36; 25:17–19; 28; 37:7), denouncing such prophets as false, asserting that their pro-Egyptian activities were contrary to God's will and would be tragic in their outcome. Undoubtedly they regarded themselves as true patriots, and hated Jeremiah as, in their judgment, a self-confessed traitor. By contrast, Jeremiah's charge against them was that Yahweh had not sent them, but they had come forward on their own initiative. Therefore their word would not come to pass. There, then, was the falsity. They spoke in Yahweh's name when He had not commissioned them. From all this it is clear that sincerity is not enough; only the divine inspiration constitutes a man a prophet (e.g. Je. 23:16, 26, 32).

Whether Nebuchadrezzar had received a direct report of disaffection or only rumours one cannot say, but Zedekiah was summoned to meet him and to report on home conditions. His return implied that he had given pledges of loyalty (cf. 2 Ch. 36:13). The pity was that, seemingly, he had not the moral courage and strength to withstand the influence of such pro-Egyptian plotters as Hananiah and his confederates. Jeremiah consistently urged him to remain faithful to his word (e.g. Je. 37:6ff.; 38:17ff.), but when Hophra became pharaoh in 589 BC, in succession to Psammetichus II, the Egyptian influence in the court gained headway and Zedekiah was finally induced to break faith with Nebuchadrezzar. Egypt was slow to move in support and the Babylonian monarch besieged Jerusalem again in 587 BC. At length the Egyptian army appeared and the Babylonians lifted the siege for the time being (cf. Je. 37:11–15).

The resumption of the siege seems to have brought matters to a head. Jeremiah was positive that his intuitions were of God, that He had revealed to him His purposes of making Babylon the instrument of His will (cf. Je. 27). Trust in Egypt, therefore, could pave the way only for disaster and exile. On the other hand, his enemies used Yahweh's name in support of their pro-Egyptian policy. Consequently they held that his attitude and word weakened the national will to fight (cf. Je. 38:4). This struggle stands out crucially in the person of Zedekiah. He stood between the two influences and was moved now to this side, now to that (cf. Je. 38:5, 10). He appeared unable to make up his mind and face the consequences, and it is clear that Jeremiah was not able to sway him sufficiently to make him abide by his oath of loyalty to Nebuchad-rezzar. The 'false prophets' won the day and Zedekiah took the plunge. For his indecision and belated action he paid bitterly. Egypt proved to be a broken reed, the resumed siege was success-ful, the Babylonian was ruthless (2 Ki. 25), and to his own heartbreak Jeremiah saw the bitter fulfilment of his prophecies.

The book gives details of Jeremiah's personal history up to his enforced departure into Egypt (Je. 43:1-7). Then the darkness sets in, relieved, if at all, only by traditional rumour. There is nothing to establish a final conclusion as to his fate. One Christian tradition is that some five years after the fall of Jerusalem he was stoned to death at Tahpanhes by the Jewish people who even then refused to share his vision and his faith.

JEREMIAH'S MESSAGE AND TEACHING

Politically, as we have seen, Jeremiah lost. But spiritually he won a major victory. He shared the faith of Amos and Hosea, that, though idolatry and disloyalty to Yahweh must invite the punishment stipulated when the Sinai covenant was made (e.g. Dt. 28:15ff.), yet Israel and Judah were not finally outcast from the grace of God (cf. Je. 5:18). He shared with those prophets too the faith that exile as a discipline would be remedial, not wholly tragic. The state, qua state, was doomed; but faith in Yahweh and Yahweh's choice of His people would abide and outlive the shock. Moreover, he saw that the old cove-nant, centring in the Temple and its ceremonial worship, was ineffective; thus he was led to see that Yahweh would write a new covenant within the heart of the 'remnant' (Je. 31:31-34), through which vital religion would persist and prove a blessing beyond national frontiers (cf. Je. 33:6-9).

When the book of the law, found by Hilkiah in the ruins of the Temple (2 Ki. 22:8), brought about reformation under Josiah in 622 BC, it seems clear that, at first, Jeremiah shared that king's enthusiasm, and lent his influence as aid (cf. Je. 11:2). It seems equally clear, however, that later he distrusted that revival as too facile and superficial to meet the demands of Yahweh (e.g. Je. 7:1-20). The great need was for a change of heart and that was feasible only in a people whose faith was in Yahweh alone. That centrality of faith the generation of Jeremiah refused to give.

It has been urged by many scholars that Jeremiah with other prophets was against all sacrificial ritual, regarding it as not commanded by Yahweh and, indeed, repugnant to Him (e.g. Je. 7:21-23; see commentary and NBD, art. 'Prophecy, Prophets'). Jeremiah's attitude, how-ever, and that of the other prophets, is better understood as teaching that a sacrifice would be invalid, and therefore contrary to Yahweh's desire and will, unless it were a true index of a worshipful and repentant heart, and set in the context of an obedient life.

THE BOOK

The authorship is a disputed issue, falling beyond the scope of a brief introduction. Denial of Jeremiah's authorship of several passages is dependant upon the uncertain criteria of style, for the most part, and so is itself uncertain. For a summary of views see E. J. Young, *Introduction to the Old Testament*.

The book actually describes how Baruch the scribe wrote down Jeremiah's prophecies (cf. 36:32) and states that 'many similar words were added to them'. Baruch seems to have acted generally as Jeremiah's amanuensis and went down into Egypt with him (43:6).

The arrangement of the prophecies is not by chronological order, and so can be confusing to the western mind with its regimented approach to such matters. In fact it is hard to discern a principle underlying the order of the book. Some indications are noted in the commentary. A scheme of possible dates for the various sec-tions is included in the analysis below. A further complication is the number of differences between the Hebrew and LXX texts of Jeremiah. These do not apply to words only but affect the order of whole passages; moreover the LXX is only seven-eighths the length of the Hebrew. How much value can be given to the LXX text is un-certain; note is taken of passages where it seems to throw light on the Hebrew text. Details of textual problems are clearly displayed by J. Bright in *The Anchor Bible*, 1965. Incisive exegesis of the book from a more conservative stand has been provided by H. L. Ellison in *EQ*, 31-40, 1959-68.

THE CHARACTER OF THE PROPHET

Jeremiah was indeed a man of God, sensitive to spiritual influence, capable of deep emotion, clear-sighted and candid in judgment. He could neither be bought nor cajoled. He followed the way of his mind, supported as it ever was by the worshipping spirit within him. He was God's man from first to last, and therefore a true patriot to the end. He was not blind to the sin and folly of his people. He read, with deep bitterness, the iron nexus of sin and penalty, and foresaw exile as the inevitable judgment, unless there was a change of heart. For that change he worked without reserve.

These two things, his insistence on a change of heart and the loneliness of his position as the prophet who stood out against the shallow optimism and political expedients of his con-temporaries, gave rise to that emphasis on personal religion which is one of the character-istics of Jeremiah's book. It must not be thought that personal religion began with him and that prior to his day people only acknowledged some sort of corporate religious awareness and responsibility (cf. H. H. Rowley, *The Unity of the Bible*, 1953, pp. 70ff.). Rather we ought to say that circumstances and temperament made

Jeremiah pre-eminently the prophet who lays bare before us the intimate dealings of his own soul with God and who therefore is the exemplar of the religious individual. This appears most tellingly in the tenderness of God's direct dealings with him at the time of his call (*cf.* 1:9; contrast Is. 6:6, 7; Ezk. 2:8ff.), and in passages of spiritual autobiography unique in Scripture (*e.g.* Je. 8:18 – 9:2; 11:18 – 12:3; 15:10, 11, 15–21; 17:14–18; 18:18–23; 20:7–18).

The idea of a close, personal walk with God lies at the heart of Jeremiah's conception of being a prophet. It stems from the distinctly personal terms in which God taught him his own call and appointment (1:5); it was thrust upon him by the isolation consequent on the preaching of an unpopular and rejected message (*e.g.* 11:19ff.); it was made a condition of genuine reception of a word from God (*e.g.* 15:19); and, above all, it became a foundation truth in his mighty polemic against false prophets. Jeremiah's own sense of personal inadequacy (1:6) made him more sensitive than any other prophet to the existence of men with an opposite message. Could he be certain that he, and not they, were inspired by God (*cf.* 1 Ki. 22:24)? Might he not be deceived (Je. 20:7)? The major treatment of this theme occurs in Je. 23:9–40. It is typical of his thought, personality and whole cast of mind that Jeremiah is unable to distinguish the true message from the false by any external criterion, such as the mode by which the alleged message was received. For him, three things substantiate the message: the quality of the life of the messenger (23:13, 14), the tendency of his message (23:17, 22), whether to encourage or to condemn sin, and the reality of his personal fellowship with God (23:18, 22; on 'council', see on Am. 3:7).

Jeremiah, however, was not a mere individualist (*cf.* H. H. Rowley, *op. cit.*; also *The Faith of Israel*, 1956, pp. 99, 148). He also understood the people of God as bound to Him in a link so intimate that only the personal terms of betrothal and marriage were accurate enough to describe the covenant relation (*e.g.* 2:2; 31:32). Out of this emerged his message of hope, characteristically described as a new covenant (31:31). In God he read promise, not hopelessness (*e.g.* 29:11), and he expected his people, no less than himself, to endure 'as seeing him who is invisible' (Heb. 11:27).

OUTLINE OF CONTENTS

Analysis of this extensive book is, in the main, a subjective exercise. A division after ch. 25 is fairly reasonable, however, as on the whole prophetic oracles govern the first half of the book, and narrative the second.

COMMENTARY

1:1 - 25:38 ORACLES CONCERNING GOD'S CHOSEN PEOPLE

1:1-19 THE PROPHET'S CALL

1:1-3 Information about the prophet

Jeremiah's call revealed the initiative of God who had predestined him to the office of prophet. **1** *Anathoth*, some 3 miles north of Jerusalem, is modern Anata. **2** *The thirteenth year* of Josiah; *i.e.* 627 BC. **3** *The captivity of Jerusalem*; *i.e.* when Nebuchadrezzar destroyed the city in 586 BC. Jeremiah's task thus continued for a few more than 40 years.

1:4-10 The consecration of the prophet

Two thoughts dominate this section: first, the insistence on the basic element of predestination in the appointment of the prophet (vv. 4, 5), and secondly, the adequacy of the divine word to equip him for every eventuality (vv. 6-10). **5** The dealings of God with Jeremiah are no divine afterthought, no panic action deriving from the need to speak a word to the nation in the present crisis. Jeremiah is rather a divine forethought, long planned as God's man for this very time. Before conception, and between conception and birth, divine intimate awareness (*knew*) and divine separating action (*consecrated*) have led up to the moment of appointment. **6-8** His commission was equally clear. The contrast drawn is that of shrinking from the task and being inspirited for it. He is the most self-questioning of all the prophets on record. He protested *I am only a youth* (v. 6), meaning that he was not qualified by training or experience. But his objection was overruled, on the grounds that authority resides not in the person of the messenger but in the divine commission (v. 7a), word (v. 7b) and presence (v. 8). **9** God *touched* his lips, thereby guaranteeing that the word spoken henceforth will be the living word of God. **10** The word will be both destructive and constructive, and herein is the clue to the pessimistic feature of his prophecies. He understood that catastrophe was the inevitable consequence of disloyalty and lack of faith among God's people. Yet should even the worst happen, Jeremiah knew that that judgment would be but God's prelude to a nobler day. Thus the message of hope is intrinsic in Jeremiah's prophecies.

1:11-16 The declaration to the prophet

The call of Jeremiah was closely connected with two visions, associated with his call to verify it, and to encourage him. Through these visions God made a declaration to the prophet and through him to the people. **11, 12** The vision of the *rod of almond* introduces the reader to Jeremiah's love and awareness of nature as a revealing agent of God. There is a play on words here: *almond* (Heb. *šāqēd*) and *watching over* . . .

to (Heb. *šōqēd*). The almond tree is the first to awake in spring; so Yahweh is always aware of events and His word heralds His action. **13** *A boiling* (lit. 'blow upon') *pot*, as RV 'caldron' implies, was a large vessel for cooking or washing; *facing away from the north* suggests that the pot was tilted, about to overflow from Syria into Palestine. **14-16** Yahweh would make a northern people the agent of His judgment (*cf.* on 3:18; 4:5), which idolatry, involving a tension of two masters, Yahweh and pagan gods, had brought upon the nation.

1:17-19 The charge to the prophet

Just as v. 5 firmly enunciates the fact of predestination, so v. 17 enunciates the requirement of obedience. Jeremiah is warned against fear of his audience; the prophet who is ashamed to stand forth with the word, will soon have no word to proclaim (v. 17). But the Lord of the word can make His servant impregnable, unlike the disloyal state of Judah (vv. 18, 19).

2:1 - 6:30 THE NATION'S SUMMONS

Jeremiah places in the forefront of his prophecies two messages which accurately state the condemnatory side of his ministry. The first (2:1 – 3:5) deals with the inexcusable apostasy of Israel from the Lord, and the second (3:6 – 6:30) states the prospect before the nation, inevitable judgment.

2:1 – 3:5 Jeremiah's first message: the sin of apostasy

2:1-3 The former state of Israel. There was once a time when Israel had been steadfast (*devotion*), loving (*love*) and committed (*followed*) to the Lord, and was thus His special portion (*holy* . . . *first fruits*; *cf.* Dt. 26:2, 10), under His watchful care (*evil* . . . *upon them*).

2:4-13 The contention with Israel. 5-7 Yahweh challenges Israel's memory of His gracious provision for them to prove that it was not He who had broken faith. It was they who *defiled my land*; **8** it was their prophets who *prophesied* by Baal, the popular Canaanite deity, officially recognized in Israel through the Phoenician alliances of Ahab (1 Ki. 16:31f.). **10** *Cyprus* represents the West; *Kedar*, in N Arabia, represents the East. Therefore, taken together, they stand for the whole pagan world. **11, 12** summarize the horror of the prophet at his people's apostasy. Unlike even pagan nations, who remained true to their gods, Israel had preferred 'profitless' gods to Yahweh, their own God. Even the heavens were aghast at such sacrilege. **13** The mention of *broken cisterns* contrasts the polluted, wasted water with that of a perennial (*living*) spring.

2:14–19 The humiliation of Israel. This paragraph shows how sin overtakes a nation. Freeborn Israel has become a slave. **14, 15** *Homeborn.* There were two kinds of slaves; those acquired by purchase became slaves through special circumstances, and those born in the house were slaves by nature. But the Lord had redeemed the formerly enslaved Israel (*cf.* Ex. 20:2). Whence, then, this new slavery, as seen in the devastated condition of the nation? **16** *Memphis and Tahpanhes.* The former is the capital of Lower Egypt, near Cairo, the latter was in the eastern Delta (*cf.* 44:1; 46:14). **17, 18** The explanation: Israel has been the architect of its own misfortunes. When the Lord would have *led,* Israel chose rather the path of apostasy. Yet the lesson has not been learned, and the nation continues to seek resources in alliances with *Egypt* and *Assyria.* **19** Disaster with all its bitterness must be the tragic teacher, since *the fear of me is not in you.*

2:20–28 The degeneration of Israel. 20 *Playing the harlot* contrasts with v. 2; unfaithfulness in a sexual relationship is a standard prophetic illustration of idolatry. **21** *A noble vine; cf.* Is. 5:1–7. The force of the metaphor is that the blame for subsequent failures is not the Lord's. **22–25** describe the ingrained nature of their iniquity and their wilful determination to continue in their sin. Jeremiah likens them to a desert creature in heat, whose desire is so great that any mate that wants it can find it without effort. It is as though the female were pursuing the male. **23** *Valley* (*cf.* 7:31) balances 'high hill' (v. 20); the whole land furnishes evidence of their apostasy. **25** *I have loved strangers* (*i.e.* other gods), *and after them I will go.* Their desire to share in the idolatrous practices of the heathen nations was so great that they were determined nothing should prevent them from doing so. **26–28** *You are my father* is indicative of complete devotion to the idol. *In the time of their trouble.* The testing hour would reveal the impotence of the gods they had made for themselves. They would be *shamed* like a caught thief (*cf.* v. 36), but could expect no aid from the God with whom they had broken faith.

2:29–37 The complacency of Israel. The nation which could say 'I am not defiled' (v. 23), when every part of the land proclaimed defilement (vv. 20, 23), now pleads *I am innocent* (v. 35), thereby showing petulant refusal of divine correction (vv. 29, 30), forgetfulness of His love (vv. 31, 32), and complacency in the face of irrefutable evidence (vv. 33–35). Judgment alone can be their portion (vv. 36, 37).

3:1–5 The wages of apostasy. Contrasting with the happy marriage of 2:1–3, Jeremiah concludes with a much broken marriage which cannot be mended (v. 1). The evidence is abundant (v. 2), but no amount of correction has produced reformation (v. 3). All this gives the lie to words which profess devotion (v. 4) and hope (v. 5a), but are set in the context of wholesale devotion to wrongdoing (v. 5b).

3 The effect of Judah's sin became apparent in the land, as stipulated when the covenant was made (Dt. 28:23f.). **5** *You have spoken, but you have done* contrasts with God who remains constant to His Word.

3:6 – 6:30 Jeremiah's second message: the prospect of judgment

In the first discourse no hint of forgiveness is given; here a distinct assurance of pardon is held out, provided repentance is genuine and heartfelt, yet the dominant note is that judgment is imminent and inevitable.

3:6–10 The unfavourable contrast between Judah and Israel. 6 The prophet saw that *that faithless one, Israel* (lit. 'apostasy Israel', signifying Israel as the personification of apostasy) had been sent into exile as a judgment on her adultery; yet Judah read no warning to herself. On the contrary, she feigned loyalty, but there was no evidence of genuine conversion (vv. 6–10). **10** *In pretence*; the reformation under Josiah did not go very deep. Judah returned, but only superficially.

3:11–18 The urgent call to Israel. Israel, broken and exiled, was told to repent. **11** *False Judah*; in spite of greater privileges, such as a succession of kings of the same family, the Temple, the Levites, the warning example of Israel, and especially her preservation hitherto, Judah proved faithless. **14** *Return, O faithless children.* The ground of the divine appeal is the gracious relationship which God had chosen to bear with His people, explained by *I am your master* (Heb. *bāʿaltî*, 'I am lord'), which makes clear that Yahweh was sovereign, and no Canaanite Baal; the people were as wilful children, turning from their master. (The translation 'I am married to you' is possible but less appropriate in this context; *cf.* on 31:32.) In line with the whole biblical revelation, Jeremiah knew that God delights in mercy. If they returned in penitence He would bring them back to worship at home in *Zion,* thus reversing Israel's great apostasy (*cf.* 1 Ki. 12:26–30). **16** *The ark* had become a talisman, its significance overlooked. In the restored worship both ark and law-tablets would be superseded (*cf.* 31:33). **17** *At that time*; when Israel returns to the Lord and from the exile, God's glory in the midst of the people would be evident to all nations. **18** *The land of the north*; the quarter from which the Babylonian armies would approach and carry away the exiles, and from which they would return. The prophet was looking forward to a time when Jerusalem would be purified from all idolatry.

3:19 – 4:2 The unconditional return of the people to Yahweh. Jeremiah continues to address Israel, the exiled northern kingdom, though his purpose is to appeal to Judah. Just as the Lord's judgment on Israel should have warned Judah (vv. 6–10), and His readiness to forgive Israel should have moved Judah's hard heart (vv. 11–18), so also the depicted total repentance of Israel provides an object lesson for Judah to copy

(3:19 – 4:2). **21, 22** Jeremiah heard a kind of weeping antiphony in the north, of the penitent children crying and the forgiving, healing God soothing in turn. *Bare heights*, not the 'high places' of pagan cult (*cf.* v. 23), but the wasted hills of the ravaged land. **24, 25** *The shameful thing*; literally 'the shame', a term used by the prophets for Baal-worship, and later as a euphemism to avoid the name Baal. The heart-broken confession touches in turn the folly (v. 24), hopelessness (v. 25a), ingratitude (*against the Lord*, v. 25b), ingrained nature (v. 25c) and disobedience (v. 25d) of sin. **4:1** The Lord instructs His people in the way of penitence, first positively, *if you return . . . to me you should return*, and then negatively, *remove your abominations*, *i.e.* the false gods and all that pertains to their worship. Thirdly, repentance involves moral determination (*not waver*) to live for God, and **2** carries the promise of a powerful influence on others.

4:3-31 The call to Judah. Jeremiah turns to apply the moral to his own people. The judgment which hangs over their heads can be averted by repentance (vv. 3-18), but it cannot be turned aside by any other means (vv. 19-31).

3, 4 The untilled land and the uncircumcised heart depict the two sides of true repentance: the outward change of a life rescued from the weeds of sin, and the inward change of the new heart; *cf.* Dt. 10:16; 30:6. **5-18** The coming invasion was probably a Babylonian attack; some see allusions in this and following passages to a historically obscure Scythian raid late in the 7th century BC. Jeremiah pleaded for a deep repentance, in the face of imminent catastrophe (v. 4b). He reinforces his plea by elaborating the threat. The appointed scourge *from the north* was already on the threshold. **7** The *lion* had come out of his lair, seeking prey. He was the fierce destroyer of nations and cities, a reference in all probability to Nebuchadrezzar. **10** *It shall be well with you.* Many read 'and they shall say', *i.e.* the false prophets of v. 9 (*cf.* 23:17); so one tradition of LXX. However, Jeremiah may refer to words of past prophets in different situations, still remembered (*e.g.* Is. 37:33-35). **11** *A hot wind* is another metaphor of destruction. It is the sirocco from the desert, a hot scorching wind, cyclonic and merciless, not the refreshing wind blowing from the coast at evening and utilized for winnowing. Such must be Yahweh's action upon the guilty land. **13** The same grave judgment appears in different figures of speech, *clouds . . . chariots* and *horses . . . swifter than eagles.* **14, 15** The efficacy of repentance is urged against the desolating doom approaching from Dan, the northern limit of the land, and the warning voice is echoed from Mt. Ephraim as near as 10 miles to Jerusalem.

In **19-31** the extent of the coming judgment appals the prophet (vv. 19-29), and in the light of it he notes the pathetic futility of worldly expedients against divine visitation (vv. 30, 31). **19-22** Note the pain of his soul (vv. 19, 20), the

question of his mind (v. 21) and the answer of his God (v. 22). His words literally writhe in the agony which tortured him. *My anguish, my anguish! I writhe in pain!* But Jeremiah was under no illusion. The judgment was just. It was the dark entail of sin upon an abandoned people. **23-28** The imagery in vv. 23-26 is so stark that a shudder vibrates throughout. World chaos has overtaken the cosmos; mountains reel, man vanishes, birds have fled out of the sky, and the fertile earth has become a desert. It is the blast of God, the reversal of creation to the shapeless meaninglessness of Gn. 1:2.

29-31 *O desolate one.* All flee before God's avenging agent (v. 29), save one who would flaunt herself in a fruitless attempt to gain his favour: so hardened was the conscience of Jerusalem. Such dread finality of sin involves the whole world. Jeremiah saw nothing but irremediable travail, bereft of hope. All these grim predictions were fulfilled in the final overthrow of Jerusalem in 586 BC.

Some authorities consider that this second message of Jeremiah begun at 3:6 is composed of several oracles, some written at Anathoth and others at Jerusalem. Be that as it may, there is a definite unity in the message which justifies a continued treatment. There is the same emphasis upon the hardened sin of a besotted nation and inevitable doom from a holy God waiting to be gracious if only the people would repent.

5:1-9 The corruption of Jerusalem. In 5:1-31 the city is seen under a relentless moral investigation. The prophet attempts a vindication of the severity of God, *i.e.* a valid theodicy. He felt that were one to search Jerusalem, no honest man would be found to avert the doom (*cf.* Gn. 18:22-32): the *poor* in the streets (v. 1) and peer (v. 5) alike are impious in life and deed. **1** *Run to and fro through the streets of Jerusalem.* The quest was in vain. **6** Hence the nation was as defenceless as a townsman in a forest of wild beasts. The inhabitants of Jerusalem, indeed, had sunk down to the level of beasts. **7, 8** When God had full-fed them they prostituted His bounty and became like full-fed stallions in their lust.

5:10-19 The call to the destroyer. The optimism of the negligent is portrayed in vv. 10-18. God's agents are to carry through the task of purging (vv. 10, 11), yet the doomed (vv. 12-17) cherish the fallacy in blind hope that Yahweh will take no action. **10** *A full end.* The Lord controls the judgment within the bounds of His promise to preserve His people. They merit judgment, and mercy triumphs ultimately. **12** *They have spoken falsely of the Lord, and have said,* '*He will do nothing*'; *i.e.* He would do nothing along the line of Jeremiah's prophecy. If this rendering of the text is correct, the people could not believe that God would punish them; **13** so they treated His prophets as false, and said that the punishment would fall on them. **15** *Whose language you do not know*; difference of speech was always a cause of dread and uneasiness in the ancient world, for appeals for mercy would be fruitless when made in an unknown tongue. **16** *Their quiver*; a remarkable comparison. Like the grave their weapons were never satisfied.

5:20–31 The stubbornness and folly of the people. This section deals on the one hand with God as the moral Governor and on the other with His rebellious people. God's world is unable to break loose from His unswerving, sovereign will (v. 22); only His people have that liberty (vv. 23, 24); a lone differential for ever characterizing man. **22** *The sea*; the prophet uses the sea to illustrate the might and majesty of God; it may not pass the bounds that He has set. Is such a God to be trifled with? If the sea is feared—and who does not fear it—is not He to be feared? **23** *Stubborn . . . rebellious*; not only are the people backsliders, they are openly hostile.

In 26–31 the prophet has three classes of people in mind: the rich who oppress the poor, the false prophets who deceive, and the priests who also misbehave (v. 31, *rule at their direction* is uncertain; 'spurn their office' has been proposed as an alternative). The nation sits loosely to the divine will, with the evil consequence that neither justice is done nor is there any desire that prophet and priest be other than what they are—liars and false guides. *My people love to have it so*. Evil, if practised long enough, is accepted by the rank and file as inevitable.

6:1–5 The investment of Jerusalem. The conclusion of Jeremiah's second message is the inevitable doom imminent upon such an impenitent and incorrigible nation. The destructive agent appointed by God was about to invest Jerusalem. **1** He was watching greedily from *the north*, ready to bring utter ruin. The warning was to be passed on from Jerusalem to *Beth-haccherem* (mod. Ramat Rahel, a height between Jerusalem and Bethlehem), an eminence from which a beacon-fire (*signal*) would be visible as far as *Tekoa* on another hill some 12 miles south of the capital. The *trumpet* and *signal* would warn and guide the city-dwellers to seek refuge in the broken terrain of the south country as the enemy approached from the north. *People of Benjamin* may mean the men of Judah (*cf.* 'Ephraim' for Israel in 7:15), the citizens of Jerusalem as a whole, peasantry whose place and practices were not with the city, or the prophet may be showing concern for his own tribe.

3 *Shepherds*; the enemy from the north is likened to shepherds with their flocks, eating up the grass on every side; everything would be devoured and nothing left. **4, 5** *Prepare war*; literally 'hallow war', *i.e.* offer sacrifices to ensure success. The exhortation calls for hostilities to begin, and it is the enemy outside the city walls that thus heartens himself. Their persistence was such that, if the day attack failed, the evening would bring victory. The prophet predicted in the name of the Lord that the victory should be absolute and final.

6:6–15 The coming ruin. 6 *Hew down her trees*;

trees were cut down to construct siege works, but this verse also indicates the devastation the enemy would cause. **9** Under the figure of a vineyard, the gatherers go over and over gleaning the very last grape and leave the vineyard desolate. This verse is addressed to Nebuchadrezzar, or in general to the leader of the besieging army. Israel had not even a 'remnant' left and Judah was facing a like extinction and exile. But the tragedy of the day was that in the gathering gloom the optimism of the religious leaders persisted. **12** *Houses . . . fields . . . wives*; these coming evils are similar to those mentioned in Dt. 28:30. **14** *Healed the wound*; the rupture between the holy God and the sinful nation was light-heartedly and superficially doctored. But the day of visitation was at hand.

6:16–21 Yahweh's appeal and Judah's disobedience. 16 An appeal came again from the Lord to the people through the prophet to seek *the ancient paths*. With the promise contained in this verse *cf.* Mt. 11:29. Jeremiah based all his appeals on the experience of the past. They refused. The nations of the earth therefore were set against them as witnesses. **20** *Sheba* lay in the south-west of Arabia and supplied incense to most of the ancient world; *cf.* 7:21. **21** *I will lay stumbling blocks*; to Jeremiah, as to his predecessors, there were no such things as intermediary causes; all was ascribed to God. Note, however, that in laying stumbling-blocks the Lord is simply bringing the 'fruit of their devices' (v. 19). It is no arbitrary or capricious act. *Cf.* Is. 8:14; Ezk. 3:20; 7:19; 18:30.

6:22–30 The enemy's cruelty and the people's incorrigibility. Once more to arouse the nation from its fatal optimistic apathy the enemy was vividly described in terrifying terms. **25** *Terror is on every side*; *cf.* 20:10; 46:5; 49:29; Jb. 18:11; Ps. 31:13; hence the fugitives are advised not to go on the road. **26** *Make mourning*; *i.e.* 'mourn for thyself'. **27–30** present the prophet's dark intuition. **27** His function was freshly realized as *an assayer and tester*. Jeremiah felt that his task would be as a 'refiner of silver', but now it was borne upon him that his 'fire' failed to refine the national silver from its dross; *i.e.* unlike the mineral refining, the human will could refuse the purging 'fire'. God gives such a soul over to its choice. Paul pictures this wilful obstinacy on the part of the Gentile nations in Rom. 1:18–32. **29** *The bellows blow fiercely* to no avail, for the lead that would draw away the dross is consumed, but the dross remains; *cf.* 9:7. **30** *Refuse silver* or 'rejected silver'. This dark shadow closes the second message of Jeremiah and the first section of his prophecy.

7:1 – 10:25 THE ILLUSIONS OF TEMPLE SECURITY

To Judah the Temple was sacrosanct and therefore impregnable to all attack. If the worst came to the worst, Yahweh would undoubtedly intervene to save the city in which He had set His name. Jeremiah here states the very reverse. Shiloh was also held to be inviolate, yet it was overthrown. The 'Temple sermon' given here makes no mention of the alarm and fury it created. In ch. 26, however, such information is given among the historical summaries of the second division of the book, together with the peril to the prophet consequent upon his fearless witness. If the assumption that ch. 26 belongs to the same period as these 'Temple sermons' is correct, then the time would be 608 BC, the beginning of the reign of Jehoiakim. This section is Jeremiah's third message, and is in two parts.

7:1 – 8:3 The Temple sermon: ritual correctness or moral rectitude

This word of the Lord is directed to two facets of behaviour that had been separated, wrongly, by Jeremiah's contemporaries: religious profession and moral conduct. The prophet reiterates the burden of the Commandments that it is impossible to respect God and disregard one's fellows.

7:1–20 A warning. 2 The message is addressed to those who *enter . . . to worship* (LXX omits this phrase), not to heedless passers-by; it is for men who make some appearance of correct belief. A great festival when people crowded the Temple courts may have been the occasion of the speech; equally, it may have been delivered to any who happened to be there on an ordinary day. **3** *Your ways and your doings* may be explained as 'settled habits and the separate acts which go to form them'. *This place*; Jerusalem as a whole (*cf.* v. 7). **4** *The temple of the Lord*. The repetition may be for emphasis or may represent the chorus of the citizens who trusted in its presence for safety. **5–7** enlarge upon vv. 3, 4; there is still opportunity for repentance. **8–10** reveal the sham of the religious as worse than James's friends whose works belied their faith (Jas. 2). **10** *This house* was officially holy, set apart geographically and ceremonially as the residence of God. By their own pollution the people contaminate it, so bringing upon themselves the appropriate penalty of expulsion and exile. *We are delivered*. Evidently the Temple rites had been degraded to the level of magic spells to ward off disaster, spells to be repeated as necessary.

11 *Den of robbers*; *i.e.* a place of retreat between acts of crime and violence; *cf.* Mk. 11:17; Lk. 19:46. **12–14** *Shiloh*, now Seilūn, lies on the road from Jerusalem to Shechem, north of Bethel. The ark was placed there in the days of Joshua (Jos. 18:1; *cf.* 1 Sa. 1:3). Its destruction, nowhere described in the OT, was carried through by the Philistines *c.* 1050 BC, according to archaeological indications. Ps. 78:60 records that God forsook it.

16–20 Addressed as a private word from the Lord to Jeremiah, these verses nevertheless continue the main theme of the Temple sermon. The people have been shown as trusting to ritual for their salvation, but now the Lord invites Jeremiah to look at the character of much of their ritual: it is pagan, abhorrent to the Lord, inviting and guaranteeing utter judgment. **18** *Queen of heaven*; probably Canaanite Ashtoreth, Babylonian Ishtar, goddess of fertility and of war. The Hebrew word 'queen' is unusual, perhaps foreign; LXX and other texts understood it as 'the host of heaven'.

7:21–28 Obedience and sacrifice. The theme of the relationship between the ritual and the moral aspects of the godly life is here brought to a climax of such force and scorn that it has often been thought that Jeremiah intended the utter repudiation of the sacrificial system. His argument, however, is directed towards the establishment of the true priorities of religion, and not towards the denial of one side of God's revelation through Moses at Sinai. **21** *Burnt offerings*, symbolizing total commitment to God (*cf.* Gn. 22:2, 12, 13), were wholly given to God (Lv. 1:6–9), and, unlike *e.g.* the peace-offerings (*cf.* Lv. 7:15), were banned from human consumption. The Lord's rejection of the superstitious ritualism of the people is here shown in that He invites them to eat the burnt-offerings also. Their meticulous ritual correctness has become, even to that extent, a matter of indifference to Him.

22 *Concerning burnt offerings and sacrifices.* All the traditions of Israel's religion available at Jeremiah's time, on any theory of the compilation of the OT, would insist that the Lord had, in fact, given commandment at the Exodus time concerning sacrifices. It is undoubtedly the case that Jeremiah would not be so rash as to jeopardize his case by calling in question the validity of the Mosaic revelation, and therefore we must understand him to be asking about the due priorities of true religion. At Sinai, was the Lord motivated by an overriding concern for sacrifices? Was He not rather looking above all for an obedient people? And were not the sacrifices a derivative legislation, designed both to express obedience (burnt-offerings), to cultivate the fellowship of an obedient people with their God (peace-offerings), and to cater for lapses from obedience (sin-offerings)? If we render the verse, as is legitimate, 'I did not speak . . . because of' or 'for the sake of', this sense is immediately clarified (*cf. NBD*, art. 'Prophecy and Prophets'). **24** *But they did not obey.* When compared with 2:2 some difference appears, yet as that passage is obviously a generalization, so is this—in the opposite direction. **27** is another word to uphold 'the prophet of doom'. Although the result of the preaching is known in advance to the prophet, he must still proclaim the word in justice to the people.

7:29 – 8:3 National mourning. The call to the people to lament is because Yahweh has rejected that generation. **29** No person is named, but the verbs are feminine in Hebrew and this points to Jerusalem or the nation personified. The symbol of deep mourning was the cutting off of the hair (lit. 'thy crown'); *cf.* Jb. 1:20; Mi.

1:16. Some have seen in this a reference to the Nazirite vow (Nu. 6:7). Jerusalem has broken her vows, and so, like a faithless Nazirite, might as well cut off the hair, which was his symbol and badge. **30** *They have set their abominations*; 2 Ki. 21:5 tells that Manasseh profaned the Temple in the manner here described.

31 *Topheth* (LXX 'high place') probably means 'fireplace'; *cf.* Is. 30:33. As a mark of horror and repudiation of the pagan concept, the vowels of the original word were replaced by those of *bōšeṭ*, 'shame', so that it was read and spoken *tōpeṭ*. Similarly, the heathen deity Molech contains the consonants of *meleḵ*, 'king' and the vowels of *bōšeṭ*; *cf.* on 3:24. It was to this Canaanite idol that human child sacrifices were offered, a thing never countenanced by Yahweh, and outlawed by Josiah, 2 Ki. 23:10. *The valley of Hinnom* (Heb. *gê' hinnōm*) lies at the southern edge of the city, and later seems to have become the municipal refuse tip, where fires burned continuously, consuming the rubbish. Thus its name came to be used as a synonym for Hell (Gehenna, *cf.* Mk. 9:47, 48, *etc.*). The exact retributive justice of God is seen in Jeremiah's vision of that foul place overflowing with dead bodies. Their sanctuary was to become their cemetery, and the scene of the covenant-breaker Judas's death (*cf.* Mt. 27:5–10; Acts 1:18–20). Fitly, therefore, in v. 31, Jeremiah says that its origin never came from God's heart. These verses are echoed in 19:3–9.

8:1 This barbarity was a deliberate insult by the enemy to the defeated (*cf.* on Am. 2:1), stemming from the pagan idea that disturbance of the burial wounded the dead man's spirit. The destruction of any physical memorial also had the effect of casting the dead into utter oblivion. All had sinned and all would be punished, including the dead. **2** *They shall be spread*. The heavenly bodies whom they have worshipped will be impotent in the day of judgment.

8:4 – 10:25 The doomed people

Jeremiah has here brought into significant connection with each other selections of his prophetic utterances, doubtless from differing periods and occasions. The purpose of the collection is both to display the inevitability of the coming doom and at the same time to offer some refuge to the truly godly man in the day of calamity.

8:4–17 Diagnosis and prognosis. 4–7 sound the note of an evil mind, stubborn against repentance. For the people of God not to repent is as unnatural as for a fallen person to fail to rise (vv. 4–6) or as for a bird to abandon its instinctive migratory patterns.

8–13 Behind the moral hardness of the people are leaders who mislead: the *wise*, whose function was to apply God's word to life in practical precepts, but who, rejecting God's word, have abandoned all hope of wisdom (vv. 8, 9); *prophet* and *priest* (vv. 10–12) who have justified moral complacency in their hearers, and brought forth no fruit for God (v. 13). **8** *Scribes*. This is the earliest mention of scribes as a professional class of interpreters of the law. They were evidently active in Josiah's time (*cf.* 2 Ch. 34:13) and may have had their origin in the reign of Hezekiah (*cf.* Pr. 25:1). **13** There is no agreed explanation of the last line of the verse; possibly it contains a sense of destruction for lack of fruit, *cf.* Mk. 11:12ff., *etc.*

14–17 A belated sense of sin (vv. 14, 15) cannot avert the inevitable doom (vv. 16, 17). The time for repentance is not everlasting (*cf.* Mt. 27:1–5; Heb. 12:17). The poisoned water (v. 14) and the *serpents* (v. 17) recall the water of Marah (Ex. 15:23ff.) and the serpents of Nu. 21:6ff., but now no divine cure is available.

8:18 – 9:22 The agony. In this deeply moving passage the prophet reflects in his own heart the anguish of God, as He shares His people's grief (8:18–22), grieves over their sin (9:1–6), and calls them to lament in the face of inevitable judgment (9:7–22). **18** is difficult; RSV is a correction. A possible rendering, involving slight emendation, is 'through lack of healing my grief mounts up . . .'. This is the mounting grief of the Lord as He sees His grieving people. **19** The voices alternate. Their despairing questions imply culpable divine inactivity, but His answering question is in terms of the alienation of God by their sin. **20** Their consternation mounts as the seasons pass without sign of deliverance. **22** *Gilead*, beyond Jordan, was among the first Israelite territories to fall to the enemy. Its *balm* was known as early as Gn. 37:25. The reference here is to the progressive failure and abandonment of every human and earthly expedient for healing the hurt of the nation.

9:1–6 The mood changes from overwhelming pity to bitter grief over sin. The people are a race of traitors. Jeremiah (figuring the divine alienation) would abandon the whole breed. Their sin shows itself socially, in corrupt relationships wherein a special emphasis lies on sins of speech, and spiritually in absence of a true intimacy with the Lord. The alteration from *do not know* (v. 3) to *refuse to know* (v. 6) shows the tendency of sin ever to become more sinful. **4** *Supplanter*. The Hebrew has a punning reference to Jacob, *cf.* Gn. 27:36. God had transformed Jacob into Israel, but Jacob's descendants insist on living the life of the unregenerate.

7–22 A divine necessity. Moved as He is over His people's plight, the Lord is none the less necessarily moved to judge them. Passages of explanation (vv. 7–9, 12–16) here alternate with calls to lamentation (vv. 10, 11, 17–22), the first of which notes the mourning of nature and the second the mourning of the women, thus denoting a total wave of despairing grief over the whole land.

9:23 – 10:25 The God of all the earth. The opening verses of this section sound its dominant note. The most important thing in life is to have intimate contact with God (9:23, 24). The significance of this is explained in stages: there is an imminent universal judgment (9:25, 26). The Lord is able to accomplish this because He alone is God (10:1-13). What a privilege and comfort, then, truly to belong to Him (10:14-16), for even in the day of calamitous exile under divine judgment (10:17, 18) the godly man can accept it from the hand of God and place blame where it belongs (10:19-21). Even in the blackest moment (10:22), such a person can commit himself to the justice of God (10:23, 24) and to His jealousy for His people's welfare (10:25).

9:25, 26 The moral incisiveness of Jeremiah: Judah, though circumcised, lacks inner dedication, and hence lies under the penalty of being a pagan, and as punishable for sin as the nations about her. Actually ritual perfection may involve ethical damnation. This passage anticipates Paul's teaching in the distinction between the circumcision of the flesh and that of the heart (*cf.* Rom. 2:25-29). *That cut the corners of their hair.* A custom of certain Arab tribes, prohibited in Lv. 19:27 because of pagan associations. Herodotus (iii.8) records the practice as honouring the chief Arabian deities.

10:1-16 This passage contains a scathing polemic against the very conception of idolatry by one who has known it at first-hand, himself being held in awe only by the monotheistic faith cherished by the best of his people. *Cf.* Is. 40:18-20; 44:6-20. The polemic itself is impressive. The prophet saw the gods as blocks of wood, inert, dumb, and scorned them as a scarecrow in a garden patch, set up by men to frighten birds, not a holy power that could discipline the rebellious human heart. Idolatry everywhere invites the same biting irony. **2** *The signs of the heavens*; *i.e.* heavenly portents, comets, meteors, *etc.* The pagan people laid great stress on these.

8 *The instruction of idols is but wood!* Such an expression is strange, the normal explanation is that idols can give nothing better than their own nature. A slight alteration could yield 'the foundation . . .' pointing to the perishable, transient basis of this wisdom, contrasted with v. 10. **9** *Tarshish* was the extreme limit of the ancient world. The LXX has 'Carthage'; many identify it with Tartessus in Spain. *Uphaz* is found only here and in Dn. 10:5. Some emend to read 'Ophir', famous for gold. Alternatively it may be a technical term 'refined', *cf.* 1 Ki. 10:18. **11** This verse, written in Aramaic, may be considered an addition, conceivably an apostrophe to the idolatrous, Aramaic-speaking nations. **17** *Gather up your bundle*; *i.e.* prepare for the flight. The Hebrew word 'bundle' occurs here only. **18** *I am slinging.* A uniquely strong metaphor, expressive of the expulsion of exile. **19, 20** This is all the dire issue of the bad leadership of the leaders (lit. 'shepherds'), who having lost touch with Yahweh were unable to shepherd the people to safety. **22** The old home was to become a jackal lair. **23** The prophet acknowledges his limitation. **24** He makes his supplication; *correct*

me. His 'me' is not the personal self, but the nation whose doom is breaking his heart. **25** He pleads for vindication. As Moses in days past, so Jeremiah intercedes for his people. This verse is repeated in Ps. 79:6, 7. The prophet appears to turn in anger upon a nation summoned by God to carry out His retributive purpose over Judah. Paradoxically, this anger is feasible and just.

11:1 – 12:17 JEREMIAH AND THE COVENANT

This section contains the fourth message of Jeremiah. The covenant here is that of Sinai, perhaps as brought to remembrance through Josiah's reform, yet not simply the book of the law (*cf.* 2 Ki. 22:8) if identified with Deuteronomy alone. To a forgetful people the prophet says that the ancient stipulations still hold force, including the curses on the unfaithful. A date in the reign of Jehoiakim is appropriate for this discourse. Apparently Jeremiah was residing in, or frequenting, his native Anathoth, for he is made aware of a plot against him (11:18-21).

11:1-8 The covenant

2 *Hear the words of this covenant* is an exhortation to the people; *and speak* is addressed to the prophet. **3** *This covenant.* Yahweh had made it with the people and they had promised obedience (*cf.* Ex. 24:7; Dt. 5:27-29). **4** It marked their deliverance *from the iron furnace*, the smelting oven being symbolic of intense suffering; *cf.* Dt. 4:20; 1 Ki. 8:51; Is. 48:10. **5** *A land flowing* . . . Outside the Pentateuch this expression occurs only here, in 32:22 and in Ezk. 20:6, 15. *So be it, Lord.* 'Amen', the prophet's obedient response. **6** *In the cities of Judah.* A touring prophet is unlikely and the phrase is more easily taken as meaning 'everybody'; *cf.* 26:2.

11:9-17 A revolt and its consequences

Whatever the people knew of their fathers' fate made no difference, they forgot both God's grace and His justice, with the result that they are doomed to worse than the 'iron furnace' of Egypt. **12** *They cannot save.* A recurrent theme; what the revered idols cannot do, the neglected God of Israel will not do. The covenant brought blessing to its observers, curses and exile to its breakers, and the people had accepted it outright. **13** *For your gods have become as many as your cities, O Judah.* A repetition of 2:28b, showing that no change of heart had taken place between the two addresses. **14** *Do not pray* . . . is also a repetition, in part, of 7:16, and for the same reason. The corruption has gone too far; only judgment can purify the nation. **15, 16** are obscure in Hebrew and so LXX is utilized for the RSV rendering. *My beloved*; *i.e.* Judah, who remains the object of Yahweh's love although she must leave His house for her hypocrisy. *Olive tree.* Despite its devoted nurturing, the slow-growing olive that promised so well is barren, fit only for burning (*cf.* Jn. 15:2, 6).

11:18–23 The anger of Anathoth

This description of plots against Jeremiah by the folk of his home town is introduced abruptly. In this short paragraph there are three scenes: in the first the people speak (v. 19); in the second the prophet speaks (v. 20); and in the third God speaks (vv. 21–23). Anathoth was the home settlement of the priestly house of Abiathar, close friend of David (*cf.* 1 Sa. 22:20–23), deposed by Solomon in favour of the younger rival house of Zadok (*cf.* 1 Ki. 2:26, 27, 35), who from that time exercised priestly dominance in Jerusalem. Here then were all the elements essential to bitterness. Wrath is incurred in a village such as Anathoth whenever a son or kinsman departs from local sentiment, especially when it favours or appears to favour the opposing side. Thus when Jeremiah, bred of the Anathoth priesthood, supported, as a prophet, the deposition of all village sanctuaries (as for a time almost surely he did; *cf.* 2 Ki. 23:8), he inferentially willed the suppression of that shrine at Anathoth. It was a deadly hurt. Abiathar had borne priestly rank and privilege before the birth of Zadok! Love can turn to hate, given adequate provocation. How bitter that hate was against Jeremiah can be inferred from the appeal he made to Yahweh's tribunal. He pleads that the desires and intentions of his village enemies be scorned and judged by that very tribunal. His own innocence was that of a tame lamb (19), unwitting of peril.

19 *That his name . . . Cf.* Is. 53:8. Several echoes of Is. 53 can be caught in 11:18 – 12:4 (the pet lamb, v. 19, the shortened life in 12:4 and here); the prophet may be consciously applying the motifs of that passage to his own suffering.

12:1–6 The problem of godless prosperity

Jeremiah concludes by addressing himself to the age-long problem of the success of the wicked. The prophet is among the boldest of any generation who have stood up in their suffering and interrogated the divine sovereignty on the issue of prosperity attending the labour of the godless and impious. Anger (vv. 3, 4) burns within him against the murderous intentions of his antagonists at Anathoth, these prosperous wicked! But God is not at the mercy of man's questionings, no matter what the anomalies of human life. Jeremiah receives no direct solution to his problem, but rather the command to gird his loins for a yet greater tax on his faith and courage. The earlier suffering, which is likened to a race against fellow-athletes, is but a preliminary discipline for a much sterner struggle. If that contest was too much for him, how will he fare if he be matched against race-horses (v. 5)? And if, when the land was peaceful, he was distressed, what will his reaction be in the difficult times ahead (signified by *the jungle of Jordan*)?

2 *Thou plantest them.* The metaphor of a tree is applied to the whole nation in 2 Sa. 7:10; here it is applied to the wicked. **4** *He will not see . . . ; i.e.* the prophet will die before, or at the hand of, his enemies, or else his prophecies of doom will not be fulfilled. **5** *The jungle of the Jordan* connotes the wild, luxuriant and beast-infested growths of the hot marshy land beside the Jordan (*cf.* 49:19; 50:44; Zc. 11:3).

12:7–17 Yahweh's lament

This section is an appendix to the message of Jeremiah just concluded. The prophet's sorrow, as that of Hosea, with whom he shares not a few characteristics, led him to feel that it had its counterpart in God. This divine lament in its historical setting is recorded in 2 Ki. 24:1, 2, where detail and date are given (*c.* 598 BC). **7** *My house.* Here the wider sense of 'my household' is intended, rather than the Temple. **8** *Like a lion.* Judah has roared against the Lord as a lion would do and has taken up a hostile attitude. **9** *Speckled bird.* As birds attack other birds of unfamiliar plumage, so Israel, differing from other nations, was attacked by them. **10** *My vineyard.* The nation is described under various metaphors in this passage—house, heritage, beloved of my soul, vineyard. 'The pastors', *i.e.* leaders, have destroyed the vineyard initially, and the enemy from without has destroyed it finally. **14–17** The *evil neighbours* are predicted to share the exile fate of Judah; these Syrian, Moabite and Ammonite aggressors will likewise be punished through the agency of the common foe, Babylon, unless they worship the living God and learn *to swear by my name.* Again the conditional character of prophecy is to be marked.

13:1–27 FIVE WARNINGS

The date of these warnings is obscure. Vv. 18, 19 probably refer to Jehoiachin and his mother, Queen Nehushta (2 Ki. 24:8–12, 597 BC). The first portion, pregnant with disaster, might cover the later years of his father, Jehoiakim, hence 600–597 BC.

13:1–11 The first warning

Where words alone had no effect, actions might speak louder, and the technique of the 'acted oracle' was often used by the prophets for the more forceful launching of the word of God into a given situation (*cf.* 2 Ki. 13:14ff.; Is. 20:1–6; Je. 19:1–15; Ezk. 4:1–3; see *NBD*, art. 'Prophecy, Prophets'). The meaning of the present act is complex. The newness of the garment stands for the nation's pride in itself which allows it to act wilfully against the Lord and seek after other gods. This pride will be humbled by Babylonian exile, just as the garment was marred by the Euphrates (vv. 9, 10). The garment itself, a short kilt, hugging the body, symbolizes the intimate nearness which Israel was intended to enjoy with the Lord (v. 11) but which their sin has destroyed.

1 *Do not dip*; do nothing to diminish its fresh

newness. 4 *The Euphrates*. Jeremiah's ordered destination could be ambiguous. Euphrates (Heb. $p^e r\bar{a}t$) may be the river of that name, some 350 miles from Jerusalem, but it could equally be Parah, about 3 miles from Jeremiah's home town, Anathoth, for in the expression *to the Euphrates* both names take on an identical form in Hebrew. The journey to the Euphrates would have symbolic value in view of the coming Babylonian captivity, but Parah could achieve much the same by means of a play on words.

13:12–14 The second warning

12 contains the parabolic warning; 13 explains it. The people complacently looked for prosperity and joy, symbolized by the full wine jar, but the imagery of the wine jar rather is made to bear the warning that just as strong drink confuses a man's walk and thought, so will Yahweh's judgment. He will fill the men of Judah with drunkenness and they shall dash against each other and be destroyed. Drunkenness is the dethronement of the alert mind essential to decision in an hour of crisis. The inhabitants of Jerusalem will have neither wits nor strength to defend themselves or to know friend from foe (*cf.* 25:15–28; Ezk. 23:31–34; Is. 51:17; Ps. 60:3).

13:15–17 The third warning

Here Jeremiah warns his people of the perils of pride. 16 *The twilight mountains* refers to the plight of travellers overtaken by night before reaching a friendly inn.

13:18, 19 The fourth warning

The contemptuous response to Jeremiah's messages was the cause, in their self-satisfaction, of the people's downfall. Hence the prophet's command to address the royal house personally and directly. 18 *The king and the queen mother* are, with little doubt, Jehoiachin and Nehushta, *cf.* 2 Ki. 24:8. The *lowly seat* which they refused to take was shortly theirs by force, for 37 years in the king's case, see 52:31. 19 *The cities of the Negeb, i.e.* the south of Judah. The cities of this territory are noted as the farthest away from the invasion, thus emphasizing the completeness of Judah's captivity, *all . . . wholly*.

13:20–27 The fifth warning

The last warning of judgment makes it plainer than ever that doom is due to obdurate sins. 21 *Friends* are intimates, trusted (the Heb. word also describes the pet lamb of 11:19), but they are the ones Judah chose, wilfully rejecting the friend of her youth (*cf.* 3:4). There were times when the Babylonians had been friends and allies of Judah. Hezekiah had eagerly accepted the friendship of Merodach-Baladan, *e.g.*, despite Isaiah's warning (*cf.* 2 Ki. 20:12–19). This verse may refer back so far, or to some later event. 23 Sin may become so habitual as to involve destiny; the nexus of sin and penalty is unchangeable and unbreakable. The appositeness of such penalty is that it shall be inflicted by those with

whom Jerusalem has coquetted. 27 Even exile did not bring Judah back to God; *cf.* the sorrowing cry of Lk. 13:34.

14:1 – 21:10 SHADOW OF DOOM

This section contains the fifth, sixth and seventh messages of Jeremiah with appendices. Events in the life of the prophet are also interspersed.

14:1 – 15:9 Jeremiah's fifth message: the rejection of intercession

This oracle deals with the plague of drought and the vicarious intercession of the prophet.

14:1–6 The drought. Drought is a deadly enemy of the Near Eastern farmer, eventually affecting the whole population, human (2 *people*; 3 *nobles, servants*; 4 *farmers*) and animal (5 *hind*; 6 *wild asses*) and the natural surroundings (4 *ground*; 5 *grass*; 6 *herbage*).

14:7–9 Prayer for relief. The drought is seen as an expression of God's displeasure. 7 Because it touches their normal life, the people are ready to repent, *we have sinned*. As the nation is still 'God's people' they claim that God must act to save His reputation, *act . . . for thy name's sake* (*cf.* v. 9). 8, 9 To them God seems to adopt the role of a passing, unconcerned visitor, despite His Temple *in the midst*.

14:10–12 The response of God. 10 The past still lives. *Now he will remember . . .* Perhaps a prophetic stock phrase; *cf.* Ho. 8:13; 9:9. **11** Jeremiah is commanded once more to cease his intercession (*cf.* 7:16; 11:14), for nothing could alter the doom of Judah. **12** *Sword . . . famine . . . pestilence.* David had to choose one of these as a punishment for sin (*cf.* 2 Sa. 24:13), Jeremiah and Ezekiel repeatedly use all three of punishment their contemporaries deserved (*e.g.* 16:4; 24:10; Ezk. 14:21).

14:13–18 Prophets and priests have misled the people. Jeremiah can only plead that other prophets have lied to the people. Such liars were not Yahweh's ambassadors; they prophesied in their own godless authority. Yet the Lord rejects the plea. Deceived the people may have been, but their wickedness (v. 16) is their own and springs back upon them to their ruin. 17 Jeremiah's tears, portraying his own and the Lord's anguish over a destroyed people, are part of his message to them and have the force of an 'acted oracle'. They show the backlash of the message of doom on him who preaches it, and none should preach destruction who cannot weep for those under its threat. **18** The political devastation (v. 18a) is traced to a spiritual cause (v. 18b). Spiritual misleaders constitute the ultimate in national disaster.

14:19–22 Jeremiah's prayer. As, in his tears, we may see his identification with a divine sorrow, so in his intercessions he takes up the people's cause. Many who never heeded the message of the false prophet (*cf.* 8:11) must yet have prayed for peace and wondered at the silence of God. Their prayer is a model for such times: confessing the divine sovereignty over the circumstance of His people (v. 19), acknowledging sin (v. 20), pleading the name, covenant (v. 21) and almightiness (v. 22) of the Lord.

20 *Our fathers.* Inherited sinfulness is never pleaded in the OT as an excuse, but always admitted as an aggravation of the offensiveness to God of the present generation (*cf.* Ps. 51:3–5). **21** *Throne*; *i.e.* the Davidic throne with which the Lord had closely associated Himself (*cf.* 1 Ch. 29:23).

15:1–9 The Lord's answer. God counted on the past, too, and found nothing to soften His verdict (v. 4). **1** Moses and Samuel had interceded with success (*cf.* Ex. 32:11–14, 30–32; Nu. 14:13–24; Dt. 9:18–20, 25–29; 1 Sa. 7:8, 9; 12:19–25; also Ps. 99:6–8), but now the Lord is as ready to turn His people from the land as the pharaoh had been after the tenth plague (Ex. 12:31). **2** The word of the Lord is final. **7** *Gates, i.e.* as the invading enemy has burst in. *Cf.* Is. 28:6. **8** RSV follows LXX. Hebrew reads 'I have brought to them against . . .'. **9** *She who bore seven.* Seven sons symbolized the height of prosperity (*cf.* 1 Sa. 2:5; Jb. 1:2); Jerusalem, which has had all she could desire, will be bereft.

15:10–21 Jeremiah's expostulation

Jeremiah becomes introspective. Anguish moves him that he has become a curse to his people, but Yahweh strengthens him and will yet vindicate him. **11** The Hebrew is difficult. As RSV understands it, the burden is that the prophet has acted in the people's interest, yet he is hated. *Cf.* RV. **12** *Iron*; a figure of the nation's obduracy in the face of God's word. **13, 14** *Cf.* 17:3, 4 whence many claim these verses have been erroneously repeated here, but their force in this context is to match the obduracy of the people towards the Lord (v. 12) with this reminiscence of the hardness of His word to them, thus preparing for the revelation of Jeremiah's loneliness (vv. 15–18). **15** *Take me not away.* The persecution is so great that Jeremiah fears for his life. The dread of death apparent in these words arises from the sense of estrangement from God which is part of his predicament (*cf.* on v. 18; Ps. 88:10). **16, 17** Jeremiah reviews his recent experience: first, his personal delight in assimilating God's word (*cf.* Ezk. 2:8 – 3:3) and his sense of God's identification with him in giving him His *name*; secondly, the distasteful alienation from men because increasingly he became the voice of the divine *indignation.* **18** There has been no compensating balm from God for his spirit. In the moment of need, the Lord (in contrast to 2:13) has been like a *brook* which has become as parched under the summer sun as the traveller who looks to it for refreshment (*cf.* Jb. 6:15–20). **19, 20** The remedy for the forlorn prophet is the same as he has been urging on others: to *return* to the Lord (*i.e.* from his rebellious self-pity), and to devote himself in utter faithfulness to His word. On this basis he will become a rallying point for the

people, and the former promises of God (1:18f.) will be fulfilled.

16:1–21 Yahweh's instructions to His servant

The prophet is ordered to behave in an eccentric manner to illustrate his message (*cf.* on 14:17; Is. 20; Ezk. 4ff.); celibacy was extremely uncommon, refusal to participate in funerary rites ill-mannered and disrespectful. Both actions had one meaning: There is no future here. **7** *Break bread . . . the cup of consolation.* A reference to a funeral feast, in some cases an annual commemoration of the dead man. **14, 15** (*cf.* 23:7, 8) sound a note of hope, abrupt and unexpected as it often is in the prophets (*cf.* Is. 28:5, 6; 29:5–8). Jeremiah's careful editing of his prophecies doubtless reflects his own clutching at the promises of God in hours of deepest darkness. *Cf.* the uprising of assured faith in vv. 19f. **16** *Fishers, hunters* replace the shepherds who had led astray (13:18ff.) and decimate the flock, for it would not recognize its master. **18** *Doubly,* perhaps 'equally' is better. *Polluted . . . with carcases.* The idols were no better than corpses, and so polluted God's land.

17:1–18 Jeremiah's sixth message: truth unchanged, unchanging

Jeremiah lays hold on snatches of proverbial truth to enforce the inevitability of the nexus between sin and punishment. He lays bare the situation: indelible sin, inevitable loss (vv. 1–4). Then he turns to establish this with reference to known truth: contrasting faiths bear contrasting fruits (vv. 5–8), and the all-knowing Lord searches both the quality of the heart (vv. 9, 10) and the life (v. 11). Because His rule is sovereign (v. 12a), He both offers sure hope to His people (vv. 12b, 13a) and sure calamity to those who reject Him (v. 13b), and Jeremiah hastens to identify himself with the former (vv. 14–18).

1 *Pen of iron.* The iron stylus was used for cutting out inscriptions on hard surfaces like rock or stone (*cf.* Jb. 19:24). The nation is in the same category of hardness. Sin is inscribed permanently upon its heart and its altars, whence no sacrifice can remove it. As durable and lasting shall be the penal fires of Yahweh (v. 4). *Their Asherim.* See *NBD*, art. 'Asherah'. **3, 4** The text was obscure; RSV translates with help from the similar passage 15:13, 14. **9** *Desperately corrupt.* In 15:18 and 30:12 the word is translated 'incurable'. It is from the same root as 'Jacob' and has related nuance; *cf.* on 9:4. **11** *Partridge.* The bird lays two clutches of eggs, one being for her mate, and so appears to hatch more than one brood. **13** *Written in the earth*; *i.e.* unenduring, like writing on sand. **16** RSV is based on a minor alteration of vowels, yielding very different sense from AV, RV. The prophet could not ask for the doom to overtake his people, but he does beg God for retribution upon his mockers.

17:19–27 Appendix about the sabbath

This prose discourse raises a problem, for

Jeremiah frequently denounced formality in worship without sincerity. Ellison points out, however, that keeping the sabbath involves the self-denial of ceasing from ordinary business, the requirements of the prophet here. **19** *The Benjamin Gate* (*cf.* 20:2; 37:13; 38:7) is substituted by RSV for the unknown 'gate of the people' of the Hebrew, which may, nevertheless, be correct. The prohibition in v. 27 suggests a city gate.

18:1–17 Jeremiah's seventh message: the ways of the sovereign Lord

1–10 This discourse is associated with the prophet's commanded visit to the potter's house, where he understood the mind of God, the divine Potter at work with His human clay. Jeremiah watched again more purposively than ever the potter working at his wheel (v. 3; lit. 'the two stones', upper and lower). He particularly noted, for it may have occurred more than once, the failure to make a vessel. This marring could be attributed to the potter's carelessness or clumsiness, the crude machine, or some flaw in the clay itself. As in the parables of Jesus, not every detail is significant. Here, the central truth is not the marring, but that the potter persevered and made the clay into another vessel. So the Lord is master of the clay, shaping it to the purpose in His mind, whether one of meanness or grandeur. The parable is a vivid picture of divine sovereignty. **6** *Can I not do with you as this potter?* The question does not ask for permission, but declares the facts. The ensuing verses clarify the terms of divine sovereign power: power to meet repentance half way (vv. 7, 8) and to punish apostasy (vv. 9, 10).

11a The message is clear. Exile is the new mould in which the nation is to be shaped. **11b, 12** *Return . . . amend.* The first draws attention to the initial process, the other to the more continuous one. The Lord's moulding will is all of grace.

13–17 Jeremiah, instructed by the Lord, warns the men of Judah and the inhabitants of Jerusalem of the evil of the stubborn mind. The sin of the people is as irrational as it is tragic. **14** Familiar elements of nature even may be cited as their judges: *the snow of Lebanon* and the running stream are perennial, but Yahweh's people forget Him and worship gods that actually have no existence. **15** *False gods*; literally 'deceit, emptiness'. In disaster, therefore, Yahweh's face is turned from them (*cf.* 2:27).

18:18–23 Reactions

At the conclusion of Jeremiah's seventh message we have recorded two reactions, first from the audience and second from the speaker. **18:18 The hostile hearers plot against the prophet.** This is the second plot against Jeremiah (*cf.* 11:19ff.). Jeremiah's enemies were confident that his dire prophecies would fail, that the present order would continue, showing his words to be false and so blasphemous as spoken in the name of the Lord. LXX has 'let us heed his words' to take evidence against him from his own lips. MT is to be preferred: the enemies will accuse or slander the prophet, ignoring his replies.

18:19–23 The prophet pleads for vindication. The retributive fury of this passage is so vehement that many think it is quite unlike Jeremiah. But the exception may prove the rule. The prophet is transparent. His very soul is laid bare. He hides nothing. The provocation is more than he can bear. The surface interpretation of egotistic imprecation may be discarded. Here is a cry that the divine cause, which the enemies so ruthlessly scorned, may be vindicated by the overthrow of their fancied security and power. In the first part of the prayer the emphasis is on himself; in the second half it is on his enemies.

19:1–15 Jeremiah's eighth message: the irretrievable shattering

19:1, 2 The setting. Like the previous oracle, this is an acted parable. The place is significant, *the valley of Ben-hinnom at the entry of the Potsherd Gate, i.e.* the rubbish tip for broken crockery. The prophet takes representatives of laity and priesthood (*elders . . . senior priests*), and a water decanter. **19:3–15 The oracle. 3–9** appear to be a summary of past oracles; vv. 4–7 occurred substantially in 7:31–33, yet this is insufficient reason for treating vv. 3–9 as an insertion. The symbolic act brought realism to the prophetic word: the flask was irreparably smashed and thrown on the rubbish heap. The deed and accompanying words probably had what we term 'magical' import to the audience. **6** *Topheth.* See on 7:31. **7** *I will make void* (lit. 'tip out'), a play on the related term 'flask'. **14, 15** The prophet returned to his habitual stand and proclaimed the gist of his message to all and sundry: the doom is inescapable.

20:1–6 Jeremiah in the stocks

1, 2 *Pashur the priest . . . chief officer in the house of the Lord* in savage reaction smites and imprisons Jeremiah in the stocks. In that priestly circle, the prophet was an incarnate menace against their reiteration that, if Babylon attacked them, Egypt would compel him to lift the siege. **3ff.** Men like Jeremiah, however, do not change their message with a change in circumstance. In his re-naming Pashur as Magor-missabib, *Terror on every side*, the meaning is that when the Babylonian victory shall prove how false was his prophecy of security, he shall be seen as responsible for such an incredible disaster, a false prophet, not only in his own eyes, but in the eyes of all his friends (v. 4).

20:7–18 Jeremiah's complaint

This is a unique psychological passage in canonical prophecy, a passage tremendous with feeling, a soul laid bare. Yahweh had drawn him to be a prophet. If he forbore the word of doom, it would be as a flame within him, a tension beyond endurance. His friends taunt him with 'terror on every side'. His perennial stimulus is that the Lord is with him as a mighty man. In the end his enemies will lose the fight. 7 *Thou hast deceived.* The Hebrew is better rendered 'seduced', 'misled', here and in v. 10. The meaning of this bold accusation is to be sought in 1:6–10 where, in response to Jeremiah's excuse that he has no personal authority for the prophetic task, the Lord peremptorily commands his obedience and promises the authoritative word. With reason, Jeremiah feels that there has been to date little compelling authority in what he has said from the Lord. People are amused but not convinced. The great promises appear as deceitful bait to lure him into an office he never desired. 10 *My familiar friends*; *i.e.* those he trusted; *cf.* Ps. 41:9; Jn. 13:18. 13 A moment of assurance in the tormented prophet's thought (*cf.* on 16:14). Was this at the instant of his release (v. 3)? 14–18 reveal the breaking-point; they suggest an even darker day, when he would be more outcast from his people than he had ever been, yet had to watch the doom engirdle them. How sure of His man God must have been when He made such a soul plough so lonely and desperate a furrow! The point is that they reveal the soul of a man of God in expostulation against his fate, but a soul yet obedient and loyal. 14 *Cursed be the day*; *cf.* Jb. 3, noting that the similarity does not demand literary dependence.

21:1–10 Jeremiah's ninth message: a divine Enemy, a desperate choice

The prophet's word here is another warning that Jerusalem will fall. In 37:3–10 there is a similar account, but it is not a doublet. It deals with the temporary raising of the siege by the Egyptians, only to be resumed later on with greater intensity. Here we have the siege in its initial phases.

1, 2 Zedekiah sends another Pashur to entreat Jeremiah's intercession. **4** The answer is that Yahweh will nullify the power of Judah (4a), prosper the arms of Babylon (4b); **5, 6** and Himself become the enemy of His people. **7** The king, his court and people, all who survive the horror of the siege, its famine and pestilence, will be handed over to Nebuchadrezzar. **8** The figure of two ways comes from Dt. 30:15, 19. **9** *A prize of war*; *i.e.* escape with his bare life.

21:11 – 25:38 KINGS AND PROPHETS OF JUDAH: THE VISION OF THE END

21:11 – 23:8 The royal house of Judah

This section contains a series of prophecies relating to contemporary kings of Judah; whether they were uttered by Jeremiah in sequence or not we cannot say.

21:11–14 Royal duty. The execution of justice was a major part of the king's activity, of the 'right' (*yāšār*) which he was expected to perform in the consciousness of God's watching (*cf.* Dt. 17:18–20). **12** *In the morning.* Regularity and primacy are most likely meant, although the normal time for a judicial sitting may be indicated. *Cf.* on Ps. 101:8. **13** *Inhabitant of the valley* could possibly be rendered 'living above the valley' as descriptive of Jerusalem, and *rock of the plain* as 'level rock'. We must take it that the reference is to the complacent sense of security found in the Judahite leaders, smugly confident in their impregnable fortifications.

22:1–9 Communal duty. King and people alike are to execute judgment and mercy, especially to the most needy: otherwise the house of David will become a waste. **5** Yahweh pledges Himself by the most solemn oath that disobedience will be punished by desolation, viz. *I swear by myself*; *cf.* Heb. 6:13–18. **6** The house of David, under the figure of a Lebanon forest, is to be gutted with fire. Again unrepentant idolatry is the reason. **7** *Your choicest cedars*; the leaders of the nation.

22:10–12 Shallum. 10 *Weep not for him who is dead.* Josiah, whose death at Megiddo (609 BC) was a major disaster to the reformation movement, is not to be mourned, but rather Shallum, *i.e.* Jehoahaz, who died in Egypt as an exile after reigning only three months (2 Ki. 23:31–34). He was the first ruler of the southern kingdom to die in exile. The whole sense is that it is better to die on the battlefield than to die in long captivity.

22:13–23 Jehoiakim. This king's father had been a reformer, but he did evil in the sight of the Lord (2 Ki. 23:34–37). Josiah was just, his son unjust; Josiah acted as the father of his people, his son faithlessly exploited their basic rights; one was a man of austerity, the other one of ostentation. **13** *Builds his house.* Excavations at Ramat Rahel (see on 6:1) have revealed ruins that may be identified with this palace. **19** *The burial of an ass.* No record of this remains (*cf.* 2 Ki. 24:6), but note the action of a victor foretold in Je. 8:1. **20–23** may speak of Jerusalem; the verbal forms are feminine as usually when the city is the subject. *Lovers*; *i.e.* 'allies'. *Lebanon, Bashan, Abarim* are the mountains bounding Israel on the north, north-east and east, symbolically the places of anxious watch for invaders.

22:24–30 Jehoiachin. The two parts of this prophecy can be understood as a formal declaration (vv. 24–27) and explanatory lament (vv. 28–30). The young king Coniah (shortened from Jeconiah, personal name of Jehoiachin) and his mother are to be exiled; Nebuchadrezzar took them to Babylon in 597 BC (2 Ki. 24:8–15) where Jehoiachin remained in prison for thirty-seven years (2 Ki. 25:27). **24** *Signet ring.* The most important private possession bearing the owner's mark and authority. **30** *Childless . . . shall not succeed.* The historian will not find place for Jehoiachin's descendants (he had seven sons, *cf.* 1 Ch. 3:17) in the list of kings. His name will not be revered by succeeding generations; his brief rule of three months witnessed no accomplishment but that 'he did evil'.

23:1–8 The rulers. While this has a general

address, Zedekiah is probably the main object of the prophecy. **1, 2** He and his princes reverse the shepherd's task; true shepherds bring together, lead, and cherish their flocks. The Lord, as Owner of the flock, will treat the false shepherds accordingly. **3, 4** He will restore *the remnant* of His flock, and install good shepherds. **5, 6** More specifically, He will *raise up* a descendant of David whose name will be indicative of his nature, *Yahweh ṣidqēnû, The Lord is our righteousness*. Again, the reverse of the current situation is depicted; Zedekiah, 'the Lord is my righteousness', had a similar name to the future king, but he was appointed by Nebuchadrezzar, and was a weakling who possessed none of the traits of a true king. *The Branch*; *i.e.* shoot, the fresh growth from the stump of a felled tree. This term for the Messianic figure is found again in 33:14–16; Zc. 3:8; 6:12; *cf.* Is. 4:2; 11:1. As a title 'Branch' is designed to trace the ancestry of the Messiah, human and divine, and in its actual use it focuses attention on the priestly and kingly aspects of the Messianic task (see references and *NBD*, art. 'Messiah'). The new king will head the nation established after a fresh 'exodus' which will be remembered as a greater saving act than that from Egypt. Contrast Zedekiah under whom many went into exile, and, in another plane, the 'exodus' mentioned in Lk. 9:31.

23:9–40 The prophets of Judah

From the leaders of state, Jeremiah turns to the leaders of religion. He probes into their life (vv. 9–15), their message (vv. 16–22) and their fate (vv. 23–40). See further Introduction.

9 *Broken . . . because of the Lord*. Jeremiah's starting-point is the holiness of the Lord, and it is the contrasting moral character of these alleged servants of God which shatters him at his heart. This observation is basic to his great discussion of false prophecy: the messenger should be like Him who sends him. In default of this similarity, his message lacks authentication (*cf.* 15:19). **10** *Adulterers*; physically and spiritually, and consequently bringing a *curse* (*cf.* Mal. 2:1, 2). *Dried up*. The experience of the drought was fresh in memory (14:1ff.) and may well provide a date for this oracle. National disasters have spiritual causes, and the chief weight of blame rests on spiritual misleaders. **11** This verse shows that the foregoing complaint is not just of general immorality but specifically of the unclean lives of religious professionals. **14** The effect of immorality in religious high places is that it strengthens the forces of moral laxity throughout the nation until the city of God epitomizes the state of *Sodom*. **16, 17** *Words* introduces the new topic: what these men are has been shown, and now we are told what they say. Their message is characterized as unfounded optimism, humanistic (*i.e.* lacking a basis in divine revelation), and encouraging to those who despise the whole idea of revelation in their insistence on their own wisdom (v. 17).

18–22 urge the essential ingredients of a true prophetic experience: an experience of intimate fellowship with God (v. 18) and a message which does not evade the truth of His wrath against sin (vv. 19–22). **18** *Council* includes the notion of the consultative assembly, as in 1 Ki. 22:19ff., and the sense of personal fellowship (the word translated 'converse' in Ps. 55:14). **20** *In the latter days*. Jeremiah is confident that it is this authentic message of wrath which will receive the seal of fulfilment (*cf.* Dt. 18:22). **21, 22** The situation of the false prophet summarized: uncommissioned (v. 21a), uninspired (v. 21b), lacking personal experience of God (v. 22a), and without a word of rebuke concerning sin (v. 22b).

23–32, which stress the distinction between the true and the pretended word from the Lord (*e.g.* vv. 28, 29), prepare the way for **33–40** with their condemnation of the pretentious pomposity of the false prophet which has only succeeded in bringing the whole idea of 'a word from the Lord' into disrepute. **23, 24** We are not necessarily to suppose any false prophet ever really thought himself free of divine scrutiny, but each, in giving as from God what he knew full well had no origin outside himself, acted as if the Lord were totally absent and unconcerned. **25** *Dreamed*. The stress on dreams is not intended to denigrate this particular means of revelation, so often experienced by the true men of God in OT times (*e.g.* Dn. 7:1), but rather to underscore that element of self-origination which marked the false prophets. **28, 29** *Wheat . . . hammer*; the nourishment and power of the true word. **30** *Steal*; another stress on the merely human origin of the false word. **33** *Burden*, often translated 'oracle' (*e.g.* Is. 21:1), was a standard word for a message received by revelation from God. The meaning of these verses is that misuse has brought the very term into disrepute, and that it should therefore be avoided lest the true prophet become associated with the false even in this way.

24:1–10 Two baskets of figs

This contrasting picture of good and bad stems from 597 BC when the cream of the population was removed to Babylonia (2 Ki. 24:10–17). Those left in Judah or seeking refuge in Egypt (*cf.* 26:20–23) were like figs 'so bad they cannot be eaten', a loathsome corrupting (v. 9) heap. The presently unfortunate exiles were, in fact, like 'good figs' which could be planted, re-establishing the land (v. 6). First, however, the exiles are to be wholly reborn of heart and become Yahweh's people (v. 7).

25:1–38 Vision of the end

Here the culmination of Jeremiah's first 23 years' ministry is reached (*c.* 627–605 BC). In the crucial battle of Carchemish (605 BC) the Babylonians put an effective end to Pharaoh Necho's domination over Palestine (*cf.* 2 Ki. 24:7). It was one of the decisive battles of history.

In it the prophet clearly read the will of the Lord; the Babylonians were the 'evil from the north' harnessed by Yahweh to carry out His judgment upon Judah (*cf.* 4:5ff., *etc.*). LXX places 46:1 - 51:64 (*q.v.*) after v. 13; some of those passages stem from this time.

25:1-14 A confirmation. 3 *Spoken persistently.* Precisely this persistence accounts for the repetitiousness of many oracles. **8, 9** Judah's obstinacy had withstood God's patience so long, now the end was beginning. Comparison may be made with Heb. 12:25. *The tribes of the north*, earlier unnamed, are here shown to be Babylonian forces, having a multitude of ethnic origins, led by *my servant* (*i.e.* 'agent'), Nebuchadrezzar. **11** The duration of exile, *seventy years*, ensures that all the original exiles would be dead before its end; this is a round figure approximately correct. **12-14** Babylon's downfall came at its capture by Cyrus the Persian in 539 BC. Although God's agent in Nebuchadrezzar's day, she was none the less under judgment for her ungodly pride. *Cf.* Is. 10:12; and the section 'God and history' in the General Article, 'OT Theology' (pp. 27f.).

25:15-29 A condemnation. The previous section was most probably delivered as soon as news reached Jerusalem that Babylon was victor at Carchemish, with these verses following soon after. Nebuchadrezzar was prevented from following up his victory immediately by the death of his father and the consequent enthronement rites in Babylon, but he returned to Syria a few months later, and began the first of a series of campaigns to subdue all of Syria and Palestine. The prophet's warnings apparently preceded these campaigns, perhaps as an antidote to a false security in the respite after Carchemish. **15** *Cup of wine* is the symbol of Yahweh's inescapable wrath over Judah and other nations (*cf.* Ps. 75:8; Is. 51:17). Babylon is His agent. **20** *Remnant of Ashdod*. The city had been reduced by Psammetichus of Egypt a decade or so earlier. **23** *Cut the corners*; *cf.* 9:26. **29** Observe that the fury of the Lord begins with Jerusalem (*cf.* v. 18) and extends to other nations who also deserve the divine chastisement.

25:30-38 The execution of justice. Fearlessly Jeremiah declares that Yahweh will take up His case against the nations and carry out his righteous verdict. **31** *The wicked he will put to the sword*. There is no place for man's concept of an entirely loving God where ingrained evil is concerned; *cf.* Mt. 13:37ff. These verses are a further demonstration of God's control over the affairs of men.

26:1 - 52:34 HISTORICAL NARRATIVES

26:1-24 THE REIGN OF JEHOIAKIM

This chapter contains the story of two prophets: Jeremiah and Uriah.

26:1-19 Jeremiah in peril

This situation is rightly linked with the more detailed account of the 'Temple sermon' in 7:1ff. *Cf.* introduction to ch. 7. The record of the unfortunate experience of Uriah (vv. 20-23) highlights the courage of Jeremiah in standing forth as he did, and gives point to his preparedness to die for the sake of God's word (vv. 12-15) as no merely theoretical devotion.

9 *Shiloh*; *cf.* 7:12-14. **10** *Gate*; the traditional place for the hearing of law-suits. **12** *The Lord sent me*; see also v. 15. Jeremiah makes no self-defence in the accepted sense. He throws all on to the divine commission which is his. Now is the moment of testing of the promises of God (*cf.* 1:8, 18, 19; 15:20, 21) and the reality of professed faith (*cf.* 16:19; 17:7, 12). **18** *Micah*. The reference is to Mi. 3:12, but the interest for us lies in the current knowledge of God's previously spoken word and the way in which scripture was used to confirm scripture. Micah had prophesied a century earlier. *Mountain of the house*; the Temple hill.

26:20-24 Uriah's death

The extradition and murder of Uriah indicate how near Jeremiah stood to death. The fickleness of the people and the loyalty of an influential friend stand out (v. 24), but so also does the contrast between the way of faith (vv. 12-15) and the way of fear (v. 21). For a number of years Jehoiakim was a vassal of Egypt and probably had extradition rights, which explains the ease with which the king 'sent to Egypt certain men' (v. 22). Ultimately Uriah was tested and found 'faithful unto death' (v. 23). Uriah was fetched from Egypt and Jeremiah was later taken into Egypt; both died for their loyalty and devotion to their God.

27:1 - 29:32 THE PROPHET'S COMMON SENSE

These three chapters, which relate to the reign of Zedekiah, may originally have been circulated among the Babylonian exiles to disabuse their mind of a speedy return from exile. Nowhere else, in the same degree, does the sane balance of Jeremiah's mind stand out so clearly as here. The background is already familiar. The first captivity in 597 BC was an accomplished fact; Zedekiah was on the throne on the sufferance of Babylon. But inside and outside the country many were plotting against Nebuchadrezzar. In these chapters Jeremiah sets himself the task of denouncing and correcting the notion that, somehow, it was possible to overthrow the power that had become supreme in the eastern world. The prophet addresses on this subject the neighbouring nations (vv. 1-11), Zedekiah the king (vv. 12-15), the priests (vv. 16-22) and prophets (28:1–16), and the exiles themselves (29:1–32).

27:1–22 The prophetic word

27:1–11 A message to neighbouring kings. In the time of Sennacherib, Hezekiah had headed a revolt in Palestine, now Zedekiah appeared to be a suitable leader for the nearby dissidents. The prophet utilized the ambassadors to convey the word of Yahweh to their pagan masters: their plot was futile, the Lord had spoken, no mere local deity but the Creator and Ruler of the world (*cf.* 10:11–13), and His prophet alone spoke the truth. **1** The date (*cf.* RSV mg.) is shown to be erroneous by v. 3; the scribe's eye may have slipped back to 26:1. See on 28:1. **6** *My servant*; *cf.* 25:9.

27:12–15 A message to Zedekiah. This consists of an exhortation to the stubborn king to submit to Nebuchadrezzar and a declaration concerning the false prophets. The falsity of these prophets lies in the fact that they speak on their own initiative, with no higher source of information.

27:16–22 A message to the priests. This message too consists of an exhortation and a declaration. MT and LXX harmonize only in the common prophecy that the sacred vessels will be carried into captivity. It is too bold to insist that the shorter form as preserved in LXX is necessarily the original. **16** *The vessels*; *i.e.* Temple equipment carried away in 597 BC. Jeremiah countered the facile optimism of the false prophets with the word that they also would experience captivity. **18** From his assurance the prophet could issue such a taunt knowing that no response would be made. **22** 'Man proposes, God disposes.'

28:1–17 An open challenge

This chapter shows large divergence between the MT and the LXX. Usually the differences are explained as expansions in the Hebrew of the terse form in the LXX. The chapter contains four speeches, two by Hananiah and two by Jeremiah.

28:1–4 Hananiah's prophecy. As here, the question is always crucial whether a prophet is true or false. Hananiah had heard Jeremiah proclaim exile for the rebellious nation. In fierce reply Hananiah said that Yahweh had spoken the contrary to him, and he symbolized that correction in the broken yoke (v. 4). **1** *That same year.* The Hebrew has a further confusion, glossed over by RSV (*cf.* AV, RV), and should probably be read, 'In that same year, in the fourth year of Zedekiah, in the fifth month . . .' and this date applied also to ch. 27. **2** *I have broken.* This refers to a fact determined upon by the Lord and therefore so certain of accomplishment that it may be said to have happened already.

28:5–9 Jeremiah's rejoinder. Jeremiah could say 'Amen' to Hananiah's words with sincerity, for the whole of his ministry aimed at the establishment of a prosperous Judah, yet he knew that it could not be so; only a change of heart

would avert disaster. In addition, Hananiah's 'oracle' was alien to the tenor of earlier, recognized prophets (a test still valid when new teachings appear; *cf.* on 26:18). The principle was tragically clear; one might be utterly sincere and yet be damned.

28:10, 11 Hananiah's demonstration. Dramatically Hananiah demonstrated his point by breaking the yoke which he had taken from Jeremiah; so would Nebuchadrezzar's power be broken within 2 years. **11** *Jeremiah went his way.* Why did Jeremiah not answer immediately? Much has been written about this. However, the true prophet could not add to his earlier declaration 'when the word of that prophet comes to pass, then it will be known that the Lord has truly sent the prophet' (v. 9). The crowd must have been greatly impressed by Hananiah's message, and a further rebuttal by Jeremiah might have endangered his life.

28:12–17 Jeremiah's verification of his message. Were there any doubt of his possession of the truth in Jeremiah's mind, it was dispelled by this oracle. **13** *I will make.* Read 'you' with Hebrew; for Hananiah's encouragement could only inspire a greater fervour among the anti-Babylon party. **15, 16** *Sent . . . remove* (lit. 'send'; see RV). Claiming a fictitious divine commission, he was in fact to receive a more terrible one. **17** Two months or less elapsed between Hananiah's false prophecy and the fulfilment of Jeremiah's (*cf.* v. 1).

29:1–32 Directions for the exiles

A large contingent of captives had been carried to Babylon in 597 BC, among them Jehoiachin the king, his household, a company of priests and some prophets (2 Ki. 24:10–17). News reached Jeremiah that certain false prophets among the exiles were prophesying a speedy return to the land. Jeremiah wrote this letter lest the exiles be carried away by the superficial, non-factual optimism of Hananiah and his friends. Patience to await Yahweh's restoration would be the great factor and it should not be endangered by precipitate action. Faith in God's tomorrow is the great principle involved—patience with its expectancy, not the inertness of despair, nor the suicide of folly. In this message the prophet first addresses an exhortation and then makes a declaration. In his exhortation to the people (vv. 4–9) he tells them to carry on the normal activities of life as far as possible. The declaration which follows (vv. 10–32) includes four groups of people: those already in captivity (vv. 10–14), those about to follow them (vv. 15–19), the false prophets in Babylon, of whom two—Ahab and Zedekiah—are named (vv. 20–23), and Shemaiah (vv. 24–32). **7** *Cf.* Gn. 18:23–33; Mt. 5:13–16. **8** *The dreams which they dream.* MT is obscure, see RSV mg.; possibly 'your dreams which you encourage (them) to dream', *i.e.* they speak what the people want to hear (*cf.* Is. 30:9–11). **10** *Cf.* 25:11; 27:7. *Seventy years* is the horizon-limit.

Yahweh will give them *a future* (lit. 'a latter end') *and a hope*. Moreover, He is accessible to them even in Babylon (*cf.* Ezk. 11:14–17). **16–20** are omitted by LXX and by many commentators. While they are reminiscent of 24:1–10, they are not simply repetition. Their position here can be interpreted as a contradiction of the optimistic pronouncements of the false prophets. **22** For the punishment see Dn. 3. A word-play may be detected in *curse* (Heb. *qᵉlālâ*), *roasted* (Heb. *qālām*) and the name of Ahab's father *Kolaiah*.

29:24–32 Reaction to the letter. The word of the Lord provoked opposition which His prophet condemned. As Hananiah had died for 'rebellion' so would Shemaiah, nor would he live to see the proof of his error.

30:1 – 34:22 THE FUTURE HOLDS HOPE

Although chs. 30–33 appear to interrupt Baruch's biography of Jeremiah, 29:11–14, 32c introduce the theme of 'the good that I will do to my people'. Previously the prevailing tone of Jeremiah's prophecies has been of judgment, though from time to time a gleam of light has fallen upon the dark path of God's people (*e.g.* 12:15; 16:14, 15; 23:1–8; 24:6, 7). These chapters present a remarkable change. The atmosphere is still charged with judgment, but a clear sky is in view, and the message is one of hope. If we accept that chs. 30 and 31 were written at the same time as chs. 32, 33, or put in their present form at that time, it is important to realize that this was the very eve of the final collapse of Judah, Zedekiah's tenth year. What an extraordinary situation! Jeremiah is in prison, famine and pestilence rage in the city, and the Babylonian army is battering against the wall of Jerusalem. This was Judah's midnight hour and the people needed hope and comfort. In this dark hour God has a message for His people. The message is that the nation is not to perish. More than that, the time will come when even the Gentile nations will acknowledge God's truth, and when a righteous Branch will arise from the house of David whose name will be the Lord our righteousness.

The whole theme is germane to the spirit of Jeremiah. The section is possibly a collection of sayings, some given earlier in other circumstances (*e.g.* 31:2–6, 18–22 about Ephraim), and others, many would claim, added to suit the exiles' situation. Affinities of style are found with the latter part of Isaiah which has brought strength to the case for later additions, yet criteria of style are too elusive to yield firm conclusions. Both spirit and expression accord with Jeremiah.

30:1–24 The book of consolation

30:1–11 Restoration assured. The chapter opens with a declaration of the restoration (vv. 1–3). There must be discipline, but not final disaster (vv. 4–11). **2** *Write. Cf.* the earlier command, 36:2; also Is. 30:8. To give a message written form implies its fixity before God and certainty of fulfilment. **8, 9** What Hananiah sought symbolically to do, but without the right or the power to accomplish it (28:10, 11), Yahweh in His great mercy would yet perform. If vv. 8, 9 are treated as an expansion in prose on the theme of vv. 10 and 11 concerning the day of the Lord, alteration of the pronouns, as in RSV, is needless. *David their king* does not mean that David the son of Jesse will be raised from the dead; it refers to an ideal king of the house of David (*cf.* Ezk. 34:23; 37:24).

30:12–17 Wounded and healed. Israel's wounds have been dealt to her by Yahweh at the hands of a merciless enemy. They are the result of her iniquity (v. 15) and are incurable (vv. 12, 15). She has been deserted by all her associates, which helps to emphasize the hopelessness of her position on the human level. But **16, 17** introduce what is almost a paradox, as so often happens in Jeremiah: God orders the affairs of all, caring especially for His chosen people. Those who have spoiled Israel shall themselves be spoiled for their arrogance, and despised Israel's wounds shall be healed.

30:18–24 Restoration. Beyond exile there is home. There is a lilt in this section, as though spring was bursting out of severe winter. This is the equivalent of Is. 35, but in the imagery and spirit of Jeremiah. There shall be laughter and children (vv. 19, 20), and their overlord shall be their own kith and kin (v. 21), both king and priest with priestly access to God (v. 21b). Thus shall be fulfilled the great covenant promise (v. 22; *cf.* Gn. 17:7; Ex. 6:7; Lv. 26:11–13; Dt. 7:6; 2 Sa. 7:24). Thus the prophet envisages a fivefold restoration—health (v. 17), the land (v. 18), prosperity (vv. 18–20), an ideal king (v. 21), and God's fellowship (v. 22). **23, 24** *Cf.* 23:19, 20. *The latter days*; *i.e.* the fulfilment of these glowing promises is not yet, but reserved for the unspecified future.

31:1–40 Restoration and the new covenant

This whole chapter deals with the restoration, prosperity and peace of Israel—both kingdoms. Vv. 1–22 concern mainly the northern kingdom; vv. 23–26 the southern kingdom; vv. 27–40 both kingdoms. There is not a dark cloud on the horizon; the vision is bright and glorious.

31:1–6 Grace in the wilderness. Northern Israel (Ephraim) is to be restored, rebuilt and cultivated anew, and there is a predicted end to the schism between north and south in a common acknowledgment of Yahweh, the God of the whole nation (v. 6).

2, 3 The general sense of these verses is clear enough: the Lord delivered Israel from Pharaoh's *sword* (Ex. 14:6ff.) and bestowed *grace* on them in their *wilderness* days. This was but the token of *everlasting love*, which has *continued* in divine *faithfulness* until the time of writing. The actual translation of the verses is, however, problematical, as comparison of RSV with RV shows.

In v. 3 RV, retaining an unemended text (see RSV mg.), suggests a grumbling comment from Israel that all the Lord's love was confined to the far distant past, eliciting the divine reply that this is by no means the case, for His love is everlasting. *From afar*; *i.e.* from His heavenly dwelling (*cf.* Ex. 3:8a).

31:7-14 Joy in anticipation. Jeremiah envisages the journey home (vv. 7-9) followed by the joy of the redeemed community (vv. 10-14). **7** *Chief*; *i.e.* in the Lord's estimation. **8** *Blind . . . lame . . . with child . . . travail.* Four categories of people personally incapacitated from making such a journey are chosen in order to show that salvation is not by inherent personal vigour but entirely by the activity of God. **9** *Weeping . . . consolations* (read rather 'supplications' with mg.; the change is needless). Repentance is ever the way home. *First-born*; *cf.* Ex. 4:22: a son, not by any process of begetting as the heathen nations supposed themselves to spring from their gods, but by historical choice and personal redemption (*cf.* Jn. 1:12; Eph. 1:3-8).

31:15-17 Rachel comforted. An imaginative prophetic touch: Rachel in her grave weeping afresh over the exile of her sons Joseph and Benjamin. But the Lord wipes away her tears in the pledge of restoration. **15** *Ramah. Cf.* 40:1; Ramah was evidently an assembly point for the captives. The site is traditionally between Jerusalem and Bethlehem (*cf.* Mt. 2:18) but is often located at Ramah near Bethel (*cf.* 1 Sa. 10:2).

31:18-22 Conscience and prayer. The same prophetic intuition hears Ephraim awaking to the call of conscience, with the Lord parentally yearning over him. **18** *Bring me back.* The first move, leading to repentance, must be made by the Lord. Only the turned heart can turn. *Cf.* La. 5:21. **21** *Set up waymarks*; signposts or stones marking the road, essential in the desert, but here also an assurance to the departing exiles of the certainty of the return journey. **22** *A woman protects a man.* Many interpretations are offered, none without difficulty. Some suggest 'a female protects a warrior', implying a peaceful paradise. It may be that we are dealing with a proverb whose meaning has been lost.

31:23-26 Judah the blessed. When these better days come, Judah will be the blessed of the Lord. **26** The prophet seems to record here how sweet to his own heart this visionary dream had been.

31:27-30 The Lord the Re-creator. Once the suffering is over, the Lord will be intent again on re-creating His people. He is the Destroyer only in the face of evil; fundamentally He is the Creator. In the foreseen future day the wilful sinner will suffer the due reward of his deed (v. 29), and the old, fatalistic proverb, which, as popularly understood, was never true to OT thought, will be given the lie (*cf.* Ezk. 18:1-3). The 'solidarity' of family, tribe and nation (*e.g.* Nu. 16:26-33; Jos. 7:1-12) is thoroughly recognized throughout the OT but was never intended to mean that any given individual, or even a whole generation, was so immersed in the sins of the past that none could now repent or that fresh moral initiative was impossible. Jeremiah looks forward to new dimensions of divine dealing with the individual (see vv. 31-34) and in the light of this foresees the disappearance of a prevalent excuse for moral indolence.

31:31-34 The new covenant. In a passage of fundamental importance, Jeremiah explains one of the central points of unity of the Bible. The NT declares the advent and establishment of the new covenant, but the idea of a new covenant belongs to the OT. **31** A *covenant*, in the meaning intended here (*cf.* Gn. 6:18; 15:18; Ex. 2:24; 6:4-6, *etc.*), signifies God's pledge to save and keep a people for Himself. Jeremiah is envisaging God's saving purposes coming to a new fruition, and, indeed (see v. 34), their final form. *Israel . . . Judah.* The new covenant will be the means of the unity of the people of God, overcoming the schisms and enmities of the past. **32** *Not like.* Wherein lies the newness of the new covenant, as compared with the great covenant-making at Sinai (*cf.* Ex. 24:3-8)? *They broke.* This is the one feature of dissimilarity which Jeremiah notes: under the former covenant, the human element was not able to live up to the covenant stipulations, notwithstanding that the Lord was *their husband.* Here Jeremiah reverts to his favourite view of the covenant relation in terms of marriage (*cf.* 2:2, 3), and by declaring the Lord as the Husband he intends to note that there was no unfaithfulness on the divine side. The former covenant needs to be succeeded by the new covenant because of human frailty (*cf.* Dt. 5:28, 29).

33 What, then, will the Lord do? He must either reduce His demands until they are within the range of human powers, or else He must change the heart of men. It is to the latter that He commits Himself. *My law.* The law reflects the nature of God, and therefore is unchanging. God cannot reduce His standards without ceasing to be Himself, but now the whole inner constitution of men, *their hearts*, is to be fashioned by God to match the requirements of His law, and in this way the great covenant promise, *I will be their God, and they shall be my people*, will be fulfilled. **34** How will this come to pass? What act of God will make it possible? Jeremiah first stresses the individualism of the new covenant. *Each* of the people of God will have independent access to God and intimate dealings with Him, such as the verb *know* in the marriage-covenant context indicates (*cf.* Gn. 4:1). This will come to pass (note the explanatory force of the word *for I will forgive*) through a full and final dealing with sin. *Iniquity . . . sin* represent respectively the inner and outer aspects of sin, and therefore, together, the totality of it in the individual life. *Remember no more* is a forcible expression of the finality of God's act. In contrast with the ritual requirements of the Mosaic covenant which faced men with incessant reminders of their guilt (*cf.* Heb. 10:3), this new divine act will drive the forgiven sins even out of the mind of God, and that for ever (*cf.* Mi. 7:18–20; Heb. 10:10–18).

31:35–37 Permanence. Two pledges are seen here that Israel shall endure, the world itself being an illustration. The perseverance of Israel rests on the persistence of Yahweh (*cf.* Heb. 13:8).

31:38–40 The polluted converted. A prophecy, the realization of which, in one sense, Nehemiah was to see and in which he was to have a share. Jerusalem would be rebuilt (vv. 38, 39), the valley of Hinnom, polluted by Baal worship and refuse, would be purified, and the city and its environment would be made sacred for life and worship (v. 40). All prefiguring the glory of the eternal city of God, yet to be (*cf.* Rev. 21:9ff.).

32:1–44 A pledge of the promised future

The next two chapters are dated in the tenth year of Zedekiah (588/7 BC), *i.e.* a short time before the final collapse of Jerusalem (*cf.* 2 Ki. 25:1–3). But, in spite of the encircling gloom, the prophet maintained a steady and impressive optimism, not in the immediate deliverance of Jerusalem but in the final purposes of God. Topically this chapter is in place here; chronologically it follows chs. 37 and 38.

The chapter can be roughly divided into two parts. In the first the prophet of God is prominent; in the second the God of the prophet is prominent.

32:1–25 The prophet of God. We note three things about him: his imprisonment, his optimism and his supplication.

1–5 describe the prophet's imprisonment. This paragraph is actually an introduction to the next one. The enemy was besieging the city and the prophet was deemed too pro-Babylonian to be left at liberty. For his realistic vision they have no room either in mind or heart. **5** *Until I visit him*; visitation may mean either consolation or punishment. As it turned out, visitation in Zedekiah's case meant penalty (*cf.* 2 Ki. 25:7).

6–15 speak of the prophet's optimism. Jeremiah had stressed that there would be no total destruction, since Yahweh had resolved on a returning remnant to serve His unchanging purpose (*e.g.* 5:10, 18; 29:11–14; 31:8–14). The test on this point of faith came through his cousin Hanamel's offer to sell the field at Anathoth, now in possession of the enemy, according to the property law of Lv. 25:25. Jeremiah felt that the revelation known to him must also be experienced by the people; hence the care he took in drawing up and safeguarding the documents of transfer and purchase. He clearly expected some relation to benefit from his action in the future. The paragraph shows three stages involving Jeremiah and others; initiative taken by God (vv. 6, 7); action taken by Hanamel (v. 8); record taken by Baruch (vv. 9–15). **9** *Seventeen shekels*. Jeremiah evidently had ample funds even in prison, for this can be reckoned as about a year's wage. **11** *The sealed deed . . . the open copy.* The former was a detailed

account folded up and sealed to prevent fraudulent alteration; the latter was an abstract or summary for ordinary consultation. Papyrus was the normal writing material. In classical history there is a similar record. When Hannibal the Carthaginian suddenly appeared within 3 miles of the gates of Rome in 211 BC, the field on which his camp stood was sold without difficulty in the Roman Forum (Livy xxvi. 11).

16–25 contain the prophet's prayer. He recollects the nature of God revealed in history (vv. 17–20), and the nature of God's people (vv. 21–23), scarcely believing that his recent purchase can really have validity. Omission of vv. 17b–23, advocated by many commentators, leaves the doubt of v. 25 without the firm-founded faith that balanced it.

32:26–44 The God of the prophet. God saw the perplexing thoughts of His servant and made a declaration concerning Judah's immediate fate, which is dark, and concerning Judah's ultimate fate, which is bright.

26–35 Judah's immediate fate was grim. The disease had advanced so far that a drastic operation was imperative. Jeremiah, as the voice of God Himself, reads out the history of His people, idolatrous the whole way through, hence the compulsion to discipline them unto righteousness. **27** stands as a reply to Jeremiah's wonderment (vv. 24, 25) at the rather incredible purchase which he has just made, and as a heading to the next two sections, vv. 28–35 depicting the coming judgment and vv. 36–44 the contrasting ultimate glory. *God of all flesh* expresses in general the Lord's sovereign sway as Creator, but in particular this sway as applied in the sphere of human life. In consequence of this almighty power nothing, whether judgment or restoration, is *too hard* for Him. **33** *Persistently* rather dulls the lustre of Jeremiah's vivid 'rising up early'; see RV.

36–44 Judah's ultimate fate was bright and glorious. Discipline there would be (v. 36), but it would not be final disaster. There would be a restoration of the people to the land (v. 37) and to the Lord (vv. 38–41), and there would be a restoration of the land to prosperity (vv. 42–44). **38** *Cf.* on 30:22. **39** *I will give*; the whole work of salvation, here viewed subjectively as touching *heart* and conduct (*way*), is the gift of God. *One heart*; *i.e.* the removal of 'double-mindedness' (*cf.* Jas. 1:6, 7); utter sincerity and singlemindedness towards God. This looks back to 31:33. *One way*; *i.e.* an outward life which is completely consistent. **40** *I will put . . . that they may not turn.* The preservation of the people of God equally depends on God (*cf.* v. 39).

33:1–26 Reiteration of restoration

This chapter continues the general theme of Israel's restoration and all that such a restoration will imply. The paragraph of vv. 14–26 is not found in the LXX; many regard it as an appendix of unknown origin. The theme of the chapter is a threefold restoration: the restoration of the people to the land; the restoration of the land to prosperity; the restoration of the Davidic king.

33:1–8 The restoration of the people to the land. These verses are dominated by the now familiar theme of the two acts of God: first, to overthrow Jerusalem in judgment, and secondly to restore and regenerate the people. But as a preface to this there is a reassuring word to Jeremiah (vv. 2, 3; cf. 32:27) that the Lord is over all. **2** *Who made the earth* adopts LXX reading; Hebrew 'who does it' is a general reference to the two-part plan of God as previously delineated (32:28–35, 36–44). Either way—whether by claiming sovereignty in general as Creator or in particular (cf. RV) as Master Planner—the words reassure concerning the divine control of history. **3** The same truth is emphasized with reference to the source of all knowledge in the mind of God. The Lord invites Jeremiah to supplicate for further revelation, thus implying that earthly events originate in the predetermined will of God. **8** *I will cleanse.* The truth of 31:34 continues to live with Jeremiah.

33:9–13 The restoration of the land to prosperity. These verses present a very striking contrast between what was and what would be, what the land had become through the sin of man, and what it would become through and by the mercy of God. Instead of desolation there would be prosperity; instead of sorrow, joy; the people in their homes, prosperity in the land, joy in their hearts, and praise in the Temple. One other thing would be needed to complete the happy picture, an ideal king, and to such an ideal king the next paragraph introduces us.

33:14–26 The restoration of the Davidic king. The whole forecast of a blessed future is made to rest on this one fundamental promise: the coming great descendant of David, the Messianic King. The promise to God's people will be kept (v. 14), but in a proper sequence of events: first, the promised Ruler (v. 15) and then the saved and secure people (v. 16). These promises are now affirmed in order: the promise of the king, associated with the Levitical priesthood (vv. 17–22); the promise of the preservation of the people (vv. 23–26). **15** *Righteous* is a frequent Messianic attribute, e.g. Is. 11:4, 5; 53:11. *Branch*; see on 23:5f. **16** *The Lord is our righteousness* was earlier the title of the king (23:6) but here of the city. As a name for the king it means that he is the source of righteousness for his people (cf. Is. 53:11; see on Ps. 24:5); as a name for the city it means that the most striking characteristic of the people of God is that they have been made the recipients of this righteousness (cf. Is. 54:17 (RSV, 'vindication'); Phil. 3:9). **17, 18** The linking of king and priest is a feature of the references to the Messianic Branch, see references at 23:5; the union of the offices was fulfilled in the Lord Jesus. **20** *Covenant with the day* (also v. 25). The OT teaches that one day follows another, not by any automatic sequence or natural necessity, but

by deliberate divine will and faithfulness (cf. Gn. 8:22).

34:1–22 King and people addressed

34:1–7 A message to King Zedekiah. In this message the prophet first makes a declaration to the effect that both the capital and the king will be delivered into Nebuchadrezzar's hands. Nebuchadrezzar, king of Babylon, will enter Jerusalem as victor, and Zedekiah, king of Judah, will enter Babylon as the vanquished. **4, 5** To the declaration the prophet adds a consolation; Zedekiah will not be killed, he will even have a ceremonial funeral, in captivity. **7** The Lachish Letters, dispatches written at this moment, vividly illuminate the situation (cf. *NBD*, art. 'Lachish').

34:8–22 A message to the people. When the city's danger came to a head in the siege, the king induced his people by solemn oath to emancipate their Hebrew slaves in the hope that such an action would effect God's blessing. When the siege was temporarily lifted by the Egyptian allies this solemn pledge was broken and the slaves were forcibly brought again into servitude. Such circumstances were the background to this prophetic message. The action of the people was a breach of faith with the 'law of release' (Dt. 15:12). It was also a profanation of the name of God, since they had pledged their action in His name. Not only had the people broken God's law but also their own promise, adding perjury to treachery. **14** *At the end of six years.* MT 'seven years' (see RSV mg.) follows Dt. 15:1, and should be retained here for it denotes the completion of the cycle, the enslavement lasting only six years, as stated. The prophet declared that the people would be removed (vv. 17–21), and that the enemy would return (v. 22). He saw at once that such a breach of faith invited the retribution of Yahweh. As they had perjured themselves by such an action and had riveted bondage again upon Hebrew kith and kin, so Yahweh would lift from them His own protection, with the result that they themselves would become slaves under such ruthless masters as sword, pestilence and famine, until their condition would become 'a horror to all the kingdoms of the earth' (v. 17). **18** *The calf.* Contracts were solemnized by the dividing of an animal as an unspoken curse (cf. 1 Sa. 11:6, 7) that retribution of similar nature should befall whoever broke the agreement (cf. Gn. 15:9–20).

35:1 – 36:32 PROPHECIES AND EVENTS DURING JEHOIAKIM'S REIGN

In these two chapters we return again to the reign of Jehoiakim. In time sequence they follow ch. 26 but other reasons have led to their present positioning. Ch. 35 is some time later than ch. 36; cf. 35:11.

35:1–19 The lesson from the Rechabites

35:1–11 The prophet and the Rechabites. The

prophet is instructed by God (vv. 1, 2) to go to the encampment of the Rechabites, to bring them (or probably their representatives) into one of the chambers in the Temple, and to give them wine to drink. Jonadab had been the ancestor of the Rechabites, and to meet, as a nomad, the Baal-worship associated with the settled agriculturist and city dweller, he had disciplined his folk to forswear vine-culture and house-building, forbidding thereby the drinking of wine (*cf.* the events of his age, 2 Ki. 10). They were to maintain the austerity of nomad life. As a Kenite tribe they had thrown in their lot with Israel. The advent of the Babylonians had driven them into the city.

Jeremiah does what he is bidden to do (vv. 3–5), and the Rechabites' reaction (vv. 6–11) is that, to a man, the people refused to drink wine.

35:12–19 The prophet and the people. That action the prophet had foreseen, and he now used it to show by way of contrast the practice of Judah. In vv. 12–15 we have the prophet's expostulation; this is followed by a declaration (vv. 16,17), which in turn leads to the pronouncement of blessing upon Jonadab's house (vv. 18, 19). **14** *I have spoken* is emphatic, putting in strong contrast the success of Jonadab with his people and the failure of Yahweh with His. The Rechabites' constancy in obeying ancestral custom, rather than their way of life, is their merit.

36:1–32 The writing of the scroll

This fascinating chapter is one of the very few indications we have of how the Scriptures achieved permanent written form. We may take it that God in His providence caused this one incident to be recorded in order to teach us of the sort of procedure which underlies all the prophetic books. In the main sections of the narrative three cardinal truths stand out: firstly (v. 4), the miraculous identity of the three sets of words: those intimated by the Lord, those spoken by Jeremiah and those written by Baruch; secondly (v. 18), the accuracy of the transfer of the word from the prophet's mind and mouth to its written form; and thirdly (vv. 23, 29–31, 32) the steadfastness with which the Lord stands by His word once given: it cannot be turned aside; on the contrary it is enforced, enlarged, and at the appropriate time fulfilled.

36:1–26 The first writing. In the fourth year of Jehoiakim (605/4 BC) God commanded the prophet to make a more permanent record of his public utterances (*cf.* Is. 8:16; 30:8), with a view to securing repentance in the hearts of the people (vv. 1–3). In response to His divine command Jeremiah secured the services of his associate, Baruch, and he recorded what the prophet dictated (v. 4). For whatever reason— political or spiritual—Jeremiah was *debarred from going to the house*, and bade Baruch act as his deputy (v. 5). His purpose in all this was that Judah should return from her evil way before judgment fell (vv. 6–8).

On a certain feast day some months later (December 604 BC), Baruch read the scroll to a large concourse of people, and we may well imagine the consternation the message caused (vv. 9, 10). Micaiah, who was present and heard what Baruch read, gave an abstract of the threatening nature of Jeremiah's prophecy to the princes of Judah (vv. 11–13). On questioning, Baruch, who had been summoned to appear before the princes with the scroll, replies that he had written the scroll at Jeremiah's dictation (vv. 14–19). The whole matter is reported to the king (vv. 20–26). Thus on one day there seem to have been three readings of the scroll—before the people, before the princes, and before the king. The inference, therefore, is that the scroll could not have been very lengthy, or that Baruch read extracts. When the matter was reported to the king, he must have felt that it was a state affair. As soon as a few columns were read, his anger was immediate, and against the intercession of the princes he flung them into the fire. The king next commanded that the prophet and his scribe be apprehended, but in vain, for 'the Lord hid them' (v. 26). Jeremiah had insisted on subordination to Babylon, and this was soon forced upon Jehoiakim, but the king would not acknowledge this as the Lord's will and concentrated on a contrary policy (*cf.* 2 Ki. 24). This strong reaction of the king seemingly banished the fear of the princes, roused as they had been by the private reading of the scroll. None appreciated that 'the word of the Lord abides for ever'.

36:27–32 The rewriting of the scroll. Prophecy, other than false, has seldom come to heel at a king's threat. Times without number the prophets of Israel had as part of their duty the discipline of king and court (*e.g.* 2 Sa. 12:1; Is. 7:1–17). So in this instance. The burning of the scroll brought but a quickened sense that a second must be written, with necessary additions, including an indication of the fate awaiting the impious king. God will have the final word. Nowhere else does prophecy provide so clear a description of its recording. The details are valued as historical evidence, the whole as revealing the purpose behind the prophecy. The first scroll might have brought repentance in the present by the cumulative force of 20 years' oracles (v. 3), the second was for the future, not to be read then and there. The written Word has relevance beyond its primary speaking, it is authoritative, and its origin, as man's, is with God. **30** *His dead body*; *cf.* 22:19.

37:1 – 39:18 PROPHECIES AND EVENTS DURING ZEDEKIAH'S REIGN

In these three chapters the emphasis first falls upon the prophet and his captivity (chs. 37–38), and then upon the king and his captivity (ch. 39).

37:1 – 38:28 The prophet's incarceration and preservation

37:1–10 A royal question and a prophetic answer. Zedekiah had been set on the throne and given a new name as vassal of Babylon. His own instability, coupled with court intrigue prompted by Egyptian agents, made him disloyal to his master. In religion, too, he evinced no loyalty, clutching for any aid without trusting wholly to it. He was a kingly Reuben unstable in all his ways (Gn. 49:3, 4). **3** *Pray for us.* Zedekiah had hopes of deliverance from the armies of Babylon, seeing only the immediate events. **5** The advance of Egyptian troops temporarily raised the siege; **9, 10** but the answer to the king's prayer simply reaffirmed Jeremiah's consistent burden of inevitable doom.

37:11–15 Arrest of the prophet. During the relief Jeremiah attempted to leave the city to attend to some property in his family. This was prior to his purchase of land from Hanamel (*cf.* 37:21; 32:2). The alert guard-officer arrested him on suspicion of desertion, a course advocated by the prophet (*cf.* 21:9; 38:2), and adopted by some (*cf.* 38:19). **16** *Dungeon cells.* Apparently make-shift quarters in the underground cisterns of Jonathan's house (v. 15). Ellison comments that there must have been widespread opposition to the ruling party to require extra prison accommodation. **17** Zedekiah still had some regard for Jeremiah, whatever his advisers told him, but he had not the faith to bring forth any more helpful prophecy than the blunt, *You shall be delivered into the hand of the king of Babylon.* Jeremiah's word had been verified by events, yet he was being treated as a traitor. **21** Zedekiah appreciated the truth of the prophet's claims enough, at least, to move him to better quarters and give him food. Bread may have run out weeks before the end of the siege (*cf.* 52:6).

38:1–6 Jeremiah is silenced. Some suggest that this chapter is a different version of the earlier events in 37:11–21. The same elements are in it: similarity of question and answer, of confinement in cisterns, of release and guard-court imprisonment. Yet the differences are considerable: the reasons for restraint, the demand for execution, the conditions of, and in, Jeremiah's answer to the king, and its setting. Jeremiah was a 'thorn in the flesh' of the king's council, it would not be surprising if he should have suffered more than one imprisonment for his consistently gloomy remarks!

1–3 Jeremiah presents the issue squarely before the people, who doubtless were able to converse with him in the busy guards' court. **4** In the eyes of the princes, however, who bore the burden of the city's welfare and survival against attack, Jeremiah's counsel of surrender to the enemy meant a weakening of morale amounting to treason. In our own time men have been executed for similar attitudes and statements. It has never been, probably never will be, easy to establish in political quarters the priority of religious prin-

ciple and vision over statecraft. The mistake the princes made was due to their failure to see that Jeremiah spoke with an authority above his own person and mind. He stood, under that authority, for the better welfare of his people, in that he stood for the divine discipline of their sin, leading on to a truer and finer life. Exile was inevitable and essential to root idolatry out of their mind and spirit. The Babylonians were the unconscious agents of Yahweh's will. How hard it is for men who have never shared such vision to accept a message of this kind. Often the history of man supplies illustrations of political expediency silencing the prophetic voice. Thus the princes, on the ground of statecraft, silenced Jeremiah, even to the extent of ordering his execution. This they did not accomplish, but they brought sufficient pressure upon Zedekiah to stop him from interfering in their imprisonment of Jeremiah in a cistern with a deep layer of mire at the bottom, whence his voice would not be heard, and where he would starve to death. This appears to have been Jeremiah's third imprisonment.

38:7–13 Jeremiah is saved. Ebed-melech, a royal Ethiopian slave-eunuch, had the faith and courage to intercede with Zedekiah to lift the prophet out of the cistern, and re-lodge him in the guard-court—the fourth imprisonment, reckoned by number of changes. Altogether these changes strike a strong note of providence (*cf.* 36:26). The Lord turns to good account the vacillation of Zedekiah, has at the ready a slave (taken into slavery under circumstances unknown to us) who has risen in royal esteem for such a time as this (*cf.* Est. 4:14b); and, on the day the greatest of the Benjaminites (1:1) is in need, the king is found in the 'Benjamin Gate' as if waiting to hear his case. Ebed-melech was promised safety when the Babylonians took Jerusalem (39:15–18).

38:14–26 Jeremiah is interviewed by Zedekiah. The desperate king again summons the prophet and swears on oath that he shall not be put to death for being candid. The prophet therefore puts before him the dread alternatives. Either go out in surrender to the Babylonians or suffer the worst when the city is captured and set on fire. Zedekiah expresses his fear of mockery if he does so surrender—the unhappy word of a weak, unstable mind. That had been the inner tragedy of Zedekiah: he could not implement in action what his own mind acknowledged as wise and sound. **22** On that Jeremiah utters a dirge in which the king is put in the position he so recently occupied (*cf.* v. 6). **23** is an extra emphasis, MT having 'thou shalt burn this city' for the last phrase. RSV follows the LXX, Syriac, Vulgate and Targum, in giving passive sense. Although this may be preferred, nevertheless it was Zedekiah's indecision and lack of courage that actually brought about the ghastly result. Quite frequently it is not positive evil that does most harm, but the weakness of an otherwise good man. Zedekiah wins our sympathy through pity roused at the massacre of his family and his own blindness (2 Ki. 25:7), but it is at the cost of respect.

38:27, 28 Jeremiah is questioned by the princes. Zedekiah pledges Jeremiah to silence as to the purport of the interview, and Jeremiah with a half-truth allays the suspicions of the princes. The truth would have betrayed the king and most likely ended Jeremiah's career. 'Sin among men often creates positions where there is no perfect solution or way out' (Ellison).

39:1-18 The collapse of Jerusalem and the captivity of Judah

39:1-3 The collapse of the city. The last hour had arrived. For some eighteen months the city had held out against the might of Babylon, but the inevitable hour could not be postponed indefinitely. Weakened by a long and merciless siege without and decimated by famine within, Jerusalem surrendered. Some difficulty attends the explanation of these verses and the following. **1, 2** appear as an insertion (*cf.* RV); **4** *Saw them* is strange if referring to the officers and could be an error for 'saw it', *i.e.* the 'breach . . . made in the city'. **3** *Nergal-sharezer . . .*; *cf.* v. 13, which implies confusion here. Most scholars read 'Nergal-sharezer, prince of Simmagir, the Rabmag; Nebushazban, the Rabsaris, with all the rest . . .'

39:4-8 The capture of the king. Though he had to give up the city, Zedekiah had not yet given up hope of life. With the few defenders who were left he escaped and made his way towards Jericho. But the hour of judgment had come for him and flight was impossible. He was overtaken near Jericho and then taken to Riblah to Nebuchadrezzar. Judgment was meted out to him and his family. His fate was a cruel one (vv. 6, 7).

39:9, 10 The captivity of the people. This was the final captivity of Judah. In 597 BC King Jehoiachin and part of Jerusalem had been carried away; now, 11 years later, the rest of the city followed suit. But not quite. **10** A small remnant, *the poor people*, are left behind to make a new start.

39:11-14 The release of the prophet. Judgment was given to the king of Judah, captivity to the remnant of Jerusalem, the country to the poor of the land, and freedom to Jeremiah the prophet. Such was Babylon's dealing with Judah. Jeremiah was set free and is given into the generous care of Gedaliah, the son of a friend, to take him home.

39:15-18 The message to Ebed-melech. This is an appendix to ch. 39, which was concerned to continue the narrative of Jeremiah and Zedekiah to its completion, the words refer to 38:7-13. As Ebed-melech rescued the prophet from death through starvation and the foulness of the cistern, so he would be preserved from his enemies (the princes, or the Babylonians to whom he might appear an Egyptian agent?), *cf.* Mt. 25:34-40. **18** *A prize of war*; *cf.* on 21:9.

40:1 – 43:7 PROPHECIES AND EVENTS IN JUDAH

The prophecies to and events among the remnant left behind by the Babylonians clearly fall into two parts: those taking place in Judah (chs. 40–42) and those taking place in Egypt (chs. 43, 44).

40:1-6 The release of the prophet

Jeremiah had remained in Jerusalem and was rounded up and put in fetters with others destined for deportation to Babylon. The watchful providence of God over the hard-pressed prophet is seen in the timely discovery of their error, and Jeremiah was released on arrival at Ramah on the authority of the Babylonian commander. Clearly information had been lodged with this officer as to the identity of Jeremiah and his king's will concerning him. He is given the choice of going to Babylon with promise of the king's special favour, or going where he would. **5** suggests that that second alternative would be to remain with Gedaliah. The first phrase of this verse is omitted from the LXX, and no clear emendation of the Hebrew is feasible. However, his choice is his own, a liberty granted to no-one else in Judah. **2, 3** need not be attributed to a Jewish writer, for such sentiments were normal among the ancients; they are spoken of the people as a whole, not of the prophet. The contrast is that all Jeremiah's work was in the name of Yahweh; on the other hand, he did yeoman service to the Babylonian cause, and his release was his reward.

40:7-12 The return of the fugitives

Gedaliah was now governor of the land, and his new task, now that the leading men had been taken into exile, was to see that farmers and peasantry settled down amicably to secure the harvest out of which the tribute money would be paid to their new masters, the Babylonians. Hence a phase of that new task would be to come to terms with the military forces scattered in the countryside, displaced garrisons, bands of deserters and so forth. That Gedaliah was a Jew would be a great factor in their pacification. His initial words (vv. 9, 10) were such as to win a measure of confidence and loyalty. His sane and cordial policy was underscored by what is reported in v. 12.

40:13-16 The warning of a plot

Gedaliah was the soul of honour, but unfortunately for him one of the escaped leaders, Ishmael, had been suborned by the Ammonite king, Baalis, to overthrow Gedaliah's policy and effect his murder. Johanan, another leader, was aware of this plot, but Gedaliah felt it was too foul to be substantial. Seemingly Gedaliah had overlooked two congruent factors: first, that Ishmael was of the royal house of David, and hence his superior in status. A slight thrown upon Ishmael may thus have created something of jealousy upon which Baalis was able to play. The other factor may have been that in Ishmael's eyes Gedaliah was a traitor to the cause by assuming this post under the Babylonians. Like many other high-souled men in history, before and after his time, Gedaliah lacked the ability to sift the spirit of treachery from that of loyalty, and thereby paved the way for the assassin's stroke.

41:1–9 The execution of the plot

1 *Seventh month* is to be understood as in the same year ('the eleventh year of Zedekiah', 39:2). The deadly nature of Ishmael's proffer of loyalty is seen in that he used the normally sacred hour of eastern hospitality to carry out the murder. Both Jews and Chaldeans who formed Gedaliah's bodyguard were wiped out by Ishmael's men. One marvels at Ishmael's lack of insight, since Gedaliah's death was a major loss to his people, but jealousy and suspicion blind and brutalize. A murderer has usually no scruples regarding life, and in vv. 4–9 we have a ruthless example of it, an action intended to prevent news of the uprising from spreading. The pilgrims were bringing meal and vegetable offerings to the site of Jerusalem on which the ruined Temple had stood. Their shaven beards and rent garments and gashed bodies symbolized their distress over the desecration and destruction of the house of God.

6 The spirit of murder is often also accompanied by that of hypocrisy (*cf.* 2 Ki. 10:6–9), as here in Ishmael's *weeping as he came*. Greed of gain also marks such a character. Ten of the pilgrims saved themselves by revealing a cache of valuable food supplies. It is remarkable that so slight a force, eleven men in all, was able to butcher seventy out of eighty men, surprise possibly being the explanation. **9** MT permits 'whom he had slain because of Gedaliah' but LXX is generally followed here, as RSV. The reference to Asa recalls that he built this cistern to supply his garrison at Mizpah with water (*cf.* 1 Ki. 15:22).

41:10 The abduction of the remnant

The uselessness of all these murders is shown by the fact that Ishmael had to flee to Ammon, taking captive with him the rest of the refugees in Mizpah entrusted to the oversight of Gedaliah, including, it is assumed, Jeremiah and Baruch. *The king's daughters* presumably refers to some relationship, direct or indirect, to the royal house.

41:11–18 The rescue of the remnant

Johanan was as prompt in his pursuit of the murderers as he had been in warning Gedaliah against them. Though he failed to capture Ishmael, he secured the release of his prisoners. **16** *Soldiers* appears to be at variance with what is in v. 3, viz. Ishmael's slaughter of them at Mizpah. Probably we should read 'men, and women, and children' as in 43:6. Fear dissipates

sound judgment, especially if, as here, it follows the murder of so important a leader as Gedaliah. **17** Presumably at the caravanserai (*Geruth*; see RV mg.) of Chimham the final intention was argued out that to go to Egypt would be safer for them than to remain and undergo examination by the Babylonians later on.

42:1–6 The remnant consults Jeremiah

1 There is confusion in MT and LXX over the names; RSV harmonizes with 43:2.

4 Jeremiah must have been gravely exercised in mind over this request, since his word *I will keep back nothing from you* is impressive. His hesitation, however, was met by the promise that they would abide by Yahweh's command, for on such obedience they felt their welfare rested. **5** Indeed, according to this verse, they invoked His judgment if they broke troth: *the Lord be a true and faithful witness against us.*

42:7–22 Jeremiah's message to the remnant

For ten days Jeremiah remained silent, but when at last he spoke he left no doubts in the minds of the people who had consulted him as to what God's message was. He began with an exhortation and assurance. They had nothing to fear from the Babylonians, and if they stayed in the land God would prosper them (vv. 7–12). Following the exhortation to remain in the land comes a solemn word of warning (vv. 13–18). Refusal to follow the divine leading involves the divine displeasure with all its dire consequences. There will be no safety in Egypt; a similar calamity to that which had overtaken their city would overtake them in Egypt. But the prophet already knew what the mind of the people would be, he had long and hard experience of them, and expostulated with the men who had asked him to inquire of Yahweh (vv. 19–21). The prophet's message ended with a solemn declaration (v. 22).

43:1–7 The rejection by the remnant of God's word

The leaders of the remnant presumably listened in silence to Jeremiah until he had finished and then gave their considered reply. Their self-assurance was such that they could reject the prophet's words, despite their earlier guarantee (42:5, 6), believing him to be little more than a Babylonian propagandist. Their prayer (42:3) was shown to be utterly insincere when the answer was not what they wanted. **2** Thus they merit the epithet *insolent*, better rendered 'presumptuous', as ranking themselves above God's word or authority. There is a small textual problem in that MT has 'saying to Jeremiah' (*cf.* AV, RV), an abnormal form and perhaps erroneous. **3** Baruch evidently argued against flight to Egypt before Jeremiah spoke. **5** *Who had returned*; *cf.* 40:11, 12. The company followed the lead of Johanan and not of Jeremiah. **7** *Tahpanhes* is now Defenneh, an Egyptian frontier town on the Palestine road (*cf.* 2:16).

43:8 – 44:30 PROPHECIES AND EVENTS IN EGYPT

43:8 – 44:14 Jeremiah's message to the remnant

This is Jeremiah's first recorded message to the remnant in Egypt. It is in four parts:

43:8–13 An announcement of what Nebuchadrezzar would do in Egypt. Jeremiah, carried to Egypt, whether by pressure from his compatriots or of his own volition, continued his ministry of warning there. He again illustrated his message. **9** *Pharaoh's palace*; read 'Pharaoh's house' with AV and RV. It was an administrative building or a fortress. The *pavement* could be a large brick paving which archaeologists have uncovered at the site (see *NBD*, art. 'Tahpanhes'). These men of Judah had fled from Nebuchadrezzar to find, as they thought, secure shelter in Egypt. **10** But all was in vain, since Nebuchadrezzar would conquer that land and upon the stones there hidden build his throne. The stones, then, represented Babylon, and the mortar Egypt. Egypt now appeared strong and hid Babylon for the moment from the eyes of the fugitives, 'but soon the mortar will vanish, and the hard stones, the Babylonian Empire will be set up in Egypt in the presence of these very men who are striving to escape from it'. This is in accordance with the LXX and Syriac approved reading 'he shall set up' (v. 10). Earlier Jeremiah had been silent at their word, and now they are silent at his; it is the silence of a new fear as they hear this note of dark destiny. A fragmentary inscription confirms the fact that Nebuchadrezzar invaded Egypt in 568 BC, Amasis then being pharaoh, and overthrew its defenders. **12** *He shall clean*. Note the change from AV, RV; the figure is of a shepherd removing lice. **13** *Heliopolis*; the Hebrew has Beth Shemesh, 'house of the sun', adding *which is in the land of Egypt* to distinguish it from Beth Shemesh in Palestine. The Egyptian city was called On (Gn. 41:45, *etc.*) and was the centre of sun-worship, celebrated with tall pillars. It lay 10 miles north-east of Cairo.

44:1–6 A reminder of what God had done in Judah. The clash of opinion was fierce. Jeremiah thrust upon the minds of the Jews then in Egypt the truth that penalty always interlocks with sin. They had burned incense to the 'queen of heaven' (Astarte, the 'Great Mother' of antiquity), and thereby the anger of Yahweh had overtaken the land of Judah. **1** *Migdol . . . Tahpanhes . . . Memphis . . . Pathros.* The first three are in Lower Egypt, north of Cairo; Pathros signifies Upper Egypt from Cairo to Aswan, and papyri of a century later give us a picture of a Jewish colony at Aswan. The message was for them all.

44:7–10 A rebuke for what the remnant was doing. In spite of all God's judgments, in spite of the many red lights of their history, the remnant had gone blindly ahead, ignoring the warnings of the past.

44:11–14 Judgment upon the remnant. The message which the prophet had to proclaim for so many years to the nation as a whole, he had now to proclaim to the small remnant in Egypt. Judgment would be their lot just as it was the lot of Jerusalem; from it there would be no escape. **14** *Some fugitives.* Ellison thinks this refers to men who reached Egypt at an earlier stage and were not under a curse as were Johanan's party. A parallel may be seen in the future prophesied for the earlier group of exiles in Babylonia (*cf.* v. 29).

44:15–19 The remnant's response

Nothing the prophet said could break their obduracy for they believed that their troubles resulted from the suppression of idolatry by Josiah; before his time, under Manasseh, they had prospered, adoring the queen of heaven. Women were prominent opponents because that cult had an especial appeal to them, but all shared in it (*cf.* 7:18). **15** *In Pathros in the land of Egypt.* No good grounds exist for deleting this phrase; it describes in general the people who had spread farther south now come together for some unstated purpose.

44:20–30 Jeremiah's final message

This is the prophet's last recorded message, and it is as realistic and relevant as any. The remnant were determined to count other deities as equal with Yahweh, not to reject Him for another but to compromise Him. The papyri from Elephantine (*cf. NBD*, art. 'Papyri and Ostraca') reveal the extent this syncretism had reached four generations later. Jeremiah went so far as to say that so dire would Yahweh's answer be to such a denial of His presence and action that, on account of such worship, His name would disappear from the mouth of every man of Judah dwelling in Egypt (v. 26). The nemesis of idolatry is that in the end a remnant shall escape to know whose word stands fulfilled—His or theirs (v. 28). As a sign, even Pharaoh, whose protection they had sought, would fall into the hands of his enemies. Herodotus (ii.161) records the fall of this monarch. He was put to death *c.* 568 BC, 2 years after his dethronement. Amasis was pharaoh in 568/7 BC when Nebuchadrezzar attacked Egypt.

This whole chapter reveals the realism of Jeremiah, based on his insight, compared with the superficial inferences of two fellow-countrymen. They argued that, in the pre-reformation, when they worshipped the Asherah, fortune favoured them; since then disaster covered the land. It was the wrath of the 'Great Mother'. To Jeremiah it was the disciplinary work of God. Although he might not see the day, Jeremiah was confident that God was in control of His creation. With this chapter also ends Baruch's biography of Jeremiah. History has left no trace of what happened to the prophet after the encounter with the remnant related in this scene.

45:1–5 JEREMIAH'S MESSAGE TO BARUCH

The date places this oracle at the time of Baruch's

first copying of Jeremiah's speeches (ch. 36). Like the oracle to Ebed-melech (39:15–18), it is placed after the main story, as an appendix to the history of Jeremiah and Judah. Baruch was stricken with sorrow, perhaps at the words of doom dictated to him, perhaps at the unpopularity of his master reflected upon him, despite his faithful hard work. He was reminded that Yahweh's sorrow vastly exceeded his own, for He was demolishing His own construction; how, then, could Baruch seek his own, individual, well-being? Enough that in the end he will win through the disaster that has overtaken the rebellious and the impious. God's gift of bare life is adequate. The *you* of v. 5 is emphatic.

46:1 – 51:64 PROPHECIES AGAINST FOREIGN NATIONS

In the LXX these chapters follow 25:13, and are in a different order. Here they move from west to east, with Babylon, the final enemy, last. Undeniably many of these oracles belong at 25:13, both historically and by formal comparison with the arrangement of Isaiah and Ezekiel. However, the Ebed-melech and Baruch oracles (39:15–18; 45:1–5) have shown already that a certain type of saying is relegated to an appendix to avoid interruption of the main themes. This position is tenable equally for these oracles. How much or little of this material was added to Jeremiah's own messages is debated; fuller commentaries supply details. As elsewhere, it can be maintained that Jeremiah's spirit and hand are pertinent here, where some of Jeremiah's finest poetry is found. The prophet was not only concerned with the lot of his own people in the currents of world politics, but also proclaimed that God is always at work among all the nations.

46:1–28 Against Egypt

The date of this oracle is 605 BC. Egypt was Israel's ancient enemy and now proving a 'broken reed of a staff' (2 Ki. 18:21).

46:1–12 The battle of Carchemish. Egypt's ambition was checked and humbled at the battle of Carchemish. This was one of the most decisive battles of history, on which bitter field the dream of Pharaoh Necho of Egypt crashed into ruin (2 Ki. 24:7). Perhaps given just before the fight, the verses first thrill as the spirit of an exultant army confronts the foe on the eve of battle; then comes the panic of a smitten army as it breaks up in flight. As nowhere else, perhaps, these verses reveal the insight of Jeremiah's mind as it bears on political implications of his day, revealing also the sanity and clarity of his thinking. He sees in the Babylonian crown prince, Nebuchadrezzar, the will and the force to overthrow the impinging enemies of Israel, Egypt included. Thus the line of Yahweh's will lay clear—peace must be made with him as Yahweh's new and strange scourge of nations. It is a day of Yahweh, a day of His vindication.

9 Egypt's army included many foreign corps (*cf*. v. 21). *Put*; the ancient name of Libya. *Lud*; Lydia in W Turkey whence Egypt drew mercenaries (*cf*. Is. 66:19; Ezk. 30:5).

46:13–26 Missing the flood-tide. With piercing insight Jeremiah saw that the overthrow at Carchemish left Egypt open to later invasion. Behind that Egyptian collapse, on foreign soil and on home soil, Jeremiah saw the will and act of God. This oracle may have followed closely after the battle of Carchemish, or belong a year or two later, even as late as chs. 43, 44. 14 These are places in Lower Egypt; *cf*. 44:1. 15 RSV follows LXX, redividing MT *nishap* (RV 'swept away') into *nās ḥap* (RSV has *Apis fled*). Apis, sacred bull, was an incarnation of Osiris. 17 *Call the name*. A minor repointing; MT has 'they called'. The pharaoh was an empty vessel; he was 'found wanting' (*cf*. 1 Cor. 13:1). 18 *Like Tabor*; *i.e*. Nebuchadrezzar towering above all others. Pharaoh must yield before him, even as other mountains must yield in majesty to Tabor and Carmel. 20 *Gadfly*; a touch of imagery for the Babylonian attack, descriptive of a biting charge causing wild flight. *Has come upon her* follows LXX and Syriac in a slight change of MT. In the crucial hour of battle, Egypt's mercenaries are but as calves in the hands of the butcher.

22–24 Here we have an effective contrast, a sound of an incredible weakness where the roar as of a lion is necessary: the snake, Egyptian symbol of royalty, creeping back into its hole. The hiss of enmity is ineffective, as the Babylonians come on as an army of woodcutters levelling Egypt as a forest appointed for timber felling. 25, 26 A summary of the oracles against Egypt. She would be given over to the Babylonian entirely, and so would those who trusted in Egypt. Yet there would be a restoration in some measure. 25 *Amon*; the chief deity of Upper Egypt.

46:27, 28 A message of comfort. These verses are a repetition of 30:10, 11, a note more in line with the thought and style of Isaiah than Jeremiah. It has been suggested that in both places they may be an addition. The main argument against their validity here is that they assume the captivity as having already taken place. But it is quite in keeping with Jeremiah's thought to look ahead and see the future as an accomplished fact. So certain was he of its fulfilment that he speaks of it as already fulfilled.

47:1–7 Against the Philistines

The Philistines were of course Israel's closest enemies. Their power had been considerably reduced in the days of David, but they apparently managed to maintain their nationhood until the days of the Babylonians. The day of their *débâcle*, then, is a phase of the day of Yahweh.

1 *Before Pharaoh smote Gaza*. Lack of evidence precludes absolute dating but the context fits well *c*. 605/4 BC. Necho's march northwards in 609 (2 Ki. 23:29) implies control at that date, but this town was liable to change hands easily. 2 *Waters are rising*. Waters sometimes signify

calamities, and sometimes multitudes of people and nations. Here they signify both. The Babylonians *out of the north* would come as a mighty flood, and that would mean calamity as far as the Philistines are concerned. **4** *Tyre and Sidon.* Phoenicia, like Judah, inclined to Egypt, and apparently was allied with Philistia. *Caphtor* is Crete whence the Philistines came (*cf.* Am. 9:7). **5** *Baldness* suggests completion of disaster, as a sign of deep mourning, as does also the *gash* or cuttings in the flesh. *Anakim*, following LXX, may be no more than a guess by the translators, although they were connected with Philistines, Jos. 11:22. The Hebrew has '*im^eqām*, which, according to the use of the root '*mq* in cognate languages, could well mean 'their strength'. The translation would then be, 'Ashkelon has perished, the remains of their strength.' The same word possibly occurs again in 49:4. **7** *How can it be quiet . . . ?* So read with LXX, Vulgate, Syriac, AV; RV had to read 'given thee a charge' next for congruence. Here is an antiphony: one voice (v. 6) is the bitter cry of the Philistines under the stroke of Yahweh, and the other (v. 7) is the prophetic intimation that the stroke is Yahweh's judgment.

48:1-47 Against Moab

The context of this group of oracles, and of those against Ammon and Edom, is not indicated. All three states apparently plotted with Judah against Babylon soon after Zedekiah's accession (*cf.* 27:1-3), and presumably fell to Nebuchadrezzar during the next decade.

The country of Moab was the elevated and rich plateau which lay east of the Dead Sea. After the Israelites conquered her northern territory (Jos. 13:15-32) there was frequent war for its possession and many cities reverted to Moab. (See *NBD* for locations of these cities.) The poetry is perhaps the most highly finished production of Jeremiah's writings. Parts of this chapter are adaptations of passages in Is. 15; 16. **48:1-10 Yahweh's judgment on Moab's god, Chemosh.** The arrogance of Moab was founded on its possession and its material strength, and thus the cities would fall and both god and priests be driven into exile (v. 7). **1** *Nebo* is the city, not the better-known mountain of the same name. *The fortress.* This is the meaning of the word which AV took as a place Misgab. **2** *In Heshbon they planned.* The Hebrew contains a play on the root *ḥšb*, 'plan'. Heshbon had been allotted to Reuben by Joshua. *Madmen*, another place-name, is unidentified. Because it is based on the three Hebrew letters *d-m-n*, it is sometimes identified with the Dimon of Is. 15:9 (RSV mg.) and this in turn with Dibon (RSV). See on 48:18; *NBD*, art. 'Madmen'. *Brought to silence*; the appropriateness of this fate rests on a word-play, the Hebrew verb *dāmam*, to be silent, being somewhat assonantal with the name. **3-6** A variation of Is. 15:5 which aids interpretation of obscurities here. **4** *Zoar. Cf.* Is. 15:5; LXX involves only repointing of MT 'her little ones'. The place lay

at the SE end of the Dead Sea, a border point of Moab. **5** *They go up weeping*; *cf.* Is. 15:5. **6** *A wild ass.* MT 'like Aroer' may play upon the place-name and the name of a desert bush. **7** *Your strongholds.* MT 'your works', *i.e.* achievements, remains a possible reading. **10** A curse is invoked upon any who might execute the Lord's anger on Moab but who hesitate in doing so. *Cf.* Dt. 7:1-5; 9:1-5; Jdg. 5:23; Mt. 5:29, 30.

48:11-17 A contrast in judgment. A distinct oracle in which Moab is masculine, whereas the feminine is employed in vv. 1-9. **13** *Israel* had trusted in the Bethel sanctuary in which Yahweh was represented by the golden bull, or deemed to mount thereon, but in vain. Moab had had an immunity from judgment, as wine that had not been changed from vessel to vessel to save it from contamination of the lees (*i.e.* dregs); but now in the judgment of exile *Moab shall be ashamed of Chemosh*, a god who in time of peril was impotence itself against the power of Yahweh, the living God. **15** The only clear meaning is that of spoliation. **17** *You who are round about him*; his neighbours, whose own security was linked with Moab's. *Sceptre, staff* are figures of strength and authority; both will disappear in the day of judgment.

48:18-25 The calamity of Moab. A picture of complete devastation, partly complementing vv. 3-9. **18** *Dibon* lay in the fertile hills some 13 miles east of the Dead Sea. **21-24** The piling up of name after name is designed to drive home the message of total judgment. Nothing will be overlooked. The Lord knows all and will judge all. **25** presents a picture of utter humiliation; *horn* symbolizes power. *Cf.* on Zc. 1:18.

48:26-34 Moab's antagonist. 26, 27 Moab is to be made drunk, not with her own wine (*cf.* Is. 16:10), but by the terror of her Antagonist, the Lord. Those who despised Israel would become despicable, a concept resumed in Rev. 1:7, *cf.* Mk. 15:27-32. In form and content these verses separate themselves from vv. 28-34, but the vivid picture is characteristic of Jeremiah. **29-33** A variant form of the passage Is. 16:6-10, whence some corrections can be made. Jeremiah could reuse these verses quite naturally. **32** *As far as Jazer.* MT 'sea of Jazer' finds support in a proposal to render *more than for Jazer* as 'fountain of Jazer' (Heb. *mbk* 'fountain' by analogy with Ugaritic). The town lay north-west of 'Ammān. **33** *No one treads them with shouts of joy.* Comparison with Is. 16:10 suggests the reading 'no treader treads them' (*shouts of joy* erroneously copied from the next line). **34** belongs with vv. 35-39 as a prose composition based on Is. 15; 16. It is taken from Is. 15:4-6, and belongs in sense with vv. 26-33. *The waters of Nimrim also have become desolate.* The life-giving streams would fail, their sources being stopped by the enemy (*cf.* 2 Ki. 3:25).

48:35-39 The wail of Moab. Is. 15; 16 are the source of this passage, as careful comparison will reveal (v. 36, *cf.* Is. 16:11; 15:7; vv. 37, 38, *cf.* Is. 15:2, 3). Of itself reuse does not mean an origin other than Jeremiah. The cause of Moab's wail is God. He would end the pagan worship, shatter the land as a useless vessel, making Moab a laughing-stock to its neighbours. **36** *My heart moans*. Jeremiah was not vindictive, the downfall of Moab touched his sensitive mind, however right it was.

48:40–47 Yahweh has the last word. 40 *Like an eagle*; a figure for Nebuchadrezzar. **43, 44** *Cf.* Is. 24:17, 18. **45, 46** *Cf.* Nu. 21:28; 24:17. Balaam's oracle against Moab would now be enacted. **47** may well reflect the pity of Jeremiah's heart as reflecting that of Yahweh. Wrath is always God's 'strange work', and mercy is ever native to His heart. Moab is to be thrust under fierce discipline, not doomed to destruction.

49:1–6 Against Ammon

This short paragraph contains two distinct thoughts: the condemnation and the restoration of Ammon. The condemnation of Ammon (vv. 1–5) is due to its greed in robbing God of some land at an unstated time, perhaps after the fall of Israel. The territory of Gad was on the east of Jordan, and the country of the Ammonites lay east of that. **1** *Milcom* was the name or title of Ammon's national god (*cf.* 1 Ki. 11:5, 33). **2** *Rabbah* (Rabbath-Ammon) was the capital of Ammon whose name survives in modern 'Ammân. *A desolate mound* of debris in Arabic is *tell*, frequent in place-names. **3** *Heshbon* was Moabite (*cf.* 48: 2) but as a frontier-town probably changed hands more than once. *Ai* is unknown and so various emendations have been postulated, but none convinces. **4** *Valleys*; Hebrew *'ᵃmāqîm*, from the root *'mq* (see on 47:5), which may, on the evidence of cognate languages, mean 'to be strong'. We could therefore possibly see here, 'Why boast of your strength? Your strength is ebbing.' (See RSV mg.) **6** The prophecy ends on the note of restoration. Once again this judgment would not annihilate, for Yahweh would bring back Ammon from captivity.

49:7–22 Against Edom

Edom, Israel's traditional foe, lay to the south of Moab. Many of the expressions used in Jeremiah's prophecy appear also in Obadiah. The common passages are evidence of either a common source, borrowing by Jeremiah from Obadiah, or by Obadiah from Jeremiah. The last possibility finds most support in close comparison of the verses. Unlike the prophecy against Ammon, there is no message of hope and restoration for Edom: judgment will be final and complete. **7** *Wisdom*; *cf.* the story of Job with one character from *Teman* (Jb. 4:1), a district of Edom. **8** *Depths*; *i.e.* the recesses of the desert and mountains. *Dedan* lay south of Edom in the Hejaz. Esau represents Edom, as Jacob Israel (*cf.* Gn. 25:30). **10** *I have stripped Esau bare*; *i.e.* all the fortresses of Edom are laid bare and he has no hiding-place. In short, there is no escape from judgment. **11, 12** Yet God is just and merciful, and spares the innocent. *Drink the cup*; *i.e.* of Yahweh's anger. If Israel had to drink of this cup, surely Edom could not hope to escape it. Indication of a date of composition after 586 BC is seen by many in this verse. **13** *Bozrah*, a city in the north of Edom, about 20 miles south-east of the Dead Sea. The physical topography is referred to poetically in v. 16.

17–22 closely resemble 50:40, 44–46. Again, there is no reason to doubt the authenticity of a reused descriptive passage. (Note that this passage is a poem, despite RSV's arrangement as prose.) **19** As a lion comes up from the thick growth of semi-tropical vegetation fringing the banks of Jordan, so the enemy would swoop upon Edom and its cities; **20** and as a lion scatters a flock, so the enemy would scatter the inhabitants of Edom. With the exile of the *little ones of the flock* contrast the Lord's promised care for the helpless children (v. 11). How and when Edom disappeared we do not know; she aided the Babylonians against Judah; *cf., e.g.*, Ps. 137:7; Ob. 10–14. During the next centuries Arab invaders gained control of the land and many Edomites settled in southern Judah, forming Idumaea.

49:23–27 Against Damascus

The scene of judgment now shifts to the north, to Damascus, the ancient capital of Syria. Assyria had subjugated the region, when she fell, Egypt held it briefly, then Babylon took over. Notices in the Babylonian Chronicle record Nebuchadrezzar taking tribute from the area, without any mention of the insurrection envisaged here. Lack of knowledge makes rejection of the oracle, as many wish, unwise; a date early in Jeremiah's career might suit this message (with chs. 4–6?). **23** *Hamath*; modern Ḥāma north of Damascus. *Arpad*; probably a little north of Aleppo (*cf.* Is. 20:9; 36:19; 37:13). Both were formerly independent states. **27** *Ben-hadad*; the name or title of several kings, among them the major Syrian antagonist of Israel (*cf.* 1 Ki. 20; 2 Ki. 7; 8).

49:28–33 Against Kedar

Even the nomad Arabs fell prey to Nebuchadrezzar, their only refuge was to scatter in the heart of the desert. The Babylonian Chronicle dates the Babylonian's campaign in 599 BC. **28** *Hazor* was read as *ḥāṣēr* 'enclosure' by LXX and refers rather to a nomadic camp-site than the great city north of Galilee (note the existence of similar names in the Negeb). **30** *A purpose against you*. MT has 'against them'. **31** is addressed to the Babylonians. **32** *Who cut the corners*; *cf.* on 9:26.

49:34–39 Against Elam

The date of this oracle (597/6 BC) separates it from the preceding words, uttered earlier. Nebuchadrezzar apparently attacked Elam, east of Babylonia, in 596/5 BC (Babylonian Chronicle), but no details are preserved. These verses may have been a warning to Zedekiah (did he receive an emissary from Elam, as from nearer states; *cf.* 27:3?) that a revolt at the opposite end of Babylon's Empire would be crushed. **39** The position of Shushan (Susa), Elam's old capital, in the Persian Empire (*cf.* Nehemiah, Esther) may embody the fulfilment.

50:1 – 51:64 Against Babylon

These two chapters contain a long and impassioned prophecy against Babylon. The oracle presents many difficulties. The critical view sees in it a miscellany of fragments, a few from Jeremiah and more from later writers. The arguments against the Jeremianic authorship of the whole can be stated as follows. First, the historical situation is after the fourth year of Zedekiah when the prophet's words were plunged into the Euphrates (51:59–63; 593 BC), for the Jews were already in exile (50:4, 17; 51:34), the Temple had been ravaged (50:28; 51:11), and the end of Babylon seemed near (50:8; 51:6, 45). Secondly, the point of view is not that of Jeremiah in 593 BC. Chs. 27–29 tell of the prophet's opposition at that time to the false prophets who spoke of Nebuchadrezzar's speedy downfall, and of the exhortation given by Jeremiah to the exiles that they should settle down for a considerable period of time. These chapters, however, assume that Babylon's fall is at hand. Thirdly, it is said that the temper is not that of Jeremiah. He was convinced that the Babylonians were God's agents for the punishment of Judah— a work which had not yet been accomplished in the fourth year of Zedekiah. These chapters on the contrary reveal an anti-Babylonian spirit and a deep satisfaction at the prospect of their approaching fate.

Therefore the suggestion is made that unknown persons compiled these chapters, incorporating some material from Jeremiah, towards the end of the Babylonian Empire, about 540 BC. A later editor of the book of Jeremiah prefixed it to 51:59–64, which was Jeremiah's original oracle against Babylon, consisting of a forecast in very general terms of Babylon's downfall.

However, the reasons for rejecting the oracle as an authentic prophecy by Jeremiah are not conclusive. If 593 BC is accepted as the year of origin, a subsequent expansion after the destruction of the Temple and the deportations, when the prophet was in Egypt, may be surmised (so E. J. Young). Mention of the Medes precludes a date later than 550 BC (see on 51:11), and the sense of imminent destruction is a vivid usage in many oracular passages. The third point confuses Jeremiah's attitude to Babylon in general with his words and counsel in a particular situation. He was ready to accept Nebuchadrezzar as God's servant to punish errant Judah, therefore he advised submission to that servant as according with the will of God. Yet the servant is never greater than the master, and so the pride of Babylon inevitably would meet its end at the

hand of the Lord, just as Assyria had done (*cf.* Is. 10:5–15).

50:1–7 Babylon's future is linked with Israel's. 2 The tense of the verbs views the action as already past; by his utterance of God's word the prophet has set it in motion. Note that vv. 2–17 are in poetry, not partly prose as RSV. *Bel*, 'Lord', was a title of Merodach or Marduk, chief god of Babylon. **3** *Out of the north*. The enemy is not identified here (a parallel to the threat to Judah in 1:13, *etc.*). **4–7** In the confusion occasioned by this disaster Israel, now moved to penitence and covenant loyalty, would be given the chance to escape. **5** *Let us join ourselves*; so LXX. MT 'they shall join themselves'. **7** *We are not guilty*; contrast 2:3.

50:8–13 Yahweh summons the spoilers against Babylon. These verses speak of the spoilers of Babylon, the sin of Babylon, and the consequences for Babylon of her sins. 'The mills of God grind slowly, yet they grind exceeding small.' **8** *He-goats*, leading the flock in orderly exodus (Ellison). **11** *As a heifer at grass*. So LXX; *cf.* RV. **12** *Your mother*. The city is mother to its citizens (*cf.* Ho. 2:5 where Israel is 'mother').

50:14–16 Encouragement to the attackers. 16 *Every one shall turn to his own people*. The many exiles and hostages escape to their homelands at the overthrow of their oppressor.

50:17–20 The result for God's people. The remainder of Israel after the depredations of Assyria and Babylonia will regain their land too. **17** *Cf.* Ezk. 37. **18** Both pagan nations had been servants, both tried to be masters and both fell, the first to the second, and the second to another servant, Cyrus. **17b, 18** are considered intrusive into the poem, and so later (dating from a revision by the prophet in Egypt?).

50:21–28 A further summons to the attack. 21 *Merathaim, Pekod* are punning forms (see mg.) of two tribal names related to the Chaldeans. **24** *You strove against the Lord*. An active excitation on Babylon's part, but neutrality would have been as reprehensible (*cf.* Mt. 12:30; Mk. 9:40). **25** *The weapons of his wrath* is a figure for the nations who unconsciously perform God's purposes. **27** *Bulls*; *i.e.* warriors defeated. *Cf.* Is. 34:7. **28** This destruction is not wanton. God's people will gain liberty and speak His praise and power. The verse, in prose, may be an addition like vv. 17b, 18.

50:29–34 Babylon's fall; Israel's restoration. This is another poetic section throughout. Israel and Judah may be enslaved, yet they have a Redeemer, and He is strong. The Lord of hosts is peace to them but disquiet to their oppressors.

50:35–40 Babylon's devastation. Here is described the doom and utter desolation of Babylon. Everyone and everything would feel the bitterness of the avenger's sword. **36** *Diviners*. Without propitious omens the Babylonian armies were leaderless. **38** *Drought*. MT reads 'drought' which has the same consonants as 'sword' in the previous verses; 'sword' is favoured by commentators and the Syriac.

50:41-46 The Lord and His agent. 41-43 are a reapplication of 6:22-24; **44-46** of 49:19-21. Babylon, the foe from the north for Judah (1:14; 6:1; 10:22, *etc.*), the 'lion' against Edom (49:19), was to face a similar enemy.

51:1-19 The Lord's plan. Babylon's destroyer would be as one winnowing chaff from grain, a synonym of judgment for that nation's crime against the Holy One of Israel. Israel and Judah had their protector. Let Israel escape when He exacts the due of guilt. **1** *Chaldea*; MT *Leb-qamai*, 'the heart of those who rise against me', is a cipher on the principle A=Z, yielding the word *kasdîm*, Chaldeans, and expressing aptly the nature of the enemy. With 'Babylon' clear beside, there is no hint of secrecy. **2** *Winnowers* follows LXX, the Targum and Vulgate repointing MT 'strangers', yet the latter could be correct. **5** The land is evidently Chaldea (see mg.). **7-10** are ironic. There may be balm in Gilead (v. 8), but none can avail Babylon (*cf.* 8:22; 46:11). Her judgment reaches up to the judgment-bar of Yahweh. **7** *The nations went mad, i.e.* lost control of themselves.

11-14 Yahweh's strange work is described in this next section. He calls a nation that knows Him not to carry out His will to wrath. It is to make an end as though it were destiny incarnate. **11b** is considered an insertion. If the theory of a revision in Egypt by the elderly prophet is permissible, this could appropriately come from that time, when the Medes had gained control in the hills to the east and north of Babylon, and were recognized by Jeremiah. Babylon was forced to recognize their power and accepted the truce between Media and Lydia in 585 BC fixing their respective boundaries. This was before Cyrus the Persian seized power about 550 BC. **12** *Watchmen* here does not mean those who 'look out', but those who blockade the city.

15-19 are an interpolation taken from 10:12-16, but adduced to show the impotence of Babylon's gods to save her.

51:20-23 The hammer of God. Here is a further reversal of Babylon's place. The description applied to Babylon (*cf.* 50:23) as well as to her conqueror, both instruments in God's hands.

51:24-33 Babylon desolate. Babylon is seen as a mountain injurious to all (a volcano?), also as part of a chain from whence it may be toppled and rendered useless. Compare the figure in Dn. 2:31-45. **27** *Prepare the nations for war*; *cf.* 6:4. *Ararat* = Urartu, ancient kingdom of Armenia; *Minni* = Mannai in NW Persia; *Ashkenaz* = the Scythians, spread over the same region. All were subject to the Medes (*cf.* v. 11b). **32** *The bulwarks*; better 'the marshes', the reed swamps of S Babylonia, a refuge for fugitives. **33** *Threshing floor.* Before the actual threshing starts, the earth is beaten down firmly; so is Babylon on the verge of her threshing.

51:34-40 Babylon judged. The drama of the eternal courtroom is given in vv. 34-37. Zion states her case against her aggressor—spoliation,

maltreatment, wrong, exile, physical injury. Yahweh makes His case His own. As a result, Babylon, the fabulous garden of the East, becomes a jackals' lair, a scorn and a desolation. **36** *I will dry up her sea* is perhaps a reference to the lakes created by Nebuchadrezzar's fortifications and waterworks. Babylon was dependent upon the state-organized canal-system for her prosperity. **39** *Swoon away.* MT 'rejoice' may be euphemistic.

51:41-44 A lament for Babylon. The final end of the city, its power and pride, is delineated. **41** *Babylon* is written in the same cipher as 25:26 (RSV mg.), and as used in 51:1. **42** *The sea*; *i.e.* the enemy army. **44** The heart of the matter. Bel, no longer 'lord', will be broken like Dagon (1 Sa. 5:1-5) before the Lord. *Wall* probably symbolizes strength.

51:45-53 Judgment and its effects. 45, 46 God's people should have no place in the city, proud, doomed. Unattached, they could disregard rumour and unrest, the rise and fall of Nebuchadrezzar's successors. **47-49** This assurance would strengthen them; Babylon faced an inexorable fate. **50, 51** In such a situation there was no place for smug complacency, the Temple remained in a state of desecration, and the name of the Lord had no visual vindication. **52, 53** In a further passage Babylon is depicted impotent against her foe, the result of the sacrilege (51). **53** An echo of the famous tower's builders is audible.

51:54-58 The fall. In the culmination of the sayings about Babylon, the writer stood in the hour of victory. The crash of doom announces the just recompense of Yahweh, with whom all destinies rest. **58** The walls of the city, up to 25 ft wide, were one of Nebuchadrezzar's greatest constructions (*cf.* Dn. 4:30), and north of the city was another great wall running between the Tigris and Euphrates. Both were eventually destroyed, the former by Xerxes in 485 BC.

51:59-64 An illustration. In this passage is found the circumstance prompting Jeremiah's first utterance of these words against Babylon. Chronologically it belongs with ch. 29, but contextually its place is here. Zedekiah was required to present himself to his overlord for reasons now unknown and included in his retinue Seraiah, apparently Baruch's brother (*cf.* 32:12) who was responsible for the royal comfort. Considerable danger surely accompanied Seraiah's mission, which inaugurated the divine plan against Babylon. The scroll will have contained the greater part of chs. 50; 51. **64** MT reads '. . . the evil that I am bringing upon her. And they weary themselves. Thus far . . .' (*cf.* RSV mg.). Generally it is believed that v. 64b, c belongs before v. 59 and has been displaced. However, it is as straightforward to see here an editorial note to the effect 'Jeremiah's words end at "And they weary themselves" ', indicating that vv. 59-64 and ch. 52 are editorial additions, perhaps after the prophet's death.

52:1-34 HISTORICAL APPENDIX

This closing chapter deals with the fate of Zedekiah and Jerusalem and of Jehoiachin. It is taken from the same source as 2 Ki. 24; 25, from which it diverges little, probably with the intention of reminding readers that Jeremiah's words had been partly fulfilled, and of encouraging, by the final paragraph, the depressed exiles.

52:1-30 Judah's fall

4–16 are abbreviated in 39:1-10 and repeated in 2 Ki. 25. **11b** is not found in the other passages. For comparison of the passages see the larger commentaries. **15** *Some of the poorest* is often deleted as erroneously taken from v. 16 (*cf.* 39:9; 2 Ki. 25:11) yet it complements that verse well. **24–27** *Cf.* 2 Ki. 25:18–21. The execution of these representatives signified the execution of the whole nation; Judah was to become extinct. **28–30** is a unique source. The variation of the dates from the earlier passage (*cf.* v. 12 and 2 Ki. 24; 25) can be explained as mistaken, or as following the Egyptian method of reckoning the king's accession year as his first. **28** refers to the deportation of 597 BC, the number 3023 may be construed as the men (*cf.* 2 Ki. 24:14, 16 covering whole families). **29** refers to 586 BC. **30** refers to 581 BC, when the Babylonian may have avenged Gedaliah's murder.

52:31-34 Hopeful conclusion

Nebuchadrezzar's son (562–560 BC) showed grace to the imprisoned king. Whereas he had previously enjoyed the fare of a menial (as texts from Babylon record), now he was recognized as royal. In the restoration to his suzerain's favour of the long-punished covenant-breaking king, the editor may have seen reflected the future restoration of covenant-breaking Judah.

F. CAWLEY
A. R. MILLARD

Lamentations

INTRODUCTION

TITLE

The fuller title, 'The Lamentations of Jeremiah', is found in the LXX and Greek Uncial MSS. But the Talmud and Rabbinical writers refer to it simply as 'Lamentations' (Heb. *qînôt*), or 'How!' (*'êkâ*), the opening word in the Hebrew.

POSITION IN CANON

In keeping with the longer title, the LXX places the book immediately after the prophecies of Jeremiah, as in our English versions. In the Hebrew Bible it is not to be found among the prophetical writings but occupies the middle position among the five Festival Rolls (Megilloth) which immediately follow the three poetical books Psalms, Job and Proverbs, in the 'Writings' or third division of the Hebrew Canon. Each of the Megilloth was read at an annual festival, Lamentations being read on the ninth day of Ab (about mid-July), the anniversary of the destruction of the Temple by Nebuchadrezzar king of Babylon. In the Talmud, the poetical books and the Megilloth are rearranged in what appears to be a chronological order, viz. Ruth, Psalms, Job, Proverbs, Ecclesiastes, Song of Solomon, Lamentations, Daniel, Esther, *etc.*

AUTHORSHIP AND DATE

The tradition that Jeremiah composed these poems goes back to the position and title of the book in the LXX, where it is introduced by the words: 'And it came to pass, after Israel had been carried away captive, and Jerusalem had become desolate, that Jeremiah sat weeping, and lamented with this lamentation over Jerusalem and said . . .' It is also asserted in the Syriac Targum and in the Talmud (*Baba Bathra*) that 'Jeremiah wrote his own book, Kings, and Lamentations'. In 2 Ch. 35:25 reference is made to this prophet's lamentations over the death of King Josiah, which are there stated to have been written down and to have become 'an ordinance in Israel'; *cf.* La. 2:6; 4:20. But our present book concerns not so much the death of a king as the destruction of a city, and 4:20 could equally well refer to Zedekiah in spite of his unworthiness (*cf.* the sentiment in 2 Sa. 1:14, 21). Nevertheless Jeremiah as the weeping prophet (see Je. 9:1; 14:17-22; 15:10-18, *etc.*) might conceivably be held to be the author also of Lamentations, were it not for the fact that there are certain difficulties in accepting this view. The style is much more elaborate and artificial than that of Jeremiah, and in chs. 2 and 4 is more like that of Ezekiel. Ch. 3 recalls Pss. 119

and 143. The attitude to foreign powers implied in 4:17 is certainly not that of the 'collaborationist' in Jeremiah and does not reflect the prophet's own experience.

Many, therefore, regard the author as a younger contemporary of Jeremiah, who, like him, was an eyewitness of the heart-rending calamities which befell Jerusalem at the time of her capture by the Babylonian armies in 587-586 BC. Others consider chs. 2 and 4 as the work of an eyewitness (note the writer's concern for the fate of the children in 2:11, 12, 19, 20; 4:4, 10), *c.* 580 BC, to which have been added, perhaps from different sources, the national lament of ch. 1, the personal lament of ch. 3, and the prayer of ch. 5. The date of this material may be about 540 BC. Some would place the whole collection much later and make the book refer to the siege of Jerusalem in 170-168 BC by Antiochus Epiphanes or even by Pompey in 63 BC, but this is very improbable. In favour of the traditional dating in the period of the Exile is the despondent note throughout which suggests a time before the rise of Cyrus the Persian. There is also the fact that this particular period of Babylonian history is noted for its threnodies, or dirges, over fallen cities. Cuneiform inscriptions are extant in which 'the daughter of . . .' is bidden lament her lot (*cf.* 2:1). The technique may thus have been learnt by the Jews in exile.

STRUCTURE

Rabbinic commentators refer to 'the seven acrostics' and it will be noticed at once that each chapter has twenty-two verses, corresponding to the number and order of letters in the Hebrew alphabet, with the exception of ch. 3 which has sixty-six, each successive letter having three verses allotted to it instead of one. This alphabetical arrangement is said to show that 'Israel had sinned from aleph to tau', *i.e.*, as we should say, from A to Z, just as in Ps. 119 the implication is that the law should command a man's whole attention and desire. In ch. 5, however, the successive letters of the alphabet are not employed, although some scholars contend that they must have been used originally.

The first four poems make use of the halting rhythm known as the dirge (Heb. *qînâ*), *i.e.* a 3:2 rhythm, which is also found in Jeremiah.

MESSAGE

The book vividly portrays God's identification in Christ with human suffering and sin. G. A. F. Knight (*TBC*) has called it the Easter eve of

659

the human soul, for in it the soul, weighed down by God's judgments, is nevertheless confident of His unconquerable mercy (see especially 3:19–25, 52–58). The keynotes of the book are, as Gottwald says, doom and hope, and it affords 'an instructive insight into the inner life of the circles faithful to Yahweh after the national collapse' (A. Weiser).

OUTLINE OF CONTENTS

COMMENTARY

1:1–22 FIRST ODE

1:1–7 The desolation of Jerusalem

The opening words of this 'political funeral song' (Gunkel) depict Jerusalem as a woman bereaved of her husband and children and from whom 'has departed all her majesty' (v. 6) through persistent sorrow. So, many years later, a Roman coin which commemorates this same city's destruction by Titus in AD 70 shows her as a woman sitting under a palm-tree, and bears the inscription '*Judaea capta*' (*cf.* v. 3). She upon whom has been centred so glorious a heritage of spiritual and prophetic religion is now brought to utter desolation 'for the multitude of her transgressions' (v. 5).

2ff. *All her friends*, those surrounding nations to whom she had looked for help, have failed her miserably, and her streets and places of assembly, whether for merchandise (*her gates*) or for the joyous solemnities of worship, are now deserted (v. 4). **6** *Her princes, i.e.* Zedekiah and his courtiers (2 Ki. 25:4; Je. 39:4, 5), have turned tail and fled away.

1:8–11 Sin brings suffering

The hint given in v. 5 is now taken up and developed, and eventually becomes one of the major themes of the book. **8** *Jerusalem . . . became filthy* because she had *sinned grievously*. **9** *She took no thought of her doom, i.e.* she failed to consider the consequences of her actions, until it became too late. Countless warnings have gone unheeded, and now she is reaping the fruits of her iniquity. But even while her plight is thus being graphically described, she is pictured as beginning to cry out to God, and her cries break in upon the poet's meditations (vv. 9b, 11b).

1:12–22 A cry for compassion

Zion's first supplicating sobs have already been overheard in the previous section. Now not only the casual passers-by (v. 12), but all nations (v. 18) and, lastly, the Lord Himself (v. 20), are asked to ponder, with sympathetic understanding, the grievous affliction which has been thus placed upon her.

12 The words in this verse have long been associated with our Lord in His passion. Although Christ deprecated sympathy for Himself (*cf*. Lk. 23:28), He identified Himself so closely with human sin and its consequences (*cf*. 2 Cor. 5:21) that, as these prophetic words suggest, He would have us consider the significance of that identification. **15** The language recalls that of the great festivals of the Jewish year. But instead of the favoured people of Israel, their enemies are summoned to a feast, the object of which is not the praises of God for His bounty in vintage or harvest, but the crushing of the Jews themselves in the wine-press of affliction. Yet there is no complaint against the divine justice, no problem of theodicy as in the book of Job. **18** *The Lord is in the right*; and so it is to Him that resort is made, for all human aid is ineffectual (vv. 17, 19, 21). He may punish, but He will bring comfort to those who are led to recognize the reasons for such punishment. And even the very instruments of the divine judgment will themselves be judged by Him whose way is perfect (*cf*. Ps. 18:30). We have here a vivid demonstration of faith in God's sovereign power, wisdom and grace.

2:1-22 SECOND ODE

2:1-9 The Lord is an enemy

With gruesome details of scenes which he himself had witnessed, the poet describes in this elegy 'the day of the anger of the Lord' (v. 22). God Himself seemed to have 'become like an enemy' to Judah, for all these terrible happenings were but the outworking of His wrath. He, and not a mere human foe, was responsible for them. **1, 2** The Temple (*the splendour of Israel*) and the ark with its mercy-seat (*his footstool*; *cf*. 1 Ch. 28:2), as well as the forts and palaces and the humble dwellings of the people, had been cast to the ground and destroyed. **6** Even his *booth* or 'tabernacle' (AV), the place of all places where mercy might confidently be awaited, had been *broken down* and *laid in ruins*, as if it were no more than a booth of the vineyards, put up temporarily in harvest time and then pulled down again, thereby showing the powerlessness of outward ritual to avert God's judgments from a guilty people. **8** God *determined to lay in ruins the wall of the daughter of Zion*; a striking testimony to His sovereign activity. Nebuchadrezzar and his Babylonian armies are completely ignored! The capture of Jerusalem, so far from being a defeat for Yahweh, was a victory for His righteousness. See Is. 42:24f. for the absolute supremacy of God. The wrath of God, His judicial displeasure against iniquity, is no idle term, but an awesome reality for those who render themselves liable to it. This fact makes the cross of Christ even more significant (*cf*. Rom. 3:25f.). **9** *The law is no more*, either because 'Israel was scattered in a heathen, unclean land, and so could no longer fulfil the precepts of the Law; or else . . . there were no priests left who were able to give ritual instruction to the people' (G. A. F. Knight).

2:10-13 The horrors of famine

The plight of innocent children (vv. 11, 12) is a theme which recurs in vv. 19-21 and in 4:4, 10. The writer evidently could not get the harrowing scenes out of his mind. The elders or heads of families who shared in the administration were powerless to do anything. Grave magistrates and light-hearted maidens alike were reduced to grief-stricken silence (v. 10). Suffering such as this is always a profound mystery; but even a child cannot be considered in isolation. 'It is monstrous to charge the providence of God with the consequences of actions that He has forbidden' (W. F. Adeney). Consider also Christ's own words in Lk. 13:1-5. The trouble which has overtaken Zion is as *vast as the sea*; there is no end to it.

2:14-17 Prophets false and true

14 *Your prophets*. This would seem to refer not to Jeremiah or Ezekiel, who were now presumably in Egypt and Babylon respectively, but to the prophets left behind in Judah who, unlike them, were visionless (*cf*. v. 9) and afraid to expose the true cause of Zion's calamity, *your iniquity*. **15, 16** They were men who had gone about saying 'bad luck' instead of crying 'repent!' Their words were mocking words, little different from the taunts of the hostile spectators of the city's desolation; **17** and they were utterly apart from the fearless messages of the true prophets in accordance with which God had now *done what he purposed* and had *carried out his threat* which *he ordained long ago*. These shallow optimists with their false oracles (v. 14) had no light to shed on the present situation.

In vv. 16, 17 the usual order of initial letters is reversed and *Pe* precedes '*Ayin*, as it does also in chs. 3 and 4, but not in ch. 1 (which may be a sign of difference of authorship). The quaint Rabbinic explanation of this feature is that 'Israel spoke with the mouth (*Pe*) what the eye ('*Ayin*) had not seen', *i.e.* illicit things.

2:18-22 A call to supplication

The suffering city is not only bidden to cry to the Lord (v. 19), but words are put into the suppliant's mouth (vv. 20-22). **18** is very uncertain, as RSV mg. shows. RSV has undertaken to correct the Hebrew text in a way that leads very well into v. 19, so that the whole is an appeal by the elegist to his countrymen to turn their sorrows into prayer. For 'godly grief produces a repentance that leads to salvation' (2 Cor. 7:10) and therein lies the hope of deliverance. In AV and RV, however, we have a close rendering of the Hebrew text as it stands. At first sight, 'their heart' ought to refer to the exulting foes of v. 17, and the 'wall' may mean those who live within it, *i.e.* the people of Zion. Thus v. 18 would open with an insolent shout of triumph on the part of Zion's enemies against the God of Israel. But the second half of the verse sounds the note of sadness rather than of spite, and it would seem therefore more appropriate (as with the altered text adopted by RSV) to regard the whole verse as a sympathetic appeal to Zion to give vent to her grief. Calvin in fact takes 'their heart' to refer to the Jews themselves, and we could well understand the second half of the verse as calling upon the very fabric of Zion to share its people's heartfelt grief (cf. Lk. 19:40). The thought would be unusual but by no means impossible, and would lead convincingly into the next verse.

19 The *night* is either the time of undisturbed reflection or a picture of sorrow itself. **22** Instead of summoning worshippers to a festival, God has called together His *terrors on every side* (cf. Je. 20:3) and so encircled His people that *none escaped or survived*.

3:1–66 THIRD ODE

This chapter with its acrostic in triplets concentrates on the personal sufferings of the writer, although he is speaking, no doubt, 'as the typical representative of his people' (T. H. Gaster). Through all his agony there breathes a spirit of quiet resignation and confidence, especially in the second section (vv. 22–39). This is a finished product of literary art, although it is possible to detect a lack of cohesion here and there owing to the exigencies of the alphabetical framework. But in more ways than one, this poem brings us to the very heart of the book. As a foreglimpse of Christ's passion it has affinities with Is. 53 and Ps. 22.

3:1–21 The cry of the afflicted

Once more, in a series of suggestive metaphors, the sufferings are directly attributed to God: **2** *he has driven and brought me into darkness.* **12, 13** One of the most striking figures here given is that of God as a huntsman, winging His arrows (Heb. 'the sons of his quiver') against the prey. **16** He has also given stones instead of bread; hence the teeth grinding on gravel. **19–21** But here the way is prepared for a different and complementary portrait of the Almighty.

3:22–39 The mercies of God

That such a beautiful expression of assurance in God's unfailing mercies should be found in Lamentations and in such a context is indeed remarkable and carries its own rich consolations. Cf. v. 57. **22** *The steadfast love of the Lord never ceases.* Targum and Syriac have: 'The Lord's mercies, verily they cease not . . .' **23** They are adapted to each day's requirements (cf. Dt. 33:25b–27). **25ff.** The poet universalizes his own experience and inculcates the duties of watchful expectancy and glad submission. **28–33** *Let him sit alone in silence, let him put his mouth in the dust like a beaten slave*; for the infliction will pass, in that it does not represent God's final will for a man. **34–36** If God is so just that He

cannot tolerate the ill-treatment of captives, the perversion of the courts of law, or sharp practices in business, then any sufferer can afford to be patient (cf. v. 26). **37, 38** *Evil* too (i.e. 'trouble', not moral wickedness) is subject to God's control and has no independent existence. God is supreme, and can use trouble for beneficent ends. **39** No man alive can contend that his sufferings are entirely undeserved. To meet them in the way suggested will turn them into means of blessing. Cf. Ps. 119:71.

3:40–42 A call for conversion

'God's kindness is meant to lead you to repentance' (Rom. 2:4). In true prophetic vein the elegist puts himself alongside his countrymen and entreats them to return to the Lord and to seek reconciliation with Him. Let them examine themselves in the light of His commandments which they have transgressed, and let the lifting up of their *hands to God in heaven* be accompanied by the lifting up of their *hearts* also, i.e. let their prayers for pardon be true and sincere. Let them know too what it feels like to be unpardoned, to be under God's judgment still (v. 42b), and they will come to appreciate all the more the wonder of His forgiveness.

3:43–54 The sorrows of sin

The sense of dereliction which precedes every genuine conversion is then described. There comes to the soul a chastening apprehension of the wrath of God against sin and of the barrier which sin has erected between it and Him (v. 44). The effects of sin are fully acknowledged and heartfelt grief ensues. But God is no longer regarded as an implacable enemy. His tender mercy is in view and is keenly awaited (v. 50) to help (vv. 52–54). These last moving verses suggest an actual physical experience on the part of the writer, but if so, it was an experience different from that of Jeremiah who was placed in a dry dungeon by his own people (cf. Je. 38:6). **51** *The maidens of my city* may be, like *the daughter of my people* (v. 48), personifications of Jerusalem in its intimate, tender aspect, or a reference to the villages outside the city which were also involved in her terrible fate.

3:55–66 Comfort and cursing

55–60 Out of the depths of self-despair the prayer of the penitent sinner reaches the heights of heaven. Casting himself upon the *name*, or character, of Yahweh, He finds that God is by his side as advocate and redeemer, with words of consolation on His gracious lips. With this section cf. Ps. 69.

But while admitting the validity of God's judgments he cannot find it in his heart to excuse those who have been the instruments of them. **61–66** They too must be punished: *Thy curse will be on them.* Such an imprecation at this juncture may strike a jarring note, but it is well to remember that the infliction of suffering upon another man may, in the providence of God, lead that man to come to a recognition of his own sins and to seek the Lord, but it does not, on that account, render the instigator of the suffering less amenable to God's laws. The writer appears to be speaking under considerable provocation, but he places the judgment in God's hands, not his own.

4:1–22 FOURTH ODE

4:1–12 Then and now

A series of bitter contrasts between Jerusalem in her glory and Jerusalem in her shame. Two parallel passages (vv. 1–5, 6–11) are brought to a conclusion in the reflection of v. 12, and the execution of this section is most artistic.

1 recalls the burning of the city by Nebuzaradan in 2 Ki. 25:9. The *holy stones* are, of course, the stones of the Temple, many of which were of *pure gold*. **2ff.** At such a time even the tender offices of motherhood were in abeyance. Children received worse treatment than the offspring of *jackals* or the young of the careless ostrich (see Jb. 39:13–17). **6** *Sodom* perished in a moment by the hand of God; Zion must undergo a long and weary punishment, meted out to her by the hands of men. **7, 8** Those normally conspicuous because of their rank or calling, *her princes* (AV has 'Nazarites'; the Heb. means lit. 'consecrated ones') are *now . . . not recognized in the streets*; they are indistinguishable from all the rest. **12** is both an illustration of arrogance and self-confidence and of subsequent disillusionment.

4:13–20 The consequences of sin

13ff. The prophets and priests who had failed to proclaim God's true word are involved in a fearful nemesis. They are treated as lepers and hurried out of the city. Even the heathen give them no shelter (v. 15), for they are guilty men, against whom the prophet Jeremiah had spoken so often (*cf.* Je. 6:13; 8:10; 23:11, 14), and they had helped to *shed . . . the blood of the righteous* (*cf.* Je. 26:20–23). The people too are brought to realize that trust in an earthly ally (such as Egypt, Je. 37:7) was doomed to disappointment (v. 17), nor could the possession of the Davidic kingship be taken as a guarantee of divine blessing and protection (v. 20). **20** *The Lord's anointed* is Zedekiah, Judah's last tragic king, whose fate is described in 2 Ki. 25:4–7. Thus ecclesiastical leaders, politicians, the king himself, have all been powerless to avert God's judgments from the guilty nation whose *end had come* (v. 18).

4:21, 22 Edom shall not escape

At the time of Jerusalem's capture, Edom had sought to enrich herself at her kinsmen's expense (*cf.* Ob. 10–16), and her conduct at that time had been bitterly resented (*cf.* Ezk. 25:12–14; Ps. 137:7–9). But the Jews could console themselves with the thought that, whereas their own punishment was now accomplished (*cf.* Is. 40:2), that of Edom was still to come: *to you also the cup shall pass*. And when it did, it would be a sign of returning mercy for Judah. *Uz*, the home of

Job, is probably mentioned here as showing the extent of Edomite domains. *He will uncover your sins.* 'Uncover' is the opposite of 'cover', the usual word for 'forgive'.

5:1–22 FIFTH ODE

5:1–10 An appeal for mercy

Although there are twenty-two verses in this chapter, the acrostic arrangement is missing. Here is a prayer which may reflect conditions a little later than the actual destruction of the city, and which is an impassioned congregational entreaty for divine mercy. Although God is responsible for the calamity, yet it is to Him that the sorrowing people instinctively turn for help. Was it not He who had given them their inheritance (v. 2)? Their present forlorn state, in which they were compelled to purchase the bare necessities of life from their captors (v. 4) and to seek their bread in the wilderness at the peril of their lives from marauding bedouin (v. 9), was a plea to God to restore them, for His own name's sake, to their rightful position in the land, so that they would no longer be under the rule of servants, *i.e.* Babylonian satraps who were often promoted slaves of the king's household (v. 8). **7** The sentiment in this verse is in line with the second commandment. Generations of mankind do not live in watertight compartments, and children normally have to bear, *i.e.* reap the consequences of, their parents' misdoing (*cf.* Ex. 20:5f.; Dt. 5:9 f.). That this does not, however, override personal responsibility is made clear in such passages as Ezk. 18:1–4.

5:11–18 The shamefulness of sin

One more glance at the awful retribution which the people of God have brought upon themselves by their persistent transgression of His laws. But the mood is one of sorrow, not resentment. All thoughts of personal revenge are absent, for the rightness of God's judgment has been freely acknowledged and the issue is left in His own hands. The poet, in the name of his people, has won through to contrite humility and patient submission. **13** For *young men . . . to grind* was dishonouring, as it was women's work (*cf.* Jdg. 16:21).

5:19–22 God's eternal throne

The last look is reserved for the throne of God which still abides, even though the throne of the Davidic dynasty has been sent crashing to the ground. Only in God is there hope for the stricken people. A great longing for reconciliation and renewal breathes through the petition of v. 21. This in turn intensifies the realization of present forsakenness (v. 20). Suffering has done its work, the prodigal has come to himself and is ready to arise and go to his Father.

22 *Hast thou utterly rejected us?* Perish the thought! *Cf.* Rom. 11:1, 2.

L. E. H. STEPHENS-HODGE

Ezekiel

INTRODUCTION

AUTHORSHIP, DATE AND CIRCUMSTANCES

On the face of it the book of Ezekiel appears to proclaim its own unity as proceeding from one author, Ezekiel, resident in one place, Babylonia. The book possesses an orderly arrangement (see outline of contents), a uniform literary style couched throughout in the first person singular, and a coherent system of dates extending from the fifth year of the captivity (*i.e.* 593 BC, 1:2) until the twenty-seventh year (29:17; 40:1). The accuracy of this system of dating is somewhat confirmed by the collateral evidence of the historical allusions made in the body of the prophecy, where, *e.g.*, Persia is mentioned only as a mercenary of Tyre (27:10) and associated with Put (Punt, on the Red Sea?) and Ethiopia (Cush, 38:5), suggesting that at the time of writing this subsequently imperial power was thought of as remote and without claim to fame. Such allusions would become increasingly impossible between 570 and 550 BC.

In the light of these facts, S. R. Driver (*Introduction to the Literature of the Old Testament*, 1891, pp. 261, 278) was able to voice the consensus of specialist opinion that 'no critical question arises in connection with the authorship of the book, the whole from beginning to end bearing unmistakably the stamp of a single mind'. Another view, however, was heralded by Kraetzschmar (*Das Buch Ezechiel*, 1900) and brought to its completion by Hermann (*Ezechiel*, 1924) and more especially by Hölscher (*Hesekiel, das Dichter und das Buch*, 1924) who so dismembered the book that he allowed no more than one seventh to Ezekiel, ascribing the remainder to a 5th-century editor. This extreme position, though matched by the views of C. C. Torrey (*Pseudo-Ezekiel and the original Prophecy*, 1930) and James Smith (*The Book of the Prophet Ezekiel: a New Introduction*, 1931), has failed to convince the majority of students. Nevertheless the same basic reasoning has led many to adopt a 'moderate' view which holds that Ezekiel's ministry was not wholly in Babylonia, as the book itself would indicate, but was partly in Jerusalem. Specialists who espouse this theory (*e.g.* Oesterley and Robinson, *Hebrew Religion, its Origin and Development*, 1930; R. H. Pfeiffer, *Introduction to the Old Testament*, 1948) differ as to whether Ezekiel or some other was the final editor of the prophecies. V. Herntrich (*Ezechielprobleme*, 1932), one of the most influential early advocates of the dual location of Ezekiel, held that a disciple of Ezekiel's edited the work

and added to it, but Pfeiffer insists that it is 'gratuitous and idle' to invent a redactor.

It is probably true, however, that the majority of present-day students of Ezekiel have reverted broadly to the tradition of one author in one location. (*Cf.* G. A. Cooke, *The Book of Ezekiel*, 1937; C. G. Howie, *Ezekiel, Daniel*, 1961; D. M. G. Stalker, *Ezekiel*, 1968; P. R. Ackroyd, however, *Exile and Restoration*, 1968, p. 106, still finds the dual location the more satisfactory; for a comprehensive review of all literature and opinions, see H. H. Rowley, *Men of God*, Essay 6, 'The Book of Ezekiel in Modern Study', 1963, first published in *BJRL* 36, 1953–54, pp. 146–190.) It would seem, indeed, that the problems undoubtedly involved in the book hardly require any of the drastic solutions suggested for them.

To Pfeiffer the attractiveness of a Jerusalem ministry rests on the fact that the command (3:4), 'Go, get you to the house of Israel' suggests a journey to Jerusalem, and the additional command to 'speak' requires the prophet's personal presence there. The death of Pelatiah (11:13) is further evidence of the actual presence of Ezekiel in Jerusalem. In addition, throughout chs. 1–24 Ezekiel displays most detailed knowledge of the state of affairs in Jerusalem, such as an eye-witness could be supposed to possess. Others add to this array of facts the rather more abstract, but deeply important, consideration that there seems not a little absurdity in supposing Ezekiel to reside in Babylonia all the while that he is hurling denunciations at a city hundreds of miles away across the desert!

The first two of these arguments seem too insubstantial to bear the weight of the theory that Ezekiel ministered in Jerusalem. In his book the command to 'go . . . to the house of Israel' is forthwith interpreted by the actual action of the Spirit of God in impelling Ezekiel to Telabib and settling him there among an exiled community (3:12–15), and it is frequent in Ezekiel that the designation 'house of Israel' means the exiles (*e.g.* 11:15; 37:16). As to the death of Pelatiah, the mystery of this event is not lessened one whit if we suppose that Ezekiel was face to face with the wretched man rather than viewing him in a visionary experience. It is just as easy to imagine that, within the context of a vision of Jerusalem such as chs. 8–11 most reasonably suggest, Ezekiel saw his word of judgment on the city take this token form in the death of someone he knew.

As regards the remaining two arguments, there is certainly more room for discussion. Taking first Ezekiel's detailed knowledge of

Jerusalem, it is necessary to say that this is not, in fact, as considerable as is sometimes alleged. We need to recall that there was a free interchange of information between Jerusalem and Babylon (cf. Jeremiah's letter, Je. 29) and it is not at all unlikely that the basic details of chs. 8–11 concerning the desecration of the Temple courts was made known to the priestly Ezekiel through normal channels prior to being woven into the fabric of the vision. At the same time, while it is not necessary to make Ezekiel's experience as unique as is often suggested, there is none the less a residuum of information that could only have been his through supernatural agency, whether we care to use the word telepathy or not. In this category, e.g., there is the foreknowledge of the death of his wife (24:15ff.). In this regard Ezekiel shares with his fellow prophets a unique experience of the miraculous, and unless we are prepared for a total re-writing of OT evidence on this point we can do no other than accept that things were supernaturally made known to the prophets which either in kind or in extent (or in both) exceeded anything which enters the customary experience of men. Cf. J. Pedersen, Israel I & II, 1926, p. 162; A. B. Davidson, Old Testament Prophecy, 1904, p. 126; W. F. Albright, From Stone Age to Christianity, 1957, p. 325.

In the last analysis, however, all depends on the fourth objection: even if Ezekiel could have so prophesied, would he have done so? Is it a justifiable exercise of the prophetic ministry to expend so much indignation on a totally absent audience? The answer to this is much more simple than the question might at first sight suggest. Ezekiel is adopting a teaching method which is found at some time or another in most of the prophets: the method of enforcing truth on a present audience by calling to mind and addressing an absent audience. When any of the prophets, including Ezekiel, addressed foreign nations, are we ever to think either that those nations were present or that the oracles so spoken were meant to be conveyed to them? Were they not rather entirely intended for the ear of Israel (whether to rebuke or to encourage) even though formally addressed to others? (Cf. W. R. Harpur, Amos and Hosea, 1910, on Am. 1:6.) Thus Ezekiel addresses Jerusalem because it is essential for his purpose at that stage of his ministry to make his fellow-exiles see the city as it really was, appreciate the justice of the coming acts of God, and thus arrive at a theology adequate to the stresses of the exile and fitted to raise a barrier against perpetuation of the sins of the past (cf. A. Lods, The Prophets and the rise of Judaism, 1937, pp. 212f.; H. L. Ellison, Ezekiel: the Man and his Message, 1956, pp. 19–21).

We may approach the book, then, in the confidence that it is what it purports to be: the record of Ezekiel's 25-year ministry in Babylonia to his fellow-exiles.

CONTENTS

As the outline of contents shows (see below), the book is constructed on a clearly defined plan, the subjects of each section being mainly adhered to. After the introductory vision of chs. 1–3, Ezekiel concentrates almost exclusively on laying bare the iniquity of his people. He pitilessly drags their sins to the light and pronounces the judgment of God on them. By symbolic actions, parables, fiery oratory and logical statement he reiterates his theme of the wickedness of the nation and its inevitable destruction. The repetition of denunciation and threat of doom is so constant as to make the reader recoil in horror, especially as, whereas other prophetic works light up their threats with promises, this element is largely lacking in the first section of Ezekiel's book. When he does allow a ray of hope to shine through, it usually glows a fiery red, so that the restoration spoken of is a shameful one and not in joy (see, e.g., 16:53–58; 20:43, 44). In this, as in other respects, Ezekiel has affinity with the author of the book of Revelation, for both works set forth, as none other in their respective Testaments, the unmitigated terror of God's wrath.

The second section (chs. 25–32) confines itself to oracles against the nations of Israel's environment, both the petty states that plundered the people in their hour of distress and the greater nations of the day. Here Ezekiel's poetic imagination soars to its height; we are given some of the most vivid word pictures of the OT in his oracles against the prince of Tyre and Pharaoh of Egypt. It is curious that Ezekiel is silent as to the fate of Babylon, the chief destroyer of Jerusalem. Some believe that, since this nation must have figured in Ezekiel's prophecies of doom, it must be symbolized by Gog in the prophecy of chs. 38, 39. There is, however, no hint of this in the text and everything seems to point against the identification. One can but feel that, like Jeremiah, Ezekiel regarded Nebuchadrezzar as a servant of Yahweh and so regarded his actions as divinely ordained; unlike Jeremiah, however, Ezekiel received no subsequent word concerning Babylon and so left the issue with God.

The turning-point in Ezekiel's ministry is occasioned by the arrival of a messenger from Jerusalem, announcing the city's fall (33:21). In face of the consistent scepticism of the people towards his preaching, this event constituted the divine confirmation of his ministry. Henceforth people flocked to hear him (33:30). He was now free to give himself to the task of rehabilitating the scattered nation and this forms the theme of chs. 33–37.

It has been a long-standing perplexity that, after the restoration of the nation in the Messianic era, Ezekiel should have spoken of a further uprising of foreign powers against Israel (38; 39). There are nevertheless cogent reasons lying behind this teaching and we cannot see any necessity for denying it to Ezekiel. See introductory notes to these two chapters in the commentary.

The conclusion of the book (40–48) is the product of a devout mind that has long and affectionately pondered over the worship of Israel in her coming age of bliss. We are here forcibly reminded that Ezekiel was a priest as well as a prophet. As such he combined in himself the two great streams of Israel's tradition. In a land purged of uncleanness, the ideal worship in an ideal Temple is set forth for the observance of an ideal people.

CHARACTERISTICS

Two features of Ezekiel's personality have already been mentioned, viz. the vividness of his imagination and his unique powers of telepathy, clairvoyance and prognosis. These combine with an overwhelming sense of the transcendence of God to produce passages of literature that in many ways seem alien to the modern mind, but which richly reward investigation. How many, for example, are so bewildered by Ezekiel's account of his inaugural vision in ch. 1 that they read no further? Yet that chapter, once grasped, is seen to be highly significant and of great spiritual value, as the Jews themselves recognized. A saying in the Mishnah records that the chariot, *i.e.* Ezk. 1, and the creation, *i.e.* Gn. 1, are the two matters to be expounded only to a prudent person (*Hagiga* 2:1, quoted by Cooke, p. 23). Similar observations could be made concerning many obscure and neglected passages in Ezekiel.

In certain directions Ezekiel pioneered movements of thought which were destined to develop into the characteristic features of later Judaism. He was the first to state with dogmatic clarity the truth of individual responsibility. By the frequency of his visions and the ecstatic nature of many of his utterances, and especially by his prophecies concerning Gog and the future kingdom, he shaped a type of prophecy that in due course led to the apocalyptic movement. Ezekiel is thus the bridge between prophecy and apocalyptic. Further, by his priestly training he was naturally more interested in worship than in evangelism; consequently the missionary spirit, so evident in the latter chapters of Isaiah, is largely absent from his writings. In all these matters, viz. individual responsibility, apocalyptic prophecy and the by-passing of the Gentile in contemplating the kingdom of God, Judaism went much further than Ezekiel and in certain directions actually produced a caricature of his teaching. (See, *e.g.*, the introductory notes to ch. 18 in the commentary.) It is as unjust, however, to blame Ezekiel for these unfortunate developments, as it is to blame Daniel for the puerilities of some apocalyptic writings, or St. Paul for the doctrine of predestination to damnation. Where Ezekiel and Daniel were silent, or at most implicit, Judaism became explicit and exaggerated, just as some people's logic drives them to a position which most Christians believe St. Paul would have disowned. It is unfortunate in the highest degree, therefore, that many biblical scholars should disparage Ezekiel as being retrogressive in its doctrine. On the contrary, this book makes an important contribution in the providence of God to the unfolding revelation of God in the Bible. It needs to be studied with a greater sympathy than some moderns are at present inclined to accord it.

Finally, it may perhaps be mentioned that in some places the text of Ezekiel has suffered badly in transmission. To sort out the difficulties would demand more space than is allowable in a commentary of this compass. Only the more important corrections have been pointed out in the exposition. The interested student is recommended to the very useful commentary by G. A. Cooke in the *ICC*. While in many respects it goes further in the matter of conjecture than conservative scholars would generally allow, it is nevertheless characterized in the main by a commendable sobriety of judgment. The present writer has not hesitated frequently to draw upon it.

OUTLINE OF CONTENTS

COMMENTARY

1:1 – 24:27 ISRAEL'S SIN AND IMPENDING JUDGMENT

1:1 – 3:27 THE CALL OF EZEKIEL

1:1–28 The vision of the glory of God

1–3 It is not known from what epoch Ezekiel dates *the thirtieth year*, whether Babylonian or Israelite. Origen thought it represented his own age. *The fifth year of the exile of king Jehoiachin*, however, fixes the date as 593 BC. Evidences of Jewish settlements have been found at Nippur on the river *Chebar*, known to the Babylonians as 'The Grand Canal'; that Ezekiel should receive in such a place *visions of God* would be revolutionary to many of his compatriots, whose feelings rather found expression in utterances such as 11:14, 15.

4–14 Like others before him, Ezekiel's call to the prophetic office came with a vision of God. But, as frequently in prophetic ecstasy (*cf.* Acts 10), the nature of the vision was conditioned by the environment of the recipient. In this case it was the approach of a storm-cloud by which God revealed Himself to Ezekiel (v. 4). The blackness of the cloud, the unnatural fiery glow and the lightning flashes provided the framework for the manifestation of the greater glory of God. (See Guillaume, *Prophecy and Divination*, pp. 155f., and *cf.* the following report of a storm on the Euphrates: 'Dense masses of black clouds, streaked with orange, red and yellow appeared coming up from the WSW, and approaching us with fearful velocity. . . . The clouds by this time were quite terrific. Below the darkest of them there was a large collection of matter, of a dark crimson colour, which was rolling towards us at an awful rate. . . . All became calm and clear as before, and barely twenty-five minutes had seen the beginning, progress and termination of this fearful hurricane.' Chesney, *Narrative of the Euphrates Expedition*, 1868, quoted by Cooke in *ICC*, p. 10.) Note the repeated term *likeness* (vv. 5, 10, *etc.*); Ezekiel can suggest only parallels to the figures of his vision. The *living creatures* (v. 5) with their wheels (vv. 15, 16) form an unearthly chariot for the throne of God. The comment of the Rabbis on the faces of the living creatures (v. 10) is frequently quoted with approval: 'Man is exalted among creatures; the eagle is exalted among birds; the ox is exalted among domestic animals; the lion is exalted among wild beasts; and all of them have received dominion, and greatness has been given them, yet they are stationed below the chariot of the Holy One' (*Midrash R. Shemoth*, 23, on Ex. 15:1). *Cf.* Rev. 4:7.

15, 16 The *wheels* enabled the chariot to travel anywhere, a needful reminder for the exiles (see on vv. 1, 2). Viewed from Ezekiel's position, they seemed to revolve within each other; their construction was as though one wheel were in the midst of another though actually there were only four wheels, each separate, standing at the four corners of a square. **17** The movement of the wheels is unimaginable if we have ordinary vehicles in mind; this is a supernatural chariot! **18** *Their rims were full of eyes.* These eyes denote intelligence, for **20** *the spirit of the living creature was in the wheels.* **22** *Likeness of a firmament*; better, 'platform'; *rāqîaʿ* is translated 'firmament' in Gn. 1, but its fundamental meaning 'something made firm and flat by stamping' is here in mind. It serves as the basis for Yahweh's throne (v. 26) and is borne by the living creatures.

26–28 Note that the prophet will not say he definitely saw Yahweh, only *a likeness as it were of a human form* or *the appearance of the likeness of the glory of the Lord*. (There is the 'large face' and the 'small face' of God, says the Talmud, and man is given to see the latter only; *cf.* Jn. 1:18.) Nevertheless that which Ezekiel saw was sufficient to overwhelm him; *cf.* Is. 6:5; Dn. 10:8, 9; Rev. 1:17.

2:1 – 3:3 The prophet's call and commission

2:1 The title *Son of man* (vv. 1, 3, *etc.*) applied to himself is characteristic of Ezekiel and emphasizes his status as mere creature over against the majesty of the Creator. It is used by God in addressing the prophet, not by Ezekiel of himself, apparently to show that his duty is to be the mouthpiece of the divine will and nothing more. **5** *They will know that there has been a prophet among them* finds its counterpart in the oft-repeated phrase 'they shall know that I am Yahweh'. Both truths are to become apparent by God fulfilling the prophet's predictions; *cf.* 33:32, 33; Dt. 18:21f.

8 The prophet is bidden not to share the rebelliousness of his nation by hiding from them the messages God will declare to him. **9** That God should have directly touched the mouth of Jeremiah (Je. 1:9) but given *a written scroll* to Ezekiel illustrates the difference between the two prophets; the former declares the immanence of God, the latter His transcendence. **10** The writing on the book *on the front and on the back*, contrary to normal usage, indicates the fullness of its contents. *Lamentation and mourning and woe* is a fair description of the major part of Ezekiel's prophecy. His message was not changed until, according to the promise of v. 5, God fulfilled his words in the destruction of Jerusalem (33:21f.).

3:1 *Eat this scroll.* There is nothing mechanical in this mode of inspiration; that Ezekiel must masticate the roll shows he must make its message his own. **3** Despite the nature of the message, its taste to the prophet was *sweet as honey*, for 'it is sweet to do the will of God and to be trusted with tasks for Him' (McFadyen). Note the variation in the experience of the NT apocalyptist (Rev. 10:10).

3:4–15 The commission emphasized

5 The prophet is not sent to a foreign nation; **6** nor to the heathen world in general. If it had been so they would have listened. **7** But Israel will listen neither to a prophet nor to God Himself. The traditional obduracy of Israel is referred to by our Lord in Mt. 11:21–24; Lk. 4:24–27. **8, 9** *Cf.* Is. 50:7; Je. 1:17–19.

11 *To the exiles, to your people.* Ezekiel's mission, although directed to all Israel (v. 4), is now specified as immediately intended for his fellow-exiles. This would be necessitated by his circumstances; but the writing of the book, or even of its separate parts, would make his message available to the whole nation.

14 The departure of the chariot of glory leaves the prophet in a reaction of *bitterness* and *heat of . . . spirit*. But he is compelled to start on his prophetic ministry. **15** He moves to *Telabib*, the 'house of green ears', a chief centre of the exiles. It takes him *seven days* to recover from the effects of the vision.

3:16–21 The prophet as watchman

17 *I have made you a watchman.* A watchman's task was to warn a city of impending danger; so Ezekiel must warn his people of the disaster shortly to overtake them. The passage has in mind the catastrophe about to fall on Jerusalem, but the prophet would no doubt apply it generally. Its importance lies in the relationship to be established between Ezekiel and his hearers; he is responsible for them individually and must warn each man as a faithful pastor (vv. 18, 20); they are individually responsible for their actions and their fate, for God will deal with them as moral persons, not as a unit (v. 19). This is a revolutionary conception and marks a significant step in the process of revelation. See on chs. 18 and 33:1–20.

3:22–27 Silence enjoined

24, 25 Ezekiel is commanded to remain in his house, perhaps owing to a threat of violence. **26, 27** Dumbness will come upon him, except when Yahweh opens his mouth in prophetic utterance. If this episode is in place here, Ezekiel's ministry is a private one, which only they receive who come to his house (*cf.* 8:1), until tidings of the fall of Jerusalem reach him (33:21, 22). Some feel that this comes strangely after the preceding commission; they suggest that this paragraph may be misplaced and belongs to a later period of Ezekiel's ministry. If that be so, v. 27 relates to a specific occasion when God shall cause the prophet's dumbness to cease (see 33:21, 22). The suggested transference is not impossible, especially as the previous paragraph finds a fuller exposition in 33:1–20. On the other hand, the passage receives a good meaning where it stands now and may be allowed to retain its place: 'his freedom of movement will be restricted by the exiles . . . God will restrain his utterance, suffering him to speak only when specially directed to do so' (Wardle).

4:1 – 5:17 FOUR ACTED PROPHECIES

4:1–3 The siege of Jerusalem

1 The *brick* used by Ezekiel would be of soft clay, and the drawing would be carved by means of a stylus; when it was finished the clay would be baked as a brick. **2** Presumably the operations described were to be inscribed on the brick. **3** The *iron plate* perhaps portrays the strong fortifications set up against the city.

4:4–8 The exile

4 The prophet lies on his side, bearing Israel's *punishment*, for the period of the exile. LXX reads 190 in vv. 5 and 9 instead of 390 and is probably correct. From vv. 5, 6, 9 we gather that Ezekiel was to lie 150 days on his left side and 40 on his right; the period from the deportation under Tiglath-pileser in 734 BC (2 Ki. 15:29) to the taking of Jerusalem in 586 was 148 years, *i.e.* roughly 150 years, while the 40 years (general designation of a generation) for Judah roughly corresponds to the period 586 to 536, the time of Judah's exile in Babylon. Cooke suggests that the figure 390 was due to a copyist interpreting *the punishment of the house of Israel* as the whole period of Israel's sinning. According to the chronology of the book of Kings, the period from the division of the kingdom under Rehoboam to 586 was $394\frac{1}{2}$ years.

4:9–17 The famine

Two thoughts about the approaching famine are to be distinguished here: the scarcity of food (vv. 9–11, 16, 17) and the uncleanness involved in eating it in a foreign land (vv. 12–15). **9** The curious mixture of grain merely implies shortage and is not to be compared with Lv. 19:19. **10** *Twenty shekels* is about 9 oz. **11** *The sixth* *part of a hin* is about 2 pints. **12** The *dung* used in the baking of bread was for fuel. **14, 15** To Ezekiel, brought up as a priest, human excrement was too revolting; in response to his prayers he was allowed to use *cow's dung*, which is still used for fuel by bedouin. **13** *Cf.* Ho. 9:3f.; Am. 7:17. All lands outside Canaan were unclean and their products likewise, for Yahweh was not worshipped in them.

5:1–4 The slaughter

1, 2 Shaving the head was a figure for catastrophe: see Is. 7:20; Je. 41:5. Here the act represents the fate of the inhabitants of Jerusalem; they were to be burned, slain and scattered (v. 2); *the sword* pursuing those that flee the city (v. 2c) indicates the completeness of the destruction. **3, 4** Of the few that truly escape (those bound in Ezekiel's skirts) some shall yet perish, so that the remnant is very small indeed. Ezekiel thus does hold to a doctrine of the remnant (see also 6:8–10; 9:8; 11:13), in spite of the asseverations of some to the contrary; but it is wholly subordinated to his message of judgment until the fall of Jerusalem, after which it becomes his dominant theme.

5:5–17 An exposition of the signs

5, 6 Jerusalem is the *centre* of the world, alike by her position and privilege (*cf.* 38:12). This makes her excess of wickedness over the nations more heinous (*cf.* 16:47f.; Je. 2:10f.). **7** The argument implies that the nations about Israel walked according to such lights as they had, but Israel had not; **8** God accordingly would requite the sins of His people *in the sight of the nations*, both as an example and vindication of His holiness. **10** *Cf.* Lv. 26:29 and Dt. 28:53, prophecies fulfilled in the event (La. 4:10). **17** *Pestilence and blood* are one plague; we thus have the four scourges of Lv. 26, *famine, wild beasts, pestilence, the sword*. They occur again in 14:21 and figure in the plagues of the book of Revelation (Rev. 6:7, 8).

6:1–14 PROPHECY AGAINST THE MOUNTAINS OF ISRAEL

2 Ezekiel addresses the country under the figure *the mountains of Israel*, since they formed its chief feature; it is, indeed, 'a central mountain range sloping down to the narrow plains by the Mediterranean and the Jordan' (Toy). **3** Moreover, *mountains* and *hills* are usually associated by the prophets with idolatry (*e.g.* Is. 65:7; Je. 3:6; Ho. 4:13). *Ravines* (AV 'rivers'; RV 'watercourses'). These and the *valleys* were used for impure rites and the worship of Molech (see Je. 7:31, 32). *High places* were originally lofty sites, but came to denote sanctuaries wherever situated; there were many of these in the land where worship was ostensibly offered to Yahweh but actually differed little from that of Israel's neighbours. Apparently the reforms of Hezekiah and Josiah had been in vain (2 Ki. 18:4; 23:5). **4** *Incense altars* (Heb. *ḥammānîm*) were either terra cotta braziers for burning incense, as discovered at Megiddo and Beth-shean, or they were like the four-horned limestone altar found at Palmyra in Syria and inscribed with the name *ḥammān* (see Albright, *Archaeology and the Religion of Israel*[3], 1953, pp. 146, 215f.). **7** *You shall know that I am the Lord.* A phrase characteristic of Ezekiel; it occurs in vv. 10, 13, 14 and about 60 times elsewhere. The motive for Yahweh's action is always the acknowledgment by the nations of His sole deity and power.

9 *I have broken their wanton heart*; not 'I am broken with their whorish heart', as AV. God breaks the heart by sorrow to bring about repentance. **11** *Clap . . . stamp.* The actions of Ezekiel seem to express exultation rather than horror (see 21:17; 22:13; 25:6). *Alas!* is better rendered 'Aha!' (LXX, *euge, euge; i.e.* 'Bravo!'), as though the prophet exults in the coming judgment. His concern is the vindication of Yahweh's honour rather than the fate of sinners. *Cf.* Rev. 19:1–4. **13** The destruction of idolaters *among their idols* will reveal the impotence of the latter and convince the survivors that Yahweh alone is God. **14** *Riblah.* RV 'Diblah' (situated east of the Dead Sea in the south) is almost certainly a misreading of Riblah (lying far north by 'the entrance of Hamath', 48:1), the Hebrew *d* and *r* being almost identical. 'From the wilderness to Riblah' thus represents an equivalent of the better-known phrase 'from Dan to Beersheba'.

7:1–27 ISRAEL'S IMMINENT DOOM

There are four short oracles in this chapter (vv. 2–4; 5–9; 10, 11; 12, 13), followed by an exposition of their common theme (vv. 14–27). **2** As *the end* is stated to be immediately impending, and the date given in 1:1 leaves 7 years to the fall of Jerusalem, it is likely that this chapter was written later. The date at the head of a section does not necessarily embrace everything that follows till the next date is given.

The oracle is directed to *the land of Israel*, yet vv. 5–7, 10, 12 appear to have the day of the Lord with its universal significance in mind. It is therefore better to translate the concluding phrase of this verse by 'the four corners of the earth' as in Is. 11:12. The judgment upon Israel is set against the background of the judgment of the nations. Note the play of words, as in v. 6, *the end* (*haqqēṣ*) *has come* or 'awakes' (*hēqîṣ*). *Cf.* Am. 8:2. **7** *The time has come, the day is near*. That this is a reference to the day of the Lord seems clear from a comparison with 30:3; Dn. 12:1; Joel 1:15; Mal. 4:1.

10, 11 record a rhythmic oracle which gives the core of the prophecy. All is ripe for judgment, 'the tree has burst into leaf and flower!' (Cooke). The 'rod' (*hammaṭṭeh*; RSV mg.) and *pride* probably refer to the king of Israel and his court. *Cf.* the frequent usage of the word 'rod' for the sceptre of Israel (*e.g.* 19:11). RSV translates *injustice* (*hammuṭṭeh*) and carries the play on words a stage further.

12, 13 The buying and selling appears to be of property, the seller either doing it against his own inclination (*cf.* 1 Ki. 21:1–16) or at a bad price. The prophet says the one need not be glad, nor the other sorry, for both will shortly be involved in catastrophe. Many have thought that v. 13 refers to the law of jubilee (Lv. 25:10f.), and it may be so. Otherwise the prophet is continuing the thought of v. 12; buying back of ancestral lands is unthinkable, for 'the nation will be broken up and questions of property will cease to have interest' (Toy).

19, 20 Comparing the last clause of v. 19 with v. 20, the uncleanness of *their silver and gold* is due to their being lavished on idols. *Cf.* Is. 30:22. **21** Such idols Yahweh will give to the invaders. **26** A threefold division of the people religiously is indicated: *the prophet* for the immediate word of Yahweh; *the priest* for instruction out of the law; *the elders* for advice on civil matters. **27** gives a threefold division socially: *the king, the prince* (*i.e.* 'princes'; the singular is collective as in 22:6) and *the people of the land.*

8:1 – 11:25 JERUSALEM'S SIN AND JUDGMENT: ITS ABANDONMENT BY GOD

8:1–18 The idolaters in the Temple

1 The date is probably August-September 592 BC, 14 months after Ezekiel's inaugural vision (1:1). **2** *The appearance of a man* (Heb. '*īš*); so LXX. *Cf.* AV, RV, RSV mg., 'the appearance of fire' (Heb. '*ēš*). Ezekiel is carried in vision to the Temple and views idolatries taking place there. Whatever information the prophet may have received from the reports of others, this is also a description of things seen by means of a supernaturally heightened gift of 'second sight'. The distance between Babylonia and Jerusalem makes the episode astonishing, but it is not without parallel in the Bible. *Cf.* 2 Ki. 5:26; 6:8–12; Is. 21:6–10. **3** The *image of jealousy* (*i.e.* an image which rouses Yahweh to jealousy) may have been an image of the Canaanite goddess, Asherah. Manasseh had set up such an image (*sēmel*, the unusual word here used) in the Temple and later removed it (2 Ch. 33:7, 15). This may have been the same idol replaced, but Albright (*Archaeology and the Religion of Israel*, pp. 165f.) understands *sēmel* as a 'figured slab' engraved with cultic scenes similar to examples found at several Near Eastern sites. **12** *Room of pictures* (Heb. *maśkīṯ*) refers to the frescoed chamber or cavern where the elders were practising strange forms of animal-worship (v. 10). It may imply that each man had his own secret room in his house where he could imagine that his doings were unseen by God.

14 *Tammuz*, a Babylonian deity, was the god of vegetation, whose death at the time of great heat was mourned annually, and whose resurrection was celebrated in spring. The traditional time of mourning was the fourth month (named, accordingly, 'Tammuz'), but as this vision took place in the sixth month the ritual may have been modified among the Jews of this time. **16** *Worshipping the sun.* Sun-worship was practised by the Canaanites, but lately had been reintroduced from Assyria (2 Ki. 23:5, 11; Je. 8:2). *Between the porch and the altar* was the place where the priests offered prayer (Joel 2:17), with their faces, of course, towards the Temple; in this spot, *with their backs to the temple*, the adoration of the sun took place, as complete a renunciation of Yahweh as possible. *Cf.* 2 Ch. 29:6.

17 *They put the branch to their nose* represents a practice which cannot with certainty be identified. Some argue from the use of the term *branch* (*zᵉmôrâ*; *cf.* 15:2; Is. 17:10) that it was associated with Tammuz-worship; some see in it an obscenity, interpreting the Hebrew word as 'stench'; others have noted that a similar action portrayed in Assyrian reliefs seems to be a mark of reverence and worship (*Iraq*, xx, p. 16).

9:1–11 The judgment of Jerusalem

1 If RSV, RV mg. be followed, the executioners are addressed directly, *Draw near, you executioners of the city.* **2** *Six men* with the man *with a writing case* make a group of seven; they are doubtless angelic beings. *Cf.* the seven angels who stand before God (Rev. 8:2, 6), who are also revealed as executors of God's wrath. **4** *Put a mark.* The righteous are marked (the word signifies, strangely, a mark in the shape of a cross) to distinguish them from idolaters and to secure for them Yahweh's protection. *Cf.* Ex. 12:23; Rev. 7:3–8; 13:16–18; 14:1. **6** *Begin at my sanctuary*; *cf.* 1 Pet. 4:17. **8** *All that remains of Israel* denotes the inhabitants of Jerusalem. The northern kingdom had gone into captivity in 722 BC, and Judah had suffered a partial captivity in 597. In contrast to his cry in 6:11, and to his usual attitude of complete sympathy with the divine judgments on Israel, Ezekiel here pleads for mercy on his erring countrymen. **9, 10** The answer is given: the guilt of the land is so heinous that its punishment cannot be averted. *The Lord has forsaken the land*; *i.e.* Yahweh has deserted His people, as is evidenced by their continual troubles. There is accordingly no obligation on their part for continued loyalty to Him. It did not occur to these apostates that their adversity was the righteous judgment of Yahweh upon their wickedness.

10:1–22 The burning of Jerusalem

1 The *throne* is empty (*cf.* 9:3); the cherubim wait for Yahweh to remount and depart. **2** The destroyer of the city is *the man clothed in linen*, who formerly marked off the faithful for preservation; all seven angels are thus ministers of vengeance, as in Rev. 8:1 – 11:15. **7** We are told nothing of the destruction of the city, other than that the commissioned angel took fire from the midst of the cherubim (cf. Is. 6:6) *and went out.* The vision was prophetic of the fires that actually destroyed Jerusalem in 587 BC (2 Ki. 25:9); but more significant than the prediction is the revelation of the identity of the Destroyer, God Himself. **9–22** The purpose of the repetition of vv. 9–22 is but to impress this very fact; for the description of the glory of God and the chariot had already been given in ch. 1. Its recurrence here in detail underlines the startling fact that the God, whom men thought to be inseparably bound to His sanctuary and city, is to destroy them both and abandon their ruins. Owing to the vagaries of later copyists, some of the description of vv. 9–22 is confused and difficult to follow. *E.g.,* v. 11a speaks of the wheels, v. 11b apparently has the cherubim in mind; v. 13 would read better after v. 6; the first face in v. 14 should be 'ox' not *cherub,* as in 1:10 (unless we follow Rabbi Resh Lakish, 'Ezekiel besought the Merciful One with regard to it (the ox face) and He changed it into a cherub'!); v. 15 interrupts the sequence and anticipates vv. 19, 20. **18, 19** *The glory of the Lord went forth.* Yahweh leaves the Temple by *the east gate;* 11:22, 23 records His departure from the city altogether. *Cf.* 43:1–5.

11:1–13 Judgment of conspirators in Jerusalem

3 *This city is the cauldron.* This statement shows the drift of these men's thoughts. The city walls would protect them as a cauldron protects flesh from the fire; the warnings of the prophets, therefore, could be ignored. The first clause may be taken to imply, 'Our present occupation must be war, not the building of houses; let us fight it out'. LXX renders, 'Have not houses recently been built?', reflecting, perhaps, the jubilation of the princes on having overcome the effects of the 597 invasion, and implying that there was no cause for worry now. If RV mg. is followed, 'Is not the time near to build houses?', we are to understand an attitude of defiance to prophetic warnings of danger and a complacent sense of security which allows time for peaceful pursuits. **7** *Your slain . . . they are the flesh.* The only people who are to enjoy the security of the city will be the slain victims of the plotters; the latter are to be led out (v. 9) and executed on the borders of the land (v. 10). See the fulfilment of this in 2 Ki. 25:18–21. **13** is an integral part of the vision but presumes that the event actually occurred while Ezekiel was 'looking on'. The phenomenon is to be compared with the vision of the idolaters in the Temple (ch. 8), that of the beginning of the siege of Jerusalem (24:2), the death of his wife (24:16), and the cessation of his dumbness (24:25, 26; *cf.* 33:21, 22).

11:14–25 Promise of restoration

15 *Your brethren* are Ezekiel's fellow-exiles from Judah; *the whole house of Israel* are the descendants of those transported from northern Israel in 722 BC (*cf.* 20:40; 36:10). *They have gone*

far from the Lord. The sneer of the remnant still in Jerusalem reflects the old notion that Yahweh's power was limited to His land; to be away from it was to be cast off from Him (*cf.* 1 Sa. 26:19). **16** The promise of God here negates such an idea. *Cf.* Je. 24:1–10; 29:4, 11. **23** *The glory of the Lord* removes entirely from the city (*cf.* 10:18, 19). Many exegetes believe the two visions in 11:1–21 occurred earlier than the rest of chs. 8–11, and have been placed here because they concern events seen in the Temple and the apostates of Jerusalem. Admittedly 11:1–13 comes strangely after the description of the destruction of the people in ch. 9 and the burning of the city in ch. 10; the message of restoration (11:14–21) would also better fit the period immediately prior to the doom of the city. It is, however, unwise to dogmatize either way on the matter.

12:1 – 24:27 PROPHECIES AGAINST JERUSALEM

12:1–20 Portrayal of the imminent exile

2 *A rebellious house; i.e.* the exiles among whom the prophet lives; they are as obtuse as the Jews at Jerusalem! **5** gives an illustration of the desperation of the besieged and of the ruin of their property; see 2 Ki. 25:4. **6** *Cover your face, that you may not see.* An allusion to Zedekiah's flight and fate. See v. 12, *that he may not see . . . with his eyes.* The LXX translates as passive, 'that he might not be seen by the eye'; *i.e.* the covering of the face serves for a disguise. But the verse is also prophetic of the punishment inflicted by the Babylonians upon the king, who was blinded at Riblah and taken captive to Babylon (2 Ki. 25:5–7). **15** *They shall know; i.e.* the escaped of Jerusalem, who will know that Yahweh is Lord when they experience these horrors according to prophecy. **16** The nations among which they travel will also know it, for this demonstration of Yahweh's might will convince them that He alone is God. The object of leaving survivors from the catastrophe is solely for the honour of Yahweh's name.

17–20 The acted prophecy of the hardships of the siege is akin to 4:9–17 (see especially 4:16, 17). The symbolic actions of the earlier passage, however, represent the scarcity that will prevail in the siege; this stresses the terror of those days.

12:21 – 14:11 Prophets and people

This passage consists of a group of five oracles dealing with prophecy, true and false, and with the attitude adopted by the people in reference to it.

12:21–28 Scepticism rebuked. Two oracles (vv. 21–25, 26–28) supply reasons for popular disbelief in prophecy. **22** The first is expressed in the proverb, *The days grow long, and every vision comes to naught; i.e.* time passes but the many threats of doom never come to pass (*cf.* 2 Pet. 3:4). The element of delay would have been aggravated by Jeremiah's ministry. For the past

30 years he had announced the coming judgment of Jerusalem; events had apparently discredited him. 23 Ezekiel's answer from God is, *The days are at hand, and the fulfilment of every vision.* 27 The second objection came from those who accepted the truth of prophecy, but regarded it as applying to *times far off.* 28 The same answer is returned to them, *None of my words will be delayed any longer.*

13:1–23 Denunciation of false prophets and prophetesses. 2, 3 False prophets were a menace by reason of their opposition to the true word of God and their propagation of untruth. Cf. Jeremiah's struggles against them (Je. 5:30, 31; 14:13–18; 23:9–40; 29:8–10, 21–23). For the test of the validity of a prophet's ministry see Dt. 13:1–5; 18:21, 22. **4** *Your prophets have been like foxes*; i.e. they were mischievous and destructive. **5** Contrast 1 Sa. 25:16. **6, 7** *Divination* is the obtaining of an oracle by the reading of omens and drawing lots; cf. 21:21. **9** *The register of the house of Israel*; i.e. the register of citizens in the coming age of blessedness. Cf. the earlier use of the idea in Ex. 32:32f. and the developed symbol in Lk. 10:20; Rev. 20:15. **10ff.** *Whitewash* (Heb. *tāpēl*); better than AV, 'untempered mortar'. False prophets merely whitewash the insecure walls (see RV mg.) of the state instead of strengthening it. When God shall shatter the wall, they will be buried beneath its ruins. **15** Read as in v. 12, 'It shall be said to you, The wall is no more . . .' **18** The false prophetesses sewed *bands* (not 'pillows', as AV) upon all wrists, a process of sympathetic magic which either fastened power upon the consulter, or symbolized the power of the sorceress to bind her victims. The head coverings (*veils*) served a similar purpose, though the derivation of the term (*mispāḥôṭ* from an Akkadian root *sapahu*, to loose) suggests the opposite power of loosing from the influence. *Souls*; i.e. 'persons'; there is no thought of distinguishing between the spirit and the man. Render the last clause of v. 18 as a statement, 'You hunt the persons of my people but your own persons you keep alive.' **19** Translate 'You have profaned me (because the sorceresses invoked Yahweh's name in their rites) with handfuls of barley and with crumbled pieces of bread'; the latter were not given as a reward but were used for divining the future, just like the liver of a sacrificial victim. **20–23** describe the fate of all those who practise divination of this kind. False prophetesses share the judgment of false prophets.

14:1–11 Idolatrous inquirers. 1 *Then came certain of the elders.* It is likely that exiles frequently came to Ezekiel, waiting for a word from God that might fall from him (cf. 33:30). **3, 4** Like the heathen, these elders thought that they could worship any god beside their own; they had not learned the meaning of 'I the Lord your God am a jealous God' (Ex. 20:5; see also Ezk. 16:38, 42). *I the Lord will answer him myself* (AV 'him that cometh'; RV 'him therein'); Yah-

weh will use no intermediary to reply to such a man. His speech will be in deeds of judgment, as in vv. 12f. **7** *Separates himself from me*; literally 'dedicates himself away from following me'; cf. Ho. 9:10. **9** As people, so prophet; both alike were corrupt. Only a *deceived* prophet would give an answer as from Yahweh to idolaters, and both would bear their punishment. Some interpret the 'deception' of a prophet by Yahweh as an instance of the OT overlooking of secondary causes; i.e. the deceived state of the prophet is due to his own perversion of conscience, but since the consequences of sin, equally with the moral law, are of God's ordering, one may say that the deception is brought about by God. Cf. Ezk. 3:20; 1 Ki. 22:21f.

14:12–23 The rationale of judgment

In vv. 12–20 a general principle is laid down, that the judgment of a wicked people is not averted by the righteousness of a few; v. 21 applies the principle to Jerusalem. To illustrate and emphasize it, three notable examples of righteousness are adduced: Noah who saved his family (Gn. 6:8), Daniel his fellows (Dn. 2:12–24) and Job his friends (Jb. 42:7–10). The achievements of these men are not to be cited as examples of the habitual leniency of God. When Yahweh sentences a guilty land, the righteous will deliver themselves only. Possibly Ezekiel had heard that the men of Jerusalem looked for the city to be spared on the basis of the story of Abraham's intercession for Sodom (Gn. 18:23f.); the prophet replies, 'This is the principle on which God acts; if it is true generally, *how much more* in Jerusalem's case (v. 21), which has no Noah, Daniel or Job!' Cf. Jeremiah's similar assertion of the uselessness of intercession for Jerusalem, even from Moses and Samuel (Je. 7:16; 15:1–4). For the principle of individual responsibility here implied, cf. ch. 18.

14 *Daniel* (and v. 20). Expositors have long questioned as to whether the man of this name is the Daniel of the book named after him, presumably a contemporary of Ezekiel, or a patriarch of similar antiquity to Noah and Job. That the Phoenicians knew of such a person is attested by the reference to him in the Ras Shamra tablets, c. 1400 BC. That his name is spelt there as in Ezekiel, and not as in Daniel, indicates it may be the patriarch who is meant here. On the other hand, vv. 12–20 mention in turn God's acts of judgment by means of natural calamity, the sword and pestilence, and the biblical Noah, Daniel (cf. Dn. 1:1–4) and Job were respectively rescued from exactly those judgments.

22 The escaped remnant would show, by their corrupt lives, how just was the judgment of Jerusalem and so set at rest the minds of the exiles. *When . . . you see . . . you will be consoled.*

15:1–8 A vine for burning

This parable suggests that certain Israelites had compared themselves, as Isaiah had done for a different purpose, to the vine among the trees, the choicest among the nations in God's sight. Ezekiel corrects such a notion. Israel is but a wild vine of the forest (not a cultivated one, as elsewhere in the OT); far from being better than other trees, it is useless for anything but fuel. As the wild vine is appointed, as it were, by nature, to be burned, so is Jerusalem destined for destruction (v. 6).

16:1–63 A faithless woman

This discourse seeks to show, in allegorical fashion, that Israel's history constitutes 'one unbroken record of black apostasy' (McFadyen). It is in four movements: *a.* An adaptation, perhaps, of a popular story concerning a foundling baby that became a queen (vv. 3–43). *b.* Jerusalem's notorious sisters, Samaria and Sodom, are righteous in comparison with her (vv. 44–52). *c.* Jerusalem can be reinstated only in conjunction with these formerly despised sister communities (vv. 53–58). *d.* Penitent Jerusalem will receive a new covenant from God (vv. 59–63). For the comparison of Jerusalem to a faithless wife, *cf.* Is. 1:21; Je. 3:1f.; Ho. 2:2–23. The allegory is developed with a candour that tends to shock the western mind, but it is normal to the oriental outlook.

3 *Amorite . . . Hittite* (3). 'The genealogy is moral, not ethnical' (Toy). Nevertheless the Aramaean ancestors of Israel were kin to the Amorites (or Canaanites) and made affinities with certain of the Hittites. **4** Normal care was denied to this child. 'Heathen by parentage, it received heathen treatment at its birth' (Cooke). **8** *I spread my skirt over you.* For this custom see Ru. 3:9. In the allegory it may be referred to the covenant at Sinai, while vv. 9–14 could be applied to the increasing prosperity of the nation up to the days of Solomon. **10** *Leather* (not 'badgers' skin' as AV or 'sealskin' as RV); *cf.* Ex. 25:5.

15 The evil process described here began when Israel adopted the Canaanite sanctuaries of Palestine (*cf.* 20:28; Je. 2:5–7). **18** The actions described represent the treatment accorded to idols on festal occasions. **20** *Your sons and your daughters . . . these you sacrificed.* Though Josiah stamped out this evil practice for a time (2 Ki. 23:10) it is likely that it was revived in the desperate days of the siege. **26** is a reference to Israel's perennial tendency to look to Egypt for help; *cf.* Is. 30:1–5; 31:1–3. **28, 29** Similarly v. 28 refers to dependence on Assyria (2 Ki. 16:7f.; Ho. 5:13; 8:9), and v. 29 to reliance on Chaldea, *i.e.* Babylonia (2 Ki. 20:12f.).

35–43 describe the punishment of Jerusalem; it will be like that of a harlot, humiliation and death (see v. 38).

44–52 Jerusalem's sin is not only as bad as that of her heathen predecessors (vv. 44, 45), not only of the same order as that of the wicked cities of Samaria and Sodom (v. 46), but even worse than these (vv. 47–51). To her unutterable shame she will later be forced to confess it (v. 52). It is not necessary to assume that Israel's deeds were of a worse character than those of Samaria and Sodom; doubtless the heinousness of her guilt was felt to be accentuated by the uniqueness of her privilege as the betrothed of Yahweh. *Cf.* Am. 3:2.

53–58 The promise of restoration is put in such a way as to be of little comfort to Jerusalem. She can be reinstated only along with Samaria and Sodom, who will be consoled by the shamefaced recognition accorded to them by their erstwhile proud and self-righteous neighbour. **60** *I will remember my covenant.* This is the one bright spot in this gloomy sky. Yahweh will make an everlasting covenant with her such as will completely restore the broken relationship and give back her former position. This is the 'new covenant' of Je. 31:31f. See also Ezk. 37:26; Is. 59:21; 61:8.

17:1–24 The vulture and the vine

3 *A great eagle*; Hebrew *nešer.* As Jb. 39:27–30 and Mi. 1:16 show, this is the griffon vulture; here it symbolizes Nebuchadrezzar. *Lebanon* is the hill country of Judah; *the top of the cedar* is Jehoiachin, king of Judah (2 Ki. 24:10–16). **4** *A land of trade* designates Babylon. Zedekiah, son of Josiah, was made king by Nebuchadrezzar in place of Jehoiachin (2 Ki. 24:17). **5** The location *beside abundant waters* denotes Palestine; *cf.* Dt. 11:11. **6** *A low spreading vine.* The metaphor changes from that of the cedar. Cooke links this sentence to v. 5 and by a change of vowels reads 'that it might grow and become a spreading vine'. Nebuchadrezzar set Zedekiah on the throne to be a submissive vassal. **7** *Another great eagle.* This other vulture is Pharaoh Hophra; see Je. 44:30.

11–21 interpret this figurative language. Zedekiah is denounced for turning to Egypt for help against Babylon (v. 15). The prophets speak unitedly against Israel resorting to Egypt for aid, though their reasons vary (see, *e.g.*, Is. 30:1–5; 31:1–3; Je. 2:36). It was not the political inexpediency of the revolt that drew forth Ezekiel's wrath, but Zedekiah's abandonment of his oath to Nebuchadrezzar (vv. 15–18). From v. 19 it is clear that Zedekiah must have invoked Yahweh's name in the oath; to break it was to disgrace the sacred Name (*cf.* Jos. 9:15–20). For another instance of Zedekiah's breaking of an oath see Je. 34:8–22.

22–24 really form an additional parable in which the figures of vv. 3, 4 are differently applied. The *tender one* taken *from the topmost of its young twigs* is the Messiah of the house of David (Je. 23:5f.; 33:15), who will be planted by Yahweh on Mt. Zion and protect the nation restored from exile. For the image of a tree sheltering beasts and birds *cf.* 31:6, 12; Dn. 4:12, 21; Mk. 4:32.

18:1–32 Retribution and responsibility

The teaching of this chapter, summarized in v. 20, needs to be set in the context of the whole book to be judged fairly. Its chief purpose is to vindicate the justice of God, and it has a particular crisis in mind. The prophet's contemporaries alleged that they were being punished for the sins of the previous generation. Ezekiel declared that God does not work in that way, but holds each man accountable for his deeds and will requite him accordingly. This is a foundation principle of revealed religion. Ezekiel gave it new emphasis and detail. That it can be abused is unquestionable, especially if men divorce the individual from society. But the prophet does not do this; he usually has the whole nation in mind, and indeed it is difficult to reconcile this chapter with his predictions of the utter destruction of Jerusalem (*e.g.* 5:12; 7:10–27; 11:7–12), so real is the unity of the nation to him. Ezekiel's teaching has many facets; they should be viewed together to be truly appreciated. The divorcing of this principle from its context led men to argue that a man's condition reflects God's judgment upon him, so that adversity is the fruit of sin and prosperity the result of righteousness. Against this distortion of Ezekiel's teaching the book of Job is directed, but none could fairly say that it was aimed at the book of Ezekiel.

2 The *proverb* was current in Jerusalem (Je. 31:29) and came from there to the exiles in Babylonia. **4** The principle is stated in brief. Then, in illustration, Ezekiel takes the case of three generations, **5–9** a righteous man who continues in his righteousness; **10–13** his son who behaves wickedly; **14–17** his grandson who repudiates the evil of his father. **20** The principle is elaborated; every man shall receive a just requital for his conduct. Ezekiel primarily has in mind the coming judgment of Jerusalem and the restoration to follow; but he would regard it as capable of general application. **21** *If a wicked man turns . . . he shall not die.* A man is not only free from the sin of his father; he may be free from his own past if he so wishes. He can repent at once. **23** Kraetzschmar declares this verse to be 'the most precious word in the whole book of Ezekiel'. *Cf.* 1 Tim. 2:4; 2 Pet. 3:9. **31** *Get yourselves a new heart*; *cf.* 36:26, 'a new heart I will give you'. The same dual truth is expressed in Phil. 2:12, 13.

19:1–14 Dirge over kings

Two elegies are joined together in this chapter; in the first the rulers of Judah are pictured as lions (vv. 1–9), in the second as branches of a vine (vv. 10–14). If the two poems were written at the same time, the second is predictive (see on v. 14); but if v. 14 describes past events, the second poem was written later, being modelled on the earlier one and so conjoined to it.

19:1–9 The lioness and her whelps. 2 *Your mother* is the nation Israel or, more strictly, Judah, as in v. 10. **3, 4** The *young lion* represents Jehoahaz, who was bound by Pharaoh Necho after a reign of only 3 months and was carried off to *Egypt* in 608 BC (see 2 Ki.

23:31–34). **5** *Another of her whelps.* Jehoiakim, brother of Jehoahaz, succeeded him on the throne, but is passed over in silence because he had a peaceful end. Jehoiachin, the son of Jehoiakim, is here described. **9** After three months as king he was taken by Nebuchadrezzar to *Babylon* in 597 BC (see 2 Ki. 24:8–16). A double application may be seen in vv. 8, 9; not only were lions captured in this manner, for the sport of Assyrian kings, but conquered princes were also confined in cages to be a public spectacle.

19:10–14 The vine and her rod. 11, 12 should be read, with the Greek, Latin and Armenian versions and RV mg. in part, as mentioning a single rod (*cf.* 'rods', AV, RV); but it is uncertain as to which ruler is meant, whether Jehoiachin, as in vv. 5–9, or Zedekiah, as in v. 14; the former interpretation seems preferable. **14** *Fire has gone out from its stem*; *i.e.* Zedekiah who is held responsible for the destruction of Jerusalem inasmuch as the city would have been spared had he submitted to the Babylonians. *Cf.* Je. 38:20–23.

20:1–44 History of apostate Israel

1 The situation is similar to that of ch. 14; elders come *to inquire of the Lord* through Ezekiel. As in 14:3 they had 'taken their idols into their hearts', so here the prophet reads their intention of conforming to the idolatry of their environment (v. 32). The answer of Yahweh on both occasions is judgment on the idolaters (14:7, 8; 20:33–39). This review of Israel's history sets forth Israel's fortunes in Egypt (vv. 5–9), in the wilderness (vv. 10–26), in Canaan (vv. 27–29), in the present (vv. 30–32), traversing another wilderness (vv. 33–39), resettled in Palestine (vv. 40–44). The date is July–August 591 BC, 11 months after that given in 8:1. **8** *They rebelled against me.* We have no information of an act of rebellion in Egypt, unless Ex. 5:21 be in view. There may have been other traditions of this period of Israel's history, current in Ezekiel's day, upon which he draws. **9** *I acted for the sake of my name*; *i.e.* so that His reputation among the nations should not suffer through apparent inability to fulfil His word (*cf.* Nu. 14:16; Dt. 9:28).

16 *Their heart went after their idols*; *cf.* Ex. 32:1–6; Nu. 25:1–3. **25** *Statutes that were not good* . . . . A reversal of the normal purpose of Yahweh's laws; see v. 11. **26** The sacrificing of children was evidently regarded as a fulfilment of the law of Ex. 13:12, an interpretation which the prophet appears to view as due to judicial blindness from God (*cf.* on 14:9; Is. 6:10–12 and Cooke's note in *ICC*, pp. 218, 219). **29** Translate 'What is the high place (*bāmâ*) to which you are the comers (*bāʾîm*)?'

33–38 Judgment is mingled with mercy. Yahweh will lead His people out from the land of exile, as He brought them out of Egypt long ago (v. 34); the guilty will perish in the desert as on the former journey (vv. 35–38; *cf.* Ho.

2:16, 17). The picture of the future redemption as a second exodus is frequent in the prophets. See, *e.g.*, Is. 41:17–20; 43:16–21; Je. 23:7, 8; Mi. 7:15–17.

40–44 The surviving righteous of Israel will return to their land and worship Yahweh. By this redeeming act Yahweh will make Himself known as God alone, both to the Gentile world (v. 41) and to Israel (v. 42). As in 16:61–63 the promise is tempered with the reminder of their former sinfulness (vv. 43, 44).

20:45 – 21:32 The sword of the Lord

A new chapter commences at 20:45 in the Hebrew text; our English translators have followed the ancient versions in their division of the chapters. Four oracles are here conjoined: the destruction of Jerusalem as by fire and sword (20:45 – 21:7); the song of the sword (21:8–17); Nebuchadrezzar at the cross-roads (21:18–27); the judgment of Ammon (21:28–32). If vv. 21, 22 afford another example of Ezekiel's clairvoyant vision (*cf.* ch. 8), the chapter dates from 588 BC, when Nebuchadrezzar marched on Jerusalem. **20:46** *The south* is Palestine; although W of Babylonia, it is so described because the caravan route traversed the Euphrates and then went southward through Syria. **49** *Is he not a maker of allegories?* This saying reflects the scepticism of the people rather than their inability to interpret what Ezekiel said to them. But in 21:3ff. the prophet uses a plainer figure to ensure that all understood the meaning of his former proverb. **21:6** *Sigh therefore.* This acted prophecy is intended to show the way the news of the catastrophe will be received; *cf.* 12:17–20.

8–17 'A wild ode to the avenging Chaldean sword' is the description given by Toy to these verses. Certain of the verses, especially 10 and 13, are difficult of elucidation owing to faulty transmission of the text. **12** *Smite therefore upon your thigh*; *i.e.* to express grief (*cf.* Je. 31:19).

19 *Mark two ways.* Ezekiel is to draw (on sand?) two roads starting from a common point, *i.e.* Babylon, and diverging outwards, one leading to Jerusalem and the other to Rabbah, capital city of Ammon. **21** Nebuchadrezzar is seen at the cross-roads. He uses divination to ascertain which road to take. *Arrows* were used in the same way as lots; one marked 'Jerusalem' and another 'Ammon' would be shaken in a quiver and one drawn out. *Liver*, owing to its connection with blood, was regarded as the seat of life; the colour and marks on that of a sacrificed sheep provided omens of the future. *Teraphim* (AV 'images') were small human-shaped images; *cf.* 1 Sa. 19:13, 16. **23** *To them*; *i.e.* to the men of Jerusalem who believe the divination is false. **25** *Cf.* v. 14. *Unhallowed* (AV 'profane'; RV 'deadly wounded': some prefer to translate this 'dishonoured'). **27** *A ruin. . . .* The monarchic succession and the state are to be brought into ruin till Messiah comes. The latter half of the verse echoes Gn.

49:10, 'until he comes to whom it belongs'; *cf.* RSV mg. 'until Shiloh comes'; see *NBD*, art. 'Shiloh'.

28–32 The language is reminiscent of vv. 9, 10; but here the sword is that of Ammon drawn against Israel at the time of Nebuchadrezzar's attack; Yahweh will blot out the memory of Ammon (v. 32), a contrast to Israel's future destiny (20:40–44).

22:1–31 Arraignment of Jerusalem

Three oracles are to be distinguished: the sins of the city of bloodshed (vv. 1–16); the smelting of Israel (vv. 17–22); the indictment of 'the classes and the masses' (McFadyen) (vv. 23–31). **4** Jerusalem by its guilt has caused its full number of days and years to draw near. *Your day* means the city's day of judgment, not the Last Day (*cf.* Jesus' use of 'my hour', Jn. 2:4, *etc.*). The *princes* abused their authority by committing judicial murders (*cf.* 2 Ki. 24:3, 4). **9** *Men who slander* (AV 'carry tales'); *i.e.* informers who got rid of their enemies by false accusations. **13** *I strike my hands together*; a sign of scorn (*cf.* 21:14, 17). **16** *I shall be profaned through you*; follow RV, which makes Jerusalem the cause of her own profanation, and *cf.* on 20:9.

18 In the second oracle Israel is unrefined ore; Yahweh smelts it in the furnace, but dross is the only result. *Bronze and tin and iron and lead* are the precipitates of the ore when first smelted, from which the silver is afterward separated. The real point of the figure is the judgment involved in the idea of smelting. Unlike other prophets who use this figure, Ezekiel excludes the possibility of refinement; his generation is but slag! (*cf.* Ps. 119:119; Mal. 3:3).

25ff. *Her princes* (Heb. *nāśî*; *cf.* LXX, 'whose princes'); AV, RSV mg. read 'there is a conspiracy of her prophets' (Heb. *nābî*'). If RSV be accepted, Ezekiel indicts the whole gamut of society in Jerusalem, the *princes* (*i.e.* members of the royal house), *priests* (v. 26), nobles (*princes*, v. 27; Heb. *śārîm*, *i.e.* officials and heads of important families), *prophets* (v. 28), and the ordinary *people* (v. 29). **30** *I sought . . . but I found none.* None of the official leaders stood for righteousness and the true welfare of Israel. Ezekiel naturally considered Jeremiah, whom those leaders persecuted, as one apart (*cf.* Is. 59:16; 63:5).

23:1–49 Oholah and Oholibah

The chapter is in two parts. Vv. 1–35 give the allegory of the two sisters, Samaria and Jerusalem, using similar figures as that in ch. 16 (see notes there). But whereas the earlier poem had in mind the evil influences of Canaanite religion, here it is the making of foreign alliances that is condemned. Vv. 36–49 are an appendix, developing the allegory in a different manner, possibly with a different situation in mind. Here the two sisters are viewed together and are indicted for Molech-worship and profaning the sanctuary and sabbath (vv. 37–39); the foreign alliances appear to be those with countries bordering on Israel (v. 42) rather than with distant empires.

4 The two names are identical in meaning, being coined feminine forms of *'ōhel*, a 'tent'. They may have in view tents associated with false worship (see 16:16). The RSV and RV forms of the names should be followed. **7** *She defiled herself with all the idols*. Political alliances usually involved the adoption of the cults of the superior power. Samaria had made alliances with Assyria (vv. 5ff.) and Egypt (v. 8); Jerusalem went further and approached the Babylonians also (vv. 14–18). Assyrian worship (v. 12) was popularized by Manasseh and remained in the city till its fall (see 2 Ki. 21:1–9; Je. 44:15–19). **16** *Sent messengers . . . in Chaldea*. The occasion is unknown, unless it be that recorded in 2 Ki. 24:1. **20** Judah's request for Egyptian aid against the Babylonians is in mind, Je. 37:7f. **23** *Pekod and Shoa and Koa* were tribes east of the Tigris. **29** *Naked and bare*. This stripping of Oholibah represents the devastation of Jerusalem.

40 describes a petition to a distant people for help, perhaps against the Babylonians. **42** *Drunkards from the wilderness* (*cf.* RV; better than AV, 'Sabeans from the wilderness'). These would be Israel's near neighbours, Arabs, Edomites, Moabites, *etc.* (*cf.* Je. 27:3f.). **45** *Righteous men* can hardly be Babylonians (*cf.* 7:21, 24); they are the few men of Jerusalem who remain faithful to Yahweh and condemn the national policy. **47** Oholah and Oholibah will be judged as adulteresses (see Dt. 22:23, 24).

24:1–27 The beginning of the end

There are three connected themes in this chapter: the parable of the rusty cauldron (vv. 1–14); the sign of the death of Ezekiel's wife (vv. 15–24); the end of the prophet's dumbness (vv. 25–27). **1** Reckoning from Jehoiachin's captivity, the date is January, 588 BC. See 2 Ki. 25:1.

2 The knowledge of the *siege* again illustrates Ezekiel's supernaturally heightened gift of clairvoyance. The setting down and announcement of this date would constitute a public confirmation of his prophetic office when news filtered through at a later date. **3** *Set on the pot*. Perhaps Ezekiel was actually preparing a meal in a cauldron when the word of God came to him, declaring this to be symbolic of the judgment of Jerusalem. The use of the figure is wholly opposite to that in 11:3. **6** *Take out of it piece after piece*. The meat is not to be eaten but thrown away, symbolic of the scattering of the people. The last clause of this verse implies that lots were drawn in 597 BC as to who should go into captivity; this time there will be no option. The city is like a cauldron whose *rust* (*i.e.* 'blood-shed'—not 'scum' as in AV) will not be removed. **11** The only recourse is to set the cauldron upside down on the fire and melt it away. **12–14** Jerusalem must be destroyed to be cleansed.

16 Ezekiel is warned that his wife is about to die, either *at a stroke, i.e.* suddenly, or 'by plague' (*cf.* Nu. 14:37). **17** He is to hide his grief and show no mourning. **18** The day following his wife's death he carried out his normal occupations. **19** That caused his fellow-exiles to ask the meaning of his conduct. **20–24** It is explained that Jerusalem and its sanctuary are as dear to them as a wife to a husband; when they hear of its destruction, and the loss of their relatives, they too must bow in silence before God; it is His just judgment.

25–27 Read as one sentence: 'On the day I take from them their stronghold . . . on that day a fugitive will come . . . on that day your mouth will be opened.' A considerable lapse of time is to occur between v. 25 and v. 26. *Cf.* Je. 52:5–7 with Ezk. 33:21. The divine restrictions on Ezekiel's ministry are to cease when the messenger from Jerusalem arrives. See on 3:26.

25:1 – 32:32 PROPHECIES AGAINST FOREIGN NATIONS

The denunciations of Jerusalem are complete. Before recounting his predictions of restoration (33–48), the prophet inserts this group of oracles against Israel's enemies (although some of them belong to a later date) to indicate that all hostile powers must be broken before Israel could be reinstated in glory.

25:1–17 PROPHECIES AGAINST SURROUNDING TRIBES

25:1–7 Ammon

Although at the Babylonian invasion Ammon joined with Edom, Moab and others in persuading Zedekiah to revolt (Je. 27:1–11), at the fall of Jerusalem they seized Israelite cities (Je. 49:1f.), and instigated the murder of Gedaliah (Je. 40:14). Ezekiel makes no mention of these things, only of their malicious joy at Israel's distress (vv. 3, 6). Note that in v. 3 the prophet speaks of the desolation of Jerusalem as a past event.

25:8–11 Moab

Jeremiah denounces Moab for its arrogancy and rebellion against Yahweh and derision of Israel (Je. 48:25f.). Zephaniah speaks of their plundering the Jews (Zp. 2:8). Ezekiel denounces them for their scornful rejection of Israel's claim to be a nation apart, in view of her relation to Yahweh (v. 8).

25:12–14 Edom

For the malice of Edom against Israel at the fall of Jerusalem *cf.* Ezk. 35:10–15; Ob. 10–16; Ps. 137:7.

25:15–17 The Philistines

We have no information of their behaviour towards Israel in this period other than this passage. Cherethites at one time had formed part of David's bodyguard (2 Sa. 8:18; 15:18; 20:7). See on Jdg. 3:3.

26:1 – 28:26 PROPHECIES AGAINST TYRE

The facts of the contemporary situation account for the prominence given by Ezekiel to Tyre. The Babylonians were about to lay siege to the city. What would be the result? 'On patriotic and religious grounds the Jewish exiles felt themselves to be involved in the issue. Ezekiel has no doubt that it will end in Tyre's overthrow and extinction (26); he anticipates its ruin in a magnificent dirge (27); and threatens its king with retribution (28)' (Cooke). *Cf.* on Am. 1:9, 10.

26:1–21 The overthrow of Tyre

2 Tyre exults over Jerusalem's fate, for she had been *the gate of the peoples.* Caravan traffic from north to south would have been subject to taxation by the Jews. **3, 4** *As the sea brings up its waves.* Tyre was built upon a rock island 'in the heart of the seas' (27:4), a position which facilitated trade and made it seemingly impregnable. **6** *Her daughters on the mainland* are Tyre's dependent mainland towns. **7** Ezekiel always spells the name of the Babylonian monarch *Nebuchadrezzar*; this approximates more closely to the Babylonian original *Nabukudurri-usur*, 'Nebo protect my boundary'.

8–12 This description of the campaign here presupposes the erection of a mole from the mainland to the island, a procedure probably adopted by Nebuchadrezzar (*cf.* on 29:18) and certainly by Alexander with complete success in 332 BC. *Your mighty pillars* (v. 11) would be those associated with the worship of Melkart, the god of Tyre. **15** *The coastlands* (AV 'isles') are coasts and islands of the Mediterranean with which Tyre traded. **20** *I will thrust you down . . . into the Pit.* Tyre is to be brought down to Sheol. *You will not . . . have a place in the land of the living.* RSV follows LXX, 'you shall not stand in the land of the living'.

27:1–36 Lament over Tyre

The elegy proper (vv. 3–9a, 25b–36) likens Tyre to an expensively equipped ship, filled with goods, which was wrecked by a storm and lamented by those that held an interest in it. The central section (9b–25a), describing the merchandise of Tyre, does not maintain the imagery; but that is insufficient reason for denying its authenticity. The whole chapter has deeply influenced the author of the book of Revelation, who applies its imagery to the anti-Christian empire of his own day (Rev. 18).

5 *Senir* was the Amorite name for Hermon (Dt. 3:9). **6** *Coasts of Cyprus* (RV 'isles of Kittim')

is a correct translation, but the phrase came to represent a wider area, covering the coastal regions of the E Mediterranean, and this may be its meaning here. **10** *Lud* (Lydia?) and *Put* (Cyrenaica in N Africa?) are placed together because of similarity of sound, not because of their supposed proximity. The three names suffice to show that Tyre's mercenaries came from all parts of the ancient world. **11** *Helech* (AV 'thine army') is Cilicia (Akk. *ḥilakku*); the *men of Gamad* probably came from Kumidi in N Syria. **12** *Tarshish* is Tartessus, a port in S Spain, or it may be Nora in Sardinia (so Albright). **13** *Javan*; Ionians in Asia Minor. *Tubal, and Meshech*; situated in E Asia Minor (see on 38:2). **14** *Beth-togarmah*; Armenia. **15** *The men of Rhodes* (AV 'Dedan') were merchants who would have traded in ivory and ebony with N African tribes. **17** The obscure 'wheat of Minnith and Pannag' (AV) is slightly emended by RSV to make the more intelligible *wheat, olives and early figs.* **19** *Uzal* is probably Sana, capital of the Yemen, but this is an unlikely source of wine. Millard's suggestion is preferable: 'and casks of wine from Izalla', a district in Anatolia famous for its wines (*JSS*, VII, 1962, pp. 201ff.). **20** *Dedan* was an Edomite caravan city. **22** *Sheba*, whence the queen came to visit Solomon, and *Raamah* were in SW Arabia (*cf.* 1 Ki. 10). **23** Towns in Mesopotamia. For further information refer to *NBD*.

25–27 The imagery of the poem is resumed; the good ship Tyre sinks with all hands lost. **26** For *the east wind cf.* Ps. 48:7, but it may be an allusion to Babylon. **29–34** describe the lamentation of the sailors at Tyre's loss. *Cf.* Rev. 18:17–19. **35, 36** *The inhabitants of the coastland* may refer particularly to *the merchants among the peoples*; *cf.* v. 3. For the lamentations of the kings and merchants *cf.* Rev. 18:9–17.

28:1–19 Dirge for the king of Tyre

2 *The prince of Tyre* (Ithobal II) is addressed as representing the city; his self-exaltation to the status of deity is typical of the pride of the people. Tyre's impregnable position on a rock reminds him of the mythical mountain of God (vv. 14, 16); as God reigns supreme there, so securely is he enthroned *in the heart of the seas.* **3** *Daniel*; see on 14:20. **8** *The death of the slain* is one without burial. **10** Since the Phoenicians practised circumcision, *the death of the uncircumcised* was shameful, involving a dishonourable position in Sheol.

11–19 Ezekiel seems to have adopted for his threnody a popular story, presumably current in Tyre as elsewhere, of a primal being who dwelt in the Garden of God in splendour and purity but was subsequently driven out through pride; so shall the king of Tyre shortly fall from his glory. It looks like a highly mythological version of the story in Gn. 3, but the prophet does not hesitate to use it since it was well known and admirably suited to his purpose. **13** *Your* *covering*; *i.e.* 'dress'; Babylonian gods were frequently dressed in robes ornamented with jewels. Nine stones are enumerated here; LXX has twelve and they are identical with those of the high priest's robe (Ex. 28:17–20); perhaps the three missing stones dropped out of the Hebrew text by accident.

14 The LXX reads 'with the cherub . . . I set you', and again in v. 16, 'the cherub destroyed you', variations which materially alter the story but which are generally adopted by expositors. **17, 18** The moral of the story is applied first to the king (v. 17) and then to the city (v. 18). Both will be brought to utter ruin.

28:20–26 Prophecy against Sidon

Sidon is to share the fate of its neighbour. Elsewhere the two cities are spoken of together (*e.g.* Is. 23; Joel 3:4f.). **24–26** state the theme not only of chs. 25–32, but also of the section dealing with Israel's restoration (chs. 34ff.); the destruction of Israel's enemies is necessary both to the establishment of Israel in the kingdom of God and the demonstration to all nations of the sole deity of Yahweh.

29:1 – 32:32 PROPHECIES AGAINST EGYPT

These oracles come from the period immediately following the siege and conquest of Jerusalem (587–585 BC), except 29:17–21 which was written in 571 BC.

29:1–16 The fall of Egypt

1 The date is January 587 BC. **2** *Pharaoh* is addressed (like the king of Tyre in ch. 18) as representing the genius of his people. **3** Gunkel argues, with considerable cogency, that Ezekiel makes Pharaoh use the speech of the chaos-dragon of the waters (see Haupt's note in Toy) and not simply of a crocodile; **4, 5** his fate is thus similar to that of the monster in the Tiamat story; see further on 32:2–8. **6, 7** Cf. Is. 36:6.

8–12 The allegory is applied. Egypt will suffer a like fate to Israel, devastation and dispersal among the nations for 40 years. **10** *Migdol to Syene*; these cities were the northern and southern limits of Egypt.

13–16 Like Israel, Egypt is to be restored, but not to a position of glory: it will be *the most lowly of the kingdoms*.

29:17–21 Nebuchadrezzar's wages

17 The date is April 571 BC. This is the latest in the book and indicates that this oracle has been added as an appendix. **18** Nebuchadrezzar worked hard to take Tyre; heads were *made bald* and shoulders sore through the toilsome construction of a mole from the mainland to the city. *Yet neither he nor his army got anything from Tyre.* The city capitulated but there was little booty; the Tyrians had plenty of time to ship away their valuables. Yahweh would recompense His 'servant' (Je. 27:6) by giving him

the spoils of Egypt. Nebuchadrezzar invaded Egypt *c.* 568 BC.

21 Israel will be restored to power once more. The fulfilment of these prophecies will open the prophet's mouth in thanksgiving and renewed prophetic ministry; and the criticism of his hearers over the incomplete fulfilment of his prophecy on Tyre would be silenced.

30:1–26 Egypt's day

In vv. 1–19 is described the approach of the day of the Lord on Egypt, in vv. 20–26 the breaking of Pharaoh's might by Nebuchadrezzar. **2** *Alas for the day!* See on 7:2 and *cf.* Joel 2:1, 2; Zp. 1:15. **5** gives a list of Egypt's provinces and allies who are to share its ruin. *All Arabia* is a slight emendation of the text for the sake of making a place-name; AV 'the mingled people' (Heb. *hāʿereḇ*) is a reference to foreign immigrants or mercenaries, and is used of Egypt (Je. 25:20), Israel (Ex. 12:38) and Babylon (Je. 50:37). *Libya*. AV 'Chub', RV 'Cub' is an unknown name; LXX reads 'Lub', *i.e.* Libya. *The people of the land that is in league* is an unknown nation confederate with Egypt; it is unlikely that it means Israel, as LXX implies and RV mg. would encourage.

13–19 The destruction of Egypt is described in detail, principal towns being singled out for particular mention. **13** Instead of *images* (RV mg. 'things of nought'; Heb. *ʾelilîm*), LXX reads 'chiefs' (Heb. *ʾēlîm*), a reading favoured by many commentators. **17** *On.* AV 'Aven' (*i.e.* 'nothingness') is a contemptuous pronunciation of 'On', the two words being spelt alike in Hebrew. It was famous for its sun temple, and hence its name 'Beth-shemesh' ('House of the Sun') in Je. 43:13 and its Greek name Heliopolis ('City of the Sun'). At *Pibeseth* the cat-headed goddess Ubastet was worshipped.

20–26 The oracle, dated April 587 BC (v. 20), takes its rise from Nebuchadrezzar's defeat of Pharaoh Hophra, characterized as a breaking of Pharaoh's arm and consequent weakening of his power (v. 21). This will be followed by a further defeat that will completely overthrow the Egyptian monarch (vv. 22f.).

31:1–18 The mighty cedar Pharaoh

The allegory has three movements: vv. 2–9 are a description of Pharaoh, representing Egypt, under the figure of a lofty cedar; vv. 10–14 describe the destruction of the great tree, and vv. 15–18 the reaction to this event on the part of the rest of the nations. Both this chapter and the next have parallels with Is. 14:4–20. Mention of *the deep* (v. 4), *the garden of God* (v. 8) and *Eden* (vv. 9, 18) indicate the probability of a background similar to that of ch. 28 (where see notes).

3 *I will liken you to a cedar* (cf. AV, 'behold, the Assyrian was a cedar'; RSV mg). The initial letter of *tᵉʾaššûr* (cedar) fell out and produced *ʾaššûr*, *i.e.* Assyria. The context clearly shows that Pharaoh is in mind. *Clouds* (as LXX and RV mg.). AV reads 'thick boughs'. **5, 6** The figurative language is frequently used to indicate the greatness of a kingdom (*cf.* 17:23; Dn. 4:11, 12; Mk. 4:32).

10 Pharaoh's sin is pride, the failing of most tyrants (*cf.* 28:6; Is. 14:13f.; Dn. 11:12). The fall of Pharaoh is to be a warning to all nations against committing the same fault (v. 14). **11, 12** *A mighty one of the nations* is Nebuchadrezzar, *the most terrible of the nations* his armies. **15, 16** The imagery portrays the effect of Pharaoh's doom on the nations left on earth. If with LXX we omit in v. 16 *in the nether world*, the figure is carried out consistently; the rival nations were *comforted* in that they were freed from Egypt's domination. **18** Pharaoh is to join in Sheol the *uncircumcised* and the *slain* in battle. Since the Egyptians practised circumcision and, even more than the rest of the Orient, paid lavish attention to burial, this involved the uttermost of disgrace—inclusion amongst the lowest ranks of the underworld.

32:1–32 Lament over Pharaoh and Egypt

The first lamentation (vv. 1–16) deals primarily with Pharaoh, the second (vv. 17–32) with the nation's descent to Sheol, though in both poems the thought passes imperceptibly from ruler to people. The former poem itself divides into two, vv. 2–10 describing the fate of the water-monster Pharaoh, vv. 11–16 the desolation of Egypt by the king of Babylon. **1** The date is the end of February 585 BC, 8 months after the fall of Jerusalem.

2 *You consider yourself a lion*; May (*IB*, vol. VI) notes that in Egypt the royal sphinx was a lion-bodied creature. *But you are like a dragon in the seas.* Most commentators believe this refers simply to the crocodile, as also 29:3–5. It is more likely an echo of the chaos-monster allegory, which told how the monster Tiamat, personification of the waters, fought against heaven and was destroyed by Marduk. From its body was made the material creation, but some of it is reserved for food for man (*2 Baruch* 29:4). The story is applied to any tyrannous peoples (*e.g.* Is. 27:1; Dn. 7), but especially to Egypt (Is. 30:7; 51:9, 10), thereby showing both their evil character and sure fate. Its use here explains the extraordinary language of vv. 4–8.

11–15 The prophet then passes from the judgment of the king (vv. 11, 12a) to that of the nation (vv. 12b–15); the allegorical language seems to be maintained in vv. 13, 14, the agitated waters settle down and become clear again; that neither man nor beast further troubles them is a sign of desolation.

17 The month is probably the same as that of v. 1, the *word* coming 14 days later, but RSV follows LXX in inserting *the first month.* **18ff.** In the verses that follow the prophet portrays Egypt going down to the land of the departed, consequent upon her destruction. Egypt must do this at the bidding of the prophet (vv. 19, 20). There they will find the armies of great nations of the past, Assyria, Elam, Meshech with Tubal (vv. 22–27), together with hostile nations of the present, Edom, *the princes of the north* (*i.e.* lands bordering on Phoenicia) and Sidon, all which are evidently to be destroyed (vv. 29, 30). When Egypt perishes from the judgment of God, then Pharaoh will at least have the cold comfort of knowing that his is not the only empire that has gone to the grave (v. 31)!

33:1 – 48:35 THE RESTORATION OF ISRAEL

33:1–20 THE RESPONSIBILITY OF PROPHET AND PEOPLE

The interpretation of this passage depends on its true context. If, as many hold, vv. 21, 22 should determine the whole chapter, then this section relates to God's judgment on sinners prior to the re-establishment of Israel in the glorious kingdom. To 'die' is to depart this life before the restoration; to 'live' is to enjoy the privileges of the kingdom. On this reading, 20:33–42 forms an excellent parallel. If, however, vv. 2ff., 10, 20 imply the last desperate stages of the siege of Jerusalem, and the consequent despair of the nation, then this constitutes a final warning to the people. Perhaps the latter is the preferable alternative.

1–6 The parable is drawn from the custom of setting a watchman on the city wall in times of danger to look for the approach of the enemy. The dread responsibility of the watchman's position is here chiefly in mind. **6** *Cf.* Gn. 9:5. **7–9** With similar seriousness Ezekiel is to view his office at this critical juncture of the nation. These verses repeat 3:17–19, on which see notes.

As the watchman has a responsibility to sound the alarm, so the people have a duty to respond. **10** implies both an admission of the justice of the nation's misfortunes and an attitude of despair. **11ff.** Ezekiel calls them to renewal of faith and hope by stressing the grace of God (v. 11), the importance of one's present state rather than one's past life (vv. 12–19) and the possibility of immediate repentance and forgiveness (vv. 11, 14–16, 19).

33:21–33 THE TURNING-POINT IN EZEKIEL'S MINISTRY

The day for which Ezekiel had waited for 7 years (*cf.* dating given in 1:2) and which he had explicitly prophesied three years before it happened (*cf.* 24:1, 25–27)! From now on he is free to devote himself to the ministry of building up instead of pulling down, and so to develop the message which he has previously no more than hinted at (*e.g.* 16:60ff.; 17:22ff.; 20:33ff.). **21** *The twelfth year.* Jerusalem in fact fell in the eleventh year of Zedekiah (*cf.* Je. 39:2) and some MSS of the Hebrew, along with LXX, are followed by many commentators (*e.g.* H. L. Ellison, *Ezekiel, the Man and his Message*, 1956, p. 118; C. G. Howie, *Ezekiel, Daniel*, 1961, p. 67; D. M. G. Stalker, *Ezekiel*, 1968, pp. 209, 240) in altering the text to read 'eleventh' here also. It is possible, however, that two systems of dating are involved, or that the news did not in fact reach Ezekiel till the twelfth year. At all events, the year of the fall of the city was 587 BC. For Ezekiel's dumbness, see on 3:26. **23–29** contain a message of judgment on the Jews left behind in the homeland. For a similar situation *cf.* 11:14ff.

30 *Talk ... about you.* Better than AV, 'against thee'. **30–33** give us a glimpse of the popularity enjoyed by the prophet, no doubt intensified by the fulfilment of his message. But the enthusiasm of the people is shallow; his word is not obeyed by them. **31** Instead of *with their lips they show much love*, LXX reads 'lies are in their mouth'. **32** Ezekiel is like one of the love-songs which they delight to hear (RV mg., RSV mg.); but probably we are to understand that he is like a singer of such, rather than the song itself, as RSV translates it. **33** *When this comes* they will realize the personal truth of his words. The reference here is not to judgment but to the redemption and conditions of its enjoyment which henceforth dominate his preaching.

34:1 – 37:28 THE RETURN OF ISRAEL TO HER OWN LAND

34:1–31 Helpless sheep and faithless shepherds

The allegory, apparently a development of Je. 23:1–4, is in two sections: the rapacious rulers of Israel, who must bear responsibility for the plight of the people (vv. 1–16); God's dealings with the nation itself (vv. 17–31).

2 *The shepherds*, as appears from the end of v. 4, are Israel's rulers, especially those who but lately had governed the nation. For the figure *cf.* Ps. 78:70ff.; Is. 44:28; 63:11; Je. 2:8; Zc. 11; 13:7. **6–8** *My sheep were scattered ... my sheep have become a prey.* A symbolic description of Israel's oppression (by such powers as Assyria, Egypt, Babylon) and of the dispersion after the fall of Jerusalem. **5** *Cf.* 1 Ki. 22:17; Mt. 9:36. **13** *I will bring them ... and gather them.* The exiles are to be brought back from all lands whither they have gone (including Egypt, Phoenicia and Arabia, as well as Babylonia) and settle down under the government of Yahweh. **14–16** The tenderness of Ezekiel, so largely concealed in his prophecies, is well seen in this description of God's beneficent rule as Shepherd of His people. *Cf.* Lk. 15:3–7; Jn. 10; Heb. 13:20; 1 Pet. 2:25; Rev. 7:17. **17** The figure changes. The prophet turns from the kings to lesser officials who nevertheless tyrannize over their fellow-countrymen.

This verse may have suggested to our Lord His parable of the sheep and goats (Mt. 25:31ff.). The teaching of the whole passage reminds us of Ezk. 20:37, 38; restoration is mingled with judgment. **23** *I will set up*; *cf.* 2 Sa. 7:12; Am. 9:11. *One shepherd* implies one flock (not two as formerly); see 37:24 and *cf.* Jn. 10:16. **24** He is to be another *David* through whom God rules; *cf.* 37:25; 46:1–18. Note that his appearing is consequent upon the salvation wrought by God. That salvation is achieved by the Messiah is a distinctively NT doctrine, adumbrated only in the latter part of Isaiah. **25** The *covenant of peace* between God and His people (*cf.* 37:26) is linked with the removal of the *wild beasts*, which would multiply in the period of exile; *cf.* Lv. 26:4–6; Ho. 2:18; Is. 35:9; 54:10; Zc. 6:13. Only then would it be safe for a man to *sleep in the woods*. **29** *Prosperous plantations* (RV 'a plantation for renown'; *cf.* RSV mg.); the word is a collective singular, implying plantations so fruitful as to become famous. **31** RSV, with LXX and Latin, omits 'men' (see AV, RV, RSV mg.). With this verse *cf.* Rev. 21:3.

35:1–15 The extirpation of Edom

The insertion of this oracle of doom in prophecies of restoration is explained by Edom's attempted occupation of Israel and Judah (v. 10). Since Israel's restoration depends on her return to the land, Edom must first be overcome; such a judgment is demanded by the cruelty (vv. 5. 6) and blasphemy (vv. 10–13) of this ancient foe of Israel. *Cf.* Is. 63:1–6 and on Am. 9:11, 12.

2 *Mount Seir* is properly the mountain range south of the Dead Sea; but it also denotes the country of the Edomites. **5** Edom's *perpetual enmity* towards Israel goes back to the origins of the two nations (Gn. 27:41). The former had evidently assisted the Babylonians in the slaughter of 586 BC, characterized as *the time of their final punishment* (*cf.* 21:25, 29). **10** Edom claimed the territory of Judah and Israel as her own possession. Since this was looked upon as Yahweh's inheritance ('the land of the Lord', Ho. 9:3) and was to be again taken up by Him (48:35), Edom's claim was nothing short of blasphemy (v. 12) in the eyes of the prophet; *cf.* v. 12 with v. 13; Ob. 12.

36:1–38 Restoration and regeneration

Israel's external recovery is dealt with in vv. 1–15, her internal renewal in vv. 16–38. **1** As in 6:1–7 *the mountains* stand for the country itself, for they are its most prominent feature. But whereas in ch. 6 the 'mountains' were denounced, here they are consoled with promises of blessing. **2** The derisive *enemy* denotes the petty states bordering on Israel (see ch. 25), but with special reference to Edom whose hatred has been the subject of ch. 35. **5** The *jealousy* of Yahweh is evoked by the nations' seizure of His land and their scorning of His people.

The same jealousy that brought requital on Israel (23:25) brings judgment upon them and leads Israel to a glorious reinstatement (39:25). **8** The end of the exile will come *soon*. This is the normal prophetic outlook on the redemption of the end-time, both in the OT and NT (*cf.* Hab. 2:3; Rom. 13:12; 1 Pet. 4:7; Rev. 1:3; 22:10). **10** *The whole house of Israel* will enjoy restitution, not one tribe only (*cf.* 37:15f.). **12** *You shall no longer bereave them.* Possibly Ezekiel recalls Nu. 13:32. A land incapable of supporting its people (*cf.* v. 30), or wherein they suffered loss through war (*cf.* 1 Sa. 31:1) or other divine scourges (*cf.* 14:21), could be said to bereave its people.

Israel's name was bound up with that of Yahweh (vv. 21, 22); their condition therefore reflected on the honour of their God. The nations thought that Israel's distress was due to Yahweh's impotence (v. 20); their restoration to blessedness in their own land would make all see that Yahweh's government was characterized by holiness, not by weakness, and so His name would be revered by all (v. 23). The conception is integral to Ezekiel's thought and is moral in the highest degree. The cleansing from sin, though described in the language of ceremonial (v. 25), is figurative for moral renewal; *cf.* Zc. 13:1. **26** The *new heart* and *new spirit* are practically synonymous, occasioned by the gift of God's Spirit; it is not to be rationalized as simply the inspiration of a new disposition, but is a supernatural gift. The bestowal of the Holy Spirit is frequently associated by the prophets with the coming of the new age (*cf.* 39:29; Is. 44:3; 59:21; Joel 2:28, 29; Acts 2:16f.). The passage is Ezekiel's counterpart to the 'new covenant' of Jeremiah (Je. 31:31f.). **30** *I will make the fruit . . . abundant.* Supernatural fertility of the land is a mark of the kingdom of God; *cf.* v. 35; see also 47:1–12; Is. 35:1, 2; 55:13; Zc. 8:12. **38** The population also will be increased, so that cities shall be as crowded as the streets of Jerusalem used to be when sacrificial animals thronged them at the great festivals.

37:1–28 Resuscitation and reunion of Israel

Ezekiel predicts the political revival of his nation (vv. 1–14) and the reunion of its two divisions (vv. 15–28).

1 Whether the prophet sees the *valley* (or 'plain') in vision, or whether he is impelled by the Spirit to go to this place to receive a vision (as in 3:22), is not clear. **2** The dry bones indicate an army slain in battle. To the despondent of Israel the nation seemed to be in a similar state. **3** Both the question and answer reflect the hopelessness of the situation (*cf.* v. 11; 33:10); nothing but a stupendous act of God could effect a restoration. **9** The same Hebrew word *rûaḥ* signifies both *breath* (or 'wind', AV) and 'spirit' (see RSV mg.). The phrase *the four winds* is an Akkadian idiom for the four quarters of the earth (see Cooke, *ICC*, p. 400). The breath of God does not come from the winds, in the sense of identity with them, but comes from the ends of the earth; translate therefore, 'Prophesy to the breath. . . . Come from the four quarters, O breath, and breathe upon these slain.' *Cf.* the Greek *pneuma* and the ambiguity in Jn. 3:8 (see RSV mg., RV mg.) arising therefrom.

12 The interpretation of the vision changes the figure by regarding the Israelites as buried in graves instead of scattered on the ground. This is a prediction of the reintegration of Israel's political life, not of a literal resurrection of the dead. Some expositors are eager to point out that the doctrine of resurrection was unknown in Israel at this time. It is pertinent to ask, however, whether it is more likely that the dogma of resurrection originated from this passage, as many believe, or whether the passage is not rather an application of the idea of resurrection with which Ezekiel was already acquainted. It seems extraordinary, in view of the later teaching on resurrection, that a prophet should coin this figure with no knowledge whatever of the doctrine. Probability would indicate that it is a figurative use of a conception already current in his circles.

15–28 Ezekiel enacts a symbol. Two sticks, representing the southern and northern kingdoms of Israel (Judah and Joseph being respectively their chief tribes), are joined to form one stick, symbolizing the unity of the nation on its return to the homeland. At that time the house of David shall rule over the united nation for ever (vv. 22, 24, 25; see on 33:23, 24). It is sometimes pointed out that this never happened in the post-exilic history of Israel; but the prophet is looking for nothing less than the advent of the Messianic kingdom, when the Tabernacle of God shall be with His people (v. 27; see Rev. 21:3). At that time the nations shall recognize the power of Yahweh through His redemption of His people (v. 28).

38:1 – 39:29 PROPHECY AGAINST GOG

These two chapters are unique in OT prophecy in that they describe an uprising of foreign powers against the people of God after the commencement of the Messianic kingdom. The prophet has already predicted the coming blessedness of Israel (33–37); he now portrays the nation as long settled in their land and transformed into a prosperous community (38:8, 11, 12, 14), a condition which, according to his earlier teaching, involves their prior repentance, regeneration and political revival (33–37). Whereas he had said that Israel's restoration would come 'soon' (36:8), he says that Gog will be mustered 'after many days . . . in the latter years' (38:8). The motive underlying the prophecy is the necessity of earlier prophecies concerning the destruction of hostile Gentile powers being fulfilled (38:17; 39:8) and for the nations of the world to learn the power, holiness and sole deity of Yahweh (see on 39:7). The author of the book of Revelation has both used these chapters to vivify his description of Armageddon prior to the millennium (Rev. 19:17, 18), and adapted their essential idea so as to make it a final rebellion of the godless of humanity at the end of the millennium, before the new creation (20:7–9). In comparing the two writings it should be remembered that Ezekiel knew nothing of a new creation nor of a new Israel which was to inherit the kingdom; if John was to incorporate the prophecy he had of necessity to change its form. In conformity with his usage of OT prophecy generally, he has not hesitated to do so.

38:2 *Gog*; perhaps from 'Gagaia', home of barbarians, mentioned in the Amarna letters. It is the name of the leader. *Magog* is both his land (as here) and people (39:6). In Rev. 20:8 Gog and Magog symbolically represent the godless nations of the whole world. *Meshech and Tubal* are always coupled together, in secular as well as biblical writings (see, *e.g.*, Gn. 10:2; Ezk. 27:13; 32:26); the reading of RSV, AV and RV mg. *chief prince of Meshech and Tubal* is therefore preferable to that of RV 'prince of Rosh, Meshech and Tubal'. Meshech and Tubal were probably E of Asia Minor and are usually identified with Phrygia and Cappadocia; their equation with Moscow and Tobolsk, and Rosh with Russia, is unsupportable. **5** *Put* (as RV; AV 'Libya') is E Africa. **6** *Gomer* is linked with Magog in Gn. 10:2. They were called Gimirrai by the Assyrians and Cimmerians by the Greeks. Originating N of the Black Sea, by Ezekiel's time they had settled in Asia Minor. Their name survives in Gamir, Armenian name for Cappadocia. *Beth-togarmah*, NE of Asia Minor, is Armenia. From Ezekiel's point of view it appears to be *in the uttermost parts of the north* just as, to the author of *Psalms of Solomon*, Rome was regarded as 'the uttermost part of the earth' (*Psalms of Solomon* 8:16).

8 *After many days*; the invasion is not to occur for a long time. *Cf.* Is. 24:22. *The latter years* indicates the period of the kingdom (*cf.* Is. 2:2). **11** Israel, long settled in peace in her own land, has no fear of attack and so dwells in *unwalled villages . . . without walls, and having no bars or gates* (*cf.* Zc. 2:4). **13** Merchants and slave dealers all over the world are interested in the forthcoming campaign.

17–23 Gog's destruction will be by earthquake (vv. 19, 20), mutual strife (v. 21) and plagues like those on Egypt at the Exodus (vv. 22, 23); it is presumed that Israel will be brought safely through these calamities as in that former time. The reference to the earlier prophets in v. 17 would be to such passages as Zp. 3:8; Je. 3:6; and perhaps, seeing that the prophets spoke *in former days*, to prophecies known to Ezekiel but which have since perished.

39:1–20 cover the same ground as 38:2–4, 14–23 (see especially the commencement of the two chapters). The repetition is made to emphasize the marvellous nature of the deliver-

ance; the number of weapons burned by the Israelites and the long time taken to bury the dead show the immensity of Gog's armies, while the feast for birds and beasts stresses the completeness of the victory. Both Israel and the nations will learn of Yahweh's greatness through this judgment (v. 7). This is a recurring theme of the prophecy (*cf.* 38:16, 23; 39:6, 13, 21–23, 25–29).

11–16 The burial of Gog and his hosts takes place in a valley E of the Dead Sea; strictly this is outside the borders of Israel in the kingdom of God (47:18), but it is sufficiently close to serve as a memorial of honour for the victorious nation. The removal of all trace of corpses is necessary for the complete cleansing of the land (*cf.* Nu. 35:33, 34; Lv. 5:2).

17–20 The picture of Yahweh's feast serves to underline the terrible destruction of Gog and his hosts. It entails a change of figure, for bodies cannot be both eaten and buried, but the inconsistency is so slight, and in any case vanishes in the light of vv. 14, 15, that it seems a hazardous ground for suggesting that the picture comes from another hand and relates to the Persian or Greek age. **21, 22** stress the supreme lesson to be learned by Israel and the nations. Israel's captivity and Gog's destruction alike reveal the holiness of God and His unfailing grace towards His people.

25–29 are a concluding summary of Ezekiel's prophecies of restoration: God will certainly perform His word to Israel and bring glory to His name in all the earth.

40:1 – 48:35 TEMPLE AND PEOPLE IN THE KINGDOM OF GOD

The concluding chapters of Ezekiel's writing form a strange contrast to the furious oratory of the earlier prophecies. In reality they are the essential complement to the judgments he had enunciated. Ezekiel was a priest as well as a prophet. It was his joyful task to balance the prophecies of the ruin of the Temple, the departure of Yahweh and the scattering of the nation with a detailed prediction of the rebuilding of the Temple, the return of Yahweh to His people and the reorganization of the national life. It was not sufficient to declare that the nation was to return and erect another Temple; they must be instructed how to build it. To ensure the holiness of Temple, people and worship alike, detailed instructions are issued by the prophet which were the fruit of both prolonged vision and reflection. If their reading is tedious to us, we must remember that, to the Jewish mind, it was impossible to bestow too much trouble and thought on the place whose name is 'Yahweh is there' (48:35). Such was the spirit in which these chapters were written. It needs little imagination to realize that among Ezekiel's companions in exile they would excite as much interest and discussion as anything he had as yet issued.

A word must be added concerning the interpretation of these chapters. It need hardly be said that Ezekiel has here advanced plans which he expected to be carried out to the letter. To make them a deliberately symbolic description of the worship of the Christian church is out of the question. Nor was the vision thought of as something to be fulfilled in normal conditions, as ch. 47 shows; it was a plan for the era of God's kingdom. Some expositors, accordingly, look for a rebuilding of the Temple at the second coming of Christ and an exact fulfilment of all Ezekiel's predictions in the kingdom of Christ.

1 THE TEMPLE AREA

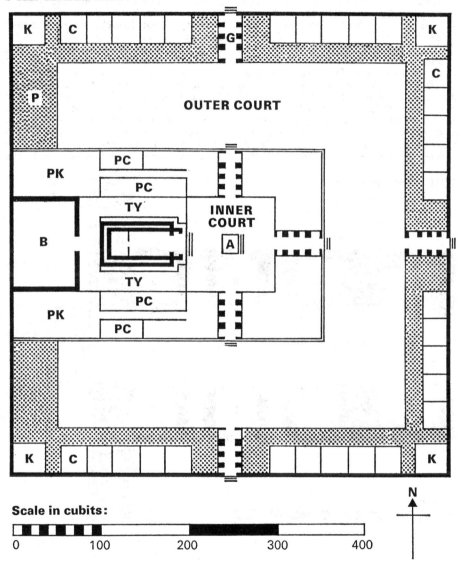

Scale in cubits:

| 0 | 100 | 200 | 300 | 400 |

N

A: Altar
B: Building
C: Chamber
G: Gateway
K: Kitchen

P: Pavement
PC: Priests' chambers
PK: Priests' kitchens
TY: Temple yard (AV separate place)

683

This view is challenged by certain fundamental principles of the NT. *a*. The atonement of our Lord has nullified all sacrifices for ever (Heb. 10:18). *b*. The heirs of the kingdom are no longer the Jewish nation but the church, the new Israel in which the old Israel may find its true place (Mt. 21:43; 1 Pet. 2:9, 10). *c*. John in the Revelation adapts these chapters to describe the church in the kingdom of God (Rev. 21:9 – 22:5) and removes from them all traces of Judaism. To speak of a 'double fulfilment' of all these things at the same time, so that there are two reigning Israels in the kingdom, two new Jerusalems, each having a river of life and trees of life, *etc.*, two rulers from David's seed, an earthly and heavenly Sovereign, and so on, is to demand credence in the incredible. The conclusion of Ezekiel's prophecy, therefore, is to be regarded as a true prediction of the kingdom of God given under the forms with which the prophet was familiar, viz. those of his own (Jewish) dispensation. Their essential truth will be em-

bodied in the new age under forms suitable to the new (Christian) dispensation. How this is to be done is outlined for us in the book of Revelation (21:1 – 22:5).

40:1 – 42:20 The plan of the new Temple

It is impossible in the limits of this commentary to attempt a full exposition of Ezekiel's description of the future Temple. This must be left to the longer works. The reading of his plans will be greatly facilitated if each paragraph is checked against the accompanying drawings.

Ezekiel is transported in vision to Mt. Zion where his angel guide greets him (40:1-4). The first thing that meets his eye is the *wall* surrounding the Temple precincts (v. 5; see Diagram 1). Passing through a massive *gateway* on the east side, built in similar style to many he had seen in Babylonian temples (vv. 6–16; see Diagram 2), he comes into the *outer court* about which was a *pavement* and thirty rooms set apart for the use of people during festivals (vv. 17–19).

2 THE EAST GATEWAY

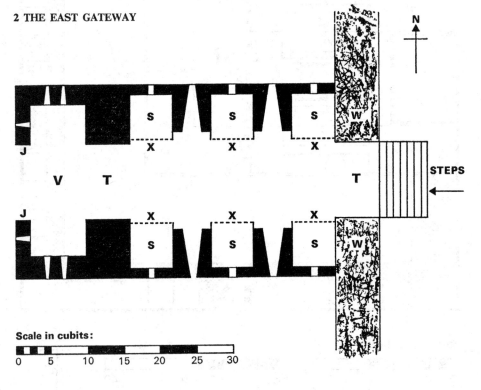

Scale in cubits:

0   5   10   15   20   25   30

	AV	RSV
J:	Posts	Jambs (of the vestibule)
S:	Chambers	Side rooms (or guard-rooms)
T:	Threshold	Threshold
V:	Porch	Vestibule
W:	Wall	Wall (surrounding temple area)
X:	Space	Barrier (probably a low wall)

3 EZEKIEL'S TEMPLE

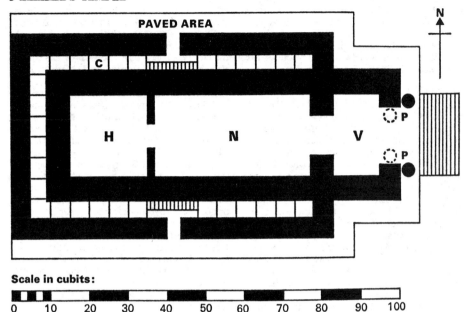

PAVED AREA

Scale in cubits:

0 10 20 30 40 50 60 70 80 90 100

C: **Side-chambers (41:5-7)**

P: **Pillars (40:49): position not certain**

V: **Vestibule (40:48, 49)**

N: **Nave, or holy place (41:1, 2)**

H: **Inner room, or holy of holies (41:3, 4)**

For the paved area, or platform, see 41:8-11.

On the north and south sides there are gateways similar to the one by which he had entered (vv. 20–26). In the four corners there are kitchens for the people (marked 'K'), but these are not described until 46:21–24. He walks through another large gateway into the inner court, which is at a higher level (note the references to *steps* in vv. 31, 34 and 37), and views the arrangements made for preparing sacrifices as well as certain rooms set apart for the priests (vv. 28–47). Here also there are gatehouses on the south (vv. 28–31) and on the north (vv. 35–37).

The Temple proper is now described, first the porch (vv. 48, 49), then the *nave* or 'holy place' (41:1, 2), then the *most holy place* (vv. 3, 4). See Diagrams 1 and 3. Round the north, west and south sides of the Temple are rooms in three storeys, thirty on each floor, presumably to be used for utensils, stores, *etc.*, needed for the service of the Temple (vv. 5–11; these rooms are marked 'C' on Diagram 3). West of the Temple lies a separate building (marked 'B' on Diagram 1) whose purpose is not mentioned, but which may have been for storage (v. 12). The total

measurements of the Temple and its immediate surroundings are supplied (vv. 13–17), and a description of the interior of the Temple follows in vv. 18–26. For *the part that was left* (v. 11) see Diagram 3 ('paved area'); for the *temple yard* (AV 'separate place') (vv. 12–14) see Diagram 1 ('TY').

North of the Temple in the inner court are two blocks of three-storey buildings, one twice the length of the other. The larger is to be used by priests for eating sacrifices (42:13), the shorter for dressing-rooms (v. 14). Similar buildings are on the south side of the Temple (42:1–14; see Diagram 1, 'PC'). Next to these are priests' kitchens (marked 'PK') but they are not described until 46:19, 20. The whole Temple enclosure is measured at 500 cubits (vv. 15–20, reading with the LXX *cubits* instead of AV 'reeds').

43:1–12 Yahweh's return to the Temple

As a fitting conclusion to his survey of the Temple, Ezekiel sees Yahweh returning in splendour by the gate through which He had earlier departed (10:19ff.; 11:23), henceforth never to leave it again (v. 7a). The prophet is told that in the future the shame of placing graves of Israelite kings next to the sanctuary must cease (v. 7b). Whereas in the past the palace had been contiguous to the Temple, separated from it only by a wall (v. 8), the whole of Mt. Zion was to be 'holy of holies' (v. 12).

43:13–27 The altar

The altar is described in vv. 13–17, the procedure of its consecration in vv. 18–27. Toy's summary of this description of the altar admirably clarifies its obscurities: 'It comprises a base twenty-seven feet square and eighteen inches high, with a moulding about nine inches wide; on this is set a square of twenty-four feet, three feet high; on this a square of twenty-one feet, six feet high; and above this the hearth, eighteen feet square and six feet high, on which the victim was laid; at the four corners are the horns, eighteen inches high, originally, perhaps, projections to which the victims were tied.' This translation of Hebrew measurements into English, however, obscures the fact that they are evidently symbolic: Cooke points out that the topmost altar-hearth was 12 cubits square and the height, including the horns, was also 12 cubits.

44:1–31 Levites and priests

After the introductory paragraph concerning the permanent closure of the east outer gate (vv. 1–4), the main topic of the chapter is discussed, viz. the status and offices of the two chief classes of priests. Formerly the menial work of the sanctuary had been done by aliens, probably prisoners of war (cf. Ezr. 8:20; Zc. 14:21). This, declared Ezekiel, had been an offence to God and must cease (vv. 6–9). Foreigners were to be replaced by the former priests of the country sanctuaries, the 'Levites', who had been responsible for much of Israel's religious declension (vv. 10–14). This procedure at once solved the problem as to how foreign labour could be avoided and pronounced a judgment on the Levites for their conduct, for they were henceforth excluded from the higher priestly functions.

15 *The Levitical priests* were of the line of Zadok, who was made principal priest by Solomon when Abiathar and his family were excommunicated from the priestly office (1 Ki. 2:26, 27, 35). They had continued ministering in the Temple of Jerusalem from that time onwards, and despite their aberrations (cf. ch. 8) were regarded as having perpetuated the true worship of Yahweh. Their obligations and duties are outlined in vv. 15–27, their rights of maintenance in vv. 28–31.

For the problems entailed in estimating the relations between Ezekiel, Deuteronomy and the 'priestly code', consult the larger commentaries.

45:1 – 46:24 Oblations and offerings

45:1ff. *A portion of the land* is to be offered to Yahweh, a territory about 8 miles square.

Of this land a strip, two-fifths of the length, was for the priests, in the centre of which was the Temple (vv. 1–4); a further strip northwards of the same size was for the Levites (v. 5) and the remaining fifth southwards was designated for the city (v. 6). **7, 8** East and west of this square, stretching to the Jordan and Mediterranean respectively, was the prince's territory. The whole scheme appears to be directed to the safeguarding of the sanctity of the Temple, making it in very truth a 'holy of holies'. **9ff.** A warning to the prince and his sons not to oppress the people as their forbears had done (v. 9; cf. 1 Sa. 26:19; 1 Ki. 21:19) is followed by a statement of the right standards for weights and measures (vv. 10–12), a source of perpetual trouble both in those and comparatively modern times. **13–17** outline the revenues to be paid to the prince for provision of the regular sacrifices. Two annual festivals are to be observed, the Passover in the first month (vv. 21–24) and the Feast of Harvest or Tabernacles in the seventh (v. 25). A kind of day of atonement is to precede each festival (vv. 18–20). **20** The quotation from the LXX in RV mg. is to be followed, 'so shalt thou do in the seventh month, on the first day of the month'.

46:1–18 Sabbath, new moon and daily offerings are detailed, with the privileges and obligations of the prince. **1, 2** While the prince, like the rest of the populace, was not permitted to enter the inner court, he was allowed to take up a position on the *threshold* of the east inner gate (*i.e.* the west end of the gate, facing the inner court) so as to observe the sacrifices more closely. **4–7** He is to make stated offerings every *sabbath* and every *new moon*. **8** It is again stressed that he is not to enter the inner court. **9** When the Temple is crowded at feasts, worshippers must pass through the Temple courts from gate to gate and not leave by the gate through which they entered; **10** this applies even to the prince.

16–18 The enactment concerning the prince's bequeathing of his property appears to be a limitation of his powers, both to ensure that his territory remains in the royal family and to prevent his seizure of commoners' lands (cf. on 45:9). **17** *The year of liberty* is more likely to be the fiftieth year, the year of jubilee (Lv. 25:13–15), than the seventh, the sabbatical year (Ex. 23:10, 11; cf. Ex. 21:2).

19ff. Kitchens for the use of priests (vv. 19, 20) and people (vv. 21–24) are now described, the former being situated at the north-west and south-west of the inner court (marked 'PK' on Diagram 1, p. 683), adjacent to the three-storey buildings running parallel to the Temple (42:1–14); the latter are placed in the four corners of the outer court (marked 'K' on Diagram 1). The kitchens for the people are themselves spoken of as *courts* (vv. 22, 23); they comprised 'a low wall surrounding each of these four corners; on the ground below and within these walls, recesses were made for the *hearths* or boiling places where the meals were cooked' (Cooke). This whole paragraph would suitably follow 42:20 and may have dropped out from that place.

47:1–12 The river of life

1ff. The prophet sees a river emerging from beneath the door of the Temple and flowing eastwards, leaving the Temple area just below the outer eastern gate. (Note that Ezekiel has to make a detour to reach that point; see 44:1, 2.) Passing along its banks, he traces its course till, from being a mere trickle (v. 3), it becomes a deep river (v. 5). In this formerly desert land trees in abundance grew on either side of the river (v. 7), yielding a perpetual cycle of fruits and healing leaves (v. 12). The water is fresh, sweetening even the waters of the Dead Sea and enabling fish to multiply wherever it flows (vv. 8–10), a point doubtless made in reference to the fact that fish carried down to the Dead Sea by the Jordan are thrown up on the shores dead.

This description is to be taken literally, but it may also have been intended to show that the source of the nation's blessing in the new age will be none other than Yahweh in His sanctuary. Many other lessons may be learned by the Christian, while John in the NT Apocalypse has characteristically used its figures to portray the spiritual blessings of the church in the age of consummation (Rev. 22:2).

47:13 – 48:35 Boundaries and allotments of the land

47:15–17 The northern border runs from the Mediterranean Sea, just north of Tyre, to a point near Damascus; **18** the eastern border is formed by the Jordan and the Dead Sea; **19** the southern from a little below the Dead Sea to the mouth of the *Brook of Egypt* (this is not the Nile; see *NBD*, art. 'Egypt, River of'); **20** western border is formed by the Mediterranean Sea. No territory east of Jordan is included, neither is the old ideal regarded that the borders of Israel stretch from the Nile to the Euphrates (see, *e.g.*, Gn. 15:18; Ex. 23:31). This may be due to Ezekiel's aiming at 'concentration rather than extension' (Cooke); the prophet was anxious that there should be no contamination of the Holy Land by Gentile influence (*cf.* 44:9). **22, 23** On the other hand the granting of full

participation in the inheritance to *the aliens who reside among you* is more generous than anything else in OT legislation in these matters (but *cf.* Lv. 19:34; 24:22; Nu. 9:14).

48:1–35 The disposition of the land is dominated by the position of the Temple and its lands; seven tribes are placed north of the portion (vv. 1–7) and five south (vv. 23–29). This, together with the transference of the 'two and a half tribes' east of Jordan to the west side, has involved a change in the allotment from that of former times (*cf.* Jos. 13–17). Especially noteworthy is the removal of Judah from south to north. It has been suggested that 'the tribes descended from Leah and Rachel are brought nearer to the oblation than those descended from the handmaids Bilhah and Zilpah (Gn. 35:23–26), as though the more privileged positions were determined by relative purity of blood' (*ICC*, p. 531).

8–22 The portion has already been described in 45:1–8. In both chapters we are right to read *cubits* instead of AV 'reeds' in the measurements: see note on 42:15–20. It is inferred that Jerusalem is to be populated by members drawn from all the tribes of Israel (v. 19). Ezekiel draws special attention to the portion, city area and city itself being 25,000 cubits *square* (v. 20). This feature also impressed John, who however added that the height of the city was also of the same measurement as the length and breadth, so making the city a perfect cube, a tremendous 'holy of holies' (Rev. 21:16). The gates similarly find a place in John's city (*cf.* vv. 30–34 with Rev. 21:12, 13), but they intersperse twelve apostolic foundations (Rev. 21:14); the city is a Christian, not a Jewish, institution!

35 The whole description of the land and people in the kingdom of God is fittingly concluded by the declaration of the name that is to be given to the City of God, *Yahweh Shammah, The Lord is there.* The unfolding of this theme is the constant delight of the NT Apocalyptist, who again and again mentions the presence of God as the chief joy of the heavenly city (Rev. 21:1 – 22:5; *cf.* especially 21:3, 4, 7, 22, 23; 22:3–5).

G. R. BEASLEY-MURRAY

Daniel

INTRODUCTION

POSITION IN CANON

In the Hebrew Bible the book of Daniel is found in the third division, the 'Writings', rather than in the second, in which the prophetical books occur. The reason for this is not that Daniel was written later than these prophetical books. In some lists, it may be noted, Daniel was included in the second division of the Canon. The reason why the book of Daniel came to be placed in the position which it now occupies lies in the status of the writer.

The authors of the prophetical books were men who occupied the technical status of prophet; *i.e.*, they were men specially raised up by God to serve as mediators between God and the nation by declaring to the people the identical words which God had revealed to them. Daniel, however, was not a prophet in this restricted, technical sense. He was rather a statesman at the court of heathen monarchs. As a statesman, he did possess the prophetical *gift*, even though he did not occupy the prophetical *office*, and it is in this sense, apparently, that the NT speaks of him as prophet (Mt. 24:15). Daniel therefore was a statesman, inspired by God to write his book, and so the book appears in the OT Canon in the third division among the writings of other inspired men who did not occupy the prophetical office.

PURPOSE

At Mt. Sinai in the wilderness the God of heaven and earth set His affection in a peculiar way upon Israel, choosing her to be His people and declaring that He would be her God. He thus entered into a covenant relationship with Israel, and manifested this relationship by a mighty act of deliverance. His purpose for the nation was that it should be a 'kingdom of priests' and that God should be its ruler. Thus the theocracy (rule of God) was established. Israel was to be a holy nation, a light to lighten the Gentiles and to bear the saving knowledge of the true God to all people.

To this high purpose, however, Israel was not faithful. After being in the promised land for a time, she exhibited dissatisfaction with the fundamental principles of the theocracy by asking for a human king so that she might be like the nations round about. An evil king was first given to her, and then a man after God's own heart. David, however, was a man of war, and so it was not until the peaceful reign of Solomon that the Temple, the external symbol of the kingdom

of God, was built . After the death of Solomon the northern tribes rebelled and renounced the covenant promises. From this time on, both in the northern and southern kingdoms, wickedness characterizes the people, and God announces His intention to destroy them (*cf.* Ho. 1:6; Am. 2:13-16; Is. 6:11, 12, *etc.*). The instruments which the sovereign God employed to carry out His purpose of bringing the theocracy to an end were the Assyrians and Babylonians. Under the power of these nations the theocratic people were carried into captivity, and the exile or period of 'indignation' came (Is. 10:25; Dn. 8:19).

The exile itself later gave way to a period of expectancy and preparation for Messiah's coming. It was revealed that a period of seventy sevens had been determined by God for the accomplishment of the Messianic work (Dn. 9:24-27). The book of Daniel, a product of the exile, serves to show that the exile itself was not to be permanent. Rather, the very nation which has conquered Israel will herself disappear from the scene of history, to be replaced by another, in fact by three more human empires. While these kingdoms were in existence, however, the God of heaven would erect another kingdom which, unlike the human kingdoms, would be both universal and eternal. It is thus the purpose of the book of Daniel to teach the truth that, even though the people of God are in bondage to a heathen nation, God Himself is the sovereign and ultimate Disposer of the destinies both of individuals and of nations.

This truth is taught by means of a rich use of symbol and imagery, and the reason for this characteristic is to be found in the fact that the revelations made to Daniel were in the form of vision. So his book may be called an apocalyptic work, but it towers far above the post-canonical apocalypses. The only work which may justly be compared with it is the NT book of Revelation. Essentially, Daniel exhibits the qualities of a truly prophetic book, and its imagery is used for a didactic purpose.

AUTHOR

The book of Daniel is a product of the exile and was written by Daniel himself. We may note that Daniel speaks in the first person and asserts that revelations were made to him (Dn. 7:2, 4ff.; 8:1ff., 15ff.; 9:2ff., *etc.*). Since, however, the book is a unity, it follows that the author of the second part (chs. 7-12) must also have composed the first (chs. 1-6). The second chapter, *e.g.*, is preparatory to chs. 7 and 8, which develop its contents more fully and which clearly presuppose it. The ideas of the book reflect one basic viewpoint, and this literary unity has been acknowledged by scholars of different schools of thought. Daniel reflects the Babylonian and Persian background, and the alleged historical objections (to be discussed in the commentary) are not really valid. Lastly, an indirect approval of the genuineness of the book seems to be found in the following NT passages: Mt. 10:23; 16:27ff.; 19:28; 24:30; 25:31; 26:64.

In the Christian church it has been traditionally maintained, because of the claims of the book itself, that the historical Daniel was the author. The first known doubt to be cast upon this view came from Porphyry of Tyre (born *c.* AD 232–233), a vigorous opponent of Christianity, who maintained that the work was the product of a Jew living at the times of the Maccabees. During the 18th and particularly the 19th centuries, Porphyry's view seemed to come into its own in the world of scholarship. It was widely maintained that the book of Daniel was the work of an unknown Jew, living at the time of Antiochus Epiphanes. The reasons for this were the remarkable accuracy with which these times are described in Daniel, the supposed historical inaccuracies in the book, and the alleged lateness of the language of the prophecy. Sometimes too, it would seem, an attitude of aversion toward the supernatural character of the book led men to seek to deny its true prophetic character. Recently, however, perhaps largely as a result of Hölscher's study ('Die Entstehung des Buches Daniel' in *Theologische Studien und Kritiken*, xcii, 1919, pp. 113–138), there has been more of a tendency to recognize the antiquity of much underlying material in Daniel. It is still maintained—wrongly, we believe—that the book in its present form comes from the 2nd century BC, but that much of the material, particularly in the first part, is very much older.

It may be well briefly to consider some of the historical objections that have been raised against the book of Daniel.

In the first place it is said that the usage of the term 'Chaldean' betrays an age later than the 6th century BC. In the book of Daniel this term is employed in an ethnic sense to denote a race of people, and it is also used in a more restricted manner to indicate a particular class, viz. the wise men. This latter usage, however, it is argued, did not arise until long after the time of Daniel. In answer it may be said that Herodotus (*c.* 440 BC) speaks of the Chaldeans as a caste in such a way as to show that this must have been the case for years before his time. Since extra-biblical references are so few, we do not know enough to assert that the representations in Daniel are in error.

It has also been charged that Daniel would never have been admitted into the Babylonian priesthood or have been made its head. A careful reading of the prophecy, however, shows that Daniel merely exercised political authority (2:48, 49). There is no evidence that he was admitted or initiated into any religious caste. If the book of Daniel really is late, how can we conceive of the late author depicting Daniel as entering a heathen caste?

It has sometimes been maintained that there are no extra-biblical allusions to the account of Nebuchadrezzar's madness and that therefore the narrative is not historical. However, the historian Eusebius quotes from Abydenus a description of the last days of Nebuchadrezzar in which the language is such that it implies that something strange had occurred toward the end of the king's life. There are certain similarities in this account with what is stated in Daniel. In Berossus also (recorded in Josephus, *Contra Apionem*, i.20) there is a reflection upon the fact of the king's madness. In Cave IV of the Qumran caves a fragment known as *The Prayer of Nabonidus* has come to light. Nabonidus states that he was smitten with a malignant disease for 7 years. This account (to be considered in detail in the exposition of ch. 4) apparently reflects upon the account of Nebuchadrezzar's madness in Dn. 4.

Objection to the Danielic authorship of the book has also been advanced on the ground that the Aramaic language in which a part of the book is written belongs to a time after that of Daniel. While there is nothing in the Aramaic usage of Daniel which in itself would preclude Danielic authorship, it seems most likely that the character of the Aramaic is that which may be called 'Reich' or 'Kingdom' Aramaic; *i.e.*, which was introduced into the Persian Empire by Darius I. Does this fact, however, rule out Daniel as the author? Not at all. It is quite possible that the Aramaic in which Daniel is written is simply a working over or modernizing of the Aramaic in which the book was originally composed. The question of the authorship of the book must be settled on grounds other than that of the language in which the book is written. A thorough discussion of Daniel's Aramaic has recently appeared in K. A. Kitchen, 'The Aramaic of Daniel', *Notes on Some Problems in the Book of Daniel*, 1965, pp. 31–79. A rejoinder appeared in a review by H. H. Rowley, *JSS*, Vol. XI, No. 1, pp. 112–116.

LITERATURE

The student will find a complete exposition of the modern point of view in the commentary by James A. Montgomery (the *ICC* Series). This same viewpoint is also expressed in the learned articles of H. H. Rowley. The views of the present writer are more fully expressed in *The Prophecy of Daniel*, 1949.

OUTLINE OF CONTENTS

COMMENTARY

1:1-21 DANIEL RAISED TO POWER

1:1, 2 Nebuchadrezzar's expedition

1 *In the third year of . . . Jehoiakim.* According to Jeremiah (25:1; 46:2) the expedition of Nebuchadrezzar (for this version of the name, see *NBD*) against Jerusalem took place in the fourth year of Jehoiakim. Daniel, however, evidently employs the Babylonian method of reckoning, in which the first year is regarded as following the year of the king's accession to the throne. Hence, the first year would equal the second year of the Palestinian reckoning, and the third year (Babylonian reckoning) and the fourth year (Palestinian) would be equated. There is therefore no conflict with Jeremiah. *Cf.* D. J. Wiseman, 'Some Historical Problems in the Book of Daniel', *Notes on Some Problems in the Book of Daniel*, pp. 16–18. *Cf.* also D. J. Wiseman, *Chronicles of Chaldaean Kings*, 1956, p. 26. *Jehoiakim king of Judah.* He was placed on the throne by the king of Egypt and was a wicked king who, in his fourth year, became a subject of Nebuchadrezzar, and three years later revolted. He reigned for eleven years and was followed by his son Jehoiachin. See 2 Ki. 23:36 – 24:9; Je. 22:18, 19; 36:30.

It is not stated that Nebuchadrezzar attacked Jerusalem as king. Rather, he is here called *king of Babylon* proleptically. Note also that Daniel does not say that Nebuchadrezzar took Jerusalem, as some critics have asserted. It may be, as Berossus (Josephus, *Contra Apionem* i.19; *Antiquities* x.11.1) has said, that word reached him of the death of his father, and he returned to Babylon to take up the kingdom.

1:3-16 The Jewish youths at the Babylonian court

3 The etymology of the word *Ashpenaz* is un-certain. The man, however, was a chief marshal or officer at the court. *People of Israel . . .* There is no reference to three different classes, as AV suggests; follow RSV. **4** Among these people the king desired those who possessed a sound mind in a sound body, and who could, therefore, the more efficiently serve at the court.

5 In order to accomplish this design, the king provided a *daily portion* of both his food and wine. **6, 7** The Hebrew youths are introduced, and we learn that their names were changed. **8** Daniel *resolved that he would not defile himself* with the daily portion, the reason being that this food and drink had evidently been consecrated by a heathen religious rite, and to have eaten it would be, in Daniel's opinion, to have been guilty of idol-worship. **9** Daniel therefore approached the chief eunuch, and God made the officer favourably disposed toward him. **11–15** The *steward* (evidently an official who was under the chief eunuch) granted Daniel's request, and at the end of the appointed time the appearance of the youths was better and they were fuller in flesh than those who had partaken of the king's food. Thus began the triumph of God's power and grace in Babylon.

1:17-21 The first triumph of grace in Babylon

17 The lives of the four youths were in the hands of God. He gave to them *learning*, that they might discern between the false and true in their instruction, which lay in the fields of *letters* (*i.e.* literature) *and wisdom* (which for them would include diplomacy or statecraft). Daniel also attained readiness or facility in the interpreting of dreams or visions. This mention of *visions and dreams* is an accurate reflection upon the Babylonian background of the book.

21 This does not mean that Daniel continued

only *until the first year of King Cyrus*. Rather, since the first year of Cyrus was the year which marked the close of the exile, it is mentioned to show that Daniel continued even to this time. The language does not imply that he did not continue beyond this time.

2:1–49 THE KING'S DREAM INTERPRETED BY DANIEL

2:1–16 Nebuchadrezzar's dream

1 *In the second year*. This phrase is thought by some to conflict with the three-year period of training mentioned in ch. 1. But the phrase 'three years' (1:5) need refer only to portions of years (*cf., e.g.,* 2 Ki. 18:9, 10; Je. 34:14; Mk. 8:31), so that the first year of training could comprise part of the year of Nebuchadrezzar's accession, and the third year part of the second year of his reign (Babylonian reckoning). The king was so disturbed by the dream that *his sleep left him*. **2–4** Hence he immediately summoned those whom he believed able to tell the meaning of his dream. These men desired to know the dream that they might interpret it. *In Aramaic* (see RSV mg., v. 4) is found in the original but is not translated in RSV. It seems designed to call attention to the fact that from this point on to the end of ch. 7 the language of the book is Aramaic. It may be, however, that the words serve to indicate the language in which the Chaldeans spoke to the king. Some critics have asserted that such a statement could not be historical, but in the light of the recently-discovered (1942) Aramaic *Letter of Adon*, such an objection can no longer stand (*cf.* F. F. Bruce, 'More Light on Daniel's First Verse' in *Bible League Quarterly*, No. 203, 1950, pp. 6–8).

With respect to the Aramaic used in the book of Daniel, it may be said that there is nothing in it which in itself could preclude usage by Daniel. If, however, the present Aramaic should prove to be later, it would not affect Danielic authorship, but would merely show that the original Aramaic had been brought up to date by a later writer. It is difficult to determine why two languages are employed in Daniel, but Daniel himself probably wrote thus, employing the Aramaic, or language of the world, for those sections of his book which deal principally with the histories of the world empires, and the Hebrew for those sections which develop the future of the people of God and His kingdom.

5 The reason why the king will not relate the dream is not that he has forgotten it, as AV implies, but that he wants to test the wise men. *You shall be torn limb from limb*. The cruelty contained in this threat was widespread in antiquity, and characterized the dealings of the Babylonian kings. **10, 11** The Chaldeans declare their inability to tell and interpret the dream, asserting that such knowledge can be found only with the gods *whose dwelling is not with flesh*. By this confession the Chaldeans make reference

to God, for even among pagans there has remained the persuasion that God exists (*cf.* Rom. 1:21). **12, 13** The king, however, was enraged and ordered the wise men to be slain. **14–16** Daniel judiciously intervenes and asks for time.

2:17–23 Daniel's prayer

18 The interpretation is called a *mystery*, since it is that which cannot be obtained by unaided human reason. **20** In response to the revelation, Daniel blesses God in prayer. To God belongs *wisdom*—He is omniscient and all-wise—and *might*, for He governs all things. **21** The course of history lies in God's hand, who changes times and seasons, and the destinies of rulers also are at His disposal. When true wisdom is found among men, it is a gift of God, and true understanding is also from Him. **22** He reveals *deep and mysterious things*, namely the wondrous works of God for the salvation of men. It is this sovereign God to whom Daniel utters his thanksgiving.

2:24–49 The interpretation of the dream

28 When Daniel reappears before the king he seeks to make clear that he has not come to the interpretation of the dream in his own power, but gives the glory to God. The dream is eschatological; *i.e.* it has to do with the *latter days* or, in other words, with the Messianic age (*cf.* Acts 2:16, 17; 1 Tim. 4:1; Heb. 1:1). **31ff.** Daniel relates the content of the dream by describing the colossus which the king saw, the various parts of which were of different metals. The head of gold is identified as Nebuchadrezzar himself, and this probably means that we are to understand the Babylonian Empire as represented by its great king. Other parts of the image are said to stand for other kingdoms.

Different interpretations of this imagery have been offered. Most critical scholars who deny the authenticity of Daniel believe that the four empires represented by the colossus are Babylon, Media, Persia and Greece. It has been maintained by some of the advocates of this position that, since Media did not exist as a separate empire after the fall of Babylon, the book of Daniel is therefore in error. There are, however, strong reasons for rejecting this identification (see the author's *The Prophecy of Daniel*, 1949, pp. 275–294). Objections to this view will be pointed out as the exposition proceeds. From time to time conservative scholars have identified the kingdoms as Babylon, Medo-Persia, Alexander's Empire, and the successors of Alexander. But for the most part the traditional conservative position has been to identify them as Babylon, Medo-Persia, Greece and Rome. This is the only position which interprets v. 44 correctly, a verse which distinctly states that the Messianic kingdom will be erected in the days of the kingdoms already mentioned. The first two views assume that the Messianic kingdom will be erected *after* the four human empires, and this is definitely counter to the teaching of v. 44.

The dispensationalist teaching interprets the ten toes of the image as representing a time when the Roman Empire will be revived and will be divided into ten kingdoms. It may be noted, however, that no mention is made of the number of toes.

34 The stone *cut out by no human hand* represents the Messiah and the growth of the Messianic kingdom, which kingdom is described as being eternal and of divine origin (v. 44), and thus standing in contrast with the human and temporal empires of the colossus.

47 *God is God of gods . . .* Nebuchadrezzar's confession does not really rise above the level of polytheism. He recognizes the superiority of Daniel's God, but does not yet adore Him as the true God. In the *Letter of Adon* (see on vv. 1-4) appears the precise Aramaic phrase, 'lord of kings', which Nebuchadrezzar applies to God. This fact supports the view that Daniel's Aramaic may date from the 6th century. It also shows that as Adon regarded the Egyptian pharaoh as a greater king than himself, so does Nebuchadrezzar regard Daniel's God as a King to whom he must do obeisance.

48 It need not be thought that Daniel's advancement would necessarily involve him in the superstitions of Babylon. We may be sure that a man of his sterling devotion to God would keep himself free from such defilement.

3:1-30 THE EPISODE OF THE FIERY FURNACE

1 *An image.* It was customary for the Assyrian kings to erect statues of themselves. That this was a statue of Nebuchadrezzar himself, however, is not expressly stated. It may be that Daniel's identification of the king as the head of gold (2:38) and his own satisfaction at the number of his conquests (among which Jerusalem itself might now probably be included) led Nebuchadrezzar to become filled with pride, and to erect this statue so as to honour both his god and himself. *Of gold.* The statue need not have been made of solid gold, but may have been gold plated. It is also possible that it may have rested upon a pedestal, and may have been in the form of an obelisk which at its base was 9 feet in breadth. The grotesqueness of the statue is no argument against the historicity of the account, and an evidence of genuineness is seen in the employment of the Babylonian sexagesimal system. *The plain of Dura.* The exact location has not been determined, although the word *duru* (an enclosing wall) is fairly common in Babylonian.

5 Objection to the authenticity of Daniel has been raised because of the presence of alleged Greek words here. The names of three of the musical instruments (viz. those translated *lyre, harp, bagpipe*) have sometimes been regarded as Greek. If they are Greek words, so the argument runs, then surely Daniel would

not have known them, since he lived so long before the rise of Greek culture. If, however, these words are really of Greek origin, it does not follow at all that Daniel could not have used them, since Greek culture had spread very early, and there were Greek soldiers in Nebuchadrezzar's armies (see *The Prophecy of Daniel,* p. 87). See also the recent discussion by T. C. Mitchell and R. Joyce in *Notes on Some Problems in the Book of Daniel,* pp. 19-27.

12 The unjust character of the charge against the companions of Daniel should be noted. They are said to be Jews, thus stressing the fact that they are foreigners, with the possible implication that, being foreigners, they would not be loyal. Note further the statement that the king has honoured these Jews, the implication being that they were lacking in gratitude. The question has been raised why Daniel is not mentioned in this chapter. Various suggestions have been offered by way of answer, but none of them is satisfactory. Since the Bible at this point does not mention Daniel it is useless to speculate upon the matter.

13-15 In rage the king commands the three accused men to be brought before him and gives them an opportunity to deny the accusation. **16** offers some difficulty, and we may best translate the latter part of it as rsv rather than av. In other words the three acknowledge the truth of the accusation and, rather than defend themselves, are willing to rest their case in the hands of God. **17** does not cast doubt upon God's ability to save, but rather stresses His *ethical* ability, *i.e.* if God in His good pleasure can deliver, He will do so.

19 In response Nebuchadrezzar orders the furnace to be heated seven times beyond what was usual, and the three were cast into the flames. **25** presents the king's astonishment when he sees in addition to the three Jews one in the furnace like *a son of the gods.* Through the opening at the bottom of the furnace the king saw a fourth Person, and, although speaking from the viewpoint of one steeped in Babylonian superstition, he recognizes the presence of a supernatural Being, one of the race of the gods. The heathen king, of course, could not recognize the true identity of the One before him. Some have thought that it was an angel who appeared in the furnace, but more likely we have to do with a pre-incarnate manifestation of the Son of God.

In the deliverance of the three a mighty miracle was performed by God. A miracle is an act, performed in the external world by the supernatural power of God, contrary to the ordinary course of nature (although not necessarily performed against the ordinary means of nature) and designed to be a sign or attestation. A miracle, therefore, is not to be regarded merely as a mighty work, but as a mighty work designed to attest God's redemptive purposes. The miraculous deliverance from the fiery furnace was designed to show the sovereignty of the true

God over the nation which had taken Israel captive. **29** Nebuchadrezzar acknowledges the superiority of Israel's God *for there is no other god who is able to deliver in this way.* Although he has advanced beyond what he said in 2:47, he has not yet spoken from a heart of true faith.

4:1-37 A SECOND DREAM INTERPRETED BY DANIEL

4:1-18 Nebuchadrezzar's dream

1-3 The doxology with which ch. 4 begins presents certain difficulties, since its language exhibits familiarity with biblical thought, and this would be strange, it is maintained, on the part of a heathen monarch. But it must be remembered that Daniel had exerted an influence upon the king, and the theocratic language of the edict is probably due to Daniel's influence.

4ff. Nebuchadrezzar states that he had dreamed a dream which the Chaldeans could not interpret, but Daniel *in whom is the spirit of the holy gods* interpreted the dream. This particular phrase may be paraphrased, 'that which pertains to true deity is to be found in Daniel'. Perhaps the reason why the king did not immediately summon Daniel was not that he had forgotten Daniel, but that he realized that the dream had to do with humiliation which he would suffer at the hands of Daniel's God. He wants to have nothing to do with Daniel's God, until driven to Him by extreme necessity.

The content of the dream is related in vv. 10-18. **10** *In the midst of the earth*; *i.e.* the tree occupied upon earth a central position so that it would attract attention. Evidently the king in this symbolism recognized himself. The language is that of paganism, for it is the king who speaks. Probably the king, in mentioning the vigilant, has reference to angels known to him from the Babylonian religion. **16** Here the stump of the tree is personified. Its heart is to be changed 'away from' that which is human. This is to be done until *seven times* (or periods of time, the length not being stated) *pass over him*. Since the length of the times is not stated, we are not warranted in identifying the duration in terms of years. **17** The king interprets the decree as of *the watchers*, but this pagan interpretation is repudiated by Daniel, who says that it is a decree of the Most High which has come upon the king (v. 24).

4:19-37 The interpretation and fulfilment of the dream

Upon hearing the dream Daniel was perplexed, for he himself wished the king well, but realized that the dream contained the announcement of a judgment upon the king from God. **19ff.** *For a moment*, not 'for a long time' as in some editions of RSV. The phrase is an idiom; AV's 'for one hour' is incorrect. We may render correctly 'for a moment'. Daniel then interprets the dream and advises the king as to what must be done if

the period of tranquillity before the judgment is to be lengthened (v. 27). It is generally assumed that, if Nebuchadrezzar repents, the threatened calamity will be averted. The text, however, does not mention an averting of the predicted judgment. The thought appears to be that the judgment threatened will come in order to bring Nebuchadrezzar to the knowledge of the true God (v. 25). However, if he repents of his sins he will enjoy a longer period of tranquillity.

27 Jerome and many following him have interpreted this verse as though it said, 'Redeem your sins by almsgiving, and your iniquities by showing mercy to the poor.' This of course teaches salvation by the merit of human works, and such a thought is foreign, not only to this verse, but to the entire Bible. Daniel's words do not mean 'Redeem your sins by almsgiving' but *break off* (*i.e.* 'cease') *your sins*, by means of doing righteously. In other words, we have to do here with a command to repent, to turn from evil and to do good. It is a perversion of the text to force it to teach the doctrine of salvation by human merit.

30 should be noted because it so accurately reflects Nebuchadrezzar's attitude. He was primarily a builder, rather than a warrior, and his own statements, preserved upon the cuneiform inscriptions, show his pride in the city and palace which he rebuilt. **31-33** The judgment came upon Nebuchadrezzar as predicted, and he was driven from men, acting like an animal, apparently suffering from the disease known as lycanthropy. **34-37** At the end of the predicted time the king's reason returned to him, and from a heart of faith he praised the true God.

Among the fragments in Qumran Cave IV (1955) was an Aramaic fragment now called *The Prayer of Nabonidus*. It is regarded as coming from the second half of the 1st century BC. On this fragment the speaker identifies himself as Nbny (probably Nabonidus), king of Assyria and Babylonia, and claims that for 7 years he was struck with an evil inflammation. When he confessed his sins, a Jew of the exile explained matters to him. The writer of this fragment, it would seem, has confused matters, attributing to Nabonidus the illness of Nebuchadrezzar. His ignorance of history appears in his identifying Nabonidus as king both of Assyria and Babylonia, whereas Nabonidus was king only of Babylonia.

5:1-30 BELSHAZZAR'S FEAST AND THE MYSTERIOUS HANDWRITING

The fifth chapter of Daniel, although it has often been attacked as inaccurate in its statements, is nevertheless noteworthy for its accuracy.

There was a time when the name Belshazzar proved to be a difficulty to expositors since his name was not known from the monuments. Hence, while some sought by various means to identify him, others denied his existence altogether. However, the name of the king, as the subsequent discussion will point out, has been found upon cuneiform tablets, and there can be no question about his historicity. The Bible is thus shown to be accurate in its mention of Belshazzar. **1** *King Belshazzar*. This statement has been criticized (most ably by Prof. H. H. Rowley, 'The Historicity of the Fifth Chapter of Daniel' in *JTS*, Vol. XXXII, pp. 12–31), since Belshazzar never reigned as sole king, and is never designated as king (*sharru*) in the cuneiform inscriptions. Furthermore, it is maintained that there is no evidence to show that Belshazzar ever ruled upon the throne as a subordinate to Nabonidus his father. In reply to these charges we may note, first of all, that the Aramaic word *malka* ('king') need not have the connotation of monarch or sole king (see R. D. Wilson, *Studies in the Book of Daniel*, 1917, pp. 83–95). Furthermore, one of the cuneiform documents expressly states that Nabonidus entrusted the kingship to Belshazzar. Now, it follows that if a kingship has been entrusted to a man and that man administers the affairs of the kingship, he is acting as a king. It is precisely that which Belshazzar did. Although on the cuneiform documents Belshazzar is consistently designated 'son of the king', yet he is also set forth as performing regal functions (see *The Prophecy of Daniel*, pp. 115–118, for evidence). In all probability there was a co-regency between Nabonidus and Belshazzar in which Belshazzar occupied a subordinate position. Since, however, he was the man upon the throne with whom Israel had to do, he is designated king in the book of Daniel. No valid objection can be raised against this usage. *Great feast*. Here again we meet the accuracy of this chapter, for great feasts were characteristic of antiquity. The word *thousand* must evidently be considered as a round number, and serves to indicate the size of the banquet. It was the custom at oriental feasts for the king to sit on a raised platform, apart from the guests. So in the statement that Belshazzar drank *in front of the thousand* we have another instance of the accuracy of the chapter. **2** Nebuchadrezzar is said to be the *father* of Belshazzar, and since this seems not to have been so, some commentators have considered the text in error. However, since the use of the word 'father' in the Semitic languages was vague, there need not be an error here. The word 'father' was capable of being employed in at least eight different ways, and it may be that it is used here merely in the sense of ancestor. **5** *The plaster of the wall*. Excavations have shown that the palace wall did have a thin coating of painted plaster. This plaster was white, so that any dark object moving across it would stand out distinctly. **6, 7** By the sight of the hand, the king was startled out of his stupor of drunkenness, and he promised that the man who could read the writing would be made *the third ruler* (or 'Triumvir') *in the kingdom*. The word translated *third ruler* means 'one of three', and

these would include, in the order of authority, Nabonidus, Belshazzar, Daniel. The use of the word implies that Belshazzar himself was only second in the kingdom. It is a mark of accuracy such as would be almost inconceivable if the book of Daniel were a product of the 2nd century BC. **10** *And the queen said*. This fact of the queen addressing the king also attests the remarkable accuracy of the present chapter. In Babylonia the queen mother held the highest rank in the royal house. **13** Because of her intervention Daniel is summoned. **17–23** He rejects the king's rewards and preaches to the king concerning his wickedness. **24–28** He then proceeds to interpret the strange writing. Each of the words is explained and then applied: MENE, 'numbered', *i.e.* God has numbered (Aram. $m^e n\bar{a}$') the days of the kingdom; TEKEL, a 'shekel', used both as a coin and as a weight, indicated that Belshazzar was weighed (in the balances) and found deficient; PERES, 'division', your kingdom is divided ($p^e r\bar{e}s$) and given to the Medes and Persians ($p\bar{a}r\bar{a}s$). The word $p\bar{a}r\bar{a}s$ would seem to point out that the Persians were the dominant power to whom Babylon would fall. When Daniel read the writing he read *and* PARSIN (v. 25), but in giving the interpretation he employed the form PERES (v. 28). The Aramaic conjunction 'and' is *u*, after which *p* becomes *ph*; hence AV's *upharsin*. *Parsîn* is a plural form, whereas $p^e r\bar{e}s$ is singular. We have thus a play upon words in which the basic idea of division is linked with the name of the conqueror.

5:31 – 6:28 DANIEL IN THE LIONS' DEN

5:31 really belongs to ch. 6, and is so treated here. The mention of *Darius the Mede* constitutes a problem, since Darius is unknown from secular history. Attempts have been made to identify him with Cambyses, Astyages, Cyaxares and Gobryas, but, in the present writer's opinion, these attempts are not convincing. The period of the downfall of Babylon is somewhat obscure, and it is possible that Darius was some hitherto unknown figure, who may have been entrusted with the kingship by Cyrus. Recently two scholarly attempts have been made to identify Darius the Mede. John C. Whitcomb (*Darius the Mede*, 1959) distinguishes Gubaru from the Gobryas of the Behistun Inscription and holds that he and Darius are identical. D. J. Wiseman (in *Notes on Some Problems in the Book of Daniel*, pp. 9–16) argues for an identification of Darius with Cyrus the Great. One can no longer say that it is not possible to identify Darius or that the writer of Daniel conceived, as has been charged, of a separately existing Median Empire after the fall of Babylon. Darius is said to be a Mede merely because he was of Median ancestry; it is not stated that he was king of the Medes. In this very context (5:28) the Medes and Persians are brought together, and in 6:8 'the law of the Medes and the Persians' (not merely the Medes) is mentioned. All the evidence in the book of Daniel points to the fact that the kingdom which followed Babylonia was Medo-Persia and not the Medes alone.

6:1 Darius appointed 120 *satraps* or 'kingdom-protectors' to care for the newly conquered country. The statement is not out of harmony with secular history. **3** Since Daniel in his position distinguished himself, jealousy appeared among the others and they sought a means of destroying him. **6** *Came by agreement*; better than AV, RSV mg. It gives the sense that they acted in harmony. **7** *Makes petition*; *i.e.* a religious request, since the king would be regarded as the sole representative of deity. Many critics, since they regard such an action as impossible during the days of the Persian kings, believe this account to be unhistorical. However, while there may be difficulties in the account, at the same time the king may very well have been overcome by the subtle flattery of the proposal and so yielded to it. The foolish and wicked action of the king, however, did not cause Daniel to be unfaithful to God. **10** In continuing to pray, Daniel was not guilty of ostentation, but evidently so prayed that he would be found out only by those who were willing to spy on him.

16ff. Objections have been raised against the account of the *den of lions* which have been based upon the assumption that the den must have been constructed in a particular way. In all probability there was an opening at the top through which Daniel had been lowered into the den, and through which the king later spoke with Daniel, and also an opening at the side through which the lions were fed. It was probably such a side entrance which was closed by the stone and seal; the entrance at the top was evidently too high for any man to escape through it.

24 In the punishment of the accusers we need not assume, as some commentators have, that 120 satraps, together with their wives and children, were cast into the den. The body of accusers was likely rather small, and these, as instigators of the attack upon Daniel, were doubtless the ones who were punished. Note the phrase, *those men who had accused* (*i.e.* 'slandered') *Daniel*, which seems to single out the guilty from the rest. We must not assume that the author of this noble account would introduce into it an absurdity, such as would be the case if all the satraps and their families had been thrown into the den, and were said to be in the power of the lions before reaching the bottom of the pit.

The accuracy of the account should be stressed, since it was in accordance with Persian custom to punish the relatives of a man because of his crime. **28** The chapter closes with the statement of Daniel's prospering *during the reign of Darius and the reign of Cyrus the Persian*. The designation of Cyrus shows that he was of different racial ancestry from Darius, who was a Mede. The kingdom, however, over which both reigned was

the same; there was not first a Median and then a Persian kingdom. It was one kingdom, administered first by a Mede and then by a Persian.

7:1-28 DANIEL'S VISION OF THE FOUR BEASTS

7:1-14 The vision described

The subject of this chapter is the same as that of ch. 2. **1** The dream which Daniel saw and the *visions of his head* were not those which originated in his head or brain, but rather those which came to his head and were intellectually apprehended. The dream and visions were special, divinely-imposed revelations, as the remainder of the chapter assumes. We are dealing, then, not with an ordinary dream of Daniel's, but with a revelation from God.

2 In the dream *the four winds of heaven were stirring up* (RV 'brake forth') *the great sea*. The sea represents humanity (*cf.* v. 17); it is not the Mediterranean or any particular sea that is intended, but simply the vast, limitless deep. The four cardinal winds symbolize heavenly powers, and these heavenly powers set the nations of the world in motion.

4 The first beast to arise from the sea corresponds to the head of gold of the image (*cf.* 2:32). The symbolism of the *lion* and *eagles' wings* represents Babylon, as may be seen from Je. 4:7; 49:19; Hab. 1:8; Ezk. 17:3. It is difficult to see how a writer, living long after the destruction of the Babylonian Empire, could have learned of this imagery. Babylon is represented by the most kingly of creatures. The change which came upon the beast evidently has reference to the event of Nebuchadrezzar's madness and his subsequent restoration. Both outwardly and inwardly, a humanizing process takes place.

5 The second beast to arise from the sea has a double-sided aspect. The feet on one side were raised for the purpose of going forward, whereas the feet on the other side were not thus raised. The beast is commanded to devour the flesh which is already in its mouth. Attempts have been made to identify the *three ribs*, but it is probably best to regard the number as a round one and not to seek for specific identifications.

6 The third beast which arises from the sea is a *leopard* or 'panther', an animal noted for speed and agility. *On its back*; the phrase may also be rendered 'on its sides', and it may be that, like the representations of winged beasts from Babylon, the beast had wings on its sides. The wings evidently denote swiftness. *Four heads*. These stand not for the four Persian kings mentioned in Dn. 11:2, nor for the four successors of Alexander's conquests, but rather, in order to symbolize the universal character of the kingdom, for the four corners of the earth. In Dn. 2:39 it was stated that this kingdom 'shall rule over all the earth'.

7 The fourth beast is introduced with particular solemnity. It is nondescript, for in the animal realm its likeness could not be found. The description stresses the beast's destructive character. *Different*. In the Aramaic a participle is employed, which we may translate 'was acting differently'. There are three points in the appearance of this fourth beast which call for special notice: first, the beast itself is mentioned; second, the ten horns upon the beast's head; and third, the little horn. It would seem, therefore, that, because of the order of statement, we have to do with the unfolding of a history. **8** After beholding the beast, Daniel was contemplating the horns, and then beheld *another horn, a little one*. The horn is described as 'little', but constantly acted as though it were big. Thus a contrast appears. This little horn does not grow in size, as does that mentioned in ch. 8. The description of the horn as little serves to call attention to the eyes and the mouth, which speaks blasphemous and presumptuous things against God.

9 introduces a heavenly scene of judgment. *Were placed*; the thought is that the thrones were placed in preparation for the judgment. *Ancient of days*; the literal meaning of the phrase is 'one advanced in days'. The Figure upon the throne therefore was that of an aged, venerable Person. The symbolism is intended to signify that God is seated upon the throne, ready to pronounce judgment. **10, 11** The scene of judgment is majestically conceived, and the tenseness with which one anticipates the pronouncement of judgment is heightened by the fact that throughout the preparation of the scene Daniel hears the mouth of the little horn speaking presumptuous things. In the vision the judgment falls first upon the fourth beast, a judgment which utterly destroys it. When the little horn is destroyed, then the power of the fourth kingdom disappears entirely. **12** The first three beasts which were seen in the vision lose their power to rule, but are nevertheless allowed to continue alive until the coming of the time which God had determined.

13 introduces a new aspect to the scene, for the judgment is not concluded by the destruction of the beasts but includes also the establishment of the kingdom of *a son of man. With the clouds*; i.e. in accompaniment with the clouds. This description is intended to express the deity of Him who comes with the clouds, for it is a symbolism expressive of judgment (*cf.* Is. 19:1; Pss. 104:3; 18:10–18; Mt. 24:30; Mk. 13:26; Rev. 1:7). Read *a son of man*, not 'the Son of man', as AV. It is a figure in human form, as distinguished from the beasts which represented the four kingdoms of men. It is not explicitly stated that the figure was a man, but that he was the likeness of a man. Thus, he is a human-like Personage, and so distinguished from the beasts which arose from the sea. The heavenly figure is escorted majestically before the Ancient of Days; **14** and an eternal and universal kingdom is given to Him.

It is now necessary to inquire as to the interpretation of the vision. Three views may be noted.

a. Among scholars who do not hold to the Danielic authorship of the book it is generally thought that the four beasts which arise from the sea stand for the following kingdoms: Babylon, Media, Persia and Greece. Since such an order of kingdoms never occurred historically, it is consequently assumed that at this point the book of Daniel is guilty of a historical error. There are several arguments adduced by those who favour the identification of the kingdoms just mentioned. For one thing it is maintained that if Rome, instead of Greece, is intended by the fourth beast, then the prophecy does not agree with history. When in AD 476 the historical Roman Empire came to an end, ten kingdoms did not arise from it. Therefore, it is argued, the fourth beast does not signify Rome. In opposition to this line of reasoning, however, it may be said that the number ten is not to be pressed and taken literally; it is a round number, and the symbolism of the ten horns merely has reference to a second phase in the history of the beast. It may further be pointed out that those who see in the fourth beast a reference to Greece have great difficulty also in identifying ten kings or kingdoms. In fact, such identification cannot be made. Attempts are usually made to discover ten *successive* kings after the death of Alexander, whereas the emphasis of the symbolism of the ten horns is not upon succession but upon contemporaneity; the ten horns exist during a second phase of the beast's history.

It is further maintained that the little horn of ch. 7 is to be identified with the little horn of ch. 8. Now this latter horn is expressly identified (8:23) as a king who shall arise from Greece, and therefore it is concluded that the little horn of ch. 7 must also arise from Greece and hence the fourth beast must represent Greece and not Rome. However, in reply to this two things may be said. In the first place, the description of the little horn of ch. 7 and that of the horn of ch. 8 show beyond any shadow of a doubt that they are not intended to be identified. If anyone will list the characteristics of each of these horns and will note carefully what is said about each, he will be impressed with the dissimilarity of the two. Secondly, if one will compare carefully all that is said in ch. 7 concerning the nondescript beast (v. 7) with the description of the he-goat (Greece) in ch. 8, he will discover how essentially different the two are. They differ with respect to origin, nature and destiny.

It is also argued that Darius is portrayed as a Median who ruled after Belshazzar and before Cyrus. However, such a charge is not quite accurate; nowhere in Daniel is it stated that Darius ruled before Cyrus. Furthermore, it has been claimed that Darius is called a Median and Cyrus a Persian, and thus a racial distinction is emphasized. However, the racial distinction has to do with the men themselves and not with the kingdom over which they reigned, which kingdom in the book of Daniel is the kingdom of the Chaldeans. Lastly, it has been argued that according to Dn. 5:28 the kingdom is to be divided between the Medes and Persians.

With respect to these arguments it should be noted that although Darius is identified as a Mede, it does not at all follow that the empire over which he ruled was Median. Such a deduction is a *non sequitur*. Also, when it is said that the kingdom will be divided (5:28), the meaning is that its present form (the form which it had when Belshazzar was king) would be broken and it would be given to the enemy, the Medes and Persians. The verse does not mean that part of the kingdom will be given to the Medes and part to the Persians. In the light of the above considerations, therefore, we feel constrained to reject the identity of the four beasts which finds Greece represented by the fourth beast. (Note: The student who wishes to read a capable defence of the identification outlined above should procure H. H. Rowley's *Darius the Mede and the Four World Empires*, 1935. For the conservative position see *The Prophecy of Daniel*, pp. 275–294.)

Advocates of the position outlined above find the identification of the heavenly Figure like a Son of man in the people of Israel, 'the saints of the Most High'. In support of this interpretation appeal is made to 7:18, 27 where it is stated that the kingdom is given to the saints. However, the saints receive it as a trust from the Son of man to hold it for ever. The Son of man is presented as a supernatural Figure and therefore He is not to be identified with the saints. Rather, they as kings reign in His kingdom.

b. The second interpretation is that held by the dispensationalist school of thought. This agrees with the traditional view in identifying the kingdoms as Babylon, Medo-Persia, Greece and Rome. It is believed, however, that there will be a revived Roman Empire which will be divided into ten kingdoms, and so the ten horns of the beast are compared with the ten toes of the image in ch. 2. This ten-kingdom period is said to occur after the return of Christ for His people. The little horn signifies a prince of the revived Roman Empire who will be satanically inspired. We must, however, leave the detailed discussion of this view for consideration in connection with 9:24–27.

c. The interpretation which the present writer believes to be correct is the following. Since the four beasts arise from the sea (mankind), they therefore represent kingdoms which are of human origin and consequently are both temporal and non-universal. The first beast stands for Babylonia. The second, as its double-sided character shows, stands for Medo-Persia, and not for Media alone. The third represents Greece. The fourth beast itself symbolizes the historical Roman Empire.

As for the ten horns, they stand for kingdoms which are to exist during the second phase of the beast's history. It does not necessarily follow that these kingdoms must arise *immediately* after

the downfall of Rome, but only that they may be able to trace their origin back to Rome. They are contemporary only in the sense that they exist during this particular period; they need not be actual contemporaries.

As this second period comes to a close a third period is introduced by the appearance of the little horn. From the symbolism it is not possible to tell whether this little horn represents a man, a government, a coalition of governments or an ideology. He will oppose the saints until the judgment of God brings about the complete destruction of the fourth beast.

The kingdom given to the Son of man is not of human, but of divine origin, and is both universal and eternal. The heavenly Figure does not represent the saints, but, as the symbolism shows, is a divine Personage. It was this vision that our Lord had in mind when He referred to Himself as the Son of man.

7:15–28 The interpretation of the vision

15 *As for me, Daniel, my spirit within me was anxious.* In the vision itself Daniel introduces himself in order to show how he was affected by what he had seen. 18 *The saints of the Most High*; not the Jews in distinction from the heathen, but the redeemed, *i.e.* true believers, who are to be a kingdom of priests, a holy nation (*cf.* Ex. 19:6). They do not found the kingdom themselves but receive it as a trust from the Son of man, to whom the kingdom was given. 22 *Judgment was given.* This verse expresses the ultimate outcome of the war which the little horn wages against the people of God. The judgment is one which God makes on behalf of His people, so that they are in eternal and secure possession of the kingdom. 25 *A time, two times, and half a time.* These words characterize the intensity of the little horn's persecution. The length of period indicated by the word *time* is not stated, and consequently we are not warranted in identifying it as a year. The expression itself is chronologically indefinite, yet the meaning is quite clear. The power of the little horn will appear for *a time*, and then for *two times*. Thus there is expressed symbolically a doubling of the intensity of the little horn's power. It would seem that this power would continue to grow, and we should expect this to be signified by the words 'four times', thus making a total of seven, symbolizing complete and perfect triumph upon the part of the persecutor. Instead, however, we find mention of *half a time*, and thus learn of the sudden end of the power of the little horn, an end brought about, we believe, by divine judgment and the return of the Lord from heaven.

8:1–27 DANIEL'S VISION OF THE RAM AND THE HE-GOAT

8:1–14 The vision described

2 *Susa the capital*; RV mg. 'Shushan the castle'. Susa, the capital of Persia, in the OT is constantly

designated the 'fortress'. We are not to think of Daniel as actually present in Persia and beholding the vision there, but rather while beholding the vision he was present in the vision in Susa. **3** *A ram.* The ram with the two horns represents Medo-Persia (see v. 20). **4** The butting of the ram symbolizes the rapid conquests of the Persian kings. **5** *A he-goat*; this stands for Greece (see v. 21), and the *conspicuous horn* represents the first king, *i.e.* Alexander (see v. 21). **7** The symbolism of the he-goat smiting the ram signifies the Grecian conquest of Medo-Persia. **8** *The great horn was broken.* By this the death of Alexander is symbolized. The four horns which arose in its place represent the four kingdoms into which Alexander's empire was broken, viz. Macedonia, Thrace, Syria and Egypt. **9** The horn which comes forth is not actually described as little, but is said to have 'gone forth from littleness'; *i.e.* the state of being little. From small beginnings the horn then grew to great power. *The glorious land* is a designation of Canaan, the promised land (*cf.* Je. 3:19). **10** *Host of heaven*; *i.e.* the stars (*cf.* Je. 33:22); the symbolism has reference to the saints, who are the objects of attack. **11** *The Prince*; *i.e.* God Himself. The 'acting greatly' (*magnified itself*) toward God consisted in the removal of the temple sacrifices. **14** The length of the desolation which the horn causes is stated as *for two thousand and three hundred evenings and mornings.* The figures given do not mean 1,150 days, but, as the AV translates, 2,300 days. The expression evening-morning (probably based upon Gn. 1) means a day. This entire period of the abominations of Antiochus would extend from about 171 BC to 165 BC, and then the sanctuary would be restored.

8:15–27 The interpretation of the vision

15 As Daniel in his mind was seeking to understand the vision an angel in the likeness of a man stood before him. **19** *The appointed time of the end* refers not to the end of all things, nor to the final judgment, but to the end of the time when afflictions will fall upon Israel. *The latter end of the indignation*; *i.e.* the end of the period when indignation has fallen upon God's people. It is the period of the appearance of Antiochus Epiphanes. **23** *Of bold countenance*; *i.e.* one of unyielding countenance; the reference is to Antiochus. *Understands riddles*; *i.e.* one who was a master of dissimulation. **25** *By no human hand.* It is God who will bring to an end the power of the tyrant.

9:1–23 DANIEL'S PRAYER

2 *Books.* This term evidently has reference to the Scriptures. From the study of Jeremiah Daniel learns that the period of exile will endure for 70 years (Je. 25:12). He therefore turns to the Lord in supplication because of the sins of his people. **4–14** Daniel makes acknowledgment of Israel's guilt, and in this acknowledgment includes himself. **15–19** constitute a plea

for God's mercy and forgiveness. **20–23** While Daniel is still engaged in prayer Gabriel comes from God to make Daniel wise in understanding.

9:24–27 THE PROPHECY OF THE SEVENTY SEVENS

This remarkable section declares that a definite period of time has been decreed by God for the accomplishment of the restoration of His people from bondage. The general theme, viz. the decreeing of a period of seventy sevens, is stated in v. 24, and the details are worked out in the three subsequent verses. It will be necessary to discuss the meaning of practically every word in this brief section.

24 *Seventy weeks of years.* The word which is usually translated *weeks* is more accurately rendered 'sevens'. It means a period divided into sevens, the precise length of this 'besevened' period not being stated. The word comes first in the Hebrew, and we may paraphrase, 'a period of sevens, in fact, seventy of them'. *Are decreed*; *i.e.* the sevens were decreed by God as the period in which the Messianic redemption was to be accomplished. *Concerning*; *i.e.* with respect to Daniel's people and Jerusalem, the holy city. The revelation of this decreed period thus has direct reference to Daniel's prayer. The time of the exile is almost concluded, what then lies in store for God's people? In answer it is revealed that with respect to these people a period of seventy sevens has been determined in which their salvation is to be accomplished.

The seventy sevens have been determined for the express purpose of bringing about six results, three of which are negative and three positive. *To finish* (RV mg. 'to restrain') *the transgression*; transgression which hitherto has lain open and bare is to be sealed up and put away, so that it may no longer be considered as in existence. *To put an end to sin, and to atone for iniquity.* The language implies that a necessary sacrifice will be offered, upon the basis of which iniquity will be forgiven. Thus, the negative result to be obtained is the abolition of the curse which separates God from man. The nature of this curse appears in the use of the words transgression, sin and iniquity (*cf.* on Ps. 32:5).

The three positive results are now described. *To bring in everlasting righteousness.* This righteousness is to be brought in from without, *i.e.* from God through the Messiah. The expression corresponds with the first; the transgression is removed and in its place is introduced the everlasting righteousness of God which, as we learn from the NT, is received by the believer through faith alone. *To seal both vision and prophet.* The reference is to the OT dispensation, during which the prophet was the representative of God before the nation, and the vision was one of the means by which God made known His revelation to the prophets. A prophet was an Israelite who was raised up by God as an accredited spokesman, to deliver God's words to the people. God made His will known to the prophets by means of dreams and visions (see Nu. 12:1–8). The entire prophetic institution was typical of the great Prophet to come, and, since it was under Moses, partook of the preparatory character of the OT age. When this method of revelation ceased, the OT dispensation itself was at an end, and it is this which is signified by the sealing of vision and prophet. *To anoint a most holy place.* This difficult phrase, which literally translated is 'a holiness of holinesses', apparently has reference to the enduing of the Messiah with the Spirit of the Lord. It will thus be seen that the six objects to be accomplished are all Messianic, and it may be noted that when our Lord ascended to heaven every one of these purposes had been fulfilled.

In vv. 25–27 the details of the period of seventy sevens are set forth. 25 states the beginning of the period and the length of time until the appearance of the Messiah. Daniel is commanded to *know* and to *understand* the message. *From the going forth of the word.* The text is referring to 'the going forth of a word' from God, not to the issuing of an edict on the part of a Persian monarch. At the same time the effects of the going forth of this word appeared in human history, and this was during the first year of Cyrus, when he permitted the Jews to return to their land. The *terminus a quo*, therefore, of the seventy sevens, was the year 538–537 BC. This word which proceeded from God had reference to restoring the city of Jerusalem to its former condition. *To the coming of an anointed one, a prince*; *i.e.* one who is both anointed and also a prince, or, in other words, one who is priest and prince. There is only One to whom these words may apply, even Jesus who is the Christ. From the *terminus a quo* of the prophecy until the appearance of an anointed one is said to be 'seven sevens and sixty-two sevens'. It is possible that the seven sevens stand for the period between the first return from exile under Zerubbabel and the completion of the work of Ezra and Nehemiah, and the sixty-two sevens for the period between that time and the first advent of Jesus Christ. The sevens should be regarded as symbolic numbers.

26 deals with that which is to take place after the expiration of the sixty-two sevens. Two events are mentioned, but it is not stated whether these are to occur during the seventieth seven or not, nor how long after the expiration of the sixty-two sevens they will be. In the first place it is said that an *anointed one* (AV 'Messiah') will *be cut off.* This anointed one is be identified with the anointed one of v. 25. The reference is to the death of Christ, who was 'cut off' by crucifixion. *And shall have nothing.* By this expression the utter rejection of the Christ, both by man and God, is set forth.

Secondly this verse mentions the fate of *the city and the sanctuary* (*i.e.* Jerusalem and the Temple), which are to be destroyed by *the people of the prince who is to come.* This seems to be a clear prophecy of the destruction of Jerusalem under Titus Vespasianus. *To the end, i.e.* of the destruction, war and desolation will continue.

27 *And he shall make a strong covenant*; better translated 'he shall cause the covenant to prevail'. The Hebrew words are unusual. They are sometimes interpreted as though they meant simply 'to make a covenant'. Such an interpretation, however, is incorrect, for it does not do justice to the original which can only mean to cause a covenant 'to prevail', or 'to make a covenant firm'. The implication is that the covenant is already in existence and that its terms and conditions are now to be made effective. Who is the one that causes the covenant to prevail? Many find the subject in 'the prince who is to come' of v. 26, and refer this, either to Antiochus, or to the Roman ruler of a future, revived Roman Empire. However, the word prince is there in a subordinate position, and it is very unlikely that this word should be the subject in v. 27. It is better to regard the subject as the Messiah, since He has been the most prominent Person in this passage. The covenant which is to prevail is the covenant of grace wherein the Messiah, by His life and death, obtains salvation for His people. The seventieth seven (a symbolical number) thus has reference to the time of our Lord's earthly life. *For half of* this seven the Messiah, by means of His death, causes the Jewish sacrifices to cease (*cf.* Heb. 8:13).

Upon the wing of abominations shall come one who makes desolate. As a result or consequence of the death of the Messiah, one making desolate (*i.e.* the Roman prince Titus) appears *upon the wing of abominations.* We may understand *wing* to signify the pinnacle of the Temple. *Cf.* the use of the Greek *pterugion* (from *pterux*, 'wing') for 'pinnacle' in Lk. 4:9. As to the description of the Temple itself (or this part of it) as *abominations*, those who associate the passage with the activities of Antiochus Epiphanes understand it to refer to his installing of heathen rites and emblems in the Temple (*cf.* 1 Macc. 1:54, 59; see J. A. Montgomery, *A Critical and Exegetical Commentary on the Book of Daniel*, 1927, *in loc.*), but it is hard to see how this event, confined as it was to the altar (see reference in 1 Macc.), would justify the specifying of the *wing*, or pinnacle. We understand, therefore, that it is the Temple itself which, following the rending of the veil (Mk. 15:38) and the consequent end of its function in the divine plan (*cf.* Heb. 10:8–18), became abominable and unacceptable to the Lord (*cf. The Prophecy of Daniel, in loc.*). By this language the complete destruction of the Temple is signified. This state of destruction will continue *even until the consummation* or 'full end', which has been determined by God, has been poured upon the desolate (*i.e.* the ruins of Jerusalem and the Temple).

This prophecy of the seventy sevens is one of the most difficult in the entire OT, and although the interpretations are almost legion, we shall confine ourselves to the discussion of three which may be regarded as of particular importance.

a. Those who do not hold to the absolute trustworthiness and divine authority of the Scriptures refer the passage to Antiochus Epiphanes. The desolation described in v. 27 is therefore one caused by Antiochus; the anointed one of v. 25 is usually thought to be the priest Onias III, and the entire passage is deprived of any Messianic character. The objections to this type of interpretation, however, are so serious that it cannot possibly be regarded as correct.

b. A very widespread interpretation today is that of the dispensationalist school of thought. The advocates of this view naturally differ among themselves in some respects, but their position is essentially as follows.

The beginning of the seventy sevens is usually taken to be the twentieth year of Artaxerxes, which is said to be 445 BC (see Ne. 2). The period of seven sevens refers to the restoration from exile and the rebuilding of Jerusalem, and the period of sixty-two sevens carries one on to the triumphal entry of Christ. This school interprets the sevens as 'weeks', each 'week' consisting of seven years and the total comprising 490 years.

The promises made in v. 24, however, according to this view, were not fulfilled at Christ's first advent, and the seventieth seven does not immediately follow the sixty-ninth. Instead there intervenes a long parenthesis which is known as 'the church age', a time that was not revealed to the OT prophets. When this parenthesis has run its course Jesus Christ will return for His people, and the seventieth seven (seven years in length) will begin. *Cf.* notes in *The Scofield Reference Bible* and, for a general presentation of a dispensational interpretation, see Robert D. Culver, *Daniel and the Latter Days,* 1954.

The seventieth seven, then (*i.e.* a week of seven years), will begin to run its course when Christ returns. His people will be taken up into the air with Him while the events of the seventieth seven transpire. The prince of v. 26 will make a covenant with many Jews for one seven. In return for allegiance to himself he will permit them to erect their Temple and perform sacrifices. In the midst of the seven (*i.e.* after 3½ years) he will violate the covenant, and a fierce persecution will break out which will last for the remaining 3½ years of the seven, when Christ will return with His saints to reign for 1,000 years. From the exposition outlined above it will be seen that the present writer considers that the difficulties which this view entails are very great.

Two points of difficulty in particular must be noted. i. The verb translated 'he shall make a strong covenant' does not refer to the making of a covenant, but to the causing of a covenant to prevail or to be strong (see *The Prophecy of Daniel* for discussion). The covenant is already in existence. ii. On the dispensationalist view the antecedent of 'he' in 'he shall make a strong

covenant' is said to be the prince of v. 26, which prince is Titus. If this is so, then the 'he' of v. 27 must refer to Titus and not to the prince of a revived Roman Empire as dispensationalism claims.

c. The traditional Messianic interpretation entails less difficulty than do the others and at the same time does justice to the language of the text. Upon this view the seventy sevens serve as a symbolical number for the period that has been decreed for the accomplishment of the Messianic salvation (v. 24). In v. 25 we are taught that two segments of time elapse from the issuing of a word from God to rebuild Jerusalem until the appearance of Christ. After these two segments have elapsed, the Messiah will be cut off by death and Jerusalem and the Temple will be destroyed by the Roman armies of Titus. The Messiah, however, will cause the Jewish sacrifice to cease by means of His death, and He will do this in the midst of the seventieth seven. As a consequence, the Temple will be destroyed, and the destruction will continue until the end appears which has been appointed by God. The precise point of termination of the period of seventy sevens is not revealed. The emphasis, rather, is not so much upon the beginning and termination of this period as it is upon the great results which the period has been set apart to accomplish.

10:1 – 11:1 THE VISION OF GOD

1 The revelation recorded in this chapter was given to Daniel in *the third year of Cyrus,* which shows that he continued in Babylon even beyond the time mentioned in 1:21. Why he did not return to Palestine with Zerubbabel is not stated. It may be noted that Daniel mentions his Babylonian name *Belteshazzar,* apparently out of a desire, now that the Babylonian Empire has been overthrown, to preserve his identity among his own people.

And it was a great conflict. In all probability the meaning is 'for a long time', since the word *ṣābā',* which is translated *conflict,* has now been found on the tablets from Mari in the sense of 'time'. At the time when the revelation was made to Daniel he was engaged in mourning, doubtless occasioned by reflection upon the sins of his own people. **5** *Behold, a man;* the revelation is a theophany or pre-incarnate appearance of the eternal Son. The language of the description reminds one of the language of Ezk. 1 (*cf.* also Rev. 1:13–15). The vision produced upon Daniel an effect of weakness (v. 8).

11 *O Daniel, man greatly beloved. Cf.* 9:23. By the assurance that he is beloved of God Daniel is encouraged and prepared to hear the message, which, he is told, has to do with the *latter days* (v. 14), *i.e.* the Messianic age. **20** It is first related that the Speaker will *fight against the prince of Persia* (*i.e.* the spiritual power behind the gods of Persia), and when the Speaker is victorious (*when I am through with him, i.e.*

victorious from the struggle), the prince of Greece will next come and must be opposed. **21, 11:1** Only Michael is at hand to help, even as, in the first year of Darius the Mede, the Speaker helped him (*cf.* v. 13). Thus, there are to be severe trials in store for God's people.

11:2–20 THE REVELATION OF THE FUTURE

2 means that three kings are to arise after Cyrus and the fourth after them will arouse all the kingdom of Greece. The kings therefore must be Cyrus, three yet to stand—Cambyses, Smerdis and Darius Hystaspis—and the fourth, Xerxes. **3, 4** *A mighty king*; *i.e.* Alexander the Great. When Alexander has come to power, his kingdom shall be broken. When he died in Babylon he was but 32 years of age. At his death his twelve generals divided the gains among themselves. For a time Aridaeus, a guardian of one of Alexander's children, ruled, but soon the Empire was broken up into four divisions.

5 *The king of the south*; *i.e.* the king of Egypt (*cf.* v. 8). The dynasty which ruled in Egypt after the breaking up of Alexander's kingdom was known as Ptolemaic, whereas that which ruled in Syria was known as Seleucid. The king of the south is Ptolemy Soter (322–305 BC), and the prince mentioned is Seleucus. **6** *The daughter of the king*; *i.e.* Berenice, the daughter of Ptolemy, who married Antiochus II, yet was unable to maintain herself against a rival wife, Laodice. Antiochus finally divorced her and Laodice encouraged her sons to murder Berenice. **7** *A branch from her roots.* Berenice's brother (*i.e.* from her ancestry) will come against the army of the north and succeed in putting Laodice to death. The scripture then continues by relating the various struggles and wars between the Ptolemies and Seleucids until the appearance of Antiochus Epiphanes.

11:21 – 12:3 THE TIMES OF ANTIOCHUS AND THE ANTICHRIST

21 *A contemptible person.* With this language Antiochus Epiphanes is introduced. By means of flattery he won to himself the kings of Pergamus, and the Syrians gave in to him. He was a master of cunning and treachery, so that his contemporaries nicknamed him *Epimanes* ('madman') instead of the title which he himself assumed, *Epiphanes* ('illustrious'). **22** *The prince of the covenant.* The identification of this prince is not certain, but the language seems to refer to some prince who stood in covenant relation with Antiochus. **23** *He shall become strong*; a general statement of Antiochus' rise to power. **24** *Without warning*; RV 'in time of security'. When men think that all is secure he will slip in. He will take *the richest parts of the province* and fortresses of the land of Egypt.

25–28 describe Antiochus' first campaign against Egypt, a campaign in which the Egyptian Ptolemy could not stand because of the treachery of those who should have supported him. Antiochus (v. 27) shows hospitality toward his enemy, but actually violates the custom of oriental hospitality by means of lying words. On his return Antiochus sets his heart *against the holy covenant, i.e.* the land of Palestine.

29 describes another campaign against Egypt, which is the third. Apparently there had been yet another campaign on which the book of Daniel is silent. It should be noted, incidentally, that this entire account is related in the future. According to the writer these events had not yet taken place, but are to occur in the future. The account, therefore, purports to be true prophecy.

30 *He shall be afraid and withdraw, and shall turn back and be enraged.* The presence of the Romans caused Antiochus to leave Egypt and so, in rage, he turned his attention toward Palestine. On the sabbath Jerusalem was attacked, and a heathen altar was erected on the altar of burnt-offering. **32** Certain apostate Jews are perverted and serve to carry out the conqueror's designs, but many among the Jews, the true elect, suffered death rather than yield to Antiochus (*cf.* 1 Macc. 1:62). **33** At this time men of true faith were able to instruct others, although they should suffer greatly.

34 The *little help* which helped the faithful apparently refers to Judas Maccabaeus. Some of the wise who follow him will stumble because of the severity of the persecution. At the same time Judas's rebellion proved to be successful, and on December 25, 165 BC, the altar of the Temple was rededicated.

Vv. **36–45** are of peculiar interest. Many expositors believe that they continue the description of Antiochus. There is a difficulty in such a position, however, since the death of Antiochus was quite different from that which is here described. The interpretation which may be called traditional in the Christian church is to regard these verses as referring to the antichrist. Antiochus who persecuted the church shortly before the first advent of Christ may be regarded as typical of the antichrist who will persecute the church before the second advent of Christ.

36 states that the king will *magnify himself above every god*, a description which does not well apply to Antiochus. **37** Likewise it is difficult to see how Antiochus showed disrespect for the gods of his fathers. **40–45** The language teaches that at the end of the present age the antichrist will engage in fierce conflict. He will finally take a stand between the sea and *the glorious holy mountain* (*i.e.* Zion) where *he shall come to his end.*

12:1 When these events take place those who are *found written in the book* will be delivered. The reference is to the elect, those predestinated to everlasting life. The persecution of the antichrist will cause many to fall. Those who are written in the book, however, will be delivered.

2 This is true also of those *who sleep*. Many of them (the reference is to those who have died during the tribulation—not to all who are dead) shall arise, some to everlasting life and some to eternal reproaches. The reference here is not to the general resurrection but rather to the fact that salvation will be not only for those who were alive but also for some who lost their lives during the persecution.

12:4-13 THE CONCLUSION OF THE PROPHECY

Daniel is commanded to protect the words just revealed until the time of the end. The knowledge of God's purposes is in the world in the Scriptures, and men shall travel to and fro in vain, not seeking in the one place where the truth may be found. **7** refers again to the length of antichrist's power and to his end (see on 7:25). The numbers of vv. 11 and 12 must be taken symbolically, the 1,290 days symbolizing the period of Antiochus' persecution, and the 1,335 days apparently symbolize the whole period of persecution unto the consummation. He who endures throughout this period will be blessed. **13** Daniel himself is assured of his salvation, and that he shall stand in his lot at the end of the days. May this same destination be that of all who read these words!

EDWARD J. YOUNG

Hosea

INTRODUCTION

The birthplace of Hosea son of Beeri is still unknown. From his familiarity with life in northern Israel, certain alleged Aramaisms in his vocabulary and the phrase 'our king' in 7:5, it has been assumed he was from the northern kingdom, but this is conjectural.

The period of his ministry is defined in the title (1:1) which implies over 30 years' activity. References to anarchy and bloodshed suggest that Hosea prophesied during the turbulent days after the death of Jeroboam II, though there is no indication that he continued after the fall of Samaria in 722. Some think the reference in 1:1 to the kings of Judah a later insertion (see below). But since Hezekiah's co-regency began in 729 it is possible that Hosea was preaching in all these reigns. The historical background is to be found in 2 Ki. 14:23 – 20:21 ('Azariah' = 'Uzziah').

Hosea's message has characteristic features. His style is 'pointed, energetic and concise. He is laconic and sententious, so as often to be obscure' (Henry and Scott). Pithy sentences are marshalled into longer passages without losing their identity or power. The long biography (chs. 1 and 3) is evidently related to the whole prophecy, experience moulding expression. The metaphors of marriage and child-rearing reflect home life.

The covenant appears in different aspects. Faithlessness to the patriarchal covenant (1:10) and Sinai (6:7; 8:1) is reflected in human relations (10:4; 12:1). The climax of reconciliation is represented as a marriage covenant (2:16–22). Covenant-love (*ḥeseḏ*) is prominent. Two other words for love occur frequently: *'ahᵃḇâ*, affection for people, things and actions (including sexual attraction), *raḥᵃmîm*, pity for the helpless, like that of a parent for a child. *Ḥeseḏ*, translated 'steadfast love, kindness, mercy' is choice-love, involving strength, gentleness, zeal and perseverance to carry out the obligations of a contractual relationship. In early married life Hosea knew *'āhᵃḇâ* and *raḥᵃmîm*; it was later in reclaiming his wife that he learned *ḥeseḏ* too.

Knowing God as a Person is important to Hosea. In this (as in 'love') he is aptly called the 'St. John of the Old Testament'. He deplores the people's ignorance (4:1–6) and expresses God's desire for communion with man rather than for any mere sacrifice as such from him (6:6). This represents the crux of the prophecy. The sacrificial system, which was intended to remind the people of their obligations in the covenant both Godwards and manwards, had been outrageously abused. A false trust in the ordinances themselves as an antidote to godless conduct or a buttress to false repentance caused Hosea to lay bare the fact that sacrifices were a means and not an end. For further discussion of this see *in loc.*

Hope (despite allegations by Harper and others) is part of Hosea's message. Snaith asserts that 'no northerner could look forward to a unified nation'; but then what man could? Through divine revelation (1:2) the prophet preached the paradoxical doctrines of justification by faith.

Past events in the nation's history are often recalled by Hosea as an encouragement (*e.g.* 12:9; 13:4) or a reminder (*e.g.* 2:15; 10:9). Hosea attacked priests, leaders and people who refused Yahweh as God and as King.

There are fourteen references to Judah in Hosea, ten of them unfavourable. Some think there were editors 'Judaizing' the prophecy: one favourably after Sennacherib's withdrawal from Jerusalem in 701 BC, the other unfavourably after the fall of Jerusalem to Nebuchadrezzar in 586. S. L. Brown, however (*The Book of Hosea*, 1932), points out that no 8th-century prophet restricted himself to one kingdom. Each prophet occasionally cast a wistful glance at the sister kingdom; it would cause surprise if not (*cf.* 2 Ki. 17:19, 20). Moreover the eschatological figure of the bride (ch. 2) necessarily included Judah. It is unthinkable that God should preach such love only to part of His people.

Chs. 1–3 and the question of Gomer have long occupied interpreters. Many interpretations of 'wife of harlotry' (1:2) have been suggested: a harlot (despite other simpler terms); a sacred prostitute, even a local 'saint'; one who dressed like a harlot; one of an apostate or immoral nation; a participant in fertility rites; a northern Israelite; a woman of illegitimate birth; one with a tendency to harlotry. The first seems the most likely (*cf.* 3:3). Some protest that God could not have commanded Hosea to marry a harlot (or one who God knew would become so). But Hosea would not have married such a woman without a special command from the Lord. The command 'have children of harlotry' (1:2) implies such a mother from the start (*cf.* Heb. 11:31). After her marriage Gomer was probably faithful during the infancy of the three children, later falling into adultery (3:1) and probably slavery (3:2).

This suggests that chs. 1 and 3 are not parallel accounts of one event (third and first person forms respectively indicating different sources) but that ch. 3, as it does not mention children,

703

is a sequel describing an event many (Gordis says 20) years later. Ch. 3 refers in the first place to an adulteress, a faithless wife (3:1). It is most natural to take this chapter as Hosea's reclamation of his wife from degradation and the slavery which would follow her disinheritance when judicially separated. Of the three children only the first, Jezreel, is explicitly stated to be to Hosea (1:3); this does not call in question his paternity of the others—after all Jezreel was his heir. He was given only one command embracing all three children (1:2). Hosea certainly named the first and second children and most probably the third (1:4, 6, 9).

Chs. 1–3 have been variously interpreted but notably (1) as a non-historical allegory, possibly even a prophetic dream. There is no evidence to justify such a view especially as it would reflect on the prophet's own integrity. Also Gomer's name has no clear meaning from which an allegory would benefit. 2. Others think it historical but symbolic, that Hosea and Gomer enacted a didactic drama. This fails to account for the historical details, especially 1:2. 3. A simple historical record of obedience to God which resulted not only in a broken marriage which was restored, but in a prophecy which speaks the truth in love.

Attempts to alter the order of chs. 1–3 gain no advantage. The most convincing is M. Scott (*The Message of Hosea*, 1921, pp. 25–30) who places ch. 3 bodily between 1:9 and 10.

The text is often difficult to determine. Yet though the details may often be obscure the message as a whole is plain. Perhaps in God's providence, the text has remained doubtful, to emphasize the revealed certainties that are discoverable only by faith. Let us, like Jerome, echo Peter's prayer: 'Lord, explain to us this parable.'

OUTLINE OF CONTENTS

COMMENTARY

1:1 TITLE

This is the title of the whole book, naming the author, dating his ministry and above all setting a divine seal on his call. Hosea did not utter his own thoughts, or even seek the thoughts of God. *The word of the Lord came* to him by divine authority and initiative, the prophet's message pre-existing in the mind of God (*cf.* Joel 1:1 *et al.*; Lk. 3:2; Gal. 1:11, 12). *Hosea the son of Beeri.* 'Hosea' is a variant of Joshua (Nu. 13:16), meaning 'Yahweh saves' (*cf.* Mt. 1:21). Ironically Hoshea, another variant, was the name of the last usurper king of Israel (2 Ki. 17:1ff.).

Why did Hosea, whose prophecy is mainly to Israel, date his book first by the kings of Judah? Hosea's message is to both Judah and Israel, concerning judgment and mercy (see

Introduction). The end of Israel is nearer but Judah's turn will come. The dynasty of Judah is of the house of David to which the promises of God were made. Hosea recognizes the supremacy of the throne in Jerusalem, prophesying a Davidic king over the ultimately reunited nation (1:11; 3:5). Judah was the kingdom of the theocracy (E. B. Pusey, *The Minor Prophets*, 1907, p. 26). Why does only Jeroboam's name appear from the seven kings of Israel living during this time? Jeroboam II, though an evil king, was God's instrument for the good of Israel (2 Ki. 14:25–27), the last saving act of God to Israel. Years before God had promised Jehu that his sons of the fourth generation would sit on the throne of Israel (2 Ki. 10:30). Jeroboam II was the last king of Israel to be succeeded by his son. Zechariah, who was assassinated by Shallum, brought Jehu's promise to fulfilment (2 Ki. 15:12). Of the six kings after Jeroboam all either succeeded or were succeeded by assassination. Although 30 more years were to pass before the nation was finally deported, its fate was sealed by the end of the reign of Jeroboam II according to the word of the Lord.

1:2 – 3:5 HOSEA MEDITATES ON HIS CALL AND HIS MINISTRY

The relationship of Hosea's private life to his public ministry is too complex for neat analysis. The two co-exist: at one time the image of the home is distinct and that of the nation blurred; at another time the reverse is true. 'It is not always clear whether the prophet's experience with Gomer is teaching him about God, or whether he is learning about his wife from his understanding of Israel. The two run on parallel lines and flash a meaning across to each other' (J. B. Phillips, *Four Prophets*, 1963, p. 53).

1:2 – 2:1 His call

As this section is in the third person some think it was compiled after Hosea's death by his disciples. However, such autobiographical use of the third person is not unknown in Hebrew and other languages (*e.g.* 2 Ki. 5:25; *cf.* Ho. 1:2).

1:2, 3 The meaning of his marriage. 2 *When the Lord first spoke* . . . ; the threshold of Hosea's ministry, who was called before his marriage. The phrase resists the attempt of some to place ch. 3 before ch. 1. *Through Hosea* could be variously construed: 'by Hosea', an ellipsis for 'by the hand (or mouth) of Hosea' as the agent; 'in Hosea', suggesting the assimilation of God's message first by the prophet: 'God enlightened him, and then others through the light in him' (Pusey, *op. cit.*; *cf.* Gal. 1:16, mg.); 'with Hosea', signifying his personal communion with the Lord. *Go, take . . . i.e.* 'marry' (*cf.* Gn. 6:2; 24:67, *etc.*). *A wife of harlotry, children of harlotry*; see Introduction. *For the land commits great harlotry*; the lesson from Hosea's marriage. *Land* means the nation, the people of the land. Possibly there are overtones of Baal-worship

in which human sexual acts were performed as religious rites, with the purpose of reminding the god to function as the divine giver of all fertility. The beginning of harlotry is *by forsaking the Lord*, as neglect of good soon leads to practice of evil.

3 *Bore him a son.* The Lord opens the womb, in contrast to the fertility rites of Baalism, in which a marriage between the god and the earth is supposed, and animal, vegetable and human fertility secured by promiscuous rites.

1:4–9 The meaning of his children's names. 4 *Jezreel* ('God sows'); a fertile valley desecrated by murder and massacre. *Yet a little while.* Thirty years were to elapse after the death of Jeroboam II before Samaria finally fell in 722 BC. The *blood* (plural, indicating much bloodshed) refers to the carnage there by Jehu including the murder of Ahaziah, king of Judah (2 Ki. 9:14 – 10:14). If Jehu was fulfilling Elijah's prophecy concerning the house of Ahab (1 Ki. 21:21, 22; 2 Ki. 10:17, 30) why was his *house* to be punished? Perhaps he exceeded his duty with misguided zeal (2 Ki. 10:16ff.), killed a king of Judah or, more likely, his own heart was not right with God (2 Ki. 10:29, 31).

5 *Break the bow of:* i.e. utterly defeat (*cf.* Ps. 46:9; Je. 49:35). There is no explicit mention of a decisive battle *in the valley of Jezreel.* The Assyrian army reached as far south as Jezreel (2 Ki. 15:29) and beyond it in the siege of Samaria (17:5). **6** *To forgive them at all*; literally 'that I should lift up in respect of them'. The phrase is elliptical: it refers to the lifting of guilt (*cf.* Nu. 14:19b). The verb is intensified. **7** *Have pity*; cognate with 'womb', the tender love of parent for child. In the case of Judah deportation to Babylon resulted in their deliverance *by the Lord their God* through the working of God's sovereign will for their return to their homeland. Concerning this reference to Judah see Introduction.

8 *Weaned*, mentioned only here, is an act of love and not of deprivation. **9** *Not my people . . . not your God.* This is a reversal of the terms of the covenant God made with Israel: 'I . . . will be your God, and you shall be my people' (Lv. 26:9, 12; Je. 11:1–5; Ezk. 37:23–27). It is repeated in more intimate terms of King David and his successors (2 Sa. 7:14 'his father . . . my son') and quoted by St. Paul in both forms (2 Cor. 6:16–18). The consequences of breaking the covenant are clearly set out in Lv. 26:14–39.

1:10 – 2:1 One God, one people—the promise on which Hosea's ministry was to be based. **10** Judgment deserved is matched by mercy undeserved, to the extent that the latter blessings not merely supersede, but actually surpass, the former. An innumerable company *like sand* was originally promised in the covenant with Abraham, reiterated to Jacob (Gn. 22:15–18; 28:13–15; *cf.* Rev. 7:9). Centuries later *in the place* of Israel's judgment the Son of God came offering the promises of divine sonship to all His believers (Jn. 1:12, 13; 3:3). **11** The reunion of the nation is foreseen in negative and positive terms: *gathered together*, an acceptance of unity; *they shall appoint for themselves one head*, an expression of unity. 'The act of God . . . then . . . the act of their own consent' (Pusey, *op. cit.*, p. 55). Some suggest that *Jezreel* belongs to the next verse, 'O Jezreel, say . . .', and that the final phrase here is 'the day of the Lord'. This removes the force of the sentence; the valley of Jezreel will be transformed; where once death reigned, now life abundant reigns, when the Son of David is enthroned.

2:1 The recovery of the family is completed. It is natural to associate this verse with chapter 1, with *brother, sister* (MT 'brothers', 'sisters'; *cf.* AV) referring to the nation. T. H. Robinson (*The Twelve Minor Prophets*, 1954, p. 8) notes that Israel is regarded as a single person, and the individual Israelites as her sons. But Rowley *et al.* think that Hosea's actual children reprove their mother. The message of reconciliation comes primarily to individuals, whose repentance is prior to and part of that of the nation.

2:2-23 His basic message

The oracle begins from Hosea's own domestic situation (v. 2), but soon fades into a picture of the nation under the figure of a marriage which has gone wrong (vv. 3-13). The reconciliation begins on the Husband's initiative and ends with a great re-enactment of the marriage witnessed by the whole universe (vv. 14-23).

2:2-5 The faithless nation. 2 Probably by now Gomer has left home and the children are grown up. *Plead* has the same root as 'controversy' (4:1) and 'contend' (4:4). It is more than an impassioned and perhaps emotional appeal. It suggests the making of a legal case. It is as if Hosea is trying to avoid a law-suit and a divorce. *Put away*. . . . Take off her adornments: either those to allure, or those given by lovers. **3** The domestic image is disappearing and the nation is coming into view. The promised land was a place of great fertility (Dt. 11:11, 12). Disloyalty to God had changed that. The Canaanites believed that the local baal could give natural fertility to the soil. The Israelites, far from condemning these practices, had actually taken part in them (*cf.* v. 5). Now God is showing His supremacy in devastating drought (*cf.* Am. 8:11). *Lest*; the final humiliation can be averted by true repentance (*cf.* 1 Cor. 11:31, 32). **4** Their *children* will enjoy neither the protection nor the provisions of the covenant (*cf.* Gn. 17:7, 8). **5** *My lovers*; the Baals, literally 'lords', local gods (*e.g.* Baal-peor) usually associated with the high places and pillars (*e.g.* 2 Ki. 18:4). The Israelites had failed to rid the land of Baalism at the conquest and later adopted syncretistic practices, worshipping Yahweh as if He were a Baal. Contrast *my* with v. 9.

2:6-13 Humiliation and punishment. 6 Israel will be discomfited by prickly thorns and dismayed by an unassailable wall. She will wander distraught as in a maze. **7** But even if she escaped from the maze she would never catch them on the open road. She is wearied and at length comes to her senses (*cf.* Lk. 15:17). *First*; 'former'. *Better . . . then than now*; Israel under judgment will look back to days of prosperity (1 Ki. 4:20, 25; 8:65, 66; Zc. 3:10; Rev. 2:4). **8** *She . . . I*; emphatic. The natural man is ignorant of the providential goodness of God. They used some things rightly but misappropriated others. *Silver and gold*; for making idols or money towards the upkeep of Baalism. **9** The Lord was about to do what had never been attributed to any Baal: to bestow a harvest and then withdraw it, by drought, pestilence or foreign tribute (*cf.* 1 Ki. 17:3-5). Grain-harvest was due in spring and the vintage in summer. *Take away*; 'snatch away', a sudden humiliating exposure of shame (contrast Gn. 3:21).

10 *Now*; logical rather than temporal. *Lewdness*; indecent exposure of the private parts of the body. The nation will be taken in the very act of adultery, in the sight of her lovers in Canaan whilst worshipping Baal. *Hand*; metaphorically 'power'. **11** The life of the nation was punctuated by regular holy seasons, times of great joy (*e.g.* Dt. 16:14): *feasts*, often occasions of pilgrimage (Dt. 16:16); *new moons* (Nu. 28:11-15); *sabbaths*, both days (Ex. 20:8-11) and years (Lv. 25:1-7); *appointed feasts* (a word translated 'seasons' in Gn. 1:14, hence an event fixed by calendar). *Put an end*; a pun on 'sabbath'.

12 *My hire*; the reward of a harlot. The vineyards will be desolated and deserted, with no-one to clear the undergrowth or to drive away the animals. **13** *Ring and jewelry*; typical both of harlots and pagans. *And forgot me*; Israel was completely devoted to the Baals and now not even trying to worship Yahweh with Baalistic rites (*cf.* 2 Sa. 5:20). *Says the Lord*; rare in Hosea, but common among his contemporary prophets.

2:14-23 Chastening and restoration. 14 Here is the beginning of the lasting reconciliation. *Therefore*; the logic of this is found only in the steadfast love (*hesed*) of the Lord. Everything before this points only to wrath righteously deserved. *I will allure her*; 'I' is emphatic. Divine initiative in love is the beginning of salvation (Jn. 3:16; 15:16). *Into the wilderness*; first must come a conviction of sin and of the need of a Saviour (*cf.* Jn. 16:8, 9), perhaps through a chastening experience (Heb. 12:7-11). *Speak tenderly to her*; literally 'speak to her heart'. We must be drawn out by fear and drawn in by love. **15** The Lord will triumph over Baal in making even the desert fertile (*cf.* Is. 35:1, 2), giving not a harlot's hire but the wedding-gifts of a husband. *The valley of Achor* recalled Achan's sin and Israel's punishment (Jos. 7:24-26). Then it was a door of foreboding but it shall be *a door of hope*.

16 *In that day*; a Messianic term. *My husband . . . My Baal*; literally 'my man . . . my lord', then a customary form of address by a wife (*cf.* 1 Pet. 3:6). **17** Israel is to be cut off from the remotest association with Baalism, even in the name (*cf.* 1 Ch. 9:39, 40; 2 Sa. 5:20). The relationship would be intimate and enduring. **18** *Covenant*; the divine marriage will bring harmony into the natural and social world. *Abolish*; literally 'break'. The test of real peace and protection is unbroken sleep, to *lie down in safety* (*cf.* Ps. 4:8; Pr. 16:7).

19, 20 Seven marks of the new marriage; *a.* Permanence (*for ever*). *b. Righteousness*; N. H. Snaith (*Mercy and Sacrifice*, 1953, p. 71) says this word in the 8th-century prophets 'shows a persistent tendency to topple into benevolence', and points out that in NT times it can actually be contrasted with strict justice (*cf.* Dt. 24:13). *c. Justice*; judgment by precedent as in case-law. God is still—even in the bestowal of grace— absolutely just (*cf.* Rom. 3:26; 1 Jn. 1:9). *d. Steadfast love* (*ḥeseḏ*; see Introduction); both marriage-partners are bound by the obligations of their covenant. *e. Mercy* (*raḥᵃmîm*, 'mercies'; see Introduction); the understanding of a God who remembers that we are but dust (Ps. 103:14). *f. Faithfulness*; loyalty. Never again shall Israel forsake her Husband, nor He her. *g. Communion* (*know the Lord*). Again we strike one of the arteries of Hosea's prophecy. Knowledge of God is not a theory but an experience, here expressed as a marriage relationship (*cf.* Gn. 4:1).

21-23 At the wedding the witnesses render their gifts in turn to the bride. The heavens give rain to the earth, the earth growth to the crops, the crops their goodness to man. *Answer*; AV 'hear' reverses the stress: 'marry' (Scott) suggests the joy of the occasion (*cf.* Ps. 65:11–13). The whole creation rejoices as God and man are joined together (*cf.* Rom. 8:19–21). *Jezreel . . . I will sow him for myself*; a play on the name. Moffatt has 'repeople' (*zāraʿ*), also of grafting (Is. 17:10; Rom. 11:23ff.) and pregnancy. As in 2:1 the curse is lifted and the complete family is restored, a promise fulfilled in the Christian church (1 Pet. 2:9, 10).

3:1-5 His marriage restored by true love

Neither mere affection ('*āhᵃḇâ*) nor even parental love (*raḥᵃmîm*) makes a marriage: a stronger, deeper love (*ḥeseḏ*) is needed. It is this that redeems Hosea's wife and teaches the manifold love of God.

3:1-3 Hosea redeems his wife. 1 *Go again*; Hosea did not go after Gomer 'because he loved her but because God sent him' (G. Campbell Morgan, *Hosea, the Heart and the Holiness of God*, 1934, p. 26). *Love* ('*ᵉhaḇ*); it was still a matter of the heart, and we need not deny Hosea an affection still for his wife. To be strictly accurate, we should, in fact, translate here, not *Go again, love*, but 'Go, love again'. Hosea was, so to speak, to resume the courtship of long ago, thus imitating the undying love of God for Israel. Being *an adulteress* implies the breaking of a marriage-bond, either by harlotry or by an illicit relationship (v. 3) with her *paramour*

('friend'). 'Beloved of her husband' is a possible translation (*cf.* Je. 3:20). A marginal reading is 'loving evil and committing adultery'. *Cakes of raisins* (AV 'flagons of wine'); products of the vintage, when feasts were held in honour of the Baals.

2 *Bought her* must mean that she had become a slave. After separation she would lose her endowment. Various calculations of the price have been made. From 2 Ki. 7:1, 16 the total value = 30 shekels, the price of a slave. But why did he pay part in kind? G. Campbell Morgan sees it as 'half-price and a day's rations (for a slave)'. To buy one who belonged to him and who owed him much, and who had sunk so low, demanded the exercise of *ḥeseḏ*.

3 The erring wife is to be disciplined before restoration to her former privileges (*cf.* Lk. 3:8) *Many days* foreshadows a long though limited period (v. 4). *So will I also be to you*; Hosea shares the trial of separation in the spirit of loyalty that he expects from his wife. A marginal reading 'so will I also not come to you' is preferred by J. Mauchline (*IB, ad loc.*), as neither Hosea's nor God's constancy are in question. It means he will deny himself a husband's rights for the present. For Israel as a whole the many days are still unended.

3:4, 5 God and Israel reunited. To be without their leaders and their religious symbols was chastening to Israel. Some were definitely condemned (*pillar*, *cf.* Ex. 23:24; *teraphim*, *cf.* Zc. 10:2) and the rest were not God's first choice. *Many days* does not necessarily mean these would be restored later but that what Israel had come to value would be taken away. **5** The reunion of Israel and Judah under a divine Davidic king. *The latter days*; the end of the age when Christ is enthroned, when every knee shall bow and every tongue confess that Jesus is Lord.

4:1 – 10:15 THE COMING OF JUDGMENT

The Lord shows what is amiss in Israel (4:1–14), and why the people cannot repent (4:15 – 6:6). He reveals His patience (6:7 – 7:16) but warns of impending judgment on the people and their leaders (8:1 – 10:15).

4:1-14 The Lord's controversy

4:1-3 With the nation as a whole. 1 *Controversy*; the same root as 'contend', 'contention' (*cf.* v. 4). It implies the lodging of a case of law against Israel. Three virtues are missing: *no faithfulness* (J. B. Phillips, 'no honesty') in daily life; *or kindness* (*ḥeseḏ*) in personal relationships; *no knowledge of God, i.e.* spiritual ignorance, one of Hosea's main burdens (*cf.* 2:8; 5:4; 6:3, 6; 7:10; 11:3; 13:4–6; 14:9). Evils quickly move in to a godless situation. **2** *Swearing*; cursing (*cf.* Jdg. 17:2) or taking false oaths (*cf.* 1 Ki. 8:31), probably both here. In Hebrew 'there is' is missing and 'swearing', *etc.* is an abrupt salvo of denunciation. Vice abounded: *they break all* *bounds* (*cf.* Pr. 29:18 (Heb.)), *i.e.* they cast off the restraint of the law. *Murder follows murder*; literally 'bloods touch bloods', an intensive plural for 'much bloodshed'.

3 Nature suffers for man's sin. *The land mourns.* either 'the people of the land' parallel to 'all who dwell', or the desolation of a neglected countryside. *Languish* ('grow feeble') can refer to loss of human fertility (*cf.* 1 Sa. 2:5; Je. 15:9), but also to a disillusioned and disappointed people who have nothing to live for (J. B. Phillips, 'have lost heart').

4:4-8 With the priests. 4 The divergence of translation rests on *with you* which by a small variation of pointing in MT would read 'your people' (as AV). The *priest* had particular responsibility for teaching the people (*cf.* Je. 2:8; 6:13; Zp. 3:4; Mal. 1:6 – 2:9; Jas. 3:1). The Lord is setting Himself up as Judge. **5** *You* (sing.); the priest. *By day*; in days of ease. *By night*; in times of affliction. A one-letter alteration of almost the same sound in the Hebrew would give 'I will destroy your people' (*cf.* JB, 'you are the ruin of your people'); see on v. 4. *Prophet*; the false prophet. *Your mother*; the tribe of Levi into which all priests were born. **6** *Are destroyed*; the prophetic perfect viewing the future as already accomplished is generally intermingled with the imperfect, the focus changing rapidly between foreground and background in the prophet's perspective. For the priest's moral responsibility, *cf.* Dt. 17:12, 13. *Forget your children*; a threat to the whole future of the priesthood.

7 For *I will change* some versions read 'they have changed' signifying a lapse into idolatry (*cf.* Ps. 106:20; Je. 2:11; Rom. 1:23). Whatever secondary agencies may be used, the Lord is the prime-mover in the downfall of the priesthood. *Their glory*; the privilege of the Levites (Lv. 3:5-13). **8** *The sin*; one word is used for 'sin' and for 'sin-offering'. It was the duty of the priests alone to eat the flesh of this sacrifice (Lv. 6:24-30): hence they were *greedy for their iniquity* (lit. 'lift up his soul'; 'lick their lips over the guilt to come', Phillips). *Cf.* 1 Sa. 2:12-17.

4:9-14 With the people as individuals. 9 *Like people, like priest*; there was nothing to choose between priest and people: as the priest has been judged so now will the people be. **10** They will not enjoy the Creator's blessing (*cf.* Hg. 1:6, 9). MT (and some translators) puts *harlotry* in v. 11, leaving *cherish* ('keep') without an object. **11** *New wine*, the potent liquor derived from the first drippings before the grapes are trodden. *Understanding* (lit. 'heart'); a common metaphor. **12** The appalling spiritual darkness of God's people leaves them groping in superstition, praying to *a thing of wood*, or 'at his tree'. This may refer to the poles set up at Baal shrines. *Their staff*; often a walking or riding stick, sometimes symbolic, possibly with pagan carvings, used in rhabdomancy (*cf.* 'arrows', Ezk. 21:21). *My people*; emphatic or exclamatory. *A spirit of harlotry* (*cf.* 5:4); a deep-seated desire

for idolatry. **13** Multiplication of altars was forbidden in Israel (Dt. 12:11-27; 14:23-26). Canaanitish shrines were situated on the high places, or near sacred trees (2 Ki. 17:10) and were to be broken down (Dt. 7:5). *Terebinth*; a tree affording pleasant shade from the heat. *Daughters . . . brides*; there was respect neither for the purity of womanhood, nor for the bond of marriage. **14** *The men themselves*; some translate 'everyone else', 'the leaders themselves'. *Cult prostitutes* (lit. 'holy women'; *i.e.* women 'set apart' for immoral religious rites) were common, but were forbidden in Israel (Dt. 23:17, 18). Lack of *understanding* ('discernment') is the slow-acting poison of a nation doomed to dissolution (*cf.* 14:9).

4:15 – 6:6 The impossibility of true repentance

Having stated His case against the people of Israel (ch. 4), God calls on the accused to answer the charge, but the sentence is given against them (ch. 5). In desperation Israel sues for mercy, but their appeal is rejected, not being based on any real change of heart (6:1-6). Hosea shows why Israel's repentance is false.

4:15-19 Bad company ruins good morals. 15 Judah is warned not to follow Israel's bad example and to keep clear of the idolatrous places (*cf.* Am. 5:5). *Gilgal* should have been a place of happy memories: it was the first encampment (Jos. 4:19-24), and the scene of the first Passover in the promised land (Jos. 5:9-12; *cf.* Mi. 6:5). But it was the place where Saul was dethroned (1 Sa. 15:21-31) and later a centre of idolatry (Ho. 9:15; 12:11; Am. 4:4). *Bethaven* ('house of iniquity'); near Bethel (Jos. 7:2). It is possibly an ironic allusion to Bethel but it most likely refers to a pagan shrine left undisturbed. *As the Lord lives*; a common formula of an oath, false (Jdg. 8:19) or true (1 Ki. 17:1; Je. 16:14, 15). **16** RSV takes this verse as a question, a decision based on the context. The *broad pasture* suggests prosperity (see Is. 30:23). Even under such ideal conditions the *stubborn* put themselves outside God's help.

17 *Ephraim*; Israel in the sense of the ten tribes of the northern kingdom. Ephraim had always held a leading position among them (Jdg. 8:2), but they should have remembered their humble beginnings (Gn. 48:14, 19). *Joined to idols*; 'wedded to idolatry' (J. B. Phillips). *Cf.* Mal. 2:14; 1 Cor. 10:20; 15:33, 34. Judah is warned not to get involved. **18** *A band of drunkards*; AV 'their drink is sour' is unlikely. 'Their drunkenness has come to an end' is possible. Thus some suggest it means 'when their carousal is over they indulge in lewdness'. Others (adding a prepositional prefix) take it with v. 17b: 'leave him alone with a band of drunkards'. RSV gives good sense. Drunkenness (*cf.* Am. 2:12; 4:1; 6:6) and sexual misconduct were rife. *Their glory* is a marginal reading, as is 'my glory'. MT has 'her coverings' giving 'they love the shame of her coverings', the hardness of the harlot's heart (*cf.* La. 3:65, 'dullness of heart').

19 A sudden gust will snatch away the covering of a dull conscience and naked shame will take its place. *Them* (lit. 'her'); possibly the female counterpart in the illicit relationship: the idols, the harlots or the coverings. *Altars*; literally 'sacrifice'.

5:1–7 Sins and sin. The whole nation is stumbling, unaware of their imminent fate. **1** Hosea sounds a warning (*hear . . . heed . . . hearken*; *cf.* v. 8). *The judgment pertains to you* (lit. 'the judgment is yours'); *i.e.* this is your sentence. The three groups correspond to the three places cited. *Mizpah* was where the first king was proclaimed (1 Sa. 10:17–19). The kings of Israel had led the people into idolatry, especially Jeroboam I, whose sin was a byword (1 Ki. 14:16 – 2 Ki. 17:23, *passim*). *Tabor*; part of Issachar (Jos. 19:22) allotted to the priests (1 Ch. 6:77). Their *net* was their carnal attitude to their ministry. *Shittim*; the last camp before Jordan (Jos. 2:1; 3:1; *cf.* Mi. 6:5). Their idolatry here was described as harlotry (Nu. 25:1–3). *Made deep the pit of Shittim*; they had exceeded their earlier grossness. MT is not certain. AV, RV have 'the revolters are profound to make slaughter', referring to human bloodshed (*cf.* 4:2) or to many sacrifices offered (*cf.* 4:13).

3 Although the people do not know the Lord, He knows them: *I*; emphatic. *Now*; logical. *Ephraim . . . Israel* are synonymous. **4** Inveterate evil habits are an obstacle to repentance (*cf.* Is. 59:2; Jn. 8:34; Rom. 6:16; Heb. 12:17). But more, there is no desire to repent because of the *spirit . . . within them*. And even if they had a desire to repent, *they know not the Lord*. *Cf.* Jn. 3:19; Rom. 1:28–32; 1 Cor. 2:14. Their sins might have been forgiven had their condition of sin not separated them from God.

5:5–7 The unforgivable sin. 5 *The pride of Israel*; possibly a word-play, a title of God (*cf.* Am. 4:2; 6:8a; 8:7) or referring to Israel's sinful pride (Am. 6:8b). In spite of warning Hosea foresees the ultimate downfall of Judah. **6** The order stresses the profusion of sacrificial animals, suggesting a shallow, probably insincere repentance (see 14:2). Such half-heartedness never finds God (*cf.* Is. 55:6, 7; Jas. 4:8) nor receives forgiveness (Lk. 12:8–10). **7** *Faithlessly* (stronger, 'treacherously'); of adultery (Je. 3:20). Israel had broken the covenant-bond with her Husband and borne strange children, a generation of people who did not know Him. *Cf.* Mal. 2:13–16. A *new moon*; another month. 'Any month now . . .' (J. B. Phillips).

5:8–12 Unsuspected corruption. 8 *The horn*; Israel's national instrument, especially in attack and defence (Jos. 6:4ff.; Ezk. 33:3). *The trumpet*; for sacred use to assemble the people (Nu. 10:1–10). Both were now to rouse the nation to a sense of aweful expectancy, referring perhaps the Syro-Ephraimitic war of 735. *Gibeah, Ramah* and *Bethaven* were near the border of the two kingdoms between Ephraim and Benjamin. *Benjamin* suggests that Judah was to see Israel's fate and repent. The last phrase is literally

'Behind you, Benjamin!', which may have been the ancient battle-cry of the tribe (*cf.* Jdg. 5:14). A one-letter change would give *tremble, O Benjamin* (*cf.* LXX, 'Benjamin is distraught'). Judah was to beware of an adversary stealing up unawares. **9** *Ephraim*; emphatic. *What is sure*; *i.e.* sure to happen.

10 A surprising switch of attention to Judah (see Introduction). Vv. 10–14 refer to both Israel and Judah. To *remove the landmark*; to interfere with personal disputes or perhaps to the annexing of Israelite territory under King Asa (1 Ki. 15:20–22; *cf.* 2 Ki. 14:25–28). **11** Some follow the margin taking *oppressed, crushed* as 'oppressor', 'crusher'. *Vanity* (AV 'commandment'); a difficult word, elsewhere only in Is. 28:10 where it represents a childish chant. Kittel suggests 'his adversary', but which? Possibly the king of Assyria (2 Ki. 17:3–6). **12** *Therefore*; not in MT. *I*; emphatic. The judgment of God is sometimes a gradual breaking down of the fabric of life.

5:13–15 The failure of human instinct. 13 The symptoms were recognized, but the remedy was wrong. No nation, however powerful, could cure the moral and spiritual sickness of Israel or Judah, nor rescue them from the judgment of God. In going to Assyria (2 Ki. 17:3–6) they were playing into God's hands. *The great king*; AV 'king Jareb', but identification is difficult. 'A king who contends' is possible: it would be just what Israel wanted. **14** Note the repeated *I*. Yahweh will tear His prey and carry it off to his lair. There will be no David to rescue (*cf.* 1 Sa. 17:35) until the Son of David comes (Mt. 15:22ff.). **15** How great is the longsuffering and goodness of the Lord! The lion will lie down with the lamb and lick its wounds. He will wait for a conviction of sin to come to His people, so that they will turn to Him. *Saying* (not in Hebrew) is better omitted as it implies that 6:1–3 is an acceptable confession.

6:1–6 Inability to grasp the truth. Hosea puts the people's shallow confession into words, probably from what he had heard and knew of them (vv. 1–3). There is no understanding or acknowledgment of guilt (5:15); on the contrary there are signs of self-interest and echoes of Baalism. The Lord's response is to reject their words and to restate His own terms of reconciliation (vv. 4–6).

1 *Come, let us return*; the impression given is of animated speech which possibly betrays a lack of awe in approaching God. **2** The resurrection-rites of the fertility-gods may be in their minds. *Third day* may not indicate a definite period of three days (*cf.* Am. 4:8; 2 Ki. 9:32). *Before him*; Moffatt, 'under his care'. They were complacently hoping for the best. **3** They knew they lacked knowledge of God but sought it unconditionally. *Press on to know*; we say 'get to know' a person. *His going . . . dawn* according to a marginal text might be 'as soon as we seek, so we shall find'. *Showers*; the 'former rain' falls in December softening the earth for ploughing and the 'latter rain' comes in spring giving growth. The country was utterly dependent on rainfall. Natural religion was all they wanted (*cf.* Jn. 6:26).

4 God sees their shallow repentance and their love for Him which would soon evaporate (*cf.* Mt. 13:21). Self-righteousness bars the way between God and man (*cf.* Lk. 18:11, 12; Rom. 10:3). *Love* (*ḥeseḏ*; AV 'goodness'); see Introduction. **5** J. Mauchline (*IB, ad loc.*) suggests the verbs *hewn, slain, goes forth* should be construed as prophetic perfects: 'will hew, slay, go forth'. This fits well with the context, although the words could be taken both prospectively and retrospectively. The words of the *prophets* had the cutting-edge of divine authority (*cf.* Heb. 4:12). For 'prophets' some read 'stones' seeing a possible allusion to the giving of the law through Moses. *Judgment . . . as the light*; *cf.* Jn. 3:19–21.

6 The glory of the new covenant is here beginning to dawn. It may at first seem that God, having given commandments concerning sacrifice through Moses, had changed His mind. *And not . . . rather than* (*cf.* Gn. 37:3) are literally translated. Some critics have seen in this (and the five other similar passages: Is. 1:11–15; 43:22–24; Je. 7:21–23; Am. 5:21–25; Mi. 6:6–8) a conflict between the prophets and the sacrificial cultus. (For fuller treatment see *NBD*, pp. 1043–44.) But nowhere do they deny the validity of sacrifice offered in the right spirit. In each case they denounce the sins of immorality, idolatry or self-righteousness which violate the covenant and invalidate the sacrifices. 'What could make repentance seem so easy as the belief that forgiveness can be won by simply offering sacrifices?' (G. A. Smith, *The Book of the Twelve Prophets*, 1903, p. 265). Lv. 26:40–45 upholds the same principle: confession, humility towards God bring reconciliation. The phrase *and not* is paralleled by *rather than*, not as expressing exclusiveness nor even mere preference but essential priority. The virtues of *steadfast love* and *the knowledge of God* (see Introduction), both essential elements of the covenant relationship (Je. 31:3, 34), are the ultimate realities which give meaning to the cultus and survive it into the new covenant. *Sacrifice*; a general term. *Burnt offerings* (lit. 'that which rises'); the dedicatory offering in which the whole animal was burnt (Lv. 1; 6:8–13; *cf.* Eph. 5:2; Phil. 4:18), but even this depends on a relationship with God expressed in knowledge (Je. 9:24) and obedience (1 Sa. 15:22). *I desire* reveals a divine longing not for the expiation of guilt but for the love which would render such expiation unnecessary. Similarly God looks for real devotion in preference to the most excellent and extravagant tokens of it. Our Lord twice quoted Ho. 6:6, in Mt. 9:13 and 12:7, in each case rebuking the Pharisees for their self-righteousness which exalted their traditions above their relationships to Christ and other people. The wise scribe (Mk. 12:32–34)

shows that he has grasped the principle of Ho. 6:6.

6:7 – 7:16 The longsuffering of God

After the sternness and strictness of the judgment seat, the Lord reveals His tenderness (ch. 7). But it is a story of 'what might have been' if Israel had responded to His patient entreaties; instead they prove rebellious or neglectful (7:1, 7, 10, 13, 15).

6:7 – 7:2 No vision, no restraint. 7 The beginning of sorrows was when Israel broke the covenant. *Adam*; possibly a place (Moff. 'Adamtown'). *Transgress*; the Hebrew word is also used of crossing a river (*cf.* Jos. 3:16). Possibly the sin of Achan is in mind (Jos. 6:18, 19; 7:1, 11; *cf.* Ho. 2:15). Other suggestions are 'in Adam (the man)' or 'like Adam' though there is no record of a covenant with him, or generally 'like men'. *There* suggests a place. It could well be that we have here a double meaning. Hosea picks the place-name, Adam, out of the Joshua narrative to show that at the very time of covenant-renewal (Jos. 3:16; 5:1–12) the sin of Achan revealed the unchanged heart of Israel. At the same time he subtly pointed back to Adam, the father of all self-seeking sin. **8** *Gilead* (*cf.* 12:11) was noted for vice. **9** *Shechem* had important associations, especially in connection with the covenant: Abram pitched there first (Gn. 12:6, 7), Joshua gathered the people there (Jos. 8:30–35; 24, especially v. 25), though later Baalism had intruded (*cf.* Jdg. 9:4—Baalberith, 'lord of the covenant'). Shechem was also a city of refuge (Jos. 20:7). These facts suggest that these crimes were committed almost on the ground hallowed by God's most gracious dealings with His people. To such villains nothing is sacred.

10 The *house of Israel*; the nation (*cf.* 1:4, 6) or a local shrine, perhaps Bethel, as *there* suggests. A *horrible thing*, to make one shudder. *Ephraim* and *Israel* are synonymous. **11a** is regarded by some as a later interpolation (see Introduction). **11b, 7:1** The Lord is waiting to bless His folk but their condition prevents it and their misdeeds intervene. *Samaria*; the capital of northern Israel, and site of an idolatrous shrine (1 Ki. 16:32). Like all capitals it may sometimes stand for the whole country. Fraud, house-breaking and highway robbery represent widespread corruption. **2** The greatest barrier to restoration is the profanity which leaves God entirely out of reckoning (*cf.* Heb. 12:16, 17).

7:3–7 No respect for godless rulers. The period was notable for assassinations and *coups d'état*. But the kings never prayed. **3** *Make glad*; they avoid suspicion by fawning and flattery which keeps the court in a happy mood. **4** The *fire* and the *baker* in vv. 4–7 can be interpreted in two ways: (*a*) when the fire is not being fanned new plots are leavening, or (*b*) the baker controls the fire to avoid over-cooking the plans. *Adulterers*; by a slight change we get 'enraged', fitting the context. **5** *On*; not in MT. The *day of* *our king* may be a personal or official anniversary. *Stretched out his hand*; became a companion, sharing the same meal with *mockers*, perhaps 'imposters'. **6** *Burn*; literally 'brought near'. Mauchline (*IB, ad loc.*) suggests transferring two Hebrew words, *like an oven* and *their hearts*, to between lines 2 and 3 giving 'But they approached (the king) with (their) intrigue . . .'. As the carousal nears its end at dawn the plot breaks. *Anger* (*'aP̄*); AV 'baker' (*'ōP̄eh*). **7** A series of short reigns ended by violence. Note the fatalism of a prayerless life.

7:8–10 National decadence. 8 Instead of being distinct from other nations, Ephraim is merely an ethnic ingredient, as useless as a cake half burnt. **9** *He* (emphatic) *knows it not*; everyone but he can see the failing of his powers. The so-called protectors Assyria and Egypt were draining the resources of the land in tribute, and Baalism was destroying the nation's spiritual and moral fibre. 'His hair is shot through with grey.' **10** *The pride of Israel* . . . ; see on 5:5. Decadence creates no desire for better things.

7:11–13 Political vacillation. 11 A double-minded man is 'unstable in all his ways' (Jas. 1:6–8). Ephraim was cooing to Egypt, fluttering to Assyria (2 Ki. 17:3, 4). 'They trimmed their foreign policy to every political wind that blew, and they were always wrong—because they were morally wrong' (John Bright, *The Kingdom of God in Bible and Church*, 1955, p. 75). This panicky dependence on foreign powers was attacked by other prophets of the time (*e.g.* Is. 30:1–7). **12** *As they go*; *i.e.* to Egypt or Assyria. The entire nation was involved in its leaders' policy. *For their wicked deeds*; 'as their congregation has heard' (as AV, RSV mg.) is based on MT; a slight emendation gives RSV. Either text would bear simple interpretation: either 'for their evil', or 'as the prophets have foretold'. **13** The possibility of redemption from their enslaved dependence on foreign aid is negatived by their blasphemy, perhaps in attributing blessings to Baal.

7:14–16 Gross ingratitude and insincerity. In spite of all the Lord has done for them, they slight Him with insincere worship or downright idolatry. **14** Moffatt has 'they never put their heart into their prayers'. They *wait upon their beds*, possibly 'beside their altars'. This might refer, like the next phrase, to the pagan rite. of Baal. *For grain and wine they gash themselves*s Baal was supposed to give fertility to the earth; gashing was a ritual extravagance to invoke Baal to act (*cf.* 1 Ki. 18:28). Human dignity is at a discount in paganism. **15** *I*; emphatic. *Cf.* Gn. 6:6. The training might refer to childhood or to manhood, *e.g.* for drawing a bow. **16** *To Baal.* Hebrew reads *lō' 'al, i.e.* '(but) not upwards' (*cf.* AV, RV; *BDB s.v. al*; T. K. Cheyne, *Hosea*, CB, 1884; also 11:7, AV, RV where *'al* occurs in the same sense). LXX translates as from *'al 'lō*, 'to nothing', *i.e.* 'to idols', but most moderns emend more extensively, *e.g.* *lelō' yō'îl*, 'to that which does not profit' (J. L. Mays, *Hosea*,

1969); *labbelîya'al*, 'to worthlessness' (Kittel, *Biblia Hebraica³*); *labba'al*, 'to Baal' (RSV; Kohler, *Lexicon in Veteris Testamenti Libris*, 1958). Insincerity is compared to a *treacherous bow* 'which is expected to shoot in one direction but actually shoots in another' (W. R. Harpur, *Amos and Hosea*, 1905). The parallel of the *sword* and the *tongue* is striking (*cf.* Rev. 1:16). Even *Egypt* may get the last laugh after all.

8:1–14 Judgment hovers overhead

Repeated refusal to repent (ch. 7) inevitably makes repentance more difficult, and ultimately impossible (8:3, 12, 14). The judgment now imminent will be swift (8:3, 7, 8 ,10, 14).

8:1–6 Broken covenant, broken calf. Israel ignored the Lord, both in their counsels and in their worship. **1** The *vulture*, silently, motionlessly hovering, was a speck in the sky but ready to swoop to the prey (*cf.* Je. 49:22). *Set the trumpet* . . . , LXX 'cast dust upon your breast . . .'; a sign of anguish. God gives the root-cause of His judgment: a positive severance of personal relationship through breaking His covenant, and incurring His displeasure through breaking His law. **2** They depended on a bygone experience of grace. *My God* (Syriac 'our God'), *we Israel know thee*; a shallow profession (*cf.* Mt. 7:22, 23). **3** The nation has had every chance. **4** *They made kings . . . princes* refers not to the divided kingship, for this fulfilled God's threat to Solomon (1 Ki. 11:9–13; *cf.* 12:24), nor to the original request for a king (1 Sa. 8:19–22) but probably to the frequent depositions by non-Davidic usurpers. **5a** As Israel spurned the good so God spurns the evil. AV follows MT, supplying object 'you'. RSV is a marginal reading. T. K. Cheyne (*The Book of Hosea*, 1913) suggests 'your calf is loathsome'. **5b, 6a** *In Israel*; from LXX. This is the cry of the God of patience. *A workman*; an engraver. Nothing man-made can either contain or represent God (*cf.* 1 Ki. 8:27; Acts 17:24, 25, 29). **6b** *Broken to pieces*; *i.e.* 'smashed to smithereens' (*cf.* Ex. 32:20).

8:7–10 God is not mocked. 7 Israel has done nothing but *sow the wind* in idolatry and in national affairs at home and abroad; now, according to both natural and spiritual law (Gal. 6:7), the harvest is due in great measure. *Whirlwind*; LXX *katastrophē*. And in the fields there is utter frustration; God is showing Israel that Baal is useless. Note the figure: if it succeeds at one stage it will fail at the next. For *aliens*, some read 'east wind', the blighting desert blast. **8** Israel has lost its identity as the people of God. A *vessel*; metaphorically a servant (*cf.* Je. 22:28; 48:38; 2 Tim. 2:20, 21). **9** The *wild ass*, Harper observes, is usually found in droves. *Wandering alone*; rather, 'going off alone', showing wilfulness. *Lovers*; literally 'loves', which some interpret as love-gifts. An alternative suggested for line 3 is 'To Egypt they give love-gifts', parallel to *Assyria*. **10** *Cease . . . anointing kings and princes*. There are various alternatives: *cease*, AV 'sorrow'; *anointing*, AV (*et al.*) 'burden';

king and princes, 'king of princes', *i.e.* the king of Assyria. Thus it means (*inter alia*): (*a*) they shall have no more kings of their own (but 'a little while' suggests eventual resumption, and princes were not anointed); (*b*) they would be released from the burden of a court that was a liability rather than an asset (Harper suggests 'this continual anointing . . .'); (*c*) they would be released from heavy tribute to the king of Assyria (2 Ki. 18:14).

8:11–14 Egypt all over again. 11 What was intended to point to forgiveness of sins (*cf.* Lv. 17:11) has become the occasion of sin (*cf.* Rom. 7:10). At any one time only one altar was to be set up for all the nation in the place which God would choose (*cf.* Dt. 12:26f.; 14:24; 27:4–8; 2 Ki. 21:4, 5). **12** No special stress on *write* suggests that Hosea already familiar with a written law (*cf.* Dt. 31:24; 2 Ki. 22:8). 4:2; 13:2, 4 may allude to the Decalogue but this is inconclusive. *By ten thousands*; RV 'in ten thousand precepts'. They were so alienated from God that they could not recognize a single detail of His commandments. **13** *They love sacrifice*; LXX suggests the ironical 'their beloved altars'. The people ate only in the peace-offering (Lv. 7:15–19); the priests also had a due in these sacrifices (Lv. 7:31–36). But their hearts were evil and their sacrifices ineffectual. God had said they should never return to Egypt (Dt. 17:16); Hosea is referring to a return to conditions of degradation and oppression such as they suffered in Egypt (*cf.* 9:3). **14** Allegedly Amos's style: why should Hosea not have caught a phrase from the older prophet of Israel? *Palaces*; large buildings, even temples. Human achievement is not always to the glory of God (*cf.* Gn. 11:1–11), who intervenes on His own behalf.

9:1–17 The beginning of the end

The sentence has been pronounced; now the method of execution is given. They shall not remain in the land but be exiled in Assyria (vv. 3–6), ultimately becoming international refugees as punishment for sinfulness over many generations (vv. 15–17).

9:1–6 Learning the hard way. Possibly Hosea was preaching at one of the great harvest festivals. **1** The *peoples*; the heathen nations. *Harlot's hire*; the Baals were thought to give grain in exchange for devotion. **2** *Winevat*; within the press into which the juice flowed. *New wine*; see on 4:11. *Fail*; deceive, play false. Though their harvest is prolific their need will exceed it. Pursuit of pleasure, or even the satisfaction of natural religious instincts rather than knowing God Himself, is sure to disappoint. **3** Yahweh is showing whose the land is. *To Egypt*; see on 8:13. The reference to Assyria indicates that Egypt is to be taken metaphorically. **4** *Wine* was offered specially at harvest and on the Day of Atonement (Lv. 23). The Lord showed His displeasure to them by reckoning *their bread* (not in MT (AV)) as defiled and defiling (Nu. 19:14) and by refusing to accept their cereal-

offerings. **6** *Memphis* had one of the largest of Egypt's many burial-grounds. *Nettles . . . thorns*; a deserted and desolated land. They would reflect in life-long exile on their home comforts.

9:7–10 The sins of the fathers upon the children. 7 *Have come*; prophetic perfect. A marginal insertion after line 1 reads 'Ephraim shall know it'. *The prophet is a fool*; either of a false prophet, or popular opinion of a true prophet. G. Campbell Morgan (*Hosea, the Heart and the Holiness of God*, 1934, p. 96) asserts that 'man of the spirit' is never used of a false prophet. If so, parallelism suggests the true is in mind in both cases. Moffatt: 'a man inspired is a man insane'. **8** The true prophet, though concerned for the highest welfare of his people, is despised and rejected (*cf.* Is. 53:3; Je. 38:4). *Watchman*; *cf.* Ezk. 33:1–9. **9** *Gibeah* was the scene of a series of atrocities (Jdg. 19, 20). Since then Israel had not changed nor could their sin be attributed to environment. **10** Israel's youth was full of fair promise. But contact with Baal soon exposed them. It was not a temporary lapse; they *consecrated themselves. Baal*; the Hebrew has *bōšeṯ* ('shame'). RV translates 'the shameful thing'. People become like their God. See Ps. 111:58 and *cf.* Rom. 8:29.

9:11–17 God-forsaken. 11 No future—no children, no hope of children, no possibility of children. What irony for a fertility-cult and for one whose name is 'fruitful' (Gn. 41:52)! **12** *When I depart from them*; the marginal reading is 'for they shall wean their boys and be ashamed'. **13** MT (AV) is difficult, though Tyre was the home of Jezebel and her god Melqart. *IB* suggests (by a one-letter change): 'Ephraim I see as a guilty man, his children are given for a prey', perhaps 'Ephraim as I have seen as a prey bereft of her sons'. This may refer to the godlessness of human sacrifice (2 Ki. 17:16–18), or to unspecified bloodshed in exile. **14** No children would be better than murdered children: so Hosea ejaculates a prayer.

15 *Gilgal*, despite its links with Israel's first king-making (1 Sa. 11:15), was the focus of the present apostasy. The cleansing of *my house* recalls Mk. 11:15–18 and may reflect Hosea's dealings with Gomer. Their *princes* (*śārêhem*), *rebels* (*sōrᵉrîm*). Of many attempts to reproduce assonance 'their nobles are rebels' (G. A. Smith) is best. *Love* ('*āhēḇ*); they have forfeited their right to God's affection; He does not like them. But *ḥeseḏ* is not exhausted. **16** *Their root*; *cf.* Mt. 3:10; Mk. 11:20. **17** This verse corresponds to 2 Ki. 17:23. The reason for God's action is their persistent disobedience. As they have wandered from Him (7:13) so they shall wander without Him. *My God*; Hosea's heart is torn between his God and his people.

10:1–15 Digging out the roots

The nation has been stricken like a diseased tree (9:16; 10:1). But God is determined that it will not sprout again to bear corrupt fruit: Baalism and the apostate monarchy will be eradicated

(10:2, 8, 15). Not content with felling the tree, God is determined to eradicate the causes lest they should sprout again.

10:1–6 No more idols. 1 The *vine* is a symbol of prosperity (1 Ki. 4:25; *cf.* Jn. 15:1). *Luxuriant*; literally 'empty' (AV), *i.e.* it yielded its fruit fully. The more God blessed Israel the more they used His gifts to worship Baal. *Altars*; see on 8:11. *Pillars*; forbidden (Dt. 16:21, 22). **2** *False*; literally 'divides' (*cf.* AV). RV mg. has 'smooth': perhaps from stones used to cast lots and hence divide. They are two-faced. The Lord will do to them what they should have done to Baal (*cf.* Dt. 7:5). **3** A completely dispirited people. *No king*; none worthy of the name, or of Davidic descent. They see their folly (*we fear not the Lord*), but immediately betray their greater folly in thinking still of what an earthly ruler might do. **4** No-one can be trusted, even in business, though it may refer to the King Hoshea's vacillations (2 Ki. 17:3, 4). *Weeds*; not wanted but inevitable especially where no crops are grown. **5** Israel's chosen champion, perhaps their last hope, will be defeated. *Calf*, MT 'heifers'; a term of derision. *Bethaven*; see on 4:15. *Idolatrous priests*; a term never used of true priests. *Wail*; for MT 'exult' (AV). **6** Hosea shows how despicable this *thing* is; it will be ceremoniously mocked. *Idol*; from margin; MT, 'counsel', *i.e.* the covenants with Egypt and especially Assyria.

10:7–15 No more kings. 8 The kings from Jeroboam I had caused Israel to sin (2 Ki. 17:21, 22) and many had not only perpetuated the Baal shrines but extended them. *Thorn and thistle* will wave in undisputed possession of the altars. *They*; Israel, or probably their altars. *Cover . . . Fall upon us* (*cf.* Lk. 23:30); *i.e.* for shame. **9** *Cf.* 9:9. **10** As the tribes once rose against Benjamin, so the nations shall rise against Israel. *Double iniquity*; their idolatry and their reliance on outside help. AV follows Targum, 'bind themselves in their two furrows'. In the East ploughing together means acting in concord as friends (*cf.* 2 Cor. 6:14). Here the reference may be to their union with Baal and the nations. **11** Ephraim in her youth loved God's will, and gained the reward of obedient service (*cf.* Dt. 25:4). *I spared* (lit. 'passed over' or 'by') *her fair neck* could mean that God spared her the burden of a yoke which would chafe her neck. The yoke, however, usually rests on the shoulders. Harper (*op. cit.*, p. 354) suggests 'I will pass on beside her fair neck', as a driver (*cf.* IB, *in loc.*). Or, 'I have passed the yoke over . . .'. Duty, once pleasure, is now drudgery (*cf.* Gn. 3:17–19). **12** Hosea appeals to the nation. The God of salvation will pour refreshing showers of grace upon those who seek Him. *Sow*; *cf.* 2:22, 23. They wanted fruit without delay but now they had to start a new cycle in faith. *Break up*; eastern husbandmen, understandably as the ground hardens, neglect ploughing and sow among thorns. They will have to go the hard way now but *steadfast love* (*ḥeseḏ*) will ensure the harvest.

13 They have sown, reaped and eaten bad fruit, dependence on defensive pacts and troops. **14** *Beth-arbel*; location unknown, probably annihilated. *Shalman*; probably not Shalmaneser V of Assyria but Salamanu, king of Moab, a tributary of Tiglath-pileser. **15** Israel can expect to fare no better than Betharbel. Two double intensives: *great wickedness . . . utterly cut off*. There is nothing arbitrary about God's judgment: every man shall be judged according to his works (1 Pet. 1:17).

11:1 – 13:16 THE TRAGEDY OF JUDGMENT

In executing judgment on Israel God was not just punishing a sinful nation, but was casting off a people on whom He had settled His inheritance. In that lay the tragedy of it all.

11:1–11 The grief and love of the Lord

The resemblance to the parable of the prodigal son (Lk. 15:11–24) is striking. Both passages reveal something of the great loving Father-heart of God.

11:1, 2 A wayward boy. 1 When Israel was a young nation (*child*, or 'boy', 'young fellow') God heard their cry of affliction and delivered them from bondage (Ex. 3:9, 10). The NT use (Mt. 2:15) indicates that as Israel had forfeited their privilege of divine sonship, the prophecy would have to be fulfilled in Another (*cf.* Rom. 11:29). **2** The high hopes of free will are soon dashed in wilfulness. *Kept sacrificing*; a confirmed practice (*cf.* 1 Cor. 10:1–12).

11:3, 4 A father's care. 3 The tender self-sacrificing care of a father to his infant children is unknown to them. Ephraim owed his ability, strength and health to the Lord. **4** *I . . . love*; 'I drove with a harness of love' (Moffatt). The Lord led them by love and understanding, rather than driving them with whips. The considerate herdsman *eases the yoke* so that they might feed more comfortably. *Bent*; perhaps ellipsis for 'bent my ear, listened'; LXX 'I kept an eye on him'.

11:5–7 Headstrong and heartless. 5 *They shall return*. The Hebrew in its most obvious meaning here reads a negative, 'They shall not return', signifying that in spite of what Israel's sin merits the Lord will not reverse His great redemptive act. Redemption is irreversible, and therefore they will not go back to Egyptian bondage, but fall to the Assyrian conqueror. This happened in 722 BC. The contradiction with 8:13 and 9:3 is apparent rather than real, for there, as 9:3 shows, *Egypt* is used in a typical sense of the place of bondage, but here in its literal reference, as in 11:1, to the place from which redemption had rescued them. Under pressure, however, from this apparent clash, many commentators would espouse the translation adopted by RSV, urging that *l'ō* means 'to him' rather than 'not', and that it properly belongs to the latter part of v. 4, where, they allege, the text is in a confused state, without, at the same time, offering any agreed or acceptable solution. 6 *The sword* is depicted as an avaricious monster. 7b MT (AV) reads 'most high' (*'al*) but RSV has *yoke* (*'ōl*). *Remove* ('raise') means then the lifting of the yoke. The determination of Israel is matched by that of God.

11:8, 9 The tension of justice and love. 8 Here we get a glimpse of the heart of God under a human figure. His heart *recoils*, His emotions are in turmoil and His *compassion* glows. He cries in anguish 'How can I?' *Admah, Zeboiim*; two cities of the plain like Sodom and Gomorrah (Gn. 14:2). **9** It is His unchanging and unchangeable character which settles the issue. To be true to Himself He must devise some just way of dealing with His people. The *Holy One* came *in your midst* to seek the lost sheep of the house of Israel (Mt. 15:24) and to give His life a ransom for many (Mt. 20:28).

11:10, 11 A tumultuous homecoming. 10 The Lion of Judah (Rev. 5:5) will roar and His cubs will come trembling and His young lions bounding across the desert. *From the west*; *i.e.* the coastlands, but perhaps it refers prophetically to the whole world at the last day. **11** The homing birds will find their way swiftly from distant migration to their own resting-place. *I will return them*; *cf.* Jn. 14:3.

11:12 – 12:14 Prosperity is through faith

The hope of restoration is beginning to dawn (11:8–11). But Hosea criticizes the nation for foreign trading-pacts (11:12 – 12:1) quoting patriarchal history (12:3, 4, 9–13). Jacob in Canaan and his successors in the wilderness were providentially sustained believing God's word through the angel and the prophets (12:4, 10, 13). In spite of these lessons Ephraim remains intransigent (12:8, 11, 14).

11:12 – 12:1 Trade is no substitute for truth. 11:12 Witnesses to Israel's dishonesty crowd around the Judge. The apparently favourable reference to *Judah*, thought by some to be the work of a Judaistic editor, may read (mg.) 'Judah roams with, or is still wayward with, God and with a Holy One who is faithful'. **12:1** *Wind*, often 'vanity' (*cf.* Ec. 1:6, 14) a wild-goose chase. *East wind*; a parching desert blast. To improve their economy they make trade pacts with godless nations.

12:2–6 Jacob became Israel. 2 *Indictment*; 'controversy' (4:1). **3** *In the womb* (Gn. 25:22, 23). From *took . . . by the heel* we get 'Jacob'; from *strove* 'Israel'. Jacob had used unscrupulous cunning to get the birthright (Gn. 27:18–29). **4** It was the blessing which changed his nature (Gn. 32:24–28). *Bethel*; the very place of Israel's idolatry. In Genesis 'Bethel' comes before 'Peniel'; **5** Hosea's purpose is to link 'Israel' with 'Jacob' and the vision of Bethel with Yahweh's name and title. *Name*; literally 'memorial'. The *hosts* may be the angels of God ascending and descending. **6** Hosea appeals to Israel to live up to their great name. But no-one can turn to God without His help. *Love* (*ḥeseḏ*); the sort of

love you can cling to. They were to be just and trustful in their God's provision.

12:7–9 Israel has become Canaan. 7 *A trader*; literally 'Canaan!' The Canaanites were proverbial for their cheating. 'Swindler!' (Moffatt). *False balances*; deceit worse than Jacob's. But even worse, 'he loves to play crooked' (*IB*). **8** God warned Israel about this pride of achievement which would be their ruin (Dt. 8:17–19). But even if Ephraim were rich, he has the wrong currency to buy off his guilt before God (*cf.* Mi. 6:7). MT (AV) difficult in v. 8b; LXX gives RSV. **9** God reminds them of His redemption, which was the purpose of the *appointed feast* (Nu. 10:10) and of His provision, as they dwelt *in tents* during the Feast of Booths (Tabernacles) (Lv. 23:39–44; Dt. 16:13–15).

12:10–14 Faith comes by hearing. God used every occasion to arrest their attention (*cf.* Je. 7:13, 25). **10** And He used every means: plain speech, visions and parables. **11** If (*'im*) does not harmonize with 6:8; a change of one letter (*'im*) gives simply 'in Gilead'. *Gilgal . . . stone heaps* (*gallīm*); a pun. 'On level ground . . . excess rocks were gathered into piles in the fields. But on the hillsides they were built into terraces to keep the good soil from washing away' (*NBD*, p. 19). The altars would resemble a pile of debris. **12** Some think this should follow v. 4, but it fits here: there is a similarity of metre with v. 13, and they both end with the same verb 'keep' (*šāmar*). **13** *A prophet*; Moses. The redeeming and preserving power of God's Word is recalled. As Jacob kept sheep for the wife he loved (Gn. 29:20) so the Lord kept Israel for love's sake (Dt. 7:7). **14** *Bitter provocation*; perhaps at Marah (Ex. 15:22–25).

13:1–16 The death of Ephraim

The end is near: a forgotten Saviour is an awful Foe (13:4–9). The last possible glimmer of repentance fades away as the nation's spirit curls up and dies in the womb of despair (13:13).

13:1–3 Sin, the cause of death. 1 The subject of all verbs may be Ephraim, the superior tribe, before whom others demur. This usage is unusual in Hosea. Sellin thinks the emphatic *he* (*was exalted*) demands a change of subject thus: 'Ephraim spoke . . . and incurred guilt, Moses bore it . . . and died.' Mauchline (*IB, ad loc.*) suggests: 'When Ephraim spoke trembling (as a child), Yahweh was exalted . . . when Ephraim incurred guilt . . . he died'. In any case it shows the connection between sin and death (Rom. 6:23). **2** Man-made gods mean more sin both in devising them and worshipping them. *Kiss*; of homage (*cf.* Ps. 2:12). **3** Four transient figures: *mist, dew* (*cf.* 6:4), *chaff* (*cf.* Ps. 1:4; Mt. 3:12), *smoke* (Is. 51:6).

13:4–11 Deliverer turns Destroyer. 4 *Cf.* 12:9; the intransient God. A god which cannot save is no god at all. No other god is knowable; **5** or knowing. *Drought*; burning thirst: the wilderness was a test for Israel and for the Lord. **6** Satisfaction of their natural appetites led to spiritual pride (cf. Dt. 8:11–17): note *therefore* (cf. Jn. 6:26). **7** *Lurk beside the way*; probably 'on the way to Assyria' (to get help) corresponding to 'there' in v. 8. **10** Yahweh challenges the kings and princes of Israel to make a case for the defence, for they shared judicial functions (cf. 1 Ki. 3:9; Je. 38:7; the gate of the city was the place where justice was administered). **11** The kings hold office only by God's consent. The verbs are iterative indicating general practice, but showing that the kingship is God's second best and subject to His will.

13:12, 13 A remote chance of life. 12 The new-born child will have a legacy of sin saved up over the years. Nothing will be forgotten (cf. Mt. 12:36). **13** But instead of facing up to reality he prefers to die. He is 'a senseless babe' (Moff.). There is a remote chance of survival if the nation will humble itself as a child.

13:14 The executioner is summoned. 14 *Ransom* refers to the payment made, *redeem* to the new relationship. The interpretation hinges on *shall I . . . where?* AV has affirmatives. *Where* probably means 'hither with' (cf. Moff. 'come with'). God is closing His eyes to them as death marches in. Paul (1 Cor. 15:55) shows that in invoking death and destruction He was not overwhelmed but has actually overcome this enemy in His Son.

13:15, 16 Guilty and innocent suffer together. 15 *Flourish,* 'be fruitful'; Ephraim (cf. Gn. 41:52). *East wind*; Assyria, commissioned by the Lord to strip the land. **16** *Samaria*; either the capital and shrine or the whole nation. Sinners never suffer alone in this world.

14:1–8 THE GOSPEL OF GRACE

The new Ephraim, a tree of beauty, fragrance and fruitfulness is planted by the Lord (vv. 5–8). At last they acknowledge their guilt and receive free pardon (vv. 1–4), becoming God's children by grace of adoption (v. 3b).

14:1–3 True repentance

1 How gentle yet firm is the invitation to return. They must acknowledge their *iniquity* in words. **2** Yahweh asks for the sacrifice of a broken and contrite heart (Ps. 51:17). *Take . . . words*; cf. Ex. 23:15. Mg., 'say to him, all of you'; a personal and national repentance is necessary. *Take away . . .* is not imperative but an imperfect

of desire: 'Please, take away . . .'. *All* has emphasis of position. *Accept . . . good*; AV 'receive (us) graciously' is better, for they have nothing good to offer except the sacrifice of praise and thanksgiving, *the fruit (p*e*rî)* or 'calves' (*pārîm*) *of our lips* (Heb. 13:15; 1 Pet. 2:5). Weiser remarks, 'The prophet . . . shows he knew, and approved, a Yahweh cult . . . in which the central portion is held by the Word (God's Word and prayer).' Here is justification by faith (cf. Rom. 3:24). **3** True repentance involves abandoning known sin. Here the double iniquity of reliance on nations (*horses* = Egypt) and idolatry is confessed. *Finds mercy (y*e*ruḥam)*; the Father-love of God for His adopted children (cf. Rom. 8:15, 17).

14:4–8 Reconciled and regenerate

4 *Faithlessness*; sin is a deep-seated malady. How graciously God alters our desires, making us both to want and to do His will (Ps. 37:4; Phil. 2:13). *Freely*; of His own will, spontaneously. This is possible because His *anger* has turned away. Hosea gives no details of this atonement, but the Gospels do. **5** *Dew*; here not transitory, but refreshing. The new Israel will have the beauty of the *lily* (cf. Mt. 6:28, 29) and the noble strength and stability of the *poplar* (lit. 'Lebanon'). **6** The *olive* was noted for its shade and its fruit and *Lebanon* for the aroma of its coniferous forests. Christians are to be attractive, stable, useful. **7** *Garden* (*gan*) may be 'corn' (*dāgān*). They, Israel, will enjoy the protection and vitality of God. All the blessings they struggled, cheated and killed for, will be forgotten in the greater blessings of His grace. **8** *Look after you*; a play on 'Assyria': the Lord will care for His own by making them fruitful ('Ephraim') as part of Himself (cf. Jn. 15:1–5). *Answer*; cf. 2:21, 22.

14:9 THE LESSON TO BE LEARNED

Cf. Ec. 12:13, 14; Ps. 107:43. This may have been added later: it is none the less part of the inspired text. *Right*; undeviating like the Lord. *Wise*; wisdom is more than and rarer than mere knowledge. Knowledge sees the way in which to walk; wisdom walks in it unerringly.

J. B. HINDLEY

Joel

INTRODUCTION

AUTHORSHIP

Nothing is known about the author of this book except his name (which may be symbolic; see the commentary) and his father's name. A very late tradition puts him down as of the tribe of Reuben, but the book itself seems to point to Judah, and in particular Jerusalem, as his background.

He may have been a priest, like Jeremiah or Ezekiel. He certainly was greatly interested in the worship at the sanctuary, like Haggai and Zechariah. But he was undoubtedly a prophet, and therefore many modern scholars and commentators have described him as a 'Temple prophet' or 'cultic prophet' meaning one who has a recognized position in relation to Israel's official religion, and one whose focus was the Temple. He shows great knowledge of farming and the plagues associated with farming life. This, however, is the rule rather than the exception in agricultural Israel, and does not necessarily prove that he was a farmer in the same sense as Amos (cf. Am. 7:14).

DATE

As to the date, most modern scholars feel that a date of about 400 BC would suit, for a variety of reasons. Israel, as the old northern kingdom, does not appear. National life is on a smaller scale, centring around Jerusalem, but there is no king mentioned. The whole life of the community centres around the worship of the Temple, as in the days after the return. Lastly, the language is tinged with Aramaisms. On the other hand the book is unlikely to be very late. While neither Assyria nor Babylon is mentioned, the Greeks are not yet a world power. The Persian vengeance has not descended on Sidon (345 BC), so that we might place the book some time before that date, and after the completion of the wall of Jerusalem by Nehemiah in 444 BC (Joel 2:7 seems to demand this).

Old scholars have placed Joel in the reign of the boy king Joash in the 9th century, but references to the captivity and literary dependence on other prophets seem to rule this out. The position of Joel in the Canon, with reference to other books, is probably not significant. We do not know upon what principle 'the twelve prophets' were arranged, but it was certainly not chronological. The reference to 'the valley of Jehoshaphat' does not help us to date the book; see the commentary on Joel 3:2.

Kapelrud compromises by suggesting the time of Jeremiah, just before the fall of Jerusalem. He does this mainly on the basis of stylistic similarities, but his view is open to the objections made above, and to maintain it he must attribute part of the book to later editions.

OCCASION

The occasion of the book was an exceptionally severe plague of locusts, possibly accompanied by a drought and followed by bush-fire. Like all true prophets, early or late, Joel interprets this historical event, and the combination of event and interpretation becomes God's revelation. In keeping with OT thought, he interprets this plague in terms of divine wrath, and therefore as intended to lead to repentance. His book thus becomes a great plea for a return by Israel to right relations with God. When these relations are restored, there follows a promise of renewed fertility, rather like that in Hg. 2:19.

From this living situation, the book moves gradually into a wider sphere. The locusts become symbols at first of an invading army (perhaps Persian or Greek) coming down from the north, and then a picture of the great complex of events that we call 'the last things', ushering in the acknowledged rule of God within a purified earth. These foreshadowings, however, appear in the distant future; the immediate occasion is the locust plague, and the spiritual and practical issues which it involves for Judah.

NATURE

The book is probably written entirely in verse, in spite of the arrangement of the RSV, which prints part as verse and part as prose. It contains no reference to written prophecy, unlike Isaiah, Jeremiah and Ezekiel. It was therefore probably delivered as a spoken message to the people of Jerusalem, much as we may imagine that of Haggai to have been. It is reasonable to suppose that Joel delivered his oracles to the crowds gathered at the Temple as Jeremiah did (cf. Je. 7:1–4) and Amos in his day (cf. Am. 7:13) and Peter in NT times. The book may even have been 'preached' at one of Israel's great agricultural festivals, when crowds would flock to the city, and when the lack of available offerings would be more conspicuous (1:9), perhaps even causing the festival to be abandoned. But it seems too far-fetched to regard it, with Kapelrud, as a 'liturgical text', either for annual Temple performance at some agricultural festival or on any occasion of visitation by locust plagues.

INTEGRITY

While the book draws heavily on older prophetic sources in the OT, the style is unified throughout and there is no reason to doubt the unity of the authorship on stylistic grounds. Nor indeed is there any marked sign of later editorial revision, and so the book may be assumed to be much as Joel composed it. When the question of authorship is raised, it is usually solely on the grounds of the break in subject-matter half-way through the book. Roughly speaking, 1:1 to 2:27 seem to deal with a practical problem of contemporary society, the locust plague. By contrast 2:28 – 3:21 pass into apocalyptic, dealing with the far distant future. The query is whether the same man could have written both sections. Kapelrud, for instance, sees in the second part an expansion and editing of Joel's earlier message by later Temple prophets. But if Kapelrud were prepared to allow a later date than 600 BC for Joel this problem would not exist. Robinson fairly represents the old school of biblical critics when he attributes the second half to various unknown hands. Pfeiffer, however, who would certainly not be reckoned as a conservative scholar, admits that the conjunction of the historic present with the apocalyptic future is typical of many prophets, and in no sense an argument against unity here.

The Hebrew text (divided into four chapters, instead of the three that appear in English) is good, and has no obvious signs of disruption.

THEOLOGY

This book is not a soul-stirring message in the style of Jeremiah, but it contains several noble calls to repentance (*e.g.* 1:13, 14) combined with an appreciation of the merciful nature of God (2:12–14). For all Joel's interest in priestly and Temple religion, he knows that repentance must be inward, not only outward. 'Rend your hearts and not your garments' (2:13) is a famous verse. Though it is often urged that he adopted an exclusivist attitude, reminiscent of Ezra and the days immediately following the return, and contrasting with the wider horizons of some other prophets, yet Joel does not believe in automatic salvation for all Israel. His strong doctrine of the remnant within Israel saves him from that (2:32). Thompson remarks that this exclusiveness may well have been a necessary stage in God's preparation for the inclusiveness of the gospel in New Testament times. Myers points out that salvation in Joel (since it is by calling on the name of the Lord) is salvation by faith and grace.

In addition the high point of the whole book should not be forgotten. This is the great promise of the universalized gift of the Spirit (2:28, 29). That the prophet's faith could rise to such heights amid the depressing conditions of the returned community is a remarkable testimony, and a supreme proof that this book came by the moving of the very Spirit of God of which it tells.

OUTLINE OF CONTENTS

COMMENTARY

1:1 – 2:27 PROPHETIC HISTORY

1:1 Title of the book

The word of the Lord that came. Cf. the opening verse of Hosea, Micah and Zephaniah. *Word* (*dābār*) does not necessarily mean a spoken word; it can also mean 'matter, subject' in a general sense. Joel wishes to stress that the source of this revelation is God Himself; this alone will give Joel his authority (*cf.*, in the NT, Mt.

7:29 and Jn. 7:17 with 1 Thes. 2:13). A similar phrase in 2:12 is *ne'um yhwh*, translated 'says the Lord' in the RSV. Elsewhere in the Prophets *kōh 'āmar yhwh*, 'thus says the Lord', is a common expression (1 Sa. 2:27, *etc.*). All these underline the same truth; the very bearer of the message was the one most conscious that its source lay outside himself.

Joel, the son of Pethuel. At least a dozen other men are mentioned in the OT as bearing the name *Joel* (*cf.* 1 Sa. 8:2; 1 Ch. 4:35; 5:4, 12; 6:36; 7:3; 11:38; 15:7; 27:20; 2 Ch. 29:12; Ezr. 10:43; Ne. 11:9). These men came from different tribes and are of very different dates; the fact that most instances are recorded in the late book of Chronicles is simply because more genealogies are contained there than in any other book. If, as is likely, the name means 'Yahweh is God' (*cf.* names like Elijah, 'my God is Yahweh', and Elihu, 'He is my God') then the distribution of these references is significant evidence for the widespread worship of Yahweh within Israel. While a name like Joel is certainly very suitable for the bringer of such a message, there is no need to see it as a mere 'pen-name' to cover anonymous authorship (a similar suggestion has been made with reference to the name 'Malachi', which means 'my messenger').

The name *Pethuel* is unknown elsewhere in Hebrew. Perhaps because of this uniqueness, the LXX and the Syriac read 'Bethuel', which is a good patriarchal name (Gn. 22:22), but does not in itself help to date the author, especially as there was a revival of archaic names in Israel's later days.

1:2–20 Description of a locust plague

Most modern commentators have felt that Joel here describes a literal plague of locusts. The wealth of detail is that of an eyewitness and a countryman. Such plagues were the scourge of the Middle East until the introduction of international locust control in recent years. The *Encyclopaedia Americana* (under 'Locust') gives account of some specific 'plagues'. At a popular level see *On the Banks of Plum Creek*, by Laura Ingalls Wilder, chs. 25 and 32, for the impression produced on a child by a similar plague. As in all the prophets, historical fact, when interpreted, becomes God's revelation, and Joel proceeds to explain this locust plague as God's judgment on His sinful people, which may be averted by repentance and turning to Him. It is just as natural for an OT writer like him that this temporal judgment should be seen as a picture of the coming 'day of the Lord' (*cf.* 2:1–11) when God will judge all under heaven; and from this Joel passes easily into the eschatology of the last part of his book (2:28 – 3:21). As many commentators old and new have pointed out, this sort of transition is too characteristic of the OT to lead us to postulate two authors.

2, 3 are typically Hebraic in their call for 'hearing'; when the prophet has himself heard God's word, he must herald it to others. God's revelation is never for our selfish enjoyment; it brings with it a responsibility for others. Perhaps that is why in the NT so much stress is laid on oral confession of Jesus Christ (*cf.* Rom. 10:9). **2** By their appeal to the *aged men*, these verses lay stress on the severity of the plague; not within living or ancestral memory has such a thing happened (*cf.* Ex. 10:6). There may also be a reference to the 'elders' (v. 14), by whom Judah was ruled in post-exilic days (*cf.* Ezr. 8:1),

though, of course, eldership was a very ancient institution (*cf.*, *e.g.*, 1 Sa. 30:26). The *inhabitants of the land* then represent the rest of the population. This locust plague is no ordinary occurrence; this, as Pharaoh's magicians confessed reluctantly, is the 'finger of God' (Ex. 8:19), God's power clearly seen at work. To the Jew, God is always at work in the universe which He has made; nowhere is this more clearly seen than in some of the great 'Nature Psalms', *e.g.* Ps. 104. What we call 'miracles' (Heb. *niplā'ôt*, 'wonders') are only instances more clear and obvious to our dull eyes. The famous 'plagues of Egypt' are one whole such series and Joel's hearers certainly would have remembered the locust plague recorded there (Ex. 10). But now God's people were being treated as God's foes; that is the peculiar sting. Israel has become like the Egyptians to God (*cf.* Am. 9:7). It was just such a locust plague that Amos foresaw, and against which he prayed (*cf.* Am. 7:1–3). Perhaps Joel's great confidence in the forgiving mercy of God comes from his knowledge that God spared Israel in the day of Amos, in answer to earnest prayer.

3 rounds off the section. Joel has heard God's word, so he must speak (*cf.* Am. 3:8). Now Israel has heard Joel's word and they must *tell* their children, and they in turn must tell the generations to come. Faith, trust in God, begins with hearing the message of what God is like (Rom. 10:14–17). We might say that faith is both begotten and nurtured by recounting the mighty acts of God. That is why Jewish and Christian religion involves so much 'recital', retelling the story of God's saving grace and, as Myers says, Joel regards the locust plague as comparable to any other mighty act of Israel's history.

4–7 describe the locust plague dramatically and poetically. **4** Four different words are used for *locust*: *gāzām*, *'arbeh*, *yeleq*, *ḥāsîl* (*cf.* 2:25), but there is no need to assume four separate plagues. There are at least nine possible words for 'locust' in Hebrew; these four are doubtless chosen for poetic variety, and perhaps because they describe various stages of the locust's growth, and thus stages of the plague's onset. Arabic has a similarly rich vocabulary to describe locusts, as it has for 'lion', 'sword' and 'camel', to give a few other instances. Few commentators today would follow the older view that here we have a veiled picture of four foreign empires who would oppress Israel (usually Assyria, Babylon, Greece and Rome; *cf.* the visions of Daniel in Dn. 2.). This would involve an unduly 'apocalyptic' approach to an historical event. Hebrew often heaps up words, in order to stress the total nature of an event (*e.g.* Is. 3:1–3), and here means, so to say, a 'plague *par excellence*'. It well represents the completeness of the judgment of God; absolutely nothing can escape.

5 It is not certain why the *drunkards* are singled out; of course such locusts would strip the grape vines with other green things, and so there would be no *sweet wine, i.e.* 'new wine', that year. It is even possible that the swarm arrived just before grape gathering, and in that case the reference would have been even more appropriate. Perhaps the *drunkards* stand for the selfish members of an affluent society; as such they are often attacked in Amos (Am. 2:8) and Hosea (Ho. 4:11, 18). Parallel to *drunkards* in the verse is *drinkers of wine*, often synonymous with those who lead a luxurious life. It may be, however, that the stress is on *awake*. A sleepiness and unreality, like that of the half intoxicated man, has come over the whole nation, and God's call through Joel is to awaken them to reality (*cf.* Eph. 5:14; 1 Thes. 5:7, 8). Another reason may be found in the pithy Jewish saying 'without wine there is no joy'; all joy and gladness are to be taken away from Israel (*cf.* Joel 1:12c). There may be a further reference to the great agricultural festivals which were normally times of rejoicing in Israel, but which could not be celebrated in this year of disaster.

6, 7 are a vivid description of the ravages of the locusts; after the leaves have been eaten they attack the bark. Vine and fig, with olive oil and grain (v. 10), are the staple crops of Palestine. The locusts are called *a nation (gôy)* as ants are called *'am*, 'a people', in Pr. 30:25, because of their numbers and apparent organization. In Joel 2:25 they are called *ḥayil*, an 'army' of God. This usage may also be the more suitable if they are not only literal locusts, but also represent a coming invasion by a Gentile (*gôy*) enemy from the north (*cf.* 2:20). *Lions' teeth* is a natural symbol, in view of the destruction of the locust. An Arab saying credits the locust with 'the chest of a lion', probably from its appearance, but perhaps also from its destructiveness. Many eyewitness accounts confirm the ghostly white of the barked trees after the passing of a locust swarm, and the bare, burnt appearance of the ground as though parched by drought.

8–20 intersperse descriptions of the plague with appeals to Israel for repentance. **8** The *virgin girded with sackcloth* is the supreme symbol of grief—the girl whose fiancé has been killed before her wedding day. As in many Eastern lands today, the formal engagement was as binding as the wedding in Israel; this explains Joseph's predicament in Mt. 1:18, 19. It was precisely to guard against this sorrow that, in Mosaic law, engaged men were exempt from military service until actually married (Dt. 24:5). *Sackcloth*, ashes and ceremonial wailing were traditional signs of grief.

9 shows us the little world of these 5th-century Jews after the return from Babylon. So severe is the drought that daily offerings in the Temple have ceased. This would not refer to the animal sacrifices—in such times, a farmer would gladly slaughter some of his herd—but to the 'cereal-' and the 'drink-offering' that should by right accompany such flesh sacrifice (*cf.* Ex. 29:38–42). Joel can imagine no greater calamity; for the tiny returned community, perhaps some 40,000

in all, living in and immediately around Jerusalem itself, their horizon was bounded by the Temple walls. The whole wellbeing and security of the nation was bound up with the wholehearted performance of Temple worship (*cf.* Hg. 1:7–11; 2:15–19), as a guarantee of the maintenance of the covenant and of right relationship with God. Haggai, Zechariah, and Malachi likewise belong to this 'day of small things' (Zc. 4:10) as does Ezra, the scribe of the law. Yet God's purpose runs through small times and small men as it does through the great days of Moses, and Joel's concern that God should receive His due in worship is a deep and abiding spiritual principle (*cf.* Mal. 1:8). Further, the correct performance of such ordained sacrifice is only in order that God's covenant may be maintained and expressed; this at once transfers Joel's concern from the ritual to the moral and truly religious realm.

The phrase *ministers of the Lord*, as parallel to *priests*, is late Hebrew, and is another pointer to the date of the book; it is used here in poetic parallelism. Because of this interest in priests and Temple, some have felt that Joel was a priest himself. Others, however, have felt that, here and in v. 13, he clearly differentiates himself from the priestly body. The distinction is not important, for, as said above, the tiny settlement around Jerusalem was like a modern religious kibbutz in Israel—all members were vitally concerned with religious questions. If Joel is a 'Temple prophet' (see Introduction) then the interest is explicable. Some would go so far as to see this book, either wholly or in part, as a liturgy or religious drama performed at public worship in the Temple. Those who hold this view stress the alternation of persons in the book between first, second, and third; but the whole idea seems too far fetched. A place in Israel's religion Joel certainly had and recognized as a prophet of Yahweh he might be. It is very possible that, like Amos at Bethel or Jeremiah at Jerusalem, he delivered some or all of his words in the Temple; but that does not make his book part of a hypothetical New Year Festival ritual in Israel.

10–12, like many other places in the book, use assonance to produce a play on words in the Hebrew. This greatly adds to the sonorous roll of the prophecy, but is virtually impossible to reproduce in English, though Moffatt tries hard. In the returned community, agriculture and the Temple were the two main sources of employment, since trade and industry hardly existed. *Tillers of the soil* and *vinedressers* virtually represent the entire secular population. V. 12, with its catalogue of agricultural failure, is a striking contrast to the buoyancy of Hab. 3:17, 18 which certainly bears some literary kinship to this passage. In spite of even greater disaster, Habbakkuk will still rejoice in the Lord. But, for Joel, the withholding of fruitfulness is not a test of faith, but a punishment for sin. This accounts for the very different attitude towards the same calamity in the two prophets. The emphasis on words like *withers* may mean that, as often, the locust plague came in time of drought. It may also refer to the bleached appearance of the country after the passing of the swarm, when nothing but bare earth and whitened branches show.

13, 14 go further than v. 9. The priests are now summoning the people to solemn fast and prayer in the Temple, as was customary in days of national calamity. Such a day, for instance, was the annual observance of the fall of Solomon's Temple (*cf.* Zc. 7:5). Lv. 16:29 shows how fasting was associated with the forgiveness of sins, in connection with the Day of Atonement.

15 is most significant. Amid another play on words, it equates this local disaster with a premonition of the *day of the Lord*. If, according to the old view, Joel had prophesied under the boy king Joash, in the 9th century, then this would have been the first occurrence of *day of the Lord* in the OT. If, as is much more likely, Joel writes in the 5th century, then he is at the end of a long succession beginning with Amos (*cf.* Am. 5:18). For *the day of the Lord* see Jenni, in *The Interpreter's Dictionary of the Bible*, 1962; Mowinckel, *He that Cometh*, 1956; *NBD*, p. 296b. In short, the phrase means God's clear vindication and manifestation of Himself in earthly history. In early popular eschatology, 'the Lord's day' meant the glorification of Israel and the punishment of her enemies; it was the task of men like Amos to show Israel that judgment began first with the house of God (*cf.* Am. 5:18–20; 1 Pet. 1:17) and that none was exempt. As always in the Bible, every act of God is at one and the same time judgment and salvation; so even in the midst of judgment, there is always a ray of hope for a humble and repentant people. To us in the new covenant 'the Lord's day' has become the weekly glad remembrance of His saving grace. In this plague, Joel sees *the day* as *near* (*cf.* Mk. 1:15, 'the kingdom of God is at hand'). One might say that the divine judgment has already begun; this disaster does not merely prefigure it—it is part of it. Older commentators seem wrong in saying that such disasters are only harbingers of 'the Day', ushering it in.

17–20 continue the vivid description. Those who have lived in a drought-stricken land like Australia will appreciate the imagery. The exact meaning of some terms in v. 17 is guesswork, but it seems to refer to the cracking of the ground in drought. The restless wandering and lowing of cattle is typical, as are the useless empty store-sheds. As for Paul in Rom. 8:19–22, all subhuman nature shares in the consequence of man's sin. Perhaps we can understand this more easily in our modern age; if there is atomic fall-out, beasts will die of leukaemia along with men. The psalter contains parallels to the sympathetic description of thirsty wild animals in v. 20 (*cf.* Ps. 104:11). God is the Lord of the

wilderness as well as of the sown land, God of the bush as well as of the city.

It is not certain whether Joel is describing an actual bush-fire here (always dreaded in dry Palestine; see 1 Ki. 19:12) or the effects of drought, or, as above, the barrenness left after the locust swarms. But in time of drought, or after the locusts, a bush-fire would be most destructive, and so perhaps a combination is meant. Earlier commentators have seen an allusion to the red wings and legs of some types of locusts. God has turned a fruitful land into a salt marsh (*cf.* Ps. 107:34) because of the sins of His people; that is why Joel passes easily into ch. 2, with its forebodings of worse judgments to come at the day of the Lord.

2:1–11 The day of the Lord

Joel returns to the thought of 1:15, the nearness of the day of the Lord. Now there is an urgency, as though doomsday has actually arrived. **1** *Blow the trumpet*. The opening verses suggest a military alarum sounded on the walls of Jerusalem; Nehemiah's men had worked with the trumpeters standing by, only a few years before, to build these walls (*cf.* Ne. 4:18). Perhaps Joel is thinking of 1:14, when the priests were called to 'sanctify' a fast. Such fasts were normally announced by the blowing of the *šôpār* or ramshorn (*cf.* Lv. 23:24), but military signals were also given in this way (*cf.* Jdg. 7:18). The eschatological phrase 'the last trumpet' ultimately belongs to this tradition (*cf.* 1 Cor. 15:52). **2** When Joel says the Lord's day is *a day of darkness* he is no doubt using the same metaphor as Amos (Am. 5:18); light is joy and salvation, while darkness is despair and judgment. It is possible that Joel remembers Ex. 10, where darkness follows the locust plague. But there may be a literal interpretation in the dark clouds of locusts, settling heavily on the hills around Jerusalem. The locusts are now pictured on a scale larger than life, and many commentators have understood them here as prefiguring some invading army from the north. If Joel had written in early days, these could have been the Assyrians, while in later days they could be Persians or Greeks.

3 raises the same question as 1:19, 20, as to whether the *fire* is literal or not. Of course, any invading army would burn and ravage the countryside as it went. The reference to *a garden of Eden* is interesting. Is. 51:3 and Ezk. 36:35 have the same metaphor in reverse, for God will 'make her wilderness like Eden'. At an earlier stage in Israel's history, she was dominated by the thought of the Exodus and conquest (*cf.* Jdg. 6:8). In and after the Babylonian captivity it was the thought of God the Creator that sustained the exiles, for only such a God could re-create His shattered people. It is not therefore surprising that the material of the early chapters of Genesis, as well as the story of the call of Abraham, filled their minds (Is. 51:2, 3 joins both ideas, *e.g.*). **4** Many nations have noted the resemblance of locusts to horses, either because of the shape of their heads, or the action of their legs; Thompson compares their German name *Heupferd*, 'hay-horse', and the Italian diminutive *cavaletta*. Other commentators have referred to the Arabic saying 'In the locust, slight as it is, is the nature of ten of the larger animals—the face of the horse . . .', etc. As Israel's northern invaders were normally cavalry or chariotry, the simile is the more apt if used of an invading army.

5, with *rumbling* and *crackling*, describes the noise of the locusts' wings. Presumably the *tops of the mountains* are ridges immediately around Jerusalem. Either locusts or invading armies would have to spill over these crests before attacking the city itself. **6–9** Subsequent verses describe the remorseless advance of the locusts, crawling up the walls of Jerusalem, as they did in the famous plague of 1915, and pouring through every crack into the houses. *On the Banks of Plum Creek*, as quoted before, is the best commentary on the terror that this 'wave attack' inspires, and the helplessness of the farmers before it. The description would equally well fit the advance of a disciplined army, marching its assault troops against Jerusalem.

10 seems to pass beyond the bounds of mere description. As in Rev. 9, the locusts have become eschatological symbols, though probably, in Joel, still only symbolizing human invaders, not supernatural beings. The earthquake and eclipse are not to be literally interpreted, though such phenomena are associated with God and His coming among men; see Ex. 19:16–18. It is better to see them as descriptions of the awfulness of the last day. Such terms recur again and again in the OT, so that it is sometimes hard to decide the direction of literary dependence. Perhaps the true answer is that there was a common stockpile of eschatological imagery, used by all. These same terms will appear again in the NT, whether in the 'little Apocalypse' of Mk. 13 (*e.g.* vv. 24, 25), or in the wider range of the book of Revelation (*e.g.* Rev. 6:12; 8:12).

11 The locusts have been compared already to an army (*ḥayil*) in 2:5 (a common Semitic simile, found in reverse in Ugaritic literature). Here, they are called God's army and His host, (*maḥⁿneh*). This is Joel's way of reasserting that all nature is in the Creator's hand. In 3:11, however, 'thy warriors, O Lord' (where *gibbôr* is used for 'warrior'), the reference seems to be either to human or angelic soldiers, not to the locusts at all. *Gibbôr* properly means 'mighty one'.

2:12–17 Call to repentance

God's summons to judgment is, in the Bible, not normally a pronouncement of irrevocable doom, but an opportunity for repentance. All the temporal judgments of God are thus also manifestations of His grace, designed to lead us to a change of heart (*cf.* Rom. 2:1–4). Israel is always called to 'return', to 'turn back' to God

because, as His people initially, she enjoyed a relationship which she has now lost. That is why, in the NT, the parable of the prodigal son (Lk. 15:11–32) had such point to a Jewish audience.

12 When the Bible says *heart* it means man's thinking powers, not his emotions. This turning back to God is thus a deliberate effort of will and an attitude of mind. Here, as in Dt. 11:13, the thought behind the phrase *with all your heart* is that of the totality of the response rather than its exact location. **13** In spite of Joel's preoccupation with the Temple and with priestly matters, the first clause of this verse shows that he belonged to the true prophetic succession: *Rend your hearts and not your garments*. The form of phrase is Semitic; he does not forbid or condemn the outward religious sign, but sets it in its true perspective. All prophets value the outward only as a sign of the presence of the inward reality. The description of God as *gracious and merciful* comes from God's self-revelation to Moses in Ex. 34:6, and is repeated in Jon. 4:2. *Steadfast love* is *ḥeseḏ*, the love that gave and maintained the covenant with Israel. It was for this sort of love in Israel that God looked (*cf.* Ho. 6:6), rather than for the ritual worship.

14 introduces (perhaps, on the basis of Am. 7:3) that hope fulfilled in vv. 18ff., where God promises to pour out His blessings on His people. *Repent* (*cf.* v. 13c 'repents of evil'), when applied to God, means that He will not carry out a threatened punishment, either in answer to intercessory prayer (*cf.* Am. 7:5) or because of a change of heart in the human involved, as here. Since God has willed that this should be, there is no conflict, nor limitation, nor inconsistency within God. Again, it is typical both of the smallness of Joel's world, and of his honest selflessness, that he first thinks of *blessing* in terms of ability to renew the interrupted daily offerings at the Temple, as an expression of an unclouded relationship with God. Dn. 8:11 shows how seriously post-exilic Jews viewed suspension of daily offerings in the Temple.

15, calling for a fast in Zion, repeats the thought, and much of the wording, of 1:14 and 2:1. **16** There are Ugaritic parallels to this list of various categories within a community—elders, children, infants, newly-wed, to indicate the total group. But in Ugarit, this is for war; here, it is for prayer. Dt. 24:5 shows that bridegrooms were normally exempt from military service, but necessity knows no law and the urgency for the need to repent is thus shown. For a bridal party to fast was, to the Hebrew, a contradiction in terms (see Mk. 2:19).

17 Those who, like Kapelrud, favour a liturgical interpretation of this book, interpret the words *between the vestibule and the altar* as a sort of 'Temple rubric', directing where the liturgy is to take place. As the phrase has exactly the same poetic rhythm as the message which follows, this is unlikely. It is better, with more literal-minded commentators, to see it as an injunction to mourn even within the inner priests' court (*cf.* 2 Ch. 4:9), for *between the vestibule and the altar* describes this area. The intercession of the priests for Israel in this verse is one of the noblest passages in Joel. It follows the tradition of the great intercessory prayers of the Bible, beginning with those of Abraham (Gn. 18:22–33) and Moses (Dt. 9:26–29). The Name, *i.e.* the revealed nature of God, is the basis of such prayer, along with the inalienable relationship that He has voluntarily established with His people. Where RSV has *a byword among the nations*, AV has 'that the heathen should rule over them'. The theological difference is not great, although the balance of linguistic probability is with the RSV. The last phrase, *Where is their God?* is an echo of Mi. 7:10 and Ps. 79:10. It finds its most poignant expression in the cry of Christ on the cross: 'My God, my God, why hast thou forsaken me?' (Mt. 27:46). 'He trusts in God; let God deliver him now', said the chief priests as they derided and mocked Him (Mt. 27:43). If Israel had been a byword, so was Israel's unrecognized Messiah, dying in apparent shame and weakness on the cross.

2:18–27 God's blessing restored

18 In this passage, Joel uses two parallel phrases to describe God, saying He *became jealous* and *had pity*; both describe the same reaction. *Jealous* would perhaps be better translated today as 'zealous', of which it is only a by-form in English. The concept as applied to God is as old as the explanation of the Ten Commandments in Ex. 20:5. It means that God is not cold or abstract or impersonal; He is love and He is the living God. In Bible thought *qannā'*, 'zealous', denotes a living personal relationship, exclusive in the sense that it will not tolerate either deviation or rival. Because God is 'zealous', there are times when He must punish His people. Equally, because He is zealous, He will turn away from His anger and come down to save His undeserving people. Both these aspects of wrath and mercy are brought out in the Exodus passage. **19** As often in the OT, especially in very early or very late prophets, God's blessing is expressed in material ways, almost understood as a sacrament of His presence. *Grain, wine and oil* are the wealth of a farming community and thus the gift of God, as in Ho. 2:8 (*cf.* Am. 9:11–15).

V. **20**, with its reference to *the northerner*, is a prophetic *double entendre* rather than a problem. Kapelrud discusses it as an eschatological symbol, and interprets this passage in the light of the last days. Thompson, however, points out that, in the past, locust plagues have frequently swept down from Jerusalem from the north, so that this verse could be quite literal. It is also true that Israel's main invaders (Aram, Assyria, Babylon, Persia, Greece, Rome) all attacked from the north; apart from Egypt, there was no major danger from other quarters. Thus the northerner, an army or king from the

north (Je. 1:13; Dn. 11:6) could well be a picture of any invader. There is no need to look for special symbolism of points of the compass here; it was a sheer fact of geography for Israel, as a glance at a map will show. In English history the same is true; for centuries 'northmen' meant enemies or raiders, irrespective of their exact country of origin. To a Chinese, 'westerner' had much the same meaning. If then we take the verses literally, God will whirl the locusts from Jerusalem to the Negeb (*a parched and desolate land*), probably by a north or north-west wind; *cf.* God's use of wind in Ex. 10:13, 19. In that case the 'locust belt' would stretch from the Philistine coast (*western sea*) to the Dead Sea (*eastern sea*), and doubtless many would drown. As to the *stench* of drowned locusts there is much recorded in the commentators. Of course this could equally well remind Israel of the odour of thousands of unburied bodies on an old battlefield; *cf.* Is. 66:24. To our modern world, one of the most refreshing things about the Bible is its frankness; a bad smell is still a bad smell, even in Scripture.

21ff. There is a description of the quick restoration of a parched and ravaged countryside by the coming of good rains. **22** Those who have lived in a land liable to drought will appreciate how quickly *the pastures of the wilderness are green.* Over the brown dust and cracked clods there spreads a fresh blur of green, and the burnt branches push out fresh leaves. Animals and men alike share in God's bounty, as they had shared in the dearth before.

23 Joel likes to use the old name *Zion*, not just for Jerusalem (*cf.* 2:15) but for all Judah (*cf.* 2:23), probably because of its Davidic associations. It is not a meaningless archaism or an escapism into the past, but a confident looking into the Messianic future. Fruitfulness in Israel, as in Australia today, depends on winter rain. The early rain was October and November, at sowing time, and the even more precious *latter rain* was March–April, when the grain was swelling, before the fierce heat of the summer. The translation of *hammôreh liṣᵉ ḏāqâ* as *the early rain for your vindication* (*cf.* AV, 'the former rain moderately') seems likely in view of Ho. 10:12 and Is. 45:8, both again with reference to rain. Presumably the thought is that, now Israel has repented, God sets His seal to their repentance by the gift of rain. The rain is, as it were, God's mark that they are justified or righteous. Thus God is now righteous to treat them so. But the word *môreh*, translated *rain* here can also mean 'teacher', and it is highly probable that the Essenes of the Qumran community derived their concept of the 'Teacher of Righteousness', or 'righteous teacher' from a typically Hebraic pun or Rabbinic exegesis of this verse. The Targum and Vulgate, not to mention some modern commentators, have preferred the translation 'the teacher', quite independently of the Dead Sea Scrolls. In that case the Essenes must have regarded the appearance of their teacher, whether historical or hypothetical, as a sign of the last days. **24, 25** Whatever the exact interpretation of v. 24, the main outline is clear; the land is flowing, not with milk and honey (that is the ideal of the nomad shepherd), but with *grain, . . . wine and oil*, the farmer's ideal. The years of the locust plague have vanished in years of plenty. This is still in the future for Joel's countrymen; but if they repent, it will surely follow. For the hard agricultural conditions after the return from Babylon, see Hg. 2:16.

26, 27 Then, in words very reminiscent of Deuteronomy (26:1-11), the prophet states God's goal in all this; Gód's people are to realize His love and power, and know that He is their God, in their véry midst. Indeed v. 27 is as strong a statement of monotheism as anything in the second half of Isaiah, or anywhere else in the OT.

2:28 - 3:21 ESCHATOLOGY

2:28, 29 Universalized gift of the Spirit

The Hebrew Bible (which makes Joel four chapters) begins its third chapter at this point, thus emphasizing its importance. It is quite clear from the word *afterward* that, while the giving of fruitfulness lies in the near future, the universalized gift of the Spirit lies in the distant future from Joel's standpoint. It was therefore a true insight of Peter's in Acts 2:16ff. to apply this promise to the gift of the Spirit at Pentecost, a feast which in origin celebrated the fullness of the harvest, and was a thanksgiving to God for the fruits of the earth. 'In the latter days' is another common phrase used in the OT to introduce descriptions of the last things.

At the risk of over-simplification, it may be said that God gave His Spirit, in OT days, to special men on special occasions for special tasks. Indeed there was almost an 'aristocracy of the Spirit', for such leaders were few in number compared with the mass of the people. The responsibility of the people was not to receive special guidance themselves but to recognize and obey God's voice, as mediated to them through these Spirit-filled leaders, rather as a Christian must recognize in the voice of Christ, the voice of God (*cf.* Jn. 7:16, 17). Now the possession of the Spirit will be the universal hall-mark of God's children, though the Spirit will find outlet in various ways. The metaphor of 'pouring' the Spirit (*cf.* Is. 32:15) is no doubt derived from the deluge of winter rains in Palestine. Numerous other prophets have spoken of this new plan of God's in their own way (Ezekiel, with reference to the Spirit, Ezk. 37:1-14, and Jeremiah with reference to the new covenant, Je. 31:31-34) but none more clearly than Joel. Even he is only reproducing the noble wish of Moses in Nu. 11:19 that all the Lord's people might be prophets, voiced in answer to Joshua's protest.

In OT (*cf.* Ex. 31:3; 35:31) and New Testament alike (*cf.* 1 Cor. 12:4-11) the gift of the Spirit has numerous forms and outlets. Here *prophesy*, *dream*, and *visions* shows that Joel, in an age when prophecy is almost dead (*cf.* Zc. 13:4), is thinking mainly of the Spirit as revealing God's will. In the Mosaic age, though not apparently in Joel's day, prophecy had been ecstatic, accompanied by unusual physical phenomena. It was therefore natural that in Peter's day, surrounded by the phenomena of Pentecost (Acts 2:1-4) his mind should go back to this passage of Joel.

2:30-32 Signs of the last days

Nowadays we tend to separate these verses from those immediately above dealing with the gift of the Spirit, but it is noteworthy that Peter, in Acts 2:16-21, continues his quotation of Joel to the end of v. 32. He equates the gift of the Spirit with the dawning of the Messianic age, which was to usher in the final judgment. Theologically this is true: factually, we recognize that, while in one sense the final judgment is always in operation, in another sense its full manifestation is yet to come. No doubt Peter and the first generation expected this full manifestation in their own day, and this should be the constant attitude of the people of God. In the Hebrew Bible, 2:28-32 is bracketed together as a separate chapter, forming ch. 3.

30, 31 The various portents given are common to both OT and NT eschatology—blood, fire, smoke and darkness. All are natural symbols, drawn from vivid memories of invading armies. Whether v. 31 is to be understood as a literal solar eclipse (often held as symbol of disaster) or metaphorically, as the collapse of world powers, is uncertain. The latter seems to be the more likely interpretation in the 'little Apocalypse' of Mk. 13:24 as well as in Rev. 6:12, where the same symbol appears. **32** Peter in Acts 2:21 uses the concept of *all who call upon the name of the Lord* as Paul does in Rom. 10:13.

V. 32 is the clearest example in the whole book of quotation from another prophet. The words *in Mount Sion . . . there shall be those who escape* are borrowed directly from Ob. 17, and the quotation is acknowledged by Joel by the addition of *as the Lord has said*. It is, however, possible that both Obadiah and Joel are quoting some earlier anonymous prophetic saying: *cf.* the allusion made in Gn. 22:14, 'on the mount of the Lord it shall be provided'. When closely examined, the OT proves to be a nexus of quotation and natural dependence, reaching far deeper than such acknowledged dependence of the later prophets on their predecessors. Dn. 9:2, referring directly to Jeremiah, is an illustration of this, as is Zc. 1:4, with its general reference to 'the former prophets'. Jeremiah's life was saved only because it was remembered that, a century before, Micah had preached the same message unscathed (Je. 26:18). For a detailed discussion of the parallel passages in Joel and the other OT books, see Thompson in *IB*. There are over twenty places where identical words are used. In all cases where the direction of the dependence can be traced, it is Joel who has borrowed from the other prophets, and not *vice versa*. This simply indicates that Joel is writing fully in the prophetic tradition, and at the end of that tradition. As Paul would say, prophecy was already passing away (see 1 Cor. 13:8). This was fully realized both in OT (Zc. 13:4) and Apocryphal days (1 Macc. 4:46). Indeed, that was why the appearance of John the Baptist caused such excitement, as heralding the rebirth of the prophetic order (*cf.* Mal. 4:5).

It has been said that Joel, short book though it is, is yet a veritable compendium of OT eschatology. It contains five references to the day of the Lord (for a similar use of 'day' with a special significance, *cf.* 'D-day'), and every major eschatological topic except those of the Messiah, the resurrection and the inclusion of the Gentiles. Ezekiel, Isaiah and Zephaniah find many echoes throughout.

3:1-15 Judgment on the nations

1 Once again, as in Je. 33:15, *in these days and at that time* points to the distant and vague future. RSV with the general phrase *restore the fortunes of Judah* may be correct, but the AV 'bring again the captivity of Judah' is the literal translation. This does not necessarily prove Joel an exilic prophet; the vast majority of the exiles never came back, even in the days of Nehemiah and Ezra, but remained in Babylonia as 'captives'. This picture now becomes that of a vast assize with *all the nations* gathered before God the Judge (*cf.* Zp. 3:8). The metaphor may have been suggested by the oft-repeated sight of multi-racial foreign armies, lying camped around Jerusalem, in the numerous sieges of her troubled history. **2** It may be that the phrase *valley of Jehoshaphat* is chosen simply for the meaning of the name, 'the Lord has judged'. The play on the verb *I will enter into judgment* in the second half of the verse, suggests this explanation, as does the synonym 'valley of decision' in v. 14. But if a geographical location is sought, from the days of Eusebius onwards the Kidron Valley has been associated with this name. Perhaps we may *cf.* the term 'the King's Valley' of Gn. 14:17, also near Jerusalem. Obviously any attacker would have to occupy this valley after seizing the Mount of Olives, before he could attack the walls of Jerusalem. The whole area would then become a great natural amphitheatre, packed with troops. The mention of *Jehoshaphat* has sometimes been used as an argument for a 9th-century date for the book of Joel. But if this is only a place-name, no argument as to date can be based on it, except that the reference can hardly antedate the king of that name.

4-8 The list of the sins of the *gôyîm*, or non-Jewish nations, reminds us of the catalogue in Am. 1:1 – 2:3. They have been merciless to the defenceless, the prisoner of war and the refugee. At this late date, the wealthy slave-merchants of Phoenicia and Philistia are the culprits singled out. Even in the days of Am. 1:6, Philistine slave-dealers had been active, but now they were actually selling Jewish slaves to the *sons of the Ionians* (v. 6). That the Greeks are a great commercial power, but not yet world rulers, helps to date the book, as does the complete absence of reference to Assyria or Babylon. The lack of reference to Persia could be explained by setting the book in the days of the early Persian Empire, when the Persian yoke was still light. In the late 4th century, Persia became decadent and oppressive. In 345 BC, after a revolt, Sidon was attacked and enslaved and, in 332 BC Alexander treated Gaza in the same way. Here was a grim fulfilment of prophecy, for doubtless Jewish middlemen, who stood in high favour at the Persian court, as Nehemiah's career shows, and enjoyed Alexander's favour, as the Jewish quarter in Alexandria demonstrates, sold these slaves in the markets of South Arabia. For the *Sabeans*, see the article by Van Beek in *The Interpreter's Dictionary of the Bible*; their importance continued into Roman days later.

Perhaps this cruelty of the Phoenicians and Philistines had taken place long before, at the time of the Babylonian sack of Jerusalem in 586 BC. We learn from Ezra and Nehemiah, however, that slavery for debt was not unknown even among the small community that returned from exile (*cf.* Ne. 5:5). We also know of Phoenician traders frequenting the Jerusalem markets in those days (*cf.* Ne. 13:16). But the reference to Temple robbing (v. 5) would fit the earlier period better. Again, there is a grim humour in v. 4. When the Phoenicians acted thus, they no doubt felt they were avenging themselves on the Lord (perhaps for the Phoenician massacres of Jehu's reign?) but now the Lord's vengeance will fall upon them. It is well to remember that in an age to which the doctrine of the resurrection had not as yet been clearly revealed, it was necessary that God should vindicate His character in this life, lest men should doubt His justice.

9-15 The RSV prints these verses as a new section, and in verse form. But the opening verses of the chapter are also poetry, and are printed as such in the Hebrew Bible. There is, however, a definite quickening of tempo, as the imaginary war token is sent to the nations. It may be that even the form of words in vv. 9, 10 is traditional on such occasions, for there are similarities in the Ugaritic texts that deal with the same subject. **10** has been called a parody of Is. 2:4 and Mi. 4:3 because it makes exactly the opposite demand, not that men 'beat swords into ploughshares' but that they *beat ploughshares into swords*. But perhaps Joel's was the original rallying call for Israel that went out along with the pieces of the slaughtered ox (or in darker days, pieces of a human body; *cf.* 1 Sa. 11:7; Jdg. 19:29). In that case it would be Isaiah and Micah who have altered the wording, not Joel. R. A. Stewart considers this possible, for other reasons.

11 The exact meaning of *bring down thy warriors, O Lord* is not clear. Thompson takes it as a reference to God's angelic armies. If so, we might compare Dn. 10:20 and Christ's words to His disciples in the garden of Gethsemane (Mt. 26:53). But perhaps it only means that God is leading these heathen hordes into a trap. **13** Supporting the first view would be the command to *put in the sickle*. Down to NT times, the eschatological harvesters are usually the angels; see Mt. 13:39; Rev. 14:14-19. Harvest and vintage, which come close together in Palestine, are natural symbols of the end of an age in any agricultural country that enjoys a seasonal climate. They are also fit symbols of the judgment because the true state of the crop is then and then only declared. Other factors that assist in the use of this image are, on one hand, the joy surrounding both harvest and grape-gathering and, on the other hand, the custom of treading out the grapes with bare feet, producing crimson stains like blood on feet and clothing. For a vivid application of this in a Messianic context see Is. 63:1. It is striking that, in the Lord's Supper, Christians still use bread and wine, the twin symbols of harvest and vintage, salvation and judgment.

3:16-21 Salvation for God's people

From now on the focus of the picture changes from God's enemies to God's people. Many features remind us of Amos, so much so that Joel may have been consciously reproducing some of the older prophet's ideas. Am. 1:2 has the simile of the Lord roaring like a lion, and Am. 9:13 supplies the picture of the mountains running with new wine, reproduced by Joel in v. 18. It may also be significant that Amos dates his prophecies by reference to an earthquake (Am. 1:1). From Mosaic days, earthquake was an outward symbol of theophany, and so in Joel the heavens and the earth shake when God speaks (v. 16). Here the goal of God's action is not only that His people may know Him for what He is, but also Jerusalem may be holy, and undefiled by outsiders. Contrast Dn. 8:13, where the tramp of foreign feet is continually to desecrate the Temple.

18 Beside the traditional pictures of agricultural fruitfulness, there is one which is typically Israelite—*all the stream beds of Judah shall flow with water* (v. 18). These are the dry wadis, the water-courses in the Negeb mentioned in Ps. 126:4. After heavy rain they become rushing torrents and, as long as they contain water, there is pasture even in the desert. The second half of the couplet, *a fountain shall come forth from the house of the Lord*, is certainly not to be taken literally, but in close connection with the symbolic river that is to flow from the Temple (*cf.* Ezk. 47:1-12; Zc. 14:8). Thompson suggests that the existence of sacred springs like Gihon in the valley below the Temple may at least have suggested the analogy. In that case the *valley of Shittim* ('Acacias') would be the lower area of the Kedron valley, where to this day there is a thin growth of acacias, although the area is very dry. But in view of Christ's use of this symbol of a spring in Jn. 4:14, and the symbolism of the 'river' in Rev. 22:1, 2 it is probably unnecessary to look for a temporal locale. Joel may well be thinking of the rivers of Paradise in Gn. 2:10-14; *cf.* Ps. 46:4. If Israel's history had been 'Paradise lost' then the Messianic age is 'Paradise regained'. Ever since Isaiah's day, 'the waters of Shiloah that flow gently' (Is. 8:6) have been a Messianic symbol, as opposed to the flood that signifies judgment.

19-21 In the closing verses, Joel turns momentarily from God's salvation to His judgment. Here are two pictures side by side. Judah has become a fruitful land instead of a wilderness, and *Egypt* and *Edom* have been turned into a wilderness from a fruitful land. This is the double aspect of God's work stressed in Ps. 107:33-36. For the threatened overthrow of Egypt, *cf.* Ezk. 29:1-12. The bitterness felt by the Jews towards Edom was very great, principally because of their siding with Babylon in the final attack on Jerusalem (*cf.* Ps. 137:7). The hatred towards Egypt may have been because, so often in the past, Egypt had proved a broken reed in time of trouble (*cf.* 2 Ki. 18:21).

No doubt Egypt shared in the general suffering and slaughter of late Persian rule, for she hailed Alexander gladly as a deliverer. Edom, though the Jews hated her for her occupation of Jewish Hebron and the Negeb, suffered far more severely herself. At this time, she lost all her old homeland (including the capital Sela, later Petra) to the new and aggressive Arab group, the Nabataeans. So soon was the 'word of the Lord' fulfilled on these lands, but Judah and Jerusalem remained, an abiding testimony to the faithfulness of God. With this triumphant assertion, *the Lord* dwells in *Zion*, the little book of Joel ends.

R. A. COLE

Amos

INTRODUCTION

THE TIMES OF AMOS

The precise date which the book of Amos supplies (1:1), 'two years before the earthquake', is unfortunately no longer ascertainable. Uzziah of Judah can be dated (767–740 BC), as can his contemporary, Jeroboam II of Israel (782–753 BC). The question remains at what point within these long reigns the internal evidence of the book makes most sense. A dating c. 760 BC is well agreed among students and suits the facts.

The reign of Jeroboam was exceedingly prosperous. Everything was conducive to Israelite expansion, and this energetic king was not slow to seize the opportunity. In 805 BC Adad-nirari III of Assyria crushed Damascus and thus disposed of Syria as a threat to the other Palestinian states. Assyria itself, however, subsequently lost momentum and made no serious attempt to exercise authority over the Mediterranean coastlands until the accession of Tiglath-pileser III in 745 BC.

Jeroboam extended the borders of his kingdom until they coincided with those of the days of Solomon, and it is very likely that Am. 6:13 (see Commentary) reflects national pride in his military prowess. Extended territory gave the nation extended control of trade routes, and this resulted in immense commercial prosperity and the establishment of a wealthy aristocracy, living in great luxury (e.g. 2:12, 15; 5:11; 6:6).

The land had known its share of troubles (e.g. 4:6–11), but worldly political wisdom saw nothing ahead but the prolongation of affluence and the banishment of serious difficulties into the remote future (5:18a; 6:3a). All these evidences agree well with a date somewhere in the middle of Jeroboam's reign.

THE TEACHING OF AMOS

God

The emphasis which Amos places on the unique privilege of Israel (2:9–11; 3:2) contrasts markedly with his failure to speak of the Lord as 'God of Israel'. In the same connection, while he clearly understands Israel to be the covenant people, he never uses the word 'covenant'. In his representation of God, in other words, everything which might foster Israelite complacency is omitted, and his favourite titles tend to be 'the Lord God' (i.e. 'the sovereign Yahweh', 1:8; 3:7, 8, 13; 4:2, 5; 5:3; 6:8; 7:1, 2, 4, 5, 6; 8:1, 3, 9, 11; 9:8), 'Lord' or 'God of hosts' (i.e. of omnipotent power, 4:13; 5:14, 15, 16, 27;

6:8, 14), 'the Lord' (i.e., when not printed in capitals, 'the Sovereign', 5:16; 7:7, 8; 9:1), and sometimes great compound designations (e.g. 5:16). We shall note later the significance of the majority occurrence of the divine name, Yahweh ('LORD' in RSV), the covenant name, and of the gracious closing description 'the Lord your God' (9:15), but it is undeniably the case that in portraying his God Amos stresses those features of His character which underly His universal rule and government.

Like the rest of the OT, Amos bases his monotheism on the facts that the Lord is the Creator (4:13; 5:8; 9:5, 6), that He is the Agent in all history (3:6; 4:6–11; 9:7), and that He alone is the moral Governor of all nations (1:3 – 2:16). At the same time it is possible for Israel to defect to other 'gods' (5:26, 27), for though there is but one God there are other objects of worship (cf. 1 Cor. 8:5, 6). Yet the monotheism of Amos is as unequivocal as that of Paul.

Judgment

The most obvious derivative from Amos's monotheism is that this great and only God is the Judge of the world. The features of his teaching which stand out are first, that crimes against humanity (see on 1:3 – 2:3), wherever, why ever and however committed, are abhorrent to God and under His judgment; second, that the privilege of being the people of God carries with it the consequence of weightier and more certain judgment (3:2), for the sins of God's people are not just against the light of nature but specifically against the light of revelation (see on 2:4ff.); and third, that there is no distinction ultimately between crimes and sins, i.e. between wrongs against our fellow-men and deliberate affronts to God's law (see on 3:9ff.).

Hope

Does Amos preach judgment to the exclusion of hope? It is quite commonly held that he does, and even that this explains why he was the first prophet whose utterances were committed to writing, because he was the first to proclaim the end of God's covenant with Israel (cf. R. E. Clements, *Prophecy and Covenant*, 1965). The view espoused in this commentary is that this is plainly not so. First, there is the clear evidence of the first two visions (7:1–6): Amos prays against total judgment, specifically on the ground that it is total, and his prayer is granted. This alone shows how mistaken it is to exclude hope from his teaching. If anything is excluded it is that God intends the final end of His people.

The commentary seeks to show that on this view chs. 7 to 9 form a coherent and persuasive whole, revealing how the sovereign justice which inevitably punishes is married to the sovereign mercy which guarantees the saving purposes of God.

Secondly, there is the fact that Amos is supremely a prophet of Yahweh, the Lord. He uses the divine name at least fifty-one times, excluding its occurrence in the compound 'the Lord God'. Even at the height of his warning, he proclaims a dire confrontation with 'your God' (4:12), and he ends with a word of promise from 'the Lord your God' (9:15). In the midst of judgment the relationship is somehow intact. And, of course, this is exactly the revelation of Yahweh which the OT enshrines, for He earned His title as 'the Lord your God, who brought you out of the land of Egypt' by a single action (the Passover) which both judged His enemies and saved His people. Amos cannot prophesy in the name of this God unless he has a message of salvation to preach.

Prophecy

Amos subscribed to the classical doctrines concerning a prophet and his functions (see on 2:11; 3:8), and gave also a personal testimony concerning his own status. In 7:14, 15 the translation of his words 'I not a prophet' (for the Hebrew expresses no verb) has occasioned much enquiry. Some urge that we must understand 'I am not a prophet' (see J. Bright, *A History of Israel*, 1960, p. 246; Y. Kaufmann, *The Religion of Israel*, 1961, p. 343; *cf.* C. Kuhl, *The Prophets of Israel*, 1961, p. 60). They hold that Amos was repudiating membership of the guilds of professional prophets. It is hard to see that this can be the case since Amos goes on to say that by divine command he has been sent to 'prophesy', literally 'to function as a prophet'. Can he both deny and affirm the same thing? Bright's rejoinder that what he meant was 'yet I am a prophet in the true sense' requires us to understand too much which Amos left unexpressed. G. R. Driver takes the words as a question: 'Am I not a prophet, and son of a prophet because I am a herdsman . . . ? And the Lord took me . . .' But was Amaziah casting doubt on Amos's prophetic vocation because he also followed a secular calling? On the whole it seems best to adopt a past tense (see on 7:14; *cf.* S. R. Driver, *Joel and Amos*, 1915; R. M. Gwynn, *Amos*, 1927): Amos looks back to a time when he was a prophet neither in fact nor in prospect, until the crucial experience of the divine appointment gave him prophetic status.

Religion

The outward appearance of Israel in Amos's day was extremely religious, but it was a religion divorced from the law of God (see on 2:7b, 8), devoid of spiritual benefit (see on 4:4, 5), incapable of sheltering its adherents (see on 3:14; 5:5, 6) and unproductive of moral and social

justice (see on 5:21–25). It was this last aspect in particular which drove Amos to ask his famous question: 'Did you bring to me sacrifices and offerings the forty years in the wilderness?' (5:25). There are still those who understand that by this question Amos was calling for a religion of ethical behaviour without any corporate cultic expression by means of sacrifices (*cf.* C. F. Whitley, *The Prophetic Achievement*, 1963, pp. 73ff.; J. Lindblom, *Prophecy in Ancient Israel*, 1963, pp. 352f.), but on the whole specialist opinion is moving rather to the view that Amos repudiated the abuse of the cult and did not question its ultimate divine authorization (*cf.* H. H. Rowley, *The Unity of the Bible*, 1953, p. 42; R. E. Clements, *op. cit.*, pp. 94ff.; 'Prophecy and Prophets', *NBD*).

The vital matter is to note that Amos makes his point by means of a question. To convey a truth by means of a question means that Amos is here expressing not only his own opinions but also those of his hearers, and there can be no doubt that those to whom he was preaching would have replied in the affirmative: sacrifices and offerings were indeed part of the wilderness (and therefore normative) religion. Amos courted disaster for his argument if he expected the answer 'No'. This position does not depend on one's acceptance of the Mosaic authorship of the Pentateuch, for, as Kaufmann points out (*op. cit.*, p. 365), if this verse repudiates the cult, 'it is not sufficient to say that Amos did not know of P's tabernacle and cult laws. One must also assume that he was ignorant of JE'—and, we may add, that his hearers were equally ignorant! The view proffered in the commentary is that v. 25 redresses any possibility of imbalance between vv. 21, 22 and vv. 23, 24: 'Was it sacrifices and offerings you brought me in the wilderness . . . ?' Was the cult the top priority of the religion stemming from Sinai? Thus Amos's rhetorical question raises the question not of the propriety of sacrifice but of its proper priority and place in Israel's religion.

THE BOOK OF AMOS

The book of Amos comes before us as a very carefully edited piece of literature, and there seems to be no good reason for doubting that Amos could have been and was his own editor. If, following 7:10–17, he was compelled to flee the north, or if, his prophetic task over, he simply returned to his home in Tekoa, this, as well as his southern origin, sufficiently explains both the Judahite element in the dating (1:1) and sporadic Judahite references throughout.

But are there parts of the book which ought to be assigned to other authors than Amos? The following are the main passages which have suggested this conclusion to some commentators: the prophecy against Judah (2:4, 5) has been suspected, first because it is against Judah and Amos was a prophet to Israel, second because it allegedly lacks the fervour characteristic of

Amos, third because its wording (*e.g.* 'to walk after' meaning to worship idols; 'to reject the law of the Lord') shows the influence of Deuteronomy. In reply it may be urged that Amos's primary task towards Israel no more rules out an oracle against Judah than against the other nations listed in ch. 1; that even if the Judah oracle lacks fervour (which at best is a matter of opinion) it is not surprising in a prophet from Judah; and that if there are links with Deuteronomy (and the suggestions are both meagre and commonplace) it is more reasonable to use this as evidence for an early date for Deuteronomy than as requiring us to dismember the prophecy of Amos.

The three similar passages, 4:13; 5:8, 9; and 9:5, 6, have been questioned. The argument is partly exegetical, that the passages are abrupt in their context. This has been dealt with in the commentary, where it has been shown that in each case the disputed passage has a vital task to perform, in showing that the Lord is capable of bringing in exactly that form of judgment which the preceding verses have threatened. The second line of objection to the integrity of these verses has been doctrinaire in the extreme: that they reflect a later theology than was possible in Amos's day (see, *e.g.*, J. P. Hyatt, 'Amos' in *Peake's Commentary on the Bible*, 1963, p. 617). The doctrine in question is that of God as Creator (*cf.* H. W. Robinson, *Inspiration and Revelation in the Old Testament*, 1946, p. 22). Apart from the fact that this theory assumes an exilic date for Is. 40–55, in which the doctrine of Yahweh the Creator is explicit, it is not now so readily accepted that one can be dogmatic about the development of doctrine in the Old Testament, and, as J. D. Smart remarks, this theology 'is not in any way inconsistent with the thought of Amos, and there seems to be no very convincing reason for denying them to him' (*IDB*, 1962, Vol. I, p. 119).

The main assault on the integrity of Amos has ever centred on 9:8b–15. It is probable that the excision of these verses stemmed from the belief that a doctrine of hope had no place in the teaching of Amos. We have shown above that this is not and cannot be the case. The argument was, however, strengthened by the allegation that the passage was too abrupt in context to be genuine: the reader must judge from the following commentary how much weight is to be attached to this. It would seem to have none at all. This leaves two other lines of attack. The first is that the language of this closing passage in the book of Amos has affinities with exilic and post-exilic writings. On examination this comes down to a mere matter of vocabulary, concerning which S. R. Driver (*op. cit.*, p. 125) was of the opinion that 'the phrases used are not linguistically suggestive of lateness; and the question is whether, it being granted that Amos might have contemplated (like other prophets) not only the exile of his people, but also its restoration, they do more than give expression

to that idea under forms which might naturally have presented themselves to him'.

The second line of attack centres on the nature of prophecy. The verses presuppose the fall of Judah, and the question (as, *e.g.*, posed by R. S. Cripps, *The Book of Amos*, 1929, pp. 67ff.) is whether it is reasonable to ask men to look forward to the restoration of the house of David while that house is still standing. The principle lying behind this approach has been persuasively stated by G. E. Wright (*Isaiah*, 1964, p. 8): 'A prophecy is earlier than what it predicts, but contemporary with, or later than what it presupposes.' If this is indeed the case, then the present passage seems to presuppose the fall of Jerusalem and must therefore be either contemporary with or later than that event. The matter is not, however, so easily settled. Can a prophet never presuppose what he has himself earlier prophesied? Could Amos, who prophesied the fall of Jerusalem (2:4, 5) not presuppose it and look beyond it? It would be to a degree unnatural if he did not. Thus the argument falls to the ground. If, of course, the reference to the fallen Tabernacle of David looks back to the division of the kingdom (see commentary, *in loc.*), then this particular argument is doubly unnecessary and mistaken.

THE BOOK IN OUTLINE

Each section of the book of Amos presents a clear message, and the three sections form a developing pattern in which answers are provided to questions raised by what has gone before. As it stands, the book is complete and well ordered.

Section 1, **The lion's roar: universal judgment and its ground** (1:2 – 3:8), proclaims imminent divine judgment (1:2) against neighbouring heathen nations (1:3 – 2:3), against Judah (2:4, 5), and Israel (2:6–16). Amos concludes this startling message by insisting that what he says is the word of the Lord (3:1–8) and the section ends as it began (1:2) with the lion's roar (3:8).

Section 2, **An enemy in the land** (3:9–6:14), reveals how the Lord will accomplish this judgment, and probes more deeply into the causes of His anger. National social crimes (3:9–11) are sins against God (3:12–15) and provoke His holiness (4:1–3). Religious formalism (4:4, 5), devoid of spiritual response to God (4:6–11), provides no safeguard and confrontation is inevitable (4:12, 13). Consequently the prophet laments over the fallen nation (5:1–3) which refused calls to spiritual (5:4–13), moral (5:14–20), and religious (5:21–27) reformation. Their complacent self-confidence (6:1–7) will collapse before the inrushing foe (6:8–14).

Section 3, **The Lord Yahweh** (7:1 – 9:15), faces the crucial question whether this judgment marks the end of God's purposes for Israel. Has He finally cast off His people? Amos records two visions of complete destruction (7:1–6) against which he prayed and prevailed. This would not be the Lord's way. A third vision (7:7–9) of discriminating judgment evoked no prayer: God will search His people through and through. Once more this startling message stirs Amos to state his credentials as a prophet (7:10–17). Judgment, though imminent (8:1–14) and inescapable (9:1–6), is discriminating (9:7–10), and beyond it lies the glorious future of a prosperous and immovable people (9:11–15).

COMMENTARY

1:1 THE TITLE

The book which lies before us consists of *the words of Amos*. Elsewhere throughout its nine chapters a more daring description is used, 'thus says the Lord'. We are in the presence of the miracle of inspiration (*cf.* Ezk. 2:8 – 3:4), that man, without losing individuality or sacrificing personality should yet speak words which originated not with himself but with his God.

Tekoa was 12 miles south of Jerusalem. The word *shepherds* appears elsewhere only as 'sheep breeder' (2 Ki. 3:4). Some have tried to give it a technical meaning, that Amos was a Temple official, but there is no shadow of evidence for such a use of the word. The Lord took one who, to all appearance, bore no marks of being His mouthpiece and made him the vehicle of a message to his day and ours. The message was one which he *saw*. This is the same as our use of 'to see' when we mean 'to understand' or 'to perceive the meaning of'. It blends revelation and inspiration, for 'seeing' implies both an object or truth revealed and also the faculty to apprehend it. God gave the truth and also the power to grasp it. (See *NBD*, art. 'Prophecy, Prophets'.)

On the historical details, see Introduction.

1:2 – 3:8 THE LION'S ROAR: UNIVERSAL JUDGMENT AND ITS GROUND

This first group of prophecies is contained within the two bracketing verses, 1:2 and 3:8: 'The Lord roars . . . The lion has roared'. Thus the message of these chapters is pronounced to be God's word in origin and a word of judgment in content.

The first three nations under condemnation, named by their capital cities, were heathen nations unrelated to Israel; the next three were 'cousins' (*cf.* Gn. 25:30; 19:36–38). Judah, the seventh, was the brother-nation to the south. Thus judgment creeps nearer until at last it falls upon Israel itself. This may have been a rhetorical device used by Amos, the open-air preacher, to catch the ear of the passing crowds and to lead them imperceptibly into hearing the Lord's word of condemnation on themselves. It may have represented the course of his own thoughts, as he contemplated the vicious social habits of his near neighbours and gradually and logically came to ask the question: What of us?

Are we not equally under the condemnation of the Holy One?

There are two distinct grounds of judgment. The heathen nations are charged with crimes against humanity: brutal methods of war (v. 3), slave-trading (v. 6), pitilessness (v. 11), *etc.* The assumption is that there are elements of moral behaviour which need no special revelation but belong to man by nature (*cf.* Rom. 2:14). On Judah and Israel, however, judgment falls for disobedience to revelation. They have 'rejected the law of the Lord' (2:4) and silenced His prophets (2:12). Amos found people sheltering under privilege (*cf.* on 5:18), and he spelled out to them the real meaning of privilege: not licence to do wrong but responsibility to do right, carrying with it the heavier judgment reserved for those to whom much is given (*cf.* Lk. 12:48).

Behind this universal condemnation of Gentile and Israelite alike there lies Amos's firm monotheism (see Introduction). It is Yahweh who declares wrath upon all alike. There is no other God in the field.

1:2 Warning

The warning is first of divine action. The name of God, 'Yahweh' (RSV, 'LORD') is emphasized, and the duplication, *Zion . . . Jerusalem*, the place of His abode, underlines the thought of the nature of the Agent: He will act in His revealed character as Israel's God. Secondly, we are warned of imminent action. *Roars* (*cf.* Jdg. 14:5) signifies that the lion is about to pounce. The more universal aspects of God's pronouncement of wrath are expressed by changing the picture to the thunderstorm, in which He *utters his voice*. The verbs could well be translated as repetitives: 'again and again He roars'. In the following series of condemnations we hear roar after roar of His voice, one thunderclap of judgment after another. Thus we are prepared for Amos's third assertion: the completeness of judgment. From *the pastures of the shepherd* in the lush valleys to the bare tops of the *Carmel* range there is no place unblighted. All lies under effective condemnation.

1:3 – 2:16 Application

The 'again and again' of the repeated roar is a continuous present tense reaching down to our own day. Wherever and whenever these crimes are committed the Lion roars again. But we learn now the immediate objects of the Lord's wrath.

1:3–5 Damascus. Syria is condemned for the expansionist military policy of Hazael (842–806 BC) who pushed the boundaries of his kingdom even across the Jordan into Israel with vicious cruelty (*cf.* 2 Ki. 8:12). Damascus fell to the Assyrians in 732 BC.

3 The numerical feature, *for three . . . four*, used throughout these oracles (*cf.* Ps. 62:11; Pr. 30:15, 18, 21, 29) probably signified that the measure of guiltiness is more than full, as if to say 'three would have been enough to warrant judgment; four makes it beyond question'. It also reveals the patience of God, who neither acts in haste or without cause, even delaying beyond the point where action was well justified (*cf.* Gn. 15:16; 18:20; 2 Pet. 3:8, 9). But when He does act His judgment is irrevocable: He says *I will not revoke the punishment* (*cf.* the same verb used in Nu. 23:20; Is. 14:27, 'turn it back'). Their crime was barbarity in war: *threshing sledges of iron*, ponderous sledges fitted underneath with points and edges, dragged back and forth over their victims.

4 *Benhadad* (*cf.* 2 Ki. 8:7–15; 13:3) signifies the dynasty of Hazael.

5 *The bar of Damascus* symbolizes all the defences of the city. *The Valley of Aven* and *Beth-eden*, identified from Assyrian sources as Bit-Adini, NE of Damascus, trace the spread of destruction through the land in a judgment of which the Lord Himself was the real Agent, whatever the instrument He used. He is the personal opponent of the barbarous and the inhuman. From *Kir* the Syrians originated (*cf.* 9:7) and to this unknown place, having blotted history with their inhumanities, they return, Tiglath-pileser of Assyria being God's instrument (*cf.* 2 Ki. 16:9).

1:6–8 Gaza. *Gaza*, representing God's judgment on the Philistines, fell to Tiglath-pileser of Assyria in 734 BC, *Ashdod* to Sargon of Assyria in 711, and *Ashkelon* and *Ekron* to Sennacherib of Assyria in 701 BC. Their crime is that they were involved in slave-trading on a grand scale with Edom as either the buyer or the middleman. Gaza was so obsessed with a simple profit motive that nothing else counted; no plea of age or sex, no appeal of parent for child or child for parent was entertained. The saleable were sold. This inhumanity is under the lash of God: indeed all the more emphatically so, for Amos significantly adds *says the Lord God*, the sovereign Yahweh, as if to say, 'Nothing calls forth the omnipotent power of the Lord more than when one person uses another simply for his own profit.'

1:9, 10 Tyre. The Tyrians were renowned for commerce (*cf.* Ezk. 27:12–25). Amos depicts them as simply handling the business side of the slave-trade. They considered themselves bound by no ties of honour. *The covenant of brotherhood* may refer to relations between Israel and Tyre in the time of David and Solomon (*cf.* 1 Ki. 5:1, 12; 9:13), but possibly it is more general. 'Covenant of brothers' (literally) would

be a good equivalent to 'human rights', and would accord well with the universal standpoint of these oracles.

Tyre became tributary to Assyria, surrendered to Nebuchadrezzar after a thirteen-year siege (585–573 BC), and was eventually destroyed by Alexander the Great in 332 BC.

1:11, 12 Edom. *Teman* is Edom (*cf.* Ob. 9; Hab. 3:3). *Bozrah* was its chief city. We do not know of any warlike activities of Edom against Israel or Judah as described here until their part in the fall of Jerusalem (*cf.* Ob. 10–15; Ezk. 25:12–14). This has led some commentators to suggest that this oracle was inserted after that date, while others solve the supposed difficulty by altering 'Edom' to 'Aram', making the reference to Syria. Our knowledge is, however, far from complete, and neighbouring states have plenty of opportunity for venting ancestral spleen. The Lord notes even unrecorded incidents. Their actions were against nature and without mercy, and their spirit was one of ceaseless, remorseless animosity (v. 11b). These things the Lord answers with fire.

1:13–15 Ammon. The Ammonite war against Gilead is not otherwise known, but the record was kept in heaven. The motive was national aggrandizement, to *enlarge their border*, and in the interests of material increase they destroyed human increase. *Cf.* 2 Ki. 8:12; 15:16. They prized the material above the human, and dealt inhuman savagery to those who more than any others merit tenderness, the pregnant woman and the unborn child. Notice the elaborate detail in v. 14 as compared with the parallel vv. 5, 7, 8, 10, 12. The crackle of the fire is accompanied by the triumphant *shouting* of the assailant, and all is set against the background of a violent storm. The *whirlwind* often signifies destruction leaving nothing remaining (*cf.*, *e.g.*, Is. 40:24), and the intervention of the forces of nature is a metaphor for the Lord Himself (*cf.* Jos. 10:11; Jdg. 5:20, 21; Ps. 18:13–15). He who is the Father of the fatherless and the widow's Defender (*cf.*, *e.g.*, Ps. 68:5) will not stand idly by while the mothers and unborn children of Gilead are violated.

2:1–3 Moab. How varied are the concerns of the God of Israel. The oppressed (1:3), the exiled refugee and slave (1:6), failure of human brotherhood (1:9), remorseless anger (1:11), ill-used women and unborn children (1:13)—and now, outside the chosen people altogether, violence to the corpse of the king of Edom. Wherever crimes against humanity are committed, and on or by whomsoever they are practised, and for whatever reason, He is their implacable foe and judge. 2 Ki. 3:26 hints some special hostility between Moab and Edom (876 BC), and we must presume that the present particular crime was committed in the interests of the same national enmity.

2:4, 5 Judah. Amos's prophecy now takes its most significant turn; the searchlight is turned on the chosen people, and first *Judah*. The repetition of the formula *for three transgressions . . . and for four* shows that they were no less guilty than the heathen nations just reviewed; the precise accusation that *they have rejected the law of the Lord* shows how much deeper was their guilt. It had four aspects: first, *law* means 'teaching', such as is personally imparted to a pupil by a teacher. They have spurned God's personal instruction. Second, they have changed the unchangeable. *His statutes* are the precepts graven upon rock for permanence (*cf.* Ex. 31:18). Third, they have replaced them with *lies* (*cf.* 2 Tim. 4:4), and fourth, their sin is deeply ingrained in them by inheritance from *their fathers*, a truth which the OT uses, never to excuse the sinner, but always to indicate that he is in the place of mounting guilt (*cf.* Ps. 51:3-5; Mt. 23:31-36).

The fulfilment of this threat is recorded in 2 Ki. 24, 25 (586 BC).

2:6-16 Israel. Amos begins with the sins of Israel (vv. 6-8), particularizing them as, first, sins against society (vv. 6, 7a), whereby they act with lawlessness against *the righteous*, unfeelingness against *the needy*, and rapacity against *the poor*.

6 *The righteous* are here the 'innocent party' at law, a significance basic to the word. Judges are open to bribery, and verdicts are sold to the highest bidder. *The needy* suggests 'those who have no recourse but to submit', the helpless, defenceless. Often in the Psalms the word means those who gladly submit to the Lord. But here it is the socially helpless who have no means of redress. Either a bribe as small as *a pair of shoes* is enough to swing the verdict, or a debt as small as that for a pair of shoes is enough to bring a man into the dock: such is the covetousness of the community.

7a This oppression of *the poor*, or 'weak', could rather point to those 'that pant after the dust of the earth upon (or at the expense of) the head of the poor', referring to covetousness for real estate, so that they grudge the poor man even the dust which he daubs on his head as a sign of mourning (*cf.* Jos. 7:6), or even go the lengths of murder ('at the expense of') to acquire landed property. *The afflicted* are the downtrodden, those who can easily be pushed around by the well-to-do.

7b Sins against revelation now follow. God's *holy name* had been revealed to Israel. The Lord had let them into the intimate secret of His real nature as the holy One. But now there is open defiance of His prohibition of adultery (*cf.* Ex. 20:14) in general and of fornication in the name of religion in particular (*cf.* Dt. 23:17, 18). Canaanite religion thought that the performance of the human actions of procreation could be used to remind the god to fertilize the earth. It is this practice which Amos sees and denounces in Israel. The holy Yahweh is being worshipped as a Canaanite Baal. The basic truth here is that God must be worshipped as He requires and not simply as we might desire

(*cf.* Mt. 15:9). *The same maiden*; literally, 'the girl'. The condemnation is not, so to say, of an aggravated immorality in which father and son use the 'same girl', but that the whole male community, 'father and son' (alike) are involved.

8 Third, Amos condemns sins against grace. The *altar*, the place of atonement for sin (*cf.* Lv. 17:11) is the place where sin is committed; *the house of their God*, the place of holy fellowship with Him, is a place of unholy revelry. *They lay themselves down* in the very act of fornication which the Lord hates. *Garments taken in pledge*, as surety against a loan, were always to be returned before nightfall (*cf.* Ex. 22:26, 27). In this, as well as in drinking *wine of those who have been fined* (paid for by fines exacted in a supposed legal trial) they show how behind their self-indulgence lie their flagrant illegalities.

We are now brought over the same ground in rather a different manner, in order to learn the sinfulness of Israel's sin (vv. 9-12). At every point at which they sinned they had been the recipients of some special assurance of His gracious favour. They possessed a society to corrupt (vv. 6, 7a) only because special grace had given them a land of their own (v. 9); they knew the holy Name which they defiled only because special grace had brought them out of Egypt (v. 10); they had a law for life and worship, which they contravened, only because God had provided special channels of revelation (vv. 11, 12). The order of the events in vv. 9-12 is therefore not chronological, but is designed to further Amos's description of a sinful people.

9 *The Amorite*; a general name for the pre-Israelite occupants of Canaan. *Fruit . . . roots* (*cf.* 'root and branch') denotes complete destruction. **10** The Exodus gave God His full style and title, 'Yahweh your God, who brought you out of the land of Egypt' (Ex. 20:2). By this they knew the holy Name which they defiled (v. 7b). **11** The *prophets* prolonged in Israel the revelation given through Moses; the *Nazirites* (*cf.* Nu. 6:1ff.) typified that consecration to God which ought to flow from the revealed knowledge of Him. **12** But the chosen people neither wanted to see the example nor hear the truth (*cf.* Is. 30:9-11).

Lastly, Amos turns to the judgment to come (vv. 13-16): a divine action (v. 13) against which neither natural ability (v. 14), military equipment (v. 15) nor outstanding courage (v. 16) will avail.

13 Israel thought of itself as living in a prosperous harvest-time. Jeroboam had raised national prosperity to a pitch unknown since the time of Solomon (*cf.* 2 Ki. 14:25-28). But there are other aspects of a good harvest. If we follow RSV we see the home-bound laden harvest waggon, pressing the earth, helpless beneath its weight. So Israel is heaping up a weight of divine wrath which will press the nation into helpless destruction. Possibly however, the verse should be translated 'as the purposely-filled cart presses the sheaves'—a picture of the weighted threshing-sledge being dragged over the ripe grain, depicting the oppressive action of a holy God against a people ripe for judgment.

3:1-8 Authentication

Sensing the solemnity of proclaiming God's judgment against God's people, Amos felt he must immediately display his credentials, and give some evidence of the authenticity of such a message. Here he authenticates his prophetic message; similarly in 7:10ff. he authenticates his status as a prophet. He pleads that nothing short of divine compulsion made him preach thus. V. 1 calls upon us to 'hear this word that the Lord has spoken', and v. 8 reiterates the claim, 'the Lord God has spoken'.

1, 2 First he recapitulates the substance of his message. It is from the Lord (v. 1a). It bears a threefold address (v. 1b): to *Israel*, to *the whole family*, and finally to all whom *I brought up out of the land of Egypt. Israel* is defined, first comprehensively and then theologically: *the whole family* includes Judah, and the reference to the Exodus make the address include the whole company of the professedly redeemed people of God. None who claims to be redeemed is exempt from what Amos says. What does he say? V. 1 exalts the privilege of God's people as His redeemed; v. 2 continues the same theme. They are not only the redeemed, but uniquely so: *You only have I known.* (*Cf.* Ex. 33:12, 13, 17.) For Him, they were the unique people, His 'own possession among all peoples' (Ex. 19:5). But now comes the moment of truth: *Therefore will I punish you for all your iniquities.* Such punishment is something belonging to the fabric of the people of God, a *therefore*, something which follows in automatic sequence. This is the inner essence of Amos' prophetic message.

But it is this very thing that he must justify to a people who confused privilege with permission to sin. Vv. 3–8 make an appeal to the law of cause and effect, first in order to prove the assertion of v. 6 that no calamity befalls a city apart from divine agency; and second that no true prophet speaks apart from divine revelation (vv. 7, 8).

3 Two people are seen habitually together (the verb could express this) only if there is agreement, but let disagreement arise and the meetings cease. Yahweh and Israel are bound together by covenant, *i.e.* by a deliberate, conditional arrangement. If, then, Israel forsakes Yahweh's way, can they continue together? The law of cause and effect operates to separate them.

4 Two illustrations from the point of view of a predator: the *lion* does not roar to the attack (*cf.* Jdg. 14:5) unless the *prey* has been selected, nor does the *young lion* growl contentedly (*cry out*) if he has captured nothing. **5** Two illustrations from the point of view of the prey: a bird goes into a snare only if bait has been laid (the narrow meaning of the word *trap*; *cf.* Ex. 23:33;

Dt. 7:16; 1 Sa. 18:21); nor does a snare snap shut unless the bait has been taken. **6** The application of the two sets of illustrations: the prey hear the warning of the predator's coming and are *afraid*; the divine Predator stands behind every terror-striking calamity. *Evil* is constantly used in this sense of historical disaster. Israel's history had contained many such (*cf.* 4:6ff.), and the thrust of Amos's argument is to ask how the people explain them. Do they accept the view of history (the only view the Bible espouses) that the Lord is the great Agent? Behind every event stands a cause; behind all history stands the Lord (*cf.* Is. 45:5-7). Maybe thus they will prepare themselves for His future acts of judgment.

7, 8 This they must do if they truly understand the nature and function of prophecy. This is the climax to which the series of questions has been leading. *Revealing his secret* means, firstly, 'opening his fellowship' (*cf.* Je. 23:18), and secondly, 'telling his plans'. Amos commits himself here to the view that the OT prophets were essentially predicters. The Lord forewarned them of what He proposed to do (*cf.* Elisha's surprise when it was not so, 2 Ki. 4:27). But if this is accepted as being the case, what of Amos's own message? In it *the lion has roared, the Lord God*, the sovereign Yahweh, *has spoken*.

3:9 – 6:14 AN ENEMY IN THE LAND: THE MORAL AND SPIRITUAL COLLAPSE OF ISRAEL AND ITS RESULTS

The theme provides the bracketing verses for the present series: 3:11, *An adversary shall surround the land;* 6:14, *I will raise up against you a nation.* In direct continuation of the concluding section of the first group of prophecies, we learn that the incoming foe is produced by a cause: it is Yahweh's 'therefore' (3:11) to Israel's oppressive and illegal ways (3:9, 10).

3:9 – 4:13 Diagnosis

3:9, 10 (keywords *oppressions, violence, robbery*), and 4:4, 5 (keywords *sacrifices, tithes, freewill offerings*) reveal that Amos first probes the social and secondly the religious state of the nation.

3:9 – 4:3 Society without justice. There are three distinct focal points in this diagnosis: first the emphasis on the crimes of the nation (vv. 9–11), social misdemeanours; second, a significant change of terminology brings in the idea of transgressions (v. 14), *i.e.* there is no crime against people which is not a sin against God (vv. 12–15); thirdly there is God's holiness (4:2), the explanation why all such crime and sin is serious: it has no place in His holy presence (4:1-3). On all three counts judgment will come.

3:9 The sins of Israel are so blatant that even the heathen would find them remarkable. *Assyria.* RSV follows LXX; Hebrew reads 'Ashdod'. Amos, however, nowhere else mentions Assyria by name. Also it is a more stinging implication that the Philistines (Ashdod) and the Egyptians, the two hated ancestral enemies, were morally superior to Israel! **10** Devotion to wrongdoing blunts moral perception so that they cease to *know how to do right* (*cf*. Is. 5:11–13), and to store ill-gotten gains is like heaping barrels of gun-powder and lighted matches together. They are storing up *violence* and havoc (*robbery*). **12** *Cf*. Ex. 22:10–13. When a shepherd brought back a few limbs of a sheep, he was in fact ridding himself of the charge of negligence: he had tried to save the sheep and had failed. The rescued parts were the evidence of a total loss. So for Samaria: what is left will only emphasize the completeness of the overthrow. The *lion* (*cf*. 1:2; 3:8) will have had the victory. *Part* (Heb. *d*e*meseq*) is otherwise unknown; possibly it is a form of the name Damascus used for damask silk. **14** Significantly the 'oppressions' and 'violence' (vv. 9, 10) of society are now *transgressions, i.e.* wilful rebellion against God. The punishment of *the altars of Bethel* suggests that false religion is the root of social decadence. It also leaves its adherents defenceless in trouble. In pagan practice (though not in Israelite, *cf*. 1 Ki. 1:51; 2:28) the horns of the altar offered asylum, but now the victims will flee to the altar to find its horns gone! **15** The main blow will fall on the affluent society—the people with *winter* and *summer* residences, with over-ostentatious *ivory* inlay, or enormous mansions. Amos had no objection to wealth; throughout he attacks ill-gotten wealth, sharp practice, and oppression. False religion and false wealth not only invite divine judgment but are defenceless against it.

4:1 What is a life that is not rich toward God? The great ladies of *Samaria*, oppressive and intolerant towards their subordinates, dominating their husbands, intent on sensual gratification—what are they but so many prime beasts from *Bashan* (*cf*. Dt. 32:14; Ps. 22:12) sunk in a purely animal existence! **2** Why is sin sinful? Here the line of thought which equated social crimes with spiritual sins comes to a head (*cf*. 3:14). The oppressive and self-seeking society (v. 1) stands before a God of *holiness*. Crime is crime and sin is sin because God is God. His holy nature erupts in wrath against all that offends Him. *Hooks . . . fishhooks.* Captives were led away by cords attached to rings in their lips. The doublet, *hooks* and *fishhooks*, stresses the impossibility of escape. **3** *Harmon*; an unknown word, one of the unsolved problems of Amos.

4:4–13 Religion without spirituality. Behind their social disease, as its cause, lay false religion (see on 3:14). Amos follows the broad outline of his diagnosis of society. Corresponding to the exposure of the outward crimes (3:9–11), he exposes the outward state of false religion, formalism (4:4, 5); corresponding to its sins (3:12–15) he sees a religion which knows no repentance (4:6–11); finally, matching the clash between the sins of men and the holiness of God

(4:1–3), he declares the coming confrontation in judgment (4:12, 13).

4 *Bethel*. *Cf*. 1 Ki. 12:29. Many places were named *Gilgal* (*cf*. Jos. 4:19; 15:7, *etc*.; see *NBD*). For this reason Amos uses the name—multiplying shrines was one of the signs of formalism. But for all their religion, the outcome is only to *multiply transgression*. Religion as such may only aggravate our disqualification for the presence of God. The evidence of formalism now heaps up. Normal practice required the main *sacrifices* once a year and *tithes* once in three years (1 Sa. 1:3; Dt. 14:28). Amos exaggerates in order to emphasize the beloved fallacy, that the religious act was the whole of religion, and therefore 'the more the merrier'! **5** Formalism has two henchmen: self-pleasing and self-advertisement. Contravening divine law (*cf*. Ex. 23:18; Lv. 2:11) they mixed leaven with their sacrifices; they also made a public performance out of private devotions like *freewill offerings* (Lv. 22:18), their guide being personal whim—*for so you love to do*.

6–11 The subject is new, the providence of God in recent history, but the aim is to expose the hollow heart of their formal show of religion. God sent His people seven warning chastisements —famine (v. 6), drought (vv. 7, 8), mildew (v. 9a), locusts (v. 9b), epidemic (v. 10a), war (v. 10b), earthquake (v. 11)—before the great threat of direct confrontation (vv. 12, 13). All these had one aim, to bring His people to repentance (vv. 6, 8, 9, 10, 11). Without repentance towards God there is no true religion. This great study of divine providence opens (v. 6) with (lit.): 'But, for my part, I . . .' The Lord contrasts Himself to their formal religiousness. While they were being religious, He was at work to bring them to repentance! **12** In the long run God will neither be fobbed off by a show of religion nor will He endlessly give warnings only. The moment of confrontation will come. No threat is made. The terror of the verse lies in its vagueness: the past, with its interim providential judgments, is as nothing to this future meeting with God Himself. **13** God is utterly inescapable because the whole universe is accessible to Him. He is sovereign over things visible, *the mountains*, things invisible, *the wind*, and things rational, *man* and *his thought*; He is in direct executive control of the world, as is evidenced when He *makes the morning darkness, i.e.* brings about the sequence of day and night; and no place is beyond His reach, even *the heights of the earth* being beneath His feet. He is the *Lord, the God of hosts, i.e.* possessing in Himself every conceivable power to do as He wills: Yahweh, God the Omnipotent.

5:1–27 The remedy, available but refused

For the most part this passage consists of calls to repentance joined to prophecies of judgment. Thus, v. 3 speaks of military overthrow, but v. 4, starting with the explanatory 'for' is a call to repent. How can a call to repent explain a defeat?

In the same way, the 'therefore' of v. 16, introducing a threat of judgment, appears to wish to explain the invitation to repent in vv. 14, 15. Then, for the third time, the call for religious reformation in vv. 24, 25 is followed at once by a forecast of deportation.

The explanation is that Amos is here recollecting the past opportunities to repent which they have rejected and therefore nothing but judgment awaits them. The chapter is a true counterpart to ch. 4. There the divine calls to the people to return to God were carried by inarticulate messengers, famine, drought, blight, war, and so on. But God did not leave His people in any doubt what He was saying. There had also been the living voice which cried: 'Seek me and live' (v. 4). . . . 'Seek the Lord and live' (v. 6) . . . 'Seek good, and not evil, that you may live' (v. 14). The message of circumstances had been interpreted in the common speech. Amos presents all this in the most dramatic way as a funeral oration in which the nation is called to attend its own obsequies and to hear the preacher not simply mourning the deceased but also explaining how he came to die.

5:1–3 The lament and its interpretation. The nation has already *fallen* in death (v. 2) and is doubly hopeless, being without internal power *to rise*, and without external aid *to raise her up*. The interpretative word follows (v. 3): what is the nature of this utterly forsaken and irretrievable collapse? It is a military defeat involving a 90 per cent loss in the armed forces. Thus the theme of the enemy in the land is brought before us again.

5:4–27 Three calls to reformation reviewed. The prostrate corpse of v. 2 is in stark contrast to the call to live in vv. 4, 6, 14. The rejection of the divine medicine of repentance has brought the patient to the grave.

The first call was to spiritual reformation (vv. 4–13), to make the Lord Himself the centre of Israel's life. We read: *Seek me* (v. 4). . . . *Seek the Lord* (v. 6). This involves an abandonment of religious (vv. 4, 5), and of moral error (vv. 6, 7). Within the call to return to Him there is the threat of exile (v. 5) and of fiery destruction (v. 6) for the unrepentant. This threat is substantiated by a description of God (vv. 8, 9) which stresses His ability to accomplish an overturning judgment. The preacher, however, has to report that the call went unheeded, the nation continued in defiance of the moral law. Their defiance was inward (v. 10, *hate . . . abhor*), manward (v. 11), and Godward (v. 12, *transgressions . . . sins*), but they carried the majority of society with them to such an extent that it was dangerous to espouse an opposite course (v. 13).

5, 6 The places mentioned were centres of the false religious cult of Israel, and we are warned of the ultimate insecurity of all false religion (v. 5b), the reality of the wrath of God against disobedience (v. 6b), and the specific inability of false religion to offer any defence in the day of the Lord's wrath, which *Bethel* can provide

none to quench. **7** Just as in religion they had overturned the whole divine intention (*cf.* 4:4–13), so in morality they had also overturned God's law. *Justice* had become a sour joke—*wormwood* typically bitter and cruel (*cf.* 6:12; Je. 9:15; La. 3:15); *righteousness*, the standard of uprightness, had been flung prostrate *to the earth*.

8 The abruptness of vv. 8, 9 in their context is rightly and well preserved in RSV. With great oratorical skill Amos switches from the men who have wrought a bitter transformation on earth (v. 7) to the great Transformer Himself (vv. 8, 9). But he does it not so much for the sake of the comparison as to invite the conclusion that human perversion cannot win against God, and that the fire of judgment promised (v. 6) against the perverters will flash out in a destruction (v. 9) well within His competence. In three pictures, Amos depicts the transforming God at work. First, the seasonal changes: the constellation of *the Pleiades* in its rising and setting marked the beginning and ending of the season of navigation, and was also used by nomads for calendar purposes. *Orion* probably has a similar significance. *HDB* (see arts. 'Pleiades', 'Orion') conjectures that loosing the cords of Orion (Jb. 38:31) has reference to God's power to release the earth from the bonds of winter. Secondly, there is the regular transformation of day and night, which Amos specifies with particular reference to darkness and light, that feature which more than any other exemplifies the totality of the change which God accomplishes. The verb *turns* is the same as used in v. 7: do they turn one thing into another? So does He, but on how much grander a scale! Even *deep darkness* must yield to His will to give light. The third picture, the *waters*, refers to floods which overthrow all man's efforts to establish his way of life on earth. So the Lord whose transforming power is chiefly shown in the 'normal' changes of days and seasons, is not bound within His own prescribed regulations. No situation is so 'established' as to make it sacrosanct, so secure as to be inviolable. It is He who is Lord. **9** Amos turns to be his own interpreter. The rulers of his day have effected a great transformation (v. 7), and none can rebuke or halt them (v. 13)—none? There is One against whose flashing destruction neither *the strong* man nor the strong place (*fortress*) can offer the least resistance. What a vision for faith this is in a day when ungodliness is rampant and the godly man is chiefly aware of his own impotent silence (v. 13)!

Vv. 10–13 follow a strict pattern: the first accusation (v. 10) is of hatred of righteous opposition; the second (v. 11a) of lawless, oppressive practice. Next is the threatened judgment by dispossession (v. 11b). Now two further accusations follow, matching the first two: the third accusation (the partner of the second) deals with lawless and oppressive practice (v. 12), and the fourth (amplifying the first) with the silencing of righteous opposition (v. 13). **10** The just judge *who reproves,* and the honest witness *who speaks the truth* are equally detested. **11** *Exactions* properly means 'gifts' or 'compulsory gifts'. 'Because you take rent from the poor (farmer) and then continue to extract "gifts" from him . . .'—according to the strict letter of the law the landlord kept within the terms of the Rent Restrictions Act, but found other means of swelling his takings! But the fruits of unjust property-management are not long enjoyed. *Cf.* Is. 5:8-10; Je. 17:11. **12** Social wrong is again referred to the court of heaven as *transgressions* and *sins* (*cf.* 3:9-15). A merely moral reformation will not do; there must be a return to God. The specific sins are the use of wealth to evade justice, and the unequal administration of justice to the rich and the poor. **13** The reign of terror puts an end to freedom of speech, and people are governed by a *prudent* expediency rather than by truth. The uninfluential man, who knows that were he to take his case to court (v. 12b) he would get no satisfaction, is obliged to *keep silent* in the face of the unredressed wrongs of others.

The second call was to moral reformation (vv. 14-20). The call to repentance (vv. 14, 15) has as its consequence ('therefore', vv. 16-20) the forecast of judgment. We see therefore that the call went unheeded. The judgment predicted here takes the matter a stage further. V. 11 predicted the negative threat of dispossession which now gives way to the positive threat of 'the day of the Lord' (v. 20). Amos did not invent the idea of the day of the Lord (*cf.* 2:16; 9:11). The present reference indicates that it was an element in popular expectation, and part of a current religious optimism. The people felt sure of the presence of God with them (v. 14) and of His grace towards them (v. 15), and consequently they looked forward to the day with confident expectation and desire (v. 18).

Amos replies along four lines. Firstly, he uses the language of hope to preach a message of catastrophe. In v. 17 'pass through' is the terminology of the Passover (*cf.* Ex. 12:12), the language of redemption, but on Amos's lips it is the language of judgment. He thus reminds the people of a forgotten dimension in the character of their God. When He passed through Egypt it was to judge and smite, and what He revealed of Himself at the Exodus is eternally true (Ex. 3:15). Secondly, Amos insists on the moral conditions of spiritual blessing (vv. 14, 15). God's presence is a reality for those whose objectives ('seek'), and hearts ('hate', 'love') match His own, and who apply these principles to their corporate lives by establishing 'justice in the gate'. Thirdly, Amos opposes any sort of cock-sureness before God. He says, 'It may be' (v. 15). When we have done all, our proper course is to confess our unprofitability (*cf.* Lk. 17:10), not to sound our trumpets. The God who is described (v. 16) as 'Yahweh, God the Omnipotent, the Sovereign' is not to be presumed

upon! Finally, Amos insists that for Israel as then constituted the day of the Lord would inevitably be one of inescapable judgment and unalleviated sorrow (vv. 16-20).

15 *Joseph* is used as a title for the tribes making up Israel because their most prominent members were his sons (*cf.* Gn. 48). **19** An illustration of inescapable judgment. Read 'and' not *or*: fleeing one way, his escape is cut off, but he thinks that safety has been secured in a providentially accessible house. However, as he leans on the wall to catch his breath the snake pounces!

The third call noted is to religious reformation (vv. 21-27). The abruptness of the introduction of the new subject shows how Amos has brought together material which did not originate at the same time, but he has imposed an impressive editorial unity on it. Vv. 4-13, recalling the nation to Yahweh showed that the symptoms of its spiritual malady were seen in its religious (vv. 4, 5) and moral (v. 7) state. Vv. 14-20 took up the matter of national morality, and now vv. 21-27 expose the sickness of the nation's religion and what is required to put it right. The threatened judgment reaches its climax also: dispossession (v. 11), and the vague threat of the day of the Lord (vv. 18, 20) now become the explicit forecast of exile (v. 27).

The section opens with the divine rejection of Israel's current religious practice (vv. 21, 22). Vv. 23, 24 seem to present an either/or, an exhortation to abandon the outward ritual of religion altogether as unacceptable to God, and to give themselves entirely to ethical obedience—a religion without services but full of service. The balance is redressed, however, by v. 25 (see Introduction): the wilderness religion was not only sacrifice and offering but also obedience and moral holiness. This is the demand which, throughout the present chapter, we have watched the doomed nation persistently refuse; now for the last time their refusal is implied, for immediately following on the plea comes the announcement of doom (vv. 26, 27). Still intent on the outward trappings of religion (v. 26), they are bound for exile (v. 27). **24** *Justice* and *righteousness,* thus associated together are respectively moral practice and moral principle.

25 Does Amos envisage a purely ethical state of affairs, without Temple, altar, priesthood, sacrifice, or congregation? The emphasis in the Hebrew suggests, 'Was it sacrifices and offerings (only) that you brought me . . . ?' The religion which had its origin in the Mosaic revelation at Sinai was one of moral response to a God who had saved His people by means of the Passover sacrifice. The offerings of the Mosaic system prolonged for Israel the benefits of that Passover sacrifice, and the moral response of nation and individual was crystallized in the Ten Commandments. It is this well-known truth which is subtly recalled by Amos's question. See further in Introduction, Amos's teaching on religion.

26 Reference is to a religious procession in which the emblems of the gods are carried.

Amos neatly touches off Israel's zest for religious parade, but underlines the sinister menace of all false religion: its end is destruction; the procession leads 'beyond Damascus' (v. 27) and into *exile*. There is a good deal of difficulty in the Hebrew text of v. 26; RSV makes excellent sense on the basis of minimal change. *Sakkuth* was the Assyrian god of war, sometimes called Adram-melech (*cf.* 2 Ki. 17:31). This god was identified with the planet Saturn, otherwise called *Kaiwan*. Amos does not leave the subject without exposing the false heart of false religion: it is blasphemous, because it replaces the true King and God with substitutes; it is man-based because these are gods which *you made for yourselves* (*cf.* Is. 2:8). 27 Processions ought always to return to base; Assyrian religion ends up in Assyria, which, according to his custom (see on 3:9), Amos does not mention but hides behind the vague *beyond Damascus*. The agency in history, however, never passes from the Lord, and it is He, God the Omnipotent, who brings upon His people the consequences of their own folly and obduracy.

6:1–14 Conclusion: the outcome of self-exaltation

Amos's diagnosis of the nation (3:9 – 4:13) stressed the social defect of the rich lording it over the poor, and the religious defect of total absence of turning to God. These two are now brought together under one common denominator: the lordly pride which can find no fault with itself.

6:1–7 Israel's estimate of itself. The link word in these verses is 'first'. They belonged to 'the first of the nations' (v. 1), they only used 'the finest (lit. first) oils' for anointing (v. 6), and just as they were 'first' in everything else, they would be 'the first of those to go into exile' (v. 7). Amos shows us pride in its complacency (vv. 1–3), luxuriousness (vv. 4–6a), moral indifference (v. 6b), and fall (v. 7).

1 The address to *Zion* is unexpected, and is expunged by those who think it impossible that a prophet to the north should address the southern capital. Others, more discerningly, note that some place-name is required here in parallel to *Samaria*, and recall that Isaiah (28:1–4) and Micah (1:5; 6:16), both southern prophets, addressed and rebuked the north also. It would clearly strengthen Amos's case if he showed that pride has the same result everywhere, that even Zion cannot escape, and that there is no partiality with God. The root of the false security which he exposes is pride—pride of person, pride of association, and pride of position. They rejoice in being *notable*, in belonging to the *first of the nations*, and in being those to whom the rest *come* deferentially for the settlement of cases. 2 The intention of this verse may be to invite a comparison so as to show how great in fact is Israel's prosperity, and therefore, by implication, what a condemnation will be theirs if they fail in gratitude to their God for such richness. But if Israel is so convinced of its superiority, what is the point of inviting a journey to prove what is not in dispute? Another interpretation takes *Gath* and the others as examples of fallen prosperity which would warn Israel not to trust in uncertain riches. It is, however, doubtful if these cities had in fact fallen in Amos's time, and those who press explanation wish to make the verses a later interpolation, though why an interpolator should defy recent chronology, and to whom he would address his words, they do not stop to explain. Amos is, however, ironically repeating the propaganda 'hand-out' of the rulers who keep up the morale of their people by drawing advantageous comparisons with reasonably distant and clearly inferior places. This interpretation leads well into v. 3, for by such deceptive and specious reasoning the rulers could hide the real dangers of the nation, and throw a sop to those who ventured to express hesitation over the injustices of Samaritan life. 3 By their own lawlessness they were hastening *the* enthronement (*seat*) *of violence*, the day when 'lawlessness will reign', 'the reign of terror'. So it must have been in the final years of the kingdom of Israel when, after Jeroboam, only one king passed the throne on to his son, and the rest ended their reigns by assassination.

5 Possibly the rulers tried to excuse their indolent and frivolous way of life by a specious comparison with David—after all was not he too a musician? Thus lesser men justify their faults by comparison with the foibles of greater men! 6 *Bowls* (*cf.* Ex. 38:3; Nu. 7:13), very large vessels indeed. As one might say, 'they drink wine by the bucket'. *Are not grieved*, literally 'have not made themselves sick': a side-long glance at the excesses of the feasts (*cf.* Is. 28:7, 8), but a straight denunciation of their failure in social and moral concern.

6:8–14 The Lord's estimate of Israel. Once again the fact of pride (v. 8), its moral indifference (v. 12) and its self-centredness (v. 13) are brought before us, but now we see the divine reaction to them. Vv. 1–7 tell us in so many words that pride goes before a fall; vv. 8–14 tell us why this is. The divine reactions are hatred (v. 8), alienation (vv. 9, 10), and enmity (vv. 11–14).

8 The dimensions of the divine reaction of hatred are immense: the whole divine nature is involved as He swears *by himself*, signifying 'by all that He is in Himself', 'with His whole heart and soul'; all the divine attributes are involved in this oath by 'the Sovereign Yahweh . . . Yahweh, God the Omnipotent'. The verb *abhor* which so suits the verse depends on a small emendation of the Hebrew, which here reads 'desire', hardly a suitable sense. 9, 10 The city is siege-bound and famine and plague are taking their toll. Finding someone hiding in the inner rooms, and asking if there is by chance anyone left, before the negative reply can bring some reaction of exasperation or of piteousness involving God's name, the mouth of the speaker is stopped, for the sense of alienation from God

is too great. The day is long past when His name may be used either lightly or seriously. God has departed from His people. **11** How has such desolation come about? By command of the Lord. We are shown in turn what the Lord commands (v. 11), why He commands it (vv. 12, 13) and how He executes His command (v. 14). *Great . . . little*, a Hebrew idiom which, by specifying two opposite types, embraces everything belonging to that class. So here, 'every house of whatsoever sort'. The Lord has commanded a total destruction.

12 The first illustration, *horses* running up a cliff face (*rocks*), is of something contrary to the nature of things; the second of something useless and not worth the effort, for the sea is first of all barren for cultivation, and secondly the water would close behind the ploughshare as if nothing had happened: doubly useless and a waste of time. But these sum up the life of the nation. They have acted contrary to the whole moral nature of things in making *justice* the *poison* instead of the preservative of society, and making moral principle a sour cynicism (*cf.* 5:7).

13 Furthermore, they have wasted time on useless pursuits, and show their lack of discernment by glorying in them. *Lo-debar* and *Karnaim* were places in Transjordan (*cf.* Gn. 14:5; 2 Sa. 9:4), and may well have been, as this verse suggests, scenes of victories by Jeroboam II when he restored the boundaries of Israel (*cf.* 2 Ki. 14:25). As a word, however, Lo-debar means 'a nothing', and Karnaim means 'horns' the symbol of strength. The verse could well have had an intentional double meaning, embracing both RSV and RV: 'Your greatest achievements are great nothings!' They perverted moral values and exalted military ones, abandoned strength of character and boasted of strength of arms. **14** But they glory in what is passing. Before the coming enemy every single thing, *from the entrance of Hamath to the Brook of the Arabah*, the whole proud achievement of Jeroboam, will vanish. For their boasting invites divine opposition. Yahweh, God the Omnipotent, is the enemy of hollow boasters and has a ready instrument of His wrath, the enemy in the land.

7:1 – 9:15 THE LORD YAHWEH: THE SOVEREIGNTY OF YAHWEH IN JUDGMENT AND MERCY

This third group of prophecies opens and closes on the same note. It begins with the intimation that the Lord does not contemplate any such judgment as excludes all hope of survival (7:1–6), and ends with a plain prediction of the same thing, a discriminating judgment (9:9, 10) which paves the way for a future glorious with Messianic hope (9:11–15). The whole passage, therefore, opens a gracious vista of the divine sovereignty where judgment and mercy are both dispensed but the purposes of God are preserved and

secured. The title 'Sovereign Yahweh' is used 9 times in chs. 1–6, but 11 times in chs. 7–9. On this as a great keynote Amos concludes.

7:1–17 Controlled judgment verified

Two visions indicate forms of divine judgment rejected in answer to prayer (vv. 1–6); a third tells of the chosen form of divine judgment (vv. 7–9); and Amos adds the narrative of his call to be a prophet (vv. 10–17).

7:1–6 The faithfulness of God to His condemned people. Intercession was an established function of the prophets (*cf.* Gn. 20:7; Je. 7:16; 11:14; 14:11). Here Amos, who never recorded any prayer against the fact that his people were to be judged by God, prays against two proposed forms of judgment which they could never hope to survive. First there is the locust plague of such intensity that national survival would be out of the question (vv. 1–3), and secondly the devouring fire which would eat up even the very land itself (vv. 4–6). Amos prayed and his prayer was heard. The significance of this cannot be overemphasized. Amos pleaded against judgment of utter destruction and the Lord granted his request. The conclusion is irresistible: neither Amos nor the Lord desired, intended or contemplated the final end of the people. We thus embark on the final group of Amos's prophecies with at least part of the answer to the question arising out of the preceding group. Will there be utter destruction, a final end? Certainly not, for Amos twice (*cf.* Gn. 41:32) prayed against it and the Lord heard him. It is notable how *the Lord God*, the Sovereign Yahweh, is the divine style used 6 times in as many verses. This great sovereign God turns away from the thought of the extinction of His people. We do not yet know what their future will be, but even now there is at least hope.

1 *The king's mowings*, of which there is no other mention, was presumably a royal levy upon the farmer. We gather that after this levy there was a 'late sowing' (*latter growth*) upon which the farmer would be specially dependent for survival. This was now threatened by locusts. **3** The gracious purpose of the sovereign God not to destroy utterly His sinful people is very evident in this verse. But how can God be said to have *repented*? A key passage on this question is 1 Sa. 15:29–35. The first verse expresses the 'absolute' truth about God—His inflexible will; but the last verse shows that this unalterable will has taken into account the fluctuations and variableness of human experience and response. Consequently it necessarily appears to us that God changes course, and the Bible speaks of Him as 'repenting', meaning that the will of God, though inflexible, is not unfeeling, but takes loving regard of all our weakness and foolishness in His perfect, sovereign ordering of the world. **6** Neither Amos nor his God can bear to contemplate the full end of the chosen people. Utter destruction is dismissed from God's planning.

7:7–9 The moral discrimination which the people of God cannot escape. A third vision follows against which Amos makes no prayer, and Yahweh, on His part, confirms the meaning of the symbol in an interpretative oracle.

7 The Lord appears in the role of the master-builder coming to inspect the work done by His labour-force. His action is deliberate; He (lit.) 'was placing Himself'. Like a wise master-builder, He had given all that was necessary for the building of a true, perpendicular wall. It had been *built with a plumb line*, and He came to test it, not by some other standard, but by the same standard which the builders had been supposed to use. Was it as perpendicular as it ought to be, and even as it may have appeared to be to the naked eye? **8** The *plumb line* is the straight edge of God's law. By it God's people were to erect upright lives and an upright society; by it He will come and judge them. There can be no plea against this form of assessment, for to possess the law of God—the knowledge of His will—and to be under obligation to obey it is part of the essential nature of the people of God. Sinai was not an incidental event: it was the object in mind from before the Exodus (*cf.* Ex. 3:12). The phrase *pass by*, used again at 8:2, appears in Mi. 7:18 in the meaning 'to forgive'. It is reminiscent of the Passover (Ex. 12:23). At the Passover, the 'passing' signified that all was well between Yahweh and the people sheltering beneath the blood of the lamb (Ex. 12:13, 23). But Yahweh can no longer view Israel with pleasure. When He comes to judge, however, it will be as discriminating as on passover night (*cf.* Ex. 11:7; 12:27).

9 Consequently the Lord now singles out certain specific objects of His displeasure, in contrast to the *carte blanche* judgments of vv. 1–6. The *high places* were the man-made centres of false religion, devoted to the worship of Baal, or else used for a perverted worship of Yahweh as though He were a Baal. Only here is *Isaac* used as a synonym for Israel. Isaac was associated with Beer-sheba (Gn. 26:33; 28:10), a well-known centre of religion in the time of Amos (5:5; 8:14). Conceivably people sought to establish the legality of such a shrine and its services by urging that after all it was associated with the venerable name of a patriarch. *Jeroboam;* see 2 Ki. 14:23–29.

7:10–17 The verification of the Word of the Lord. For the second time Amos displays his credentials (*cf.* 3:1–8), and for the same reason: in order to verify the terms of his message of judgment upon the chosen people, and to vouch for his own right to proclaim such a message.

10 Amaziah, *the priest of Bethel*, was understandably stung by the prophet's strictures on contemporary religion, in which, indeed, Bethel had featured, and not to its advantage (*cf.* 4:4; 5:5), and by his prediction against the royal house itself (7:9). **12** *O seer* is not a sarcasm—the word is perfectly honourable (*cf.* Is. 29:10)—but the advice to *go . . . to . . . Judah, and eat bread*

there certainly suggests that Amos is in the job for the money and that he will welcome news that oracles against Israel's royal house attract more custom in the south.

14 For a discussion of Amos's dignified and courteous reply, see Introduction, p. 727. RSV in using the present tense, *am*, makes Amos deny in v. 14 what he wishes to affirm in v. 15, namely that by the act of God he has become what once he was not, a genuine prophet. 'I was . . . was' (*cf.* RV) is the simplest and best understanding of it. Amos outlines the nature of the office of a prophet in three implied negatives, followed by three positives. First, it is not based on human capacity, *I . . . no prophet.* Second, it was not a matter of human choice and enrolment, *nor a prophet's son.* The 'schools' of the 'sons of the prophets' gathered round a great prophet to hear his instruction and to share his work (*cf.* 2 Ki. 2:3, 5; 6:1–7; 9:1–3). But Amos was not such a one. He had followed the secular vocation of a *herdsman* and fruit-farmer, tending *sycamore trees* which produced a type of fig. Consequently, the prophetic office was not, thirdly, based on any human pre-conditioning or preparation. **15** It rested in fact, fourthly, on divine choice: *the Lord took me.* Fifthly, the primary privilege of the prophet was to enjoy fellowship with God: *the Lord said to me*, and then, sixthly, to minister in the appointed place, which, for Amos, was *my people Israel.* These last three features appear in all the prophets who have left us testimonies of their call: the divine initiative (Is. 6:1; Je. 1:5; Ezk. 1); the divine fellowship (Is. 6:6–8; Je. 1:6–16; Ezk. 2:1, 2); the divine appointment (Is. 6:9; Je. 1:5b, 10, 17–19; Ezk. 2:3ff.).

17 The personal and national aspects of the exile. Within the family of Amaziah there will be degradation (*harlot*), bereavement (*fall by the sword*), and defilement (*unclean land*). Truly it is not enough to be religious! Amaziah was the prime example of that religion without repentance which Amos saw throughout the whole people. But in the day of the accounting it can only show an utter loss.

8:1–14 Imminent judgment justified

First (vv. 1–3) there is the vision with its explanation, stressing that the end has come upon the people, the judgment is imminent; secondly (vv. 4–14) the theme of crime and punishment justifies the foretold imminent divine action.

8:1–3 Vision and explanation. The harvest metaphor is well suited to this passage. The crop comes to harvest as the climax of its own inner development. So God's judgment coincides exactly with the moral fitness of the people to be judged in this way. The metaphor also suits the wider context of chs. 7–9, for the harvest is a time of discrimination (9:9, 10; *cf.* Mt. 13:24–30; Rev. 14:14–16).

8:4–14 Crime and punishment. The crime (vv. 4–6) is characteristically summed up as oppression of those who have no means of redress (v. 4).

Amos cannot be accused of mere opposition to wealth and the wealthy. Antagonism is reserved for unjust, rapacious and unscrupulous gain. He indicts a community in which everything was subordinated to money-making and covetousness (vv. 5, 6). Religion is resented when it hinders commerce (v. 5a); honesty is sacrificed to the profit-motive (v. 5b); other people become pawns in the commercial racket (v. 6a); and standards are disregarded as long as trade flourishes (v. 6b). Self-advantage and greed for gain mark the society ripe for judgment.

5 *The ephah*, a dry measure of 8 gallons, was used to measure out the corn for the purchaser, and *the shekel* was used to weigh the money he paid for it. They sold less than they promised for more than they stated. In smaller transactions they adjusted the scales to their own advantage. 6 The *silver* here is probably a loan made to a poor man; the *pair of sandals* a purchase which he has been allowed to make on credit. But in the mind of the creditor each aims at taking the poor man himself into slavery when he defaults in payment (*cf.* 2 Ki. 4:1).

The punishment is elaborated in vv. 7–14. Just as vv. 4–6 were full of the 'we' of human sharp practice, so these verses are full of the 'I' of divine reaction and judgment. The nation-wide scale of the coming judgment is figured by an earthquake (vv. 7, 8). Another natural illustration opens up the first facet of the day of the Lord, the reversal of worldly enjoyments (vv. 9,10). The end of the feasting forecasts the next aspect, the exposure of true needs in terms of unsatisfied hunger and thirst for God's Word (vv. 11, 12). The third facet of the day of the Lord is linked to the second by the idea of thirst: false religion will be seen in its inability to satisfy human need (vv. 13, 14).

7 *The pride of Jacob* must be understood sarcastically. Every oath requires some unalterable object by which to swear. Nothing seems more mountainously stable than the nation's pride in itself! 8 The earthquake, conveying the idea of an upset affecting the entire land, is compared to the annual rise and fall of *the Nile*. The reference to the Nile may also have been intended to remind Israel of God's acts of judgment against the whole of Egypt in the plagues. This same God must now set Himself on the same scale against the people He once laboured to redeem (*cf.* Is. 28:21). Furthermore a truth much emphasized in the Old Testament is that the relationship between God and His people, for good or ill, is reflected in the natural order. The very land mourns for the sin of its inhabitants (*cf.* Ho. 4:3), is defiled by their iniquities (Je. 3:9), and 'vomits them out' in disgust (Lv. 18:28; 20:22). 9 The natural imagery continues. The irregular and supernatural darkness typifies the deliberate extinguishing of all the light of rejoicing. Factually, this darkness has been associated with the eclipse of the sun which coincided with an earthquake recorded in June 763 BC. 10 Once Egypt knew such a mourning as

this (*cf.* Ex. 12:30). Now it is Israel. How easily the redeemed forget the holy nature of their God and sit loose to His requirements! There is such a thing as the 'vengeance' of the covenant (Lv. 26:25).

11 The day of trouble reveals how strong are the inner springs and resources, and a life solely nourished on the sweetmeats of this world is soon stripped to the bone when they are gone. Then comes the hunger for an authoritative spiritual 'word'. 12 Round the compass they go: from the Dead *sea* in the south to the Mediterranean *sea* in the west, and so to the *north* and *east*, completing the circuit. No journey too great, no distance too far if only spiritual satisfaction comes at the end. Yet mere desire was not enough, for *they shall not find it*, not, in this case, by divine unreadiness to give them the word, but because they search in the wrong way and the wrong places. The word was near them (*cf.* Dt. 30:11–14), the word through Moses and the prophets, the word of Amos and Hosea. Sometimes the pride of a lifetime remains (see v. 7) and makes even the person who knows his hunger unwilling to face the repentance and self-humbling needed for coming to what he had so long and haughtily rejected.

13 What is the source of this thirst? Vv. 13 and 14 should be seen together: *Fair virgins and the young men shall faint for thirst* (namely) *those who swear. . . .* The day of the Lord will bring experience of the insufficiency of false religion. The hope of the future seems to be held in mortgage for the sins of the past as the youth of the nation perishes in the snares of false cults. 14 The worship of *Ashimah* is found later in Samaria (*cf.* 2 Ki. 17:30), cultivated by the men of Hamath. Since Hamath had been captured in Jeroboam's reign (2 Ki. 14:28) there is no problem of dating involved in finding the cult already established in Amos's day. The Hebrew text makes play upon the fact that Ashimah is very near to the word meaning 'guilt', and we may well hold to the double meaning: in swearing by Ashimah they are not aiding their souls but incurring further guilt (*cf.* 4:4). *As the way of Beer-sheba lives* is not understood. Some quote the Arab custom of swearing by the sacred road to Mecca. Did the pilgrims' way to Beer-sheba itself become an object of veneration?

9:1–6 Inescapable judgment divinely enforced

The fifth of Amos's visions reveals the Lord Himself superintending the destruction of the shrine. Total destruction is commanded, involving all the fabric and all the people (v. 1a); no way of escape is left, neither Sheol, nor heaven offer escape; the top of Carmel, the depths of the sea, and the ends of the earth are equally useless. Thus they have no spiritual refuge (Sheol, heaven), no earthly security (Carmel, sea), and no future expectation as they go into exile. This appalling vision of overthrow is finally substantiated by viewing the universal power of a God great enough to put His threats into effect (vv. 5, 6).

2 *Sheol*; the place-name for the abode of the dead. **3** *The serpent* was a mythological monster of contemporary paganism, living in the deep, whose storms showed it to be in opposition to the creator-god. Amos uses this, first, imaginatively. For the sake of argument, just as he allows the possibility of climbing to heaven (v. 2), he allows the possibility of such a monster as this to cut off their escape in the dark deep. But, more important, he uses the reference theologically. What in pagan religion was the implacable and often not unsuccessful foe of the creator, is utterly at the bidding of Yahweh, subservient to His purposes. Thus Amos compels mythology to serve the truth and to display the omnipresence and omnipotence of the only God.

5, 6 See Introduction, p. 728 for a discussion of these verses along with their companions, 4:13 and 5:8, 9. God is displayed in terms which show Him as equal to the task of implementing the judgment He has threatened. We see His universal and sovereign power first (v. 5) horizontally: the whole earth is subject to His touch; it offers no resistance, but *melts* before Him; *all* its inhabitants are affected; it loses stability and rises and falls like a river. No wonder then that neither in Carmel nor in captivity is there a hiding-place from such a God. Second, the power of God is displayed vertically (v. 6): the heavens, for all their lofty inaccessibility, are no more than His 'stairs' (preferable to *upper chambers*), His ways of movement and access; from another view the heavens are His *vault* encircling the earth and binding it—the word elsewhere means a 'bond' (*cf.*, *e.g.*, Is. 58:6). Cf. Is. 40:22. *The waters of the sea* are also at His command. No wonder then that neither heaven nor sea offers an avenue of escape. In the Hebrew, these verses are not as abrupt as the RSV suggests. In v. 1 Amos opened up a vision of 'the Sovereign' (*ʾaḏōnāy*); in v. 5 he rounds it off: 'And the Sovereign (*ʾaḏōnāy*) is Yahweh the Omnipotent. . . . ' There is a compelling unity in this portrayal of judgment.

9:7-15 Controlled judgment and ultimate blessing

Amos now allows the third group of prophecies, opening at 7:1, to come full circle. He began by describing two visions of utter destruction (7:1-6), against which he prayed and the Lord relented. But the substance of the intervening verses has seemingly implied that the state of the nation called for complete overthrow. Thus there has been created a tension between 'it shall not be' in 7:3, 6 and the mounting tide of destruction in 8:1 – 9:6. We need the present section to resolve the tension and to offer final explanations. For the view that the genuine words of Amos end with 9:8a and a reply to it, see Introduction.

The two sections which make up this final division of the prophecy are carefully balanced and contrasted: v. 7, Israel's equality and identity with the nations, is balanced by vv. 11, 12, Israel's ultimate possession of the nations; v. 8, the dimensions of divine judgment, is balanced by v. 13, the dimensions of the Messianic blessing; vv. 9, 10, the act of God in sifting Israel, are balanced by vv. 14, 15, the act of God in planting Israel (see Introduction).

9:7-10 The insufficiency of privilege. Amos begins to examine this topic by stressing God's moral concern (vv. 7-8a). All nations are equally under the executive control of God. He has organized every migration of peoples: not just Israel, but the Syrians (their recent opponents), the Philistines (their ancestral foes), and even as far as Ethiopia—*i.e.* to the world's end. But we make Amos contradict himself if we conclude that all nations are exactly equal in the sight of God. In chs. 1 and 2 Israel and the nations were equally under judgment, but Israel was under judgment within the closed circle of revelation (2:11) and election (3:2). Amos is not now suggesting that Israel's 'speciality' has been abandoned. What he is teaching is this: Israel is associating privilege—the privilege of being God's people—with the historical past. They are the whole family which He brought up out of Egypt (3:2). But there is nothing special about this unless they are manifesting a proper response to God's historical dealings in terms of daily holiness. It is not past experiences which the Lord gazes upon but present sinfulness (v. 8a), and if He sees sin instead of holiness in Israel then their claim to a privilege will only bring them greater condemnation because they alone of all people ought to have known and been better.

Nevertheless (vv. 8b-10), the Lord will not proceed blindly against His people. In ch. 7 the abandonment of the notion of total destruction (vv. 1-6) was followed by a vision of discriminating judgment (vv. 7-9). Amos does not now say that all sinners must perish, or that only the sinless will be preserved. Spiritual complacency is the main issue: doom awaits sinners who go blithely on, presuming on God's acquiescence in their sinfulness, as they say 'Evil shall not overtake or meet us' (v. 10). The people of God are all of them sinners, but the mark of the true as distinct from the merely professing is that they mourn over their sins (*cf.* Ezk. 9:4-6; contrast Ps. 50:16-21).

8 *Except that. Cf.* Je. 4:27; 5:10, 18; 30:11. **9** *Pebble.* Only elsewhere in 2 Sa. 17:13. Most assume that grain is being sieved. Some urge that 'pebble' means firm, good grain—an entirely unexemplified meaning—and that v. 9 stresses the preservation of the good, balancing the destruction of the bad in v. 10. Apart from the lack of evidence for the required meaning, this would contradict the normal use of a sieve, which in fact collects the refuse and allows the good through. Other commentators suggest that pebbles were included with grain to assist the winnowing. In this case the pebbles would certainly be part of the reject material, and vv.

9, 10 would concentrate on the removal of waste material from the nation. But the word 'pebble', rather suggests the sieving of soil or gravel. The sieve as a metaphor points to the gathering out of impurities. This coincides well with the emphasis of the passage where (v. 8) the Lord's eyes are 'upon the sinful', and (v. 10) 'all the sinners of my people shall die'. We have therefore a distinct insistence on the discriminatory nature of divine judgment: not a final end but a guarded purging.

10 *Who say.* The Hebrew suggests 'who characteristically say'. The one person whom the Lord cannot tolerate is the person who avers that sin is an allowable way of life.

9:11–15 The certainty of hope. The other side of the discriminatory judgments of God is now opened. The first feature is the restoration of the Davidic rule (vv. 11, 12).

11 *Fallen.* This may point to the schism of the ten northern tribes which quite undid the whole accomplishment of David (1 Ki. 12). On the other hand, Amos was under no illusions about the future of Judah (*cf.* 2:4, 5; see also on 3:2), and he may be 'ideally' looking back to the fall of Jerusalem to the Babylonians, as if it had already taken place, and seeing the ultimate restoration of the kingdom from that crushing blow. Again, the verb could be translated, 'which is about to fall', in which case he is looking forward to the fall of Jerusalem and then beyond it to the Messianic restoration.

12 *Edom.* The full conquest of Edom was accomplished only by David (2 Sa. 8:14). It rebelled against Solomon (1 Ki. 11:14); under Jehoshaphat some sort of Edomite monarchy was recognized (1 Ki. 22:47; 2 Ki. 3:8ff.); under Joram Edomite sovereignty was fully re-established (2 Ki. 8:20). The bitter hostility of Edom, from the very first (Nu. 20:14) probably contributed to the use of Edom typically and eschatologically as the figure *par excellence* of enmity to the people of God (*cf.* Is. 63:1ff.; Ezk. 35) to be overthrown finally by David's greater successor, the Messiah Himself. Thus, here, the possession of Edom is one of the signs of the presence of the Messianic Kingdom. *And all the nations.* In the great Davidic expansion many heathen nations had been claimed in the name of Yahweh (*cf.* 2 Sa. 12:18). The world-wide rule of the Davidic Messiah is a regular prophetic feature (*e.g.*, Is. 9:6, 7; 11:1–16) and figures prominently in the royal Psalms (*e.g.* 2:7–9; 72:8–11; 110:5–7). The warlike metaphor in many of these passages is, of course, to be understood in terms of the kingship of the Lord Jesus Christ and the missionary expansion of the church. This is the interpretation authorized by the NT in Acts 15:12–19.

13–15 Amos brings his prophecy to a conclusion on the note of the enjoyment of secure prosperity (vv. 13–15). The prosperity (v. 13) will be so abundant that the ploughman going out to prepare the ground for the next year's sowing will find the harvester still at work gathering last year's crop, and likewise the vintage will over-run its allotted time until it trespasses into the season of planting. And this will not be all, for the very soil itself will seem to run with productivity, a prosperity enjoyed (v. 14) by the people of the land in unbroken tenure for ever (v. 15).

The truth expressed through this imagery tells of the total reversal of the effects of sin. It was through sin that people were insecure in their tenure of the land and lived under threat of eviction and exile (5:26, 27); it was through sin that people were disappointed in their expectation of enjoyment of the fruits of the earth (5:11); it was sin which perverted nature itself away from its proper plenty and its full benevolence toward man. Adam was king in Eden (*cf.* Gn. 1:28; 2:15ff.), heir and monarch of the abundance implied in the permission to eat freely of every tree in the garden save one. But with the entrance of sin the liberality dried up to become a trickle, and that hard won (Gn. 3:17–19) and grudgingly given. When, however, its rightful King returns to Eden (*cf.* Is. 11:6–9) all the energies, pent up for the centuries during which sin abounded and death reigned, will explode in one triumphant burgeoning as nature hastens to lay its tribute at the feet of Him whose right it is to reign.

The great seal, guaranteeing the vision as certain to be fulfilled was affixed in the very last words Amos transmitted to us: *Says the Lord your God.* It is the word of Yahweh, the Exodus-God, the God whose eternal nature (Ex. 3:15) is to judge His enemies and redeem His people; it is the word of *your God*, ours not by our choice but by His sovereign choice (*cf.* Dt. 7:7, 8; Ezk. 20:5–7; Jn. 15:16; Eph. 1:4, 11); it is a word utterly reliable, for without more than a hint of paraphrase it takes all the Messianic promises and blessings and affirms them saying, 'On these the Lord your God has made up His mind.'

J. A. MOTYER

Obadiah

INTRODUCTION

AUTHOR AND DATE

The title of this little prophecy—the shortest book in the OT—is 'The vision of Obadiah' (v. 1). Who this Obadiah was we have no means of knowing. The name means 'servant of Yahweh' and occurs a number of times in the OT, but there is nothing to connect this prophet with any of the others so called. For the use of the word 'vision' to describe the contents of a prophecy, and as throwing light on the way in which the prophet received his message, *cf.* the opening verses of Isaiah, Ezekiel, Amos, Micah, Nahum and Habakkuk; see also Nu. 12:6.

The prophecy is 'concerning Edom'. Edom is denounced for her pride, especially for her lack of brotherly kindness towards Judah, and her judgment in the day of Yahweh is predicted along with that of all the nations.

As for the date of the prophecy, we may refer it to some time after the destruction of Jerusalem by Nebuchadrezzar, king of Babylon, in 587 BC. This event seems to be clearly alluded to in vv. 11-14. There are scholars, however, who place the prophecy before the fall of Jerusalem, and refer to 2 Ch. 21:16, 17 or 2 Ch. 28:17 as providing the possible historical context for the attack on Jerusalem to which the book alludes.

There are marked similarities both in ideas and phraseology between the first part of Obadiah (vv. 1–8) and Je. 49:7–22, a passage which belongs to the years *before* the fall of Jerusalem. Literary critics do not agree on the exact relationship between the two passages. Some argue for the direct dependence of one on the other. But while Je. 49 is almost certainly earlier than Obadiah, and while the passage in Obadiah shows some signs of having been derived from another source, yet in certain respects the Obadiah passage appears the more original of the two. For this reason many critics hold the hypothesis that *both* Jeremiah and Obadiah are making use of an earlier prophecy. This is not inherently unlikely, as the character and doom of Edom was a constantly recurring theme among Hebrew prophets.

EDOM AND JUDAH

The ancestor who gave his name to the Edomites was Esau (see Gn. 36:1, 8, 9). His relations with his twin brother Jacob, father of Judah, are described in Gn. 25–36. Even while the children struggled together within the womb of their mother it was told her by the Lord that 'two nations are in your womb, and . . . the elder shall serve the younger' (Gn. 25:22f.). Subsequently Esau is portrayed as one 'who sold his birthright for a single meal' and who thus became the type of 'irreligious' man (Heb. 12:16), insensitive to spiritual values. He was born within the covenant, but he failed to appreciate the privilege which was his by right, and he failed also to enjoy the accompanying blessing. God's estimate of Jacob and Esau respectively is most succinctly expressed in the declaration 'I have loved Jacob but I have hated Esau' (Mal. 1:2f.; *cf.* Rom. 9:13).

The Herods of the NT were Edomites, and were true to type. Notice how they showed themselves insensitive to spiritual truth, especially as it was embodied in Jesus Christ, the perfect representative of Jacob and Judah. (See especially Mt. 2; Lk. 13:31f.; 23:8ff.; Acts 12:21ff.)

Gn. 36:8 tells us that 'Esau dwelt in the hill country of Seir'. Seir, the chief mountain range of Edom, is often used as a synonym for the whole land, which became the land of Esau's descendants. Edom is the area directly south of the Dead Sea, especially the mountainous country east of the Arabah (*i.e.* the depression connecting the Dead Sea with the Gulf of Aqabah). The southern part of Edom is the region of Teman, also sometimes used in the OT as a synonym for the whole land (*e.g.* Hab. 3:3), and Edom's two principal cities are Bozrah and Sela. The latter (which means 'crag' or 'rock') is now identified with Umm el-Biyara, the rocky eminence dominating the enclosed valley in which the famous city of Petra (also meaning 'rock') was built by the Nabateans in later times (4th century BC).

From Ezion-geber on the Gulf of Aqabah, 'the king's highway' ran through Edom northwards. It was along this highway that Moses wanted to lead the children of Israel. The account of Edom's refusal to give the necessary permission is found in Nu. 20:14–21 (*cf.* Dt. 2:1–18). The antagonism continued after the settlement in Canaan (see, *e.g.*, 2 Sa. 8:14; 2 Ki. 14:7; 2 Ch. 28:17), and we find the prophets denouncing Edom continually. For the principal anti-Edom prophecies, see Is. 34:5; Je. 49:7–22; La. 4:21f.; Ezk. 25:12–14; 35; Joel 3:19; Am. 1:11f. A vivid picture of judgment is given in Is. 63:1–6, Edom being used to typify the world's hostility to God's people and purposes, and its overthrow as typical of the universal Messianic conquest (*cf.* Is. 34:8ff.; Ezk. 35). Some time later we find a backward look to Edom's destruction in Mal. 1:2–5. There were recrudescences of the power and influence of Edom after the close of the OT period, but today the remarkable ruins at Petra are all that is left of Edom's greatness.

For Edom's part in the sack of Jerusalem in 587 BC see especially Ezk. 35:5, 12, 15 and Ps. 137:7. This participation by Edom is not mentioned in the historical books, though it would easily fit into the picture as we see it, *e.g.*, in the marauding raids described in 2 Ki. 24:2.

Esau and Edom occupy a place of profound significance in the divine revelation of truth. That significance is brought into sharp focus in this small prophecy of Obadiah. 'The background of the picture presented to us by Obadiah is Jacob; the foreground is Esau. Jacob and those descended from him are seen passing through suffering, which is of the nature of chastisement, to ultimate restoration. Esau is seen proud, rebellious, defiant, moving towards ultimate destruction' (G. C. Morgan). We may rejoice that, in the day of the Lord, 'the kingdom shall be the Lord's' (v. 21), but we should no less be warned by Esau's example, for, after all, 'is not Esau Jacob's brother?' (Mal. 1:2). In the NT the writer to the Hebrews exhorts us to 'see to it that no-one fail to obtain the grace of God; that no "root of bitterness" spring up and cause trouble, and by it the many become defiled; that no one be . . . irreligious like Esau. . . . For you know that afterward, when he desired to inherit the blessing, he was rejected' (Heb. 12:15ff.).

OUTLINE OF CONTENTS

1–9 Impending doom on Edom

10–14 Edom's behaviour towards Judah

15–21 Judgment on Edom and all nations in the day of the Lord: Judah's restoration

COMMENTARY

1–9 IMPENDING DOOM ON EDOM

1, 2 This opening section of the prophecy of Obadiah, which describes some terrible disaster apparently about to overtake Edom, is prefaced by the words: *Thus says the Lord God concerning Edom.* Yahweh does not actually speak until v. 2, and the form of the intervening passage, *We have heard tidings from the Lord . . .* , suggests that Obadiah is here quoting an earlier prophetic oracle which he believes has come near to fulfilment. It is interesting, therefore, that most of this section appears almost word for word (though not in the same order) in Je. 49:7ff. Obadiah is perhaps quoting from Jeremiah, whom he may have heard preaching in Jerusalem, or both prophets may be employing an earlier prophecy; Jeremiah and Obadiah were assuredly not the first to speak of Edom in such a way. (See also Introduction.)

The immediate occasion of Obadiah's utterance, and for which he draws on the words of an earlier prophet, seems to be indicated in v. 7. This verse, which has no parallel in Jeremiah, gives the idea (though the Hebrew is somewhat obscure in details) that Edom's own neighbours and confederates were turning against her. 'The men of your covenant' and 'the men of your peace', to give a literal rendering, were either treacherously hostile or were yielding none of their expected assistance. In this situation Obadiah saw the appropriateness of the former oracle . . . *a messenger has been sent among the nations: "Rise up! let us rise against her* (Edom) *for battle!"*

3 The chief ground of Edom's proud confidence was her almost impregnable position. The Edomites were not the first nor the last to put their trust in a rocky fortress city. But neither their strong position nor their wit (Edom was renowned in antiquity also for her wisdom) could deliver them now. No matter how high Edom should go, to inaccessible eagle's eyrie, or among the very stars, yet God would bring her *down to the ground. The rock* is the capital Sela (see Introduction).

5 A picture of the completeness of Edom's coming destruction. Had it been a case of an ordinary raid by a band of robbers, there would have been plenty left to salvage. *Plunderers by night*, depending on speed and surprise, would take only a limited amount of booty, and so steal *only enough for themselves*, much as grape-gathers leave plenty of gleanings behind them. But Edom, by contrast, is 'cleaned right out', as we should say, and the utter devastation evokes the prophet's exclamation: *how you have been destroyed!*

6ff. Another picture of the completeness of Edom's destruction is in the exposure of all the *treasures* contained in her inaccessible and mysterious strongholds. All is *sought out* and laid bare. Since the judgment of Edom is here seen in the context of the final judgment of *the day of the Lord* (v. 15), its characteristics are the more worthy of study. It is always part of the judgment of God to 'bring to light the things now hidden in darkness' (1 Cor. 4:5). Edom gloried in her wisdom, might and riches (*cf.* Je. 9:23ff.). But her 'hidden treasures' (RV) will be *sought out*, her *wise men* destroyed (v. 8), and her *mighty men* dismayed (v. 9).

743

10-14 EDOM'S BEHAVIOUR TOWARDS JUDAH

10 Why was all this to befall Edom? The reason is given in vv. 10, 11: *For the violence done to your brother Jacob.* 'The name *Jacob* is expressly used (in place of Israel or Judah) in order to recall the relationship between the nations. In Dt. 23:7 the claims of kinship between the two peoples are urged upon Israel; but Edom had shown no reciprocal sense of brotherly relationship' (G. W. Wade). Not only did this age-long antagonism date back to the time in the wilderness when Edom refused to give Israel passage through his border (Nu. 20:20f.), but, as v. 11 shows, it reached a head in the sack of Jerusalem by Nebuchadrezzar in 587 BC. The participation of Edom on this occasion was long and bitterly remembered by the Jews. In exile by the rivers of Babylon they cried: 'Remember, O Lord, against the Edomites the day of Jerusalem, how they said, "Rase it, rase it! Down to its foundations!" ' (Ps. 137:7).

11 clearly looks back on the destruction of Jerusalem, when Edom had *stood aloof* instead of coming to his brother's assistance against attack by foreigners. For *aloof* RV has, more literally, 'on the other side'. One is reminded of the unbrotherly conduct of the priest and Levite in Lk. 10:31f.

12-14 appear in RSV as a series of reproofs, *you should not have gloated . . . you should not have rejoiced*, etc., whereas RV renders as prohibitions, 'look not . . . rejoice not', etc. The latter represents the actual construction of the Hebrew, but this is a rhetorical device, and RSV is right in seeing that in fact they have a past reference. These verses, then, may be taken as describing the actual part taken by the Edomites in the sack of Jerusalem.

First they gloated insolently and without pity over the fall of Jerusalem (v. 12). Then they *entered the gate* of the city and joined in the looting (v. 13). Finally they took up positions where they prevented fugitive Jews from escaping and even rounded up any they could find unapprehended (v. 14).

Note the use of the word 'day', especially in such phrases as *the day of your brother* (v. 12). *Cf.* 'the day of Jerusalem', as already quoted in the passage from Ps. 137:7. 'The expression *day* is often thus used to denote the occurrence of either good or bad fortune in connection with some place or person' (Wade). Jerusalem was to have another 'day' (Lk. 19:42), the time of her visitation, but she knew it not. *The day of the Lord*, on the other hand, which the next section of Obadiah introduces, is the day of Yahweh's final and uninhibited vindication of His own righteousness.

15-21 JUDGMENT ON EDOM AND ALL NATIONS IN THE DAY OF THE LORD: JUDAH'S RESTORATION

15 *The day of the Lord* is one of the great themes of the OT. Its character is emphasized rather than its exact time, although it is the ultimate issue of history and is often spoken of as imminent. Since 'the Lord alone will be exalted in that day' (Is. 2:11) it is a day of just retribution on all 'the nations that forget God' (Ps. 9:17). Among these Edom shall suffer: *as you have done, it shall be done to you.*

16 seems to be an ironical thrust. The prophet, recalling the way in which the Edomites caroused and drank in Jerusalem after the plunder of the city, declares that the heathen nations shall drink indeed, but it shall be such a drinking and swallowing down as shall make them *as though they had not been.*

17 In Yahweh's judgment on the nations, however, there shall be one safe place: *Mount Zion.* Here, *those that escape* of the exiles of Judah shall congregate. The phrase *it shall be holy* refers not to moral quality but to security from defilement and so from assault of the heathen, as in Joel 3:17. Best of all, the saved remnant of *the house of Jacob* will be reinstated in the territories which God had given them of old.

18 It is interesting to notice that *the house of Joseph* is mentioned alongside *the house of Jacob.* This means that there is to be a restoration of the northern kingdom of Israel as well as of the southern kingdom of Judah. Historically, it was only through a faithful remnant of the single tribe of Judah—indeed through the single faithful Israelite. Jesus Christ, 'the Lion of the tribe of Judah' (Rev. 5:5)—that God's saving purposes were carried out. But by His death the Christ of God was to 'gather into one the children of God who are scattered abroad' (Jn. 11:52), and in God's purposes His chosen people, 'the Israel of God' (Gal. 6:16) will ultimately stand complete in all its tribes. It is the fully restored nation of the children of Israel which will consume as a flame the whole house of Esau (*cf.* Dn. 7:22; 1 Cor. 6:2).

19 Vv. 19, 20 describe the full extent of Israel's 'possession' of its inheritance. Not all the details are clear, and the passage may be somewhat corrupt in Hebrew, but a glance at the main physical divisions of the kingdom on a map and at such a passage as Je. 33:13 will help to give the general sense well enough. *The Negeb* (meaning 'the south') is the area south of Hebron towards the wilderness of Paran. The second division, *the Shephelah*, is the lowland lying roughly west of Hebron towards the sea. The actual seaboard was occupied by the Philistines who had come there in the 12th century, after the Israelite entry into Canaan. The third division of Judah ought to be the hill country, and it has been conjectured that the next sentence of v. 19 has lost its original subject and that (here with some support from the LXX) it should be restored to read 'they of the hill country shall possess Ephraim and the hills of Samaria'.

20 The text of this verse is even more uncertain, but on the whole it seems best to take it as a reference to the future of the two principal groups of exiled Hebrews: first, those deported from the northern kingdom of Israel by Sargon after the fall of Samaria in 722 BC (*the exiles . . . of the people of Israel*), and secondly, the exiles of Jerusalem, *i.e.* those carried off from Judah by Nebuchadrezzar in 587 BC. *Halah* is a conjectured emendation in the RSV of the Hebrew text ('this army'), Halah being a place in Assyria to which Israelites were deported from Samaria in 722 BC (2 Ki. 17:6). This group will occupy *Phoenicia*, since their original area is now occupied by Jews from the southern kingdom. The latter group will occupy the cities of the Negeb, which the Jews who occupy Edom have vacated (v. 19). *Sepharad* has been variously located. Ancient identifications included Spain and the Bosphorus. More plausible modern suggestions include Sardis, capital of Lydia in Asia Minor, and, more likely, Saparda (probably the Persian Sparda), mentioned in Assyrian annals as a neighbouring country in Mesopotamia. It was no doubt a group of exiled Jews in which Obadiah and his hearers had some special interest.

21 gathers together the main themes of the book in two fine affirmations. First, there is the actual execution of judgment on Edom by *saviours*, whose headquarters are in Jerusalem. In regard to the Jews they are deliverers or defenders (*cf.* Jdg. 2:16 and Is. 19:20), and with regard to the Edomites they are executors of justice.

Finally, *the kingdom shall be the Lord's.* The people of God never doubted that Yahweh was ruling as King, 'be the earth never so unquiet' (Ps. 99:1, Prayer Book Version), but they awaited the full expression and acknowledgment of His sovereign rule. See Dn. 2:44 and 7:27, and especially Rev. 11:15, where the people of God still rejoice in the assurance that 'the kingdom of the world has become the kingdom of our Lord, and of his Christ, and he shall reign for ever and ever'.

D. W. B. ROBINSON

Jonah

INTRODUCTION

The book of Jonah is entirely concerned with the personal dealings between Yahweh and His servant Jonah the son of Amittai. These dealings arise out of a prophetic commission and its attempted evasion. Jonah finds that God's thoughts are not his thoughts, and that his ways are not God's ways. But God will not leave Jonah to himself. In the first half of the story He lets him go to the extremity of almost losing his life, only to restore him to where he was before he attempted, by physical means, to evade Yahweh's command. In the second half of the story He lets him go to the extremity of both mental and spiritual depression only to reveal to him the essential rightness of His merciful purposes.

THE MESSAGE AND ITS FORM

The form of the book is that of a piece of biographical narrative, similar (in style, language, atmosphere and miraculous content) to the various incidents in 1 and 2 Kings concerning Elijah and Elisha, who, indeed, were Jonah's immediate predecessors as prophets in the northern kingdom of Israel, and who, like him, performed part of their work in relation to heathen peoples: Elijah to Sidon (1 Ki. 17:8ff.), Elisha to Syria (2 Ki. 5:1ff.), Jonah to Nineveh.

Indeed, if we are looking for literary parallels (which we must do if we are to determine the literary *genre* to which the book of Jonah belongs) there are marked similarities between Jonah and the episode of Elijah's encounter with Baal-worship in 1 Ki. 17–19: a terse oracle of judgment (1 Ki. 17:1 = Jon. 3:4); God's intimate protective dealings with His prophet; a series of miraculous occurrences; after the prophet's great moment, his solitary depression, accompanied by God's provision for him and His confrontation of him; the final utterance of God, rebuking the prophet's narrowness and vindicating the divine sovereignty (1 Ki. 19:18 = Jon. 4:11). If Jonah does not actually belong to the same cycle of stories as those of Elijah and Elisha, it could well have been modelled on them. The latter possibility would be compatible with the story itself being a literary invention (whatever purpose the writer may have had in view). The fact that Jonah comes to us as part of the prophetic Canon, however, means that it owes its place in the Bible to its acceptance by the Jews as recording the experience of the actual prophet Jonah, a belief obviously endorsed by Jesus (see below). Is there sufficient reason to reject this view? The popular modern view is

that Jonah was written as an imaginative tale, either as an allegory of the exile and mission of Israel (*cf.* Je. 51:34), or to teach the truth of God's universal love by way of parable. The difficulty of accepting this view in preference to the traditional view is that it rests on subjective impression rather than on comparative literary tests: no other biblical book can be classed as either parable or allegory, and where these literary forms appear within larger books there is always some internal or contextual indication that it is parable or allegory we are dealing with. But there is no positive evidence, either internal or external, to show that Jonah is allegory or parable.

The allegorical view is not, in fact, held by many, owing to the difficulty of finding a consistent allegorical interpretation in detail. The parabolic view is more favoured, partly no doubt because it seems to relieve the reader of the necessity of accepting as factual the miraculous events of the story. This, however, increases the difficulty of determining the literary *genre* of Jonah, for, in the case of most biblical parables, the cogency of the parable depends on its verisimilitude as portraying a human situation. This means that, if the miraculous will not do in history, it equally will lend no conviction to a parable. There is still the possibility that Jonah is a deliberate imitation of the Elijah–Elisha type of prophetic episode, designed to teach a certain truth. If this view is taken, however, much of the ground for thinking Jonah a literary invention (*i.e.* the miraculous element) is removed, unless the whole prophetic cycle is to be classified as similarly didactic invention. Are we to argue that there was no encounter between Elijah and the prophets of Baal at Mt. Carmel, and no encounter between Elijah and God at Horeb, on the ground that the episode includes miraculous interventions, exhibits Elijah's exclusiveness and teaches a doctrine of the remnant?

The particular revelation with which the book of Jonah is concerned may be expressed in the words which form the conclusion of the story of Peter and the Gentiles in Acts 11:18: 'Then to the Gentiles also God has granted repentance unto life.' This revelation is so given as to emphasize, on the one hand, God's supreme mercy and justice in granting Nineveh 'repentance unto life', and, on the other hand, the sinful particularism of God's servant, Jonah, in resisting this manifestation of His will.

While this truth might well be conveyed in a number of literary forms in inspired Scripture, it is not necessary to suppose that it cannot be conveyed by the medium of historical narrative. God's revelation is regularly conveyed by means of the record of events and of the prophetic interpretation of those events. *E.g.* Acts 10 – 11:18, which, we have already suggested, is in some respects the NT counterpart of Jonah, has a similar didactic motive. But we are not therefore to infer that Luke thought he was writing parable or homiletic fiction. Similarly, the presence of miracle in a story is no evidence that it was not recorded as, and intended to be accepted as, historical narrative.

Any assessment of the literary character of Jonah must take into account the following facts. First, Jonah himself was an historical figure, a prophet of Yahweh in Israel (2 Ki. 14:25). Secondly, the work is *prima facie* historical narrative, without any positive indication that it is to be interpreted otherwise. Thirdly, neither Jews nor Christians have ever, until quite recently, regarded Jonah as anything but a record of the prophet's experience, whatever they may have taken its message to be. Fourthly, our Lord Jesus Christ clearly believed that the repentance of the men of Nineveh was a real occurrence, and it is most natural to take His allusion to Jonah's 'three days and three nights in the belly of the whale' (Mt. 12:40, 41) in the same way. In addition it may be urged that the whole force of Yahweh's self-vindication to Jonah demands an actual mission to a heathen city with an actual repentance and 'sparing' of it. It is not easy to believe that the challenge 'Should not I pity Nineveh?' was presented to the people of Israel through the inspired writer as a purely hypothetical consideration.

DATE AND AUTHORSHIP

No certainty can be reached as regards the date of the book. Some have argued that the entire story would have no meaning after Nineveh had actually been destroyed (612 BC). There is force in this argument. 'Should not I pity Nineveh?' would then be not only a hypothetical consideration, but a particularly ill-chosen one. (Jon. 3:3 will be considered in the commentary.) The book has actually been assigned, by various prominent scholars, to every century from the 8th to the 2nd BC. But it should be pointed out that the chief reason why many scholars hold the book to be a product of the post-exilic period is that 'the general thought and tenor of the book . . . presupposes the teaching of the great prophets' including Jeremiah (S. R. Driver). With this highly subjective judgment we see no compelling reason to concur.

'The presence of Aramaisms in the book cannot be made a criterion for determining the date, since Aramaisms occur in Old Testament books from both early and late periods' (E. J. Young, *Introduction to the Old Testament*, 1953, p. 255). Indeed, L. Morris is able to quote learned opinion that ' "Aramaic" words are now

known from the Middle Babylonian and Middle Assyrian period, *c.* 1400 BC' and that 'the evidence of early Aramaisms is abundant' (L. Morris, *Ruth*, *TOTC*, 1968, p. 233 n. 2). With the linguistic evidence must also be reckoned the fact that 'there is not in them (Jonah, Joel, *etc.*) one certainly Persian word, nor a single Greek word' and 'not a Babylonian word not already found in the earlier literature' (R. D. Wilson, 'The Authenticity of Israel', *PTR*, Vol. XVI, pp. 280–298, 430–456). This evidence does not support the theory that Jonah belongs to the post-exilic period. S. R. Driver, who himself held the post-exilic view, admitted as a possibility that 'some of the linguistic features might be consistent with a pre-exilic origin in northern Israel' (*Introduction to the Literature of the Old Testament*, 1909, p. 322).

Jonah exercised his ministry in the reign of Jeroboam II (793–753 BC), and it seems most natural to suppose that the story was first committed to writing some time before the fall of the northern kingdom in 722 BC, though there may easily have been circumstances occurring between 722 BC and 612 BC, when Israel was governed from Nineveh, which prompted the wider publication of the book in that period.

Nothing is said in the book of Jonah about its author. Although Jonah himself must obviously have been the main ultimate source of information for the story, there is no reason why he should have been the writer. No doubt the story soon became known in Israel, and we may presume that the sailors did their share of the telling. There were schools of prophets in Israel in the 9th century (2 Ki. 3:13; 6:1) and in Judah in the 8th century (Is. 8:16ff.) among whom such prophetic stories may first have circulated.

JONAH AND JESUS

A number of important scriptures should be studied alongside Jonah. In the OT, *e.g.*, Je. 1:4–10 (for the prophetic commission); Je. 18:7–10 (for the effect of repentance on God's proclamation); Pss. 16:8–11; 139 (for the prophet's experience). In the NT, Acts 10:1 – 11:18 and Rom. 9–11 illustrate the missionary message of Jonah, and *vice versa*. But, in particular, the Gospel passages which refer to Jonah should be compared and studied (Mt. 12:38–41; Lk. 11:29–32). Some points will be dealt with in the commentary. But here we may notice that Jonah is the only OT prophet with whom Jesus directly compared Himself. Jesus obviously regarded Jonah's experience and mission as of great significance. It is the more interesting, therefore, to recall that both Jesus and Jonah were 'prophets of Galilee'. Jonah's town, Gath-hepher, was only a few miles to the north of Nazareth, Jesus' town. It was less than an hour's walk away. Jesus must often have gone there. Perhaps even in His day the tomb of Jonah was pointed out there, as it was later in Jerome's day. Was it here that, in the days of His obscurity, Jesus began to meditate on the significance of Jonah and of His own mission?

According to the usual text of Jn. 7:52, the Pharisees taunted Nicodemus with the claim that 'no prophet is to rise from Galilee'. A recently discovered manuscript, P 66, gives the sense '*the* prophet does not rise from Galilee' (*cf.* Jn. 6:14; 7:41; Dt. 18:18). They failed to perceive that 'something greater than Jonah is here' (Mt. 12:41).

OUTLINE OF CONTENTS

COMMENTARY

1:1-3 THE COMMISSION GIVEN TO JONAH AND REJECTED

1 Jonah appears as one to whom *the word of the Lord came*, *i.e.* as a prophet. (*Cf.* 2 Ki. 14:25 for other details of Jonah.) **2** His assignment was as unusual as it was unwelcome, for *Nineveh*, mighty and famous, was capital of the heathen Empire of Assyria, the constant enemy of Israel. The phrase *has come up before me* pictures Yahweh as 'Judge of all the earth' (Gn. 18:25; *cf.* Gn. 6:13; 18:20, 21).

3 Jonah's resignation of his prophetic commission is immediate and deliberate. The emphasis on his fleeing *from the presence of the Lord* (see also v. 10) does not imply a belief, like that of Naaman in 2 Ki. 5:17, that the presence of Yahweh was restricted to the soil of Israel. Vv. 2b and 9 prove the contrary. Rather it indicates a withdrawal from the prophet's intimacy with Yahweh. No longer could the prophet say of his God, 'before whom I stand' (1 Ki. 17:1). Jonah did what Moses feared to do (*cf.* Ex. 33:14, 15), and he forfeited also the 'rest' which accompanies the presence of God. With a gesture of independence, the servant of Yahweh selects his own destination. *Tarshish* apparently refers to more than one place in the OT (*cf.* 1 Ki. 22:48). Here it may be Tartessus, a mining port in Spain, far away at the western end of the Mediterranean Sea. Relying now on his own resources, *he paid the fare* of the ship and embarked. *Joppa*, modern Jaffa, was the only considerable port on the coast of Palestine. It is interesting that Joppa also plays a part in the NT story of Peter and the Gentiles in Acts 10:1 – 11:18.

1:4-17 JONAH'S FLIGHT AND THE LORD'S PURSUIT

Jonah's desperate attempt to evade God, even to the point of accepting death by drowning, and God's reclaiming of Jonah, occupy the largest section of the narrative. The disobedient prophet cannot escape from Yahweh. We have not yet been told why it was that Jonah chose to disobey Yahweh's command; that will be disclosed later in its appropriate place.

Here we are confronted with a fundamental fact of God's elective purposes, viz. that 'the gifts and call of God are irrevocable' (Rom. 11:29). To all His prophets He said, as Jesus said to His apostles, 'You did not choose me, but I chose you' (Jn. 15:16).

4 Yahweh took two steps to recover Jonah. First, He *hurled a great wind upon the sea*. This resulted in the terror of the sailors, the exposure of Jonah and his being thrown overboard. Secondly, 'the Lord appointed a great fish to swallow up Jonah' (v. 17; see note below). This was the means of preserving him from death and of causing him to throw himself on the mercy of God. God's instruments here were *a great wind* and 'a great fish'. *Cf.* other occasions when God works for His people through the manoeuvring of His creatures, *e.g.* in the Exodus (see Ex. 14:21; Nu. 11:31).

It is instructive to study Jonah's experience in the light of Ps. 139. The writer's thoughts, words and every movement are known to Yahweh. 'Whither shall I flee from thy presence?' he asks. 'If I make my bed in Sheol, thou art there! If I . . . dwell in the uttermost parts of the sea, even there thy hand shall lead me, and thy right hand shall hold me' (Ps. 139:7-10). So Jonah found it.

5-16 The account of the ship in distress is graphic and realistic—the violent gale, the *mariners* of many races and religions, their panic, the excited questioning of Jonah, their reluctance to take the desperate step he suggests, their frantic rowing. The LXX adds the detail that it was Jonah's snoring as he lay asleep in *the inner part of the ship* that first attracted the shipmaster's attention to the suspicious traveller!

Jonah's behaviour is set off against the behaviour of the heathen sailors. They have a strong sense of religious obligation and are amazed at Jonah's temerity in fleeing from the presence of his God (v. 10). They are scrupulous when the ejection of Jonah appears inevitable; and when the sea is finally calmed, they show proper fear towards Yahweh (v. 16). Yet the incident clearly shows that Jonah is no coward. He is comparatively calm and self-possessed. He professes his faith and his guilt deliberately, and as deliberately chooses to drown rather than let others perish on his account. No doubt he regarded his impending death as Yahweh's punishment. A comparison of Jonah's behaviour with that of the characters in Acts 27 and Mk. 4:35-41 (and parallels) will be found instructive.

It ought not to be overlooked that Jonah testified to one God only over all the earth (v. 9). To him, Yahweh is the transcendent *God of heaven*, the Creator and Sovereign of *the sea and the dry land* alike. Yet Jonah, in his religion and devotion, cramped this glorious doctrine of God into the narrow confines of a jealous exclusivism. It is thus part of the purpose of the book to warn against a life and practice which falls below our grasp of the truth.

17 Speculation as to the nature of the *great fish* is needless. Our Lord's reference to this same incident in Mt. 12:40 carefully adopts the same designation, emphasizing the entombment rather than the creature itself (Gk. *kētos*, 'a large sea-monster', translated and interpreted by AV, RV and RSV as 'whale'). For theories concerning the fish the reader is referred to A. J. Wilson's article in *PTR*, Vol. XXV, pp. 630-642. It may not be without significance that the Sumerian and Akkadian ideogram for the city of Nineveh is *nina* written with a sign compounded of a fish within a large dwelling-place or tomb. The information that Jonah was incarcerated for *three days and three nights*, if intended literally, is not likely to have been supplied by Jonah himself, who, even he had been conscious for the whole time, would hardly have had any means of marking the passage of time. It must then have been calculated from information supplied by the sailors. On the other hand, this may be only a conventional expression for a shortish period of time (*cf.* 3:3 and Jos. 2:16). The addition of *three nights* does not necessarily add to the accuracy of the expression, and we know that elsewhere 'after three days' is equivalent to 'on the third day'. *Cf.* the NT references to the duration of Jesus' entombment (*e.g.* 1 Cor. 15:4). Mt. 12:40 shows that 'three days and three nights' was regarded then as sufficiently accurate to denote a period of not more than 36 hours.

2:1-10 JONAH'S PRAYER FROM THE FISH'S BELLY

In this section Jonah describes his experience, ascribing salvation to Yahweh, and is restored to land. We are perhaps meant to observe the contrast of Jonah's position: he who, in the ship, apparently declined to arise and call upon his God (1:6) is now constrained to pray 'to the Lord his God from the belly of the fish' (2:1).

Jonah's prayer, a psalm in Hebrew elegiac metre, has often been declared to be an extraneous insertion. It has, however, a real appropriateness in its context, and we need not doubt that its sentiment belongs to the occasion to which it is ascribed, even if its poetic form should belong to the period of reflection after the deliverance from death ('Sheol'), and not, as some seem to think it ought to have been, a prayer to be saved from the fish.

The sequence of thought in vv. 2-7 suggests that after his desperate prayer Jonah was overcome by the water and pressure of the depths, and that the next thing he was conscious of was simply that he was still alive. If we are to take it that his thanksgiving was uttered near the end of the three-day period, we may suppose that for most of the preceding time he was insensible, as perhaps he was already insensible when swallowed by the great fish. In that case, his was the further experience of Ps. 139:18, 'when I awake, I am still with thee'. Yahweh had heard Jonah's prayer and had brought up his life 'from the Pit' (v. 6; *i.e.* Sheol). Jonah promises a sacrifice of thanksgiving, for 'deliverance belongs to the Lord' (v. 9).

We should note, however, that although Jonah is no doubt ready now to obey God's command, there is no evidence that he feels any compassion for the Ninevites. His experience of God's mercy only confirms him in his belief that those who 'pay regard to vain idols forsake their true loyalty' (*i.e.* cut themselves off from Yahweh, the only true source of succour for them) (v. 8). This evidence of Jonah's exclusiveness, even in the midst of Yahweh's mercy, gives further point to Yahweh's remonstrance in ch. 4. But this attitude was not peculiar to Jonah. Again Ps. 139 has a parallel; note the similar transition of thought there from v. 18 to vv. 19ff.

This psalm of Jonah is of especial importance in the light of Jesus' reference to him in Mt. 12:40; for the nature of the similarity between Jonah's experience and that of Christ is most clearly seen here. Thus, Jesus, the greater than Jonah, the true Servant and Prophet of Yahweh, went to the extremity of human suffering (because of the disobedience of others). What Jonah endured 'figuratively' (Heb. 11:19—a similar figure of death) Jesus endured in reality. In His 'distress' He went to 'the belly of Sheol'; all God's waves and billows passed over Him (*cf.* Is. 53). As Jonah cried, 'I am cast out from thy presence' (v. 4), so Christ was constrained to cry, 'My God, my God, why hast thou forsaken me?' (Mt. 27:46).

And yet the entombment of Jesus not only denoted the extremity of His passion (as the Creed states, 'He descended into hell', *i.e.* Hades, or Sheol); it also emphasized the reality of His deliverance from death to life. Study Peter's Pentecostal sermon in Acts 2, especially vv. 24ff.: 'But God raised him up, having loosed the pangs of death, because it was not possible for him to be held by it.' Jonah's testimony, 'yet thou didst bring up my life from the Pit' (v. 6), has a striking parallel in the verse from Ps. 16:10 quoted by Peter in Acts 2:27: 'Thou wilt not abandon my soul to Hades, nor let thy Holy One see corruption.'

2, 3 First Jonah describes how in his extremity his voluntary resistance to Yahweh broke down, and as the awfulness of his fate impressed itself on him he cried in desperation to his God. (*Cf.* Peter's spontaneous cry in Mt. 14:30.) *The belly of Sheol* is the place of the dead (the word for 'belly' is different from that used for 'belly of the fish'), whose inhabitants, if they had died as Jonah was in danger of dying, estranged from God and unforgiven, were thought of as being cut off from God's hand and remembered no more by Him (*cf.* Ps. 88:5; read the whole of this Psalm for an understanding of Jonah's horror).

4 *Thy holy temple*, here and in v. 7, symbolizes the place of Yahweh's presence, whence Jonah had fled. It is in extreme contrast to 'the belly of Sheol'. At whatever shrine Jonah may have been accustomed to worship in Israel, it is probable that he who worships the God of heaven is here thinking of *thy holy temple* as 'heaven thy dwelling place' (1 Ki. 8:39).

3:1–9 THE PROPHETIC COMMISSION RENEWED AND DISCHARGED

1 Jonah, having been restored to land at Yahweh's commandment, is commissioned a second time. Chastened by his experiences he obeys, although he is not apparently more charitably disposed towards Nineveh than before. **2** *The message that I tell you* emphasizes that the preacher speaks not of himself, but 'oracles of God' (1 Pet. 4:11). What is true of Christ the Son, the eternal Word, must also be true of all His servants: 'He whom God has sent utters the words of God' (Jn. 3:34). *Cf.* also the case of Moses (Ex. 4:10–16), Jeremiah (Je. 1:6–9) and Jesus' disciples (Mt. 10:19, 20). Jonah knew from the beginning that he must preach the preaching that God bade him; he was a disobedient, not a false, prophet.

3 A note here draws attention to the magnitude of Nineveh, and thus of Jonah's task. *Exceedingly great* is lit. 'great to God' or 'great before God', which is a regular way of expressing a superlative. This, however, has caused difficulty to some people on two scores. First the verb *was* is in the perfect tense in Hebrew, and has been thought to imply that Nineveh had long since perished (thus supporting a late date for that book). Secondly, modern archaeological research does not altogether confirm the great size of Nineveh. The first difficulty is not decisive, for since the whole narrative is cast in the past, the statement that *Nineveh was an exceedingly great city* need imply no more than that this is how it was when Jonah went there. *Cf.* 'now the famine was severe in Samaria' in the Elijah

story in 1 Ki. 18:2, referred to in the Introduction. Alternatively, the note may be a gloss inserted later by a scribe to explain the following verse. The second difficulty is likewise capable of solution. Nineveh city itself, according to the dimensions given by Sennacherib and modern surveys of its ruins (*c.* 12 miles), was considerably smaller than the language of Jonah implies. Gn. 10:12, however, applies the title 'the great city' to four cities in the area, of which Nineveh proper is first named and most important. Recent archaeological discoveries show that one of these, Calah, had a population of 70,000; and as this city is known by its walls to have been about half the size of Nineveh, the much doubted figure of 'a hundred and twenty thousand persons' (4:11) is seen to be most likely a census figure of Nineveh in its prime. In later times Nineveh was calculated (by Ktesias and Diodorus) to have had a circuit of some 480 stadia, or about 60 miles, and this seems to reflect the tradition of a very large city area (though it was never bounded by a single wall, as Diodorus seems to think it was). The entire circuit of the four seats of the Nineveh district is, in fact $61\frac{1}{2}$ miles, or about *three days' journey*. Now, in addition to this note in 3:3 which we are considering, Nineveh is on three separate occasions described as 'that great city' (1:2; 3:2; 4:11) and the addition of this term may indicate that the larger area or 'district' is deliberately intended. We may compare such modern appellations as 'Greater London'. It may be significant that the term is not added in 4:5; 'the city' here is no doubt Nineveh proper, the city of 'a day's journey' where Jonah had first entered (3:4). Here the word of Jonah's preaching came to the king of Nineveh, by whose proclamation the fast of repentance extended to all the people of Nineveh.

4–7 We do not know what other circumstances in Nineveh may have been favourable to the producing of contrition, but Jonah's preaching of imminent doom—the only actual 'prophecy' in this prophetic book—resulted in an immediate and widespread repentance. The king himself ordered a national fast. Note the curious inclusion of animals in the fast (v. 7), as in Judith 4:9ff., and as in the famine of Joel 1:19, 20. The very beasts of the field who cry unto the Lord are in turn the objects of His compassion, as the last words of Jonah tell us.

'The sign of Jonah' (Mt. 16:4) includes not only his 'death' and 'resurrection', but also his preaching, by virtue of that 'resurrection', to Gentile Nineveh. Ponder the great importance of this sign for Christ's generation (*cf.* Lk. 11:29ff. and Mt. 12:38ff.) and for our own.

3:10 – 4:11 TWO REACTIONS TO NINEVEH'S REPENTANCE: THE LORD CHALLENGES JONAH

3:10, 4:1 *God repented of the evil . . . But it displeased Jonah exceedingly.* God's 'repentance' and averting of judgment is, of course, not arbitrary. It is a basic postulate of the book of Jonah that God repents of evil (*cf.* on Joel 2:13, 14 and especially Je. 18:6–10). But we have reached the core of Jonah's problem. Jonah now explicitly confesses the reason, hitherto unexplained, for his first attempt to evade Yahweh's command. The question which forms the climax of the book here comes directly into view: 'Should Yahweh have pity on Nineveh?'

2, 3 It was in the certain knowledge that God would spare Nineveh if she repented that Jonah fled to Tarshish. Now that Nineveh has repented, Jonah knows that judgment will not fall, and this he cannot face. He cannot reconcile himself to what he knows is the unchangeable character of God. Again he seeks death rather than see God's face and live. *Take my life from me . . . for it is better for me to die than to live. Cf.* Elijah's prayer in 1 Ki. 19:4 and the grounds for it.

4 But Yahweh directly challenges Jonah. His question may be construed as 'Are you rightly angry?' or 'Are you very angry?' The force is not very different. The first is an explicit challenge to the righteousness of Jonah's behaviour. The second is more in the nature of an exclamation of surprise that Jonah should be at variance with God's mind.

5–11 In the final passage of the book, God presents His challenge to Jonah in dramatic form, in the acted parable of the gourd. By means of this parable God elicits from Jonah a confession in the matter of the gourd which carries a condemnation of his unrighteousness in the matter of Nineveh.

Jonah, awaiting in forlorn hope the expiry of the 'forty days' of his prediction (3:4), is again the object of God's 'preparations'. This time a *plant*, a *worm* and a *sultry east wind* are employed. In his depression God dealt with him thus: first He relieved Jonah's grief by providing additional shelter in the thick leafage of the tropical gourd. Next day He reversed the situation and allowed Jonah to suffer acute physical distress by destroying the gourd. Jonah was angry because the gourd perished. Though it was in no sense 'his' gourd, and was by nature short-lived, yet Jonah would have spared it, because it brought comfort to him.

11 *And should not I pity Nineveh?* asks Yahweh. Cannot Jonah see some ground for pity in the 120,000 ignorant people and the dumb beasts therein? *Persons who do not know their right hand from their left* is probably a reference to their ignorance, as compared with the Israelite, of the law of God. The ignorance of the people and the helplessness of the cattle are not, of course, the sole ground for the exercise of Yahweh's mercy, but they are mentioned to show how lacking, even in common sympathy, Jonah's religious exclusiveness has made him. Selfishness, blindness, unrighteousness: these are progressively revealed by the parable as Jonah's sins.

The last word is with God, 'whose property is always to have mercy', and the book of Jonah is another signpost to the full revelation of the salvation of God, which, in His sovereign mercy and grace, was to be 'a light for revelation to the Gentiles' (Lk. 2:32). The evangelical message of the book may be expressed in the words of Paul: 'What shall we say then? Is there injustice on God's part? By no means! For he says to Moses, "I will have mercy on whom I have mercy, and I will have compassion on whom I have compassion"' (Rom. 9:14, 15).

D. W. B. ROBINSON

Micah

INTRODUCTION

The prophet Micah was probably from an obscure family, since his father's name is not given. Certainly he came from an outlying provincial town, Moresheth, bordering upon the Philistine territory of Gath. His concern and interest seem to be centred a little more upon the plight of the oppressed lower classes than was the case with his contemporary, Isaiah (who was apparently a citizen of Jerusalem itself).

His career began in the reign of Jotham, perhaps after Ahaz had already become co-regent with his father in 743, but before Jotham's death or deposition in 736. Ahaz ruled on until 728, when Hezekiah his son came into power, and Micah continued his ministry well into his reign. (Exact dating in this period is notoriously difficult. For a slightly variant view, see Introduc-

tion to 1 and 2 Kings, pp. 321ff.) We have no reliable evidence for a *terminus ad quem* to his career. Certainly he received revelations concerning the Babylonian captivity and the subsequent restoration, just as Isaiah did (and for this reason it is customary for some critics to deny the authenticity of such passages in both prophets). This may possibly suggest a date after the Assyrian invasion of 701 BC, but the criteria for this are quite tenuous.

Some analysts regard this book as a series of disconnected and miscellaneous discourses but, as the Outline below will demonstrate, a logical progression and interconnection of thought can be made out between the successive units of the book of Micah, and there is no strong case tor heterogeneity.

OUTLINE OF CONTENTS

COMMENTARY

1:1–16 GOD'S SENTENCE UPON BOTH IDOLATROUS KINGDOMS

1 Micah's ministry extended from the reign of *Jotham* (751–736 BC) to that of *Ahaz* (743–728) and *Hezekiah* (728–696). Apparently even ch. 6 was delivered before 724, since any later appeal to the northern kingdom of Israel would have been pointless. **2** *You peoples, all of you* suggests that God's dealings with Israel had an important bearing upon the destiny of all the surrounding nations as well. His proclamation comes *from*

752

his holy temple (*cf.* Am. 1:2) as the one valid meeting-place between God and man, with its altar of substitutionary atonement. The universal validity of the unique OT revelation is here implied. **3, 4** Destruction (at the hands of future Assyrian and Chaldean invaders) awaits the idolatrous *high places* in both Samaria and Judah, a catastrophic devastation like volcano and earthquake, or avalanches caused by torrential rains. **5** This disaster will be brought on by Israel's moral degeneracy, for both the capital cities, Samaria and Jerusalem, have become centres of idol-worship.

6, 7 Jerusalem's destruction is still 150 years off, but Samaria's is imminent (722 BC), and will be so thorough as to leave her a deserted mound of ruins, with her stone walls tumbling down into the valley through erosion and neglect. The Assyrian troops of Sargon would smash her idols and destroy the dedicated treasures and votive monuments (her harlot's *hires* from her false lovers, the heathen gods) in her temples. All the materialistic gains and advantages (such as the political alliance with Phoenicia engineered by Jezebel's marriage to Ahab) will be wiped out or carried off as spoil by the enemy.

Now follows (vv. 8–16) an anguished lament by the prophet as he foresees the inexorable march of the Assyrian host under Shalmaneser V, and the Chaldeans under Nebuchadrezzar a century and a half later. Twelve cities are mentioned, chiefly those whose names contain elements of ill omen.

8 *Jackals* (more accurate for *tannîm* than AV's 'dragons') have a peculiar howl at night, beginning with a high-pitched, long drawn-out cry repeated at a successively higher pitch, and finishing with a series of loud yelps. The *ostriches* (rather than AV's 'owls') had an eerie, doleful cry. **9** Samaria's *wound* (AV 'wounds') is *incurable* (or 'desperately ill': the same word is figuratively applied to man's heart in Je. 17:9), and is destined to be inflicted on Jerusalem also in time to come (the Chaldean invasion is especially in view here).

10 *Gath* was the nearest Philistine city to Judah, and would be most apt to hear with joy about the disaster to the Hebrews, their hereditary foes. Hence the Jews must not weep aloud when calamity strikes, but keep it secret as long as possible. *Beth-le-aphrah* (possibly the same as Ophrah in Benjamin near Bethel) means 'House unto Dust', suggesting the dust in which the mourning Hebrew will *roll* in despair. **11** *Shaphir* (possibly Sawafir, SE of Ashdod) meant 'Beautiful', which accentuated the pathos of her naked, stripped condition as the Chaldeans would lead her inhabitants into exile. *Zaanan* (perhaps Zanan in the Shephelah; *cf.* Jos. 15:37) suggested the verb *yāṣāʾ* 'go or come forth', which is what its hapless people would not be able to do under siege. *Beth-ezel* ('House of Nearness', perhaps the same as Azal in Zc. 14:5 (AV), E of Jerusalem) suggests the ominous proximity of the besieging invaders to the

beleaguered capital. *The wailing of Beth-ezel shall take away from you its standing place* (rather than AV's 'receive of you his standing') means that in their despairing lamentation the defenders of Beth-ezel retreat to Jerusalem, taking along with them the refugees from Zaanan and Shaphir, who have briefly made it their *standing place* or abiding-place.

12 *Maroth* was doubtless another suburb of Jerusalem; its name meant 'Bitterness'. **13** *Lachish*, in SW Judah, was apparently one of its first cities to permit the N Israelite cults to be established in it; now its inhabitants must harness their horses and flee with their goods as the invaders approach. **14** Lachish will have to give *parting gifts* or a 'dowry' (suggested by Heb. *môreshet*, 'a betrothed woman') as *Moresheth-gath* (Micah's own home town) is given up to the enemy. *The house of Achzib* (suggesting *ʾakzāb*, 'deceitful'), a town SW of Adullam, proves a *deceitful* hope for the Judean forces attempting to stem the advance of the foe.

15 The conqueror will take possession of *Mareshah* ('possession' from Heb. *yāraš*, 'take possession of'), NE of Lachish (according to Aharoni), pushing back the *glory of Israel* (*i.e.* the flower of army and nobility) toward *Adullam*, site of a famous cave in which David hid out from Saul (1 Sa. 22:1) to the E of Achzib. **16** The plucking out or shearing off of hair in a paroxysm of grief was customary for mothers who had received tidings of the death of their sons. Since the Hebrew *nešer* could mean 'vulture' as well as 'eagle', it may have been the former which Micah had in mind here, since the carrion vulture has neither feathers nor hair around its head and neck. The *exile* here foretold is more likely to be the Babylonian (*cf.* Mi. 4:10) than the Assyrian (which involved only the provinces, not Jerusalem itself). (J. Aharoni, *The Land of the Bible*, 1967, prefers the Sennacherib invasion; *cf.* the map on p. 338 of his book.) Perhaps both invasions (701 BC and 587 BC) are in view.

2:1 – 3:12 THE UPPER CLASSES GUILTY OF OPPRESSION

2:1–11 Exploitation of the poor and defenceless by the idle rich

1 These grasping land-owners and money-lenders are so obsessed with acquiring wealth by foreclosure or fraud that they even lie awake at night thinking up new schemes for exploiting the poor. *In the power of their hand* may also be rendered, 'Their hand is as a god (to them)'; *i.e.* they make their own power the highest force they will recognize. (It is unusual to render *ʾēl* as 'strength' rather than 'god'.) **2** *They covet* (Heb. *ḥāmaḏ* is the same verb as in the tenth commandment, which they deliberately and cynically violate) the property of others, as Ahab coveted Naboth's vineyard (1 Ki. 21). This meant depriving Israelite families of their ancestral inheritance conferred upon them by the Lord Himself back in the days of Joshua.

3 In punishment for this disregard of their obligations of brotherhood under God's covenant with Israel, God will 'devise' or counterplot against these ruthless plotters, who have succeeded in evading justice from human authorities. He will bring down calamity upon them all as a yoke pressing down upon their necks. The *family* meant here is the family of the rich oppressor (although Keil would equate it with the whole nation of Israel; *cf.* Am. 3:1). 4 *In that day* (*i.e.* the day of God's intervention to punish or redeem) 'one shall take up' (more accurate than RSV's *they*) *a taunt song*, or more likely 'a proverbial utterance' (Heb. *māšāl*), since the lamenting speakers must be the Israelites themselves (*We are utterly ruined*), rather than their jeering foes. They will deplore God's removal of their ancestral portion in the land of promise as they are driven off by their enemies. Render the final clause: 'To the rebellious (Heb. *šôḇēḇ*) He is dividing our fields' (rather than AV's 'turning away he hath divided', or RSV's *among our captors* which implies a different word, *lešôḇēnû*, for which there is no textual support). The 'rebellious' in this case would refer to the heathen invaders who have never entered into covenant relation with Yahweh or recognized His sovereignty. 5 These unscrupulous oppressors will have no descendants to cast lots for the apportionment of the land, as their forebears had done back in the days of Joshua (*cf.* Jos. 14:1, 2). The *line* here is the surveyor's measuring cord used in determining the bounds of real estate.

6 Micah's warning is scornfully rejected by his public: *Do not preach* ('prophesy', AV, RV, *BDB*, *GB*; 'drivel', Kleinert). Literally, 'cause to drop down, drip'; perhaps 'prate' brings out best what the word connotes here. The cynical Jews refuse to listen to the old-fashioned ranting of Micah and his colleagues: 'They shall not prate to them.' 'Disgrace shall not overtake' (there is no *us* expressed in the Heb.) is the hope of these hardened materialists. RSV's *overtake* assumes a change in the Hebrew text from *yissag*, 'will draw back', or 'depart', to *yassîg*, 'will overtake'. It is better to render: 'Reproaches (*i.e.* by these tiresome prophets) will not depart', or 'cease' (so *BDB*). (AV's 'that they shall not take shame' is no truer to the Heb. grammar than this latter rendering, and does not fit in with the context as well.) 7 *Should this be said* (*cf.* RV) understands the Hebrew *he'āmûr* as a question, but it could also be, 'The one who is called'. *Cf.* AV's 'O thou that art named' (so Keil). Or else *he'āmûr* could mean, 'That which is spoken' (so Kleinert, who inserts ' "in" the house of Israel'). *Is the Spirit of the Lord impatient?* (Heb. *qāṣar*, lit. 'is short'; rendered 'straitened' in AV and RV). The question here implies a negative: God's Spirit is certainly not impatient. *Are these his doings?* refers to His deeds of punishment, which are not His characteristic or congenial dealings with His covenant

people, Israel. Normally His words have a benevolent intention towards them, as they lead a righteous life.

8 *But you rise against my people as an enemy* implies reading Hebrew *eṭmûl* as a compound preposition, 'against', or else as *attem le-*, 'Ye against . . .'. AV's 'of late' (so RV) implies equating *eṭmûl* with *eṭmôl*, 'yesterday' or 'recently', which is far more likely. Render: 'But of late My people rise up as an enemy (*sc.* against Me).' Their crime is, 'You strip the broad-dress-cloak (Heb. *'eḏer*) from off (*mimmûl*) the upper-garment (*śalmâ*, a by-form of *śimlâ*) from those who pass by trustingly, turning away from war' (*i.e.* peaceably disposed). The RSV rendering implies several changes in the Hebrew text. Presumably they committed this robbery against travellers or strangers passing through their territory, in blatant disregard of the Torah (*cf.* Ex. 22:21). 9 The ruthless mortgage-holders expel widows and orphans from their homes, and deprive these children of their dignity and *glory* as members of the commonwealth of Israel by selling them into life-long slavery to foreign owners in heathen lands, to secure payment for their loans to the helpless survivors of the deceased. This means depriving Yahweh of His *glory*, for they belong to Him. 10 The ungodly Hebrews are bidden to leave and *go* off into captivity, for the Holy Land cannot bear the defilement of their abominable crimes. 11 Literally, 'If a man walking in vanity (lit. according to wind) and falsehood should lie: "I will preach (or prate, prophesy) to you with reference to wine and strong drink", then he would be the preacher of this people.' These false prophets stand ready to preach a popular message of earthly blessings and sensual enjoyment, disregarding completely the spiritual and moral conditions necessary for any lasting prosperity and safety as a nation.

2:12, 13 The eventual regathering of the dispersed of Judah

In contrast to that false message of carnal security, the Lord has a true word of encouragement to the remnant of sincere believers who still heed His revelation. 12 Israel's hope is not to be found in any immediate political success or moral reformation; her apostasy has gone too far under King Ahaz for anything but temporary respites under Hezekiah and Josiah. But her future is bound up with the minority of true believers who will remain faithful to God through the coming ordeals of military disaster and captivity. *I will surely gather* (rather than AV's 'assemble') *all of you, O Jacob, i.e. the remnant of Israel . . .* 'as the sheep of Bozrah'. (RSV's *sheep in a fold* assumes a noun *boṣrâ*, meaning 'fold', for which there is no real evidence and which never occurs elsewhere. The town of Bozrah in Edom was a well-known sheep-raising centre.) *A noisy multitude of man* lacks textual support. 'They shall make a land noise from (*i.e.* by reason of) men': *i.e.* the remnant returning to Palestine will become a large *multitude* under the care of the divine Shepherd.

13 *He who opens the breach* (AV 'the breaker'), from *pāraṣ*, 'make a breach through a wall', refers to God as Deliverer of His people from the prison-house of Babylonian captivity. (It first appeared as a Messianic title in Ob. 21, back in the 9th century.) Probably *their king* also refers to Yahweh or His Messiah. This promise, then, is an encouraging revelation from God, rather than the vain optimism of some unnamed false prophet (as Ewald, Kleinert and Orelli suppose).

3:1-4 The government devours its people instead of defending them

Keil regards this as the commencement of a separate address by the prophet; yet the chapter begins with the Hebrew connective *wᵉ-* which means 'and' or 'but'. **1** *And I said: Hear, you heads of Jacob* introduces an address to the ruling classes of government and society in Judah under the rule of Ahaz. **2, 3** They who have been entrusted with the faithful administration of justice and the carrying out of God's law have used their power only for injustice and the heartless exploitation of the governed. They are like cannibals who prey upon their brethren, as things rather than as people, mercilessly devouring all their substance like ravenous beasts and reducing them to absolute destitution, starvation and death. *Is it not for you to know justice?* (Hebrew *mišpāṭ* ('justice') is the application of the principles of righteousness to concrete situations, as administrative decisions are made or judgments are rendered in the lawcourts.) They have not simply been deflected by considerations of expediency or personal gain; they have taken up arms against justice and conceived a bitter hatred for goodness and virtue.

4 When the coming judgment befalls the nation, and invaders threaten to destroy all their possessions or even their very lives, these leaders of Israel will look in vain to Yahweh for deliverance, 'according as (which is better for Heb. *ka'ᵃšer* than *because*) they have made their deeds evil'. Because they have turned their back on God's law, He will turn His back on their cry for help (as it turned out later in 587 BC).

3:5-8 The corrupt state religion confronted by the Spirit-empowered prophet

5 The unscrupulous governors and judges have received support and encouragement from the venal clergy, the popular prophets who preach messages of false reassurance and optimism to those who pay them well. But those who are of no financial benefit to them or who exert no influence in their favour become the objects of their scathing condemnation. RSV without justification omits 'who bite with their teeth' after *who lead my people astray*. The Hebrew word for 'bite', incidentally, is *nāšak*, which is ordinarily used

of the bite of a serpent. Instead of being men of God and standing out against the sins of the people, these faithless prophets have become professionalistic career men who cherish only worldly values. **6, 7** Literally, 'Therefore night unto you away from (or, without) vision.' Here, as in Am. 5:18 and Zp. 1:15 the darkening of the sky symbolizes terrible judgment and despair. The *seers* (*ḥōzîm*) and *diviners* (*qōsᵉmîm*; a class of soothsayers strictly forbidden for Israel by Dt. 18:14) will become completely discredited and humiliated in the coming day of national emergency, because they will be utterly unable to tell their countrymen what is going to happen. God will grant them no revelation whatever, despite their most anguished entreaties. *They shall all cover their lips* by covering up their faces up to the nose, a customary gesture of mourning and despair in ancient Israel (*cf.* Lv. 13:45; Ezk. 24:17).

8 In contrast to these false prophets with their self-invented messages, Micah, for all his unpopularity and outdated emphasis on righteousness and justice, nevertheless has one quality that they lack. He is *filled with power* by God's Holy Spirit, for what he says is the truth of God, not the speculation of man. With the authority of a herald from the king he proclaims God's judgment upon guilty Israel. He has no time for dialogue with scholars of differing theological insights, but what he foretells has power behind it, for it actually comes to pass. Rather than going along with the fashionable new morality, Micah thunders forth the sanctions of the unaltered and unalterable Ten Commandments and pronounces 'guilty and condemned' upon his countrymen, for all their suave sophistication, and makes them tremble.

3:9-12 Utter destruction impends for all three: rulers, priests and prophets

9, 10 *Hear this* is better rendered, 'Pray hear this' (since the Heb. precative *-nā'* is used here). The utter perversity of Israel's rulers is here stressed, as defenders against crime who have themselves become criminals, and who imagine that they can build security for themselves and their state upon a foundation of 'bloodshed' (more accurate for the plural *dāmîm* than *blood*, which is the singular *dām*). *Who build* implies the Hebrew *bōnê* instead of *bōneh* (which probably means 'one is building'); but the LXX, Targum and Syriac Versions seem to support *bōnê* (lit. 'builders of'). **11** The judges had the sacred responsibility of rendering decisions impartially, not influenced by personal motives, but these judges were willing to sell their verdict to the highest bidder. The priests were required to give instruction concerning God's law (Lv. 10:11; Dt. 17:11; 33:10), but these priests demanded a fee, which meant that their services were not available to the poor. Yet they have the effrontery to claim God's protection and care, simply because His Temple was in their midst; on that account they suppose that He is obliged to safeguard them from evil, no matter how wickedly they live.

12 On the contrary, because of their flagrant ungodliness God will not only withdraw His protection from them against their heathen foes, but He will see to it that the holy Temple (which they suppose He is obliged to defend) is reduced to rubble, and the sacred precinct to a ploughed field, or a neglected hill overgrown with trees. (*Cf.* Je. 26:18, 19, where this verse is quoted verbatim, with the added information that Ahaz's son, Hezekiah, trembled at these words and besought the Lord's mercy to defer imposing this dreadful judgment upon Jerusalem.) It is interesting to observe that in later times, even after the return from Babylon, Mt. Zion was apparently left outside the city walls, and still is to this day, for it was dug down and deprived of defensive value in the 2nd century BC and the name 'Zion' was later transferred to the southwestern eminence of the Upper City.

4:1 – 5:15 THE ULTIMATE TRIUMPH OF GOD'S GRACE TOWARDS ISRAEL

4:1-8 The triumph of the Messianic kingdom over the Gentile world

The first three verses of this chapter are nearly identical with Is. 2:2–4. It may have been that the same revelation was granted to both prophets at about the same time; it is hardly likely that one would have copied from the other.

1a *In the latter days* is literally 'at the end of the days', an expression used by the prophets to refer to the last days, or the times of the Messiah (*cf.* Je. 23:20; Ezk. 38:16; Ho. 3:5). If this was a symbolic vision, Micah may have seen Mt. Moriah lifted up above all other mountains on earth, but the import of this symbol was surely the exaltation of the kingdom of God to a supreme position above all the kingdoms of this earth. *As the highest of the mountains*; more accurately, as RV, 'on top of the mountains'. **1b, 2** *Peoples . . . many nations* (Heb. *gôyîm*), *i.e.* Gentiles, shall come to God's kingdom, His holy Mt. Zion, which symbolizes the uniquely authoritative revelation of God through the Scriptures. *Flow.* They will come, not merely as individual proselytes, but like a flowing river (the verb translated *flow* is the same root as *nāhār*, 'river') in order to be taught by Yahweh concerning His saving truth, so that they may lead God-pleasing, God-serving lives. *For out of Zion shall go forth the law and the word of the Lord from Jerusalem.* These Gentile converts will recognize God's revelation from the altar and the ark of the covenant as uniquely authoritative. They will embrace the gospel and the sacrifice of Christ on their behalf, and His salvation will become known throughout the Gentile world.

3 *He shall judge between many people*; *i.e.* He shall become the absolute Arbiter for all moral and ethical questions among all the nations of the earth. But this is so reinforced by the next clause (*and shall decide*—or 'reprove', or 'exercise the judge's office'—*for strong nations afar off*) that an established sovereignty of Christ upon earth is clearly suggested, beyond anything which now obtains in this present church age. For when He assumes this supreme and effective authority among the nations of the earth, then a warless society will commence: *they shall beat their swords into ploughshares.* Under His rule men will turn their energies from manufacturing weapons of war to tools of fruitful production, and the nations shall not *learn war any more.* Clearly this points beyond this present age to a future era when Christ will have complete control here on earth (there would be no employment for ploughshares or pruning-hooks in heaven!) and the uninterrupted peace and harmony of the millennium will prevail all over the world. No nation will lift up a sword against any other nation. **4** Accompanying this universal peace will be universal security and prosperity: *every man under his vine and under his fig tree, and none shall make them afraid.* This indicates that the final world order will not be any kind of socialist or Marxist state ownership of all property, but every man will remain undisturbed in the enjoyment of his own personal property. (*Cf.* 1 Ki. 4:25 where this ideal condition is said to have obtained for a time, at least, during the prosperous, well-ordered reign of Solomon. This v. 4, incidentally, was not included in Isaiah's form of this revelation.)

5 Comforted and encouraged by this assurance of the ultimate triumph of God's truth and grace, Micah and his fellow-believers express a new confidence and commitment to Yahweh: *For all the* (non-Israelite) *peoples walk each in the name of its god, but we will walk in the name of the Lord our God for ever.* To *walk in the name of* a deity means to live in conformity to the will and character of the one whom they serve. The *name* of God includes all His self-disclosures to His believers, all that by which He makes Himself known. **6** *In that day* points to the future age of Messianic fulfilment once more. In the coming age of the restoration of God's people, *the lame* and *those whom I have afflicted* will come back to God; *i.e.* those who are lame and wretched in soul, miserable because of the chastening of the Lord and the afflictions of exile. **7** And yet it is these who, confessing themselves to be spiritually crippled and in need, make up the remnant of true, repentant believers among national Israel. After their conversion to Christ He will assume the throne and *reign over them* directly and personally, and on a permanent basis, *from this time forth and for evermore.* **8** The *hill* (Heb. *'ōpel*) of Zion was apparently the southern end of the eminence of Zion (which lay due south of Mt. Moriah). It was fortified by a great tower, probably in the reign of Jotham, Hezekiah's grandfather (2 Ch. 27:3). It is here termed the *tower of the flock* because from it the dynasty of David watched protectively over the flock of Israel, just like a watch-tower erected by shepherds to keep an eye on predatory beasts or human poachers who might endanger their sheep. *Cf.* 7:14, where Israel is represented as the sheep of Yahweh's inheritance.

4:9–13 First must come suffering, exile, restoration, and judgment upon Israel's foes

9, 10 The prophet reverts to the present situation. Because of Judah's unfaithfulness and apostasy, the kingdom will be bereft of effective leadership by David's descendants. Lacking a king with God's blessing and power to support him, having no leader who had access to God's will and plan (as David did) and could be their wise *counsellor*, the commonwelath is reduced to utmost anguish (like the physical anguish of a woman in labour). Inexorably the chastening judgment of God closes in upon them, their city is destroyed and their land laid waste, and their survivors are driven off into captivity in a foreign land. Amazingly enough, the prophet foretells the land of their captivity: not Assyria (which was then mistress of the Middle East), but *Babylon*, which in Micah's day was only a subject province of Assyria. As in the case of Micah's contemporary, Isaiah, supernatural revelation disclosed 130 years in advance the triumph of the Chaldean power under Nebuchadrezzar. More than that, it also foretold the eventual release of the captives and their return to the land of promise, which was fulfilled under Zerubbabel and Jeshua in 538 BC. Commentators who resist this evidence of predictive prophecy are compelled by their own presuppositions to classify this verse as a later insertion, and they are nearly unanimous in doing so. *Groan* (Heb. *gōḥî*) rests upon a purely conjectural emendation; it should be rendered 'burst forth' (of the expulsion of the foetus from the womb, from the verb *gûaḥ*). AV's 'labour to bring forth' is quite justified.

11 The scene is depicted of the gathering of Nebuchadrezzar's Chaldean and allied troops encircling besieged Jerusalem in 588 BC (2 Ki. 24:1f.) and planning to plunder and destroy not only the city itself but the Temple on Mt. Moriah as well. *Let our eyes gaze upon Zion* is a literal rendering of the Hebrew, but in actual usage the verbs 'to see' (*rā'ah*) and (as here) 'gaze at' (*ḥāzâ*), when followed by the preposition *be-*, always implies a keen satisfaction in the heart of the beholder, and usually a malicious or spiteful satisfaction. Render: 'May our eye gloat over Zion!' **12** Little do these exultant troops of Nebuchadrezzar realize that they are only being used as instruments of Yahweh. But here their own doom is foretold in such a way as to suggest that these Chaldean forces prophetically symbolize the combined armies of the world powers that will converge upon Jerusalem in the last days (*cf.* Zc. 14:1–3), only to be completely crushed and annihilated by God's special intervention, as sheaves of grain are trampled out by oxen on the threshing-floor. Some commentators regard Sennacherib's invasion in 701 BC as the fulfilment of this, but their disaster did not occur

near Jerusalem, nor did it involve a crushing military defeat, as this implies. **13** The agents for the destruction of Jerusalem's besiegers will apparently be the *daughter of Zion*, for it is she who will do the 'threshing' with hoofs of *bronze* (symbolic of the irresistible hardness of their destructive force) and equipped with iron horns (for the *horn* was a customary figure for offensive power, like the lowered horns of a charging bull). The Hebrew text makes the Lord Himself the subject of *devote*: 'and I will devote their gain unto the Lord' (RV mg.). The LXX, Syriac and Vulgate support the RSV emendation of *haḥᵃramtî* to *haḥᵃrmt*, 'you (feminine singular) will devote', yet it should be noted that God is occasionally quoted in the OT as referring to Himself in the third person, as here. In other words, victorious Israel will not appropriate the spoil of its heathen foes to her own use, but lay it all under the ban (*ḥērem*), as Joshua did in the case of Jericho (*cf.* Jos. 6:17–19). Yahweh will therefore sanctify the wealth of the fallen foe to Himself by its complete destruction.

5:1–6 The divine-human Victor will defend His flock and destroy the world powers

1 is numbered as 4:14 in the Hebrew Bible, but improperly so, since this verse introduces a new movement in the thought: the coming of the Messiah. Translate (with RV), 'Now shalt thou gather thyself in troops, O daughter of troops' (RSV's *Now you are walled about with a wall* involves extensive and unwarranted emendations of the Hebrew text). Besieged Jerusalem gathers its various detachments and troops of defenders (hence its title here *baṭ gᵉdûd*, 'daughter of a troop') in the great national crisis which now looms up (presumably the assault of Nebuchadrezzar's armies in 587)—the word *now* ('*attâ*) here indicates a new point in time—the preliminary series of events leading up to the advent of Christ. As the *ruler of Israel* (*i.e.* her executive head) is to be smitten on the cheek, he will be defeated and crushed (as Zedekiah was by the Chaldeans, 2 Ki. 24). Possibly the defeat of the Jewish king, Aristobulus II, by Pompey's forces in 63 BC is also had in view. **2** In contrast to this vanquished king of Israel, a new *ruler* is to rise over God's people, and He is going to come from a town almost too small to be included among the 1,000-family towns of Judah, namely *Bethlehem* (which for the sake of added solemnity is here addressed by its ancient name of Ephrath or *Ephrathah* (*cf.* Gn. 35:19; Ru. 1:1, 2) meaning, perhaps, 'Fruitful'). RSV renders '*alᵉp̄ê* by 'clans of', rather than 'thousands of' (RV), but even though this is a possible rendering for '*elep̄*, it does not seem appropriate as a term for a municipal unit. This new *ruler* from Bethlehem is no mere human being, for His *origin* (better, as RV, 'goings forth', since *môṣā' ōṭāyw* is plural) has been from the remotest age, *from ancient days* (AV and RV retain 'from everlasting'). This phrase, *yᵉmê 'ôlām*, means literally 'the days of the age', and is elsewhere used of the earliest beginnings of human history (Dt. 32:7f.), or of the days of Moses and Joshua (Is. 63:9), or even of the time of David (Am. 9:11). In Mi. 7:14 it refers to the time of David. When used without *yᵉmê*, '*ôlām* may mean 'eternity'. *Cf.* Ps. 90:2 where *mēʿôlām* ('from eternity') refers to beginningless eternity. But with 'days of' it refers only to antiquity. In the present context, therefore, it views the Messiah's ancestry as reaching back to the early founders of Israel, the promises and predictions of Him as dating from the earliest times, and Himself as pre-existing the actual date of His appearing.

3 Since this Ruler is to redeem God's people in due time, Yahweh will *give up* the Israelites to disciplinary judgments in order to prepare them for His coming. He will be brought forth by a woman who will give birth. *She who is in travail* (*yôlēḏâ*; *cf.* Is. 7:14) is probably the virgin Mary, although it may possibly refer to the nation Israel. *His brethren* as a believing remnant (*the rest of*, *yeṯer*) will return to Him from the captivity of sin and judgment. In the first instance the Jews who would be converted to the Christian faith, although possibly also the Gentile believers (children of Abraham by faith, *cf.* the 'sheep . . . not of this fold', Jn. 10:16), are intended. **4** As the good Shepherd, Christ will feed His flock on the bread of life, defending them from the malice and deceit of Satan, guaranteeing them an eternal security (Jn. 10:28), and extending His saving power *to the ends of the earth* as the church carries out the great commission. **5** Christ will constitute the peace and welfare of His people as they come under the attack of their foes, who are (very appropriately for Micah's time) represented by *the Assyrian*, but doubtless this term here includes all the future enemies of Israel and the church: the Seleucid Syrians, the Romans, the Inquisition, the Modernists and the Marxists. All these will be checked and repulsed by Spirit-empowered leaders: the Maccabean patriots, the apostles, Athanasius, Augustine, Wycliffe and Luther, and whoever else would be needed to preserve the community of true believers from conquest or extinction. The number *seven* represents the full and perfect work of God, and would be quite sufficient, but one more (*eight*) is added to ensure that there will be more than enough to furnish the proper leadership against all assailants. Instead of *upon our soil*, which rests upon a reading of the LXX and Syriac, RV reads, 'shall tread in our palaces', which faithfully renders the Hebrew text, and fits in perfectly well with the context.

6 The tone of this verse is more definitely eschatological, and lends support to the view that v. 5 may also refer to the conflict of the last days and the overthrow of the world powers at Armageddon. *They shall rule* (*rāʿâ* means 'govern the flock as a shepherd') *with the sword* would seem to point to the imposition of Christ's authority by force as His millennial kingdom is established. *Assyria*, symbolic of the area

formerly held by the hostile world power, was called the *land of Nimrod* because he was the original founder of historic Assyria (Gn. 10:8–11). Render with RV, 'and he shall deliver us', referring to Christ's irresistible power at His second coming. There is no textual warrant for RSV's *they shall deliver*, nor for its substitution of *the drawn sword* for the 'in the entrances therefore' of the Hebrew text.

5:7–15 The triumph of Israel after it is purged of idolatry

7 *The remnant* (*šᵉʾērît*) of true believers in Israel will bring showers of refreshment and blessing (the liberating truths of Christ's gospel) to the *many peoples* of Gentile mankind, and that on the initiative of God rather than of man. **8** In the last days the Lord's battle champions will carry the field before them, and the destruction of the enemy (at Armageddon; *cf.* Rev. 16:16) will be irresistible and complete. **9** *Shall be lifted up* ignores the jussive form of the verb *tārōm*. Render with RV, 'Let thine hand be lifted up above'; so also, 'and let all thine enemies be cut off'. This is a summons of encouragement to God's victorious people in the day of final conflict. **10, 11** This victory by the Israel of God will not be accomplished through any human strength or military resources; all their horses and chariots (or the latter-day military equivalents of horses and chariots) and fortifications will be stripped away from them before they spring upon the astonished foe (like an unarmed Samson upon the Philistines) and utterly crush them.

12–14 God's people will also be purged of all idolatry and heresy before that day of triumph comes. Every form and type of idol is here enumerated in 8th-century BC terms: cultic *pillars* (AV's 'standing images'), or stone uprights which represented the male god on the pagan 'high places'; and the *Asherim* (AV's 'groves'), or cultic wooden pillars representing the female consort of the male god. Note the indication that astrology and spiritism will be especially rampant in the degenerate 'post-Christian' society of the last days. **15** The wrath of God will pour out irreversible judgment in that final day upon the rebellious world, a destruction far transcending anything that history has ever recorded (*cf.* Rev. 16).

6:1–16 GOD'S CONTROVERSY WITH UNGRATEFUL ISRAEL

6:1–5 Israel summoned to repent, recalling God's mercy at the Exodus

This chapter contains a separate discourse, which is generally thought to be addressed to the northern kingdom of Israel in the declining years of Hoshea's reign (730–722 BC; 2 Ki. 17), because of the reference to Omri and Ahab in v. 16. Yet there was a sense in which the malign influence of Ahab's dynasty infected Judah as well, through his daughter Athaliah, queen of Judah (841–835 BC; 2 Ki. 11), whose example of Baalism helped to prepare the way for the apostasy of Ahaz (743–728 BC; 2 Ki. 14). Therefore these admonitions were intended for the southern kingdom as well.

1, 2 The *mountains* and *hills* (referred to as the *enduring foundations*) have witnessed God's abiding mercies to Israel ever since the Exodus and conquest; hence they are appropriately invoked here (as in Is. 1:2 and elsewhere) as Yahweh remonstrates with His covenant people for their ingratitude and faithlessness. **3, 4** They have treated the Lord as if He had been guilty of injustice towards them; yet they cannot cite any wrong He has done to them except perhaps His loading them with undeserved benefits and mercifully delivering from all their dangers and foes since the days of Moses and Aaron, whom He sent to lead from Egyptian bondage to the land of promise. **5** They should remember how God turned the malignity of *Balak King of Moab* into their benefit, as the prophet *Balaam*, whom he had hired to curse them, was compelled to pronounce their blessing and triumph over all their foes, while they were encamped at Shittim (Nu. 22–24). RSV supplies the words *and what happened* (*cf.* RV 'remember') before *from Shittim to Gilgal*; the Hebrew text is elliptical here, apparently (although AV is content to render it quite literally as it stands). *Saving acts* is too inexact and interpretative for *ṣidᵉqôṯ Yahweh*, 'the righteous acts of the Lord' (*cf.* RV).

6:6–16 Response to repentant Israel: valid worship must be accompanied by a godly life

6, 7 The prophet imagines the idolatrous Israelites moved to fear and repentance by his warnings (as some of them doubtless were; *cf.* Je. 26:18, 19, at least in Judah), and they show a basic misconception of the purpose of sacrificial worship as they propose to buy God's mercy and favour by lavish and extravagant sacrifice: *thousands of rams, with ten thousands of rivers of oil*, going far beyond anything specified in the law of Moses. They even offer to appease His wrath by the pagan practice of infant-sacrifice (as followed by the kings of Israel and by Ahaz of Judah *cf.* 2 Ki. 16:3; 17:17), even though this was sternly denounced in the Pentateuch as an abomination to Yahweh (*e.g.* Lv. 18:21; Dt. 18:10; *cf.* Gn. 22). But they, of course, have long since 'outgrown' and therefore neglected the Holy Scriptures in their search for an up-to-date and 'relevant' theology, and would therefore ignore Ex. 13:13 as they contemplated reconciliation with God.

8 This prophetic answer to those who seek to bypass true repentance and self-surrender by lavish gifts to the Lord is a stern but loving reminder that valid sacrifice and acceptable worship must include a presentation of their own bodies as living sacrifices to Him. 'Be holy, for I am the Lord your God.' It would be a gross misinterpretation of this verse, a violent wrenching of the text out of its context, to construe this as a mere pronouncement that the whole point of religion is a virtuous life, without the need of atonement or of faith in God's revealed word. On the contrary, it is a reminder to those who are under the covenant that God requires a true and living faith which manifests itself by obedience and love. The Israelites are addressed as *O man*, not in any universalistic sense that would include unbelieving pagans the world over, but only as mere human beings (*'āḏām*) standing before the infinite and eternal God. A true and living faith, then, will be evidenced by a will, firstly, to carry out *justice* (*mišpāṭ*) in accordance with the principles of Scripture revealed as God's will: secondly to love *kindness*, or 'steadfast love', *i.e.* the covenant loyalty and covenant love (*ḥesed*) which involves honouring the commitment of loyalty and love subsisting between husband and wife, parent and child, subject and king, and, most especially, between the believer and his God; and, thirdly, *to walk humbly* (lit. 'making humble to walk') with (or in fellowship with) the Lord Himself, in utter dependence upon His enablement to lead a godly life, and in full recognition of the total lack of personal ability or merit which might furnish a base for pride or self-justification. This last verse, by the way, is quoted from Dt. 10:12, or is at least a paraphrase of it.

9–11 These verses contain many unwarranted textual corrections in the RSV; it is safer to follow RV in rendering, 'Hear (or, give heed to) the rod (*maṭṭeh*, which may also mean 'tribe', although it hardly does so here), and Him who appoints it.' *I.e.* give heed to the warning of disciplinary judgment, and the God who has appointed it to be used for the chastening and correction of His people. Likewise read, 'Are there still treasures of wickedness', rather than RSV's completely unfounded *Can I forget the treasures . . . ?* Also (v. 11) the correct translation of the Hebrew text is 'Shall I be pure with . . . ?' (the repentant Israelite is here speaking), rather than *Shall I acquit the man with . . . ?* (which implies that God is speaking, but requires reading *'azakkeh* rather than *'ezkeh*). These verses teach that God is the faithful Protector and Enforcer of the moral law, and no-one who has failed to make restitution for sin can possibly hope for His forgiveness and favour. **12, 13** Because Micah's countrymen have abandoned the biblical standards of morality and have given themselves over to dishonesty and deceit, God has brought calamity and disaster upon them in order to bring them to repentance.

14, 15 The Lord promises depression to their agricultural economy, and consequent shortages and famine, later to be followed by invasion and slaughter at the hands of the enemy. For RSV's *there shall be hunger*, RV has 'thy humiliation shall be in the midst of thee'. The word here, *yešaḥ*, is uncertain, for it occurs nowhere else in the OT. *BDB* suggests that it means 'emptiness', which would favour the RSV rendering. **16** *For you have kept the statutes* assumes an unnecessary alteration of the text. RV is preferable, 'For the statutes of Omri are kept'. The *statutes of Omri* included unbridled wickedness and Baal-worship (*cf.* 1 Ki. 16:25); *the works of the house of Ahab* involved the slaughter of God's prophets and of citizens like Naboth who stood in the way of his greed (1 Ki. 16:29 onwards). For *the scorn of the peoples* read 'the scorn of my people' (*cf.* RV), *i.e.* the shame which God's people will have to bear as they go down to defeat and are carried off captive by the Chaldeans.

7:1-20 COVENANT PROMISES WILL BE FULFILLED TO THE FAITHFUL REMNANT

7:1-6 True Israel laments the sins of selfishness and corruption

Here the prophet speaks, not in his own name, but in the name of spiritual Israel, which confesses and deplores its rebellion against God.

1 Backslidden and disobedient believers mourn over their fruitlessness, like some field or orchard from which the crops and fruits have been removed, or a vine bereft of all its grapes. **2** Israelite society has so degenerated morally that the old-fashioned virtues of integrity and honesty have all but disappeared, and crime and gang warfare run rampant in the cities. The *net* was used in traps to catch unwary birds or beasts; hence it stands for malicious craftiness which seeks to overreach and defraud one's neighbour. **3** They are all eager to make a dishonest living, and the administration (*prince*) and judiciary are both honeycombed with corruption, so that wealthy criminals can buy protection. **4** *A thorn hedge.* RSV has omitted any attempt to translate the preposition *min* ('from', 'than') prefixed to this word. RV reads *min* as 'worse than a thorn hedge'. The Hebrew text reads 'your watchmen' rather than *their watchmen*, and 'your punishment' rather than *their punishment* (so RV). The *watchmen* are of course God's prophets, who have denounced and warned their backsliding countrymen in vain, until the threatened disasters overtake them. They fall into *confusion* or 'perplexity' (RV) because they have lost their wager that divine justice would not catch up with them, and they cannot now turn to God for deliverance after they have all their lives despised or ignored Him. **5** So thorough and pervasive is the general depravity that no one can trust anyone else, not even the members of the same family: here we see the breakdown of the home.

7:7-10 True Israel will continue trusting in God's mercy

7 The repentant remnant now turn with horror from the morass of sin into which their nation has fallen, and cast themselves wholly upon God, whose promises never fail. They *look to* Him to deliver them somehow from the dreadful judgments that are to befall their people. **8** Israel's foes have already counted her out and expect her complete extinction; but they reckon without

Israel's God, who knows how to rescue His faithful remnant from destruction even through national disaster and the Babylonian captivity. He still has a future for His covenant people, which He will reveal in due time. **9** Because this believing remnant perceives Yahweh's faithfulness and consistency in fulfilling all His promises of punishment for apostasy, they can trust Him to deal with their foes and oppressors in His own time and way. *Deliverance* is more accurately 'righteousness' (RV), here in the specific sense of promise-keeping righteousness with redemptive results. **10** Thus the cynical scepticism of the worldly wise, who spurn the revelation of Holy Scripture and despise the biblical faith, and who jeer at those who are simple-minded enough to embrace it, will be shown up to be tragic folly. As Assyria and Babylon each in turn fell beneath the blows of their invaders and were trampled in the mire of their own streets, so it will be with every world power, or system of religion or philosophy that raises itself up against the God of Scripture, Not so much because of malice but because of joy that God has vindicated His own righteousness and truth, the remnant are pictured here as looking with pleasure upon the fall of the apostate and the God-blaspheming heathen.

7:11-20 The triumph of Christ through the church age and the millennium

11 The *walls* of God's kingdom are to be built, and its *boundary* (*ḥōq*) will become *extended* (*yirḥaq*) beyond the diminutive area of Palestine, where it was confined before Christ's coming. Others interpret *ḥōq* ('prescription, statute, ordinance') to refer to the restrictive law of Moses, which will be 'removed' (*yirḥaq*) when the gospel is proclaimed to the Gentiles. But *rāḥaq* occurs nowhere else with such a passive meaning. **12** *To Egypt* should rather be, with RV, 'and the cities of Egypt' (implying '*ārê* instead of RSV's '*adê*). From all over the earth converts to the true faith will come to the Lord and join themselves with believing Israel. **13** After this ingathering of converts will come the terrible destruction of the tribulation and the last days, as a judgment upon the wickedness of mankind.

14 After this destruction of the rebellious world powers the good Shepherd will personally take control as Defender of Christian Israel, fulfilling for them all of the promises of God concerning a prosperous and undisturbed enjoyment of the entire territory promised to Abraham and his seed, all the way from Mt. Carmel in the west (so render *garden land*, Heb. *karmel*) to Bashan and Gilead in the east (*i.e.* Transjordania), *as in the days of old* (*yᵉmê 'ôlām*), *i.e.* the time of David and Solomon. **15** For the re-establishment of this millennial kingdom of Israel the Lord will spare no miracles of intervention necessary for the purpose, just as He had done back in the days of the Exodus. **16** All the Gentile *nations* will be reduced to impotence before this display of divine power, and will surrender unconditionally to Yahweh's reign, so that Christ's empire will extend over all the earth.

18–20 Lifted up to a pinnacle of joyous thanksgiving by this disclosure of the ultimate triumph of God's grace, the prophet breaks into a paean of praise. He adores God for His *pardoning* grace and *steadfast love* (or 'loving-kindness', Heb. *ḥeseḏ*; *cf.* on 6:8) in language reminiscent of Ex. 34:6, 7. Yahweh's forgiveness will mean the complete removal of sin and guilt, so that He will remember them no more. Thus He will fulfil completely all of His gracious promises to Abraham and the patriarchs of old, without compromising His holiness or tarnishing His glory. On this triumphant note these remarkable prophecies come to a close.

GLEASON L. ARCHER, JR.

Nahum

INTRODUCTION

THE DATE

The prophecy of Nahum anticipates the fall of Nineveh. The prophet speaks of the fall of the city with a clarity and an intimacy which suggests that the event is almost immediate. This would date the prophecy of Nahum shortly before the fall of the city in 612 BC. The prophet also mentions the sack of Thebes (3:8) as an accomplished fact. This city was pillaged by King Ashurbanipal of Assyria in 663 BC. The prophecy may therefore be dated between these two events. Another small piece of internal evidence suggests that the date may be fixed more precisely as being shortly after the Josianic reformation of 621 BC. There is one reference (1:15) which suggests that the importance of observing religious ceremonies was fresh in the minds of the people of Judah at this time. We may therefore tentatively place the prophecy between 621 and 612 BC. The prophet was therefore a contemporary of Zephaniah, Habakkuk and Jeremiah.

THE MAN

The writer is described as 'Nahum of Elkosh'. The name Nahum means 'consolation', 'comfort', or 'relief'. While the primary message of Nahum is the impending doom of Nineveh, a necessary consequence of the fall of the Assyrian tyrant was the relief of the oppressed Judah. In that sense, the message of Nahum justified the name of the prophet. He had no word of judgment or of condemnation for his own people, but only of comfort. He declares in the name of the Lord, 'Though I have afflicted you, I will afflict you no more. And now I will break his yoke from off you and will burst your bonds asunder' (1:12, 13).

The title of the prophet indicates that he was closely connected with a locality known as Elkosh. Of the four locations suggested for this place— Elkasch, a little village of Galilee; Capernaum in Galilee; Alqush near Mosul in Assyria; and Elcesei, a village of Judah—the last is the least difficult. Nahum may therefore have come from Judah and have delivered his prophecies in Jerusalem, perhaps in the Temple itself.

HIS MESSAGE

The primary note of Nahum's message is 'Vengeance is mine, I will repay, says the Lord'. 'The Lord is a jealous God and avenging' (1:2). The word 'jealous' here means the zeal, or the intense feeling, of God towards His enemies. Nahum apprehended and declared with passionate insistence the one truth that the wrath of God is provoked by wickedness. He bears long with men, but His anger is eventually aroused. Then He punishes those who have provoked Him. He strikes and makes an utter end. The wrath of God is terrible and inescapable. He who divides the storm-darkened sky with spears of lightning and cracks the rocks is an awful adversary. Puny man is nothing before Him. Men may take counsel with themselves. They may say, 'We are strong. Who can throw us down?' God will deal with them. No matter how strong they may be, no matter how many helpers they may have, God will inflict upon them a death-blow. There have been others stronger than they. These were overthrown. So shall the enemies of God always be overthrown.

Nahum singles out two sins in particular for denunciation. There is first the sin of ruthless military power. As a result of this evil, blood is shed in rivers, nations are annihilated, institutions are destroyed, and war is waged with every kind of ferocity (2:11–13). The track of Assyrian conquerors, e.g. Ashurnasirpal, was marked by impalements, by pyramids of human heads, and by other barbarities too horrible to be described. Of the people who so violate the decencies of human life, it is declared, 'Behold I am against you, says the Lord of hosts'

The other sin which Nahum denounces is unscrupulous commerce. The surrounding nations are corrupted so that they may minister to the luxuries and vices of the conquering city. Merchants, motivated by greed for gold, sell their wares in a city lusting for fine things. Morality and honesty are allowed to perish so that wealth may be acquired and pleasures enjoyed (3:1–4).

To his own people Nahum declares that messengers with good tidings are already on their way. As an expression of gratitude for the destruction of the oppressor, the people of Judah are to observe the religious seasons and scrupulously to discharge the obligations of their faith (1:15).

HIS SIGNIFICANCE AS A PROPHET

Like Cato, the Roman senator, who closed every speech in the senate with the words *Carthago delenda est* ('Carthage must be destroyed'), Nahum is dominated by one idea, *Nineve delenda est*. His gaze is fixed on Nineveh and her sins, almost to the exclusion of all else. His heart and prophecy are full of exultation at the thought of the vengeance which is coming upon her. He has little to say of the inwardness of true religion. He does not call for a personal and national return to righteousness, rather than the observance of religious fasts, as does Amos (Am. 4:4, 5). He does not seek to win his own people with the tenderness of Micah (Mi. 6:3). He does not warn Judah that she also will be judged, as Zephaniah warns her (Zp. 1:4). He does not proclaim mercy for all men, even for Nineveh, with the breadth of vision and the wide charity of the book of Jonah. He sees only the evil-doing of Nineveh and her doom, and he believes that this doom will result in deliverance for Judah. He does not pause to require from his own nation the moral standard which he so sternly demanded from others. For this reason, some scholars have regarded Nahum as a type of the 'false' prophet, and have argued that his ethics are poor. It has been said that he is narrow and nationalistic in his outlook; that he proclaims judgment on Nineveh, and leaves his own people with the impression that, provided they observe the worship of Yahweh, all will be well with them. It might even be said that Nahum was like the prophet Hananiah, the opponent of Jeremiah, who spoke peace to his people where there was no peace for them (Je. 28).

But this is to do Nahum less than justice. There are reasons for the apparent limitations of Nahum's message. The date at which his prophecy was composed may help to explain his apparent lack of concern over the sins of his own people, his omission of their moral and spiritual obligations, and his seeming lack of charity towards Nineveh itself. If the prophecy were composed just before 612 BC (the fall of Nineveh), then it was not long after the Josianic reformation (621 BC). It is true that Jeremiah saw that the reforms were not sufficient; but possibly at the time of his prophecy, indications were still favourable enough for Nahum to have felt that the nation was now on the right road. The disillusionment brought about by Josiah's untimely death in 609 BC had not yet taken place, and the relief felt at the impending destruction of Nineveh was for Nahum the over-riding consideration. Equally, however, it should not be overlooked that 1:1–8, e.g., while it belongs to 'the oracle concerning Nineveh', is couched in general terms and makes no direct reference to Assyrian misdeeds. Its clear reminiscence of such passages as Ex. 34:6, 7, and Dt. 4:24 means that the applicability of its truth to the covenant people themselves is direct and inescapable. Nahum would thus not altogether lack a moral and spiritual message to his countrymen.

The prophecy of Nahum has been well called 'the cry of an outraged conscience'. It is a passionate assertion that justice in its stern retribution will prevail. This truth he declares with insistence. He proclaims its moral necessity. He envisages its accomplishment with unrivalled lucidity. He foresees the completeness of its fulfilment. In the great corpus of truth taught by the twelve prophets, this truth is particularly the property of Nahum, and if his prophecy is the prophecy of one idea, at least he presents that idea with much power and complete effectiveness. Limited as the message of Nahum may have been, his place among the prophets is secure.

OUTLINE OF CONTENTS

1:1–15 An alphabetic acrostic
1:1 The book's title
1:2–8 The poem: the vengeance of our God
1:9–15 The punishment of enemies

2:1–13 A threefold picture
2:1–6 The siege
2:7–10 The sack
2:11–13 The overthrow

3:1–19 A war song
3:1–7 The wickedness of Nineveh
3:8–15 Comparison with Egypt
3:16–19 The irremediable doom

COMMENTARY

1:1–15 AN ALPHABETIC ACROSTIC

1:1 The book's title

An oracle concerning Nineveh. This is an exact description of the contents of the prophecy, and is a better translation of the original text than the AV 'the burden of Nineveh'. The book of the vision of Nahum of Elkosh. The word book does not necessarily mean that the message of the prophet was prepared in written form and that it was not orally delivered, but it does suggest that it was early committed to writing. *The vision of Nahum* signifies the revelation of Nahum, as the vision of Isaiah (1:1) is the revelation of Isaiah.

1:2-8 The poem: the vengeance of our God

There are a number of poems in the Bible which have each verse, or perhaps each line, beginning with successive letters of the alphabet. Pss. 111; 112; and notably 119 are examples of this arrangement, the purpose of which was probably to act as a kind of *aide-memoire*. In some cases, as here, the whole alphabet is not employed.

The distinctive peculiarity of the poem, with its successive initial letters is of course lost in translation. An indication of the working out of the scheme, however, may be given here. *'Alep*; 'The Lord is a jealous God' (v. 2). *Bêt*; 'His way is in whirlwind and storm' (v. 3). *Gîmel*; 'He rebukes the sea and makes it dry' (v. 4). The letter *dālet* cannot be traced. *Hē*; 'The mountains quake before him' (v. 5a). *Waw*; 'the earth is laid waste before him' (v. 5b). *Zayin*; 'Who can stand before his indignation?' (v. 6a). *Ḥêt*; 'His wrath is poured out like fire' (v. 6b). *Ṭêt*; 'The Lord is good' (v. 7a). *Yôd*; 'he knows those who take refuge in him' (v. 7b). *Kap*; 'he will make a full end of his adversaries' (v. 8).

Some critics make the liturgical hymn include v. 9. If that be the case, the order of the clauses requires to be reversed, as at present the first begins with *mēm* and the second with *lāmed*. In the revised order, they read *lāmed*; 'he will not take vengeance twice on his foes'. *Mēm*; 'what do you plot against the Lord? He will make a full end'.

2 The theme of this poem is the certainty and the severity of God's vengeance upon the heathen, and it begins with a very forceful statement of this fact. With cumulative repetition, the prophet affirms and reaffirms that the Lord *takes vengeance*. He declares that just because the anger of the Lord is slow to gather, it will be slow to dissipate. **3** *The Lord will by no means clear the guilty,* but will hold them responsible and will judge them. It is all too easy to lose sight of these moral truths. Only too readily do men think that, because wickedness is allowed for a time, it is therefore condoned. A passage such as this is a reminder that God's anger is directed against all unrighteousness and that, without repentance, there is no cheap and easy forgiveness.

4, 5 To convince his audience of the terror of the Lord, Nahum points to the phenomena of physical nature and in vivid language paints a picture of storm, whirlwind, drought, earthquake and destruction. These all reveal the power of the mighty God and, confronted with them, even the boldest of men become aware of their own insignificance. **6** *Who can stand before his indignation?* asks Nahum. *Who can endure the heat of his anger? His wrath is poured out like fire, and the rocks are broken asunder by him.*

7 Nahum then states the moral implications of the power of God, both for the righteous and for the wicked. Just because God is so strong, He is a safe refuge. He knows them who trust in Him. He delivers them. **8** On the other hand, He is mighty to smite those that rise up against Him. He knows them also, and His vengeance will not fail. Their doom is certain.

A note may be added on the textual point of v. 8. The text of this verse may be incomplete. The first phrase, *But with an overflowing flood,* may be completed by supplying some such sentence as 'He delivers them'. It is better to read *his adversaries,* or 'those that rise up against him', with the RSV, following the Greek text. To read 'her place', or 'the place thereof' with the AV, following the Hebrew text, is to employ an expression for which there has been no preparation. The last line may equally well be translated 'darkness shall pursue his enemies' or *he will pursue his enemies into darkness.* The latter translation is preferable, because it does not involve a change of subject from the previous line.

1:9-15 The punishment of enemies

9-11 In this arrangement we have separated v. 9 from the liturgical hymn, although, as we have pointed out above, a number of critics include it in the hymn. Working on the theory that Nahum did not compose the alphabetic acrostic, but that it was added later to his prophecy, these commentators consider that vv. 10 and 11 are the first genuine verses of Nahum. Some, indeed, wish to place 1:10, 11 after v. 1 of ch. 2, thus making these verses part of the war song describing the attack upon Nineveh. There is, however, a close connection between these verses and those which have preceded them. The same theme is handled and the two thoughts previously noticed are worked out, *i.e.* the punishment of the enemies of the Lord and the consequent relief to those whom they have oppressed.

While the vengeance of God threatens them, God's enemies are not yet subdued in mind. They still refuse to believe that He will smite. But He is about to deal with them. His punishment of them will be complete and final. He will not need to strike *twice* (v. 9). In describing this judgment Nahum uses a metaphor which is a favourite with the prophets (*cf.* Is. 5:24; Joel 2:5; Ob. 18) and one likely to appeal to the imagination of an agricultural people. God's enemies will be gathered together as thorns and consumed as fire burns the dry straw after harvest (v. 10; *cf.* Mt. 13:30).

11 *Did one not come out from you, who plotted evil against the Lord . . . ?* Nahum seems to see the evil of the Assyrian people summed up in the person of one of their leaders. He is so contemptible that especial shame is reserved for him (v. 14). His family will cease to be, his gods will be thrown down and he himself will be put to death. **12, 13** As a consequence of the overthrow of the enemies of the Lord there is relief for His oppressed people. **15** The arrival of this good news is declared in a picturesque and beautiful fashion. Perhaps it was because good news must of necessity be brought to Jerusalem over mountain roads that it was announced by the prophets in this form (*cf*. Is. 52:7). *Behold, on the mountains the feet of him who brings good tidings, who proclaims peace!* In gratitude for this deliverance, Judah is exhorted to cultivate her religious life (v. 15b). Along with this section may be taken 2:2, where AV is obscure. It is better to read with RSV, *For the Lord is restoring the majesty of Jacob* . . . The meaning might be expressed thus: 'The vine of Judah shall bloom afresh as the vine of Israel, although the spoilers have spoiled him and destroyed his tendrils.'

Thus Nahum deals with his theme of the overthrow of Nineveh in a general and introductory manner. He has given the setting in relation to the justice of God and to the oppressed people of Judah. In the remaining two chapters he turns to his subject in particular and in detail, setting forth its accomplishment in word-pictures of battle, unrivalled in Hebrew literature.

2:1–13 A THREEFOLD PICTURE

2:1–6 The siege

1 The enemy is come up against Nineveh. These verses may be dated after the death of the great Assyrian ruler Ashurbanipal in 627 or 626 BC. Nineveh was beset by many enemies. Among these were the Scythians, wandering bands of horsemen in search of plunder; the Chaldeans from the edge of the Persian Gulf, whose king, Nabopolassar, had seized Babylon; and the Medes from the area of the Caspian Sea, led by their king, Cyaxares. In 616 BC the allies appeared before the gates of Nineveh. Nahum, with bitter mockery, exhorts the Ninevites to prepare defensive measures. **2** See above. **3** *Scarlet* was a favourite colour with the fighting men of Media. Their shields are red, as are their cloaks. The whole scene is lit by the light of torches, carried by the chariots in the darkness of the early morning before the assault. 'Fir trees' (AV); RSV corrects the text and translates *the chargers prance*. **4** The chariots roll along the broad ways in the large built-up areas which surround the central fortifications of Nineveh. **5** *Officers* are called to lead the attack. The attackers come forward at a stumbling run. *The mantelet*, a movable defence under cover of which they make ready for the final assault, is set up. **6** Then, having captured the sluices and water-gates controlling the river Chaser which flowed through the city, they suddenly open them, so allowing a great flood of water to pour down on the buildings and increase the terror. The AV rendering 'dissolved' suggests an even more arresting picture. A great flood of water pours down on the buildings. Foundations are loosened and in this way the palace is literally dissolved.

2:7–10 The sack

7 *Its mistress is stripped*; *i.e.* the queen, or perhaps the female representative of the goddess Ishtar, goddess of Nineveh. The AV reads 'and Huzzab shall be led away captive'. The word 'Huzzab' is difficult. It has been variously translated as a verb (see AV and RV mgs.) and as a noun: a symbolic name for the city, like Rahab for Egypt; a name for the image of the goddess of Assyria; or even a name for the car in which the image of the goddess was carried. It seems simpler just to accept the RSV mg., 'The meaning of the Hebrew word is uncertain', and to render the word as *mistress*, signifying perhaps the female representative of the goddess. Her female attendants follow her as she is *carried off*. They moan in their distress *like doves* cooing in a wood and beat upon their breasts. **8** Nineveh has been a reservoir of trade and wealth into which have been flowing from all quarters streams of goods and gold and has thus become *like a pool* fed by many tributaries. She has a heterogeneous population, held together only by the opportunities to acquire wealth which the power of Nineveh gives. When the blow falls there is nothing to make these people cohere. They rush in every direction, as waters break out when a dam bursts. A few try to rally the defence crying *Halt! Halt!*, but the inhabitants flee wildly, without looking back. **9** House-to-house plunder begins. *Silver . . . gold . . . every precious thing*, the accumulated wealth of centuries, are looted. **10** The sacked city stands desolate. The few terrified survivors look sadly on the ruins.

2:11–13 The overthrow

Nahum closes the ode with a magnificent picture of a pride of lions which has been destroyed. *Where is the lions' den?* In vivid words he describes their fearlessness, strength and rapacity. But now the den is forsaken and the menace a thing of the past. So the Lord has finally dealt with Nineveh. She also was cruel and bloodthirsty. But her brood has been smoked out and slain with the sword. She will not prey upon the surrounding nations any more.

Thus ends the first of two powerful odes on the fall of Nineveh. In the closing verses of this poem the emphasis seems to be laid on the ruthlessness and aggressiveness of Nineveh. Of all empires, Nineveh has been one most unashamedly founded on force and cruelty. Nahum teaches that force will be destroyed by superior force; 'for all who take the sword will perish by the sword' (Mt. 26:52).

3:1–19 A WAR SONG

3:1–7 The wickedness of Nineveh

1 Other aspects of Nineveh's wickedness are indicated, namely her commercial unscrupulousness and evil influence. **2, 3** Her sins are punished in 'the battle of the streets'. These verses are a superlative example of Nahum's powers of description, and form one of the most vivid battle scenes in Hebrew literature. The confusion and noise as the chariots and horsemen attack, the glint of the sun on armour and weapons, the huddled dead lying in heaps about the streets, so thickly strewn that the advancing troops stumble over the bodies. A grim picture!

4–7 Nahum then speaks of the city of Nineveh under the simile of a *harlot*. This metaphor for sinful nations and cities was a favourite one with biblical writers. Sometimes it was used to describe idolatry. The people of Israel worshipping other gods were compared to an adulterous woman (*cf.* Lv. 17:7). It was also used of their action in imitating the ways of the Gentiles (*cf.* Ezk. 23:30). It condemned the practice of superstitions associated with idolatry (Lv. 20:6). Finally, as here, it was applied to the exchanges of trade which the Gentile peoples carried on among themselves. It is evident that after her conquests Nineveh endeavoured to build herself up as a centre of world commerce. Presumably this was for the sake of the wealth and luxuries to be gained thereby. She approached people with her wares. She deceived them by her lies. She enervated them with her luxuries. Like a harlot she corrupted them with her immoralities. For these sins also will she be punished. Instead of honour, she will be a *gazingstock*. Instead of fine living and soft clothing, she will be humiliated with every circumstance of degradation.

3:8–15 Comparison with Egypt

8 To convince Nineveh of the certainty of her doom, Nahum reminds her of the fate of Thebes, which fell despite its strength. This town, described by Homer (*Iliad* IX. 383) as hundred-gated, was the most ancient and most honourable in Upper Egypt. Of great extent, it was beautiful with temples, obelisks and sphinxes. It was situated on both banks of the Nile, the waters of which were led to the gateways of its temples by canals. The wonders of this mighty place may still be seen by visiting Karnak and Luxor. Nahum refers to its river and canals when he writes that she *sat by the Nile, with water around her.* **9** In addition to her natural strength, Thebes was at the centre of a strong political alliance. Egypt was united under one dynasty with *Ethiopia*, the latter a poor and backward country, but producing vigorous Sudanese warriors. The whole length of Egypt lay between Thebes and her Assyrian foes in the north. She was also helped by *Put and the Libyans*. Put may be identified with the Punt of the Egyptian inscriptions (the present Somalia on the Red Sea). **10** Yet in spite of all this total strength of Egypt and her allies, the cruel Assyrians themselves under Ashurbanipal overthrew Thebes in 663 BC. **11** A like fate shall overtake Nineveh. She will reel and stagger under her misfortunes. The brightness of her glory will be clouded over. *You will seek a refuge from the enemy*; *i.e.* she will attempt to form defensive alliances, just as Thebes did, or the people of Nineveh may proclaim public fasts and prayers to the gods, as indeed the last Assyrian king did, but nothing will save her. **12** The forts of her outer ring of defences are ready to fall. Just as a man shakes a fruit-tree and collects the over-ripe fruit which falls easily, so will the enemy gather up her forts.

Her people have no stomach for resistance. The strongholds in the passes which led to Nineveh have been forsaken. **13** As the Assyrians were wont to do those who attack Assyria have already burned her defences with fire. The city of Calah was burned before Nineveh was destroyed.

14 As in 2:1, Nahum then ironically bids the city make ready for war. Let them lay in a water supply that will not become exhausted during a long siege. Let them build ramparts and repair the breaches in the towers. Let them go to the clay-pits, dig out the clay, mix it with straw, set it in moulds, fire it in the kilns, and repair the walls with it. **15** Such measures, though very necessary, were somewhat late, when the enemy was at hand. The great buildings of Nineveh will be given to the flames. The sword will cut down her chief men. The city will be stripped bare as a field is denuded by the locust.

3:16–19 The irremediable doom

16, 17 The prophet takes up this image of *the locust*, one of the facts of nature familiar to oriental minds, and serving for a favourite literary illustration. Having already applied it to the ravages of the invading army (v. 15a), he now uses it to describe the numbers of Nineveh's citizens (vv. 15b, 16). Nineveh had grown to be a great community: there were innumerable *merchants*; persons of wealth and authority were as common as grasshoppers, or perhaps as voracious as locusts; there were great companies of scribes employed in keeping accounts and records. All these had gathered within the city, like a swarm of locusts gathering together for warmth on a wall or fence in winter. But when the sun shines forth, the locusts scatter. There is not one to be seen. They suddenly disappear, rising in clouds to seek new fields. So the men who were attracted to Nineveh by self-interest will take flight in every direction, when her evil day comes.

18 *Your shepherds are asleep.* Hence the people are scattered on the mountains like lost sheep with none to gather them into the fold. The picture is of a helpless nation deprived of all its leaders. **19** *There is no assuaging your hurt.* For Assyria there is no hope of a 'remnant'. This is the end. And the *news* of her overthrow will cause satisfaction in all places where her wickedness has been experienced.

The striking fulfilment of Nahum's prophecy in the disappearance of Nineveh from the face of the earth is a seal upon the abiding truth of his message. Here is no mere piece of antiquity, but a confirmed word of God. To be sure, God gives opportunity to repent (Jon. 3), but when succeeding years expose the hollow unreality of professed repentance, and godless cruelty continues as though God had never spoken, then the time of repentance passes, giving place to the time of wrath. The government of the earth rests, not with wicked men, but with the righteous God.

ALEXANDER FRASER

Habakkuk

INTRODUCTION

THE AUTHOR

We know nothing about Habakkuk apart from his book, and even here he does not give us his genealogy or tell us when he prophesied. The name itself is akin to an Assyrian word which signifies a plant or vegetable. In the LXX it appears as *Ambakoum*. Jerome derived it from a Hebrew root meaning 'to clasp' and said 'he is called "Embrace", either because of his love to the Lord, or because he wrestles with God'. Luther and many modern commentators have favoured the same derivation. It is certainly not unfitting, for in this little book we see a man, in deadly earnest, wrestling with the mighty problem of theodicy—the divine justice—in a topsy-turvy world. The same sort of conflict meets us in the larger book of Job.

Habakkuk is the first prophet to arraign not Israel but God. The book contains a soliloquy between himself and the Almighty. What baffles him is the apparent discrepancy between revelation and experience. He seeks an explanation. No direct answer is given to his query, but he is assured that patient faith will win the day (2:4). He expresses this faith very vividly in 3:17–19, where the sentiment finds a more recent echo in William Cowper's hymn: 'God is His own interpreter, and He will make it plain.'

Because of the musical arrangement of ch. 3, some have thought that Habakkuk was a Levite. It may be that he was a member of a professional guild of prophets attached to the Temple (1 Ch. 25:1). He is the only one of the canonical prophets who is styled a 'prophet' in the title verse of his book (1:1), and this is thought to indicate professional status. For the contrast with Amos see Am. 7:14f. Certainly he helps us to see what the office of a prophet entailed; in 2:1ff. we see him preparing to receive a vision, and in 3:16 we note some of the physical and spiritual symptoms which accompanied the process. *Cf.* Is. 21:1–10.

Habakkuk appears in the Apocryphal story of Bel and the Dragon as the one who rescued Daniel from the lions' den for the second time; but this is only legend.

DATE AND OCCASION

In 1:6 we are told that God is raising up the Chaldeans (*i.e.* the Babylonians) as an instrument of punishment. This no doubt refers to the revived kingdom of Babylonia which overthrew the weakened Assyrian Empire at the close of the 7th century BC. Nineveh was destroyed in 612 BC and Nebuchadrezzar king of Babylon defeated Pharaoh Necho of Egypt at Carchemish in 605.

Three years before this battle, Pharaoh Necho slew Josiah king of Judah at Megiddo (2 Ki. 23:29, 30; 2 Ch. 35:20ff.) and set up puppet kings on the throne of Judah, but neither he nor they were any match for the growing power of Babylon, and so, for the next 20 years, Judah was at the mercy of the Chaldeans and was finally carried away into captivity in 586 BC.

The prophecies of Habakkuk clearly refer to this period and may have been delivered either before or after the battle of Carchemish. In both cases Habakkuk would be a contemporary of Jeremiah (626–587 BC).

In favour of the earlier date is the suggestion in 1:5 that the raising up of the Chaldeans is still future and, at the time of the prophet's speaking, is still a thing to be wondered at; in favour of a date after 605 is the detailed description of Chaldean methods of warfare as something already well known (1:7–11).

The reign of the evil king Manasseh had been 'an age to try the faith of pious souls' (Kirkpatrick). The reformation under King Josiah (639–609 BC) had proved ineffectual and so the iniquity and perverseness (1:3) of backsliding Judah must be punished. For this God is raising up the Chaldeans.

This is the general view of scholars. Some, however, refer 1:2–4 not to backsliding Judah but to some heathen oppressor. The oppressor may be Chaldea herself; if so, the text must be rearranged so that vv. 5–11 precede vv. 2–4 (Giesebrecht) or are eliminated (Wellhausen). Or the oppressor may be Assyria; so Budde, who places vv. 6–11 after 2:2–4 and dates the prophecy just after 625 BC when Nabopolassar the Chaldean made himself independent of Assyria. But in this case why is Assyria not mentioned? Thirdly there is Egypt: so G. Adam Smith, who compares 1:2–4 with 2 Ki. 23:33–35. But Habakkuk's complaint in 1:12 – 2:1 is not that God is using one heathen nation to punish another, but that He is using a heathen nation to punish Judah. In spite of the rediscovery of the law in the Temple in 621 BC (2 Ki. 22:8; *cf.* Hab. 1:4), the people of Judah are bent on violence and injustice. The rearrangement of the text to suit a particular theory is always a questionable expedient. It seems safer to take the text as it stands and refer 1:2–4 to the people of Judah.

Others, however, with a certain amount of support from the Greek versions, omit the word 'Chaldeans' in 1:6 altogether, or else, with

Duhm, substitute for it the word 'Kittim', *i.e.* Cypriot Greeks, and so place the book in the days of Alexander the Great, *c.* 333 BC. Such views demand considerable tinkering with the text and are not very feasible. But it is interesting to note that the Dead Sea Scroll which contains the Habakkuk commentary, although lacking the first half of 1:6, has this note about it: 'Interpret (this) of the Kitti'im, whose fear is upon all the nations.' This, however, may only be a 'modern application' of an older situation. As Eissfeldt says, Qumran's identification of 'Chaldeans' with Kitti'im presupposes 'Chaldeans' in the text, and is an argument against Duhm's contention rather than for it. In no circumstances must 'Chaldeans' be excised or explained away.

It seems best, then, to put the date of Habakkuk at about 600 BC, or a little earlier.

The Qumran commentary on Habakkuk, found near the Dead Sea in 1947, deals with the first two chapters only. Into the text, which shows a few variants from MT, are inserted 'interpretations' linking the words of Habakkuk with events contemporary with the commentator, viz. the 1st century BC. Some of these are noted here. Whoever the Dead Sea sectaries were, they certainly 'gave the status of canonical Scripture to the biblical texts they used' and showed that 'for them the Bible of their day was authoritative in all matters of faith and conduct' (J. G. Harris).

TEXT AND COMPOSITION

The meaning of the Hebrew text is not always clear and the LXX has a few interesting variations, *e.g.* the great assertion in 2:4 is in one text of the LXX 'through and through Messianic' (T. W. Manson). See note *in loco*. Uncertainty as to

whom various passages refer to has led many critics to rearrange the text, and, in some cases, to divide the authorship. To some, Habakkuk is the author of ch. 3 and the compiler of chs. 1 and 2, to others he is the author of ch. 1 and most of ch. 2, whereas ch. 3 is a late poem of the Persian or Maccabean period. But many prefer to look upon the book as an artistic and connected whole. Kuhl, for instance, says that the style and conception of ch. 3 are so similar to those of the previous two chapters that 'it is quite unnecessary to postulate a different authorship'. As a cult-prophet, Habakkuk would be well able to add the liturgical and musical notes which are to be found in ch. 3.

As to the Qumran commentary, 'its corroborating evidence of the primitiveness of the traditional form adds considerable weight to the view that the traditional text of this prophecy has been transmitted with remarkable fidelity from early times' (J. G. Harris).

MESSAGE

Like Nahum, Habakkuk is not out to reproach his own people (except in 1:2–4 if this be taken to refer to the ungodly within the nation). But there is no complacency about him. The book reveals 'an agony of spirit at the evil which follows from the world-rule of an unjust and immoral power' (Eissfeldt). It is no accident that a greater than Habakkuk, the apostle Paul, chose a saying from this book to express his new and deeper religious experience. What William Temple said of the author of Ps. 73 is true also of Habakkuk: 'In his fellowship with God he has found that nothing matters in comparison with that fellowship' (*Nature, Man and God*, p. 43).

OUTLINE OF CONTENTS

COMMENTARY

1:1 INTRODUCTION

The theme is greater than the man; hence the briefest mention of the prophet's name and status together with his *oracle, i.e.* prophetic utterance (AV 'burden'). The word is practically synonymous with 'revelation': thus *saw* (as a 'seer'). *Cf.* 2 Ki. 9:25.

1:2–4 THE FIRST COMPLAINT

2 *How long shall I cry for help?* The prophet speaks as the conscience of the nation. He is troubled at the presence of iniquity among God's people to the detriment of all religious institutions. **4** *The law* (*i.e. tôrâ*) *is slacked, i.e.* is numb, ineffectual. It *never goes forth, i.e.* it is never put into practice. Why does not God intervene? Such a question could arise only in Israel. Only to men who believe in one God who is both holy and good and is at the same time the omnipotent Creator and Upholder of the universe can there be any real problem of theodicy. The dilemma 'if God, then why evil?' is no dilemma to those who believe in a pantheon of warring deities whose morals are hardly different from those of men and women. But if there is one only God, of undeviating righteousness and irresistible power, then the demand is created for an explanation of the conflicting experiences of life. There are times in some men's lives when this tension becomes particularly acute, as here. *The wicked surround the righteous* as an enemy with a view to causing his ruin.

1:5–11 GOD'S ANSWER

The Chaldeans, who are already wreaking destruction on surrounding nations, are to be turned against Judah and to become, in God's hands, an instrument of chastisement. This is the *work* which the people of Judah *would not believe* if told (v. 5), so incredible would it appear that God should so act towards His people and should use so unlikely an agent. For the Chaldeans are a law unto themselves (v. 7b) and mock all authority (v. 10); they worship their own strength (v. 11) and with them might is right.

5 For *among the nations* (Heb. *baggôyyîm*) LXX reads 'you despisers' which probably reflects the Hebrew *bogᵉdîm*, 'you traitors', a reading found also in the Qumran commentary. Qumran adds: 'The interpretation of this word refers to the betrayers with the man of falsehood, for they have not believed the words of the Teacher of Righteousness' (presumably the leader of the Qumran community). The 'man of falsehood' would be the Jerusalem high priest whose corrupt ways were abominable to the sectaries. This is an interesting though uncompelling 'application'. Nevertheless 'you betrayers', the faithless Judahites of Habakkuk's day, may be the

preferable reading. *Cf.* Moffatt, 'faithless creatures'.

9–11 are difficult. **9** *Terror* is a translation of an emended Hebrew word, which, in its present form, is not found elsewhere. Duhm, emending differently, translates, 'From Gomer (*i.e.* Cappadocia) they marched towards the east', and applies it to the campaigns of Alexander the Great, and makes the heaping up of earth or dust (v. 10) refer to the siege of Tyre. This extensive adaptation of the Hebrew is, however, unnecessary. RSV achieves the most sense by the smallest alteration. **11** For *guilty men* (*cf.* RV 'and be guilty'; AV 'and offend'), the Qumran text following a slightly different Hebrew reads 'and he makes', viz. a god of his own strength. Though this makes good sense, it is not necessary to adopt the alteration.

1:12 – 2:1 THE SECOND COMPLAINT

1:12–17 If the Chaldeans idolize their own brute strength, how can they be used by a God who cannot, by His very nature, *look on wrong* (v. 13). If He uses them, then He must be like them, treating men as if they were the *fish of the sea* (v. 14) to be captured and slaughtered at will, the only consideration being the pleasure derived from their destruction (vv. 15ff.). The revealed nature of God and the actual object of Chaldean worship seem dead against the assumption that God can use the Chaldeans. The prophet can see no possibility of contact from either side. In seeking to solve this dilemma, Habakkuk starts from a position of faith (*cf.* Je. 12:1). Since God is unchangeable, the preservation of His people is certain (v. 12). But how can a God who is unchangeable in holiness tolerate to use such vile instruments (v. 13)? The question is given point by considering the wickedness (v. 13b) of the Chaldeans; their inhumanity (v. 14) in treating others as a disposable commodity; their joy in conquest (v. 15) and devotion to their own instruments of self-advancement (v. 16). The *seine* (vv. 15, 16) is the dragnet. We are not to understand that the Chaldeans actually treated this as a religious object. The language is metaphorical: they 'idolized' their pitiless power of conquest. Does Israel's God look on in silent complacency while His people are treated as though He were not their king (*cf.* v. 14b), and while the Chaldeans appear to be set for an unending career of domination (v. 17)?

2:1 Habakkuk is conscious of the urgency of getting an answer, and therefore *I will . . . look forth to see what he will say.* Some have suggested that we should read 'and what He will answer', but the thought of holding dialogue with God, though daring, is suitable. Habakkuk is determined not to be fobbed off, but to receive satisfaction for his *complaint.*

2:2–4 GOD'S ANSWER

Chaldaea, God's instrument of chastisement, is itself under God's judgment and will not escape the just penalty of its misdeeds. Arrogance and faithlessness each has its own reward, as those who wait will see.

At first sight, there does not seem to be anything very inspiring about this assertion. Some have even doubted whether it constitutes a 'revelation' at all. Some, *e.g.* Budde and Eissfeldt, regard 1:5–11 as part of the revelation and place it after 2:3. Weiser thinks that the mention of several 'tablets' demands something longer than the epigram in v. 4 and that therefore the answer of God is contained in ch. 3, which may originally have followed immediately after 2:1–3 and was then placed at the end of the book for liturgical reasons. 2:4 would then belong to the Woes (see note below). But there is more here than meets the eye, and the use of this passage in the NT shows it to be indeed a pregnant one. It is 'a saying which was only fathomed in its utter profundity by St. Paul' (Kuhl).

But whatever treasures the statement in v. 4b was later made to disclose, one thing is immediately clear, and that is that the prophet himself has been given the realization that the only lasting element in an unstable, wicked world is character. Tyranny, greed and pride are all self-doomed; only integrity lasts on.

2 *Make it plain upon tablets.* Clay tablets were used in Babylonia (*cf.* Is. 8:1) and we also hear of tablets of wood or ivory (see *NBD*, p. 1343, section *b*). *So he may run who reads it*; a Hebrew idiom. The meaning is: 'that he may read it quickly (whoever sees it)'. **4** *The righteous shall live by his faith.* This great theme is developed by St. Paul in Rom. 1:17; Gal. 3:11, and by the author of the Epistle to the Hebrews in Heb. 10:38. The first half of the verse is differently rendered by the LXX which has: 'If he, *i.e.* the promised deliverer who *will surely come* (v. 3), draw back, my soul hath no pleasure in him.' This version is reproduced in Heb. 10:38 but the clauses are there inverted. LXX continues 'but the just shall live by my faith'. The 'my' is omitted in Heb. 10:38. The Hebrew text of Habakkuk (*cf.* also Rom. 1:17; Gal. 3:11) has 'his faith' (so also AV, RV) and the reference is not to the Messiah who is to prove His identity by courageous fidelity to His commission, but to the believing soul who in 'faith' has the touchstone of perseverance. *Live* is used in the pregnant sense of enjoying God's favour with or without temporal benefits.

Here 'faithfulness' as well as *faith* is in view; the term is wider than in Paul or Hebrews. But 'this faithfulness must spring from faith: hence Paul's insight is a true one' (Kirkpatrick). 'Faithfulness' (Heb. *'ĕmûnâ*) is used of the steadiness of Moses' arms in Ex. 17:12, and in Je. 5:3 it signifies fidelity ('truth') as opposed to falsehood. In Is. 11:5 it is parallel to righteousness. Its general meaning is therefore moral steadfastness. 'The upright man will survive, will win through, if he maintains his integrity.' But how can he do that? Habakkuk opened his 'complaint' by asserting the truth about God (see on 1:12). The 'faithfulness' of which he now speaks is not only moral endurance to the end (Mk. 13:13) but persistent belief that God will be true to Himself. 'Faith' in this narrower sense is an essential element in the wider fidelity, as Paul and Luther clearly saw.

2:5–20 THE FIVE WOES

These verses contain five predictions of the doom of the man 'whose soul is not upright in him' (v. 4). *Cf.* the six woes of Is. 5:8ff. Note the recurring phrase *for the blood of men* in vv. 8, 17, which may originally have been a refrain concluding each of the five woes. Some regard the last three woes as later additions, but S. R. Driver regards all five as authentic.

5, 6a are introductory, and the meaning of v. 5 has been a long-standing problem. Instead of *wine*, Qumran has 'wealth'. Some have urged the possibility of reading 'woe', making this the first of six woes. Duhm reads 'Ionian' (*i.e.* 'Greek'), making the phrase refer to Alexander who 'neither keepeth at home' (AV) but *collects as his own all peoples*. J. H. Eaton (*TBC, ad loc.*), on the other hand, urges that the puzzling nature of this opening verse was part of Habakkuk's purpose. He made use of a proverbial utterance concerning 'wine' in which, though 'the words were aimed obliquely, they would nevertheless find their target; where the cap fitted, it would in this case descend of its own accord, for it was the sure justice of God which had been invoked'. Thus he figures and denounces the deceitful and insatiable Assyrian.

2:6–8 Woe against aggression

Some see here a reference to King Jehoiakim (609–597 BC; see 2 Ki. 23:36ff.) but the application to the plunderer of many nations (v. 8) makes the Assyrian the likelier target, and so throughout these woes. But the principle laid down in v. 5, that if the cap fits then any may wear it, remains in operation. Habakkuk asserts not just the doom of a bygone Assyrian war-lord but of all who at any time behave in this way. He uses now the metaphor of a merciless money-lender, causing his victims to cry out *How long?* in their despair of relief, while he takes more and more of their belongings as pledges against his loans (v. 6) and endlessly pauperizes them. Exact retribution will be his lot (vv. 7, 8).

2:9–11 Woe against self-assertion

9 *Set his nest on high.* As birds built in the tops of tall trees, so he would put himself out of harm's way. Jehoiakim engaged in building projects (*cf.* Je. 22:13), but again the cock-sure Assyrian (*cf.* Is. 36:18ff.) may be more in mind, figured here as a rogue who uses his ill-gotten wealth to 'feather his own nest'. **10, 11** But the house has been built by *shame*, and even its very material fabric will in the end witness against him; *cf.* Am. 3:10.

2:12–14 Woe against violence

12 *Cf.* Mi. 3:10. Habakkuk may be quoting from this passage. **13** The meaning is that since God alone can establish a city (Ps. 127:1) all human attempts to do so, however violent, are foredoomed. It will only be *for fire*, or, as we might say 'go up in smoke'! **14** quotes freely from Is. 11:9, and means that the future is with God, not with any human achievement. *Cf.* Is. 2:17.

2:15–17 Woe against inhumanity

15 The second clause has been variously rendered. AV has 'that puttest thy bottle to him'; RV 'that addest thy venom thereto'; RSV, omitting one letter of the Hebrew, makes best sense. Of this cup of the divine wrath (*cf.* Ob. 16; Is. 51:17; Ps. 75:8) Assyria had been the bearer to the nations, but had used the opportunity for base self-advantage (*cf.* Is. 10:5–15). **16** reiterates the principle of exact retribution, and that from the Lord, **17** for the violence done by invading armies to nature (*Lebanon*), animals, men, and property.

2:18–20 Woe against idolatry

18, 19 With v. 18 we expect another woe, and, because of its absence, some have wished to transpose vv. 18 and 19; others have labelled v. 18 a scribe's comment, but Eaton (*op. cit.*) is to be heard when he says that 'the doom-laden "woe" is held back, heightening the tension, while two rhetorical questions prepare the way'. The questions touch on the Assyrian's idolatry, and therefore expose his greatest offence, failure to bow to the glory of God. With v. 18, *cf.* Is. 44:6–20, and with v. 19, *cf.* 1 Ki. 18:26; Ps. 115:4–8. **20** In contrast to this helplessness of man-made gods, and completing the series of woes with a cry which prepares us for the theophany of ch. 3, v. 20 describes *the Lord in his holy temple*. The *temple* is heaven, the place of power and authority. As in v. 4 we are encouraged to wait upon the Lord, before whom no other attitude is proper but to *keep silence* whether in submissive, patient faith, or in speechless terror.

3:1–19 A VISION OF JUDGMENT

'For sublimity of poetic conception and splendour of diction', says S. R. Driver, this chapter 'ranks with the finest which Hebrew poetry has produced.' It contains reminiscences of the Babylonian creation myth (see on v. 10) but 'the mythological elements have been tamed to liturgical use' (*IB*). The prophet also draws on the great events of Israelite history, particularly the Exodus and the defeat of the Canaanites at the river Kishon (Jdg. 4, 5).

The genuineness of this chapter, as coming from the pen of Habakkuk, has been questioned. *E.g.*, there are no features in it which connect it specially with either the Assyrians or the Chaldeans; the calamities in vv. 17ff. are due to natural causes rather than to enemy action. But such details can be overpressed, making the contrast too sharp, and it is better to see this chapter as an example of that 'faithfulness' by which the just man is enabled to look beyond present frustrations to eternal justice ceaselessly at work in the world. In fact, it bears the same marks as those Psalms which, in the Psalter, are associated with historical events: they do not set out to describe details but to enunciate principles, and in this light ch. 3 could hardly be more suitable to what has preceded. Eaton energetically espouses the view that 'ch. 3 was deliberately designed by Habakkuk as crown of his whole composition'. The omission of ch. 3 from the Qumran commentary need not mean that it was not thought to belong to Habakkuk. More likely, it did not suit the purpose and style of the commentator.

1 *Shigionoth*, *cf.* the title of Ps. 7, is apparently an indication of the musical setting to be employed for this poem. It may derive from a verbal root meaning 'to reel' or 'to err', and if so points to some irregular rhythmic mode. At all events, as when such words occur in Psalm titles, it points to the use of this hymn in Temple worship. **2** God's action of old, of which Habakkuk has *heard the report*, while its immensity makes him tremble, yet is the basis of his prayer for a present divine intervention. But if any are to escape, it will only be because *in wrath* He remembers to be merciful. While this is the more probable meaning, Habakkuk could have intended 'In the wrath which we are suffering, come in mercy and help us'.

3 *God came from Teman*. Teman was a district of Edom and here, poetically, the part means the whole; *cf.* Am. 1:12. *Paran* was the hilly country between Edom and Sinai along the Gulf of Aqabah, and was regarded as the cradle of Israelite religion (*cf.* Dt. 33:2). The implied prayer is, therefore, that God will come now in the fullness of that revealed nature which once He showed to Israel at Sinai. See also Jdg. 4, 5; Ps. 68:7, 8. *Selah* (see also vv. 9, 13) is a direction for the liturgical use of the hymn, but its significance is not known. **4, 5** We now turn to the power of His coming. It is pictured as a storm. The *rays* allude to the lightning flashes, for, as often, the theophany is pictured in terms of a gathering storm. His coming is also inescapable. Those who may escape the preceding *pestilence* will be overtaken by the following *plague*; **6** and this is reinforced by the deliberate acts of God whereby He *stood* and *looked*, taking deliberate aim, so to speak, before He released His thunders. **7** *Cushan* was a Midianite or Arabian tribe (*cf.* Nu. 12:1); *in affliction* means 'torn to shreds'; to *tremble* is to 'flutter wildly'. **8** asks, 'What was the purpose of it all?' and the answer is given in v. 13. **9** is very obscure. Delitzsch says that 'nearly a hundred translations of this verse have been offered'. Thackeray sees in the 'oaths', 'tribes' (or 'rods') and 'word' of AV and RV a reference to the three passages of Scripture read during Pentecost, viz. Dt. 16:9–12; Nu. 17:1ff., Gn. 12:1ff., each known by these catchwords. This is, however, over subtle. These older versions, attempting the best that may be done with the unemended Hebrew text, rather suggest this, that when God's bow is bared for action it is not an uncontrolled force of destruction, but acts according to His Word: that is to say, in faithfulness to His chosen tribes, and with all the power of the Creator's word over His created world. RSV, attempting to correct the Hebrew for easier understanding, makes the verse throughout speak of the power of the divine judgment: when the bow is readied for action, it possesses all the cutting force of that creative action which once made ways through the earth for rivers.

10 Before such a One all creation is helpless. *The deep* (Heb. *t^ehôm*) is the Tiamat of Babylonian mythology, the chaos which forcibly opposes the Creator's purposes, but the use of such language does not, of course, imply acceptance of the ideas behind it, and is simply used to enhance the truth of the divine Creator's irresistible power. **11** *The sun and moon stood still* either as hidden by the storm-clouds, or as eclipsed by the glory of God's appearing (*cf.* Acts 26:13) or, as in Jos. 10:12f., where the regularities of nature are suspended in order to guarantee the fullness of the Lord's victory. **12–14** The picture of the Warrior-Creator continues as we see Him *bestride the earth*; nothing is beyond His reach or above His power, but yet, as the prophet had prayed, in wrath He does remember mercy, for all this energy of victory is *for the salvation of thy people*, those whom He had *anointed* for Himself (*cf.* Ps. 105:15). RSV mg. reveals the problems of translating vv. 13b, 14, but the text makes the best possible rendering of them, as the prophet continues the tale of complete divine conquest. **15** He returns to metaphor: the *sea* is often the picture of restless power in opposition to God; *cf.* Ps. 93:3, 4.

16 With this verse Habakkuk's hymn comes full circle. He who confessed to being terror-struck at the report of God's past acts (v. 2) now trembles and melts with fear as he seems to hear the on-coming march of such a God. The end of the verse seems full of paradox. How can he *tremble* and *totter* and at the same time *quietly wait* with an apparently assured calm? **17, 18** His assurance is born of the living faith which these verses so beautifully express. Though everything which, humanly speaking, supports life may fail, yet he can now *rejoice in the Lord*. Personal faith is the practical answer to life's discontents. The contemplation of the history of God with His people, that all His deeds are 'for the salvation of thy people' (v. 13) now leads the prophet to rejoice *in the God of my salvation*. **19** Thus Habakkuk has discovered the answer to his initial questioning, and his deep contentment with the answer is expressed in the testimony that *he makes my feet like hinds' feet*. He feels as if he is 'walking on air', so light-hearted and sure-footed is he. Not even the most trying *high places* (*cf.* Dt. 32:13) through which life's path may lead can daunt the man of faith.

The concluding words of v. 19 are further liturgical directions. The hymn is assigned to the Choirmaster's Collection, and is to be accompanied by the Temple strings.

L. E. H. STEPHENS-HODGE

Zephaniah

INTRODUCTION

AUTHOR AND DATE

The book of Zephaniah is the ninth of the books of Hebrew prophetic literature. It is typical in that it sounds the usual prophetic notes of judgment, renewal, and prediction, but it stands out as important in that its prophecies broke a prophetic silence of two generations and it marks 'the first tingeing of prophecy with apocalypse'. Zephaniah was obviously a plain-spoken man, sober and restrained but also employing impressive powers of imagination and vivid, realistic figures of speech. It is almost certain that he was a young man when he began to prophesy. He was a contemporary of Jeremiah among the prophets and of the good Josiah (640–609 BC) among the kings. Some would say that Nahum also belonged to Zephaniah's time or that he actually preceded him. Nahum's prophecies were solely concerned with the city of Nineveh, and since the destruction of Nineveh did not take place till 612 BC it may be that Nahum prophesied nearer to that date than in the period covered by 640–621 BC, which is the period within which Zephaniah must have appeared (Ellison, *Men Spake from God*, 1958, p. 70).

It was some 70 years since Isaiah and Micah, the prophets of the period of Assyrian ascendancy, had been heard. The fate of Samaria in 722 BC had brought a solemn reminder of God's might and majesty and righteousness. The 50 years before the reign of Josiah had sounded a new depth of degeneracy and barrenness in the history of Judah, and so Zephaniah's youthful vigour and zeal were qualities needed by the situation in which he was called to serve, and they are easily discernible in his book. The forthrightness and the unsparing tone of the pronouncements of judgment are typical of a young man possessing strong convictions and manifesting an unusual degree of moral sensitiveness and earnestness. The reforming zeal of the young King Josiah (640–609) was well matched by the earnest preaching of the new young prophet. They were both 'come to the kingdom for such a time as this' and their youthfulness and the difficult years which moulded them fitted them well to play a worthy role in this new era.

G. A. Smith suggests that Zephaniah's name, which means 'Yahweh has guarded (or hidden)', may indicate that his birth took place in the killing time of Manasseh (*The Book of the Twelve Prophets*, 1900, Vol. II, p. 47). It is certain, at any rate, that when, in the providence of God, Zephaniah stepped to the front of the stage of events in Judah, he marked the beginning of a new line of prophets which was to contain Jeremiah, Habakkuk, Obadiah and Ezekiel (and Nahum, if the later date for that prophet is accepted), all of whom were to seek to save Judah from the fate which had already overtaken the northern kingdom. It is therefore possible to say with certainty that the main body of the book is to be associated with the reformation connected with Josiah which took place in 621 BC, and it is reasonable to suppose that Zephaniah's preaching was one of the contributory causes of it. We may conclude, therefore, that the probable date of utterance was *c.* 627 BC.

It would appear that Jeremiah began his work soon after Zephaniah. It has been claimed that they were around the same age, but there is no proof that this is so, or that there was any close collusion between them. Indeed, at certain points, Jeremiah seems to detect weakness and danger in Zephaniah's sweeping and lightning-like revival. Doubtless he rejoiced in the reforms which Zephaniah's preaching caused Josiah to make, but Jeremiah seemed to see further and deeper—perhaps because he lived longer—and he viewed some of the reformation as an outward form, a fashionable gesture to a popular movement, and not a sincere, spiritual purification with qualities of permanence about it.

CIRCUMSTANCES OF ITS UTTERANCE

As already indicated, the circumstances in which Zephaniah was called to prophesy were, at one and the same time, perilous and promising. During the long reign of Manasseh (696–642), the evil son of the good king Hezekiah, the moral and religious state of Judah had sadly deteriorated (2 Ki. 23:11, 12; 2 Ch. 33:1–11). Although Judah had a certain independence, it came in reality to be little more than a vassal state of the Assyrian Empire, and Manasseh was both unable and unwilling to resist the cultic and ethical changes which came from Nineveh. Throughout his reign Manasseh had opposed the revival of religion which had marked his father's reign. He had built again the altars which his father had thrown down and restored the debasing nature-worship associated with Baal. Superstition, worship of the stars and even human sacrifice became part of a religion of outward form and ceremony devoid of inward reality, and without spiritual or ethical convictions. It is possible to construe all this as a sincere, though fanatical, return to the religion of his grandfather, Ahaz (2 Ki. 16), but it was nevertheless a religious syncretism which paid too much deference to the Assyrian overlords, and in the eyes of the prophets it was sheer, headlong wickedness. Those who had tried to preserve the purity of the worship of Yahweh were rewarded for their pains with persecution and even death, for 'Manasseh shed very much innocent blood, till he had filled Jerusalem from one end to another' (2 Ki. 21:16).

It is true, of course, that Manasseh repented from this attitude before his death in 642 BC, and 'humbled himself greatly before the God of his fathers' (2 Ch. 33:12). His son Amon who succeeded him as king showed no desire to reject the gross idolatry of his father's reign and he fell a victim to intrigue and treachery on the part of his palace officials (2 Ki. 21:19–24).

It is apparent, however, that the evil tendencies of these two reigns had not completely won the support of the people. Once again a remnant had not bowed the knee; there were those who wished and worked for better times. It was this factor which made the times promising as well as perilous. When Josiah came to the throne in 640 BC, there were many who yearned for a purer religion, and were ready both to hear Zephaniah and to follow the king in his reforming zeal.

Mention must also be made of the Scythian invasions in and after 630 BC. This tribe of horse-riding nomads (cf. NBD, art. 'Scythians') had been held in check by the Assyrian Empire when at the height of its power, but it was a mark of waning Assyrian ascendancy that they began to make vigorous and disruptive inroads into the Fertile Crescent. They assisted Assyria, nevertheless, against the Medes. They also pushed southwards to the very borders of Egypt, and were deterred from invading that land only by large bribes from Pharaoh Psammetichus I. They are credited at this time with the destruction of Ashkelon and Ashdod, and their activities in this direction may even have sharpened Zephaniah's awareness of the power of the Lord to inflict universal judgment (cf. IDB, 'Scythians', 'Zephaniah').

The account of this invasion, which is given by Herodotus in Book IV of his History, serves to explain the waning power of Assyria, and when Ashurbanipal died in 627 BC the way was open for Josiah to press on energetically with his reforms unhindered by his erstwhile masters. Some scholars, on the other hand, doubt the accuracy of Herodotus's account because of the demonstrable errors which it contains, and because it is our only authority for the story that they swept as far south and west as the Egyptian border (cf. J. Bright, A History of Israel, 1960, p. 293). Moreover, it is argued that, since we are here dealing with 'the typical vague language of eschatology, where everything is seen through a haze of dust', the judgments here announced cannot refer to this invasion (Ellison, op. cit., pp. 81, 68).

It is not essential, however, to suppose that the Scythian invasion is actually portrayed, but it is reasonable to hold that, knowing of it as he most certainly would, Zephaniah should see in it a picture of what would happen if Judah persisted in her present course of rebellion against the Lord. As a matter of fact the Scythian invasion does not seem to have touched Judah at all; her ultimate oppressor and instrument of God's judgment was Babylon.

ZEPHANIAH'S MESSAGE

Zephaniah was an inhabitant of Jerusalem, as is obvious from references to specific parts of the city which could have been made only by one well acquainted with them (cf. 1:4, 10, 11, 12). In the city he observes people bent on living by force and fraud among themselves, and idolatrous and sceptical towards God. His early prophecies are, on that account, of almost unrelieved gloom; the dark line in the face of God is very clearly seen in the picture given in 1:1 – 3:8. From that point onward, however, a new note is sounded: the hope of universal salvation and ultimate restoration for Judah. The section 3:9–20 is so different from what precedes it that some scholars would dissociate it from the rest of the book (cf. IDB, 'Zephaniah'), but there is no real reason why this should be done (cf. J. H. Eaton, TBC, 1961). It is true that the great burden of Zephaniah's prophetic preaching was about judgment, swift, imminent and disastrous, on Judah and the surrounding nations. Yet we often find that those who discern most clearly God's judgments abroad in the world are those who also see the rainbow of His love and mercy arching the horizon of the future. And while Zephaniah foretold the judgments upon Judah, he foresaw them as a purgative essential to Judah's becoming the blessed of the Lord and His handmaiden to the whole world.

THE INTEGRITY OF THE BOOK

Recent study of this prophecy has resulted in a much more conservative attitude on the unity and consistency of the book as a whole. Formerly the authenticity of very many verses had been called in question by one commentator or another. This was done on various counts: the break in the elegiac measure after ch. 1; the presence of certain words which were in more frequent use in post-exilic writings; the difference in tone between the general message of universal judgment and destruction and the notes of hope sounded in 2:7b, 9b; 3:8–20. These points have been fairly met and answered. The presence here and there of a word which came into wider use in later years does indeed occur, but this need not invalidate the work as being Zephaniah's. 'Meek' and 'meekness', e.g., are Hebrew words which occur often in the later psalms and prophets, but they also occur in Ex. 10:3; Nu. 12:3; Is. 2:9; Mi. 6:8.

Other difficulties were concerned with the historical accuracy of the details of the prophecies, *e.g.* that the Scythian invasion did not affect Moab and Ammon since it did not come through their country at all; or that a destruction of Jerusalem is presupposed in 2:8, 10; or again, that the prophecy is inconsistent in its attitude towards Judah as evidenced by comparing ch. 1 with 2:9, 10. The first two problems are hypothetical in origin. The invasion which

punished Moab and Ammon need not have been that of the Scythians. Furthermore, 2:8, 10 do not in fact actually demand the destruction of Jerusalem, while the blessed hope of the emergence of a remnant of God's people, spared and redeemed from the general destruction, is always breaking through in the prophetic writings. The promise of salvation was not nationalistic but proffered to the humble and penitent in the nation.

OUTLINE OF CONTENTS

COMMENTARY

1:1 THE TITLE: ZEPHANIAH INTRODUCED

A biographical introduction such as this is not unusual (*cf.*, *e.g.*, Ho. 1:1; Am. 1:1; Zc. 1:1). It informs us about the prophet himself, about his genealogy and the times in which he prophesied. The significant thing to note here is that it is unusually long. When this occurs it may indicate some epic achievement or some ancestor of note (*cf.* G. A. Smith, *The Twelve Prophets*, 1900, Vol. II, p. 47). Here it may even draw attention to the fact that Zephaniah came of royal lineage and that four generations separated him from King Hezekiah (*cf.* J. H. Eaton, *TBC*, 1961, p. 121). If this is so, then the conclusion seems sound that Zephaniah cannot have been much more than twenty by the time Josiah came to the throne. It would also add interest to his outright condemnation of the royal house for their aping of foreign manners and for the high-handed wrongs practised by their retainers.

Notes. On *the word of the Lord*, see Am. 1:1. *Cushi*. The name of Zephaniah's father means 'Ethiopian' and may indicate some African mixture of race, or some strong pro-Egyptian bias on Gedaliah's part to give such a name to his son. *Cf.* Je. 38:7–13; 39:15–18 for the presence of an Ethiopian at court a little later than Zephaniah's time. It has also been suggested

that in view of the fact that in Dt. 23:8 no Egyptian or Ethiopian could be admitted into the Jewish community unless he could show a pure Jewish pedigree for at least three generations, Zephaniah's genealogy here is unusually full in order to meet any opposition on this score. *Hezekiah*. In spite of the fact that no mention is made of him as 'King of Judah' it is generally thought that it is the good King Hezekiah (715–687 BC; 2 Ki. 18; 2 Ch. 29) who was so outstandingly great as to need no tag to indicate who he was. *In the days of Josiah*. This could mean anything from 640 to 609 BC, but the whole tone of the book indicates that the prophecies must have been delivered before Josiah's great reformation (621 BC; 2 Ki. 22–23). The particular vices condemned in this book are exactly those which Josiah wiped out. These events must therefore be placed within the period 630–621 BC.

1:2 – 2:3 THE DAY OF THE LORD ANNOUNCED

This is a warning of universal judgment (1:2, 3) spoken as by the Lord Himself: 'I will sweep away . . . I will overthrow'. It is then concentrated on Judah and especially the inhabitants of Jerusalem (vv. 4–13). The meaning of this for the whole world (vv. 14–18) is described as

Zephaniah takes up again the theme with which he opened. In stark, vivid language the prophet tries to arouse and awaken a sinful people and world to the approaching crisis and to a possible catastrophe. Nevertheless in the midst of all this denunciation and warning the prophet holds out in God's name a hand of mercy and a promise of salvation from the day of the wrath of the Lord (2:1-3).

1:2, 3 Its universality

2 This is an assertion of God's sovereign right and power to judge the whole *earth* (not 'land' as in AV) rather than an announcement of an impending doom. **3** The cataloguing of all the various forms of life is designed to stress the totality of the scope of judgment and the concluding reference to *the wicked* of *mankind* concentrates attention on the central point at issue: sin and its inevitable reward.

1:4-13 Its focus on Jerusalem

4 *Jerusalem* is regarded by Zephaniah as the fountainhead of the rampant evil and idolatry of the period. Judgment must begin at the house of God and, as he will show, the salvation which God intends must be effected in germ at Jerusalem. There must be a complete disappearance of the Baal-worship which had flourished in the days of Manasseh and Amon (2 Ki. 21:1-9, 16, 21), and the name of the *idolatrous priests* must disappear. The persistence of the Canaanitish religion in the life of God's people was phenomenal. **5** There was also the worship of the host of heaven, of the sun, moon and stars, practised on the rooftops. This does not seem to be alluded to by prophets to the northern kingdom and owed its strength in Jerusalem to the time of the Assyrian overlordship (2 Ki. 21:3, 5, 21; Je. 7:18; 44:17-19). From the same source and equally abhorrent to God originated the attempt to combine the worship of God and of Milcom, 'the god of the Ammonites' (*cf.* 1 Ki. 11:5). No man can serve two masters and such an attempt to divide their loyalties had disastrous results. The prophet foretold its destruction and Josiah saw to it that it was swept away when the reformation took place (2 Ki. 23:13). **6** In addition many were wilfully or through sheer neglect ignoring the worship of God. This was their crowning sin and it would not go unpunished. Compromise can be appealed to but studied indifference slams the door in God's face. **7** Consequently the prophet solemnly announces that the Lord is ready to act in judgment. The *sacrifice* is prepared and the Lord has consecrated (not 'bid', AV) His guests.

8, 9 The prophet now turns from the sphere of worship to the life of the royal court. The king is not specifically named but he, his courtiers (*officials*) and his sons had aped the ways, the dress and the customs of an alien faith. The religious significance of this to the prophet was disloyalty to God. The court was obviously full

of cruel and dishonest practices and had apparently grown immensely rich by means of them. **10–13** The commercial life of the city was no better. Zephaniah obviously knew the city well and he knew it to be full of covetousness and dishonesty. The vast majority of the merchant class had done well out of the people's poverty. They had grown inordinately wealthy, lazy and indifferent to God and men. They had survived many a crisis and had even begun to think they could hoodwink God, that He was morally indifferent to what they did. But Zephaniah declared that their hidden assets would be discovered, their magnificent houses would fall into disorder, their grandiose schemes would be unproductive and yield them no satisfaction, but only bitterness and ruin.

Notes. 4 *The remnant of Baal.* The use of this phrase is sometimes thought to prove that Zephaniah spoke after Josiah's reforms and not before them. This does not necessarily follow, however, and the bulk of the book is against it. What is intended rather is that the very last sign of Baal-worship should disappear. *The idolatrous priests* (AV 'Chemarims', see *NBD, s.v.*) were the non-Yahwistic priests. The term was used somewhat contemptuously, and especially of those who tried to combine true and false worship at the high places. **5** *Milcom* (AV 'Malcham') was the national God of the Ammonites (1 Ki. 11:5, 33; 2 Ki. 23:13) and this worship received much encouragement when Solomon built high places for it in order to please his foreign wives (1 Ki. 11:7f.).

7 *Be silent before the Lord God!* God's judgment is here shown as a sacrificial feast and this phrase from the Temple liturgy, calling for a breathless silence as the climactic moment approaches, is certainly vivid enough. J. H. Eaton has also suggested that the arrangement, ideas and language of the book could have been influenced by the intention to recite it in the course of Temple services. **9** *Leaps over the threshold.* This is thought by some to refer to some pagan superstition (*cf.* 1 Sa. 5:5). In view of the sentence which follows it is perhaps better to regard it as a proverbial term for anyone bent on plunder by oppression. The threshold was considered the domain of the household gods who guarded the dwellers against intrusion. 'Leaping the threshold' was the phrase used to describe anyone who would try to avoid them in order to enrich themselves. **10, 11** The topographical references may indicate the route of the traders into the city. The *Fish Gate* (also referred to in Ne. 12:39) in the north wall was the entrance into the area of the city known as *the Second Quarter* (*cf.* 2 Ki. 22:14). *The Mortar* (AV 'Maktesh'), so called because it seemed to be a hollowed-out piece of ground, is thought to be that part of the Tyropoeon Valley ('valley of the cheesemakers') where foreign merchants congregated (*ISBE*, p. 1969). *The hills* may be another sector or industrial landmark within the city.

12 *Thickening upon their lees*. The allusion here is to the process of wine-making. The wine must not be allowed to settle or else it thickens with sediment. It has to be poured from one vessel to another in order to mature properly. Character degenerates when it ceases to be disciplined. When men have all they need and become independent of God moral decay soon sets in and contaminates society. *Lamps* (not 'candles', av); God is shown here as a night watchman. No-one can hide from Him and no sin escape. This figure of speech moved mediaeval artists painting Zephaniah to show him as the man with the lamp. It was in many ways the correct picture of the man, his character and his mission.

1:14–18 Its imminence

14ff. Zephaniah returns now to the thought of the universal scope of the judgment which the day of the Lord will bring, but the specific emphasis here, adding to the information sketched out in vv. 2, 3, is that the day is *near and hastening fast*.

There is no favouritism with God and He has an appointment to keep with all men. This passage recalls the famous hymn of Thomas of Celano, the 'Dies Irae' (the wrath of God). The language is apocalyptic in character but the urgency of the situation strikes home with every phrase and is true in every age when men forget or defy God. He will break down the walled fortifications, which suggest those defences behind which men feel safe from God. **16** may suggest an actual invasion of Jerusalem by an enemy already poised to invade, such as could have been prompted by the example of the Scythians, and which was fulfilled by the Babylonians who arrived in 597, and sacked Jerusalem in 587 BC. In any case it is to be clearly the day of the Lord. His wrath has been aroused through the false worship and dishonesty of Jerusalem and its people. **17** When it dawns, men who think they can be independent of God soon discover that they are as helpless as blind men to get away from Him. The whole value will go out of life and the futility but worthlessness of a godless existence is conjured up in the use of the word *dung*. **18** Neither an abundance of wealth nor the security of vaunted privileges can save from the fire of the jealousy of the Lord, and this will fall on all impartially.

Notes. **14ff.** *The . . . day of the Lord*. According to Von Rad (*Old Testament Theology*, Vol. II, 1965, p. 119), there are sixteen OT passages which refer to this important idea, and Zephaniah's prophecy concerning it is 'certainly one of the most important sources of material at our disposal'. Prophets such as Isaiah, Amos, Ezekiel, Joel and Zephaniah saw in their current dilemmas situations which called for the intervention of God in judgment. They read back into the story of Israel and believed that God's final uprising would take much the same form as in the days of old. They expected the day of the Lord to bring war in its train, *e.g.*, and they looked at a predicament that was of local or national importance as a phenomenon of cosmic and universal significance. By whatever instrument it was brought to pass, the day of God's zealous anger was largely aroused by His abhorrence of the worship of foreign deities, and His judgment was carried out with unquenchable zeal. (*Cf.* on Am. 5:18.)

18 The jealousy of God is a familiar OT concept. God is to be worshipped exclusively, and with all the ardour of a thwarted lover He resists the unfaithfulness of His sinning people. We must not, however, think of His jealousy as identical to our human emotion so often charged with anger and sin. God could not be a jealous God if He were not a God of love. God's jealousy is the measure of His love. That is why He wants to possess His people all to Himself. *Earth* ('land', av). This change in translation is regretted by some who still think Zephaniah speaks only of Judah and Jerusalem. Some even suggest that v. 18b is not Zephaniah's phrase because of the universal destruction it visualizes. But we have seen above, the near and the distant often merge as the prophets survey the horizon of events. Events which are historically separate are often seen in a timeless sequence. (See S. Winward, *A Guide to the Prophets*, 1968, p. 107.)

2:1–3 The door of hope

1 Zephaniah now calls for a halt and a final reflection. There may still be a chance. Those who see the worst in human nature are often the first to see a gleam of hope. Following the gloom, unmitigated and unrelieved in any way, Zephaniah sends one shaft of light into the darkness. A remnant may yet be saved. **2, 3** He does not see any way of escape for any but for the *humble*, whom He mentions in contrast to the proud who have provoked the jealous wrath of God. There is no mention of the mercy of God here, it is true. Zephaniah's gospel appears sternly moral as he commands them to seek righteousness and humility. But we are not to understand that he thinks otherwise than that all our hopes of ultimate salvation begin in the mercy and grace of God.

Notes. **1** *Come together and hold assembly*. The text is difficult and has been variously translated: 'Gather for yourselves stubble and be stubble' (Wade, *WC*, 1929); 'Pull yourselves together and collect yourselves' (Eaton, *TBC*); 'Be ashamed together and feel shame' (J. P. Hyatt, *Peake's Commentary*, 1962). Whatever the best rendering may be, the sense is clearly a call to humiliation and repentance. It reminds the nation that they are no more able to stand against God than chaff is to withstand the storm. **3** *Humble* (Heb. *ānāw*) is the word used so often to describe the devout worshipper of Yahweh. It carried with it the suggestion of an attitude towards God rather than towards men. The meek man is not necessarily the weak man but one who humbles himself before God as opposed to the 'proud' and the 'evildoers'. *Who do his commands* (*cf.* 'which have wrought his judgment', av; 'do right', LXX). Humility expresses itself in obedience to God's will, whatever it may be.

2:4 – 3:8 THE DAY OF THE LORD IMPLEMENTED

2:4-15 Against the nations

This whole passage is a series of prophecies about certain neighbouring nations. The prophet deals in turn with those on the western (vv. 4–7), eastern (vv. 8–11), southern (v. 12) and northern (vv. 13–15) borders of Judah, and the formal way in which this is done suggests a primary didactic intention. In other words, these nations were undoubtedly enemies of God's people yet they are summoned here and addressed as being typical of all the enemies everywhere who oppose God's people and defy His rule. Then, as now, God took steps to pull down the mighty from their seats and to lift up the humble. The proud are humiliated and it makes no difference whether they are in the land of Judah, or of Judah's heathen neighbours.

2:4–7 Philistia. 4 First, the enemy on Judah's western side is mentioned. Through this gateway there had come successive waves of invaders from Europe, from as early as 1200 BC. Commerce came this way and the coastal cities were large and prosperous. The whole area was ruled by a league of five cities (Jos. 13:3) and of these, four are mentioned here: *Gaza, Ashkelon, Ashdod*, and *Ekron*. The destruction of the other one, Gath, is mentioned in 2 Ch. 26:6. The area would be depopulated (*deserted*) as the result of a swift, surprise attack, *at noon; i.e.* either it would occur when least expected, or it would be over in half a day.

5, 6 The character of the coastal plain (*sea coast*) would be drastically changed. That it should become a place of pasturage is basically a metaphor for depopulation (*cf.* Is. 5:14–17), for the shepherd leads his sheep away from busy and peopled areas, but it conceivably also suggests that the materialistic civilization of Philistia could only be reformed by returning to simpler and less sophisticated ways. Behind it all may lie the defeat of Goliath, the Philistine champion, by the shepherd lad, David (1 Sa. 17). This, more than anything else, prepares for the revelation of **7** that this land was then to be given to the *remnant of the house of Judah*. God always preserves something out of catastrophe on which to rebuild. It is not simply that Judah will be restored nationally but that looking on down the centuries of time God's chosen people, the new Israel of God, will arise. This conception of the remnant pushes back the limitations of race and privilege until at last 'the full number of the Gentiles come in, and so all Israel will be saved' (Rom. 11:25f.).

Notes. 4 The Scythian invasion aimed at Egypt certainly passed through the coastal plain (Herodotus i. 103–106). Nebuchadrezzar captured and destroyed Ashkelon in 604 BC (D. J. Wiseman, *Chronicles of Chaldaean Kings*, 1956,

p. 69). **5** The *Cherethites* were a Philistine clan occupying the sea coast. They were said to come from Caphtor (Je. 47:4; Am. 9:7) which is generally taken to be Crete. *O Canaan, land of the Philistines.* The use of the name Canaan as synonymous with Philistia occurs nowhere else in the OT, although in Egyptian inscriptions it is used in different ways. At an earlier time, when the Assyrians occupied all land west of the Jordan except Judah, Canaan was practically confined to what was Philistia. 'Canaanite' was also a term used of merchants, and it could well be that the rich commerce of this land was in the hands of the old original families who controlled the life and industry of the newcomers.

7 Much of this verse is sometimes classed as post-exilic editorial addition because it speaks of the coming glory of the remnant of Judah whose fortunes are to be restored (*cf.* Hyatt, *op. cit.*). This rests on a somewhat odd view of the prophets as men who could see the coming divine judgments of the people of God but who then made no attempt to resolve the resulting tension between God's wrathful acts and His previously stated covenant promises. Furthermore, in the present context (*cf.* Eaton), the victory of the people of God over the Philistines has the deep symbolic value of showing the victory of the godly humble over proud ungodliness, foreshadowed, as we suggested above, in the triumph of David over Goliath. In the same way David's people will ultimately possess all the nations. Any apparent nationalism in the prospect of possessing the nations is smoothed away in the due development of Zephaniah's teaching, wherein he shows that in fact 'the peoples' will be transformed so as to call upon the name of the Lord (3:9).

2:8–11 Moab and Ammon. 8 These two nations are linked together because they were both on the eastern side of Judah, both Semitic in origin and descended from Lot (*cf.* Gn. 19:36–38). Their reproaches and revilings of God's people were exceedingly bitter, and their desolation would be thorough and permanent. (*Cf.* Is. 16:6; Je. 48:25–27; Ezk. 25:3, 6, 8.) **9, 10** The seriousness of their offence is reflected in the solemn terms in which this prophecy is announced; *As I live, says the Lord of hosts, the God of Israel*, indicating 'the living nature of the affronted Lord and the certainty of His retribution' (J. G. Gailey).

Notes. 9 *Sodom* and *Gomorrah* are often used as outstanding examples of utter overthrow (*cf.* Dt. 29:23; Is. 13:19; Je. 49:18). In the present context the reference is all the more apt because of the connection of Lot with these nations (*cf.* Gn. 19). Indeed, the fact that Lot was so mercifully saved from the overthrow even serves to add emphasis to the pronouncement of utter doom on his descendants. *Nettles* (Heb. *ḥārûl, cf.* Jb. 30:7; Pr. 24:31) is properly chickling or vetch, a plant of the pea family. The picture is one of a land run wild. This again is a frequent prophetic metaphor for depopulation (*cf.* Is. 7:23–25).

10, 11 Four thoughts emerge in turn in these verses as Zephaniah reveals the inner motives of the divine wrath against Moab and Ammon. First, it is the due and just reward of their pride (v. 10a). The Lord's acts are always in opposition to sin and directed against guilty sinners. Against this background we are able to see that when the prophet reveals the Lord's second motive as the vindication of His chosen people (v. 10b), this is not a bare act of favouritism. The Moabites invited wrath because of what they were, quite apart from what they did. Yet the truth is precious that the Lord does intervene on behalf of His people. Thirdly (v. 11a), the Lord acts in pursuance of a spiritual conflict with *the gods of the earth* whom He will not permit to possess for ever what is rightfully His. Fourthly, He designs in thus acting to bring *all lands* to Himself (v. 11b).

2:12 Ethiopia. The prophet now turns his gaze south. It may be that he is here sarcastically referring to Egypt, because Egypt was ruled by an Ethiopian dynasty 715–663 BC (*cf.* Hyatt). Alternatively, since this situation in Egypt considerably antedates Zephaniah, it may be that he is using Ethiopia (Heb. *kûš*) simply as a cypher for the remotest parts of the earth, and thus continuing the vision of the Lord's worldrule from v. 11. If the reference is to Egypt, it may have found fulfilment in Nebuchadrezzar's punitive invasion of Egypt in 568 BC (*cf.* J. Bright, *op. cit.*, p. 333). This would certainly match the threat that they would be *slain by my sword*.

2:13–15 Assyria. Assyria was undoubtedly Judah's worst and most bitter and cruel enemy. It was described as 'the climax and fount of heathendom' over 200 years before Israel first felt the weight of bondage to her. About 100 years earlier her hosts swept through the land, and for at least 50 of these this supremacy had been accepted by Judah and expensively paid for. But as she had menaced, so she was now menaced herself. 'It was the close of an epoch' (G. A. Smith, *op. cit.*, p. 66). It is also certain that nothing seemed less likely when it was first prophesied, yet so it was. The nation that ruled the world was brought to nothing, *a dry waste like the desert, a lair for wild beasts*, and the haunt of beasts and birds. Assyria flaunted her strength and boasted her self-confidence: *I am and there is none else* (v. 15b; *cf.* 'I am the Lord, and there is no other', Is. 45:5, 6, 18, 21). The place that was once the centre of pride and glory became nothing more than 'a few mounds and monuments in a wilderness, at which a traveller shakes his head'. So fickle is earthly glory, so uncertain her rewards, and so exact and true the vengeance of God.

Notes. **13** *Nineveh* was the capital of Assyria. *Cf.* Nahum *passim* for the loathsomeness of Nineveh to the people of God, as expressive of all that they had suffered at Assyrian hands. **15** *Hisses and shakes his fist*, *i.e.* as an expression of intense scorn and contempt. *Cf.* Ezk. 27:36; Na. 3:19.

3:1–8 Against Jerusalem

No city is mentioned by name, but it is quite clear that Jerusalem is intended. Up to this point social sins have not been mentioned much in Zephaniah's prophecies, but here he shows that they are far from being forgotten. Indeed it would seem even that he had held off until now in order to give them a special emphasis. Social sins are specially unpardonable in the people of God, they represent the height of iniquity, the supreme sin, the unanswerable indictment of their corrupt worship of God.

1 The impartial wrath of God fastens upon the evil which is all too evident among His own people. The city is charged with active disloyalty (*rebellious*; better than 'filthy', AV). This is the fundamental tragedy of being out of tune with God and actively engaged against Him. The city has shed innocence and holiness and is *defiled*. Furthermore, such moral decay had overtaken the city that injustice ruled the day and *the oppressing city* earned a reputation for injustice and wrong. **2** This attitude was carried over into the religious realm: she behaved with haughtiness and disobedience towards the prophets, acting independently of God and with indifference towards His law. She neither acknowledged His claims nor sought His mercy, neglecting the opportunity to *draw near* in worship of Him.

3, 4 Four kinds of leaders are mentioned, each found, under the scrutiny of divine judgment, to be wanting and therefore solemnly warned: the rapacious *officials*, the chief executives; the *judges*, other rulers and civil servants, who were as fast to pursue injustice as *wolves* after their prey, and too greedy to leave anything over for another time; the *prophets*, who trimmed their message in order to court popularity; and the *priests*, who profaned their sacred task of teaching *the law* (*cf.* Mal. 2:5–7), violently altering its precepts. *Wanton* arises from a verb meaning 'to gush (like water)' (*cf.* Gn. 49:4, 'unstable'; Jdg. 9:4, 'reckless'). The ideas, therefore, of untrustworthiness and garrulity are combined. 'It characterises the prophets as vapourers, extravagant and arrogant in their own imaginations and conceits' (A. B. Davidson, *CBSC*, 1920).

5–7 In stark contrast to all this is the unchanging righteousness and justice of the Lord. He is daily showing what is right and good, but the ungodly never learn from it. Indeed, the punishment of other nations was meant to be a warning to Judah, but she was all the more eager to be corrupt. **7** *Eager to make their deeds corrupt. Cf.* 'rose early, and corrupted', AV; Je. 7:13, 25; 11:7; 26:5, contrast RSV with AV. **8** Zephaniah pleads finally for Jerusalem to return to God. He will surely destroy everything that rises up against Him. This verse has been variously interpreted: by some as an ironical call to Judah to await the predicted universal judgment; by others as an encouragement to bear up until God decides to act. The latter undoubtedly provides the straightforward sense in which it is to be taken. There is, however, little doubt that the 'tinges of apocalypse' are beginning to appear. Zephaniah sees beyond the events that are near, beyond the iniquities of Judah and her neighbours, even beyond the events of the impending future to the time and the judgment of the End. The immediate events are not themselves the end, but 'heralds of the climax' (Winward, *op. cit.*).

3:9–20 THE VICTORY OF THE LORD

From this point forward there is a new note of victory in the prophecies of Zephaniah. Indeed, the change is so marked that some commentators insist that this section must belong to a much later period, *i.e.* after the Exile, when optimism might possibly promote a note of triumph. The reality of these verses as the Word of God would not, of course, be imperilled if it were proved to be a later editorial addition, but this has not, in fact, been done, and in these verses Zephaniah can still be heard, singing a new song above and beyond the din of disaster and the dust of judgment.

Eaton rightly points out that the dramatic rituals of the Temple, as reflected in the Psalter, held together the contrasting themes of a judgment which appeared final and an abrupt dawning of mercy and hope when all hope seemed gone (*op. cit.*, pp. 150f.; *cf.* Introduction to Psalms). To him, as clearly also to Zephaniah, it is 'of fundamental importance . . . that the Day of the Lord must have two necessary aspects: punishment and peace. The conquest of opposition to God's rule is thus matched by the resultant perfection of his kingdom.'

3:9–13 The new Jerusalem

The order of the announcement of judgment (1:2–6) is repeated in the order of the revelation of hope. **9, 10** There is a world-wide vision of redeemed *peoples* which **11–13** almost at once concentrates its focus upon the new Jerusalem wherein a chastened and humble remnant will no longer be troubled by the proudly exultant and haughty, who had brought nothing but trouble and shame to the city.

Notes. **9** *Change the speech of the peoples to a pure speech.* This means not that they will worship God with better Hebrew but with purer hearts. *Cf.* Is. 19:18, 'In that day there will be five cities in . . . Egypt which speak the language of Canaan and swear allegiance to the Lord of hosts.' The divisive curse of Babel (Gn. 11:9) will be gone. **10** The use of *Ethiopia* here is to include the most distant nations of all, Ethiopia being considered as far away as they could imagine (*cf.* on 2:12). *My suppliants, the daughter of my dispersed ones.* Some small textual difficulty does not obscure the essential clarity of this phrase, but the assumption that it refers to the regathering of a Judahite dispersion has led some to assume that we are dealing with a late addition to Zephaniah. Even were this the meaning of the phrase, the conclusion drawn would still be far from necessary, but in fact 'my dispersed peoples' (as the idiom involved could be translated) may well be taken to refer to those whom God purposes to bring to Himself out of every nation. *Cf.* the 'other sheep' of Jn. 10:16, and 'the children of God who are scattered abroad' of Jn. 11:52. Once more, Zephaniah is looking back to the initial 'dispersion' of Gn. 11:9.

12 *Humble* (Heb. *ānî*) means one humbled by misfortune, as compared with *ānāw* (2:3), which is one who is humble in character. *Seek refuge in the name of the Lord*; *i.e.* in contrast with their former, fatal alliances with pagan nations. **13** Two further marks of the people of the new Jerusalem are given. Corresponding to their new-found humility (v. 12) there is their new tongue and speech, ever a prime mark of the regenerate (*cf.* Jas. 3:2ff.), and matching their seeking of refuge in the Lord (v. 12b) is their unbroken security and peace.

3:14–20 The new Israel

14 This verse commences a series of three distinct pictures of the Lord in relation to His people, which are then followed by three matching statements of their transformation by grace. **15** The Lord is *the King of Israel*, seen here performing the distinctively kingly acts of pronouncing an acquittal over His people (v. 15a), driving out their foes (v. 15b), and guaranteeing their security (v. 15d). **16, 17a** Continuing the theme of security from the end of v. 15, we now see the Lord as *a warrior*, encouraging the spirit of His people (v. 16) and giving victory (v. 17a). **17b, 18a** The third picture now follows. RSV agrees with many commentators in assuming some need to read a different text here. Consequently we read that *he will renew you in his love* (following LXX). Wade (*op. cit.*) emends to 'He will be stirred in his love', as being more in keeping with the Lord's exuberant joy. The Hebrew, however, reads, 'He will be silent in his love' (RSV mg.). Eaton comments: 'He is further represented as the Bridegroom, who in his love for his bride, Zion, now proclaims his joy, now falls into rapt silence.' **18b** Now comes the first of the matching statements of a transformed people. Corresponding to the work of the King (vv. 14f.), there is a people freed from reproach and *disaster*, if this is indeed the meaning of a most difficult text.

19 The divine warrior who called for an end to despondency (v. 16b) is matched by a people changed from the helplessness of lameness and banishment to *praise* and *renown*. **20** Finally, the Bridegroom brings home His bride and she sees at last with her own *eyes* all that her Lover and Lord has done for her. And lest for us, the Bride of Christ, the tarrying of the vision should provoke any lingering doubt of the promise, Zephaniah ends his prophecy with words which provide a divine countersignature upon its authority and a shout of triumphant assurance echoing out of his heart and into ours: 'The Lord has said it.'

JOHN T. CARSON

Haggai

INTRODUCTION

AUTHOR

Haggai, the earliest prophet of the post-exilic restoration of Judah, is known, apart from this book, only from references made to him in Ezra. These show him as a contemporary of Zechariah, serving in Judah and Jerusalem. As a result of their joint ministry the work of rebuilding the Temple was resumed and completed (Ezr. 5:1; 6:14). Nothing is stated about the private life of Haggai and it is generally assumed that he was one of the main group of exiles who returned from Babylonia following the decree of Cyrus in 538/7 BC, which allowed the rebuilding of the Jerusalem Temple. If so he would have witnessed the initial work then undertaken and the subsequent lapse of effort in the face of opposition. Since he employs a technical ritual argument (Hg. 2:11–14) it has been suggested that he was in some way connected with the Temple service. Such a general interpretation of the law, however, made as a result of an inquiry, and the allusion to the covenant promise made at the time of the Exodus (Hg. 2:5), would be known to any devout Jew. His name Haggai (Lat. Festus, Gk. Hilary) could simply imply that he was born or dedicated on a festal day. The name could be similar to that borne by several Levites (Gn. 46:16; Nu. 26:15) or a variant of Haggiah (1 Ch. 6:30). Tradition (Epiphanius) describes him as a young man on the return from Babylon; there is no evidence for the view that he was of great age, having seen the Solomonic Temple before its destruction in 587 BC (as some assume from Hg. 2:3) or that he reached the city with a special party under Zerubbabel only briefly before his recorded prophecies. The LXX links Haggai and Zechariah with Pss. 137; 144–148.

DATE

The prophecies are introduced by date formulae which ascribe them to precise days in the sixth (1:1, 15), seventh (2:1) and ninth months (2:10, 20) of the second regnal year of Darius I (Hystaspes) of Persia who ruled 522–486 BC, *i.e.* 29 August–19 November, 520 BC. The language and style is consistent with this date.

This was a time when the outlying provinces of the Persian Empire, each under their appointed governor (1:1), were deprived of direct help from the central government. The enlightened policy of encouraging local autonomy in secular and religious affairs initiated by Cyrus, by whose decree the first return of Jews had begun in 536 BC, had ceased with his death some 6 years

later. His son Cambyses (530–522) showed less sympathy to vassal states and this doubtless contributed to the failure of the Jewish people to press forward with the reconstruction of the Temple at Jerusalem where work had come to a standstill soon after the arrival of the first returnees under Sheshbazzar, the Judean governor nominated by the Persians. This interruption was prolonged by the opposition of the Samaritans and local landowners which led to a prohibition of further work. Cambyses failed to use his powers to uphold the lost building permit originally granted by his father (Ezr. 4). On the death of Cambyses revolts broke out, one leading to the seizure of the throne by Bardiya until his death at the hand of Darius three months later. In Babylonia a local revolt brought Nidintu-Bel (Nebuchadrezzar III) to the throne (3 October–18 December, 522). On his defeat Darius gained control there for almost a year. Then Araka (Nebuchadrezzar IV) led another rebellion, and it was late in 521 BC before Darius could restore order there. The effect of these disturbances on the economy and on communications with the west was worsened by a series of famines. Haggai is the sole direct evidence for these troubled conditions in Judah at this time (*cf.* Zc. 1:11), though archaeological evidence supports his statements concerning the prevalence of poverty (1:9–11; 2:16, 17). Morale was low and men concentrated on the betterment of their own circumstances. To them it was an inappropriate time to spend effort and wealth on God's house (1:2).

MESSAGE

Haggai is designated 'the prophet' (1:1, *etc.*, also Ezr. 5:1; 6:14) by whom came the word of the Lord (1:1, 3, 5, 7, 9; 2:1, 10). He claimed to be sent by the Lord (1:12, 13) and to be under His authority (Ezr. 5:1). His single objective was to encourage the people to complete an unfinished task, the building of the Temple. Although his public work as recorded covered only about three months, he was to be one of the few prophets who lived to see the fulfilment of his words, the work being finished in the sixth year of Darius (6 October, 516; Ezr. 6:15). His words were expressly stated to have greatly helped the work forward (Ezr. 5:1).

He concentrates thought upon the Temple of the Lord as the place of the divine presence and glory (1:8; 2:3; note also the frequent reference to 'I am with you', 'among you', 1:13; 2:5, *etc.*). This was in no way to encourage dependence on the physical Temple, and in this he followed Jeremiah (Je. 7:4). Haggai clearly stated that the failure to complete the House of God was the direct cause of the unfavourable economic conditions. The Law taught that such conditions resulted from national sin (1:11; Dt. 11:17; Am. 4:7). Thus directly, as indirectly in the analogy of levitical uncleanness (2:11–14), Haggai followed the earlier prophets in diagnosing the cause of the present low spiritual and economic state of the people. Unlike Amos, who uses the prevailing distress as the basis for a call to repentance (Am. 4:6–11), Haggai stresses it as a call to works meet for repentance. It was left to his contemporary to call directly for repentance (Zc. 1:3f.). Though different in presentation, Haggai's message is identical in purpose with that of Zechariah and follows the same general arrangement and dating. The book of Haggai reminds us that God's will and work must always take priority. 'Seek first his kingdom and his righteousness, and all these things shall be yours as well' (Mt. 6:33).

It has been argued that Haggai marks the change from prophet to teacher. In practice these roles are always combined in OT prophecy. His recurrent use of brief quotations introduced as 'Thus says the Lord' or of questions (1:4, 9; 2:3, 12, 15, 19) have been taken to foreshadow the later rabbinic style of teaching, but these can equally be found in the earlier prophets. The style and brevity of the prophecies may also be

explained by taking them as but a selection related expressly to the work on the Temple from the prophet's fuller sayings. His style is terse, direct and forceful and thus admirably suited to his purpose. He preaches for a decision and response to God's demands' (1:12) and throughout appeals to the mind and emotions. He employs a rhythmic prose style rather than the common poetic form often characteristic of the prophets (but cf. 2:4, 5, 14). Most scholars accept the integrity of the book and message though a few consider the introductory formulae as artificial and some material as out of place (e.g. 1:15a), but this often requires emendation of the text which is not supported by any internal or external evidence. The message is consistent and unified.

In keeping with the rising feelings of nationalism encouraged by the external political situation, Haggai looks forward to the ultimate glory of the finished Temple. Like Isaiah before him, he sees it as a place of international significance (2:6–9; cf. Is. 2:2–4). At the same time he points ahead to the Messianic hopes revived in the new 'shoot' of the Davidic line to spring up from the barren earth (2:20–23; cf. Je. 23:5). Zerubbabel would continue the promised royal line in Zion; he was to be the ruling authority (signet) of the new age marked by the completed Temple. Man-wrought economic distress would be replaced by divinely-given prosperity.

OUTLINE OF CONTENTS

COMMENTARY

1:1, 2 THE MESSAGE TO THE LEADERS

The principal subject of the whole collection of prophecies—the building of the Temple—is introduced by a statement of the problem which hinders the work. The civil and religious leaders are told of the people's doubts that it was an appropriate time to take action.

1 The use of a precise date to introduce a specific prophecy is common in post-exilic writings (e.g. Zc. 1:1, 7; Dn. 7:1; 8:1; 9:1; Ezk. 8:1). *Zerubbabel, i.e.* 'seed of Babylon', was thus born in exile. He was *son of Shealtiel* and thus grandson of the last rightful ruler of Judah, Jehoiachin (cf. Ezr. 3:2; Mt. 1:12). In 1 Ch. 3:19 he is said to be son of Pedaiah, perhaps by

levirate marriage (but LXX here agrees with Hg. 1:1). The special term (district-) *governor (peḥah)* is a reminder of foreign domination. It accords with Ezra's 'governor of the Jews' (Ezr. 6:7). Both civil and religious leaders are equally responsible to God. **2** *This people* implies that Haggai considered himself their spokesman. *The time has not yet come* (cf. v. 4). The tense indicates their low morale for it implies that they also did not see a future appropriate time coming. Their excuse could not be occupation with harvest for that was now past (first and fifth months) or the opposition of the Samaritans and Persian government, for that was 16 years previously (cf. Ezr. 4:1–5). It is noteworthy that none of these factors delayed the work when once there was the will to do it.

1:3–11 THE CHALLENGE TO THE PEOPLE

The people are asked the same question as their leaders since they are equally responsible and guilty of neglecting God's house. The underlying cause of their failure and of their feeble circumstances is shown to be selfishness. This sin is emphasized by the withholding of divine blessing.

4 *Is it a time for you . . .?* This could be a rhetorical question, in effect an emphatic denial. Haggai goes straight to the point. What are our priorities? Should people live in *panelled houses* while wood is in short supply for the House of God (*this house*)? The technical term (*sāpan*) is used of decorative panels (1 Ki. 7:7) and of roofing beams (1 Ki. 6:9) and might have been chosen as a play on the identically spelt Aramaic/Babylonian verb (*sāpānu*) meaning 'flattened (crushed)', a sidelong glance at the contrasting state of the Lord's House. The latter verb is used also of ground prepared for sowing seed. **5** 'Consider your ways' (AV; *cf.* v. 7; 2:15, 18), *consider how you have fared* (RSV). The former is preferable since the challenge is to decide on the future ways (plur.), meaning 'way of life'. **6** *Cf.* vv. 9–11. A description of the barrenness of life and ineffectual work as a pointer to spiritual need. **8** *Bring wood* may indicate that this was the main commodity required, since stone would be at hand. As with the Solomonic Temple, the design may have followed the Syrian style with wood beams laid as courses between the stones. The reference to 'ruins' (v. 4) may preclude the view that all that was still needed was wood from the mountains (*i.e.* large logs) for roofing. On either interpretation the major need required sacrifice and effort if it was to be met. God's *glory* was always thought to be expressed visually (*cf.* Ex. 16:7) especially in His House (*cf.* 2 Ch. 7:1–3) and in the body of His people as a temple (*cf.* 1 Cor. 3:16; 6:19). All material things are to be used for His glory and not for selfish ends. **9** *Brought it home*; to your own house as opposed to Mine. **10** The heavens withholding their *dew* was set as a direct sign of God's displeasure on sin (*cf.* Dt. 11:10–12; 28:23, 28; Am. 4:7) and as such was to be regarded as a call to repentance.

1:12–15 THE RESPONSE OF THE PEOPLE

Obedience to God's Word through His messenger brings unity of purpose, a further word from the Lord, encouragement and stimulus to right action.

12 *The remnant of the people* (*cf.* v. 14; 2:2, 3) is used as in Isaiah's eschatology (*cf.* Is. 10:20f.) of all those who would keep true faith and righteousness (*cf.* Zc. 8:6–8, 12). It does not refer only to the returned exiles or those left in the land.

The phrase cannot be dismissed as a gloss since it defines the necessary subject for the final sentence, *the people . . . the Lord. The voice of the Lord* and *the words of Haggai the prophet* are shown to be identical. This is true prophecy. The source of the words in God and their consequent authority over men is acknowledged in the obedience of the people. This always results in the fear of the Lord, *i.e.* an attitude of heart and mind which leads to worship, wisdom and the renunciation of evil (*cf.* Pr. 1:7; 8:13). **13** The *messenger of the Lord* follows from his being 'sent' by the Lord (v. 12). The term is used by Isaiah (42:19; 44:26) and in the name of Malachi (1:1; 3:1; 'My messenger'). He was this because he acted 'in the commission of the Lord' (rather than *with the Lord's message*). The word could be used also of an 'angel' (*cf.* Gn. 19:1) or of any messenger (hence the qualifying words here), the derivative noun being commonly used for 'occupation, work'. *I am with you* is an unchanging promise by an unchanging God. These words have always stirred men to faith and action, so Moses (Ex. 3:12), Gideon (Jdg. 6:16) and the disciples of Christ (Mt. 28:20). **14** Obedience to the commands of God always results in, and is witnessed by, the Spirit of God working on the spirit of man (*cf.* 2:5). **15** The unexpected date can best be explained as an indication of the time (23 days) taken to respond to the call of v. 1. Before work could begin time would be needed for the acquisition of materials and personnel. The proposition that it is an out-of-place preface to 2:15–19 would require an emendation of the text to 'ninth' month, the date of the new foundation (2:18), and would imply that the prophecies have not been arranged in chronological order. A considerable rearrangement of the whole text would be needed to give logical sense to the whole new idea and is unnecessary.

2:1–9 THE WORD OF ENCOURAGEMENT

After one month's hard toil God graciously sends a further word of encouragement to all the team as they work. This time any despondency is dispelled by a reminder of the previous word (v. 4, 'I am with you'), an exhortation to renewed effort (v. 4, 'take courage', 'work') and a promise of unfailing power (v. 6, 'I will shake'), provision (v. 8) and ultimate splendour and prosperity (v. 9).

1 *The seventh month . . . the twenty-first day* was the last day of the Feast of Tabernacles and preceded the day of solemn assembly (*cf.* Lv. 23:34–36). **3** Despite the joyful occasion a few were downcast at the contrast between their puny efforts and Solomon's great building (*cf.* Ezr. 3:12). **4** *Take courage.* The word means to be or grow firm. *The people of the land* here is not a special term for peasants or any particular class, but denotes all citizens. God's presence is the source and strength of all true work (*cf.*

Jos. 1:6, 9). 5 *The promise* was traditionally known and repeated by all devout Jews (*cf.* Ex. 29:45; Ne. 9:20; Zc. 4:6). 6 *Once again* is another reference back to the Sinai events (*cf.* Ex. 19:18). *A little while*—to encourage steadfast hope (*cf.* Jn. 16:16). *I will shake the heavens*; quoted in Heb. 12:26, 27. 7 *All nations* points to the future when, as at the Lord's coming, all nations will pay tribute to His people (*cf.* Is. 60:9-11). The present disturbances in the Persian lands might well have occasioned the thought. *The treasures.* RSV here follows LXX. RV 'the desirable things' is preferable to AV 'the desire', since the following verb is plural. Or read possibly 'that which is desired (by the Lord)'. There is not necessarily a reference here to the Messiah. Rather it points to the gifts to be brought by the Gentile rulers to adorn the Temple. This would have a first fulfilment soon (v. 9; *cf.* Ezr. 6:8, 9) but not completely so until Christ's reign (*cf.* Eph. 2:17-22). Zechariah emphasized the eagerness with which men would desire to associate themselves with God's people in Jerusalem (Zc. 8:20-23).

8 The splendour of the Temple, though from one point of view the result of man's wealth and labour, is nevertheless God-given. This is the biblical answer to man's claim of absolute possession. 9 *I will give prosperity.* Thus RSV translates a word often found as 'peace' (*cf.* AV, RV). It is in fact more comprehensive than either translation, signifying total spiritual, mental and physical well-being. This is the opposite of the conditions then experienced by the builders. *The Lord of hosts*, a title of God which stresses His universal dominion and control of the forces of heaven and earth, is particularly appropriate here. Note its frequent use (15 times) in this short book. The occurrence throughout Isaiah (49 times) and Jeremiah (76 times) shows that it cannot be used for dating sections of the text (*cf.* 1 Sa. 1:3, 11).

2:10-19 THE PROMISE OF BLESSING

Between this and the last message Zechariah had called for repentance (Zc. 1:3-6). Haggai now underlines that demand by a public question to the priests (vv. 12-15). This aimed, by analogy with the levitical law, to remind the people that the fact that they were engaged in work on a holy place did not of itself make them holy. The sin which had led God to judge His people and allow the destruction of the very place they were rebuilding persisted. Contact with holy peoples, places or things will not make a man holy (*cf.* 2 Tim. 2:22). By realizing the true state of affairs they would be ready to take the first step, showing the reality of their repentance by their work, which would be followed by immediate blessing (vv. 16-19).

2:10-15 The reality and realization of sin

Failure to free themselves from dead works had brought failure just as contact with a dead body

(failed life) rendered anyone touching it unclean (Nu. 19:13). Sin is contagious in the human race and can continue to be infectious even when a holy life has begun.

11 *Ask the priests*; their ritual had been continued amid the building activities. This question is insufficient evidence to class Haggai himself as a ritualist; rather it identifies him with the earlier prophets who upheld the traditional law. 13 *Unclean* may well have been applied by the newly returned exiles to the hostile Samaritans and to those locals who had maintained a ritual at the altar set up in the ruins (the dead thing; *cf.* Ezr. 4-5) which to them would be imperfect. Haggai makes it clear that it refers to the people, nation and work (v. 14). 15 *Stone . . . upon a stone* refers either to the present reconstruction or back to the earlier work begun 16 years before. If to the latter, the following verses (15, 16) hark back to the perilous state of the economy discussed in 1:9-11.

2:16-19 The need for repentance and work

17 *Blight* and *mildew* were given as signs that the Law had been broken (*cf.* Dt. 28:22; Am. 4:9). *Yet you did not return to me* renders a difficult text in the light of Am. 4:9. 18 *The twenty-fourth day* picks up v. 10 to emphasize *from this day onward* (*cf.* vv. 15, 19), a phrase customary in drawing up ancient legal documents involving new pledges. *The day that the foundation . . . was laid* may well relate to the ritual act to mark a new start (as Ezr. 3:10). If this and the date given in this verse are accepted there need be no clash with the Ezra account. More than one foundation ritual was commonly employed for temples (J. S. Wright, *Building of the Second Temple*, 1958, p. 17). It is likely that the first marked the subterranean foundation-laying and the second the first building at ground level as in ancient Mesopotamian practice. This phrase could also be a simple reference to work continued on the foundations laid by Sheshbazzar (*cf.* Ezr. 5:16).

2:20-23 THE PREDICTION TO THE PRINCE

A special message is sent to Zerubbabel, heir to the throne of David and a link in the line to Jesus Christ (*cf.* Mt. 1:13). It tells of the dominion of the Lord of hosts (v. 21), already the subject of the second prophecy (vv. 6, 7), and of the choice of the Judean prince to bear the authority of kingship (signet).

Some have criticized this section as it bears the same date as the preceding prophecy, repeats 2:6, 7 and does not seem to correspond to Zc. 6:11 which describes the coronation of Joshua the high priest as 'Messiah'. But this involves the unlikely assumptions that no more than one prophetic message could be given in a single day or a phrase be used by more than one prophet (Is. 13:13; Joel 3:16; *cf.* Heb. 12:26). The reclothing and coronation of Joshua is a separate incident emphasizing the priestly function of Messiah (J. Davies, *Princeton Theological Review* 18, 1920, pp. 256–268) which in Christ was to be combined with the royal powers here vested in Zerubbabel. The latter's rule was real though little is known about it, as is the case of others in the Messianic line. He was closely associated with Joshua (Hg. 1:1, 12; 2:4). Both were 'typical' (so Zc. 3:8). There are thus no grounds for asserting that Zerubbabel's designation as Messiah is a case of unfulfilled prophecy.

20 For the *second time* in a single day Haggai has to speak, this time to an individual. *To Haggai*. When compared with the earlier 'by Haggai' (1:1, 3; 2:1, 10) this is slender evidence for the view that demands a change in the role from prophet to teacher. **21** Once again God will intervene in human affairs (*shake the heavens and the earth*, so v. 6). As the former promise of the same action (v. 6) resulted in the universal recognition of the Temple, so now all would see in the overthrow of Judah's opponents Zerubbabel's authority continuing the Davidic line as a new, independent and authoritative leader. **23** Zerubbabel would be recognized publicly. The *signet ring* was the official mark of supreme authority as well as of the pledge and favour of the Lord towards His own people (*cf*. Ct. 8:6). The imagery of the ring had been used of Zerubbabel's grandfather (Je. 22:24). While Haggai may have foreseen the violent end of the Persian Empire, it has been suggested that the silence concerning the fate of Zerubbabel might mean that he was subsequently demoted by the Persians for his aspirations of independence. Against this, Haggai was himself still active when the Temple was completed (*cf*. Ezr. 6:14).

These brief prophecies close on a spiritual note. All human activity which is to build and not pull down must be the result of divine action in that He 'will take . . . will make . . . has chosen'. As Haggai's contemporary wrote, 'This is the word of the Lord to Zerubbabel: Not by might, nor by power, but by my Spirit, says the Lord of hosts' (Zc. 4:6).

D. J. WISEMAN

Zechariah

INTRODUCTION

THE BOOK

Luther described the book of Zechariah as 'the quintessence of the prophets'. This term, from ancient philosophy, was used of a heavenly substance latent in all things, and so has come to mean the essential nature of a thing, the refined extract, the pure and perfect form. Allowing for a modicum of overstatement in Luther's estimate, it remains true that Zechariah exhibits many links with earlier prophecy. Thus, the four horns in 1:18 reflect Dn. 7:7, *etc.*; the measuring line in 2:1 reminds us of Je. 31:39 and Ezk. 40:3; the brand plucked from the burning in 3:2 of Am. 4:11; the seven eyes in 4:10 of 2 Ch. 16:9; the call to righteousness in 7:9, 10 of the language of the book of Exodus (*e.g.* 22:21–24); the penalty of scattering in 7:14 of Lv. 26:33 and Dt. 4:27, 28; 28:36, 37; the prospect of Jerusalem in 8:3–13 of Is. 2:2–4; 54:1–17; Je. 3:17, 18; 50:4, 5; and the oracles against surrounding nations in 9:1ff. of Am. 1:2 – 2:3. The promise of restoration in 1:17; 2:10 recalls Is. 40:1; Ho. 2:23; Mi. 7:14; and the living waters flowing from Jerusalem in 14:8 recall the new Jerusalem of Ezekiel's theocracy (Ezk. 40–48, especially 47:1ff.). As Zechariah claims in 1:1–7 and 7:1ff., he is in the strict prophetical succession, and his pure Hebrew echoes the language of his predecessors in the sacred office. Zechariah's far-reaching acquaintance with all parts of the OT was due to his priestly duty of interpreter of the sacred writings.

The second and third sections of the book (chs. 9–11, 12–14), consisting of a series of predictions, must be read in the light of the NT as Messianic, either directly or indirectly. The Apocalypse of the NT is coloured by images taken from this book.

THE PROPHET

The title 'prophet' in Zc. 1:1 comes at the end of his genealogy and belongs naturally to him as the chief person named. Brackets are really required after the names Zechariah and Iddo, contrary to the Hebrew punctuation, however, which connects the title with Iddo, his grandfather.

We know nothing about Zechariah's life except what is revealed here. His ancestor, Iddo (Ezr. 5:1; 6:14), head of a returned priestly family (Ne. 12:4), was part of the captivity led back by Zerubbabel and Joshua (*cf.* Ne. 12:16). The inference is that Zechariah was both a priest and a prophet.

Evidently Zechariah's father died while he was still young, so that he was reared by the head of the clan and brought to Jerusalem while a boy. The suggestion is often repeated that the reference to Berechiah, his father, is an insertion here from Is. 8:2 (Jeberechiah), but this is unnecessary. The link between Zechariah and Berechiah persists in Mt. 23:35 (*cf.* Lk. 11:51) which certainly points to the fact that the combination of the two names was a familiar one. Does it also suggest that Zechariah was actually martyred, and thus throw light on the mysterious reference to the smitten shepherd in Zc. 13:7?

The prophet's name means 'Jah remembers', and was a common one in the OT, being found twenty-eight times. He probably returned from exile with his grandparents in 537 BC and grew up in the rampartless city while the Temple foundations were being laid and while the building operations were in abeyance. In 520 BC, in company with his fellow-prophet Haggai, he sought to arouse the remnant of the returned exiles to recommence the work. The 'man with a measuring line' in 2:1ff. may be his own image projected into the night vision.

The peculiar nature of these night visions in chs. 1–8 marks a transition stage between the older type of prediction and national diagnosis, and what is called apocalyptic, with its lurid portrayal of the future in terms of catastrophic imagery. Affinities have been sought in the Akkadian oracular dreams of Ashurbanipal (*ANET*, 451), but the links are slender. The prophet in fact always retained his self-consciousness and remained alert to question the angelic medium concerning the significance of the events revealed.

HISTORICAL BACKGROUND

The period covered by chs. 1–8 is that of Ezr. 5 and 6. In the first year of Cyrus the Great of Persia, a decree had permitted the return of the Jews from exile in Babylon, with a licence to rebuild the Temple of the Lord at Jerusalem; *cf.* 2 Ch. 36:22f.; Ezr. 1:1f.; Is. 44:28. Zerubbabel, son of Shealtiel and legal heir to the throne of David, led the return; *cf.* Ezr. 3:8; 5:16 (where he is named Sheshbazzar; see further on Ezr. 1:8; Hg. 1:1, 12; Mt. 1:12; Lk. 3:27. In 1 Ch. 3:19 he is called the son of Pedaiah (son of Jeconiah, son of Jehoiakim). Shealtiel probably died without male issue, and his brother Pedaiah (in accordance with Dt. 25:5–10) had taken his deceased brother's wife (*cf.* Je. 22:18; 28:30).

A feeble response had hindered the work of

rebuilding and local opposition had also delayed it. The two prophets provoked the people to renewed activity and the Temple site was completed. Unlike Solomon's Temple, and the Tabernacle previously, the new edifice did not contain the Shekinah glory (*cf.* Ex. 40:34; 1 Ki. 8:10, 11; 2 Ch. 5:13f.; Hg. 2:7-9). The references in Zechariah to glory (*e.g.* 2:5, 8, 10) may be due to this omission. There is instead a Messianic significance to the term; *cf.* Hg. 2:7, 8.

TEXT AND CANON

Ecclus. 49:10 (*c.* 180 BC) refers to 'the twelve prophets', and probably implies that the prophetic canon was already fixed by that date. According to C. D. Ginsburg, the order of the twelve is not the same in every MS, nor in the earliest editions of the printed Hebrew Bible. It is, however, an essential preliminary to the subject-matter of the next section to note that in them all, chs. 9-14 appear as an essential part of Zechariah, separate from the roll of Malachi. There is no MS evidence that they were ever considered to be an addition from an unknown source. For fuller references to the Talmudim see W. H. Lowe, *Hebrew Students' Commentary*, 1882, p. xvii. No doubt was ever cast on the genuineness of the last six chapters by the Rabbis. The language is good classical Hebrew, free from Aramaisms which might have been expected in a returned exile, but which may have been avoided on purpose to show the spiritual lineage with the former prophets. The text is obscure in parts and there may be minor displacements (*e.g.* 13:7-9) and possibly an occasional gloss. An obscure text, however, is not necessarily a corrupt one. In textual studies the harder reading is often to be preferred, in view of the tendency of scribes to simplify the rendering.

THE COMPILATION

The prevailing tendency among scholars is to divide Zc. 1-8 from Zc. 9-11 and 12-14, and to introduce each section with the title, 'An Oracle'. *Cf.* Zc. 9:1; 12:1; Mal. 1:1. The night visions and their two appendices (2:6-13; 3:6-10) are thus severed from the verbal predictions. The first scholar to question the genuineness of chs. 9-14 was Mede, the great exponent of prophecy, who died in 1638. He questioned it on the ground that Mt. 27:9 (evidently from Zc. 11:12, 13) ascribed it to Jeremiah. Also the pre-exilic allusions in chs. 9-11 convinced him of a different authorship. No-one today argues for a pre-exilic authorship, however. E. J. Young (*Introduction to the Old Testament*, 1958, pp. 278ff.) gives an interesting account of the history of interpretation and shows that scholarship is divided on the issue. In view of the great variety of dates proposed for the different strands within the section 9-14, no confidence can be placed in any one of the proposed solutions. This particular period of Jewish history

is meagre in data and our knowledge of it is limited. It is hazardous to be dogmatic. P. R. Ackroyd (*Peake's Commentary on the Bible*, 1962, p. 651) says, 'It may be wondered whether the attempt to date the allusions is the most useful method of approach.'

Three main arguments are employed against the unity of authorship. First, it is argued that there is a different atmosphere in chs. 1-8 from that of 9-11 and 12-14. The first section is concerned with the rebuilding of the Temple and the restoration of the nation. The second and third sections face a different situation altogether. Neighbouring peoples, a discredited prophetic institution, and discord between Judah and Jerusalem fill the canvas. Second, 9:13 refers to the sons of Javan (Greece) as the dominant power in the Middle East, whereas in Zechariah's day Persia predominated. Third, the changed form of the prophecy points to a later era.

In reply, traditional defenders of Zechariah's authorship affirm that difference of style, language and form can be fairly explained on two grounds. *a.* When chs. 9-14 were written, the situation had changed radically from that of 520 BC. Also Zechariah was older. His message, therefore, was aligned to face a new age. *b.* Visions are bound to take a different structure from verbal predictions. Van Hoonacker in 1908 argued that the subject determines the nature of the media to be employed. L. G. Rignell (*Die Nachtgesichte des Sacharja*, 1950) argued that Zechariah prophesied at three different times and was also editor of his own work. Literature, like music, can differ in form and yet emerge from the same mind. Even within the same composition changes of form may be devised to convey the complex features of the work, but subtle links will be found to unify the whole.

These are not lacking in Zechariah. *E.g.*, *a.* an expression is found in both parts of the book, which only elsewhere occurs in Ezk. 35:7: literally, 'from passing through and from returning', 7:14; 9:8. *b.* The formula 'says the Lord' is common to the whole book, appearing in 10:12, 12:1, 4; 13:2, 7, 8 as well as throughout part one. *c.* 'The eyes of the Lord' occurs in 4:10 (*cf.* 3:9); 9:8; 12:4. *d.* 'Lord of hosts' as a title of deity occurs in 1:6, 12; 2:9; 9:15; 10:3; 13:2. *e.* The active verb *yāšaḇ* ('to sit', 'dwell') is used in the passive sense in 2:4; 7:7; 12:6; 14:10, and rarely elsewhere. *f. Cf.* 2:10 with 9:9 for resemblance of language and ideas. In both parts of Zechariah there is a fullness of language as the writer lingers on a word, phrase or idea; *e.g.* 6:13; 9:5; 12:4. *g.* Five sections to a verse are rare in Hebrew, yet in both 6:13 and 9:5, 7 this feature is found. *h.* In both parts no mention is made of any earthly ruler except the Messiah.

The strand that runs through the whole like a thread is the habit of incorporating quotations from the other books of the OT. Suggestive images, dominant ideas, particular words all echo a single mind. The unity is thus deeper than appears at first sight. These are not proofs in themselves, but they are pointers towards the reasonableness of accepting the MS evidence of the unity of authorship. The lack of agreement in critical analysis shows up the difficulty of providing a satisfactory alternative.

The strongest argument for post-exilic authorship is the reference to the sons of Javan (Greece) in 9:13. 'From about 520 BC onwards the Greeks in Asia Minor were a continual source of trouble to Darius, and in 500 BC a great Ionian revolt occurred. In 499 BC the Athenians burnt the Persian stronghold of Sardis, and in 490 BC and 480 BC, the Persians, in full-scale invasion of Greece, were defeated at Marathon and Salamis' (NBD, art. 'Zechariah, Book of'). The prophet could have seen Greece as a menace to the Persian Empire, and accordingly it fits Zechariah's day as well as any later time. Indeed the defeat of Greece is also foreseen, in company with other nations, in the purpose of God.

THE CHARACTER OF GOD

The prophet's messages to the people, like every sermon, were conditioned by a particular situation. Except by inference these situations are unknown to us now. The compilers of the Canon preserved these utterances as authentic words of God because they felt such messages were readily applicable to a wider audience and to new needs in the worshipping community. Every truth in the book hinges on the character of God revealed to the prophet and portrayed by him in his declarations.

The Lord had a supreme purpose in making Jerusalem the centre of the world and the city of His presence (Zc. 1:1–6; 8:7). But this goal could not be achieved without His people being prepared for such bliss. The prophet, therefore, had to warn men of the punishability of sin and to promise deliverance to the penitent (cf. 3:2, 9; 5:3, 4, 8). His control extended to all nations and to the whole of creation (cf. 8:23; 12:1). Ultimately all nations will recognize Him as King (cf. 2:13; 6:1–8; 14:16–21).

His will is communicated in a variety of ways. His Word is given through angelic agents, oracular media and the pressure of a burden upon a sensitive spirit. God's Spirit is the controlling agency and the energizing force (cf. 4:6). His character is just and no ritual observance can appease His righteousness (cf. 7:5–14). Yet due seemliness in worship is required (cf. 2:13; 14:16–21). Acceptance of man by the Lord of hosts is dependent upon repentance, and the cleansing fires of judgment and grace and the divine promise to bless (cf. 3:2; 12:10; 13:1–9).

The Lord's purpose is centred on the Messiah. In part one He is lowly (cf. 3:8, 'my servant'), of Davidic origin (cf. 6:12, 'the Branch'; see also Is. 4:2; Je. 23:5; cf. Is. 11:1). In part two He follows the Davidic pattern as Shepherd (cf. 11:4; 12:10; 13:7) and as the King (cf. 9:9; 14:9).

The early Christians saw a fulfilment of some of these predictions in the life and passion of Jesus (cf. 11:13 with Mt. 27:9). His ministry was patterned on these oracles (cf. 13:7 with Mt. 26:31). He also provided them with the key to unlock the Messianic secret and to interpret the allusions in Scripture to His own Person (cf. Lk. 24:44, 45). Other links are to be found between this book and the NT. Additional to the bare reference to Zechariah in Mt. 23:35, a wide range of apocalyptic imagery is quarried from his book (cf. Mt. 24:30 with Zc. 12:12; Mt. 24:36 and Mk. 13:32 with Zc. 14:7; Mt. 26:15 with Zc. 11:12). In addition Acts 1:11 must be linked with Zc. 14:4, and 1 Thes. 3:13 with Zc. 14:5; cf. Jude 14.

John in the Apocalypse also drew upon this source for material (cf. Zc. 1:8 with Rev. 6:4, 5; Zc. 1:18, 19, 21 with Rev. 17:3, 16; Zc. 3:4 with Rev. 7:14; Zc. 3:9 with Rev. 5:6; Zc. 4:2 with Rev. 1:12; 11:4; note the phrase, 'Sir, you know', in Rev. 7:14 as an echo of Zc. 4:13; cf. Zc. 6:2, 3 with Rev. 6:2; Zc. 6:11 and 9:16 with Rev. 6:2; Zc. 12:10 with Rev. 1:7; Zc. 14:7 with Rev. 21:23, 25; Zc. 14:8 with Rev. 22:1; Zc. 14:11 with Rev. 22:3). The ultimate fulfilment of many of these realities lies in the unknown future, but it is a day 'known to the Lord' (cf. 14:7).

ANALYSIS OF CONTENTS

Zechariah belonged to the prophetic succession (1:1). In the prologue (1:2–6) the lesson of history is spelled out and becomes the divine word to the returned exiles.

Then follow eight visions (1:7 – 6:15) to portray the divine zeal for the rebuilding of Zion. The Lord has intervened in the events of the times to deliver His own people from their oppressors, and to resettle them in their own land (1:7–21). Zion will be rebuilt (2:1–13) and the Temple restored with a consecrated high priest (3:1–5). He will typify the Messiah, whose special name here is the Branch, to signify both His humble human origin and His supernatural growth

(3:6–10). Israel will be like the golden candlestick in the Temple, a lampstand for the divine light to shine into the darkness of the world (4:1–14). In order to achieve this position the nation must be purged of guilt by its recognition and its removal (5:1–11). These two visions of the flying scroll and the women in the barrel are linked with the chariots of the Lord (6:1–8) by a key phrase 'going forth'. The heavenly patrol represents the divine control of the nations. The section concludes with a symbolic crowning of Joshua and a further oracle concerning the Branch (6:9–15).

In the second section (7:1 – 8:23) the same

themes are covered in a different way. The lessons to be learned from the past history of the nation are the material for the prophetic word of exhortation, followed by a tenfold promise of restoration, which has remarkable parallels to the preceding chapters.

In the third section (9:1 – 14:21) the Messianic theme is further elaborated. Once again the neighbouring nations come under divine judgment (9:1–8) and this is aptly concluded with a lyric on the coming of Zion's King (9:9–17). The scattered Israelites are recalled to their own land (10:1–12) and a taunt song is taken up against their enemies (11:1–3). This is extended into an allegory against worthless rulers (11:4–17). An oracle for Judah and Jerusalem outlines the nature of deliverance after a period of setback (12:1–9) followed by the purification of the city to make it holy, and of the land to make it fit for God's presence (12:10 – 13:6). Then a mysterious oracle is uttered concerning the smitten Shepherd which the Gospels link with Jesus Christ and His passion (13:7-9). Like most prophetic narratives the last chapter is concerned with the final rout of Zion's foes, and the arrival of their King to dwell among a dedicated people (14:1–21).

COMMENTARY

1:1-6 THE PROLOGUE

The opening message is an appeal for obedience to God. The people of God find security when they put God first. The flagging zeal of the returned exiles was a clear symptom of a deterioration in their spiritual condition (cf. Hg. 1). Zechariah's remonstration warned them that a great work claimed their allegiance, with no time left for postponement, or they would commit the same folly as their forefathers.

1 This may be editorial framework. Emphasis is placed on the date, October–November 520 BC, 18 years after the return of the first contingent of exiles from Babylon (cf. 2 Ch. 36:22; Ezr. 1:1; Is. 44:28). *Darius* is Darius I (522–486 BC). *Eighth month*; i.e. between Hg. 2:1–9 (seventh month) and Hg. 2:10–23 (ninth month). **4** *Former prophets* implies a succession of witnesses. 'God buries His workmen but continues His work.' The divine Word has thus an enduring quality, and its fulfilment in every age confirms its truth.

1:7 – 6:15 EIGHT VISIONS
(AND THEIR TWO APPENDICES)

Before launching upon the admittedly complex details of these visions, it is advantageous to try to chart the over-all course which they follow. They fall into two groups: visions 1–3 (1:7 – 2:13), and visions 4–8 (3:1 – 6:8). The first group is focused on Zion and the future glory which the Lord will bring to it; the second group is focused on the Messiah as Priest-King and on the various steps by which the Lord will bring about the promised glory. The sequence is as follows: the Lord will return in blessing to Zion (1:7–17); its opponents will be overthrown (1:18–21); and the city, indwelt and guarded by the Lord Himself, will extend its unwalled boundaries (2:1–13). But if this is to come to pass and the Lord is really to dwell with His people, then sin must be dealt with. Hence there is need of a perfect priestly mediator, the Messianic Branch (3:1–10), who, being King as well as Priest, is the complete means of blessing to the people (4:1–14). His work, likewise, is total: sinners are purged out of the land (5:1–4), wickedness itself is removed (5:5–11), and, in a final confrontation between God and the world-system in which wickedness has found a resting-place, evil is overthrown and God's wrath appeased (6:1–8). The symbolic crowning of the Priest-King (6:9–15) looks forward to the consummation of the kingdom of God.

1:7–17 The first vision

The call to repentance is followed by a series of night visions, all apparently seen in one night, early in 519 BC. They are not direct from the Lord, in the sense that an angel mediates them and interprets them to the prophet. The theme of the first vision is the zeal of the Lord for the rebuilding of Jerusalem. The earth was now at rest after the people and their land had enjoyed a compulsory sabbath of 70 years.

8 *A man riding upon a red horse* is probably the angel of the Lord (cf. v. 11; see also Introduction to Exodus, p. 116). In this scene, enacted in the valley bottom, he is the protector of God's people. Aspects of the divine providence are represented in the colours of the heavenly scouts. *Red* depicts battle and bloodshed (cf. Rev. 6:4); *white* represents victory and peace (cf. Rev. 6:2); *sorrel*, i.e. reddish brown, is the aftermath of confusion in the unsettled period after the end of hostilities (cf. Rev. 6:5–8). **9ff.** The prophet is puzzled by the vision. The interpretation fits the contemporary situation. Darius's Empire was being shaken by revolt, and only a temporary peace had been secured at that moment. **12** *Seventy years* may be a round number, or the period which expired with the return of the exiles (see on 2 Ch. 36:21). **16** *Thus says the Lord.* Four years later when the Temple was rebuilt, v. 16a was fulfilled. The rebuilding of the city by Nehemiah in 445 BC saw the fulfilment of v. 16b. **17a** This prosperity waited until the victorious reigns of the Maccabean princes in 165 BC (see *NBD*, art. 'Maccabees', p. 762), while **17b** is Messianic and awaits realization. Chs. 9–14 are thus anticipated.

1:18–21 The second vision

The end of heathen supremacy is foretold. Four horns, perhaps on the heads of four beasts, symbolize the power of the nations which have scattered Israel and Judah. They are frightened away by four craftsmen, who may represent the Temple workmen. This vision was an additional assurance that God's purpose would be fulfilled. The scattering experience was completed, and now nothing could hinder God's people in their task of restoration.

18 *Four*. Many attempts have been made to identify four historical foes, *e.g.* Assyria, Babylon, Medo-Persia, and Greece (see, *e.g.*, C. H. H. Wright, *Zechariah and his Prophecies*, 1879), but possibly the numeral is symbolic rather than danger 'on every side', just as we speak of the 'four' points of the compass. The people of God are ever surrounded by a menacing world. *Horns* are symbolic of power. **20** *Four smiths*, or craftsmen, indicate that the victory of the people of God would be achieved by peaceful means as they responded to the call to engage in the craftsman's work of Temple-building (*cf.* Hg. 1:8, 13; 2:4–9, 15–19). As the danger had been 'fourfold' so the remedy is 'fourfold'; the divine strategy is sufficient to meet the peril from every quarter.

2:1–13 The third vision

1–5 This follows directly from the first two visions. The foreshadowing of the city yet to be is provided in the rebuilding and restoration of Jerusalem. Josephus regarded the building works of Herod Agrippa as its literal fulfilment. But the final chapters of the book envisage a more glorious future with Zion as the central metropolis of the world. In the first part of the vision the angel stops the young man from measuring the old boundaries of the city because the new limits will overspill the ancient landmarks. Within an all-embracing divine omnipotence, its inhabitants will dwell safely. The Shekinah glory that departed with the deportation of the people into exile in 586 BC had now returned in some measure to the city to dwell there, and to make it a holy abode once more (*cf.* Ezk. 11:22, 23; 43:1–9; 48:35).

6–13 The second part of the vision is a lyric poem of triumph. A summons is issued to the Jews still in Babylon to return to their own land. Haste is urged lest they should be engulfed in the doom of Babylon and also that they might share in the promised prosperity of Jerusalem.

8 *After his glory sent me.* The translation is difficult because the Hebrew reads simply 'after glory' (*cf.* RV). This could be the war-cry of the Lord for His host (*cf.* Jdg. 5:14, RV). The speaker is the Messiah, who is sent to the Jews, to whom pertains the *glory* (*cf.* Rom. 9:4), to be their Protector and to perfect their salvation. The *glory* of Zechariah's time was the restoration of Jerusalem, mentioned in v. 5, which foreshadowed a greater glory to come in the Person of the Messiah. *After* in this case means in search of the glory. The phrase *sent me* is repeated in v. 9 to emphasize the importance of the commission. *The apple of his eye* (*cf.* Ps. 17:8). From every angle the pupil of the eye is safely guarded against attack. This is symbolic of God's protection of His own from all hostile powers that menace this precious possession. Others, however, think that the pronoun refers to the enemies of Israel and means that they endanger their own safety by hostility toward the elect.

9 *Then you will know.* The requital of their oppressors, as instruments of His chastisement, is proof of the prophet's mission. *Shake my hand* is the attitude of threatening (*cf.* Is. 10:32). **10** *Daughter of Zion.* Cf. 9:9 for a similar term, and evidence of the stylistic links between the three parts of the prophecy. **11** *Many nations . . . in that day* also anticipates the later chapters of the book (*e.g.* 8:22; 14:16). **12** *The holy land* is used only here in Scripture, although the idea is found elsewhere (*cf.* Is. 11:9; 27:13). **13** *Be silent* (*cf.* Hab. 2:20) is an impressive announcement of the advent of the Lord that implies more than the ordinary divine activity in history. He has invested Himself to partake in a holy war on behalf of His people (*cf.* 14:4ff.). *His holy dwelling* is heaven itself and not the Temple in Jerusalem.

3:1–10 The fourth vision

From the promises of a glorious future for the city and people of God, Zechariah turns to the means by which they are to be achieved. God will raise up a perfect priestly Mediator, of whom Joshua and his fellow-priests are a foreshadowing (*cf.* 3:8). This is followed by the vision of the golden lampstand (4:1–14), which symbolized the bestowal of the power of the Spirit of God upon His people to spread the light of the gospel throughout the earth. They need first to be purged of all iniquity (5:1–11) before the universal sovereignty of the Lord can be acknowledged (6:1–8). The setting up of this Messianic kingdom is symbolized by the crowning of Joshua (6:9–15).

In the fourth vision Joshua is vindicated and the promise of the Messianic Branch is made. The high priest probably signifies the chosen representative of the nation, whose misfortunes are due to a super-human adversary, as well as to their own ceremonial defilement. This uncleanness may also be due to the people's failure to rebuild the Temple (*cf.* Hg. 2:14), or to the limitations of the priesthood (*cf.* Mal. 3:1–4). The Targum interprets it as the sin of marrying foreign wives, which characterized the period 60 years later (*cf.* Ezr. 10:18). Joshua is arraigned like a criminal before the angel of the Lord. In the presence of supernatural witnesses the adversary accuses him. Joshua was laden with personal iniquity (v. 4) as well as the guilt of the land (*cf.* 5:6). His pardon, therefore, had to be both personal and representative.

2 *Satan.* W. E. Barnes (*Zechariah, CBSC,* 1917, *in loc.*) treats this person as no more than a prosecutor, acting under orders from the Judge, in the sacred court. The use of the article (Heb. 'the Satan') shows that it is not a proper name, but the fact that Satan is rebuked by the Lord implies that his designs are contrary to the divine purpose. *A brand.* Perhaps a proverbial expression. Israel as a nation had been rescued from the furnace of Babylon (*cf.* Am. 4:11) to become a torch to enlighten the nations. This idea is further enlarged under the figure of the lampstand in the next vision. **4** *Rich apparel* signifies the white robe of cleanliness, and the plural in the Hebrew points to the different articles of dress in the robe of state. **5** The *clean turban* is to the high priest what the headstone is to the Temple, its crowning glory and the evidence of its renovation. Atonement has been accepted by God for His people (*cf.* Ex. 28:36ff.; Is. 62:3; Zc. 14:20). *And I said.* The prophet intervenes, enthusiastic to see the complete establishment of a full and acceptable priesthood.

6, 7 *Enjoined.* The angel of the Lord gives a solemn charge to Joshua concerning his personal holiness and his faithful discharge of his sacred office. Consequent upon his obedience, he is promised the principal charge of the rebuilt Temple, and the prospect of access to the heavenly council. Like the angels he will be a co-worker in the fulfilment of the divine purposes for Zion and Israel. Peaceful security would lead to settled conditions and prosperity. Perhaps there is also the suggestion of a rejuvenated earth like the pictures in 8:12; 9:17; 14:6. **8** *Men of good omen.* Joshua and his fellow-priests who *sit before* him as subordinates are those for whom the miracle of renovation has been wrought. They thus become a pledge of the approach of Messiah's kingdom in which the perfect priestly mediation and reconciliation will be achieved. *My servant, the Branch.* This is a technical term in the prophets to portray the coming Davidic Prince (*cf.* Is. 4:2-6; Je. 23:3-5; 33:14-26; Zc. 6:9-15; Is. 11:1 uses a different word, but involves the same idea). From obscurity He would arise to become the builder of the Temple, and combine in Himself the offices of King and Priest. Joshua knew that he could not be the Branch because he was not of the Davidic line. Zerubbabel, the civic head, was not present, neither was he a priest, so he did not qualify for the office.

9 *A single stone with seven facets* (lit. 'seven eyes') is another Messianic title. Whereas 'the Branch' is the kingly-priestly Messiah (mainly in relation to His human lineage with David), 'the Stone' with its seven engraved eyes (*cf.* Ex. 28:11, 12, 36-38; Ps. 118:22; Is. 28:16) suggests His divine omniscience (*cf.* the eye as the organ of knowledge, 2 Ch. 16:9; Ps. 94:9). Thus as the perfect Priest, endowed with divine knowledge (*cf.* Is. 53:11), He brings about the perfect cleansing (v. 9b). *Seven facets,* literally 'seven

eyes', are wrought on the stone, and one of this character was actually found at Gezer. The same general symbolism appears again in Rev. 5:6. The sacred number 'seven', signifying completeness and perfection (*cf.* Rev. 1:4; 3:1) here depicts God's all-knowing character and all-inclusive rule, while the 'eyes' (*cf.* Rev. 1:14; 4:6b) speak of God's watchfulness over the Temple, its worshippers and the events yet to come. A single day anticipates the making of a complete atonement (*cf.* Heb. 10:12) and the full enjoyment of its benefits in the regeneration of all things (*cf.* Zc. 14:7).

4:1-14 The lampstand and the two olive trees

The deep significance of this vision is implied by the manner in which it was brought to the prophet's notice. He was aroused out of his sleep by the question from the angel, *What do you see?* The object that attracted his notice was a golden lampstand.

The structure of the lampstand resembled that which stood in the Tabernacle (*cf.* Ex. 25:31-40), but certain features were different. Those common to both are omitted in the description, and only the peculiar features are mentioned here. In Solomon's Temple ten candlesticks (*cf.* 1 Ki. 7:49) of the Tabernacle type were provided, and were probably deported into captivity (*cf.* Je. 52:19). In the second Temple only one such lampstand was used (*cf.* 1 Macc. 1:21; 4:49, 50; Josephus, *Antiquities* xiv.4.4). Each one was similar in form to the Mosaic pattern if the Arch of Titus can be relied upon for accurate details, but they were not identical with it (*cf.* C. H. H. Wright, *op. cit.,* p. 82).

There is a close connection between the work of rebuilding the Temple and the ministry of the congregation of the Lord as a spiritual light in the world around them. This characterized the NT church also (*cf.* Mt. 5:14-16; Mk. 4:21, 22; Lk. 12:35; Jn. 8:12; Phil. 2:15; Rev. 1:20; 2:5). The church of the old covenant and of the new, purified by divine grace, should show forth God's glory throughout the nations.

The peculiar features in the vision point beyond the 'earthly sanctuary' (*cf.* Heb. 9:1) to the reality it foreshadowed. No priest was required to trim the wicks nor to supply the reservoir with oil, which came directly from the two fruit-bearing trees, positioned on the right and left sides of the golden candlestick.

More than God's providence is expressed by the imagery of the vision. There is an advance in thought from the continual watchfulness of the all-seeing God (*cf.* the association of the seven lamps with the seven eyes of the Lord in vv. 2, 10b with vv. 12, 13, 14) to the coming of the Messiah.

The answer of the interpreting angel is intentionally obscure because the two mysterious agents are Joshua and Zerubbabel, who as Spirit-filled men convey blessing from God to church and state, and are a type of the Messiah as Priest and King. These 'two anointed ones' thus replace the ministers of the sanctuary as a sign of Messiah's coming ministry. It envisages the Light of the world shining through lesser lights amid the darkness that covers the nations (*cf.* Is. 9:2).

2 *Seven lips*; a curious, fantastic detail which causes problems in exegesis. Such things are possible only in dreams. The seven is repeated in MT for emphasis and corresponds to the seven eyes of the Lord (v. 10). The lips are the 'nozzles to contain the wicks, rather than "pipes" as RV' (P. R. Ackroyd, *op. cit.*, p. 648). **6** *Not by might* (RV mg., 'an army'). Possibly there had been some loose talk about a revolt against Darius. The reference could also be to the opposition encountered from local groups of different nationality (*cf.* Ezr. 5). **7** *Grace, grace to it* may be an exclamation of admiration from the multitude at the completion of the Temple, with the implication that divine favour had enabled them to complete the task. **10** *Whoever has despised the day of small things* is a caution against a human failing. An answer is implied in the question, which amounts to a prohibition, 'Let none despise it', since God does not scorn meagre beginnings. All such work proceeds under the watchful eye of the Lord God. Superhuman energy is promised to Joshua and Zerubbabel for the finishing of this tremendous undertaking.

14 It is a matter of some difficulty to decide, throughout this vision, what is the source and the direction of flow of the oil. It would seem more natural to take the two trees as the source, therefore standing for the all-providing Lord, and the *two anointed* (the 'two branches' of v. 12) would thus be the kingly and priestly rulers mediating the Spirit of God, via the central reservoir, to the people, the seven lamps, shining into the world. It is difficult to see, however, why trees, rooted as they are on earth, could well symbolize the divine source. Elsewhere the planted tree is either the godly man (*cf.* Ps. 1) or the established kingdom (*cf.* Ps. 80:8ff.). Maybe, therefore, the central reservoir stands for the self-sufficient God, the eternal, self-replenishing fount of life. The trees represent the people of God securely established on earth, and the lamps represent them in their function as witnesses. There are two trees in order to reflect the two distinct Messianic functions by which they are sustained: the priestly work of cleansing and the kingly work of ruling, and in this the existing functionaries, Joshua and Zerubbabel, foreshadow the single, Messianic royal Priest who was yet to be.

5:1–11 The sixth and seventh visions: the flying scroll and the large barrel

The two visions together take up the theme of 3:9b and follow naturally after the cleansing of the high priest as the nation's representative (3:4). The flying scroll appears to represent the main provisions of the law, both moral and religious, and symbolizes the divine standard of holiness. Its flight in the heavens shows from which quarter judgment comes and also the speed of its execution. Two particular sins are condemned, one on each side of the scroll, according to the force of the Hebrew. The curse lights upon every thief and perjuror, theft and lying being typical sins of a poor community (*cf.* 7:9, 10; 8:17). So penetrating and permanent is the penalty that it enters and consumes the very structure of the house of the wrongdoer as though the building were defiled by leprosy (*cf.* Lv. 14:45).

The large barrel (*ephah*) with its leaden lid contains a woman who is the personification of wickedness. As she tries to escape, the angel thrusts her back into the barrel. Two windborne women transport the barrel with its contents into the land of Shinar, S Babylonia, where mankind first organized a revolt against God (*cf.* Gn. 11:2ff.). The living power of evil must yet be banished from Israel, and this operation can successfully be achieved only by the power of God.

In the sixth vision the land was purged of social evils, but in the seventh of apostasy. 'Sin not only finds a natural home in Babylon, but worship is paid to it' (*IB*, p. 107).

6 *Iniquity*; RSV accepts LXX text. MT has 'their eye', *i.e.* their appearance, which is a better reading. Two interpretations have been suggested for the phrase. 'Their desire', the longing eye towards the female, as the inclination towards wickedness of which she is the symbol. Many prefer to take the weights and measures as typifying the sometimes abused (*cf.* Am. 8:5) fondness for commerce which increased during the period in captivity and which had dominated them ever since the exile. *Ephah* is a measure containing over 7 gallons. There may be a play on words here (Heb. *'āpâ*, 'flying', and *'ēpâ*). **8** *Wickedness* was also applied to Athaliah in 2 Ch. 24:7. **9** *Stork* is a migratory bird with powerful wings, and capable of flying long distances. There may be another play on words here: 'pious' (Heb. *ḥāsîd*), and 'stork' (*ḥᵃsîdâ*). **11** *They will set the ephah down* when the house for ungodly worship is ready.

6:1–8 The eighth vision: the universal sovereignty of the Lord of the whole earth

The final vision resembles the first, and anticipates ch. 14. Four chariots, drawn by horses of different colours, represent the servants of the Lord in the ministry of subduing the nations. They are held in check before being released upon the world powers to fulfil the divine purpose of universal dominion.

1 *Two mountains*; literally 'the two mountains'. The article suggests that they were well known. Zechariah may here be drawing upon some current mode of thought concerning the last days, and possibly we may discern a similar reference in 'the valley of my mountains' (14:5).

2–8 The general teaching of these verses is clear in spite of much difficulty in explaining the details. The chariots represent the exercise of divine rule over the whole earth, and in the sequence of visions they foreshadow the final ordering of all things in conformity with the will of God (see introduction to 1:7). Consequently, since 'the land of Shinar' (5:11) was the final stronghold of wickedness, so the report that the Spirit of God is 'at rest in the north country' (6:8), *i.e.* Shinar (Babylon), signals the completion of God's universal victory. Thus the scene is set for the crowning of the Messiah as universal King (6:9ff.).

2 *Red.* It is likely that the four colours mentioned have no significance other than that they serve to differentiate four chariots to match the 'four winds' (v. 5), *i.e.* the four cardinal points of the compass. But this does not explain why the red horses are not specified in v. 6. It seems arbitrary and unsatisfactory to say that possibly their work was already done, and to instance some historical fact (as, *e.g.*, that the Chaldean Empire had already fallen to the Persian). It is better to urge that we are dealing with symbols of divine government rather than references to historical events. While, therefore, the red horses (presumably detailed to patrol eastwards—the compass-point unmentioned in v. 6) are necessary to complete the symbolism of world-wide rule, in fact no enemy ever attacked the people of God from the east. Enemies marched in from the south (Egypt), the west (the Philistines) and especially the north (Assyrians, Babylonians, Greeks). The prophet naturally concentrates on these. **3** *Dappled grey.* The translation is not at all certain (*cf.* RSV. mg.; RV mg.). Nothing of vital consequence appears at stake, however. **5** *Four* (*cf.* on 1:18) symbolizes 'on every side'. **8** *Have set my Spirit at rest. Cf.* 'have quieted my spirit' (RV), *i.e.* have removed all cause of offence and grief to the Spirit of God (*cf.* Is. 63:10; Eph. 4:30). *The north country.* Babylonia (Shinar, in 5:11, the archaic name being used because Zechariah is consciously dealing with symbols) was geographically due E of Judah, but since attacking armies from the various eastern empires never made frontal assaults across the desert but always marched round the Fertile Crescent and attacked from the north, they were popularly called 'the kingdoms of the north' (*e.g.* Je. 1:15).

6:9–15 The symbolic crowning: the harmonious rule of priest and king

Zechariah is commanded by God to take gifts of silver and gold from a deputation of returned exiles and to make a composite crown of circlets for Joshua. This coronation of the high priest took place in the house of Josiah. Three men were witnesses of this symbolic act (*cf.* 3:8). No mention is made in MT of the Davidic prince, Zerubbabel. Most modern commentators, following Ewald, insert his name here, and assert that the crown is a royal diadem. Another theory claims that blanks were left in the text for the names of the leaders, but owing to the fear of treason charges they were never actually

inserted until the priestly rulers of Maccabean times were instrumental in inserting Joshua's name. There is no MS evidence for this ingenious but unnecessary theory, disproved by the careful wording of the passage. False hopes of the restoration of the temporal kingdom would have fostered revolt. The oracle points to someone other than the two men, Joshua and Zerubbabel, as the fulfilment. 'Behold, a man of distinction, his name is the Branch', draws a sharp contrast between the present leaders and the One to come. This is achieved by the emphatic pronouns used. The offices of king and priest will be combined in the person of the Messiah.

12 *The Branch* is used here as if the title were part of the accepted terminology of Messianic expectation. This is what we would expect from its previous use by Isaiah and Jeremiah (see on 3:8 for the references). Signifying that which shoots from a parent root, it invites enquiry into Messiah's ancestry, and thus becomes one of the OT evidences for the expectation of a divine-human Messiah (see *NBD*, art. 'Messiah'; J. G. Baldwin, '*ṣemaḥ* as a Technical Term in the Prophets', *VT*, Vol. XIV, 1, 1964). The reference to growth here recalls Is. 53:2, stressing the humanity of the coming One.

13, 14 *Royal honour*; literally 'majesty', but not necessarily regal. 'It may be that the crown here is a sign of special honour, and not necessarily of kingship' (J. G. Baldwin, *art. cit.*). The repetitive element in this verse is deliberate, and foreshadows a greater Temple than the work of the exiles, and a vaster kingdom than the land of Israel. In the light of Christ's offices of Priest and King, their significance is spiritual and heavenly. *Between them both.* If two leaders had been meant, then harmony would reign between the civil and religious heads of the nation, as against the possibility of jealousy under dual leadership. But it points to the perfect union of Yahweh and the Branch. Was the crown placed in the Temple to invest it with spiritual meaning and safeguard the donors from a charge of treason?

15 *Help to build.* The crown of gold was put aside until the Temple was completed, and then deposited there as a memorial to the men who had formed the deputation. An assurance was thus given that those who were afar off should come to add their strength to that of the returned exiles (*cf.* Hg. 2:6–9). *If you will diligently obey.* The sentence ends rather abruptly, although it is not necessarily incomplete. This sentence structure could be deliberate, with its potential promise, conditional upon obedience.

7:1 – 8:23 THE DEPUTATION FROM BETHEL

7:1–3 Questions about fasts

An interval of 2 years stands between the night visions and the events which are recorded in chs. 7 and 8. After the deputation from Babylon came another from Bethel in December–January,

518 BC. RSV takes the names of the men as the deputation, and not those of the chief citizens of Bethel. The motive of enquiry is whether fasts which had been instituted as memorials to tragedy should continue to be observed in the new economy. In an era of peace and prosperity, should the destruction of the Temple in 586 BC (the fast of the fifth month, v. 3; cf. Je. 52:12ff.), and later the murder of Gedaliah its governor (the fast of the seventh month, v. 5; cf. 2 Ki. 25:8–25), be worthy of commemoration?

7:4–14 The negative answer: severity

Four parts complete the answer to the delegates' questions (7:4, 8; 8:1, 18). The negative answer is given in ch. 7, the positive answer in ch. 8, and the result is the conversion of fasts into feasts. The negative answer is marked by severity.

3 RSV omits 'separating myself' (RV), following the best Greek MSS. This is a loss. Like a Nazirite under religious and ceremonial vows, they had practised self-denial (cf. Nu. 6:1ff.). **4–7** The searching enquiries by the Lord imply that the fasts were self-imposed, devoid of true religious motive and therefore unacceptable to God. The calamities which the fasts were instituted to commemorate were the direct consequence of disregarding the former prophets who had in fact expressed the true mind of the Lord regarding fasting (cf. Is. 58:1–10; Joel 2:12, 13). **8–10** A summary of their teaching is then provided, to indicate that a religion in pre-exilic times which was never short of ritual observance (cf. Is. 1:11ff.) yet failed to register a true moral response to the Lord, and that this failure was manifested in social carelessness over the needy among men. Thus fasting as such is religiously inconsequential compared with the Lord's demand for moral obedience (see on Je. 7:21ff.; Am. 5:25). **11** Like a beast fighting against the yoke, the people had resisted the claims of the law. **12–14** The punishment matched the crime. God had called them by His law but they had rebelled; in their turn, when adversity came, they called to Him but He refused their cry for help. Ch. 7 is thus an extended comment on 6:15, enforcing by harsh lessons from the past the necessity to obey the word of God. **12** *Adamant.* When men turn from doing the will of God they become progressively insensitive and opposed to His truth. The adamant heart speaks of the final hardening and depicts the terrible moral consequences of disobedience. **14** *Was made desolate.* The Hebrew is active, not passive, attributing blame to the people (cf. RV).

8:1–23 The positive answer: promises

Ten promises are now uttered, each introduced by the usual formula by which the prophets authenticated their messages (vv. 2, 3, 4, 6, 7, 9, 14, 19, 20, 23). They spoke from the mouth of the Lord, not their own (Ex. 4:16; 7:1, 2), Most of the promises are concerned with the future prosperity of Jerusalem, making a marked con-trast between the present times of the prophet and the times to come. The chapter looks beyond the immediate future to the glorious era of Messiah's reign and forms a glowing prelude to chs. 9–14. Some of the themes, indeed, of those chapters begin to appear here, *e.g.* the dwelling of God in Jerusalem (v. 3; cf. 9:9; 14:9, 16), family life no longer disrupted by war (vv. 4, 5; cf. 10:6, 7; 12:5–8), the return of the exiles (vv. 7, 8; cf. 9:11–17; 10:6, 8–10), the enjoyment of harvests with no hostile despoiler (vv. 9–12; cf. 9:16, 17), the incorporation of the nations into the people of God (vv. 20–23; cf. 9:10b; 14:9, 16). The Messianic reference here is not direct but it features the true development of OT religion and faith in Christianity. The mission to the Gentiles by the Christian church was an initial fulfilment of this prediction.

3 *I will return* (cf. Ezk. 11:22f. with 48:35). The restoration of the exiles did not exhaust this promise, which spoke of the invisible splendour of the presence of the Lord in a city which was faithful to Him. Its new name is 'The city of the truth' as the seat of the God of Truth, and 'The mount of holiness' as the abode of the Holy One of Israel (cf. 14:20, 21). **6** *Marvellous in my sight.* The picture is too brilliant for the returned remnant to visualize. God's question to them implies a negative answer. 'With God nothing will be impossible' (cf. Lk. 1:37; Gn. 18:14). He repeated His promise in order to renew His former favour toward them.

9 *Let your hands be strong* (cf. v. 13). This is designed to encourage the Temple builders. As the foundation had been laid according to promise, so the completion was assured by promise, but, like all promises, dependent upon their faith in God's enabling power. Such a purpose could be achieved only by loyalty in the community itself. Dishonesty and selfishness would destroy their very unity and resolve. **12** *A sowing of peace and prosperity*, literally a seed (which flourishes in times) of peace, *i.e.* the vine, *etc.* **18, 19** *Fast . . . feasts*; a more particular answer is given to the enquiry of the Bethel deputation (see 7:2). *Fourth*; cf. Je. 39:2. *Tenth*; cf. 2 Ki. 25:1. Their failure to love truth and peace had led to their past sorrows. **21** *I am going* is the eager reply of the citizen invited to belong to Zion (cf. Mi. 4:2, 3; Is. 2:2–4). **23** *Ten men* stands for an indefinitely large number (cf. Gn. 31:7; Lv. 26:26). *A Jew*, literally 'a man, a Jew', is to contrast the nature of the believer in the true God with the mass of Gentiles. *God is with you*, declare these Gentile converts to the true worship of the Lord. The general title for God, not the special one, is used by them, and is an echo of the Immanuel prophecy (cf. Is. 7:14; 45:14). *Take hold of the robe* means to become a disciple of their religion and to embrace the Jewish ways of living. Such men were called proselytes, or 'God-fearers', in NT times.

9:1 - 13:9 THE WORLD-WIDE RULE OF ZION'S KING

9:1-8 An oracle of judgment on surrounding peoples

As we approach this difficult section of the book we do well to heed the salutary warning of H. S. Nurnburg (*The Man of Sorrows*, 1942): 'We have no right to assume that an obscure text is the same thing as a corrupt text.' There are reasons normally for the obscurity.

Israel, in its entirety, looks for divine deliverance from powerful enemies and is not disappointed. Syrians, Phoenicians, and Philistines are named, which suggests a pre-exilic situation. But the primary reference of the passage is to the conquests of Alexander the Great in 332 BC, and to similar campaigns by his successors, the Seleucids.

1 *Oracle.* RSV makes this a title, whereas the Hebrew by its system of accents connects it closely with *the word of the Lord* (*cf.* RV). It is thus a formula for presenting the divine will (*cf.* 12:1; Mal. 1:1). 'The phrase is part of the oracle and not a further title' (P. R. Ackroyd, *op. cit.*, p. 652). This divine word is portrayed vividly as resting heavily upon the land of Hadrach like a burden of wrath. *Hadrach* is mentioned only here in the OT but the Assyrian inscriptions refer to it. Probably it was near Damascus. The rabbinic interpretation of it was Messianic. By dividing the name into two words, 'sharp-gentle', they forced a meaning from it: 'Messiah is sharp toward the nations of the world, and gentle toward Israel.' *The cities of Aram.* This is a conjectural emendation, found in the margin of Kittel's *Biblica Hebraica*, and incorporated into the text of the RSV without any support from the other Versions. MT has 'the eye of Adam (mankind) is toward the Lord'. D. R. Jones (*Haggai, Zechariah and Malachi*, 1962, *in loc.*) says, 'RSV ought not to be accepted and is unnecessary'. The point of the reference is that God's judgments will cause both Jew and Gentile to turn to Him (*cf.* Is. 17:7). This future recognition of the sovereignty of the Lord has just been mentioned in 8:23. **2** *Tyre* was the bastion for Philistia. Her destruction meant that the five cities of the Philistines were vulnerable to attack. **6** *A mongrel people.* Two views are proposed; that this refers either to the occupation of Ashdod by a Jewish community, or to the end of the Philistines' independence by their becoming Jewish proselytes. After the conquests of Alexander the Philistines disappeared as a separate people. **7** *Abominations.* The consumption of unclean foods, which were often sacrificial offerings to alien gods, will cease. Like the Jebusites of old, the Philistines will be amalgamated into the holy people (*cf.* Ps. 87:4). According to Josephus such an incorporation of the Philistines among the Jews did actually take place (*cf. Antiquities* xi.8.3). Moreover they gave their name to Palestine (*cf.* Joel 3:4, AV). **8** *As a guard.* RSV follows LXX. MT has 'on account of

an army'. Alexander passed by with his army *en route* for Egypt, and having founded Alexandria, he returned this way. *No oppressor shall again overrun them.* Alexander spared Jerusalem and gave the Jews special favours. His successors, the Seleucid dynasty, did not succeed in enslaving them. *With my own eyes* (*cf.* 4:10; Ex. 3:7). This is both the promise of a speedy execution of the prediction and also the assurance of God's watchful care over His city and Temple.

9:9-17 The coming of Zion's King

V. 8 is now further expounded beyond the nearer limits. Ibn Ezra saw in the passage, which is like a psalm about a monarch (*cf.* Pss. 2; 72), the figure of Judas Maccabeus. Rashi, another mediaeval Jewish commentator, regarded the picture as that of King Messiah. Modern expositors adopt one position or the other. If we accept the unity of the book, and there are no reasons sufficiently weighty against such a view, then the passage elaborates 6:13. In the strict context it refers to the theophany of the Lord God (see vv. 14, 15, 16). It echoes the prediction of Zephaniah delivered in 630 BC (*cf.* Zp. 3:14-20). Israel will not use earthly weapons to establish the Messianic kingdom (*cf.* Zc. 4:6).

9 The speaker is the Lord and the prophet is His mouthpiece. The ideal Israel is personified as the audience. *Rejoice greatly; cf.* 2:10; Is. 62:11; Mt. 21:5; Jn. 12:15. *Your King.* The long-expected, long-promised, legitimate heir of David, their very own monarch. *Triumphant* (lit. 'righteous') is a mark of the suffering Servant of the Lord (Is. 53:11; *cf.* 32:1; Je. 23:5, 6). *Victorious*; literally 'the recipient of salvation'. LXX has 'Saviour'. He is vindicated by the Lord after His rejection by men and restored to rightful honour. This is another mark of the suffering Servant (*cf.* Is. 53:10-12). *Humble*; *i.e.* in the sense of oppressed, humiliated, poor and lowly. The idea is further elaborated by the description of His advent upon an untamed colt. The allusion to Gn. 49:10, 11 is clear. Judah will produce a mysterious ruler, who is not a worldly conqueror but will maintain His right by peaceful means. The contrast is strongly marked between the ass and the war-horse, the emblems of peace and war respectively. In the Messianic age weapons of destruction will be banished (*cf.* Is. 2:2-4; Mi. 5:10; Zc. 8:2-23).

10 *Dominion*; the language resembles Ps. 72 (especially vv. 7-11) and the reign of David's great son, Solomon. There the primary reference is to well-known geographical boundaries. Its ultimate reference is to universal sovereignty. **11** *Blood of my covenant.* Zion is addressed (*cf.* Ex. 24:8). The exiles are hailed with emphasis (*as for you also*), and reminded that their charter of redemption is the covenant. This same ground of confidence inspired other prophets also (*cf.* Is. 42:5-7; 51:14-18; Je. 31:31; *cf.* Heb. 10:29; 13:20). **12** *Restore . . . double.* According to Is. 40:2 it is the full quota which had to be paid for the sins of the nation. Now a recompense is to be made and the portion of the heir is to be bequeathed to them (*cf.* Is. 61:7).

13 *O Greece.* This prediction was largely fulfilled during the Maccabean struggle for independence from Syrian overlords in 165 BC. They tried to impose Hellenistic practices upon the Jews in Palestine. The prophecy also prefigures the warfare between the hosts of God and His foes. The language is graphic as it describes God engaging the enemy and taking His people as weapons of attack. *Greece* (Heb. *yāwān*) may only be a poetic rendering and an archaic way of describing Gentile and distant peoples. In the next century it received a literal fulfilment at the battles of Sardis in 499 BC, and at Marathon in 490 BC, when the Greek power challenged the Persian for world supremacy. This verse is no evidence of late authorship except when prediction has been ruled out as impossible.

14 *The Lord will appear* (lit. 'reveal Himself on their behalf') as champion with the thunder for His war-trumpet, the forked lightning as His arrows, and the whirlwinds of the desert as the fury of His might. *Cf.* Jdg. 5:4; Hab. 3:3. **15** *Slingers* (lit. 'slingstones', which recalls David's unconventional weapons of victory; *cf.* 1 Sa. 17:40, 49, 50). The imagery is that of Israel's battles of the past. It also recalls the battle feast of Ezk. 39:17–20; Is. 25:6. *Drink their blood.* RSV gives an impression of unheard-of ferocity, based on emendations of the text. But the very idea of drinking blood would be abhorrent to a Jew as forbidden in the law. Hence the translation must be rejected as unsuitable. Israel's enemies (see RV) will fall under them like slingstones which have missed their mark and lie trodden down in the victor's onward rush. So complete is the victory that the celebration is both exhilarating and sacred. The instruments which God will use are to be as consecrated as any holy vessel because it is a holy war that He wages. The unusual metaphor expresses the fullness of victory.

16 *Jewels of a crown.* His people now glitter like a flock of sheep on the Judean foothills. The stones in the Messiah's diadem portray a people consecrated to the divine will, like the high priest's mitre. **17** *How fair it shall be!* seems to be a sigh of wonder by the prophet as he contemplates that which is unutterable. The revelation granted him is beyond words. How good is the Lord's salvation and how fair is His crown of beauty! (*Cf.* Ps. 45:2; Is. 28:5; 33:17.) *Flourish.* The fertility of the soil will increase the population. This is a familiar theme in the prophets (*cf.* Ezk. 36:29; Joel 2:19; Zc. 3:10; 8:4–6).

10:1–12 The recall of the scattered flock

1, 2 are a connecting link with the previous chapter. In Palestine the fertility of the land is dependent upon the rainfall. The lightning heralds the spring rains that mature the crops. The storm-clouds provide 'the pourer' (as the type of rain is so aptly named) which breaks up the

hard dry ground after the summer drought in readiness for the autumn ploughing. Thus prepared, the seed can be sown. Blessing is promised when the people seek the Lord and not the diviners for the rainfall upon which everything else depends. No longer now will there be recourse to the superstitions of the heathen nations around them. Such boons will be God's gift to a people enjoying His salvation.

Teraphim were probably household gods, connected with ancestor-worship, and used as oracles. Four strong terms are employed in v. 2 to show how such practices fall into disrepute. The imagery is apt. For lack of true guidance the people had lived aimlessly and drifted into calamity. There was no shepherd to lead them, *i.e.* no Davidic king with powers to rule justly (*cf.* Ezk. 34:5–8). The true shepherd of Israel had ceased to guide and protect them. *Afflicted.* Diviners and dreamers reply to their pathetic enquiries for help and only add to their plight. The blind lead the blind.

3–12 As through a second Exodus, Israel and Judah are to be re-united, and restored to the land of promise. **3** *Leaders* (lit. 'he-goats'; *cf.* Ezk. 34:17); *i.e.* the principal men of the nation. There is no need to regard them as the Ptolemies, or any foreign rulers, but the unsatisfactory government which they then experienced. In their dire straits the Lord Himself will become the Shepherd of the flock. Suddenly the metaphor changes. Judah will become His proud steed for battle, and majestically lead Him to victory.

4 *Out of them* is repeated four times in this verse. Judah will provide the corner-stone for security. In Is. 28:16 this is a figure for the Davidic king. The *tent peg*, or nail, was the hooked peg built into a wall to hold the implements of war as well as the household utensils. This is the attribute of reliability (*cf.* Is. 22:23). The *battle bow* refers to effective power in leadership (*cf.* Ho. 1:5). *Every ruler* (lit. 'oppressor'); usually the word is employed in a bad sense, but here it is used positively. Their prince-leader will not oppress by unjust taxation or impose crushing burdens too great for the poor to bear, but will exact tribute from their vanquished enemies. Oesterley ascribed the above titles to Simon, Judas, and Jonathan Maccabeus, but each one of the four is undoubtedly Messianic. The ultimate reference is to the Lion of the tribe of Judah, by whose aid His people will conquer every foe. Christians have read these words as the missionary expansion of the church in every age.

5 Historically the formidable might of the Syrians was put to flight by the Maccabeans. Judah's success is due to the presence of the Lord. Notice the figurative nature of the verse in the little word *like.* **6** *Not rejected.* A favourite theme of the prophets is mentioned, viz. the restoration of the northern kingdom to the Davidic Prince (*cf.* Je. 3:18; Ezk. 37:21; Ho. 1:10). *I will answer* contrasts with v. 2. This is the sole ground of the prophet's confidence. **7** *Their children.* Posterity will see the fulfilment of this promise. Ephraim shall share the same elevation as Judah and promotion will be equal.

8 *Signal*; *i.e.* as a shepherd for his flock or a beekeeper for his swarm (*cf.* Is. 5:26; 7:18). *As many as of old* is an allusion to the rapid increase of the people at the time of the Exodus (*cf.* Ex. 1:12). The promise is that of Jeremiah (*cf.* Je. 23:3; Ezk. 36:11). **9** *Scattered.* Contrast RV 'and I will sow'. The former rests on minimal emendation of the Hebrew, but the difference between scattering and sowing hardly affects the meaning of the verse. Common to both is the idea that Israel will bear fruit among the nations. The real difference between the two is found in the tenses: RSV looks back to the scattering of the Exile, whereas RV looks forward to a time when the dispersed people will blossom spiritually and return to the Lord. **10** *Egypt, Assyria, Gilead, and Lebanon* are the countries where the ten tribes spent their exile. Gilead is mentioned because it was the first to be taken by Assyria (*cf.* 2 Ki. 15:29). Lebanon was the symbol of pride, to be abased on the day of the Lord (*cf.* Is. 2:13). The reference may also be to the eastern and northern boundaries (*cf.* Dt. 11:24).

11 *Egypt.* RSV here emends the Hebrew which reads 'distress' (see RSV mg.) and which ought to be retained (*cf.* RV). The 'distress' of that time will be to those involved in it as was *the* (Red) *sea* to the generation of the Exodus, *i.e.* a seemingly insoluble problem which, none the less, vanished before the power of the Lord (*cf.* Is. 43:2). The point of the prediction is the new redemptive act which will be like a second Exodus. The distressing waves are parted to give them passage to safety (*cf.* Is. 11:15, 16). Assyria and Egypt are symbols of world powers and possibly 'cover terms' for the present oppressors. **12** *Glory* (MT 'walk'; see RSV mg.). The MT means that the returned exiles will conduct their manner of life in accordance with God's code of conduct, and hence they will bring glory to His name. *Says the Lord* ends the statement and it is a solemn oracular utterance. Throughout this section the emphasis has been on the Lord's speech and His operation. With this characteristic touch the whole message is terminated.

11:1-3 The wail of the shepherds

David Baron (*The Visions and Prophecies of Zechariah*, 1918, p. 375) draws an interesting parallel between the visions (chs. 1-8) and the verbal prophecies (chs. 9-14) in the book of Zechariah. Ch. 11 stands to chs. 9-14 as ch. 5 to chs. 1-8. Five visions have given the promise of restoration. Then follows the obverse side of the message in the vision of the flying scroll and large barrel, depicting apostasy and judgment. Yet in ch. 6 the nation emerges from the valley of sin, and Israel's Messiah is crowned as Ruler and Priest on His throne. Jew and Gentile are included in his Temple. So in the verbal prophecies is the same sequence found. After the

promise of restoration, suddenly in ch. 11 the nation is brought to a precipice of national apostasy and consequent judgment.

There is a reason for this order. To prevent the complacent misuse of the promises of salvation by the godless majority of the people, the gulf of sin and apostasy is revealed. From the deep abyss the land and people emerge in the next three chapters and see the glorious conclusion in the reign of King Messiah over all the earth.

In the opening three verses of the chapter characteristic notes of judgment are sounded: fire (*cf.* Am. 5:6), the felled forest (*cf.* Is. 10:33, 34), the wail (*cf.* Am. 5:16, 17). If we were to view these verses in the light of the rest of the chapter we would see that their most significant content is 'the wail of the shepherds' who have been despoiled of all they ever gloried in (v. 3). The whole chapter centres on this point: worthless rulers have exploited the people of God for blatant self-advantage, but the hour of their condemnation and judgment is approaching. *Cf.* Ezk. 34.

1 *Lebanon . . . cedars.* As aristocrats of the forest, the cedars of Lebanon are apt symbols of worldly pride (*cf.* Is. 2:13; 10:33; Ezk. 31:1ff.). *Fire* is the emblem of divine judgment. **2** *Cypress.* If the great cedar has fallen, how much more the lesser trees should fear. Not even the *oak* in its strength has ground of confidence if *the thick forest* has fallen. Thus, symbolically, the prophet shows that neither worldly place nor worldly strength avails in the day of divine visitation. **3** *Shepherds.* The metaphor is now brought home to its human centre of reference, the national leaders. But the prophet returns at once to metaphor: even *the lions* in *the jungle of the Jordan* cannot resist the onslaught which deprives them of cover and security. Zechariah thus builds up, in picture form, the vision of total, irresistible catastrophe, but the centre of his vision is unelaborated: the judgment is destined to fall on the national leaders. It remains for the rest of the chapter to show how and why this shall be.

11:4-17 An allegory: the true shepherd and the worthless shepherds

Many of the details of this section are obscure. Consequently, it will be to our advantage to try to grasp the main outline of the narrative. Zechariah may be describing the contents of a visionary, or, more likely (*cf.* D. R. Jones), a series of acted oracles which he performed by divine command. First, he is cast by the Lord into the role of the true shepherd (vv. 4-8a), even though (vv. 4-6) the Lord forewarns him that his shepherding activities will not save the people from the doom which hangs over them. Nevertheless, he takes up the emblems of his office and engages in his work, even to the extent of opposing false shepherds and destroying them (vv. 7, 8a). Secondly, however, finding that his shepherding work provoked nothing but hate against him (v. 8b), he gave up his work, signifying its end by breaking his staff (vv. 9–11), and asked for his wages, which he cast down in the house of the Lord (vv. 12, 13), and then completed his symbolic conclusion of his office as true shepherd by breaking the second staff (v. 14). His third acted oracle (vv. 15–17) was to garb himself as a worthless shepherd, symbolizing the shepherds whom the Lord would impose as an act of judgment on the people (v. 16), and by whom they would be despoiled. Finally, the chapter fittingly returns to its point of departure: the proclamation of a curse on the worthless shepherd (v. 17; cf. v. 3a).

However much this recital may reflect the rejection of any or all the prophets whom the Lord sent to His people, it is obviously and truly fulfilled only in the Lord Jesus Christ, His coming as the true shepherd, His exposure of the existing 'shepherds' as false, His rejection and the shameful payment of 30 pieces of silver, and the subsequent delivery of the people into the hands of leaders who brought them into conflict with Rome and the horrors of the fall of Jerusalem in AD 70.

4 *Doomed.* The Lord sees the end from the beginning. The only means of saving them will be the sending of the true shepherd, but his rejection by them will be the occasion of their irretrievable condemnation. **5** With this picture of self-seeking rulers using their position for personal gain, cf. Ezk. 34:2, 3. **6** In rejecting the true shepherd, the people automatically choose for themselves shepherds of the opposite sort, and thus become the architects of their own destruction.

7 *Those who trafficked*: LXX for a difficult expression of MT. Johanon Aharoni (*The Land of the Bible*, 1967, p. 61) says that 'Canaanite' in ancient times had the meaning 'merchant', and here it is preserved in this sense (cf. Ho. 12:7, RV and RV mg.). P. R. Ackroyd (*op. cit.*) renders it as 'tax-gatherer' and regards it as a reference to the Roman oppression. *Two staffs* (cf. Ps. 23:4); maybe the standard equipment of the shepherd. *Grace . . . union.* The former speaks of the covenant relation of grace between God and His people, the latter (cf. v. 14) of the consequent union obtaining among the people of God. Zechariah thus casts himself into the role of the great shepherd-king, David, under whom the people of God had been knit together, and in doing this deliberately foreshadows the coming greater David (cf. Ezk. 34:23, 24).

8 *One month . . . three shepherds.* Commentators go to great pains to establish the symbolic value of the 'month' and to identify the three shepherds, and may well be right in doing so, but nothing like a consensus of opinion has been reached (see Baron, *op. cit., in loc.* for a useful summary of opinion among the older commentators). It may well be, however, that in the 'month' we are to see no more than that the activity of the true shepherd was short-lived indeed. He received no acceptance among his people. And as

to the 'three' shepherds whom he *destroyed*, the OT often recognizes a threefold division of authority in the nation: kings, priests and prophets (*e.g.* Je. 13:13).

10 *The covenant which I had made.* It is clear that in acting the part of the Messiah, Zechariah knew himself to be acting the part of the Lord Himself, for no other could annul the divine covenant as is symbolically done here. *All the peoples* is an unexpected phrase. Does it stress the northern and southern kingdoms, Israel *in toto*? **11** The *traffickers*. RV here preserves the Hebrew intact: 'the poor of the flock that gave heed unto me', and the change seems both needless and improbable. One would not expect the perception indicated here to be found among the self-centred rulers. **12** *Thirty shekels*; a contemptuous sum, the compensation money for an injured slave (Ex. 21:32)! **13** *Treasury.* See RSV mg., 'potter', which accurately reads the Hebrew. No satisfactory explanation of the reference to the 'potter' has been advanced, and it may be that we are dealing with a proverbial but otherwise unknown expression of extreme contempt: 'To the potter with it!' The casting down of the price *in the house of the Lord* has had various explanations attached to it: that since the shepherd was acting for the Lord, he must bring back to the Lord evidence of his rejection; or, since the real rejection was of the Lord Himself, it had to be signalized in this way, *etc.* **14** Peace among men is a by-product of peace with God, and when the latter is gone (*cf.* v. 10) the former inevitably follows. Civil strife and anarchy characterized the nation under foreign domination. In AD 70, *e.g.*, when the holy city was besieged by the armies of Titus, four separate Jewish groups fought within the city for control of it.

15, 16 *Worthless shepherd*, because of his unworthy character, which is outlined in the fivefold defection (v. 16). His identity is not disclosed. It was so typical of the many that one portrayed the rest. Behind the neglect of the healthy, the merciless treatment of the weak, and the voracious devouring of the wealth of the flock, was the lack of care for them. **17** *My worthless shepherd.* Eli Cashdan (*The Twelve Prophets*, 1948, *in loc.*) aptly comments, 'The instruments that fail are punished: the arm of strength is completely enfeebled, the right eye that lacked discernment is utterly darkened by judicial blindness.' The principle that privilege carries responsibility is here set forth (*cf.* Am. 3:2). The chapter foreshadows the terrible afflictions of the Jews, subsequent to their rejection of the Messiah, and the ultimate downfall of their overlords. That this ruler is spoken of as *my* shepherd offers significant light on the sovereignty of the divine rule over history. He is where he is by divine appointment (v. 16) and the scandalous acts which his wicked heart teaches him to perform are the Lord's dread judgment on a people which rejected the true shepherd. See General Article, 'Old Testament

Theology', under 'God and history' (pp. 27f.).

12:1-9 The deliverance of Jerusalem and Judah

In the preceding chapter we were made aware of the crucial test through which the people were to pass: the coming of the true Shepherd, consequent upon whose rejection there would be a colossal act of divine judgment upon the chosen false shepherds and their flock. How this judgment would be inflicted, we were not informed. In the present chapter we find Jerusalem and Judah under the heel of the nations and internally disunited. We are thus invited to understand that, as so often, the Lord has used the power of the nations against His people. But this is a situation which He will not suffer to continue indefinitely, for to do so would be to go back on His promises.

The main theme of the verses is the overthrow of the nations which fight against Jerusalem. The historical background to the concept of Jerusalem as the scene of the final battle is found in incidents like the divine overthrow of Sennacherib (2 Ki. 19); it may also be that the abiding hostility of the kings of the earth to the people of God, and the eleventh-hour deliverance of the city from their grasp, formed part of an annual liturgical drama in the Temple in pre-exilic times (cf. Introduction to Psalms; D. R. Jones, op. cit., in loc.) and that for this reason also Zechariah is handling a well-known group of ideas.

A somewhat unexpected feature of these verses is the apparent quarrel between Jerusalem and Judah (vv. 2, 7; cf. 14:14). No historical occasion affords a parallel for the references, and nothing in apocalyptic writings offers a clue to its meaning.

The verses open with a brief hymn to the Creator (v. 1; cf. Am. 4:13; 5:8; 9:5, 6). The purpose of this is to authenticate the vision of world conquest which is to follow. The God of whom Zechariah speaks has the inherent authority and power to bring this to pass. In consequence of this universal power, Jerusalem will not fall to the nations but will be their destruction (vv. 2, 3). Far from the nations having their way, the Lord will render them impotent (v. 4a), but will bring spiritual illumination (vv. 4b, 5) and victory (vv. 6, 7) to Judah, protection and glory to Jerusalem (v. 8) and destruction to the nations (v. 9).

1 The affirmation of the divine origin of this message is very strong. An Oracle should not really stand as a heading but be joined to what follows: 'The oracle of the word of the Lord . . . the Lord's utterance.' Heavens . . . earth . . . man. The totality of the divine sovereign sway, embracing height, depth, and inwardness; or, things invisible, things visible and things spiritual. **2** A cup of reeling. Cf. Is. 51:22, 23; Je. 25:17f. The metaphor of the cup is used to denote the Lord's sovereign disposing of the lot of men and nations (cf. Ps. 75:8). It will be against. This suggests that Judah is linked with

the enemies of Jerusalem and with them receives the cup of reeling. D. R. Jones offers the alternative translation: 'And Judah also shall be involved in the siege that is laid against Jerusalem.' This postpones the revelation of disunity between the two and here simply prepares the way for the fact that the first movement of divine deliverance is towards Judah (vv. 4-7). **3** A heavy stone. The metaphor of the 'cup of reeling', implying the fuddling of the minds of the attackers, is matched by that of the heavy stone, beyond their physical prowess. Thus, in every way, Jerusalem is beyond their reach.

4 Horse . . . rider. To the insufficiency of their mental and physical powers is now added the immobilization of their military force. Open my eyes; i.e. in favour, protection. Cf. the metaphor of the uplifted countenance of blessing, Nu. 6:26. Eyes . . . blindness. There is a contrast between the stupefied eyes of the panic-stricken attackers and the protective eyes of the Lord, watchful over the attacked. **5** Then. Behind this verse lies the implication of some disaffection between the country and the city, but the day of deliverance is also a day of enlightenment, in which the alienated Judahites will recognize that Jerusalem and its inhabitants will possess a genuine access of divine strength, and a special relationship whereby the Lord can be called, with some distinct implication, their God. The truth behind this is that the promises of David were also promises centred in Jerusalem. **6** In consequence of this new mind, Judah turns upon the attackers. **7** Another sidelight on the implied hostility between Judah and Jerusalem: it would seem that some spiritual pride on the part of the Jerusalemites had given offence to Judah. But the Lord's award of prior victory to Judah would be a corrective of this. **8** Nevertheless there would be no abandonment, but rather a new affirmation, of the Davidic and Jerusalem promises, and the royal house and city would come into new splendour and even divine dignity. Like God, like the angel of the Lord looks forward to the actual divinity of 'great David's greater Son'. On 'the angel of the Lord', see General Article, 'Old Testament Theology' (p. 29); also Introduction to Exodus (pp. 116f.).

12:10-14 The purification of Jerusalem

Just as victory is a sovereign gift of God, so is repentance. To this spiritual aspect of the Lord's activity for His people the prophet now turns.

10 Compassion and supplication; i.e. the Spirit of God, sent forth in consequence of the divine compassion for His people, creates in them a new spirit of supplication to God concerning their needs. If we adopt the probably more correct rendering 'grace' instead of compassion, the essential meaning remains unaltered but the picture becomes one of God's bestowal of the particular grace of supplication. Supplication is, in Hebrew, a plural of intensification: intense and efficacious prayer. Look on him; Hebrew 'on me'. All the ancient Versions and the best

Hebrew MSS read the first person singular. The change to the third person in RSV is prompted by the immediate switch to the third person in the following phrase *mourn for him*. It has a harmonistic motive, and possibly also proceeds from the unsuitability of thinking that the Lord Himself is pierced and mourned for. In pursuance of this line of thought, various suggestions of historical personages have been made in an attempt to identify the pierced one—the brother of Johanan, Onias III, *c.* 170 BC, or Simon the Maccabee, *c.* 134 BC, or the Teacher of Righteousness mentioned in the Dead Sea Scrolls, or even Zerubbabel, and others. But the traditional identification with the suffering Messiah remains the best understanding. Just as in 11:10, the prophet, posing as the true Shepherd, also acted in the person of the Lord Himself, so here there is an identity of the Sender and the Messiah whom He has sent (*cf.* Mal. 3:1; Mk. 9:37; Lk. 10:16). The verse is really another form of the prophecy of the Servant of the Lord (Is. 52:13 – 53:12): He who is 'the arm of the Lord', God Himself come down to save, and who is yet smitten by God for the people's transgressions. Pusey (*The Minor Prophets*, 1907, Vol. 8, *in loc.*) says that Zechariah has concentrated in a few words the tenderest devotion of the gospel. To look on the pierced form of Christ by faith is to discover what we owe to Him for His suffering on our behalf. See D. R. Jones for a different interpretation with supporting translation of the verse: Jones holds that the 'pierced' are those who died in the war of the foregoing verses. In contemplating their death, the survivors learn the costliness of salvation. From this point, Jones proceeds to relate the verse to Is. 53.

11 *Hadad-rimmon*. The allusion is obscure to us. Hadad was a Canaanite god; Rimmon (*cf.* 2 Ki. 5:18) belonged to the Assyro-Babylonian pantheon. We must assume that Zechariah refers to some heathen rite of lamentation, like, *e.g.*, the mourning for Tammuz (*cf.* Ezk. 8:14). *Megiddo* recalls the death of Josiah (*cf.* 2 Ch. 35:22–25) and the mourning which followed. The lamentation over the death of a good and loved king is an apt reference in a passage which centres on the death of the true Ruler and only Saviour. **12** *David . . . Nathan . . . Levi . . . Shimeites*. Two views are possible here. Either these names represent leading classes in the nation, *i.e.* royal, prophetic, priestly, and scribal, and the groups are separated from each other from the greatest to the least, or else David stands for the chief ruler and Nathan for the subordinate ruler (*cf.* 2 Sa. 5:14); Levi the chief of the priests with Shimei as the subordinate priest (*cf.* Nu. 3:18–21), or as representing the associated tribe of Benjamin (*cf.* 2 Sa. 19:16). *Their wives by themselves*. This custom need not be an indication of a late date. It is intended to elaborate the distinction between personal and private grief and the public expression of it. The whole context denotes a very great mourning by the land, the family, and the individual.

13:1-6 The purified land and the disannulment of false prophecy

Moral reformation is the inevitable consequence of national repentance. Mourning for sin is a preparation for cleansing from sin. A spring will be opened permanently for such purification (v. 1). It will be like one of the 'rivers of paradise' which flow from the city of God (*cf.* Ps. 46:4; Ezk. 36:25). In Zc. 12:1 the 'doors' had been opened to admit the fire of judgment. The nation's uncleanness had compelled them to be separated as a sign of contrition. Now the means for removal of defilement had been provided by God: a living fountain ever flowing free. Idolatry was the prime cause of the land's defilement. But without the false prophet such substitute-gods could not have flourished. Hence with the cleansing ritual must also come the exclusion of the false principle. Ungodly inspiration had to be removed (v. 2). Whenever anyone tried to revive the institution of the prophetic guilds, his parents were to remember the injunction of the Mosaic code in Dt. 13:1–11, and chastise him for the folly of his ways and the error into which he would lead the nation (v. 3). This parental correction would hold in check the foremost cause of the adulteration of true religion. Such discredit would be cast on the false prophet by his own kin that he would be ashamed to wear the tokens of which he had formerly boasted (v. 4). His garb and his dream would be discredited (*cf.* 1 Ki. 19:19; 2 Ki. 2:2–13). To avoid the suspicion of being a false prophet, the deceiver would try to pass himself as a serf in the fields, engaged from his youth in the humble tasks of husbandry (v. 5; *cf.* Am. 7:14).

5 Contrast the challenge to Amos and his reply, Am. 7:10ff. *The land has been my possession*; rather, 'Man has possessed me', *i.e.* I have been a slave. Jones (*op. cit.*) tellingly remarks 'The word for man, '*adham*, is one which designedly contrasts man with God, and the vivid antithesis is with Amos' "*the LORD* took me*". Such will be the exposure and humiliation of the false prophets, that they will disclaim any connection with Yahweh, and prefer to call themselves slaves of *man*.' **6** *Wounds on your back*, literally 'between your hands', which could signify anywhere on the hands, arms or chest. The point of the question is that self-inflicted wounds would have been one of the tell-tale marks of the false prophet (*cf.* 1 Ki. 18:28) and may have been the thing which first prompted the enquiry whether or not this person belonged to one of the prophetic guilds. *The house of my friends* may be a subtle prevarication. By his 'friends' the dissembling false prophet would intend the false gods to whom he is devoted, but in the ears of his questioner it would sound as if he was saying that these were (perhaps) marks left by loving parental discipline, or (as Jones urges) 'the result of a private brawl'.

13:7–9 The purified land: separation of the unworthy

These verses are related by association of ideas to what has immediately preceded, and also by way of explanation of some bare hints earlier dropped by the prophet. In the smiting of the Lord's shepherd we cannot but see an incredible counterpart of the treatment which the false prophet (v. 6) claimed to have been meted out to him. Here is a most unexpected and undeserved smiting of the true Shepherd in the house of His friends. Furthermore, we learn here of the inner meaning of the piercing of the divine One, mentioned at 12:10. A sword awakes against the Lord's Shepherd, and as a result there is a sifting out among the people and, in the end, a purified company in fellowship with the Lord.

7 *My shepherd.* A Messianic stamp has been given to this by Jesus in Mk. 14:27, but even apart from this authoritative directive as to the meaning of the passage, it is the sense which best suits it and relates it to its context, as above. *The man who stands next to me.* The additional description is given in order to distinguish 'my shepherd' in this passage from the personage who, for other reasons, and in another sense, was the Lord's shepherd in 11:16 (*q.v.*). Here a true intimacy and fellowship is intended, and the relationship is reminiscent of 6:13 (*q.v.*). *Turn my hand.* As the Lord is the Agent here in sifting the flock, so we understand Him to be the Agent wielding the awakened sword which smites the shepherd. *Cf.* Is. 53:6, 10; Acts 2:23. **9** *Refine* is the same picture as that painted by Ezekiel in 22:17–22, linked with Zc. 11:13, as a removal of the ignoble and rebellious elements where they still exist. *Call . . . answer* are the two attitudes of the suppliant and the Supplier and depict a relationship of mutual harmony and cordiality between the purified remnant and its God. *My God* is a personal affirmation and the climax of the renunciation of idolatry. Such mutual responsiveness in prayer, worship, and service is the heart of the covenant. This has always been the secret life of the city of God.

14:1–21 THE DAY OF THE LORD

14:1–15 The rout of Jerusalem's foes

In this chapter the theme of the previous section is expanded in outline. It opens with a characteristic formula that is slightly different and is therefore particularly emphatic. 'Lo! there is a day coming that belongs exclusively to the Lord', *i.e.* for His glory. Yet strangely it features the last siege of the holy city (*cf.* vv. 2–4, 12–14). Previous chapters have already described the event in some detail, and now it is set forth in lurid imagery. The words are addressed to Jerusalem whose capture, with the horrors attendant upon such an event, is outlined vividly with a few strokes of the pen. So complete is the sack of the city that the united nations will sit down in the midst of it to divide the inviting spoil.

The judgment of God against Jerusalem will recoil eventually upon the very ministers of His wrath. Such world powers as Babylon and Rome have already experienced it in full measure. They are types of the future oppressors of the church. As the captives go forth from the gates to face unspeakable misery, so the Lord goes forth to the battle (v. 3). The divine intervention will be neither too soon nor too late for deliverance. The war is not for conquest but a holy engagement (*cf.* Dt. 7:17–26; 9:1–5), and the imagery employed is that of the Red Sea escape (*cf.* Ex. 14:14). Now the mountains will be divided to provide the preservation of Israel from their heathen foes.

The direction of the flight is also indicated by the cleaving of the Mount of Olives. By His demonstrated power in thus cleaving the mount the Lord will again establish His claim as Lord of all natural forces. The valley of safety will be created by the removal of the mountain toward the north and toward the south. The former valley that intervenes between Olivet and Jerusalem will thus be stopped up (v. 5), and this new valley will be named (lit.) 'my valley of the mountains'.

5 For the awkward expressions in this verse, various solutions have been proposed. RSV has aimed at a smooth translation. From the MT the translators have extracted a preposition, translated *the side of it*, from the Hebrew '*āṣal* (which appears as a place-name, Azel, in RV); they have also altered the three verbs which are alike in form, as though the repetition was a mistake, and changed the meanings of the first to *stopped up*. The place *Azal* (MT) is unknown, but according to Cyril of Jerusalem (*c.* AD 315–386) it was a village on the extremity of the mountain and destroyed by the Romans when they besieged Jerusalem in AD 70 (see Pusey, *op. cit.*, p. 340). The Hebrew could also be rendered 'God will withdraw Himself' to become the rearguard of the fleeing multitude as He did when the Egyptians pursued the host into the cul-de-sac by the Red Sea (*cf.* Ex. 14:19f.). Other names have also been suggested by Ackroyd (*op. cit.*).

Further amplification is made in the reference to the earthquake. According to Am. 1:1 such a disaster of some magnitude furnished a date from which other events were sometimes reckoned in Israel. Beside the cleft mountain two other features describe the theophany: *His feet shall stand* (v. 4) as a symbol of domination over every foe, and *He shall come with His host* (v. 5). *Holy ones* come as attendants upon the divine majesty. RSV has altered the possessive pronouns to *your* and *with him*. 'My' and 'you' are relegated to the margin. Who are these attendants? They could be saints, angels, or celestial beings (*cf.* Dt. 33:2, 3; Ps. 89:5–7). Is it not the return to the city of the fleeing host with the angel of the Lord as their vanguard?

A break occurs here in the Hebrew text between vv. 5 and 6. What follows in v. 6 is a description of the unique day. To the eye of the prophet the events are being unfolded as though they are happening before his very eyes.

6 *On that day.* RSV mg. says that the MT is uncertain and to obtain a suitable translation has resorted to the Greek, Syriac, Latin, and Aramaic Versions. Three different interpretations have been proposed for this allusion. The first suggests a contrast between the judgments in the days of Noah and the radical revision of the covenant which emerged from that era (*cf.* Gn. 8:22). So the rendering must be, 'There shall not be heat and congealing cold, but there shall be continuous day.' It is urged, secondly, that the imagery is that of the universe clothed in darkness after the intense light of the theophany. The heavenly bodies will contract their spendour and wane (*cf.* Is. 13:10). This will be like day one in the creation narrative. The Hebrew has 'It is day one'. A third possibility is the comparison with the long day recorded in Jos. 10:12–14, 'There has been no day like it before or since.' The three views need not cancel out one another.

7 *Continuous day* suggests a transformation of nature after the victory over the heathen confederacy against the hosts of God; the world will bask in continual springtide (*cf.* Rev. 21:25). *It is known to the Lord* is placed in brackets in RSV because it sounds like the wistful sigh of the prophet, or his scribes, or like the warning given in parenthesis in Mt. 24:15. But Mt. 24:36 seems to be a closer parallel. **8** *Living waters* picture the river of God in paradise regained (*cf.* Gn. 2:10 with Ezk. 47:8 and Rev. 22:1). The figure is more than a mere solution of the land's chief problem, that of water supply: it is the satisfaction and sustenance of the city of God for ever.

9 *Become king.* If we accept the unity of the book, then there is a progression of ideas concerning kingship. It begins with the anointed representative of the Lord, whether priest or monarch (6:12), and advances finally to the majesty of the Eternal as Sovereign over all His renewed creation. *His name one.* Jewish exegetes said that the ineffable name of Yahweh will be written as it is pronounced and will be found in the mouths of all men. This will mean universal monotheism. The one day and the one name speak of the harmony restored, in contrast with the babel and chaos of the old, fallen creation (*cf.* Phil. 2:9–11).

10 *Geba* is the mountainous district 6 miles north of Jerusalem, and *Rimmon* is 35 miles southwest of the city. The new *plain* will be lowered to the level of the plain of the Arabah so that Jerusalem will tower above all the area (*cf.* Is. 2:2). **11** *No more curse* (mg. 'ban'). The 'ban' is the utter destruction which happened in a holy war (*cf.* Dt. 7; Jos. 6; Mal. 4:6). All things will have returned to a state of primitive perfection. The picture is ideal.

14 *Even Judah will fight against Jerusalem.* The preposition *against* is literally 'in'. Confusion is caused as the verb 'to fight' uses the same preposition for two different meanings, 'to fight

against a foe', and 'to fight in a place' (*cf.* Ex. 1:10 with 17:8). The place of the contest gives the better sense here and this is the rendering in the LXX. Eli Cashdan (*op. cit.*) aptly comments 'at that time the city will be in the hands of the enemy'.

14:16–21 The glories of the king's abode

16 *The feast of booths* (Tabernacles). Passover was the chief Jewish festival because it commemorated the Exodus from Egypt. The Feast of Weeks also celebrated the giving of the law. The Feast of Tabernacles concluded the agricultural year with the celebration for the ingathering of summer fruits. It will be the appropriate festival, therefore, to commemorate the final ingathering of nations and the renewal of nature into a harmonious whole. Men who have long dwelt in the wilderness of ignorance and idolatry will then acknowledge their return to the true God. Of the three festivals, Booths seems to be the most fitting for the inclusion of the Gentiles. **17** *If any . . . do not go up* recognizes the possibility of a recalcitrant element within the spared remnant. The same sequence of ideas appears again in Rev. 21:8. **18** *Egypt* is singled out because the rainfall was not the vital factor in the economy of the land. Its prosperity was bound up with the inundation of the Nile, which provided seasonable irrigation for cultivation. So an equivalent alternative to the withdrawal of the rains vital to Palestine is named. Instead of drought there will come upon Egypt its dreaded plague (*cf.* Ex. 15:26; Dt. 28:27).

20 *Horses.* The old distinction between secular and sacred will have been abolished. Everything will have become holy because it will be dedicated to a holy purpose. The instruments of war, looked upon with such disfavour by the prophets, will be converted to better use (*cf.* Mi. 4:3, 4). They are even to bear the same inscription as the mitre on the head of the high priest (*cf.* Ex. 28:38). *Pots* are mentioned as the commonest of vessels, and like everything else they will be transformed by their consecration to the Lord. This recalls Ezk. 40–48. **21** *Trader* (lit. 'a Canaanite'); one who might exploit the pilgrims, mar the glory of the consecration and be unworthy of the golden age (*cf.* 11:11 for the same word, and the commentary on 11:4–17 for its meaning). There is a play on words here. The ancient inhabitants of Canaan had been a corrupt people. Their name had become a byword for all that was profane and unholy (*cf.* Ezk. 16:3). *Sacrifice.* Christians naturally understand the reference to the offering of animals in worship in the light of the NT (*cf.* Heb. 10:1–4, 10). Animal sacrifice, however, is not one of the main features of the imagery. Throughout the prediction existing institutions are used to illustrate the wonder of the age to come. The chief point is the exclusion of all unworthy elements from the holy worship of the universal King.

The vision defies any historical identification.

It must be regarded as ideal. Everywhere the figurative and the Messianic predominate. Such a unique day, of which everything we know is but a shadow, is known only to the Lord (v. 7).

The vision is the assurance that it will become a reality when God shall be 'all in all' (*cf.* 1 Cor. 15:28, RV; Rev. 11:15).

R. E. HIGGINSON

Malachi

INTRODUCTION

DATE

It is not possible to fix the date of Malachi with any exactness. We know from his reference to the Temple and the priests that he lived after the rebuilding of the Temple (516 BC). The reference in 1:3 to a raid on Edom is not helpful as many such raids occurred in the 5th and 4th centuries. Nor is the 'governor' in 1:8 necessarily a Persian governor. However, the state of affairs during the prophet's ministry is similar to that presupposed by the reforms of Ezra and Nehemiah, and scholars are of the opinion that the book was written shortly before their coming to Jerusalem. This date (c. 460 BC) is very generally accepted.

HISTORICAL BACKGROUND

The Persian Empire succeeded the Babylonian in 539 BC, and lasted until the time of Alexander the Great. Little is known of the Jews during the period 515 to 450 BC. The Persian kingdom was ruled by satraps, to whom local governors were responsible. Apparently Judah did not have a governor to itself and was administered from Samaria. The Temple had been rebuilt at the beginning of the period, and possibly the high priests were the local representatives. There was considerable friction between the subject Jews and the Samaritan officials, and, when in the reign of Artaxerxes I (464–423) the dwellers of Jerusalem began to rebuild the walls of their city, they were accused of sedition by the Samaritans. The reply of the king, who was afraid of rebellion and of the loss of tribute, brought the work to a halt. See Ezr. 4:6–23.

For the Jews, relations were strained also with neighbouring peoples, among whom were to be found the Edomites and the Arabs. The Edomites had taken advantage of the weakness of Judah after the fall of Jerusalem in 587 BC and had made inroads into the country. Powerful Arab tribes were also on the move along the southern borders. See on 1:3.

POPULAR MORALE

The Jews, had returned from exile with high hopes. Inspired by Haggai and Zechariah, they had rebuilt the Temple. This building did not have the glory of the original one which had been destroyed by the Babylonians, but it served its purpose. As the years passed, the Jews became disillusioned. The promised prosperity did not return. Life was hard. They were surrounded by enemies, who sought to thwart them at every opportunity. They suffered from drought and bad crops and famine (3:11). They began to doubt the love of God (1:2). They questioned the justice of His moral rule (2:17). The evil-doer is good in the sight of the Lord, they said. They argued that there was no profit in obeying His commandments and walking penitently before Him, for it was the evil and self-reliant who prospered (3:14f.).

THE PROPHET'S MESSAGE

The prophet proceeded to answer them and to show them that this scepticism was hypocritical. If adversity was their lot, it had befallen them not in spite of their godliness, but because of their sinfulness. There was, e.g., the corrupt worship of the priests (1:6). They were irreverent and extremely perfunctory in their Temple duties (1:13). They gave a bad lead to the people who brought blemished offerings, even after promising good ones (1:13f.). The very Gentiles offered worthier sacrifice (1:11). The people were also transgressing, the men divorcing the wives of their youth, and contracting foreign marriages (2:14). Sins of all kinds prevailed: sorcery, adultery, dishonesty, oppression of the weak and general ungodliness (3:5). How could they expect to prosper when the country was rotten with such practices?

Malachi, in true prophetic strain, condemned these sins and summoned the people to repentance (3:7). If they would purify their worship, obey the law and pay their tithes in full, God's blessing would follow (3:10). In sounding forth this call, the prophet revealed that he had a lofty conception of God. God was the majestic Lord of hosts (1:4, etc.); His decrees and judgments were irresistible (1:5); His love was holy and unchanging (3:6).

Malachi found ultimate salvation for his people not in their repentance but in the Lord's action. The great day of the Lord would dawn. It would purify and vindicate the godly and destroy the wicked (3:2; 4:1). That day would be prepared for by the coming of the prophet Elijah (4:5).

THE MAN

All that we know of the prophet himself we have to infer from his utterances. He was a true prophet. He spoke with full authority. He could say 'Thus says the Lord of hosts'. He had an intense love for Israel and for the services of the Temple, and a high conception of the tradition and duties of the priests. It has often been said that, while the other prophets emphasized morality and inward religion, Malachi laid stress on worship and ritual. While this is true on the whole, we have to note that he was not altogether forgetful of Israel's moral obligations (see the formidable list at 3:5), and that for him ritual was not an end in itself, but the expression of the people's faith in the Lord (for the unity of priest and prophet in Israel's religion, see *NBD*, art. 'Prophecy', especially p. 1044). Some have drawn attention to his limitations, but he was no mere uninspired expounder of traditional law. Like a true prophet, he was strong enough to resist the current of popular thinking, and some of his viewpoints are well in advance of his time, *e.g.* his respect for Gentile worship (1:11), and his daring condemnation of divorce (2:16). His sense of the all-embracing Fatherhood of God is finely expressed in 2:10.

His style is simple and direct, and marked by the frequent occurrence of the words 'Yet you say'. Perhaps this is more than the rhetorical method of the writer; it may have had its origin in the protesting and questioning cries of the hecklers, when he first delivered his message on the streets.

NEW TESTAMENT QUOTATIONS

Only three passages are referred to or quoted in the NT, viz. 1:2; 3:1; 4:5f.

The first of these, 'I have loved Jacob but I have hated Esau', contains an idea that has proved somewhat offensive to modern taste. Yet it is difficult to avoid holding some doctrine of election in view of the many statements in the Bible and of the facts of human experience. Truly one is often taken and another left. Further, like Abraham, Israel was chosen that it might bring blessing to all the families of the earth. It is in support of the doctrine of the election of the true Israel that Paul quotes the verse in Rom. 9:13.

Mal. 3:1 is about the messenger who will prepare the way for the Lord; 4:5f. identifies the messenger with Elijah and describes his function as effecting reconciliation between father and children. In this conception of the precursor we have a new note in Jewish eschatology, and there are indications that this became an element in the subsequent thinking about the day of the Lord (see on 4:5f.). In Mt. 17:10 the disciples mention the current view of the scribes that Elijah must first come, and in Mt. 11:10, 14 Jesus applies the words of the prophet to John the Baptist: John is the preparer of the way and the Elijah who was to come. The identification does not mean that John is Elijah come back to earth according to some principle of reincarnation. The two were distinct personalities. Rather does it mean that John ministered in the spirit and power of Elijah. *Cf.* Lk. 1:17. The mantle of the true prophet rested on John as much as it did on Elijah's earliest successor, Elisha. John was responsible for the revival of prophecy before the coming of the Lord.

THE CESSATION OF PROPHECY

With Malachi the curtain was rung down on prophecy until the coming of the Baptist. The living and powerful words of the prophets were heard no more. The scribes and the priests became the central religious figures. The age of creativeness had given way to the age of learning. The Jews had now a large body of literature, and its exegetes, those who expounded it, were the new channel of the voice of God. Of this coming situation, in which religion was mainly legalistic, we have a clear sign in the book of Malachi.

THE UNITY OF THE THOUGHT

The Lord God has a great love for Israel (1:2–5), but the people have not made an appropriate response. On the contrary, they have dishonoured the Lord in their careless and blemished worship, their broken vows, and their culpable partiality. Both priests and people are involved (1:6 – 2:9). This faithlessness is revealed also in the prevalence of divorce and of foreign marriages (2:10–16).

Such sin can lead only to the judgment of a holy God, but because it is the judgment of a faithful and loving God it will involve deep purging but not complete destruction (2:17 – 3:6). There is still time for repentance, which should be expressed in the giving of tithes and which would change the threatened curse to blessing (3:7–12).

Though Israel has been on the whole faithless, there are those who have consistently reverenced the Lord and in the day of judgment they shall experience new life (3:13–18). Salvation will eventually be found in the day of the Lord, and the people are exhorted to prepare for it by keeping the law of Moses and awaiting the coming of Elijah (4:1–6).

OUTLINE OF CONTENTS

COMMENTARY

1:1 THE SUPERSCRIPTION

The oracle of the word of the Lord. The Hebrew phrase appears also in Zc. 9:1; 12:1. *Oracle.* Something taken up solemnly on the lips (AV, 'burden'). *Malachi.* The word means 'my messenger or angel'. There has been considerable discussion as to whether this was the real name of the prophet. If so, it may be the contracted form of Malachiah, 'the Lord's messenger', on the analogy of Abi for Abijah ('Yahweh is my father') and Uri for Urijah ('Yahweh is my light'). Calvin took the word as a title. It is now more generally taken as a common noun. The proper name does not occur elsewhere. The LXX reads 'by the hand of his messenger', and the Targum has 'by the hand of my messenger, whose name is called Ezra the scribe', a tradition which is accepted by Jerome. One conjecture is that the oracle was originally anonymous and that a compiler took 'malachi' from 3:1, and that the word was elevated to the plane of a proper name to provide a title analogous to the other prophetical books.

1:2–5 THE LORD'S LOVE FOR ISRAEL

This love is seen in the Lord's choice and care of Israel and in the devastation of Edom.

2 *But you say.* The prophet employs the vivid method of question and answer eight times (*cf.* 1:6, 7; 2:14, 17; 3:7, 8, 13). Men are asking for a proof of the Lord's love. It is to be found in the favour He has shown *Jacob* (*i.e.* Israel), and in the overthrow of Edom, a people originally sprung from Jacob's twin brother *Esau*, but in recent years Israel's hated foe. **3** Edom has suffered utter and final desolation, and in the future her waste places will be a witness of her wickedness and of the Lord's anger. The reference in this verse is to some recent calamity that had befallen Edom.

Edomites took advantage of the calamity of the fall of Jerusalem in 587 to migrate to southern Judah. Those who remained in their homeland in Mt. Seir were driven out by subsequent Arab pressure and occupied most of south Palestine to a point north of Hebron, an area eventually called Idumea. By the 5th century Arab tribes had overrun Edom completely, and even begun to mingle with the Edomites in south Palestine. Edom remained without settled population through the Persian period. The explorations of Glueck have shown that when Edom was re-settled it was by a new people, the Nabateans.

4 *The Lord of hosts.* This title occurs twenty-four times in the book. The *hosts* are heavenly powers, and the phrase speaks of the universal and sovereign rule of God. *The wicked country.* The thought is that when men of a future generation see the desolation, they will conclude that Edom must have been desperately wicked to merit such punishment. Israel, on the other hand, will have indisputable proof of God's sovereign care. **5** *You shall say.* 'You' is emphatic in Hebrew. *Beyond the border of Israel* may also be translated 'above the territory of Israel'. The first rendering shows us God's sovereignty over all nations, the second, His special care over Israel.

1:6 – 2:9 ISRAEL'S DISHONOUR OF THE LORD

Sacrifices are blemished and worship is perfunctory. Deception is practised in the fulfilling of vows, and partiality is shown in the administering of the law. The priests fall far below the dignity of their calling, and the people are involved in the irreverence.

1:6 *A son honours his father.* In Israel this attitude towards one's father was stressed above all others. To think of God as Father, therefore, should result in honouring His authority and majesty. *My fear*; *i.e.* reverence for Me, of the sort that is due to a master from a servant. **7** *By offering polluted food* . . . Follow AV. This is not an answer to the preceding question, but a second predicate descriptive of the priests, which is explained in v. 8: they despise His name in thinking that the Lord's table may be treated with contempt, and they pollute Him by their blemished offerings. **8** *Blind . . . lame or sick.* Every sacrificial victim had to be without blemish (see Dt. 15:21). *Governor*; Hebrew *peḥâ.* The word is used for the governorship of Zerubbabel in Hg. 1:1, and of Nehemiah in Ne. 5:14. The governors instanced by Nehemiah in Ne. 5:15, who made heavy exactions and whose very servants behaved with insolence towards the Jews, might well have been governors in Malachi's time. The word *peḥâ* appears also in earlier literature, *e.g.* 2 Ki. 18:24; Je. 51:23. In v. 8 the governor could be the governor in Samaria, and the point is that the priests were bringing offerings to the altar which they would not dare present to the civil ruler. Their efforts to entreat God's favour will avail nothing if they bring such gifts to Him. *Show you favour*; literally 'lift up your face', to assure you of acceptance.

10 It is better to close the Temple doors and have no sacrifice at all than offer this vain worship.

11 In the prophet's day the very Gentiles were offering worship which was more sincere than that in Jerusalem. This estimate of Gentile worship may have been due to Malachi's understanding of Persian religion, which seems to have been purer than most heathen religions, and is similar to the thought of Acts 10:34f. Some think that the contemporary reference is to the worship of Jews living in foreign lands, those of the Dispersion, especially as *my name* suggests the divine revelation to Israel. But this view would require an understanding of *incense* and *offering* in a spiritual sense, whereas the terms suggest sacrificial worship. Further, the picture of this worship as *from the rising of the sun to its setting* would be an exaggeration in Malachi's time. The verse has also been understood as applying to the future, whether of the acceptance of Israel's religion by the nations, or of the universal response to the gospel, or of the Lord's Supper. But there is no verb in the Hebrew phrase *my name is great*, and so it is natural to render it by a present; *cf.* v. 14 ('my name is feared'). Nor is it reasonable to use a fact from the future to express disapproval of the current worship in Jerusalem. What is required is a contrast with a contemporary reality. **12** *When you say. Cf.* v. 7; it is their attitude rather than their actual utterance that the prophet has in mind. **13** The priests find the Temple services boring, and the people, following their example, are stingy and deceitful. **14** *Cursed be the cheat.* We are reminded of the story of Ananias and Sapphira in Acts 5. Dr M. Dods quotes appositely from *Pirqe Aboth* 1:16, 'Say little and do much. Be like Abraham, who only promised a morsel of bread, but fetched a calf tender and good.' *And vows it.* The reference here is not to one of the regular offerings, but to a free-will offering of the type that a man might vow to pay when he was in trouble. *Cf.* Lv. 22:18-20. But God is *a great King*, and so is not to be trifled with.

2:1 *This command*; *i.e.* the teaching of the subsequent verses. *For you.* The 'you' is emphatic. **2** *Glory.* The word that is translated 'honour' in 1:6. *The curse.* The Hebrew has the definite article, and the allusion may be to such a verse as Dt. 28:20. In Scripture the curse is more than an expression of displeasure; it is a potent instrument of God's judgment, travelling like a well-aimed missile against the wrongdoer. *Your blessings.* Probably the priestly benedictions, a most solemn part of the divine service (*cf.* Nu. 6:22-27), though some would understand the phrase as meaning the personal advantages enjoyed by the priests. **3** *Dung.* Not excrement but the contents of the bowels of the slain animals (*cf.* Lv. 4:11). *I will put you out of my presence.* The LXX reads 'Behold, I remove the shoulder from you', *i.e.* incapacitate you from your function of blessing. The German Bible has the interesting reading, 'It shall remain stuck to you'. The obvious meaning of v. 3 is that the

priests will be openly disgraced and thoroughly discredited unless they learn to be worthy representatives of God's *covenant with Levi* (v. 4). See Nu. 25:12, 13 and Dt. 33:9.

5-7 The nature of the true priestly service is indicated. These verses give a remarkable picture of the qualifications, duties and dignity of the priest and need to be noted, especially as the popular view of Malachi is that he was wholly a formalist and a ritualist. The true priest is among men as a messenger of God. He is not simply a professional expert in the minutiae of ceremonial observances. He is a teacher, able to instruct men in the knowledge of God and of His will. He is a man of devotion and integrity. The peace of God is in his heart and he is a strong moral influence on the lives of men. It is a mistaken view that contrasts the OT priest with the prophet to the disparagement of the former. In Malachi there are indications of the future and perfect union of prophet and priest in the Son of God. *Peace* means here general prosperity. The covenant of God promised prosperity in return for true reverence. *Instruction* (RSV mg., 'law'; Heb. *tôrâ*) is authoritative teaching acquired by revelation. Priestly duty included the exposition of what God had taught His people. *He is the messenger.* The priest, as well as the prophet, is the Lord's messenger with the duty of imparting *knowledge*, *i.e.* of the Lord and of His commandments.

8 *But you*; 'you' is emphatic. *You have corrupted the covenant*; *i.e.* 'broken' it. This they have done by showing partiality towards the rich and influential and generally doing the opposite of what was expected of them. Little wonder that they were despised by the people.

2:10-16 CONDEMNATION OF DIVORCES AND FOREIGN MARRIAGES

The holiness of the Lord's people has been profaned by marriages with foreign women and God Himself outraged by the practice of divorce.

10 *Have we not all one father?* The fact that Israel has in God a common Father and Creator ought to bind them closely together, and make them despise any treachery that tends to break the unity. *The covenant of our fathers* contains a prohibition of marriage with non-Israelites (Ex. 34:15, 16; Dt. 7:3, 4). **11** *Judah has been faithless* and profaned the Lord's sanctuary with her foreign marriages. *Sanctuary* means either the Temple or the holy people (*cf.* Je. 2:3). *The daughter of a foreign god* is a woman of another religion. Such mixed marriages involved the very real and ever-present danger of apostasy. **12** *Any to witness or answer.* This phrase in the Hebrew (*cf.* mg.) may be idiomatic and mean everyone belonging to him. The RSV is based on an emendation and signifies 'anyone to defend him in a court of law'. This suggests the loss of civil rights, and the last phrase in the verse suggests the loss of all religious rights.

13 There are two ways of understanding the

verse. The *weeping* may be that of the divorced wives, as a consequence of which the worship of the people is not acceptable before the Lord. Or the weeping may betoken the renewed efforts of the zealous but impenitent people to procure the Lord's favour, after their offerings have been rejected by Him. **14** *Your wife by covenant*; *i.e.* the wife to whom you have vowed loyalty. The marriage contract is understood as having been made when the men were youthful. Monogamy is obviously here assumed as the rightful practice. **15** The meaning of the first half of the verse is obscure. A closer rendering of the Hebrew would be: 'Has not one made and a remnant of spirit was his? And what does the one seek? A godly seed. So take heed to your spirit . . .' The key words appear to be 'óne' and 'spirit'. 'One' seems to echo the one God of v. 10, and the Spirit of God seems to be understood as the source of the spirit of life in man. We are reminded of passages like Gn. 2:24; Is. 42:5; Mt. 19:4–6. There have been many interpretations of this passage. The general sense seems to be that the one Fatherhood demands loyalty among the members of the family. When Israelites put away their wives they are guilty of disloyalty. Faithlessness to the tradition of their religion is especially in evidence when they proceed to marry non-Israelitish women, for the religion of the seed or offspring is more likely to be that of the mother than that of the father. Godliness is therefore more likely to be ensured by marriage within the covenant people. **16** *For I hate divorce.* God's opposition to divorce is nowhere else found in the OT. Malachi leaves his hearers in no doubt as to the Lord's attitude to this putting away of their wives, so justifying his call to them to *take heed. Covering one's garment with violence.* When a man claimed a woman as his wife, he cast his garment over her (*cf.* Ru. 3:9). In this verse, therefore, *garment* has to be understood in the sense of 'marriage relationship', and the reference is to the brutal treatment involved in divorce.

2:17 – 3:6 THE COMING JUDGMENT

God's righteousness will be vindicated in the coming judgment, for which He will prepare by the sending of His messenger. There will be an extensive purging, but the Lord's faithfulness will prevent the destruction of Israel.

2:17 The people have *wearied the Lord* by saying that He delights in the evil-doer and by doubting the justice of His rule. The attitude expressed in this verse has to be understood against the background of the hardships of the post-exilic years. The prophet announces a day of judgment, when they will learn that the Lord is indeed holy, and that He acts in righteousness. **3:1** *My messenger.* See Introduction, p. 805 and 4:5. The messenger will remove obstacles from the way, and, like the herald who announces the approach of an earthly monarch, will prepare men to receive the Lord. *Whom you seek* refers back to the last question in 2:17. *Messenger*

of the covenant. Some understand this as another description of 'my messenger', and hold that vv. 2–4 describe the activity of the messenger. But it is better to take *the messenger of the covenant in whom you delight* as in apposition to *the Lord whom you seek.* The messenger of Yahweh or the Angel of the covenant is not a created angel but One who 'not only bears the divine name but has divine dignity and power, dispenses divine deliverance and accepts homage and adoration proper only to God'. See *NBD*, art. 'Trinity', p. 1298. Christ's cleansing of the Temple comes to mind when we read this section. *Covenant.* This is the sixth occurrence of the word in Malachi (*cf.* 2:4, 5, 8, 10, 14). The concept is distinctively a scriptural one and speaks of the relationship that God establishes with His people, a relationship of sovereign and redemptive grace, of divine faithfulness and of eternal blessing, demanding holiness and obedience on the people's side. All the covenants of the OT find their fulfilment in the new covenant of Christ.

2 The day of the Lord is a day of darkness and not light (*cf.* Am. 5:20), yet its purpose is to purify rather than to destroy. Contrast 4:1. *Fullers' soap.* A 'fuller' was a bleacher of cloth. In the Anglo-Saxon Gospels John the Baptist is called 'the Fuller'. **3** *He will sit as a refiner.* The silver refiner sits over his crucible until the impurities are burnt away and the surface shines like a mirror. *The sons of Levi.* Judgment will begin at the house of the Lord in the person of the priests, purifying them to fit them for their high function (v. 4).

5 shows that the prophet is concerned about the social morality of the people as well as their worship. The coming Judge will expose and condemn evil-doers of all kinds. *Swift witness.* He will be resolute in action when the time comes. *Sorcerers.* They use curses, magic spells and charms in order to exercise a malign influence over people and events. See Ex. 22:18. *Those who swear falsely.* Those who, while making a solemn affirmation or promise under oath, are guilty of lying. The sinners in the second part of the list are those who take selfish advantage of the defenceless, *e.g.* of *the sojourner.* As the stranger was liable to have few friends to protect him and to ensure that he received justice, special concern was shown for him in the Law (*cf.* Lv. 19:10, 33). **6** *I the Lord do not change.* The Lord's love for Israel is unchanging, and so Israel is not destroyed (*cf.* La. 3:22). This verse may go equally well with the following section; so RSV.

3:7–12 REPENTANCE BY TITHES WILL BRING BLESSING

Their disobedience has been revealed in their withholding of tithes. Repentance and payment of these would lead to an overflowing abundance.

7 *From the days of your fathers.* Their apostasy has been deep-rooted, and the prophet now calls them to return to the Lord and to the observance of His ordinances. **8** *Rob*. The Hebrew word is a rare one occurring elsewhere only in Pr. 22:22 (*qābāʻ*). They are well named *the sons of Jacob* (v. 6). As Jacob cheated his brother and deceived his father, so they rob God. *Tithes.* See Lv. 27:30; Nu. 18:21. They have been robbing God by withholding from Him His dues. This has brought down a curse upon them. **9** *Me* is emphatic in Hebrew. *Nation.* The word here is normally used only of the heathen, and so it reminds them that their conduct was unworthy of a covenant people. **10** *The full tithes.* The people had been keeping back part of what they should bring. Times were admittedly bad, but Malachi calls them to prove God by bringing to His house what the law demanded. Then the *windows of heaven* (*cf.* Gn. 7:11; 2 Ki. 7:2) would be opened, a phrase which suggests that they had been experiencing drought and bad crops, and there would be more than enough for all. *Storehouse.* See Ne. 13:5. **11** *The devourer*; *i.e.* the locust. See Joel 1. *Fail to bear.* The cause of this would be mildew and blasting (*ICC*). **12** When the surrounding nations see the prosperity which will follow liberality towards God, they will rightly judge that it is the Lord's action in blessing His people. *You* is emphatic in both places. *A land of delight. Cf.* Is. 62:4.

3:13 – 4:3 THE COMING VINDICATION OF THE GODLY

In a time of great cynicism there have been those who have truly feared the Lord, and they will be spared, and animated by gladness in the day of judgment.

3:13 *Stout*; *i.e.* unyielding, insistent. The attitude of the people to God has been one of defiance. *Spoken.* The form of the verb in Hebrew is the Niphal, which is used of reciprocal action. The meaning is that they have spoken to one another, perhaps in little groups. Among themselves they have questioned the profitableness of serving God loyally, and have imagined that it is the evil-doers who are prosperous. **14** *As in mourning*; *i.e.* in penitence for any failures to obey the Lord's commands. **15** *We* is emphatic. **16** Some, following the LXX, would read, 'Such things spoke they that feared the Lord to each other'. But it is better to follow the Hebrew as in AV and RSV. The words in v. 14 are the complaints of the sceptics. The faithful refuse to be moved by these arguments and seek to deepen their fellowship with each other and

to reassure themselves of God's justice. Their names and records were written down in the Lord's *book of remembrance* (*cf.* Ex. 32:32, etc.). Malachi seems to be the first to link this book with eschatology. **17** *My special possession. Cf.* Ex. 19:5; Dt. 7:6, *etc.* As God's special treasure the faithful will be spared the judgment which will fall on the ungodly. **18** *Distinguish between.* There will be a restoration of the moral order that obtained in the pre-exilic days. **4:1, 2** The wicked shall be punished, burnt up like *stubble*; the godly, on the other hand, shall be justified and healed, as in the rays of the sun. *Leaping like calves.* The picture is of a joyful, vigorous and carefree life. **3** describes the triumph of the righteous. *Cf.* Am. 9:12; Mi. 4:13; 7:17; Jos. 10:24.

4:4–6 CONCLUSION

They are exhorted to keep the law of Moses, and promised the coming of the prophet Elijah before the day of the Lord.

4 appears in the LXX after v. 6. *Horeb.* The name given to Sinai in Deuteronomy; there are several traces of the influence of Deuteronomy in our book. With this exhortation to remember the law of Moses, we might compare the ending of Ecclesiastes: 'Let us hear the conclusion of the whole matter: Fear God and keep his commandments' (AV). **5** *Elijah.* See Introduction, p. 805 and on 3:1. There is a reference to 4:5f. in Ecclus. 48:9f. (*c.* 180 BC); it speaks of Elijah, the unique prophet taken up to heaven in a chariot of fire, who is 'ready at the appointed time, it is written, to calm the wrath of God before it breaks out in fury, to turn the heart of the father to the son, and to restore the tribes of Jacob'. The coming of Elijah is a popular theme in the Jewish Mishnah. According to Josephus some 1st-century Jews believed that Elijah had been hidden by God until the time of his return. The coming of this prophet will reconcile fathers and children, and avert the threatened curse. **6** The vision would be inspired in part by the conditions in the prophet's day; there was an estrangement between the older and younger generations, probably not unconnected with the laxity about the marriage bond and the subsequent weakening of family life.

These closing verses indicate that both the Law and the Prophets have their part to play in preparing for the coming of the Lord. *Cf.* Mk. 9:4; Lk. 24:44.

JAMES T. H. ADAMSON

PART THREE

The New Testament

Matthew

INTRODUCTION

IMPORTANCE OF THE GOSPEL

The Gospel according to Matthew has probably had more influence upon Christian thinking than any of the other three canonical Gospels. It was long thought to have been the first one written, and its position at the beginning of the Canon helped to establish its importance. We find it to be the most quoted of the Gospels from the 2nd century onwards, and the one which enjoyed the greatest liturgical use. Its systematic arrangement and the collections of the teaching of Jesus, such as the Sermon on the Mount, have particularly proved their usefulness to generations of Christians everywhere. The emphasis on the priority of Mark in the last 100 years or so has tended to discount the importance of Matthew in the opinion of scholars, but it is much to be desired that the particular contribution of Matthew should once . again receive full recognition.

SOURCES OF THE GOSPEL

The question of the relationship between the Synoptic Gospels is dealt with in the General Article, 'The Fourfold Gospel', p. 64. In this commentary it is assumed that Mark is the basic source of Matthew, which is almost a revised version of Mark. Matthew omits only fifty-five verses of Mark altogether, but he compresses many Markan stories. His alterations are normally concerned with making the narrative smoother and tidying up the style and vocabulary or with guarding against misunderstanding of some of the blunter statements in Mark.

In addition to what comes from Mark, there is in Matthew a good deal of material which is also found in Luke. It is assumed here that this comes from a common source used by both evangelists, known to modern scholars as Q. The exact nature and content of Q are by no means established. It appears that Matthew, with his emphasis on collecting the teaching of Jesus, has been rather freer with the order of this source, as it consists largely of sayings, than with that of Mark, which is basically narrative.

Besides the verses coming from the two major sources (Mark, 500 verses; Q, 250 verses), there are just over 300 more verses in Matthew. These are peculiar to him and are known as M. The particular characteristics of the Gospel spring largely from the content of these verses. They may depend upon some grouping of oral material handed down to Matthew. The 'formula quotations' (see below, p. 814) from the OT may have come from a separate source but we do not have enough evidence to postulate a 'testimony book'.

STRUCTURE AND CONTENTS

It is clear that Matthew has taken considerable care over the arrangement of his material, but scholars are nonetheless divided about the exact nature of his plan. It is evident that there are five discourses in the Gospel (5:1 – 7:27, 'The Sermon on the Mount'; 10:1–42, the mission charge to the Twelve; 13:1–52, the parables of the kingdom; 18:1–35, relationship in the kingdom; 24:1 – 25:46, the second coming). Each of these is followed by a note stating that when Jesus had finished this teaching He went on to further action. It has been suggested that the blocks of narrative and teaching are akin to the *kērygma* and *didachē* of the apostolic church.

As far as the teaching is concerned, there is no question about its topical arrangement. The first discourse is basically ethical, the second missionary, the third kergymatic, the fourth ecclesiastical and the last eschatological. It is probable that ch. 23 (the denunciation of the religious leaders) should be taken as part of the final discourse.

For the over-all plan of the Gospel, numerous solutions have been proposed, but the most promising is that suggested by J. C. Fenton (*Saint Matthew*, 1963). He sees the arrangement as *chiasmus*, *i.e.* a, b:b, a. There is then found to be a similarity in length, and to some extent in subject-matter, between the first discourse (chs. 5–7) and the last (chs. 23–25) and between the second (ch. 10) and the fourth (ch. 18). The third discourse, the parables of the kingdom (ch. 13), is the central point. It is not apparent that there is any particular parallel between the narrative sections, as far as the third (chs. 11, 12) and the fourth (chs. 14–17), or the second (chs. 8, 9) and the fifth (chs. 19–22) are concerned. But there is parallelism between the beginning and the end of the Gospel. While it is not clear that Matthew intended the baptism (ch. 3) and the death (ch. 27) of Jesus to match up to each other (but *cf.* Mk. 10:38f.; Lk. 12:50), it is striking how the birth of Jesus is followed by the first quotation from the OT, 'God with us' (1:23) and the rebirth of Jesus from the dead is followed by His last word, 'I am with you always' (28:20). This commentary will assume that Matthew had some such outline plan and that there are a good number of smaller numerical groupings within the Gospel which show evidence of a desire for a systematic presentation of the facts of the gospel.

CHARACTERISTICS

What special features belong to Matthew as distinct from the other Synoptic Gospels? They may be classified as stylistic and theological. As has been shown, the Evangelist is careful in arranging and grouping his material, with the result that he presents a much more systematic work than Mark. Together with that goes a tendency to abbreviate the narratives of Mark and to touch them up a little in the interests of good Greek, or to avoid misunderstandings. Also noteworthy is Matthew's use of the reverential Jewish expression 'kingdom of heaven', where the other Gospels speak of the 'kingdom of God'.

More important, however, are his theological interests. Perhaps the most striking thing is his interest in the fulfilment of the OT and his repeated use of 'formula quotations' to bring this out (1:22f.; 2:15, 17f., 23; 4:14–16; 8:17; 12:17–21; 13:35; 21:4f.; 27:9f.). Careful study of the context shows these to be much less arbitrary than is often alleged. (See R. H. Gundry, *The Use of the Old Testament in St. Matthew's Gospel*, 1967.) This involves fulfilment of the law (but not its destruction) by Christ (5:17–20), and consequently a new ethic which goes further than the current interpretation of the OT (5:21–24, 27–30, 33–37). Jesus is represented clearly as the Messiah, the Son of David (the phrase occurs eight times) and is shown to have royal authority at the time of His passion (26:53) as well as supremely after His resurrection (28:18). Yet, at the same time, Matthew makes it plain that He is the Servant of the Lord who took men's infirmities (8:17) and who dealt gently with people (12:17–21).

One who is concerned about the relation of the old covenant and the new inevitably gives prominence to the place of Israel in God's plan. The genealogy of Jesus is taken back to Abraham (1:1f.). Matthew alone records that Jesus' mission was only to the lost sheep of the house of Israel (15:24), as was that of the Twelve (10:5f.). But it is the people of God, and in particular their religious leaders, who receive the most severe condemnation for their failure to see the law in perspective and for their hostility to and rejection of the prophets and the Messiah Himself (23:1–39). The murderers were to be destroyed and their city burnt (22:7). The Servant of God was to proclaim justice to the Gentiles and they were to hope in His name (12:17–21). The final charge of Jesus recorded in the Gospel is to go and make disciples of all nations (28:19f.). The old people of God has lost its inheritance to a new one (21:43). There is therefore considerable emphasis in Matthew on the church. It is only in this Gospel that the word *ekklēsia* occurs; and it is clear that the evangelist is concerned about authority and order in the Christian community (16:17–19; 18:15–18).

In this Gospel there is also emphasis on the miraculous. It alone records the finding of the coin in the fish's mouth (17:24–27). But this interest is particularly prominent in the last two chapters, where the raising of the saints (27:51–53) and the action of the angel at the tomb (28:2–4) are described. Matthew also contains a good deal of teaching about the *parousia* or second coming of Christ. The word itself is found only in Matthew's Gospel (24:3, 27, 37, 39) and there are a number of occasions where he inserts apocalyptic sayings into the Markan material (*e.g.* 24:30f.). A number of the parables peculiar to Matthew deal with this theme (13:24–30, 36–43, 47–50; 25:1–46). He records as much as the other Gospels sayings which relate to the present activity of the kingdom in the person of Jesus, but he clearly has a special interest in the future consummation.

DATE AND PLACE OF ORIGIN

The first unmistakable quotation of Matthew is found in the writings of Ignatius (c. AD 115), and it is generally agreed that it was written some years before that. A decision about the earliest date at which it could have been written depends, in the first place, upon the view taken of its relationship to Mark. If, as seems most likely, Matthew is dependent upon Mark in its present form and Mark was published after Peter's death (c. 65), then Matthew must clearly be dated later than that.

A second factor is its relationship to the fall of Jerusalem in AD 70. Some have argued that the Gospel must be dated before AD 70, for it would have been very strange for Matthew not to have made explicit reference to the destruction of the Temple if it had occurred, because it would clearly have marked the end of the old covenant. But Matthew would be less concerned to make such a point than would the writer to the Hebrews. On the other hand, the majority of scholars have suggested that the indirect references to the fall of Jerusalem demand a date after AD 70. Such an argument loses much of its force, however, if its basic assumption, that Jesus could not have predicted such an event, is challenged. (Yet it must be conceded that the reference to the burning of the city in 22:7 could be a 'footnote' bringing the parable up to date after the event.)

There are certain features of the teaching in the Gospel, such as the assumed development of church order (16:19; 18:17f.), conditions of persecution (10:22; 24:9ff.), the emphasis on the certainty of the *parousia* after delay (24:37–51; 25:1–12), and the Gospel's general 'theological atmosphere', which are generally assumed to reflect a period towards the end of the 1st century. A few scholars have supposed that references to 'their synagogues' (4:23; 9:35; 10:17; 12:9; 13:54) demand a date after the exclusion of Christians from Jewish synagogues c. AD 85, but the evidence for this is not compelling. Any attempt at the precise dating of a Gospel is precarious, unless its publication can be shown to be closely connected with some known historical event. It is wiser, therefore, to say that Matthew should be dated somewhere between AD 65 and 110, with the Jewish nature of the Gospel and its many parallels with the Dead Sea Scrolls suggesting a date well within the first half of the period.

There is no certainty either about the place of origin of the Gospel. Its Jewish character is undoubted and the absence of explanation of Jewish customs (*e.g.* 15:2; 23:27) suggests a centre where Judaism was strong. It must, however have been a place where Greek was the normal language spoken as it is clear that our Gospel is not a translation from the Aramaic, and does not include some Aramaic words found in Mark. Most scholars therefore hold that it was not written for a community in Palestine. Some suggest Phoenicia as a likely place of origin, but most would favour somewhere in Syria, probably Antioch. Here there seem to have been Greek-speaking Christians, most of them of Jewish origin. It was a meeting-place between Jews and Jewish and Gentile Christians, and it was a centre of the Gentile mission. The interest of the Gospel in Peter and its use by Ignatius support this suggestion. This is probably the best hypothesis, but its acceptance does not involve the belief that all the material in the Gospel was necessarily collected at Antioch. The true place of origin of the Gospel may still have been Galilee and Jerusalem.

AUTHORSHIP

It was the unanimous tradition of the early church that the Gospel was written by the apostle Matthew in Hebrew (or Aramaic) and that it preceded the others. This view is now very widely challenged. The most serious difficulty is the supposition involved that an apostle, who was an eyewitness of the events recorded, should have made such use of Mark's Gospel, whose author was not an apostle. This does seem unlikely, yet if Mark preserves the Petrine tradition it could be seen that this would be taken as authoritative even by the other apostles, and Matthew could have edited Mark's version of it with touches based on his own experience. It is further alleged that some of the stories, usually of a miraculous nature, in Matthew's special material, and some of the teaching, particularly the emphasis on futurist eschatology, could not have come from an apostle. This is a problem, though to some extent it may beg the question of how far Mark is really the norm and whether the special emphases of the other Gospels do not give us a fuller picture of what Jesus in fact said and did.

Of particular importance is the saying of Papias: 'Matthew composed the Logia in the Hebrew tongue and everyone interpreted them as he was able.' This assumes an Aramaic origin for the Gospel which has been generally abandoned on account of the use made of Mark and of the LXX version of the OT. Those who do accept it have to suppose that our Gospel was based on a thorough revision of this Aramaic original with frequent reference to Mark, and this seems most improbable. Papias is therefore assumed to be wrong about the language, but right about Matthew's authorship of the Gospel, or to be referring to something else. If the latter is the case, what is meant by 'the Logia'? There have been two suggestions which have gained support. First is the possibility that it refers to a collection of 'testimonies' or proof-texts from the OT, but there is very little evidence that there was ever such a collection in book form. Secondly, the reference may be to a collection of sayings and, if this is so, it is tempting to identify it with Q. But again we do not know whether Q was written or oral and if written whether it was one document or more. In any event the term 'Logia' can mean more than a collection of sayings and is used elsewhere in early Christian literature and possibly by Papias himself in the sense of 'Gospel'.

It seems undeniable that the apostle Matthew is connected in some way with the Gospel which bears his name, not in the text but in the title, which was probably affixed early in the 2nd century and is evidence of the widespread belief in his authorship. He was not prominent enough to be an obvious choice for having a Gospel fathered on him if its paternity were unknown. The fact that he is named 'Matthew' not 'Levi' at his call is hardly basis enough for this (9:9; Mk. 2:14). Precisely what the connection is we cannot tell, but if the apostle did not actually write the Gospel, it is likely that he was a leader in the community out of which it emerged (perhaps a sort of catechetical school), or had played a prominent part in collecting and transmitting much of the material which is included in it. The systematic nature of the Gospel has often been thought to bear the mark of a revenue official. At any rate, the author may well have his own function in mind when he records the saying of Jesus that 'every scribe who has been trained for the kingdom of heaven is like a householder who brings out of his treasure what is new and what is old' (13:52).

PURPOSE

The general purpose of any Gospel is well summed up by John (Jn. 20:31). It is to make a selection of the deeds and words of Christ to induce faith in Him and life through Him. The basic contents of a Gospel are the contents of the apostolic *kērygma*, 'beginning from the baptism of John until the day when he was taken up from us' (Acts 1:22). The special purpose of Matthew can be sought by examining again the special characteristics of his Gospel.

The Jewish nature of the Gospel, with its emphasis on the fulfilment of the OT, suggests that it was intended as apologetic against unbelieving Jews. Six of the 'formula quotations' deal with either the birth and infancy or the death of Jesus, both obstacles to faith in Him for most Jews, because of rumours of illegitimacy and the scandal of a crucified Messiah. Emphasis is also laid on the reality of the resurrection against Jewish attempts to explain it away (27:62–66; 28:11–15). Yet it does not give the impression of being written directly for the outsider so much as for the Christian to use to deepen his own understanding of the fact of Christ, and then to be able to use its material in apologetic for the faith.

Because of its systematic arrangement, Matthew's Gospel has always been the most useful for teaching. Whether or not this was the product of a rabbinic type of 'school' (see K. Stendahl, *The School of St. Matthew*, 1954), it bears some of the marks of a 'manual of discipline' for a local church, with its emphasis on casuistic ethics and church order. It has also enjoyed

more use in the liturgy of the church than any of the other Gospels, but this does not mean that it had its origin in the worship of a Christian community. (*Cf.* G. D. Kilpatrick, *The Origins of the Gospel according to St. Matthew*, 1946.)

We may conclude that the Gospel was probably written by a Jewish Christian for Jewish Christians in close contact with unbelieving Jews somewhere near to Palestine in the latter part of the 1st century AD. It was intended to instruct them carefully in the way in which Jesus had fulfilled the prophecies of the OT and had laid the foundations of the Christian church, continuous with the people of God in the old covenant and yet reformed and constituted from among all men on a spiritual basis. This instruction was to enable them to refute the attacks of the non-Christian Jews and to present to them also Jesus as their true King.

OUTLINE OF CONTENTS

COMMENTARY

1:1 – 2:23 THE BIRTH AND INFANCY OF THE CHRIST

The essential starting-point of the Gospels, as of the *kērygma*, is the baptism of John. Matthew, like Luke, has two preliminary chapters to explain Jesus' identity and to show how even in His birth and infancy prophecy was being fulfilled. The material here is all peculiar to Matthew. It seems to represent Joseph's story of the events, while Luke gives Mary's.

1:1–17 The genealogy of Jesus

The systematic arrangement of the genealogy is important as it shows at once the way in which Matthew approaches the gospel events.

1, 2 *The book of the genealogy* means literally 'the book of the genesis'. It is unlikely to be an attempt to parallel the first book of the OT as a whole. The phrase is, however, probably influenced by 'the book of the generations' of Gn. 5:1. *Jesus* is the normal name by which our Lord

was known during His earthly life. Its significance is given in v. 21. *Christ*, literally 'anointed', was the title of the Messianic King of Israel. *David* was the greatest of the kings of Israel, with whom a covenant was made that his son should sit on his throne (2 Sa. 7:12–16; Pss. 89:29, 36, 37; 132:11). This came to be understood in a Messianic sense. Jesus is referred to as *son of David* also in 9:27; 12:23; 15:22; 20:30f.; 21:9, 15; 22:42, 45. This shows the royal emphasis of the Gospel. *Abraham* was the father of the Israelite race, with whom God also made a covenant of blessing through his descendants (Gn. 12:1–3; 17:1–8). The true fulfilment of this was likewise through the Christ. Luke goes back to Adam (Lk. 3:38) showing his universalism, Matthew starts with Abraham demonstrating his emphasis on God's working through the chosen people.

3 *Tamar* is one of four women mentioned to show that irregular unions had been part of the royal ancestry. This may have been done be-

817

cause of slanders about Jesus' origin. She was an adulteress (Gn. 38). **5** *Rahab* had been a harlot and was a foreigner (Jos. 2). *Ruth* was a Moabitess (Ru. 1–4). **6** *The wife of Uriah* was Bathsheba with whom David committed adultery (2 Sa. 12). **11** *The deportation to Babylon* is important because it marked the end of the Davidic succession and pointed on to a greater king. **16** *Joseph the husband of Mary*: it seems as if Matthew has been tracing the legal descent down to Joseph while Luke may be giving the natural descent. The lists diverge after David, coincide for Shealtiel and Zerubbabel, then diverge again until Joseph. There is no suggestion in this verse that Joseph was the natural father of Jesus. The mention of Mary and the story which follows make that quite clear. Even the Sinaitic Syriac MS, which makes Joseph the father of Jesus, does not necessarily mean anything more than the legal father. **17** *Fourteen generations* is a stylized presentation, because three names have been left out from the first group, and the third group contains only thirteen generations (hardly an indication of a separation between Jesus at His birth and at His becoming *the Christ* later on). Perhaps Mary was supposed to be included. The numerical value of the letters of the Hebrew form of David is fourteen, and thus the royalty of Jesus is further stressed.

1:18–25 The birth of Jesus

The details given here are quite different from those in Luke, though both agree on the basic points that Jesus was conceived without a human father and was born at Bethlehem. In the nature of the case, it is hardly surprising that the details were treated with reserve by Joseph and Mary and were not part of the primitive Christian proclamation. Matthew's account of the birth and infancy emphasizes the guidance of God given in dreams and the fulfilment of OT prophecy.

18 *Betrothed*: this was a binding relationship and unfaithfulness during it was regarded as adultery. *The Holy Spirit* takes the initiative in the conception of Jesus (*cf.* Lk. 1:35). There were occasions in the OT where God's action brought about the birth of a man of God (Gn. 18:11–14; 1 Sa. 1:4–20) and the same happened in the case of John the Baptist (Lk. 1:5–25). But nowhere is it suggested that both parents were not involved in the act of procreation. Here and in v. 25 it is specifically denied that Joseph had intercourse with Mary before the birth of Jesus. **19** *Husband* was a term which could be used of a fiancé. Because the engagement was binding a divorce would be necessary. Joseph, as a just man, wished to do the correct legal thing. Of the alternatives of a court action and simply giving her a writ in the presence of two witnesses, he chose the latter. Justice should be tempered with mercy. **20** *A dream* was the means of guidance also in 2:12, 13, 19, 22. *Son of David* is a reminder of the legal Messianic descent of

Jesus via Joseph. **21** *Jesus* is the Greek form of the Hebrew Joshua, 'the Lord saves'. It is possible that Joshua, as well as Moses, provides a type for some of the actions and sayings of Jesus in the Gospel, but this is nowhere made explicit. The removal of sin was one of the features expected in the Messianic age, but the way in which Jesus was to do it was totally unexpected.

22 is the first of the 'formulas' which introduce special OT quotations (see Introduction). **23** *A virgin*: Hebrew *'almâ* does not normally mean anything more than a young woman. In the context of the quotation in Isaiah (Is. 7:10–17), it seems that the woman referred to may have been a wife of King Ahaz. LXX translated the word by the Greek *parthenos* ('virgin') for reasons which are uncertain. There was no expectation of a virgin birth in Israel, and it is clear that for Matthew the fact leads on to the prophecy rather than *vice versa*. It is useful to him that LXX has used this word, but the point is subsidiary to the name *Emmanuel*. The sign given to Ahaz was the pledge, through the birth of a son, that God was faithful to the covenant made with David by delivering His people from their enemies and being with them in His living presence (2 Sa. 7:4–17). This new sign fulfils all this and more, for God's presence is with men not in the Temple but in something greater, the person of His Son (12:6). This note is taken up more clearly in the promise of the perpetual presence of the risen Christ (28:20). **24, 25** imply that Joseph and Mary had normal sexual relations after the birth of Jesus, though RSV rightly omits AV's 'firstborn'. It is natural to suppose that the brothers and sisters of Jesus (13:55f.) were children of Joseph and Mary.

2:1–12 The visit of the Magi

This story has often been dismissed as legendary, partly because of parallels in other literature and partly because of the unusual features involved. But it seems that Matthew is treating it as factual and it would not be surprising that, if Jesus was God incarnate, His infancy as well as His birth and ministry should have been attended by remarkable phenomena.

1 *Bethlehem* was the birthplace of David (1 Sa. 16:1) and the census had taken Joseph and Mary there because of their Davidic descent (Lk. 2:1–6). *Judea* was the name of the Roman province, but it is probably mentioned here as a reminder of the descent of Jesus from the royal line of Judah. *Herod* was an Idumaean, known as 'Herod the Great'. He was a puppet king under the Romans and was given the title 'King of the Jews' in 40 BC. He died in 4 BC, and this fact is the only help we get from Matthew in dating the birth of Jesus. *Wise men* (Gk. *magoi*) were astrologers, probably from Persia or thereabouts. There is no reason to suppose that they were thought of as evil men practising black magic.

2 *King of the Jews*: the royalty of Jesus runs right through the Gospel as far as the cross (27:11, 29, 37). Here it is set in contrast to Herod's kingship over the Jews. (Luke on a broader canvas contrasts Caesar Augustus, who claimed the titles 'Saviour' and 'Lord', with the 'Saviour, who is Christ the Lord' (Lk. 2:1-11).) The title is equally misunderstood by Herod who feels threatened by it, and Pilate who feels bewildered by it (27:11-14). *His star*: it was thought that the star signified the presence of a great man. As it denoted someone great in Judea, they naturally went through the official channels, never expecting the obscurity which surrounded the One whom they sought. There is no certainty about the astronomical phenomenon but it may have been the close conjunction of Jupiter and Saturn in 7 BC. **3** While the Gentiles come to worship (*cf.* 12:18-21), those in control of Jerusalem, the city of God, are *troubled*. **4** Herod recognizes that a person of such importance to the Magi is likely to be the Messiah. **5** For the belief that the Messiah would be born in Bethlehem, *cf.* also Jn. 7:42. **6** This 'formula quotation' of Mi. 5:2 agrees neither with MT nor LXX. It should probably be taken as the comment of the Evangelist rather than part of the words of the priests and scribes. Matthew takes as a starting-point the assertion that Bethlehem is least (though clearly the prophet only considered it least in the eyes of the world) and shows that now it is by no means least. *Rulers* is a possible translation of Hebrew *'elep̄*, 'thousands' or 'clans' in LXX. *Who will govern*: Greek *poimanei* literally means 'shepherd'. The thought is found in Mi. 5:3f., but this clause is in fact quoting 2 Sa. 5:2 where the tribes of Israel came to make David king over them in Hebron. **10** It is interesting that Matthew does not link *the star* with the prophecy of the star from Jacob (Nu. 24:17) which was taken as Messianic in Judaism and the early church. This suggests that this prophecy had no part in shaping the story. **11** The reference to *the child* suggests that this may have been a considerable number of months after His birth. The Magi probably told Herod when they first saw the star, and his killing of the children under two years old (v. 16) suggests that there was a fair period of time involved. They *worshipped*, even though they would not have full understanding at this stage of the one who was 'God with us' (1:23). The background of Ps. 72:10; Is. 49:7; 60:10, brings out some of the significance which was later attached to the gifts, and explains why the Magi came to be thought of as kings. The mention of three gifts is the basis on which the Magi were believed to number three. None of these points is made by Matthew and they are purely speculative. The Son of God, having been revealed first to Mary and Joseph, two humble and poor Jews, is now revealed to representatives of the learned and rich among the Gentiles.

2:13-23 The flight to Egypt and the return

This section has likewise been seen as having a legendary character and as being inspired by the desire to demonstrate the fulfilment of Scripture both by type and by prophecy. Our attitude to it will again be determined by what we believe Matthew is trying to do and by whether we accept the divine overruling of history.

13 There is irony in the fact that *Egypt*, the place of bondage (Ex. 20:2), is now the place of safety. It is here that Jesus must be taken to escape the wrath of the king (*cf.* Heb. 11:27) in the promised land. **15** The quotation in its original context (Ho. 11:1) refers to the people of Israel as God's *son* (*cf.* Ex. 4:22). Matthew uses it here because he sees that Jesus is not only the Son of God in a unique way, but also the embodiment in Himself of the people of God. He is soon to go through the water and the desert, as did the people at the Exodus (Mt. 3:13 – 4:11). **16** This action is quite typical of what is known about Herod. There may have been only a score or so children of that age-group in the area, so that there is no reason why this should have been recorded by secular historians in comparison with some of his more notorious deeds. His action is similar to that of Pharaoh (Ex. 1:15-22) and the comparison of Jesus with Moses (as well as with Israel as a whole) is clear in this passage. Yet the differences are such that there is clearly no attempt to make the pattern of Jesus' experience the same as that of Moses. **18** The connection of this quotation (Je. 31:15) with the events does not lie on the surface and it is further evidence that for Matthew learning of the event comes first and finding the appropriate scripture follows. *Rachel* is the mother-figure of Israel and her tomb at *Ramah*, some 5 miles north of Jerusalem, was near the route that the Israelites took on their way to exile in Babylon. She is said to have died 'on the way to Ephrath (that is, Bethlehem)' (Gn. 35:19; *cf.* 48:7), and the Bethlehem allusion may also be in mind. The context of Je. 31 shows that the taking away of the 'children' of Israel into captivity, while a matter for profound sorrow and mourning, was in fact the prelude of a new era for the people of God, in which 'There is hope for your future, says the Lord' (Je. 31:17). So the weeping of the mothers of Israel is here a prelude to the saving work of the Messiah. **20** *Cf.* Ex. 4:19. **22** *Archelaus* succeeded to Herod's territory in Judea, Samaria and Idumaea. Herod Antipas became tetrarch of Galilee and Peraea, and Philip of the area north and east of Galilee. Archelaus was seen to be a greater threat to the safety of the infant Christ than was Antipas. **23** This is the most difficult of the 'formula quotations' to trace. *The prophets* (plural) suggests that several passages may be in mind. It is usual to relate it particularly to the *nēṣer* ('branch') of Is. 11:1. This was taken to be a Messianic passage fore-telling the lowly origin of the Christ despite His

Davidic ancestry. It seems that the name *Nazareth* brings this point to the mind of the evangelist. There is no real reason to see any connection with Nazirites. For the contempt of Nazareth, *cf.* Jn. 1:46. Matthew must show that the fact that Jesus lived in Galilee did not mean that He was not born in Bethlehem (*cf.* Jn. 7:41f.).

3:1 - 4:25 THE BAPTISM AND TEMPTATION OF THE CHRIST

Matthew has shown us the royal, Messianic, divine origin of Jesus and the way in which the Scriptures were fulfilled in His birth and infancy. There follows a long gap and the story is not picked up again for some 30 years (*cf.* Lk. 3:23). The saving events are connected with His ministry, death and resurrection, and it is these that form the main content of the *kērygma*. John the Baptist stood at the beginning of the *kērygma* (Acts 1:22; 10:37; 13:24f.) and at the beginning, therefore, of the main part of the Gospels (*cf.* Mk. 1:2ff.; Lk. 3:1ff.; Jn. 1:6ff.). He was the last of the prophets of the old covenant (Mt. 11:13), who came as the forerunner of the Messiah (11:11; Mk. 1:2) and was a witness to the incarnation (Jn. 1:7f.) rather in the way that the apostles were witnesses to the resurrection. He is an antitype of Elijah (Mt. 11:14) and may also be compared to Moses, bringing his people to the borders of the promised land but not being able to enter it himself (11:11). Here we move from the voice of the prophets in Scripture (chs. 1, 2) to the voice of the living contemporary prophet teaching us the truth about Jesus.

The baptism of Jesus, in which He was commissioned for His Messianic ministry, leads on naturally to His temptation, where His vocation is thoroughly tested. Once that has been done and John's ministry has been brought to an end (4:12), the way is open for Jesus to begin His own ministry and call men to share with Him in it.

3:1-12 The ministry of John

This section partly follows Mk. 1:2-8, but for vv. 7-10, 12, *cf.* Lk. 3:2-9, 16f. It describes the general tenor of John's ministry before he was called to his supreme task of baptizing the Christ.

1, 2 *In those days* is perhaps a rather vague time note (Luke alone of the Evangelists gives dates), but it may mean 'in those momentous days'. *John the Baptist* is well enough known to readers of the Gospel not to need any further introduction. *The wilderness of Judea* embraced a large area which was not cultivated, but much of which was suitable for grazing. Traditionally the wilderness stood for the simplicity of life with God as against the corruption of city life, and some prophets and ascetic groups operated in or from it. Any connection of John with an Essene group is purely speculative, but his object was quite different from theirs. He did not try to

withdraw people from the main body of Judaism but to create a spiritual remnant within it. The content of John's *preaching* is summarized by Matthew in the same terms as that of Jesus (4:17). *Repent* meant a change of attitude to self and to God. The call is made because of the imminence of the Messianic kingdom. Matthew uses the reverential expression *kingdom of heaven* while the other Evangelists all speak of the 'kingdom of God'.

3 In MT of Is. 40:3 there should probably be a colon after 'crying'. The evangelists have taken over the quotation in the form here and see *the Lord* as a reference to Christ. This oracle originally calling for preparation for God's deliverance of His people from the Exile is appropriate for this new act of deliverance which is about to happen. **4** The sartorial model is clearly Elijah (*cf.* 2 Ki. 1:8). **5** John evidently caused a great stir at the very heart of Judaism. **6** The exact procedure of baptism is uncertain. The Qumran community made repentance a condition for receiving its rite of baptism.

7 His clientele was surprisingly far-ranging. The *Pharisees* might have been expected to think that their legalism, and the *Sadducees* that their ritualism, would be sufficient passport to heaven. But many of them came from a sense of fear like snakes fleeing from a forest fire. John's bluntness is characteristic. **9** The danger of relying on pedigree, rather than on spiritual conformity, is an ever-present one (*cf.* Jn. 8:39f.). It is not stated whether they were in fact baptized, but it seems unlikely at least for most of them (*cf.* 21:25f.). **11** John's baptism was to point not only to the person of the Messiah but also to His activity. John admits himself unfit to be His slave. As Jesus is greater than John, so will His baptism be greater than John's. *The Holy Spirit* should probably not be understood here in the fully personal sense in which the third person of the Trinity was revealed at Pentecost. There was to be an inward work of God in their hearts. **12** The wind of the Spirit and the fire were alike agents of decisive judgment.

3:13-17 The baptism of Jesus

This is close to Mk. 1:9-11 (*cf.* Lk. 3:21f.), but vv. 14, 15 are peculiar to Matthew. Most commentators see the baptism of Jesus not only as a commissioning for His ministry (*cf.* 21:23-27) but also as a symbolic recapitulation of the Exodus from Egypt, performed by Jesus the new Israel and bringer of the new Exodus of salvation (*cf.* 1 Cor. 10:1-4). As Matthew alone records John's hesitation about baptizing Jesus, vv. 14f. have often been regarded as unauthentic and as an addition to meet objections that Jesus' acceptance of baptism at the hands of John implied both sinfulness and also inferiority to John. It is thought unlikely that John recognized Him as the Messiah (*cf.* Jn. 1:31). For this does not mention any such recognition but only John's sense that he was dealing with someone morally superior. John would have known Jesus' character, and His bearing on this occasion would confirm that here was no sinner in need of repentance. It would appear from Jn. 1:31–34 that through what happened at Jesus' baptism, John himself realized who He was, or came more deeply to appreciate the work He had come to do.

15 *To fulfil all righteousness*: this seems to mean that He accepted the divine plan and vocation and identified Himself with the remnant within Israel. **16** *Went up*: the same word is used of the Exodus (*e.g.* Ex. 13:18) and of the entry into the promised land (*e.g.* Dt. 1:21), and this may be significant in the context, though it is, of course, a common descriptive word. The opening of the heavens may be in fulfilment of Is. 64:1 and symbolizes the coming of God into the world in Christ (*cf.* Jn. 1:51). The Spirit's descent *like a dove* was something which only Jesus is said to have seen. **17** The *voice* was the voice of God (the *baṯ qôl*). The words are generally taken to be a combination of Is. 42:1 and Ps. 2:7. This would show that Jesus was the Messiah but that His Messiahship is to be interpreted in the light of the prophecies of the Servant of the Lord. *This is . . .* does not mean that Jesus became Son of God at this moment but that He was commissioned for His work as Son of God (*cf.* 17:5). *My beloved Son* is a phrase which suggests a unique relationship (*cf.* Jn. 1:18) and Jesus is referred to as 'the Beloved' in Eph. 1:6. *With whom I am well pleased*: not only in His obedience thus far but also as the agent by whom God will fulfil His plan of salvation.

4:1–11 The temptations of Jesus

These are referred to briefly in Mk. 1:12f. For this account, *cf.* Lk. 4:1–13. The only substantial difference from Luke is the order of the second and third temptations. Matthew's account works to a psychological climax; Luke's seems to be governed more by geography. Only the Synoptic Gospels and Hebrews mention the temptations (*cf.* Heb. 2:18; 4:15). There is no doubt at all about the Exodus typology here. The answers which Jesus gives from Deuteronomy, which is a theological commentary on Israel's time in the wilderness, show that He has entered into an understanding of His recapitulation of the role of Israel in His own person. The temptations are basically the same as those of God's people (*cf.* also 1 Cor. 10:1–13) and come to test both the person and the programme of Jesus. There is a further parallel with the temptations of Adam and Eve (Gn. 3), described as 'the lust of the flesh and the lust of the eyes and the pride of life' (1 Jn. 2:16), which suggests that the temptations were typical of those which mankind as a whole has to face.

1 This was a work of *the Spirit* because it was necessary for Jesus to overcome temptation. **2–4** The *forty days* in the wilderness after His baptism are a miniature of the 40 years of Israel in the wilderness after their baptism at the Exodus, when as God's son they were called

out of Egypt (Ho. 11:1). *If you are the Son of God*: *cf.* v. 6; 27:40, 43. The declaration of God (3:17) is put to the test (*cf.* Gn. 3:1). To turn stones into bread would have been quite inconsistent with the creative power of God who made these things different. *It is written . . .* The scripture is Dt. 8:3, referring back to Israel's grumbling about the manna (Nu. 11:4–9). This, then, is a temptation to the body ('the lust of the flesh'; *cf.* Gn. 3:6, 'good for food'), to be dissatisfied with God's provision and to embark on a programme of miraculous feeding in order to achieve His ends. **5–7** *The pinnacle* was probably some projecting turret or buttress. The ascent does not seem to be literally intended. Satan's quotation of Scripture is subtle but out of context. Jesus' reply is from Dt. 6:16, meaning not that the devil should not tempt Him but that He should not put God the Father to the test. This refers to the incident at Massah where the people demanded signs of God's presence (Ex. 17:1–7). This is therefore a temptation to the mind ('the lust of the eyes'; *cf.* Gn. 3:6 'a delight to the eyes'), to be dissatisfied with God's methods and to embark on a programme of spectacular wonder-working in order to achieve His ends. **8–10** *A very high mountain* seems to be symbolic. The scripture quoted is Dt. 6:13 which refers back to the incident of the golden calf (Ex. 32:1–6). This is the culminating temptation—to the soul ('the pride of life'; *cf.* Gn. 3:5 'you will be like God') to be dissatisfied with God Himself and to embark on a programme of unscrupulous manipulation to achieve His ends. **11** This does not mean that He was never tempted again (*cf.* Lk. 4:13: 'until an opportune time').

4:12–25 The beginning of the ministry

Vv. 12, 17–22 are parallel to Mk. 1:14–20 (*cf.* Lk. 4:14). Vv. 13–16, 24f. are peculiar to Matthew. Matthew omits the story of Jesus in the synagogue at Capernaum (Mk. 1:21–28), and places the healing of Peter's mother-in-law and of the sick at evening (Mk. 1:29–34) in 8:14–16. He also omits the reference to Jesus' withdrawal (Mk. 1:35–38) and again parallels Mk. 1:39 in v. 23. In this section the Messiah, who has been commissioned for His work, now begins it in Galilee and begins to call to Himself disciples to be associated with Him in it. A general summary is given of His work in Galilee.

12 The arrest of John is the signal for Jesus' ministry to begin. **13** *Nazareth* was apparently not *in the territory of Zebulun and Naphtali* while *Capernaum* was. This becomes 'his own city' (9:1) and the move is seen to be a fulfilment of prophecy. **15, 16** quote Is. 9:1f., where the contrast is made between the darkness of the northern regions subjugated by the Assyrians and the light of deliverance which would shine on them. So it is in the despised provinces that the Messianic King begins His work unknown. **17** is the summary of Jesus' message in the first part of His ministry (*cf.* 16:21 for His message in the second part). The message is the same as John's in outline (*cf.* 3:2). **18** The call of the disciples and their immediate response may be accounted for by the fact that Jesus had met them before (*cf.* Jn. 1:35-42). **19** *Follow me* was a command to be obeyed literally and figuratively. **23** is a general summary of Jesus' Galilean ministry. *Teaching* and *preaching* follow in chs. 5-7, and healing in chs. 8, 9. The disciples are to be associated with this threefold work (*cf.* 9:35-37). **24** *Syria* may be used in the sense of the Roman province to which Palestine belonged, rather than specifically the territory north of Galilee. The area had a mixed population and some contact with Gentiles must have occurred.

5:1 - 7:29 THE SERMON ON THE MOUNT

Matthew is shown here *par excellence* as the collector and systematic arranger of the teaching of Jesus. While much of the Sermon is his own material, there is a certain amount found also in Luke, but in different places in his Gospel. If Matthew is indeed a handbook of Christian instruction, we should expect him to lay more stress on the subject-matter than on the occasion of utterance of many of Jesus' sayings. It is natural to see Jesus as the new Moses delivering the new Torah (Law) with a new authority (5:21f., 27f., 31-34, 38f., 43f.). But it is not a new legalism, despite the emphasis on the importance of law and the danger of antinomianism (5:17-20). The real criticism is directed not against the OT law but against the rabbinic interpretation of it. Matthew shows how Jesus 'radicalizes' the demand of God, revealing it to be something that deals with the inward man and which can be worked out only through the power of love (5:21-48). It is *didachē* (moral teaching) but it is set within the framework of *kērygma*. It can be attempted only by the man who has responded to the challenge of the kingdom presented by Jesus, and who seeks to obey on the basis of grace. The perfection demanded (5:48) does not mean that there is a double standard, but that the new life of sonship in Christ is the only basis on which the principles set out are in any way attainable. Only that can give the right outlook and attitudes, and it is these, particularly as they are expressed in personal relationships, rather than the outward actions, which have the primary significance. Yet no divorce is expected between the two.

5:1-16 Characteristics of discipleship

This section is peculiar to Matthew in this form, but there are parallels to vv. 3, 5, 6, 11, 12 in Lk. 6:20-26. Matthew does not include the woes given by Luke. This is a 'programmatic' discourse (like the sermon at Nazareth in Lk. 4:16-30) setting the tone of the teaching ministry of Jesus. The emphasis is on the Messianic bliss of the poor and oppressed. For vv. 13-16, *cf.* Mk. 9:50; 4:21-23; Lk. 14:34f.; 8:16-18; 11:33.

1 *The mountain* has not been identified; the word does not signify a peak but a place withdrawn enough for Him to escape from the crowds and to be with His disciples. There is no apparent emphasis on the comparison with Moses giving the law from the mountain. He *sat down*, as was the custom of teachers in the synagogues (*cf.* Lk. 4:20). **3** *Blessed*: the 'Beatitudes' received their name from the Latin word *beatus*, 'blessed'. The sense is 'Oh, the blessedness of . . . ' (*cf.* Ps. 1:1). Many of the Beatitudes have close OT parallels. Jesus, however, unites them into one integrated Christian character. Some ancient versions place v. 5 before v. 4 and, if that is the correct order, the Beatitudes fall naturally into four pairs with v. 11 expanding the eighth in v. 10. *The poor* in the OT were often the pious (*cf.* Ps. 69:29-36; Is. 61:1). **4** *Mourn*: *cf.* Is. 61:2. The comfort is Messianic. **5** This statement is very similar to Ps. 37:11. The *earth* may simply mean the 'land', with the idea of the promised land. **6** *Cf.* Is. 55:1f. *Righteousness* may mean not only right ethical conduct but vindication by God. **7** There does not seem to be a clear OT parallel to this Beatitude. **8** *See God*: *cf.* Ps. 24:3f. **9** *Peacemakers* is a rare word. In Is. 27:5 there is the idea of making peace with God.

10 The Beatitudes are rounded off as they were begun with the promise of the Kingdom. Here *righteousness* must mean right conduct and it is only when this is involved that the persecuted can be regarded as blessed. All the Beatitudes upset human calculations, but this one more than most. It is expanded and personalized in vv. 11, 12. **11** Matthew makes a point of the evil being spoken *falsely* (cf. Lk. 6:22). **12** *Rejoice*, because of, rather than in spite of, persecution. The *reward* offered is not something for mere selfish enjoyment but a greater capacity to enjoy and serve God. Persecution is the mark of the prophetic succession (*cf.* 23:37). **13** *Salt* is of value as a preservative. To the Rabbis it denoted wisdom (*cf.* Col. 4:6). The wise life and speech of the disciple should have their effect on society, but contact without dilution is necessary. **14** *The light of the world* was said by the Rabbis to be God, Adam, Israel, the law, the Temple or Jerusalem. The Jews, at least in their own estimate of themselves, and Christians are both referred to in such terms by Paul (Rom. 2:19; Phil. 2:15). But for the NT, Jesus is supremely the Light of the world (Jn. 8:12). **16** Where the motives are really good, public doing of right is much to be commended (but *cf.* 6:1). *Your Father*: a very important concept in the teaching of Jesus. He never identifies the relationship of the disciples to God with His own relationship to God (*cf.* Jn. 20:17).

5:17-48 The old and the new law

This section is largely peculiar to Matthew, but there are some parallels to vv. 38-48 in Lk. 6:27-36 and to vv. 18, 32 in Lk. 16:17f. For vv. 25f., *cf.* Lk. 12:57-59. After an initial statement of His attitude towards the law and the prophets (vv. 17-20), Jesus then gives examples of the application of His principles to various OT precepts and their normal rabbinic interpretation.

5:17-20 The validity of the law. These verses have caused considerable difficulty because they seem to demand a total acceptance of the OT law in a way which was neither practised by the early church nor apparently advocated in the rest of the Sermon on the Mount. Their very difficulty should make us less ready to write them off as unauthentic. Nor is there any objective ground for calling v. 19 'anti-Pauline polemic'. The verses seem to be basically a criticism of the position of the Pharisees with a warning against antinomianism.

17 *Think not*: some of His early actions might have caused them to think this (*cf.* Mk. 2:23–28). *Abolish* may mean rather to 'break up' the divinely-given unity of *law* and *prophets* as a whole in Scripture. To *fulfil* (Gk. *plēroō*) is probably not so much to obey them as to 'give them their full meaning'. This is the way in which the word is used in the 'formula quotations'. Law and prophets find their deepest significance when the Messiah comes. **18** Some have tried to take this as referring to the attitude of the Pharisees, but this seems unnatural. *Iota* probably refers to the Hebrew *yôḏ* which may often be omitted. *Dot* probably refers to the small strokes on certain Hebrew letters, but it may signify the Hebrew *waw* which was also dispensable. *Till heaven and earth pass away* means 'during the present age', stressing its relative permanence. *Pass* (Gk. *parerchomai*) is the same word as *pass away*. *All is accomplished*: the Greek word *ginomai* is frequently used in Matthew of something which happens in fulfilment of prophecy (*cf.* 1:22; 21:4; 24:6; 26:54, 56). There is a close parallel to this verse in 24:34f. where *ginomai* and *parerchomai* are both used. The sense may well be that in this age nothing shall pass away from the OT until everything which it predicts about the Messiah has happened and so been given its full significance.

19 extends the principle from what is 'fulfilled' in the coming of Christ to the attitude of disciples to the law. *Relaxes*: this is what the Qumran sect and others thought the Pharisees did. By their casuistry they made the law practicable and therefore blunted its moral force. *These commandments* are usually taken as referring to the OT law, but it may be that *these* looks forward to what follows—Christ's deeper interpretation of the law, which indicates the way to its true fulfilment. **20** *Exceeds*: in quality rather than quantity. The scribes were those who claimed to teach the law, and the Pharisees those who claimed to do it. Entry into the kingdom depends on a new relationship with God (*righteousness* and 'justification' are cognate words) which must be demonstrated by lives and teaching of a new depth and power.

5:21-26 Killing and anger. The commandment from the Decalogue is extended to deal with the motive of anger. There is a similar pattern in the following five paragraphs also. The repeated

I say to you emphasizes Jesus' authority in giving moral principles more radical than the rabbinic *hălāḵâ* (*cf.* 7:28f.).

22 'Without cause' (RSV mg.) is not in the best MSS. The prohibition is absolute. It is hard to see a clearly ascending scale of wrongs and penalties, even if *judgment* simply means a human court. It may be that they said that *whoever insults his brother shall be liable to the council*. This would mean that Jesus twice contrasts an eternal punishment with a temporal one (judgment human: judgment divine; council: hell of fire) though this is not the most natural way to take the Greek. It is possible, on the other hand, that the Greek *more* (*fool*) is a transliteration of the Hebrew *môreh*, 'apostate' (Je. 5:23; Ps. 78:8). **23, 24** move on from being angry with others to others being angry with the disciples. *Offering your gift at the altar* implies a situation within Judaism rather than the church. The Day of Atonement was held not to cover offences against a man's neighbour unless there was reconciliation. **25, 26** were probably originally in an eschatological context, as in Lk. 12:57–59. The principle of getting right with God is here extended to getting right with one's neighbour. It is the realization of human bankruptcy towards God and the need to keep short accounts with Him that should underlie dealings with one's neighbour (*cf.* 18:23–35).

5:27-32 Adultery and lust. Here there is a similar extension of the Decalogue followed by a statement about divorce.

27, 28 *Adultery* meant in the first instance a man's taking another man's wife, and was similar to taking his property or his life. The principle is probably to be extended to all forms of sexual relations outside marriage. The desire has the same nature as the action. **29, 30** are also found in 18:8f., *cf.* Mk. 9:43–48. Metaphorically the *eye* is the organ through which the wrong thought is stimulated and the *hand* the limb by which it is put into action. A limitation of certain areas of experience is preferable to having the whole body, which represents the whole personality, thrown into hell, the place of final destruction. **31** This instruction was given in Dt. 24:1–4. It was a limitation on unfettered divorce without proper safeguards. Jesus supports the stricter school of Shammai. **32** *Except on the ground of unchastity*: there is a parallel to this passage in 19:1–9; *cf.* Mk. 10:2–12; Lk. 16:18. Only Matthew includes the exception, but he may only be making explicit what was implicit in the other Gospels. *Unchastity* (Gk. *porneia*) originally meant sexual relations before marriage, but it came to have a wider connotation of all sexual irregularity. *Makes her an adulteress*: presumably because she will remarry. If she has been divorced for unchastity then she has already made herself an adulteress. This is the absolute ethic of the kingdom which is no more meant to be a subject for legislation than anything else in this passage.

5:33-37 Oaths and truthfulness. This is based

upon the ninth commandment. The prohibition of false witness was extended to an obligation to keep oaths which were sworn (Nu. 30:2; Dt. 23:21; *cf.* also Jas. 5:12). **33** *Swear*: not necessarily to God. What is sworn to a neighbour in His name a man must *perform to the Lord*. **34, 35** All the things used for oaths were in some way related to God, despite the fact that the Rabbis did not regard them as binding (*cf.* 23:16–22). **36** Oaths sometimes presume a power of the swearer which is quite lacking. **37** A man's word should be capable of being trusted without any verbal ritual to give it validity. *Evil*: probably in the sense of fallen human society, but it may mean 'the evil one'.

5:38–48 Revenge and grace. There are parallels in Lk. 6:27–36. The legalistic basis of 'tit for tat' which must provide a general framework for society, must also yield within the kingdom to the principle of grace.

38 The *lex talionis* (principle of revenge) stated in Ex. 21:23f. was a restriction on unlimited revenge (*cf.* Gn. 4:23f.). Jesus carries the principle further. **39** *Do not resist*: the context suggests that it is applicable to wrongs done to a person himself and not a prohibition of the defence of others. The disciple is ready to give extra rather than to demand restitution. **40** *Coat*: the undergarment which could be demanded as a legal fine or pledge. The *cloak* was the outer garment which had to be returned to the poor man (Ex. 22:26f.; Dt. 24:12f.). **41** The Romans could press those who were not Roman citizens to carry equipment for a mile (*cf.* 27:32). **42** The obligation to *give* is one to which the disciple is open without limitation, though there is no command to give precisely what is asked for (*cf.* Acts 3:6). **43** The law only commanded *love* to the *neighbour* (Lv. 19:18). Sectarian groups in particular extended this to hatred of those who did not belong to the righteous. **44** The law in fact provided for kindness to enemies (Ex. 23:4f.). Persecutors are the most difficult enemies to love. Prayer is an essential step towards loving them. **45** This attitude comes from a quality of life which depends on a family relationship to God (*cf.* 5:9). He is indiscriminate in his general undeserved blessings ('common grace') to mankind. **46, 47** *What reward . . . ?* is probably to be taken in the sense of 'What have you done for which you would deserve a reward?' and is parallel to the expression in v. 47, *what more . . . ?* The disciple does extra in response to the God who gives extra far beyond deserts. (*Cf.* Lk. 6:32–34 where Gk. *poia charis* probably means 'what sort of grace are you showing?') **48** The perfection demanded springs from this relationship which revolutionizes attitudes. It is a perfection which is unattainable and therefore continually to be aimed at.

6:1–18 Religious observance

If the last section (5:21–48) has been mainly dealing with the teaching of the scribes, this one deals with the practice of the Pharisees. It is peculiar to Matthew, except for the Lord's Prayer (vv. 9–13; *cf.* Lk. 11:2–4). V. 1 links up the idea of reward with the preceding passage. It shows that the motive is what counts in religious observance as well as in morals. It demonstrates that these must be undertaken in the spirit of sonship. Vv. 2–4 deal with almsgiving—the obligation towards men. Vv. 5–15 deal with prayer—the obligation towards God. Vv. 16–18 deal with fasting—the obligation towards oneself.

2 *Alms* were thought by many Jews to atone for sin. *Hypocrites* literally means 'actors'. They were not necessarily insincere, but they had such a wrong idea of what religion was about that their usually correct outward acts did not correspond to any inward spiritual reality. People with such an attitude *have their reward*. They have achieved what they wanted, human praise. They have been paid in full and there is no further reward to come. **4** The almsgiving not seen by men is seen by God and He alone provides a reward of a truly satisfying kind. (The word 'openly' in AV here and in vv. 6, 18 does not occur in the best MSS.) **5, 6** The same principles apply to ostentatious prayer. It is even more reprehensible that something supposed to be directed towards God is so flagrantly directed towards men. **7, 8** *Heap up empty phrases*: or, 'gabble'. This is the 'slot-machine' principle. You put in words and get out answers. Prayer is not really like that but springs out of personal relationship to the Father. His prescience does not destroy the point of personal requests which deepen the sense of dependence and gratitude.

9–13 The Lord's Prayer occurs also in Luke. Jesus may have given it in slightly different forms on two separate occasions, but, if it is taken as the same utterance of His, then it appears that Matthew has expanded a number of the points in it in order to make the meaning plainer. The doxology (v. 13, AV) is no part of the original text but came into it through its use in the worship of the early church. As with much else about the teaching of Jesus, it can be paralleled from Jewish sources. Its originality lies in its compact arrangement, its sense of the Fatherhood of God and its emphasis on the coming of the kingdom. It treats first of God's will and glory and then of human need.

9 *Like this*: it is a model as well as something to use itself (*cf.* Lk. 11:2). *Our Father . . .* : Luke has simply 'Father'. 'Heavenly Father' is a common phrase in Matthew (*cf.* 5:48; 6:14, 26, 32; 15:13; 18:35; 23:9). The use of the Aramaic *abba* (Rom. 8:15; Gal. 4:6) shows the impact made by this teaching (*cf.* also Mk. 14:36). *Hallowed be thy name* is in the passive which was used to express reverence in Jewish prayers. It involves the revelation and acknowledgment of the holy character of God. **10** The coming of the *kingdom* means bringing into human life the eternal reign of God. It was 'at hand' when the ministry of Jesus began (4:17) and every significant event in His career was a further step in its coming until the final consummation. *Thy will be done . . .* is peculiar to Matthew and seems explanatory of the previous phrase. It involves present ethical response but is in the context of God's eschatological activity. **11** *This day*: Luke has 'each day'. *Daily* (Gk. *epiousion*) is a very unusual word, with several possible derivations. The most likely meaning is 'for tomorrow'. The idea may be based on Ex. 16:22f. A prayer of this kind would be good reason for lack of anxiety about tomorrow (*cf.* v. 34). But it must almost certainly carry overtones of the Messianic feast, and the bread of the eucharist could be thought of as a token and pledge of that banquet. **12** *Debts*: Jews thought of sins (the word 'sins' occurs in Luke) as debts. **13** seems to mean 'Do not let us be put to the ultimate test' (*cf.* 24:22), with *deliver us from evil* (not in Luke) an explanation of that. *Evil* may mean the evil one. It is in the final trial that men are particularly tempted to apostasy (*cf.* 24:9–13).

14, 15 draw out the point about forgiveness and drive it home (*cf.* 18:23–35). Human forgiveness is not the basis of divine forgiveness, but it is evidence of a life lived on the principle of divine grace (*cf.* 5:44f.). **16** The same principle of secrecy and spiritual reward applies to fasting. There is no idea of its complete abrogation nor on the other hand of its formalization. How sadly the point was missed by a 2nd-century writer: 'Let not your fasts be with the hypocrites, for they fast on Mondays and Thursdays, but do you fast on Wednesdays and Fridays' (*Didache* 8:1).

6:19–34 Material possessions

This section is closely paralleled in Lk. 11:34–36; 12:22–34; 16:13. It takes on the thought from concern about reputation to concern about material provision and shows the need of right motives (vv. 19–24) and of faith (vv. 25–34).

19 *Rust* (Gk. *brōsis*) means 'eating' and could be rendered 'worm' with RSV mg. The Pharisees thought of wealth as a reward for keeping the law. **20** When the reward is spiritual this is not selfish. **21** is a searching truth. **22** *Sound*: Greek *haplous* probably means not 'single' but 'generous' (*cf.* the noun in Rom. 12:8; 2 Cor. 8:2; 9:11, 13). A wide-ranging outlook means a greater intake of light in the spiritual sphere. **23** *Not sound*: Greek *ponēros* means 'grudging' (*cf.* 20:15 RSV mg.). A restricted outlook has the opposite effect of a lesser intake of light. **24** *Mammon* means wealth in all its forms. The claims of Jesus reach to the bottom of a man's bank account.

25 *Life* (Gk. *psychē*, often rendered 'soul') and *body* are more important than *food* and *clothing*. The man himself is more important than his trappings. **26** God provides food for the lesser creation without their worrying; all the more will He do it for men. **27** *Span of life* is probably the meaning rather than *stature* (RSV mg.). **28–30** God provides clothing also for the lesser creation, and so all the more for men. **31** It is

anxiety rather than proper stewardship and forethought which is condemned. **32** *The Gentiles* represent those who do not know a personal, loving, provident God (*cf.* vv. 7f.). **33** Material provision is not unimportant but the first motive must be the will of God (*cf.* vv. 10f.). **34** may be a combination of two proverbs. There may be an ironic touch about it. The saying occurs only in Matthew.

7:1–12 Attitudes to man and God

This section is largely paralleled in Lk. 6:31, 37–42; 11:9–13. It deals first with a right estimation of the character of others (vv. 1–6), then with a right estimation of the character of God (vv. 7–11), and ends with the golden rule (v. 12).

1 A censorious attitude towards others will bring a divine judgment (*cf.* 6:15). **2** Men can in a sense set their own standards for God to judge them by. **3** The contrast between *the speck* and *the log* is meant to be ridiculous. **4, 5** The need for helping others even in the correction of a fault is not denied (*cf.* Gal. 6:1f.). But self-examination and reformation will stop a man being a mere do-gooder, approaching from a position of assumed superiority. **6** is peculiar to Matthew. It suggests a right-minded discrimination in spiritual matters. *Dogs* and *swine* were descriptions of Gentiles and the meaning has probably been transferred to dealings with those outside the Christian community. The *Didache* (9:5) applied it to the eucharist. **7, 8** These are confident promises that God will answer the requests of His people, though not necessarily in just the way they ask (*cf.* 5:42). **9, 10** On the other hand, a useless or dangerous thing will not be given when something beneficial is requested. **11** *Who are evil* probably has the sense of 'for all your meanness' (*cf.* 6:23). Despite our grudging human nature, we provide for our children. *A fortiori* the gracious and omnipotent God will give His children *good things*. *Cf.* Lk. 11:13 where the reference is seen to be to the supreme 'good thing', the Holy Spirit. **12** The golden rule was found in Judaism, though it was expressed in the negative form. The positive form reaches much further. Here Jesus describes it as the summary of the OT.

7:13–29 The demands of the kingdom

This section is partly peculiar to Matthew but has parallels also in Lk. 6:43–49. There is the challenge of entry into the kingdom (vv. 13f.), the danger of false prophets (vv. 15–23) and the need for obedience to the words of Christ (vv. 24–27). The Sermon on the Mount is then rounded off with a reminder of the impact which the teaching of Jesus had on the crowds (vv. 28f.).

13, 14 This was probably uttered on a different occasion from the saying in Lk. 13:23f. The idea of the two ways is found also in, *e.g.*, Je. 21:8; Ps. 1:6; Pr. 14:12. Some MSS omit the second mention of *the gate* but it should probably be retained. There are two gates and two roads.

The wide gate leads on to a 'broad' (rather than *easy*) *way*, and is therefore popular. The narrow gate leads on to a 'restricted' (rather than *hard*) *way* which only a minority choose. The decision between *life* or *destruction* is made in response to the gospel. **15** *False prophets* were always a danger (*cf.* 24:11, 24) and often smoothed over the issues of life and death (*cf.* Je. 6:13f.). **16** Deeds must be the test of words and the true indication of character. **17** For the metaphor of *tree* and *fruit* and its connection with judgment, *cf.* 3:10; 12:33–35; 15:13. **21** shows again that words are no substitute for deeds. **22, 23** On the judgment *day* even the claim to have used this name and to have exercised charismatic gifts will be useless. The decisive distinction then will be between those whom He recognizes as His, and those on whom He passes judgment as doers of lawlessness (Gk. *anomia*). The role of Christ in judgment is shown strikingly here by the way in which it is stated without arguing. **24–27** If words without action have just been condemned, now hearing without action is condemned also. The two ways of preservation and destruction are vividly portrayed. This combined exhortation and warning is a fitting conclusion to the Sermon on the Mount (*cf.* Lv. 26; Dt. 28). **28** This concluding formula is basically the same for all five discourses in Matthew (see Introduction). **29** The *authority* of Jesus came from His person and His fresh, unitary and penetrating treatment of the OT.

8:1 – 9:34 THE WORKS OF THE CHRIST

Having finished his first major collection of the teaching of Christ, Matthew now goes on to a collection of the deeds of Christ. Of the thirteen paragraphs in this part of the Gospel, ten are paralleled in Mark (*i.e.* all but 8:5–13, 18–22; 9:32–34, all of which are paralleled in Luke). This shows how close Matthew and Mark are in their record of the deeds of Jesus, as compared with Matthew's independent collection of the words of Jesus as shown in the Sermon. The incidents are found in various places in Mk. 1–10. There are nine mighty works divided into three groups of three with non-miraculous paragraphs in between. The healings of the leper, the centurion's servant and Peter's mother-in-law are followed by the scribe's promise to follow Jesus. The stilling of the storm, and the healings of the demoniacs and the paralytic are followed by the call of Matthew and the teaching on fasting. The raising of Jairus's daughter and the healings of the woman with a haemorrhage, the blind men and the dumb man finish with a warning of the Beelzebub controversy ahead. Problems have been raised by the inclusion of a second demoniac in 8:28 and a second blind man in 9:27 (*cf.* Mk. 5:2; 10:46). This may be because Matthew had more details, but it seems possible that he is collecting the deeds of Jesus (as he did His sayings) and telling them with an economy of words. He may therefore be indicating that

Jesus did these healings more than once (possibly referring to Mk. 1:21–28; 8:22–26 which he does not include). This is less likely in the case of the blind men because two men are also healed in 20:29–34. There is possibly significance in the double witness (*cf.* Dt. 19:15).

8:1–17 Acts of healing

This section includes the first three miracles— the healing of the leper (vv. 1–4; Mk. 1:40–44; *cf.* Lk. 5:12–14), the centurion's servant (vv. 5–13; *cf.* Lk. 7:1–10) and Peter's mother-in-law (vv. 14f.; Mk. 1:29–31; *cf.* Lk. 4:38f.). It closes with a summary verse about general healings (v. 16; Mk. 1:32–34; *cf.* Lk. 4:40f.) and a quotation from Isaiah (v. 17).

1 is a link with the Sermon on the Mount but does not demand that all the healings happened in exact chronological order after all the teaching. **2** The healing of the *leper* may come first as indicating Jesus' attitude to the OT ceremonial law. **3** Matthew and Luke do not include Mark's 'moved with pity'. The miracles of healing are immediate in their results in response to the expression of personal need and faith. **4** Jesus observes this law, which was an important rule of public health and a reminder of the need of giving thanks to God (Lv. 14:2–32). The law was of course impotent to effect the cure. *To the people*, to show that Jesus was not against the law; or 'to them' (RSV mg.), literally, meaning the priests, as a witness of his cure.

5 Matthew and Luke agree in the dialogue of this story but each has given the setting in his own words. **8, 9** This was a remarkable statement of humility and faith in the power of Jesus to heal at a distance, reached through a comparison with the centurion's own position in the army. **10** It is a Gentile who first acknowledges the authority of Christ in this way. **11, 12** are paralleled by Lk. 13:28f. *Sit at table*: at the Messianic banquet. *Abraham, Isaac, and Jacob* are of course the Jewish patriarchs. *The sons of the kingdom* rely only on their natural descent, and so the whole concept of the phrase will have to be redefined.

16 Matthew emphasizes that they brought *many* and Jesus healed *all* (reversing the use of the words in Mark). **17** The 'formula quotation' is from Is. 53:4. Some of the Rabbis took this literally, though most spiritualized it. The NT as a whole refers the suffering Servant passages to the redemptive death of Christ. The Hebrew text is followed here and the point is made that the healings are not just works of mercy, but are part of the all-out attack of the Messiah on every kind of evil in God's world (*cf.* 12:29). *He took our infirmities and bore our diseases*, not in the sense of transferring them to Himself but of removing them. This was a foretaste of the new age when, by His dealing with sin, the physical ailments belonging to the fallen state of mankind would also be done away (*cf.* Rev. 21:4).

8:18-27 Faith put to the test

This section contains the scribe's promise to follow Jesus (vv. 19–22; *cf.* Lk. 9:57–60) and the stilling of the storm (vv. 18, 23–27; Mk. 4:36–41). The first is a challenge to the non-disciple to commit himself absolutely to following Jesus; the second a challenge to the disciples to trust absolutely in Jesus.

18 Jesus often avoided the *crowds* because they were liable to misunderstand His mission. **20** Jesus points out the insecurity of a life of wandering discipleship. It is not recorded whether or not the man faced up to the challenge. *The Son of man* is the term which Jesus undoubtedly used most frequently to describe Himself. It is based on Ps. 8 and Dn. 7 (which are both probably inspired by Gn. 1). Sometimes Jesus uses it to mean 'I' (*e.g.* 16:13), sometimes He refers the term to His suffering (*e.g.* 17:12) and sometimes to His glory (*e.g.* 16:27). The term was meant to stimulate faith. **21** The father may not yet have been dead and the son may have wished to wait until he could receive his inheritance. **22** The claims of the kingdom are absolute and immediate. Those who are spiritually alive will react to the situation quite differently from those who are spiritually dead (*cf.* 10:37f.). Again, we do not know the response of the man. **26** While there are a number of differences in detail from Mark, this verse shows Jesus exercising the power of the Creator (*cf.* Ps. 89:9; 107:23–32) and rebuking the lack of faith of the disciples. **27** They must not only follow Him as their teacher and leader but also trust in Him as someone different from ordinary men.

8:28 – 9:8 Further acts of healing

This section contains the healing of the demoniacs (8:28–34; *cf.* Mk. 5:1–20) and of the paralytic (9:1–8; *cf.* Mk. 2:1–12). Jesus is shown to be capable not only of physical healing but also of psychological and spiritual healing.

28 *Gadarenes* is probably the right reading in Matthew's account. The town of Gadara itself was about 6 miles from the lake and the term was probably used here because Gadara was the metropolis of the region. If 'Gergesenes' (RSV mg.) is correct, then the town in question may be the modern Khersa on the eastern shore of the lake. *So fierce* . . . Matthew summarizes where Mark gives much more detail. **29** *O Son of God*: the demons are shown to have recognized the supernatural power and person of Jesus long before most men did (*cf.* Mk. 3:11) because of His assault on the realm of Satan (12:22–29). *Before the time*: Jewish apocalyptic literature taught that the destruction of demons would take place at the last judgment. In Jesus the kingdom is breaking in now (*cf.* 12:28). **30** The reference to *swine* shows that it was an area with a mainly Gentile population. **31** Not enough is known about demon-possession for us to be sure what this verse means. It seems as if the

demons wished to be reincarnated. **32** This provided the man with convincing proof that his affliction had been cured. It also showed that human life is of more value than that of animals. **34** Economic interests take precedence over spiritual (*cf.* Acts 19:23–27). They no more wished for the 'interference' of the Son of God in their affairs than did the demons (v. 29).

9:1 *His own city* is now Capernaum (*cf.* 4:13). **2** In this story spiritual healing precedes physical. *Their faith* may include that of the patient as well as of his friends. There is a great power in corporate faith (*cf.* 18:19). **3** *Blaspheming* because forgiveness was a divine prerogative (*cf.* Mk. 2:7). **4** *Knowing* need not imply a supernatural knowledge, but simply a keen spiritual discernment. **6** It was easier to speak of forgiveness because it could not be tested. Yet the actual provision of forgiveness required a greater authority even than of healing a paralysed man. As in the previous story something physical was a sign of a psychological cure, so here something physical is a sign of a spiritual cure. There is no suggestion that the man had suffered as a direct result of his sin (*cf.* Jn. 9:2f.). **8** *They glorified God* (*cf.* 5:16) in contrast to the Gadarenes' reaction (8:34). *To men*: Jesus was seen as a man, yet one who was able to exercise the authority of God as the true Son of man (v. 6; *cf.* Ps. 8:5f.).

9:9-17 The call of Matthew and questions about fasting

For the two stories here, *cf.* Mk. 2:13–22; Lk. 5:27–39. They follow the healing of the paralytic in Mark.

9 The name *Matthew* occurs in this connexion only in this Gospel. Mark and Luke have 'Levi'. While all have Matthew in the list of the apostles, only this Gospel describes him as a 'tax collector' (10:3). While it would be unusual for a man to have two Jewish names, it may be that *Matthew* was a 'Christian' name, probably meaning 'gift of the Lord'. If Matthew were the Evangelist, or were in some way closely connected with the Gospel, it would be natural to include his new name here. The change of name in itself is hardly likely to be the basis for the tradition that Matthew was the Evangelist.

10 It is noteworthy that Matthew included two of the three challenging sayings to would-be disciples which are in Luke (8:19–22; Lk. 9:57–62). He did not record the saying about going to bid farewell to the people at home, perhaps because this story showed that there was a right way of doing this. *In the house* is almost certainly Matthew's house. *Tax collectors* were normally Jewish and were employees of the *publicani*, who may have been Roman citizens. They were very unpopular because of the nature of their work and the way in which it easily led to corruption and extortion. *Sinners* included outcasts of every kind, from the morally degraded to those who did not keep the full ceremonial law. It was the tragedy of much Pharisaism that it could not distinguish between them. Jesus treated people as individuals. **12** The reply is a model of common sense as well as a heartening expression of divine grace. **13** The quotation is from Ho. 6:6, and occurs again in Mt. 12:7. *Mercy* (Heb. ḥeseḏ) means 'covenant love', a mutual relationship between God and His people, defined in the second half of the verse in Hosea (not quoted) as 'the knowledge of God'. On the basis of this conception of religion the Pharisees can only be called *the righteous* ironically. (AV 'to repentance' is not part of the original text.)

14 *The disciples of John* may have been a considerable group of people (*cf.* Acts 19:1–7). Only Matthew records that they asked the question. **15** *The bridegroom* was a Messianic figure (*cf.* 22:2; 25:1). *Taken away*: probably by the ascension rather than the crucifixion. Fasting seems to have been practised on a regular basis by John's disciples as well as by the Pharisees. The apostolic church seems to have followed Jesus' habit of fasting for special occasions (*cf.* 4:2; 6:16–18; Acts 9:9; 13:2f.; 14:23). It was recognized as important but could lead to dangers of ostentation (Mt. 6:16) or self-righteousness, as here. **16, 17** There is a radical newness about Jesus' message which needs new forms of expression. Patching up Judaism will not do. *New wine*: *cf.* Jn. 2:1–11.

9:18–34 Further healings

There are three more healing stories here, that of the raising of the ruler's daughter (vv. 18–26; *cf.* Mk. 5:21–43; Lk. 8:40–56), within which is also included the cure of the woman with a haemorrhage, that of the two blind men (vv. 27–31) which is in a form peculiar to Matthew, and the dumb demoniac (vv. 32–34; *cf.* Lk. 11:14–16). Stories similar to the last two occur in Mt. 20:29–34; 12:22–24.

18 The *ruler* was an office-holder in the synagogue (*cf.* Mk. 5:22). *Cf.* and contrast Mk. 5:23; Lk. 8:41f. It would appear that Jairus meant that his daughter was already as good as dead, and that the actual occurrence of death was shortly confirmed. See Mk. 5:35; Lk. 8:49. **20** The woman seems to have suffered from continuous menstruation and would therefore be unclean (Lv. 15:25). This probably explains her coming up *behind* Jesus. The *fringe* was probably the tassel (Nu. 15:38). **21** There is a combination of superstition and faith. **22** *Made you well*: Greek *sesōken* is the usual word for 'saved' in the spiritual sense. Even if the physical cure took place by touching the garment (*cf.* Mk. 5:29), wholeness of the personality can only come through face-to-face confrontation with Jesus. **23** *Flute players* were hired with other mourners after a death had occurred. **24** *Depart*, because there was no need for people who were only putting on a show of mourning for money. *Sleeping*: it is usual to take this as metaphorical, but it may be literal if she was in a coma, but see the doctor's account in Lk. 8:53, 55. **25** Matthew gives only the action of Jesus and not His words. **26** Matthew alone emphasizes the way in which

His reputation spread. **27** *Son of David*: the Messiah was expected to restore sight to the blind (Is. 35:5). **28** *The house* is probably His own house rather than Matthew's (9:10). *Yes, Lord* implies faith in the power and the person of Jesus, though the term 'Lord' would not here have its full Christian sense. *Sternly charged*, because it was important not to receive the wrong sort of publicity arousing wrong expectations. **31** It was hardly possible to keep such a happening quiet, human nature being what it is. **33** Again there is emphasis on the crowd's reaction. *In Israel*: even among the people of God with their sacred history. **34** This is a foretaste of controversy to come (*cf.* 12:24).

9:35 – 10:42 THE MISSION OF THE TWELVE

After a preliminary section which describes the motives of Jesus and His calling of His disciples for mission, the bulk of this part of the Gospel is the mission charge. It forms the second of the five discourses which make up the teaching material of the Gospel.

9:35 – 10:4 Jesus' compassion and call

These verses are found in a number of different places in the other Synoptic Gospels (*cf.* Mk. 3:14–19; 6:6b, 7; Lk. 9:1; 10:2; 13:22). **35** *Teaching*, *preaching* and *healing* are the three characteristics of the ministry of Jesus (*cf.* 4:23); **36** the motive is compassion for the people of Israel without a God-given leader (*cf.* Nu. 27:17–20; 1 Ki. 22:17). The aim of His mission was to help them to recognize Him as such. **37, 38** The metaphor of *harvest* was used more with evangelism and preaching than with teaching. This was a work where others had to be associated with Jesus.

10:1 This is the first mention of *his twelve disciples*. Though healing authority may have been recognized as having been given 'to men' (9:8), the Mediator of this divine authority is Jesus. *Every disease and every infirmity*: the scope of their ministry of healing is to be as wide as His (*cf.* 9:35). **2** *Apostles*: the term 'disciple' means a learner. Only after they had been this could they be 'apostles', men sent out from Jesus with His authority (Heb. šᵉlûḥîm). The term is mainly kept for the Twelve and Paul, but in some instances has a wider use. They are named here to show the connection of their calling with their sending out (v. 5). There are twelve as representing the twelve tribes of Israel (19:28; *cf.* the Qumran MS, 1 QS 8). Only Matthew gives them in pairs, perhaps for easy memorization. *First* denotes his leadership. Matthew has considerable interest in Peter (*cf.* 16:17–19). *The tax collector*: Matthew alone records this. If the Evangelist is the apostle it would be a recalling of his once having been an outcast. *Thaddaeus*: as in Mark. Luke has 'Judas . . . of James'. **4** *Cananaean*: as in Mark. Luke calls him 'the Zealot'. The word probably comes from Aramaic *qan'ān* ('zealot'). The Zealots were a militantly nationalist party. *Iscariot* has usually been taken to mean 'man of Kerioth' but may come from Aramaic *'išqaryā'* ('the false'). *Who betrayed him* would then be seen to follow naturally from his name. He is presumably placed last because he was the traitor (probably the only Judean and bearing the very name of the royal tribe), but it may be that he was associated with Simon as a Zealot.

10:5-42 The mission charge

The material here again seems to have been collected by Matthew from a number of different places, and a number of things which were probably said by Jesus on other occasions are gathered for convenience of reference into this teaching on mission. For vv. 9-16, *cf.* Mk. 6:8-11; Lk. 9:1-5; 10:1-12. Vv. 17-25 have parallels in the eschatological chapters Mk. 13 and Lk. 21. Vv. 26-39 are similar to Lk. 12:2-9, 51-53; 14:26f.; 17:33. Vv. 5-8 and 40-42 are peculiar to Matthew.

5 The order of priority in evangelism in the apostolic age was 'to the Jew first and also to the Greek' (Rom. 1:16). This was even more so in the case of Jesus whose task was to call God's people to repentance and to the recognition of their own vocation through the Messiah to take the gospel to all men (28:18-20; *cf.* Acts 1:8). **6** *The lost sheep* are probably *'am hā'āreṣ* (the people of the land), who were despised as ignorant. **7** The substance of their preaching was to be the same as that of John (3:2) and of Jesus (4:17). **8** Healing was part of the work of evangelism, and was associated here with preaching. The third of Jesus' activities, teaching, was hardly possible for them at this stage of their understanding. *Raise the dead* is not in some good MSS but is probably a correct reading. There is to be no restriction on the power of the apostles to do what their Master did (*cf.* Jn. 14:12). *You received without pay, give without pay*: they had received the gift of forgiveness and the power to heal from Jesus gratis. So they were to proclaim forgiveness and exercise the powers to heal gratis. **9, 10** They were to travel light, both because of their need for haste and also because of the obligation of the people to support them; for *the labourer deserves his food*. The fact that the gospel is free means that its proclamation is not on a business basis, but there is an obligation, inspired by gratitude, on local believers to extend hospitality to travelling evangelists (*cf.* 1 Cor. 9:14; 1 Tim. 5:18). *Nor a staff*: one is permitted in Mk. 6:8. Luke agrees with Matthew. It is possible that a 'Q' saying from another context is being used here. At any rate, they are to have the minimum of encumbrance. **11** *Worthy*: probably in the sense of responsive to the preaching and willing to offer hospitality. **12** *Salute it*: with some such greeting as 'Peace be to this house'. **13** The greeting would not be something merely conventional. Peace would be brought at a new level to those who responded.

14 *Shake off the dust*: as a sign of complete rejection of them in their turn. **15** *Sodom and Gomorrah* were types of spiritual wickedness and refusal to listen to God's messengers (Gn. 19:4-9; Ezk. 16:48-50; Mt. 11:23f.). *The day of judgment* presumably means the last day, but there may be at least some hint at the coming temporal judgment in the horrors of the Jewish War of AD 66-70.

16 The defencelessness of *sheep in the midst of wolves* means that their position must be supported by both wisdom (the subtlety of the serpent—*cf.* Gn. 3:1) and innocence (which would mean that as they were doing God's will they would have His protection). **17** *Men*: it seems that they were warned against the reaction of the human race as a whole. *Councils* were local sanhedrins. The flogging would be the traditional thirty-nine lashes (2 Cor. 11:24). **18** The scope of the mission was to extend beyond Judaism. Their testimony to the truth of the gospel would often have to be given as prisoners (*cf.* Acts 23:11; 25:11). **19** *Do not be anxious*: *cf.* 6:25-34. It is God's provision which should allay anxiety, whether concerning material things or words. **21** The gospel will divide families (*cf.* vv. 34-36). **22** The universal hatred experienced by those who brought a message of love to the world was particularly hard to bear, as was the charge that they themselves hated the human race. *For my name's sake*: *i.e.* because you belong to Me and bear the name of Christian (*cf.* 1 Pet. 4:14). *To the end* probably means to the end of his life, through persecution, rather than to the end of time (*cf.* 24:9, 13).

23 is a very difficult verse. Schweitzer based much of his 'thoroughgoing eschatology' on it, saying that Jesus expected the end at this time. Clearly Matthew did not think of it in this way. A possible solution is that they would not have completed the rounds of the *towns of Israel* before the *Son of man* came in judgment through the Romans in the Jewish War (*cf.* Cyrus the Persian king as God's shepherd and anointed in Is. 44:28; 45:1). **24, 25** explain the reason for the hatred which the apostles would receive (*cf.* Jn. 15:18-21). *Beelzebul*: see 12:22-32.

26 *Have no fear of them* probably refers to what follows, the need to preach openly, rather than to what precedes, slander of the apostles. **27** In some ways the apostles were to have more of a public ministry than did Jesus Himself. **28** *Him who can destroy both soul and body in hell* must refer to God, rather than to Satan. The soul in biblical thought is not immortal, except when new life is conferred upon it through Christ (1 Tim. 6:16; 2 Tim. 1:10). Hell is therefore the place of its destruction as Gehenna, the valley of Hinnom, was the rubbish of Jerusalem. **29** God who is the terrible Judge of all is also the loving Father of those who trust Him (*cf.* 6:26). **30** is a vivid picture of the detailed loving care of the Father. **31** For the *a fortiori* argument, *cf.* 6:30. **32** Mark and Luke in parallel sayings both refer to the Son of man.

Matthew shows that Jesus meant to refer to Himself when using the expression in this context. Open confession is an essential mark of discipleship (cf. Rom. 10:9-11). *My Father* is parallel to 'your Father' (v. 29), but there is always a distinction in the relationship. 'Our Father' (6:9) is for the disciples, not for Jesus too.

34 Jesus came as the Prince of peace, and *peace* on earth was His ultimate goal (cf. Lk. 2:14). But because of the variety of human response to the gospel, the immediate result was *a sword*, which Luke rightly interprets as 'division'. **35, 36** are based on Mi. 7:5f. which depicts the breakdown of trust in human relationships and contrasts it with the faithfulness of God. The object of the coming of Elijah was reconciliation in families (Mal. 4:6), but in the short term the reverse is often the case. **37, 38** are similar to Lk. 14:25-27, where the comparative is made absolute by the use of the word 'hate'. *Worthy of me*: to belong to Me and to be called My disciple. *Take his cross*: in sacrificing his whole personality. **39** *His life* (Gk. *psychē*) is his soul or real self. Only the man who is in a right relationship to God in Christ has become what he was created to be. Vv. 38, 39 are repeated in 16:24f.

40 shows the solemnity of their commission as apostles or agents (*šelûḥîm*) of Jesus, for 'a man's *šālîaḥ* ('agent') is as the man himself' (*Berakoth* 5:5). **41** *Receives a prophet*: cf. 1 Ki. 17:9-24; 2 Ki. 4:8-37. *Righteous man*: presumably one whose witness is primarily by his life. For prophets and righteous men see 13:17. **42** *Little ones* probably refers to the humble believers. The smallest act of kindness is truly significant (cf. 25:40).

11:1 - 12:50 THE CLAIMS OF THE CHRIST

After the mission charge, which was teaching contained within a narrative, Matthew gives us two chapters of narrative which contain a good deal of teaching. The stories collected here are designed to show the nature of the Messiahship of Jesus and the fact of the unbelief of Israel. The kingdom has been announced to Israel by John the Baptist (ch. 3), by the words (chs. 5-7) and deeds (chs. 8, 9) of Jesus and the apostles (ch. 10). Israel is shown here, in the person of the Pharisees, to reject the Messiah and so the first step is taken towards the presentation of the gospel to the Gentiles (12:18-21).

11:1-19 Jesus and John

After a linking verse, Matthew gives the story of the visit of John's disciples to Jesus and His teaching the crowds about John. This section is closely parallel to Lk. 7:18-35, apart from vv. 12, 13 which are similar to Lk. 16:16.

1 This verse is more clearly connected with the preceding than with the following section (cf. 7:28f.). **2** John was arrested by Herod Antipas (4:12) and kept, according to Josephus, at Machaerus, a fortress on the east side of the Dead Sea. He was later executed on Herod's orders (14:1-12). *The deeds of the Christ* are the Evangelist's way of putting it. John had doubts about their significance. **3** *He who is to come* was probably a general Messianic term. John himself had spoken of the coming one (3:11). There is no doubt in his mind about the fact of the Messiah's coming, only about the identity of the Messiah. Perhaps John expected Him to begin to put the judgment into effect already (cf. 3:12) and also to release him from prison. **4** Luke records healings done 'in that hour'. But the words and works of Jesus as a whole are the evidence. **5** These are Messianic works as foretold in Is. 29:18f.; 35:5f.; 61:1. They are a reminder to John, the accent of whose ministry was on judgment, that basically the ministry of the Messiah is one of mercy. **6** *Offence* might be taken because Jesus did not conform to people's ideas of what the Messiah should be (cf. 13:21, 57; 15:12).

7, 8 John was neither one who bowed to popular opinion nor one who sought an easy life. **9, 10** He was a *prophet*, a man who by his words of judgment and life of asceticism in the wilderness stood out against the easy-going society of his day. But he was *more than a prophet* because he had to identify the Messiah of whom the other prophets had simply spoken in general terms. He was the *messenger* and forerunner of whom Malachi had spoken (Mal. 3:1; cf. Ex. 23:20). **11** *No one greater*: because of his divinely-appointed role. Yet he belongs to the old covenant and therefore even *he who is least in the kingdom of heaven is greater than he*, in the sense of having a more privileged position (cf. 13:16f.). **12** is one of the most difficult verses in the Gospel. Lk. 16:16 is similar but not identical in wording and the order is different, and so may have been spoken on another occasion. *Has suffered violence* represents the Greek *biazetai*. This may be passive, as in RSV. It would mean that Zealots and others had been trying to take hold of the kingdom (cf. Jn. 6:15f.), or that it was being violently stormed by people eager to enter it, though despite the marvelling of the crowds we are not given the impression that many had responded to the claims of the kingdom at a deep level. But *biazetai* may be in the middle voice, as in RSV mg. It would then mean 'has been coming violently'. The radical claims of the kingdom had a disruptive effect on Jewish life. It is probable that the passive rendering should be adopted. **14, 15** are peculiar to Matthew. John was not Elijah reincarnate (cf. Jn. 1:21) but he fulfilled the role of Elijah prophesied by Malachi.

16 *This generation* were the privileged witnesses of the redemptive acts of the new covenant, as had been the generation of the Exodus in the old covenant (Dt. 1:35; 32:5, 20; Ps. 95:10; Mt. 12:39, 41f., 45; 16:4; 17:17; 23:36; 24:34; Acts 2:40; Heb. 3:10). They are therefore in a particularly responsible position in their reaction to the gospel. **17** They were sulky and unwilling to 'play weddings' with Jesus or 'funerals' with John. **18, 19** For the issue of fasting, *cf.* 9:14–17. For Jesus' association with sinners, *cf.* 9:10–13. *Yet wisdom is justified by her deeds*: Luke has 'children' for 'deeds' and that may be the more literal rendering. *Justified* seems to mean 'proved right', though this may be only in the long term. 'Deeds' or 'children' would mean the actions taken by John and Jesus respectively, which gave the proof to their words. There is almost a personification of wisdom here (*cf.* Lk. 11:49). (For further teaching about John see Mt. 3:1–17; 14:1–12; 21:23–32.)

11:20–30 The refusal and offer of the gospel

This section consists of an oracle of judgment against the towns which had rejected the good news of the kingdom (vv. 20–24; *cf.* Lk. 10:13–15), a prayer of thanks to God for His revelation of the truth (vv. 25–27; *cf.* Lk. 10:21f.), and a statement of what Christ offers to those who respond to Him (vv. 28–30), found only in Matthew.

20 *Most of his mighty works* are said to have been performed in a small area at the north end of the Sea of Galilee. **21** *Woe* means 'Alas'. *Chorazin* was about 3 miles north of Capernaum, and *Bethsaida* a little farther away from Capernaum to the west. *Tyre and Sidon* were Phoenician cities treated in the OT as pictures of wickedness and spiritual pride (Is. 23; Ezk. 26–28). **22** *Day of judgment* may have a temporal as well as an eternal significance (*cf.* 10:15). **23** is based on Is. 14:12–15, which refers to Babylon under the figure of Lucifer (but see also the similar reference to Tyre in Ezk. 28:2–8). The attitude and the fate of Jesus' own city (9:1) will be worse than that of the oppressor of God's people, the 'foreign land' in which it was so hard to sing the Lord's song (Ps. 137:4). *Sodom* was another city which was a by-word for wickedness and the rejection of God's messengers (Gn. 19:1–29; Mt. 10:15).

25–27 The style of this saying is very similar to that of John's Gospel (*cf.* Jn. 3:35; 17:2). It has been called 'an erratic block of Johannine rock'. While many scholars are inclined to make it secondary and late because of its similarity to John, it could be equally well argued that this provides important evidence that Jesus could have taught in the style used in John. There are many Semitic turns of phrase and it looks to have been a rhythmical oracle in Aramaic. The terms 'Father' and 'Son' are used absolutely also in 24:36, denoting a unique relationship between God and Jesus. The *Father* has complete authority in *heaven and earth* and He delegates that to *the Son* (*cf.* 28:18). He has, therefore, complete power of revelation and has chosen to hide *these things* (the meaning of Christ's words and deeds) *from the wise and understanding* (or those who are such by human standards) and to reveal them to *babes* (those who are spiritually dependent enough to be able to receive them; *cf.* 18:3). The

whole sum of divine truth is transmitted from Father to Son (*cf.* Jn. 5:20). The central part which comes only by the gift of God is the knowledge of the Father and the Son, something which goes beyond facts to a personal relationship (*cf.* Jn. 17:3). The sovereignty of the Father and the Son is shown by the words *gracious will* and *chooses*. For the revelation of the Son by the Father see 16:16f. **28–30** have affinities with the invitation of Wisdom in Ecclus. 51:23–25. *Come to me* is similar to Is. 55:1–3. *All*: the sovereign invitation is not a restricted one. The *rest* promised is not mere idleness but means a new *yoke* for service. The yoke of the law, as the Rabbis called it (*cf. Pirqe Aboth* 3:5), was something that proved heavy and burdensome because of its impersonal and external nature (*cf.* 23:4). The acceptance of the yoke of Christ (His *hālāḵâ* or moral instruction) was different because of His character. Like the suffering Servant He was *gentle and lowly in heart* (*cf.* Is. 42:2f.; 53:6f.). In a paradoxical sense, despite the absoluteness of His claims, His was the easy way (*cf.* 6:13f.). Such is the wonder of the divine offer.

12:1–14 Controversy about the sabbath

For this section, *cf.* Mk. 2:28 – 3:6; Lk. 6:1–11. The regulations about the sabbath were one place where the yoke of the law as interpreted by the Pharisees was particularly burdensome. The two stories show different examples of meeting human need through preparing food and healing.

1, 2 It was permissible to *pluck ears of grain* in another man's cornfield normally (Dt. 23:25) but the Rabbis had made restrictions on the practice on the sabbath (*Mishnah Shabbath* 7). **3, 4** The account of David's eating the *bread of the Presence* is in 1 Sa. 21:1–6. He broke a minor law in order to meet a human need. **5** *The priests* had to offer some sacrifices on the sabbath (Nu. 28:9f.). The Rabbis allowed this to overrule the sabbath law. **6** *Something greater* is the kingdom of God in the person of Jesus. The argument is *a fortiori*. If David and the priests can break sabbath technicalities to meet human need, how much more can the bringer of the kingdom? **7** Ho. 6:6, which is quoted here, contains an important prophetic principle. It is also quoted in 9:13. *Guiltless*: as the Rabbis held the priests to be (v. 5). **8** Matthew and Luke omit Mark's phrase 'the sabbath was made for man . . .'. The *Son of man* here means the ideal man, Jesus. If David was able to do what he did without condemnation, how much more was the Messiah able to decide the real meaning of the sabbath law? **10** Jesus obviously had a reputation for fresh interpretation of the law, and it seems that there was almost a plot here to see how far He would go. It was held to be *lawful to heal on the sabbath* where a man's life was in danger, but this sort of healing could have waited without undue harm. **11, 12** Only Matthew records this argument, but *cf.* Lk. 13:15. The Pharisees permitted the rescue of an animal, but at Qumran the rule was 'If (a man's beast) should fall into a cistern or pit, he shall not lift it out on the sabbath' (CD 11). By the *a fortiori* argument based on the superiority of man to the animals (*cf.* 10:31), Jesus justifies His action. Though there is no emergency, it is an opportunity *to do good on the sabbath.* **14** Mark tells us that the Pharisees *took counsel* with the Herodians. The leading representatives of these two very different parties were united in their desire to *destroy* the life of the Giver of healing and life.

12:15–37 Further healings and controversy

In this section, vv. 15, 16 are very much shorter than the parallel passage in Mk. 3:7–12 (*cf.* Lk. 6:17–19). Vv. 17–21 are a 'formula quotation' peculiar to Matthew. For vv. 22–32, *cf.* Mk. 3:22–30; Lk. 11:17–23; 12:10. For vv. 33–37, *cf.* 7:16–20; Lk. 6:43–45. The plot made by the Pharisees leads on to further healings by Jesus and a justification of His approach from the OT. The allegation that Jesus' healings are inspired by the devil leads to a head-on clash and a stern warning about the relationship of words and character.

15 Jesus' knowledge of the plot made Him move on. Again He is followed by a large crowd and again His healing is universal (*cf.* 8:16). Again He seeks not to have unnecessary publicity (*cf.* 8:4; 9:30). **18–21** quotes Is. 42:1–4 (mainly following the Hebrew text), which is probably alluded to both at the baptism (3:17) and the transfiguration (17:5) of Jesus. A longer passage is quoted here in order to bring out His gentle ministry to the outcast and its further extension to the Gentiles. *My servant* has been identified with Israel as a whole, with the faithful remnant and with the Messiah. It is probable that all three references overlapped in the prophet's mind. In any event, Matthew sees Jesus as the embodiment of the true Israel (2:15). *He will not wrangle or cry aloud* explains that Jesus did not seek controversy, though He sometimes had to engage in it, and that He did not wish to publish His Messiahship in the wrong way. *Brings justice to victory*: the vindication of the ways of God is something seen to be of great importance. This vindication occurs partly through the mission to the outcast and ultimately to the Gentiles.

22 Luke gives the occasion of the following controversy, but Matthew alone says that *the dumb man* was also *blind*. **23** Matthew alone states that the crowds were wondering if Jesus was *Son of David* (*cf.* 9:27). **24** It is always possible to find a perverse explanation for any good thing. *Beelzebul* probably comes from *ba'al z^eḇûl*, 'Lord of the house' or 'exalted Lord'. In 2 Ki. 1:2 the god of Ekron is called 'Baal-zebub' or 'Lord of flies', presumably as a Hebrew estimate of his worth. But the ending in '1' may also be derogatory in Hebrew usage if it were derived from *zebel* 'dung'. He was not regarded by the Jews as a god but as *the prince of*

demons. **25, 26** Jesus makes a *reductio ad absurdum* of their argument.

27 Another powerful refutation of the charge is provided by the fact that the *sons* (presumably disciples) of the Pharisees also practised exorcism, though perhaps with notably less success than Jesus (*cf.* Acts 19:13–16). **28** *The Spirit of God* seems to be an interpretative rendering while Luke has preserved the saying more literally as 'the finger of God'. This would refer to the miracles performed before the great act of redemption in the OT (Ex. 8:19). The miracles of Jesus are a prelude to the great act of redemption of the new covenant. *Has come upon you*: the Greek (*ephthasen*) almost means 'has come by anticipation'. It has just arrived, but not yet in its fullness. The cross and resurrection are essential for its power to be revealed. **29** The ministry of Jesus is a process of binding Satan and stopping his activity, preparatory to entering his realm of death and freeing his captives (Heb. 2:14f.). **30** The conflict with Satan demands wholehearted dedication to the cause of Christ. It is perhaps significant that He speaks of those *with me* (the loyalty being to Himself), while in the converse statement (Mk. 9:40; Lk. 9:50) it is *us* or *you* (the loyalty being to the disciples).

31 *The blasphemy against the Spirit* seems to be the deliberate labelling of good as evil (*cf.* Mk. 3:30). That *will not be forgiven* because those who persist in it are putting themselves in a position where they cannot receive forgiveness (*cf.* Jn. 3:19f.). **32** *The Son of man* may be misunderstood as a human being and people may fail to see His divine character, but that is different from the deliberate quenching of conscience. **33** The nature of *the tree* determines *its fruit.* The Pharisees thought that by making the fruit good the tree would be made good. Jesus shows the essential priority. **34** Evil sayings were the inevitable result of evil character. The Pharisees are also described as *vipers* in 3:7; 23:33. **36, 37** It is often the *careless word* which reveals the true character of a man. The careless words of the Pharisees about Jesus had shown them up and would in the end be evidence on which they would be *justified* or *condemned.* (For judgment based also on apparently trivial deeds, *cf.* 25:31–46.)

12:38–50 Challenges to commitment

In this section, with vv. 38–42 *cf.* Lk. 11:16, 29–32; with vv. 43–45 *cf.* Lk. 11:24–26; with vv. 46–50 *cf.* Mk. 3:31–35; Lk. 8:19–21. The inevitably divisive nature of the ministry, leading to controversy with Jewish religious leaders and the foreshadowing of the Gentile mission, is further illustrated in three calls to repentance and discipleship.

38, 39 *A sign* would have been something spectacular, which Jesus would not do for them (*cf.* 4:5–7; Jn. 4:48; 1 Cor. 1:22). They had already seen a number of miracles (called 'signs' in John's Gospel), but the appetite for the spectacular is insatiable and was hardly likely to lead to faith (*cf*. Lk. 16:30f.). They were *adulterous* in turning away from God to this sort of religion. *The sign of the prophet Jonah* was primarily his preaching which led men to repentance (Jon. 3:2–5), though in some way he provided a sign in his own person, having escaped from 'the belly of Sheol' (Jon. 2:2; *cf*. 1 Pet. 3:18–20). **40** This brings out the full meaning of the Jonah story. Only the more general statement has been retained in Luke. *The whale* was a 'great fish' (Jon. 1:17). *Three days and three nights* seems to be a Semitic idiom and need not be supposed to contradict the resurrection on the third day (16:21). **41** *Something greater* is the kingdom of God, as present in the person of the Messiah. *The men of Nineveh* were Gentiles and oppressors of the people of God. **42** *The queen of the South* made the long journey from Sheba in Arabia because of her desire to know the truth (1 Ki. 10:1–10). The men of *this generation* did not respond to a far greater spiritual revelation which was occurring in their very midst.

43–45 The context suggests that this refers to Judaism as a whole, though the truth applies also to individuals. There was a certain movement for reformation highlighted by the ministry of John. Then there was the exorcizing work of Jesus. But repentance without possession by the Spirit of God meant the danger of relapse into a much worse spiritual state than previously. The *waterless places* of the desert were thought of as the abode of demons. **46** *His brothers* were presumably younger children of Joseph and Mary. It is usually thought that Joseph was dead by this time. RSV rightly omits v. 47 on MS evidence. **50** The relationship that counts is not physical, but moral and spiritual. It is to belong with Him to the family of the one *Father in heaven* and to do His will (*cf*. 5:43–48; 6:9f.; Lk. 11:28).

13:1–52 THE PARABLES OF THE KINGDOM

The stories in the previous section have brought into focus the crisis of faith and unbelief. Now there is a collection of seven parables of the kingdom which explain different aspects of this crisis. The parable of the sower and its explanation, together with the reason for teaching in parables (vv. 1–23), agrees with Mark (*cf*. Mk. 4:1–20; Lk. 8:4–15; but for vv. 16f., *cf*. Lk. 10:23f.). The parable of the weeds (vv. 24–30) and its explanation (vv. 36–43) is peculiar to Matthew. The mustard seed (vv. 31f.) is found also in Mark (*cf*. Mk. 4:30–32; Lk. 13:18f.), the leaven (v. 33) is found also in Luke (Lk. 13:20f.) and the habit of using parables occurs in Mark, and is expanded by a quotation (vv. 34f.; *cf*. Mk. 4:33f.). The treasure (v. 44), the pearl (vv. 45f.) and the net (vv. 47–50) with the concluding verses (vv. 51f.) are all peculiar to Matthew.

In this, the third great discourse, Matthew makes it plain that there was a distinction between the teaching which Jesus gave publicly and privately. A parable was a story to illustrate a spiritual or moral truth. It was different from an allegory where every detail had to be decoded. There was usually one main thrust to a parable, though there were often subsidiary points and it is absurd to deny that Jesus may have used the occasional allegorical touch. But the main point of a parable was to bring men into a judgment on a situation often by ridicule (7:3–5) or by indignation (*cf*. 2 Sa. 12:1–7a; Mt. 21:33–41). The parables in this chapter are concerned with the response which must be made to the coming of the reign of God among men in the person of Jesus. Because of an over-emphasis on the difference of a parable from an allegory, there has been a widespread tendency amongst recent scholars to dismiss the explanations of the parables of the sower and of the weeds as unauthentic and to suggest that the early church missed the real point. This only adds to the problem because it assumes that even the closest disciples did not understand the parables. We can agree that the main emphasis is on the coming and the triumph of the kingdom, without holding that references to the different kinds of response are necessarily to be excised.

1–9 Comment on these verses will be found under vv. 18–23, where the explanation of the parable is given. **10–15** The sheer difficulty of these verses is proof enough of their authenticity, although v. 12 may originally have been in another context (*cf*. Mk. 4:25). *Given*: the sovereignty of God in revelation must be maintained (*cf*. 11:27). The corollary of *not been given* is brought out only in Matthew. *Because seeing they do not see*: Mark and Luke have 'so that', and it may be that both are possible translations of the underlying Aramaic. The sense in the context is no different. It seems that parables are in a sense to prevent revelation. Matthew alone quotes Is. 6:9f. (LXX) to back this up (but *cf*. Jn. 12:39–41; Acts 28:26f.). It is not to be assumed that the parables stopped people from believing who otherwise would have done, but probably that they served to harden dispositions already formed (*cf*. Jn. 9:39; 3:17–19). The suggestion that it means they see the parables though they do not see the truth, and that therefore the parables are a pictorial method of evangelism, does not seem to meet all the points in the context, which clearly shows the great moral problems of unbelief and judgment. **16, 17** are a reminder of the privileged position of the disciples over against the saints of the old covenant (*cf*. Heb. 11:39f.). Luke has 'kings' for *righteous men*. **18–23** describe the different sorts of people who come in contact with the gospel: the casual, the shallow, the worldly and the responsive. The seed is the same; the soils are different. The point is made that there will be antagonism from the *evil one* (*cf*. 6:13), and from the world both in *tribulation* and *persecution* (*cf*. 24:9–13) and in its cares and pleasures (*cf*. 19:23f.). The sower, whether it be Jesus in the first instance or a disciple later, can be assured that, although much of his seed is wasted, there will be an abundant harvest.

24 *The kingdom of heaven may be compared to a man*: there is not meant to be an exact comparison of the kingdom and the man, but a comparable situation. There are some parallels to the parable of the seed growing secretly (Mk. 4:26–29), but enough differences to make it more likely that they are separate parables. (For further comment on vv. 24–30, see on vv. 36–43 where the explanation of the parable is given.) **31, 32** The point is that from small beginnings there are eventually enormous results. The mustard plant can grow to 10 ft or more. *The birds of the air* are generally taken to be the Gentile nations (*cf.* Dn. 4:20–22). The extent of the spread of the gospel could hardly have been imagined by Jesus' contemporaries. **33** The influence of the kingdom is intensive as well as extensive. It affects the whole society with which it comes in contact. *Leaven* normally has a bad meaning in the NT but this seems unlikely here.

34, 35 The use of parables is again defended on the basis of fulfilment of prophecy. While some MSS read 'Isaiah' instead of *prophet*, this is unlikely. Matthew may have had in mind that Asaph, to whom Ps. 78 is ascribed, was described as a prophet (1 Ch. 25:2), but in any event the psalmists speak prophetically. The writer was revealing the inside story of God's dealings with His people in redemption and judgment under the old covenant. The quotation is based on the Hebrew text. **36–43** *The weeds* refers to darnel which looked very like wheat. *So will it be at the close of the age*: the parable is a warning against an attempt to make a premature harvest (vv. 28–30; *cf.* 1 Cor. 4:5). There is bound to be a 'mixed' community, caused by the actions of the *Son of man* sowing *good seed* and *the devil* sowing *weeds*, but in the end the truth will be revealed and men will be divided into two classes, the *evildoers* and the *righteous*. This will be a final division made by the *Son of man* with His *angels* (*cf.* 24:30f.; 25:31–46), leading to anguish on being rejected (*cf.* 8:12; 22:13; 25:30) or the radiance of being accepted (*cf.* Dn. 12:3).

44–46 While it has been suggested that these two parables refer to Jesus' giving all for mankind, this seems unlikely. Rather does it stress the infinite worth of the kingdom for which any sacrifice is not too great (*cf.* 16:24–27). If there is any distinction in meaning between the two it may be that the first shows how a man can stumble upon the kingdom without really seeking it, while another may be searching through all sorts of substitutes before his quest succeeds. **47–50** The parable of the *net* has a similar meaning to that of the weeds. There will be a great harvest of the sea (*cf.* Jn. 21:11) but it will be a mixed catch to be sorted out at *the close of the age*. **51, 52** show the importance of understanding on the part of the disciples. Those who have understood are like scribes (knowing the law) who have been *trained for the kingdom of heaven* (instructed in the gospel). This is often thought

to have been the evangelist's self-portrait, as he *brings out of his treasure what is new and what is old*.

13:53 – 17:27 THE REJECTION OF THE CHRIST

After the collection of parables which explain the issues of faith and unbelief, Matthew follows the narrative of Mark showing the build-up of conflict with the Jewish leaders which is to lead to the rejection and death of Jesus. The order of Mark is followed throughout and the only additions are 14:28–31, Peter walking on the water; 15:12–14, a comment about the Pharisees; 16:17–19, the promise to Peter; and 17:24–27, the Temple tax. It will be noted that in three of these passages Peter plays a prominent part. This part of the Gospel on the one hand shows the build-up through the miracles and the confession of Jesus as the Christ to the high point of the transfiguration, and on the other shows His rejection at home, the rejection of John, the disputes with the Pharisees, the faithlessness of the disciples and the predictions of His suffering and death.

13:53 – 14:12 The rejection of Jesus and the execution of John

For this section *cf.* Mk. 6:1–6a, 14–29; Lk. 9:7–9. Matthew is close to Mark in the story of the rejection of Jesus but gives a briefer account of the execution of John. Luke does not include the story of the rejection, for he has already told a similar story at the beginning of the ministry (Lk. 4:16–30) and he alludes only in passing to the execution (Lk. 9:7–9).

53 is a linking verse following a discourse (*cf.* 11:1). **54** *His own country* seems to be Nazareth, where He had been brought up (2:23). Any Jewish man might be invited to teach *in their synagogue*. The *wisdom* was presumably that of His teaching, but it is not clear whether He performed *mighty works* there. **55** *The carpenter's son*: Mark has 'the carpenter'. The Greek (*tektōn*) could mean a mason. The mention of names other than Joseph's suggests that he was dead (*cf.* 12:46). **56** *Where then did this man get all this?* The fact of His local and humble origin made it impossible in their eyes to account for what Jesus was doing. **57** *They took offence at him*, therefore, and looked for some explanation which would not involve commitment to Him. *A prophet*: though the saying may have been proverbial, Jesus did at least claim for Himself this title. *His own house*: for the unbelief of His brothers, *cf.* Jn. 7:5. **58** Mark records more bluntly that 'he could do no mighty work there', but qualifies this with reference to the healing of a few sick people.

14:1 Even if His own people would not believe, *the fame of Jesus* reached as far as *Herod the tetrarch*. This was Herod Antipas, son of Herod the Great, who had succeeded to part of his father's realm, the provinces of Galilee and Perea. **2** suggests that the ministries of Jesus and

John did not overlap (cf. 4:12), for if Herod had heard of their both working simultaneously, he could not have formed this view. Luke says that others held what seems to have been a superstitious belief in John's resurrection. *These powers* seem to refer to the miracles of Jesus. John did not perform signs (Jn. 10:41). Herod's guilty conscience could have confused him concerning two men of God. **3** Josephus says that John was arrested because he was suspected of possible revolutionary activity (*Antiquities* xviii.5.2). That may well have been the pretext while the greater reason was more personal. *Philip* was not the same as Philip the tetrarch (Lk. 3:1). **4** For the law see Lv. 18:16; 20:21. This would be regarded as incest. **5** *He wanted to put him to death*: Mark makes the point that it was Herodias who wanted to put him to death, while Herod heard him gladly. The mixture of motives is not uncommon in such a guilt-ridden situation. The chief priests and elders were similarly afraid because of John's reputation (21:26). **6** The party would normally be an all-male affair. It may be assumed that the dance was of a suggestive nature. The only known *daughter of Herodias* was Salome, who later married her uncle, Philip the tetrarch. **7** Such a rash oath was probably made in a state of inebriation. **8** Herodias was clearly waiting for such an opportunity. **10** Josephus says that John was imprisoned at Machaerus east of the Dead Sea, and presumably the prison was part of the castle there. **12** A courageous action by John's disciples. Only Matthew records that *they went and told Jesus*. For many of them He would now be their leader, though groups of John's disciples remained (cf. Acts 18:24 – 19:7).

14:13–36 The feeding of the five thousand and the walking on the water

For this section, cf. Mk. 6:31–56; Lk. 9:10b–17 (Luke has only the feeding). These miracles are recorded also in Jn. 6:1–21, and this provides the most substantial convergence of the Synoptic and Johannine traditions before the passion narrative. This suggests that they may be of special importance.
13 This takes up the story from v. 2. Vv. 3–12 have been an explanation of why Herod was so worried. Jesus was not ready for a confrontation with Herod at this stage. (Luke suggests that Herod had been given his last chance of responding to the truth. See Lk. 13:31–33; 23:6–12.) But He could not get away from the crowds. **14** Mark explains the reason for His compassion as being that 'they were like sheep without a shepherd'.
15–18 indicate how difficult it was to arouse faith in the disciples, but at least they did what they were told. The *five loaves* were probably of barley, the normal food of poor people. The fish may have been smoked or pickled and would be a delicacy. **19** The threefold action of taking, blessing and breaking would be the normal action at a Jewish meal; it also shows a

connection with the last supper (cf. 26:26). *Blessed*: 'gave thanks to God'.
20 The provision of enough and to spare is important (cf. 2 Ki. 4:42–44). This was a miracle performed out of concern for the needs of the hungry, but essentially as a sign of Jesus' exercising the power of the Creator who is always multiplying bread and fish. Here the action is localized and speeded up. It also points forward to the Messianic banquet at the end of the age. John, in the discourse which follows, records the parallels with the feeding of the people of Israel with manna in the desert. Mark's reference to the greenness of the grass, and the companies in which they were made to sit down and his emphasis on the *men*, have been taken to suggest that this was an attempted Messianic uprising, as the Messiah was expected to appear at Passover time. John's account lends strong support to this suggestion, but there is little hint of this aspect in Matthew's account. **21** *Besides*: Greek *chōris* could mean 'without', but it is more naturally taken as it is here.
22, 23 Cf. v. 13. It was a constant struggle for Jesus to find privacy with the opportunity for prayer. *The other side*: it is not quite certain what part of the lake they were crossing. **25** *The fourth watch* was between 3 and 6 a.m. *Walking on the sea*: it is possible for the expression to mean 'on the sea shore', but this is unlikely in the context. It seems as if His power over the natural order was being vividly demonstrated to the disciples. **27** *It is I*: Greek *egō eimi* can mean 'I am' (cf. Ex. 3:14) or 'I am He' (cf. Is. 41:4). It seems to be frequently used in John as a claim to divinity, but this is not the primary sense here.
28 This is typical of the impetuous Peter. **30, 31** As on other occasions, Peter had forgotten the difficulties and had committed himself beyond what he was able to achieve (cf. 26:33–35). While some have seen these verses as an allegory of Peter's life, there is no reason to think that the Evangelist did not intend it to be taken as fact. **32** Cf. 8:26. **33** *You are the Son of God* does not occur in Mark. It seems to be a groping after a title for One who can do such wonders (cf. 8:27) and does not imply commitment in the same way as Peter's confession at Caesarea Philippi (16:16). *Gennesaret* was just south-west of Capernaum. **36** *Touch the fringe of his garment*: this was probably the tassel (cf. 9:20). Presumably this was not mere superstition but a symbolic act accompanying an encounter with Him.

15:1–20 The tradition of the elders

This section is paralleled in Mk. 7:1–23, but includes in addition vv. 12–14, paralleled in Lk. 6:39. It is an important development in the growing conflict with the Pharisees over the nature of true religion.
1 *From Jerusalem*: the Galilaean ministry seems to have caused a stir even in the capital. Perhaps Jesus was being consulted as leader of a rabbinic school who might have a special teaching on the points at issue. **2** *The tradition of the elder*

was the oral tradition handed down by the great Rabbis and regarded as a supplement to, and often as an interpreter of, Scripture. Much of it was codified and written down in the Mishnah at a later date. It was treated as of equal authority with the law.

Wash their hands: the law laid down for the priests that they should make themselves clean from defilement (Lv. 22:1–16), and it may have been in an attempt to assert the priesthood of all that the Pharisees had adopted this rule about washing. **3** This question of Jesus struck at the very heart of Pharisaism and showed its inner self-contradiction. **4** The quotations are from Ex. 20:12; 21:17.

5 Matthew omits the technical word 'Corban' which occurs in Mark, as he does also the explanation of Jewish customs. Something could be dedicated to the Temple and the owner could still enjoy the proceeds of it, rather than having any obligation towards his parents. By the end of the 1st century the Rabbis accepted Jesus' position on the conflict of vows with obligations under the law. **6** *Made void*: cancelled, in practice at least. The opposite to Jesus' intention to 'fulfil' it (5:17). **7–9** The quotation is based on LXX of Is. 29:13. It shows the vanity of the externalism which results from man-made religion. **10** The action and words emphasize the importance of the principle about to be stated. **11** As the comment in Mk. 7:19 confirms, this statement implied that the ceremonial laws concerning clean and unclean foods (Lv. 11) had no absolute moral validity. **13** *Every plant* refers to the Pharisees rather than their teaching (*cf.* Is. 60:21). **14** The Pharisees' claim to light was ironic when they in fact obscured the light of the Torah (*cf.* Rom. 2:17–24). They and their disciples were on the road to spiritual disaster. **15** *The parable* must be the saying of verse 11. **18** The *mouth* is here connected with spiritual defilement, not as an entrance for physical food, but as an organ of expression for the thoughts and attitudes of a man's *heart*, *i.e.* his imagination and will. **19** Matthew has only seven vices to Mark's thirteen, and *false witness* is not mentioned in Mark. **20** *But to eat* . . . : this conclusion occurs only in Matthew, and may be an editorial note.

15:21–39 Further healings and the feeding of the four thousand

This section is parallel to Mk. 7:24 – 8:10 with some variations and some abbreviations. There is no parallel in Luke. There is the healing of a Gentile and a general description of healings followed by a further example of feeding the crowd.

21 Jesus withdrew from the legalism of His own people to Gentile territory, near to two notoriously ungodly cities (*cf.* 11:22). **22** *Canaanite*: descended from the inhabitants of Palestine before the Conquest under Joshua, who were regarded as likely to corrupt the Israelites (Ezr. 9:1). Such an outsider can never-

theless call on the *Son of David*. **24** This was the general policy of Jesus (*cf.* 10:5f.) but He allowed exceptions, as here. **26** Perhaps this was said half-humorously as He saw her faith developing. Many Jews referred to Gentiles as *dogs* (*cf.* 7:6). **27** Her reply shows her faith and humility. **28** As in the other Gentile healing, the cure is effected at a distance (8:13). **30, 31** Mark has only the healing of one deaf and dumb man. For other general healings, *cf.* 4:23; 9:35; 19:2. *The God of Israel*: this particular phrase suggests that these healings took place in an area where there was a considerable number of Gentiles. **32–39** While many scholars suppose that this is a 'doublet' of the feeding of the 5,000, there are many differences and the fact that Mark includes both in his relatively short Gospel is evidence that he at least believed there were two separate incidents. In the narrative as it stands it is hard to see why the disciples ask where they are to get bread when they know that Jesus has already fed an even larger number with even less food, but there may have been reasons for their obtuseness (*cf.* 16:9f.). It may be that this second feeding was mainly of Gentiles. *The region of Magadan* is unknown.

16:1–12 Pharisees and Sadducees

In this section Matthew parallels Mk. 8:11–21, with the addition of a saying about signs (*cf.* Lk. 12:54–56) and an explanatory note at the end.

1 There had been a request before in similar terms (12:38f.). Now the Sadducees are involved. **2b–3** do not occur in some MSS and NEB omits. Rather different weather phenomena are described from those in Luke, but the point is the same. Their sensitivity to meteorological signs makes a mockery of their insensitivity to spiritual crisis. **6** *Leaven* usually has a bad connotation in the NT (*cf.* 1 Cor. 5:8). **7** The misunderstanding of spiritual metaphors arising from the feeding miracle is even more clearly described in Jn. 6:25–58. **8–10** There was no need to worry about literal bread when they had experienced two feeding miracles. **11, 12** The point at issue must therefore be *teaching*. The Pharisaic and Sadducean approach has often enough corrupted the thought and life of the church.

16:13–28 The confession and challenge of Messiahship

This section is closely parallel to Mk. 8:27 – 9:1 (*cf.* Lk. 9:18–27), with the insertion of the promise to Peter (vv. 17–19) and the omission of the saying about being ashamed of Jesus, to which there was a parallel in 10:32f. The confession by Peter of Jesus' Messiahship is in many ways the turning-point of the Synoptic Gospels, because it is from this point that the shadow of the cross falls over the ministry.

13 *Caesarea Philippi* was formerly called Paneas after the Greek god Pan. It was rebuilt by Philip the tetrarch and called Caesarea in honour of Augustus, and Philippi to distinguish it from other towns named in honour of the emperor. It is ironical that it was in such a district that the first true confession of the Messiah of the Jews was made. *Son of man* is here equivalent to 'I'. **14** For confusion with *John the Baptist*, cf. 14:2. *Elijah* was expected to return (Mal. 4:5). Only Matthew mentions *Jeremiah* (cf. quotations from Jeremiah in 2:17; 27:9). Jesus was acknowledged to be the prophet like Moses (Dt. 18:15; Acts 3:22f.). **15** More important than other people's opinions is their own response to the challenge of His person. **16** *You are the Christ*: despite foreshadowings (especially 14:33) this is the first considered affirmation of such faith in Jesus. Matthew alone includes the words *the Son of the living God*, though Luke has 'the Christ of God'. The Messiahship thus confessed was something more than current Jewish expectation, though it is doubtful whether the phrase 'Son of God' would have had its full Christian meaning at this stage. *Simon Peter* took the lead as so often, but may only have been the spokesman for the Twelve who must often have discussed the Messianic characteristics of Jesus among themselves.

17-19 have in the past been considered by some scholars not to be a genuine utterance of Jesus. The word 'church' does not occur in the Gospels apart from here and 18:17, and its inclusion has been taken as evidence of Matthew's ecclesiastical bias; also the rest of the NT does not seem to attribute to Peter the primacy which is given him here. The discoveries at Qumran have, however, removed many of the difficulties about attributing to Jesus the idea of founding a community, and a careful exegesis of the promise to Peter shows that there is no necessary conflict with other references to him in the NT. It has also been pointed out that there is a sort of parallelism between the commendation of Peter in vv. 17, 18a and the rebuke to him in v. 23.

17 *Simon Bar-Jona* was his full Aramaic name, meaning 'Simon, son of Jonah'. *Flesh and blood*: human nature (cf. the revelation to Paul, Gal. 1:16f.). **18** *Peter*: Greek *Petros*, meaning 'stone', is here linked with *rock* (Gk. *petra*). The play on words would be brought out even better in Aramaic where one word *kepha* lies behind *Petros* and *petra*. (For the use of Cephas as a proper name, cf. Jn. 1:42; 1 Cor. 1:12; 3:22; 9:5; 15:5; Gal. 2:9.) The name need not have been given to Simon here for the first time (cf. Jn. 1:42; Mk. 3:16), but it receives a new significance. Some have wished to place this saying after the resurrection, but it would be strange if Jesus had given Simon this name during the ministry and never explained the reason for it. Abraham is spoken of as 'the rock from which you were hewn' (Is. 51:1) but the metaphor is rather different from this. Jesus is also referred to as the corner-stone (Is. 28:16; cf. 1 Pet. 2:8; Eph. 2:20) and the rejected stone (Ps. 118:22; Mt. 21:42; 1 Pet. 2:7), as well as the stone of

stumbling (Is. 8:14f.; Rom. 9:32f.; 1 Pet. 2:8), and the foundation (1 Cor. 3:11). Some interpreters have therefore referred to Jesus as the rock here, but the context is against this. Nor is it likely that Peter's faith or Peter's confession is meant. It is undoubtedly Peter himself who is to be the rock, but Peter confessing, faithful and obedient. There is no suggestion of any kind that the promise was made to his successors in office and the situation involved hardly allows for further foundations in the post-apostolic age. That Peter is to exercise his authority in conjunction with the rest of the apostles is made plain in 18:18. The leading role which Peter played is shown throughout the early chapters of Acts. *My church* does not necessarily mean the universal church as a distinct entity from the people of Israel. It may refer in the first instance to Jesus' own community, intended to act as a remnant within the people of God, though He would see how it would inevitably develop. *The powers of death*: literally 'the gates of Hades or Sheol'. The phrase occurs in the writing of Hezekiah (Is. 38:10). The gates suggest the picture of a fortress or prison which lock in the dead and lock out their rescuers. This would imply that the church is on the offensive, and its Master will plunder the domain of Satan (cf. 12:29; 1 Pet. 3:18-20).

19 *The keys of the kingdom of heaven*: the phrase is almost certainly based on Is. 22:22 where Shebna the steward is displaced by Eliakim and his authority is transferred to him. 'And I will place on his shoulder the key of the house of David; he shall open, and none shall shut; and he shall shut, and none shall open.' (This is applied directly to Jesus in Rev. 3:7.) In rabbinic usage the terms 'bind' and 'loose' signified the promulgation of rules of conduct (*hālāḵâ*) and most commentators therefore believe that the keys represent internal authority in the church rather than the power to open it up to outsiders. If this is so it would give Peter, and the apostles associated with him (18:18), not only the power to preach the *kērygma* but also to formulate the *didachē*. The promise does not of course mean that God will be bound by anything that Peter says (cf. Gal. 2:11), but that things done according to the will of Christ will have binding validity. It may be significant that these verses seem to have so many allusions to Isaiah on the one hand and so many connections with 1 Peter on the other hand. **20** Despite this momentous confession, the news was not to be blazed abroad. It was still better that men should make the discovery for themselves.

21 *From that time*: a new depth of teaching is possible when they have recognized who He is. As soon as the confession has been made it must be reinterpreted in terms of suffering. *He must go*: because it was written of Him. The fact that the disciples were bewildered when the crucifixion and resurrection took place is hardly surprising, even if they had been previously warned. **22** *Took him*: perhaps drew Jesus to him with a gesture implying superior knowledge. Already the blessing has gone to his head and he has failed to understand. **23** *Satan*: for a moment Peter is almost an incarnation of Satan (*cf.* Mk. 5:9), just as previously he has been given the authority to do the work of God (v. 19). He was repeating the temptations to avoid the cross (4:1–11). *Hindrance*: RSV mg. 'stumbling-block'. The rock of foundation has already become an obstacle, though this was due to a change in Peter's attitude. Jesus is both foundation and obstacle to men but that is due to *their* different attitudes (1 Pet. 2:6–8). Despite the revelation which was from God and not man (v. 17), his outlook now was purely human.

24 The way of the disciple must be that of the master. *Deny himself* means to say 'No' to his own assertion of independence. *Take up his cross*: on the way to crucifixion (*cf.* 27:32). **25** *Life* (Gk. *psychē*) also means 'soul' (*cf.* 10:39). The verse means that a man finds his real self when he abandons his own self-assertion and self-seeking for the sake of Christ. **26** There is no comparison of any kind between what a man is and what he has (*cf.* 6:25). **27** *He will repay every man for what he has done*: only Matthew has these words, which are taken from Ps. 62:12; Pr. 24:12. Deeds are the evidence of attitudes (*cf.* 7:21). **28** *The Son of man coming in his kingdom*: Mark has 'the kingdom of God come with power'. This must refer to a very significant event which will vindicate the new sense of values in the preceding verses. Many scholars refer it to the *parousia*, and state that Jesus was mistaken about its date. But His unwillingness to predict its time may make us wary about supposing that He even said it would happen before some of His audience had died (*cf.* 24:36). Some have referred it to the transfiguration but the reference to death when this followed only six days later seems strange. It is more likely to be a major event constituting a stage in the coming of the kingdom after Jesus Himself had tasted death and others had expressed their willingness to (26:35). Mark's 'power' is connected with both the resurrection (Rom. 1:4) and Pentecost (Acts 1:8) and either of these could be in mind.

17:1–27 The transfiguration and its consequences

This section is closely parallel to Mk. 9:2–32 (*cf.* Lk. 9:28–44; 17:5f.) with some minor additions and some substantial abbreviations, but vv. 24–27 are peculiar to Matthew. The transfiguration in all the Synoptic Gospels follows Peter's confession and is a foretaste of the glory of the Messiah. There are connecting links back to the baptism and forward to the resurrection, exaltation and *parousia* of Christ. Some scholars have dismissed the transfiguration as entirely unhistorical, and others have suggested that it is a resurrection appearance read back into the ministry of Jesus. The exclusive revelation to the three disciples makes it unlikely to be a post-resurrection appearance, and there are good reasons why Jesus should have wished to be

revealed to them in this way before His death. The transfiguration story leads on to a saying about Elijah, a healing and a further prediction of the passion. Then Matthew adds the story about the Temple tax.

1 *After six days*: cf. Ex. 24:9–18, where the cloud covers the mountain for six days and God speaks on the seventh. *Peter and James and John* were the inner circle (*cf.* 26:37; 20:20). The *mountain* may have been Tabor or Hermon, which was near to Caesarea Philippi. It was the place of divine revelation. **2** *Transfigured* (Gk. *metemorphōthē*): *cf.* Rom. 12:2; 2 Cor. 3:18. Something of Jesus' true *morphē* (or 'form') as God (Phil. 2:6f.) was revealed. *His face shone like the sun*: He was the source of light, while Moses' face shone with the reflection of the divine light (Ex. 34:29–35). *His garments became white* perhaps as the Messianic high priest's garments. **3** *Moses and Elijah* represented the law and the prophets. Neither of them had a known grave (Dt. 34:6; 2 Ki. 2:11). Each of them had conversed with God on a high mountain (Ex. 31:18; 1 Ki. 19:9–18).

4 Peter seems to wish to make the experience more lasting. Mark alone comments 'for he did not know what to say, for they were exceedingly afraid'. There may be some connection with the Feast of Tabernacles which was thought of as a time when the nations would come up to Jerusalem to worship (Zc. 14:16–19). **5** The *bright cloud* was a symbol of the divine presence. *This is my beloved Son*: this recalls the voice at His baptism (3:17). Only Matthew records *with whom I am well pleased* which makes the link explicit. *Listen to him* is generally taken to be an echo of the promise that one day a prophet like Moses should come (Dt. 18:15). Elijah in his day had also been in some ways a prophet like Moses. **6, 7** are peculiar to Matthew, but Mark also stresses the awe which this revelation of the glory of Jesus inspired.

9 *The vision* suggests something more than a merely subjective experience. It would be meaningless to others before the risen Christ had appeared. **10–13** It has been argued that Jesus really filled the role of *Elijah* preparing in His coming in humility for His coming in glory. Even if some facets of Elijah are types of Jesus rather than of John, the gospel tradition as a whole sees John as fulfilling the role of forerunner (Mal. 3:1; 4:5). Matthew makes this quite explicit in v. 13.

14 The pattern of the ministry is a continual one of withdrawal and involvement. From Jesus alone (v. 8), they return to the crowd. **16** From the glory of the mountain, they return to the suffering and impotence of the plain. **17** *Faithless and perverse generation* seems to echo Moses' comment on the generation of the first Exodus (Dt. 32:5; *cf.* Mt. 11:16). He is disappointed at their failure to cope without His being on the spot, for His physical presence will not be with them for long, and then they will have to learn to rely upon Him spiritually.

18 *Rebuked him*: the demon. **19, 20** Matthew, whose story is shorter, brings out more clearly than Mark the lack of faith of the disciples. It is interesting that this is an occasion where the apostle Matthew was involved in the rebuke, but Peter, who stands behind Mark's Gospel, was not. *This mountain* must be taken figuratively of any seemingly immovable obstacle (*cf.* 21:21f.). **21** is absent from the best MSS.

22, 23 He has to keep emphasizing the coming passion because they are quite unable to see its necessity (*cf.* 16:21; 20:18f.). **24–27** This story emphasizes the fact that Jesus was a loyal Jew who accepted the imposition of the Temple tax, but was under no theological obligation to pay it. The analogy of the Roman government taxing aliens heavily would be well understood. **26** *The sons are free*: *cf.* Gal. 4:21–31. **27** *Not to give offence*: to avoid causing difficulties for those with a less emancipated conscience (*cf.* 1 Cor. 8:9–13). He was willing to identify Himself with His people in their religious obligations (*cf.* 3:15) though He was Himself greater than the Temple (*cf.* 12:6). *A shekel*: the half-shekel was not in general use so two men paid a shekel. A miracle seems to be implied, but it is the only case in the Gospels where a miracle is not made explicit. Various attempts have been made to explain the incident in other ways, but without much success. The story would have more point if the Gospel were written before AD 70, but it does not demand an early date for the Gospel.

18:1-35 LIFE IN THE MESSIANIC COMMUNITY

This is the fourth of Matthew's discourses and it deals with relationships within the Christian brotherhood, laying particular stress on humility and forgiveness as two vital attributes. Vv. 1–5 are parallel to Mk. 9:33–37; *cf.* Lk. 9:46–48. Vv. 6–9 are parallel to Mk. 9:42–48; *cf.* Lk. 17:1f. Vv. 10–14 have a parallel in Lk. 15:1–10 and 15–22 in Lk. 17:3f. Vv. 23–35 are a parable peculiar to Matthew.

1 *At that time* seems to be more than a formal link as the order is the same as that of Mark, and in addition the question is appropriate in view of Matthew's story about the tax. Matthew omits the record of the disciples' quarrelling. The idea of rank was a prominent one at Qumran, 'that every Israelite may know his place in the community of God according to the everlasting design. No man shall move down from his place nor move up from his allotted position' (1 QS 2:19–25). Greatness in the kingdom is attributed to those who observe and teach the least of the commandments (5:19; *cf.* also 11:11). **3** *Turn*: a complete reorientation of the life towards God. *Become like children*: in respect of dependence and humility rather than innocence (*cf.* Mk. 10:15). *Never enter*: this is necessary not only for greatness in the kingdom but for entry into it (*cf.* Jn. 3:3, 5). **4** Jesus reverses all human ideas of greatness (*cf.* 5:3–12; 20:25–28).

5 Not only must the disciple be like a child receiving the kingdom, he must also be able to receive a child in Jesus' name. He must treat the weakest as a person to be respected, not as a thing to be manipulated (*cf.* 10:40; 25:40). **6** *Causes to . . . sin*: literally 'to stumble' (RSV mg.). The Rabbis regarded Jeroboam the son of Nebat as the greatest of sinners, because he caused Israel to sin (1 Ki. 14:16). Any terrible physical punishment would be preferable to the spiritual responsibility of upsetting others. **7** preserves the biblical balance between the inevitability of evil and the moral responsibility of those who perform it. **8, 9** The substance of these verses is found in 5:29f. Here Matthew, like Mark, groups a number of sayings connected with Greek *skandalon* ('stumbling-block'). This one deals with the individual's need for care in his own spiritual life.

10 occurs only in Matthew. The *little ones* are not necessarily children. They may be those weak in faith. Every believer may have been thought to have a guardian angel with access to God to report on his charge (*cf.* Ps. 91:11; Acts 12:15). **12, 13** The emphasis here is on the worth of each individual, while in Lk. 15:1–7 it is on the joy over the repentant. The sayings were probably given on different occasions. **14** This emphasizes the pastoral concern for every member of the Messianic community, none of whom God wishes to *perish*.

15 *Your brother*: presumably within the community of those who recognize God as their Father. *Against you* is omitted by good MSS, which NEB follows. If this is correct, then any kind of sin will be in mind. Private reasoning with an offender is the first step of love (*cf.* Lv. 19:17f.). *Gained your brother*: probably in the sense of keeping him as a member of the community. **16** The refusal to listen to a private word means that it has become a corporate affair, and so *two or three witnesses* must be called, presumably to try to establish the facts and conciliate. But if that fails they are then to give evidence of the offence to the community publicly (*cf.* Dt. 19:15). **17** *The church* is the local community of believers. Failure to listen to the church means excommunication (*cf.* 1 Cor. 5:4f.; 1 Tim. 1:20). The Gentiles and tax-collectors are the types of outcasts from God's people, though in fact they were responding to the gospel (21:31, 43). For Qumran procedure see 1 QS 5:25 – 6:1. **18** See 16:19. Judicial rulings, like the promulgation of rules of conduct, are binding. **19, 20** The conditions for what is done on earth being ratified in heaven are real agreement in prayer, gathering in the name of Christ and His presence in the midst. The Christian community has a solemn duty to exercise discipline in this pastoral and spiritual way. Where it is done according to the will of Christ it will have the authority of Christ.

21, 22 *Seventy times seven* may be as in RSV mg. 'seventy-seven times'. This is a complete reversal of the situation before the law laid down equivalent revenge (Ex. 21:24; *cf.* Mt. 5:38). 'If Cain is avenged sevenfold, truly Lamech seventy-sevenfold' (Gn. 4:24). Now forgiveness is to be equally unlimited. **23** This parable vividly illustrates the point of the extent (rather than the frequency) of forgiveness. It also expounds the petition in the Lord's Prayer about forgiveness (6:12, 14f.). **24** *Ten thousand talents*: NEB 'ran into millions'. The figure is unrealistic in a human story but it sharpens the point of the extent of human sin and divine forgiveness. **28** *A hundred denarii*: NEB 'a few pounds'. **32** *Wicked*: 'mean'. A natural action was here inexcusable. The contrast is really immeasurable. **33** The divine mercy is the only true basis for human mercy (*cf.* 5:43–48). **35** *So also*: not all the details of the parable are to be pressed. But the point is clear that the unforgiving man cannot be in a position of forgiveness before God. The man forgiven by God through what Christ has done will give in his treatment of others unmistakable evidence of His gratitude to and dependence upon Him.

19:1 – 22:46 CHRIST'S JOURNEY AND CHALLENGE TO JERUSALEM

Having shown something of the life which will be possible within the Messianic community, the Messiah now moves away from Galilee to Jerusalem to present to the holy city and the Jewish leaders the challenge to become the centre and nucleus of the renewed people of God. Matthew is parallel to Mk. 10:1 – 12:37, but has in addition 19:10–12 (celibacy and the kingdom), 20:1–16 (the labourers in the vineyard), 21:14–17 (the children crying out in the Temple), 21:28–32 (the two sons) and 22:1–14 (the royal wedding). There is an atmosphere of crisis, for men must decide about Jesus and their decision is connected with temporal and eternal judgment (to which theme the teaching collected in chapters 23–25 is devoted).

19:1–15 Marriage and children

This section is parallel to Mk. 10:1–16 with the addition of the saying about celibacy (vv. 10–12). The saying about the children is also in Lk. 18:15–17. Jesus had already made a pronouncement about divorce in the Sermon on the Mount (5:31f.), and here similar issues are raised again in controversy.

1 *When Jesus had finished these sayings*: *cf.* 7:28; 11:1; 13:53; 26:1. **2** The *large crowds* may have been on their way to the Passover. **3** *For any cause*: there was a difference in the interpretation of the reference to 'some indecency' in Dt. 24:1 by the main rabbinic schools. Hillel allowed it to be anything which displeased the husband, while Shammai limited it to unchastity by the wife. **4** Jesus takes them back behind the law (*cf.* Gal. 3:17) to the creation which showed that the two sexes were according to the purpose of God (Gn. 1:27). **5** *And said*: it is natural to take this as the words of Scripture

(Gn. 2:24) being attributed to God. But it is possible that NEB 'and he added' is right. *One*: literally 'one flesh'. A consummated union means such a deep relationship between the two partners 'knowing' each other (*cf.* Gn. 4:1, *etc.*) that they become one on the human level corresponding to the oneness between Christ and the Christian (1 Cor. 6:16f.). **6** The ideal is plain. *Man* must not undo the work of *God*.

7 Jesus' pronouncement has seemed to rule out divorce altogether. This would seem to be an assault on the law (Dt. 24:1–4). **8** *For your hardness of heart*: Moses had to legislate for those already involved in disobedience. He *allowed* (contrast their view in v. 7 that he 'commanded') them to divorce their wives, but in fact this was a restriction on the unlimited freedom of the husband. **9** Jesus in effect accepts the interpretation of Shammai. Some difficulty has been caused by the fact that Mark does not include the phrase 'except for unchastity' (*cf.* 5:32). Here we have explicit what may be implicit in the saying recorded in Mark. Matthew does not include Mark's reference to the wife divorcing her husband, which was not a Jewish custom but a Greek and Roman one. The moral principle of monogamy is clearly stated here, but there is no reason to suppose that civil legislation should not permit divorce in cases where the ideal has not been attained. **10** shows how far short men fell of the ideal in practice. **11, 12** For most Jews marriage was a duty. Some Essene groups included people who had voluntarily undertaken celibacy. *Who have made themselves eunuchs*: this was understood literally by some early Christians, including Origen. The claims of *the kingdom of heaven* are such that even the most desirable human experiences ordained for mankind by God may need to be sacrificed. But this is *given* (v. 11) to those able to *receive it*; it is not a 'superior' way of life but a special vocation (*cf.* 1 Cor. 7:7).

13–15 Parents may have thought that there would be special blessing from a great Rabbi. *The disciples* may have *rebuked the people*, not because they thought this was not the right thing to do, but because they felt He was too busy. *To such belongs the kingdom of heaven*: to children and to those who have a childlike faith (*cf.* 18:3f.; Matthew omits the similar verse which appears here in Mark). This provides a justification for treating children as members of the Christian community (*cf.* 1 Cor. 7:14). The word *hinder* (Gk. *kōluō*) was used as a technical term with reference to baptism later (*cf.* 3:14; Acts 8:36; 10:47), but the incident by itself is not a blueprint for infant baptism.

19:16 – 20:16 Riches and rewards

19:16–30 is parallel to Mk. 10:17–31 (*cf.* Lk. 18:18–30), but includes a saying about the disciples judging Israel (v. 28) similar to one which occurs in Lk. 22:28–30. 20:1–16, the parable of the labourers in the vineyard, is peculiar to Matthew. The dangers of material wealth are emphasized and the reality and unexpectedness of spiritual rewards.

19:16, 17 The story is introduced by Matthew with a rather different question and answer than are found in Mark and Luke. Mark has 'Good Teacher' and 'Why do you call me good?' In Matthew the emphasis is not on the goodness of Jesus in Himself but on His authority as a teacher of goodness. The law has already revealed *what is good* (*cf.* Mi. 6:8). *Keep the commandments*: obedience to them is not normally given as the way to *enter life*. It may be that Jesus is meeting him on his own terms in order to show him that this was not the way. **18, 19** *Which?* suggests both the idea that some were more important than others and that he was better at keeping some than others. Jesus gives the five commandments which deal with actions towards others (omitting that on coveting) and adds (in Matthew alone) *you shall love your neighbour as yourself* (Lv. 19:18), which sums up the others (*cf.* 22:37–39; Rom. 13:9). **20** *What do I still lack?* probably is an expression of felt need rather than of complacency. **21** *Perfect*: it has sometimes been suggested that this is an instance of Matthew's tendency to create a double standard (the other Evangelists do not include the word). But perfection is something at which it is the obligation of all disciples to aim (5:48). The challenge was to prove his love for his neighbour through his pocket and through wholehearted commitment to Jesus. As with the saying about celibacy (v. 11), this was a command to one person, and while the principle of Christ's Lordship over money is binding on all, the practice of selling up and giving the proceeds to the poor may apply only to some.

23 Many Jews thought that wealth was a reward for the righteous (Ecclus. 44:6), though there was also a tradition of the rich as oppressors (Lk. 1:53). **24** There have been attempts to interpret this saying either by supposing that *camel* (Gk. *kamēlos*) should really be 'rope' (Gk. *kamilos*) or that there was a small gate known as 'The Needle's Eye' to pass through which a camel would need to stoop. Either of these is possible but they are simply speculations. Jesus may well have used a ridiculous figure to make His point (*cf.* 7:4f.; 23:24 where 'camel' is used presumably because of its size). **25** The disciples must have thought of wealth as a reward for piety. **26** Salvation is the gift of God unattainable by human effort; therefore He can bestow it upon any who will receive it.

27 seems rather a complacent remark by Peter (*cf.* 4:18–22). **28** *New world*: literally 'new birth' of the world (*cf.* Is. 65:17; 66:22; Rom. 8:18–22; Rev. 21:1–5). Josephus uses the word of a new birth of the land of Israel (*Antiquities* xi.3.9). *The Son of man* is judge of all (25:31) and the Twelve are associated with Him as patriarchs of the new Israel. *Judging* can mean 'ruling' (*cf.* Ps. 2:10). **29** There are far more satisfying possessions and relationships in the spiritual realm when these things are done *for my name's sake*. *Eternal*

life is not itself a reward but a gift, but those who have made such sacrifices are able to enjoy its full outworking. There is nothing 'unspiritual' about desiring such rewards (*cf.* 6:4). **30** The divine perspective upsets human values, and this will be made plain in the world to come (*cf.* 20:16).

20:1–16 This parable tells a story involving absurd economics, to get home a truth of the kingdom. As in other parables, many of the details are to give colour to the story and are not to be pressed for a theological meaning. The point is that in the kingdom men receive what they need (the *denarius* was a day's wage for a labourer), and this is eternal life (for there are differences in spiritual privileges, 19:29). This is given by God, who is continually calling men of different degrees of moral attainment and spiritual privilege to His service, and therefore no-one has any claim on Him for more than anyone else. There is nothing unjust about God's dealings for He gives what He promises (v. 13). He has sovereign freedom to do as He pleases for generosity may be added to justice (vv. 14f.). The self-righteous, no doubt particularly those with leading positions in Israel, were only upset because His generosity was given to others (vv. 12, 15). The grateful are better off than the grumblers (v. 16). The theme is similar to the story of the elder brother of the prodigal (Lk. 15:25–32).

20:17–34 The suffering and love of the Messiah

This section closely follows Mk. 10:32–52 (*cf.* Lk. 18:31–43), except that there are a number of differences in the healing of the blind men. The teaching about the reversal of human values continues—a crucified Messiah and greatness in service—and a sad human need is relieved.

17–19 *He took the twelve disciples aside*: because this was private teaching to those who had acknowledged His Messiahship. This is the third prediction of the passion and resurrection (*cf.* 16:21; 17:22f.). Here there is specific mention for the first time of deliverance to the Gentiles and of crucifixion. **20** *The mother of the sons of Zebedee* is not mentioned by Mark, who refers only to James and John themselves. There can be no serious attempt here to shift the onus from the sons, as many scholars allege, since the others are indignant at them (v. 24). **21** They thought that exaltation could be obtained without suffering, and that Jesus could dispose the places in the kingdom. **22** The first misapprehension was that suffering might be bypassed. *The cup* is one of suffering (26:39; *cf.* Is. 51:17). Mark refers also to His baptism of suffering. **23** James was put to death as a martyr (Acts 12:2). It is probable that John lived on to an old age. Neither of them was ready to face up to martyrdom with Jesus at the coming Passover. It is the *Father* who has *prepared* places in the kingdom, and Jesus does not state whether He knows the order of precedence.

24 The others show the same ambitious spirit as James and John. **25** In most human societies power is sought for personal ends. **26** *It shall not be so among you*: the standards of the kingdom are quite different. Greatness is shown in service. The word for *servant* (Gk. *diakonos*) was adopted as the most common one for Christian ministry in the NT and every 'minister' should remember its true meaning. **28** The basis of such an approach is the example and atoning death of *the Son of man*. The Jews thought of the death of the righteous atoning for others. Here Is. 53:10–12 probably lies in the background. *Ransom* (Gk. *lytron*) means a costly act of deliverance without specifying to whom the price is paid. *Many* is inclusive rather than restrictive (*cf.* 26:28). The Greek preposition *anti* suggests an equivalence or substitution. Even in an ethical context great theological truths can be taught (*cf.* Phil. 2:1–11). Here are set side by side the humility of Jesus, the suffering Servant of the Lord, and His greatness in being able in the sacrifice of Himself to provide for all a means of deliverance from their sins.

29–34 *Cf.* 9:27–31. Matthew's account is briefer than Mark's. He records a second blind man but does not include the name Bartimaeus. The cry *Son of David* is now full of extra significance (*cf.* 9:27). *Jesus in pity touched their eyes* comes in Matthew only. Here is the selfgiving love of Jesus which is soon to lead Him to His death.

21:1–17 The triumphal entry and cleansing of the Temple

In this section Matthew continues to agree with Mark closely, but the cursing of the fig-tree occurs a few verses later in Matthew, and he includes the children crying out in the Temple (*cf.* Mk. 11:1–11, 15–17; Lk. 19:28–40, 45f.). He also introduces a formula quotation. The Messiah's entry into His capital causes enormous popular enthusiasm, but the peaceful, yet stern, nature of His Messiahship was shown by His riding on an ass and by His driving the exploiters out of the Temple.

1 *The Mount of Olives* was the place where the Jews expected the Messiah to appear. *Bethphage* was probably on the east side of the hill and not in view of Jerusalem. **2** *The village opposite you* may have been Bethphage or Bethany. *You will find*: probably by previous arrangement with friends. **3** *The Lord* may be Jesus or God or simply the owner of the ass. **5** The 'formula quotation' is from Is. 62:11 and Zc. 9:9. There is no doubt that the quotation refers to only one beast, as it is an example of Hebrew parallelism. It is asserted by most commentators that Matthew misunderstood this and therefore introduced a second animal (vv. 2, 7). This seems *a priori* most unlikely when it is remembered what a knowledge of the Hebrew OT, as well as LXX, the Evangelist has. He does not include Mark's phrase 'on which no one has ever sat' and it may be assumed that he mentions the mother because she would be needed to calm the colt in the crowd. The word *ass* (Gk. *hypozygion*) in the last line of the quotation refers to a male ass, and if Matthew realized this when translating LXX it is clear that he was not equating this with the female ass (Gk. *onos*) in the narrative.

7 *He sat thereon*: it is amazing how many

commentators seem to have referred this to the two animals and not to the garments. **8** *Spread their garments*: *cf.* 2 Ki. 9:13. The *branches* were a further sign of a royal welcome. *Hosanna* originally meant 'save now' but it had become a shout of praise. *Blessed be he who comes in the name of the Lord* is a quotation from Ps. 118:26. This was part of the Hallel (Pss. 113–118) sung at the Feast of Tabernacles and the Feast of Dedication, as well as at Passover. The blessing of the psalm was on all pilgrims coming up to the feast. It is especially appropriate for *the Son of David*, who came as the supreme Pilgrim to enter His kingdom. The question has been raised whether this did not take place at one of the other festivals, but the impression given is that it occurred just before the Passover. **10, 11** *All the city was stirred*: this statement and the question and answer of the crowds are peculiar to Matthew. The Galilaean crowds acclaim Him as the local prophet, but the whole symbolism of the occasion marks Him out as Messiah and the context of the quotation from Zechariah indicates His world-wide dominion of peace.

12 *The temple* means the whole Temple area, and the particular part of it was the court of the Gentiles. *The money-changers* were those who changed foreign coins for those in which the Temple dues might be paid. Presumably they made a profit on the transaction. *Those who sold pigeons* did so to the poor as offerings (*cf.* Lk. 2:24). A good deal of extortion went on in this field. **13** This is a prophetic act symbolizing the coming of the Messiah in judgment (Mal. 3:1–5) and Jesus quotes Is. 56:7 and Je. 7:11. The words 'for all peoples' from the first quotation are omitted by Matthew, but Jewish readers would have known that this was the court of the Gentiles. The context of the second quotation is one of judgment and destruction upon the people and the Temple. Between them they point to the replacement of the old order by the new (*cf.* v. 43). **14–16** *The blind and the lame* had been hated by David (2 Sa. 5:8), but the Son of David heals them. *The children* were still using the words of the crowds without fully understanding them, yet this could not be stopped because it was an expression of praise to God the Creator (*cf.* Lk. 19:39f.; Ps. 8:2). Jesus by His action and His acceptance of the acclamation of the crowds and the children had presented a direct challenge to the whole established order of things. **17** At this stage *he went out of the city* as many pilgrims did because of the shortage of accommodation.

21:18 – 22:14 Judgment on the Jewish leaders and nation

In this section Matthew is parallel to Mk. 11:12–14, 20–33 (*cf.* Lk. 20:1–8) in the cursing of the fig-tree (21:18–22, though the order is different) and the question about the Baptist (vv. 23–27). The parable of the two sons and the reference to the Baptist (vv. 28–32) are peculiar to Matthew. He parallels Mk. 12:1–12 in the parable of the wicked tenants (vv. 33–46; *cf.* Lk. 20:9–19), but the royal marriage (22:1–14), though showing some resemblances to Lk. 14:15–24, is peculiar to him. The theme of judgment on God's people is symbolically acted first and then strongly pressed home in three parables.

18, 19 The *fig tree* would not be expected to have full-grown figs on it at this time, but there should have been some small edible growth. The fig-tree represented Israel in Ho. 9:10, where the context was one of judgment for breaking the covenant. Matthew emphasizes that this happened *at once*. Immediate results were usual in the case of miracles (*cf.* 8:3; 20:34). There is little doubt that this action, unusual as it was, symbolized the coming judgment on a faithless Israel (*cf.* the parable of Lk. 13:6–9). **20–22** emphasize the unlimited power of God available to faith (*cf.* 17:19f.). **23** *These things* probably refers mainly to the cleansing of the Temple and the events associated with it, but could include His teaching. His actions and words had been in the style of a prophet. They wish to know His authority as they would the credentials of any other Rabbi or prophet. **25** *The baptism of John*: it is sometimes taken as an evasive counter-question. But it is more likely to mean that just as John was called direct by God so was Jesus, or that His baptism was the moment of com-missioning when the divine authority was given to Him by John representing the law and the prophets and the divine voice acknowledging Him (3:13–17). **27** They confess themselves incompetent as teachers and there is no point in the circumstances in Jesus' saying anything more about His authority.

28–32 The context shows clearly the contrast between the professedly religious and the out-casts. The ministry of John as well as that of Jesus divided men on this score and expectations were overthrown. Again the last are first and the first last (20:16). **33–46** There is little doubt that this parable has allegorical features, as Israel is seen as a vineyard in Is. 5:1–7 (*cf.* Ps. 80:8–11). **33–36** *The tenants* are presumably the leaders of the Jews who kill God's *servants*, the prophets (*cf.* Je. 7:25). **37** *Afterward* suggests the last appeal to them through *his son*. **38** The *inherit-ance* was used in the OT to refer to Israel as a nation (Ps. 33:12) or to the promised land (Ps. 105:11). **41** Only Matthew records that the answer to Jesus' question was spoken by His audience. Here is a vivid example of a parable moving people to indignation (*cf.* 2 Sa. 12:1–6). **42** The quotation is from Ps. 118:22f. (part of the Hallel, *cf.* v. 9). For the idea of Jesus as the *stone*, *cf.* Acts 4:11; Rom. 9:33; Eph. 2:20; 1 Pet. 2:7. **43** In Matthew the meaning of the parable is made explicit—*the kingdom of God* would be taken away from the people of God constituted on a national basis, and given to the people of God constituted on a spiritual basis, who would produce *the fruits of it*. **45, 46** The issues were now clear to the *chief priests and the*

Pharisees, but they had the same reservations about taking action against Jesus as they had about speaking against John (v. 26).

22:1–14 The parable is very similar to that of the wicked tenants. **1ff.** *The marriage feast* gives the idea of the Messianic banquet. The invita-tions are sent out more than once but those invited prefer to get on with the everyday things of life. **6, 7** Commentators have pointed out that these verses do not go naturally in the parable. With the parallel verses 21:35, 36 in mind, they may have been introduced as an interpretative marginal note referring to the fall of Jerusalem and then later been incorporated into the text. **9** The invitation is therefore extended to the outcasts (not necessarily Gentiles). **10** *Both bad and good; cf.* 13:47f. **11** It is not clear whether the *wedding garment* was something which the guest should have brought (presumably rep-resenting good deeds as evidence of a true heart) or something which the host supplied (represent-ing forgiveness). **14** *Many are called, but few are chosen*: the calling must refer to the gospel message to which they make a merely outward response, not being chosen by God.

22:15–46 Controversy with the Pharisees and Sadducees

This section follows fairly closely Mk. 12:13–37 (*cf.* Lk. 20:20–44), but Matthew abbreviates the account of the lawyer's question. In the final round of controversies with the Jewish leaders, Jesus faces questions about taxation (vv. 15–22), life after death (vv. 23–33), and the greatest commandment (vv. 34–40). In His turn He poses to them the last question concerning their views about the Messiah (vv. 41–46).

15–22 The presence of *the Herodians* would be no doubt to take advantage of any remark Jesus made which might appear treasonable. **17** *Is it lawful . . . ?* This question of taxation was hotly debated among the Jews. **20** The *likeness and inscription* were offensive to the Jews because of the tendency to deify Caesar. **21** *Render there-fore to Caesar the things that are Caesar's, and to God the things that are God's*: this was a bril-liant answer, getting to the heart of the problem. Caesar represented the legal government and in that sense owned the coinage and therefore had a right to taxes. But man bears the image and likeness of God (Gn. 1:26) and therefore the whole of his life has a higher loyalty to the divine will.

23–33 The *Sadducees* based their faith entirely on the five books of the Law. Their question was based on the law of levirate marriage (*levir* is Latin for brother-in-law) which was an attempt to perpetuate the race on the physical level (Dt. 25:5). **29ff.** Their attempt at a *reductio ad absurdum* of the doctrine of resurrection was refuted by the explanation that the life to come will be of a different order from the present one. *The angels* (in which they did not believe either, *cf.* Acts 23:8) are spiritual beings and show that the life to come will not be physical, though there will be a body (*cf.* 1 Cor. 15). The Sadducees did not in fact know their Pentateuch, from which Jesus quotes Ex. 3:6. God spoke of Himself as the God of the patriarchs long after their physical death, and so they must still be in some sense alive. The phrase *God of Abraham, etc.* is used with special reference to His keeping His promises in redemption, and therefore is specially relevant to the subject.

34–40 The question at issue was one that was keenly debated but the attempt *to test him* was probably with hostile intent. The combination of Dt. 6:5; Lv. 19:18 was not unknown in Judaism (*cf. Testament of Issachar* 5:2). Jesus shows that love is at the heart of the OT. **41–45** The challenge has to be put to them as to what their views of the Messiah really are. Matthew has given great prominence to the idea of Jesus as *the son of David* (1:1, *etc.*). But this is not a sufficient designation for Him. He is in some sense Lord as well. There is some difficulty about the use of Ps. 110:1. Though this was entitled 'A Psalm of David', it looks as if it were more a psalm in praise of the Davidic king, who was the psalmist's lord. But the Rabbis understood the Psalm in a Messianic sense, and it had its true fulfilment in one greater than David. Considerable use of the Psalm is made in Hebrews. **46** The time for questioning has ended. They cannot defeat Him in the field of argument. When next they appear on the scene it will be with force (26:47).

23:1 – 25:46 CHRIST'S WARNINGS AND PROPHECIES OF JUDGMENT

At this stage Matthew gives us the fifth discourse of Jesus—on judgment. Ch. 23 consists of a detailed criticism of the scribes and Pharisees and a warning of judgment coming on that generation. It contains much that is peculiar to Matthew and appropriate to a Jewish–Christian Gospel. Ch. 24 resembles Mark's apocalyptic discourse with some additions, mostly paralleled in Luke. It deals with both the coming judgment on the Jews and also the final judgment. Ch. 25 consists of three parables peculiar to Matthew about the final judgment. If the emphasis in these chapters is on the future coming of Christ, the Gospel as a whole shows a balance between that and the present coming of the kingdom in the ministry. Matthew is not one-sided in his eschatology and it would be arbitrary to reject as unauthentic anything which heightened it, though one may allow that each evangelist had a particular viewpoint in his selection of the sayings of Jesus.

23:1–39 Woes against the scribes and Pharisees

This section is a collection of sayings which takes the place of the summary warning against the scribes which comes in Mk. 12:38–40. There are parallels to many of them in Lk. 11:37–52 and the last three verses are almost the same as Lk. 13:34f. There is a warning against the practice of the scribes and Pharisees (vv. 1–12), then seven woes on them (vv. 13–36), followed by the lament over Jerusalem (vv. 37–39). The chapter may have been based on the 'Song of Moses' (Dt. 32).

1 *Then said Jesus*: this chapter is probably to be regarded as the start of a new discourse rather than simply the continuation of the controversy in the previous chapter. **2** *Moses' seat* was the teaching chair of the synagogues. **3** *Practise and observe whatever they tell you*: it is very hard to take this at its face value in view of 15:1–20. It is likely to refer to everything consistent with the law of Moses. *They preach but do not practise*: this is not likely to be a wholesale condemnation of all Pharisees, many of whom were well aware of the danger of inconsistency. **4** With their burden and yoke, *cf.* that of Christ (11:28–30). **5** *To be seen by men*: *cf.* 6:1, 5, 16. *Phylacteries* were small amulets containing passages of the Pentateuch (*cf.* Ex. 13:16; Dt. 6:8; 11:18). They were normally worn only at prayer. *Fringes* were tassels worn on the outer garment (*cf.* 9:20). **6, 7** All these things were meant to mark out the man with a superior knowledge of the law. **8–10** *Rabbi* meant 'my great one'. *Father* was probably mainly applied to great Rabbis of the past. *Master* means something more like 'professor'. None of these terms has any finality because it is God and Christ who have true spiritual authority. It is doubtful if the use of the terms themselves is intended to be forbidden, but rather the attitude of mind of those who seek to be dependent on others and those who like to receive that dependence. **11, 12** The reversal of human values is again emphasized (*cf.* 20:25–28).

13 *Woe to you*: 'alas for you'. This is a very searching condemnation of the Pharisees, but it is done in love. There are affinities between the 'woes' here and the Beatitudes (5:1–12). Not to enter the kingdom was bad enough. To prevent others from entering was far worse. **14** is probably to be omitted on MS evidence. **15** Despite their missing the kingdom, there was still a proselytizing zeal among many of them, with disastrous results. *Proselytes* were Gentiles who had received proselyte baptism and circumcision and become Jews fully. Many 'God-fearers' would not take this step. **16–22** The intention of the Rabbis was good—to discourage rash oaths by sacred things. But because of popular custom they had to make some rules allowing certain oaths. This led to such abuse, when everything in fact derives from God, that Jesus forbade the use of oaths (5:33–37). **23, 24** They went beyond the requirements of the law (Dt. 14:22f.). But they missed the true requirements of God (*cf.* Mi. 6:8). Their lack of proportion in spiritual matters is as ridiculous as *straining out a gnat* (to avoid defilement, Lv. 11:41) *and swallowing a camel* (*cf.* 19:24).

25, 26 The Pharisees not only lacked proportion, they tended to treat religion as a matter of external observance (*cf.* 15:10f.). **27, 28** are similar in their contrast of appearance and reality. The *tombs* were *whitewashed* in order to prevent people bumping into them and becoming defiled. *Iniquity* means 'lawlessness', when they were apparently keeping the law in all its minutiae.

29-33 For the putting to death of God's messengers, *cf.* 21:33-43; Heb. 11:32-38. It is always easier to honour a dead prophet than to heed a living one. They witness against themselves that they are the physical sons of the prophets' murderers. What they do not realize is that they are the spiritual sons also. **32** *Fill up*: they were to bring it to fulfilment (Gk. *plēroō*) in the supreme murdering of the Prophet and righteous One. **33** *Cf.* 3:7. Their judgment is a final one.

34-36 Luke introduces this with 'the Wisdom of God said', but it is not clear what he is quoting. *Prophets and wise men and scribes* presumably all belong to the Christian church (*cf.* 1 Cor. 12:28f.). Their fate will be as Jesus warned the disciples (Mt. 10:17, 23). *Zechariah* mentioned here is generally thought to be the son of Jehoiada (2 Ch. 24:20-22). As 2 Chronicles was the last book in the Hebrew canon, Abel (Gn. 4:8) was the first martyr and Zechariah the last. Zechariah *the son of Barachiah* was the prophet (Zc. 1:1). There is no tradition that he was murdered. It seems likely that the two have been confused at some stage. There was also a Zechariah the son of Baris killed in the middle of the Temple just before the siege of Jerusalem (Josephus, *Jewish War* iv.5.4). *This generation* (*cf.* 11:16) brought unbelief to its culmination in the murder of the Messiah, and the crimes of centuries were in a sense avenged in the horrors of the Jewish war.

37-39 A sad and loving prophetic oracle. For *Jerusalem* as the centre of rejection, *cf.* Lk. 13:33f. *How often* implies previous visits to Jerusalem such as John records. The rejection of the protection of God incarnate, in favour of the outward trappings of religion in which they had a vested interest (*your house*), could only have the result of their losing those as well (*cf.* Jn. 11:47-53). For the desolation of the Temple, *cf.* 1 Ki. 9:7f.; Je. 12:7; 22:5. The One who could have saved it will not be seen again until the end when *Blessed is he who comes in the name of the Lord* will have a new meaning altogether (*cf.* 21:9).

24:1-42 The fall of Jerusalem and the coming of the Son of man

This section is close to Mk. 13:1-32 (*cf.* Lk. 21:5-33) with divergences in vv. 10-13 and the addition of vv. 26-28, 37-42, which have parallels in Lk. 17:23-37. After the introduction (vv. 1-3), there is teaching on disturbances (vv. 4-8), persecution and evangelism (vv. 9-14) and the great tribulation (vv. 15-28). These refer mainly to temporal judgment. There follows the coming of the Son of man in final judgment (vv. 29-31) and the linking of the two phases of judgment

together (vv. 32-36). There are then a number of warnings in the form of illustrations of sudden disaster.

1, 2 The disciples look at the buildings of *the temple* with the awe of provincial pilgrims. Jesus saw far more clearly the judgment to come upon it because men had not used it as they ought (21:12f.). **3** shows that there are two things involved in the chapter: *this* (the destruction of the Temple) and *the sign of your coming and of the close of the age*. It seems that Matthew makes explicit the two signs of the end. Both *parousia* (*coming*; *cf.* vv. 27, 37, 39) and *the close of the age* (*cf.* 13:39, 49; 28:20) only occur in Matthew of the Gospels. **5** There were a number of Messianic pretenders in the 1st century (*cf.* 7:15). **6** *Wars* may be more than just the Jewish war of AD 66-70. There was a programme of events but this was not *the end*. **8** It was *the beginning of the sufferings*: 'of the birth-pangs' of the new age (*cf.* Is. 26:16-19; Mi. 4:9f.).

9 summarizes Mk. 13:9-13 (*cf.* 10:17-21). **10-12** are peculiar to Matthew and list most of the spiritual disasters which can come on the Christian community—apostasy, treachery, internal hatred, heresy, lovelessness. **13** Full salvation nevertheless comes to those who stand fast. **14** The world-wide proclamation of the gospel is an essential preliminary to the end. **15** *The desolating sacrilege* (Dn. 9:27) seems to refer to the Roman standards (which were often worshipped) preparing for the siege of Jerusalem (*cf.* Lk. 21:20). *Let the reader understand*: the Evangelists thus show that this is a cryptogram to be solved and Matthew tells them the book to turn to. **16** On the basis of this saying many Christians fled to Pella in AD 68. **17-20** stress the urgency and the suffering that there will be. *Sabbath* does not occur in Mark, but this is a subject in which Jewish Christians would be interested. **21** This was the eschatological suffering coming upon this generation (23:36). The horrors of the Jewish War were indescribable, though in quantity at least they have been exceeded since.

22 The idea of a definite length of tribulation *shortened for the sake of the elect* is found in *2 Baruch* 20:1f. **23-25** In such times of stress there are always counterfeit deliverers. **26, 27** *The coming of the Son of man* will not be secret but open and sudden. **28** *The eagles* may well be the Roman standards about to swoop on the rotting corpse of Judaism. **29-31** *Immediately* might suggest that the end was to come straight after the fall of Jerusalem. Some have assumed that vv. 29-31 refer to that event in vivid symbolic language. But they are more naturally taken as referring to the end, and 'immediately' (Gk. *eutheōs*) might have a weakened sense (*euthys*), as it often has in Mark. There will be cosmic disorder, the appearance of *the Son of man* (*cf.* Dn. 7:13f.), the mourning of despair by those who were taking their side with the crucifiers of the Messiah (Zc. 12:10-14) and the gathering of the *elect* from all over (Dt. 30:4) at the sound of the trumpet (Is. 27:13; cf. 1 Thes. 4:16).

32, 33 This seems to mean that the sufferings of the Jewish War are a sure sign of the imminence of the end. It is unlikely that the *fig tree* is to be taken allegorically of Israel and the reference to its putting forth its leaves as meaning her repentance. **34** *This generation* has been interpreted as the Jewish race (Gk. *genea* may mean 'generation' or 'race'), or as the human race, or as the generation which sees the signs of the end. It is much more likely that it should be taken in its normal sense of the generation of Jesus' own day, the generation of the second Exodus (12:41f., 45; 23:34–36). *These things* will then refer to the events connected with the fall of Jerusalem, which occurred almost exactly 40 years (a round figure for a generation—cf. Ps. 95:10f.) after Jesus' words. **35** emphasizes the permanence of Jesus' words even in the most extreme cosmic disaster (*cf.* 5:18).

36 *That day* seems to refer to the end. If it is true that Jesus does not know the date of it, it seems unlikely that we should refer His prediction of v. 34 to the same event. *Nor the Son* should probably be retained and occurs anyway in Mark. An attribution of ignorance of this kind to Jesus could hardly have been invented. A distinction must be made between His ignorance which He confessed on such an occasion and the possibility of error when He taught things authoritatively. **37–39** The story of *Noah* (Gn. 6–9) is not used typologically (*cf.* 1 Pet. 3:19–21) but simply as a warning of the suddenness of disaster for the unprepared. **40, 41** The *parousia* will make a sharp division between people outwardly similar who are working together. **42** All this makes it essential to *watch*.

24:43 – 25:46 Five parables about the judgment

In this section the first parable, the householder and the thief (vv. 43f.) is closely paralleled in Lk. 12:39f., and the faithful servant (vv. 45–51) in Lk. 12:42–46. The same ideas are found in Mk. 13:33–37. Those of the ten maidens (25:1–13), the talents (vv. 14–30) and the sheep and the goats (vv. 31–46) are all peculiar to Matthew, though there are a few similarities in the parable of the talents with the Lucan parable of the pounds. Each emphasizes the need for faithfulness or alertness in view of the coming judgment.

24:43, 44 This is a warning to those who will be condemned by the *Son of man* at His sudden coming unless they repent (*cf.* 1 Thes. 5:2–6; Rev. 3:3). **45–51** It is not certain whether any definite group is in mind, and it may refer to disciples generally. The reward of faithfulness and responsible service to others is further responsibility. The punishment (RSV mg. 'cut him in pieces') for abuse of power in the church seems to be irrevocable.

25:1–13 There are certain allegorical features to this parable. *The bridegroom* (probably we should omit 'and the bride' of RSV mg.) represents the Messiah, and the *maidens*, who were to meet

him and join in escorting the couple to his home for the wedding feast, represent professing Christians. *Lamps* (Gk. *lampadas*) are almost certainly torches (*cf.* Rev. 4:5; 8:10). If this is so, the torches would be *going out* (v. 8), not because the oil had been burnt up but because they never had any oil and they could not get their torches going at all. *All slumbered and slept* (v. 5): the distinction was between those that made preparations at the right time and those who did not and tried to rely on others when the crisis came. Spiritual preparedness is not something which can be distributed round in a crisis, and the *wise* are not being selfish but realistic when they point this out. The foolish were shut out because the bridegroom did not know them in a personal way (*cf.* 7:21–23).

14–30 show the need for responsible use of the gifts of God in His service during the time when Jesus is not present. The first two servants were *good and faithful* (vv. 21, 23), for they made the most of their opportunities for their master's sake. The third saw no point in trying to get a profit which would go to the master at the risk of making a loss for which he would be punished. He is condemned (v. 26) as a *wicked* (Gk. *ponēros* probably has the force of 'mean'; *cf.* 20:15) *and slothful servant* (the opposite of the *good and faithful* servants). *You knew . . .* (v. 26) is rightly given as a question. On the supposition that he was right, he ought all the same to have acted differently. The parable concludes that different spiritual opportunities are given to different people. Those who take them will have further ones (presumably especially in the life to come) and those who do not will be thrown out as useless.

31–46 This is not strictly speaking a parable, but a pictorial description of the last judgment. It will be a universal affair of *all the nations* (v. 32), though the separation into *sheep* and *goats* looks like the judgment of individuals (*cf.* Ezk. 34:17). The small acts of kindness done to the least important of Christ's *brethren* (which seems to mean all men rather than just Christians) are done to Him, and *vice versa* (v. 40; *cf.* 10:40–42). These small things have not been remembered as meritorious by the righteous (for presumably they are the outcome of a living faith and not the basis of acceptance), and have been neglected by the others. The division is absolute between inheriting *the kingdom prepared for you from the foundation of the world* (v. 34) and going *into the eternal fire prepared for the devil and his angels* (v. 41; not for men). *Eternal punishment* and *eternal life* (v. 46) are not necessarily the same in duration. *Eternal* (Gk. *aiōnios*) simply refers to the age to come and makes the point that the division is final for men's destiny.

26:1 – 27:66 THE PASSION AND DEATH OF THE CHRIST

There is great emphasis in all the Gospels on the death and resurrection of Christ, the central point of the *kērygma*. The fact that they occurred at the Passover gave them particular significance as a fulfilment of all that had been foreshadowed through the Exodus in the OT. Here were the events which ushered in the kingdom of God, not yet in its consummation, but in the demonstration of love and power which was sufficient to place life on a new plane. The paradoxes found already in the Gospel reach a climax here, as it is through the death of the Messiah at the hands of the Romans and at the instigation of His own people that life is won for the world. Matthew parallels Mark quite closely (Luke is more independent) with the inclusion of a number of short pieces of which the most important are the saying about the sword and the angels (26:52–54), the death of Judas (27:3–10), some references to Pilate (27:19, 24f.), the resurrection of the saints (27:51b–53) and the watch over the tomb (27:62–66).

26:1–16 The anointing and betrayal

This section closely agrees with Mk. 14:1–11 (*cf.* Lk. 22:1–6; Luke does not give the story of the anointing as he has a different anointing in Lk. 7:36–50). The actions of all the protagonists come into sharper relief as Jesus goes knowingly to His death which the chief priests and elders are plotting in detail, and to which Judas is preparing to betray Him.

1 With this link-verse, *cf.* 7:28; 11:1; 13:53; 19:1. **2** Matthew alone draws attention to Jesus' knowledge of the connection between *the Passover* and His death. The Passover was the major Jewish festival. It was a commemoration every year of the deliverance of the people of Israel from Egypt, with all that this implied for Israel becoming a nation with its own land, and a source of blessing to the world (see Ex. 12; *cf.* 1 Cor. 5:7). *After two days* indicates that this was Wednesday. **3** *Caiaphas* was high priest from *c*. AD 18 to 36. **5** *Not during the feast*: probably this intention was overruled by events. The reason given is political rather than religious. There was considerable danger of a popular uprising with the large number of Galilaean pilgrims at the festival.

6–13 The woman seems to have anointed Jesus with *very expensive ointment* (v. 7) as a mark of devotion, but possibly also as private acknowledgment of His Kingship (*cf.* 1 Sa. 10:1; 1 Ki. 1:38f.; 2 Ki. 9:4–10). Jesus interprets it as being done to prepare Him *for burial* (v. 12), for that is the immediate destiny of the Messiah. The reaction of the disciples, *Why this waste?*, is understandable enough. Yet devotion to the person of Jesus has often in the long run produced the greatest benefit for the poor. Her deed would be an inspiration to others because it would be remembered in the world-wide proclamation of the gospel, of which the central point was Jesus' death and resurrection.

14–16 *One of the twelve*: this sad phrase highlights the tragedy of the betrayal. No motive is ascribed to Judas in the Synoptic Gospels (but

see Jn. 12:4–6). Matthew alone records his question *What will you give me?* and the exact price of *thirty pieces of silver* (*cf.* Zc. 11:12; for other citations of or allusions drawn from Zechariah's prophecy, see on 21:5; 24:30f.; 26:31; 27:9).

26:17–29 The Last Supper

In this section Matthew is close to Mk. 14:12–27 (*cf.* Lk. 22:7–30). Through the Passover meal Jesus interprets His coming death and Judas is identified as the traitor.

17–19 *The first day of Unleavened Bread* was the same as the Passover day and was followed by a further seven days of Unleavened Bread. There seems little doubt that the Synoptic Gospels present Jesus as eating a Passover meal. There is some difficulty in reconciling this with John, but it is possible that there may have been two different calendars in use, and it seems very unlikely that any of the Evangelists would not have accurate information about the dating of the last few days of Jesus' life or that he should feel free to alter it for supposedly 'theological' reasons. *My time is at hand* indicates the sense of destiny which Jesus had. **20** *The twelve* seem to have been there alone with Jesus. **22** *They were very sorrowful*, partly because Jesus was to be betrayed and partly because one of them was to do it. *Is it I, Lord?* is an incredulous question which yet allows the possibility that it is so. **24** For this blend of predestination and moral responsibility, *cf.* 18:7. **25** *Master* means 'Rabbi' (RSV mg.). The others call Him 'Lord'. *You have said so* may lay the emphasis on Judas' saying it himself or it may simply mean 'Yes'. There is no mention of the departure of Judas.

26 Jesus performed the action of the head of the household at an ordinary Jewish meal. He *blessed* God for providing the bread. The words of institution are very brief in Matthew and Mark, and the command to eat is not in Mark. *This is my body*: in the context of the breaking and eating it suggests His coming death and the way in which His incarnation and passion will sustain their lives (*cf.* Jn. 6:53–58). The bread cannot be identical with His body, but it is an effective sign of it when received in faith. **28** *This is my blood of the covenant* has echoes of Ex. 24:8, where the old covenant is connected with the great act of redemption. The word 'new' (RSV mg.) was probably added to emphasize the parallel. *Many* is inclusive rather than exclusive (*cf.* 20:28; Is. 53:11). *For the forgiveness of sins*: this is in Matthew alone, and, as he alone omits it with reference to John's baptism in 3:2, it looks as if he wishes to emphasize that the true basis of forgiveness is the redeeming death of Christ. **29** The Supper looks forward to the Messianic banquet (*cf.* 14:13–21) as well as backward to the mighty act of redemption.

26:30–56 Gethsemane

This section parallels closely Mk. 14:26–52 (*cf.* Lk. 22:31–53). The prediction of the failure of the disciples (vv. 30–35) is followed by Jesus' acceptance of the will of His Father (vv. 36–46) and His arrest (vv. 47–56).

30 The *hymn* was probably the second half of the Hallel (Pss. 115–118). **31** *I will strike*: the quotation is from Zc. 13:7 and Jesus has changed it from an imperative to a future indicative. This is probably intended to show that God is in control of all that is about to take place. **32** For reference to *Galilee, cf.* 28:7, 10. **33–35** *Peter* is the leader in vain boasting as he had been in the confession of Jesus as Christ (16:13–19). The first to confess also becomes the first to deny. **36** *Gethsemane* means 'oil-press'. It was an olive grove just east of the Kidron. **37** *Peter and the two sons of Zebedee* witnessed His glory (17:1ff.) as now they witness His agony. **37, 38** The sorrow was caused partly by His rejection by His own people and partly by the horrors of the atoning death which lay before Him. *With me* is included only by Matthew here and in v. 40. Jesus needed human companionship in His hour of trial. **39** The *cup* represented suffering and death (*cf.* 20:22; Is. 51:22). **41, 42** There are many features here reminiscent of the Lord's Prayer: *My Father; thy will be done; not enter into temptation* (*cf.* 6:9–13). He Himself in His incarnation faced the problems which He knew His disciples would also have to face. *The flesh is weak*: for His own experience of the weakness of the flesh see Heb. 5:7–10. **45** *Are you still sleeping?*: RSV is almost certainly right in making this a question.

47 *One of the twelve* emphasizes both the fact that he would know where to find Jesus and the enormity of his treachery (*cf.* v. 14). **48** The *sign* was necessary as there were probably many pilgrims about, and if there had been a struggle the wrong man might have been arrested in the darkness. **49** This would be the way in which a pupil would greet a Rabbi. **50** *Friend, why are you here?* would be a loving rebuke by implication. But it may be rendered with RSV mg. 'do that for which you have come'. In any event there is love and peace, for the struggle has been fought out in prayer with His Father. **51** The one who *drew his sword* was Peter, according to Jn. 18:10. Luke and John relate that Jesus healed the servant. **52–54** Matthew alone records these sayings. *All who take the sword will perish by the sword* means that in general terms violence will always beget violence. The deliberate resort of the Jewish leaders to violence here reaped its due reward (*cf.* 27:25). **53** If the angels looked after the little ones (18:10), how much more could they come in force to wait upon the Son of God. **54** *The scriptures* are probably the passages referred to frequently in the passion narrative, such as Ps. 22; Is. 53. **55** *A robber* was probably a terrorist, a role which Jesus may have been suspected of taking and which Judas may well have betrayed Him for not taking. **56** *The prophets* may be a wider term which could include the Psalms, as in 13:35. Jesus is left to face His ordeal alone.

26:57–75 The trial before Caiaphas

This section is closely parallel to Mk. 14:53–72 (*cf.* Lk. 22:54–71), though Matthew's account is shorter in places. There is now a confrontation between the religious leaders and the unrecognized and rejected Messiah. He confesses to His Messiahship, only to be met by the sentence of death from the court and denial by His leading disciple.

57 A number of difficulties have arisen about this meeting of the Sanhedrin, as it was not supposed to reach a verdict in a capital case at night-time, nor was it supposed to meet on the eve of a sabbath or of a festival. It seems likely, therefore, that this was an informal meeting hastily summoned with the intention of passing Jesus on to Pilate as a dangerous Messianic claimant. **59–61** Two witnesses were needed to sustain a charge (Dt. 19:15). In this case their testimony was not exactly false, for Jesus had made a statement about the destruction and raising again of the temple of His body (Jn. 2:19). The wrong implication was taken (*cf.* Acts 6:13f.). **63** For the majestic silence of Jesus, *cf.* Is. 53:7. He is then put on oath to say whether He is *the Christ, the Son of God.* **64, 65** *You have said so* presumably means the same as the more straightforward 'I am' in Mark. His assertion is a combination of Ps. 110:1 and Dn. 7:14. *Hereafter* (Gk. *ap' arti*) suggests something soon to happen. The whole sentence may refer to the exaltation and vindication of Jesus (as in Dn. 7 the Son of man goes to God). It is more likely to refer to something in two parts—an immediate exaltation followed inevitably by a return in glory (*cf.* 24:30). The *blasphemy* lay in the claim to be *seated at the right hand of Power*, a reverential periphrasis for 'God'. **66–68** seems to show that there was no legal verdict, but simply a decision accompanied by abuse of the prisoner.

69–75 There seems little doubt that this story must go back to Peter himself. His boasts had proved vain and Jesus' prediction had come true (vv. 33–35). Peter was given away as a disciple of Jesus, not by the quality of his life (*cf.* Acts 4:13) but by his provincial accent. The man called by Jesus to be a rock twice denied that he knew his Master, to servant girls and once to by-standers. No wonder that *he went out and wept bitterly.*

27:1–31 The death of Judas and the trial before Pilate

This section closely parallels Mk. 15:1–20 (*cf.* Lk. 23:2–5, 17–25). There is the addition of the death of Judas (vv. 3–10) and references to Pilate in 19, 24f. While the chief priests and elders take the final steps in handing Jesus over for crucifixion, the one who handed Him over to them in remorse commits suicide. Pilate is baffled by the silence of the supposed Messianic claimant. He tries to release Him by a special annual amnesty but in the end gives in to the pressure of the Jews who say that Jesus has claimed to be their King.

2 *Pilate* was *the governor* of Judea and Samaria from AD 26 to 36. His official headquarters were at Caesarea but he had to be present in Jerusalem on any occasions when there might be disorder. **3–10** For another account of Judas' death, *cf.* Acts 1:16–20. The word here translated *repented* is not the normal word for a whole-hearted turning to God. It seems more like remorse. **4** The chief priests seem to have no spark of humanity, let alone morality. **9, 10** This is a composite quotation from Jeremiah and Zechariah. The main passage referred to is Zc. 11:12f. where the wages of thirty pieces of silver were cast into the treasury, though MT reads 'to the potter'. There is some disagreement about the reference to *Jeremiah*, who may have been named because the allusion to Zechariah was so obvious. Most commentators look to Je. 32:6–15, where the purchase of a field is a token that God's people will return from exile to their own land. Both passages are near to references to the new covenant (Je. 31:31–34; Zc. 11:10). But there may also be allusion to Je. 19:1–13, in which the prophet breaks a potter's vessel in the valley of Hinnom as a token of judgment on the people of Judah who 'have filled this place with the blood of innocents'.

11–14 *King of the Jews* was a title with clearly seditious overtones. There is no point at this stage in Jesus' explaining what the real meaning of it is in His case. **16** Matthew does not mention, as do Mark and Luke, the terrorist activities of *Barabbas*. Some MSS read 'Jesus Barabbas' (RSV mg.). If this is correct, there is an ironical choice between the two who are 'Saviour', for that is what 'Jesus' means (*cf.* 1:23) and 'Son of the Father', which is what 'Barabbas' means (*cf.* 11:27). **19** For dreams, *cf.* 1:20; 2:12, 13, 19. **20** It is not certain what arguments were used to persuade the people, but probably Jesus was said to be against the Temple and the law (*cf.* 26:61; Acts 6:13f.).

24, 25 Only Matthew includes these verses. The hand-washing was a Jewish custom to signify the removal of guilt (Dt. 21:6; Ps. 73:13) but Pilate may have used it either in desperation or in mockery. The people make a terrible cry, accepting the consequences of Jesus' death, which was fulfilled in the horrors of the Jewish War (23:34–36). This most Jewish Gospel affirms that it was *all the people*. The saying has been wrongly used in later generations to persecute the Jews. **26** Pilate probably gave in in the end because of the need to keep in with the emperor (Jn. 19:12). **27–31** This is a combination of physical and mental cruelty. *Battalion* suggests more men than were likely to be involved. The *scarlet robe* was probably a soldier's cloak. The *crown of thorns* was probably a 'radiate' crown, a symbol of divinity.

27:32–56 The crucifixion

This section is closely parallel to Mk. 15:21–41 (*cf.* Lk. 23:26–49), with the addition of the reference to the resurrection of the saints (vv.

51b–53). The mockery, the suffering and the rejection of Jesus reach their climax in His crucifixion as a criminal and His separation from His Father. Yet even in this tragic scene there are signs of life and faith, hope and love.

32 The naming of *Simon* suggests that he became a Christian. Mark refers to him as 'the father of Alexander and Rufus', who were probably well known in the church to which Mark wrote. The part of the *cross* which had to be carried was probably the horizontal piece. **34** Drugged *wine* was offered to those about to be crucified to deaden the pain. Matthew describes the drug as *gall* to show the fulfilment of Ps. 69:21. Jesus presumably preferred to drink the cup of suffering to the dregs (26:39) by remaining conscious on the cross. **35** This fulfilled Ps. 22:18. It was customary for the soldiers to have prisoners' garments as perquisites of the job. **37, 38** The 'crime' of Jesus is specified, but not that of the *robbers*. They were probably Zealot terrorists with whom Jesus may have been associated in the Romans' minds. **40** For the charge about the Temple, *cf.* 26:61; Jn. 2:19. *If you are the Son of God*: *cf.* 4:3, 6. **42** It was only by not saving Himself that He could save others at the deepest level (*cf.* 20:28). **43** *He trusts in God . . .* is based on Ps. 22:8.

45 *All the land* presumably means the promised land (*cf.* the darkness over Egypt at the Exodus, Ex. 10:21f.). The period was from noon until 3 p.m. At the paschal full moon it could not have been caused by an eclipse of the sun. **46** *Eli, Eli, lama sabach-thani* seems to be a mixture of the Hebrew and Aramaic versions of Ps. 22:1. The repeated *Eli* is more like a transliteration of the Hebrew than of the Aramaic. The best MSS read 'lema sabachthani', which is Aramaic. Jesus does not address God as Father as is usual. He enters fully into the anguished distress expressed by the psalmist as He bears the sins of the world. The Psalm goes on to speak of vindication later. **48** The *vinegar* may have been a soldier's drink but it is also in fulfilment of Ps. 69:21. **50** Jesus is triumphant even in death.

51–53 While Mark records the tearing of the Temple curtain, signifying access into the presence of God (*cf.* Heb. 10:19f.), only Matthew refers to the resurrection of the saints. It is most natural to take the Greek as meaning that they *were raised* at this time but did not come *out of the tombs* until *after his resurrection*. Christ is 'the first-born from the dead' (Col. 1:18; 1 Cor. 15:20), and there is some difficulty about an anticipation of His resurrection unless it is intended to be something like the raising of Lazarus. The claim that they *appeared to many* makes it almost certain that Matthew means these verses to be taken literally and to refer to some anticipation of the general resurrection at the last day. **54** *The centurion*, though a Gentile, because he observes what is happening makes a confession of Jesus, though with limited understanding, in terms which the leaders of His own people have only used in mockery (vv. 40, 43).

56 *The mother of the sons of Zebedee* is presumably to be identified with Mark's 'Salome' (see also 20:20).

27:57–66 The burial, and setting of the guard

In this section Matthew has a shorter story of the burial than that in Mk. 15:42–47 (*cf.* Lk. 23:50–56), and includes the story of the setting of the watch. The emphasis here is on the reality of the death of Jesus, against Jewish denials of the resurrection.

57 *Joseph* is clearly described as *a disciple* here and in Jn. 19:38. It seems as if the crucifixion had given him the necessary boldness to go and see Pilate. Bodies had not to be left overnight on crosses because of the danger of polluting the land (Dt. 21:22f.). **60** *New tomb*: rich people would often have these built during their lifetime. Jesus would be the first to occupy this as He was the first to occupy Mary's womb (1:18–25). The *great stone* was put there to prevent possible rifling of the tomb. **61** This showed courage and devotion and also made it unlikely that they would go to the wrong tomb later. **62–66** Matthew seems deliberately to avoid mentioning that it was the sabbath. *After three days I will rise again* may be the Christian way of putting what they said. *You have a guard*: if this is the right translation it will refer to the Temple police. If it is imperative (RSV mg.) then he is offering them Roman troops.

28:1–20 THE RESURRECTION OF THE CHRIST

The second half of the Gospel has been leading up to the cross and all the shattered hopes involved in the shameful death of the Messiah at the instigation of His own people. But while Jesus has been speaking of His death, He has also been promising that He will rise again (16:21; 17:9, 23; 20:19). Now, in a brief final chapter, Matthew shows how tragedy is turned into triumph through the empty tomb, the appearances to the disciples and the world-wide mission of the church.

28:1–10 The resurrection

The narrative has some affinities with Mk. 16:1–8 but also considerable independence (*cf.* Lk. 24:1–11). Matthew makes explicit the miraculous nature of the event.

1 Matthew continues to emphasize the watch being kept on the tomb by the women as well as by the guards. **2–4** Matthew alone mentions the details of how the stone was rolled back. It is not suggested that the earthquake and the angel were involved in the rolling away of the stone to let Jesus out, but only in making it possible for the women to see that the tomb was empty. **5** *The angel* is the same as the 'young man' 'dressed in a white robe' of Mark. *Do not be afraid*: there was an impressive display of divine majesty and power, but the faithful women were not to be frightened like the unbelieving

guards. **6** *As he said*: see 16:21; 17:9, 23; 20:19. **7** The news must be communicated quickly. *Going before you to Galilee*: this does not rule out any Jerusalem appearances (*cf.* 26:32). **8** Contrast the initial awe-struck silence recorded in Mk. 16:8. **9** *Them* is the women, not the disciples. Their response was a recognition of His divine power. **10** *My brethren*: *cf.* 12:49; 25:40. The term seems to be wider than just the eleven. *There they will see me*: this was to be Jesus' main appearance to commission them as His witnesses.

28:11–15 The bribing of the guard

This is peculiar to Matthew. It is here included to meet Jewish denials of the resurrection, just as the birth stories were to refute Jewish rumours.

11 *All that had taken place*: all the phenomena they had seen (vv. 2–4). **13** This was the only way of explaining the fact of the empty tomb. **14** If they were Roman soldiers, Pilate may have handed over responsibility for them on this duty to the Sanhedrin, and therefore he might be persuaded not to punish this offence of sleeping on duty. **15** This does not help us much in the dating of the Gospel.

28:16–20 The final commission

This section is peculiar to Matthew.

16 It is not clear which *mountain* is indicated. It may be the same as that from which He had given the Sermon (5:1) or that on which He was transfigured (17:1). **17, 18** There seems to be a division between faith and doubt even among the disciples, but it may be only that they were uncertain until *Jesus came*. Jesus has now received universal *authority* as a gift from His Father, not as something wrongly grasped by worshipping Satan (4:8f.). The Messiah has come into His own, though His inheritance had not yet reached its full consummation (*cf.* 24:30f.). **19** *Make disciples of all nations*: the universal authority of the Lord leads to the universal mission of the church. Here is the authority for Christian baptism. It would not have been likely that it would have been practised so early after Pentecost (see Acts 2:38–41) if it had not been commanded by Jesus. It was administered 'in the name of Jesus' (Acts 2:38; 8:16, *etc.*), the name indicating ownership. In due course it came to be administered in the name of the Trinity. The reference to the Trinity here may not be intended as a baptismal formula but as a theological description of the meaning of the sacrament. **20** As a new Moses, Jesus stresses the importance of obedience to His commandments. One of the functions of His servants was to teach obedience, just as Jesus Himself had a ministry of teaching. Emmanuel, 'God with us' (1:23) in humiliation, is now glorified and with His disciples until *the close of the age* (*cf.* 13:39, 40, 49; 24:3). He has accomplished His work in His incarnation. He gives us His presence so that we may accomplish ours.

R. E. NIXON

Mark

INTRODUCTION

AUTHORSHIP

The Gospel does not refer to its author. Yet the authorship of Mark, the associate of Peter, has never been seriously questioned. Although Mark (Marcus) was one of the commonest of Latin names, there is little doubt that this Mark is the 'John whose other name is Mark', who is mentioned 8 times in the NT. He was a relative of Barnabas (Col. 4:10) and the statement in 1 Pet. 5:13 may mean that he was converted through Peter.

Evidence for the Markan authorship is abundant in the writings of the church Fathers of the first four centuries. Papias, Justin Martyr, Irenaeus, Clement of Alexandria, Tertullian, Origen, Eusebius and Jerome all refer to it.

DATE AND PLACE OF WRITING

In fixing the date of the Second Gospel, opinion differs widely within the limits of the 35 years from AD 40 to 75. But it is now almost universally agreed that Mark's Gospel is the earliest of the four. On the one hand, the statement of Irenaeus that Mark composed his Gospel 'after the departure (exodos) of Peter and Paul' would indicate a date not earlier than AD 68, assuming that 'departure' here means death, which it possibly may not; while the discourse of Mark 13, reflecting the situation before the investment of Jerusalem, suggests one not later than AD 70, when Jerusalem was destroyed. Vincent Taylor favours AD 65–67, and thinks 'attempts to date the Gospel earlier are precarious'. On the other hand, the relation of Mark to the other Synoptics, particularly Luke which antedates Acts (Acts 1:1), tends to throw the date back into the fifties. A date somewhere between AD 55 and 60 would represent a position midway between extremes.

Most scholars, following ancient testimony, favour Rome as the place of writing. Peter's greeting in 1 Pet. 5:13 tends to confirm this, if indeed 'Babylon' is a code-word for Rome, as a number of commentators have concluded, such as H. B. Swete, F. W. Beare, A. M. Stibbs. Other suggestions have included Alexandria, Caesarea and Syrian Antioch.

The Gospel was probably written for Gentile readers in general, but particularly for Romans. OT quotations and allusions are relatively few; Aramaic expressions are interpreted (e.g. 5:41); Jewish customs are explained (e.g. 7:3, 11); there are some Latin words. The general tone, depicting the Lord's ceaseless activity and His power over demons, disease and death, is such as would appeal to Roman readers, whose interest was in deeds rather than words. The writer's purpose was doubtless to provide for the needs of the church in Rome, to strengthen its faith in view of impending persecution and to supply material for evangelists.

MARK AND PETER

A tradition which dates from Papias (AD 70–130) says that behind the record of Mark's Gospel there is in fact the preaching and authority of the apostle Peter. The statement of Papias (preserved by Eusebius) is that 'Mark, having become the interpreter of Peter, wrote down accurately all that he remembered of the things said and done by the Lord, but not however in order'. This tradition has been called in question by some of the most recent scholars (e.g. A. M. Farrer), but it is confirmed by other patristic writers and 'is so sound', says Vincent Taylor, 'that if we did not possess it, we should be compelled to postulate something very much like it' (Gospel According to St. Mark, 1952, Preface, p. vii). This does not mean that Mark was little more than a scribe or amanuensis, or that he did not make use of material from other sources, including his own reminiscences; for it is evident that the author, though not an apostle, was nevertheless very close to the events he narrates, and there are all the marks of originality in his record. His order or arrangement of the material is evidently criticized in the Papias tradition; and it appears from the Gospel itself that in some places this is homiletical rather than chronological; although C. H. Dodd goes so far as to say that 'there is good reason to believe that in broad lines the Marcan order does represent a genuine succession of events, within which movement and development can be traced' (C. E. B. Cranfield, St. Mark, CGT, p. 18, quoting C. H. Dodd, ExpT, XLIII, 1932, pp. 396–400).

The internal evidence for the influence of Peter is equally clear:

The Gospel begins at the point where Peter became a disciple, and gives no account of the nativity.

The Galilaean ministry is prominent, centring particularly on the district around Capernaum, Peter's home.

The vividness of the narrative suggests the first-hand acquaintance of an eyewitness.

Details such as the benediction at Caesarea Philippi and the walking on the water, which tend to present Peter in a favourable light, are omitted; while others less favourable, such as the denial, are related with exceptional fullness.

SOURCES

In view of the established priority of Mark, inquiries into the sources which lie behind this Gospel have not been nearly so successful as in the case of Matthew and Luke. In regard to the oral tradition, much work has been done in the last 50 years in the field of form-criticism, of which Martin Dibelius is one of the originators. Form-criticism postulates the existence, prior to any written Gospel, of comparatively small tradition cycles (mostly oral, though some may have been written and be such as Luke's preface mentions). The nomenclature for these cycles differs with various critics. B. S. Easton divides the material into Sayings-groups, Parables, Dialogues, Miracle Narratives and Passion Narratives. Vincent Taylor distinguishes Pronouncement Stories, Miracle Stories and Stories about Jesus. The very diversity of these analyses points to the danger that lies within them, namely that the isolation of these groups must be purely subjective, since there is no external check such as textual criticism supplies. If we are to explore behind the documents, any plausible hypothesis may be put forward. On the other hand, there is value in the claim of the form-critics that the gospel was 'preaching' before it was a written record. Much of the material tended in the course of time to assume well-defined forms for mnemonic and catechetical purposes, and there may be traces of this in Mark's topical grouping.

This oral tradition is largely Semitic in its colouring and atmosphere. The presence of a quite considerable Aramaic element in Mark's Greek indicates this, though it is probably insufficient to justify the conclusion, strongly maintained by C. C. Torrey and others, that the Gospel is a translation from an Aramaic original. What is of importance is that this fact undoubtedly enhances the historical value of the record, inasmuch as Mark, though Gentile in his sympathies, nevertheless stood very near to the original Jewish Christian tradition.

In regard to documentary sources, the main question is whether Mark knew of and used the elusive document known as Q. In the opinion of B. H. Streeter, it almost certainly antedated Mark, and some consider there are traces of it in Mark's Gospel. Beyond this vague possibility, however, nothing more can be said. Attempts have been made to show the existence of an earlier edition or draft behind our Gospel, known as 'Ur-Markus', or Original Mark, in order to account for some of the alleged phenomena, such as 'doublets', 'extracts' from a sayings-source, and the apparent use made of Mark by Luke; but these may be dismissed as at best hypothetical and highly subjective.

Summarizing, we may say that the principal source of this Gospel is the preaching and teaching of Peter, whose sermon at Caesarea (Acts 10:34–43) is practically a résumé of it. This was supplemented by other oral tradition of a general kind and by Mark's own reminiscences, together with perhaps some documentary material.

HISTORICAL RELIABILITY

More recently there has been a change of emphasis in NT investigations, and scholarship has become less occupied with documentary and historical problems and has devoted more attention to theological and religious matters. We are warned against treating the Gospels as biographies, and it is pointed out that the purpose of the Evangelist is not biographical but theological. The material handled by Mark 'bears all the signs of having been community tradition and cannot therefore be derived directly from St Peter or any other eyewitness', and Mark's 'understanding of Christ was for the most part simply that of the church to which he belonged, and he was not conscious of doing anything more than commit the "gospel" of that church to writing' (so D. E. Nineham). This, of course, at once calls in question the Papias tradition. The most extreme form of this scepticism is that represented by Rudolf Bultmann, whose contention is that the Gospel narratives, even of such historical events as the incarnation, resurrection and ascension, contain a mythological element unacceptable to the modern mind, and therefore need to be 'demythologized'.

Now it is vital to Christian faith that its foundations rest not upon any myth, philosophy or teaching, however lofty, but upon these mighty acts of God in history, and to call them in question 'is in our view, whether it proves attractive to modern man or not, an example of *heteron euangelion ho ouk estin allo*' (a different gospel which is not another: Gal. 1:6, 7) (C. E. B. Cranfield). It is of importance to us to know, not merely what Jesus had come to mean to Christian faith in the closing decades of the 1st century, but what He actually was and said and did historically. The Gospels are, indeed, not biographies and should not be read as such; if they purported to be, they would be fragmentary and ill-proportioned. But this is not to say, with Nineham, that if the modern reader approaches them without adequate knowledge of their origins and consequent character, positive misunderstanding is likely to result. In that case many generations of believers, who were unfortunate enough to be born too soon, have already been terribly misled. One is tempted to observe that the ultimate expert in these matters is not the theologian or scholar but the saint.

The Gospels are a revelation of the Person and teaching and work of Christ, as far as these things affect our life and godliness, and there is good reason to believe, as we have already seen, 'that in Mark we have an authority of first rank for our knowledge of the Story of Jesus'; this Gospel 'sets at the centre the personality of Jesus Himself and His redemptive work for men' (Vincent Taylor).

THEOLOGY

The Person of Christ

It has frequently been said that Mark's presentation of the Person of Christ is that of the Servant of God (cf. Is. 52:13 – 53:12), while, correspondingly, Matthew presents the King, Luke the Man and John the Son of God. Several features suggest this, such as the absence of genealogy and the predominance of deeds over teaching. The title 'Son of man', which occurs 14 times, is in most cases (e.g. 8:31; 9:9, 12, 31; 10:33, 45; 14:21, 41) to be interpreted in terms of this conception. Nevertheless, as Mark asserts in his very first verse, the lowly Servant is also beyond all doubt the Son of God, whose ministry was authenticated by mighty works. The divine attestation of this at the baptism and the transfiguration (1:11; 9:7) is unequivocal. Vincent Taylor considers this the most fundamental element in Mark's Christology, which, he says, 'is a high Christology, as high as any in the New Testament, not excluding that of John'.

The Messiahship of Jesus is seen in Mark's Gospel to be in the nature of a carefully guarded secret, at least until the confession of Peter (8:30). This was doubtless to avoid the peril of the popular national and materialistic conceptions with which the expectations of the Jews invested the title, and to secure for it an ethical as well as an apocalyptic content. The term 'Christ' occurs only 7 times, and in no instance does Jesus use it of Himself.

The work of Christ

The two metaphors of 10:45 and 14:24 indicate the two main lines of teaching. Our Lord's life, laid down sacrificially, is 'a ransom for many' and the 'blood of the covenant'. The former effects deliverance from sin and judgment, while the latter provides covenant relationship and fellowship between God and men. This is not to say that in Mark's Gospel these conceptions are worked out into anything like a developed doctrine. Still less is there any justification for thinking that the ransom saying is an indication of Pauline influence. 'If we find the same thought in Paul', says James Denney, 'we shall not say that the evangelist has Paulinized, but that St Paul has sat at the feet of Jesus.' All the Synoptists mention the three occasions when Jesus made deliberate attempts to initiate the disciples into His approaching passion; but Mark especially notes the varying attitude of the disciples (8:31f.; 9:31f.; 10:32).

Eschatology

The eschatology of the Gospel is contained chiefly in two passages, 8:38 – 9:1 and 13:1–37, where Jesus seems to have had in view two widely separated events, the destruction of Jerusalem in AD 70 and His personal return in glory. Nevertheless it has also to be said that Mark's view of the kingdom of God is predominantly eschatological. The primary ideas in this conception are, first, of the kingly rule or sovereignty of God, and then of a realm or community which may be entered (9:47; 10:23). Sayings of the latter kind may carry a future meaning as well, but in others, such as 14:25 and 15:43, the reference to a future consummation is unmistakable.

Affinities with Pauline teaching

Reference has been made above to the suggestion that Mark was subject to Pauline influence. This has been strongly debated for many years. An examination of the vocabulary and ideas of this Gospel undoubtedly betrays much that is common to Mark and Paul, but it could with equal truth be claimed that such common ground belongs in fact to early Christianity as a whole. And it still remains that many of the distinctively Pauline words and doctrinal concepts, such as righteousness, justification by faith, union with Christ, life in the Spirit, and others are entirely absent from Mark. The most we are entitled to say is that Mark lived and wrote in a Roman and Pauline environment, and may have been acquainted with some of the earlier Epistles. But, as Vincent Taylor says, 'he has neither recast nor obscured the historic tradition. His Jesus is the Jesus of Galilee.'

OUTLINE OF CONTENTS

COMMENTARY

1:1–13 THE PREPARATION

1:1–8 John the Baptist

1 The opening verse is probably intended by Mark as a title to the whole book. *The gospel*, however, is not the book itself but its contents, 'the good news about Jesus Christ'. It is possible to treat vv. 2, 3 as a parenthesis, thus connecting v. 1 directly with v. 4: 'The beginning of the good news about Jesus Christ the Son of God . . . was John who baptized in the desert . . .' This is attractive, and brings out the suggestion that good news of the Messiah's coming began in a religious revival, not, as was commonly expected, in a political upheaval. It tends, however, to subordinate the importance of the OT quotation; and the RSV arrangement, which places a full stop at the end of v. 1, leaving it as the title, is to be preferred.

2, 3 *In Isaiah the prophet*; the quotation is actually a composite one, v. 2b embodying the LXX of Ex. 23:20 and the Hebrew of Mal. 3:1, while v. 3 is substantially from Is. 40:3. The important phrase is *in the wilderness* (v. 3), which is taken up in v. 4. Mark may have named Isaiah as the author of this, at the same time including the previous quotation for its obvious suitability—unless v. 2a (as in 9:13; 14:21) refers back to v. 1—for Isaiah is the prophet of good tidings (see Is. 40:9; 52:7; 61:1). Both prophecies are introduced to show the nature of John the Baptist's mission, as a preparation for the coming of the Messiah. Both speak in their original setting of a drawing near of God to His people, yet they are here significantly applied to Jesus Christ. **4** The quality and influence of John's preparatory ministry are further indicated. It was a preparation of the hearts of men, and notable for its moral power; *a baptism of repentance* with a view to *the forgiveness of sins*. The Greek word for repentance (*metanoia*) originally denoted change of mind, but in the NT it assumes the deeper meaning of a deliberate coming to one's senses, resulting in a change of conduct. This aspect of John's ministry is more fully described in Lk. 3:1–20 (see commentary *in loc.*). **5** The whole province of Judea was affected; Jesus Himself came from Galilee (v. 9), but that Judea should be so deeply stirred was a measure of the power of John's mission. The confession of sins was probably oral, an open avowal, after which the one who confessed was plunged (*baptizō*, the intensive form of *baptō*) in the waters of the river, as a representative action. **6** John's clothing and food indicated frugality and separation from worldly interests. His dress was characteristic of the prophets, and particularly of Elijah (2 Ki. 1:8) whom John resembled in other respects also (see on Mk. 9:11ff.). Locusts, though tolerated as food only by the poorest, are said still to be eaten roasted or salted by the bedouin. **7** The testimony of John is centred in the One *who is mightier than I* who was at hand, and **8** whose baptism should be not with water but with the Holy Spirit. That this would characterize the days of the Messiah was also in accord with OT teaching (Is. 44:3; Ezk. 36:26f.; Joel 2:28f.).

1:9-11 The baptism of Jesus

9 Jesus appeared at Jordan simply as one of the many who came to John's baptism. Matthew records the surprise and diffidence of John (Mt. 3:14, 15), but upon our Lord's insistence John took the sacred body and immersed it in the waters. It is noteworthy that Jesus made no confession of sin, and although He received John's baptism, the early church remained unshaken in its faith in His absolute sinlessness. For Him, the baptism was, first, the fulfilment of all righteousness; secondly, an act of identification, in which He was 'numbered with the transgressors' (Is. 53:12); thirdly, an act of dedication to His ministry. In the record of these opening events, we are provided, as it were, with 'essential clues to the understanding of what follows'. Mark records our Lord's 'submission to the baptism of repentance, the messianic gift of the Spirit, and the declaration of divine Sonship, thus putting the reader in the way to know the secret of his person—the Servant, the Messiah, the Son of God' (Cranfield).

10 *Immediately*; the first instance of Mark's favourite adverb, occurring 41 times. As Jesus emerged, a threefold experience set Him apart from all others and marked Him as having a unique relation to God. First, He saw *the heavens opened, i.e.* being rent asunder (Gk. *schizomenous,* present participle), signifying open vision of heavenly things (*cf.* Jn. 3:12, 13; Is. 64:1). Secondly, He saw *the Spirit descending upon him like a dove.* That the dove was something visible, and more than a poetic simile of the gentleness of the phenomenon, is clear from Luke's addition, 'in bodily form' (Lk. 3:22). An interesting suggestion connects this with Gn. 1:2, where the Spirit is seen hovering like a bird over the primaeval waters. **11** Thirdly, the *voice* of the Father was heard from heaven, bearing witness to His Son; so also in Mk. 9:7 and Jn. 12:28. The words are reminiscent of Ps. 2:7 and Is. 42:1. There is thus a clear revelation of the Trinity here, but the final focus is on the Son; for, although God is a Trinity, man's first encounter with Him must always be in Christ.

1:12, 13 The temptation of Jesus

Information about this must have come from Jesus Himself. Mark's account is exceptionally brief, which is the more remarkable in view of his evident interest in the victory of the Son of God over the powers of darkness. **12** All the Synoptists agree in emphasizing the close proximity of the baptism and the temptation. Edersheim (*Life and Times of Jesus the Messiah,* 1, p. 281) suggests that in the former, Jesus was active, in the latter, passive, driven by the Spirit; in the former case He fulfilled righteousness, in the latter His righteousness was tried. Before ever He entered upon a ministry whose purpose

was to challenge and ultimately to break the power of Satan in others, that enemy had to be met and defeated on the battle-ground of His own life (*cf.* Heb. 2:18; 4:15). **13** The loneliness of the struggle is reflected in the words *he was with the wild beasts* (a detail noted only by Mark), and its severity in the fact that *the angels ministered to him* (*cf.* Lk. 22:43). No merely psychological explanation is adequate. The encounter was real; Satan was real, seeking to divert his opponent from the path of the obedient Servant to some less costly way; the angels were real. In a lesser degree, every disciple, called to some high task, must expect similar conflict and may enjoy similar victory. Mark considers it unnecessary to say who was the victor.

1:14 – 9:50 THE GALILAEAN MINISTRY

1:14-20 The call of the first disciples

1:14, 15 The ministry of Jesus. According to Mark this began *after John was arrested,* which implies that there was an interval between Jesus' baptism and His Galilaean ministry. But what Jesus did in that period Mark does not say. The Gospel of John, in this as in other matters, supplements the Synoptic record (see Jn. 1:19 – 4:42).

14 *Arrested*; this word, which means simply 'handed over', seems to be used by Mark, and indeed elsewhere, with the underlying suggestion that the purpose of God is being fulfilled in what is done (*cf.* 9:31; 14:18; Rom. 8:32). **15** Jesus began to proclaim the good news from God, that the time of waiting was at an end and the long-expected kingdom of God was at hand. In view of its advent, men everywhere were required to *repent, and believe.* These are the two key words of the Gospel on its human side. *The kingdom of God* is the rule of God in the hearts of men and in society; clearly it is intimately connected with the actual Person and presence of Jesus; He is Himself the kingdom, so that we are able to say that it has both come and is still to come, since Jesus has already come and yet is to come again.

1:16-20 The call of Peter, Andrew, James and John. The choosing and training of the Twelve, who were to share with Him the proclamation of the good news and to continue it after His ascension, was a matter of vital importance in the ministry of Jesus. The two pairs of brothers here had all met Jesus before (see Jn. 1:35-42), and had believed that He was the Messiah. Now He calls them to the further step of leaving their fishing in order to follow Him wholly. Their previous work as fishermen would have provided good training in the patient endurance necessary for the work of winning men for Christ. Nevertheless more is needed, and if they will now follow Him, He declares *I will make you become fishers of men.* Christ calls men, not so much for what they are, as for what He is able to make them become, if they are prepared to obey Him.

1:21-45 The first sabbath in Capernaum

This compact account of the day when Jesus first came forward in Peter's own town (*cf.* Mt. 9:1) and ministered in his home would be related with especial personal interest by Peter. It bears all the marks of personal reminiscence and of the evidence of an eyewitness. A parallel account is given in Lk. 4:31-44.

1:21-28 The cure of a demoniac in the synagogue. Though but little of the actual teaching of Jesus is recorded by Mark, much emphasis is placed upon His teaching ministry (see 2:13; 4:1; 6:2, 6, 34). **21** *Synagogue* is strictly a Greek word meaning 'a bringing together' or 'an assembly'; but it was often used, as here, for the building in which the congregation met. Of the origin of synagogues nothing is known. The service in them was largely instructional: but they were also courts of justice (Lk. 12:11; 21:12), where punishment could be inflicted (Mt. 10:17). It was the custom for the president of the synagogue (Gk. *archisynagōgos*) to arrange who should read and expound the Scriptures each sabbath, and at this stage of His ministry this provided Jesus with manifold opportunities, for wherever He went He would be invited to teach. Paul was similarly invited later. **22** The authoritative tone of Jesus' teaching contrasted sharply with the utterances of Jewish teachers whose knowledge was entirely derivative and who invariably appealed to tradition or to the sayings of famous rabbis. **23, 24** While Jesus was thus speaking, either His very presence or His utterance, or both, provoked an outburst from a demon-possessed man. Demon-possession is a subject that presents many difficulties to the modern mind, which tends to dismiss it as an outgrown superstition. It is, however, a phenomenon specially associated with the period of our Lord's presence on earth. It is referred to only twice in the OT, and twice in the NT outside the Gospels; and it is clearly distinguished from mental disorders. 'The question whether the spread of a confident certainty of the demons' non-existence has not been their greatest triumph gets tragic urgency from such twentieth-century features as Nazism' (Cranfield). The demons were real, and knew of the Messianic office of Jesus long before the disciples were aware of it, although they were never allowed to proclaim the fact (see v. 34 and Jas. 2:19). Jesus had but lately challenged the prince of evil; little wonder that the subordinate spirits of wickedness realized they had now met their conqueror. **25, 26** The authority of the Saviour's word is now seen not only in the quality of His doctrine but in His power to command; for at His word the unclean spirit, having convulsed the man, *came out of him*; though, as Luke the physician tells us (Lk. 4:35), it had 'done him no harm'. Jesus never touched a demoniac in order to deliver him; the spoken word sufficed. **27** The people watched in awe, and then broke out into a buzz of conversation (*cf.* RV). **28**

Quickly the fame of Jesus spread throughout the region.

1:29-31 Peter's mother-in-law healed. *The house of Simon and Andrew* became almost a headquarters for Jesus from this point, when He was in Galilee (see 2:1; 3:19; 9:33; 10:10). In Jn. 1:44 we are told that these two brothers belonged to Bethsaida. They may have moved in the meantime. On the other hand there are some who think that this Bethsaida was the fishing quarter of Capernaum. 1 Cor. 9:5 confirms that Peter was married, and that later, possibly, his wife accompanied him in the ministry. To him, this occasion in his own home was unforgettable. The rapidity and completeness of the cure is indicated by the fact that, without any of the exhaustion and debility generally consequent upon such a fever, the restored woman *served them* at the sabbath meal after the synagogue service.

1:32-34 Healing after sunset. The sabbath ended at sunset; it then became possible to move the sick without infringement of the law. The physically sick are classified separately from the demon-possessed. People began flocking towards the door of the house, and soon a dense crowd was formed. Jesus did not fail them, for the divine compassion and power are always put forth in response to the appeal and acknowledgment of human need. The awareness of these evil spirits concerning the Person of Christ is an example of the truth stated in Jas. 2:19: 'Even the demons believe—and shudder.' There are no atheists in the realms of evil!

1:35-39 Departure to solitude and a tour in Galilee. 35 It was an unexpected development that from the midst of such scenes Jesus should arise *a great while before day* (lit. 'very much at night') and slip out of the town before others were awake. The story is related from the point of view of those within the house who discovered He was gone, and who at once felt He was discarding valuable opportunities in Capernaum without realizing how widely He was sought after. **36** Simon Peter at once began to lead and with his friends *followed him* (lit. 'hunted Him down'—a strong word occurring only here in the NT but frequently in LXX, *e.g.* Ps. 23:6). **38** The determining motives of Jesus' withdrawal were desire for communion with His Father and the need to preach elsewhere. He could not be monopolized in Capernaum. *That is why I came out* probably refers not to His departure from the town but to His mission from the Father (Lk. 4:43). The RSV rendering unfortunately tends to obscure this.

1:40-45 The cleansing of a leper. The miracles of healing apparently aroused particular excitement, and there was the danger, so common in our own day, that this type of ministry would eclipse the more fundamentally spiritual work of the gospel. So we find no mention of healing in v. 39. This case of a leper, however, evoked the Lord's compassion and was of a type that cannot be explained on any basis of 'suggestion' or 'faith-healing' so called. The leprosy of the Bible varied considerably in malignity, some skin diseases being classed as such.

40 With the leper's *If you will* should be compared the father's 'if you can' in 9:22. Leprosy is never said to be healed in Scripture, always cleansed. **41** *Moved with pity, he stretched out his hand.* 'It was owing to His compassion for mankind that He had a hand with which to lay hold' (Plummer). An alternative reading, however, found in many MSS, has 'moved with anger'; this would suggest the strength of His emotion as He confronted the forces of disease, death, sin and Satan in the man. **44** Having first experienced the power of Christ, the man is then able to fulfil the requirements of the law (Lv. 14:2–20). This is the order of Christian experience (Rom. 8:1–4). His ability to do so is *a proof to the people.* See RSV mg., 'Greek *to them*'; *i.e.* either to the priests or to the people in general. The leper was strictly bound to silence. **45** His disobedience necessitated a temporary change in the Lord's sphere of ministry from town to country.

2:1 – 3:6 The beginnings of opposition

2:1–12 The paralytic and forgiveness. This incident is the first of a series in this section, showing the gradually mounting hostility to Jesus which was now appearing among the scribes and Pharisees. **1** The rumour went round Capernaum that Jesus had returned and was *at home* again. It was almost certainly the home of Peter and Andrew, the one previously mentioned (1:29). Like many Palestinian houses, it would have an outside staircase leading to a flat roof. **2** While Jesus was within, *preaching the word* (almost a technical term for the 'good news'; *cf.* 4:14, 33; Acts 8:4; 11:19, *etc.*) to the crowd who had gathered again, **3** four men arrived carrying their paralysed friend, **4** and with commendable earnestness and resolution to overcome all obstacles mounted the roof and began to break through it. Luke mentions the 'tiles' (Lk. 5:19). Then they lowered the man on his mattress to the feet of Jesus. The plight of some needy souls is such that the sympathetic faith of believing friends is required to bring them to Christ (*cf.* 5:36; 9:24). Their common task of mercy would also have created an interesting bond between the four friends themselves.

5 *When Jesus saw their faith, i.e.* the faith of all five, He immediately responded, but in an unexpected way. He by no means taught that every case of affliction results from sin (*cf.* Jn. 9:2; Lk. 13:1–5), but as the Great Physician He diagnosed this case unerringly. The man's physical condition had a fundamentally spiritual cause. The conclusions of much modern psychotherapy are thus anticipated. Jesus' pronouncement, *your sins are forgiven*, was not a mere declaration that God had forgiven his sins; it was an authoritative action. Jesus Himself forgave the man, exercising the divine preroga-

tive. That the scribes understood it so is clear from the sequel. His authority to do so is the crucial point of the story. **6, 7** The scribes were right when they asked *Who can forgive sins but God alone?*; but their question was a challenge to the implied deity of Christ. **8** He answered this first by replying to their thoughts without anything being said; He who knows the hearts of men can pardon their sins. **9, 10** Secondly, He provided a test. The claim to forgive sins could not be substantiated by any visible result; but the power to heal could be demonstrated at once. If therefore He can cause the man to walk, let them *know that the Son of man has authority on earth to forgive sins. Son of man* is a title used exclusively by our Lord of Himself, and originating probably in Dn. 7:13. Opinions differ widely as to its precise meaning, though most expositors believe it had Messianic significance. At least it seems to convey the idea of the essential and representative humanity of Christ. But that the Son of man has authority *on earth* to forgive indicates that He had not, by incarnation, been emptied of divine prerogatives. **12** The forgiven man was then enabled to arise and walk, for divine forgiveness is always accompanied by power to discontinue sinning, *i.e.* to 'walk in newness of life' (Rom. 6:4).

2:13–17 The call of Levi. The identification of Levi with Matthew the publican (Mt. 9:9) and author of the First Gospel is practically beyond doubt, though none of the four lists of apostles gives the name Levi. His renunciation of a lucrative calling was greater than that of the fishermen, since it was final, whereas they could on occasion return to their fishing. His call illustrates the grace of the Lord in choosing a despised tax collector to be an apostle, but also the wisdom of the Lord, for Levi probably knew both Aramaic and Greek; and 'the only thing he took with him out of his old occupation was his pen and ink' (Alexander Whyte).

13 That Jesus *went out again beside the sea* suggests a recurrence of the circumstances of 1:16 in which yet another is called to join the apostolic company. **14** *Levi* was an official in the service of the tetrarch of Galilee, Herod Antipas. **15** His first missionary act was to entertain Jesus in his house and invite his colleagues and acquaintances to meet Him. Lk. 5:29 confirms that the house was in fact Levi's, and there is the suggestion that it was spacious by comparison with the humbler home of Peter. The meal table is regarded in the East as the place of most intimate fellowship. **16** The next ground of offence therefore to the Pharisees is the close association of Jesus with moral and social reprobates in this way. This time they voice their objection to the disciples. **17** Jesus' answer reveals the irreconcilable difference between Himself and them, and precipitates the conflict which is eventually to end in His death. The message of Christ is essentially redemptive, a message to the masses of the unwashed, ignorant and erring. He is the physician to the sin-sick soul, and He looks for the response of confidence and committal (Rom. 3:21–24).

2:18–22 The question of fasting. Only one fast day, the great Day of Atonement, was prescribed by the law (Lv. 23:27–29; Acts 27:9). Others, however, had been added to such an extent that fasting had become a feature of religious life in our Lord's day (*cf.* Lk. 18:12). **18** While the disciples of John were actually engaged in such a fast, along with the Pharisees, and in answer to this third objection Jesus points out the incongruity of such behaviour for His disciples. **19** His companionship with the disciples constitutes a situation as joyous as a wedding feast. *Wedding guests*, or groomsmen; NEB 'the bridegroom's friends'. **20** *Taken away from them*; *i.e.* violently (Gk. *aparthē*). This word is found only here and in the parallel passages in the NT, but the simple verb occurs twice, significantly, in the LXX of Is. 53:8. That there is a reference here to a violent death can scarcely be doubted, and we thus have the first hint of the passion from the lips of Jesus Himself. **21, 22** To impose upon this new situation of the gospel the religious observances of the old Judaism is as incongruous as applying a patch of new-made cloth to an old garment, or pouring unfermented wine into hard, inelastic wineskins, and as disastrous in its results. This was precisely the mistake of the later Judaistic teachers, against whom Paul's polemic is directed in the Epistle to the Galatians (*e.g.* Gal. 4:9, 10). On the subject of fasting, it may be said that Jesus sanctions it without enjoining it (Mt. 6:16–18). The essence of it is self-discipline; not the formalism of the ascetic or monastic, but the voluntary subordination of the physical to the spiritual (*cf.* 1 Cor. 9:24–27).

2:23 – 3:6 Jesus' attitude to the sabbath. Two incidents illustrate the fourth objection, one which is frequently levelled against Jesus in the Gospels (*cf.* Lk. 13:10–17; 14:1–6; Jn. 5:1–18; 9:1–41), namely His attitude to the sabbath. The disciples walking through the cornfields were doing what was quite allowable on any other day (Dt. 23:25); but the Pharisees classed it as reaping, which was forbidden on the sabbath (Ex. 34:21). In answer, Jesus quoted as a precedent no less a person than David, whose greatness was acknowledged. The fourth commandment (like all the rest) was given, not for the sake of imposing religious restrictions, but to meet man's physical and spiritual need. **26** *When Abiathar was high priest*; this is thought by most commentators to be incorrect and a possible later addition, since the high priest in question was actually Ahimelech, father of Abiathar (1 Sa. 21:1ff.). But textual evidence is not decisive against the reading 'Abiathar'. The OT context suggests that Abiathar was one of a considerable number who exercised priestly functions at Nob during Ahimelech's high-priesthood, and most of whom were slain by command of Saul very shortly after the occasion here referred to. **27** *And he said to them* rather

indicates the conclusion of the cornfield incident and that Mark has here appended the saying of Jesus as generally relevant. The sabbath has been given for man's benefit. Therefore the Representative Man may decide how it can best be used. Under His influence it has been changed to another day of the week and made available to all nations. We disregard it to our loss and peril.

3:1–6 The second incident introduces a positive note. The sabbath should be devoted not merely to rest and passive inactivity, but to works of love and mercy (*cf.* Jn. 5:16, 17). **4** *To save life or to kill* has a double significance. The rabbis themselves admitted that relief might be given to a sufferer when life was in danger, and being in danger was interpreted liberally. On the other hand they were using the sabbath with murderous intentions, plotting to kill Jesus. Which was more appropriate to the day, His healing or their plotting? In this case there was, in fact, no danger to life. Could the man therefore not have waited until the next day? It has been suggested that our Lord felt a sense of urgency in His confrontation of the forces of evil of which sickness was but one manifestation. 'Evil works seven days a week. And the warfare against Satan must go on on the sabbath as well as on the other six days' (T. W. Manson). The healing of this man provoked the final cleavage between Jesus and the religious authorities; it was the parting of the ways. **5** *Hardness of heart* is rather 'blindness' (Gk. *pōrōsis*) of heart (*cf.* Rom. 11:25; Eph. 4:18); NEB 'obstinate stupidity'. **6** So bitter was the opposition aroused that *the Pharisees*, ardent nationalists, were ready to join forces with their deadliest opponents, *the Herodians* (who were quislings of a kind), in a common effort to destroy Jesus.

3:7–19 The Twelve appointed

7 Perhaps because of the imminent danger, Jesus with His disciples withdrew to the Sea of Galilee. He never adventured Himself into danger unnecessarily, and in the interests of His ministry such precaution was right and proper. **8** A graphic and lifelike description follows of the crowds who were attracted by His works of healing. Two multitudes seem to be indicated, one from Galilee and the other from remoter places. Almost the whole of Palestine is represented in the latter group, with the exception of Samaria; which shows how widespread the fame and influence of Jesus had by this time become. **9** The purpose of the *boat* was probably the purely practical one of enabling Him to cope with the situation. He did not apparently use it on this occasion as a pulpit; but *cf.* 4:1. **10** The crowds almost fell upon Him (Gk. *epipiptein*) in their eagerness to touch Him, especially *all who had diseases* (Gk. *mastigas*, lit. 'scourges'). The word (which occurs also in 5:29, 34; Lk. 7:21; Heb. 11:36) suggests distressing bodily diseases inflicted as a divine chastisement. It is a wholesome thing when such affliction drives people to Christ.

11, 12 Reference is again made to works of exorcism, and for the third time we learn that the demons who recognized Jesus were forbidden to make Him known (*cf.* 1:24, 25, 34). Great happenings draw great multitudes, and where human need is truly met there is no lack of seeking souls. Moreover, Jesus was never unequal to the increasing demands made upon Him.

13 From the lake Jesus went into the surrounding hill country, where Luke tells us (Lk. 6:12) He spent the whole night praying in preparation for the momentous task of choosing the Twelve. This was the first step in organizing the church, and from this point the teaching and training of these men became a matter of paramount importance to our Lord. They were chosen in absolute sovereignty; Jesus *called to him those whom he desired, i.e.* according to His pleasure, not theirs. But in free will they responded and *came to him.* **14** The 'Twelve' quickly became an official designation, used sometimes even when not all were present (1 Cor. 15:5). Some important MSS insert the words 'whom he named apostles'; but they may be an interpolation from Lk. 6:13. Their appointment involved communion and companionship, *to be with him*; commission, *to be sent out to preach*; **15** and delegated authority, *to cast out demons.* **16–19** The list is given four times in the NT (*cf.* Mt. 10:2–4; Lk. 6:14–16; Acts 1:13) with slight variations in the order. But three groups of four are distinguishable, headed in each list by Peter, Philip and James the son of Alphaeus. Judas Iscariot is always last. Five of the twelve (Peter, Andrew, James, John, Matthew) have appeared in the narrative before (1:16, 19; 2:14). **17** The origin of the name *Boanerges* is obscure, most explanations being in the nature of attempts to account for Mark's phrase *sons of thunder*, which at least has the merit of appropriateness in the light of Lk. 9:54. **18** *Philip's* first contact with Jesus is recorded in Jn. 1:43. *Bartholomew* is a patronymic (*i.e.* son of Talmai, a name which occurs in 2 Sa. 3:3). He has anciently been identified with Nathanael (Jn. 1:45), for John never mentions Bartholomew, and the Synoptists never mention Nathanael. But the identification, though probable, is not certain. All that we know of *Thomas* comes from the Fourth Gospel. *James the son of Alphaeus* is so called to distinguish him from James the son of Zebedee; he may be the same as 'James the younger' (Mk. 15:40). Nothing is known of *Thaddaeus*, for whom Luke substitutes the name of another Judas (Lk. 6:16; Acts 1:13); the two may, of course, be the same. *Simon the Cananaean* is derived probably from the Hebrew *qanna*, 'jealous' or 'zealous', and is correctly interpreted in Lk. 6:15 as 'the Zealot'; NEB 'a member of the Zealot party'. **19** The title *Iscariot* (lit. 'man of Kerioth', a place whose site is uncertain) applied to Judas indicates that he was the only apostle who was not a Galilaean.

Here were twelve typical men, no two alike, and all imperfect; yet, with one exception, there was a place for each in the fellowship of Christ.

3:20–35 Charges against Jesus

20 The lake and the mountain are left, and Jesus with His disciples enters 'a house' (NEB). RSV *he went home* is perhaps too strong. It may have been the house of Simon and Andrew in Capernaum once again. Here opposition arises from two quite different sources: from His family (vv. 20, 21, 31–35) and from the scribes (vv. 22–30). **21** It is evident that we are to understand *his friends* (lit. 'those belonging to Him') to be the same as the relatives mentioned in v. 31. So that vv. 22–30 represent an interlude going on in the house, while His family were outside seeking contact with Him. This at least is a more natural and satisfactory explanation than that the material has been editorially assembled in this way by the Evangelist. The opposition from the family was in the nature of well-intentioned, but misguided, remonstrance. *He is beside himself* means not that He has lost His reason, but that He is suffering, as we would say, from religious mania and has become eccentric. A similar charge was more than once brought against Paul (Acts 26:24; 2 Cor. 5:13), and is often made against an earnest Christian.

22 The opposition from the scribes was more serious and resulted from bitter hatred and jealousy. They were attributing the work of the Holy Spirit to Satan. *Beelzebul.* The name is of uncertain spelling and derivation; it may originate in 2 Ki. 1:2, 16, where Baal-zebub means 'Lord of flies'. It is no less uncertain whether the name is another name for Satan or represents an inferior evil power. The charge seems to have been made behind the Saviour's back, for **23** *he called them to him* in order to answer them. In reply, He showed first the sheer absurdity of such an allegation, then warned of the awful consequences which would result. There is nothing so illogical as unbelief. **24–26** The gradation is noteworthy: kingdom, house, Satan. The smaller the community the more fatal the division. In an individual, division is a contradiction in terms. **29** The saying about blasphemy against the Holy Spirit is one of the most challenging utterances of Jesus. Wrongly understood it has caused untold distress. On the other hand it must not be explained away. The unpardonable sin is not an isolated act or utterance, but an attitude of defiant and deliberate rejection of light, a preference of darkness to light (Jn. 3:19). Jesus did not say the scribes had committed it; only that they came perilously near; *guilty of an eternal sin* would perhaps be better rendered 'involved' in it, or 'liable' for it (Gk. *enochos*). Such an attitude of wilful unbelief might rapidly harden into a condition where repentance, and therefore forgiveness, became impossible. But 'Of all religious teachers no one was less inclined than He to minimize possibilities of forgiveness and amendment and the boundless resources of divine grace' (Vincent Taylor). The very fact that anyone is overcome by the fear that he may have committed this sin is itself, surely, clear evidence that he has not committed it.

31 On the subject of *his brothers* the literature is extensive, but three main views have been held. They were either Jesus' own brothers by blood; or half-brothers, the sons of Joseph by a former wife; or cousins, the sons of Mary the wife of Clopas and sister of the Virgin Mary. The second and third alternatives have been argued by some, principally Roman Catholic writers, in the interests of the dogma of the perpetual virginity of Mary. The available evidence is unfortunately not conclusive; but the fact that Jesus had His own brothers is the most natural inference from such passages as Mt. 1:25 and Lk. 2:7. From a doctrinal point of view it would, moreover, emphasize the reality and completeness of the incarnation. Mary the mother of our Lord appears only here in Mark, and the absence of any reference to Joseph suggests that he was dead.

33-35 The answer given by Jesus, when at last the message from without reached Him, does not in any way depreciate the sacredness of family relationships, but asserts that the ties which bind the spiritual family of God are even deeper and dearer, and are based upon obedience to the will of God. This is, so to speak, the germ truth out of which grew the early church.

4:1-34 Parabolic teaching

This chapter introduces a new departure in the teaching ministry of Jesus, namely His adoption of the parabolic method. The change coincides significantly with a shifting of the principal objective of His teaching from the multitudes to the Twelve, whose training He is now taking in hand. The people are still in view, but they have hitherto been far more attracted by His works than by His words. They came for physical healing, but are as yet unresponsive to His spiritual teaching.

1 *Beside the sea* once more, therefore, Jesus first secured a measure of detachment by withdrawing into a boat (possibly the same one as in 3:9), and using it as a pulpit from which to address the crowd assembled on the shore facing the sea. **2** The word 'parable' means literally the placing of two things side by side for purposes of comparison; hence, the illustration of truth in the spiritual realm by a story in the earthly or natural realm. This, according to Aristotle, was its meaning in classical Greek; and it is predominantly so in the NT also. There are, however, instances where it seems to represent the equivalent of the Hebrew *māšāl*, which in fact is frequently translates in the LXX. This was often no more than a wise saying or aphorism. *Cf.* Lk. 4:23 where 'proverb' (RSV) is the same word; and Mk. 7:14-17. **3** Yet a parable was more than a mere illustration to enlighten. The word *Listen* (preserved by Mark alone), followed by the repeated injunctions to hear (vv. 9, 23, 24), suggests that parables were designed to provoke serious thought. They were also moral weapons to surprise and stir the conscience. Nathan's

parable to David (2 Sa. 12:1-14) may be compared as an OT example of this.

The parable of the sower, recorded by all three Synoptists, reflects the immediate situation in which Jesus found Himself in His preaching, and at the same time enunciates principles which hold good for all time in regard to the preaching of the word. **5** *Rocky ground* is not ground full of stones, but with rock close to the surface so that there is *no depth of soil*. Such ground is common in Galilee. **8** The emphasis of the story is on the abundant harvest, despite initial discouragement (*cf.* Jn. 4:35; Mt. 9:37). Mark alone of the Evangelists preserves this emphasis by using the singular (*some seed fell* . . .) of the three failures, and the plural (*other seeds fell* . . .) of the one success (Gk. *ho men*, v. 4; *allo*, v. 5; *allo*, v. 7; *alla*, v. 8). The seed on the good ground was the most abundant.

10 Before giving the explanation of the parable to the Twelve alone, Jesus makes a further statement about the purpose of parabolic teaching in answer to their question. **11, 12** These verses have for long presented a difficulty to expositors. The OT reference is to Is. 6:9, 10, and on the face of it it seems to suggest that the purpose of parables is twofold, first to reveal the truth to disciples, secondly to conceal it from *those outside*, as judgment or chastisement upon their blindness (*cf.* vv. 24, 25). And certainly this receives support from the reference to *the secret of the kingdom of God* (Gk. *mystērion*, a word which in the Pauline Epistles has the sense of an 'open secret', made known by revelation, but previously hidden; *cf.* Eph. 3:3, 4; Col. 1:27). Nevertheless this interpretation has been felt to be so intolerable by some expositors that they have preferred to surrender the verse as an authentic saying of Jesus, regarding it and the explanation which follows as secondary tradition enshrining later Christian beliefs. Other attempted interpretations are that this judgment upon unresponsive hearers is in fact merciful, delivering them from the guilt of rejecting plain truth; or that Mark's compressed style here creates the difficulty, and that the words *so that* are a loose equivalent for 'in order that the scripture might be fulfilled which says . . .' (*cf.* Mt. 13:14). NEB adds in parenthesis 'as Scripture says'. Or, more probably, Cranfield: 'God's self-revelation is veiled, in order that men may be left sufficient room in which to make a personal decision. A real turning to God or repentance is made possible by the inward divine enabling of the Holy Spirit, but would be rendered impossible by the external compulsion of a manifestation of the unveiled divine majesty. The revelation is veiled for the sake of man's freedom to believe.' The basic assumption which all expositors seem anxious to secure is certainly right, namely that the ultimate purpose of a parable is to help and not to hinder the apprehension of the truth. But beyond this we may say that it belongs to the very nature of revelation that the capacity to receive it depends upon the prior surrender and obedience of the will. 'Come and see' (Jn. 1:39) is the order of Christian experience; moral conquest must come before intellectual enlightenment. The disciples had so surrendered to the sovereignty of Jesus and could therefore know. If temporarily parables concealed the truths of the kingdom from the outsider on the intellectual plane, it was only in order that moral conviction might first be secured with a view to intellectual enlightenment afterwards. There are many who through intellectual pride would like to have it otherwise, but it cannot be (*cf.* Mt. 11:25ff.).

13 So far from being a specimen of the work of the early church exhibiting its excessive tendency towards allegorization, this interpretation is clearly given as an example, to provide canons of interpretation for all parables, much after the manner of a teacher who, when teaching something new, works an example or two on the blackboard. The first part of this verse should probably be taken as a statement, and the distinction preserved between the two words *understand* which are different in Greek. 'You do not understand (*ouk oidate*) this parable; how then will you come to know (*gnōsesthe*) all My parables?' **14** The kingdom is to be propagated by the sowing of the word. This conception is fundamental to all evangelism; the task of the evangelist is not merely by means of cogent argument or persuasive eloquence to induce others to think in a certain way, but to sow living seed of the word of God in the soil of human hearts. The germ of the new life is in the word, and without its implantation no-one ever became a Christian (1 Pet. 1:23). **15–20** There are things that hinder the reception of the word: hard-hearted indifference (v. 15), lack of spiritual depth (vv. 16f.), preoccupation with the cares and riches of the world (vv. 18f.). But where the word is heard, understood and believed, the harvest is sure (v. 20). **15** The reference to *Satan* is strong evidence that Jesus taught the existence of a personal power of evil, for He could easily have explained the birds in v. 4 as impersonal temptations. **16** There is no confusion between the seed and the soil. We commonly speak of land being sown, *i.e.* planted with seed, which is the sense here.

21–25 Two groups of sayings, each introduced by the formula *And he said to them*, further explain the parabolic method with special reference to the moral responsibility of the hearers. The statement about the *lamp* confirms the view of v. 12 taken above, that the ultimate purpose of a parable is to enlighten and reveal, even if it temporarily conceals. A *bushel* is a vessel for measuring seed. The second group teaches that response to the truth is the condition of receiving further truth. Where there is no response, even the power to respond is diminished; like the atrophy of a physical faculty through disuse.

26–29 The parable of the seed growing secretly is the only one peculiar to Mark. Its principal emphasis is upon the fact that the word of God will do its own work in human hearts if given the opportunity in right conditions, in exactly the same way as *the earth produces of itself* (Gk. *automatē*) (*cf.* Is. 55:10f.; 1 Cor. 3:6f.). Outside instrumentality is limited to two things, first sowing and finally reaping (Jn. 4:35, 38). Between these initial and final activities it is a matter of confidence in the vitality of the seed and in the fruitfulness of the interaction between seed and soil.

30–32 The expression used to introduce the third parable of the kingdom, that of the mustard seed, is unique: *what parable shall we use for it?*, lit. 'in what parable are we to place it?', as though the parable were a kind of wrapper to contain the truth. This parable may be viewed in one of two ways, as showing either the expansion of the kingdom from insignificant beginnings, or (as Campbell Morgan held) its development into abnormal proportions so that the fowls of the air (spirits of wickedness) find lodgment in it. The latter view has the merit of a certain consistency in the use of the symbols (*e.g.* the birds represent evil both here and in the parable of the sower, and it may be said that history supports it. For it was when, under the Emperor Constantine, the church gained an imperial position and patronage it was never intended to have, that it became corrupt). On the other hand the traditional view is the simpler, and accords better with the general atmosphere of the chapter which is one of optimism and confidence in the ultimate prosperity of the word of God.

33, 34 A statement by the Evangelist finally summarizes the purpose and principle of parabolic teaching. The kingdom of God was so different from prevalent notions about it, and the parables were well fitted to dislodge these popular ideas where direct statements would not have been received. The nature of the kingdom was declared to the people by comparison rather than by definition. But to His private disciples privately (Gk. *kat' idian de tois idiois mathētais*) Jesus gave fuller instruction.

4:35 – 5:43 Mighty works

The series of parables is followed by a series of miracles, as though to suggest that the works of Jesus vindicate His words. What He does confirms what He says. A similar arrangement is found in Matthew, where these and earlier miracles are recorded as following the Sermon on the Mount.

4:35–41 The stilling of the storm. 35 Jesus decided to cross the lake from west to east. This may have been either to disperse the crowd or to find a new sphere for His ministry, or perhaps for both reasons. **36** *Just as he was* refers back to v. 1. After some hours of teaching the multitude and the disciples, He was too weary even to help in sending the people away. **37** The sudden storm is characteristic of the region round the Sea of Galilee, where the movement of the air currents causes the wind to sweep with tremendous violence down the narrow gorges that descend to the shore from the surrounding hills. **38** It is Mark alone who preserves the vivid detail that *he was in the stern, asleep on the cushion.* The cushion was probably a rower's wooden or leather seat used as a head-rest. There is a note of resentment and reproach in the disciples' question paraphrased by Moffatt, 'Teacher, are we to drown, for all you care?' **39** Jesus therefore awoke, and said to the sea, *Peace! Be still!* (lit. 'be silent, be muzzled'; the latter word is the same as in 1:25).

The story illustrates, first, the divine authority of Jesus over the forces of nature; He is superior even to a storm which caused experienced fishermen to panic with alarm. It also shows His true and real humanity, for He had evidently toiled up to and almost beyond the limit of His strength. On no other occasion is His sleeping mentioned; but He needed sleep, just as He needed food. Again, some have thought the story was intended to bring a message of peace to a storm-tossed church in a time of persecution. The disciples were in the path of obedience, but even obedience brings no immunity from trouble. Dangers beset the church even when engaged in carrying out the Master's commands. Nevertheless there is no ground for cowardice or craven fear. They should have known enough of Him by now to enable them to trust and believe that neither could the Messiah perish in a storm, nor would He allow them to perish because they had obeyed Him. 'Have you no faith even now?' (NEB).

5:1–20 The Gerasene demoniac. 1 It is not clear to what part of the opposite shore Jesus crossed. *The country of the Gerasenes* represents the best reading, though 'Gadarenes' is found in Matthew. At only one point on the E shore of the lake is there a *steep bank* (v. 13), and there are no rock-hewn tombs in the vicinity of this; but tombs built on the ground (*cf.* Lk. 11:44) may possibly be meant.

The fullness of detail in this account illustrates Mark's particular interest in this type of miracle of exorcism, which exhibits the power and authority of the Lord Jesus Christ even in the spirit realm. It has also been pointed out how the narrative seems to be arranged in scenes in which the centre of interest shifts from the man (vv. 1–10) to the herd of swine (vv. 11–13), then to the townspeople (vv. 14–17) and back again to the man (vv. 18–20), almost like a little drama in four acts. **4** First the demoniac is described as to his strength. Man had tried to tame him as a beast is tamed, but the external remedies of coercion and restraint had failed. **5** His life was one of misery to himself, for he knew neither rest nor sleep, but only ceaseless outcry and self-laceration. **6** His recognition of Jesus and acknowledgment of His authority seem to have been a common feature of these cases (*cf.* 1:24; 3:11), and show that no merely psychological explanation can account for the facts. This

man was more than a case for the psychiatrist.

7 The expression *the Most High God* is one used repeatedly in Scripture by Gentiles (Gn. 14:18; Is. 14:14; Dn. 3:26; Acts 16:17) and suggests that the man was not a Jew. The population on this side of the lake was probably of a mixed character, for Jews would not have been found keeping swine. It is remarkable that in a frantic appeal to Jesus not to inflict immediate punishment the unclean spirit used the same formula, *I adjure you by God,* that was employed in exorcisms. **9** Two explanations have been given of the question, *What is your name?* First, the ancient belief that knowledge of the name gave power over an adversary. Alternatively, and more probably, it was to recall the man to a sense of his own personality apart from the demon. *Legion* was a Latin word, which to people under Roman domination would suggest numbers, strength and oppression. He felt himself to be a conglomeration of evil forces, without moral unity, and this divided personality is reflected in the alternating singular and plural pronouns on his lips. **10** For the expression *out of the country,* Lk. 8:31 has 'into the abyss', which suggests that what the spirits feared was complete disembodiment. **11–13** The ethical implication of Jesus' action in regard to the swine has given rise to much discussion. Was it not wanton destruction of property with consequent heavy loss to the owners, and did Jesus anticipate the result, or did He not? Those who accept a psychological explanation of demon possession are obliged to account for the panic of the swine by saying that in the paroxysm which accompanied his deliverance the man struck terror into the herd and drove them down the cliff. 'But, supposing we are right in suggesting that there may be more in the NT view of the demons than has for some time been generally allowed, we must then take seriously the possibility that Jesus permitted real demons to enter the herd of swine, and the question "Why"? becomes pressing' (Cranfield). The most satisfactory view is that the destruction of the swine was permitted by the Lord as an ocular demonstration to the demoniac that the demons had in fact departed from him, and to confirm his faith. The sacrifice of brutes and property is justifiable where the sanity and lives of persons are at stake. One man is of more value than many swine.

15 Three phrases describe the completeness of the transformation wrought in the man by the grace and power of Christ; he was *sitting* instead of restless, *clothed* instead of naked, *and in his right mind,* sober instead of raging. Thus does Jesus expel the spirits of anger, pride, selfishness, impurity and the like from the lives of men, restoring them to spiritual health and clothing them with the garments of salvation. **17** But the townspeople, filled with alarm in the presence of the supernatural, and probably fearing, as so many have done since, that if Jesus stayed yet other things might have to go, *began to beg Jesus to depart*; and He will never stay unwanted. **18** The prayer of the man was very different; but Jesus' answer was contrary to His usual practice of enjoining silence in such cases (*cf.* 3:12). The reason was probably that, in this country beyond Jordan, there was not the danger of the miracle being used for political purposes, as in Judea. **20** *Decapolis* was, as the name implies, a group of ten Greek cities, all except one being east of the lake.

5:21–43 The raising of the daughter of Jairus and the healing of the woman with an issue of blood. These two miracle stories, the one within the other, illustrate the Lord's authority over disease and death. It will be convenient to consider the story of the woman first. Her malady was one which made her ceremonially unclean and would convey the uncleanness to all who came in touch with her (Lv. 15:25). **27** For this reason, probably, she approached Jesus from behind, in order not to be seen. **28** It was an ancient belief that even handkerchiefs and aprons carried from the person of a healer possessed healing power (*cf.* Acts 19:12), and similarly his shadow (Acts 5:15). **29** Having touched the Lord's garment, the woman was instantly cured, **30** but He would not allow her to escape without a fuller understanding of what had taken place. His inquiry *Who touched my garments?* seems therefore to have had a twofold purpose. First He desired the information; for although He was aware that the power proceeding from Him had gone forth in conscious response to the touch of faith, there is no need to suppose that He exhibited supernatural knowledge where information could be obtained without it. Secondly, He wished to elicit her open confession (*cf.* Rom. 10:9, 10). What follows is an interesting lesson in the nature of true faith.

31 The impatient remonstrance of the disciples shows that there is a world of difference between thronging Jesus and touching Him in personal faith out of a deep sense of need and a conviction of His saving power. It is still true that, while multitudes throng Jesus, it is the few who touch Him. **34** Calvin pointed out that the words of this verse do not encourage a belief in the efficacy of relics! We may go further and say that no outward 'sacrament' is efficacious apart from faith in the living Christ. There was no magical power resident in the garment. Again, although Jesus attributes the woman's cure to her *faith*, nevertheless in the NT view faith is no mere subjective experience, but something which derives its virtue from the object in which it rests, 'a spiritual experience which begins in a venture of spirit and is constituted and made effective by God Himself' (Vincent Taylor). The Greek of this verse is ambiguous, perhaps intentionally so; we could equally well translate, 'Your faith has brought you salvation.' The whole story is a parable of salvation by faith.

35 The delay caused by the intrusion of the woman must have been an agonizing test of faith to the ruler of the synagogue, who had approached Jesus by the lakeside and, casting aside his dignity in the acuteness of his distress, had fallen at His feet (v. 22). This was only intensified when a message from his house suggested that it was already too late, *Your daughter is dead.* **36** It is not quite clear whether Jesus overheard this message or ignored it. RV and RSV take the latter view (but see RSV mg.). The word *ignoring* (Gk. *parakousas*) means 'to refuse to listen' in the LXX and in Mt. 18:17. Perhaps both meanings are implicit here. Jesus overheard the message and deliberately set it aside in giving a word of assurance to Jairus. *Only believe.* The present imperative to denote continued action. Jairus was called not to a single act but a steady attitude of faith. **37** For the first time Jesus took with Him *Peter and James and John*, who were later present also at the transfiguration (9:2) and in Gethsemane (14:33). This was not for favouritism; but first, because in sovereignty He had chosen them for special service; and secondly, perhaps, because they emerged as a nucleus of the most responsive among the apostolic band. **39** The crucial question in the story is the meaning of the words *The child is not dead but sleeping.* Some expositors take the view that whereas Matthew (9:18) and particularly Luke (8:53, 55) plainly imply that the child was dead, the Markan saying, which is earliest, is ambiguous and could mean that she was only in a coma or trance-like sleep. In which case, 'the miracle is reduced to a penetrating diagnosis that saved the girl from being buried alive' (Cranfield). This is, however, by no means decisive. The scorn of the people points to the contrary. So also does the injunction to silence, which may among other reasons have been designed to forestall the suggestion that He was right after all; she was only asleep. It is better to conclude that here in fact is the germinal truth of later Christian teaching about death. As God sees it, it is a sleep from which there is to be an awakening (1 Thes. 4:13, 14). Our knowledge of the other world is limited, but it is within reach of the Saviour's voice and our dead are safe in His keeping. His authority extends beyond the grave. This is particularly true in regard to little children. The apostle Peter evidently observed his Master's technique on this occasion very closely, and the story of Dorcas in Acts 9:36–43 not only invites an interesting comparison, but well illustrates the great truth of Jn. 14:12.

6:1–13 Rejection at Nazareth and the mission of the Twelve

1 *His own country* is clearly Nazareth, as the context indicates. This visit is to be distinguished from that described in Lk. 4:16–30, which took place a year earlier. Jesus had left Nazareth as a private individual; now He returned as a Rabbi, surrounded by His scholars, presumably to give His own folk a further opportunity. But the result was the same as before; their jealousy was aroused. It was inconceivable that one of their fellow-villagers could have any mission from heaven. The reason for this attitude is stated as *their unbelief* (v. 6). **2** The fact of His wisdom and power was undeniable, but they questioned the divine origin of these things, the implication being that when the obviously supernatural does not come from God it must emanate from the devil. This is the essence of unbelief, the stubborn refusal to accept the evidence and admit the presence and power of God; and nothing so inhibits the power of God. That *he could do no mighty work there* (v. 5) is one of the boldest statements in the Gospels, but it clearly shows that our Lord's miracles were no mere magic; they were vitally related to the moral condition and faith of the people. Though He is omnipotent, God in His sovereignty will not act for blessing in the face of human rebellion. **3** Of the family mentioned, *James* afterwards became president of the church in Jerusalem (Acts 15:13; Gal. 2:9, 12) and author of the Epistle of James; *Judas* the author of the Epistle of Jude. Little is known of the others or of the sisters. **5** Matthew (13:58) modifies the statement to read 'he did not do', instead of Mark's *could do no mighty work there*. Mark's statement, however, does not imply that Jesus was in any sense powerless, but that He could not proceed in accordance with His purpose where faith was absent. Vincent Taylor refers to Holtzmann, who 'comments on the deep impression of historical accuracy left by verse 5'.

7–13 This mission of the Twelve is said by Matthew (9:35–38) to have originated in the Master's compassion for the people, which led Him to bring in at this point as 'fellow-labourers' those whom He had chosen and was training for the purpose. At the same time this first preaching tour may have been in the nature of an experiment forming part of the training itself. They would learn much from it, as, *e.g.*, that Christ's power extended beyond His presence and could even be delegated to them; that God could supply their temporal needs; that their commission was one of moral dignity and authority. They were to go in twos for the sake of witness (Dt. 19:15; 2 Cor. 13:1) and fellowship. Their equipment was to be simple and serviceable, avoiding either extreme of slovenliness or extravagance. **8, 9** The exception of the *staff* is peculiar to Mark as is also that of the *sandals*. Both these items are expressly forbidden in Mt. 10:10, and the sandals in Lk. 10:4. The tendency of modern commentators is to suggest that Mark has modified the instruction to suit western conditions of travelling and missionary work. Plummer, however, thought that the discrepancies were of no moment. The *bag* was a begging-wallet; they were not to beg. **10, 11** Hospitality was to be accepted where offered; but where it was refused they were to 'shake the dust off . . . as a warning to them' (NEB). This action did not express personal resentment; it was symbolic of the fact that the place was to be regarded as heathen, the intention being to provoke thought and lead to repentance. **12, 13** The threefold ministry of the

Twelve is summarized as preaching repentance, exorcizing demons and healing the sick. Anointing with oil is mentioned only here, Lk. 10:34 (a case of medicinal use) and Jas. 5:14. It is probably to be thought of here as an accessory to miraculous healing and a stimulus to faith.

6:14–29 Herod and John the Baptist

14 Herod Antipas was the son of Herod the Great (Mt. 2:1ff.) and Malthace. The title *king* as applied to him is at best one of courtesy or local custom. He was actually 'tetrarch', or ruler of a fourth part, in Galilee and Peraea, under the overlordship of Rome, and is invariably so described by Luke. Of the varying reports of Jesus which reached the ears of Herod, pangs of conscience probably led him to fix on the first as the most likely, *John the baptizer has been raised from the dead*, and that was why supernatural powers were at work in Him. **17ff.** Mark now narrates retrospectively and with some fullness the circumstances which led to the murder of John. This not only throws light upon the character of Herod, but seems to be a kind of interlude before proceeding to the acount of Jesus' further ministry in Galilee, within Herod's jurisdiction, and beyond it into Gentile territory. According to Josephus, the scene of John's imprisonment was Machaerus, a combined fortress, palace and prison just NE of the Dead Sea. *Herodias* was in fact the niece of Antipas, being the daughter of Aristobulus his half-brother; she had married yet another half-brother whom Josephus calls Herod, but who may also have borne the name Philip. **18** John had repeatedly rebuked Antipas for this union on the grounds of Lv. 18:16; 20:21, with the result **19** that Herodias nursed a grudge and was only restrained from carrying out her fell desire by Herod himself, whose conscience was evidently not yet completely dead. **20** presents the picture of a vacillating moral weakling, torn between his respect for John and his passion for Herodias. The story is told after the manner of the oriental potentate and should be compared with Est. 5:2f. There is reason for thinking that Herod Antipas is an example of one who had committed the unpardonable sin (Mk. 3:29). He had persistently and deliberately trifled with the truth as John gave it to him, and when later Jesus Himself appeared before him for the first and only time (Lk. 23:7–11) Jesus had nothing to say to him. That silence is most significant, for, had he been responsive to any entreaty, the Lord would surely have spoken.

22 The identity of *Herodias' daughter* here is uncertain. There are three MS variations: *a.* The best attested has the reading 'when his daughter Herodias came in'. This is felt, however, by most commentators to be intolerable, since it would imply either that Herod had a daughter of his own of this name and that 'mother' in v. 24 is used very loosely, or that the union of Herod and Herodias was of longer standing than the story seems to suggest. *b.* The second reading, accepted by most scholars, is: 'when the daughter of Herodias herself came in.' This would presumably refer to Salome, Herodias' daughter by her first husband, Herod Philip. It could also be translated 'when her daughter Herodias . . .', but this would involve the daughter having the same name as her mother. *c.* The reading represented by RSV omits the possessive pronoun altogether. The real difficulty is that of believing that a Herodian princess would thus dance before the court of Antipas.

6:30 – 8:26 Miracles and teaching in Galilee and beyond

6:30–34 The return of the disciples. 30 Here and here only in this Gospel are the Twelve called *apostles*. 'Having discharged a temporary commission, they went back to school to make greater advances in learning' (Calvin). **31** They report to the Master and are taken aside to recuperate. *Cf.* Lk. 9:10. **32** The position of the *lonely place* is thought by most commentators to have been the NE side of the lake. There is a time for rest as well as for work in the service of Christ. **33, 34** But, as so often, the seclusion of both the Master and His disciples is invaded by the claims of human need, and once more His deep *compassion* is the source of the events which follow. This compassion reflects the very heart of God in a picture of surpassing tenderness (*cf.* Je. 23:1–4; Ezk. 34).

6:35–44 The feeding of the five thousand. This miracle has the distinction of being the only one recorded by all four Evangelists. See Mt. 14:13–21; Lk. 9:10–17; Jn. 6:1–15. **36** The suggestion of the disciples was perhaps not wholly in the interest of the people. They had been disappointed of their time apart with Jesus and may have been hungry themselves (v. 31). **37** The answer of Jesus must therefore have come as a seemingly impossible challenge; and the word *you* is very emphatic: 'they are not to go away; you are the ones to feed them.' Such words come as a lasting rebuke to the helplessness of the church in face of a starving world, and regarding her own paltry resources with dismay. Yet it is evident that the need can be met if the Lord is allowed to direct the use of those resources. Estimates of the worth of a *denarius* or penny necessarily vary owing to the changing values in the purchasing power of money; but it was a day's wage for a working man, and the point of the computation here is that a sum far greater than the disciples had with them would be hopelessly insufficient. Mark's description of what followed is singularly vivid. **39** The people were arranged in an orderly fashion *by companies* (Gk. *symposia symposia*, lit. 'drinking parties') *upon the green grass . . .* **40** *in groups* (Gk. *prasiai prasiai*, lit. 'garden beds'). They resembled garden beds in their bright colours against the green background. The purpose of this, however, was rather the practical one of dividing up the assembly into manageable groups so as to avoid confusion and secure that all were served 'decently and in order'

(1 Cor. 14:40). **41** Attention has been drawn to the similarity of this verse to 14:22, as though to suggest that the meal in the wilderness was in some sense an anticipation of the Last Supper. That may be so, but probably the safer view is that these simple actions were usually associated with any meal on the part of the host, and were later invested with new and richer meaning by the Lord in the fellowship of His disciples. **42** The manner of the miracle alone is left unrevealed, as to whether the multiplication took place in the hands of the Lord or of His disciples. Various attempts have been made by the rationalists to dispose of the miraculous element altogether, by supposing that the numbers are exaggerated, or that the crowd were persuaded to share their provisions; in which case it is difficult to see why so ordinary an event has been preserved in a fourfold record. Everything depends upon the view we take of our Lord's Person. If He was in fact incarnate Deity, there is no real difficulty in believing that He wrought on this occasion a creative act, as the Evangelists clearly supposed. In the light of John's account, which leads on directly to the great discourse about the bread of life, we are left in no doubt as to the meaning of the story. Jesus is not only the Giver of life; He is the Support and Sustainer of it, as indispensable for Christian living as daily bread for the body, the complete satisfaction and nourishment of the believing soul who daily, hourly feeds upon Him in the heart by faith. **43** The *baskets* (Gk. *kophinoi*) were provision-baskets carried by travelling Jews to avoid eating Gentile food (*cf.* 8:8, 19, 20). *Broken pieces* were not crumbs, but surplus portions.

6:45–52 The walking on the water. By comparison with the earlier story of the stilling of the storm (4:35–41), the central feature here is the fact that Jesus walked upon the sea. There He was in the boat with the disciples; **45** here they were alone, having been compelled by Him to embark *while he dismissed the crowd*. The reason for this compulsion appears from John's remark (Jn. 6:15) 'that they were about to come and take him by force to make him king'. The disciples would have been delighted if they had done so, for this was precisely what they had always hoped for. **46** But Jesus recognized it to be a moment of supreme peril necessitating the immediate dispatch of the disciples and His own retirement into solitude and prayer. It was the temptation of Lk. 4:5–8 all over again. There is a geographical difficulty about Bethsaida (*cf.* v. 53 and Jn. 6:17), which led some older scholars to conjecture the existence of a western Bethsaida as a kind of fishing suburb of Capernaum and distinguishable from Bethsaida Julias to the NE. But the simplest solution seems to be that the disciples set out to cross the bay, and were blown off course and out to sea, eventually making for Gennesaret on the western shore. **48** It is remarkable that Jesus did not immediately intervene. The disciples struggled for some hours until *the fourth watch of the night*; or three o'clock in the morning according to the Roman reckoning which Mark is using. Even then Jesus *meant to pass by them.* This is entirely after the manner of His conduct on other occasions (*cf.* Lk. 24:28; Jn. 11:6) and we may infer that His purpose was to test their faith. **49, 50** Mark is careful to tell us that *they all saw him;* it was no subjective delusion or hallucination, but someone objectively visible to the whole company. **51, 52** Yet such was their blindness of heart (see on 3:5) that even the miracle of the loaves afforded them no basis for further understanding. The human heart can be unbelievably obtuse in spiritual matters.

Here once more objections have been raised to the miraculous element: first, on the ground that the intervention of Jesus does not meet any desperate need, for the disciples were not in jeopardy; secondly, and more seriously, because the story has been held to support a Docetic view of the Person of Christ, that His body was heavenly and not truly human. But if Jesus was only wading through the surf, there was no cause for terror, neither could He have conversed with them, nor is there any adequate explanation of the words *out on the sea* (v. 47). Furthermore we cannot dogmatize upon what would be possible or impossible for a unique Personality such as His.

The omission of the story of Peter's stepping from the boat (Mt. 14:28–31) points to the influence of the apostle himself on the Markan narrative. As we have seen (Introduction, p. 851), he is careful to avoid incidents which might tend to magnify him. Many of the Christians at Rome and elsewhere probably felt they were making little headway against the contrary winds of persecution, and the record of this incident would bring untold consolation to them, assuring them of the presence and power of their Lord.

6:53–56 Ministry at Gennesaret. 53 *Gennesaret* was a fertile and populous plain, lying S of Capernaum. The scene here so graphically described marks the climax of the Galilaean ministry. **54, 55** As Jesus moved through the district, the people followed Him, carrying around their sick upon pallets. Sometimes they were too late and missed Him; then they carried the sufferers from place to place until they overtook Him. **56** Their desires apparently did not rise above the healing of the body; and as there is no mention of any further teaching here, it seems that Jesus gave Himself unreservedly to them to do as much as they would let Him. *The fringe of his garment* was that worn by a pious Jew according to Nu. 15:37ff.; Dt. 22:12.

7:1–23 Teaching about cleansing. 1–4 The first four verses provide further evidence that this Gospel was written for Gentile readers, for the Jewish customs in regard to ceremonial ablutions are carefully explained. **2** *Defiled* (Gk. *koinais,* translated 'common', Acts 10:14, 28, and 'unclean', Rom. 14:14) was a technical term for what was ceremonially unclean to Jews. **3** *All the Jews* has been thought by some to be an

exaggeration, since the earliest Jewish authority on the subject, the Talmud (*c.* AD 450), makes these ablutions obligatory only on the priests in the time of Jesus. 'Accordingly', says Nineham, 'the story as it stands can hardly be historical.' But, in the first place, the Synoptic Gospels may be regarded as 'at least as good an authority for the customs prevalent during the period A.D. 1–70 as the Talmud' (Vincent Taylor, quoting G. Margoliouth), and secondly, Mark may have had in mind Jews of the Dispersion. Moreover, recent light on the subject from the Dead Sea Scrolls, particularly the Manual of Discipline, suggests that in fact these rules were widely observed. They were not for the purpose of cleansing in the hygienic sense but for the removal of ceremonial defilement. The untranslated Greek word referred to in the RSV mg. is *pygmē*, 'with the fist', as RV mg. This has been variously rendered 'diligently' (RV), 'up to the wrist' (Moffatt). The Talmud refers to 'dipping up to the wrist' as a minor ablution, 'plunging up to the wrist' as more extensive. Some MSS read *pykna*, 'frequently'; *cf.* AV 'oft'.

In this section three groups of people are addressed ; a hostile group of critics (v. 1), the people (v. 14) and the disciples (vv. 17f.). **5** The Pharisees raised the question of *the tradition of the elders.* **6–8** In reply Jesus stated that human tradition can never have the same authority as the Word of God. There were times when the scribes made even more of it than of the commandments, preferring, as so many still do, religious ritual to that which is inwardly moral and spiritual. It is an ancient attitude of the human heart, aptly described by Isaiah (Is. 29:13), for human nature is basically the same in every generation. **9–13** Jesus then cited an outstanding example which is not necessarily hypothetical; some think there may have been some contemporary *cause célèbre* of the kind which was current gossip. It related to the Corban vow. The law concerning duty to parents was plain, being doubly emphasized in the OT, but the Jews, with characteristic sophistry, had devised a means of evading it, even under the cloak of piety. A son could pledge his money to be paid into the Temple treasury. This could be done in an ideal sense without any actual payment being made, or the payment could be deferred until after his death. He could even do it in a fit of anger, and could then tell his old parents in their time of need that he could offer them no help, since his money was *Corban, i.e.* dedicated under oath. *Corban* is a transliteration of a Hebrew word meaning an offering or gift devoted to God. The Jews, being determined to establish their own righteousness, 'must needs attempt to render the Law something they could live on other terms than the forgiveness of sins, something compatible with their self-righteousness and complacency. In so doing they substituted for the Law of God a human legalism. "It is characteristic of all those who would find their justification in the Law", says

H. Roux, "that they always end by modifying it or perverting it, in order to escape from it and to make void its authority" ' (Cranfield).

14, 15 Having answered the Pharisees on the subject of tradition versus commandment, Jesus now turned to the whole company to deal with the question of defilement. This He did in a parabolic saying which is revolutionary in its religious implications and was destined to liberate Christianity from the bondage of legalism. On the one hand, nothing external can pollute a man; on the other, the real source of all impurity is within, a matter not of the hands but of the heart. **17** The disciples did not at the time understand, and therefore asked the Lord privately about it. **18–23** are an expansion of the two parts of the saying in v. 15. The comment in parenthesis (v. 19) may well be a reflection of Peter's in the light of his experience at Joppa (Acts 10:9–16). Jesus had ended the old distinction between meats clean and unclean. **21, 22** In the catalogue of vices that follows, Mark begins where all sin begins, in the realm of thought. Gal. 5:19–21 may be compared. It is a thoroughly Jewish catalogue, with an OT flavour about it, rather than a mark of Pauline influence. *Foolishness* is that moral inanity that considers 'sin is a joke, and mocks at those who treat it seriously' (Plummer).

This whole section, 'with its message of emancipation from Jewish particularism, is a fitting prelude to the account which follows of Jesus' ministry on Gentile soil' (Nineham).

7:24–30 The Syro-Phoenician woman. The significance of this and the following two miracles is that they took place on Gentile or pagan territory, whither Jesus had gone not only to avoid a premature clash with the hostile Jews, but primarily to secure some privacy with His disciples. His undertaking of a brief Gentile ministry also foreshadows the universal scope of the gospel. **26** The woman is introduced by her religion, as *a Greek, i.e.* either Greek-speaking or 'Gentile', and so 'pagan'; and by her nationality, a Phoenician of Syria, *Syrophoenician* being a term used in distinction from Liby-Phoenician or Carthaginian. These Phoenicians came from the Canaanites, and Matthew (Mt. 15:22) so describes her. We might indeed ask, Was she the first heathen convert to Christ? **27** The apparent roughness of the Lord's answer to her plea for the healing of her daughter admittedly arises from the fact that she was a stranger to the covenant, but none the less brings into focus the question of the sovereign grace of God in election, which at first sight looks like divine favouritism. But election is merely the method of God's initiative in salvation. 'Particularism is a stage towards a wider universalism in God's plan' (E. Y. Mullins). *Cf.* Eph. 2:11–18. God seeks to save not as few but as many as possible. The stage of the wider universalism has not yet been reached, but it is foreshadowed in Christ's treatment of the woman. **28** Her answer, which so clearly evinced

her faith and earnestness, seized upon two things. First, the term *dogs* (Gk. diminutive *kynaria*, 'little dogs', household companions, not outside scavengers) has not the opprobrium we associate with it. She assented to His estimate and drew her own conclusion. Secondly, His word *Let the children first be fed* led her to expect that her own turn would come eventually. **29, 30** Some modern expositors regard this story as a case of supernatural or telepathic knowledge rather than miraculous healing. But it seems clear that Mark, followed by Matthew, intended us to understand that Jesus healed at a distance, the only example in this Gospel of His doing so.

7:31–37 The healing of the deaf mute. 31 The geography is difficult, as a glance at the map will show. In involves a long detour proceeding first northward, then eastward and southward. Most of the attempts that have been made to account for this long journey are speculative and unsatisfactory. We cannot do more than surmise that Jesus may thus have tried to gain the necessary seclusion for the instruction of the Twelve, which He had twice previously failed to secure (*cf.* 6:31–34; 7:24). For *Decapolis*, see on 5:20. Once more Jesus was near the country of the Gerasenes, where in the meantime the healed demoniac had been bearing his testimony (*cf.* 5:19) and thus acting as a pioneer. **32** The people of the district accordingly brought to Jesus another helpless soul, *who was deaf and had an impediment in his speech* (Gk. *kōphon kai mogilalon*; the latter is a rare word occurring only here and in Is. 35:6 LXX, which was almost certainly in Mark's mind). He was not necessarily dumb, but a stammerer. A well-supported variant reading, *moggilalon*, which Vincent Taylor thinks cannot be dismissed, describes him as 'harsh of speech'. The account is full of vivid and interesting detail of the method employed to restore him; **33** first the retirement from the crowd, perhaps to avoid distraction and unnecessary publicity (*cf.* v. 36); secondly, the various means of contact, including the use of saliva which was supposed to be remedial, but in this case was designed to evoke in the man the co-operation of faith (*cf.* 8:23; Jn. 9:6); **34** thirdly, the upward look and the sigh or groan, an indication of the Lord's deep feeling and compassion and an example of those human emotions in Him which Mark delights to record; fourthly, the actual Aramaic word used, *Ephphatha*, which could easily be read from the lips by a deaf person. **35** Dumbness usually results from deafness. If our ears are open to listen to the word of the Lord, then our tongues will surely be unloosed in praise, prayer and testimony. Furthermore, only as the church hears the Word of God has it anything worth while to say.

8:1–10 The feeding of the four thousand. The chief question which arises is whether this narrative is a doublet of the feeding of the five thousand (6:35–44). There is admittedly considerable agreement, even verbally; and it is argued that the disciples must have been incredibly stupid to have asked such a question as that in v. 4, in the light of their earlier experience. On the other hand there are differences which ought not to be minimized. **2** The period of *three days* is much longer than in the case of the 5,000, which occupied hardly a day. **3** In the earlier narrative the dismissal of the crowd is urged by the disciples; here it is rejected by Jesus on His own initiative. The variation in numbers, though not of the same importance, is nevertheless not negligible. **8** But particularly striking is the difference in the word used for *baskets*. Here this is *spyris*, an affair woven of twigs or rushes, of the kind carried by Gentile merchants and large enough to contain a man (Acts 9:25). The basket of the earlier occasion was the Jewish provision basket (Gk. *kophinos*; see on 6:43). These two kinds are carefully distinguished by Jesus in vv. 19, 20. It is scarcely satisfactory therefore to dismiss these differences as mere modifications of the tradition, and we may be pardoned for suspecting that some commentators are finding themselves in difficulties when they admit that Mark indeed usually adheres closely to the original tradition, but that this is an exception where he has allowed homiletical or other impulses to colour the record of the Lord's words. The significance of this occasion seems to be that Jesus was still among the Gentiles, to whom the bread of life is to be offered as well as to the Jews. **10** The identity of *Dalmanutha*, a name which occurs only here, is not known. Mt. 15:39 has 'Magadan' (RSV) or 'Magdala', which suggests a crossing once more to the western side of the lake.

8:11–21 The demand for a sign from heaven. 11–13 should be compared with Mt. 16:1–4, where Jesus condemns the Pharisees for their failure to discern the signs of the times. They were insincere in their demand, and far more anxious to secure material for proving that Jesus was not the Messiah than to be convinced that He was. *Cf.* also Mt. 12:38–42; Lk. 11:29–32. Signs on earth were not wanting, and Jesus' saying to the disciples (vv. 17–21) implies that both miracles of feeding were of that order. But it is *a sign from heaven* that is required; a voice, or a wonder in the sun or moon, would be more convincing, so they suggest, than the meeting of human need. Yet would it? There is none so blind as those who refuse to see, and to the moral perversity that shows itself in these Pharisees Jesus has nothing more to say. **13** The words *And he left them* mark a tragic abandonment.

14ff. The occasion is used to warn the disciples of those corrupting influences which more than anything cause blindness of heart. *Cf.* Mt. 16:5–12. **15** We learn from Lk. 12:1 that *the leaven of the Pharisees* was hypocrisy; *the leaven of Herod* was probably worldliness and sensuality. But even the disciples were completely missing the inner spiritual meaning of their Master's teaching and supposed that He was

referring to some specific kind of leaven about which the Pharisees were very punctilious. Of the perplexity of the disciples, Trench (*Notes on the Miracles, in loc.*) appropriately says: 'It is only the man of a full-formed faith, of a faith which the apostles themselves at this time did not possess, who argues from the past to the future, and truly derives confidence from God's former dealings of faithfulness and love (*cf.* 1 Sam. 17:34–37; 2 Ch. 16:7, 8).' The stubbornness and dullness of the human heart frequently appears in Scripture (*cf.* Ex. 14:31 with 16:2, 3) and was evidently a source of grief to the Lord here. The disciples' condition, however, was not that of the Pharisees, for which there was nothing but abandonment (*cf.* v. 13); it was rather their spiritual dullness which called for and met with infinite patience from the Lord. There is consolation in this. The keynote of this passage therefore is the all-important one of spiritual discernment, a faculty all too rarely possessed even by disciples. It is a matter of the heart rather than the head (v. 17), of moral sympathy rather than intellectual erudition. *Cf.* 1 Cor. 2:9–16; Eph. 1:17f.

8:22–26 A blind man healed at Bethsaida. There are remarkable similarities between this miracle and that of the deaf mute (7:31–37). They are the only miracles peculiar to Mark. In each case, the sufferer was isolated from the crowd, spittle and the touch of the hand were used and undue publicity was to be avoided. But in one notable feature this work of healing was unique, in that the cure was gradual. **24** The man looked up and said, *I see men; but they look like trees, walking*; and a second touch was required to restore his sight completely. This highly distinctive detail alone confirms the historical character of the incident. It is difficult to resist the conclusion that Mark has introduced the narrative here with a purpose. The disciples were at this time rather like the blind man in the first stage of his recovery. But a note of hope is sounded. There is thoroughness in every work of Jesus and He will not be satisfied short of perfection. What He has begun He will finish; and presently, after the second touch of His Spirit at Pentecost, they will see all things clearly.

8:27 – 9:29 Messiahship and suffering

From this point the narrative becomes dominated by the thought of the approaching passion, of which there are three definite predictions (8:31; 9:31; 10:33f.).

8:27–33 The confession of Peter and the first prediction. 27 *Caesarea Philippi* was the most northerly town reached by Christ. It is to be distinguished from Caesarea Stratonis on the W coast, the seat of Roman government frequently mentioned in Acts. There Jesus put to the disciples two questions: first a general one which elicited the information that men recognized in Him someone outstanding, but no more. **29** The second challenged them personally, and Peter, as spokesman for them all, made the tremendous affirmation that He was *the Christ*, the Messiah, promised and predicted of old. Significantly the Lord's benediction upon Peter at this point is omitted. Peter had doubtless preserved a modest silence about it. But the parallel account in Mt. 16:13–23 should again be compared. After the blindness of the Pharisees and the dullness of the disciples, Jesus rejoiced to find the light of revelation beginning to dawn. They were beginning to see; but, as the sequel shows, their vision like that of the blind man was by no means clear yet. Nevertheless those who knew Jesus best reverenced Him most. With human characters it is not always so; familiarity often breeds contempt; on approach the halo often becomes dim. The reverse was the case with Christ.

This confession is the crisis-point of the teaching of Jesus and the watershed which divides the Gospel record in two. Jesus Himself had been aware of His Messianic mission at least from the beginning of His public ministry and probably before (*cf.* Lk. 2:49); aware too of the suffering involved and of the necessity of the cross which had shadowed His pathway from the first (Jn. 2:19; 3:14). But only at this decisive point did He begin to speak of it plainly. And from this point Mark's narrative becomes governed by the one purpose of establishing the thesis that Jesus was not taken unawares, but that the course of events was foreknown, and indeed was part of the predetermined counsel of God (Acts 4:28).

The disciples were right as to the fact, but wrong in what they understood by it. The OT prophets foreshadowed the Messiah in two ways, as triumphant (Is. 11) and as suffering (Is. 53); *cf.* Lk. 24:26; 1 Pet. 1:10, 11. The Jews cherished the material and political implications of the former and conveniently ignored or rejected the spiritual implications of the latter. And at this stage even the disciples shared the common view. **31** Jesus therefore *began to teach them that the Son of man must* (Gk. *dei*, of the divine decree) *suffer*. The disciples were obviously staggered by this revelation, and **32** Peter, probably after some deliberation on the matter, drew the Lord aside and *began to rebuke him*. **33** Through Peter's lips Jesus recognized a voice He had heard before (Lk. 4:5–8). It is a solemn reflection that a well-meaning but unspiritual disciple can become the tool of Satan. The goal of true discipleship is complete conformity to the divine mind, as revealed in Jesus. NEB renders v. 33, 'you think as men think, not as God thinks' (Gk. *phroneis ta tou theou*). Paul uses a similar expression in Col. 3:2. This is further developed in what follows.

8:34 – 9:1 The conditions of discipleship. 34 The first mention in Mark of the *cross* is here, and with its familiar Roman associations the word must have fallen upon apostolic ears far more startlingly than it does upon ours. For the follower it means precisely what it meant for the Lord; not mere inconvenience or discomfort,

but death. The mind of the disciple in relation to the world is defined in this way. He will experience an essential antagonism resulting in persecution, and he will exhibit non-resistance to that persecution (Jn. 15:19; Gal. 6:14). He will accept the last consequences of obedience and take the last risk. In relation to himself his attitude will be that of self-denial, which means the complete dethronement of self that the life may be Christ-centred. In relation to his Lord, he will follow in submission to His will. **35, 36** Paradoxically such surrender and submission is the surest and most abiding gain; whereas the self-realization and self-expression so dear to the modern mind is to lose one's own soul. **37** And once lost, what has a man to *give in return* (Gk. *antallagma*, a marketable equivalent) to redeem it? The loss is irrevocable.

But lest such stern doctrine should utterly discourage, Jesus went on to speak of His coming (8:38) and His kingdom (9:1). Although suffering awaited the Son of man, nevertheless that other strand of Messianic prophecy which spoke of His victorious reign should not go unfulfilled. **9:1** The precise meaning of this verse remains somewhat uncertain. Four possible interpretations which have been suggested are: the transfiguration; the resurrection and ascension; the destruction of Jerusalem in AD 70; Pentecost and the beginning of missionary enterprise. If the first of these be accepted the words amount to little more than an assertion that some of the disciples would still be alive six days hence, which seems pointless. Of the other three the last is probably most satisfactory. The disciples eventually came to see that the cross, which was now such a stumbling-block to them, was in fact the sign and secret of conquest over the hearts of men, and thus of the coming of the kingdom. On the basis of the rather speculative idea that the designation 'Son of man' denotes the elect community (a view advanced by some expositors), Vincent Taylor (*The Gospel according to St Mark, in loc.*) says: 'A visible manifestation of the rule of God displayed in the life of an Elect Community is the most probable form of His expectation.' This may be so in this particular context, though we prefer to think that 'the Son of man' should be interpreted personally rather than communally.

9:2–8 The transfiguration. 2 This is the second occasion on which the Lord took the three disciples into special intimacy with Himself (*cf.* 5:37). The *high mountain* is nowhere named but is generally conjectured to have been Mt. Hermon (9,200 ft), about 12 miles NE of Caesarea Philippi. The time was probably at night (Lk. 9:32), though Luke is careful to emphasize that the disciples were thoroughly awake when it happened. **3, 4** Hypotheses advanced in explanation of the phenomena of this event differ widely, ranging from those which attribute no more than a legendary or symbolic value to the story, or explain it as a resurrection story read back into the earthly life of Jesus, to the other extreme of the spiritualists who claim it as a seance. In reply to the latter it may be pointed out that there was no communication from Moses and Elijah to the disciples, and the subject of discussion was the cross (Lk. 9:31), not usually a topic at seances! **5, 6** The behaviour of Peter is thoroughly true to life and argues strongly for the historical character of the narrative, as does also the appropriateness of the story in its context. Campbell Morgan considered that what the disciples saw was not the effulgence of deity but the glory of sinless and perfected humanity, that the Lord at that moment was ready to return into heaven again without dying (for death is the result of sin, and He was sinless), but 'for the second time turned His back upon heaven, in order that, as perfected Man, He might share in the mystery of human death'. But the transfiguration, while an event of tremendous significance in itself touching the Person of Jesus, also played an important part in the spiritual education of the disciples and profoundly impressed the early church (2 Pet. 1:16–18). It confirmed their faith, which may well have begun to waver after the revelations of 8:31, 34. It showed that in fact the conception of a suffering Messiah was not contrary to the OT revelation, but accorded well with the testimony of the Law and the Prophets, of whom Moses and Elijah were representatives. **7** It urged the importance of listening to the Lord when He spoke of His approaching passion (*cf.* Dt. 18:15); this Peter had been unwilling to do (8:32).

9:9–13 The descent from the mount. 9, 10 For the last time we meet the command to keep silence, this time with the resurrection as a time limit. The concealment of the Lord's Messiahship had been necessary because of the current political and materialistic expectations. But once He had died and risen again, the danger of seeing in Him a Messiah of this world was over. Also, what the three had seen would help them to understand what had happened to Christ's body, when the tomb was found empty (see Jn. 20:8). **11** The question arose from the presence of Elijah at the transfiguration. **12** In reply the Lord made two things clear: first, that 'Elijah' had already come in the person of John the Baptist and had been rejected and killed; secondly, the Son of man would suffer the same fate as His forerunner. **13** *As it is written of him* must refer to the persecutions Elijah endured (1 Ki. 19:1–3). John had found his Ahab and Jezebel in Herod and Herodias.

9:14–29 The epileptic boy. The contrast between the glory of the mountain and the scene of human tragedy and failure in the valley has often been observed and is probably intentional. The group in the valley represents the world in miniature: youth in the grip of evil, parental anguish, nine disciples to whom the necessary power had been given (6:7) so that they ought not to have failed, but who, for certain reasons they were later to learn, were helpless before the challenge of

this need, and finally *scribes arguing with them*, a collection of critical and hostile religionists. It is easy to criticize the failure of others and do nothing ourselves. **15** In view of v. 9 we conclude that it was the opportuneness of the Lord's unexpected arrival that occasioned the amazement of the people, rather than any remaining traces of the celestial glory. **17, 18** Modern medical science would probably regard the case as one of epilepsy; but that is not incompatible with the view that the malady was caused by the presence of a demon with whom Christ directly deals. We have already noted Mark's special interest in such miracles of exorcism (see on 1:20–28 and 5:1–20), and his account here is distinctive for its wealth of vivid detail. **19** Before such a situation the Lord first expresses His distress, describing the whole company as an unbelieving generation (*cf.* Heb. 12:3). Nevertheless infinite forbearance is His, *How long am I to bear with you?* and infinite compassion, *Bring him to me.* **20–22** It is remarkable that Jesus should have left the boy in his distress while He engaged in conversation with the father. This was evidently to lead the father to the point of faith first. **23** Jesus takes up his doubting words *if you can* and flings them back at him. **24** He responds to the challenge, *I believe*, but feeling the very weakness of his faith casts himself all the more upon Jesus. **25** The *crowd* in this verse is not necessarily the same as that in v. 14 from which apparently Christ and the father had withdrawn while the boy was being fetched.

28 If we have failed, the wisest thing is not to set up a committee of enquiry, or even to discuss our problems among ourselves, but to ask the Master, privately. This the disciples did. **29** Comparing Matthew's account here (Mt. 17:19–21) we find the Lord gave three reasons for failure: lack of faith—unbelief deterred them from using the power they had been given; lack of prayer—perhaps they were so stunned by the announcement of the cross that they forgot to pray and were thus out of touch with God; lack of self-discipline (fasting). The words 'and fasting' referred to in the margin are omitted by Codices Sinaiticus and Vaticanus, and are said by some to have been added in the interests of early asceticism. But the evidence against them is not conclusive. The meaning is that only prayerfulness and strict self-discipline can make a man competent to deal with such cases.

9:30–50 Rebukes and warnings

9:30–37 Second prediction of the passion. At this point begins the final journey southward towards Jerusalem and the passion. **30** The reason for the secrecy preserved was probably twofold: first, the fact that the Galilaean ministry was now ended; secondly, the desire to instruct the disciples. **31** *For he was teaching his disciples*; *i.e.* His coming passion was the constant theme along the road. The second prediction of the cross follows (*cf.* 8:29–31). *Delivered* has reference to the divine action rather than the treachery of Judas. The thought is that of Paul in Rom. 8:32. **32** Once more the disciples failed to comprehend, and *were afraid to ask him.* Undoubtedly the reason was their preoccupation with prospects of political power. **34** Their dispute may have arisen out of the privilege accorded to the three who were specially chosen to witness the transfiguration. Such is human nature that even the highest spiritual privileges may engender pride. The cardinal sin is pride, and there are times when God has to take drastic steps to secure that humility in us which is of paramount worth to Him (*cf.* 2 Cor. 12:7). 'Humility is the ornament of angels, and pride the deformity of devils,' wrote William Jenkyn, an old Puritan. **35–37** The Lord's answer, first in plain words, then by means of a child as an object-lesson, is at once an encouragement to all parents and teachers and any who have the care of little children, and at the same time a rebuke to proud ambition.

9:38–50 Lessons in discipleship. These verses contain a miscellaneous collection of sayings of Jesus, which are distributed in various forms and different contexts in the other Gospels. This suggests that, while they are all genuine, they have nevertheless been assembled editorially here by Mark and were not necessarily spoken on the same occasion. If we look for some common theme linking them together, we may say that there are two groups, the first (vv. 38–42) dealing with the duty of mutual charity and toleration, and the second (vv. 43–50) dealing with the need for personal discipline. The first governs the disciple's attitude to others, the second his attitude to himself. Towards others he must be charitable, towards himself strict.

38 Unlike the exorcists of Acts 19:13–16, the man described by John was at least sincere and successful, in however defective a way; **39** and if lives are being blessed and delivered from the power of evil, such work ought not to be hindered. There is no more forthright rebuke of ecclesiastical intolerance than this. **40** Mt. 12:30 should be compared. The two sayings are complementary, not contradictory. 'While the principle of Mk. 9:40 should govern the attitude of the Church toward those without, the principle of Mt. 12:30 must be part of the Church's preaching both to those without and to those within' (Cranfield); to be neutral toward Christ is to decide against Him. **41** Even a much less spectacular service than exorcism shall earn its reward if it be from the right motive. **42** Possibly the disciples' discouragement of the man had in fact caused him to stumble and this accounts for the stern warning. *A great millstone* (Gk. *mylos onikos*) is one large enough to require an ass to turn it.

43 The language of this second group of sayings is obviously figurative. 'We must shrink from no spiritual surgery to save the life of the soul' (J. D. Jones). The word *hell* (also in vv. 45, 47) is the Greek *geenna*; this is a loose trans-

literation of the Hebrew *gê-hinnōm*, 'the valley of Hinnom', a gorge just outside Jerusalem which had in ancient times been the scene of human sacrifices (Je. 7:31), but later, during the reforms of Josiah (2 Ki. 23:10), became the refuse-heap of the city. It was a natural metaphor for the place of future punishment. **49** At least fourteen or fifteen possible explanations have been advanced of this obscure verse, the latter half of which, referred to in the margin, should probably be omitted on the textual evidence, as being an attempt to explain the preceding statement on the basis of Lv. 2:13. It is probably a challenging word on the purifying value of suffering, which would be particularly relevant to the church at Rome facing persecution. In which case the fire of v. 49 has nothing to do with that of v. 48 (which is destructive rather than purificatory), and *every one* means every disciple. **50** The connection seems to be purely verbal and artificial, for *salt* here is used in its more familiar sense of the grace of Christian character.

10:1–52 THE JOURNEY TO JERUSALEM

1 The geography of this verse is complicated somewhat by textual uncertainty. *The region of Judea and beyond the Jordan*, which is probably the best reading, may mean the region of S Palestine on both sides of the river. At all events, the teaching and incidents here described are to be thought of as taking place in the course of the journey.

10:2–12 On marriage and divorce

2 Once again the question put by the Pharisees was malicious, *in order to test him.* Divorce was a matter of dispute at the time, and there were two distinct schools of thought. **4** The Mosaic enactment (Dt. 24:1–4) stated that a husband was allowed to give his wife a writing of divorcement if he had found some unseemly thing in her. The question turned upon what constituted an unseemly thing. The school of Shammai maintained the strict interpretation of this, that the marriage bond was indissoluble except in the event of the wife's infidelity. That of Hillel took the liberal view allowing divorce for almost any cause. **5** In reply, Jesus first pointed out that Moses' legislation was a concession to human weakness and rightly introduced to regulate divorce in a defective state of society. **6–9** Secondly, He took them back beyond Moses to God's ideal at the beginning, from which we discover that marriage was instituted as the divine ideal for man and woman, and that the bond is permanent and indissoluble. **10–12** When, later, His disciples questioned Him in private about the matter, He took them further in order to indicate that in this particular the sexes are on equal terms. Jewish law did not allow a wife to divorce her husband. 12 is therefore an innovation.

It is not possible to comment exhaustively on this complicated question as it affects modern society. Something depends upon the view we take of the exceptive clause introduced by Matthew (Mt. 5:32; 19:9). Suffice it to say that, while the teaching of Jesus to unbelievers moves on one level and, without in any way lowering the divine ideal, can be interpreted as endorsing the Mosaic concession, yet to the disciples it moves on a higher level at which, undoubtedly, the individual believer must reckon with it. Paul's development of the subject in 1 Cor. 7:10-16 is designed to meet the new situation in the church of the post-marital conversion of one partner. The individual Christian need not be left in doubt. But 'for its own protection and well-being society will do well to be guided by His positive teaching in defining grounds for divorce which threaten personal and family life' (Vincent Taylor).

10:13-16 On childhood

The subject follows naturally from that of marriage, which leads modern commentators to think that its insertion here is topical. It is difficult to resist the attractiveness of the older suggestion, however, which associates the children with the house in v. 10. They 'were brought to Him to say good-night and receive His blessing before being sent to bed' (Salmon). The Lord is the Defender both of womanhood and of childhood; and when the disciples, true to their materialistic ideas of the kingdom, attempted to drive the children away **14** *he was indignant*. This is the only occasion where this word (Gk. *aganaktein*, implying anger) is predicated of Jesus. *Do not hinder them*. Some scholars suggest that this is an allusion to the baptismal rite of the early church, in which the question: 'What hinders?' was asked before the candidates were baptized. *Cf.* Acts 8:36. It is, however, to be noted that the Lord's invitation was *Let the children come*, not 'let them be brought'.

The disciples had a wrong estimate both of the worth of a child and of the nature of the kingdom. As to the first, it is not necessary for a child to become an adult before participating in the kingdom; rather the reverse is the case, the adult must be converted, turn back and become a child (*cf.* Mt. 18:3). **15** As to the second, the kingdom is not a matter of achievement or merit; we must *receive the kingdom of God* as a gift, and this is where the child has the advantage. The point is not that it is innocent or humble, which it may not be, but that it is receptive and willing to be dependent upon others. **16** And so Jesus took up the children *and blessed them*. It is a delightful picture conveyed by the strong compound word in Greek (*katēulogei*), occurring nowhere else in the NT: 'He blessed them fervently, again and again.'

10:17-31 On riches

17 It is Luke (18:18) who tells us that this man was a 'ruler', though of what seems uncertain. His youth is rather against his being ruler of a synagogue. There are several indications of the attractiveness of his character, apart from his own words which constitute no mean claim (*cf.* Phil. 3:6). Mark adds the details that he *ran up and knelt*, which suggests both eagerness and respect. But his form of address, *Good Teacher*, was a very unusual one, quite unknown among Jews to a Rabbi, and perhaps intended as a fulsome compliment. In Mark the expression *eternal life*, so common in the Johannine writings, occurs only here and at v. 30, and whether it has in this passage the full Johannine connotation of a present possession is at least doubtful. In the mind of the young man it probably had an eschatological meaning of life in the age to come, which a man inherits. V. 30 confirms this. Of such life he could feel no sense of security despite all he had attempted to do. **18** In answer, Jesus took up a word the man had used, and threw it back upon him for consideration (*cf.* on 9:23). The theological implications of this answer have been variously understood. Many of the Fathers and some modern commentators have taken the view that Jesus was trying to lead him to a perception of His divinity; as much as to say, 'God alone is really good; and as you do not believe I am God, but only a teacher, I cannot accept that epithet from you.' But it is extremely doubtful whether the man would have understood this at all. Strictly, the theological implications are secondary; and in so far as there are such, the meaning probably is that in an absolute sense goodness belongs to God the Father alone. By contrast, the goodness of Jesus was in some sense subject to growth and testing in the circumstances of the incarnation wherein He 'learned obedience through what he suffered' (Heb. 5:8). So H. R. Mackintosh (*The Doctrine of the Person of Christ*, p. 37). But the primary bearing of the words is upon the need of the man who, despite his sense of insecurity for the future, **20** nevertheless felt himself to have attained a measure of goodness judged by the standards of the law. What he now expected was to be told to undertake something difficult and exceptionally meritorious, to make good anything that might be lacking. It is this popular idea of meritorious goodness—and there is no sin more subtle than this—that our Lord attacks. The lesson to be learnt is that human attainment, such as he relied upon, can produce nothing 'good' in God's sight (Rom. 7:18). It is still true that perfect obedience to the law without failure or deviation would mean eternal life; but see Jas. 2:10, 11. In fact this man was breaking the first and greatest commandment; for his possessions were his god. **21** Therefore Jesus administers to him a liberal dose of the law as his 'schoolmaster' to bring him to Christ that he might be justified not by works but by faith (Gal. 3:24). The command to sell his possessions is accordingly not of general application; it concerned this man in particular. Neither did Jesus promise him eternal life in return for the sacrifice of his riches; but only a secure treasure in return for an insecure one. The way of life is to dispose of anything that hinders and then to *follow* continuously (Gk. *akolouthei*—present imperative). It is quite possible to part with one's possessions in some good cause without becoming a follower (1 Cor. 13:3). **22** We do not know whether this man ever thought better of it and returned. An interesting conjecture is that he did, and that his name was Barnabas.

23, 24 The disciples were astonished when Jesus pointed out how difficult it is for a rich man to enter the kingdom, for it was the prevalent opinion in Judaism that riches were a mark of divine favour, as with Job. When He went on to repeat the statement in tender tone (*Children*, . . .) but **25** stronger form, that it is difficult for anyone, rich or poor, **26** they were even more amazed. **27** But, after all, it is the fundamental proposition of the gospel that salvation is with men impossible, but not with God. It is the gift of God which money cannot buy; for rich and poor alike it is a miracle of divine grace (*cf*. Eph. 2:8). The Western Text reverses the order of vv. 24, 25, with the result that the conversation then moves smoothly and logically to the climactic statement in v. 27.

28 In the meantime Peter had been making some characteristic mental calculations and began to compare himself and his fellows favourably with the rich man. *We* is emphatic. **29, 30** Jesus in reply used figurative language to state the truth that He will be no man's debtor either in time or eternity; but neither will He encourage a bargaining spirit among those who profess to follow and serve Him. **31** Hence the warning added, which may be compared with Mt. 20:1–16 in the same context.

10:32–34 The third prediction of the passion

The journey draws near to its close, and we have depicted here, in an atmosphere of deepening solemnity, a striking procession—Jesus walking ahead, after the manner of an oriental shepherd (*cf*. Jn. 10:4); then apparently two separate companies, the Twelve, awestruck, and farther back a group of casual followers who have an indefinite presentiment that something is impending. Once more the Twelve are drawn aside and the unwelcome subject renewed, this time in the most explicit terms of all. For the first time it is made clear that both Jews and Gentiles are to have a hand in this thing, the Jews to condemn and the Gentiles to execute. The latter, had the disciples understood it, is tantamount to a disclosure that His death would be by crucifixion. Matthew (Mt. 20:19) so records it.

10:35–45 The request of James and John

From such solemn reflections the transition to this ambitious request is almost abrupt. Nothing could better illustrate the danger of having a mind preoccupied with petty thoughts of self at a time when big things are happening in the spiritual realm. Matthew (20:20, 21) puts the request into the mouth of the mother of James and John. She was Salome, and seems to have

been the sister of Christ's mother (15:40; Mt. 27:56; Jn. 19:25). James and John would therefore be first cousins to Jesus. What has been well described as 'the first ecclesiastical intrigue for high places in the Church' doubtless began as a family attempt to steal a march on Peter, the third member of the inner trio. But Jesus, as Bengel finely put it, was dwelling on His passion, knowing that He was first to have others on His right hand and on His left; and all the time their minds were in another world. **38** Using therefore the poetic terms of *the cup* and *the baptism*, familiar from the OT (Ps. 11:6; Is. 51:17; Pss. 42:7; 69:1; 124:4, 5), as descriptions of suffering and immersion in overwhelming sorrow, He tried to lead them to see what lay between Him and His glory and therefore between them and the realization of their desire. **39** Their bold assertion *We are able* is as ignorant as their request; but Jesus took them at their word, as they both lived to discover afterwards (Acts 12:2; Rev. 1:9). **40** Nevertheless the place of their ambition was in the right of the Father alone to bestow, and that not by favouritism but on the basis of fitness of character. As little could an umpire promise the first two prizes to two runners in a race, as could Jesus promise to them the chief places in the kingdom. They might indeed obtain them, but it would be because they were worthy and not as a personal favour.

41 *When the ten heard it* they displayed little better grace than the ambitious two, for they were by no means content to be last. **42ff.** Yet again, therefore, Jesus took them all aside to repeat the lesson they had already been taught (9:33ff.) and to put to them in plainest terms the essential difference between worldly greatness and spiritual greatness. In the world—and the words are as true a reflection of society in this modern age as in any—men delight to domineer and *lord it* over one another, using personal influence to secure private advancement. In the kingdom, true greatness flows from lowly and voluntary service.

45 But the unique fact about Jesus is that without any exception He practised what He preached; He is the embodiment of His own ethic. We therefore find these principles gathered up now in a saying concerning Himself which is one of the most important in the Gospels, and certainly the key verse of this Gospel. (For the suggestion that this saying is unhistorical and a product of Pauline influence see Introduction, p. 853.) It is one of the earliest explicit statements of the purpose of Christ's coming, and defines His work as being in two parts: first *to serve* and secondly *to give*. This, we may note in passing, also provides a simple division of this Gospel, the first part as far as 10:31 dealing with the service or ministry of the Son, and the remainder dealing with the ransom or sacrifice of the Son. Our main interest, however, centres in the remarkable phrase *a ransom for many* (Gk. *lytron anti pollōn*). There is little doubt that Jesus has in mind the predictions of Is. 53, which tell of the work of the suffering Servant of God in order to redeem men from evil. The figure of *ransom* means to deliver by paying a price and should be understood in the light of other sayings of Jesus which imply that the soul of man may become lost or forfeit. Here, for example, is the divine answer to the humanly unanswerable question of 8:37. Jesus came 'to lay down His own life as a ransom price that those to whom these forfeited lives belonged might obtain them again' (James Denney, *The Death of Christ*, 1951, p. 33). The word *ransom* (Gk. *lytron*) occurs elsewhere only in compounds; *e.g.* 1 Tim. 2:6 (*antilytron hyper pantōn*), where also it is followed by a different preposition of less intensive force. The use of the Greek preposition *anti* in this case clearly indicates the substitutionary character of the work of Christ. The force of the two prepositions together may be well illustrated by the action of a signatory for an illiterate person. He does what the other cannot do (*hyper*, on behalf of) and what the other therefore need not do (*anti*, instead of). The word *many* (Gk. *pollōn*) is a probable allusion to Is. 53:11, 12, and is intended not to limit the scope of the atoning work of Christ as though it applied to many but not all, but to show how a multitude shall derive blessing from the solitary offering of the One (*cf.* Rom. 5:19). The Early Fathers pressed the analogy of this ransom saying too far, by speculating as to who received the price, God or the Evil One. The results were grotesque, even as the speculation is illegitimate. A metaphor is intended to convey only a fragment of the truth.

10:46-52 Blind Bartimaeus restored to sight

Cf. Mt. 20:29-34; Lk. 18:35-43. There are divergent details in the three accounts of this incident which have for long exercised the ingenuity of the harmonizers. Matthew (Mt. 20:30) speaks of two blind men, while Luke (Lk. 18:35) places the incident at the approach to Jericho instead of when Jesus was leaving the city. These differences do not affect anything vital, being such as one would expect to find in all evidence given by trustworthy eyewitnesses. And this is doubtless a case where, if all the facts were known, there would be no difficulty of reconciliation.

Besides being in all its details an excellent parable of the gospel, the healing of the blind man was a work of Messianic significance (Is. 35:5), and is evidently introduced here by Mark with that in mind. **47, 48** Bartimaeus addressed Jesus by a Messianic title, *Son of David*, and is the first in this Gospel to do so. The whole incident was a prelude to the public presentation of the Messiah. Yet despite this movement of the divine programme and purpose which took Jesus steadily towards Jerusalem, it is remarkable that He was halted by the impassioned cry of need. God is always responsive to such a cry characterized, as this was, by determination (v. 48), definiteness (v. 51) and faith (v. 52).

50 The vivid picture drawn here in a few rapid strokes is peculiar to Mark. **51** At first the question put by Jesus, *What do you want me to do for you?* sounds superfluous to a blind man; but it probably had the twofold purpose of making him define his need and of demonstrating to the crowd that this time he was not merely begging for money. The same question had been put previously to James and John (10:36), but there received a very different response. *Master* (Gk. *Rhabbounei*). This is stronger than 'Rabbi', and means 'my lord', 'my master'. It occurs only here and from the lips of Mary Magdalene in Jn. 20:16.

11:1 – 15:47 THE PASSION WEEK

11:1-26 The entry into Jerusalem and opening events

With the exception of the last few verses dealing with the ascension, the entire remainder of the Gospel from this point is occupied with the narration of events which took place within the space of 8 days. By comparison, the events recorded hitherto cover a space of 3 years. The same literary ratio is preserved more or less by all the Evangelists, and is an indication of where the emphasis lay in the gospel of the early church. In the language of Dr James Denney, the centre of gravity in apostolic preaching was not Bethlehem but Calvary; not the life of our Lord, but His death; not His example but His expiation; not His teaching but His atonement.

11:1-11 The triumphal entry. The Messianic significance of this event is clear to us from the Gospel accounts. It represented, first, a fulfilment of Zc. 9:9; secondly, an open and deliberate assertion of Messiahship: the hour was approaching when He would be rejected and the issue must now be made plain. Either He is King, or a mistake lies at the roots of His life. He must be rejected as Messiah-King. It seems doubtful, however, whether this was understood either by the disciples or by the crowd at the time. Mark's account here is singularly restrained by comparison with the others, and there are those who consider that it was his intention still to maintain the hiddenness of our Lord's Messiahship. Furthermore John tells us (Jn. 12:16) that at first the disciples did not understand, but realized the significance of these events only after the resurrection. They were 'a veiled assertion of His Messiahship, which would not be recognized at the time, though it would afterwards be luminous for His disciples' (Cranfield). The manner of His entry expressed the character of His Messiahship, for here was in fact no military conqueror upon a war-horse, or political revolutionary of the kind the Jews expected. His purpose was not the overthrow of Rome but the breaking of the power of sin. On arrival in the capital city Jesus went at once to the Temple, which He is depicted as surveying with authority. His work had to do not with the politics and wars of Israel, but with its religion.

Finally, He retired to Bethany for the night. This was His procedure every night of the passion week.

1 *Bethphage* is named by all Synoptists in this connection, but the name occurs nowhere else in the OT or NT, although it is frequent in rabbinic literature, and means 'house of figs'. Its locality is uncertain. **2** It is not clear whether *the village opposite you* is Bethphage or Bethany, though it might well be either. There is no need to understand this verse as indicating supernatural knowledge on the part of Jesus; the simpler view, which is not just an easy rationalization, is that He had an arrangement with the owner, who was perhaps an anonymous disciple like 'the householder' (14:14). *On which no one has ever sat* was one of the general conditions of consecration to God (*cf.* Nu. 19:2; 1 Sa. 6:7). Plummer points out that the virgin birth and the burial in a new tomb are facts of the same kind. **3** Some expositors prefer to regard *The Lord* (Gk. *ho kyrios*) as referring to the owner of the animal, as we might say 'its master', on the ground that the title is not used of Jesus at all until after the resurrection, and then only by Luke and John. But there is an air of artificiality about such a message put into the mouths of the disciples, and it was after all Jesus Himself who needed the colt. He regards Himself as having a certain sovereignty over the possessions of His followers even though He will not take them by force. He promised to return the colt as soon as possible. Such was His poverty that even for this occasion He had to borrow an animal to ride upon. But it was not a mark of His humiliation that the animal was an ass, for an ass is quite in keeping in biblical thought with a royal personage coming peaceably, and this is indeed the real significance of the triumphal entry. **9** The cry *Hosanna* is a transliteration of the Hebrew of Ps. 118:25, 'Save now'. It is remarkable that Mark does not translate it, but it had probably become a general expression of praise and salutation, as familiar in common parlance as 'Rabbi'.

11:12–14, 20–26 The barren fig tree. *Cf.* Mt. 21:18–22. In Mark this story is in two parts, divided by that of the Temple cleansing. **12–14** The miracle has aroused criticism from modern scholars on two grounds: first, the unreasonableness of our Lord's action in looking for figs at Passover time; secondly, that such an action associated with His own hunger is both unlikely and unworthy of Him. The usual explanation is to say that a parable like that of the fig tree in Lk. 13:6–9 has reappeared in factual form. As to the first of the two objections, the probable explanation is that the fig tree in Palestine bears an early crop of immature fruit, like green knobs, which appears before the leaves, These are known as *taksh* and are the common food of the *fellahin*, or peasants. Their absence was clear indication of the barrenness of the tree. As to the second objection, we may note that this was Christ's only miracle of judgment, performed 'in mercy

to man, on an inanimate object, to teach a moral lesson' (T. M. Lindsay). The fig tree was a symbol of the Jewish nation, which abounded in the leaves of religious profession but was barren of the fruits of righteousness. Its cursing was prophetic of the fate of the Jewish authorities who were now about to reject their Messiah.

20–26 The following day, Peter was startled by the rapidity with which the Lord's word had taken effect, and from the incident Jesus drew for His disciples a lesson on the effectiveness of prayer. Prevailing prayer turns upon two conditions, one governing our relation to God and the other our relation to our fellows. **22** The first is faith. *Have faith in God* (Gk. *echete pistin theou*) means 'Have a faith which rests on God'. **23** With such you will be able to challenge and remove mountains of obstacles in the way of God's purpose. *Cf.* Zc. 4:7. **25** The second is forgiveness. The words apply, of course, to the spirit and attitude of the believer when he prays. They do not make God's forgiveness of the sinner, in the evangelical sense, depend upon the sinner's forgiveness of others first (see Eph. 4:32). **26** On good MS authority, this verse is relegated to the margin in RSV and NEB. It is found in Mt. 6:15.

11:15–19 The cleansing of the Temple. The tendency among some modern scholars is to identify this incident, recorded by all the Synoptists at the beginning of passion week, with that placed by John right at the beginning of the ministry (Jn. 2:13–17), though whether Mark's or John's placing of it is the correct one is a matter upon which opinion is sharply divided. By far the most satisfactory solution is that Jesus cleansed the Temple twice. There is nothing improbable about this; indeed it is likely that the evil would revive after a first cleansing. It would agree also with John's general plan of supplementing the Synoptists, and would account for important differences of detail (*e.g.* the scourge) in his narrative.

The sight that met His eyes the previous evening must have led Jesus to take this course. But it was also yet another function of the Messiah (see Mal. 3:1–4). **15** The scene of action was the Court of the Gentiles where there was a market for the sale of Temple requisites and an exchange to provide Tyrian coinage in which the Temple dues had to be paid. These apparently reasonable amenities had opened the door to extortion by the hierarchy and to all the contentious bargaining of an oriental bazaar where the pilgrims were defrauded. **16** There were also those, apparently, who used the precinct as a short cut between the city and the Mount of Olives, a detail noted only by Mark. We may well picture the confusion caused by Jesus' action, and just as we are entering upon the period when He meekly surrendered to His foes it is valuable to be thus vividly reminded of His capacity for moral indignation. **17** Having cleared the market, He began to teach, basing His teaching upon two OT passages, Is. 56:7 and Je. 7:11, the former of which, significantly, has special reference to the provision of a place of prayer and worship for the Gentiles. **18** Yet in face of this, the authorities were still powerless to take any immediate action because of the popularity of Jesus with the multitude. **19** Also, every day during this last week, when He was a 'wanted man', He went out of the city as evening fell.

11:27 – 12:44 Teaching in Jerusalem

11:27-33 The question of authority. 27 *They came again to Jerusalem*, probably later in the same day as v. 20. It was the Tuesday, and, in view of all that follows, it has been called 'The day of questions'. **28** Such drastic interference as the cleansing of the Temple quite naturally led the Jewish leaders to call Jesus to account on the question of His *authority*. If He claimed Messiahship, He should in their view have attacked the Romans first, not the Jews. *These things* refers not only to the events of the previous day, but also to the whole career of Jesus which they considered had been one continual conflict with lawful authority. Yet their question was put not from the motive of protecting the public from an impostor. They sought to trap Him fatally. For Him to claim divine authority would, so they thought, amount to blasphemy; to claim authority as Son of David would be treason against Rome; to disclaim all authority would prove Him an impostor. **29, 30** His reply was in no sense an evasion or clever piece of fencing. It was merely tracing the issue a stage further back, for the right answer to His question would also answer theirs and would, moreover, show whether they had any capacity to test moral authority. **31, 32** John the Baptist had borne testimony to Jesus as the Messiah. If they acknowledged him to be a prophet with divine authority, the answer to their question was plain, and they would see that the authority of Jesus was derived from the same source. The ministry of John was one of high public importance upon which men in their position should be competent to pronounce. **33** When therefore they pleaded ignorance on a matter of such magnitude they virtually abdicated from their office as teachers of the nation, and had no further right to question the authority of Jesus. Our Lord, therefore, did not reply to their question directly. Instead He provided the complete answer in the parable that follows.

12:1-12 The parable of the wicked husbandmen. The chapter division here is unfortunate, since the parable arises out of the challenge of the chief priests. Its scope is remarkably comprehensive, covering the centuries of Israel's past history, depicting the present situation of conflict and pointing to its future issues. **1** As a national symbol of Israel, the *vineyard* was familiar from the OT (*e.g.* Is. 5:1-7) and would quickly be so understood. The *hedge* (Gk. *phragmos*) to give protection from wild animals, the *pit for the wine press* (Gk. *hypolēnion*), a vessel or trough to gather the juice of the pressed grapes, and the *tower* (Gk. *pyrgos*), a wooden

booth on a high platform for a watchman (all of them words represented in the LXX of Is. 5), are all necessary elements in the story exhibiting collectively the care bestowed by the landlord, but without further significance individually. **2-5** The lesson is, first, that to this nation has been sent through the centuries a succession of servants in the OT prophets, culminating in John the Baptist, all of whom have looked for the fruits of repentance and righteousness (*cf.* Lk. 3:8). **6** Last of all has come One who is not merely another in the line of servants, but the only begotten and beloved Son and Heir, invested with all the authority of His Father. **7ff.** At v. 7 the parable becomes prophetic: first, of the cross involving the rejection of the Messiah by His own people; secondly, of the judgment that would overtake the nation at the destruction of Jerusalem in AD 70; thirdly, of the final triumph and exaltation of the Son. **9** The words *He will . . . give the vineyard to others* refer to the extension of Israel's privileges to the Gentiles (*cf.* Mt. 8:11, 12; 21:43). **10, 11** The change of figure from the vineyard to the corner-stone makes possible the allusion to the resurrection, for where the slain son could not be revived, the rejected stone can be exalted. The OT reference is to Ps. 118, the 'Hosanna' psalm, part of which had been sung at the triumphal entry (11:9, 10). *Builders* are experts who should have known better. It has been objected against the parable that the behaviour of the husbandmen is contrary to natural probability. But is it any more unnatural or unreasonable than the unbelief it is meant to illustrate?

12:13-17 On tribute to Caesar. 13 For the second time the Pharisees are found in alliance with the Herodians who were their political opponents (see on 3:6). Their common purpose was *to entrap* (Gk. *agreusōsin*, a hunting metaphor) *him in his talk*. **14** Their question, put with flattery, concerned the Roman taxes so hateful to the Jews as a sign of their subjection. It involved the usual dilemma wherein an affirmative reply would disgust the people and a negative one would bring Him into trouble with the Romans. **15-17** Jesus' answer is one of several on this 'day of questions' which display His unassailable and perfect wisdom, and one which has profoundly influenced all subsequent thought on the ethical problem of the attitude of the Christian to the state. The whole principle laid down turns on the change of wording from *pay* (v. 15) to *render* (v. 17). In the former, AV 'give' is better than either RSV or NEB. For 'it was not a question of giving what might lawfully be refused, but of paying what was lawfully claimed. The tribute was not a gift but a debt. Caesar gave them the inestimable benefit of stable government; were they to take it and decline to pay anything towards its maintenance?' (Plummer). Duty to God and duty to the state are not incompatible; we owe a debt to both. The Pharisees admitted their debt to Caesar by using his coinage; this was why Jesus asked for the coin. If they could produce it, they had the answer to their own question. This answer would be of particular interest to Mark's Roman readers, since it acquits Christianity from the charge of disloyalty to the state. We may compare the teaching of Paul in Rom. 13:1-7.

12:18-27 On the resurrection. 18 This is Mark's only reference to the *Sadducees*, whom he introduces with a word of explanation. They were a priestly aristocracy, less numerous than the Pharisees and less popular. Religiously they were the rationalists of the day, although conservative in their attitude to the Scriptures in the sense that they denied the validity of the oral tradition which the Pharisees held to be binding. They took their stand particularly upon the authority of the Pentateuch. They were therefore as obnoxious to the Pharisees on religious grounds as were the Herodians on political grounds. But the Pharisees were willing to work with either for the destruction of Jesus. It may be, however, that the Sadducees now hoped to succeed where their adversaries had failed. **19-23** Their question was less dangerous than the previous one, being a matter of exegesis and speculation rather than politics, doctrinal rather than ethical. The fantastic story they told was doubtless intended to draw Jesus into ridicule. It was based on the law of levirate marriage in Dt. 25:5-10, the purpose of which was to prevent the eventuality of a man dying without posterity—a calamity of the first order to a Jew. **24-27** Our Lord's reply deals first with the manner of the resurrection, pointing out that marriage on the physical side, to which the levirate law relates, is relevant only in the world where death prevails and so makes necessary the perpetuation of the race. Life in the next world is not a mere repetition of present conditions. In one sense, the particular question of the Sadducees is of little concern to us today, but objections arising from the difficulty of conceiving a resurrection are still current. It is argued that a resurrection would involve conditions that are incredible. The answer to all such objections is the plain one, *you know neither the scriptures nor the power of God.* The Lord then proceeds from the manner to the fact of the resurrection, **26** skilfully drawing His proof from the Pentateuch so greatly cherished by the Sadducees. Long after the patriarchs had died, God spoke of Himself as enjoying a relationship with them which remained intimate and permanent. 'The passage suggests the one consideration which above all others confirms the modern Christian in his belief in life after death; for to him this hope is based, not on Platonic arguments concerning the nature of the soul, but upon the experience of communion with God' (Vincent Taylor, *in loc.*).

12:28-34 On the first commandment. Lk. 10:25-28 is considered by Manson and Cranfield to be neither parallel to, nor a doublet of, this passage, but to refer to a different occasion. This further question, a moral one, is obviously introduced here by Mark as having been asked on the same occasion; it is not inserted merely for topical reasons although belonging chronologically to the Galilaean ministry, as some have suggested. The scribe exhibited qualities not apparent in other questioners. He was sincere and intelligent; yet this did not suffice to bring him into the kingdom (v. 34). **28** His question—literally 'What kind of commandment (Gk. *poia entolē*) is first of all?'—presupposes a difference in importance between commandments or classes of commandments. Rabbis divided the precepts of the law into 'weighty' and 'light', but the allocation of them into these categories caused much debate. Or possibly the scribe had in mind the distinction between moral and ritual commands. **29-31** The answer of Jesus is remarkable for the fact that it brings together two widely separated scriptures to sum up the duty of man. Yet both were very familiar. The first, Dt. 6:4, 5, was the *Shema*, or creed of Israel, and would normally be recited twice daily by the questioner himself. It was the commandment actually worn in phylacteries, and sometimes nailed to doorposts in literal obedience to Dt. 6:8, 9. The second is given in the exact words of the LXX from Lv. 19:18. The two are summed up in the one word 'love', first toward God, then toward man; love conceived not as an emotional sentiment but as an active principle embracing the entire personality. It is probably true to say that in modern times men lay great emphasis on love to man, or philanthropy, but are inclined to forget the requirement of love to God. Our Lord links the two and gives primacy to the latter. Philanthropy is no substitute for religion, but should flow from it.

12:35-37a On the Son of David. It is the turn of Jesus Himself to ask a question. The reason He does so is not, as some have suggested, to deny His birth in Bethlehem from the line of David, but to teach that He is in fact far more than 'son of David'; He is Lord. To do this He quotes from Ps. 110:1, the Davidic authorship of which is generally denied by modern criticism. An interesting critical problem is therefore raised, and it is surprising to what subtleties of argument critics will allow themselves to be driven rather than jettison the theory that the psalm is not Davidic. It is impossible to state the position fully here (see the introduction to Ps. 110, p. 521 above), but we may observe that, whereas in other instances the validity of our Lord's pronouncements on questions of OT authorship may be held not to affect His argument, in this case His whole argument turns upon it. It 'is not drawn from the august language of the Psalm, but from David's relationship to the Messiah, and crumbles to pieces if he is not the singer' (Alexander Maclaren). We hold, therefore, that our Lord's attribution of the psalm to David must foreclose the question of authorship for all who accept His authority. (*Cf.* Acts 2:34. See also Edersheim, *Life and Times of Jesus the Messiah,* ii, pp. 405f.)

12:37b–40 A warning against the scribes. That *the great throng*, or 'the mass of the people' (Moffatt), *heard him gladly* is a statement which belongs probably to what follows rather than to what precedes. His teaching still attracted crowds. They were fascinated by His wisdom and perhaps enjoyed seeing the rout of the professional teachers. But nearly all, under pressure, were later prepared to consent to His death. Not all the scribes were equally bad (*cf.* v. 34), but the general tendency of their class was in the direction of ostentation, avarice and hypocrisy. Let simple folk *beware* of religion of this kind; moral and spiritual power counts for far more than *long robes* and officialdom.

12:41–44 The widow's two mites. This choice story brings welcome relief after the heat of controversy, for here is one who, in the simplicity of her lowly worship, gave to God her all. It is no doubt in place here as to its historical setting, but possibly the saying about devouring widows' houses (v. 40) gave it a topical appropriateness as well. **41** It is not certain that there was a building called *the treasury* (Gk. *gazophylakion*; *cf.* Jn. 8:20); but along the colonnade which surrounded the Court of the Women there were thirteen chests with trumpet-shaped openings (Heb. *šôp̄ārôṯ*) provided for the offerings of the worshippers. At some vantage-point in full view of this part of the Temple Jesus sat, probably wearied by the prolonged disputations of the day.

The lesson of the whole story is that our Lord's first concern is not what men give but how they give it. Money in itself has no value in the kingdom of God; so Jesus refused to count totals but looked at the motives of the donor (*cf.* 2 Cor. 8:12). **42** Therefore when His eye fell upon the solitary figure of a poor widow who *put in two copper coins* (Gk. *lepta*, the smallest copper coin in use) which Mark, for the benefit of his Roman readers, computes in terms of Roman coinage as equivalent to a *penny* (Gk. *kodrantēs*, a transliteration of the Latin *quadrans;* NEB 'a farthing'), **43, 44** He called the attention of the disciples to her. In answer to the question how Jesus came to know the amount of her gift, we reply that He may have discovered by quite ordinary means which are not disclosed, or, as some prefer to think, by supernatural knowledge; but in any case the question is irrelevant to the story. The essence of all true giving is sacrifice, and the value of every gift relative, not absolute.

13:1–37 The prophetic discourse

It is not possible within the scope of our present purpose to discuss at any length that form of criticism in regard to this great chapter, in which it has been called the 'Little Apocalypse'. For some time it was a widely-accepted hypothesis that the core of the chapter was a small Jewish or Jewish-Christian apocalyptic writing. Two considerations, however, tend to discredit the idea. First, certain characteristics of true apocalyptic are wanting. There is none of the highly figurative language of Daniel or Revelation, featuring strange beasts and visions; also, while apocalyptic is predictive to the almost entire exclusion of moral exhortation, the latter is present here in a marked degree throughout. Secondly, as Edersheim has shown, contemporary Jewish opinion regarding the end-time was utterly different from anything expressed here. Moreover, it is significant that this discourse of our Lord on Mt. Olivet is recorded by all the Synoptists at considerable length and with substantial agreement as to the main details; they further agree in placing it at the same point in our Lord's ministry (see Mt. 24:1–51; Lk. 21:5–38). This indicates that the early church recognized and accepted it as part of the original gospel tradition.

13:1–4 The question of the four disciples. 1 As was His custom at the close of the day, Jesus left the Temple and the city. On the way, an unnamed disciple drew attention to the magnificence of the Temple buildings. We may imagine that the Temple, larger than York Minster, and having a façade of gold, would present a most imposing spectacle from the Mount of Olives. Some of the stones measured as much as 30 ft in length. To the Jew nothing seemed so stable as this building, the symbol of God's presence with His people. **2** Little wonder that the disciples were astounded to be told that the great edifice should be completely overthrown. **3** Four of them, therefore, the two pairs of brothers who were called at the beginning (1:16–20), **4** put to Jesus in private a twofold question as to the time and the sign of this terrible calamity. It is not quite clear what *these things* refers to, and Matthew (Mt. 24:3) expands the question into a threefold one looking on to the end of the age. In any case, from this question flows the discourse that follows in which two major events seem to be in view throughout: first, the immediate event in the fall of Jerusalem in AD 70, and secondly, the ultimate event of the return of Christ in glory. It has frequently been observed that there is a kind of perspective in the point of view of prophecy, whereby crises of history are seen like mountain ranges portrayed upon a canvas, one behind another, without any cognizance of the tracts of territory between. This chapter, with its two great crises in view between which already 1,900 years have intervened, is an illustration of this principle, and this fact should be borne in mind when seeking to interpret it.

13:5–13 Warnings to disciples. Some take the view that this section derives from a group of sayings relating to the 'coming' of Christ, or *parousia* (a word found only in Mt. 24 in the Gospels), rather than to AD 70, and that therefore it is no part of the original answer to the question in v. 4. It is obvious, however, that Mark intends us to take it as the answer, and we prefer to think that Jesus spoke these words, as He so often did, first for the disciples there present, but also with an eye to the future needs of the church. He is, as it were, using the events associated with the immediate crisis to foreshadow those connected with the ultimate crisis, and this explains why the two are interwoven so closely.

5 *Jesus began to say to them, Take heed.* The words not only state the main lesson of the chapter (*cf.* vv. 9, 23, 33) but also emphasize the true purpose of all biblical prophecy, which is not speculative but practical, not to enable us to forecast the future but to interpret the present, not to satisfy curiosity but to deliver from perplexity and to encourage watchfulness. **6–8** The disciples are warned against deception. There would be impostors in the religious sphere, commotions in the political and international field and calamities in the physical realm; but such things are incidental to the course of the age, and are not necessarily to be taken as the signs of the end. Rather are they *the beginning of the sufferings* (Gk. *ōdinōn*, 'birthpangs'). **9–13** A second warning follows against spiritual failure in view of what will happen to them personally and within the Christian community. This paragraph brings vividly before us a truth which is often lost sight of in modern times, namely that the role of the Christian church during this age is unquestionably one of suffering. Indeed the church has never flourished better than at those times when it has been an illicit society driven underground. Worldly favour and prosperity, as in the days of Constantine, have always had an enervating and enfeebling effect upon it. **9** One of the first to fulfil the prediction of this verse was Saul of Tarsus, as a persecuting Jew and then as a persecuted Christian (Acts 9:1, 2; 2 Cor. 11:24). **10, 11** significantly place the preaching of the gospel in this context of suffering, a context which it undoubtedly has in the book of Acts, where the greater part of apostolic preaching was not before respectable congregations gathered for the purpose, but in courts of justice. **11** offers no encouragement to the unprepared preacher; it is a promise to those suddenly called upon to defend their faith in the face of persecution, that they may count upon the moment-to-moment guidance and inspiration of the Holy Spirit. **13** To endure *to the end* probably means not to the end of the age, as in v. 7, but to the uttermost (*cf.* Jn. 13:1), an endurance which is complete. Endurance, therefore, is one of the keynotes of Christian life and witness in this age. It is very often much easier to be busily engaged in work and action than it is to endure with patience (*cf.* Heb. 10:32–39; 12:3, 4; Rev. 1:9). The expression *will be saved* is used here, of course, in an eschatological sense (*cf.* Heb. 9:28).

13:14–27 The two crises of the future. A new section of the prophecy seems to begin here. Having answered the questions of v. 4 thus far in a general, rather negative manner, pointing to certain phenomena which are not signs of the end, Jesus now speaks of a particular notable event, and of the proper behaviour of the disciples when such an event shall come to pass.

14 *The desolating sacrilege* (Gk. *to bdelygma tēs erēmōseōs*) is an expression which comes from Dn. 9:27; 11:31; 12:11. In OT usage this is any idolatrous person or object such as would excite the disgust and abhorrence of the Jew. *Cf.* 1 Ki. 21:26; 2 Ki. 16:3, where the same Greek word occurs in the LXX. The fact that Mark here deliberately, though ungrammatically, connects a masculine participle, *set up* (Gk. *hestēkota*), with this neuter noun indicates that a person is in view. We conclude therefore that the first reference in this verse is to the profanation of the Temple by the Romans in AD 70; this is confirmed by Lk. 21:20. Nevertheless the meaning of the words is not exhausted by this, and Jesus was probably referring in a secondary sense, for the benefit of the future church, to the appearing of antichrist. The context supports this, for the language of vv. 19, 20 is certainly eschatological and far too emphatic to apply only to the circumstances of the siege of Jerusalem, however terrible. *Where it ought not to be* is an intentionally vague expression, since more precise terms would perhaps have been politically dangerous for Mark's readers. *Let the reader understand* may be either the words of Jesus calling attention to the passage in Daniel, or those of Mark calling attention to this saying of Jesus. **15–18** A series of vivid illustrations of the need for instant flight as in conditions of war. Prayer for temporal advantages to facilitate escape is enjoined. **18** *Winter* may perhaps better be rendered 'stormy weather'. Just prior to AD 70 the Christians of Jerusalem did in fact make their escape in this way and Eusebius, the church historian, tells us that they fled to Pella, in Peraea, E of Jordan. **21–23** These verses are thought by some to be a doublet of vv. 5, 6, derived from a different source and reflecting a doctrinal situation in the early church similar to that of 2 Thes. 2:9. There is, however, no inherent improbability in the suggestion that what is undoubtedly the chief practical lesson of these prophetic utterances should have been thus reiterated and expanded by our Lord. His technique as a teacher is no less perfect than His technique as a physician. **24, 25** From this point Jesus goes on to speak of the second great crisis yet future, namely the return in glory of the Son of man. The impression is conveyed that this follows soon upon the tribulation of vv. 14–23, which again leads us to think that the latter has an eschatological significance and was by no means limited to the happenings of AD 70. How far the language here is to be understood symbolically of political and international convulsions, as most commentators of the past 60 years have understood it, is difficult to decide. Much that used to be relegated unhesitatingly to the realm of apocalyptic may now, in an atomic age, be seen to have rather the semblance of sober truth and grim reality; and it would be unscientific, to say the least, to affirm that these words may not refer to objective phenomena in the form of cosmic disturbances prior to the return of Christ. **26** *The Son of man coming in clouds* is a clear reference to Dn. 7:13. Early in His ministry Jesus began to use the title 'Son of man' of Himself (see on 2:10), but here for the first time the connection with the prophecy in Daniel is apparent. Amid much that is perplexing in the details of such a chapter as this, the one fact that stands out with crystal clarity is the ultimate triumph of Jesus; the suffering Messiah shall eventually enter into His glory, although the use of the third person here, *then they will see*, rather intimates that those whom He is addressing will not live to see it. **27** The gathering together of the *elect* by the angels (*cf*. Heb. 1:14) suggests that the divine purpose in v. 10 will have been accomplished in the meantime.

13:28–37 Parables and sayings on watchfulness. This is the practical application of all that has gone before. The chapter concludes with a plain assertion that these injunctions belong not to that generation alone, but to every generation of the Christian church. 'What the Church of the New Testament has been and is, that her Lord and Master made her, and by no agency more effectually than by leaving undetermined the precise time of His return' (Edersheim).

28 The *lesson* of the fig tree draws attention once more to what is the true purpose of prophecy (see on v. 5), not that disciples may prophesy, but that they may with spiritual insight discern the unfolding of God's purpose in the moving spectacle of events. **30** This is a saying of acknowledged difficulty, preserved by all three Synoptists. Two meanings seem possible: either that the Jewish race will survive until the end of the age, or that Jerusalem would be destroyed within the lifetime of the generation then living. This latter actually happened and is the more probable meaning; although Swete (*in loc*.) concedes in regard to the word *generation* (Gk. *genea*) that it may have been purposely employed because it was capable of being understood in a narrower or a wider sense. Clearly we are to learn from this and **31** the following verse that the fact of Christ's personal return is unalterably sure. **32** The time alone is uncertain, being locked in the counsels of the Father, so that even the Son, in the voluntarily-accepted limitations of His incarnation, does not share the secret. The absolute use of *the Son* is specially significant. 'It is an important piece of evidence against the view that Jesus could not have thought of himself as the unique Son of God' (Cranfield). **33** The necessity for vigilance and prayerfulness is therefore reiterated. **34, 35** The parable of *the master of the house* helps to define vigilance not as a leaving of our duties, but a faithful doing of them, in the expectation that the Master will one day examine our work (1 Cor. 3:13–15; 2 Cor. 5:10). Our duty is to use the time that remains in the work of winning others for Him.

14:1 – 15:47 The passion narrative

14:1–11 The plot to betray Jesus. We treat this paragraph as a whole, because vv. 10, 11 are directly connected with vv. 1, 2, and the intervening story of the anointing has evidently been introduced here by Mark with the twofold purpose of throwing into relief the treachery and avarice of Judas and of showing that the incident was at least one factor in his turning traitor. For here he heard Jesus speak quite plainly of His burial, and perhaps at last realized that his cherished hopes of material power and advancement were doomed.

The chronology of events on the Thursday and Friday of passion week presents one of the most difficult problems in the Gospels. What is clear is that those events moved according to divine programme, not human design. The priests evidently planned to arrest Jesus after the Feast of the Passover to avoid an insurrection. But the unexpected offer of Judas Iscariot simplified matters considerably, so that they were able to act without further delay. They had secured a competent agent whose responsibility it now was, instead of theirs, to find an opportunity to arrest Him. Thus it came to pass that the divine plan was followed, and Jesus, 'the Lamb of God', yielded up His life on the great festival day. There is therefore discernible in Judas an amazing fusion of divine sovereignty and human free will. The latter must not be surrendered in an attempt to soften his guilt. Jesus must suffer; but Judas need not have been the traitor; he opened the door to Satan (Jn. 13:27) and well illustrates the solemn principle enunciated in Heb. 6:4–8 that there is a supreme peril in enjoying spiritual privileges and failing to respond.

3–9 The lovely story of the anointing is placed by John 'six days before the Passover' (Jn. 12:1). His precision in dating it is not likely to be erroneous, and we conclude that Mark, followed by Matthew (Mt. 26:6–13), has sacrificed the chronological order for homiletical reasons. It is John also who identifies the woman with Mary of Bethany. *Simon the leper* was probably one who had been healed; he may have been related to Lazarus and his sisters. The identity of name has led some, even as far back as Origen's time, to confuse this narrative with that in Lk. 7:36–50. But whereas the difficulty of believing in two such anointings is infinitesimal, that of believing that Mary of Bethany was ever 'a woman of the city, who was a sinner' is enormous. Moreover Simon was one of the commonest of names. C. C. Torrey makes the interesting suggestion on the basis of the Aramaic that the word for *leper* should in fact be 'jar-merchant', the two words in Aramaic having identical consonants. The meal was probably the special festive meal of the sabbath. At that last feast of fellowship Mary alone among the disciples and guests seemed to discern how near the end was. *An alabaster jar* would probably be a fragile unguent flask with a long narrow neck. The precise meaning of the expression *ointment of pure* (Gk. *pistikēs*, 'genuine') *nard* is uncertain. That it was of special quality and value is clear.

Whether Mary fully appreciated the significance of her action at the time may be questioned; for it is probably true of most service and worship offered in pure devotion to Christ that it possesses a worth and meaning beyond our understanding. So far as we know, Jesus' body received no other anointing for burial; *cf.* 16:1. When therefore this fact came home to her, how great would be her joy! In humility, love and faith she exemplifies 'the fellowship of his sufferings' (Phil. 3:10). 5 *Three hundred denarii* represents a sum of money roughly equivalent to a labourer's wage for the greater part of a year, the 'denarius' being a day's wage.

14:12–25 The Last Supper. 12 *The first day of Unleavened Bread, when they sacrificed the passover lamb* was the day we know as Good Friday, 14th Nisan. But according to Jewish reckoning this day began at sunset the day before. The events of this paragraph therefore took place on the Thursday evening. The question of whether the supper was in fact the Passover meal remains unsettled despite prolonged discussion on both sides. The Synoptic tradition, as here, clearly indicates that it was. On the other hand John, with precision and consistency (Jn. 18:28b; 19:31), places the Passover on the Friday evening after the crucifixion. There is hardly likely to be any better solution than to conclude that Jesus, knowing that He could not observe the Passover at the proper time, kept it a day in advance. It is attractive to believe, accordingly, that 'Christ, our paschal lamb' (1 Cor. 5:7) was sacrificed for us at the very hour when the Passover lambs were slain in the Temple. **13** In preparation for the feast, Jesus *sent two of his disciples*, whom Luke names as Peter and John (Lk. 22:8), into the city to look for *a man carrying a jar of water*. This was unusual, since normally only women carried such jars (Jn. 4:7). The man would evidently be a servant, and on following him they would be led to the owner, with whom it seems Jesus had a previously arranged understanding about the use of the room. **14** This is rather implied in the question *The Teacher says, Where is my guest room?* 'There is perhaps a hint of messianic sovereignty in the word' *my* (Nineham). For security reasons it was necessary that both the identity of this anonymous disciple and the location of the venue should be a well-kept secret. **15** The *large upper room* would be furnished with such necessities as table, couches for reclining, basin, water and towel (Jn. 13:4f.). **16** The disciples would complete the preparations for food. Perhaps the most significant detail is that there is no mention of a lamb being provided or consumed, and it is very improbable that there was one. There would be no need of a typical lamb when the true Lamb of God was present and about to be offered the very next day.

Originally the Passover lamb was eaten standing (Ex. 12:11), but this custom had long been abandoned, and the feast was now celebrated reclining, in token that the people were no longer slaves but free, enjoying the security of the land of promise. **18** The disclosure of the betrayal is made with startling plainness, yet not, according to Mark's account, in such a manner as to name the traitor. We depend upon John (Jn. 13:26) for the knowledge that this information was secretly given to the beloved disciple. The enormity of the crime is indicated by the fact that, to the oriental, the fellowship of a meal was specially sacred, and hostile action against one with whom one ate bread was absolutely precluded (*cf.* Ps. 41:9). **20** In this case Judas not only ate with Jesus; even more intimately, he dipped with Him in the dish. *The dish* (Gk. *tryblion*) was probably the bowl of sauce into which pieces of unleavened bread were dipped, assuming that the meal was in fact the Passover. **21** clearly states both the divine sovereignty and human responsibility to which we have already referred (see on vv. 1, 2, 10, 11), and places the latter squarely on the shoulders of Judas. 'The divine necessity for the Passion was no excuse for the free agent who brought it about' (Swete).

22–25 Mark's account of the institution of the Lord's Supper is concise almost to the point of obscurity, but it brings before us the second main line of teaching in the Gospel concerning the work of Christ (see Introduction, p. 853, and on 10:45). The following points are clear. First, *Take* indicates that His death with its benefits was a gift which His disciples must appropriate, and that this appropriation is of a most intimate kind comparable with the assimilation of food and a partaking of its nourishment and efficacy. Secondly, His death is the inauguration of the *covenant* of grace prophesied by Jeremiah (Je. 31:31–34). Moses had spoken of the 'blood of the covenant' (Ex. 24:8) in connection with the old covenant which God made with Israel at Sinai. Centuries later Jeremiah revealed the terms of the new covenant, namely divine forgiveness and indwelling, but he said nothing about its ratification by blood. This would strike Hebrew ears as unusual, for among oriental peoples any kind of covenant or agreement between two persons, such as, for example, two bedouin of the desert, would be sealed in some way by blood. It is as though Jesus now completed the picture outlined by Jeremiah; the new covenant would be sealed in His blood. *Poured out for many* (*cf.* again 10:45) once more echoes Is. 53:11, 12. Jesus thought of His death as a vicarious sacrifice for men. The expressions *this is my body* and *this is my blood*, though literally rendered in the RSV, are perhaps as well translated by Moffatt as by any: 'Take this, it means my body . . . This means my covenant blood.' 'Our Lord's human body was present and His blood had not yet been shed. Therefore all carnal ideas respecting the meaning of these words are excluded' (Plummer). Thirdly, Jesus looked forward beyond His death to His risen life and to the perfect fellowship of the consummated kingdom. The table of the Lord has a forward aspect towards the consummation as well as a backward reference to the cross. **25** The vocabulary and ideas of this verse are strongly Semitic. Barth connects the refusal to *drink again of the fruit of the vine* with the Nazirite vow (Nu. 6:1–21), by making which 'Jesus consecrates Himself for the imminent sacrificial offering of His life'. Or the words may imply a final break with the Jewish dispensation under which He had hitherto lived. The eschatological interest appears also in Paul's account (1 Cor. 11:26), while the idea of a Messianic banquet in the kingdom of God belongs to both OT and NT. *Cf.* Is. 25:6; Mt. 8:11; Lk. 14:15; Rev. 19:9.

14:26–31 Peter's denial foretold. 26 *When they had sung a hymn*; it was probably the second part of the Hallel (Pss. 115–118). **27** As Jesus foretold the betrayal, so now, on the way from the upper room to the Mount of Olives, He foretells the denial by Peter. The words of Zc. 13:7 will find fulfilment in the case of Himself and His disciples. A time of testing will come upon them as a result of which the faith of them all will give way. **28** Nevertheless beyond the dark hour He will meet them again in Galilee. Jesus scarcely ever referred to His death without looking beyond it. **29** Peter protested, as once before (8:32f.), and **30** Jesus' reply is in the most solemn terms, *Truly, I say to you. . . . This very night* brings the denial within the space of the next few hours. **31** It is well to remember that all the disciples associated themselves with Peter's vehement protestations.

14:32–42 The agony in Gethsemane. Again the privileged three are taken and there are several points of similarity between this scene and the transfiguration. With vv. 37–40 *cf.* 9:5f.; Lk. 9:32. **32** *Sit here* is spoken to the eight who are left near the entrance. **33** While still in the company of the three He *began to be greatly distressed and troubled* (Gk. *ekthambeisthai kai adēmonein*). These are words supremely difficult to translate. They express the utmost degree of unbounded horror and suffering. **34** Little is said in Scripture about the soul of the Lord Jesus, but when He says *My soul is very sorrowful, even to death*, the deep anguish of His humanity becomes evident. **35** So great was it that He was driven from them a short distance—Luke says 'about a stone's throw' (Lk. 22:41), where they could both see and hear—to seek the face of His Father. **36** *Abba* is Aramaic for 'Father'. The addition of the Greek *patēr* is probably not a translation by Mark. Some think the two words together are a very early liturgical formula of address in prayer. But it is more likely that they reflect a natural prayer habit of Jesus Himself, which some of His disciples caught and transmitted (*cf.* Rom. 8:15; Gal. 4:6). In any case they are a reminder that our faith had its origin among a bilingual people.

We shall never know exactly what *this cup* was from which Jesus shrank in such horror. It was certainly more than physical suffering, otherwise many a martyr has since shown greater

courage than He. We may say that it was the agony to His sinless soul of being 'made sin' (2 Cor. 5:21) and exposed to the divine judgment on sin, of tasting in all its bitterness that death which is the wages of sin, that those who trust in Him might never taste it (Heb. 2:9). This is something beyond the range of human experience altogether, since He alone was sinless. The words *yet not what I will, but what thou wilt* are the crucial point in Gethsemane. Doctrinally they illustrate the important truth that there was in Jesus a real human will, distinct from, but always submissive to, the will of His Father. Experimentally they mark the point of His triumph, so that the victory of the cross was in fact won in prayer in the garden beforehand and Jesus went to Calvary victoriously. Man's arch-enemy wrought sin and death by asserting his will against God (Is. 14:13, 14); Jesus wrought salvation by submitting His will to God. Acceptance of the will of God is always victory, whereas self-will inevitably leads to defeat. **37** The picture of the sleeping disciples is in sharp contrast with that of Jesus at prayer. Peter is addressed as the one who had protested that he would die with Jesus; yet now he had not the strength to watch for an hour. There was clearly an element of conflict with Satanic powers in the garden. The earlier temptations of our Lord's ministry were here renewed in a last titanic assault, the intensity of which He felt. **38** Knowing full well that victory in temptation was to be won only at the price of vigilance and prayer, He warned the slumbering disciples of their own need. **41** It is possible that between the question here and what follows we are to understand an interval of time during which Jesus Himself watched over them.

14:43–52 The arrest of Jesus. Few details in history have so powerfully impressed the minds of men as the fact that Judas betrayed the Son of God with a kiss. **45** An emphatic form of the verb (*katephilēsen*; RV mg. 'kissed him much') is used, as though to suggest more than usual fervour and affection. **47** *One of those who stood by*. This anonymous person is referred to by John (Jn. 18:10) as Peter, and the servant's name is given as Malchus. Luke alone (Lk. 22:51) records the healing of the ear. **49** *Day after day* 'suggests a longer ministry in Jerusalem than Mark has recorded and is perhaps evidence in support of the Johannine tradition in this respect' (Cranfield). **50** *All* is emphatic in the Greek. Without exception the disciples failed Jesus and He was completely forsaken. **51** *A young man.* Why is this curious incident mentioned? Many commentators favour the suggestion that the young man was Mark himself, who thus, as it were, 'paints a small picture of himself in the corner of his work' (Zahn). If, as some also have conjectured, he was the son of 'the householder' in v. 14 (*cf.* Acts 12:12), his appearance at this juncture is even more intelligible. Becoming aware of the noise and the lights in the garden near at hand, he took the first thing that came to hand as a covering and ran out to see what was happening. No good reason can be shown for the recording of the incident unless it is based on personal reminiscence.

14:53–65 The trial before the high priest. The combined Synoptic record makes it plain that the trial of Jesus was in two parts, one ecclesiastical before the Jewish authorities as here related, the other civil before the Roman governor as related in the next chapter. Again, the ecclesiastical trial seems to have been in two parts, the first of an informal and preliminary character at midnight, and the second before a full official meeting of the Sanhedrin in the early morning (15:1). Luke's account (Lk. 22:54–71) is clearer than Mark's in this respect. The whole proceeding transgressed the requirements of Jewish law in several particulars. The meeting of the Sanhedrin by night was in itself illegal, as was also the suborning of witnesses. **53** *The high priest* was Caiaphas (Mt. 26:57) who held office AD 18–36. Nothing is said by Mark about Annas (*cf.* Jn. 18:13). **54** Peter's affection for his Lord evidently reasserted itself to a degree, but to follow *at a distance* is in any circumstances to invite disaster. **55ff.** From this point the narrative consists almost entirely of sayings, questions and answers, and seems to lack the usual artless details which characterize the record of eye-witnesses. This may be due to the fact that no disciple was an immediate witness of the trial, though Jn. 18:15f. suggests that the beloved disciple and Peter were in the vicinity. The efforts of the council were at first unavailing. **56, 59** The witnesses did not agree, and **61** Jesus kept silence. The high priest therefore sought to force an issue, and put to Jesus a point-blank question about His claim to Messiahship. **62** Thus challenged, Jesus for the first time in the Gospel acknowledged who He was, using the language of Ps. 110:1 and Dn. 7:13.

63 *Tore his mantle.* For his own misfortunes the high priest was forbidden to do this (Lv. 21:10), but in his official capacity he protested in this way against any utterance regarded as blasphemous. The Talmud prescribes the exact manner in which it must be done. His question reveals 'the satisfaction of the conspirator . . . through the distress of the official' (Plummer). **64** *They all condemned him as deserving* (Gk. *enochon*, 'worthy of'; RV mg. 'liable to') *death*, but had no power to inflict the penalty; only Pilate could do that. **65** That members of the supreme court could behave in this manner shows the malignity with which they had come to judge their prisoner.

14:66–72 Peter's denial. It is well to remember that this particular account comes without doubt from the recollections of Peter himself and is accordingly related with singular fullness and vividness. **71** That *he began to invoke a curse on himself and to swear* (Gk. *anathematizein kai omnynai*) does not, however, mean that he used profanity; but rather that he affirmed on oath. He called down the 'anathema' of God

upon his head if what he said was not true. **72** *He broke down and wept* (Gk. *kai epibalōn eklaien*); the exact meaning of the Greek words has long constituted a difficulty. RSV here is perhaps the best attempt.

15:1–15 The trial before Pilate. 1 *As soon as it was morning*, *i.e.* as soon as it was lawful to transact business, a brief and formal meeting of the Sanhedrin was convened to confirm the proceedings of the irregular midnight session and to get the matter dealt with by the Roman governor before the paschal lambs were killed in the afternoon. The delivering of Jesus to Pilate initiated the civil trial. Pontius Pilate was procurator of Judea under the legatus of Syria from AD 26 to 36. Normally he resided in Caesarea but came to Jerusalem for the Passover season to ensure order at a time when national feeling ran high. He is represented in secular history as corrupt and cruel, but the Gospels seem to take a less unfavourable view of him. Mark's account here does not hide the deplorable weakness of the man but, at the same time, seems designed to exonerate him as far as possible and to place the ultimate responsibility for the crucifixion upon the Jews. It would be of particular importance to Roman readers to learn that, in the eyes of the Roman officer, Jesus was held to be innocent and could not be condemned as a political agitator.

2 *King of the Jews.* The hierarchy had evidently framed the charge with this political flavour, since a claim to Messiahship would be meaningless to Pilate. *You have said so* is an answer which assents without necessarily agreeing to the meaning which Pilate would attach to his question. The general course of the proceedings becomes more intelligible if we compare the more detailed account given by John (Jn. 18:28 – 19:16). There we discover that Jesus explained to Pilate in private that His kingdom was not of this world. **3** The priests felt their case was not going too well, so they multiplied accusations. **6** Nothing is known of this custom beyond what is told us in the NT. **7** *Barabbas* means 'son of a father' and the name invites a contrast with 'the Son of the Father'. In the parallel passage (Mt. 27:16) there is an interesting variant reading 'Jesus Barabbas', which was originally rejected by Hort as a corruption. At that time, however, the Koridethi manuscript of the Gospels and the Sinaitic Syriac Version, both of which contain it, were unknown. Vincent Taylor therefore concludes that 'There is good reason to think that it is original in Matthew . . . and to conjecture that it was read in Mark'. Barabbas was just the type of political insurgent the hierarchy had wanted to see in the Messiah, one who would use force where Jesus had refused to do so. **8–10** Here the crowd comes into view. Pilate began to discern that the real crime of Jesus was not hostility to Rome, which Jews would not normally resent, but that He had been too popular and the priests were envious of Him. He therefore hoped that a proposal to release

Jesus in honour of the feast would be welcomed by the people. **11** The amazing fickleness of the crowd, stirred up as they were by the chief priests, is thought by some to be almost incredible. But it was undoubtedly a profound shock to them to see the supposed Messiah a helpless prisoner in the hands of the heathen procurator. There was a violent change of feeling, psychologically characteristic of a mob, and they were quickly ready to clamour for the punishment of the impostor. **15** *Wishing to satisfy the crowd.* The lasting shame of Pilate is that he chose expediency above principle. Multitudes have done, and are doing, precisely the same thing since. The punishment of scourging usually preceded crucifixion. It was a brutal torture, inflicted with whips of leather loaded with metal or bone. One infliction of it often proved fatal. John seems to suggest that Pilate resorted to it in the hope that the Jews could be satisfied (Jn. 19:1). Even so it was a flagrant breach of Roman justice in the case of an uncondemned man.

15:16-41 The crucifixion. In all the Gospels the actual crucifixion is narrated in the most straightforward manner and with marked restraint. Our Lord's physical sufferings are not dwelt upon, for nothing is gained by gruesomeness. Moreover the physical pain was only secondary to the bitter desolation of spirit which He experienced because of sin. The comment of Calvin is noteworthy here: 'These matters call for secret meditation, rather than for the ornament of words.'

16 Jesus was handed over to the soldiers who made sport with Him. *The praetorium* is translated 'hall of judgment' in Jn. 18:28 (AV); it was probably part of the residence of the procurator, which some think was in Herod's palace in Jerusalem. **17** The *purple cloak* may have been a soldier's faded garment which looked like purple. In all this they acted out of contempt, not so much for Jesus, perhaps, as for the Jewish nation whose King He claimed to be. **20** It is not said that they eventually removed the crown of thorns as well as the purple, but it is probable that they did. Plummer points out that the centurion would not have allowed the mockery to continue when the march to the place of execution began. Pictures of the crucifixion are therefore misleading when they represent the Saviour as wearing the crown of thorns. Perhaps the dominant impression left upon the mind by this account of the mockery is that of the intense loneliness of Jesus.

21 *Cyrene* is in N Africa. There was a strong colony of Jews there and Simon may have been one of them, arriving in Jerusalem for the Passover; or he may have been a Gentile stranger. The mention of his sons indicates that they had become disciples. We know nothing further of *Alexander*, but *Rufus* may be the Rufus of Rom. 16:13, a member of the church in Rome. **22** *The place of a skull* was probably so called from the contour of the ground. **23** *Wine mingled with*

myrrh was an opiate or anaesthetic. But Jesus refused to meet death with His mental faculties clouded. Had He received the potion, we might never have had the words from the cross. **25** *The third hour* was 9 o'clock in the morning. Various explanations have been advanced to explain the apparent disagreement with Jn. 19:14. But John is probably reckoning from midnight, in which case he merely states that Jesus was still before Pilate at 6 a.m. **26** *The inscription* accords with Roman custom; all four Evangelists record it, but no two agree exactly as to the wording. Mark's version, however, is basic to all and preserves the words that were so particularly offensive to the Jews (*cf.* Jn. 19:21). **27** The *robbers* occupied the places for which James and John had asked (10:37). **31** The mocking words of the chief priests constitute 'one of the supreme ironies of history' (Vincent Taylor). He could have come down from the cross, but did not. His staying there was our salvation; and that salvation costs us nothing because it cost Him everything.

33 All the Synoptists record the darkness from noon until 3 p.m. Though brought about by natural causes, the timing of it was clearly supernatural. It could not have been the darkness of a solar eclipse, for, as Origen pointed out, it was full moon. **34** The cry of dereliction is the only word from the cross recorded by Mark and Matthew. It is preserved in the Aramaic, but it is not improbable that Jesus actually quoted the words of Ps. 22:1 in the Hebrew. Mark translates the Aramaic into Greek for the benefit of his readers. We may not fathom the depths of the saying, for it brings us to the very heart of the atonement. But it is important that we do not interpret the words merely of the feeling and subjective consciousness of Jesus, as though the dereliction were not a fact. This is the tendency among some modern scholars. But the view of the older theologians (*e.g.* R. W. Dale, *The Atonement*, pp. 61f.) is to be preferred, namely that since God cannot look upon sin (Hab. 1:13) He hid His face when our sin was laid upon His sinless Son. Jesus, the sinner's substitute and sin-bearer, was in fact forsaken that we might never be (Heb. 13:5). This was indeed the supreme and unparalleled sorrow from which He shrank. To affirm that such a view is inconsistent with the love of God (so Vincent Taylor, *in loc.*) is to emphasize the love of God at the expense of His holiness. 'It is, of course, theologically important to maintain the paradox that, while this God-forsakenness was utterly real, the unity of the Blessed Trinity was even then unbroken' (Cranfield). **37** None of the Evangelists says He died. Mark's expression is simplest: He *breathed his last*; *i.e.* 'expired' (Gk. *exepneusen*). But even here the *loud cry* confirms what is even more clearly expressed by the others, that His death was not the result of natural causes or of exhaustion. It was a voluntary act and therefore unique. Before any natural cause became fatal, and at the moment of His own choosing, He delivered up His spirit, so that Pilate marvelled that He was already dead (v. 44, AV; *cf.* Jn. 10:17f.). **38** This again is recorded by all the Synoptists. It would be observed and reported by the priests, of whom afterwards many believed (Acts 6:7). Upon the Hebrew mind such a momentous happening must have made a tremendous impression after centuries of Tabernacle and Temple worship in which the Holy of Holies had been closed to all except the high priest on the Day of Atonement. Its meaning for us is clearly set out in Heb. 10:19ff. **39** *The centurion*, whom tradition has named as Longinus, and who was stationed directly opposite the cross where he saw all that happened, was evidently impressed by precisely those peculiarities about our Lord's death that we have noted above. Though his words may not have meant for him all that we read into them, nevertheless he stands at the close of the Gospel story as the first among the heathen to be drawn to faith in Christ by the power of His death. **40, 41** The women at the cross surpassed the disciples in their devotion, and may even have supplied to the Evangelist some of his information concerning the crucifixion. *Salome* was the mother of James and John (Mt. 27:56). Mark does not mention the mother of our Lord.

15:42–47 The burial. The burial of Jesus occupied an important place in the creeds of the early church because it proved the reality of His death (see 1 Cor. 15:3f.).

42 *The day of Preparation* is the technical term for the Friday before the Jewish sabbath, as Mark explains for his Gentile readers. An additional reason for urgency in burying the body of Jesus was the law of Dt. 21:22f., commanding the burial of criminals before nightfall on the day of execution. **43** *Joseph* is described as 'from' Arimathea (Gk. *apo*). He had probably ceased to reside there, and had settled in Jerusalem. The location of Arimathea is uncertain. The tomb (Mt. 27:60), and possibly also the garden containing it, were his. As a member of the Sanhedrin that had driven Pilate to condemn an innocent person to death, his action would indeed require courage. But reverence and love for the Master prevailed in him. **44** Mark alone records the questioning of the centurion.

16:1–20 THE CONSUMMATION

16:1–8 The resurrection

Evidence for the resurrection is unimpeachable. The tomb was empty and no-one could produce the body. His friends could not have stolen it and His foes would not have done so. If further evidence is needed we may find it in the very existence and survival of the Christian church. We may with profit compare here Paul's enumeration of the consequences that result from the dire hypothesis, 'If Christ be not risen . . .' (1 Cor. 15:14–19).

1 *When the sabbath was past.* Complete silence hangs over this sabbath except for the brief statement of Lk. 23:56 that they rested that day. The accounts of the resurrection differ in details as all genuine eyewitness evidence does; but the main outlines of the day's events are clear. **2** The first visit was made by women who came *very early. When the sun had risen* is thought to be difficult in view of Jn. 20:1, 'while it was still dark'. Torrey repunctuates and connects the phrase with v. 3: 'When the sun was risen and they were saying . . .' But something depends upon the point of view from which the events are narrated. The actual resurrection was unseen by human eyes, and **4** the first sign of it was the removal of the stone. **5** Angels appeared before Jesus Himself was seen. Mark leaves us to infer that the *young man* was an angel. **7** The words *and Peter* are peculiar to Mark and constitute one of the evidences of the connection between this Gospel and the apostle. Peter would cherish the fact that, despite his grievous fall, his risen Lord showed special remembrance of him.

16:9–20 The epilogue

These last 12 verses, relegated to the margin in RSV, present one of the major textual problems of the NT. The principal facts are as follows. The two Codices Sinaiticus and Vaticanus omit the whole section, though their scribes possibly knew of it. Four other MSS of less weight supply an alternative and much shorter ending also given in the margin, and three of them add an explanatory note. Most other uncial and cursive MSS, together with versions and patristic writers, support the inclusion of 16:9–20. Conybeare found in an Armenian MS of the 10th century a note ascribing the verses to Aristion, the disciple of John of whom Papias speaks. This would mean that they are at least very early (perhaps AD 100), even if non-Markan, and have something of the authority of John. The transition from v. 8 to v. 9 is abrupt and there is a change of subject. Mary Magdalene is introduced as a stranger in v. 9, despite her appearance in v. 1. Instead of the vividness of detail so characteristic of Mark, we have here a kind of résumé or summary of the resurrection appearances.

The generally accepted view is either that the Gospel was, very early on, mutilated at the last page, or that Mark was unable to finish, perhaps owing to the rising tide of persecution. There remains the possibility, however, that Mark intended to end abruptly at v. 8 and this has been argued with some force by R. H. Lightfoot (*The Gospel Message of St Mark*, 1950, ch. vii).

An interesting theory, which would fit the facts, is that when the Gospels of Matthew and Luke appeared, by reason of their greater detail and interest they eclipsed Mark in popularity, with the result that the latter was discarded in obscurity for a time. Shortly afterwards, when the church at Rome began to be interested in the preservation of its records, the only copy of Mark which could be found was mutilated at the end and this became the parent of future copies, the present conclusion being supplied to round it off. Yet although the question of literary authenticity must remain uncertain, all scholars agree that these verses are canonically authentic. They are part of the Canon of Holy Scripture. The passage contains four sections. The appearance to Mary Magdalene (vv. 9–11); the appearance to two travellers (vv. 12, 13; cf. Lk. 24:13–35); the appearance to the eleven (vv. 14–18); the ascension and the session on high (vv. 19, 20).

12 *In another form*: the risen body of Christ had powers which it did not possess before the passion. **14** The term *the eleven* is used in a collective sense to designate the apostolic company irrespective of the exact number. Though upbraided for their unbelief, **15** they are given the great missionary commission. **16** It is noteworthy that no mention of baptism is made in the negative member of the pair of clauses. It is unbelief which leads to condemnation, not absence of any ritual observance. **17, 18** Instances of all these signs may be found in the NT, with the exception of drinking poison. See, *e.g.*, Acts 8:7; 2:4; 28:3–5; 28:8. **19, 20** From one point of view our Lord's work on earth, of which this Gospel is the record, is finished: He *sat down at the right hand of God*; from another point of view it is to continue through the church which is His mystical body: *they went forth . . . while the Lord worked with them.* And so the Gospel which pre-eminently sets forth the power and activity of the Son of God on earth closes with the revelation of the unfinished task of the church on earth. That task still awaits completion, but the same Lord still works with those who obey His command, confirming the message by the signs that attend it.

C. E. GRAHAM SWIFT

Luke

INTRODUCTION

THE THEOLOGY OF LUKE

The Gospel according to Luke differs from the other three Gospels in that, while they are each independent, self-contained writings, Luke is part of a two-volume work which has as its theme the beginnings of Christianity. In his opening dedication (1:1–4), written in the style of a secular historian, Luke has expressed his concern to give an orderly narrative for the benefit of those who have learned something already about the Christian faith. For Luke this story is a piece of history, and he is much more of a self-conscious historian than the other Evangelists. He believed that Christian faith was based on historical events which could be regarded as the acts of God, and he was trying to establish a firm historical foundation for the faith of his readers. He had his own characteristic understanding of the faith, complementary to that of the other Evangelists; by his methods of selection and emphasis he has drawn attention to those aspects of the life of Jesus which he considered to be of especial importance. He possessed fine literary gifts and used them to the full in the telling of his story.

1. Luke narrates the story of Jesus as *a piece of history*. Of all the Evangelists he comes the nearest to writing a biography of Jesus, although he has recorded the facts that are vital for faith rather than the general details of appearance, character, psychological development, and so on, which would interest a modern biographer. He traces out the continuity between the ministry of Jesus and the rise of the early church, thus making the story of Jesus part of the history of the church. This is not unimportant, for even Paul does not place so much emphasis on the earthly life of Jesus as part of the gospel. Luke, of course, does not mean that the life of Jesus is merely a part of church history. Rather it is the central era in God's gracious dealings with men, preceded by the history of Israel and inaugurating the period of the church; history will be wound up by the return of 'this same Jesus' whose earthly life is the central act in redemption.

2. The keynote of the ministry of Jesus is the *gospel of salvation*. Two of Luke's favourite words are 'preach the gospel', and 'salvation'. The former sums up the character of the ministry of Jesus; His teaching, healing and acts of compassion were all part of the proclamation of the good news that God was visiting His people. The latter word sums up the content of Jesus' message; it is contained *in nuce* in 19:10: 'The Son of man is come to seek and to save that which was lost.' In Mark the message of Jesus was that the kingdom of God had drawn near (Mk. 1:14f.). Luke brings out more clearly the fact that the ministry of Jesus was the era in which men actually received the salvation associated with the kingdom of God. Indeed, it is God Himself who has come to men in Jesus, a fact expressed in Luke's frequent use of the title of 'Lord' (the name for God in the Greek OT) for Jesus.

3. If salvation is for the lost, it is *for all men*, since all are lost. No-one can fail to observe that Luke shows particularly how Jesus brought salvation to the less privileged people in Judea— the poor, women, children and notorious sinners —and how, although for the most part He confined His ministry to the Jews, He indicated plainly that the gospel embraced the Gentiles, and in particular the despised Samaritans.

4. It is a curious feature of Luke's Gospel that it has very little to say about *the significance of the cross* as the place of salvation. Luke shows that suffering and death form the divinely appointed path which Jesus must tread before entering His heavenly glory, but only in Lk. 22:19f. and Acts 20:28 does he speak clearly of the sacrificial nature of the death of Jesus.

5. If no writer has emphasized more than Luke the 'wideness in God's mercy', at the same time in no other Gospel are *the claims of Jesus* expressed more stringently. Jesus summoned men to be disciples, and would-be disciples had to be prepared to count the cost, to deny themselves and to follow Jesus. The grace of God is not 'cheap grace'; the sinner must be prepared for repentance and renunciation of his sin.

6. Luke has reserved for his second volume the story of the church, but already in the Gospel he has indicated the characteristics of that period. It is the time during which Jesus, having ascended to heaven, sits at the right hand of God. His servants must continue His work of preaching the gospel of salvation to all nations, and they are enabled to do this by the power of the same *Holy Spirit* who equipped Jesus for His ministry, and as they call upon God in *prayer*, just as Jesus prayed. Only when this task is complete will Jesus suddenly return as the Judge of mankind and set up His heavenly kingdom.

THE SOURCES OF LUKE

Luke himself has expressed his indebtedness to his predecessors who had written about the life of Jesus and to the early eyewitnesses and Christian preachers. Speculation enters when we try to identify these sources more precisely. The most commonly accepted theory of Gospel origins is that Luke and Matthew each had access to the earlier Gospel of Mark and to a further written document or (more probably) a collection of traditions (generally designated 'Q') which has not survived. In addition to this material shared with Matthew, Luke had a considerable amount of further information of his own (generally indicated by the symbol 'L').

Two theories of the way in which he went to work are held. The older view is that he made Mark the basis of his work and inserted into it at appropriate places large blocks of additional material from Q and L. A more recent view is that Luke first combined the Q and L material into one document, and then later combined this 'proto-Luke' with Mark; one may plausibly associate the first stage of this process with Luke's period in Palestine while Paul was a prisoner there, and the second stage with his arrival with Paul in Rome, where Mark very probably wrote his Gospel. The arguments for and against these theories are highly technical, and any theory of composition must remain very hypothetical at the moment, but of the two the proto-Luke theory is perhaps less open to objection.

What is more important is whether we can be sure that the sources employed were reliable and that the author used them faithfully. The former question can be answered only in a general study of Gospel origins, but it may be said here that Luke's sources have high claims to reliability. In particular, the L material is of high worth, and the contacts between it and traditions independently preserved in the Gospel of John indicate its strong attestation. As regards the author's use of his sources, scholarship is very much divided at present. A growing body of radical opinion has stressed the creative ability of Luke and holds that he has manipulated the sources in the interests of his own theology. For example, where Luke records an incident also told by Mark in very different wording or tells of a similar but apparently different incident, such scholars are inclined to attribute the differences to Luke's rewriting of his sources rather than to his possession of additional, authentic information. Now it must be admitted that Luke has made a thorough stylistic recasting of his sources and has made many changes of a minor character in his narrative, but against this must be set his expressed intention of faithfully recording his story, his great accuracy in portraying the geographical and political background of events, and the way in which he makes very little alteration when reproducing the actual words of Jesus. To say, as some scholars have done, that Luke was not concerned with historical accuracy, is to fly in the face of his own expressed intentions. When these things are borne in mind, the case for Luke's fidelity to his sources is seen to be a strong one. If, like John, he has given us an artist's portrait of Jesus rather than a photograph (and even photographs are taken from a particular point of view and contain an element of interpretation), he has given us a true portrait.

THE AUTHORSHIP AND DATE OF THE GOSPEL

If the Gospel rests on sound tradition faithfully recorded, the question of its author's name is one of secondary importance. That he was Luke, the 'beloved physician' and companion of Paul, is the clear and consistent verdict of writers in the early church from the latter half of the 2nd century onwards. It is sometimes argued that this tradition is simply an intelligent deduction from the NT evidence that Luke-Acts was written by a companion of Paul, who is most likely to have been Luke, and that consequently the tradition possesses no independent value. The matter is not so simple. The tradition is unequivocal in singling out Luke from among several possible companions of Paul; we can trace it back to a fairly early date (possibly even to c. AD 120); and there is no sign of any other tradition in the early church. Attempts have been made to strengthen the argument for Lucan authorship by finding examples of medical language, such as a physician might readily use, in Luke-Acts, but the indications are perhaps too slight to provide anything more than corroboration of a view already held on other grounds.

Two arguments are commonly brought against the traditional view of the authorship. One is that the portrayal of Paul in Acts is too far removed from historical reality to be the work of a contemporary and companion; see the discussion of this point in the Introduction to Acts. The other is that the Gospel breathes the atmosphere of the sub-apostolic period. It is said that Luke gives the impression of being written at a time when the early church had had to come to terms with the fact that the second coming of Jesus had not taken place as soon as was expected, and when the early church had settled down into 'early catholicism'.

Neither of these last two points is convincing. The former assumes that at first the early Christians expected the *parousia* almost hourly and that only later its continued delay brought them to the point (reached in Luke) of transferring it to the distant future and thereby depriving it of its significance for the Christian life. But the evidence is decisively against the view that the early Christians expected the *parousia* to happen immediately, and it is simply not true that the *parousia* has lost all significance in Luke; see 12:35–40; 17:20–37; 18:8; 21:5–36. As for the second suggestion, that in Luke the church has developed into an institution for dispensing salvation, it is sufficient to compare Luke's writings with the Apostolic Fathers, in which this type of theology begins to find expression, to see that it entirely fails to carry conviction. In short, the burden of proof still rests upon those who would deny the Lucan authorship of the Gospel.

The date of composition is uncertain. It is closely bound up with the problem of the dates of Mark and of Acts. There are two serious possibilities, a date in the early sixties or in the later decades of the 1st century. The latter is the view most commonly held, and AD 80 is often given as a round figure. This view presupposes that Luke was not dependent upon the writings of Josephus (c. AD 93), but that he did write after the fall of Jerusalem (AD 70). This last point, however, is uncertain, and a date before AD 70 can certainly not be ruled out.

The place of composition is also uncertain. Early tradition suggests that Luke wrote in Achaia (Greece), but the relation of the Gospel to Mark suggests a connection with Rome. It is possible that Luke wrote in Rome but intended his Gospel for Achaia; if we knew who Theophilus was, the matter would be solved, but his identity remains a mystery.

OUTLINE OF CONTENTS

The structure of Luke closely resembles that of Mark and Matthew in which the ministry of Jesus is broadly divided into a Galilaean period and a Judean period. Luke differs from Mark in prefixing to the ministry an account of the birth of Jesus, and in developing at great length the account of the final journey of Jesus to Jerusalem.

COMMENTARY

1:1–4 PREFACE

Unlike the other Evangelists, Luke begins his Gospel with a brief preface in excellent Greek, such as one would find in the work of a secular writer. He was addressing the world at large and claiming a place for Christianity on the stage of world history. He justifies his venture by referring to the precedent of earlier Gospels, to the trustworthy nature of his sources and to his own qualifications to produce an orderly narrative based on careful research. His purpose was to give a reliable historical account which would form a sound basis for Christian faith.

1 *Many* should not be taken too literally. *The things . . . accomplished among us* include all that is related in both Luke and Acts. **2** The apostles and their immediate circle were the original transmitters of an authoritative tradition, and their testimony was based on personal experience. **3** *Theophilus* is otherwise unknown. *Most excellent* may be simply a piece of politeness or may indicate his official status (*cf.* Acts 23:26; 26:25). **4** Whether Theophilus was already a Christian depends upon whether *informed* means the reception of catechetical instruction; this remains uncertain.

1:5–2:52 THE BIRTH AND CHILDHOOD OF JESUS

As a prologue to the ministry of Jesus, Luke relates the story of His birth and shows how He was born as the Son of God (1:35). Closely linked with this story is the parallel narrative of the birth of His forerunner who prepared the people for the coming of the Lord (1:16f., 76f.). The account is characterized by frequent allusion to OT parallels and prophecies which show how God's new acts were entirely consonant with His earlier deeds and promises; and by various supernatural elements which marked out the two children as God's servant and Son respectively. The origins of the narrative must lie in traditions handed down by the parents of John and of Jesus, but Luke has written up his sources in his own style.

1:5–25 The prophecy of John's birth

The story of Jesus begins with the prophecy of the birth of His cousin. His coming is announced in words almost as majestic as those reserved for Jesus, since John was the greatest man of his generation (7:28). His parents were devout members of the old dispensation (*cf.* Gn. 17:1; 1 Ki. 9:4), and it was while his father was engaged in his priestly duties that he had a vision of an angel who told him that his prayer for a son was to be answered. The boy was to be called John ('God is gracious') and he was to prepare for that final coming of God to visit His people, which was the hope of Judaism. He would be separated to God's service like a Nazirite and empowered for his task by the Spirit. He would bring joy to the people, for his role as the new Elijah (*cf.* Mal. 4:5) would assure them that God's day was at hand. Like Abraham before him (Gn. 15:8), Zechariah could not believe the word of God and asked for confirmation. The angel replied by giving his name and divine commission, and added that Zechariah would be dumb (and deaf, 1:62) until the child's birth. When the priest reappeared outside, the people attributed his speechlessness to shock at the vision which they assumed he must have experienced. In due time God fulfilled His promise, and the child was conceived.

5 Herod the 'Great' ruled until 4 BC; *cf.* 2:1. **6, 7** Childlessness was a great reproach to a Jewish woman (1:25; Gn. 30:23), and was sometimes regarded as a punishment for sin. But v. 6 shows that this was not so here; indeed the birth of a child to a previously barren woman was sometimes an indication of great blessing for the people (*e.g.* through Isaac, Gideon and Samuel). **8–12** The large priestly tribe of Levi was subdivided into twenty-four *divisions*, that of Abijah (v. 5) being the eighth (1 Ch. 24:10). Each division did priestly duty at the Temple for two weeks in the year, and many of the priests spent the rest of the year away from Jerusalem (v. 23) following secular occupations. *Incense* was offered twice daily, and the choice of the individual to perform the actual offering in the Holy Place was a matter of *lot*, no priest being allowed to have this supreme honour more than once in his lifetime and many never having the opportunity. The priest was alone during the actual offering; *the people* prayed outside until he reappeared and gave them his blessing. **13** Giving a *name* was the father's duty. When God took over this task, it was a sign that He was making the child His responsibility. **24** Elizabeth *hid herself* during the period when her pregnancy would not be especially obvious and she would still be liable to reproach for childlessness. The news was first broken to Mary, and the miracle remained a secret from the people at large.

1:26–38 The prophecy of Jesus' birth

The story of the announcement of the birth of Jesus is very similar to the preceding narrative, but this time interest is centred on the mother of the child. Mary was engaged to Joseph, but their marriage had not yet taken place. Like Zechariah she was filled with fear by the angelic vision and perplexed by being addressed as 'favoured'. The angel's reply was that she was favoured by God, for she was to bear a son who was to be the Messiah (Is. 7:14). Mary's question to the angel (v. 34) has caused much difficulty: if she was engaged to a descendant of David, why should she protest that she had no husband? The view of some Roman Catholics that she had taken a vow of virginity can be safely discarded. Probably Mary understood the angel to be referring to an immediate conception and could not imagine how this was possible before her marriage; it is said that usually a year elapsed between engagement and marriage. The angel's reply made it clear that her Son was not to be an earthly Messiah, merely adopted by God as His Son (cf. 2 Sa. 7:12–14), but truly and really the Son of God; His birth would be due to the power of the Spirit coming upon Mary so that her child would be 'holy', i.e. divine. In confirmation of his word the angel spoke of the miracle already experienced by Elizabeth, and Mary quietly accepted her high honour.

26 Sixth: cf. v. 36. **27** The emphasis of the narrative is not so much upon the negative fact that Mary was a virgin as upon the positive fact that her child was born of God. Of the house of David refers to Joseph; as his adopted son, Jesus was legally a descendant of David. **28** Favoured means simply that God graciously chose Mary to be the mother of Jesus and not that she was 'full of grace'. **31** Jesus (Heb. Joshua) means 'Saviour'. **32, 33** The description is based on OT language and describes the significance of Jesus as the Jewish Messiah or anointed king in the line of David who would rule over an everlasting kingdom. **35** The coming of the Spirit is described in words reminiscent of the resting of the glory of God on the Tabernacle (Ex. 40:35). Overshadow is not a euphemism for 'beget'. The basic meaning of holy is 'separated to God' rather than 'morally pure'; hence it can mean 'divine' (cf. Ps. 89:5, 7).

Note. The historicity of the virgin birth

The story of the virgin birth is one of a miraculous, supernatural occurrence. We cannot here spend time on those criticisms of it which reject the supernatural on principle. Such doubts are part of a general outlook which must be discussed in a different context. Other factors are more important: a. The silence of most of the NT writers. The fact that the virgin birth is scarcely mentioned is not a strong objection to its his-

toricity, for the story, if true, can have come only from the family of Jesus, and was not one to be publicly proclaimed. Jewish slanders regarding the illegitimacy of Jesus' birth indicate that there was known to be something out of the ordinary about it. b. Pagan parallels. Critics have adduced pagan stories of great heroes being the offspring of the gods, and of mortal women being visited by gods who had intercourse with them. It has therefore been argued that the story of the virgin birth represents an admixture of Jewish or Hellenistic myth into the Christian faith in an attempt to express poetically or mythologically the divine origin of Jesus. But there is a world of difference between the atmosphere of the pagan stories and that of Lk. 1–2; and a precise parallel to the Christian story can be gained only by some elaborate and highly speculative jigsaw work on the sources. The force of the argument should not be underestimated, but in the end it fails to carry conviction. c. Details in the narrative. Historical difficulties over such matters as the census will be treated below. In any case, they do not affect the central matter at issue. d. Doctrinal objections. Such arguments as that Jesus is not truly like us if He were not born in the normal, human manner lie beyond our present scope. The reader may be referred to J. G. Machen, The Virgin Birth of Christ, 1958, for a full, masterly and satisfying discussion of the problem.

1:39–56 Mary's visit to Elizabeth

Mary's reaction to the angelic message was to fulfil the implied command to visit Elizabeth; she stayed until the birth of Elizabeth's child. Further confirmation of the angel's promise was given by Elizabeth, who was filled with prophetic inspiration and burst forth into a benediction. She realized that Mary was to be the mother of the Messiah and was overjoyed that she should visit her; she praised Mary for accepting the angel's word. The very movements of the child in her womb were a response to Mary's arrival.

Mary's poetic reply is known as the Magnificat. It is filled with echoes of OT praise, especially from Hannah's psalm (1 Sa. 2:1–10), and the best commentary on it (as on the whole of this chapter) is the margin of a good reference Bible. The wording, as in the other hymns in these chapters, is rather general, and Jewish rather than Christian. It is probable that Mary employed words already familiar in Jewish praise (she will hardly have composed the hymn extempore) and that what she said has been written up and elaborated later. Her hymn praised God for His personal blessing to her, a merciful act which was thoroughly in line with the way in which He cared for the humble and brought down their haughty oppressors.

41 In later life John apparently did not know Jesus very closely (Jn. 1:31; Lk. 7:19). This is in harmony with this passage, where nothing is said about the two boys subsequently coming into contact with each other. **46** Some MSS read 'Elizabeth' instead of Mary, and hence it has been conjectured that it was really she who spoke the Magnificat. But the textual evidence is extremely weak, and the hymn fits Mary better. Elizabeth's sentiments are fully expressed in vv. 42–45, and a comment by Mary, expressing her reactions, is a fitting and necessary conclusion to this scene (*cf.* v. 38). **48** The *low estate* (lit. humiliation) is Mary's feeling of unworthiness for her great honour. **49** God shows that He is *holy* by saving His people and acting mightily on their behalf (Ps. 111:9). **51–55** The past tenses indicate what God always *is* doing.

1:57–80 The birth of John

Elizabeth's neighbours rejoiced that God had shown His mercy to this previously barren woman. They expected that the child would be called after his father, but his mother insisted that he be called John, and the dumb father confirmed her choice. It is not certain whether she had been told by Zechariah about his vision or chose the name independently and hence miraculously; probably the former view is correct. Thereupon Zechariah regained his speech, and his first words were the hymn of praise which follows in vv. 67–79. The whole event made a tremendous impression upon the neighbours, who foresaw an unusual future for a child whose birth was accompanied by such signs.

Zechariah's prophetic hymn, the Benedictus, resembles Mary's hymn in its sentiments and fits equally well into this Jewish context. It begins by praising God for bringing redemption to His people through a scion of David in accordance with the ancient prophecies and covenant made by God. The second part is specifically directed to the future mission of John as the prophet who would prepare the way of the Lord by assuring the people of forgiveness of sins when His salvation was at hand.

For the moment the record of the fulfilment of the prophecy is delayed as attention is again focused on Jesus; a brief note speaks of John's upbringing. **59** The *eighth day* was the appointed date for circumcision (Lv. 12:3), but the naming of the child on this occasion is unusual, as in the OT names were given at birth. **63** *His name is John*: not 'will be', for the angel had already commanded it. **65** *Fear* is the normal human reaction in the Bible to the supernatural (*cf.* v. 12). **66** The people resolved to see whether what had happened was confirmed by later events. *For the hand . . .* is Luke's comment, not the people's. **67–79** The hymn is a prophecy, as is shown by vv. 76–79. There is a change in tone between the more general sentiments in vv. 68–75 and the specific language in the prophecy, but this does not detract from the unity of the hymn. **68** To *visit* is to come in order to save (1:78, see mg.; 7:16). **69** An animal's *horn* is a symbol of strength. Zechariah, like his wife, would know that Mary's child was to be the Davidic Messiah. **70** The prophecies include 2 Sa. 7:12; Is. 9:11; *cf.* Acts 3:21. **71** Zechariah's hymn, like Mary's,

has the flavour of the Jewish Messianic hope. Note, however, that there is here no thought of vengeance upon the enemies of the Jews. **73** The *oath* of Gn. 22:16–18; 26:3; Ps. 105:9–11 is understood to mean that God will make it possible for His people to serve Him in holiness and righteousness. **76** John is given the rank of a *prophet* (*cf.* Is. 40:3; Mal. 3:1). By the *Lord* is meant not Jesus (contrast 1:43) but God—a God, however, who acts through Jesus. **77–79** John's preaching of forgiveness was the sign that God had begun to act. *Through the tender mercy of our God* (v. 78) qualifies *knowledge of salvation* (v. 77), which is to be understood in a moral, not political, sense. In the second half of the verse follow rsv mg: 'whereby the dayspring will visit'. 'Dayspring' (Gk. *anatolē*) is either a translation of the Hebrew 'shoot' or 'branch', used as a Messianic title in Zc. 3:8; 6:12, or (more probably) refers to the rising sun (Mal. 4:2; *cf.* Nu. 24:17). In either case the reference is to the Messiah and not to John. It is not clear whether v. 79 is parallel to v. 77 or dependent on v. 78.

In this section John's mission is described in lofty terms; this contrasts with the subordinate position he occupies in the Gospel and shows that Luke did not invent the hymn; on the other hand, the view that the hymn was preserved by a group of John's followers who regarded him as the Messiah ignores the way in which John is plainly differentiated from the Messiah in the hymn. **80** *In the wilderness* could mean that John lived near Qumran where a Jewish sect practised an ascetic regimen with ritual baths and looked forward to the coming salvation of God. John may well have acted later in conscious correction of their outlook.

2:1–20 The birth of Jesus

(*Cf.* Mt. 1:18–25.) During the reign of Augustus (31 bc–ad 14) the Romans reorganized their administration in several parts of the Empire and carried out fresh censuses of the population for purposes of taxation. The execution of such an imperial decree in Syria (of which Judea formed a part) brought Joseph and Mary to Bethlehem, long ago prophesied as the Messiah's place of birth. The fact that Mary travelled with Joseph means that they were now married, but the description of her as *betrothed* (v. 5) to him (if this is the correct text—some mss, followed by av, have 'his wife') shows that they had not yet consummated the marriage (*cf.* Mt. 1:25). A 2nd-century tradition gives a cave as the scene of the birth, but Luke appears to mean an outhouse of the inn. The child's birth was heralded to an unexpected and even a despised group of people, shepherds. They had a vision of an angel who announced the significance of the birth: a Saviour had come. His message was confirmed by a chorus of angels who sang: 'Glory to God in highest heaven, And on earth his peace for men on whom his favour rests' (neb). Of the older renderings 'good will toward men' (av) and 'men of good will', the former is based on an incorrect text, and the latter reflects a theological misunderstanding. God's peace is not given to men because they deserve it, but to the undeserving whom He has freely and graciously chosen to favour.

2 The *enrolment* or census (not 'taxing', AV) of Augustus is surrounded by numerous problems. There is, however, sufficient evidence to show that a census of this nature was possible, that it could have taken place within the kingdom of a Roman client king, and that it was based on where one resided or held property. The real problem is the date. Quirinius was governor of Syria from AD 6, and during this time there was a rebellion over the imposition of the census (Acts 5:37 and Josephus). Jesus, however, was born before the death of Herod (4 BC). Possible solutions are: *a.* 'Quirinius' is a textual error for 'Saturninus', governor 9–6 BC. *b.* Quirinius may have held an earlier post in the East, during which he initiated the census. This could not, however, have been the governorship of Syria, as W. Ramsay held. E. Stauffer has argued that he had a 'roving commission' in the eastern Empire. *c.* Since this was the first enrolment in Judea, the process of listing the people and then actually taxing them would take several years. Luke mentions the name of Quirinius as the well-known governor under whom the process was completed after Herod's death; and the rising in Acts 5:37 will then have taken place when the new tax was first collected.

7 *Swaddling cloths* were the normal dress for a new-born child. **8** Flocks were kept *out in the field by night* from April to November, but this was apparently possible in winter also. There is, however, no evidence that Jesus was born in December. **10** *All the people* means Israel; only in v. 32 is the world-wide significance of Jesus revealed. **11** *Christ the Lord*: some think that this is a slip for 'the Lord's Christ' (*cf.* v. 26), but the wording is probably as Luke intended it to be. **12** The *sign* is the confirmation of the unusual significance of the child as Saviour by the unusual place where He was to be found. Earlier critics held that the finding of a miraculous child in a manger by shepherds was a theme drawn from pagan myth, but more recent criticism has shown that this view rested on an erroneous interpretation of inadequate evidence. **19** This verse probably points to the source of the story. Some readers may feel that the narrative has been poetically embellished, but, as B. S. Easton remarked, 'critical discussion of this perfect story is idle'.

2:21-40 The presentation of Jesus in the Temple

V. 21 briefly relates how Jesus was circumcised and named, the stress falling on the significant name which He was given before His conception. Prophecies regarding John's future had been made at his circumcision, but in the case of Jesus these took place later at the Temple. Three distinct elements must be unravelled in the background to the prophecies. *a.* After the birth of a male child, the mother was unclean for seven days and had to remain at home for a further thirty-three, after which on the fortieth day a purification sacrifice had to be offered (Lv. 12:1–8). This is described in v. 24. *b.* A firstborn child had to be 'redeemed'. All firstborn were regarded as holy or consecrated to God; the firstborn of animals were sacrificed, but the firstborn of men were redeemed by a payment of 5 shekels when they were one month old (Ex. 13:13; Nu. 18:15, 16). The law did not require the child's presence at the Temple when payment was made, but on this occasion the two ceremonies were simultaneous. *c.* A third consideration entered in also: Mary seems to have made a special dedication of her child to God, just as Hannah had earlier given Samuel to God at the Tabernacle (1 Sa. 1:11, 21–28).

The main theme, however, is the reception given to Jesus by Simeon and Anna. Simeon was a godly Israelite who looked forward to God's redemption of His people and had received His promise that he would not die before the coming of the Messiah. When he came into the Temple at the impulse of the Spirit and received the baby into his arms, he did not need any further confirmation that this was the Messiah, but expressed his gratitude to God and his readiness to die now that the promise had been fulfilled. He had seen the coming of a Saviour for all mankind, and not merely for the Jews; here is struck the note of universal redemption promised in the OT (see Ps. 98; Is. 49:6). Simeon then pronounced God's blessing upon Mary and Joseph and made a further prophecy. The child's coming would bring judgment as well as salvation, for men would be revealed as they really were in their hearts, and Mary herself would suffer anguish at the treatment meted out to her Son. Simeon's words were confirmed by the arrival of Anna, who gave thanks to God for the coming of the Messiah and prophesied the redemption that God would bring to His people through Him. Thereafter the family returned to Nazareth (but *cf.* Mt. 2), where Jesus grew up with the evident blessing of God upon Him.

22 *Their purification* should strictly be 'her purification' (as in AV, based on inferior MSS); Luke, however, included Jesus with Mary since he was thinking of the redemption of the firstborn at the same time. **24** Joseph offered the cheaper sacrifice permitted for poor people. **25** *Consolation; cf.* Is. 40:1; 61:2. **27** Joseph and Mary are called His *parents* here and elsewhere because Jesus was the adopted son of Joseph; the usage in no way contradicts the fact of the virgin birth. **33** Some scholars have argued that the wonder of Mary and Joseph at Simeon's words is incomprehensible if they had already heard the angelic messages about Jesus, and that therefore the two stories are independent and even contradictory. This is being extremely pedantic. The parents' surprise is psychologically probable, as they were given fresh confirmation of the significance of their Son. **34** It is not certain whether this verse refers to the *fall* of some persons and the *rising* of others or to the penitence and restoration of the same persons (so AV, NEB mg.). **36** *Asher* was one of the northern tribes, the so-called lost ten tribes. **37** Anna was *eighty-four* years old. But the Greek could mean that she had been a widow for that period (RV, NEB mg.). The second part of the verse should not be pressed to mean that she never left the Temple (*cf.* 24:53). **38** *Jerusalem* means the same as Israel (*cf.* v. 25) in this context. It is the place from which redemption started (Acts 1:8). **39** The sojourn in Egypt (Mt. 2:13–23) must be fitted in at this point. **40** The *wisdom* of Jesus is demonstrated in the next incident.

2:41–52 The Passover visit of Jesus to the Temple

Of the three great festivals which Jewish men were required to keep in Jerusalem, only the Passover was strictly observed; whole families went up to Jerusalem, and an estimated 60,000 to 100,000 visitors packed themselves into a town whose normal population was about 25,000. Large caravans of people travelled together for companionship and security, and it is not surprising that Mary and Joseph did not bother unduly about Jesus on the first day's journey home. A second day was spent in returning to Jerusalem, and on the third day He was found in the Temple. His intelligent discussion with the Rabbis was an earnest of His later teaching, but the passage does not mean that Jesus was trying to instruct them, but only that they were impressed by His unusual promise as a pupil. Jesus' reply to His parents was in effect: 'You ought to have known where to find me—in my Father's house.' Thus from an early age Jesus was aware of an intimate filial relationship to God, a relationship which went beyond the normal religious consciousness of a devout Jew, as His later teaching made clear (10:21, 22). One should not see here a criticism of His parents; He sought to be obedient to them (v. 51). The final verse indicates how His perfect growth as a boy (v. 40) continued during His adolescence (*cf.* 1 Sa. 2:26).

42 At the age of *twelve* a boy was prepared for entry to the religious community as an adult; it was not necessarily Jesus' first visit to Jerusalem. **46** Teaching took place in the environs of the Temple (*cf.* Acts 5:25). **49** The alternative translation 'about my Father's business' (AV, JB) is less apt.

3:1 – 4:13 JOHN THE BAPTIST AND JESUS

3:1–20 The preaching of John

(See Mt. 3:1–12; Mk. 1:1–8; Jn. 1:19–28.) Like the first Christian preachers, Luke saw the real beginning of the gospel in the appearance of John the Baptist (*cf.* Acts 10:37). He places this important event in its historical context by giving its date and a brief description of the political situation in Palestine. The ministry of John marked the end of the old era (*cf.* Lk. 16:16) as well as the beginning of the new. He was not only the fulfiller of prophecy but also the last of the

prophets, and is described as a prophet (*cf.* vv. 1f. with Je. 1:1f.). His coming was in fulfilment of Is. 40:3–5, a text which the Qumran sect also saw fulfilled in their activities, and his task was to proclaim a baptism which pledged forgiveness of sins.

This proclamation is expanded in three brief sections. In the first (vv. 7–9) John warned the people that it was no use being baptized without a true repentance that showed itself in deeds. A mere claim to physical descent from Abraham was no defence against imminent judgment. The axe was already poised, ready to chop down the unfruitful tree, but there was just time for repentance before it was too late. A second paragraph (vv. 10–14), peculiar to Luke, gives specific instructions to the people. The multitudes, composed of poorer people, must practise generosity, a work of love as opposed to the works of the law. Tax collectors ('publicans', AV) and soldiers were to act honestly and justly in their professions. There is here no radical upheaval of the existing social order, but an insistence on those moral principles which will lead to a transformation of society from within rather than by the path of violent revolution. A third paragraph (vv. 15–17; *cf.* Jn. 1:19–34) brings the vital point. Many people asked during John's lifetime and after whether he was the Messiah. Whatever his followers thought, John knew his own subordinate position. A mightier One would follow him. John cleansed men ceremonially with the sacramental symbol of water, but the coming One would cleanse men's hearts with the fire of the Holy Spirit; He would carry through the great separation among men, like a harvester who preserves the wheat and destroys the chaff. Therefore let men repent without delay.

This message is summed up as 'good news' (v. 18), and the force of this word should not be weakened, for the coming of John meant that the coming of Jesus was near. But before His arrival is described, the story of John is rounded off with the story of His arrest (*cf.* Mk. 6:17–29), and the stage is left clear for Jesus.

1 There are two alternative ways of reckoning the chronology of Tiberius' reign (AD 14–37) which make his *fifteenth year* either AD 27–28 or AD 28–29. *Pilate* was governor of Judea AD 26–36; a recently discovered inscription shows that his proper title was prefect and not procurator. *Abilene* lay to the north-east, within the general bounds of Palestine; *Lysanias* is mentioned in inscriptions. **2** There was only one high priest at a time. Caiaphas held office AD 18–37, but his father-in-law, Annas, who held office AD 6–15, remained very influential. **7** *Vipers* were regarded as evil and destructive. According to Matthew, this choice epithet was addressed to the Pharisees and Sadducees. *Who warned you . . . ?* i.e. 'Did somebody tell you that you could escape judgment simply by being baptized (*sc.* without repenting)?' **8** *Stones* and *children* give a pun in Aramaic. **11** A man might wear *two coats* to keep warm on a journey or in the open at night. **14** The *soldiers* may have been members of Herod's police force. **16** It is debatable whether *fire* is a symbol of final judgment or of present cleansing by the Spirit; if the metaphor in **17** supports the former view, Acts 1:5 is decisive in favour of the latter.

3:21, 22 The baptism of Jesus

(See Mt. 3:13–17; Mk. 1:9–11; *cf.* Jn. 1:32, 33.) Luke mentions the actual baptism almost parenthetically and lays all the stress on the accompanying revelation. The words *in bodily form* emphasize the reality of the coming of the Spirit to equip Jesus for His ministry (*cf.* 4:18). The heavenly *voice*, its words reminiscent of Gn. 22:2; Ps. 2:7; Is. 42:1, does not indicate the adoption of Jesus as God's Son but the divine approval with which He began His work as God's Servant and Son.

3:23–38 The genealogy of Jesus

(See Mt. 1:1–17.) It may seem odd that the genealogy is inserted at this point where it interrupts the developing narrative, instead of coming somewhere in the birth stories. (Was it part of 'proto-Luke' before the birth stories were added to it?) But ancient writers did not have the device of removing material from the main text by using footnotes.

The purpose of the genealogy is to establish that Jesus was *legally* a descendant of David (*cf.* 1:27, 32, 69) and to assign Him a place in the Jewish branch of the human race. It is nonsensical to say that v. 38 is meant to prove that Jesus was the Son of God. The existence of a genealogical table going back through Joseph is no argument against the historicity of the virgin birth. It has been observed that the list contains 77 (*i.e.* 11×7) human names, but grouping of the names in this way does not lead to any very useful results.

The genealogy differs from that in Matthew. Apart from being in reverse order and tracing back the line beyond Abraham to Adam, it contains a quite different and longer set of names between David and Jesus (only Zerubbabel and Shealtiel occur in both lists). Both lists give the descent of Jesus through his adopted father Joseph ('as was supposed', v. 23), and the theory that one of the genealogies is really that of Mary has little to commend it. The least difficult explanation is that Matthew gives the legal descendants of David down the royal line (*i.e.* who was heir to the throne at any given time), whereas Luke gives the particular line to which Joseph belonged (so J. G. Machen), but it must be confessed that in the absence of fuller information the problems of explanation and harmonization are insoluble.

23 *The son of* does not imply strict paternity any more than Matthew's 'was the father of', and allows for gaps in the line. For *Heli*, Matthew has 'Jacob'. **24** It is uncertain whether *Matthat* should be identified with Matthan (Mt. 1:15). **27** *Zerubbabel* was the leader of the Jewish community after the Exile; for *Shealtiel* see Hg. 1:1,

but in 1 Ch. 3:19 (Heb., not LXX) Zerubbabel's father is Pedaiah. According to 1 Ch. 3:17; Mt. 1:12 Shealtiel was the son of Jeconiah, and not of *Neri*; an adoption may have taken place. **31** *Nathan*: not the prophet; *cf.* 2 Sa. 5:14. From v. 32 onwards the names are in agreement with the LXX, except for minor spelling differences. They are drawn from Gn. 5:1–32; 11:10–26; Ru. 4:18–22; 1 Ch. 1:1–34; 2:1–15; 3:5–19. **33** *Admin* and *Arni* do not occur in the OT; 1 Ch. 2:10 has Ram. **36** *Cainan* is found in the LXX but not in the Hebrew text.

4:1–13 The temptation of Jesus

(See Mt. 4:1–11; Mk. 1:12, 13.) The final episode in the preparation of Jesus for His ministry was a period of testing by Satan. The experience came to Jesus as He followed the guidance of the Spirit, and He resisted every temptation in the power of the Spirit. **3, 4** The first temptation urged Jesus to use His newly confirmed status as the Son of God (3:22) to perform an act of power in order to satisfy His hunger. The temptation was directed against Jesus' obedience to God, and implied that the satisfaction of His bodily desires was more important than the spiritual experience which produces a steadfast character (Rom. 5:3). Jesus resisted it by quoting the scriptural principle that a man's real life does not depend on the satisfaction of physical hunger (Dt. 8:3; AV, following inferior MSS, completes the quotation).

5–8 Then Jesus was taken up on high and given a vision of the entire world. Its ruler (Jn. 12:31) offered to surrender dominion over it to Him if He would acknowledge his higher authority. But ultimately the world does not belong to the devil; his promise was not to be trusted; and to bow to his will was incompatible with worshipping and serving God (Dt. 6:13).

9–12 Finally, the devil, defeated by Scripture, tried to enlist its service in his own cause, and suggested that Ps. 91:11f. justified Jesus in leaping down from the high colonnade of the Temple which overlooked the ravine of the Kidron valley. The act was presented as one of filial trust in God, but in reality it would have been one of disbelief. To have yielded to the temptation would have been to doubt the reality of His Sonship and His relationship to the Father, for a person tests the faithfulness of God (Dt. 6:16) only when he doubts and no longer trusts Him. Thus the devil was repulsed each time and departed from the fray.

The temptations were all directed against the divine Sonship of Jesus. They encouraged Him to misuse His divine powers, to gain His purpose in the world by obeying the devil instead of His Father, and to doubt the reality of His Father's love and care. The temptations were therefore not directed specifically against the Messianic office of Jesus, encouraging Him to win the people by performing spectacular miracles, but rather against the inner relationship of Sonship on which His Messiahship rested. There are some parallels with the experience of Israel in the wilderness (Dt. 6-8), but these should not be pressed too far.

13 The devil does not reappear until 22:3, but it would be rash to assume that he was inactive in the intervening period (*cf.*, *e.g.* 13:16; 22:28).

4:14 – 9:50 THE MINISTRY IN GALILEE

4:14 – 5:11 The good news of the kingdom

4:14, 15 Introductory summary. (See Mt. 4:12-17; Mk. 1:14, 15.) Luke opens his account of the work of Jesus in Galilee with a brief summary which stresses His activity as a teacher and the great impression which He made on His immediate hearers and in a wider area.

4:16-30 Jesus teaches at Nazareth. (*Cf.* Mt. 13:53-58; Mk. 6:1-6.) It is widely agreed that Luke has placed this incident ahead of its proper chronological position (v. 23) because it provided an ideal opening summary of the message of Jesus. In the synagogue of His home town Jesus read the 'second lesson' from Is. 61:1, 2 and gave a discourse on its fulfilment. There was the note of *present* fulfilment: what the prophet had foretold was now finally coming true. There was also *personal* fulfilment: the One anointed with the Spirit was Jesus Himself. There was finally *gracious* fulfilment: the era of God's salvation had arrived, and it may well be significant that Jesus did not go on to finish the quotation with its reference to 'the day of vengeance of our God'.

Apparently the people were at first amazed by what Jesus said, but their response quickly became hostile as they took exception to one of their own number making such pretentious claims. Jesus saw their attitude as one of disbelief. They would have liked some tangible proof of His claims before their own eyes: let the physician perform some cures at home as well as at Capernaum! So they failed to recognize in Jesus a prophet, and He could only tell them that when the prophets of Israel had been faced by similar disbelief they had wrought their wonders among the heathen (1 Ki. 17:8-16; 2 Ki. 5:1-14). Thus the word of judgment *was* spoken—against themselves—and Jesus implied that the gospel would ultimately go to the Gentiles. In their wrath the people would have lynched Him for making such a suggestion.

16, 17 The synagogue service consisted of prayers, readings from the law and the prophets, and a sermon. The leader of the service stood to pray and read, and sat to teach. Any competent person present could be invited to take part (*cf.* Acts 13:15). There was at this time a set lectionary for the readings from the law, but Jesus was probably able to choose His own reading from the prophets. **18, 19** The text includes a phrase from Is. 58:6, probably included by the narrator because of its obvious fitness to describe the ministry of Jesus. The various acts described are to be taken spiritually rather than literally. The *acceptable year* is the one graciously chosen by God as the era of His favour to men. **22** The

swift transition from praise to disbelief is perhaps strange. Some scholars have therefore thought that two or even three distinct incidents (vv. 16-22, 23f., 25-30) have been run together as one here. Others retranslate this verse: *spoke well* (lit. 'bore witness') could mean 'bore witness against', and *wondered* may indicate annoyance rather than acceptance. *Gracious words* are words speaking of God's grace. Jesus would be known locally as *Joseph's son* (but see Mk. 6:3). **25** *Three years and six months*: *cf.* Jas. 5:17. **30** A miraculous disappearance is probably not meant.

4:31-44 Successful work at Capernaum. (See Mt. 8:14-17; Mk. 1:21-39.) From the hill country Jesus went down to Capernaum on the lakeside. His main activity was teaching in the synagogue at worship on the sabbath. On one occasion He was interrupted by a demoniac who possessed supernatural insight into His Person and purpose: Jesus had come from God to destroy all that was unholy. Perhaps the demoniac hoped to overpower Jesus by using His name—this was a common ancient superstition—but Jesus peremptorily ordered the demon to be silent and leave the man. The healing confirmed the impression of tremendous authority already made by Jesus' teaching, and the people were not slow to spread the news.

Illness too was seen to be subject to His authority. On leaving the synagogue, Jesus healed both Simon's mother-in-law and many other people. He silenced the cries of the demoniacs because He wanted people to learn for themselves who He was. In the morning He could scarcely escape the crowds, but nevertheless left them. The task for which He had been sent by God was to proclaim the good news of God's rule far and wide, and He could not stay in one place and become the idol of an admiring throng.

33 A person possessed by a *demon* would undoubtedly be regarded today as suffering from mental illness. This, however, is not a full diagnosis of the phenomena in the Gospels, where the demoniacs also possessed a supernatural knowledge of things unknown to ordinary men. The presence of an evil, supernatural power cannot be rationalized away, and, just as theologians speak of the 'concursive' action of the Holy Spirit in men, so we may perhaps argue for a like action by evil spirits. **34** The *Holy One of God* means the same as 'the Son of God' (v. 41) or 'Christ' (v. 42), and stresses the opposition of Jesus to evil, perhaps as the bearer of the *Holy* Spirit. **38, 39** A *high fever* may be a technical medical term. Jesus *rebuked* it almost as if it were a person.

40 Once the new Jewish day had begun at sunset, the sabbath restrictions were lifted, and the sick could be carried to Jesus. By laying His hands on the sick, Jesus showed that He was bestowing God's power upon them. **42** Luke does not mention here that Jesus was at prayer (Mk. 1:35), but see 5:16. **43** *Kingdom of God*: see Mk. 1:15. **44** *Judea* here means Palestine as a whole, including Galilee (which some MSS have here); Jesus did not enter Judea proper for a settled ministry until later.

5:1-11 The call of the disciples. (*Cf.* Mt. 4:18-22; Mk. 1:16-20.) Mark's briefer account of the call of the first disciples concentrates attention on the basic fact that the proper response to the message of the kingdom of God is instant obedience to the call to discipleship. Luke's longer account shows that the call took place only after Jesus had won the friendship of Simon and revealed His heavenly power to him. Although Simon, as an experienced fisherman, knew that there was little likelihood of a catch, he was already sufficiently impressed by Jesus to obey His command. When the full revelation of Jesus' power came to him, he was overcome with a profound sense of fear and unworthiness in the presence of One who displayed heavenly power and was thereby demonstrated to be holy in His nature. Jesus, however, bade him not to be afraid (*cf.* 1:13, 30), and issued His call to discipleship in words obviously suggested by Simon's present occupation. All the attention is focused on Simon as the leader of the Twelve; we are left to infer Andrew's presence from v. 6.

1 *Gennesaret* ('Chinnereth' in the OT) is an alternative name for Galilee, and refers specifically to the district immediately south of Capernaum (*cf.* Mk. 6:53). **3** *Cf.* Mk. 2:13; 4:1f. **4, 5** The best fishing was done by night in deep water; during the day-time they fished in the shallows. **8** *Simon Peter* receives his full name only here in Luke (*cf.* 6:14), since his call was the moment which made his new name possible. He was not necessarily any more *sinful* than other men, but he felt that fear which all sinful men ought to feel in the presence of the divine (*cf.* Jdg. 13:21f.). **10** Critics who argue that Jesus could not have used this metaphor in a good sense, because it occurs only with a bad sense in the OT, are preferring a far-fetched explanation to the obvious one. **11** Theories that the great catch of fish was meant to provide provision for the dependants of the disciples during their travels with Jesus or is an allegory of the catch of men which they would take (*cf.* Jn. 21:1-14) are alike speculative.

5:12 – 6:11 The beginning of controversy with the Pharisees

In this section Luke recounts five incidents in all of which (apart from the first) various actions of Jesus and His disciples led to criticism from the Pharisees and showed up the nature of the new faith in contrast with the old legalism.

5:12-16 The healing of a leper. (See Mt. 8:1-4; Mk. 1:40-45.) The first story stands in contrast to the ensuing narratives, for it illustrates how Jesus normally abided by the OT law. If a man who had previously been certified as a leper claimed to be cured, he had to go through the proper form of discharge from the priest before being allowed to move freely in society again (Lv. 14:1-32), and Jesus instructed this man to obey the law. The story also makes clear how

Jesus wrought cures in response to faith (though the word itself is not used), and indicates how His reputation was growing, both as a teacher and a healer.

12 *Leprosy* can mean any of several skin diseases, not all of them infectious.

5:17-26 Jesus' authority to forgive sins. (See Mt. 9:1-8; Mk. 2:1-12.) Luke (unlike Mark) indicates at the outset the presence of the Pharisees and teachers of the law, and prepares the reader for their hostile reaction to Jesus. When Jesus did not immediately heal the paralysed man but declared that his sins were forgiven, the unspoken thought of the onlookers was that this was a blasphemous declaration: only God could forgive sins, and Jesus had no authority to speak in His name. Jesus' response was to give indirect proof of His authority to forgive sins by showing that He possessed divine authority (v. 17) to heal; performance of the visible act should convince them that He also possessed authority for the invisible, and therefore unprovable, act. What the Pharisees said, however, was lost in the chorus of praise from the healed man and the bystanders alike which testified to the reality of Jesus' power.

17 The *Pharisees* were a religious party who placed great stress on punctilious observance of the unwritten law. The *teachers of the law* (or scribes) were a professional class of lawyers and teachers, usually but not exclusively members of the Pharisaic party. **19** Mark's description of a roof made of mud and wattle is in accord with Palestinian house construction; Luke has retold the story in terms of the Hellenistic roofing with *tiles* with which his readers would be more familiar. **20** The fact that Jesus singled out this man for a declaration of forgiveness *may* imply that he was guilty of some particularly culpable sin; it certainly does not mean that disaster is *always* due to sin (*cf.* 13:1-5). **21** A prophet or priest could forgive sin in God's name; the question, therefore, was whether Jesus possessed prophetic authority. In fact He claimed the higher authority of the Son of man who is associated with God's final judgment on men (*cf.* Dn. 7:9-22; Lk. 9:26; 12:8f.).

5:27-32 Jesus' attitude to sinners. (See Mt. 9:9-13; Mk. 2:13-17.) Unlike the story in 5:1-11, the story of Levi tells only incidentally what is implied in discipleship. Its main purpose is to show the kind of people Jesus called and to justify His action. He was glad to bring the gospel to Levi and his former companions, and His justification of His action was unimpeachable. No more than a doctor could He be expected to keep His hands clean. His duty lay with the needy whom He invited to repent; those who thought themselves to be righteous were not His primary concern.

30 *Tax collectors* were religiously unclean because they worked for the Romans, and hated because they fleeced their fellow-Jews and lined their own pockets with conspicuous success. *Sinners* included prostitutes and their kind, criminals and ne'er-do-wells, all of whom were beyond the pale for the Pharisees.

5:33–39 Jesus' attitude to fasting. (See Mt. 9:14–17; Mk. 2:18–22.) **33–35** The OT required fasting only on the annual Day of Atonement. Jesus disregarded the Pharisaic innovation of fasting twice a week. He argued, first, that it would be as fitting for His disciples to fast as for the groomsmen at a wedding to mourn instead of leading the festivities. The plain implication is that the new era of salvation has come, and the mournful rites of the old era are incompatible with it; only during the sad days between the death of Jesus and His resurrection would mourning be fitting. **36–39** Second, it is futile to try to combine the new religion with man-made legalism; the new religion will be debased, and in any case the two ways cannot be mixed, just as an unshrunk patch of cloth will pull away from an old garment or fermenting wine will burst old skins that have lost their elasticity. (**38** The addition in AV misses the point.) **39** is probably an ironic comment on Jews who rejected the *new wine* of the gospel and held that the old ways were better.

6:1–11 Jesus' attitude to the sabbath. (See Mt. 12:1–14; Mk. 2:23 – 3:6.) The first of this pair of stories deals with the rigid sabbatarianism which prescribed meticulously what men must not do on the sabbath, even down to rubbing ears of grain in their hands. When the Pharisees heard (no doubt from some tell-tale) that Jesus was breaking their man-made law and criticized Him, He referred them to the example of David, who was allowed by the priest to give the bread of the Presence to his men, although it was normally reserved for the priests to eat (1 Sa. 21:1–6). It is important to observe that David was *not* breaking the OT law, and that Jesus was not citing his action as a precedent for doing so. Rather Jesus was showing that the OT itself does not uphold the rigorous legalism which the Pharisees had developed in their man-made traditions. The sabbath was made for man, and consequently the Son of man is its Lord. Since the sabbath is the Lord's day, this statement of Jesus is a veiled claim to equality with God.

In the second incident it looks as though the opponents of Jesus 'planted' the sick man in the synagogue to see what Jesus would do. He at once accepted the unspoken challenge and posed His searching question: if His action in healing a man on the sabbath was to be considered sinful, how much more sinful was their plotting of His death. For the penalty for transgression of the sabbath law was death, and Mark tells us that from this time the Pharisees began to plot the death of Jesus.

1 The AV and RSV mg. text 'the second sabbath after the first' is unexplained; it may be a technical term of the Jewish calendar or a scribal error. **2** In the Mishnah there is a list of thirty-nine occupations forbidden on the sabbath, including threshing. **9** The view that *to do harm* and *to destroy* life refer simply to not healing the sick

man is less likely than that suggested above.

6:12–49 The teaching of Jesus to His disciples

Having given us a sketch of the general character of the ministry of Jesus and depicted the relationship of Jesus to His opponents, Luke now describes the relationship of Jesus to His disciples. After narrating the call of the Twelve, he presents the teaching which Jesus gave to all who wished to follow Him.

6:12–16 The call of the Twelve. (See Mt. 10:1–4; Mk. 3:13–19.) Luke alone draws attention to the way in which Jesus prayed all night before making the momentous choice of the Twelve. Out of the larger company who had responded to His teaching He chose His apostles. The use of this title is often regarded as an anachronism from the time after the resurrection, but it is entirely in harmony with the way in which Jesus spoke of sending (Gk. *apostellō*) them out on mission (10:3).

14 Luke does not tell when *Simon* received his new name of 'rock' (*cf.* Mt. 16:18; Jn. 1:42). *Bartholomew* is probably the same as Nathanael (Jn. 1:45–51). **15** *Matthew* and Levi (5:27) are the same person. It was not uncommon for Jews to have two names. A *Zealot* was one of the extreme Jewish nationalists who eventually took up arms against Rome. **16** *Judas* (*cf.* Jn. 14:22) is the Thaddaeus of Mark's list. *Iscariot* may mean 'man of Kerioth' or 'assassin' (Latin *sicarius*) or 'false one'.

6:17–19 The assembling of the people. (Mt. 4:23–25; Mk. 3:7–12.) From the hills Jesus returned to a level place where the people could more easily reach Him as they swarmed together from all over the area surrounding Galilee. They may have been especially attracted by His healing power, but Jesus did not lose the opportunity to teach them. **17** The same scene is described in Mark *before* the call of the Twelve. The Evangelists were obviously not concerned to give an exact chronological record. Luke's arrangement shows that there was a substantial crowd to hear the following sermon (*cf.* 7:1) and that it was not delivered solely to the Twelve. **19** *Cf.* 8:46.

6:20–26 Two kinds of men. (See Mt. 5:1–12.) The 'Sermon on the Plain', so called to distinguish it from the 'Sermon on the Mount' (Mt. 5–7), is basically a shorter version of the latter, and it is generally agreed that Matthew has enlarged the sermon found in Luke by adding to it other sayings of Jesus on the same or related topics.

The Sermon here begins with a contrast between two types of men. The first group are those who by all outward appearance are to be pitied, but in the judgment of Jesus are *blessed* or happy because of what is promised to them. They are poor and needy, hungry and sad. This can hardly refer purely to their literal condition, and must be understand spiritually (as Matthew indicates) of those who feel dissatisfied with this present world and long for what God has to give to them. They are promised that He will hear them and fulfil their longings in the coming kingdom which was the theme of Jesus' message. Men may *hate* and *revile* them for putting their trust in God's representative, the Son of man, but, like the prophets, they will receive their reward from God. This fourth 'beatitude' shows that the persons whom Jesus has in mind are His disciples, and that what He is speaking of are the privileges and implications of disciple-ship. The other group of men are those who have what the present can offer—satisfaction of their desires for material goods, happiness and a good reputation among men—and do not want anything more: no need for them to cry out to God in prayer, for they think they have enough. The time will come, says Jesus, when they will have nothing; many in Israel will fall (2:34).

6:27–38 Love and mercy. (See Mt. 5:39–48; 7:12, 1f.) If the first part of the sermon dealt with the disciples' relationship to God, this second part now deals with their relationship to other men. It is summed up in the idea of love for one's enemies. The general principle is laid down in vv. 27f., where it is made clear that the *enemies* meant are especially those who perse-cute the disciples. Two brief examples of such love are given—refraining from retaliation when struck a blow and readiness to give a footpad who robs you more than he demands. The disciples must be prepared to give away their possessions freely, and their conduct is summed up in the 'golden rule' of v. 31.

This sort of behaviour is revolutionary. Most people are quite ready to do good to those who have helped them or from whom they expect some benefit in return. But if sinners can do that, disciples ought to go further and abandon this principle of mutuality; their love should not simply repay love or expect something in return. There may well be no earthly *credit* or reward (AV 'thank'), but there will be a heavenly reward, and they will be accounted as true sons of the God who shows mercy to the undeserving.

What the reward is is shown in vv. 37f. The man who loves like this will receive a like love—and more—from God. He who does not judge his fellow-men will not be judged by God, and he who gives will receive ample return, like a meas-ure of meal so well filled that it is running over.

Notice again that all this is spoken to disciples. Jesus is not saying that all a man has to do to inherit a heavenly reward is to love his neighbour.

29, 30 Jesus is not of course advocating the kind of indiscriminate generosity which would encourage lazy and parasitical good-for-nothings. **34** Probably *sinners* hoped to get even more back by charging a fat rate of interest.

6:39–49 Pictures of discipleship. (See Mt. 15:14; 10:24f.; 7:3–5, 16, 21, 24–27; 12:33–35; *cf.* Jn. 13:16; 15:20.) In the final part of the sermon a series of parabolic sayings brings out the character that disciples should show.

39–42 The first group speaks of spiritual sight. The disciple must learn before he can be a teacher. For one who is taught is not better

than his teacher, and if the teacher himself falls the pupils will fall also. The disciple must also see himself clearly before he can point out the faults of others. Jesus makes His points with humorous exaggeration.

43–45 A second group of sayings shows that good conduct can come only from a good heart. It is as foolish to expect good fruit from a bad tree as to expect good deeds from a bad man. Only the man whose heart is richly stored with good will bring forth good teaching.

46–49 Finally, what ultimately matters is not simply hearing Jesus but obeying His words. The man who hears and does not obey is as foolish as the man who builds a house without care to secure a good foundation; the man who hears and obeys will be as secure on the day of judgment as the man who takes care to build his house with strong foundations on the rock.

7:1–50 The compassion of the Messiah

7:1–10 The healing of a centurion's servant. (See Mt. 8:5–13; Jn. 4:46–53.) The central figure in this story is a Gentile, possibly in the employ of Herod Antipas (*cf.* 3:14). He had sufficient money to help in the building of the synagogue in Capernaum; even an honest man could readily make money in the police force. He is presented as a man of the highest character in his concern for his slave, his attitude to the Jews and his consciousness of unworthiness in the presence of Jesus. What shines out especially is the quality of his faith. As one who himself had been given such authority from his superior officers that he could enforce the obedience of his subordinates, he recognized in Jesus one who had the authority of God to quell disease, and he was prepared to trust Jesus to heal even by a simple word of command. Well did Jesus com-mend such faith, and note that a Gentile had surpassed the Jews in showing it.

The story as told by Luke differs somewhat from Matthew's version in that here the centurion sends two groups of messengers to Jesus instead of appearing personally; it may be that through abbreviation (*cf.* Mt. 9:18–26 with Mk. 5:22–43) Matthew has given a different impression. There is a very similar story in John about an official whose son was ill in Capernaum. The similarity is greater if the word *pais* (used in Lk. 7:7 and Matthew) is translated as 'boy' (= son) rather than as 'boy' (= servant), and if it is assumed that Luke's use of 'slave' (vv. 2, 10) is mistaken. But there is nothing in Matthew or Luke which suggests that a son is meant, and the details of the story in John are very different.

3 The *elders* were the leading men in a small community, and would be closely associated with the synagogue. **6–8** The messengers would report the centurion's message verbatim.

7:11–17 The healing of the widow's son. The story of the healing of a person at the point of death is followed by that of the resurrection of a dead man. His death especially aroused the sympathy of Jesus because his mother was a widow and he would be her only means of support. The funeral procession was already going out of the town to a cemetery with the dead man carried on an open bier. Ignoring ritual contamination with the dead body, Jesus stopped the bier and commanded the young man to arise. His simple word of command sufficed to work the miracle, and the people were filled with mingled terror and joy in the presence of the supernatural. They remembered that Elijah and Elisha had worked similar wonders (1 Ki. 17:17–24; 2 Ki. 4:18–37) and glorified God far and wide.

11, 12 *Nain* was a village to the south of Nazareth. Archaeologists suggest that since it was never fortified it may not have had a *gate*, and it is possible that here Luke describes the scene in terms of the kind of city with which his readers were familiar. **13** Luke alone of the Evangelists makes frequent use of the title *Lord* to designate Jesus. Jesus was probably not known generally as 'the Lord' during His lifetime (see Mk. 11:3); when He was addressed as 'Lord', it meant no more than 'Sir' as a common title of respect. **16** *Cf.* 1:68, 78.

7:18–35 Jesus and John the Baptist. (See Mt. 11:2–19.) In his prison John was perplexed by the news that filtered through from his followers about Jesus: Jesus did not seem to be setting the heather on fire in quite the way that John had anticipated. So he sent messengers to ask Jesus plainly whether He was the promised One or not. Jesus' reply was to draw attention to the works of mercy which He was performing and to send messengers back to John with words drawn from Is. 26:19; 29:18f.; 35:5f.; 61:1. This should show John that the signs of the age of salvation were being performed. Let not John miss their point and 'lose faith in Jesus' (JB). Whether the message confirmed John's faith we are not told directly. Perhaps there is a hint in the way in which Jesus went on to praise John. Here was no easy-going or fickle person who lived in comfort. This was the greatest of the prophets, the greatest man ever born, the forerunner of the Messiah. The praise is unstinted, and then comes the surprise: even the most insignificant person in the kingdom of God is superior to John, for John lived just outside the era of salvation. In vv. 29f. we are told in parenthesis how the supporters of John in the crowd praised God that their prophet had been vindicated by Jesus, but the Pharisees and lawyers rejected John and Jesus alike.

Then Jesus commented on the attitude of the Pharisees and their followers. They were like children playing games. When one group of children suggest playing at weddings and play merry music, the other group refuse to dance; and when the first group suggest playing at funerals instead and sing a dirge, the others still refuse to play and will not join in the mourning. The Jews did not find the ascetic John to their liking, and they bitterly criticized Jesus for mixing with frivolous people and joining in their revels; we may be sure that their pictures of both men were over-drawn and exaggerated. Despite them all, said Jesus, God's wisdom is shown to be right by her children, *i.e.* those who responded to John and Himself.

19 *He who is to come* may have been a title. Jn. 6:14; 11:27 might suggest that a coming prophet was in mind, but it is more likely that the Messiah was meant (*cf.* Heb. 10:37). **22** Since the signs were those of the actual coming of salvation, Jesus was not merely the prophet of the new age, but the actual bringer of it. **23** Perhaps John was offended by the absence of judgment from the message of Jesus (*cf.* 4:18f.). **24, 25** The *reed* represents an easy-going person. The fact that John did not *live in luxury* meant that he was not likely to condone easy-going ways in his hearers. **27** *Cf.* Mk. 1:2. The quotation is based on Ex. 23:20 and Mal. 3:1 where God promises to send His messenger to His people. **34** The title of *Son of man* here refers to Jesus in the humble character of His earthly life as one rejected by His generation. Some hold that the Aramaic phrase could be used as a periphrasis for 'I', so that Jesus' hearers may not necessarily have realized that He was using a title. It is extremely unlikely that anyone would have invented this saying and then ascribed it to Jesus. **35** For *children* Matthew has 'works'. *Wisdom* is a periphrasis for the name of God.

7:36–50 The woman who was a sinner. (*Cf.* Mt. 26:6–13; Mk. 14:3–9; Jn. 12:1–8.) The immediately following story gives point to the accusation made in v. 34. Jesus had been invited to the home of a Pharisee, probably for a meal after a synagogue service. It was not uncommon for uninvited guests to be found at a banquet, and among them was a woman well known as a prostitute. She proceeded to anoint Jesus with ointment, very possibly bought with her immoral earnings, but the fulfilment of her intention was interrupted by her tears. The Pharisee was disturbed by the way in which Jesus accepted this respect given in so embarrassing a manner from so undesirable a person; his feelings that Jesus might be a prophet (possibly *the* prophet, RV mg.) were being contradicted by the latter's apparent ignorance of the person of the woman. But Jesus knew what He was doing. He made His point with a crystal-clear parable. Love is the proof of the reception of forgiveness, and the more a person is forgiven, the more he will love. There is no need at all to read supercilious indifference into Simon's reply (v. 43), and it is unnecessary to suppose that his treatment of Jesus had been discourteous; he had performed the duties of hospitality but had not gone out of his way to give Jesus a special welcome. By contrast the sinful woman had lavished her devotion upon Jesus. This was proof that she had been forgiven many sins (*cf.* v. 47, NEB).

Jesus then proceeded to confirm her forgiveness by a clear declaration and to assert that her faith had brought her salvation. Many commentators, especially an older generation of

Roman Catholics, have held that the woman's love for Jesus was the *cause* of her forgiveness rather than its result. They would interpret v. 47 as 'the reason why her sins are forgiven is because she loved much' and see in v. 48 the first intimation of forgiveness to her. This interpretation is unquestionably wrong. It makes nonsense of the parable (vv. 41f.) which shows that love *follows* forgiveness, and it ignores the stress on faith in v. 50. It arises from failure to recognize that 'to love' is the Hebrew phrase for 'to show gratitude'. We must assume rather that the woman had already heard and received the gospel from Jesus.

The story is not to be identified with that in the other Gospels.

37 The woman would easily be able to reach Jesus as He reclined on a couch at the table. **38** The woman's actions were unseemly, but she was too much under emotional stress to care what people thought. **41** The *denarius* was roughly an agricultural worker's daily wage. **46** Olive *oil* was vastly cheaper than *ointment*. **50** *Saved* must be taken spiritually.

8:1-21 Jesus teaches in parables

8:1-3 Travelling arrangements. This brief paragraph notes how Jesus began to travel round the countryside after a period of fairly settled ministry. Various women took part in the campaign and helped to provide for the necessities of the missionaries (*cf.* Mk. 15:40f.); there is a thematic link between v. 2 and the story of the woman who anointed Jesus, but nothing suggests that it was Mary Magdalene who anointed Jesus.

1 *Cf.* 4:44; Mt. 9:35. **2** Magdala was a village near Capernaum. *Seven* is a round number, indicating the worst possible state of corruption; *cf.* 11:26. **3** Joanna: *cf.* on 9:9; 24:10.

8:4-8 The parable of the sower. (See Mt. 13:1-9; Mk. 4:1-9.) After giving us stories not found in Mark (6:20 – 8:3), Luke now returns to the general framework in Mark and follows it to 9:50, omitting many details found in Mark. Thus he has not mentioned the lakeside scene in which Mark sets the parables of Jesus. The first parable is a simple description of the varying fortunes of seeds sown broadcast over a field which contains different kinds of soil. Nothing is said regarding the meaning of the parable: the people were meant to ask themselves: 'What is all this about?'

4 The word *parable* is used in the OT to describe any kind of non-literal utterance, including oracles, similes, fables and stories, and riddles. Similar stories were told by Jewish teachers, although their parables fell far below those of Jesus in quality. The 'parables' of Jesus included metaphors and similes (*e.g.* 5:36-39), proverbs (*e.g.* 4:23), typical happenings (as here) and particular events (*e.g.* 10:30-37) which were used to illustrate the nature of God's acts (*e.g.* 13:18-21) and the kind of response that men ought to make to them (*e.g.* 16:1-9).

8:9-15 The meaning of the parable. (See Mt. 13:10-23; Mk. 4:10-20.) When the disciples later asked Jesus what the parable meant, He began by giving a general statement on the use of parables. Those who responded to His teaching had been given a knowledge of His purposes by God: *secrets* means the plans of God for the outworking of His kingdom which had long been hidden from men but were now made known to those whom He chose. Other people refused to accept Jesus' message, and therefore it was presented to them in a veiled form, so that, if they did not make the effort to understand it, they would be none the wiser; thus they would fulfil the prophecy in Is. 6:9f. about men who do not understand the meaning of what they hear.

The wording of the explanation of the parable of the sower differs from that in Mark, and Luke has no doubt stressed certain elements that were important for his readers. He brings out the need for the coming of God's word to be met by faith and perseverance if the hearers are to be the kind of ground which produces good fruit. In some men's hearts the seed may never get a chance to germinate, in others its growth is arrested because they fail to endure.

8:16-18 The parable of the lamp. (See Mk. 4:21-25.) The audience is presumably again the general public. The application of the parable of the lamp is obscure. It may refer to the need for the disciples to reveal to others the light they have received, or to the way in which the teaching of Jesus, now conveyed obscurely in parables, will one day be clearly expressed. *Those who enter* may be the Gentiles. **18** brings out the meaning of v. 10: receptive listening leads to fuller understanding, but refusal to listen will mean deprivation of even the opportunity to listen.

8:19-21 Jesus' true relatives. (See Mt. 12:46-50; Mk. 3:31-35.) Luke has placed this incident here (in Mark it *precedes* the parables) to illustrate how men should respond to the teaching of Jesus. Those who receive it obediently are accepted by Him as on a level with physical relatives. The saying does not of course imply any denigration of His relatives; their presence simply provided Him with an object lesson.

19 The *brothers* were Mary's later children by Joseph (*cf.* 2:7; Mt. 1:25) who was probably now dead.

8:22-56 A group of mighty works

8:22-25 The master of the storm. (See Mt. 8:23-27; Mk. 4:35-41.) The lake of Galilee is surrounded by steep mountains with narrow valleys down which the wind is funnelled in sudden, strong squalls. When Jesus lay unconcernedly asleep while the boat was awash, the disciples roused Him, apparently in the hope that He would do something to help them. His answer implied that they should have known that, even if He was asleep, no harm could come to them, but nevertheless He arose and masterfully addressed the elements. The disciples rightly asked, *Who then is this . . . ?* The answer is that God rules the waves, and His power was at work in Jesus (Ps. 89:8f.; 93:3f.; 106:8f.; 107:23ff.; Is. 51:9f.). But they did not yet fully realize this.

8:26–39 The Gerasene demoniac. (See Mt. 8:28–34; Mk. 5:1–20.) On arrival at the other side Jesus was met by a man suffering from a manic-depressive psychosis associated with demonic possession, which gave him an uncanny insight into who Jesus was. Human medicine knew no better cure for the mentally ill than to keep them under the severest restraint, but this man had eluded all attempts to control him. He was driven by such a mass of conflicting impulses that he felt himself to be possessed by a legion of some 5,000 demons. Jesus had compassion on him and freed him from the demons who entered into a herd of swine. Critics have demurred at the loss of the swine, but it is an adequate reply that one man is worth many swine. Others have suggested that the rational explanation of the incident is that it was the rampagings of the demoniac which frightened the herd into a stampede. If, however, the fact of demon-possession is accepted (*cf.* on 4:33), it would be unwise to brush aside the explanation given by the Evangelists when we have no means of knowing whether any other theory is true.

The people around were alarmed and frightened by the whole affair, and besought Jesus to depart. Their minds were so filled with fear at the incursion of the supernatural into their daily life that they could not see through to the grace and mercy of God. This was surely why Jesus urged the cured man to stay at home; if the people were frightened of Him personally, they would listen to a man whom they knew and hear from him of God's goodness revealed in Jesus.

26 The name of the place varies in the MSS. The best authorities treat it as Gerasa, a city some 30 miles south-east of the lake; its territory could have reached to the lakeside. Others refer to Gadara (only 6 miles from the lake) or to Gergesa (modern Khersa) on the lakeside, which was probably the actual site of the incident. **27** The *tombs* were caves in which a man might shelter. **31** The *abyss* is the abode of demons (Rev. 9:1–11). Here it is a place of confinement or punishment. **32** In a largely Gentile area the keeping of *swine* would not be strange.

8:40–56 The healings of Jairus's daughter and the woman with a haemorrhage. (See Mt. 9:18–26; Mk. 5:21–43.) Back on the Jewish side of the lake Jesus found a ruler of the synagogue anxious for His help for his sick daughter. His journey to Jairus's house was interrupted by an incident which should have confirmed the nascent faith of Jairus, but perhaps simply made him impatient at the delay. The newcomer was a woman with a haemorrhage which refused to yield to treatment. Since her disease made her religiously unclean, she was afraid to approach Jesus openly, but she had sufficient faith to hope that mere physical contact with Him would heal

her. We may be tempted to dismiss her belief as superstitious, but Jesus did not. His healing power (v. 46, AV 'virtue') did not flow from Him automatically at a touch, but was under His control, and He responded instinctively to the faith which He felt to be present. Then He summoned the woman into the open so that He might complete the cure by restoring her self-respect and making her relationship with Him one that was fully personal and free from the suspicion of superstition.

The delay seemed to spell doom for Jairus's hopes, for now news came that Jesus was going to be too late. But Jesus assured him that this was not the end. At the house He went in quietly to the dead girl, and a word from Him restored her to life. The fact of her recovery could hardly be kept secret, but Jesus wished for the privacy to be as great as possible; nobody need know just what had happened in the sick-room. It was His occupational hazard in performing miracles that people might believe in Him as a wonder-worker because of the power which He displayed instead of believing in Him as the Son of God and the Saviour of the world because of the revelation of divine love in Him.

41 The *ruler of the synagogue* arranged the synagogue services and its other affairs; his wishes were executed by the attendant (4:20). **42** Attempts to deny that the girl really died go against the whole tenor of the story (*cf.* v. 49). **43** Luke does not mention that the woman had tried many doctors in vain; but it is not clear whether this is simply due to his habit of abbreviation or to a desire to remove a possible slur from his profession. **52** Funeral rites took place with great speed in the ancient East (*cf.* Acts 5:5–7), and the mourning would have commenced as soon as the girl died. **55** The command to give food may be a demonstration that the girl was really alive, but more probably shows the human compassion of Jesus.

9:1–50 Jesus and the Twelve

9:1–9 The mission of the Twelve. (See Mt. 10:5–15; 14:1–12; Mk. 6:7–29.) The expansion of Jesus' work (8:1) gave Him the opportunity to give the Twelve practical training. Equipped with His authority they were to do His work of preaching and healing. They were to live frugally, perhaps so as to avoid the reproach of making a good thing out of their mission, and to avoid being mistaken for other less reputable types of wandering preacher. They were not to go from house to house seeking hospitality; if a town did not receive them, they were to do what Jews did when leaving a Gentile town, so as to indicate by an acted parable that the inhabitants were cutting themselves off from the true Israel.

Between the missionaries' departure and return Luke notes the opinions which men were now holding about Jesus, and thus prepares for the question in v. 18. Herod Antipas was inclined by his guilty conscience to accept the view that perhaps John the Baptist had returned from the dead. But his longing to see Jesus was scarcely motivated by a lofty purpose (23:8).

1 Luke omits the story in Mk. 6:1–6; see 4:16–30. 3 Mk. 6:8 allows the use of a *staff*; this will be an adaptation of Jesus' teaching for more rigorous conditions outside Galilee. AV 'scrip' means 'bag'. 8 For the return of *Elijah* see 1:17. 9 Here Herod comes short of identifying John and Jesus; contrast Mk. 6:16. Luke seems to have had fuller details about Herod, possibly from Joanna (*cf.* 8:3).

9:10–17 The feeding of the five thousand. (See Mt. 14:13–21; Mk. 6:30–44; Jn. 6:1–14.) Jesus had hoped to take the Twelve away for rest after their mission, but the crowds thwarted the scheme, and Jesus took the opportunity to teach them. At the end of the day the disciples were anxious about the crowds; they themselves had a pitifully small amount of food and certainly not the money to provide for such numbers. Jesus, however, took what was available, and having given thanks in the normal Jewish way He broke and distributed the food. The story is told simply as an indication of the power of Jesus; Mark and John bring out more clearly that it reveals Jesus as the Supplier of human needs, the Giver of bread from heaven.

10 *Bethsaida*, at the head of the lake, was the destination of the disciples after the feeding (Mk. 6:45); the feeding must have taken place in its vicinity. 12 Luke alone mentions the need to find somewhere *to lodge*; the people would camp out or seek near-by hamlets. 16 Jesus *blessed* not the loaves (as AV implies) but God; the Jewish grace is 'Blessed art thou, O Lord our God, King of the world, who bringest forth bread from the earth.'

9:18–27 The Person and destiny of Jesus. (See Mt. 16:13–28; Mk. 8:27 – 9:1.) Luke omits the stories about Jesus which occur in Matthew and Mark between the feeding of the five thousand and Peter's confession; he may have felt that they added nothing distinctive to the picture of Jesus which has already been given. The reader has seen sufficient to be able to appreciate why Peter, speaking on behalf of the disciples, confessed that Jesus was the Christ (or Messiah) rather than simply a prophet, even a prophet raised from the dead. The fact that Jesus told them not to reveal this to anybody means that He accepted Peter's estimate of Himself. The reason for this command to secrecy was to prevent misunderstanding of the Messianic claim in a political sense.

But now a new fact must be learned. He must endure suffering and death and be raised from the dead. The Jews do not seem to have thought of anything like this happening to the Messiah, and the disciples themselves never grasped the meaning of Jesus' words that He must suffer as many righteous men suffered and above all perfectly fulfil the prophecy of the suffering Servant of Yahweh. It consequently took them a long time to realize also that the disciples of the Messiah must be prepared to suffer. If they

seek to save their (earthly) lives, they will lose the life that really matters, but if they are prepared to lay down their lives for Jesus, they will know real life. For on the day of judgment those who loved their earthly lives so much that they despised Jesus will find themselves rejected. 22 Jesus' favourite title for Himself was *the Son of man* (5:24; 6:5, 22; 7:34). The Jewish Messiah was a human figure, but the Son of man (Dn. 7:9–22) is a heavenly figure and is better fitted to express the role of Jesus. Jesus' concept of His function was so different from that of popular Messianism that He avoided open use of the title. He also reinterpreted the functions of the Son of man by speaking not only of His activity on the day of judgment (v. 26) but also of His suffering (Is. 52:13 – 53:12). 27 The reference of this saying is somewhat uncertain. It can hardly mean that Jesus expected the end of the world within the lifetime of His hearers; it may refer to the coming of the kingdom in His own ministry or in the life of the church, but the position of the saying suggests that it refers to the transfiguration as an event prophetic of Jesus' future exaltation.

9:28–36 The transfiguration of Jesus. (See Mt. 17:1–8; Mk. 9:2–8.) The very precise time note shows that the transfiguration must be linked closely with the preceding saying (v. 27). As Jesus was praying on a mountain, His appearance and garments took on a heavenly lustre, and He was joined by two men, long before departed from this world, who spoke with Him about His departure (Gk. *exodos*), *i.e.* His death (AV 'decease') and resurrection, thus confirming the prophecy made in v. 22. Peter felt that they should make three 'booths' or tabernacles for the heavenly visitors, either to honour them or to prolong their stay. But the narrator expressly comments that Peter had misunderstood the occasion. The true significance is to be found in the heavenly voice which assured the disciples that the Jesus whom they confessed to be the Messiah was indeed the Son of God, not despite His coming passion but because of it; they were to obey Him—and Him alone.

28 *Eight days* means 'a week'; Mk. 9:2 has 'six days'. 29 Luke alone records that Jesus was *praying* and thus in contact with the heavenly world. Is the story an account of how the disciples' eyes were opened to see what was happening when Jesus communed with His Father (*cf.* 2 Ki. 6:17)? 30 Jewish tradition expected both *Moses* and *Elijah* to reappear at the end of time. They represented the law and the prophets, and both had unusual departures from this world. 34 A *cloud* regularly symbolizes the presence of God. 35 The *voice* repeats the address at the baptism of Jesus, but this time speaks to the disciples. 36 Luke has omitted the conversation on the way down from the mountain, as well as all geographical indications.

9:37–50 Experiences in the valley. (See Mt. 17:14–23; 18:1–5; Mk. 9:14–41.) In this final section on the work of Jesus in Galilee a number of incidents all show the need of the disciples for power and instruction. **37–43a** In the first story a boy suffering from epilepsy and demonic possession had been brought to the disciples who had not accompanied Jesus on the mountain, and the case had proved to be beyond their healing powers (9:1). The boy was then brought to Jesus who expressed His sorrow at the faithlessness and perversity of men who required His personal presence before the power of God could operate. The act of healing amazed the people with its revelation of the greatness of God's power.

43b–45 A swift contrast to this revelation was given by the words of Jesus in which He again told the disciples that the Son of man must suffer rather than make His way through the world in triumph. Like Mark, Luke stresses the obtuseness of the disciples who found this teaching beyond their grasp and attributes it to the purpose of God.

46–48 Two further incidents stress this lack of comprehension. The first shows the disciples quarrelling about rank and position among themselves. Even disciples could have ambitions of this kind, and Jesus was able to penetrate to the elemental motives that struggled for mastery in their hearts. Setting a child—the most insignificant member of society in Jewish eyes—in their midst, He said that the person who was humble enough to receive a child would receive Himself and His Father. When men have that kind of attitude, questions of precedence will not arise.

In this connection John remembered how they had treated a man who was casting out demons in the power of the name of Jesus and yet was not one of the Twelve (vv. 49f.). He was not to be despised, said Jesus, for a man who is not against Him is on His side; the saying in 11:23 shows that there is another side to this truth.

9:51 – 19:10 THE JOURNEY TO JERUSALEM

Luke omits the incidents recorded in Mk. 9:42 – 10:12 and does not return to the outline of events in Mark until 18:15. Instead he gives much material which is not in Mark. The impression is given of a journey to Jerusalem which covers the next chapters (contrast the briefer account in Mk. 10), but it is difficult to believe that all that is recorded here took place on one journey. Some of the incidents and sayings given here seem to belong to Galilee or Jerusalem, and it is likely that Luke has gathered together material from various periods in the ministry of Jesus and grouped it thematically at this point. (Compare the procedure of Matthew in his 'great discourses'.) We also know from John that Jesus paid several visits to Jerusalem, and it is probable that this section of Luke reflects details of a number of journeys to Jerusalem rather than just one. The general theme of the section is discipleship, and this is expressed against the background of following Jesus to Jerusalem.

9:51 – 10:24 The duties and privileges of discipleship

9:51–56 The Samaritan village. Jews and Samaritans deeply hated each other, but Jesus refused to meet human opposition with judgment (*cf.* 2 Ki. 1:10f.). The additional words recorded in RSV mg. (and AV) in v. 56 are not a true part of Luke's text, but express accurately the mind of Jesus: He suffered opposition without retaliation because He had come to save.

51 *To be received up* is used of the total event of passion, death and ascension. *He set his face*: Is. 50:7. **52** Were the messengers to arrange an evangelistic meeting?

9:57–62 Readiness for discipleship. (See Mt. 8:19–22.) Many men wish to follow Jesus, even to Jerusalem, until they find out what is involved. Jesus' reply to the first would-be disciple speaks of the homelessness of the Son of man and His disciples. Since many friends provided for the material needs of Jesus, the saying refers metaphorically to His being rejected by men. A second man was told that he must not make any excuses for delay. The third had to be told that there can be no turning back in the service of Jesus, any more than a backward-looking ploughman can expect to produce a straight furrow. All three sayings stress the idea of absolute commitment to Jesus.

60 means 'Let that duty look after itself' or 'Leave that task to the spiritually dead'. **61** is more rigorous than 1 Ki. 19:19–21.

10:1–16 The mission of the Seventy. (*Cf.* Mt. 9:37f.; 10:7–16; 11:21–23.) Only Luke records that in addition to the Twelve Jesus sent out a further group to do mission work for Him. He addressed them in words similar to those with which He sent out the Twelve (9:1–6). After speaking of the richness of the harvest to be gathered, He indicated paradoxically that they were going out in simplicity among a ravenous horde of wolves who would frustrate their work. They were to travel lightly like the Twelve and not to waste time in long, oriental salutations. They were to accept the hospitality given to them as their 'wages', but were not to seek for better conditions by going from one house to another. Their message was that the kingdom of God had arrived; the tokens of its presence were the works of healing which they performed. Where the message was not received, a warning of divine judgment was to be uttered. As if in parenthesis, Jesus then alluded to the towns which had refused His own preaching and soliloquized upon their fate at the day of judgment. Heathen towns of old would have given a warmer response to the gospel than these Jewish towns; their pride would experience a swift downfall. Then, finally, He emphasized that the disciples were to be His personal representatives and consequently God's representatives.

1 The MSS here and in v. 17 (and in other passages also) are divided in reading *seventy* or 'seventy-two', with the latter having slightly better support. The number may allude to the number of nations in Gn. 10 or to the seventy elders (Ex. 24:1). **6** A *son of peace* is a peace-loving man, one worthy of the Messianic gift of peace. Note how real power resides in a word of blessing. **7** See 1 Cor. 9:14. Jesus taught that those who receive the gospel should provide for the evangelist. The early church carried out the principle by providing for its teachers and evangelists so that they would not be dependent on those whom they evangelized (3 Jn. 7f.). Paul sought to impose no burden at all on his churches, although he was fully entitled to do so (1 Cor. 9:14) and quoted this text in connection with the rights of elders (1 Tim. 5:18). **9** *Has come near* (Gk. *ēngiken*): when the gospel is proclaimed, the blessings of God's rule are within the grasp of all who will accept them; cf. Mk. 1:15. **11** The missionaries disclaim further responsibility after having clearly presented the message. **13** *Chorazin*, a town north of Capernaum, not mentioned elsewhere in the Gospels. **16** Cf. 9:48; Jn. 15:23.

10:17–24 The return of the Seventy. (See Mt. 11:25–27; 13:16f.) When the missionaries joyfully returned, having found that their healing powers even extended to exorcism, Jesus saw a sign that Satan's throne was toppling. Yet it would be wrong to rejoice too much over this; men may cast out demons and yet be excluded from the kingdom (cf. Mt. 7:22f.). Far better to rejoice that one's name is recorded in God's book.

Then Jesus rejoiced and thanked God for His revelation given to ordinary men in accordance with His purpose which does not take account of human wisdom. His prayer culminates in the great saying confessing that all such knowledge has been given to Him by His Father; there is an exclusive, mutual bond of personal knowledge between the Father and the Son, so that only the Son can make the Father known to men. The disciples have received this knowledge from the Son; the men of the past would gladly have seen the coming of the kingdom, but only the disciples had been granted to see and hear the Son of God.

18 Cf. Rev. 12:7–10. Jesus is speaking metaphorically. He has a vision of the spiritual defeat of Satan which took place at the cross; and the exorcisms, the defeat of Satan's minions, confirm His certainty of the coming victory over their master. **19** *Serpents and scorpions* are symbolical of spiritual wickedness: Dt. 8:15; Ps. 91:13. **20** Cf. Phil. 4:3. **22** The slight difference in wording from Mt. 11:27 does not affect the meaning. The authenticity of the saying has been much attacked, but it is being increasingly recognized that the language is thoroughly Jewish. *All things* means 'all revelation' rather than 'all power'. The word *know* is used in Hebrew to express personal knowledge (*e.g.* Gn. 4:1 of the marriage relationship) or choice (Am. 3:2); here it expresses the personal communion between Jesus and His Father, reflected in the prayer of Jesus

(cf. Mk. 14:36), as a result of which Jesus alone is qualified to reveal the Father to men. The saying is thoroughly in keeping with Jesus' teaching in John (e.g. Jn. 10:15).

10:25 – 11:13 The characteristics of disciples

10:25–37 The good Samaritan. The story is not to be confused with the different one in Mk. 12:28–31. Here Jesus is asked about how a man may qualify for eternal life (cf. 18:18) and He replies by referring His questioner in good Jewish fashion to the law. The question then becomes one of summarizing the essence and purport of the law. The lawyer gives the same reply as that given by Jesus in Mk. 12:29–31, a fact which should not surprise us, since there is evidence that the Jews had already coupled Dt. 6:5 and Lv. 19:18 before the time of Jesus. In view of Gal. 3:12 Jesus' answer may sound legalistic, but it is not so when considered in the total content of His teaching.

The lawyer had 'lost face' by being given this textbook answer, and tried to regain the initiative by demanding a more precise definition of his neighbour. The parable given in reply is most remarkable. One commentator has suggested that we would expect to hear a parable which tells how a Jew should show love to anybody, even to a Samaritan, but in fact Jesus shows how even a Samaritan may be nearer to the kingdom than a pious, but merciless, Jew. For although the lawyer asked '*Who* is my neighbour (passively understood)?' Jesus suggests that the real question is rather 'Do *I* behave as a neighbour (active sense)?' In other words, Jesus does not supply information as to whom one should help, for failure to keep the commandment does not spring from lack of information but from lack of love. It was not fresh knowledge that the lawyer needed, but a new heart—in plain English, conversion.

30 A steep road, 17 miles long, descended the 3,300 ft from Jerusalem to Jericho, which was a country dwelling of priests (cf. 1:23). The story may well be based on fact. **31, 32** The priest and Levite may have feared defilement by touching a corpse. **33** The audience no doubt expected that the third character would be a Jewish layman, thus giving an anti-clerical point to the story. **37** The lawyer could not bring himself to say 'the Samaritan'!

10:38–42 Serving Jesus. Martha was busily preparing supper while Mary listened to the teaching of Jesus. When Martha rudely complained to the guest about her lazy sister, Jesus replied gently but firmly. Martha, He said, was busy trying to provide an elaborate supper with many dishes when only one course would be sufficient. Mary had chosen to listen to Jesus, and that was more important than preparing a large supper. The story is not meant to show the value of the contemplative life compared with the life of action, but to teach that service to Jesus must not be misdirected to such an extent that a person has no time to learn from

Him; one honours Him more by listening to Him than by providing excessively for His needs. *Cf.* Jn. 6:27.

38 Since the *village* was Bethany on the outskirts of Jerusalem (Jn. 11:1), the incident took place before Jesus' last visit to Jerusalem or is not recorded in chronological order. **41** The text is uncertain, but the meaning is clear. **42** *Good* is Semitic for 'better'.

11:1-13 How to pray. (See Mt. 6:9-13; 7:7-11.) Christian prayer goes back to the example and precept of Jesus Himself. His own prayer was the occasion for the disciples to ask Him how to pray. He replied with the Lord's Prayer which appears here in a different form from the more familiar version in Matthew. It is not certain whether Jesus gave His disciples two versions of the prayer or the early church adapted His original words in different ways to meet its needs. Luke's form is the shorter; it contains an address and two sets of petitions. **2** *Father* is the translation of the Aramaic *Abba* used by Jesus (*cf.* 10:21; Mk. 14:36); here, therefore, Jesus introduces His disciples to the same intimate relationship with the Father which He enjoyed. *Hallowed be thy name* is the first of two petitions concerned with God Himself. May His name, which represents His Person, be honoured and accepted in the world of men. Such hallowing forms the basis for the second petition: *Thy kingdom come.* May God's rule in peace and righteousness swiftly come about. It is a prayer for God to act by hastening the coming of the day of the Lord. Only after these petitions are the needs of the petitioner mentioned. **3** First, there is a prayer for the supply of *daily bread each day*. Commentators increasingly see here a petition not simply for ordinary food (though this is included) but for the bread of life, the gift of God without which man cannot live. (*Daily* (Gk. *epiousios*) is a word of uncertain meaning: 'for the morrow' or 'necessary' are possible renderings. The former brings out the way in which the prayer asks for a foretaste of the blessings of the kingdom now.) **4** Second, there is the prayer for daily forgiveness, which is granted only to those who forgive others. Finally, the petitioner asks to be preserved from tribulation and testing which would weaken his faith and exclude him from God's kingdom.

The prayer is followed by parables whose purpose is to encourage men to pray. **5ff.** Although the friend who has *bread* (*cf.* v. 3!) in his house is asleep and unwilling to get up, yet because of the unblushing persistence of the caller the bread will be supplied. It is a parable of contrast: if even a human friend will respond to importunity, how much more will God respond *without importunity*, even if He seems to delay (*cf.* 18:1-8)? **7** A one-roomed house is envisaged. **11ff.** Just as earthly fathers do not deceive their children in their gifts, so God will give His good gift of the Spirit to all who ask. With these assurances confident prayer can be a reality. *Fish* and *serpents*, and *eggs* and

scorpions resemble one another in appearance.

11:14-54 Opposition to Jesus

11:14-28 In league with the devil? (See Mt. 12:22-30, 43-45; Mk. 3:22-27.) **14-23** The performance of miracles does not automatically lead to belief. The Pharisees thought that they could explain away the exorcisms performed by Jesus by attributing them to the devil and demanded some more certain sign from Him. Jesus replied that a kingdom or household divided against itself soon comes to nothing. It was, therefore, preposterous to suggest that Satan, alias Beelzebul, was promoting civil war in his own kingdom. Moreover, the argument could equally well be turned against Jesus' opponents themselves, for their own 'sons', *i.e.* pupils, also performed exorcisms. In fact the casting out of demons was an act of divine power and a sure token that God's era of salvation had come. One stronger than Satan was stripping him of his armour and delivering his captives. In this situation to refuse support to Jesus was not to take up a position of neutrality but to join the opposition.

14 *Cf.* Mt. 9:32-34. **15** Beelzebul (AV 'Beelzebub' is due to the influence of 1 Ki. 1:2f.) was a name for the devil. **20** *Cf.* Ex. 8:19; Ps. 8:3.

24-26 The following parable of the empty house is added at this point because of its subject-matter. Dry *waterless places* were regarded as the normal abode of demons, but they preferred human habitation. The point of the story, however, is not to give interesting facts about demonic ecology but to warn against the fearful danger of a repentance that is purely negative. A relapse can lead to dreadful danger. What is needed is 'the expulsive power of a new affection'.

Opinions differ as to whether this story is meant to be taken literally or as a parable of spiritual deterioration. For *seven* see on 8:2.

27, 28 Mark has a different story at this point (Mk. 3:31-35), which Luke has told already (8:19-21) and which teaches the same lesson as the brief incident now recorded. The woman's rather sentimental benediction on Jesus' mother meant, 'If only I had such a son as this.' Jesus' reply is that something else matters far more—namely, to hear the message He proclaimed and to obey it (*cf.* 6:46-49). The Pharisees should have perceived that He was speaking God's word without wonderful signs to confirm it, and acceptance of it would prevent the kind of relapse described in v. 26.

11:29-32 The sign of Jonah. (See Mt. 12:38-42.) Jesus has now answered the charge made in v. 15, and the present section forms a reply to the question in v. 16. **29** The people wanted some miraculous demonstration to attest the message of Jesus, but He was unwilling to accredit Himself or His words by deeds of power that would overawe men, but only by works that would reveal the character of His Father as Judge and Saviour. He therefore refused to give any sign at all (Mk. 8:11f.) except for *the sign of Jonah*. **30** Only in the way in which Jonah was a sign to Nineveh would He be a sign to the Jews. **31** The meaning of this sign is explained by the parallel saying about the *queen of the South* (*cf.* 1 Ki. 10:1–10, where she came from Sheba in SW Arabia); she would be a witness against the Jews of Jesus' time, for she made great efforts to hear Solomon and yet the Jews were not impressed by the wisdom of one greater than Solomon. Similarly, the men of Nineveh responded to the preaching of Jonah, and yet the Jews failed to respond to the preaching of Jesus. The 'sign of Jonah' is thus the preaching of Jesus. But there is a deeper implication. The use of the future tense in v. 30 and the way in which Mt. 12:39f. mentions the resurrection of Jesus as a parallel to the resuscitation of Jonah suggest that the sign is the preaching of the *risen* Jesus or possibly the *parousia*.

11:33–36 Light and darkness. (See Mt. 5:15; 6:22f.) This little group of sayings is not easy to understand. In v. 34 the eye is regarded as the means by which light reaches a man's personality; a healthy eye lets light in, but an unhealthy eye leaves a man in darkness. The hearers of Jesus must be sure that what they accept as light really is light and not darkness (v. 35). Then v. 36 may mean that the person who is full of true light will himself illuminate others. But what about v. 33 (*cf.* 8:16–18)? The saying may urge the hearers not to hide the light which they have received (Mt. 5:15), or may refer to Israel which had hidden the light God gave her (*cf.* v. 52), or (most probably) it may be a reference to the light shining from Jesus which the people were unwilling to receive. The whole paragraph, therefore, is a warning against spiritual blindness and hardness of heart.

11:37–54 The hypocrisy of the Pharisees and scribes. (See Mt. 23:4–7, 13, 23–36; *cf.* Lk. 20:46.) More than once in Luke Jesus visited the homes of Pharisees (*cf.* 7:36; 14:1), here for one of the two daily meals. He did not wash before eating, a practice that was not primarily connected with hygiene but with removing sinful defilement through contact with Gentiles and other sinners (Mk. 7:1–5). He justified His conduct in a speech that was very critical of the Pharisees and what they stood for. In cleansing their bodies (v. 39), the Pharisees resembled a man cleaning only the outside of a vessel full of filth. If God made both the inside and the outside of man, surely both demanded cleansing. Instead of showing rapacity and wickedness, the Pharisees should give alms and then they would be truly clean in their hearts.

In a series of three woes (vv. 42–44) the failings of the Pharisees are exposed. They so concentrated on the tiny details of religion that they forgot the great moral principles. They had grown to love the respect of men for their religiosity. They were as a result hypocrites who misled men, just like hidden graves which men might tread on and hence be contaminated.

The lawyers (see on 5:17), condemned by what Jesus had already said, had further charges brought against them. They created the pettifogging regulations of the law, and either did nothing to relieve the burden or failed to shoulder it themselves. Although they built elaborate tombs for the prophets, they were really at one with their ancestors who had killed them by making sure that they stayed dead! God in His wisdom had foreseen what they would do; their attitude to the prophets and apostles of the church would simply be the culmination of a long history of persecution of His messengers, and judgment would follow. Finally, the lawyers stood condemned for obscuring God's revelation and keeping men out of His kingdom. It is no wonder that after this denunciation they plotted against Jesus.

41 *Give for alms* may be Luke's interpretation of 'cleanse' (Mt. 23:26). **42** The Pharisees went beyond the law's requirements in their tithes. **43** This saying must refer to Pharisees who were scribes (*cf.* 20:46). **48** Building tombs is scarcely sympathy with murder; the saying is metaphorical and ironical. **49–51** Probably a saying from a different context, since it disturbs the structure of the three 'woes'. **51** For *Zechariah* see 2 Ch. 24:20f. and on Mt. 23:35.

12:1 – 13:9 Readiness for the coming crisis

In this and later sections (17:20 – 18:8; 21:5–38) Luke has gathered together teaching in which Jesus spoke of the crisis that was coming upon men as a result of His ministry. The gospel of salvation had its dark side for those who refused the message. Jesus warned the Jews of the fearful consequences of rejecting Him, both in terms of political destruction and in terms of rejection by God on the day of judgment. At the same time He warned His disciples to stand firm in the days of trial that lay ahead and to be ready for the coming of their Master. In the event, destruction came upon Judea in the war with Rome (AD 66–70), but the return of the Lord is still awaited. Difficulties of interpretation arise because Jesus closely linked these two events as parts of one great act of God, but it should be remembered that Jesus confessed ignorance of the precise times settled by the Father (Mk. 13:32).

12:1–12 Fearless confession. (See Mt. 10:26–33; 12:31f.; 10:19f.; *cf.* Mk. 3:28f.) The opening verse links with the previous section on the Pharisees; their teaching acted like leaven or yeast in its penetrating effects upon society, and had a corrupting influence because of its hypocrisy. But all men must beware of hypocrisy, for one day the hidden thoughts of men will be revealed.

Disciples, however, might be tempted to a different kind of dissimulation, that of hiding their allegiance to Jesus out of fear. But it is far worse to be hypocritical and then have to face the judgment of God, who can cast men into Gehenna, than to suffer at the hands of men. There is indeed no reason to fear men, for not even the worst that persecution can devise can take place without God's knowledge and care for men.

Men, therefore, have the alternatives of confessing or denying Jesus, and corresponding to their choice will be the decision of the Son of man to be witness for or against them at the heavenly judgment seat. In v. 10, however, it is stated that denial of the Son of man is a pardonable offence. It would seem that v. 9 is addressed to disciples who have no excuse for ignorance about the significance of Jesus, but v. 10 is addressed to the crowds for whom the Son of man was a phrase which did not necessarily disclose who Jesus really was. If, however, they refused to accept the clear evidence of the working of God's Holy Spirit in Jesus (*e.g.* by attributing His power to Satan), then they were sinning against the light and liable to judgment. But if a man does confess Jesus, then the Holy Spirit will sustain him when on trial before men whom he would otherwise fear.

1 *First*: the sayings are addressed especially to disciples. **2** *Cf.* 8:17. **6** Mt. 10:29 has 'two sparrows for a penny'; the point is the same. **8, 9** Jesus appears to speak of the Son of man as somebody different from Himself. That this was the case is most unlikely, and it is probable that this was part of His attempt to avoid making open declarations about the divine significance of His Person to the crowds. **10** A change of audience at this point (see above) is not explicitly mentioned, but is not unlikely in view of the way in which the Evangelists gathered together Jesus' teaching thematically.

12:13–34 Material possessions. (See Mt. 6:25–33, 19–21.) Since Jesus was commonly regarded as a Rabbi, it is not surprising that His opinion was sought upon a legal matter, a dispute over property; probably a younger brother was being defrauded of his share in an inheritance. Jesus refused to decide the matter, for He was not an ordained Rabbi. He did, however, go to the root of the matter by giving a stern warning against covetousness, which may well have been motivated by His personal knowledge of the man in question. Covetousness, or the desire to have more than one has (not necessarily through envy of somebody else) not only leads to strife but also expresses a fundamentally wrong philosophy of life, according to which possessions are all that really matter. It only needs God to take away the life of a man who thinks that he can retire in comfort and ease thanks to a bumper harvest, and at once it becomes apparent how useless possessions can be. Money cannot buy everything. The rich man had failed to acquire the true riches of a right relationship to God (one step in which would certainly be to give to the poor, v. 33!), and so he was a fool, a godless and therefore a senseless man.

How, then, should possessions be regarded? The disciples should not worry about food and clothing (the two essential requirements of the body) as if they were the most important things in the world. The man himself is more important. If God feeds even carefree birds and clothes the flowers, surely He will all the more provide what is necessary for His children. In any case, what good is it to be anxious about these things, when worry cannot make a man live any longer? In a world in which men are set on the rat-race for superior living conditions, let the disciples first seek God's will and His salvation, and they will find that bodily needs are taken care of. Let them sell their possessions and give to the needy, and set their hearts on a heavenly treasure that will not pass away.

Such teaching may seem to encourage laziness and lack of concern about worldly things— 'God will provide; I don't need to do anything.' It is, however, not addressed to the lazy but to the worried and to those who are tempted to join the rat-race. They are urged to trust in God and to get their priorities right.

13 The lawyers or Rabbis dealt with both religious and civil matters. **25** *Span of life* and 'stature' (AV, RSV mg.) are equally valid translations, but the former fits the context better. **31** To *seek* God's *kingdom* is to set one's aim in life on God Himself and the accomplishment of His purpose of bringing in His rule with all its blessings. To all such seekers God has promised that He will fulfil their longings.

12:35–48 The coming of the Son of man. (See Mt. 24:43–51.) From the thought of the way in which men should set their minds on the kingdom of God Jesus turns to consider their attitude to the future. The great event to which they look forward, bringing with it both the judgment (vv. 8f.) and the kingdom, is the coming of the Son of man (v. 40) at an unexpected and unknown hour. The disciples must be ready for this event by being diligently engaged in the service of their Master. Like servants left in charge of the household, they must be ready to greet Him when He appears. If they are ready, He Himself will reward them by serving them. A second, extremely brief parable speaks of the situation of a householder who is surprised by the invasion of a burglar. This depicts the other side of the expectation, and illustrates the serious effects of the coming of the Son of man for those who are not ready.

But for whom is this teaching meant? Speaking as it does of the Master's servants, does it refer to all of them or merely to the leaders of them? Jesus appears to have the latter principally in mind. A servant who is set over a household and does his duty properly will be rewarded with fuller responsibility. But if the servant left in charge takes advantage of his master's absence to behave irresponsibly, he will get a shock when the master comes unexpectedly and find that his lot is with the unbelievers. His punishment will depend upon his knowledge and consequent measure of responsibility. The implication is that the heavenly judgment is not a matter of a simple verdict of guilty or not guilty; there are varying degrees of judgment and reward.

35 Girding the loins meant kilting up a flowing eastern garment for ease of movement; 'roll up your sleeves' is the modern equivalent. The imagery of night is used to stress the need for wakefulness. **42** The future tense *will set* suggests a reference to positions of responsibility in the church after the departure of Jesus. Note that all the parables in this section refer allegorically to the period after the resurrection and before the second advent. Many scholars argue that this is a reinterpretation by the early church of parables originally meant to arouse the Jews to awareness of the coming crisis. But the arguments for this view are far from compelling, and it is altogether likely that Jesus did warn His disciples against the danger of backsliding.

12:49–59 The crisis for Israel. (*Cf.* Mt. 10:34–36; 16:2f.; 5:25f.) Finally, Jesus returns to the crisis actually upon men as a result of His ministry; it is the period in which they must decide whether or not to confess Him as their Lord. His coming means that there will be division among men. His coming is meant to set the world on fire, and He longs that the fire might be kindled and burst into flame. It entails suffering for Jesus Himself, and He longs that it might soon be accomplished. For His ministry and response to it do not mean peace and ease, but strife as opposition is set up even within families to the progress of the gospel.

And in this situation men fail to realize that the time is up. They know how to tell a change in the weather from the direction of the wind, but they cannot read the signs of the times and act accordingly. They fail to realize that they are like a man being haled to court by his accuser. The wise man will make sure that he comes to a settlement long before he arrives at court and finds a watertight case being presented against him and then is cast into prison. Now is the time to respond to Jesus; soon it will be too late.

49 The *fire* symbolizes the spread of the message or of the power of the Spirit, and Jesus longs that it might spread the more quickly. **50** In the OT, being plunged into water is a metaphor for distress and suffering (*cf.* Ps. 69:1–3). Here, therefore, *baptism* is a metaphor for the passion of Jesus (*cf.* Mk. 10:38f.). *Constrained: cf.* 2 Cor. 5:14; Phil. 1:23. **56** *Hypocrites* has here the Hebrew sense of 'godless' rather than the Greek sense of 'acting a part'. **58** Luke has put the scene into Greek terminology; Matthew describes it in the language of Jewish law. **59** A doctrine of purgatory can be read out of this verse only if it is first read into it.

13:1–9 The need for repentance. Two brief concluding pieces of teaching further stress the need for response to the crisis brought about by the coming of Jesus. Some Passover pilgrims from Galilee had been butchered by Roman troops in the Temple while they were slaying their sacrifices, and the matter was reported to Jesus to see what His reaction would be. His response was to contradict the orthodox Jewish view that the greatness of the calamity suffered by these men showed that they were unusually wicked sinners; with equally scant justification could one say that men accidentally crushed to death by falling debris were exceptionally sinful. Rather, the Jewish nation as a whole was sinful in God's sight, and its members would all suffer the fate of sinners if they did not repent.

And God had graciously provided opportunity for repentance. The situation of the nation resembled that of an unfruitful tree which was ripe only for destruction; the ground it occupied could be well utilized for something more fruitful. But just as the owner was prepared to feed it and give it a chance, so God was prepared to appoint a further limit for Israel to repent. If they failed to respond, their fate would be their own responsibility. Perhaps the vine-dresser represents Jesus as an advocate to God for undeserving Israel.

1 The story is thoroughly in keeping with Pilate's character, although this particular act of murder was evidently too slight to excite the comment of a historian like Josephus. **4** Likewise, the accident at Siloam was no more likely to figure in a history book than any one of the countless road accidents in our own time. **6** Trees of all kinds were planted in vineyards. For the metaphorical use of the *fig tree* see Ho. 9:10. **7** Since fruit could not be taken from a tree during the first three years (Lv. 19:23), the tree was presumably six years old; there is no allegorical meaning in the *three years*.

13:10–35 The saving effects of God's rule

13:10–17 The bent woman. In the previous section, the ministry of Jesus appeared as a period of crisis; the accent now falls again on the coming of salvation. The story is of a woman suffering from a spinal deformity who was 'freed' (v. 12) by Jesus on a sabbath in the synagogue. The ruler of the synagogue argued that healing in a case like this where her life was not at stake could equally well have waited until a weekday. Jesus' reply was that if cattle could be loosed on the sabbath to be watered a woman could all the more be loosed from an infirmity. Note how the disability is said to be due to 'a spirit of infirmity' (v. 11), a state of being bound by Satan (v. 16). Human suffering is due to the same cosmic power as human sin. The final note brings out how the people rejoiced at the salvation revealed in Jesus while His opponents had nothing to say.

15 The Rabbis argued as to which kinds of knots could be tied and untied on the sabbath.

13:18–21 Two parables of the rule of God. (See Mt. 13:31–33; Mk. 4:30–32). Whatever their original context may have been, these parables are here connected with the coming of God's saving rule in Jesus. They contain the promise that God's work would come to a glorious fulfilment, no matter how small its beginnings seemed to be. Just as a mustard seed grows to tree-like proportions and a small amount of leaven (or yeast) permeates a large mass of dough and makes it expand, so what begins as a small influence will increase and spread widely. Attempts to distinguish between the meaning of the two parables are risky, and the view that leaven represents evil here is certainly wrong.

13:22–30 Entry to the kingdom. (*Cf.* Mt. 7:13f.; 22f.; 8:11f.) The mention of Jerusalem (where the reader knows that Jesus was crucified) gives an abrupt reminder of the context of Jesus' teaching. Would many men be *saved, i.e.* enter the heavenly kingdom of God? The orthodox answer was that all Jews—except of course for gross sinners and heretics—would find entry. But Jesus refused to speculate on the issue. It is far more important, He said, to ensure that one gets in personally. The kingdom is like a house with a *narrow door* (AV 'gate' rests on inferior MSS) offering limited admission; it is shut when the feast begins (Mt. 25:10), and then it will be too late to seek entry. It will be no use pleading acquaintance with Jesus if there has been no response to His message. On that day there will be no question of automatic admission for Jews. Some Jews will be excluded, and in their place will be found Gentiles from all over the earth alongside the saints of the OT. Those who thought that they ought to be first will find themselves placed last. Once again the lesson of the need for repentance (chs. 12, 13) is emphasized; salvation and judgment cannot be separated from each other.

13:31–35 The fate of Jerusalem. (See Mt. 23:37–39.) The primary point of this section lies in vv. 34f. The preceding verses tell how some Pharisees warned Jesus to flee from Herod's dominions. Whether they were friends warning Jesus of possible danger or hypocrites acting in collusion with Herod to frighten Jesus away is not clear. In any case Jesus had nothing but contempt for the murderer of John the Baptist and his threats. Herod could not harm Jesus, for the divinely appointed path for Jesus led to Jerusalem, and there at God's appointed time He would suffer. For the present He would continue His work, and then finish His course as a prophet in Jerusalem. The thought made Him break out in sorrow over the city which had so persistently rejected the messengers of God and would in the end find itself locked out of the kingdom. Even before the love and compassion of Jesus Jerusalem remained adamant. Therefore its Temple would be empty of God's presence, and it would not see Jesus until it was prepared to welcome Him as the Messiah or was visited by Him as its Judge.

31 Herod's dominions included Galilee and Peraea. **32** The *fox* probably typifies cunning, or possibly insignificance. *Today and tomorrow* is to be understood from Ho. 6:2 where 'two days' represents a short period of time before a crisis ('the third day'). Jesus expresses His determination to carry on His work until either it is complete or the time of His martyrdom comes (*cf.* 2 Tim. 4:7). **33** The Syriac Peshitta version has 'I must work today and tomorrow

and go on my way (*i.e.* die) the day following' which gives parallelism with v. 32. The text, however, gives a good sense without this emendation. **34** *How often* implies that Jesus visited Jerusalem more than once before His passion. **35** *Blessed* . . . is echoed in 19:38, but the reference here is to the second advent.

14:1–24 Jesus at table

14:1–6 The man with dropsy. The setting of this section is a visit by Jesus to the home of a Pharisee for a meal after the synagogue service on the sabbath. The meal provided an opportunity for teaching in which Jesus made use of the imagery of a banquet, but first of all there occurred a healing miracle which aroused the anger of a suspicious and hostile audience by being performed on the sabbath. Jesus justified His action by claiming that it was not different in principle from rescuing an animal which had fallen into a pit. The story makes a similar point to that recorded earlier in 13:11–17, and it is possible that the two stories were originally told as a pair (like the two parables in 13:18f.). Here, however, the main point may be the way in which Jesus showed compassion to an uninvited guest (*cf.* vv. 13, 21).

1 *A ruler* . . .: perhaps 'a leading Pharisee' (NEB). **2** *Dropsy* is a swelling of parts of the body as a result of fluid collecting in the tissues. **5** The text is uncertain; the best MSS have 'son' instead of *ass*, but the latter fits the context better. What Jesus here regards as permissible by orthodox Jewish law was forbidden in the austere rules of the Qumran community: 'Let no beast be helped to give birth on the sabbath day; and if it fall into a cistern or into a pit, let it not be lifted out on the sabbath' (*CDC*, 11:13f.).

14:7–11 Places of honour. The teaching given here by Jesus is not to be regarded simply as good advice for guests similar to that given in Pr. 25:6f. It is described as *a parable*, which means that it has a spiritual significance, and it refers to *a marriage feast*, which was a recognized symbol for the kingdom of God and heavenly bliss (v. 15). The parable is based on the practice of seating guests at table by rank and distinction. The more important guests no doubt arrived last (as they often still do!), and an unwary early arrival might have to move to a lower place (AV 'room' is archaic) so as to accommodate them. Far better to adopt an attitude of modesty and wait to be invited to a better seat. For God exalts the humble and debases the proud. It needs no saying that Jesus is not commending the false modesty which takes a lower place simply in order to be publicly exalted later.

11 The passive form of the verbs *will be humbled* and *will be exalted* is a circumlocution for naming God as the subject.

14:12–14 The choice of guests. This plain piece of advice is in line with Jesus' other teaching about deeds which receive their full recompense in this life: see Mt. 6:1f., 5, 16. Men ought to do those deeds which God will reward. This, however, can easily be misunderstood. On the one hand, Jesus is not making a down-right condemnation of holding a party for one's family or friends; this would have conflicted with His own practice (*e.g.* Jn. 2:1–11). Rather He is condemning the attitude which does good simply for the sake of a tangible, earthly reward. But, on the other hand, He is not saying that one should do good simply in order to receive a heavenly reward. The point is that men should seek to do good to those who cannot give any-thing in return, and leave the whole question of recompense to God.

14 To speak of *the resurrection of the just* (*cf.* 20:35) does not exclude a resurrection of the unjust for judgment (Acts 24:15). The implica-tion is that only for the just has the resurrection a positive character.

14:15–24 The heavenly banquet. (*Cf.* Mt. 22:1–10.) The mention of the resurrection caused one of the guests to utter a blessing on those who would share in the heavenly banquet. Jesus at once took up the statement with a parable which discussed the kind of people who would be present. The double invitation (vv. 16, 17) was characteristic of Jewish practice. It has been suggested that the parable was deliberately modelled by Jesus on a Jewish story of a *nouveau riche* tax collector who tried to gain social stand-ing among the aristocrats by inviting them to dinner but was harshly rebuffed by them. The upper-class audience addressed by Jesus would have thoroughly appreciated the story—until it was borne in upon them that this was how they were treating God's invitation given to them by Jesus. So that his meal might not be wasted, the tax collector in the story invited the poor in, and so, implied Jesus, does God seek out the needy and poor from both inside and outside the city to receive His largesse. It is, therefore, all very well to express the kind of pious sentiment found in v. 15; the vital point is whether one has accepted the heavenly invitation. The story foreshadows the defence given by Jesus for bringing the gospel to the 'tax collectors and sinners' in 15:1–32.

A very similar story occurs in Mt. 22:1–10; it is a moot point whether Jesus originally told one parable, developed by His disciples into two different forms, or told two similar but distinct parables.

16, 17 There may be an allegorical allusion to the invitations from God in the OT and through Jesus. **18** *To make excuses* does not necessarily imply the falsity of the pretexts put forward, but there can be little doubt that the guests could have come if they had wanted to. **23** The inclu-sion of the Gentiles is probably implied.

14:25–35 The cost of discipleship

(*Cf.* Mt. 10:37f.; 5:13; Mk. 9:50.) Before taking up the theme of 'the gospel for the outcast', foreshadowed in vv. 21–24, Jesus indicates the stringency of the claims which are implicit in His invitation to men to come to God's banquet. He warned the multitudes who flocked after Him that discipleship meant readiness to place His claims above those of both family and self. The disciple must be prepared even to face death for the sake of Jesus. Let men therefore count the cost of total self-renunciation before embark-ing upon a course which they may not be able to sustain. Even today men speak of a building left unfinished for lack of funds as a 'folly'. How foolish too is the army commander who does not reckon up the strength of his army before engaging a superior foe in battle. A disciple who gives up in midstream because the going is too tough is like salt which has lost its taste and is unfit for seasoning food or even for fertilizer; it cannot be made useful again.

26 *Hate* means 'love less' (*cf.* Mt. 10:37). **27** *Cf.* 9:23. Crucifixion was a sufficiently common event in Palestine to account for Jesus' saying, but He may have had His own coming fate in mind. **34** The impure mixture used as *salt* could lose its salt content and become useless.

15:1–32 The gospel for the outcast

15:1–10 The lost sheep and the lost coin. (*Cf.* Mt. 18:12–14.) The theme of the parable of the heavenly banquet (14:15–24) receives fuller treatment in the three parables which are told here. Their lesson, which is crystal clear, is indicated in vv. 1f. Jesus' ministry to the mem-bers of society commonly regarded as sinful and unrepentant by the Pharisees had earned Him their continual criticism. 'Let not a man associate with the wicked, not even to bring him to the Law' is a saying in the rabbinic literature which sums up their attitude. Jesus had already defended His attitude by pointing to the need of these people (5:29f.). In the parable of the heavenly banquet He had declared that He would issue God's invitation to such people rather than to religious people who spurned it. Now He presents the highest reason of all, that God rejoices over the recovery of a lost sinner. It is His pleasure to seek and to save the lost, and therefore it is Jesus' supreme desire to do the same (19:10). This divine attitude is illustrated by the willingness of a shepherd to go out over the moors and hills so that not even one sheep may be missing from his flock. There may well be shepherds who ask 'What does one lost sheep matter compared with ninety-nine safe in the fold?' and ignore the value of the individual. Not so with God. He rejoices even more over the return of the lost than the safety of those at home. In precisely the same way the housewife who has lost one coin out of ten rejoices when it is found, and summons her friends to share in her rejoic-ing. In the same way, it is implied, the Pharisees should share in God's rejoicing over the salva-tion of the outcasts.

The parable of the lost sheep is also found in Mt. 18:12–14, but there it serves as an object lesson to the members of the church to care for the weaker members of the flock of God. **7, 10**

Joy in heaven and *before the angels of God* are both circumlocutions for saying that God Himself rejoices. At the same time, it is implied that God's people share in His rejoicing. **8** The *ten silver coins* may have formed the woman's headdress. Their intrinsic value was not great and suggests that the woman was comparatively poor. She had to *light a lamp* because she lived in a typical Palestinian peasant house with a low door and no windows.

15:11–32 The lost sons. The third parable makes the same point at greater length, so that the main character in it is really the father himself. The dramatic situation is that the younger son demanded immediately full rights of possession over the portion (about one-third) of his father's estate which he could expect to inherit in the normal course of events when the father died. While the elder son remained at home, and his father retained his rights over the produce of his portion of the estate, the younger son turned his share into cash and departed to enjoy the proceeds away from home and parental control. When extravagant and dissolute living had reduced him to penury, and his erstwhile friends had deserted him, he was forced to take the most menial form of employment, one that was particularly loathsome to a Jew who regarded swine as unclean animals. He would gladly have eked out his miserable wages by sharing the carob pods which the swine ate but, it is implied, he was too disgusted to do so. His desperate state brought him to repentance. He realized not only that he had landed himself in sorry straits but also that he was unworthy to be called his father's son; he was fit only to be a servant, and he was prepared to humble himself and seek reinstatement at that level. But before he reached home his father was already looking for his arrival, and before he could blurt out the whole of his intended confession, his father had welcomed him back into the family circle, treated him with great honour, and given orders for a feast of rejoicing over the return of one who had been as good as dead.

One person refused to join in the celebration, and grumbled at the lavish care being expended on a ne'er-do-well. He accused his father of failing to treat him in the same free and joyous manner, only to be reminded that all the resources of the home were his. One can be lost even at home. The discovery of the lost and the resurrection of the dead were occasions for joy. One question is left unanswered: did the elder brother eventually join in the celebration and accept his brother back as a member of the family? The omission is deliberate. For the elder brother represents the Pharisees and their spiritual kin, and the parable is an appeal to them to receive the outcasts. Jesus was waiting for their verdict.

But although this is the primary purpose of the parable, one cannot help but feel that the pardoning love of God, which should have shamed the Pharisees into response, is the centre of attention. It is true that there is no mention

of His seeking the lost (as in 15:3–10) or of atonement for sin, but this story is a parable, not a detailed allegory, and these other manifestations of divine love are sufficiently plain elsewhere in the teaching of Jesus.

12 The legal position is correctly depicted. Property could be disposed of either by a will or by a gift during one's lifetime. **18** *Heaven* is again a periphrasis for 'God'. Note that there is no suggestion that the son's repentance was in any way insincere, even if it required a desperate situation to induce it. **21** The addition in RSV mg. (also in AV and RV) is by a scribe who failed to realize that the father interrupted the son's statement before he could finish it. **22** The gifts are all signs of honour and authority. *Shoes* were the prerogative of free men, not of slaves. **29, 30** The elder brother's complaints are expressed extravagantly. He could not bring himself to say 'my brother' but spoke contemptuously of *this son of yours*.

16:1–31 Warnings to the rich

Having vindicated His preaching to the poor and outcasts, Jesus now issued warnings to those whose avarice and wealth (vv. 14, 19) blinded them to the need for response to the gospel before it was too late. They should in any case have heeded the teaching of the OT Scriptures about the moral law of God, which remains permanently valid. Various sayings on these and allied themes have been collected together, so that the chapter also discusses the disciples' attitude to wealth.

16:1–9 The prudent steward. A steward, entrusted with his master's estate and accounts, was suspected of mismanaging his affairs, if not of actually behaving dishonestly. When he realized that he was in danger of dismissal, he summoned his master's debtors and allowed each one to enter a lower figure on his IOU or promissory note. The debtors would thus feel indebted to the steward and help him when he was out of a job. He had acted with commendable astuteness in providing for his own interests.

There are various interpretations of the parable. *a.* The parable may simply urge men to prepare for the crisis brought about by the ministry of Jesus with the same zeal of the steward facing an uncertain future. *b.* Jesus commented that astuteness is shown much more by worldly people than by those who belong to the new era. Men should learn from the steward and use their wealth to make God their friend, so that, when money is no longer of any help to them, God may receive them into His presence (v. 9). As such, the parable may be giving advice to the disciples ('the sons of light', v. 8), or to the Pharisees whose greed was excluding them from God's friendship (v. 14; *cf.* 11:39–41). *c.* Recent study of Jewish law has suggested that the steward may not have been acting dishonestly at this point. He was merely releasing the debtors from the huge interest payments which had been imposed (quite illegally) when the loans were made to them. Keeping the law and showing generosity are the ways for wealthy people to gain God's approval. None of these interpretations can be excluded; the original story possibly ended at v. 8a, and the ensuing verses contain sayings of Jesus bringing out a series of different points from the parable.

6, 7 The measure of oil (*bath*) was 4–5 gallons, the measure of wheat (*kor*) about 12 bushels. Since oil was cheaper, the reductions were about equal. **8, 9** *The master* may be the steward's master or Jesus Himself (in which case 'master' means 'Lord'; *cf.* 18:6); in any case it was the steward's astuteness and not his morality which was commended. *Dishonest* (AV 'unjust') and *unrighteous* typify the people and money (*mammon*) of this present, evil age. *They* (v. 9) means 'God'.

16:10–13 Faithful stewardship. (See Mt. 6:24.) Various general principles of stewardship for disciples follow. First, the way in which a man acts as steward of a little shows how he will act as a steward of much (v. 10). Therefore, if a man is a poor steward of money, he will hardly be entrusted with spiritual riches (v. 11). And if a man cannot exercise proper care over a trust given to him, for which he can be brought to account, he will not be given wealth of his own to use as he pleases (v. 12). Second, it is impossible to be committed to two masters, God and wealth (v. 13). The ancient idea of slavery did not envisage such a division of labour or devotion as might be practised by a man who works, say, for one employer in the morning and another in the afternoon. God makes exclusive claims.

16:14–18 The Pharisees and the law. (*Cf.* Mt. 11:12f.; 5:18, 32.) Jesus' teaching did not appeal to those who tried to combine the pursuit of wealth with piety, and He warned the Pharisees that, while they may have given the appearance of piety to men, in fact the secret avarice of their hearts made them an abomination to God.

Vv. 16–18 present an antidote to the antinomian attitude which argued that the message of Jesus made the OT law and its moral demands out of date; Jesus stated that this was not so, and that men would find God's will still expressed in the OT (v. 29). It was true that the era of the law and prophets had ended, and now the new era of the kingdom had come. But this did not mean that the law had been countermanded. For example, divorce followed by remarriage is adultery. This particular example in fact sharpened the law; the Jews thought of adultery as a sin by a woman against her husband or by one man against another; Jesus taught that a man may commit adultery against a woman.

16 Luke's version (*the good news . . . preached*) is probably a (correct) interpretation of Matthew's difficult 'the kingdom of heaven has been coming violently' (Mt. 11:12, RSV mg.). *Every one enters* probably refers to ordinary people eager to enter the kingdom rather than to demons or men opposing the kingdom violently or to zealots attempting to force God's hand.

16:19–31 The rich man and Lazarus. Egyptian and Jewish sources have furnished stories similar to this one in describing the reversed fates of rich and poor men in the next world. The parable implies that the rich man did scarcely anything to alleviate the beggar's distress. When the latter died, he found a place of honour beside Abraham, the father of the Jewish race and the friend of God. The rich man found himself in Hades (AV 'hell') in torment and agony. He called upon Abraham as 'father' for mercy, but the reply of Abraham, though it called him 'son', offered no hope. Thus far the story follows traditional lines, but now there is a fresh element. Could the rich man's brothers, presumably rich and careless themselves, be warned before they reached Hades? The reply was that the teaching they possessed in the OT should be enough. Not even the miracle of somebody returning from the dead to warn them would have any effect on those who had shut their ears to the voice of God in the Scriptures. Failure to practise the love and mercy taught in the OT will lead to loss in the next life.

It is a moot point whether the parable is intended to give literal information about the next world, and, if so, whether it refers to an intermediate state before the final judgment or to a lasting state. But, although the language (*e.g.* Abraham's bosom) is surely symbolical, it speaks of real destinies for men.

19 A recently discovered MS gives the rich man's name as Neues. **20** We are to infer that *Lazarus* ('he whom God helps') was a pious man. **21** *Dogs* were unclean animals. **26** The imagery expresses with all clarity the irreversibility of God's verdict upon men.

17:1–19 Teaching for disciples

17:1–4 Stumbling-blocks. (*Cf.* Mt. 18:6f., 15, 21f.; Mk. 9:42.) Various pieces of teaching for disciples are collected together here. While Jesus knew that 'stumbling blocks' (RSV mg.) are inevitable in this world, He warned sternly against the danger of being the cause of another person's sin. It would be better for a tempter to suffer drowning than the fate reserved for tempters. Let each man, therefore, take heed to himself in this matter. On the contrary, the disciples should help any brother who does fall into sin both by warning him as to what he has done and by being ready to forgive, no matter how often this may be necessary.

2, 3 The NEB punctuation, with a full stop after *yourselves* so that v. 3a is linked to v. 2 rather than to v. 3b, is preferable.

17:5, 6 Faith. (*Cf.* Mt. 17:20; Mk. 11:22f.) Jesus commended the desire for the *faith* necessary to enable disciples to obey His commands; even a tiny 'amount' of faith can do great wonders.

5 *Increase our faith* may simply mean 'give us faith'. **6** *Sycamine*: the black mulberry (*Morus nigra*). Jesus was speaking metaphorically.

17:7–10 Duty. Once a servant has done his

duty, he has no right to expect any more than his normal wage and remains 'unworthy', *i.e.* has nothing of which to boast. Elsewhere Jesus taught and demonstrated a different attitude by Himself serving His disciples (Jn. 13:1–16; *cf.* Lk. 12:35–38; 22:27). This fact shows that He is not here teaching that God's dealings with men are on a basis of law and duty rather than of grace and faith; instead He is giving a necessary lesson to all who are tempted to feel proud of their 'work of faith' (1 Thes. 1:3) for God.

7 The fact that Jesus here uses an illustration from slavery is no proof that He would have commended slavery as an institution any more than dishonesty (16:8).

17:11–19 The healing of ten lepers. When some lepers sought healing from Jesus, He simply commanded them to go and show themselves to a priest (5:14). The implication is that their faith would be shown by obedience. All showed faith and were cleansed, but only one both praised God and thanked Jesus for his cure. Jesus commented on the ungratefulness of the others (all presumably Jews) and confirmed that the Samaritan's faith had made him well in body and soul. The story is both an illustration of wonder-working faith (*cf.* v. 6) and a lesson on the need for gratitude as an aspect of faith.

11 The location on the border explains the mixed character of the group of men. The geography is not clear; perhaps *Galilee* here includes Peraea (also ruled by Herod). 14 The story is similar to that in 5:12–16, but there is no good reason to believe that it is based upon it.

17:20 – 18:8 The coming of the Son of man

17:20–37 The kingdom and the Son of man. (*Cf.* Mt. 24:23–28, 37–41.) In previous episodes Jesus had spoken of the coming of the kingdom and the Son of man. The natural question to ask was when this would happen. Would there be some indication that it was about to take place, so that men might prepare themselves for it? Jesus' reply was that the coming of the kingdom is not something accompanied by observable signs (AV 'with observation'). Men will not be able to say, 'Here it is.' But the second part of Jesus' statement is not easy (v. 21b). The words translated *in the midst of you* may mean 'within your grasp' (NEB mg.) or 'within you' (RSV mg., AV, RV). The third rendering is to be rejected, not simply because the kingdom was hardly within the Pharisees, but rather because Jesus never elsewhere spoke of the kingdom as an inward, spiritual state of affairs. A decision between the first two translations is less important. A further difficulty is whether the saying means that the kingdom *is* or *will be* in the midst of you. The analogy of such a passage as 11:20 supports the former possibility, in which case Jesus is saying that the working of God is already present in His ministry for those with eyes to see it; salvation is within their grasp.

In the following verses, however, Jesus is looking to the future and saying that God will suddenly intervene in history without any premonitory signs. He warns His hearers that they will long to see the coming of the Son of man and the new age, no doubt because of their tribulation and distress. That will be the time when they must not be misled by false signs. When the Son of man does come, His glorious appearance will be sufficiently clear for all to see—in marked contrast to the suffering and humiliation which He must first undergo. It will come as a surprise to the godless world (and therefore it behoves men to prepare now for it). Just as the flood overtook the world and the fire devoured Sodom by surprise, despite the witness of Noah and Lot (2 Pet. 2:5–8), so will it be when the Son of man comes in judgment. It will be too late to escape then; men must therefore beware of attachment to earthly things, remembering the terrifying example of Lot's wife. Only the man who has given up living for himself will escape. There will be separation even between members of the same families and groups of workers. When Jesus is asked where it will happen, He makes no concessions to those who want a map as well as a timetable: just as the location of a corpse in the desert is obvious from the crowd of circling vultures, so it will be quite obvious where the Son of man is.

20 Jesus' warning against looking for signs seems at first to be out of harmony with His own words in 21:5–36, and some scholars have rashly concluded that one or other strand of His teaching is not authentic. But premonitory signs were a recognized part of apocalyptic teaching, and Jesus had to warn people against trusting to them for security. At the same time, He had to prepare His followers for the troubles that lay ahead of them, lest they should lose faith (*cf.* 18:8). 22 *Days of the Son of man* seems to mean the period immediately before the coming of the Son of man, but there is no agreed interpretation of this unique phrase. 34 *Two men*: *i.e.* two persons (*e.g.* man and wife, *cf.* on 24:25). 36 is omitted by the best MSS; it is a gloss from Mt. 24:40.

18:1–8 The unjust judge. Although we think of this parable as being about prayer, it really forms the closing part of the teaching about the future given in 17:20–37. Like the very similar parable in 11:5–8, it makes its point by contrast. If even a judge who honours the laws neither of God nor of men can be induced to act by the incessant appeals of a widow, how much more will God act to vindicate His elect when they cry to Him. The last clause of v. 7 is difficult. The NEB gives the alternatives 'while he listens patiently to them' and (in the mg.) 'while he delays to help them'. Another possibility, which assumes that the original Aramaic has been slightly obscured in the Greek translation, is 'even if he keeps them waiting for him'. The point is that even if God gives the appearance of unwillingness to answer, like the unjust judge, yet He will certainly answer prayer without the need for importunity. He will vindicate His elect *speedily* ('soon enough' NEB) or perhaps 'suddenly and unexpectedly'. The vital question is not whether He will respond to importunity but whether there will be faithful men, who have *persisted* in prayer, when the Son of man comes. Luke has rightly characterized the parable as one to encourage men to continue in prayer without losing heart before the end comes. There is an interesting parallel in Ecclus. 35:14–19.

2 The mention of a single judge probably means that the woman was seeking satisfaction in a financial matter. **4** The judge would be waiting for a bribe, but the woman was too poor to pay; persistence was her only weapon. **7** The *elect* are the people who have heard God's call and responded to it. Here they are in a situation of persecution and long to be vindicated; they pray, 'Thy kingdom come.'

18:9 – 19:10 The scope of salvation

18:9–14 The Pharisee and the publican. Like the preceding parable this one too deals with prayer, but its purpose is different. Here the prayers recorded are reflections of two characters. The Pharisee was a pious man living an honest and upright life. He more than observed the law by fasting regularly on Mondays and Thursdays, although the law required fasting only once annually on the Day of Atonement, and by giving tithes of all his possessions. His sin was that he commended himself for his piety, despised his neighbours and was self-sufficient in God's presence. By contrast, the tax collector stood far from the Holy Place and did not dare to lift up his eyes, still less his hands, in prayer, but simply poured out a confession of sinfulness and an appeal for God's mercy. Jesus' verdict was that he went home justified and accepted by God, but the Pharisee was not accepted. The parable thus vindicates 'the gospel for the outcast' once again by stressing that God is always ready to receive the unrighteous when they call to Him and closes His ears to those whose pride in their piety makes them self-sufficient.

11 The *Pharisee* here was not untypical of his sect, although it did contain many excellent men. Prayers very similar to this one are preserved in rabbinic sources. *Prayed thus with himself*: better 'took up a prominent position and prayed'. **14** *Rather than* is too weak: 'and not' gives the true meaning.

18:15–17 Jesus and children. (See Mt. 19:13–15; Mk. 10:13–16.) After a long section (9:51 – 18:14) without parallels in Mark, we now come to a series of incidents in which Luke again keeps in step with the older Gospel. The first of these tells how Jesus received the 'infants' (Luke alone uses this word) whom His disciples would have prevented from bothering Him, and pronounced that the kingdom of God belongs to such as they. In Mark this is the main point of the story, and it is emphasized by Jesus taking the children in His arms. Luke omits this feature,

not because he felt it was an improper thing to record, but because he wished to concentrate attention on the lesson that the kingdom of God is only for those who are prepared to receive it like children in a humble and receptive frame of mind (*cf.* 18:14).

15 *Touch* implies 'bless', *i.e.* pray to God to bless them. **16** The kingdom is for children as well as for the childlike.

18:18–34 The rich ruler. (See Mt. 19:16–30; 20:17–19; Mk. 10:17–34.) The same theme of the attitude accepted by God from men continues. A ruler addressed Jesus as 'Good teacher' and asked the way to inherit eternal life (*i.e.* to enter the kingdom of God (v. 24) or to be saved (v. 26)). Jesus asked if he really knew what he meant by using the word 'good' indiscriminately. Note that He did not repudiate the address; there is hidden here a consciousness of divine Sonship. Then He answered the question in the orthodox Jewish manner by citing the commandments, the 'second table' of the law which could be tested by a man's outward conduct. When the man claimed to have kept them, He probed deeper. Let the ruler realize his not inconsiderable assets, give to the poor and become a disciple. The man's failure to respond showed that he did not truly love his neighbour as himself, and that he worshipped himself and his wealth rather than God. Outward conformity to the law was again a mask for a sinful heart. Here was clear proof that it is extremely hard for a rich man—and, we may add, for any man whose heart is set on riches—to enter the kingdom. In fact, it is as impossible for a rich man to be saved as for a camel to go through the eye of a needle. Indeed, it is not too much to say that it is impossible for any man to be saved. There is only one way. Although man cannot overcome his sinful heart, God intervenes to save those who will respond to His call. Peter suggested that the Twelve had made this response and given up everything for Jesus. And Jesus made His promise that those who were prepared for the sacrifices involved in the path of discipleship would receive far greater blessings both now, in the fellowship of God's people, and in the world to come.

In Mk. 10:30 the disciples are also promised persecution. This is omitted here, but is surely implied in the prophecy of the fate of the Son of man with its details of the shameful treatment which He would receive from the Gentiles. The Twelve, however, failed to understand. As is clear from Mark's story of the ugly struggle for precedence which followed, they rejected the idea; see 9:45 for their earlier, identical reaction.

18 The man's status as a *ruler* is uncertain. **20** The peculiar order of the commandments is also found in the LXX. The command against covetousness is omitted, perhaps because this is not an outwardly observable attitude. **25** A similar Jewish proverb speaks of an elephant. **31** See Is. 49:7; 50:5f.; 52:13–53:12 and also Pss. 22; 69.

18:35–43 The healing of a blind man. (See Mt. 20:29–34; Mk. 10:46–52.) The final two stories in this section are both examples of men who responded to the call of God given by Jesus. A blind man, hearing that Jesus was in the vicinity, called upon Him as the Son of David to help him. He showed persistence (*cf.* 18:1) in continuing to call for help, despite those who would silence him, and Jesus responded to his faith. He received his sight and became a follower of Jesus. The crowds joined him in praising God for revealing His power in Jesus.

35 In Mark the healing of Bartimaeus took place as Jesus was leaving Jericho, but here as He was entering the town. It has been suggested that two towns, Old and New Jericho, lay near to each other and that the incident took place between the two. Luke may have inserted the story of Zacchaeus (not recorded in Mark) last, to gain a climax, and altered the historical order slightly for this purpose (*cf.* on 6:12–19). **38** *Son of David* was a Messianic title: see Is. 11:1–10; Je. 23:5f.; Ezk. 34:23f.; Lk. 20:41–44.

19:1–10 Zacchaeus the tax collector. Not all rich men departed from Jesus sadly. Zacchaeus is an example of what is 'possible with God' (18:27). The Romans farmed out the task of collecting the taxes in any particular area to the highest bidder. The man did not receive any salary for his work but collected as much money as he could so that he would have a handsome rake-off after paying the government the appointed sum. Zacchaeus was such a tax farmer. His attempt to see Jesus, the man known as the friend of tax collectors (7:34), indicates his interest in Him. Whether he hoped to be hidden from view is not certain, but in any case Jesus summoned him before Him with a request that he would provide lodging. The command was obeyed, and Zacchaeus showed both repentance and joy as he welcomed Jesus. Outside there were great murmurings about Jesus' fraternizing with such a man, but Jesus was able to justify His action; salvation had come to the house of Zacchaeus, a son of Abraham who was as much entitled to hear the gospel as any other Jew. In this event the purpose of the coming of Jesus is fully and finally summed up; as a shepherd seeks for the lost sheep (*cf.* 15:3–7; Ezk. 34:16), so the Son of man seeks and saves the lost of humanity.

8 *I give* and *I restore* are present forms having, as often in Greek, future significance. The resolve corresponds to the penitence expressed in 18:13. **9** The saying does not imply the omission of the Gentiles from Jesus' concern, but stresses that one Jew is no more or less valuable than another in God's sight.

19:11 – 21:38 THE MINISTRY IN JERUSALEM

19:11–27 The parable of the pounds

As Jesus' ministry moved to its climax and Jerusalem came in sight, the Twelve continued to hope that a successful worldly type of revolution was about to take place and inaugurate the promised reign of God. They bickered about the places which they would occupy in the new order (*cf.* Mk. 10:35–45). The present parable was meant to be a corrective to this attitude by warning that the Messiah was going to be rejected by men and by teaching that there lies ahead a period when the disciples of Jesus must engage in faithful service during their Master's absence until He returns in kingly power. Two strands of thought are thus intertwined.

As an 'earthly story' the parable reflects the action of various members of the Herodian family in going to Rome to petition for, or to be confirmed in, royal power over their realm. In particular, Archelaus, the son of Herod the Great, went to Rome in 4 BC to have the provisions of his father's will confirmed, but an embassy of Jews followed close on his heels to protest to Augustus, 'We do not want this man to rule over us', and as a result Augustus severely limited his powers. Jesus was probably using this incident as a basis for His parable. The fate of the rebellious citizens was thoroughly in accordance with ancient despotic ways (though there is no record that Archelaus himself actually behaved thus).

The centre of interest, however, is not the rebellious citizens but the ten servants (a round number), each of whom was given a pound with which to trade (AV 'occupy') and make a profit. The first servant, having successfully demonstrated his faithful and competent stewardship, received the privilege of high office. The second servant, less successful, received a correspondingly lesser privilege. A third, however, had not done his duty, not even to the extent of letting a banker do the work for him. He criticized his master for his harshness in unjustly appropriating the fruit of other men's labours, and perhaps he was afraid to trade lest he incurred a loss and consequent punishment. He was rebuked for his laziness and his money was confiscated. So the need for faithful service is taught, and the prospect of reward and loss put before the servants.

The parable has a family resemblance to that of the talents. Moreover, it contains some curious inconsistencies. In v. 20 the Greek text has *the* other (so JB), as if there were originally only three servants, as in Matthew. Again, it is curious that an extra *pound* should be given to a man who has just been given ten *cities* and that this should arouse a protest (v. 25). Finally, the part of the story about the ruler and his rebellious citizens is not in the parable of the talents and is perhaps slightly inconsistent with a story of trade transactions. Many scholars therefore hold that two independent parables of Jesus have been fused into one here and that some of the details have been changed in the telling of the stories. Something similar has probably happened in Mt. 22:1–14. These facts, however, in no way affect the basic truths taught in the parable.

13 The *pound* (Gk. *mna*) is said to be worth £5, but it would have a much larger purchasing power. **21** The description of the master as *severe* and the account of his use of harsh ancient cruelty in v. 27 should not be pressed to give false conclusions about the character of God, but at the same time the reality and seriousness of divine judgment cannot be evaded.

19:28–40 Jesus rides on a colt

(See Mt. 21:1–9; Mk. 11:1–10; Jn. 12:12–19.) Having warned His disciples against false expectations of what would happen in Jerusalem, Jesus prepared for His distinctive entry to the city. Taking His seat on a colt He rode down the slope of the Mt. of Olives towards the city. His companions spread their clothes on the road as a sign of acclamation (*cf.* 2 Ki. 9:13). Those who had come from Galilee with Him broke into praise over the mighty works which they had seen, no doubt in anticipation of more to follow in Jerusalem itself. They hailed Jesus as the coming One, the King possessed of divine authority. Only Luke records how the Pharisees, fearful of the consequences, warned Jesus to quieten His enthusiastic followers. He was not prepared to do so, for in a deeper sense than the crowds realized their words were true: the Messiah had come. In hyperbolical fashion He told the Pharisees that the crowds could not but welcome Him. The Pharisees do not seem at this point to have been opposed to Jesus (see perhaps 13:31). Was it Jesus' refusal to repudiate the acclamation of His followers that made them begin to turn against Him?

29 *Bethphage* and *Bethany* were villages east of the Mt. of Olives, which itself was east of Jerusalem. **31** It is not certain whether *the Lord* means Jesus Himself or the colt's owner ('the boss'!). The latter view is possible if 'its owners' (v. 33) refers to the underlings looking after the colt for its real master, with whom Jesus will have made a previous arrangement. But Jesus may have referred uniquely to Himself as 'the Lord' on this occasion. **38** The wording differs from that in Mk. 11:9f. where the kingdom rather than the King is welcomed, but the difference is trivial. In either case the crowds seem to have expected some kind of *coup* by Jesus despite all He had said to the contrary. *Peace in heaven* . . . is probably Luke's paraphrase of 'Hosanna . . .' for Gentile readers: does it imply that peace is no longer possible on *earth* for Jerusalem (2:14; 19:42)?

19:41–48 The destruction of Jerusalem

(See Mt. 21:12f.; Mk. 11:15–18.) There is a sudden change of tone as Jesus turns to look at the city spread before Him and utters a sorrowful prophecy about its fate. He longed that even at this late stage it might repent and seek what would be for its welfare: how little did the conduct of Jerusalem, the city of peace (Heb. 7:2), resemble its name! The time would come when the city would be besieged with a bank (AV 'trench') round it and captured with tremendous loss of life, and all because it had failed to recognize that God was visiting it and longing to save it.

Then Jesus entered the Temple and drove out the people who carried on commerce within its precincts. Their trade was associated with the needs of pilgrims, like a modern souvenir shop under the shadow of a cathedral selling Bibles along with picture postcards, but it was conducted in a manner that was not beyond reproach and had grown to alarming proportions. The Court of the Gentiles had become a thieves' kitchen instead of a place of prayer.

So began a brief period in which Jesus taught daily in the Temple to the accompaniment of rising opposition from the authorities and strong sympathy from the crowds who appreciated His words.

42 These words strongly imply that, as we know from John, this was not Jesus' first visit to Jerusalem but that had He ministered there earlier. See on 13:34.

20:1 – 21:4 The growth of opposition

20:1–8 The authority of Jesus. (See Mt. 21:23–27; Mk. 11:27–33.) As in Matthew and Mark the story of Jesus' last visit to Jerusalem is filled with a series of incidents in which the points of difference between Him and the Jewish leaders became ever more clear, and they were encouraged to take action against Him. In the first of these incidents His preaching of the good news was interrupted by a deputation from the Sanhedrin. What was His authority for setting Himself up as a teacher, they asked? Or was it that He claimed to be a prophet with divine authority? Jesus replied with a counter-question. Let them first tell Him whether John the Baptist had received his authority from heaven, *i.e.* God (*cf.* 15:7), or from men. To have answered 'From heaven' would have raised the awkward question why they had not responded to his message (Mt. 21:32) and would have implicitly indicated that Jesus too had divine authority. But to deny the divine authority of John was to run the risk of alienating the people for whom John had certainly ranked as a prophet. Their pitifully weak 'We do not know' earned a crushing rebuke. It would be wrong to see in this story a clever piece of logic-chopping by Jesus. Rather it brings out the character of the questioners, unwilling to recognize divine authority and vacillating in fear of public opinion.

1 Representatives from the three groups of leaders mentioned here constituted the Sanhedrin, the Jewish 'parliament' composed of 71 persons and chaired by the high priest. The *chief priests* were either the members of the high-priestly families or the holders of various special priestly offices (*e.g.* the ruler of the Temple, the leaders of the weekly and daily courses, the captains and the treasurers). The *elders* were the lay leaders of the people.

20:9-19 The parable of the wicked husbandmen.
(See Mt. 21:33–46; Mk. 12:1–21.) Jesus next
took the offensive with a parable whose meaning
was but thinly veiled. Any Jew who knew his
Scriptures would be reminded of Is. 5:1–7, where
a vineyard expressly represents Israel. In the
owner's absence the tenants decided first to
withhold the fruits from him and then to ensure
that the vineyard would pass into their possession. They killed the heir and sat tight on the
property. The picture is based on the law of the
time, but it portrays the history of Israel and its
leaders who had continually rejected the messengers of God. We know that 'the beloved son'
represents Jesus, but whether the first hearers
would have realized this is uncertain. They may
possibly have seen in the title of Son a Messianic
designation or known that Jesus claimed a
unique filial relationship to God. Certainly
Jesus had in mind His own identity and fate,
but it would have been thoroughly in keeping
with the manner of His public teaching for Him
to have been designedly ambiguous in this
parable. It required no skill to guess what a
landlord would do with such tenants. Nevertheless, the hearers said 'God forbid!', a reaction
which indicates that they were already applying
the parable to 'the vineyard of the Lord of hosts'
and were aghast at the suggestion of the Gentiles
taking possession. But Jesus claimed scriptural
support for what He said. What else could be
meant by the metaphor of the rejected stone
being given the chief place in the building but
that the One whose authority they refused
(20:1–7) was the person of God's choice. Anybody who rejected Him would suffer judgment
(see Is. 8:14f.; Dn. 2:34, 45).

9ff. The slight differences in wording in the
Gospels reflect the minor adaptations made by
Christian preachers in telling the story. **14** In
certain conditions the property of a Gentile or
proselyte who died intestate would pass to
whoever was first to gain possession of it.

20:20-26 Tribute to Caesar. (See Mt. 22:15–22;
Mk. 12:13–17.) The message of the parable was
so plain that the scribes and chief priests would
have arrested Jesus on the spot, but the time was
not propitious. They contented themselves with
collecting further evidence against Him and trying to put Him into a position which would make
Him lose favour with the populace or incur the
suspicion of the Romans. They therefore asked
directly about the relationship of Jews to the
Roman government. The poll tax imposed
by Rome (see on 2:2) had been accompanied
by riots at its imposition (Acts 5:37) and
remained exceedingly unpopular. Would Jesus
oppose it, and perhaps be arrested as a rebel, or
uphold it and lose popular support? He demanded
whether His questioners could produce a coin,
not necessarily because He did not possess one,
but so that He might demonstrate that they
themselves used Caesar's money. To use his
coinage obliged them to pay back his property
to him. At the same time, said Jesus, going

beyond the original question, there is a parallel
debt to God. Perhaps there is the thought that
men are God's 'coinage' for they bear His
image. The respective spheres of Caesar and
God are not defined here. Jesus' point was simply
that those who benefit from Caesar must
pay him for it. It looks as though His wise
answer impressed His hearers, at least for the
moment.

24 The *coin*, a silver denarius, bore Caesar's
image on the obverse and the goddess of peace
on the reverse, with an inscription which read,
'Tiberius Caesar Augustus, son of the divine
Augustus, Chief Priest'.

20:27-40 The problem of the resurrection.
(See Mt. 22:23–33; Mk. 12:18–27.) The Sadducees were the next to test Jesus. They were a
party chiefly drawn from the priesthood and the
wealthy aristocracy, perfectly happy with the
status quo and willing to fraternize with the
Romans. They professed a traditional, conservative religion based solely on the five books of
Moses, but it was empty and formal. They were
materialists and denied the resurrection, angels
and spirits (Acts 23:8). Their question took the
form of an absurd story based on the principle of
levirate marriage (from Latin *levir*, a brother-in-
law; see Gn. 38:8; Dt. 25:5f.): how could a
wife have seven husbands in the resurrection?
Jesus' reply had two parts. First, He asserted
that conditions in the resurrection are not like
those on earth. Since there is no death and
hence no need to replenish the race, there is no
need for procreation. This should not be taken
to mean that earthly relationships like marriage
will come to an end in heaven. Rather, *all*
relationships will be taken up to such a high
level that the exclusiveness of marriage will not
be a factor in heaven as it is on earth. The
continuance of earthly relationships is surely
implied in 1 Thes. 4:17f.

Second, Jesus gave an argument for the fact
of the resurrection based on the law of Moses.
At the bush God had said to Moses, 'I—the
God of Abraham' (Ex. 3:6). As is normal in this
type of Hebrew sentence, there is no verb, and
Jesus implies that the present form 'am' must be
supplied (as is done in the LXX), showing that
God was still the God of Abraham centuries
after his death and that consequently Abraham
must still be alive. He who was Abraham's God
in his lifetime would not let death interrupt the
relationship but would resurrect him. The
scribes, who believed in the resurrection, could
not but applaud the discomfiture of their rivals.
35 See on 14:14.

20:41-47 The Person of the Messiah. (See
Mt. 22:41–46; 23:6; Mk. 12:35–40.) The final
episode in these conflict stories shows Jesus
taking the initiative in criticizing inadequate
views of the Christ or Messiah. The Jews looked
forward to the coming of an *earthly* deliverer
and king, a descendant of David (see on 18:38).
But in Ps. 110 David called the Messiah 'My
Lord': how could he thus speak of his son? A

purely earthly Messiah was an inadequate conception of God's deliverer.

The implications of the argument are not pressed home. Instead, Jesus turned to expose the inadequacies of scribal religion. The scribes had become proud of their robes and loved the respect of the people. They were hypocrites who cheated the poor and put up an empty show of piety. They who of all men should have known God's will would receive the greater condemnation. Note, however, that there were individual exceptions (Mk. 12:28–34).

21:1–4 The widow's offering. (See Mk. 12:41–44.) In sharpest contrast to the false religiosity of the scribes is placed the attitude of a poor widow who gave two of the tiniest coins in circulation (AV 'mites') as her offering alongside the large gifts of the rich. In the sight of Jesus her gift was the greatest, for what God measures is not so much the size of the gift as what remains after it has been given. In this particular case the donor had given her whole income.

1 The *treasury*: *i.e.* the place where free-will gifts were received in the Temple.

21:5–38 The destruction of the Temple, and the last things

21:5–7 The fate of the Temple. (See Mt. 24:1–3; Mk. 13:1–4.) Like many other Jews, the disciples were filled with admiration for the lavish and flamboyant architecture of Herod's new Temple which was the main scene of Jesus' ministry in Jerusalem. Jesus, however, did not share their enthusiasm, but used the opportunity to prophesy that it would be razed to the ground. The disciples then asked when this would happen and what indications there would be that it was about to happen. In posing their question in this form, they appear to have associated the destruction of the Temple with the end of the age, and in the ensuing discourse Jesus certainly linked these two events.

The discourse which follows differs considerably in wording from that in Mk. 13. Scholars debate whether Luke rewrote the discourse in Mark to make certain lessons clearer for his readers or had access to different traditions of the words of Jesus. The latter is the more likely theory, although some interpretation by the Evangelist cannot be excluded. Like the Sermon on the Mount, it contains sayings of Jesus probably spoken on several occasions (see on 6:20–26).

5 *Some*: *i.e.* the disciples.

21:8–11 Signs of the end. (See Mt. 24:4–7; Mk. 13:5–8.) Jesus' first words were a warning not to expect the end immediately. The disciples were not to be misled by false messiahs. Nor were they to be tempted to despair by the dreadful events which would precede the end. There would be both human conflict and cosmic disaster before the end.

8 The false prophets declared 'I am', meaning 'I am the Messiah' or 'I am Jesus', and announced the coming of the end in words reminiscent of Jesus' own preaching (*cf.* Mk. 1:15).

21:12–19 The fate of the disciples. (*Cf.* Mt. 10:17–22; 24:9–14; Mk. 13:9–13.) The course of events is not given in chronological order, and discourages any attempt to work out an 'apocalyptic timetable'. Before all this (see v. 12; *i.e.* before the cosmic signs just mentioned) there will be tribulation for the disciples themselves as they suffer persecution from both the Jews and the Romans. This apparent disaster will be an opportunity to witness to the gospel. They need not be worried about preparing speeches beforehand, for in the hour of crisis Jesus Himself will inspire them for bold and incontrovertible witness. Persecution will come even from family and friends and lead to martyrdom and universal hatred. But in all this they will be under the hand of God, and whatever happens to them, those who endure faithfully to the end will gain eternal life.

14, 15 This saying plainly applies to Christians suddenly arrested and brought into court, not to preachers going peacefully to their pulpits! *I will give. . . .* In 12:11f. the Holy Spirit is to be the teacher of the disciples; Jn. 16:7 shows that He is sent by Jesus. **18, 19** In view of the preceding teaching, these verses can hardly mean that the disciples will be saved from physical harm and martyrdom; they contain the promise of divine control over their fate and a summons to perseverance.

21:20–24 The fall of Jerusalem. (*Cf.* Mt. 24:15–22; Mk. 13:14–20.) Two distinct stages in the coming of the end are now described. The first is the encirclement of Jerusalem by armies. Men who value their lives will flee before it is too late, for it will be the time of God's judgment upon the city. At the thought of the inevitable suffering, especially for the women, Jesus again broke out in sorrow. The city would be depopulated and handed over to Gentile domination for a fixed period.

20 Although the language describes a siege much more clearly than the corresponding section in Mark, this does not mean that Luke was writing after the event. The wording is familiar from OT prophecy, especially the passages foretelling the fall of Jerusalem in 587 BC. But whether Jesus used the words in Mark or Luke (or both) or Luke has brought out the meaning of His cryptic words more clearly as coming events were casting their shadows in the air is hard to determine. **24** The *times of the Gentiles* are the period of Gentile domination of Jerusalem; some scholars regard them as the period of the conversion of Gentiles (Rom. 11:25), but this is a thought alien to the present context, whatever its scriptural justification elsewhere. Jesus says nothing about whether Jerusalem would be reinstated at the end of the period.

21:25–28 The coming of the Son of man. (See Mt. 24:29–31; Mk. 13:24–27.) The second stage in the coming of the end is the cosmic disorders (21:11) prophesied in the OT. Some scholars think that this description is metaphorical of the overthrow of the Gentile powers. After this final prelude the coming of the Son of man is announced in language based on Dn. 7:13f. where the coming is associated with the day of judgment and the final, visible establishment of God's rule. Because the disasters ahead are the prelude to this divine act of release, the disciples should be filled with hope, in contrast to the fear which will characterize the rest of men.

21:29–33 The certainty of the end. (See Mt. 24:32–35; Mk. 13:28–31.) **29** In Palestine the *fig tree* is the first to show its leaves and act as the harbinger of spring; in other countries *all the trees* join it in announcing that summer is at hand. So the dreadful events prophesied by Jesus are in reality a sign of hope that the coming of the kingdom is near.

32, 33 What is the meaning of this saying, so strongly affirmed (v. 33) by Jesus? *All*, He said, was to happen in *this generation*. We are to understand by 'all' the premonitory signs, including the fall of Jerusalem in AD 70, which took place as prophesied, rather than as including the coming of the Son of man (*cf.* v. 36 for this distinction). But the fulfilment of these signs was to be proof that His coming was *near*, and this has not yet taken place. We dare not assume that Jesus was mistaken, especially in view of v. 33, but must take into account Mk. 13:32 (with its Lucan equivalent in Acts 1:7), and admit that a full understanding of His words is hidden from us. What can be affirmed with certainty is that the first coming of Jesus and the judgment upon Jerusalem have brought the coming of the kingdom near, even if God's understanding of 'near' has proved to be different from our expectations. It is worth asking whether the coming of the end is not dependent in some way upon the church's fulfilment of the command to evangelize the world.

21:34–38 Preparation for the end. Meanwhile, the vital thing is not speculation or despair but readiness for the end. The day will mean judgment for those who fall prey to worldly temptations, and so the disciples must pray for strength to persevere to the end.

A final statement notes that Jesus was lodging outside Jerusalem, as many pilgrims had to do at passover time when the city was overcrowded.

22:1 – 24:53 THE PASSION AND RESURRECTION

22:1–38 The Last Supper

22:1–6 The treachery of Judas. (See Mt. 26:1–5, 14–16; Mk. 14:1f., 10f.; *cf.* Jn. 11:45–53.) Once the Jewish leaders had decided to do away with Jesus, their main problem was how to avoid an uprising by His supporters; chs. 19–20 have shown that Jesus had much sympathy among the common people, many of whom would have been ready to take up arms on His behalf. The offer of Judas was to provide an opportunity to arrest Jesus quietly. Since there could be

about 100,000 people in and around Jerusalem at the Passover season, the chances of tracking down an individual who wished to remain hidden would be slight.

1 The feasts of *Unleavened Bread* and the *Passover*, originally separate, were regarded as one in practice. The Passover was celebrated on the 14th and 15th of the month Nisan. During the afternoon of the 14th the Passover lambs were slaughtered at the Temple; in the evening of the same day (by our reckoning) the feast was held. Since, however, the Jewish day began at sunset, the feast was in fact held in the early hours of the 15th. The days of Unleavened Bread lasted from the 15th to the 21st of Nisan inclusive. In 22:7 the 14th is described as the first day of Unleavened Bread, possibly because the feasts were closely linked or because Luke was writing for readers who followed our reckoning of the day starting at midnight. Note that Luke agrees with the Markan chronology of the Last Supper and crucifixion; this is significant because, although Luke's passion narrative shows a number of important links with John, he does not suggest that Jesus held His supper a day earlier than the official Passover; see also on Jn. 13:1. **2** Luke does not tell us why the Jewish leaders wished to execute Jesus. **3** This is the first mention of *Satan* since 4:13; see note there. **4** The *captains* were the leaders of the Temple police.

22:7–13 Preparation for the Supper. (See Mt. 26:17–19; Mk. 14:12–16.) On the appropriate day Jesus sent two of His disciples to prepare for the Passover meal. They would need to secure a suitably furnished room within Jerusalem itself and the food—a lamb, bread, bitter herbs and wine. The arrangements made suggest that Jesus had already planned where to meet without being disturbed and made a secret arrangement with a friend in Jerusalem. The room was quite probably that mentioned in Acts 1:13, possibly in the house of Mary (Acts 12:12). A man carrying a water jar would be an unusual sight.

22:14–23 The significance of the meal. (See Mt. 26:20, 26–29, 23f.; Mk. 14:17, 22–25, 20f.; *cf.* Jn. 13:21–30.) The normal course of the Passover meal was: *a.* An inaugural blessing and prayer were followed by the first of four cups of wine and a dish of herbs and sauce. *b.* The story of the institution of the Passover was recited, Ps. 113 was sung, and the second cup drunk. *c.* After a grace the main meal of roast lamb with unleavened bread and bitter herbs was eaten, and after a further prayer the third cup of wine was drunk. *d.* Pss. 114–118 were sung, and the fourth cup was drunk.

Jesus began with words expressing His knowledge that He would shortly suffer and His desire to eat this last meal undisturbed. It would be the *last* supper, for the next occasion for Him would be the fulfilment of the meal in the kingdom of God. The reference is probably to the Messianic banquet rather than to the church's observance of the Lord's Supper. Then Jesus took a cup of wine (the first or second in the series), and reaffirmed that this would be the last occasion on which He would drink before the coming of the kingdom; thus He clearly linked His death to the coming of the kingdom. Next He gave thanks for the bread eaten with the main course and distributed it, saying 'This represents my body'. According to vv. 19b-20 (RSV mg.; see below), He indicated that His body was about to be given for the disciples in sacrificial, vicarious death, and bade them repeat the rite in remembrance of Him. Similarly, He interpreted the third cup of wine to mean His blood by which the new covenant was sacrificially inaugurated (Ex. 24:8; Je. 31:31-34). Finally, He spoke of His imminent betrayal, bringing together in one enigmatic sentence the facts of the divinely ordained course which He must follow and the free responsibility and consequent guilt of His betrayer.

15-18 Luke has put the prophecy of betrayal, recorded by Mark at this point, at the end of the meal, and has brought forward the 'vow of abstinence'. This and much other evidence show that for the passion story Luke had access to other traditions in addition to the one recorded in Mark. The words seem to mean that Jesus Himself did not share in the meal or at least in the fourth cup of wine. **19, 20** The words recorded in RSV mg. are omitted by only one Greek MS (Codex Bezae) out of nearly 3,000, and a number of Latin and Syriac MSS. If the omission is correct, Luke has given an account of a supper in which the wine preceded the bread and which had no sacrificial significance. But there is no evidence in early church order for such a sequence at the Lord's Supper. Despite the support given to the 'short text' by the RSV and NEB, the longer text is to be preferred (see on 24:3). It has links with the tradition recorded by Paul in 1 Cor. 11:23-26, but is not interpolated from there. The shorter text may have arisen through misunderstanding or in an attempt to keep the central Christian 'mystery' as a secret from pagans.

22:24-38 Sayings of Jesus at table. (Cf. Mt. 26:31-35; Mk. 14:27-31; Jn. 13:36-38.) Four sets of sayings by Jesus complete the narrative. **24-27** First, a dispute among the disciples as to which of them would be the greatest led Jesus to tell them that the question of status does not arise in the kingdom of God, whatever may happen in the world. In human society the one who is waited upon is reckoned the greatest, but the example of Jesus who served His disciples shows that this is not so in the kingdom. The story reminds us of the narrative about the feet-washing in Jn. 13 and also of the dispute recorded in Mk. 10:35-45; it seems simplest to suppose that Luke and Mark are recording two different incidents. **28-30** But the second saying of Jesus does allow some honour to the Twelve. They were supporting Jesus in His trials and would both share in the Messianic banquet and act as rulers over the tribes of Israel in the kingdom of Jesus.

It is strange that the saying takes no account of the defection of Judas and that it allots places of honour after Jesus has just rebuked self-seeking (cf. Mk. 10:28-31 for the same problem). What is probably the same saying is found in Mt. 19:28, and it may be that this is the better context. The difficulty about the *twelve* tribes disappears if the saying refers metaphorically to the 'new Israel'. **31-34** In the third section Jesus tells how Satan had sought to have the disciples in order to *sift* them (cf. Jb. 1-2; Dn. 10:13) and lead them into apostasy. Jesus had permitted this, but at the same time He had prayed for Peter that he would not fail in faith and so be able to strengthen the others. Nevertheless, Peter himself would fall like the others and deny his Master. The sequel shows that he did not fall away completely. **35-38** Finally, Jesus spoke of the new situation. Formerly, when the disciples had gone out on mission, they had not lacked anything. Now they would need a purse, a bag and even a sword. The saying is heavily ironical, for Jesus knew that now He would have to face universal opposition and be put to death. But the disciples misunderstood Him and produced weapons. 'That's enough', said Jesus, to end a conversation which they had failed to understand. The way of Jesus, as they should have known, was not the way of the sword, but of love.

22:39-53 The prayer and the arrest of Jesus

(See Mt. 26:36-56; Mk. 14:32-50; Jn. 18:1-11.) After the meal Jesus went out to the Garden of Gethsemane at the foot of the Mt. of Olives. Conscious of the temptations surrounding them all, He urged His disciples to pray and then withdrew by Himself and prayed that, if possible, the cup of suffering and wrath (cf. Is. 51:22; Mk. 10:38) which lay ahead of Him might be averted. Nevertheless, as an obedient Son, He freely put Himself at His Father's disposal. After intense strain, He rose to find His disciples asleep, and again urged them to pray. It was only the One who had prayed who remained strong during the next few hours. Already the betrayer—contemptuously designated 'the man called Judas' (v. 47)—had arrived and given his traitorous greeting. The disciples realized what was about to happen and one of the two swords (v. 38) was promptly produced and used. Jesus restrained His followers and then turned to the mob: was this the way to arrest a peaceable teacher? The hour of evil's sway had come! **40** If *the place* was one visited regularly by Jesus (cf. v. 39), this would explain how Judas knew where to find Him. **43, 44** These verses are omitted by some of the best MSS, but their language is Lucan and they are probably genuine. It is not clear whether the *sweat* was in great drops like drops of blood or was literally blood, but *like* implies the former view. **52** The people mentioned were the proper persons to deal with disturbances in the Temple.

22:54-71 The Jewish trial

(See Mt. 26:57-75; Mk. 14:53-72; Jn. 18:12-27.) Jesus was taken first to the high priest's official residence. Peter slunk in and joined the servants at the warm fire. The big fisherman had no doubt been a conspicuous companion of Jesus earlier, and now he had to run the gauntlet as one person after another accused him of being a friend of Jesus. The fact that he came from Galilee, evidenced by his speech (Mt. 26:73), was regarded as positive proof. In fear for his life Peter yielded to temptation. Luke alone records how Jesus gave him a searching glance, and Peter, full of remorse, broke down completely.

Meanwhile, Jesus had His own load to bear. He claimed to be a prophet: very well, let Him show His powers in a grim game of blind man's buff for the amusement of the guards.

At daybreak the Sanhedrin was convened and Jesus was brought before it. The preliminaries are passed over; the decisive question was whether Jesus claimed to be the Messiah. At first He hesitated to reply, for His hearers would not believe an affirmation from His own lips, and they would not answer if He were to seek their opinion. Nevertheless, He declared that from now onwards the Son of man would be seated at God's right hand. Did that mean that He claimed to be the Son of God? 'That is your way of putting it', said Jesus. It was enough; He was guilty of blasphemy.

In Mark there is a description of a lengthy trial by night in the high priest's house, at which substantially the same dialogue as that recorded by Luke took place; this was followed by a brief morning meeting of the Sanhedrin. Luke records no trial by night, but confines his attention to the morning trial. It is clear that there was an unofficial enquiry at night at the high priest's house, which Luke has passed over in silence, and this was followed in the morning by an official session of the Sanhedrin (which Mark passes over hurriedly) at which the earlier decisions were ratified. It is uncertain whether the dialogue reported by Luke really took place at night, or whether Jesus was subjected to a brief re-examination in the morning. This explains why the accounts of Peter's denial and the mockery by the servants occur *before* the (morning) trial in Luke but *after* the (night) trial in Mark.

55 The house had an open central *courtyard* off which the various rooms opened. **60** A literal *cock crow* is probably meant, rather than the Roman bugle call at 3 a.m. (*gallicinium*). **66** See on 20:1. **69, 70** The words of Jesus differ from those recorded in Mark. Where Mark has one question addressed to Jesus and one answer, Luke has two, separating the titles of Christ, Son of man and Son of God. More important is the fact that where in Mark Jesus says that His judges will see the Son of man sitting at God's right hand and coming as the Judge, here He speaks of the present enthronement of the Son

of man. The two accounts are complementary rather than contradictory. The sitting of the Son of man at God's right hand as judge implies a previous exaltation to that position, which is stressed more in Luke's version. Note how Jesus again substitutes Son of man for the title of Christ (9:20-22). **71** The charge against Jesus was thus that He claimed to be the Messiah or Son of God; probably the latter was regarded as a Messianic title, or else some garbled version of Jesus' private teaching to His disciples had reached their ears. To claim to sit at God's right hand was blasphemy (Mk. 14:64).

23:1-25 The Roman trial

23:1-5 Jesus before Pilate. (See Mt. 27:1f., 11-14; Mk. 15:1-5; *cf.* Jn. 18:28-38.) Since the Jews had in general no power to carry out a death sentence (Jn. 18:31), it was necessary to take the case before the Roman authorities. A Roman governor would not listen to 'questions about words and names' (*cf.* Acts 18:14f.), and therefore the charge against Jesus had to be reformulated as one of sedition against Rome. Of the two particular charges made, the first was false (*cf.* 20:25), but the second was true, although not in the sense in which the Jews meant it (*cf.* Jn. 18:36f.). So, when Pilate asked Jesus if He claimed to be a king, He answered in a non-committal way. Pilate will have questioned Jesus more closely before reaching his verdict that there were no grounds for a political charge against him.

1 Pilate was normally resident in the administrative capital of Caesarea (Acts 23:33; not to be confused with Caesarea Philippi), but (like Herod) visited Jerusalem at the Passover season. **2** *A king* is elucidation of 'Christ' for Roman ears.

23:6-12 Jesus before Herod. The mention of Galilee by the Jews (v. 5) gave Pilate his cue. Throughout the trial he gives the impression of baiting the Jews. He was well aware that Jesus had committed no crime, and deliberately played with the Jews as he tried to thwart their purpose. In the end, when the situation was getting out of control, he was quite prepared to sacrifice an innocent man in order to keep the peace. For the moment, it would do no harm to send Jesus across to Herod Antipas, the tetrarch of Galilee. Herod is presented as a trifler, hoping to see some amusing tricks performed by One whom he probably regarded as some kind of magician, but to such a man Jesus had nothing to say. He and his soldiers descended to rough mockery before returning the problem prisoner to Pilate. Later in the day they amused themselves by chatting over their experiences.

6, 7 Pilate was not necessarily trying to rid himself of the case; he may simply have been taking a second opinion. There is no good reason to think that the incident has been fabricated from Acts 4:25f.; see on 9:9. **10** Some Jewish representatives went across to Herod's residence to ensure that their case did not go by default.

11 The mockery is very similar to that by Pilate's soldiers, but one set of troops could easily have copied the other's example.

23:13-25 The sentence of death. (See Mt. 27:15-26; Mk. 15:6-15; Jn. 18:38 – 19:16.) Pilate perhaps hoped that the people (v. 13) might side with him in resisting the Jewish leaders when he delivered his verdict. No doubt the prisoner had been something of a public nuisance, but for this a scourging would be an adequate penalty. But the crowd had been swayed by the priests and they shouted for Barabbas, a well-known revolutionary, to be released instead of Jesus. Pilate was naturally ill-disposed to a suggestion which involved not only the death of an innocent man but also the release of a dangerous, convicted criminal, but the intensity of the public uproar was such that he deemed it prudent to yield. Pilate's character was summed up by Agrippa I as 'inflexible, merciless and obstinate'; it is borne out by this scene, for the common view that Pilate here shows vacillation and weakness is certainly an over-statement. One thing is certain, that Pilate showed no mercy.

16 Scourging was both a punishment in itself and a normal preliminary to crucifixion (Mk. 15:15). **18** Luke does not explain what led the people to ask for Barabbas, unless v. 17 be accepted as part of the original text, against the evidence of the best MSS.

23:26-49 The crucifixion of Jesus

(See Mt. 27:32-56; Mk. 15:21-41; Jn. 19:17-30.) A condemned man usually carried the cross himself to the place of execution (Jn. 19:17), but in this case a passer-by was requisitioned to help with the load; 'behind' (v. 26) may be a conscious echo of 9:23; 14:27. A crowd always attended executions out of compassion or curiosity. The women among them raised a death-wail for Jesus, but He raised, as it were, a death-wail for Jerusalem. Let them have pity for themselves, for a day would come when they would rue having borne children who were to endure such terrible suffering and long for some mighty convulsion of nature to put an end to their sufferings (cf. Ho. 10:8; Rev. 6:16). For if this is how the Romans treat the innocent Jesus, how much worse will be the fate of guilty Jerusalem. The words are of pity rather than of condemnation.

After being crucified between two criminals (cf. Is. 53:9, 12), Jesus' first recorded words in this Gospel are a prayer for forgiveness for His executioners. The division of the dead man's clothes among the executioners was a recognized custom. Meanwhile, the rulers sneered at Jesus with unconscious irony; the Christian reader knows that it was the death on the cross which decisively showed that Jesus was the Christ and the Saviour. The soldiers also joined in the mockery, taking their cue from the Jews and making use of the words in the *titulus*, or charge-sheet, nailed on the cross. Even one of the criminals repeated the same taunt. Luke alone records how the other criminal, perhaps after initially taunting Jesus also, was of a different mind and uttered a confession of his own sin and Jesus' innocence. Turning to Jesus he asked that He would remember him when He came in His kingly power to reign. Even at this late hour his faith was accepted and he was promised a place in Paradise instead of Sheol, with the justified instead of the condemned.

From noon (the 'sixth hour', v. 44, by Roman reckoning) there was darkness for three hours. The Greek word used need not mean an eclipse of the sun, and cannot mean one, since it was the Passover season of full moon. The cause of the darkness was perhaps a dust-laden sirocco wind, strong enough to split the curtain of the Temple. The significance of this is not indicated by the Evangelists: was it regarded as a prophecy of the forthcoming destruction of the Temple or as an indication that the way into God's presence was now open for all men (Heb. 9:8-14; 10:19f.)?

Then at the ninth hour came the end as Jesus committed Himself into God's hands with the words of Ps. 31:5. The manner of His death led the officiating centurion to glorify God by saying, 'Certainly this man was just'. The words declare the innocence of Jesus, and perhaps allude to His sharing the frequent fate of the just (cf. Wisdom 2:12-20). But why did the centurion *praise* God? Was it because God had sustained Jesus to die nobly after living nobly? The mourning by the crowds is dismissed by some critics as imaginary, but this is surely perverse. The final note emphasizes that Jesus' friends saw Him really die.

33 The place of the crucifixion, here called *The Skull* (Aramaic *Golgotha*) is still uncertain, but was probably near the Church of the Holy Sepulchre on the north of the city; the identification of the site with the skull-shaped hill known as Gordon's Calvary is today generally rejected. **34a** is omitted by a formidable list of early MSS, but it should be retained either as a genuine part of Luke (cf. Acts 7:60) or as a reliable piece of extraneous tradition. It would be omitted by scribes who felt that it was unseemly or not answered. **36** This action seems to be distinct from the kind act in Mk. 15:36. *Vinegar* was the cheap wine drunk by soldiers. **39, 40** It is unnecessary to suppose that the criminal's words were ironic but nevertheless accepted by Jesus, still less that the whole incident is legendary. Here, as elsewhere, Luke had access to other traditions than those recorded in Mark. **42** *In your kingly power* means 'when you return as King'. The variant text 'into your kingly power', expressing Jesus' vindication by God, is less likely. **43** *Paradise* is the resting-place of the redeemed before the final judgment, and is opened to those who trust in Jesus. There is some tension with other statements which imply that Jesus visited Hades (Mt. 12:40; Acts 2:27, 31; 1 Pet. 3:19f.) before His resurrection. The difficulty is perhaps due to our inability to think of the after-life in any other than spatial categories; perhaps *today* means the new era inaugurated by the resurrection. **47** For *innocent* Mark has 'the Son of God'. Luke may have wished to avoid giving the impression that the centurion thought of Jesus in pagan fashion as a demi-god.

23:50–56 The burial of Jesus

(See Mt. 27:57–61; Mk. 15:42–47; Jn. 19:38–42.) The bodies of crucified criminals were usually left hanging and then cast into a common grave. A friend and disciple of Jesus spared Him this indignity. Joseph, a member of the Sanhedrin who had not agreed with its verdict upon Jesus, gained permission from Pilate to bury the body. He wrapped it, according to Jewish custom, in a shroud and placed it in a new grave. Jewish graves were caves, natural or man-made, in the sides of hills, large enough for a man to enter, and sealed by a sliding stone across the entrance. Joseph, however, did not embalm the body, and the women from Galilee decided to repair this omission as soon as possible after the sabbath which they observed in the normal manner.

50 *Arimathaea* was about 20 miles north-west of Jerusalem on the border between Judea and Samaria. **51** Since all Jews were *looking for the kingdom of God*, the phrase here must mean that Joseph held the particular form of expectation taught by Jesus and lived in accordance with this hope. **52** Death by crucifixion was normally slow and drawn out; Luke does not mention Pilate's surprise at the rapid death of Jesus. **54** The *day of Preparation* for the weekly sabbath extended from sunset on Thursday to sunset on Friday. But *the sabbath* 'was dawning' (RSV mg.; Gk. *epiphōskō*) implies not sunset but sunrise (*cf.* Mt. 28:1); here, however, the word should perhaps be taken to mean that the lights were being lit on the Friday evening when the sabbath was imminent (JB).

24:1–53 The resurrection of Jesus

24:1–12 The empty tomb. (*Cf.* Mt. 28:1–10; Mk. 16:1–8; Jn. 20:1–10.) Very early on Sunday morning an unspecified number of the women from Galilee came to the tomb of Jesus, found it open and went inside, only to discover that there was no body there. Two 'men', clothed in the white garments associated with heavenly beings (*cf.* 9:29) appeared and spoke to them, gently criticizing them for expecting to find in a tomb One who had prophesied His resurrection from the dead (9:22; 18:33). They therefore made their way back from the tomb and told the story to the other disciples of Jesus. The naming of some of the women (v. 10) is perhaps an indication that they ought to have been regarded as credible witnesses, but nevertheless for the moment the apostles were not disposed to believe the story. Peter, however, went to the tomb and confirmed that it was empty (v. 12, RSV mg.).

The historicity of the story has often been called in question. It has been argued, *e.g.*, that the women went to the wrong tomb, but it is quite incredible that both they and the later visitors to the scene could have been mistaken on such a point. The argument that, while there may have been 'resurrection appearances', the story of the empty tomb is both late and mythical is exposed to the fundamental objections that in fact the tradition of the empty tomb is early (it is presupposed in 1 Cor. 15:3–7), and that the NT understanding of resurrection is of a *bodily* resurrection; to hold that the bones of Jesus are still somewhere in Palestine is to disbelieve in the NT doctrine of the resurrection and is at the same time to adopt what is historically a very tenuous hypothesis. But if the basic facts are certain, it must be confessed that it is as difficult to harmonize fully the various versions of what happened on Easter morning as it is to frame a coherent account of any modern cataclysmic event witnessed by a number of individuals. If this absolves the witnesses from any possible charge of collusion, it does leave a number of loose ends which it is difficult to tie up satisfactorily.

1 *They* stands in contrast to the visit of Mary Magdalene to the tomb by herself in Jn. 20:1–10; it is possible that two or more separate visits have been telescoped in Luke's account. **3** Here and in a number of places in this chapter (vv. 5, 12, 36, 40, 51, 52) RSV has removed phrases to the margin. With one exception, the evidence for omission is confined to one Greek MS (Codex Bezae) and some Latin authorities (*cf.* on 22:19f.). Although Westcott and Hort omitted the phrases, it is being increasingly recognized that they are probably a true part of the text. **4** Mark mentions only one young man at the tomb and his words are different. In particular, Luke does not record the command to go to Galilee (Mk. 16:7; *cf.* 14:28), very probably because he has not described any appearances of Jesus in Galilee. **9** The statement in Mk. 16:8 that the women said nothing to anybody out of fear should not be regarded as contradicting this verse, since it is uncertain what Mark may have gone on to record at this point, and in any case he probably meant that they said nothing to anybody except the Eleven. **10** For *Joanna* see 8:3. **12** A summary of the story in Jn. 20:1–10.

24:13–35 The walk to Emmaus. (*Cf.* Mk. 16:12f.) On the same Sunday afternoon two of the disciples were walking to Emmaus and discussing the recent events. When the risen Jesus joined them on the road they did not recognize Him; a supernatural failure to perceive His identity is meant, rather than that He had a different form (though this is possibly implied in Mk. 16:12). By professing ignorance He learned what had saddened them and that His tomb was rumoured to be empty. They remembered that there had been a prophecy of His resurrection on the third day, but they had not heard of anybody seeing Him. They had expected Jesus to be the redeemer of Israel, but they could not understand how He had been rejected by the rulers. Jesus' reply was that suffering was the necessary prelude to the Messiah's entry into kingly glory, and He directed them to the scriptures which prophesied this (see on 18:31, for references). When they arrived at their destination they pressed Him to accept their hospitality for the night. They prepared an evening meal, but at the table He assumed the position of host, took up the bread, gave thanks to God, broke it and gave it to them. The language used is reminiscent of that describing the action of Jesus at the feeding miracles and the Last Supper (9:16; 22:19; Mk. 8:6). But whether or not the disciples were reminded of these acts (there is no evidence that they were present on any of those occasions), the veil immediately fell from their eyes and they recognized Jesus, who immediately vanished from their sight. Then they realized that they had felt a strange elation as their unknown companion had spoken with them on the way. They must tell the others what had happened, and promptly rose to go back to Jerusalem to tell them. But before they could tell their story, they were greeted with the exciting news that Jesus had appeared to Simon. He was risen!

13 *Emmaus* is usually identified with Kubeibeh, some 7 miles north-west of Jerusalem. Mozah, in the same vicinity, is another possibility. **18** *Cleopas* may be the Clopas of Jn. 19:25. **19** This describes the most that Jesus can be to those who do not believe that He is risen. **21** The disciples knew that Jesus had spoken about something significant happening on the third day, and that His tomb was said to be empty. But this was not adequate evidence for the resurrection; this could be provided only by the appearance of the Lord Himself. **25** *Men* is too strong a translation. Greek idiom would use the masculine form to address a mixed company (*cf.* 17:34), and it is likely that the unnamed disciple was Cleopas's wife. **27** The Jewish Scriptures consisted of three parts: the Law of Moses (Genesis–Deuteronomy); the Prophets (Joshua, Judges, 1 and 2 Samuel, 1 and 2 Kings, and the prophets, with the exception of Daniel); and the Writings (the remaining books of our OT). The first two groups were complete and closed by the time of Jesus. The third (sometimes called 'the Psalms', v. 44, from its chief component) was virtually closed, but doubt still existed about the status of two or three books. The omission of the third group here is not significant, the OT writings are here considered from the point of view of their prophetic content. **34** For the appearance to Simon see 1 Cor. 15:5. The brief summary in Mk. 16:12f. which says that the disciples did not believe them refers to the incredulity and disbelief later in the story at vv. 37, 41.

24:36–53 Jesus appears again to the disciples. (*Cf.* Mt. 28:16–20; Mk. 16:14–20; Jn. 20:19–23; Acts 1:6–11.) The excited story of the two travellers was interrupted by the sudden appearance of Jesus in the room and His greeting 'Peace

to you'. The disciples were very naturally filled with panic at this supernatural manifestation, but He spoke so as to relieve their distress. It was really He Himself, and He showed them His physical body with its flesh and bones, and His hands and feet with the nailprints in them. To give further proof of the reality of His presence He ate some food in their presence.

What follows need not necessarily have happened on the same occasion or on the same day. If the account is taken literally, it would imply that the resurrection and ascension both occurred on Easter Sunday. Luke's own account in Acts 1 shows that this was not the case, and therefore what he has here described briefly and compactly must have taken place over a longer period. There was a repetition of the instruction given to the two disciples on the road to Emmaus, so as to enable all the disciples to understand the OT prophecies of His coming. Two new factors are introduced. The command to preach repentance and faith to all nations was issued, and those who had been witnesses of His resurrection appearances (a much larger group than the Eleven) were promised that God's power would enable them to be His witnesses. Finally, He led them out of Jerusalem to Bethany where He gave them His parting blessing and was then carried away from them into heaven. They returned to Jerusalem and waited there in joyful expectation of the fulfilment of His promise.

The story bears resemblances not only to that in Jn. 20:19–23 but also to that in Mt. 28:16–20 where Jesus gives the mission charge on a mountain in Galilee. There need be no doubt that Jesus appeared to His disciples both in Jerusalem (as in Luke, Acts and Jn. 20) and in Galilee (as in Matthew and Jn. 21), but it is more difficult to harmonize the mission charge in Luke with that in Matthew. It should, however, be noted that Mt. 28 is not a record of the ascension but of a resurrection appearance, and it is by no means unlikely that Jesus repeated His last commands more than once to His disciples.

39–43 The description of the resurrection body of Jesus in strongly physical terms has worried many scholars, but it is hard to see why He may not have appeared in this form. The mention of 'honeycomb' alongside the broiled fish in v. 42 AV is not upheld by the best MSS. **47** For prophecy of the preaching to the Gentiles, *cf.* Is. 2:3; 42:6; 49:6; 51:4f.; Rom. 15:9–12. **50** *Bethany* lay at the foot of the Mt. of Olives (*cf.* Acts 1:12). The various uncertainties in the text of vv. 51f. (*cf.* on 24:3) may be due to alterations made in the text of Luke and Acts after these two books, originally meant to be read as one, were separated from each other when John was inserted between them. Some MSS may have tried to avoid an apparent contradiction with the forty days' period in Acts 1. **53** *Continually* should not be taken too literally (*cf.* 2:37), as Acts 1:13f. indicates.

I. H. MARSHALL

John

INTRODUCTION

AUTHORSHIP

It is not possible in brief compass to give more than a bare outline of the discussion over authorship of this Gospel. But the main features of the discussion may be summarized as follows.

a. There is a very strong tradition, supported by early evidence from patristic sources, that the author was the apostle John. There are no specific references to the identity of the author in the Gospel itself. It is necessary therefore to weigh carefully the external evidence to decide how reliable it is. At least as early as Irenaeus there was belief in the apostolic authorship, and his witness is strengthened by the possibility that he may have had access to authentic tradition through his earlier acquaintance with Polycarp. The latter did not himself refer to or cite from this Gospel when writing his epistle to the Philippians, but this need not lead to the conclusion that he was ignorant of it. The sole opposition to the apostolic authorship came from a group known as the Alogoi, who appear to have been a small splinter group in Rome. Their views were opposed by Hippolytus who wrote a defence of this Gospel. The history of the book before Irenaeus is not easy to determine, but it must have been regarded as authoritative for some considerable time to have been placed indisputably on a level with the other three as part of the fourfold Gospel.

b. Some internal considerations corroborate, although they do not prove, the veracity of the tradition, as, *e.g.*, 1:14; 19:35; 21:24. Although all of these references have been otherwise understood by some scholars, it is most natural to see them as evidence of the author's own claim to be an eyewitness. Moreover, John, son of Zebedee, is nowhere mentioned by name in this Gospel, while John the Baptist is named simply as John without further description. This would certainly be more intelligible if the author were himself the other John. A further consideration is the mention anonymously of the 'disciple whom Jesus loved', which may well be a reference to John the apostle. Some dispute that John would have described himself in this way and prefer to regard this as evidence that the apostle was *not* the author. Others identify the beloved disciple as Lazarus or some other follower of Jesus. It is impossible to be sure, but his close association with Peter would support the view that he was John, as would the fact that some of the references to him show his very close association with Jesus in the upper room.

c. The author appears to possess detailed knowledge of Palestine and of Jewish customs. This would be most intelligible if he were a Palestinian Jew, although the evidence does not demand this. He may have obtained his information from another source.

d. Many incidental details also suggest that an eyewitness account lay behind the Gospel, as, *e.g.*, the number of waterpots at Cana and the number of fish caught in the Sea of Galilee when Jesus appeared to His disciples after His resurrection. Such details are not essential to the narrative, but add a certain vividness to the account.

e. The Hellenistic characteristics of this Gospel are, nevertheless, said to militate against the correctness of the early tradition, since John the apostle was not a Hellenistic Jew. Moreover, parallels with the non-Christian philosophical tractates known as the *Hermetica* are said to support this contention. There are certainly parallels in terminology with both Philo of Alexandria and Hermes, but this factor does not conclusively show that the author was a Hellenist. Some similar parallels in thought are found also in the Jewish literature from Qumran.

f. The close acquaintance of the author with rabbinical methods of argument is another reason why some have rejected the apostolic authorship, since John was a Galilaean fisherman. But due allowance must be made for the fact that the rabbinical arguments are found in the teaching of Jesus, not in the author's own comments.

g. The Evangelist, moreover, appears to adopt a polemical attitude towards the Jews, as if they are a race apart from himself, a feature which would be surprising if John the apostle were the author. But this may be evidence of the deep feeling of a Jewish Christian over the bitter hostility of his own people towards Jesus.

h. Alternative theories regarding authorship generally attempt to retain some connection of John the apostle with the Gospel by regarding him as the witness, while at the same time postulating another author. The most widely held theory is that another John, known as John the Elder, was the author. If there were two Johns so closely associated in the production of the Gospel, it is not impossible that confusion may have arisen between them in the early tradition. But the existence of John the Elder depends on a somewhat ambiguous statement of Papias, who makes no mention in any case of a Gospel being written by him.

i. Some deny all connection of John the

apostle with the Gospel and suppose that it was attributed to him to gain apostolic authority for the work.

j. In face of all these various opinions it is difficult to be dogmatic, but it would appear reasonable to suppose that the apostolic authorship accounts best for all the evidence, internal and external.

PURPOSE

We cannot do better than examine the author's own statement of purpose in Jn. 20:31. That purpose was specifically evangelistic. It was aimed to produce faith in Jesus as Christ and as Son of God. The record of the various signs was intended to produce this result, and with this in mind the many references throughout the Gospel to believing and to non-believing become significant. Both the historical narratives and the didactic discourses were chosen because of their power to focus attention on the specific claims of Jesus. John has no thought, therefore, of producing a biographical or psychological study. It must not be supposed that an evangelistic purpose weakens the historical veracity. To be effective the theological motive needs an authentic historical basis. This is not to exclude the possibility that John regarded some at least of his material as possessing symbolic significance.

There may well have been some subsidiary aims, such as a presentation of the true relationship between Jesus and John the Baptist, or a refutation of Docetic views about Christ (*i.e.* theories which draw a distinction between the heavenly Christ and the human Jesus). Some have supposed an eschatological or a sacramental corrective against misunderstandings.

A strong body of opinion regards the Gospel as a presentation of Christianity in a Hellenized form. The prologue (1:1–18) may seem to lend support to this theory. But the crucial factor is the extent to which the prologue determines the purpose of the Gospel as a whole. It is better to suppose that the body of the Gospel supplies the key to the understanding of the prologue, rather than *vice versa*. The teaching of Jesus was sufficiently comprehensive to be intelligible to Greek as well as Jew without the necessity to posit such thoroughgoing interpretation as the Hellenistic school supposes.

THE RELATION TO
THE SYNOPTIC GOSPELS

A comparison with the other Gospels shows a marked difference in John in the substance and in the method of presentation. A large amount of material included in the others is lacking from John, whereas a considerable amount of the Johannine material is lacking from the Synoptics. In fact there is little material common to all four Gospels, apart from the passion narratives. A major difference is that the Synoptics concentrate on the Galilaean ministry, whereas John fixes his attention on the Jerusalem ministry. This largely accounts for the difference in style of Jesus' teaching, the parabolic teaching of the Synoptics giving way to the dialogue and discourse style of John. Certain historical differences have also been noted, such as the setting of the cleansing of the Temple, the events which precipitated the arrest of Jesus, the duration of the ministry and the date of the Last Supper. From these considerations some have concluded that John aims to correct and supersede the Synoptics, but this is difficult to maintain, for on so many occasions he assumes knowledge of the Synoptic traditions as a basis for his own. It is better to regard John as complementary to the Synoptics, although this does not in itself explain all the differences. The most difficult problem is the chronology of the passion events. The solution may lie in the use of different calendars by John and the Synoptics, but the data are not sufficient to point to a completely satisfying answer.

It may at first seem that the Johannine presentation of Jesus differs so completely from that of the Synoptics that both portraits cannot be of the same person. But this would be a wrong deduction. When sufficient attention is paid to the different purposes of the separate Gospels, and to the different types of audiences to which Jesus addressed His teaching, the contrast is more intelligible. Some have attributed the difference in John to the probability that the material had for a long period been adapted to the Evangelist's own teaching ministry. But a more probable explanation is that the Evangelist was himself drawn to the more reflective style of the discourses and allowed his own style to be considerably moulded by his model.

DATE AND PLACE OF WRITING

There is some dispute whether or not any certain traces of John's Gospel can be found in writers before the time of Irenaeus. But there is good ground for supposing that Justin (*c.* AD 150) knew and used the Gospel and a possibility that Ignatius also knew of it. Apart from patristic citations there are two early 2nd-century papyrus MSS which show the early existence and circulation of the Gospel. The Rylands papyrus contains a scrap of John's Gospel and the Egerton papyrus echoes the language of John and the other Gospels. It is impossible therefore to date this Gospel much later than the end of the first century at the latest. If the apostle was the author, a date a few years before the end of the century would almost certainly be required as the latest possible date. Since the Gospel must have come after the Synoptic Gospels, a date fairly late in the first century is generally preferred (*c.* AD 90), although some have suggested an earlier date.

As for the place of origin, tradition has it that John was resident in Ephesus and there seem to be no real grounds for disputing this. Some who do not maintain apostolic authorship suggest not only that this Ephesus tradition is unreliable, but also that John did not live to old age. The evidence which is claimed to support this view consists of scanty and none too reliable clues that John died a martyr's death much earlier than the Gospel could have been written. But the tradition of his long life and of his writing the Gospel is much stronger.

THEOLOGY

John has many characteristic features, particularly in his presentation of Christ, and this may be said to be the most significant feature of his theology. It has already been pointed out that his major purpose was theological, and indeed Christological. The focus of attention was on Messiahship and Sonship. The Messianic status of Jesus more than once formed the topic of discussion among the Jews (7:26ff.; 10:24). Moreover, three times in this Gospel there are recorded confessions of the Messiahship of Jesus (1:41; 4:29; 11:27). To the Evangelist Jesus was the fulfiller of all the Messianic hopes of the Jewish people. In full harmony with this is the frequent appeal to the OT testimony.

Jesus as Son of God is far more characteristic of the Gospel. Many times does Jesus bring out His own filial relationship with the Father. Whereas this aspect is not absent from the Synoptics, it is specially noteworthy in John because of the frequent occurrence of the term 'Son' without further description. The plan of salvation was effected by the Father through the Son. It was through love for the world that God sent His Son (3:16). The Son is the agent through whom the Father reveals Himself (1:18). The claim of Jesus to be Son of God was the basis of the charge before Pilate that according to Jewish law He ought to die (19:7).

The most characteristic feature of the Synoptic Gospels is Jesus as Son of man, and although it is not quite so prominent in John, it is still basic to his presentation. It is the Son of man who not only reveals the Father but who will be lifted up (3:13, 14). This process of lifting up will result in the glorification of the Son of man (12:23). Moreover, there are many indications of the perfect humanity of Jesus in this Gospel. He can experience human emotions, can hunger and thirst, can be tired through a journey. The exalted Christology is never allowed to detract from the perfect humanity of Jesus.

In the prologue the pre-existence and deity of Christ are expressed explicitly. The *Logos* was not only with God in the beginning, but was God (1:1), and it was this *Logos* who became flesh and is identified with Christ. Whatever the origins of the idea of the *Logos* for the Evangelist, his own Christology is clear. The narrative which follows is not that of a mere man but of the pre-existent Son who shared with the Father the creation of the world (1:3).

A further feature of the Johannine Christology is the number of statements of Jesus introduced by the significant 'I am'. In this way He described Himself as the Way, the Truth, the Life, the Resurrection, the Bread, the Shepherd, the Door, the Vine. All of these suggestive titles explain different aspects of what He came to be and to do for men.

There are many figures of speech used to describe the nature of the work of Christ. The sacrificial lamb (1:29), the temple of His body (2:21), the serpent in the wilderness (3:14), the shepherd giving his life for his sheep (10:11), the grain of wheat (12:24). The death of Jesus was even recognized as expedient by the high priest that year, but John sees a deeper meaning in it than Caiaphas (11:51). There is throughout the Gospel a sense of the inevitable as Jesus' hour draws gradually nearer.

One further important factor in Johannine theology is the frequent mention of the Holy Spirit. His work in regeneration (3:5ff.), His promised outpouring following the glorification of Jesus (7:37ff.), and the five sayings about Him in the farewell discourses (chs. 14–16) are all found only in John's Gospel. In the latter sayings, He is described as Counsellor, as dwelling in the believer, as the Teacher, as a witness to Christ, as convicter of the world and as guide into all truth for Christ's people. Of all the Gospels John shows most clearly that the continuation of the ministry of Jesus would be through the agency of the Spirit.

This is a Gospel which contributes much to the theology of the NT and repays the most diligent study. Its language is often simple but its thought is profound.

OUTLINE OF CONTENTS

COMMENTARY

1:1–18 THE PROLOGUE

Unlike the other Evangelists, John does not begin his Gospel with an immediate introduction of the historical Jesus. Instead he introduces his readers to the Word (Gk. *logos*), whom he does not identify with Jesus Christ until the end of his prologue. There can be no doubt that his method of leading up to the historical events has considerable bearing on the interpretation of the whole. For this reason an appreciation of the meaning of the 'Word' as it would have struck the earliest readers of the Gospel is essential, but on this question there have been varying points of view. A strong body of opinion has maintained the Greek associations of the idea.

The term *Logos* was used among the Stoics in describing the principle of divine reason (*logos spermatikos*) which caused the natural creation to grow. This idea was much more fully developed as a distinct entity in the writings of Philo where it is used of the instrument through which the world was created. Any similarity between this concept and the statement in Jn. 1:3 is more than offset by the fact that there are crucial differences in the use of the term in the two writers. Philo never conceived of the *Logos* as a person, nor did he explicitly claim its preexistence to the world. But the most significant distinction between the two is Philo's denial of any incarnation of the Word and John's express assertion that the Word had become flesh. Some similarities of expression may be found between this Gospel and the syncretistic philosophical literature current during the early centuries of the Christian era known as the *Hermetica*, but the essential thought is quite different. It will be seen, therefore, that although Greek thought can be regarded as part of the background of John's prologue it by no means furnishes a complete or even adequate explanation.

In view of the similarity of the opening of John's prologue to the opening of the book of Genesis, and in view of the constant appeal throughout the Gospel to the OT, it would seem reasonable to assume that Jewish thought contributed a major part of the significance of the *Logos*. The notion of the creative activity of God being effected through His word or wisdom is particularly dominant in the Jewish wisdom literature (*cf.* Pr. 8 and Wisdom 18:15, 16). Closely linked to this is the rabbinical practice of attributing to the law some agency in creation. The Dead Sea Scrolls, which have shown some combinations of ideas similar to those of John's prologue, have led to a more sympathetic consideration of the Jewish *milieu* behind the prologue.

But John's prologue must be considered on its own merits. It is distinctively Christian. It is designed to prepare the way for the record of the activities and teachings of a unique Person. For this reason the prologue must be interpreted in terms of the remainder of the Gospel, not *vice versa*. If any readers began reading the Gospel convinced that there could be no incarnate link between God and man, they would soon discover that John's conviction is quite different and that the life of Jesus must be conceived as a unique phenomenon. A careful analysis of the prologue will show how integral it is with the recurrent ideas of the Gospel.

1:1–5 The pre-existent Word

1, 2 When the opening words of Genesis and John are compared, there is enough similarity to show the close connection in the latter writer's mind between the two, although John's distinctive contribution is to show that before creation the Word existed. *In the beginning was the Word.*

Here the verb used, although referring to the past, emphasizes continuity. The Word that is now was the Word before creation began. *With God.* The form in which this is stated is suggestive, for the preposition (Gk. *pros*) conveys the idea of communion. The literal idea is 'towards God', which at once requires some distinctiveness between God and the Word, a feature which has significance for the interpretation of the next clause. *The Word was God.* Some translators have incorrectly rendered this 'The Word was divine', but this is an unwarranted weakening of the statement. As there is no article in the Greek (*theos*), the term must be taken as a predicate, in which case it states the characteristic of the Word; but since it is a noun and not an adjective it must assert the Godhead of the Word. It involves not merely divinity but deity.

3 The thought next turns to the creative activity of the Word. The Greek draws attention to the agency of the Word (*through*, Gk. *dia*) and then goes on to exclude all possibility of creation apart from Him. The close connection between the Father and the Son, which has already been stressed in Their essential relationships, is seen also in Their part in creation. Any conception of creation which does not take account of this is not in harmony with NT teaching generally. This would certainly exclude Gnostic ideas of intermediaries in creation, which were designed to protect God from direct contamination with an essentially evil world. John's assertion that the Word was *life* is a logical sequence from His creative activity. This view of the Word as the source of life is basic to this Gospel, for John states his purpose as being that his readers might have life in Him (Jn. 20:31).

4 The close connection between *life* and *light* is not unexpected. In the physical world, life is dependent on light (*cf.* the creation narrative) and John transfers the idea to the spiritual world. An alternative reading (see mg.) connects the end statement in v. 3 with the phrase 'in him was life' in v. 4, but this is a more difficult punctuation and the other is to be preferred.

5 *The light shines in the darkness.* There can be no doubt that the light here must be interpreted by means of v. 4. There it is an illumination which comes to man generally and would seem to refer to the light of conscience and reason. But here the idea is developed, for the light is focused on its environment, which John describes as darkness. Since in this case the light is personal it is not external as the light from a lamp. Rather, the light of spiritual enlightenment which mankind has received is exclusively derived from the divine Word. The following statement that *the darkness has not overcome it* could also be rendered 'has not apprehended it', but the former fits the context better for it draws attention to the superior quality of the light.

1:6–8 The witness of John to the Word

Having stated that light has shone in darkness,

John moves nearer to the historical setting of the ministry of the Word by appealing to the witness of John the Baptist. 6 The important feature about John's testimony is that it was divinely appointed. The verb *sent* is characteristic of this Gospel, especially in describing the mission of Jesus. Even the herald was specifically sent. 7, 8 The purpose was *to bear witness to the light*. It is not improbable that the Evangelist knew of some who attached more importance to John's teaching than to that of Jesus and he designed therefore to clarify at once the relationship between them (*cf.* also vv. 15, 26ff.). The express repudiation of any idea that he was the light and the double assertion of his character as a witness focus attention on John's true position. The ultimate purpose of all true Christian testimony is to lead to faith, the scope of which is universal as the *all* shows.

1:9-13 The light coming to men

The subject of the witness is more important than the witness. Hence the greater concentration upon it. 9 *The true light . . . was coming into the world*. This gives a better connection of thought than AV which relates the latter phrase to 'every man' and gives the impression that all men receive light at the time of birth. The following verse makes clear that this could not be true of light in the specific, personal sense in which John clearly intends it. Before the coming of Christ some light certainly existed, but when He came He was constituted as the only true illumination from whom all existing light was derived. 10 There was a general lack of recognition of Him by *the world*, by which John evidently meant not so much the physical creation as the world of men. It is characteristic of this Gospel to contrast the mission of Jesus with the world, which generally symbolizes people adversely disposed towards God.

11 *He came to his own home*. RSV is justified in rendering the text in this way, rather than relating the neuter plural adjective to 'things'. In the next clause John leaves no doubt that he is dealing with people. Failure to receive Christ is a personal responsibility. *His own home* would presumably, therefore, relate to Israel. That His own nation were opposed to Him is amply illustrated in the body of the Gospel. It is the Jews who are consistently seen to be at enmity with Christ. John does not intend his readers to suppose that none of His own people received Him, for he makes this clear in the next statement. Another possible interpretation takes *his own* to mean His own world in the sense of His own property. 12 For the Evangelist there is a close connection between receiving and believing, indeed they are identical. *He gave power to become children of God*. Through the divine Word a new relationship is possible. The word *power* (Gk. *exousia*) describes a rightful authority. It is clear that sonship once received is in no jeopardy of being dispossessed for it originates from God and not from man. This supernatural characteristic is particularly evident in John's next statement about the divine origin of the new birth. 13 *Not of blood nor of the will of the flesh*. This at once excludes all idea of natural process. Since the word *blood* is in the plural in Greek, some exegetes suppose that the blood of both parents in natural birth is alluded to (so C. K. Barrett), but others maintain that the singular would for Christians suggest the blood of Christ, which would make the statement less valid (*cf.* E. C. Hoskyns). Another suggestion sees in the whole verse an allusion to the virgin birth, but this requires an extension of the plain literal meaning.

1:14-18 The incarnation of the Word

At this point in his prologue John describes the coming of the Word into human life. It is here that the record of Jesus' life really begins. 14 The statement, *the Word became flesh*, distinguishes John's use of the word *Logos* from all others, especially its emphasis on flesh, which is here used as a symbol of humanity. He who was God then became truly man. The wording, *dwelt among us*, draws special attention to the residence of Christ in our midst for a limited period of time. It is significant that *grace* and *truth* are singled out as characteristics of Him, for these are biblical rather than philosophical terms, and show that John has no intention of treating the theme of his story in a speculative way. *We have beheld his glory*. At its face value this statement would be assumed to refer to an eyewitness observation, but some scholars take the first person plural to refer to Christians generally. Yet if glory was visibly seen, the former interpretation must be right. It may be that the glory was the transfiguration scene, but more likely that it was the moral splendour of the whole ministry, including especially the signs (*cf.* 2:11). John himself defines the glory as that of an *only Son*, which highlights the unique Sonship of Jesus. 15 *He who comes after me*. The parenthesis about John the Baptist is unexpected, but is intended to add greater strength to the witness. *Ranks before me* means that Jesus is superior to John in respect of His office. John was only the herald, whereas Jesus was the Messiah. *He was before me*. Cf. 8:58 as a testimony to Christ's pre-existence.

16 After the parenthesis of v. 15 the thought returns to the idea of fullness which must be compared with the similar idea in v. 14. While it is a Gnostic term, *fullness* is not here used in a technical sense. *Grace upon grace* seems to mean continuous grace, showing its inexhaustible quality. The preposition in the Greek is *anti*, which means 'in place of' or 'in exchange for', and this has led some to suppose that OT grace is exchanged for NT grace; but since John draws a distinction between law and grace this interpretation is unlikely. 17 The contrast between Moses and Jesus Christ lies in the method of approach to God. Obedience to law is clearly inferior to the simple acceptance

of grace and truth. In this verse John identifies the *Logos* for the first time specifically as *Jesus Christ*.

18 The comparison between Moses and Christ is carried on, for it was inherent in the law that God was too holy to be approached directly and certainly could not be seen. Yet Christ has made Him known. *The only Son.* There is an alternative reading here, which has 'God' in place of 'Son', and this undoubtedly has the stronger MS support. Yet in view of the subsequent statement, 'who is in the bosom of the Father', the reading 'Son' seems more intelligible, especially with the adjective *only* (Gk. *monogenēs*). The alternative reading would have to be understood as an assertion of the deity of Jesus Christ. *He has made him known.* The verb means literally 'interpreted' or 'narrated'. Jesus Christ is the perfect exegete of God.

1:19 – 2:11 INTRODUCTORY EVENTS

1:19–34 The testimony of the Baptist

The witness of John has already twice been referred to in the prologue, but is now placed in a specific historical setting. **19** The occasion chosen is a deputation from some of the Jerusalem Jews with the challenge to John to declare his identity. **20** *I am not the Christ.* Importance is clearly attached to distinguishing the forerunner from the Messianic Person he had come to announce. **21** *Are you Elijah?* Some see in John's answer to this question a correction of the Synoptic tradition, since Matthew records our Lord's identification of John the Baptist with Elijah (Mt. 11:14; 17:12). But Jesus' comment shows that He was not identifying John with Elijah in the generally accepted sense of the term. John denies that he is the Elijah of current popular expectation; but Jesus asserts that he is Elijah in the true spiritual sense. *Are you the prophet?* It seems best to refer this to the expectation found in Dt. 18:15, of one who was to come. It does not appear to have been a Messianic title (*cf.* 7:40, 41). The enquirers were examining all the popular possibilities. **22, 23** *What do you say about yourself?* It is interesting to note that here John the Baptist is said to cite Is. 40:3, but in the Synoptics the words are not found on John's own lips. The difference is understandable, for in this Gospel the herald is obliged to give a self-identification, whereas each of the other Evangelists gives his own comment. There is no contradiction. *Make straight the way of the Lord.* The imagery is drawn from the practice of heralds clearing a path for the approaching king, an office of considerable importance. Although John is no more than a voice, he is herald of the Messiah Himself. **24** *Now they had been sent from the Pharisees.* John identifies the senders, referred to in v. 19 as Jews. The Pharisees were the party concerned about Messianic speculations. **25** The question now turns away from the Baptist himself to a demand for an explanation of his baptizing mission.

The form of the question shows that the rite was being understood in the sense of an official sign of authority. But John the Baptist did not fit into any of the current expectations. This is why the official mind instinctively turned to the question of John's authority. **26** John's answer draws attention once again to the distinction between his work and Christ's. *I baptize with water.* Since water was the natural medium of baptism, this statement must be intended to contrast with a different kind of baptism to be practised by the Messiah. It is not, however, until v. 32 that the spiritual nature of His baptism is brought out. **27** *The thong of whose sandal I am not worthy to untie.* This remarkable self-effacement of John the Baptist bears eloquent testimony to his awareness of the tremendous superiority of the Messiah. To loose his master's latchet was a slave's task, which John does not consider himself worthy to perform. **28** *Bethany beyond the Jordan*, the place of John's baptizing activity, is carefully distinguished from another place of the same name mentioned in 11:1 as the village of Mary and Martha.

29 It is noticeable that in John 1 and 2 a series of chronological allusions are made which suggest that events covering six days are being recorded (*cf.* 1:29, 35, 43; 2:1). At the conclusion of the ministry John records another sequence covering six days (*cf.* the time reference in 12:1). *Behold, the Lamb of God.* Since this is John the Baptist's first personal introduction of Jesus to his followers, it is a startling statement. It is necessary to enquire what it meant to the hearers, to John and to Jesus Himself. To the hearers the idea of a lamb must at once have suggested the paschal lamb. The offering of lambs in Temple sacrifices was so familiar to Jewish minds that it would be difficult to think of the concept 'Lamb of God' apart from this. But the real difficulty occurs in the transference of the lamb imagery to a person. Whether the hearers connected this up with the servant concept in Is. 53 is doubtful, but it is by no means improbable that John himself did so. Indeed the full statement can only be fully understood against the background of both Ex. 29:38–46 and Is. 53:4–12. Such a synthesis must have been in the mind of Jesus as He listened to and accepted John's testimony concerning Him. Regarding the further statement, *who takes away the sin of the world*, there is some debate about the significance of the verb. The most natural understanding of the word would be in an expiatory sense. This would be supported by the evidence from Is. 53, where the idea of vicarious suffering is inescapable. It has been objected that the notion of 'bearing away' sin cannot here be present in view of the fact that the paschal lamb was not sacrificed as a sin-offering (*cf.* C. H. Dodd). Yet there is no need to suppose that John's statement must be rigidly interpreted in terms of the paschal lamb. It is clear that in the mind of the Evangelist this formed an important key to the ministry of

Jesus which historically begins at this point. The baptism of Jesus, which John does not record, had already taken place (cf. v. 32). The impression is at once created of a universal redemptive mission of the most far-reaching kind.

Some scholars find difficulty in believing that John the Baptist spoke these words, particularly because at a later stage in the ministry of Jesus he expressed doubts about the Messiahship of Jesus. Various alternative suggestions have been proposed. Vincent Taylor sees a dramatic representation, R. H. Strachan an echo of an early Christian liturgical formula, and others an idea of the Evangelist attributed to John the Baptist. Yet it cannot be said to be impossible as a genuine utterance of John the Baptist unless it be denied that he could have had a passing glimpse of the majesty of Christ's mission consequent upon the enlightenment gained when Jesus was baptized. So penetrating a concept of Messiah's work would explain John's self-effacing devotedness to his own task. **30** There follows a repetition of the same statement as in v. 15, evidently intended to emphasize Jesus' superiority to John. **31** John's words, *I myself did not know him* (cf. v. 33), must be limited to knowledge of Him as the 'Coming One'. In stating the purpose of his baptizing mission, John shows that Messiah is to be *revealed to Israel*. It is significant that in this Gospel 'Israel' is never used in the adverse sense in which the word 'Jews' is used. **32** John's own testimony to the descent of the Spirit is marked by a more distinctive objective note than is found in the Synoptic accounts, for the Baptist claims here to have seen the bodily form. The *dove* may symbolize gentleness of character or may be used as an emblem of flight to show the reality of the Spirit's descent. The contrast between this and the visible manifestations of the Spirit's descent at Pentecost is striking (cf. Acts 2:2, 3). Both descents were intended to be extraordinary attestations to divine missions. **33** The baptizing with the Holy Spirit is specifically contrasted with baptizing with water in order to show the essentially different character of the Messiah's mission. **34** John the Baptist affirms that his testimony, based on what he has seen, is that Jesus is *the Son of God*. This links up with the conclusion of the prologue and shows again the divine status of the Messiah whose ministry is about to be recorded.

1:35–51 The calling of the first disciples

35, 36 The same announcement concerning *the Lamb of God* follows the next day without the descriptive clause (cf. v. 29). In this case it was the effect which the statement had on two of John's disciples which is brought into focus. No doubt the Baptist gave them more information about Jesus than his brief recorded statement contains. Yet brief as it is, its implications as mentioned above are far-reaching. The identity of one only of the two disciples is given, *i.e.* Andrew (see v. 40). The other may perhaps

have been John. **37** *They followed Jesus.* Although sometimes used in a technical sense of becoming a disciple, the word 'follow' is here neutral and means 'pursuing'. **38** Jesus' question and the further question of the men in reply shows the latter's seriousness of purpose. Their clear intention was to attend on the mission and teaching of Jesus. They called Him *Rabbi*, which was a title generally given to scholars and teachers. This has led some to question whether it would have been used of one who was untrained in the official schools. But it is probably used here only in a general sense as a mark of respect. **39** The fact that *it was about the tenth hour* is stated as the reason for their staying with Jesus, but the note of time is strange. It would have been late afternoon, if John's reckoning is according to normal Jewish custom. If this were so the statement would perhaps imply a stay until next day. But on Roman reckoning it would be 10 a.m., which makes a stay 'that day' more intelligible. The point of John's reference to the hour, however, is more to draw attention to the serious contact between Jesus and His disciples than to provide precise chronological data. **40** *Andrew, Simon Peter's brother.* On two other occasions John mentions Andrew (cf. 6:8, 9; 12:22), in both of which flashes of insight are given into his character. **41** *We have found the Messiah.* It is noticeable that both here and in v. 38, John gives an interpretation of Jewish terms for the benefit of non-Jewish readers. No doubt the two disciples differed from Jesus in their ideas of what Messiahship involved. Some have seen here a contradiction of the Synoptic accounts which suggest that not until Caesarea Philippi was the Messiahship of Jesus recognized and even after this, especially in Mark's record, there were repeated exhortations to secrecy. Yet there is no need to suppose that the disciples had a fully developed notion of what Messiahship actually meant. **42** There is a marked emphasis on personal relationships in this next development related, involving Andrew, Simon and Jesus. Clearly John is inferring here that Peter received his special name *Cephas* at his first meeting with Jesus, although both Mark and Matthew mention it later in their accounts. Cephas was the Aramaic form equivalent to the Greek *Peter*. It should be noted that Jesus uses a future form of the verb, which could relate to the more official occasion referred to in Mt. 16:18. More probably, however, the Matthaean account is intended to bring out the theological significance of the name. Simon did not, in fact, become 'a stone' till he confessed Jesus as Christ. Cf. the way in which others become stones (see 1 Pet. 2:4, 5).

43 Another day sees more disciples added to the group of Jesus' followers, on this occasion in Galilee. In the case of Philip, Jesus takes the initiative. He is another disciple mentioned several times in John (cf. 6:5; 12:21; 14:8). He appears to have been a man with a practical frame of mind. There is no knowing whether

Philip had met Jesus before, but if not, the call to follow must have come very abruptly to him. **44** The fact that *Bethsaida* is specially mentioned as the city from which Philip, Andrew and Peter all came suggests that Jesus was acquainted with them all previously and knew where to look for Philip. **45** *We have found him of whom Moses in the law and also the prophets wrote.* Many passages in the Pentateuch were regarded as Messianic by the Rabbis and the Christians interpreted various other passages in the same way. Philip had soon grasped the fact that Jesus of Nazareth, the One whom he knew as Joseph's son, was the expected Messiah. *Nathanael* has often been identified with Bartholomew, who is mentioned in the Synoptic list of apostles next to Philip. Since Nathanael is named with other apostles in Jn. 21:2, it is not improbable that this identification is correct. At the same time there is no certain knowledge that Nathanael was definitely an apostle. He was certainly highly esteemed by Jesus. **46** *Can anything good come out of Nazareth?* appears to be a proverbial saying, although no such saying appears elsewhere. It may at first seem strange that a Galilaean should repeat a saying derogatory to a Galilaean city. But Nazarenes appear to have had the type of character to give rise to such a proverb, if their treatment of Jesus is anything to go by.

47 The guilelessness of Nathanael is specifically mentioned as characteristic of a genuine Israelite. The statement, *Behold, an Israelite indeed, in whom is no guile!*, implies that many Israelites were not guileless. Jesus may have been comparing him with Jacob, who was clearly in His mind in the statement in v. 51. **48** Nathanael's response is one of surprise, which deepens as Jesus converses with him. His question, *How do you know me?*, shows that his surprise springs from the fact that he had had no previous acquaintance with Jesus. In view of this, Jesus' answer shows a foreknowledge which deeply impressed Nathanael and led to the conviction that He was of supernatural origin. *When you were under the fig tree, I saw you.* The phrase may be illuminated by the rabbinic use of a similar expression for those who studied the Torah at home. On the other hand, the reference to the precise location may be mentioned simply to draw attention to the remarkable acquaintance of Jesus with Nathanael's movements. **49** *Son of God . . . King of Israel.* The order of these ascriptions is interesting, as it might have been supposed that they would have been reversed. But the combination of the two names significantly focuses on Kingship, since a true Israelite is seen to recognize at once his true King. The idea of divine Sonship was probably only rudimentary as far as Nathanael was concerned, but for the Evangelist this early testimony was important. It was to be often reiterated throughout the Gospel.

50 *Greater things.* These things are elucidated by v. 51, which points to a development of spiritual vision. **51** The double *Truly, truly,*

which occurs several times in John, gives additional emphasis to the following statement. The vision of angels *ascending and descending upon the Son of man* is probably an echo from the story of Jacob (Gn. 28:12), but applied in a specific sense to our Lord. The meaning of this statement seems to be that heaven is now opened for continuous communication with men, the representative of whom is Christ Himself under the title of *Son of man*. It is remarkable that this title is substituted for Nathanael's 'Son of God'. The link between heaven and earth depends as much on the Mediator's human character as on the divine.

2:1–11 Revelation through signs

In John's Gospel various miracles are described as *signs*. There is a sequence of seven such signs which are narrated. Most of these lead into a discourse on a related theme. It is clear, therefore, that these signs are an integral part of the structure of the Gospel. The first one in some senses sets the stage for the rest. They are all interpreted as manifestations of Christ's glory (2:11).

1, 2 *Cana in Galilee*, where Jesus performed His first miracle at a village marriage feast, would have been about three days' journey from where John was baptizing. **3** *They have no wine.* It would have been regarded as an act of discourtesy for an eastern host to fail to provide wine for his guests. **4** *O woman, what have you to do with me? My hour has not yet come.* It may seem strange that Jesus should have spoken to His mother in this way, but His purpose is to correct an impression that must have been in Mary's mind, that Jesus might take His directions from her. His commands came only from the Father (as John's Gospel so frequently demonstrates). But the remark may alternatively be regarded as idiomatic, meaning 'Your ideas and interests are not Mine. My time for acting in the way you suggest has not yet come'. (*Cf.* Jn. 7:2–6, 10; Is. 55:8, 9.) The reference to the *hour* of Jesus is another characteristic of this Gospel (*cf.* 7:30; 8:20; 12:23, 27; 13:1; 17:1). It reveals an awareness of approaching crisis and climax, not only in the mind of the Evangelist, but also in the mind of Jesus. **6** *Six stone jars.* The fact that John explains the connection of the jars with Jewish purification rites suggests that a symbolic meaning may be intended. Some see the whole incident as a symbolic rather than a factual account, to portray the superiority of Christianity over Judaism. In this view, the water would represent the Torah, for which there is some warrant in rabbinic tradition. But it is better to see in the incident a demonstration of divine power in a domestic setting. *Twenty or thirty gallons.* The total quantity of water when all the jars were filled would have been over 100 gallons. It is not stated whether all the water was changed to wine, or only the water which was drawn off for the feast, but the latter is the more likely.

8, 9 *The steward of the feast* was the official in

charge of the festivities. It has been suggested that sometimes one of the guests was appointed wine-taster (*arbiter bibendi*), in which case his ignorance of the source of the wine would have been more intelligible. 10 *You have kept the good wine until now*. This ran contrary to custom. But why is it referred to at all? The main point is the unexpected quality of the wine which may suggest the superiority of the Messianic provision over previous provision. 11 *The first of his signs*. The fact that John mentions the beginning (Gk. *archē*) of signs is important, because it shows that the apocryphal miracles of Jesus' childhood cannot be authentic. On the other hand, the 'first' here must be related to 4:54 where a 'second' sign is mentioned, also in Cana. It may be that the 'first' is the first of a series in Cana. In view, however, of the importance of 'signs' in this Gospel, a wider reference to all the miracles of Jesus is more probable. The two results of this sign are typical of all the 'signs' which John records, namely the manifestation of the glory of Jesus and the development of faith in the disciples. Signs are of no significance to those who have no readiness to see and hear.

2:12 – 4:54 EARLY ENCOUNTERS IN JERUSALEM, SAMARIA AND GALILEE

2:12–25 At Capernaum and Jerusalem

12 *His brothers*. There is no reason to suppose that these were other than the children of Mary subsequent to the birth of Jesus. This verse serves only as a link with the following passage, in which the time reference is more specific. 13 *The Passover of the Jews*. Some see here a description intended to distinguish the feast from the Christian Passover, but it is probably added for the benefit of non-Jewish readers. 14 *In the temple*. This would here refer to the outer court where animals were prepared for sacrifice. The details of the incident are graphically described, and differ in some respects from the record of the similar event in the Synoptic Gospels. It is only John who mentions that Jesus drove out oxen and sheep. The *money-changers* were the people who exchanged other currency for the official Temple currency. This was a legitimate pursuit, but was open to abuse since it offered opportunity for exorbitant exchange rates. 15 Jesus' use of *a whip of cords* was a symbolic act, for the scourge was a symbol of judgment. 16 *You shall not make my Father's house a house of trade*. Our Lord's claim that the Temple was His Father's house is a distinctive claim which fits in with His Messianic office. It was the threat that the traffickers made to true worship that Jesus challenged. 17 The appeal to Scripture (*cf.* Ps. 69:9) in support is characteristic of the early Christian approach. 18 *What sign . . . ?* The word 'sign' is here used in the general sense of 'miracle' and not in the more specific Johannine sense. 19 *Destroy this temple, and in three days I will raise it up*. It is not surprising that the Jews misunderstood, for the state-

ment is enigmatic. The explanation is given in v. 21, although even the disciples did not recognize this until after the resurrection of Jesus. 20 The statement was perplexing for the Jews, because of the considerable time taken to build the Temple thus far. It was not in fact completed until 36 years later. The contrast between *forty-six years* and *three days* was ludicrous to those who never imagined that Jesus was speaking symbolically. 21 *But he spoke of the temple of his body*. The application of the concept of a Temple to the body of Jesus is suggestive. Both were the dwelling-place of God. Some find difficulty in supposing that Jesus is referring to His own body, because there is no parallel reference to Jesus raising His own body. Accordingly the body is interpreted of the church. But the three days clearly refer to the resurrection of Christ. At the same time there is a close connection between the resurrection of Christ and the emergence of the church. 22 *His disciples remembered*. After the resurrection the disciples not only recalled but understood the significance of many things not previously grasped. It is worth noting that memory led to faith both in Scripture and in the statement of Jesus, a reminder of the close connection of these in the thought of the early Christians. The *word* of Jesus was placed on a level with Scripture in the faith of the disciples.

23–25 The passage closes with a general statement regarding happenings at the Passover Feast and the emphasis is again on the close connection between signs and faith. John's purpose, stated in 20:30, 31, furnishes the key. The signs recorded are in order that the readers might come to faith in Jesus as the Christ and Son of God. But here there is an unexpected consideration—Jesus' hesitation to trust them. Although some faith had been exercised, Jesus knew its unworthy character and its fickleness. The statement, *he knew all men*, draws attention to a supernatural knowledge of human motives. Jesus did not need advice from others, because His own knowledge was already perfect. The Nicodemus incident which immediately follows this illustrates the statement.

3:1–21 The new birth

1 *A man of the Pharisees*. John has much to say about the Pharisees throughout the Gospel, generally in an adverse sense. But here he writes about a Pharisee who had a serious purpose in seeking Jesus. He was, moreover, a man of some importance, since he was a member of the Sanhedrin. This would account for his reluctance to be seen openly approaching Jesus. 2 He addressed Him as *a teacher come from God*. Not all Jewish teachers had the evidence of a divine commissioning, for their authority was derived from the tradition of the Schools. It is noticeable that Nicodemus recognized the stamp of God upon Jesus by the character of the *signs*. They were, in fact, authenticating. 3 *Unless one is born anew*. The word translated

'anew' could be rendered 'from above' (see mg.), which would draw attention not only to the need for rebirth, but also to the spiritual character of it. It is probable that Jesus had in mind this latter significance, but that Nicodemus missed the force of it, as his reply suggests. Many of the early Fathers understood the statement to refer to baptism, supported by the further statement in v. 5. *The kingdom of God.* An expression not used much in John but occurring frequently in the Synoptics in the teaching of Jesus. It primarily refers not to the sphere over which God rules, but to the sovereignty which He exercises. The connection of the kingdom idea with regeneration is important, because it describes the essentially spiritual character of God's kingdom. In an age when many materialistic and political notions of kingship were predominant, this idea of a spiritual kingdom would have been difficult for a Jew to accept. It should be noted that 'seeing the kingdom' here and 'entering the kingdom' in v. 5 are so closely parallel as to be inseparable. If any distinction is to be made it must be that 'entering' is a positive development from 'seeing', involving a definite decision. On the other hand only those who take the step of faith to enter can be said in any real sense to 'see' the kingdom. 'Seeing' in this sense may be understood as experiencing (*cf.* v. 36). The new birth is prior to and not consequent upon the 'seeing'.

4 *Can he enter a second time into his mother's womb?* It is surprising to find so literalistic an interpretation of Jesus' statement in the mind of a Jewish leader, who could not have been entirely ignorant of the concept of spiritual regeneration. Was he being serious? Or was he desiring to make Jesus' statement look absurd? It is more probable that he was in a genuine difficulty, because the transformation of people who have reached the age of maturity and have settled into fixed habits cannot be imagined along natural lines. The only alternative that Nicodemus could think of was an entirely new beginning, which was nevertheless a physical impossibility. **5** *Unless one is born of water and the Spirit.* Some consider that 'water' refers to baptism and 'the Spirit' to regeneration. If this is correct, it must have been connected in the mind of Nicodemus with the baptism of repentance practised by John the Baptist. If those who submitted to John's baptism considered themselves reborn, it was necessary for them to learn that the outward rite was insufficient without spiritual regeneration. Another possibility is that 'water' refers to natural birth, and if this interpretation is correct it would follow naturally from Nicodemus' question. But the major difficulty with this exegesis is that no parallel exists to support the connection of water-birth with physical birth. Moreover, the former view is more in keeping with the close connection between water-baptism and Spirit-baptism elsewhere (*cf.* 1:33; Mt. 3:11). There is little doubt that the emphasis in the present statement lies on 'Spirit' and not on

'water', as vv. 6–8 show, but the connection between the two is close. **6** *Flesh . . . Spirit.* Here is an antithesis which frequently occurs in the Epistles of Paul, although the word 'flesh' is not here used, as so often in Paul, in a moral sense. It seems rather to refer to the physical and external as contrasted with the spiritual and essential. Our Lord is pointing out that the character of those born is determined by the source that gives them birth. **7** *You must be born anew.* In this repetition of the need for spiritual regeneration the statement assumes an imperative force. There is nothing optional about spiritual rebirth.

8 *The wind blows where it wills.* There are two ways of understanding this statement, since the word for 'wind' is the same as that for 'Spirit'. When understood in this latter sense it would imply that the Spirit breathes where He wills, so stressing the sovereign character of His operation. But to recognize a reference to the wind is the more natural interpretation, since both in its apparent unpredictability and in its invisibility the wind serves as a useful illustration of the activities of the Spirit. The miracle of new birth cannot be arranged by human ingenuity. Its operation is beyond human control. **10** *A teacher of Israel.* Since the Greek has the definite article, the 'teacher' must be taken in a representative sense. The whole class of those who claimed to be teachers of Israel is represented by Nicodemus, who ought to have understood but failed to do so. **11** It is significant how often in John's Gospel misunderstandings lead to further elucidations, as here. *We speak of what we know.* Jesus clearly distinguishes Himself from the rabbinical teachers and implies the lack of authoritative teaching on their part. But why does He use the plural instead of the singular? It may be that He is including His disciples, although at this stage they had come to know very little. It is possible to regard the plural as adding strength to the statement, in the style used sometimes by the apostle Paul. Some have suggested that the 'we' includes the prophetical witnesses, but this seems unnatural. Others consider the Father and the Spirit are included and there is less objection to this. The words, *you do not receive,* illustrate the general statements of 1:5, 10, 11. **12** *Earthly things . . . heavenly things.* The 'earthly things' must be related to the previous disclosures, in which case they include spiritual truths, such as the new birth. The 'heavenly things' would then be those truths which cannot be fully revealed on earth. **13** *No one has ascended . . . but he who descended.* Since the first verb is in the perfect and not in the future, it cannot easily refer to the ascension of Jesus. Most scholars take it therefore to refer to the state from which Jesus descended and to which He returned at His ascension. The descending certainly refers to the incarnation. The concluding statement is in some MSS 'the Son of man who is in heaven', but the best MSS have 'Son of man' without further description. The additional phrase does not readily fit into the context. It could be interpreted only as a reference to the pre-existence of Christ and could underline His heavenly authority which nevertheless has already been emphasized. **14** *As Moses*. The incident in the OT of Moses and the brazen serpent (Nu. 21:8, 9) is cited to illustrate the earthly work of the Son of man. The uplifting clearly refers to the cross and not to glorification. **15** The real force of the analogy is in the necessity for faith. It is important to notice that the uplifting of the Son of man is stated as an imperative necessity. It was for this purpose that He came. The reference to eternal life may be compared with 'life in his name' (20:31), which John mentions in stating the purpose of his Gospel. The adjective *eternal* expresses the indestructibility of the life received.

16ff. There is some dispute as to whether the next passage is a continuation of Jesus' discourse or a comment by the Evangelist. The conjunction 'for' would seem to suggest a connection with the previous discourse and rather favours the view that it is Jesus speaking. **16** The statement that *God so loved the world* shows the object of God's love to be universal. The expression of that love is sacrificial. The purpose of it is eternal life for believers, who must otherwise perish. It is no wonder that this verse has been described as 'the gospel in a nutshell'. The tense used for the verb *have* shows that believers have a present possession of life. The two following verses elucidate the same theme. **17** The purpose of the Son's mission was not condemnation but salvation; **18** but this salvation is available only for those who believe. The specific object of faith is stated to be *the name of the only Son of God*. This again connects with the purpose of the Gospel (20:31), while the adjective *only* (*cf*. v. 16) echoes the prologue (*cf*. 1:18). **19** Another allusion to the prologue is seen in the introduction of the antithesis between *light* and *darkness* (*cf*. 1:5). Evil deeds are specifically linked with darkness, and judgment follows as a result of men's preference for darkness rather than light. There is an implied contrast between God loving the world (*cf*. v. 16) and men loving darkness. **20** *Lest his deeds should be exposed*. Man's love of darkness is not for its own sake, but because of what it can hide. On the other hand, those whose deeds are true welcome light because of what it can reveal. **21** *He who does what is true*. Such phraseology is found in rabbinic writings. It implies worthy moral actions. The last clause of v. 21 can be understood as expressing either the content of what is seen, *i.e. that his deeds have been wrought in God*, or the reason why he comes to the light, *i.e.* because his deeds have been wrought in God. The former presents a better parallel to v. 20.

3:22 – 4:3 Jesus and John the Baptist

22–24 Here the narrative resumes and a historical connection is stated between John's activity and

that of Jesus. It is significant that at this period of the mission John's baptizing runs concurrent with that of Jesus and His disciples. The Synoptic Gospels, with which John at this point runs parallel, show that Jesus continued the same message of repentance that John had preached. The fact that John's imprisonment had not yet taken place makes clear that the events so far recalled were prior to the Synoptic narratives (*cf*. Mk. 1:14).

25–30 John's testimony to Jesus is called forth by a dispute. His disciples are mystified by the apparent competition caused by the baptismal activity of Jesus and His followers. **27** *No one can receive anything except what is given him from heaven*. What connection has this with the comment of John's disciples? It may draw attention to the fact that John's disciples are giving him more supremacy than God intended, which would well suit the context. Or it may express the divine authority of Jesus, which John could not take away. **28, 29** John shows his own function to be merely preparatory, like the work of the bridegroom's friend. His task is to attend to the happiness of the bridegroom. The bridal imagery is found in Jesus' teaching in the Synoptics (*cf*. Mt. 22:1ff.; 25:1ff.). The idea of the church as the bride of Christ is found explicitly elsewhere, especially in Eph. 5:22ff. **30** *He must increase*. This reiterates the superiority of Jesus already emphasized in ch. 1. It is not only John who must decrease, but the whole of the old order which he represented.

31ff. The concluding section of the chapter could be either the words of John the Baptist or of the Evangelist. The latter is the preferable interpretation. The passage sets out the superiority of the One whom God has sent. *a.* **31** He is *from above* and *above all*, *i.e.* in distinction from the earth, which means that earthly methods of assessing His importance are invalid; *b.* **32** His testimony is based on personal experience; *c.* His testimony is generally rejected, **33** but those who receive it not only give credence to the message of Jesus, but also authenticate the source of the message as utterly trustworthy. **34** God can commission His Son to speak only what is in accord with His own nature. *For it is not by measure that he gives the Spirit*. It is not clear from the Greek whether it is God who gives the Spirit, or Christ, or whether it is the Spirit who does the giving. In the last case the gift must be the words of God. It seems best to take God as the subject, in the sense that He endues those whom He sends with the Holy Spirit in abundant measure. 'Not by measure' would then mean 'unrestrictedly'. This interpretation is supported by v. 35, which speaks of the Father's gifts to the Son. **35** The fact that God has given *all things into his hand* shows the supremacy of Christ, not only in the created order, but in all spheres (*cf*. 5:22, 27; 5:26; 12:49; 17:2; 17:24). **36** The concluding sentence in this chapter is an echo with some variations of v. 15. The disobedient are here said not only to lack the possession of life ('seeing life' is idiomatic for experiencing it), but also to incur *the wrath of God*. The result is thus stated both negatively and positively. The idea of wrath is active and its occurrence here should be compared with John the Baptist's use of it in Mt. 3:7 and Lk. 3:7. It is God's judgment in action. In the phrase *rests upon him* the verb suggests a present and continuous abiding.

4:1-3 There is a return to the historic situation to account for Jesus' departure from Judea. It was because of probable repercussions from Pharisaic sources over Jesus' having greater impact than John the Baptist. John they just tolerated, but Jesus was clearly going to be a more serious threat to them. The use of the title *Lord* is unexpected and perplexing in view of the following use of the name *Jesus*. The variant text which reads 'Jesus' in both places is understandable, but may have arisen through the desire to remove the title 'Lord' from the narrative because it is unfamiliar in John. If the title is original it reflects the high esteem of the Evangelist for Jesus. **2** (*Jesus himself did not baptize . . .*) This parenthesis is added to correct the Pharisees' report.

4:4-42 Jesus in Samaria

4 *He had to pass through Samaria.* The verb suggests necessity. It was the quick route from Jerusalem to Galilee and anyone taking this route could not avoid Samaria. **6** *Jacob's well was there.* This was at Sychar, commonly identified as Shechem. The significance of Jacob to the Samaritans is seen in v. 12. *And so Jesus, wearied as he was with his journey, sat down beside the well.* The importance of this statement lies in the human tiredness of Jesus. In a Gospel setting out to lead to faith in the Son of God, the human touches have more than usual meaning. The mention of the hour adds colour to the story. On Jewish reckoning *the sixth hour* would be noon.

7 *A woman of Samaria.* To a Jew there would be a double prejudice in this encounter—on grounds of sex and of race. **8** John mentions the absence of the disciples in order to throw into greater relief the uniqueness of the following conversation between Jesus and such a woman. **9** The strangeness of Jesus' request for a drink prompts the woman to ask a reason and leads immediately to Jesus' comment about the gift of God. The woman would no doubt have recognized that Jesus was a Jew by His speech. *For Jews have no dealings with Samaritans.* This may be regarded either as the Evangelist's comment or as a continuation of the woman's question. In either case it explains the surprise of the woman. The verb means 'to use together with' and some scholars have supposed that this refers to the prohibition of common use of vessels. But a Jewish regulation to this effect is no earlier than AD 65 or 66. Relations between the two races were certainly not good. **10** *If you knew the gift of God.* The word for *gift* (Gk. *dōrea*), whenever it is used in Acts or in the

Epistles, is always used of a divine gift. The gift in mind here is the Spirit of God, as always in the book of Acts. There is a close connection between living water and the Spirit in 7:37-39. *And who it is.* The gift of the Spirit can be bestowed only by Jesus. If only the woman had known that He had power to impart such a gift, she would have changed her request. *Living water.* The Rabbis spoke of the law in terms of water and the figurative use of the idea is found in the OT (*cf.* Pr. 13:14; Je. 17:13; Zc. 14:8). **11** But the woman fails to understand and takes the expression literally. *The well is deep.* It was incongruous to her that Jesus could offer her water without the use of a bucket. **12** Such a feat would outdo Jacob who dug the well in the first place. It is always difficult for people to conceive that anyone could be greater than a venerated patriarch from the distant past (*cf.* 8:53 for a similar remark regarding Abraham). There is here a touch of fanatical veneration of a sacred site because of its associations rather than its abundant supply. The word for 'well' used by the woman (Gk. *phrear*) describes the masonry construction, but Jesus uses in v. 14 the word for 'spring' (Gk. *pēgē*), thus describing the water itself. **13, 14** Jesus brings out the contrast between water which temporarily quenches thirst and that which does so permanently. The latter is infinitely superior, particularly as it leads to eternal life. With unerring insight Jesus perceived the basic spiritual character of the woman's need. **15** But any understanding of His teaching on her part was non-existent, for she conjured up the possibility of never again coming to draw from Jacob's well. There was, in fact, a moral blockage in her understanding.

In the next section of the story the dialogue becomes more personal. **16** *Go, call your husband, and come here* is intentionally abrupt. It precipitated a crisis in the conversation. The woman was obliged to face reality. **17** *You are right in saying, 'I have no husband'* is Jesus' commendation of her confession, although in some respects it involved an evasion. It enabled Him to face her with both her past and her present life. **18** *Five husbands.* The Rabbis did not approve of more than three marriages. **19** *Sir, I perceive that you are a prophet.* She acknowledges at once the insight of Jesus and considers that He must be a seer to know so much. **20** *Our fathers worshipped on this mountain.* The woman turns the conversation from her own moral problem to a fundamental religious problem. Worship was closely linked to a sacred place; to a Samaritan it was Mt. Gerizim and to a Jew, Jerusalem. Why should one be preferable to the other? It was more comfortable to turn from a matter of conscience to a matter of religious controversy. **21** Yet Jesus graciously takes up the point. *The hour is coming.* The present hour may be one of controversy, but an hour of certainty is imminent, an hour when it will be realized that the aspect which gives genuineness to worship is spiritual, not local (*cf.* v. 23). The controversy over locality is entirely irrelevant. **22** Of more importance was the object of worship and here the Jews were superior to the Samaritans in their spiritual comprehension. *We worship what we know, for salvation is from the Jews.* The Jews had a much fuller revelation than the Samaritans, since the latter restricted themselves to the Pentateuch. Since the neuter 'what' is used, attention is drawn more to the essence than to the person of the object of worship. **23** *But the hour . . . now is.* This brings the previous statement in v. 21 to the present. There is nothing now to prevent anyone, Jew or Samaritan, from worshipping *in spirit and truth.* The linking of spirit with truth throws light on the meaning of 'true worshippers'. These are genuine worshippers as opposed to those who merely appear to be so by participating only in outward ceremonies. The main emphasis is on spirit, as the following verse shows. *For such the Father seeks to worship him.* The basic reason why true worship must be spiritual is found in the nature of God. He can seek as worshippers only those who accord with His own nature. **24** Hence the next profound statement about that nature: *God is spirit.* This must refer to His essential character. The spirituality of God was not an alien idea to the Jews, but they had not recognized the need for correspondence between worshippers and the One worshipped. **25** It was probably because the Samaritan woman found herself out of her depth that she self-consciously introduced the subject of the *Messiah* as one who will be able to clarify these issues. There is some question about the extent to which Samaritans were acquainted with Messianic hopes. Their ideas may have been vague, but this woman was, at least, looking for a Revealer, *i.e.* a Prophet (*cf.* Dt. 18:15). **26** *I who speak to you am he.* There is no reserve on Jesus' part in admitting that He was a Messiah of that kind, although the Synoptics often record such reserve. There was no fear of political repercussions when Jesus was among Samaritans as there may well have been among Jews. This would sufficiently account for the difference of approach. Here was a personal revelation of the Messiah to one who clearly had some expectancy and was therefore prepared for such a revelation.

27, 28 The return of the disciples from their errand to buy food (*cf.* v. 8) had a double effect. It caused them to marvel at what they saw—Jesus talking to a woman—and it caused the woman to leave her jar and go to the city. The marvelling may have been occasioned by the disciples' knowledge that Jewish Rabbis were not permitted to speak to women in the street. *What do you wish?* more literally means 'What do you seek?', implying that the only reason for the conversation must have been because Jesus was asking the woman for something (*cf.* v. 7). The disciples seem too embarrassed to enquire. Their eventual somewhat nervous exhortation that Jesus should eat (v. 31) bears this out. **29** *Come, see a man who told me all that I ever did.* It was the Lord's penetrating discernment of her moral condition which had impressed her most, in spite of the fact that she had sidetracked the issue. Conscience became more awakened as conversation had proceeded on other lines, as so often happens. *Can this be the Christ?* The form of the question in the Greek suggests that she cannot bring herself to believe it. It might be translated, 'Surely this cannot be the Christ?' **30** The question, however, aroused immediate interest in the hearers.

31ff. Jesus' discussion with the disciples forms a sort of interlude which is nonetheless closely linked to the main narrative. **32** In reply to the offer of food Jesus turns the conversation to spiritual issues: *I have food to eat of which you do not know.* Both pronouns are emphatic and draw attention to the strong contrast between Jesus and His disciples. **33** They can think only in materialistic terms. Since Jesus had no food when they left, someone else must have given Him some. Perhaps they thought the woman had done so. **34** *My food is to do the will of him who sent me, and to accomplish his work.* The principle here enunciated seems to be that doing God's will must take precedence over physical food, although Jesus is not here advocating neglect of physical needs. As so often in this Gospel, the Lord's deep consciousness of His mission comes to the fore. He cannot be satisfied until He has accomplished it, *i.e.* brought it to completion. **35** The reference to the harvest is intended to illustrate the accomplishing of the work. It is not predictable on a chronological basis like the natural harvest, in which the time of harvest can be calculated after the seed has been sown. But there is a spiritual harvest which is not governed by seasons. *Lift up your eyes, and see.* Did Jesus mean this literally or not? If He did, what were the whitened fields? It may be that He and the disciples could see the Samaritans coming towards them up the hill and He regarded them as the spiritual harvest from the seed already sown in the mind of the woman. Otherwise the words can be taken metaphorically as an exhortation to use spiritual discernment in seeking opportunity of bringing others. **36, 37** *He who reaps receives wages, and gathers fruit for eternal life.* Our Lord is here elucidating the illustration by pointing out a fundamental spiritual principle, *i.e.* that the reaper deserves a reward, but He links this with the reminder that no reaper can reap apart from the sower. **38** *I sent you to reap.* Jesus reminds the disciples that their recent and present experiences owe much to the labours of others. The word for *labour* is that used for heavy toil. The *others* to whom Jesus refers are those who have prepared the way for Christ. This principle means that no single individual can claim all the credit in a spiritual mission.

39 *Many Samaritans from that city believed in him.* Since the message of the woman was mainly based on the extraordinary insight of Jesus, the content of the faith of these Samaritans was necessarily limited. **40, 41** Yet after a further *two days* of personal contact with Jesus *many more believed* and it must be supposed that their faith was deeper in content. **42** Indeed this fuller faith is seen from their confession, *we know that this is indeed the Saviour of the world.* No doubt Jesus had explained much to them about the essential purpose of His mission, but their idea of Saviourhood would naturally fall far short of the more developed ideas of Paul (*cf.* his use of the same title in Phil. 3:20).

4:43–54 Return to Galilee

43–45 The section is intended to mark the transition from Samaria to Galilee and to comment on the reception that Jesus received in Galilee. The saying about a prophet's *honour in his own country*, which is clearly proverbial, occurs also in the Synoptic Gospels, but there his own country is Galilee, while here it appears to be Judea. The warm reception given to Jesus by the Galilaeans supports the interpretation. It should be noted that in Mk. 6:4 and Mt. 13:57 the saying is given as our Lord's words in direct speech, but here the Evangelist gives a reported statement. Alternatively the Evangelist may be contrasting the success in Samaria and in Jerusalem with the general reception in Galilee, and especially in Nazareth, as known from the Synoptics. In that case there is special point in John's mentioning that He was welcomed by those who had been at the feast, *i.e.* who had had experience of Jesus outside His own country. On the other hand, for a Jew a prophet's country was generally regarded to be Jerusalem. Hence signs in Jerusalem would deeply impress the Galilaeans.

The second recorded sign also takes place at Cana. **46** *An official whose son was ill.* Both the word for *official* (Gk. *basilikos*), an officer in the king's service, and the reference to his *son* distinguish this miracle from the similar healing of the centurion's servant (Mt. 8:5–10; Lk. 7:2–10). There are other differences which make identification of the incidents difficult. It is better, therefore, to treat them separately. **47, 48** The official's urgent pleading for Jesus to go to his son brings a surprising response: *Unless you see signs and wonders you will not believe.* Jesus knew the man's mind. He knew that true faith was not present. Perhaps there was a kind of magical belief which could exist only if propped up by sight. This statement shows the ineffectiveness of signs which are regarded as no more than wonders.

49 It is astonishing how quickly the man responds to Jesus' challenge. After a further respectful request that Jesus should come, **50** he at once reacts when Jesus tells him to go, for his son lives. *The man believed the word that Jesus spoke to him.* No longer did he require to see anything. The rebuff of v. 48 had been wholly effective.

51–53 The conclusion of the incident draws attention both to the timing of the healing and more particularly to its completeness. The effect of the father's discovery that the healing was at the precise hour of Jesus' assurance, and was also instantaneous, was faith for himself and his household. The sign had, in fact, led to more faith in Jesus. **52** *The seventh hour.* On Jewish reckoning this would be 1 p.m., but on Roman reckoning 7 p.m., which is more probable in view of the reference to 'yesterday'.

5:1–47 HEALING AND DISCOURSE IN JERUSALEM

5:1–18 Christ makes the lame to walk

1 *After this there was a feast of the Jews.* Since the feast is unnamed, it is impossible to be certain of its identity. The reason for its being mentioned here is probably to account for Jesus' presence in Jerusalem after being for so short a time in Galilee. **2** There is some dispute about the identity of the *pool*, for some suggest the Pool of Siloam, and others the Virgin's Well. Some texts call the place the Sheep Pool. The most important detail is the number of *porticoes* which could hold a great many ill people waiting for healing from the medicinal waters. **3, 4** It should be noted that the latter part of v. 3 and the whole of v. 4 in AV is omitted from RSV on the basis of good textual authority. **5, 6** *When Jesus saw him and knew that he had been lying there a long time.* John tells us the illness was of *thirty-eight years*' standing. It was evidently common knowledge. Perhaps the man was in the habit of advertising the fact to rouse the sympathy of the bystanders. Jesus' question, *Do you want to be healed?* suggests the need for a pointed challenge to rouse him from apathy. **7** It is striking that he gives no direct answer to the question. *When the water is troubled.* Although there is no other evidence to support the view that the waters when disturbed possessed curative properties, it is certainly not impossible that many people believed that they did. The point of the man's complaint was the impossibility of getting himself into the pool during the brief spells when the waters were believed to be curative. **8** *Rise, take up your pallet, and walk.* Jesus does not comment on the popular belief. His command would have seemed incredible to the curious bystanders, **9** but the man must immediately have felt new strength come to him which made response possible.

Now that day was the sabbath. This statement supplies the key to the sequel. Here was the first open violation of the sabbath by Jesus in Jerusalem. **10** Jewish casuistry is vividly seen in the objection made by the Jewish critics. To carry the pallet was regarded as an act of work. According to the Mishnah, a couch could be carried only if it had a man on it. Although it is the healed man who is here criticized, it is, in fact, an indirect attack on Jesus Himself (*cf.* v. 16). **11, 12** The discussion between the healed man and the Jews over the identity of the healer is interesting because of his complete ignorance. He gets no nearer than to describe Jesus as *the* *man who healed me*. So far the miracle was not a means of revelation to him. **13** *For Jesus had withdrawn*. His withdrawal from the crowds was most probably to avoid popular acclaim. **14** It also gave Him an opportunity to seek out the man for a personal encounter. *See, you are well! Sin no more, that nothing worse befall you*. There appears to be here a distinction between physical healing and moral disorder. It could be that there was a definite connection between the man's illness and his moral life, although this is left undefined. Alternatively, the moral disorder may have had nothing to do with the illness, and the worse thing may be understood as spiritual lameness. The imperative is in the present tense—'do not continue in sin'. **15** *The man went away and told the Jews*. What was his motive in doing this? Probably it was his Jewish sense of duty in obeying instructions. He knew the hostility of the Jews, but his action shows little sense of gratitude to Jesus. **16** The immediate result was persecution. **17** The position was further aggravated by Jesus' statement: *My Father is working still, and I am working*. The connection of thought seems to be that the healing act was evidence of divine activity, which supersedes human regulations. There is no difference between the works of the Father and the works of Jesus. They are exactly similar in character. **18** The Jewish objectors recognized this as a claim to equality with God. To the Jewish mind this would, of course, be a more serious offence than breaking the sabbath. It challenged their basic monotheism.

5:19-47 The Father and the Son

The implications of the statement in v. 17 are now worked out more fully. Jesus' teaching is aimed to show the essential unity between the Father and the Son. **19** *Truly, truly*. This gives solemn endorsement to the following statement. It should be noted that the absolute use of *Son* in this passage follows from the relationship implied in the words of v. 17. The reasons why the Son does nothing of His own accord are stated in four steps: *a*. **19** the Son acts precisely like the Father; *b*. **20** the Father shows the Son His plans; *c*. **21** the Son, like the Father, has power to give life; *d*. **22** the Son has been given authority for judgment by the Father. Two specific purposes of all this co-ordinate activity are mentioned—**20** *that you may marvel* and **23** *that all may honour the Son, even as they honour the Father*. The first of these would be misleading apart from the second. Jesus was no sensational wonder-worker, but some of the Jews to whom He was speaking had not yet even reached the position of marvelling at His works. **20** *For the Father loves the Son*. It is important to note that the basis of unity between the Father and Son is love. This is the reason for the sharing of all plans. **21** *As the Father raises the dead*. In both the OT and rabbinical literature, this power is attributed to God. In this statement either physical or spiritual resurrection may be intended, but v. 25 must be understood spiritually and vv. 28, 29

physically. **23** *He who does not honour the Son does not honour the Father who sent him*. This was a pointed challenge to the Jews, who were nonetheless professing to honour the Father.

24 A second important utterance is introduced by another *Truly, truly*. This relates to the effect of hearing and believing, *i.e.* eternal life. There is a close link between hearing the teaching of Jesus and believing Him who sent Jesus. Faith springs from a recognition of the divine mission of Jesus and therefore the divine authority of His words. *From death to life*. The Greek is more vivid: 'out of death'. Death and life are thought of as two distinct spheres. Faith is the means by which men pass from one to the other.

25ff. Another statement is introduced by the same strong formula, in this case concerning the coming resurrection. It is just possible that the reference to the dead may include those raised physically by Jesus, but the words *and now is* seem to be against that interpretation. It is noticeable that Jesus uses the title *Son of God* when speaking of resurrection and **27** *Son of man* when speaking of judgment. The second title, unlike the first, has no articles in the Greek, and must be interpreted generally of His character as true man. Judgment will be executed by One who knows man. **28** *The hour is coming*. This 'hour' is evidently different from the 'hour' in v. 25, for here it is the final physical resurrection which is in mind. **29** There is a contrast between *resurrection of life* and *resurrection of judgment*, the reason for which is the fact that those who possess life are considered to have been judged already, whereas evil-doers have nothing but judgment to anticipate.

The concluding section of the chapter gives a discourse of Jesus on the subject of the nature of the testimony to Himself. It is set forth in various steps. **5:30, 31 Jesus disclaims self-testimony.** This is excluded as far as He is concerned because His will is identical to the will of Him who sent Him. Indeed, self-witness would be false witness. The statement in 8:14 does not contradict this, for there Jesus is not considering, as here, the impossible hypothesis of a witness by the Son which conflicted with the witness of the Father. **5:33-35 The testimony of John is valuable but insufficient. 33** *He has borne witness to the truth*. John's testimony, because it was true, led men to Jesus. Such testimony cannot be decried. **35** The witness was through a brilliant *lamp*, which must nevertheless be distinguished from the light itself. There was a popular rejoicing—yet over John's own light. **34** Even so, had men believed his testimony they would have been saved. **5:36-38 Testimony to Jesus comes from a greater witness. 36** Jesus next appeals to the testimony of His *works*. These works are of a special nature because the Father had commissioned them. The works should bear witness, therefore, to the One who commissioned. This is why the witness of Jesus' doings is greater than that of John's words. Yet the testimony had fallen on unproductive soil. **37** In spite of the Father's voice which had spoken through the Son's deeds, they had not heard it nor seen any evidence of Him in those deeds. **38** The plain fact was that, through unbelief, God's word did not abide in them. The 'word' refers primarily to the Scriptures, as the next verse shows.

5:39–47 Testimony to Jesus comes also through the Scriptures. 39 *You search the scriptures.* The words could be understood as an imperative. The indicative is better, however, because Jesus proceeds to show their ignorance of the true meaning of Scripture. The word 'search' is strong and means thorough investigation, an appropriate description of the Jewish approach to the law. Yet they missed the real aim of Scripture—to bear witness to Christ. **40** *You refuse to come to me.* This implies a deliberate rejection of the testimony. **41** *I do not receive glory from men* is stated to explain the absence of official sanction for His mission. This idea is elucidated in v. 43. **42** *You have not the love of God within you* could mean man's love for God or God's love for man, or perhaps both. **44** Those who love God will seek God's glory, not their own, but by their attitude to Jesus it is clear that the Jews were not doing this. Indeed, it is a moral impossibility to seek one's own glory and God's glory at one and the same time. **45** *It is Moses who accuses you.* For the Torah-loving Jews, this was a bitter statement. The very Torah itself exposed their inconsistency. There were Messianic germs in the Pentateuch which pointed to Christ. **46** *For he wrote of me.* The Jews did not lack enthusiasm in studying the Torah, but they lacked insight into its true significance. **47** It was no wonder they did not believe the words of Jesus.

6:1–71 FURTHER SIGNS AND DISCOURSES IN GALILEE

6:1–15 The feeding of the multitude

This is the only miracle performed by Jesus recorded in all four Gospels. For this reason only the salient features of John's account will be mentioned. **1** *The Sea of Tiberias.* It was probably not popularly known by this name in Jesus' day as the town by that name was not established until AD 22, but John is familiar with it. **2** *Because they saw the signs.* John accounts for the dimension of the crowd on the basis of signs, in which he has special interest. The signs led men to seek for Jesus. **3** *Jesus went up into the hills.* It would seem from v. 15 that He must have come down again to perform the miracle. The expression is probably used generally of hilly districts. **4** *The Passover.* The reason why John mentions this is not at once apparent. He probably attached significance to the connection of the miracle with the spiritual teaching about the heavenly bread which formed the basis of the Christian 'Passover' (*cf.* v. 51).

5 One difference from the Synoptic accounts is that they record the disciples taking the initiative,

whereas John records that Jesus Himself first drew attention to the need for food. His question was addressed to *Philip*, who is mentioned on three other occasions in this Gospel (1:43ff.; 12:21f.; 14:8f.). **6** John's comment here should not be regarded as the Evangelist's attempt to avoid the imputation of ignorance to Jesus, but as an instance of his insight into the divine nature of Jesus. The details of the arrangements for the crowds to sit down and for the multiplication of the loaves are closely parallel to the Synoptic accounts. **8** A distinctive feature of John is the special mention of *Andrew.* One tradition had it that Andrew was associated with John in the production of the Gospel (*cf.* 1:44; 12:21, where he is also mentioned in connection with Philip).

11 *When he had given thanks.* All the Synoptic Gospels say that Jesus looked up to heaven, then blessed and broke the bread. John's term seems to summarize the first two actions, while definitely omitting the third. The verb used here (Gk. *eucharisteō*) is used by all the other Evangelists in their account of the institution of the Lord's Supper. This is the more noteworthy because John himself does not record that institution. **13** The *baskets*, which were light wicker baskets, were easily carried. **14** *When the people saw the sign.* Here John uses his special word to describe the miracle, but it need not be supposed that the people themselves recognized it as a sign in the fullest sense. They certainly were impressed, however, as their reference to *the prophet* shows. The coming prophet is an allusion to Dt. 18:15. For these people it probably had Messianic connections, as v. 15 indicates. **15** The plan to make Jesus King is not recorded in the other Gospels, but it explains features of Matthew's and Mark's narratives, *e.g.* the necessity for Jesus to constrain His disciples to get into the boat. Jesus is again seen to have powers of perceiving human motives.

6:16–21 The walking on the water

This is not specifically described by John as a sign, nor is any indication given of any results which followed it. Yet it seems reasonable to regard it as one of John's sequence of seven signs. **17** The fact that *Jesus had not yet come to them* suggests that they had a prearranged *rendez-vous* with Him. **19** *They saw Jesus walking on the sea.* It is indisputable that John intends his readers to understand a miraculous happening in spite of certain interpretations of v. 21 (*q.v.*). **20** *It is I, do not be afraid.* This is not one of the great 'I am' statements, although it shares the same form in the Greek. The message is clear—fear is banished by the realization of the presence of Jesus. **21** *Immediately the boat was at the land.* Some have suggested that Jesus was on the shore all along, but that the disciples thought He was on the sea. But would they have been frightened had this been the case? They were no doubt nearer the shore than they thought.

6:22–59 Discussions at Capernaum

22–24 These verses form a link in the narrative

to explain how many of those who witnessed the feeding of the multitudes were present at Capernaum to hear the discussions. John intends his readers to connect the discussions with the sign.

25 *Rabbi, when did you come here?* This opening question reveals their surprise. They had no notion that Jesus was beyond material limitations as the walking on the water had shown. **26** But He in His answer goes deeper, by charging them with seeking Him for the sake of food. Jesus here uses the word *signs* because He is speaking of the people's attitude. They saw no more than the food, so the miracle had failed to convey its full significance. **27** *Do not labour for the food which perishes.* These words of Jesus must have seemed strange, for His hearers were seeking to avoid labour, but this is His gracious way of declining their quest. Enduring food is a gift, not the result of labour. The *seal*, which God has set upon the Son of man, is the mark of authentication. He who holds the seal acts on behalf of the owner of the seal. What Jesus does and what He says are the deeds and words of God. It should be noted that it is upon Jesus as Son of man that the seal is set. **28** In the question, *What must we do, to be doing the works of God?* the questioners conceive of work in terms of earning merit, but **29** Jesus at once draws attention to the need for faith. **30** *Then what sign do you do?* For them faith can be based only on sight. But they had already seen a sign and had not recognized its true significance. **31** Their concept of 'sign' was limited to a reproduction of manna as in the time of their fathers, *i.e.* the supply of physical and material needs. The implication seems to be that one miracle of feeding a multitude does not compare with Moses' provision of food throughout the wilderness wanderings. Messiah must surely outdo Moses. *Bread from heaven.* The Jews cite from Ps. 78 and **32** Jesus takes up the phrase and applies it spiritually. First, He denies that it was Moses who provided the heavenly bread; it was the Father. Then He indicates that the real heavenly bread was not manna, but Christ Himself. **33** *Gives life to the world.* This comprehensive spiritual food contrasts vividly with the manna which sustained only the Israelites and that for a limited period. **34** The request, *Lord, give us this bread always*, does not rise above material provision.

35 *I am the bread of life.* It was necessary for Jesus at once to dispel the materialistic idea and to turn the conversation towards Himself. Note that, in each verse from 35 to 40, the first person is stressed. In this great introductory affirmation, *bread of life* means bread which gives life. Coming to Christ and believing in Him are seen to be synonymous, as the only means of securing spiritual satisfaction. **36** *You have seen me and yet do not believe.* The importance of faith is again stressed, this time by a pointed reference to their refusal to give it. **37** In this next verse there is a combination of divine sovereignty (*All that the Father gives*) and human response (*him*

who comes), but the major stress is on the divine side. There is a distinction between the comprehensive *all* (neuter) and the personal *him who comes*. Response is an activity of individuals. In the statement, *I will not cast out*, the negative is emphatic. **38, 39** There follows another reminder of the complete harmony between the Father and the Son, which ensures that nothing of what the Father has given the Son can be lost (*cf.* 5:19ff.). Again the neuter *all* is used, as in v. 37, for the total gifts given to the Son. **39, 40** Twice Jesus here speaks of resurrection *at the last day*, an emphasis which adds strength to the claim that the Father's will would be accomplished.

41ff. At this point in the discussion, Jewish objections are interjected. **42** The main problem was Jesus' claim to be from heaven, for they knew His humble origins. **43, 44** Jesus does not directly answer them, but once again appeals to the close connection between His claims and the Father's purpose. Logically His claims seemed inconceivable, but discernment needed a spiritual impulse (*unless the Father . . . draws him*). **45** Confidence that such a divine impulse is to be expected is supported from the prophets. The quotation is from Is. 54:13, which describes the triumphs of the Servant in His kingdom. The direct implication of this statement is that the divine initiative is again stressed. **46** Yet only Jesus (*him who is from God*) has seen the Father. Others must accept His testimony.

48 The theme changes back to the discussion about the 'bread of life' with the repetition of Jesus' self-identification. **49, 50** The superiority of this heavenly bread over the manna is seen in its effects. One leads to eternal life, the other failed to prevent death. **51** Jesus follows up His comment on this with what is one of the most important statements in the whole discourse. *If any one eats of this bread, he will live for ever* is a further elucidation of v. 50. All real life is unending. *And the bread which I shall give for the life of the world is my flesh.* It is Jesus Himself who now gives, whereas previously it was the Father. The word for *flesh* (Gk. *sarx*) is used without the moral sense it so often has in Paul's writings. It refers here to the human life of Jesus which He gave up for (Gk. *huper*) the world. By *world* is meant the world of men. **52-54** Because the Jews put a literalistic interpretation on His words, Jesus gives a fuller explanation in the following words—*unless you eat the flesh of the Son of man and drink his blood, you have no life in you.* The metaphor of eating and drinking prepares the way for the later institution of the Lord's Supper. It is understandable that the Jews would not have grasped the spiritual meaning of these words, which can be understood only in the light of the subsequent sacrifice of Jesus upon the cross. The eating and drinking become symbolical of the appropriation of the effects of that sacrifice. **55, 56** Two further aspects of the same thought are then stressed. Such food and drink are real (*food indeed* and *drink indeed*) and those who partake of them are really abiding in

Jesus. **57** The believer's life is in fact intimately bound up with Christ's. **58** The whole discussion then closes with a repetition of the comparison between the true heavenly bread and the Israelites' manna (*cf.* vv. 49, 50). **59** *In the synagogue.* This is the first mention of the place (*i.e.* the synagogue) where the discussion took place. Clearly not all the discourse took place there, since at first too many people were involved. Perhaps the discussions between 'the Jews' (vv. 41ff.) and Jesus were within the synagogue and the preceding discussions outside.

6:60–71 The disciples' reactions to Jesus' teaching and work

John includes samples of reaction on the part of the general following and then more specifically of the Twelve. **60** *This is a hard saying; who can listen to it?* The *saying* here is probably the whole of the preceding discourse. By describing it as *hard*, they meant 'difficult to accept'. **61ff.** Jesus' answer does not appear to be specifically related to their question, but since John draws attention to His knowledge of their murmuring it must be supposed that Jesus is giving an answer to the inner motives that prompted their question. It was perhaps the saying about eating His flesh which provided the main stumbling-block, especially as 'flesh' is explained in v. 63. **62** *Then what if you were to see the Son of man ascending where he was before?* The sentence is incomplete, but it implies that there will be greater cause for offence than the idea of eating Christ's flesh, *i.e.* the lifting up of the Son of man and His ascension through a path of suffering. In that event any literal eating of His flesh would be impossible. **63–65** As yet these disciples had not learned to distinguish the physical from the spiritual. This is what Jesus makes clear in these verses. They were concentrating on the *flesh*, but He urges them to consider the real meaning of the words *spirit and life. But there are some of you that do not believe.* In spite of the fact that they considered themselves disciples, Jesus knew their true state.

66ff. The contrast in the reaction of the Twelve is striking. Many *drew back*, but the Twelve, through Simon Peter as their spokesman, affirmed a deepening faith. **68** *You have the words of eternal life.* So often eternal life had been the theme of Jesus' earlier discussions that the disciples had come to recognize it as the distinctive feature of His teaching. **69** Their reaction consisted of both faith and knowledge. *The Holy One of God.* There are various other readings with other titles, but this is to be preferred since it is the most unusual. In Mk. 1:24 and Lk. 4:34 it is used by demons. It is less complete than Peter's confession in Mt. 16:16. **70** It is clear that the 'we' of Peter's confession here needed qualifying in view of the reference to the betrayer. Nothing is said about the disturbing effect of this news of the betrayal upon the Twelve. **71** merely gives John's comment identifying the betrayer.

7:1 – 8:59 JESUS AT THE FEAST OF TABERNACLES

7:1–9 Jesus moves from Galilee to Jerusalem

After the discussions of the last chapter, the scene shifts again to Jerusalem. The first section of ch. 7 gives an insight into Jesus' relationship to His brethren. **1** The scene is set here in an atmosphere of hostility in Judea. **2** The Feast of Tabernacles was near and would provide an admirable opportunity for Jesus to display Himself publicly to a large number of people. **3** At least, this was according to the brothers' reckoning. **4** Their statement, *For no man works in secret if he seeks to be known openly,* shows an evident lack of sympathy with Jesus' true aims. The brothers thought His purpose was to be in the public eye. **5** gives the reason—their lack of faith in Jesus. **6** In declining their suggestion, Jesus again asserts that His time has not come. This brings out vividly His consciousness that all His movements were according to a timetable. **7** *The world cannot hate you.* Clearly *world* must here refer to unbelievers. Since those addressed are also unbelievers there is no cause for hatred. *But it hates me,* since Christ unveils the world's evil by turning the searching light of truth upon it. **8** *I am not going up to the feast.* Some texts have 'not yet', which probably arose from a desire to avoid the seeming difficulty of v. 10. There must have been an interval of a day or two, which might account for the different plan. But in favour of the alternative reading, it should be noted that 'not yet' occurs in the second clause (*for my time has not yet fully come*) which gives the reason for Jesus' decision. It is at least possible that the two Greek words involved (*ouk, oupō*) may have been confused by scribes. Nevertheless, 'not' has the strongest MS support. It could be regarded as a negation of the brothers' public demonstration idea, but not of Jesus' ultimate intention to go. *Cf.* Jn. 2:3, 4.

7:10–52 The Feast of Tabernacles

Jesus' plan was different from the brothers' scheme. There was certainly some basis for their suggestion, in that much speculation was going on in Jerusalem regarding Jesus' presence at the feast (*cf.* 11:55ff.). **10** *Not publicly but in private.* Such unobtrusiveness was unintelligible to His brothers. **12** The different opinions expressed concerning Jesus are typical of reactions towards Him, not only in His own age but in all subsequent ages. Goodness and deception are mutually exclusive opposites. **13** Neither Jesus nor the general populace, at this stage, could be 'open'.

14 It was in *the middle of the feast* that Jesus' action became more public. **15** The quality of His teaching caused investigations regarding His training. *Never studied* must be understood in the technical sense of not having passed through the rabbinical schools. **16** In answer to their question Jesus does not refer to *learning* (Gk. *grammata*), but speaks of His *teaching* (Gk.

didachē), which consists of God's revelation. Our Lord then proceeds to elucidate His teaching. *a.* It is not His own, but God's who sent Him; *b.* **17** it is available to those who desire to do God's will; *c.* **18** it is not based on the desire for self-glory; *d.* it is true. **19** The conclusion to Jesus' answer is abrupt. He appeals to Moses and to the fact that none of His questioners keep the law and then challenges them, *Why do you seek to kill me?* The connection of thought is missing. The only conclusion to which one can come is that Jesus looks beyond their immediate questioning to their deeper motives. He possessed perfect intuitive knowledge (*cf.* 2:24, 25). **20** In self-defence the Jews resort to the charge of demonology. **21–23** But Jesus points out their inconsistency in interpreting the law by demanding circumcision while criticizing an act of mercy on the sabbath day. **24** *Do not judge by appearances, but judge with right judgment.* Jesus criticizes their whole basis of judgment. They were using the wrong criteria.

25, 26 This leads to a discussion about the Messiah. Some of the people are perplexed because the authorities are taking no action. Can the explanation be that the authorities suppose Jesus to be the Christ? But the form of the question implies improbability. **27** Yet there is a problem in the minds of these questioners: the origin of Messiah was supposed to be secret, whereas Jesus' origin was known. It was a Jewish belief that Messiah's advent would be unexpected (*cf.* 1 Enoch 48:6; Ezra 13:51f.). **28, 29** At this point Jesus *proclaimed* (lit. 'cried out') in the Temple, thus banishing all thought of secrecy. He challenges their assumption that they know His true origin, on the grounds that they do not know the One who sent Him. **30** *So they sought to arrest him.* John impresses on his narrative the impotence of any human agency to forestall the 'hour' of Jesus. There is a deep sense of destiny in these incidents. **31** Again the Evangelist mentions that many believed and the connection between faith and signs should once more be noted.

32 Another attempt is made to arrest Jesus, with official backing. *The chief priests and Pharisees* probably convened an informal Sanhedrin meeting. **33, 34** Jesus' response is enigmatic. *I shall be with you a little longer, and then I go to him who sent me.* This shows that the Lord's mind is already on His passion. His consciousness of the divine mission again comes to the fore. **35, 36** The perplexity of the Jews is understandable, but it arises yet again from over-literalism. The statement of Jesus, *Where I am you cannot come,* is not intelligible to the Jews because they cannot think in spiritual terms. All they can think of is *the Dispersion, i.e.* those Jews who lived away from Palestine. There is an element of scorn in the reference to *the Greeks.*

37–39 The next passage is important because of its teaching about the Spirit. It is set *on the last day of the feast, the great day.* This was the climax of the celebrations. At this feast there was a daily water ritual which was specially stressed on the eighth and final day. The ritual was connected with the need for rain during the following year. In saying, *If any one thirst, let him come to me and drink,* Jesus is claiming to provide a better alternative to the water of the ritual. Again He uses the physical in a spiritual sense. **38** His further comment, *Out of his heart shall flow rivers of living water,* makes clear that the refreshment is available only to believers. There is a problem about the reference to *the scripture* here, for the singular form usually refers to a specific passage, but there is nothing which exactly corresponds to this. It must therefore be considered as a general reference to such passages as Is. 58:11; Zc. 14:8; Ezk. 47:1. The idea of the waters flowing out of a person is a vivid reminder of the way in which truth may be communicated (*cf.* the imagery in 1 Cor. 10:4, where the reference is to men drinking from the Rock, *i.e.* Christ). The Mishnah refers similarly to a man devoted to the law. **39** John, however, sees something distinctive—the coming of the Spirit. *For as yet the Spirit had not been given, because Jesus was not yet glorified.* This explanation of the Spirit's coming identifies the coming as subsequent to the resurrection and ascension. However much the water libation may have been understood by the more pious as symbolic of the Spirit, the statement of Jesus pointed to truth beyond the grasp of the Jews who were listening to Him.

40–52 The discourse had certain repercussions. The first obvious result was schism, caused by an inability to agree about the nature of Jesus. There were three views—a prophet, the Christ, not the Christ. **42** For only the last is the basis given— they thought the Scriptures were against it. They appear to be unaware of how precisely Jesus did, in fact, fulfil this prediction (Mi. 5:2). **44** Again the desire and yet the failure to arrest Jesus is mentioned. **45, 46** The officers return empty-handed, because of the deep impression that the teaching methods of Jesus had made upon them. No doubt they realized that Jesus' teaching had won support and they feared a dangerous situation. **47–49** The Pharisees' answer shows their arrogance. *The authorities* and *the Pharisees* are set over against *this crowd.* The Pharisaic contempt is clearly shown in the idea that the common people were accursed. **50, 51** Nicodemus' protest shows that the earlier interview (ch. 3) had not been in vain. He ventures to point out an inconsistency in their approach to the law. Their attitude was out of harmony with the true spirit of the law. **52** This is too much for the Pharisees and a jibe about Galilee is flung at Nicodemus, revealing a further contempt for the provincials by the Jerusalem authorities.

7:53 – 8:11 The woman taken in adultery

It is generally agreed that this section does not belong to this context in John. Most MSS either omit it from this context or mark it with asterisks to indicate doubt. A few MSS place it at the end of the Gospel and a few others after Lk. 21:38. At the same time it has ancient attestation and there is no reason to suppose that it does not represent genuine tradition.

2 The incident took place as Jesus was teaching at the Temple. The scribes and Pharisees sought out Jesus at a time when He was surrounded by a crowd of people. **5, 6** Their intention was to make Him publicly fall foul of the authorities, either religious or civil. The real crux was Jesus' attitude to the Mosaic law. The religious leaders lost no time in drawing attention to the command of Moses in the case of a flagrant act of adultery. Would Jesus condemn the woman and uphold the Mosaic law? If He did, the scribes and Pharisees knew that the civil authorities would not permit sentence to be executed. Or would He evade the issue and by so doing condone the woman's sin? **7** He did neither, but turned the challenge towards His accusers: *Let him who is without sin among you be the first to throw a stone at her.* The Lord leaves the matter to their own consciences. He transforms a legal quibble into a moral issue. **9** The withdrawal of the accusers from the eldest downwards heightens the point of the story. There is no need to debate what Jesus wrote with His finger on the ground. His presence was sufficient to make all His accusers uneasy, until at length only Jesus and the woman were left.

11 *Jesus said, 'Neither do I condemn you; go, and do not sin again.'* Here is compassion linked with strong exhortation, a fitting example of the true treatment of offenders. That there is no question of condoning adultery is clear from Jesus' attitude to the woman.

8:12–59 Jesus the light of the world

12 This discourse is a continuation of the discourse in chapter 7 and Jesus is, therefore, addressing the same people. Now He uses the analogy of *light*, a theme which is found in the prologue (*cf.* 1:4, 5, 9, 10). Here Jesus makes His own claim in the form of an 'I am' statement. It is noteworthy that light is linked with life, again as in the prologue. In the spiritual world, as in the physical, life cannot thrive in darkness. But the unique feature of Jesus' claim is the personal character of the illumination.

The light of the world. There is an obvious connection here with the prologue, where the Word is said to be light. The immediate occasion which led Jesus to select this imagery may have been the lighting of candelabra in the Court of the Women, to symbolize the pillar of fire. *Will not walk in darkness.* The imagery is here extended. The picture is of a path shrouded in darkness along which people are walking behind a bright lamp which dispels the darkness as it proceeds. Any who do not keep behind it will soon lose their way. In the spiritual sense it is necessary to follow the light of the world. The idea of walking as figurative of progress is a characteristic of John's writings.

13 This declaration led to a discussion on testimony between Jesus and the Pharisees. Our Lord's self-witness was a stumbling-block to them because they were not prepared to accept it. They conclude, therefore, that it cannot be true. **14** But self-testimony, as Jesus points out, is not in itself necessarily untrue. It depends on what it is based, and in His case it was based on personal knowledge of His mission, of which they were ignorant and were therefore in no position to pass judgment on His testimony (*cf.* 7:28). **15** *You judge according to the flesh, I judge no one.* The word *flesh* is here used of external appearances. The Lord implies that their judgment is superficial. The last part of the statement could either mean 'I do not judge according to the flesh', or 'The purpose of my mission is not primarily judgment'. **16** supplies the key to v. 15, and suggests that the former alternative is preferable. The antithesis of judgment according to the flesh is judgment in harmony with the mind of the Father. *I and he who sent me* brings out the mission-consciousness of Jesus. His is not isolated judgment, but judgment within His whole life purpose, and it is therefore true. **17** Appeal is then made to the law in support of the greater strength of dual testimony. The description of the law as *your law* is not evidence of an anti-Jewish approach, but an argument based on the principles accepted by Jesus' critics. He proceeds to show that the Mosaic law conflicts with their method of assessing what testimony is true. **18** There were in fact two witnesses, and not one as the Pharisees supposed, —Jesus' own testimony and the Father. Again the Father is described as the One *who sent me.*

19 The critics pose the question, *Where is your Father?*, in which the use of *your* suggests that natural fatherhood is in their minds. Without any perception on their part of the divine mission of Jesus it is not surprising that they were unconvinced by the claim of Jesus to a corroborating witness, for an absent witness would, in their eyes, be invalid. It is for this reason that they asked 'Where?' and not 'Who?'. But Jesus' answer is to the latter question rather than the former. *If you knew me.* Their whole attitude towards Jesus showed that they had not penetrated to a real knowledge of Him. Jesus shows that His close relationship with the Father would have become apparent to them had they only understood Him. In no clearer way could Jesus have claimed that He was the means for men to attain a knowledge of God. **20** *The treasury* was the treasury hall, situated in the Court of the Women. It was a place of public assembly and it is for this reason that it is mentioned here. *His hour had not yet come.* John by-passes any circumstantial human explanation of Jesus not being arrested and goes for a theological reason. This is a sequel to 7:44 where the desire to arrest Him is emphasized, and to 7:46, which records the report of the officers who returned from an earlier but fruitless attempt to arrest Jesus. The thwarting of human designs is an important factor which John explicitly mentions to show that the events of Jesus' life were under divine control.

21 *I go away.* Cf. 7:34, where the idea of going away equally mystified the hearers. *You will seek me and die in your sin.* The point of this statement seems to be that they will seek for Jesus as Messiah too late and will not therefore receive the benefit of His redeeming work. In that case the seeking must be understood in a spiritual sense and so must the following statement, that they cannot go where Jesus is going (*cf.* 7:34). Since the same idea is later expressed to the disciples (13:33), it draws attention to the uniqueness of the mission of Jesus. **22** The chasm which divided Him from the Jews is seen clearly in the following passage. Their misunderstanding is based on a literal understanding of Jesus' words. All they could think of was suicide, **23** but Jesus points out the essential contrast between His approach and theirs. *Below* is contrasted with *above* and *this world* with *not this world.* It was the difference between an earthly and a heavenly view of things. **24** Jesus gives His own explanation of v. 21. Dying in sins can be avoided only by faith in Jesus. *Unless you believe that I am he* shows what the content of the faith must be. It is believing in the full revelation of Jesus. *I am he* is analogous to the great 'I am' assertions found in the OT and must imply the self-existence of the Messiah. Jesus demands a comprehensive faith in His Person. **25** The 'I am' statement was clearly not intelligible to the hearers, otherwise they would not have asked, *Who are you?* The person of Christ is the touchstone in matters of Christian faith. The answer of Jesus to their question is, however, enigmatical. The problem lies in the interpretation of the Greek phrase translated *from the beginning.* If this is the correct translation, the statement implies that Jesus has been consistently declaring His identity from the first, both in word and deed. RSV mg. gives an alternative rendering, 'Why do I talk to you at all?' which is possible on grammatical grounds, but is inconsistent with the context. Another possibility is to understand the words as implying, 'Primarily or essentially I am what I am telling you', which has the advantage of taking the verb as present, which it is in the Greek. Such an interpretation fits well into the context and adds emphasis to the 'I am' assertion preceding it.

26 *I have much to say about you and much to judge.* In this way Jesus leaves their question to return to the main theme of the preceding conversation, *i.e.* judgment. He has twice reminded them that they will die in their sins, and there are further strongly adverse comments that He has to make. He again asserts the truth of His testimony on the grounds that He who sent Him is true. What He declared to the world (lit. 'into the world') was only what He had heard from the Father, which again draws attention to His divinely initiated mission. **27** John's comment, *They did not understand that he spoke to them of the Father,* shows insight into the perplexity of their minds. The whole Gospel is full of instances of pathetic misunderstandings. **28** Our Lord's answer to their perplexity, which must have been only too evident, is surprising. *When you have lifted up the Son of man* would appear to refer to the cross, but how does this relate to the context? In all probability our Lord has in mind the revelation of the Father which will come as a result of His crucifixion. It would then be evident to those who had eyes to behold and ears to hear that what Jesus had spoken was not only true, but was stamped with the authority of the Father. *Then you will know that I am he. Cf.* v. 24, where the same expression occurs, only there with the verb 'believe'. Such knowledge as this will come as a result of the resurrection of Jesus, which is understood, although not mentioned, here. **29** *He has not left me alone.* As in the opening part of the prologue, so here the close relation of the Son to the Father is brought out. The present statement may be contrasted with the cry of abandonment (Mk. 15:34; Mt. 27:46). It does not conflict, for here the emphasis is on an abiding relationship, but there on a temporary experience. *I always do what is pleasing to him.* The comprehensiveness of this claim shows the measure of oneness between the Father and Son. **30** *Many believed in him.* This implies faith of a personal kind.

The next section discusses the nature of true freedom. **31** *The Jews who had believed in him* needed to progress beyond their present condition of faith. Continuing in the word of Jesus implies a full committal to His teaching, which is indispensable for true discipleship. **32** *You will know the truth, and the truth will make you free.* The connection between truth and freedom is important. Truth never leads to bondage. The whole idea is perplexing to the Pharisees, who are not in the least convinced that they need freedom. In spite of the heavy yokes imposed on others by their casuistry, they never conceived of it as bondage. **33** The appeal to *Abraham* is considered sufficient to justify their claim to freedom. But this showed that their concept of freedom was deficient in moral content. **34** In answer, Jesus makes a comment to which He attaches great importance, as the introductory formula shows. He proceeds to show the true nature of moral slavery, in order to bring out the true nature of freedom. **35** There is an obvious contrast between a slave and a son in the rights that each possesses and this illustrates the chasm between bondage and freedom. **36** *You will be free indeed.* Freedom obtained through the Son is real. The idea in the *if*-clause is that freedom can come only through One who is Himself free. The Son is free and can therefore make free. **37** At this point Jesus refers to their appeal to *Abraham.* He points out the incongruity of Abraham's descendants seeking to kill One who speaks from God. The basic reason for this incongruity is said to be that Jesus' word *finds no place* in them. The word used is unusual in this context. It means 'making room for' in order to allow for development. The Pharisees' trouble was that their minds were closed. **38** *My Father . . . your father.* Although there are textual variants, the reading in the text seems best supported with its specific contrast between Jesus and His disputants. If *your father* is to be interpreted by means of v. 44, Jesus is meaning to refer to the devil.

39 *Abraham is our father.* So important to them was their connection with Abraham, that they could not get away from it. This reflects the general belief in the great merits of Abraham, which were believed to become available to Abraham's seed. But Jesus corrects the popular misconception by challenging its basis. Abraham's children must be defined on moral, not on genetic, grounds. **40** But the intentions and actions of these Jews are most clearly un-Abrahamic. To seek to kill anyone who declares God's truth can find no warrant in Abraham's example. **41** The second reference to *your father* is intended to challenge them further and draws out from them an indignant protest. Because their lineage from Abraham has been called in question, they resort to claiming that God Himself is their father. *We were not born of fornication.* The most natural interpretation of this statement is to understand *fornication* in a spiritual sense (as apostasy from God) as used in the OT (as, *e.g.*, in Hosea). This is more likely than to see here an indirect allusion to slanders regarding the birth of Jesus. **42** *If God were your Father* is an unfulfilled condition parallel to v. 39. *You would love me* is an advance on 'you would do what Abraham did' of v. 39. True children of God could not fail to love the Son of God. This thought leads Jesus to assert again the divine origin of His mission. He will not allow His hearers to forget this. **43** *You cannot bear to hear my word.* The Greek here expresses more vividly a moral impossibility—'You are not able to hear'. The word (*logos*) is closely linked to the Person of Jesus (*cf.* the prologue). With the Pharisees' presuppositions, it was impossible to appreciate the message and mission of Jesus. **44** But the next statement reinforces the idea of moral impossibility—*You are of your father the devil.* The implications of this are far-reaching. The connection of thought is in three steps: first, the devil is a murderer; second, you are seeking to kill Me; third, therefore you are his children. The most characteristic feature about the devil is his opposition to truth. This is expressed in various ways in this verse: he *has nothing to do with the truth*, no *truth* is *in him*, he is *a liar and the father of lies.* The latter expression could mean 'the father of the liar', which would have a similar but more personal meaning. It would, however, fit better the charge that the opponents of Jesus were of their father the devil. **45** The sequence in this verse moreover suggests that their rejection of the truth shows their basic allegiance to falsehood. *You do not believe me.* Once again the attitude towards Jesus Himself is made the touchstone. Since He speaks truth, all

that is contrary to Him must be false. **46** His opponents' attitude of unbelief implies that Jesus does not speak the truth—hence the double challenge. **47** There is a syllogism in this verse, the steps of which are as follows: first, he who hears the words of God is of God; second, you do not hear the words of God; third, therefore you are not of God. It is the second step in the argument which the hearers would challenge, for Jesus' estimate of their piety was very different from their own. Their strong reaction is understandable.

48 The next section shows the nature of the opposition which the words of Jesus aroused. *Are we not right in saying that you are a Samaritan and have a demon?* The question expresses strong contempt, although there is no evidence that *Samaritan* was generally used in this sense. The Jews denied any spiritual kinship with Samaritans, although the latter also claimed Abraham as their father. The charge of demon-possession is a much more bitter charge and is their reaction to Jesus' statement in v. 44. **49–51** The answer of Jesus brings out, first, that honouring the Father is incongruous with demon-possession, and second, that the judge of the matter is not Jesus but the Father, and therefore it is not a question merely of His opinion against theirs. *He will never see death* may either be understood to mean 'he will never see the terrors of death', *i.e.* death as it was understood in the contemporary world; or it may be taken more literally with the implication that no-one can ever completely keep the word of Jesus. The former is preferable. **52** The Jews, however, took the words literally. It is significant that they changed the words to *taste death.* **53** *Are you greater than our father Abraham?* To the devout Jew none could be greater. Moreover, even *the prophets* gained much greater status than the Jews were ready to grant to Jesus.

54–56 Jesus' answer to the question *Who do you claim to be?* is indirect. He virtually declines to answer, but rather infers that the Father has shown that Jesus is greater than Abraham. He strongly asserts His knowledge of the Father. *Your father Abraham rejoiced that he was to see my day.* The *your* draws attention to their constant appeal to Abraham in argument. But when did Abraham rejoice over such a prospect? Some sort of vision must be in mind. A Jewish tradition held that Abraham saw the whole history of his descendants (*cf.* Gn. 15:6). But this is not likely to be the meaning behind the words here. The reason for Abraham's rejoicing was the promise that all the peoples of the earth were to be blessed through his seed (*cf.* Paul's interpretation of this promise in Rom. 4 and Gal. 3). This was supremely fulfilled in Christ. *He saw it and was glad.* Some regard this as referring to Abraham in Hades, others as referring to his insight when offering Isaac, and yet others to a foreseeing in faith. The last seems best to fit the context. **57** The Jews distort the expression by asking *Have you seen Abraham?*,

58 but Jesus makes an emphatic declaration in answer. *Before Abraham was, I am* must refer to absolute existence. The two verbs vividly bring out a contrast and point to the superiority of Christ. That this statement must be regarded as making an exalted claim is clear from the violent reaction. **59** The Jews could think of no other treatment for anyone so indisputably claiming a pre-existence to Abraham. *Jesus hid himself* may have some symbolic significance for John. Withdrawal was not only from the Temple but from all that it represented. The Jewish leaders were rejecting Him.

9:1 – 10:42 FURTHER HEALING AND TEACHING

9:1–41 The blind man receives his sight

This incident provides an illustration of the theme of the previous chapter. Here is a specific example of Jesus as the light of the world. In view of this it is not impossible than John sees in the incident a symbolic significance. Some scholars regard this as evidence that John is giving an interpretation of Christ, but it is clear that all the Gospels record instances of blind men receiving sight from Christ. What is characteristic in John is his record of the discussion which it provoked.

1 *A man blind from his birth.* It is worth noting that the healing miracles in John are specifically stated to concern people in a chronic state (*cf.* 5:5). The power of Jesus is thus seen to be capable of acts of restoration even in extreme cases. **2** *Rabbi, who sinned?* There was much current discussion about the connection between suffering and sin. The disciples' conclusion that the man's blindness must be due to his own sin or his parents' is typical of current opinion. The idea that a congenital condition could be the result of sin naturally presents difficulties. It may be that the disciples knew nothing about the man and did not know that he was born blind. If they did know, it must be supposed that they conceived the possibility of sin before birth, as in fact some of the Rabbis taught (*cf. Bereshith* R xxxiv). **3** But Jesus' reply gives no support to either of the disciples' alternatives. *But that the works of God might be made manifest in him.* This was a possibility which was given little consideration in our Lord's day. That suffering could be used for God's glory was difficult to believe, although it is inherent in the Christian approach to the problem. This miracle, however, is not concerned with that problem. It is aimed to show the illuminating power of Christ, not only in the physical but also in the spiritual sphere. Restored sight led to a developing faith. **4** *We must work the works of him who sent me.* Some MSS read 'I' instead of *we*, and this would certainly agree better with the context, since the disciples were not associated with Jesus in the sign of the healing of the blind man. If the plural is retained the statement becomes more general. *Night comes.*

The contrast between day and night appears to be used symbolically, if the reference is to the mission of Jesus, for *night* would represent the close of that mission. Some, however, have understood the night to refer to the spiritual blindness of our Lord's enemies. The former seems preferable. **5** is a repetition of 8:12 and a further parallel with the prologue. But it is important to note that in this case Jesus announces His claims before performing the miracle. **6** *Made clay . . . and anointed.* Another instance of healing accompanied by the use of spittle is recorded by Mark (7:33). It was a current belief that saliva was curative, especially for diseased eyes. Jesus clearly used currently understood means, but there is no need to assume that He attached superstitious value to them. **7** Indeed, the healing took place only when the man washed in the pool of Siloam. The interpretation of the name as *Sent* must have significance, but the purpose is not clear. Some have supposed that there is reference to Christ as the 'Sent One' and this would fit well into the phrase in v. 4. But the interpretation is more probably a note added for the benefit of John's Greek readers in agreement with his characteristic procedure with Hebrew names (*cf.* 1:42). *And came back seeing.* Obedience was rewarded with healing. The delay in the cure may well have been to test the man's faith.

8–12 The account of the interchange of conversation between the man and his neighbours is marked by exceptional vividness. The argument about the man's identity, the vagueness of his own knowledge of Jesus and the certainty of the cure are all clearly brought out. Each of those points finds elaboration in the man's subsequent discussion with the Pharisees. **13** *They brought to the Pharisees the man who had formerly been blind.* What prompted the neighbours to do this is not stated. It is not even certain that it is the neighbours who are referred to. Obviously the people concerned were some who were somewhat hostile to Jesus and were themselves sticklers for the Jewish law. **14** This is supported by the statement that the cure was effected on the *sabbath day.* Jewish casuistry could regard the making of clay as work which was forbidden on the sabbath. That it was an act of mercy was irrelevant. **15** The man's answer to further questioning shows impatience, which adds further vividness to the account. **16** The Pharisees show a similar division of opinion as the neighbours, although in their case it was a dispute between the extreme legalists, whose only concern was over sabbath regulations, and others who were so impressed with the signs that they could not imagine a sinner performing them. These latter implied that the legalists must be judging wrongly. **17** *He is a prophet.* This statement from the blind man himself is an advance on his answer to the neighbours' enquiries, on which occasion (*cf.* v. 11) he speaks of 'the man called Jesus'. A prophet would be considered of greater importance than a Rabbi.

18-23 The next section brings into sharp focus the sheer obstinacy of unbelief. Not only did the Jews disbelieve the man's own words, but also Jesus' power to heal. They demanded the supporting testimony of the man's parents, but their enquiries do not appear to be made in the spirit of impartial examination. They were definitely prejudiced against the possibility of a man born blind ever receiving his sight. It was reasonable to seek confirmation of the identity and previous condition of the man, but unreasonable to expect an explanation of the phenomenon from the parents. Their response to the last demand reflects the fear which conditioned their whole approach to the Pharisees. Threat of excommunication appears to have been a powerful ecclesiastical weapon. At the same time it was justifiable for the parents to pass the question back to the son, who alone could speak from personal experience. Indeed the whole incident shows the clash between academic quibbling and personal testimony (cf. v. 25).

24 *Give God the praise.* This cannot mean that they were urging him to praise God for the cure, for they still appear doubtful about its veracity. It was a common Jewish oath and must be regarded as a solemn exhortation to the man to speak the truth. **24, 25** *We know* contrasts with the man's *I know.* Their knowledge of Jesus was based on a technical breach of sabbath regulations, but his on a personal experience. He cannot debate on the technical question, but he refuses to be put off on a matter of experience. **26** *What did he do to you?* Baffled by the assertion of fact, they return to the theoretical problem of method, **27** which understandably caused the man no little irritation. The man's question to them, *Do you too want to become his disciples?* is ironical. He suggests that their desire to hear the evidence all over again shows such eagerness that he can only conclude that they would make good disciples! **28** But his irony only drew out their scorn. *We are disciples of Moses.* Their legalistic position comes to the fore here. Moses to them is infinitely superior to Jesus. **29** They claim knowledge of Moses and ignorance of Jesus. The contrast implies an unwillingness to give credence to the actions of anyone of whose origins they were ignorant. This would be particularly so for one whom some claimed to be a prophet. **30ff.** It is no wonder that the man himself becomes increasingly cutting in his remarks. For him facts were more telling than theories of origin. But he ventures to reason the matter in the following steps. **30** First, his sight has been restored. **31** Second, God hears only those who do His will. Third, hence, by inference, the man's healer cannot be a sinner. **32** Fourth, that a mere man could have opened the eyes of a man born blind is without precedent. **33** Fifth, therefore the healer of the man must be from God. **34** The theologically-minded Jews at last see that they can make no headway with a man who can reason in such a manner and so they finally eject him. *You were born in*

utter sin seems to be an admission on their part that the man really had been born blind, which in their theory of suffering meant a deeper condition of sin (cf. v. 2). They are, therefore, more concerned to show contempt for his former condition than pleasure in his present restoration. This reveals how very blind they were and illustrates the comment of Jesus in v. 41.

35ff. The concluding section focuses upon the man's personal interview with Jesus and reaches its climax in his declaration of faith. **35** *Jesus heard . . . and having found him he said.* By this sequence of verbs, John brings out vividly that the initiative was taken by Jesus. The challenge given to the man is significant for its emphasis on faith and for the title used by Jesus of Himself. It is characteristic of the Johannine signs that they lead to faith and the idea of faith in the Son of man is found elsewhere in the Gospel (cf. 3:14, 15). **36** Yet the man did not without further comment from Jesus understand the term—hence his request for more explanation. **37, 38** As soon as Jesus makes clear that He is the Son of man, the restored man at once believes, which suggests that he already had the seeds of faith in him. Indeed, the earlier account shows a distinct progression of faith. *Lord, I believe.* There is no need to suppose that the word translated *Lord* is used in any theological sense, for it is unlikely that the man had come to an understanding of the Lordship of Christ. Most probably it was no more than a title of respect.

39 *For judgment I came into this world.* It is surprising that Jesus should respond to the man's confession of faith by referring to judgment. The statement cannot be regarded as comprehensive, for judgment was not the primary mission of the Lord. It was rather the inevitable effect of His coming. It brings men to the point of crisis. The cured man had in fact sealed his own excommunication by his act of worship. The antitheses—non-seeing and seeing, seeing and becoming blind—are one of the characteristic features of this Gospel. The notion of sight is used in different ways. The blind man had received both physical and spiritual sight. The Pharisees possessed natural sight and thought they possessed spiritual sight, but their reaction to Jesus shows they were really blind. In this sense His coming brought judgment. **40, 41** Jesus' answer to the Pharisees' question, *Are we also blind?* is somewhat enigmatic. *If you were blind* might be regarded as meaning 'If you were conscious of your blindness', with the implication that they would have responded and would therefore have been without guilt. Another interpretation would be to take the if-clause as meaning 'If you were really blind', in which case the then-clause (*you would have no guilt*) would follow because they could not be held responsible. But they were claiming to be responsible people by saying 'We see', while their rejection of the claims of Jesus proved their guilt. The former interpretation of the if-clause is to be preferred.

10:1-18 Jesus as the shepherd

This section of the Gospel records an allegory, which while akin to the Synoptic parables is nevertheless distinguished from them. But the allegory must not be pressed in its details even here. It is broad principles which are illustrated.

1-10 The opening illustration concentrates on the door, which leads naturally into the shepherd imagery. But the two ideas are inseparably connected. The imagery of the shepherd is often found in the OT (*cf.* Ps. 23; Ezk. 34; Zc. 10; Je. 23). **1** *Truly, truly* probably shows a continuation from chapter 9, in which case the teaching about the good shepherd is intended to contrast with the bad shepherding of the Pharisees. Eastern sheepfolds had only one door which was guarded by the shepherd. Those who entered by any other means were false, described in these verses both as thieves and robbers and also as strangers (or aliens). **3** *To him the gatekeeper opens.* There is no need to attempt to interpret the gatekeeper, who is not identified in the allegory. The focus of attention is on the accessibility of the shepherd to the sheep. Some have seen an allusion to God or to the Holy Spirit. It is the relationship between the sheep and shepherd which is specially emphasized. **4** The calling of the sheep by name and the leading of them out is characteristic of a true shepherd. **5** No such personal relationship exists between strangers and the flock. Although Jesus had at this stage given no interpretation, He clearly intended a spiritual meaning. **6** John characteristically notes the hearers' inability to understand, **7** before recording the specific claim of Jesus to be the door. **8** Then follows another statement which has caused difficulties. *All who came before me are thieves and robbers.* Some MSS omit the words *before me* which would lessen the difficulties of interpretation, but the words are probably original. If understood in a temporal sense, the statement implies that others who had before His time claimed to be the door, *i.e.* the way of access, were impostors (*i.e.* pseudo-Messiahs). It is unlikely that Jesus is referring to the OT prophets. If *before me* relates to position and not time, the statement could refer to the present Jewish leaders. The Pharisees' treatment of the man born blind illustrated what alien shepherds of God's flock they were. **9** Jesus' own claim to be the door is repeated in a more extended form, promising not only salvation, but also spiritual sustenance. **10** *I came that they may have life, and have it abundantly.* The contrast between Jesus and the false shepherds here is vivid. He brings life; they bring death. The abundance of life is characteristic of the Johannine portrait of Christ.

11-18 The next section concentrates on Jesus as the good shepherd. If the metaphors are mixed the spiritual implications are nevertheless transparent. **11** *The good shepherd lays down his life for the sheep.* Having just claimed to give abundant life to others, Jesus now speaks of sacrificing His own. The verb used could mean 'laying aside', which would draw attention to the voluntary character of the sacrificial act. The main emphasis lies on the fact that the act is on behalf of others. **12** The contrast with the hired shepherd who has no personal interest in the sheep is again vivid. **13** It is the lack of care which is particularly noted. **14ff.** The assertion of v. 11 is repeated with additional details in these verses. There is a significant emphasis on personal knowledge; Christ's knowledge of His own people and their knowledge of Him, the Father's knowledge of the Son and the Son's knowledge of the Father. This is a development of the introductory illustration concerning a shepherd's knowledge of his sheep (*cf.* vv. 3-5). Where no such personal relationships exist, there can be no true shepherd. **16** *I have other sheep, that are not of this fold.* This is a further development of thought. If the *other sheep* are Gentiles as differentiated from the Jewish fold, this statement is an important witness to the universalism of Jesus. The distinction between *fold* here and *flock* in the next sentence shows the variety which exists within the people of God. There are many folds, but one flock. *I must bring them also.* The form of the Greek draws attention to a divine necessity. This is the purpose for which Jesus came. The initiative is seen to be with the shepherd. *One flock, one shepherd.* The unity of the flock arises from the unifying factor of the shepherd. Ecumenical unity could have no other basis. **17** *For this reason* could refer to the preceding verses with the meaning 'The Father loves Me because I am the good shepherd'. Or it could refer to the following statement, *because I lay down my life.* The love of the Father is not to be regarded as having its basis in the action of the Son, but it does find its fullest manifestation in that action. *That I may take it again.* This gives the purpose of the voluntary life-giving, *i.e.* a self-willed resurrection. **18** So remarkable is this claim that Jesus proceeds to vindicate it. The emphasis is on Jesus' own authority, as the word translated *power* could well be rendered. But it is an authority received from the Father—another example of the delegated character of the mission of Jesus.

10:19-21 The effects of this teaching

19 *A division.* Cf. other examples of the same result in 7:43 and 9:16. **20** The demon-possession charge is found also in 7:20; 8:48, 52. The close connection between demon-possession and madness in contemporary thought is reflected here. **21** *Can a demon open the eyes of the blind?* The force of the Greek question implies a negative answer. Not all the Jews were equally credulous.

10:22-42 Dialogue at the Feast of Dedication

22 There is no particular significance in the mention of this feast, which was first instituted by Judas Maccabaeus, except in so far as John shows special interest in connecting events with feasts. **23** The season of the year, *winter*, accounts for Jesus walking and discussing in Solomon's portico. **24** *How long will you keep us in suspense?* In all probability an interval of some weeks separated this incident from the preceding discourse, in which case much further discussion may have taken place regarding the claims of Jesus. Their request implies perplexity. **25** But Jesus' answer draws attention to their lack of faith. They do not even believe the works of Jesus. **26, 27** Reference is again made to the shepherd imagery. These Jews showed that they did not belong because they did not recognize the shepherd's voice. **28** *I give them eternal life.* The tense of the verb is present, which shows that the people of God have already entered into possession of eternal life. *No one shall snatch them out of my hand.* There can be no doubt Jesus means to imply by this statement the security of His people in face of any adversary. **29** This security is reinforced by the fact that they are the Father's gift to the Son, and there can be no greater security than this. **30** *I and the Father are one.* Much discussion has ranged around the significance of this statement, but it is difficult to avoid the conclusion that unity of essence is in mind. It is insufficient to regard the meaning as moral agreement. The identity of security in both the Son and the Father bears testimony to a more basic identity.

31 At this point of the dialogue comes the threat of stoning, which turns the discussion to the consideration of motives. **32, 33** Jesus challenges the Jews to cite the 'good' works for which He is being stoned, which brings forth their retort about blasphemy. *I have shown you many good works* points to the evidential purpose of Jesus' deeds. This is in harmony with the purpose of the Gospel. *Because you, being a man, make yourself God* is a charge which conveys a sense of contempt, especially in the emphasis on 'you'. A similar charge is found in 5:18. According to the Levitical law (Lv. 24:16) blasphemy was punishable by stoning. **34** *Is it not written in your law, 'I said, you are gods'?* The word *law* here embraces all three parts of the Jewish Scriptures so that a citation from Ps. 82:6 is not out of place. The method of exegesis which Jesus used is typically Jewish and illustrates again how He took up the same approach as His hearers when He was contending with them. The argument is *a fortiori*: since even unjust rulers are called 'gods', how much more reason for the Father's special representative to be called Son of God. How can He be charged with blasphemy? By this means Jesus shows the fallacy of their charge. **35** *Scripture cannot be broken.* The use of the singular (Gk. *graphē*) draws attention to this particular passage as inviolable, but the principle is generally applicable. Because of this the truth of Ps. 82:6 has abiding validity. **36** *Whom the Father consecrated.* Many times in this Gospel Jesus refers to the fact that He was sent, but here

the word 'consecrate' is used in addition. It means 'set apart', is frequently used in the OT for the setting apart of a man for a specific office and is used in the NT of Christian believers (*cf.* Jn. 17:19).

37 The discussion concludes with a statement of Jesus about works and faith. *The works of my Father* are evidently special works and are connected with, if not identical with, the 'signs'. But the works must have evidence of divine origin, otherwise they should not be believed. **38** The following verse implies that faith based on works is inferior to faith based on what Jesus has said. This statement is in harmony with the purpose of the whole Gospel. The works (or signs) are for a theological purpose—to bring understanding of the relationship between Jesus and the Father. The form of the Greek in this verse is significant—that you may come to know and continually know. Some texts, however, read 'believe' in place of the second verb. Those who had come to understand the intimate relation between the Father and the Son would not have stumbled over the statement of v. 30. *The Father is in me* relates primarily to the works. It is impossible to differentiate between the Son and the Father in these. **39** The Jews' reaction is still violent, but their attempt to arrest failed.

40–42 A concluding historical note mentions Jordan as the scene of John's baptism. There seems no special reason for the reference, except to give validity to John's witness concerning Jesus. The statement, *John did no sign*, is clearly intended to contrast with Jesus. The response of faith across Jordan also contrasts with the lack of it in Jerusalem.

11:1–57 DEATH AND RAISING OF LAZARUS

11:1–44 Jesus the overcomer of death

For two main reasons the account of the raising of Lazarus has been objected to; the first is its extraordinary character, the second the silence of the other Gospels concerning it. Basically this story is no more extraordinary than any of the miracles, once the possibility of a divine breaking into the natural world is admitted. The latter condition can hardly be denied if the resurrection of Christ Himself is given credence. It surely becomes more credible to regard the narrative as historical than to view it as an idealized illustration of the statement of Jesus, 'I am the resurrection and the life' (11:25), or, as some have supposed, a development of the story of the widow's son at Nain.

1–4 The occasion of the miracle is briefly stated. John is concerned to make clear the identity of Lazarus and especially his relation to the Mary who anointed Jesus, although he does not relate this incident until later (ch. 12). When John wrote the incident was, of course, in the past and it is for this reason that the past tense is used in v. 2. **3** *Lord, he whom you love is ill.* It is noticeable that the verb used in the sisters' report is *phileō*, whereas John uses the fuller word *agapaō* in v. 5. These statements have been used by some scholars as the basis of the claim that Lazarus is the beloved disciple who is referred to several times in the latter portion of the Gospel. But it is unlikely that Lazarus was present in the upper room. **4** *This illness is not unto death.* By this Jesus means that the purpose of the sickness is not death, but the glorification of the Son of God. This may be compared with other signs in this Gospel (*e.g.* 2:11; 9:3). The glory of God is more significant than the sickness. The sickness is conceived of as a means to a greater end (*cf.* v. 15).

5-16 The report sent to Jesus and the consequent discussion between Jesus and His disciples raises an important theological problem. Why did Jesus delay? **6** *So when he heard that he was ill, he stayed two days longer in the place where he was.* It is important to notice that there is a definite connection between v. 6 and the previous statement. The delay must be understood in terms of Jesus' love for the Bethany family. This excludes any possibility of regarding the delay as evidence of lack of care or concern. A more dominating purpose must be found and this is indicated both in v. 4 ('for the glory of God') and v. 15 ('that you may believe').

7, 8 In reply to Jesus' suggestion that they should go to Judea, the disciples remind Him that even at that very time the Jews were seeking to stone Him. This recalls what was stated in 10:31, 39. The whole situation was fraught with danger. The Transjordan district where they were at that time was less hostile than Judea. No doubt the disciples were relieved that Jesus delayed His journey and appear to have hoped that He would abandon it altogether. **9** *Are there not twelve hours in the day?* This response of Jesus to the disciples' panic is surprising. How does it answer their fears? The connection of thought is that the hours of day are not affected by external circumstances. They are there to be used. The implication is that Jesus' hour has not come (*i.e.* the twelfth hour) and until God wills that it should come, the only course to adopt is to go about one's mission. The reference to a twelve-hour day is based on Jewish reckoning, which divided the period between sunrise and sunset into twelve equal parts. These parts varied in length according to the time of year. **9, 10** The figures of light and darkness and the ideas of walking and stumbling all go to show the contrast between Jesus' unerring progress and the Jews' fumbling attempts to stop it.

In the further discussion over Lazarus' death, there occurs another instance of misunderstanding through taking a metaphorical statement literally. **11** The idea of death being described in terms of *sleep* was not unknown, but when Jesus stated His purpose as being to arouse Lazarus out of sleep **12** the disciples became convinced that He meant it literally. *He will recover.* In the minds of the disciples, sleep was a

hopeful sign in any illness. All was not lost. Restoration would come independent of any action of Jesus. **13** John explains how the confusion arose and **14** this leads to the plain statement that *Lazarus is dead.* The tense of the verb here (aorist) is more abrupt than that in v. 11 (perfect), drawing attention to the finality of it. **15** *And for your sake I am glad that I was not there.* Once again Jesus draws attention to the higher spiritual purpose behind His acts. It is almost as if our Lord's mind was concentrating more specifically on the training of the Twelve than on the two sisters or Lazarus. The effect on the disciples would have a more far-reaching outcome. *So that you may believe.* This must mean 'in a fuller way than you have so far done'. Again the connection between signs and faith comes into focus. **16** Thomas' response to Jesus' repeated *Let us go* (*cf.* v. 7) sounds like a resigned act of despair rather than an act of courage.

17-27 The next scene in this vivid drama is a conversation between Jesus and Martha on the outskirts of Bethany. This is the most theological section of the whole narrative and draws attention to the spiritual truths. **17** *Now when Jesus came.* From v. 30 it is evident that Jesus remained on the outskirts of the village, perhaps in the vicinity of the tomb (but *cf.* v. 34). He received a report of the time that Lazarus had been in the tomb. The verb *found* need not imply a previously limited knowledge. It suggests the completion of the journey (*cf.* similar use in 2:14). **18, 19** The nearness of Bethany to Jerusalem is mentioned to account for the presence of so many Jews who had come to comfort the sisters. **20** *When Martha heard that Jesus was coming.* It is characteristic of the Synoptic picture of Martha that she did not wait for Jesus to reach the house. Here was the same bustling, impetuous person whose major interest was action. Mary sitting at home is the same reflective, rather inactive person as in the Synoptic records. **21** *Lord, if you had been here, my brother would not have died.* Martha and Mary must have speculated much in this vein, for Mary says identical words later (*cf.* v. 32). It shows a loving faith in Jesus' power to heal. Indeed, v. 22 shows the possibility of a deeper faith. **22** *And even now I know* suggests some kind of conviction that Jesus would do something. At least Martha affirms her faith that God would grant any request from Jesus. She appears to be reaching out for some ray of hope. Martha manages to hide her grief behind a calm exterior, but Mary weeps until the miracle is performed. **23, 24** *Your brother will rise again.* It is understandable that Martha regarded this as no more than a conventional statement of consolation relating to the end of the age, as her answer shows. It is probable that her understanding of resurrection was vague and was certainly not applied by her in any personal way.

25 The crux in the whole narrative comes with Jesus' great 'I am' assertion, *I am the* *resurrection and the life.* It shows first that Jesus' statement in v. 23 was intended in a double sense. It further reveals Jesus' own approach to His mission. He identifies Himself with the climax of His work, as if the resurrection had already taken place. The greatest possible source of comfort in the hour of bereavement is the risen Lord. It should be noted that resurrection comes before life, because for mortal men new life is the product of resurrection. **26** The availability of this life is by means of faith, which leads Jesus to the direct challenge, *Do you believe this?* It should be noted that Jesus does not invite a confession of faith in Himself, but in His statement. The two ideas are essentially inseparable, but the emphasis here falls on the content of belief. **27** Martha's response bears a striking resemblance to John's statement of purpose (20:31), as if her confession of faith forms the pattern which the whole Gospel is intended to support. To what extent she understood the Messiahship or Sonship of Jesus it is impossible to say. But there is no doubt that to the Evangelist the content of her faith was highly significant. Faith which fell short of so exalted a concept of Christ was inadequate.

28–37 The next section portrays first the reaction of Mary and then that of the Jews who had come to mourn with the sisters. The salient features of Mary's part in the story may be summarized as follows: *a.* **28** Jesus sent Martha for her; *b.* **29** she immediately responded; *c.* **32** she fell down at Jesus' feet and repeated the same statement that Martha had made on meeting Him (*cf.* v. 21); *d.* **33–35** her tears caused Jesus to be distressed and to weep. In this narrative Mary stands out as more emotional than Martha. Even the Jewish observers add to the pathos of the scene. They are shown **31** as consoling Mary, as following her, supposedly to the tomb, **33** as weeping with her, **36** as being touched by the sight of Jesus' tears, **37** as speculating on why Jesus had not prevented this sad happening. **33** The climax of this part of the narrative is in the sentence *he was deeply moved in spirit and troubled.* The first verb is strongly expressed, meaning 'to show anger', and a problem arises concerning its cause. Some have suggested moral indignation at the result of human sin, *i.e.* death, and at the sorrow caused by death. But this must have been present to our Lord's mind constantly, whereas His emotion here appears to belong to the specific occasion. Was His distress, on the other hand, caused by His sympathy for the sisters? The verb seems too strong for that. Was it because the Jewish display of grief was unreal? This is a possibility, for any show of hypocrisy must have aroused His anger. It may well be that something of the pathos of human suffering was bearing upon Jesus as He knew His own cup of suffering was so close. The troubling of His spirit proceeded from within. Perhaps it was due to His knowledge of the strength of the unbelief of some of them which would cause them to oppose Him even after they had witnessed the stupendous sign. **37** The question, which links the present incident with the last sign (ch. 9), may well have been asked in mockery.

38–44 The actual account of the miracle itself is relatively brief and is marked by its reserve. The repetition of Jesus' distress, the objection of Martha to the request that the tomb be opened, Jesus' reminder to her that she would see God's glory, the acquiescence in the removal of the stone, the prayer of Jesus, His command to the dead man and the simple instruction to loose him and let him go: all these details have about them the ring of truth. **40** *Did I not tell you?* It was to the disciples (*cf.* v. 4) that Jesus had mentioned God's glory, but it was implicit in what He had said to Martha. **41, 42** The prayer of Jesus is significant because of its emphasis on faith and on the authentication of His mission. **44** The reserve in the account is particularly brought out in Lazarus' coming forth, presumably with each limb bound separately, but without saying a word.

11:45–57 The results of the miracle

There were different reactions to the sign. **45** Some believed, **46** some reported the matter, **47–53** the Pharisees discussed the matter in council and decided to plot for Jesus' death, **54** while Jesus Himself withdrew towards the wilderness. Even the most remarkable sign will not convince some men. **47** *What are we to do? For this man performs signs.* The signs are seen as a threat to their position. They believe that most people (they actually say *every one*) will believe, but they clearly intend to exclude themselves. **48** *The Romans will come and destroy both our holy place and our nation.* Their concept of people believing in Jesus is dominated by political considerations. The 'place' is either the Temple or the city, and the nation is the administration, which to some extent was still in Jewish hands. **49** *Caiaphas, who was high priest that year.* John clearly attaches importance to this because he repeats his comment about 'that year' in v. 51, where he explains its significance. In that fateful year the high priest spoke a prophecy in his representative capacity. **50** *It is expedient for you that one man should die for the people.* The principle that one should be a substitute for the many is fundamental to the NT doctrine of atonement. Its statement here is all the more noteworthy because uttered, unwittingly, by the very Jewish high priest who helped to execute it. **51** John's comment shows how the early Christians viewed it—as a prophecy which went far beyond Caiaphas's statement, for the application was to be universal. **52** *To gather into one the children of God who are scattered abroad.* Christ's death was seen to have a unifying purpose, the term 'children of God' being used proleptically of those who would believe.

55–57 The setting was the pre-Passover activity, which consisted of purification rites.

Reports had been passed round about Jesus' signs and the Pharisees' plot. Inevitably speculation followed as to Jesus' movements. John mentions the official plot in order to set the scene for the anointing and the entry into Jerusalem.

12:1-50 CLOSE OF THE PUBLIC MINISTRY IN JERUSALEM

12:1-8 The devotion of Mary

1 The incident of the anointing at Bethany is important because of its connection with the miracle of the raising of Lazarus. *Six days before the Passover.* The specific time reference is significant for John and may be compared with the six days mentioned in chs. 1 and 2 at the commencement of the ministry. It has been suggested that John may have had in his mind a comparison with the six days of creation, but this seems highly improbable. 3 *Mary took a pound of costly ointment of pure nard.* There is some doubt about the meaning of the word translated 'pure' as its root meaning is 'persuasive' or 'trustworthy', but the idea of genuineness is no doubt correct. The ointment was probably a liquid perfume. *And anointed the feet of Jesus.* The normal procedure was to anoint the head, not the feet, as a sign of honour. In the parallel case of anointing in Lk. 7:38 it was also the feet that were anointed. There are many similarities between John's and Luke's narrative, but it is unlikely that the two women concerned should be identified. The woman in Luke's narrative was a sinful woman who is portrayed as deeply penitent, whereas this woman is deeply devoted to Jesus and agrees completely with Luke's own picture of Mary of Bethany. In both instances Jesus' feet are wiped by the woman's *hair.* It would have been against Jewish convention for a hostess to appear in the presence of men with unbound hair, but in the case of Mary love was stronger than convention. John's mention of the odour filling the house is a vivid detail which would not easily be forgotten by one who was present.

4-6 Judas's complaint about this expensive waste is fully in character with the Synoptic portrait of him. He was stricken not only with the deadly sins of greed and covetousness, but also with dishonesty. 5 *Three hundred denarii* would, in modern currency, be quite a considerable sum of money. A labourer's rate of pay was one denarius per day. 7 Jesus' answer is *Let her alone, let her keep it for the day of my burial.* This translation assumes that Mary had some perfume still unused and that Jesus suggested that this remainder should be kept to anoint His body at the burial. But this does not fit well into the context, for Judas is concerned about the perfume already used. In the light of Mk. 14:8, it is better to understand the meaning as in the AV, which suggests that Mary's present act was in fact anticipatory of His burial. There may be the suggestion here that what she had

given she had really retained, since her action had become a memorial to her. 8 clearly implies the uniqueness of Jesus.

12:9-11 Reactions to Jesus' presence at Bethany

9, 10 The crowd showed curiosity, which is contrasted with the hostility of the official party. Lazarus was a draw to the former and a threat to the latter. 11 The plot against Jesus and Lazarus was spurred on by many coming to faith.

12:12-19 The entry into Jerusalem

12 One day nearer the Passover pilgrims were increasing in numbers. The desire of such a crowd not only to meet Jesus, but to honour Him, is in marked contrast to the official ecclesiastical line. 13 *Branches of palm trees.* The practice of carrying palm leaves was an act of honour to a victorious person. *Hosanna! Blessed be he who comes in the name of the Lord.* The chant of the people comes from Ps. 118:25, one of the psalms sung by pilgrims on the ascent towards Jerusalem. The description, *the King of Israel,* makes clear the Messianic significance of the cry. 14, 15 John cites Zc. 9:9 in support of the fact that Jesus rode into Jerusalem on a young ass. 16 He does not mean that this occurred to him or any of the disciples at this time. It was only after the resurrection, here referred to as the glorification of Jesus, that any of them understood.

17, 18 These verses appear to refer to two different crowds. One group had seen the miracle of Lazarus' restoration, and the other group had only *heard* of it. 19 The Pharisees' reaction is one of despair from their point of view—*Look, the world has gone after him.* They seem to be given to exaggerations (*cf.* the Sadducean Caiaphas' remark that all would believe in Him, 11:48). Perhaps they feared that Jesus had gained too much popular support for their plot to succeed as easily as they had hoped.

12:20-26 The quest of the Greeks

20 *Now among those who went up to worship at the feast were some Greeks.* These were evidently Greek proselytes who would be able to join the Jews in the Temple worship. The fact that they had come to worship shows the seriousness of their purpose. 21 The mention of Philip's home town is probably to account for the Greeks addressing their request to him. The men may well have come from the Decapolis, which was within easy reach of Bethsaida. 22 John does not specifically state that the Greeks were actually brought to Jesus by Philip and Andrew, but the narrative gives that impression.

23 *The hour has come for the Son of man to be glorified.* This is a strange response to the request. The Greeks may have interpreted it in terms of the triumphal entry, but Jesus has His mind on the cross, as v. 24 shows. This reference to the *hour* points also to the approaching crisis. 24 To explain Himself more clearly Jesus uses the

imagery of *a grain of wheat*. The formula, *Truly truly*, shows its importance. The principle in nature that death is essential for further life is applied by Jesus to Himself by inference. *It bears much fruit.* Wheat reproduces its own kind, and Jesus regards His passion in the same light. His death would bring many sons to life. **25** 'Loving' and 'hating' life are relative terms which bring out in sharp relief the choice and consequence in which personal reaction to Jesus involves men. **26** To follow Him is to serve Him, not to serve oneself. The Father honours only those who honour the Son.

12:27–50 Attestation and withdrawal

27 *Now is my soul troubled.* At this point begins our Lord's consciousness of the *hour* to which the whole Gospel narrative has been moving. There is a clear connection between our Lord's soul-trouble here and the agony in the garden of Gethsemane as recorded in the Synoptic Gospels (*cf.* Mt. 26:38; Mk. 14:34). It shows that the experience in the garden was the climax to earlier stresses. *What shall I say?* There appear to be two alternatives—deliverance out of (Gk. *ek*) the hour, or **28** glorification through it. Jesus was deeply aware that this particular 'hour' was the crucial experience of His whole redemptive work. He could not for a moment entertain escaping from it. At this point the heavenly voice supplies the divine authentication of the choice made by Jesus: *I have glorified it, and I will glorify it again.* The idea of the whole of Jesus' mission, but especially its climax, as a process of glorification is characteristic of this Gospel. **29, 30** There were three reactions to the heavenly voice. Some heard a noise like thunder, which shows they were not well attuned to receive a revelation. Others distinguished some kind of communication but thought of nothing higher than the angels. Jesus alone recognized the voice as being for the sake of the hearers.

31 *Now is the judgment of this world.* The repetition of the 'now' (*cf.* v. 27) shows the more precise definition of the 'hour'. It consisted, in fact, of judgment for the world, by which must be understood the general condemnation of the present world-order through the cross. **32, 33** *And I, when I am lifted up from the earth, will draw all men to myself.* John's comment on Jesus' words shows clearly how the uplifting is to be understood. But in what sense is the drawing to be taken? The same word (Gk. *helkō*) occurs in 6:44 of the drawing by the Father of men to Christ. Here it is Christ crucified that acts as a magnet whose influence none can escape. The statement leaves open the result of the drawing. The idea of drawing to judgment cannot be excluded in view of v. 31, but clearly not all will be drawn for this purpose. **34** The reaction of the crowd shows that they understood the uplifting in some sense which was incompatible with the eternal character of the Messiah. In answer to the question, *Who is this Son of man?*, **35** Jesus draws attention again to the truth which

is also a theme of the prologue, that He is the light. This light is again contrasted with darkness. It is not without considerable meaning that immediately after saying, *Walk while you have the light*, **36** Jesus departed and hid Himself. The light was not Jesus in His presence, but Jesus in His teaching which they had already heard.

37–43 The next paragraph gives John's summing-up of the effect of Jesus' ministry upon the people. The signs had not generally led to faith and Isaiah's prophecy is cited in support of this fact. There is emphasis here on the divine initiative, although in the LXX the statement has the form 'they closed their own eyes'. John's philosophy of history is that God is the First Cause of events and it is in this sense that he understands Isaiah's words. **38** The first citation, from Is. 53:1, draws attention to the tendency for the prophet's report not to be believed, **40** and the second, from Is. 6:10, points out the obdurateness and hardness of heart with which Isaiah had to contend. John is clearly thinking of the occasion of the statement in Is. 6:10, *i.e.* the vision of glory in the Temple. **41** *Because he saw his glory* suggests that the vision was the cause of the prediction, in the sense that it provided the occasion. It is important to notice that John regards the Jewish unbelief in Jesus as a direct fulfilment of prophecy (vv. 37, 38), which shows that he believed that what happened to Isaiah might be expected to happen also to Jesus, a view supported by v. 41. **42** *Nevertheless many even of the authorities believed in him.* John never tires of matching up instances of unbelief with instances of faith. This present statement strikingly complements v. 37. Yet John admits that motives of self-interest were an inhibiting factor in their faith. All too often fear of men has cramped the testimony of faith.

44–50 The concluding passage of this chapter is a kind of summary of the main themes of the ministry. It is as if Jesus, having withdrawn (*cf.* v. 36), returns to make one last public announcement before devoting Himself more specifically to the disciples. Or else, the words *Jesus cried out* may refer to His general teaching rather than to a specific occasion. Three times in this passage Jesus refers to 'him who sent me'. Faith is again stressed, as is also the claim of Jesus to be the light. **47, 48** The concept of judgment is further enlarged upon: *I did not come to judge the world but to save the world.* Although judgment is determined by the word of Christ, His mission was not primarily for this purpose. Salvation was the objective, judgment but the consequence. **49, 50** *For I have not spoken on my own authority.* When it comes to judgment, authority (Gk. *exousia*) is of supreme importance, and once again Jesus claims to have received this from the Father. The theme of eternal life mentioned in v. 50 is but a reiteration of teaching already given by Jesus as recorded earlier in this Gospel. This section prepares the way for the events in the upper room which follow (13:1ff.).

13:1 – 17:26 JESUS WITH THE DISCIPLES

13:1-38 The feet-washing and its sequel

13:1-20 Jesus' symbolic action. The events of this section clearly belong to the day before the Passover (as v. 1 shows), *i.e.* Nisan 13. There is some difficulty over the fact that the Synoptic Gospels seem to imply that Jesus was crucified on Nisan 15. It is just possible that the difference may be accounted for by assuming that the references are to two different calendars. But the problem is a difficult one and cannot be resolved with complete certainty because of lack of sufficient data about the use of these different calendars (see my *New Testament Introduction: Gospels and Acts*, 1965, pp. 271ff.).

1-3 The opening section gives a concise statement of the spiritual importance of the events about to happen. Note especially the deep consciousness on the part of Jesus of the dawning of the *hour*, His constant love for His own people, the work of the devil in Judas resulting in betrayal and the awareness of Jesus of the divine origin and destiny of His work. This is a brief epitome of the drama of the Gospel. **2** *When the devil had already put it into the heart of Judas Iscariot.* The striking antithesis between the Father's love and the devil's designs is clearly brought out. **3** Yet John is convinced that the hour of sorrow was in the Father's hands, because Jesus was unmistakably convinced of this. **4, 5** The girding and washing that followed were prompted by this conviction. It was clearly a studied symbolic act. It was a totally unexpected act of humility, the meaning of which is given in vv. 12ff.

6 *He came to Simon Peter.* This suggests that Peter was first, but the Greek does not seem to support this (*oun*, 'therefore', is omitted from RSV, but would make v. 6 subsequent to the action in v. 5). Peter's question, Jesus' assurance that he would later understand, Peter's emphatic refusal followed by Jesus' statement that unless permission were given Peter would have no share in Jesus' work, and Peter's impetuous and extravagant reversal of attitude are all thoroughly characteristic of Peter and of the Lord's dealing with him as recorded elsewhere. **7** *Afterward you will understand* refers to the post-resurrection understanding. Many of Jesus' deeds must have been enigmatic until after that event. **10** *He who has bathed does not need to wash, except for his feet, but he is clean all over.* The washing of the feet was more than an example. It was a means by which the disciples could participate in the Lord's humiliation. This brings cleansing. Nothing more is needed. Peter's impulsive request (v. 9) is irrelevant. **11** *You are not all clean.* John repeats this statement of Jesus, with an explanation, which was not immediately apparent to the disciples. But John desires to draw attention to our Lord's divine insight.

The next paragraph emphasizes the same theme. **12** *Do you know what I have done to you?* Jesus challenges them because He knows how

limited their understanding is. In answering His own question, **13** Jesus appeals first to His relationship to them (*Teacher and Lord*), **14, 15** and then to the example He has given. The authoritative nature of His approach is unmistakable, but the surprising character of the exhortation becomes even more striking when it is remembered that humility was despised in the ancient world as a sign of weakness. This action of Jesus was revolutionary in the realm of human relationships. *You also ought to wash one another's feet* is specific in the context of Jesus' own act and some Christians have literally observed it. Others have considered the principle to be more important than the act, stressing as it does the honourable character of lowly service to others. **16** *A servant* is literally a slave, who had no rights at all in his master's house. *He who is sent* represents the Greek word *apostolos* and is a reminder that apostles held a position of great challenge, being commissioned to conform to the nature of the One who sent them, even if it led to humiliation. **17** *If you know . . . if you do.* Knowing without doing finds no sanction anywhere in the teaching of Jesus. **18** At this point the dark cloud of the betrayal once more appears. Judas was a man who did not do what he knew to be true. His heel was raised against his Master, and scripture (Ps. 41:9) is cited in support to show that such betrayal did not take Jesus unawares. Even such an action came within the divine providence. **19** The present announcement was intended to lead to faith in our Lord's person. **20** This section closes with a saying, which occurs in Mt. 10:40 at the sending out of the Twelve. Our Lord's meaning here is that too much should not be made of one man who did not receive Him. The positive aspect of receiving those whom Jesus had commissioned is more important.

13:21-30 The exclusion of the betrayer. 21 The mounting tension in the mind of Jesus over the betrayer is seen in John's comment, *he was troubled in spirit* (*cf.* 11:33; 12:27, where the same verb is used). It expresses strong distress. **22** The reaction of the disciples is even more vividly described in the Synoptics (*cf.* Mt. 26:22; Mk. 14:19; Lk. 22:23). This was a tense moment not easily forgotten. The details—the disciples looking at one another, the beloved disciple lying close to Jesus, the beckoning action of Peter, the whispered conversation and the Lord's deliberate and symbolic response—are so vividly told that an eyewitness must be presupposed. **23** *One of his disciples, whom Jesus loved.* Because of the vivid details, it is a reasonable conclusion that the author is here referring to himself. He was deeply conscious of the love which Jesus showed to His disciples. Some consider it more probable, however, that another is here describing John, and yet others that Lazarus is meant (*cf.* 11:3, 5). But the first interpretation is preferable. **26** *So when he had dipped the morsel.* This was a gesture of honour and must be regarded as a final appeal to Judas. **27** John's comment that after this *Satan entered into him* was no doubt the result of considerable subsequent reflection. Anyone who could act like Judas must be under Satanic influence. **28, 29** The immediate reactions of the disciples at Judas's withdrawal were connected only with financial matters, since he was treasurer for the Twelve. When Jesus said to Judas, *What you are going to do, do quickly,* no-one can tell what passed through the mind of Jesus or of Judas. **30** John simply states that the latter *immediately went out; and it was night.* It may well be that John intends more than a comment on the time. It was spiritually night for the soul of Judas.

13:31–35 A new commandment given. 31 *Now is the Son of man glorified.* Judas's act is but a step in the process of glorification, **32** which involves also the glorification of God. *And glorify him at once* points to the cross and shows our Lord's triumphant estimate of it. **33** *Little children.* A diminutive term is here used when Jesus turns His attention to His disciples, in much the same way as a Rabbi would address his pupils. The message which the Jews had misunderstood (*cf.* 7:33) needed clarification for the disciples. Glorification would involve separation; **34, 35** but love would overcome all difficulties and would show men who were the true disciples of Jesus. *A new commandment.* Commands to love were already known in the sense of the highest devotion to God, but Jesus' command that the disciples should *love one another* was new in its scope and in the fact that its motive power sprang from a new source— *even as I have loved you.* Jesus could never have set a higher pattern before His people than this.

13:36–38 Peter's fall foretold. Peter's curiosity gets the better of him and he seeks an elucidation of the Lord's enigmatic statement of v. 33. In answer Jesus predicts that he will follow later, which causes the impulsive Peter to protest his present whole-hearted allegiance. In Mt. 26:33 a similar confident assertion of Peter's is uttered on the way to Gethsemane. It is the kind of assertion that may well have been repeated. **38** No doubt the prediction of the denial seemed quite incredible to Peter. Indeed it was not until the denial had happened that Peter recognized the truth of the prediction.

14:1 – 16:33 The discourse to the disciples

14:1–11 Assurances and questionings. 1 *Let not your hearts be troubled.* Forebodings of betrayal and denial must have proved deeply disturbing. Jesus' answer is *believe, i.e.* an exhortation, or less probably a statement (*cf.* AV). But He also gives assurances. **2** *In my Father's house are many rooms.* Because Jesus Himself will soon leave them, He turns their thought towards the Father. The *rooms* represent abiding-places, symbolic of the ample spiritual provision which God makes for His children. This includes room for His disciples—Jesus will see to that. **3** *I will come again and will take you to myself.* This future coming most naturally refers to the second

advent, but some have interpreted it as referring to the resurrection or to Pentecost or even to a coming at the death of believers (*cf.* Acts 7:59; 2 Cor. 5:8; Phil. 1:23). **4** *And you know the way where I am going.* The subsequent questionings show a lack of appreciation of spiritual values on their part, but they had no excuse. **5** Thomas suffers from literalism, which closes his eyes to possibilities. **6** But Jesus gives a spiritual answer to his perplexity, by the great assertion, *I am the way, and the truth, and the life.* The latter two ideas are both mentioned in the prologue; the first follows from them in spiritual experience. The three ideas may be linked—to mean 'the true and living way'—just as Heb. 10:19, 20 speak of 'the new and living way'—*i.e.* with two of the nouns, following Aramaic idiom, being understood as adjectives. This assertion is our Lord's answer to Thomas's 'How can we know the way?', as if He had said, 'It is enough that you know Me.' The way to God, personified as it is in Jesus, was a way of suffering and of triumph through humiliation. **7** It is a profound truth that knowledge of Jesus conveys knowledge of the Father. **8** Yet this was something difficult to grasp, as Philip's request shows. Was he thinking of a direct vision of God as the only means of satisfaction? **9** He is rebuked by Jesus for his lack of faith. *Have I been with you so long, and yet you do not know me?* Philip had had ample opportunity, but had never perceived the true nature of Jesus as the revelation of the Father. **10, 11** Jesus appeals to him to believe the close connection between Himself and the Father. *Or else believe me for the sake of the works themselves.* This is addressed not only to Philip, but to them all. They had seen Jesus' works. They should have known that He possessed extraordinary power, which could have come only from God.

14:12–31 Exhortations to the disciples. In the following discourse Jesus concentrates on exhortation and encouragement. **12** The words are addressed to the disciples who believe and are therefore timeless in their application to all other believers. *Greater works than these will he do.* Not only are Jesus' own works to be the pattern for the disciples, but they are actually to exceed them. Clearly the 'works' must here be understood in terms of God-given mission, and 'greater works' would then relate to the wider opportunities which the disciples would have when Jesus had returned to the Father. **13, 14** It would then be possible for Jesus to work through His people. The book of Acts is a commentary on this promise. **15** Faith must be linked with love which will lead to obedience. *My commandments* refers to all the content of the Lord's teaching. This principle of observance of commandments through the motive of love is a revolutionary advance over the Jewish approach to the Mosaic law. **16** The promise which immediately follows is intended to be closely linked with loving obedience: *he will give you another Counsellor.* This is the first of five important statements regarding the Holy Spirit in these discourses. The Greek word translated 'Counsellor' (*paraklētos*) includes the idea of one called in to help, but is not to be restricted to a legal advocate. The more general idea of counselling better expresses the meaning. The counsellor's help is not intermittent, but continuous. **17** *Even the Spirit of truth* (*cf.* 15:26; 16:13). Our Lord lays special emphasis on the characteristic of the Spirit as truth because of its obvious importance for a counsellor. The Spirit brings out the antithesis between the world and the disciples, which is further developed in the next paragraph.

18, 19 Jesus next assures His disciples of His continued presence with them, even when the world can no longer see Him. The word *desolate* literally means 'orphans' and adds special point to Jesus' promise about the Father's love (*cf.* v. 21). *Yet a little while* points to the resurrection when the disciples would see Jesus in a new light. **21** Loving Christ and keeping His commandments are inseparable. Moreover Christ's love for us is said to be the basis of His self-revelation to us. **22** But this raised a problem for Judas (not Iscariot). Why not love for all men? And how could Jesus be manifested to some and not to others, if Jesus' words be interpreted on a literal plane? **23, 24** In answer Jesus again draws attention to the love motive, as if declining to be deflected by Judas's question. But it was nevertheless a true answer, for wherever there are believers the Father and the Son make Their home with them and others by this means receive a manifestation. But many do not want either Jesus or His words.

25, 26 The work of the Spirit is again referred to in order to give confidence to the disciples to face the departure of Jesus. These men have heard the teaching of Jesus. They will not only be aided by the Spirit in recalling all that Jesus had said, but they will also receive the Spirit's own interpretation. This Paraclete statement is important for determining ideas about the preservation of the tradition of the teaching of Jesus. No view of Gospel origins which is not in harmony with the promised aid of the Spirit can be considered valid. **27** Jesus goes on to speak of peace and reiterates some of the thoughts already expressed in this discourse. *My peace I give to you*. The possessive idea is strong. It might be rendered, 'The peace that is mine'. It is a peace which has been put to the test. It was completely unparalleled in the world. The antithesis between Christ's way and the world's way is a frequent theme of these discourses. **28** *If you loved me, you would have rejoiced, because I go to the Father*. This is a mild challenge to them to recognize the inadequacy of their love, for if they really loved Jesus they would not be troubled, as they obviously are, by the thought of His departure. *For the Father is greater than I*. There is no need to go into the subtleties of patristic exposition of this statement. It must be regarded in its context,

i.e. in the light of the thought that Jesus was going to the Father, which was a process of glorification. His future position would be greater than His present position because of the greatness of the Father. This verse should be compared with 10:30. **29** is closely paralleled in 13:19, and again the end in view is faith. **30** *The ruler of this world is coming*. The same description of Satan is found in 12:31. It is of significance here because Jesus is deeply conscious of the powerful forces arrayed against Him. Yet He asserts, *He has no power over me*, or literally, 'He has nothing in me', no point of contact. Instead Jesus is wholly devoted to the Father's plans. It was His aim that the world might know of His love to the Father. In this Jesus is an example of the most effective method of overcoming the devil. **31** This part of the discourses closes with an exhortation, *Rise, let us go hence*, which has led some scholars to place chs. 15 and 16 before 14, in which case the exhortation marks the conclusion of the sequence of teaching in the upper room. As it stands, however, it must imply that His teaching in chs. 15 and 16 must have been given in the open air on the way to Kidron.

15:1-17 The vine allegory. It is not clear from the narrative where Jesus was when He gave this teaching. If 14:31 marks the point of departure from the upper room, it is possible that Jesus and His disciples were passing by a vine which was then used as a spiritual illustration. **1** *I am the true vine*. This is another of the great assertions of Jesus. It needs to be considered against the OT concept of Israel as a vine or vineyard (*cf.* Is. 5:1-7; Ezk. 15:1-6; 19:10-14; Ps. 80:8-16). Jesus may be describing Himself as *true* (Gk. *alēthinē*) to mark Himself off from all counterfeits, *i.e.* He is genuine. But the adjective is more probably used with the meaning that Jesus is the reality of which the Vine of Israel is but the type. *My Father is the vinedresser*. The reference is to the owner who cares for his vines. **2** The purpose of any vine is to bear fruit, hence the vine cannot be considered apart from its fruit-bearing branches. *He takes away . . . he prunes*. A good dresser looks at the usefulness of each branch. A completely fruitless branch is not worthy of a place in the vine, while pruning can improve branches with a poor yield. Among the disciples, Judas proved no true part of the vine, while all the others underwent 'pruning' experiences before producing much fruit at Pentecost. **3** Jesus regards the 'pruning' as if already complete: *you are already made clean*. This purifying action has been effected by means of Jesus' own teaching, the importance of which cannot be overstressed. **4** *Abide in me, and I in you*. The allegory illuminates this spiritual principle. The branch can receive no sap from the vine unless there is constant and unimpeded contact between them. **5** Jesus makes clear the identification of the branches and brings out the principle of the utter dependence of the disciples upon Him. **6** *He is cast forth*. This is an explanation of v. 2, for the cast-out branches are those not 'abiding' in the vine, *i.e.* those not essentially a part of the vine. As details of the allegory must not be pushed too far, it is unnecessary to treat *the fire* as symbolic.

In the next passage, Jesus draws out some of the implications of the spiritual truth which He has just illustrated. **7** Abiding gives assurance of answered prayer, for those who abide will desire to do the Father's will. **8** Fruit-bearing is not an end in itself; it glorifies the Father. In the statement, *and so prove to be my disciples,* the verb literally means 'become', which points forward to the completeness of discipleship. **9** The Father's love for Christ is the pattern of Christ's love for His disciples. **10** A similar parallel in the form of an exhortation occurs here, regarding the keeping of commandments. The disciples are not left without an exalted pattern. **11** The whole purpose of this teaching is summed up in joy: *my joy . . . your joy.* The disciples' joy is dependent on the Master's joy, a joy which results from utter self-sacrificial service. Several times in this passage Jesus stresses the motive power of love. **12, 13** Another high example is set before the disciples. When Jesus said, *Greater love has no man than this,* there is no doubt that here He was referring to His own approaching death, conceived of as an act of sacrifice on behalf of others. **14, 15** The change of relationship from *servants* to *friends* is significant because of what friends are able to share. It is strongly expressed as *all that I have heard from my Father.* Although this is stated as a completed act, the revelation was not completely understood until after the death and resurrection of Jesus (*cf.* 16:12). The Spirit would be the interpreter. **16** is a development from v. 7, with the important addition of the divine choice. The initiative is with Christ—*I chose you and appointed you.* The appointment is to specific tasks, the choosing to discipleship. *In my name* qualifies the *whatever you ask,* for it must be in harmony with Christ's nature. **17** Both here and in v. 12 love is said to be a command, which shows its essential character.

15:18 – 16:11 The hostility of the world to Jesus and His disciples. The mind of Jesus again reverts to the impending clash with the forces of this world and considers the further position of the disciples. **18, 19** The first principle is the essential hatred of the world. Hate is the antithesis of love and involves hostility. The second principle is that in spiritual matters like attracts like and repels opposites. Hate is inevitable *because you are not of the world.* From this it is clear that 'world' is to be understood in a moral sense of the world-order under the control of adverse spiritual forces. **20** Recalling a statement made earlier (13:16), Jesus shows that the disciples, as servants (Gk. *douloi*), could expect no less persecution than their Master. *If they kept my word, they will keep yours also.* Since this is an unfulfilled condition, it is equivalent to saying that the world will not heed the disciples' teach-

ing. This does not mean, of course, that none in the world will respond. **21** The reason for the persecution is stated to be ignorance of the true mission of Jesus. **22** *But now they have no excuse for their sin.* The idea seems to be that the coming of Jesus should have been recognized as from God, throwing a moral responsibility on the hearers which would not have been so had He not come. **23–25** These verses return to the theme of hate. Hate towards Jesus must involve the Father. Hate exists because of deliberate rejection of Jesus' works. Hate in this sense is predicted in Scripture (*cf.* Pss. 35:19; 69:4).

26 To offset any gloom that might have descended on the disciples, Jesus reassures them with another promise about the Paraclete. The most important aspect of this promise is the repeated assertion that the Spirit *proceeds from the Father.* The preposition used in the Greek (*para*) in both statements suggests mission from the Father, rather than external procession as understood by the Greek fathers. The Spirit's main function is witness to Christ. **27** *And you also are witnesses, because you have been with me from the beginning.* The witness of the Spirit is closely linked with the witness of the disciples. They too, in a special way, can testify to Christ because of their experience of Him. They were eyewitnesses of the historic events.

16:1–4 The coming persecution is here referred to more specifically. To be forewarned is to be forearmed. The main purpose of the warning which Jesus gives is to prepare the disciples. **1** *To keep you from falling away* is lit. 'to prevent you from being caused to stumble' as by an obstacle. In this case the obstacle was Jewish opposition. **2** *They will put you out of the synagogues.* Excommunication was something that every devout Jew would understand and dread, for it meant turning away from that cherished heritage which he held dear. But all the early Jewish Christians had to come to terms with this threat. *Offering service to God.* Much persecution has been prompted by the same deluded motive as here. Saul of Tarsus was a notable example (*cf.* Acts 9:1, 2; 26:9–11). **3** Jesus points out that the basic reason for this inconsistency is that the persecutors have never really known God.

4 There is a distinction drawn between the earlier and later teaching of Jesus. **5** Now that His going is imminent He has had to give some clearer indications of what is to take place. But He points out that no-one asks *Where are you going?* The disciples have not as yet attained sufficient spiritual insight to ask this question or even to understand the true mission of Jesus. **6** In spite of His own impending sorrow, Jesus shows Himself deeply sensitive to the disciples' feelings. **7** The answer once again lies in the promise of the Counsellor, for unless Jesus departs the Spirit will not come. **8** *And when he comes, he will convince the world of sin and of righteousness and of judgment.* This is an aspect of the Spirit's work which has not been previously stressed. The convincing or convicting work of the Spirit through the disciples is directed here towards the world, which the Lord has already shown to be hostile to Him. The convicting does not necessarily involve a recognition of the Spirit's action on the world's part. Whatever conscience the world might display is the Spirit's work. The sequence of sin, righteousness and judgment is significant. **9** The Spirit will show that men are sinners because of their unbelief in Christ; **10** that Jesus is righteous and has been vindicated by His exaltation; **11** and that the ruler of this world (*i.e.* Satan) is evil and has been judged (*i.e.* at the cross). The judgment of the ruler of this world shows the operation of divine judgment generally. With this assurance of the Spirit's activity, the disciples need not fear what lies in store for them.

16:12-33 Special promises to the disciples. The next section deals with yet another aspect of the Spirit's work. **12** Jesus has not told them everything, **13** so the Spirit will complete the work. *He will guide you into all the truth.* The masculine pronoun and the idea of a guide both point to the personality of the Spirit. He can guide only in harmony with His own nature, *i.e.* truth. It is the *authority* of the speaker which gives importance to any statement, but the Spirit's authority is one with the Father and the Son. **14** *He will glorify me.* There is no question of the Spirit's activity being directed to any other end but the glorification of Christ. **15** The repetition draws special attention to this.

16 Already in the upper room discourse Jesus has mentioned His departure (14:18-24) and a similar statement is now repeated. *You will see me* refers initially to the resurrection. Earlier Jesus had made clear that the world would see nothing of Him (14:19). **17, 18** The perplexity of the disciples is again expressed, although no specific question was addressed to Him (*cf.* v. 19). It was the expression *a little while* which bothered them most, while the reference to the Father was also clearly not understood. *We do not know what he means.* This frank confession suggests the comment of one who was well acquainted with the disciples' private questionings. **19** The perceptiveness of Jesus with regard to their inner motives is vividly brought out, although outward signs of their perplexity were no doubt not lacking. The repetition of the former statement, which had perplexed them, focuses special attention upon it. **20** In reply the Lord stresses again what is in store for the disciples. He thus turns their thoughts away from Himself to them, but the main theme is joy not sorrow. *The world will rejoice . . . your sorrow will turn into joy.* The believer's sorrow is but an avenue to true joy, which is contrasted with the world's rejoicing over the subject of the believer's lamentations, *i.e.* the crucifixion of Christ. Sorrow will mark the first little while, but joy will mark the second. **21** *When a woman is in travail.* In the Greek the definite article is used, which shows that the illustration is based

on a universal law. Child-birth is accompanied by anguish, but the joy over a new-born human life far transcends the anguish. **22** The same principle of transformation of sorrow into joy is then applied to the disciples, and the main characteristic of the joy is said to be its security. The transformation is to be effected through Christ's seeing them again, *i.e.* at the resurrection. This will bring a lasting joy which no amount of opposition will ever destroy. The book of Acts furnishes examples of this (see Acts 2:46; 16:23-25, 34). **23** *In that day* refers to the time when the full implications of the resurrection have dawned upon them, in which case questions such as the meaning of Jesus' enigmatic statements regarding His departure would be unnecessary. In any case questions will not then be put to Jesus, but to the Father in His name. This reference to prayer is important in view of Jesus' departure and special attention is drawn to it by the formula, *Truly, truly.* **24** Communion with the Father ensures the completeness of joy. The form of the Greek in the last phrase of the verse shows that Jesus has in mind a constant fullness.

25 *I have said this to you in figures.* The word for 'figures' has already been used in 10:6 to describe the allegory of the sheepfold. As Jesus chose to speak to the Galilaean crowds in parables, so His teaching to His disciples was necessarily at the moment veiled. The revelation of the Father is not naturally comprehended by men. *The hour is coming* refers to the Day of Pentecost, after which event Jesus through the Spirit will plainly reveal the truth to the disciples. The meaning of the figures used before the resurrection will then become clear. **26** *I do not say to you that I shall pray the Father for you.* Jesus returns to the theme of prayer and in this statement suggests that no need will remain for his intercession. **27** *For the Father himself loves you.* This is the reason for the believer's direct access to the Father. But it is remarkable that the disciples' love is said to be the cause of the Father's love. It would be expected to be the reverse. Yet their love towards Christ and their faith in Him is a striking evidence of God's love towards them. There is a close connection here between love and faith, but no significance can be attached to the order of mention since love connects with the Father's love just mentioned. **28** puts into brief compass Jesus' mission and its consummation.

29-33 The concluding section reveals a further case of inadequate understanding on the part of the disciples. They thought they understood, but Jesus has again to make them aware of their coming failure to support Him. **30** *By this we believe that you came from God.* Faith in the divine origin of Jesus is here said to be based on His deep understanding of their motives, but their confession must have received a shock following His further revelation. **33** Jesus gives a reassurance to them on the ground of His victory over the world. He regards His work as if it were already complete (the perfect tense is used).

17:1-26 The prayer of Jesus

No indication is given of the place where Jesus prayed and from John's point of view this is unimportant. The prayer may be divided into three sections.

17:1-5 Jesus' prayer for Himself. The main theme of this prayer is glory. **1** *Father, the hour has come.* Cf. 12:23, where a similar statement is made to enquiring Greeks. The glory of the Son contributes to the glory of the Father. **2** *Power over all flesh.* This authority given to the Son is fully comprehensive (*cf.* 5:27). The giving of eternal life is introduced as the main purpose of the Son. **3** What the gift involved is further defined: *that* (Gk. *hina) they know thee the only true God, and Jesus Christ.* The knowing here is progressive and its object is true as contrasted with false deities. Both titles used here are not found elsewhere in John. In fact this is the only occasion on which our Lord is reported to have used the title 'Jesus Christ'. **4** *I glorified* relates to the mission of Jesus which is now regarded as *accomplished,* but doubtless He is including in His own thought the approaching passion. **5** The concluding request for the Father to glorify the Son is important because of the words *with the glory which I had with thee before the world was made.* These words can be understood only in terms of Christ's pre-existence. The glory is that which He possessed before and to which He returned after the ascension.

17:6-19 Jesus' prayer for His disciples. The first section of this prayer deals with Jesus' revelation to the disciples. **6** *I have manifested thy name.* This contrasts with the Jewish refusal to pronounce the name of Yahweh. In Christ the disciples have learned to use the name Father. *They have kept thy word.* Here is our Lord's description of the disciples' approach to the message, to distinguish them from the many who have rejected it. **8** explains the meaning here, for the words of Christ are identified with the word of God. The frequently recurring idea of *giving* in these verses shows how important this concept was for the mind of Jesus. *They have received them.* The evidence for this took two forms—knowledge and faith, in both cases centred on the divine origin of the mission of Jesus.

9 This prayer for the disciples is specifically distinguished from prayer for the world. **10** Again the idea of gift and possession is emphasized as well as the fact that Jesus is glorified in the disciples. This is a lesser glorifying than that spoken of in vv. 1 and 5. **11** *But they are in the world.* It is because the disciples are placed in such an adverse environment that the prayer is so vital. *Holy Father, keep them.* Here only is the Father addressed by Jesus in this way. The adjective *Holy* is the antithesis of all that the world stood for. *Thy name which thou hast given me.* Other readings have 'whom' or 'what', thus avoiding the strangeness of the idea of a name

being given to Christ (yet *cf.* Phil. 2:9, 10). *That they may be one, even as we are one.* The basis of the unity of God's people is the unity of God Himself. The oneness springs from a unity of nature.

The prayer next turns to past achievements and future prospects. **12** *I kept them... I have guarded them.* Jesus claims the security of the disciples except for Judas, who is called *the son of perdition,* a description of his character as wholly given to the way which must end in total loss. In the Greek there is a solemn play on words between 'lost' and 'perdition'. *That the scripture might be fulfilled.* Probably an allusion to Ps. 41:9 (*cf.* Jn. 13:18). **13** The future prospect is expressed in the phrase, *that they may have my joy fulfilled in themselves.* No more exalted prospect could be conceived. The possessive 'my' is emphatic. **14** *I have given them thy word* refers to the whole message and mission which Jesus imparted by what He taught. The world could only hate what did not belong to it. **15** Yet Jesus is not wanting an escape-route for the disciples, but preservation in an adverse environment. *From the evil one.* The Greek preposition (*ek*) means 'out of', suggesting that the world lies in the grasp of the evil one. **17** *Sanctify them in the truth; thy word is truth.* The meaning is that the disciples are to be set apart for a holy purpose, the sphere of which is truth. *Thy word* refers to the message of God in the teaching of Christ. **19** *For their sake I consecrate myself.* There is a close correspondence between the mission of Jesus and the mission of the disciples. Jesus' consecration consisted in the determination to carry through the work of redemption.

17:20-26 Jesus' prayer for the church. 20 The prayer is now extended to include those who are to believe in Christ through the disciples' word. **21** *That they may all be one.* This unity is applicable only to those who have believed in Jesus Christ. There can be no distinction made between those who had personally heard Jesus and those who would hear only second-hand. The unity is exemplified in the unity of Father and Son and is maintained by abiding in both Father and Son. The purpose of such unity is said to be *that the world may believe that thou hast sent me.* There is a cycle here—faith leads to unity which leads others to faith. **22** The same idea of unity is expressed, but here it is connected with the theme of *glory,* which has already been prominent in the first part of the prayer. When believers manifest the glory of Christ this engenders a basic unity. **23** *That they may become perfectly one.* Nothing short of complete unity is in mind and Jesus makes clear that this must be evident to the world, so that the world may recognize its source.

24-26 The concluding verses are a specific prayer that the disciples may behold the glory of Jesus received before the foundation of the world. Again the pre-existence of Christ comes into view (*cf.* v. 5). In this prayer Jesus asserts that He has made known the Father's love to the disciples. The plea is based on the righteousness of the Father. The prayer ends with the assurance of the indwelling of Christ in believers.

18:1 – 21:25 PASSION AND RESURRECTION NARRATIVES

18:1 – 19:16 The betrayal and trial of Jesus

18:1-11 The betrayal. Although there are certain points of contact between John's account and the Synoptics, this record of the betrayal is mainly peculiar to John. **1** *The Kidron valley, where there was a garden.* John alone mentions the name of the valley, whereas the Synoptics name the garden as Gethsemane. John does not mention the agony in the garden, yet knows of it, as v. 11 shows. **2** *Judas . . . also knew the place.* Jesus must have known this, but made no move to avoid it. **3** *A band of soldiers.* Although the word used might denote a cohort, John clearly intends only a detachment of troops sent to maintain order. They would accompany the Temple police. **4** Jesus does not wait for Judas to single Him out, but steps forward Himself and addresses the soldiers and the police. **5** *Jesus said to them, 'I am he.'* This may simply be Jesus' identification of Himself as Jesus of Nazareth, or it may carry with it the implications of the divine nature. The latter seems preferable in view of the reaction. **6** The falling back may be due to the moral supremacy of Jesus, or it may be that His presence struck dread into those concerned. **8** Jesus' request that the disciples should be allowed to go free is another feature found only in John. **9** is seen as a fulfilment of the statement of Jesus in 17:12. **10** *Then Simon Peter . . . struck the high priest's slave.* The fact that Peter carried *a sword* is surprising, but suggests that he and the other disciples had anticipated trouble. His act was one of desperation. John alone mentions the slave's name. **11** *Shall I not drink the cup which the Father has given me?* This seems to be a clear allusion to the cup referred to in the Synoptic accounts of the experience in Gethsemane (*cf.* Mt. 26:39, 40). There is no thought of withdrawal in Jesus' mind.

18:12-27 The ecclesiastical trial. 12-14 The arrest is concisely related, the chief interest of these verses lying in John's specific reference to Caiaphas as *high priest that year*, which recalls his earlier important statement to the same effect (11:49-51). Annas, Caiaphas's father-in-law, had previously held the high-priestly office, and still exercised considerable influence.

15, 16 The reaction of only two disciples is mentioned, Peter and *another disciple*, who may well have been John, although his acquaintance with the high priest is difficult to explain. Nevertheless, had it not been John his name would most likely have been mentioned. It was through this other disciple's agency that Peter gained access to the courtyard, **17** but it led at once to the first denial. **18** *Because it was cold.* This is specially noted by John because it had

deeply impressed itself upon his mind. Luke is the only other Evangelist who mentions the fire and he suggests that the maid recognized Peter by the light from the fire (Lk. 22:56).

19-24 John's account of the denial is split by an account of the preliminary questioning before the high priest. The reply of Jesus to this questioning suggests that the high priest was probing for some secret teaching which Jesus had given to the disciples. **20** *I have spoken openly to the world* is in emphatic contrast to this suggestion. **21** If the high priest wanted evidence there was ample opportunity for him to seek it from witnesses. Indeed, if any trial were to be conducted according to proper procedure, the defence witnesses should have been called first. Clearly the high priest was not proceeding by legal rules. **22, 23** The blow from the officer's hand and Jesus' calm and reasoned reaction also focus attention on the irregularity of the examination. **24** raises difficulties, if the high priest already mentioned in v. 19 was Caiaphas, unless he was present at the examination before Annas, who although no longer high priest may still have retained the title.

25-27 The account of Peter's denial is resumed. Certainly Peter was putting himself in the place of temptation. The reference to Malchus's kinsman shows the author's close knowledge of the event.

18:28 – 19:16 The trial before Pilate. 28-32 The first episode in the trial takes place outside the praetorium. Pilate examines the accused and His accusers. **28** *So that they might not be defiled.* The irony of the Jewish scruples is highlighted by John. They were already defiled in their hearts by their plot to kill Jesus. **29** *What accusation . . . ?* To this reasonable question, **30** the accusers give an answer which both evades the issue and reveals their insolence. **31** *It is not lawful for us to put any man to death.* The Sanhedrin had power to condemn a man to death, but were required to obtain the sanction of the Roman authorities. **32** It is implied that, since Jesus had predicted death by crucifixion, events were overruled in the fulfilment of the prediction.

33-38 The second incident is set inside the praetorium and consists of an interview between Pilate and Jesus. **33** *Are you the King of the Jews?* Probably Pilate means by this, 'Do you claim this position?' **34** Jesus' answer is designed to show that He does not have the same idea of kingship as Pilate and it was essential that this should be clearly understood if proper judgment was to be made. **36** Hence Jesus' further comment: *My kingship is not of this world.* Kingship in the political sense must be supported by power, but spiritual kingship needs no such aid. **37** Pilate's perplexity is revealed in his further question, *So you are a king?* which cannot be divorced from scorn. Spiritual realities were unintelligible to him. Jesus leaves Pilate to decide the answer for himself, since it was he who had first used the word 'king'. *For this I was born . . .*

to bear witness to the truth. This makes transparently clear the spiritual character of the Kingship of Jesus. The royalty of the world was not generally linked to the idea of truth. Because of this Pilate's question **38** *What is truth?* is understandable as well as revealing his impatience.

Pilate's own judgment about the innocence of Jesus and yet **39** his proposition to the Jews about the custom of release show his appalling weakness of character. His suggestion was made in sarcasm, for he calls Jesus *King of the Jews.* **40** The Jews' request for Barabbas is related in all the Gospels, but in none so concisely and poignantly as here. A robber was preferred to the King of truth.

19:1–3 Pilate gives in and scourging and mockery immediately follow. Scourging was normally part of the examination, but Pilate's use of it was utterly arbitrary and unjustified. It is most probable, in view of Lk. 23:16, that Pilate regarded the scourging as an alternative to crucifixion and **4** this is supported by his action here in again declaring the innocence of Jesus. **3** The tense of the verbs is the imperfect, suggesting a succession of mock acts of homage.

5 The belated attempt of the governor to appeal to the people's pity is another pathetic evidence of his inconsistency and weakness. *Here is the man!* There is no knowing what significance Pilate attached to this statement. But the statement was more important than he knew, for in his humiliation Jesus stands in place of man as the true man. **6** *Crucify him, crucify him!* In all the records this clamour follows Pilate's offer to release Jesus. *Take him yourselves and crucify him, for I find no crime in him.* This is said ironically, for Pilate knew the Jews had no power to carry out crucifixion. **7** The accusers now introduce a religious charge based on an appeal to law. It was not the charge that *he has made himself the Son of God* which perturbed Pilate, but the reference to *a law,* for the Romans had committed themselves to maintain Jewish customs and laws. **8** It was probably aggravated by a superstitious fear of the description 'Son of God', which clearly mystified him and **9** prompted the question, *Where are you from?* The question was irrelevant to the charge and was met by silence. **10** Such silence stings Pilate into reminding Jesus of his authority, but **11** Jesus takes up and corrects Pilate's concept of authority. *You would have no power over me unless it had been given you from above.* Although Pilate possessed the imperial authority, this did not reach to ultimate destinies. Our Lord is conscious that the whole work of redemption does not rest on the despotic action of the Roman governor. *He who delivered me to you* is Caiaphas, who is held to be more responsible than Pilate.

12–16 Pilate's further attempt to release Jesus and his capitulation under the threat of being disloyal to Caesar bring the account of the trial to an end. **12** *You are not Caesar's friend.* Although sometimes used as a title of honour for provincial governors, it is here used as a sign of loyalty. Pilate's record was such that he could not afford to risk any report of this kind reaching the emperor (*cf.* Lk. 13:1). This seems to have clinched the issue for him. **13** *The Pavement* was a tessellated area near to the castle of Antonia. **14** *Now it was the day of Preparation for the Passover.* This is mentioned, together with the precise timing (*sixth hour*), because for John the relation of the death of Jesus to the Jewish Passover was important. In this Gospel the Passover was not held until after the crucifixion, although the Synoptic Gospels seem to imply that the Last Supper was Passover time (*cf.* Mk. 14:12). **15** *Shall I crucify your King?* Pilate addresses his question scornfully, but draws out from the chief priests such a confession of loyalty to Caesar that he could not ignore. The confession was the final apostasy of the official representatives of theocratic Israel.

19:17–37 The crucifixion

17 Jesus was regarded as a common criminal in that He bore His own cross. John does not mention Simon's help in bearing the cross (*cf.* Mt. 27:32; Mk. 15:21; Lk. 23:26), but the transfer must have happened on the way to Golgotha. **18** Nor does John mention that the other two were crucified on charges of sedition. **19** On the other hand John alone relates that it was Pilate who prepared and caused the title to be placed on the cross. Whereas there are slight variations in the different records in the form of the title, all agree that the inscription contained the words, *The King of the Jews.* **20–22** It was this statement which caused resentful protests among the Jews, but which revealed the obstinacy of Pilate. It is significant that John refers here to *the chief priests of the Jews,* clearly by way of contrast to the title given to Jesus.

23 The garments of a condemned man were the perquisite of the soldiers on duty. **24** Here John sees a fulfilment of Ps. 22:18, but the Synoptics do not mention this. **25** Watching the operation were certain women, including the mother of Jesus. Comparison with the other Gospels raises the question whether there were three or four women, including Salome, who is not here mentioned by name. It seems most reasonable to suppose that there were two pairs, in which case Salome was Mary's sister and *Mary the wife of Clopas* was mother of James of Alphaeus (*cf.* Mk. 15:40). **26** *Woman, behold, your son!* This was a tender consideration for the mother of Jesus. If the identification of Salome mentioned above is correct, John was related to Jesus and **27** this would throw light on Jesus' words and John's subsequent action.

28, 30 The concluding moments of Jesus' earthly life are marked by two further cries, one relating to His own human need (*I thirst*), the other to His completion of His task (*It is finished*). John again notes a fulfilment of Scripture. **29** *So they put a sponge full of the vinegar on* *hyssop*. Since hyssop has only a slender stalk, something else must have been used to support it. Mk. 15:36 refers to vinegar being offered on a reed. Some scholars consider that the original here may have been *hyssos*, a soldier's javelin. The vinegar would give some strength for the concluding cry.

31 *For that sabbath was a high day*. It was doubly important to the Jews to observe their ritual requirements on a day which was both sabbath and festival. **32, 33** The brutal procedure of the leg-breaking was not part of the punishment of crucifixion but was resorted to in order to hasten death. **34, 35** The spear-thrust and the flowing out of blood and water evidently had particular importance for the Evangelist, as the latter verse suggests. Without going into the various views regarding the *blood and water*, it is sufficient to note that these prove the physical reality of Christ's death in contrast to the views held by the Docetists, who claimed that He only appeared to die. *He who saw it* has been interpreted as a reference either to the author himself, or to a third party. It would not be unnatural for an author, who has carefully concealed his identity, to use the third person when authenticating his personal knowledge of the event. His desire to stress the truth of the matter is to lead to faith. The same adjective for *true* is used here as in the description of the Vine in 15:1 (*q.v.*). **36, 37** In harmony with his usual practice John again finds support from the Scriptures, one from Ex. 12:46 and the other from Zc. 12:10.

19:38–42 The burial

John's account of the burial is important mainly for its mention of the part played by Nicodemus. Both he and Joseph of Arimathea were members of the Sanhedrin. **38** Although a secret disciple, Joseph became bold to pay his last devoted service to Jesus. Pilate's granting of permission for burial was in accordance with general Roman procedure. **39** When mentioning *Nicodemus* the Evangelist for the second time recalls his earlier interview with Jesus (*cf.* 3:1ff.; 7:50). *A mixture of myrrh and aloes, about a hundred pounds' weight* was a very costly evidence of Nicodemus' devotion. **41** The tomb in which Jesus was placed was situated in *a garden*, a feature which John alone mentions. *Where no one had ever been laid*. Luke also mentions this fact (Lk. 23:53) and Matthew refers to the tomb as being new. The significance of this is that Jesus' body was not brought into contact with corruption.

20:1–31 The resurrection

20:1–10 The empty tomb. Clearly in his resurrection narrative John is selective over the incidents he relates. He intends to illustrate some of the spiritual lessons to be derived from the fact of the resurrection. **1** *Mary Magdalene came to the tomb early*. She was evidently the first to arrive at the tomb. According to Matthew and Mark an angel gave a message to the two Marys

and to Salome. This incident must have preceded that. **2** *We do not know where they have laid him*. By using the plural Mary is including in her thought the other women who had gone with her, or else is including those to whom she is speaking. She is convinced that they will have no more clue than she has. **3–5** The Evangelist gives a vivid touch to the story as he recalls how *the other disciple* outran Peter but did not enter the tomb. Of both men it is recorded that they *saw the linen cloths lying*, but different verbs are used in the Greek, a stronger one to denote intentness of gaze being attributed to Peter. **7** The precise positioning of the different cloths is carefully noted. The isolated napkin suggests that Jesus left the grave clothes without disturbing them. **8** *Then the other disciple . . . saw and believed*. He interpreted what he saw. The mention of faith here must surely be the touch of an eyewitness. The 'other disciple' is the only one who would know the precise moment of faith. **9** *For as yet*. A specific knowledge (*i.e.* understanding) of a specific portion of Scripture is referred to here (presumably Ps. 16:10). It is deeply ingrained in Gospel records that understanding did not come even to the disciples until after the resurrection, and even then only gradually.

20:11–18 The revelation to Mary. Faith had come to the 'other disciple', but not as yet to Mary. **11** She *stood weeping*, having interpreted the empty tomb as evidence of theft of the body (*cf.* v. 13). **12, 13** The function of the *angels* here is to challenge Mary over her weeping. They have no words of comfort or encouragement to offer. **14, 15** In Mary's mind there could be only one person who might have removed the body, *i.e.* the gardener. When Jesus posed the same question as the angels, she blurted out her worst fears, thinking that she was addressing the gardener. **16** *Jesus said to her, 'Mary.'* By now she was looking away, but the voice of Jesus, which she at once recognized, called her to turn again to Him. *Rabboni!* (*which means Teacher*). In this incident there is an emphasis on personal relationships (*cf.* 'my Lord' in v. 13). **17** *Do not hold me, for I have not yet ascended to the Father*. There is no contradiction between this statement and the invitation to Thomas to touch Him. Mary was evidently trying to cling to Him and this He disallows. The introduction of the ascension here is to mark the approaching change of relationship between Jesus and His disciples. Mary is told to announce to the brethren, *I am ascending to my Father and your Father, to my God and your God*. Does this mean that John places the other appearances (*cf.* vv. 19ff.) after the ascension assuming a descent? It is better to regard the sequence of appearances as constituting a process of ascending. The present tense of the verb would support this. The distinction between *my Father* and *your Father* distinguishes Jesus from others who are children of God. **18** It is noteworthy that Mary's announcement was concerned with her meeting with the Lord, not so much with the ascension.

20:19–31 The revelation to the disciples. 19 Before the end of the same day Jesus appeared to the assembled disciples who were still gripped by fear. *Peace be with you.* Although this was the ordinary salutation, it means more here, for the words conveyed the Master's own gift of peace. **20** There was no denying His identity, for He showed the marks of crucifixion. Even the risen body carried the proofs. **21** The repetition of the gift of peace brings special emphasis to it. **22** *Receive the Holy Spirit.* The breathing upon them of the Spirit is understandable, since the Greek *pneuma* means both breath and spirit. This would appear to be in anticipation of Pentecost, although some specific assurance of the conveyance of the gift is clearly given here. **23** The purpose is stated here. *If you forgive . . . if you retain.* This is addressed to the disciples as a group (the verbs are plural). Although it is not in the power of man to forgive sins, man can pronounce forgiveness on the basis of what God has done in Christ. This is through the agency of the Holy Spirit within him, making him Christ's ambassador. Those who refuse to accept forgiveness inevitably retain their sins. Because v. 23 follows the reference to the gift of the Spirit, and the words were not confined to the apostles, the authority given is general and not confined in its exercise to special ministers. With this verse, *cf.* Mt. 16:18, 19; 18:18, 19.

24–29 Thomas's unbelief and subsequent leap to faith are no doubt included in John's story to illuminate the main purpose—to lead to faith in Jesus as Son of God. **24** No reason for Thomas's absence is given, **25** but his emphatic unbelief of their testimony reflects his uneasiness at not having been present. **26, 27** Jesus' return after eight days is marked by a repetition of the salutation of peace and a personal challenge to Thomas. The precise repetition of Thomas's own words must have made a deep impression on the man. The Lord showed sympathy for Thomas's misgivings, but there was no need for him to fulfil his own request. **28** *Thomas answered him, 'My Lord and my God!'* This marks the highest level of faith recorded in this Gospel. The high conception of the divine nature of Jesus is unmistakable and provides a fitting conclusion to John's record of the path of faith. **29** *Blessed are those who have not seen and yet believe.* This statement of Jesus is for those whose faith rests on the report of others. Such faith is of a nobler order than Thomas's. It is the kind of faith which has sustained the Christian church to the present time. Ultimately true faith must always be independent of sight.

30, 31 Here the author states his purpose. He makes clear that his record is selective (*many other signs . . . which are not written in this book*) and that its purpose is to inculcate a specific kind of faith, *i.e.* in the Messiahship and divine Sonship of Jesus, which will lead to an inheritance of life in His name.

21:1–25 The epilogue

Some scholars have supposed that this chapter is by another author, but there is no MS evidence of the circulation of the Gospel without it. It certainly appears to be something in the nature of an afterthought, perhaps to correct a misunderstanding about a saying of Jesus regarding John (21:23). Unlike those in ch. 20, the incidents here are set in Galilee.

1 *After this Jesus revealed himself . . . by the Sea of Tiberias.* This clearly places this Galilaean appearance after the Jerusalem appearances. **2** *The sons of Zebedee.* Since these are unnamed, it is support for John's influence behind the Gospel. **3** The fishing episode here shows some interesting similarity to Luke's account of the call of the first disciples (Lk. 5:1–11). But Peter's *I am going fishing* suggests an action of despair, a return to his former occupation. The fruitless night's toil is paralleled in Lk. 5:5. **4–8** John sees a spiritual principle here, for he proceeds to show the difference when Jesus is on the scene. **6** At Jesus' command the net is cast over again *on the right side of the boat* and the result is an unusually large haul (see v. 11). **7** It is the beloved disciple who first recognizes the Lord but does nothing other than telling Peter, who acts on what he heard without attempting to verify its truth by sight. Peter's impulsive action is wholly consistent with the general representation of him in the Gospels. **9, 10** There is a vivid touch in the description of the charcoal fire with its fish and the command of Jesus to bring more fish. **11** *A hundred and fifty-three of them.* Many fanciful explanations of the precise number have been given, but the best solution is to see the vivid recollection of an eyewitness who recalled the counting of the fish. **12** The invitation from Jesus to the disciples to join Him at breakfast supports the contention that this was an ordinary meal.

15–19 The breakfast leads into the interview between Jesus and Peter. The threefold challenge to Peter may well have been designed to parallel his threefold denial. The differences in the three questions are significant. In the third question the verb used for love (Gk. *phileō*) is the same as that used in all Peter's answers, but differs from that of the first two questions (Gk. *agapaō*, which is the nobler type of love). There are slight differences also in the three exhortations to Peter. The first and third use the word *feed*, whereas the second uses the word *tend* (Gk. *poimainō*) which involves all the responsibilities of shepherding the sheep. The second and third are, moreover, directed to the *sheep* and the first to the *lambs*. **17** *Lord, you know everything; you know that I love you.* This is the strongest assertion of the three called out by Peter's grief at being asked three times. The second word for 'know' (Gk. *ginōskō*) in this statement differs from the first (Gk. *oida*), which is also used in the other two assertions, and may convey the idea of knowledge gained by experience. **18** *When you* *are old ... another will gird you.* Tradition has it that Peter was crucified upside-down. **19** John clearly knows of some report concerning Peter's death. *Follow me* (*cf.* v. 22) recalls the initial commissioning of Peter (Mt. 4:19).

20-23 The brief interchange between Jesus and Peter regarding John seems intended to correct a misunderstanding. The rather elaborate and somewhat self-conscious way in which John is referred to suggests that it is the author himself. Peter is rebuked for his inquisitiveness and the form of this rebuke led to the misunderstanding.

24, 25 The comment would be most relevant if the disciple concerned were still alive, and this is borne out by the additional note. *This is the disciple who is bearing witness to these things, and who has written these things.* In no clearer way could the author claim to have been an eye-witness. Others are prepared to authenticate the truth of his testimony (as the plural verb shows). The last verse is intended to emphasize again the selective character of the whole Gospel.

DONALD GUTHRIE

The Acts of the Apostles

INTRODUCTION

The book of the Acts is the sequel to the third Gospel, and written traditionally by the same author, Luke, the beloved physician and companion of Paul (*cf.* Col. 4:14). The external evidence from the 2nd century onwards, which is unanimous on this point, is corroborated by the internal evidence of the style, outlook and subject-matter of the two books. (See *The Acts of the Apostles; The Greek Text with Introduction and Commentary*[2], by F. F. Bruce, 1952, pp. 1ff.)

Acts, like the third Gospel, is dedicated to a certain Theophilus (*cf.* Lk. 1:3 with Acts 1:1). The third Gospel is the 'first book' of the opening sentence of Acts. Theophilus appears to have been a person of some distinction, as he is accorded the title 'most excellent', elsewhere given to the Roman governors of Judea (Acts 23:26; 24:2; 26:25). He had already acquired some information about the Christian faith, and it was to provide him with a more accurate account of its trustworthiness that Luke in the first instance wrote his history of Christian beginnings, carrying the story from the nativity of John the Baptist and Jesus (*c.* 8–6 BC) to the end of Paul's two years' detention at Rome (*c.* AD 61).

Thus, Luke and Acts are not really two works, but two parts of one work; and the brief preface to the Gospel (Lk. 1:1–4) is intended to apply to both parts. Arguments advanced for the belief that Luke projected a third volume are not conclusive.

DATE

The date of the twofold work is a matter of dispute; some would put it as late as AD 90; but the weight of evidence seems to the present writer to favour an earlier date, probably not long after the last event of which Acts tells. Acts ends on a note of triumph, as has often been pointed out, with Paul proclaiming the gospel at Rome, in the heart of the Empire, without let or hindrance.

Would such a note of triumph have been sounded if, indeed, Paul had been executed by the time Luke wrote, or if the Neronian persecution had already taken place? As it is, there is no hint either of that persecution or of Paul's death (unless Acts 20:25, 38 be interpreted in the latter sense). Again, should we not have expected some reflection of the Jewish revolt of AD 66 and the destruction of the Temple and city of Jerusalem four years later if these had been events of the past when Acts was written? Considerations such as these have suggested a date for the composition of Acts practically coincident with the last event it mentions, the termination of Paul's two years of house-arrest in Rome.

On the other hand, the theological outlook of the book has been felt to point to a later date. One scholar has gone so far as to envisage a date towards the middle of the 2nd century, on the ground of affinities between the attitude of Acts and that of Justin Martyr (J. C. O'Neill, *The Theology of Acts*, 1961). To this it may be said *a.* that the narrative of Acts is so true to its 'dramatic date' that a date of composition a century later is on that score improbable; and *b.* that the affinities between Luke and Justin are accounted for in that Luke in several respects serves as the 1st-century prototype for the 2nd-century apologists. More generally, the 'early catholicism' of Acts has been held to be a sufficient argument for its post-apostolic dating. Not only is the 'delay of the *parousia*' no longer an acute problem and the current 'age of the Spirit' viewed as an independent chapter in the unfolding of the divine purpose on earth; the Jewish–Gentile tension in the church is a thing of the past, resolved once for all by the Jerusalem decree of Acts 15. Paul and the Twelve are brothers-in-arms, not leaders of two separate missionary enterprises, the former orientated to Gentiles and the latter to Jews; Peter preaches to Gentiles (as in Acts 10:34–43) and Paul to Jews (as in Acts 13:16–41) without any feeling that the one is trespassing on the other's mission-field. In this regard, it is said, Acts reflects not the turbulent situation of Paul's Galatian and Corinthian correspondence, where Paul has to contend with Judaizers on one front as energetically and vigilantly as with gnosticizing libertines on the other, but the calmer waters of Ephesians, which from this point of view is self-evidently sub-Pauline, where Jewish and Gentile believers are happily reconciled to each other in Christ, the old hostility having died out. (See, *e.g.*, E. Käsemann, 'Ephesians and Acts', in *Studies in Luke–Acts*, ed. L. E. Keck and J. L. Martyn, 1966, pp. 288–297.)

With regard to these arguments it must be said that the presuppositions on which they are based call for critical appraisal. In particular, the belief that Pauline Christianity and 'early catholicism' are mutually exclusive is perhaps not so axiomatic as Lutheran scholars especially are prone to assume. Luke has his own distinctive presentation of Christianity, which is not identical with Paul's, and in that presentation 'early catholicism' of the kind we find in Acts was an important element; but there is nothing in this 'early catholicism' which a man of Luke's outlook could not have held in the late sixties. It was one of his concerns to bridge the gap between Jewish and Gentile Christianity, and to show that the Gentile mission (to which he himself presumably owed his faith) was the legitimate development of the ministry of Jesus and original Jerusalem Christianity.

An earlier draft than our present Luke–Acts may have been prepared by Luke, if not to serve as one of the 'documents in the case' when Paul's appeal came up for hearing before the Emperor, then to supply the intelligent middle-class public of Rome, of whom Theophilus was a representative, with reliable information about the origin and character of Christianity. Paul's case must have made it necessary for some Roman officials to acquaint themselves with the peculiarities of this 'Way' which had won for Paul such animosity on the part of his fellow-Jews, but where were they to turn for a trustworthy account? Luke made it his business to provide them with the very thing they sought.

But later Luke expanded this preliminary and *ad hoc* draft by the inclusion of material which would not have been immediately relevant to that apologetic purpose. If, at the time of publication of the completed work, the Neronian persecution had come and gone, and Paul was now dead, no matter: Nero's *damnatio memoriae* might stamp his persecution as a horrible aberration from the path of true Roman justice. What the path of true Roman justice was could be shown from the record of Paul's apostolic activities in the eastern provinces—activities which (albeit in restricted circumstances) the authorities allowed him to pursue freely for two years in Rome itself. If, at the same time, Luke seized the opportunity to make a clear distinction between Judaism and Christianity, that would be no handicap to Christianity, but rather the reverse, at a time when Judea was in revolt against the Empire. A date towards AD 70 for Acts in its present form might thus be indicated.

The date of Acts cannot be considered in isolation from the date of Luke. If Acts does not obviously presuppose that Jerusalem has fallen, in the opinion of many this is certainly presupposed in Luke, especially in the eschatological discourse of Lk. 21. It is not so certain as many think that the fall of Jerusalem is in fact presupposed in Lk. 21, but a possibility to be borne in mind in this regard is that the original two-volume work comprised Proto–Luke (see the General Article, 'The fourfold Gospel', pp. 68f.) and Acts, and that those features in Luke which point to a date after AD 70 were not present in Proto–Luke (see C. S. C. Williams, *The Acts of the Apostles*, 1957, pp. 12ff.).

Very early in the 2nd century, the four Gospels, which hitherto had circulated separately, began to be bound up together in one collection. This led to the separation of the two parts of Luke's history. The second part soon began to circulate independently, under the title 'The Acts of the Apostles'. There is some textual evidence that the separation of the two parts led to a slight readjustment at the end of Luke and the beginning of Acts; possibly at this time the former was rounded off by the addition of the words 'and was carried up into heaven' in Lk. 24:51 (mg.), which naturally involved the addition of 'was taken up' in Acts 1:2. If this be so, some discrepancies which have been noted between the ascension stories of Luke and Acts disappear, for there would then be no record of the ascension in the former.

LUKE THE PHYSICIAN

Luke was not himself a personal companion of Jesus before the cross. He was, according to a tradition going back to the Anti-Marcionite Gospel Prologues at the end of the 2nd century, and even earlier to the formation of the 'western' text (see on 11:27), a native of Syrian Antioch, and in that case his acquaintance with Christianity may have dated from the early days of Christian witness in that city, when the gospel was first preached on a large scale to Gentiles and the first Gentile church was established. For Luke appears to have been a Gentile. In Col. 4:10f. Paul sends greetings from three friends, Aristarchus, Mark and Jesus Justus, whom he calls his only Jewish fellow-workers. And as he then goes on in vv. 12–14 to send greetings from three others—Epaphras, Luke and Demas—we conclude that they were Gentile Christians.

There are several touches about Luke's history which betoken the Greek outlook. Sir William Ramsay suggested that he was a brother of Titus, and although this suggestion can hardly be based on 2 Cor. 8:17–19 (where Origen thought the 'brother, whose praise is in the gospel in all the churches', as AV has it, to be Luke: *cf.* the Collect for St. Luke's Day), it is at least a possibility. Titus also was a Greek from Antioch (Gal. 2:1–3), and although it is evident from the Epistles that he played a very important part among Paul's companions, he is never mentioned in Acts.

SOURCES AND COMPOSITION

What, then, were Luke's sources of information as he traced the course of all things accurately from the very first? For part of the narrative of Acts, of course, he was himself present at the events. This he indicates delicately but unmistakably by his sudden transition from the third person to the first person plural in 16:10; 20:5; 27:1, three verses which mark the commencement of what we call the 'we' sections. It is, of course, possible to suppose that the author of Acts incorporated in his work the travel-diary of some eyewitness, not himself, but in this case the simplest hypothesis—that the author incorporated part of his own diary, that the 'we' of the diary includes the 'I' of 1:1—is also on general grounds the most satisfactory. And as most of the second half of Acts, even apart from these 'we' sections, is devoted to the activity of Paul, Paul's beloved physician had ample opportunity for first-hand information about these events. While the narrative of the Ephesian ministry, for example, does not fall in one of the 'we' sections, some parts of it exhibit the vividness of an eyewitness account, especially the description of the riot in the theatre (19:23–41), for which Luke was probably indebted to Gaius and Aristarchus, who were present.

He had many other possible informants about events in the earlier days of the church's life, before Paul's conversion, as well as about the events narrated in his Gospel. A native of Antioch must have met many who could tell him about those beginnings, such as Barnabas and even possibly Peter (cf. Gal. 2:11); and he had special opportunities of amplifying his knowledge during the two years when Paul was kept in custody in Caesarea (Acts 24:27). In that city lived Philip the evangelist, with his four prophesying daughters, who are mentioned by later writers as informants about persons and events in the infant church. In Jerusalem, Luke stayed with Mnason, one of the original disciples (Acts 21:16), he met James the Lord's brother, and this contact with the holy family may suggest a possible source for the nativity narrative of Lk. 1 and 2.

The question of written sources, apart from the travel-diary on which the 'we' sections are based, is entirely problematical. One or more Jerusalem sources, a Caesarean source, an Antiochene source and some others have been discerned, but it cannot be established that any of these was available to the author in written form. Some form-critical study has been devoted to certain parts of the book, especially the narratives of escapes from prison and the voyage and shipwreck narrative of ch. 27, but the upshot of this is little more than that these narratives conform in measure to well-recognized patterns widely followed in the relating of such incidents. (See M. Dibelius, *Studies in the Acts of the Apostles*, 1956.)

One branch of the source-criticism of Acts canvasses the possibility that an Aramaic document or documents may underlie the first half of the book. Here too it must be said that the evidence for *written* sources is not conclusive. Certainly the earlier chapters of Acts breathe a different atmosphere from the later chapters. When Paul sets out on his missionary journeys, we breathe the fresh air of the wide spaces of the Roman Empire; but in the earlier part of the book, which deals mainly with events in Jerusalem and other parts of Palestine, there is (as might be expected) a clearly discernible Semitic atmosphere. Some sections of these earlier chapters, especially some reports of apostolic preaching, not only reflect an Aramaic-speaking environment but present evidence of an oral Aramaic substratum. (See M. Black, *An Aramaic Approach to the Gospels and Acts*³, 1967; M.

Wilcox, *The Semitisms of Acts*, 1965.)

Luke probably employed a good part of the two years of Paul's imprisonment in Caesarea setting in order the material which he had gathered thus far. On the Proto–Luke hypothesis (see the General Article, 'The fourfold Gospel', p. 68), this material, so far as it related to the life and ministry of Jesus, constituted the first draft of the Gospel of Luke, and we may surmise that, so far as it related to the subsequent period, and especially to the career of Paul, it was designed to provide background information which might be helpful when Paul's appeal was heard in Rome. Later, Luke amplified both parts of his work. The Proto–Luke hypothesis envisages the amplification of the first draft of the Gospel by the incorporation (among other things) of a good deal of the substance of Mark's Gospel, and it has been held that Luke was also indebted to Mark for some of the 'Jerusalem' information appearing in the first twelve chapters of Acts. (For a judicious appraisal of the source-criticism of Acts see J. Dupont, *The Sources of Acts*, 1964.)

HISTORICAL CHARACTER

Luke's sources of information were second to none in value, and he well knew how to use them. The resultant work is a masterpiece of historical accuracy. Unlike the other NT writers, Luke sets his work in the framework of contemporary imperial events. He is the only NT writer who so much as mentions a Roman emperor's name. His pages are full of references to provincial governors and client kings. A historian who does this sort of thing must do it carefully if he does not wish to be exposed as inaccurate; Luke emerges from the severest test with flying colours. What has struck several critics most is the familiar way in which he moves among the multiplicity of varying titles borne by officials in the cities and provinces of the Empire, getting them right every time. Almost as striking is the deft way in which, with a few touches, he paints the true local colour of the widely differing places mentioned in his narrative.

A detailed and thoroughgoing vindication of the historical accuracy of Acts, especially in relation to Asia Minor, was provided by Sir William Ramsay, who devoted many years to intensive archaeological research in that area. When he went out there first in the eighties of last century, he accepted the then current Tübingen theory that Acts was a late and unhistorical production of the middle of the 2nd century; and it was not apologetic interests, but the evidence of archaeology, that compelled him to recognize that Luke's writings reflect the conditions, not of the 2nd century but of the 1st, which were very different, and reflect these with unsurpassed accuracy. Ramsay sums up Luke's qualities as a historian in these words:

'Luke's history is unsurpassed in respect of its trustworthiness. . . . Luke is a historian of the first rank: not merely are his statements of fact trustworthy, he is possessed of the true historic sense; he fixes his mind on the idea and plan that rules in the evolution of history; and proportions the scale of his treatment to the importance of each incident. He seizes the important and critical events and shows their true nature at greater length, while he touches lightly or omits entirely much that was valueless for his purpose. In short, this author should be placed along with the very greatest of historians' (*The Bearing of Recent Discovery on the Trustworthiness of the New Testament*, 1915, pp. 81, 222). When it is said that Luke 'touches lightly or omits entirely much that was valueless for his purpose', we should observe (perhaps more clearly than Ramsay did) that Luke's main purpose in his finished work is to relate the on-going story of salvation as the gospel advances along the road to Rome, and not necessarily to answer a modern historian's questions— *e.g.* what happened in the end to Paul and Peter. The 'critical events' for him are those which, like the conversion of Paul and the first evangelization of Gentiles, are epoch-making in the history of salvation.

Ramsay's estimate is frequently regarded as exaggerated, but students of Acts who ignore his unique contributions to the study of that book impoverish themselves and their pupils. 'Every reader of *St. Paul the Traveller* knows with what a wealth of detail Ramsay brings out the historical value of innumerable passages in Acts' (W. F. Howard, *The Romance of New Testament Scholarship*, 1949, p. 151). (A more recent assessment of Acts in this regard is provided by H. J. Cadbury in *The Book of Acts in History*, 1955; see also A. N. Sherwin-White, *Roman Society and Roman Law in the New Testament*, 1963.)

It has been held against Luke's standing as a historian that he is too fond of miracles. But he does not relate miracles for the sake of the miraculous; to him, as to the other Evangelists, they are important because they are signs as well as wonders—signs, that is, of the inauguration of the New Age, signs of the Messiahship of Jesus. For just as Jesus in the Gospels performs these signs and mighty works in His own Person, so it is He who, in Acts, performs them from heaven by His Spirit in His representatives, as they act in His name and by His authority.

It is noteworthy, too, that the miraculous element is not scattered at random throughout the book; it is more prominent at the beginning than at the end, and that is what we should expect in any case. 'Thus we have a steady reduction of the emphasis on the miraculous aspect of the working of the Spirit which corresponds to the development in the Pauline Epistles; it seems reasonable to suppose that Luke is here reproducing his sources faithfully.' (*Cf.* W. L. Knox, *The Acts of the Apostles*, 1948, p. 91.)

When we consider how scanty is our knowledge of the progress of Christianity in other directions during the years AD 30–60, and in all directions during the decades that followed those 30 years, we may estimate our indebtedness to Acts for our relatively detailed knowledge of its expansion along the road from Jerusalem to Rome during the period which it covers.

APOLOGETIC INTEREST

While the primary and stated object of Luke's history was to provide Theophilus (and the class of reader represented by him) with a trustworthy account of the origin of the gospel, and its progress from Palestine to Italy, other aims can be discerned. One obvious one is to demonstrate that the Christian movement was not a menace to law and order throughout the Roman Empire. Luke demonstrates this by citing the testimonies of imperial representatives. As Pilate pronounces our Lord 'not guilty' of the threefold charges of rebellion, sedition and treason (Lk. 23:4, 14, 22), so, when similar charges are brought against His followers, Luke shows what ill success they meet. The praetors of Philippi, it is true, imprison Paul and Silas because of a threat to property interests, but have to release them with a humble apology for their high-handed excess of jurisdiction (Acts 16:19ff., 35ff.). The politarchs of Thessalonica are content to find citizens of that place who will be guarantors for the missionaries' good behaviour (Acts 17:6–9). Gallio, the proconsul of Achaia, the brother of the influential Seneca, who was Nero's tutor and adviser in the early years of his rule, refuses to listen to the charges made against Paul by the Corinthian Jews, recognizing that they are not charges of which Roman law takes cognizance, but internal questions of Jewish theology (Acts 18:12–17). At Ephesus, Paul enjoys the goodwill of the Asiarchs, the chief men of the cities of the province of Asia (Acts 19:31); and when a riot is aroused by the outcry of property interests *versus* the threat implicit in Christianity against the cult of Ephesian Artemis, the town clerk of the city testifies that Paul and his companions have been guilty of no indictable offence in relation to the worship of the great goddess (19:35–41). At Jerusalem, Paul's bitterest enemies do their best to procure his condemnation by the Roman governors Felix and Festus, with conspicuous ill success; Festus and the petty king Agrippa II agree that he has committed no offence worthy of death or imprisonment, and that he might have been set free had he not, in order to secure a fairer trial than he feared he might receive in Palestine, appealed to the supreme tribunal of the Emperor in Rome (Acts 26:32). And Acts ends on a triumphant note, with Paul in custody, it is true, but yet prosecuting his missionary work unmolested in the Imperial City itself. The implication of all this is that fair-minded judges, reaching a decision in accordance with the impartial ideals of

Roman law, could not accept the misrepresentations of those who charged Christianity and its preachers with subversive activity inimical to the interests of the imperial administration.

It could not be denied, however, that wherever Paul and his companions had gone, trouble had risen. If the new movement was really as innocent as Luke maintained, how had it so invariably been attended with so much unrest? In taking up this argument, Luke shows himself a pioneer in another form of Christian apologetic which was to become very popular—the defence of the gospel against the Jews, conducted in such a way as to present Christianity, not Judaism, as the true fulfilment of the faith of the patriarchs and prophets. With the exception of the incident at Philippi and the riot at Ephesus, Luke explains that the trouble encountered by the gospel was due to the opposition fomented in almost every place by the Jews. In the Gospel it is the Jewish Sanhedrin, led by the Sadducean chief priests, who overbear Pilate's desire to acquit Jesus and force him to condemn Him. So in Acts it is Jews who are the fiercest enemies of the gospel in almost every place visited by Paul. In Damascus, Jerusalem, Pisidian Antioch, Iconium, Lystra, Thessalonica, Beroea, Corinth, it is his own fellow-countrymen who form the greatest hindrance to his work. They deeply resented the way in which Paul, as it seemed to them, poached on their preserves by visiting the synagogues and enticing away those Gentiles who attended worship there, and who, the Jews hoped, would one day become full proselytes. The bulk of the Jews, in city after city to which Paul went, would not have Jesus as the Messiah themselves, and were enraged when the Gentiles accepted Him; and while Acts records the steady advance of the gospel in the great Gentile communities of the Empire, it records at the same time its progressive rejection by that nation to which it was first offered.

Yet another branch of early Christian apologetic is adumbrated in Acts—the defence of the gospel against pagan religion, accompanied by an exposure of the folly of idol worship. This apologetic strain appears in Barnabas and Paul's remonstrance with the men of Lystra (14:15–18) and in Paul's speech before the Athenian Areopagus (17:22–31), early Christian expositions of the theme of natural revelation.

THEOLOGICAL EMPHASIS

Luke's historical competence is compromised neither by his apologetic interest nor by his status—increasingly recognized nowadays—as one of the theologians of the NT, standing in his own right alongside the others. Certain features of his theology (*e.g.* his 'early catholicism') have been mentioned above in the discussion of the date of Acts. But the dominating theological motif of Acts is the presence and work of the Holy Spirit. At the beginning of the book, the promise of the Spirit is made by the

risen Lord, and this promise is fulfilled for the Jews in ch. 2, and for Gentiles in ch. 10. The apostles proclaim their message in the power of the Spirit, manifested by outward supernatural signs; the converts' acceptance of the message is likewise attended by visible manifestations of the Spirit's power. This probably explains what some have felt to be a difficulty in Acts—that the Spirit is received by some believers after repentance and baptism (as by the Jews who believed on the Day of Pentecost, 2:38), by some after baptism and the imposition of apostolic hands (as by the Samaritans in 8:15ff. and the Ephesian disciples in 19:6), and by others immediately on believing, before baptism (as by Cornelius's household, 10:44). What Luke is thinking of in each case is not so much the invisible operation of the Spirit in the soul as His outward manifestation in speaking with tongues and prophesying.

Indeed, the whole book might well be called, as A. T. Pierson called it in the title of his exposition, 'The Acts of the Holy Spirit'. The Holy Spirit controls the whole work; He guides the messengers, such as Philip in ch. 8 and Peter in ch. 10; He directs the Antiochene church to set Barnabas and Saul apart for the work to which He Himself has called them (13:2); He guides them from place to place, forbidding them to preach in Asia or enter Bithynia, but giving them clear indications that they must cross to Europe (16:6–10); He receives pride of place in the letter from the Apostolic Council to the churches of Syria and Cilicia: 'it has seemed good to the Holy Spirit and to us' (15:28). He speaks through prophets, foretelling for example the famine of the days of Claudius and Paul's arrest at Jerusalem (11:28; 21:11), just as He spoke through the prophets of OT days (1:16; 28:25). It is He primarily who appoints the elders of a church to be its overseers (20:28). He can be lied to (5:3), tempted (5:9), and resisted (7:51). He is the primary Witness to the truth of the gospel (5:32).

In short, for Luke, as for Paul, the present age is the age of the Spirit, during which the work accomplished by Christ for His people is made effective in them by the Spirit, while the 'powers of the age to come' operate already through the same Spirit. Luke envisages the age of the Spirit as a distinct and substantial phase of the history of salvation, and discourages over-enthusiastic eagerness for an imminent *parousia*. As in his Gospel he relates how the parable of the pounds was told because some 'supposed that the kingdom of God was to appear immediately' (Lk. 19:11), so at an early point in his second volume he tells of the angelic direction to the apostles not to 'stand looking into heaven' (Acts 1:11). The accompanying words imply that Jesus would return in due course, but none the sooner for their standing and looking; meanwhile there was work for them to do, so let them return to Jerusalem and get on with it. For this Lucan perspective see H. Conzelmann,

The Theology of St. Luke, Eng. tr. 1960; the title of the German original, *Die Mitte der Zeit* (1954), defines his thesis, according to which the age of Jesus is for Luke 'the middle of time', preceded by the age of Israel and the law and followed by the age of the church and the Spirit. To Conzelmann's contribution should be added the insight of D. P. Fuller (*Easter Faith and History*, 1965), that Luke sees the events which he records in Acts, and especially the Gentile mission, as the fulfilment, out-working and verification of the act of God which culminated in the resurrection and ascension of Christ—an act of God both redemptive and creative, accomplished with a purpose of love for mankind without distinction and attested by apostolic witnesses. Such a perspective does not require more than a generation from the resurrection to take form and expression.

OUTLINE OF CONTENTS

COMMENTARY

1:1 – 5:42 THE BIRTH OF THE CHURCH

1:1–26 The forty days and after

In the first five chapters we have a series of pictures of the primitive Christian community in Jerusalem. The book opens where Luke's Gospel left off, with the risen Lord appearing to His disciples at intervals during forty days, directing them to wait in Jerusalem until they should receive heavenly power, and then to act as His witnesses in Jerusalem, Judea and Samaria, and to the ends of the earth. It has been pointed out that this threefold geographical indication (1:8) forms a sort of Index of Contents to Acts, for this is the order in which Luke describes the gospel spreading. The words of Christ, *you shall be my witnesses*, are noteworthy as being a quotation from Is. 43:10; the implication is that these words of the great OT prophet are fulfilled in the disciples of Jesus; they form both the remnant of the old Israel and the nucleus of the new.

Then comes the account of the ascension, after which the disciples, 120 strong, wait in Jerusalem for the fulfilment of the promise of the Spirit, and meanwhile fill the vacancy left in the number of the Twelve by the defection of Judas, for whose fall they find OT prediction (*cf.* Mt. 27:9f.; Jn. 17:12).

1 *The first book; i.e.* the third Gospel, also addressed to Theophilus (Lk. 1:3). Who *Theophilus* was we cannot be sure, but he appears to have been a Roman citizen of equestrian rank, and possibly of administrative position, as the title 'most excellent' (Lk. 1:3) suggests. *All that Jesus began to do and teach.* Since the subject-matter of the third Gospel is summed up thus, the implication is that this new volume is to deal with what Jesus continued to do and teach after His ascension—by His Spirit in His followers. **3** *Appearing to them during forty days.* Hence in the Christian calendar Ascension Day falls on the fortieth day after Easter. But Jesus' exaltation to God's right hand, which is what Ascension Day really commemorates, did not await the fortieth day after His triumph over death. In the primitive apostolic message His resurrection and ascension, which together constitute His exaltation, are viewed as one continuous movement. The fortieth day marked the last time on which He vanished from His disciples' sight after a resurrection appearance: the series of frequent though intermittent visitations was now brought to an end with a scene which brought home to them their Master's heavenly glory. We should not imagine that the intervals between these appearances were spent by Him in some earth-bound condition. *Speaking of the kingdom of God.* This brief statement was expanded by the Gnostics to represent Jesus as imparting esoteric teaching such as the Gnostic schools maintained. But 'the kingdom of God is conceived as coming in the events of the life, death, and resurrection of Jesus, and to proclaim these facts, in their proper setting, is to preach the Gospel of the Kingdom of God' (C. H. Dodd). No doubt the bearing of Jesus' passion and triumph on the message of the kingdom was now made plain to the disciples. **4** *Staying with them.* Or 'eating with (Gk. *synalizomenos*) them' (RSV mg.). **5** *You shall be baptized with the Holy Spirit.* Cf. John's own prediction in Mk. 1:8; Lk. 3:16, which is nowhere

mentioned explicitly in Acts. **9** *A cloud,* such as enveloped the glory of God in the OT; *cf.* Ex. 40:34; 1 Ki. 8:10f. The farewell appearance of the risen Lord took the form of a theophany. **11** *In the same way.* Possibly with particular reference to the *cloud* (v. 9); *cf.* Lk. 21:27 (Mk. 13:26); Mk. 14:62. **13** The list of apostles agrees with that in Lk. 6:14ff., with some variation in order, and the omission here of Judas Iscariot. **14** *Mary the mother of Jesus.* Her last appearance in the NT. *His brothers.* Now for the first time associated with the disciples (contrast Jn. 7:5); at least one of them, James, had seen the risen Lord (1 Cor. 15:7).

18 *Now this man. . . .* Vv. 18 and 19 must be regarded as Luke's parenthesis, not as part of Peter's words to his fellow-disciples. *Falling headlong,* or 'swelling up' (mg.); the adjective *prēnēs* is founded in both senses. **19** *Field of Blood. Cf.* Mt. 27:8.

20 The quotations are from Pss. 69:25 and 109:8. **22** *Beginning from the baptism of John. . . .* The period is that of Jesus' public ministry, covered by the apostolic preaching (*cf.* Acts 10:37) and by the Gospel of Mark. The outstanding qualification is that the new recruit to the Twelve must be *a witness to his resurrection.* **23** *Joseph called Barsabbas.* Of him Papias relates, on the authority of Philip's daughters, that he suffered no harm after drinking snake-venom (*cf.* Mk. 16:18). *Matthias.* There is no further record of him to which any serious attention need be paid. **26** *And they cast lots.* Deliberate selection and prayer played their parts in this appointment as well as the lot. The lot was a sacred institution in ancient Israel and was a well-established means for ascertaining the divine will (*cf.* Pr. 16:33), being in fact the principle of decision by Urim and Thummim (see *NBD*, art. 'Divination'). This is the first and last occasion of the employment of the lot by the apostles; it belongs, significantly enough, to the period between the ascension and Pentecost; Jesus had gone, and the Holy Spirit had not yet come. But if there are better ways of appointing the right men to ecclesiastical responsibilities, there are also worse ways. *And he was enrolled with the eleven apostles.* The idea that Paul was divinely intended to be the twelfth, and that the apostles here wrongly anticipated God's plan, betrays a misunderstanding of the unique character of Paul's apostleship.

2:1–13 The Day of Pentecost

1 The Day of Pentecost, the Feast of Weeks (*cf.* Lv. 23:15; Dt. 16:9), which fell on the fiftieth day after the passion Passover, found the little community gathered together in one place. Suddenly the Holy Spirit took possession of them while visible and audible signs accompanied the effusion of the promised heavenly Gift. **2** There was a sound as of *a mighty wind;* **3** and *tongues as of fire* appeared, *resting on each one of them.* **4** But more impressive was the outburst of *glossolalia,* speaking *in other tongues,* as the disciples were heard praising God in languages and dialects diverse from their native Galilaean Aramaic, but recognizable by visitors to the feast as those which some of them spoke. Most of the visitors would speak the common Greek dialect (the *Koinē*) except those from eastern parts (Parthia, Media, Persia, Mesopotamia, Syria), who would speak in Aramaic dialects.

5 *There were dwelling in Jerusalem Jews, devout men from every nation under heaven.* According to rabbinical tradition, the Feast of Weeks was the anniversary of the giving of the law at Sinai, and on that occasion the voice of God was heard by every nation on earth (seventy in all, by rabbinical reckoning). But Gentiles are not in view here; even if, with Codex Sinaiticus, we omit *Jews* from this verse, the word *devout* (Gk. *eulabēs*) is used in the NT only of Jews; it is Jews from every land of the Dispersion that are intended. **11** *We hear them telling in our own tongues the mighty works of God.* The reversal of the curse of Babel is probably in the narrator's mind.

2:14-36 The apostolic preaching

The Galilaean dialect was so distinctive and difficult for non-Galilaeans to follow that the disciples' release from the peculiarities of their local speech and their sudden capacity for speaking in a variety of tongues could not fail to be remarked. **14** When once the attention of the people had thus been attracted, Peter seized the opportunity to stand up with the other apostles, and address all who were within earshot. The words of his address are noteworthy, for they show the pattern regularly followed in the primitive apostolic preaching, or *kērygma*, the pattern or outline which can also be traced as the original framework of our gospel tradition. This pattern shows four main features: *a.* a narrative of the public ministry and passion of Jesus; *b.* the divine attestation of His Messiahship in the resurrection, of which the speakers claim to be eyewitnesses; *c.* 'testimonies' from the OT proving Jesus to be the Messiah; and *d.* exhortation to repentance and faith.

These features can be traced fairly clearly in this speech of Peter, delivered at a time when the events leading up to the crucifixion were fresh in the minds of his audience. The change in Peter since the night of the betrayal has often been remarked upon; here he straightly charges his audience with the guilt of delivering their Messiah over to *the hands of lawless men* (*i.e.* the Romans) and putting Him to death.

The use made by Peter of OT testimonies is striking: his *This is what was spoken* (v. 16) proclaims that the time has now come of which the prophets testified. For example, the words of Ps. 16:10 (LXX), *Thou wilt not abandon my soul to Hades, nor let thy Holy One see corruption* (v. 27), ascribed by the Hebrew and LXX texts to David's authorship, cannot, he argues, refer to David himself, for everyone knows that David did die, his soul *was* left in Hades, the

abode of the dead, and his body did see corruption. To whom, then, do the words refer? Not to David, but to Him whom David prefigured, 'great David's greater Son', the Messianic King.

Thus far, every Rabbi in Jerusalem would have agreed with Peter. But, he goes on, there has been only one Person of whom these words could be truly spoken—Jesus of Nazareth; for although (as all knew) He died, yet His soul was not left to Hades, nor did His flesh undergo corruption; He rose from the dead, 'and we are witnesses of this', he adds; 'we saw Him alive.' Therefore Jesus of Nazareth, crucified by men, raised from the dead by God, is the true Messiah; the stone which the builders rejected has become head of the corner. Later we find the same argument drawn from Ps. 16 by Paul at Pisidian Antioch (Acts 13:35-37). But Jesus not only died and rose; He also ascended into heaven; Peter and his companions had seen Him go up. And this fulfilled another Davidic psalm, Ps. 110: *The Lord said to my Lord, Sit at my right hand, till I make thy enemies a stool for thy feet* (vv. 34, 35). Who was raised to God's right hand? Not David, but King Messiah: that this psalm was Messianically interpreted at that time is plain from its quotation in Lk. 20:42f. and parallels. This, too, corresponded with the actual facts about Jesus of Nazareth; He was therefore undoubtedly Lord and Messiah.

16 *The prophet Joel.* The quotation is from Joel 2:28-32. The physical phenomena of vv. 18, 19 may have reminded the hearers of the strange darkness of Good Friday afternoon and its accompaniments. **17** But, while the whole section of Joel's prophecy of the Day of the Lord is quoted, the outstanding point of comparison with the present situation is *I will pour out my Spirit upon all flesh.* **23** *The definite plan and foreknowledge of God*; *i.e.* as revealed in OT Scripture, especially, no doubt, in Is. 53 (*cf.* Lk. 24:26, 46). The guilt of those who engineered Christ's death was none the less, but it was overruled by God for the achievement of His saving purpose. **25** *For David says.* The following quotation, from Ps. 16:8-11, is given for the sake of the words *Thou wilt not abandon my soul to Hades, nor let thy Holy One see corruption,* which were fulfilled in the resurrection of Jesus. **33** *He has poured out this, i.e.* the Holy Spirit, upon His disciples. **34** *David did not ascend*; better, 'It was not David that ascended . . .' **36** *Both Lord and Christ.* For the triumph and exaltation of Jesus as confirming His Messianic sovereignty *cf.* Rom. 1:4; Phil. 2:9-11.

2:37-47 The first Christian church

37 Convinced by the power of Peter's argument, the multitude were conscience-stricken; realizing that they were guilty of the blood of the Lord's Anointed, they cried, *Brethren, what shall we do?* and received from Peter the assurance that forgiveness and the gift of the Holy Spirit would be granted them by God if they repented and were baptized in the name of Jesus as

Messiah. The generation as a whole had proved perverse, but there was a place for a believing remnant; having previously quoted from Joel 2:32 the words 'whoever calls on the name of the Lord shall be saved' (v. 21), Peter now urged his hearers to save themselves thus from that perverse generation, and so effective was his exhortation that three thousand believed the good news and were baptized, thus forming the first Christian church.

Then follows a picture of the primitive Christian community, gathered daily in various homes to break the bread, meeting publicly in the Temple precincts (apparently in the colonnade called Solomon's, to judge from 3:11 and 5:12), adhering to the apostolic teaching and fellowship, and increasing in number day by day, praising God and enjoying the favour of all the people. The miracles which, when wrought by Jesus in His own Person, had been 'signs' of the advent of the Messianic age, continued to be performed by Him from heaven through His disciples as they acted in His name, providing additional proof that the divine kingdom had invaded the present age, for these mighty works were indeed 'powers of the age to come'.

38 *Repent, and be baptized.* This command seems to have caused no surprise to Peter's hearers; they had probably some familiarity with the practice of baptism. Christian baptism is, like John's, baptism in water, accompanied by repentance, but it is administered in the name of Jesus and associated with the gift of the Spirit. Like John's, it has an eschatological reference, but it betokens the realization of that to which John's baptism pointed forward. **39** *Cf.* Is. 57:19; Joel 2:32. **42** *The apostles' teaching and fellowship.* The fellowship was shown in *the breaking of bread and the prayers* and also in the community of goods (v. 45). **46** *Day by day.* This adverbial phrase modifies every verb in the sentence. **47** *And the Lord added to their number day by day those who were being saved.* Not that a continuous process of salvation in each individual is here in view, but a continuous procession of individuals who, one after another, accept the offered salvation and are incorporated in the saved community.

3:1 – 5:42 A miracle and its consequences

3:1–26 The cripple cured. In ch. 3 Luke goes on to give an example of these 'wonders and signs' (2:43), narrating one which had interesting consequences. The apostles and the other believers continued to be observant Jews, and attended the Temple regularly. One afternoon, as Peter and John went to the Temple at the time of the evening oblation (about 3 p.m.), they were about to pass through the 'Beautiful Gate', which probably led from the Court of the Gentiles to the Women's Court, when their attention was attracted by a man lame from birth, who lay there to ask alms from people who passed through the gate. Peter commanded him to stand up and walk, invoking the author-ity of Jesus the Messiah of Nazareth. When he had helped him to rise to his feet, the cripple walked, and, overjoyed with his new-found strength, he raised his voice in praise to God, jumping about so that all the people round about noticed him. Naturally, it created a great sensation, as everybody knew the cripple who had sat so long begging at his usual station. When a crowd had collected in Solomon's colonnade, Peter improved the occasion by proclaiming Jesus as the Messiah, rejected and crucified by the Jewish people, but now risen from the dead and offering remission of sins and fulfilment of the prophetic promises to Israel. And the healed man stood by, a powerful witness to the truth of Peter's words, for it was by the power of the name of Jesus that he had been cured, and his cure was a patent Messianic 'sign', for they could remember how Isaiah had prophesied of the Messianic age: 'Then shall the lame man leap like a hart' (Is. 35:6).

1 *At the hour of prayer.* The stated times for prayer were early morning, the time of the morning sacrifice; afternoon, the time of the evening sacrifice; and sunset. Josephus (*Ant.* xiv. 4. 3) says that sacrifices were offered in the Temple 'twice daily, in the morning and about the ninth hour'. **2** *Which is called Beautiful.* The gate is probably to be identified with what the Mishna calls 'Nicanor's Gate' and with the gate of Corinthian bronze described by Josephus as 'far exceeding in value those plated with silver and set in gold' (*Jewish War* v. 5. 3). **11** *The portico called Solomon's* ran the whole length of the east side of the outer court (*cf.* Jn. 10:23).

13 *His servant Jesus* (Gk. *pais*; so in v. 26 and 4:27, 30). The expression harks back to the Servant of Yahweh portrayed in Is. 42:1ff.; 52:13ff. With the present statement that God glorified his servant, cf. Is. 52:13, 'Behold, my servant . . . shall be exalted and *lifted up*' (LXX *doxazō*, the same verb as is used here). **14** *The Holy and Righteous One*; two Messianic designations. **15** *The Author of life.* 'Author' represents Greek *archēgos*, 'pioneer', appearing also in Acts 5:31; Heb. 2:10; 12:2. **16** *And his name. . . .* Perhaps render: 'And by faith in His name He has healed this man whom you see and know.'

17 *In ignorance*; *i.e.* they did not know that it was their Messiah who was thus being put to death. **18** *That his Christ should suffer.* It is not explicitly prophesied in the OT that the Messiah will suffer; this statement is based on Jesus' own identification of the suffering Servant with the Messiah and His acceptance and fulfilment of Messiahship in that sense (see on 2:23). **19** *That times of refreshing may come.* The sense probably is that their acceptance of Jesus as Messiah would speedily be followed by His *parousia* and by those conditions of world-wide blessing which the prophets had described as characteristic of the Messianic age. **20** *The Christ appointed.* This does not mean that between His resurrection and *parousia* Jesus is only Messiah-designate; it means that by raising

Him from the dead and exalting Him to His throne God has already installed Him as 'Lord and Christ' (2:36; *cf.* Rom. 1:4). Nevertheless this passage expresses a very early phase of the *kērygma*, if not 'the most primitive Christology of all' (J. A. T. Robinson). Its perspective is different from Luke's own (see p. 969). **22** *Moses said.* The quotation is from Dt. 18:15ff., a favourite Messianic 'testimony' in the early church; *cf.* 7:37; also Jn. 1:21; 6:14; 7:40. (It appears also as a 'testimony', though not a Messianic one, in the Qumran texts.) Jewish Christians in particular in the early centuries AD looked on Jesus as a second Moses. *You shall listen to him.* The words 'listen to him' in the heavenly Voice at the transfiguration (Mk. 9:7; Lk. 9:35) probably echo this Deuteronomic injunction. **24** *All the prophets . . . from Samuel.* Samuel is here regarded as first of a series of prophets (*cf.* 1 Sa. 3:20). There is no record of any Messianic prophecy by Samuel, but the general sense here is that the days which had now arrived marked the consummation of all that the prophets had foretold. **25** *Saying to Abraham.* The following words are a free quotation from Gn. 12:3; 18:18; 22:18. **26** *Having raised up his servant.* Here (as in v. 22) *raised up* may refer, not to Christ's resurrection, but to God's raising Him up as a Deliverer to Israel, as in 13:22 He is said to have 'raised up David' (see also on 13:33).

4:1-22 The rise of persecution. But such a commotion was by no means to the liking of the Temple authorities, who seized the two apostles and put them in custody till the following day, when they were brought for examination before the Sanhedrin. The high-priestly party, who dominated the Sanhedrin, were mostly Sadducees, and it is noteworthy that their grievance was that the apostles *were teaching the people and proclaiming in* (the case of) *Jesus the resurrection from the dead.* Besides, the ruling caste, anxious to maintain peaceable relations with the Romans, looked with great disfavour on every Messianic movement, whether political or spiritual. But they could find no legal fault with the apostles, especially in the presence of the once-lame man, whose cure was a strong testimony in their defence.

Peter, bold as ever, pressed home his accusation where it most properly belonged, warning the supreme court that the same name by which the cripple had received bodily health was the only name through which they could receive from God spiritual health. This boldness was the more surprising on the part of 'laymen', untrained in the rabbinical schools; but these men had been disciples of no ordinary teacher, who had Himself excited the surprised comment: 'How is it that this man has learning, when he has never studied?' (Jn. 7:15).

1 *The captain of the temple*; the *sāgān*, who was head of the Temple police and superintended arrangements for the preservation of order in and around the buildings. **2** *Proclaiming in Jesus*

the resurrection from the dead. It is significant that it was adherents of the Sadducean party who objected most strongly to the apostles' preaching, in view of their insistence on the resurrection of Jesus, which naturally involved the general principle of resurrection, repudiated by the Sadducees (see 23:8). **4** *The number of the men,* i.e. of the males. **5** *Their rulers and elders and scribes.* In other words, the Sanhedrin, the supreme court of the Jewish nation, consisting of seventy-one elders, including the high priest, who was president by virtue of his office. **6** *Annas the high priest and Caiaphas. Cf.* Lk. 3:2. Annas was senior ex-high priest, having held the office from AD 6 to 15; his son-in-law Caiaphas (*cf.* Jn. 18:13) was now high priest (AD 18–36). But Greek *archiereus* is used not only of the high priest strictly so called, but also of the chief priests in general, i.e. members of the wealthy families from which the high priests at this time were regularly selected. *And John and Alexander.* Neither of these can be identified with certainty. **11** *This is the stone. . . .* Quoted from Ps. 118:22, another common early Christian 'testimony', used in this sense by Jesus Himself (Mk. 12:10; Lk. 20:17). **13** *Common men.* The Greek word here used, *idiōtēs*, appears in later Hebrew and Aramaic as a loanword (*hedyôt*) meaning 'unskilled', 'untrained', which is no doubt the sense here. *They recognized that they had been with Jesus*; i.e. they recognized that this was the explanation of the otherwise inexplicable boldness and eloquence of men who had enjoyed no rabbinical education. **15** *They conferred with one another.* It is noteworthy that no effective attempt seems to have been made by the Sanhedrin to disprove the central affirmation of the apostles' proclamation, the resurrection of Jesus; yet, if they thought there was a reasonable chance of success, would they not have done so? **19** *Whether it is right in the sight of God to listen to you rather than to God, you must judge. Cf.* 5:29. Human authorities must be respected (*cf.* Rom. 13:1–7), except when their law conflicts with God's. **20** *We cannot but speak of what we have seen and heard.* Because of their commission (1:8) 'necessity' was 'laid upon' them as later on Paul (1 Cor. 9:16).

4:23-37 Continuous expansion. In the absence of any reasonable ground for punishing Peter and John, the Sanhedrin dismissed them, forbidding them with threats to speak any more in the name of Jesus. But the net result was a further increase in the church, which now numbered five thousand men, not to speak of women. The original pooling of property continued, by which the richer members made provision for the needs of the poorer. Among these richer members Barnabas, a Levite of Cyprus, receives special mention for liberality.

24 *Sovereign Lord, . . .* The opening words of this prayer probably illustrate early Christian liturgical practice, based on Jewish liturgical forms. The phraseology of the exordium echoes such OT passages as Ex. 20:11; Ne. 9:6; Ps. 146:6. **25** *Who by the mouth of our father David, thy servant, didst say by the Holy Spirit.* The text may be rendered: 'Who didst say through thy servant David our father, the mouthpiece of the Holy Spirit.' *Why did the Gentiles rage . . .?* Quoted from Ps. 2:1, 2. The application of this psalm to the future Messiah appears first in the seventeenth 'Psalm of Solomon' (*c.* 50 BC). **27** *Thy holy servant Jesus.* See on 3:13. *Whom thou didst anoint*; *i.e.* 'whom Thou hast made Messiah'. *Both Herod and Pontius Pilate*, representing 'the kings . . . and the rulers' of v. 26 respectively, as *the Gentiles and the peoples of Israel* correspond to 'the Gentiles . . . and the peoples' of v. 25. *Herod* is Herod Antipas, tetrarch of Galilee (4 BC – AD 39); the occasion referred to is that of Lk. 23:7-12. **28** *To do whatever. . . . Cf.* 2:23 for the foreordained character of the death of Christ. **31** *The place . . . was shaken.* The phenomena of Pentecost were repeated (*cf.* 2:2f.).

32 *They had everything in common.* The reference to the community of goods (*cf.* 2:44f.) is repeated here to introduce the incidents of Barnabas and of Ananias and Sapphira. **36** *Barnabas (which means, Son of encouragement).* This is the idiomatic Semitic use of 'son' in a phrase indicating a man's character. How apt the designation was is evident from the record of Barnabas's subsequent career.

5:1-16 Ananias and Sapphira. But in such a large company, especially at such a time of enthusiasm, there must almost inevitably be some black sheep; and the case of Ananias and Sapphira illustrates the temptations to which less spiritual members were liable. That the pooling of property was purely voluntary is plain from Peter's question to Ananias: *While it remained unsold, did it not remain your own?* The sin consisted not in keeping back part of the money received for their estate, but in pretending that the part which they handed over was the whole. And the lie told to the church was reckoned as told to God the Holy Spirit.

The story has given offence to many; one commentator, for example, finds it 'frankly repulsive'. But we need not make Peter guilty of their death; he told them plainly that they had been trying to cheat God, and the shock produced by the sudden sense of the enormity of such a crime caused their death. Sapphira had the additional shock of having the news of her husband's sudden death so bluntly broken to her. The whole story fits exactly into the picture of spiritual exaltation prevailing in the infant church. The tragedy had a salutary effect on those who might light-heartedly have joined the popular movement; but even so the progress continued.

2 *He kept back some of the proceeds.* The Greek verb *nosphizomai*, used here, is the verb used in the LXX of Jos. 7:1, of Achan's misappropriation of part of the consecrated spoil of Jericho. If the Gospels are the 'Torah' of the NT, Acts is its book of Joshua, and there are a number of striking parallels between Joshua and Acts, though beneath rather than on the surface. **3** *To lie to the Holy Spirit.* The sovereign presence of the Holy Spirit in the church is so real that any action done to the church is regarded as done to the Spirit, just as any action taken by the church is predicated of the Spirit (*cf.* 15:28). The language of vv. 3 and 4 makes it clear that the Holy Spirit is viewed as a divine Person. **9** *To tempt the Spirit of the Lord.* The idea is that of seeing how far one can go with impunity. Ananias and Sapphira discovered that they had gone too far. **11** *Upon the whole church.* This is the first occurrence of *church* in Acts (the word is absent from the best texts of 2:47). The word (Gk. *ekklēsia*) has its background in the LXX, where it is sometimes used of the 'congregation' (Heb. *qāhāl*) of Israel: see on 7:38. The followers of Jesus are the new people of God, continuators and successors of the old 'congregation of the Lord', formerly restricted to one nation, but now about to be thrown open to all believers everywhere. **13** *The rest.* It is difficult to determine who these are, since they are distinguished from *the people*; emendations have therefore been suggested, such as Dibelius's 'the rulers'.

5:17-42 A further attempt at persecution. A second attempt by the priestly authorities about this time to inhibit the Christians met with as little success as the previous one. Gamaliel's moderating advice to let the new movement alone, lest it might prove to be of God, was followed for the time being, although the apostles this time had an opportunity of rejoicing that they had been counted worthy to endure stripes for the honourable name which they proclaimed. But before long a new departure within the Christian community gave the authorities an opportunity to institute a really thoroughgoing policy of suppression.

19 *But at night an angel of the Lord opened the prison doors.* The *angel of the Lord* represents Gk. *angelos Kyriou*, the phrase which in LXX renders Heb. *mal'ak Yahweh*, the supernatural messenger who manifests God's presence to men (see on 7:32). It is unlikely that Luke has this particular idea in mind. Certainly he wishes to indicate that the agency of God was behind this opening of the prison doors, but this would be as true if the doors were opened by secret sympathizers with the apostles as if an angel came down from heaven to let them out. *Cf.* 12:7ff. for the similar experience of Peter himself. On the present occasion all the apostles appear to have been locked up. **20** *All the words of this Life.* In Aramaic one word represents both 'life' and 'salvation'; the expression used here is thus almost identical with that in 13:26. **21** *All the senate; i.e.* the Sanhedrin (Gk. *gerousia*, 'body of elders'). **22** *The officers.* Probably Levites of the Temple police force. **28** *This man's blood.* We can probably trace thus early a reluctance on the part of the Jewish religious leaders to refer to Jesus by His personal name (*cf.* J. Jocz,

The Jewish People and Jesus Christ, 1949, p. 111, for the persistence of this tendency). **29** *We must obey God rather than men.* Cf. 4:19; cf. also the words of Socrates to his judges: 'I shall obey God rather than you' (Plato, *Apology* 29d). **30** *The God of our fathers raised Jesus.* See on 3:26 for the sense of 'raised' here. These words introduce the fourth summary of the primitive apostolic preaching in Acts; the three previous ones come in 2:22-36; 3:13-26; 4:10-12. Note how the emphasis is regularly pointed on the contrast between the hearers' action and God's, so here: *whom you killed . . . God exalted him. Hanging him on a tree*; harking back to Dt. 21:22, 23, where the divine curse attaches to such a death (*cf.* Acts 10:39; Gal. 3:13). **32** *We are witnesses to these things, and so is the Holy Spirit.* Note the continued existence of the apostles' personal testimony (*cf.* 1:8, 22; 2:32; 3:15; 4:33), with which the witness of the Spirit in them is here combined (see on 5:3). **34** *Gamaliel.* The most illustrious Rabbi of his day, disciple of Hillel (and now head of the school of Hillel), teacher of Saul of Tarsus (22:3) and leader of the Pharisaic party in the Sanhedrin. The Pharisees were a minority in that body, but they enjoyed the support and confidence of the people to such a degree that their judgment had to be respected by the Sadducean majority. **36** *Theudas.* The only insurgent named Theudas of whom we know from any other source was a magician who, according to Josephus (*Ant.* xx. 5. 1), led a band of his adherents to the Jordan, promising to divide it that they might cross dryshod, but was attacked and killed by soldiers sent against him by the procurator Fadus. This incident is to be dated *c.* AD 44, whereas Gamaliel's speech was delivered 10 or 12 years earlier. Gamaliel's Theudas (who in any case antedates the revolt of Judas in AD 6) is probably one of the innumerable insurgents who infested Palestine after Herod the Great's death in 4 BC. **37** *Judas the Galilean arose in the days of the census.* When Judea was reduced to the status of a Roman province in AD 6, Quirinius, imperial legate of Syria, held a census there with a view to assessing the amount of tribute to which the new province would be liable. Judas and others, regarding this action as a prelude to enslavement and as a dishonour to God, the only true King of Israel, raised the standard of revolt. The revolt was crushed, but the party of the Zealots kept its spirit alive until the outbreak of the Romano–Jewish War in AD 66. **38** *Keep away from these men and let them alone.* 'The doctrine preached by Gamaliel is sound Pharisaic teaching; God is over all, and needs no help from men for the fulfilment of His purposes; all men must do is to obey, and leave the issue to Him' (J. A. Findlay). *Cf.* the dictum of a later Rabbi: 'Every assembly which is in the name of heaven will ultimately be established, but that which is not in the name of heaven will not ultimately be established.'

6:1 – 9:31 PERSECUTION LEADS TO EXPANSION

6:1-15 Appointment of the seven and the activity of Stephen

A new departure in the narrative of Acts is marked by the introduction of the name of Stephen. Stephen appears first as one of the seven officers who were appointed to supervise the distribution of largesse from the common fund to the poorer members of the community. At a very early stage, the church attracted Hellenistic Jews (*i.e.* Greek-speaking Jews from outside Palestine) as well as Aramaic-speaking Palestine-born Jews; and before long complaints arose that the widows of the latter group were being favoured in the daily 'hand-reaching'. It is significant that the seven officers chosen by the community and appointed by the apostles to supervise this business all bore Greek names, being probably themselves Hellenistic Jews. Two of the seven, Stephen and Philip, were destined to leave their mark on the church far beyond the bounds of this special function to which they were appointed. Stephen seems to have had an exceptionally far-sighted comprehension of the total breach with Judaic worship which the new movement logically and ultimately involved. In this he blazed a trail later trodden by Paul and especially by the writer to the Hebrews.

The Twelve had kept the respect and goodwill of the Jerusalem populace; they attended the Temple services regularly, and appeared outwardly to be observant Jews whose only distinction from others was that they believed and proclaimed Jesus to be the Messiah. But a new note was heard in the debates in the Hellenistic synagogue which Stephen attended, a note which envisaged the abolition of the Temple cultus and the institution of a new and more spiritual form of worship. If the charges made by Stephen's accusers are garbled, yet we are not at a loss to discover the real trend of his arguments; the speech preserved for us in ch. 7 is not so much a speech by the defence aimed at procuring an acquittal as a reasoned exposition of his teaching about the transitory nature of the Jewish worship. An attack on the Temple, as Stephen's teaching was construed to be, ranked as blasphemy of the worst kind (so too Jeremiah had earlier found to his cost); there was also the subordinate consideration that the economy of Jerusalem was based on the Temple. The rulers at once saw their opportunity, and arraigned Stephen on a popular charge. The indictment against him was practically the same as that against his Master at an earlier date (Mk. 14:58), and against Paul at a later date (Acts 21:28); it was alleged that he meditated the destruction of *this holy place.*

1 *The Hellenists murmured against the Hebrews.* The *Hellenists* were Greek-speaking Jews, mainly belonging to the lands of the Dispersion; the *Hebrews* were Aramaic-speaking Jews, most of whom, like the apostles themselves, were native-born Palestinians. *Their widows were neglected in the daily distribution.* From the common pool in which the property of the wealthier members had been placed (2:45; 4:34, 35) daily distribution was made to those who were needy, among whom widows would naturally figure prominently. 3 *Pick out from among you seven men.* It is evident from the names of the seven that they were Hellenists; one of them, indeed, was not even a Jew by birth, but a proselyte from the Gentile city of Antioch. They were probably recognized as leaders of the Hellenistic community in the primitive Jerusalem church. Note that even for such practical duties as fell to their lot spiritual endowment is required as well as a good reputation and general wisdom. While they were appointed on this occasion as almoners, the ministry of those of their number of whom we have any further account was not restricted to this form of service. 5 *Nicolaus.* According to Irenaeus (who may depend on Papias), the Nicolaitans of Rev. 2:6, 15 took their name from him; the truth of this cannot be determined. 6 *They . . . laid their hands upon them.* The seven were selected by the rank and file; the imposition of apostolic hands confirmed this selection, commissioned the seven for their special work, and expressed the apostles' fellowship with them in the matter. 7 *A great many of the priests.* Many of the ordinary priests were humble and pious men, unlike the wealthy ecclesiastical politicians of the high-priestly families. If members of the Temple staff were attaching themselves to the church, such activity as Stephen's was bound to produce tension with his more conservative fellow-Christians as well as with the Jewish rulers. 9 *Some of those who belonged to the synagogue. . . .* Probably one synagogue is meant, although five, four, three and two have been understood by various commentators. As it was attended by *those from Cilicia,* it may have included Saul of Tarsus among its members. *Freedmen* (Gk. *libertinoi*). Probably Jewish freedmen or descendants of freedmen from the various places mentioned; Deissmann suggests freedmen of the imperial household. There is not sufficient reason to reject the text here for the attractive emendation 'Libyans' suggested by Beza, Tischendorf and Dibelius. 12 *Brought him before the council, i.e.* the Sanhedrin.

7:1 – 8:1a Stephen's defence and death

Arrested and put on trial before the Sanhedrin, the supreme court of the Jewish nation, over which in those days the high priest presided, Stephen stated his case in the form of a historical review, a form not uncommon among the Jews. The two chief themes of his speech are, first, that the nation, from the days of Abraham onwards, had always been intended to sit loose to any one locality of earth; a movable tent was therefore a fitter shrine than a permanent building; and second, that the nation, from the time of Moses onwards, had always rebelled against

God and opposed His messengers, a course of action which had culminated in their slaying of *the Righteous One.* Any line of argument less likely to conciliate his judges could hardly be imagined. After one or two angry interruptions, which Stephen countered in true prophetic vein, he was prevented from finishing his speech, thrown out of the building and stoned. Whether his death was an act of lynch-law or an excess of jurisdiction on the part of the Sanhedrin is not quite clear; probably it partook of the nature of both.

1 *And the high priest said,* acting as president of the court. 2 *When he was in Mesopotamia, before he lived in Haran.* Haran was a flourishing city in the first half of the 2nd millennium BC, to which the life of Abraham belongs. According to the MT and LXX of Gn. 11:31 – 12:5 (see RSV for correct translation), it was after Abraham's arrival in Haran that the words quoted here in v. 3 were spoken. But Philo and Josephus agree with Stephen that Abraham received a divine communication before going to Haran (*cf.* Gn. 15:7; Ne. 9:7). 5 *But promised . . .*; *cf.* Gn. 17:8. 6 *And God spoke to this effect . . .*; quoted from Gn. 15:13f. *Four hundred years.* Rabbinical exegesis reckoned 400 years from the birth of Isaac to the Exodus. 7 *And worship me in this place.* These words come from Ex. 3:12, where they are spoken to Moses and where the place referred to is Horeb. The conflation of separate quotations is characteristic of Stephen's speech as here summarized. 8 *And he gave him the covenant of circumcision; cf.* Gn. 17:10; 21:4. 'Thus, while there was still no holy place, all the essential conditions for the religion of Israel were fulfilled' (Lake and Cadbury).

9 *And the patriarchs, jealous of Joseph, sold him into Egypt.* The narrative from here to v. 34 consists largely of a cento of passages from Gn. 37 – Ex. 3. 12 *He sent forth our fathers the first time,* as distinct from *the second visit* (v. 13). 14 *Seventy-five souls.* The MT of Gn. 46:27; Ex. 1:5; Dt. 10:22 enumerates seventy persons, including Jacob himself and Joseph and his two sons; the number *seventy-five* comes from the LXX of Gn. 46:27 and Ex. 1:5 and is found in a Hebrew MS of Exodus from Qumran; it omits Jacob and Joseph, but reckons nine sons to Joseph. 16 *And they were carried back to Shechem.* Jacob was buried in the cave of Machpelah at Hebron (Gn. 49:29ff.); Joseph was buried at Shechem (Jos. 24:32). *In the tomb that Abraham had bought for a sum of silver from the sons of Hamor in Shechem.* Abraham bought the cave of Machpelah at Hebron from the Hittites (Gn. 23:16); Jacob bought the land at Shechem which he gave to Joseph (and where Joseph was buried) from the sons of Hamor (Jos. 24:32). Not only separate quotations (see on v. 7) but separate incidents are conflated in Luke's summary of Stephen's speech.

18 *Till there arose over Egypt another king who had not known Joseph;* probably a reference to

the foundation of the XIX Dynasty (*c.* 1320 BC). **20** *Beautiful before God*; probably a Semitism, meaning 'very beautiful'. **21** *Pharaoh's daughter adopted him*. A daughter of Seti I or Rameses II. **22** *And Moses was instructed in all the wisdom of the Egyptians.* Stephen is more moderate than the generality of Hellenistic Jewish writers, who represent Moses as the founder of all science and culture, and indeed of the whole civilization of Egypt. *And he was mighty in his words and deeds.* Moses disclaims eloquence in Ex. 4:10, but the reference here may be to written words. Josephus (*Ant.* ii. 10) preserves a legend of his prowess in martial deeds. **23** *When he was forty years old.* Ex. 2:11 says simply 'when Moses had grown up'. **25** *He supposed that his brethren understood. . . .* This explanation of his action is not given in the OT. Philo, like Stephen, regards Moses' championship of the Israelites at this point in his career as a settled policy. And note the parallel here: Moses appeared as a messenger of peace and deliverance and was rejected; Jesus in due course was treated the same way. **29** *He became the father of two sons*; *i.e.* Gershom and Eliezer (Ex. 2:22; 18:3, 4).

30 *An angel appeared to him in the wilderness of Mount Sinai.* Stephen emphasizes that God is not tied to one city or land; He appeared to Abraham in Mesopotamia, was with Joseph in Egypt and revealed Himself to Moses in the wilderness, in the land where he was *an exile* (v. 29). This *angel* is a messenger of the Presence, an extension of the divine personality, **32** who speaks and is spoken to as God.

35 *God sent as both ruler and deliverer.* The rejected one is God's appointed saviour: this pattern recurs in the careers of Joseph, Moses and Jesus. *By the hand*; *i.e.* by the agency. **37** *God will raise up for you a prophet.* This citation from Dt. 18:15 (see on 3:22 above) helps further to point the parallel between Moses and Christ. **38** *This is he who was in the congregation in the wilderness.* Probably an allusion to Dt. 18:16 (immediately following the words quoted in the previous verse), where mention is made of 'the day of the assembly' (Heb. *qāhāl*, LXX *ekklēsia*) at Horeb. As Moses was with the old *ekklēsia*, so Christ is with the new *ekklēsia*, but it is still a pilgrim church, 'the church in the wilderness'. *With the angel who spoke to him.* In Ex. 32:34 God says to Moses, 'My angel shall go before you'; but later, at Moses' persistent request, He makes a more personal promise, 'My presence (*i.e.* 'I myself', so LXX *autos*) will go with you' (Ex. 33:14). In *Jubilees* 1:27; 2:1, however, an angel speaks with Moses at Sinai (see on v. 53 below). **41** *And they made a calf in those days.* See Ex. 32 for the narrative of this. **42** *But God turned and gave them over to worship the host of heaven.* This statement is not based, apparently, on the OT narrative of the wilderness wanderings, but seems to be an inference from the passage from Am. 5:25–27 quoted in vv. 42, 43. In the MT of Amos, the people of

Israel are warned that the Assyrian king will deport them 'beyond Damascus', and that they will carry thither the very instruments of that idolatry for which this calamity is about to overtake them. In the LXX (quoted here with variations) this idolatry—the worship of the heavenly host, especially of the planet Saturn—is dated as early as the wilderness period. *Did you offer to me . . . in the wilderness?* The Greek wording makes it plain that the answer is 'No'. It was not Yahweh but heathen astral deities that they worshipped. **43** *The tent of Moloch*, in contrast to *the tent of witness* (v. 44). The Hebrew means 'Sakkut your king', Sakkut being an Akkadian name of the god of the planet Saturn. *The star of the god Rephan.* The RSV of Amos has 'Kaiwan', an Assyrian name of Saturn; in the LXX (quoted here) the Assyrian name is replaced by an Egyptian name for the same planetary god, represented here by *Rephan. Beyond Babylon.* Stephen has the Babylonian captivity in mind, as was natural for one speaking in Jerusalem, and therefore substitutes *beyond Babylon* for Amos's 'beyond Damascus', which referred to the earlier Assyrian captivity.

44 *The tent of witness.* So called because it enshrined the 'witness' or 'testimony' which God gave to Israel, consisting of the tables of the Law—whence the ark which housed them is also called 'the ark of the testimony' (*e.g.* Ex. 25:22). *According to the pattern that he had seen*; quoted from Ex. 25:40 (*cf.* the development of this idea in Heb. 9:1ff.). **45** *Until the days of David.* The process of dispossessing the Canaanites, begun under Joshua, was not completed until David's time; besides, and more especially, successive generations had the tent handed on to them until the reign of David (2 Sa. 7:6; *cf.* 1 Ch. 17:5). **46** *Asked leave to find a habitation for the God of Jacob.* Cf. Ps. 132:5. Several excellent textual authorities have 'the house of Jacob' here, but this reading gives awkward connection with v. 47, *But it was Solomon who built a house for him.* There is emphasis upon *house*—a fixed house as distinct from a movable tent. **48–50** Stephen regards the building of the Temple as a retrograde step, and counters the idea that God could dwell in a house with the quotation from Is. 66:1, 2. Other divinities might be so conceived of, but not *the Most High.* This unmistakable attack on the most cherished centre of the national religion probably caused an explosion of anger, which drew forth the denunciation of v. 51.

51 *You stiff-necked people. . . .* The language of the denunciation is thoroughly OT; *cf.* Ex. 33:5; Lv. 26:41; Dt. 10:16; Is. 63:10; Je. 4:4; 6:10; 9:26; Ezk. 44:7. **52** *They killed those who announced beforehand the coming of the Righteous One.* Cf. our Lord's accusation in Mt. 23:29–37 and the implication of His words in Mk. 12:2–8; Lk. 13:33, 34. **53** *Who received the law as delivered by angels* (lit. 'by angelic ordinance'). For the mediation of the law through angels *cf.* Gal. 3:19; Heb. 2:2. The idea does not appear in the

OT, but is found in *Jubilees* 1:29, *Testament of Dan* 6:2, Josephus (*Ant.* xv. 5. 3), and Philo (*On Dreams*, i. 141ff.).

54 *When they heard these things. . . .* They cut his speech short; they had heard more than they desired. **55** *Jesus standing at the right hand of God.* If there is special significance in His *standing*, it is probably because He appears as Stephen's advocate in the heavenly court, to which Stephen appeals from the judgment of the earthly court. The reference to *the right hand of God* is based on Ps. 110:1 (see 2:34f.). **56** *I see the heavens opened, and the Son of man standing at the right hand of God.* This is the only NT occurrence of the title 'the Son of man' outside the Gospels (the expression in Rev. 1:13; 14:14 is different). Many members of the Sanhedrin must have been reminded of the words of Jesus Himself (Mk. 14:62) which drew forth their verdict of blasphemy. Stephen's vision is a fulfilment of Jesus' promise in Lk. 12:8: 'every one who acknowledges me before men, the Son of man also will acknowledge before the angels of God.' **58** *The witnesses laid down their garments at the feet of a young man named Saul.* It was the witnesses' duty to cast the first stones. The mention of Saul suggests that he played some responsible part in the proceedings, which is confirmed by 8:1a. **60** *Lord, do not hold this sin against them.* Contrast the dying prayer of Zechariah in a similar situation (2 Ch. 24:22). **8:1a** *And Saul was consenting to his death.* This could, but does not necessarily, mean that he was a member of the Sanhedrin. *Cf.* 22:20; 26:10.

8:1b–25 Philip and the Samaritans

The execution of Stephen was now the signal for a much more thorough campaign of repression. The large community of believers in Jerusalem was scattered throughout Palestine and even beyond its borders, although the apostles, who perhaps were not identified in the popular mind with the activity of Stephen, stayed in Jerusalem. The dispersion, however, did much more good than harm to the cause; those who were thus scattered carried the good news with them and disseminated it everywhere, even as far north as Syrian Antioch, which led to a remarkable development in that city in a few years' time. But nearer home a fresh departure was made almost immediately, for another member of the seven, Philip, left Jerusalem for Samaria, and began to evangelize its schismatic, half-heathen population (as the Samaritans were in Jewish eyes). Hitherto the gospel had been preached to pure Jews only. But Philip's evangelism was remarkably successful and, when news of it came to the apostles, Peter and John were sent there on a mission of inquiry. (Did John remember his earlier proposition with regard to the Samaritans in Lk. 9:54?) After the arrival of the two apostles the Samaritans who had believed were seen to have received the Holy Spirit. This confirmed the reality of their participation in Christ.

1b *They were all scattered . . . except the apostles.* It appears from the sequel that the Hellenistic believers were the chief target of the persecution, perhaps as being more closely associated with Stephen. From this time until AD 135 the church of Jerusalem seems to have been composed mainly of 'Hebrews' (but see 21:16 for one surviving Hellenist). **3** *Laid waste*; *i.e.* 'ravaged', as a wild beast does the body of its victim. **5** *A city of Samaria.* The city in question might be Gitta, said by Justin to have been the native place of Simon Magus. A variant reading, 'The city of Samaria', appears in several authorities; it would indicate the ancient city of Samaria, restored by Herod with the new name Sebaste. In any case, the preaching of the gospel to Samaritans represented a widening of its scope (*cf.* 1:8). **9** *A man named Simon.* Simon Magus is said in later times to have visited Rome and other parts, where he secured a large following; the Simonians are known to have survived to the 3rd century at least. **10** *That power of God which is called Great.* This may mean that he claimed to be the Grand Vizier of the Most High. **13** *Even Simon himself believed.* Theologians may discuss whether or not he exercised 'saving faith'. Although (for a time at least) *he continued with Philip*, Peter judged that the root of the matter was not in him. Perhaps he was simply convinced of the potency of the name of Jesus when he saw the mighty works wrought by its means.

14 *They sent to them Peter and John.* For some time the Jerusalem apostles exercised general supervision over the widespread work of evangelization. **15** *Prayed for them that they might receive the Holy Spirit.* Evidently at their baptism there had been no immediately discernible manifestation of the coming of the Spirit—which is what Luke means by saying **16** *it had not yet fallen on any of them.* But they *had only been baptized in the name of the Lord Jesus* (lit. 'into the name of the Lord Jesus'), an expression found in Acts only here and at 19:5. The person so baptized bears public witness that he has passed into Christ's ownership. **17** *Then they laid their hands on them and they received the Holy Spirit.* It has frequently been held that this action was apostolic confirmation, considered as a sacramental act, distinct from baptism, in which the gift of the Spirit is bestowed. But the evidence of the NT is against this interpretation; Paul, *e.g.*, takes it for granted that all baptized believers (in other words, all believers) have the Spirit of God (*cf.* Rom. 5:5; 8:9; 1 Cor. 12:13). Not until the rite of Christian initiation itself became divided was any separation between baptism and confirmation envisaged. On this occasion we probably have an act of recognition and incorporation of the new community of Samaritan believers into the larger community of the apostolic church, the imposition of apostolic hands being an act of fellowship, which was attended by manifestations of the Holy Spirit in the new converts. (See G. W. H.

Lampe, *The Seal of the Spirit*, 1952, pp. 64ff.)
18 *He offered them money.* He thereby gave the
term 'simony' to the ecclesiastical vocabulary.
23 *The gall of bitterness*; probably a Semitizing
genitive, meaning 'bitter gall'; quoted from Dt.
29:18 (*cf.* Heb. 12:15). *The bond of iniquity*; *cf.*
Is. 58:6. 24 *Come upon me.* The 'western' text
adds 'who never stopped weeping copiously',
an adjectival clause which is tacked on awkwardly
at the end of the sentence instead of coming
immediately after its antecedent 'Simon'. Simon
figures in later Christian literature as the father
of all heresies.

8:26–40 Philip and the Ethiopian chamberlain

Once the work in Samaria was well established,
Philip was sent by the Holy Spirit to make contact with the treasurer of the kingdom of Ethiopia
(Nubia). He had been on pilgrimage to Jerusalem,
and was now returning south in his chariot. His
perplexed reading of the great prophecy of the
suffering Servant in Isaiah gave Philip the opportunity of preaching Jesus to him from this very
passage—most appropriately, because this, more
than any other part of the OT, colours our
Lord's language about His life mission, as well
as the language of a number of the NT writers.
When this new convert had been sent on his way
rejoicing, Philip continued his northward journey
along the coast road to Caesarea.

26 *But an angel of the Lord said to Philip.*
The language of this section is curiously reminiscent in places of the Elijah and Elisha
narratives of the OT. *Gaza.* Old Gaza had lain
deserted since its destruction in 93 BC; New
Gaza, built in 57 BC, was by the sea, a little south
of the old city. 27 *Candace the queen of the
Ethiopians.* The kingdom of Ethiopia lay on
the Nile between Aswan and Khartoum; its
capital was Meroe. The king was deified as child
of the sun-god and regarded as too holy for
secular functions; these were discharged for
him by his mother, who bore the dynastic title
Candace. Had come to Jerusalem to worship;
probably as a 'God-fearer' (see on 10:2 below).
30 *Heard him reading Isaiah the prophet.* The
ancients habitually read aloud. 32 *The passage
of the scripture which he was reading was this.*
The words are from Is. 53:7, 8, in the LXX (this
explains the differences between the rendering
here and in the English OT, which represents the
MT). He had no doubt procured a scroll of
Isaiah in Greek in Jerusalem. 34 *About whom,
pray, does the prophet say this, about himself
or about some one else?* The answers that have
been given to this question throughout the
centuries would fill a volume. 35 Yet no answer
is so satisfying as that which Philip gave when,
*beginning with this scripture, he told him the
good news of Jesus.* 36 *What is to prevent my
being baptized?* Philip's stipulation and the
eunuch's response (appearing in v. 37 in AV) do
not form part of the original text (they first
appear in the 'western' recension); but they do
reflect early Christian baptismal procedure.

39 *The Spirit of the Lord caught up Philip.* The
'western' text has: 'the Spirit of the Lord fell
upon the eunuch, and the angel of the Lord
caught away Philip'. But even if the best attested
text does not explicitly speak of the eunuch's
receiving the Spirit, this is probably implicit in
the statement that he *went on his way rejoicing.*
40 *Azotus.* The OT Ashdod, 20 miles N of Gaza.
Till he came to Caesarea. The seaport on the
Mediterranean coast, *c.* 50 miles N of Ashdod,
built by Herod the Great *c.* 13 BC. Here Philip
appears to have settled down and brought up a
family (*cf.* 21:8).

9:1–31 Conversion of Saul of Tarsus

The ringleader of the campaign of repression
which followed Stephen's death was Saul of
Tarsus, one of the greatest men of all time.
Although born a Roman citizen in the Greek
city of Tarsus in Asia Minor, he was brought
up by his Jewish parents not as a Hellenist but
as 'a Hebrew born of Hebrews' (Phil. 3:5),
and was educated in Jerusalem at the feet of
Gamaliel, the great leader of the Pharisees
whom we have already met as a counsellor of
moderation. The pupil showed little of his
teacher's moderation. As a Jew of Cilicia, he
may well have attended the synagogue where
Stephen debated, and heard those arguments
which were bound to undermine the whole
religious structure of Judaism. Saul's mind, as
penetrating as Stephen's, saw the irreconcila-
bility of the old order and the new, and he set
out on his career as a vigorous champion of the
ancestral traditions of his people, resolved to
stamp out the revolutionary movement.

At Stephen's martyrdom he played a responsible part (see on 7:58), and thereafter, wherever the believers fled in their dispersion, he
pursued them, not only in Palestine itself, but
even to Damascus. To the synagogues of that
city he carried a letter from the high priest,
authorizing him to arrest and bring to Jerusalem
any who might have sought refuge in the ancient
Syrian city. The writ of the high priest was
respected in the synagogues of the Empire, and
his authority in religious matters was upheld by
the Roman power. It was on his journey to
Damascus that Saul was confronted by the
vision of the risen Christ which wrought such a
revolution in his life, and made him thenceforward the most zealous champion of the faith he
had hitherto sought to destroy. 'The conversion
and apostleship of St. Paul alone,' in the view
of the 18th-century statesman George, Lord
Lyttelton, 'duly considered, was of itself a
demonstration sufficient to prove Christianity to
be a divine revelation.' Luke realized the importance of Paul's conversion in the history of
salvation for, despite his limited space, he relates
it in some detail three times, once in the third
person (ch. 9), and twice as narrated by Paul
himself (ch. 22 and 26).

The way was prepared for Paul's entertain-
ment by Christians in Damascus by the Lord's

appearing to Ananias. The Lord's words to him describing Paul as *a chosen instrument* have stuck to Paul ever since. In later years he recognized that, without his knowing it, he had been set apart by God for the work of the gospel even before his birth (Gal. 1:15f.; Rom. 1:1). Jewish by birth and education, he was also a Roman citizen, and his privileges as such stood him in good stead more than once. While the influence of the educational atmosphere of his native Tarsus upon him has often been exaggerated, it need not be minimized to the point of vanishing altogether (see on 22:3).

His conversion and baptism were immediately followed by his bold proclamation of Jesus as the Son of God in those very Damascus synagogues to which he had been accredited by the high priest for a very different purpose. But his activities there and in the neighbouring territory of the Nabataean king Aretas IV (the 'Arabia' of Gal. 1:17) roused so much opposition that at last he had to be smuggled out of a city which had become too hot for him to stay in.

On his return to Jerusalem in the third year from his conversion, he spent a fortnight with Peter, and also met James the Lord's brother (Gal. 1:18f.). His contact with these and other Christians was facilitated by Barnabas, who presumably knew him before and could vouch for his sincerity. But when he began to do in the Jerusalem synagogues what he had done at Damascus, he had again to be got away for his own safety, and was escorted to the coast and shipped off to Tarsus; and then, says Luke, *the church . . . had peace* (9:31). The first wave of persecution seems to have died down with the conversion of the leading persecutor.

1 *The high priest.* Still, probably, Caiaphas. **2** *If he found any belonging to the Way.* 'The Way' was a primitive Jewish-Christian idiom denoting Christianity (*cf.* 19:9, 23; 22:4; 24:14, 22). It was probably in the main refugees from Judea, rather than native Damascene believers like Ananias, that Saul went to arrest. The evidence of the 'Damascus Document', first discovered in the synagogue *genizah* of Old Cairo early in the present century, suggests that a branch of the Qumran community lived in Damascus; it would be interesting to know what contact, if any, there was between this group and the Damascene disciples of whom Ananias was one. **7** *Hearing the voice*; *i.e.* hearing Paul's voice: 'but they did not hear the voice of the one who was speaking to me', he says in 22:9. **10** *Ananias.* His character is described by Paul in 22:12. He appears to have been a native of Damascus, who knew of the outbreak of persecution in Jerusalem only by hearsay (v. 13). We have no account of the establishment of Christianity in Damascus; it may have been carried there from Galilee. **11** *The street called Straight*; still called the Darb al-Mustaqim. **12** *He has seen.* We can distinguish three early visions of Paul: on the way to Damascus (vv. 4ff.); in the house of Judas (v. 12); and on his return to Jerusalem (22:17ff.).

14 *From the chief priests.* See on 4:6 above. *All who call upon thy name*; *i.e.* those who invoked Jesus as Lord (*cf.* 2:21). **16** *How much he must suffer for the sake of my name.* He was to endure many times over what he had made others endure, and that for the sake of the same name. But in the kingdom of Christ suffering for the King is a sure sign of His favour and an earnest of His reward. **17** *Laying his hands on him* not only as a token of fellowship, greeting him as a fellow-Christian (*Brother Saul*), but also because Ananias, albeit a 'private' Christian, was acting for the time being as the Lord's duly appointed commissioner to Saul. *Be filled with the Holy Spirit.* Such filling was necessary for the prophetic ministry described in v. 15; the sequel (vv. 20–22) makes it plain that the particular manifestation of the Spirit shown in Saul was the power of his missionary preaching. **18** *Something like scales*; better, 'a scaly (or flaky) substance'. *He rose and was baptized.* We are probably to infer that (unlike the Samaritans in 8:16) Saul had received the Holy Spirit before he was actually baptized.

19 *For several days he was . . . at Damascus.* Whether this was before or after his visit to Arabia (the Nabataean kingdom) mentioned in Gal. 1:17 cannot be ascertained. Luke's chronological indications here are vague; we know from Gal. 1:18 that the events of vv. 26ff. took place in the third year after Paul's conversion. **20** *He is the Son of God.* It is significant that the only occurrence of this title in Acts should be in the report of Saul's first preaching. While the divine Sonship of Messiah is a corollary of Ps. 2:7, Paul's use of the title here probably marks an advance on the designation of Jesus as Lord and Messiah hitherto (*e.g.* 2:36). **22** *Proving.* The Greek word (*symbibazō*) probably suggests that his method of proof was to place the prophetic Scriptures alongside the events which fulfilled them. **23** *The Jews plotted to kill him.* According to Paul himself, in 2 Cor. 11:32, 'the governor under King Aretas guarded the city of Damascus in order to seize me'. The leaders of the local Jewish community appear to have made common cause with the representative of Aretas. **27** *Brought him to the apostles.* The term *apostles* is used in a wider sense here. According to Gal. 1:18, 19, the only apostles (in a stricter sense) whom he saw were Peter and James the Lord's brother. **29** *Disputed against the Hellenists*; no doubt in the very synagogue or synagogues which had witnessed Stephen's similar activity. **31** *So the church throughout all Judea and Galilee and Samaria had peace.* This was the church of Jerusalem, now in dispersion because of the recent persecution.

9:32 – 12:24 ACTS OF PETER: THE GENTILES BROUGHT IN

9:32–43 Peter in Western Palestine

A sign of the peace (v. 31) is seen in Peter's evangelization of the semi-Gentile territory in the Plain of Sharon and his visits to Lydda and Joppa, in both of which he performed miracles of healing.

32 *The saints that lived at Lydda. Lydda* is modern Lod. Obviously there were Christians at Lydda and Joppa before Peter visited these places (*cf.* v. 36). **34** *Make your bed.* The Greek might alternatively mean 'get ready to eat'; this would accord with the interest which Luke and other NT writers elsewhere show in the nourishment of convalescents. **35** *Sharon*; the coastal plain. **36** *Tabitha*; Aramaic for *Gazelle*; in Greek, *Dorcas*. **37** *When they had washed.* A reference to the Jewish custom of 'purification of the dead'. **39** *Showing coats and garments.* The middle voice of the Greek verb indicates that they were wearing them at the time. **43** *He stayed . . . with one Simon, a tanner.* Simon lived by the shore (10:6), perhaps because he required sea-water for his tanning, and Peter, as a fisherman, might naturally choose a lodging in this part of the town. But that he lodged with a man who followed the 'unclean' occupation of a tanner may suggest that he already enjoyed some sense of emancipation from ceremonial convention.

10:1–48 Peter and Cornelius

A great step forward had still to be taken, and it was at Joppa that Peter learned the lesson that nothing cleansed by God should be called common or unclean. Was it in the light of this lesson that he added to our Lord's teaching on meats the comment, 'Thus he declared all foods clean', reported in Mk. 7:19? At any rate, having learned this lesson, he had immediately to put it into practice when he was invited to visit the Roman centurion Cornelius at Caesarea and make known the good news to him and his household. This is another episode to which Luke obviously attached high importance, for, after telling it in ch. 10, he repeats it in ch. 11, where Peter himself tells the story, and reverts to it in ch. 15, again in the mouth of Peter.

Cornelius as well as Peter had been divinely prepared for the new move. Cornelius, a member of the class referred to by Luke as 'God-fearers', who attached themselves to the spiritual and monotheistic Jewish worship in the synagogues without becoming converts to Judaism, was instructed in a vision to send for Peter. When Peter entered his house and began to proclaim the divine action in the cross and resurrection of Christ, a further proof of divine guidance was afforded in the sudden possession of the Gentile household by the Holy Spirit, manifested by the same outward signs as on the Day of Pentecost. There was this difference: at Pentecost those who were baptized received the Spirit; now Cornelius and his family were baptized because they had already received the Spirit. Without this obvious mark of God's favour, Peter might have hesitated to go so far as to baptize them.

1 *A centurion of what was known as the Italian Cohort.* A centurion had the status of a non-commissioned officer with the responsibility of a captain. Centurions were the backbone of the Roman army; it is striking that something is recorded to the credit of all the centurions mentioned in the NT. *The Italian Cohort* (Gk. *speira*) may be identical with the 'second Italian cohort of Roman citizens' for which there is inscriptional evidence in Syria in AD 69. **2** *A devout man who feared God*; *i.e.* a 'God-fearer', one of a class of Gentiles who gave general adherence to the Jewish faith, worship and practice without submitting to circumcision and becoming full proselytes. **4** *Have ascended as a memorial.* The verb 'have ascended' may suggest the burnt-offering (Heb. *'ôlāh*, lit. 'ascending'). The Greek word *mnēmosynon*, rendered 'memorial', is used in Lv. 2:2ff., LXX, for that part of the meal-offering which was presented to God. For the sacrificial character of such conduct as that of Cornelius *cf.* Ps. 141:2; Phil. 4:18; Heb. 13:15, 16.

9 *About the sixth hour*; *i.e.* midday. **10** *Trance*, or 'ecstasy' (Gk. *ekstasis*); a state in which a man, so to speak, 'stands outside' himself. **11** *Something* (lit. 'a certain object'); the Greek word (*skeuos*) is quite indefinite. *A great sheet* was suggested to Peter's subconscious mind possibly by the awning spread over the roof or a sail on the western horizon. *Four corners.* The Greek word *archē*, here rendered 'corner' (lit. 'beginning'), was used in medical parlance for the end of a bandage, and in nautical language in the sense of 'rope'. **12** *All kinds of animals and reptiles and birds of the air.* For the threefold division of the animal world *cf.* Gn. 6:20. **14** *No, Lord . . .* ; *cf.* Ezekiel's protest (Ezk. 4:14). The Jewish food laws were based on Lv. 11. These laws, in their ceremonial application, were now abrogated explicitly as they had been implicitly in Jesus' teaching in Mk. 7:14ff.

19 *The Spirit said to him.* The Spirit of inner prophetic monition. **20** *I have sent them.* This raises a question about the relation between the Spirit now speaking within Peter and the apparently external angelic manifestation to Cornelius. **22** *Was directed*; lit. 'received an oracular communication' (Gk. *chrēmatizō*). **23** *Some of the brethren from Joppa.* They were six in number (11:12). **25** *When Peter. . . .* The 'western' text amplifies this verse: 'And as Peter was drawing near to Caesarea, one of the servants ran ahead and announced that he had arrived. Then Cornelius ran out and met him. . . .' *Worshipped him*, or 'paid homage to him' (Gk. *proskyneō*), does not necessarily connote divine honours. **30** *Four days ago*; by inclusive reckoning. On day one Cornelius received his vision; on day two Peter received his, and Cornelius's messengers came to him; on day three Peter and the others set out from Joppa; on day four they arrived at Caesarea. **33** *You have been kind enough to come*; an expression of gratitude; *i.e.* 'Thank you for coming'.

34 *God shows no partiality.* Cf. Dt. 10:17; Rom. 2:11; Eph. 6:9; Col. 3:25. Divine election does not imply favouritism; God's grace extends to Gentiles as freely as to Jews. To us this is a truism, but it was a revolutionary thought to Peter. **36** *The word which he sent to Israel.* From here to the end of v. 43 we have the fullest summary of the apostolic message in Acts. Its scope extends from the ministry of John the Baptist to the resurrection, and looks on to the judgment. The present summary bears the marks of fairly literal translation from Aramaic. **37** *Throughout all Judea*; here used in the wider sense of Palestine (*cf.* Lk. 4:44, RV mg.). **38** *God anointed Jesus of Nazareth with the Holy Spirit.* Anointed carries with it the more formal idea 'made Messiah'; the occasion intended is our Lord's baptism, when the Spirit descended on Him (Lk. 3:21f.). *Cf.* Is. 61:1, quoted in Lk. 4:18. **39** *In the country of the Jews*; *i.e.* all Palestine, like 'Judea' in v. 37. **41** *Who ate and drank with him.* This emphasized the reality of His bodily resurrection. *Cf.* Lk. 24:41, 43 (and see on Acts 1:4). **42** *Ordained by God to be judge of the living and the dead.* This goes back to the 'Son of man' vision of Dn. 7:9ff. **43** *Forgiveness of sins.* The chief OT prophecy promising remission of sins through Christ is Is. 53.

44 *The Holy Spirit fell on all who heard the word.* As Peter himself suggests in v. 47 (*cf.* 11:15), this event reproduced the descent of the Spirit on the original band of disciples in Acts 2. The occasion has been well described as 'the Pentecost of the Gentile world'. No routine procedure would have availed for so unprecedented a situation as the acceptance of the gospel by Gentiles; an unmediated act of God was required. **46** *Extolling God*; *cf.* 2:11, 'telling . . . the mighty works of God'. **48** *He commanded them to be baptized in the name of Jesus Christ*; the same expression as in 2:38. It is nowhere hinted that anything was said to these Gentiles about the necessity, or even the desirability, of circumcision.

11:1-18 The other apostles approve Peter's action

The news travelled quickly to Jerusalem, and when Peter arrived back there he found himself obliged to answer the criticisms of his fellow-apostles. Stephen's activity had been bad enough, in the eyes of men who, while followers of Jesus, were still orthodox Jews; but that the prince of the apostles himself should so outrage sacred convention was too bad altogether. The apostles apparently still enjoyed a measure of popular favour, but they were likely to lose it, too, if it became known that their leader had fraternized with the uncircumcised. It is probably more than a coincidence that, not long after this, Herod Agrippa I made a bid for popularity by laying violent hands on two of the apostles, and also that very soon James, the Lord's brother, appears as leader of the Jerusalem church.

However, when Peter told of his experience of the Lord's guidance, and of the outpouring of the Holy Spirit in the house of Cornelius, asking, *Who was I that I could withstand God?*, the apostles were convinced that he had acted rightly and praised God for His grace to Gentiles.

2 *The circumcision party.* The more 'rigorist' party in the Jerusalem church is probably intended here, although the same phrase in 10:45 (lit. 'those of the circumcision') means simply Jewish Christians. **14** *By which you will be saved, you and all your household.* Additional to the version in 10:22. The 'household' included not only the family in the modern sense, but all who were under the authority of the head of the house—slaves, attendants, and so forth. *Cf.* 16:15, 31ff.; 18:8. **16** *John baptized with water. . . .* The words of the Lord in 1:5. **18** *Then to the Gentiles*; better, 'even to the Gentiles' (in Jewish eyes, the most astounding token of divine grace).

11:19-30 The first Gentile church

The other apostles might well approve Peter's action, for about the same time there took place a great work with far-reaching results at Antioch, in the north of Syria, to which some Hellenistic Jews had made their way in the course of the dispersion which followed Stephen's death. The atmosphere of Antioch was as different as could be from that of Jerusalem. In this busy northern capital, a commercial city where European and Asiatic met, where Greek civilization touched the Syrian desert, men naturally got their rough corners rubbed off, and religious differences which loomed so large in Judea began to look far less important. It was here, then, that some of these Hellenists, not content with preaching Jesus in the synagogues to their fellow-Hellenists, began to preach Him to Gentile Greeks as well, with the result that a great number of these embraced the new faith, so that the second Christian church to be founded had a considerable Gentile element, and the disciples first received the name 'Christians' there.

When news of this innovation reached Jerusalem, the apostles, wishing to look into it, sent just the right man for the job, Barnabas, 'the son of encouragement' (see 4:36). He went to Antioch, and, instead of being scandalized at the mingling of Jew and Gentile, he rejoiced at so astounding a token of God's grace, settled down among them, and did all he could to help this new church and build it up. But the work grew apace, and Barnabas, casting about in his mind for a suitable helper, bethought himself of Saul, who had been for some years now in Tarsus and the surrounding regions. So he went and fetched Saul, and made him his fellow-worker, and both of them continued to promote the great work which God had inaugurated in Antioch.

It was about this time that the prophet Agabus announced in the church at Antioch that great and widespread dearth was to be expected. In consequence of this announcement Barnabas and Saul were sent to Jerusalem by the Antioch church, bearing to the mother church the proceeds of a special collection which the daughter church had made to help the Palestinian Christians in their distress. The Jerusalem church seems to have been afflicted with chronic poverty; later on we find Paul organizing collections in the Gentile churches founded by him for its relief. It was possibly during this famine-relief visit of Barnabas and Saul that the events of Gal. 2:1-10 took place; the 'revelation' according to which they went up (Gal. 2:2) might then be the prophecy of Agabus (Acts 11:28), and the words of Gal. 2:10 are specially applicable to this visit: 'They would have us remember the poor, which very thing I was eager to do.'

19 *Now those who were scattered.* These words take us back to the same point of departure as we have in 8:4, which begins with the same expression. *Phoenicia; i.e.* Tyre, Sidon, *etc.; cf.* 21:3ff.; 27:3. **20** *Antioch.* The former capital of the Seleucid kingdom, now the seat of government of the Roman province of Syria, and the third largest city in the world (Rome and Alexandria being first and second). *Spoke to the Greeks.* Whether the true reading here be 'Greeks' (Gk. *Hellēnes*) or 'Grecians' (AV), *i.e.* Hellenists, the meaning certainly is that Greek-speaking Gentiles were now evangelized. **22** *They sent Barnabas,* just as they sent Peter and John to Samaria (8:14). **25** *So Barnabas went to Tarsus to look for Saul.* Saul had spent the time since 9:30 in various parts of the united province of Syria-Cilicia, in which Tarsus and Antioch were both situated (Gal. 1:21). **26** *And in Antioch the disciples were for the first time called Christians;* lit. 'they did business (Gk. *chrēmatizō*) under the name of Christians', *i.e.* became commonly known by this name. Only from Gentiles could they have received this name (meaning 'Christ's people'), for 'Christ' was a mere personal name in Gentile ears, whereas to Jews it meant 'Messiah' and they would not have called the followers of Jesus 'Messiah's people'.

27 *In these days; i.e.* during the year that Barnabas and Saul spent in Antioch (v. 26). *From Jerusalem to Antioch.* The 'western' text goes on: 'and there was much rejoicing; and when we were gathered together, one of them ...' —thus providing an additional 'we' section which is our earliest witness for the tradition of Luke's Antiochene origin. **28** *Agabus.* He reappears in 21:10 in a 'we' section of Acts. *Over all the world; i.e.* the Roman world. *In the days of Claudius.* Claudius was Emperor from AD 41 to 54. Suetonius confirms that his reign was marked by constant seasons of unfruitfulness. Josephus tells us that about the year 46 Palestine was hard hit by famine, and that the Jewish queen-mother of Adiabene, in North-eastern Mesopotamia, bought corn in Egypt and figs in Cyprus to relieve the necessities of the Palestinian Jews. It is not clear how long before the famine Agabus's prediction was made. Probably the Antiochene Christians set aside money systematically until the time of need actually came, and then sent Barnabas and Saul as their delegates to take the accumulated sum to the Christians at Jerusalem.

12:1-24 Herod Agrippa and the church

A new wave of persecution broke over the Jerusalem church, and this time the apostles, far from being immune, were the chief object of attack. Herod Agrippa I, the grandson of Herod the Great, had received a large grant of territory in and near Palestine from his lifelong friend the Emperor Gaius, commonly called Caligula (37-41), together with the title of king; and Claudius (41-54) added to that territory the regions of Judea and Samaria. During his brief reign over Judea (41-44), Herod, despite his faults, proved a studious patron of the Jewish faith, and maintained friendly relations with the religious leaders of the people. It is said that on one occasion, when reading the law at the Feast of Tabernacles, he burst into tears as he read Dt. 17:15 ('one from among your brethren you shall set as king over you; you may not put a foreigner over you, who is not your brother'), for he remembered the Edomite origin of the Herod family; but the populace cried out: 'Be not distressed; you are our brother!'

His execution of James the Zebedean, and his arrest of Peter, are related here. The words, *he saw that it pleased the Jews,* are significant, for reasons already suggested (see introduction to 11:1-18). The idea that John suffered martyrdom at the same time as James rests on the flimsiest foundations, in spite of the vigour with which it has sometimes been pressed. Peter's escape from prison, and his unexpected visit to the house of Mary, where the believers were praying for him, are narrated with a masterly vividness.

Soon after this, Herod's death took place under circumstances of dramatic impressiveness which are related by both Luke and Josephus. The two historians differ in details, but agree on the main features; as for their differences, we may quote the German historian Eduard Meyer: 'In outline, in date, and in the general conception, both accounts are in full agreement. By its very interesting details, which are by no means to be explained as due to a "tendency" or popular tradition, Luke's account affords a guarantee that it is at least as reliable as that of Josephus.'

3 *This was during the days of Unleavened Bread.* The days of Unleavened Bread commenced on Passover eve, Nisan 14, and lasted till Nisan 21 (*cf.* 20:6). Nisan 14 fell in that year (AD 44) on May 1—an unusually late date owing to the intercalation of a second month of Adar that year from March 19 to April 17 inclusive. **4** *Four squads of soldiers.* One squad for each watch of the night. Peter was in the custody of four soldiers at a time, of whom two were probably on guard at either side of him, and two at the door. *After the Passover.* The Passover strictly speaking was celebrated on Nisan 14, but the term was sometimes used in a more general sense, to cover the Festival of Unleavened Bread as well (*cf.* Lk. 22:1); that is the sense here. **7** *And behold, an angel of the Lord appeared*; *cf.* v. 10. Probably the most remarkable modern parallel to Peter's release is the story of Sadhu Sundar Singh's mysterious release from a well in which he was locked by a Tibetan ruler (told by Streeter and Appasamy, *The Sadhu*, pp. 30f.). But 'Peter thought it was all a vision until he found himself safe and sound. The Sadhu thought the rescuer was a man until he disappeared' (L. E. Browne). **10** *When they had passed the first and the second guard, they came to the iron gate leading into the city.* 'There were obviously three gates and three wards to pass (Peter was allowed to pass the first and the second, being taken presumably as a servant; but no servant would be expected to pass beyond the outermost ward at night, and a different course was needed there)' (Ramsay). So the street-gate opened *of its own accord* (lit. 'automatically'; Gk. *automatē*); how, we are not told. But the whole inserted description reflects the account of an eyewitness, including the 'western' addition 'and went down the seven steps' inserted after *they went out.* Peter was probably imprisoned in the fortress Antonia, NW of the Temple area. **12** *He went to the house of Mary, the mother of John whose other name was Mark.* This house appears to have served as a meeting-place for one group of Jerusalem Christians; it is an attractive conjecture that it was the house in which the Last Supper was held. The group associated with James the Lord's brother seems to have had another meeting-place (v. 17). **15** *It is his angel!*; *i.e.* his guardian angel or spirit counterpart, capable of assuming his appearance and of being mistaken for him. The Iranian *fravashi* conception is a parallel. *Cf.* also the reference to children's angels who behold the face of God (Mt. 18:10). **17** *Motioning to them with his hand to be silent*; another eyewitness touch. *Tell this to James and to the brethren.* Evidently by this time James the Lord's brother had attained a special status in the Jerusalem church (*cf.* 15:13ff.; 21:18). *Went to another place.* This may simply mean that he went into hiding, 'went underground'. He told nobody at the time where he was going, and Luke could not find out in later years where he had actually gone. **19** *That they should be put to death*; lit. 'led off' (presumably to execution). Herod probably suspected them of collusion in a plot to rescue Peter. **20** *Their country depended on the king's country for food.* The Phoenician seaboard depended on Galilee for its food supply, as in the days of Hiram and Solomon (1 Ki. 5:9ff.). **21** *On an appointed day.* Josephus says it was a festival in honour of the Emperor Claudius (*Ant.* xix. 8. 2), possibly on his birthday, August 1. This might well have afforded an occasion for public reconciliation between Herod Agrippa and his Phoenician neighbours. *Herod put on his royal robes.* 'He put on a robe made of silver throughout, of marvellous weaving' (Josephus). **22** *The people* (Gk. *dēmos*); *i.e.* the city populace

of Caesarea. *The voice of a god, and not of man!* According to Josephus, his flatterers, addressing him as a god, said: 'Be gracious to us: hitherto we have reverenced you as a man, but henceforth we acknowledge you to be more than mortal.' **23** *An angel of the Lord smote him.* For this OT expression *cf.* 2 Ki. 19:35. *Because he did not give God the glory.* He accepted the divine honours from his flatterers, instead of ascribing them to God. *He was eaten by worms.* A medical colleague diagnoses his malady as a hydatid cyst. *And died*; five days later, at the age of fifty-four. The persecutor dies; **24** the cause he persecuted survives in increasing vigour.

12:25 – 16:5 ANTIOCH BECOMES A MISSIONARY CHURCH

12:25 – 13:12 The evangelization of Cyprus

On the return of Barnabas and Saul from Jerusalem to Antioch, they took with them Barnabas's cousin John Mark, and continued for some time to minister to the church as had been their custom. In addition to Barnabas and Saul, the most gifted teachers of that church, there were three others, whose identity opens up fascinating vistas (see on 13:1).

But the Holy Spirit had further work for the Antioch church to do, and He called upon them to release Barnabas and Saul for the special work to which He had called them. It is worth noticing that it was the two ablest ministers of the church who were thus set apart for what we should call 'foreign missions', though such an expression is not really applicable to a time when almost all the civilized world was politically united under Rome.

Acquiescing in the divine will thus expressed, the church sent forth the two men, expressing their fellowship with them by the imposition of hands. Having set sail from Seleucia, the port of

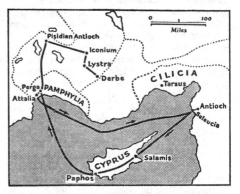

PAUL'S FIRST MISSIONARY JOURNEY

Antioch, with Mark in attendance on them, they landed in Cyprus, Barnabas's native island, and traversed it from east to west. When they came to Paphos, the western capital, there occurred a passage-of-arms between Paul and the magician

Bar-Jesus, who belonged to the entourage of Sergius Paulus, the proconsul of the province. Bar-Jesus was probably afraid that, if Sergius paid too much attention to the missionaries, his own days as court magician would be numbered. Ancient commentators delighted to point out that the magician's temporary blinding was intended by Paul to have the same effect as his own three days' blindness at Damascus had. Ramsay argues that some members of Sergius's family were Christians in later generations.

12:25 *Barnabas and Saul returned from Jerusalem; i.e.* to Antioch. A problem is presented by the strong early attestation of the reading '*to* Jerusalem'. **13:1** *Symeon who was called Niger; i.e.* 'the Black'. It is tempting to identify him with Simon of Cyrene (Mk. 15:21; Lk. 23:26); his wife might in that case be the mother of Rufus who showed herself a mother to Paul (Rom. 16:13). *Lucius of Cyrene.* There is no evidence for associating him with Lucius of Rom. 16:21 or with Luke the Evangelist, although the latter identification was made in antiquity. *Manaen a member of the court of Herod the tetrarch*; lit. 'foster-brother (Gk. *syntrophos*) of Herod' (*i.e.* Herod Antipas; see on 4:27). This Manaen was possibly the grandson of another Manaen, an Essene mentioned by Josephus as a favourite of Herod the Great. It was perhaps from him that Luke received much of his special information about the family of the Herods. **2** *The Holy Spirit said*; probably through one of the prophets. **5** *Salamis*. On the E coast of Cyprus, the chief town of the island, and the seat of government of the eastern half. *They had John to assist them*; lit. 'as their attendant' (Gk. *hypēretēs*). John Mark was probably one of the 'ministers (Gk. *hypēretai*) of the word' in Lk. 1:2; his first-hand acquaintance with certain phases of the gospel story would be useful to the missionaries. **7** *The proconsul*. The Romans had annexed Cyprus in 57 BC: it was a senatorial province from 22 BC onwards. *Sergius Paulus*. Probably identical with a man of the same name who appears on a Roman inscription as a curator of the Tiber earlier in Claudius's reign. **8** *Elymas the magician (for that is the meaning of his name)*. This does not mean that 'Elymas' is equivalent to 'Bar-Jesus', but that Elymas, being a Semitic word, means 'magician' (Gk. *magos*). **9** *Saul, who is also called Paul*. From this point the apostle is regularly given his Roman cognomen Paul (Lat. *Paullus*) instead of his Hebrew birth-name, Saul, the former being more appropriate when the story is moving into a predominantly Gentile environment. **12** *The proconsul believed, . . . for he was astonished at the teaching of the Lord*. It has been suggested that the proconsul's courtesy was mistaken for conversion, but a matter-of-fact Roman official was the very man to be convinced by the act of power which accompanied the teaching (*cf.* Lk. 4:32).

13:13-41 Paul's address at Pisidian Antioch

From Cyprus the company sailed across to Asia Minor, where Mark left them and returned to Jerusalem. His reasons are not given; perhaps he resented the way in which his cousin Barnabas was falling into second place. When they set out from Antioch, it was *Barnabas and Saul* (v. 2); when they left Cyprus, it was *Paul and his company* (v. 13). Whatever his reason, Mark went back; Barnabas himself seems not to have minded; he was an outstanding example of the old saying:

It takes more grace than I can tell
To play the second fiddle well.

Barnabas and Paul, left alone, now struck up country (Ramsay thought this was because Paul had caught malaria in the low-lying country near the coast, though this is only speculative). They arrived at Pisidian Antioch, a Roman colony in the province of Galatia, and stayed there some time. Roman colonies played an important part in Paul's plan of campaign in all his missionary journeys. With true strategic instinct he picked out for intensive evangelization the important points along the main highways between Jerusalem and Rome. Another constant feature of his method is seen at Pisidian Antioch, where they tackled the local Jewish synagogue first. 'To the Jew first' was Paul's constant programme everywhere.

On the first sabbath after arriving at Pisidian Antioch they went into the synagogue; and after the reading of the law and the prophets the rulers of the synagogue invited the strangers to pass on any word of exhortation they might have for the company. Paul stood up to speak, and the summary of his address is given at some length, probably to show the sort of synagogue sermon he was accustomed to preach throughout the Empire. He narrated the deliverance wrought by God for the nation of Israel at the Exodus, and outlined their history from Moses to David. Then he passed from David to the promised Messiah of David's seed, and declared that the promised Messiah had appeared in their day in the Person of Jesus, whose death and well-attested resurrection proved Him to be the Messiah foretold in Hebrew Scripture. Like Peter at Pentecost, he argued that the words of Ps. 16:10, *Thou wilt not let thy Holy One see corruption*, could not apply to David himself, who did 'see corruption', but to the descendant of David who had in these last days, as a matter of evidence, risen from the dead. The sermon ended with an application to the present situation of the warning of the prophet Habakkuk on the eve of the Chaldean invasion.

14 *Antioch of Pisidia*. It was not 'in' (AV) but near the border of Pisidia (one of the regions of the province of Galatia); render 'Pisidian Antioch'. **15** *After the reading of the law and the prophets*. The law was read through according to a fixed lectionary; readings were selected from the prophets with some resemblance or relation to the preceding lesson from the law. *The rulers of the synagogue*. These made arrangements for public worship, and invited suitable members of the congregation to read the lessons and give the address.

16 *Men of Israel, and you that fear God.* These words indicate the two elements in the congregation, the Jews and the Gentile 'God-fearers' (see on 10:2). **18** *He bore with them.* Some texts, with a change of one letter in the Greek verb thus translated, read 'he carried them like a nurse' (*cf.* Dt. 1:31). **19** *Seven nations.* See Dt. 7:1. **20** *For about four hundred and fifty years.* This time-note probably denotes the interval between the beginning of the patriarchal sojourning and the occupation of the land. **22** *I have found in David . . .* ; quoted from Ps. 89:20 and 1 Sa. 13:14. The narrative thus far covers the scope of the recurring OT confession of faith or rehearsal of God's gracious dealings with His people: *cf.* Dt. 26:5–9; Ps. 78. **24–31** contain an outline of the apostolic preaching similar to that in 10:36–43. **25** *I am not he*; *i.e.* the Messiah. *Cf.* Jn. 1:20, 21. **29** *They took him down*; a generalizing plural. In the Gospels Joseph of Arimathea and Nicodemus are said to have done this. **33** *To us their children.* Read 'to us and to our children' (F. H. Chase). *By raising Jesus.* The reference here is to God's raising up Jesus as Messiah in the sense in which He *raised up* David as king (v. 22; *cf.* 3:26; 5:30); contrast v. 34, where the resurrection is in view: *he raised him from the dead. Thou art my Son, today I have begotten thee*; quoted from Ps. 2:7. The day of the king's anointing 'was ideally the day in which he, the nation's representative, was born into a new relation of sonship towards Jehovah' (F. H. Chase); the day of Jesus' baptism is probably intended here (when He was addressed by God, 'Thou art my Son . . .'). **34** *I will give you the holy and sure blessings of David*; quoted from Is. 55:3. The 'sure mercies' (AV) promised to David find their fulfilment in Christ through His resurrection. **39** *Every one that believes is freed.* It is noteworthy that only in this sermon of Paul's does the concept of justification (Gk. *dikaioō*) find explicit expression in Acts. Faith in Christ brings a completely righteous status in God's presence, such as the law could never afford. **41** *Behold, you scoffers . . .*; *cf.* Hab. 1:5 (which itself echoes Is. 29:14). The word *scoffers* is quoted from LXX, where it replaces 'among the nations' of MT.

13:42–52 Reaction to the gospel at Pisidian Antioch

Paul's address had been listened to with special interest by the Gentiles who attended the Jewish place of worship, the 'God-fearers', as Luke calls them, who, without becoming proselytes, were attracted by the pure worship of Judaism, and even kept the Jewish law to some extent, *e.g.* by observing the sabbath. These were greatly attracted by Paul's proclamation of forgiveness of sins through Christ, and begged that he should address them again next sabbath. These people, indeed, formed the main nucleus of Paul's converts in most of the cities he went to, as he offered

them through Christ equal rights before God with Jewish believers, without the necessity of observing the Jewish ceremonial law and becoming proselytes.

Their adhesion to Paul naturally aroused the envy of the Jews of the Dispersion, who resented his drawing after him these Gentiles for whose ultimate conversion to Judaism they hoped. Such envy was speedily aroused at Pisidian Antioch, for the 'God-fearers' spread the news around, and next sabbath nearly the whole Gentile population of the colony attended the synagogue. When the Jews manifested their annoyance, Paul announced that since they reckoned themselves unworthy of the eternal life which he proclaimed, he would concentrate on the Gentiles—a process which was to be repeated in city after city. But such opposition was stirred up by the Jews that Paul and Barnabas had to leave the city, not, however, before a number of the 'God-fearers' had confessed Christ and been formed into a church.

43 *Devout converts to Judaism.* It is disputed whether actual proselytes or 'God-fearers' are meant, but if it be the latter (as is suggested by the word rendered *devout*, Gk. *sebomenoi*), then this is the only place where such people are called *converts to Judaism*, *i.e.* 'proselytes' (Gk. *prosēlytoi*), a word elsewhere used in its strict sense. **46** *Eternal life* (Gk. *zōē aiōnios*) represents the Jewish expression 'the life of the age to come (the resurrection age)', which believers in Christ receive while still living temporally in the present age. **47** *I have set you to be a light for the Gentiles. . . .* This quotation from one of the Isaianic Servant Songs (Is. 49:6) implies that the mission of the Servant of the Lord, inaugurated by Jesus, is continued by His followers. **48** *As many as were ordained to eternal life*; *cf.* v. 46. The verb rendered *ordained* may here have the sense of 'inscribed', 'enrolled'. *Cf.* Rev. 13:8; 17:8.

14:1–28 Iconium, Lystra and Derbe

The next city to be visited was Iconium where, in the same manner, the apostles entered the synagogue, and as a result of their preaching a large number both of Jews and Gentiles believed. But they were soon forced to leave Iconium in the same way as Antioch. Persecuted in one city, however, they fled to another, and betook themselves to Lystra, another Roman colony, where the healing of a lame man by Paul provoked an outburst of religious enthusiasm among the native Anatolian population. Fancying that their city was again being favoured by a visit from the supreme god and his chief herald, as it had been in mythological narrative, they prepared to pay the missionaries divine honours.

When the apostles discovered what was afoot (the use of the Lycaonian vernacular had prevented their grasping the full situation at first), they succeeded with much ado in dissuading them, and Paul improved the occasion by instructing them in the truth about the one true

Creator who had revealed Himself in creation and providence. This short summary of his speech resembles the longer account of his Athenian speech (17:22–31); and if in ch. 13 we have a sample synagogue sermon of Paul, we have here a sample sermon delivered to pagans which, when taken along with the Athenian speech of ch. 17 and the arguments of Rom. 1:18 – 2:16, shows us the proper function of 'natural revelation' as a *praeparatio evangelica*.

The visit to Lystra was abruptly cut short by a visit from Jews of Pisidian Antioch and Iconium, who stirred up a riot in which Paul, so recently acclaimed as the messenger of the Immortals, was manhandled and cast out of the city as dead. When he revived (this is narrated in such a way as to suggest miraculous intervention), they went on to the neighbouring city of Derbe. After repeating their programme there and founding another church, they made their way back through Lystra, Iconium and Pisidian Antioch, encouraging the new disciples and placing the young churches on a stable basis by the appointment of elders in each. Some modern missionaries would think it hardly wise to confer presbyteral ordination on 'native' Christians so recently converted from heathenism! But we should not overlook the pluck of the apostles in revisiting cities from which they had so lately been expelled with every circumstance of outrage and brutality. From these cities they made their way to the coast, preaching the gospel *en route*, until they reached Attalia, from which they took ship for the River Orontes and Syrian Antioch. See map on p. 988 for the complete outline of this first missionary journey.

1 *Iconium.* The modern rail-junction of Konya, then the easternmost city of the Phrygian region of the province of Galatia. *Together*; better, 'in the same way' (as in Pisidian Antioch). **2** is recast in the 'western' text: 'But the Jews' synagogue-leaders and rulers stirred up persecution against the righteous, and made the Gentiles' minds ill-disposed towards the brethren. But the Lord soon gave peace.' This recasting is no doubt intended to smooth the transition from v. 2 to v. 3, but it involves a double persecution. V. 2 is really parenthetical, preparing the way for v. 5, and *So* (*i.e.* 'So, then') at the beginning of v. 3 is resumptive. **4** *With the apostles.* Barnabas was no more one of the Twelve than Paul was, but he was probably, like him, a witness of the resurrection. **6** *Fled to Lystra and Derbe, cities of Lycaonia*; *i.e.* they crossed the regional frontier from Phrygia into Lycaonia, another region of Roman Galatia. **12** *Barnabas they called Zeus, and Paul . . . they called Hermes.* The names of the two gods given by Luke have the Greek forms; *in Lycaonian* (v. 11) native Anatolian names were no doubt used. An altar near Lystra records the dedication to Zeus of a statue of Hermes by men with Lycaonian names; another altar in the vicinity is dedicated to the 'Hearer of prayer' (presumably Zeus) and Hermes. Ovid's tale of how these two gods were

hospitably entertained unawares by Philemon and Baucis has also its setting in these parts. *Because he was the chief speaker.* Hermes had a title similar to this in the Egyptian mysteries. **13** *The priest of Zeus, whose temple was in front of the city*; *i.e.* in front of the city gate (the temple of Zeus Propolis). **15** *That you should turn from these vain things to a living God. Cf.* 1 Thes. 1:9 for very similar language. **16** *In past generations. Cf.* the reference to 'the times of ignorance' in 17:30.

19 *But Jews came there from Antioch*; *i.e.* Pisidian Antioch. *They stoned Paul*; *cf.* 2 Cor. 11:25, 'once I was stoned'. **20** *He went on with Barnabas to Derbe*; near Kerti Hüyük, *c.* 13 miles NNE of Laranda, and so *c.* 60 miles from Lystra; render therefore: 'he set out . . . for Derbe'. **22** *And saying that through many tribulations we must enter the kingdom of God*; a transition from indirect to direct speech. Here 'the kingdom of God' is something yet to be realized. **23** *In every church.* The churches planted by Paul and Barnabas during this journey are those to which the Epistle to the Galatians was later addressed. **25** *Attalia*; modern Antalya, at the mouth of the Cataractes; it was the chief port of Pamphylia. **27** *All that God had done with them.* An expression emphasizing that the apostles were but God's agents, or even instruments. (*Cf.* the title of Müller's *Narrative of the Lord's Dealings with George Müller*.) **28** *No little time*, a characteristic Lucan idiom; probably about a year.

15:1 – 16:5 The apostolic letter from the Council of Jerusalem

15:1–29 The letter issued. The Gentile mission was bound to result in predominantly Gentile churches and an excess of Gentile Christians over those of Jewish birth and background; and the more extreme Jewish party in the Jerusalem church saw that they must act at once if they were to act at all. So a campaign was organized in Antioch, the citadel of Gentile Christianity, urging the wholesale adoption of the Jewish law by all Christians as an indispensable condition of salvation and of fellowship with their Jewish fellow-believers.

What happened at Antioch is described by Paul in Gal. 2:11ff.; so vigorously did the Judaizers press their point of view that even Peter, who was in Antioch at the time and knew perfectly what the rights and wrongs of the matter were, was drawn into an alarming appearance of 'play-acting', as Paul calls it, for he withdrew from the society of Gentile Christians. This action, though Peter may have justified it on grounds of expediency, was bound to have a devastating effect; even Barnabas of all people was inclined to follow suit, and Paul dealt drastically with the situation, charging Peter outright with dissimulation. His rebuke had a salutary effect; at the ensuing Council of Jerusalem Peter supported Paul's arguments in an uncompromising manner.

But the problem raised by the Judaizers had to be dealt with and settled, if the Christian church was to avoid the risk of being split right at the beginning into two bodies, a Jewish and a Gentile. So the church at Antioch sent delegates to the apostles and elders at Jerusalem, and the question was thoroughly discussed by them in the meeting known as the Council of Jerusalem. In spite of the arguments of the Pharisaic party in the church, the weight of Peter's authority, supported by Barnabas and Paul's narrative of God's blessing on the Gentile mission, and finally by James's judicious summing-up, swayed the mind of the Council in the liberal direction.

No conditions were to be imposed on the Gentile Christians for salvation or admission to full Christian fellowship, save that condition which God Himself had accepted as sufficient, faith in Christ. Once that principle had been established, it was easier to deal with the practical question of social intercourse. It would manifestly be an act of courtesy and grace on the part of Gentile Christians to respect certain Jewish scruples; and the finding of the meeting was therefore conveyed in a letter to the church at Antioch and her daughter churches, asking them to abstain from food which had been sacrificed to idols, from blood and from flesh from which the blood had not been properly drained (*what is strangled*), and to conform to the lofty and divinely appointed Jewish code of relations between the sexes. It is nonsense to say, as some have said, that Paul would never have accepted such conditions for his Gentile churches. Where principles were at stake, Paul was uncompromising; where these were not compromised, he was the most conciliatory of men, and there are several places in his letters where he urges upon his converts and others this very duty of respecting the scruples and consciences of others (*cf.* 1 Cor. 8:1ff.; Rom. 14:1ff.).

1 *Some men came down from Judea.* Probably the same as those referred to in Gal. 2:12, 'certain men came from James' (though there is MS authority for reading 'certain' there as singular: 'someone came from James'). *Cf.* v. 24. **5** *Some believers who belonged to the party of the Pharisees.* There was nothing to prevent a Pharisee from accepting Jesus as Messiah while retaining the distinctive Pharisaic tenets, but he tended to be a legally minded Christian. (Paul, of course, was the great exception to this tendency.) *It is necessary to circumcise them, and to charge them to keep the law of Moses.* By 'them', of course, Gentile converts are meant. It is not clear whether 'necessary' means 'necessary for salvation absolutely' or 'necessary for recognition by and fellowship with Jewish Christians'. Probably these Pharisees would have considered this a distinction without a difference.

6 *The apostles and the elders were gathered together.* It seems from v. 12 (*all the assembly*) that other members of the Jerusalem church were

present, although deliberation and decision rested with the leaders. **7** *That by my mouth the Gentiles should hear the word of the gospel*; a reference to the Cornelius incident (see ch. 10). **8** *Giving them the Holy Spirit just as he did to us*; *cf.* 10:47; 11:15–17. **9** *Cleansed their hearts by faith. Cleansed* (lit. 'cleansing'), like *giving* in v. 8, is in Greek a simultaneous aorist participle, and both participles denote the same event: as those Gentiles believed the gospel, the Holy Spirit came upon them, cleansing their hearts (*cf.* 10:15, 'what God has cleansed'). **10** *A yoke . . . which neither our fathers nor we have been able to bear.* The obligations of the Jewish religion are frequently referred to as a 'yoke' by the Rabbis (*cf.* the words of Jesus, 'my yoke', Mt. 11:29, 30). Peter's words probably represent the general attitude of the Jewish rank and file (as distinct from people like the Pharisees) towards the practicability of keeping the law. **11** *But we believe. . . .* This verse probably means: 'But by the grace of the Lord Jesus we are saved by faith just as they are.'

13 *James replied.* James appears by this time to be the acknowledged leader of the Jerusalem church, and one who commanded the loyalty of the legalists. **14** *Symeon, i.e.* Peter; *Symeon* represents Heb. *šim'ôn* more accurately than Simon does. *To take out of them a people for his name*; from among the Gentiles, that is, as well as from the Jews. **15** *With this the words of the prophets agree.* The main quotation is from Am. 9:11, 12 (LXX), with additions at the beginning and the end from Je. 12:15 and Is. 45:21. The prophecy of the restoration of David's house and the extension of its rule over Gentiles is now fulfilled in that not only Jewish believers but many Gentiles farther afield have yielded allegiance to the Son of David.

20 *To abstain.* The conditions laid down for social intercourse are in the main food laws; the *unchastity* (Gk. *porneia*, lit. 'fornication') here prohibited may denote breaches of the Jewish marriage law of Lv. 18 (fornication in the general sense was in any case absolutely forbidden to all Christians). The 'western' text, here and in v. 29 (and 21:25), turns these conditions into ethical regulations—abstinence from idolatry, fornication (in the general sense) and bloodshed—and adds a negative form of the golden rule: 'and that they should not do to others what they do not wish to have done to themselves.' The 'western' reading reflects a time when the Judaizing controversy was gone and forgotten. **21** *For from early generations Moses has . . . ; i.e.* there is no danger that the Mosaic law will be forgotten, as it is regularly made known in synagogues throughout the Gentile world. **28** *It has seemed good to the Holy Spirit and to us.* So completely Spirit-possessed is their consciousness that the community is regarded as the very mouthpiece or vehicle of the Spirit.

15:30 – 16:5 The letter received. The letter was taken to Antioch by two Jerusalem Christians, Judas and Silas, who accompanied the delegates from Antioch on their return journey. The reception of the letter at Antioch caused great satisfaction.

Then Paul and Barnabas agreed to revisit the churches evangelized on their former journey, but disagreed about Mark. Barnabas refused to forgo the company of his cousin, and the upshot of the dissension was that instead of one missionary tour there were two: Barnabas and Mark going to Cyprus again, while Paul took Silas, who had the double advantage of being a member of the Jerusalem church and a Roman citizen, and with him went through the cities of Asia Minor visited on the previous journey.

34 (AV), taken over by the Received Text from the 'western' text, is no part of the original, and is therefore rightly omitted; it contradicts v. 33, but was interpolated in an effort to explain why Silas appears again at Antioch in v. 40; it is simple, however, to suppose that Paul sent for

16:1 *A disciple was there*; *i.e.* in Lystra, the common factor in *Derbe and Lystra* (v. 1) and *Lystra and Iconium* (v. 2). *A Jewish woman who was a believer*. She is called Eunice in 2 Tim. 1:5. On her 'mixed' marriage, Ramsay suggests that the Phrygian Jews were less exclusive than those of Palestine. **3** *Paul . . . circumcised him*; so that he might be the more useful in the work of the gospel. Lesser minds have not been slow to charge Paul with inconsistency here (or else to deny the truth of Luke's statement); but Paul was in truth loyal to a higher consistency, the consistency described in 1 Cor. 9:19–23. He fought against any suggestion that Christians should be circumcised in order to complete their salvation; but circumcision in itself, he held, was religiously indifferent (1 Cor. 7:19; Gal. 5:6; 6:15). Timothy had been brought up by his Jewish mother and grandmother to be a Jew religiously in every point but circumcision. More-

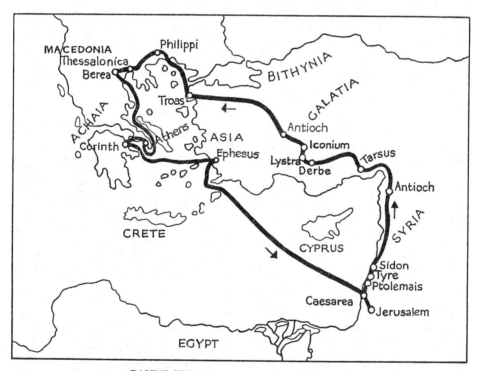

PAUL'S SECOND MISSIONARY JOURNEY

him to Jerusalem. **39** *There arose a sharp contention* (Gk. *paroxysmos*). It is idle to apportion blame between the two apostles; Mark's later development proved that Barnabas had right on his side, but probably Mark would not have developed thus in Paul's company. **40** *Paul chose Silas*, who is called Silvanus in the Pauline Epistles and in 1 Pet. 5:12. It appears from 16:37 that he was, like Paul, a Roman citizen. **41** *Syria and Cilicia*. The double province mentioned in the address of the apostolic letter in v. 23.

over, as his mother was a Jewess, he ranked as a Jew in Jewish eyes, albeit an irregular one because, his father having been a Greek, he was not circumcised. Therefore to regularize his position Paul circumcised him; it was better that he should be clearly one thing or the other than betwixt and between. **4** *They delivered to them. . . .* The substance of this statement appears in the 'western' text also in 15:41, and that may be its sole original context, since the *decisions* were addressed to the churches of

Syria and Cilicia, mentioned there, and not to those of S Galatia, which are now in view.

16:6 – 19:41 THE AEGEAN SHORES EVANGELIZED

16:6–40 Over to Europe: the gospel in Philippi

As the three made their way in the direction of Ephesus, they were conscious of a succession of heaven-sent inhibitions which barred other roads to them, and turned them north until they found themselves in the Aegean port of Troas, another Roman colony, where they were joined by a fourth companion, Luke, the writer of the narrative.

At Troas Paul had the night vision which led the whole company to conclude that God was calling them to go across to the European mainland with the gospel. So they sailed across the north Aegean, landed in Macedonia and went inland to the colony of Philippi. Here they settled, for Paul saw the value of planting a church here, near the eastern end of a great Roman highway, the *Via Egnatia*, which connected the Aegean with the Adriatic. The city's status as a Roman colony was perhaps in Paul's mind when at a later date he reminded the Philippian Christians that they were 'a colony of heaven' (Phil. 3:20).

There was apparently no synagogue in Philippi, presumably owing to the lack of the requisite quorum of ten men; but by the River Gangites they found *a place of prayer* (v. 13)—or, as AV has it, a place 'where prayer was wont to be made'—and spoke to the women who came together there. One of these, Lydia from Thyatira, traded in the purple dye for which her native town had long been famed. When she heard the gospel, she believed, was baptized with her household, and persuaded the four missionaries to accept the hospitality of her home.

Lydia is the first of three people in Philippi whose experience of the power of Christ in their lives is specially mentioned; and the three are so different that they might almost have been deliberately chosen to show how that power was able to bring peace and deliverance to the most diverse types. The second was the fortune-telling slave-girl who persisted in shouting unsolicited testimonials after Paul and his friends in the Philippian streets until Paul in the name of Christ exorcized the spirit that possessed her. Unfortunately from her owners' viewpoint, he exorcized their means of gain as well, and this led to Paul and Silas being dragged before the praetors—the grandiloquent name by which the two chief magistrates of this and other Roman colonies liked to call themselves—with the complaint: 'These men are Jews and they are disturbing our city. They advocate customs which it is not lawful for us Romans to accept or practise.' It is noteworthy that on the two chief occasions in Acts where Gentiles oppose the gospel, it is because of its threat to vested financial interests, the other occasion being at Ephesus (19:23ff.).

Paul and Silas were seized not only because they were the two leaders of the party, but also possibly because they looked much more Jewish than did Timothy, who was Greek on his father's side, or Luke, who was probably a complete Greek. The praetors, without inquiring carefully into the allegations, commanded the two men to be beaten with the rods of the lictors, the attendants of senior Roman magistrates, and to be securely imprisoned. But while the two missionaries were praising God aloud at midnight, in spite of their cramped and painful situation, an earthquake loosened the bars of the prison and the bonds of the prisoners, and the jailer, probably an ex-soldier, awakened in spirit as well as in body, found himself indebted for the preservation of his life and the salvation of his soul to the men whom a few hours previously he had locked in the stocks. (Vv. 25–34 form a pericope which can be removed without doing violence to the sequence of the narrative, but it does not follow that it was not from the first incorporated in Luke's account.)

The praetors, sending next morning to release the prisoners, found the tables turned on them, for they learned what in yesterday's excitement they had omitted to ascertain, that the men were Roman citizens, and therefore legally protected against such shameful treatment as had been meted out to them. So they had to eat humble pie and ceremoniously conduct the two missionaries out of prison. Soon afterwards Paul, Silas and Timothy left, apparently leaving Luke behind to help the new church, which quickly became a church worthy of emulation.

6 *The region of Phrygia and Galatia*; i.e. the Phrygian region of the province of Galatia. They turned northwards through this territory after the way into the province of Asia was barred. Their original intention probably had been to follow the main road westwards to Ephesus. **9** *A man of Macedonia*. It is idle to inquire how Paul knew him to be a Macedonian; his words, *Come over to Macedonia and help us*, were sufficient indication. **10** *Immediately we sought. . . .* These words mark the beginning of the first 'we' section of Acts, which continues to v. 17.

11 *Neapolis*; the port of Philippi, modern Kavalla. **12** *Philippi*; so called after Philip of Macedon who refounded it as a fortified city, c. 350 BC. It was made *a Roman colony* when Antony and Octavian settled their veterans there after the battle of Philippi in 42 BC. *The leading city of the district of Macedonia*. Read 'a city of the first division of Macedonia' (Macedonia was divided by the Romans into four administrative areas). **13** *A place of prayer*; this would normally mean a synagogue, but not here, since there were no men to constitute a synagogue congregation. **14** *A worshipper of God*; i.e. a 'God-fearer'.

16 *Who had a spirit of divination* (lit. 'having a python-spirit'). 'Pythons' were people supposed to be inspired by Apollo, the 'Pythian' god, whose chief oracle was at Delphi (also called

Pytho), where he was believed to be embodied in a snake (the 'Python'). 17 *Servants of the Most High God, who proclaim to you the way of salvation.* These religious terms were as current in Greek as in Jewish circles at this time. Among the Gentiles 'salvation' (Gk. *sōtēria*) was the object of many vows and prayers to the 'Most High God' (Gk. *theos hypsistos*) and other 'saviour gods' (Gk. *theoi sōtēres*), and was held out to initiates in the mystery religions. 20 *The magistrates*; more accurately, 'the praetors' (which is the sense of Greek *stratēgoi* used as a civil title). They were the two senior collegiate magistrates of the colony. The more general Greek term for magistrates (*archontes*) is translated *rulers* at the end of v. 19. 22 *Gave orders to beat them with rods.* Cf. 2 Cor. 11:25, where Paul says he received this treatment on two other occasions as well. The rods were those which the praetors' attendants, the lictors, carried in bundles (*fasces*) as a badge of office. 24 *Fastened their feet in the stocks.* This served as an instrument of torture, as well as of security, for it had more than two holes for the legs, which could thus be forced far apart, causing great discomfort and pain.

25 *Paul and Silas were praying and singing hymns to God.* 'The legs feel no pain in the stocks when the heart is in heaven,' says Tertullian. 27 *Was about to kill himself*; since, presumably, he was answerable for the prisoners' safe keeping, and not even an earthquake could relieve him of his responsibility. 28 *We are all here.* This suggests that the two missionaries were able to exercise some moral control over the other prisoners. The jailer and his actions could be seen from within, silhouetted in the doorway, although the prisoners in the darkness were invisible to him. 30 *What must I do to be saved?* It is difficult to say how much he meant by this expression, but the salvation he actually received was full salvation, resulting from his acceptance of *the word of the Lord* (v. 32). 33 *Washed their wounds, and he was baptized.* 'He washed them from their wounds, and was himself washed from his sins' (Chrysostom). 34 *With all his household* is an adverb (Gk. *panoikei*) which modifies *rejoiced* as well as *had believed.* For the whole household's becoming Christian cf. the stories of Cornelius (11:14), of Lydia (16:15), and of Crispus (18:8). 35 *The police*; i.e. the lictors; lit. 'rod-bearers' (Gk. *rhabdouchoi*). 37 *Uncondemned*; Greek *akatakritos*, which probably represents here Latin *re incognita*, 'without investigating our case'. By a series of laws (extending from the earliest days of the republic to c. 23 BC) Roman citizens were exempt from all degrading forms of punishment. 39 *Asked them to leave the city.* They could not expel Roman citizens from a Roman city, but only request them to leave; the responsibility of protecting two unpopular Roman citizens was apparently more than they felt able to undertake.

17:1-15 Thessalonica and Beroea

Paul and his company continued along the Egnatian road to Thessalonica, the capital of Macedonia, where they stayed long enough to found a new church. The message on which this church was founded is made plain in 1 Thes. 1:9, 10. Paul first made known the gospel in the synagogue for three successive sabbaths, showing from the Scripture lessons that Jesus was the Messiah. But when the Jews who opposed him accused him of sedition before the politarchs, Paul had to leave the city in a hurry. Continuing south, he came to Beroea, and found its Jewish community more amenable than that of Thessalonica; but Thessalonian Jews followed him there and stirred up the people against him. So he left Beroea for Athens, where he waited for Silas and Timothy, who had remained behind. (The course of events at this juncture must be reconstructed by comparing this passage of Acts with 1 Thes. 2:17 – 3:8.)

1 *Amphipolis*, a bridgehead position on the Struma, and *Apollonia*, between the Struma and the Vardar, were Macedonian cities on the Egnatian Way. *Thessalonica*, made a free city by the Romans in 42 BC, was the capital of the Roman province of Macedonia. 3 *Explaining and proving*; i.e. opening the prophetic scriptures and setting alongside them the recent historic events which fulfilled them. *It was necessary for the Christ to suffer.* For this emphasis cf. Lk. 24:26, 46. 4 *The devout Greeks*; i.e. the 'God-fearers'. 5 *Wicked fellows of the rabble*; i.e. 'loafers', 'corner-boys'. 6 *The city authorities.* Greek *politarchai*, a word not found in classic literature, but attested epigraphically in this sense in a number of Macedonian cities. Thessalonica was governed by a board of five magistrates so named in the Augustan Age. *These men who have turned the world upside down.* The verb (Gk. *anastatoō*) suggests subversive revolutionary agitation; there is some evidence of militant Jewish Messianism in a number of places throughout the Empire about this time. 7 *Another king*; or 'another emperor'. The charge as framed was of the most serious character and could not be ignored. 9 *When they had taken security from Jason.* Jason and his associates went bail for Paul's good behaviour, which in this case involved his leaving Thessalonica, a situation referred to in 1 Thes. 2:18.

10 *Beroea*; a city of Thessaly. 11 *More noble*; i.e. more liberal or open-minded. 14 *To the sea*; perhaps to Methone or Dium, where he took ship for Piraeus, the port of Athens.

17:16-34 Paul in Athens

Paul's residence in Athens is reported by Luke in a manner which rings true in the ears of classical students. Several centuries earlier this city had been reproached by its statesmen for being more interested in hearing the latest news than in attending to matters of more pressing importance (cf. 17:21). Nothing is said of

Paul's aesthetic appreciation of the sculptures of Pheidias, or of any feelings stirred in the breast of this champion of Christian liberty by the knowledge that this was the cradle of democracy; to him the sight of the beautiful city of Cecrops brought sorrow as he beheld it so full of idols. Here he discoursed not only with the Jews in the synagogue, but also with the Athenians in the market-place, the *Agora*, the centre of Athenian life, where he disputed with followers of two leading philosophical schools, the Stoics and the Epicureans, the former of whom pursued self-sufficiency as the highest good, the latter pleasure. To these Paul appeared as *a preacher of foreign divinities* (v. 18) and they brought him before the Court of the Areopagus to expound his teaching.

This was the most ancient institution of Athens, founded, according to tradition, over 1,000 years before by the city's patron goddess Athene. When Athens became a democracy in the 5th century BC, much of the power of this court was broken, but it retained great moral prestige, which tended to increase under the Romans; and there is evidence that at this time one of its functions was to examine and license public lectures.

Paul's speech before this body, as reported by Luke, followed lines not unlike those of his speech at Lystra (14:15–17). Beginning with a reference to an altar dedicated '*To an unknown god*', Paul declared that his mission was to make this unknown God known to them; and he went on to describe His work in creation and providence, using language borrowed from some of the Greek poets.

Paul then argued that God should not be worshipped after the idolatrous fashion of Athens and the pagan world in general, and that, whereas hitherto God had overlooked the ignorance of men, a change had come now in that He was commanding all men everywhere to repent, in view of the coming judgment of the world, proof of which had been publicly given, seeing that the Man appointed to execute this judgment had been raised from the dead. The audience listened interestedly enough until Paul spoke of resurrection. This they could not stomach. The immortality of the soul was a commonplace of several of their philosophical schools, but the resurrection of the body was to them as absurd as it was undesirable. It is still as much a stumbling-block to many as it was to the Athenians, but it is integral to the Christian faith. (See B. Gärtner, *The Areopagus Speech and Natural Revelation*, 1955.)

16 *Full of idols*; *i.e.* full of temples and images of pagan deities. **17** *Devout persons*; *i.e.* 'God-fearers'. **18** *Epicurean*. The Epicureans took their name from Epicurus, the founder of this school (341–270 BC); *Stoic philosophers* were so called from the Painted Stoa (colonnade) where Zeno, their founder (340–265 BC), taught his disciples. *Babbler* (Gk. *spermologos*); an intellectual cheap-jack, a retailer of scraps of second-

hand philosophy (a word of characteristic Athenian slang). *Jesus and the resurrection.* These may have been taken by the Athenian populace as the names of two new-fangled divinities. **19** *Areopagus.* Not here a place, but a body of men, the Court of the Areopagus, so called from the Hill of Ares (*Areios pagos*), on which it originally met; now it met in the Royal Stoa in the Agora (market-place). **21** *Now all the Athenians . . . spent their time in nothing except telling or hearing something new.* Several examples of this characterization of the ancient Athenians can be found in classical literature. **22** *The Areopagus*; here, as in v. 19, the men, not a place, should be understood. *Very religious.* Josephus calls the Athenians 'the most religious of the Greeks'; similar testimonies are provided by Sophocles, Pausanias, *etc.* **23** '*To an unknown God.*' Pausanias and Philostratus attest the presence at Athens of altars to 'unknown' deities. **24** *Does not live in shrines made by man.* Cf. 7:48. The higher paganism agreed with the affirmation which Paul based on OT revelation, that no 'house built by craftsmen could enclose the form divine within enfolding walls' (Euripides). **25** *Nor is he served. . . .* The true emphasis is excellently conveyed in NEB: 'It is not because he lacks anything that he accepts service at men's hands.' Here the Epicureans would find confirmation of their view that the divine Being has no need of anything that men can give, and the Stoics of their view that He is the source of all life. **26** *Made from one*; presumably from Adam, the 'one man' from whom, in the Bible, all men are descended. This contradicted the cherished Athenian belief that they themselves were sprung from the soil of Attica. *Having determined allotted periods.* Cf. the 'fruitful seasons' of 14:17. *The boundaries of their habitation.* Cf. Dt. 32:8. **28** *In him we live and move. . . .* This quotation from Epimenides of Crete is interesting for several reasons. For one thing, Epimenides was supposed in Greek legend to have advised the erection of 'anonymous altars' in and around Athens; for another, a further line from the same context is quoted in Tit. 1:12. In the context referred to, Epimenides addresses the Supreme God:

'*They fashioned a tomb for Thee, O holy and high One,*
The Cretans, always liars, evil beasts, idle bellies!
But Thou art not dead; for ever Thou art risen and alive,
For in Thee we live and move and have our being.'

For we are indeed his offspring; quoted from the poem on *Phenomena* by Aratus of Cilicia.

30 *Overlooked*; *cf.* Rom. 3:25, 'he had passed over former sins'. **31** *He will judge the world in righteousness*; based on such OT passages as Ps. 96:13. *A man whom he has appointed*; *cf.* 10:42. For this emphasis on the manhood of the coming Judge *cf.* Jn. 5:27, which harks back to the 'one like a son of man' of Dn. 7:13. **32** *When they heard of the resurrection of the dead.* The tragedian Aeschylus had described the god Apollo as saying, on the occasion when the Court of the Areopagus was founded by the city's patron goddess Athene, 'But when the earth has drunk up a man's blood, once he is dead there is no resurrection' (the same Greek word *anastasis* being used as in Paul's preaching). This, in Athenian eyes, was higher authority than Paul's. **34** *Dionysius the Areopagite.* A member of the Areopagus Court. The body of Neoplatonic literature ascribed to this Dionysius is actually several centuries later than his time.

18:1–28 Paul in Corinth

18:1–17 The church founded. Paul's next move was to Corinth, a great commercial city with a double harbour. After its destruction by the Roman general Mummius in 146 BC, it had lain in ruins for 100 years, until Julius Caesar refounded it as a Roman colony in 46 BC. It had long enjoyed an unenviable reputation for loose morality, and it was only with difficulty that the church soon to be founded there kept this at bay; yet Paul knew the importance of leaving a strong 'cell' of the new community in this city, and he spent 18 months there. There he met Aquila and his wife Priscilla, who were to prove such a help to him in his subsequent labours.

At first, with some success, he made the local synagogue his base of operation, but when Jewish opposition made it impossible to continue there, he availed himself of the hospitality of Titius Justus, a 'God-fearer' who lived next door to the synagogue.

As Paul went on proclaiming the good news at Corinth, many believed, including the ruler of the synagogue, Crispus (*cf.* 1 Cor. 1:14). His Jewish opponents, however, did not slacken their efforts to hinder him, and soon accused him before Junius Gallio, the Roman proconsul of Achaia, of illegal religious propaganda. Gallio is an interesting figure; he was the much-loved brother of Seneca, the Stoic philosopher and tutor of Nero. He saw through the specious pleas of Paul's accusers. If Paul had contravened Roman law, he said, he would listen to them, but as the question seemed to concern only Jewish beliefs and interpretations, it did not fall within his jurisdiction. Ramsay emphasizes the importance of Gallio's decision both as a precedent for other governors and as a sign in Paul's eyes that Roman government could be relied upon to protect the liberty of Christian preachers, in which confidence he later appealed to Caesar himself.

The scene which followed Gallio's rebuff to the Jews, the beating of the ruler of the synagogue by the Greek mob, shows how near the surface anti-Jewish feeling lay in those days. If this Sosthenes is the same as that of 1 Cor. 1:1, then he, like his predecessor Crispus, ultimately became a Christian. Another eminent Corinthian convert was Erastus, the city treasurer (Rom. 16:23), whose name has been identified with great probability in a Corinthian inscription.

2 *Pontus.* A province of northern Asia Minor, on the S shore of the Black Sea. *Priscilla;* the more familiar form of her name; Paul regularly refers to her, more formally, as 'Prisca'. *Claudius had commanded all the Jews to leave Rome;* all Jews, that is, who were not Roman citizens. According to Suetonius, he expelled them 'because they were constantly rioting at the instigation of Chrestus', probably a distorted allusion to disputes between Christian and non-Christian Jews at Rome. The expulsion may be dated *c.* 49–50. **3** *Tentmakers.* The word may mean, more broadly, 'leather-workers'. It was regarded as proper for a Rabbi to practise a manual occupation, so as not to make monetary profit out of his sacred teaching. **4** *Every sabbath.* The 'western' text adds, 'inserting the name of the Lord Jesus' (*i.e.* as an interpretative expansion in the readings from the prophets). **5** *Was occupied with preaching; i.e.* 'proceeded to devote himself entirely to the preaching', his material necessities being supplied by gifts which Silas and Timothy brought from the Macedonian churches. **6** *Reviled him;* or 'spoke evil of the name of Jesus'. **7** *Titius Justus, a worshipper of God; i.e.* a 'God-fearer'. He may be identical with 'Gaius' of Rom. 16:23; 1 Cor. 1:14; in that case his full name as a Roman citizen was Gaius Titius Justus. **8** *With all his household.* Cf. 11:14; 16:15, 31ff. **10** *No man shall attack you to harm you.* This promise was fulfilled in the failure of the attack described in vv. 12–17. **11** *A year and six months.* Probably from autumn 50 to spring 52.

12 *When Gallio was proconsul of Achaia.* An inscription at Delphi, recording a proclamation of Claudius, makes it probable that Gallio was appointed to his proconsulship in July 51. The Roman province of Achaia included all Greece south of Macedonia; it was a senatorial province of second rank, governed by a proconsul from 27 BC to AD 15 and again from AD 44 onwards. **13** *This man is persuading men to worship God contrary to the law; i.e.* he propagates a *religio illicita,* a cult not licensed by Roman law. **14** *I should have reason to bear with you.* Better, 'I should naturally have taken up your case' (Gk. *anechomai* is used in this legal sense of 'taking up'). **15** *I refuse to be a judge of these things.* Previously Jewish opposition had had recourse to mob violence or to city magistrates; it now attempted to influence a higher court, the provincial magistrate, against the apostles. Gallio's decision that the gospel was a form of Judaism, which was a religion specifically protected by Roman law, could not enjoy undisputed validity for long, but as a precedent it did afford protection to Christianity for ten vital years. **17** *Gallio paid no attention to this; i.e.* he turned a blind eye to the behaviour of the pagan crowd, who followed up the proconsul's snub to the local Jews by assaulting one of their leading representatives.

18:18–28 Paul leaves Corinth and Apollos arrives. In the spring of 52 Paul left Corinth and paid a short visit to Jerusalem, at the Passover season. On the way he called at Ephesus, but could not stay there at the time, in spite of the pressing invitation of the synagogue. He promised, however, to return, and kept his promise in the autumn. Meanwhile great interest was aroused in the synagogue at Ephesus by an Alexandrian Jew named Apollos, well versed in the OT Scriptures and also in the story of Jesus, comparison of which with the OT convinced him that Jesus was indeed the Messiah; and with his powerful reasoning he expounded this teaching in the synagogue. Aquila and Priscilla, who had accompanied Paul from Corinth to Ephesus, heard him and, as he knew only of the baptism of John, they taught him the way of the Lord more accurately, benefiting from the teaching they themselves had received from Paul. When Apollos was about to pursue his journey to Greece, they commended him to the church of Corinth; and so powerful was the assistance he gave the Christians there that Paul could write to them later: 'I planted, Apollos watered' (1 Cor. 3:6). Although some Corinthians tried to make him a party leader in rivalry to Paul, it is clear that there was no party feeling between Paul and Apollos themselves (*cf.* 1 Cor. 16:12).

18 *At Cenchreae he cut his hair, for he had a vow*; *i.e.* Paul. The vow was a temporary Nazirite vow, perhaps one of gratitude for the promise of vv. 9, 10. The full discharge of the vow demanded a visit to the Temple in Jerusalem. *Cf.* Acts 21:23, 24. *Cenchreae* was the eastern (Aegean) port of Corinth: *cf.* Rom. 16:1. **19** *Ephesus.* An ancient Greek city, at this time capital of the province of Asia and chief commercial centre of Asia Minor. **21** *He said.* The following words in AV, 'I must by all means keep this feast that cometh in Jerusalem', represent a 'western' addition to the text. The feast was probably Passover, which in AD 52 fell early in April, and as the seas were closed for navigation until March 10 there was the less time to spare. **22** *He went up*; *i.e.* to Jerusalem. **23** *Went from place to place through the region of Galatia and Phrygia* (lit. 'the Galatian region and Phrygia'), revisiting the churches founded on his first missionary journey in Asia Minor.

24 *A native of Alexandria*, and perhaps therefore given to the allegorizing interpretation of Scripture, like Philo. *An eloquent man*; or 'a learned man' (RV). **25** *Fervent in spirit*; *i.e.* full of enthusiasm. *The things concerning Jesus*; *i.e.* the gospel story. *He knew only the baptism of John.* His knowledge of the gospel may have come from a Galilaean source rather than from the Jerusalem apostles. **27** *When he wished to cross to Achaia.* According to the 'western' text, some Corinthian visitors in Ephesus heard him there and persuaded him to accompany them back to Corinth.

19:1–41 Ephesus and the province of Asia

19:1–20 Ephesus evangelized. Paul, having paid his visit to Palestine, returned overland to Ephesus and settled down there for some two and a half years, from the autumn of 52 to the spring of 55. There a great work was accomplished, radiating out from Ephesus to other cities of the province of Asia. The effect of the preaching is vividly portrayed by Luke in a few scenes.

In the first scene we meet the twelve 'disciples' who knew only John's baptism and had never heard of the Holy Spirit. Then we have Paul's withdrawal from the synagogue to the lecture-hall of Tyrannus where, according to one textual tradition, he lectured daily from 11 a.m. to 4 p.m., during the heat of the day, after having presumably spent the earlier hours of the morning tent-making. The mighty works wrought through Paul at Ephesus led to encounters with the local magicians, and we have the vivid description of the sons of Sceva and of the bonfire of the magic scrolls.

1 *Passed through the upper country.* Paul, instead of taking the main route to Ephesus by the Lycus and Maeander valleys, appears to have taken a higher road farther north, approaching the city from the north side of Mt. Messogis. *Disciples.* This word standing alone means not 'disciples of John' but 'disciples of Jesus', whatever the defects in their knowledge might be. **2** *Did you receive the Holy Spirit when you believed?* The question may have been provoked by a suspicion that there was something defective about their 'discipleship'. *We have never even heard that there is a Holy Spirit*, with special reference to the Holy Spirit as sent at Pentecost with outward manifestation (so regularly in Acts). **4** *John baptized . . . ; cf.* 1:5; 11:16. *The baptism of repentance. Cf.* not only Lk. 3:3; Acts 13:24, but also the apostolic baptism of Acts 2:38. *To believe in the one who was to come after him; cf.* Jn. 1:26ff.; 3:25ff. There are striking agreements between John and Acts in their accounts of John the Baptist and of the Holy Spirit. But no reference is made here (or anywhere else in Acts) to the fact that John himself promised that the Coming One would 'baptize with the Holy Spirit' (Mk. 1:8; Lk. 3:16; *cf.* Jn. 1:33; see Acts 1:5; 10:37; 11:16; 13:24f.). **5** *They were baptized in* (into) *the name of the Lord Jesus.* The same expression as in 8:16. This is the only instance of re-baptism recorded in the NT. **6** *And when Paul had laid his hands upon them, the Holy Spirit came on them*, as happened to the Samaritan converts in 8:17.

9 *Speaking evil of the Way, i.e.* the gospel, as in 9:2. *Argued; i.e.* 'conducted discussions' (Gk. *dialegomai*). *In the hall of Tyrannus*, which thus served much the same purpose in Ephesus as the house of Titius Justus did in Corinth. The 'western' text adds 'from the fifth to the tenth hour', the midday recess when Tyrannus himself did not use his lecture-room. **10** *Two years.* Probably two years and a few months, which with the *three months* of v. 8 approximate to the *three years* of 20:31. *All the residents of Asia*; *i.e.* in the Roman province of that name, and especially in the area round Ephesus. Probably all seven churches addressed in Revelation (Rev. 1:11), as well as those at Colossae and Hierapolis (Col. 4:13), were founded in these years.

12 *Handkerchiefs or aprons.* Two words of Latin origin: *sudaria* (lit. 'sweat-rags'; *cf.* Lk. 19:20; also Jn. 11:44; 20:7) and *semicinctia* (articles which Paul would use while engaged in 'tent-making'). **13** *I adjure you by the Jesus.* The use of this name and other Jewish names in pagan exorcisms is attested by papyrus scrolls

'Ephesian letters'. *Pieces of silver*; drachmae ('shillings').

19:21–41 The riot at Ephesus. The most vivid scene of all in Luke's narrative of Paul's Ephesian ministry is the riotous assembly in the great open-air theatre of the city. The local guild of silversmiths, who drew a comfortable income from the sale of silver images of the great goddess Artemis set in silver niches, were alarmed for the prospects of their craft at the sight of so many people becoming Christians and, disguising this alarm as concern for the honour of the goddess, they called an indignation meeting. The indignation spread to the general public, who ran into the theatre and staged a pro-Artemis and anti-Jewish riot. Paul himself was prevented from

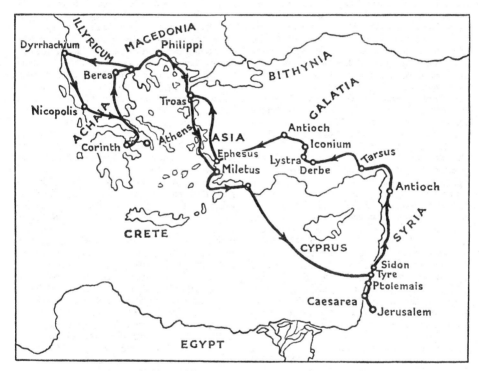

PAUL'S THIRD MISSIONARY JOURNEY

of magic spells which have come down to us. **14** *High priest.* Luke is probably quoting, but not confirming, Sceva's account of himself. A Jewish high priest was believed to know the secret pronunciation of the ineffable name of Israel's God, and so to be in command of a specially potent spell. **18** *Confessing and divulging their practices*; *i.e.* their spells. To divulge these was to render them useless. **19** *Books*; *i.e.* scrolls of papyrus or parchment, like the famous magical papyri, full of spells and 'abracadabra', in the London, Paris and Leiden collections. Such scrolls were so closely associated with Ephesus in Graeco-Roman antiquity that they were commonly called *Ephesia grammata*,

entering the theatre. Alexander, a local Jew, tried to address the mob, perhaps in order to dissociate the Jewish community from the objects of the popular resentment. But the mob, in no mood to make fine distinctions, howled him down, and kept up for two hours the cry, 'Great is Artemis of the Ephesians!' At last the town clerk, greatly agitated lest the Roman authorities should lay severe penalties on the city for this riotous behaviour, persuaded them to be quiet and go home, telling them that if they had any complaint against these men they should lay it before the authorities in the proper manner.

21 *Go to Jerusalem*, along with the delegates of his Gentile churches who were carrying gifts from these churches to the Jerusalem Christians (*cf.* 1 Cor. 16:1-4; 2 Cor. 8;9; Rom. 15:25ff.), to mark the completion of his Aegean ministry. Of these gifts Luke has nothing to say, apart from a general allusion in 24:17. *I must also see Rome.* Cf. Rom. 1:11ff.; 15:23ff. for Paul's plans. Ramsay finds here 'the clear conception of a far-reaching plan' to visit Rome on his way to evangelize 'the chief seat of Roman civilization in the West' (*i.e.* Spain), and regards this decision as a crisis in Paul's career. While Rome is Luke's goal, it was but a transit-point in Paul's programme. **22** *Timothy.* Cf. Phil. 2:19 for this mission of Timothy to Macedonia. **23** *The Way*, as in v. 9. **24** *Artemis.* Not the Greek virgin-goddess of that name, sister to Apollo, but the great goddess of Ephesus (a local form of the great mother-goddess worshipped from time immemorial in Asia Minor), whose temple was one of the seven wonders of the ancient world. **27** *She whom all Asia and the world worship.* Over thirty places throughout the world have been enumerated where the cult of Ephesian Artemis was venerated.

29 *Dragging with them Gaius and Aristarchus, Macedonians.* Read with some MSS, 'a Macedonian', referring to Aristarchus; Gaius belonged to Derbe in Asia Minor (20:4). These two may have been Luke's informants for this incident. *Into the theatre.* The open-air theatre of Ephesus could accommodate 25,000 persons and was a convenient place for meetings of the citizen body, regular or irregular. **31** *Asiarchs.* The chief citizens of Ephesus and of other cities in the province, who constituted the 'council (*koinon*) of Asia'. From their ranks also the high-priesthood of the provincial cult of 'Rome and Augustus' was recruited. It is noteworthy that Paul found sympathizers in the highest ranks of Ephesian society. **32** *Most of them did not know why they had come together.* A good example of Luke's quiet humour. **35** *The town clerk* (Gk. *grammateus*). He was head of the free municipal administration of Ephesus and the chief liaison officer between it and the Roman provincial government. *Temple keeper of the great Artemis*; 'Temple Warden (Gk. *neokoros*) of Great Artemis' was a much prized title borne by the city. *The sacred stone that fell from the sky*; presumably a meteorite, in which the semblance of the 'many-breasted' goddess was discerned. **37** *Sacrilegious*; lit. 'temple-robbers'. **38** *There are proconsuls.* The generalizing plural is used because Junius Silanus, proconsul of the province, had recently been assassinated (late in 54) and his successor had not yet arrived. *Cf.* NEB: 'there are such people as proconsuls.' The proconsul presided at the assizes (*the courts are open* means 'assizes are held'). **39** *In the regular assembly.* The regular assembly (Gk. *ekklēsia*) of the citizens met three times a month. Rome would not tolerate an irregular and riotous assembly like the present one. **40** *Being charged with rioting*; *i.e.* by the Romans.

20:1 – 28:31 HOW PAUL REALIZED HIS HOPE OF SEEING ROME

20:1-38 Paul sets out for Palestine

20:1-16 The apostle sails with the delegates. After the conclusion of his time in Ephesus, Paul spent some time in Macedonia and Greece, during which he travelled to the borders of Illyricum (the modern Albania and Yugoslavia), as we learn from Rom. 15:19. He had organized collections, as an outward sign of fellowship, in his Gentile churches, for the poor Christians in the Jerusalem church; and in the spring of 57 he set sail for Palestine with the delegates whom these Gentile churches had appointed to present their gifts. His intention was, after paying this visit to Jerusalem, to leave the Eastern Mediterranean for the Western, calling on the Roman church on his way to Spain (19:21; Rom. 15:23ff.). Luke rejoined him at Philippi and accompanied him to Jerusalem, and we have a detailed narrative in the first person plural of the voyage to Palestine. The visit to Troas throws some interesting light on Paul's practice when he visited a church; we notice incidentally that his sermons (or rather dialogues) were not of the 20-minute order, and even if his discourse was interrupted by a momentarily fatal accident, yet, after Paul's reassuring words about the young man, the meeting went on till daybreak.

2 *He came to Greece*; *i.e.* into the province of Achaia (*cf.* 19:21 and see on 18:12). **3** *There he spent three months*; mainly perhaps at Corinth, where early in AD 57 he wrote his Epistle to the Romans. **4** *Sopater . . . Trophimus.* The names are those of delegates from the Pauline churches on both sides of the Aegean, who were carrying their churches' gifts to the Christians at Jerusalem (*cf.* 24:17; 1 Cor. 16:1ff.; 2 Cor. 8:1ff.; Rom. 15:25ff.). The churches which they represented are probably 'the churches of Christ' of Rom. 16:16. *Sopater*; perhaps the Sosipater of Rom. 16:21. **5** *These went on and were waiting for us at Troas.* They crossed from Cenchreae, presumably, while Paul and Luke crossed from Philippi.

6 *We sailed away from Philippi.* It is noteworthy that this new 'we' section (20:5 – 21:18) begins where the former one finished (16:17)— at Philippi, where Luke may have spent the whole intervening period. *After the days of Unleavened Bread.* In AD 57 they ended on Thursday, April 14. **7** *On the first day of the week, when we were gathered together to break bread*; *i.e.* to celebrate the Eucharist; probably it was their practice to do this each Sunday evening. In the event it was Monday morning before they 'broke the bread' (v. 11), for Paul *prolonged his speech until midnight.* **8** *There were many lights*; *i.e.* torches. The resultant smoky, oily atmosphere would increase Eutychus's proneness to sleep. **9** *Was taken up dead.* Luke, as a physician, presumably satisfied himself that this was so. **10** *His life is in him*; probably implying that life had returned to him. Cf. 1 Ki. 17:22; 2 Ki. 4:34, 35. **11** *Broken bread* (lit. 'broken the bread'); the article points back to v. 7 and indicates that now at last they celebrated the Eucharist as they had intended to do. *And eaten*. This refers to their taking food in addition to the eucharistic breaking of the bread. **12** *They took the lad away alive*. Eutychus evidently recovered consciousness just before Paul's departure.

13 *Paul . . . intending himself to go by land*. The sea route from Troas to Assos was longer than the land route, as it involved the rounding of Cape Lectum. **14** *Mitylene*. The chief town of the island of Lesbos. **15** *Samos*. The following clause, 'and after remaining at Trogyllium' (mg.), is absent from the best texts, but the statement is inherently probable. **16** *Paul had decided to sail past Ephesus*. He probably made this decision at Troas, and so chose a fast ship which took the straight course across the mouth of the Ephesian gulf, in order to reach Palestine in time.

20:17–38 Paul's address to the elders of Ephesus. The meeting at Miletus between Paul and the elders of the Ephesian church is important because it contains the one record in Acts of Paul's addressing a Christian audience. Its authenticity is strongly supported by its similarity to hortatory passages in Paul's Epistles, the more so as there is no evidence that Luke was acquainted with these. The address throws light both on the course of events in the recent past and on Paul's misgivings for the future, although nothing shifted him from his determination to carry out the work divinely allotted to him and to finish his course with joy.

17 *From Miletus he sent to Ephesus*. A distance of some 30 miles. **19** *Trials which befell me through the plots of the Jews*. *Cf.* the reference to Alexander the coppersmith in 2 Tim. 4:14, which may be relevant here if he is the Alexander of 19:33. It is plain, besides, from references in the Corinthian Epistles (*cf.* 1 Cor. 15:30–32; 2 Cor. 1:8–10) that Paul was exposed to serious danger during his Ephesian ministry, over and above the danger occasioned by the riot of 19:23ff. **21** *Both to Jews and to Greeks*; *cf.* Rom. 1:14ff.; 3:9. *Repentance to God and faith in our Lord Jesus Christ*. For this summary of Paul's message *cf.* 26:20; Rom. 10:9ff.; 2 Cor. 5:20f. **22** *Bound in the Spirit*; *i.e.* under the constraint of the Spirit (*cf.* 16:6, 7). **23** *The Holy Spirit testifies to me in every city*. Speaking through the prophets in various churches (*cf.* 21:4, 11). Compare the apprehensions expressed in Rom. 15:31a. **24** *To testify to the gospel of the grace of God*. This is evidently identical with *preaching the kingdom* (v. 25). **25** *I know that all you . . . will see my face no more*. His intention, if he survived the foreseen dangers at Jerusalem, was to go to Spain. Whether in fact they did see him again must remain uncertain. **26** *I am innocent of the blood of all of you*. For the general idea *cf.* Ezk. 33:1–9. **28** *The Holy Spirit has made you guardians*; *i.e.* 'bishops' (Gk. *episkopos*). In the 1st century AD 'elder' (*cf.* v. 17) and 'bishop' are

practically interchangeable terms. *Which he obtained with his own blood*. Or '. . . with the blood of His own One', '. . . of His Well-beloved'. **29** *Fierce wolves*. This refers to one class of false teachers (invaders from outside); another class (those from within) is indicated in v. 30. **31** *Three years*; see on 19:10. **32** *The word of his grace*. 'This message of the free bounty of God is the word which has the greatest effect on the heart of man, and so it is *able to build up* the church' (Rackham). *The inheritance among all those who are sanctified*; *cf.* 26:18; Eph. 1:14; Col. 3:24. **34** *These hands ministered to my necessities*. Spoken no doubt with an appropriate gesture. *Cf.* 1 Cor. 9:15ff.; 2 Cor. 11:7ff.; 1 Thes. 2:9; 2 Thes. 3:7ff. **35** *It is more blessed to give than to receive*. This saying is not recorded in the Gospels, though its general sense can be paralleled there. It seems that collections of the sayings of Jesus were already current.

21:1–14 Miletus to Caesarea

When Paul and his companions left Miletus they continued the journey to Palestine and landed at Tyre, where their ship was to unload. The picture of their departure from Tyre, escorted to the ship by the Christian families of that city, fast friends after a week's acquaintance, shows how firm a bond primitive Christianity was. As Paul went from one port to another, indications of the danger lying ahead of him in Jerusalem became more and more ominous; the Tyrian disciples, speaking by inspiration, begged him not to continue his journey there, and at Caesarea the prophet Agabus reappears to foretell plainly what is going to happen to him. But Paul would not be dissuaded from his course. We must not infer that he was wrong in going on; these friends tried to dissuade him because they foresaw the risks to which he would be exposed at Jerusalem, but they seem to have recognized that Paul's movements were divinely guided when they acquiesced in his decision, saying, *The will of the Lord be done* (v. 14).

At Caesarea we meet Philip again, after leaving him there at the end of ch. 8. Now we find him at home with his four prophesying daughters; Luke was probably indebted to them for some of his information about the gospel story and the history of the early church, if not during the few days they spent in Caesarea at this time, then during Paul's 2 years' detention there.

1 *Cos*; an island of the Dodecanese; *Rhodes* is the largest island of that group; *Patara* is a port of SW Asia Minor. **3** *Come in sight of Cyprus*; Gk. *anaphainō*, apparently a nautical term for sighting land. **4** *And having sought out the disciples*. T e Tyrian church was probably planted during the Phoenician mission of 11:19. **7** *Ptolemais*; OT Acco, modern Acre or Akka. At this time it was a Roman colony. **9** *Four unmarried daughters*. Some at least of Philip's daughters spent their old age at Hierapolis in Phrygia, where they were renowned as authorities on persons and events belonging to the earliest days of Christianity (*cf.* Eusebius, *Eccl. Hist.* iii. 31, 39, v. 24).

10 *Agabus. Cf.* 11:27, 28. His sudden appearances and disappearances are 'not fiction, but real life' (Lake and Cadbury). **11** *He took Paul's girdle and bound his own feet and hands.* Acted prophecy of this kind was common in the OT (*cf.* 1 Ki. 11:29ff.). *So shall the Jews at Jerusalem bind the man . . . and deliver him into the hands of the Gentiles. Cf.* Jesus' prediction in Mk. 10:33; Lk. 18:32. The general sense, but not each detail of Agabus's prophecy, was fulfilled; in the event Paul was delivered by the Gentiles from the Jews. **14** *The will of the Lord be done. Cf.* the words of Jesus in Gethsemane (Lk. 22:42). There is a (probably intentional) series of parallels between this account of Paul's last journey to Jerusalem and our Lord's last journey thither.

21:15 – 23:35 Paul in Jerusalem

21:15–30 The apostle in trouble. From Caesarea Paul and his companions went up to Jerusalem, and the party lodged with Mnason, one of the original believers, probably a Hellenist, in whose house the Gentile Christians would be sure of a welcome. When the delegates called on James and the elders of the Jerusalem church they were welcomed; but these good men were clearly troubled because of the exaggerated rumours that had reached Jerusalem about Paul's attitude to the law. They admitted that the position with regard to Gentile believers had been defined at the apostolic Council, but they wished Paul to give the lie in a practical manner to the report that he was dissuading *Jewish* Christians from keeping the law and from circumcising their children. Paul himself, so far as we can tell, continued to observe the law throughout his life, especially in Jewish company, and his consent to take the advice of James on this occasion and share the purificatory ceremony of four men who had taken a temporary Nazirite vow and pay their expenses was entirely in keeping with his settled principle: 'To the Jews I became as a Jew, in order to win Jews' (1 Cor. 9:20). We may compare his own vow of Acts 18:18, which involved the shearing of his hair. He has been quite unnecessarily castigated for such actions by people whose ideal seems to be that lower brand of consistency which has been called 'the virtue of small minds'.

The carrying out of this duty involved his presence in the Temple, and there he became the object of a hue and cry raised by some Jews from the province of Asia who recognized him. Having seen him in the city with a Gentile Christian from Ephesus, they imagined that he had taken this man into the Temple. A riot broke out at once, the mob dragged Paul out of the Temple, beating him all the time, and as soon as they were outside, the gates were shut.

15 *We made ready.* The single Greek word *episkeuasamenoi* might mean here 'having hired horses'. **16** *An early disciple* (Gk. *archaios*).

The adjective suggests that he was a foundation member of the church. Since he was a Cypriot, we infer that a few Hellenists were left in the church of Jerusalem after the dispersion that followed Stephen's death. **18** *Paul went in with us to James; and all the elders were present.* Apparently none of the original apostles was now resident in Jerusalem. James (the Lord's brother) is the undisputed leader of the Jerusalem church.

20 *How many thousands*; lit. 'how many myriads (tens of thousands)'. We may too easily underestimate the strength of early Jewish Christianity. But as the entire population of Jerusalem in normal times was about 55,000 (J. Jeremias), 'thousands' is the more realistic rendering. *Zealous for the law*; lit. 'zealots for the law'. **21** *The customs*; *i.e.* those ordained by Jewish law, 'received by tradition from Moses' (*cf.* 6:14; Gal. 1:14). **24** *Pay their expenses.* To perform this service for Nazirites was a pious duty. *Cf.* Nu. 6:14, 15 for the nature of these expenses. **25** *We have sent a letter.* A reference to the apostolic letter of 15:23–29. This reference to it does not necessarily mean that Paul is now being made acquainted with it for the first time.

27 *Were almost completed.* Rather, 'were going to be fulfilled'; the following events took place about the beginning, not the end, of the 7 days. **28** *Who is teaching men everywhere against . . . this place. Cf.* the charge brought against Stephen (6:13). *Brought Greeks into the temple, and he has defiled this holy place.* Into the outer court anybody might go; but further penetration was forbidden to Gentiles on pain of death. The Roman government ratified the death sentence passed by the Sanhedrin for this offence even when the trespasser was a Roman citizen. Notices in Greek and Latin were fixed to the barriers separating the outer and inner courts, warning Gentile visitors against further ingress; one of these notices, found in 1871, is now in Istanbul, while another, found in 1935, is in the Palestine Museum. By the letter of the law, Trophimus (v. 29) would have been the guilty party had the charge been true, although Paul would have been guilty of aiding and abetting him.

21:31 – 22:29 Paul fails to pacify the Jerusalem mob. Above the Temple stood the fortress of Antonia, in which a Roman garrison was stationed. Hearing of the riot the captain of the garrison sent down soldiers, who rescued Paul from being lynched. Even so, the mob thronged them to such an extent as they ascended the steps to the fortress that they had to carry Paul to prevent him from being pulled down. At the top of the steps stood the captain, who imagined that Paul was an Egyptian agitator, who had presented himself to the people some time previously in the guise of a second Moses, and who had aroused deep popular resentment when he left his followers to be cut to pieces by Felix's soldiery while he himself escaped. He was, therefore, surprised when Paul addressed him in Greek, and requested leave to speak to the people.

Having obtained leave, Paul stood on the steps and addressed the people below, not in Greek but in the Aramaic vernacular. Silence fell as they heard themselves addressed in their native tongue, and Paul told them of his up-bringing at the feet of Gamaliel in that very city, his persecution of the Christians, his conversion near Damascus, where he stressed the part played by Ananias, *a devout man according to the law* (22:12). They listened to all this with quiet interest, but when Paul went on to tell of his commission to evangelize the Gentiles their fury burst out afresh, and the captain, at his wits' end, ordered Paul to be scourged, so that he might find out the true reason for the trouble. Paul, however, protested his Roman citizenship and thus escaped the scourge, which was a much more murderous instrument than the lictors' rods of Philippi.

31 *The tribune of the cohort*; *i.e.* the military tribune in charge of the auxiliary cohort which was stationed in the fortress Antonia (*the barracks* of v. 34). **35** *When he came to the steps.* Two flights of steps led down from the fortress to the outer court of the Temple. **38** *Are you not the Egyptian . . . ?* The story of this Egyptian agitator is told by Josephus in his *Jewish War*, ii. 13. 4f., and *Jewish Antiquities*, xx. 8. 6. *Four thousand men of the Assassins.* The reference is to the *sicarii* ('dagger-men') who specialized in assassinating Romans and pro-Roman Jews. This figure of 'four thousand' is more probable than Josephus's 30,000. **40** *In the Hebrew language*; *i.e.*, probably, in Aramaic.

22:2 *They were the more quiet*; as though a bilingual Irish or Welsh audience, expecting to be addressed by an unpopular politician in English, suddenly realized that he was using the Celtic vernacular. **3** *I am a Jew. . . .* The following phrases should probably be punctuated 'born at Tarsus in Cilicia, brought up in this city, educated at the feet of Gamaliel . . .' (*cf.* BFBS Gk. Testament); this implies that while Tarsus was his native place, he spent his boyhood not there but in Jerusalem, where in due course (presumably in his teens) he entered the school of Gamaliel. (See W. C. van Unnik, *Tarsus or Jerusalem: The City of Paul's Youth*, 1962.) *According to the strict manner of the law of our fathers.* Paul here emphasizes all those features in his career which would appeal to their religious nationalism. **5** *The whole council of elders*; *i.e.* the Sanhedrin. **9** *Did not hear the voice of the one who was speaking.* See on 9:7. **14** *The God of our fathers appointed you. . . .* These words of Ananias are not given in the other accounts of Paul's conversion, but we may compare the words spoken by the Lord to Ananias in 9:15, 16. Ananias communicated to Paul the revelation he had received from the Lord concerning him. There is no basic contradiction between this account and Gal. 1:1, 12, where Paul maintains that he did not receive his apostolic com-

mission from man. There Paul is concerned to show that he received his gospel and the authority to proclaim it directly from God, not from the Jerusalem apostles. Ananias acted simply as the mouthpiece, or messenger, of Christ to Paul. *To see the Just One.* The 'Righteous One' of 3:14; 7:52, where the same Greek adjective (*dikaios*) is used. Here, as in 26:16, we have evidence in Acts parallel to the more emphatic assertions in the Epistles that Paul actually saw the risen Lord (*cf.* 1 Cor. 9:1; 15:8). **16** *Be baptized, and wash away your sins.* These verbs are in the Greek middle voice and might be rendered: 'Get yourself baptized and get your sins washed away.' *Calling on his name*; *i.e.* 'invoking His name' by confessing it in baptism; such invoking the name of Christ appears to have been involved in baptism in (or 'with') that name (*cf.* 2:38; 10:48; *cf.* the 'word' of Eph. 5:26). **17** *When I had returned to Jerusalem.* This was in the third year from his conversion (see 9:26; Gal. 1:18). **18** *Make haste and get quickly out of Jerusalem.* In 9:29, 30 the Jerusalem brethren, getting wind of a plot against Paul, take him to Caesarea. This is not the only place in Acts where action is taken in simultaneous response to divine revelation and human advice. **19** *And I said, Lord, they themselves know. . . .* Paul argues that he is the very man to persuade the Jews, because they must remember how whole-heartedly he persecuted the Christians and must therefore realize that the reasons for his change of attitude are overwhelmingly cogent. **21** *I will send you far away to the Gentiles.* And so he went back to Tarsus, and in that neighbourhood and later in Antioch he had ample opportunity to fulfil his commission to evangelize Gentiles.

22 *Up to this word they listened to him*; *i.e.* to the word 'Gentiles'; this reminded them of their grievance. **23** *Threw dust into the air.* 'In England mud is more frequently available' (Lake and Cadbury). **25** *Is it lawful for you to scourge a man who is a Roman citizen, and uncondemned?* Paul at once protests his Roman citizenship, which exempted him from this treatment. (Thus far he had mentioned only his Tarsian citizenship; 21:39.) A non-citizen might be scourged in order to make him admit the truth. As in 16:37, *uncondemned* means 'without having my case investigated'. **28** *I bought this citizenship for a large sum.* This may be sarcastic: 'I know how much it cost me to buy Roman citizenship; if a man like you can claim it, it must have become cheap of late.' The officer's gentile name 'Claudius' (23:26) suggests that he had become a citizen in the reign of Claudius. *But I was born a citizen.* How Paul's father or earlier ancestor acquired Roman citizenship we do not know. A man of Paul's status might prove his Roman citizenship by producing a diptych containing a certified copy of his birth registration—if he had it ready to hand.

22:30 – 23:35 Paul before the Sanhedrin: he is sent to Caesarea. A Roman citizen must be treated with scrupulous regard to the due processes of law, so next day the captain brought Paul face to face with the Sanhedrin. Ananias, the high priest, behaved in a thoroughly disgraceful manner; and it is excessively squeamish to censure Paul for his plain speaking to him (for which, indeed, he apologized to the official, if not to the man), or for his throwing the apple of discord between the Sadducees and Pharisees. It was just the question of resurrection that made all the difference, for to Paul the general resurrection in which Pharisees believed hung upon the resurrection of Christ. A Pharisee might become a Christian without ceasing to be a Pharisee (*cf.* 15:5); a Sadducee could not become a Christian and remain a Sadducee.

The captain, as far as ever from learning what the real cause of the trouble was, dismissed the meeting and ordered Paul to be taken back to the fortress. His troubles were not lessened when he learned of a plot against Paul's life, and so he sent him off to Caesarea at dead of night, under a well-armed escort, to Felix, the Roman procurator of Judea.

30 *The chief priests and all the council*; *i.e.* the Sanhedrin, in which the chief-priestly Sadducean families played an influential part. If Paul had broken the Jewish law in a matter of which Rome took cognizance, it was the Sanhedrin's business to try and sentence him, and the Roman governor's to ratify a capital sentence. **23:1** *I have lived before God in all good conscience.* Cf. Phil. 3:6. **2** *The high priest Ananias.* Ananias, son of Nedebaeus, a notoriously unscrupulous and avaricious politician, was high priest from 47 to 58. **3** *God shall strike you.* Some have seen the fulfilment of these words in Ananias's assassination by Zealots in 66. *Contrary to the law.* Jewish law presumed a man's innocence until his guilt was proved. **5** *I did not know . . . that he was the high priest.* Does he mean 'I didn't think that a man who spoke like that could possibly be the high priest'? *You shall not speak evil of a ruler of your people.* Quoted from Ex. 22:28. **6** *With respect to the hope and the resurrection of the dead I am on trial.* The resurrection of Christ, the foundation of Israel's hope, as he saw it, was central to Paul's gospel. **8** *The Sadducees say that there is no resurrection.* Cf. Mk. 12:18 and parallels. *Nor angel, nor spirit.* 'What they rejected was the developed doctrine of the two kingdoms with their hierarchies of good and evil spirits' (T. W. Manson). *The Pharisees acknowledge them all*; *i.e.* both resurrection and angels and spirits. **11** *So you must bear witness also at Rome*, thus confirming Paul's own purpose. **12** *By an oath*, breach of which would automatically incur the divine wrath against perjurers. **14** *The chief priests and elders.* Not the whole Sanhedrin, as appears from v. 15 (*with the council*), but that part of it which was most hostile to Paul.

16 *The son of Paul's sister.* The first reference to any member of Paul's family; we wish that we knew more about them. **23** *Get ready . . . to go as far as Caesarea.* The escort consisted of

heavy-armed infantry, cavalry, and light-armed troops, the three constituents of the Roman army. Caesarea was the headquarters of the provincial administration of Judea. **24** *Felix the governor*; *i.e.* Antonius Felix, procurator of Judea AD 52–59. **26** *His Excellency the governor.* The title 'most excellent' (Gk. *kratistos*, equivalent of Lat. *egregius*) was given primarily to members of the equestrian order, from which such procurators were normally drawn (Felix was an exception). It is given in Acts also to Festus (26:25) and in Lk. 1:3 to Theophilus. **27** *Having learned that he was a Roman citizen.* A delicate manipulation of the truth; it was rather later that Lysias learned this fact! **30** *I sent.* The 'epistolary aorist' in Greek. The English idiom requires 'I am sending'. **31** *Antipatris* was about 10 miles N of Lydda and 25 miles S of Caesarea (mod. Ras el-'Ain or Rosh ha-'Ayin). **32** *Leaving the horsemen to go on with him.* The road from Antipatris ran through open country, inhabited mainly by Gentiles. **35** *Herod's praetorium*; a palace in Caesarea, built for himself by Herod the Great, and now serving as official headquarters for the procurator.

24:1 – 26:32 Paul in Caesarea

24:1–27 Paul and Felix. Felix, a man of ignoble birth, a freedman who had attained high station because his brother Pallas was an influential favourite at the imperial court, has been pilloried for all time in the cutting epigram of Tacitus: 'he exercised the authority of a king with the mind of a slave.' His present wife was Drusilla, the younger daughter of Herod Agrippa I, and they both knew something of Christianity, though their interest was strictly academic.

A few days later, a delegation from the Sanhedrin, led by the high priest and assisted by the services of a second-rate orator called Tertullus, went down to Caesarea to state their case against Paul. Tertullus began his speech with a magnificent flourish, but it tailed away in a very lame and impotent conclusion, Paul being indicted only in general terms, not unlike those in which Christ was accused before Pilate (Lk. 23:2).

To each of Tertullus's charges Paul opposed a categorical negative, telling exactly why he had come to Jerusalem and what he had done since coming there, insisting again that the whole difference between him and his opponents hinged on this question of resurrection, which was no new-fangled notion of his own, but one which had been handed down from his fathers. If we realize the centrality of the resurrection in Paul's gospel, we shall not quibble at this statement of his case.

Felix adjourned proceedings until Lysias, the captain, could come down from Jerusalem to give his evidence. Meanwhile he and his wife Drusilla availed themselves of Paul's presence in Caesarea to summon him frequently to their presence for theological discussion. Although their interest was academic, Paul's was not, for he seized the opportunity to discourse on three subjects which both his hearers badly needed to hear about—*justice and self-control and future judgment* (v. 25)—so much so that Felix trembled, but did no more about it. He kept on postponing a decision on Paul's case, hoping to receive money for releasing him, until after two years he was recalled to Rome; and knowing that the Jews were likely in any case to send an adverse report of his term of office to imperial headquarters, he decided to ingratiate himself with them at least to the extent of not releasing Paul, but leaving him in custody for his successor Festus to deal with.

2 *Since through you we enjoy much peace.* Felix's procuratorship was marked by severe attempts to suppress insurgent bands, and so great was the consequent disaffection that only by courtesy could the ensuing conditions be described as 'peace'. Some Jewish nationalists would have been inclined, in words attributed to a later opponent of the Romans, to charge them with 'making a desert and calling it peace'. The Jews of Jerusalem had, however, co-operated with Felix in putting down the Egyptian mentioned in 21:38. **5** *A pestilent fellow, an agitator among all the Jews throughout the world.* Tertullus represents Paul as a disturber of the peace in terms which were calculated to suggest that he was another insurgent leader of the class that Felix had so energetically suppressed, but more dangerous than most, because his activities were of wider range. It was easy to portray the spiritual Messianism of the gospel as a form of militant and political Messianism (*cf.* 17:6, 7). *The sect of the Nazarenes.* The most natural explanation is that the Christians received this appellation after Jesus the Nazarene; but other explanations are current, such as that the term means 'observants'. In Hebrew and Arabic Christians are still known as 'Nazarenes'. **6** *We seized him.* The words which are supplied in RSV mg., 'and we would have judged him according to our law. But the chief captain Lysias came and with great violence took him out of our hands, commanding his accusers to come before you' (*cf.* AV text), represent a 'western' reading which has found its way into the Received Text; although not attested by the best authorities, it bears strong marks of genuineness. The reproachful reference to the 'great violence' with which Lysias took Paul away from his Jewish enemies when they were about to judge him according to their law is an even grosser manipulation of the facts than Lysias himself had practised in his letter to Felix (23:27). **11** *Twelve days.* From the time-notes which are fairly full in this part of Acts (*cf.* 21:15, 18, 26, 27; 22:30; 23:11, 12, 23, 32; 24:1), we conclude that the seven days of 21:27 were only beginning when Paul was arrested. **14** *The Way, which they call a sect.* Christians spoke of their movement as 'the Way', for to them it was the true fulfilment of

Israel's faith and the one way of salvation. Non-Christians called it *a sect*—a party within Judaism (but much less respectable than the parties of Sadducees, Pharisees, and so forth). The Greek word is *hairesis*, used of 'the party of the Sadducees' (5:17) and of 'the party of the Pharisees' (15:5). **15** *Of both the just and the unjust.* This is the only place in the NT where Paul refers definitely to a resurrection of the unjust (*cf.* Jn. 5:28, 29; Rev. 20:12ff.). **17** *To bring to my nation alms and offerings.* The sums contributed by Gentile churches for the relief of the Jerusalem Christians. This is the only reference to the collection in Acts, and it is expressed in such general and allusive terms as to suggest that Luke's reticence has some apologetic motivation. **21** *Except this one thing.* He is not blaming himself for his words before the Sanhedrin (he has just repeated the same argument before Felix, vv. 14, 15); but he maintains that the one charge that can properly be brought against him is a theological one. **22** *Having a rather accurate knowledge of the Way*—possibly derived from *his wife Drusilla, who was a Jewess* (v. 24), a daughter, in fact, of 'Herod the king' of 12:1. (Felix, despite his low birth, married into distinguished families; his three successive wives were all princesses, one of them a granddaughter of Antony and Cleopatra. Drusilla was his third. They had a son, Agrippa, who perished in the eruption of Vesuvius of AD 79.) **25** *When I have an opportunity I will summon you.* He did this rather frequently, moved partly by theological interest of a strictly detached character, and partly by financial expectations (v. 26). Laws against bribery were more often violated than observed by Roman provincial administrators. Ramsay argued that there must have been a considerable improvement in Paul's financial position about this time; there is not much evidence for this, but he no doubt received gifts of money from the Gentile churches which he had founded. **27** *But when two years had elapsed, Felix was succeeded by Porcius Festus.* Felix was recalled because of his violent but ineffective intervention in riots between the Jewish and Gentile inhabitants of Caesarea. A new provincial coinage in AD 59 suggests that this was the year of the change of procurators.

25:1-12 Paul appeals to Caesar. Festus, a more upright man than Felix, arrived in his province some time in AD 59; and after a few days went up from Caesarea, the seat of government, to Jerusalem to meet the high priest and Sanhedrin. These lost no time in bringing up Paul's case, hoping that Festus in his inexperience would allow them to have their way with Paul. Festus did not accede to their request that Paul should be sent up to Jerusalem, but invited them to come down to Caesarea and state their case against him. This they did after 8 or 10 days, making charges which they could not substantiate, and to which Paul returned uncompromising negatives. Then Festus, perplexed and wishing to do the Jews a favour at the outset of his term of office, asked Paul if he were willing to go up to Jerusalem to be tried before him there; and Paul, afraid lest the weakness of Festus might again expose him to danger from his bitterest enemies, made a far-reaching decision: availing himself of his privilege as a Roman citizen, he appealed from the provincial tribunal to Caesar himself to be tried before the supreme court of the Empire. His previous experience of Roman justice probably made him confident of getting an impartial hearing there, and perhaps a verdict which would carry with it independent recognition as a *religio licita*. Festus gladly seized this opportunity of avoiding the responsibility of making a difficult decision; his only trouble now was to know how to frame the report which he should send to Rome with Paul.

1 *When Festus had come into his province.* We have no information about Festus outside the writings of Luke and Josephus. His administration was not marked by the excesses of his predecessor and successor, but it was of short duration, being terminated by his death in AD 62. **8** *Nor against Caesar.* In addition to answering the old charges of offences against the Jewish law in general and of profaning the Temple in particular, he also rebuts the charge of activity against the emperor's interests (see 24:5). **9** *Do you wish to go up to Jerusalem?* The suggestion seemed reasonable enough; as the alleged crime was committed at Jerusalem, Jerusalem might seem the most appropriate place to have the charge examined, and Festus himself proposed to act as judge. But Paul was afraid that this one concession to the Sanhedrin might lead to others. **10** *I am standing before Caesar's tribunal*, the procurator being the Emperor's representative. **11** *I appeal to Caesar.* The right to appeal to the emperor, which every Roman citizen enjoyed, arose out of the earlier right of appeal to the sovereign Roman people. The right might be exercised by appealing against a magistrate's verdict or at any earlier stage in the proceedings, 'claiming that the investigation be carried out at Rome and the judgment pronounced by the Emperor himself' (Schürer). The present emperor was Nero (AD 54–68).

25:13–27 Agrippa the Younger visits Festus. A way out of his difficulty soon presented itself to Festus. On the NE borders of his province was the petty kingdom of Herod Agrippa II (son of the Herod of Acts 12:1), whose capital was at Caesarea Philippi, famed in Gospel story. He and his sister Bernice, the elder sister of Drusilla, were about to pay their respects to the new imperial representative, and Agrippa was known to be an expert in all matters affecting the Jewish religion. Among other things, he had the right of appointing (and deposing) the Jewish high priests, and hence has sometimes been called, not very accurately, 'the secular head of the Jewish church'. So when he and his sister came to Caesarea, Festus sought help from Agrippa in framing his report on

Paul; it was necessary that he should grasp the gravamen of the Sanhedrin's accusation in order to communicate it to the emperor, but all that he could make out was that the trouble concerned *one Jesus, who was dead, but whom Paul asserted to be alive* (v. 19). Paul had made his main point clear enough, in spite of the procurator's lack of comprehension! Agrippa was interested and expressed a desire to see the man himself. So next day Festus, Agrippa and Bernice seated themselves in state, in the company of the procurator's entourage and the chief men of Caesarea. Paul was then brought before them, introduced by Festus to Agrippa, who gave him permission to state his case.

13 *Agrippa the king and Bernice.* This Agrippa was only 17 at the time of his father's death in AD 44, and so Claudius was dissuaded from appointing him to succeed his father as king of Judea, but a few years later gave him as a kingdom the former territory of Philip the tetrarch (Lk. 3:1), which Nero enlarged. Bernice figures later in Roman history, when the crown prince Titus wished to marry her (*c.* AD 75) but changed his mind in view of popular disapproval at Rome. **19** *Their own superstition*; RV 'their own religion'. As Agrippa professed the Jewish religion himself, Festus would hardly have referred to it before him in disparaging terms. **21** *The emperor* (Gk. *Sebastos*, Lat. *Augustus*); a title of honour, 'His Majesty'. **23** *Military tribunes*; there were five cohorts at Caesarea, each in the charge of a military tribune. **26** *My lord*; *i.e.* the emperor.

26:1–23 Paul's speech before Agrippa. Paul proceeded to state his case with no reluctance, saluting the distinguished audience and congratulating himself on so illustrious an opportunity of making known the message which it was his life's mission to proclaim. This speech may well be called Paul's *Apologia Pro Vita Sua*. Here for the third time we have the story of his conversion, told for the second time by himself. The differences between his narration here and that to the Jerusalem mob in ch. 22 are mainly differences of emphasis; on each occasion he emphasized those aspects of the story which were likely to interest his audience at the time. The present speech may be divided into exordium (vv. 2, 3); his stand as a Pharisee for the hope of Israel, which involves the belief in resurrection (vv. 4–8); the account of his persecuting zeal (vv. 9–11); the heavenly vision (vv. 12–18); his life of obedience thereto (vv. 19, 20); his arrest (v. 21); the substance of his preaching (vv. 22, 23). The Greek style of the original is unusually elegant, as befitting this distinguished audience.

Point by point Paul tells his story, insisting throughout that he is guilty of no innovation, that the hope which he proclaims is the ancestral hope of his whole people, that he preaches no other things than what Moses and the prophets said would happen, namely, that the Messiah was to suffer and rise from the dead, and that light and salvation were thereby to be offered both to the Jews and to the Gentiles.

1 *Paul stretched out his hand*; *i.e.* in a gesture of salutation. **2** *Before you* is emphatic. **5** *Our religion* (Gk. *thrēskeia*); *i.e.* 'cultus', 'ritual' (referring to the external manifestations of religion); a different word from that used by Festus in 25:19 (Gk. *deisidaimonia*). **6** *The promise made by God to our fathers.* Paul has in mind the promise made in particular to Abraham, Isaac and Jacob, of world-wide blessing to come through their progeny. This promise was fulfilled in Jesus, and especially by His resurrection. **7** *Our twelve tribes.* Cf. Jas. 1:1. Paul knows nothing of the figment of ten 'lost' tribes. *For this hope I am accused by Jews.* That Jews, of all people, should show hostility to one who proclaimed that on which the fulfilment of their ancestral hope depended was preposterous. **8** *Why is it thought incredible by any of you that God raises the dead?* There is no textual or contextual justification for moving this verse to a position between vv. 22 and 23. *By any of you* is again emphatic: 'by any of you Jews'. The hope of Israel was bound up with the resurrection of Christ. **10** *When they were put to death I cast my vote against them.* As in the case of Stephen (8:1). **11** *Blaspheme*; *i.e.* to say 'Jesus is anathema' (1 Cor. 12:3) or something to the same effect. *To foreign cities*; *i.e.* cities outside Palestine, such as Damascus. **14** *When we had all fallen to the ground.* In the other version of the incident, only Paul is said to have fallen. *In the Hebrew language*; *i.e.* in his Aramaic mother-tongue. *It hurts you to kick against the goads.* The picture is that of an ox kicking out against the goad and only causing itself more trouble by doing so. The expression is proverbial and can be paralleled in several places in Greek literature. *The goads* are the pressure now compelling Paul to turn round in his tracks and travel in the opposite direction to that which he had been pursuing hitherto. **16–18** summarize the communication which Paul received from the Lord on the Damascus road, through Ananias in the house of Judas, and later in the Jerusalem Temple. **16** *Stand upon your feet.* Cf. Ezk. 2:1, where Ezekiel's commission contains these words. Ezekiel, too, had fallen to the ground when he first saw 'visions of God'. *You have seen me.* Cf. on 22:14. **17** *Delivering you.* Cf. Je. 1:8, where Jeremiah hears similar words when receiving his prophetic commission. **18** *To open their eyes.* Cf. Is. 42:7. Paul is called to continue the mission of the obedient Servant inaugurated by his Master (*cf.* 13:47). These echoes of OT prophetic commissions show that in Acts, as in his own writings, Paul is 'a figure of eschatological significance' (J. Munck). The remaining words of v. 18 are characteristically Pauline and can be abundantly paralleled from his Epistles. **20** *Deeds worthy of their repentance*; *i.e.* works which would show that their repentance was genuine. Cf. Mt. 3:8; Lk. 3:8. **23** *That the Christ must suffer, and that, by being the first to rise*

from the dead. . . . This verse seems to consist of headings from a collection of Messianic 'testimonies': 'Is the Messiah to suffer? Is He first by the resurrection of the dead to proclaim light to the (Jewish) people and to the Gentiles?' By these headings Luke summarizes the arguments from the OT which Paul pressed upon Agrippa to demonstrate the truth of his gospel. *Cf.* 3:18; 17:3.

26:24–32 Festus, Agrippa and Bernice make up their minds about Paul. As Paul went on in this vein, Festus, who had been vainly trying to follow the drift of his argument, interjected the observation that his great learning must have driven him mad. Paul was quick to defend himself against the charge of madness, and assured Festus that Agrippa could, if he would, bear witness to the truth of his words, since the subject of all his preaching was also the subject of OT prophecy, and Agrippa himself believed the prophets. His direct appeal to the king put that gentleman in a dilemma. He had followed Paul's talk with interest enough, but he did not want even to appear to commit himself to agreement with Paul and thus lose face with Festus and the others. On the other hand, he did not wish to forfeit Jewish favour by appearing not to believe the prophets. So he laughed off Paul's appeal.

The court then rose, and Festus, Agrippa and Bernice, conferring with one another, agreed that at any rate Paul had done nothing deserving either death or even imprisonment, and that he might have been liberated there and then had he not appealed to Caesar.

24 *Your great learning is turning you mad.* Festus found himself completely out of his depth, and could only conclude that Paul, while obviously extremely learned, had been carried by his learning over the narrow frontier that divides erudition from insanity. **26** *This was not done in a corner*; a proverbial tag. The early Christian preachers regularly insisted that the historical foundations of their gospel were matters of public knowledge (*cf.* 2:22). **27** *I know that you believe.* The implication is that anyone who knows and accepts the truth of the prophetic writings, as Paul is persuaded Agrippa does, must inevitably agree with Paul's conclusions. But Agrippa is not to be manoeuvred into an appearance of supporting Paul's case, nor can he afford to disclaim belief in the prophets. **28** So he says, 'In short, you are trying to persuade me to play the Christian'—for that is the true sense of his words. **29** And Paul replies: 'The short and the long of it is, I could pray that you and all the others here today were what I am, apart from these manacles' (holding out his chained hand). **31** *This man is doing nothing to deserve death or imprisonment.* Luke emphasizes again this official testimony of the law-abiding nature of Christianity and its preachers. **32** *This man could have been set free if he had not appealed to Caesar.* But as he had appealed, the legal procedure must take its course. We need not, with J. V. Bartlet, detect an ominous note in the 'if' clause.

27:1 – 28:31 Paul's journey to Rome

27:1–12 The voyage begins. The narrative of the voyage and shipwreck of Paul is as graphic a piece of descriptive writing as any in the Bible. It has been called 'one of the most instructive documents for the knowledge of ancient seamanship'. (James Smith, *The Voyage and Shipwreck of St. Paul*, 4th edition, 1880, remains an indispensable handbook to the study of this chapter.) We need not allegorize it as a picture of the rise and progress of religion in the soul or of the history of the Christian church in order to derive spiritual profit from it.

the command of a centurion. Paul, with his ready capacity for making friends, soon won the favour of this Roman officer (it is remarkable how the centurions in the NT are uniformly presented in a favourable light); and this favour was to stand him in good stead not only at Sidon at the beginning of the voyage, but to even better purpose at the journey's end, when the soldiers were for killing the prisoners to prevent their escape.

They sailed to Myra in their first ship, which was calling at the ports of the province of Asia. There they transhipped to a vessel of the Alexandrian grain fleet. Egypt was the great granary of Rome, and the fleet which served the corn trade between these two places was a State

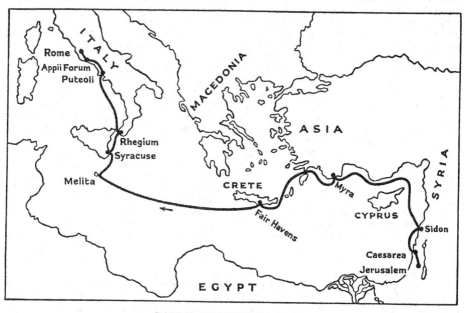

PAUL'S JOURNEY TO ROME

It is, above all, valuable to us for its portrayal of the character of Paul in circumstances in which the real man is most likely to be revealed. We have seen him in many roles, but here we see him as the practical man in an emergency. Not once or twice the world has had to thank the great saints and mystics for providing that help in critical times which realistic, practical men of affairs were unable to give. When Lot had to be rescued from Chedorlaomer and his allies, it was Abraham—Abraham the man of faith, Abraham the 'unpractical' man from the viewpoint of secular business methods—who seized the opportunity and proved himself to be the man of the moment.

Luke, Paul's fellow-traveller on this occasion, looked at the sea with the eye of a Greek, and tells us what he saw. Together with Luke and Aristarchus, Paul set sail from Palestine under

service. Sailing became dangerous in the Mediterranean after 14 September, and ceased altogether for the winter after 11 November; and before they reached Fair Havens, a harbour on the south of Crete, the Day of Atonement (*the fast* of v. 9) was already past; it fell on 5 October in AD 59. As it was thus getting late for safe sailing, a ship's council was called, at which Paul, as a distinguished passenger and experienced traveller, was apparently present. He urged them strongly to remain where they were, at Fair Havens, but the shipowner and the helmsman thought they might be able to make Phoenix, another and more commodious port farther west along the S coast of Crete. The centurion, who, as the principal officer on board, had the last word, naturally accepted the advice of the experts rather than Paul's, and so they set sail for Phoenix.

1 *That we should sail for Italy.* The 'we' narrative is resumed, and continues to 28:16, but Luke was probably not far away from Paul during his 2 years' custody in Palestine. *The Augustan Cohort*; 'The Emperor's Cohort'. We have evidence that a similarly named cohort (*Cohors I Augusta*) was in Syria in the time of Augustus; but here we may have to do with the corps of *frumentarii* charged with the organization of the Roman grain-supply. **2** *A ship of Adramyttium*, a port in Mysia, opposite Lesbos. The ship was a coaster; Julius expected that at one of the ports which it touched he would find a ship bound for Rome. *Aristarchus*. Cf. 19:29; 20:4. **4** *We sailed under the lee of Cyprus*; east and north of it, the prevailing winds in the Levant throughout the summer months being from the west. **5** *Myra* was an important centre for cross-sea traffic and one of the chief ports of the Egyptian grain service. **6** *A ship of Alexandria.* With a steady wind from the west, the best route from Alexandria to Rome was by Myra. **7** *Cnidus* lay at the extremity of the Triopian promontory of SW Asia Minor. *We sailed under the lee of Crete*; i.e. east and south of the island. **8** *Coasting along it with difficulty*; perhaps because of the rocks round Cape Salmone (at the east end of Crete). *Fair Havens*. Modern Kalolimonias. After Fair Havens the coast tends northwards, and would therefore no longer afford such good protection from a north-west wind. **11** *The captain*; i.e. the helmsman (Gk. *kybernētēs*). **12** *Phoenix*; perhaps identical with modern Phineka. The more popular identification with Lutro (so J. Smith) is probably responsible for the doubtful RSV rendering of the closing words of the verse: *looking northeast and southeast.* RSV mg. reads 'southwest and northwest', which represents the Greek more accurately.

27:13–44 Storm and shipwreck. Before they could make the port of Phoenix, however, a typhonic wind blew down upon them from Mt. Ida, in Crete, from the north-east, and drove them away from the Cretan coast. With great difficulty they got the dinghy on board (in normal weather it was towed astern), and, having jettisoned part of the cargo, they contrived, by careful tacking, to avoid being driven on the quicksands off the Libyan shore. They continued for a fortnight in a west-north-west direction through the central Mediterranean, until all hope of safety was given up—by all except Paul, who stands out as the one man on board able to take charge of this hopeless situation and inspire his fellow-passengers with encouragement and fresh hope. The confidence which he had derived from an angelic visitant he sought to pass on to them, and encouraged them to take food.

Paul's confidence was justified; they found that they were approaching land, and although, by reason of the ship's prow being caught fast in a spit of sand and the stern being beaten by the waves, the vessel broke amidships, yet all on board escaped safe to shore, 276 in all.

14 *A tempestuous wind*; lit. 'a typhonic wind'. *Called the northeaster* (RV 'Euraquilo'); a hybrid formation, from Greek *Euros* ('east wind') and Latin *Aquilo* ('north wind'). *Struck down from the land*; i.e. from Crete. **15** *We gave way to it and were driven*; 'we scudded before it'. **16** *Cauda*; modern Gavdho, Italian Gozzo, in the vicinity of which the Battle of Cape Matapan was fought on 28 March, 1941. *We managed with difficulty to secure the boat*; i.e. to get the dinghy aboard. **17** *They took measures to undergird the ship.* The *measures* (Gk. *boētheiai*, 'helps') were apparently cables for bracing the ship. Smith quotes from Falconer's *Marine Dictionary*: 'To frap a ship is to pass four or five turns of a large cable-laid rope round the hull or frame of a ship, to support her . . . when it is apprehended that she is not strong enough to resist the violent efforts of the sea.' *The Syrtis*; i.e. the quicksands off the north coast of Africa. *Lowered the gear.* Smith takes the phrase to mean that they sent down on deck the 'top-hamper'. *So were driven*; on the starboard tack, according to Smith. **18** *The cargo*; i.e. the grain which the ship was taking to Italy. **19** *The tackle*; i.e. the spare gear. **20** *Neither sun nor stars appeared.* They were thus left in ignorance of their course.

21 *Without food.* This would be due to various reasons, such as the difficulty of cooking, spoiling of food by sea-water, sea-sickness, *etc.* Cf. v. 33. *You should have listened to me.* We appreciate Paul's inability to avoid saying 'I told you so'; but he now proves a tower of strength to his despairing shipmates. **24** *God has granted you all those who sail with you.* Cf. Gn. 18:26 for the principle that the presence of good men is a protection to a community. **27** *We were drifting across the sea of Adria*; i.e. the central Mediterranean. (This is not the Adriatic Sea, which was then known as the 'Gulf of Adria'.) *They were nearing land*; lit. 'some land was approaching'. Possibly they could hear the breakers. **28** *They sounded. . . .* The soundings agree with the direction of a ship passing Koura on her way into St. Paul's Bay, Malta. **29** *They let out four anchors from the stern*; i.e. to act as a brake. Anchoring by the stern on this occasion meant that the prows kept pointing to the shore. **31** *Unless these men stay in the ship.* Paul's presence of mind appears again. Had the sailors made good their escape, there would not have been enough skilled hands to work the ship. **32** *Cut away the ropes of the boat*; i.e. 'cut away the falls of the dinghy', possibly misunderstanding Paul's advice. They certainly prevented the sailors from getting away, but also made the business of getting ashore more difficult.

33 *You have continued . . . without food.* Cf. v. 21. **35** *Giving thanks* (Gk. *eucharisteō*). Some have conjectured that the Christians on board made this meal a Eucharist, but there is no proof of this. **37** *Two hundred and seventy-six.* The Vatican MS says 'seventy-six', but there is no improbability in the larger figure. In AD 63

Josephus sailed for Rome in a ship which had 600 on board (and it too was wrecked in the Sea of Adria). **38** *They lightened the ship*; *i.e.* by jettisoning the rest of the grain cargo (*cf.* v. 18). **39** *A bay with a beach* (lit. 'with a sandy beach'). This sandy beach is the only feature of Luke's narrative now missing from the traditional site in St. Paul's Bay; Smith considers that it was 'worn away by the wasting action of the sea'. **40** *The ropes that tied the rudders*; *i.e.* the lashings of the steering-paddles. *The foresail* (Gk. *artemōn*), a small sail on the foremast. **41** *A shoal*; lit. 'a place of two seas' (mg.). This was the narrow channel between Malta and Salmonetta (Smith). **44** *On pieces of the ship*; or possibly (but less probably), 'on the backs of members of the crew' (lit. 'on some of those from the ship').

28:1-10 Winter in Malta. When the shipwrecked party landed, they found that they had arrived at the island of Malta, an appropriate name, for it is a Phoenician word meaning 'refuge'. The natives received them hospitably, and lit a fire to warm and dry them. Paul again shows a practical turn of mind; he gathers sticks to keep the fire going, even though one of the sticks turned out to be a snake, torpid through the cold. When the heat of the fire thawed it, it fixed on Paul's hand, and there is quiet humour in Luke's description of the natives' reaction, first thinking he was a murderer whom Justice had resolved to destroy, if not by the sea, then by the snake, and then seeing no harm come to him after he shook the beast into the fire, changing their minds and concluding that he was a god.

But although he was not a god, yet both Paul and Luke proved very useful guests during the three winter months they spent in Malta. First Paul healed of dysentery the father of Publius, the chief man of the island. Then others were tended by Paul and Luke and, when at last they left, the islanders loaded them with gifts.

1 *We then learned that the island was called Malta*. If the sailors did not recognize Malta at first, it may have been because they were accustomed to landing at Valletta. **2** *The natives* (lit. 'the barbarians'). Greeks and Romans used the term 'barbarians' of all who did not share their civilization. **3** *A viper came out because of the heat. Cf.* T. E. Lawrence, *Revolt in the Desert*, p. 107: 'When the fire grew hot a long black snake wound slowly out into our group; we must have gathered it, torpid, with the twigs.' It has been suggested that the snake was a *Coronella leopardinus*, which is found in Malta and looks like a viper but is not poisonous. There are now no poisonous snakes in Malta. **4** *Justice* (Gk. *dikē*), personified as a deity. **6** *Said that he was a god*. M. Dibelius finds a different attitude in the narrative here from that shown in 14:14ff., where Paul and Barnabas cry out with horror at the ascription to them of divine honours. This overlooks the humour of the situation as Luke sees and describes it. **7** *The chief man of the island*; lit. 'the first man (Gk. *prōtos*) of the island'.

Both Greek and Latin inscriptions confirm the accuracy of this title in a Maltese context. **9** *Came and were cured*. 'The whole story of the abode of the narrator in Malta is displayed in a medical light' (Harnack). **10** *Many gifts*. Gk. *timē* (lit. 'honour') may mean 'honorarium' here, as in 1 Tim. 5:17.

28:11-16 The last lap. The voyage to Italy was completed early in AD 60 in another ship of the Alexandrian grain service. They disembarked at Puteoli, where they were entertained for some days by Christians. Then they proceeded to Rome, and as they travelled along the *Via Appia*, they were met, while still 40 miles away from the city, by a delegation of Roman Christians who had walked that distance to greet the apostle and escort him to the capital. There he was handed over to the appropriate authorities.

11 *A ship of Alexandria*. Probably it also belonged to the grain fleet. *Which had wintered in the island*; probably in the harbour at Valletta. *The Twin Brothers* (Gk. *Dioskouroi*, 'The Heavenly Twins'), *i.e.* Castor and Pollux. Ships, like inns, took their names from their figureheads. **12** *Syracuse* was on the E coast of Sicily. It was the chief city of that island, with a double harbour. **13** *We made a circuit*; better, as in RV mg., 'we cast loose'. *Rhegium*. This was Reggio di Calabria, a Greek colony in the toe of Italy. *Puteoli*, modern Pozzuoli, then the principal port of S Italy, and one of the two chief ports of arrival of the Alexandrian grain fleet (the other being Ostia). **15** *The Forum of Appius and Three Taverns*. Both these places were situated on the Appian Way; Appii Forum was a market-town *c.* 43 miles S of Rome, Three Taverns (*Tres Tabernae*) was a station *c.* 33 miles from Rome. *Paul thanked God and took courage*. He might well be glad for this assurance that he was not friendless in the Eternal City. He had assured the Roman Christians 3 years previously of his desire to see them; now, in circumstances then unforeseen, he found his desire fulfilled. **16** *When we came into Rome*. AV adds 'the centurion delivered the prisoners to the captain of the guard'. This clause, which came into the Byzantine text from the 'western' text, is absent from other texts and therefore from RSV. The 'captain of the guard' (Gk. *stratopedarchos*) might be the camp-commandant of the emperor's praetorian guard. *Paul was allowed to stay by himself, with the soldier that guarded him*, to whom he would be lightly handcuffed.

28:17-31 Paul in Rome. Paul's interview with the Roman Jews sums up one of the themes of Acts, the general rejection of the gospel by the Jews. Paul, as usual, gets the last word, 'generally with devastating effect', says one commentator, and the last word on this occasion is that quotation from Is. 6:9, 10 which our Lord similarly used in the days of His flesh (*cf.* Mk. 4:12; Jn. 12:40).

The other and chief theme of Acts is summed up in the closing words of the book, which depict Paul spending 2 years at the heart of the Empire, under house-arrest but free to receive visitors, and proclaiming the gospel without let or hindrance. At last, by mysterious paths, his desire had had its fulfilment: 'I am eager to preach the gospel to you also who are in Rome' (Rom. 1:15). 'The victory of the Word of God,' says Bengel, 'Paul at Rome, the apex of the Gospel, the end of Acts. ... It began at Jerusalem; it ends at Rome. Here, O Church, thou hast thy pattern; it is thine to preserve it and guard thy deposit.'

19 *Though I had no charge to bring against my nation.* He confines himself strictly to the defensive; he will make no complaint against the Jewish people. **20** *It is because of the hope of Israel that I am bound with this chain.* For his constant emphasis on this point *cf.* 23:6; 24:14, 15; 26:6, 7. **21** *We have received no letters. . . .* The Roman Jews would be anxious to dissociate themselves as far as possible from the prosecution of a Roman citizen who had won favourable verdicts from Festus and Agrippa. **22** *With regard to this sect we know that everywhere it is spoken against.* They had probably had more experience of Christianity in Rome itself than they were prepared to admit at the moment (see on 18:2). **25** *They departed*; better, 'they began to break up'. **28** *This salvation of God has been sent to the Gentiles; they will listen.* This is a recurrent theme from first to last in the record of Paul's ministry in Acts (*cf.* 13:46). What appears in AV as v. 29 is a 'western' reading which was taken over by the Byzantine text. **30** *Two whole years.* They were the years AD 60 and 61. What happened at the end of them we can only surmise. 'Perhaps Paul benefited from the clemency of Nero, and secured a merely casual release. But there is no necessity to construe Acts to mean that he was released at all' (A. N. Sherwin-White). *At his own expense*, 'on his own earnings'. **31** *Preaching the kingdom of God and teaching about the Lord Jesus Christ. Cf.* v. 23. 'In the conjunction of these words the progress of doctrine appears. All is founded upon the old Jewish expectation of a kingdom of God; but it is now explained how that expectation is fulfilled in the person of Jesus, and the account of its realization consists in the unfolding of the truth concerning Him. The manifestation of Christ being finished, the kingdom is already begun. Those who receive *Him* enter into *it*. Having overcome the sharpness of death, He has opened the kingdom of heaven to all believers' (T. D. Bernard).

F. F. BRUCE

Romans

INTRODUCTION

See also the General Article, 'The Pauline Epistles', p. 71.

THE CHRISTIAN CHURCH AT ROME

Its origin

The fellowship of saints in Rome is expressly stated by Paul not to be of his own founding (1:10–15; 15:20–22). It is the exception to the apostle's rule not to build on another man's foundation (2 Cor. 10:16). Churches established by his co-workers Paul reckons as his own. By whom, how and when the church at Rome came into being forms one of the problems of early ecclesiastical history. The tradition that Peter was the founder is not accepted, but the denial does not exclude the fact that this leading apostle was certainly at some time or other in Rome and there suffered martyrdom. But when Paul wrote his letter to the Roman church it is evident that Peter was not in the city. Had this alleged head of the church been in Rome surely Paul would have mentioned the fact, or indeed never addressed an Epistle to this church at all. It is believed that the church at Rome must have originated in the witness and labours of Christians who were Empire citizens in the habit of travelling to and from the metropolis. It is not unlikely that the work of evangelization was commenced by the 'visitors from Rome, both Jews and proselytes' (Acts 2:10). These witnesses of Pentecost would in after days be assisted by Christians from Syrian Antioch, Ephesus and Corinth and thus augment the fellowship. By the year AD 49 the presence of an active Christian group in the imperial city is attested if, as is likely, the edict of Claudius in that year has in view the disturbance caused by Jewish-Christian debates (Claudius, Suetonius reports, 'expelled the Jews from Rome, since they were continually making disturbances fomented by Chrestus'). By the time Paul wrote his letter to the church at Rome the Christian community would be of a goodly size. This supposition is confirmed by what Clement of Rome (AD 96) says of the martyrs who suffered in Nero's pogrom in the mid-sixties: 'a great multitude of the elect'.

Its character

The church at Rome was evidently composed of both Jews and Gentiles. As Paul does not address any special ecclesiastical dignitary or any persons with recognized authority, it is deduced that there was no central organization.

If Palestinian Christian Jews founded the fellowship they would evangelize first among their own countrymen, who formed a colony in Rome and had many synagogues. The apostle throughout the Epistle implies Jewish readers by addressing them particularly and by many allusions to the OT (there are about 60 direct quotations) and to the history of the children of Israel.

Again Paul certainly has in mind Gentile readers who would form the majority of the Christian community. He addresses such in the opening chapter (1:1–15). *Cf.* also 15:14–16; 11:13, where there is the unambiguous statement 'I am speaking to you Gentiles. Inasmuch then as I am an apostle to the Gentiles'. It is also significant that the greater number of the names cited in ch. 16 are of Greek or Roman origin. Thus the Roman Christian church was composed of both Jewish and Gentile members, the latter being the more numerous and possibly to a great extent accepting Christianity by way of previous conversion to Judaism. Hence Paul was justified in quoting from the OT and engaging in the problem of the Jewish race.

THE PLACE AND DATE OF WRITING

There is no doubt about the place where this Epistle was written. In his third missionary journey Paul waited at Corinth (see Acts 20:2, 3) for the delegates from the Gentile churches, who bore the offerings for the relief of the destitute Jewish Christians in Jerusalem. We read of this collection in 1 Cor. 16:1–4 and 2 Cor. 8, and of the apostles' last visit to Jerusalem in Acts 24:17, after all the delegates had arrived at Corinth. Some of the names given in the last chapter of the Epistle, such as 'Phoebe, a deaconess of the church at Cenchreae', the port of Corinth, 'Gaius, who is host to me' (*cf.* 1 Cor. 1:14), 'Timothy, my fellow worker' (*cf.* 2 Cor. 1:1), 'Erastus, the city treasurer' (*cf.* 2 Tim. 4:20), have a very definite association with Corinth. Such a careful and well-reasoned Epistle as Romans could have been penned only when Paul was able to stay in a comparatively fixed abode for some period of time. He remained at Corinth for 3 months, according to the testimony of the historian Luke (Acts 20:3), which fulfils the necessary conditions for writing.

An indication of the time of composition is given in ch. 15, where the apostle reveals that he is about to sail to Palestine, bringing with him the 'contribution for the poor', and that then he hopes to be free to visit Rome, and afterwards Spain. This points to the close of the third missionary journey and the last visit to Jerusalem.

It was on the eve of his departure to Jerusalem that Paul finished his letter and addressed it to Rome. Regarding the exact chronology of Paul's life and work no authority can be dogmatic, but depending on the date determined for Gallio's appointment at Corinth (in AD 51 or 52), we may date Paul's residence in that city during the winter of AD 54–55, and fix the writing of the letter in the spring of the later year, AD 55.

THE OCCASION OF WRITING

Why did Paul write to the church at Rome, especially as neither he nor any of his fellow-workers had founded it, nor had he ever previously visited it? The answer to this question involves the question of the form of the Epistle. Is it a theological treatise or simply a letter occasioned by circumstances in the career of Paul? It may be both in some degree, but the point is whether the apostle originally sat down to expound the gospel he preached or took up his pen to write a letter which imminent affairs dictated. The view has been held that Paul felt that his days were numbered and he wished to leave to posterity a definite and final statement of his teaching. That the apostle's doctrine in his day was misunderstood and assailed, that it never lacked critics (especially from the ranks of Judaism), and that it had never had a systematic presentation, may be conceded. The suggestion is, therefore, that Romans was the last will and testament of the great apostle to the Gentiles. Moreover, it is argued that the Roman church was just the right repository for this authoritative document. The logical and theological form of the Epistle, which is the most systematic and closely reasoned, the most doctrinal of all Paul's letters, affords no little ground for the formal theory. But that Romans is a theological treatise is going too far. Note the following arguments against this hypothesis of a studied manifesto of Pauline theology as though it were 'a compendium of Christian doctrine' (Melanchthon).

There is every indication in the Epistle that Paul was addressing a live Christian community out of circumstances which gave reality to his letter.

There is no real justification for suggesting that the apostle felt that 'the sands of time were sinking' and his career about to close so that he must leave his theological system to posterity. Rather, at the time at which he wrote, Paul's eyes were looking to the future of a new missionary enterprise.

Does Romans, in any case, set forth the complete teaching of the apostle? Is there not more of the Pauline theology in his other Epistles which the occasion of writing to the Romans did not immediately educe?

Paul's purpose in writing is definitely stated in the letter and he has no reason to conceal any theological ambition. He writes to intimate his true intention to visit the Roman Christians (see 1:10–13) in order to impart to them as an apostle of Jesus Christ 'some spiritual gift' (cf. 15:29). He makes the best of all his available contacts as ch. 16 reveals. Paul also plainly declares that his coming to Rome falls within a larger plan (see 15:15–24). He has completed as far as lies within his power the evangelization of the Gentiles eastward; now he sets his face to a new missionary enterprise westward. He writes to engage their co-operation in this scheme since Rome is a real strategic centre and the Roman fellowship an influential group in that direction. All the doctrinal part of the Epistle was penned for this very purpose, that the Roman church might apprehend the greatness of divine grace and the wideness of God's mercy, so amazing and so all-embracing that evangelization on his part (and on theirs also) was absolutely imperative.

We may conclude, therefore, that Paul wishes to introduce himself to the readers by a careful statement of what he considers the essence of the apostolic preaching to the Gentiles. 'Romans is the theological self-confession of Paul, which arose out of a concrete necessity of his missionary work' (W. G. Kümmel, *Introduction to the New Testament*, ET 1966, p. 221). An alternative proposal may be mentioned and considered after the textual question of the letter has been looked at.

THE TEXTUAL PROBLEM

The question here is whether the letter is a complete whole and composed all at the same time by the apostle, or whether any other author has had his writing incorporated at an earlier or later date. The problem arises from four points:

A short form of Romans was in circulation during the 2nd and 3rd centuries. Textual evidence shows that we have MSS, in particular, represented by Marcion's *Apostolikon*, ending with ch. 14.

The Epistle as we now read it has various endings. 'The God of peace be with you all. Amen' (15:33). 'The grace of our Lord Jesus Christ be with you all. Amen' (16:24), not found in RSV which omits with the best MSS. 'To the only wise God be glory for evermore through Jesus Christ! Amen' (16:27).

In the shorter recension the doxology which appears in our English versions at 16:25–27 is found at the close of ch. 14. Some MSS insert it at the close of both ch. 14 and ch. 16. Intrinsically also its genuineness has been doubted by some as not being in Paul's usual style.

The personal greetings of ch. 16 are alleged to be inappropriate to the circumstances since Paul was a comparative stranger to the Roman church. They suit rather the church at Ephesus.

In the face of these objections the integrity of the Epistle is still maintained. The solution of the textual problem is probably found in the belief that the heretic Marcion (who flourished at Rome AD 154–166) deliberately expunged the last two chapters because ch. 15 gave Judaism a preparatory function in the furtherance of the gospel. See, *e.g.*, v. 4: 'For whatever was written in former days was written for our instruction, that by steadfastness and by the encouragement of the scriptures we might have hope.' Moreover, ch. 15 has at least five quotations from the OT, while ch. 16 was of no importance to Marcion's views, being neither for them nor against. The longer version, according as we now read it, is accepted as the original version, since the shorter version ending at ch. 14 manifests a bias against the OT. It is possible, however, that Marcion's shortened text is explained not by the heretic's abbreviating work but by the fact that he found the text already mutilated, and this version of the textual history may well account for the presence of 16:25–27 after 14:23 and 15:33 in some traditions as well as after 16:23. As for ch. 16 with its list of names, there appears a certain fitness in their mention considering that Paul's purpose was to create as many contacts as possible, while Rome was as suitable for the home of Paul's friends as Ephesus, even apart from the hypothesis of Ephesus as the origin of many of the Pauline Epistles. The view here accepted is that we have in Romans a complete letter written at one time by the apostle from Corinth. T. W. Manson's theory (set out in reprinted form in *Studies in the Gospels and Epistles*, 1962, pp. 225–241) accepts 1:1 – 15:33 as Paul's letter in its original form. This was subsequently rounded off by the addition of the doxology, 16:25–27. Manson was able to appeal to P46 (which contains the oldest available copy of Romans) for support, for this is how P46 has the text. He proceeded to argue that this was the version of the letter sent to Rome. Ch. 16 contains (on his view) items which connect it with Ephesus; and the letter (1–16) is a version which found its way into the archives of the Ephesian church. A third version (comprising 1:1 – 14:23; 16:25–27), he suggested, was sent to other Pauline churches (*e.g.* in Syria).

From this reconstruction of the textual ancestry of the letter, Manson went on to maintain that Romans was originally conceived not as a pastoral letter intended for Christians at Rome but 'a summing up of the position reached by Paul and his friends at the end of the long controversy' reflected in Galatians, 1 and 2 Corinthians and Philippians. The letter is best understood as a charter of Gentile freedom over against the Judaizers, though its immediate occasion was to prepare the way for Paul's visit to Rome from where the next phase of the Gentile mission westwards would be launched. By this suggested origin, Manson was able to explain the reason for and relevance of the letter's transmission to other centres of Pauline Christianity as well as Rome.

Commentaries mentioned by authors' names

Barrett, C. K. *The Epistle to the Romans* (*Black's New Testament Commentaries*), 1957.

Barrett, C. K. *Reading through Romans*, 1963.

Bruce, F. F. *The Epistle of Paul to the Romans* (*TNTC*), 1963.

Dodd, C. H. *The Epistle of Paul to the Romans* (*MNTC*), 1932.

Leenhardt, F. J. *The Epistle to the Romans*, ET 1961.

Manson, W. 'Notes on the Argument of Romans I–VIII' in *New Testament Essays* in memory of T. W. Manson, ed. A. J. B. Higgins, 1959.

Moule, H. C. G. *The Epistle to the Romans* (*Expositor's Bible*), 1890.

Sanday, W. and Headlam, A. C. *A Critical and Exegetical Commentary on the Epistle to the Romans* (*ICC*), 1902.

OUTLINE OF CONTENTS

COMMENTARY

1:1-17 THE PROLOGUE

1:1-7 The address

The salutation is briefly 'Paul to all the saints, *i.e.* God's chosen and holy people, in Rome'. The form is similar to that adopted in all the Pauline letters as it was the regular epistolary style of the 1st century. We have many examples of such letter-writing in the Greek, and all follow the same pattern; first the writer's name, then the reader's, followed by the greeting. This formula is varied in the Pauline literature according to circumstances. Here, as addressing a church which he has neither founded nor hitherto visited, Paul presents his credentials. **1** He is *a servant of Jesus Christ* (lit. 'a slave'), one whose very life is that of unwavering loyalty and undisputed obedience. Yet, on its OT background, the word stood for an honoured calling and office, gladly accepted by those (such as Israel's kings and prophets) summoned to be God's representatives. *Called to be an apostle*; lit. 'one sent', 'a messenger', and so rendered in 2 Cor. 8:23; Phil 2:25. The special calling here is apostleship. Paul consistently maintained his direct call to this high office (*cf.* 'not from men nor through man', Gal. 1:1). The dignity was normally mediated through the living church in response to the will of the living Christ. The title belonged primarily to the Twelve whose distinction was that they were with Jesus in the days of His flesh. Later it was given to other church leaders and preachers (*cf.* Acts 14:14). *Set apart for the gospel of God.* Thus Paul further introduces himself, harking back (as in Gal. 1:15) to the commission he received from the risen Jesus (Acts 26:15ff.; *cf.* Acts 9:15; 22:14ff.). *The gospel* is God's good news of salvation in Christ, shortly to be expounded in this letter. Occasionally Paul uses the same term to mean 'Christian service' (*e.g.* Phil. 1:5); and this may

be the meaning here. At his conversion-call Paul knew that his future life was to be devoted to Christ's work.

We now have an example of Paul's habit of 'going off at a tangent'. In most of his salutations and elsewhere he expands his thought as ideas chase after each other in swift succession. Here the word 'apostle' leads to the 'gospel' which, in its turn, leads him into a passage of great Christological value. He proceeds to define the gospel of God as divine (v. 1), predicted (v. 2), and Christocentric (vv. 3–5). **2** Before proceeding to describe what the gospel is about, the apostle affirms the continuity of his message with the revelation given previously to the Jewish people. It is in line with all the promises of the prophets of old; it is rooted *in the holy scriptures, i.e.* the OT, which describes God's liberating of His exiled people as His announcement of 'good news' (*cf.* Is. 40:9; 52:7; 61:1). **3–5** The main feature of the gospel is that Jesus Christ is its central theme. In this Christological passage Paul stresses first the incarnation, since that must be the starting-point of the gospel message. But His coming *according to the flesh* was a fulfilment of Messianic prophecy, which looked forward to God's deliverer as a descendant of David's family (2 Sa. 7:12ff.: a Messianic testimony whose importance was seen in the intertestamental Jewish literature, both of the Rabbis and Qumran community, and in the NT church; *cf.* Heb. 1:5; 2 Tim. 2:8); and so his statement in v. 2 is justified. Secondly, *according to the Spirit of holiness, i.e.* in respect of His exaltation by the Holy Spirit's power, following *his resurrection from the dead.* The two phrases containing 'flesh', 'Spirit' denote the two states of Christ (incarnate, exalted). In His earthly life He fulfilled the office of Israel's Messiah (David's Son); risen and exalted by the Spirit's power

(Rom. 8:11), He is now to be acknowledged as the divine Son (Ps. 2:7) ruling in manifest authority. What was hidden in His incarnate life is now openly displayed (2 Cor. 13:4) in His office as the church's *Lord*, *i.e.* sovereign ruler (Rom. 14:9). It is likely that Paul is here using an early credal statement which set out in rhythmical form the substance of Christological faith, expanded in Phil. 2:6-11.

This great gospel, divine, predicted and Christocentric, becomes the rule for Christians as such. The unity of writer and readers is *Jesus Christ our Lord*. Note Paul's use of the personal, the official and the universal names of God's Son who is Saviour, Messiah and King. *Grace*, which normally means, for Paul, God's undeserved favour shown to sinful men, can also be a synonym for 'power, ability' from God (as in Rom. 12:3, 6; 15:15; 2 Cor. 12:9). So here it qualifies *apostleship*, and signifies 'the God-given ability to perform the role of apostleship'. Paul ever marvelled at this calling he had received, viz. to bring the Gentiles to faith in Christ (Eph. 3:1-13; 1 Tim. 2:7; 2 Tim. 1:11), as he will remark later in the letter (Rom. 15:16). The end of the Pauline endowment of apostleship is the *obedience of faith*, or trusting submission, of all the Gentiles to the Saviour of the world. Paul is the apostle of the Gentiles and hence interested in the Romans both as potential and actual sharers of divine grace. Thus he infers his claim to address them. **7** *To all God's beloved in Rome, who are called to be saints*. There is evidently a Christian fellowship in the metropolis, composed of believing Jews and Gentiles. By the use of terms (*beloved, called, saints*) which the OT uses in reference to Israel as God's special people, Paul claims that Israel's place and vocation are now offered to a world-wide church. *Saints* looks back to Dt. 33:2, 3; Pss.; Dn. 7:22, 27 where the term describes Israel or a remnant as God's holy people, called to His service. That designation now fits the whole church at Rome and elsewhere. The address proper concludes with a benediction which is the combination of Greek and Hebrew ideas, *grace* and *peace*.

1:8-15 Thanksgiving and Paul's hopes

The apostle expresses his gratification concerning the Roman Christians, every one of them, because their faith is not hid in a secret corner but is public property. They have been faith's heralds to such an extent that God, whom he so worships in his spirit by preaching His Son, is witness to his continual mention of them in his prayers. The burden of his petitions is that God would speed him in due course to a meeting with them, if it be His will, the reason underlying the request being twofold. He wishes to establish them by imparting to them a spiritual gift, and also to share with them the comfort of mutual faith, theirs and his. **10** The implication (which is explicitly stated in v. 13) that Paul had tried unsuccessfully to pay a visit to Rome is not elaborated; we do not know, from any other

source, of such frustrated attempts. The Roman Christians must know that, though so far prevented from doing so, Paul had often proposed to visit them in order to see the same spiritual work done among them as had already been done among other Gentiles. He feels his debt to civilized as well as to uncivilized, to wise as well as to fools. His commission is to preach the gospel to all men and, so far as his personal eagerness is concerned, he feels that he owes Rome a debt of evangelization, for he is proud (note the meiosis, *not ashamed*, in v. 16) of preaching the gospel, which is able to save everyone who believes, Jew or Greek, though the Jew has the first claim and interest.

1:16, 17 The theme of the gospel

This short paragraph is the seed-plot of the subsequent chapters. In brief compass the 'Gospel according to Paul' is set out, using the characteristic terms which match the outline of the Epistle: 'righteousness of God. . . . through faith' (chs. 1-8); 'the Jew first and also . . . the Greek' (chs. 9-11); 'he who through faith is righteous shall live' (chs. 12-15; ch. 16 is an appendix). Moreover, as this correspondence shows, 'righteous-(ness)' in this letter carries a double sense, which may be labelled forensic and moral, though in Pauline thought no strict division should be pressed.

Righteousness is pre-eminently in Scripture a divine attribute which sets a lofty standard for human behaviour. Indeed, it is too lofty for man's unaided attainment; hence the confession of failure in the Psalms (quoted in Rom. 3:10ff.). But the term equally describes God's activity in setting His people 'in the right' with Himself; its outworking brings salvation (see Is. 51:5, 6). So it can be 'revealed', *i.e.* brought by God within the sphere of human experience, and received by faith. As a third extension, righteousness becomes the quality of life expected of the believer in his personal relationships; and the standard, hitherto unattainable by a man's native powers, becomes possible by the indwelling and energizing Holy Spirit (Rom. 8:2-4).

17 *Through faith for faith*. By a cryptic use of Greek prepositions Paul writes a phrase which can have a variety of meanings. Probably, however, we should refuse to speculate too closely and should see here a rhetorical expansion meaning 'based on faith and addressed to faith' (so Bruce, Lohse). The appeal to Hab. 2:4 recalls the rabbinic use of this verse as a quintessence of the Jewish faith. Paul goes to the heart of the prophet's message, re-interprets *faith* as personal trust in God, and insists that a right relationship with God on that basis will work itself out in practical affairs ('shall live'). It is likely, however, that the verb 'to live' looks back to Paul's Aramaic background in which the same Semitic term *ḥayyē* means both 'life' and 'salvation' (*cf.* Acts 3:15 for this double sense). In that case, *shall live* implies the gaining of salvation, and is equivalent to the phrase in the Gospels, 'inherit (eternal) life'.

1:18 – 5:21 THE PRINCIPLES OF THE GOSPEL

The apostle now begins at once the doctrinal part of his letter and so embarks upon a discussion of the principles of his gospel. The subject of the treatise was stated in v. 17 as *the* (RV 'a') *righteousness of God . . . revealed through faith for faith*. This great theme is the very heart of the Epistle, even as it was of the gospel which Paul preached. Simply expressed, it is 'justification by faith alone'. The apostle's personal problem, not primarily of his mind but of his practice, was the question, 'How can I be right with God?' Before the arresting experience of the Damascus road Paul had essayed to solve the problem in the Jewish way, by doing right, *i.e.* by establishing right relations with God by fulfilling the law of God. The method had proved hopeless. No mortal man has ever been sinless, much less positively holy, keeping all the commandments of God. All Paul's theology was experiential, and he discovered that by the way of faith in the finished work of Christ he was set right with God. He was not rectified or put right by himself; he did not get right with God, but was put right by 'a righteousness of God'. This is the meaning of justification. The apostle's terms for 'just', 'justification' and 'righteousness' (Gk. *dikaios, dikaiōsis* and *dikaiosynē*) all come from the same root. Justification by faith, therefore, means righteousness by believing, the entrance into a proper relationship with God through faith in Jesus Christ as revealed in the gospel.

It is for this blessed reason in his own experience that Paul is not ashamed of the gospel of God. Some Jews at Rome might stumble at it and some Gentiles think it foolishness (1 Cor. 1:23); but to the apostle this selfsame gospel is real dynamite (*power*), a spiritual force, a manifest activity of God in his own life, bringing salvation in its most comprehensive sense to body, mind and soul, both here and hereafter. This divine activity within human experience, this entrance into and maintenance of a right relationship with God, is the gist of the apostle's whole message. As the theme of the righteousness of God is developed it involves, in the course of the letter, the doctrines of justification, sanctification and predestination, which emerge from Paul's exposition and defence of it.

1:18–32 Gentile 'righteousness'

The 'righteousness' of the human race is in fact unrighteousness. The absolute moral ideal is the righteousness of God which can come only from God and be revealed, or made known, only through the gospel of Jesus Christ. **18** Paul accordingly draws a vivid picture of the unrighteousness of the Gentile world, describing both heathen religion (*ungodliness*) and heathen morality (*wickedness*). Upon both *the wrath of God is revealed* equally as His righteousness is revealed (see v. 17). The idea of judgment is frequent in the OT as an integral part of the righteousness of God in dealing uprightly with His own people and with the Gentile world. Paul's Jewish readers, at least, would be well aware of the implications of this term 'the wrath of God', which is used, in both Testaments, of God's displeasure at moral evil in His world. The notion of an impersonal principle of retribution (familiar to Paul's Greek audience as *nemesis*) is not the same as divine wrath which involves an exercise of personal will (though not including anything vindictive or capricious in God's nature).

1:18–25 Heathen religion. The pagan world of Paul's day worshipped idols after the likeness of both men (Athens) and beasts (Egypt). This polytheism was the religious outcome of rationalism, *i.e.* man's trust in his ability to know God apart from divine revelation. **21** The Gentiles became *futile in their thinking*; *i.e.* futile in their philosophies. This section has an importance in Paul's thought and teaching on the moral state of the world of his day. It underlines *a.* human responsibility which is seen in the way men 'by their wickedness suppress the truth' (v. 18), and so have only themselves to thank for their futility and mental aberrations in regard to the knowledge of God (v. 21). They deliberately chose to accept a falsehood about God and preferred to represent Him in the form of one of His creation—because (we may infer) such a representation seemed more tangible and 'real', and made no moral demands upon them, so leaving them free to indulge their passions at whim (vv. 23–25); *b.* human pride is exposed as the seat of the strange practice of deifying the creature, for it is a bid to claim 'wisdom' (v. 22) that leads to this result, and a reluctance to confess to any sense of obligation to God which would naturally express itself in thankfulness (v. 21); *c.* human accountability which Paul is anxious to underline leaves men 'without excuse' (v. 20). This verdict comes as the conclusion of the argument in vv. 19, 20 to which appeal is often made as support for 'natural theology'. That God may be known from His works in creation is a belief found in Stoic philosophy as well as in those parts of Jewish literature (especially the Wisdom of Solomon) which stand under Greek influence. It may be doubted, however, if Paul is simply accepting this conclusion. Perhaps he is agreeing with the best in pagan and Greek religious belief for the sake of the argument (as in Acts 17); more characteristically he insists that such 'natural knowledge' of God leaves men conscious only of their fallen condition and condemned for perverting such knowledge as they have to ignoble ends and so landing them only in the morass of idolatry in the crudest and most ludicrous form (vv. 21–25). So men, left to themselves, 'have rejected the inference (of God's true nature, manifest in His works) and so forfeited this knowledge. The knowledge of

God in creation remains an objective possibility, as it were, but the subjective condition for receiving it has been lost. And the consequence is that when man, alienated from God, yet haunted by the lost knowledge of God, attempts to recover it by himself, he reaches only distortions and perversions' (G. S. Hendry, 'Reveal', in *A Theological Wordbook of the Bible*, ed. A. Richardson, p. 198).

Paul's thought has its background more in the Genesis account of Adam than in Stoic philosophy or the intertestamental literature. See Gn. 1:20–25 for the classification of the species, and Gn. 1:26 for man's creation in the divine 'image and likeness' which he disowned by his bid for independence. The logical outcome was idolatry (vv. 23, 25), symptomatic of man's cherishing a 'heart that enthrones itself in God's place' (Barrett).

1:26–32 Heathen morality. An impure religion results in an impure life. This ghastly picture of heathenism is corroborated by the writers of Paul's day. It was an age of unabashed vice and anti-social sin, a period of unspeakable moral decadence. The inevitable judgment of God fell upon those who preferred human reason to divine revelation. The apostle three times asserts the divine abandonment, *God gave them up* (vv. 24, 26, 28). It has been observed that this desertion is definitely punitive, not merely permissive in the sense that God allowed the heathen idolaters to give Him up, nor just privative in that He quietly withdrew His grace. It is a positive punishment for culpable ignorance and wilful sinfulness.

26, 27 The divine judgment was an inevitable sequence, a harvest of the seed sown. The heathen world was given over to lust in the unnatural use of their bodies in sexual perversions and finally **28** to *a base mind*. Observe the play upon the words here. Even as the heathen *did not see fit* (Gk. *edokimasan*) *to acknowledge God, God gave them up to a base mind* (Gk. *adokimon noun*); *i.e.* just as these foolish and filthy idolaters disapproved of God, so God abandoned them to a disapproved conscience. **29–31** As we study the fearful list of human turpitude we see 'what happens when a man dethrones God and puts himself at the centre of his own life; he fails to recognize his obligations to others, and exploits their property and even their bodies to serve his desire' (Barrett). **32** indicates that the sins which are condemned are not the result of sudden yielding to temptation, but are indulged in deliberately and are encouraged in others, whether by complicity or condoning the sin. Paul's verdict implicates both the doer and the spectator who nods his approving head or gains a vicarious satisfaction from what he sees or hears of in others.

2:1 – 3:20 Jewish 'righteousness'

Like the 'righteousness' of the heathen world, the 'righteousness' of the Jews is also a miserable unreality and failure. With greater privileges than the Gentile, the Jew nevertheless has not attained to justification. Before entering upon his indictment of Israel, the apostle declares two preliminary principles—the impartial judgment of God (2:1–11) and the universality of moral obligation (2:12–16).

2:1–11 The impartial judgment of God. 11 sums up the first principle upon which Paul bases his charge against his own people. **1** When the Jews act as critics of righteousness, as they are always doing, they condemn themselves, for as judges they do the same things themselves. **2** It is a postulate with Paul that all the Jews acknowledge the undisputed righteousness of God in judgment. Hence the divine verdict is according to the moral reality of the case (*rightly*, lit. 'according to truth'), quite apart from privilege or profession. **3** The apostle undermines the false assumption that the Jewish people are exempt from universal judgment on the ground of integrity or because they are less sinful than the pagan world. Even the fact of national privilege does not exempt them from judgment (*cf.* Mt. 3:9; Jn. 8:33; Gal. 2:15). **4** If this has not yet fallen upon the Jewish practitioners of the selfsame sins as the heathen it is only because of the divine *forbearance*. God's seeming indifference to sin is due wholly to His *patience*, the aim of which is to induce repentance. The wealth of grace—*the riches of his kindness*—and **5** the wealth of wrath—*you are storing up wrath for yourself*—are set in solemn contrast. Every man will be judged according to his deeds, Jew and Gentile alike. Hard impenitence is an investment in divine wrath at compound interest to be realized on *the day of wrath. Cf.* Is. 13:6; Ezk. 30:3; Zp. 1:7; see also NT references to 'the day of the Lord' (*e.g.* Acts 2:20; 1 Cor. 1:8; 2 Cor. 1:14; 1 Thes. 5:2). **6** On that day the divine righteousness in judgment will be manifest as strictly just, recompensing every man according to his works. **7** If these are the fruit of patient well-doing in search of glory, honour and incorruption, the result is eternal life. **8, 9** But factiousness, disobedience to the truth and obedience to wickedness culminate in wrath and passion, in trouble and anguish, for every soul of man that works evil, particularly for the Jew (who should know better), but also for the Greek. **11** Thus the impartiality of the divine judgment is demonstrated. None is exempt.

Notes. 1 Paul's style of writing, in which his argument takes on an imaginary disputant with whom he conducts a running debate, is fashioned on the 1st-century literary convention known as *diatribē*. This method of writing explains the question-and-answer procedure of the following verses (3, 4) as Paul has alternately in view both a Jewish religionist and a pagan moralist, each of whom adopted a stance of moral self-congratulation and criticism of the failures and foibles of 'lesser breeds' who respected no moral code. The apostle turns upon this proud display by exposing its underlying error. **3** The key-phrase is *and yet do them yourself*, which does not necessarily imply that these moralists were guilty of overt acts; rather Paul, like his Master (Mt. 5:21–48), is searching the hidden depths of the human heart, and scrutinizing the secret thoughts which give rise to the outward actions. **7** No salvation by good living is taught here, but Paul is stating the principle at the heart of Jesus' teaching (Mt. 7:16–20), just as his earlier verse picks up the Lord's condemnation of censoriousness and a critical spirit (v. 3; Mt. 7:1ff.). **11** *Partiality* translates a Greek composite expression drawn from an OT metaphor, 'to lift up the face', *i.e.* to show favour to a person. The Jews claimed a leniency from God on the ground of a 'most favoured nation' clause in their covenant relationship with God. Paul, like the Hebrew prophets before him (*e.g.* Am. 3:2; 9:7, 8) denies this.

2:12–16 The universality of moral obligation. All are accountable to God for judgment whether, like the Jews, they possess the Mosaic law or, like the Gentiles, the 'natural' law written on the conscience of men who are all made after the divine image. All have a valid standard for trial, for it is not he who possesses law that is reckoned righteous but he who practises it. The Jews may not pride themselves in their Torah, for it does not matter whether one has or has not a law. Our actions, which reflect our true character, are the criteria of judgment. **15** Every man has a *conscience* (Gk. *syneidēsis*), a moral consciousness, a co-knowledge between the act and its ethical value, or between man and God as ultimate truth or reality. (Paul uses the term in this Epistle also in 9:1 and 13:5, and several times in his other letters.) If he attends to this conscience it will infallibly accuse or acquit him, **16** particularly when on the day of God all secrets shall be read and judged by Jesus Christ. Paul's gospel is here again affirmed to be Christocentric, which is indeed its chief characteristic.

2:17–29 The indictment against the Jews. Having thus prepared the way by affirming both impartiality and universality in divine judgment, the apostle proceeds to his specific charge against the self-assumed righteousness of the Jews. They, equally with the Gentiles, have not lived up to their light, and their light was greater than that of the Gentiles. In fact the Jewish gift of divine revelation was reckoned to mean privileged practice as well as privileged possession. Paul refers to two things in which the Jews prided themselves, the law (vv. 17–24) and circumcision (vv. 25–29), although they neither obeyed the law nor were really circumcised in heart.

17 *But if you call yourself a Jew.* The emphasis is upon their nationality. The name 'Hebrew' implies origin and language; 'Israelite' recalls their relation to God and religion; 'Jew' speaks of the race in distinction from the Gentiles. The enumeration which follows of advantages included in the gift of the law is somewhat satirical, for the apostle implies that the Jew has perverted his privileges. *Rely upon the law.* Paul's word

(Gk. *epanapauomai*) suggests complacency. The Jew was the chosen of God, and the gift of the Torah was a proof of the fact. Hence possession was considered to be enough without worrying about practice. *Boast of your relation to God* (Moff. 'priding yourself in God'). He is charged with a wrong idea of his relationship with God. True, he might glory in God (*cf.* Je. 9:24) but not arrogantly. The Jew behaved with a conscious superiority over other races which were regarded as 'lesser breeds without the law'. He claimed to be so intimate with God through his possession of the law that he knew the divine will. **18** *Approve what is excellent* renders one meaning which the Greek allows. 'Things that differ' (RV mg.; Gk. *ta diapheronta*) may be taken in a comparative sense as well as a superlative one (which RV, RSV accept). The former possibility is adopted by NEB ('you are aware of moral distinction') and JB ('can tell what is right'). The meaning is that the Jew claims to be able to discern right and wrong and the shades of moral value between lesser and greater good (*cf.* Phil. 1:10). Because of all these advantages of the law the Jew prided himself upon his ability to guide, teach and judge others. **19** *A guide to the blind* (*cf.* Mt. 15:14; 23:16) was probably a proverbial phrase. **20** *A corrector of the foolish*; *i.e.* the infants in religious knowledge such as the Gentiles appeared to the Jews. Such proud claims all rested upon the possession of *the embodiment of knowledge and truth* contained *in the law* of Moses and its rabbinical interpretation which made it cover every facet of human experience. Did Paul mean that the Jew really had the secret of the Lord, the fount of all knowledge and truth, for the term *embodiment* (Gk. *morphōsis*) implies the outline, delineation, 'the full embodiment', of the essential form (Gk. *morphē*; *cf.* Phil. 2:6, 7)? Or did he imply here, as the context would suggest, that the Jew had only the semblance of the true *morphē* through his own failure to fulfil it? The apostle uses the term *morphōsis* only in this passage and in 2 Tim. 3:5 where it is put in contrast to *dynamis*, 'power'. Certainly the gift of revelation was real; but the point is that the Jew, by his obedience, could have had a fuller insight into it, and, in spite of his boast, was in fact but a poor guide, light, corrector and teacher of the heathen.

21–24 Arising from this there follows a fearless exposure of the unrighteousness of the Jews. 'Well, Mr Teacher-of-others, do you teach yourself? You preach against stealing, are you a thief yourself?' *etc.* **22** *Do you rob temples?* This was evidently a crime for which the Jew was sometimes blamed (*cf.* Acts 19:37), though explicitly condemned by the best Jewish opinion (Josephus, *Ant.* iv. 8. 10). There may be an allusion, however, to an incident in AD 19 when some renegade Jews at Rome absconded with a sum of money, donated by a Roman lady to the Jerusalem Temple (see Bruce). **24** Paul quotes freely from Is. 52:5 (LXX). Jewish inconsistency of profession and practice and their boasting of God's favour while showing an utter disregard for His standard of morality must cause God's name to be dishonoured among the Gentiles. A similar admonition not to cause Gentiles to blaspheme God by disreputable conduct is found in the literature of the Dead Sea community. **25** *Circumcision indeed is of value.* Paul admits the advantages of this peculiar and distinguishing rite in which the Jew also boasted and for which he was despised by the Gentiles. Circumcision has its points, but only if the law is kept (Gal. 5:3). If that is transgressed, then circumcision becomes uncircumcision. Similarly, if the uncircumcised man keeps the requirements of the law, surely his uncircumcision should be accounted to him for circumcision? The man who is by nature uncircumcised (as was the non-Jew), and fulfils the law, shall judge the Jewish transgressor of the law. Paul bluntly declares that the upright Gentile in his uncircumcised state is as good as the disobedient, though circumcised, Jew. His teaching should be related to the OT statements (Dt. 10:16; 30:6; Je. 4:4; 9:25f.) which stress the inadequacy of circumcision simply as an outward sign or surgical operation. Its value as a mark of a covenant relationship between God and Israel is forfeited by Israel's defection. Paul insists, moreover, that it belongs to the nonessentials of a spiritual religion and so uses the term of an inner disposition and obedience (Phil. 3:3). **27** *The written code* (AV 'by the letter'); **29** *literal* (AV 'in the letter'); Gk. *gramma.* In the first case the reference may be to the letter of circumcision, the literal commandment; but it probably means the letter of the law which is definitely the meaning in v. 29, thus emphasizing the outwardness of the law. Paul has in mind here 'the written word as an external authority in contrast with the direct influence of the Spirit as manifested in the new covenant' (G. Abbott-Smith, *Greek Lexicon*). Paul employs the same contrast in 7:6 and 2 Cor. 3:6; *cf.* Acts 7:51. The idea of a *heart* circumcision belongs also to the OT (*cf.* Dt. 10:16; Je. 4:4; 9:26; Ezk. 44:7). **28** Hence, *he is not a real Jew who is one outwardly.* Thus Paul clearly demolishes the alleged righteousness of the Jew. **29** *His praise*: a play on the word 'Jew' which derives from Judah, a tribal name linked with the Hebrew (*yadah*) 'to praise' (Gn. 29:35; 49:8).

3:1–20 Jewish objections answered. Such reduction of Jewish righteousness to unrighteousness could not pass unchallenged. **1–8** The criticism of the apostle's condemnation may come from his opponents, or perhaps arose in Paul's own mind, as he reasoned out his grave charge against his race. From the earlier references in the argumentative diatribe style, the latter reason may be supposed; but we may take note of the recent view of the Epistle which sees it as a summing-up of Paul's case against the Judaizers (see Introduction). If this description is true, then Paul makes clear the sort of answers he was accustomed to give in debate

with the Jewish Christians who dogged his footsteps continually. The unseen heckler's objections are four.

a. **1, 2** If the Jews are equally condemned with the Gentiles and are as grievous sinners, what is the good of their privileges, what profit is there in circumcision? Paul replies that in spite of the fact that the Jews abuse their favours, nevertheless such remain for their proper acceptance and world-wide witness. Here he refers only to the highest of all their blessings (he lists others in 9:4, 5); they are entrusted by God to be 'the repository of revelation'. **2** The term *logia* (*oracles*; *cf.* Acts 7:38; Heb. 5:12, AV; 1 Pet. 4:11) refers particularly to the utterances of God on Mt. Sinai and His promises of a coming Messiah.

b. **3, 4** If the Jews are not right with God, what of all God's oracles and promises to them? Is not God going back upon His word? Paul repudiates the argument. The faithlessness of *some* (Paul is charitable in saying 'some', which is his customary way of referring to opponents whom he does not wish to identify more closely; *cf.* v. 8; 1 Cor. 15:12, 34; Phil. 1:15, *etc.*) does not impugn the faithfulness of God. It is obvious that if a covenant is broken by the unfaithfulness of one party, the honour of the other is unimpaired. **4** *As it is written.* The quotation is from Ps. 51:4 (LXX). While human faithlessness prevails, nevertheless the divine character is vindicated in all God's pronouncements about sin.

c. **5, 6** One objection grows out of the other. The heckler continues questioning *the justice of God* in punishing sinners. If the unrighteousness of the Jews is only a foil to set off the righteousness of God, and if the failure of the Jewish nation serves only to accentuate by contrast the uprightness of God, can God honourably condemn such serviceable sinners? Paul dismisses the idea as preposterous and declares it to be virtually a denial of God's prerogative to bring the world to righteous judgment. If our wrongdoing commends God's righteousness, are we to say that God is unjust in applying wrath to us? *I speak in a human way; i.e.* 'Pardon my very human expression; it is perhaps too bold an anthropomorphism'.

d. **7, 8** If my sinfulness, persists the objector, serves to glorify the holiness of God, this fact not only strikes at the root of the divine title to judge me, but condones my sin. Note how, in Paul's presentation of the objection, *God's truthfulness* is contrasted with the *falsehood* of the Jews; *i.e.* the divine fidelity to all promises and revelation is set over against Israel's unbelieving faithlessness and practical falsehood. Why am I still adjudged a sinner? the objector argues. **8** The logical conclusion surely is *Why not do evil that good may come?* Paul reveals here that some had slandered him in declaring this immoral maxim to be part of his doctrine. These traducers are dismissed in a word: *their condemnation is just, i.e.* that such men stand clearly in the wrong and under God's judgment is as it should be. They have perverted Paul's teaching in order to make it appear both ludicrous and immoral by their false logic, *Why not do evil that good may come?* Paul will not stay to rebut them now; that comes later in his insistence on union with Christ and the believer's fulfilment of the law's requirement by the Spirit's aid.

These four questions are not handled by the apostle at any length here, but they crop up again later. Objections *a.*, *b.* and *c.* are treated in ch. 9, while objection *d.* is dealt with in ch. 6.

9–20 In the remainder of this section Paul continues his exposure of Jewish unrighteousness. He points out that it is condemned by Scripture as sternly as the Gentile unrighteousness. Both Jews and Gentiles are sinners. The apostle appeals to the absolute authority of the Word of God, universally admitted by the Jews, and gives a mosaic of Scripture verses in proof, which may have been put together to suggest that the entire human person (*throat, tongue, feet, eyes*) has shared in sin. With two exceptions these are all taken from the Psalms and are quoted from the LXX. These passages of Scripture represent the law, and they mostly apply to the Jew in his unrighteousness. **20** The conclusion of this section is stated here. The failure of the Jew to find justification was due to his adopting the wrong method; indeed no-one living can hope to get right with God in this way, for *no human being* (whether Jew or Gentile) *will be justified in his sight by works of the law*; for the inference is that if the Jews, with their immeasurable privileges, are accounted guilty before God, there can be no other verdict possible for the rest of mankind (*cf.* v. 23). Truly, the law brings hopelessness, for it creates a consciousness of sin, a realization of what it means to God and man, to the Judge and the judged. 'And this way, Paul says, will not work. Our own piety, our own good deeds, our own churchmanship; all in the end count for nothing. "*Nothing* in my hand I bring" ' (Barrett).

3:21–31 The way of righteousness

Paul now proceeds to describe *the righteousness of God* (*cf.* 1:17), the method by which he himself became right with God. Note the following characteristics.

21 It is *apart from law*. The law reveals what duty God requires of man (whether it be contained in the Law, the Prophets and the Writings, or more specifically in the Law or Pentateuch) and demands moral effort or works for man's justification. God's saving righteousness must come independently of the law because *a.* religion based on a code can easily be twisted into legalism and merit-seeking; and *b.* the moral dynamic needed by sinners to break free from their egocentric world and attain the requirement of obedience to God on which the law insists cannot come that way. A new principle of relationship to God is needed (8:2–4). Only on the basis of a faith-principle can the law's

true purpose (viz. to order human lives in conformity with God's will and intention) be achieved; hence the conclusion of Paul's discussion in v. 31.

Secondly, it is attested by the law. The previous mosaic of Scripture passages (3:10–18) was taken chiefly from the Writings, the third section of the complete Hebrew Bible: now the apostle makes the testimony of the law complete by referring to *the law and the prophets*. The new way of being right with God is really not new at all, but was actually foretold in rites, types and predictions throughout the OT.

Rabbinical thought divided the time-periods of human history into three epochs: the period before the law of Moses was given; the age of the law; the Messianic age. Paul, as a Christian, assumes that the world's history has entered the third phase—where the law's authority as an instrument of gaining favour with God now no longer runs. This daring conviction explains the intense antagonism of his Jewish compatriots (see Leo Baeck, 'The Faith of Paul', *Journal of Jewish Studies*, 3, 1952, pp. 93ff.); and accounts for the emphatic adverb in v. 21: *but now*.

22–25 In the third place God's righteousness is provided in Christ through faith. It is for all who believe, *through faith in Jesus Christ*. The Greek has the genitive case here and is thus capable of being rendered either subjectively or objectively. The divine righteousness may be achieved by the faith of the Saviour even up to the cross, which strong faith was an integral element in the atoning value of His supreme sacrifice. Again, and in harmony with the NT usages, this faith is projected towards Jesus as object, and so becomes faith in the Redeemer. **23** *All have sinned and fall short of the glory of God. Glory* (Gk. *doxa*) is the visible brightness and splendour which emanates from the perfect character of God. This is the Shekinah glory of the OT (*cf.* 9:4; Ex. 16:10; 24:16f.; 29:43; 33:18, 22, *etc.*) and in the NT is expressed in the incarnate life of Jesus, the Word or expression of the Father (see Jn. 1:14; 2 Cor. 3:18; 4:6). In respect of God's glory all men *fall short*. The Greek *hysterein* means 'to fall behind', 'to be inferior', 'to suffer want' (*cf.* Mt. 19:20; 1 Cor. 8:8; 2 Cor. 11:5; Phil. 4:12). This universal deficiency is one view of sin. Both in reality and consciousness all are far removed from the blazing light of the divine perfection. The biblical background to this verse is suggested by the references to *sinned . . . the glory of God*, which recall Adam's original state (Gn. 1:26f.) as made in the divine image and his forfeiture of that honour as he sinned by disobedience. Men generally, sprung from Adam's stock, have failed to reach their God-intended destiny and in that sense 'all fall short of the glory of God'. Only in the second Adam is the image restored. Rabbinic Judaism held that Adam, at his fall, lost the image of God.

24, 25 But in face of this universal sinfulness,

justification is free or *by . . . grace.* Christ is a propitiation provided by God, to be received by faith. Christ's blood is the price accepted, in the divine forbearance, in virtue of which man's sins to date are passed over. Paul expresses the ground of righteousness in two pregnant phrases: *through the redemption which is in Christ Jesus* and *an expiation by his blood, to be received by faith.* The Greek *apolytrōsis* means 'release effected by payment of a ransom', hence *redemption*, emancipation or deliverance. The word for *expiation* (*hilastērion*) is the neuter of an adjective derived from the verb *hilaskomai*, which has three meanings: to placate, conciliate or appease someone; to be propitious or merciful; or to make propitiation for. The NT uses the two last renderings (see Lk. 18:13 and 1 Jn. 2:2). The idea is not that of conciliation of an angry God by sinful humanity, but of expiation of sin by a merciful God through the atoning death of His Son. It does not necessarily exclude, however, the reality of righteous wrath because of sin. Christ is therefore a means of satisfaction for sin, this expiation being effected by the death of Jesus, the *blood* signifying the principle of life sacrificed (*cf.* Gn. 9:4; Lv. 17:11; Dt. 12:23). Hence the RSV *by his blood, to be received by faith* is preferred to the AV 'in his blood'. Justification on such grounds has nothing to do with man's moral effort nor his spiritual merit. It is bestowed *by his grace as a gift.* In other words we are acquitted for nothing, without price, and out of the undeserved love of God towards sinners. Because of this once-for-all method of dealing with sin, men's sins in the past were temporarily overlooked; and the punishment of sins in the present is likewise delayed; all with perfect righteousness on God's part.

Much discussion has centred on a possible specific setting for the Pauline reference to 'expiation', aside from the more important issue of the most adequate translation of the Greek term. L. Morris has argued forcefully for an 'objective', God-ward application of the benefit of Christ's death mentioned here and has insisted that the word includes a removal by God Himself of His wrath which justly rests on sinners (1:18) and once vicariously was borne by His Son to save them (5:9). On the question of background, a suggestive view sees an allusion to the 'mercy seat' at which God met His people (Ex. 25:22) and which was especially prominent in the annual Day of Atonement ritual (Lv. 16). Atonement was made for Israel's sins as blood was sprinkled on the lid of the ark and confession made. Both LXX and Paul's text use the same Greek word, and a series of contrasts between the two atoning rites (centred on the mercy seat and the cross) has been impressively made by T. W. Manson (*JTS*, 46 (o.s.), 1945, 1ff.).

26–31 The fourth characteristic of God's righteousness is that it is divinely just. The apostle now expands his last phrase *to prove . . . that he himself is righteous.* God is not only just, as always; He can also justify, or put into right relationship, those who have faith in Jesus, though apart from Christ they have no right to such justification. God is righteous; and because of His eternal and intrinsic righteousness (not in spite of it) reckons righteous the sinner who *has faith in Jesus.* On this basis of justification by faith alone the apostle challenges the boasting of the Jew. There is no room for it. **27** *On what principle?*; *i.e.* on what grounds is it excluded? Paul uses the term 'law' in a number of different ways. It stands for the Torah and for the Pentateuch; here it means an established principle. The rule *of works* does not banish boasting, for many a Pharisee was full of self-glorification. But the rule of faith does absolutely exclude any such exultation. **28** The definite conclusion of the whole matter is that a man is put right with God by faith quite apart from any confidence in the law as a way of salvation. Paul does not overthrow the claims of the law (as his traducers suggested, v. 8); rather he rejects its place as an instrument of salvation, and insists that it is *by faith, i.e.* by trustful acceptance of the proffered mercy of God in Christ and obedience to His word, that salvation is received. But the goal of what the law set out to achieve is not forgotten or changed, though it is reached by another route than law-keeping (see 8:3, 4). In that sense 'we uphold the law' (v. 31). **29** This principle of faith at once abolishes the wall of partition between Jew and Gentile; God is the God of both if they believe. And such belief is the *sine qua non* which only God can bestow. **30** *On the ground of their faith . . . because of their faith.* The expressions merely emphasize the contrast between circumcision and uncircumcision. There is no difference in the quality or in the method of faith. So, if there is one God, there is one people whose hallmark is faith. God looks past circumcision to faith in the Jew, and equally past uncircumcision to faith on the part of the Gentile. Both really display the same 'trade mark'. Moreover, Paul adds, in such faith the law is not side-stepped but established. God is not being soft or sentimental. His justice is satisfied.

4:1–25 Abrahamic righteousness

Paul now takes Abraham as a test case, in which he shows the relation of the new system of justification to the OT teaching. He imagines the objector asking where in this discussion Abraham stands. Is he a 'faith' man or a 'works' man? This is a crucial point, but the apostle demonstrates beyond doubt that the patriarch was justified by faith and not by deeds of the law. The ground of the argument is Gn. 15:6: 'And he believed in the Lord; and he reckoned it to him as righteousness.' This quotation from Gn. 15:6 focuses attention on the special relation to God held by Abraham, Israel's great ancestor and founder. Paul chooses this case and verse because precisely this scripture was a basic text for the rabbinical doctrine of merit (*z[e]kût 'abôt*, lit.

the merits of the Fathers). To the specific question, 'What merit did the Israelites possess that God divided the sea before them?' Rabbi Shemaiah (in 1st century BC) taught: 'Sufficient is the faith, with which Abraham their father believed in Me that I should divide the sea before them, as it is said, And he believed in God and He counted it unto him (*i.e.* at the sea) for (doing) charity (with his children).' (See, for an illuminating discussion of this chapter, C. K. Barrett, *From First Adam to Last*, 1962, pp. 22ff.) The review of Abraham's life reveals three realities.

4:1-8 His righteousness was wholly by faith. It was universally accepted by the Jews that Abraham was uniquely righteous and had better grounds than most to boast. 2 But such glorying is inadmissible in the sight of God. 3 Scripture says *Abraham believed God*, and that was reckoned to him *as righteousness* (see Gn. 15:6). 4 Now, if a man works, his wages do not depend on his employer's goodwill, but on his employer's indebtedness to him. 5 But if he doesn't work, merely believing in Him who justifies the sinner, his faith is counted as righteousness.

The sacred writer to the Hebrews echoes the OT view in Heb. 11:8-19. Abraham's faith is outstanding and he had an illustrious niche in this author's temple of fame. It is noteworthy that James in his Epistle (Jas. 2:23) also quotes Gn. 15:6, adding 'and he was called the friend of God'. Paul and James arrive at the same conclusion from entirely different points of view. When James declares 'Was not Abraham our father justified by works?' (Jas. 2:21), his aim is to commend good works as the necessary proof and essential fruit of faith. Paul's task, on the other hand, is to condemn good works as the ultimate ground of salvation and to deny to them any merit in getting right with God. The apostle continues to emphasize that this new system of justification, which is his gospel, has its roots in the OT by showing that David is also a 'faith' man; for he expresses the blessedness of those who are reckoned righteous apart from any merit accrued by works (Ps. 32:1, 2). This state of the highest happiness is not pronounced upon the forgiven by David, but by God Himself. The psalmist is merely recording the blessed fact, even though with personal exultation, out of his own experience.

Paul's rebuttal of the claim to merit on the ground of 'works' (v. 2) draws upon an accepted rabbinical principle of scriptural interpretation, viz. that when the same word appears in two separate passages the one can be used to explain the other. The common term is 'reckon', used of Abraham (v. 3) and David (v. 6). This correspondence shows that 'to reckon righteousness' equals 'not to reckon sin' (v. 7), and proves Paul's point that as forgiveness cannot be earned, so righteousness comes only as a gift bestowed, not a right to be claimed (v. 4).

4:9-12 Abraham's righteousness was independent of circumcision. The order in the experience of

the patriarch was first faith, then justification, then circumcision. Jewish practice reversed the order, putting the rite first. 10 Taking the idea of blessedness as his link, the apostle shows that Abraham possessed this fruit of faith previous to his circumcision. 11 *He received circumcision as a sign or seal.* The rite itself was the token, or confirmation, of the covenant made by God with Abraham (*cf.* Gn. 17:1-14; Acts 7:8). On this ground the patriarch is the father of all who believe, whether circumcised or uncircumcised (*cf.* 2 Pet. 1:1). In the face of orthodox Jewish teaching, Paul asserts one of the vital principles of his doctrine, the open door for the Gentiles, the universal privilege of justification by faith.

4:13-22 Abraham's righteousness was independent of the Mosaic law. Paul's next point is that Abraham was reckoned right with God some 400 years before the law came into existence, before ever it was promulgated from Mt. Sinai. 13 *The promise ... that they should inherit the world* was not given to either the patriarch or his posterity by way of law, but by way of *the righteousness of faith.* That 'they should inherit the world' is interpreted as the sum of all the promises which Abraham received as revealed in Gn. 12:3, 7; 13:15, 16; 15:1, 5, 18; 17:8, 19, and mentioned in Acts 3:25 and Gal. 3:8. These promises included the gift of a son and heir, a countless posterity, the Messiah, and His universal kingdom. Observe the way in which our Lord, in one of the beatitudes, spiritualized the idea of world inheritance by stating that the meek should inherit the earth (Mt. 5:5). 14 Had those of the law inherited it, faith would have been *null* and the promise *void* in securing righteousness. 15 Law, however, can bring only the sense of sin, guilt and penalty; for remove the law and sin is gone. Accordingly faith, not law, is the basis of Abraham's righteousness in the sight of God.

'In laying the supreme emphasis on (the promise to Abraham) Paul parts company with Judaism. For Judaism the great thing was the deliverance from Egypt together with the giving of the law ... Paul reverses the emphasis. Judaism would read the patriarchal narratives in the light of Sinai. Paul insists on looking at Sinai from the standpoint of the promise to Abraham' (T. W. Manson, *On Paul and John,* 1963, p. 45).

The apostle argues similarly in Gal. 3:17ff., but the logic there is more legal and historical, whereas here it is more doctrinal. Law and grace are two incompatible spheres. 16 Hence the promise is confirmed to all the seed, not just to that sprung from the law, but also that sprung from faith. By this faith Abraham becomes the father of all believers, Gentiles as well as Jews. 17 In a physical sense the promise is given that he shall be father of all (Gn. 17:5); but Paul is thinking here of a universal spiritual fatherhood. Abraham, the father of the faithful, appears before God as the representative of all believers, Jew or Gentile. Gn. 17:5 is quoted, the significance of which is that 'the LXX renders the word "nations" by the word which to Paul regularly means "Gentiles" (Gk. *ethnē*). Abraham is thus proved by Scripture itself to be the father of non-Jews' (C. K. Barrett). There may also be a play on words in the Hebrew text of Gn. 17:5 where 'father of a multitude (*'ab hamôn*) of nations' is similar in sound to the last syllable of Abram's expanded name (*'abrāhām*).

Note the two arresting and apposite divine attributes which Paul adds here: *God . . . who gives life to the dead and calls into existence the things that do not exist.* **19** God's life-giving power is seen in the miracles of Abraham's procreation of Isaac (*cf.* Heb. 11:12, 'and him as good as dead'), by the deliverance of Isaac upon the sacrificial altar (*cf.* Heb. 11:19, 'God was able to raise men even from the dead') and by the resurrection of Christ (v. 24). The second attribute may be rendered, 'Who also speaks of, or summons, non-existents as if they were really existents.' The reference is to the unborn sons, the future posterity of father Abraham, when historically he was childless.

20 Again Paul eulogizes the faith of the patriarch. *No distrust made him waver . . . but he grew strong in his faith,* meaning that in reference to the divine promise Abraham did not vacillate in unbelief but was empowered by faith (RV 'waxed strong through faith'), thus bringing glory to God's name by his full faith in the divine ability to fulfil this promise. **22** The conclusion of this test case of Abraham is the assertion with which it began, that his faith was imputed to him for righteousness (*cf.* v. 3).

4:23–25 The apostle now prepares for his greatest theme, the believer's righteousness. This acceptance of Abraham, the father of the faithful, is recorded that we might also believe and claim the righteousness of God through Jesus, who was offered up for our transgressions and resurrected for our justification. **25** The conclusion of Paul's argument picks up the two earlier convictions that forgiveness and justification are offered freely as gifts of God's grace. Abraham's acceptance with God (which, as Ps. 32 shows, includes the promise of pardon) and his assurance of a continuing posterity (likened to a resurrection from the dead) depend on God's grace and were received by faith. Christians benefit in exactly these ways, and on precisely the same terms. This verse makes use of a pre-Pauline confession of faith in the form of a couplet and betraying by its Semitic structure its Palestinian origin. Its background is Is. 53 with a picture of Christ as the Servant who atoned for His people's sins and who is the guarantee by His living presence of their acceptance with God.

5:1–21 Believer's righteousness

The apostle now passes more into the subjective or experimental sphere. Some consider this chapter to be a devotional parenthesis since it is based on Paul's own experience of God's dealings with him. But the great theme of justification by faith is being here further developed. 'Paul never contemplates the possibility of a justification which was not invariably followed by a sanctification: justification and sanctification are for him inseparably connected in fact.' The one is the wicket-gate, introductory absolution; the other the long road to the heavenly Jerusalem. The apostle unites himself with all believers and speaks for them. On the firm foundation of being right with God the blessed effects of justification are declared (vv. 1–5). Then, in poetic style, there follows the guarantee of such blessedness (vv. 6–11). To this is added the method of justification as men of faith realize it through the new Head of the race (vv. 12–21).

5:1–5 The benefits which justification brings. 1 *We have peace with God.* Those justified by faith secure peace with God. The best attested texts have the subjunctive instead of the indicative mood in the verb *echōmen*, the only difference being the long or the short vowel. Hence the hortative rendering of the RV, 'let us have'. But as Paul seldom mingles his teaching and his preaching, the meaning is the milder exhortation 'we should have', and so 'we do have' (*cf.* Sanday and Headlam, p. 120). We actually enjoy, as men of faith, peace with God; we may approve the NEB rendering: 'let us continue at peace with God.' It is a new relationship with God which is not a question of mere feeling but of fact. Second, **2** *we have obtained access.* The believer does not enter into favour with God on his own merit. The idea of access is introduction into the presence-chamber of the king. This presentation before the royal throne is effected by one near the monarch himself. Here it is Jesus who leads us to God (*cf.* Eph. 2:18; 3:12). The apostle describes the active favour of the Father to believers by the term *grace* (*cf.* Gal. 5:4; 1 Pet. 5:12). The justified are ushered into a state of grace which brings security and confidence. **2, 3** A third blessed result of being right with God is joy, a triumph based on hope and victorious over tribulation. Believers exult *in our hope of sharing the glory of God.* They rejoice in the glory (*cf.* 3:23) which one day will be the crown and consummation of all things for the justified. They also boast even in trial, because trouble is productive of many fine qualities in believers, who know that sufferings produce patience, and **4** this endurance (*cf.* 2:7) leads to a tested character, and this proved experience (*cf.* 2 Tim. 2:3) brings forth hope. (Paul uses this 'chain-catalogue' style again in 10:13–15; *cf.* also 2 Pet. 1:5–7.) **5** This high hope does not carry disgrace nor prove illusory (*cf.* 2 Cor. 7:14; 9:4) because the souls of believers are flooded with God's love, which is in fact the presence of the Paraclete. The justified become conscious of God's love toward them through the indwelling Spirit. (*Cf.* the blessedness of the man to whom God reckons righteousness apart from works; 4:5–8.)

5:6-11 The security of the believer. The believers who are set right with God enjoy their new relation with God, their standing in grace, with perfect security. It is guaranteed on the one hand through the death of Jesus Christ upon the cross (vv. 6-8), and on the other through the risen life of the same Saviour (vv. 9-11). **6** *Christ died for the ungodly* (*cf.* v. 8). Christ's death on the cross was for us first *while we were yet helpless*; *i.e.* when we were weak and impotent to save ourselves by legal merit (though the description of Abraham as impotent by human standards, in 4:19, may have suggested Paul's thought here) and were indeed the ungodly (v. 6), sinners (v. 8) and enemies (v. 10). Secondly it was for us *at the right time*. This right season, the 'psychological moment' of the world's clock, is frequently expressed by Paul (*cf.* Gal. 4:4; Eph. 1:10; 1 Tim. 2:6; 6:15; Tit. 1:3). For us, then, in the fullness of time, Christ died, even though we not only had nothing to commend us, but in very truth had everything to condemn us. **7** The apostle makes a verbal contrast between the *righteous* and the *good man*. But no hard-and-fast distinction should be drawn. Paul's use of analogy runs: 'You would scarcely bring yourself to die for a righteous man, would you? Well, perhaps for a really good man you might. . . . But now see what Christ has done. We were neither good nor righteous, but still sinners when He died for us' (Barrett). **8** Behind this display of saving mercy stands God's *love* which is proved to us by the cross.

9 *Much more.* Paul continues his assertion of the security of the believer's righteousness with a triumphant *a fortiori* argument. The love of God toward us as undeserving and rebellious sinners is testified by the sacrifice of His Son on our behalf, a death upon the cross which brings us into a completely new relation with Him. This amazing love of God in putting us right with Himself is the greatest fact of our salvation. **10** God achieved reconciliation *by the death of his Son* when we were in a state of unbelieving hostility. Much more, then, shall God be able to keep us in peace with Himself as His friends by the risen *life* of His Son. If God can accomplish our justification, beyond doubt He can also accomplish our sanctification. The idea is all of life, the believer's life through the Saviour's life. Paul does not use the term 'sanctification' in his measuring of the greater and the great. His contrast is between justification and salvation. But the latter term has just this meaning of progressive holiness. In union with Christ as a living Lord we are empowered to live the holy life of moral and spiritual overcoming so that we, in our sanctified personality, escape the wrath of God on the judgment day through the completed and efficacious work of Jesus Christ. **11** This finished work upon the cross, which puts believers right with God and involves their being kept right through the life of Jesus, is the constant spring of intense joy. This relationship

is termed *our reconciliation*. The Greek *katallagē* means 'change' or 'exchange'; hence, when predicated of persons, a change from enmity to friendship, a reconciliation. This implies a change of attitude on the part of both God and man. The necessity of change on the human side is obvious; but many theologians deny any need for such on the divine side. God's love is abiding and He in Himself is unchangeable. But note that the apostle speaks of a reception by us (Gk. *elabomen*) of a reconciliation freely given to us by God. Implicit in the doctrine of justification is the changed attitude of God toward the sinner on the ground of the work of Jesus Christ, which does 'not mean that He changed God's *feeling* to the race. That was grace always, the grace that sent Him. But He did change the *relation* between God and man. The reconciliation of one always means a great change for both parties' (P. T. Forsyth).

5:12-21 A righteousness of grace. The apostle now concludes this section on the believer's righteousness by emphasizing that it is in truth a standing in grace, for it is accomplished through grace (vv. 15, 20). The channel of justification is through one Person by the free gift of God, a principle which leads Paul to discuss the two heads of the human race, Adam and Christ (*cf.* 1 Cor. 15:21f.). Note the construction of the passage. After stating the truth of the universality of sin and its penalty through Adam (v. 12), the apostle digresses in a parenthesis (vv. 13-17), and resumes his argument in vv. 18, 19. We have in v. 12 a grammatical anacoluthon. There is no sequel to the 'as' clause which depicts Adam as the type of Him who was to come. This 'as' does not find its sequel until v. 18, after the parenthesis had dealt with some difficulties.

The typological contrast between Adam and Christ has a twofold objective. First it is used to show how the activities of an individual can affect the lives of others who are intimately connected with the former; and then, Paul uses the Fall of Adam as a foil to set forth the excellence of God's renewal of lost humanity in Christ. Paul is employing two exegetic methods known in the Judaism of his day: *a.* the principle of solidarity by which Adam represented the whole of mankind. Paul builds on this, and extends it to include the notion of the 'whole Christ', *i.e.* Christ and His people who are one with Him in His acceptance by God. Also, *b.* Paul learnt from his Jewish faith the close tie-up between events at the beginning of the world and a setting right of earth's wrongs at the end of the age. This principle (known as *restitutio in integrum*) permitted him to teach that as the old creation had been ruined by Adam's Fall and paradise lost, so Christ's obedience and vindication by God would lead to a new order of harmony and reconciliation, with paradise regained. But he does not say simply, 'The second Adam restores what the first Adam lost', although that is included. By his use of the 'much more' contrast (vv. 17, 20) he goes on to demonstrate that the ultimate Adam gains for His people far more than ever their connection with the old order could have meant. Hence the explanation in v. 15, 'But the free gift is not like the trespass' on two counts, viz. Christ's work undoes the mischief caused by Adam's transgression, and lifts His people on to a new plane altogether (v. 16).

12 is the crucial verse of the passage. Here the doctrine of the relation of the one to the many is set forth. Special emphasis is laid upon the two prepositions used in the Greek, *dia*, 'through', and *eis*, 'into', whereby a channel and a passage are indicated. Through one man as channel sin passed into the world (*kosmos*), and through sin, as its penalty, death. The world hitherto had been pronounced by the Creator 'very good', but now, by Adam's transgression, both sin and death had entered in. The point which Paul makes is that all are involved in the sin of Adam, all have sinned in him and with him. Humanity is not simply accounted as having sinned and just legally charged with Adam's sin, but all are declared to have actually and actively sinned with Adam.

13 This dogmatic statement leads the apostle into a parenthesis where he faces two difficulties. The first is that up to the time of Moses the law had not been declared. As there was no law there could be no sin. He lets that go, admitting that *sin is not counted where there is no law*; i.e. is not regarded as guilt involving penalty. **14** In the second place he argues that, law or no law, sin's penalty was in operation from Adam's time. The universality of death nobody could deny, and Paul adheres to the doctrine that death is the sentence of God upon sin, although there was no law until Moses' day, and although those penalized did not sin after the likeness of Adam's sin, i.e. eating the forbidden fruit. Commenting upon this v. 14 some argue for the universality of sin but not for its Adamic origin. This would be to deny our oneness in Adam, which is the type of the oneness of the redeemed in Christ.

15 Up to this point Paul is describing the comparison between Adam and Christ. Both by a single act influenced the whole race. Now follows the contrast. The effect of Adam's sin is death; the effect of Christ's righteousness is life. But Paul has more to say than that. He states that the result is abounding, or overflowing, grace or *the free gift*, which is further defined in v. 17 as *the free gift of righteousness*. **16** The sentence was of one to the condemnation of all; the free gift was of many transgressions to a pronouncement of *justification*. The Greek *dikaiōma*, not the usual *dikaiōsis*, rendered simply *justification*, means a judicial utterance, or decree, or act of justification or putting right with God. The same Greek word occurs in 1:32; 2:26; 8:4. **17** The contrast between Adam and Christ is further developed in this verse where the one establishes a reign of sin and death, the other a reign of grace and life. The connec-

tion with Christ annuls for eternity the sinful connection with Adam, and makes possible a new relationship with God undreamt of in Adam.

18 Paul now links up with the principle posited in v. 12, restating it and adding the other limb of the parallelism, *so one man's act of righteousness leads to acquittal and life for all men*. Christ's life of perfect submission to His Father's will (Jn. 8:29) was crowned by His acceptance of the cup of suffering and death, and so may be summed up as His obedience (v. 19; *cf*. Phil. 2:8) or *righteousness* indifferently.

19 *Obedience* may look back to Is. 53:11, especially if the Hebrew text (translated '*By his knowledge* shall the righteous one, my servant, make many to be accounted righteous' in RSV) means 'By his submission (in obedience to God's will)'. Clearly, it seems, Paul is fusing the two ideas of Christ as the second Adam and Christ as the obedient Servant of the Lord. The latter part of the picture is most obviously to be seen in the recurrence of the term 'many' (vv. 15, 16, 19), drawn from Is. 53:11. The expression is a Semitic way of saying that 'all' are included with the assurance that 'the all' are not a few in number.

The sum of the whole comparison and contrast between Adam and Christ is stated here as the conclusion of the argument that the believer's righteousness is one of grace. It leaves us, however, with the problem of the relation of Adam and Christ to mankind whereby sin on the one hand and grace on the other are transmitted. Imputation is a legal conception and does not completely satisfy. The theory of federal headship is helpful, which lies in the thought of both Adam and Servant of Yahweh typologies. The former is based on a racial interdependence, the latter on a faith-relationship (Is. 53:4–12). Paul elsewhere teaches that this spiritual headship of Christ antedates the physical headship of Adam (*cf*. Eph. 1:4; Col. 1:15–17; see also Jn. 1:1–5). Yet by his deductions from it the apostle indicates a closer relationship, for humanity has no power of choice to commission its representative. The scientific fact of the solidarity of the race gives the best solution. As the whole lies in the germ, the oak in the acorn, so all humanity resides in Adam and, by grace through faith, also in Christ. As we are a physical, so also are we a spiritual organism.

20, 21 Paul concludes this section of the believer's righteousness with an appended note on the function of the law. Gal. 3:19 explains more fully; and both verses attribute to the law a parenthetic and provisional character. Indeed, the entry of law serves only to exacerbate the sinner's plight by giving legal definitions which both multiply offences and (human nature being what it is) actually provoke transgressions by inciting man's rebellious instinct. Yet even an increase of sin cannot overwhelm God's grace; indeed the latter rises with every fresh tide of lawlessness. **21** Grace is not the end. It leads through righteousness to its consummation, *eternal life*.

6:1-23 ETHICAL PROBLEMS RAISED BY THE GOSPEL

Paul now proceeds to defend the doctrine of justification by faith against the charge that it is incompatible with morality. He does so by affirming the doctrine of sanctification. This is not merely a theoretical sequence to justification; it is a vivid fact in the apostle's experience. It is equally a common message of all the NT writers 'that we are justified by the faith that works through love' (Gal. 5:6), and the link uniting justification by faith with justification by works is the obedience of faith expressed in 'works of love' (A. B. Crabtree, *The Restored Relationship*, 1963, p. 77). This ethical problem takes two forms. First, does not being reckoned righteous by God simply encourage sin? Secondly, does it not result in lawlessness?

6:1-14 The charge of licence

Paul's doctrine of justification, the objector argues, implies 'the more sin, the more grace'. If more sin means more grace, why not continue to live in sin? Paul's reply centres in the fact of the believer's union with Christ. This mystical relationship with the Saviour is here set forth for the first time in this Epistle. The apostle's characteristic thought is illustrated by the rite of baptism in the mode of immersion. The three actions therein are symbolic: into the water—death; under the water—burial; out of the water—resurrection. 3 To be *baptized into Jesus Christ* is to be brought into union with His death, 4 His burial and 5 His resurrection. Burial is really a confirmation of the fact of death. Christ's death was concerned with sin. It was a sacrifice by which sin was put away (*cf.* Heb. 9:26). 10 *He died to sin, once for all*; *cf.* 1 Pet. 3:18; Heb. 7:27; 9:12, 28; 10:10. His resurrection marked His entrance upon a new life 'apart from sin'. 11 The believer, accordingly, passes through the same experiences. It is the way of sanctification, the destined issue of justification. God not only puts us right, but keeps us right with Himself. His righteousness is first imputed, then imparted to us.

12, 13 Paul has been dealing so far with the Godward side of sanctification through faith-union with Christ. Now he declares the manward aspect. Moral effort is necessary in the progressive righteousness of the believer. The believer must not present his members as *instruments of wickedness*. This would mean continual sinning (Gk. *paristanete*; continuous present tense). The second presentation, as *instruments of righteousness*, is 'an act of choice' (Gk. *parastēsate*; completed past tense) whereby believers definitely yield themselves to a life of holiness, although such cannot be continually sinless. 'Do not go on presenting your limbs to sin as

weapons of unrighteousness. Present yourselves outright (once for all) to God.'

14 The transition to the next aspect of the ethical problem is found in this verse, where Paul exults in the certainty of progressive righteousness, and cries: 'Sin shall not lord it over you. You are not under law, but under grace.' The 'Thou shalt not' of the law must give place to the power of the Spirit.

Notes. 3 Paul's appeal to baptism as the event in a believer's life which marked his union with Christ and acceptance of His Lordship is amplified in Gal. 3:27; 1 Cor. 12:13. In NT times the baptismal experience must have made an indelible impression on the newly converted man or woman, signifying the passage from the thraldom of sin to a new life of incorporation into Christ and the church (see Eph. 5:14 as a baptismal chant). 6 *Our old self was crucified with him* relates to the effect of Christ's death which frees the believer from the tyranny of *the sinful body*, *i.e.* his unregenerate nature, inherited from his membership in the fallen creation 'in Adam'. Christ's sacrifice and victory (v. 8), while accomplished by Him as a historical fact at Calvary and on Easter morning, have far-reaching ramifications; for they involve His people whom He inclusively represented in His obedience and triumph. The precise question posed by the verse is: granted that the general sense is clear, that all that Christ did He did to liberate His people from sin's dominion (v. 6c), when exactly was it that *our old self was crucified with him*? When the Christian died with Christ long ago at Calvary? Or, at the moment of baptism when by faith he identifies himself with the past act of salvation and makes it his very own? Some verses in Paul's exposition (vv. 9, 10) suggest the former; others (vv. 3, 4, 8) the latter alternative. But 'is it not apparent that both these views are inadequate (on their own) and that both are embraced at once by Paul? ... It is the old problem in a new guise of relating the objective work of redemption to the personal appropriation of it' (G. R. Beasley-Murray). Our controlling guide should be that Paul's doctrine of baptism is ethically oriented, with his chief insistence on the fact 'We were baptized into Christ' (v. 3) and its inseparable purpose, in order that 'we too might walk in newness of life'. 7 NEB suggests a proverbial expression by its translation: 'a dead man is no longer answerable for his sin.' 'Death pays all debts', so the man who has died with Christ has his slate wiped clean (Bruce).

6:15-23 The charge of lawlessness

'Not under law but under grace' (v. 14) was the triumphant conclusion of Paul's argument; but it was capable (as 3:8, 31; 6:1 shows) of being misused and the false deduction being drawn: 'If we are no longer under the law, which forbids us to sin, we can do as we please and sin without compunction. Indeed (Paul's enemies were insinuating) the more we sin, the greater opportunity we give for God's grace to be displayed in forgiving us; and now that the law as our master is dead, we are at liberty to enjoy our independence.'

Paul's answer to this objection against free grace is that, while it is true that the believer is not under law but under grace, this does not mean that he is lawless (*cf.* 1 Cor. 9:21). He owes allegiance to God. **16** There are two possible masters to lord it over us—sin or God. To make his point the apostle takes an illustration from the slave-law of the time. (He is using the term *doulos, slave*, throughout.) A slave could buy his freedom by paying his price to the temple, *i.e.* he gave his purchase money to some god or goddess and in this way claimed his freedom; but the gold actually went, via the temple, to the master. Thus the deity ransomed the slave from the owner and the slave went free, although still the slave of the god. In a similar way the believer is free in the sense that he has become God's slave. He is not an irresponsible person without a master, for Jesus is Lord of all his life. **19** The apostle realizes the inadequacy of the analogy but reminds his readers that he speaks *in human terms* (*cf.* 1 Cor. 15:32; Gal. 3:15) and owing to *your natural limitations, i.e.* their immaturity. **20–23** Paul closes his argument by an appeal to the results or fruits of the two services, sin or righteousness. The one issues in shame and death; the other in sanctification and life eternal.

Notes. **17** *The standard of teaching to which you were committed.* 'The creed you were taught' is the JB translation, which is an acceptable rendering provided we think of a code of moral instructions and guidelines (such as Paul alludes to in Eph. 4:5) available to early Christians. Elsewhere Paul refers to 'the traditions' in the same sense of a pattern of ethical counsels to regulate believers' conduct (1 Cor. 11:2; 2 Thes. 2:15; 3:6; Phil. 4:9; Col. 2:6).

7:1 – 8:39 THE CHRISTIAN AND THE LAW

Another difficulty involved in the apostle's doctrine of 'the righteousness of God' as a free gift, or 'justification by faith alone', was the position of the law. The law was almost worshipped by the Jews and it was sheer blasphemy to assert that faith should take its place. To this question of the abrogation of the law Paul now addresses himself.

7:1–6 Law is valid only in lifetime

1–3 The illustration is used of the emancipated widow released from the law of the husband on his death. She is free to marry again. The law is superseded and is no longer valid or operative in this case. **4** Similarly believers *have died to the law through the body of Christ; i.e.* through Christ as crucified in the body (see E. Best, *One Body in Christ*, 1955, pp. 52f. for discussion). The 'you' becomes 'we' by coming to belong to the body of Christ, the totality of whose members, or limbs, constitutes the body

of which Christ is the Head. The point of the analogy is that the believer, being dead to the law, is free to be united to the risen Lord. The apostle here substitutes the law for sin, deadness to which, accompanied by life unto righteousness, was his teaching in the previous chapter. **5, 6** He stresses now the emancipation through death. *In the flesh*, the contrast to which is 'in the spirit', describes the life of sinful indulgence. The two states of slavery are again contrasted in the phrases *the new life of the Spirit* (*cf.* 8:9) and *the old written code*; and they represent the state of grace and the state of law and describe the antithesis between 'spirit' and 'letter' (as in 2 Cor. 3:6) which is taken from Je. 31:31ff.

7:7–25 Law and sin are not synonymous

Paul, as we have seen, has substituted 'law' for 'sin' in his argument. This fact gave rise, either in his own mind or in that of his critics, to the question, *That the law is sin?* (v. 7). Are these two things identical? The regenerate man dies to sin and self, and so to law. What then is the relation between sin and law? The apostle defines the connection between the two from his own personal experience. This section has been understood as autobiographical, although some commentators have thought that Paul is speaking quite generally. The better view is that it is the regenerate man who is speaking from his own experience. We have no picture of unregenerate experience *per se*, but rather the righteous man's retrospect, for he alone is in a position to assess the slavery of sin. 'The chapter should be taken as a dialectical analysis of the state of the naturally sin-enslaved soul "under law" ' (W. Manson). Paul regards his own experience as typical. The true relationship between law and sin is set forth as threefold.

7:7, 8 The law reveals sin. *I should not have known what it is to covet if the law had not said*. . . . Were there no law we would be unconscious of sin's vitality, and so of sin's existence. This is really an ethical commonplace, so very commonplace that it is ignored. *Sin, finding opportunity* (*cf.* v. 11). Sin, like a military strategist, made the law a sort of 'base of operations'. This is the literal sense of the Greek word *aphormē* when applied to warfare. It means a 'starting-point', and so, metaphorically, an 'occasion', 'claim', 'opportunity' (*cf.* 2 Cor. 11:12; Gal. 5:13. The soul, ignorant of the prohibitions of the law, is happy in unrecognized sin; but when the knowledge of sin comes then sin arouses rebellion against the law, which keeps on saying 'Thou shalt not', and so sin works *all kinds of covetousness*.

Scholars have drawn attention to the allusions to the Genesis account of man's temptation and fall: *a.* 'commandment' recalls the divine command in Gn. 2:16; 3:11, 17; *b.* sin is personalized, if not actually personified, here as in Gn. 3; *c.* 'The suggestion that sin is "dead" apart from the law reminds us of the serpent lying inactive, motionless, hidden, and as it were dead in the garden: nothing resembles a dead serpent more than a living serpent so long as it does not move' (Leenhardt); *d.* the verb *to covet* may cover any evil desire (as it does in 1 Cor. 10:6ff.) and Paul may have in mind Gn. 3:6. This reference could throw light on v. 10.

7:9–13 The law stimulates sin. Once, says Paul, I lived free from any consciousness of sin. I really lived apart from the law. *But when the commandment came* (*i.e.* a particular injunction of the law; perhaps represented in Paul's experience when, as a boy of 13 years, he accepted membership of the covenant-community of his people), *sin revived* (Gk. *anazēn*, 'to leap into life') *and I died.* 10 The apostle's experience was that the law, decreed to promote life (*cf.* 10:5; Lv. 18:5) by obedience, turned out to be death to him. 11 Indeed, through the law, sin beguiling him (*cf.* Gn. 3:13; 2 Cor. 11:3; 1 Tim. 2:14) slew him. This death does not mean atrophy or paralysis of this or that living function. It means wholesale death, the kind of thing that drove Paul to a frenzied persecution of the Way, to a mania of hatred towards it, which the Lord alone 'cured' by the vision on the Damascus road. Every law-begotten covetousness (*i.e.* evil 'concupiscence') must have leapt into a new heinousness as the Christian looked back upon the frenzied baiter and persecutor, as Paul indeed looked back upon Saul, and understood the misery of his hatred. 12 The apostle will not allow that the law, in whole or in part, is anything but holy, just and good. Its purposed effect is life. 13 Only when perverted by sin and made subservient to its deceit does the law work death. Sin is the mischief that waylaid and slew Saul. The divine intention was to show sin in its true colours, as already declared (see vv. 7, 8). But sin turned God's blessing, the law, into a curse.

Notes. 10 Some particular part of God's law seems intended; if so, the prohibition of the tree was intended for Adam's good and obedience would have brought 'life' (Gn. 3:3). As it happened, disobedience to that very commandment incurred death. **11** The verb *deceived* (as in 2 Cor. 11:3; 1 Tim. 2:14) matches the same word in its simple form in Gn. 3:13 (LXX): 'The serpent beguiled me.'

7:14–25 The law creates a conflict with sin. The apostle reaches now the very core of his bitter experience. He confesses that he sees the better way, and approves thereof; but he follows the worse. He realizes the difference between the nature of the law and his own nature. *Spiritual* and *carnal* are opposites: one is of the Spirit, the other of the flesh. **15–19** Paul continues in a classical picture of divided consciousness to sketch his inner conflict between what psychologists term the organized and disorganized self. The real self centres in an ideal, in Paul's case Christ, or the good and holy law. Sin, personified in the graphic and emotional portrait, is the disorganized self and definitely not Paul as he longs to be. **20** When doing what he does not approve he declares *it is no longer I that do*

it, but sin, identified here with his lower or disorganized self. **21** The apostle's experience provides a principle, enunciated here, which operates all through life. 'To be saved from sin a man must at the same time own it and disown it; it is this practical paradox which is reflected in this verse' (James Denney). **24** The emotional expression of this inner conflict and divided consciousness culminates in a cry of distress or despair. Paul lives again his experience, which he presents as typical, of being the convicted sinner. *Wretched man that I am! Who will deliver me from this body of death?* The body is the instrument of sin and destined to die; so repulsive is sin, and death so much its synonym, that Paul agonizes to be rescued from this death's body which, in his horror, he feels it to be. **25** Then follows the swift reaction in a paean of praise, as salvation floods his soul: *Thanks be to God through Jesus Christ our Lord!*

Notes. 14 *Sold under sin; cf.* Wisdom of Solomon 1:4, 'wisdom will not enter a deceitful soul, nor dwell in a body enslaved to sin.' **15** Ovid's dictum, 'I see and approve the better life, but I follow the worse one' is often quoted as parallel, but the correspondence is not exact, mainly because Paul's self-estimate is viewed in the light of God's law, and he looks upon sin as an alien intruder into his life (v. 20), setting up an inner conflict (*cf.* Gal. 5:17). **24** *This body of death.* Paul is not describing his physical frame as evil; no disparagement of the human body, made by God, is intended. Rather, it is the 'heritage of human nature subject to the law of sin and death which he shares with all the sons of Adam' (Bruce) that he refers to in this phrase. **25** *I of myself,* or 'I, left to myself', 'when I rely on my own unaided effort'. Then the result is this unequal conflict between his aspiration and achievement. But this is not the final word nor the whole of the picture, as the next chapter will show.

8:1–39 Sin is vanquished by Christ and the Spirit

The law, while thus exposing and exciting sin and splitting the self, is still in its purpose holy and good. The law is the friend of men if it could be allowed to operate, but it is *weakened by the flesh* (v. 3). However, through Christ, it is strong and condemns sin in the flesh, for Christ is absolutely righteous and He dwells within us. We are also in Christ and by this union fulfil the law (vv. 1, 4). Christ's obedience is our obedience. We satisfy in this way the claims of the law and render it powerless. So in this chapter the apostle proceeds to chart the course of the Christian life in which believers are set free from the law of sin and death by the law of the Spirit of life in Christ (v. 2).

8:1–4 The failure of law. The previous system of life through obedience to the law had manifestly never been successful. Now it is made good by the incarnation of Jesus and the presence of the Spirit. Law is unable to confer benefits, but what the law failed to do, grace accomplished through Christ and the Holy Spirit. The overcoming life begins here and now in the absence of any sentence for being in the wrong with God. **1** United with Christ, the believer is acquitted and is free for ever from the tyranny imposed by the law of sin and death. The term *condemnation* refers, as a legal expression, to the sentence which the guilty and convicted man receives and his ensuing punishment. The believer is set free from both the law's power over him and any punishment it could inflict upon him as a condemned 'law-breaker'. The just requirement of the law, a righteous life, is accomplished not 'by' us but *in* us (v. 4). **3** This is *what the law . . . could not do*. The idea is more of the inherent inability of the law to do anything in the direction of a holy life, than merely of its impotence to do what Christ accomplished. The failure of the law is absolute. **2** The new law under which we are brought is *the law of the Spirit of life in Christ Jesus*, and this law emancipates us *from the law of sin and death.* 'This verse contains a complete picture of the Christian life as Paul understood it' (Barrett). Sin is foreign to human life. It is an intrusion. By sending His Son *in the likeness of sinful flesh* God dealt with sin. Paul does not here imply that Jesus was incarnate in sinful flesh, as if all flesh were tainted or corrupt with sin. The Evangelists are very definite about the advent of our Lord as regards the manner of His birth. The holiness of the child is marked both as originated by the Holy Spirit and as itself holy (*cf.* Lk. 1:35). Our Saviour's flesh was the true, unfallen humanity of the divine intention. Our Lord's body was only 'in the guise of sinful flesh' (Moff.), not in sinful flesh itself which is our legacy from Adam. The Pauline point here is that the Father sent His son to deal with sin in the very same circumstance and sphere in which our human race in Adam had been worsted. This engagement with sin implies all that Jesus was, said and did to condemn sin in His own body on the tree (*cf.* v. 3, RSV mg. 'as a sin offering', reminiscent of Is. 53:10; *cf.* also Rom. 3:25; 2 Cor. 5:21). Flesh was the realm of sin; but in the case of believers God put that sphere of influence out of court, the death of the Son annulling the power of sin over saints completely and permanently. Man in Christ is free for ever from the law of sin and death. **4** *The just requirement of the law*, a righteous life, is accomplished not through the law (for it has failed) but through grace; and the grace of God makes available to the man renewed in Christ the power he needs to translate the law's 'righteous requirement' into action. 'God's commands have now become God's enablings' (Bruce) because the law's exactions, now placed within the Christian as his guide and mentor (fulfilling Je. 31:31ff.), are matched by the promise of the new spirit (also placed within the Christian; Ezk. 36:26f.) which loves to do God's will, and by the indwelling Spirit is enabled to do it.

Notes. **3** *The likeness of sinful flesh* is a composite phrase which guards against the twin false notions of *a.* denying a real taking of our human life by the incarnate Son of God (the heresy of Docetism), for one sense of 'likeness' stresses a similarity which borders on identity (as in Rom. 5:14; men did not sin just as Adam did); and *b.* too close an identity of the incarnate Lord with our *fallen* nature which would incapacitate Him from being man's Redeemer. Hence the qualifying *sinful* flesh, which He did not share, else He would not have been 'without sin'. 'The flesh of Christ is "like" ours inasmuch as it is flesh; "like", and only "like", because it is not sinful' (Sanday and Headlam).

8:5-11 The triumph of grace. The apostle proceeds to describe the grace-life as one of the Spirit and to contrast it with the life of the flesh under the law. The old life has its interests and absorptions in fleshly things, but the new in spiritual things. If our life accords with the flesh, the carnal streak will run through our mental outlook. If the spiritual element prevails, the analogous results will be seen in our spiritual alignments. **6** The sum of the matter is *to set the mind on the flesh is death, but to set the mind on the Spirit is life and peace.* On the one hand death is the result of the flesh-life: on the other life flows from the Spirit-life. The underlying reason is plain. **7** The carnal life is *hostile to God*, frustrating the divine ideals for humanity. It is self-centred and at war with God. By its very nature it is powerless to submit itself to the law of God. **8** Living in the world of self as supreme it *cannot please God*. The flesh, in fact, is the seat of revolt against God. John's synonym for the flesh in this Pauline sense is 'the world' (*cf.* Jn. 16:8-11; 17:6, 9). It is life without God in it: one of egotism, self-indulgence and disobedience to the light of conscience.

9 Paul now turns directly to his readers and addresses them as Christians in whom the Spirit dwells. The motive power behind the spiritual life is the indwelling Holy Spirit. Hence the victory of grace over law; for by grace, through faith, the Spirit is in them and they in the Spirit. Here mark Paul's characteristic preposition 'in', which he uses in the metaphorical sense of union or communion with God in Christ through faith (*e.g.* 8:11; 9:1; 1 Cor. 3:16; *cf.* 1 Thes. 4:8). *The Spirit of God . . . the Spirit of Christ* are used interchangeably, showing the equality and functions of the one Godhead. The Father is the source of all grace; the Son, the channel; the Spirit, proceeding from both the Father and the Son, the agent. The criterion of the Christian is this indwelling, divine motive power, apart from which dynamic there can be no communion with God. **10** *Your bodies are dead because of sin.* This is true 'in the sense that it is "mortal", "subject to death" ' (Bruce), but not to shed as a useless clog, for the Lord has a purpose for the body, sanctified by His incarnation (Heb. 10:5ff.), indwelt by His Spirit and useful in His service (1 Cor. 6:15ff.), and at last to be raised in a manner patterned on His resurrection (1 Cor. 15:35-55; Phil. 3:21). This teaching may suggest an alternative interpretation of Paul's phrase, making 'dead' refer to the believer's passage out of sin's domain, so that he no longer employs his body as a tool for evil, but regards it as a vehicle of his true life, viz. his spirit which is alive (to God) as conversely his body is dead to sin. *Cf.* 7:6. This view necessitates the taking of *spirits* (Gk. is singular, *pneuma*) of the human spirit, enlivened by the Holy Spirit, though some (*e.g.* Bruce) prefer to see the Holy Spirit's activity directly mentioned here. *Because of sin . . . because of righteousness.* This is another way of expressing the triumph of grace over law. Nothing but death is in the old way of sin, but all life pulses through the new way of righteousness, or justification, that stupendous thing which God does for us, in the doing of which we ourselves have neither part nor competence. Such justification, the pure judicial assignment of righteousness to us on God's part, is the basis of such moral righteousness as results from receipt of the blessings of Christ. **11** The statements made about *the Spirit* are analogous to those made in v. 10 about Christ. This makes the verse most important for the Trinitarian conception of God, so vital and indispensable to true Christian knowledge.

8:12–17 The goal of grace. Vv. 12 and 13 form a hortatory aside. The brethren at Rome are admonished, along with the preacher himself, not to go on living to the lower self, as if that were a necessity (*cf.* 1:14; 13:8), but to engage in living to the Spirit, causing death to all selfish actions and so gaining, not death, but real life.

14 Sonship with God is the glorious end of all grace's triumph. *Led by the Spirit of God*; *cf.* Gal. 5:18. The contrast of slavery – freedom is worked out in Gal. 3:23 – 5:1. The dangers of reverting to a state of slavery to fear (v. 15) are very real. In this Epistle Paul simply assumes that his readers are aware of these tendencies, and will resist them. Those whose lives are controlled by the Spirit are in fact, from the moment of their reception of the Spirit, in filial relationship with the Father. They hold a rank which entitles them to privilege. (*Cf.* Peter's conception of Christians as a royal priesthood in 1 Pet. 2:9.) **15** *The spirit of slavery* is neither the human nor the divine spirit, but rather a temper, mood or state. The corresponding phrase *the Spirit of sonship* is a phrase framed to contrast with 'spirit of slavery', yet in spite of this formal similarity a reference to the Holy Spirit is evidently intended. It is the Spirit who imparts the assurance of sonship and enables believers to call God their Father. *Sonship* means an adopted state, a position conferred upon one to whom it is not natural. It is by Christ's act of grace that Christians are in such a relationship. The Jews had no such custom of adoption, but it was common to both Romans and Greeks.

Paul does not go out of his way to deny any doctrine of universal fatherhood, but definitely teaches the necessity of Christian sonship, the relationship to God as Father in Jesus Christ

through the Holy Spirit. This sonship is no mere official recognition of a filial tie, a title only. It is an actual fact. We are sons with a right to say *Abba! Father!*, as sharing the sonship of the eternal Son. *When we cry*—in prayer, though the unusual verb may suggest some public utterance in congregational worship in the early church. *Abba*, meaning 'dear Father' as an invocation of God, may conceivably be the opening word of the Lord's Prayer (as in Lk. 11:2); whether this is so or not, the name of God as Father certainly goes back to Jesus' own usage of the familiar title which Jewish children used of their earthly father. The precise Aramaic form *Abba* was avoided in both synagogue and private prayers out of reverential motives, some alternative form (*e.g. Abinu*, 'our Father') being substituted. Yet Jesus calls God by the homely title (Mk. 14:36); this usage became indelibly fixed upon the prayer-speech even of Greek-speaking Christians. **16** The cry under intellectual or spiritual emotion reveals the naked soul of the believer and is spontaneously accompanied by the corroborating testimony of the Holy Spirit to real sonship.

17 Paul now advances in his exultant thought, *and if children, then heirs* (*cf.* 4:14). The idea of inheritance runs through both OT and NT (*cf.* Nu. 26:56; Ps. 25:13; Is. 60:21; Mt. 5:5; 21:38; Gal. 3:29; 4:7). The advent of the indwelling Spirit is the earnest, or guarantee, of the believer's inheritance (*cf.* 2 Cor. 1:22; 5:5; Eph. 1:14). Christ is God's Son, hence we are His fellow-heirs, *heirs of God, and fellow heirs with Christ*. Christians have a common inheritance with Christ, which they will share in due course. In v. 17b Paul may be quoting a familiar saying of the early church (*cf.* 2 Tim. 2:11–13) that believers experiencing adoption are co-heirs with Christ if indeed 'they share His sufferings that they may share His glory too'. The Christian's life is a reproduction of the life of Christ. *We suffer with him* implies the communion of cross-bearing or self-sacrifice; not that our experiences are redemptive in themselves, but we 'complete what is lacking in Christ's afflictions' (see on Col. 1:24).

8:18–27 The glory which shall be revealed. In his ecstasy over the victory of grace Paul has soared far beyond the richest possibilities of law. He is entranced in a realm which the law could never know. **18** The apostle has no doubt about the 'hardness' needed for following Christ (*cf.* Paul's sufferings in Acts 19:23–41; 20:18–35; 2 Cor. 1:3–11; 6:4–10; 11:23–33). As little does he doubt that the glory to come will far outbalance present sufferings. This future glory or ultimate manifestation of God in Christ will be no mere objective vision alone, but a subjective transformation of the believer's character (*cf.* 2 Cor. 3:18; 1 Jn. 3:2). The assurance of future glory is not a passing emotion of optimism. Paul confirms his confidence with three testifying facts.

19–22 First he points to the organic unity of

creation. Paul here states a scientific fact viewed theologically. Man and nature are so closely related that, as by man's sin nature suffered with him, so by free grace in putting man right with God nature also shares the hope of righteous readjustment or perfect completion. **20** *The creation was subject to futility, not of its own will.* Man fell of his own free will, but the universe automatically and not voluntarily was corrupted with him, according to the decree of God. Its fate was to be *subjected to futility* or cursed with dissatisfaction or incompleteness, yet not without hope of deliverance. *By the will of him* refers most naturally to God, although some scholars argue for an allusion to Adam or Satan; but the concluding mention of *hope* can really be explained only if it is God who intends creation's final deliverance and restored harmony. **21** The content of that hope is given in the words 'that the creation itself also shall be delivered from the bondage of corruption' (RV). Man's redemption will mean for the whole of groaning nature the fulfilment of the prophecy that the desert shall blossom as the rose. **23** The apostle strikes again the main theme of the passage, that this present grace of possession of *the first fruits of the Spirit* awaits the future *redemption of our bodies. Adoption,* already a fact as the Spirit imparts the witness of our sonship (vv. 15, 16), will one day be fully realized at the resurrection. The present possession of the Spirit is a sample (*first fruits*) of the full harvest to be reaped at *the redemption of our bodies.* In a like earnest expectation to that of the visible world, Christians who experience the 'first instalment' (the same word is found in 2 Cor. 1:22; 5:5; Eph. 1:14) of the Spirit, the foretaste of His transforming power, also sigh for the deliverance of the body from sin and sin's environment. The resurrection will be the final stage of sonship with God. The passage in 2 Cor. 5:1–10 is closely parallel. *Cf.* Eph. 4:30.

24, 25 Paul now proceeds to call as his second witness the Christian's conscious *hope,* which by its very nature proves the reality of future glory. It is another ground of assurance. *For in this hope we were saved.* Paul, by emphasizing hope in this way, does not thereby discard or minimize the pre-eminent function of faith in the believer's salvation. Some prefer to render 'in hope' (as RSV) so as to avoid misunderstanding, but 'by hope' (AV) and 'through faith' serve the same purpose. Faith is the definite means of salvation and hope can emerge only within the faith-attitude. The point which the apostle is making here is that by its very nature hope testifies to the fact of future glory. Hope is no longer hope if it can realize the consummation for which it looks. Our duty, then, is to wait for the end, to endure, to exercise patience. We are saved, yet full salvation still lies ahead.

26, 27 The help of the Holy Spirit is the third witness to the full realization of adoption, the third ground of assurance that grace will become glory. *Likewise the Spirit helps us in our weakness.*

Paul is fortified in his faith in the believer's final glory by the experience common to all Christians of the Spirit's operation in furthering prayerful aspiration towards the realization of complete adoption as sons of God. If God is thus involved in our movement towards the glorious consummation, then the end is no delusion but a wonderful reality. The term *helps* (Gk. *synantilambanetai*) is in the original a very forcible word, being compounded with two prepositions, *syn,* 'along with' and *anti,* 'over against', as prefixes to the verb, *lambanein,* 'to take hold of'. The metaphor is of a helper supporting the weight in co-operation with the bearer and at the opposite end of the burden. *Weakness* refers to the frailty of the Christian in his ignorance or part comprehension of the will of God, *for we do not know how to pray as we ought.* Here the specific help of the Spirit is realized. His intercession is within us; the intercession of the Saviour is at God's right hand (Heb. 7:25). The Paraclete, not merely beside us but dwelling within us, strengthens us by energizing and inspiring the inarticulate longings of the soul towards a full sonship of imparted righteousness as the fruit of imputed righteousness. Divine intercession gives utterance to our sighs and the intervention prevails: our great longing for the consummation is borne to the Father's throne. *He who searches the hearts* is God Himself who is omniscient, knowing the direction and movement of the Spirit in His inspiration of human aspirations. But even more specifically the Father knows this *mind of the Spirit,* for it is His own mind.

8:28–30 The sovereign will of God guarantees grace. The human and divine Spirit, harmonized into one will, are in fact, Paul asserts in this paragraph, realizing the all-embracing will of God. **28** In view of such divine working in us and on our behalf, we are aware that to them that love God all things co-operate for good, that is, to those who are effectually *called according to his purpose.* The eternal will is behind the called, who not only hear the call but obey it. The subject of the verb *works* can hardly be 'all things' as in the familiar AV. The best alternative is to regard the Spirit as subject in both vv. 27, 28 (so NEB, 'he pleads for God's own people in God's own way; and in everything, as we know, he co-operates for good with those who love God'). What is established in the divine foreknowledge and foreordination inevitably reaches the divine goal for the divine glory, which includes the blessed state of the elect. **29** This eternal purpose and plan is to make believers *conformed to the image of his Son,* who is Himself the perfect image of the Father (*cf.* 1 Cor. 15:49; 2 Cor. 3:18; 4:4; Col. 1:15), so that He is the firstborn among a host of brethren. *First-born* implies not mere priority but pre-eminence within the host of redeemed brethren. Paul reveals the stages of the divine decree and its accomplishment. The eternal order operating in space is foreknowledge, then foreordination. The predestination is based upon the 'knowing beforehand'. The several stages thus develop one from another. The term 'to foreknow' (Gk. *proginōskō*) means 'to unite oneself before with someone' (Cremer, p. 161). The idea is a personal and pre-temporal association, and in the dynamic not static sense, for it is the prolific origin of subsequent activities. Thus 'to foreknow' anyone is to enter into communion with a view to conferring special favour upon him. Here 'to foreordain' decides that this special favour will take the shape of sonship in Christ. Foreknowledge according to the biblical usage of the verb 'know' (*cf.* Pss. 1:6; 144:3; Ho. 13:5; Am. 3:2; Mt. 7:23; Jn. 10:27; 1 Cor. 8:3; Gal. 4:9) implies favour or grace as the eternal beginning of all the other processes of salvation, an interpretation which accords with the whole Pauline theology. 30 Then the divine decree passes over into time and is manifested as calling, justification by faith, and finally glorification. This miraculous consummation, planned in eternity, is worked out in our earthly experience. It holds promise of an issue in our creaturely praises in the state of sanctification here and glory hereafter. *He also glorified.* The past tense used of a future event is remarkable; it is probably to be explained as an example of the 'prophetic past', common in the OT to describe the fulfilment of an event which, to the eye of faith, is so certain that it can be regarded as having already occurred even though it belongs to the prophet's future.

8:31–39 A hymn of praise. With a triumphant paean of praise Paul concludes his review of the course of the Christian life, which is lived in a realm beyond the grasp and power of law. If God be in our destiny nothing else matters. To us who are of the faith-family He gave His own Son, and with the greatest gift all else is certainly included. 32 *Did not spare his own Son* is reminiscent of Abraham's sacrifice (Gn. 22:16). Isaac's willingness to be bound on Mt. Moriah was invested by the Rabbis with atoning efficacy; and Paul draws upon the analogy to emphasize the Father's love and the Son's obedience, which make available a full provision for all the church's need. The apostle continues from this all-inclusive promise of limitless blessing by reverting to his first statement in v. 1. 'There is therefore now no condemnation.' There are two main questions to which the thought of the hymn is subordinated. First, 33 *Who shall bring any charge against God's elect?* and second, 35 *Who shall separate us from the love of Christ?* If God justifies, can anyone dare to accuse the chosen of God? And again, if Christ Himself died for the faithful, rose again for them, and now at God's right hand is their continual Advocate, is there any possible power to sever the love-link between the Saviour and the saved? There can be no charges and there can be no dissolution of redemptive bonds. 34 *Who is to condemn?* is a question answered by the rhetorical *Is it Christ Jesus who died . . . ? Cf.* Is. 50:8f. *Who is at the right hand of God* draws upon the oft-quoted testimony of Ps. 110:1, used in the NT of

the enthronement and consequent supremacy of Christ over all the church's foes, and the guarantee of God's supply for every need (Eph. 1:20–23).

Paul in his ecstatic confidence now defies every conceivable antagonism. There are two classes of frustrating opponents. 35 First he lists temporal adversities experienced generally by those professing Christ who, suffering with Him, shall also share His glory. The sufferings are real indeed, as the apostle well knows (*cf.* 16:4; 1 Cor. 4:11; 15:30; 2 Cor. 11:23–27; *cf.* Acts 12:2), and 36 he quotes to prove his case Ps. 44:22 (LXX). 37 *In all these things*; *i.e.* 'despite all these adversities'. Secondly, 38, 39 there are spiritual powers recorded almost with derision because of the futility of their attempts to separate from the love of Christ. AV reads 'powers' after 'principalities', but most modern versions put 'powers' after 'things to come' (*cf.* NEB). These terms signify the enemies which 1st-century Hellenistic man most feared, summed up in the malevolent control exercised over human life and destiny by the stars and heavenly bodies in the sublunar region. From the tyranny of astrology and the 'loss of nerve' that feared all life was in the grip of a pitiless 'fate', the gospel of God's love and care in Christ came as a great deliverance. Christ has conquered all enemies and put them under His feet. The glorious consummation of this victory is 'that God may be everything to every one' (*cf.* 1 Cor. 15:24–28).

9:1 – 11:36 THE PROBLEM OF JEWISH RIGHTS AND PRIVILEGE

Paul at this point appears to have reached his climax and all is ready for the practical application of his teaching on how to be right with God and how to keep in the same reconciled relationship. He has successively expounded the doctrines of justification, sanctification and glorification. But there emerges another problem, the Jewish question. The apostle must have faced this difficulty many times. Stated simply it is this: This new gospel of 'faith-righteousness' in place of 'law-righteousness', which opens the door of salvation for the Gentiles, abolishes the covenant rights and privileges of the Jewish race and, moreover, passes them by as the channels of revelation. The Jews are not only reduced in the order of grace but altogether rejected. What value has their history been and what is their future to be? Historical facts and the Pauline gospel do not appear to agree; hence the apostle's gospel of a new way of life must be false. No preaching could alter the place of the Jews in God's revelation.

Paul felt this objection keenly. It meant that he was accused of being no genuine apostle and his gospel was being treated as entirely untrue. This was not, however, the sharpest sorrow. The tragedy of the Jews was that they had been left outside the progressive revelation of God and cut off from the economy of grace. He therefore addresses himself to this historical problem. It was obvious that the people of God were losing their place in the kingdom and that the Gentiles were now filling it. The gospel given to the heathen people was being readily received and it appeared as if Israel was now neither being saved nor being serviceable. When the Gentiles were in their sin, Israel had the revelation of God. They were God's own chosen people. Elected and rejected! How can this be? He essays the solution in three assertions. The first deals with the absolute sovereignty of God (9:1–29), the second with Jewish responsibility in the historical situation (9:30 – 10:21), and the third with the merciful purpose of God (11:1–36).

9:1-29 The absolute sovereignty of God

9:1-5 Paul's personal sorrow. As a preface to dealing with the main problem, Paul expresses his own anguish at the state of the Jews. **1** *I am speaking the truth in Christ.* This is the apostle's solemn oath. His Judaistic adversaries charged him with insincerity; hence his vehement defence. In it he reveals himself as a true patriot. **3** Moses' solemn adjuration (Ex. 32:32) may be in the apostle's mind. He loved his race and was unashamed to call them *my brethren, my kinsmen by race.* **4, 5** He is proud of the Jewish privileges and recounts them with a certain flourish, the greatest of all being that Christ sprang from the Jewish stock. *The sonship* refers to Israel's place as Yahweh's people (Ex. 4:22f.; Ho. 11:1). *The glory*, the OT Shekinah, denotes God's radiant presence with His people in their pilgrimage and at worship. *The promises* are presumably the Messianic prefigurations of what God intended for His people, especially the provision of a righteousness-by-faith, exemplified in the promise to Abraham and his family and now made good in Christ and His church (*cf.* 4:13–21). **5** *God who is over all be blessed for ever.* Cf. AV and contrast RSV mg. and RV mg. 'Beyond all fair question, the Greek here (in view of the usual order of words in ascriptions of praise) is certainly best rendered as in AV; had it not been for controversy, probably, no other rendering would have been suggested' (Moule). An even more telling point in favour of the ascription of the phrase to Christ is that some such designation of the Lord as 'God over all' seems required to balance *according to the flesh, i.e.* as regards His human descent. Paul complements this with a statement: as regards His eternal being, He is *God . . . over all* (so Bruce, and Cullmann, *The Christology of the New Testament*, 1959, p. 313).

9:6-13 God is not unfaithful in His promises. This is the substance of the first objection. **6** Paul begins his reply by denying that *the word of God had failed.* The promises which he has already mentioned (v. 4) are not broken but fulfilled to the true Israel. The distinction between a racial and a real claim to belong to the elect people of Israel has already been registered in 2:28f.; and the distinction between the patriarchal lines through Abraham–Isaac and Abraham–Ishmael

is elaborated in Gal. 4:22–31, with the same contrast (v. 8) between 'children of the flesh' and 'children of the promise' (*cf.* on v. 4). God's Israel is henceforth contrasted with Judaism, hitherto the official heir of Abraham, but now rejected owing to its lack of faith and its refusal to accept the claims of the Messiah. **7, 8** The apostle makes his point by distinguishing between spiritual and carnal sonship with illustrations from the patriarchal history. Had history given the whole Jewish race a claim upon God, reversing what seems more normal, God's claim upon them? Because they were the seed of Abraham are all Jews the children of God? Paul declares that God in the exercise of His sovereign will has decreed that faith, not heredity, is the eternal principle of sonship. **9, 10** Within God's redemptive purpose the actual promises of God to Sarah and Rebecca were fulfilled. God was free to exercise His selective grace in the case of the patriarchs, for He alone is the originator of its purpose. **11, 12** Righteousness then is *not because of works but because of his call*, thus excluding all human merit. Jacob and Esau were not differentiated on the ground of their life and character, for Jacob was chosen before the twins were born. **13** *Jacob I loved, but Esau I hated* must be interpreted in the sense of nations, not individuals, which is the original reference in the two OT quotations (Gn. 25:23; Mal. 1:2, 3). The nations of Israel and Edom are in view, not Jacob and Esau as individual men, whose names occur as eponymous ancestors of the later tribes. Edom had called down on itself the divine judgment, as the OT makes plain (Ps. 137:7; Is. 34:5ff.; Je. 49:7ff.; Ezk. 25:12ff.; 35:1ff.; Ob. 10ff.). Moreover, 'love' and 'hate' are not the grounds of election as we understand these subjective feelings. God is not arbitrary in His choice and cannot be charged with irrational favouritism. The emotional terms indicate rather a special function and destiny. Judah, not Edom, was elected for progressive revelation in history. This meaning may be supported by the rendering 'Jacob have I loved, but Esau have I loved less' (*cf.* Gn. 29:30–33; Mt. 10:37; Lk. 14:26; Jn. 12:25).

9:14-24 God is not unrighteous in His dealing. The Judaistic objector (real or imaginary) now advances his accusation that if Paul's gospel is true then God has been unrighteous. **14–18** Paul deals first with the suggestion that God is unfair in His choice. **14** He expresses himself vehemently in his categorical denial of this charge: *By no means!* (AV 'God forbid'). Let no-one say this! **15** Mercy and pity are entirely of God. So much is this so that we cannot understand, but can only accept their incidence as being His will. This is no new doctrine. It was revealed of old time to Moses (Ex. 33:19, LXX). **16** Neither human purpose nor human effort enters into divine election. *It depends not upon man's will or exertion.* God alone acts alone. It just is, and no human can hinder it! **17** *The scripture*, almost personified here, in mind is

Ex. 9:16 referring to the Egyptian ruler *Pharaoh* Rameses II, whom God *raised up* so that he played a positive part in His purpose. 'How could God's power be revealed, and how could His name be spread abroad, if it were not for Pharaoh?' (Barrett). Pharaoh is but a medium to enable God to display His power in that monarch and to publish His own holy name far and near. Of His own will absolutely God shows mercy; of the same will He hardens men. **18** Echoing Ex. 33:19 as well as Ex. 7:3; 9:12; 14:4, 17, Paul's references to God's actions of mercy and judgment must be taken together. No-one objects when God is merciful; by parity of reasoning, no-one should boggle if His mercy, rejected and disowned, wears an aspect of wrath. Note that the verb used for *wills* is *thelō*, not *boulomai*. The latter is the firm term for will denoting determined purpose. Paul uses it sparingly and prefers the former word, as here, which permits a bigger background in the divine character than bare volition (*cf.* Eph. 1:5, 11). It is God as our Father in Christ Jesus who wills one way or the other, not stark, cold, divine will. In a word it is God who wills, not an unknown Will that wills.

19–24 Paul now proceeds to deal with the charge that, if what he has said is true, then God is unjust to blame. If God is absolutely free to elect for better or worse, as Paul has now demonstrated, what of human responsibility? **19** 'Since none can withstand this omnipotent divine will, sin is not voluntary; hence the sinner is not blameworthy'; so ran the implied objection. **20** Paul replies that this argument is out of court. The creature may not find fault with the Creator, although the reverse stands. Who is anyone to 'speak back' to God? The thing moulded simply cannot quarrel with God over its formation. **21** The apostle introduces the illustration of the potter and the clay (*cf.* Is. 29:16; 45:9, 10; 64:8; Je. 18:6). It is the potter's prerogative to make out of the same lump of clay *one vessel for beauty and another for menial use*, one a work of supreme art and another a homely article. *Cf.* 2 Tim. 2:20. 'What answer will you make now?' Paul challenges his opponent. If God wishes, on the one hand, to display His wrath and manifest His power, that is His will and He will await His time to reveal it. If God wishes, on the other hand, to publish His mercy in His election to salvation, that is again a matter of His good pleasure.

22, 23 The contrast is vividly expressed in the terms *vessels of wrath* and *vessels of mercy*. The sovereign will of God in relation to the latter is an eternal preparation for glory. Can it be likewise interpreted that the former are predestined pre-temporally to destruction? The vessels of wrath are the disobedient, with whom God is justly angry and upon whom there comes the nemesis for sin. Are they also prepared beforehand for eternal loss? Note, in the first place, that the two verbs are themselves different. The vessels of mercy are *prepared beforehand*

(Gk. *proëtoimasen*), while the vessels of wrath are *made for* (Gk. *katērtismena*; lit. to render 'fit' or 'complete', with the perfect participle giving a sense of 'equipped' or 'perfected'). God is not stated to be the agent of the 'fitting'. The condition is stated simply as historical fact. Hence some would prefer the rendering 'fit for destruction', *i.e.* 'ripe and ready for destruction' (Moff.). Secondly, note that the prefixes of the two parallel verbs are different—*pro*, signifying beforehand, and *kata*, signifying intensity of the action of the verb. It is legitimate to deduce from this that in the case of the disobedient the stress on the eternal aspect is missing. The mystery of predestination must remain, yet there appears here no warrant for any dogma of predestination to damnation, while the parallel foreordination to glory is stated with no uncertainty. In the third place it seems clear from Paul's language and thought that, while in the case of the vessels of mercy God's action was pre-preparation, in the case of the vessels of wrath He took no action but *endured with much patience*. He was active on the one hand and passive on the other. 'God has tolerated most patiently the objects of his anger' (Moff.). Paul thus leaves his opponent without an answer; for no mortal man can reply either to the right of God in election or to His exercise of that right. There is no answer; but nevertheless the character of God remains irreproachable.

9:25–29 God's election confirmed by the Scriptures. In this whole section dealing with the Jewish question the apostle probably has in mind more particularly the Jewish Christians in Rome. He therefore turns naturally to the law and the testimony for confirmation of the statements he has made. To corroborate his conclusion that the divine will is absolutely free to include Gentiles and reject Jews, and to create an election within the election, Paul quotes freely first from Ho. 2:23 (LXX) and 1:10 (LXX) and secondly from Is. 10:22, 23 (LXX) and 1:9. Here the doctrine of 'the remnant' is introduced to be treated further in 11:1–10 (where see notes).

9:30 – 10:21 Jewish responsibility in the historical situation

In this defence of the legitimacy of his gospel, the gist of which was the new way of justification by faith, not works, Paul has routed all charges by the thunder of a high and inscrutable predestination. His opponent is silenced, but the apostle feels that the Jew will now take refuge in an attitude of fatalism. To avoid a drift into determinism Paul now turns to examine the question of human responsibility. The Jewish question is therefore reviewed, not now from the divine standpoint as previously, but from the human standpoint. Paul asserts that the Jews themselves are to blame for their rejection by God as the media of revelation to the world and (which is even more tragic) as sons of God themselves.

9:30 – 10:13 The Jews sought law-righteousness instead of faith-righteousness. The Jews are responsible for their own apostasy. It is they who reject God, not God who rejects them. A vivid contrast is drawn between the Gentiles who had only the light of conscience and the Jews who possessed a special revelation. The one secured salvation by faith, even acceptance by God; the other lost the way of life by relying upon the observance of law. **32** *They have stumbled over* (*i.e.* 'took active offence at' or 'showed irritation at') *the stumbling stone* (*i.e.* 'the stone which causes stumbling or offence'). The reference is partly to the cross (1 Cor. 1:23), a seeming shame which the Jews could not endure as being the destiny of their Messiah (because of the rubric which pronounced a crucified man under God's curse, Dt. 21:23; *cf.* Gal. 3:13); more likely, however, Paul's conclusion embraces the failure of the Jews to understand the offer of righteousness-by-faith, apart from the law. **33** The historical background to this citation is Is. 8:13–15, where the Assyrian invasion is foretold and the one place of refuge promised is God Himself whose word is to be trusted (Is. 8:17). The alternative is to court national and personal disaster as the invader sweeps down on the people; then the very provision of God, once spurned, becomes an occasion of ruin as God's faithless people are dashed against the rock which He had appointed for safety. A similar setting is to be understood in Is. 28:16.

Paul cannot get over the plight of the Jews. **10:1** His *heart's desire*, longingly laid before God, is for their salvation. **2** Their appetite for religion is strong. But this zest is *not enlightened*; **3** their action arises from their *being ignorant*. Paul does not mean that the Jews are unenlightened (RSV is misleading here; NEB 'ill-informed' is only a slight improvement. Moff. 'ignorant' is what is needed) and without revelation of the righteousness of God. Rather they have not paid careful attention to (Gk. *epignōsis*) and have ignored (Gk. *agnoeō*) God's righteousness. Their ignorance is culpable. Their keenness is not in question; but they have not fully grasped the crucial point that God has a righteousness above the righteousness of the law. **4** They do not see that *Christ is the end of the law*, now superseding its sway and gaining its goal. Christ is the real righteousness; that of the Mosaic law might be enough if it could be kept, for law-righteousness must be kept (see v. 5). But faith-righteousness is a thing totally other. It is applied righteousness when applied by God to man.

Christ is the end (Gk. *telos*) *of the law* is an important Pauline dictum, capable of diverse meanings. The crux is whether the Greek words rendered 'for righteousness' (AV) go with 'Christ' who thus fulfils the law and provides a righteousness available to all believers, or with 'law' (so NEB mg. 'Christ is the end of the law as a way to righteousness for everyone who has faith'). The latter would make Paul utter a truism, viz. Christ makes an end (*telos*) of legalism; but

legalism has never been viable for Christ to terminate it, except in the preaching of Judaizers. The former interpretation makes Christ the goal to which the law points (as in 3:21). He ushers in a new era, and so renders the law as a way to obtain righteousness otiose. Obviously there is ambiguity here and it is hard to decide between the two views, but the NEB text ('Christ ends the law and brings righteousness for everyone who has faith') seems preferable. (See C. F. D. Moule in *Christian History and its Interpretation*, 1967, pp. 401ff. In this volume there is also a good discussion of Paul's use of Dt. 30:11–14 (in vv. 6–8) in the light of his Christ–wisdom contrast.) The Jews equated law and wisdom as media of divine revelation; Paul counters the implied claim by associating Christ with heavenly wisdom (thought to be inaccessible to mortals but entrusted to Israel as a precious heritage). So 'righteousness based on faith does not annul the law but brings it to its true goal, for "the word of faith which we preach" is Jesus Christ, incarnate wisdom', *the goal of the law* (M. J. Suggs, *op. cit.*, p. 311). So NEB text (quoted above). C. E. B. Cranfield's rendering (cited by Moule) is even clearer: 'for Christ is the goal of the law, so that righteousness is available to everyone that believeth.'

Paul now portrays for his readers the divine method. **5–10** His first point is that the way of salvation is not difficult and remote but near and easy. He quotes from Dt. 30:11–14 and places an interpretation on the words with reference to Christ which he is careful to indicate. Christ is ever available to faith and so likewise is the gospel. **9, 10** indicate the form taken by the earliest Christian creed. *Cf.* Paul's reply to the question of the Philippian jailer in Acts 16:31. Salvation is a matter of personal trust in a living Saviour, which will be evidenced by open confession made in baptism. These actions of belief and witness are complementary and Paul could hardly envisage one existing without the other. **11** The quotation is repeated from 9:33 and is itself taken from Is. 28:16. It follows naturally on the thought that those who believe will also be proud to confess. **11–13** Paul then picks on the word *No one . . . will be put to shame* to introduce his second point, that the way of salvation is within the reach of all, Jew and Gentile alike. **13** This universality of the gospel is emphasized by a further quotation from Joel 2:32 which leads inevitably to the conclusion that, if they do not *call upon the name of the Lord*, the Jews are themselves responsible for their fate.

10:14–21 The Jews are without excuse in their unbelief. Israel cannot validly object that there has been lack of opportunity or warning. **14–18** In the first place the gospel, this righteousness of God by faith, has been universally preached. The Jews may allege, by way of exoneration of their unbelief, that the preaching of the gospel has never reached them. **14** *Call upon* picks up the phrase of v. 13 (from Joel 2:32). To invoke the name of God is no formality nor 'knowing how to use the right religious formula' (Barrett); it means trusting the Person whose name is invoked and (as an OT phrase) committing one's way of life to God's service (Gn. 4:26; 21:33). Paul replies by a series of questions and answers laced with the words of prophecy (see Is. 52:7; 53:1; Ps. 19:4). **15** The first quotation is drawn from Is. 52:7 which Paul freely translates from the Hebrew text. The picture of the herald announcing the promise of Israel's restoration from Babylonian exile becomes, for him, an adumbration of the good news of God's mercy in reclaiming sinners and restoring them to His family through Christ. **16** But, as in Israel's history, good news is often met with incredulity, especially when it is unexpected and dramatic. The 'suffering Servant' of Is. 52:13 – 53:12 had to endure rejection and humiliation; and Paul sees a re-enactment of this failure to understand and accept God's message in the obduracy of the Jews of his day. **17** The desired response to *the preaching of Christ* (*i.e.* the gospel proclamation) is *faith*, noticeably lacking in the Jews' claim to a righteousness before God (9:31, 32). **19-21** In the second place lawgiver and prophet alike have issued a warning that Israel would reject God's message. The Jews cannot plead ignorance of their attitude. They cannot say it was not told them. God provoked this nation and angered it by what was not a nation, a nation void of understanding. *Not a nation* is a subtle play on words, combining Dt. 32:21 and Ho. 2:23. The Gentiles are meant, who are also spoken of as *foolish*, *i.e.* denied the true knowledge of God. **20** And Isaiah, who asserts that God was found by them that sought Him not, and revealed to them that did not ask for Him (Is. 65:1), has recorded that Israel, on the contrary, rebuffed God's approach by their disobedience and contradiction.

11:1-36 The merciful purpose of God

Paul now proceeds to consider more carefully whether the historical fact of the apostasy of the Jews and their consequent dereliction by God does necessarily amount to a final, absolute rejection of Israel. He comes to the conclusion that it does not, and glows with hope as he reasserts the fact of the believing remnant, the election within the election. Further, he is confident that, as the Jews have led to the conversion of the Gentiles, so the Gentiles will be the agents of the conversion of the Jews. The issue of the divine purpose will be to include all under grace.

11:1-10 The rejection of the Jews is partial, not complete. 1 *Has God rejected his people? By no means!* The apostle with some heat repudiates the very idea that the disobedience of Israel was tantamount to God's rejection of His own people. It may have appeared as if this were indeed the end of Paul's argument, but the apostle rejects it in strong language. The idea of an all-inclusive casting away of God's own

chosen and favoured people is as blasphemous to him as to the Judaizers. God did not wholly reject. The issue of a total abandonment, which the historical situation seemed also to uphold, was avoided by reference to the past as well as a plain insistence that Paul himself bore witness to a continuing remnant of believing Jews. His autobiography elsewhere confirms these details (2 Cor. 11:22; Phil. 3:5). **2** Paul then selects the case of Elijah (1 Ki. 19). *Of Elijah* (lit. 'in Elijah') can mean either 'in the passage of the OT to do with Elijah' or (more likely) 'in regard to Elijah's case', which is held up as a pattern. It is parallel to the present situation. The prophet had good cause to condemn Israel then and to despair of its destiny; but God corrected his pessimism by the revelation of the remnant. **4** However stubborn a people may be at any time, there is always room for God's elected remnant. The faithful in Israel at the time of Ahab's apostasy are appealed to as proof that God never totally abandons His people. **5** And that He does reserve a nucleus is a sign of *grace*, not human deserving. God still had grace for Israel. Election is by grace. **6** If it were of works, there could be no grace. **7** *The elect obtained it, but the rest were hardened.* Israel as a whole failed to get right with God, but the true election secured this righteousness of God. *The rest were hardened* according to the purpose of God (*cf.* 9:18); *i.e.* **8** *a spirit of stupor* (*cf.* Is. 29:10) was given them, a sort of spiritual insensibility. **9, 10** By quoting Ps. 69:22, 23 Paul places them on a level with David's own adversaries. The use of Ps. 69 is amply attested in the early church, especially in reference to the Lord's passion. The point here is that, as David knew enemies whose evil plans needed to be checked, so the greater David encounters in His offer to Israel through the church a spirit of rejection, except for the response of the believing remnant. But, Paul goes on, this is not the final verdict on Israel.

11:11-15 The rejection of the Jews is only temporary, not final. 11 Again pressing the high predestination of God, the objector seems to ask, 'Was it the purpose of God to make the Jews stumble in order that they might fall? Did the Almighty cause this irretrievable tragedy?' Paul once more protests *By no means!* The fall was not an end in itself but had in view a larger issue. The ruin of Israel was not final. One great result of their defection is the salvation of the Gentiles which is, in its turn, a goad to Israel's jealousy. The apostle still abjured any facile dogmatism such as his adversaries would spin from the situation. He still falls back upon an ultimate justification of God against plain appearances. **12** If Israel's *trespass* is the world's wealth and their loss the Gentiles' gain, then, *a fortiori*, a much greater blessing may be anticipated from their return. The word *trespass* (Gk. *paraptōma*) is a moral concept; hence *full inclusion* (Gk. *plērōma*) must also have an ethical meaning, although the Greek term is quite neutral, signifying 'completeness'. The context suggests a perfect consummation of faith, a spiritual goal which does not exclude material success. **13** What Paul is saying is addressed to the Gentiles. But he wants them to understand that one of the reasons why he makes so much of his special commission as an apostle to them is that his brethren may be made jealous and in this way find salvation for themselves. 'The large-scale conversion of the Gentile world is to be followed by the large-scale conversion of Israel (*cf.* verse 26)' (Bruce). **13–15** thus repeat the thought of vv. 11 and 12. **15** The description of this recovery of Israel as *life from the dead* may suggest that it will take place as part of the preparatory events leading up to Christ's return and the resurrection of the dead. *Cf.* Ezk. 37:1–14. This idea of the interaction between Jews and Gentiles is then further enlarged by an illustration.

11:16–24 The figure of the olive-tree. Paul begins with two metaphors in his mind: the piece of dough offered as a heave-offering (Nu. 15:17–21) consecrating the whole, and the holy root consecrating the branches. He passes over the first, however, and develops only the second (*cf.* Je. 11:16; Ho. 14:6). **16** The metaphor of the *first fruits* (in Lv. 23:10ff. as well as in Nu. 15) is taken by Paul to apply to the risen life of Christ, which promises the resurrection of all His people (1 Cor. 15:20ff.). Here the application is to the Jewish-Christian *ecclēsiola* which presages the full *ecclēsia* of God to be realized when God's purposes for Jews and Gentiles are completed. **17–24** The figure of the *olive tree* serves the twofold purpose of warning the Gentiles against boastful pride, and of substantiating Paul's Jewish optimism. The Gentiles are prone to adopt a supercilious attitude towards the Jews because of the gift of the righteousness of God by faith which they have received. Paul therefore applies the illustration first to them. **17** It happens that branches are broken off, and wild olive strains are grafted in their place. *A wild olive shoot, i.e.* Gentile Christians, inserted into the purpose of God's redeeming grace. **18** In consequence the grafted shoots feed on the fatness of the original roots. Hence Paul insists that Gentiles should not *boast* themselves as the olive's branches, for the branches are supported by the root and not *vice versa*. Gentile believers were evidently prone to congratulate themselves on their good fortune in being incorporated into the church, and **19** despised the faithless Jews whose place they were taking. **20** Paul counters this false spirit, as in Eph. 2:11ff. *So do not become proud, but stand in awe.* **21** God punished the Jews, the natural branches. **22** Therefore the apostle warns the Gentiles, the grafted branches, lest this severity take the place of His goodness toward them. All Christians hold their place in God's family by His grace, the counterpart of which is an obedience to Him which shows itself in continuance in that grace. *Cf.* 1 Cor. 10:12.

23, 24 Paul then applies his illustration to the Jews. His hope for their future is presented as being perfectly natural by the *a fortiori* argument of *how much more* can the natural branches, once cut off, be grafted back into their own olive-tree. If only Israel would give up their persistent unbelief, *God has the power to graft them in again.* Here Paul implies a spiritual, if not a horticultural, reality; the original branches are more akin to the tree than the wild shoots and should therefore be easier to graft into the stock from which they were originally taken. *Contrary to nature.* Ordinarily a farmer would take slips from a cultivated tree and graft them into a wild plant, thus producing a new fruit-bearing plant. Paul pictures God working the other way; and admits to the strangeness of this procedure. 'He is arguing from God to nature, not from nature to God' (Barrett).

11:25–32 The fullness of both Jew and Gentile. Thus may be seen, Paul continues, the purpose of God working upwards through apparent severity to a beneficent goal, the restoration of all. **25** He calls attention to *this mystery.* In Paul's period, the age of 'the mystery religions', the meaning of the word was a secret known only by the initiated. But by the term as applied to the Christian faith Paul means a secret, hidden in the past, but now revealed openly (*cf.* 16:25; 1 Cor. 2:7; Eph. 6:19; Col. 2:2; 1 Tim. 3:9). Here the particular sense of the mystery is the new light shed upon the unbelief of the Jews, as in Eph. 3:3ff.; Col. 1:26f. where the 'mystery' entails the special revelation to Paul of the universal church, comprising Jews and Gentiles in one body. The historical situation was now to be viewed with a different interpretation. This defect of Israel was not to be their last condition; for restoration was the divine will. The apostle desires the Jews to mark well this issue, lest in the pride of their own wisdom they arrive at the wrong conclusion. *A hardening*; Gk. *pōrōsis*, from *pōros*, a stone, hence 'a covering with a callus'. Here the agent of the hardening is not mentioned. It is merely a historical fact morally interpreted. The partial hardening of Israel finally issues in their salvation as eternally decreed. *Until the full number of the Gentiles*; *i.e.* until the 'great multitude' of Rev. 7:9 is complete. The suggestion is that there will be little response to the gospel on the part of the Jews while the Gentiles are being brought into the kingdom. **26** *And so all Israel will be saved.* This conclusion taken together with v. 32, *that he may have mercy upon all*, is not infrequently interpreted as Pauline universalism. In what sense does the apostle use such terms? In v. 32 the word *all* evidently refers to the unbelieving Jews and the unbelieving Gentiles who have now come into the kingdom by their repentance and faith. In v. 26 *all Israel* could mean either the true spiritual Israel or the people taken as a race. Some commentators, bearing in mind statements such as those in 9:6–8 in which Paul stresses the spiritual nature of the true Israel, interpret the word here as referring to the true and eternal seed of Abraham which includes, of course, both Jews and Gentiles (*cf.* Gal. 6:16). Others point out that in the following verses Paul seems to have clearly in mind the Jews as a race and feel that 'Israel' must therefore be interpreted in this sense in v. 26. In that case Paul is envisaging a future from the 'present time' of v. 5 until the historical Israel is saved. Some, again, would interpret this of the Jewish nation as a whole. Others feel that the phrase should not be regarded as so all-embracing and that it has the same meaning in relation to the Jews as has the term 'fullness of the Gentiles' in relation to non-Jews; *i.e. all* means 'all those who, in the purpose of God, will turn in faith to Christ'. Evidence for this view is found in the use of the phrase, current in Paul's day, 'All Israel'. The Rabbis used this to stress the totality of Israel without necessarily implying every single individual in the whole. It means 'all—except those not included' for various reasons, usually because they chose to contract out by their sinful practices (as in Mishnah, *Sanhedrin* 10:1ff.). This view seems to be the best background of Paul's thinking (so Sanday and Headlam; J. Munck, *Christ and Israel*, ET 1967, p. 136). To interpret it as referring to a universal salvation conferred upon men and women in view of their physical birth irrespective of their belief would be to contradict what Paul has plainly taught elsewhere (see, *e.g.*, 2:28, 29). **29** *The gifts and the call of God are irrevocable*; *i.e.* the unchanging God never regrets His promises or falters in His purpose, a fact which in vv. 26 and 27 Paul corroborates from Is. 59:20, 21 and 27:9. From the gospel standpoint the Jews are objects of God's hostility, *they are enemies* (v. 28); but from the point of view of 'the election' *they are beloved*. Actively and at the 'present time' the Jews are against Christ in the Gentile interest; passively, *i.e.* on historical considerations, they are beloved in the covenant sense. Disobedience characterizes both Jews and Gentiles in God's sight and even in this there is a purpose; it is so that God may have mercy on both, for neither party can really claim any pre-eminence over the other. Mercy apart, there is nothing for either Jew or Gentile. **32** *All men . . . upon all*. The universalistic references are probably to be understood in a representative sense, as in Col. 1:23, *i.e.* all without distinction, not all without exception (*cf.* Jn. 12:32; 1 Tim. 2:4). See on v. 26 above.

11:33–36 Doxology. The apostle has now ended his argument. He has vindicated the justice and mercy of God in the rejection of the Jews and the election of the Gentiles on the basis of the merciful purpose of God. He has shown how even unbelief and sin are overruled for good. Paul ceases his arguing and concludes with praise. The eternal decrees of God are beyond man's understanding, but they are both wise and good. The divine acts are all-mysterious. If God condemns, who shall question or annul the

decree? We behold His works in redemption, but the 'how' of them utterly baffles; for, after all, He is God unsearchable, inscrutable. All things originate from Him, continue through Him, and find their consummation in or for Him, for His glory. This ascription of praise is called forth from the apostle's heart, though the language he employs is drawn **34, 35** partly from the OT (Is. 40:13; Jb. 35:7; 41:11) and **36** partly from the liturgical vocabulary of the early church, which veils a Trinitarian ascription (see G. Bornkamm's study of the verse in *Das Ende des Gesetzes*, 1961, pp. 70–75).

12:1 – 15:13 CHRISTIANITY IN PRACTICE

12:1, 2 Introduction

The apostle has completed the doctrinal sections of the Epistle dealing with principles and problems. He has set forth how to get right and how to keep right with God. He has defended this free righteousness of God against all objections. Now he seeks to explain the life of faith in practice and to impress upon his readers the duty of Christian living. The righteousness of God accepted by the believer is an inward experience which must have an outward expression. The *therefore* of v. 1 marks the transition from the defended doctrines of justification, sanctification and election to applied Christianity. At root the Christian life is one consecrated to God, lived not in conformity to the world but in 'transformity' to God. The apostle's approach to the Roman Christians is a model for all true preachers. **1** *I appeal to you therefore, brethren*; *cf.* for the same appeal Eph. 4:1; 1 Tim. 2:1; 1 Cor. 4:16. Note that *the mercies of God* form the ground of the appeal. They are collectively all that Paul has described in God's compassionate dealing with sinners of both parties, Jews and Gentiles. The demand is for a *spiritual worship* in contrast to the sacrifice of brute beasts, a moral rather than a ceremonial surrender to God (*cf.* 1 Pet. 2:5). Paul is contrasting the worship which expresses the gospel under the new covenant with 'the externalities of Israel's temple worship' (Bruce), but this statement of true worship as embracing the whole of the Christian's life from day to day does not exclude the importance of congregational assembly which is worship's focal point. This consecration involves both body and mind. Paul urges the Roman Christians to *present* their *bodies*, *i.e.* themselves as living persons; but the use of the verb *present* (which is the same as 'yield' in 6:13, 19) may be occasioned by an existing tendency to belittle the flesh and to abuse the earthly temple as evil in essence. The Christian view of the body as sacred and as the servant of the soul is unique among the religions of the world, Judaism excepted. The yielding of the life in holy living is well-pleasing to God (*cf.* 14:18; Phil. 4:18). **2** This *living sacrifice* also includes the *mind* which, however, must first be renewed before it can be offered. This is a miracle of transformation, a readjustment to both temporal and eternal realities. The ideas conveyed by the terms used to express nonconformity and transformation are striking. The first has the root *schēma*, implying external semblance; the other is derived from *morphē*, meaning essential and radical likeness. But it is doubtful if a rigid distinction between these Greek terms ought to be pressed. AV and RSV 'conform' and 'transform' adequately represent Paul's meaning (see C. E. B. Cranfield, *A Commentary on Romans 12-13*, 1965, pp. 15ff.). The consequence is the recognition of God's will as right and fit and ideal.

After this exordium dealing with the fundamental principle of Christian living, self-sacrifice and devotion to God, the apostle proceeds to apply the law in four main sections of exhortation.

12:3-21 Personal ethics

In this section the apostle evidently has in mind relations with both Christians and pagans. His admonitions are given spontaneously without any attempt at logical presentation; yet many characteristically group themselves together.

12:3-8 The exercise of gifts. 3 *By the grace given to me*; Moff. 'in virtue of my office'. Paul declares that talents which come from God ought to be used with humility. He who is specially endowed is tempted to fancy himself and become self-important; hence the apostle warns that such must take himself seriously and avoid conceit. The sane view is grounded on the fact of the givenness of gifts from God and on the truth of mutual interdependence, *each according to the measure of faith which God has assigned him*; *i.e.* every Christian ought not to be conceited in his self-estimate, but to think of himself and his gift *with sober judgment*, measuring himself by the standard which God has given him in his faith. **4, 5** This latter idea of faith-distribution as the norm of endowments leads the apostle to refer to the figure of the *body* and its *members* (*cf.* 1 Cor. 12:12; Eph. 4:16; Col. 1:18). He is clearly thinking of the Christian community as a social organism with the various members co-operating in mutual service. **6-8** There follows a list of seven illustrative gifts functionally correlated. *Prophecy, i.e.* inspired utterance of truth, or preaching (*cf.* 1 Cor. 14:3), is to be exercised *in proportion to our faith*. This phrase may be taken in two ways: either 'drawing upon the prophetic inspiration of the Spirit' and so controlling the utterance to the limits of that inspiration, or 'in agreement with the standard of faith' contained in the apostolic gospel. The latter is preferable. *Service (i.e.* deacons' work, service in things material rather than spiritual), *teaching* and *exhortation* are three gifts which are to be used each in its place; otherwise they will be ineffectual. Giving or contributing is to be exercised *in liberality, i.e.* without any parade (*cf.* 2 Cor. 9:7, 13; Jas. 1:5) and purely because of the need for the gift. *He who gives aid* (Gk. *ho proistamenos*) represents a term which older

commentators (Origen, Calvin) took to mean 'a ruler over congregational life' (so AV 'he that ruleth'); but more probably it stands for 'the administrator in charge of the charitable work of the congregation' (Cranfield; RSV agrees). *He who does acts of mercy, i.e.* is active in glad ministry to others (Moff. renders 'the sick visitor must be cheerful'). The phrase expresses the general idea of Christian kindness, as do no fewer than four of the seven 'special gifts' referred to in vv. 6-8.

12:9-13 The law of love expressed in various activities. Love, which is really the ruling principle of Christian living, is more than an emotion and of firmer nature than mere sentimentality or pure philanthropy. The Greek term *agapē* implies a quota of intellect and volition as well as feeling. It is akin to the divine quality behind 'the mercies of God' (v. 1) and all His redemptive intervention in the destinies of a lost world. **9** If this love be *genuine, i.e.* void of hypocrisy and pure and sincere in its outflowing, then it will find activity in various forms. Love will produce loathing of evil and hungering after good. **10** Also it will inspire a mutual affection for kindred souls. *Outdo one another in showing honour* is a phrase capable of several possible interpretations. It may mean putting the interests of others before our own, or being forward to pay honour to others, or eagerly surpassing others in praiseworthy works. The first meaning—'honour your fellow-Christian above yourself'—is argued for by Cranfield on the (theological) ground that the fellow-believer is the representative of Christ to me, or rather the one in whom Christ is mysteriously present for me. **11** *Never flag in zeal* appears to refer to the service of God and our neighbours, linked as a common responsibility. The idea is that love, if allowed to rule, will never allow enthusiasm to flag. *Be aglow with the Spirit* is memorably rendered by Moffatt as 'maintain the spiritual glow', the reference being not to the divine but the human spirit. But RSV assumes the divine Spirit, and some scholars rightly relate this fervency (*cf.* AV) to the Spirit's action in the believer (so Calvin, Bruce, Cranfield; *cf.* Acts 18:25; 1 Thes. 5:19). *Serve the Lord; i.e.* the Lord Jesus Christ. Some MSS read *tō(i) kairō(i)* for *tō(i) Kyriō(i)*, hence the rendering 'serving the opportunity' (RV mg.; *cf.* Eph. 5:16). But this reading of the Western textual tradition is certainly to be rejected and regarded as 'a purely accidental error, perhaps due to the use of abbreviations' when the Greek consonants only were written (Cranfield). **12, 13** The apostle continues the manifold manifestations of the dynamic of love in Christian living by citing cheerfulness in the reality of the Christian hope, endurance in suffering, perseverance in prayer, sharing the needs of Christian brethren and the practice of hospitality.

12:14-21 Additional maxims of Christian ethics. In this further list of moral precepts Paul may have non-Christians more in mind. Some certainly are definitely relative to those outside the fellowship of the church. **14** echoes our Lord's teaching in the Sermon on the Mount (Mt. 5:44). **15** 'Share your fellows' joys and sorrows' admonishes the apostle. **16** *Live in harmony with one another*; lit. 'mind the same things' (Barrett); *cf.* 2 Cor. 13:11; Phil. 2:2; 4:2), *i.e.* never alter your Christian attitude to your fellows. Beware of selfish ambition. 'Aspire not to lofty tasks but follow the stream of lowly duties' (David Smith). Beware of self-conceit (*cf.* Pr. 3:7). **17** Never return ill for ill (*cf.* Mt. 5:43, 44; 1 Cor. 13:5, 6; 1 Thes. 5:15; 1 Pet. 3:9). *Take thought for what is noble in the sight of all*; *i.e.* either consider the best things of any philosophy or religion in your cosmopolitan environment (*cf.* Pr. 3:4; 2 Cor. 4:2; 8:21), or think nobly of all men, or aim to be above reproach in the eyes of all (Moff., NEB). But it is more likely that Paul regards as the criterion of what is noble and good, not human philosophy or opinion, but the gospel by which the fallen human mind is renewed (12:2). **18** To be at peace with all men is the next admonition, attached to which is the concession *so far as it depends upon you*. The other man may make it impossible.

19 The last injunction on *vengeance* is an important point, he seems to say, by the introduction of a stylized *Beloved. Leave it to the wrath of God.* This means either that we should leave it to God to exercise wrath as declared in Dt. 32:35, or that we should let the principle of retribution inherent in the moral universe pursue its course (*cf.* 1:18). The first affords the best interpretation. **20, 21** The attitude of the Christian under the rule of love must be one of mercy, the very opposite of retaliation. *You will heap burning coals upon his head*; *i.e.* give him a burning sense of shame; though some writers want to see a specific reference, *e.g.* in Egyptian ritual a man purged his offence by carrying on his head a dish containing burning charcoal on a bed of ashes. The verse is a quotation from Pr. 25:21, 22 (LXX), but omitting the closing words, 'and the Lord shall reward thee'. Paul gives a nobler meaning: 'Treat your enemy kindly; this may soften his hard heart and take away his evil disposition.' 'The best way to get rid of an enemy is to turn him into a friend' (Bruce). Therefore let good triumph over evil.

13:1-7 Political ethics

In this second section of admonitions Paul passes from purely personal matters to the realm of political ethics, and declares the Christian's duty to the state, a subject most revelant to his Roman readers. The apostle's view of the state in relation to the believer presents the principle of Christian submission which has ever been recognized as the mind of God and obligatory upon the church. The grounds of this obedience to secular powers can be expressed under three headings.

13:1, 2 Civil government is a divine institution.

1 *Every person.* Paul exhorts the Roman Christians, not as a social community merely, but as individuals, to be subject to the Roman rule. The apostle had always found the Roman high officials to be just and helpful, but this fact does not wholly account for an inspired dictum on political relations. It is the divine revelation for the church in all ages, for which rational grounds are afforded. The teaching here falls into two parts. First, God is sovereign ruler of nations. It is He who sets up rulers and behind all earthly dominion lies His authority (2 Sa. 12:8; Je. 27:5f.; Dn. 2:21, 37f.; 4:17, 25, 32; 5:21). Then, every Christian has a duty to recognize the state (*be subject to* implies the recognition of a claim laid upon us), to obey lawful authority so far as such obedience does not conflict with God's law or Christ's authority, and to intercede for those who hold such responsible posts (1 Tim. 2:1ff.). More problematical is the precise meaning of *the governing authorities*. All agree that civil authorities represented by the Roman Empire in Paul's day are in view; and a novel modern view sees a further allusion in the phrase to the angelic powers, thought to stand behind and to act through these members of civil government (see Cranfield for a full discussion sympathetic to this double reference). **2** The believer who resists lawful earthly authority is, in fact, disobeying God. For such disaffection the rebel *will incur judgment.* It has been plausibly suggested that in Paul's thought here both Jew and Gentile are visualized as possible, if not actual, resisters. The Jew in his religious assertiveness and the Gentile believer in his Christian dogmatism might both indulge in some hotheaded fanaticism against the authorities. Such conduct is condemned.

13:3, 4 Civil government is ordained to promote good and to prevent evil. Obedience to secular powers is further commanded because of its service to the very righteousness of God which is the Epistle's theme. Twice here Paul describes the secular authority as *God's servant*, continuing the idea of divine appointment into that of its purpose. A Christian must obey the magistrate because, in God's hand, his business is to keep order, commending the good and punishing the evil. Only evil-doers need tremble before the judges of the earth, for they are on the side of right-doers. *Bear the sword*: an allusion to the Roman *ius gladii*, by which a Roman citizen serving in the army could be condemned to death, has been seen (Barrett), but this is doubtful. Paul rather has a general statement in mind, that the state has power to quell resistance when civil order is in peril. The magistrate is appointed by divine providence to conserve good order (*for your good*) and to restrain and punish evil (*to execute his wrath on the wrongdoer*), as *the servant of God*.

13:5-7 Civil government has the approval of the Christian conscience. Obedience to the powers that be is a Christian's duty, not only because of the inevitable penal consequences of resistance, but *for the sake of conscience, i.e.* lest, by seditious disobedience to a God-ordained authority, he should incur a guilty conscience. The moral constitution of the believer approves of the workings of the moral constitution of the state. 6 Hence, *taxes* due as citizens of Rome or as a subject people must be paid. 7 Indeed the apostle, enlarging the scope of the obligation, declares that all *dues*, taxes and tolls are to be honoured (*cf.* Mt. 17:24ff.; 22:21; Mk. 12:17; Lk. 20:25).

13:8–14 Personal ethics

Paul at this point reverts to exhortations in relation to one another after the style of ch. 12. He has just said 'Pay all of them their dues', which carries him back to the fundamental principle of all ethics, the law of *love*. 8 The Christian has one debt, spoken of by Bengel as 'his immortal debt', which suggests that we owe it to all men indiscriminately rather than to fellow-Christians exclusively. Origen says, 'It is our duty always to pay and always to owe this debt of love.' Love is the one obligation which fulfils all obligations. *For he who loves his neighbour has fulfilled the law* could be translated 'for he who loves has fulfilled the other law' (*i.e.* the Mosaic law, as well as the civil obligation imposed by Rome) or 'the rest of the law' (*i.e.* the second part of love to one's neighbour, Mt. 22:39). But we should stay with RSV, being careful to give to *neighbour* the NT sense of 'anyone who is needy and is thrown across my path in life' (*cf.* Lk. 10:25–37). 9 A summary of the Decalogue spelt out in terms of Lv. 19:18. 10 This conclusion does not invalidate the Ten Commandments in the interest of a nebulous, existential 'Love, and do as you please' (as Augustine's dictum is popularly misunderstood and misapplied). Love realizes the end of all law (*cf.* Gal. 5:14) and is the spirit in which we are to keep the law; but we need the law's particulars and prescriptions to give body and definition to love's 'situational' approach to ethical obligation.

11 To reinforce this exhortation to love Paul reminds his readers of the approaching return of our Lord. The imminence of the *parousia* is cited as one of the strongest motives for Christian living, as in Phil. 4:4–7; 1 Thes. 5; Heb. 10:24f.; Jas. 5:7–11; 1 Pet. 4:7–11; and in the Gospels, Mt. 25:31–46; Mk. 13:33–37. *You know what hour* (Gk. *kairos*, time of crisis and challenge) *it is.* It is the definite age before the second coming, the period yet to pass until the Lord appears again according to promise (*cf.* Mk. 1:15; 1 Cor. 7:29). The admonition is to *wake from sleep*, to be up and doing, living more intensely the Christian life in its dynamic love. The end of the 'opportunity' is near, drawing ever nearer every day. The introduction of the word *first* before *believed* emphasizes rightly the aorist tense of a definite time, that of conversion. 12 . . . *night . . . day . . . darkness . . . light.* These contrasts are found elsewhere (Ps. 43:3; Is. 2:5; 9:2; 42:6f.; 60:1ff.; Lk. 16:8; Jn. 1:4ff.; 3:19ff.; 8:12; Acts 26:18; 2 Cor. 6:14; Eph. 5:8; 1 Thes. 5:4f.) and 'children of light' was a self-designation of the Dead Sea

community in opposition to the 'sons of darkness' against whom they protested. The aroused condition of the believer under the stimulus of the signs of the times will result in three resolute duties of higher living. First, *put on the armour of light* (*cf.* 2 Cor. 6:7; Eph. 6:13; 1 Thes. 5:8), the negative of which is abjuring all evil deeds which are associated with the night-time of ignorance. *Cast off* (lit. 'put off') *. . . put on* represent two Greek terms which played an important part in NT ethical patterns, especially in the training of new Christians and in preparation for baptism. The baptism actions of stripping and re-clothing may have suggested these calls to moral decision (Eph. 4:22ff.). Secondly, 13 *let us conduct ourselves becomingly.* Conduct must be as seemly as in the open day. Light is contrasted with darkness in v. 12, and here again day with night, since the admonitions are being based on the passing of night-time and the nearness of the day of the Lord. Thirdly, 14 *put on the Lord Jesus Christ,* the negative of which is refusing all provision for the lower man and his lusts. Christ is here conceived as the complete panoply of the believer (*cf.* Gal. 3:27).

14:1 – 15:13 The strong and the weak

Paul now addresses himself to the special situation in the Roman fellowship of which he had been reliably informed. There are always brethren in every church who entertain imperfect conceptions of Christian truth combined usually with a certain doggedness for their defective creed. These are not to be browbeaten. Their conscience, partially enlightened as to the liberty which Christians enjoy in Christ, must be reverenced, and the conduct of the other members of the society of believers must not hurt them. On the other hand such troublesome brethren must not criticize the rest, advance their views as standards and demand uniformity. Evidently the apostle was familiar with this type of mind, as such men were found in other churches under his inspection, especially in Corinth (*cf.* 1 Cor. 8:1 – 10:33) and Colossae (*cf.* Col. 2:16–23). Two of the vexed questions upon which difference of opinion arose in Paul's time were the keeping of the sabbath and the eating of flesh. Probably the church at Rome refused membership to those who held eccentric views and Paul was endeavouring to advance the milder policy that they should be accepted upon confession of the essentials of the Christian faith and afterwards instructed in the Lord. Many had scruples in these matters and the apostle seeks to avoid schism in the church and to counsel toleration under the law of love.

14:1–12 The weaker brother is not to be despised. Paul first of all stresses the point that every man must have his own reasoned convictions. Let him regulate his conduct thereby with intellectual and moral honesty and suffer his neighbour to do likewise. He lives not in the presence of his fellow-men, but before the Lord at whose judgment seat we shall all stand. 1 *Weak in faith* implies a lack of balance in discerning between the essentials and non-essentials of saving and sanctifying faith. Paul with apostolic authority commands the reception of such weak brethren into the Christian fellowship, but *not for disputes over opinions*; *i.e.* without entering into critical discussions or condemning their scruples by 'attempting to settle doubtful points' (NEB). Prejudices of such minor importance are not sufficient grounds for denying sacramental privileges. Paul proceeds to note the two problems at issue, flesh-eating and holy days. **2** *Eat anything . . . eats only vegetables.* The former group rejoiced in their freedom from Jewish dietary rules, on the basis of Ps. 24:1 (*cf.* 1 Cor. 10:26); the latter maintained vegetarian principles, fearing an unconscious infringement of the law which forbade the eating of animal blood or defilement because of their touching food formerly used in pagan sacrifice, only a token part of which was consumed in the idol-shrine. It is not clear here whether flesh is abstained from simply *per se*, or whether there is the added taint of consecration to idols (1 Cor. 10:25; for the background to the problem at Corinth, see *NBD*, art. 'Idols, Meat offered to'). It is likely that both elements entered into the prejudice. **3** At any rate there must be no criticism between eater and non-eater. **4** Before God alone and not his fellow-men the eater *stands or falls*, *i.e.* is acquitted or condemned, or, if taken subjectively, is morally unshaken in his liberty or becomes immoral in licence. But Paul adds that the free man shall be in no danger, for the Lord can preserve him, having already *welcomed him*.

The other question is to be solved in the same spirit of liberty and toleration. **5** One man holds by the sanctity of special days, another considers all are the same. The groups were divided over the observance (presumably by the practice of fasting) of certain 'holy days'. *Cf.* Col. 2:16. **6, 7** The observance or non-observance of such days, provided Christians think through their decisions, is non-consequential for fellowship; it should not be made a matter for refusing to accept a fellow-Christian; it is a decision which affects only the Christian and his Lord. Hence the warning in vv. 10, 13. Each should settle his own way of regarding such matters so long as it is *in honour of the Lord*. This motive of service justifies observance or non-observance. **7–12** Paul becomes gripped with this normative principle of the inspiration of service and expands it in these verses. The Lordship of Christ is supreme and all-inclusive of life and death and judgment. **12** When Christians remember that each *shall give account of himself to God*, other matters will assume the right perspective.

14:13–23 The weaker brother's conscience must be respected. Paul passes from his wise counsel to the Roman Christians not to judge one another to the suggestion that their critical faculty could be better employed by being turned upon themselves. They ought never to put temptation in the way of the weaker brethren by parading their own liberty in the matter of eating and drinking.

13 Such freedom in the presence of those whose conscience disapproved might become a hindrance or *a stumbling block*, *i.e.* a snare in the path of moral progress. Action taken against the light of conscience, however poor that light may be, is moral failure. **14** When the apostle states that he believes that no meat is *unclean in itself* and he appeals to the teaching of *the Lord Jesus* (in Mk. 7:14–19) for his authority, he is referring simply to edible food under the ban of the ceremonial law or custom. Some think differently and for them, as for all, their view must regulate their conduct. This principle again picks up the teaching of Jesus in Mk. 7:20–23 (*cf.* Tit. 1:15). **15** The motive for deferring in this way to a weak brother's opinion is the ruling principle of *love* which Paul has already expounded (12:9–13), and to which he now joins the fact that such a one is beloved of the Lord and a sharer in the benefits of His atoning death. *Do not . . . cause the ruin.* Paul uses this strong term to describe the final result when a weak brother is caused to act against his own conscience. **16** To allow one's *good*, *i.e.* one's liberty, to grieve and destroy others in this way would cause the gospel to be evil spoken of or 'become an occasion for slanderous talk' (NEB). **17** As far as *the kingdom of God* is concerned love is more important than questions of eating and drinking, and its expression in righteousness, peace and joy is the thing which matters most. Paul here is evidently combating the Jewish materialist conceptions of the Messianic kingdom. **20** *Do not . . . destroy*, *i.e.* 'pull down'. It is the opposite of *upbuilding* in v. 19. The principle of total abstinence in all things that give offence is commended as the Christian's rule in living the life of faith-righteousness, lest a brother be tempted, not so much to carnal degradation, as to moral and spiritual ruin by suppressing his conscience. **22** *The faith that you have* is the Christian's stance and conviction in controversial issues, reached by intelligent thought, careful consideration of all interests involved, his brother's included, and in obedience to the Lord's will for him (earlier key-verses in the chapter: 5, 6, 8, 15 combine to form these 'controls'). *Cf.* 1 Cor. 8:9–13; 10:29–33. In some circumstances our faith may have to be expressed not openly but secretly in our communion with God. The happy man is the one whose conscience is clear. But the one who acts against his conscience condemns himself. **23** Faith, *i.e.*, in this context, conviction and fixed principle, is the all-important factor. To change one's behaviour in such a matter without believing that it is the right thing to do is, in fact, sin.

15:1–13 A plea for unity. The apostle now warns against the unwisdom of division, urging unity within the church at Rome, especially as regards the questions of Christian liberty and Gentile privilege. Basing his counsels upon the teaching already given, he pleads for mutual understanding and helpfulness between those whose views and practice differ in the matters he has discussed. **1** *We who are strong.* This is the first time that the apostle uses this term to describe those whose conscience enjoys the greater light, although the idea was implicit in his use of the term 'the weak' (cf. 14:1; 1 Cor. 8:11) to describe their opposites. The idea is one of moral ability, which serves not only its possessor but also others who may need support. True oneness of heart can be achieved in two ways, both of which are essential. First, it is the duty of the strong to *bear with* the weak and not to assert themselves. Egotism must be shunned. **3** The life of self-sacrifice was the example set us by Christ, for even He *did not please himself.* In confirmation of the point he is making Paul quotes from a Messianic psalm (69:9); **4** this leads him to assert the value of Scripture in its inspiration for present Christian living (cf. 1 Cor. 10:6, 11; 2 Tim. 3:16).

7 The second way of achieving unity is for the strong, representing the authorities of the church, to admit the weak into their fellowship. This duty the apostle had already urged (14:1), using the same term, *Welcome*; for after all it is Christ who *welcomed* us all (cf. 14:3), strong or weak, into the fellowship of His people, at our conversion when we had nothing to commend us to Him save our need. Glory then be to God! **8** *For I tell you* is an unusual opening in this context, and what follows probably means 'I am telling you "strong" Christians to put up with the religious oddness of the "weak", and this is precisely what Christ did; for He made Himself the servant of the oddest of all religious people—the Jews' (so Barrett).

9 Paul then reminds the church at Rome that the *mercy* of God is extended to both Jew and Gentile alike. On this ground he exhorts to unity between circumcised and uncircumcised. That the fellowship at Rome should be split, or in any wise suffer, because of this universalism of the gospel is unthinkable. Christ was equally a servant to Jew and Gentile alike. By His life and work our Lord confirmed to the circumcision the promises made to the patriarchs (cf. 9:4, 5). But the promises made to the uncircumcision in the OT are similarly confirmed so that *the Gentiles might glorify God for his mercy.* Paul avers that all are 'one in Christ Jesus' (cf. Gal. 3:28). To prove to the Jews this sublime truth, the 'mystery' of his Epistle, Paul adds several OT quotations; see Ps. 18:49 (LXX); **10** Dt. 32:43; **11** Ps. 117:1 (LXX); **12** Is. 11:10 (LXX). **13** Paul then concludes the section by a benedictory prayer. *The God of hope*; cf. v. 5, 'the God of steadfastness and encouragement' (RV 'comfort'), and v. 33, 'the God of peace'. The reference to *hope* connects with the promise drawn from Is. 11:10 in v. 12, that Messiah's blessing will cause the Gentiles to *hope* in God's mercy.

15:14 – 16:27 EPILOGUE

15:14–21 Paul's justification for writing

The apostle has now come to the conclusion of his noble Epistle. He begins his closing section

with a reference to his own vocation as the explanation of his writing to the Roman Christians. **14** With supreme tact he commends their spiritual maturity and ability in mutual self-help. He is persuaded that they are *full of goodness.* Paul did not know the Christians at Rome at first hand; hence this tribute to their solid Christian profession. His letter is simply a reminder of truths they have learnt already, even though he had not been their teacher. **15** His boldness in addressing them arises from the fact of his apostleship to the Gentiles. **16** Paul describes his divine commission in terms of the priesthood: *a minister* (Gk. *leitourgos*; lit. 'a priest'; cf. Heb. 8:2), *in the priestly service* (Gk. *hierourgōn*) and *offering* (Gk. *prosphora*) are three sacerdotal terms. In the exercise of his preaching ministry as the prophet of God he is also a priest, offering the sacrifice of the Gentiles made righteous to God and consecrated by the Holy Spirit. The same metaphor of offered sacrifice is used in 12:1, 2 and Phil. 2:17 with the same association of assured acceptance. There is perhaps a polemic slant in the use of these sacral terms drawn from the sacrificial cult of Judaism, especially in the reference to *the offering of the Gentiles* as *sanctified.* Paul's Jewish enemies might have argued exactly to the contrary on the ground that Gentiles were regarded as 'unclean' in God's sight (cf. Acts 10:14, 15, 28).

16, 17 An indirect allusion to his whole Gentile mission, using language which recalls Phil. 1:26; 2:16. **18** The success of his work among the Gentiles is another mark of his apostolic commission upon which Paul rests his authority to write this Epistle. His mission has prospered, not through himself but through Christ working in him. **19** These miracles wrought *by the power of the Holy Spirit* are the only ones of which he is free to speak. He refers to his field of labour as *from Jerusalem and as far round as Illyricum*; i.e. 'the north-west coast of the Adriatic with its hinterland, extending perhaps even into the Roman province of Macedonia'. Most of the Roman eastern provinces are meant, although there is no record in the Acts of Paul's missionary travels in Illyria. *From Jerusalem* is mentioned as a *terminus a quo* of Paul's missionary labours partly because in a vision there (Acts 22:17–21) the call came, but more likely because of his theological conviction that OT prophecy (e.g. Is. 2:1–4) promised salvation for the Gentiles as 'the word of the Lord' proceeded from Jerusalem. **20** The apostle, while not an individualist, is diffident about mentioning the labours of others; his policy had always been to pioneer with the gospel and not to *build on another man's foundation*, a rule he also states in 2 Cor. 10:15, 16. The figure of a foundation he also uses in 1 Cor. 3:10 and Eph. 2:20. Paul justifies his missionary strategy to go to the regions beyond by a citation from Is. 52:15 (LXX).

15:22–33 Plans for future journeys

Dealing with more personal affairs, Paul now

alludes to his future plans. **22** The breaking of all this new ground has hitherto prevented a visit to Rome. **23** But now the work has been covered and, having for many years longed to visit them, **24** he hopes soon to come *en route* to Spain. Indeed the apostle expects the assistance of the Roman Christians to further his missionary enterprise in the West. If ever he was to fulfil this cherished ambition and reach Spain he would need a new base. Antioch and Ephesus were too remote; it would have to be Rome. Hence *once I have enjoyed your company for a little*. He will not leave them until he has had the opportunity of satisfying some of the longing to have fellowship with them which he has already expressed in v. 23.

25–27 Meanwhile Jerusalem calls for his ministry as the bearer of alms from Macedonia and Achaia for the poor. The Hebrew Christians have shared with the Gentiles their spiritual treasures; it is therefore the duty of the new converts to contribute in temporal things to the needs of the mother church. *Contribution* (Gk. *koinōnia*) emphasizes the sense of sharing in a common cause (in this case, the relief of the needy Christians in Jerusalem) at some cost (see *NBD*, art. 'Communion'). The generosity of the churches in Macedonia is stated in 2 Cor. 8:1ff. and the same generous spirit is advocated as an incentive to the Corinthians (2 Cor. 8:7). The effectiveness of Paul's earlier plea is evidenced by this tribute to *Achaia*, *i.e.* churches in southern Greece, including Corinth (2 Cor. 9:2). **28** With this charitable commission fulfilled, Paul plans to visit Rome on his journey to Spain. RSV mg. offers a literal translation of some obscure words: 'having sealed to them (the church in Palestine) this fruit.' The last word clearly means the collection, but Paul elsewhere uses the figure of 'fruit' (1:13; Phil. 1:22; 4:17) of his ministry to the Gentiles. This application is confirmed by his use of the commercial term 'seal', again employed elsewhere (1 Cor. 9:2; 2 Cor. 1:22) to affirm that his ministry as apostle to the Gentiles was authenticated by God. So we should see in this passage 'Paul's hope that the collection would move the Jerusalem Christians to recognize the full and present validity of his mission to the Gentiles' (K. F. Nickle, *The Collection*, 1966, p. 129). **29** He arrived at Rome in circumstances never envisaged in his plans; but this confidence that his coming would be *in the fullness of the blessing of Christ* was abundantly fulfilled. We do not know whether he ever reached Spain, though it is just possible that *1 Clement* (5:6, 7) refers to a wider ministry than is given in Acts: 'he (Paul) was a herald both in the east and in the west . . . he taught righteousness to all the world, and when he had reached the limits of the west, he gave his testimony before the rulers.'

30–33 This more personal section ends with an apostolic charge that they should pray to God for him. His requests are, first, that he might be *delivered from the unbelievers in Judea, i.e.* the Jews who were still rejecting the claims of their

Messiah; secondly, that he might find his missionary contribution acceptable to the Jerusalem saints; thirdly, that his western visit might be unto edification by God's will, with the blessed result of refreshment both for the Roman Christians and for himself. As later events show, Paul's wish was far from being fulfilled. His experience, both in Jerusalem and Rome, was very different from his peaceful dreams. With v. 33 *cf.* vv. 5 and 13.

16:1–16 Greetings to friends in Rome

As Heb. 11 has been termed the 'picture gallery' of OT saints, so we may call Rom. 16 the 'picture gallery' of NT believers. It may be thought strange that Paul, who had never been to Rome, should yet have so many friends there. This remarkable list in a letter sent to a church Paul had never visited lends weight to the theory that ch. 16 does not belong to the letter to the Romans, but is a fragment of a Pauline letter to the Ephesian church. Up to 1935 this hypothesis remained a conjecture for which there was no MS evidence. But with the publication of the Chester Beatty Codex leaves of Pauline Epistles (P46: 3rd century) it has been clear that the oldest known MS of Romans ended with the doxology at the close of ch. 15. This means that the view of a separate origin of ch. 16, which earlier commentators like Lietzmann and Dodd had not felt free to accept (in default of tangible MS evidence), 'has a stronger claim than ever before to the most serious consideration' (T. W. Manson). But F. F. Bruce (*in loc.*), who presents a balanced picture of the *pro* and *con*, opts for retaining ch. 16 as integral to the letter to the Romans, chiefly on the ground of the large number of inscriptions containing personal names connected with Rome (see the full discussion in Dodd, pp. xx ff.) as well as the fact that travel was frequent and swift, thanks to Roman roads and world peace. The Jews of the 1st century (as of every century afterwards) were a commercial and migratory people. They moved along the trade routes and followed the markets. The commendations and salutations were to saints either going to, or living at, Rome. The greetings are varied, each giving a true index of the work performed and of the character won. One third of the names on this historical roll are those of women, revealing the prominent place women held in the church at Rome. Paul was a pioneer in the recognition of the function of women in Christian service and his attitude has been much misunderstood in this sphere.

1, 2 His testimonial to *Phoebe* is most honourable. She is described as *our sister, i.e.* in the spiritual family of the Lord, suggesting equality of privilege with the brotherhood: as *a deaconess* of the church at Cenchreae (*cf.* 1 Tim. 3:11, NEB mg., for this order of ministry in the early church); and as *a helper* (Gk. *prostatis*, 'patroness'), implying 'probably some measure of wealth or social position' (Dodd). It is believed that Phoebe was on her way to Rome and Paul entrusted his precious Epistle to her care for safe delivery. **3** *Prisca and Aquila* are a married couple whom Paul met at Corinth (Acts 18:1–3) on his first visit there; being of the same trade (they were tentmakers), the apostle lodged with them. We read of them further in Acts 18:18, 19, 26; 1 Cor. 16:19; 2 Tim. 4:19. **4** Apparently they had risked their lives for Paul's sake at or near Ephesus in some unrecorded incident which was well known to *all the churches*. Note how these churches are united with Paul in this expression of gratitude. Here, as in four out of the six instances in the NT, the wife's name (AV 'Priscilla') precedes her husband's, the reason being unknown. **5** *The church in their house* is included in Paul's salutation. In the early church there were at first few, if any, church buildings. Groups of Christians met in houses of prominent believers or in other available rooms (*cf.* Mt. 26:18; Acts 12:12; 1 Cor. 16:19; Col. 4:15; Phm. 2). This is the first of five groups of believers in Paul's list, but the only one referred to definitely as a church (see vv. 5, 10, 11, 14, 15). *Epaenetus* is marked as a special friend and one of the first of Paul's converts in the Roman province of *Asia*. 'What a tremendous thing it was, when for the first time, in a vast area and a huge population, a man had the grace and the courage to say "Jesus is Lord"!' (Barrett). **6** *Mary* is mentioned for her conspicuous service to the Roman church (*among you*). Paul may have gleaned this scrap of information from Prisca, but it is remarkable that he knows a small detail about the church at Rome. The difficulty would be eased if the reference were to Ephesus. **7** *Andronicus and Junias* are *kinsmen* or, rather, fellow-countrymen (*cf.* 9:3), *i.e.* Jewish Christians like Paul. Three interesting pieces of further information are given. They had been *fellow prisoners* with Paul, probably implying simply imprisonment for Christ's sake and maybe a period of confinement with the apostle in the same prison, possibly at Ephesus. They were *of note among the apostles*, *i.e.* outstanding apostles themselves in the wider sense of mission-preachers (*cf.* Acts 14:14; 1 Cor. 15:7; 2 Cor. 8:23; 11:13). They were *in Christ before me*, *i.e.* they became converts to the new way of faith-righteousness before Paul had his own experience of the Damascus road. Their non-Hebraic names suggest that they may have belonged to the Hellenists of Acts 6:1. **8** *Ampliatus*, a slave name, is unknown, but it has been suggested (by C. H. Dodd) that this man's name on a tomb inscription in the cemetery of Domitilla in Rome is a silent witness to him. **9** *Urbanus*, also a slave name, and *Stachys* are likewise unknown. **10** *Apelles* is distinguished as a well-tried Christian (*cf.* 1 Cor. 11:19; 2 Cor. 10:18; 13:7). *The family of Aristobulus* is the second group of Christians listed. This noble was a grandson of Herod the Great, who lived privately at Rome. Those belonging to him, aptly rendered 'his family', including officials and slaves, had a Christian fellowship among them. **11** *Herodion*,

as his name implies, belongs to Herod and probably is included in the household of Aristobulus. He may have been a leader in the group already mentioned in v. 10. Along with Andronicus and Junias he is described as a *kinsman* of Paul. Hence, if we exclude Mary, who may have been a Jewess, there are only three Jews of the church at Rome in the catalogue of commendation. Similarly among the greetings from Corinth given later in this chapter (vv. 21–23) there are only three other Hebrews. *The family of Narcissus* contains the third group of Christians mentioned. **12** *Tryphaena and Tryphosa* were probably twin sisters. Another lady, *Persis*, is honoured in this verse. The name occurs in an inscription as that of a freed woman. **13** *Rufus* is perhaps the Cyrenian noted in Mk. 15:21. The apostle refers to him as *eminent* (AV 'chosen', NEB 'an outstanding follower of the Lord'), in the sense of being set apart for distinguished service. *His mother* at some time or other evidently 'mothered' Paul (possibly when Paul was brought to Antioch, Acts 11:25f.) and so is included in the greeting. **14** Now follows another group of believers, the fourth in this roll of honour, the most important of them being named—*Asyncritus, Phlegon, Hermes, Patrobas, Hermas*. **15** A fifth company of saints, if not actually a church, comes next. The prominent members are mentioned—*Philologus* (lit. 'lover of wisdom'), *Julia*, supposed to be husband and wife, with their family, *Nereus* (whom the tradition of the church at Rome associates with Domitilla, a Christian who was exiled by her cousin, the emperor Domitian, in AD 95) *and his sister, and Olympas*. **16** *A holy kiss* is referred to by Paul in 1 Cor. 16:20; 2 Cor. 13:12; 1 Thes. 5:26. Another name is 'the kiss of love' (1 Pet. 5:14). In all cases, as we know from Justin's description of Christian worship in the middle of the 2nd century, the setting is that of the church assembled for public praise and worship. To salute with a kiss was the usual Eastern manner of greeting. The apostle now closes his roll of honour by greetings to the Roman saints from *all the churches of Christ*. This is the more general phrase which Paul adopts. He claims to speak sometimes in their collective name (*cf.* 16:4; 1 Cor. 7:17; 2 Cor. 8:18; 11:28). His practice, however, is to localize the fellowship, while generalizing the members, *e.g.* 'all the saints' of such and such a church (*e.g.* 2 Cor. 13:13; Phil. 4:22). Once he writes 'the churches of Asia' (1 Cor. 16:19). Here he sends greetings in the name of the whole Gentile mission to the believers in the imperial city, which held a special place in the world.

16:17–20 A final admonition

This warning against false teachers is as surprising in its interruption as that inserted in the Philippian letter (3:2). It is suggested that at this point of the Epistle Paul took the pen from his scribe to add his name as its credential of genuineness (*cf.* 1 Cor. 16:21–24; Gal. 6:11–18; 2 Thes.

3:17, 18). Then the pastoral emotion arose in the apostle's heart and he could not refrain from a last word of exhortation. Such an interpretation would suit a normal situation. On the other hand some advance the idea, as in the case of the church at Philippi, that something unusual had happened, perhaps the advent to Rome of the very false teachers against whom Paul feels urged to warn. It is not definitely known who these were, though the closest parallel would be the type of false teaching castigated in Phil. 3:18f. and would suggest a Gnosticizing tendency in both cases. The basic idea began with a dualistic conception of God and the world which was held to be alien to Him. The human body, as part of the material order, could safely be ignored or indulged without restraint or conscience. **17** Paul exhorts the Roman saints with an impressive imperative, *take note*; *i.e.* so as not to follow them. In Phil. 3:17 the term is used positively as a call to follow a good example. The evil of these false teachers lies not merely in their doctrine but in their divisive influence. They cause *dissensions and difficulties*; *i.e.* by introducing teaching subversive of the apostolic gospel. Paul's experience in other churches leads him anxiously to this warning. **18** He appears to know these disturbers well. Their aim is not to glorify the Lord but to benefit themselves. He charges these deceivers with selfish egotism: *their own appetites*. RSV mg. is less euphemistic and recalls Phil. 3:19 which uses the same Greek word. Indiscriminate indulgence is implied, and not simply food but all the sensuous appetites were given free rein on an acceptance of the Gnostic principle that the human body is a useless and irrelevant vehicle of the spirit. They also exercise the accomplished art of flattery and trap the unwary. Paul commends the fidelity of the Roman church to the traditional Christian faith which is already widely known. **19** Further his ideal for them (*cf.* Mt. 10:16) is his motive in this warning. **20** The appropriate title *God of peace* (*cf.* 15:33) is used in this exhortation to beware of those who cause divisions and offences. Paul is confident that the Maker of peace is stronger than the destroyer of peace and soon Satan shall be thrown under the feet of the Roman saints that they may trample upon him (*cf.* Gn. 3:25; *cf.* also 2 Cor. 11:13–15).

16:21–23 Greetings from Corinthian brethren

Paul had interrupted his long list of salutations with a warning he felt a strong urge to give. Now he seeks to conclude. His companions at Corinth, where he is writing, wish to associate themselves with the apostle's greetings. Whether it is because they are prominent saints or have some connection with Rome is not revealed. **21** *Timothy* is well known as an intimate associate and *fellow worker* in the gospel. *Lucius and Jason and Sosipater* are three of Paul's fellow-countrymen who are with him at Corinth, just as he has three Hebrew friends in Rome (see on v. 11).

The three Corinthian Jews (if we assume that *my kinsmen*, *i.e.* fellow Jewish Christians, applies to all three names) may be identified as Lucius of Cyrene, connected with Antioch (Acts 13:1)— but this is only a guess; Jason, Paul's host at Thessalonica (Acts 17:5–9); and Sopater of Beroea who went with Paul from Corinth to Asia (Acts 20:4). **22** It appeared to the amanuensis that Paul had now finished and so he added his own name *Tertius* to the salutations. The use of a scribe by authors of NT books is attested also by 1 Pet. 5:12, though Tertius and Silvanus (Silas) are the only two names preserved (*cf.* Gal. 6:11, marking Paul's own epilogue in his own handwriting). Amanuenses employed to write 1st-century letters were highly regarded and had a share in arranging the sender's thoughts. **23** However, the apostle remembers some more people interested in the brethren at Rome and so he puts in a postscript. *Gaius* is described as *host to me*; clearly Paul had found a lodging with him during his stay at Corinth. He is probably the same person whom Paul baptized along with Crispus (1 Cor. 1:14), and almost certainly the man known as Titius Justus in Acts 18:7. The name is found in Acts 19:29; 20:4; 3 Jn. 1. But he is also host of *the whole church*, *i.e.* the church at Corinth. Its gatherings were, presumably, held in his house. *Erastus* is a high official in Corinth, the treasurer of the city, and certainly a Christian. He is most likely to have had some civil connection with the imperial city. The same name is mentioned in Acts 19:22 and 2 Tim. 4:20, but no certain identification is possible. A more promising link is with the Erastus who is mentioned in a Latin inscription found at Corinth ('Erastus, commissioner for public works, laid this pavement at his own expense'). But the term in the inscription ('commissioner' or 'aedile') is not the same as Paul's Greek *oikonomos tēs poleōs* (*the city treasurer*). *Quartus* is an unknown brother. The benediction of v. 24 is omitted by RSV in accordance with the best MSS. See the Introduction, p. 1013.

16:25–27 A concluding doxology

While not always concluding an Epistle with a doxology, Paul has composed several (*cf.* 11:36; Gal. 1:5; Eph. 3:20; Phil. 4:20; 1 Tim. 1:17). The ascription of praise is here offered to God in two aspects of His perfection. He is *able to strengthen* and is also *the only wise God*. This divine ability has already been referred to in the Epistle (1:16; 14:4). God's omnipotence is redemptive through the gospel for it is 'the power of God unto salvation'. This conception, which was early emphasized in the Epistle, is now, at its close, proclaimed after the inspired exposition of the gospel entrusted to the apostle. The appropriateness of the wording in this doxology answers the objection, occasionally brought against these verses, that they represent an addition to the letter made by the 2nd-century heretic, Marcion, or at least a Marcionite follower. But it has to be admitted that some of the key terms are unusual. **25** This *gospel* is described as *the preaching of Jesus Christ*; *i.e.* the offer of a faith-righteousness in place of a works-righteousness on the ground of the finished work of reconciliation through the life, death and resurrection of Jesus Christ. It is also *the mystery, which* . . . *is now disclosed*, a reference to the inclusion of the Gentiles in the privileges of the righteousness of God (11:25; Eph. 3:3ff.; Col. 1:26f.). **26** It is also *through the prophetic writings . . . made known, i.e.* attested. The gospel, Paul all along maintained, had been foretold by the Scriptures of the OT (*cf.* 1:2; 3:21; 9:1 – 11:36). The prophets of old were commissioned by the eternal God to declare His will of salvation to all men, *to bring about the obedience of faith*. Paul also throughout his Epistle conceives of the divine omnipotence in its redemptive aspect as an inward force in the believer whereby he is able to stand. The power to establish the Roman saints is an inner experience whereby he is upheld (14:4). Thus, in this concluding doxology, the characteristic concepts of Paul's teaching are repeated: the new way as the real consummation of the old, the effectual call of God to His servants in both dispensations to reveal His will, the universalism of the gospel, and the one condition, 'faith'. *Only wise* is another phase of the divine character which evokes the adoration of the apostle. The wisdom of God in the Pauline thought is not mere speculation, or philosophy, beyond the ken of human understanding. It is rather an attribute wherein Paul sees the mercies of God toward sinful men, practically designed and achieved through Jesus Christ. Such wisdom is the sole prerogative and property of God. Hence eternal glory be to God! *Laus deo*. Amen.

F. DAVIDSON
RALPH P. MARTIN

1 and 2 Corinthians

INTRODUCTION

CORINTH

Paul first reached Corinth in the autumn of AD 50, in the course of his second missionary journey. His stay of more than 18 months (Acts 18:11, 18) was unusually long for him, but he did so on the direct instruction of the Lord (Acts 18:9, 10). Even apart from this, Paul would have appreciated the city's strategic value for the gospel. Astride the Isthmus of Corinth, the land-bridge linking N Greece with the Peloponnese, and with sea routes to east and west, Corinth was splendidly placed for commerce and communications. Julius Caesar rebuilt the earlier city, left in ruins by other Romans 100 years before, and raised it to the status of a Roman colony. The famous commercial prosperity of the first Corinth soon returned, and so did its notorious reputation for sexual licence, which had spawned a new word, to 'Corinthianize'. The temple of Aphrodite, the goddess of love, perched 1,875 ft up on the Corinthian acropolis, about 1,500 ft above the town, provided an attractive religious excuse for a city remarkable even by ancient standards for its vice. The lot of the infant Corinthian church had indeed fallen in a foul place.

The city's importance was enhanced in 27 BC when Corinth became the Roman governor's seat and the administrative capital of the province of Achaia; this covered the whole of Greece south of Macedonia. Paul was the first to seize the opportunity which Corinth offered (1 Cor. 3:5f.; 4:15), for with all its coming and going, anything preached there would quickly be spread abroad in all directions and among all sorts and conditions of people. Thus within 25 years of the crucifixion, the gospel was being proclaimed in the first and worst city of S Greece, with its teeming cosmopolitan population of half a million Greeks, Roman colonists and Jews.

THE CHURCH AT CORINTH

The Corinthian church seems to have been fairly large (Acts 18:8, 10), and secure from the threat of persecution (1 Cor. 4:10). There were some Jews in its membership (Acts 18:7, 8); but it was predominantly Gentile and ex-pagan in character, and included many who had been rescued from the very dregs of society (1 Cor. 6:9–11). Judaizing tendencies, which troubled other churches with Jewish members, seem to have been only a minor problem in Corinth (1 Cor. 7:18). The 'super-apostles' of 2 Corinthians with their 'other gospel' appear to be more concerned to undermine Paul's authority than to drag converts back into Jewish practices. On the other hand, the pagan world blankets the whole of life in Corinth, and Paul has to deal extensively with the practical problems the Corinthian Christians were meeting every day. Purity was an odd novelty in the pagan world, and even more so in Corinth (1 Cor. 5:9; 6:9–11, 15). Christians too had to decide on their attitude towards pagan clubs (1 Cor. 8 and 10) and about such matters as invitations to dine with pagan neighbours (1 Cor. 10:27).

Socially, the church ranged from the well-to-do city treasurer (Rom. 16:23) to Jewish refugees (Acts 18:2) and former thugs (1 Cor. 6:10f.). Not many in the church were cultured or clever (1 Cor. 1:26), and there was some striving after airs and graces (1 Cor. 4:10). Many were delighting in cheap rhetoric (1 Cor. 1:20f.; 2:1ff.), boasting about their teachers (1 Cor. 3:4), and even modifying some of Paul's 'cruder' doctrines to make them more 'contemporary' (1 Cor. 15:12).

The instability of the Corinthians is not surprising in view of the novel tensions to which their utterly anti-Christian religious and moral environment exposed them, not to mention the multi-racial character of the church membership. Their lack of OT background was another factor, although Apollos was able to remedy this in some measure (Acts 18:27f.), and Paul appreciated his efforts (1 Cor. 16:12). The divisions in the church are marked by party-cries (1 Cor. 1:12) and the existence of opposite perversions—witness the attitudes towards incest on the one hand (1 Cor. 5) and celibacy on the other (1 Cor. 7). Paul rarely suggests, however, that the divisions were doctrinal. It was rather that the Corinthians were behaving 'just like men of the world' (1 Cor. 3:3, Phillips). James Stalker once said that Paul's letters take the lid off the meeting-places of the early Christians and let us look inside. This is particularly true of his Corinthian correspondence.

PAUL'S LINKS WITH CORINTH

We have a record in Acts of two of the visits Paul made to Corinth (Acts 18, 20), and know that he exchanged letters with the church he planted there (1 Cor. 7:1a; 2 Cor. 2:4). Judging by his own Epistles, Paul's relations with the Corinthians were close and personal. He stayed with Aquila and Priscilla, leather-workers like himself, who had taken up residence in Corinth (Acts 18:1–3). Although Paul arrived very uncertain about his reception in the city (1 Cor.

2:3), several notable converts were won, including Crispus, the ruler of the synagogue (Acts 18:8), with his household, and Sosthenes (1 Cor. 1:1), probably the same man who succeeded Crispus in the synagogue (Acts 18:17). There were many conversions, too, among the ordinary folk of the city (Acts 18:8, 10; 1 Cor. 1:26).

The arrival of Timothy and Silas encouraged Paul to an even greater effort, and this aroused strong opposition from the Jewish quarter. But the new Roman proconsul, Gallio, dismissed the Jews' attempts to bring a charge against Paul, and indeed their action provoked a popular anti-Semitic demonstration by the Greek towns-people (Acts 18:12–17). So Paul stayed, turned to the Gentiles, and built up the church under the implicit protection of the Roman authorities. After 'many days' (Acts 18:18) he embarked upon another missionary tour to Ephesus, Jerusalem and Antioch, through Asia Minor, and back to Ephesus. There he remained for 2 years (Acts 18:11, 18–23; 19:1).

Aquila and Priscilla had left Corinth with Paul. In Ephesus they were able to be of con-siderable spiritual help to a promising Jewish convert named Apollos, who went across to Corinth and filled the gap left by Paul's absence (Acts 18:28; 1 Cor. 3:6). Other teachers were not lacking (1 Cor 4:15), though the 'Cephas party' (1 Cor. 1:12) need not imply a visit by Peter. Soon afterwards Paul revisited Corinth from Macedonia and stayed a further 3 months, before leaving (for the last time, so far as we know) by the overland route instead of going by sea, thus avoiding another Jewish plot (Acts 20:3). But some of the details of all this programme are not clear.

HOW MANY LETTERS AND VISITS?

1 and 2 Corinthians pose more problems than do most of Paul's letters, about the sequence of events to which he alludes as he writes. Earlier commentators assumed that the apostle had paid only one visit to Corinth before writing 2 Corinthians, that an earlier letter mentioned in 2 Cor. 2:3 and 7:8 is our 1 Corinthians, and that the offender in 2 Cor. 2:5–11 was involved in the case of incest in 1 Cor. 5. None of these suppositions is now considered likely by the majority of commentators, who feel that the character of 1 Corinthians as a whole hardly suits a letter said to have been written 'out of much affliction and anguish of heart' and 'with many tears' (2 Cor. 2:4). If this view is correct, then the 'severe letter' has not been preserved.

There is less agreement, however, on another problem. This concerns chs. 10–13 of 2 Corinth-ians. The abrupt change of tone is thought to indicate that this section has been attached to 2 Corinthians by a later hand and is really part of the 'severe letter' mentioned in 2 Cor. 2:3. In addition, fragments of a lost letter are supposed by some scholars to be preserved in 1 Cor. 6:12–20 and 2 Cor. 6:14 – 7:1. It must

be made clear, however, that there is no evidence whatever from MSS or patristic sources for any of these conjectures. Early church editors with scissors and paste are a modern imagination. The ancients used papyrus rolls, not sheets, for important long letters, and it is hardly likely that self-contained sensible portions of such rolls conveniently survived for a later editor to join together.

Recently scholars have been more ready to accept the unity of 2 Corinthians, a unity which can be observed, despite the variations in subject and tone, in the common theme of Paul's intended third visit. 'In spirit the reader follows Paul from Ephesus through Troas to Macedonia (2 Cor. 1–7); then he lingers with him for a moment in the churches of Macedonia (chs. 8, 9); finally, he is led to the consideration of conditions in the church at Corinth from the point of view of Paul's coming visit there' (Zahn).

The sequence of events is perhaps as follows: 1. The 'previous letter' sent from Ephesus (1 Cor. 5:9). This has probably disappeared, though some writers think part is preserved in 2 Cor. 6:14 – 7:1. 2. The Corinthians' reply, asking further questions (1 Cor. 7:1). 3. Our 1 Corinth-ians written from Ephesus (1 Cor. 16:8) in answer to the Corinthians' letter. 4. Paul's brief and 'painful visit' (2 Cor. 2:1). 5. The 'severe letter' (2 Cor. 2:3, 4, 9; 7:8) written from Ephesus. Some scholars consider part of this forms 2 Cor. 10–13. Probably, however, this letter too has not survived. The Corinthians would hardly be keen to preserve it. 6. The letter of reconcilia-tion (our 2 Corinthians) written from Macedonia. 7. Paul's third and last visit to Corinth, where he winters before going on to Judea via Macedonia with the collection for the Jerusalem church.

DATES

The 18 months that Paul spent in Corinth at the end of his second missionary journey (Acts 18:11) probably stretched from the early days of AD 50 to the spring of 52. We can accurately date this period of Paul's life from an inscription at Delphi. This reveals that Gallio, a brother of Seneca the philosopher, came to Corinth as pro-consul of Achaia in July 51 (Acts 18:12–17). Gallio's *bēma*, or judgment seat (Acts 18:12), and the *makellon*, or meat-market (1 Cor. 10:25; AV 'shambles'), have also been identified. The arrival of Gallio for his 1-year appointment appears to have inspired the Jews to attempt to bring Paul to trial. But his opponents were confounded without the apostle having to say a word (Acts 18:14), and then routed by a popular demonstration. So Paul remained 'many days' longer (Acts 18:18) before going off on another missionary journey.

Some 5 or 6 years later, Paul returned to Achaia for 3 months (Acts 20:3) and almost certainly must have spent part of that time in Corinth. Then he left on what turned out to be his last visit to Jerusalem. The outside dates for the two canonical Epistles are therefore AD 51 and 57. 1 Cor. 16:8 indicates that the first letter was written in Ephesus towards the end of his stay there. This would date 1 Corinthians about the spring of AD 54. It is likely that Titus delivered this letter in order, among other things, to set in motion the arrangements for the collection intended for the poverty-stricken Christian Jews in Jerusalem. If this is so, then 2 Cor. 8:10 suggests that the second letter should be dated a year or so later. It was composed somewhere in Macedonia (2 Cor. 2:13; 7:5–7; 8:1; 9:2–4). The subscription 'from Philippi' in some MSS is early and a likely conjecture, though if Paul wrote the letter piecemeal while on his travels through the province this might go some way to explain sudden changes of tone which worry the commentators.

At all events the Corinthian letters are among the earliest documents in the NT, compiled about twenty-five years after the crucifixion. Hundreds were still alive who had vivid memories of Christ's life and ministry, and Paul indeed draws attention to this very point in his famous list of our Lord's resurrection appearances (1 Cor. 15:6).

AUTHENTICITY

None of the books which make up the NT comes to us with better credentials than 1 and 2 Corinthians. The internal evidence of both is so strong that commentators usually accept it without debate. Besides the writer's claim to be Paul (1 Cor. 1:1; 16:21; 2 Cor. 1:1; 10:1), the letters are unmistakably Pauline in the tone and character of their teaching and in their vocabulary and style. The mention of the many survivors of the 500 who had seen Christ after His resurrection (1 Cor. 15:6) would indeed be a 'bad joke' (Godet), if it be the work of a 2nd-century forger. The many coincidences with Acts and with the other Pauline letters are together beyond chance or invention.

The external evidence is also impressive. In his own letter to the church at Corinth, Clement of Rome appeals to the authority of 1 Corinthians as the 'epistle of the blessed Paul the apostle' (*1 Clement* 47:1). This was about AD 95. It is the first time any NT writer is quoted in literature outside the Bible. Ignatius (AD 110) seems to have known much of 1 Corinthians by heart. Polycarp (martyred *c*. AD 156) provides the earliest quotations from 2 Corinthians, in his letter to the Philippians. But the genuineness of both Corinthian letters as the work of Paul has never seriously been questioned. The heretic Marcion (AD 150) found them a place in his rather select canon.

PAUL'S PURPOSE IN WRITING

Corinth lay almost opposite Ephesus, less than 300 miles across the Aegean. Ordinary cargo-boats averaged two or three knots and took only a few days for such a trip. Communications between the two ports, therefore, must have been constant, and no doubt from time to time Christians went to and fro. Among the travellers were 'Chloe's people' (1 Cor. 1:11), possibly her slaves or freedmen (but see commentary). They brought Paul disturbing news. The Corinthian Christians were splitting into factions, not on doctrinal grounds but merely because some were becoming 'fans' of one teacher or another. Paul's homelier and more direct expressions, *e.g.*, were being compared unfavourably with the polished speech of Apollos (1 Cor. 1:12; 3:4; 4:6). Perhaps this was not surprising since Greeks had long enjoyed literary refinements from Stoic preachers. It seems possible too that Judaizing Christian teachers had come from Jerusalem (1 Cor. 7:18), as in the case of the Galatians. Chloe's people had even more serious reports. One man had married his widowed stepmother (1 Cor. 5). Corinthian Christians were bringing business disputes before pagan courts (1 Cor. 6). Gatherings for the Lord's Supper were degenerating into convivial cliques which left some members out in the cold (1 Cor. 11:17ff.).

While Paul was grieving over this news, a letter arrived from the Corinthians themselves (1 Cor. 7:1; 16:7). This is the only letter we know for sure that Paul received; but the papyri reveal that the Greeks were great letter-writers, and undoubtedly Paul had his share of mail. The Corinthians had little Christian experience and no literature to guide them in practical Christian living. So they put their questions to Paul. What were the right Christian principles about sex, marriage, and divorce? Should they do their shopping at meat-markets associated with the great pagan temples? Should a woman dress for services as for a private or for a public function? (There were no church buildings, of course, and Christians met for worship in some large private house.) Should capable women take a leading part in those services? (Greek women were used to far more liberty than Jewish, and the Corinthian church included both cultures.) The worship itself was sometimes disturbed by uncontrolled ecstatic speaking. What guide-lines should be followed? And finally, while to the Greek mind immortality was a familiar notion, what was meant by 'resurrection' (a Jewish concept)?

Our 1 Corinthians is Paul's response, first to the alarming reports brought by Chloe's people (1 Cor. 1–6), and then to the problems raised by the Corinthians in their letters. However precious subsequent readers have found Paul's first letter, we are not altogether surprised, from a 'public-relations' point of view, that the Christians in Corinth were upset by the apostle's reply. Paul at first completely ignores their own letter and vigorously attacks the evils reported to him by Chloe's people. Whatever steps Paul may have taken to check the truth of the hearsay, we can readily imagine that his listening to tales from some third party would cause resentment. No-one likes being spoken to deprecatingly (1 Cor. 1:26), or addressed like a child (1 Cor. 3:1; 4:21), or put in his place (1 Cor. 11:16; 14:36). Compared with what Paul intended in his love and fervour, 1 Corinthians was not altogether appreciated by its first recipients.

The next stage in the relationship of Paul with the Corinthian church is revealed in the earlier verses of our 2 Corinthians. It seems that the situation in Corinth had deteriorated and Paul interrupted his work in Ephesus to pay them a hurried visit. But the trip proved a painful failure. So at great personal cost, but in duty bound, he wrote another letter (2 Cor. 2:3, 4), even though he regretted that its plain speaking would hurt their feelings further (2 Cor. 7:8). Titus took the letter, and Paul arranged to meet him at Troas to hear what the reaction had been (2 Cor. 2:12, 13). But Titus did not appear, and though there were plenty of evangelistic opportunities in Troas, a worried Paul could not settle and he went on into Macedonia (2 Cor.

2:12–14). There to his relief he met Titus and was overjoyed to learn of a complete change of heart among most of the Corinthians (2 Cor. 7:5–7). So Paul wrote to them again (our 2 Corinthians) to express his thankfulness at the reconciliation which had been brought about. But even now he has to speak forcefully about certain self-styled 'super-apostles' who had arrived on the scene to try to undermine Paul's authority (2 Cor. 10–13). Yet still the apostle's love shines through his sternness: 'I will most gladly spend and be spent for your souls' (2 Cor. 12:15). 'Remembering the background of the membership, it is difficult to know as we read 1 Corinthians and its sequel whether to be more astonished at the dauntless faith and magnificent courage of the apostle, who might have given up in despair, or whether to be more heartened that it was upon such unpromising foundations that God built a world church' (William Neil).

See also the General Article, 'The Pauline Epistles', p. 71.

1 Corinthians

OUTLINE OF CONTENTS

COMMENTARY

1:1-9 INTRODUCTION

1:1-3 Greeting

1 Paul follows 1st-century custom: writer, intended recipient, greeting. But each item is given a Christian elaboration. *Called, i.e.* 'to be a Christian', is in the NT always a call obeyed. *The will of God* can refer to Paul's conversion (Acts 22:10; Gal. 1:15) and to his unique appointment to take God's message to the Gentiles (Acts 9:15; Rom. 15:15f.). Paul underlines his divine authority, a claim some Corinthians challenged (see, *e.g.,* 1 Cor. 9:1f.). *Sosthenes*; perhaps the synagogue leader (Acts 18:17), now a Christian *brother* (*cf.* Mt. 23:8). Believers are now on a level as sons of the one Father (*cf.* Gal. 3:28; Col. 3:11). **2** *The church of God*; *i.e.* formed by God and belonging to God, not to some party (*cf.* 1:12). *At Corinth*; the local expression of a universal society (see Introduction, 'Corinth'). *Sanctified*; *i.e.* set apart by the Spirit, not by human action. *Saints*; *i.e.* 'holy persons', not primarily in the ethical sense, but 'separated as God's people' (*cf.* Ex. 19:6; see on 2 Cor. 1:1), with great moral consequences. *All . . . who in every place call on the name, i.e.* in trust and worship (*cf.* Rom. 10:12, 13); a significant description indicating who belong to the universal church. **3** *Grace* is the God-given basis of all Christian life; *peace* is the outcome of God's redemption in Christ (see on 2 Cor. 1:2). *The Lord Jesus Christ*, living in Palestine only 25 years before, is now wondrously resident in God's church everywhere, including Corinth as Paul's letter is read. He is also regarded as one with God as the source of blessing.

1:4-9 Thanksgiving

4 *Thanks.* Paul is ever mindful of what God has done. Although severe criticism will follow, Paul genuinely encourages his converts whenever he can. *The grace of God* is the source of all they have. **5** Paul mentions two gifts which the Corinthians as Greeks highly prized: *speech*, the telling forth of truth; and *knowledge*, the grasp of truth. **6** *Testimony*; borne *to Christ* by Paul while he ministered among them, and confirmed as true by their transformed lives.

7, 8 *Spiritual gift.* The term is used of salvation (Rom. 5:15), God's gifts in general (Rom. 11:29), and (as here, and particularly chs. 12, 14) of the special gifts of the Spirit. Paul himself did not lack spiritual gifts (*cf., e.g.,* 14:18); but his confidence is in *Christ*. It is He who will *sustain . . . to the end*—a gentle reminder that the Corinthians had not yet 'arrived' at perfection, despite their many gifts. Full redemption awaits *the day* of Christ's return in triumph; but then they will be declared *guiltless* and found unimpeachable (*cf.* Rom. 8:33). **9** God's character guarantees the outcome of His call (*cf.* 1:2). *Fellowship*; created by Christians' common participation in Christ. The Lordship of Christ is mentioned many times in these opening verses as Paul sets the scene.

1:10 – 4:21 DIVISIONS IN THE CHURCH

Chs. 1-6 give Paul's vigorous reaction to reports of scandals in Corinth (1:11). See Introduction, 'Paul's purpose in writing'.

1:10-17 Rival cliques

10 Paul appeals to their common relationship in Christ; they are *brethren* to him and to each other. By invoking *the name* of Jesus the apostles healed (Acts 3:6), baptized (Acts 2:38), pronounced judgment (1 Cor. 5:3). This one authoritative name, standing over against party labels (v. 12), can heal wounds that rend a church. *Agree*; literally 'say the same thing', *i.e.* avoid party cries. *United*; Greek 'mended', the word used in Mt. 4:21; 2 Cor. 13:11. *Judgment*; opinion. *Reported*; made clear (*cf.* 3:13, 'disclose'), so leaving no room for doubt. **11** *Chloe's people*; possibly someone's slaves. But Chloe was the popular name for the goddess Demeter (the Roman Ceres). She had 56 temples in Greece, including one at Corinth. *Chloe's people* appear as disinterested critics outside the church parties mentioned. They may therefore be devotees of Chloe, and would be sympathetic to Paul, for they worshipped a pure deity and had baptismal rites, sacramental cake, and a belief in an after-life. They would hate the orgies practised by the rabble as much as Paul did. *Quarrelling . . . brethren.* The juxtaposition is pointed.

12 *Each one.* Not necessarily everyone, but the majority. The reason for this personality cult can only be guessed. *I belong to Paul*; probably the claim of some of his converts. Loyalty he appreciated (2 Tim. 4:11), but not partisanship. *Apollos* succeeded Paul in Corinth (Acts 18:24; 19:1). His eloquence doubtless appealed to Greeks and his Bible knowledge to Jews. Paul always speaks highly of him. *Cephas*; Aramaic form of Peter (*cf.* Jn. 1:42). Some unrecorded visit to Corinth is possible (1 Cor. 9:5 suggests itinerant preaching); or the personal attachment may be due to his standing among the Twelve, or to his special interest in work among the Jews (Gal. 2:7). A *Christ* sect is surprising. Possibly it refers to some who boasted of spiritual independence. *I belong to Christ* could be Paul's own corrective comment (there is no *or* in the Greek), but the parallel form of words makes this unlikely. **13** Note Paul's decisive appeal to the Person, work, and name of Christ. Rightly understood these all unite and leave no room for attachment to Paul or anyone else. **14, 15** Paul is not decrying baptism, but expressing relief that by practising it he has not unwittingly recruited devotees to himself. *Crispus*; *cf.* Acts 18:8. *Gaius*; *cf.* Rom. 16:23. **16** The family of *Stephanus* was the first to be converted in Achaia province. This verse is doubtful evidence of infant baptism since this *household* appears from 16:15 to have been adult. **17** *To baptize* was not Paul's primary commission. *Eloquent wisdom*, beloved by Greeks, would merely dazzle, and obscure the meaning of the cross.

1:18 – 2:16 God's wisdom

18, 19 Paul contrasts human wisdom, which leaves God out of account and is man-centred, with the wisdom of God. *Word*; *i.e.* preaching. It is *folly*; *cf.* Gal. 5:11. It appears to be 'nonsense' (Phillips) that the Son of Almighty God should go unrecognized and be so ill-treated. Men would expect the Lord to destroy sin, but not apparently to be destroyed by it. *Perishing . . . being saved.* The process of division is going on. Destruction and salvation will be consummated in the last day. God's *power* (*cf.* Rom. 1:16; Gk. *dynamis*); 'dynamite' to shatter human pride and human 'wisdom', *i.e.* good advice about what to do (*cf.* 1 Cor. 2:5). *I will destroy . . .* ; from Is. 29:14, LXX. This antithesis between God's wisdom and man's was revealed in the OT. **20** 'What have the philosopher, the writer, and the critic of this world to show for all their wisdom?' (Phillips). Each Corinthian party argues for its greater cleverness. But true 'rightness' comes from a broken heart, not from brains.

21 *In the wisdom of God*; in God's providential ordering of human affairs (Acts 14:16; 17:30). To *know God* implies harmony with His mind and character (Je. 22:15, 16), something alien to the world (Pr. 1:7; 3:7). *Through wisdom*; *i.e.* self-chosen ways (Rom. 1:21f.). *Pleased* emphasizes God's love and sovereign choice. *Folly*;

because of its unexpected contrast with human expectation. *What we preach*; *i.e.* the content of the message. *Believe*; present continuous tense indicating constant attitude. **22** The demand for *signs* (*cf.* Nu. 14:11; Mt. 16:1–4) implies distrust of God, and also the Jews' false expectation of a spectacular Messiah. The seeking of *wisdom* illustrates the effort to discover God through human speculation. **23** A *crucified* Messiah was to Jews unthinkable (Dt. 21:23; *cf.* Gal. 3:13), while for God to take human form and then be put to death was to Greeks incomprehensible. **24** To those responding to God's call the cross makes available *the power of God* to overcome sin, and reveals the true *wisdom of God* in offering men the only effective scheme for their salvation. All man's unaided attempts to know God or to defeat sin prove futile. **25** *Foolishness* (*i.e.* in the world's eyes); not the abstract noun, as in vv. 18, 21, 23, but a neuter adjective: 'foolish act'. God's apparent *weakness* (neuter adjective again) shown in allowing His Son to hang on the cross is *stronger*, more effective, than any human effort (*cf.* 2 Cor. 13:4).

26 The paradox of God's method is further seen in the socially despised membership of the Corinthian church (see Introduction, 'The church at Corinth'). *Your call*; *i.e.* from God to be Christians: not 'vocation' in our sense. **27, 28** Few Corinthian Christians were outstanding according to the sophisticated society of the day; but their transformed lives demonstrated how God was overturning the world's standards. *God chose.* Three times His initiative is emphasized. *What is foolish . . . weak . . . low.* God has not merely chosen to confound what the world considers wise and strong. He has used for the purpose what the world deems of no account. *Low*; in birth (slaves) and in morals. *Things that are not.* Once there was no church in Corinth, save in God's mind (*cf.* Rom. 4:17). Despite opposition and its own weakness that church now existed, even though its members count as nothing in the eyes of the world. **29** God's purpose is to remove any occasion for human self-congratulation in His presence, however much men may boast to one another (*cf.* 1:12). **30** *Source.* The believer's new life derives from God (*cf.* 2 Cor. 5:18; Eph. 2:8). *In Christ*; *cf.* 2 Cor. 5:17. This is a favourite phrase of Paul's to describe the believer's intimate relationship with the Person of the risen Saviour. The Greek suggests that *wisdom* (*cf.* Col. 2:3) is defined by what follows. *Our righteousness* (*cf.* 2 Cor. 5:21); as sinners our right relationship with God is secured only because of Christ's death on the cross. Similarly, *sanctification*, holiness of life, is a divine work. The ground of all these blessings is Christ's act of *redemption*, *i.e.* of liberation by purchase, effected for us by His death on the cross (*cf.* 6:20; 1 Pet. 1:18, 19). The full fruits of His action will be experienced by the believer in the last day (Rom. 8:23). **31** The only boasting permitted the Christian is in what Christ has done for him. Paul's application of Je. 9:23f. to Christ points to His deity.

2:1 *When I came.* See Acts 18:1f. and Introduction, 'Paul's links with Corinth'. *Testimony*; bearing witness to God's work in Christ for men's salvation (*cf.* 1:6). **2** *I decided.* Paul is not suggesting that following apparent lack of response in Athens (Acts 17:32f.) he changed his method on moving to Corinth. He is here stating his invariable practice, the more positively because he addresses those who prize 'wisdom', and also in contrast to others in Corinth. Paul concentrates on the central truths: who *Jesus* is—the *Christ* or promised Messiah; and where hope of salvation lies, viz. in what He did: in the Messiah *crucified* (the *him* is emphatic). **3** *Weakness*; *cf.* 2 Cor. 10:10; 12:10. *Fear*; see Acts 18:9, 10. **4** The Corinthians might not appreciate plain *speech*, but flights of oratory or philosophy were not for Paul. *Message*; *i.e.* the content of what he said and the way he said it. *Demonstration*; convincing proof, brought about solely by the power of the *Spirit*. **5** Paul's purpose from the outset was to ensure that their *faith* was divinely based and not due in any sense to human persuasiveness. For faith to survive in a city like Corinth it needed a supernatural basis.

6 *Mature.* There are spiritual 'babies' at Corinth (3:1; *cf.* Heb. 6:1), but others who have grown in the Christian life will understand what Paul means by the revealed divine *wisdom* (defined in 1:30). *Not a wisdom of this age*; *i.e.* not simply the clever use of words, which is no substitute for true Christian preaching. Worldly wisdom obstructs the work of the Spirit, and puts forward man-centred values which readily suggest that the cross is foolishness. *Rulers of this age.* Behind the evil designs of the earthly authorities (*e.g.* Pilate, Caiaphas) were the supernatural powers of darkness (*cf.* Col. 2:15). **7** AV follows the Greek literally: 'We speak the wisdom of God in a mystery.' 'Mystery' (Gk. *mystērion*) in the NT is a 'secret revealed to faith', as RSV brings out. *Hidden*; impossible for men to discover by reasoning. *Before the ages.* God's wise plan of salvation (1:18) is no afterthought (2 Thes. 2:13, 14). **8** The earthly *rulers* of the time showed their complete lack of understanding in the way they treated Christ (*cf.* Acts 4:27). In His love God has all along had our glorification in mind; hence Christ is described as the *Lord of glory.* **9** *As it is written*; a free adaptation of Is. 64:4 and 65:17. The natural man is unable to perceive or imagine what God has in view to do.

10 *To us*; emphatic in the Greek. The divine plan about Christ's work has been revealed to Christians. The whole process is the work of the Spirit (*cf.* 12:3). *Searches everything.* Not in the sense of needing information but rather of 'penetrating' into all things. *Depths of God*; 'unfathomable' to human minds. **11** A human analogy is helpful. Only a man's spirit (his 'self-

consciousness') knows that man's thoughts. How much less can a mere human being know the inward truths of God, unless the Spirit of God takes the initiative and reveals them to him? **12** But Christians are privileged to have God's Spirit and thereby can *understand* all the blessings freely bestowed by the gospel. *The spirit of the world* may inspire geniuses in human fields, but not apostles for the spreading of the knowledge of God. **13** *We impart this.* No-one can pass on this secret to others except as he is *taught by the Spirit*, and even then the ground must be prepared by the Spirit. 'God alone can speak truth about God' (Pascal). The very words, not merely the ideas, are provided by the Spirit. The perpetual problem of communication is here answered. Two translation problems obscure the latter part of this verse. *To those who possess the Spirit* paraphrases one Greek adjective, which RSV takes as masculine. It could be neuter, however: 'with spiritual things' (RSV mg.). *Interpreting.* The Greek usually means 'combining'. L. Morris (*The First Epistle of Paul to the Corinthians*, TNTC, 1958) suggests: 'combining spiritual things (the words spoken) with spiritual things (the truths expressed)'. C. K. Barrett (*The First Epistle to the Corinthians*, 1968) prefers: 'interpreting spiritual truths by means of spiritual words'.

14, 15 *Unspiritual*; 'natural' (AV, RSV mg., RV), one lacking the Spirit and the spiritual insight He alone can give (*cf.* Eph. 2:1; 4:17f.). *Receive*; welcome as a guest. *Discerned.* The Greek verb means 'to scrutinize, sift', the word used of the Beroeans examining the Scriptures (Acts 17:11). The same verb is translated *judges . . . judged* in v. 15. *The spiritual man*; one with the Spirit within him, *i.e.* a Christian. *All things*; *i.e.* both secular and spiritual. *No one*; no man lacking the Spirit. The Christian's source of inspiration and strength is a mystery to the natural man, who therefore finds him an enigma. **16** *Who has known . . . ?* is from Is. 40:13. This declares the natural man's ignorance of the mind of God. What is otherwise impossible has now come to pass. *Mind of Christ.* The Holy Spirit enables the Christian to see things from Christ's point of view (*cf.* Phil. 2:5).

3:1 – 4:21 God's servants

1 During Paul's first stay in Corinth he could not address the Christians there as *spiritual men*, those who had matured (*cf.* Eph. 4:13–16) as they were but young in the faith (*cf.* 1 Pet. 1:23). Unhappily they have failed to grow spiritually since then. **2** *Milk*; *i.e.* elementary teaching (*cf.* Heb. 5:11f.), but not a 'watered-down' message. Its content was defined in 2:1, 2. **3** The Corinthians are *still of the flesh, i.e.* though Christians, they are dominated by their lower nature (Rom. 13:14; Gal. 5:16–24), and so in practice are little better than *ordinary men* who know nothing of the Spirit (*cf.* Jas. 3:14f.). **4** *One says*; taking up again the party cries of 1:12. *Merely men*;

arguing like worldly people, an attitude completely unspiritual and therefore un-Christian.

5 *What*, rather than 'who' (AV), fixes attention upon the function of those named, and their relative insignificance—*servants* of the one *Lord. As the Lord assigned.* The apportioning of the work is His responsibility. The servants are merely the agents *through whom* He works. **6, 7** The agricultural symbolism stresses the limited and subordinate character of what Paul and Apollos have done. *I planted.* Paul was the first evangelist in Corinth (*cf.* Rom. 15:20). *Apollos* watered; *cf.* Acts 18:27 – 19:1. *God gave the growth.* The creation and fostering of faith is the work of God alone. Without Him there would be no result from men's efforts. **8** *Equal*; literally 'one'. Their activities, whether 'planting' or 'watering', are one and complementary; so they ought not to be the cause of dissensions. Each has his own responsibility and each will *receive his wages* (*cf.* Mt. 20:8). The controlling factor is *according to his labour*, not 'his success' (*cf.* Mt. 25:21). The Corinthians are in effect quarrelling about which of the 'under-gardeners' is more important. **9** RSV takes *fellow workmen* as 'those co-operating together in God's service', but the Greek is probably as AV, 'together with God' (*cf.* RSV mg.; Mk. 16:20). In the Greek the word *God's* is very emphatic, being thrice repeated as the first word of three phrases. The apostle now changes the picture from work in a field to work on a *building*.

10 *Commission*; Greek *charis*, 'grace'. Paul glories in an undeserved privilege enjoyed by God's free gift (*cf.* Rom. 12:3; Eph. 3:8). *Skilled* (Gk. *sophos*, 'wise'); used of the workmen who erected and adorned the Tabernacle (Ex. 35:10). The *master builder* (Gk. *architectōn*) superintended the building operation, contributing knowledge rather than labour. *I laid*; *i.e.* on Paul's first visit to Corinth. *Another man is building.* In the establishment of the church in Corinth different workmen have co-operated (v. 6a). *Each man* is answerable to God for his share in the work. The phrase comes four times in vv. 8–13. **11** Men have no choice about the *foundation*, which must be the Person and work of Jesus Christ (*cf.* 2:2; 1 Pet. 2:5). Any other foundation would not produce the church (Gal. 1:7). **12** What is built upon the foundation may be durable: *gold, silver, precious stones*; or perishable: *wood, hay, stubble.* The *precious stones* are either costly, as marble or granite, or suitable for ornamentation (*cf.* Is. 54:11f.; Rev. 21:18ff.). **13** *The Day, i.e.* of judgment, when Christ returns (*cf.* 4:5), will be the occasion when each man's work will be shown up in its true character. *It will be revealed.* The subject is probably *the Day* rather than a man's *work* (*cf.* Mal. 4:1). *Fire* illumines as well as burns (*cf.* 2 Thes. 1:7). It is frequently a symbol of divine activity (*e.g.* Ex. 3:2; 13:21; 19:18; Acts 2:3). *Work . . . done*; *i.e.* in building on the foundation of Jesus Christ. Only those who minister in the church of God are in view here.

14 *The reward* (*cf.* 3:8) is undefined, but cannot be salvation itself (see v. 15). The parable of the pounds (Lk. 19:11–27) suggests opportunites of higher service. **15** *Loss*; *i.e.* of his reward (*cf.* 9:27). 'He personally will be safe, though rather like a man rescued from a fire' (Phillips). *Through* means 'out of the midst of', not 'by means of' (*cf.* 'through water', 1 Pet. 3:20). There is no suggestion here of a purifying fire or 'purgatory'. The fire reveals the quality of work done here on earth; it is not a means of improving the character of him who did it.

16 *Do you not know?* appeals to an acknowledged fact; the phrase occurs ten times in this letter. *Temple*; not the Greek *hieron*, which includes the temple precincts, but *naos*, 'sanctuary', suggesting the very dwelling-place of God (*cf.* 1 Pet. 2:4–10). *You* is plural, *i.e.* the local church, the worshipping community of believers (*cf.* 2 Cor. 6:16; Eph. 2:21f.). **17** *If any one destroys*; *i.e.* by false teaching or by causing grievous division, thus driving out the Spirit of God. *God's temple* is not the church of God in general (*cf.* Mt. 18:17) but as represented by the local congregation. Such local churches have indeed vanished in history (*e.g.* those of Rev. 2, 3). *God will destroy him.* Retribution is not vindictive but inevitable, for the one responsible reveals by his activity that he rejects God's salvation. *Holy; i.e.* set apart for God's use, and sanctified by His presence.

18 Paul reverts to the subject of the folly of worldly wisdom. In this connection it is fatally easy for anyone to *deceive himself* (*cf.* 6:9; 15:33; Gal. 6:3, 7). *Wise in this age* hints at changing fashions. *Become a fool; i.e.* in the eyes of the world, by becoming a Christian, but thereby gaining spiritual insight which is true wisdom (*cf.* 2:6; Col. 2:3). **19** Paul quotes Jb. 5:13 to drive home his point—quotations from Job are rare in the NT. *Catches* expresses the secure grip God has upon the slippery cleverness of the wicked. Though *craftiness* may deceive men, it cannot deceive God. **20** *The Lord knows . . .* is quoted from Ps. 94:11. *Thoughts* (Gk. *dialogismoi*); often in a bad sense of men questioning God's ways (*cf.* Lk. 5:22; 6:8). *Futile*; without lasting result (*cf.* Rom. 1:21). **21, 22** Far from needing to *boast of men* and their wisdom and ability, as the Corinthians were doing (1:12; *cf.* 1:31), they were as Christians possessors of *all things* (*cf.* Rom. 8:32). This includes all Christian teachers (inverting 1:12) and their gifts of ministry. By each following one favoured teacher, the Corinthian parties were impoverishing themselves. *The world*; not merely in the ethical sense (v. 19), but the whole of creation viewed as the Christian's rightful inheritance (*cf.* Gn. 1:26; Rom. 4:13). **23** *You are Christ's*; not Paul's (*cf.* 1:12). Each believer belongs to and is responsible to Christ (*cf.* 1:30; 6:19f.). The Christian's life must reflect this community of interest and duty of service. *Christ is God's*; *cf.* 11:3; 15:28. No subordination within the Godhead is intended. Messiah and His people are viewed as one entity belonging to God. The incarnate Son voluntarily took a lowly place among men to bring about man's salvation. Christ 'has all, because He is content to belong to the Father (Jn. 14:28; 1 Cor. 11:3); and we have all, while we are content to belong to Him' (H. L. Goudge, *The First Epistle to the Corinthians'*, *WC*, 1915).

4:1, 2 The apostles are not rival party-leaders (*cf.* 1:2), but Christ's *servants* (Gk. *hypēretai*, 'under-rowers', those who rowed in the lower bank of oars on a large ship) and *stewards*. A 'steward' had the responsible oversight of his master's household (*cf.* 1 Tim. 3:15). By *stewards* Paul is not suggesting that apostles should be ecclesiastical administrators (*cf.* Acts 6:2) but emphasizing the need to be absolutely *trustworthy*. They are stewards of *the mysteries of God* (see on 2:7), *i.e.* responsible for proclaiming unblemished the clear facts of the gospel (*cf.* 1:17; 2:2), not their own views. **3** *Judged by you.* Paul is answerable to his Master (Rom. 14:4), not to any amateur *human court* raked together by his Corinthian opponents. *Judge myself.* It is impossible rightly to assess even one's own achievements. To attempt this may result in improper elation or depression. 'Judging' in the sense of self-examination to improve one's Christian life and service is not in view here (*cf.* 11:31). **4** Paul is *not aware* of any failure in his service, but he is not relying upon a clear conscience to be *acquitted*, absolved by God's tribunal, which alone is competent to reach a correct verdict. **5** *Things now hidden*; *i.e.* facts of men's conduct now unknown or forgotten. *Darkness* in the NT often refers to evil deeds (Jn. 3:19). *Purposes*; only God can rightly assess motives (Rom. 2:16). *Commendation from God* is the only praise that matters (Mt. 25:21; Rom. 2:29); and being *from God* the award is final.

Three judgments (evaluations) are mentioned in this section: *a.* Judgment others pass on us (v. 3). This must be without full knowledge and can be disregarded. *b.* Judgment of one's own conscience (v. 4). This also lacks some factors, and although very important cannot be perfect. *c.* Only the Lord's judgment (v. 4) can be complete and final (*cf.* Jn. 3:20).

6 *For your benefit.* Paul has talked of himself and Apollos. The Corinthians know to whom also (as unworthy ministers in Corinth) these standards of judgment ought to be applied. *According to scripture* (lit. 'what is written'); *i.e.* according to its general sense. Parry in *CGT* argues that the Greek means 'not to go beyond the terms', *i.e.* of their commission as teachers, but, as the RSV translation brings out, Paul probably had the OT in mind. *Puffed up.* Their conceit and arrogance is mentioned several times (4:18f.; 5:2; 8:1; 13:4). **7** Their supposed superiority is self-assumed. All is owed to God's grace, and so boasting is out of place. **8** With heavy irony Paul contrasts apostolic truth with Corinthian illusion. *Already . . . filled.* The Corinthians are perilously self-satisfied (Rev.

3:17; *cf.* Mt. 5:6). *Without us*; not 'without our help' but 'without our company'. *Kings*; they have already 'arrived' while apostles still struggle! **9** *Exhibited.* 'God meant us apostles to come in at the very end, like doomed gladiators in the arena' (Moffatt). Condemned criminals were often paraded in public. This corresponds to the condition of discipleship—the real meaning of bearing one's cross (Mt. 16:24). Note that this condition is God-given. The apostles, not the Corinthians, exhibited what God intends Christ's followers to be. *Spectacle*; Greek *theatron*, 'seen as in a theatre'. *To angels*; *cf.* 1 Pet. 1:12.

10–13 pungently depict the harsh facts of life for the apostles (*cf.* 2 Cor. 6:4–10; 11:23–29). **10** *Fools*; *i.e.* in the eyes of the world. *Wise in Christ*; or so the Corinthians complacently think. *Held in honour*; eminent. *In disrepute* (Gk. *atimos*); used of one deprived of citizenship (*cf.* 2 Cor. 12:10–12). **11** *Present hour*; not past and perhaps exaggerated memories, but an up-to-date report. Paul and his companions are treated like tramps. **12** *Working*; 'slogging'. The Greeks despised manual labour, but Paul gloried in it (*cf.* 9:6; 1 Thes. 2:9). Paul highlights the Corinthians' failure to appreciate true Christian values, for to *bless* (*cf.* Lk. 6:28) . . . *endure* . . . *conciliate* were all responses alien to the worldly-wise Greeks. **13** The Greek words for *refuse* ('sweepings') and *offscouring* were used with reference to human sacrifice. Worthless members of society were chosen in such cases, which adds point to Paul's remarks.

14 No doubt Paul's words did make the Corinthians blush, yet his purpose was rather to *admonish*. The cognate noun in Eph. 6:4 describes a father's 'instruction' of his children. *Beloved children* emphasizes his tender parental relationship. **15** *Countless guides* ironically implies too many! A 'guide' (Gk. *paidagōgos*) was a slave who escorted his master's child to school. Though he might love his charge, he could never be as close to him as the *father*, a relationship Paul claims to the Corinthians (*cf.* 9:2). **16** *Imitators.* Not personal following (*cf.* 1:12), but as defined in 11:1. Paul boldly accepts that preaching and practice must tally. **17** Paul exercised his right as their spiritual father to exhort them. The visit *Timothy* made was evidently short, for he is back when Paul begins 2 Corinthians. *My . . . child.* He was converted through Paul at Lystra (Acts 14:6, 7; 16:1). *Everywhere in every church.* Paul is not treating the Corinthians differently. *Cf.* 7:17; 11:16; 14:33b, 36. **18, 19** *Arrogant*; confident that as Paul had sent a substitute before (v. 17), so he would still not dare to come himself. Possibly the 'Christ' party (*cf.* 1:12; 2 Cor. 10:7–11), who despised apostolic authority, is meant. **20** *The kingdom of God*; mentioned in 1 Cor. 6:9, 10; 15:24, 50, but rarely outside the Gospels. God's rule is not a matter of fine *talk* (*cf.* v. 8) and good advice. Men often know what they ought to do; they need God's *power* to do it. **21** Love must sometimes wield *a rod*, ready to chastise and rebuke (*cf.* 2 Sa. 7:14).

5:1 – 6:20 MORAL FAILURE

5:1–13 Incest

1 Another example of conceited self-satisfaction among the Corinthians is their condoning incest (*cf.* Lv. 18:8), presumably on the ground of their 'liberty' in Christ (*cf.* 1 Cor. 6:12; 10:23). Corinth was notorious for its sexual licence (see Introduction, 'Corinth'), but this case scandalized even the pagans. *Father's wife.* Presumably the culprit's pagan stepmother, otherwise Paul would have said 'mother' and included her, if a Christian, in the indictment. **2** *Mourn* suggests that the church is bereaved of a member. The offender should have been *removed*, excommunicated (see v. 13).

3, 4 Absence from Corinth does not prevent Paul from condemning the 'new morality'. He calls for a solemn church meeting to be held and disciplinary judgment passed. He indicates the sanctions which give its action authority— the *power* and the name of the *Lord Jesus* (*cf.* Acts 3:16). **5** The Corinthians are to expel the culprit from the church and thus back into the domain of *Satan* (*cf.* Col. 1:13; 1 Tim. 1:20; 1 Jn. 5:19). *Flesh* is man's lower nature, the seat of evil; but here doubtless includes the body, for *destruction* is physical. Illness often appears in the Bible as Satan's work (see Jb. 2:7; Lk. 13:16). He is here to be made to serve God's purposes. Moral disorders were thus sometimes followed by sickness and death (*cf.* 1 Cor. 11:30). Paul's intention is clearly disciplinary and remedial, and ultimately for the man's spiritual benefit. **6** By their laxity the Corinthians betray their ignorance of the nature of Christian life. *Boasting* is aptly portrayed by the swelling of dough. *Leaven* (yeast) in Scripture symbolizes evil (*cf.* Ex. 12:15; Mt. 16:11, 12). One evildoer is enough to defile the whole Christian fellowship. **7** *Cleanse out.* Evil must be removed entirely, for it is by nature corrupting. *Fresh dough.* The church is a society of those whose lives have been radically and divinely recreated (*cf.* 2 Cor. 5:17). The Israelites had to remove all leaven from their houses before the Passover festival (Ex. 12:15, 19f.). Their *paschal lamb* prefigured Christ (1 Pet. 1:19). (The crucifixion probably took place on Nisan 14, the day the paschal lambs were slain.) His sacrificial death, by taking away sin, makes Christians, the new Israel, *unleavened*, *i.e.* free from evil. **8** *Let us celebrate*; continuous present tense. The Christian life is likened to a constant *festival*; so believers must continuously keep 'leaven' out of their lives and fellowship.

9, 10 If some Corinthians were too lax, others were too rigid, refusing all contact with unbelievers. *I wrote.* The 'previous letter', which has not survived (see Introduction, 'How many letters and visits?'). Paul's instruction not to mix *with immoral men* had been misunderstood.

Of course in this world it is impossible not to mix with some evil men. The command to cease fellowship applies only to professing Christians (church members) who become immoral. **11** He may bear *the name of brother*, but he is not living the life of a Christian. The catalogue of sins vividly sketches the background from which many early converts came. *Not even to eat; i.e.* social meals, but the Lord's Supper is included. Note the stern view taken, *e.g.*, of covetousness and abusive language, and the open and severe character of the disciplinary action. **12** It is not a Christian's function to pass judgment on the heathen behaviour of *outsiders* (*cf.* 6:2). But those *inside the church* are certainly the church's responsibility. **13** *Drive out.* In the OT (*e.g.* Dt. 17:7) this instruction always has a singular verb. Paul uses the plural: excommunication concerns the whole church community, with whom, under Christ, authority is vested. The old covenant ordained death for gross sinners, and so the penalty under the new covenant is not excessive.

6:1–11 Litigation

1 Paul now deals with another cause of scandal. *Grievance against* renders a Greek phrase used in the papyri for 'lawsuit'. *Does he dare? i.e.* 'How dare he!' Paul was deeply shocked. Even Jews living in heathen cities did not take such cases before Gentile courts. *Unrighteous; i.e.* not Christian. Paul is not suggesting that pagan courts are corrupt. As a good citizen the Christian acknowledges civil law (Rom. 13:1–7). Paul himself claimed its protection (Acts 18:12f.; 25:16). But to invoke pagan courts to settle lawsuits between believers was a confession of Christian failure. When a dispute between brethren could not be amicably settled by them, the matter should be decided before the *saints*, the church (*cf.* Mt. 18:17). **2** *Do you not know?* An appeal to a recognized fact. The words occur six times in this chapter. *Judge the world*; not now (see 5:12) but in the next age (*cf.* Dn. 7:22; Mt. 19:28; Rev. 3:21; 20:4). **3** The inclusion of *angels* (*cf.* Jude 6; 2 Pet. 2:4) indicates that *world* here means the universe, not just human society. This is based perhaps on Dn. 7:18, where sharing the kingdom would involve sharing the king's authority. **4** *Least esteemed; i.e.* pagans, those whose standards and judgments are worthless compared with those of Christians. Or, as AV, RV mg.: If judgment on such matters is necessary, let those thought least of in the church tackle them. **5** *Shame; cf.* 4:14. *Wise enough.* A stinging reference to the Corinthians' claim to wisdom (*cf.* 4:10). Surely without setting up a court to conduct a trial a fellow-Christian could be asked to give his decision. **6** *Goes to law.* Lawsuits against one another should anyway be avoided by Christians; and to engage in them with unbelievers as judges was surely unthinkable. **7** *Defeat; i.e.* in the spiritual contest, whatever the legal verdict. *Suffer wrong;* a principle laid down by Jesus (Mt. 5:39f.). **8** *Defraud.* Sharp practice, unethical in any company, was doubly sinful in a society based on brotherly love.

9, 10 *Unrighteous*; those who are not Christians (*cf.* 6:1). They are defined in type and character by the lists which follow. *Inherit*; *i.e.* be citizens of the future kingdom of God and enjoy its benefits and privileges (*cf.* 15:50; Gal. 5:21). The inclusion of *idolaters* among sexual offenders recalls the immoral nature of much contemporary heathen worship (see Introduction, 'Corinth'). **11** Paul frankly recognizes the pre-Christian character of the Corinthian converts. Three times a strong adversative 'but' (Gk., AV) stresses the contrasts. Such unpromising material required the mighty power of God to recreate characters and attitudes (*cf.* Rom. 6:17). *In the name of . . . Christ . . . Spirit . . . God.* Note the unconscious Trinitarianism. The words may recall the actual formula used in baptism and the complementary baptism of the Spirit which effects the vital change. Lightfoot considers there is reference here to the external and internal essential of baptism. Thus association with the sinners of v. 10 is all the more intolerable. *Justified*; *i.e.* declared righteous before God's tribunal because of Christ's atoning sacrifice. To jeopardize the 'inheritance' (vv. 9, 10) by a return to the evil practices listed is unthinkable (*cf.* Tit. 3:3–7).

6:12–20 Fornication condemned

Paul dealt with a particular case of immorality in ch. 5. Now he turns to the basic principle, and incidentally provides Christian teaching about the body. Redeemed by Christ's sacrifice (v. 20) and indwelt by the Spirit (v. 19), the Christian's body forms part of Christ's body, the church (v. 15); after death it will be raised (v. 14) and so continue God's purposes.

12 *All things. . . .* Perhaps a current slogan (repeated in 10:23), claimed by the Corinthians to justify their loose behaviour. The maxim needs careful qualification (*cf.* 1 Pet. 2:16). Liberty is not licence. *Helpful*; *i.e.* towards Christlikeness. Only actions motivated by love build up (*cf.* 8:1). It is possible so to use liberty as to become *enslaved* by one's desires (*cf.* 2 Pet. 2:19; Gal. 5:1, 13). **13** *Food is meant. . . .* Perhaps another slogan. The implied comparison is that sex is as natural and transient as eating. Paul replies that God did not design the body for fornication or passing sexual 'satisfaction', as He did the stomach simply for food. For Paul, *body* is much more than the physical: it includes the whole personality. As the stomach requires food for its proper function, so the 'body' requires *the Lord* to fulfil its God-intended purpose of service and sacrifice (*cf.* Phil. 1:20; Heb. 10:5), and can find its true satisfaction only in Him (Jn. 6:54). **14** The resurrection of the Lord and of Christians is intimately linked (*cf.* 1 Cor. 15:20; Rom. 8:11; Phil. 3:21). The present physical body must be properly valued and used (*cf.* 2 Cor. 5:10). As a resurrected body (*cf.* 15:35f.) it will still be needed for God's purposes.

15 *Members of Christ.* Paul develops the thought of Christians as the body of Christ in 12:12f.; Rom. 12:5; Eph. 5:23; Col. 1:18. *Take* ('take away'); *i.e.* from their proper Lord and their proper use. **16, 17** *Prostitute*; *i.e.* attached to a pagan temple: not a 'call-girl'. In both Testaments resort to a temple prostitute meant resort to a strange god. *As it is written*; in Gn. 2:54. *Cf.* Mt. 19:5; Eph. 5:31. *Joins* (v. 16) and *united* (v. 17) translate the same verb, which literally means 'glued'. The bond is as close as it can be. *Becomes one spirit.* The Christian's body and personality are controlled by the Holy Spirit, a position brought about by the work of the Lord (Christ). **18** *Shun* ('flee from') *immorality*; present imperative, indicating a constant attitude and reaction (*cf.* 10:14; 1 Thes. 4:3). Disapproval is insufficient: evasive action is required. *Every other sin* against the body (*e.g.* gluttony, drunkenness), as Tasker points out (*TNTC*, p. 102), involves 'the use of that which comes from without the body. The sexual appetite rises from within. . . . They are sinful in the excess. This is sinful in itself.' *Against his own body*, and therefore against his own personality (v. 13). **19** *Do you not know?*—for the sixth time in this chapter. *Temple.* The individual Christian is the personal shrine of the *Holy Spirit*, who is not concerned simply with a man's soul. *From God.* Since the temple belongs to God, the Christian is not independent. **20** *Bought*; aorist tense, pointing to Christ's one decisive action on the cross (*cf.* 7:22f.; 2 Pet. 2:1). The language reflects a contemporary custom. By paying the price of his liberty into a god's temple, a slave became the god's property; but society now considered him free. Our redemption by Christ from the enslavement of sin was no such pious fiction, but at the cost of His sacrifice (1 Pet. 1:18, 19; Gal. 5:1; Tit. 2:14). *Glorify God*; but not simply by refraining from immorality: the *body*, *i.e.* the whole person, is to be used positively in Christian service (*cf.* Rom. 12:1).

7:1–40 MARRIAGE PROBLEMS

In chs. 7–15 Paul deals with matters raised in a letter from Corinth (see Introduction, 'How many letters and visits?'). Ch. 7 is not a treatise on marriage, but answers six questions on the subject, with a general governing principle in vv. 17–24. The problems posed by the Corinthians would be prompted by the different cultures represented in their church—Jewish, Greek, Roman—each with an accepted approach to marriage. Paul distinguishes between commands of Jesus during His ministry and his own apostolic rulings, for which inspiration is claimed (v. 40); and between divinely ordained principles obligatory upon all and points into which personal choice may enter (see, *e.g.*, vv. 7, 36f.), for men's gifts and calling differ, and circumstances vary.

7:1–7 Question one

Are couples to continue normal sexual relations

after conversion? Yes; they owe it to one another to do so.

1, 2 *Now concerning* (repeated 7:25; 8:1; 12:1; 16:1) introduces Paul's replies to the Corinthians' questions. *It is well . . . woman* is probably a quotation from their letter (*cf.* 6:12), for Paul goes on to disagree. *Touch a woman*; a euphemism for sexual intercourse (*cf.* Gn. 20:6). Some were probably urging complete abstinence. Having opposed licence in 6:13–20, Paul now opposes asceticism. The two extremes were encouraged by Gnostic views of matter as evil (*cf.* 1 Tim. 4:3). Paul argues that marriage is the norm. Celibacy, as some say, is good. But *temptation* to immoral acts (the Greek is plural) abounds, especially in Corinth (see Introduction, 'Corinth'). Marriage was the divinely appointed safeguard; so each *should have* (*i.e.* 'must', not 'may') his own spouse—an incidental reference to monogamy. **3, 4** Marriage must be real, not 'spiritual'. *Should give*; the Greek indicates the paying of a debt rather than the conferring of a favour (*cf.* Mk. 12:17). Husband and wife have equal sex rights, a novelty in antiquity. **5, 6** *Do not refuse* (Gk. 'defraud'), *i.e.* withhold what is owed. Any abstention must be mutually agreed, temporary, and have a spiritual objective (*cf.* 1 Pet. 3:7). *Devote yourselves*; literally 'have leisure for'. *Cf.* Ec. 3:5; Joel 2:15, 16. Paul's *concession* shows wise balance. Abstinence carried to extreme may only expose one to temptation—to satisfy the appetite wrongly. **7** *As I myself am*; *i.e.* by God's *special gift* not in need of a marriage partner. If Paul was once married, he is now widowed. Celibacy and marriage alike are special gifts. Every Christian is called to serve God in one state or the other (*cf.* Mt. 19:11f.). Different courses are in consequence God's will for different individuals.

7:8, 9 Question two

Should the unmarried marry? Paul commends celibacy—but only for those with that gift.

8 *Single* has been inserted by RSV. But *unmarried* (Gk. *agamos*) covers divorcee (as v. 11), bachelor and widower. So probably *unmarried* here means 'widowers' (pairing with widows), otherwise the omission of bereaved husbands is strange. (Greek has no special word for widower.) Only exceptionally did a Jew remain unmarried (*cf.* Je. 16:2). Probably the apostle was a widower. If 'I cast my vote' (Acts 26:10) indicates Paul belonged to the Sanhedrin, he must have been married. *It is well for them*; see vv. 26, 32. **9** *Self-control*. If they lack the gift of celibacy, they should marry. Enforced abstinence is valueless if it means being *aflame with passion*, *i.e.* emotionally distracted by unsatisfied appetite. Sexual desire is natural and marriage is provided for its fulfilment.

7:10, 11 Question three

Is divorce permitted to a Christian couple? No. **10** *Not I but the Lord*; *i.e.* Jesus (*cf.* Mk. 10:1–12). These are not simply Paul's own views.

11 *Should not divorce*. Christ's exception in a case of fornication (Mt. 5:32; 19:9) is not mentioned; but Paul is not composing a full treatise on the subject. If two Christians who have separated find they cannot happily live a *single* life, the only course properly open to them is to *be reconciled*. *Remain single*. Remarriage is excluded while the other spouse is alive (*cf.* Rom. 7:3). Separated partners are thus still subject to church discipline; they are not expelled from the fellowship.

7:12–16 Question four

When one partner gets converted, should old relationships continue with the pagan spouse? Yes. The Christian is not to leave the unbelieving partner unless the latter desires separation. **12, 13** The problem of mixed marriages would hardly have arisen during Christ's ministry, and so Paul cannot quote a specific word of *the Lord*. But his own judgment is given authoritatively. **14** *The unbelieving husband is consecrated*, *i.e.* not 'made personally holy' (*cf.* 6:11), for he is still unsaved (v. 16), but treated as in a special relationship with God solely for the purpose of the marriage. *Children* of such a union are similarly covered, presumably until a responsible age. Scripture teaches that divine blessings extend to individuals' children and to their sphere of life (Gn. 17:7; 39:5). Some would contend that since the children *are holy* this means they should be treated as members of the people of God, and therefore baptized. Logically, however, this would also apply to the pagan spouse, for *consecrated* and *holy* derive from the same Greek root. Paul's aim is doubtless to reassure Christians that there is for them nothing in a mixed marriage contrary to Christian holiness. **15** But if, following the other's conversion, the unbelieving partner desires to discontinue the marriage, separation may follow. *The brother or sister*, *i.e.* the Christian partner, is *not bound* to maintain the union against the other's wishes. Since one is now converted, there is a new and fundamental difference between them, with social as well as spiritual consequences. Separation in this case presumably means that the Christian is free to marry someone else—provided he or she is a Christian (v. 39). The guiding principle must be what tends to promote *peace*, for this is God's general will and purpose for Christians. **16** *Whether you will*; *i.e.* 'perhaps you will'. If the believer views the mixed marriage, with its inevitable difficulties, as a missionary situation, it is possible that the heathen partner will ultimately be converted (*cf.* 1 Pet. 3:1f.).

7:17–24 A general principle

17 The conditional liberty allowed in the matter of mixed marriages is exceptional. Normally a Christian is to continue to *lead the life* he was living when God's call to become a Christian came to him; *i.e.* he is socially, *etc.*, to stay put. No violent changes should be made simply because of conversion; this applies to differences of racial custom and social status. Paul twice underlines this principle (vv. 20, 24) as he discusses the great dividing factors in religion and society in his day, circumcision and slavery. **18, 19** *Circumcision* was the distinctive sign of the divine covenant (Gn. 17:10ff.). Now Christ has come the mark is valueless (Gal. 5:6; 6:15). Paradoxically (for circumcision was itself a divine commandment) Paul now adds that what is all-important is *keeping the commandments of God*. By this Paul means obeying God's will as now revealed in Jesus (Jn. 14:21; Gal. 6:2). The point is developed in 9:20ff. (*cf.* Rom. 2:25ff.; 13:8ff.). **20, 21** If a slave is converted, he is not to mind his social status (*cf.* 1:26ff.). His Christian calling is to serve God where he is (Eph. 6:5), although if he can legitimately gain his freedom he should do so. **22** Relationship to the Lord alters everything. When a slave becomes a Christian, he becomes the Lord's *freedman*, *i.e.* he is delivered from bondage to sin and death. When someone not a slave becomes a Christian, he becomes Christ's *slave*, *i.e.* he owes Him complete loyalty and service. **23, 24** Believers belong to Christ, for they have been *bought* at the *price* of His life (*cf.* 1 Pet. 1:18f.). So Christians should not be *slaves of men*, *i.e.* dragooned by others in the way they are to live. For Christ is now their owner; and His will is that *in whatever state* each became a Christian, there he should remain—with this difference: that in Christ he now faces life in fellowship *with God*.

7:25–38 Question five

Ought Christian fathers to give their daughters in marriage? Each father should make his own decision. 'But bear in mind the passing nature of the world and the greater liberty to serve Christ that being single offers.'

25 *The unmarried*; 'virgins' (AV) can include both sexes (*cf.* Rev. 14:4). Paul first discusses in general terms the advisability of not marrying, before turning to the specific problem about daughters in vv. 36–38. While Paul again cannot quote a direct *command of the Lord* (*cf.* 7:12), he gives an opinion which by the witness of the Spirit he is sure is in line with God's thought (*cf.* 7:40). Though aware of his human frailties, Paul claims that *by the Lord's mercy* (*cf.* 2 Cor. 4:1; 1 Tim. 1:15f.) he speaks authoritatively. *Trustworthy.* The Greek *pistos* expresses both faithfulness and the possession of Christian faith; one follows the other. **26** Paul may again be quoting from the Corinthians' letter: '*In view of the impending distress* there is much sense, as you say, in a person not changing his status.' *The impending distress* was evidently more than ordinary antagonism (*cf.* 2 Tim. 3:12), but probably not the portents presaging the second advent (Lk. 21:23), for Paul never mentions these signs in his many references to Christ's return. This event, however, is not far from his mind (v. 29). **28** Remaining single avoids many *worldly troubles* (*cf.* Mk. 4:19), *i.e.* cares and problems

inevitably involved in family life. **29, 30** Apart from the local distress apparently pressing upon the Corinthians, *the appointed time* for the return of the Lord is imminent. From now on, therefore, they should no longer be engrossed in whatever would normally absorb their attention, be it earthly relationships, *e.g.* with their *wives*, or day-to-day experiences like *mourning*, *rejoicing*, or trading. **31** Christians are to hold loosely to all that concerns *this world* (*cf.* Col. 3:2), *as though they had no dealings with it*; or rather, 'not using it to the full', *i.e.* not being absorbed with its affairs (*form*).

32 Paul commends the unmarried state because a single person can give himself wholly to *the affairs of the Lord*, *i.e.* make it his one business to please Him. **33, 34** *The married man* must of necessity concern himself also with the needs of wife and children. So *his interests are divided*, *i.e.* he wants to please both his wife (as a good husband) and the Lord (as a good Christian). A similar difficulty faces a woman. If unmarried, she can serve the Lord wholeheartedly and without family distractions, however legitimate in themselves (*cf.* Lk. 10:38–42). She can devote herself to personal holiness or full consecration *in body and spirit* (*cf.* Rom. 12:1, 2). **35** Paul's advice is intended as wise guidance, *not to lay any restraint* (Gk. 'put a halter') upon the Corinthians, *i.e.* coerce them into a course of action like so many farm animals (*cf.* 2 Cor. 1:24).

RSV assumes that vv. 36–38 refer to engaged couples. This would reflect a more recent and western situation. In Paul's day marriages were arranged by parents. As in **36** *betrothed* renders *parthenos*, 'virgin' (AV), the verse could mean, 'If any father decides that he is not doing his duty by his unmarried daughter. . . .' It was a disgrace for a maiden to have 'no marriage song' (Ps. 78:63). The perils in Corinth for an unmarried girl would weigh with a Christian father. 'If she pass the flower of her age', *i.e.* the usual marrying age (AV; Gk. *hyperakmos*), is applied by RSV to the supposed fiancé, and translated *if his passions are strong. And it has to be* may refer to the absence of the gift of continence, or to an existing marriage contract. In such a situation the father should *do as he wishes*, *i.e.* act on his conviction that his daughter ought to be married. **37** But another father is *firmly established*, convinced that there is no necessity for his daughter to be married; *but having his desire under control*, being free to act in accordance with his judgment, he *has determined*, made up his mind, to keep her unmarried (RSV, *betrothed*)—a decision Paul commends. **38** So Paul judges that he who marries off his daughter does well; but he who refrains from doing so, having in mind the contemporary situation, *will do better*, *i.e.* act more wisely.

7:39, 40 Question six

May a Christian widow remarry? Yes—with qualifications.

39 Marriage is indissoluble until death. (Here, as in Rom. 7:1–3, the position of women is considered; but men are equally bound: vv. 11, 27.) The Christian widow is free to marry *whom she wishes, i.e.* unfettered by the law of levirate marriage (Dt. 25:5–10). But only *in the Lord, i.e.* to another Christian; for she is a member of Christ's body (*cf.* 6:15). **40** Yet in Paul's *judgment* not to remarry would make her *happier, i.e.* with fewer 'troubles' (v. 28), 'anxieties' (v. 32), and distractions from serving Christ (*cf.* 1 Tim. 5:5). '*I think*', Paul adds with a touch of irony, 'that I too (Gk.) can claim to be in tune with the mind of *the Spirit of God* as much as any of my opponents.'

8:1 – 11:1 CHRISTIAN FREEDOM AND ITS LIMITATIONS

Another problem raised by the Corinthians concerned the Christian attitude towards the use of food previously offered to idols. This included most of the meat sold in the shops. Was it wrong to eat it? Furthermore in 1st-century Corinth it was customary on sociable occasions to gather for a meal in a pagan temple. Might Christians go? Paul answers by reference to the general principles involved. The Christian is free: but other considerations should limit his use of his freedom.

8:1–13 Respect for the consciences of others

1–3 True, we may have *knowledge*; but it easily breeds conceit, provides glib answers, and at best is incomplete. What matters more is *love*. This promotes the good of others, and means being *known* by God, *i.e.* acknowledged by Him as His (*cf.* Mt. 7:23; 2 Tim. 2:19). **4, 5** The truth about God that '*there is no God but one*' (Dt. 6:4) is fundamental to right understanding and practice. For in spite of the many *so-called gods*, an idol has no existence as a god. It is a 'nothing' or a 'vain thing' (*cf.* Dt. 32:17, 21; Acts 14:15). Later (10:20) Paul will add that evil spirits certainly exist, and it is they who promote idol-worship to lure men away from the true God. **6** It is distinctive of *us* as Christians to acknowledge the *one God* as *Father*, and as the first and final cause of the universe; and with Him to acknowledge *Jesus Christ* also as *Lord* (*i.e.* God), and as the agent of all creation.

7 Some were 'weak' as believers in Christ since they were still unconvinced that an idol had no real existence as a god. They felt they were doing wrong when they ate meat offered to it. Their *conscience* was *defiled* not by the food in itself (see Mk. 7:18, 19) but by doing something which their so far unenlightened conscience still said was (for them) wrong (*cf.* Rom. 14:23). **8** Partaking of or abstinence from food makes no difference to a man's standing with God. **9, 10** But *a man of knowledge*, an enlightened Christian, who uses his *liberty* to eat at a social occasion held *in an idol's temple*, could by his example induce a fellow-believer

whose *conscience is weak, i.e.* unenlightened, to do what was still for him wrong; and this would be to trip him up (*cf.* Rom. 14:23). **11** By using his knowledge carelessly the maturer Christian could bring spiritual disaster to the other; he will be *destroyed*, not built up (*cf.* 8:1). 'The last clause (of v. 11) could hardly be more forcible in its appeal; every word tells: "the brother," not a mere stranger; "for the sake of whom," precisely to rescue him from destruction; "Christ," no less than He; "died," no less than that' (A. Robertson and A. Plummer, *The First Epistle of St. Paul to the Corinthians*[2], *ICC*, 1914). Such sinning is doubly wrong. It is both against a Christian *brother* and against *Christ*. **12** Also it involved heartlessly wounding the weak. **13** Therefore, Paul summarizes, if some otherwise innocent action by a mature Christian proves to be a cause of involving another believer in defiling his conscience, the former must surrender his right to do it. Yet Paul's declaration is conditional, not absolute. He does not say he will henceforth always be a total abstainer, but only *if* and when such eating may *cause* his *brother to fall.*

9:1–27 Forgoing rights

The principle of self-sacrifice brought out in ch. 8 is now illustrated from Paul's own life. He lists his positions, all of which carry rights. **1** As an ordinary Christian he is *free*. By divine appointment he is an *apostle* (*cf.* 1:1). On the Damascus road (Acts 9) he had the privilege of seeing the Lord Jesus (*cf.* 2 Cor. 12:1), an essential qualification for an apostle (Acts 1:21f.). **2** Though others may challenge his claim to be an apostle, at least he is one to the Corinthians. They themselves are living proof of his divinely-owned ministry (*cf.* 2 Cor. 3:2; 12:2).

3 The words *This is my defence* go more appropriately with the preceding two verses. Paul has put his case. Now he lists the rights which are consequently his. **4** As a Christian minister, the church should provide his food and drink. **5, 6** Had he a wife like others, he could, in his ministerial travels, rightly expect support for two. There is surely nothing which disqualifies him and Barnabas from receiving support? **7** The principle is illustrated in ordinary life. A soldier who draws pay, a landowner who plants a vineyard, or a slave who tends a flock, all obtain sustenance from their occupations. The examples are appropriate. The Christian minister fights evil, plants churches, and shepherds congregations (*cf.* 2 Tim. 2:3–6; 1 Cor. 3:6, 7; Jn. 21:15–17). **8, 9** It was not just human wisdom but a specific divine command (Dt. 25:4) that forbade the muzzling of an ox to prevent it from eating any of the grain it was treading out. The lesson of this commandment is not exclusively to teach God's concern for oxen, though that is not denied (*cf.* Mt. 6:26). **10, 11** The word was *for our sake.* (*Entirely*: Gk. can mean 'assuredly'.) So it has a higher significance: it indicates that the needs of those who toil should be recognized and their labours recompensed. Similarly, the Christian minister, pictured as a ploughman (*i.e.* one who begins the cycle of work) or a thresher (one who completes the harvest) should rightly expect *material* maintenance in return for his *spiritual* work. In vv. 11, 12 the *we* is emphatic, in contrast to the *others*. As the founder or father of the Corinthian church, Paul has *still more* right than they. The *others* are not Paul's opponents—no wrong is suggested—but other Christian teachers in general who serve the church. **12** The determining concern which made Paul willing for any hardship was not to interrupt the progress of the gospel. He would give his opponents no excuse for personal attack which would hinder God's work (2 Cor. 6:3; 11:9). **13** In both Jewish and pagan religious practice those who were employed in temple service received subsistence from the temple (Nu. 18:8f., 21f.). **14** By the Lord's (*i.e.* Christ's) explicit command the same rule applies to those who preach the gospel (see Mt. 10:10; Lk. 10:7).

15, 16 His *ground for boasting* (see on v. 18) is not that he is a preacher. *Necessity* presses upon him to proclaim the gospel to others. **17** He did not choose the task. The Lord has commissioned him. Such disinterested self-denial was a proof of his integrity and an answer to any who accused him of mercenary motives. To preach is therefore for him an obligation, not an optional personal interest. **18** His *reward*, his ground for boasting, is to *make the gospel free of charge*. 'What pay do I get? The pleasure of refusing pay!' This is why he will not make full use of his right in the gospel.

19 Paul has surrendered more than his right to personal subsistence. Though he is *free from all men*, *i.e.* in no sense bound by the standards or fashions of others, he is prepared to make himself *a slave to all*, and conform to their standards or fashions, providing no real principle is at stake, in order to win as many as possible to saving faith in Christ. **20** So when among Jews he acts *as a Jew*, conforming to their customs *under the* Mosaic *law* (Acts 16:3; 18:18; 21:26), though as a Christian he himself is no longer obliged to keep that law (*cf.* Gal. 2:11–21). **21** Similarly he is ready to identify himself with those who are not bound by the Jewish law, *i.e.* Gentiles; though he adds an important proviso. Gentiles not only disregard the Mosaic law, but may also refuse to recognize any divine commandment. Paul, on the other hand, is always under the authority of the true God and of His Christ (7:22). Subject to this overriding consideration, he is prepared to conform to the practice of Gentiles as far as is necessary to win them to Christ. **22** To sum up: Paul is willing to *become all things to all men* (*cf.* 2 Cor. 11:29). This does not mean that he will act in an unprincipled manner, or compromise on Christian principles; but he will sacrifice his own legitimate interests and preferences completely, if thereby he may save some. **23** His reason is twofold: *for the sake*

of the gospel, *i.e.* because it is so precious to him; and that he may not fail himself to *share in its blessings* (*cf.* v. 27). NEB renders the last clause 'bear my part in proclaiming it'.

24 The need for rigid self-discipline is illustrated by athletes in training, a familiar sight to every Greek. The Isthmian Games, second only to the Olympics, were held every 3 years in Corinth, and drew immense crowds. To win was to be immortalized by the Greek public. **25** *Every athlete*, literally 'every one that agonizes', *exercises self-control in all things*, giving up not only unhealthy pleasures, but even legitimate occupations if they tend to make body or will flabby. Greek athletes were prepared to carry out the 10-month training for a mere *wreath* of leaves. How much more worth while the Christian's prize! And that prize is imperishable (2 Tim. 4:8). **26** The Christian does not *run aimlessly*, not knowing the point of the race or where the finishing post is. Nor is he like a shadow-boxer, *beating the air* without purpose (*cf.* 14:9). **27** On the contrary, Paul realizes he must, so to speak, *pommel* (Gk. 'give a black eye to') *his body and subdue* it; *i.e.* he must be master of himself in every department. Otherwise Paul fears that *after preaching to others*, like the herald at the games proclaiming the rules of the contest and calling the competitors together, he himself should be *disqualified* (Gk. *adokimos*; *cf.* 2 Tim. 2:15, where the positive *dokimos* is used). His own salvation is not in question, but his reward for acceptable service (*cf.* 3:15).

Note. 5 *The brothers of the Lord* were evidently active in Christian service. The phrase is remarkable incidental witness to the deity and humanity of Jesus; *cf.* Gal. 1:19. Nothing in the NT forbids the natural interpretation that they were children of Joseph and Mary born after Jesus.

10:1–13 Warnings of perils to be avoided

The Corinthians' shallow view of Christian liberty (exposed in ch. 8) stemmed from their taking idolatry lightly; and this in turn (so Paul now explains) arose from misunderstanding the nature of Christian baptism and the Lord's Supper. They were not charms. Even an apostle had to persevere in his Christian life (9:27). Paul illustrates his point from the OT. The fivefold repetition of 'all' in vv. 1–4 emphasizes that the Israelites without exception received high privileges. This throws v. 5 into relief (*cf.* 9:24).

1, 2 The expression *our fathers* points to the continuation of the church of God from its OT foundations. The cover given by the divine *cloud* (Ps. 105:39) and the miraculous deliverance through the water of the Red Sea (Ex. 14) are described as the means whereby the Israelites *were baptized into Moses*, *i.e.* brought under his authority and leadership, language obviously designed to parallel to some extent the Christian's baptism into Christ (Rom. 6:3; Gal. 3:27). **3, 4** The Israelites were sustained by supernaturally-given *food*, the manna of Ex. 16:4 (*cf.* Jn.

6:31f.). *The supernatural Rock* which provided their water (Ex. 17:6; *cf.* Jn. 7:37f.) is said to have *followed* ('accompanied'; *cf.* Mt. 9:9) them. Paul is speaking metaphorically; *i.e.* wherever the Israelites were, the supply never failed. (Jewish tradition, however, took Nu. 20:11; 21:16, *etc.*, to refer to a movable rock with its well.) More important is the explicit reference to Christ as pre-existent, and to His being the source of the people's blessings at all times. Note the clear statement that *the Rock was Christ.* Paul thus gives to Christ a title used in the OT of God Himself (*e.g.* Dt. 32:15; Is. 26:4). **5** Despite their spiritual privileges, however, *most of them, i.e.* all the adults except Caleb and Joshua (Nu. 14:30), displeased the Lord (*cf.* Heb. 11:6); and so by His sentence *they were overthrown* (*cf.* 11:30). The Greek graphically suggests a desert strewn with corpses (*cf.* Nu. 14:16).

6 *These things* are historical facts recorded as *warnings* against sinful desires for evil things. *For us*: Paul is not exempt (*cf.* 9:27). **7** The temptation to idolatry was as much before the Corinthians as the ancient Israelites. *As it is written*; see Ex. 32:6. *The people sat down to eat and drink*; *i.e.* taking part in the sacrifices offered to God before the golden calf (Ex. 32:4; *cf.* 1 Cor. 10:20). *And rose up to dance*; *i.e.* ritually. **8** Such activities were also common to idol-worship in Corinth (see Introduction, 'Corinth'), and were accompanied by, or inevitably led to, *immorality* (*cf.* Rev. 2:14, 20). Paul quotes an example of a consequent judgment by plague which swept off thousands (see Nu. 25:1–9). **9** Neither must the Corinthians *put the Lord to the test* (the Greek implies prolonged and severe testing), *i.e.* see how far they can go in defying His requirements. **10** *Nor grumble* (*cf.* Nu. 16); for this many Israelites were *destroyed* (*cf.* Nu. 14:2; 21:6). *The Destroyer* (*cf.* Ex. 12:23), or 'Angel of Death' (Phillips), is not mentioned in this context in the OT, but the point is plain: rebellion against God invokes divine judgment (*cf.* 5:5; 11:30).

11 The judgments fell upon the Israelites of the day *as a warning* (lit. 'typically'). God has caused them to be *written down for our* (*i.e.* Christians') *instruction.* (Modern zeal for ascertaining the meaning of the OT for its first readers forgets what is here taught.) Similar temptations faced the Corinthians, and in different guise face all Christians. *The end, i.e.* the culmination, of all past *ages* has arrived (*cf.* Gal. 4:4; Heb. 1:2). All that happened before Christ came was provisional and symbolical. We have the advantage of learning from the Israelites' experiences, and supremely of knowing the full revelation given by Christ. **12** But as with the Israelites, self-confidence, which saps wholehearted devotion to the Lord, easily leads to a *fall*. **13** A Christian is not exempt from temptation. But neither is he subject to unique temptations *not common to* all men everywhere and at all times. *Temptation* here includes testing and trials.

God allows these experiences (*cf.* Jb. 1:12; 2:6) to stretch and strengthen faith (Gn. 22:1). *God is faithful; i.e.* to His promise of full salvation. Over against v. 12, which speaks to the careless or overconfident, this is a word to the fearful and despondent—a word of assurance and encouragement. *Provide* (lit. 'make') *the way of escape.* The Greek suggests an army trapped in the mountains slipping out through a narrow pass.

Note. 8 *Twenty-three thousand fell.* Nu. 25:9, Philo and Josephus quote 24,000. Both figures are obviously round numbers, though Paul's additional words *in a single day* may hint at an explanation. Jewish tradition ascribed 1,000 deaths to the action of the judges described in Nu. 25:5.

10:14–22 The impossibility of compromise

14 *My beloved.* The affectionate address turns command into entreaty. *Shun* ('flee from'); present imperative—'Make it your habitual practice' (*cf.* 6:18). Deliberate avoidance is often the best defence against temptation. The Corinthians were playing with fire by attending pagan festivities. Paul has already said that they might mislead others (8:10). **15** He now gives a deeper reason for avoiding idolatrous practices, and one he expects the Corinthians *as sensible men* to appreciate. **16** *The cup of blessing*; the third cup in the Passover festival, so called because a Jewish father pronounced a blessing, *i.e.* a prayer of thanksgiving (*cf.* Mt. 26:26 with Lk. 22:17), before passing it round the family. It was quite possibly the cup used by Jesus when instituting the Lord's Supper (Lk. 22:17). The mention of the cup first (contrast 11:26, 28) may be due to the prominence of the cup in pagan sacrifices, for Paul's allusion to the Lord's Supper is for the purpose of warning against idolatry. To share rightly (*cf.* 11:29) in the bread and wine is a *participation* (Gk. *koinōnia*, a common sharing) in the benefits won by the sacrifice of *the body* and *blood of Christ* (*cf.* Rom. 3:25; 5:9). The worshippers are thereby bound in fellowship with the living Christ, and so with one another. **17** That unity is symbolized by the use of the *one loaf* (*cf.* 5:7).

18 Paul finds parallels in *the practice of Israel.* AV adds, with Greek, 'after the flesh', *i.e.* unbelieving Israel (*cf.* Rom. 2:28f.; Gal. 6:15f.). Jewish sacrifices were consumed by priests (*e.g.* Lv. 10:12–15) and by other worshippers (*e.g.* 1 Sa. 9:11–24). Such actions were acknowledged to be a sharing *in the altar* and all it represented. **19** Paul is not implying by the illustration that idol's food is anything other than food, or that a stone or wooden idol has any reality (*cf.* 8:4f.). **20** But communion can be only with the living. Thus *what pagans sacrifice*, whether they realize it or not, *they offer to demons* (*cf.* Dt. 32:17), who take advantage of men's leaning towards idolatry. Paul would save the Corinthians (*cf.* 7:28) from being unwitting *partners with demons* (Eph. 6:12). **21** On such an issue there can be no compromise. Fellowship with *the Lord* and fellowship with *demons* are utterly incompatible (*cf.* Is. 65:11). **22** Consequently to join in heathen festivities is inevitably to *provoke the Lord to jealousy* (*cf.* Dt. 32:21), for devotion to Him must be exclusive.

10:23 – 11:1 Summary of guiding principles

Paul rounds off his treatment of the subject which has occupied him from 8:1 by considering two practical points: shopping (v. 25) and social meals in private houses (v. 27). Though Christians may not attend idol-feasts, Paul agrees that in itself the eating of food previously offered to idols is immaterial (*cf.* 6:12f.; 8:8). **23** To the Christian *all things are lawful, i.e.* he has full liberty of action; but that liberty must be used to *build up* spiritual life (*cf.* Rom. 14:20). **24** This can be done only by his considering not his own rights and privileges but the spiritual *good of his neighbour.* **25, 26** He may eat food bought at the meat-market (*cf.* 8:1f.) without asking if it has been formally offered in a pagan temple. Food is from God, and all His gifts are good (Ps. 24:1). Being offered in idol-worship cannot affect the divine origin of food. It remains, therefore, fit for God's people to eat, if received with thanksgiving to Him (v. 30; 1 Tim. 4:4f.).

27 Attendance at functions in heathen temples is barred to the Christian. But whether to go *to dinner* in a pagan home is a personal decision. The Christian is not expected to forgo all social intercourse with unbelievers (*cf.* 5:9f.). The food provided is to be eaten without asking where it came from (*cf.* Lk. 10:8). **28, 29a** *But if some one* (evidently a weaker Christian; a pagan would not mind) declares that the food has previously been *offered in sacrifice,* the enlightened Christian is not to eat it. The principle to follow is again *consideration* for others (*cf.* vv. 24, 32, 33), by avoiding hurt to their conscience (*cf.* 8:7; Rom. 14:13–16). **29b, 30** After the parenthesis of vv. 28, 29a, Paul continues his positive exposition of principles: 'But I am under no obligation to let my liberty be permanently limited by other people's scruples. Since I can partake with thankfulness to God, I ought not to be denounced as doing wrong.'

31, 32 Liberty can become selfish and thankfulness Pharisaic (Lk. 18:11), so the regular rules to follow are: positively, *do all to the glory of God; i.e.* 'show my fellowmen the love and holiness of my heavenly Father' (F. Godet, *Commentary on 1 Corinthians*, 2 vols., ET 1893); and, negatively, avoid giving unnecessary offence to *Jews* with their food laws or to *Greeks* (*i.e.* Gentiles outside the church) or to weaker consciences within *the church of God.* Let Christianity offend only for the right reasons (*cf.* 1:23). **33** It is Paul's over-riding principle to *try to please all men,* not personally to curry favour or to avoid persecution, but to set forward the *advantage . . . of many, i.e.* their salvation (9:19, 22). **11:1** Finally Paul can boldly offer himself

as the Corinthians' example, but for the one reason that he imitates *Christ* (*cf.* Phil. 3:17; 1 Thes. 1:6; 2 Thes. 3:7, 9).

11:2 – 14:40 PUBLIC WORSHIP AND ITS WORTHY CONDUCT

11:2–16 The veiling of women

When praying, Jewish men and women both used veils (*cf.* 2 Cor. 3:14). So did Romans. Greeks, without the same awe of God, sacrificed bareheaded. With differing traditions represented in the Corinthian church, the Christian attitude needed defining in the interests of orderly worship (14:40). Believers should not unnecessarily flout social conventions, yet their view must be based on biblical principles. In this case Paul appeals to the relative status of men and women in the created order.

2 Paul praises the Corinthians for maintaining *the traditions* (*cf.* 15:1–3; 2 Thes. 2:15), *i.e.* the oral teaching about Christian doctrine and practice, which Paul had (not invented but) *delivered, i.e.* faithfully handed on from the Lord or the earlier apostles. **3** He first stresses the new Christian principle of union in subordination. Although the *woman* is subject to *her husband* (and decidedly so in ancient days), his authority is significantly modified because of his own subjection to *Christ* (*cf.* Eph. 5:23). The principle does not interfere with the personal relationships of men and women to Christ (*cf.* Gal. 3:28; 1 Pet. 3:7). It must be applied today against the background of the different sociological situation. (Otherwise we must revert to the clothes—and slavery—of those times.) **4** The Christian man is not to pray in public (or to prophesy: see on 12:10), as the Jew did, *with his head covered,* a sign of submission to another person (*cf.* Gn. 24:65). To do so *dishonours his 'head', i.e.* Christ, the only one to whom he owes submission. **5, 6** A Christian woman praying unveiled in public *dishonours her 'head', i.e.* her husband. In Paul's day this meant she repudiated his authority. Paul is outspoken. But for a woman in Corinth to be unveiled in public was as shocking in its social significance as being *shorn,* the contemporary punishment for a prostitute.

7–9 A man ought to be unveiled when praying to God since he is His *image and glory.* Gn. 1:26, 27 includes both sexes with regard to the *image, i.e.* 'constitution as a rational and morally responsible being' (D. Kidner, *Genesis, TOTC,* 1967), but does not mention *glory.* Paul derives this from the prior creation of the man (Gn. 2:18–22). For a woman to pray uncovered would display the *glory of man,* and in God's presence this must inevitably turn to shame. The 'glory of man', *i.e.* the woman, must therefore be covered, lest dishonour be brought upon the woman's 'head', *i.e.* the man (see M. D. Hooker, 'Authority on her head: An examination of 1 Cor. xi. 10', in *NTS,* X, 1963–64, pp. 410–416). **10** A woman should (lit.) 'have authority on her head' (*cf.* RSV mg.), *i.e.* wear the veil in public, to symbolize submission to her husband, and to protect her honour and dignity before other men. An unveiled woman in public would be despised and insulted. *Because of the angels* probably means that a woman who shocks men will shock angels, as guardians of the created order (vv. 8, 9) and who were present at public worship (*cf.* 1 Tim. 5:21). At Qumran men with physical blemishes were excluded from 'the assembly of God', for 'the holy angels are present'; *i.e.* nothing unseemly must come before them (G. Vermes, *The Dead Sea Scrolls in English*, 1962). Or possibly it means 'because the angels do', *i.e.* reverently veil their faces before God (Is. 6:2). Tertullian considered that bad angels were meant here and that Paul was warning against a repetition of the sin of Gn. 6:1-4.

11, 12 Paul qualifies what is meant by 'subordination'. *In the Lord*, *i.e.* in the Lord's intention in the created order (Gn. 2:23), man and woman are interdependent. **13-15** The Corinthians can see for themselves the fitness of Paul's arguments, supported by the accepted convention that women should be veiled in public, and also by *nature*—which expresses the will of the Creator. A woman's hair is distinctively longer than a man's. For her to wear it so indicates a willingness to fulfil what God intended her to be. **16** Paul's teaching is not peculiar to him but common to all other local *churches* (*cf.* 14:33, 36). As churches *of God* they are under His government. To dress with decorum is a Christian principle of permanent validity, for the outward appearance reflects the inner attitude. How this principle finds expression in detail will vary from place to place and from age to age.

11:17-34 The Lord's Supper

In the early days the observance of the sacramental acts of the Holy Communion took place in connection with a common meal or 'love feast' (Jude 12), in imitation of the Last Supper. Such opportunity for fellowship was welcomed by Christians from the first (Acts 2:46). But at Corinth the sacred harmony intended to be expressed thereby had been scandalously disrupted.

17 In Paul's judgment the matter is serious. He sends no more advice but authoritative *instructions*. He cannot *commend* (contrast 11:2) actions which ruin Christian life and witness. **18** The root of the trouble is in their *divisions* (not necessarily those of 1:10). *I hear*, presumably from Chloe's people (1:11) or Stephanas, *etc.* (16:17). **19** *Factions* are unedifying but to some extent inevitable; so divine providence makes them serve a positive purpose—they expose men's true characters. **20** When the Corinthians assemble for worship it is impossible to eat *the Lord's* (emphatic) *supper*, with all that it is intended to express. **21** Their manner is utterly selfish. They do not wait for latecomers (*e.g.* slaves) nor share what they have. Each is interested

only in *his own* (emphatic) supper, not the Lord's. The divisions of v. 18 are obviously based on money and class. **22** The Corinthians are despising both the dignity and brotherhood of the *church*, and its creator, *God*. So there is nothing whatever for Paul to commend.

23 Paul makes straight for bed-rock. He recounts the institution of the Lord's Supper. (This is our earliest record, and includes some features not found elsewhere; *cf.* Mt. 26:26f.; Mk. 14:22f.; Lk. 22:17f.) *Received* and *delivered* are terms often applied to oral Christian teaching (*cf.* 11:2; 15:3). But the emphatic *I* and *of the Lord* suggest a special revelation to Paul (Gal. 1:12; 2:2). He reminds the thoughtless Corinthians of the poignant setting of the first Lord's Supper—on the night of being handed over (by God) to death. **24** *When he had given thanks* (*cf.* 10:16) translates one Greek word from which comes 'eucharist'. This is how food is consecrated for us: by thanksgiving to God the Giver (1 Tim. 4:4, 5). 'Broken' (RSV mg.) *for you*. The interest is focused on what happened to His body on the cross and why. So the bread is not equated to His body as it then was in the upper room, or as it now is in glory. *Do this*. This is the chief, if not the sole, authentic place in the NT where the command to repeat the Lord's Supper occurs. The Greek words for *Do this* can only mean 'perform this action', not 'offer this (sacrifice)'. Again the Greek for *in remembrance of me* cannot bear the sense 'to remind God of Me', but only 'to remind yourselves of the death *I* (emphatic) suffered to win your redemption'. **25** *The cup, after supper*. In the upper room the bread and wine were deliberately separated by an interval, just as the pieces of slain animals were divided in covenant-making (Gn. 15:9f.) to represent the violent death of the covenant-maker, should he break the covenant. *Covenant*. The Greek word (*diathēkē*) means not a mutual compact but (as with a will) a solemn disposition by one party for the benefit of others. Jesus is referring to the 'new covenant' of Je. 31:31f. (replacing that described in Ex. 24) established through the shedding of His blood. The benefits flowing therefrom are all by His gift. **26** *Proclaim the Lord's death* can only mean 'to men' and not 'to God'. The Greek verb occurs 17 times and always concerns the proclamation of the gospel before men. The action that does it is eating and drinking, not offering, and is only to be used *until he comes*. Then He will drink with them in person at the triumph feast (Mt. 26:29).

27 This solemn rite demands a reverent approach. To take part *in an unworthy manner*, *i.e.* carelessly (*cf.* vv. 21, 29), is to deny the purpose of Christ's self-offering. It is thus to share the guilt of those responsible for the crucifixion, rather than by faith to receive the benefits of His sacrifice. **28** The worshipper must *examine himself*, *i.e.* his spiritual condition and motives (2 Cor. 13:5), for he is answerable directly to his Lord. **29** Every Christian is *unworthy*, but Paul defines his meaning as not *discerning* (lit. 'not distinguishing') this bread as signifying *the body . . . of the Lord*. Some think *body* here refers to the church (*cf.* 10:17), but a change of meaning from v. 27 seems unlikely. **30** Such carelessness invites *judgment*, *i.e.* not eternal damnation but divine chastisement, expressed physically in illness and death (*cf.* 5:5). **31, 32** *If we judged ourselves*, *i.e.* 'distinguished' between what we are and what we should be, there would be no need to be *judged by the Lord*; *i.e. chastened*, as children of the Father, not in the sense of being eternally *condemned along with the* unbelieving *world* (*cf.* 3:15).

33, 34 Consequently when the Corinthians meet for the Lord's Supper, they are to *wait* considerately *for one another* (*cf.* v. 21). This is a time of togetherness. If they forget the true purpose of this sacred meal (which is not for the satisfying of physical hunger), their misbehaviour will be *condemned* by God and by their fellows.

12:1-31 Gifts of the Spirit

Characteristically Paul begins his discussion of the gifts of the Holy Spirit (chs. 12–14) with a basic reminder of the Lordship of Christ. Their use must always be subject to Him; and, when exercised publicly, in a manner making for order and harmony, not confusion (14:40). Some gifts are admittedly spectacular and exciting, but they are less important than the outworking of divine love (ch. 13) in Christian character (*cf.* Gal. 5:22f.).

1, 2 The Corinthians knew from pre-Christian experience the dangers of being *led astray* ('carried away'), *i.e.* under undesirable and unprofitable constraint. *Dumb idols* (Ps. 115:4–8), unable to reveal spiritual truth (Hab. 2:19). Paul accepts that the Corinthians were *moved*. Behind lifeless idols were evil spirits (*cf.* 10:20); they were still active. **3** Hence the blasphemous cry *Jesus be cursed!*—perhaps an ecstatic utterance by an uninstructed worshipper who had misunderstood teaching about Christ being made 'a curse' (Gal. 3:13). *Cursed* (*cf.* 16:22; Gk. *anathema*, meaning 'devoted' like Jericho was, set apart for destruction (Jos. 6:17). *The Spirit of God* bears witness to the Lordship of Christ. He alone can or will do this (*cf.* 1 Jn. 4:1–3).

4–6 Competition among the Corinthians over the use of the gifts had split the church. This was a false rivalry, for Christians differ in their gifts, in opportunities for service, and in the way God's power is applied through them. But behind all the variety is the one unifying author, *God* Himself. The doctrine of the Trinity is unconsciously but clearly expressed in these verses. **7** Gifts were not for private individual enrichment nor for rivalry and jealousy, but for the benefit of all.

Paul lists nine gifts. **8** *The utterance* (lit. 'a word') of *wisdom* (*cf.* 2:6–10). What is divinely imparted is the power of communicating to others. Paul associates *knowledge* with mysteries, revelations, and prophecy (13:2; 14:6), and it evidently means knowledge supernaturally given

(*cf.* that of Peter in Acts 5:3). **9** *Faith* (*cf.* 13:2) is distinct from saving faith, though that too is divinely given (Eph. 2:8). George Müller is a modern example of one with the special gift of faith. *Gifts of healing* (lit. 'healings'); the plurals suggest different gifts for different diseases. **10** *The working* (Gk. plural) *of miracles* (Gal. 3:5; Heb. 2:4) is distinguished from acts of healing (*cf.* Mk. 16:17f.; Acts 5:5, 10; 13:11). *Prophecy* in Scripture includes foretelling future events (Acts 11:27f.; 21:10), but more often refers to 'forthtelling' God's message in inspired words (*cf.* Lk. 1:67ff.; Acts 19:6; 21:9). Some thus outstandingly gifted were recognized as 'prophets' (1 Cor. 12:28f.). *The ability to distinguish between spirits*, good and evil, was specially needed in the palpable paganism of Paul's day. But the battle still continues (Eph. 6:12; 2 Thes. 2:2). 1 Jn. 4:1 suggests a more general ability bestowed upon all Christians (as with 'faith', v. 9). *Various kinds of tongues* (*cf.* 14:1f.); *i.e.* ecstatic speech in languages usually unknown (14:9; *cf.* Acts 2:6), apart from the gift of *interpretation* (14:13). **11** *All these* gifts have one Author and Distributor, the *Spirit*, who acts not as men may demand (though *cf.* v. 31) but *as he wills* (Heb. 2:4), words which imply the personality of the Spirit as having a mind of His own.

12 The functioning of the physical *body* provides an appropriate analogy of variety in unity within the church, the body of *Christ* (v. 27). **13** *We were all baptized*. The rite of baptism is one and the same for all professing Christians, from whatever cultural background (Col. 3:10f.). The common application of water externally symbolizes the converts' vital incorporation by the Holy Spirit into the living unity of the body of Christ. The Spirit is around us (the figure of immersion in water) and within us (the figure of drinking). All Christians have been 'saturated with one Spirit' (Goodspeed).

14 The very idea of a *body* implies *many* members which are complementary and interdependent. Perhaps some Corinthians felt second class, because they lacked spectacular gifts possessed by others. **15, 16** *Foot* is contrasted with *hand*, not with *eye*, 'because we are wont to envy not those who are very far above us, but those who are a little higher' (Chrysostom). A 'foot' bearing the weight of the body might easily envy a 'hand' swinging free and unencumbered. *I do not belong.* A Christian lacking, say, the gift of tongues is not *any less a part of the body* of Christ. **17, 18** A body needs many components to carry out its varied functions. God in His wisdom provides them all and fits and places them for their own tasks. The emphasis is on God's plan, choice, and appointment. **19** If all organs were alike, the result would be 'a creature with only one sense organ, such as is found in the lowest forms of animal life' (Godet). **20** Others in Corinth evidently considered that they alone were capable, and wanted to do everything. But all the different parts of a body need one another. 21 For example, *the eye*, though naturally placed 'above' *the hand*, cannot do without it. Boasting is quite inappropriate. 22 Moreover, what in one way are *weaker* parts. *e.g.* the eyes, are in fact indispensable. 23 *Less honourable*. Far from despising the humbler members of the church, they should be given special consideration. 24, 25 God has so arranged the interrelation of organs within the human body that they operate not only without conflict but also in positive co-operation and interdependence. 26 In so far as the Christian church is functioning properly as a body, all its members will feel involved in the misfortune or prosperity of fellow-Christians, with sympathy but without envy.

27 Paul's simile of the body applies directly to the local church in Corinth, for in *Christ* they constitute a *body*—His body—in which they are *individually members*, each with a responsible part to play. 28 *God has appointed in the church*; *i.e.* He has chosen their character and given them their place to further His own purpose (Eph. 4:11f.). *Apostles* had a unique primary ministry as custodians of the authentic gospel (Eph. 2:20). *Prophets* were particularly needed until the NT was written and in general circulation. The fact that some may render a primary or more fundamental service does not make them lords over God's heritage. Their function is ministerial, not magisterial. Then follow lesser necessary but complementary ministries. The gift of *tongues*, excessively prized by the Corinthians, is twice placed last (vv. 28, 30), after the more prosaic yet necessary *helpers* and *administrators* (*cf.* Rom. 12:6–8; Eph. 4:11f.). 29, 30 *Are all apostles? . . . prophets? . . . teachers?* These questions, all expecting the answer 'No', emphasize once more diversity and interdependence. 'God did not want any one to be self-sufficient. He so arranged things that all the brethren should need each other' (Godet). 31 *The higher gifts* are to be sought by prayer and self-preparation (14:1). But there is *a still more excellent way* of service, the way of love (ch. 13). 'A little love is worth more than any amount of eloquence, learning, or ecstasy' (G. Deluz, *A Companion to 1 Corinthians*, ET 1963).

13:1–13 Divine love

This famous hymn in praise of love is 'the greatest, strongest, deepest thing Paul ever wrote' (Harnack). It has a literary and rhythmic beauty. *Agapē* was rare in Greek before Christians made it their characteristic word for 'love'. The usual terms; *erōs* (sexual love) and *philia* (a more general term meaning affection) are essentially 'love of the deserving', coupled with the desire to possess. By contrast, *agapē* is 'love of the undeserving', love which gives. Its classical expression is in Rom. 5:8: 'God shows his love for us in that while we were yet sinners Christ died for us.' Paul's exposition is in three parts: vv. 1–3, the futility (for their possessor) of spiritual gifts without love; vv. 4–7, love's

characteristics (an incidental portrait of Christ); vv. 8–13, love's permanence.

1 By *tongues* Paul doubtless means the gift (*cf.* 12:10; 14:18); but human eloquence, however 'angelic', is likewise censured as mere noise, disturbing and unhelpful, if it lacks love. The *noisy gong* and *clanging cymbal* were familiar in Corinthian temples to Dionysus and Cybele. 2 Similarly, one who possesses *prophetic powers* (*cf.* 14:3), however important (12:28) or desirable (14:39), and understands *all mysteries* (see on 2:7) and *all knowledge* (12:8; *cf.* 8:1f.), and has the special gift of wonder-working *faith* (12:9; *cf.* Mt. 17:20), yet lacks love—is himself valueless for all his valuable gifts. 3 The rashest philanthropy or the most painful self-immolation without the love-motive, gains no credit at the judgment, whatever material benefits others may reap.

The moral excellences named as love's virtues (vv. 4–7) are aimed at the special faults exhibited by the Corinthians. 4 They include being *patient*, passively 'long-tempered' with people, and *kind*, actively generous and helpful. Eight negatives follow. *Love is not jealous* at the success, or because of the gifts, of others (12:26; *cf.* 3:3); not *boastful*, a 'wind-bag' (*cf.* Mt. 26:33 with Jn. 21:17), ostentatious, out for applause. 5 Love is *not arrogant* (*cf.* 4:6; 8:1), inflated with empty conceit; *or rude* ('not behaving properly' in 7:36). 'Love does nothing to raise a blush.' Love is not out for *its own way*, not self-seeking (*cf.* 11:21), but disinterested (10:33). It is *not irritable*, touchy, ready to take offence. It is not *resentful*; literally 'it reckons (accountancy term) not the evil thing', *i.e.* it keeps no register of wrongs, and so harbours no resentment. 6 *Love does not rejoice* in the opportunity to censure *wrong*; or, 'cannot share in the glee of the successful transgressor'. *But* 'joins in rejoicing' (a stronger expression) *in the right*, literally 'truth' (1 Jn. 1:6). 7 Positively, love *bears*, *i.e.* either covers (1 Pet. 4:8), or endures (1 Thes. 3:1, 5), *all things*. Love credits others with good intentions; or, 'never loses faith' (Barrett). Love *hopes*, not with unreasoning optimism, but in expecting ultimate triumph by the grace of God. Love *endures*, *i.e.* in an active positive sense. 'When love has no evidence, it believes the best. When the evidence is adverse, it hopes for the best. And when hopes are repeatedly disappointed, it still courageously waits' (Robertson and Plummer). Come what may it is undismayed.

8, 9 Love *never ends*, literally 'never collapses'. It is eternal by nature (1 Jn. 4:16), unlike the gifts, which are designed for the present life. *Prophecy* and *tongues* (see on 12:10) will be unnecessary in the immediate presence of God. *Knowledge*, human and divinely revealed (*cf.* 12:8), will be superseded by fuller light and understanding. 10 *When the perfect comes*: not perfection in quality so much as totality; *i.e.* full knowledge about God. *The imperfect*, the partial (*cf.* Je. 31:34), that which is characteristic of our present experience. 11 Childish reckoning and speaking are naturally replaced with maturity. But Paul says he *gave up* childish ways, *i.e.* he determined no longer to be governed by childish attitudes. By overstressing tongues and undervaluing love the Corinthians were displaying immaturity. **12** Our present understanding is like peering into a primitive metal *mirror* with its imperfect reflection (*cf.* 2 Cor. 5:7). *But then*, in the next life, we shall see *face to face* (*cf.* 1 Jn. 3:2). Similarly with *knowledge*: partial *now*, perfect *then*—even as God's knowledge of each Christian is perfect already. **13** *Faith*, trustful acceptance of God as He is, *hope*, 'perseverance in faith' (Calvin), and *love*, are eternal, as present gifts of the Spirit are not. *Abide* is singular and suggests *these three* graces form a unity (*cf.* Col. 1:4, 5; 1 Thes. 1:3). Only the final *agapē* in v. 13 has the definite article; greatest is the Greek comparative (normally taken as superlative). R. P. Martin (*1 Corinthians–Galatians*, Scripture Union Bible Study Books, 1968) therefore suggests: 'Faith, hope, love abide—the well-known trio; but greater than these is the love (of God)' shed in our hearts (Rom. 5:5).

14:1-40 The gifts of prophecy and tongues

1 Paul now resumes (from 12:31) his discussion of the gifts of the Spirit. Assuming that the Corinthians now appreciate the supreme importance of *love*, they are to go on to seek the very best God offers. While acknowledging the Spirit's sovereign will in distributing His *gifts* (12:11), the Corinthians should *earnestly desire* to receive them—particularly the higher gifts (12:31) and most of all prophecy. **2** *A tongue* is ecstatic speaking in a language usually unintelligible to speaker and hearer (see on 12:10). Some consider the gift in Acts 2:6f. is different, since some or other of those present did understand what was said. But in both cases *God* not man is primarily addressed (Acts 2:4, 11). *Mysteries, i.e.* things not understood by unaided human reason. *In the Spirit, i.e.* through the gift bestowed by the Holy Spirit. Or the reference may be to the man's own spirit, *i.e.* he is not using his mind. **3** The gift of prophecy (see on 12:10) builds up believers in their faith by giving *encouragement, i.e.* counsel to the mind, and *consolation, i.e.* comfort to the heart. **4** Tongues are for the personal blessing of the speaker. He is edified, not indeed in his understanding (*cf.* v. 14), but by what has been called 'the glow of soul associated with the exercise of the gift' (*cf.* Acts 2:13). By contrast, prophecy benefits not simply the speaker but *the church, i.e.* the assembled congregation (*cf.* v. 19; 11:18; 14:23). **5** Paul encourages the proper use of tongues for personal edification through the worship of God (*cf.* v. 28). Tongues may not be used in public services unless another believer present has the gift of interpretation. *He who prophesies is greater, i.e.* as a better servant (Mt. 20:26) he has something more to offer the church than merely his own spiritual advancement.

6 *Revelation* is the source of *prophecy* (*cf.*

vv. 29–31). *Knowledge* (see on 12:8) is the source of *teaching*. **7, 8** Paul illustrates the need for 'tongues' in public to be interpreted. A melody cannot be recognized if the notes are indistinct. An army is baffled if *the bugle* calls uncertainly (*cf.* Nu. 10:9). **9** *So with yourselves* (pronoun emphatic). Intelligible communication is vital, however highly the Corinthians may prize the gift of 'tongues'. **10, 11** The languages of the world all have *meaning*, for their whole purpose is for intelligent communication. But if the language is not understood, speaker and listener are foreigners to each other. *Foreigner* is Greek *barbaros*, 'barbarian', one whose speech sounds like 'bar-bar' to another, *i.e.* makes no sense. **12** The Corinthians are rightly *eager for manifestations of the Spirit* through His gifts, for these demonstrate the presence and activity of God. But only some gifts are valuable *in building up the church* in worship and service. These are the gifts to seek, for the motive must be the general benefit of the church (12:7), not unspiritual self-gratification.

13 *Therefore*, for the good of the church, the further gift of interpretation should be sought to widen the usefulness of 'tongues'. Spiritual gifts additional to those received on any one occasion are thus obtainable. **14, 15** The gift of interpretation also benefits the one who speaks in a tongue. Without it his *mind* lacks understanding, and thus remains *unfruitful, i.e.* produces and contributes nothing. Worship must be intelligent as well as fervent. **16, 17** *With the spirit* (only), *i.e.* without the mind, and so unintelligibly. *Outsider* (*cf.* vv. 23, 24); *idiotēs* was used in some religious associations for 'non-members who may participate'. Note that apparently such interested enquirers had a recognized 'place' in the Christian community. Where 'tongues' are concerned Paul implies that even committed Christians, if lacking the gifts, might feel themselves in the position of 'outsiders'. *Amen*; from Hebrew 'to confirm'. Christians followed Jewish practice in adding *Amen* to make a prayer their own (Ne. 8:6). **18** Paul is not without experience of *tongues*. Perhaps this was not generally known because he exercised the gift in private. **19** *In church, i.e.* wherever Christians gather for worship, *five* understandable *words* addressed to men edify far more than a torrent in 'tongues' addressed to God.

20 The spectacular nature of 'tongues' appealed to the Corinthians, but Paul gently implies that their attitude is childish. **21, 22** 'Tongues' can have another purpose, besides blessing the user in private or, in conjunction with the gift of interpretation, believers in general. *The law* (here, Scripture generally—as, *e.g.*, Rom. 3:19— not the Pentateuch only) shows that 'tongues' have significance for *unbelievers* too, in their case as a sign of judgment (*cf.* Heb. 4:2). Paul's quotation is freely taken from Is. 28:11f. Israel has spurned the prophet's message as fit only for children. Since God's people refuse to listen in obedience and faith to His plain word, they will hear words they cannot understand, *i.e.* be punished by exile among *men of strange tongues*, the Assyrians, and be hardened in their unbelief (Is. 6:9f.). **23** Paul evidently has this last point particularly in mind. The use of 'tongues' in a public service could well confirm non-Christian visitors in their unbelief, instead of persuading them of the reality of Christianity. The use of 'tongues' in a gathering of believers is, therefore, inappropriate. *Outsiders* (see on v. 16) *or unbelievers*; *i.e.* interested non-Christians attending the service out of curiosity or spiritual concern. **24, 25** *If all prophesy.* In church the thing that should make non-members conscious of God's presence and bring them under deep inner conviction is the prophetic word given by the Holy Spirit (*cf.* Acts 5:3f.)—not sensational 'tongues', or liturgical ritual, or even elaborate visual aids!

26–33 reveal some of the activities in an early church service. Note their varied and spontaneous character. **26** Paul's list suggests the eagerness of *each one* to use his gift in public worship. Any member present might take part. *A hymn* (*cf.* v. 15; Eph. 5:19) might be one composed by a member. *A lesson*, literally 'teaching', would be some exposition of a text from the OT, following Jewish custom, rather than just a reading from Scripture (*cf.* Col. 3:16). Prophesying is omitted, but is perhaps the same as *a revelation*. The overriding principle controlling the use of the manifestations of the Spirit in public worship is again stressed: the edification of all present. **27** *In turn*; literally 'by shares', *i.e.* sharing the time. The exercise of the gift is under the control of the speaker's will, even if the language is not understood by the mind. **28** 'Tongues' may be used publicly only if someone present can *interpret*. **29, 30** The use of prophecy is qualified. Messages through this medium are not to be accepted uncritically, but tested against Scripture (*cf.* 1 Thes. 5:21), *e.g.* to ensure that the source is divine and not Satanic (*cf.* 12:10; Dt. 18:22; 1 Jn. 4:1). **31** Despite the limitations imposed by Paul, *all* who *can prophesy* will have an opportunity to use their gift at some time so that all the church may benefit fully from this ministry of the Holy Spirit. **32** Just as those who speak in tongues are able to keep silence if necessary (v. 28), so prophesying is under the control of the one possessing that ability. **33** *God* is the source and inspiration behind all these gifts, and so any *confusion* or lack of self-control occurring in church services cannot be according to His will or due to His Spirit.

34, 35 Paul's famous instruction that *women should keep silence in the churches* and *not . . . speak* is still much misunderstood by being divorced from its local and contemporary context. Paul has earlier discussed what is meant by the *subordinate* status of women (see on 11:3, 11). He is keenly aware of the need for emancipated Christian women to avoid unnecessary scandal through flouting the social conventions of the day. Women had to be wise in using their newly-given liberty in Christ. Paul is here protesting against the disturbance of services by feminine chatter—the meaning of *speak* in vv. 34, 35. Some women (they sat apart from men) were perhaps calling out questions, and commenting knowingly on things said in the service. Paul did not condemn women to complete silence in church for he mentions some able to prophesy (11:5; *cf.* Acts 21:9), and this was a gift exercised in public. Paul's injunction also has positive value. A woman's femininity and so her influence (*cf.* 1 Pet. 3:2) are alike enhanced by the practice of silence. Men too are told to be silent on occasions (vv. 28, 30). Only in quietness could the word of God be heard and absorbed.

36 Paul ironically enquires if the Corinthians alone possess *the word of God* and know proper Christian practice. Due weight must be given to the experience of *all the churches of the saints* (*cf.* v. 33). **37** Anyone claiming to be *a prophet, or spiritual*, *i.e.* in tune with the Lord's mind, should be the first to recognize the correctness of what Paul has been expounding. **38** If such a man *does not recognize* divine truth when he hears it, *he* himself *is not recognized* as authoritative (*cf.* 11:16), either by God or by the other churches; *i.e.* he stands self-condemned. **39** Paul's conclusion is positive. The gift of prophecy is to be sought eagerly; 'tongues', with due safeguards, are to continue. These are God's good gifts. **40** *All things* in public worship should be carried on in a manner which is (lit.) 'well formed', *i.e.* with beauty and harmony, and *in order*, a military metaphor (*cf.* v. 33).

15:1–58 THE RESURRECTION

15:1–11 The resurrection of Christ

The last major subject Paul discusses is doctrinal and fundamental to Christianity. To deny the resurrection of the dead (15:12) is to evacuate the gospel of all its worth. So Paul restates the essentials of the gospel. He shows how the truth of the resurrection of Christ is an assured part of it (vv. 1–11), and that it implies the resurrection of Christians (vv. 12–34). Finally certain difficulties raised against the doctrine are resolved (vv. 35–58).

1, 2 Paul feels it necessary to *remind* them of the essentials of *the gospel* itself—the truth which was the subject of his preaching and the sole grounds of their salvation as Christians. The need to do this makes him question whether they have forgotten it or never really embraced it. Note the measure of implied rebuke and the radical character of the apostle's concern. **3, 4** This is a very early summary of the preaching and shows a tendency to set it forth in brief credal form (note the fourfold *that* in vv. 3–5; also the vocabulary is not Paul's usual style). Far from being ideas of human origin, they are objective facts concerning God's Christ which were long ago divinely anticipated and have recently been historically fulfilled. Here is what happened—death, burial, resurrection; and why —*for our sins*. That *he was buried* and did not rise till *the third day* emphasizes the reality of Christ's death and excludes the possibility of swooning. The repeated phrase *in accordance with the scriptures* draws attention to the further divinely inspired witness provided by written prophecies. In v. 4 the phrase probably applies to the fact of Christ's resurrection (*cf.* Is. 53:10–12; and Ps. 16:10 was often used in early preaching) rather than *on the third day*, for which only Jon. 1:17 and Ho. 6:2 can be cited (*cf.* Lk. 24:46). **5** This list of appearances by the risen Lord is selective; *e.g.* no women are included. This also suggests a tendency towards a recognized and widely used (official) list of divinely chosen witnesses. The appearances to *Cephas* (*cf.* 1:12; 9:5) and to *the twelve* (a nominal, and official, title—Judas and Thomas were missing) are recorded in Lk. 24:34–36. **6** The *five hundred brethren* may be linked with Mt. 28:10, 16ff. Most of them were still alive when Paul wrote: their testimony could still be verified by doubters. Note too how the death of Christians is described as sleep (*cf.* 1 Thes. 4:14). **7** *James* is probably the Lord's brother, an unbeliever during Jesus' ministry (Jn. 7:5), but converted soon after the resurrection (Acts 1:14), and later a pillar of the Jerusalem church (Gal. 2:9). The assured truth of Christ's resurrection is the firm and essential basis for Paul's classic exposition of the doctrine of the resurrection in this chapter.

8, 9 *Last of all* in the series of the resurrection appearances, which otherwise ceased at the ascension, came that to Paul himself on the Damascus road (Acts 9), *as to one untimely born. Ektrōma* is not a 'late birth' as the context might suggest, but the opposite, an 'abortion' (NEB, 'monstrosity'). The expression refers not to the timing of Paul's conversion, but either to the sudden intervention by which he was torn from opposition to become an apostle or to his sense of utter unworthiness—'as unworthy *to be called an apostle* as an abortion is to be considered a man'. Though Paul here describes himself as *the least of the apostles*, he is not suggesting his ministry is inferior to that of others (*cf.* 2 Cor. 11:5; Gal. 2:11), for he has actually laboured more abundantly; but because he had *persecuted the church of God* (Acts 26:9f.; Gal. 1:13) he was not fit to be an apostle at all (1 Tim. 1:15). **10** He owes everything solely to *the grace of God*—his life as a Christian, his apostolic ministry, and the way he has been enabled to persevere in the work. All this too is evidence that Christ is risen indeed. **11** *So we preach.* This gospel thus authenticated continues without variation to be preached by all the apostles, including Paul. It is the one and only foundation of the decisive self-committal of faith.

15:12–34 The resurrection of Christians

In vv. 12–19 Paul indicates the fatal consequences for Christian believers of denying all possibility of resurrection; viz. it makes apostolic preaching a lie, and faith a delusion; dead Christians are lost, living Christians pitiable in the extreme.

12 Some Corinthians were still maintaining Greek ideas about the immortality of the soul, *i.e.* that after death the soul escaped from the body, to be absorbed into the divine or to continue a shadowy existence in the underworld. To Greeks physical resurrection was impossible (*cf.* Acts 17:18f., 32). **13, 14** But to accept this would rule out Christ's resurrection and destroy the whole foundation of Christian *preaching*; any so-called *faith* in Christ would then be *vain, i.e.* empty of meaning or practical effect since He is not alive to save. **15** Also it would mean that the apostles have been *found* ('caught out') deliberately lying about their supposed good news. **16, 17** If this is so, then the redemptive work of Christ lacks vital proof, and anyone's claim to know forgiveness is mere self-deception. **18** There is no hope either of further life for Christians who have died (*cf.* Rom. 6:1–11). **19** *If in this life* Christians have only 'hope' and no 'next life' to follow, all their purposeless struggling makes them supreme objects of pity for being deluded. Another reading (RSV mg.) applies the *only* to *this life*: 'If Christianity means simply hoping in Christ in this life, that and nothing beside. . .'.

20–28 Here over against the negative consequences of denial are the positive consequences flowing from Christ's resurrection. **20** *But in fact*, overthrowing the six hypothetical 'ifs' just listed, *Christ has been raised* (perfect tense: a past event with continuing consequences), never to die again. So faith is established, forgiveness a genuine experience, and the after-life for Christians assured (*cf.* Heb. 6:19f.). *First fruits* implies community of nature with the 'harvest' to follow; *i.e.* Christ's resurrection promises the ultimate home-gathering of all God's people. The full harvest was foreshadowed and consecrated by the first sheaf brought as an offering on the day following the sabbath after the Passover (Lv. 23:10f.), *i.e.* on Easter Day, the day of Christ's resurrection. Death with its sting gone (v. 55) is for Christians no more than falling *asleep.* **21, 22** It is *in Adam* as the representative man or federal head that all die; it is *in Christ* as Himself truly man that all Christians are resurrected (*cf.* Rom. 5:18f.; see further on vv. 45–49). (Note that Paul treats Adam as an historical figure; *cf.* Rom. 5:12.) Physical and spiritual *death* entered the world through Adam's sin (Gn. 2:17). *All* men, as members of the human race, inherit the inclination to sin, and thereby the penalty of sin, death. The second *all* in v. 22 is limited by v. 23 to *those who belong to Christ* (*cf.* 1 Thes. 4:16); a universal resurrection (including that of unbelievers) is not here in view (*cf.* Dn. 12:2). *Be made alive* suggests not simply physical resurrection but abundant spiritual life (*cf.* Jn. 10:10).

23 *Each in his own order*; a military metaphor. The resurrection was begun, not completed, when Christ was raised (*cf.* 2 Tim. 2:18); that of believers will follow (*cf.* vv. 51–53; 1 Thes. 4:15f.). *At his coming*; Greek *parousia* (commonly in the papyri of a royal visit), used by Christians as a technical term for the Lord's return. **24** *Then*; how soon is not indicated. Paul means when these things happen; *i.e.* the *parousia* of Christ and the resurrection of Christians will usher in *the end*, viz. the climax of the ages. When Christ thus returns to assert His full and direct authority (2 Thes. 1:7f.) every rival power will be destroyed ('rendered inoperative'). With His commission fulfilled (Mt. 28:18) Christ then *delivers* His authority back *to God the Father*. *The kingdom*; *i.e.* not territory but 'kingly power' (see Lk. 19:12; *cf.* RSV with AV). **25** *He must reign.* Christ is exercising kingly rule now—before the end—but not till every rival power has been put down will the end come. God has already promised to His Christ the final and complete overthrow of opposing powers. *Under his feet* alludes to the promise in Ps. 110:1, the verse most quoted in the NT. **26** *Death* is personified (*cf.* Is. 25:8). It was defeated by Christ's resurrection (*cf.* 2 Tim. 1:10); and, although still at work in the world, at His return it will openly be *destroyed* (*cf.* Rev. 20:14), *i.e.* 'robbed of all power' (as v. 24), when all its captives are raised. **27** Ps. 8:6ff., which speaks of the subjection of all things to man, is fulfilled in the representative Man, Jesus Christ (*cf.* Heb. 2:6–9). **28** Christ's total triumph is in no sense in competition with the Father's rule, to which the Son Himself is *subjected*, *i.e.* is obedient (*cf.* Jn. 6:38; Heb. 10:7). The goal is that *God may be everything to every one* (*cf.* Rom. 11:36). This does not mean loss of all distinction by absorption into God, but the perfectly acknowledged rule of the God of love over all His creatures. It is noteworthy (in contrast to some prophetic interpretations that Christ is coming to reign and that this reign will follow the *parousia*) that here Christ's special exercise of sovereignty ends with the overthrow of the last enemy, and He can report to His Father that His work is complete (*cf.* Mt. 13:41, 'his kingdom'; 13:43, 'the kingdom of their Father').

29 *Baptized on behalf of the dead* is possibly proxy-baptism on behalf of friends who had died unbaptized. The Greek can also mean 'baptized because of the dead', *i.e.* the reference is to the baptism of those influenced by the testimony of a Christian who had recently died, and in the hope of being re-united with him at the resurrection. In either case, if death is the end the future is hopeless. **30** Similarly, Paul's mortal risks would be foolhardy and pointless (*cf.* 4:9; 2 Cor. 11:23f.). **31** *My pride in you* (*cf.* Phil. 4:1). The winning of the Corinthians from the pagan world is worth many deaths. **32** Paul's fighting *with beasts at Ephesus* is evidently metaphorical (sentence to the arena involved loss of citizenship—which Paul still retained in Acts 22:25). The occasion was one of intense peril (*cf.* 2 Cor.

1:8f.). *Let us eat* . . . ; from Is. 22:13. **33** *Bad company* . . . ; a proverb found in Menander's lost comedy *Thais*. The Corinthians will ruin their Christian lives by mixing with those who live merely for selfish pleasures because they deny any resurrection or final judgment. **34** *Come to your right mind*; 'wake up properly from your drunken stupor'. 'Some of you claim to be agnostics. But ignorance of God while natural to pagans is shameful to Christians.'

15:35–58 The nature of the resurrection body

35 *With what kind of body do they come?*; *i.e.* out of graves. Greeks thought only of soul-survival and denied any resurrection of the physical body. Consequently some Corinthian believers assumed that Christianity taught that corpses were resuscitated, and resurrection-life was simply a prolongation of material existence. Paul takes up two points. **36** First, how can death give rise to life? The seed analogy indicates that death can be necessary to perpetuate life (*cf.* Jn. 12:24). Note how Paul appeals here to their individual experience and exposes their lack of sense and observation. **37** Secondly, what is the nature of the resurrection body? It is intimately linked with the old but not identical with it. **38** *God gives.* The new life is not automatic but dependent upon the predetermined will and the creative act of God. **39–41** *Not all flesh is alike.* Different forms of existence imply different spheres and modes of operation, for which each form is suited by the Creator; and there is obviously very great variety in such differentiation.

42 *So it is.* The Christian's resurrection body will be fitted to its radically new sphere (*cf.* 2 Cor. 5:1–4). *Resurrection* means re-appearance or restoration to function in a new form (Phil. 3:21), and Paul describes this in a series of couplets. *What is sown* can apply both to the body during life and to its lying in the grave. *Perishable*; subject to decay. This basic fact was why Greeks objected to any doctrine of resurrection. **43** *Dishonour* (Gk. *atimia*, 'without rights of citizenship'), and *weakness* (*cf.* 2 Cor. 13:4), *i.e.* powerlessness (*cf.* Ps. 115:17; Is. 14:10) are both characteristic of a corpse. **44** *If there is*; *i.e.* 'since there is'. *Physical body*; *i.e.* subject to the conditions of natural life; literally 'psychic', formed to be the organ of the *psychē*, 'soul'. *Spiritual body*; *i.e.* controlled by man's spirit in perfect harmony with the Spirit of God. *Physical* and *spiritual* indicate the spheres or forms of existence for which the bodies respectively are fitted. **45, 46** Further support is found in Gn. 2:7. *A living being.* Man is distinct by being made 'a living soul' (AV). It is characteristic of man in his present form of existence that he has a soul-governed body. *The last Adam*; *i.e.* Christ, the progenitor of the new race of redeemed men. He is their *life-giving spirit* (*cf.* Jn. 6:63). It will be characteristic of the life to be that we shall have a spirit-controlled body. **47** *Man of dust* again alludes to Gn. 2:7. *Of dust* implies liable to decay and dissolution. *From heaven* means of a higher, imperishable order. Christ is 'from heaven', originally as God become man, and eschatologically in the glory of His resurrection body. **48, 49** *Who are of the dust.* All men share in the corruption which is characteristic of the human race. Christians because of their relation to, and new life in, Christ are already 'of heaven'. This holds the promise of ultimate bodily likeness to *the man of heaven* (1 Jn. 3:2). *We shall . . . bear.* The Greek can mean 'wear' (*cf.* 2 Cor. 5:3). **50** *Flesh and blood*; *i.e.* man's present kind of mortal physical body. Paul is contradicting crude notions of physical resurrection (see on v. 35). A new type of body is needed for the new conditions of the next life.

51 *Mystery*; a divine secret now revealed to Paul to declare (*cf.* 1 Thes. 4:15). On Christ's return the bodies of Christians still living on earth will be transformed without experiencing death (Phil. 3:21). Dead Christians will be raised and given new bodies. **52** *In a moment*; instantaneously. *The last trumpet* (*cf.* Mt. 24:31; 1 Thes. 4:16); not the *last* of a series (as in Rev. 8:2) but the call announcing 'the end' (v. 24). The *trumpet* sometimes accompanies divine interventions in history (*e.g.* Ex. 19:16). **53** *Must put on*, as clothes; *cf.* 2 Cor. 5:1-4. **54-56** *Death is swallowed up . . .* (*cf.* v. 26); a free quotation from Is. 25:8, folowed by one from Ho. 13:14. Paul speaks of the ultimate destruction of death. At present death is still operative; it retains its *sting*, *i.e.* sin, which gives death its power of wounding mortally. Death follows sin not simply as a biological but as a moral consequence. Paul frequently connects *sin*, *law*, and *death*, though he does not develop the theme here (see, *e.g.*, Rom. 5:13; 7:7-25). **57** *Who gives us.* The believers' sharing in the fruits of Christ's triumph is so certain that Paul can use the present tense. The sting of death is sin, and so *victory* over death is forgiveness and participation in resurrection life. Note the full title: *our Lord Jesus Christ*, emphasizing the majesty of His Person. **58** *Therefore* (as a consequence now comes the practical application) *be steadfast.* The Corinthians needed such exhortation because of their instability. Their *labour* ('wearisome toil'), *i.e.* in building up the church, if it is *in the Lord*, *i.e.* in His wisdom and power, cannot perish or be *in vain* ('never be thrown away', Moffatt). The firm and clear grasp of the great doctrine of the resurrection provides the motive-power for always abounding in the Lord's work.

16:1-24 OTHER BUSINESS

Characteristically Paul can now turn from the consideration of lofty themes to practical everyday matters and personal news. Saint and theologian though he is, he keeps his feet firmly on the ground when it comes to details of administration.

16:1-4 A special collection

1 *The contribution* is a gift which Paul is arranging from a number of Gentile churches to poverty-stricken Jewish Christians in Jerusalem (v. 3; Acts 11:29; Rom. 15:25). A year later Paul had to urge the Corinthians to greater efforts (2 Cor. 8, 9), but finally their contribution was completed (Acts 24:17; Rom. 15:26). Although the collection is not mentioned in our canonical letter to the Galatians (*cf.* Gal. 2:10), the Corinthians apparently heard about the proposal from the Galatian Christians. **2** *The first day* suggests that Sunday was already the day when Christians met for worship (*cf.* Acts 20:7; Rev. 1:10). In readiness for Paul's arrival *each* Christian, whatever his means, is regularly to set aside a proportion of his weekly income (2 Cor. 8:12). (Note the assumption that of course everyone will do so.) This would avoid a last-minute scramble, underline personal responsibility over a period, and probably raise far more money. **3** *When I arrive*; Greek 'whenever': Paul's plans are still uncertain. The Corinthians, however, are to select and authorize their own delegates (see 2 Cor. 3:1f., and commentary) to take the gift to Jerusalem. Paul will neither handle the money nor himself appoint their representatives. He thus wisely safeguards his position (2 Cor. 8:19-21). **4** *If it seems advisable*; *i.e.* if the sum raised warrants an apostolic escort (so Moffatt, NEB); or, if Paul's plans allow him to go.

16:5-12 Paul's plans

5 Paul now confirms his proposed visit to Corinth (4:19) after travelling through the province of Macedonia (see Introduction, 'How many letters and visits?'). *For I intend* implies that the Macedonia trip will be news to the Corinthians. **6** Paul expects to remain in Ephesus until Pentecost (May–June) and possibly to *winter* at Corinth. When the bad weather has passed and ships are able to sail again (*cf.* Acts 28:11; Tit. 3:12), the Corinthians can *speed* Paul on his *journey* (*cf.* v. 11; Rom. 15:24; 3 Jn. 6), *e.g.* assist in finding a suitable ship and travelling companions; money would not be in mind on this occasion (*cf.* v. 2; 2 Cor. 12:17). *Wherever I go.* Paul's further plans, more clearly settled later (Acts 19:22), have not been fixed at the time of writing. **7** Paul emphasizes his desire to spend a longer period with the Corinthians and not just to give them, like the Macedonian churches, a brief *passing* visit. He seeks to avoid any delay on his part being misunderstood or misrepresented as unloving or fearful (*cf.* 2 Cor. 1:15). *If the Lord permits* (*cf.* Jas. 4:15); the apostle's arrangements are always subject to his Master's overruling. **8, 9** Paul explains why he cannot come sooner. He intends to remain in Ephesus *until Pentecost* (the great festival 50 days after Passover; *cf.* 5:7; 15:20), because evangelistic opportunities are many and, as a spiritual consequence, the opposition is great (Acts 19:9, 23f.). Thus it will be a little while before he can reach Corinth. This is not to contradict the promise of 4:19 to 'come soon'. In ch. 4 Paul is rebuking those who wanted to ignore the apostle: 'Anyone would think I was never going to set foot in Corinth again; but look out! I'll be there sooner than you think' (Barrett).

10, 11 *When Timothy comes*; overland through Macedonia (4:17f.; Acts 19:22), thus taking longer than Paul's letter by sea. Timothy's unease is due perhaps to timidity—some Corinthians could be overbearing (*cf.* 2 Cor. 10:10; 11:5; 12:11). Years later his 'youthfulness' is still evident (1 Tim. 4:12). Yet Paul obviously thinks highly of him, entrusting him with personal commissions. The Corinthians are told to treat him worthily because he too is engaged in the same *work of the Lord* as Paul, in evangelism and building up the churches (*cf.* 1 Tim. 4:13). *The brethren* may include Erastus (Acts 19:22). **12** The Corinthians had apparently enquired about another visit from *Apollos* (Acts 19:1; see Introduction, 'Paul's links with Corinth'). Despite Paul's urging, Apollos perhaps decided that Christian unity at Corinth would better be served by his staying away for the present (*cf.* 1:12). No further visit is recorded, nor is Apollos mentioned in 2 Corinthians.

16:13-24 Final greetings

13, 14 *Be watchful*. Not enjoining vigilance generally, but referring to imminent eschatological events (as Mk. 13:34f.; Rev. 3:3). Christian conduct should be constantly governed by two factors: one is Christ's return, the certainty of which should encourage the Christian to be *courageous* and *strong* (*cf.* 15:58) in facing temptation, persecution, and everyday troubles. The other is Christian *love* (*cf.* 8:1; 13; 14:1).

15 *The household of Stephanas* (*cf.* 1:16) is described as *the first converts in Achaia*, the province including Corinth and Athens. Paul presumably means the first complete family, as distinct from individuals (*cf.* Acts 17:34; Rom. 16:5). 'To the apostle's mind the pledge of a future Church came not in Athens but in Corinth' (T. C. Edwards, *The First Epistle to the Corinthians*, 1885). *Devoted themselves* (lit. 'appointed themselves'); *i.e.* spontaneously on the Spirit's direct prompting, without waiting to be told by Paul or the church (*cf.* 2 Cor. 8:17). *Saints* (*cf.* 1:2); *i.e.* Christians generally, both in the local church and those visiting Corinth. **16** The spiritual calibre of *such men* as Stephanas should be recognized and their lead followed. *Labourer*; *i.e.* 'one who toils to the point of weariness' (*cf.* 1 Thes. 2:9; 1 Tim. 4:10). 'Many work, a few toil' (Edwards). **17, 18** We know nothing about *Fortunatus* and *Achaicus*. They probably brought Paul the Corinthians' letter

(see Introduction, 'How many letters and visits?') to which the present Epistle is in part a reply. Paul had been *refreshed* (*cf.* 2 Cor. 7:13) by their visit. The verb is used of 'giving rest' in Mt. 11:28 and suggests Paul's anxiety for news from Corinth. *As well as yours*. Evidently these three men were noted for their ability to encourage.

19 *The churches*. Paul writes from Ephesus (v. 8), but is in close touch with Christian groups elsewhere in the province of *Asia* (*cf.* Acts 19:10, 26). *Aquila* and his wife *Prisca* left Rome (Rom. 16:3) after the emperor Claudius' edict against Jews in AD 49. Paul met them in Corinth (Acts 18:2) and they accompanied him to Ephesus (Acts 18:18f.), where they willingly opened *their house* for *church* worship (*cf.* Rom. 16:5). They were a courageous couple (Rom. 16:4), and evidently well instructed Christians (Acts 18:26). *Hearty greetings* suggests real affection for the Corinthians, based on their common faith *in the Lord*. **20** Paul invites the Corinthians to *greet one another*, when his letter is read to the congregation, as he would have done had he been present. The contemporary practice of the *holy kiss* (of peace) would further unity among them (*cf.* 1 Pet. 5:14). So Paul is implicitly exhorting them once more to abandon their unhappy divisions.

21 *With my own hand*. Paul usually dictated his letters (*cf.* Rom. 16:22), then added a concluding word himself to show their authenticity (*cf.* 2 Thes. 3:17). **22** *Accursed*; *i.e.* by separation from God (Gk. *anathema*; *cf.* 12:3). Paul declares the final condemnation of traitors to Christ (*cf.* 1 Thes. 2:16). True devotion to Him would correct party-spirit and moral laxity in Corinth. *Our Lord, come! Maranatha*, which is Aramaic, the language of the earliest Palestinian church, here appears untranslated in the Greek text. The catchword's preservation by Greek-speaking Christians suggests its frequent use to express their eager longing for the Lord's return (*cf.* Rev. 22:20). AV divides the phrase *Maran atha*, 'Our Lord has come', *i.e.* at the incarnation. **23, 24** Paul ends with the usual prayer for *grace* (*cf.* 2 Cor. 13:14) and by sending his Christian *love to all*, including the troublers (*cf.* 2 Cor. 11:11; 12:15).

Notes. 22-24 Paul's letter would be read aloud when the Christians met for worship. NEB, following recent scholarship, arranges the closing verses as a liturgical dialogue. The characteristic notes of a communion service are sounded: fraternal love having been established (v. 20), the table is 'fenced' by the dismissal of those who are not committed believers. *Our Lord, come!* invokes the risen Lord's presence with His people at the meal. The concluding grace is pronounced, and Paul adds an affectionate greeting (Martin).

2 Corinthians

OUTLINE OF CONTENTS

For the general introduction to this Epistle see p. 1049.

COMMENTARY

Much of this letter, written some 12 months after 1 Corinthians, is intensely personal, 'a pouring out of the man himself'. Though including several doctrinal matters (*e.g.* 5:1–10 on the resurrection; chs. 8, 9 on Christian giving), the letter vividly reveals Paul's feelings—and his faith—as he faces peril and disappointment, and counters slander and disloyalty, while he carries out his commission as an apostle. Often we are puzzled by unexplained references and allusions to people and events, doubtless familiar to the Corinthians, yet tantalizingly obscure to us. But in general the letter is Paul's spirited refutation of certain sham 'apostles' who had infiltrated the Corinthian church for their own ends, and in the process were busily discrediting Paul and the true gospel he preached.

1:1 – 2:17 PAUL'S RECENT EXPERIENCES

After greeting his readers (vv. 1, 2), Paul tells how his knowledge of God has been intensely deepened (vv. 3–7) through certain recent fearful experiences (vv. 8–11).

1:1, 2 Greetings

1 Paul's greetings are never perfunctory. Al-

though his opening words are similar to those in 1 Corinthians, a year or so earlier, Paul again carefully lays down the ground of his authority. He writes as *an apostle of Jesus Christ, i.e.* as His commissioned representative. This is no self-appointment, but one made *by the will of God* (*cf.* Gal. 1:1). Though generously associating colleagues with him in his greetings, it is Paul who is the *apostle*, while Sosthenes (1 Cor. 1:1) and *Timothy* are each simply described as a *brother*, a fellow-believer. **2** *Grace . . . peace* could suggest a Christian linking of the common Greek and Jewish greetings. More probably the words reflect the ancient Aaronic blessing (Nu. 6:24f.).

1:3–7 The value of suffering

3 Paul at once praises God for His great mercies. Being brought through the desperate situation mentioned in vv. 8, 9 has deeply enriched his understanding of God's character. God is *the Father of mercies, i.e.* the most merciful Father, one whose outstanding characteristic is mercy (Ps. 86:5, 15; Mi. 7:18), and *God of all comfort, i.e.* encouragement and cheer. **4, 5** Through unusually severe trouble Paul had had a profound experience of divine comfort. He describes his afflictions as a sharing of *Christ's suffering*. While the latter are unique (2 Cor. 5:14f.; *cf.* 1 Cor. 1:13), possibly Paul's were too. At his conversion he was warned of the sufferings he would face as the apostle to the Gentiles (Acts 9:15, 16; Col. 1:24). Paul's *as . . . so* clause indicates that he means only sufferings which Christians endure in virtue of their union with Christ (*cf.* 2 Cor. 4:10), and not those due to their own sin. The same union explains why we can *share abundantly in comfort too*. 6 The apostle's sufferings and comfort would doubly benefit the Corinthians. First, Paul himself was now better fitted to serve them, for experiences which come to a Christian are not for the individual alone but also for the profit of others (v. 4). 7 Secondly, the Corinthians too could learn to draw from the same source of comfort. This is one practical illustration of what is meant by the communion (*koinōnia*, 'fellowship', 'sharing') of the saints. Christians should thus encourage one another.

1:8–11 Paul's providential deliverance

8, 9 Paul explains why he feels so moved about divine comfort. In Asia Minor he had been in such desperate straits that even he had decided his end had come; and the apostle was no stranger to perils (*cf.* 2 Cor. 11:23–27). His unexpected deliverance was to him virtually a resurrection (*cf.* 4:10f.; Eph. 1:19f.). **10, 11** But all danger was still not over, and so he asks the Corinthians to help by praying. When those prayers are answered, they will be able to share in the thanksgiving (*cf.* 4:15; 9:11). Thus in Christian fellowship God can use us to involve and enrich one another, to His own greater glory.

Note. **10** *So deadly a peril* (lit. 'so great a death') is not defined. It happened after the First Letter was written (v. 8 indicates that the 'peril' was news to the Corinthians), which excludes whatever is meant by 'fighting with beasts' at Ephesus (1 Cor. 15:32). Nor does Acts 19:23–41 seem to provide an answer, for the riot at Ephesus did not apparently involve Paul in direct personal danger. The 'peril' could have been a desperate illness, but more probably it refers to mobviolence or the near-success of some plot against him (*cf.* 1 Cor. 16:9).

1:12 – 2:17 Why his plans were changed

1:12–18 evidently reflects allegations being made in Corinth against Paul because a promised visit had been postponed. The real reason for the changed plan (1:23) was to avoid 'another painful visit' (2:1). At the centre of the trouble then was some prominent antagonist of Paul's (2:5–11). A sharp letter (2:9; *cf.* 7:8) from the apostle had brought the man to repentance and Paul assures the Corinthians of his forgiveness. The section concludes (2:12–17) with reference to Paul's activities after the Ephesus riot (Acts 19; 20:1) and to the effect of the gospel.

12 Paul claims their sympathetic prayers with a clear conscience, for with God's help his conduct in Corinth before pagan and Christian alike had been irreproachable. **13** It is the same straightforward Paul who now writes. He is not a man who speaks or writes one thing while meaning another, as some in Corinth were apparently alleging. **14** When everything was finally revealed *on the day of the Lord Jesus*, i.e. when He appears as Judge, both Paul and the Corinthians would rejoice to discover how much each had in fact profited the other (*cf.* 1 Thes. 2:19).

15, 16 Originally Paul intended to visit Corinth after passing through Macedonia (1 Cor. 16:5). Later he had apparently told the Corinthians he would visit them both before and after the Macedonia trip, to give them *double pleasure*. But then hostile reports from Corinth made Paul change his mind a second time and he decided to go straight to Macedonia. **17** Normally a change of plan would have disappointed his friends, but nothing worse. His opponents, however, charged Paul with *vacillating* (AV, using 'lightness', suggests a ship without ballast) and acting like an unprincipled pagan; 'such unreliability must affect his teaching too'. Paul retorts that his life has been perfectly consistent, and well they know it. **18** His emphatic *as surely as God is faithful* inspires a little homily. **19, 20** Paul argues that anyone who like himself wholeheartedly proclaims Jesus Christ, who is truth, and the utter reliability of *the promises of God* in the OT, must so absorb this positive attitude as to be incapable of practising double-dealing in other matters. *Find their Yes*; their full and satisfying endorsement in Christ (Rom. 11:36). *Yes* represents the Greek and *Amen* the Hebrew form of affirmation. Paul characteristically brings together the two languages. The clear preaching of Christ and the hearty acceptance of that message are alike *to the glory of God*. **21, 22** God's gift of constancy is not limited to apostles. Neither is His gift of the Holy Spirit. He is bestowed upon all believers as a mark of His ownership (1 Jn. 2:20, 27). *Establishes . . . commissioned . . . put his seal* are all expressions of the divine affirmation. All the Trinity is active: *God* the Father *establishes* the believer, i.e. in his faith, *in Christ*. At the same time he is *commissioned* (AV 'anointed', lit. 'christed'), i.e. by the Spirit, for the service of Christ. In the ancient world a *seal* was a sign of ownership or genuine production ('trademark'), and a pledge of security. *Guarantee* is another commercial term, meaning deposit, first instalment, and in modern Greek an engagement ring (*cf.* Eph. 1:13; 4:30). The *Spirit* guarantees the believer's security in Christ and the full blessings of salvation (*cf.* 5:1; Eph. 1:14). **23, 24** Paul had changed his mind about coming, not from fickleness or cowardice, but to avoid another painful and profitless visit. Because of the hostility some had stirred up against him in Corinth, he would have had to come 'with a rod' (*cf.* 1 Cor. 4:21). The phrase *to spare you* could imply authority to punish, so Paul carefully disclaims any desire to *lord it* over them in matters of individual faith (1 Pet. 5:3). As a true pastor he works together with his converts *for their joy* (Phil. 1:25), so that spiritually they learn to stand on their feet (Rom. 14:4; 1 Pet. 1:21).

2:1 *Another painful visit.* See Introduction, 'How many letters and visits?'. The Greek order suggests that Paul had paid one such visit, of which Acts says nothing (2 Cor. 12:14; 13:2). **2-4** It would give Paul no pleasure to cause his converts further distress. Already in duty bound he has had to rebuke them sharply in a letter, though it cost him a great deal. Tough though he is, he does not hide his tears (Acts 20:19, 31) but reveals 'the essential qualification of the Christian minister—a heart pledged to his brethren in the love of Christ' (J. Denney, *The Second Epistle to the Corinthians, EB*, 1894).

5 *If any one.* This is not a hypothetical case, but one notorious to the Corinthians. Neither does it concern the culprit of 1 Cor. 5:1, for something personal against Paul is implied (vv. 5, 10, and 7:12). All the same, Paul insists that the offence is really one against the whole church (1 Cor. 12:26). *Not to put it too severely*, *i.e.* not to exaggerate. **6** As Paul has since learned from Titus, the church had sharply disciplined the offender, unlike their earlier failure (1 Cor. 5:4), and the apostle considers that the punishment given is sufficient. It appears that the sentence was decided only by a *majority*; Paul's next remarks suggest the rest wanted sterner measures. **7, 8** But the penitent must not be allowed to despair utterly and left to drift away (Gal. 6:1; 1 Thes. 5:14). He must be brought back into the church fellowship. 'The cure of souls is the art of arts and the whole body must take its share in it' (H. L. Goudge, *The Second Epistle to the Corinthians, WC*, 1927). Pastoral discipline among the early Christians was always remedial. The temporary exclusion of an impenitent offender was to safeguard the fellowship from being implicated in his sin, and to secure his repentance and subsequent return. **9** The reason *why* Paul *wrote* was to see if the Corinthians would acknowledge his authority, first by disciplining the man and then by restoring him when he repented. **10** Now that the church has taken action successfully, Paul reassures them that the matter is closed as far as he is concerned. **11** If an unforgiving spirit were kept up after the offender had repented, only *Satan* would benefit. Now the breach has been healed the members of the church must stand together. Unity in Christ is 'the final security against the devices of Satan' (Denney).

12, 13 The narrative of 1:8-10 is now briefly resumed. When Paul decided against going to Corinth and instead wrote the 'severe letter', he asked Titus to report on the Corinthians' reaction (8:6; 12:18). Paul moved northward (Acts 20:1) to *Troas*, the port of embarkation for Macedonia, to meet *Titus* on his return. Although his preaching met with much response in Troas, Paul could not settle down as he awaited news

from Corinth. So Paul left Troas, crossed the Aegean Sea and entered *Macedonia*, hoping to find Titus. At last he did.

14 Paul characteristically breaks off the narrative to praise God as he recalls the good news which Titus eventually brought (*cf.* 7:6). God had indeed won the victory in Corinth. This sets Paul reflecting on the conquests of the gospel generally. *Leads us in triumph.* Paul is visualizing a Roman 'triumph', the technical term used of a victorious general parading through the packed streets of Rome. As the long and wretched procession of captives and booty (Col. 2:15) revealed the greatness of the Roman victory, so Paul sees his own hardships (Acts 9:16) as glorifying God. **15, 16a** The once proud Pharisee is, as it were, being led in Christ's 'triumph', spreading the knowledge of Christ like the *aroma* scattered by the incense-bearers who accompanied triumphal processions. That aroma was certainly sweet to those praising the victory, but smelled of *death* to the doomed prisoners. **16b, 17** *Who is sufficient* for such a responsibility of proclaiming the gospel with its awesome consequences to the hearers? No man is—in his own strength. And certainly not those in Corinth who were preaching a watered-down gospel (*cf.* 11:4, 12-15), as mere *pedlars of God's word, i.e.* simply in the business for selfish gain. Unlike these false teachers, Paul and his colleagues were men of *sincerity* with the purest of motives (1:12); neither were they self-appointed, but *commissioned by God* (*cf.* 1:1).

Notes. **2:3** *I wrote; i.e.* the 'severe letter' (between 1 Corinthians and 2 Corinthians), which has probably not survived (see Introduction, 'How many letters and visits?'). Earlier commentators took this letter to be 1 Corinthians, but v. 4 hardly suits the first canonical Epistle. **6** *By the majority* (lit. 'by the more'); from the use of a similar expression at Qumran, a reference to the assembly of the church could be intended. **11** *Satan* (also 11:14; 12:7), 'the god of this world' (4:4), 'Belial' (6:15), and 'the serpent' (11:3), all stress the personal nature of the evil power. **13** *Titus* is mentioned nine times in 2 Corinthians and highly praised. According to Eusebius, Titus became the first bishop of Crete. W. M. Ramsay (*St. Paul the Traveller and the Roman Citizen*, 1895), thought he was Luke's brother, for surprisingly he is not named in Acts. **16** *Fragrance.* The Rabbis likened the Mosaic law to a drug: its effects were either deadly (to the ungodly) or life-giving (to the righteous). *From death to death . . . from life to life.* The expressions probably represent a Semitic idiom whereby verbal repetition conveys emphasis.

3:1 – 7:16 PAUL'S MINISTRY

3:1-18 Ministries old and new

The preaching ministry Paul has been discussing prompts an exposition of the complete superiority of the gospel over the old covenant founded by Moses.

1 *Commend ourselves again* does not imply earlier self-praise, but carries on the thought of 2:14–17. *Letters of recommendation* (*cf.* Acts 9:2; 18:27; Rom. 16:1); Paul does not need them in Corinth—*as some do*. Jewish opponents armed with such letters had gone to Corinth to discredit him. **2, 3** The Corinthians themselves are authentic testimony to Paul's work, for their astounding transformation (1 Cor. 6:9–11) is *known* everywhere. Each Christian in that profligate city is *a letter from Christ . . . , written not with ink*, which was washable (*cf.* Nu. 5:23) and the tool of men, but with the life-giving Spirit. The authentic gospel, as preached by Paul, inscribed the new covenant *not on tablets of stone*, as in the case of the old covenant (Ex. 31:18), *but on tablets* that are human hearts (Je. 31:33; Ezk. 36:26); and hearts that are reachable only by divine action. The law has not been cancelled by the gospel, for this indeed now provides the means of fulfilling it, through the power of the risen Christ within the believer (Rom. 10:4f.).

4 The changed lives at Corinth confirm Paul's *confidence* concerning his divine appointment. **5** But he declines to *claim* any credit for the content of the gospel or for its effect. What he is and what he does are the work of grace (1 Cor. 15:10; 2 Cor. 4:7). **6** *New*; Greek *kainos* (new in quality), not *neos* (new in time). The biblical *covenant* is a relationship offered by God to man. Man cannot initiate or alter it, but only accept or reject it. The new covenant requires ministers *qualified* by God's Spirit (1 Tim. 1:12). The old *written code* (Ex. 24) demanded a standard impossible to reach unaided. But the new covenant inaugurated by Christ (1 Cor. 11:25) also offers man the spiritual ability to keep it. **7–11** Paul makes three contrasts between the dispensations: letter and Spirit (vv. 7, 8); condemning and justifying (v. 9); passing and permanent (v. 11). **7** The function of the Mosaic *dispensation* ('administration') was the education of man's moral sense (Gal. 3:24). But it lead to *death*, for unless the moral law it laid down was kept, men's relationship with God was severed (Rom. 7:9–11). The *brightness* on *Moses'* face (Ex. 34:29), gained from being with God on Mt. Sinai for the giving of the law, did not last. That very fact symbolized the transience of the old dispensation, brought in only until the time came to supersede it with that which is final (Rom. 5:20; Gal. 3:19). The old dispensation, by which God demonstrated man's moral impotence, was accompanied by *splendour*, because it had a divine origin. **8** Since the new *dispensation* also has God as its active agent, *i.e. the Spirit* within men's hearts, it is *attended with greater splendour* than the earlier dispensation (*cf.* 4:6). By it God freely provides men with a right standing with Himself, otherwise impossible for them to attain. **10** The old dispensation *has come to have no splendour*, as the moon loses its brightness when the sun has risen.

12 Paul can rightly be *very bold*, for his gospel will not pass away. **13** Neither has he anything to hide, unlike *Moses* who had to put *a veil over his face* lest the fading radiance suggested to the Israelites the impermanence of the dispensation he was inaugurating (Ex. 34:32f.). Yet its very insufficiency pointed to the greater dispensation to follow (Heb. 8:13). **14** *Read the old covenant, i.e.* the Jewish Scriptures; this is the first time they are so described. *Only through Christ* is the OT fully intelligible. Paul's special mission was to proclaim Christ as the 'end', the perfect fulfilment, of the law (Rom. 10:3f.).

15, 16 *To this day*; *i.e.* as Paul writes. But the truth still holds. *A man, i.e.* a Jew, cannot 'see' this truth (Rom. 11:7–9) *whenever Moses* (the Pentateuch) *is read*, until he *turns to the Lord*, and so finds in Jesus the Christ all the righteousness demanded by the law. This theme is worked out in Romans and Galatians, and loomed large in Paul's own experience (Acts 9:20). **17** *Freedom*; *i.e.* from every kind of bondage, to fear (Rom. 8:15), to sin (Rom. 7:6), to corruption (Rom. 8:21–23), and especially to the law (Gal. 5:18). **18** *We all*, Hebrew and Gentile Christians alike, prominent or obscure, have the privilege of looking upon *the glory of the Lord, i.e.* of the Father as revealed in Christ (*cf.* 4:6; Jn. 17:24). *With unveiled face*; *i.e.* as did Moses, though in the earlier dispensation he alone was permitted to do that (Ex. 34:34). Nevertheless, in the present life even Christians see but imperfectly, *beholding* God's glory as if looking in a primitive metal mirror (1 Cor. 13:12). But by contrast with Moses' experience, this glory for the Christian goes on increasing *from one degree* to another, as his knowledge of the Lord increases (*cf.* 1 Jn. 3:2). Neither is the glory superficial, but inward, the work of *the Spirit*, here described explicitly as *the Lord* (*cf.* the Nicene Creed), *i.e.* Yahweh Himself.

Notes. 16–18 In English these verses seemingly confuse Christ with the Holy Spirit. *a.* Some who take *Lord* to mean Christ interpret v. 17 in terms of v. 6, where 'Spirit' is set over against 'letter'; *i.e.* if Christ is recognized as present in the Mosaic law, that law is living and life-giving (*cf.* 1 Cor. 15:45); without Christ the law is dead and death-dispensing (*cf.* 2 Cor. 2:15, 16). *b.* Others take the *Lord* to mean Yahweh, the God of Israel revealed in the OT. Paul normally uses the Greek definite article with 'Lord' when he means Christ, and omits it when he means Yahweh. In this passage only the first 'Lord' in v. 17 has the article, and there it is probably retrospective: 'Now *that* Lord (*i.e.* Yahweh, v. 16) whom Moses approached, means for us Christians *the Spirit*.' (In the OT theophanies Yahweh is sometimes the pre-existent Lord Jesus and sometimes the Holy Spirit; see N. Turner, *Grammatical Insights into the New Testament*, 1965.)

4:1–15 Human weakness and divine glory

1 The splendour of Paul's God-given *ministry*

of the new covenant, superior to that of Moses (3:6–18), spurs him on. It is the undeserved gift of God's *mercy*, for Paul fully realizes his own unworthiness (1 Tim. 1:12–17). **2** *Renounced.* Paul is not implying that he did practice *cunning* (Gk. *panourgia*, used in 11:3 of Satan's deceit of Eve), though he was accused of this (12:16). Neither did Paul *tamper with God's word*, i.e. by misapplying it (*cf.* 2:17) or even ignoring it (*cf.* 1 Cor. 9:21; 14:21), as Judaizers in Corinth were apparently alleging. *God's word* is here primarily the OT, but includes the Christian revelation. For those whose minds are not darkened (3:14), the *open statement of the truth* in Paul's preaching is plain enough to reach *every man's conscience.* The Greek can mean 'human conscience in all its forms'. 'The truth' is often almost a technical term for 'Christ' or 'gospel'.

3, 4 Paul concedes that many fail to respond. The parable of the sower (Mk. 4) suggests the same point. The 'seed' is not at fault, but the 'soil'. *Those who are perishing* (Gk. present participle); not yet 'are lost', as AV, but 'losing the way'. *The god* (i.e. Satan; *cf.* Is. 14:14) *of this world* (lit. 'age'); i.e. of the present dispensation (*cf.* 1 Jn. 5:19). Satan is a mere 'squatter' in the world (*cf.* Mt. 4:8f.) and his apparent power but temporary. Christ's *likeness of God* (*cf.* Col. 1:15) means, in Paul, not 'a pale imitation' but the visible representation of the invisible God. The phrase is amplified in v. 6. **5** *What we preach is not ourselves*; i.e. not for personal advantage or following. Those who reject 'our gospel' (v. 3) refuse not the preacher but the subject, Christ. *Your servants* invites contrast with Corinth's 'super-apostles' (2 Cor. 10–13). **6** In the first creation God's fiat brought light (Gn. 1:3). In re-creation *light* comes personally (Heb. 1:2f.), an aspect of the gospel vividly impressed upon Paul by his Damascus road experience (Acts 26:13).

7 Paul likens Christians to *earthen vessels* (*cf.* Is. 64:8; La. 4:2), i.e. cheap pottery lamps, which carry Christ's light (*cf.* v. 6). The same Greek word was used of Paul at his conversion when he was appointed a 'vessel' (RSV 'instrument') to carry Christ's name to others (Acts 9:15). Or the 'triumph' (2:14) may still be in mind; valuable booty was often paraded in earthen vessels to show up its glory. The frail meanness of the gospel's human 'containers' magnifies God's *power.* **8, 9** The present tenses, and 'always' (v. 10), speak of Paul's incessant experience (*cf.* 11:23f.). The four contrasts can be paraphrased: 'Hemmed in, but not hamstrung; not knowing what to do, but never bereft of all hope; hunted by men, but never abandoned by God; often felled, but never finished.' The end of man's resources is not the end of God's. More than any other Christian, Paul demonstrated that human extremity was the best position in which to prove divine power. **10, 11** Paul's 'dying' day after day (1 Cor. 15:30f.; Rom. 8:36) was a sharing of his Master's earthly experience as a man. This is

stressed by the reiteration of the personal name *Jesus.* Through such excessive sufferings the powerful *life of Jesus* was also being more clearly revealed in him (Phil. 3:10). **12** The paradox of v. 11 is repeated; Paul points out that the Corinthians reap the benefit of what he is going through. This is not irony, but sober fact (1:4).

13 Paul realizes that he could well die through one of these experiences (1:9; *cf.* 5:1). In the face of that possibility the apostle expresses his faith by an apt quotation from Ps. 116:10. **14** Even if death should come, the resurrection of Jesus by God guarantees the resurrection of Christians (1 Cor. 15:20f.). So death will not separate Paul either from Jesus or from the Corinthians. *Bring us*; i.e. present us as to a sovereign (Col. 1:22). **15** As *more and more people* come to know what Christ is doing in and through Paul, so more will learn the art of *thanksgiving*, a practice which glorifies God (1:11; 9:11; Ps. 50:23; *cf.* Rom. 1:21).

4:16 – 5:10 Earthly decline and heavenly renewal

16 *Our outer nature*, earlier described as 'earthen vessels' (v. 7), 'bodies' (v. 10), 'mortal flesh' (v. 11), ought not to be confused with the 'old self' (Rom. 6:6) and the 'old nature' (Eph. 4:22; Col. 3:9), which are ethical connotations referring to the old unregenerate nature. *Wasting away.* Sufferings are taking their physical toll. This would be true of anyone. But they cannot touch the Christian's *inner nature*, 'the highest part of our immaterial being, which is capable of being the home of the Holy Spirit and of being ruled by Him' (A. Plummer, *The Second Epistle to the Corinthians, ICC,* 1915). Humanly speaking, Paul's sufferings were intense and unending. **17** But taking the heavenly standpoint, he counts them as light and *momentary* compared with the consequent *eternal weight* (i.e. 'solid worth') *of glory* (1 Cor. 2:9; Rom. 8:18). **18** His afflictions and their physical effects, though plain for all to see, are after all only *transient*, i.e. for the length of this life. He is occupied rather with the *unseen* and *eternal* (*cf.* Heb. 11:1).

5:1 Paul now naturally turns to the provision of a new type of body, fitted for the next life (see also on 1 Cor. 15:35f.). *We know*; i.e. not by human reasoning, but by divine revelation (*cf.* 1 Cor. 15:51). The doctrine goes far beyond the Greek idea of the immortality of the soul. *Earthly tent*, although a usual Greek expression for body, is for Paul an appropriate symbol of transitoriness, alluding to Israel's pilgrim life in the wilderness (*cf.* 1 Pet. 2:11). *Destroyed*; dismantled as a tent or booth (*cf.* Lv. 23:42, 43). *We have*; not yet, but awaiting us. *Not made with hands*; not belonging to the perishable natural order, but *from God*, supernatural, heavenly, *eternal.* **2** *We groan*; not in complaint but in prayer (Rom. 8:23, 26). **3** *Found naked.* Hebrew and earlier Greek thought considered that disembodied spirits were under the earth and incapable of taking part in life in any region of the universe. **4** *Further clothed.* Paul longs that the return of Christ may take place in his own life-time and that the heavenly body may arrive before *what is mortal* is gone. Some consider that since writing 1 Cor. 15 Paul had changed his views on this subject because of the delay in Christ's return and his own physical extremity. But Paul's earliest letter (see 1 Thes. 4:13f.) recognized that some Christians would die before the Lord came back. *Swallowed up*; Is. 25:8; 1 Cor. 15:54. **5** *Prepared.* God has had this end in view from the beginning. *Guarantee*; see on 1:21.

6, 7 *Away from the Lord*; but only in the sense of being unable to see Him. **8** *We would rather.* Paul's own preference is clear (*cf.* Phil. 1:21–23), though as a 'runner' he intends to complete (not abandon) his earthly course (see on 10:13; *cf.* 2 Tim. 4:7). **9** But whether *at home or away*, *i.e.* living or dead when the Lord comes (*cf.* Rom. 14:8), the Christian's *aim* or ambition must be to be well pleasing to Him then. **10** *We must all*; *i.e.* all Christians, not unbelievers. *Appear*; be made manifest, laid bare. The teaching here about the judgment of actions is not at variance with the doctrine of justification by faith alone. Professor G. E. Ladd comments in *NBD* (p. 389) that this *judgment seat of Christ* is also the judgment seat of God (Rom. 14:10, RV, RSV). However, because of the redemption in Christ, the day of judgment has lost its terror for the man in Christ (1 Jn. 4:17). But this tribunal will assess, with complete justice and impartiality, the worth of our Christian lives, *i.e.* our actions after conversion; it will disclose both what has been *good*, *i.e.* valuable to God's kingdom, and what has been *evil*, *i.e.* worthless (*cf.* Jn. 15:8; 1 Cor. 3:10–15).

5:11 – 6:10 The ministry of reconciliation

11 *The fear of the Lord*; solemn awe prompted by the thought of rendering account to Him, *i.e.* Christ (v. 10), at His judgment seat. *We persuade men.* The reference is not to preaching the gospel to the unconverted (as vv. 19, 20), but to the need to convince certain Christians of Paul's integrity as a Christian and an apostle. **12** *Not commending ourselves*; *cf.* 3:1. *Giving you cause*; *i.e.* providing his Corinthian friends with material with which to refute Paul's denigrators. **13** *If we are beside ourselves.* Paul's detractors are evidently making such a charge aginst him (*cf.* Mk. 3:21). In both his intense enthusiasm and times of spiritual ecstasy (12:1f.), and in his more sober moments, Paul is never out for his own ends; *it is for God* and His glory and *for you* and your spiritual benefit. **14** *The love of Christ*, *i.e.* his love for Paul as a sinner, *controls* or constrains him; it shuts him up to one course of action. The same Greek verb is used in Lk. 12:50 of the compulsion felt by Jesus. *One has died for all; therefore all have died.* The reasoning here implies that Christ died not only on their behalf but in their place, *i.e.* He died the death they should have died. **15** This fact should impel those who realize it to spend the rest of their lives for Him and *no longer for themselves* (*cf.* 1 Cor. 6:19). *And was raised.* In the NT the death and resurrection of Jesus are always linked (*cf.* 1 Thes. 4:14). Death without resurrection would evacuate Calvary of all meaning.

16, 17 Paul's outlook has been transformed and made *new* by his being *in Christ*, his favourite expression for a Christian, and one denoting the most intimate faith-union with Jesus in His death and resurrection (Gal. 2:20). *From a human point of view*; *i.e.* from worldly considerations. Applied to Christ, however, modern radical theologians assume that Paul is here discarding 'the human Jesus of the Gospels' and exalting 'the glorified Christ of faith'; but so to interpret his words would destroy the essential historical basis of Christianity. More probably Paul means that before his conversion he had assumed that Jesus was merely a Messianic pretender. Now as a Christian he worships Him as the Christ of God and Lord of the universe (Phil. 2:9–11).

18 *God . . . reconciled us to himself.* He is both the initiator and the goal of reconciliation. *Reconciliation* in the NT sense is not something brought about by man dropping his antagonism towards God. It is something accomplished by God when through the death of Christ He put away everything that on His side meant this estrangement from man. The obstacle which God had to remove was His wrath 'against all ungodliness and wickedness of men' (Rom. 1:16–18). *The ministry of reconciliation* is the preaching of the good news that at infinite cost God's wrath has been put away by His only beloved Son bearing it upon the cross. The priceless peace won thereby is now freely offered to men. (See J. Denney's magnificent exposition in *The Second Epistle to the Corinthians.*) **19** *God was in Christ reconciling the world to himself.* AV wrongly inserts a comma after Christ, whereas *was* taken with *reconciling* gives: 'God was by means of Christ reconciling the world to Himself' (*cf.* RSV mg.). **20** *We beseech you.* The very conception of *ambassadors* descending to entreaty is, as Calvin says, an incomparable commendation of the grace of Christ. Paul preaches the gospel in the spirit of the Gospel (Denney). *Be reconciled to God*; *i.e.* accept the reconciliation already made by God through Christ's death on the cross (Rom. 5:11).

6:1 *Working together with him*; a consciousness confessed in 5:18–20; *cf.* 1 Cor. 3:9. *The grace of God*; God's provision in Christ described in the previous passage, and entirely His work. But men have the responsibility of receiving it. *In vain*; either superficially (Mt. 13:20f.; *cf.* 1 Cor. 15:2) or because false apostles had subsequently misled them into supposing that they themselves could contribute something towards their own salvation (2:17; 11:4). Either way the results which should follow in Christian living would be lacking. Paul may still have the judgment seat in mind (5:10). **2** *For he says*; Is. 49:8. *The acceptable time* means the season acceptable (not to man but) to God (*cf.* Is. 61:2) because it is *the day of salvation* decreed by Him, *i.e.* a period of grace giving men the opportunity to respond to God's message through Christ. Implied also are the responsibility of men to respond and the limitation of God's offer of reconciliation to a certain time. **3** *No fault*; no cause for blame or ridicule. 'There are people who will be glad of an excuse not to listen to the gospel, or to take it seriously, and they will look for such an excuse in the conduct of its ministers' (Denney). **4, 5** Nine trials are listed in three groups of three, preceded by the supreme quality of *great endurance*, needful for them all. The first group of general testings are *afflictions*, pressures physical, mental, and spiritual; unmitigated *hardships*; and *calamities*, frustrating situations. The second lists hardships caused by other men; *beatings* (11:24f.), *imprisonments* (Acts 16:23), *tumults* (Acts 13:50; 14:5, 19, *etc.*). The third concerns hardships Paul accepted to undergo to further the gospel: *labours*, physical and spiritual fatigue (*i.e.* he was 'overworked' NEB); *sleepless nights* (Acts 20:31; 2 Thes. 3:8) and *hunger* (*i.e.* sometimes 'starving', NEB).

Paul's list of tribulations is now, in vv. 6–10, matched by a catalogue of spiritual qualities which enable him to endure triumphantly. Even in translation the literary structure of these verses is impressive. **6** *Purity*; *i.e.* in moral life, and single-heartedness in motive. *Knowledge*; *i.e.* of the truth as it is in Jesus (Col. 2:2f.). Saving knowledge, not intellectual, is meant. *Forbearance*; unprovoked by hurts inflicted. Christian *kindness* (Gk. *chrēstotēs*, appropriately close in sound to *Christos*, Christ) is the response of God's kindness toward us in Christ Jesus (Eph. 2:7; Tit. 3:4). *Forbearance* and *kindness* are also linked in Gal. 5:22 and 1 Cor. 13:4. The inconspicuous place here given to *the Holy Spirit* appears surprising. The meaning can be 'a spirit that is holy'. H. B. Sweete concludes, 'It is not the person of the Spirit but the gift that is intended.' **7** Paul now turns to the conditions of his ministry. *Weapons of righteousness.* The genitive defines the origin of the weapons; one result of justification is the provision by the Holy Spirit of weapons for the spiritual battle (*cf.* Eph. 6:16f.; Is. 59:17).

8–10 reflect the calumnies being spread about Paul by his opponents at Corinth. **9** He was dismissed by some *as unknown*, a nobody, not 'recognized'; *yet well known*, making an unforgettable impression upon others. *As dying*; 'finished' (*cf.* 1:9)—*and behold*, much to everyone's surprise, *we live*, 'we still keep going' (1:9; Acts 14:19). *Punished* can refer to sentences by human authorities or to 'chastening' by God (Ps. 118:18). **10** *Always rejoicing*; ever conscious of an unquenchable joy in the Lord (Rom. 8:35f.; Phil. 4:4). *Poor* materially, *yet making many rich* in what really counts, the knowledge of Christ (Eph. 3:14f.; Phil. 3:7f.) *Possessing everything*; *i.e.* all that matters (Rom. 8:17, 32; 1 Cor. 3:21f.).

6:11 – 7:1 Keep clear of ungodly attachments

Some scholars consider that the abrupt change of subject and tone at 6:14, and the fact that the thought of 6:13 is carried on by 7:2, suggests that 6:14 – 7:1 is misplaced. But MS evidence for this is absent, and no editor would insert an incongruous passage carelessly (see Introduction, 'How many letters and visits?'). It would not be unnatural for Paul at this point to bring up briefly and sharply some critical affair known to the Corinthians, if not to us. He has just invited them to 'widen' their hearts (6:13) and here is a practical reason for doing so. We can only guess the point at issue. Paul recognized that Christians could not isolate themselves from human society (1 Cor. 5:9f.). Existing mixed marriages were not to be broken (1 Cor. 7:12f.), though the Christian must not marry an unbeliever (1 Cor. 7:39). Dining with heathen neighbours was not impossible (1 Cor. 10:27). (See Introduction, 'Paul's purpose in writing'.) In this passage Paul prohibits some particular though unspecified relationship with unbelievers (v. 14). The veto somehow concerns heathen sacrifices; and certainly any association with heathen worship involved immorality of the worst kind (see Introduction, 'Corinth').

11 *Corinthians*. Paul addresses his readers by name only when his feelings are stirred; *cf.* Gal. 3:1; Phil. 4:15. *Our heart is wide*; open-heartedness is for friends (*cf.* Mt. 12:34). **12, 13** He is speaking intimately as to those he trusts, and appeals for a similar loving response in return. Indeed, he speaks *as to children*, in whose affections their father should have a special place.

In a series of antitheses in vv. 14–16 Paul brings out the principle of the incongruity of believers being paired with unbelievers; fundamentally they have nothing in common. **14** *Mismated*; unequally yoked (Lv. 19:19; Dt. 22:10; *cf.* Phil. 4:3). **15** The climax is reached in naming the chief figures on the two sides, *Christ* and *Belial* (Satan). No harmony between them is possible. **16a** *With idols*. Conversion for Gentiles meant an absolute break with Corinth's entire way of life, which revolved around idol-worship. *We*, the Christian community, *are the temple of the living God* (1 Cor. 3:16; Eph. 2:19–22; 1 Pet. 2:5). **16b–18** *As God said*. Paul presses home his argument by citing, as one statement, words culled from all over the OT (see RSV mg.). Separation may mean loss of relatives, friends, and livelihood, and giving up apparently innocent involvements. But the holy God promises to dwell among His people, and there can be no compromise with anything contrary to His interests. **7:1** With such *promises*, given repeatedly down history, what does earthly loss matter? The recompense will be out of all proportion: the privilege of personal membership of God's own family (Mk. 10:29). *Let us cleanse ourselves.* The moral demand of the passage is finally expressed positively. *Make holiness perfect.* Personal sanctification demands persistent effort.

The fear of God is the regulating standard; *i.e.* reverence for God as Himself holy and demanding holiness in His people (*cf.* 1 Pet. 1:14–17).

7:2–16 Paul's confidence in the Corinthians

2 resumes the thought of 6:13. **3** *I said before*; in 6:11–13. 'You are in my very heart, and you will be there in death and life alike' (Moffatt). **4** The cheerful statements are due to the good news Titus has brought from Corinth (vv. 6, 7); see Introduction, 'Paul's purpose in writing'.

5 At 2:13 Paul spoke of his restlessness at Troas waiting for Titus to return with a situation-report from Corinth (see Introduction, 'Paul's links with Corinth'). Now he resumes the narrative. He had crossed the Aegean *into Macedonia* to meet Titus. There an anxious Paul had to face additional troubles, of which Acts (20:1–3) says nothing; but these were apparently unconnected with Corinth. **6, 7** *God, who comforts*; *cf.* Is. 49:13b. See on 2 Cor. 1:3, 4. Titus had conveyed Paul's 'severe letter' to Corinth (see Introduction, 'How many letters and visits?'). Now at last Titus brings his reassuring report, and Paul is overjoyed with relief. **8, 9** Though his *letter* had made them *sorry*, and Paul regretted hurting them, it had had the desired effect, because they were *grieved into repenting*. So Paul had no continuing regret about it. Repentance means submitting conduct to God's standard and seeking His forgiveness. **10** By doing this the Corinthians had truly shown *godly grief*; and this, far from bringing lasting *regret, leads to salvation. Worldly grief* is merely remorse; it has no place for hope, forgiveness, or grace, and simply *produces death* and despair, because it cannot result in positive action. **11** On the other hand, *this godly grief* has really stirred the Corinthians to set their house in order; so Paul can now pronounce them *guiltless in the matter*. **12** *Not on account*; rather, 'not so much on account'. Paul uses a Semitic idiom to express a comparison by a contrast. (For a similar usage see Lk. 14:26 and *cf.* Mt. 10:37.) The most important object of the 'severe letter' had been achieved in bringing the Corinthians to a radical change of heart in their attitude towards the apostle; but it had also been necessary for the *one who did the wrong* to be punished (*cf.* 2:5).

13 Paul's own satisfaction is increased by *the joy* given to *Titus* through the success of his errand. **14** Paul's forecast of the Corinthians' reaction had proved correct. **15** Titus had grown to love the Corinthians during his stay. *The fear and trembling*; *i.e.* not fright but a 'solicitous anxiety lest love should fail in doing all that is required' (C. Hodge, *The Second Epistle to the Corinthians*, 1959). **16** *Perfect confidence in you.* Paul writes as any proud father whose children have not disappointed his expectations (6:13). But Paul is also leading up to the delicate question of collecting money for the poor Christians in Jerusalem (8:1 – 9:15).

8:1 – 9:15 THE LOVE-GIFT FOR THE JERUSALEM CHRISTIANS

Relief for the Jerusalem Christians is first mentioned in Acts 11:27–29 and Gal. 2:10; the story ends in Rom. 15:25–29. Paul laid the duty on the conscience of his churches to express the loving concern of Gentile Christians for their Jewish brothers and sisters in Christ in the mother church at Jerusalem (Rom. 15:27). The acute poverty of the large Christian community there stemmed from the day the first Jewish converts were inevitably cut off from relatives, society, employment, and Temple. Those better off had at once responded (Acts 4:32f.); so later did Christians at Antioch when famine increased their plight (Acts 11:27f.). Paul had evidently raised the question with the Corinthians before writing 1 Cor. 16; by the following year (2 Cor. 8:10) not much progress had been made. With their change of heart, however, the moment seems ripe to press the matter further. In doing so Paul provides us with two chapters (8 and 9) on the philosophy of Christian giving.

8:1–24 The collection

1, 2 To encourage the Corinthians to respond to his appeal for support for the Jerusalem poor, Paul sketches the fine example set by *the churches of Macedonia*. Their generosity is a demonstration of *the grace of God*, for they themselves were suffering some *severe test of affliction* and were in *extreme poverty*. The Corinthians were not in this plight (8:14). **3, 4** Furthermore, the Macedonians gave *of their own free will*, even *begging* Paul *for the favour* of sending aid. **5** *Not as we expected.* Even Paul was surprised at their fervour. The explanation was that they first had given themselves *to the Lord, i.e.* put themselves entirely at Christ's disposal in the matter; and consequently, says Paul, they gave themselves *to us*, understanding this to be *the will of God*. Such spontaneity, thoroughness, Christian spirit, and confidence in Paul, were all lessons for the Corinthians. **6** *Titus . . . made a beginning.* Paul wants the Corinthian collection (1 Cor. 16:1f.) to be speedily completed and added to the Macedonians' gift now ready. *Titus* has agreed to return to Corinth for the purpose (8:17). *This gracious work.* Will the Corinthians too reveal the working of God's grace (8:1) in their liberality? **7** *As you excel in everything* (*cf.* 1 Cor. 1:4–7). God had bestowed special spiritual gifts upon the Corinthian church (1 Cor. 12–14). *Faith*; probably not saving faith, but the charismatic gift; so also with *utterance* and *knowledge* (see 1 Cor. 12:8–10). *Earnestness . . . love for us; i.e.* now, after their change of heart (7:7–12).

8 *Others; i.e.* the Macedonians (8:1), whose generosity has demonstrated their love. **9** *Our Lord Jesus Christ*; named in full for solemn emphasis. His example is enough to assert the principle: the haves must provide for the have-nots. *He was rich*; sharing His Father's glory

(Jn. 17:5). *Became poor*; referring to the incarnation (Phil. 2:7). Paul does not here refer to the poverty of the earthly life of Jesus (Lk. 9:58), but rather to His willingness to leave heaven, to limit Himself to a human body, and to die for men's sins on the cross (2 Cor. 5:21). **10** He gives *advice*, for a *command* (v. 8) is unnecessary; the Corinthians know their duty and indeed *began* the collection a *year ago* (rather, 'last year' —which could mean only a few months before), though others have outstripped them. **11, 12** *Out of what you have*. Perhaps the Corinthians had made promises larger that they can now fulfil. **13** They are not to get into debt, and so need relief themselves. **14, 15** The sharing of means, first practised in the earliest days (Acts 2:44; 4:34f.), is laid down by Paul as a guiding principle. This *equality*, *i.e.* fair shares for all, is illustrated by citing the lessons the Israelites learnt in the wilderness (Ex. 16:18) that hoarding did not pay, yet frugality proved sufficient.

16, 17 Paul now deals with the method of taking up the collection. *Titus* has responded to the challenge to visit them for this purpose. Not that he had to be persuaded; for already God had prompted him to take up the task *of his own accord*. Paul delicately underlines Titus' *care for you*, *i.e.* the Corinthians, though the love-gift is for others. **18** *The brother*. Luke is a widely-held guess, but Paul refrains from naming either him or the second delegate in v. 22. *Gospel*; no written Gospel was yet in existence. To make this clear, RSV paraphrases by supplying the words *for his preaching of*. **19** *Appointed by the churches*; *i.e.* not simply by Paul. *In this gracious work*. AV 'with this grace', *i.e.* 'gift', now has better MS support. The dual object of the exercise is *the glory of the Lord* (*cf.* v. 9), *i.e.* by reflecting something of God's generosity, and *to show our good will*, or 'readiness' (9:2; *cf.* Gal. 2:20), particularly towards Jewish Christians.

20 *Blame us*. By getting delegates appointed by the churches to collect the money, Paul safeguards against giving Satan any excuse to prompt his enemies to attack him (12:17, 18). 'There is nothing which is more apt to lay one open to sinister imputations than the handling of public money' (Calvin). *Liberal gift*; AV 'abundance'. Paul expects a large sum to be raised. Mentioning it is a compliment and a challenge to the Corinthians' generosity. **21** *We aim*. Paul is out to avoid all chance of misunderstanding. Besides having a clear conscience *in the Lord's sight*, the Christian must openly appear to be utterly straightforward *in the sight of men*. 'It is a foolish pride which leads to a disregard of public opinion' (Hodge). This verse is a free quotation from Pr. 3:4, LXX. Paul is concerned for his own name only because his Master's reputation is bound up with it. **22** *Our brother*. This second delegate (see v. 18) has not been identified. **23** *Titus . . . my partner*. Paul wants them to know that Titus fully represents the apostle's own views and authority. The

other two *messengers* (lit. 'apostles', 'sent ones') derive their authority from *the churches* sending them. 'Apostles' *of the churches* does not put them into the same category as Paul and Peter, who are 'apostles of Jesus Christ by the will of God'. But Paul boldly describes them as *the glory of Christ*, *i.e.* as 'shining examples' (Phillips) of His grace, in their discharge of such ministry. **24** *Give proof* (practical demonstration) *before the churches*, *i.e.* before the delegates, as if the congregations they represent are present. The latter would in any case quickly hear what the result had been.

9:1-15 Principles of Christian giving

1 *To write*; *i.e.* to go on writing. Paul is probably continuing the subject of ch. 8 and 1 Cor. 16:1-4, though some consider ch. 9 is a separate note from Paul written earlier than ch. 8 and taken by Titus, whose (hypothetical) mission as the bearer of ch. 9 is mentioned in 8:6. Most scholars prefer the first and simpler solution. **2** The apostle had stayed in Corinth for 18 months (Acts 18:11; see Introduction, 'Corinth'); he knows their 'eagerness' to help. *I boast*; present tense. He is still confidently doing so. *Achaia* was the Roman province stretching from the Isthmus of Corinth southwards. *Has been ready*; rather 'was making preparations'. The collection is not yet complete. *Since last year*; 8:10. **3** *I am sending*; not 'I sent' (AV). The Corinthians' generosity is not in doubt, only their ability to be ready with the collection in time. Paul naturally wants to avoid being discredited; for what he has told others about the Corinthians' intentions has, under God (8:1), 'stirred up' (v. 2) generous giving among the Macedonians. **4** Paul himself will soon be arriving with *some Macedonians* to receive the Corinthians' contribution and convey it to Jerusalem (Rom. 15:25f.). **5** *To go on before me*. Paul gives the Corinthians a chance to press ahead with the collection before he and his party arrive. Paul is also anxious to avoid any slander which might arise if he had a hand in the collecting personally. *Not as an exaction but as a willing gift*. AV more closely renders 'as a matter of bounty, and not as of covetousness', *i.e.* sharing in the collection not with an eye to retaining as much as possible for self, but with a genuine concern to bless or benefit the recipients. **6** Thus they are to give *bountifully* not *sparingly*. The principle of reaping what is sown (Pr. 11:24f.; 19:17) is applied in Gal. 6:7-10 to a spiritual harvest, and in Mt. 6:14f. to forgiveness; *cf.* Mt. 7:1, 2; 10:42; Lk. 6:34-38. 'It is right to present to men the divinely-ordained consequences of their actions as motives to control their conduct' (Hodge). **7** *Not reluctantly*, *i.e.* not thinking, 'How little will do?' 'The source of giving is not the purse but the heart' (P. E. Hughes, *Paul's Second Epistle to the Corinthians*, NLC, 1962); *cf.* Mk. 12:41ff. *A cheerful giver*. Genuine giving is exhilarating. The quotation is from Pr. 22:8, LXX; it is not in the Hebrew. *Cf.* Rom. 12:8.

8 *God is able* to make our remaining resources more than adequate. *Enough* ('content', Phil. 4:11; 'contentment', 1 Tim. 6:6); a characteristic result of God's response to faith. The title El Shaddai (Gn. 17:1, RSV mg.) could signify 'the God who is enough'. God provides materially and spiritually *for every good work* in His service (Phil. 4:19). Note the repeated 'every'. **9, 10** Scriptural support is drawn from Ps. 112:9; Is. 55:10; Ho. 10:12. AV takes v. 10 as a prayer; RSV, following earlier MSS, states a divine principle. *He who supplies*. Is. 55:10 simply says 'giving'. Paul uses a richer term ('furnishes'), as in Gal. 3:5. *Seed*, that may be sown, is also from God (5:18). The sowing God thus prospers is the giving of vv. 6–8. *Will supply*; *cf.* Phil. 4:15, 19. *Multiply*. A seed's potential is, under God, out of all proportion to its size. *Righteousness*; right action, in this case 'liberality'. **11, 12** *Enriched*. Giving is an enriching experience (*cf.* on v. 7). Paul is disinterested in his encouragement of almsgiving, for he had already refused to take anything for himself from the Corinthians (11:7–9). *Service*. The Greek word *leitourgia* ('liturgy') was used of public services paid for by wealthy Athenian citizens. *Great generosity* not only meets the material needs *of the saints* but does much more. Spiritually it *also overflows in many thanksgivings* of the recipients *to God* (1:11) and promotes mutual love and prayer (v. 14). **13** *Test*. By their aid Gentile converts would be demonstrating the genuineness of their Christian profession to Jewish converts and expressing their oneness with them in Christ. *Contribution* (Gk. *koinonia*); fellowship, sharing; *cf.* 1:7. **15** Paul closes this section on giving by returning to 'the divine gift which inspires all gifts' (R. V. G. Tasker, *The Second Epistle of Paul to the Corinthians*, TNTC, 1958), Jesus the Saviour (8:9; 1 Jn. 4:11). *Inexpressible*. Human language is inadequate to describe the full extent of either the *gift* or its consequences (Rom. 8:32).

10:1 – 13:14 PAUL'S APOSTOLIC AUTHORITY

On the changed tone and subject of the remaining chapters (10–13) see Introduction, 'How many letters and visits?'

10:1-18 His credentials

1 Turning to more personal matters, Paul stops writing as 'we'. The parenthesis, *I who am humble . . . when I am away*, evidently echoes calumny against Paul by his critics in Corinth (10:10). *Meekness*; willing acceptance of God's will. *Gentleness*; clemency (Jn. 8:11). This is the attitude for even an apostle. **2** But gentleness is not timidity. If necessary, Paul will *show boldness* by speaking severely *against some*, his traducers. *In worldly fashion*; inconsistently, governed by self-interest (1:17; Rom. 8:4f.). **3, 4** Christians have to live *in the world* with its troubles, and 'in the flesh' (AV) with its frailties (1 Cor. 2:3–5). But the real battle is spiritual.

Worldly, i.e. human, qualities are impotent *to destroy strongholds* of evil within either society or the individual. The only effective *weapons* are those which *have divine power*, literally 'are rendered powerful by God' (*cf.* Eph. 6:11f.). **5** Men fortify themselves against the gospel with their intellect and will, *i.e.* with *arguments* ('reasonings'), and pride, self-sufficiency. It is humbling to accept the implications of *the knowledge of God* as revealed in the gospel. *Thought* (*cf.* 11:3), also translated 'design' (2:11) and 'mind' (3:14; 4:4), is in 2 Corinthians always used in a bad sense. *Captive*. Not even a thought is outside the sphere of obedience claimed by Christ. **6** *Punish*; 'court-martial' (Moffatt); another military metaphor. *Complete*. Paul anticipates the majority will submit. Only any defiant remnant will then need sentencing. Paul now goes on to justify his threats.

7 The Greek can be a question (AV), statement (RV), or command (RSV). The last is best: 'Face the facts before you.' *He is Christ's* is not a reference to the clique of 1 Cor. 1:12, nor to personal faith, but to divinely-given authority. Paul's authorization by Christ, not his faith, is under attack. **8** His 'boasting' is never self-centred but always magnifies what God has done. *Building you up*. Paul's credentials are proved by positive results in the lives of his converts (1 Cor. 15:10). **9, 10** They also refute the charge that he writes his *letters* to terrorize his converts. *Seem*; put on a show. The reported comments testify to the effect his writing produced. By contrast his opponents considered that Paul in person was ineffective. The allegation concerns character rather than physique. **11** Paul does not threaten only words when he arrives, but rigorous action. 'There was no doubt a great difference between Paul in his ordinary frame of mind, not very ready to be hard, not very fluent in speech, and Paul inspired, when there was a great principle to fight for, or a great wrong to remove' (A. Menzies, *The Second Epistle of the Apostle Paul to the Corinthians*, 1912). **12** *Venture to class or compare ourselves*. Paul's heavy irony clothes an important principle. The only true comparison must be with a standard which is external and unchanging. Paul knows this can only be Christ.

13-18 enlarge on the point. **13** *Beyond limit*. The conceit of these 'super-apostles' (11:5) is boundless. Paul's ministry, however, has certain divinely imposed *limits*: Paul is the apostle to the Gentiles (Acts 9:15; Rom. 1:5; Gal. 2:9), and he is a pioneer missionary (Rom. 15:20). *Apportioned*. Paul is 'in the lane' (athletics metaphor) of service marked out by God. **14** *We are not overextending ourselves*, 'not going beyond our sphere of authorized activity'; *i.e.* as though Paul's mandate did not reach to Corinth. *First to come*; *cf.* 1 Cor. 3:6; 4:15. **15, 16** *As the* Corinthians' *faith increases*, and provides more settled conditions in the church there, Paul will be able to go on to pioneer *in lands beyond* Corinth. Perhaps he has Rome and Spain in mind (Acts 19:21; Rom. 1:13; 15:24, 28). But he will never claim credit for work he finds *already done* by others (Rom. 15:20). **17** To *boast* of what *the Lord* has done is alone permissible to the Christian (*cf.* Je. 9:23, 24; 1 Cor. 1:31). **18** *Accepted*; 'tested and approved'. Man cannot give such a verdict upon himself.

Note. **15** *That . . . our field among you may be greatly enlarged* can hardly be the meaning. The point at issue was not an increase in Paul's service at Corinth but beyond it. The wording is clarified if for *among you* we read 'by you' (AV). The Corinthians can help to open up a wider ministry for the apostle by stabilizing the conditions in their church.

11:1-33 Misrepresentations answered

Paul has shown (10:13-18) that at Corinth he kept to his divine brief, while his opponents exceeded theirs. **1** Now, though it is *foolishness*, not the thing to do normally, he draws other comparisons with them. **2** The church is to be Christ's *bride*. The picture is used frequently (Mt. 25:1-13; Jn. 3:29; Eph. 5:25f.; Rev. 19:7). Paul views himself as the arranger of the marriage, since he founded the Corinthian church (1 Cor. 4:15). The work is God's, however, and so Paul describes his own intense feelings as a *jealousy* which is *divine*. *One husband*. The loyalty Christ claims is exclusive, as in the marriage relationship. 'Paul was very far from despising marriage, since he makes it the symbol of the ideal consummation' (E. B. Allo, *Saint Paul: Deuxième Epitre aux Corinthiens*, 1937); *cf.* Eph. 5:32. **3** Paul *is afraid* that the Corinthian church is being *led astray* by *thoughts* (*cf.* 10:5) inconsistent with her first loyalty *to Christ*. **4** Satan is up to his old tricks again (Gn. 3:1; *cf.* Rev. 12:9; 20:2), through those who have been preaching *another* sort of *Jesus* (Gal. 1:6; *cf.* Mk. 8:33), *i.e.* either simply a human Jesus or, like the later Gnostics, a sort of demi-god. *Comes*; of his own accord, as distinct from being *sent* by *God*. *Readily enough*; no doubt because such a *different gospel* is alluring (Gal. 3:1). **5, 6** Paul denies that he is *inferior to these superlative apostles*, fine oratory apart (1 Cor. 2:4); certainly not *in knowledge* of Christ, *i.e.* in spiritual qualifications. The Corinthians must realize on reflection that Paul's claim is true. When Paul refers to *superlative apostles* (*cf.* 12:11), some earlier commentators thought he meant that he had as much right to be heard as the 'very chiefest apostles' (AV), *i.e.* the Twelve. But this is ruled out by vv. 13 ('disguising') and 15 (Satan's 'servants'). These 'super-apostles' were intruders to Corinth needing instruction (3:1) and even self-commendation (10:12). They were Hebrews (11:22) and mercenary-minded (*cf.* 11:7, 9; 12:13-18). Their message was not Paul's (11:4, 15), but sought to lure the Corinthian Christians into Mosaic bondage (3:6f.; 11:15).

7 *Abasing myself*, *i.e.* in not claiming the material support due to genuine Christian preachers (1 Cor. 9:11-14). Professional Greek rhetoricians (alluded to in v. 6) would be suspect if they failed to demand fees (*cf.* 2:17). **8, 9** *Without cost*. In Corinth Paul had kept himself by his tent-making (Acts 18:1ff.), and by accepting support from *other churches*. Thus no one could accuse him of exploiting the Corinthians. *Robbed* (pillaged) and *support* (ration-money) are military metaphors. 'Robbery' colourfully expresses Paul's acceptance of gifts from churches where he no longer ministered. He could not expect maintenance from them of right. *With you and . . . in want*. A vivid sidelight. But God had not overlooked him. *Macedonia*. Another reminder of their generosity (8:1). **10, 11** Paul will not keep quiet about his decision not to take money from the Corinthian church, because it demonstrates his very real love for them. **12** His refusal to accept support must *undermine* his rivals' claims to *work on the same terms* as Paul. **13, 14** Paul now plainly asserts that these 'super-apostles' are in fact Satan's agents. *Disguises himself as an angel* from the kingdom *of light*. One of Satan's principal methods is that of imitation, as Jesus reveals in the parable of the weeds (Mt. 13:24-30, 36-43). **15** *Servants of righteousness*, *i.e.* those who give the appearance of serving the cause of the gospel, but for other ends. Paul may be alluding to their Judaizing efforts to teach salvation by works (see on 11:5); *cf.* Gal. 2:21. *Their end*. Paul never shrinks from declaring the destiny of those who oppose the true gospel of Jesus Christ (Rom. 3:8; Phil. 3:19; 2 Thes. 1:8; 2 Tim. 4:14). He recognizes a limit to toleration. *Deeds*. Their emphasis on 'works' at the expense of free grace means that they will ultimately get the 'works' they deserve.

16 *I repeat*; resuming v. 1. The awkwardness revealed in what follows shows Paul's embarrassment at being forced to speak in this distasteful manner. **17** *Not with the Lord's authority*; literally 'not after the Lord' (AV), not a method He would have adopted (*cf.* 1 Pet. 2:23). Paul's purpose, is not self-praise, *as a fool*, but to challenge his opponents on their own ground. Some waverers at Corinth would appreciate only this sort of approach. **18** *Worldly things*; external appearances, accidents of birth, and so on, as in vv. 22f. **19** *Bear with fools*; *i.e.* with the boastful false apostles, or with Paul (vv. 17, 21). *Being wise*. Paul's continued irony aims at stabbing the Corinthians awake to the real situation. **20** *If a man*. These things are evidently happening. *Makes slaves*. The verb is used elsewhere only in Gal. 2:4 of efforts to compel converts to submit to Jewish legal restrictions. *Preys*; uses every means of extorting money (Lk. 20:47 employs the same verb). *Strikes*; literally, or metaphorically of bullying treatment. **21** *Weak*. If genuine apostleship is defined by tyranny, greed, falsity, arrogance, and violence, then Paul admits he was a failure in Corinth. But now he will match any claim others can make.

22 The false apostles were evidently boasting

that they were pure *Hebrews*; although born outside Judea, Paul's pedigree too was impeccable (Phil. 3:5). *Israelites*; the title of privilege, which now belongs to Christians (Rom. 9:6). *Abraham*; *cf.* Gn. 22:17; Rom. 9:7. 'There was not an Israelite in the world prouder of his birth, with a more magnificent sense of his country's glories, than the apostle to the Gentiles: and it provoked him beyond endurance to see the things in which he gloried debased, as they were debased, by his rivals—made the symbols of a paltry vanity which he despised, made barriers to the universal love of God by which all the families of the earth were to be blessed' (Denney). **23** *Servants*. 'Where the ministry is concerned, Paul's is something beyond their horizon' (Hughes). Few of the sufferings now listed are in Acts, a reminder of how little we know of Paul's biography (6:4). *Labours*, arduous campaigns. *Imprisonments*. Acts 16 records only one, at Philippi, before 2 Corinthians was written. Three other instances in Acts, at Jerusalem, Caesarea, and Rome, are later. *Near death*; 1:9; *cf.* 1 Cor. 15:31. **24** *Forty lashes less one*; to keep within the limit of Dt. 25:3. This barbarous flogging (Mt. 10:17) was sometimes fatal. **25** Being *beaten with rods* by Roman lictors was less fearful. Only two examples of all the sufferings in vv. 24 and 25 are mentioned in Acts (14:19; 16:22). *Shipwrecked*; Acts 27 is still to come. **26, 27** Few *rivers* had bridges. *My own people*, Jews, and *Gentiles* alike attacked him from time to time, as Acts often confirms. The ceaseless travelling, adventure and toil portray this tough character of immense courage and determination. **28** *Daily pressure*. Constant claims are made upon his time and thought concerning the affairs of *all the churches*. **29** *Weak*. No-one appeals to this sensitive apostle in vain.

30 Paul looks back to the experiences he has just catalogued. A 'boastful' person, in the ordinary sense, would never have mentioned such things. **31** Incredible though the record is, Paul swears he does *not lie*. **32, 33** Then he recalls another incident, at the outset of his ministry, mentioned perhaps to counter a slander that he had deserted (*cf.* Acts 9:23–25). *Governor*; or ethnarch, literally 'ruler of a tribe or race', *i.e.* one charged with overseeing a certain racial section of a population—in this case, no doubt, the Jews. *Aretas* was king of Nabataea from 9 BC to AD 40. Between AD 37 and 54 there are no Damascus coins bearing the Roman emperor's image. It seems likely that Caligula granted the city to Aretas on acceding as emperor in 37. The fish-basket incident must have taken place between AD 37 and Aretas's death in 40.

12:1–13 Paul's experiences of glory and weakness

1 Paul counters his opponents' boasts about their spiritual experiences with one example of his own. *Of the Lord*; subjective genitive, 'given by the Lord'. *Revelations* may not involve

something visible, as do *visions*. **2** *A man in Christ* well suggests Paul's reluctance to speak of himself. *Fourteen years ago*, about AD 41–42, *i.e.* some years after the Damascus escape (11:33), probably as he began his great missions. *Caught up* (Gk. *harpazo*, to snatch away); used in Acts 8:39 of the Spirit catching away Philip, and in 1 Thes. 4:17 of the 'rapture' of Christians at the second advent. *Third heaven* (only here in the NT) is a Jewish expression for the immediate presence of God, and for Paul a phrase to convey the idea of the most sublime blessedness. *I do not know*; *i.e.* do not remember (as 1 Cor. 1:16). Only *God knows* how the transfer to heaven was made. **3, 4** *Paradise*, from a Persian word meaning 'park'; used in LXX for the Garden of Eden, and in the NT for the place where the glory lost in Eden is regained by Christians (Lk. 23:43; Rev. 2:7). Paul says nothing about what he *saw*, and declines to reveal what he *heard*. The NT deliberately veils the next life, though it makes plain what is needful for our salvation. **5, 6** *On behalf*. Paul claims no credit, although what he relates is the *truth*. *Sees in me*. The Corinthians are to take him as he is, not as someone special because of his experiences. *Hears from me*; in letters.

7 *To keep me*. Whatever golden opinions some may hold of themselves, Paul is in no danger of conceit. The *thorn . . . in the flesh* is not defined. *Thorn*; *cf.* Nu. 33:55. The Greek probably means 'for' rather than literally *in* the flesh. Paul's extraordinary stamina hardly supports the view that he constantly suffered from some physical ailment, though Ramsay's proposal is possible: 'In some constitutions malaria fever tends to recur in very distressing and prostrating paroxysms, whenever one's energies are taxed for a great effort.' The accompanying headache was 'like a red-hot bar thrust through the forehead'. In this verse 'thorn' balances 'elation' and so includes intense depression, whatever the cause. Doubtless the lack of explanation is, under God, deliberate. Define the 'thorn', and any believer lacking that particular affliction would dismiss Paul's experience as remote from his own. 'Is there a single servant of Christ who cannot point to some "thorn in the flesh", visible or private, physical or psychological, from which he has prayed to be released, but which has been given him by God to keep him humble, and therefore fruitful in His service? Every believer must learn that human weakness and divine grace go hand in hand together. Hence Paul's "thorn in the flesh" is, by its very lack of definition, a type of every Christian's "thorn in the flesh", not with regard to externals but by its spiritual significance' (Hughes). *Satan* is concerned with physical disease in Jb. 2:5; Lk. 13:16 (*cf.* 1 Cor. 5:5); but in the last resort he is merely an agent of God's saving purposes. *Harass*; literally 'punch'.

8 *Three times*; *cf.* Mk. 14:30. *The Lord*; *i.e.* Jesus. Paul usually addresses prayer to the Father. *Leave me*. The attacks recurred. **9** *But he* *said*; only after the third prayer. The Lord's 'No' was a rich positive which empowered the rest of Paul's ministry. *Rest*; 'pitch tent' (Ex. 40:34). **10** So sure is Paul of God's power that even troubles make him *content*, for what happens glorifies God. *Strong*. Divine power is unfailing and invincible (Phil. 4:11–13).

11 *Commended by you*. After Paul's 18 months among them, the Corinthians themselves (3:1f.) should have promptly refuted his opponents' allegations that he was *nothing*, *i.e.* of no real standing. *Superlative apostles*; see on 11:5. **12** *The signs* (*i.e.* credentials) *of a true apostle* (*cf.* Mt. 7:15–20) were to be seen in Paul's evangelistic successes in bringing men to Christ and in establishing churches (*cf.* 1 Cor. 2:4; 9:2; 2 Cor. 3:2, 3). The second reference to *signs* is evidently in the sense of miracles (*cf.* Jn. 2:11). *Wonders* and *mighty works* are also miracles, but seen from a different standpoint. *Signs* 'are not empty shows, but are appointed for the instruction of mankind'; *wonders* 'by their novelty arouse men and strike them with astonishment'; *mighty works* 'are more signal tokens of divine power than what we behold in the ordinary course of nature' (Calvin); *cf.* Acts 2:22; Heb. 2:4; 2 Thes. 2:9. *Were performed*; not 'I performed'. No mere modesty, but an acknowledgment that God was at work through him. *In all patience*, *i.e.* with unflagging persistence. **13** *Burden you*, *i.e.* by requiring keep (see on 11:9).

12:14 - 13:4 The third visit imminent

Paul's purpose in this letter is to smooth the way for his third visit (12:14). He explains why he declined to accept support from them—his motive had been misunderstood (12:14, 15) or misrepresented (12:16–19). The sins of the Corinthian church (12:20, 21) must be set right, and the falseness of allegations against him exposed (13:1). Far from seeking peace at any price, Paul is determined to see that all these wrongs are corrected. But paradoxically it will be through his own weakness, for that is how Christ's power is demonstrated (13:2–4).

14 *Third time*; *i.e.* the third visit, not the third time Paul has made ready. The first visit was to found the Corinthian church; the second was the 'painful visit' of 2:1; 7:12. (See Introduction, 'How many letters and visits?') As their spiritual father Paul claims the privilege of supporting them, rather than requiring due support from them as their minister. **15** *Spend . . . be spent*; 'all that I have and all that I am'. *Loved the less*. Naturally a hurtful response, but Paul's aim is to bind them to Christ, not to himself. **16** *But granting* that Paul accepts no direct support, some insinuate that being *crafty* he will obtain money by filching funds collected in Corinth by his agents. **17, 18** The Corinthians are challenged to recall anything from Titus' first visit (8:6) which suggested that Paul would benefit personally. In 8:16–24 safeguards are made to forestall a repetition of the charge on Titus'

next visit to speed the collection for Jerusalem. *Same spirit . . . same steps*. They know Paul and they know Titus. Neither has given cause for suspicion.

19 *Defending ourselves*; as in a court. *Before you*; as judges (1 Cor. 4:3). But Paul softens his charge—no judge is called *beloved*. All along Paul has been speaking as *in the sight of God* (2:17) and conscious of his responsible position *in Christ* and His service. Paul's consistent purpose is their *upbuilding* into what the body of Christ should be. **20** Christian growth involves the elimination of the poisons he now lists (*cf.* Mk. 7:21f.; Gal. 5:19f.). These sins are the very ones which provoked him to write 1 Corinthians. *Perhaps they may be* delicately hints that the ills can be put right before he arrives. **21** *Humble me before you*; *i.e.* 'in connection with you'. Paul took great pride in his converts (1:14; 3:2; 7:4; 8:24; 9:2). Anything that disgraced them was a humiliation to him. *Mourn*; as over those spiritually dead.

13:1 *Any charge*; *i.e.* any still being made against Paul when he arrives will need substantiating by *witnesses*, in accordance with Dt. 19:15; *cf.* Mt. 18:16; Jn. 8:17. A proper and thorough investigation is to clear the air. **2** *Second visit*; the 'painful visit'. (See Introduction, 'How many letters and visits?') *If I come*; *i.e.* 'when' (as Jn. 16:7). *I will not spare*. If necessary, Paul will take severe action; but he is not vindictive. Discipline in the early church was pastoral rather than penal, and intended to reform, not to outlaw the sinner (*cf.* 2:5–11).

3 *In you*; among you. Christ will make His presence known through Paul. **4** While in a human body Jesus shared its limitations and *weakness*. On the cross He appeared to be at the mercy of sinners. The cross and the resurrection, the heart of the gospel, enshrine the paradoxical principle of power out of weakness (12:9). Those who are *in him* can be said to share His weakness. *In dealing with you*, unlike on the 'painful visit' (2:1), *we shall live*, *i.e.* demonstrate the powerful presence of the living Christ. Paul is not referring to the after-life.

13:5-14 Final charge and word of cheer

Paul's goal is the unity and mature development of the Corinthian church. The Corinthians' part is, through self-examination (v. 5), to recognize and so repent of their sins. On his side, Paul will meanwhile use prayer (vv. 7, 8) and even threat (v. 10), pending his arrival in person. But he is completely confident about the outcome.

5 'You have been examining Paul. Now *examine yourselves*' (*cf.* 1 Cor. 11:28–32). *Do you not realize . . . ?* The question expects an affirmative answer. *Unless . . . you fail*. 'But this is unthinkable.' **6** *Find out*; *i.e.* recognize. Their very faith is evidence of the validity of Paul's ministry (3:2). **7** The Corinthians must not *do wrong*, *i.e.* fail to acknowledge what their consciences must tell them is true. Paul is not primarily concerned with his own exoneration, but with the Corinthians' doing *what is right*. *Failed*; literally 'have not stood the test', because no test was required. The meaning is that if, as Paul hopes, the Corinthians have put their house in order by the time he arrives, there will be no need for him to prove his authority. **8** *We cannot do anything*, *i.e.* we have no occasion to exercise power, *against the truth*, against what is right and proper. A vigorous demonstration of power when all was in fact well, would be sheer tyranny. **9** *When we are weak*; *i.e.* when there is no need to enforce authority. *You are strong*, self-disciplined. Spiritual power would naturally follow. Paul's whole object is their *improvement*, a word which denotes a restoring of disordered limbs and joints. **10** *I write this*. Paul hopes that a warning now will avoid the need for strong disciplinary action when he comes. *Authority*. A display of force might impress the world, but it would hardly build up the church (*cf.* 10:8).

11 The closing fourfold appeal aptly summarizes his letter. By acting upon it, their Christian fellowship would become what God intended, and He who was *love and peace* would be 'at home' there. **12** The *holy kiss*, their customary greeting and symbol of Christian brotherhood, must be heartfelt, and so reflect a new loving confidence in one another. **13** *All the saints*; *i.e.* the Christians with Paul, though almost all unknown personally to the Corinthians. **14** Some of the most quoted words in all Scripture conclude Paul's letter. *Grace*, chronologically first in Christian experience, brings the believer to know *the love* shown by *God*, and thence to share in *the fellowship* of Christians brought about and maintained by and in the *Holy Spirit*. The unexpected order of the three Persons prompts Tasker to comment: 'There can be no adequate understanding of God's love apart from the cross; and the only lasting fellowship between men is the fellowship of sinners redeemed by the blood of Jesus.' It would accord with Paul's virile faith to take his closing verse not as a prayer but as a statement: 'Grace, *etc.*, are with you all! So—go forward on this foundation!'

NORMAN HILLYER

Galatians

INTRODUCTION

See also the General Article, 'The Pauline Epistles', p. 71.

ARGUMENT

One of the greatest expositors of Galatians, Martin Luther, said in his introduction to the Epistle, 'St. Paul goeth about to establish the doctrine of faith, grace, forgiveness of sins, or Christian righteousness, to the end that we may have a perfect knowledge and difference between Christian righteousness and all other kinds of righteousness.' Against those who allow or demand human works as contributing towards salvation, Paul pits the gratuitousness of the divine initiative and act in Jesus Christ, the completeness and sufficiency of the cross, the adequacy of faith without works as man's proper response to the work of Christ, and the demand of actual righteousness in men who are justified by faith, through the help of the Holy Spirit as the complement of imputed righteousness.

HISTORICAL SETTING

At the climax of 19th-century biblical scholarship, there emerged what were felt to be assured results of biblical studies, including a chronology of the apostolic period (C. H. Turner, 'Chronology of the New Testament' in *HDB*). At that time no date in Paul's life could be fixed with certainty by reference to any extra-biblical source. The Gallio inscription at Delphi has since established at least one, that Gallio, before whom Paul appeared (Acts 18:12–17), arrived at Corinth in AD 51.

Turner accepted J. B. Lightfoot's identification of Gal. 2:1–10 with Acts 15, who said that Galatia was North Galatia, which had been the traditional view. But already Sir William Ramsay was challenging the North Galatian Theory, by arguing that 'Galatia' meant the southern region and coastal cities of the province. Data which have come to light since have served only to make the puzzle more intractable. Scholars of eminent reputation are ranged on both sides. While the weight of opinion favours Ramsay's conclusion, scholars do not dismiss lightly the alternative interpretation. (For excellent summaries of the data see Donald Guthrie, *New Testament Introduction: The Pauline Epistles*; and G. B. Caird, *The Apostolic Age*.) Two sets of questions are involved. First, which part of Galatia is intended by the term 'Galatia', the north or the south? Second, which visits of Paul recorded in Acts coincide with those mentioned in Gal. 1 and 2?

Location of readers

North Galatia identifies the old kingdom in the central mountainous area of Asia Minor, which was established by Celts from Gaul (hence the name Galatia) in the 3rd century BC. It included the cities of Ancyra, Tavium, and Pessinus. In 25 BC for administration purposes Rome added to it the southern districts of Pisidia and Lycaonia, including the cities of Antioch and Iconium which, along with Lystra and Derbe in Cilicia, are mentioned in connection with Paul's missionary journeys. This enlarged Roman province raises the question of whether Paul visited the north as well as the south, and particularly the location of those to whom this letter is addressed.

Argument to support the North Galatian Theory includes chiefly the following points. It has long been the traditional view, and is buttressed by the reputation of J. B. Lightfoot, James Moffatt, and several outstanding European scholars. Luke employs local regional titles for the southern cities (Pisidia for Antioch in Acts 13:14; and Lycaonia for Derbe and Lystra in 14:6); therefore the term Galatia is employed for Old Galatia, rather than for the Roman province of Galatia. Paul was proud of his Roman citizenship and employed the proper Roman provincial title to include the north. Further, it is urged that the terms Pisidia and Galatia denote two districts, not one (Acts 16:6); and that the same applies in Acts 18:23. Moffatt argued on grammatical grounds that the term translated 'went through' (Acts 16:6) and 'went from' (18:23) denotes not simply travel but preaching and establishing churches. Since Paul had been forbidden by the Spirit to preach in the province of Asia, this could occur only in the north. However, this argument has been strongly disputed (Askwith), and the more so as it has to find support in a dubious grammatical point. Even if Acts 13 and 14 allow the interpretation that for a time Paul suffered physical weakness, it has been argued that this would have discouraged his making the difficult journey northward; but others have countered that Paul travelled to the mountainous northern region specifically to convalesce from illness (Gal. 4:13). Finally, on the South Galatian Theory, the Epistle is often regarded as the earliest one. This destroys the traditional order of placing Galatians between 2 Corinthians and Romans, as a doctrinal stage moving towards the more fully developed theological position of Romans after the polemics of 2 Corinthians. This would necessitate re-casting our understanding of the course of development of Pauline theology.

The South Galatian Theory has had widespread support since the end of the last century. A highly readable account of events when this theory is adopted is given by F. F. Bruce in his book *The Spreading Flame*. Argument in favour of the theory is chiefly the following: Ramsay said that Acts 16:6 and 18:23 means the Phrygic-Galatic area, which was inhabited by Phrygians and known as Phrygia. Thus Acts does not support the idea that Paul visited North Galatia. Crucial to this point is that Luke nowhere mentions churches of the north, though it has been answered that he also does not mention other activities of Paul, including trips to Syria and Dalmatia. On the use of titles, Paul could as well have followed Luke in using geographical locations when detailing travel, but provincial areas when grouping churches. Furthermore, besides pride of place by use of the Roman title in the coast areas, it is difficult to see, said Ramsay, what other common title besides Galatia could have been used to embrace the variety of people in the southern district. The references to Barnabas in Gal. 2:1, 9, 13 have greater force if he was known to the Galatians, which is possible only on the Southern Theory, for Barnabas was Paul's fellow-worker only on Paul's first journey. Also, the relief-money delegation to Jerusalem includes no representative from the North (Acts 20:4); however, the Galatian churches did participate (1 Cor. 16:1). Certain details in Galatians may be allusions to the first missionary journey. These include the 'marks' as results of the Lystra incident (Gal. 6:17; Acts 14:12, 19). The struggle of Gal. 2:5 may allude to post-Galatian church planting, because the Jerusalem meeting occurred before Paul's alleged journey to North Galatia. Then, too, it is highly unlikely that the Judaizing Christians would trail Paul into the obscure northern areas, but it is easy to account for their presence in Pisidian Antioch. Many scholars feel that the historical and critical problems are best accounted for by means of the Southern Theory, because a more coherent account of events and theological development can be given, especially in relation to the Jerusalem meeting.

Date and relation to Acts

We turn to the question of Paul's visits. The difficulties of correlating the data of Acts and Galatians are no less formidable. In Galatians Paul mentions one visit to Jerusalem 3 years after his conversion; another after 14 years along with Barnabas and Titus to meet James, Peter and John concerning admission of Gentiles to the church; and an incident at Antioch when he rebuked Peter. Where do Paul's Galatian journeys and the Epistle fit among these events? Are the 3 years included in the 14 years, or are

they in addition? In Acts, Luke mentions five visits by Paul to Jerusalem: 9:26–30; 11:30 and 12:25; 15:1–30; 18:22; 21:17. The text of 15:20, 29 presents difficulties due to significant variations between the Greek texts. Most scholars, however, follow the reading of the RSV. The visits mentioned in 9:26–30 and Gal. 1:18–24 are usually identified. But which visit in Acts corresponds with Gal. 2:1–10?

The theory that Gal. 2:1–10 should be identified with both Acts 11:30 and 15:1–30 (A. D. Nock) may be dismissed. It rests on the unjustified premise of Luke's inaccuracy in separating what in fact are different reports of one visit, and does not deal with the central questions. Similarly, we may reject the theory (John Knox) which jettisons the Lucan chronology completely in favour of what can be gleaned only from the Pauline Epistles, thereby simply avoiding the difficulties of harmonizing the Acts and Galatians accounts.

The traditional view identifies Gal. 2:1–10 and the Jerusalem meeting of Acts 15; indeed, advocates of the North Galatian Theory are bound to do so. In maintaining this, Lightfoot argued from the similarity of the places (Antioch and Jerusalem), persons, topic of discussion, and decision reached in each instance; and also that it was not to Paul's point in Galatians to mention the visit of Acts 11:30. Scholars who defend the South Galatian Theory challenge the argument point by point (see Guthrie and Caird). A crucial matter is the absence in Galatians of any allusion to the decision of Acts 15, which is reinforced by the statement in Gal. 2:6 that no addition to the message would be tolerated. Also, Paul's rebuke of Peter (Gal. 2:11ff.) is held to be more likely before, rather than after, the Jerusalem meeting. On these and other grounds the two visits cannot be identified without attacking the accuracy of either Luke or Paul, it is held.

Advocates of the South Galatian Theory, especially in Britain, widely support identifying the visits of Gal. 2:1–10 and Acts 11:30. This would mean that agreement was reached between Paul and the Jerusalem leaders on the admission of Gentiles to church membership during the famine-relief visit to Jerusalem, and prior to Paul's first mission to the Gentiles. It mitigates the problem of the omission of the Acts 15 decision from Galatians, and puts the confrontation of Peter by Paul at Antioch in a new light, *i.e.* before the Jerusalem decision. On this understanding the course of events would be approximately as follows: Paul and Barnabas, already engaged in Gentile work at Antioch, took the opportunity of the famine-relief visit to Jerusalem (AD 46) to discuss with the apostles the question of Jewish-Gentile fellowship. The presence of Titus with them sharpened the issue, but he was not compelled to be circumcised. The apostles agreed that Paul's apostleship was valid, and asked him to assist the poor, which he already had done

(Gal. 2:10). At Antioch Paul resumed his Gentile work. On a visit there Peter acknowledged the work of grace by sharing fellowship at the joint Jewish-Gentile table. But the arrival of Jewish-oriented representatives from Jerusalem embarrassed Peter, who withdrew, as did Barnabas. Paul challenged Peter and rebuked him before the whole church. Thereafter Paul and Barnabas were commissioned from Antioch to the first missionary journey, which quickly turned into a Gentile mission. Christians from Judea, while agreeing that Gentiles could become Christians, refused to give up claims that all Christians must abide by Jewish customs, including circumcision, as essential to salvation. Presumably, also, because such Judaizers were already reported to be influencing adversely Paul's converts in South Galatia, he at once wrote this Epistle to them. In addition, in order to settle the dispute, Paul and Barnabas were sent from Antioch to Jerusalem, where the Acts 15 meeting was convened. There James, with the support of Peter, tipped the balance in favour of Paul, but not without asking Gentiles to respect Jewish scruples to a certain degree. On this view Galatians is the earliest of Paul's extant Epistles (Duncan).

Proponents of the North Galatian Theory are bound by the traditional date of 54–56 AD, which places the Epistle during Paul's third missionary journey. The early date of 48–49 AD is not universally held by South Galatian Theory scholars. All that seems possible at present is to develop relative patterns of sequence and dating, but it is apparent that in the first place the date adopted depends on the destination. On the Northern Theory it is assumed that the Galatian churches knew about the Acts 15 meeting but, lacking vigilance, had been swayed from the truth. The same applies to the Southern Theory if it is combined with a late date (AD 54–56). The Northern Theory also preserves the view that in language, style, subject-matter and general atmosphere, Galatians is the natural link between 2 Corinthians and Romans. The Southern Theory combined with the early date (AD 48–49), while previously thought improbable chronologically, is possible. It provides an intelligible account of the sequence of events, especially of Paul's early ministry in relation to those who opposed him, and of the relationship of Peter and Paul to the Antioch confrontation and the Jerusalem meeting. On the early dating, Paul sees clearly and at once the theological implications of the Judaizing position and writes hurriedly and heatedly to his South Galatian converts to head off the trouble, pending later formal church action. To group the Epistle 6 or 8 years later, in the interests of the literary and logical coherence of 2 Corinthians, Galatians and Romans, seems to miss the likelihood that Judaizers were active from the outset of Paul's powerful evangelizing activity, and that Paul would not have remained silent so long when the future of the gospel was at stake. The Southern Theory combined with the early date is preferred here, though in the present state of our knowledge such a conclusion must be held with a certain reserve.

Jewish opposition to Paul was of two kinds. First, there were the Jews in the Gentile centres who incited the population against Paul's mission, as in Acts 17:5–7. Second, there were the Jewish Christians, probably from Judea, who ardently but erroneously tried to impose Jewish ceremonials, including circumcision, upon the Gentile converts; and who may have had no scruples about using non-Christian Jews to support their opposition to Paul. It is certain that standards of conduct under Jewish and Gentile law differed, and that beyond this the character of Gentile converts had to be transformed. Paul saw that the gospel alone was equal to this, and that imposition of the law on Gentiles destroyed the gospel because it frustrated the grace of God.

TEACHING

The Pauline authorship and the authenticity of Galatians have scarcely been questioned, either by ancients, as Marcion, or by modern critical schools. It is a highly personal and controversial letter. We may epitomize the themes under four headings:

Paul's own defence. Galatians is an intimately personal expression of Paul's own faith in Christ who 'gave himself for me', he says; and a powerful defence of his apostleship, of the true gospel, and of his right to preach the gospel, to plant churches, and to exercise care of them.

The gospel of grace. The central issue of Christianity is salvation by grace alone. How can the Galatians who began in grace continue under law (1:6; 3:3; 5:4)? Law condemns; it cannot justify. Ritual acts and good works offered as the basis for salvation destroy grace. No man can win acceptance with God on terms other than God's grace given freely. Anything less amounts to a denial of the completeness and finality of the cross of Christ.

Justification by faith. Faith on man's part is the only proper response to God's movement towards him in grace (2:16; 3:24). Hence the famous dictum of the Reformation: *sola gratia, sola fidei* ('by grace alone, by faith alone'). These are irreducible and crucial elements of the gospel. They are hallmarks of evangelical Christianity without which the gospel ceases to be of Christ (1:6, 7).

The fruit of grace and faith. The freedom of grace and faith is not an invitation to false security or to careless standards of living (5:1). The Christian begins under grace, continues under grace, and is not under law. The works of the flesh (which cannot be bridled by law) are evident, but the fruit of grace is the fruit of a Spirit-possessed life (5:22). God vindicates His grace and the life of faith in the proper use of liberty by His sons in Christ.

OUTLINE OF CONTENTS

COMMENTARY

1:1–5 INTRODUCTION

1, 2 *Paul an apostle.* In the opening sentence of the Epistle Paul at once expresses the apologetic and polemic tone which dominates the entire letter. Galatians has the character of an official document as well as of a personal letter. His apostleship has been challenged. He vigorously defends it on historical and theological grounds. The pre-resurrection function of the apostles (Mk. 3:14, 15) parallels their new, post-resurrection function as appointed by Christ to proclaim His words, deeds and resurrection. Paul refers elsewhere to the marks of his apostleship (1 Cor. 9:1, 2; 2 Cor. 12:12), but his primary claims are stated in Galatians: he was divinely commissioned by Christ and the Father, not by men; he has founded churches, especially among the Gentiles such as the Galatians, through the gospel; and his authority is independent of men by virtue of his commission and the gospel he preaches. His declaration is not an argument, but an incontrovertible statement. While he does not deny the apostleship of others, he will not submit to them, nor will he submit disputed questions to them. Paul recognizes no college of apostles above him, only Christ and the gospel. His reference to *all the brethren who are with me*

is an appeal to their concurrence with his views and claim, though they are unidentified. If the early dating of the Epistle is accepted (see Introduction, above) they may be his fellow-Christians and co-workers in the church at Antioch in Syria.

Not . . . nor . . . denies that his apostleship originated from men or was mediated through men. Conversely, it came directly and jointly *through Jesus Christ and God the Father*, with the added emphasis on the resurrection of Christ by the Father (*cf.* Rom. 1:4; Acts 13:36, 37). Paul also was a witness of the risen Christ (1 Cor. 15:8), who had commissioned him. That God is Father was no new doctrine (*cf.* Dt. 32:6), but that God is the God and Father of our Lord Jesus Christ (1 Pet. 1:3), with all that this conveys personally to NT Christians, is new to the NT era (*cf.* Rom. 8:15).

The churches of Galatia are those of Derbe, Lystra, Iconium and (Pisidian) Antioch (see Introduction, above). **3** *Grace* and *peace* are traditional Greek and Hebrew forms of greeting adapted to Christian usage and are commonly used by Paul. They point to God's loving-kindness in Jesus Christ, through which God is now by redemption 'our' Father, which reading is preferred to the RSV which connects 'our' with

Christ. *Grace* is God's unmerited favour towards sinners which is the basis of salvation. *Peace* is the state of well-being in which the recipients of grace are kept. The title *Lord* puts Christ on equal terms with the Father, and points to the common confession of Christians (*cf.* Acts 2:36; Rom. 10:9; Phil. 2:9–11).

4, 5 *Who gave himself for our sins* emphasizes the all-sufficient work Christ came to accomplish, and is complementary to the Father's raising Christ from the dead (Rom. 4:25). The sense is Christ's voluntary surrender to death in relation to our sins. In Paul this is to deal first with the condemnation (Gal. 3:13, 14; Rom. 3:23–26; 5:9, 10), and then the power of sin (Gal. 2:20; Rom. 6:1–11). The death of Christ was not a historical accident or expedient, but *according to the will of our God* to deliver us. The initiative was God's. The cross is central to Christian faith, not peripheral or simply a stumbling-block (Rom. 5:6; 1 Cor. 15:3). *The present evil age* means present evil world-system, or way of life, alienated from God (Gal. 4:3, 9; Rom. 12:2). The deliverance is rescue from the power of the world, not removal from it (note Jn. 17:15; Col. 2:13). To deal with sin is *to deliver us*. The action of rescue, which relates to our life, complements the action of atonement which deals with our sins. The inclusion of the statement in v. 4 in the introduction is significant. The importance of the death of Christ for the salvation of men is declared at the outset in order to challenge the error of the Judaizers who taught that works of men can save.

1:6 – 2:21 GOSPEL AUTHORITY

1:6–10 No other gospel

Paul casts aside his usual thanksgiving to express amazement at their defection and anger at those who deceive them.

6, 7 *So quickly deserting* shows that it is not long after their conversion. Their new life in Christ is probably at an early and critical stage of development, and Paul writes in great anxiety to head off spiritual disaster. They are, the wording implies, in the act of turning, but have not yet done so completely. As the gospel is not Paul's, so their call was not his, but God's; hence their defection is doubly bad. To desert the grace of Christ for law is also to desert God. Paul's opponents claimed for their message the designation of *gospel*, or 'good news', and they may have contrasted their message with his. *A different gospel* is a specious gospel, which is *another gospel* only in the absurd sense of one invented to confuse them (*cf.* 2 Cor. 11:4). *The gospel of Christ* stands *in the grace of Christ* The term *grace* holds the primary position in the sentence. Paul's astonishment is due to their so quickly turning away from grace (*i.e.* that of Christ), to be ensnared by law. The two are mutually exclusive options. **8** Even if Paul himself or *an angel* should preach a gospel different from that which he and others originally preached

to them (which suggests that such an option can exist), *let him be accursed.* **9** Hence, if *anyone* is now preaching to them such an option (therefore the urgency of Paul's letter), *let him be accursed* (*cf.* Rom. 9:3), which means 'condemned by God'.

10 shows that the Judaizers attacked Paul personally by alleging that he compromised by appealing to the interests of men in order to seek their favour. Such a charge is contrary to his purpose, as stated in 1 Cor. 9:19–23; 10:23–33. The tone of this letter itself contradicts the charge that he curries favour. To please men Paul would have remained a Pharisee and would not have entered the service of Christ as His slave. The primary issue is not pride, but the truth of the gospel and the true nature of salvation, involving free grace and faith in contrast to keeping the law.

1:11–17 The gospel divinely revealed

The divine, not human, origin of the gospel is Paul's crucial point in his vindication of its truth, of the validity of his apostleship, and of his independence as an apostle.

11 It is *not man's gospel; i.e.,* lit. 'the gospel preached by me is not according to man'. **12** Nor did it have a human source (which would make Paul's apostleship inferior). Nor did he receive it by instruction. But *it came through a revelation of Jesus Christ.* It is Christ who was revealed to Paul, which disclosure carried along with it the conviction of the truth of the Christian gospel (*cf.* 2:5, 14). The *revelation* included for him divinely prompted re-interpretation of the Christian facts, which he before held to be punishable blasphemy (Acts 9:1, 2, 5, 20–22); and divinely given new insights on the Christian realities (Eph. 3:3–5). Paul thus got a true understanding of who Jesus Christ is and of what He came to do. So Paul received the gospel. **13** We do not know fully the extent and locations of Paul's persecuting activity, but his name struck terror to Christians (*cf.* v. 23). He states that his activity was against *the church of God*, which here significantly identifies the whole body of Christians. **14** Paul's extreme zeal was born of early dedication to Judaism when, as a young man, he had blazed a trail of commitment to the Pharisaic traditions far ahead of his contemporaries. **15, 16** But from this Paul was turned by God. Significant textual evidence supports the AV 'but when it pleased God'; however, by omitting 'God' RSV correctly gives the reading of more weighty MS evidence. On either reading the hand of God in Paul's life is clear. So completely is Paul's conversion by *grace*, that he acknowledges the divine purpose for him prior to his birth and the divine initiative to call him and to *reveal his Son* within him. The phrases are forceful and carefully chosen: *set me apart, called me through his grace,* and *was pleased to reveal.* To me is properly 'in me' or 'within me', *i.e.* with no reference to others. This highly personal testimony and confession of indebtedness to grace alone is a powerful apologetic for the gratuitous and decisive character of the saving act of God in Christ. Paul's apostolic commission to preach Christ *among the Gentiles* was unique and independent. Jewish Christians acknowledged the unqualified extension of the gospel to non-Jews only grudgingly at the first, as Acts 10, 11, 15 show. **17** Since the gospel, Paul's conversion and his commission were all independent of men, he did not seek counsel from men nor a briefing by the original apostles. What Paul experienced and knew came directly from Christ. The visit to *Arabia* refers probably to the area eastward from Damascus (*cf.* Acts 9:25; 2 Cor. 11:32, 33). We do not know what Paul did in Arabia. Perhaps he pondered his new experience and knowledge in the light of the OT teaching on the Messiah, and began his preaching career.

1:18–24 Human approval unsought

Paul reinforces the foregoing points by alluding to the private, fraternal character of his first visit to Jerusalem, which did not occur until three years after his conversion (*cf.* Acts 9:26–30).

18 *To visit Cephas* (Peter) means 'to get acquainted with', not to seek the instruction or approval of Peter. It may also mean 'to get information from Cephas', *i.e.* possibly information about Jesus' life and ministry which Peter knew at first hand; or to satisfy his curiosity to meet Peter. **19** Paul did not meet the other apostles; hence he had not sought their approval. He did meet *James*, our Lord's younger brother (not James the son of Zebedee, Acts 12:2), though it is not clear whether at this time James was regarded as an apostle. Paul means, 'I visited Peter, casually met James, but met no other person of importance.' **20** Paul stresses the truth of his narrative, that this initial visit would have been crucial to any apostolic approval, had he sought it. He remained unknown outside Jerusalem, and probably only later preached in Judea (*cf.* Acts 26:20), which points to the personal nature of his initial visit. **21–24** The report of his conversion and preaching reached the Judean churches, causing them to give glory to God. Actually, he exercised his apostolic ministry in *Syria and Cilicia*, which corresponds to our knowledge of his connection with the Antioch church (*cf.* Acts 9:30; 11:25). For this he had not been commissioned by the apostles at Jerusalem nor by the Judean churches. Thus, neither the purpose of his first visit to Jerusalem, nor his meeting with Peter and James, nor the reputation which his ministry had in Judea, nor his activity in Syria and Cilicia evoked any question about his gospel or his commission to preach it. Likewise, his second, more formal visit to Jerusalem, to which he now turns (2:1), yields the same conclusion. In the interval, too, he had felt no need of a consultative visit to Jerusalem.

It is not possible to solve the problem of the relationship of the 3 years to the 14, nor of how the 14 or 17 years fit into Paul's early career as a Christian and apostle. However, the differences between 1:19–22 and Acts 9:26–30 are not irreconcilable if the general character of the narrative in Acts in contrast to the very specific detail in Galatians is borne in mind (see Introduction).

2:1–10 The priority of gospel authority

1, 2 In the light of the Introduction, the meeting mentioned in these verses should be identified with Acts 11:29, 30. If we include the 3 years of 1:18 in the 14, Paul's conversion occurred probably in AD 35; otherwise it would be in AD 32. Paul's visit to Jerusalem was not in response to an apostolic summons, but by reason of inner divine urging. Or Paul may be referring to the prophecy of Agabus (see Acts 11:27–30). At a private meeting Paul outlined to the Christian leaders in Jerusalem the gospel he preached to Gentiles. The passage indicates that troublesome persons did cavil at his claims to freedom from Jewish custom, but there is no hint that this was ever true of the apostles. Paul writes, knowing he has the prominent leaders of the church on his side. The meeting also shows that a considerable body of Jewish-oriented opinion against Paul had developed within the church. This identification of the meeting rather than the traditional connection with Acts 15 mitigates somewhat the problem of the qualifications enjoined on Gentile converts in Acts 15:19–21, 28, 29, as against the complete absence of them in Gal. 2:9, 10. The Acts 15 agreement thus becomes a later concession to Jewish-Christian sensibilities without compromising the essential nature of the gospel, on which all the leaders were agreed. Paul's concern is to reconfirm this understanding, lest his past and present work, set here in the figure of *running* a race, should be to no purpose if the Jerusalem church opposed him. The integrity and unity of the Christian movement were at stake.

3–5 The sentence structure is notoriously difficult to unravel. Paul condemns the despicable spying on their persons by traitors who falsely presented themselves as Christian brethren, and he resists strenuously their attempts to impose the Jewish custom of circumcision on Titus. Paul aimed in principle to preserve the purity, simplicity and freedom of the gospel not only for the Galatians, but by implication for all Gentiles. Should we understand that Titus was not compelled to be circumcised and in fact remained uncircumcised; or that, though not compelled, he submitted to the rite for the sake of Jewish-Christian scruples? Many commentators hold that Titus did submit to circumcision as a practical matter of association with Jewish Christians (*cf.* Acts 16:3), but not on the theological grounds of circumcision being necessary for salvation. However, in view of Paul's emphatic statement in v. 5 Titus probably did not submit, for if he had done so it would have proved embarrassing to Paul both theologically and as an act of compromise. While some texts omit 'not' most key ones contain it, as in RSV. Paul did not and would not yield on 'the submission issue', not even for an hour.

6–10 Paul's reference to the Jerusalem leadership as men *of repute* (*cf.* v. 2) included the three apostles designated *pillars*. He acknowledges their position but not their suzerainty. His words in v. 6 can also be interpreted as irony: what these men were mattered nothing to him nor to the truth of his message. They added or taught nothing new. To substitute 'Peter' for *Cephas* and to put his name before that of James, as some western texts do in v. 9, is suspect as an attempt to elevate Peter. The points of similarity between them and Paul are threefold: the same gospel, equally valid commissioning, and equally vindicating results by the Spirit. These were never in question. Only now they publicly acknowledged that, just as they were appointed to Jewish evangelism, Paul was divinely entrusted with the work among Gentiles. But the message of both was identical. Hence the hand given to Paul and Barnabas in fellowship was also a pledge of agreement. Their only request (not demand) was not theological but practical, namely help for *the poor*, which Paul had been eager to give. Crucial to the argument is their acknowledgment that Paul's gospel is true, his calling and work equally as valid as Peter's, and that his accomplishments were due to divine *grace* given to him.

This significant incident publicly confirms a new phase of Christian understanding. If not theologically (except for a small minority; *cf.* Acts 15:1, 24), at least socially, Christians were divided into two groups over questions of foods, circumcision and other ceremonial rites of Jewish tradition. Paul insisted that the true gospel is of grace, not law, that it liberates men from law, and that liberated men in the fellowship of the one church must not be subjected to Jewish scruples. Otherwise the gospel is undercut and unity is destroyed. The new faith is morally life-transforming and barrier-breaking on the basis of grace and faith, and is not based on belonging to a particular race and observing certain rules. It is a freedom 'in Christ' in contrast to bondage 'under law'. Theologically, the apostles were in agreement. But the new reality must now revise the thought-categories of the Jewish Christians as well as transform the moral life of Gentile converts.

2:11–14 Paul rebukes Peter at Antioch

11, 12 The confrontation with Peter vindicates Paul on the nature of the gospel, but it shows Peter's conduct to be inconsistent with his faith. Prior to the Acts 15 meeting the theological issue had been settled between the apostles; only practical questions concerning Jewish-Christian scruples remained. Since Barnabas was associated with Paul on only the first missionary journey, this incident and the writing of Galatians may be dated early in Paul's career. The connection

of the incident with Acts 15:1, 24 seems assured. While visiting Antioch, Peter had shared fellowship with Gentile Christians at meals, presumably including the Lord's Supper, but when the *men . . . from James* arrived, whose views James did not share, Peter withdrew. Significant textual evidence allows a singular indefinite pronoun (note the indefiniteness of AV), instead of the plural *certain men* of RSV. But the latter is the preferred reading. This event is not to be construed as a repudiation of the earlier apostolic agreement, but the natural emergence of conflicting views which are superseded only gradually and not without controversy.

The face-to-face encounter suggests that its purpose was to clear the issue, not personal hostility. *Stood condemned* means that Peter indicted himself by his own actions (Moff. 'self-condemned'). Since arriving, Peter had been eating habitually with Gentiles; but because opposition appeared he cautiously and probably gradually retreated, fearing the circumcision party. **13** His example, which was not only theologically inconsistent (*cf.* Acts 11:1–18) but ethically hypocritical, influenced other Jewish Christians, including Barnabas. Involved were traditional Jewish scruples about eating with Gentiles (the circumcised Jew avoided the uncircumcised Gentile, where circumcision was seen as a mark of obedience to the Mosaic laws; *cf.* Acts 10:28). It is known that Jews drew up forms of ethical instruction for Gentile converts. Even though these may be similar at some points to Christian virtues, the point of the gospel is that no man is saved by formal religious obedience but by grace, and no man is bound by another's religious scruples but by Christ (*cf.* 1 Cor. 10:20–33).

14 The issue again is the nature of *the gospel*, but as expressed in its results, which can be only the common, equal fellowship of Christians redeemed by grace. Anything less would make of Christians party groups, not the one body of Christ. *Straightforward* here means 'correct', or 'on the right road', rather than morally right; they were not going straight towards *the truth of the gospel* (*cf.* Acts 11:17) at the point where they altered course and withdrew from Gentiles. While knowing the truth, they acted inconsistently with the truth. Paul's actual words quoted in v. 14 pointedly remind Peter of his freedom in the gospel: how can he, as a converted Jew who enjoys the freedom to ignore Jewish scruples, especially on questions of foods, compel Gentiles to submit to non-essential Jewish religious *mores*?

2:15–21 At issue: Christ or law?

Key terms of this passage, such as sin, works, justification, grace, the cross, faith, and union with Christ, comprise the heart of the gospel and of Christian experience. Paul shows that legalism, or confidence in one's own observance of moral standards, no less than religious formalism, is the enemy of the gospel, because both come under the heading of 'works'. Sin is coming short of God's standard, not man's; righteousness depends on God's acquittal of sinners through Christ, not on man's efforts to be saved. Justification by faith is the touchstone of the gospel. Though a legal term, it expresses a moral and spiritual reality. It should be studied with the parallel passages in Romans in mind. In view is the sinner's standing before God (Rom. 4:22 – 5:2). Justification by God is God's free acquittal of condemned men in undeserved grace (Rom. 5:17). It is to account righteous, not to make righteous, and rests justly on the atoning death of Christ (Rom. 3:26). Christ died our death. Men are justified by faith alone (2:16), *i.e.* by the grace of God in Christ on which faith lays hold. To respond in faith means to put complete reliance on Christ. It is radical and unreserved trust that God has acted in Christ to save, and that He acts through Christ to justify. Condemnation and guilt are removed through absolute pardon. The new standing with God in Christ is the condition of the new spiritual life. Once it is clear that salvation is based on grace alone, then the life of faith yields appropriate works of grace. James Denney wrote, 'The miracle of the Gospel is that God comes to the ungodly, with a mercy which is righteous altogether, and enables them through faith, in spite of what they are, to enter into a new relation to himself, in which goodness becomes possible for them' (*Expositor's Greek Testament*, II, p. 616).

15, 16 Paul turns quickly to the vital theological issue. The *we ourselves*, in contrast to *Gentile sinners*, is a jibe, *i.e.* born Jews like himself and Peter, who are not *sinners* by being born Gentiles, already know that no-one is *justified by works of the law*. In view are differing Jewish and Christian conceptions of sin. Law-works are acts of obedience to Jewish law, involving moral and religious rules thought to be necessary for salvation. He quotes the OT for added proof (Ps. 143:2). All men are sinners in a sense far greater than any cultic or ethnic meaning. The decisive issue is that men cannot be justified by law-works, but only *through faith in Jesus Christ*. This passage epitomizes the remaining argument of the book, which Paul develops later in identical fashion (*cf.* Rom. 3:21–31). We put our faith in Christ for justification, says Paul, because experience and knowledge both showed us that a man is unable to be justified by law-works. Men cannot be delivered from their guilt and condemnation by their own self-adjudged good deeds. The issue concerns God's righteousness, not man's. Justification and righteousness are interchangeable terms which translate the same Greek word group.

17, 18 Still speaking from the standpoint of a Jew, Paul extends the argument with brotherly feeling, having Peter in mind, but with a double-play of meaning. Against Paul it was said that by their acceptance of faith-justification Jews

became *sinners* (violators of the law), which they never were previously, by fraternizing with Gentiles. All Christians, including Jewish ones, agreed that Christ could not encourage sin, but this is not the same as to say that Christ approves Jewish scruples. Rather, Paul says, if he as a Christian should now allow the law to dictate to him, as one who has been released from it through Christ, then he stands self-convicted. To turn back to law is the real sin (as Peter well knows); to cling to Christ by faith is the only salvation. Jewish and Christian meanings of sin and righteousness are sharply contrasted. Christ has allegedly furthered their sinning, *i.e.* their falling short of law-righteousness. Paul's teaching is thus claimed to degrade righteousness (of the law) and to disgrace Christ. But, to be a violator of Jewish law is not equivalent to being a wrongdoer or violator of God's will. The emphatic *Certainly not!*—a sharp repudiation translated 'God forbid' in AV (*cf.* 3:21)—tears at this specious argument. In v. 18 Paul tactfully applies to himself the net effect of Peter's conduct: to *build up again* the wall of laws and ordinances, which he had before torn down, is really by these very standards to make oneself a sinner. Men are totally and unconditionally indebted to Christ for salvation.

19 The nature of the law compels a sinner to abandon it as a means of salvation. Paul may mean that he *died to the law* because in Christ he is in a new realm no longer related to the law (*cf.* Rom. 8:2); or, more likely, he means that the law could only condemn him to death which, when he saw his true situation, compelled him to cast himself upon God's grace rather than rely on his own works (*cf.* Rom. 7:9–12). **20** There follows the gem of personal testimony on the nature of salvation and of Christian experience. *I have been crucified with Christ* points to a decisive act of faith in the past when Paul had committed life and destiny to Christ. It happened then, but continues in effect now and henceforth. He was in that act identified with Christ in His death, a fact symbolized in baptism (*cf.* Rom. 6:3, 4). Christ died the death that Paul was condemned to die for sin and in that death Paul died (*cf.* 2 Cor. 5:14; Rom. 6:3). Here he says he died to self and all pretensions to self-salvation, and elsewhere he says he died to sin and the sinful world (*cf.* Gal. 6:14; Rom. 6:1–11). No longer does self rule in Paul, but Christ lives within his life. This is union with Christ. It is the supremely personal relation the Christian has with the Lord Jesus. Only by the interpenetration of personal lives do men become personal. Through Christ's own presence in them they become true spiritual persons. Though dead with Christ, the Christian lives in Christ and Christ in him. *The life I now live* is the present life every Christian must live, but he lives it by trust in Christ, just as he committed himself by faith to Christ initially. *Son of God* is a direct reference to Christ's divinity (*cf.* Phil. 2:6). The redemption comes not by a mere verbal protestation of love, but through Christ's love for us which brought Him to self-sacrificing death. This death was not merely an act of human violence or an accident of history, but the self-giving of Christ on behalf of sinners (Gal. 3:13; cf. Mk. 10:45; Rom. 5:6; 1 Jn. 4:10). **21** By this Paul neither sets aside grace nor breaks faith with it, for if justification can come through obedience to the law, the death of Christ is *to no purpose*. There is therefore an immediate and necessary connection between the death of Christ and the justification of sinful men before God. There is an equally necessary connection between godliness and the presence of Christ in the Christian's life.

3:1 – 4:31 DOCTRINAL ARGUMENT

3:1–5 Appeal to history and experience

Paul develops the foregoing statement in greater detail referring directly to the Galatian situation.

1 To begin with, their own conversion experience should have prevented them from being so *foolish* (*i.e.* gullible or unperceptive, not naturally stupid) as to turn to law. *Bewitched* means 'as if blinded by malicious magic', but metaphorically not literally, which to Paul is the more remarkable when those same eyes had been fastened upon Christ, who had been *publicly* placarded or advertised to them *as crucified* (*cf.* Jn. 3:14, 15; 1 Cor. 1:18–25; 2:2). They have been hoodwinked. The early Christians rejected esoteric mysteries and sorcery. They insisted on the public character of God's revelation in Christ, of the cross, the gospel, and Christian fellowship. The tense of *crucified* indicates not just a past event, but one accomplished in the past, the results of which continue to the present. **2–5** The rhetorical questions drive the point home by relating their receiving of the Spirit to Christ crucified and faith, not to ritual observances. To trust Christ, who was put to death on the cross and rose again, and to receive the gift of the Spirit, are indivisible aspects of NT salvation (*cf.* Acts 2:38; Eph. 1:13). But the Spirit is God's gift in response to faith, not works. Therefore, he asks, did you receive the Spirit by obeying the law, or by believing the gospel? Are you so unperceptive as to suppose you could begin with the Spirit of God, but be completed or perfected by external acts? The antithesis is twofold: beginning . . . ending; Spirit . . . flesh (*cf.* 2 Cor. 3:6; Phil. 1:6). The 'experiences' may mean what they have already suffered as Christians, or, more likely, spiritual benefits of their faith. Whether these are *in vain* is still in doubt, depending on whether they lapse completely into legalism. Finally, did God give His Spirit and accomplish actual signs among them (*cf.* 1 Cor. 12:1–11) on the ground of works of law, or hearing and believing the gospel message? As with the gift of the cross, so with the Spirit; the initiative is God's, to which the only appropriate human response is faith.

Paul contrasts Spirit and flesh sharply (*cf.* Rom. 8:1–17). Used variously, *flesh* sometimes designates simply a human being or the material body of a living creature (Gal. 1:16; 2:16 (AV); 2 Cor. 12:7), the basis of natural reproduction (Rom. 9:5), and secular or corporeally conditioned life (Gal. 2:20; 4:13, 14 (AV); 6:12). The main line of usage, however, is to identify and characterize what natural generation produces and what natural sinful life is, apart from the regenerating power of the Spirit of God (*cf.* Jn. 3:6; 1 Pet. 1:23–25). Hence *flesh* stands for man's fallen nature and its sinful deeds (Gal. 5:13–24; 6:8; Rom. 13:14). It is the force which opposes good and which corrupts. The flesh produces vices; the Spirit, virtues. This includes ritual religion seen as external acts which leave the inner life untouched (Gal. 3:3; 6:12, 13). Paul does not denigrate the body or the material world which God has created, but the natural unregenerate life with its sinful propensities (*cf.* Rom. 8:8).

3:6–9 The witness of Abraham

To a Jew, the authority of Abraham was decisive. Paul shows that, theologically, Abraham was accepted by God through faith, not works. Scripture thus corroborates Paul's gospel and their own experience.

6 'Hearing with faith' (*cf.* v. 5) is illustrated in *Abraham* who, as the father of the Jews, antedates Moses, and whose faith is compared with the Galatians' faith. Abraham's importance to the argument shows in the next two chapters also. It is crucial that Abraham not only acted rightly, but that through believing God's promise, righteousness was *reckoned* (or imputed) *to him* (*cf.* Gn. 15:6). In answer to his opponents at Galatia, Paul declares that Abraham's faith, not his circumcision (Gn. 17:14), was reckoned to him as the ground of acceptance with God and is the deeper basis of the covenant. Answering faith takes God at His word. **7** Therefore, not Jews as natural descendants, but *men of faith* are Abraham's true descendants, *i.e.* men whose standing before God and whose life derive from faith. **8** Further, the OT anticipated the inclusion of Gentiles in the promise (Gn. 12:3), but through faith (note Rom. 4), not circumcision as the Judaizers claimed. **9** *Men of faith* are blessed now, along with believing Abraham. The faith-basis of the gospel is the same, then or now. In response to God's promise, Abraham believed; in response to God's word in Christ through the gospel, men today are called to believe, and thereby to receive the blessing of righteousness put to their account. When Paul speaks of righteousness as being *reckoned* to the Christian he is using legal terminology; but there is nothing of legal fiction about it. Christ's righteousness is imputed to believing sinners (*cf.* Acts 13:39; Rom. 5:1, 9; 10:4). The Christian stands in a new relation to God in a righteousness not his own. The forensic sense is clear from Rom. 3:20–28; 4:5–7; as well as from this passage and elsewhere in Galatians (2:16; 3:11; 5:4). Imputed righteousness is antithetical to condemnation (*cf.* Rom. 8:33, 34), and interchangeable ideas convey an equivalent sense (*cf.* Jn. 3:18; Rom. 4:6–8, 24; 2 Cor. 5:19).

3:10–14 The law curses, but faith makes alive

From the Galatians' experience and the biblical argument based on Abraham, the argument moves to examine the logic of reliance on the law.

10 First, law can only condemn, hence to rely on it is to incur the curse of Dt. 27:26. While this is the verdict of law, Paul means to deny (2:16) the affirmative proposition (v. 12) derived from it by the Jews, namely that he who fulfils all the law shall live. Paul is distinguishing verdicts of law, derived by the legalist, and the judgment of God. The purpose of law is to exhibit and judge the guilty, not to acquit them. **11** To the Galatians the specific point is that, Judaizers to the contrary, Christians are not obliged to keep the law for salvation. Christ frees us from the law. Righteousness, the Spirit and life come not through the law, but through Christ by faith. *It is evident* that no man, *i.e.* no human by human achievement, can be justified before the holy God, for, as Paul shows, even the OT testifies that the righteous man shall live by faith (Hab. 2:4; *cf.* Rom. 1:17). The passage from Habakkuk is not used as a proof-text exegetically, but as an apt illustration of a broadly-based biblical principle, which is proved from God's dealings with Abraham. In this context, as elsewhere in Paul's writings, the *righteous* means the man who has a standing of saving righteousness before God, *i.e.* the man accepted or approved by God for the sake of Christ. This happens only through believing. **12** Now the law is not based on a response of faith, but on our actions. It cannot deal with our sin and guilt. Besides, no man can do all that the law requires. Legalism and belief in the work of Christ exclude each other as bases of justification. **13, 14** In sharp contrast, *Christ redeemed us* from the just condemnation which the law imposed on our sin. 'To redeem' means to deliver by payment of the cost of deliverance, *i.e.* a ransom, which is the death of Christ (*cf.* 1 Cor. 6:19, 20; 7:22, 23; Mk. 10:45; 1 Tim. 2:6; Tit. 2:14). Christ bore our judgment and died our death (2 Cor. 5:14, 20, 21) vicariously, as our Substitute and Representative. *For us* cannot mean less than both 'in our place' and 'for our sake'. Christ entered into the area of death caused by our sin, taking to Himself our judgment and satisfying its demands completely under the conditions of holy obedience to God. Sin's penalty was borne in a substitutionary way. He bore our curse, the curse cited from Dt. 21:23, which is equivalent to the wrath of Rom. 1:18 and 2:8. In his Christian understanding of sin and guilt, this text from Deuteronomy no longer left room to Paul, as it did in the Pharisaic

tradition, for a ritual or ethical obedience which could justify a religious man.

3:15–18 Law cannot annul promise

15 To illustrate the priority of promise over law, Paul employs the analogy of a last will and testament. The same Greek word is translated *will* here and *covenant* in v. 17. Under some ancient legal systems, even a testator could not cancel a valid will nor add a codicil. **16** The divine agreement referred, says Paul, not to the plurality of Abraham's natural descendants, but *to his offspring*, seen to be *Christ* as the head of a new race. The sense is not to successive generations of men, but fulfilment in one kind of offspring, which is summed up in Christ. This interpretation is not evident in the language of Gn. 12:7; 13:15; 17:7, 8 and 22:18, but neither is it excluded. Paul's teaching gives us a key to history in its movement towards fulfilment in Christ, and in the union with Christ of those who are 'men of faith' (*cf.* vv. 7, 9) and who inherit the promise. **17** The exact period of time between the promise and the giving of the law is not germane to Paul's argument (see Gn. 15:13; Ex. 12:40; Acts 7:6), though we note that Paul usually quotes the LXX, and that here he gives the actual duration of Israelitish stay in Egypt. He means, rather, that the later giving of the law did not and could not annul the covenant to Abraham. Law cannot make the promise of no account, and neither can works displace faith. **18** If the inheritance now comes by law, promise and faith are cancelled. However, God gave the blessing to Abraham by promise and faith. This does not undercut the validity of law, nor is the law to be regarded as a codicil which displaces promise, because law is not the condition of receiving the promise. As a later addition in the history of God's dealings with man, it serves to uncover and to judge sin, as Paul proceeds to show.

3:19–29 The custodial function of law

19 The subordinate position of the law to the covenant is seen in the supplementary and temporary character of the law, for it was given till the offspring should arrive to whom the promise was made; and because it was enacted by angels (*cf.* Acts 7:53; Heb. 2:2) through Moses as the intermediary, it was therefore not given directly as was the covenant to Abraham. This view was a prevailing rabbinic tradition. *Because of transgressions* points to what follows the giving of the law. In addition to sin seen as evil impulse, Paul speaks here of sin as violation of known law. The overt, rebellious character of sin which makes men doubly culpable is in view. The law furnished a norm by which transgressions were produced (*cf.* Rom. 3:20; 4:15; 5:13, 14, 20; 7:7–12). **20** Wherever there is *an intermediary*, a plurality of persons exists, whereas *God is one*. Paul depreciates the law because it came from God indirectly, rather than directly as did the covenant of promise. In the latter God acted directly in the sovereign freedom of His grace.

21 While this is so, the law is not contrary to God's promises. If law had the power to give life, righteousness would be due to law; but to put sinful men right with God is neither the function nor the power of law, as already stated. **22** Rather, the truth is that Scripture has shut up everything under sin (Dt. 27:26; *cf.* Rom. 3:10–18), *i.e.* under condemnation, which is the verdict of the law against sinners. This occurred so that the promise, which comes to faith, might be given to those who believe in Jesus Christ. Paul affirms again the gratuitous character of the promise and gift to men of faith, not to men of works. God's main, final, and direct way of dealing with men is through grace and faith.

23–25 Stated more positively, the law functioned as a *custodian* until the gospel came. The custodial function is not educative, but restraining or disciplining. What is meant is not progress in religion, but being in custody awaiting the Redeemer. Men were kept like wards under guard, not (as in RSV) until *faith* came, but until they could obtain 'the faith' (23b, AV) which was to be revealed. 'Faith' as the proper human response to God is certainly intended here, but Paul has already argued that faith was the basis of the OT covenant also. Here 'the faith' or 'the event by which faith came' is equivalent to the Christian gospel, in contrast to the law. We were wards under the law like children under prohibitions, which is all that the law could do, until Christ came, in order that we might be acquitted by faith. One historical period succeeds another. The era of the law is succeeded and displaced by the new age of the free gospel of Christ. 'The faith' having thus come, we are free of the custodian.

In the Graeco–Roman world the child-custodian (pedagogue), or attendant, fulfilled certain clearly-defined functions. He was often a slave appointed by the parent to conduct the child to school and to have general charge of him until he came of age, even to imparting ethical instruction to him. If the child must travel abroad for his education, it was the attendant's responsibility to put him under a suitable teacher. Competent attendants were highly esteemed by parents, and children were required to respect them.

26 In contrast to the status of wards, *in Christ Jesus* you are all *sons of God, through faith*. It is full sonship, not custody. The characteristic Pauline phrase 'in Christ' means united to Christ personally (2 Cor. 5:17). There follows a climactic passage. **27** The only way to share the inheritance of promise is faith-union with Christ. The happening is wrought by God in baptism (*cf.* Rom. 6:1–11), not as an outward act (1 Pet. 3:21), but through the response of each man's own faith in Christ. In baptism we *put on Christ*. The figure of changing garments attests to the inner spiritual change. We strip off the clothes of the old life to be clothed with the garments of Christ's righteousness through

faith-baptism (note the same figure in Ps. 132:9; Is. 61:10; 64:6; Zc. 3:3). **28** In this new life all ethnic, caste and other old distinctions are destroyed, in favour of complete equality within union with Christ. **29** Being Christ's, who is Abraham's true offspring, Christians are heirs of the promise along with Christ.

4:1-7 Analogy of the heir

The analogy of the child-heir continues, the chapter division being arbitrary.

1, 2 The sharpness of the argument is maintained in the threefold characterization of the heir as *child* (immature), *no better than a slave*, and *under guardians* (for his welfare) *and trustees* (for his estate). Traditions in the ancient world varied on the matter of transition from childhood to social and legal coming of age (probably age 17 or 18), hence the precise legal situation Paul had in mind is uncertain, though it probably was a definite one. The term *date set* does not require the death of the father. The sense may be that parentally designated guardianship and legally established trusteeship were concurrent, though the duration of social and legal coming of age may have differed. In this passage what goes beyond the point of 3:24 is that the subservience looks to emancipation. God Himself always had in view a future time for our deliverance from the law. **3** Similarly Christians generally, like the immature child, were under controls, but in the far worse state of slavery to *the elemental spirits of the universe* (see vv. 8, 9).

The point of vv. 3 and 8–11 is that Gentiles as much as Jews are under bondage; however, the argument slips back in vv. 4–7 to the question of the Jewish law.

4 The possibility of our new relation as sons rests on God's purpose, the incarnation, the atonement, and the Holy Spirit. The sense of providential intervention characterizes God's saving action (*cf.* Rom. 5:6; Eph. 1:9, 10), on a date set by Him. *Time . . . fully come* is a metaphor of year added to year, like an unfilled measure filled drop by drop, until the fullness of it came. *God sent forth his Son* points to Christ's pre-existence, deity, incarnation, and mission, *i.e.* to His whole saving mission. The Son came forth from God. *Born of woman* concerns His true humanity, *i.e.* a man among men (*cf.* Phil. 2:6–8). In this passage the term *woman* is neither confirmation nor denial of the virgin birth of Jesus. *Born under the law* is that system the curse of which He takes to Himself (*cf.* 3:13), and the restraints of which He experiences (*cf.* 3:23; Heb. 2:15). **5** *To redeem* (see on 3:13) *those . . . under the law* includes in this passage strictly not only Jews, but Gentiles also, for Christ delivers them from bondage as well, and Paul sees Gentiles under law (*cf.* Rom. 2:14, 15). *Receive adoption as sons* says that those who are not natural heirs acquire the status of sonship by sheer grace and gift. Sonship is vouchsafed to us through the indwelling Spirit (*cf.* 1 Cor. 6:19; Rom. 5:5; 8:11) who makes Christ a reality in our lives (*cf.* Jn. 15:26). **6** *The Spirit of his Son* (*cf.* Rom. 8:9) is cited often in support of the Spirit's procession from the Father and from the Son. The filial cry *Abba!* is the childish 'Daddy' in Aramaic, to which is joined the Greek translation *Father*. The familiar form was introduced to Christians by our Lord (*cf.* Mk. 14:36), and indicates trust and liberty, as against the strictures of legalism. **7** To conclude, the result is to be *a son*, not *a slave*; and, if a son, then *an heir*, made so by God.

4:8–11 The bondage of custom and tradition

8, 9 The *elemental spirits* (*cf.* v. 3) may be rudiments of knowledge or of the nature of things in the sense that the ABCs are the rudiments of language. To others, they are the beings designated *no gods*, *i.e.* celestial and demonic powers which control destiny, as in ancient astrology and mythology (*cf.* 1 Cor. 8:4–6). The devotee was related to these as a slave, not like the Christian to the true God as a son. The elemental spirits are by nature excluded from being God, and were served only because the Galatians did not formerly know God. *But now* marks the dramatic transition *to know God* through the gospel, indeed, *to be known by God*. The initiative was God's: they became the objects of His gracious concern. How totally irrational and unthinkable therefore to turn back to, or to wish to be enslaved again by, powers proved to be impotent (they cannot save men) and impoverished (in comparison to the heirs of God in Christ)! **10, 11** Paul is concerned lest his work should be frustrated because they have returned to legalistic religious play-acting. Such mummery included *days* (sabbath), *months* (new moons), *seasons* (recurrent festivals), and *years* (jubilee years). Are these Jewish or pagan observances? In writing to the Galatians, Paul clearly has Judaizers in mind. Did these worship elemental spirits? Astrological elements were at times infused into Jewish as well as pagan practices. The *elemental spirits* of this passage refer probably to the ethos of an age traceable in part to pagan astrological mythology, but which had become a religious habit as much as, and perhaps more than, a metaphysical system (*cf.* Col. 2:8).

4:12–20 Appeal to first love

12 Paul drops the argument, which is resumed in vv. 21–31, to make a personal appeal, especially noted in the affectionate terms *Brethren* and *I beseech*, or entreat, *you*. The grammatical form of the entreaty is doubtful, but the meaning is not. The second clause of the comparison is without a verb, hence we might translate: 'become as I (am, or have become), because I (am, or have become) as you (are).' He urges them to be free of the law, as he is; for he, having been a zealous Jew, jettisoned the law to put himself on their level (*cf.* 1 Cor. 9:22). He means 'take my stance' or 'adopt my outlook', *i.e.* do not seek to become Jews. *You did*

me no wrong may point to their original warm welcome, or to their freedom to hear alternative viewpoints; only he now begs that they return to their affection for him.

13 The occasion of his *first*, or a former, visit raises the chronological and geographical questions mentioned in the Introduction. On the view adopted here, the visit occurred when Paul and Barnabas arrived in Asia Minor from Cyprus on the first missionary journey. However, it is felt by some that the natural sense of this passage points to two visits prior to his writing Galatians. Whether Paul experienced a recurrent illness which can be identified with 2 Cor. 12:7, or a weakening disability, or an illness such as malaria contracted in Pamphylia (Acts 13:13), is uncertain. However, the illness compelled him to seek a different climate, hence his visit to them and his initial evangelistic efforts among them. **14** Despite his weakened, even repulsive, condition, which might have tempted the Galatians to reject or despise him, they received him as if he were a super-human being, even as Christ Jesus Himself. This may allude wryly to what is recorded in Acts 14:12. **15** *Satisfaction* suggests, rather, self-congratulation at their good fortune. Where is that feeling now, asks Paul? Their happiness had been so great that, had it been possible, they would have given him their own *eyes*. This is not a likely reference to his poor eyesight, but a common eastern metaphor expressing personal indebtedness to a benefactor.

16 is more an ironical exclamation than a question: 'So I have become hated for telling you the truth!' **17** The Judaizers zealously pursue them, but seditiously, in an effort to capture their interest, *i.e.* to make the Galatians jealous of the Judaizers' doctrines. **18** It is good to be courted always, Paul adds, so long as it is done in a good way; for he does not wish them to be dependent on his presence. But the intention of the false teachers is not honourable. **19** He expresses deep emotion over them in the diminutive *my little children*, as if he must again experience the pain of childbirth to win them. *Until Christ be formed in you*, *i.e.* until maturity of Christian character and comprehension result from their initial turning to Christ. Here Paul likens himself to a mother, elsewhere to a father (*cf.* 1 Cor. 4:15). The Christian at his conversion is 'in Christ' (Gal. 5:6; *cf.* Rom. 16:7; 2 Cor. 5:17; Eph. 2:13), and Christ is in the Christian as the pattern and power of his new life (*cf.* Rom. 8:10, 11, 29; 2 Cor. 3:18; 13:5; Col. 1:27). **20** Paul wishes he could be with them, for that would radically change their present strained relations. He would drop the language of censure for the language of reunion and restoration. As it is, he is at his wit's end what to think of them.

4:21–31 Allegory of Sarah and Hagar

21 In resuming the argument, Paul challenges those who are keen to remain under the law (chiefly the Judaizers, but not excluding the vacillating Galatians) that they have misunderstood the meaning of the law which they hear read sabbath after sabbath. They are not hearing what it is actually saying. Paul invokes rabbinical argument against those who rest on the rabbinical tradition. The argument is in three parts: the historical situation is identified (vv. 22, 23), interpreted by Paul (vv. 24–27), and applied to Christians including the Galatians (vv. 28–31). While the comparison is called an *allegory* (v. 24) it is not allegory in the Philonic sense. Key elements are aspects of the historical narrative, especially the contrast between the bondwoman and the free, and between law and promise (grace). It is more in the nature of typology, but the major points derive from Paul's understanding of the OT in relation to the covenant of grace in Jesus Christ, rather than from a historical interpretation of the Genesis account.

22, 23 The setting concerns Abraham's two sons, Ishmael from Hagar, and Isaac from Sarah (*cf.* Gn. 16; 17; 21). When it appeared that she would remain childless, Sarah had given Hagar her servant-woman to Abraham to conceive in her stead (a not uncommon practice in those days), but once the child was on the way, Hagar despised Sarah. Subsequently the divine promise that Sarah would bear a son in her old age was fulfilled, but the tension between the two women increased. Sarah's ejection of Hagar and Ishmael was in keeping with the legal code of the times. Paul anticipates his major conclusions: Ishmael was the son of bondage but Isaac was free-born; Ishmael was a natural descendant but Isaac was born of *promise*, beyond the usual child-bearing age, and is therefore of grace. The stinging implication is that Jews who take pride in their natural descent from Abraham (as he himself did; *cf.* 2 Cor. 11:22; Phil. 3:4) are really no better than Ishmael. The sons of grace are the true heirs of Abraham.

24–27 The interpretation follows. The two women represent two covenants (Hagar: law; Sarah: grace). The first bears a son to bondage, the second son is free-born of promise. The first represents Mt. Sinai in Arabia where the law was given and *corresponds to the present Jerusalem, i.e.* the Jerusalem under Judaism, whose descendants are in bondage. The text of v. 25 is uncertain, but it reads either that Mt. Sinai or Hagar or both are of Arabia, hence outside the land of promise. *The Jerusalem above* means the spiritual Jerusalem, of God's heavenly kingdom, a community of children of faith (*cf.* Phil. 3:20; Heb. 11:16; 12:22). Its members are heirs through the promise of grace, not because of earthly nationality. Paul's meaning is that the heirs of promise are both supernatural and supranational. As to covenant, generation and citizenship, the two Jerusalems represent qualitatively differing realms. The text from Is. 54:1 serves to reinforce the point that not natural generation, but divine promise fulfilled, will produce the progeny of the new Jerusalem.

28–31 Like Isaac, Christians are children of promise, not law. Their standing with God depends not on natural descent, but on the covenant of grace. Just as in Genesis the son of law mocked the free-born, it is not surprising that heirs of the law should now persecute the sons of grace. In keeping with the action of Sarah, they are to rid themselves decisively of any tendency to legalism or the dominance of the Judaizing teachers (*cf.* Gn. 21:10), for they have been begotten from freedom for freedom. The true heirs of Abraham are not those who claim the suzerainty of the law, but those who know the freedom in Jesus Christ.

5:1 – 6:10 FREEDOM VINDICATED

5:1–12 The freedom of faith

1 While this verse logically concludes the preceding argument, it has a connection with this following section. The sense of the verse is clear, but whether *stand fast* attaches to the first or the second clause has tempted textual editors to make emendations. The translation option given in RSV is probably the best. There is a word-play on freedom: 'for freedom Christ has freed us; therefore, stand to and don't knuckle under again to bondage.' This is freedom based on redemption through grace, which must be contrasted with the condition of men who, like the Jews of Paul's day, are chained to a treadmill of religious ritual.

2, 3 The particular issue is *circumcision*. A mark of the orthodox Jew, it was regarded as absolutely essential for obedience to the law and for salvation. However, circumcision is man's act for righteousness, therefore what Christ is and has done is of little use to him who counts on his own fulfilling of the law. Salvation does not come by Christ plus the law, but by Christ alone. *If you receive circumcision* may indicate that they have not yet done so. Paul protests from his own experience that to submit to circumcision is no isolated ritual. It puts one again under *the whole law* which demands perfect obedience (which is impossible). **4** By such submission, and such a desire to be justified by works of law, a man in principle and in fact cuts himself off from the sphere of *grace* and of the obedience of faith in Jesus Christ. Thereby one makes grace ineffective. *Fallen away from grace* does not mean what it means to some today, *i.e.* fallen away from salvation; rather, they have dropped away from a life bound up with grace to an existence bogged down in legalism. The two ways exclude one another. To adopt legalism is to repudiate Christ. One cannot be trying to save himself, and at the same time be trusting Christ wholly for salvation. **5** Christians, by *the Spirit* and by *faith*, await the hoped-for righteousness (*cf.* Rom. 5:2). Righteousness is not achieved by us but is God's gift in Christ. **6** *In Christ Jesus* means the way of life of those who are united to Christ by faith. It is the sphere of those who are united to Christ and to one another. There *neither circumcision nor uncircum-*

cision is of any avail; indeed, they are hindrances if depended upon for salvation. Only *faith* coming to effective expression in *love* avails (*cf.* v. 13). For Paul, the controlling principle of life is faith expressed in love, as in the life of Christ (*cf.* Rom. 5:5–8; 8:35–39). The essence of Christianity is not legalism, but a personal relationship to Jesus Christ which is characterized by faith and love.

7 Paul breaks off the argument to remind them that they had progressed well, until impeded, or cut in on, by the Judaizers. The content of the gospel as revealed truth is again in view. **8** The persuasion they have does not derive from God who called them. **9** Compare this verse with 1 Cor. 5:6; as an ancient proverbial saying. **10** Paul sets himself over against the unknown seditious person, and expresses confidence that they will heed him, taking no other viewpoint than his. The troubler, or unsettler of their faith, will suffer his due judgment, whoever he may be. **11** As for Paul, if some slander him by alleging ridiculously that he continues to preach the necessity to be circumcised, why is he still persecuted? In such a case the offence of the cross vanishes, *i.e.* of the indispensable, unique nature of the cross, whose efficiency cannot be supplemented by human merit. The scandal (*stumbling-block*) of the cross is found in its explanation as a suffering for sin and in its totally gratuitous character. The cross alone is the divine way of redemption. If human works or rites can avail, salvation ceases to be of grace (*cf.* 1 Cor. 1:18–25). **12** So crucial is this issue that Paul caustically remarks he wishes the Judaizers would not stop at circumcision, but go on to castrate themselves. Some heathen rites (*e.g.* the worship of Cybele) ended with the priests mutilating themselves.

5:13–15 Right use of freedom

Like 5:1, this first sentence is transitional. The strong feeling expressed in v. 12 relates also to Paul's defence of Christian freedom which now follows. **13** *Freedom* includes freedom from legalistically imposed religious ordinances, but its positive meaning is the essential spiritual liberty of the Christian man, which liberty is God's purpose for men (*cf.* Jn. 8:32, 36; Rom. 8:2). The use of freedom ought to be morally qualified. True freedom implies service to others. It cannot be used *as an opportunity* (pretext) *for the flesh*. Paul does not denigrate the physical world or body. The term *flesh* was used previously as a physical term, but in this chapter (vv. 16, 17, 19, 24) it has the definite ethical connotation of fallen human nature which urges to evil (*cf.* Rom. 8). On the contrary, *love* expressed in benevolent action for the well-being of others, which results in mutual service, should be the fruit of Christian freedom. Here is love's concern, equally for all men as for fellow-Christians, as the fitting result of faith in Christ. This is in contrast to certain sects who claimed the law yet also depreciated the body only to exploit

carnal desires. There is a Christian bondage, but not to law. It is a joyous and willing servitude to one another in the liberty of the gospel. **14** Even the law itself epitomizes this truth in the dictum *You shall love your neighbour as yourself* (Lv. 19:18). Gal. 3:28 shows that Paul does not limit *neighbour* to Jews. The paradox does not intend to convey that salvation comes by Christian service; but that once he is free in Christ through the cross, the Christian devotes himself to the ethical principles of God's Word. Fulfilment of the law is achieved not through servile obedience for self-justification, but through justification by Christ and the obedience of love thereafter (*cf.* Rom. 8:4; 13:8–10; Heb. 10:5–10). For the Christian, Jew or Gentile, freedom from law cannot result in lawless living. The obligations of Christian charity and morality are greater under grace (*cf.* Rom. 6:1–15). **15** The problem to which this verse is directed is unknown. It may refer to petty interpersonal strife, or to deep differences occasioned by the Judaizing teaching. The strong language indicates that their fellowship is in danger of dissolution.

5:16–26 Antagonism between flesh and Spirit

The contrast between life in the Spirit and under the law is now expounded.

16 The metaphor *walk* means way of life taken, and is an imperative denoting action in progress. *The Spirit* is the Spirit of God (*cf.* v. 5). The command to *walk by the Spirit* is the proper antidote for Judaistic teaching, which included the allegation that without the pressure of the law they would fall into sin. Paul urges them to let their conduct be controlled by the inward impetus of the Spirit. To do so is the sure way not to yield to the inner power which makes for evil. RSV translates the concluding clause as a command (*do not gratify*), but it is better to follow the conjunction with a confident declaration: 'and you will never fulfil the desires of the flesh.' **17** This principle, that to live the life in the Spirit is confidently the way to overcome the desires (impulses) of the flesh, governs the way this verse should be understood. Paul does not envisage an indecisive, lingering battle between equally balanced contestants (Spirit and flesh), whose struggle cancels our freedom of action. The key is the principle of the previous verse: 'You will never satisfy the impulses of the flesh.' Spirit and flesh are in combat. To walk by the Spirit of God ensures that we do no longer as we please (*i.e.* fall to the false freedom of carnal impulse). Rather, we live in freedom which triumphs over such impulses. This is not freedom which steers an uncertain middle course between evil impulses and obedience to religious rules, but a new way which transcends them both. **18** Hence, to be *led by the Spirit* is to be no longer subject to the law. The life under the law (legalistic obedience) cannot be imported into the life by the Spirit (faith and love). The former involves externally imposed rules, while the latter involves the new dynamic of the indwelling Spirit. The two are a universe of meaning apart.

19–21 What *the works* of carnal impulse are is common knowledge (these are not in principle the same as the works of the law): sexual sins (fornication, impurity, wantonness); pagan practices (idolatry, witchcraft); sins of passion and sedition (enmities, strife, jealousy, anger, self-seekings, dissension, divisions, envyings); and sins of indulgence (drunkenness, carousing). The verb translated *do* conveys the sense of 'wont to practise'. Such are not of the Spirit of God, hence they cannot *inherit the kingdom*.

22 What *the Spirit* produces in the life of the Christian follows. It is a spiritual harvest appropriate to the new divine life within Christians. Contrast this with the gifts of the Spirit in 1 Cor. 12. *Fruit* is a collective noun designating crop, or harvest, and suggests the many-sided character of virtuous life. It is not clear whether to Paul these fell into classes, but they include inner personal qualities, qualities governing social relations, and principles of conduct. The pattern of *love* is God's love revealed in Christ, which love enables us to love God (*cf.* 2 Thes. 3:5) and others (Gal. 5:13, 14). Love does not seek its own selfish ends, but the good of others. *Joy* is deep happiness born of a personal relation to God (see Phil. 4:4), which includes a sense of our fulfilling His will (*cf.* Jn. 15:11; 17:13). *Peace* in the NT is primarily tranquillity of mind, or spiritual well-being, based on forgiveness (*cf.* Rom. 5:1; 15:13; Phil. 4:7). Peace with God affects our relationships with others significantly (*cf.* Rom. 14:17, 19). *Patience* is AV 'longsuffering'. Other uses of the word include 'steadfastness' and 'forbearance'. The latter is the sense of *patience* here. God has been forbearing to us in Christ (*cf.* 1 Tim. 1:16), so we should be patient with one another (*cf.* 2 Tim. 4:2). *Kindness* (AV 'gentleness') denotes excellence of character in the sense of a due regard for the fragile nature of human personality and for human need (*cf.* Rom. 2:4; 11:22; Eph. 2:7). *Goodness*, occurring in addition to *kindness*, suggests the general sense of ideal character, but with righteousness softened by love. It is a term which Paul employs elsewhere in his writings only in Rom. 15:14; Eph. 5:9; 2 Thes. 1:11. *Faithfulness* translates the Greek word 'faith' (so AV). As employed here it denotes 'fidelity' as a fundamental trait of Christian character, especially in relation to other men. **23** *Gentleness* (AV 'meekness') is used in the NT in two related senses, submissiveness to the divine will (*cf.* Jas. 1:21) and considerateness towards men (*cf.* Gal. 6:1; 1 Cor. 4:21; 2 Cor. 10:1). *Self-control* (AV 'temperance') translates a Greek term used to denote self-mastery or continence. In this passage it relates particularly to curbing the fleshly impulses, though lack of restraint in any behaviour may be in view (*cf.* 1 Cor. 7:9; 9:25). That there are self-evidently no prohibitions against such virtues is Paul's way of reinforcing their value by understatement. **24** On one side, victory over sin is due to

the new life in the Spirit; but, on the other side, it is due to the Christian having died in Christ's death, which marks the death of the power of the flesh (*cf.* Gal. 2:20).

25 The reality of their having been made alive by the Spirit (*cf.* Rom. 8:1–11) should also lead them to *walk by the Spirit*. For Christian experience not only begins through the Spirit, it continues by the Spirit. **26** Therefore conceit, provocation and envy should have no place.

6:1–5 Ethical responsibility

The moral responsibility of Spirit-led Christians for those of their own number who fall into sin and also of each man for himself next comes into view.

1 The forbearance of grace in contrast to legalistic censoriousness should be expressed, for example, even in the case where a man is taken unawares in a lapse: guilty as he obviously is, those *who are spiritual*, *i.e.* men and women of the Spirit, should aim to restore him. *If* should be rendered 'even if' to indicate the serious nature of the contingency Paul has in mind. *Restore* means 'to complete' or 'put into proper condition', like a mason repairing a wall or a physician setting a broken limb. The lapse is antithetical to walking by the Spirit (Gal. 5:25). In regard to the lapsed, Paul pleads that they restore him to his former condition (note 'mending', the same Gk. word, in Mk. 1:19) in a (human) *spirit of gentleness* (*cf.* Gal. 5:23). The law of Christ operates within the body of Christian fellowship not as a set of statutes but through all-embracing love. The restorer should help in a 'spirit of meekness' (AV) having regard to his own human limitations and proneness to succumb to temptation. *Tempted* here refers to 'solicitation to sin', not to 'testing the righteous'. Sin has been slain in principle, though the Christian must still reckon with it as a power. **2** *Burdens*. The word denotes a heavy weight and is the reproach Christians all bear when one of their number falls. Such expression of concern and mutual support issues from love as the new principle revealed in Jesus Christ (*cf.* Jn. 15:12), rather than from the old way of counting good deeds (*cf.* Mt. 18:21). **3** Self-deception catches only the unwary, the unself-conscious. **4** The alert man gives attention to proper testing of his own work. Then his basis of self-congratulation will rest validly on his achievement, not on imagined superiority over the lapsed brother. **5** The term *load* designates what each man must bear for himself, like a soldier his own knapsack, which is his own responsibility, and is to be distinguished from the additional burdens of v. 2.

6:6–10 Sowing and reaping

6 The verb 'to teach', which occurs twice in this verse, translates the Greek verb from which we derive 'to catechize', showing how early in the church's history oral instruction of Christian truth figured prominently. Here the second practical way of showing Christian charity is identified (the first being the restoration of a fallen brother). Those who are taught ought to respond by sharing the blessings of their livelihood with Christian workers and supporting them financially (*cf.* Rom. 15:27; 1 Cor. 9:11). He appeals to them to maintain the ministry adequately. An application follows. Just as the incident of another's fall ought to sober us to the realities of our own propensities to sin, so the generosity of those who teach ought to be living proof that man reaps only what he has sown.

7 As valid as may be the application by Christians generally of this verse to the unconverted, let us note that Paul applied it first to Christians. **8** The general principle is clearly that unreceptiveness to gospel teaching and indulgence in carnal pursuits will bear its own fruit. What a man sows he will reap. From fleshly indulgence issues decay leading to destruction. On the contrary, to sow *to the Spirit* means devoting the energies of life to values of the Spirit of God revealed in and by Jesus Christ (*cf.* Rom. 6:19–23; 1 Tim. 6:12; Tit. 3:7). That which is of the Spirit yields life eternal (*cf.* 1 Jn. 2:15–17). A man deceives only himself when he supposes that he can turn up his nose at God with impunity. No-one can hoodwink God. **9** *Grow weary* may have the added thought of being neglectful. The final harvest comes; therefore sow well in expectation of it. *Well-doing* includes the sense of beauty and grace, as well as of intrinsic goodness. It is important to remember that in this passage two fields are in view (flesh and Spirit) as well as two sowings. *Lose heart* has the added force of relaxing effort (*cf.* Heb. 12:3–5), or of becoming exhausted (*cf.* Mt. 15:32). **10** The principle which follows marks the true character of the life under grace, namely, as occasion allows, *let us do good to all men.* Christians have a special obligation to one another. The word translated *household* means that something is 'one's own' or belongs to one's family. Those who through faith have been born into God's family are members of the same household and are therefore related to us with all that that implies in the way of claims upon us.

This passage may indicate Paul's concern that the Galatians neither ignore nor cease from assisting in the collection for the afflicted Christians at Jerusalem because of the troublesome Judaizers. The Near East, especially Palestine, was beset by bad harvests and famine during the fifth and sixth decades of the first century. Government relief projects were organized to relieve the distress, and the churches made collections also (*cf.* Rom. 15:24–27; 1 Cor. 16:1–4; 2 Cor. 8; 9).

6:11–18 CONCLUSION

11 Paul often dictated his letters to a scribe, but added a personal footnote himself (*cf.* 1 Cor. 16:21; Col. 4:18; 2 Thes. 3:17). *With what large letters* has evoked conflicting opinion. This conclusion is the longest Paul wrote (he may even have begun it at 5:2). Does he write the conclusion in large letters for emphasis, so that it can be displayed, or because he writes awkwardly, or because of weak or diseased eyes? Probably the meaning is 'with such bold letters' to emphasize their danger from the Judaizers and the cruciality of salvation by the cross alone.

12 The issue compels him to question their motive. Submission to circumcision (this now includes all who receive it, and not the Judaizers only) is a ritual act in which it is possible to glory; hence it spares a man from the offence of looking for salvation to the cross alone. Such are more concerned about externals. There is an analogy between their boasting in the external physical rite of circumcision and their carnal appetites. It is in total contrast to the nature of the gospel, faith, and the true spiritual life. The Judaizers were prepared to tolerate the offensive cross, but only within the prescribed forms of Judaism. **13** Paul repeats a theological conclusion (*cf.* 3:10, 11) as an accusation: the circumcision party are themselves not law-abiding in all points. Paul probably means that they are insincere, as their actions show. They demand circumcision of the Galatians only to exult in an external mark of religious conformity.

14 But for Paul there is no exulting, *except in the cross of our Lord Jesus Christ.* By using Christ's full title Paul intends to reaffirm not only the indispensable redemptive act, but the divine nature of Christ, hence of the act. The cross is God's cross, therefore God's way, therefore the only way of salvation (*cf.* Rom. 5:18–21). Through the cross Paul's life has been revolutionized. That by it the world has been crucified to Paul, and he to the world, reaffirms his having died in the death Christ died (*cf.* 3:26, 27; Rom. 6:3, 4), by which event he is reckoned dead to the world, *i.e.* the world-system as life ordered in alienation from God. **15** The attractions of the unredeemed life have become dead things to him. No outward symbol of religious conformity or non-conformity avails, only *a new creation* (*cf.* 2 Cor. 5:17), which is the spiritual re-creation of man. **16** If one should speak of religious rules, then let a benediction rest on those who live by the principle of new life in Christ. These are the true Israel of God, heirs of Abraham (*cf.* 3:14; Phil. 3:3).

17 is an appeal born of deep feeling that he be spared the further distress of persecution in view of the sufferings he has already experienced (*cf.* Acts 14:8, 19; 2 Cor. 11:23–28), which are sufficient evidence of his devotion to Christ.

18 The benediction is similar to others. Here the occurrences of *grace* and *spirit* peculiarly reinforce major themes of the book which are tied to the centrality of the Lord Jesus Christ, and to Paul's fraternal feeling for the Galatians.

SAMUEL J. MIKOLASKI

Ephesians

INTRODUCTION

THE PLACE AND PURPOSE OF EPHESIANS IN PAULINE LITERATURE

Two features of this Epistle stand out clearly. First, except for the closing paragraph in 6:21, 22 the argument and appeal of the document are strangely impersonal and indirect. The apostle has heard of his readers' Christian profession through indirect channels (1:15) and knows that it is only in this way that they have heard of his apostolic ministry for the Gentiles (3:1, 2). His bond with his readers is that of an author to his recipients (3:4) rather than one of first-hand acquaintance.

The second feature is one of literary usage. Both choice of words and employment of a studied style mark out this Epistle as unusual in the Pauline literature. There are many words not used elsewhere in the NT, long ponderous sentences complicated by involved relative clauses, a profusion of abstract nouns, *etc*. These traits seem to be far removed from the style of a pastoral letter, addressed to the church at Ephesus by the apostle Paul whose letter-writing habits involve the use of rhetorical questions and a pointed, direct approach (*e.g.* Galatians).

These two features have been used in modern criticism to cast a doubt on the Pauline authorship of the letter. But before this question is looked at, it will be well to draw some conclusions from the above data. First, from the evidence of the writer's unusual relationship with his addressees it becomes clear that 'Ephesians' is no ordinary pastoral letter sent to a specific congregation or group of churches. This fact is confirmed by the textual uncertainty in 1:1. The two words translated in AV as 'at Ephesus' are lacking in the leading MSS, both codices and cursives, including the important papyrus P46 dated AD 200. Moreover early Christian writers endorse the view that 'at Ephesus' was not found in the earliest texts. Two suggestions have been offered to explain this textual irregularity. One possibility is that the letter never had a place-name but was composed as a general tract or essay and not as a letter intended for a particular readership. A 2nd-century scribe is thought to have supplied 'at Ephesus' to bring the document which later Christians claimed as a Pauline composition into conformity with the other Pauline letters to the churches of the 1st-century Christian world.

Against this view and in support of the second submission is the fact that, while the letter does read more like a sermon than a pastoral letter addressed to a church with specific needs, the author does have a certain group of persons in mind and speaks to them in the second person. It is more likely, then, that this document was composed as a circular letter to the churches in a wide region—Asia Minor is the most probable location—and either carried from one place to another in the area by a courier or (in view of the later textual authority for the place-name of Ephesus) left by the author with a blank in the superscription, to be filled in as the messenger handed over the particular copy to the church. There are some difficulties with this reconstruction, but on balance it seems to be the most plausible view.

The author is gripped by his subject which runs as a main thread through his treatise. In a style which seems to be influenced by possible liturgical and hymnic speech he marvels at the grace of God which has brought into being a united church in which Jews and Gentiles together find their true place (2:11–22). The unity of this universal society which is nothing less than Christ's body (1:23; 3:6; 4:4; 5:30) is his great concern (4:3ff.). He starts from the premise of 'one new man' (2:15) in which a new humanity has been created by God through Christ's reconciling work on the cross (2:16). By this work Jews and Gentiles are brought into God's family (1:5; 2:19; 4:6; 5:1) as brothers. The coming into existence of this one family where all barriers of race, culture and social status are broken down is the wonder which fills his vision. The earlier Pauline teaching of Gal. 3:28, 29 is now filled out and its lessons drawn and applied.

The letter to the Galatians had fought and won the battle for the recognition of Gentiles as members of the church of Christ. This Epistle builds upon that charter of Gentile liberty and offers a double warning to Gentile believers now that their place within the family of God has been secured. First, the readers are counselled against allowing their pre-Christian moral standards to determine their conduct (4:17ff.), and are put on their guard against pagan teachers who would undermine the Christian ethic which they have accepted as part of their new life in Christ (5:3ff.). Then they are reminded that Jewish Christians are fellow-believers with them; that Jesus came as Israel's Messiah through whom the entire world is blessed; and that they can never deny the Jewish participation in the gospel message without severing that message from its historical roots (*cf.* Jn. 4:22). This explains the appeal made to the OT and the demonstration the author gives that the Messianic hope of Israel meets all the needs of his Gentile Christian readers (2:11ff.; 3:6) who, converted to Christ later in time than the Jewish believers (1:12, 13) but in no way inferior on that account, came to share with them the Holy Spirit of (Messianic) promise (1:13; 4:30).

If we imagine a situation in the NT period of church history when the Gentile mission had prospered and Gentiles were streaming into the church; when they were boasting of their supposed independence of Israel, and were becoming intolerant of their Jewish Christian brethren (adopting the attitude reflected in Rom. 11:33ff.); when they needed a reminder of the Jewish past of the church—then we have a life-setting which makes this Epistle understandable in the Pauline literature.

AUTHORSHIP AND DATING

Evidence taken from the letter itself (1:1; 3:1) and from the attestation of the church Fathers (Irenaeus, Clement of Alexandria, Tertullian) supports the traditional view that this Epistle came from Paul's hand. But denials of authenticity are frequently made, partly on the score that both vocabulary and style are non-Pauline, and partly on the ground that the situation in the document could have arisen only in the post-Pauline period.

If Paul is drawing upon the liturgical language of the churches' worship and composing in a style which is lyrical and exalted, the unusual features are well explained. The second line of attack on apostolic authorship is now conceded to be the more important and decisive, especially the claim that Ephesians confronts a situation which could have appeared only when the church had become institutionalized and more developed in its structure and life. Marks of 'early catholicism' have been detected in this Epistle: *e.g.* the apostles are looked upon as a closed group (2:20; 3:5; 4:11); the unity of the church in which the Gentiles have taken their settled place is a matter for concern; the expectation of an imminent return of Christ is fading (*e.g.* 4:13–16, on which Masson comments: 'the church grows towards Christ. She no longer waits for Him to come to her') as the church settled down in the world. But none of this evidence points indubitably to a period later than the mid-sixties, and there are counterbalancing data (*e.g.* 5:16; 6:13 do stress the life of the church 'between the times' of the advents of Christ). F. F. Bruce has shown how ideas which are stated in outline in the earlier Pauline Epistles are developed and continued in this Epistle (art. 'St Paul in Rome: 4. The Epistle to the Ephesians', *BJRL* 49, 2, 1967, pp. 303ff.).

The date of Ephesians belongs to the period of the apostle's imprisonment in Rome, *c.* AD 60–61. The letter has many points of similarity with Colossians, especially at 6:21, 22 (= Col. 4:7ff.) from which it is clear that Tychicus was the bearer of both documents. It is true that both Epistles have thoughts which overlap and amplify one another, and attempts to play off one Epistle against the other—to support the view that Colossians is authentic and Ephesians non-authentic—are not very impressive. Both letters belong to the same time of composition; Ephesians is best regarded as the last letter in the group of imprisonment Epistles.

For guidance regarding the debate over authorship and purpose, see D. Guthrie, *New Testament Introduction: The Pauline Epistles*, 1961, pp. 99ff.; E. F. Harrison, *Introduction to the New Testament*, 1964, pp. 310ff.; and the present writer's forthcoming *The Epistle to the Ephesians*, with a summary of the discussion on the purpose of the letter in *ExpT*, LXXIX, 10, 1968, pp. 296–302.

OUTLINE OF CONTENTS

COMMENTARY

1:1-14 INTRODUCTION

1:1, 2 Address and salutation

Following the pattern of 1st-century letter-writing practices and of his earlier correspondence with the churches, Paul begins the letter with his own name and greets his readers under their Christian vocations as 'the saints' and the 'faithful in Christ Jesus' (v. 1). He then invokes upon them the twin blessings of grace and peace which are the gift of the Father and His Son (v. 2).

Notes. 1 *An apostle of Christ Jesus.* Paul is implying that his writing is authoritative, for apostleship meant the exercise of a God-given authority within the life of the churches (*cf.* 2 Cor. 13:10). *By the will of God.* Paul acknowledges that his calling is not self-derived or conferred upon him by other Christians. Rather his apostolic authority and status are traced solely to the call and commission of the risen Christ. *The saints who are also faithful.* The following phrase *in Christ Jesus* is best taken to cover both terms which are adjectives. *Saints* is literally 'holy ones', but this may be a misleading title if it is thought of exclusively in terms of personal piety. The meaning of 'sainthood' is dedication to God and usefulness in His service. Hence the explanatory *faithful, i.e.* devoted to their calling as the people of God who serve Him *in Christ Jesus, i.e.* in union with Him, or, possibly, in the fellowship of the church. For the omission of 'at Ephesus' from RSV see the Introduction. 2 *Grace . . . and peace.* A familiar Pauline prayer (*cf., e.g.*, 1 Thes. 1:1). Both gifts are ascribed to *God . . . and the Lord Jesus Christ* as joint-Authors. By sure Christian instinct, even in the apostolic age, the foundations of the credal doctrine of the Godhead are being laid.

1:3-14 The purposes of God in eternity and time

There are two ways in which these stately verses may be approached. We may discover in them a trinitarian pattern corresponding to the purposes and activities of the Godhead of Father who chooses His people (vv. 3-5), Son who redeems at the cost of His own sacrificial death (v. 7), and Holy Spirit who applies the work of Christ to the church and so makes real, in human experience, the eternal purpose of the Trinity (vv. 13, 14). An alternative proposal suggests that Paul's thought flows along temporal channels as he views the entire range of God's redeeming purpose from a past eternity (v. 4) to its future realization (v. 14). These two approaches are not mutually exclusive, however, and in either case the central point of this statement of divine enterprise is in v. 7.

1:3-6 The Father's choice. 3 Paul breaks out in an exultant doxology in praise of God as the Father of our Lord Jesus Christ, His beloved Son (v. 6), recalling that all spiritual good is placed at the disposal of the church which exists in, and draws its life from, Christ its Head, who now reigns *in the heavenly places. Cf.* v. 22, where the Headship of the risen Christ over His people is traced to God's appointment. 4 The church now lives *in Christ* because of God's pre-mundane choice which ensures that those who hear the gospel in its historical context will respond in faith (v. 13; *cf.* 2 Thes. 2:13). Here we confront the mystery of divine election which the NT consistently proclaims not as a conundrum to tease our minds but as a wonder to evoke our praise; not as an element in God's character to be minimized but as an assurance that our lives are in His powerful hands, not in the grip of fate; and never as an excuse for carelessness in spiritual matters, but always as a reminder that Christians have a responsibility 'to confirm your call and election' (2 Pet. 1:10). We are chosen *that we should be holy and blameless.*

5 God's electing purpose is an expression of His *love* and has as its design the fulfilment of His purpose that there should be many sons in His family, all sharing the likeness of their elder Brother (*cf.* Rom. 8:29; Heb. 2:10). 6 It is through the beloved Son who conveyed the grace of God in His life and death (*cf.* Jn. 1:17b) that the Father's grand intention is realized; and the stress on the freeness of that grace shows that Paul's thought of God's sovereign action looks back to the OT (*cf.* Dt. 7:6-8).

Notes. 3 *Blessed*; the Greek word (*eulogētos*, as in 1 Pet. 1:3) picks up the Hebrew term (*berāḵâ*) which plays an important part in Jewish worship. 5 RSV associates *in love* with *he destined us* rather than with the preceding verse (as AV, NEB), and is preferable. 6 *The Beloved* recalls Mk. 1:11 as a title for the Messiah; but the closest OT background reference is Gn. 22:1-8, which Paul has in mind in Rom. 8:32.

1:7-10 The Father's plan accomplished in Christ. 7, 8 Mention of God's grace leads on to a larger treatment of this theme. Sonship and membership of the divine family are made possible on the ground of redemption (v. 7); and it is by the offering of His blood in sacrificial death that Christ obtains His people's liberation (*redemption* was exactly what captive Israel needed; *cf.* Dt. 15:15) from the tyranny of evil and gives them the assurance of pardon.

9, 10 Redemption and forgiveness are but a part of the entire work of God in Christ. What Paul terms *the mystery of his will* embraces the universe in its scope, for it is *a plan for the fullness of time, i.e.* a plan which God will fulfil in His own way and according to His invincible will (v. 11). This plan has as its great objective the summing up of all things in Christ—a difficult phrase which probably means that in Christ the entire universe finds its full explanation and rationale. Christ gives meaning to the cosmos when it is perceived that He is not only the source and sustainer of all that is (Col. 1:15ff.; *cf.* Jn. 1:3, 4; Heb. 1:2, 3) but the goal towards which the whole creation is moving.

Notes. 7 The background here is the OT, as in 5:2. **9** The prominent terms here, *wisdom*, *insight*, *he has made known* (Gk. *gnōrisas*), *mystery*, may well have been used by the false teachers in Asia Minor, whom Paul addressed in the letter to the Colossians. They were claiming a secret teaching, open only to initiates, which gave them a clue to the understanding of the universe. Paul counters this specious pretension. The 'secret' of the divine purpose is in Christ—and is accessible to all who believe in Him. It is a 'mystery' in the sense that no human intelligence could have guessed what God intended to do in Christ, but it is now made known to Christians (*cf.* 3:3–6). Its content is 'the inclusion of the Gentiles as well as the Jews in a common human hope in Christ' and even more 'the unification of humanity in the Christ' (J. Armitage Robinson, *St Paul's Epistle to the Ephesians*, 1904). In this light we should interpret the next verse. **10** The Greek verb translated *to unite* poses a problem; it recurs in Rom. 13:9 ('summed up'), which is our clue. Love is the all-embracing command which includes, intergrates and gives coherence to all other commands. Christ performs this role on a cosmic scale by gathering the fragmented parts of human life into a whole, so forming a uni-verse.

1:11–14 The Holy Spirit's ministry. 11, 12 Paul's mind turns to consider the process by which God's plan comes to effectual outworking in human lives. He joins together both himself (in v. 12), as representing the Jewish people who had long been sustained by the hope of Messiah's coming, and his readers who were of Gentile origin (v. 13; *cf.* 3:1; 4:17). Now in Christ these ethnic and religious connotations have lost their meaning inasmuch as both Jews and Gentiles are 'members of the same body' (3:6); but they did come into that body from different cultures.

13, 14 The way to Christ, however, is the same for both Jews and Gentiles. The outline is described in these verses. Hearing *the word of truth*, *i.e.* the gospel (*cf.* Col. 1:5) is the first step, to be followed by a trustful acceptance of Him of whom it speaks. The third term is that of 'sealing', which is associated with *the promised Holy Spirit* who indwells all those who *have believed in him* and who gives His own witness in terms of an assurance to the believer that he belongs to God's chosen people, just as Israel was God's inheritance under the old covenant (*cf.* Col. 1:12). The seal for Israel was circumcision (see Rom. 4:11). This may be why many commentators from the 2nd century onwards have taken the sealing here to refer to baptism as the outward attestation of the Christian's resolve to follow in the way of Christ and in the fellowship of His church. Others interpret it simply as referring to the gift of the Holy Spirit

at conversion (*cf.* 4:30). This indwelling of the Spirit is again compared with Israel's experience (v. 14). She became God's elect nation by adoption and covenant but did not enter her full possession of the divine promises until the time of Joshua and the conquest of Canaan. The Christian receives the *guarantee*, the 'first instalment' (Gk. *arrabōn*) of the Spirit at conversion and awaits the final consummation of God's purpose.

Notes. 11 RV gives the more literal translation: 'in whom also we were made a heritage.' The same thought is continued in v. 18, and connects with the OT designation of Israel as God's inheritance (*cf.* Dt. 32:9). **12** *Appointed* also contains the notion of divine election (RV 'having been foreordained': the verbs 'chose' in v. 4 and 'foreordained' are coincident but have different nuances, as F. Davidson has shown in his Tyndale monograph, *Pauline Predestination*, 1946). **13** The verbs in this verse are also coincident in time. The actions of believing and sealing by the Spirit happen simultaneously (*cf.* Acts 19:2). The full experience of redemption, of which the Spirit's presence in the church is now a token (*cf.* 2 Cor. 5:5), awaits the fulfilment of Rom. 8:23.

1:15 – 3:21 THE CHURCH'S LIFE IN CHRIST

1:15–23 Paul's intercession for the church

In this section the apostle expresses his thankfulness that the readers have come to share in the blessings of God's saving plan; and he does so in his characteristic way as he prays for them (vv. 15, 16). The theme of his intercession picks up some equally characteristic Pauline thoughts which we can find re-echoed in his other letters, viz. a desire that his Christian friends may be grounded in the knowledge of God and His ways (vv. 17, 18); a confidence that they may lay hold more firmly upon the hope to which they have been called (v. 18); and above all, an assurance which he wants to share with them that God's power is available for their needs (v. 19). The signal exhibition of that power is seen in the mightiest of all God's acts in history when He raised Christ from the defeat of death and installed Him in His presence. This enthronement of the risen Lord (vv. 20ff.) not only confers on Him personal dignity and honour but also has far-reaching consequences for the world (which now receives a new Ruler) and for the church (which is given a sovereign Head under whom its life is secure).

15 This is the opening of what forms one connected, if lengthy, sentence which runs on to the end of the chapter division. From the way Paul writes it seems clear that he does not know his readers personally; and in this respect they compare with the Colossians (*cf.* Col. 1:3, 4; 2:1). But the news of their faith in Christ and its expression in active love to their fellow-believers has reached him at a distance; this interlocking of faith and love is a factor in Christian living by which Paul set a considerable store (*cf.* Gal. 5:6). **16** Paul's prayers are often expressed in language similar to this (see, *e.g.*, Rom. 1:9).

17 The address and subject of this verse form the first part of his intercession as he calls upon God to grant the requisites for the acquirement of the most vital of all knowledge, viz. God Himself. These are the *spirit of wisdom and revelation*. Both terms are to be understood in an OT background (*e.g.* Jb. 28:12ff.; Je. 9:23ff.) and underline the biblical teaching that *wisdom* does not come by human ingenuity and cleverness in excogitating divine truth from man's mind but is the gift of God (*cf.* Lk. 10:21); and that *revelation* is the name for this gracious self-disclosure of God who always takes the initiative in this action. **18** He prepares human minds to receive the revelation; and this receptivity is expressed in terms of illumination. The second element in Paul's petition is now given: that to the illumined minds of his readers God would make known *the hope to which he has called you* (*cf.* 4:4, an identical phrase in the Gk.). God's calling is His summons to salvation (as in Phil. 3:14) rather than His appointing His servants to some specific task, though the latter idea is found elsewhere in Paul. A third constituent in the apostle's prayer touches upon the theme of the church's wealthy heritage as the people of God and looks both backward to 1:11ff. and forward to Paul's exposition of the church's enrichment by the exaltation of Christ. *His inheritance* is 'the inheritance from God the Father which Christians share with His Son Jesus Christ (Rom. 8:17)' (Foulkes, *TNTC*, p. 62). **19, 20** Two phases of Christ's elevation by God are in view: His resurrection (vv. 19b, 20a), and His subsequent enthronement (vv. 20b, 21). The power on which believers lay hold is that which was deployed in God's act in vindicating His Son (*cf.* Rom. 6:4) when men had done their worst. Thereafter He set Him in the place of world authority, which is what the pictorial *at his right hand* means.

21, 22 The lordly Christ is Master not only of the visible world of nature and men; He has command as well of all those spirit-forces which were regarded as controlling the destiny of men. Christ, Paul teaches, is Lord of all the cosmic agencies that men may care to name because He is both their Creator (*cf.* Col. 1:16) and rightful Ruler (*cf.* Phil. 2:9-11). His name excels all these forces, both in the present age and in the age to come, *i.e.* throughout the entire time-span of the universe. Nor is this all that is bound up with the vindication of Christ, for He has been accorded an authority by God to exercise a *de facto* rule over these spiritual powers which until His victory at the cross and empty tomb held men in bondage (*cf.* Gal. 4:3; Col. 2:15). *He has put all things under his feet*; here Christ is seen as the ultimate Adam who enters upon His promised reign as Lord of creation (*cf.* Ps.

8:6, which is interpreted in this way in Heb. 2:5ff.). Paul's thought thus reaches forward in anticipation of His final triumph (*cf.* 1 Cor. 15:25) which faith claims now as a present reality. Paul claims the unrivalled control of the Lord over the church as a fact of present experience. The Head-to-body relationship is found described in less detail in the earlier Pauline Epistles (*cf.* Rom. 12:4, 5; 1 Cor. 12:12ff.; Col. 1:18; 2:10, 19). In Ephesians the earlier hints and adumbrations are made explicit, as Christ's Headship over His body, the church, is spelled out in some exciting, if enigmatic, ways. The present verse contains the key-term, *head . . . for the church*, which S. F. B. Bedale (*Studies in Ephesians*, 1956, pp. 69f.) has shown carries the sense 'ruler of the church'.

23 The church is His body as the instrument of His purpose in the world. That much is plain, but Paul's emphasis here is rather to show that Christ has authority in His church, just as the head controls the movements of the human body (so 5:23ff.). The final phrase, though much controverted, confirms this, if we accept the more probable interpretation of the Greek participle here accordingly translated *who fills*. The question posed here is, Is it Christ that fills the church, or the church that fills Christ as His complement? Stig Hanson (in *The Unity of the Church in the New Testament. Colossians and Ephesians*, 1951, pp. 126ff.) has offered conclusive reasons for preferring the former alternative, concluding 'all that Christ has from God, the power, the gifts, the grace, He passes on to the Church . . . the Church has nothing to give Christ of herself, by which what is lacking in Him could be filled up. Instead, it is the Church that is filled with Him (3:19), becoming a partaker of all that He owns and is, for the purpose of continuing His work'.

Notes. 15 Some important textual authorities miss out *and your love*. E. F. Scott (*MNTC*) tries to construct an alternative meaning on the basis of this omission: 'your loyalty as manifested in your individual Christian lives and in your relations towards the church'. But this gives an unnatural sense to the Gk. *pistis* (*faith* which he takes as meaning 'fidelity'). **18** *In the saints*; better 'among the saints' (*cf.* Acts 20:32). **20** The OT 'testimony' or Messianic proof-text in mind here is Ps. 110:1. Exaltation at God's right hand connotes co-regency and the exercise of cosmic authority. **21** This division of time is based on a Jewish concept: 'The Most High created not one Age, but two' (4 *Ezra* 7:50; see also Mt. 12:32). **23** See *NBD*, art. 'Fulness'.

2:1-10 The church's history—past, present and future

This passage takes a broad sweep in its survey of the plight of human life outside Christ and untouched by the influence of His gospel (vv. 1-3) and then it goes on to relate the saving action of God in some of its vital (*i.e.* life-giving) applications as the life of God in Christ is brought into touch with the spiritual death caused by sin (vv. 4–6). The closing part of Paul's description (in v. 7) reaches into the future as he shows that God's work, begun now in this age, will gain in lustre in the coming ages, and that while salvation is a fact of past experience for the Christian (v. 5) it introduces the believer to a new way of life which stretches out into the future (v. 10). What God has begun to do for His people has an eternal dimension, in both the temporal (v. 7) and local (see 3:10) senses. His saving grace, present now, extends into the future; and also, enacted on earth by His saving historical events in Jesus Christ, it has repercussions which affect non-human agencies. Hence the double allusion (in v. 6 and 3:10) to 'the heavenly places'.

2:1–3 Humanity outside Christ. 1 The risen and exalted One (*cf.* 1:20ff.) has become the Giver of spiritual life (*cf.* 1 Cor. 15:45). This vivifying power is the prime need of men outside Christ who are *dead*. 'Death' in this sense has to be understood in the light of 4:18: 'cut off from the life of God' because of human alienation from God (*cf.* Col. 2:13 and Rom. 6:13, 23; 1 Tim. 5:6) and so standing under His just condemnation of sin, whose most deadly effect is that it separates God and man (*cf.* Is. 59:2).

2 A twofold characterization of society in Paul's day follows here, as Graeco-Roman life is viewed from a Christian viewpoint. *Course of this world*; lit. 'according to the age (Gk. *aiōn*) of this world-order (Gk. *kosmos*)', suggesting that human life is seen under the malign influence of celestial powers which hold man in a tyrannical grip (so Gal. 1:4; 4:3; Col. 2:8; Heb. 2:15). *Prince of the power of the air*. This description answers to the devil who, as ruler of the demonic agencies in the upper regions, controls human action by goading men into sin. In ancient cosmology the inter-stellar region, especially that between the moon and the earth, was thought to be the place of constant demonic activity, with baneful effects upon all earth-dwellers (*cf.* 1 Jn. 5:19). *Disobedience* was Satan's downfall (*cf.* Is. 14:12ff. which was widely believed by the later Jewish writers to be linked with Satan's rebellion against God). His rebellious spirit is still active in men who have pitted themselves against God in their blindness (*cf.* 2 Cor. 4:4). **3** The sad fruit of this disobedience to God's gracious will for mankind is seen in the moral turpitude of human society. Perhaps saddest of all descriptions is the solemn sentence: *by nature children of wrath*, *i.e.* under divine judgment by reason of moral choice which in turn is dictated by man's warped nature.

Notes. 1 *Trespasses and sins* are here almost synonyms (so H. Schlier, *Der Brief an die Epheser*, 1965). **3** *Children of wrath* is a Hebraism (= deserving of God's judicial condemnation). The verse gives no support for the doctrine of original guilt or for thinking of wrath as a fitful emotion.

2:4–6 Humanity in Christ. 4 The darkness of hopelessness and desperate need serves only as a backcloth to make the love and grace of God shine more brightly. **5, 6** The evidence of that loving concern of God who does not leave man to perish in his own deserved plight is seen in a double action. He has both made alive the spiritually dead and raised up those who were held down by the servitude of that same death. Both verbs are found together in Jn. 5:21 and Rom. 8:11; and this context confirms the view that both actions are uniquely predicated of God (as in the OT and the synagogue liturgy, where it is God alone who can both quicken and raise up the dead), but with this distinction that while in the OT teaching the raising of the physically dead is in view, here it is a spiritual renewal that is stressed. The former hope of resurrection is clear elsewhere in Paul (*e.g.* 2 Cor. 4:14). The best parallel to Paul's thought here is one by contrast, viz. Gal. 3:21. The very thing which the law cannot do—give life to those dead in their alienation from God—is achieved in the gospel (*cf.* 2 Cor. 3:6). And this promise is bound up with Christ's own resurrection which, in turn, was followed by His exaltation; so believers are lifted *with him* to a new plane of living, sharing His life (so 1 Cor. 6:17).

Note. 4 The richness of divine mercy stands in contrast to the sentence of doom passed on a fallen creation (v. 3). Paul exults in the love of God, as in Rom. 5:8; the past (aorist) tense of *loved* focusing on the specific act of His giving His Son.

2:7–10 What it means to be in Christ. 7 The purpose of God's action in lifting the church out of the condemned realm of sin and death is one which only the future will disclose. For it is with the consummation of His redemptive plan *in the coming ages* that the full extent of His bounty will be known.

8 Paul's summary of past, present and future is epitomized in this creed-like, pregnant sentence. Salvation is complete (hence the perfect tense) in the sense that no defect or inadequacy mars God's purpose; it originates in the grace or saving love of God expressed to sinners; and it enters human experience by the receptivity of faith or trustful acceptance. Indeed, the whole process is God's doing (as 2 Cor. 5:18 insists), not man's; and it comes to him as a freely-offered gift (*cf.* Rom. 6:23). **9** The reason why there is no room for a human contribution is given: lest any person should make a proud claim, thus subverting the divine sovereignty (*cf.* 1 Cor. 1:29–31).

10 Salvation *sola gratia, sola fide* (by grace alone, by faith alone) can be misrepresented, as Rom. 6:1ff. makes only too painfully clear. Paul's teaching is travestied when righteousness of living and a high moral tone to life become forgotten on the mistaken assumption that Christians can live carelessly, for if they sin their lapses only give the grace of God more room for display. Hence the call now to *good works*, not as a ground for claiming God's favour (denied in v. 9), but as the necessary consequence of their new life in Christ as His new creation (*cf.* 2 Cor. 5:17). Tit. 2:14 is the best commentary.

Notes. 7 *Coming ages*: the plural is non-significant (M. Dibelius, revised by H. Greeven, *An die Epheser, HNT*, 1953). **8** On the relation between *grace* and *faith*, see Rom. 4:16. *This* is neuter in the Greek and cannot look back to *faith* (Gk. *pistis*, a feminine noun), however true it may be that we come to believe only because of God's prevenient or causative grace. It is the whole process of salvation that forms the antecedent to the word 'this', as in 2 Cor. 5:18. **9** *Boast*; a pivotal Pauline term in his salvation teaching. Comparing the LXX's references in Ps. 97:7 and Is. 42:17 we can show that boasting in idols means trusting in them; and this self-confidence (which Paul would consider no better than idolatry) is the antithesis of a self-distrust which casts itself wholly upon God and His mercy; so Phil. 3:3-11. **10** Having rebutted a moralism which trusts in 'works' (as in Rom. 4:1ff.; Gal. 2:14ff.), Paul turns to an equally pernicious danger: libertinism which throws off all moral discipline. The contrast with vv. 1-3 is striking, for while unredeemed man lives according to his nature, the Christian lives according to his (new) nature, for which God has prepared him by inserting him into the realm of grace (so C. Masson, *L'épître de S. Paul aux Éphésiens*, 1953).

2:11-22 The unity of the church

A new section begins with v. 11 and these verses form an extended exposition of the theme of the church's essential oneness in spite of the barriers of race and culture which kept the Jews and the Gentiles apart in the ancient world. The kernel of Paul's argument is in 1 Cor. 12:13; Gal. 3:28; Col. 3:11; and these verses offer an elaborate extension of the unity theme stated earlier. It is this fact of an elaborate discussion which has suggested to some scholars that Paul is using material drawn from Christian worship (especially baptismal hymns) in order to spell out fully the importance of the church's unity (*cf.* 1 Cor. 12:13 for the 'one Christ – one baptism' lesson, as in 4:4ff.).

The centre of the discussion is v. 14: 'he is our peace, who has made us both one'. It combines the elements of the surrounding verses, viz. the enmity between Jews and Gentiles has been cancelled; the disparate sections of the 1st-century world are now called to a harmony in the fellowship of the church; and both Jews and Gentiles, having lost their ethnic and cultural identity, gain something in return which is far better—a place in Christ's body. They thus form a new race of men, and are privileged to enjoy an access to God which they could never know in their previous and unreconciled state.

2:11-13 The Gentiles before and after Christ's coming. 11, 12 The appeal is directed specially to the non-Jews who were the apostle's readers

in this letter. They were classed by the Jews as 'uncircumcised' because they stood outside God's covenant in a threefold way. To the Jews the condition of the Gentiles was *a.* characterized by a lack of Messianic hope. Indeed, the usually-attested Jewish hope of Messiah's coming entailed the destruction of the Gentile foreigners or at best their subjugation to Israel; *b.* one of deprivation in that they did not share in the privileges and advantages of belonging to the most favoured nation; *c.* described by the saddest of all misfortunes, viz. an ignorance of God and so a denial of hope which can only be engendered by a knowledge of the living God and His presence in the world. **13** With Christ's coming a new era has opened for them.

Notes. 11 *Gentiles in the flesh* means 'Gentiles because of not having the marks of circumcision on your bodies'. *Uncircumcision* (Gk. *akrobystia*, lit. 'foreskin') was, in the OT, the equivalent of being outside God's covenant with Israel (*cf.* Je. 9:26; but this verse points forward to a distinction within Israel which Paul was later to elaborate in Rom. 2:25-29). **12** *The commonwealth of Israel*. The right of citizenship within the elect nation is meant (so Masson), a sense confirmed by v. 19. *The covenants of promise* are those solemn assurances of Israel's destiny given to the patriarchs (*cf.* Gn. 15:18; 17; 26:2ff.) and to Moses (*cf.* Ex. 19:5, 6). Paul sees these covenant promises fulfilled in Christ and the church (*cf.* Gal. 3:16ff.). *Without God*; not in the sense of denying His existence (there were few atheists in the ancient world), but, as Gal. 4:8 explains, as ignorant of the one, true God (*cf.* Acts 17:22ff.).

13 Two expressions—first, *but now*, answering to 'at one time' (v. 11) and 'at that time' (v. 12); and second, *in Christ Jesus*, which fills the lack suggested in the phrase 'separated from Christ' (v. 12)—show how the Gentiles' position has changed with their inclusion in the covenant of grace. The contrast *far off . . . brought near* is borrowed from Is. 57:19, LXX; and the means by which the underprivileged Gentiles have come into the inheritance is Messiah's death. So the intention of this verse which is explained in detail (see on vv. 14-18) is to show how, in transforming radically the state of Jews and Gentiles before God, Christ has transformed their mutual relations (so Masson).

2:14-18 Jews and Gentiles are now one body— in Christ. 14 *Peace* carries a double sense. In uniting sinners to God by cancelling the enmity set up by sin (v. 16b) Christ has brought Jews and Gentiles together in a unity and amity otherwise unknown in the 1st-century world. Reconciliation is the application of Christ's work in His breaking down *the dividing wall of hostility* between the two rival groups, as in Gal. 3:28; Col. 3:11. That *wall* which set up *hostility* is best understood as the Mosaic law and its scribal interpretation, which both protected Israel by keeping her separate from the other nations, and prevented the Gentiles from having access to God because of Judaism's particularism (so Masson, Schlier: see the Notes below for other possibilities of background to this cryptic phrase). This view is confirmed if in v. 13 *far off* means that the Gentiles were kept at a distance from Israel which alone was a people near to God (*cf*. Ps. 148:14).

15 The key-thought of the whole passage is *one new man in place of the two*, *i.e.* one Christian church instead of two ethnic groups of Jews and Gentiles separated by an 'iron curtain' of animosity. The way by which this reconciliation is accomplished is now set out. Jesus as Israel's Messiah abolishes the law by fulfilling it (*cf*. Mt. 5:17), and vicariously endures the penalty of that law which the Jews had broken (*cf*. Gal. 3:10–13; Rom. 8:3). He also brings in a new age of righteousness on a basis quite independent of law-keeping (*cf*. Rom. 3:21ff.) and because it has this character the Gentiles are as much the beneficiaries as the covenant people of Israel (so Gal. 3:14, clearly). He is the Creator of a new race in which the age-old distinctions of Jew and Gentile have lost their relevance and force. **16** The *one body* can hardly be a reference to the crucified body of Jesus. The sense is more likely that when He died His purpose was to embrace the disparate sections of humanity in that saving deed and in reconciling men without distinction to God to kill the hostility which up to that point had kept them apart and at war.

17 *He came* in the person of His apostolic messengers who carry the gospel of peace (*cf*. Rom. 10:15) which is freely offered to all races, both Gentiles afar off and Jews formerly God's chosen race. **18** The experimental token of the reality of the 'one new man' is shown in the freeness of access to God by the Holy Spirit who is the author of unity within the church (so 1 Cor. 12:13).

Notes. **14** *Peace* recalls the description of Messiah as 'Prince of peace' (Is. 9:6). The Hebrew word for 'peace', *šālôm*, means much more than an absence of hostility, like an armed truce; it connotes well-being and security at every level. *Both*; *i.e.* both Jews and Gentiles together. Mark the recurrence of this term (vv. 14, 16, 18). *The dividing wall*; the commonest illustration of the imagery behind this phrase adopted by commentators is the Temple balustrade which separated the Court of Gentiles and the Court of Women, referred to by Josephus (*Ant*. xv.11; *Jewish War* v. 5). This fence with its warning inscription served to remind the Gentiles that they must keep their distance from Israel's sacred shrine (*cf*. Acts 21:27ff.). This barrier, the verse declares, has been broken down in the sense that access to God is no longer restricted to Jews. Another suggestion looks to Gnostic images of a wall which separates the aeons and divides the heavenly *plērōma* from the earthly world as the most suitable background to this verse. The thought, then, is that the Gnostic redeemer's re-entry from the terrestrial to the celestial regions has opened a way by which his followers may gain access to the *plērōma*. But

the barrier in the text is a vertical one denoting a division between two groups of people resident in this world rather than a horizontal division between the upper and lower world. And the verb *has broken down* more naturally refers to a vertical structure. The suggestion that the *wall* which caused *hostility* (taking the second term as an explanation of the first) is an allusion to the Mosaic law finds confirmation from the teaching of the *Letter of Aristeas*, 139, and from the wording of this verse where the demolition of the wall is explained as the abolishing (*i.e.* rendering void) of the law's enactments which, in the rabbinical view, served to isolate the Jew from his neighbour. The law's abrogation was necessary for the creation of a universal church.

16 *Cf*. Rom. 7:4. The *hostility* spoken of is either that between God and man (*cf*. Rom. 5:10) or that between the two races (as in v. 14); but possibly both ideas are in the writer's mind.

2:19–22 The one church on the one foundation. 19 The promise here cancels out the disability under which Gentiles suffered (*cf*. v. 12). Their admission to the church implies no second-class status within the covenant community, but full membership as *fellow citizens* with the *saints* (here probably meaning Jewish–Christians, as often in the Acts); both classes then constitute, as a single entity, *the household of God*, as members with equal rights and privileges. **20** The church as a house (*cf*. Heb. 3:6) means in Paul that the church takes over Israel's vocation as God's holy house (*cf*. 1 Cor. 3:10, 16), *i.e.* His Temple. This is endorsed by v. 21. Christians are then likened to living stones (as in 1 Pet. 2:5) built into the framework which, in turn, rests upon a foundation which is Christ (*cf*. 1 Cor. 3:10) and which is laid by the apostles and prophets (so NEB). It is their witness to Christ which God uses to build up the edifice (*cf*. 1 Tim. 3:15). **21** The result of the church's being settled on a foundation-stone and growing as a living organism (Paul's verb brings in a change of metaphor) is that a *holy temple* is taking shape as a consequence of the apostolic mission (*cf*. 4:11–16). **22** The dwelling-place is realized in the formation of a spiritual community in whom His Spirit dwells (*cf*. 1 Cor. 3:16).

Notes. **19** On the experimental ground of a common fellowship with God (at the Lord's table?) Gentiles are not debarred from any of the privileges which belong to members of God's household. **20** The Greek is ambiguous. *Apostles and prophets* (prophets in the NT church are intended, as in 3:5; men like Agabus, Acts 11:27ff.; 21:10; *cf*. Acts 13:1–3; 15:32) could conceivably constitute the foundation of the church (as Rev. 21:14) in the sense that they were the primary and unique witnesses to the saving events of the gospel and later became inspired interpreters whose literary deposits are found in the NT. But NEB: 'the foundation laid by the apostles and prophets' gives a preferable alternative. Christ's designation as *corner-stone* (Gk. *akrogōniaios*) is also capable of diverse interpretation. The best view is that taken by G. H. Whitaker (*Expositor*, VIII, 1921, pp. 470ff.), who argues on the basis of Is. 28:16 for the meaning 'corner-stone' by which the architect determines the 'lie' of the whole building. See, too, R. J. McKelvey, *NTS*, 8, 1961–2, pp. 359ff. **21** Jewish expectation (especially at Qumran) looked for a new Temple. **22** *Dwelling place* of God: *cf.* Ex. 15:17; 1 Ki. 8:13.

3:1–21 Paul's apostleship and his prayer for the church

Paul held his commission to be Christ's special messenger to the Gentiles in high regard; and the calls to service recorded in Acts 9:15, 16; 22:21; 26:17 brought together the twin elements of a vocation to be an apostle to the Gentiles and the warning that this task would not be undertaken without personal risk and exposure to danger. These same notes are sounded in this chapter (vv. 1, 2, 8 are a glad acknowledgment of his special ministry to the Gentiles; v. 13 is a reminder of his suffering on their behalf). The autobiographical introduction merges into a statement of the content of his preaching in the light of the special destiny which he was charged to fulfil (vv. 3–6), viz. that his apostolic ministry to the Gentiles is based on the place which they have in the economy of God's saving purpose for the world through the church (vv. 9–11). The personal note creeps in again as an interlude (vv. 7, 8), and is resumed as Paul offers a memorable pastoral prayer for the Christian congregations in the world (vv. 14–19), concluding with an equally notable ascription of praise (vv. 20, 21).

3:1–6 Paul's calling and how he understood it. **1** The apostle's own name, coupled with his writing in the first person singular and his self-description as *a prisoner for Christ Jesus on behalf of you Gentiles*, is intended to give emphasis to the prayer which will follow in vv. 14ff. In fact, there is no verb to follow his name until that section, which is introduced at v. 13. The passage, therefore, of vv. 1–12, is a statement of his ministry with his name standing at the head of it. **2** Paul writes to a company of believers to whom he is unknown (*cf.* 1:15), but who are certain to have heard that he was well known in the churches as the apostle to the Gentiles (*cf.* Rom. 15:16; Gal. 2:7). **3** He came to understand the truth of God's intention early in his Christian life (see the references in Acts given above); and the mention of this *revelation* harks back to the Damascus road encounter and its sequel (*cf.* Gal. 1:16). **4** *The mystery* (*cf.* 1:9) is the divinely revealed truth which relates to the inclusion of the Gentiles in a church wherein all barriers of race are broken down (*cf.* 2:14, 17, 18). **5** Earlier periods of history, even within the life of the Jewish people, failed to recognize the embracing purpose of God, although hints had been given as, *e.g.*, in the promise to Abraham which Paul

exploits in his argument with the Judaizers at Galatia (*cf.* Gal. 3:8, 9). What was once hidden and unrecognized—viz. that there should be one, holy, catholic (= universal), apostolic church—is now entrusted to the preachers of the Gentile mission by the Holy Spirit. **6** The content of this truth, of which Paul himself was the chief custodian as a teacher of the Gentiles (*cf.* 1 Tim. 2:7), is spelled out clearly by the use of a triad of terms all of which have the same prefix (Gk. *syn*); so J. Armitage Robinson aptly translates 'the Gentiles are co-heirs, concorporate, co-partakers of the Promise'.

Notes. 3 *Have written* (Gk. *proegrapsa*); the tense of the verb would be classed as epistolary aorist, *i.e.* the writer puts himself in the place of his readers at the time when the composition is actually read by them. So the notion of an earlier letter (as suggested by E. J. Goodspeed, *The Meaning of Ephesians*, 1933) is not required; and Paul has in view what he has just written (so Schlier, citing for *briefly* Heb. 13:22; 1 Pet. 5:12). **5** The *apostles and prophets* are Christian leaders (as in 2:20), and the force of *holy* (*cf.* Lk. 1:70; 2 Pet. 1:21) is not to invest them with an aura of sanctity—a trait of a later age, and so taken by some scholars as a mark of the lateness of this Epistle in its witness to 'incipient catholicism'—but to distinguish them from *the sons of men* (*i.e.* mankind in general). **6** By contrast with 2:12, 19a the Gentiles are now sharers in all the blessings promised to the Jews (*cf.* 1:18). *Partakers* here stands also in contrast with the negative use of the same term in 5:7.

3:7–12 Paul's calling and how he fulfilled it. **7** For the fulfilment of his God-appointed service (*cf.* 2 Tim. 1:11) Paul, like all who are called to Christ's service in His church in every age, needed the gift of divine grace (*cf.* Phil. 1:7).

8 In a telling snatch of autobiography and self-revelation Paul confesses to his own inadequacy and need, yet rejoices in the supply of God's power to enable him to accomplish his task of preaching *to the Gentiles* a message which he describes as one of unfathomable wealth (*cf.* 1:18), viz. that **9** all men may be enlightened by the unveiling of God's plan, once concealed (*cf.* v. 5) but now brought out into the light. **10** The church on earth is the witness to and the vehicle of this revealed 'mystery'; and the hostile angelic powers are not only held in wonder at this but their death-knell is sounded with the proclamation that God in Christ has decisively acted for cosmic salvation and so brought their malign régime over human life to an end (see on 1:21, 22).

11, 12 God's age-old plan is thus realized in a proof to which Paul has earlier alluded (*cf.* 2:18), the confident approach of the reconciled to God the Father through the Christ whose victory spells the end of the devil's control over man's destiny.

Notes. 8 The Greek is a reinforced superlative: 'the most insignificant of all God's people', a self-confession written out of his painful recollection of his past persecution of the church (*cf.* 1 Tim. 1:13). If the sight of his past infamy flashed at that moment before his mind's eye, this may explain a phrase often regarded as 'calmly deliberate, even self-conscious, and a little theatrical' (C. L. Mitton, *The Epistle to the Ephesians*, 1951). **9, 10** *Hidden for ages* is usually taken in the time-sense ('from all eternity' is F. F. Bruce's translation), but the reference to God as Creator of all things, together with v. 10, suggests that Paul may be speaking of God's plan as a *mystery* concealed from the angelic intelligences ('the aeons') and made known to them only to sound their defeat (so 1 Cor. 2:8; Col. 2:15). Certainly later in this letter (see 6:12) Paul will write realistically of the church's conflict with these (potentially defeated) enemies. To these cosmic forces God's wisdom in Christ's cross displays His *manifold* (lit. 'multi-coloured') *wisdom*—to dazzle them the more because of its sheer simplicity and apparent weakness (*cf.* 1 Cor. 2:6ff.). **11, 12** But this 'weakness' of God (*cf.* 1 Cor. 1:25) which allowed His Son to be crucified by the design of these agencies was the divine strategy, the triumphant purpose of which is displayed in Christ enthroned (1:20, 21) and in the church given through Him grace and access. Christians are reminded that 'they owe to Jesus Christ their Lord the distinctive characteristics of their new spiritual state' (Masson) by *faith in him.*

3:13–21 Paul's prayer for the church. 13 RSV offers one possibility of translation out of many (see Notes) because the Greek is cryptic and compressed. In any event, Paul is requesting the prayers of his readers partly on the ground of the freedom of access to God which they, as Gentiles, now enjoy, and also because they have a special place in his ministry, for he is 'their' apostle. He knows that he can confidently count on their intercession.

14, 15 The opening words take us back to v. 1 which they complete. God's fatherhood is the archetype of all family life, but the exact nature of His fatherly relationship in this context is not clear. Jewish literature spoke of two aspects of divine fatherhood: 'the chief family', *i.e.* the angelic world (a reference which would explain *every family in heaven*) and 'our family', *i.e.* Israel. The phrase *on earth* is best understood in this light, as Paul's bold appropriation of a title proudly claimed by Jews but which he re-interprets in the light of 2:18. Both Jews and Gentiles now make up God's family in the fellowship of a united church.

16, 17 The content of this petition is twofold: *a.* the empowering of the Spirit whom Paul calls in to fortify the Christian's 'inner life' especially under trial (*cf.* Phil. 1:19; Col. 1:11; and 2 Cor. 4:16 for the phrase); *b.* the indwelling of Christ who comes to make His home in the believer's heart. The two verbs *to be strengthened* and *may dwell* are parallel, and so there is no great difference between the action of the Spirit on the inner man and Christ's habitation in our hearts. The indwelling Christ is the assurance to the Christian of moral strength (*cf.* Phil. 4:13). Certain consequences follow from the fulfilment of the apostle's prayer which has, as its frontispiece, a combination of metaphors which are found together at Eph. 2:21 and Col. 2:7. *Rooted* is a horticultural term denoting the firm bed in which plants are set; *grounded* (from the Gk. verb *themelioō*; *cf.* Gk. *themelios*, 'foundation', in 2:20) borrows from the language of architecture and ensures a strong base on which a superstructure rises. *Love* is both the soil in which the plant thrives and the firm ground on which the building rests.

18, 19 *Comprehend . . . know.* The two verses combine verbs of apprehension, the objects of which are *a.* God's redemptive plan in all its richness and profundity (hence the quadratic dimensions, *breadth, length, etc.*); and *b.* Christ's love of which this redemptive plan is the consummate expression; indeed, so amazing is that love which God's purpose for His church in the world reveals that it eludes our full grasp. It *surpasses knowledge*, yet at the same time beckons us on to a progressive experience as we are more and more filled 'up to the measure of' (Gk. *eis*) God's fullness.

20, 21 The doxology celebrates the church's confidence that God is both able and willing to do all that Paul's prayer asks for; indeed, by the use of a rare adverb *abundantly* (Gk. *hyperekperissou*; a translation like 'infinitely more' as popularly used brings out the sense) Paul knows that God's intention is to exceed by His answer even the far-reaching petitions of his prayer and the aspirations which have prompted them. The secret of this confidence is that God's power is *at work* in the church in which His fullness dwells by the presence of Christ (*cf.* Col. 1:27). Fittingly, at the conclusion of this lofty thought, praise is ascribed to God who is present both in Christ (uniquely, as the embodiment of His deity; *cf.* Col. 2:9) and the church (as Christ's body, intimately associated with Him; *cf.* 1:23; 4:15, 16; 5:30). But for Paul in this letter Christ and His church are not two separate entities but so closely conjoined that it would be permissible to write of one corporate whole, Christ-in-His-church. It is because of this indwelling and empowering presence that *glory* can be offered to God eternally.

Notes. 13 The exegetical difficulty centres on the proper subject of the verb *lose heart.* Is Paul praying that he himself will not become discouraged (see RSV mg.)? Or is he praying that they may not be despondent because of his imprisonment on their behalf (*cf.* 3:1)? Some scholars argue for the second meaning on the (dubious) ground that the pronoun 'you' (Gk. *hymas*) has fallen out of the text by accident. **14** Jews normally stood to pray (*cf.* Mt. 6:5; Lk. 18:11, 13); kneeling for prayer was a sign of great urgency and distress (see the discussion in the present writer's *Carmen Christi*, 1967, pp.

264f.). *Father* is the distinctively Christian name for God, derived from Jesus' use of the Aramaic *'Abbâ* ('dear Father') (*cf.*, *e.g.*, Mk. 14:36). **17** The verb *dwell* (Gk. *katoikeō*) looks back to 2:22 ('dwelling place', Gk. *katoikētērion*). **18** *Saints*; *i.e.* 'all God's people' (NEB); no special class of Christians is intended. Nor does Paul know of any private mystical experience in isolation from the company of believers. **20, 21** *Cf.* doxologies in Rom. 16:25ff.; Heb. 13:20, 21; Jude 24f. God's glory is here reflected in the church's worship; Eph. 5:27 (the church in its glory) gives the complementary thought.

4:1 – 6:9 THE CHURCH'S LIFE IN SOCIETY

4:1–16 The church's vocation as Christ's body

So far in his address to his Gentile congregations Paul has expounded the way in which God's purpose was conceived and executed. This intention of God to have Jews and Gentiles as one people united to one Head, Christ, began to be actually realized chiefly through Paul's mission, and he has here looked back on the accomplishment of it during his life-time of Christian service. But the ideal of one Head – one body needs an empirical application to the churches made up of ordinary men and women in the Graeco–Roman world. So from the exposition of his 'ecclesiology' in which he has had the ideal relation between Christ and His people in view, Paul now turns to the practical outworking of this ideal in everyday living. His writing takes on a practical purpose as he sets before his readers the guidelines of Christian conduct and deportment in the world. But before he gets to grips with details he must first give an over-all picture of what is to be the church's calling in the world. This is the theme of vv. 1–16.

The characteristic note is struck in v. 1 as he calls them to be true to their destiny in the light of *a.* their place within a church which by definition is one (vv. 2–6); *b.* yet unity does not mean a monochrome, dead-pan uniformity which would be true if the church were a thing, an inert object. But the church is an organism, pulsating with life and made up of living persons who are responsible for growth of character and personality, according to their use of the gifts which Christ has bestowed (v. 7); *c.* His purpose is that His church shall reach 'mature manhood' (v. 13), and towards this end He has provided gifts to be exercised through His servants (vv. 8–12); *d.* the church's progress should therefore be marked by a growth out of infanthood into maturity as it takes on the character of its Head, Christ (vv. 14–16).

4:1–6 The church's calling in the light of its unity. 1 The Christian's *calling* is God's summons answered at conversion (*cf.* Phil. 3:14); and his response is to be worked out in his subsequent behaviour. *Worthy* (*cf.* Phil. 1:27) shows the connection between God's plan and the

Christian's acceptance of it in terms of his daily living. See too Col. 1:10; 1 Thes. 2:12, for the same ethical incentive. **2** *Cf.* Gal. 5:22, 23. **3** Two matters are stated here, both significantly connected with church fellowship. There is a unity which the Holy Spirit creates; and Christians have a responsibility to cherish it by their harmonious relationships (*in the bond of peace*).

4–6 The Holy Spirit's gift of unity to the church is further defined in a series of creed-like formulations, all of them being given emphasis by the repetition (seven times) of *one*. Moreover, the three parts of v. 4 are matched by corresponding partners in the next verse, thus forming a triad of couplets: *one body*, the church, answers to *one Lord*, the church's Head; *one Spirit* inspires *one faith* as He calls men to acknowledge that Jesus is Lord (*cf.* 1 Cor. 12:3) and baptizes them into one body (*cf.* 1 Cor. 12:13); *one hope that belongs to your call*—a call, acceptance of which was marked in the early church by participation in the *one baptism*. After this 'trinity of unities' Paul seals this credal statement with a Trinitarian allusion to *one God* who is known in His self-revelation as Father *above all*, Son *through all* (the use of the preposition here answers to the same idea of mediation in 2:18), and Spirit who is *in all* the family of God. *Cf.* 1 Pet. 1:2 and *NBD*, art. 'Creed'.

Notes. **3** *The unity of the Spirit* should be understood as 'unity which the Spirit makes possible' by His gift and activity (so v. 4 and 1 Cor. 12:13). The church's task which requires diligence is to guard that oneness already imparted by the Spirit and implied in their being one body of Christ (see 1 Cor. 1:10ff. for a NT illustration of a forgetfulness of this fact). The means by which the unity is preserved is stated: it is made fast (NEB) by the bond which God's peace in Christ's reconciliation established (so Hanson, p. 149; *cf.* Eph. 2:17). **5** This triad is often regarded as a baptismal creed, confessing the *one Lord* (over against the polytheism of the pagan world which the new convert renounced; *cf.* 1 Cor. 8:6), *one faith* (which is the act of believing as in Eph. 2:8, leading to the substance of the confession—in its most elemental form, 'Jesus Christ is Lord', but later expanded—made in baptism), *one baptism* (in contrast to the lustrations of the pagan mystery religions or Jewish proselyte baptism, or possibly a deviationist baptism like that practised by John's disciples near Ephesus; *cf.* Acts 19:1–7). **6** *One God* picks up the OT and Jewish creed of the unity of God (*cf.* Dt. 6:4; 1 Cor. 8:4; 1 Tim. 2:5) but Christianizes it by the addition of *Father* revealed in Jesus and applied to *us all* (*i.e.* Christians), though *us* is a scribal addition absent from the best texts and probably has crept in from 1 Cor. 8:6. Nonetheless the following *all* is in every case to be understood as a personal and not a neuter reference (so Masson).

4:7–12 Christ's gift and the church's gifts.

7 The singular *gift* is the key to this difficult passage. Paul has in mind the part which all Christians are to play in the life of the church; there are no exceptions (so 1 Cor. 12:4ff.), for all in the body of Christ as His members are endowed with some gift-by-grace (Gk. *charisma*). And it is the ascended Lord who bestows these gifts by first sending His gift *par excellence*, viz. the Holy Spirit (*cf.* Jn. 7:39; 20:22; Acts 2:33). 8–10 The quotation from Ps. 67:19 (LXX; EVV Ps. 68:18) is adapted to produce a reading which closely follows the Syriac version known as the Peshitta: 'Thou didst ascend on high, and take captivity captive; and thou gavest gifts to men'; and a similar version in the Aramaic Targum (*i.e.* paraphrase of the OT text) shows that the sense of 'He gave unto men' was an old Jewish interpretation on which Paul is evidently drawing in this citation. The apostle's application of this text is to Christ's ascension. Scholars are divided over the logical connection between the descent and ascent of Christ (see Notes). Following G. B. Caird, we prefer the view that Paul's sequence is that Christ's ascent (*cf.* Lk. 24:49ff.) is followed by the descent of the Spirit at Pentecost when, in the realistic sense of 2 Cor. 3:17 (*cf.* Jn. 14:15–18), the Lord returned to earth, laden with gifts for His church. Acts 2:33 speaks of the Holy Spirit as the gift of the exalted Lord; and it is He who has given to the church all the varied ministries which serve to upbuild the church's life (vv. 11, 12). Christ's enthronement over the universe is the guarantee that nothing needful for the church is lacking (exactly the sense of 1:22, 23).

11 Paul's emphatic pronoun (Gk. *autos*) should be brought out: 'And it was He—the One who fulfilled the prediction of the Psalm—who gave.' The 'grace-gifts' of v. 7 are now spelled out in terms of the church's ministries, with *apostles* and *prophets* in first place (for the reason given in 2:20; *cf.* 1 Cor. 12:28). *Evangelists* are men like Philip (*cf.* Acts 21:8) and Timothy (*cf.* 2 Tim. 4:5) in the apostolic church, though the term denotes a function more than an office. The construction of the phrase *pastors and teachers* with one definite article covering both words suggests that there were two functions shared by the same individuals whose chief task is described in Acts 20:28. These men would be local congregational leaders in charge of established churches brought into existence by the preaching of the apostles and others (*cf.* Acts 14:23 where 'elders' corresponds to those addressed in Acts 20:17). 12 The bestowal of Christ's gifts of the ministry has a specific purpose in view, viz. that all God's people (the meaning of *the saints*) may be equipped by the functions which God's servants perform in order that they in turn may discharge their service as Christians in the world; and so by the complementary functions of both a regular ministry, ordained and appointed by the Head of the church, and of the rank and file of the church, Christ's body may be edified. Only on the basis of this render-

ing can we do justice to the subtle use of prepositions and make sense of such admonitions as 1 Thes. 5:11–13 and Heb. 13:17 as well as the calls to respect the pastoral office in the letters to Timothy and Titus.

Notes. 7 The *grace* here is not an allusion to 2:8, but rather to the Spirit's gifts as in Rom. 12:3ff.; 1 Cor. 12:4ff. 8 Paul's text reads *he gave* (Gk. *edōken*) for the LXX 'thou didst receive' (Gk. *elabes*). Other possibilities of explanation are given in E. E. Ellis (*Paul's Use of the Old Testament*, 1957, pp.15f.). The Targum mentioned above reads 'thou (*i.e.* Moses) hast given it (the Torah) as gifts to men'. G. B. Caird's view (stated in *Studia Evangelica*, II, i, 1964, pp. 535ff.) is built on the following assumptions: *a.* that AV's addition of 'first' (in v. 9) is to be rejected, as it must be on insufficient textual grounds; *b.* that *the lower parts of the earth* refers to a coming from heaven to earth (so NEB) and not to a descent to the underworld; *c.* that Ps. 68 has a Pentecostal setting as a psalm appointed to be read in the Jewish liturgy at Pentecost or the Feast of Weeks which in later Judaism celebrated the giving of the Law. As Moses brought down the Torah as God's gift, the exalted Christ at Pentecost came down as the Spirit and brought gifts to His church. 12 The punctuation in RSV is to be noted; and it is clear that of the three practical results mentioned, the last two are dependent on the first. NEB reads: 'to equip God's people for work in his service, to the building up of the body of Christ.'

4:13–16 The church's path to maturity. 13 'The unity of the Spirit' (v. 3) is a present possession, but *the unity of the faith* is clearly here an object of hope one day to be attained. The work of the ministers who are Christ's gift (vv. 11f.) has this end in view, viz. that the church will be upbuilt until its final state is reached. That goal is denoted by the phrase *mature manhood* (Gk. *anēr teleios*, 'complete man') and is reached as Christians make progress in their united (*we all* sounds the death knell of all party spirit and factiousness) apprehension of the riches which are theirs in Christ. The connecting word *and* is best understood as explanatory so that *the unity of the faith* consists in a deeper insight (Gk. *epignōsis* which RSV translates *knowledge*) into Christ Himself as the embodiment of God's treasure (*cf.* Col. 2:3 and Eph. 1:18; 2:4; 3:8) and the supplier of the church's needs as its Head (*cf.* 1:22, 23). Christ's care for His people promotes their growth and ensures that they develop into a *stature* which is measured only by the fullness of Christ, *i.e.* by the availability of His grace and resources which are made over to the church and which aid its growth until it reaches His designed end, which is a fully completed church embodying all His fullness (*cf.* the parallel thought in Rom. 11:25, 26).

14 Certain tests of the church's increasing maturity are given: Christians will no longer remain infantile (Gk. *nēpios* which is the opposite of *teleios* in v. 13), nor be lacking in stability

when storms rage against them (the Gk. participle translated *tossed to and fro* suggests the picture of the church as a ship battered by angry seas; *cf.* Lk. 8:24), nor led astray into false teaching which heretical leaders will seek to promote. **15** By contrast, the church will maintain the truth (better than RSV *speaking the truth* which is only one sense of the verb) in its resistance to pernicious propaganda and will grow up in love as it conforms its life more and more to that of its *head*, Christ Himself. **16** Guided by Col. 2:19 we may interpret the line of thought as the church's growth *into Christ* in the sense that it derives its life from Him who supplies all its need. The growing is both from and towards the Head; this striking paradox should put us on our guard against expecting a neat, logical analogy between Christ's body and the human body. What can be seen is that *a*. Christ's body is made up of many members (*cf.* Rom. 12:4, 5; 1 Cor. 12:12) who, although different in obvious ways, yet are connected to the one body (*i.e.* the universal church, likened in 2:21 to a holy temple built by many stones); *b*. the church grows by the action of Christ on its behalf; and He exerts a unifying action on the body by means of His work through *every joint* which He supplies. This last thought takes us back to v. 11 and makes possible the equation of *every joint* with Christ's gift of the ministry; *c*. by this chain-reaction of Christ – His servants – His people the whole body is edified as *love* becomes the 'atmosphere' in which this process of mutual encouragement and responsibility is exercised, with each part of the church playing the role appointed for it. Christ the Head imparts His risen life and bestows by the Spirit His gifts of ministries; His servants fulfil their mission by equipping the saints (v. 12) and by being the ligaments of the church's cohesion to Christ and one another; Christ's people making the contribution (the meaning of Gk. *meros*, RSV *part*) needful for Christ's design to be realized for the body's upbuilding and growth into Him.

Notes. **14** *Cf.* 1 Cor. 2:6; 3:1. Paul had been accused of cunning ways (*cf.* 2 Cor. 4:2) and in rebuttal he gives a notable statement of his clear motives, so different from those of the false teachers here condemned. **15** *Speaking the truth* (Gk. *alētheuontes*) means 'dealing truly' (RV mg.) and the following phrase *in love* may be taken with the words *grow up*.

4:17-32 The Christian's personal conduct

One form of ethical challenge in the NT is based on the contrast between the old life, characterized by pagan ways, and the new outlook and behaviour pattern which Christians accept at their conversion and baptism, which should therefore mark a clean break. 2 Cor. 5:17 states this contrast clearly; elsewhere it is expressed by the phrase 'no longer . . . but now'. Here its practical implications are pressed home with great effect by an appeal couched in the form: 'Put off the old nature . . . put on the new nature';

and Gal. 3:27 roots this call in the baptismal experience.

This section of the letter in which Paul turns more specifically to the actual congregations of the Gentile churches illustrates in detail this type of moral appeal. Formerly his readers adopted the only way of life they knew, viz. the pagan outlook and practice (vv. 17-19). But at conversion they exchanged—for many of them in a dramatic renunciation—these evil practices and took on a new deportment which vitally affected their character and manners. Vv. 28-32 vividly recall the change with an insistent summons not to relapse into former ways. The 'put off . . . put on' form of appeal is explicitly expressed in the terms Paul uses (vv. 22-25), and has an obvious, pointed application to Christian conduct which exemplifies the new life imparted by the living Christ to His people.

4:17-24 Some principles which govern Christian conduct. 17 The Gentile way of life is painted in some sombre colours which recall Rom. 1:18-32. Paul fastens here on the root cause of the idolatry and excesses which disfigured life in the 1st-century Graeco–Roman world: *the futility of their minds*; *cf.* Rom. 1:28 which uses the same Gk. word *nous* of a 'depraved reason', which 'leads them to break all rules of conduct', NEB; and God's provision for this 'depravity', *i.e.* being turned aside from His truth, is given in v. 23 (*cf.* Rom. 12:2). **18** Two consequences follow. Unregenerate man has his understanding (*i.e.* of spiritual realities; Gk. *dianoia*; *cf.* the same word, 'mind', in 2:3) darkened, and he suffers alienation from God caused by his culpable ignorance of God and refusal to submit himself to God; this process of resistance leads inevitably to a deadness and insensitivity to God, called by Paul *hardness of heart.* **19** Man's relationship with God as a sinner has its direct repercussions on his daily behaviour and his relations with his fellow-men.

20 The Greek implies a contrast, not represented in RSV. 'But that way of life doesn't fit in with a life in Christ', begun when you became His disciple (*learn Christ* means this). **21** 'Just as you heard in the preaching of the gospel and in the instruction you received in the fellowship of His people.' **22** The last part of v. 21 may (accepting C. A. A. Scott's suggestion, *Christianity according to St Paul*, 1961 ed., p. 36) be connected with this call to abandon old ways. The *old nature* which dictated the tendencies of believers' *former manner of life* (*cf.* 1 Pet. 1:18) is the willing victim of a seduction which appeals to it and leads it into evil desire; and this seduction is made all the more easy because man's nature in Adam is twisted and so a prey to evil.

23 The summons to put off the old nature as a suit of clothes is shed may sound like a counsel of despair, for fallen man is in helpless plight. But Paul's appeal is to Christians who have known the renewal of the Spirit which, begun decisively at conversion, is a process to be continued. Hence the present tense of his admonition which calls upon his readers to *be renewed* in their minds (answering the need stated in vv. 17, 18) by the action of the Holy Spirit. **24** Grace, as nature, abhors a vacuum. To divest oneself of evil habits is not enough; this must be followed by the donning of *the new nature*, imparted at the new birth by the Spirit and to be increasingly recognized as the dominant moral force in the Christian's life as he faces an inner conflict (*cf.* Gal. 5:16ff.). The new birth and the Spirit's control restore the image of God broken by sin (*cf.* Gn. 1:27), and so give back to man the sinner, now redeemed by Christ and renovated by the Holy Spirit, what he lost in Adam, viz. *righteousness* (*i.e.* a right relationship with his Creator) and *holiness* (*i.e.* a requisite for fellowship with a holy God) demanded by the truth of God.

Notes. 17 *Futility* may be the apostle's estimate of idol-worship as the veneration of lifeless vanities (*cf.* Acts 14:15, which picks up the OT condemnation of worthless idols; *cf.* Ps. 115, *etc.*). **18** The *ignorance* here is not an intellectual deficiency, but a wilful refusal to know God and to honour Him (*cf.* Rom. 1:21). **19** *Given themselves up*; the converse of Rom. 1:24, 26, 28. *Greedy* represents a Greek noun (*pleonexia*) often linked with immoral ways (*cf.* 1 Cor. 5:10, 11; 6:10; Col. 3:5), and this may be the sense here especially as *licentiousness* (NEB 'vice') and *uncleanness* have been mentioned. *Cf.* 5:3 for the same association of *pleonexia* (there translated 'covetousness') with irresponsible sexual excesses. **23** The reference to *the spirit* is better taken as pointing to the Holy Spirit's work; *cf.* similar wording in Tit. 3:5.

4:25-32 A continuation of Christian social ethics. 25 Paul here begins a section which applies to concrete situations the principles stated earlier. Opposed to truth-telling which is the mark of a character fashioned in likeness to God (v. 24) is lying, which has to be discarded. Two reasons are implicit: *a.* lying is condemned in the OT (Zc. 8:16 is quoted in Paul's words) and *b.* failure to honour one's word leads to a breach of Christian fellowship because it breeds distrust and suspicion, and so destroys the common life in the body of Christ (*cf.* Rom. 12:5). **26** The force of Paul's language is: 'In your wrath—provoked by the presence of evil and injustice—don't give the devil a loophole by persisting in it.' He is again turning to the OT (Ps. 4:4, LXX) for illustration, and adds a comment to show how Christian indignation must be kept in firm check. Personal pique and outbursts of emotional temper are not in view (see v. 31); rather Paul is thinking of a provocation caused by a miscarriage of justice (as in 2 Cor. 11:29). But even then, such proper indignation must not be allowed to simmer until it becomes a fixation. **27** For the devil uses all devices, even by exploiting our good intentions and social concerns, to bring the church into disrepute (hence his name here is *diabolos*, 'slanderer', in

place of the more usual Pauline preference for 'Satan'; 2 Cor. 2:5–11 gives an apt example of how he works in this way). **28** Let the thief renounce his occupation (*cf.* 1 Cor. 6:10, 11) now that he has become a new man in Christ, and has a social conscience for the needs of the poor, especially within the fellowship of his new circle (*cf.* Gal. 6:10). **29** Words are an index of character (*cf.* Mt. 12:33, 34. The Greek word 'bad' (*sapros*) is the same as Paul's *evil talk*). *Good* words may be tested by this criterion: do they build up the hearer's character and make him a better man for having heard our speaking? Do they meet his need (*as fits the occasion* is a paraphrase of this requirement; *cf.* 5:4 for the negative side)? And do they in this way 'bring a blessing' (so NEB) by supplying that need? **30** Foul or inappropriate language is not only an insult to the hearer; it saddens the Holy Spirit by wounding Him and denying in practice the meaning of His indwelling and sanctifying presence in the believer, which is a token of his final redemption (*cf.* 1:13, 14). **31, 32** Mention of the misuse of the tongue leads on to a full statement of vices to be avoided and virtues to be cultivated, with the use of the spoken word running through all these admonitions. *Malice* (Gk. *kakos*, 'evil') is the parent of the unhappy brood of earlier terms. But, as befits that new quality of life in Christ (Gk. *Christos*), the Christian should seek to be kind (Gk. *chrēstos*) with a compassionate and forgiving disposition which is based on the simple but amazing fact that this is the disposition which has been shown to him in God's forgiveness, offered *in Christ* (*cf.* 2 Cor. 5:19 for the sense of this phrase).

Note. 32 The positive injunctions are amplified in Col. 3:12ff.

5:1-20 The Christians' conduct in the world

If a change of perspective and proportion may be rightly detected, this section of social ethics moves away from the Christians' behaviour within the church fellowship (described both in principle and by precept in 4:17–32) and relates that conduct more to their bearing and actions in the world around them. From this standpoint we may pick out some of the salient features of Paul's guidance. He is addressing his readers as God's children (v. 1) and God's chosen people (v. 3: their vocation is one of sainthood), but both these descriptions need the qualification that their lives are set, not in isolation from the world of men, but in the midst of a society which is alien to God (*cf.* 1 Jn. 2:15–17) and hostile to the Christian spirit (*cf.* 2 Cor. 6:14ff.). Hence the warning of v. 6: 'Let no one deceive you' and the call of v. 7: 'Do not associate with them.' The antidote to these viruses to which the body of Christ in the world is exposed is hinted at by Paul in a number of his references in this section.

In addition to the ethical maxims we have already noted Paul recalls the churches to their

God-appointed destiny as children of light (v. 8) who, at baptism, have been brought into the full light of Christ (v. 14 contains a snatch of a baptismal chant); as followers of wisdom whose practices show up the folly of an immoral and materialistic society around them (vv. 15ff.); as men and women whose lives reflect a dependence on God and who turn to Him in grateful acknowledgment of His goodness (vv. 4, 20 repeat a characteristic Christian response in thanksgiving, both in private life and public worship, v. 19). In all, the Christian life is shown in this section as possessing a distinctive pattern, intended to be both a challenge to and a rebuke of contemporary society. But Paul offers no mandate for Christians to contract out of the world as though they were ascetics or fanatics.

1, 2 Forgiveness within the family of God (*cf.* 4:32) is but one aspect of what life ought to be like. For Christian character finds its pattern and exemplar in God Himself, the Father (*cf.* 3:14, 15; Mt. 5:48). *Beloved children* finds its natural sequence of thought in a reference to the Father's well-beloved Son (*cf.* 1:6; Mk. 1:11, *etc.*) who in turn demonstrated His love for the church (*cf.* 5:25) as well as His loving acceptance of the Father's will, which included the cross, by His sacrificial death. His self-offering at Calvary pleased the Father as an acceptable offering (*cf.* Ps. 40:6, 7) and has the effect of eliciting from Christians a desire to 'live in love' to Him and their fellow-believers.

3, 4 This astringent ethic reflects the need for the church to retain its identity in the 1st-century world and by the purity of its life (as *saints*; see on 1:1) to give no countenance to the immoral practices which were the accepted norm of Graeco–Roman society. *Silly talk* (Gk. *mōrologia*) and *levity* do not condemn light-hearted merriment or good-humoured fun; but, in association with *filthiness* (*i.e.* coarseness of speech), refer to slanderous name-calling (the best commentary on *mōrologia* is Mt. 5:22 which repeats the sneering remark, 'You fool' (Gk. *mōre*), which incurs a fearful penalty) and flippant buffoonery which goes beyond the bound of good taste. On Christian lips the note of praise to God is more appropriate.

5, 6 A clear statement of warning, drawing upon accepted Christian teaching (*cf.* 1 Cor. 6:9, 10; Gal. 5:21; Heb. 13:4; Rev. 21:8; 22:15). *Covetous* may have in mind immoral excesses (as in v. 3) which are produced when men live for the gratification of their appetite and so become idolaters (exactly the sin of Phil. 3:19: 'appetite is their god', NEB). No distinction is to be drawn between *the kingdom of Christ* and that *of God*. The serious consequences of playing fast and loose with God's moral law speak for themselves; and Paul found it needful to spell out this warning in view of contrary views to which Christians were listening: *Let no one deceive you.* Whether these sentiments are directed against pagans who were urging believers to do what they did or misguided Christians (like the anti-

nomians of Rom. 6:1ff. who had perverted Pauline teaching) cannot be decided. *Sons of disobedience* is an OT expression for men of disobedient character, *i.e.* by their wilful infringement of God's law (*cf.* Rom. 1:32).

7, 8 They are what Christians formerly were— children of darkness; but by God's grace the church has been brought into the light (*cf.* 1 Pet. 2:9). The calling of believers is then to live as *children of light*, *i.e.* true to their place in God's family. Again Paul is drawing upon common Christian teaching (see Rom. 13:12; 2 Cor. 6:14; 1 Thes. 5:5; *cf.* Jn. 12:35f.; 1 Jn. 1:5f.); and the contrast of light and darkness runs through this section up to v. 14. **9** A parenthetic note added to show what are the qualities of living in the light. **10** This 'intention to please God in all things' (as William Law phrased it in his *Serious Call*) is a Pauline ethical rubric often found: *cf.* Rom. 12:2 (the will of God which is well-pleasing to Him); 14:18; 2 Cor. 5:9; Col. 3:20; 1 Thes. 4:1. It is a reminder that Christian ethics cannot be stereotyped as a legalistic 'bundle of prohibitions' but in essence represent a positive ambition to be pleasing to a loving God whose character His children long to share (5:1).

11, 12 Not only do Christians steer clear of evil practices and pursuits; they have a responsibility to show up by a contrasting way of life the nature of the world around them and its culpability. So *expose* is explained by **13** *exposed by the light*, *i.e.* Christians as children of light in the world (*cf.* Phil. 2:15) cast an illuminating beam into the dark corners of human society where evil practices are conducted in the darkness of secrecy (a veiled hint at immoral and magical pursuits in the pagan world?). Christian influence has a reproving effect as Christ's light shines 'not merely "to display", but "to show to be evil", so that we do best to keep to the rendering "to correct", especially as deeds and doers are closely related' (Büchsel, *TDNT*, ii, 474). *Cf.* Jn. 3:20. **14** The encouragement given in these verses is backed home by the citation of a hymn of three lines:

> 'Awake, O sleeper,
> From the grave arise.
> The light of Christ upon you shines.'

Clearly the setting of this exhortation is baptism, known in the later church as 'enlightenment' and depicted as the rising of the convert from the death of sin to union with the living Lord (*cf.* Rom. 6:4ff.). Paul harks back to this experience as a reminder to his readers to fulfil now their baptismal profession by walking in Christ's light and by stirring themselves to active witness.

15–17 This witness is now the subject of Paul's admonition, which here takes a positive turn. In the earlier verses (3–13) his directions have been mainly negative, warning the churches of the threat of complicity with evil in the world. Now he issues a call to wisdom which is set over against the folly of a pagan environment. The path taken by *wise* men has to be understood on its OT background where wisdom is not an intellectual achievement, but an attitude to life which begins with a knowledge of God and an avoidance of all that displeases Him (*cf.* Jb. 28:28; Ps. 1; Pr. 4:5ff.; 8:1ff.). The practice of wisdom in everyday conduct involves *a.* a buying up (Gk. *exagorazomenoi*—a commercial term straight from the market-place (*agora*); the prefix *ex* denoting an intensive activity, a snapping up of all the opportunities which are available) of every chance of *making the most of the time* (*cf.* Rom. 12:11, NEB mg.); *b.* a recognition that *the days are evil*, probably as days which precede the final crisis of the end of the Age (so E. F. Scott); *c.* a call to self-knowledge in the light of God's will, which is the outstanding mark of a wise man who lives in fellowship with God (*cf.* 2 Tim. 2:7).

18 Another sign of wisdom is the maintenance of self-control which sees the danger of intoxication through which the vigilance of the moral censor is lifted and a gate is opened to immorality. In a daring contrast Paul goes on to apply the lesson: let the infilling you seek be not of wine but of the Spirit; and as drunkenness is a common occurrence in the world around you and over-indulgence in wine a daily experience, let the fullness of the Holy Spirit be your constant preoccupation (Gk. *plērousthe*, 'be filled', is in the present tense). **19, 20** One hallmark of the Spirit's filling will be a desire to give vocal expression to the heart's devotion *to the Lord* by the use of canticles and songs which the Spirit inspires. In this way Christians both edify one another (hence *addressing one another*) and give vent to their emotional stirrings by the spiritual exercise of thanksgiving to God. Paul has a congregational assembly (as in 1 Cor. 14) in mind; and this recalling of the scenes of their corporate worship is a bridge which links the ethical teaching of these verses with what follows in his letter.

Notes. 2 AV's 'sweetsmelling savour' gives a more literal translation which shows the link with the Mosaic sacrifices so described (*e.g.* Ex. 29:18, 25). **3** Paul's reticence to name certain vices stands in contrast with present-day trends of a permissive society. 'Western culture, in all the mass-media, calls a spade a spade with a crudity that is corrupting. The present age has a filthy tongue' (G. Johnston, *Ephesians, Philippians, Colossians and Philemon, CB*, 1967).

7 *Do not associate* (Gk. *synmetochoi*) *with them* is a sentence obviously framed to stand in contrast with 3:6. Christian detachment from the evil-doers arises from the prior commitment which has been made to Christ in the fellowship of His church. The closest parallel is Paul's teaching in 1 Cor. 10:14–21. **8** *Children of light* was a self-description claimed by the people of the Dead Sea Scrolls in their hatred of 'the sons of darkness'; and their withdrawal to the Qumran monastery was a protest movement,

for which the NT ethical teaching offers no parallel. **11** See on v. 7.

14 *It is said* (lit. 'he/it says': attempts to trace this verse to an unwritten saying of the Lord or an OT quotation are not successful; the introduction must be, 'Therefore it—the hymn—says'). The following words are rhythmical and arranged so as to form a rhetorical device of assonance at the end of lines one and two. The summons to awake and be quickened into life in response to Christ's call, answered at baptism, is best taken in a metaphorical sense; but one suggestion gives a futuristic application by relating the call to the *parousia* when the returning Lord will summon His people to the resurrection. Paul uses this eschatological hope to call Christians to their present duties (as in 1 Thes. 5:1–11).

18 *Do not get drunk with wine* quotes Pr. 23:31 (LXX), a vice equally reprobated in the list of Gal. 5:19–21. The positive injunction poses a nice difficulty in translation. Paul's Greek is compressed. ' "By the Spirit" is too precise; "in the Spirit" is too vague. We propose: "seek the fulness which the Spirit gives" ' (Masson). **19** *Cf.* Col. 3:16. The classification of these terms into OT psalms, Christian hymns used in early church worship, and songs employed by the heavenly worshippers (*cf.* Rev. 5:9; 14:3; 15:3) is too neat. Probably distinctively Christian compositions are intended for all three types. Full discussion of the background here and the place of this rubric in the development of church worship is offered by the present writer in *Worship in the Early Church*, 1964, chs. 4 and 12.

5:21 – 6:4 Christ, the church, and the family

Mention of the church at worship invites a consideration by Paul of the place of women, first in the church service and then, as a natural sequel, in the family relationship with their husbands and children. From this opening statement of the true ordering of the husband-wife relationship Paul proceeds to appeal to the analogy of Christ and the church, using Gn. 2:24 as a text applicable, first to human relations, but also—and for him more significantly—prefiguring the nuptial union between the heavenly Bridegroom and His bride the church, which is one with Him (v. 31). In this correspondence between the Christ – His church and man - woman relationship four lessons are drawn: *a.* Christ is the Head of the church, His body; and in the ordering of creation man occupies the place of headship over woman (*cf.* 1 Cor. 11:3; 1 Tim. 2:13); *b.* Christ requires the obedience of His people who are rightly subject to Him (v. 24); and the inference is made that the wife too is to be submissive to her husband in all things (v. 24) and not simply in the ordering of public worship (to which v. 22 seems naturally to refer); *c.* Christ has set His love upon the church and shown the extent of that love in all He has done for the church's redemption (vv. 25ff.); while much of the foregoing belongs uniquely to the Christ - church relation the chief point is made in v. 28: let husbands love their wives with a love that is akin to His love; *d.* Christ who looks upon His church as a part of Himself, as His body, cares for it (vv. 29, 30); in the marriage bond too the husband has a responsibility for his spouse. V. 33 sums up the Pauline discussion, the emphasis on 'respect' in that verse answering to the emphasis on 'reverence' (the same word in the Greek with a change of grammatical form) in v. 21.

5:21–33 Marriage in the light of the sacred marriage of Christ and the church. 21 This verse belongs as much to the preceding section as to what follows; it is a bridge between the two passages. The submission (Gk. *hypotassomenoi*) belongs to the description given of the structure of the church at worship (*cf.* 5:19, 20) when the presence of the Lord was powerfully felt (1 Cor. 5:4 gives one example of what *out of reverence for Christ* meant). It also carries over into **22** which has no verb in the Greek, but clearly 'be submissive' is understood. The background may, however, still be that of congregational worship in view of the use of the same verb in 1 Cor. 14:34; and the cognate noun in 1 Tim. 2:11 may indicate that that passage too is to be seen in the light of the place of women members of the congregation. **23** The first correspondence in the analogy is drawn. Headship belongs to both Christ and man-as-a-husband (Gk. *anēr* is used, not the generic term for man, *anthrōpos*; but the usage is not hard and fast, as the occurrence of *anthrōpos* in the quotation in v. 31 shows). Christ is also the church's *Saviour*. The verb underlying 'Saviour' (Gk. *sōzō*) in 1 Tim. 2:15 may suggest the meaning that Christ preserves the church; and that thought would prepare for vv. 29, 30 in the analogy. **24** *In everything* extends the limited reference of the submission given in v. 22 by inference.

25 The true meaning of obligation, expressed by the verb rendered *be subject* in the earlier verses, is now made plain; it is an obligation in love. The husband's love is patterned on that greater love of Christ for His bride (for further references see 2 Cor. 11:2, 3; Rev. 19:7ff.; 21:2). The background here is OT. Paul in particular is drawing upon Yahweh's marriage with Israel described in Ho. 2:16; Is. 54:4f.; 62:4f.; Ezk. 16:7f. in the light of the rabbinic practice of eulogizing the covenant at Sinai as a marriage between Yahweh and His people. The Torah became the marriage contract, with Moses as the one who led the bride to God. Christ's relationship to His bride, the church, is for Paul one further way of saying that the Torah-age has given place to the new Age of Messiah's fulfilment. The apostle now plays the part of the lawgiver Moses in leading Christ's spouse to Him. (See *NBD*, art. 'Bride, Bridegroom'.) The heavenly Bridegroom's actions for His bride are traced back to His love and self-giving on the cross (Gal. 2:20 combines the same verbs). **26** The purpose and effect of His work for the church

are given in terms of sanctification, *i.e.* the church is taken out of the sphere of sin and placed in that of holiness. The means by which this is accomplished is cryptically described as *having cleansed her by the washing of water with the word.* 'This washing . . . can scarcely be anything other than baptism' (F. F. Bruce, *The Epistle to the Ephesians,* 1961), the allusion to *the word* being understood as the convert's affirmation of faith, mentioned in Acts 22:16 and illustrated in the question-and-answer dialogue of Acts 8:36ff., RSV mg. Examples of this baptismal interrogation in the later church are given in the writer's *Worship in the Early Church,* pp. 60f. **27** looks forward to the ultimate realization of His purpose when the Bridegroom comes to claim His bride (*cf.* Rev. 19:7, 9). Then the church will attain its full *splendour* as *holy and without blemish* (*cf.* Col. 1:22).

28 The application of the teaching is now made. The strange wording *as their own bodies* used of the husbands' love of wives probably is explained by the desire to keep close to the analogy: Christ loves His body, the church. **29** Two verbs are borrowed from the nursery with a possible OT background (*e.g.* Is. 1:2). Both *nourishes* and *cherishes* (*cf.* the same word in 1 Thes. 2:7) mean great solicitude and as used of a husband's care of his wife imply 'protection, affection and tangible and practical maintenance' (Masson). Similarly Christ cares for the church. **31** A citation from Gn. 2:24 (slightly different from LXX) is taken by Paul *to mean Christ and the church.* Jesus used this OT verse (in Mk. 10:7f.) to establish the permanent nature of the marriage bond; Paul, following the insight accorded him into the nature of the church (*cf.* 3:4 which also speaks of the *mystery, i.e.* God's plan for the world through the church; *cf.* 1:9) applies the text analogically to the union, not of man with woman, but of Christ and His body which is one with Him. **33** The line of reasoning adopted by Paul and stated in v. 32 accounts for the conclusion. He is arguing from the Christ - church relationship to the human marriage tie, not *vice versa.* This is why he 'never tells wives that they are to love their husbands. . . . The reason is that which he gives: Christ loves the Church, but it is for the Church to obey and submit to Christ' (C. Chavasse, *The Bride of Christ,* 1939, p. 77).

Notes. 26 *Sanctify* carries here a pregnant sense (= 'consecrate by committing the life to God') as in Jn. 10:36; 17:17; *cf.* Je. 1:5. It points to the commencement of the Christian life; and the following reference to baptism agrees. *The washing of water* recalls Tit. 3:5, but more especially 1 Cor. 6:11 where washing and sanctification are side by side.

6:1–4 Family duties. 1 Attention is switched to family relations as *children* are called to accept their place in obedience to parents. It is *right, i.e.* in line with God's will (as in 4:24), that they should. **2** A further reason is supplied by this quotation from Ex. 20:12 with which is coupled

3 an adaptation of Dt. 5:16, possibly influenced by Dt. 22:7. *The first commandment* means either that this is the first requirement of the Decalogue to have a promise attached or that *first* is not a reference to numerical order but is used adverbially = 'a very important commandment' (*cf.* 1 Cor. 15:3 where the word is rendered 'of first importance'). **4** A father's duties are displayed both negatively and positively. First there is a warning against irritating children (by nagging at them?) and so leading to their exasperation; then an injunction to train them in the disciplinary education (Gk. *paideia* is properly education by discipline; *nouthesia* is education by word of mouth) of the Christian life (*of the Lord* means this).

6:5–9 Relations of masters and slaves

This section of Paul's 'household code' deals with a very real problem for 1st-century Christians in their social responsibilities, viz. the way slaves were to accept their status, and the treatment Christian slave-owners were to give to slaves in their control.

5 The call to obey, not to revolt (a suicidal action, unsuited to the 1st-century world of the Roman Empire where slavery was established by law), is the hallmark of the NT generally. Instead the sting is partly drawn from this inhuman institution by the slaves' attitude as Christians. *As to Christ* sounds a distinctively Christian note, thereby transforming all work and recalling Mt. 25:31ff. **6, 7** The same thought is repeated in the play on words *as slaves of Christ* (RSV mg.), who serve Him by doing the will of God *from the heart*, *i.e.* not in a dilatory or listless fashion, and *with a good will*, *i.e.* with an eagerness 'which does not wait to be compelled' (J. A. Robinson). **8** Present opportunities of service point forward to the future when Christ will assess the worth of the Christian's life at His judgment-seat (see Rom. 14:12; 1 Cor. 4:5; 2 Cor. 5:10). **9** Slave-owners too are bidden to act in a way which befits their Christian calling, with a caution against an overbearing disposition and a reminder that, though they are masters (Gk. *kyrioi*) of their slaves, they too have a heavenly Master (Gk. *kyrios*) who cannot be bribed or corrupted in any way. Col. 3:25 uses the same idea of impartiality of treatment as part of a call to slaves not to exploit their Christian owners – a slant perhaps inspired, as E. Percy suggests (*Die Probleme der Kolosser- und Epheserbriefe*, 1946), by the case of Onesimus who had cheated and run away from his master Philemon at Colossae.

Notes. 7 *With a good will* (Gk. *met' eunoias*). Dibelius-Greeven cite an interesting commentary on this phrase from a papyrus dated a century or so later than Paul in which a slave is set free in his master's will because of his 'cheerfulness and affection' in service rendered. Not all slave-owners were the monsters of popular imagination, however degrading the principle of the institution seems to us today. **9** *Partiality*;

i.e. favouritism which can be bought. The OT is Paul's authority here (*e.g.* 2 Ch. 19:7).

6:10–24 CONCLUSION

6:10–20 The Christian's warfare and the apostle's plea

In this concluding admonition the actual situation of the church in the world is faced with a call to steadfastness under trial and a summons to prepare for conflict. The enemies Paul has in mind are, however, not simply the human agents which oppress the churches; behind them he sees the malign forces of evil. Demonic powers can be faced only with heavenly aid which God places at the Christians' disposal by the provision of His armament (v. 13). This panoply is listed in a description drawn from the equipment worn and used by the Roman soldier ready for battle. A representative soldier may well have been at Paul's side as he wrote or dictated this letter, for he speaks of himself as 'an ambassador in chains' (v. 20). As a Christian apostle he looks to his friends in the Asian churches to stand by him with their prayers, for he is a special target of attack and so in special need of the encouragement which their intercessions can bring (vv. 18, 19). In particular, he wants to be faithful in the discharge of his apostolic work (v. 20; *cf.* 3:8, 13).

10 The two exhortations set side by side interpret each other. 'Find your strength in the Lord, in his mighty power' (NEB). The Greek words are all variants of the idea of power, and recall a similar piling up of synonyms in 1:19. **11** The battle motif is now introduced, as the Christian lives as it were in a no-man's-land between the opposing forces of *God* and *the devil*. He is called to align himself with God and against His enemy by wearing the armour which God Himself wears (as the sources of Paul's thought in Is. 59:17 and Wisdom of Solomon 5:17–20 make clear). Moreover the devil in his capacity as 'slanderer' (Gk. *diabolos*) is the sworn foe of the church which cannot be neutral in any case (*cf.* Rev. 12:10), in view of the evil machinations (Gk. *methodeia*; both here and at 4:14 translated *wiles*) of the devil and his minions.

12 Paul lifts the veil over the church's struggle in the world. The struggle is not against human powers (*flesh and blood*: see Mt. 16:17 for the phrase in this sense) but is directed against the real power behind the persecutors on earth, demonic agencies which also were the prime movers in the events which led to Jesus' death (*cf.* 1 Cor. 2:8). The spiritual hierarchy of evil is described in some detail: *principalities, powers* are the terms used elsewhere for the orders of creation of which Christ is both the origin and the head (*cf.* Col. 1:16), but they are thought of here as having detached themselves in rebellion against the cosmic Lord and so as being in active opposition to Him and His people. *World rulers* belong to the same company but the derivation of the term (which is not found in LXX) is uncertain. The Rabbis used a Semitic form of the term to denote the angel of death; and later Gnostics within Christendom applied the word to the devil. Paul's word is plural and denotes evil forces which are implacably opposed to the church as *darkness* is opposed to light. This contrast picks up the earlier teaching of 4:18; 5:7ff. with its stark antithesis. The final phrase in this cluster of malevolent agencies is *the spiritual hosts of wickedness in the heavenly places*. The nearest parallel is 2:2; and in both texts the church's conflict is seen to be located in the upper air regions (Gk. *en tois epouraniois*). But this precise region is also the sphere of Christ's rule (*cf.* 1:20), the consequent fountainhead of God's blessings upon His people (*cf.* 1:3), and the place where the wonders of what God is doing through the church are being made known (*cf.* 3:10). In spite, therefore, of the tremendous hostility from demonic powers which the church encounters the assurance is given in this phrase that because 'these powers are competing against God' (G. H. P. Thompson, *The Letters of Paul to the Ephesians, etc., CBC,* 1967) they are doomed to failure and defeat.

13 Because of the church's confidence in its struggle against a foe which already is under sentence of doom—this is the logical connection of *therefore*—the Christian soldier is bidden to take up his battle position with high courage, standing his ground *in the evil day, i.e.* in an age when the pressure of persecution against the church mounts (*cf.* 5:16). *Having done all* carries the natural sense of a total preparedness in the light of a fresh onslaught of evil, but a secondary meaning (attested by Herodotus) of 'having defeated all' is just possible; the *all* will then look back to the spiritual hosts of v. 12. The important part is clear: get ready for battle and be ready when the fighting breaks out.

14 The clarion call to alertness involves the soldier's ability to equip himself adequately. But as the armour is God's (v. 11), no provision is lacking. Paul, using the model of the Roman soldier on duty, draws an implication from each piece of armament. The belt is a sign of active duty; the *miles accinctus* (Lat. *cingulum* = 'belt') is the soldier at the ready. *The breastplate* imagery is taken from Is. 59:17 with Paul's reference to *righteousness* following the prophetic sense of vindication and action which redresses all wrong. **15** *Feet* equipped with shoes for marching (Lat. *caliga*) also recall Is. 52:7 as an OT allusion, and in the light of Rom. 10:15 may suggest a promptitude of service in evangelistic endeavour. **16** *Above all* is ambiguous in English as in Greek (*en pasin*). Does it mean 'with all these' (NEB) or 'to cover all parts of the body'? The latter idea is certainly possible because it is matched by Paul's choice of *scutum* (*shield*, the Latin term behind his Gk. *thureos*) for the soldier's defence against all the flaming darts thrown by the devil (2 Thes. 3:3, RSV mg.). The *scutum* 'was a large quadrangular shield devised to catch and extinguish ignited arrows' (Thompson); and in

the spiritual warfare it is a shield *of faith* in God's final victory, already achieved in principle by Christ's resurrection and exaltation over all evil powers (*cf.* 1:20-22).

17 Two further items of equipment are mentioned: *helmet of salvation* is drawn from Is. 59:17 where Yahweh wears this on His head as He goes forth to vindicate His oppressed people. The Rabbis, however, applied this to Messiah's work and Christian interpretation of the OT may well have followed suit, as we know was the case with a similar passage in Is. 11:1-5. Taking the helmet, then, means availing oneself of all that Christ in His saving work offers. *The sword* is wielded with cutting power when *the word of God* is preached (here Is. 11:4 seems in view; it describes Messiah's conquest as in Rev. 19:15). *Cf.* Heb. 4:12. The Greek *rhēma theou*, rendered *the word of God*, by the omission in the Greek of definite articles suggests a LXX usage, where the term relates to some words spoken by God. An apt illustration of what this verse implies is seen in the temptations of Jesus who, 'full of the Holy Spirit', met the enemy's insinuations with some appropriate part of Scripture which became to Him *the sword of the Spirit* (*cf.* Lk. 4:1-13).

18 Although having no counterpart in a soldier's equipment, *prayer and supplication* are evidently intended to be included in Paul's list. The link-thought is *the Spirit* who inspires Christian prayer (*cf.* Rom. 8:26ff.) here defined as *prayer* in general (Gk. *proseuchē*) and prayer as the offering of some specific request (Gk. *deēsis*). The same terms are brought together in Phil. 4:6 and 1 Tim. 5:5. Paul spells out one object of Christian *supplication*, viz. *for all the saints* who form God's people of the new covenant (*cf.* 1:1). The call to intercession for fellow-Christians requires both a watchfulness and a resolution (Gk. *proskarterēsis*; the cognate verb 'to persevere' is found in Acts 1:14; Rom. 12:12; Col. 4:2 in a similar context). **19** A personal plea, re-echoed in 2 Cor. 1:11. But here it is directly connected with the apostolic ministry committed to Paul as apostle to the Gentiles (*cf.* 3:1). He asks for co-operation in prayer that his ministry of proclaiming *the mystery of the gospel* (explained in this letter as the uniting in one church of both Jews and Gentiles) may be fulfilled. **20** For such a task he needs above all courage in time of trial (*cf.* Phil. 1:19ff. for a similar request in similar circumstances) as a prisoner whose witness will not be muted. He is Christ's *ambassador* (*cf.* 2 Cor. 5:20) but enjoys no diplomatic immunity. Quite the contrary; he is *in chains* (Col. 4:18).

6:21-24 Personal remarks and final greeting

Vv. 21, 22 contain 'the most extensive verbal connection' (Dibelius–Greeven) between Ephesians and Colossians; and Col. 4:7, 8 should be compared. Tychicus is to be the informant of Paul's immediate circumstances to the Asian churches; and he is warmly commended with the apostle's excellent character reference. By bringing news of Paul's situation in Rome he will put fresh heart into these Christians.

The letter which opened with a salutation of grace and peace now closes with the same terms in inverse order and with the addition of love and faith. The final grace embraces all believers in its scope, especially its first readers and its readers in every age.

21 The unusual *you also* has posed a difficulty, for Paul seems to have another group in mind with whom he is linking the addressees of Ephesians. F. Foulkes accounts for this allusion and for the close correspondence of wording with Col. 4:7f. by the 'supposition that the apostle wrote the two conclusions together, when both letters had been written and were about to be despatched' (*TNTC*, p. 23). *What I am doing* is not to be taken literally. NEB captures the Greek idiom with 'how I am', *i.e.* 'how I am getting on', in colloquial English. *Tychicus* is described as a *faithful minister* (lit. 'helper', or, if the Gk. *diakonos* carries its technical sense, 'minister', as in 3:7. But the latter meaning is not certain). **22** *I have sent him* too literally translates the Greek 'epistolary' aorist tense (see on 3:3). NEB improves with 'I am sending', *i.e.* Tychicus is to be the bearer of the letter

to its destination; and he will be able to give a personal report of the apostle's condition and so encourage the churches.

23, 24 The closing greeting is slightly longer than in other Pauline letters (*cf.*, *e.g.*, Phil. 4:23) and of a more general character by the use of an impersonal term (*the brethren*) instead of the normal 'you'. Paul ends on his favourite note, with a prayer for God's *grace* to be with the universal church described as *all who love our Lord Jesus Christ with love undying*. The last three words in RSV represent the Greek *en aphtharsia*, literally 'with immortality'. This 'immortality' could go with *grace* as the theme of Paul's prayer for his readers (so NEB), but the order of words is against this view. Dibelius–Greeven suggest a different interpretation by taking the preposition locally: the Lord Jesus Christ who (lives) in imperishable (glory). In support Jas. 2:1 as well as 1 Tim. 1:17 may be quoted; and the solemn character of the conclusion is another reason for accepting this view. The Epistle which began with the church's blessings 'in heavenly places' (1:3), where the enthroned Christ rules (1:20) and to which He calls His people (2:6), concludes fittingly on the same note.

RALPH P. MARTIN

Philippians

INTRODUCTION

PAUL, PHILIPPI AND THE CHURCH THERE

Before 360 BC a small Thracian village stood on the site of later Philippi. The city was founded and its name was given by Philip of Macedon, the father of Alexander the Great, who realized the strategic nature of the site. Philippi came into the hands of the Romans after the battle of Pydna in 168 BC, and subsequently became part of the Roman province of Macedonia. In 42 BC Antony, after he with Octavian had defeated Brutus and Cassius, settled some of his disbanded veterans in Philippi, making the city a 'colony'. Then in 30 BC, when Octavian had defeated Antony and Cleopatra at the battle of Actium, he sent further 'colonists' from Italy to Philippi, to make room nearer home for the settlement of his own war veterans. A Roman 'colony' was like a little piece of Rome abroad. The Latin language was used; Roman law controlled local administration and taxes; many aspects of public life went on as in Rome itself; most of the officials had the same titles as in Rome. The strong consciousness of the privileges of Roman citizenship in Philippi is seen in Acts 16:20f., 35–39 and probably reflected in the Epistle in 1:27 and 3:20. In the 1st century AD Philippi could be described not only as 'a Roman colony' but as 'the leading city of . . . Macedonia' (Acts 16:12), though Thessalonica was the actual capital of the province.

Paul must have been well aware of the strategic significance of Philippi when he came there, on his second missionary journey, and thus preached the gospel for the first time in Europe. He came (together with Silas and Timothy), as Acts 16:9f. tells us, in response to his vision in the night of 'a man of Macedonia . . . standing beseeching him . . . , "Come over to Macedonia and help us." ' At Philippi Paul found no synagogue, but a small group of women gathered 'on the sabbath day' at 'a place of prayer' by the riverside. One of these, Lydia, 'a seller of purple goods' from Thyatira, appears to have been the first convert, and she opened her home to Paul. We see something of the pagan background of Philippi when we read of 'a slave girl who had a spirit of divination and brought her owners much gain by soothsaying'. Paul and Silas were condemned to prison through the anger of the slave owners, when with the evil spirit exorcized they 'saw that their hope of gain was gone', though the pretext for the condemnation of Paul and Silas was that they as Jews disturbed the city and advocated customs which, their accusers said, 'it is not lawful for us Romans to accept or practise'. The partnership in the gospel, the persecution, and the largely Gentile background of the Philippian Christians, all of which are brought out in the Epistle, are thus seen in this record in Acts 16 of Paul's first visit to Philippi.

Manifestly Paul left a devoted group of Christians when he went on from Philippi. On his third missionary journey we read in the first place of his spending time in Macedonia (Acts 20:1) and that doubtless included a visit to Philippi; then, after a time in Greece, he was back in Macedonia, and Acts 20:6 tells us specifically that Paul set sail from Philippi to return to Jerusalem.

THE TIME AND PLACE OF THE WRITING OF THE EPISTLE

That Paul wrote this letter from imprisonment is made clear in 1:12–26 and 2:17. Traditionally Philippians has been linked with Colossians and Philemon and Ephesians, and believed to have been written in Rome in the imprisonment which Acts 28 records. Two other suggestions have been made, that the letter might have been written while the apostle was imprisoned in Caesarea or Ephesus.

Little can be said in favour of *Caesarea* as the place of writing of Philippians, and much against. In Caesarea Paul was not facing the immediate threat of execution, but a journey to Rome to stand on trial before the emperor, in consequence of his 'appeal to Caesar' recorded in Acts 25:11. No such situation was contemplated when Paul wrote Philippians, but the alternatives of death and release, and in the case of the latter the hope of a visit to Philippi (2:24). Nearly all of the circumstances associated with Paul's imprisonment, described in ch. 1 of the Epistle, would be most difficult to account for from what we know of Paul's Caesarean imprisonment.

Adolf Deissmann in 1897 suggested *Ephesus* as the place of writing of Philippians, and since then many have felt the force of the reasons given in favour of this and against a Roman origin of the letter. It is true that we have no proof that the apostle was imprisoned in Ephesus; nevertheless such passages as Acts 20:18f.; 1 Cor. 4:9–13; 15:31f.; and 2 Cor. 1:8–10; 4:8–12; 6:4–10 and 11:23–27 make it very probable that he faced such opposition that led to imprisonment and the threat of death. The following arguments for the Ephesian origin of Philippians may be noted.

a. The Epistle indicates at least four journeys between Philippi and the place of Paul's imprisonment—the first took news of his condition, then Epaphroditus came to Paul from Philippi, a message went back to tell of the illness of Epaphroditus, and subsequently news was received of the Philippians' concern (2:25f.). The journey from Philippi to Ephesus would take 7 to 10 days, that to Rome much longer.

b. Acts 19:22 tells us that Timothy was sent from Ephesus to Macedonia, and this would fit in with 2:19–22.

c. Whereas Paul certainly faced the threat of death during his time in Ephesus (as the passages quoted above show), it is questioned whether he did in Rome.

d. It is argued, further, that beyond his Roman imprisonment Paul's eyes were turned westwards and he did not expect to come eastwards again (Acts 20:25; Rom. 15:18–29) and so could hardly have written 2:24 from Rome. When in Ephesus, however, Paul certainly contemplated and indeed fulfilled the hope of travel to Macedonia and Greece.

e. There are said to be similarities between this letter and Paul's earlier letters rather than his later ones, and in particular the problem of the Judaizers remains as a paramount concern.

f. It is thought that such passages as 1:30 and 4:15f. view the first preaching of the gospel in Philippi as much more recent than the 11 or 12 years which would be required if Paul wrote from Rome.

If the letter was written from Ephesus, its date of writing would be about 54–55 AD. Against Ephesus and in favour of *Rome* there are the following arguments.

a. The journeys between Rome and Philippi would have been much longer, but need not have taken more than 7 or 8 weeks each.

b. It is not difficult to imagine that circumstances in Paul's confinement in Rome changed from those described in Acts 28:30f., which may have caused him to see death as the probable outcome of his imprisonment.

c. It may also have been the case—and there is evidence to suggest it—that while in Rome the apostle turned his thoughts away from Spain back to the lands east of him where he had laboured already, and where the churches he had founded were in great need of further help from him.

d. If there are similarities, there are also considerable differences from the earlier Pauline Epistles. The church was still in danger of the Judaizers' legalism at the time of the writing of the Pastoral Epistles.

e. It may be questioned whether the Philippians would be as likely to wish or to need to send help to Paul in Ephesus, where he had many friends, as to him in Rome.

f. Although explanation can be given of the 'praetorian guard' (1:13) and 'Caesar's household' (4:22) in relation to Ephesus (or even

Caesarea), both expressions would more naturally be used in Rome.

g. A final argument suffers through being an argument from silence, but may not be irrelevant. In Ephesus Paul was greatly concerned with the collection for the Jerusalem Christians (as the Corinthian letters show). It would be strange if it found no mention in Philippians, if that letter were written from Ephesus, especially when we realize from 2 Cor. 8:1–5 and 9:1–4 the involvement of the Macedonian Christians in the whole undertaking.

We cannot be dogmatic, but the arguments on the whole seem to favour Rome rather than Ephesus, and if this is the case, we should date the letter about 63 AD, that is towards the end of the period of Paul's imprisonment of which Acts 28 speaks.

THE PURPOSES OF THE EPISTLE

From its contents Paul appears to have had a number of reasons for writing to the Philippians as he did.

a. He wanted to acknowledge the gifts that they had sent to him (see especially 4:10, 14–18).

b. He wanted to give news of his own circumstances and to take away their concern that his imprisonment might have been a set-back for the gospel (1:12–26). He wished to tell them of his plan to send Timothy to them, and subsequently to come himself (2:19–24).

c. He felt it was necessary to explain why he was sending Epaphroditus back to them, when apparently they had intended that he should remain with the apostle and minister to him (2:25–30).

d. News brought to him indicated the dangers of divisions and party spirit among the Philippian Christians, and he wanted to exhort them to live and act and witness in the unity of the Spirit (see 1:27; 2:1–11; 4:2f.).

e. He was also made aware of the danger of their being influenced by the Judaizers and he wanted to remind them and demonstrate to them that legalism was a basic contradiction of the gospel (3:3–11), and perhaps at the same time to warn them of the danger of a false perfectionism (3:12–16).

f. Finally, his writing provided an opportunity for him to encourage the Philippian Christians to suffer bravely, to live in single-mindedness and to trust their lives to their Lord in all things and under all circumstances (see especially 1:27–30; 2:12–18; 3:17–21; 4:4–9).

THE SPECIAL FEATURES OF THE EPISTLE

a. It has often been commented that *joy* is a great theme of this letter. Sixteen times the noun or the verb is used. We see the apostle rejoicing in prayer (1:4) and in the fruit of his own labours (4:1), rejoicing in the knowledge of the preaching of the gospel (1:18), rejoicing in suffering even if it should mean death (2:17). He exhorts his readers to 'rejoice in the Lord' (3:1 and 4:4). He wants them to have joy in believing (1:25), joy in fellowship (2:28), and like him to rejoice even in trial and suffering (1:29).

b. Fellowship is also a keynote of the Epistle, and understandably so in that it is part of the apostle's reason for writing to express his appreciation of the Philippians' gift, and he can also speak of their sharing with him in the proclamation of the gospel from the very beginning (1:5-7). We have seen that it was also an important part of the apostle's purpose to stir the church at Philippi not to allow its fellowship to be marred by selfishness, pride or party spirit (2:1-4).

c. The *gospel* is also a great theme of this letter. Paul rejoices that with these Philippians he had not only the joy of fellowship in Christ, but 'partnership in the gospel' (1:5, 7; *cf.* 2:22 and 4:3). He was content to suffer at the hand of enemies, and even of fellow-Christians, as long as the gospel was preached and Christ was made known. He wanted his readers to 'strive side by side for the faith of the gospel' (1:27). It may be said also that he deliberately dealt with practical and doctrinal problems by going to the very heart of the gospel (as chs. 2 and 3 indicate).

d. Finally we may say that no letter shows more clearly the *spiritual ambition of the apostle* than this. We see the completeness of his commitment to Jesus Christ, and his single-minded desire to know Him and make Him known. 3:7-14 shows this most clearly, but alongside this passage we should place his statement in 1:20 of his 'eager expectation and hope' that, whatever his circumstances, Christ would be magnified in him. We find also (in 4:11, 13) his sense of utter contentment with any conditions, any deprivations, any difficulties, as long as Christ strengthened him to bear them and Christ was being glorified through them.

THE UNITY AND AUTHENTICITY OF THE EPISTLE

In general there has been no questioning of the Pauline authorship of Philippians. It is quoted by most of the 2nd-century Christian writers and referred to as Paul's from the time of Irenaeus. There are, however, three points that require consideration under this heading.

a. There is little doubt that we should regard 2:6-11 as a hymn with the humiliation and exaltation of Christ as its theme. It is rhythmic in form, and can be arranged in 6 stanzas of 3 lines each. We have highly poetic passages in Paul's letters (such as 1 Cor. 13), but these verses read as a quotation, deeply relevant to the purpose of the section but not originally composed for it, 'a "purple patch" stitched into the fabric of the exhortation' (A. M. Hunter). We have other instances of hymns or credal fragments being used in NT Epistles, in Eph.

4:4-6; 5:14; 1 Tim. 1:17; 3:16; 6:15f. and 2 Tim. 2:11-13. This appears to be a similar though longer example of such a quotation. There are words here not used elsewhere by Paul, some not otherwise in the NT. If the hymn were composed by someone other than the apostle himself, this would also account for the incarnation and the work of Christ being described in a different way from that with which we are familiar from Paul's writings. On the other hand, we cannot rule out the alternative that Paul himself was the author. It is difficult to find sufficient evidence to assure us that originally the hymn was in Aramaic, or that necessarily it was composed for baptismal use or use at the Lord's Supper, as some have rather too dogmatically maintained. We see it best as a hymn in praise of Christ, perhaps by Paul, perhaps by another, aptly taken and used in this context.

b. It has been suggested that the section beginning at 3:1b belonged originally to another letter. Certainly 3:1b represents a break in the apostle's argument. E. J. Goodspeed has suggested that 3:2 – 4:20 is from another letter written at a different time but to the same church. Others see 3:1b-19 or 3:1b-4:3 as coming from another letter. The difficulty of finding a conclusion of the supposed interpolation, and the equal difficulty of accounting for its being thrown in after 3:1a, in addition to the absence of any textual evidence in support, make more probable the view that the apostle's writing was interrupted after he began 3:1. Perhaps fresh news came to hand making the apostle aware afresh of the menace of the Judaizers, and in consequence he wrote of the peril of legalism and the glory of the righteousness of God in Christ before he brought his letter to a close.

c. With still less probability it has been suggested that two other sections of the Epistle belonged originally to other letters. J. H. Michael finds the section concerning Timothy (2:19-24) as containing things incongruous with the rest of the Epistle, but not many have agreed with him in this view. It has been suggested also that 4:10-20 belongs to an earlier letter, on the grounds that Paul would not have waited as long to acknowledge the gift brought from Philippi by Epaphroditus. There is no need to suppose, however, that Paul had done nothing to express his gratitude to the Philippians for their gift before he wrote 4:10-20.

The arguments for these interpolations from other letters are not insignificant, but they fall far short of probability. It is to be noted that in no case is Pauline authorship doubted, and if 2:6-11 did not originally come from the apostle's hand, it cannot be doubted that Paul in this letter takes up this wonderful hymn and makes it his own; through it the central facts of the gospel as preached by Paul are revealed, and by it an example is given relevant to any situation where Christians are divided through pride and party spirit.

OUTLINE OF CONTENTS

COMMENTARY

1:1–11 INTRODUCTION

In this letter, as in most of Paul's letters, the apostle follows the conventional pattern of letter-writing of the day, 'A to B, greeting', followed frequently by a thanksgiving and a prayer. With Paul, however, what is said about writer and readers and in greeting is lifted far above the conventional by the thought of their life in Christ; and the thanksgiving and prayer come from the apostle's heart, an expression of his praise for the working of God, and of his concern for those things which were constantly in his intercessions for the churches.

1:1, 2 Greeting

1 In the form of address three things are significant. First, *Timothy* is graciously linked with Paul (as in 2 Cor., Col., 1 and 2 Thes. and Phm.), although from v. 3 we have first person singular used. Timothy had been with Paul when the gospel was first preached in Philippi, he had continued to have a close association with the Philippian Christians, and he remained a close colleague of Paul (see on 2:19–23). Secondly, Paul stresses that he is writing to *all* the Philippian Christians; this repeated emphasis (see 1:4, 7f., 25; 2:17, 26; 4:21) suggests that there was danger of factions among them (*cf.* 2:1–4). Thirdly, he mentions in particular their ministers, possibly because there was a danger of their being slighted (*cf.* 1 Thes. 5:12f.), possibly because they were instrumental in arranging for the gifts sent to Paul (4:14–18). **2** The greeting is exactly that of several other letters (*e.g.* Rom. 1:7; 1 Cor. 1:3), the combination of Greek and Hebrew traditional greetings, but it is more than just a greeting—it has the full significance of Christian prayer.

Notes. 1 *Servants.* More literally the word is 'slaves'—they reckoned themselves to belong, body, mind and spirit, to Christ, and were subject to Him in everything. *Saints.* The reference is to all Christians, set apart to live for God (the basic meaning of the word), called to live in holiness (*cf.* Rom. 1:7). *In Christ Jesus.* This phrase or its equivalent is used many times in this letter. Christ is the very environment of the Christian's life; the believer lives and moves within the orbit of His will, His grace, His complete provision. He finds life as he is united by faith to Him, and cannot live as he should for a moment apart from Him (see Jn. 15:1–11). *Bishops.* There were more bishops than one at Philippi; it is widely agreed that in the NT elders and bishops (*i.e.* overseers; see RSV mg.) are alternative names for the same people (*cf.* Acts 20:17, 28; Tit. 1:5–7). *Deacons* are mentioned elsewhere only in 1 Tim. 3:8, 12f. (although the Greek word is often used in the sense of 'servant' or 'minister'); possibly their work is to be traced back to Acts 6:2 where the seven were appointed to 'serve' (Gk. *diakonein*) in a way like the later deacons. **2** *Grace* is the undeserved favour of God, which reconciles us to Himself through Christ, supplies our every need, and allows us the privilege of serving Him. *Peace* in Scripture is more than the absence of conflict; it is complete well-being, and like grace comes only *from God our Father* through *the Lord Jesus Christ.*

1:3–7 Thanksgiving and confidence

3, 4 Paul, as regularly was both his precept and practice (see 4:6), joins praise and prayer. **5, 7** Most particularly he gives thanks for the way in which the Philippian Christians have shared with him in the work of the gospel; as he worked to defend the gospel and strengthen its hold on the lives of others, and as for the sake of this work he was in prison, he knew that they were partners with him. **6** More deeply he sees this as a sign of God's working in them; and in this he rejoices, and finds cause for confidence that such working of God in their lives will continue right on to its goal and culmination at the coming of Christ.

Notes. **3** The word *remembrance* may indicate the fact that he remembers them constantly for what they are, or that he mentions them before God in prayer. **4** *Always . . . every . . . all.* It is typical of Paul to speak like this; but for the *all* here and twice more in v. 7, see on v. 1. *Joy*, it has been noted (see Introduction, p. 1126) is one of the great key-notes of this letter, the noun occurring 5 times, and the verb or its compound 11 times. **5** *Partnership* is the regular NT word for fellowship. It is noteworthy that the fellowship between Paul and the Philippians is not simply fellowship in Christ, but *in the gospel.* All who are concerned to serve Christ must be concerned in the task of making known His gospel (*cf.* Mk. 8:35). The word *partnership* may express the sharing which is involved in the bestowing of material gifts (*cf.* 2 Cor. 8:4; 9:13); the Philippian Christians did make such gifts to the apostle to provide for him as a messenger of the gospel (4:10, 14–18), but the context indicates that they shared in the actual work. The Greek preposition (*eis*) led to the RV translation 'in furtherance of the gospel'. *The first day* may mean the beginning of Paul's time in

Philippi, when Lydia opened her home to him, and thus helped forward the preaching of the gospel. **6** Their work is evidence of the *good work* of God in them. Because it is clear that God has begun to work in them, Paul is confident of the continuance of this, and in this confidence he prays. Man may give up a work he undertakes, but not God (*cf.* Rom. 11:29). As he thinks of his own life and service and also the spiritual progress of those to whom he ministers, Paul's eyes are constantly turned to *the day of Jesus Christ.* His constant aim is that he and his fellow-Christians may be presented before God mature and unashamed in that day (*cf.* 2 Cor. 1:14; 5:9f.; Eph. 5:27; Col. 1:28). **7** *Grace* here has perhaps two of the three meanings which we have noted on v. 2; there is the privilege of being called to make the gospel known to others (*cf.* Eph. 3:7f.), and there is strength to enable Paul and the Philippian Christians alike to do this. Such enabling is necessary because the work of the gospel is costing Paul *imprisonment.* But his more constant task—and need of grace—one that continues even in prison is *the defence and confirmation of the gospel.* The first part of this task is mentioned again in v. 16, and 1 Pet. 3:15 shows it to be the responsibility of all Christians; the second involves helping to make men more sure of its truth and its power (*cf.* Lk. 1:4; 1 Cor. 1:6).

1:8–11 Prayer

8 The apostle can say that God knows the reality of his prayer for the Christians at Philippi, and the love which inspires that prayer. **9–11** He asks three things for them: *a. Love*, increasing and overflowing. *b. Knowledge*, in particular 'the gift of true discrimination' (NEB) where there is need to distinguish different values. *c. Righteousness*, for with the day of Christ in view he wants them to be living at no lower standard than that of absolute purity, their whole lives filled with goodness.

Notes. **8** *God is my witness. Cf.* Rom. 1:9; 2 Cor. 1:23; 1 Thes. 2:5, 10. He yearns for them not just with his own love, but *with the affection of Christ Jesus* in him (*cf.* NEB). 'The believer has no yearnings apart from his Lord; his pulse beats with the pulse of Christ . . .' (Lightfoot). *All* once again; see on v. 1. **9** They had already shown love for their Lord and for others, but it is the apostle's prayer that that love might *abound more and more*; *cf.* 2 Cor. 9:8; 1 Thes. 3:12. He was concerned however, that that love should not be a blind and misguided enthusiasm. It needed to be directed with *knowledge* (*cf.* Col. 1:9) and *discernment*, a sensitivity to the truth of God, to the needs of others and to the situation. **10** *That you may approve what is excellent.* This is one way of translating these words; the other way is to speak of 'testing things that differ' (Weymouth). But in either case the dominant thought is that of discrimination. The verb often means approving by testing (*cf.* Eph. 5:10), and the things to be approved are those things that are highest and best. The true wisdom is the knowledge of what is honourable and just and lovely (*cf.* 4:8) and it must lead to corresponding action. Paul prays that they may be *pure and blameless*; the first of these words suggests 'sincerity', 'transparent character' (Weymouth), while the second can mean either 'not stumbling' (*cf.* Acts 24:16) or 'not causing offence' (*cf.* 1 Cor. 10:32), perhaps both. For *the day of Christ* see on v. 6. **11** The original here has 'fruit', not *fruits*; probably it is that *righteousness* is the fruit that the apostle prays will fill these Christians' lives (*cf.* Heb. 12:11; Jas. 3:18), but the reference could be to the good deeds and qualities which result when God's righteousness indwells their lives. All of these things for which he prays *come through Jesus Christ* and through Him alone; and the purpose and goal of them all is nothing but *the glory and praise of God* (*cf.* Eph. 1:6, 12, 14).

1:12–26 THE APOSTLE'S CIRCUMSTANCES

Paul knows the concern of the Philippian Christians for him, and thus, as often in his letters, he sends news of himself. He is able to tell how his imprisonment has meant the advance of the gospel, how Christ is being proclaimed where he is, and how he views the possible issues of his imprisonment, release and further service, or death. With reference to the past, the present and the possibilities for the future he could say 'I rejoice'.

1:12–14 The results of his imprisonment

12 His imprisonment had not been loss but gain as far as the gospel was concerned, for two reasons. **13** First, the fact that he was imprisoned for the sake of Christ became widely known, and so the gospel was made known. **14** Secondly, the Christians around him who had been fearful before had gained courage and confidence through Paul's example.

Notes. **12** The apostle does not dwell on his sufferings. Behind the words *what has happened to me* lies all that it meant to one who had been free to range far and wide preaching the gospel, to be confined and in all probability to be chained day and night to a Roman soldier. **13** *The whole praetorian guard.* This is probably the right translation, not 'all the palace' (AV). The 'praetorium' was originally the praetor's tent in the camp. Hence it came to mean the governor's residence (as in Mt. 27:27), or the soldiers' barracks, or the body of soldiers themselves. It is most likely that the soldiers going to and from the apostle spoke about him to others, and told that he was imprisoned *for Christ* (lit. 'in Christ', and perhaps the thought is not only of the reason for his being in prison, but also the spirit in which he bore imprisonment). **14** The fact that these Christians became *much more bold* was in its turn a significant example for the Christians at Philippi, as vv. 27–30 will show.

1:15–18 Christ is proclaimed, though from differing motives

15, 17 The next great fact on which the apostle would dwell was that Christ was being proclaimed. He must report, however, that there were differing motives in the proclamation. Some think that those who preached Christ *from envy and rivalry* were the Judaizers who are mentioned in 3:2. Paul does not, however, criticize the content of their preaching. These people did not proclaim wrong doctrine, but they had a wrong spirit of partisanship (*cf.* 1 Cor. 1). Perhaps they were the Christians who were in Rome before Paul came, and now they were jealous of the success of his preaching, determined to outdo him, and willing to cause him anguish and offence in his imprisonment. **16** On the other hand there were those who proclaimed Christ with single-minded love for their Lord, and love for the apostle, realizing that he was in prison for his own faithfulness to the gospel. **18** Paul 'had lifted the matter beyond all personalities; all that mattered was that Christ was preached' (Barclay).

Notes. **16** *I am put here.* The word used could mean 'appointed' (Way), or 'I am where I am' (NEB). *For the defence of the gospel.* Cf. v. 7. **17** In origin and usage the word translated *partisanship* conveys the idea of selfish ambition, rivalry and party spirit. **18** *Pretence.* The same word is used for the prayers of the scribes in Mk. 12:40 (*cf.* also Acts 27:30); it is the opposite of sincerity.

1:19–26 The alternatives of life and death

19 Paul faced imprisonment and the threat of death, and from fellow-Christians animosity and provocation, and yet he was confident that all would turn out well (*cf.* Rom. 8:28). Humanly speaking he relied on the prayers of his friends, and in answer to them on the unfailing help of the Holy Spirit. **20** It was his one earnest desire and anticipation that whatever the circumstances, whether the issue of his imprisonment was release or death, he would magnify Christ. In practical terms this meant showing courage, and in nothing being ashamed of his Lord. **21–23** He weighs up in his mind now the two alternatives and can rejoice in both. To go on living in this world is to live in constant enjoyment of Christ Himself, and there will be further fruitful toil in his Master's service. He knows, on the other hand, that death is sheer gain, because beyond death is the immediate presence of Christ. **24, 25** He contemplates the alternatives, and although he does not say that he knows which God will grant, he begins to feel that he is being called to remain for further service. It was more advantageous to him to go to be with his Lord; it was more advantageous (even *more necessary*) for others that he should continue in this life. By so doing he would help them to make spiritual progress, and to be more truly joyous and triumphant in their faith. **26** In particular, the

Philippian Christians will be able to give thanks to God for him, if he is spared to come to them again.

Notes. 19 *Help*. The Greek word used indicates both a generous provision and an undergirding strength. *Deliverance*. This does not mean liberation from prison. Paul is uncertain whether this will be granted, but he is confident that 'the Lord will rescue (him) from every evil and save (him) for his heavenly kingdom' (2 Tim. 4:18). The words of Jb. 13:16 (and no doubt the context of that verse) seem to be in the apostle's mind. 20 *Eager expectation* is one word in the Greek, which literally means straining forward with outstretched head, and its prepositional prefix implies a turning aside from all other interests. *Honoured*. AV 'magnified' is nearer to the original, Paul's great longing being to cause Christ to be seen by others more clearly and in His true greatness. 23 *Depart*. The Greek word is used for a ship weighing anchor, or for striking camp; the corresponding noun is used in 2 Tim. 4:6. There is not necessarily any contradiction between thinking of death as 'sleep' (as in 1 Thes. 4:13–15) and as departing to *be with Christ*. It may be only the limitation of our thinking in terms of space and time that makes it impossible for us to understand at all fully what lies beyond the gateway of death. It is enough to say that to die is gain because it is to be with Christ. 25 *Remain and continue with you all*. These words stand for two Greek verbs, one the compound form of the other; NEB translates 'stay, and stand by you all'. *Progress*. This is the apostle's great desire for himself (*cf.* 3:12–14), and for others (*cf.* 1 Tim. 4:15). His desire was also that they should have the same *joy* in their *faith* as he had himself. 26 *Glory* is another great Pauline word, used frequently by the apostle for one Christian exulting in the work of God in another. He refers more specifically to his *coming . . . again* to Philippi in 2:24.

1:27 – 2:18 EXHORTATIONS CONCERNING CHRISTIAN LIVING AND FELLOWSHIP

Paul has told of his own circumstances. Now he has matters of special importance to deal with concerning the life of the Christians at Philippi. They are being called to suffer; they must count it a privilege, and endure with courage. In their trials and in every aspect of their common life they must stand united. Pride hinders that unity and fellowship which they should demonstrate, and the only remedy for selfishness and faction is to look long and often at Christ Himself till His way of thinking and acting is theirs. He is Example, and He is Saviour, but His salvation must be worked out in lives of obedience, lives that shine as lights in the world, and that will not be counted as loss in the day of Christ.

1:27–30 The call to live worthily of the gospel (united in spirit and courageous in suffering)

27 As Paul has said already, he may return to Philippi or he may remain a prisoner till he dies. He may see them, or hear report of them. In either case he hopes that he will know of the unity and courage of their witness. 28 Trust in their Lord and forgetfulness of themselves will mean that they will not be terrified by their opponents. Their fearlessness will show their enemies that they are not fortified merely by human courage, and that to oppose the servants of Christ is to fight against God (*cf.* Acts 5:39), and to take the path that leads to *destruction* (*cf.* 2 Thes. 1:4–8). Perhaps as he wrote Paul recalled the voice of God in his own conscience indicating this when he persecuted the Christians (Acts 26:10f., 14). At the same time the presence of God with them will assure the Philippians themselves that they are God's and blessed with His *salvation*. 29 It is their privilege to believe in Christ; but also (by that strange contradiction of the world's standards found in what the NT, and not least this Epistle, says so often) to suffer for Christ (*cf.* Mt. 5:11f.; Acts 5:41). 30 Their calling is to accept that toil and struggle, and its cost, as the apostle himself had accepted it, as they had seen when he was in Philippi (Acts 16:19–25) and heard of him now.

Notes. 27 *Your manner of life*. AV translated 'conversation', in the old sense of 'behaviour'. The verb used here speaks of the discharge of obligation as citizens; it would have had special force for those in Philippi where Roman citizenship was prized (see Introduction). In addition to earthly duties and privileges, Christians in Philippi had the responsibility to live individually and corporately as heavenly citizens (*cf.* 3:20). *The gospel* of Christ is twice mentioned here, and we see again (*cf.* v. 5) how central it was in the apostle's thinking. *Stand firm* is a repeated exhortation in Paul's letters (*cf.* 1 Cor. 16:13; Gal. 5:1; Eph. 6:11–14; 1 Thes. 3:8; 2 Thes. 2:15). *In one spirit, with one mind*, he says for emphasis and in the verb translated *striving side by side* we have one of those words, so frequent in Paul, with the Greek prefix *syn-*, 'together'. From the verb itself (Gk. *athleō*) we derive our word 'athlete', and thus it signifies the Christian conflict. 28 *Frightened*. The word is used of startled horses; 'never be scared' is Moffatt's translation. 29 The verb *granted* conveys the thought of a gift of grace: 'to you has the privilege been freely given' (Way). 30 *Conflict* translates the Greek word from which we have 'agony'. The use of the noun and corresponding verb is frequent in Paul (*e.g.* Rom. 15:30; Col. 1:29; 2:1; 1 Thes. 2:2). It so deeply expressed the nature of his Christian service.

2:1–4 Appeal for unity, through personal humility

1 Paul now addresses himself directly to the need of greater unity and stronger fellowship in the church at Philippi, and he sets down four

grounds for his appeal. *a.* In Christ Himself there is every *encouragement* to unity; disunity is rejection of His will and purpose. *b.* Those who have known the blessing of *love* should manifest that love to others without reserve or discrimination (*cf.* 1 Jn. 4:7–12). *c.* All have the same *Spirit*, and so belong together as one. *d.* The knowledge of the mercy and compassion of God should lead them to show this to others in *affection and sympathy.* 2 It will *complete* the *joy* that Paul already has in the Philippians (1:4; 4:1) if only he can hear that they are standing together in harmony and concord. 3 *Selfishness* and *conceit* are the inevitable enemies of fellowship and hindrances to unity. There are two practical ways of overcoming them. First, they should *count others better than* themselves, seeing the strengths and gifts of others, and realizing their own weaknesses, failures and limitations (*cf.* Rom. 12:10, RV). 4 Secondly, they should make a habit of thinking and speaking of the interests of others, and not just of their own (*cf.* Rom. 15:2f.; 1 Cor. 10:24, 33; Gal. 6:2).

Notes. 1 The word translated *encouragement* may mean 'comfort' (RV), 'consolation' (AV) or 'appeal', 'exhortation'. The force of it here may be that the comfort found in Christ is to be shown towards others, or that there is appeal and *encouragement* in the word of Christ to seek unity (*e.g.* in Jn. 15:1–11; 17:20–23). RSV translates the next phrase *participation in the Spirit* (*cf.* NEB) and thus makes it an appeal on the basis of the common possession of the Spirit (*cf.* Eph. 4:4); it could refer to the 'fellowship' which is the work of the Spirit (see AV and RV). *Affection.* AV translated literally 'bowels' (the seat of emotions to the Greek, as the heart is to us). 2 There is not any great difference in the four phrases in this verse that express unity, though distinctions are possible. Paul uses twice the verb 'think' (here *mind*) that is used more frequently in Philippians than in any other NT book. The apostle knows that thoughts and attitudes are the basis of speech and action, and direct the whole course of the life (*cf.* especially 2:5; 3:15; 4:8). 3 *Selfishness.* This word (Gk. *eritheia*) has been used in 1:17 and here, as there, denotes self-seeking, personal ambition, party spirit. *Humility* translates a word which to the Greek conveyed the thought of a base and servile spirit. To the Christian it is a high virtue, because it was the way of Christ Himself (as vv. 5–8 are to show), and because it is the essential prerequisite of serving others and uplifting the Lord, as well as being vital for the maintaining of unity in the church (*cf.* Eph. 4:1–3). 4 *Each* in the Greek is plural, and the force may be 'each group' and thus refer to their factions, or it may mean simply 'each and all' (Lightfoot).

2:5–11 The example of Christ

5 The best way Paul can inculcate humility is by turning his friends in Philippi to the example of Christ, that they may let the thought of His condescension and self-giving shape all their attitudes. 6 As we have seen, it appears that Paul here quotes a previously composed hymn in praise of the pre-existent, incarnate, exalted Lord, and whether Paul's own or the work of another, it is used aptly here (see Introduction). The first stanza speaks of His glory and greatness before His incarnation. 7 The second tells of three steps in His humbling of Himself— emptying Himself of His glory, acting as a slave rather than as Lord of all, and, though truly God, taking on Himself our humanity. 8 The third stanza traces His descent to the depths, for having abased Himself to become man, He lived 'a life of utter obedience' (*cf.* Rom. 5:19; Heb. 5:8f.; 10:5–14), 'even to the extent of dying' (Phillips). That death, moreover, was *death on a cross*, 'that death of unimaginable pain and of utter shame' (Moule) which to the Jew meant that the victim was placed outside God's covenant people (Dt. 21:23; Gal. 3:13), and of which the Roman Cicero says, 'Far be the very name of the cross, not only from the body, but even from the thought, the eyes, the ears of Roman citizens.'

9–11 The remaining three stanzas speak of His exaltation by the Father in consequence of His humiliation and self-sacrifice (*cf.* Heb. 2:9). He is given a *name which is above every name*; it is not a title that is meant, but the highest honour and authority over all creation (*cf.* Eph. 1:20–22; 4:8–10; Rev. 5:13). To express this Is. 45:23 is quoted in application to Christ, and also the earliest and most fundamental Christian creed, 'Jesus is Lord' (1 Cor. 12:3; *cf.* Rom. 10:9). We read this great passage and not wrongly use its statements, along with those of other parts of the NT, to express our doctrine of the Person of Christ; but we should not forget that the purpose of these tremendous statements in their context is the very practical one of using the example of Christ 'to persuade . . . the Philippians to live a life in which disunity, discord and personal ambition were dead' (Barclay).

Notes. 5 *Have this mind.* See on v. 2. If RSV is right, the meaning of this verse is that the kind of life that we have *in Christ Jesus* is to shape our attitudes in the fellowship that we have *among* ourselves (*cf.* NEB). On the other hand AV and RV may be right in calling us to think 'in' our minds according to the pattern revealed in Christ Himself. Ultimately the difference is not a great one. 6 *Though he was in the form of God.* Two significant Greek words are used here. There is a participle (*hyparchōn*), a strong word, stronger than that of the usual verb 'to be', and it speaks of what was and is unchangeably His. Then the Greek *morphē* speaks of permanent *form*, a word very close in meaning to our more philosophical word 'nature', found in many translations here. *A thing to be grasped* translates a single word that occurs only here in the NT, and the varied translations indicate the difficulty of rendering it. It is difficult also to determine precisely the meaning of *equality with God.*

There are two main ways in which we can understand the thought. *Equality with God* may be essentially the same as being *in the form of God*. This, then, was inalienably His; but He 'did not cling to his prerogatives as God's equal' (Phillips); it was not a 'prize' to seize (RV), an act of 'robbery' to take those prerogatives. Therefore in trust and without fear He humbled Himself, and laid aside His glory. On the other hand *equality with God* may not be identical with *the form of God* but may speak directly of the glory and honour of a position alongside of God. He rejected the kind of temptation to which the first Adam fell, who was persuaded to seize that which he wrongly thought would make him 'like God' (Gn. 3:5). So Christ 'did not think to snatch at' (NEB) what would in fact finally and fully be His by the Father's own appointment beyond a human cradle and a human grave. In either case the meaning is that He 'laid His glory by'. 7 He *emptied himself*. It has been suggested that there is an allusion here to Is. 53:12, and thus to the death of Christ rather than to His incarnation. These verses do not necessarily give a chronological sequence; yet the supreme humiliation of the death of the cross seems the subject of v. 8 rather than this verse. The reference seems to be to the incarnation. It is important, however, not to read into the word more than is intended. It gives no justification for the Kenotic Christology, that He *emptied himself* in some sense of His essential deity. The terms of v. 6 imply that 'He took the form of servant while He retained the form of God' (Hendriksen). The context, moreover, indicates the force of the word to be that 'He stripped Himself of His glory' (Weymouth), He 'made himself of no reputation' (AV); *cf.* 2 Cor. 8:9. It is status, not nature, which is involved, as the next phrase shows: *taking the form of a servant* ('slave', RSV mg.). The word *form* is the same as that in v. 6, and indicates He was in reality and not merely in appearance a servant (*cf.* Mk. 10:45). *Likeness* must not be taken to mean similarity without full reality; He was truly man (*cf.* Paul's statements in Rom. 8:3 and Gal. 4:4), but the expression 'leaves room for the thought that the human likeness is not the whole story' (Beare). 8 His was a truly *human form*, but here *form* translates a different Greek word, one which speaks of something more temporary (*cf.* 1 Cor. 7:31). The *form of God* (*morphē*) was His from the beginning; He later took the *form* (*schēma*) of man. *He humbled himself*. The verb used is cognate with the noun of v. 3 (see note). 9 *Therefore*. In furtherance of the practical exhortation of which these verses are a part, the implication here for Christian people is that true exaltation comes only by the way of humility (*cf.* Mt. 23:12; Jas. 4:10; 1 Pet. 5:5f.). 11 *To the glory of God the Father*. Perhaps this is added to indicate that the glory to which Christ is raised is in no way independent of the Father (*cf.* 1 Cor. 15:28).

2:12-18 The practical outworking of salvation

12 The example of Jesus Christ is not only one of humility; it is also one of obedience (v. 8). To such obedience—irrespective of whether or not Paul is with them (*cf.* 1:27)—the Philippians are called. Christ is Example, but supremely He is the Giver of salvation. Yet that salvation is not to be accepted complacently, but worked out in life in a spirit of reverence and fear by men who know that they live in His holy sight and must give account to Him. 13 Man's striving in the Christian life is nevertheless by God's enabling, His work in the Christian giving both desire and strength to do what is pleasing to Him. 14 In this life, moreover, it is not only the deeds done that matter but the spirit in which they are done: 'on . . . guard against a grudging and contentious spirit' (Weymouth). 15 The highest standards must prevail if Christians are to live 'in the midst of a society morally warped, spiritually perverted' (Way), as those who are children of God. For to be called children of God indicates not only their privilege (Jn. 1:12), but also their responsibility (Eph. 5:1). In the sight of men they must be pure, utterly sincere and without reproach; then they will *shine as lights*, thus fulfilling God's purpose for them (*cf.* Mt. 5:14-16; 1 Pet. 2:9). 16 They have the gospel which is the very *word of life* for a perishing world (*cf.* Jn. 3:16; 6:68; Acts 5:20; 2 Cor. 2:15f.). Again, as Paul thinks of the lives of his Philippian converts, his eyes turn to the *day of Christ*. He longs to be able to present them before his Master then in such a way that he will be able to rejoice not to have run the Christian race and toiled in Christian service *in vain*. 17 The thought of death as the possible outcome of his imprisonment comes to the apostle again; that death would be as an offering to God, but he would think of it just as a *libation poured* on the much more significant *sacrificial offering*, their *faith* and the quality of life and service produced by faith. At such a thought he rejoices, and it is a rejoicing with them in the fruit to be seen in their lives. 18 He trusts that they in turn will rejoice, and that with him in his fruitful service.

Notes. 12 *Work out* is a fair translation of the Greek verb here (*katergazesthe*). It conveys the idea of bringing to completion; Paul says in effect, 'Go on until the work of salvation is fully and finally wrought out in you' (Barclay). This does not mean that we can and must effect our own salvation. The very word *salvation* signifies that we cannot save ourselves (*cf.* Jn. 15:4f.; 1 Cor. 15:10; Eph. 2:5, 8); the next verse stresses the essential work of God. We can and must live lives that experience and show forth God's saving power which is made our own. 13 *At work in you*. Paul loved to use this verb, and the corresponding noun (*energeia*, from which comes our 'energy'), to speak of God's working in the believer, and (except for Eph. 2:2; 2 Thes. 2:9, 11 where it is used of the working of Satan and the powers of evil) they are used in the NT only of what God does (*cf.* Phil. 3:21; Eph. 3:20). **15** *Without blemish.* The Greek adjective (*amōma*) was used of animals for sacrifice in the OT; it is used in a moral and spiritual sense of our Lord Himself (Heb. 9:14; 1 Pet. 1:19); it presents here the standard for Christian living (*cf.* Eph. 1:4). *A crooked and perverse generation.* A quotation of Dt. 32:5. *Lights.* The word here is used for the heavenly bodies; hence NEB 'stars'. Perhaps the thought is that Christians are light-bearers rather than actually the light of men (*cf.* Jn. 1:8f.; 8:12). **16** *Holding fast.* It may be right to accept this translation, and assume a change of metaphor. Although it is not the basic meaning, the verb can have the sense of 'hold towards', and hence AV and RV 'holding forth', or NEB 'proffer'. *That . . . I may be proud.* The same word is translated 'glory' in 1:26. *Labour.* This is another word that typically describes Paul's Christian service. It denotes toil to the point of utter exhaustion (for its use note Mt. 11:28; Col. 1:29; 1 Tim. 4:10; 5:17). *In vain.* There is, apparently, an allusion to Is. 49:4 and perhaps also Is. 65:23. **17** *Poured as a libation.* The only other use of the verb in the NT is in 2 Tim. 4:6, where the reference is also to Paul's death. *Sacrificial offering.* The stricter translation of AV and RV is 'sacrifice and service'. The first of the two Greek words (*thysia*) is a regular word for an offering to God. The second (*leitourgia*) was originally a service performed by an individual for the state; it came to be applied to the service of God (Lk. 1:23; 2 Cor. 9:12; Heb. 8:6; 9:21). Clearly the Christian life and service of the Philippians is here considered as sacrifice offered to God (*cf.* Rom. 12:1).

2:19-30 FUTURE PLANS

At this point in the letter the subject-matter changes. From exhortation the apostle turns to speak of his two fellow-workers, Timothy and Epaphroditus, and his plans for them—and his hope for himself too—to go to Philippi. In the process he speaks of these two men in deeply affectionate terms and gives a glowing testimony to their devoted and selfless service.

2:19-24 Commendation of Timothy

19 We have seen that Timothy was with Paul when he wrote this letter (1:1). He had been with him when the gospel was first preached in Philippi. Dependent on the date and place of the writing of the Epistle (see Introduction), he had sent or was to send Timothy to Philippi again. Paul says tactfully that his first desire with respect to Timothy's mission was that he might be *cheered by news* of the Philippian Christians. Doubtless, however, he had also in view a ministry that Timothy would have in Philippi. Therefore he speaks to them of Timothy in terms of highest commendation. **20, 21** There was no other whom Paul could send like Timothy. He would be *genuinely anxious* for their

welfare. With deep sadness the apostle had to say that when he thought of others around him whom he might send they were 'all bent on their own ends, not on the cause of Christ Jesus' (NEB). *Cf.* 2:4. **22** *Timothy's worth* was known at Philippi, as it was certainly known to the apostle with whom Timothy had now served for years in the ministry of the gospel 'like a son helping his father' (Moffatt). **23** Paul has a further reason for sending Timothy, and it will involve a delay in his departure. He wants his messenger to be able to carry news as to which of the two alternatives concerning which he has written (1:23f.)—release or death—is to be fulfilled in him. **24** He is not certain, but he is led to think that the outcome may be release (*cf.* 1:25f.), and in this case Paul hopes that he may himself soon come to Philippi.

Notes. **19** *In the Lord Jesus.* Cf. v. 24, *in the Lord.* All Paul's hopes and plans for the future were referred to the Lord to whom his life was united (*cf.* 1 Cor. 16:7; Jas. 4:13-15). **20** *No one like him.* AV more literally translates the Greek 'no man likeminded'; Way paraphrases 'no one else who is heart and soul with me'. **21** *All.* Paul must have been discouraged; he had so few genuine colleagues, no others whom he could send; he was surrounded by those who, while professing to serve Christ, put their own advantage first (1:15, 17; 3:18f.). **22** *Worth.* The Greek means 'proof' (AV), and speaks of the approval that is the result of testing: the corresponding verb has been used in 1:10. *Served.* Paul might have said 'he has served me' but intentionally says that he *served* (as a slave) *with* him. *In the gospel.* The Greek uses the preposition *eis* (meaning literally 'to') which is thus translated by RV here, as in 1:5, 'in furtherance of the gospel'.

2:25-30 Explanations concerning Epaphroditus

25 Of Epaphroditus we read nowhere else in the NT except this Epistle. The Philippian church had sent him to Paul with their gifts (4:18), and it appears that he was intended not only to be their messenger, but to stay on to help him, 'commissioned to minister to (his) needs' (NEB). He had indeed done what they expected him to do, and Paul could call him his *brother and fellow worker and fellow soldier.* **26-28** But something had happened that made it wise for Paul to send him back to Philippi rather than keep him at his side. He had been critically ill, but by the mercy of God (mercy to Paul, as he sees it), he had recovered. The report of the seriousness of his illness had gone to Philippi, and news had come back of the anxiety of his friends there. This caused distress to Epaphroditus, and brought into his heart a longing for those at home, so that Paul recognized that it was best that he should return. **29** Paul, however, was sensitive to the situation. He appreciated the fact that there was some danger that the Philippians might misunderstand the reason for their messenger's return. So he called on them to receive Epaphroditus with a warm-hearted Christian welcome, not merely as one of their own fellowship returned from abroad, but as a man to be highly honoured for the faithfulness and costliness of the service he had rendered. **30** He had come near to death, willingly risking his life in the work of Christ, and indeed in the process of giving that service which the Philippians themselves could not give to the apostle.

Notes. **25** *Messenger*. This is an example of the NT use of the word *apostolos* in a sense other than that of the foundation apostles of Christ. Most likely the meaning is that he is their authorized messenger (*cf.* 2 Cor. 8:23). It could mean that he had an apostolic function in being a missionary working (with and after Paul) to lay the foundations of the church in Philippi. *Minister*. The word (Gk. *leitourgos*) is cognate to that used in v. 17 (see note). **26** *Distressed*. This is a very strong word in the Greek; its only other NT use is in relation to our Lord's anguish in Gethsemane (Mt. 26:37; Mk. 14:33). **28** *That I may be less anxious*. This is revealing of the selflessness of Paul. 'Easing the mind of his dearly beloved Philippians and imparting to them gladness of heart meant more to him than any personal service he might be able to derive from Epaphroditus' (Hendriksen). **30** *Risking his life*. The reference may be to the illness mentioned, or it may be that attending to Paul in prison led him into a position of danger of suffering the same fate as that with which the apostle himself was threatened. The actual word used is a gambling term. He 'staked his life for the service of Christ' (Martin).

3:1–21 SPIRITUAL AMBITIONS

It seems that Paul is about to close his letter at this point. *Finally, my brethren*, he writes, *rejoice in the Lord*. Then, whatever the reason (see Introduction), he feels he must give warning concerning the Judaizing Christians. This leads him to speak of his reliance on Jesus Christ alone for acceptance with God, and to speak of his ultimate ambitions for his spiritual life, and also for the lives of his Christian friends at Philippi.

3:1–3 Warning against the circumcision party

1 Apparently to conclude his letter, Paul now strikes again a great key-note of his writing, *rejoice*, and find your joy *in the Lord*. It is not quite clear what is the significance of the second part of the verse—perhaps that it is not inappropriate to repeat the call to rejoice (so Way and Moffatt translate); more likely it refers to what follows, and the present infinitive should be given full force. Lightfoot paraphrases, 'Forgive me, if I speak once more on an old topic.' To do so was not *irksome* for Paul, as it led to the heart of the gospel in which he rejoiced. For them it was the *safe* course, because they were tempted to turn from the gospel to legalism. **2** The warning was necessary, and three times

he says *look out*. Jews regarded Gentiles as *dogs*, but these Judaizers were more deserving of the name than any Gentile for the way they liked to 'prowl round the Christian congregations, seeking to win Gentile converts over to Judaism' (Beare). They were *workers*, but in an *evil* cause, turning men aside from truth and freedom (*cf.* Mt. 23:15; 2 Cor. 11:13; Gal. 1:7–9). The rite that they advocated was no longer spiritually meaningful but a mere mutilation of the flesh. **3** There was a *true circumcision*, but it was not of the letter, but of the spirit (*cf.* Rom. 2:27–29). It involved glorying in Jesus as the Christ, the Fulfiller of every institution of Judaism. There never was any real basis of confidence in the external rite alone (Lv. 26:41; Dt. 10:16; 30:6; Je. 4:4; Ezk. 44:7); now to try to impose this on Gentiles, when all that God required was faith and obedience, was the confidence of fools.

Notes. **2** *Mutilate the flesh*. AV and RV translate 'concision' to bring out the force of the Greek word (*katatomē*), cognate with that for circumcision (*peritomē*); but RSV gives the actual meaning. **3** *We are the true circumcision*. Some think that Paul is speaking just of Jewish Christians. The evidence is rather that Paul, and NT writers generally, take up all the titles and privileges of the people of God in OT days and apply them to Christians, whether Jewish or Gentile (*e.g.* Eph. 2:11–22; 1 Pet. 2:4–10). *In spirit*. This probably represents the true text, and the contrast of the verse is between *flesh* and *spirit*. (RV 'by the Spirit of God' could be the meaning, but it is likely that 'of God' was not in the original text.) *Flesh* is a word with different facets of meaning for Paul, but in this verse and the next it clearly refers to reliance on external ordinances to the neglect of the inner state of the heart before God.

3:4–7 Paul's previous life and aims

4 Paul could, if he chose, argue with the Judaizers on their own ground. 'If anyone thinks to base his claims on externals,' he says, 'I could make a stronger case for myself' (NEB). **5, 6** Seven things he could list: *a*. He was circumcised on the eighth day as the law required (Gn. 17:12). *b*. He was born and bred an Israelite, a member of the people of God. *c*. He could name his tribe (that of Israel's first king, after whom he was named), *Benjamin*. *d*. He was not only a true Jew, but a *Hebrew*, an Aramaic-speaker (*cf.* Acts 6:1; 22:2; 2 Cor. 11:22), son of *Hebrew* parents, not like so many who had lost the use of their native tongue. *e*. His devotion to the *law* was signified by his being a devout *Pharisee* (Acts 23:6; 26:5; *cf.* Gal. 1:14). *f*. His *zeal* was shown by what he did to persecute the Christians (Acts 8:3; 9:1). *g*. He could say that as far as the external demands of the *law* were concerned, by which he had tried to live, he was *blameless* (*cf.* Mt. 19:20). **7** All these things he put on the credit side as long as his terms of reference were those of the Judaizers; but now he could only say, 'All such assets I have written off because of Christ' (NEB). He had come to see them as a false basis of confidence and even a hindrance.

Notes. 6 *Righteousness.* In this and the following verses *righteousness* means a way of being reckoned righteous, of being accepted as in right relationship with God. Prior to his conversion Paul depended on *a righteousness of his own, based on law,* as he describes it in v. 9. He came to reject this for *the righteousness from God that depends on faith.* 7 *Gain.* The original has the plural. Paul had listed his gains individually, but now writes them off as one great *loss.* The contrast between *gain* and *loss* goes back to the Rabbis, and Paul's use of it may be dependent on our Lord Himself (*e.g.* Mk. 8:35f.).

3:8–14 The renunciation of the old, and the assuming of new ambitions

8 Because he had found the way of acceptance with God in Christ, Paul reckoned all those things on which he had relied before as *loss*; he decided, moreover, that all was 'far outweighed' by the single 'gain of knowing Christ' (NEB). He not only has counted and does count his previous assets as *loss*, but for Christ's sake has *suffered the loss* of everything that mattered most in his previous life—his place in Judaism, among the Pharisees, perhaps even in his home. He had lost much, but he did not grieve; everything else was 'useless rubbish compared with being able to win Christ' (Phillips). **9** Now his desire, first, is to be accepted on the basis of the *righteousness* which is God's gift, offered on the simple condition of believing (*cf.* Rom. 3:21 – 4:25; Gal. 2:15 – 3:29; Eph. 2:4–9), laying aside that so-called *righteousness* of his own works on which he had relied before. **10** Secondly, he wants to live in that knowledge of Him, which is fellowship, obedience, service. To have fellowship with Christ is to know *the power of his resurrection* in daily experience (*cf.* Rom. 8:10f.; 2 Cor. 4:10f.; Eph. 1:19f.). Thirdly, his aim is to *share* Christ's *sufferings.* Paul spoke of his being associated with his Lord in His death in two ways. There is that identification with Christ in His death and resurrection that baptism signifies, a death with Him to sin, and new life with Him and in Him to righteousness (*cf.* Rom. 6:1–6; Gal. 2:20; 5:24). Leading on from that into the whole of Christian life and service, there is a sharing of His sufferings and death, in that death to self of which Jesus himself spoke (Mk. 8:34f.), and in the willingness to suffer that His saving gospel may go out to all men. Paul often spoke of this (*e.g.* 2 Cor. 4:7–12; Gal. 6:17; Col. 1:24f.); here he describes it as his great ambition and longing. **11** This verse comes to us strangely now. Does not attaining to the resurrection depend on faith alone? Could the apostle be in doubt about his final salvation? He never lacked assurance that he was a child of God, accepted with Him (Rom. 8:15–17; Gal. 4:6f.). Yet he was never complacent. Faith must endure to the end (*cf.* Heb. 3:14); the identification with Christ at baptism must lead

to continual dying with Christ and life in His risen power, right to the end. Alternatively the phrase 'if by any means' (AV, RV) may be regarded as 'an expression not so much of doubt, as of humility' (C. J. Ellicott) in view of the goal contemplated (see also v. 21). **12, 13** It seems that there were in Philippi those who thought they had reached the goal of Christian perfection. Paul would never think of himself as having 'arrived' (Phillips), nor use of himself the word *perfect.* To the end he must *press on,* a man of *one* ambition. Christ has laid hold of him; he must, therefore, lay hold of that which is his Lord's purpose for him. He must forget the past —the failures and sins of the past, and also its achievements in the service of Christ—so that he may always be *straining forward to what lies ahead* in work for Christ and likeness to Christ. **14** He has one *goal* to which he must *press on,* the *prize* that is the fulfilment of *the upward call of God in Christ Jesus,* the 'imperishable wreath' of which he speaks in 1 Cor. 9:25.

Notes. 8 *Refuse.* The Greek word can mean 'garbage' (NEB) or 'dung' (AV). 11 *Attain.* Nine times in Acts the Greek verb is used for arriving at a place. *Cf.* Eph. 4:13 for a similar use to that here. 12 *Perfect.* The Greek uses a verb that can mean 'complete', 'fulfil', or 'make perfect', one used in relation to initiation in the mystery cults which may have influenced the thought and expression of the Philippian Christians. There is a Christian perfection (Eph. 4:13–16), but Paul must speak of it as a goal he set himself and had not attained. *Press on.* The word means literally 'pursue', and has been used in v. 6 for Paul's persecuting the Christians. 13 *Straining forward.* The picture, so often used by Paul, is that of a race, perhaps a chariot race, perhaps an athletic contest. 14 *The prize.* The word (Gk. *brabeion*) is used in the NT only here and in 1 Cor. 9:24. It is possible to think of the *prize* as Christ Himself (*cf.* v. 8), as 'God's call to the life above' (NEB), or as 'the crown of life' (Jas. 1:12), the gift of His grace to those who persevere faithfully in their calling to the end.

3:15–17 Exhortation to such Christian living

15 Paul has spoken of his own spiritual ambitions. He longs that those who would be *mature* in Christ, or who would call themselves 'perfect' (AV), would think in these terms. He can only rely on God to reveal to them what is mistaken in their thinking or deficient in their living. **16** From what has been *attained,* in them or in himself, he trusts that there will be no turning back. **17** He can only say that he has tried to provide a pattern of Christian living, and he desires to see that way of life, accepted already by genuine Christians around them, noted and followed by others also.

Notes. 15 *Mature.* This is the adjective cognate with the verb translated in v. 12 by the use of the word *perfect.* Since Paul will not apply that word to himself, it seems that here he is particularly addressing himself to those who (mistakenly) claimed perfection. *Be thus minded.* This is the same verb again as in 2:2, 5 (see notes). **17** We should not regard Paul's words as presumptuous. There was no NT at this time to be a guide for Christian conduct. The apostle knew, moreover, that ultimately Christian standards of behaviour must be embodied in life rather than code. So it was as much his duty to live a pure Christian life for others to follow, as it was to preach the pure gospel for them to believe. Then those who saw the example faithfully given had the responsibility of living by it themselves (*cf.* 1 Cor. 4:16; 11:1; 1 Thes. 1:6; 2:10; 2 Thes. 3:7, 9). Phillips paraphrases, 'let my example be the standard by which you tell who are the genuine Christians among those about you'; and in the light of what follows we can realize that this was Paul's meaning.

3:18–21 Warning concerning worldly living, and a call to the heavenly

18 From the thought of his own great ambitions fired by the love of Christ, and from the thought of those with a misguided concept of perfection, he turns to think of others within the Christian fold whose lives he can contemplate only with pain and grief. They may have been antinomian in thinking that they could hold the faith of Christ and be indifferent to moral issues; more likely they were like those whom Paul has described in 2:21 as looking after 'their own interests, not those of Jesus Christ'. They were *enemies of the cross of Christ*, not opposing its doctrinal significance (*cf.* Gal. 5:11; 6:12), but rejecting it as the central principle of the Christian's living (see on v. 10). **19** In fact it meant that instead of finding in the cross both salvation and their way of life, they were on the path to *destruction*, and they had chosen a life of self-indulgence. They took pride in the things which in fact were shameful (*cf.* Rom. 6:21); their *minds* were *set on earthly things*, and so inevitably they lived for earthly things. **20** The true Christian, in contrast, knows that his life and citizenship are even now in heaven with Christ (*cf.* Eph. 1:3; 2:6; Col. 3:1–4). He waits 'with longing expectation' (Weymouth) for his Lord from heaven, but he knows that a heavenly life now is a foretaste and pledge of what will be his (2 Cor. 5:5), and the hope that he has transforms his life (*cf.* 1 Jn. 3:2f.). **21** Christ's coming will mean the transformation of *our lowly body* to be like Him in His glory (*cf.* 1 Cor. 15:35–50; 2 Cor. 4:16 – 5:4; 1 Jn. 3:2), and that by the power of God, to whose working there can ultimately be no limitation or hindrance.

Notes. 19 *The belly.* The satisfaction of carnal appetites and selfish desires stands first in their lives. **20** *Commonwealth.* The corresponding Greek verb has been used in 1:27, and there as here AV has 'conversation' in the sense of 'behaviour'. The noun can be taken to mean their way of life as citizens—hence RV 'citizenship'. More literally the word means 'state' or commonwealth; it may have had special signi-

ficance for the Philippians; as citizens of a Roman military colony (see Introduction), they looked to Rome and thought of Rome constantly—so as Christians they were to regard themselves as 'a colony of heaven' (Moffatt). **21** *Our lowly body.* AV 'vile' and Phillips 'wretched' are unfortunate renderings. The body is not despised, but it is a sign of 'our present lowly state' (Way)—the same word is used in Lk. 1:48. Now it is subject to passions and pains and limitations. It will be transformed to 'His glorious state' (Way).

4:1–23 EXHORTATIONS, THANKS AND GREETINGS

Paul's final paragraphs include exhortations, personal messages, and the acknowledgment of the Philippians' gifts. His grateful remembrance of the gifts from Philippi leads him to speak of the spiritual blessings that come from generous giving, and to say to his Philippian friends that for himself he has learnt to live with little or much, enabled in all things by the Lord who will also surely supply fully all their needs.

4:1–3 Personal appeals

1 First, there is a general appeal. The word *therefore* shows that it is based on what has gone before—the danger of the Judaizers, and the disappointment of the worldly-minded. The five words Paul uses in addressing his friends show his depth of feeling; he longs that they should *stand firm in the Lord* (*cf.* 1:27). **2** Then there is a special appeal. In 2:1–5 he has dealt in general terms with divisions and party-spirit in the church at Philippi. He knows, however, of one particular quarrel that is marring the witness of that church. He addresses himself directly to these two women, *Euodia* and *Syntyche*, and in such terms that neither could think the apostle had given her priority. **3** Moreover, he asks one of his closest and most trusty colleagues (unnamed, and so unknown to us) to help them, doubtless meaning him to help them *to agree in the Lord*. Yet he has words of encouragement for these women, as well as criticism; they 'shared' Paul's 'struggles in the cause of the Gospel' (NEB). Then, speaking like this of them, he must say the same of one other in particular, *Clement*. He is aware that there are many others of whom he might speak in commendation; they may not be mentioned here, but they can be assured of the one thing that matters supremely, their *names are in the book of life* (*cf.* Lk. 10:20).

Notes. 1 *Long for. Cf.* 1:8; 2:26. *Crown. Cf.* 1 Thes. 2:19. **2** *Euodia* and *Syntyche* are not otherwise known. **3** *Laboured side by side.* See on 1:27, where the same word is used. *Clement* is not otherwise known in the NT; it was quite a common name, and it is unlikely that this was the Clement who was important in the church in Rome at the end of the century. *The book of life.* The OT several times refers to a book in which names are writen of those accepted with God (*e.g.* Ex. 32:32; Dn. 12:1); because of God's gift of life to them it is called 'the book of life' in Ps. 69:28 (RV). In the NT it is spoken of most frequently in the book of Revelation.

4:4–7 A call to joy and prayerfulness

4 Yet again this call to joy is sounded (*cf.* 3:1)— joy *in the Lord*, united to Him, glorying in Him, doing His will. **5** The Christian is to be characterized by an attitude of *forbearance*, patience, gentleness towards all people, and this prompted by the realization of the nearness of the Lord. **6** Anxiety is to have no place in his life because *in everything* there can be *prayer* (*cf.* Mt. 6:25–34; 7:7–11; 1 Pet. 5:7). 'Anxiety and prayer are more opposed to each other than fire and water' (Bengel). *Thanksgiving* should always accompany prayer (see 1:3), because praise is always due to God, and because faith is quickened by the thought of what God has done already. **7** When prayer replaces worry, God's gift of the peace 'which transcends human understanding' (Phillips) comes in, and that peace acts as a sentry guarding the Christian's mind and emotions from being overwhelmed by the sudden onrush of fear, anxiety, or temptation.

Notes. **5** *The Lord is at hand.* This may refer to the nearness of the Lord to the believer, or the nearness of His coming, or both. **6** First there is here the general word for *prayer*, then *supplication* or 'petition' (NEB); the *requests* are the particular objects of *supplication*.

4:8, 9 A call to hold to the true and lovely

8 Paul uses eight words here to characterize the things which should fill the Christian's thought-life—the *true* and honest; things worthy and noble; *just* and right; *pure* and holy; *lovely* and beautiful; the things that are 'of good report' (AV), pleasant to hear about; the things that possess moral *excellence* (the best word for virtue in classical Greek thought); the things that are praiseworthy. Often the word *think* has been used in this Epistle (Gk. *phroneō*; see especially 2:2, 5; 3:15, 19); here the strong *logizomai* is used. 'Take such things into account,' Paul is saying, 'let them shape your attitudes'. **9** 'Then translate such thinking into action' (*cf.* Rom. 12:2). The result will be the kind of life that follows the example seen and known from the apostle himself (see on 3:17); and not only will the peace of God be found, but the unfailing presence of 'the author and fountain of peace' (Michael). (*Cf.* 2 Cor. 13:11; 2 Thes. 3:16.)

4:10–20 Paul's attitude concerning the gifts from Philippi

10 The apostle now must speak of the gifts received. Probably he had acknowledged them already, but he is sending back Epaphroditus who brought them, and so he refers to them again. He rejoiced in their gifts. They represent a fresh blossoming (NEB) of their earlier ministry of giving to him—for a long time they *had no opportunity* to send. **11–13** Paul wants to make it clear, however, that he is not dependent on their gifts or seeking further provision. He has learnt the secret of contentment with outward circumstances, whether he has little or much. He knows his Lord will not fail to give what He sees to be necessary, and to strengthen him to face every situation.

14–16 Nevertheless he appreciated the kindness of the Philippians in expressing this *partnership* with him; indeed from the time when he was *in Thessalonica*, and when he *left Macedonia* (Acts 16; 17), no other church in the area did as they did. **17, 18** He would reiterate that he is not seeking gifts for himself; much more he rejoices in the spiritual blessing that they receive in giving. Such was the spirit of their gifts, that they were as an *offering* and *sacrifice* to God, fragrant as the OT described sacrifices (Ex. 29:18; Ezk. 20:41) and as was the incense that accompanied sacrifice (*cf.* Jn. 12:3; 2 Cor. 2:16). **19** Giving in such a spirit will never impoverish, for it is an expression of love and trust in the God—*my God*, Paul says from his experience—who *will supply every need*, and that in the measure of *his riches in glory in Christ Jesus*. **20** For this fact, and for all that He is and has done, God is worthy to be praised *for ever and ever*.

Notes. **11** *Content.* The Greek word (*autarkēs*) literally means 'self-sufficient'. It was regarded by the Stoics as high virtue to be detached from outward circumstances, and to have resources in oneself to meet every situation. Paul uses the word in the sense of his being independent of circumstances, but his all-sufficient resources are by the grace of Christ who lives in him (*cf.* 2 Cor. 9:8; 1 Tim. 6:6). **12** *I have learned the secret.* The word for initiation into the mystery cults is used. **15** Paul feels it wise to remind them that the partnership was in both *giving and receiving*—1 Cor. 9:11 explains. **17** *To your credit.* Here and in v. 15 the word for an account is used, and other expressions indicate that Paul is using metaphors from business transactions: 'profit' (NEB) or 'interest' (Moffatt) in this verse, and *full payment* in v. 18. The apostle, however, would have repudiated the least thought of earning anything from God; everything received is a gift of His grace.

4:21–23 Concluding greetings

21 The letter closes with mutual good wishes in *Christ Jesus*. **22** It is significant that there were Christians in *Caesar's household*, especially if this was the imperial palace in Rome; the expression means not members of Caesar's family, but 'persons employed in the domestic and administrative establishment of the Emperor' (Beare). **23** The Epistle closes as it began with that prayer, which embraces every other petition, for *the grace of the Lord Jesus Christ*.

F. FOULKES

Colossians

INTRODUCTION

DESTINATION

This Epistle was sent to Colossae (1:2), which was a small, relatively unimportant city in the Lycus valley. The place was situated about 100 miles E of Ephesus and was in a group with two other cities. Laodicea and Hierapolis, both of which were more flourishing than Colossae. In all three centres Christian churches had been established (see 4:13). It would appear, however, that Paul himself had not visited them (*cf.* 1:4; 2:1). He mentions Epaphras as one from whom the Colossians had learned (1:7, 8) and it seems reasonable to conjecture that he was the founder of the church at Colossae. Paul's connection with these Christians is second-hand, yet nonetheless real. As Gentiles he regarded them as coming within the sphere of his personal responsibility, and in 1:7 (see note *in loc.*) speaks of Epaphras as acting as his representative. There is no definite knowledge as to what earlier contact Epaphras had had with the apostle. In all probability he had become a Christian through Paul's influence. If this supposition is correct, it would be highly probable that it was during Paul's ministry at Ephesus that this occurred, for we know that during this time 'all the residents of Asia heard the word of the Lord' (Acts 19:10). It would be natural for a man like Epaphras to turn to his spiritual adviser when faced with difficulties in the course of his ministry.

AUTHORSHIP

The Epistle makes clear that the apostle Paul is the writer, not only by means of the opening greeting, but also in the body of the letter (1:23) and in the conclusion (4:18). The personality of the apostle shines through the whole letter. Moreover, as far as we know from extant records, no-one in ancient times ever had doubts about the authenticity of the Epistle. It was included in the earliest list of Pauline Epistles, even that compiled by the heretical Marcion. Yet in spite of this strong internal and external evidence, some objections have been raised against Pauline authorship. Those who take this line must first explain the references to Paul within the Epistle. It is suggested, therefore, that these references are pseudepigraphic devices used by some other author to give the impression of a Pauline Epistle. The main objections to authenticity are literary and historical, but it should be noted that advocates of non-Pauline authorship are in the minority. Some find

stylistic differences from Paul's other letters, but the criteria for judging style are not accurate enough to place the authenticity in jeopardy (for details see my *New Testament Introduction: the Pauline Epistles*, 1961, pp. 168ff.).

The other problem relates to the supposed allusions in the Epistle to the Gnostic ideas of the 2nd century. This will be more fully dealt with under 'Occasion' below, but it should here be noted that a distinction needs to be drawn between incipient Gnosticism and fully-developed Gnosticism. (*Cf.* R. McL. Wilson, *The Gnostic Problem*, 1958.) There are no doubt points of contact with the former but not with the latter. Opponents of authenticity have invariably confused the two things. Moreover it has been thought that the Christology of Colossians shows features more developed than those found in Paul's other Epistles (as, for instance, the idea of cosmic reconciliation, *cf.* Col. 1:20), but when due allowance is made for the different purpose of the various letters there is nothing in this Epistle which could not have been written by the apostle.

A major consideration in support of authenticity is the close connection between this Epistle and Philemon. They both mention a number of people who were associated with Paul (*cf.* Col. 4:7-17; Phm. 2, 23, 24). Of special importance is the fact that Onesimus, the chief subject of the Philemon letter, is mentioned in Col.4:9 as being 'one of yourselves'. The conclusion is inescapable that both Epistles were written at the same time. But the authenticity of Philemon remains unchallenged and furnishes a strong probability that Colossians is equally reliable. We may therefore with confidence accept the ascription of the Epistle to Paul as genuine.

OCCASION

Nowhere in this Epistle does the apostle specifically state the situation which caused him to write, but this may be inferred from the contents with a fair degree of detail. Evidently Epaphras, who was one of the Colossians (Col. 4:12) and, as mentioned above, may well have been the founder of the church, had sought out Paul to tell him of the situation which had arisen at Colossae. In Col. 1:8 Paul states that Epaphras had made known to him the Colossians' love in the Spirit. He seems to have given him a favourable report of the healthy state of the church, but from various references to some who were trying to persuade the Colossians to pursue devious teachings it appears certain that false teachers of some kind were active in the vicinity. It was important for the apostle to fortify the Christians against this threat.

To obtain a clear picture of the occasion, it is therefore necessary to put together as far as possible the various threads, traceable in the Epistle, which had connection with the heresy. It is always more difficult to reconstruct the tenets of a heresy where our only data are those provided by the Christian answer to it. Care must be taken to avoid reading back too much into the positive approach which Paul gives. Some of the more leading features may be isolated without hesitation. In view of the great stress that Paul places on Christology in this Epistle, it is reasonable to suppose that the false teaching was defective in this respect. Any view of Christ which denied Him the pre-eminence in everything (*cf.* 1:18) would be inferior to Paul's view of Him. Indeed it is a fair inference that the exalted view of Christ set out in the whole section 1:15–20 was called out by the opposite tendencies of false teachers. Gnosticism in the 2nd century supplies a parallel in which Christ had become so far deteriorated that He had become no more than the last of a long series of intermediaries connecting man with God. There is no evidence that such an advanced deterioration in Christology had occurred as early as this Epistle was written, nor is the evidence which exists sufficient to prove that this Epistle was a product of the 2nd century (see under 'Authorship' above).

Another feature of the heresy is what Paul calls 'philosophy and empty deceit, according to human tradition, according to the elemental spirits of the universe' (2:8). These allusions seem to be based on two main streams of thought, one Gentile, the other Jewish. The word 'philosophy' is very general. Paul's concentration on its emptiness suggests that he had little time for its precepts. It may well have been a mixture of ideas drawn from Greek sources. It is worth noting that such words as *fullness* (1:19; 2:9) and *knowledge* (2:3) were familiar terms in contemporary speculative thought, although Paul uses them in a thoroughly Christian way. Again these words were current in 2nd-century Gnosticism. The 'fullness' was an abstract name for the absolute God who could have no direct contact with earth (known as the Emptiness or *Kenōma*). But these developed ideas are found at Colossae only in embryo, if at all. For a discussion of the probable meaning of *elemental spirits*, see the commentary *in loc*. It appears to be an allusion to the powerful spirit-world which was believed to exert influence on human affairs.

To add to the complexity of the Colossian situation there was the Jewish stream, seen most probably in the above reference to *human tradition*, since Judaism was notorious for its insistence on the importance of the tradition of the elders. In addition to this there were questions

of *food and drink* (apparently a reference to food taboos) and of *festivals, new moons* and *sabbaths* (2:16). All these are easily intelligible in a Jewish setting. Twice in the Epistle circumcision is mentioned (2:11; 3:11). Moreover, there was some stress on asceticism as is clear from 2:21, another feature which would well fit into a Jewish setting. One element in the heresy which is not easy to place is angel-worship (2:18). While there was great respect for angels among the Jews, there is no evidence that during this period angels were the objects of worship. This development may have been the result of the fusion of Greek and Jewish elements.

It is clear from this brief survey that some kind of syncretistic movement was on foot and was threatening to affect the Colossians. There are features which show parallels in Gnosticism and it may be surmised therefore that this was a kind of pre-Gnostic Gnosticizing tendency. An example of the confluence of Jewish and Hellenistic ideas, more contemporary with the apostolic period, is to be seen in the Qumran Community, whose library contained MSS of Gentile origin. The Community itself, however, remained essentially Jewish. It is not possible to define the Colossian heresy more closely, but enough has been said to describe the background to the Epistle and to enable a reasonable assessment of its purpose.

PURPOSE

Bearing in mind the nature of the false teaching, it is evident that Paul regarded it as an urgent matter to warn the Colossians about the danger and this subject forms the main purpose of the first half of the Epistle. Paul's clear insight into the nature of Christian doctrine never shows more clearly than when he is countering wrong emphases or definite errors. In writing the Epistle, he may have been doing so at the request of Epaphras, who was himself apparently unable to cope with the situation. At all events, an answer from so authoritative a Christian apostle as Paul would carry great weight with the Colossians. Another subsidiary purpose was to give a series of practical exhortations calculated to develop in them a more healthy Christian life. This is done in chs. 3 and 4 in two ways, first by giving general principles and then by adding specific examples affecting the homelife of the Christians.

The most important section is that which sets out Paul's Christological position. The pre-eminence of Christ is the focal point (1:18) and the various aspects of this pre-eminence are seen in the fact that He is the image of God (1:15), the fullness of God (1:19), the Creator (1:16) and the head of the church (1:18). Not only does Paul aim to give an exalted view of Christ's Person, but also of His work, for He has delivered from darkness (1:13), has redeemed from sin (1:14), has reconciled men through the blood of His cross (1:20ff.) and has disarmed spiritual forces (2:15). Moreover, He has become the believer's life (3:4), having shared with him the effects of His own death and resurrection. In this Epistle, therefore, Paul succinctly gives to the Colossians a remarkable and comprehensive view of the Christian's inheritance 'in Christ'.

PLACE AND DATE OF ORIGIN

It has been traditionally held that this Epistle was written during Paul's imprisonment at Rome. The apostle makes little comment on his captivity, although he requests the readers to remember his fetters (4:18). Of those imprisonments of which we learn in Acts, Rome seems the only reasonable choice, although a few scholars have preferred Caesarea. The greetings from Paul's associates in ch. 4 suggest that, in spite of Paul being imprisoned, they had direct access to him, and this feature supports the view that the Roman imprisonment of Acts 28:30 furnishes the setting for this Epistle. Since the letter to Philemon, however, was sent at the same time (see Introduction to that Epistle), the place of origin of both letters is affected by the position of Onesimus who had run away from his master. In view of the distance between Colossae and Rome, this is considered an obstacle to a Roman origin. Some scholars have suggested Ephesus, on the assumption that there was an Ephesian imprisonment which, however, must be recognized as no more than an inference. Certainly if Paul were at Ephesus, it would be easier to conceive of Onesimus absconding there—a distance of 100 miles. But it might be argued that a runaway slave would get as far away as possible to escape detection. The balance of evidence still favours a Roman origin.

What part of the Roman imprisonment makes the best setting for this Epistle is impossible to decide, and we must be content with this approximate dating.

OUTLINE OF CONTENTS

COMMENTARY

1:1-8 SALUTATION AND THANKSGIVING

1, 2 In most of his Epistles Paul introduces himself as *an apostle of Jesus Christ*. This is no formal title, but a claim to a God-given authority, which is supported by the further phrase *by the will of God*. Some see this as evidence that Paul is on the defensive, but since there is no indication in the Epistle that his authority had been challenged, it is more reasonable to see this as a reflection of his deep awareness of his high calling. He writes to these Colossians, not as a self-appointed teacher, but as a man called to a special office by God. A similar introduction is found in the Epistle to the Ephesians, but without the salutation from *Timothy our brother*, who is nevertheless mentioned in several other Pauline Epistles and was one of his closest associates. The addressing of the Epistle *to the saints* is also characteristic (*cf.* 1 Cor. 1:2; 2 Cor. 1:1; Eph. 1:1; Phil. 1:1). The word is used in the sense of 'set apart', here qualified by the expression *in Christ*, which suggests a closely knit community linked by the common bond of allegiance to Christ. The deeper idea of incorporation in Christ is probably also in Paul's mind in view of the important discussion on the glory of Christ's Person in vv. 15–23. The joining of *grace* and *peace* in the greeting, which is also a characteristic of Paul, not only links the familiar Greek and Hebrew salutations but invests both with a spiritual meaning.

3–8 Paul follows the usual pattern of giving thanks for his readers, but this is no mere convention on his part. His thanksgiving here is full of spiritual reminders, which were calculated to inspire his readers. It also gives some indication of the way in which the apostle became acquainted with the situation in the church at Colossae, which he had not yet visited.

3 *We always thank God.* The plural may include both Paul and Timothy, or may be a stylistic plural. Since from 1:23 Paul uses the singular when referring to his own experience, the former alternative is to be preferred. The word *always*, reflecting the warm enthusiasm of Paul for those for whom he feels responsibility, is to be taken with the following phrase, *when we pray for you.* In vv. 4, 5 Paul proceeds to give the content of his thanksgiving. **4** It is based on reliable information about their *faith* and *love*, the former in relation to Christ, the latter in relation to other Christians. Neither without the other would be complete. **5** Moreover, both are motivated by *hope.* This is not a merely pious desire, but a robust certainty *laid up . . . in heaven.* The Christian is not bound by this life only. Even his attitude to Christ and to others is affected by what he knows will take place in the future, although its precise nature is still not clearly seen. *Cf.* 1 Cor. 13 for the linking of faith, love and hope; also 1 Thes. 1:3; 5:8. *You have heard before* refers to the knowledge they gained of the Christian hope at the time of their conversion. This was *before* they heard any false teaching. The twofold description of what they have heard is significant. It identifies the *gospel* with *the word of the truth* and is probably intended to contrast with the 'gospel' of the false teachers. **6** *Bearing fruit and growing.* It is because Paul recognizes that the gospel has within it the latent capacity for growth that he can speak of it coming to *the whole world*, although as yet only a small part of the known world had been evangelized. By *bearing fruit*, Paul means showing evidence of some spiritual maturity and of the practical effects of Christianity. He is confident that such growth has taken place in his readers. Another description of the gospel is given as *the grace of God in truth*, which, while again stressing the reliability of the gospel, draws attention to its essential basis in grace, *i.e.* in the unmerited favour of God towards those who believe. It is one of the apostle's favourite words. The expression *in truth* could alternatively be understood in the sense 'as it truly is', 'untravestied' (C. F. D. Moule, *The Epistles of Paul the Apostle to the Colossians and to Philemon*, 1957). Any other interpretation of the gospel which denied its basis in grace would be false.

7, 8 It was through one of the Colossians, *Epaphras*, that Paul had received knowledge of their faith and love. He has two complementary descriptions of Epaphras—*our beloved fellow servant* and *a faithful minister of Christ.* Both 'servant' and 'minister' were words that Paul delighted to use of himself, and wherever possible to use of others. The first word means literally 'bond-slave' and Paul's idea is that he and Epaphras are both owned by the same master. The second word (Gk. *diakonos*) relates more specifically to the task, an attendance to the duties laid upon him by Christ. *On our behalf* is a well supported reading, although some authorities read 'on your behalf'. The former is to be preferred, drawing attention as it does to the fact that Epaphras was acting as Paul's representative when preaching at Colossae. He was not therefore a free lance, but an authorized minister. Once again Paul draws attention to the Colossians' *love*, which he clearly regards as of great importance (*cf.* 1 Cor. 13). The words *in the Spirit* are best applied as in RSV to the Holy Spirit, but the Greek could sustain the meaning 'in the spiritual sphere'. Paul would never have conceived the possibility of this kind of love apart from the Holy Spirit. It was essentially one of the fruits of the Spirit (*cf.* Gal. 5:22).

1:9–14 PRAYER

The prayers of Paul are a rewarding study and none more so than this one. Not only does it tell us much about Paul's desire for these Colossians, but provides a valuable pattern for the prayer-life of the believer.

9 *From the day we heard of it* echoes the language of v. 6, and shows that Paul still has in mind all he has said in the preceding passage. Prayer and thanksgiving are closely linked in his Epistles. Paul is never tired of stressing the constancy of his prayer for those committed to his charge. The first petition is for true *knowledge . . . wisdom and understanding.* This knowledge is centred in the *will* of God, thus distinguishing it from all other knowledge, particularly from the kind being vaunted by the false teachers (*cf.* 2:8). All these words depicting a reasoning approach were current intellectual catchwords which Paul uses in a new and thoroughly Christian way; hence the use of the adjective *spiritual.* There can be no doubt that knowledge of God's will is the basic need of every Christian. The prayer echoes that of our Lord, 'Thy will be done'.

10 The second petition concentrates on the outcome, the putting into practical effect of the knowledge concerning God's will. *A life worthy of the Lord* brings out the noble ideal of Christian living. *The Lord* is best understood as a reference to Christ. The ideal is made even nobler by the addition of the words *fully pleasing to him.* Although the word translated *pleasing* (*areskeia*) originally conveyed a cringing attitude towards superiors, when related to God it implies complete and willing submission to His sovereign purpose. Paul leaves no room for self to have any say in the religious ideal. Two specific outcomes of such committal to the pleasing of God are constant fruit-bearing and further *knowledge.* The apostle's emphasis on *good work* is an important corrective for those who thought his rejection of salvation by works (*cf.* especially Romans and Galatians) meant his disinterest in Christian good works. Such works are the means by which others can see the fruitfulness of the Christian life. The reiteration of *knowledge* is important as showing that this is a progressive activity. Knowledge of God's will is a means of attaining more knowledge of God Himself. The repetition of the idea of fruit-bearing and growth (*cf.* v. 6) shows how strongly this idea appealed to the apostle. For him Christianity was no static concept.

11 The third request is for spiritual strength. Such a request at once draws attention to man's inability to produce good work or acquire true knowledge in his own strength. *Strengthened with all power* sounds comprehensive enough, but becomes doubly so when linked with the further phrase *according to his glorious might*. As Lightfoot remarks, 'The power communicated to the faithful corresponds to, and is a function of, the Divine might whence it comes' (J. B. Lightfoot, *Saint Paul's Epistles to the Colossians and to Philemon*, 1900). The expression suggests that the might of God is an aspect of His glory. Although men cannot see God and live, they can see the evidences of His power and can share in it. But the outworking is not in spectacular wonders, but in *endurance* under trial. When Paul adds *with joy*, he clearly distinguishes the Christian from the Stoic in his attitude towards affliction.

12–14 The prayer ends with a remarkable petition that the Colossians should give thanks for their hope. Paul is not content merely to .thank God himself. He wants others to do the same. **12** *The Father, who has qualified us.* Some strong ancient authorities read 'you' instead of 'us', but this is difficult in view of the next verse which must read 'us'. On the other hand, since Paul is wanting the Colossians themselves to give thanks, it would not be pointless to remind them of their *share in the inheritance*. His mind goes to the imagery of the inheritance of the Israelites in the promised land. The Jews regarded all other nations as dwelling in darkness but held out no hope that they would ever come to the light. But the gospel is different. The expression, *the inheritance of the saints in light*, contrasts the hope of the people of God (whether Jew or Gentile) with the darkness of the unbelieving world around. This inheritance is not to be attained through human effort. It is God who takes the initiative, as is clear from the following verses.

13, 14 The conclusion of the prayer makes some statements of deep theological significance, which leads naturally into the profound view of Jesus Christ contained in the next section. The word *delivered* (v. 13) conjures up the picture of a conqueror who has overcome the enemy and has set free the people previously enslaved by him (as, for example, at the Exodus). Paul thinks of two kingdoms at war with one another. *The dominion of darkness* is contrasted with *the kingdom of his beloved Son*, but different words are used to express the contrasted ideas. The first word (*exousia*) means 'authority' and seems to draw attention to demonic authorities. These were the agents of evil, for which darkness was an accepted symbol. The contrast between

light and darkness is familiar in NT thought (*cf.* Johannine literature). It was prominent also in the Jewish community at Qumran, where the initiates were called the sons of light, and their mission in life was to battle with the sons of darkness. The word translated *kingdom* (*basileia*) is used in the sense of 'reign', *i.e.* in an essentially personal sense. The Colossian converts had experienced a transformation from slavery to freedom. The words translated *his beloved Son* mean literally 'son of His love', which throws the emphasis on the Father's love, of which the Son is the perfect expression. The transference to the Son's kingdom is defined in v. 14 in two important terms, *redemption* (*apolytrōsis*) and *forgiveness* (*aphesin*). The former idea has its basis for Paul's thinking in the release of slaves on payment of a ransom price. Such a work was performed by Christ and involves forgiveness. Redemption releases from the power of sin and forgiveness from its guilt. There can be no finer motive for thanksgiving than remembrance of what God in Christ has done.

1:15–23 A REVELATION OF JESUS CHRIST

Nowhere else in the Epistle does the apostle express such profound theological ideas as in this passage. There has been much debate whether he has here incorporated an existing hymn to Christ (*cf.* the discussion of the evidence by R. P. Martin, *EQ*, Oct.–Dec. 1964). Whatever the conclusion which is reached, all would agree that Paul sees the need at this point to appeal to the supremacy of Jesus Christ, which may well be an indication that the false teachers in question were advancing an inadequate view of Him. In this section there are some evidences of OT background, particularly the wisdom passage of Pr. 8:22ff., but the section itself cannot be interpreted from the OT point of view, since its key is the historic fact of Christ.

15 *The image of the invisible God.* This description of Christ follows immediately on Paul's reference to 'the beloved Son' and must be interpreted accordingly. This will immediately indicate an understanding of *image* (*eikōn*) in the sense of personal relationship. The Son is the image of His Father. But more precise discussion of the significance of the word is necessary. A parallel with Gn. 1:26f. immediately springs to mind. Man was created in the image of God, which relates to his moral nature. Even more essentially is Christ the image of God. The importance of the parallel has some bearing on the doctrine of incarnation (as Bruce points out, E. K. Simpson and F. F. Bruce, *Commentary on the Epistles to the Ephesians and the Colossians*, 1957). It is because man bore God's image that it was possible for God to become man. In this way what otherwise would be invisible becomes visible to man. These words are difficult to understand except against the background of the pre-existence of Christ. They are, in fact, illuminated by the following phrase. For other NT statements of a similar kind, *cf.* Jn. 1:18; Heb. 1:3.

The first-born of all creation. The meaning of the word *first-born* (*prōtotokos*) is crucial for a right understanding of Paul's conception of Christ. The real problem is whether or not this word implies that Christ was included in creation, whether in other words there is any sense in which Christ can be described as a created being. If the word is considered out of context, it would be possible to make a case for the inclusive meaning as paralleled, for instance, in Rom. 8:29. But the context makes clear that Christ is the agent of creation, which at once places Him above it. In this case the word *first-born* must be understood in the sense of 'supreme' rather than in the temporal sense of 'born before'. The sovereignty of Christ over the created world is supported by other NT statements (*cf.* Jn. 1:3; Heb. 1:2). On the other hand some meaning would be missed if the term were emptied of any inclusive meaning. There is a sense in which the incarnate Christ became part of the creation over which He is sovereign. See the comment on v. 18 for further light on the use of the same term.

16 *For in him all things were created.* This is an important elucidation of the preceding statement. The conjunction *for* (*hoti*) supplies the basis for that statement and supports the contention that *first-born* does not include Christ in the creation. The *all things* here are identical to the 'all creation' in v. 15 and since all things are *in him*, He cannot Himself be part of the 'all things'. The words *in him* can be understood either as instrumental (by means of) or as local (within Him). The latter idea would see the created order as having its abode in Christ. There is some parallel for this idea in the Stoic doctrine of the Logos and in Philo. But the present statement of Paul's presents a fully Christian interpretation of the creation as finding its essential unity in Christ.

The rest of this verse makes the first statement more explicit, especially enlarging it against the background of the false teaching being combatted. *In heaven and on earth* links the two aspects of creation and excludes the possibility of any separation between them. The heretics may well have placed too much stress on heavenly beings as instrumental in influencing human actions. For Paul there could be no beings outside the sovereignty of Christ whether *visible or invisible*. There are several words used in the NT to describe angelic agencies and the four mentioned in this verse—*thrones, dominions, principalities, authorities*—may be regarded as different ranks of supernatural beings. Such an interpretation would fit in with current speculation regarding such beings. Paul is not only convinced that such unseen agencies exist, but also that all are subordinate to Christ. The last statement that *all things were created through him and for him* contains an important development of the first

statement in the verse. Instead of 'in him', Paul now says *through him* (*dia*) and *for him* (*eis*), the first stressing that Christ was agent in creation, the second that He was its goal. From start to finish the created order is bound up with the Person of Christ. In no more vivid way could Paul express his exalted view of Christ.

17 He sums it all up by making two further statements which underline Christ's supremacy over all creation. In saying that *he is before all things*, Paul may mean (*a*) exists before, or (*b*) exists superior to, or (*c*) is before, or (*d*) is superior to. Although all are possible, the first seems to accord best with the context and is supported by the more usual meaning of the Greek *pro* (*before*). The thought that *all things hold together* in Christ again brings out the idea that Christ is the unifying and cohering factor in creation (*cf.* Heb. 1:3).

18, 19 So far in this statement about Christ, the thought has been concentrated on creation generally, but now Paul deals with Christ's relationship with the church. The idea of the church as a body has parallels elsewhere (*cf.* Eph. 1:22, 23; 4:15; Col. 2:19). In 1 Cor. 10 and 12 and Rom. 12:5 the figure of the body is rather differently applied because there in those cases Paul is thinking of the relation of the members to each other. Here it is the Headship of Christ which is prominent. **18** *Head of the body* is an expression which brings out the supreme importance of Christ in His church. No member of the body can even exist and certainly cannot function without the head. The figure of the body is moreover valuable in stressing the oneness of the *church*. The word translated *beginning* (*archē*) has a variety of possible meanings which may be summarized, as Moule suggests, as supremacy in rank, precedence in time or creative initiative. He inclines to the latter, but in view of the following statement that Christ is *first-born from the dead*, the second interpretation seems also in view (*cf.* Lightfoot). Here the same word, *first-born*, occurs as in v. 15, but here must be understood in an inclusive sense, since others will rise from the dead in consequence of Christ's resurrection. The repetition of the same word shows that in Paul's mind a direct parallelism exists between Christ's relation to the creation and to the church. The new creation came into existence by the same principles as the old. Paul's aim in all these statements comes to focus when he speaks of Christ as pre-eminent. The goal of both old and new creations is to show the supremacy of Christ. This evidently was a truth inadequately held or else denied by the heretics.

19 *Fullness of God.* When the apostle connects Christ with *the fullness* (*plērōma*) he is making another statement which directly bears on the Colossian heresy. The word was later used in Gnostic thought to describe the absolute being of God, but it cannot be established that the Colossians were using it in the same sense. If they were, Paul would be saying that there is no gulf, as the Gnostics maintained, between God and Christ, for the fullness of God dwells in Christ. But if the Colossian heresy, as is most probable, was not as advanced as this, Paul would be saying that all that can be conceived of God dwells in Christ, thus expressing the highest possible view of the Person of Christ. *Was pleased to dwell.* RSV here makes 'fullness' the subject of the verb, but there is much to be said for making God the subject, since the verb is used in a personal sense. On the other hand the subject of all the preceding statements is Christ and it seems strange suddenly to introduce God as subject. The verb expresses the Father's delight in the incarnation.

20–23 The thought now turns to the idea of reconciliation. Paul recognizes that in spite of what he has said about all things holding together in Christ, there is considerable disharmony in creation. The necessity for reconciliation is not questioned or discussed. It is assumed. But the means for reconciliation needs stressing. *Through him* points to Christ as the exclusive agent for such reconciling work. The verb 'reconcile' (*apokatallassein*) is elsewhere used only of persons and it seems strange for Paul to be speaking here of the reconciliation of things. It is a bold concept. But Paul was probably thinking of things in terms of the personal agencies which were believed to control them. More important is the method of reconciliation expressed in the words *making peace by the blood of his cross.* There can be no denying that by this Paul is thinking of the work of Christ in sacrificial terms. The importance of this for the apostle is evident from the many other occasions when he speaks of the blood of Christ (*cf.* Rom. 3:25; 5:9; 1 Cor. 11:25; Eph. 1:7). The whole expression sums up the effective meaning of the passion of Christ. The making of peace is a fitting interpretation of Christian reconciliation, involving as it does the removal of all obstacles between creature and Creator.

21 Already in v. 13 the apostle has dwelt on the remarkable transformations which are effected by Christ and he returns to the same theme here. Reconciliation involves a change of attitude on the part of the offending party. Hence a full recognition of the offence (here stated in the terms *estranged and hostile in mind, doing evil deeds*) will put in clearest perspective the wonder of the reconciling work of God. It is noteworthy that Paul describes the former state of these Colossian Christians in terms of thought as well as deed. Some moderns whose behaviour is relatively upright are nevertheless blameworthy in that they have rejected the authority of God. Man in his natural state is in revolt against God, estranged and hostile.

22 *His body of flesh.* There was probably a good reason for Paul expressing himself in this rather full manner. If he has in mind the type of error which came to fruition in Docetism, there would be an implied criticism of the view that Christ's body was not physical but apparent. But the word *flesh* may be added to distinguish

body from its metaphorical use in v. 18. *By his death* would refute the view that Christ did not suffer. The purpose or perhaps the result of the reconciling work of Christ is next stated—*to present you holy.* The idea behind the verb is the presentation of sacrifice. Of the three adjectives here, *holy* is used in the sense of 'sacred' or separated to God, *blameless* in the sense of 'without blemish' (*cf.* Lightfoot), and *irreproachable* in the sense of 'not open to any charge'.

23 This moving passage is concluded by a condition—the need for stability. Firmness of faith will be evidence of the reality of the reconciliation. *Not shifting from the hope of the gospel* is another challenge to those tempted to fall for false teaching. The apostle considers it to be unnecessary to define *gospel* any further except to say it is that which had been preached, not only to them, but to *every creature under heaven*, a phrase which shows that Paul is dwelling on possibilities rather than actualities. The same gospel is the subject of Paul's ministry.

1:24 – 2:3 THE APOSTLE'S MINISTRY

In one sense this section is a digression in which Paul refers to his own calling. Yet it is not wholly unrelated to what precedes and what follows. Having just dwelt on the person and work of Christ, he is reminded of his high privilege in being a minister of such a gospel. And as he thinks of exposing some of the errors threatening these Colossians, he is reminded of the need to make clear his credentials before doing so.

24 *My sufferings for your sake.* Paul thinks of the hardships which he has had to endure in the preaching of the gospel as being in a sense on behalf of the whole church. Hence he can say *for your sake*, although he has never worked among the people of Colossae. Paul regards his sufferings as a means to an end. *I complete what remains of Christ's afflictions.* This statement raises difficulties for the interpreter. First, as to the meaning of the verb (*antanaplēroō*): this word suggests the supply of a deficiency from whatever source. But in what sense can Paul be thinking of a deficiency in the sufferings of Christ? He could not mean that Christ's death was inadequate and needed supplementing as a saving act. He must be thinking of afflictions in a different sense. Bruce appeals to the servant passages in Isaiah to supply the key, since he sees there, as here, an alternation between the servant as an individual and the servant as a corporate personality. In other words, Christ is still suffering through the sufferings of His people. What Paul endures is therefore an extension of the sufferings of Christ. These sufferings are on behalf of the *body*, the church as a whole, not just the local community.

25, 26 Paul's deep awareness of *the divine office* to which he was called (note again the divine initiative in this) comes to the forefront here, with its special purpose in the making known of the word of God. The word *fully* suggests 'bringing to completion', as if Paul's preaching was contributing to the ultimate consummation of God's purpose revealed in His Word. It is characteristic of Paul to describe the revelation as a *mystery*, which although long hidden is *now made manifest*. Some take the words *ages and generations* in a personal sense as does RSV mg. ('angels and men'), but the interpretation in the text is a closer rendering of the Greek. The manifestation is not unlimited, since it is restricted *to his saints*, *i.e.* to those capable of appreciating it. But there is no question here of Christian revelation being purposely hidden from the uninitiated, yet the plain fact is that its value cannot be recognized by those still in a state of hostility to God. **27** Indeed, Paul again points out the divine initiative in making the revelation known. *The riches of the glory of this mystery*. The stress falls on the word 'glory' as is clear from the further expression *the hope of glory*. It is a word which in the NT is inseparably bound up with the nature and activity of God. To Paul this is a treasure of inestimable wealth. The key to his thinking is found in the words *Christ in you*. It is not simply the glory of Christ in itself, but the revelation of Christ 'among' men, as the phrase could be understood, rather than in a mystical sense. 'Among you' would then be exactly parallel to 'among the Gentiles'.

28 Here Paul shares more specifically some of his thoughts regarding the ministry. He sees it as proclamation, exhortation and instruction, with the ultimate aim of presenting *every man mature in Christ*. All three activities of the minister of Christ are thus bent to a common spiritual end. The word for *mature (teleios)* means 'complete, fully developed'. It was later used among Gnostics for those privileged to be initiated into the higher realms of knowledge, a sense alien to the conception of Paul. It is not impossible that at this stage some of the false teachers were setting themselves up as an élite clique. If so the threefold occurrence of *every man* in this verse would contain a significant counterbalance.

29; 2:1 The apostle is desirous that the Colossians know how much effort he is putting into his ministry, even for those whom he has never met. But Paul does not rely on his own energy, for he recognizes that his real source of power is in Christ. There is a constant combination of human and divine energy in the Christian ministry. *Those at Laodicea*. The church in this place is mentioned again in Rev. 3. Paul had clearly not visited any of the churches in the Lycus Valley, in which case the words *and for all who have not seen my face* should be regarded as including the Colossians and Laodiceans (see Introduction).

2, 3 The apostle ends this section with a definition of his purpose, again expressed in a deeply spiritual manner. It involves encouragement towards brotherly love. The words *knit together in love* are suggestive, since the verb seems here to mean 'united, compacted', although it could mean 'instructed' as in LXX. The former brings out more vividly the essential unity of believers in Christ. *The riches of assured understanding*. Paul returns to the same word used in 1:27 for spiritual wealth, but here the wealth consists of an informed conviction and knowledge of God's mystery in Christ. The metaphor of wealth is continued in the expression *all the treasures of wisdom and knowledge*, which is a repetition of ideas already expressed. The concept of all knowledge being hidden in Christ brings out His uniqueness. According to Lightfoot, wisdom involves the power of reasoning concerning those truths apprehended by knowledge. But Paul is probably not intending any fine distinction. In this whole passage he is like a man searching for words to express the value of the revelation which formed the basis of his gospel. No doubt he also had his eye on the false teachers as much as to say that the only kind of hidden knowledge (*gnōsis*) that he would countenance was what was hidden in Christ.

2:4–15 FALSE TEACHING AND THE CHRISTIAN ANSWER

The previous section leads naturally into this passage dealing with false teaching. **4** There were those using *beguiling speech* and what Paul is about to say is to prevent anyone being deluded. It is worth noting that the error arose from false speech rather than false practice. It is possible that the singular *no one* may indicate that the chief source of false teaching was an individual, but it is more likely that Paul is using the term generally in the sense of 'anyone'. **5** More than once in his Epistles Paul mentions his spiritual presence in churches when he is absent from them (*cf.* especially 1 Cor. 5:3–5). This is all the more significant when it is a church he has never visited. When speaking of *your good order*, Paul is using a military metaphor describing their preparation for the spiritual battle. The word *firmness* is similarly used to denote a solid front in matters of faith. Before challenging them to resist the false teaching, he rejoices over what he knows of them.

6 To receive Christ is but the beginning. The follow-up is to *live in him*, which is described as involving four aspects, the first three very similar. **7** *Rooted, built up, established* all probably borrow from a building metaphor, but express the same idea of reliability as is seen in the previous military metaphor. *Just as you were taught* reminds them of their Christian origins and contrasts them with those who had listened to a different type of teaching. The fourth aspect is *abounding in thanksgiving*, which echoes the apostle's own enthusiasm to give thanks.

8–15 It is here that the main allusions to the false teaching occur, although Paul gives nothing approaching a systematic analysis of it. **8** *No one.* See on v. 4. *Philosophy and empty deceit.* The apostle loses no time in summing up the teaching. Though seemingly intellectual, it was hollow —a vivid and almost contemptuous contrast with the riches in Christ. For the meaning of philosophy here see the Introduction. *Human tradition.* In all probability this is a reference to Jewish tradition. It was a poor substitute for divine revelation. *The elemental spirits of the universe* are placed in direct contrast to Christ. For this reason RSV is here undoubtedly correct in rendering the word (*stoicheia*) as spirits, although it could mean elementary ideas. It is not possible to be more specific but the power to delude would fit well into contemporary notions of the adverse influence of spirits on human actions.

9 The contrast with Christ leads Paul to make a profound theological statement about Him— *For in him dwells the whole fullness of deity bodily.* Every word here is significant. Christ is the focal point. The *fullness* (*plērōma*) may well be a catchword used by the false teachers to describe the transcendent God, as later Gnostics did. It was believed that the Pleroma was so transcendent that it was necessary for a long succession of intermediaries to connect man with God, of which the last in the succession was Christ. But in Paul's view no intermediaries are necessary. The Pleroma dwells directly in Him. The word *deity* (*theotētos*) occurs only here in the NT and denotes the divine essence. There is some dispute about the sense in which the word *bodily* is to be understood. Moule gives five interpretations, but the most probable are (*a*) 'as an organized body' referring to the totality of the Godhead as distinct from the hierarchy of spiritual beings, or (*b*) 'assuming a bodily form', referring to the incarnation. Common usage favours the second. It is because the fullness took on some visible form in Christ that it became knowable to man. It is worth noting that the verb is in the present tense which points to the continuing effect of the incarnation as an act of revelation. **10** The fullness in Christ is next transferred to the fullness of the salvation He brings. The Greek behind the words *fullness of life in him* is literally 'you are fulfilled in Him', which vividly draws attention to the inadequacy of life apart from Him. Paul is still bearing the false teaching in mind for he next asserts that Christ is *the head of all rule and authority*, which would include those spiritual agencies to which the false teachers were appealing. This is an extension of the Headship of Christ referred to in 1:18.

11 Paul is more concerned to point out the positive teaching about Christ than the negative teaching of the false teachers. *In him also you were circumcised.* The abrupt introduction of the theme of circumcision suggests that there was some confusion on this subject among the Colossians. Some of the false teachers were possibly making it a condition of salvation as happened among the Galatian churches. Paul is thinking of a new kind of circumcision, which

he calls the *circumcision of Christ*, by which he means not Christ's Jewish circumcision, but His passion, which was essentially *putting off the body of flesh.* Alternatively the latter phrase could be understood in a spiritual sense of putting away of self. In view of the fact that Paul next deals with Christian baptism as an identification with Christ's burial, it seems better to accept the former interpretation, especially as in vv. 14, 15 the reference to the passion is specific. **12** The figure of *baptism* is seen by Paul to be illustrative of death and resurrection, but has no meaning apart from the identification of the believer with Christ. The additional words, *through faith in the working of God*, make clear that the external rite is dependent on a right approach, in the same way that Christ Himself depended on the activity of God in His resurrection (*cf.* 1 Pet. 3:21).

13, 14 To draw attention to the transformation which had already taken place in these Colossians, Paul contrasts their past with their present. *Dead in trespasses.* Men who live without God do not readily admit that they were dead in trespasses. But once new life comes in Christ, the character of their previous state of sin becomes increasingly clear. Paul is speaking to Gentiles; hence the expression, *the uncircumcision of your flesh.* True life is inseparable from a right relationship with God and for this reason Paul dwells on God's method of forgiveness. He uses the metaphor of a *bond* (*cheirographon*), which Moule describes as 'an "IOU", a statement of indebtedness' which had to be signed by the debtor as an acknowledgment of his debt. The debt was impossible to pay. Moreover it was backed by *legal demands*, since every trespass is a violation of the law of God. The only hope was for someone to cancel the debt. Paul imagines God taking the statement of debts and nailing it to the cross of Christ, a vivid way of saying that the death of Christ is the basis of God's forgiveness of man's sin.

15 The metaphor changes again as Paul thinks of God's master-stroke in Christ. He is reminded of a conqueror's triumphal procession in which the captives of war are exhibited to enhance the conqueror's own glory. The enemies here are spiritual—*principalities and powers*—which have nevertheless been *disarmed, i.e.* robbed of all further opportunity to do harm. God made a *public example of them*, not only in the sense that all can see, but also as an act of defiance against those powers which were challenging His authority. They now presented a sorry spectacle, utterly defeated. *In him* (*i.e.* 'in Christ') is better than 'in it' (*i.e.* in the cross), since God is the subject of the whole sentence.

2:16 – 3:4 A RIGHT APPROACH TO LIFE AND WORSHIP

In the last section Paul has dealt with some basic principles arising from the false teaching. In this he comes to more practical matters.

16, 17 *Therefore* links the two sections together. In view of Christ's triumph over all spiritual adversaries, it would be foolish to allow anyone to pass judgment over such matters as *food* and *festivals*. Paul is here referring to any system which makes salvation dependent on the observance of certain food taboos or rigid adherence to the observance of certain days as sacred. The Jews were guilty of doing this and such an approach may well have been shared by the false teachers. Paul thinks of the contrast between a *shadow* and its *substance* as a fitting illustration of the relationship between a ritual religion and Jesus Christ. Whatever symbols are used, they must never be mistaken for the real thing.

18 Another practical matter concerned modes of worship. The statement in this verse raises some difficulties because of our lack of sufficient knowledge of the practices being combatted. *Let no one disqualify you* seems to mean 'Let no-one deprive you of your rightful prize', an illustration from the athletic arena. But who could deprive them? Paul goes on to speak of *self-abasement and worship of angels* as being required, as if these things were encumbrances preventing the athlete from running. An underestimate of oneself is a serious impediment in a race, but what is meant by angel-worship? It seems best to regard this as a reference to the usurping by angels of the true place of Christ as the only Mediator. This would be tantamount to the athlete going off course altogether. The meaning of the words *taking his stand on visions* has been much debated. The Colossians would probably associate the verb which Paul uses with the mystery religions, where it was used of the entry of the initiate to a higher stage of knowledge. In this case, the Colossians were being pressed by nothing more substantial than ecstatic visions to pursue spiritual advancement. The difficulty is that the visions are spoken of in the past tense (*ha heōraken*). Some have suggested emendations to the text, assuming a corruption, but without MS evidence. Yet the above interpretation seems to make reasonable sense. The words *his sensuous mind* literally represent 'the mind of his flesh', but no doubt RSV captures Paul's basic meaning. Those relying on visions and the like are placing more reliance than they should on their own mental powers, which results in spiritual pride.

19 Already in 1:18 Paul has introduced the metaphor of a body to describe the church with Christ as its Head, and he returns to the figure here to develop the imagery. Those who are seeking to lead the Colossians astray show by that fact that they are out of harmony with the Head. One of the signs that a body is wholly under the direction of the head is that all parts of it, joints and muscles, act as a unity. It is a remarkable picture of the essential oneness of the church of Christ. The words *nourished* and *knit together* are worth noting. The former means 'equipped', in the sense that the body, if it is to function as a body, must be furnished with joints and ligaments which facilitate healthy growth. For the other word, see 2:2 where the same close unity is in view. *Growth that is from God* (lit. 'the growth of God') shows the pattern for the true development of the church.

20–23 Paul's argument proceeds on the basis of what should follow if the Colossians had been identified with Christ in His death. **20** *If with Christ you died* should be compared with the if-clause of 3:1. The death involved the overthrow of the elemental spirits (*cf.* v. 14). The Christian can no longer view the world as if the spirits still controlled it. Paul appeals to them on this ground not to be inconsistent. If the regulations were tied up with things now done away with in Christ, it would be equally unreasonable to submit to them. **21, 22** The apostle cites some examples of such outworn regulations. They have a strongly Jewish flavour, since taboos of various kinds were integral to Judaism, but asceticism was not confined to Judaism in the ancient world. The Pythagoreans, *e.g.*, were given to ascetic practices. Paul is clearly quoting the precise prohibitions and then comments that they concern perishable (as contrasted with eternal) things, and are anyway based on human (rather than divine) teaching. **23** This verse is difficult. *These have indeed an appearance of wisdom* refers back to food taboos. The word for *appearance* (*logos*) is used here in the sense of 'reputation'. Outwardly they were regarded as wise. Their aims appeared good, involving considerable self-discipline. Yet Paul's comment is that *they are of no value in checking the indulgence of the flesh*. An alternative reading, given in RSV mg., has 'serving only to indulge the flesh', but this is less probable when linked with the previous phrase *severity to the body*. What Paul appears to mean is that in spite of rigid self-discipline, taboos of the kind mentioned leave untouched the moral problems of sensual indulgence. He finds the answer in the Christian's higher life, to which he next turns.

3:1–4 This paragraph is intended to parallel the last. Both are introduced with an if-clause, the first, 'if with Christ you died', being inseparably linked with the second, *if then you have been raised with Christ*. In the former section the emphasis was mainly negative; in this it is positive. In fact Paul proceeds with this double view in his next sections—'Put off' and 'Put on'. Christian living always has both negative and positive aspects.

1 *Raised with Christ*. There appears to be an allusion here to baptism, in view of 2:12. In that act is symbolized being both 'buried' and 'raised' with Christ. Since baptism may be regarded as representing the entry point into the Christian church, it serves as a picture of Paul's thought here. 2:20–23 speaks of dying with Christ, and this section of 'resurrection' with Christ. This kind of resurrection-life clearly involves transformation, an essentially new beginning which brings responsibilities and challenges. Lightfoot calls it 'a removal into a new sphere of being'. It is fitting, therefore, that the more practical section of the Epistle should be introduced in this way. *Seek the things that are above, where Christ is.* In v. 2 the word 'above' is seen as the opposite of 'things that are on earth', and denotes the spiritual as contrasted with the merely material. Paul is aware that this might result in nebulous ideas, if not linked with Christ, and hence his addition here. He conceives of Christian life as a constant quest with Christ Himself as the goal. The place of Christ *at the right hand of God* is a familiar NT theme (*cf.* Acts 2:33; 5:31; 7:55; Rom. 8:34; Eph. 1:20; Heb. 1:3, 13; 8:1; 10:12; 12:2; 1 Pet. 3:22; Rev. 3:21). In many of these references, especially in Hebrews, he is said, as here, to be *seated*, an idea which is borrowed from the imagery of enthronement, which comes from Ps. 110:1. It speaks of the glory and triumph of Christ.

2 The change from 'seek' in v. 1 to *set your minds* (*phronein*) in this verse emphasizes even more vividly the mental re-orientation which new life in Christ necessitates. The verb is a favourite one with Paul, denoting the whole mental activity, not simply an occasional thought. **3** Here again is the idea of union with Christ in death and new life. But why does the apostle return to this? No doubt because he feared that it was difficult for the Colossians to grasp that the old life had no more hold upon them. They now had a new centre. Their whole existence was to be God-orientated. The hiddenness is as far as the world is concerned, which cannot fail to cause misunderstanding on its part. **4** In this verse is the sole reference in this Epistle to the second coming, but it forms an essential part of Paul's thought here. Although the new life-secret is now hidden, it will not always be so. *When Christ . . . appears, . . . you also will appear.* Throughout this portion of the Epistle Paul is constantly stressing the close identification of the believer with Christ and he now relates this to the return of Christ. *Christ who is our life* is a development of v. 3 in that Christ is now seen as the centre of life, rather than simply associated with our life. It is also noticeable that Paul says *our* to include himself, although some texts have *your*, no doubt influenced by the previous verse. *In glory.* Paul is reminded of the believer's glorious hope (*cf.* Rom. 8:17). Whatever the present experiences, the future holds out nothing less than a share in the glory of Christ Himself.

3:5–17 THE PRINCIPLES OF CHRISTIAN LIVING

This exposition may be subdivided into two parts, vv. 5–11 setting out the negative side—what must be put away; and vv. 12–17 dealing with the positive side—what must be put on. In both sections are found lists of qualities which were a familiar feature of the ancient world, but in Paul's hands become invested with new meaning.

5 *Put to death.* Bruce renders this 'reckon as dead', but the verb is probably stronger than that. The only other occasions when the same verb is used (Rom. 4:19; Heb. 11:12) relate to Sarah and Abraham when the Isaac promise was given. But here it is used metaphorically. It suggests that some effort is needed to deal the death blow to evil habits. *What is earthly in you* would more literally be rendered 'the members which are upon earth'. The word for 'members' (*melē*) is the same word used elsewhere for limbs of the body, but clearly Paul is here using it in a moral and not a physical sense. One's limbs can be used in either a right or wrong way. Examples of the latter are seen in the following list of vices. Nevertheless the identification of the limbs with the vices is rather strained and has drawn out a variety of explanations. It seems best to suppose with Lightfoot that some such verb as 'put off' (as in v. 9 and parallel with the 'put on' of v. 10) should be assumed to introduce the list of vices. *Immorality . . . evil desire.* In the first four vices Paul moves from a particular sin to general tendencies of the same kind. Although the main emphasis falls on sexual sins, the last word is sufficiently general to include all base desires. In stressing the inner motives in addition to the outward acts, Paul is doing the same as Jesus (in the Sermon on the Mount). *Covetousness, which is idolatry.* This fifth sin is more subtle than the others. The ancient world was no stranger to the idea of idolatry, but would have been unaccustomed to think of covetousness in such a category. This sin sums up all sins of the mind centred in self. It is a particularly needy field for Christian transformation.

6 *The wrath of God.* The argument here parallels that in Rom. 1:18ff., where Paul uses the same phrase and illustrates the objects of the divine wrath by reference to an even fuller list of vices. *Wrath* must not be confused with a vindictive reaction. It is rather the negative side of holiness, the revulsion of righteousness towards all unrighteousness. *Is coming* is capable of being understood either of the present or of the future. There is some doubt about the reading 'upon the sons of disobedience' (rsv mg.). Since it is paralleled in Eph. 5:6 it may have been introduced from such a source. Even if the reading is not original, it expresses what was probably in Paul's mind. **7** Paul again takes the opportunity of reminding his readers of their former condition to highlight their present transformation. The idea of life as a walk is also characteristic of the apostle and of other NT writers.

8, 9a *Put . . . away.* Paul uses a verb applied to the taking off of clothes and is thinking of certain moral characteristics as garments which can now be discarded, because ill-fitting. He lists another five vices of a different kind, all affecting other people and all centring in wrong attitudes. There is no need to interpret the first four by the last as if all were sins of speech, although words are clearly the channel through which they have impact on others. There is little distinction between anger and wrath, although Lightfoot says the former 'denotes a more or less settled feeling of hatred' and the latter 'a tumultuous outburst of passion'. The transference of thought from God's anger (*orgē*) to man's anger is suggestive. The fitful outbursts associated with man's anger are wholly absent from God's anger and sets it on a wholly different plane. *Malice* (*kakia*) is a word implying vicious or malignant action against others, while *slander* and *foul talk* denote malicious and evil speech. It is a formidable list, but Paul is particularly impressed by the evils of speech which can cause havoc even within the Christian community. *Do not lie* may be rendered 'Do not continue to lie'—in other words, put an end to a habit which is a hang-over from the old life.

9b, 10 The basic reason why these evils must be excluded from Christian behaviour is because they belong to *the old nature* and are alien to *the new nature*. Here the 'putting off' of the one is precisely matched by the 'putting on' of the other, a reminder that there could be no middle position. Some scholars, however, take the participles in vv. 9 and 10 as dependent on the imperative, which is grammatically more usual. In this case the 'putting off' and 'putting on' are commands rather than reasons for ceasing to lie. Since Paul is addressing a Christian church, however, it is better to assume that their understanding of the implications of this was defective. There is an implied contrast between the static *practices* of the old nature and the new nature *being renewed*. The latter is continuous and dynamic. A similar idea of the continual renewal of the inner man in contrast to the outer man is found in 2 Cor. 4:16. The words *in knowledge after the image of its creator* need some comment. *Knowledge* is set out as the target of the renewal process, in which case it denotes full understanding of Christian obligations as the end-product. This emphasis on Christian knowledge would be a valuable antidote to any error which claimed, as Gnostics did, to be in possession of the inner key to knowledge. The word *image* has already been used in 1:15 of Christ and could mean the same here. But this would be more obscure than regarding the whole phrase as analogous to Gn. 1:26. The standard for the believer in Christ is no less than the standard which God set Himself at the creation, no less than His own likeness.

11 Paul next shows how national and social distinctions disappear in Christ. That such a theme should suddenly be introduced is evidence that the apostle was deeply conscious of the scandal of such distinctions in the world of his time. The division between *Greek* and *Jew* was virtually unbridgeable, at least from the Jewish side. The *circumcised* would not acknowledge the *uncircumcised*. Greeks regarded a foreigner as a *barbarian* and Romans regarded him as a *Scythian*. These distinctions were deep rooted in a strongly nationalistic era. Moreover, the divi-

sion between *slave* and *freeman* could not have been more sharply defined. Paul marvels at the power of Christ to do away with such divisions as these. The racial and social divisions have changed in their form, but not in their intensity, nor has the solution altered. The assertion that *Christ is all, and in all* effectively excludes all partial views of Christ, such as the false teachers appear to have had. There is probably no intention to distinguish between *all* and *in all*. The expression points to the complete adequacy of Christ as the supreme unifying agent.

12–17 Having spoken of the new nature in v. 10, Paul proceeds to define more precisely what he means. To offset the two lists of vices he gives a list of virtues. **12** *As God's chosen ones.* This description focuses attention on God's choice, because of the high spiritual qualities that Paul is about to introduce. As special objects of God's choice, they were also, by that fact, objects of His love (*cf.* Rom. 8:33ff.). The further descriptions, *holy and beloved*, are characteristic NT words and, together with the word *chosen*, are drawn from old covenant language. They effectively describe the men of the new covenant, because they are invested with new meaning in Christ. The qualities mentioned form the counterpart of the list of vices in v. 8. Those are social irritants; these are social 'ointments'. Those are aimed at harming others, whereas these imply a desire to care for others and to put them first. Three of the qualities mentioned here, *kindness, meekness* and *patience*, occur in Paul's list of the fruits of the Spirit in Gal. 5:22. *Lowliness* was not a quality admired in Paul's day, yet Christ was the supreme example of it. The same may be said of *compassion* (*cf.* the use of the same Greek word in Phil. 1:8, where Paul uses it of Christ).

13 Here Paul turns away from abstract nouns to mention two positive activities, *forbearing* and *forgiving*. Both verbs are frequent in his Epistles. He recognized the importance of these activities in enabling peaceable relations to be established. A readiness to make allowance for the weakness of others and a readiness to forgive in cases of just complaint are possible only on the strength of Christ's own example. There is an echo here of the Lord's Prayer in the close link between God's forgiveness of us and our forgiveness of others. The phrase *as the Lord has forgiven you* provides a powerful motive. There is a variant reading which substitutes 'Christ' in place of 'Lord' and this has strong support. But whichever is right does not alter the force of the argument. **14** In saying *above all these put on love* is Paul thinking of an over-garment or a girdle? In view of the allusion to binding it is not impossible that the latter idea is correct, although there is no support for the use of the word in this sense. On the other hand, *above all* may mean 'especially', in the sense of 'more than all these'. The existence of the other qualities cannot guarantee *perfect harmony*, but love can. The word rendered *perfect harmony* (*teleiotēs*) really means 'perfectness', a state which cannot be improved on. Since Christ, who is our life, is perfect, no lesser aim is permissible for us.

15 The theme of peace, like love, finds a notable place in the teaching of Jesus (*cf.* Jn. 14:27, His legacy of peace) and recurs frequently in the Epistles of Paul. The expression *peace of Christ* can mean either the peace which Christ bestows or the peace which belongs to Christ. Both probably merge here, if the words are interpreted in the light of Jn. 14:27. The word *rule* (*brabeuetō*) comes from the imagery of the athletic arena and means 'umpire'. Paul seems to mean that those who have peace have an umpire, which maintains order and harmony within the life. *To which . . . you were called in the one body.* The Christian body, already mentioned in this Epistle, was designed for peace, and anything promoting discord is clearly not in tune with Christ. This is a sound principle for the umpire's decisions. It may be wondered why Paul suddenly includes an exhortation to *be thankful.* Perhaps he recognized the difficulty of maintaining peace, and further recognized that any such achievement must elicit special gratitude to God. But Paul's Epistles supply abundant evidence of the importance of thanksgiving (*cf.* 1:3ff. and vv. 16, 17 below).

16 The next exhortation centres on the need for assimilating the Word. But when Paul says, *Let the word of Christ dwell in you richly,* two problems of interpretation arise. What does he mean by the *word of Christ?* It could be understood either of the word which Christ speaks, or the word about Christ. The former is the more natural, but even this is capable of different interpretations. Lightfoot considered that the expression represents 'the presence of Christ in the heart as an inward monitor'. Yet the *word* suggests more than presence. It implies specific teaching, and Bruce is nearer the point when he says that 'Christian teaching must be based on the teaching of Jesus Himself'. Since the expression occurs nowhere else it is impossible to be certain, but Paul may well have chosen it to include a variety of meanings, with their emphasis on Christ. Some texts read 'Lord' and others 'God' instead of 'Christ', but these look like alterations from the less to the more familiar. The word *richly* occurs in only three other places in the NT (1 Tim. 6:17; Tit. 3:6; 2 Pet. 1:11), in all of which it describes the richness of God's provision for man, and can bear the same meaning here. Another problem arises in the next part of the verse. RSV joins the words *in all wisdom* to the teaching and admonishing, but they could equally well be attached to the first part of the verse, in which case a wise handling of the word of Christ would be indicated. Moreover, RSV has separated the singing from the teaching, but the Greek would more naturally be understood to mean that the teaching was with the singing of psalms. What Paul may have meant is that in Christian assemblies teaching and admonition should be conveyed by means of

various types of singing (as Eph. 5:19 more explicitly states). By *psalms* is presumably meant the OT Psalms, but what distinction can be made between *hymns* and *spiritual songs* is not clear. Bruce suggests that the former might be Christian canticles (like the Magnificat) and the later unpremeditated songs. It seems more likely, however, that *hymns* are ascriptions to Christ (*cf.* Rev. 4, 5). The words *with thankfulness* are literally 'with grace' (*en chariti*) and could be understood in the sense 'by the grace of God'. In any case the thanksgiving is directed to God, which contains an acknowledgment of His grace.

17 is a general summary of the Christian philosophy of living. It has its focus in the relating of *everything* to the *name of the Lord Jesus*. In the NT church this would be regarded as no mere superstitious uttering of the name as a magical formula in the manner of many contemporary heathen cults, but as a recognition of the Lordship of Christ in everything. It is a noble principle to subject all *word* as well as *deed* to the name, and therefore to the nature of Christ. The note of *thanks* with which this section closes completes its threefold exhortation to gratitude.

3:18 – 4:1 ADVICE FOR HOUSEHOLDS

Having discussed spiritual principles, Paul now comes to specific relationships within households. The section may be conveniently divided into two, the first dealing with family relationships (3:18–21) and the second with slave–master relationships (3:19 – 4:1). Similar advice is found in Ephesians, Titus, 1 Timothy and 1 Peter. It also occurs in several of the early church writers.

18, 19 Paul's teaching regarding husbands and wives must be approached against the background of both Jewish and pagan ethics, in neither of which were wives granted any rights. His positive contribution is not therefore the injunction for wives to submit, but for the submission to be *fitting in the Lord.* The word rendered *fitting* (*anēken*) is thoroughly Stoical, but the addition is thoroughly Christian. This would at once transform current ideas and would invest the wife's position with an adequate safeguard. Support for this is found in the injunction that husbands should *love* their wives. There is no suggestion in Paul's language of any inferiority being attached to the wife. **20** The pagan approach to children left much to be desired, although Jewish home life was on a higher level. Nevertheless, in the exhortation to children, *obey your parents,* the new element as before is in the notion of doing it to please the Lord (or more literally to be 'pleasing' or 'commendable' in the Lord). **21** Home discipline, as this verse shows, is no longer a matter of rigid enforcement, but of relating the parent–child relationship to Christ. In an age when parental authority is everywhere being challenged the

Christian home should be an example of healthy discipline. Paul recognizes that this is possible only if fathers avoid provocation. The word he uses means 'irritate' suggesting a friction which could be avoided. Harshness in men was widespread in Paul's day, but he recognized that it should find no place in a Christian household. Children could only be discouraged by such an approach.

3:22 – 4:1 In the ancient world slavery was an accepted institution and carried with it inevitable evils. Paul's advice here aims to transform the master–slave relationship from within, not to launch a frontal attack upon it, a course which would have involved political action and which for this reason was quite impractical for the small emerging churches. **22** *Obey in everything* is a sweeping command to slaves who could not call their souls their own. Why should they obey? If the whole structure was illegitimate, what right had masters to expect implicit obedience? Paul does not deal with the wrongs of the system. He is concerned with human attitudes. He gives a series of practical advice, which would be as relevant for employees today as for slaves then. *Not with eyeservice, as men-pleasers.* Paul means them to avoid governing their action by whether they could be seen or not. The alternative provides a nobler motive. *Singleness* points to a consistency of action, and *fearing the Lord* to a religious approach even to secular work, an idea fully developed in **23, 24**: twice in these verses work is directly related to the Lord and it is from the Lord that the reward will come. The injunction to *work heartily* would be a real challenge for slaves who worked without wages. Though Paul makes clear that some reward will be gained, what he calls *the inheritance* shows that the idea is intended in a spiritual sense. **25** Dishonest dealings will rule out the inheritance, since with the Lord *there is no partiality*, no judging merely according to outward appearances. The judgment will fit the offence.

4:1 Having mentioned the absence of partiality in the Lord, Paul reminds masters to show similar fairness. This address to masters is significant because it recognizes that obligation does not rest only with servants. It is well to note that Paul places the responsibility of Christian masters on the highest level—they are to remember that they too have a *Master in heaven*, which means that they themselves are His servants.

4:2–6 MORE GENERAL ADVICE

This brief section forms the concluding exhortation in the Epistle, followed as it is with various personal allusions. Paul mentions two main points, one an appeal for prayer-support and the other a final plea for right conduct and speech.

2–4 He had begun the Epistle by assuring the readers of his constant prayer for them. He now closes by eliciting their constant prayer for him. **2** The verb behind the words *continue steadfastly* (*proskartereō*) is several times used with the same construction as here (followed by the dative) and always in relation to prayer (Acts 1:14; 2:42; 6:4; Rom. 12:12). The expression evidently denotes an attitude of consistent piety, rather than uninterrupted prayer. *Being watchful* is reminiscent of the injunction of Jesus to His disciples in the garden of Gethsemane. Note the returning of the *thanksgiving* theme (*cf.* Phil. 4:6). **3** *Pray for us.* Paul here includes others associated with him in the Gentile mission (Timothy is included in Col. 1:1 and may be more particularly in mind). The request is specific—*that God may open to us a door for the word.* Paul uses the same imagery in 1 Cor. 16:9; 2 Cor. 2:12, in both of which cases it refers to preaching opportunities. The request here suggests that Paul for the time being is denied such opportunity through being in prison, but he believes that prayer can overcome even such a circumstance. The *word* is defined as *the mystery of Christ,* and reference must be made to the earlier use of the same word in this Epistle (see 1:26ff.; 2:2). **4** The apostle adds a further target for their prayers which is an elucidation of the earlier. An open door would be useless without clarity of speech and the conviction of saying the right thing, as the phrase *as I ought to speak* must be understood. The request is not misplaced, since many opportunities are wasted through garbled utterance.

5, 6 The second section concentrates on the Christian's attitude towards outsiders. *Conduct yourselves wisely* is literally 'walk in wisdom', as much as to say, 'Let outsiders see that your chosen path is a wise one'. This can be done in two ways: in the use of time and the manner of speech. *Making the most of the time* (*kairos*) is a paraphrase of words that mean literally 'redeeming the time'. If the verb is the key to the imagery, reference must be made to the slave market. In this case Christians are to buy up every opportunity, an idea which would supplement the open door imagery of v. 3. The word for *time* means a specific opportunity for action, not time generally. When Paul urges that speech should *be gracious,* he uses the same Greek phrase as in 3:16 where it is rendered 'with thanksgiving' (see on 3:16). Here it means more than charm of expression. It means speech permeated with the grace which has been received in Christ. *Seasoned with salt.* Parallels exist for the metaphor of salt in relation to conversation, although it is unlikely that Paul is using it to describe witty speech as many ancient writers did. It is suggestive here for two reasons: it gives flavour and it preserves in a wholesome state. Both are valuable assets for Christians wishing to commend their message to others. Part of right flavouring consists of suiting conversation to the hearers. Christians must learn to choose the best manner of answering questions about the faith.

4:7–18 PERSONAL NEWS

7, 8 This note about Tychicus is repeated almost verbatim in Eph. 6:21, 22 and suggests that Colossians was sent at the same time by the same messenger. 7 Paul's high opinion of Tychicus is reflected in the adjectives used here (*beloved* and *faithful*, the same used of Onesimus in v. 9 and of Epaphras in 1:7), obviously favourite descriptions with the apostle. Tychicus's function is described in a twofold way: as *minister* (*diakonos*) and *fellow servant* (*syndoulos*). The former word recalls Paul's own use of it of himself in 1:23, and the latter also finds a parallel earlier in the Epistle (1:7) with reference to Epaphras. The bond between Paul and those who have shared so much with him is strong. **8** Tychicus is the link-man between Paul and the Colossians. His mission is one of encouragement, with which *cf.* the statement of 2:2. **9** *Onesimus* is described as *one of yourselves*, which is valuable evidence for the fact that the Epistle to Philemon, which also mentions Onesimus, must have been sent to a member of the Colossian church. For a description of the circumstances in which Onesimus was placed, see the commentary on that Epistle. Here it is sufficient to note that the runaway slave is being sent back with Tychicus.

10, 11 Three Jewish Christians send greetings. One of them, *Aristarchus*, is named as a *fellow prisoner*, a word which literally means 'fellow-prisoner-of-war' (*cf.* Acts 19:29, where he was seized by the mob at Ephesus). But some scholars prefer to take the word metaphorically of those engaged in Christian warfare. There is no reason, however, why the literal meaning should be discarded. *Mark the cousin of Barnabas*. Only here is Mark's relationship to Barnabas noted, although Acts speaks of his association with Barnabas on the second missionary journey, after his defection on the first (Acts 15:36ff.). Paul has clearly been reconciled to him by this time. What were the *instructions* the Colossians had received? They were probably from Paul, but could have been passed on by another. Nothing else is known of *Jesus who is called Justus*. The *kingdom* idea is mentioned earlier in 1:13 as part of the theme of the ministry of Paul, and these associates are now said to share the same mission.

12–14 Next Paul mentions three others who, in the light of v. 11, must be Gentiles. *Epaphras* (*cf.* 1:7, 8) is warmly commended as a *servant of Christ Jesus* who never lets up in his prayer for the Colossians. The word used is 'agonize' and may be some kind of allusion to the prayer of Jesus in Gethsemane. That kind of praying ranks a man high in spiritual stature. The expression *that you may stand mature* (*teleioi*) reminds us of 3:14. What Epaphras prays for is what Paul has already exhorted. *Fully assured* may be rendered 'fulfilled or completed', in which case it adds little to the other word. But the RSV here is probably right, particularly as the words *in all the will of God* are linked to it. No greater request for the Colossians could be made than this. Epaphras had evidently not spared himself on behalf of the three churches in the Lycus Valley (see Introduction). Only here do we learn that *Luke* was a doctor, while all that is known elsewhere about *Demas* is that he left Paul for the 'present world' (2 Tim. 4:10).

15–18 The last section sends greetings to various people. **15** *The brethren at Laodicea* are presumably the church there, as in v. 16. House churches, like the one in Nymphas's house, are frequently mentioned by Paul (see on Phm. 1).

16 This verse provides valuable evidence for what was probably a common practice in the early churches—an interchange of letters. *The letter from Laodicea* has now been lost, but presumably it was a letter written by Paul to that church which would be forwarded from there to Colossae. If the heresy was threatening Colossae, it would be salutary for the neighbouring church at Laodicea to have access to Paul's answer to it. The statement here is also support for the view that Paul's letters were publicly read in Christian assemblies. **17** *Archippus* is mentioned again in Phm. 1. What the *ministry* was that he was to fulfil is not clear, but he may have been standing in for Epaphras as leader of the church in his absence.

18 As usual, Paul closes in his own handwriting. The fact that he notes it suggests that he had used an amanuensis up to this point. *Remember my fetters* is a touching reminder of his present circumstances. But he nevertheless ends with his usual greeting, *Grace be with you.*

DONALD GUTHRIE

1 and 2 Thessalonians

INTRODUCTION

BACKGROUND

Thessalonica (Saloniki) was originally called Therme, but was refounded by Cassander *c.* 315 BC and named Thessalonica after his wife, a step-sister of Alexander the Great. Alike in Macedonian and Roman times it was an important city. The Romans made it the capital of the province of Macedonia in 164 BC and a free city after the battle of Philippi in 42 BC. Through it ran the great Egnatian Road, on its way from Neapolis on the Aegean to Dyrrhachium on the Adriatic.

Paul's first visit to Thessalonica—to be dated probably in the early summer of AD 50—is narrated in Acts 17:1-9. It was the first city where he and his companions, Silas (Silvanus) and Timothy, spent any length of time after their departure from Philippi, in the course of his 'second missionary journey'. In accordance with their regular practice, they visited the local synagogue. For three successive sabbaths Paul attempted to convince the synagogue congregation from their OT scriptures that the Messiah was bound to suffer and rise again from the dead, and that Jesus was therefore the Messiah. Several of his hearers believed his message, including a large number of 'God-fearing' Gentiles. But the consequent opposition of the synagogue authorities to the missionaries led to Paul's quitting the synagogue. He had to find another base for his teaching, which was provided in the house of a Thessalonian citizen named Jason. Here he continued a few weeks more, after which his opponents stirred up public disorder. The city magistrates, or 'politarchs' as Luke calls them (a title which they shared with the chief magistrates of other Macedonian cities), received information that Paul and his companions were Messianic agitators, such as had recently caused disturbances in many other places throughout the Roman Empire where there were Jewish communities, and that they proclaimed another king in rivalry to the emperor. Such a charge was necessarily regarded with the utmost gravity. But Jason, Paul's host, and other friends whom the missionaries had made in Thessalonica, went bail for them, undertaking that they would leave the city quietly, and sent them away by night.

The young church which they were thus forced to leave behind in Thessalonica was exposed to some active persecution. Paul was very anxious for his converts' welfare, and wondered how they would stand, especially as his sudden departure prevented him from giving them all the instruction that he regarded as adequate for the establishment of an infant Christian community (*cf.* 1 Thes. 3:10). But his hands were tied by his Thessalonian friends' guarantee; he could not go back at present. From Thessalonica he went on to Beroea with Silas, and Timothy later rejoined him. He sent Timothy back to Thessalonica, and Silas to other parts of Macedonia, while he went on from Athens to Corinth. Here, after some weeks, Silas and Timothy returned to him, and Timothy was able to report that the Thessalonian Christians, far from succumbing to the persecution with which they had been tested, were standing firm and actually propagating the gospel on their own initiative. But there were several matters on which they desired further enlightenment, especially with regard to what Paul had taught them about the return of Christ. In particular, some of their number had died since Paul left their city, and they were eager to know if these would in consequence suffer any disadvantage at Christ's return in comparison with those who would still be alive when it happened.

Paul was overjoyed at Timothy's good news, and wrote at once to congratulate and encourage his Thessalonian converts, and to deal with their practical problems. The letter which he wrote has come down to us as the first Epistle to the Thessalonians.

1 Thessalonians

INTRODUCTION

DATE, AUTHORSHIP, CANONICITY

It follows from what has been said in the Intro-duction above that 1 Thessalonians was written in the earlier part of Paul's stay at Corinth—say towards the end of AD 50. For Timothy's return from Macedonia to Corinth (bringing Paul the news from Thessalonica) see Acts 18:5.

Paul associates his two travel-companions with himself in the salutation (1:1). Such variation in literary style as may be revealed by statistical analysis between this letter and Paul's 'capital letters' (Romans, 1 and 2 Corinthians, Galatians) could easily be accounted for if one or the other of these companions were in some degree responsible for the wording. But the substance of the letter is Paul's (*cf.* 2:18; 3:5; 5:27 for the first person singular). There has been little serious doubt of its genuineness. F. C. Baur's idea that it was written after AD 70 by a disciple of Paul in order to arouse interest in the return of Christ rests on subjective arguments which have failed to win general agreement. The personal note of pastoral concern and affection speaks strongly for the letter's authenticity. It was included in Marcion's Canon (*c.* AD 140) and in the orthodox Roman Canon preserved in the Muratorian fragment (late 2nd century).

TEACHING

Paul is not concerned in this Epistle to give instruction on any one doctrine or to correct any one error—apart from his desire to complete the eschatological teaching which he had given the Thessalonian Christians during his curtailed visit to their city, and thus remove some misunderstandings and perplexities in this field. It is first and foremost a missionary's letter to his converts, and references to Christian doctrine are incidental rather than central. But for that very reason the way in which they are introduced and expressed is the more significant. We may note the following points.

God the Father

Paul is completely and continuously God-conscious. It is basic to his whole thought that God is the source of all and the goal of all, the One in whose presence he lives and works moment by moment. It is He who has chosen His people (1:4); He is the object of their faith (1:8) as the living and true God to whom they turned from unreal gods (1:9). He imparts the authority for the apostle's bold confidence (2:2); it is by His permission that the gospel has been entrusted to their charge (2:4); it is His pleasure that they must seek and His witness that they ought to be able to invoke (2:5, 10). It is His will that must be done (4:3; 5:18); His guidance that must be followed (3:11). He has called His people to holy living (4:7) and He alone can impart to them the sanctification to which He has called them (5:23). It is He who raised up Jesus and will bring His people back with Him from the dead (4:14), thus consummating the salvation to which He has appointed them (5:9).

The Lord Jesus Christ

The spontaneous and almost unconscious way in which Christ is associated with God the Father is even more eloquent testimony to Paul's conception of the Person of Christ than a formal statement of His deity would be. The church at Thessalonica is 'in God the Father and the Lord Jesus Christ' (1:1). So also in 3:11 'our Lord Jesus' is directly and actively associated with 'our God and Father' in His direction of the apostles' footsteps. (*Cf.* also 2 Thes. 1:1; 2:16.)

The Holy Spirit

The Holy Spirit is all-pervasive in the Christian life, which indeed is His creation. The gospel is proclaimed by His power (1:5); not only is His joy imparted to those who believe it (1:6), but He Himself is given to them (4:8) to accomplish His sanctifying work in their lives (2 Thes. 2:13). In church life too He plays His part by communicating the divine will through prophetic utterances; to despise or inhibit such utterances is to 'quench the Spirit' (5:19).

The apostolic preaching

The references to the message which had brought salvation to the Thessalonian Christians show that it was the same message as that attested elsewhere in the NT. Its basic facts are Jesus' death ('for us', 5:10) and resurrection, which have already taken place (4:14; 1:10), and His coming again, which is to take place at the day of the Lord, when His people, delivered by Him from the wrath to come (and sharing His resurrection if they have already died), are to live for ever with Him (1:10; 4:15ff.; 5:1ff.). Those who believe this message turn from unrealities to the living and true God, to serve Him in the light of Christ's second advent (1:9f.). And it is plainly shown what this serving God involves, by the plain instruction in practical Christian living here and there throughout this Epistle and the following one (*e.g.* 4:1–12; 5:6ff.).

Pastoral responsibility

Paul reveals himself in every sentence of this letter as a true and faithful pastor, rejoicing in his flock but anxious for their welfare, confident and concerned, thanking God for them and simultaneously praying to God for them, tirelessly caring for them as a father for his children, straining his strength to the limit in order not to be a burden to them. 'Here was a new phenomenon in history, a man to whom the religious steadfastness and ethical progress of other men was a matter of life and death (see especially ii. 8, 9, iii. 6–8)' (C. A. A. Scott).

OUTLINE OF CONTENTS

COMMENTARY

1:1 SALUTATION

Paul, Silvanus, and Timothy. Associated with Paul in the salutation are his two friends who had collaborated with him in the evangelization of Thessalonica and were now with him at Corinth. *Silvanus*, the Silas of Acts 15:22ff., was a Hellenistic member of the Jerusalem church and a Roman citizen who joined Paul as his travel-companion after the Council of Jerusalem, at the outset of the second missionary journey. (Paul gives his friends their formal names when writing about them; Luke prefers the more homely pet-names.) *Timothy*, a native of Lystra in Asia Minor, joined Paul and Silvanus when they passed through his home town early in their journey (Acts 16:1ff.). *To the church of the Thessalonians in God the Father and the Lord Jesus Christ.* The expression *the church . . . in God* (also in 2 Thes. 1:1) is exceptional; *cf.*, however, Col. 3:3. (Acts 17:28, 'In him we live . . .', is not a true parallel, for there the reference is to the natural order of the old creation.) The close and spontaneous collocation of *God the Father* and *the Lord Jesus Christ* is eloquent of the apostolic understanding of the supremacy to which God had exalted the crucified and risen Christ along with Himself (*cf.* Eph. 1:20ff.; Phil. 2:9–11). *Grace to you and peace.* This is the only Pauline letter in which these familiar words of salutation are not followed by 'from God the Father' or a comparable phrase.

1:2–10 THANKSGIVING

2 Paul and his friends express their joy at the Thessalonian converts' steadfastness and energy in Christian grace and witness. The facts were known widespread, and spoke for themselves. **3** *Faith . . . love . . . hope.* This triad of graces reappears in 5:8 and Col. 1:4f. as well as in the famous passage 1 Cor. 13:13. The writers rejoice that these graces are manifested in the life and activity of the Thessalonians. **4** *We know . . that he has chosen you.* They had recognized the genuineness of the Thessalonians' Christianity

by the way in which they received the gospel in the beginning, and this was confirmed by the news which Timothy had brought back. Their conduct and witness bore undeniable witness to their being truly among the 'elect of God'; **5** theirs was no superficial conversion but, as the sequel proved, the work of *the Holy Spirit* who both convinced them of the truth of the gospel and enabled them to embrace it and translate it into real life. **6** *You became imitators of us*; in Christian behaviour as well as in the endurance of persecution. *With joy inspired by the Holy Spirit.* For joy as the fruit of the Spirit *cf.* Gal. 5:22; also Rom. 5:2f., 11; 14:17. **7** *Macedonia and . . . Achaia.* These two Roman provinces together covered most of the area of modern Greece. Apart from Thessalonica itself, Philippi was the principal church in Macedonia; Corinth was the outstanding church in Achaia. **8** *Everywhere.* Had Priscilla and Aquila (*cf.* Acts 18:1–3) told Paul that news of the church in Thessalonica had travelled as far as Rome? **9** *They themselves*; *i.e.* the people of Macedonia and Achaia and so forth. *You turned to God from idols, to serve a living and true God.* Cf. the apostolic admonition to the pagans of Lystra 'that you should turn from these vain things (*i.e.* idolatry) to a living God' (Acts 14:15). This was a primary necessity when the gospel was proclaimed to Gentiles. **10** *And to wait for his Son from heaven, whom he raised from the dead.* The words in which the Thessalonians are reminded of their conversion show us that the message delivered to them followed the regular lines of the primitive apostolic preaching. For the close connection of Christ's resurrection with His coming again in this preaching *cf.* Acts 17:31. The return of Christ had plainly occupied a prominent place in the apostolic preaching at Thessalonica, as it did elsewhere in the earliest days of Christianity (*cf.* Acts 3:20; 10:42). *Jesus who delivers us from the wrath to come.* This might be rendered more personally 'Jesus, our deliverer from the coming wrath', *i.e.* the divine judgment to be poured upon the earth at the end of the age.

2:1-16 APOLOGIA

Paul's conduct had been represented in an unfavourable light to the converts whom he had left behind at Thessalonica, and he now defends himself. He and his companions had made no attempt to exploit them or live at their expense; on the contrary, they had shown all gentleness and care towards them. They had worked night and day in order to earn their own living while they were busy preaching the good news and building up the new-born Christian community. And the Thessalonian Christians in turn had proved worthy converts, persevering in face of persecution just like the Christians of Palestine.

2 *We had already suffered . . . at Philippi*; a reference to the well-known events related in Acts 16:19ff. **3** *Not . . . from error or uncleanness, nor is it made with guile.* So many wandering charlatans made their way about the Roman world, peddling their religious or philosophical nostrums, that it was necessary for the apostles to emphasize the purity of their motives and procedure by contrast with these. **4** *As we have been approved by God to be entrusted with the gospel, so we speak, not to please men, but to please God who tests our hearts.* Every phrase and clause here expresses Paul's sense of responsibility in regard to his apostolic commission; *cf.* Rom. 1:1, 14; 1 Cor. 4:1-4; 9:16f.; 15:9f.; 2 Cor. 2:17; 4:1ff.; Gal. 1:10; 2:7ff.; Eph. 3:7ff.; Col. 1:23ff. Paul was frequently charged with adapting his message to please his constituency, of being 'all things to all men' in an unworthy sense; this is his answer. **6** *We might have made demands as apostles of Christ.* For Paul's voluntary forgoing of his undoubted right to have his material requirements met by those for whose spiritual welfare he cared *cf.* 2 Thes. 3:9; 1 Cor. 9:4ff.; 2 Cor. 11:7ff. Here he associates Silvanus and Timothy with himself as *apostles*, in the wider sense of the term (*i.e.* missionaries). *Cf.* Acts 14:4, of Barnabas as well as Paul. **7** *We were gentle* (Gk. *ēpioi*). There is a variant reading 'we were babes' (Gk. *nēpioi*); but *gentle* seems preferable, and more appropriate in the context.

9 *We worked night and day*; *cf.* 4:11; 2 Thes. 3:7ff.; Acts 18:3; 20:34. This policy not only reflected a desire to be financially independent of those among whom they ministered; it also marked them off from the ordinary religious traffickers of the day, and showed the converts a good example. **12** *To lead a life worthy of God, who calls you into his own kingdom and glory.* The highest of all incentives for holy living is set before them. In the NT as in the OT the people of God must display the character of God. By faith they had already entered the kingdom of God, but the revelation of its full glory belonged to a day yet future; they were, however, heirs of that glory, and must live accordingly. **13** *Not as the word of men but . . . the word of God.* Paul was so accustomed to hearing his message denounced as man-made, not only by non-Christian Jews, but by many Jewish

Christians as well, that he found it specially encouraging when it was sincerely welcomed as the good news of God. *Cf.* Gal. 1:11, 12. **14** *The churches of God in Christ Jesus which are in Judea*; the original church of Jerusalem in dispersion (*cf.* Acts 9:31; Gal. 1:22). *Your own countrymen*; *i.e.* fellow-townsmen, both Gentiles and Jews (Acts 17:5). **15** *Who killed both the Lord Jesus and the prophets.* The bitterness of this reference to *the Jews* (v. 14) is unparalleled in Paul's writings and it has been suspected of being an interpolation. There is no textual basis for this suspicion, however, and the summary of their behaviour is closely in accord with the narrative of Acts. The primary reference is to the Jews of Judea, but in addition the trouble stirred up by the leaders of the Jewish communities of Thessalonica and Beroea was fresh in Paul's mind. It would be foolish to imagine that the author of vv. 14–16 could not also have expressed himself in the language of Rom. 9:1–5. **16** *Hindering us from speaking to the Gentiles*; *cf.* Acts 13:45. *So as always to fill up the measure of their sins.* For the same idea *cf.* Mt. 23:32. *God's wrath has come upon them at last!* This has been thought by some to anticipate the destruction of Jerusalem in AD 70 (*cf.* NEB, 'and now retribution has overtaken them for good and all'). The Jews of the Dispersion were not for the most part involved in that disaster. Paul means that by their persistent opposition to the gospel they had already ensured for themselves that eschatological judgment which they might have averted by accepting it (*cf.* Acts 2:38ff.; 3:19ff.). In Christian literature before AD 70 no very clear distinction is drawn between the destruction of Jerusalem which, taught by their Lord, Christians knew to be impending as the beginning of the end-time 'birth-pangs' (Mk. 13:8), and the final judgments of the day of the Lord. On vv. 14–16 see H. L. Ellison, *The Mystery of Israel*, 1966, pp. 13ff.

2:17 – 3:10 NARRATIVE OF EVENTS SINCE PAUL LEFT THESSALONICA

It was not lack of interest that prevented Paul from staying longer with them or going back to see them; it was circumstances over which he had no control. He assures them of his longing for them and his joyful confidence in them in view of the return of Christ. It was his impatience to know how they fared that made him send Timothy back to visit them, together with his concern that their faith should be strengthened amid their afflictions. Timothy's report of their welfare and steadfastness had filled him with joy, and also with fresh longing to see them once more.

18 *I, Paul.* Of the other signatories Timothy had actually visited them, and Silvanus had paid a short visit to Macedonia (Acts 18:5), if not to Thessalonica itself. *Satan hindered us.* W. M. Ramsay supposed that Paul detected this subtle agency behind the politarchs' action in exacting security from Jason (Acts 17:9) and binding him over to prevent Paul, the alleged cause of the disturbance, from coming back to Thessalonica. 19 *What is our hope . . . before our Lord Jesus at his coming? Is it not you?* If Paul's converts do him credit, he will face with joy the review of his service to take place at Christ's return (*cf.* Phil. 2:16; 4:1). This is the first occurrence of Greek *parousia* (translated *coming*) in the Pauline Epistles. Its ordinary sense is 'presence' (*cf.* 2 Cor. 10:10; Phil. 1:26; 2:12); but its eschatological sense is akin to its idiomatic usage in the Hellenistic vernacular, of the arrival of some dignitary to pay an official visit to a place. It is so used of the return of Christ 18 times in the NT; the Thessalonian Epistles account for 7 of these.

3:1 *We were willing to be left behind at Athens alone.* Here the *we* is purely epistolary, referring to Paul himself. *Cf.* v. 5. For the occasion, see Acts 17:15ff. **2** *God's servant.* For *servant* (Gk. *diakonon*) there is a well-attested and probably original variant 'fellow-worker' (Gk. *synergon*); *cf.* 1 Cor. 3:9. AV 'minister of God, and our fellow labourer' represents a later conflation of the two readings. **3** *This is to be our lot.* It is taken for granted throughout the NT that affliction is the normal lot of Christians; it is, in fact, an evidence of the genuineness of their faith and an earnest of their part in the coming glory. *Cf.* Acts 14:22; Rom. 8:17f.; 2 Tim. 2:12. **4** It is noteworthy that the inevitability of *affliction* had formed part of the apostles' instruction to the Thessalonian Christians as to others. What had been an acute problem to faith in OT times—the suffering of the righteous—had come to be recognized as an essential element in God's purpose for His people. Since their Lord Himself had suffered, they need expect nothing else; let them rather glory in tribulation (*cf.* Jn. 15:20; 16:33; Rom. 5:3).

7 *In all our distress and affliction we have been comforted.* *Cf.* the similar language of 2 Cor. 1:3-7, written in response to similar good news of his converts' spiritual health brought from Corinth by Titus. **8** *Now we live, if you stand fast in the Lord.* Paul's concern for his converts breathes through all his correspondence; *cf.* 2 Cor. 11:28f. When they were led astray, he was indignant; when they slipped back, he was distressed; when they gave signs of living worthily of the gospel, he was overjoyed (*cf.* 2 Cor. 7:6ff.).

3:11–13 PRAYER FOR A SPEEDY REUNION

Paul prays for a speedy reunion with his Thessalonian friends and for their increase in love and holiness in view of the return of Christ.

11 *Now may our God and Father himself, and our Lord Jesus, direct our way to you.* The fact that the verb *direct* is singular in Greek, despite its compound subject, has no particular theological significance in itself; in such a construction the verb commonly agrees with the nearer subject. But it is significant that Christ is thus associated in action with God the Father. **13** *So that he may establish your hearts unblamable in holiness.* The second coming of Christ should provide the Thessalonian Christians, as it did Paul himself (2:19), with an incentive to holy living. *Cf.* 5:23; 1 Jn. 2:28; 3:3. The day of Christ's return is the day when He reviews His people's record. *At the coming of our Lord Jesus with all his saints*; or 'with all his holy ones'. *Cf.* the description of the day of the Lord in Zc. 14:5 (LXX): 'The Lord my God will come and all his holy ones (Gk. *hagioi*, as here) with him.' This description is based on the earlier theophanic vocabulary of the OT such as Dt. 33:2; Ps. 68:17 (*cf.* also Dn. 7:10 and the words of Enoch quoted in Jude 14f., and such words in the NT as those of Jesus in Mk. 8:38; Mt. 25:31). Primarily therefore here, as in 2 Thes. 1:7, we may regard the 'holy ones' as attendant angels, though we may find cause in 2 Thes. 1:10 to see departed believers associated with them. The unobtrusiveness with which language used of Yahweh in the OT is applied to Jesus in the NT should not make us overlook the startling implications of such a practice on the part of one with Paul's orthodox Jewish and Pharisaic upbringing.

4:1-12 EXHORTATION TO HOLY LIVING AND BROTHERLY LOVE

Paul exhorts them to personal consecration and purity, especially in sexual relations. To this he adds an admonition to maintain brotherly love —superfluous as such an admonition may be in their case—and to go on diligently with their daily work and not to become a charge on others.

1 *In the Lord Jesus*; *i.e.* by His authority; so also *through the Lord Jesus* (v. 2). The whole 'tradition' of ethical instruction in the NT letters derives from His teaching and example (*cf.* on 2 Thes. 2:15). *How you ought to live* (lit. 'to walk'); this ethical sense of 'walk' is common in the NT. **3** *Your sanctification: that you abstain from immorality.* Paul lays special emphasis on this particular aspect of practical holiness because it was in the sphere of relations between the sexes that even the highest pagan ethic of the time fell far short of the Jewish and Christian standard. Fornication was widely regarded in the Graeco-Roman world as almost on the same level of ethical indifference as food and drink. Experience proved that insistent injunctions of this kind were by no means superfluous for Christians converted from paganism. **4** *To take a wife for himself*; RV 'to possess himself of his own vessel' (Gk. *skeuos*); *i.e.* to keep control of his body, rather than to live with his wife; the latter interpretation is not so appropriate here, despite the sense of 'vessel' in 1 Pet. 3:7. **5** *Like heathen who do not know God*; *cf.* Rom. 1:24ff.; 2 Thes. 1:8. **6** *That no man transgress, and wrong his brother in this matter*; *i.e.* in the matter already referred to. Paul seems to be thinking of a trespass of this kind even within the family circle of a fellow-Christian. *Because the Lord is an avenger in all these things*; cf. Eph. 5:6. **7** *God has not called us for uncleanness, but in holiness*. In one sense believers are already 'saints', set apart by God for Himself; in another sense they must manifest this sanctification in daily life. **8** *Whoever disregards this*; *i.e.* he who disregards these apostolic precepts about practical purity. *God, who gives his Holy Spirit to you*. This reference to the indwelling Spirit is specially relevant here, because He is the divine agent in sanctification (*cf.* on 2 Thes. 2:13).

9 *Taught by God*; *cf.* Is. 54:13; Jn. 6:45; 1 Jn. 2:20. **11** *Aspire to live quietly, to mind your own affairs, and to work with your hands*. This is not a new subject, but belongs to the duty of brotherly love; the behaviour of one member affects the welfare of the whole community. *Cf.* 2:9 for the apostolic example. The Greek word rendered *aspire* is *philotimeisthai* (lit. 'be ambitious'). It is usually supposed that exaggerated eschatological expectation (*cf.* 2 Thes. 2:2; 3:6ff.) tended to make some of them excited and restless and neglectful of their ordinary business; this would make them a charge on others and would bring the whole group into disrepute. Brotherly love therefore demanded sober and industrious habits. Paul's idea of readiness for the coming of Christ is in line with the gospel injunction, 'Let your loins be girded and your lamps burning' (Lk. 12:35). He himself had taught them this lesson by example as well as by precept.

4:13 – 5:11 CONCERNING THE SECOND ADVENT

He reassures their anxiety about the position of those of their number who have died; they will suffer no disadvantage at Christ's return, but will be raised from the dead and joined by those who are still alive, to form a united escort for their Lord. The time of His return is unknown; it is therefore necessary for His people to be continually ready and watchful. **13** *Concerning those who are asleep*. Some of their number had died since Paul's departure (possibly as a result of persecution); would these forfeit a share in the glory to be bestowed upon Christians at the second advent? *As others do*; *i.e.* non-Christians; *cf.* Eph. 2:3. *Who have no hope*; *cf.* Eph. 2:12. The hopelessness of the pagan world in face of death can be illustrated by much contemporary literary and inscriptional material. **14** *Since we believe that Jesus died and rose again*; the quintessence of the gospel (*cf.* 1 Cor. 15:3f.). *Even so, through Jesus, God will bring with him those who have fallen asleep*; *i.e.* bring them back from death, by resurrection, as He brought Jesus back. Albeit at a later date, they will rise with Jesus, sharing His resurrection (*cf.* 1 Cor. 15:20ff.). The prepositional phrase *through* (by means of) *Jesus*

(Gk. *dia tou Iēsou*) 'points to Jesus as the mediating link between His people's sleep and their resurrection at the hands of God' (G. Milligan). *Cf.* Rom. 8:11; 1 Cor. 15:18. Death through Jesus is but the prelude to resurrection with Jesus.

15 *By the word of the Lord*; *i.e.* on the authority of an utterance of Christ Himself. We do not find an exact equivalent to what follows in any of His sayings preserved in the Gospels, but that need not imply that Paul is quoting a private revelation made to himself as a prophet. *We who are alive, who are left until the coming of the Lord*. If here Paul groups himself with those who would be alive at that date, yet a few years later, in 1 Cor. 6:14 and 2 Cor. 4:14, he groups himself with those who would be raised from the dead. His estimate of the probability one way or the other might vary from time to time, but as he did not know when the *parousia* would take place, he could not know whether he would in fact be alive or dead when it happened. *Shall not precede* or 'have any advantage over'. **16** *The Lord himself*; for the emphasis *cf.* Acts 1:11, 'this same Jesus'. *With a cry of command* (Gk. *keleusma*; *cf.* its solitary LXX occurrence in Pr. 30:27, 'the locust marches at one word of command'). *With the archangel's call*; it is doubtful if we should think of Michael or any other individual archangel here. *And with the sound of the trumpet of God*; *cf.* Mt. 24:31; 1 Cor. 15:52 ('the last trump'). The command, the call and the trumpet may be different figures for the same event. The language reflects the theophanic passages of the OT; *cf.* Joel 2:1ff., especially v. 11. *The dead in Christ*; *cf.* on v. 14; 1 Cor. 15:18; Rev. 14:13. **17** *Shall be caught up*; Greek *harpagēsometha*, Latin *rapiemur*, whence the event is sometimes called the 'rapture' or snatching away of the saints. *In the clouds*; *cf.* Dn. 7:13; Mk. 13:26; 14:62; Rev. 1:7. The clouds which invest the advent of the Son of man, like those at the transfiguration (Mk. 9:7) and the ascension (Acts 1:9), betoken a theophany, the presence of the divine glory or *šeķînâ* (*cf.* also Ex. 24:15ff.; 40:34ff.; 1 Ki. 8:10f.). *To meet the Lord* (Gk. *eis apantēsin tou kyriou*). When a dignitary paid an official visit or *parousia* to a city in Hellenistic times, the action of the leading citizens in going out to meet him and escorting him on the final stage of his journey was called the *apantēsis*; it is similarly used in Mt. 25:6; Acts 28:15. So the Lord is pictured as escorted to the earth by His people—those newly raised from death and those who have remained alive. *And so we shall always be with the Lord*; the climax of blessedness.

5:1 *But as to the times and the seasons*; Greek *chronoi* and *kairoi*, denoting respectively the ages to elapse before the *parousia* and the critical epochs marking these ages (so Milligan). **2** *The day of the Lord will come like a thief in the night*. For the simile *cf.* Mt. 24:43; Lk. 12:39; Rev. 3:3; 16:15. See also Lk. 21:34ff. for a parallel simile, and Lk. 17:24ff. for the general teaching.

From his words *you yourselves know well* we may infer that Paul had already given them some oral teaching to this effect, based on the words of Jesus. Paul here identifies the OT *day of the Lord* with the second coming of Christ. 3 *As travail comes upon a woman with child*. The woes preceding the inauguration of the Messianic age are called in Jewish literature *ḥeḇlô šel māšîaḥ* ('the birthpangs of Messiah'); *cf.* Mk. 13:8, 'the beginning of travail'. 5 *Sons of light*; *cf.* Lk. 16:8. The terms 'sons of light' and 'sons of darkness' for the elect and non-elect figure prominently in the Qumran literature. *Sons of the day*; not merely a synonym for *sons of light*, but marking believers out as partakers of the glory to be revealed on the day of the Lord. 6 *Let us not sleep*. If we are *sons of light* and *sons of the day*, let us behave accordingly.

The following verses present a close parallel to Lk. 21:34–36. 8 *The breastplate of faith and love, and for a helmet the hope of salvation*. See 1:3 for the triad of graces, and for an elaboration of the armour metaphor *cf.* Eph. 6:11ff. Is. 59:17 is a background for both passages. 9 *God has not destined us for wrath, but to obtain salvation*; *cf.* 1:10 and Rom. 5:9. There, as here, the *wrath* is the judgment of the day of the Lord. *Whether we wake or sleep*; *i.e.* whether we survive to His coming or have died. The words are the same as those above for moral watchfulness and carelessness respectively, but Paul does not mean that it will not matter in the end whether we have been watchful and sober or not! He means, as in 4:15ff., that no difference will be made between living and dead saints at Christ's appearing; both groups will live together, and live with Christ, since He died for them. *Cf.* Rom. 14:9. 'The real point of this whole paragraph, whose motto, Watch and Pray, should be graven on the shield of every Christian warrior, is the paradox so difficult to us, but much less difficult to minds schooled in the prophets, of stressing the imminence of the Parousia while denying its immediacy' (W. Neil).

5:12–22 GENERAL EXHORTATIONS

They are exhorted to lead orderly and peaceable lives, active in well-doing.

12 *Respect those who labour among you and are over you in the Lord and admonish you*; *i.e.* give them practical acknowledgment by submitting to their guidance. The term *pro-istamenoi* ('those who are over you', 'leaders') used here appears also in Rom. 12:8 of the leaders of the Roman church; they are no doubt identical with those elsewhere called pastors, elders and bishops. Presumably they had been appointed by the missionaries, like the elders of the Galatian churches (Acts 14:23), but there is no record of this. 14 *And we exhort you, brethren*. It may be that in this verse the leaders themselves are addressed. *Admonish the idle*; RV 'the disorderly', lit. 'those who do not remain in the ranks' or 'those who play truant' (Gk. *ataktous*),

referring here to 'loafers' (Moffatt), who neglected their daily duty and lived in idleness; *cf.* 4:11. 15 *See that none of you repays evil for evil*. The ethical injunctions of the Pauline Epistles contain clear echoes of the teaching of Jesus; *cf.* Rom. 12:17. 16–18 *Rejoice . . . pray . . . give thanks*. Christian life is to be lived in an atmosphere of continual joy, prayer and gratitude to God. 19–21 *Do not quench the Spirit, do not despise prophesying, but test everything*. The reference here is to the exercise of the gift of prophecy, under the impulse of the Holy Spirit, a common phenomenon in the church of apostolic days. The gift was easily counterfeited, and called for discernment (*test everything*), especially on the part of the leaders. The gift itself was not to be disdained, and genuine prophecy was not to be repressed, for that would amount to 'quenching the Spirit'. 21, 22 *Hold fast what is good, abstain from every form of evil*. These clauses should probably be taken together as a pair of complementary injunctions. *Form of evil* is lit. 'species (Gk. *eidos*) of evil'. The AV 'appearance of evil' is based on the other sense of *eidos*.

5:23–28 PRAYER, FINAL GREETING AND BENEDICTION

23 *The God of peace himself*; *cf.* Rom. 15:33 and other references in note on 2 Thes. 3:16. *Sanctify you wholly*; *i.e.* bring to completion the work of sanctification already begun (*cf.* on 4:7); the aorist optative *hagiasai* here indicates 'a "process seen in perspective", and so contemplated as a complete act' (Hogg and Vine). *May your spirit and soul and body be kept sound and blameless*. This clause expresses the same prayer in a new way; the aorist optative is again used with the same force (*tērētheiē*). It is not certain that *spirit and soul and body* should be interpreted as teaching a formal tripartite doctrine of human nature, *spirit* being the 'God-conscious' aspect and *soul* the 'self-conscious' aspect of the inner life. One might as well deduce a formal quadripartite doctrine from Mk. 12:30. *At the coming of our Lord Jesus Christ. Cf.* 3:13 for the same emphasis. 24 probably means that He who calls His people to holiness is He who also makes them holy. 27 *I adjure you by the Lord that this letter be read to all the brethren*. It is not clear why Paul so solemnly puts the recipients on oath to read the letter to every member of the community. Harnack's theory that there were two distinct groups in the Thessalonian church, one Gentile and the other Jewish, and that, while this Epistle was primarily directed to the Gentile group, Paul wished its contents to be communicated to the Jewish group as well, cannot be maintained. Possibly he wished to make sure that those members who were 'playing truant' (v. 14) heard what he had to say. But his words may be no more than a solemn direction to read the letter at a meeting of the whole church.

2 Thessalonians

INTRODUCTION

DATE, AUTHORSHIP, CANONICITY

The second Epistle to the Thessalonians, like the first, is addressed 'to the church of the Thessalonians' by 'Paul, Silvanus, and Timothy'. The situation with which it deals is to a large degree similar to that dealt with by the first Epistle. This suggests that it also was sent from Corinth, and not long after the despatch of the earlier letter. Like 1 Thessalonians, this letter appears too in the earliest lists of Pauline letters that have come down to us. The external evidence for its canonicity is as good as for that of the first Epistle. It is quoted by Polycarp (c. AD 120).

Yet several difficulties have been felt to stand in the way of accepting this internal and external evidence at face value. The style of 2 Thessalonians is said to be formal and official by contrast with that of 1 Thessalonians. This point does not amount to much; it arises from such expressions as 'we are bound' and 'as is fitting' in 1:3, which really call for no special explanation—certainly not that offered by Dibelius, that 2 Thessalonians, unlike 1 Thessalonians, was written specifically to be read in church (see 1 Thes. 5:27).

More serious is the argument that 2 Thessalonians insists that certain events must precede the day of the Lord (ch. 2), whereas 1 Thessalonians stresses the unexpectedness of that day's arrival, 'like a thief in the night'. But a distinction should be made between suddenness and immediacy; Paul's words about the suddenness of Christ's return in 1 Thessalonians had been interpreted to imply its immediacy, and this made it necessary to point out that a number of things must happen first.

In describing these things, however, 2 Thessalonians uses apocalyptic language unparalleled elsewhere in the Pauline letters. We have, in fact, a tiny apocalypse in 2 Thes. 2:3–12. This is not an adequate argument against the authenticity of the letter, and, indeed, present-day knowledge of apocalyptic beliefs at that time, with special reference to the manifestation of antichrist, has done much to reduce what was once felt to be a great difficulty here (see Commentary below).

The similarities between the two Thessalonian Epistles have also been felt to constitute, in their way, almost as great a problem as the differences. In spite of the first Epistle's warning against restless idleness arising from excessive eschatological expectation, the same situation is implied by the second Epistle. However, if the first Epistle's emphasis on the suddenness of the *parousia* had been understood to mean its immediacy, the tendency for some to 'play truant' would have been strengthened, in spite of all the admonitions to remain calm and get on with the ordinary business of life.

RELATION TO 1 THESSALONIANS

There are real difficulties in the relation between the two Epistles, and they are largely due to our very inadequate information about the circumstances at Thessalonica. Apart from the attempt to cut the knot by regarding 2 Thessalonians as pseudonymous, various theories have been propounded to account for the difficulty in relating the two Epistles to each other.

One of these makes 2 Thessalonians earlier than 1 Thessalonians. There is no *a priori* objection to this; Paul's letters to churches are arranged in descending order of length, not in chronological order. This theory does indeed help in some respects (*cf.* T. W. Manson, *Studies in the Gospels and Epistles*, 1962, pp. 268ff., for the view that 2 Thessalonians was taken to Thessalonica by Timothy on the occasion mentioned in 1 Thes. 3:2). But 2 Thessalonians does seem to imply some previous correspondence by letter (*cf.* 2:2, 15; 3:17), whereas 1 Thessalonians certainly appears to be the first letter written to the Thessalonian church after Paul's departure (see 2:17 – 3:10).

Harnack's theory has already been mentioned —that 1 Thessalonians was written to the Gentile section of the Thessalonian church and 2 Thessalonians to the Jewish section. The apocalyptic teaching of 2 Thes. 2, it was supposed, would be more intelligible to Jews. But it is incredible that Paul of all people would have acquiesced in such a division between Gentile and Jewish Christians to the extent of writing a separate letter to each; we should certainly have found him taking the line he took at Antioch when a division of that sort began to appear there (see Gal. 2:11ff.) and making the inculcation of Christian unity his first concern in writing to them.

Yet another suggestion is F. C. Burkitt's— 'that both Letters were drafted by Silvanus– Silas, that they were read to Paul, who approved them and added 1 Thess. ii 18 and 2 Thess. iii 17 with his own hand'. This suggestion does not greatly help us—in any case Burkitt intended it as a supplement to Harnack's hypothesis—and 2 Thes. 3:17 seems rather intended to authenticate the whole letter as Paul's own (despite Burkitt's idea that the terms of Paul's autographed postscript 'suggest that he is not wholly responsible for all the rest').

In fine, all these suggestions raise greater difficulties than the view that 2 Thessalonians was sent by Paul (in association with his two companions) to the whole Thessalonian church no long time after the despatch of 1 Thessalonians, to deal with a development of the earlier situation of which fresh news had come to him. The persecution of the Christians seems to have died down, and there appears to have been no occasion to repeat his previous warning about moral purity. But the eschatological excitement had not abated—partly because Paul's words in 1 Thessalonians were misunderstood and partly through some teaching which they had received from other quarters, and which was perhaps represented as having Paul's authority. It was therefore necessary to deal more explicitly and sharply with this particular question.

OUTLINE OF CONTENTS

COMMENTARY

1:1, 2 SALUTATION

1 *Paul, Silvanus, and Timothy, To the church of the Thessalonians . . . .* A comparison with the salutation of the first Epistle makes it as certain as anything can be that both Epistles were written to the whole Thessalonian church. *In God our Father and the Lord Jesus Christ.* See on 1 Thes. 1:1 for this expression. **2** *From God the Father and the Lord Jesus Christ.* Common in Paul's epistolary salutations, but not in 1 Thes. 1:1.

1:3–12 THANKSGIVING AND ENCOURAGEMENT

3 *We are bound to give thanks to God . . . as is fitting.* The alleged formality of this language has been contrasted with the language of 1 Thes. 1:2ff. and used as an argument against the authenticity of 2 Thessalonians. But if the Thessalonian Christians had protested against what they considered the excessive commendation expressed in the previous letter, Paul might well reply: 'But it is only right that we should thank God for you; it is the least we can do'; and that is the force of the wording here. **4** *We ourselves boast of you in the churches of God.* This is not inconsistent with 1 Thes. 1:8, 'we need not say anything'; even if there was no need, they would speak all the same. *Cf.* 1 Thes. 2:20.
5 *Evidence of the righteous judgment of God.* As in 1 Thes. 3:3f., so here, he points out that their affliction is a proof of the genuineness of their faith, and that their steadfast endurance of it marks them as worthy to inherit the divine kingdom: in them, as in their persecutors, God's righteousness will be vindicated. **6, 7** *To repay with affliction those who afflict you, and to grant*

rest with us to you who are afflicted. The day of Christ's return will be the day of equitable retribution and reward. The *rest* is relaxation or relief (Gk. *anesis*) after toil and conflict. *When the Lord Jesus is revealed from heaven.* The reference is to His manifestation in glory (*cf.* Lk. 17:30; 1 Cor. 1:7). *With his mighty angels.* *Cf.* Mt. 25:31; Mk. 8:38; and other passages mentioned in the note on 1 Thes. 3:13. *In flaming fire.* This again reflects the theophanic language of the OT (*cf.* Ps. 18:8ff.; Is. 66:15). **8** *Inflicting vengeance.* The exercise of judgment by Christ in the NT is based on Dn. 7:13f.; *cf.* Jn. 5:27; Acts 17:31. *Who do not know God*; *i.e.* who ignore Him, 'refuse to have God in their knowledge' (*cf.* Rom. 1:28; 1 Thes. 4:5). **9** *Eternal destruction*; *i.e.* the destruction which belongs to the age to come, with the decisive implication of finality. It consists in *exclusion from the presence of the Lord*, with whom alone is 'the fountain of life'. **10** *To be glorified in his saints.* This might mean His holy angels (see on 1 Thes. 3:13), but the parallelism with the following words, *and to be marvelled at in all who have believed*, suggests that Christian men and women are meant here. They are to share His glory; the 'revealing of the Lord Jesus from heaven' (v. 7) is also the day of 'the revealing of the sons of God' (Rom. 8:19).
11 *That our God may make you worthy of his call.* This probably looks forward to the day of recompense at the *parousia*, that they may on that day be adjudged to have acquitted themselves worthily of their calling; even so, it implies a prayer for their present spiritual progress. *And may fulfil every good resolve*; RV, 'every desire of goodness'. This refers to their own desires, while it is of course true that every such desire, like every *work of faith*, is produced in them by the Holy Spirit (*cf.* Gal. 5:22; Phil.

2:13). **12** *So that the name of our Lord Jesus may be glorified in you, and you in him.* The reference again is primarily to the *parousia*, but Paul's prayer would be fulfilled then only if the Lord's name were glorified in them day by day through life.

2:1–12 EVENTS TO PRECEDE THE DAY OF THE LORD

Some of the Thessalonian Christians had somehow got it into their heads that the day of the Lord had already begun. Paul explains that it must be preceded by the great apostasy, led by the antichrist, who is to be brought to nought by the advent of the day of the Lord.

1 *Concerning the coming;* the Greek preposition is *hyper*. *Our assembling to meet him;* a reference probably to the event described in 1 Thes. 4:17, when those who survive to the *parousia* will be 'caught up together' with those who are raised from the dead 'to meet the Lord in the air'. **2** *Either by spirit or by word, or by letter purporting to be from us; i.e.* neither prophetic utterance, nor more ordinary oral communication, nor a letter purporting to come from Paul or his companions must be allowed to mislead them. It is not plain whether Paul suspected that a letter in his name had actually been sent to the Thessalonians without his authorization. Certainly it would be unwarranted to suppose that this remark casts any doubt on the authenticity of 1 Thessalonians. Even if 2 Thessalonians were pseudonymous, it is unlikely that its author would have intended to throw suspicion on 1 Thessalonians. Possibly the reference to the *letter purporting to be from us* alludes to false conclusions drawn from the wording of 1 Thessalonians. But more probably Paul suspected that the idea that the day of the Lord had already started had been conveyed to the Thessalonians' minds by some kind of communication claiming his authority, but he had no certain information on this point. *That the day of the Lord has come;* RV 'is now present', *i.e.* 'has already set in' (Gk. *enestēken*). *Cf.* 1 Thes. 5:2. **3** *That day will not come.* This apodosis to the conditional clause has to be supplied; it means, 'the day of the Lord will not begin'. *Unless the rebellion comes first;* Gk. *apostasia* (whence our 'apostasy'), here used of the end-time revolt against the rule of God. *And the man of lawlessness is revealed.* 'The lawless one' (*cf.* v. 8), otherwise called antichrist and Belial and 'the beast from the abyss' (*cf.* Rev. 11:7), is the leader of the great eschatological rebellion against God. *The son of perdition;* a Hebraism, meaning here 'he who is doomed to destruction'; the same phrase is used of Judas Iscariot in Jn. 17:12 where it means rather 'the lost boy'. **4** *Who opposes and exalts himself against every so-called god or object of worship.* The language here echoes the description of the pre-Christian 'antichrist', Antiochus Epiphanes, in Dn. 7:25; 8:9ff.; 11:36ff.; *cf.* also Rev. 13.

So that he takes his seat in the temple of God. This part of the picture of antichrist probably reflects the attempt by the Emperor Gaius in AD 40 to have his statue set up in the Temple at Jerusalem. That crisis brought vividly to the minds of Christians the eschatological discourse of Jesus preserved in Mk. 13. The words 'when ye see the abomination of desolation standing where he ought not' (Mk. 13:14, RV; note that a person is referred to) seemed specially applicable to the emperor's policy. **5** *Do you not remember . . . ?* An interesting sidelight on the element of apocalyptic in the early *kērygma*.

6 may be paraphrased: 'You know what holds him back, so that he will not make a public appearance before the time appointed for him.' *What is restraining him* is impersonal here, but personal in v. 7; this throws light on the meaning. The apostle is intentionally vague in writing this, but he appears to have been more explicit in his oral teaching at Thessalonica. This supports the view that the Roman Empire is the restraining agency, since it may be considered either as an impersonal power, or as embodied personally in the emperor. After the accusation brought against Paul at Thessalonica (Acts 17:6f.), any allusion to the imperial power—especially to its prospective abolition—had best be as vague as possible lest the letter fall into the wrong hands. **7** *For the mystery of lawlessness is already at work.* The principle of rebellion against God is already operating (*e.g.* in the opposition offered to the gospel in Thessalonica and elsewhere), but it is not openly enthroned in the world as it will be for the brief duration of antichrist's domination, because of him *who now restrains it.* Here the agency that holds the spirit of godless revolt in check is personal, indicating the emperor himself. Others, however, have regarded the restrainer as being as much an apocalyptic figure as antichrist, *e.g.* the angel of the abyss (Rev. 9:1; 20:1); in that case, however, Paul's reference might have been more explicit. Even less plausible is the suggestion that the Holy Spirit is intended, or the theory that Paul refers to his apostolic ministry as due to be completed before the End. But if the restrainer is the emperor, we need not think that the reigning Emperor Claudius (AD 41–54) is specifically referred to, or that Paul was thinking of Nero as Claudius's heir whose accession was held in check so long as Claudius lived. Nero was only 12 years old in AD 50, and some of Paul's warmest tributes to the Roman power (especially Rom. 13:1–7) were written after Nero came to the throne. But Paul had frequent reason to be grateful for the protection of the imperial authorities, who restrained the forces most opposed to the gospel. When such protection was withdrawn, the forces of antichrist would be able to work their will. How the same political power could at one stage restrain the anarchic forces which threatened the gospel and at another appear as the chief of those forces may be appreciated by comparing Rom. 13:1–7 with Rev. 13 (cf. also 1 Pet. 2:13–17; 3:13, alongside 4:12ff.).

Until he is out of the way. The subject of this clause is the restrainer, but it would be considered seditious to speak explicitly of the removal of the emperor; hence Paul's vagueness. The Greek *ek mesou genesthai*, 'to be taken out of the way', is a quasi-passive form corresponding to the active *ek mesou airein*, 'to take out of the way' (1 Cor. 5:2; Col. 2:14; and *cf.* Lat. *e medio tollere*). Failure to recognize this idiom has led some to force upon the words here a literalist translation, 'until he (antichrist) become (*i.e.* appear) out of the midst'; but that is not Paul's meaning. **8** *And then the lawless one will be revealed.* Here we have the normal Greek construction (*ho anomos*) corresponding to the Semitizing 'man of lawlessness' of v. 3. His revealing or unveiling precedes that of the true Christ. *With the breath of his mouth*; *i.e.* by His Word; *cf.* Is. 11:4; Rev. 19:15. *By his appearing and his coming*; *i.e.* 'by the manifestation (Gk. *epiphaneia*) of His *parousia*'. 9 Antichrist also has his *parousia* (*coming*). For his being energized by Satan *with all power and with pretended signs and wonders cf.* Rev. 13:2, 13ff. **10** *Because they refused to love the truth.* That refusal to accept God's truth is the certain precursor of infatuation by error is similarly taught in Rom. 1:18ff. **11** *To make them believe what is false*; lit., 'the lie', the false counterpart of *the truth* of vv. 10, 12; *cf.* again Rom. 1:25, which is literally 'who exchanged the truth of God for the lie'. In Zoroastrianism, too, 'The Lie' (Avestan *druj*) denotes the whole system of evil.

On this whole section (vv. 1–12) Geerhardus Vos's chapter 'The Man of Sin' in *The Pauline Eschatology*, 1930 (pp. 94ff.), is specially deserving of study.

2:13 – 3:5 FURTHER THANKSGIVING AND ENCOURAGEMENT

13 *But we are bound to give thanks to God always for you*; *cf.* 1:3. *Brethren beloved by the Lord*; *cf.* 1 Thes. 1:4. *God chose you from the beginning*; see on 1 Thes. 1:4, where Paul indicates the ground of his certainty that they were chosen by God. We should probably understand *from the beginning* to denote the eternity of God's choice, as in Eph. 1:4. Had Paul meant the earliest days of his preaching at Thessalonica he would probably have used such an expression as 'the beginning of the gospel' (Phil. 4:15). We should note the variant reading 'firstfruits' (Gk. *aparchēn*) for *from the beginning* (Gk. *ap' archēs*); both are well attested, but *ap' archēs* is probably to be preferred. If 'firstfruits' were read, the idea might be that of Jas. 1:18, a carrying over into Christian phraseology of the Jewish idea of Israel as God's firstfruits among the nations. Harnack, in line with his theory of the destination of this Epistle, took *aparchēn* to imply that the Jewish believers were the 'firstfruits' of

Paul's mission at Thessalonica. *To be saved.* 'The thirteenth and fourteenth verses of this chapter are a system of theology in miniature. The apostle's thanksgiving covers the whole work of salvation from the eternal choice of God to the obtaining of the glory of our Lord Jesus Christ in the world to come' (J. Denney). *Through sanctification by the Spirit*; *cf.* 1 Thes. 4:3ff.; the Holy Spirit is the Sanctifier, in that He sets believers apart for God, unites them to Christ, and reproduces the likeness of Christ in their lives, in view of the day when they are publicly to share Christ's glory. **14** *So that you may obtain the glory of our Lord Jesus Christ*; *i.e.* at His *parousia*. *Cf.* 1 Thes. 3:13; 5:23; Rom. 2:6ff.; 8:18ff., 30.

15 *Hold to the traditions*; *i.e.* the things handed on to you (Gk. *paradosis*). With this term are associated two Greek verbs *paralambanein*, 'to receive in turn', 'to have handed down to one' (*cf.* 1 Thes. 2:13; 4:1; 2 Thes. 3:6), and *paradidonai*, 'to hand on in turn', both being found in conjunction, *e.g.*, in 1 Cor. 11:23; 15:3. Emphasis is laid on the continuity of the transmission of the truth of Christianity; the tradition is identical with the apostolic testimony, resting on the authority of Christ Himself. (See O. Cullmann, *The Early Church*, 1956, pp. 59–99.) *Either by word of mouth or by letter*; 'whether by our oral or written teaching'. The *letter* he has in mind is doubtless 1 Thessalonians. **16, 17** *Now may our Lord Jesus Christ himself, and God our Father, . . . comfort your hearts.* As frequently (*cf.* 1 Thes. 3:11), the Lord Jesus and God the Father are united in action. Here, as in 2 Cor. 13:14, the Lord Jesus Christ is placed first. 'The only theological significance to be attached to the variations in order is that there is complete equality in the apostle's mind between the Father and the Son' (W. Neil).

3:1 *Finally, brethren, pray for us*; *cf.* 1 Thes. 5:25. *That the word of the Lord may speed on and triumph*; *cf.* Ps. 147:15 ('His word runs swiftly'). The reference here, of course, is to the gospel, which Paul and his companions were proclaiming at Corinth. **2** It is probably with special reference to dangers at Corinth that he requests prayer *that we may be delivered from wicked and evil men*. The Greek word *atopos*, here rendered *wicked*, means literally 'out of place', hence 'untoward', 'improper', 'perverse'. Paul is thinking primarily of his Jewish opponents. *For not all have faith.* This may mean 'all men do not exercise faith' (in Christ), or 'all men do not hold the faith' (*i.e.* the gospel). It makes no difference to the general sense here whether we understand *faith* as subjective (*fides quâ creditur*) or as objective (*fides quae creditur*), but the former is more probable at this stage. **3** *But the Lord is faithful*; Gk. *pistos*, an easy transition from *pistis*, the last word of the preceding sentence; *pistos* is the first word of the new sentence in the Greek. *Cf.* 1 Thes. 5:24. *Guard you from evil*; RSV mg., 'guard you from the evil one'. Here, as in the Lord's Prayer (Mt.

6:13), we should probably understand the evil (Gk. *ponēros*) as personal. **4** *And we have confidence.* For similar expressions of confidence *cf.* 1 Thes. 4:1, 9f.; 5:11. **5** *May the Lord direct your hearts to the love of God.* The Lord Jesus is the subject. *The love of God* may be either their (increasing) love for Him or (a fuller appreciation of) His love for them. It would be natural to suppose that the construction is the same as that of the following phrase, *and to the steadfastness of Christ*; to suppose, in other words, that both genitives are subjective. The *steadfastness* is an attribute of Christ Himself which the writer desires to see reproduced in His people; we should therefore take *the love of God* to be the love which God shows to men. The AV translation, 'the patient waiting for Christ', is a less natural way of understanding the words; if it were right, it would suggest that *the love of God* similarly is our love for Him (which indeed is but the response called forth by His love; *cf.* Rom. 5:5; 1 Jn. 4:19).

3:6–15 THE NEED FOR DISCIPLINE

They must dissociate themselves from those of their number who refuse to work for their living.

6 *We command you . . . in the name of our Lord Jesus Christ.* Apostolic authority is fundamentally the authority of Christ; the apostles are His accredited ambassadors. *Any brother who is living in idleness* (Gk. *ataktōs*); *cf.* the adj. *ataktous* in 1 Thes. 5:14; here, as there, we have a military metaphor, denoting those who 'break rank' or 'play truant'. He reverts to the problem of those who neglect to earn their own living, instead of following *the tradition . . . received from us.* This practical aspect of the *tradition* was emphasized by example as well as by precept; **7–9** for the words of these verses, drawing attention to the apostles' own behaviour in this regard, *cf.* 1 Thes. 2:6ff. and other passages cited in our notes there. **10** *If any one will not work, let him not eat.* This may be a Jewish proverb based on Gn. 3:17ff. Even Rabbis were expected to earn their living by manual labour and not to make the teaching of the law a means of gain; thus Paul maintained himself by working in leather. **11** *Living in idleness, mere busybodies.* There

is a word-play here in the Greek, *mēden ergazomenous alla periergazomenous*: 'Busybodies instead of busy' (Moffatt); 'neglecting their own business to mind other people's' (Knox); 'minding everybody's business but their own'. **12** *To do their work in quietness and to earn their own living*; lit. 'eat their own bread' (AV), *i.e.* the bread they have earned themselves. 'Stop fussing, stop idling, and stop sponging' (W. Neil). *Cf.* 1 Thes. 4:11. **13** *Do not be weary in well-doing*; *cf.* Gal. 6:9.

14 *If any one refuses to obey what we say in this letter, note that man.* Again the apostolic authority is stressed (*cf.* v. 12). It is not formal excommunication that is enjoined, but such practical expression of disapproval as will make the 'loafers' ashamed of themselves and mend their ways. **15** But they are not to be treated as outsiders, 'as a Gentile and a tax collector' (Mt. 18:17); they are still brethren, members of the Christian community, responsive (it is hoped) to this brotherly discipline.

3:16–18 PRAYER, FINAL GREETING AND BENEDICTION

Paul takes his leave of the Thessalonians with a prayer for their blessing, pointing out that his personal signature authenticates this and other letters as genuinely his.

16 *The Lord of peace*; He who is 'the author of peace and lover of concord'; *cf.* 'the God of peace' in 1 Thes. 5:23; Rom. 15:33; 16:20; Phil. 4:9; Heb. 13:20; also 1 Cor. 14:33; 2 Cor. 13:11. **17** *I, Paul, write this greeting with my own hand. This is the mark in every letter of mine*; *it is the way I write.* Lest they should be misled by a letter purporting to come from him, he draws their attention to the fact that all his letters are authenticated by some words in his own handwriting at the end. For the most part, he made use of amanuenses in writing his letters (*cf.* Tertius, Rom. 16:22). There is a reference to the character of his own handwriting in Gal. 6:11. **18** *The grace of our Lord Jesus Christ be with you all*; the same benediction (with the addition of *all*) as in 1 Thes. 5:28 (and Rom. 16:20).

F. F. BRUCE

The Pastoral Epistles

INTRODUCTION

OCCASION AND PURPOSE

Behind these three Epistles there is a specific historical situation which is nevertheless not easy to piece together. In 1 Timothy Paul has recently left Timothy at Ephesus (1 Tim. 1:3). In Titus he has recently been with Titus in Crete (Tit. 1:5) and appears to be, at the time of writing, at Nicopolis where he requests Titus to join him (Tit. 3:12). This latter city was in all probability the place of that name in Epirus. By the time 2 Timothy was written the apostle is a prisoner who anticipates that his end is not far off. He has at some time been in Rome (2 Tim. 1:17) and has recently left some of his belongings at Troas (2 Tim. 4:13). Moreover, he has been to Miletus where he had to leave behind his companion Trophimus, who was ill (2 Tim. 4:20), while another associate, Erastus, has remained behind at Corinth. From all these allusions it is evident that, shortly before writing these Epistles, Paul has travelled respectively in Asia, in Crete and in parts of Europe. He appears to be back at Rome by the time that 2 Timothy was written.

In spite of various attempts, these historical data cannot be fitted into the framework of Acts and it seems highly probable, therefore, that Paul's movements reflected in these Epistles must be placed subsequent to his house imprisonment in Rome mentioned in Acts 28:30. This involves the assumption that he was released from this imprisonment, which some consider to be highly unlikely (but see discussion below on this point). There is good reason to believe that he could have expected a release on the basis of the charges preferred against him in Acts. If such a release be assumed, it must be supposed that he was later rearrested, perhaps in the region of Nicopolis, and taken back to Rome, where tradition has it that he suffered martyrdom.

If the historical occasion has thus been correctly understood, it is possible to define the purpose of these Epistles with some precision. Clearly Paul realizes that his time on earth is nearly done, and his mind is set upon giving guidance to those who are to follow him in positions of responsibility. He is considering the demands of church organization and writes to confirm certain matters, mainly about church officials, which he must already have imparted orally to his associates (cf. Tit. 1:5). In all probability Timothy, who was timid by nature, needed the authoritative written instructions of the apostle in order to put them into practice.

He could then appeal to the apostle's letter in any case of dispute (cf. 1 Tim. 3:14, 15). These Epistles contain a variety of topics, not all of which are concerned with ecclesiastical discipline. There were certain problems about false teachers over which his associates needed advice, but they are not told how to answer the heresies. The main injunction is to avoid them because of their irrelevancies (see section below on the false teachers). In writing to Timothy, the apostle on more than one occasion issues a solemn charge to him, which suggests that he had some apprehension about Timothy's resolution.

A more specific purpose lies behind 2 Timothy than behind the others, for this Epistle is undoubtedly the apostle's last letter. He urges Timothy to stir up the gift he has already received (2 Tim. 1:3–7), reminds him of his own example (3:10ff.) and exhorts him to preach the word (4:2f.). The concluding chapter of this Epistle is particularly revealing of the mind of Paul at the conclusion of his life. He knows that he has fought a good fight (4:7) and is ready to depart. He refers to his first defence (4:16) and poignantly remarks that all had deserted him, but that the Lord stood by him. There is a touching request for some books, parchments and a cloak which he had left behind at Troas (4:13). This Epistle has been described as Paul's swan-song.

AUTHORSHIP

Many scholars do not regard these Epistles as authentic Pauline letters, and the reasons for this must be briefly mentioned, although they cannot be fully discussed. Each of these Epistles makes the claim to have been written by the apostle Paul, but those who dispute his authorship regard this as merely a literary device. As the following indications will show, there are strong reasons for regarding the claims to apostolic authorship to be authentic.

The *historical* situation mentioned above has led some to treat the personal allusions either as non-authentic, because they will not fit into the Acts story, or else as fragments of genuine Pauline letters which have been incorporated into pseudonymous epistles. As pointed out already, there is strong possibility that Paul was released from the Roman imprisonment of Acts 28, and if so the difficulty disappears. Any theory which postulates that genuine fragments were incorporated into fictitious epistles raises more problems than it solves.

The *ecclesiastical* situation reflected in these Epistles is said by some to reveal a time too late for the apostle Paul. But the organization is certainly less developed than that in the time of the earliest apostolic Fathers and points to a definitely more primitive period. At the same time more interest is shown in ecclesiastical organization than in the other Pauline Epistles. An objection on this ground would carry some weight if it could be shown that Paul was the kind of man who would not have concerned himself with the qualities of the men to be appointed; yet this cannot be shown. Since, on the first missionary journey, Paul and Barnabas appointed elders, they could not have been unmindful of the need for care in choosing those who were to lead God's people.

Another factor which has been claimed as non-Pauline is the *heresy* alluded to in these Epistles, because of its supposed connection with 2nd-century Gnosticism. But two considerations make this objection most inconclusive. The references in these Epistles are too general and too undeveloped in form to be connected immediately with the period of developed Gnosticism in the 2nd century. The second factor is the increasing recognition that Gnosticism had earlier forms which had their rise in the 1st century. There is therefore nothing intrinsically impossible in supposing that the Pastorals' heresy existed in the time of Paul. He does not refute the errors point by point as some claim that Paul would have done, because his associates, Timothy and Titus, knew his teaching well enough to do that when necessary. What they needed was advice not to waste time refuting idle chatter.

In the matter of *doctrine* another difficulty has been found in the fact that most of the major themes of the Pauline Epistles are lacking from the Pastorals. Moreover, there is a tendency in these Epistles for doctrine to be formalized into 'the truth' or 'the faith' or 'the deposit', which contrasts with the creative thinking of the apostle Paul. But allowance must be made both for the time when these Epistles were written (*i.e.* at the conclusion of Paul's work) and for the difference in the recipients (*i.e.* his trusted associates as compared with church groups who would need more detailed teaching). It is not impossible to imagine that the apostle could have written in this manner to those who had worked closely with him for some time.

More have been influenced to reject Pauline authorship by *linguistic* considerations than by any of the other arguments. It has been noted that many of the words in these Epistles are not used in Paul's other Epistles, and a large proportion of them not even elsewhere in the NT. Moreover, the style is said to be non-Pauline. Various statistical methods have been used in an attempt to demonstrate the differences of style between the Pastorals and the other Epistles. But such methods require bigger samples than those available within the group of Pauline

Epistles. The problem of language cannot be passed over, but two possibilities exist and both support belief in Pauline authorship. Either Paul had a greater range of vocabulary and variety of style than many scholars allow; or else he made use of an amanuensis in the writing of these letters, to whom he granted some liberty of expression.

No doubt there will continue to be much dispute about the authorship of these Epistles, but their authenticity has the greatest probability and is supported by strong external evidence.

THE FALSE TEACHERS

It is not surprising that errors arose in some of the early churches. Such an occurrence was foretold by our Lord. There was error in the church at Colossae and also among those groups addressed in the Johannine Epistles and in the Apocalypse. The false teachers in the Pastorals show certain tendencies, but the evidence does not support the view that they belong to a highly organized sect. As pointed out above, their tendencies have some affinities with Gnosticism, but show nothing of the development of that movement during the 2nd century.

The most striking feature is the apparent irrelevance of much of the teaching. Paul refers to 'stupid, senseless controversies' (2 Tim. 2:23), and these he considers to be 'unprofitable and futile' (Tit. 3:9). There was much disputing about words (2 Tim. 2:14) which does no good. 1 Tim. 6:20 and 2 Tim. 2:16 refer to 'godless chatter'. These teachers, therefore, were not so much propagating errors as wasting time on things which do not matter.

There was among some a tendency towards undue asceticism, in the form both of celibacy and of abstinence from meats (1 Tim. 4:1–4). There was a desire to be outwardly religious, but a lack of real power in the religious life (2 Tim. 3:1ff.). On the other hand some were giving way to licence and it is to be noted that Timothy himself is warned to guard his personal purity (1 Tim. 5:22; 2 Tim, 2:22).

One or two specific features may be noted. There was an interest in genealogies (see comment on 1 Tim. 1:4; *cf.* Tit. 3:9). Moreover, appeal to myths was prominent (*cf.* 1 Tim. 1:4; Tit. 1:14) and these appear to have been Jewish. In 1 Tim. 6:20 reference is made to 'contradictions of what is falsely called knowledge'. Although Marcion in the 2nd century published a book with the title *Antitheses* (Contradictions), there can be no connection, unless Marcion was influenced by 1 Tim. 6:20, which is highly unlikely. The word was in common use in reference to any subjects under dispute. At least two of the false teachers were spreading error about the resurrection (*cf.* 2 Tim. 2:18).

It is noteworthy that Paul's main advice to his associates is 'avoid!' He is concerned that they should not be side-tracked from their major calling of preaching the gospel. Much of his advice in these Epistles has relevance in the modern church's conflict with deviations.

DEVELOPING FORMS OF CHRISTIAN DOCTRINE AND CHURCH ORDER

There are significant signs in these Epistles of a process of development. The content of the faith is clearly becoming crystallized in brief confessional summaries, often so framed as to present a moral challenge. So we find numerous 'faithful sayings' (1 Tim. 1:15; 4:9; 2 Tim. 2:11; Tit. 3:8), which are said to be worthy of active appropriation and believing response. We find essential principles expounded and applied to particular practical problems in a form which not only can be clearly taught, but which is also meant to be pressed upon the faithful with exhortation to act accordingly.

Some points of fundamental Christian theology are explicitly emphasized in a new way in order to counter the prevalent false teaching. There is, for example, the marked emphasis on the essential nature, attributes and unity of God as the sovereign Creator and Saviour of all (see 1 Tim. 1:1, 17; 2:3–5; 4:4, 10; 6:13, 15, 16; 2 Tim. 2:13; Tit. 1:2, 3); on Christ as the only Mediator between God and men, on His Person and work, on His humanity and on His death, endured as a substitutionary ransom price, as the one and all-sufficient way of redemption,

spiritual renewal and consecration to God and His service (see 1 Tim. 1:1; 2:5, 6; 3:16; 2 Tim. 1:10; Tit. 2:13, 14; 3:5, 6).

There are evidences of an ordered and more regulated congregational worship, found in references to the necessary place of reading of Scripture, exhortation and teaching (1 Tim. 4:13), and of supplications, prayers, intercessions, thanksgivings (1 Tim. 2:1). There are traces of hymns, of credal and liturgical fragments, of doxologies (see 1 Tim. 3:16; 6:13–16; 2 Tim. 1:9, 10; 2:8, 11–13; 4:1; Tit. 2:11–14; 3:4–7). Guidance is given for the proper appointment of individuals to responsible oversight and ministry, in pastoral care and exposition of the Word; and plain and detailed warning is given of the dangers latent in unwise appointments. Each local congregation, or church, is recognized as a household of God, and a divinely intended warden of, and witness for, the truth. And such congregations are likely to prove steadfast and faithful in the face of perils from within as well as from without only if diligent attention is paid to such proper procedure (1 Tim. 3:15, RV). Yet underlying all such detailed guidance, and predominantly expressed through it, is the compelling awareness that what matters most of all is not the system but the men; the main stress is not on office and form but on genuine Christian character and on conscientious and consistent behaviour.

1 Timothy

OUTLINE OF CONTENTS

COMMENTARY

1:1, 2 PERSONAL ADDRESS AND GREETING

1 Paul writes as *an apostle*, as one conscious of a mission given to him by divine appointment. He writes as a servant of Jesus, recognized as Messiah or the Lord's anointed; he writes, therefore, as a man under orders, as an ambassador of 'King Jesus'. The form *Christ Jesus* is characteristic of this letter (*cf.* 1:12, 14, 15). This commission given to Paul is an expression of God's own activity to save men, and is directed towards helping men to find sure *hope* of this salvation in Christ. Such language indicates at once that this is more than a private, personal letter. **2** It is written to Timothy as to a genuine second-generation Christian, one of the true children in the faith of Christ, to whom Paul can look to carry on the work and witness of the gospel. Its contents concern Timothy's activity as a minister in the church, household or family of God (see 3:14, 15). The spontaneous way in which Christ is twice coupled with God Himself in these verses implies a significant recognition of His place in the Godhead.

1:3–20 A FORMER CHARGE REITERATED

1:3–11 A call to oppose false doctrine

3 Paul reminds Timothy of the particular task committed to him when he urged him to remain at Ephesus. He was to admonish those who are tending to turn aside to false and profitless teaching, and to recall them to sincere and devoted Christian living. It is noteworthy how quickly the churches were troubled from within by false teachers, and how Paul viewed such men with the most solemn gravity, and took deliberate and sustained precaution against their potentially fatal influence. *Cf.* 6:3–5; Acts 20:28–30; Gal. 1:6–9. The varied errors are all comprehensively described as the teaching of *different doctrine*. Note that this implies a recognized 'form of doctrine' or 'pattern of teaching' (Rom. 6:17) already generally accepted. **4** Here the danger is lest wrong attention be paid to (probably Jewish) *myths* and *genealogies*, possibly fanciful additions to, and interpretations of, the OT. To try to find hope in human descent or succession is inconclusive and unsatisfying, *i.e. endless*. Such inquiries give rise only to controversial questionings and *speculations*. *Divine training*; Gk. 'dispensation', 'stewardship' or 'order' (see RSV mg.). The meaning is either that they cannot further that dispensation of God in the gospel which offers men salvation by faith; or that they do not promote that effectual discharge of the stewardship of life, to which we are called as believers.

5 In contrast to these mistaken activities of some, the practical teaching of the gospel demands a response which is expressed in inner sincerity and active goodwill. The four characteristics of v. 5 are acquired in the reverse order. *Faith*, which is no mere pretence, is the foundation. This issues in the inward enjoyment of *a pure heart*, and the concern to preserve *a good conscience* (*cf.* Acts 24:16), and in the outward practice of *love* towards God and men. Such love is the end in view, the proper goal or completion of saving faith. *Cf.* Acts 15:9; 24:16; Gal. 5:6. **6** The aforementioned *certain persons* have not only failed to aim at and pursue this

end; they also *have wandered away into vain discussion*, or idle chatter, into an activity which is valueless instead of fruitful. **7** They are dominated by the desire to be authorities or *teachers of the law*, like Jewish Rabbis. Actually they have no proper understanding of the things concerning which they thus not only talk but even make self-confident assertions. They are, therefore, a serious danger to the Christian community, capable of deceiving and misleading many.

8–11 Lest his derogatory reference to would-be law-teachers should be misunderstood, Paul introduces a statement declaring that the law is good, and that it supports and complements the gospel by forbidding everything that is opposed to its wholesome teaching. The fault lies with the false teachers, who do not use the law as God intended it to be used, *i.e.* to restrain and convict evil-doers. It is not intended as material for fanciful interpretation and profitless speculation on the part of the righteous or justified man. Evil-doers are here described as lacking moral standards, reverence for God, a sense of the holy, and without regard for family relations, human life, sexual purity and social good faith. As a consequence they are unruly, sinful, profane, merciless. **9, 10** Paul obviously here follows the order of the Ten Commandments and bluntly specifies violations in their most extreme form. The *sound doctrine*, or wholesome, healthful teaching, is a phrase characteristic of, and peculiar to, the Pastoral Epistles. By contrast, false teaching is like gangrene (2 Tim. 2:17); and devotion to it a sign of spiritual sickness (1 Tim. 6:3, 4). **11** *The glorious gospel*; RV 'the gospel of the glory'. The genitive is one of content rather than of quality. God's glory is revealed to men in the gospel which tells men of Christ; 'the glory' is virtually a reference to Christ Himself. *Cf.* Jn. 1:14, 18; 2 Cor. 4:4, 6. *Blessed* here 'describes God as experiencing within Himself the perfection of bliss' (*TNTC*, p. 62).

1:12–17 Paul's own experience of salvation

12 Paul proceeds indirectly to encourage Timothy to a high yet humble view of his calling and to a sustained devotion to its discharge. This he does by a typical, parenthetical doxology to Christ and to God for his own amazing experience of divine mercy, and for his appointment by Christ to a stewardship of that gospel (note also v. 11), to which he first owed his own salvation. In the Christian experience the complement to trusting Christ and to being inwardly empowered by Him is to be trusted or treated as trustworthy by Him to fulfil some appointed *service*. The word here (Gk. *diakonia*, without the definite article) is potentially very general in reference, though Paul often uses it (and 'minister', Gk. *diakonos*), as no 2nd-century writer would have been likely to do, to refer to his apostolic office (*cf.* Rom. 11:13; 2 Cor. 3:6; 5:18; 6:3). **13** 'Injurious' (AV, RV; Gk. *hybristēs*) describes a doer of outrage, a man given to violence. It was when Paul was showing no mercy, as one strong in the conviction that he knew what was right, that he was treated mercifully, as one whose active unbelief prevented him from understanding the truth. **14** Such is the overflowing excess of divine *grace* (*cf.* Rom. 5:8, 10, 20), given to us in Christ Jesus, and moving us to live the characteristic Christian life of *faith and love,* instead of the typical sinful life of unbelief and enmity (so violently expressed in Saul before his conversion). **15** Thus it was through a deep, personal experience of its benefit that Paul both learned and exemplified the character and the trustworthiness of that gospel which he was appointed to beseech all men to believe (as *sure*) and to receive (as *worthy*). For he still (note the significant present tense, *I am*) knew himself as *the foremost* of sinners. He knew that the purpose of the incarnation of God's Son as Messiah Jesus was to save sinners like himself. This truth is here summed up by quoting a current primitive credal phrase. **16** Paul knew, too, that God's purpose in showing such a chief sinner as himself such utterly undeserved mercy was to make his life *an example,* or exhibit, of the full extent of Christ's long-suffering kindness (*i.e.* towards such a violent opponent). Such an exhibit would encourage others in the future to put their confidence in the same Saviour, and thus enter into the enjoyment of life eternal. **17** The doxology is noteworthy for the attributes ascribed to God. He is eternally sovereign, immune from decay, not observable by human eyes, the one and only true God. And when such words were publicly uttered it was for all to assent and to say, *Amen.*

1:18–20 A reminder and a warning

Paul appeals to the inspired words, which at the beginning of Timothy's ministry indicated the work and spiritual warfare to which he is called (*cf.* 4:14). He then warns him of the underlying cause of that spiritual disaster to which some have already come. **18** *The prophetic utterances* marked Timothy out as chosen of God for special service. He was meant to find *by them* (lit. 'in them') inspiration or fortification to wage a good campaign for God. Comparison of vv. 18, 19 with v. 5 suggests that Paul is repeating a charge originally given to Timothy concerning the importance of moral sincerity. **19** It is because some have failed just here, and deliberately thrust away from themselves the good conscience to which they should have held fast, that they have made shipwreck with regard to the Christian faith and become heretical in their teaching. **20** Their error is so serious that for their own good they have had to be severely disciplined. *Delivered to Satan*; *cf.* Jb. 2:6; 1 Cor. 5:5. This seems to mean to excommunicate. By putting such a one outside the sphere of Christ's kingdom or protection, he was exposed to the dominion of Satan, and particularly to his power to inflict physical disease. (For more detail about *Hymenaeus* see 2 Tim. 2:17, 18.)

2:1–7 AN EXHORTATION TO PRAYER FOR ALL MEN

Paul begins here to indicate the particular items of his general charge. He treats as of first importance the full practice of prayer *for all men* (v. 1). It seems probable that Jewish or Gnostic heretical teaching was suggesting the restriction of salvation to a particular race, or to certain classes only. Paul, therefore, justifies his universal exhortation by a sixfold assertion. He points to the character and will of God as the universal Saviour; to His unity as the one God of all men; to His provision of the human Christ Jesus as the single Mediator between Himself and the whole human race; to the universal scope of Christ's redeeming act which was *for all* (v. 6); to the consequent testimony to God's purpose to save all men which is provided by the accomplishment of the promised redemption at the appointed time; and to his own divine appointment to a share in its proclamation as none other than *a teacher of the Gentiles* (v. 7), *i.e.* one called to evangelize men of all nations alike.

1 The four words used for prayer may be progressive as well as comprehensive, indicating the supplication of one in need, the general outgoing of prayer to God alone, confident boldness of access to God's presence to make known one's requests, accompanied by thanksgiving for mercies enjoyed and prayers answered. The word *intercessions* has no necessary reference to others; its primary idea is of approach to a superior to make request. Such prayers should primarily be for all men's salvation; **2** but a complementary duty, if Christians are to be free to live as they ought in this world, is to pray for rulers and for *all who are in high positions,* that by their government they may preserve peace and order. *Godly and respectful* means with due reverence for God and with a proper sense of the seriousness of life. RV renders 'in all godliness and gravity'. **3** *This* (*i.e.* such praying) is intrinsically good, and pleasing to God because in harmony with His will for men. **4** does not say that God has determined that every single man must be saved; but simply that His general desire for mankind is that all alike shall enjoy salvation (*cf.* Rev. 7:9, 10) by coming to *the knowledge of the truth* (*cf.* 2 Tim. 2:25; Tit. 1:1). **5** This universality arises from God's oneness. As the only God, He deals directly and in the same way with all men (see Rom. 3:29, 30; 10:12). *The man* (Gk. *anthrōpos*, 'a human being', without the definite article); RV renders 'himself man'. The very humanity of Christ and His appointment as the only mediator between God and men supply added indication that the salvation provided in Him is for men, and for all men alike. **6** *Ransom* (Gk. *antilytron*) indicates a price paid for release. The preposition *anti*, 'instead of', suggests substitution; *cf.* Mk. 8:37; 10:45 (Gk.). Note that what Christ thus gave was *himself.* **7** *In faith and truth* may indicate Paul's sincerity or, more probably, the subject of his teaching; *cf.* v. 4.

2:8–15 GUIDANCE CONCERNING PRAYING AND TEACHING IN THE CONGREGATION

In all congregations it should generally be the men who lead in prayer, and those who do it should be careful to do it worthily. Similarly, Christian women should abstain from lavish adornment, and seek to commend themselves by their good works. They should display a becoming modesty and restraint, a quiet and submissive readiness to learn, rather than a self-assertive desire to teach. The proper place of woman in relation to man is indicated by the original order of creation; and her unfitness as a guide of the man is demonstrated by the way in which Eve was deceived and transgressed God's commandment. Woman's special calling is to motherhood; and, although there are now pain and peril in childbirth (see Gn. 3:16), those women will be brought safely through who respond fully to the demands of the gospel.

8 Paul gives authoritative counsel which is to apply *in every place*, *i.e.* wherever Christians meet for worship. To 'lift up the hands' was a recognized outward expression of the attitude of prayer (see Ex. 17:11, 12; 1 Ki. 8:22; Ps. 28:2). The conditions of effective praying are *holy hands*, *i.e.* personal purity, and freedom from ill-will towards others and consequent wrong motives. **9, 10** Women are to give a silent witness by their seemly dress and deportment, and by lives of active good works. *Cf.* 1 Pet. 3:1–6. *Modestly* (Gk. *aidōs*) signifies an appropriate reserve or sense of shame which preserves from all unbecoming behaviour. *Sensibly* (Gk. *sōphrosynē*) describes a balanced and discreet self-restraint. **11,12** In public worship it becomes the woman to be silent and submissive—that is part of her true dignity—not to try to take over the reins and direct the man. So Paul does not permit this; to do so would be to encourage something bad for both sexes, and to violate the created order. **13, 14** This appeal to the mind and purpose of the Creator shows clearly that Paul is not basing what he says simply on the position assigned to woman in the society of that day. He is appealing rather to a guiding principle of universal and abiding application (*cf.* 1 Cor. 11:2–16). Further, the tragedy of the Fall establishes the general truth that a woman is more easily deceived than a man; so it is out of place for her to take the lead in settling either doctrine or practice for the Christian community. (Note that it is, however, a woman's privilege to teach children and younger women; see 2 Tim. 1:5; 3:14, 15; Tit. 2:3, 4.) **15** The change to the plural 'they' (so AV, RV and Gk.) follows a reference to 'woman' in vv. 11–14 which is generic and collective. The concluding sentence indicates what each particular woman must actively do in order to experience the blessings of salvation in relation to the discharge of her function of

motherhood. *Cf.* 1:5; these words *in faith, etc.*, indicate the pathway of Christian obedience.

3:1–16 QUALIFICATIONS FOR THE CHRISTIAN MINISTRY

The function of oversight in, *i.e.* managing or caring for, the church of God (see v. 5) is a worthy task that should be well discharged. It requires a man of blameless, pure, disciplined and generous character, who manages his own home well; and particularly no recent convert, but one whose established good conduct as a Christian is well spoken of, so that he may give no occasion to the devil to accuse or ensnare him either because of his own pride, or because of the reproaches of those outside the church. Similarly, those who are to serve as deacons ought first to have approved themselves by their consistent and conscientious Christian behaviour, particularly in matters of self-discipline and home management. For this similarly is a ministry which ought to be discharged well, and those who fulfil it worthily will thereby both ensure their own good standing as Christians, and generally increase the outspoken confidence with which they can commend the Christian faith.

3:1–7 The office of a bishop

1 Paul's first concern here is to encourage a proper regard for the task of oversight or episcopacy (Gk. *episkopē*), and the corresponding recognition that those who are to undertake it ought to be men above reproach. *Bishop* (Gk. *episkopos*) and 'elder' (Gk. *presbyteros*) were in NT times alternative names for the same officer (see Tit. 1:5, 7; Acts 20:17, 28), the first term indicating function or duty, and the second dignity or status. Each local congregation had several. The translation 'bishop' must therefore not be understood in its developed monarchical and diocesan sense. **2** 'Married only once' seems more likely to be the meaning here than *the husband of one wife*, *i.e.* not practising polygamy. *Cf.* 5:9. It doubtless means a man free, as many converts to the faith were not, from all unsatisfactory sexual history or associa· tions. **3** *Gentle, not quarrelsome*; the Greek words mean 'forbearing', or 'considerate', and 'not contentious'. **4, 5** Capacity for effectively controlling others will not find expression in church oversight if it is lacking in a man's handling of his own children. **6** *Puffed up with conceit*; the Greek participle means 'beclouded', and so in a confused state of mind, here due to conceit because of sudden elevation to office. *The condemnation of the devil* probably refers to the judgment under which the devil came because of his insensate pride. Though, as the Greek word *diabolos* occurs in these Epistles in the sense of 'slanderer' or 'accuser' (see v. 11), some would interpret it in vv. 6 and 7 in this sense. Then the phrase in v. 6 would mean 'the judgment passed upon him by the typical slanderer'; and vv. 6 and 7 together would reinforce at the end the first qualification for a bishop mentioned in v. 2, *i.e.* 'above reproach', having a good reputation, and so not open to obvious or easy attack from 'the slanderer'.

3:8–13 The office of a deacon

8 *Deacons.* The Greek word has a very general meaning, 'ministers'. But in the Christian fellowship it obviously became the special term for a class of helpers subordinate to bishops or elders; *cf.* Phil. 1:1. As the qualifications emphasized in this whole section are moral, and are such as ought to characterize all good Christians, much the same are required in deacons as in bishops. If, however, as seems likely, deacons did house-to-house visitation and looked after church funds, there is special appropriateness in the qualifications stressed in v. 8. *Double-tongued* means saying different things to different people to suit the occasion; or the Greek word *dilogos* can mean simply 'given to repetition', *i.e.* a tale-bearer. *Greedy for gain*; the Greek word means disposed to seek gain in base and shameful ways; *cf.* Tit. 1:7, 11. **9** A *mystery* is something hidden from men in general, but openly revealed to the privileged, in this case to those who have faith (*cf.* v. 16). Such faith and understanding can be healthily maintained only where there is active conscientious obedience; *cf.* 1:5, 19; 2:15. **10** None should be allowed to serve as deacons unless they have first thus openly approved themselves as worthy in the eyes of all.

11 The Greek word translated *women* is ambiguous. It could mean the deacons' *wives* (AV). Here it may refer to women workers or deaconesses (*cf.* Rom. 16:1). The four qualifications demanded are closely parallel to those demanded of men in v. 8; in the misuse of the tongue women are more prone to be *slanderers* (Gk. *diaboloi*). **13** *A good standing* has been interpreted as the first step on the ladder of promotion; but this does not suit the context. Some regard the 'good standing and great boldness' (RV) thus gained as pointing Godward, particularly with reference to the day of judgment and reward; *cf.* 6:19; 1 Jn. 2:28; 3:21; 4:17. It seems more appropriate, however, to interpret the words manward, for the main emphasis of this whole section is on the need for a worthy reputation to be gained and maintained in the eyes of men by all who are to hold office in the church. This will increase their *confidence* or 'boldness' in preaching the gospel.

3:14–16 The purpose of these instructions

15 *How one ought.* Paul is concerned to guide the behaviour of all church members, not of Timothy only, and that because of the character of the company to which they belong. The reference is to each local congregation; there are no definite articles. Every such congregation is a genuine *household* or 'family' and *church* of God, not occupied like a heathen temple by a lifeless idol, but enjoying the manifested presence *of the living God*. Also, its corporate existence and

regular public meetings provide for the truth in that locality a visible witness, or *pillar*, and an enduring support or *bulwark*. **16** summarizes this *truth* as a *mystery* revealed to those who have a spirit of true piety or 'godliness' (AV, RV), which is of the essence of true *religion*. The common Christian confession of this mystery indicates its greatness (the Greek says it is 'confessedly' great, *i.e.* great by common consent). There follows a quotation from such a confession, abruptly introduced in the Greek by a masculine relative pronoun, obviously referring to Christ; for this 'mystery' is a Person (*cf.* Col. 1:27). The rhythmical and antithetical phrases suggest a quotation from an early credal hymn. Christ's pre-existence is implied and His incarnation asserted. It is by what happened in the realm of His spirit (RV) that His true identity was vindicated (*cf.* Rom. 1:3). This manifestation of God in history disclosed new wonders even to angels (*cf.* Eph. 3:10; 1 Pet. 1:12), and has provided a gospel to be preached to all nations. His consequent rewards are a company of believers gathered from earth, and His own exaltation into the realm of the divine glory in heaven.

4:1–5 A SOLEMN WARNING REGARDING FALSE TEACHING

In surprising contrast to these things (3:15, 16), Paul testifies that unmistakable witness has been given by the Spirit that there will be in the future, on the part of some in the church, an abandonment of revealed truth. This will be due fundamentally to the influence of evil spirits, and more immediately to the false teaching of insincere men, who will be the instruments of these evil spirits, and who will improperly insist on the necessity of abstaining from marriage and from certain foods. Such teaching directly contradicts the purpose of the Creator, particularly His purpose for fully instructed believers. For everything which God made is not only good in itself, but intended to be used by men. Nothing, therefore, is to be rejected as absolutely unusable. Rather we need to learn how we may properly and continuously sanctify things to our use in a spirit of thanksgiving, expressed to God in appropriate prayer, particularly prayer itself learnt from the written Word of God.

1 *The Spirit expressly says*; probably through Christian prophets, or possibly through Paul himself (*cf.* Acts 20:23; 21:11; see also Mt. 24:11). *In later times*; the Greek means subsequent to the time of writing, not 'last' as in 2 Tim. 3:1. *The faith*, with the definite article, indicates the body of revealed truth (*cf.* 1:19, RV; Jude 3). The *doctrines* are not about demons, but they emanate from demons. Over against the Spirit and the mystery of godliness stand misleading spirits and their false teaching. **2** The *liars whose consciences are seared* are either men lacking in moral sensitivity, or men bearing the brand-mark of demonic ownership. **3–5** The assertions of these verses are significant when studied in relation to the Gnostic and dualistic views that matter is evil and not created by God. But, while God created everything for use by men, right use depends on faith, full knowledge of the truth and an actively expressed spirit of thanksgiving. **5** *The word of God* is a common phrase for divinely inspired utterance, especially as found in Scripture. Here it suggests the use in saying 'grace' of actual OT phraseology; or it may mean that such eating is sanctioned by explicit divine direction.

4:6–16 TIMOTHY'S TEACHING AND PERSONAL BEHAVIOUR

Paul makes plain to Timothy that his calling to the service of Christ demands faithful devotion, both in his own living and in his ministry to his fellow-Christians. He must be careful both to preach what is true and profitable and himself to practise and pursue the same. The various aspects of the ministry of the Word must all be diligently discharged, and the God-given gift for such service fully exercised. Such ministry demands utter devotion. To live in this way leads to the double reward of salvation fully enjoyed by both preacher and hearers alike.

6 It is Timothy's responsibility to set these truths (see vv. 4, 5) before the Christians, to lay them down as the foundation of right practice (Gk. *hypotithemenos*). This he will be able to do only if he continually feeds himself (Gk. present participle) on the gospel truths to whose practice he is committed. This, therefore, is how to approve himself as *a good minister of Christ Jesus*. **7** The ideas of the two halves of this verse stand in opposition. One can give oneself to the good only by having nothing to do with the bad. The *myths* are *silly* because (Gk.) characteristic of superstitious old women. Christ's minister must keep himself spiritually fit by appropriate nourishment (v. 6) and exercise (v. 7). Instead of the misleading self-discipline of asceticism (v. 3), let him engage in proper and strenuous Christian training (*cf.* 1 Cor. 9:25–27). **8** Even at its best, bodily discipline as an end in itself is of only limited value. In his training the Christian minister ought rather to make *godliness*, or the devotion of his life to the proper worship of God, his dominant aim. The benefit thus to be gained is without limit or all-embracing; it concerns one's true spiritual *life* rather than one's physical existence (Gk. *zōē*, not *bios* as in 2 Tim. 2:4; see AV, RV), and it promotes its future as well as its present well-being or full enjoyment. **9** Such teaching is worthy to be believed and received, *i.e.* acted on, by all Christians. **10** It indicates the *end* that Paul himself has in view (note the use of *we*) in continuing to face the physical effort and endurance demanded by his apostolic labours. Also, *hope* of this benefit is settled and continuous (Gk. perfect tense) because it is grounded, not on any power in the physical exertion to

produce such a result, but on God in His revealed character as *living* (Gk. *zōn*) and as *Saviour*. These characteristics assure men of His ability and His readiness to give them true life (Gk. *zōē*). While God, by His gracious providences, shows Himself active to save in His dealings with all (*cf.* Mt. 5:45; 6:26), the full exhibition of all that His saving activity can mean is especially realized in the experience of believers.

11 This proper practice of Christian living Timothy is both to enjoin and explain, in order to lead his hearers to engage in it with full understanding. **12** His relative youthfulness and natural diffidence must not be allowed to encourage any to look down on him (*cf.* 1 Cor. 16:10, 11). Rather, he should openly set himself before all as a model to be imitated (*cf.* Phil. 3:17; 2 Thes. 3:9), not only in his teaching, but also in his conduct and in the underlying love, faithfulness and integrity to which it obviously gives expression. **13** Also, as one called to public ministry in the congregation, he must give sustained attention to its three main responsibilities: *the public reading of scripture*; exhortation or *preaching* based upon it (*i.e.* sermons); *teaching* or catechetical instruction (*cf.* Lk. 4:16–21; Acts 13:15; 15:21; 17:2, 3).

14 Nor should he forget and leave unexercised the special *gift* he has within him for such ministry. Note that such God-given enablement demands human co-operation for its full exercise (*cf.* Phil. 2:12, 13; 2 Tim. 1:6). Timothy had been assured of the character and of the impartation of this gift by the complementary witness of both a prophetic word and a solemn ordination (*cf.* Acts 13:1–3). Note the significant reference to the corporate function of a body of local *elders* acting together; and the combination in significant order of prophecy and symbolic action directed towards the recipient (*i.e.* 'word' and 'sacrament'). **15** The minister must continually give his whole mind and self to these things. Not only should he thus make *progress*, **16** but also it should be obvious to all that he is thus growing in grace of personal character and in the fullness and quality of his teaching. These are the things to which he must unceasingly apply himself. Such practice by the minister is the way to ensure the full salvation of himself and his hearers alike. Note how the minister not only fulfils his ministry by what he says (those he serves are described as *your hearers*), but also necessarily completes it, or spoils its effectiveness, by how he himself lives.

5:1 – 6:2 SPECIAL GROUPS WITHIN THE CHURCH

5:1, 2 General instructions

Ministry like Timothy's involved dealing with people and solemnly confronting them with the truth, and this duty must be discharged; but it should be fittingly done in true affection and with sober restraint. **1** It does not become a relatively young minister like Timothy sharply to reprimand anyone older than himself. The word 'elder' (AV) refers here simply to age, not office, *i.e. an older man.* 2 The qualification *in all purity* refers particularly to Timothy's ministry to the young women. It is part of his responsibility to exhort them, but he must watch against any development, or even suggestion, of improper interest or intimacy. In Tit. 2:3–5 the actual training of young women is explicitly entrusted to older Christians of their own sex.

5:3–16 Instructions about widows

In rightly marking widows out for appropriate regard and care, those should be distinguished for such honour and help who are both really destitute and truly worthy. Whenever possible, widows should be provided for by their own children or families; this is an obvious Christian duty, and the church ought not to be needlessly burdened. Only those widows should be enrolled among those who fulfil ministry and receive maintenance who are 60 or over, who have been married only once and do not intend to remarry, and who are well spoken of as active in good works. Younger women are unsuitable for such appointment. They may be tempted to remarry, or fall into the snare of making house-to-house visitation an occasion for idle and harmful gossip. It is better for such to remarry and to shoulder the responsibilities of having children and running a home. In this way they may be able themselves to help widows whom the church would otherwise have to relieve.

3 *Honour.* This may include the provision of necessary material assistance; see v. 17 and Mt. 15:5, 6. *A real widow* (v. 5) who needs such assistance is one without either means or relatives to support her; she is *left all alone.* 4 Every widow with relatives should be supported by them. This means that they must, as a primary duty, *learn* (*i.e.* make it their regular practice) to show filial piety towards members of their own family, and to give back proper recompense to their parents or forbears. Such conduct is *acceptable* not only to those who thus benefit, but also *in the sight of God.*

5 The genuine widow, in addition to being *left all alone,* will commend herself as worthy of support as one who has acquired the habits of looking hopefully to God, not men, and devoting herself to long and frequent praying. 6 In contrast to this, the type of woman who wastefully or prodigally spends life and all that it brings is not to be reckoned as actually a widow for, though living, she is in God's sight already dead. 7 The need to make these distinctions and to maintain a worthy standard must be definitely enforced by Timothy, with a view, not to shutting some widows out of benefit, but rather to securing that all will live irreproachable lives. 8 Every Christian ought to take thought for the needs of his relatives, and most of all for those of the members of his own family. Not to do so is by act to deny the faith which with the mouth

one professes. It would even make one worse than the unbelieving heathen, for he recognizes a duty in such matters.

9, 10 Some find here the earliest and a significant scriptural reference to an 'order · of widows' (often mentioned in other early Christian writings). These seem to have been 'women elders' rather than 'women deacons' or 'deaconesses' (see on 3:11), who can scarcely all have been over 60. Their particular responsibilities appear to have been to care for children, particularly orphans, and the younger women; this would involve house-to-house visitation. The qualifications for enrolment are obviously strict. Such conditions seem clearly those for ministry rather than merely maintenance, unless the reference is to specially selected as well as needy widows, who are guaranteed permanent lifelong support by the local church.

Paul gives two reasons for not enrolling younger widows. 11, 12 In the first place it is unwise to make them pledge not to remarry. For, should they later wish to do so, such desire, otherwise innocent, will then be a rebellion against the yoke of Christ, and will make them stand self-condemned *for having violated their first pledge.* 13 Secondly, it would give them an undesirable opportunity to become talkative busybodies rather than active workers. The suggestion seems to be that still active, younger women, who as wives have been occupied with home management, if they are suddenly given maintenance, and possibly a ministry largely to be fulfilled by visiting other homes and by words of exhortation, may fall into the temptation to be lazy and to become talkers who make mischief by betraying confidences. 14 Therefore, to avoid the danger of giving opponents a ground for reproaching Christians, it is better that such women should remarry and be fully occupied again with family responsibilities. Some would say that this passage implies that the experience of married life develops a woman's aptitude . for some tasks and lessens it for others; that younger women who are maintained by the church to do work as deaconesses should be spinsters, not widows; or, alternatively, that any healthy widow under 60 ought to find some kind of employment (if not a husband) rather than be given full maintenance, even as a church worker. *The enemy* seems here to mean the typical human opponent, not the devil. *Occasion.* The Greek word is a military word meaning 'a base of operations'. 15 Paul appeals to the witness of experience to confirm his judgment. This kind of departure from the way of Christ (v. 11) to follow Satan has thus occurred in some cases. The insertion of *already* suggests that it has happened in the short time which has elapsed since such appointments of younger widows were first made. It is also significant as indicating that the probable date of such a reference to church organization is therefore not so late as might at first seem probable.

5:17-25 The proper treatment, discipline and appointment of presbyters

Timothy was charged with special responsibilities in connection with *the elders*, who were the leaders of the local churches. For other references to such officials see Acts 14:23; 15:6; 20:17, 28; Tit. 1:5. Some of these were also active in preaching and teaching. He is, in particular, solemnly charged (v. 21; see RV) to beware both of wrong prejudice against, or undue partiality for, particular individuals. First, he must see that the value of the elders' service is recognized and they themselves amply recompensed (v. 17). Secondly, discipline of some who fail may be necessary: but no accusation should be treated seriously unless it is properly supported by confirming witnesses (v. 19); and those proved guilty of sinful practices should be openly reproved (v. 20). Thirdly, he should make no hasty appointments, lest his own position be compromised by connection with the sinful, and he himself be defiled (v. 22). For neither all the bad nor all the good of any man's character is immediately obvious. There are other things not so conspicuous, but discoverable by the patient and watchful investigator. In appointments to the presbyterate, therefore, it is a mistake either to receive or to reject anyone too quickly.

17 *Elders.* In contrast with v. 1 the reference here is to those who are set over a local church as its leaders. The following verse makes plain that the *honour* they ought to be given includes material support (*cf.* v. 3); also it should be *double* or 'ample'. Not only should they be given it, they should also be truly recognized as worthy of it. **18** Paul quotes Dt. 25:4, not to enforce the letter of the law, but to appeal to the moral principle which it illustrates. Note *when it is treading*, *i.e.* while he is actually working (Gk. present participle). Some have wondered whether the phrase *the scripture says* covers the second quotation, because it is found in Lk. 10:7. If so, it would be a remarkable reference to the third Gospel as Scripture. The words are more probably a well-known proverbial saying, quoted by our Lord, and here used by Paul to indicate the point of his preceding OT quotation. **19** *Cf.* Dt. 19:15. **20** *Them* and *all* are perhaps best taken as both referring to the elders only, though the second, and some think the first also, may refer to church members in general. **22** *The laying on of hands.* For the practice *cf.* 4:14; 2 Tim. 1:6. The meaning is, 'Ordain no-one with undue haste,' an injunction appropriately applying the preceding warning against partiality. Timothy will serve God and the churches well only if he keeps himself pure, and refuses to welcome the unworthy to partake in the leadership. **23** In a personal parenthesis—a striking sign of the Epistle's genuineness—Paul indicates that this exhortation to keep himself undefiled need not prevent Timothy, in the interests of his health, from ceasing to be a total abstainer (note the force of *no longer*) and taking wine in moderation. *A little wine*: contrast 3:3. Note the indication that Timothy's health was poor. **24, 25** *Conspicuous*; *i.e.* 'clearly evident', 'immediately obvious'. *Pointing*; the Greek means 'leading the way'. Some men are pursued later by the after-effects of their sins, which in due course find them out.

6:1, 2 The duty of Christian slaves

These verses provide more teaching for Timothy to pass on concerning due *honour* (*cf.* 5:3, 17) to be given, this time by slaves to their masters. **1** It will bring only dishonour on the name and gospel of God, as apparently subversive of the existing social order, if Christians who happen to be slaves fail to be good slaves. **2** Nor, if their masters happen to be fellow-believers, ought they to cease properly to respect them as their human masters. They ought rather to serve them the better, just because those who get the benefit of their improved service are Christians. *All honour* means 'full honour', honour in every form and way in which it is due.

6:3-10 SOME FURTHER WARNINGS

It is easy to be led astray by the worldly attractiveness of some men's teaching; and yet it stands condemned as 'different' (v. 3, RV), or heterodox, because those who give it have clearly abandoned the fundamental spiritual loyalties, and their personal condition and conduct are unworthy. Also their teaching causes violent social strife, because it serves only to pervert men's moral judgment, to rob them of the truth, and to obsess them with the idea that the purpose of the practice of godliness is material gain (vv. 4, 5). Not that there is not great gain in true godliness, but only if one is free from covetousness (v. 6). Since we cannot amass wealth and take it with us when we leave this world, it is for us to be satisfied here as long as we have food and clothing (vv. 7, 8). For such as set their desire on the acquisition of wealth get enticed, ensnared, obsessed and utterly overwhelmed (v. 9). Such love for money is a root which, if allowed to grow, produces only evils of every kind (v. 10). Those who allow themselves to be occupied with it are commonly led astray from the faith, and cause themselves many troubles.

3, 4 There is a contrast here between teaching which is 'healthful' and teachers who are 'sick' (see RV mg.). Teaching is confirmed as *sound* or 'wholesome' (AV), first, by having Christ as its author and, second, by the God-fearing spirit and conduct of the teacher. By contrast the false teacher stands self-condemned by his air of conceit, by his lack of understanding, and by his unhealthy obsession with the kind of discussion which only produces strife and all its accompanying evil thought and speech about others. **5** In the Greek the participles (not adjectives) by which such men are described indicate permanent losses which have happened to them; their powers of moral judgment are destroyed, and they are deprived of the truth. So they now habitually suppose that godliness is a means to material gain. *Gain*; the Greek *porismos* means virtually 'good business', *i.e.* a source of profit or way of gain. **6** Paradoxically *godliness* is then said to be a great source of profit, but not in terms of material wealth, and only if it is accompanied by *contentment*. The Greek word means 'self-sufficiency'. It describes an independence of changing circumstances. *Cf.* Phil. 4:11. **7** The statements of this verse confirm the implied attitude of the passage to material things; they are of only secondary and passing importance, not part of the true and abiding self, not transferable to the life beyond. **8** The Greek verb is future indicative. It is not so much an exhortation as a dogmatic assertion that this is the way of realized contentment—in contrast to setting one's mind on acquiring wealth. **9** *Senseless and hurtful*; *i.e.* passionate *desires* which are doubly condemned as negatively senseless and positively injurious. **10** The occupation of the mind with getting rich and the consequent stretching out of oneself in its pursuit result in both negative loss (being 'led astray from the faith', RV) and positive damage. In contrast to the 'good business' of godliness it does not pay.

6:11–16 A SOLEMN PERSONAL CHARGE

Paul exhorts Timothy to be true to his Christian calling, to keep clear of such ensnaring things as the love of money, and to sustain the pursuit of Christian virtues (v. 11). Let him maintain the contest worthily to the end, that he may gain the prize. He is committed to such a course by his Christian *confession* (v. 12). Let the recollection that God sees and will not fail to sustain, that Christ Jesus Himself has confirmed the truth Timothy has confessed by the witness of His sufferings, and is going to be manifested openly as the Judge by the all-sovereign God—let such awareness enforce Paul's charge to him not to defile or expose to reproach his Christian obedience (vv. 13–16).

It is possible here to give some of the phrases a particular interpretation. **11** *Man of God* may refer to Timothy's status as a worker; the phrase was a recognized OT description for a prophet (see 1 Sa. 9:6). **12b** may refer to Timothy's ordination, and **13** to our Lord's own faithful testimony before Pilate. Then **14** will be a specific exhortation to Timothy to discharge his particular ministry. However, it seems preferable to give the phrases a more general reference. *Man of God* may describe any mature Christian (see 2 Tim. 3:17). **12b** may refer to Timothy's baptism. The *good confession* (note the definite article) is 'the faith' or truth then confessed; *good* describing 'the faith confessed', not Timothy's confession of it. **13** This same *good confession* Timothy is reminded was attested as true by our Lord Himself by His death and resurrection, which took place 'under Pontius Pilate' (an equally possible interpretation of the

Greek phrase, as in the Apostles' Creed). Some of the accompanying phraseology may well echo confessions of faith used in baptism. Note the reference to God as the Life-giver or Creator, and to the passion and second coming of Christ. This then means that Paul knows no better way to exhort Timothy than to address to him words applicable not only to him as a special worker but to him (as to all) as a Christian believer. In v. 12 the difference of the Greek tenses suggests *fight* as a sustained activity and *take hold* as a decisive act. **14** Christ's *appearing* (Gk. *epiphaneia*), or 'manifestation', will occur at its own proper time by the pleasure and act of God, and as a 'showing' (see AV, RV) or sign from His hand (*cf.* Jn. 2:18). **15, 16** provide a significant description of the unique sovereignty of God. In His absolute bliss and unending life He is completely self-contained. Such things belong wholly to Him, and to Him alone. He is thus the exclusive Lord of all else. So to Him should all honour be rendered and all power or rule ascribed.

6:17–19 THE RIGHT USE OF MATERIAL THINGS

Paul here completes his teaching concerning material wealth by adding to his previous negative warnings against desire for gain (vv. 6–10) some positive instruction concerning the right use of wealth by those who have it.

Rich Christians need to beware lest the possession of material wealth make them over-confident. Their settled hope should rest, not in their wealth and its characteristic insecurity, but in God the Giver (v. 17). They need, too, to remember that such wealth is given not to be hoarded, but to be enjoyed (*cf.* 4:3–5) and used to *do good* (v. 18). Thus to share one's good things liberally with others is the way to put by for the future something more enduring than earthly riches, and thus to possess true life (Gk. *zōē*) rather than just to have in abundance the present earthly means of livelihood (Gk. *bios*). See 1 Jn. 3:17; Lk. 12:15.

17 Note the contrast between *this* (RV 'present') *world* and *the future* (v. 19); *cf.* Mt. 6:19–21. In v. 17 (see RV) to 'have their hope set on' brings out the force of the Greek perfect; also the warning is enforced by giving prominence in thought not to the amount of the 'riches' but to their 'uncertainty'. Those with earthly riches are exhorted to use them to acquire better and more enduring wealth. **18** For this they need paradoxically in deed and heart a readiness to share their material riches with others—to be *liberal and generous*.

6:20, 21 A FINAL EXHORTATION

In an emphatic personal word to Timothy Paul here briefly sums up his chief, twofold concern in writing—to secure that Timothy preserves and hands on unimpaired the deposit of truth, and avoids the impious and arrogantly assertive false teaching, which has already fatally side-tracked some.

20 Timothy is here addressed as a steward who has been entrusted with 'the deposit' (RV mg.; *cf.* 2 Tim. 1:12, 14, RV mg.; 2:2), *i.e.* what Jude (v. 3) calls 'the faith delivered to the saints'. The *falsely called knowledge* suggests an un-justified pretentiousness, which consequently attracts adherents to their own undoing as believers. **21** *Grace be with you* is Paul's distinctive form of Christian salutation to end an Epistle; see 2 Thes. 3:17, 18. The *you* is in the plural and so includes the local congregation.

2 Timothy

OUTLINE OF CONTENTS

For the General Introduction to this Epistle see p. 1166.

COMMENTARY

1:1, 2 PERSONAL ADDRESS AND GREETING

1 Compare and see notes on 1 Tim. 1:1, 2; Tit. 1:1–4. It is typical of Paul to ascribe his apostle-ship to *the will of God* (*cf.* the opening verse of 1 and 2 Corinthians, Ephesians and Colossians). He was overwhelmingly conscious that his appointment was of God; see Gal. 1:1, 15, 16. *According to the promise of the life . . . in Christ Jesus.* This expresses the concern of Paul's apostleship; it was to make this promise known, and to bring men to embrace it, that he was commissioned (*cf.* Tit. 1:1–3). **2** *My beloved child*; an affectionate indication of intimate association, particularly as leader and follower in work for God (*cf.* 1 Cor. 4:17). Paul often spoke thus of his converts; see 1 Cor. 4:14, 15; Gal. 4:19; Phm. 10.

1:3–5 THANKSGIVING FOR TIMOTHY'S FAITH

Paul confesses the depth of his feeling towards Timothy, feeling to which he continually gives expression in his prayers, feeling which includes the eager yearning to have the joy of seeing Timothy again, instead of the recollection of the tears which he shed when they parted. Above all, Paul says, he thanks God as he is reminded in his prayers of the sincerity of Timothy's faith, and of the similar faith of his grandmother and mother before him. In the context of this thought about Timothy Paul becomes conscious how much he too owes to his forbears, from whom he learned to serve or worship God with conscientious sincerity. Both these references may be regarded, therefore, as Christian testimonies to the value of a good Jewish religious upbringing. For when Timothy was taught the OT as a small child (3:15) his teachers had probably not yet believed in Christ.

1:6–14 THE NEED FOR COURAGE AND FIDELITY

Paul reminds Timothy that he has a spiritual gift, and that God's endowments are not given to make men cowardly, but strong, loving and self-controlled. Therefore he ought to stir up into flame the God-given fire, and in the strength of God to take his share in any suffering in which the gospel may involve him, by not hesitating to associate himself with witness concerning our Lord, and with Paul as one who suffers imprisonment on Christ's account. To enforce this appeal Paul reminds Timothy how wonderful the gospel is. For according to His own gracious purpose, and not because of anything which we have done, God has saved us. This gift of grace, already given to us before world history began, has now been openly manifested through the advent of Jesus Christ to be our Saviour and through His victory over death. In consequence, through the gospel now being preached, incorruptible life has been brought out into the light (for men to see as a reality and embrace as a possession, in contrast to previous dark uncertainty about its existence and despair of its enjoyment). This is the gospel, says Paul, which I am commissioned to preach; and it is through discharging this commission that I suffer as I do. Nor (in spite of imprisonment and the prospect of martyrdom) do I see any reason for being ashamed of it. For God is faithful and able; so (although my day of fulfilling a stewardship in the gospel is done) I am sure He will preserve what He has thus entrusted to me so that a good account may be given on the final day of reckoning. It is this outline of wholesome teaching, says Paul to Timothy, passed on by me to you, which you must make your own and preserve, in responsive faith and love to Christ Himself. Remember also that God's Spirit dwells in us to enable this stewardship to be discharged.

6 *Hence*, or 'for the which cause' (RV); reference to Timothy's *sincere faith* (v. 5). Note how Timothy is not exhorted to seek fresh grace; he is rather reminded of grace already given and exhorted to stir it up into flame (see RV mg. and on 1 Tim. 4:14). 7 *Spirit* may be interpreted as 'Holy Spirit', or it may describe the human spirit as wrought on by the Holy Spirit. The two are complementary; *cf.* Rom. 8:14–16. 8 *His prisoner*; *i.e.* by His doing; *cf.* Eph. 3:1; Phm. 9. 9 Those who are saved are first called by God according to His own freely predetermined *purpose* (*cf.* Rom. 8:28); this *calling* is *holy* because by it we are called to holiness or Godlikeness; *cf.* 1 Cor. 1:2; 1 Pet. 1:15, 16. While these Pastoral Epistles repeatedly insist that good works are an intended fruit of salvation, they also make equally plain, in characteristic Pauline fashion, that human good works are not its cause; *cf.* Tit. 3:5; Eph. 2:8–10. *Ages ago*; RV, following the Greek, 'before times eternal'. *Cf.* Tit. 1:2; Rom. 16:25. This implies Christ's pre-existence. 10 *Abolished death*; *i.e.* brought it to nought as a power holding men in its grip; the Greek *katargein* means 'to render inoperative'. *Life and immortality* (RV 'incorruption'). The latter indicates the character of the former; *i.e.* life completely exempt from destruction. 12 *I have believed*. The Greek perfect tense used here implies a continuing attitude of trust consequent upon its decisive adoption. *What has been entrusted to me* (Gk. 'my deposit'). The same word clearly refers in 1:14; 1 Tim. 6:20 to 'the deposit' of the gospel, with which the steward is entrusted. So that sense seems preferable here. But the AV interpretation is possible. An assertion by Paul of his hope of final personal salvation (*cf.* 1 Thes. 5:23) suits the context. His use of 'guard' and 'deposit' may have suggested

their further use in a contrasted sense in v. 14. 13 *Pattern*; the Greek word means an 'outline sketch' demanding to be followed and filled in in greater detail. *Faith and love* indicate the Christian spirit and manner in which Timothy is to do this—an activity dependent upon being personally *in*, *i.e.* in intimate union with, *Christ Jesus*.

1:15–18 PAUL COMMENDS THE DEVOTION OF ONESIPHORUS

Paul enforces his appeal to Timothy not to be ashamed of the gospel and its apostle (1:8) in a day of persecution by reminding him both of the many who have been ashamed to be openly associated with Paul the prisoner and of one who outstandingly was not. Since Onesiphorus has shown such kindness to Paul in his need, Paul prays that the Lord will recompense him by showing kindness both to Onesiphorus's household now, and to Onesiphorus himself in the coming day of divine judgment and reward. 15 *All . . . turned away from me*. It was a decisive act of repudiation; they disowned Paul. 16, 17 By contrast Onesiphorus not only acknowledged and helped Paul after his arrest, but later, when he arrived in Rome, he took extra trouble to find Paul (apparently no easy task) in order again to encourage him. 18 Timothy, too, is well acquainted with the many ministries he performed in Ephesus. Onesiphorus appears here as one separated from his household, either by absence from home, or quite possibly by death (*cf.* 4:19). This does not mean, however, that Paul is praying for his present well-being as one dead, a practice completely unsupported elsewhere in Scripture. The prayer concerns not the intermediate state at all, but conduct in this life, and reward on the future day of judgment. Such desire for adequate and appropriate recompense then is one that can equally be expressed for living or dead, and is in harmony with the plain teaching of our Lord and the NT. See Mt. 10:32, 33; and compare and contrast 2 Tim. 4:14, RV.

2:1–13 A FURTHER EXHORTATION TO STEADFASTNESS AND DILIGENCE

Following the example of Onesiphorus, and in contrast to the failure of others, Paul exhorts Timothy to find his strength in Christ and to be prepared to suffer hardship. Two tasks supremely matter: first, that the deposit of truth, the full gospel, should be faithfully handed on to faithful men, who will in their turn teach others; and secondly, that God's purpose in giving the gospel should be fulfilled in the eternal salvation of the elect. These tasks demand for their discharge such devotion, discipline and diligence as may be seen in the soldier (vv. 3, 4), the athlete (v. 5) and the farmer (v. 6). They may also involve suffering, as may be seen in the actual Christian experience of the aged apostle himself. In the face of possible martyrdom, which is Paul's prospect and may become Timothy's, it is good to remember the faithfulness of God and the sure heavenly reward of present earthly sacrifice and steadfastness, as well as the corresponding shame that must follow failure.

1 *Be strong.* The Greek present tense and passive voice means 'be continually strengthened'. *In the grace that is in Christ Jesus*; *i.e.* by means of the divine help of which all who are joined to Christ are assured. **2** *Entrust*; Gk. *paratithenai*, from the same root as 'deposit' (Gk. *parathēkē*) in 1:14 (see RV mg.). Timothy had been solemnly entrusted with the gospel by Paul. He is charged similarly to commit it to those who will in their turn pass it on to others. Note the qualifications to be looked for in such ministers—trustworthiness and ability to teach. *Before* (*i.e.* in the presence of) *many witnesses* may refer to those present when Timothy was set apart to this ministry; or the phrase may mean that the content of Paul's gospel had been confirmed to Timothy 'through' (Gk. *dia*) the testimony of many others. **4** Such *service* of the *soldier* demands complete detachment from ordinary worldly business, single, whole-hearted devotion to obeying one's commanding officer, and fulfilment of the purpose of one's enrolment. **5** In ancient times the winner in an athletic contest was given a crown or garland as his prize. *According to the rules*, in strict conformity to what the particular contest demands, first in training and then in actual performance. **6** *Hardworking* and *first* are significant words added to an otherwise general statement about the *farmer*. Such partaking is in contrast to the rightly inferior participation of the indolent. These three illustrations (vv. 3–6) enforce different aspects of the challenge to utter devotion to the worthy discharge of gospel ministry.

7 *Think over what I say*; *i.e.* grasp the meaning of what has just been said, and its practical application to your own ministry. This is no empty exhortation, because the *understanding*, *i.e.* the ability to pass right judgment, the Lord will give. **8** *Remember Jesus Christ.* The following two phrases are credal. Timothy is to find inspiration in the recollection of *Jesus* vindicated as 'Messiah' (*Christ*) not only by His human birth *descended from David* in fulfilment of prophecy, but much more by His resurrection from the dead; *cf.* Acts 2:36; Rom. 1:1–4. He can, therefore, be called to mind as the living Lord. Such essential truth about Him is part of the gospel entrusted to Paul (and through him to Timothy) to be preached. *My gospel*; *cf.* Rom. 2:16; 16:25; 1 Cor. 15:1.

9 The word *gospel* refers to the evangelizing as well as to the evangel. *Wearing fetters like a criminal.* These words emphasize the extremity of utterly undeserved indignity and shame which Paul was suffering and which Timothy must be ready to share. *Is not fettered*; *i.e.* as Paul is. God's word cannot thus be confined. **10** *Therefore*; *i.e.* on this account,

for the sake of the gospel and its propagation. *I endure everything*; *i.e.* I patiently submit to every kind of experience, even the worst; *cf.* Heb. 12:2. The goal in view is that those whom God has freely chosen for such a destiny may also themselves actually encounter His salvation—the salvation which is to be found in Messiah Jesus (above referred to, 2:8) and which possesses a glory whose quality and full manifestation are eternal, not temporal.

11–13 *The saying is sure.* The following phrases, quoted as worthy of credence, were possibly taken from a familiar hymn, or string of aphorisms, intended to inspire faithfulness unto death and hope of sharing in Christ's eternal glory. Our entrance into that glory will correspond to our share in His sufferings here; *cf.* Rom. 8:17. **11** *If we have died with him* (Gk. aorist tense) refers to a decisive past-event, and may have in mind Christian baptism rather than martyrdom. *Cf.* Rom. 6:3, 4, 8. **12** Contrast *if we endure* (Gk. present tense, *i.e.* a sustained activity). Note the paradoxical contrast between the pathway and the goal—through death to life, through patient submission to sovereign sway. *If we deny him* (Gk. future tense); a more remote possibility is suggested; *cf.* Mt. 10:33. While men's failure to confess Him now will affect Christ's future acknowledgment of them, **13** their failure to trust Him and to be true to Him does not alter His abiding trustworthiness and faithfulness; *cf.* Rom. 3:3. To be false to Himself is something which even omnipotent God cannot be.

2:14–26 SOME RULES OF CONDUCT

There was increasing danger of attention being diverted to profitless and damaging speculation and controversy. Two men are mentioned by name who were propagating wrong doctrine about the resurrection. Timothy, therefore, must remind the Christians, and particularly those 'faithful men' (v. 2) to whom he entrusts the gospel to be preached, of such truths as Paul has just enumerated (vv. 4–13). And he must solemnly charge them not to become involved in the prevalent controversies. For his own part let him rather adhere to the straightforward presentation of the truth in a way which will win God's approval, and give him, as a workman, no cause for shame in God's sight, particularly in the coming day of judgment. Let him avoid irreverent fancies, which are capable of being as harmful as an eating sore. If the overturning of the faith of some tempt him to tremble for the very survival of the Christian community, let him remember that the true church is God's own firm foundation, but that not all who profess to acknowledge Christ as Lord are its true members. For only God knows who are truly His. Profession of the name involves the demand (to which some do not respond) to give up sin. Just as the many articles in a large house vary in quality, and some are of little or no value and unfit for honourable use, so the visible community of professing Christians is a mixed company. The individual believer, like Timothy, who has the discernment to recognize this, should seek, by diligent self-purification, to cease to belong to the class of the unworthy, and thus to become fit for honourable use in the Master's service. He should abandon self-indulgence and share the company and spiritual ambitions of sincere believers. He should refuse to engage in senseless investigations which promote only violent disagreement. As one called to the Lord's service he should not engage in controversy with those ensnared by error, but show them gentle forbearance, and meekly seek to instruct them in the truth in the hope that God may bring them to a better mind, and so they may escape from the devil who has ensnared them, and devote themselves to doing God's will.

14 *Avoid disputing about* (or 'with') *words*; *i.e.* not to engage in controversy. The following phrases indicate its results. Negatively it is without profit; positively, instead of edifying the hearers, it overturns them, or involves them in spiritual 'catastrophe' (Gk.). **15** *Who has no need to be ashamed*; the Greek word may have a passive force, viz. 'not to be put to shame'; *cf.* Phil. 1:20, RV. *Rightly handling* (lit. 'cutting straightly'; see RV mg.); possibly a metaphor from cutting a straight road or furrow, and so not deviating from *the word of truth*, *i.e.* the gospel; *cf.* Gal. 2:14. **16** *Avoid*; *i.e.* 'stand clear of', 'withdraw from'. *Godless chatter*; *i.e.* talk empty of value and irreverent in spirit. Those who give themselves to such talk make progress only in the wrong direction, in ungodliness; the spirit of irreverence grows. **17** Such talking, when given the opportunity through their indulgence in it, spreads like a malignant sore eating away healthy tissue. *Hymenaeus* is also mentioned in 1 Tim. 1:20. **18** Belief in a physical resurrection was a difficulty to many (*cf.* 1 Cor. 15), especially to those who regarded all matter as evil. So they interpreted *the resurrection* as a spiritual quickening or initiation already experienced, thus missing the truth themselves and *upsetting the faith* of others. **19** *God's firm foundation stands*; *i.e.* it cannot be overturned. The reference is to the true church of God's building; *cf.* Eph. 2:19–22. Its double attestation indicates, from God's side and from man's, how its genuine members are to be distinguished and separated from the false. For light on the virtual quotations see Nu. 16: esp. 5, 26; *cf.* Is. 52:11. Note that the genuineness of others is fully known only to God, and that it is for each one who professes to acknowledge Christ as Lord to make his own election sure by appropriate action.

21 reiterates the individual's responsibility to separate himself from the defilement of association with the unworthy. Note the obvious reference for Timothy to the false teachers. **22** indicates complementary truths. Defilement from within, as well as from without, must be avoided, and fellowship with the sincere is to be pursued. **23** Note the repeated indication that some inquiries are foolish and inept, or unenlightened, because they generate not edification but contention. **24** *The Lord's servant*; RV mg. 'the Lord's bondservant'. The term applies to any Christian (1 Cor. 7:22), but particularly to one called to special ministry like Timothy; *cf.* Tit. 1:1. *Cf.* also Is. 42:2, 3. *An apt teacher, forbearing*, **25** *correcting . . . with gentleness*; *i.e.* devoted to positive exposition of the truth rather than to controversy with those who oppose it. This is how those ensnared by false teaching ought to be treated (contrast the more drastic handling of its deliberate propagators, Tit. 3:10); for such can be won back only as God grants to them a change of mind and to enter into full knowledge of the truth. **26** See RV and RV mg. Of the three interpretations suggested RV mg. seems the best, viz. that those who have been taken alive by the devil may return to soberness, escape from his trap, and enter instead into the pursuit of God's will.

3:1-9 A WARNING OF COMING APOSTASY

If Timothy thinks it strange that so much of evil should arise within the visible church, Paul now desires him to learn that worse is to follow as the end approaches. The sinfulness of human self-will will find full, unrestrained expression in deed, word and thought. The practice of reverence, dutifulness, gratitude, love of kindred and covenant-keeping will cease. Men will become diabolical, uncontrolled, violent, enemies of virtue, ready to betray their fellows, reckless, misled by their own conceit. Those who profess religion will put love of pleasure before love of God; they will outwardly affect a form of reverence for God but deliberately repudiate or gainsay its actual transforming power. Men of this kind must be avoided. They are the sort who stealthily impose on and mislead weak women, who because of their sensitive conscience about wrongdoing, their readiness to be moved by emotion, their love of novelty, and their inability to grasp the truth, are an easy prey. Such men must be recognized in their true character as opponents of the truth, of a depraved mind, and in God's eyes rejected in relation to the very faith which they profess (*cf.* Mt. 7:22, 23). Nevertheless there will be a limit to the progress they make; for all will see that their behaviour is manifestly senseless.

1 *In the last days.* The Christian era as a whole is sometimes so described (see Heb. 1:2), but the reference here is explicitly to the consummation of the age. Note the future tense *will come*; though the present tenses in vv. 5, 6 indicate that the evil later to mature was already at work. *Cf.* Mt. 13:24–30; 2 Thes. 2:7, 8. *Times of stress* (Gk. *chalepos*); *i.e.* 'difficult', 'hard to live in'. **2** *Men*; the Greek has the definite article, *i.e.* not men or mankind generally. The whole context, especially v. 5, suggests that this moral decline and manifestation of evil is to occur within the sphere of professed Christianity. It is not unenlightened heathen, but those who resist the truth and repudiate the power of the gospel who become corrupt. *Cf.* 2 Thes. 2:3 where Paul teaches that 'a falling away' (Gk. *apostasia*), *i.e.* religious apostasy, must happen first. In vv. 2–4 note how the description begins and ends: *lovers of self, lovers of money . . . lovers of pleasure rather than lovers of God*; *i.e.* they are men who put devotion to self-satisfaction in the place of pleasing God. Moral corruption inevitably follows. *Proud, arrogant*; *i.e.* boastful and haughty, prone to swagger and scornful of others. *Abusive*; *i.e.* those who speak disrespectfully, whether of God or man. 3 *Implacable.* The Greek *aspondos* describes not so much one who breaks contracts (AV) as one who will not make any. *Haters of good*; *i.e.* of all good, whether in things or people. 5 *Denying*; *cf.* 1 Tim. 5:8; Tit. 1:16. *Avoid such people*; contrast 2:25. These are apparently to be regarded as past redemption, and capable of doing only harm. 6 *Weak women*; Gk. *gunaikaria*, a diminutive expressing contempt. For the greater ease with which women are misled *cf.* 1 Tim. 2:14. 8 *Jannes and Jambres* are mentioned in a Hebrew Targum on Ex. 7:11 as magicians who opposed Moses. This comparison may imply similar use of occult powers; see on 3:13 ('impostors'). *Of corrupt mind*; *i.e.* no longer able to understand the truth (*cf.* Rom. 1:21, 22; Eph. 4:17, 18). 9 Contrast 2:16; 3:13. While such men will get worse in their own depravity and in their power to deceive, they will not be able to do so without their folly being generally recognized.

3:10 – 4:5 A CALL TO PREACH THE WORD IN SPITE OF PERSECUTION

3:10–13 The example of Paul's own experience

How different is Timothy's previous history from all this (*i.e.* 3:1–9)! Paul reminds Timothy of his own faith and practice, and of the persecution and suffering in which his Christian service has involved him, not least in his early missionary work in Timothy's home neighbourhood. Let Timothy take to heart that this experience was typical. All who determine to live lives of true Christian devotion must expect persecution; and the more so as the contrast between the good and the evil increases, and evil men get worse, both in their own blind departure from the truth, and in their power to mislead others.

10 *Now you have observed*; lit., as in RV, 'didst follow', *i.e.* in responsive discipleship; *cf.* 1 Tim. 4:6. Paul is not boasting but reminding his devoted follower of the essentials of devotion to Christ. Note the significance of each of these. **11** *What . . . what*; lit. 'such (as)'. In illustration of his point Paul selects trials specially well known to Timothy, from which he first learned that such afflictions are part of the inevitable experience of all true Christians (see Acts 14:19–

22). This is the lesson enforced in v. 12 (*cf.* Mt. 5:10; 10:22; Jn. 15:20). **12** *All who desire*; lit. 'all who are so minded or determined'. *Godly . . . in Christ Jesus* is a significant description of the spirit and sphere of true Christian living, *i.e.* responding in reverent devotion as one enabled and constrained by a vital personal relation. **13** *Impostors.* The Greek *goētes* means 'wizards', lit. 'wailers', referring to incantation by howling; it may imply, therefore, the use of magical arts.

3:14–17 The value of the Scriptures

What is more, Timothy knows the revealed truth of God and has been assured of its value from those who taught him as a child. His duty, therefore, is steadfastly to adhere to these things. For the sacred Scriptures in which he was taught are uniquely qualified to guide men into the experience of that salvation of God which is to be enjoyed through faith in Messiah Jesus. Not only so, every single Scripture (v. 16), because it owes its origin to the creative breath or Spirit of God (Gk. *theopneustos*, 'God-breathed'; *cf.* Ps. 33:6), has its value for the moral education of the man of God and his thorough equipment for every kind of good work.

14 *But as for you*; in sharp contrast to the *evil men* (v. 13). **15** *From childhood* (lit. 'from a babe'); a reference to Timothy's instruction from very early infancy (see 1:5). *The sacred writings.* Used with the definite article this is a virtual technical expression (found also in Philo and Josephus) for the OT. Note the significant Christian description of their theme and purpose. They afford not just knowledge or information, but practical instruction. *Able.* In Greek the word is a present participle, indicating a permanent enduring quality. **16** See RV and RV mg. The meaning is that every single scripture (of those just referred to), because it is inspired of God, is also profitable; so none should be neglected. *Training in righteousness*; *i.e.* discipline, or education, in the way (or life) of righteousness. **17** *The man of God*: here with special reference to the Christian minister who, like Timothy, has preaching and pastoral responsibility (see 4:1, 2). *Complete, equipped.* In Greek the adjective and the participle reiterate the same root, enforcing the idea of 'fully equipped and adapted'.

4:1–5 Paul's charge to Timothy

In view, therefore, of his calling to ministry Paul solemnly charges Timothy before God, and in the light of the account he must render to King Jesus when He comes to judge, to preach the word, to be on the alert to do so on all occasions, whether favourable or not, and to apply its challenge to his hearers both in rebuke and in encouragement with unfailing patience and comprehensive instruction. Timothy ought to do this the more because a time is coming when men will not tolerate this kind of profitable teaching, but will turn from the truth to fiction and to teachers who say things to tickle their fancy. Timothy must, therefore, be always sober, prepared to suffer hardship, active in declaring the Christian good news, discharging to the full his ministry.

1 Paul adjures Timothy by God, by Christ the future Judge, by His 'epiphany', or second advent, and by His kingdom. It is an important feature of the NT gospel that Jesus is to judge all men, and that a day is coming when He will thus be manifested. *Cf.* Acts 17:31; Rom. 2:16. The phrase, *judge the living and the dead,* is found in early Christian creeds. **2** *Preach the word;* i.e. the gospel; cf. Acts 6:4; Col. 4:3. *Be urgent;* i.e. be attentive, as one standing by ready to fulfil this ministry. *Convince, rebuke, and exhort.* Note how the word and its preacher must hurt before they can heal. *Be unfailing in patience and in teaching.* This indicates how the minister is to handle both his hearers and his subject-matter. He should give varied and positive teaching, not monotonous and negative condemnation. **3, 4** The future prospect described here provides added reason for such preaching. *Endure; i.e.* 'put up with', 'have the mind or patience to receive'. Note how this hearing is wrong both in motive and interest; it is determined by selfish caprice or desire to be entertained; and deliberately directed away from the truth toward more fascinating *myths.* **5** Timothy greatly needs, therefore, *always* to *be steady* or 'sober' (RV)—'to steer clear of the heady wine of heretical teaching' (J. N. D. Kelly).

4:6–22 A DESCRIPTION OF PAUL'S OWN CIRCUMSTANCES: FINAL GREETINGS

Paul declares that he is ready to die a martyr's death, which he knows is imminent. His life work is done; he has been true to his trust. He can look forward to that consummation of salvation which the Lord will give, in that day when He comes as Judge, to all who have their hope thus fixed on His appearing. Of Paul's intimate friends and fellow-workers only Luke is now with him. So Paul urges Timothy to endeavour to come to him quickly, and to bring with him Mark and some of Paul's personal belongings which he left at Troas. In his imprisonment and trial Paul has had his disappointments. Demas forsook him. Alexander actually did him injury and spoke against him. No-one was prepared publicly to take his side. But the Lord did not fail to enable him fully to declare the substance of what he preached for all to hear. He was preserved from being overwhelmed and silenced, and is persuaded that the Lord will bring him safely through what now lies ahead into His kingdom above. To Him is eternal glory due. Timothy is to give Paul's greetings to his special friends, and himself to accept greetings from some who wish to send them to him. Because Paul is without those whom Timothy might imagine to be with him, let him come before winter. May he know the Lord's presence in his heart; and may the saving grace of God be with all in whose midst he is. (*Your* (v. 22) is singular, *you* is plural.)

6 Paul's circumstances provide added reason why Timothy should fulfil his ministry. Pouring out of blood (Dt. 12:27) or wine (Nu. 28:7) unto the Lord accompanied sacrifice; Paul so speaks of the shedding of his own blood (RV mg.). *Cf.* Phil. 2:17. Note that what was then a remote possibility is now an immediate certainty, indeed, has already begun. *My departure;* the Greek word is used of the loosing of a ship from its moorings. **7** *The good fight* is the one fought for *the faith* (cf. 1 Tim. 6:12). *The race.* 'My course' (AV) expresses better the idea; cf. Acts 13:25; 20:24. *The faith; i.e.* the gospel, or deposit of doctrine, entrusted to Paul. This he has successfully guarded (*cf.* 1:14). **8** *Laid up; i.e.* reserved, set aside. *The crown of righteousness;* either the crown is the reward for righteousness, or righteousness is the content of the crown (*cf.* 1 Pet. 5:4). The two ideas may be combined in that heavenly consummation of the God-given righteousness or justification, of which believers enjoy now only the firstfruits (*cf.* Rom. 5:1, 2). This interpretation seems to be confirmed by the fact that the crown is to be shared in equally by all who have had their love set on this coming manifestation of the Lord in righteous judgment at His second advent.

10 *Demas* is not charged with apostasy, but with unwillingness to face the possibility of physical suffering and death through further association with Paul the prisoner and likely martyr. Contrast his love of *this present world* with others' love of the Lord's appearing (v. 8). **11** *Get* or 'pick up' *Mark, i.e.* add him to your company for, or on, the journey; cf. Acts 20:13. In spite of serious early misgivings about his fitness (Acts 15:38), Paul here (*cf.* Col. 4:10) commends Mark as *very useful* for ministering, perhaps in the gospel, or more probably to Paul's more personal needs. Some think Mark's probable knowledge of Latin made him particularly useful in Rome. **12** implies, perhaps, that Paul needs Mark to take Tychicus's place. Paul trusted the latter more than once to carry messages and act on his behalf (see Eph. 6:21, 22; Col. 4:7, 8; Tit. 3:12). **13** *The cloak; i.e.* a large outer garment, apparently needed by Paul for use during the cold of the coming winter; see v. 21. *The parchments;* Gk. *membranai,* in origin a Latin word and meaning prepared skins of vellum, preferred to papyrus for important documents. These were especially precious to Paul. They were presumably either copies of OT scriptures or proof-texts, or possibly valuable personal documents of Paul's own. **14** *Did me great harm; i.e.* 'shewed' (RV mg.) me much ill-treatment. *The Lord will requite him;* a virtual quotation of Ps. 62:12 (*cf.* Pr. 24:12), implying 'It is for the Lord to recompense him accordingly (not me or you)'; cf. Rom. 12:19. **15** 'Meanwhile', says Paul to Timothy, 'there is need for you to beware of him.'

16 *At my first defence.* According to Roman

legal procedure Paul had appeared once in court to present his defence. On that occasion he had to plead his cause alone. He had no advocate or supporting witnesses. Those who might have been such all deserted him, presumably through fear, not deliberate malice, as in the case of Alexander. So Paul prays that God in mercy will not reckon such failure against them. **17** 'That through me the message might be fully proclaimed' (RV) expresses well the sense of Paul's concern, namely that the proclamation of the gospel should be faithfully discharged by him there in the capital city for all to hear. *All the Gentiles* refers to the cosmopolitan character of Paul's audience, corresponding to the scope of the gospel and of his commission to preach it. See Rom. 16:26; 1:5. 'To be rescued out of a lion's mouth' may have been a current phrase for deliverance out of apparently overwhelming peril. Or 'lion' may refer, either to the beasts of the amphitheatre, or to the Emperor Nero, or to the devil. In 1 Pet. 5:8 to be devoured by the lion seems to mean to have one's faithful testimony silenced by surrender through fear to the devil. *Cf.* also the Lord's Prayer— 'deliver us from the evil (one)'—of which there seem to be further reminiscences in v. 18. **18** *Save me for*; Gk. *eis*, a pregnant construction. Paul's salvation is to be completed by his being brought safely 'into' *his heavenly kingdom.* The deliverance he expects from all evil is not from death, but through it. Note that the doxology is addressed to Christ as God.

22 The benediction is twofold: the first is addressed to Timothy personally, the second is the distinctive Pauline 'signature' (see 2 Thes. 3:17, 18).

Titus

OUTLINE OF CONTENTS

For the General Introduction to this Epistle see p. 1166.

COMMENTARY

1:1-4 PERSONAL ADDRESS AND GREETING

Compare and see notes on 1 Tim. 1:1, 2. Paul writes as one constrained by the obligation of bond-service to God and by the authority of the commission of Christ. This service and commission concern, and are directed towards, the bringing of those whom God has chosen to save to faith in Him (*cf.* Acts 13:48; 1 Thes. 1:4-8) and to the full knowledge of the truth. **1** Note that full instruction in the truth is an essential part of the apostolic task and that such truth is disclosed in Christ. See Mt. 28:19, 20; Jn. 1:14; Eph. 1:13; 4:20, 21. Both for its understanding and for its enjoyment this truth demands a spirit of *godliness*, or active reverence Godward. **2** Such truth gives to men nothing less than a *hope of eternal life*, a hope guaranteed by a promise made before world history began by God, who cannot deceive or utter falsehood. *Cf.* Nu. 23:19; Heb. 6:18. Note the sure guarantee afforded by the word of such a God. **3** God's announcement of this word of His to men has been openly made, when the proper time for this came (*cf.* 1 Tim. 2:6), in the gospel message. It is with its proclamation, says Paul, that *I have been entrusted* by the direct appointment of God Himself, as the One active to save us. **4** Paul, by natural birth a Jew, greets Titus, a Greek (see Gal. 2:3), as one brought by the faith which they now share into an intimacy of family relationship. The wording may well mean that Titus owed his conversion to Paul.

1:5-9 THE QUALIFICATIONS OF ELDERS OR BISHOPS

Paul left Titus in Crete to complete the establishment of their missionary work there, and particularly to see to the appointment of elders in each local congregation (*cf.* Acts 14:23). He had not only charged him to do this, but had also indicated how to do it properly by stating what kind of men should be appointed. These instructions he now repeats and enforces. Anyone who is to be appointed ought in character and conduct to be beyond reproach, free from incongruous moral weakness, actively given to good works and to the disciplined pursuit of personal holiness, and so unswerving in his loyalty to the truth which he has received that he can encourage many by his healthy teaching and expose the error of any who speak contrary to it. *Cf.* 1 Tim. 3:1–7 and see notes there.

5 Titus was to *amend* any things which were *defective*. Note that the same officers are called *elders* (Gk. *presbyteroi*), describing status as 'seniors', and *bishops* (Gk. *episkopoi*), describing function as 'overseers'. One congregation might have several; *cf.* Acts 20:17, 28. **6** A man's personal and family life and previous history are all important as indicating his character and determining his fitness for appointment. *Not open to the charge of being profligate or insubordinate* refers to the *children*. Note the plain indication that children of a true Christian home should not be dissolute or undisciplined, but rather themselves responsive to the gospel as believers. **7** Irreproachable character is indispensable because the elder has to be *a bishop*; *i.e.* to exercise oversight as one answerable to God as His steward. For 'the house', or church, for which he cares is God's. **7, 8** Note the relevance to the task to be done of the vices from which a bishop should be free, and of the virtues which he should possess. **9** The word that is *sure*, or trustworthy, and essential to the giving of *instruction in sound doctrine* and to the refuting of any who speak against it, is the 'word which is according to the teaching' (RV), or apostolic doctrine. Paul, who has himself been entrusted with that word, is supremely concerned that others, appointed to its stewardship, should first hold fast to it themselves, and then faithfully preserve and propagate it. *Cf.* 2 Tim. 2:2.

1:10–16 A WARNING AGAINST FALSE TEACHERS

Note the significant correspondence with our Lord's similar warnings in Mk. 7:1–23. There is need for 'bishops' who can expose the error of those who oppose the truth (v. 9). There are many who are active in misleading men by their false teaching, and they must be silenced. Also, Cretans readily fall for things untrue and sensual, as a true testimony of one of their own poets makes plain. So severe exposure of the false teachers and of their fanciful and man-made teaching is the more necessary if the Cretan Christians are to maintain their spiritual health. In these matters the response of the heart and the practice of the life go together. Those who through heart unbelief become inwardly corrupt defile everything they touch by the way they use it. Though they may confess God with their lips, their deeds proclaim that they do not know

Him. Rather in His sight they are detestable, because disobedient, and so disqualified for any good work.

10 The false teachers are *insubordinate*; *i.e.* they do not submit their minds to divinely revealed truth; and as church members they are undisciplined and rebellious. *Empty talkers and deceivers*. They teach things which have no substance or corresponding reality (*cf.* Rom. 1:21, 22), and are capable of misleading the minds of men. Those who are the greatest danger are Jews and Judaizers, propagating teaching which has its roots in Judaism (*cf.* v. 14). They must be silenced, both because of the damage they can do—they are the sort who can overturn the faith of whole families—and because they stand doubly condemned as teaching what is wrong and as doing it for material gain.

12 Paul here quotes a hexameter line of the Cretan philosopher Epimenides, who wrote about 600 BC. In remarkable language Paul calls him *a prophet* and **13** endorses his *testimony* as *true*. This affords scriptural authority for believing that in some small degree Gentile nations have had their own prophets. The quotation was probably well known. Certainly Cretans had in the Greek world a proverbial reputation as *liars*. The character of the false teaching and of those who propagate it is then radically exposed and condemned. **14** In contrast to the gospel, which is 'of God' and *the truth*, this teaching is *of men* and consists of *myths* or mere fiction. Those who teach it have turned their backs on the truth. Therefore, to give heed to their teaching is to do likewise (*cf.* Is. 29:13; Mk. 7:6–9). These *commands* probably prohibited the use of certain things as unclean (*cf.* 1 Tim. 4:3; Col. 2:16, 21). **15** refers to *things* (*cf.* 1 Tim. 4:4), not to actions which are always morally wrong. It declares that such *things* are pure or not in men's use (not in their judgment) of them according to their inner spiritual and moral condition. Defilement takes its rise within, not through things from without (*cf.* Mk. 7:15). **16** *Unfit*; Gk. *adokimoi*, a word often used by Paul; it means 'unapproved of', 'rejected after testing'.

2:1–10 INSTRUCTIONS FOR VARIOUS GROUPS IN THE CHURCH

Having shown (1:10–16) why the error of opponents of the truth needs exposing, Paul now indicates how to exhort in 'the healthful teaching' (see 1:9; 2:1, RV mg.). The injunctions here given personally to Titus and the detailed exhortations he is to give to others all concern conduct. The best antidote to wrong teaching is positive moral exhortation and teaching which promotes spiritual health and consequent worthy behaviour. It has already been shown that those who follow wrong teaching are first corrupt in heart, and then become so in life. Therefore those who desire by their teaching to maintain the true spiritual well-being of others must demand the consistent expression in conduct of heart-soundness within. This is the kind of teaching to which Titus must publicly give utterance. He must direct appropriate exhortations of this kind to the different age-groups in the church. He should exhort the older women similarly to teach the younger women. He should enforce what he demands, particularly to the young men, by the example of his own personal behaviour. Thus, by the serious sincerity and irreproachable character of his ministry, he should put to shame and silence potential opponents. Those who as slaves have to serve human masters need special exhortation to show themselves obedient and faithful in order thus attractively to exhibit the worth of the gospel which declares that God is the Saviour of men.

2 *Temperate*; *i.e.* practising restraint. *Serious*; *i.e.* dignified, and worthy of respect. *Sensible*; *i.e.* prudent, thoughtful, self-controlled. *Sound*; *i.e.* healthy, in contrast to being sick: see 1 Tim. 6:4, RV mg.; Rom. 14:1. 3 *Reverent*; the Greek means 'as befits a holy person'. *Slanderers* (Gk. *diaboloi*); *cf.* 1 Tim. 3:6, 11. 4 The older women are to fulfil an active teaching ministry in the home and among the younger women, but not in the congregation generally; see 1 Tim. 2:11, 12. 4, 5 teach that Christian married women are to find their sphere of service in the family and the home as good wives and mothers, submissively recognizing their husbands as the head of the house, lest the God-given gospel be reproached for encouraging an improper freedom and disturbing domestic life (*cf.* 1 Tim. 6:1). *Kind*; *i.e.* not hard or mean in their management of the home. *Cf.* the use of the word in Mt. 20:15 (AV, RV 'good').

7 *Show yourself . . . a model*; the personal reference is emphatic; the practical 'model' (Gk. *typos*) of good living which Titus is to provide for others to look upon is himself. *Integrity, gravity*; *i.e.* purity of motive and seriousness of manner, describing characteristics of the teacher, not the teaching. 8 Further, what Titus teaches should be not only intrinsically 'healthful' but also so expressed as to be 'irreproachable'. The opponent of the truth, whose aim is to slander its teachers and to propagate error, is to be put to shame by this ministry of the health-giving word and by his own inability to say anything bad about the Christians' manner of life. 9 *Refractory*; RV 'gainsaying'. The Greek *antilegein*, lit. 'to contradict', can mean 'to oppose', 'to show active enmity against'. 10 *Pilfer*; the Greek literally means 'putting on one side for themselves'. *Entire*; Gk. *pas*, 'all', has here an extensive force and signifies 'on every possible occasion'. *Adorn*; the Greek verb *kosmein* can be used of the 'setting' of a jewel, a process by which it is favourably displayed. *The doctrine of God* (not Christ) *our Saviour*; *i.e.* not the ethical precepts of our Lord, but the gospel of our salvation; see v. 11.

2:11 – 3:11 THE CHRISTIAN'S DUTY TO MAINTAIN GOOD WORKS

Paul has just indicated that it is the gospel of God's salvation which ought to be attractively set forth by the appropriate good works or Christian behaviour of those who believe it (2:5, 10). He now introduces two remarkable doctrinal summaries of essential features of this gospel (2:11–14; 3:3–7), both of which are directed to show that a life of good works is God's purpose and the only appropriate behaviour for all who enjoy the benefits of His redeeming grace and saving mercy. Titus is told, therefore, that it is his responsibility confidently to proclaim this gospel, which is so worthy of being believed, and then authoritatively to apply its practical challenge in exhortation and rebuke to all who profess to have believed it, in order to move them to give the most careful attention to the matter of good living. This is the teaching, says Paul, which is both virtuous in itself and profitable to men. Foolish inquiries and subjects which, by contrast, are productive of nothing but strife and division should be avoided because they are obviously so unhelpful. So should any who show a perverse interest in them and will not give them up after being admonished.

11 *Has appeared* (Gk. aorist tense) points to one definite act, *i.e.* the incarnation and atoning work of Christ (*cf.* 3:4). In character and purpose the grace thus manifested is 'saving' or 'bringing salvation' (see RV), and that not to Jews only, but to *all men*. Its scope is worldwide. 12 God's saving grace brings us under a discipline or instruction which makes plain that we must live our present lives differently. Negatively, we must decisively abandon the kind of life which is dominated by lack of reverence for God and by mere worldly interests; positively, we must seek to live rightly in relation to ourselves, to others, and to God—*i.e.* sober, upright, and godly lives. 13 This gospel also gives us a hope beyond this life which is to be anticipated as *blessed*; *i.e.* the consummation of bliss. For Christ's second advent will be an appearing (Gk. *epiphaneia*) of God's 'glory' as the first was of His 'grace' (v. 11). Then Jesus will be openly manifested not only as *our Saviour* but also in all the glory of His majesty or greatness as *God*. Or the phraseology may mean that Christ's appearing will be accompanied by a manifestation of the divine glory. 14 Christ's ability to be *our Saviour* depends on His one accomplished act of self-sacrifice on our behalf as a ransom price (*cf.* Mk. 10:45; 1 Tim. 2:6). The full salvation which He thus procured means, negatively, our release from every kind of lawlessness, and, positively, our purification to be His own chosen people (*cf.* Ps. 130:8; Ezk. 37:23), devoted to good works. So transformed living is intended and possible for those who know God and His Christ as their Saviour. It is therefore rightly expected from them both by God and by men. 15 *Let no one disregard you*;

i.e. when you thus speak, do not allow anyone to treat what you say as unworthy of their attention.

3:1, 2 These verses give detailed instruction how, in this world, appropriate Christian good conduct should express itself in relation both to civil authorities and one's fellowmen. Christians ought to be dutiful citizens, prepared to take an active share in every kind of good activity—a particularly significant injunction here as Cretans had a reputation for being seditious. Christians ought also to act towards all with whom they come into contact in positive goodwill, refraining from attacking any by word or deed, and actively displaying a considerate and yielding spirit towards all.

What should inspire such conduct is the recollection that we ourselves were by nature as bad as any, and that God has treated us kindly and saved us when we did not deserve it. The gospel of saving grace is therefore again pregnantly stated. **3** provides a general description of sinful and unredeemed human nature— what *we ourselves were once. Foolish*; lit. 'senseless', 'without understanding'. Sinners show how completely abhorrent their sinful condition must be to God, because they even hate one another. **4** shows that the change in our condition is due entirely to God, to His initiative, to His kindness and active love (contrast our hate and active enmity), to His open intervention to save. **5** makes it still more explicit. Our salvation is not due to any righteous works of our doing, but is wholly determined by God's mercy; the *not, us* and *his own* are all emphatic. In status this salvation is made ours through the outward seal of baptism, *i.e. the washing of regeneration*; in vital experience it comes through the inner quickening or making new by the Spirit. (*Cf.* Jn. 3:5, 'born of water and the Spirit'.) **6** This gift of the quickening and indwelling Spirit has been made ours by God through Christ and His saving work (*cf.* Jn. 7:39; Acts 2:33). So the whole Trinity is active to make salvation ours. **7** And the full gospel includes not only the gift of God's Son for our justification, but also the gift of God's Spirit to make us heirs who can, by the life which He makes ours, hope to enjoy salvation eternally. *Cf.* 1:2; Rom. 8:11, 15–17, 23, 24. Alternatively, following RSV or RV rather than AV in v. 5, one may interpret the *washing* of baptism as a mediating token of two benefits, *regeneration* and spiritual *renewal*, benefits which are possibly again referred to as being *justified* and becoming *heirs in hope of eternal life*, the one giving a new status of acceptance with God (elsewhere called 'adoption', *e.g.* Gal. 4:5), and the other giving the complementary blessing of new Spirit-born life. Note that *regeneration* (Gk. *palingenesia*), like our word 'naturalization', though it suggests a new birth or nature, may rather signify a change of status.

8 The gospel thus summarized in vv. 4–7 is trustworthy doctrine and justifies Titus in confidently making the strongest assertions with regard to it (see RV) in order that those who have thereby come to trust in God may give attention to the practice of *good deeds*. The Greek *proistasthai* may mean 'to be forward in', 'to devote themselves before all else to' (*cf.* 2:14). **9** Note how similar are the descriptions of harmful teaching given here and in 1 Tim. 1:4; 6:4, 20; 2 Tim. 2:23. **10** *Factious* (Gk. *hairetikos*, and so RV 'heretical') primarily describes one who causes divisions. This he does by 'choosing on his own' (the root idea) to depart from the truth, and to follow and propagate different teaching. So 'heretical' comes to mean 'holding false doctrine'. But note the fundamental references of the word, first to the moral cause, self-will, and then to the evil consequence, division. Such a man needs not argument but admonition. **11** *Perverted.* What makes his completely unsatisfactory moral (not intellectual) condition plain is his refusal to heed admonition.

3:12–15 PERSONAL MESSAGES AND FAREWELL GREETINGS

Paul instructs Titus to join him at Nicopolis, where he intends to spend the winter. Titus is to leave as soon as either Artemas or Tychicus arrives, whom Paul says he will send—probably to take over the work in Crete for which Titus was responsible. Practical help is also to be given to expedite the journey of Zenas and Apollos, who likewise may have been going to join Paul. This instruction brings Paul back in thought to a final reiteration of his main injunction, that the Christians in Crete should learn to use every opportunity to do good works and to supply the needs of others. Only so will they be truly fruitful. Paul then sends greetings from all his companions to Titus; he himself greets all in Crete who have true Christian love for himself and his fellow-workers in the gospel. Then he adds his characteristic benediction.

12 *Nicopolis.* There are three cities so called, in Cilicia, in Thrace or Macedonia, and in Epirus. The last is most probably the one here referred to. *There* (not 'here') implies that Paul was not at Nicopolis when he wrote. **13** *Do your best to speed . . . on their way.* There are several indications in the Epistles that Christians were taught and expected to entertain and provide for Christian travellers, particularly those active in preaching. See Rom. 15:24; 1 Cor. 16:6; 3 Jn. 5–8. **15** *In the faith*; RV 'in faith'. This was the bond that united them. It was Christian not natural love. *Cf.* 1 Tim. 1:2. *Grace be with you all.* See on 1 Tim. 6:21.

A. M. STIBBS

Philemon

INTRODUCTION

AUTHORSHIP

Not only is Paul stated to be the author of this letter, but this ascription has rarely been questioned. It breathes too obviously the genuine Paul to be disputed. Of all his Epistles, in spite of its brevity, it is the most revealing of the character of the apostle. It may be wondered why so brief a personal letter was preserved among the NT books, but the answer must surely be that it provided an exquisite example of one Christian man's petition for another. The fact that the author was no less a man than the apostle Paul must have warmly commended it to the early Christians.

OCCASION AND PURPOSE

The Epistle is addressed to Philemon, who, according to the most natural understanding of v. 2, was host to a church group in his house. He also appears to have been the owner of a slave, Onesimus (v. 10), who had run away from him, having apparently absconded with some of his belongings. By some means which is not disclosed Onesimus came into contact with Paul, as a result of which he became a Christian. Paul can therefore speak of him as 'my child, Onesimus'. The apostle had clearly been told the full circumstances which caused Onesimus to be away from his master. He recognized that it was his Christian duty to return to Philemon, although, since being with Paul, he had been useful in ministering to him. But the duty to return carried with it a considerable hazard, for in a society which not only accepted slavery, but was widely dependent upon it, there were severe penalties for slaves who defected. Although Philemon was a Christian he may still have considered it advisable to administer punishment. The letter is a plea for leniency. Armed with so potent a petition, Onesimus would have a weapon of defence which Philemon as a true Christian man would find it difficult to resist. Indeed, Paul not only pleads for leniency, but seems to suggest far more. He was expecting Philemon to receive Onesimus in a new relationship, as a brother instead of a slave, in the same way, in fact, as he would receive Paul himself had he been coming. All this makes good sense of the letter which closes with a request for lodgings when he visits the area, which he evidently expects will be soon.

An alternative proposal has been put forward, which warrants some mention, although based on certain assumptions which are open to question.

J. Knox (*Philemon Among the Letters of Paul*, 1935) suggested that Onesimus was owned by Archippus who, according to him, was the host of the house-church, not Philemon. The latter was an overseer of the Lycus Valley churches based on Laodicea. The further suggestion is made that Archippus's ministry, mentioned in Col. 4:17, was to release his slave Onesimus and to send him back to Paul as a kind of missionary service. Moreover, Knox proposed that this letter to Philemon was 'the letter from Laodicea' which the Colossians are urged to read (Col. 4:16). The reason for this is that Archippus would be less inclined to refuse if the matter had been brought before the whole church. The theory is ingenious but fails to convince. It is unnatural for an epistle to mention first a person who is not its main recipient. Moreover, the evidence to which Knox appeals is better explained by the traditional interpretation. The one feature about the theory which makes a positive contribution is the thought that Paul was asking for the services of Onesimus, but it can hardly be supposed that this was the main subject of the letter. He may have hoped that it would be a by-product.

DATE

The close connection between this Epistle and Colossians has already been mentioned. For a fuller discussion of the date, reference should therefore be made to the Introduction to Colossians. All that applies to that Epistle applies to this. It may reasonably be maintained that Philemon was sent from Rome during Paul's imprisonment there.

SLAVERY IN EARLY CHRISTIAN THOUGHT

Although slaves are mentioned in several Pauline Epistles, in none does slavery appear so vividly as in this, since the whole Epistle revolves around a runaway slave. The question arises why Paul did not take the opportunity of pointing out in a more direct manner the evils of the whole system. Certain factors must be borne in mind before an answer is suggested. Slavery was so integral a part in the social system that a direct confrontation with the State to abolish it, even if it had been possible for the Christian church to embark on such a crusade, would have resulted in nothing short of revolution. Paul was certainly no revolutionary and clearly believed that alleviation of the system could best come some other way. Although the Christians could not have hoped to make abolition of slavery a political platform, they could set an example to the world at large concerning the way in which Christianity could transform the system from within, and by this means could mitigate its evils. This brief letter is a notable example of such an approach in that Paul argues that a new relationship must develop between Philemon and Onesimus, since both master and slave were now Christians. Had the Christian church acted upon the apostle's advice it would not have been so many centuries before campaigns were launched against the evils of slavery. Whether men of his own day saw the real point of Paul's method of undermining the system cannot be determined. But there can be no doubt that this brief letter supplied not a little inspiration to later campaigners for the abolition of the slave trade.

OUTLINE OF CONTENTS

COMMENTARY

This brief Epistle falls into four sections: Greetings, thanksgiving, petition for Onesimus and conclusion. It will be seen, therefore, that although it is essentially a personal letter it conforms to the same pattern as the church Epistles.

1-3 GREETINGS

1 *Paul, a prisoner for Christ Jesus.* Paul makes no reference to his apostolic office as he does in writing to Colossians. He confines himself to a description of his present state, no doubt to impress on Philemon that his request for Onesimus was small compared with the hardships he himself had endured for Christ's sake. A man who has suffered much for the cause has a right to be heard. The linking with *Timothy* is identical with the Colossian letter. Philemon is described as *our beloved fellow worker*, a description which Paul frequently used to make others conscious of their share in his work. 2 Nothing else is known about *Apphia*. She may have been Philemon's wife. *Archippus*, mentioned in Col. 4:17 in connection with the ministry, is here described as *our fellow soldier*, used elsewhere only in Phil. 2:25 of Epaphroditus. Many commentators suggest that he was the son of Philemon and Apphia. 3 The salutation is in a form frequently used by Paul.

4-7 THANKSGIVING

This thanksgiving is specially instructive because of its personal character.

4 *My God.* The possessive pronoun draws attention to Paul's special awareness of his own relationship with God. The word *always* is characteristic of Paul when referring to his prayer for his readers (*cf* 1 Cor. 1:4; Phil. 1:4; Col. 1:3; 1 Thes. 1:2). Remembrance of Philemon meant thanksgiving for him. 5 When Paul says, *because I hear*, it seems reasonable to suppose that he has received this information from Epaphras (*cf.* Col. 1:4, 8). There is some question how the four parts of the rest of the sentence are to be understood. There are three possibilities *a. Love* may be linked with *toward . . . all the saints*, and *faith* linked with *toward the Lord Jesus*. In that case the order would be unusual, but not unknown in the writings of Paul. *b.* Both *love* and *faith* could be taken with both the other expressions, in which case *faith* would indicate the source of the *love*. It would not be faith towards all saints, but a faith expressed in love. This is more difficult than *a. c.* Another possibility is to interpret *faith* as meaning 'faithfulness', but the word could not be so readily understood in this sense in v. 6.

6 *The sharing of your faith.* The interpretation of this whole verse is difficult. Paul seems to have compressed his thoughts to such an extent that various renderings are possible. The present phrase can be taken to mean a sharing of what comes as a result of faith, *i.e.* perhaps Christian almsgiving, or a sharing of the faith itself, *i.e.* faith as the content of Christian belief, or less likely communion (with God) based on faith. The general Pauline usage of the Greek word involved (*koinōnia*) favours the first of these (*cf., e.g.,* Phil. 1:5). But the next words, *may promote the knowledge of all the good*, are even more obscure. A literal rendering might be 'may become effective in the sphere of knowledge of every good thing'. Perhaps Paul is preparing Philemon to examine his 'knowledge', because he wants it to grow in his dealings with Onesimus. In this case *knowledge of all the good* will mean a fuller understanding of the good in Christ, an understanding of the blessings which Christ brings. But this interpretation must be governed

by the concluding phrase, *that is ours in Christ.* The form of the Greek here suggests the meaning 'unto Christ' (*eis*), *i.e.* as the aim of the activity prayed for. This means that Paul is praying that Philemon's 'fellowship' may be directed towards Christ.

7 The words, *For I have derived much joy and comfort,* show what a deep impression reports of Philemon have had upon him. Both qualities mentioned are particularly recurrent in the letters of Paul. The word *comfort* may better be understood in the sense of 'encouragement'. It is significant that Paul returns here to the thought of Philemon's *love,* as in v. 5. *The hearts of the saints have been refreshed.* There is no knowing what Philemon had done to produce this result, but it is generally supposed that it was some act of benevolence which benefited the Colossian Christians. In the Greek the warm address, *brother,* comes at the end, throwing even more emphasis on it than in the RSV text.

8–20 THE PLEA ON BEHALF OF ONESIMUS

The approach of the apostle in this section shows a highly developed sense of Christian tact, to which the various steps in his petition for Onesimus bear witness. These will be noted in the following comments.

8 *Accordingly.* This is a significant connecting link between the petition and the introductory section. It is Paul's knowledge of the character of Philemon which encourages him to plead along the lines of appeal rather than *command.* There is here an indirect allusion to his apostolic authority, although he omits reference to it in the opening verse. Boldness *in Christ* is a boldness which comes through being in a special sense an authorized representative of Christ. Paul assumes that he could exercise this boldness as a right. *What is required* is literally 'what is fitting' (*cf.* Col. 3:18). **9** Having twice mentioned Philemon's love, the apostle now bases his own appeal on love. He could not adopt an authoritative attitude in view of Philemon's own approach. But he makes his appeal thoroughly personal—*Paul, an ambassador and now a prisoner.* The word *ambassador* could be understood in the sense of 'old man', but the RSV translation is almost certainly correct in view of the almost identical use of the metaphor in Eph. 6:20. The plea comes from an ambassador who has been arrested for Christ's sake—a powerful plea. **10** *My child, Onesimus.* There are other occasions on which Paul speaks of his spiritual children (*e.g.* 1 Cor. 4:15; 1 Tim. 1:2). The metaphor is vivid, introducing a new relationship in Christ. A slave who has become the spiritual offspring of the apostle had ceased to be regarded as a slave by him. **11** The parenthesis in this verse contains a play on words, since the name of Onesimus means *useful.* Paul's point is that not till now had he begun to live up to his name. *To you and to me* is another delicate hint, the

inference being that even as far as his relationship to Philemon was concerned there had been a radical transformation—although Philemon is only now being informed about it. **12** In no more forceful way could Paul have shown his attachment to Onesimus than he does here by equating Onesimus with his own *heart.* In sending him back Paul is performing an act of self-sacrifice and is actually conferring a favour on Philemon. What the apostle asks in return must be measured against his loss of a dear friend. Some have suggested that the verb *sending . . . back* may be understood as 'referring back' and that the meaning is that Paul is not intending Philemon to retain Onesimus but is referring the matter to him for a decision in the hope that he will be allowed to return to Paul. The only other occurrence of the same verb in the NT would support this alternative suggestion. Moreover the next verse would seem to confirm this view. But if the Epistle is sent from Rome, this raises the difficulty of the long journey back to Paul. **13** The apostle here expresses as a wish what he hopes Philemon will concede—that Onesimus might serve him with Philemon's consent. No hint is given as to the nature of this service, but since the apostle is imprisoned, the usefulness of having a loyal associate close at hand needs no demonstrating. **14** Again the apostle presses the point about Philemon's *consent* and contrasts it, as if it were the only live alternative, with *compulsion. Your own free will* adds further emphasis to the idea of *consent.*

15–20 In this paragraph Paul at last specifies his request. The remaining steps in his petition are perhaps the most telling of all. **15** This verse makes it difficult to suppose that the apostle was asking for the services of Onesimus. The contrast between *for a while* and *for ever* seems against that suggestion, unless the latter word refers, not to Philemon having Onesimus back as a slave, but as a Christian (as in v. 16). It is better, however, to suppose that Paul is using an argument to mitigate the loss by Philemon of the services of Onesimus, over which he might justly have complained. **16** Paul edges still nearer the point when he contrasts Onesimus as he was with Onesimus as he now is—the transformation from *a slave* to *a beloved brother* (*cf.* Col. 4:9, where the same ascription is used of him). It is tactfully suggested that he should mean more to Philemon than to Paul. The distinction between *in the flesh* and *in the Lord* is between his material status (a slave) and his spiritual standing (a Christian). **17** *If you consider.* There is a subtle tactfulness in this clause. There is no doubt that Philemon regarded Paul as a *partner.* The then-clause should therefore follow without question. The words, *as you would receive me,* show that Paul regards himself as a sort of pattern for Philemon's approach to Onesimus. **18, 19** At this stage in his petition, he refers to any debts which Onesimus might owe. The fact that this subject is mentioned suggests that Onesimus had told Paul that he had robbed his master. Paul's generous offer to pay the debts for Onesimus raises problems in view of various references in his Epistles to his poverty and to his need for working with his own hands. He may, of course, have inherited some resources. On the other hand this may have been a delicate way of reminding Philemon that his spiritual debt to Paul exceeded anything that Onesimus owed him. Nevertheless, the fact that Paul drew attention to his own signature shows that he intended Philemon to treat his I O U seriously. He could not imagine that he would take him up on his offer. **20** Here is the final step—a personal appeal for *some benefit* for himself. This is more effective than ending with a plea for Onesimus. The word *refresh* is used by Paul in a similar sense in 1 Cor. 16:18 of others who had performed some service for him.

21–25 CONCLUSION

21 The apostle is confident of the complete success of the letter. What he expects Philemon to do is implied rather than stated. If the above-mentioned suggestion, that he wanted the services of Onesimus for himself, is correct, he may have been hinting here that the slave should be freed. **22** The mention of the *guest room* shows that Paul regarded his imprisonment as temporary and expected release in the not too distant future. **23** All those mentioned here are also mentioned in Col. 4:10ff. *Epaphras* is not there called a *fellow prisoner*, although the term is applied to *Aristarchus*. **25** This conclusion is the same as at the close of Galatians.

DONALD GUTHRIE

Hebrews

INTRODUCTION

There are several questions which it is natural to ask concerning the writing of a document of the NT, and which in the case of this Epistle it is impossible to answer with any certainty. While possible answers may be suggested and to some extent reasonably supported, the simple truth is that we do not know either who wrote this Epistle or to whom it was first written.

Our ignorance on such points does not, however, prevent right understanding or minimize the spiritual and theological value of a document which has from the first commended itself as authoritative by its own intrinsic worth. Indeed, the only adequate answer of Christian faith to these very questions is that God Himself is the primary author and Christians of every age are the divinely intended readers. For through this Epistle God unquestionably has spoken, and still speaks, by His Spirit to His people. This is ultimately the most important vindication of its place in the Canon of the NT.

AUTHORSHIP

In the Epistle itself there is no explicit indication who wrote it. Nor do early Christian writers provide us with any unanimous or convincing testimony. Tertullian is definite in his witness; he says that Barnabas wrote it. But this witness is unconfirmed, though there is still a little to be said in its favour. The man who was given a Christian name meaning 'son of exhortation' (Acts 4:36, RV) may well be responsible for this 'word of exhortation' (Heb. 13:22). As a Levite he would have more than an ordinary interest in the sacrificial ritual; as a Jew from Cyprus he quite possibly had intimate contact with the Hellenistic and philosophical teaching of Alexandrian Judaism with which both the writer and his readers seem to have had some acquaintance; as one of those converted immediately after Pentecost (which may be what Heb. 2:3, 4 refers to), he doubtless came under the influence of the teaching of Stephen, an influence which seems to persist in this Epistle.

In Alexandria, where the Epistle was accepted on its own merits, there is evidence of a growing tendency in the 3rd century to connect it with Paul, but only rather indirectly. Clement suggested that Paul wrote it in Hebrew and that Luke translated it into Greek. Origen was prepared to think that the original thoughts were the apostle's but not the final written form and language. Such connection of the Epistle with the name of Paul commended itself widely because it gave it welcome apostolic authority, for lack of which many hesitated to accept it as canonical. Consequently many manuscript copies came to be headed with the title 'The Epistle *of Paul* to the Hebrews'. This ascription to the apostle, however, most present-day students are not prepared to accept. The internal evidence of the Epistle itself, its language, style and contents, are regarded as conclusive against it (*e.g.* contrast 2:3 and Gal. 1:12; 2:6).

Other suggestions are wholly speculative. They include Apollos, Silas, Aquila (or Priscilla and Aquila) and Philip the evangelist. Of these Luther's suggestion of Apollos is perhaps the best. From what we know of him (see Acts 18:24–28) he is exactly the kind of man who might have written such an Epistle. But there is no other evidence to prove that he did. When a human writer of Scripture was providentially led to hide his identity there is no need to try, and possibly little or no hope of success in trying, to discover it. It is wiser to be content not to know.

THE FIRST RECIPIENTS

There is no clear indication in the Epistle itself to whom it was originally written. The familiar title *To the Hebrews* goes back to the 2nd century. The contents strongly confirm that the Epistle was written to Jewish Christians. In it there is no reference to heathenism at all; 9:15 seems to imply that those referred to had been 'under the first covenant'; and the Old Testament Scriptures, the Sinaitic covenant and the Levitical sacrificial ritual are treated with marked respect as possessing God-given sanction and authority. Nevertheless, for this very reason that the references to the Jewish background are all to what is written, and to what God thus says, rather than to Judaism and to current practice in the Temple in Jerusalem, several attempts have recently been made to suggest that the Epistle was written to Gentile Christians. (*Cf.* the way in which in 1 Cor. 10:1–11, in writing to a predominantly Gentile church, Paul appeals to the OT, and refers to 'our fathers'. See also 1 Cor. 5:7, 8.)

There is a lack of information in the Epistle concerning the location of its original readers. Jerusalem, Caesarea, Antioch in Syria, Ephesus, Alexandria and Rome have all been suggested. The fact that the readers had not themselves heard Christ (2:3) tells against their being lifelong residents in Jerusalem. Their general background, while unquestionably Jewish, seems to have been Hellenistic and somewhat

Alexandrian rather than exclusively Palestinian and rabbinical. They seem to have been Jews of the Dispersion, whose Scriptures were the OT in Greek. The phrase 'They of (literally 'from') Italy salute you' (13:24) may be interpreted to mean people away from Italy sending greetings to their homeland. If this interpretation be correct (see notes *ad loc.*) it favours the view that the recipients were a Jewish section of the Christian community in Rome. It is perhaps significant that the earliest known quotations from this Epistle occur in a letter written by Clement of Rome about AD 95. Also, the reference to persecution in 10:32–34 might be a reference to the expulsion from Rome of (Christian) Jews by the emperor Claudius about AD 50. See Acts 18:2.

In form the Epistle appears more like a sermon than a letter. The style is oratorical, the argumentation logical, the literary structure elaborate. There are periodic exhortations. The writer even says, 'Time would fail me to tell' (11:32). But, even if it was first composed as a sermon, in the form in which we have it it was clearly sent as a letter to a definite group of readers. See 2:3; 5:11, 12; 6:9, 10; 10:25, 32–36; 13:7, 19, 23, 24. They knew the writer and Timothy. The writer hopes to come and see them. They had been Christians for a long time, and had been known to the writer from the beginnings of their Christian faith. From the references in the Epistle (see 13:24) they seem to have been a limited circle, who perhaps had a special 'house-church' meeting of their own rather than a large community which would presumably have included many more recent converts.

It seems possible to suggest (but it is only a suggestion) that the particular recipients of this Epistle were a group of Jews who had originally been members of a synagogue of the Dispersion. They were men zealously devoted to Judaism, and to Judaism as they understood it, not from lifelong residence in Palestine, but from the study of the OT in Greek. They were not unacquainted with Alexandrian thought. As Jews they were originally zealous in visiting Jerusalem for the great annual feasts. Possibly it was when, as a group, they were on such a visit to Jerusalem, at or soon after the great Christian Pentecost, that they, as well as the writer, were converted to faith in Jesus as the Christ through hearing the preaching of the apostles and through seeing the visible signs of the power of the Holy Spirit (2:3, 4). They may even have seen and shared in the persecution that was stirred up against the church in Jerusalem by the Jewish authorities and by zealous Jews like Saul of Tarsus; which may be to what 10:32–34 refers (see Acts 5:41; 8:3; 9:13, 14). It may well be to the poor saints in Jerusalem that they subsequently ministered from their home base (6:10).

Such a background to their entrance into the experience of new life in Christ would give added significance to the writer's assertion that the followers of Jesus have no earthly Jerusalem as their continuing city; rather they must go forth to Him outside the camp (13:12–14). As Christians they are 'come to Mount Zion and to the city of the living God, the heavenly Jerusalem' (12:22). Here they need no longer stand in the court outside the shrine into which the high priest alone enters, and that only once a year, but can themselves freely and continuously enter boldly through the now rent curtain into the very sanctuary of God's presence.

DATE

This it is impossible to fix with absolute certainty, though one may say with considerable confidence that the Epistle was most probably written between AD 60 and 70. Its readers had been Christians quite a long time (5:12; 10:32). Some of their original leaders had passed away (13:7). On the other hand, Timothy was still alive (13:23). It seems possible to argue that had the destruction of Jerusalem taken place the writer would not have omitted to refer to it, particularly as it was such a significant judgment of God on the old order of Jewish worship.

OCCASION AND PURPOSE

In order to be able to assess the occasion and purpose of the Epistle we need first to appreciate the circumstances of those to whom it was written. In this connection their spiritual condition is of much greater significance than their geographical location. For knowledge about this we depend entirely on the evidence of the Epistle itself. The writer clearly contrasts the state in which his readers are with what they have been, what they ought to be, and what they seem to be in danger of becoming.

As Christians they are slothful (5:11; 6:12) and despondent (12:3, 12). They have lost their initial enthusiasm for the faith (3:6, 14; 10:23, 35). They have failed to grow or to progress, and are seriously deficient in spiritual understanding and discernment (5:12–14). They are ceasing to attend Christian meetings (10:25) and to be actively loyal to their Christian leaders (13:17). They need afresh to be exhorted to imitate the faith of those who have gone before (13:7). They tend to be easily carried away by new and strange teachings (13:9; some think these were Gnostic in character and similar to those which troubled the church in Colossae. See the Introduction to that Epistle, p. 1140). They are in danger of coming short of God's promises (4:1), and drifting away from the things which they have heard (2:1). They are even in danger of completely abandoning the faith in deliberate and persistent apostasy (3:12; 10:26); and this danger will be the greater if they fail to check any one of their number who may be moving in that direction (3:13; 12:15). If they yield to such temptation and actually reject the gospel of Christ they can expect nothing but judgment (10:26–31).

Particularly as those who had once been zealous adherents of Judaism, it seems very probable that they had become personally disappointed with Christianity because it had brought to them no visible earthly kingdom, and because it had been decisively rejected by the great majority of their fellow-Jews. Further, continued attachment to it seemed only to involve them in sharing the offensive reproach of a suffering and crucified Messiah, and in having to face the increasing prospect of violent anti-Christian persecution. It may well be, therefore, that they were being seriously tempted to disown Jesus as the Messiah and to go back to re-embrace the visible and preferable good which Judaism still seemed to offer to them.

That it was Judaism which thus attracted them afresh as preferable to Christianity seems confirmed by the obvious way in which the writer sets himself from the first to demonstrate the superiority of the new covenant over the old, and to set forth particularly the outstanding excellence of Jesus, the Son of God, as compared with the prophets and angels, leaders and high priests, who functioned in the old economy. So he shows that, while the old order was imperfect and provisional, Christianity brings perfection (7:19), and perfection which is eternal (5:9; 9:12, 15; 13:20).

The writer and his readers were apparently Hellenistic Jews with some acquaintance with Greek philosophical thought, and he seems to be using ideas from these sources when he declares that the old order contained merely 'figures' or 'a copy of the true' (9:24), 'a shadow of the good things to come instead of the true form of these realities' (10:1). Christianity is the truth itself, the heavenly and ideal reality, which actually and absolutely possesses all those inherent values which these other things can at their best only reflect or prefigure. Nevertheless, since his readers recognize the divine authority of the OT Scriptures, his final argument for recognizing the superiority of Christ over angels and over the Levitical priesthood, and the superiority of His sacrifice of Himself over that of bulls and goats, is the prophetic testimony of the OT itself. See 1:5–13; 7:15–22; 10:5–10.

The writer's purpose, therefore, is to make his readers fully aware, first, of the amazing revelation and salvation given by God to men in Christ; secondly, of the true heavenly and eternal character of the blessings thus freely offered to the appropriation of faith; thirdly, of the place of suffering and patient endurance by faith in the present earthly pathway to the goal of God's purpose, as shown in the experience and work of the Captain of our salvation, and in God's discipline of all His children; fourthly, of the awful judgment which must befall any who, knowing all this, reject it. Having striven to make them aware of these things, his complementary purpose is to stir them to act accordingly. These purposes are pursued throughout the Epistle by the use in turn of reasoned exposition, challenging exhortation and solemn warning.

CONTENTS

As already indicated, the contents of this Epistle are to be properly appreciated only in relation to its occasion and purpose. The writer obviously regards the OT Scriptures as the authoritative Word of God Himself, full of figures and anticipations of the true realities of God's purpose. Therefore he continually uses them to support, illustrate and develop his own theme. He recalls, for instance, how God brought a people out of Egypt, established a covenant with them at Sinai, and provided a priesthood and Tabernacle worship for the maintenance of covenant relationship. He remembers how many who thus began with God perished in the wilderness (3:16, 17). On the one hand they failed through unbelief to embrace God's promise and to enter into the inheritance (3:18, 19; 4:2, 6). On the other hand they came under the divine judgment by disobeying the covenant regulations (2:2). For instance, the punishment for those who committed spiritual adultery and worshipped other gods was death (10:28). Or, similarly, when Esau, born and brought up within the family of privilege, despised his birthright and sold it, it was lost beyond recall; there was for him no place for repentance (12:16, 17). From such scriptures the writer is aware that those to whom God's light is given and God's call comes either go on with God in faith and obedience to possess the full inheritance, or by rejecting the light and disobeying the call come under judgment.

So he longs and fears for his readers; longs that they may all go on to maturity or perfection (6:1); fears lest any fall back from or fail to obtain the grace of God (12:15). For they have tasted the benefits (6:4, 5) of the greater 'exodus' (Gk. exodos, Lk. 9:31) accomplished by Jesus at Jerusalem. They have been sealed and sanctified by the blood of the new covenant (see 10:29). As with the Israelites at Sinai, these things not only place upon them obligations to faith and obedience, but also set before them the opportunity to inherit the divine promises. But the dangers besetting them are also exactly similar to those besetting the Israelites under the first covenant. There is the danger of unbelief; there is the complementary danger of disobedience and apostasy, of deliberately rejecting the light and departing from the living God (3:12; 10:26, 38). They need, therefore, encouragement to go forward, and warning against turning back; and of these the Epistle is full.

The writer is no less persuaded that, in contrast to the first covenant, the revelation and the redemption given to men in Christ are the final truth of God. The obligation to pay heed and the assurance of complete divine provision are, therefore, absolute. These things settle either one's full salvation or one's final condemnation. So his urgent concern is to exhort his readers fully to respond, to warn them properly to take heed.

He provides a solid basis for such exhortations and warnings by an exposition in some detail of the superiority of Christ and of what is given under the new covenant to everything used or given under the old covenant. In Christ there is the final revelation of God, greater than anything hitherto given through prophets and angels, because He is Himself God the Son. In Christ there is the final reconciliation to God, because, having condescended to become true man, a partaker of flesh and blood, He went even lower and tasted death for every man, thus putting away sin by making Himself the sin offering. So the true house, or community, of God's people is being built of which Christ is the Head, and to which all who believe in Him are called to belong. They will become partakers in it only if they hold fast to their confidence through this testing wilderness experience which lies between the great 'exodus' of redemption and the coming inheritance of the promise.

Further, this community is called to share in a new covenant, which is full of better promises, and of which Jesus has become the effective mediator by His decisive redeeming work and by His never-ending administration of its benefits. As their High Priest He has dealt with sin once for all by the one offering of His earthly, human life upon the cross. This has secured for Him as their representative not only entrance into God's presence but also enthronement at God's right hand.

The separating curtain which kept them out of the sanctuary is decisively rent. So they can come to the very throne of God and find it a throne of grace, with One there ever waiting to speak to God on their behalf. So they can look to their High Priest on the throne for grace to meet their every need and fully to perfect their salvation. So they can count on the fulfilment in them as His people of all the divine promises of the amazing new covenant. With the wonder of such privileges open before them let them hold fast to their confidence and its open confession, and press forward to a fuller experience and enjoyment of the available benefits.

One other important truth they also needed more effectively to learn. Those who would thus have dealings with God must have them by faith. He is the great unseen One, and His greatest rewards lie in the future. Indeed, the immediate outlook and one's present experience may seem both to deny His presence and to contradict the hope of His reward. Faith, therefore, is indispensable to right awareness and to steadfast continuance. Here, once again, the OT Scriptures, as a God-given handbook of instruction, show by the witness of men's lives and achievements that this has continuously been true in the experience of all who have in any way pleased God and become heirs of His promises. So the writer would encourage his readers not to be turned aside by the lack in Christianity of visible glory and immediate, earthly triumph. Rather, he says, 'let us hold fast the confession of our hope without wavering, for he who promised is faithful' (10:23). 'For here we have no lasting city, but we seek the city which is to come' (13:14). The kingdom we are given to enjoy will stand fully disclosed only when this temporal order has passed away in judgment.

Let them, therefore, find their all in Christ, in His unchanging Person (13:8), in His abiding companionship (13:5, 6) and in the all-sufficiency of His one atoning act outside the gate of Jerusalem (13:12). Instead of yielding to the temptation to abandon Christianity and to return to Judaism, let them once for all, whatever the reproach involved, stand clear of Judaism and openly associate themselves with Jesus the crucified as their only hope (13:13). For, says the writer in his final benediction, this Jesus is 'our Lord'; He is the 'great shepherd of the sheep' (13:20). All our hopes are rightly fixed on Him. Nor is such confidence vain. God has raised Him from the dead. The covenant which His death sealed is already in operation. God Himself is active to fulfil it. We may, therefore, count on Him to make perfect that which concerns us. So, while others may draw back— and it is well that the awful warning should be sounded—it is inconceivable that we should. Nay, 'we are not of them who draw back unto perdition; but of them that believe to the saving of the soul' (10:39, AV).

For further notes on the new covenant, on the priesthood of Christ and on the warning passages see Appendices 1, 2 and 3, pp. 1217–1221.

OUTLINE OF CONTENTS

Note the alternation of exposition and exhortation and the closely linked sequence of thought in the expository sections.

COMMENTARY

1:1–4 INTRODUCTION: GOD'S FINAL WORD THROUGH HIS SON

This grand opening statement indicates the great theme of the writer (*cf*. 3:1). This vision of the absolute supremacy and sufficiency of Christ dominates the thought of the whole Epistle. He is superior to and supersedes all other mediators between God and men, such as prophets (v. 1) and angels (v. 4). Note the continuity between the OT revelation and that now given in Christ. The first prepares for the second; the second consummates the first (*cf*. 10:8, 9). Note also that this final revelation of God is given to men not only in the incarnation of the Son, but in the Son as the Fulfiller of the work of atonement for sin (*cf*. 1 Jn. 4:9, 10), and that the full significance of this revelation and redemptive work is appreciated only by those who see by faith that the Christ once crucified is now enthroned, and so able to save completely or to the uttermost all who draw near to God through Him (see 8:1; 7:25).

2–4 There are eight successive statements about Christ. In His eternal being He is genuine, absolute Deity, the visible outshining of God's glory, Himself an exact expression of the divine nature, the eternal *Son* of the Father, 'very God of very God'. In the divine ordering of the universe He is its Creator, Sustainer and End. By Him it was made. He upholds it. He is its *heir*. Note that the end is seen from the beginning; the divine appointment of the Son to be the Heir of the universe precedes its creation. In relation to men He is men's Prophet, Priest and King. In Him God spoke His final word of revelation; so He brings God to men (*cf*. Jn. 1:14, 18). In His own Person He purged our sins and finished the

work of reconciliation; so He brings men to God. He now sits enthroned at God's right hand. As the exalted God-Man He has obtained by inheritance a position far above all others (*cf*. Eph. 1:20, 21; Phil. 2:9–11).

1:5–14 THE SON'S SUPERIORITY TO ANGELS

In Jewish thought angels held a very important place as the mediators of God's revelation to His people. Therefore the writer sets out to demonstrate Christ's superiority to angels in order to establish the superiority of the message which He brings (*cf*. 2:1–4). This he does by introducing seven quotations from the OT. The whole method is very significant. It implies, first, that the OT possesses a direct relevance and a decisive authority for Christian believers. Secondly, the words quoted are ascribed not to the human psalmists and prophets, but directly to God as their Author. *Cf*. the statement of v. 1. Thirdly, it is now possible for those who are acquainted with the final revelation in Christ to see in the words of the OT a meaning and significance with reference to Christ, which could not possibly have been seen in the same way, either by those who wrote them, or by any before Christ came. *Cf*. 1 Pet. 1:10–12.

5 *Son* is the 'more excellent' name (v. 4) by which Christ's superiority to angels is measured. The Son is superior to the angels, first, because of what He is eternally as God; secondly, because of what He has now become as the exalted God-Man. The first quotation from Ps. 2:7 introduces both thoughts. There never was a time when the Father could not say to Him, *Thou art my*

Son. But there came a day in time when by resurrection in glorified humanity He was begotten to a new status as the exalted Man. So in Acts 13:33 this quotation from Ps. 2 is explicitly applied to Christ's resurrection. In consequence, He is not only Son in virtue of His deity; he is now exalted to be as a son ('the first-born among many brethren', Rom. 8:29) in virtue of His humanity. The second quotation, the promise to David concerning his seed (2 Sa. 7:14), is fulfilled in Christ as it never was, nor could be, in Solomon.

6 Similarly, He is 'the first-born' in a double sense (*cf.* Col. 1:15, 18), first as the only-begotten of the Father, existing before the created universe and Lord over it (see Ps. 89:27), and now as the firstborn from the dead, who has, as the great path-maker of salvation, opened the way for the many to enter as sons into glory (2:10). The third quotation is made to indicate that this office of His in relation to men, both as Creator and Redeemer, will be consummated at His second coming, when He will be brought again into this 'inhabited earth' (RV and mg.). For the prophetic vision of God coming to judge will be fulfilled in the Person of His Son. Then His deity will be openly manifested. Then all the angels shall worship Him. See Ps. 97:7 (the Hebrew word 'gods' becomes 'angels' in the Greek of the LXX).

7–9 The fourth and fifth quotations show that while angels fulfil their service (*e.g.* at Sinai) through wind and fire, *i.e.* in the material sphere, in transitory fashion, in creaturely subservience to the divine pleasure, the Son is a free moral personality, Himself occupying the throne of God, as God, in righteousness for ever. Because of His righteousness as the God-Man, He has, too, been exalted and anointed as the One to whom belongs the pre-eminence. The quotations are from Pss. 104:4 and 45:6, 7. For subsequent reference to His *comrades* see 2:10–13; 3:14 (RV). 10–12 The sixth quotation shows that, in contrast to created things, the Son is the Creator, the sovereign, unchangeable Lord. Words from Ps. 102:25–27 are quoted (from the LXX version) as addressed by the Father to the Son indicating that He is God 'the Lord'; and that there will be with Him no decay nor decease. *Cf.* 13:8.

13 Finally, as the seventh quotation shows (*cf.* vv. 3, 4) the Son is superior to the angels not only in what He is as God but also in what God is now doing for Him as the exalted Man or enthroned Messiah. By divine appointment He is to continue to occupy the throne in sure hope of complete triumph (Ps. 110:1). 14 The angels, by contrast, are sent forth from the throne as servants to fulfil ministries on behalf of those who are to share in this glorious consummation of man's full salvation. *Those who are to obtain salvation*; the first of a variety of expressions used by the writer to describe the people of God and their destiny.

2:1–4 PRACTICAL APPLICATION AND WARNING

The writer here introduces the first of his characteristic words of urgent exhortation and solemn warning (see Appendix 3, 'The Warning Passages', p. 1219). This new revelation places on all who hear it a supreme obligation to give heed, an obligation which, for a number of reasons, is greater than that of obedience to the law of Moses. 2 First, there is the known authority of that law. It was a word which could not be defied or disregarded with impunity. Under it every sin of commission (*i.e. transgression*), and every sin of omission (*i.e. disobedience* or 'failure to hear'), received its *just retribution*.

3, 4 Secondly, there is the character of the new message which is *salvation*, so great and of such a kind as to be amazing (*cf.* Jn. 1:17). The third reason is the Person of the Messenger. On the Godward side the Sinaitic law was given to Moses by angels (*cf.* Acts 7:53; Gal. 3:19); it was a mediated revelation. This new revelation is direct and immediate, given by the Lord Himself in Person. In the fourth place there is the decisive confirmation of the message. In addition to having been first spoken by the Lord Himself it has been *attested to us* by the evidence of eyewitnesses, and also by the superadded testimony of a great variety of God-given miraculous *signs* and *by gifts of the Holy Spirit*, which in their distribution are clearly not of man's appointing but wholly according to the divine pleasure. *Cf.* Mk. 16:20; 1 Cor. 12:11. Finally, there is the inevitable consequence of *neglect.* To drift past out of reach (v. 1) when we have the opportunity to pay heed must leave us without excuse and with no prospect but judgment. This point is made still more explicit later (see 10:26, 27). *How shall we escape?* (future indicative). Note here the implied certainty of judgment to come.

2:5–18 THE INCARNATION, SUFFERING AND DEATH OF THE SON OF GOD

In this chapter the writer deals with a difficulty which his readers might find in his teaching regarding the superiority of Jesus to angels, for to Jewish minds the place of angels was of no small importance. To them it was clear that, in the present order, angels are superior to men. For example, they stood between God and men at the giving of the law (v. 2). If Jesus was a man, and still more if He suffered and died, how can He be said to be superior to the angels as a mediator (1:4)?

In answer these verses indicate first the fact and significance of His exaltation as man—'we see Jesus . . . crowned' (v. 9); note the use of the unqualified human name. Secondly, they describe the divinely ordained and saving purpose of His preceding humiliation, together with (for God) its moral fitness and (for men) its beneficial consequences. Further, these verses indicate that not only Jesus but men—through Jesus as their High Priest and Author of salvation—are called to inherit a destiny of glory and dominion.

2:5–8 Not angels, but men, are the divinely destined lords of the coming age

All this is prophetically anticipated in Scripture. In Ps. 8 it is made plain that, although man in this present world-order begins by being made *for a little while lower than the angels* (v. 7), God's ultimate purpose is to give him glory and dominion, even over the angels. For the *everything* (v. 8) includes the angels. *Cf.* 1 Cor. 6:3. This consummation is clearly not yet fully realized (v. 8c). It must, therefore, still be spoken of as future; it is *the world to come* (v. 5); *i.e.* 'the coming world-order' (*cf.* 6:5). It is this coming consummation or completed salvation which is the writer's theme (v. 5), and ought to be the Christian's constant object of hope (see 10:37–39; 11:13–16; 13:14).

2:9–18 The purpose of the incarnation, suffering and death of Christ

9 On the other hand, there is to be seen in the Person of *Jesus* a present realization of man's destiny. He, as a true man, began, like men, by being *made* (for a little while) *lower than the angels*. He is now *crowned with glory and honour*. Ps. 8, therefore, is thus seen to be Messianic. God's purpose for man is fulfilled only through the one Man, *i.e.* Christ (*cf.* Gal. 3:16).

Also, in relation to God's intended purpose for men, it is possible to see why the Son of God was humbled to the form of a servant. For, as man, He is *crowned with glory and honour* only because He has suffered death. By a wonderful manifestation of *the grace of God* He became man in order that, for the benefit of mankind as a whole (*i.e. for everyone*), He might thus enter into death.

10 It was, indeed, supremely *fitting*, and an act worthy of God Himself, who is the first cause and final end of *all things*, that in order to bring sinful men into the true glory of manhood, which they had irretrievably lost, God should provide for men a Saviour of this kind. By entering into His own glory through suffering He opened up the way by which the *many* (*cf.* Is. 53:12; Mk. 10:45) can now be brought in to share the same human glory as sons of God and joint-heirs with Christ (*cf.* Rom. 3:23; 5:2; 8:29, 30). Jesus' suffering of death, therefore, was necessary completely to qualify Him to function as men's Saviour. *Pioneer*; *cf.* 12:2. The same Greek word is rendered 'Author' (Acts 3:15) and 'Leader' (Acts 5:31). It describes an originator without whom the resulting benefit would not exist. Our Lord's work issues in His becoming the Head of a saved company or community, *i.e.* those whom God has given Him through and because of what He has done (*cf.* Jn. 17:2, 6, 26). The OT quotations used to confirm this are remarkable. 12 The first is from Ps. 22, a Psalm which foreshadows the cross. The constitution

of the *congregation* or 'church' (Gk. *ekklēsia*), with Christ in the midst revealing God to His brethren, is possible only because of His sacrifice. 13 The other two quotations are from Is. 8:17, 18. The first is often said to be from Ps. 18:2; but the LXX of Is. 8:17, 18 suggests that this one passage is the source of both quotations. It is a place in the OT where the thought of the believing remnant or 'church' distinctly emerges.

14, 15 These elect *children* of the divine purpose were, as men, sharers *in flesh and blood*, and, as sinners, subject to bondage and fear, held under by the devil and the power of death. There was no hope of a redeemed community being raised up to enjoy man's intended destiny, unless this hold of the devil and of 'the gates of Hades' could be broken (see Mt. 16:18; Mk. 3:26, 27; 1 Cor. 15:17–19). This was done when the Son of God became incarnate and entered into death, not as a helpless victim but as the decisive victor. (*Cf.* Rev. 1:18; Rom. 14:9.)

16 This salvation is meant for men, not angels. Christ came to redeem *the descendants of Abraham*, *i.e.* men of faith (*cf.* Gal. 3:7, 9, 29). Note that 'doth he take hold' (RV) refers not to His becoming man, but to His work of rescue and redemption. *Cf.* 8:9, quoted from Je. 31:32 where the same Greek word describes a gracious 'laying hold' in order to take out of a state of bondage. 17, 18 Christ could fully help them in this way only by entering completely as a true man into their human experience of trial. What they needed was one who could put them right with God by making atonement for sin; and also help them to triumph over life's continuing temptations (v. 18). So as 'the author of their salvation' (v. 10, RV) the Son of God became a High Priest who was *faithful* in His discharge of the work of making *expiation* (RV 'propitiation') for the sins of the whole people of God; and *merciful*, *i.e.* 'compassionate', or ready to sympathize with and help the tempted, because of His own experience of human temptation. This, then, is why He trod the path of incarnation, suffering and death.

3:1–6 THE SUPERIORITY OF CHRIST JESUS TO MOSES

Moses was the human mediator of the old covenant; he was called in a unique way to be God's servant. See Nu. 12:5–8. The Israelites traced back to him their sense of status and calling as the consecrated people of God. The Christian brotherhood is similarly consecrated and called through Jesus (2:11), the Mediator of the new covenant. 1 Christians, therefore, should *consider*, *i.e.* fix all their gaze, their steadfast mental attention, upon *Jesus*, whom they have confessed to be their *apostle and high priest*. He combines in His own Person both these offices. As God, He has been 'sent forth' to reveal God to men; as Man, He has become High Priest to reconcile men to God. *Who share in a heavenly call*. There is an implied contrast with the earthly inheritance set before those who came out of Egypt under Moses.

2 Jesus is like Moses in a number of ways. God made or *appointed him*; *i.e.* His status and function are divinely constituted (*cf.* 1 Sa. 12:6). He was *faithful*. The sphere of His work was the whole house of God (vv. 2 mg., 6). *Cf.* Nu. 12:7. **3** Jesus also surpasses Moses and is worthy of more glory and honour. For Moses was himself part of the house in which he served, himself one of the people of God. **4** But Christ is the builder of the house, Himself God. It was the declared task of God's anointed king to build a house for His name (2 Sa. 7:13); and the church which Jesus said He would build is this 'house of God' or new 'Israel' (*cf.* 1 Tim. 3:15; Gal. 6:16).

5, 6 Therefore it is we Christians who are this 'house of God' (v. 6). Again, Moses was only a *servant* in the house (v. 5). Christ is set as the Son over His Father's house (v. 6). He is its Head; by virtue of His Sonship the house is *his* (*cf.* Mt. 1:21: 'his people'). Note that He is here called Son in reference to God (*cf.* 1:2); there is definite implication of Godhead. Again, Moses' work was one of preparation (v. 5); it pointed forward to that which should come after; it witnessed to the kind of work that the coming One would do. See Dt. 18:15-19. Christ is the fulfilment of all that Moses foresaw and foreshadowed. He points to none but Himself. No wonder this Epistle emphasizes so strongly, 'Consider him' (3:1; 12:3). Similarly, the OT house or people of God, in which Moses served, pointed forward to the Christian church, that present house of God, over which Christ is set as Son.

In the latter half of v. 6 the thought turns to the personal application of what has been said. These privileges can be fully possessed only if those who have embraced the hope set before them in Christ remain steadfast until the hope is realized. They must continue in that outspoken *confidence* and *pride* or exulting testimony (RV 'boldness' and 'glorying') which are characteristic of the new-born believer.

3:7 – 4:13 PERSONAL APPLICATION AND WARNING

3:7-19 The danger of unbelief

See Appendix 3, p. 1219. The warning here is enforced by the solemn example of the failure of the Israelites in the wilderness. The comparison between Moses and Jesus given in vv. 1-6 is followed by a comparison between the promise and the people under the old covenant and under the new. Moses and Christ were both faithful to the end (v. 2). But the great majority of those who followed Moses were faithless. They all shared in the great deliverances of the Passover and the Red Sea, but later they hardened their hearts against God and perished in the wilderness. *Cf.* 1 Cor. 10:1-5. This provided an eloquent warning to those Jews of the 1st century AD who had seen in Jesus the Passover Lamb

sacrificed and God's power manifested in His resurrection from the dead. It was clearly no new thing for the majority of the nation not to believe. Also, many of the Israelites under Moses saw God's works for 'forty years' (v. 9) and still hardened their hearts. So, at the very doors of the promised land, they failed to enter in. Similarly, at the time this Epistle was written, about 40 years had possibly elapsed since the first proclamation of salvation by the Lord Himself. The divine origin of the gospel had been signally confirmed to these Hebrews (2:3, 4). Let them fear lest they, also, take offence at God's ways and come short of the promised consummation (4:1).

7 This exhortation is introduced in words from Ps. 95:7-11, which are quoted as spoken by *the Holy Spirit*, and as spoken for *today* to those who are now confronted in this new era of redemption by the new revelation given by God's voice spoken in Christ. Note the implied divine authorship and Christian purpose of the OT Scriptures. Everything depends on how men hear. It is not just words but the living God who here confronts men. *Cf.* 4:12, 13. To refuse to hear is to reject Him (v. 12).

8 *Rebellion* and *testing* are translations of the Hebrew names Meribah and Massah. See Nu. 20:1-13; Ex. 17:1-7. The latter instance of Israel's unbelief occurred in the first, and the former instance in the fortieth, year of the wilderness wanderings. They are evidence that the hardening of heart persisted from beginning to end of the 40 years. **9** To *put God to the test* seems to mean seeing how far one can go in disobeying Him. **10** Though God in His displeasure rebuked them and made them aware of their error, they still showed no understanding of the purpose of His dealings with them. They refused to repent. **11** So God solemnly declared that it was impossible for people in such a condition to enjoy the promised inheritance.

12-15 These words from Ps. 95 are taken to indicate that *today*, while there is fresh opportunity to hear God's voice in the gospel (*cf.* 2 Cor. 6:2), there is danger of the same peril as beset the Israelites. For God's Word calls forth an inevitable reaction; men either respond in obedience to it or stubbornly reject it. The causes of failure, which ought to be avoided, are the *deceitfulness of sin*, through which men's hearts are *hardened* against God (v. 13); and consequent unbelief, which leads men *to fall away* or 'apostasize' (Gk.) from God, *i.e.* to abandon response to God altogether (v. 12). Protection against these evils is to be found in daily, mutual exhortation (v. 13). *Every day* Christians should speak words of encouragement to *one another*. The many are responsible for the one; every member of the Christian community should *take care* lest any one of their number becomes infected. For full participation in the Messianic blessings is given only to those who are steadfast in their *confidence* (v. 14) from start to finish. It is faith that provides such a 'conviction' or 'assurance' (such an underlying foundation, Gk. *hypostasis*) of things hoped for (11:1). It must be held *firm to the end*, in all the intensity of its first manifestation (*cf.* 3:6), and in the face of delay, suffering and temporary disappointment (*cf.* 10:35, 36), *i.e.* in the face of 'testing in the wilderness' (v. 8).

16-19 The solemn significance of the example of the Israelites' failure is further enforced by a series of questions. Those who provoked God for 40 years in the wilderness by their rebellion were none other than those who shared in the deliverance from Egypt, a surprising anticlimax. The reason why they were overthrown in judgment was sin. The reason why they failed to enter the promised land was disobedience due to unbelief. Lack of faith, then, or 'an evil, unbelieving heart' (v. 12), is the obvious and fatal peril of which to beware.

4:1-13 Exhortation to enter into rest

There is urgent reason to pay heed to the warning both because the divine promise of entering into God's rest still stands open, and because failure to embrace it may result in a loss that cannot be remedied, a permanent missing of God's best. **1** It is possible to *fail to reach it* or to be 'left behind'. The writer again stresses that the whole company should be on its guard lest any single individual drop out. *Cf.* 3:12, 13; 12:15.

2 This promise of entrance into God's rest is offered to men afresh in the preaching of the gospel of Christ. It is this which gives to men 'today' opportunity to 'hear his voice'. But, as the OT Scriptures make plain, when men hear the God-given Word they can enjoy the blessings He promises only if they become vitally united to it by means of the response of faith or, following an alternative MS reading, if they believingly associate themselves with those who obey it (see mg.). And although God swore that the unbelieving Israelites should not enter in, it is clear from the present experience of Christian believers that Christ has brought this rest within the reach of His people. **3** For those who have become believers are actually entering into this very rest.

4 This rest of God has been in existence for men to share since the creation of the world was finished. In Gn. 2:2 we read that *God rested on the seventh day from all his works.* This rest does not consist merely of inactivity; the word describes the satisfaction and repose of successful achievement. Further, the words of Scripture which speak of this subject (Gn. 2:2; Ps. 95:11) are to be regarded as God's own word and witness on the matter. These words show, first, that God Himself rested. Secondly, and by implication, they indicate that it is clearly His purpose that men should enter into and share His rest. His word about it guarantees its certainty; God never speaks empty words. **6** Thirdly, we are told that those to whom the opportunity was first offered failed to embrace it because of *disobedience*, and were by the word of the same

God solemnly forbidden all hope of entrance (vv. 3, 5). **7, 8** Also we see that the inheritance into which Joshua led the people cannot really be the promised rest because, long after the time of Joshua in the days of David, God speaks of a fresh opportunity ('today') to hear His voice and to enter in.

9 It is clear, therefore, that God intends His people to share His own *sabbath rest*. This is the reward that He has reserved for them. **10** Entrance into it means a cessation from their own works (*cf.* Rev. 14:13), just as God rested from the work of creation on His sabbath. In its fullness such a goal is, therefore, something which lies beyond this life. Yet those who find salvation and new life in Christ do begin to experience it here and now (see Mt. 11:28, 29). So, as the writer has already said (v. 3), those who take the decisive step and become Christian believers are entering into rest. They have begun to enjoy a blessing which is yet to be consummated. Its possession is both now and not yet.

11 There is need, therefore, for us all to exhibit zeal and earnest endeavour in its continual pursuit, lest any single one of our number fall by the way, and become, like the Israelites in the wilderness (*cf.* Lot's wife), yet another similar example of unbelieving disobedience. It is a solemn thing to become a negative witness to the truth of God's promises by being 'left behind'. It is better to be a positive witness and to enter in. Those who have opportunity to hear His voice must become one or the other (*cf.* Mt. 7:24-27).

It is well, therefore, to consider the character of the Word that confronts us, the Word of Scripture and of the gospel, if we are fully to appreciate the responsibility under which hearing it puts us. **12** For this Word is God's Word. It shares the very attributes of God Himself. It is living, and full of activity and power to achieve. In it God Himself is active, and so it is never without result (see Is. 55:11); it brings either salvation or judgment. It penetrates into a man's inmost being and, like a dissecting knife, forces open a radical division and distinction between things that differ in human life. It brings under judgment the thoughts and ideas of man's mind and will (*cf.* 1 Cor. 4:5). It is the 'critic' (Gk. *kritikos*; AV *discerner*) by which all are judged. **13** Confronted by it, man is confronted by God, before whom nothing can be concealed. Indeed, it makes us aware that all things stand stripped and bare and fully exposed to His searching glance. And it is to Him, the God from whom this Word comes, that all who hear the Word (Gk. *logos*) have ultimately to give back in answer their own 'word' or 'account' (Gk. *logos*). *Laid bare.* The Greek word means 'with the head thrown back and the neck bare'. It suggests the impossibility of hiding one's face. In the final giving of account all must look at God and be looked upon by Him face to face.

4:14–5:10 CHRIST OUR GREAT HIGH PRIEST

4:14-16 The Epistle's main theme stated

Here the urgent warning already given is complemented by positive encouragement. **14** As Christians *we have* (the words are emphatic) *a great high priest, i.e.* great in His essential nature, for He is both truly man and truly God. In the fulfilment of His work as High Priest, He has *passed through the heavens* into the very presence of God Himself, where He sits enthroned (*cf.* Eph. 4:10). Note that this enthronement is implied in v. 16; it is explicitly stated several times (see 1:3, 13; 8:1; 10:12). Because of His humanity and earthly experience He is able sympathetically to appreciate our human limitations and trials. We ought, therefore, to hold firmly to the open confession of faith in Him; and enter into the enjoyment of the benefits that His priestly work has made available. **15, 16** 'Boldly' (v. 16, AV) or *with confidence, i.e.* with outspoken expression of our faith and our need, we may now come to the very throne of God Himself, there to find that it is a throne of grace and divine bounty, where we may always obtain compassion or mercy in relation to our weakness and sin, and where we may discover grace that will afford us timely help, *i.e.* help suited to the need of the present hour. *Our weaknesses* (v. 15) are those due to our finite creaturely existence, *e.g.* weariness, shrinking from pain, *etc.* These are things which the incarnate Son Himself experienced. *Yet without sinning.* This phrase may describe either the issue of His temptations (*i.e.* He never fell into sin), or a difference in the way in which He was tempted (*i.e.* there was in Him no sinful nature, no sinful promptings from within). *Draw near* (v. 16); the Greek word here is commonly used of priestly approach to God. This privilege, formerly restricted to a select few, is now extended to all the people of God. Also, it is not just a symbolic earthly shrine that we can enter, but the very presence of God.

5:1-10 Our Lord's qualifications and work as High Priest described

A high priest is appointed to act for men in matters of Godward reference, especially to present offerings to God which deal with sins (v. 1; *cf.* 9:7). He must be chosen from among men and be able, as a true man, fully to sympathize with men's weaknesses (v. 2). (This qualification has already been declared to be true of our Christian High Priest; see 2:18; 4:15.) Also, he must not presume to take such an office upon himself; he must for such a task be called and appointed by God (v. 4). All this (in reverse order) is declared to be true of Christ as the writer considers His divine appointment, His perfect humanity and consequent ability to sympathize, and His office and work. For it is God who, raising Him from the dead, acknowledged Him as His Son (v. 5) and openly declared His appointment to an eternal priesthood after an order different from that of Aaron, 'the order of Melchizedek' (v. 6). He is also able fully to sympathize with men in their life in the flesh. For He Himself, though He were God the Son, learnt as man in the experience of His earthly life the full meaning of obedient submission to the will of God in the face of extreme human suffering and the power of death (vv. 7, 8). This is how He reached that human perfection, which qualified Him to enter upon His work (v. 9). It is as thus qualified that God has solemnly ascribed to Him the title which is His due, the title of High Priest after a new eternal order (v. 10). And it is as thus fully competent to act that He has become the one sufficient cause of 'eternal salvation' to all who learn from Him to make a similar believing and obedient response to the will and way of God for men (v. 9).

1, 2 The *sins* covered by the sacrifices of the law were sins due to human infirmity, occasions of going astray through ignorance (v. 2), not wilful sins done with a high hand (see Nu. 15:28-30). A human high priest would be able to show understanding sympathy towards such wrongdoing because, as a man, he himself suffers from the same weakness. **3** Also, for a similar reason, he must of necessity offer expiatory sacrifice for his own sins. Christ's case is, of course, different on this last point; for He was undefiled (7:26). But His sympathy is none the less real. One does not need to yield to temptation to be fully aware of its pressure upon the natural man. Indeed, only He who resisted to the end felt its full weight. *Cf.* 2:18; 4:15.

5, 6 The OT quotations of these verses come from two important Messianic Psalms (Pss. 2:7 and 110:4). They very significantly emphasize by this juxtaposition that the exalted Jesus is both the enthroned King, and the eternal Priest. (See also on 1:5; 7:1ff., and Appendix 2, p. 1218).

7 *Jesus offered up prayers.* Christ prayed, particularly in Gethsemane, with earnest and urgent entreaty to be saved from having to die. But even though His human nature shrank from such a way forward (Mk. 14:33-36), He prayed in a spirit of reverent submission and obedient response to the will of God, as one prepared to learn—such was *his godly fear*—that every circumstance and experience had its place in the Father's plan. Such praying was heard. He was strengthened to go through with God's will, and to 'drink the cup'. **8** Also by the experience of such a discipline He, Son of God though He was, learnt the full meaning and cost of human obedience, and was thereby perfected in His human character, and in His fitness to be the cause to men of salvation eternal in quality. Men can enjoy the full benefit of His saving work only if they, too, are baptized into the same spirit, and become those who at any cost make active obedience to Christ their continual practice.

5:11 – 6:20 AN EXHORTATION TO PROGRESS AND TO PERSIST

This rebuke and exhortation are prompted by the writer's subject (which only the mature can fully understand), by his awareness of his readers' backward condition, by his recognition of God's purpose for His children, and by the contemplation of the only ultimate alternative, namely, complete relapse and terrifying judgment. For those who share to the full in a God-given opportunity to receive His Word, and then knowingly and deliberately reject it, can expect nothing but judgment. It is impossible to do anything further to move such to repentance; they openly take sides with those who crucified the Son of God. Here (6:9) the writer, alarmed by such thoughts, is careful at once to state, in tender affection for his readers, that their condition is not hopeless. Their lives show the fruit of good works. But they need to be awakened to the dangers of sloth, and they need to learn to put devotion (similar to that which they have put into their good works) into persisting in believing hope until the day of full possession (6:11, 12). Further, God Himself, in order to remove from men's minds all possibility of doubt, has pledged His sure word by a confirming covenant oath (6:17).

So men have in their dealings with God by faith a double ground of confidence—God's word and God's oath, both of which are incapable of being proved false (6:18). Finally, Jesus Himself has entered, as 'a forerunner' (6:20) into the holy of holies, *i.e.* the very presence of God, having become men's High Priest after the new eternal Melchizedek order. There is, therefore, every reason and 'strong encouragement' (6:18) for seeking to progress into the full possession of God's promises, and for laying hold of 'the hope set before us', by following Jesus the forerunner into God's very presence.

5:11 – 6:12 An urgent call to go on to spiritual maturity

The truths concerning Christ's Melchizedek priesthood (5:11) require much detailed exposition. They are 'solid food' (5:12, 14), which can be understood or digested only by the spiritually mature. The whole subject, therefore, is difficult to expound to these particular readers because, although they are Christians of long standing, they have become slack and backward in their response to the God-given Word.

5:11 The same Greek word, *nōthroi*, is translated as both *dull* and 'sluggish' (6:12). **12** See below on 6:1, 2. In **13, 14** note the detailed contrast between the two types (*a child* and *the mature*), their condition (*unskilled* and *faculties trained by practice*), and their diet (*milk* and *solid food*). Note that ability acquired, through *the word of righteousness, to distinguish good* from evil is evidence of maturity. *Cf.* 1 Ki. 3:7–9; Is. 7:16.

6:1, 2 *The first principles of God's word* (5:12) and *the elementary doctrines of Christ* (6:1) which provide a foundation are indicated in detail in 6:1, 2. Here are steps which new converts would be expected to take, and essential truths which they would be required to believe. *Ablutions*; since this word is in the plural and, in Greek, not the usual word for Christian baptism, Jewish ceremonial washings may be meant; *cf.* 9:13. Indeed, some think that the fundamentals here listed could all be learnt by Jews from the OT. If so, this may be why it was undesirable (v. 1) that those here addressed should treat them as enough. They urgently need to *go on* from such Jewish *foundations* to full Christian *maturity*. This requires deliberate and decisive action. Yet, paradoxically, *let us go on* is in the Greek a passive verb and means literally 'let us be borne along' (*cf.* Acts 26:15, 17; 2 Pet. 1:21). 'The thought is not primarily of personal effort, but of personal surrender to an active influence. The power is working; we have only to yield ourselves to it' (B. F. Westcott, *The Epistle to the Hebrews*, 1950). *Cf.* Eph. 3:20; Phil. 2:13. So the writer exhorts his readers to respond and in v. 3, speaking for himself not for them, expresses the decision thus to act.

3 There is one necessary and very solemn qualification. Men can so act only *if God permits*. **4ff.** Some actions by the very divine constitution of things are morally *impossible*. If men share within the visible church in all the blessings of the gospel, if (like those at the Red Sea deliverance, who later perished through unbelief in the wilderness) they have actually been in the company of the people who have experienced the mighty workings of God's Spirit, and so have themselves *tasted* of its character, and then deliberately turn from it all and reject Christ, it is impossible to begin all over again with them and lay once more the foundation of repentance. As those who have decisively failed, or deliberately refused, to respond to divine grace there is nothing for them but judgment. *Cf.* 1 Cor. 10:1–5 and especially Lk. 20:13–16. Scripture consistently teaches that the same actions of divine grace, which bring within men's grasp salvation and life, also finally settle the condemnation of those who, after sharing in the revelation, deliberately reject it. *Cf.* 2 Cor. 2:15, 16. Also, it is impossible in the early stages to distinguish between the wheat and the tares, or between the seed that will wither or be choked and the seed that will bring forth fruit unto life eternal. *Cf.* 1 Cor. 10:12; 2 Tim. 2:18, 19. Judgment is determined not by the beginning but by the *end* or fruit (vv. 7, 8). That is why this writer is so concerned that those who have begun to experience the grace of Christ should prove their genuineness by going on to its true end. *Cf.* 2 Pet. 1:5–11.

Once enlightened (v. 4). The word *once* suggests a certain absoluteness and finality, indicating something done once for all in such a way that it is of necessity incapable of repetition. It is in contrast to *again*. *Cf*. its use in 9:26, 28; 10:2; 12:26, 27. Those so enlightened could never again become as those who had never received the light. 6 *Commit apostasy*. This is what is here meant by 'falling away' (AV, RV), *i.e.* a complete rejection and disowning of the faith of Christ. As far as they are concerned (*i.e. on their own account*, or 'to themselves', AV, RV), such people put Christ out of their lives, or reject His claim to be the Son of God, by an action similar to that of those who got rid of Him by crucifying Him. Thus they publicly *hold* Christ *up to contempt*. See also Appendix 3, p. 1219.

9 After such a solemn picture of inevitable doom (v. 8), the writer hastens with real affection (only in this place does he call his readers *beloved*) to assure his readers that he is convinced that they are in no such hopeless state. (Some therefore regard the type described in vv. 4–8 as hypothetical rather than real.) 10–12 From these verses we learn what is indicative of true spiritual life and needful for full spiritual progress, namely, *earnestness*, or all-absorbing zeal, not only in works of *love* (v. 10), in ministering to Christians for God's sake, *i.e.* because they are His people, but also *in realizing the full assurance of hope* (v. 11) by holding on to it *until the end* or the day of its fulfilment; and in exhibiting that kind of patient *faith* (v. 12) that equally persists until the day of realized possession. Only so can we join the company of those who *inherit the promises*.

6:13–20 Grounds of confidence to inspire steadfastness

13, 14 God's promises of salvation are the more sure because they are confirmed by an oath by God Himself. This was true from the first. When the promises were made to Abraham, God at the same time swore to fulfil them. 15 Abraham's confidence in God's word enabled him patiently to endure until the promise was fulfilled. 16 The significance of oath-taking one may learn from the common practice of men. Its purpose is to put an end to all doubt or misgiving about a promise and to silence those who would gainsay its certainty. Its veracity and sure fulfilment are therefore confirmed by the most solemn of pledges. This commonly involves swearing by Almighty God. When men thus pledge their word to one another they virtually call upon God Himself to mediate or stand between them as a witness of their promises (*cf.* Jdg. 11:10; Rom. 1:9) and to watch over their fulfilment (*cf.* Ru. 1:17). As Someone *greater* He is able to take vengeance if either party fails to keep his word. This certainty of divine vengeance makes swearing by God *final* as a way of confirming promises.

17, 18 In order to make men doubly sure of His promise God has condescended to use this method of oath-taking. So *he interposed with an oath*; He made Himself (since there was none greater to appeal to) a kind of third party or mediator between Himself and men. So *we* (note the present personal reference) are meant to gain thereby *strong encouragement* (v. 18); for we have a double ground of confidence, in God the Promiser who gives us His word and in God the Guarantor who confirms it by His oath. There is therefore no possibility of being deceived or disappointed.

19 An *anchor* provides a peculiarly appropriate illustration. It was a recognized symbol of hope. It suggests a confidence to turn to and to lay hold of, a confidence which will hold fast and never fail because it enters into the unseen depths, the holiest of all, or *inner shrine*. 20 Also, this line of thought brings back the minds of the readers to *Jesus* and to His high-priestly office *after the order of Melchizedek*, the great theme which the writer has already indicated his eagerness to expound (5:10, 11). Jesus offers us new hope because He has entered the innermost sanctuary not only *on our behalf* but also *as a forerunner*, opening the way for us to follow Him and thus enabling us to draw near to God. *Cf.* 7:19 and 10:19–22. Also, like an anchor, He offers us a sure and an abiding confidence because in the innermost sanctuary of God's presence He abides, or remains enthroned, in contrast to the Levitical high priest who came out and was removed by death. So He is *a high priest for ever*. It is this eternal quality which distinguishes the Melchizedek order of priesthood from that of Aaron.

7:1–28 THE CHARACTERISTICS AND EFFICACY OF CHRIST'S ETERNAL PRIESTHOOD

The writer has already asserted that Jesus can be, to all who obey Him, 'the source of eternal salvation' because He has become on their behalf 'a high priest after the order of Melchizedek' (see 5:6, 9, 10). It is this new and distinctive priestly office and work of Jesus about which he has 'much to say' (5:11), and which he now sets himself fully to expound. The OT Scriptures themselves both provide and authorize the use of this illustration or pattern, namely, the priesthood of Melchizedek, after whose order the Messiah is by divine oath declared to be a priest for ever (see Gn. 14:17–20; Ps. 110:4). It is the implications of these Scriptures and the significance of this divinely ordained pattern that the writer now expounds. This new order of priesthood implies and involves difference from, superiority over, and the supersession of, the old Levitical order. Also, it makes possible (as the Levitical priesthood failed to do) the realization of the hope of all religion, namely, free access to God and full and complete personal salvation (7:19, 25).

3, 4 (On vv. 1, 2, see below.) The record in Genesis indicates two things about *this Melchizedek*—his continuance for ever and his greatness. It indicates the first figuratively by its silence, and the second factually by its statements.

This means that in Scripture both what is said and what is omitted are alike important. It is very remarkable that in Genesis nothing is said about Melchizedek's ancestry; for in the OT great importance is attached to genealogies, particularly of priests. Melchizedek is simply presented as a priest in his own right, not by reason of physical descent. Also, his birth and death are not mentioned. He simply appears once in the record as a living figure, and is left to abide alone and *for ever* in the minds of readers as Melchizedek the priest. Nor is anything said of any successor to him. In all this he is made, by the very silence of Scripture, to resemble *the Son of God* (note the divine title and contrast v. 22), who appeared once in history, but who *has neither beginning of days nor end of life*. Jesus is a High Priest after this order, unique and *for ever*.

Further, the Genesis record makes plain Melchizedek's greatness (v. 4). For no other than Abraham, the patriarch, gave him a tenth or *tithe*, and selected it from the very best of the spoil. And he did this in the hour of his own victory when he might have claimed to be second to none in the land. 6 Also, Melchizedek actually *blessed* Abraham which proves that, signally favoured by God as Abraham was, Melchizedek was even greater than he. Similarly, Melchizedek is greater than the Levitical priests. They have only a legal right to take tithes from their equals. Abraham acknowledged that Melchizedek possessed an inherent right to be regarded as his superior. 9 Also, *one might even say* (*i.e.* though some may think such reasoning rather unusual), that in what Abraham did Levi his descendant was involved, and so shared in acknowledging the greatness and superiority of Melchizedek. 1, 2 Note that Scripture pictures him as one who is a *king* as well as a *priest*. The combination of these two offices was to be a distinguishing characteristic of the Messiah. *Cf.* 8:1 and Zc. 6:13. Also, the meanings of the Hebrew words suggest that as 'Melchi-zedek' he is *King of righteousness*, and as King of 'Salem' he is *King of peace* (v. 2). Note, too, the moral significance of the order here emphasized, *first* righteousness, *and then* peace. *Cf.* 12:11; Is. 32:17; Jas. 3:17, 18.

There is, moreover, independent proof that this Melchizedek priesthood, to which order our Lord belongs, is radically different from, and far superior to, the Levitical priesthood. For there is the scriptural prophecy (Ps. 110:4) that the Messiah is to be a priest divinely appointed according to this Melchizedek order. 11 This scriptural indication of the need for a new order of priesthood clearly implies that the existing Levitical order has failed to achieve its intended end or true *perfection*. 12 Also, the priesthood was so fundamental to the old covenant between God and His people (the whole relationship was constituted in dependence upon its ministry), that any change in the order of priesthood must of necessity involve a change in the whole constitution; *i.e.* it implies nothing less than an accompanying new, and indeed 'better covenant' (v. 22).

13, 14 One of the distinctive features of the new order is then noted. Priests of the old order had to be descendants of Levi. But we know, not only from Scripture prophecy but also from the historical facts about Jesus, that He whom (so the writer implies) we confess to be the Messiah has been pleased to become a member of another tribe. For it is public knowledge that Jesus was *descended from Judah*, a tribe with no claim to the order of priesthood appointed by Moses. Note the striking description of Jesus as *our Lord*. It corresponds here to the thought of Ps. 110:1, in which David called Him 'my Lord'.

15ff. Further, the ground on which our Lord has made good His right to be Priest makes it still more obvious that there has been a complete change in the law governing the priesthood. Under the old order the necessary qualifications both for being a priest and for performing priestly functions were all physical and external, depending on conformity to law (v. 16). It was a matter of proper ancestry and of physical purity by means of appropriate ritual. Under the new order Christ's necessary qualifications to be Priest and successfully to complete His priestly work are essentially spiritual and internal. They depend on the personal possession of life which cannot be destroyed (v. 16), and on the consequent ability to complete to its finish or full perfection His work of saving men (v. 25). This difference is made unmistakably clear by the description of the new Priest as one who *arises in the likeness of Melchizedek* (v. 15). The distinctive feature of the Melchizedek priesthood which is now emphasized is that it is *for ever* (v. 17). The One who is to be a Priest of this order must have life which not only never does end, but never can be brought to an end, *i.e.* *indestructible* (v. 16). This is why He is able to do what no Levitical priest could do. He can both bring men to God (v. 19) and save them to the uttermost (v. 25, RV and mg.). For Christ's physical death as Man was no dissolution of His eternal life as God. He entered heaven as the living One and is there alive for ever more. In other words, His indissoluble life made it possible for Him in and through His human death still to act and to enter in, and thus to present Himself to God as the Lamb slain. Also, it makes it certain that in God's presence He now continues alive for evermore.

18, 19 Further, such a solemn introduction by God of a new priest itself sets aside or cancels out the old order and proves that it was only *former* or 'foregoing' (RV), *i.e.* temporary and provisional. Indeed, in the light of what Christ has now done, we can see that the old law was completely powerless and useless. Indirectly, therefore, the writer is teaching his Jewish readers as Christians to recognize this and not to be so foolish as to trust any longer in the old Jewish order; for it has been divinely superseded by 'the bringing in thereupon' (v. 19, RV, *i.e.* on top of it) by God Himself of something better which does do what the old order could not do and gives us full access to God's presence.

20–22 Again, the new priesthood is superior to the old because it has been constituted with *an oath* of God. This is witness that the new order of priesthood is a divine undertaking, and one that is thus doubly pledged by God's Word and God's oath (*cf.* 6:13–18). Therefore it cannot fail like the old. Also, being thus divinely instituted, this priesthood is *for ever*. The day will never come when this Priest will cease to be or His ministry cease to be effective. The divine oath implies something final, eternal, unchangeable. Therefore Jesus, who is thus given to us as the Priest of the new covenant, is to us the Guarantor of a covenant which is clearly far *better* than the old one. Note that 'draw near' (v. 19) and *surety* (v. 22) probably come in the Greek from the same root. Jesus is 'the One who ensures permanently near relations with God'.

23–25 Because this Priest continues for ever, His priesthood will never, like the Levitical, pass to someone else by reason of His death (vv. 23, 24). It is a priesthood which death cannot encroach upon. It is 'inviolable' (v. 24, RV mg.), and unsupersedable. No-one will ever draw near to God, looking to Jesus to save, and fail to find Him there, still alive and active to intervene to support their cause. And, because He thus lives for ever to function as Mediator and Priest on behalf of His people, He is able to bring to its final completion the salvation of all who thus draw near to God, trusting in Him. The present tenses of the verbs *save* and *draw near* (v. 25) may well suggest a sustained experience resulting from a continuous practice. He is able 'to be saving' those who are 'continually coming', *i.e.* those who make it a regular habit thus to draw near to God.

26–28 sum up what the writer has been saying. Our Christian High Priest is outstandingly great. Only one as great as this was fitted to meet our need and secure our full salvation. In character, He is towards God *holy*, towards man *blameless*, and in Himself *unstained*. He is free from any pollution which would incapacitate Him for the work of His office. As regards His sphere of operation, He is lifted out from among sinful men by His removal to heaven, and there He is exalted to a position of the highest dignity, at the right hand of God. In contrast to the Levitical priests, He has no need repeatedly to offer sacrifices for sins. If He had, He would have to offer them *daily*, for His priestly work is going on every day. But all the offering necessary for sins He made *once for all when he offered up himself*. This is a new thought (although it has already been suggested) which is to be developed later. As one whose life was not dissolved by human dying, He was able, as no other could, to be both Priest and Victim; He offered *himself*. Similarly, the new covenant is vastly superior to the old. The old was a law which appointed as

high priests weak men unable to achieve the true end of priestly ministry. The new order, which has superseded the law, is constituted by an oath of God Himself. It appoints as High Priest One who is divine, a veritable Son of God, and One who by reason of His incarnation, death, resurrection and ascension has become perfectly and permanently competent to discharge His office *for ever* for all who 'draw near to God through him' (v. 25).

8:1–6 THE EXCELLENCE OF CHRIST'S HIGH-PRIESTLY MINISTRY

The writer now comes to the crowning truth of all that he has to say, namely, that we Christians (in contrast to the Jews of the OT order) have a High Priest of this outstanding kind: One who is Himself the reality, who answers to and fulfils the God-given pattern of priesthood; One whose ministry is therefore fulfilled in the heavenly sphere and not the earthly: One whose work has been consummated in enthronement at the right hand of God; and One who is therefore able to fulfil a more excellent ministry as the mediator of a new and better covenant.

It is important to recognize that because Christ is a *minister* of the *true tent* or 'Tabernacle' (v. 2), and has entered for us not into some earthly shrine but into the very presence of God, the whole sphere of His ministry is to be thought of as *in heaven* (v. 1) and not *on earth* (v. 4). This explains why He is invisible and not consummating His work, like the Jewish high priest, with elaborate ceremonies in some grand and visible earthly Temple—an important truth for Jewish readers to grasp. The Jewish priests who served on earth belonged to a different order, to which Jesus did not belong (v. 4). Also, the order of their service, while God-given, was only *a copy and shadow* of the heavenly truth (v. 5). It was Christ's work to fulfil this heavenly truth. This explains also why it was necessary for Him to die. For the pattern shows that he who would approach God as High Priest for men must *have something to offer* (v. 3). So Christ offered Himself. *Cf.* 7:27; 9:14; 10:10. This offering was all accomplished and finished in one decisive action. In the Greek the aorist tense of the verb to *offer* suggests a single finished act, not a continuous activity. Jesus, therefore, is not now offering. Indeed, the fact that His one offering was accepted as eternally sufficient is demonstrated by the fact that He is permanently enthroned in the place of all power (*cf.* 10:12, 13), and so able fully to save all who draw near to God by Him. It is this heavenly achievement and its successful consummation in enthronement which make Him the effective Mediator of the wonderful new covenant (v. 6). No wonder that the writer describes His ministry as being very different from the Levitical. No wonder that the possession as ours (*we have*) of *such a high priest* is called 'the chief point' (v. 1, RV), the mountain peak of revelation and redemption, the crowning truth of all.

Notice carefully the writer's distinction between the heavenly realities and their earthly copy or figurative representation (vv.2, 5; cf. 9:23, 24; 10:1). Because Jesus belonged to the heavenly order and not to that on earth (v. 4) His offering of Himself (though He died as Man on earth) can be properly appreciated only if it is understood as done in relation to the heavenly Tabernacle, and as having its consummation at the throne of God (cf. 1:3; 10:12; 12:2). Compare the way in which Christians, though they still live on earth, are to regard themselves as belonging to heaven (see 3:1; 12:22, 23); and are exhorted, by following Jesus, to pass into the heavens and to come boldly to the throne of grace (see 4:14, 16). Christian worship, like Christ's priestly work, is not 'on earth'.

8:7–13 THE TWO COVENANTS

7 The very presence in the OT of a promise of a new covenant is itself witness that the first covenant was not wholly satisfactory and free from fault. 8ff. This promise (quoted in vv. 8ff.) is found in Je. 31:31–34. What is there said indicates how the first covenant failed because the Israelites failed to abide by its conditions. This covenant, though genuine and good, was deficient in that it provided no guarantee that sinful men would continue in its faithful observance. So God declared His intention to make a new covenant by whose terms or 'better promises' (v. 6) He Himself undertook to make good the deficiency and to ensure the realization of His purpose. This purpose is that a company of people should be separated from the world, and brought into fellowship with Himself to be His people, to delight in His company, and to do His will.

10 God is to secure this end by making His law no longer an external restraint from which men only break away, but an inner constraint. This change is to be effected by putting the Spirit of obedience into men's hearts, so that, like the incarnate Son, they will say, 'I delight to do thy will, O my God; thy law is within my heart' (Ps. 40:8). Such intimacy of personal dealing will give to each individual direct personal knowledge of God. 11 No privileged intermediate class, whether of priests or prophets, will be needed to teach men about God. For all shall know Him directly. Knowing Him and being taught by Him personally in this way are thus to become the distinctive marks of God's true children. Cf. Is. 54:13; Jn. 6:45. 12 And all this will happen because God in His mercy towards them (instead of judgment against them) will so put away their sins (cf. 9:28) that perfect unhindered fellowship between them and Himself will become possible.

The foundation act of divine mercy on which all else is built is therefore the priestly work of putting away sin. The High Priest who does this,

and makes it possible for men to draw near to God, thus becomes the one who mediates this new covenant (v. 6). 13 This very promise of a new covenant means that, since the days of Jeremiah, the first covenant has to be recognized as already made old; and this description of anything as getting ancient and becoming aged means that it may be expected soon to pass away. Thus, from their own Jewish OT Scriptures, the writer provides his readers with a further decisive indication that the old covenant was only temporary, and that it was the divine intention that it should be superseded by the new covenant and itself cease to be.

9:1–10 THE MINISTRY OF THE FIRST COVENANT DESCRIBED

1 The first covenant had its divinely appointed regulations for worship and a sanctuary for their performance, an earthly one. 2–5 A Tabernacle was prepared with two sections, each richly and elaborately provided with furniture necessary for the ritual ceremonies, and with symbols of God's presence, of His past dealings with His people, and of His revealed will for their lives. It is impossible here, says the writer, to comment on all these features in detail (v. 5). The important thing on which to concentrate attention is the way in which this order of 'divine service' (v. 1, RV) furthered the one great purpose of its existence, namely, to enable men to draw near to God. 4 Having the golden altar of incense. The wording here (cf. 1 Ki. 6:22) probably means not that it was itself kept in the inner shrine, but rather that it was specially connected with the ministry carried out there on the Day of Atonement. See Ex. 30:1–10; Lv. 16:12, 13, 18–20.

6 These ordinances of the first covenant allowed a select class—the priests—to go continually into the outer tent, the holy place. 7 But into the inner shrine, or holiest sanctuary of all, where the cherubim (v. 5) over the ark symbolized the dwelling-place and manifested glory of God Himself, access was very severely restricted. One man only could enter, the high priest, on one day only each year, and only if he took with him the shed blood of atoning sacrifice. 8 An order of worship so arranged by divine direction was a witness given by the Spirit of God Himself that the way for all God's people to enter freely into the immediate presence of God is not yet opened. Note here the contrast between the divinely ordained splendour of the old order of worship, so dear to the writer's Jewish readers, and its disappointing, spiritual ineffectiveness. It 'made nothing perfect' (7:19, RV). Yet, far from being valueless, it had a deep spiritual significance. For, by providing 'figures of the true' (9:24, RV), it foreshadowed the character, the necessity and the benefits of the 'good things that have (now) come' (v. 11), when Christ, the true High Priest, appeared.

9 The limited and provisional character of the

first covenant is still further demonstrated by the very nature of its forms of worship. For the *gifts and sacrifices* which were ordained by it have no moral power to purge away the defilement of sin and to make those who bring them properly fit to reach the desired goal, *i.e.* to approach and to enjoy God's presence. **10** All that they can do as *regulations for the body* is to give those who submit to them a certain external or physical 'purification' (13), a formal or ritual status of ceremonial 'holiness'. They are, therefore, clearly temporary and provisional and meant to serve a purpose only until the time comes for them to be superseded by the realities whose character they foreshadow.

It is these 'good things' (v. 11) which are now made available for all to enjoy through Christ's coming and His high-priestly work. For the very forms which showed symbolically, *i.e.* in 'figure' (v. 9, AV) or 'parable' (RV), what was necessary to make access possible also showed that as yet the barriers were not removed for all to enter into the sanctuary (v. 8). As long as men were kept at a distance by a veil and an outer shrine placed between them and the holiest of all, clearly they could not enjoy access to God's presence. This meant, therefore, that only by the removal of this existing order, by the rending of the veil, and the doing away with a separate outer shrine, could the people outside have open access to God's presence. The writer is, therefore, suggesting to his Jewish readers that the realization of those hopes to which the first covenant pointed forward must involve the complete abolition of the old order. As he says later of the two kinds of sacrifice (see 10:9), God has abolished the first in order to establish the second—the new and living way into the sanctuary of His presence (see 10:19, 20). The writer has prepared his readers' minds for this extremely radical conclusion by suggesting earlier (8:13) that, since the first covenant has now been made old, it may be expected to disappear.

9:11 – 10:18 THE CHARACTERISTICS OF THE SACRIFICE OF CHRIST

The writer now describes the distinctive characteristics of the sacrifice of Christ and the great eternal benefits which are made ours by it. Following his now familiar method he illustrates and enforces these truths, first by both comparison and contrast with the Levitical forms of service and sacrifice, and then by quotation and exposition of some of the God-given prophetic words of the OT Scriptures.

9:11–15 Its far-reaching consequences

These consequences are briefly summarized. **11** First, by His offering of Himself Christ made a decisive entrance into the presence of God as the High Priest of sinful men. The goal of all priestly ministry is to secure access to, and acceptance in, God's presence; to restore, and to secure the

unbroken maintenance of, communion with God. Because Christ has appeared, *the good things have come*; they are no longer, as 'they were, still 'to come' (mg., AV, RV).

12–14 Secondly, Christ thus secured *eternal redemption*. He wrought a work of deliverance which set God's people permanently free from the defilement and doom to which they were otherwise subject because of sin. So His entrance, like His sacrifice (7:27), was *once for all*, never to be repeated. Thirdly, through His bloodshedding (*i.e.* by reason of the inexhaustible and abiding virtue of His one sacrifice of Himself) Christ is able to purge the conscience from the paralysing power of guilt and to set men free to *serve the living God*. For His sacrifice has a moral value and inner efficacy to cleanse not possessed by the ceremonies of the Jewish ritual (vv. 13, 14).

Taking . . . his own blood (v. 12); this is exactly what the Greek does not say (see mg.). 'Through' *his own blood* means on the ground of His already accomplished sacrificial death. *Through the eternal Spirit* (v. 14); recognition that as God's servant He was divinely enabled (*cf.* Is. 42:1); or possibly an indication that, since as God He was eternal or undying Spirit, He was able still to act at the time of His death as Man, and to 'offer Himself'.

15 Fourthly, such achievements mean that He is *the mediator* (or executor) *of a new covenant, i.e.* One who personally establishes all whom God calls in the actual possession of the eternal inheritance which He promises. Lastly, this result is the more sure because His death secures release from the penalty of *transgressions under* the *first* covenant. It clears the field for a new work of divine grace by fully settling the outstanding issues between God and His people. It blots out all the sins of the past.

9:16–23 Its necessity

Jesus had said of His death, 'It must be so' (Mt. 26:54). But the crucifixion of the Messiah continued to be a stumbling-block to Jews. They needed much help if they were to see why it was necessary. So the writer here stresses two reasons for its necessity. First, it was required in order to dedicate, institute or ratify the new covenant. Solemnly it sanctified or set apart the person making the covenant to the keeping of its terms by thus pledging (and in this case actually performing) obedience unto death. Secondly, it was needed in order to cleanse or purify the people who are covered by the covenant and to secure for them release or remission from the sin which would otherwise estrange them from God. For 'without the shedding of blood there is no forgiveness of sins' (v. 22). So a sacrifice of this unique and surprising kind, a better sacrifice than under the law (v. 23), the death of Christ Himself, was necessary to secure a better (moral) purification and to establish the better (and really effective) covenant. Note that men's hearts and consciences which are thus cleansed (v. 14) are called 'the heavenly things themselves' (v. 23).

16, 17 In the references here to the necessity for death to take place in connection with a testament or covenant, two or three different ideas are probably combined. According to ancient practice, covenants were sealed in blood (v. 18) by the symbolic introduction of the death of the party or parties making it. So vv. 16, 17 (see RV mg.) speak of 'death' being 'brought in' and of a covenant having validity only 'over dead bodies', *i.e.* probably over the divided pieces of the sacrificed victims between which such covenant-makers passed. See Gn. 15:7-21; Je. 34:18, 19. This gave visible confirmation to a vow of faithfulness unto death, and was probably accompanied by the prayer that one's life might be similarly taken in penalty (see, *e.g.*, Ru. 1:17, 'May the Lord do so to me') if the promise thus sealed was broken. Once the transgression of a covenant obligation had been committed, therefore, death became necessary for a second reason, to pay the penalty of such failure. So **22** asserts that under the old law this was the common price of redemption.

Further, since God's new covenant spoke of an inheritance which included the full forgiveness (or forgetting by God) of sins, this could not become available for men to enjoy until an actual death had taken place for the remission of sins, *i.e.* to redeem them 'from the transgressions under the first covenant' (v. 15). In this connection, therefore, the new covenant operates like *a will* or testament (in the Greek the word used signifies both 'covenant' and 'testament'). Its good things become available for enjoyment only after the death has taken place of the benefactor who is making the disposition. For He (*i.e.* Christ) could make forgiveness of our sins possible only by dying and Himself paying the penalty of our sins.

9:24 – 10:18 Its finality

This offering of Himself to God which Christ has made once for all in His human death is also perfect and final. It has achieved in full completion the true end of such sacrifice. Therefore, none greater is possible; and no other is necessary. As Jesus Himself said, 'It is finished' (Jn. 19:30). So 'there is no longer any offering for sin' (10:18).

9:24 By it He entered into heaven itself. His one act achieved what the sacrifices of the law only figuratively suggested. For the Levitical high priest entered only an earthly, man-made shrine. Through His death Christ has won an entrance *on our behalf* as our High Priest into the immediate presence of God (*cf.* vv. 11, 12). There He is now openly manifested before the very face of God as our representative, guaranteeing that we shall be accepted and our prayer answered when we come. It is because He is there to support our cause that full salvation is assured to all who come unto God by Him. *Cf.* 4:14, 16; 7:25; 1 Jn. 2:1, 2.

9:25, 26 He offered Himself. *Cf.* 7:27; 9:14. This was in contrast to the Levitical high priest who entered the holiest of all *with blood not his own*. He had no power himself to perform this act as a sacrifice to God; *i.e.* he could not offer himself. His presentation of the blood of a slain animal before God was an acknowledgment that something was necessary which he not only could not do himself, but also needed to have done on his behalf. Christ doubly excelled him. Not only did He not need any *blood not his own* shed on His behalf to give Him entrance (for He was sinless); but also He made His decisive appearance on the field of human history to put away the sin of others *by the sacrifice of himself.* This He was able to do because, as man, He was 'without blemish' (9:14), and as God He could as 'eternal Spirit' (9:14), by the power of His 'indestructible life' (7:16), still Himself act in death and offer the sacrifice of His human life to the Father. So He was both Priest and Victim; He offered Himself to God.

9:25-28 He offered Himself once only and once for all. This is proved by His non-appearance in earlier ages. For, as it is very important to recognize, He offered Himself to God on the field of history by becoming Man and offering His human body to die to bear the sins of many. We are saved by the earthly sacrifice of His flesh and blood. Therefore, had frequent offerings been necessary, similar to the yearly repetitions of the sacrifice of the Day of Atonement, it would have been necessary for Christ to have had many incarnations in order to suffer death many times. Also, if one offering availed only for a limited number, such as the generation then alive, it would 'now' (v. 26, AV, RV) (*i.e.* in the 1st century AD) be too late to offer sacrifice for the sins of earlier generations; and so it would have been necessary soon after the creation and the Fall of man for a series of incarnations to begin (v. 26). No such series has occurred. This is objective proof that it was not necessary, and clear indication that the one incarnation and death are sufficient and final for all history—past, present and future. Christ's one appearance *at the end of the age* (v. 26) is all that is necessary to remove completely the sins of the whole world by His one sacrifice of His single human life. As He said Himself, His one soul (or human life) thus given is enough to provide ransom for the many (Mk. 10:45).

Further, this final settlement of eternal destiny by the decisive action of a single life and death in human history corresponds with, and is confirmed by, all that is revealed by God concerning the solemn responsible character and eternal consequences of all human life in this present world. For all men live and die once, and according to the deeds done in that one lifetime their eternal judgment is settled (v. 27; *cf.* Rev. 20:12, 13). Similarly Christ's single appearance in history, and His one decisive action in atonement for sin, is sufficient to secure eternal redemption and the possession of an eternal inheritance (v. 28). There is no need of repetition. Any idea that either on earth or in heaven He must repeat or continue His offering is completely out of place. The redemption is eternal, and it has been obtained finally and for ever, not by an eternally continuous offering, but by the single decisiveness of one act in history. There is, however, a complementary event which is still future. The Christ who was once offered *will appear a second time* (v. 28), to complete the salvation of His people, who will, or ought to be, *eagerly waiting for him*.

9:26b – 10:4 By this sacrifice of Himself He actually put away sin. This was something which it was absolutely impossible for the Levitical sacrifices to do. The purpose and the consequence of His sacrifice of Himself was to bring sin to nought, to cancel it out, to set it on one side (v. 26b, Gk.; the old covenant is similarly 'disannulled'; see 7:18, Gk.). Christ was offered *to bear* (or 'bear away') *the sins of many* (v. 28; *cf.* Is. 53:12). He took the burden upon Himself and removed it. It is, therefore, completely gone. When He appears the second time it will be *not to deal with sin*, but as One able to complete the salvation of those who have their hopes fixed on Him (v. 28).

In contrast to this substantial reality—*the true form of these realities* (10:1)—all that the old Jewish law had to offer was a *shadow*, or representation in outline, *of good things* (yet) *to come*. Its sacrifices, yearly repeated, had no power to effect a permanent benefit for those who thus drew nigh to God. Rather their continued repetition was first a witness of their own ineffectiveness to complete the work of cleansing, and second a witness to the fact that those who thus used them did not gain from their use any real deliverance from a sense of guilt (10:1, 2). For such animal sacrifices can never *take away sins* (v. 4). What they cannot do, Christ has actually done.

10:5–10 His offering fulfilled the will of God with regard to sacrifice. It was thus that He effected the sanctification of God's people. For His offering of Himself was the reality of which the sacrifices of the law were but a shadow. Because of the ineffectiveness of those sacrifices, there was an important sense (to which the OT Scriptures gave expression: see Ps. 40:6–8, quoted here), in which God was not satisfied with them and did not desire them. In their place they served a purpose. But the same Scriptures, which spoke of God's lack of pleasure in them, also indicated that ultimately God contemplated a better sacrifice (vv. 6–9). His will with regard to sacrifice would be fulfilled when a person, in the full freedom of personal moral choice and qualified so to act, would devote himself and his human life to doing God's will by offering his own body. Also, the prophetic Scripture teaches that this is what the Christ of God will choose to do and come to do (v. 7) in fulfilment of the pattern, and in obedience to the principles, set forth in Holy Scripture. For He will recognize that what is there written concerns Him and the God-given work which He is to do.

Further, the way in which the disowning of animal sacrifices and the promise of a person to come to do God's will precede and follow one another in the same Psalm (40:6–8) plainly indicates that it is God's purpose that the second should take the place of the first (vv. 8, 9). For the writer's first readers this meant again that, as Jews, they must recognize that, in fulfilment of the will of God, the Levitical order was now 'abolished' and openly superseded by God's own establishment of a new order in which is to be found the full and final realization of all towards which the older order pointed. For, by Christ's one offering of His human body (v. 10), the people of God are eternally made fit for God's presence and consecrated to His service.

10:11–14 In consequence of His one finished sacrifice Christ sits enthroned and assured of complete victory. There is a striking contrast between Christ's present position and prospect and that of the Levitical priests. They continue to stand in order to continue offering their repeated sacrifices, but with no hope that they will ever *take away sins* (v. 11). Christ is already seated, a sign that His work of offering is finished (v. 12). What is more, He is enthroned in the place of sovereignty and power at God's right hand with the sure hope, based on the Father's own word to Him (see Ps. 110:1; Heb. 1:13), that all His enemies are to be subdued beneath His feet (v. 13). All this has come about through His *single offering* (v. 14) which is eternal in its efficacy. By it *he has perfected for all time those who are sanctified, i.e.* He has secured the permanent continuance in right relation to God (perfected) of all whom it serves to cleanse from sin and to dedicate as God's people (sanctified).

10:15–18 There is no further need or place for any more offering for sin. Such a conclusion is here based on the witness to us of the Holy Spirit given in the words of a prophecy which declares the blessings of the new covenant (see Je. 31:31–34). For its crowning promise is the declaration by God Himself that, once the new covenant is ratified, He will remember the sins of His people no more (v. 17). And if sins are so completely remitted that God Himself ceases to remember them, there is obviously no need or place for any further offering to be made to secure their removal. This, then, is the conclusive proof from God's own new covenant promise that Christ's redemptive act which has established the new covenant is in itself all-sufficient and absolutely final. Henceforth there is no longer any place for any kind of offering for sin or presentation before God of Christ's one sin-offering (v. 18). Reconciliation has not to be made or completed by any further propitiatory offering or memorial of Christ's sacrifice; it has simply to be received by penitent faith as an already complete and available benefit of the finished work of Christ (see Rom. 5:11).

10:19–39 PRACTICAL EXHORTATION

10:19–25 A call to steadfastness in faith, hope and love

These verses summarize the positive appeal of the whole Epistle. It is based (note the *therefore* of v. 19) on the doctrinal teaching already given about the absolute efficacy of Christ's one sacrifice and His abiding continuance in the place of sovereign ability as our High Priest. It is a call first of all to enter into the realized presence of God in confident, appropriating faith (v. 22). Here the writer reinforces an appeal already made in 4:14–16, when he introduced these themes. This is complemented by exhortations to be steadfast in the open confession of Christian hope (v. 23) and to be active towards fellow-Christians in love, fellowship and mutual encouragement (v. 24). This brief, threefold exhortation is virtually expanded in the remainder of the Epistle. Chs. 11, 12 and 13 emphasize in turn the same three themes, the expression of faith, the patience of hope, and love and good works.

19, 20 The new possibility open to all Christians is that of free access to God's presence. There is a way which has been inaugurated for us by Jesus, the forerunner. This way is *new*, *i.e.* it did not exist under the old covenant, and it is *living* or effective. (*Cf.* Jn. 14:6, where the meaning probably is 'I am the true and living way'.) The *curtain* or 'veil' through which Jesus opened up this way was His human *flesh*. For when it was broken in sacrificial death the symbolic Temple veil was rent asunder. See Mt. 27:51–53; Col. 1:20–22. So we can have joyous *confidence* or 'boldness' (AV, RV) to enter God's presence through *the blood* (*i.e.* the death, or accomplished and effectual sacrifice) *of Jesus*. Note it does not say 'with the blood of Jesus'. Christians have no longer to seek to win entrance by a fresh presentation of the sacrifice. The way stands open and unbarred. **21** Further, as we thus enter God's dwelling-place and join the company of His family (*the house*, or household, *of God*), we find we have the same Jesus as our enthroned and ever-living *priest*, *great* in this ability to support our case and meet all our need (*cf.* 7:25). **22** What is required of all who thus come is sincerity of purpose (*a true heart*) and absolute confidence (*full assurance of faith*) that what Christ has done avails to make ours that full purification both within and without which was symbolized under the old ritual forms by sprinkled blood and freshly washed bodies (see, *e.g.*, Lv. 8:6, 23). **23** In the face of temptations to abandon their confidence because some promises remained unfulfilled, the writer appeals for a steadfast persistence in openly confessing their Christian hope; for they have the sure guarantee of the faithfulness of the Promiser. **24** There should also be among Christians mutual 'provocation' (Gk.; see AV, RV: a striking word because commonly used with a bad sense) to active good works by deliberately taking notice of each other's needs.

The Greek here says 'consider one another' (so AV, RV). **25** They should not, therefore, copy the custom of some and cease attendance at Christian meetings, but rather use such opportunities for mutual encouragement, and the more so in the light of the approaching consummation and judgment of *the Day* that is coming.

10:26–31 The consequences of deliberate rebellion

The writer sees for those in the position occupied by himself and his readers only two possibilities: either to make full response, or to become deliberate rebels. Having exhorted his readers fully to respond (vv. 19–25) he now considers, at least hypothetically (this may be the force of *if we*), the only alternative. Suppose that, persistently and by deliberate choice, we completely turn aside from what has been brought within our knowledge and our reach; what else remains for us to enjoy?

The solemn answer is, first, that there is no second, alternative way of atonement for sin (v. 26), and, second, that nothing awaits us but the terrifying prospect of judgment as objects of that divine wrath which is to be displayed against all who oppose God (v. 27). For even under the old covenant (see Dt. 17:2–7) a man who completely set its demands on one side in active rebellion (*e.g.* idolatry) suffered the extreme penalty of death without mercy (v. 28). Does it not commend itself as fitting, even to our judgment, that an apostate from the new covenant (*i.e.* an 'enlightened' (v. 32) person who deliberately renounces and opposes the Christian faith), ought to suffer a much worse penalty (v. 29)? For consider the gravity of his offence. He has trampled down the person of Him who is, and has been confessed as, the Son of God. He has denied sacred significance to that blood which had been to him the covenant seal of his own sanctification. He has treated with proud insolence that Spirit who is Himself the author of the whole work of grace in the experience of which he had shared. Do not God's spoken words (*i.e.* in Scripture) make plain, also, His character as a God who executes judgment, and who will certainly show by His judgments who are His people and who are the traitors and rebels against Him (v. 30)? Can any prospect be more terrifying than thus to have this God against one in judgment (v. 31)? See also Appendix 3, p. 1219.

26 *Sin* must mean here apostasy or rebellion (*cf.* Is. 1:2, 19, 20; Heb. 3:12, 13; 2 Pet. 2:21). The present tense indicates sustained persistence; the emphatic adverb, put first in the Greek, stresses that it is done *deliberately*. There *no longer remains a sacrifice for sins*; not only because the one final sacrifice has been rejected, but also because such sin is unforgivable; there is no divine provision for its remission. **30** *The Lord will judge his people.* The OT idea is that God will execute judgment for or on behalf of His people. The meaning here is that He will vindicate the true by removing the false. *Cf.* Nu. 16, especially v. 5.

10:32–39 An encouragement to steadfast persistence

Having contemplated the worst, the writer now finds ground to expect and appeal for the best. If his readers are tempted to abandon Christianity because it involves them in suffering and reproach rather than fulfilment of their natural hopes, let them find inspiration to continue first in looking back, and then in looking forward. Let them remember from their own early experience as Christians that public exposure to reproach and trial has been, from the first, the lot of those who share this enlightenment.

It is therefore no new and unexpected development. At that time their own attitude in the face of such trials showed that they fully realized that these were experiences in which, as Christians, they were called to share, and that any physical pain or material loss could be accepted with joy when compared with their heavenly and eternal gain (vv. 32–34; *cf.* 2 Cor. 4:16–18). Let them also look forward and realize that their joyous Christian confidence has not been misplaced. It holds sure promise of a full reward and ought by no means to be abandoned (v. 35). They must realize, however, that in the will of God there is a period of waiting and working and trial before the promised fulfilment can be enjoyed (v. 36). This fulfilment will be very soon. It will be consummated by the appearance of the Coming One (v. 37). His advent is certain; nor will He be behind His time. For those who know these things there are only two possible attitudes: to find acceptance with God and life by holding on in faith; or to withdraw one's confidence and come under God's displeasure (v. 38). For us, says this writer, the latter alternative is unthinkable. We are not (v. 39) the sort to depart from the faith to our own destruction; we are the kind who go on believing until we reach the goal of gaining our souls, *i.e.* enjoying full salvation. (*Keep their souls* (v. 39): RV mg. 'the gaining of the soul'. *Cf.* Lk. 21:19, AV, RV, RSV, NEB: *cf.* also Jn. 12:25.)

37, 38 The writer does not claim to be specifically quoting Scripture; but there is obviously a free use of OT phrases. *A little while* is probably an echo of Is. 26:20. The other sentences are from Hab. 2:3, 4. There, according to the Hebrew and the OT translation, what is coming is either the vision or the advent of God thus visualized. The LXX makes the subject a person. This personal reference is made still more definite here by the addition in Greek of the definite article to the participle. Hence *the coming one*, a Messianic title (*cf.* Mt. 11:2). In using the statements of Hab. 2:4 the writer not only follows the LXX, which is a statement very different from the Hebrew, but also he transposes the two sentences. Also, here the subject of both statements is the same person, suggesting that the true believer may apostatize.

The second statement is, however, only hypothetical. The resulting couplet states the plain alternatives: to live by faith, to perish by apostasy. Just as before God there is justification and life by faith, so, if a believer deliberately withdraws from the faith attitude, he can only encounter divine displeasure and perdition. 39 No wonder the writer adds that neither he nor they can have any intention of committing such spiritual suicide.

11:1–40 THE TRIUMPHANT ACHIEVEMENTS OF FAITH

In 10:38, 39 the writer has enunciated the scriptural principle of faith as a way of life pleasing to God and has expressed the resolution to persist in it until the full possession of its reward is received. He now enforces this by many scriptural illustrations, showing that, from the very beginning and throughout all subsequent history, faith has been in God's sight the one indispensable condition of worth-while achievement and hopeful endurance.

Faith, he declares, deals essentially with things of two types, things future (or 'hoped for') and things 'not seen' (v. 1). It is equally sure of the coming fulfilment of the one and of the present reality of the other. Without such an active attitude of awareness and assurance towards God 'it is impossible to please him' (v. 6), or indeed to have personal dealings with Him (*i.e.* to 'draw near to God'). For the very being of God Himself is the supreme unseen reality with which faith has to do; and His faithful fulfilment of His promises (*cf.* v. 11) and His certain rewarding of those who seek Him (v. 6) are the great future good for which faith hopes. The one requires 'conviction' (Gk. *elenchos*), *i.e.* 'proving' (RV) or certification; the other requires 'assurance', or 'substance' (AV, NEB, Gk. *hypostasis*, of which a possible meaning is 'title deed'), *i.e.* the faith of assured confidence and settled expectation (v. 1). It is because they manifested a faith of this sort (v. 2, see AV, RV) that those who have gone before have had their deeds and sufferings approved by God as worthy to be recorded in Scripture. It was by their faith that they joined the company of God's witnesses (12:1) or 'martyrs' (Gk.). For God witnessed for them (vv. 2, 4, 5); and they thus still witness for Him. The activity of such a faith as theirs afforded something to be recorded which has an abiding message for men; it continues to provide encouragement and examples for others. Such witness, therefore, outlives the individual who gives it; and through the record of his doings his faith still speaks to others after he is dead (v. 4).

The many witnesses of the OT record are then surveyed in chronological order and in some detail. Throughout there is emphasis on their conviction concerning the unseen divine realities and on their assurance of the coming divine fulfilments, both in striking contrast to the visible appearance and immediate natural outlook, which seemed often completely to contradict their confidence (vv. 9, 11, 17, 18). The one sure and all-sufficient certainty was, and is, the living God and His faithful doing. So, for instance, Moses 'endured as seeing him who is invisible' (v. 27); he counted earthly suffering and reproach preferable to worldly enjoyment and wealth, because he looked for God's sure payment of worth-while reward (vv. 25, 26). The common experience of all these pilgrims was to see from a distance promised rewards, which they never enjoyed in this life (v. 13). Yet they never withdrew and turned back to the world which they had left behind, because they believed in a fulfilment that was heavenly rather than earthly (vv. 14-16). These are the people whom God owns as His, condescending to be called their God.

The final emphasis is upon rewards beyond this life. True, many reached faith's goal here in open triumph (vv. 29-35a), and such victories have been of all kinds—material, moral and spiritual. Yet faith's most outstanding witnesses are the martyrs (vv. 35b-38), those who, for faith's sake, have endured great suffering, those who have died painful and shameful deaths rather than deny their faith. In them faith has shown itself victorious in indomitable endurance, in refusal to accept deliverance. Their reward, which they thus chose, lies beyond death in 'a better resurrection' (v. 35, AV, RV, *i.e.* better than restoration to life in this world such as was granted to the sons of the women of Zarephath and Shunem). Indeed none of these old heroes of faith, worthy as they are of their place in Scripture, ever enjoyed the complete fulfilment of God's promises, because God in His providence ordained that we Christian believers should enjoy even greater privileges and share with them in the consummation (vv. 39, 40).

1 The order of the words in Greek puts the emphasis on the objects of faith, *i.e.* the *things hoped for* and *things not seen*; and the inclusion of a noun (Gk. *pragmata*) in the second phrase, making explicit that these unseen things are realities, is itself a proof or 'evidence' (AV) of their existence. **3** Such faith is a primary condition of knowledge, particularly knowledge of the scriptural witness. It is essential to the understanding of the origin of the universe as described in Gn. 1. It is the foundation of all right thinking about those 'worlds' or 'ages' which form the stage and setting of human history. For it is impossible to provide an adequate explanation simply by reasoning from what can be observed by the senses. One needs to recognize the prior and independent existence of the living God and His creative activity as the first cause. With the phrase *by the word of God, cf.* 'And God said' used ten times in Gn. 1; *cf.* also Ps. 33:6. **4** It was the faith in which he offered it that made Abel's sacrifice better than Cain's. He made a more appropriate response to the truth about God of which he was aware. It was because of

his faith, thus expressed by what he gave, that he was reckoned *righteous*. It is through his faith that he still speaks (*i.e.* through the pages of Scripture; note the present tense, *is still speaking*) witnessing to men how to please God. Note that *which* refers back to *faith*.

5 *Enoch* witnesses that faith, active in a man's heart in this life, so pleases God that He gives finally to the true believer escape from death and a fuller enjoyment of His own presence and glory. **6** Such examples are sufficient to justify the generalization of v. 6, 'Without faith it is impossible to be well-pleasing unto God' (RV). For how can a man have dealings with One who is unseen, and whose chief rewards lie beyond this present life, unless he believes both that God exists and that, whenever a man thus sets himself wholeheartedly to *draw near* to God, God never fails to become his rewarder or payer-back of recompense (*cf.* Jas. 4:8a)?

7 *Noah* is a peculiarly significant example for those privileged to hear the gospel. Out of reverence for a word from God, which spoke of impending judgment and indicated a way of salvation, he acted in obedience to the divine command, because he believed that what God said would be fulfilled. By such faith he not only himself inherited that *righteousness* which is God's gift to believers (note the implication that this is a thought familiar to the readers of the Epistle; *cf.* Rom. 1:17); he was also used as God's witness and worker to the condemnation of his generation and the salvation of others of his family.

8 *Abraham* obeyed the divine call to go forth to possess an inheritance, though he did not know to what land he was going, still less what it was like. His faith was in a marked way a conviction concerning the unseen and a guarantee of something to be enjoyed in the future (*cf.* v. 1). **9** When he actually entered the land of divine promise it was to reside in it only as an outsider living in a land belonging to others. He learnt also to make his home in tents, as a man always on the move. His son and grandson entered into the heritage of the same divine promise, but no more saw its actual fulfilment than he. Yet this experience did not cause him to give up believing. **10** Rather he looked for a supernatural fulfilment, an abiding city, built according to the design (note RV mg. 'architect') and by the working of God (*cf.* 12:22; 13:14). **11** The triumph of faith in Sarah's experience was the more remarkable not only because she had been long barren (Gn. 11:30), but still more because any such fulfilment was no longer normally to be expected at the time of life she had now reached. Her faith rested on God's word of promise and on His active faithfulness in fulfilling His Word (*cf.* Rom. 4:20, 21). **12** The *one man* from whom such a vast progeny sprang was Abraham; see Gn. 15:5; Is. 51:1, 2; Ezk. 33:24.

13-16 This experience of deferred fulfilment in the lives of the patriarchs enabled them eventually to triumph by faith over death itself.

For they learned to look beyond death for a larger fulfilment than that which their own lifetime and earthly experience could afford. So they came to realize that this life is not an end in itself but a pilgrimage (see Gn. 23:4; 47:9) towards a better (*i.e.* a heavenly) goal beyond it. It is such people with whom God has condescended openly to associate Himself and to be known as *their God* (v. 16); *cf.* Mk. 12:26, 27, and note the similar reference there to life beyond death.

17, 18 Abraham's faith was tried in the demand to offer up Isaac not only because he was peculiarly beloved as Sarah's only child (*his only son*), but most of all because the demand seemed to oppose the fulfilment in Isaac of the God-given promise which Abraham had already embraced, *i.e.* that through him Abraham's family was to be continued and multiplied. Abraham's faith triumphed because he refused to see inconsistency or faithlessness in God. He believed God could and must resolve the problem. No solution seemed possible unless God gave Isaac back from death to become the father of children. **19** This Abraham therefore reckoned as fully possible with God; his faith thus triumphing in a fresh way over death by the hope of resurrection. Such faith turned a way of darkness into a pathway of hope. *Figuratively speaking*, RV 'in a parable', may mean 'as it were' or it may suggest 'for a lesson', *i.e.* one from which Abraham learnt the kind of working to expect from God as His way of solving life's darkest problems (*cf.* Rom. 4:17). Some think the reference is to such a lesson already learnt from the manner of Isaac's birth (*cf.* v. 12).

20 *Isaac* expressed his faith in God's sovereign providence by accepting, contrary to his own natural preference and intention, that Jacob should come before Esau in blessing (*cf.* Gn. 27:33), and in anticipating blessings of the future for their descendants. **21, 22** Similarly *Jacob* and *Joseph* looked beyond their own deaths and anticipated the *exodus* of the Israelites from Egypt and their return to Canaan (*cf.* Gn. 48:21; 50:24). Jacob gave to Joseph instead of to Reuben the privilege of the firstborn, *i.e.* a double share, divided between his two sons. Jacob also showed his awareness of the reality and sovereignty of God by the way in which, in spite of his age and infirmity, he bowed or prostrated himself in worship on his staff (LXX) or bed (Heb.) (Gn. 47:31). Joseph, like Jacob, out of regard for God's sure purpose, was concerned ultimately to be buried not amid the wealth of Egypt but in the land of divine promise. See Ex. 13:19; Jos. 24:32.

23 Moses' *parents* apparently saw something in their child which made them sure that it was God's purpose to preserve and use him. So, instead of killing the child through fear of Pharaoh and his order, they saved him through faith in God and His co-operating providence. **24, 25** What Moses *refused* to enjoy was the princely status of a son of a daughter of the

royal house. He did this because he deliberately preferred publicly to be known as one of the Hebrews, who were to his faith not a race of slaves but *the people of God*, *i.e.* a people with a divinely ordained destiny. Inevitably this meant choosing to share their hardships rather than, at the cost of apostasy from the God of the Hebrews, to enjoy the immediate but shortlived comfort and luxury of the Egyptian court. Note here the significance for the original readers of the word *sin* (*cf.* 10:26) and of Moses' choice to suffer rather than commit it. **26** So, having regard to the ultimate reward it would bring at God's hand, he reckoned that to suffer *abuse* in such a cause would be a greater personal enrichment than all the Egyptians' wealth so obviously within his grasp. Such reproach is 'the reproach of the Christ' (AV, RV and mg.; *cf.* 13:13) because it is the typical lot in the world primarily of the Lord's anointed or Messiah (Ps. 89:50, 51; Rom. 15:3), but also and inevitably of all associated with Him as God's elect people (*cf.* 1 Pet. 4:12–16). **27** *Not being afraid of the anger of the king.* Ex. 2:14 seems to contradict this; but the two are not irreconcilable. For, although Moses felt natural alarm and the need for flight, his spiritual awareness of God and of His purposes both for the Israelites and for Moses' own life made him sure that Pharaoh's enmity would not be allowed to prevail. Also, while the words *he left Egypt* may refer to Moses' flight to Midian, it is more likely that they refer to the Exodus, an event calculated in a much bigger way to provoke Pharaoh's anger. Note that the two reasons why Moses chose as he did, and persisted in his choice, were his awareness of the unseen One (v. 27), and his confident expectation of future reward (v. 26).

28 Moses' faith helped the whole people to respond to God's words of warning and promise (note RV mg. rendering). Inspired by his leadership, they believed beforehand in the certainty of an impending divine judgment upon the firstborn, and in the sufficient shelter from such judgment afforded by the one divinely appointed provision, 'the sprinkling of the blood' (RV). It was thus in judgment and salvation that the Lord showed who were His (*cf.* Ex. 8:22). **29** *The Red Sea* presented a naturally impassable barrier. It was impossible first to conceive and then to avail themselves of a way through except *by faith*. The attempt by the Egyptian forces simply to 'try it out', without any confidence of faith in God's control, resulted only in their being overwhelmed (see RV). **30** The manner of Jericho's capture is another striking example of that obedience and endurance of faith, to the practice of which the writer wished to exhort his readers. The Israelites acted throughout in confidence in the unseen, and they held on till God's time was fulfilled (*for seven days*) in the sure expectation of His certain action; nor were they disappointed. **31** *Rahab* acted as she did because she recognized the power of the God of Israel (*i.e.* things unseen) and the certain coming victory of His people (*i.e.* things future). See Jos. 2:8–13. Her response is significant because as a woman, a Gentile and an open sinner she joined the company of those who were saved by faith. By contrast the other inhabitants of Jericho are described as *disobedient*, *i.e.* actively unbelieving.

32–34 Forced to summarize, the writer now limits himself to a selection of typical names and a list of characteristic and outstanding achievements. Among the latter there seem to be obvious references to Daniel (viz. *stopped the mouths of lions*; *cf.* Dn. 6:22, 23) and to the three who were cast into the fiery furnace (viz. *quenched raging fire*; *cf.* Dn. 3:25–28). But while many deeds which fit the other phrases used can be found in the OT, it seems possible that this and the subsequent survey (vv. 35–38) also include some intended references to the doings of faithful Jews in the centuries between the Testaments, particularly in Maccabean times.

The supreme achievement of faith is victory over death in resurrection. **35–38** Some experienced this reward in this life (v. 35); their dead were restored to them (see 1 Ki. 17:17–24; 2 Ki. 4:17–37). (Note that in Scripture the recorded raisings from the dead are mostly for women; *cf.* Lk. 7:11–17; Jn. 11:1–46.) Others had the faith to hold on in unconquered but outwardly unrewarded endurance, through imprisonment and torture, and as fugitives and exiles (vv. 35–38). They accepted no earthly deliverance because it would have been enjoyed only at the price of denying their faith. Their reward lies in 'a better (*i.e.* a heavenly) resurrection' in the life beyond (v. 35). *Of whom the world was not worthy* (v. 38). This is the actual but paradoxical truth. The world of their day treated them as not worthy to live in it; actually the world was not worthy of such men. It is for such that God has 'prepared a city' (v. 16). **39** The goal towards which all these heroes of faith were moving in confident hope was one which they never reached. **40** For God in His providence had reserved *for us* (*i.e.* Christian believers) the crowning blessing and had ordained that they should not enjoy the consummation until we had been brought in to share it. Note the implication that the men of faith of OT and NT times alike are all called to belong to the one company of God's purpose who are to be *made perfect* together (*cf.* 12:22–24).

12:1–29 PERSONAL APPLICATION: A CALL TO SERVE GOD ACCEPTABLY

This exhortation is based first on the supreme example and complete sufficiency of Jesus Himself as the pioneer and perfecter of our faith (vv. 1–3); secondly, on the positive purpose and profit of trials under the providence of a loving heavenly Father (vv. 4–11); thirdly, on the dangers of the greater (and even fatal) failure to which the slack and careless expose themselves (vv. 12–17); fourthly, on the amazing privileges of grace to be enjoyed under the new covenant compared with the experiences of those who first participated in the old covenant (vv. 18–24); and finally on the impending and inescapable consummation of God's dealings with men (vv. 25–29).

12:1–3 The supreme example of Jesus Christ

Having surveyed the achievements of the past heroes of faith, the writer confronts his readers with the inspiration and challenge of their example (v. 1); let them face their contest with similar concentration and endurance. Above all, he exhorts them to find encouragement to face reproach and persecution by deliberately filling their minds with thoughts of Jesus and His triumphant achievement (vv. 2, 3). Let them fortify themselves against despondency and collapse by recalling what He endured and by recognizing that, in the face of the extreme shame and suffering of crucifixion, He had regard for the joy of the heavenly reward which He now permanently enjoys as One who is enthroned at God's right hand. Also, the manner and success of His achievement not only make possible our pursuit of the same pathway of faith, but also guarantee that He will enable us to complete what He enables us to begin. In this way, therefore, He is both the initiator and consummator, 'author and finisher' (v. 2, AV), of our faith. *Cf.* 2:10; 5:8, 9; 7:25.

1 *A cloud of witnesses.* While the idea of an encompassing crowd of spectators may be included (see 1 Tim. 6:12), the primary reference is to their testimony. They are God's witnesses to us, who encourage us by their example. *Sin* (vv. 1, 4), in the mind of this writer, seems often to be an act of apostasy. Here the temptation is to give up the race altogether, one which is constantly put in their way, and so needing decisive rejection and unflinching resistance (*cf.* 3:12–14; 10:26, 38; 11:25). *Perseverance*; or 'endurance'. Note the recurrence of 'endure' (vv. 2, 3, 7). **2** *Jesus.* Note the significance of the unqualified human name (*cf.* 2:9; 6:20; 7:22; 12:24; 13:12); He is One who has Himself sustained the conflict. **3** The *hostility* (RV 'gainsaying') *from sinners* means nothing less than the rejection of His claims in defiant rebellion. *Cf.* 'sets himself against (AV, RV, more literally 'speaketh against') Caesar' (Jn. 19:12).

12:4–11 The purpose of suffering

They need to remember, he says, that their sufferings are so far light compared with those of Jesus; faithfulness has not yet cost any of them his life (v. 4). What is more, they have forgotten the teaching of Scripture which makes plain that, as a loving Father, God uses the trials which men have to endure in their earthly experience, for their spiritual discipline and education as His children (v. 5). The very experience of such trials is, therefore, practical proof that God is dealing with them as sons (vv. 6, 7); it is those who are without such experiences who may well question their status in God's family (v. 8). Admittedly such experiences are at the time unpleasant (v. 11). It is important, therefore, to recognize the unseen hand that controls them, and to submit in reverence to a spiritual or heavenly Father's pleasure, as children often do in their way to their earthly parents (v. 9). It is equally important to recognize God's purpose in these trials, and the consequent profit that, in the end, they will unquestionably gain from them. This divinely intended fruit is nothing less than the increase in the life of practical righteousness and godliness (v. 10), *i.e.* 'that we may share his holiness'. Such results ensue in the experience only of 'those who have been trained by it' (v. 11), *i.e.* those who in responsive and persistent faith are prepared to submit to the unseen God, and actively to co-operate in letting the discipline do its work in the hope of worth-while benefit.

5ff. *The discipline*; the Greek word *paideia* means 'education', the training of a child, with particular reference here (as in Pr. 3:11, 12) to discipline and reproof. Note how the OT is quoted as of practical relevance to our present experiences as Christians. **7** *It is for discipline that you have to endure.* This indicates why God allows trials to befall men and makes men endure them—in order to further their education as His children. **9** *The Father of spirits*; a reference to God as the Creator of the human spirit; contrast 'fathers of our flesh' (AV, RV). The verse implies that beings thus created can know true life only by submission to God's control. **10** *For a short time.* Discipline by human parents has its limits. It is administered only during childhood; it depends upon men's uncertain judgment or mood. Divine discipline is infinitely superior; it is always imposed in men's interest and aims to make them sharers in the very holiness of God Himself.

12:12–17 Grave danger to be avoided

They ought, therefore, to throw off despondency and face life as Christians with courage and confidence (v. 12). For if they do not thus help one another to go forward the imminent danger is that some who are halting in their response will completely abandon the way of faith (v. 13). Let them therefore seek in their fellowship to promote true holiness as well as peace with one another (v. 14). Let them all be on the watch lest any one of their number should not only himself turn aside from God's way of salvation by grace, but also be allowed in their midst to become a perverting influence injuring the whole community (v. 15). For this kind of failure needs to be recognized as nothing less than spiritual profanity and apostasy. It means acting like Esau and vilely giving up one's God-given inheritance for some trifling material gain (v. 16). Still worse, Esau's history shows that, once a God-given inheritance has been thus deliberately rejected, there can be no further opportunity of regaining it. A man who acts in such a way stands permanently condemned (v. 17).

12–15 The full significance of vv. 12, 13 is best appreciated by comparing Is. 35:3; Pr. 4:25–27; 1 Ki. 18:21. The whole community is exhorted to advance, to walk in an even, or straight-forward, path and to avoid inconsistencies in order to help the halting to make headway (*cf.* Rom. 15:1, 2). The *lame* were possibly those halting between Christianity and Judaism. The danger was lest they should completely abandon faith in Christ, an action described in v. 15 as 'falling back from' (RV mg.) or *failing to obtain the grace of God.* The description in v. 13 is figurative. It stresses that unless those limping find healing, they may soon become completely disabled, and unable to make any further progress. *See to it that no one fail* (v. 15). The Greek verb here means 'exercising oversight' or acting as 'bishops'. But the reference is to the whole community, not to special ministers. In the Christian congregation the many should care for and deal with the one. *Cf.* 3:12, 13; 4:1 (RV); Gal. 6:1, 2. *That no root of bitterness . . . trouble you* (v. 15). *Cf.* Dt. 29:18, where similar phraseology is used to describe the man who turns from the Lord to serve other gods, *i.e.* the apostate. Note also that such a person can bring defilement on the whole congregation. *Cf.* the story of Achan; see Jos. 6:18; 7:25. **16, 17** Esau's folly ended in despair (*cf.* Judas); it was impossible to alter what he had done. He had made the decisive choice which settled his destiny. Also, his profanity, or lack of reverence for the things of God, was such that he was incapable of true repentance. He wept for what he had lost (the blessing), not for the sin he had committed.

12:18–24 The privileges of the old and new covenants contrasted

As Christians they have entered under the new covenant into the enjoyment of things very different from those experienced under the old covenant by those who came out of Egypt. Those things were earthly, visible, terrifying and forbidding; these are heavenly, unseen, all-glorious and all-gracious. In the wilderness the Israelites stood in the presence of a tangible mountain and actual burning fire. The place was overshadowed by clouds and intense darkness and the violence of storm (v. 18). They heard a trumpet sound and a voice speaking words (v. 19). The whole experience was so terrifying that the people asked that it might cease (Ex. 20:18, 19). Since even an animal, venturing too near, had to be stoned for sacrilege, they feared for their lives (v. 20; see Ex. 19:12, 13; Dt. 5:25). Even Moses himself was overwhelmed with fright (v. 21). How different is the experience of drawing nigh to God in which, as Christians, they are called to share! They come to the unseen heavenly realities, which correspond to and actually fulfil the mere earthly types. They come to the true mountain and city of God, where God actually dwells; to hosts of angels in festal array (v. 22); to the church of the privileged with the heavenly inheritance; to the one all-sovereign God as their Vindicator; to the spirits of the righteous (*i.e.* either OT saints or all the faithful departed), whose bliss is consummated (v. 23); to Jesus the Mediator of this recently established (Gk. *nea*, not *kainē*, as is usual) covenant; and to the blood of sprinkling which speaks of remission of sins in contrast to Abel's blood which cried out for vengeance (Gn. 4:10), and so (in contrast to the voice at Sinai) offering them welcome and assured peace (v. 24).

In the Greek none of the terms used in the two descriptive lists given in these verses is preceded by the definite article. The writer is simply describing general distinctive characteristics of the two covenants. **18** The word 'mount' does not occur in the best Greek MSS. The primary stress is on the whole character of the revelation at Sinai as something tangible (*cf.* 1 Jn. 1:1), rather than on its particular locality on a mountain. On the other hand, since there is an obvious opening contrast between Mt. Sinai and Mt. Zion, the insertion of 'mount' is appropriate and not misleading.

22 *Innumerable angels.* The description 'tens of thousands' or 'myriads' (Gk.) is commonly used of angels (*cf.* Dt. 33:2; Dn. 7:10). *In festal gathering.* This is in contrast to their terrifying manifestation on Sinai. **23** *The assembly*; Greek *ekklēsia*, so 'church', AV, RV. The *first-born* expresses the idea of privilege and heirship, blessings such as those which Esau despised (v. 16). In Egypt, and subsequently in Israel, the firstborn were redeemed by blood (Ex. 12:12, 13; 13:2, 13, 15). In Greek the word is in the plural, *i.e.* 'firstborns'; it describes all who belong to the church. They are the company who have peculiar rights in the heavenly Jerusalem and whose names are, therefore, enrolled in the register of its citizens (*cf.* Lk. 10:20; Rev. 21:27). Note that it is to this 'church', the one true church in heaven, that these Hebrew Christians are come. **24** Jesus' crowning and comprehensive work, as our great High Priest enthroned in heaven, is to minister to all who come to Him all the promised blessings of the covenant now established and sealed for ever by His shed and sprinkled blood. *Cf.* 7:20–22; 8:6; 13:20, 21.

12:25–29 All must have dealings with God

25, 26 Let them take heed, therefore, not to seek (like those at Sinai) to withdraw from listening to Him who speaks. (Note the present tense; it is an abiding ever-present revelation. Also, from the previous verse (v. 24), we know that He now speaks in mercy through the sprinkled blood.) For it is impossible to escape having dealings with Him. Those who tried to withdraw from the earthly manifestation at Sinai found that His voice literally *shook the earth*. Christians, by contrast, are confronted by One who speaks to them in the heavenly realms disclosing the final realities. But note that, in whatever way He speaks, it is the same God who speaks throughout (v. 26; *cf.* 1:1, 2). Let them realize that it

is much more impossible now to turn aside and escape having dealings with Him. For, as He has declared in prophecy (see Hg. 2:6), God will in Christ bring His dealings with the universe to a head in a single decisive act of judgment by finally shaking both heaven and earth. *Cf.* Mk. 13:31; and note that it is his words that abide, not the universe; see also 2 Pet. 3:7. **27** Then this transient, temporal order will pass, and the abiding eternal order will stand revealed. **28** We Christians are destined to share in a kingdom or sovereignty belonging to this abiding eternal order (*cf.* Dn. 2:44; 7:18–27). *Let us be grateful.* Sheer gratitude to God ought therefore to constrain us (or, following AV, let us appropriate the 'grace' so abundantly available) to serve God in ways well pleasing in His sight, *i.e.* to *offer to God acceptable worship.* In the presence of such a God and in the face of such a prospect this will be with a real sense of unworthiness and awe (*cf.* 2 Pet. 3:9–14). **29** For the God whom we are thus privileged to call *our God* is *a consuming fire* (*cf.* Dt. 4:24; Is. 33:14–17), both of zeal for holiness and of zeal against sin. Only those who thus follow after holiness will survive His judgment, see the Lord, and reign eternally with Him. See also Appendix 3, p. 1219.

13:1–17 VARIOUS ADDITIONAL EXHORTATIONS

The writer now adds (quite in the manner of Paul, *cf.* Rom. 12:4–13) a variety of brief statements containing pointed practical exhortations to worthy Christian living. He includes also a warning against prevalent misleading teaching, and issues an urgent challenge to his readers finally to abandon Judaism and the earthly Jerusalem, and to find in the unchanging Jesus Christ and in His one sacrifice outside the city gate both inevitable earthly reproach and abiding heavenly gain.

He knew that his readers had been active in the past in sympathy and kindness towards their fellow-Christians (see 6:10; 10:33, 34). He urges, therefore, the importance of maintaining such practical love between fellow-members of the Christian brotherhood (v. 1). This should be practised not only towards familiar local brethren but also towards 'strangers' (v. 2) or visitors from elsewhere, a ministry sometimes rewarded by enriching surprises, *e.g.* in the experiences of Abraham and Lot. (See Gn. 18, 19.) Let them be particularly mindful of any in prison or suffering physical illness or ill-treatment; for Christians ought to share each other's trials, and to recognize that in this life they are all equally liable to suffer physical affliction (v. 3). Let them also recognize that (since God has ordained it) there is nothing dishonourable about the marriage relationship (v. 4) and that its physical intimacy, when rightly practised, brings no defilement. But those who engage in improper sexual relationship, whether they are unmarried or married, will find that they have God Himself against them in judgment.

In relation to material things (v. 5) the right attitude is not covetousness but contentment, learning to make do rather than always wanting more. This attitude is possible because one never faces life alone. The Lord has promised each one His personal help. He will never leave any in the lurch. It is therefore possible to face life with cheerfulness, *i.e.* confidently (v. 6), and openly to confess that, with the Lord at one's side, there is nothing to fear, and no-one who can harm us. These two verses show how OT Scriptures can be quoted, and how the believer may use their words to tell his soul what God has promised, as if the assurance were addressed to him personally and individually (see Dt. 31:6; Jos. 1:5); and also to confess his confidence before God and men (see Ps. 118:6).

Let them find inspiration to be steadfast in the faith by remembering their former Christian leaders (v. 7), by whom they were instructed in the truth of God and the gospel. Fresh consideration of the lives they lived and of the way such lives ended will help them to copy their faith. For Jesus Christ, whom they trusted and followed, is the same today as He was then, and will continue the same for ever (v. 8). He is the one all-sufficient guarantee of salvation (*cf.* 12:2).

Let them beware, therefore, of the perverting influence of other very varied and strange doctrines which are in circulation (v. 9), particularly the teaching that one cannot become properly established except by partaking of special, sacred or sacrificial food. Such teaching stands completely condemned. It is unspiritual in principle. The good way for the heart to be established is by God's own working in grace, not by man's physical eating of food. Also its professed value is denied by experience. Those who have devoted themselves to such things have gained from them no spiritual profit. Our Christian altar (v. 10) or sacrifice (to use the familiar language suggested by OT figures; *cf.* 10:19-22) is not one of which the worshippers (*i.e.* those who serve the true Tabernacle; *cf.* 8:4, 5) have any right to eat. Even in the corresponding Levitical figure of the earthly Tabernacle the bodies of those animals, whose blood was used to make atonement for sin by being brought into the inner shrine, were never eaten; they were burnt outside the camp (v. 11). That, therefore, is how Jesus, as our great High Priest, consummated the work of saving or sanctifying the people on whose behalf He was acting: He suffered outside the gate (v. 12). This indicates in figure that those who would embrace the benefits of His work must not trust in eating sacrificial meat, nor cling to the earthly Jerusalem (v. 13). Rather they must be prepared to go forth from the camp of Israel after the flesh; to bear the abuse or reproach of associating themselves with One who in Jewish eyes was rightly rejected because He hung crucified under the curse of God; to find their all not in food but in Him, the living Lord of

grace; to find their hope not in any city of the present earthly order which must pass away, but in the true city of the living God, which is a city of the coming heavenly order which will remain (v. 14; *cf.* 12:27). Henceforth Christian worship needs no earthly holy city, no special visible Temple, no priestly caste. There are sacrifices to be offered, but we are to offer them in the heavenly Tabernacle through Jesus as our one great High Priest (v. 15); everything is done through Him. These sacrifices, too, are not sacrifices of beasts but continual offerings of praise and thanksgiving to God (v. 15; *cf.* Ps. 50:14, 23; Ho. 14:2, RV) together with ministries of practical kindness to men (v. 16; *cf.* Ho. 6:6).

Instead of allowing themselves, therefore, to be perverted by strange doctrines, let them with a ready confidence and compliance follow the teaching of their leaders (v. 17). For the latter have a solemn responsibility to discharge on their behalf and an account to render. Their lead is, therefore, worthy of respect. Not to follow them now is to make the leaders' task on that great day of reckoning a painful rather than a joyful one. Also it will result in loss for themselves.

9, 10 raise questions of interpretation on which opinions differ radically. In contrast to the exposition given above some think the reference to eating *foods* has to do with distinctions between clean and unclean foods (see NEB, and *cf.* Rom. 14:14-21; 1 Cor. 8:4-13; Col. 2:16; 1 Tim. 4:3-5). But in such cases holiness would be promoted by proper abstinence from that which is unclean (so NEB reads into the text the sense 'not from scruples about what we eat'); here the idea seems rather to be of a misleading suggestion of some spiritual benefit to be gained by eating meat offered in sacrifice. The Christian *altar* is generally recognized to be the cross *i.e.* the sacrifice of Christ. But, as the NT teaches that the sacrifice of Christ is something of which Christians spiritually partake (see Jn. 6:53-56; 1 Cor. 5:7, 8; 10:16), many prefer the interpretation that what the priests of the Jewish Tabernacle could not do physically all Christians can do spiritually, *i.e.* partake of their sin-offering. 11 Further, the details of the Levitical ritual and of Christ's crucifixion (12) figuratively imply that it is impossible thus to partake of Christ without completely abandoning Judaism. 16 *To communicate* (AV, RV, Gk. *koinōnia, i.e.* 'fellowship') describes (as RSV makes plain) the act of sharing with others material things. In Rom. 15:26 the sense is rendered by 'contribution'; *cf.* 2 Cor. 9:13.

13:18-25 PERSONAL MESSAGES AND FINAL BENEDICTION

18, 19 For the first time the writer speaks of himself, and in the first person singular. His request for prayer and his profession of integrity (v. 18) imply an awareness that his action and attitude may be misjudged. He is personally particularly eager for their prayer that he may be enabled to rejoin them as soon as possible (v. 19). This seems clearly to imply that he had been in the past in some way closely connected with them. **20, 21** His benediction is remarkable for its significant details and its comprehensive sweep; again it is quite Pauline in character. His words focus their thoughts on the doings of God. For them as well as for him what God has done is the ground of assurance and hope. Therefore, what God may be counted upon to do for them is the substance of his prayer. God brought up Jesus from the dead ('up' seems here the force of the Greek prefix *ana* rather than *again*). He did this to Him not only personally as His Son, but more particularly as the Leader of His people (*cf.* 2:10; 12:2), *i.e.* as *the great shepherd of the sheep*, and as *our Lord*. He did it to Him in relation to the new and *eternal covenant* secured and ratified by His death or *blood*. His resurrection is, therefore, decisive proof that man is reconciled to God, or able to enter glory, and that God is now active to fulfil for His people all that is promised to them under the new covenant (*cf.* Zc. 9:11). He will bring them up also, as He brought up Israel with Moses their shepherd out of the Red Sea (see Is. 63:11). So the writer prays for his readers that through this Jesus, acknowledged as God's *Christ*, they may know God both personally and corporately as *the*

God of peace and experience His working in their lives and fellowship, enabling them fully to co-operate in the doing of His will. *Equip you*, or 'make you perfect' (AV, RV); the Greek verb *katartizō* is very suggestive. It includes the ideas of harmonious combination (*cf.* 10:24, 25; 12:13, 14), the supply of what is lacking (see 1 Thes. 3:10), and the rectification of what is wrong or damaged (*e.g.* it is translated 'restore' in Gal. 6:1 and 'mending' in Mk. 1:19). **22** The writer claims to have written *briefly*, *i.e.* considering the vastness of the themes dealt with, and so ventures to ask for their patient attention. **23** He sends them news of *Timothy*'s liberation; this provides yet another indication of possible close connection with the apostle Paul. **24** His special greetings to their *leaders* and to the whole Christian community suggests that the letter was actually sent to a limited group of ordinary Christians. 'They of Italy' (AV, RV). This reference indicates plainly that the writer was in the company of Italian Christians; but the wording is not sufficiently explicit to decide whether he was writing from or to Italy, though either is possible; and RSV opts for the latter. **25** Finally, the simple and sufficient Christian 'farewell', indeed its guarantee, is found in the one word *grace* and in the assurance that it is fully available for all.

Appendix 1
THE NEW COVENANT

According to this Epistle God has for His people a destiny which is variously depicted. It is described as inheriting salvation (1:14, RV), as lordship in the world to come (2:5–10), as participation in God's house and in or with His Christ (3:6, 14, RV mg.), as entering into the rest of God (4:1, 11), as going on to maturity or perfection (6:1), as inheriting the promises (6:12; 10:36; 11:13), as receiving the eternal inheritance (9:15), as gaining the soul (10:39, RV mg.), as reaching the heavenly country and the divinely prepared city (11:10, 16; 12:22; 13:14), as receiving the kingdom which cannot be shaken (12:28). This destiny is to be theirs simply because they are His people and He is (and is not ashamed to be called, 11:16) their God.

In order first to establish, and then to preserve, this special relation between Himself and those whom He is pleased to call His people, God has not only given His word of promise, but has also solemnly pledged Himself in covenant under the recognized covenant seal of shed blood. It is into this covenanted relation to Himself that God calls men to enter; it is with this immediately in view that He redeems them. Henceforth, for those who respond, it is according to the promises

thus covenanted that men have dealings with God, obligations towards Him, and an assured ground of confidence in Him.

Although there are two distinct covenants of this kind there is in them an essential unity and continuity. The same ultimate end is contemplated in both. The second has been introduced only because the first was ineffectual, and was, indeed, never intended to be more than a provisional anticipation of better things to come (see, *e.g.*, 9:9, 10; 10:1). The second supersedes the first because it completely achieves what the first failed to accomplish. Because this achievement is eternal the second covenant is the final covenant. There is no hope of, or need for, some further provision of God beyond it. One of the great purposes of the writer of this Epistle is to make this plain. Christianity not only supersedes Judaism; it is God's last word to men.

The first covenant failed for two reasons. On the one hand, the people brought under it did not fulfil its conditions; they did not continue in God's covenant (8:7–9). On the other hand, its institutions did not avail to give men true release from sin and consequent access to God's presence (10:1–4). The very order and ritual of its Tabernacle was a witness that the way into the sanctuary was not yet opened (9:8); its Tabernacle was only a figure for the time then present (9:9). As a covenant it was weak and useless (7:18). So, even while it obtained as the divinely ordained order, the same Scriptures which acknowledged its divine origin also prophetically anticipated the provision of something better. The very mention of a 'new' covenant was itself witness that the first covenant was to be disannulled, and was shortly to pass away (7:11–19; 8:1–13; 10:5–9).

The new covenant is 'a better covenant', and one 'enacted on better promises' (8:6). It is effective in ways in which the first covenant was not because it provides a real redemption from transgressions (9:15), or putting away of sin (10:15–18), and so makes possible full and free access to God's presence (10:19–22). Also, it provides an all-competent High Priest who, because of His 'once-for-all' finished sacrifice (10:10–14) and His 'indestructible life' (7:15, 16), has not only gained entrance for Himself and those He represents into God's presence, but sits for ever enthroned by God in the place of all power (1:13), able to complete to its full perfection the salvation of all those who make Him their Mediator between God and

themselves (7:25). What God has done for Him in raising Him from the dead and bidding Him sit at His own right hand in sure hope of complete triumph (10:12, 13), is pledge and proof of the final victory of His people. For it was done by God to Him as 'our Lord Jesus, the great shepherd of the sheep'; and it was done 'by the blood of the eternal covenant' (13:20). There is, therefore, through this covenant, sealed by Christ's death, full and final remission of sins and completely assured perfection for all Christ's people (10:8–18). There is no need for, and indeed no possibility of, failure. For under this covenant God puts His law in His people's hearts (8:10); and Himself works to equip them with everything good that they may do His will (13:20, 21).

The one all-sufficient guarantee of this new covenant is to be found in the Person and work of its Surety and Mediator (7:21, 22; 8:6; 9:14, 15). Its benefits are administered by One who is enthroned on high, and who never dies: Jesus Christ, 'the same yesterday and today and for ever' (13:8). It is, therefore, the outstanding theme or 'chief point' of this Epistle to declare that, as Christians under the new covenant, 'we have such a high priest, one who is seated at the right hand of the throne of the Majesty in heaven' (8:1).

Appendix 2
THE PRIESTHOOD OF CHRIST

In this Epistle the writer connects with Christ the ideas of 'truth' and 'perfection'. What elsewhere is only figuratively hinted at, or but partially realized, is in Christ found in actuality and fullness. Henceforth, therefore, we must not limit our Christian idea of priesthood to what we learn from the Levitical priesthood. Although the latter did foreshadow or figuratively indicate many of the fundamental essentials of all true priesthoods, there are other complementary and distinctive characteristics which, in as far as they were foreshadowed at all in the OT revelation, were foreshadowed not by Aaron but by Melchizedek. These distinctive characteristics, which belong of necessity to the perfection of Christ's priesthood, are to be appreciated over against the Levitical priesthood in terms more of contrast than of comparison.

The Levitical high priests were weak men, sinful and mortal, needing first to offer sacrifices for their own sins, and unable to continue in office because they were inevitably removed by death (7:23, 27, 28). They served in an earthly shrine, a mere figure of the true (8:4, 5; 9:1, 9, 23, 24). Their sacrifices were sacrifices of animals, which could never remove sin (10:1–4); and so, under the old order, the dividing curtain which

shut men out from the Holy of Holies was never rent and done away (9:7, 8). The sacrifices of the Day of Atonement gave one man only temporary, symbolic access once a year to the inmost shrine of the divine presence; they did not give to the whole people full and abiding access to God. Also, these sacrifices had to be incessantly repeated (10:11), and served only as a sobering reminder that something still needed to be done fully and finally to put away sin (10:1–3). The way into the sanctuary was not yet opened (9:8).

Our Christian High Priest is 'Jesus the Son of God' (4:14). His priesthood is of a different order because of the difference in the Person of the Priest. He is, first of all, very God of very God (1:3), able 'through eternal Spirit' (9:14) to act as deity and to do things completely beyond the power of weak men. He is, on the other hand, truly Man, One who not only genuinely partook of human nature, but who also, through the experience of earthly trial and suffering, has reached a final perfection in His manhood, which has qualified Him to be for His fellow-men the author or cause of an eternal salvation (2:9, 10, 14–18; 4:15; 5:7–9). He could do what no Levitical high priest was able to attempt. Because, as Man, He was Himself without sin, He did not need to offer sacrifice for His own sin. What is more, He was in a position to offer His own spotless human life as the sin-offering for others, that is, for sinful men. Being, as God, undying Spirit, and acting in the power of an indestructible life (7:16), He was able in His one Person and two natures to act both as Priest and Victim, and in the experience of the death of His human nature deliberately to offer Himself to God (9:14), and to claim, as One still alive in death, entrance thereby as men's High Priest into the actual presence of God. As He thus offered Himself in His physical human death upon the cross (10:10), symbolically 'the curtain of the Temple was torn in two from top to bottom' (Mk. 15:37, 38; cf. Heb. 10:19, 20). Actually, as One acting in the true heavenly sanctuary (8:2; 9:11, 12, 24) and not in the figurative Tabernacle (or Temple) on earth (8:4, 5), He thereby 'through his own blood' (9:12, RV), or by the act of laying down His physical human life (cf. again 10:19, 20), entered decisively and once for all into the true sanctuary there 'to appear before the face of God' (9:24, RV) on our behalf. When He did this He was immediately accepted, hailed as victor and invited to occupy the throne at God's right hand. God further sealed His acceptance of His work as a work on behalf of sinful men by raising Him up in His humanity from the dead (13:20). It is, however, probably significant that Christ's resurrection is mentioned only once in this Epistle, and that right at the end. This is because, in the earlier consideration of His offering of Himself, He is thought of, not as rising on the third day and ascending after another 40 days, but as acting in the heavenly sanctuary and immediately entering the presence of God.

The enthronement in heaven of the One who entered through His own death as our High Priest is the divine proof and pledge that He has by this one act of sacrifice obtained eternal redemption for us (1:3; 10:12, 13; 12:2). Also, He was then declared by God, not only by His word, but by His solemn oath, to be a Priest for ever after the order of Melchizedek (5:9, 10; 6:19, 20; 7:21, 22), which means, in other words, that His priesthood is royal in power

because of His finished sacrificial work, and also unceasing in duration because of His divine Person. For He was seated at once upon the throne, and remains there, placed by God in the position of supreme power, able to give gifts to men (4:14–16), and assured by God of final victory over all His foes (1:13).

Through such achievement as High Priest, far surpassing anything accomplished by the old order of Levitical priests, He is able to engage in a more excellent ministry as the mediator of the new covenant (8:6), under which sinful men who come to Him, or to God through Him (7:20–25), are assured in the possession of forgiveness of sins, intimate personal knowledge of God, and the transforming inner quickening of the indwelling Spirit (8:10–12). His ability thus to proclaim absolution and to assure His people that their sins are actually forgiven and forgotten by God is itself proof that no further offering for sin is necessary (10:14–18). As One exalted above the heaven, our Christian High Priest has no need to make fresh or further offering of Himself, or of His blood or earthly sacrifice, to God (7:26–28). But, as One who never dies, He is always at God's right hand to intervene on men's behalf, to speak for them to the Father (or against the adversary who would condemn them, Rom. 8:33, 34) whenever they come to the throne of God, and thus to secure the full completion of their salvation (Heb. 7:25). All who come can also be sure of understanding sympathy and appropriate help because He is thoroughly qualified to discharge such compassionate ministry by His own earthly experiences of suffering and trial (2:17, 18; 4:15, 16; 5:2, 7, 8).

Those, therefore, who come to Him as their Mediator are assured by the royal and eternal order of His priesthood of participating in a salvation which is (like His Person and work as Priest) perfect, final and eternal. For His one sacrifice gives to all who trust Him eternal fitness for unhindered approach to God's presence (9:13, 14; 10:10, 14); and the final completion of the work of salvation which He has begun in them is assured by the blood of the eternal covenant, by God's resurrection of our Lord Jesus from the dead (13:20, 21), and by His own undying presence as our advocate at God's right hand (7:25).

Appendix 3
THE WARNING PASSAGES

See 2:1–4; 3:7 – 4:1; 6:4–8; 10:26–31, 38, 39; 12:15–17, 25. As Jews these Hebrew Christians had been used to the ideas of a succession of prophets and a continuous repetition of sacrifices for sin. They needed to be made aware of the once-for-all and final character of the revelation

of God and the reconciliation to God given to men in Christ. Because the incarnate Son is God's last word to men, and because there is offered to men in Him amazing salvation by grace, those who pass Him by cannot expect to escape the coming judgment of God (cf. Mk. 12:6–9). No further word of saving intervention from God is to be expected. Also, since Christ's sacrifice of Himself was a decisive, 'once-for-all' achievement, there is no more offering for sin (10:18) either by Christ in heaven or by men on earth. Neither can there be repetition of this one sacrifice (9:25–28), nor will there be the introduction by God of any other sacrifice (10:26). This one sacrifice for sin, wrought once for all, is all-sufficient for ever for all God's people (10:10–14).

Enjoyment by men of the benefit of Christ's sacrifice is similarly 'once for all' (6:4, Gk. *hapax*); it is decisive, final and eternal. Therefore (to follow one interpretation of these passages) any who have been consciously confronted by this offer of grace, and have personally shared in the proofs of its origin, and then deliberately reject the gospel of Jesus as the Christ (without of course ever truly believing and becoming regenerate), cannot be similarly brought a second time to the opportunity of repentance and faith (see 12:16, 17). Or, alternatively (to follow another interpretation), those who have experienced all the characteristic blessings of God's saving grace through Christ's atoning sacrifice, and by the Spirit's work in their hearts, and have then turned aside from it all and tried to settle down to live as if such things were not true and had never happened, cannot be brought back a second time to the initial and decisive Christian response of repentance and faith. The meaning of 6:6 may be that even to suggest that Christ virtually needs crucifying again to bring such an apostate or backslider for the second time to the place of decisive repentance and quickening by the Spirit is to put Christ and the efficacy of His one sacrifice to an open shame. The whole thing is unthinkable. Such renewal of enlightenment and repentance a second time is therefore absolutely impossible, just as, when many Israelites departed from God in unbelief in the wilderness, it was impossible to take them through the Passover and Red Sea deliverances a second time in order to awaken or renew their faith. For such apostates or unbelievers there was, and still is, no prospect but judgment (*cf.* 1 Cor. 10:1–5).

The kind of failure here in view (to follow one interpretation) is nothing less than a conscious, deliberate and persistent abandonment of the Christian way of salvation, an abandonment which involves nothing less than apostasy from the living God (3:12), rejection of the Word and confirming witness of God, Father, Son and Holy Spirit, treating the Son of God, as the Jews had done in Jerusalem, as One who ought to be disowned and crucified, and thus brought publicly under the curse of heaven, denying the covenant significance before God of His shed blood, and doing open insult to the Spirit who in grace pleads with men to acknowledge Jesus as Lord (10:29). Such actions are surely what our Lord called the sin of blasphemy against the Holy Spirit, which is eternal sin and never has forgiveness (Mk. 3:28, 29). Yet it was to nothing less than a sin of this character that these

Hebrew Christians were exposed, if they were being tempted to go back to where they were before in Judaism (although actually to do this was impossible), and in doing so publicly to repudiate Jesus as the Messiah and the Son of God.

It may be, however (to follow an alternative interpretation), that the writer is concerned to make plain to his unquestionably Christian readers that their present tendency to become slack, and to settle down halfway in the imagined possession of what their faith in Christ has already made theirs, is a fatal self-deception. The reason is that for those who have thus made a beginning in the way of Christian discipleship the only possible alternatives are either to go on to the full possession of faith's inheritance, or to draw back from this forward movement of God in their lives and to come under His inevitable judgment, like the Israelites who became the objects of God's wrath and were overthrown in the wilderness, because they were not prepared by faith in God to go forward into the promised land. In that case the kind of failure here in view is that of those who, having been taken by grace into covenant relation with God, completely fail to regard its amazing privileges and overwhelming obligations with due seriousness. If those, already redeemed from Egypt, who failed to obey God's word under the first Sinaitic covenant, were removed in judgment from the company of God's people, may not those who fail to respond to the demands of the new covenant in Christ rightly expect even more severe and drastic treatment? For while, in the Christian life, God's discipline, however painful, is profitable and to be welcomed as a proof that He is dealing with us as His sons for our progress in holiness (12:5–11), can anything be more terrible in the life of one who is already by grace a child of God than that, in relation to his subsequent earthly conduct, God should have to deal with him in fiery and even fatal judgment?

The theological questions here involved are whether those who may thus apostatize or come under judgment ever were regenerate, and whether any man once saved can finally be lost. In answer to both questions some say emphatically, 'No'. They would compare the types mentioned in Mt. 7:22, 23; 12:22–32. They would argue that the very apostasy of these individuals is proof that they were never regenerate. Others say that those described in 6:4, 5 must be regenerate; for no more decisive description of the regenerate could be given. Some would then argue that the consequent judgment on their complete degeneracy and unfruitfulness does not necessarily involve them in the loss of eternal salvation. They are, for instance, only 'near to being cursed' (6:8). *Cf.* 1 Cor. 3:15; 5:5. Others, again, suppose that this suggestion that the regenerate can thus become apostate, and be finally lost, is actually only hypothetical and theoretical. Even on the human side it is much more unlikely than physical suicide, and so only to be thought of as a remote possibility; and actually on the divine side it can by grace never happen. See Jn. 10:28.

Yet Christians, and all who share in the knowledge of the truth, will do well to treat such solemn warnings with due seriousness. Let us remember that John Bunyan wrote, 'Then I saw there was a way to hell even from the gates of heaven, as well as from the City of Destruc-tion.' Let us remember, also, that Paul the apostle feared lest by any means after he had preached to others, and been used to bring them to Christ, he himself should be 'rejected' (1 Cor. 9:27, RV; the Greek is literally 'disapproved', which AV renders a 'castaway', *i.e.* a 'throw-out'; see Mk. 12:10; and *cf.* 2 Pet. 2:20, 21).

A. M. STIBBS

James

INTRODUCTION

Luther's criticism is well known: it is 'a right strawy Epistle . . . for it has no evangelical manner about it' (cf. 1 Cor. 3:12). This shows a failure to appreciate that it is a spiritual corrective and not a theological source-book. We must first listen to our Lord and to His servant Paul, and then let His other servant James be a stimulus to hear and obey all that is already given in the Word. For James does not write an evangelistic tract but exhortation addressed to believers. As soon as the gospel has been received the Christian life has to be lived. The disciple has blessings and privileges. He also has duties. James seeks therefore to teach the duties of discipleship and to urge his readers to fulfil them: to be doers of the Word. His exhortation is based on the teaching.

This will explain the absence of much of the proclamation, the gospel message, the *kērygma*. It may not be explicitly stated in detail, but behind the reference to the Word (1:21) are large theological presuppositions. Jesus is the Christ, the Lord of glory, who is coming again and whose honourable name is not to be blasphemed. James understands the language and experience of conversion and salvation (1:1, 18, 21; 2:1, 7; 5:8).

The apparent lack of any continuous argument in the Epistle creates a staccato effect. It may be explained in part by its affinities with the Greek diatribe though this argument must not be pressed to extreme. The diatribe was an ethical lecture on the popular level, even a secular sermon, with marked characteristics—terse dialogue, question and answer, argument with an imaginary objector, and other vivid literary expedients calculated to impress. But the Epistle is more than a mere diatribe. Its Greek is good indeed, giving no immediate impression of 'translation Greek'; but it has some Semitic features and a Jewish background; and at its heart is the gospel.

The letter begins with simple majesty and there can be only one candidate from the NT for the rank of author—James, the Lord's brother (cf. Mk. 6:3; Acts 15:13; Gal. 1:19). Authenticity cannot be demonstrated finally and various difficulties have been raised. The Greek, we are told, is too good; no claim is made to be the Lord's brother; the *kērygma* is missing; ritual (as opposed to moral) law is not as prominent as might have been expected. There is also the problem of the relation to Paul and the interpretation of the external evidence. It is not impossible to give answers to these criticisms, and alternative theories such as pseudonymity, anonymity, an original Jewish document with the addition of 1:1 and 2:1, a 'patriarchal pattern' (cf. Gn. 49) and others, do not carry complete conviction.

The Jewish background of this 'Christian Amos', as he has been called, the Semitic elements, the parallels to Acts 15 and the similarities to (though not literary dependence on) the Sermon on the Mount may not prove, but they accord with, the traditional view of authorship. Until this is cogently disproved and an opposing theory satisfactorily established it has the right to stand.

If James the Lord's brother is indeed the author, the Epistle must be dated not later than AD 62. (Some place it even before AD 50.) This is supported by the following: there is no reference to the fall of Jerusalem in AD 70; the social conditions (large landowners) did not apply after the fall; nothing is said about the Jewish-Gentile controversy; the eager expectation of the second advent is primitive; it is not necessary to assume that James had read the Gospels or Paul's letters; and the church order is primitive. These facts do not in themselves prove an early date but their evidential value is strong. It is likely that advocates of a late 1st-century or of a 2nd-century date are to some extent influenced by their views of authorship.

The letter is sent to Christians, not excluding Jewish Christians. It is perhaps worth noticing that James was hardly an enthusiastic believer before the resurrection (cf. Jn. 7:3–5). Yet the Lord appeared to him (cf. 1 Cor. 15:7) in His mercy, despite Acts 10:41.

OUTLINE OF CONTENTS

COMMENTARY

1:1 Salutation

The beginning is conventional: from whom, to whom and greeting (*cf.* Acts 15:23–29; 23:26–30). James does not elaborate as Paul sometimes does (*cf.* Rom. 1:1–7) but he makes it plain that he is a Christian. He has the right to address Christians, for whom he feels a pastoral responsibility. At the same time he speaks as a Jew to Jews.

Servant is strictly slave (Gk. *doulos*). It implies the absence of rights, total dependence on the master and complete obedience. The term aptly describes what should be the Christian's attitude to God, though slavishness is ruled out (*cf.* Jn. 15:14f.). In Judaism, *servant of God* was largely used of men who served God in a special way. James thus quietly takes his place with patriarchs and prophets. When a Jew was at prayer he spoke of himself in the presence of God as a servant. The expression is thus religious. James combines both leadership and piety.

Note the unobtrusive effectiveness with which James places *Lord Jesus Christ* beside *God*. Behind *Jesus* stands the whole gospel tradition of the historic Man of Nazareth. *Christ* (Gk. form of the Heb. *Messiah*, 'the anointed one': Ps. 2:2; Acts 4:26, AV, RSV) shows that James believed in the Messiahship of Jesus. *Lord* is used in the LXX to translate the ineffable Name (Yahweh) and implies the sovereignty of God, personally exercised. God has the right to rule and nothing and nobody in the created universe can escape His control. Now James applies the term to Jesus. He can regard himself as the slave of his new Owner because he interprets the Messiah's work as redemption. The Lordship of Jesus is no innovation; the teaching goes back to Jesus Himself (*cf.* Mt. 22:41–45; 28:18). *Cf.* 1 Cor. 7:23.

The twelve tribes . . . seems at first to refer to Jews scattered throughout the world. The term is used for the living nation in Acts 26:7, though it is already an anachronism. The contents of the Epistle are, however, hardly limited to Jews. The Christian community is the new Israel of God and may therefore have this term 'twelve tribes', descriptive of the old Israel, applied to them. *Cf.* Acts 15:16f. Christians are thus 'scattered abroad' from their home and at best are temporary visitors (*cf.* 1 Pet. 1:1; 2:11). James perhaps saw an illustration in Acts 8:4; 11:19. It is fitting that in such a context James did not refer to himself as the Lord's brother but as His slave, ministering to 'the integrity of the nation Israel' (J. H. Ropes, *ICC*), *the twelve tribes* of the believing church. *Cf.* 1 Pet. 2:9f.

1:2–4 Dealing with trials

2 James links this paragraph with v. 1 by similarity of sound. *Greeting* is Greek *chairein* and *joy* is *chara*. Moffatt neatly turns it by: '. . . greeting. Greet it as pure joy. . . .' M. Dibelius regards the resemblance as intentional (see *Der Brief des Jakobus*, 1964). The author can write in literary style. James does not mean that the only *joy* in the Christian life comes from adversity. He is advocating an attitude. 'Count it nothing but joy.' 'Joy' here means 'ground of rejoicing', as in 'good news of a great joy' (Lk. 2:10). The address, *brethren*, is common in the OT and was widespread in Judaism, but has a deeper note among Christians. It expresses devotion to Jesus (*cf.* Mt. 12:50) and in Him membership of God's family (*cf.* Rom. 8:29). It is thus related to the doctrine of adoption (*cf.* Rom. 8:15f.). James deftly reminds his readers of their unity with him. Contrast here the OT wisdom literature, *e.g.* Pr. 1:8 'my son', and *cf.* Mt. 23:8f. *Meet* implies an external source of the trial (contrast v. 14), as with the man who 'fell among' robbers (Lk. 10:30).

3 The secret lies not in Stoic courage or in weak collapse (*cf.* Heb. 12:5f.) but in knowledge. James is sure that his readers *know*. If they are to profit by their knowledge they should remember that the trials which embody *the testing of your faith* bring to light its reality and its power. This they know already. Let them dwell on it, realizing that faith preserved and practised in trials leads on to victory and deeper joy. The outcome is *steadfastness*, the quality of 'staying put'—under 'the slings and arrows of outrageous fortune'. *Cf.* Rom. 5:3.

4 James is not limiting himself to a single, isolated trial. Active resistance must continue always. The *full effect* is personal, for it means that through their steadfastness they will be *perfect and complete. Perfect* suggests a ripeness and maturity in contrast to an earlier weakness; *complete* implies a wholeness and freedom from blemish with no Christian virtue absent; but the two words should be taken together. Note that James has anticipated 2:14. Faith 'works' (*cf.* Gal. 5:6). *Lacking* is the keyword or cue by which the following section is linked on to this one.

1:5-8 Gaining wisdom

5 To forestall any possible disclaimer of knowledge (*cf.* v. 3) James advocates prayer. But he advances one step ahead of the objector. He advocates praying not only for knowledge but for *wisdom*, which includes knowledge and its application. Right prayer (*cf.* 4:3) does not deal with One who is unaccustomed to giving. God *gives* regularly, frequently (not 'will give'), *to all men* even when they do not ask Him (*cf.* Mt. 5:45). *Generously* suggests the scale, purpose and speed of the divine answer. When God thus gives He does so *without reproaching*. In this He is consistent. He does not scold the recipient any more than He scolds the returning penitent (*cf.* Lk. 15:20; 18:14). James will speak again about wisdom (*cf.* 3:13-18). In the meantime, in response to prayer by a believer, *it will be given him.*

6 If a man lacks wisdom he should pray and *ask in faith* for it. *Faith* here means trust in God through Christ, without which a person is only a nominal Christian. (See on 2:22 for its constituents.) The characteristic attitude of James is apparent once more. For him true faith is not a quiescent intellectual assent. It is to be exercised. All the time the man is asking he should be trusting. *Doubting* is not disbelief or philosophical scepticism. Its characteristic is an inner cleavage. The doubter both affirms and denies; he clings to the promise—and is sure it will not be fulfilled. He is vividly described in the picture of the surge of the sea. He 'mounted up to heaven' to receive the promised wisdom; he 'went down to the depths' (into the trough of the wave), sure that he would never attain it. (*Cf.* Ps. 107:26 and context.)

7, 8 *For* gives the reason for asking in faith. *That person* is the doubter. James does not say

'this person', although he has only just mentioned him. It is because *that* is the more remote. James keeps the doubter at a distance, in disapproval. He is aptly termed *a double-minded man*, for in a sense he is a divided personality, a man with two souls. (See on v. 6.) He ought to love the Lord with all his one soul (*cf.* Mk. 12:30). James obviously has no room for compromise: 'one thing I do' (*cf.* **Phil.** 3:13; Jas. 4:8). *Unstable in all his ways* continues the characterization of v. 6. The doubter is tossed in vacillation when he ought to 'stand' (*cf.* 1 Cor. 16:13). *Ways* is a Hebraism for conduct (*cf.* Acts 14:16). He does not follow the fixed road of trust but constantly changes route, and even then cannot stand. *The Lord*, from whom he must not suppose that he will receive anything, appears from v. 5 to mean God. But 5:14f. has the same term in connection with the elders of the church and prayer, and it must there mean Christ. In 5:7, 10, however, it has both senses. The absence of precision in 1:7f. reflects the fact that God deals with men through the Mediator.

1:9-11 Assessing wealth

The lowly brother and *the rich* (man) are both generic, denoting in each case a class, not an individual. Two interpretations of the paragraph are possible. On the one hand James may have the day of judgment in mind. *The lowly brother* will then be exalted and *the rich* man, who is regarded as a non-Christian, will be brought low. The advocacy of boasting by *the rich* is then ironical and the best comment is Lk. 16:25. On the other hand James may be thinking of the present moment. *The rich* man is a Christian and his wealth is transitory (*cf.* Mt. 6:19f.; 1 Tim. 6:17f.). This seems to be the better view. It is *the rich* as such, not the mere man, who *will pass away*. He will *fade away* in his 'business journeys' (*cf.* 4:13). Even so he can join the poor man in his boasting: God gives more than the poor man lacks (*cf.* 2:5) or the rich man possesses. This is already *the lowly brother's . . . exaltation.* It needed Christ's *humiliation* to reveal it to *the rich.*

James draws his vivid figure of *the sun . . . with its scorching heat* from Is. 40:6ff., with a possible allusion to Ps. 102:4, 11, but he restricts it to *the rich.* 1 Pet. 1:24 uses it in a way which should cheer the once rich Christian: this gospel now preached to you abides for ever. You really can boast in your humiliation; against its dark background the treasure in heaven stands out brilliantly.

1:12-15 Recognizing temptation

12 The beatitude follows the form of Ps. 1:1 LXX (*cf.* Dn. 12:12) and recalls Jas. 1:2. James is still thinking of *trial* but he soon passes on to the thought of moral trial, which may be occasioned (not caused) by poverty or wealth. Affliction from outside is to be endured but inner temptation must be resisted (*cf.* 4:7; 5:11). James does not suggest any definite temptation but proceeds at once to give the reason for the blessedness or happiness. *The man who endures trial* and has thereby passed his examination *will receive the crown of life*. It is *the crown* of victory and is the gift of God, being due to divine grace and not to human right. In spite of the imagery (*cf.* 1 Cor. 9:24-27) it is no mere adornment, for it consists *of life*, eternal life. The fact that *God has promised* it shows that it is a gift. *God* is an emendation; the Greek simply has 'He'. The meaning would be self-evident to James's readers. *Those who love him* is used both in the OT (*e.g.* Ex. 20:6) and in the NT (*e.g.* Rom. 8:28) as a description of God's own people. It here suggests the motive power of the man who *has stood the test*.

13 Resentment at the intensity of trial may produce questions about its origin; or a man may seek to excuse himself for feeling attracted by evil *when he is tempted*. He forgets 1 Cor. 10:13. In the midst of his moral trial the man speaks, for to the Palestinians thinking was saying, and he traces its origin to God. But God is exalted above sin and feels no pull towards evil. He can neither tempt nor be tempted. This is not divine ignorance or indifference but holiness. God understands human temptation, however, both by His omniscience and by the incarnation, and can help the tempted: *cf.* Heb. 2:18; 4:15. **14, 15** *Desire* in itself is a term which can be neutral or even good (*cf.* Lk. 22:15; Phil. 1:23). Here it is used with verbs suggesting force ('taken in tow', Arndt) and attractiveness ('bait'). Some translate, 'hooked and trapped'. There is a distinction between the *ego* and the desire (*cf.* Rom. 7:17; Jas. 1:8). The dominant theme of v. 15 is the idea of birth, with desire as a harlot. The *ego* fertilizes the desire, *sin* is born and when grown up (*i.e.* completed in action) in turn gives birth to death. *Cf.* Rom. 6:23; 7:5. *Death* includes everything from present spiritual condition to God's final verdict at the last judgment. Contrast Jas. 1:12.

1:16-18 Ascribing all good to God

16, 17 *Do not be deceived*, because wrong thoughts lead to wrong conduct. If God tempted men, He would be nullifying His own work. He is the author of nothing but good. James expresses this in his picture of an unending shower of *good* and *perfect* gifts. We need not distinguish between the different kinds of gift. The two words, which are in the context of a hexameter, have a rhetorical effect. *Father of lights* means that God is their Creator. Obviously the heavenly bodies are indicated, but *lights* is charged with deeper meaning: they declare the glory of Him who is Light (*cf.* Ps. 19:1f.). For a majestic picture, *cf.* Is. 40:26. But for all the blessings brought by sun and stars, they are subject to change. They follow their prescribed orbit: in consequence night follows day and though the stars may set, God does not. On Him falls no *shadow*, as when a man finds himself in the shade through the 'movement' of the sun; and He is no insubstantial shadow but eternal reality. God is

unchangeable in nature and consistent in character; He is always holy, righteous, loving, wise. He will never tempt.

18 As further evidence to dispel the deception that God tempts men, James refers to the action of the unchanging God in regeneration, which has moral implications. It would not be consistent for God to incite men to evil when His purpose in giving them the new life is moral and spiritual. Regeneration is neither an accident nor a natural development. It is of God's *own will* that believers are born again. *Brought us forth* is a term of maternity though it is not subject to the normal limitations. Its reference to the reception of salvation as a new birth reflects NT thought and experience (*cf.*, *e.g.*, Jn. 1:12f.; 3:3; 1 Pet. 1:23). If James has creation in mind at all he is thinking of the new creation. God's instrument in regeneration is *the word of truth*, the preached gospel—a 'perfect gift' indeed (v. 17). God's purpose is expressed metaphorically in *a kind of first fruits*. *First fruits* is the name of the first part of the produce to be gathered, 'all the best of the oil, and . . . of the wine and of the grain' (Nu. 18:12). The term suggests that the quality is of the finest and that the rest of the harvest will follow. The Greek (*aparchē*) is used of 'first convert(s)' in Rom. 16:5 and 1 Cor. 16:15. Christians should thus be models to the world and should expect to increase in number as the rest of the spiritual harvest is brought in.

1:19-27 Hearing and doing

19 The Word which regenerates also brings us under obligation. *Know* (Gk. *iste*) may be indicative or imperative, and scholars are divided. If it is indicative, the readers know ('us', v. 18) the content of the Word, the wealth of the gospel. If it is a command, it recalls the attention, perhaps of listeners as well as of readers, to the coming weighty utterance. James now switches to the third person imperative in his call for individual obedience. Such a command does not come naturally in English except when a man issues it through a neutral party, as when, for example, the president tells his secretary 'let the manager come and see me'. Three phrases follow, to which the rest of the section corresponds: *quick to hear* (vv. 21-25); *slow to speak* (vv. 26f.); *slow to anger* (v. 20). The widest application is possible. Each should be quick to hear the Word of God, the message of the preacher or teacher, the contribution of 'the other man' to any discussion. (The secret is to abide in Christ; *cf.* Jn. 15:1-10.) Each should refrain from hurried proclamation and swift retort, and from anger. The word for *anger* (Gk. *orgē*, not *thymos*) has some significance as used of the divine wrath. It is not an uncontrolled outburst of passion (*slow to anger*) and a period of reflection is thus suggested.

20 *The anger of man* has consequences. It disobeys Mt. 7:1 and is unrighteous. *The righteousness of God* is (strangely!) a quality of man and should be brought into being through the action of man. From one point of view it is the standard of human conduct which God demands and thus is an ideal; from the other point of view it is the work of a man who meets His demands. He is indeed obedient to the righteousness of God (*cf.* Rom. 10:3) and in his obedience he does work it.

21 *Therefore*: note the causal connection. *Put away* is a metaphor from dress and means 'take off' (the dirty clothes). The exhortation may reflect the teaching regularly given (the catechism) to candidates for church membership. *Cf.* 1 Pet. 2:1 and see E. G. Selwyn, *The First Epistle of St. Peter*, 1946, pp. 393f. The moral outweighs the metaphorical. The readers should repudiate in principle, and disentangle themselves in fact from, their past non-Christian behaviour: the uncleanness and the *wickedness* which is both abundant and superfluous. *Meekness* or gentleness implies 'strength restrained'. When the Word is *implanted*, do not receive it roughly and resist it. It should take deep root. It may be asserted that the readers have received it already and indeed they have (v. 18); but they must constantly take it to heart afresh. *Meekness* is in contrast with the anger of v. 19, and suggests the receptivity of faith. It is not the merely scattered but *the implanted word*, the received word, *which is able to save your souls* both now and at the judgment.

22 Note the three stages: they should be *hearers* of the word; they should receive it; and they should be *doers of the word*. This recalls the teaching of Jesus; *cf.*, *e.g.*, Mt. 7:24-27; and of Paul; *cf.*, *e.g.*, Rom. 2:13. In full: consciousness is informed; belief and faith exercised; and the will moved. Without action the mere hearers are *deceiving* themselves, for they do not realize what piety really is.

23, 24 The reason is now given. The mere *hearer* is like a man who sees himself *in a mirror*. The *word* is compared to a mirror, for it shows a man to himself as he is and the sight is not pleasing. *His natural face* is the rendering of the difficult expression 'the face of his *genesis*'. Of the various possible translations of this word the best seems to be 'birth'. 'The face of his birth' must then mean 'the face he has had all the time', *i.e.* his own. The language recognizes that the Word addresses the individual and he knows that it does. But the mere *hearer* gives himself a glance and hurries off; and away from the mirror he *at once forgets* what he saw—though his face was dirty (*cf.* v. 21). He does not receive the Word and act on it.

25 In contrast to a momentary glimpse James now shows us an intense gaze. *Looks into* (Gk. *parakypsas*) pictures a person bending over something because he wants to see it better, like Mary who 'stooped to look into the tomb' (Jn. 20:11). Schlatter is struck by the attitude of the attentive and eager reader as he bows down over the roll of the Torah. James sees a man similarly looking into *the perfect law*. The law in question is not the law of ancient Israel but

the gospel in its obligatory aspect, the standard of all Christian behaviour. For the gospel is both gift and demand. It is *perfect* in comparison with Gentile codes of law; and, better still, perfect as coming from Jesus. In its demands it may be called a *law* for Christians, but in its first impact it liberates and hence is *the law of liberty*. It is the charter of freedom throughout the Christian life. It does not support antinomianism but is still 'without the yoke of compulsion' (*Epistle of Barnabas* 2:6). The man who *looks into* it seriously is the man who perseveres. This quickly changes the metaphor. He so plunges into the Word and becomes steeped in it that he proves to be not a *hearer that forgets* but *a doer that acts*. Such a man will be *blessed* not only at the judgment but 'when he does it'. He shares the blessedness of the man who endures (*cf.* v. 12).

26, 27 These verses, misunderstood, are the secularist's paradise. But James is not thinking of 'religion without God'. He has in mind the external aspect of religion, the practice of religious observances. As we should say today, *religion* in this sense is what the observer sees taking place in church. The term may be summed up in the word 'ritual'. There is a valid distinction between the inner religious disposition and its outer expression in worship. But the man who *thinks he is religious* and does not control his speech but only *deceives* himself is not showing the true spirit of faith. At first sight it would seem that for James the complete outer expression of inner faith is the ethical, *to visit* the needy and to be morally *unstained*. He is not, however, blind to the place of worship. He is manifesting the spirit of protest. If, as here, moral duty is neglected, the ethical is put forward as the true ritual. If worship had been neglected in favour of secular morality and the care of the poor and defenceless, we may suspect that James would have called his readers to worship as the true morality. Protests inevitably tend to be one-sided. But both worship and morality are essential expressions of Christian faith: *cf.* Heb. 10:23-25.

Religion that is pure is free from sin, and it is *undefiled* when the worshippers are fit to draw near to *God and the Father*. The men in Jn. 18:28 were hardly *undefiled* in a manner to satisfy James. How not to *visit* is given in Jas. 2:16. To be *unstained*, which recalls the dirty clothes of v. 21, is possible only if we *keep* ourselves from too close an association with *the world*, which is hostile to God (*cf.* 4:4).

2:1-13 Discriminating

1 James continues the theme of the previous section by describing a situation which cries out for men to be doers of the Word (*cf.* 1:22). He calls his readers to refrain from acting with *partiality*. His Greek plural noun means 'acts of partiality'. Although he visualizes only one, partiality is shown in many ways, all of them valuing a man according to what he has and seems, rather than what he is. Such conduct does not befit Christians, who *hold the faith of our Lord Jesus Christ*. James wants to see their faith in action, effective. This is not the faith which the Lord Himself exercised. The phrase *of our Lord Jesus Christ* represents a Greek objective genitive which is more naturally rendered by '(faith) in our Lord . . .' (RSV rightly uses 'in' for the same Gk. construction in Mk. 11:22; Rom. 3:22; Gal. 2:16).

A worthy interpretation which goes back to Bengel (1687-1752) sees an apposition, 'our Lord . . . the glory'. Jesus *is* the glory. Glory means *a*. God as He has revealed Himself, His being, character, majesty and might; and *b*. the 'physical radiance' which symbolizes the divine presence (*cf*. Ex. 24:16f.; 40:34f.), the rabbinic Shekinah. Both are fulfilled in Jesus (*cf*. Jn. 1:14; 2 Cor. 4:6). Glory is not unrelated to 'Emmanuel'; *cf*. Mt. 1:23; 28:20. F. Mussner (*Der Jakobusbrief*, 1964) aptly points out that partiality acts as if Jesus were no longer the glory; the entrance of the rich is celebrated as if it were an appearing of the Lord Jesus Himself.

2 Notice the *if*. James is illustrating. Both men seem to be strangers and probably non-Christians. Both are judged by appearance. The Greek *synagōgē* may be an *assembly* or a place of assembly. We seem to be on Jewish soil but Christians predominate. *Cf*. Dt. 1:17. **3** The rich man is deemed worthy of a *seat*, perhaps a special one (*cf*. Mt. 23:6), and a *please*. The poor man is denied both and has to stand or to sit on the floor while the speaker sits in his own seat, which he might have courteously given up. *You pay attention . . . and say . . . while you say . . .* : these are plural; the 'sidesman' voices the thoughts of the congregation, which has gazed in awestruck wonder at the fine clothes. **4** James does not object to the courtesy shown by the dazzled congregation to the rich man; but he does criticize the unequal treatment given to both. The poor man is hardly likely to believe the preached Word now. *Made distinctions* is the same Greek verb as in 1:6 (*diakrinō*, translated 'doubt'). (See on 1:6.) The *distinctions* (doubt) consist in the fact that faith is manifested by attendance at the assembly and worldliness by contempt of the poor. The inconsistency is analogous to that of the doubter, the man with two souls. *Among yourselves*; *i.e.* these feelings are in their hearts, not openly expressed. They have proved to be *judges* directed by *evil thoughts*. *Cf*. 4:11.

5 James continues with vigour and affection. What a contrast is suggested between God's attitude and treatment, and theirs! The *poor* in this world's goods and therefore in the eyes of *the world* have been chosen to be *rich* in the realm of *faith*. They become rich indeed through faith. But the expression does not mean that they are *rich in faith* in the sense that they have great 'quantities' of it as a sort of compensation for their earthly poverty. They are rich now; and rich they will be, for they are *heirs*. *Cf*. 1:12. The man in shabby clothing can be a kind of

sacramental sign of God's election. *Cf*. Dt. 7:6-8. **6** *But you have dishonoured* him; and, by implication, favoured *the rich*. But these are the very people who exploit you! Though James is illustrating by means of a typical example ('a man', v. 2) he is thinking of a class and he remembers the oppressive conduct of wealthy non-Christians. It is a familiar OT theme. **7** Further *they . . . blaspheme* the fair *name* of Jesus. In the OT the name of God was named over a man and he was in this way God's possession. The suggestion of the name of Jesus is therefore highly significant for Jewish Christians, for it re-affirms His glory. The *name by which you are called* may be the name 'Christian'. But a strict translation renders 'the name which was invoked over you' and a reference to baptism is possible. The name of Jesus was certainly invoked when men were baptized in His name. The citation of Am. 9:12 in Acts 15:17, from the LXX, by James himself shows that he was of broader vision than some have supposed: Gentiles have civic rights in the church of Christ. Over them the name is invoked.

8 *The royal law* (*cf*. Lv. 19:18) is 'kingly' as coming from God the King, to be observed by the subjects of His kingdom; and it has royal rank over the other commandments. It might be argued that the members of the congregation do *love* their *neighbour*—the rich man. **9** But they have not loved the poor man. James may be thinking of the context (*cf*. Lv. 19:15) of the scripture quoted in v. 8. If they show *partiality*, it is sheer disobedience to God's known will and it incurs His displeasure, for they *commit sin* (*cf*. 4:17). *The law*, like a judge, convicts them: 'you are *transgressors*'.

10 *Cf*. Dt. 27:26 (LXX) quoted in Gal. 3:10, and note the 'all things written' in relation to *guilty of all*. The law is a unity. The detailed laws express the detailed manner of loving one's neighbour. To fail in any one point is to fail in love. It does not mean that a man who steals a sum of money is automatically guilty of murder or adultery. The law is more than the sum of its commandments, and to obey one does not cancel the disobedience to another. Dishonouring the poor man is not covered by courtesy toward the rich. (To illustrate: a roof is supported by pillars; remove one and the roof still stands. A chain is constituted by links; break one and the whole chain is broken. The latter is the point.) The whole law expresses the whole will of God for man. This is how we should love our neighbour: with all the light thrown on to the law by the Sermon on the Mount (Mt. 5-7). **11** James drives this home by quoting Ex. 20:13, 14; Dt. 5:17, 18. Behind every commandment is *he who said*, the living God. J. Schneider helpfully says that 'he who gets over the fence in one place has got over it' (*Die Briefe des Jakobus, Petrus, Judas und Johannes*, 1961). Note that for James the scripture is decisive. It is relevant to say that the Decalogue is as binding today as it was to the early church.

12 The emphasis placed by James on conduct (*cf.* 1:22–27) is not merely 'practical Christianity'. Christian conduct is motivated. The readers are to receive the Word and to *act as those who are to be judged . . .*, *i.e.* they are to keep in mind that they are to be judged. Judgment will be *under the law of liberty*: it will be exercised through or by means of it. *Cf.* 1:25. Man wants to be his own master. The consequence is seen in 1:14f. Desire is deaf to the law. But in the gospel (*cf.* 1:21) the law has already been fulfilled. Jesus Christ fulfilled it for us. The reception of the gospel means regeneration (*cf.* 1:18) and the regenerated man wants to please God. The law shows him what he wants to do. The Christian is not like a dog tied to the chariot of Zeus. He gladly chooses to 'follow Me' without being 'tied'. He is thus free, and the gospel, in its demands on those who have accepted it, is well called a *law of liberty*. The 'new morality', by contrast, drives men into bondage.

13 *For* obviously gives an explanation. The thought is compressed by the omission of a whole clause. By a normal Greek idiom the *for* introduces the explanation of the omitted clause. The thought in full is thus: 'You are going to be judged—v. 12. (This is a fearful threat.) *For judgment is without mercy. . . .*' *Cf.* Mt. 18:33. *Mercy* is a feeling of compassion expressed in action (*cf.* vv. 15f.). It implies here at least the love of neighbour, to be shown in the right attitude to the poor man. The unmerciful do not understand mercy and in spite of any claim to faith they do not realize that they themselves are in debt to the mercy of Christ. Their alleged faith is not faith at all and they are ripe for *judgment*. The absolute statement that *judgment is without mercy* appears vindictive and sub-Christian. But this is not so. Judgment, as judgment, is merciless. The moment it shows mercy it ceases to be pure judgment. James is stating a general principle and he can match it with another general principle. To be unmerciful in a given case, to fail to love one's neighbour and to show partiality, is a particular case of sin (*cf.* v. 9) and James has a gospel which deals with all sin—the other general principle. He knows of a saving word (*cf.* 1:21) of grace (*cf.* 4:6) and forgiveness and sins covered (*cf.* 5:15, 20) and he can look forward to the second advent, which he would hardly do if the only prospect were judgment. And he speaks from personal experience. The law had not helped him but he had found mercy in Jesus. Through the cross he found that *mercy triumphs over judgment.*

2:14–26 Faith working

14 The rhetorical question, *What does it profit . . . ?* with its implied admonition (*cf.* 2:1ff.; 3:1ff.) states the theme of the section. Again notice the *if* (*cf.* 2:2). James supposes an example, no doubt drawing on his experience of pseudo-Paulinists. The careful wording suggests a claim to faith, a comment and a question. A man says, 'I have

faith.' But, comments James, in actual fact he is without works. The claim and the comment constitute the hypothesis. If this is the situation, says James, nothing can be gained from it. 'Faith of that kind cannot *save him,* can it?' (The implied answer is 'No'.) The claim to faith is unsupported by evidence of its reality, for there is no discernible evidence: he *has not works.* For James, salvation depends on the word received and obeyed (1:21f.). **15, 16** This is not an actual event: James still says *if* and he thinks of *a brother or sister.* An actual event would require a specific person. James is using his imagination and is making a comparison from what we should call social work. His point is that goodwill or a friendly attitude is not enough. He therefore repeats his question. 'What's the good?'—sociologically, in the realm of human welfare, not that of eternal salvation. Contrast Mk. 5:34b.

17 *So:* as in social work goodwill without works is dead, so in religion *faith* without works *is dead.* The dead do not do anything! Faith *by itself* corresponds to 'faith alone' in v. 24 and to 'faith apart from works' in v. 26. It is perhaps tautological to translate by 'inwardly' (J. B. Mayor, *The Epistle of St. James,* 1913) as it has no 'externals'. It is instructive here to consider Lk. 23:43. The penitent thief had no time left for works; and faith had no time in which to die. James would not have dissented from this. He sees faith as having had time for expression in works but the opportunity was not taken.

18 This verse is notoriously difficult. It is largely a question of who speaks and where the marks of quotation are to be put. *But some one* (Gk. *tis*) *will say* is the mark of an objection; and the *tis* belongs to the style. There are two possibilities. *a.* The *some one* might be *a man* (*tis*) of v. 14 or his representative. He merely says, *You* (James) *have faith.* He means: 'You are in the same position as we are; you are one of us.' James sharply replies, *and I* (emphasized) *have works,* and continues with his attack, *Show me. . . . b.* On the other hand James may be keeping himself in the background and the *some one* may be speaking on his behalf and answering the *tis, a man* of v. 14. He begins by saying, *You have faith* (as you say, v. 14) *and I have works.* He continues his offensive. Knowing that faith is an inner attitude and that the man claims to have it, he says, '*Show* it.' At the back of his mind is the thought, 'if you can. I doubt it.' For it is impossible to *show* it without *works,* which the man does not have. He finishes the round with a heavy blow: *I by my works will show you my faith.* This is possible because the works express the faith.

19 The attack is resumed and pressed home. Perhaps the man will try to show his faith by reference to its contents. 'You are a monotheist in belief? (The Gk. may be interrogative.) Good!' This is a sincere comment (*cf.* Dt. 6:4), for the doctrine is basic; but it becomes ironical. You have not demonstrated your Christian faith; indeed you keep strange company: *the demons* *believe* just as you do, *and shudder* at the exorcistic formula, 'one God', in fear of His power. Your 'faith' is merely the popular, intellectual (though not necessarily learned) idea, and it can be combined with evil. Just as *the demons believe* and continue their wickedness; so you too can *believe* and go on sinning. The point is not that the content of faith was wrong but that it was inadequate. We might fitly compare Tit. 1:16; Heb. 11:6.

20 James speaks in his own name here. Is proof desired? He adds Scripture (v. 21) to reason to show that *faith apart from works is barren, i.e.* idle (*cf.* Mt. 20:3, 6), inoperative, useless. The vocative is characteristic of the diatribe (see Introduction). *Foolish* (vocative of Gk. *kenos*, empty) is like the 'Raca' of Mt. 5:22 (AV, RSV mg.); *i.e.* 'empty simpleton'. *Cf.* our modern 'There's nothing in him'. 21 The expected answer is 'Yes'. *His son Isaac upon the altar* is from Gn. 22:9 (LXX) with 'laid' changed to *offered. Abraham . . . offered his son* in principle. If *justified* means 'deemed righteous' it can be used in two ways. It can be used of a man who has actually lived righteously (*cf.* Gn. 18:19) and is therefore righteous 'as a result of works'. This is what James means. Or it can be used of a man who is not thus righteous (*cf.* Rom. 3:10) but is deemed righteous by the mercy of God. This is Paul's doctrine of justification.

22 *You* (singular) is the *man* of v. 14 and an appeal is made to his insight and his desire 'to be shown' (v. 20). Observe the same notes: *faith* 'worked' *along with his works* (and not *vice versa*). The *works* were not secular morality but deeds of faith; as a result of *works, faith* is shown really to exist (v. 18), to be living or 'vital' (v. 17) and fruitful (v. 20), *i.e.* completed, perfected, mature. True *faith* thus combines belief (of doctrine), trust (in Christ) and moral action (works of love).

Surprising as it may seem, Pauline justification is abstract. The doctrine has been sharpened, emphasized and isolated in thought as a result of the conflict of faith and works. But justification itself is abstract in the sense that though we may consider it by itself as a doctrine, the experience does not occur by itself. There is no case of 'pure' justification. No man ever existed who was justified without something else happening at the same time. At the moment of justification he is born again, receives a new nature and is incorporated in Christ. So far James would not be unsympathetic.

But now a new factor enters—the time element. At least some period must elapse, however small, between 'first faith' and good works. Paul's point is that God accepts a man as soon as he believes. James is considering a man who believes but who has neglected every opportunity for good works from the time of his 'first faith'. James looks for fruit and finds only leaves. Paul would understand this (*cf.* Gal. 5:6). But at the moment of conversion faith, for him, is

everything; and James says that the Word must be received (Jas. 1:21). During the subsequent Christian life the believer's 'walk' must avoid sin, which is not merely the negative 'sins of omission'; he should positively obey God (*cf.* Rom. 6:1-4, 13; Eph. 2:8-10). This Pauline emphasis on good works is reflected in the view of James that faith without works is worthless (*cf.* 2:14); it is not faith at all, certainly not Christian faith. These two positions are not inconsistent. Paul thinks especially of the beginning of the Christian life; James thinks of its continuance. At the beginning all that is needed is faith; if faith is genuine, works will follow.

23 James sees in all this the fulfilment of Gn. 15:6. Abraham really *believed*. If this is regarded as in some sense a prophecy, it was *fulfilled* in Abraham's actual readiness to offer (a sacrificial technical term) his son. It was a work of faith. The rest of the citation from Gn. 15:6 (*it was reckoned . . .*) and the allusion to *friend of God* (Is. 41:8; *cf.* 2 Ch. 20:7), one who loves Him and is loved by Him (*cf.* Dn. 3:35, LXX), are the divine verdicts on Abraham. (Notice Paul's complementary use of this same text, Gn. 15:6, in Rom. 4:1-5; *cf.* Gal. 3:6f.)

24 *You* (readers) *see*; plural. The thought is now general and not restricted to Abraham; contrast v. 21. Paul and James present different 'causes' or instruments of justification, which are not alternatives. To illustrate: an owner of a large estate invites the unemployed and their families to enter his park, to walk (with him) to his mansion and he will feed, clothe and house them. Two old friends meet in the house. 'How did you get here?' they ask each other. 'I came in through the gate, as invited', says one. 'I walked up the drive', says the other. This is what Paul and James are saying. How does a man get in? By accepting the invitation and going through the gate (Paul); by the walk from the gate to the house (James). Paul also believes in the driveway; and James also believes in the gate; but their emphases are different. Both gate and driveway are necessary though either may be given as the method. Similarly a man is *justified* by faith, and *justified by works*. The faith must be living and the works inspired by faith. They are distinguished in thought and must be united in fact. J. Jeremias neatly picks up the salient points of emphases thus: Christian faith and Jewish deeds (Paul); Jewish faith and Christian deeds (James). Paul insists on Christian faith, not Jewish deeds, works of the law, to justify (*cf.* Rom. 3:28). James will not consider Jewish faith (monotheism; *cf.* v. 19) but requires Christian deeds as evidence of being justified.

25 See Jos. 2:1-24; 6:15-25; Mt. 1:5; Heb. 11:31. Paul could have used this example (*cf.* 1 Cor. 6:9-11). 26 A dead theism or even a dead orthodoxy has little value in the eyes of James. *Cf.* v. 17 and 4:17. Without pressing the parallelism too far we may say that the unity of *body* and *spirit* aptly points to the unity of *faith* and *works.*

3:1–18 Teaching with reticence and wisdom

1 James, true to his emphasis on a living faith, takes up his references to speaking in 1:19, 26 (*cf.* 2:12), and expresses himself in a very direct way that is difficult to render into English. 'Do not become teachers in great numbers.' The position of teacher was esteemed in the Christian community and was therefore attractive; and it could be dangerous to the church. Well-meaning but unqualified men, or even self-righteous men, might seize opportunities for teaching, with disastrous results. Teachers inevitably talk, but they do not all talk wisely (*cf.* v. 13) or peaceably. They must have a sense of responsibility. James appeals to what is definitely known already, by using a Pauline formula *you know* (Gk. *eidotes*; *cf.*, *e.g.*, Rom. 13:11), and includes himself with the teachers in the liability to 'greater condemnation'. He does not forget forgiveness (*cf.* 5:15) though the reminder of judgment is wholesome. The comparative adjective *greater* suggests 'degrees' of treatment at the judgment and accords with our Lord's teaching (*cf.*, *e.g.*, Lk. 12:47f.). James shows the same serious attitude to speech that his Master did (*cf.* Mt. 12:36f.) and is close to His Greek language (*cf.* Lk. 20:47; both there and in Jas. 3:1 the Greek is *lambanō krima*, 'to receive condemnation', in the future tense).

2 *For* gives the reason for giving the warning. Translate: 'We all stumble (*cf.* 2:10) (including James) in many ways (or, often).' James may already have the picture of the horse in mind. This is general, but he turns to sins of speech and his words are applicable to others besides teachers. Speech is a test case: absence of failure here implies *a perfect man*, a finished character. As regards teachers the sin would be not so much false doctrine as disputatiousness and 'knowing better'. Even the teacher can learn. If *perfect* he can *bridle* not only his tongue but also the whole realm of impulse expressed through the body. This is not the asceticism which kills but the discipline which controls.

3, 4 James gives two simple illustrations of what the 'perfect man' is able to do. Note the contrast of small and great. The *strong winds* suggest the violence of the impulses which the perfect man controls. **5** The small bridle or bit and the small rudder can direct large objects because they themselves are controlled. But the unbridled *tongue*, though only *a little member*, can have large effects which continue without restraint. It *boasts* of great achievements, done or promised. Like the rudder, it ought to be controlled by the will (v. 4) and further guided by reason (*cf.* 1:26) and the Word. But it is no more under control than a spark in dry brushwood. A tiny spark can kindle a *forest* fire which may blaze for weeks and go on smouldering for months. Speech is equally dangerous and hence its effects run riot. A little book of heresy can set the church *ablaze*; a whisper of gossip can inflame a city.

6 *And the tongue is* indeed *a fire. An unrighteous world* represents (not incorrectly) the Greek 'the world of unrighteousness'. In the light of Lk. 16:8 (Gk. 'the steward of unrighteousness') and Lk. 18:6 (Gk. 'the judge of unrighteousness') we can say that the world does unrighteousness. It also stains (*cf.* Jas. 1:27) and is hostile to God (*cf.* 4:4). This has points of contact with John (*cf.* Jn. 7:7; 15:18f.; 17:14f.). It seems plain that the tongue is a world in miniature. 'The tongue is settled in our members as the world of unrighteousness, (the tongue) that stains the whole personality. . . .' James goes on to think not only of the individual but of humanity at large. The tongue inflames *the cycle of nature*, i.e. 'the wheel of *genesis*' (*cf.* on 1:23). We can dismiss doctrines of reincarnation from the exposition of the robust Jewish Christian James. He loosely uses a Hellenistic expression associated with the Orphic mysteries and ultimately with Indian thought. It seems to mean here 'course of life'. Now the tongue is concerned with communication. Each speaker may be seen standing in *the cycle* or 'circle' of humanity and *setting* it *on fire* with desire, suspicion, rivalry, hatred and war. (The picture may be that of the red-hot axle setting the wheel alight.) The tongue itself is *set on fire by hell*, or 'Gehenna' (RSV mg.). The term 'Gehenna' is used for the devil; analogous to this is the use of 'heaven' for God in 'kingdom of heaven'. Gehenna is the Greek form of the Hebrew 'Gehinnom', 'valley of Hinnom'. As a result of threats of judgment over it in Je. 7:32; 19:6, apocalyptic literature came to regard it as the *hell* of the last judgment. (See *NBD*, arts. 'Eschatology' and 'Hell'.) James sees a Satanic origin for evil speech.

7, 8 These verses justify the previous verse. *Cf.* Gn. 1:26f.; 9:2. It is an element in the nature of man to subdue all members of the animal creation. This is confirmed by past experience and present practice: *can be tamed* should be rendered 'is being tamed'; the process continues. It is similarly the nature of animals to be subdued by man. But no man *can tame the tongue*. The Pelagians, who laid stress on human effort in salvation, read v. 8 as a question. The tongue is *a restless evil*: it will not stay still. Even its echoes can kill, when the original speaker is silent. *Cf.* Ps. 140:3.

9 *Cf.* Gn. 1:27; Ps. 62:4. James is thinking either of humanity or of Christians. In the former case he means that *we* churchmen and *we* worldlings use the same instrument, the tongue. '*We* worldlings' is not a happy expression but it is inevitable on the present interpretation. James then identifies himself with humanity, though not necessarily with its cursing. If, however, he is thinking of Christians only he means that *we* Christians 'attend church' and quarrel socially. The *we* of pastoral tact shows how far James could go in his desire to win rather than repel. It is pure speculation to ask if James himself ever could *curse men*, even though he says *we curse men*. The next verse shows his attitude, which is like that of Paul (*cf.* Rom. 12:14).

A quite different matter is raised by 1 Cor. 16:22; Gal. 1:8f.

10 Not necessarily at the same time. The inconsistency raises questions about the reality of the worship, both public and private. **11, 12** James is sure of the answers to his questions even as he asks them. These are more than apt illustrations. Nature itself in its consistency has a lesson for man, especially as he (not nature) is made in the image of God; and the final statement suggests the need of regeneration (*cf.* 1:18) and a living faith (*cf.* 2:17). A grapevine produces grapes, not figs; the tongue should produce that which accords with the gospel. If it produces both blessing and cursing, its owner is a man of two souls (*cf.* 1:7f.).

13 James now turns to the teachers, for in late Judaism they (Rabbis) were identified with the wise. The question is pointed (*understanding* is almost our 'scholar') but the force is conditional: if there is a man who applies his knowledge to the production of good behaviour.... Wisdom is analogous to faith (*cf.* 2:18) and must be shown by *works*. The temptation of teachers is to be purely theoretical; and arrogant (*cf.* Jn. 7:49). James wants the knowledge to issue in good conduct and not to be roughly hurled at simple souls. They must not be always 'putting people right' nor engaging in controversy with 'rivals' in the work of teaching. Some of the churches may be suffering from the activities of Pauline or pseudo-Pauline extremists.

14 *But if you have . . . selfish ambition*: the *ambition* (Gk. *eritheia*) savours of selfish canvassing and election intrigue, illegal manipulation for one's own advantage, the base self-seeking of those who cannot aspire to higher pursuits. Such behaviour is no qualification for a teacher or for any Christian; therefore *do not boast* of your wisdom. Inasmuch as to *boast* is to use speech, to *be false to the truth* is to lie against it, and 'against' involves a measure of hostility to it. But *truth* is God's instrument in regeneration (*cf.* 1:18). If the words of James are applicable to any readers they have wandered from *the truth* in its demands if not in its doctrines (*cf.* 5:19; 1:21f.).

15 This sort of wisdom is *not . . . from above* (*cf.* 1:5, 17). Its range is *earthly* and secular; its nature is non-supernatural, without the characteristic touch of regeneration (*cf.* 1 Cor. 2:14; Jude 19); and its source and home is the devil. The teachers are short-sighted, belie their own conversion experience and play into the hands of the enemy. **16** *Disorder* means the disruption of the peace of the community. James does not mean that every local church will have *every vile practice* but that there is a causal connection between *jealousy and selfish ambition* on the one hand and *disorder . . .* on the other. *Cf.* Gal. 5:19f. The *practice* includes that which caused it, *i.e.* the *jealousy and selfish ambition* perpetuate themselves both as causes and results.

17 This verse describes what the heavenly wisdom does for men—not only teachers: *cf.* 1:5, where the 'any man' may not be of great intellect. *Wisdom* which is *pure* controls the thoughts (*cf.* Phil. 4:8); as *peaceable* it counteracts those who are 'spoiling for a fight' and as *gentle* (Gk. *epieikes*) it does not insist on its rights or the letter of the law. In being *open to reason* it will consider any sound argument, not merely one from a limited field; it wants to yield if in good conscience it can. It is always animated by *mercy*, a compassion which acts as well as feels, with good results: it produces *good fruits*. It has no *uncertainty* for it has no inner cleavage (*cf.* 1:6) and makes no unworthy distinctions (*cf.* 2:4). At its heart is no *insincerity* and it adopts no pose.

18 The unusual 'sowing the harvest' is not impossible. A farmer might point to a fine field and say that 'the crop was sown in bad weather'. Here *righteousness* has a crop. *Righteousness* is described in v. 17. Those with wisdom from above act as in v. 17 and it requires thought and effort (*cf.* Mt. 5:9): they have to *make peace*. It is not the peace of the cemetery. Such 'good life' (v. 13) or behaviour tends to reproduce itself. If *peace* is the motive and the atmosphere, the local church will not be divided, and in large measure it will be due to the mastery of the tongue.

4:1–17 Breaking the peace and loving the world

1 James cannot be thinking of *wars* and *fightings* between nations. *Cf.* 3:14, 16. If the whole letter is indeed steeped in the thought of Jesus, it is natural to think of Mt. 5:21f. 'War' implies continued hostility; 'battle' the occasional outburst. There may possibly be a further distinction. 'To battle' is used in Greek for violent verbal dispute and for 'making a scene'. In prolonged disputes which are *wars* actual weapons may be envisaged. The immediate cause of dissension may be doctrinal difference or social distinction: theological or economic (*cf.* 2:1f., 6; 3:1, 13). Peace is not 'natural' but has to be created: *cf.* Eph. 4:2f. The source of strife is *passions*, literally 'pleasures', which Dibelius acutely identifies with 'desires' (*cf.* v. 2 'you desire', not 'you enjoy'). Here they do not war against the soul (as in 1 Pet. 2:11) but against reason (*cf.* Rom. 7:23) and love of one's neighbour (*cf.* 2:8), using guile as well as force (*cf.* 1:14). Notice the unity of body and soul: the tongue is a member (*cf.* 3:5f.).

2 The desiring and the not-having are continuous: there is no lasting possession. *Covet* may not be an anticlimax as it shows the inner motive of the 'killing'. See RSV mg. It includes envy and jealousy—the cause of some evil crimes. The momentary satisfaction leaves a gaping emptiness. So you go on killing and fighting and warring. This may be interpreted figuratively. R. V. G. Tasker (*TNTC*, p. 87), points out that the sentences may be taken as virtually conditional. 'If you desire . . . the result is you kill. And if you covet . . . the result is you fight and wage war.'

3 Their great failure is in the life of prayer. Do they *ask* or do they not? Some see here an afterthought, a swift admission: 'yes, you do pray, but . . .'. It may, however, reflect the Hebraic difficulty of expressing an exception. *Cf.* Gn. 2:16f. They *do not receive* because they always ask for things; and they are wrong things requested with the wrong motive: *to spend . . . on* (and 'in') their pleasures. *Spend* covers more than money and has an air of lavish waste. Murder and prodigality: some will wonder if Christians can be thus guilty. Perhaps race riots reveal how thin the lid may be which holds down the desire to kill and waste. Note that it is possible for men to pray wrongly.

4 *Unfaithful creatures* is literally 'adulteresses' and is used for spiritual unfaithfulness. The marriage metaphor is found in the OT (*cf., e.g.,* Is. 54:5) and is used by our Lord (*cf.* Mt. 12:39) and by Paul (*cf.* 2 Cor. 11:2). James implies the doctrine of the church as the bride of Christ. He passes on, however, to the thought of friendship. *Friendship with the world* is logically and spiritually incompatible with friendship with God: logically because both God and the world make total demands and spiritually because to ally oneself with the world is to take the world's point of view, which is *enmity with God*. James is clear-cut, black or white; he is no man of two souls (*cf.* 1:8). *Whoever wishes to be a friend of the world* exercises his choice and 'prefers' the world rather than God as friend. He thereby *makes himself an enemy of God* whether he at first realizes it or not. James expects his readers at any rate to, follow him here: *do you not know . . . ? Therefore. . . .*

5 *The scripture* has not been identified in the OT. There may be a general allusion to such passages as Ho. 11:8. Either the two friendships are incompatible or the scripture is *in vain* and has no meaning. The *jealously* is as noble as that of a true husband for a faithless wife. The 'yearning' is illustrated in Phil. 1:8. *He who yearns* is God, as the tenor of vv. 5, 6 suggests. *The spirit* can hardly be the Holy Spirit, in view of v. 6a: God does not give grace to the Holy Spirit, who is Himself the Spirit of grace (Heb. 10:29). *The spirit* is the breath of life of Gn. 2:7 (*cf.* Jas. 2:26). It would be difficult to make it the subject (though linguistically possible) owing to the absence of an object and the unnecessary emendation of the verb *made to dwell*. In the 'yearning' God makes a claim for Himself alone.

6 *Gives . . . grace* is an anticipation of the fuller quotation introduced by *it says* (*cf.* Pr. 3:34, LXX). James calls it a 'greater' *grace*, which is greater than that already given in the breath of life (Mussner); and greater in view of the greater requirement (Ropes), which recalls Rom. 5:20. Some feel that *grace* has not for James the rich meaning that it had for Paul. But before accepting this we should consider the dark picture of sin presented by James and his belief about forgiveness (*cf.* 5:15). *Grace* must be received

with humility; independence before God involves the divine opposition. James is still clear-cut: either pride or humility from man and opposition or grace from God. *Cf.* 1 Pet. 5:5f.

7 *Therefore* James calls for humility: *submit . . . to God*. His motive is that they may receive grace: the judgment may be avoided, or at least the judgment of condemnation. He then shows how to *submit* and gives encouragement with a promise. Negatively, he urges his readers to *submit . . . to God* by opposing His enemy: *resist the devil . . .* (*cf.* Lk. 4:13). The battle is constantly renewed and the promise holds. *Cf.* Lk. 22:28 AV which has 'temptations' instead of RSV and NEB 'trial(s)'. Note how James removes any possible misunderstanding. In v. 4 he spoke of the world and God. Now he shows what is involved in this opposition: it is between *the devil* and God.

8 James wants more than a negative submission. Positively, he desires his readers to *draw near to God*. This was a characteristically priestly act in the OT (*cf.* Ex. 19:22; Ezk. 44:13) but it is now spread over the whole company of believing men (*cf.* Heb. 7:19). The best comment on *he will draw near to you* is Lk. 15:20. The first step in man's salvation is taken by God, because to *draw near to God* is itself a response to His prior call. Having given encouragement James gives a strong call to repentance in a series of sharp and urgent imperatives. He is the surgeon who cuts rather than the masseur. *Cleanse . . . and purify . . .* is the language of religious approach to God, with moral intent (*cf.* Ex. 30:19f.; 40:31f.). The purified man is 'religiously qualified', *i.e.* is in a state of holiness for encounter with God. The *hands* symbolize the outer act and the *hearts* the inner intention. It is not without significance that Levitical cleansing of the hands is necessary at times of prayer. Note the means of cleansing in Acts 15:9 (and who was listening then, in Acts 15:12, 13). We should not separate too widely the cleansing and the purifying, the hands and the heart, the *sinners* and the men of two souls (*cf.* 1:8). *Cf.* Ps. 24:4.

9 *Be wretched . . . :* if repentance is real, let it show itself. This is the very opposite of nominal religion. According to Rengstorf the Rabbis did not often speak of laughter. It comes from enemies and from fools and in the rabbinic view marks the rejection of God's universal control and the affirmation of human autonomy. There is no room for frivolity in repentance, and joy should await the divine renewal. 10 The severe words are followed by encouragement. *The Lord . . . will exalt* those who *humble* themselves before Him. If the laughter is secular, the humbling should not be: it should be *before the Lord*. The consequent exaltation is the only one to be prized (*cf.* Lk. 16:15).

11 Still mindful of the wars and battles and the hot words which flow (*cf.* 4:1) and of the uncontrolled tongue generally (*cf.* 3:8), James seriously (and now affectionately, *brethren*) urges his

readers *not* to *speak evil against one another*, to 'cease from mutual slander'. Defamation of character judges a man unheard and is forbidden. It is an offence against the law, against the whole law (*cf.* 2:8, 10), and it actually defames and *judges the law*. For the speaker implies superior knowledge and an independent position, as if he himself were not under the law. When he ought to be *a doer of the law* by obeying it, he is putting himself above it as well as above his brother. He has made himself *a judge*; and not merely *a judge* who administers the law but something further.

12 He has made himself a *lawgiver*. He has really set up another law by which he judges his brother. This denies God, sins against God and arrogantly usurps His position. Solemnly James asserts: *There is one lawgiver and judge*. (The word *one* would raise emotions in many a Jew; *cf.* Dt. 6:4.) He does not weakly advise; He commands, judges and implements His decisions. For all power is His to match His righteousness. He can *save* and He can *destroy*. The rhetorical question, *who are you . . . ?* needs no answer by James. If there is any Christian conscience left, the answer will come. Note the final echo in *neighbour* (*cf.* 2:8). Whoever he is, he is to be loved, whether he is in the world or in the church. The repeated 'brethren' . . . 'brother' in v. 11 shows that James is speaking to the church, but the spirit of the loveless world has broken into it.

13 James now turns to other 'superior' people, those who set themselves above (not the law but) providence or destiny. He begins brusquely: 'Now then, *you who say . . . we will go* into the city of So-and-so. . . .' Their attitude is not merely decision or even determination. It is secular independence (who or what is to stop us?). James is not attacking the profit motive so much as the failure to take God into their thinking. They act as if they control the future. They do not say 'let us go . . .' but exhibit the cold, merciless confidence of grand administration with a whole year in prospect. Relentless bureaucracy could hardly go further. **14** But even *tomorrow* is hidden from their eyes. The answer to the question, '*What* sort of a *life* is yours?' (*cf.* the French *comment est . . . ?*) is not expressed but it is implied, and *for* gives the reason for it. *What is your life?* Cannot you see that it is a thing of futility? *For you are a mist*, or vapour, which *appears . . .* and then '*disappears*'. In place of their self-security there is nothing but transitoriness: a vapour ends in a rainbow or a drain. *Cf.* 1:10f. and, in literature, William Shakespeare, *The Tempest* IV.1.156.

> *. . . the great globe itself,*
> *Yea, all which it inherit, shall dissolve*
> *And, like this insubstantial pageant faded,*
> *Leave not a rack behind.* (*rack* = cloud)

15 *If the Lord wills* is the familiar DV (*Deo volente*), which is the decisive factor to be remembered in all planning. *Cf.* Acts 18:21;

1 Cor. 4:19. Life itself (*we shall live*) as well as planning is dependent on God. A possible Semitic interpretation is: 'If the Lord wills that we go on living, we shall do this or that', but it is not so convincing. **16** *As it is*, when you ought to say 'God willing', *you boast* in what you say in v. 13. The *arrogance* here lies in deliberately claiming to be more than you are, the proud master of life and of time. *All such boasting is evil* because God is Lord of creation, of nature and of history and time.

17 This verse should begin with 'therefore'. James is stating the sin of omission, and it is universally applicable. The merchants know their duty but suppress the knowledge. This is relevant sometimes for 'big business'. Note the transition from 'evil' in v. 16 to *sin* and the Christian answer to the unbeliever who says that he 'has done nobody any harm'. To fail to do *what is right* includes failure to receive and obey the word.

5:1–6 Accusing the rich

1 James now turns from the merchants to the great landed proprietors, the owners of vast estates. He writes like a prophet, not so much calling to repentance as announcing a doom, and addressing the rich directly and with vigour. 'Now then, *you rich, weep and howl* in mourning' because of your impending experiences of wretchedness.

2, 3 The ruin of their wealth is expressed in the perfect tense, which some have supposed to be the 'prophetic perfect'—the future event is so certain that it can be described in a past tense. But it can be argued that these men have so much wealth that they cannot use it all. Consequently their grain has *rotted*; their 'changes of raiment' have become *moth-eaten*; their coins and ornaments of *gold and silver* have tarnished. (*Rust* must not be pressed here. James is not writing as a scientist; and anyway the Greek *ios* means 'poison' as well as rust, as in 3:8.) The diction is traditional: *cf.* Ecclus. 29:10; *Gospel of Thomas*, 76; Mt. 6:19f.; literary dependence on Matthew is not established (*cf.* D. Guthrie, *New Testament Introduction: Hebrews to Revelation*, 1962; W. G. Kümmel, *Introduction to the New Testament*, 1966). The very *rust*—and the moth holes and the mouldy grain—will be *evidence*, at the judgment, of economic carelessness and social callousness. *Will eat your flesh*: Mussner tentatively compares the *rust* with the leprosy of hell which consumes the *flesh* of the condemned: *cf.* Nu. 12:12; and for the association of leprosy and burning *cf.* Lv. 13:24f. *For the last days*: read 'in (Gk. *en*) the last days', as in Acts 2:16f. The estate owners are blind or unconcerned.

4 And worse: with all their resources they have not paid their men. The *fields* here must imply something like 'broad acres'. The verse is in the form of synthetic parallelism. The withheld pay which shouts (now—not at the judgment) is therefore linked with *the cries of the harvesters* ('pay us our money!'). Both parties are heard by *the Lord of hosts*. *Cf.* Am. 4:13. *Hosts*, or armies, has been taken to mean: *a.* the armies of Israel (*cf.* 1 Sa. 17:45); *b.* the armies of heaven, *i.e.* the stars and the forces of nature (*cf.* Gn. 2:1); *c.* the armies of angels (*cf.* 1 Ki. 22:19; Is. 6:1–5). History, nature and the supernatural are tools in the divine hand to vindicate the oppressed.

5 And not only the oppressed but righteousness itself will be vindicated. From the standpoint of the coming judgment James looks back upon their whole life *on the earth* as *luxury* and voluptuousness. *Cf.* Lk. 16:19, 'every day'. He presses home his charge with prophetic vigour. *You have fattened—your hearts!* They were like the rich fool who wanted his soul to eat and drink (*cf.* Lk. 12:19), and they were equally blind to their imminent doom. They continue in their sins to the very end, absorbed in them, oblivious of the fact that they are *in a day of slaughter*. Observe how delicately and dramatically James has made use of Jeremiah's phrase, 'for the day of slaughter' (Je. 12:3).

6 Change to the staccato: 'You condemned! You slew the righteous man!' *The righteous* is here collective and it is thus best to omit *man*. *Cf.* Ps. 37:12, 'the righteous', 'him', in the singular; and Ps. 37:17, where 'the righteous' is plural. As *the righteous* is a Messianic title (*cf.* Acts 7:52), James seems to see the condemnation of the Messiah repeated in the experience of His righteous servants. In both cases the rich may have controlled the courts. Ropes, following the text of Westcott and Hort, takes the last clause as a question: 'Does not the Righteous One *resist you*?' (*sc.* 'Yes, He does').

5:7–11 Waiting patiently for the Lord

7 *Patient* here has reference to time rather than to pain. *Therefore* links with the preceding section and reveals the connection between the judgment and the *parousia*, *the coming of the Lord*. Any poor *brethren* can be encouraged. It is unlikely that James has the coming destruction of Jerusalem in mind. He aids his admonition by an example which would be familiar to all. A problem in geometry may be solved slowly or quickly, even instantaneously by a genius; but the farmer has to accept the necessary elapse of time. *Early* and *late* remind us of the germination of the seed and the maturing of the grain respectively. *Cf.* Dt. 11:14.

8 James 'applies' the lesson. The farmer exercises patience: *you also be patient. Establish*, *i.e.* strengthen, *your hearts* (not 'fatten', v. 5) with the thought that *the coming of the Lord is at hand*. This is the true cure for double-mindedness (Mayor; *cf.* 1:8). The verb *is at hand* (Gk. *ēngiken*) implies nearness but not actual 'arrival'. *The coming* had obviously not yet taken place. This is important evidence in the interpretation of Mk. 1:15, where the same verb is used. The kingdom of God is similarly *at hand* in Jesus but there is still room for its final coming in the

second advent. If this is not so, James was completely wrong.

9 James knows that distress or anxiety can embitter, and so loosen tongues. He therefore gives an affectionate exhortation to the *brethren*: *do not grumble*. He is well aware that grumbling *against one another* is a form of judging, which has its own consequences (*cf.* Mt. 7:1; Rom. 2:1). The nearness of *the Judge* adds to the solemnity of the warning. The bare statement, *the Judge is standing at the doors*, is striking and effective. Contrast the same Figure in Rev. 3:20. In James He just stands; in Revelation He speaks, even before the man inside opens the door. The fact that James says nothing to indicate who opens the door adds to the tension. *Cf.* 4:11f.

10 James assumes the readers' familiarity with biblical tradition and their knowledge of the national 'roll of honour', the classical expression of which we find in Heb. 11. In particular they knew of the prophets as martyrs. This helps to explain why James asks his readers to *take the prophets* rather than our Lord as *an example*, in contrast with Peter (*cf.* 1 Pet. 2:21). Christians knew that He was more than a martyr. *Suffering and patience* imply that *the prophets* endured what was imposed on them. The idea of time (v. 7) is now merging with endurance. *Prophets* are well defined as men who speak *in the name of the Lord*.

11 *We call those happy who were steadfast* is an appropriate attitude to national heroes. *Cf.* Ecclus. 44 beginning 'let us now praise famous men'. The recipients *have heard of the steadfastness of Job*, not only in common talk but also in the public reading of the OT Scriptures. The RSV rendering of the Greek *telos* as *purpose* is open to question. The word may mean 'end' in the sense of termination (*cf.* Mk. 3:26; Heb. 7:3); 'goal' (*cf.* 1 Tim. 1:5); or 'result' (*cf.* Rom. 6:21). James means 'the end which the Lord brought about' and the expression is a Hebraism. Dibelius helpfully points to Mt. 26:58. Peter went to see, not 'the end of Jesus', but 'how it would turn out'. Render *how the Lord is compassionate . . .* by 'because *the Lord is compassionate . . .'. Cf.* Pss. 103:8; 111:4.

5:12 Swearing forbidden

Cf. Mt. 5:34–37. The link with the previous section is provided by the thought of judgment (*cf.* v. 9). The prohibition is absolute. No compromise (*cf.* 1:8)! *Above all is* a mark of epistolary style: '*Above all* I ought not to forget' (Mussner) to urge you. . . . *Cf.* 1 Pet. 4:8.

5:13–20 Applying spiritual principles

13 The vivacious questions are really hypothetical, in the style of the diatribe (see Introduction). *Cf.* 3:13; 1 Cor. 7:18, 21, 27. The verb *suffering* is cognate with the noun in v. 10. It means 'being at the receiving end' of something unpleasant. The sufferer should 'keep on praying'. The *cheerful* man is not frivolous but 'of good heart', 'with good morale', like soldiers before

a battle. He should *sing praise*. To *pray* and to *praise* are both positive responses to experience. **14** Note that the patient is conscious: he is to summon *the elders*, the presbyters who hold office in the local *church*. The anointing may be before or during the time of prayer. *Oil* was regarded as therapeutic and it may be here suggested as an 'aid to faith', or a stimulus to faith. Charismatic gifts are not suggested (*cf.* 1 Cor. 12:9, 28, 30). *In the name* may mean 'in the context of (the invocation of) the name' or 'in the power of the name'.

15 There is ambiguity here and in v. 14. *Sick* renders two Greek words, *astheneō* (v. 14) and *kamnō* (v. 15). The former refers to illness but is also cognate with the Greek adjective *asthenēs*, 'helpless' (*cf.* Rom. 5:6), which is used as a description of sinners. *Save* is concerned with salvation from wrath in Rom. 5:9f. but the same Greek word (*sōzō*) is used medically in Mk. 6:56, 'made well'. *The sick man* is indicated by a verb (Gk. *kamnō*) which is used of exertion and of illness and even of the dead (*cf.* Wisdom 4:16) but never apparently of the dying (Mussner). It is used of wearying, both literally and spiritually: '. . . that you may not weary and (like runners) crack up in your souls' (Heb. 12:3). *Raise* is used of resurrection, but far from exclusively: it can mean 'rouse from sleep' or 'lift up' from bed or floor. The perfect tense of the Greek verb rendered *has committed sins* implies something like 'is still in (the power of unforgiven) sin' (*cf.* Jn. 8:21, 24; 1 Cor. 15:17). The ambiguity caused by the different meanings of all these words can hardly be denied. It is possible to give a consistent medical or a consistent religious interpretation. Either the patient is ill and *the prayer of faith* will heal him and *the Lord will raise him* from his bed; or he is helpless and weary spiritually and he will be saved in a spiritual resurrection. James may be ambiguous deliberately, leaving his readers to choose the interpretation which accords with the outcome of the elders' visit. For everything is subject to God's will. He may heal: the medical terms will then fit. If He does not heal, the gospel terms are appropriate, for a Christian man ('any among you', v. 14) when conscious would not refrain from adding a sincere 'Amen' to *the prayer of faith*. In either case the concluding reference to being *forgiven* is relevant.

This verse is a very precarious foundation for the Extreme Unction of Roman Catholicism. The first known author to employ the expression was Peter Lombard (*c.* 1100–1160) and from his time Extreme Unction has been one of the Seven Sacraments, according to Roman theology. The patient usually receives the anointing when he is on the point of death, and recovery is normally not expected. By contrast there is little in James to commend the Roman practice. He says nothing explicit about a sacrament or about anointing the five senses, nothing about the mediaeval necessity of using oil consecrated by the bishop. The elders are presbyters rather than priests. For the first seven centuries it was generally expected that as a result of the anointing the patient would recover. This is more in accordance with what James says than is the view which regards Extreme Unction as provisions for the journey into eternity given to those who are already *in extremis*.

16 '*Therefore* (in view of the encouragement of v. 15) admit *your sins . . .*' for it is conceivable that you have been wrong. In some sense they are all apparently ill, since James is desirous that they *may be healed*. James is back at the wars and battles of the tongue (*cf.* 4:1). He then individualizes, for intercession must begin with someone: the petition of *a righteous man has great power*. *In its effects* means 'when it is at work'. Even *a righteous man* is not always praying, for he must sleep. This clause reflects the Aristotelian doctrine of potentiality and actuality. **17, 18** *Of like nature*: Elijah was 'one of us'. *Cf.* Acts 14:15. *He prayed . . . that it might not rain*: *cf.* 1 Ki. 17:1; 18:1, 41–46. The 3½ years is Jewish tradition. *Cf.* Lk. 4:25. The hint is plain: the readers may not be prophets but it was not the prophecy but the prayer of the righteous which prevailed. Be righteous—and pray.

19, 20 The interpretation here turns on whether *any one* who *wanders* is to be a subject of reclamation or conversion. In favour of the former is the fact that the wanderer is *one among you*, *i.e.* a church member. In that case *brings back* tells of the pastor who sought and found the *sinner*. But we might wonder if a Christian, even when wandering, needs *some one* who *will save his soul from death*. The difficulty is not in the salvation by a fellow Christian, who is only a means (*cf.* 1 Cor. 9:22), but in the thought of the doom of a Christian. It would seem therefore that James has conversion in mind. *Among you* does not then imply believing church membership. The readers were a mixed crowd, spiritually, and there must have been some unconverted people among them (*cf.* 4:1), to judge by their description. If they were under the sound of the gospel, such people were near to the truth. James sees that someone *wanders* farther away *from* (Gk. *apo*) *the truth*, not out of (Gk. *ek*) it. He is increasingly unlike the man who was 'not far from the kingdom of God' (Mk. 12:34). *Brings back* will then mean 'converts' (*cf.* RV). The Christian worker is the means of the wanderer's salvation and by the preaching of the cross he removes his many *sins*.

RONALD A. WARD

1 Peter

INTRODUCTION

AUTHORSHIP

The writer claims to be 'Peter, an apostle of Jesus Christ' (1:1), and to have been 'a witness of the sufferings of Christ' (5:1). He writes by the agency of Silvanus from a place he calls Babylon, where his son Mark is with him (5:12, 13). Apart from this direct evidence the letter contains many allusions to the life and teaching of Jesus: see the references below in the Commentary. The verdict of F. H. Chase (*HDB*, III, p. 780) is that 'No epistle has caught so much of the spirit of Jesus'.

The letter was well attested by references and quotations in early authors, but of recent years its authenticity has been called into question on five main counts.

a. It is held that the style and language, which are admittedly good, but not really so classical as some would like to make out, are far too good for Peter, who was described in Acts 4:13 as 'uneducated'. Objectors also point out that the OT quotations are from the LXX. Against this it must be remembered that in Peter's day Galilee was probably bi-lingual: the Greek language would have been familiar to Peter from boyhood (his own brother's name is a Greek one), and being a fisherman and living on one of the great trade routes would have made it necessary for him to speak it regularly. Thirty years' work of evangelism and Christian teaching in a church which contained an increasing proportion of Gentiles would have made Greek his usual language and the LXX his 'Authorized Version'. In any case, we know from 5:12 that Silvanus acted as the apostle's amanuensis for this letter, and this may have meant that he was given a fair amount of freedom with regard to the style and language while receiving from Peter the contents of the letter. It is generally agreed that he is to be identified with the Silvanus mentioned in a number of Paul's letters and called Silas in Acts. As a Roman citizen (see Acts 16:37), Silvanus appears to have been a man of some background and breeding, and there are certain affinities between this Epistle, 1 and 2 Thessalonians and the apostolic decree of Acts 15 which suggest that he may have had a hand in drafting all four documents.

b. Much has been built on the language of 4:14, 16 to suggest that it was written when the very fact of being a Christian was a crime, and the first evidence of this generally-known situation is found in the correspondence of Pliny, governor of Bithynia, with Trajan, who was emperor from AD 98 to 117. Peter's argument,

however, in chs. 2–4 is that the Christian must take care to live an innocent life, so that, if he is slandered and attacked, such calumny will be without foundation. The book of Acts shows that from the earliest days misunderstanding, vested interests, and rejection of the gospel could lead to persecution 'for the name of Christ': 1 Pet. 4:14, 16 need have no further implications than similar phrases in Mt. 10:22; Acts 5:41. In fact, Peter's reference to the role of the state in 2:13, 14 suggests that he did not expect persecution from that quarter: the situation of the church *vis-à-vis* the authorities is basically the same as in the Acts.

c. The presence of ideas found in Paul, and particularly the affinity with Ephesians, is felt by some to be an objection. This holds only if one feels that the two apostles were never finally reconciled, and that their teaching must have been different. The basic content of Christian teaching in the early church is fairly standard, and it would have been strange if there were no similarities. If we allow that Peter and Paul may have been together in Rome just before this letter was written, they would doubtless have talked together over many of the issues considered in this letter.

d. Some hold that the area to which the letter was written was one evangelized by Paul, and so this would have been a breach of the arrangement made in Gal. 2:9. Here again such agreement was probably made at least 10 years previously, and in the interval the distinction between Jewish and Gentile churches would have become less clear. 1:12 suggests that Peter had not initially evangelized these areas, but it is far from certain that Paul had been originally responsible for bringing the gospel to them either —Acts 16:6, 7 suggest not.

e. It is alleged that there is in this letter a lack of personal reference to Jesus such as would be expected of Peter. This is a very arbitrary statement, and many commentators reach the opposite conclusion—see 1:13; 2:20, 22–25; 3:14; 4:14; 5:1, 2 and other references in the Commentary below. It is best for the reader to make up his own mind on reading the letter.

Taken in all, none of these objections is conclusive, and in view of the overwhelming evidence, both external and internal, there would seem no valid reason for rejecting the traditional Petrine authorship.

DATE AND PLACE OF WRITING

In view of what was said above under argument

b., a date in the reign of Nero would seem best. In view of 2:13 it would seem likely to have been written before the outburst of persecution at Rome in AD 64, especially if Paul had perished at that time, since Peter makes no allusion to Paul's martyrdom. The literary affinities are considered by some to suggest a date post-60, and so as far as we can draw any conclusions from the evidence it was probably written *c.* AD 63–64.

The argument for a Roman origin is based on the fact that in Rev. 16:19; 17:5, *etc.* Babylon is a cryptic reference to Rome. It is argued from the order of the places listed in 1:1 that the writer had in mind the bearer of the letter travelling by boat (as he would if he came from Rome) to a port in Pontus, and then travelling in a wide circuit of the addressees in order to return from the same port again, or from some point of the coast of Bithynia. Col. 4:10 shows that Mark was then in Rome with Paul, but intending to go to Asia Minor, and in 2 Tim. 4:11 he is in Asia Minor and sent for to return to Paul in Rome. In 1 Pet. 5:13 he is with Peter, and this could well have been in Rome, though some argue that on the death of Paul at Rome Mark fled to Babylon in Mesopotamia to take refuge with Peter. In view of the fact that most of our evidence links both Peter and the letter with Rome, this seems the most reasonable conclusion.

DESTINATION OF THE LETTER

Reference to a map in the light of 1:1 shows that the letter was addressed to a number of churches in the part of Asia Minor north of the Taurus mountains. Their precise location is difficult as the place-names were used to refer to ancient kingdoms as well as to contemporary Roman provinces, and the two were not always co-terminous. Some have argued from the language of 1:1; 2:6–10 and the use of the OT that it was written to Jewish believers. There is, however, plenty of other evidence (see 1:14, 18; 2:9, 18ff.; 4:3–5) that the writer had Gentiles in mind, and it is most unlikely that at this stage in the area in question there would have been separate Jewish and Gentile churches. By then they were no doubt mixed churches: confusion arises because Peter writes from a Jewish background, and is full of the truth that the Christian church is the true Israel of God.

THE UNITY OF THE LETTER

Those who reject the Petrine authorship have suggested that 1:1 and 5:12–14 could have been added to the letter at a date subsequent to its writing. This may suit their theories, but it is more difficult to expunge the personal reference in 5:1, and certainly no MS evidence supports such an idea.

Another view put forward is that the original letter ended with the doxology at 4:11. This is said to be a natural conclusion for a letter, and

then it is suggested that 4:12 to the end was added later as the situation appears to be different. In 3:17, it is said, the possibility of suffering is viewed as being remote, and in 4:12 the fiery trial is coming upon the readers. This is not so strong an argument as it seems at face value, for most scholars accept the unity of 1:3 – 4:11, and yet the situation of 1:6 is more akin to that of 4:12 than to that of 3:17. What seems more likely is that Peter's mind is moving between the church as a corporate body and its individual members. Persecution will most likely involve every church in the near future, and to that extent all the members will suffer with one another, but in each church there may be only a few called on actually to suffer in each wave of persecution, so that the likelihood of 3:17 applying to each individual reader is less great. Others suggest that by the time Peter reached 4:12 fresh news had reached him which caused him to alter the tenor of his letter, but this is less satisfactory in view of 1:6.

On the other argument, the doxology of 4:11 is not necessarily a conclusion, and it is understandable that at the end of a train of thought which has stirred deep emotion the writer should burst into an ascription of praise. This literary style is paralleled in Rom. 11:33–36; 15:33; Eph. 3:20, 21, *etc.* Again, the absence of any MS evidence for such piecemeal manufacture of the letter should make us very chary of adopting such conclusions.

THE PURPOSE OF THE LETTER

Of recent years it has been fashionable to trace from the references to baptism and spiritual beginnings in the letter (3:21; 1:22; 2:2) the possibility that it is either a homily delivered at a baptism service, or even a baptism or paschal liturgy. Ingenious theories have been built up along these lines, analysing either 1:3 – 4:11 or 1:3 – 5:11 into such a structure, and the reader who wishes to explore them will need to refer to a fuller work of reference (such as A. M. Stibbs and A. F. Walls, *TNTC* or D. Guthrie, *New Testament Introduction: Hebrews to Revelation*). For present purposes it is sufficient to note that while such theories are not impossible, there is no direct evidence for them, and it is best under the circumstances to take the letter at its face value. This would suggest that Peter is writing to scattered groups of believers, some of whom have not long been Christians, to instruct them in the practical consequences of living out the Christian faith, and to warn them how to cope with trials and suffering. Such themes have obviously been treated by the writer for use in sermons, and so it is understandable if some of the material should bear the mark of the homiletical approach.

THE AFFINITIES OF THE LETTER

The Epistle is much indebted to the OT, especially to Isaiah and the Psalms (cf. 1:18–20, 24, 25; 2:6–8, 22ff.; 3:10–12; 4:17, 18). The writer gives no indication of any knowledge of the Gospels, but there are numerous allusions to incidents in the life of Jesus. Similarities can also be traced to Peter's speeches in the Acts.

There are many verbal affinities with Romans and Hebrews: here it is well said that the writers 'breathed the same spiritual atmosphere'. By this time certain words and phrases would any-way have tended to become the accepted language of Christian experience. Again there are strong connections of theme with Ephesians and James, and while these are interesting to note (and a fuller commentary or introduction should be consulted for the details) it is dangerous to build any theories on them.

THE THEOLOGY OF THE LETTER

Peter writes from the standpoint of the practical theologian. The letter abounds in Christian doctrine, but it is doctrine related to life, as may be seen from the following summary.

Doctrine of God

The practical relationship between the three Persons of the Trinity is clearly set out in 1:1, 2. God is sovereign, and so can be trusted (4:19); He is holy, and so is to be copied (1:15, 16); He is a Father, and so His sons must live up to the family name (1:17); and the fact that He has predestined His people is a ground for assurance (1:2).

Doctrine of Christ

He was sinless, obedient, and prepared to suffer to the limit—this is an example for us (2:21–24). He died and rose again: we must die to sin and live by His risen power (2:24; 4:1). His work is seen in terms of redemption (1:18, 19), reconciliation, the sin-offering and the substitute (all in 3:18), and He was predestined for this very purpose by the Father's love (1:20, 21). This is at once the ground of faith and hope, and the incentive to holiness and love (1:21, 22).

Doctrine of the Holy Spirit

He is seen both as the agent of sanctification (1:2), the author of Scripture (1:11) and the one who enables the preachers of the gospel to carry out their work (1:12).

Doctrine of Scripture

Its authoritative nature is stressed by the way the writer appeals to the OT for confirmation of his teaching (1:24, 25; 2:6–8; 3:10–12). Its source is seen to be in the guiding of the writers by the Holy Spirit (1:11) and its enduring quality is stressed by quotation from the OT (1:23, 25). It is also depicted as a seed, by which the new birth is effected in human lives as men hear and respond to the preaching of the gospel (cf. 1:23 with 25).

Doctrine of the church

Peter has a high regard for the corporate nature of the people of God, entered by the individual believer at the new birth (2:2–5; cf. 1:22, 23). This is God's building, on the foundation of Christ Himself (2:6–8), and as such it is the inheritor of the blessings promised to Israel (2:9, 10). Its twofold function is to offer worship to God and to witness before men (2:5, 9) and already it has a ministry which is a very responsible and sacred office (5:1–4).

Doctrine of eschatology

The writer lives under the shadow of the great unveiling, and he prefers to use this Greek root (apocalyp-) to describe the return of Christ. Thus he reminds his readers that the unseen Christ is never far away, and points them to the glories they will share when He re-appears. It will be the consummation of salvation and entry into the full inheritance (1:5), the moment when faith is finally honoured (1:7; 4:13), and the full extent of God's grace discovered (1:13), Christ's glory shared (5:1) and faithful service rewarded (5:4). Expectancy of His return is a most compelling argument for holy living and careful stewardship now (4:7–11, 17, 18).

This is a challenging letter, written by one whose heart had lost none of the fire of love stirred up by the Master's own challenge by the Sea of Tiberias (cf. Jn. 21:1, 15–19). In its lines there is all the vividness of the personal recollections of a follower of Jesus Christ.

OUTLINE OF CONTENTS

COMMENTARY

1:1, 2 OPENING ADDRESS

In accordance with contemporary custom, Peter begins by declaring his identity and authority, and names those to whom the letter is addressed. These are Christians by now scattered throughout the Roman provinces of Asia Minor, who have been brought by God into a relationship to each Person of the Trinity. The Father has *chosen* them and set them apart by the Spirit that they might live a life of *obedience to Jesus Christ*, being cleansed for such a walk by the *sprinkling with his blood*. To such Peter sends greetings for the increase upon them of the characteristic blessings of Old (*peace, i.e.* well-being) and New (*grace*) Covenants.

Notes. 1 *Apostle*: Gk. 'one sent'. *Exiles of the Dispersion* would seem best understood as referring to mixed churches of Jewish and Gentile Christians (see Introduction, under 'Destination of the letter'). 2 *Sprinkling with his blood* may refer to obtaining the benefits of Christ's death (Heb. 9:13, 14), participating in the benefits of the New Covenant (*cf.* Ex. 24:3–8 with Mk. 14:24), or the regular cleansing needed during our earthly pilgrimage (see 1 Jn. 1:7). The position lends weight to the last reference, but Peter may well have had all in mind: at the commencement of the Old Covenant the promise of obedience by God's people is ratified by the sprinkling of the blood of the covenant sacrifice on the altar and on the people (Ex. 24:1–11). The Greek *charis* (*grace*) comes from the same root as the customary Hellenistic introduction to a letter (*chaire*—'greetings') and is a deliberate play on words, giving greetings to Gentile and Jew, to whom *peace* was the normal greeting.

1:3–9 SALVATION: ITS NATURE

Mention of the Christian's position before God leads Peter, following the pattern of some of Paul's Epistles, to pour out thanksgiving to God as he elaborates these benefits. So great are they that it is possible to pass joyfully through times of testing holding by faith to a Christ they have not seen: such faith is the road to full and final salvation.

3–5 As Peter surveys the richness of the salvation believers enjoy, he cites its source (*his great mercy*), its scope (*born anew*; *cf.* Jn. 3:1–21), its effect (*a living hope*), its means (*through the resurrection . . . from the dead*), its Agent (*of*

Jesus Christ) and its goal (*to an inheritance*). In these verses salvation is seen in all its tenses: Christians have been born anew by the mercy of God, are being guarded by the power of God and look forward to obtaining complete deliverance from all evil *in the last time*. 6, 7 Such blessings from God should lead to rejoicing in spite of difficulties, for the purpose of earthly trials is to sift out what is really genuine in our faith. 8, 9 This triumphant faith in the unseen Christ has two results for the believer: at present an inexpressible joy even in the midst of adversity, and for the future the prospect of the fuller realization and enjoyment of salvation.

Notes. 4 *Imperishable, undefiled, and unfading; i.e.* liable neither to destruction nor defilement from without, nor to decay from within. 5 The supreme cause of the Christian's preservation is *God's power*, the subordinate means, *faith*. 6 The marginal reading shows that the verb here could be imperative, but is better as a statement of fact. *In this* is the wrong gender to refer to salvation, and probably looks back to the fact stated in the past three verses rather than to *the last time*. The connection with the next clause could be causal rather than concessive: we rejoice because we are suffering *various trials* (see Mt. 5:11, 12). The Greek word for *various* emphasizes their diversity, and is used again in this letter to describe the grace of God, which alone can meet these trials (4:10). Peter stresses that such trials will be relatively brief, *for a little while*, and do not fall outside the permissive will of God (AV 'if need be' is closer to the original Greek here). 7 The genuine and deepened faith which results from such trials will, at His revelation (*i.e.* 'unveiling'), bring glory both to Jesus Christ and to the one who has been thus tested. The theme of suffering is resumed later in the Epistle at 2:19–23; 3:14–17; 4:1–6, 12–19; 5:10. 8 Compare the Lord's beatitude to Thomas in Jn. 20:29.

1:10–12 SALVATION: ITS REVELATION

This salvation was the subject of careful investigation by the prophets who foretold it, and they were shown that the things they were proclaiming would be finally understood only by those to whom the *good news* of Jesus Christ was preached. So wonderful is this salvation that it has not yet been fully revealed even to the *angels* (see Rom. 8:19).

Notes. **10, 11** *The prophets* most naturally refers to the writers of the OT whose twofold theme was *the grace* that was destined for God's people and the *sufferings* and *subsequent glory* that were destined for Christ (there is a vivid parallelism here). It is a forced interpretation to take this as a reference to Christian prophets of the NT age. Note the statement here of the inspiration of the OT writers: *cf.* Lk. 24:25–27, 44–47; Jn. 5:39, 45–47; Mt. 5:17. The same Spirit who guided the OT prophets guided the NT preachers in declaring this good news effectively to Peter's readers.

1:13 – 5:4 SALVATION: ITS PRACTICAL OUTWORKINGS

The whole of the rest of this letter is concerned with showing how these great truths of the Christian faith are to be applied by those who believe them to all kinds of situations. As the content becomes mainly ethical, we are constantly referred back to the great themes of the gospel as the reasons behind such Christian behaviour, and Peter takes pains to show how the salvation described so magnificently in the opening paragraphs can and should result in men and women living out the life of Christ's disciples even in the most adverse circumstances.

1:13–21 Holiness of life

13 In view of such a salvation and such good news, Christians are called to exercise mental diligence and moral discipline: this is to be done by looking joyfully and confidently forward to the *grace* that *the revelation of Jesus Christ* will bring. **14–16** Living thus in the light of His return will call for obedience of life (*cf.* Lk. 12:35–48), and this obedience will be worked out by modelling their behaviour on the holiness of the God who has called them to Himself (*cf.* Mt. 5:48). This is the only positive antidote to having their lives moulded by the often conflicting desires of their previously unenlightened state. Unbridled passions are the product of spiritual ignorance, but God's pattern of behaviour for His people is based on His own revealed character. **17** To claim to be the children of such a heavenly Father, who is also an utterly just Judge, calls for reverent behaviour during one's earthly life, which is to be regarded as but a brief exile from His presence. **18, 19** A further motive for such behaviour lies in the fact that the Christian's freedom from the emptiness of pagan superstition or Pharisaic formalism was purchased at such immense cost. **20, 21** Reference to Christ leads Peter at once to develop the theme of the greatness of His work and its results: He stresses the pre-historical and transcendent nature of this and the phrase *at the end of the times*, referring to Christ's appearing, stresses His finality. Such a mighty work of Christ, coupled with the fact that God subsequently *raised* and glorified Him, provides the Christian with more than adequate grounds for entire *confidence* in

such a God as the object both of our faith in the present and our hope for the future.

Notes. **13** *That is coming* (Gk. 'being conferred'): the present participle indicates certainty. *At the revelation.* See v. 7 for other concomitants of Christ's return. **14** *Obedient children* is a Hebraism suggesting that Obedience is their mother whose character they should have inherited. *Conformed*; *cf.* Rom. 12:2. **16** *You shall be holy*; see Lv. 11:44, 45; 19:2; *cf.* Ex. 19:5, 6. The meaning of this in terms of human behaviour was, of course, made plain in the life of Jesus (Jn. 1:18). **17** On God's justice as Judge see Peter's words in Acts 10:34; *cf.* also Dt. 10:17. **18, 19** The language used here is reminiscent of that in both Mark (10:45) and John (1:29, 36; *cf.* Rev. 5:6 with Is. 53:7, where LXX uses the same word for 'lamb') on the atonement. *Without blemish* refers to the moral and without *spot* to the physical perfection of the sacrificial victim (see Lv. 22:17–25 and Ex. 12:5 for these requirements). **21** RSV translates the final clause of this verse as a consequence, and this is preferable to the AV and RV which make it a purpose clause, 'so that your faith and hope might be in God.' In fact, faith and hope in God are both the purpose and the result of Christ's resurrection and ascension: the reading of RSV mg. is grammatically possible, but does not appear to follow the argument so well.

1:22–25 Love for the brethren

22 The life of obedience already referred to (vv. 2, 14) will result in the purity required before God of those who are to reflect the Father's holiness, and should lead to a genuine love for one's fellow-Christians: the reality of this should be evidenced by its intensity (*earnestly*) and depth (*from the heart*). **23–25** Such love is motivated by the sharing of a new and heavenly birth, mediated by the *living and abiding word of God*. Peter identifies this regenerating Word with the preaching of the gospel.

Notes. **22** *Earnestly* (Gk. *ektenōs*). This word is used in the NT here and in 4:8 (of love), and in Lk. 22:44 and Acts 12:5 (of prayer). It denotes supreme effort, 'with every muscle strained'. **24, 25** Is. 40:6, 8 stresses the enduring and dynamic quality of the Word of God.

2:1–3 Desire for spiritual growth

Such a wonderful new birth calls for a consequent concern for growth, for its subjects are now spiritual *babes*. This is to be achieved negatively by putting away all forms of evil, and positively by fostering the desire for *spiritual milk*, and keeping in mind the goal of full and final salvation as the end for which the new life is given.

Notes. **2** *Spiritual* is the Greek *logikon*, which can equally well mean 'of the word', as AV. Heb. 5:12 contains the same idea, and the OT and rabbinical writings are rich in allusions to the Law or the Word of God as spiritual sustenance. **3** Quotation of Ps. 34:8 may be understood either as a motive for the desire of v. 2, or the desire may be an evidence that one has *tasted the kindness of the Lord.*

2:4–10 Membership of God's people

Christian growth must be seen in its corporate as well as its individual aspect, and Peter now turns to that. **4, 5** The thought this provokes is so thrilling that Peter mixes his metaphors, but the thread is fairly easy to follow. By constant communion with Christ, the living Stone, Christians will become like Him, living stones. The purpose of stones is not to be kept in isolation, but so to be joined together as to form a building. This, however, describes only one aspect of the corporate life, and by itself is insufficient as a description, for, once built into the edifice, the stone's role is passive. So Peter switches thought from the structure, presumably of the Temple, to those who actively function inside the building in corporate worship: here is the active side of the life of the Christian family. **6–8** In a parenthesis he takes up the references to the living stone, and shows how both have been fulfilled in Christ, one in the case of believers, and the other of unbelievers. Whatever men's reactions, whether they come in faith to the living Stone, or reject Him like the builders, God's purposes are supreme: Christ becomes the Head of the corner, the Keystone of the building, and those who *disobey the word* can only stumble and fall against Him, as God decreed such should. **9, 10** In contrast to the position of the unbelievers last referred to, Peter shows how the Christian church has inherited the privileges promised to the people of God in the OT: *you are . . . that you may* is a salutary reiteration of the biblical principle that such privilege involves responsibility. Those who inherit Israel's blessings have Israel's work to do, and must publish abroad the greatness of the God who has done so much for them.

Notes. **4, 6–8** Two strands of prophecy are drawn together here: the precious foundation stone of Is. 28:16 (v. 6 quotes LXX, as does Paul in Rom. 9:33) and the rejected keystone of Ps. 118:22. Jesus applied the latter reference to Himself in Mk. 12:10 and parallels, and Peter quoted it of Him before the Sanhedrin in Acts 4:11. Jesus Christ is both the Foundation on which the Christian church is built, and the Keystone into which it grows up (see 1 Cor. 3:11; Eph. 4:11–13). By bringing the two metaphors together Peter emphasizes that Christ is precious only to believers (as the original context showed), and that those who refuse to believe find Him a Stone which causes them to *stumble*—here is added a quotation from Is. 8:14. **5** *Be yourselves built* is difficult unless taken as NEB 'let yourselves be built', but the AV and RV indicative 'you are being built' (the form is the same) is better. *Priesthood* is collective rather than abstract: *i.e.* 'body of priests'. V. 9 below emphasizes that this is the privilege of all believers. The idea of *spiritual sacrifices* is

elaborated in Rom. 12:1, 2 and Heb. 13:15, 16. *Through Jesus Christ* can be taken either to explain how the sacrifices are offered, or why they are acceptable. **8** *Destined* need not imply more than that those who disobey the Word of God, both written and living, are bound to find that instead of being the foundation on which to build He is embarrassingly in their way and will sooner or later cause them to trip and fall. (For further discussion of the doctrine of predestination implicit here, see *NBD*, art. 'Predestination'.)

9 appropriates to Christian believers the promises of Ex. 19:5, 6; Is. 43:20, 21, for which Paul argued in Rom. 9. *Race* implies physical descent, and may refer to the Godward and manward relationship brought about by the new birth. The root from which *priesthood* (Gk. *hieratyma*) is derived is never used in the NT to describe the Christian ministry, but rather the corporate function of all believers (*cf.* Rev. 1:6). Throughout the OT the kingship and the priesthood were never united, except in Melchizedek and Messiah (Saul sinned when he attempted to combine both functions; 1 Sa. 13:5–15). The Christian enjoys both through being 'in Christ'. *A holy nation*; *i.e.* called to reflect the character of the God who has called them (*cf.* 1:16). *God's own people* draws on the imagery of the Eastern potentate, who kept a treasure-chamber apart from the exchequer he shared with his government ministers. This was his own privy purse, and the idea originates in Ex. 19:5, being mentioned also by Paul in Tit. 2:14. The latter part of this verse links with vv. 5, 6 to stress the twofold ministry to which God's people are called: offering spiritual sacrifices to God and declaring His *wonderful deeds* (RV 'excellencies' is closer to the original abstract noun) to men. **10** Such a response, both Godward and manward, will be natural and spontaneous when the Christian has grasped that all these blessings spring directly from the free grace and mercy of God. To bring this point home Peter quotes the theme of Ho. 1:8 – 2:1; 2:23.

2:11 – 3:12 Witness in the world

Since Christians are in this very special way God's people, their true home is with Him, and so their conduct in this world and in its relationships is to be that of those who are only passing through it, but in doing so they are to show by their behaviour that they are citizens of a better country.

2:11, 12 General principles. From 1:15 Peter has been dealing with the positive side of holiness, living to God. Now he takes up briefly the negative side, abstinence, which he will resume at 4:1 in the light of the theology of 3:18–22. Such abstinence silences the allegations against Christians which the non-Christian world was already making. Here Peter echoes our Lord's instructions in Mt. 5:16.

Notes. **11** *Aliens and exiles.* This language, reminiscent of 1:1, 17 and Heb. 11:13, derives originally from Gn. 23:4. *Passions of the flesh.* The latter term is not synonymous with 'physical', but is to be understood in its ethical sense, as in Gal. 5:19ff. These passions are to be refused, as they militate against the immortal part of our being. **12** *Gentiles* is used in view of the church's relation to Israel shown in vv. 9, 10. *The day of visitation* is the day when God will visit the earth and search out men's hearts in judgment.

2:13–25 In society. 13–15 Such good conduct is to be expressed in a submissive acceptance of the demands of *every human institution*, and it is striking that Peter, writing probably in the age of Nero, still sees the state as the God-appointed society for the maintenance of moral values, in which the Christian's uprightness should raise him or her above the slanders or suspicions of the ignorant. Christians must render to Caesar what is his due, and although Peter knew well what it meant to refuse Caesar when the latter claimed what is God's (Acts 4:19, 20; 5:29), he does not lay emphasis on that duty here. **16** The Christian's freedom is the liberty to live as the *servants of God*, doing what He wishes, and not the licence to do as one pleases, indulging sinful lusts under the pretext of 'permissiveness'. **17** The practical outworkings of this are outlined in the four brief commands which follow. *All men* are to be honoured, as those for whom Christ died and in whom the divine likeness can be restored, while there is a special relationship of *love* within the Christian brotherhood. *God* is to be approached with worship, and *the emperor* with respect.

18–25 Peter follows these principles with detailed instructions for two groups of people whose inferior position in the ancient world could make life, particularly as a Christian, very difficult for them. The lot of *servants* would be easy under a good master, but they were often treated *unjustly*. Patience while suffering a deserved punishment is no virtue, but the Christian is called to accept the harsh treatment of an unkind master gracefully, and so to win God's approval. Such perseverance in doing good, and patience under suffering, are even the Christian's vocation, for it is part of the fellowship of Christ's sufferings (*cf.* Phil. 3:10). This reference at once leads Peter to describe vividly the Lord's behaviour during His sufferings, and inevitably he goes on to remind his readers of the benefits we enjoy as a result of them.

Notes. 13 *For the Lord's sake* is a reminder both of the example and the teaching of Jesus (*cf.* Mt. 22:21). *Supreme*; *i.e.* over human institutions. **17** quotes Pr. 24:21, but Peter will not apply the same word to our attitude both to God and to the emperor as the former writer does. **18** *Servants*: the household slaves found regularly in Greek and Roman families. **19** *Mindful of God* is literally 'on account of the knowledge of God', and may indicate either the master's reason for inflicting the undeserved punishment, annoyance at the slave's Christian faith, or the slave's

motive for accepting it, awareness that God knows and shares his sufferings. Peter probably had in mind the words of Jesus in Mt. 5:11f., 46f.; Lk. 6:22f., 32–35; Jn. 15:18–21. **21** *Example* (Gk. *hypogrammos*) is used only here in the NT, and refers to an outline drawing or copy-book letters to be followed by the pupil. **22, 23** See Mk. 14:61, 65; 15:29; Jn. 19:1–9, *etc.* Peter quotes Is. 53:9 and 7. **24, 25** This description might be that of an eyewitness, the words are so graphic. *Bore*: literally 'carried up', as RSV mg. The language is vivid and deliberately sacrificial (*cf.* Heb. 7:27). The reference to the purpose of Jesus' sufferings, citing Is. 53:12 and 5, gives the motive for ours. The response to the sin-bearing Saviour can only be to return to Him as *Shepherd* and to *die to sin and live to righteousness.* The imagery again reflects Is. 53:6 and Jn. 10. *Guardian*, or 'overseer', is the word used regularly to describe the function of a shepherd, and so of a spiritual pastor, and the English 'bishop' (so AV) is derived from this root.

3:1–7 In the family. Similar submissive conduct is now enjoined of wives, for the ancient world classed women and slaves together as 'inferior beings'. Christianity ennobled the status of both, and Peter stresses the spiritual equality of man and wife as *joint heirs*, while maintaining the wife's subordination to her husband within the economy of God, demonstrated by her physical weakness and the example of Sarah. Christian women were often married to unbelieving husbands, and Peter stresses the importance of Christlike behaviour to win such. Finally, marriage is lifted to its highest plane by the call to husbands to treat their wives with consideration and respect, on the basis of their shared faith, and with the practical purpose of being a praying partnership, which must not be hindered by any misunderstanding between them. These last instructions are obviously directed to Christian couples, graphically described as sharing the inheritance of God's gracious gift of eternal life.

Notes. 3 *Outward adorning.* . . . The nouns which follow contrast sharply with the attitude of v. 2, as they are all active and stress the time and energy spent on such personal adornment: God prefers to see beauty of character which will never fade. **4** *A gentle and quiet spirit* is one which puts up with the impositions of others without causing any itself. Such a character has a good pedigree within the people of God—Sarah, Rebecca, Ruth, Hannah, *etc.*—and makes its possessor the true daughter, by spiritual descent and likeness, of Sarah. **6** *Calling him lord* may refer to Gn. 18:12, where the word 'husband' can also mean 'lord' or 'master'. **7** *Likewise* (*i.e.* 'in the same spirit') may refer back to 2:17, to the general admonition to 'honour all men', or it may look to the wife's behaviour and urge husbands to reciprocate with mutual love and understanding. Phillips translates RSV's *live considerately* as 'try to understand'. *Weaker sex*: see Gn. 2:18; 3:16.

3:8–12 In the fellowship. Peter now leaves the

realm of special relationships and concludes this section with a summary of the attitudes which Christians should display both in their actions and reactions. This is all contained in the one word *blessing*, i.e. calling down God's gracious power and love on all men, even on those who wish or do us harm. Such behaviour is encouraged by the Christian's knowledge that he himself will ultimately inherit God's blessing, and this argument is supported by quotation of Ps. 34:12-16. The Christian is called, no less than his OT counterpart, to walk the way of blamelessness and uprightness, actively pursuing peace with all men, and for the same reason, that God watches over and blesses such behaviour, but sets Himself against its opposite.

Notes. 8 *Unity of spirit* is not the best translation as the word, used only here in the NT, means literally 'of the same mind' (*cf.* AV, RV) and refers to the unity Christians should experience through sharing the mind of Christ (see Phil. 2:5; Col. 3:2). This will enable them to enter into the feelings of others (*sympathy* is derived from the Greek word used here) and to experience His love for their fellow-Christians. This quality has been mentioned before in 1:22 and is emphasized again in 4:8. It should be the hallmark of a Christian fellowship. The *tender heart* brings a new Christian meaning to an old Greek word for 'courageous', and the *humble mind* enjoined with it (see also 5:5, 6) emphasizes that the secret of the character described in this verse lies in a low estimate of oneself and a high concern for others. **9** is reminiscent of 2:23. See the references there to the example of Jesus in this respect, together with Lk. 6:27f.; 23:34. *This* could refer to the role of blessing as our inheritance, in which case the inheritance is viewed as the purpose of such behaviour, almost suggesting that it is a reward to be earned. It seems more in line with NT teaching and the spirit of the passage to take the clause *that you may obtain a blessing* as an expansion of *this*, defining the nature of our vocation. This then complements the earlier statement of 2:21, that the Christian's vocation is to follow his Lord's example of suffering and with Him inherit the blessings God has prepared for him (*cf.* Rom. 8:17, 18). **10-12** The opening of the quotation from Ps. 34:12-16 is altered here to fit the context, changing the verb from the second to the third person imperative. *Life* was probably intended by the psalmist to refer to temporal existence on earth: in the present context Peter may well be using the word of eternal life, giving it the same connotation as in v. 7, especially as he changes the original 'desires life, and covets many days' to (lit.) 'he who wishes to love life and to see good days'.

3:13 - 4:6 Witness under persecution

13-17 Because Peter was assured of God's sovereignty as well as His justice, he follows this last remark with a rhetorical question and comment which suggest that zeal on the Christ-

ian's part for what is right is not likely to lead to persecution. This seems strangely inconsistent with the warnings of Jesus (*cf.* Mt. 5:10-12; 10:17-22; 24:9; Jn. 15:18 - 16:4), the teaching and experience of Paul (Acts 14:22; 16:19ff.; 19:23ff., *etc.*) and Peter's own words in the next chapter (4:12-19) or even vv. 16 and 17 of this very chapter. In view of this it is probably right to lay the stress in this question on the verb *to harm* (Gk. *kakōsōn*). Persecution may well come upon the Christian, but it cannot ultimately do him injury, for the experience can lead to blessing (v. 14; *cf.* 1:6-9), and the final issue can be left with God (4:19), who watches over His own and their persecutors (3:12). In consequence believers are urged not to be afraid: the positive antidote to fear is to be found in giving to Christ the special place that is His due right at the centre of our lives, where He is to reign as Lord. Such true fear of the Lord, expressing itself both in upright behaviour and in a reasoned statement of faith, will drive out all lesser fears and eventually shame the detractors.

18-22 This kind of suffering on the part of the innocent could be the will of God, and mention of this leads Peter to elaborate how the divinely-ordained suffering of the innocent Christ not only resulted in the benefits of salvation, but also culminated in His vindication and glorification at the hands of the Father. It is not easy to follow the thread of the argument here: so anxious is the writer to bring out the fact that suffering was purposeful in the case of Jesus, that he adduces two consequences of His death. The first is familiar to all Christians: it opened for man the way to God. The second is not so familiar, but it appears from this verse that when, by death, Christ's spirit was separated from His body, He was enabled to go and preach in the spirit world. Reference to this sphere links the writer in thought with Noah, whose experience of salvation is a striking parallel with that which baptism symbolizes. The faith which is the believer's response to God in baptism is made possible by the resurrection of Jesus from the dead, and Peter is now linking both strands of thought together again by seeing the glorification of Jesus not only as the divine sequel to His sacrificial death, but the compelling reason for men to respond to Him in faith. See further comments in the Notes below.

4:1-6 Suffering in the flesh is therefore to be accepted, not merely in order to follow the example of Christ, but also because such behaviour makes it easier for the sufferer to follow the will of God, especially as he is thereby more closely united with Christ. Here the mention of baptism in 3:21 may have prompted Peter to follow the same sort of argument as Paul follows in Rom. 6. Baptism symbolizes the believer's entry into the benefits obtained by Christ's sufferings and death, and in undergoing it the subject is regarded as mystically sharing those sufferings and death. The consequence of such a death in Rom. 6:11 is that 'you also must consider yourselves dead to sin and alive to God in Christ Jesus', and this is the consequence Peter is stating here, adding a note of urgency by contrasting time spent in the past on selfish indulgence with the opportunity for serving God in the future. Such changed behaviour on the Christian's part often leads to persecution by those who resent their withdrawal from their previous habits, but the Christian must remember that it is to God that all must give account of their conduct. The comprehensiveness of this judgment leads Peter (v. 6) to make in parenthesis the point that the death of Christians proves the value of preaching the gospel to men while they are alive, since though they have now received in their bodies God's judgment on sin, their spirits are still alive with Him (for other interpretations of this verse see Notes below).

Notes. 3:14 The quotation from Is. 8:12, 13 suggests that the genitive *of them* should be taken as subjective ('do not share the fears felt by them') rather than objective, as RSV ('do not experience the fear which they inspire'). There is also a possibility that the command here and in Isaiah could be a warning against apostasy, which was often encouraged by fear of persecution— 'do not share their objects of religious reverence' (Gk. *phobeisthai* is used in this cultic sense in Lk. 1:50; 18:2, 4; Acts 13:16, 26, *etc.*). 17 The mood of the verb *should be* is optative in the Greek. This suggests that the possibility of suffering *for doing right* is rather remote. Peter may have expressed himself thus to allay the fears of his readers. *God's will*; *i.e.* that you suffer.

18 This verse is one of the most succinct and yet profound statements of the doctrine of the atonement. Jesus is seen as dealing with the fundamental problem of man's broken relationship with God in three ways: *a.* He made the perfect offering for sin (*cf.* Heb. 9:11–14; 10:1–10), thereby fulfilling the requirements of the law; *b.* He endured the death due to unrighteousness as the penalty imposed by the law on sinners (*cf.* 2 Cor. 5:21; Rom. 6:23); and *c.* He thereby removed the barrier between man and God which had been caused by sin. *Died.* The RSV mg. reading 'suffered' is well attested but would make no difference to the argument. *For sins.* Having stressed so much the value of Christ's sufferings as our Example (see 2:21), Peter is anxious to redress the balance by stating also their uniqueness and efficacy. He uses the term here (Gk. *peri hamartiōn*) which is used in the singular in the LXX of Lv. 5:11; 7:37 to describe the sin-offering. Other NT writers use the phrase with similar reference: *e.g.* Rom. 8:3; Heb. 10:18; *cf.* Heb. 5:3; 13:11. A. M. Stibbs comments: 'Since Christ Himself was sinless this kind of phraseology implies here that His suffering was atoning or propitiatory' (*TNTC, 1 Peter*, p. 141). *Once for all* is the Greek *hapax*, which stresses the finality of the work of Christ (*cf.* Heb. 9:28). *The righteous for the unrighteous* contains the

preposition *hyper*, 'on behalf of', and shows that Christ's suffering was vicarious. The one Man, whose perfect righteousness meant that He never deserved to die, endured the pains of death on behalf of those who deserved to die. In this way He took our place and endured our punishment: the language reflects strongly that of Is. 53:6. *Bring us to God* is again technical language, the Greek verb *prosagō* having the idea of admitting a person to an audience with a king: from this root comes the noun translated 'access' in Rom. 5:2; Eph. 2:18; 3:12. *Spirit* contrasts here with the *flesh*: Jesus died physically, in that His bodily functions (respiration and circulation of the blood, *etc.*) ceased, and He died spiritually, in that He underwent the separation from God consequent on bearing the sins of the world and expressed by the cry of dereliction (Mk. 15:34 and parallels). But spiritual death is not annihilation, and once He had undergone in full God's judgment on sin His spirit was released from the body: the Greek of Mk. 15:37 and parallels uses the common but vivid metaphor of 'breathing out' His spirit.

19 This verse poses two inter-related questions: when did Jesus preach *to the spirits in prison*, and who were they? Traditionally the verse has been taken to refer to the chronological sequel to Jesus' death, when His spirit passed into the realms of the departed: this verse is taken with Acts 2:31 and Eph. 4:9 to establish the clause in the Creeds referring to the descent into hell. Some would, however, deny this reference here, and suggest rather that it was either the pre-incarnation Spirit of Christ preaching through Noah to his contemporaries, or the post-Pentecost Spirit of Christ preaching through the apostles to Jews and Gentiles: in both cases the *prison* is interpreted as the body, or for the former interpretation it could refer to their present habitation. Either of these views involves a harsh transference of thought and subject. If we follow the other view that Jesus did go and proclaim (the basic meaning of *preached*) His triumph to the spirit-world, we are then faced with a further two lines of thought. Some suggest that this was a proclamation of the gospel to those who had died before the time of Christ and had not had the chance to hear, repent and believe: of this class those who perished in the Flood are a notorious example. The use of *spirits* in this sense can be supported by the usage of Heb. 12:23. On the other hand it can be argued from such passages as 2 Pet. 2:4–10; Jude 6 and reference to Gn. 6:1–8 that the spirits in prison are the fallen angels, and that this interpretation is more consistent with the usage of the word *pneumata*, spirits, in Scripture when it occurs without qualification. This would seem on the whole the best interpretation of a difficult passage, and the thought is then taken up again in v. 22 where Christ's triumph is seen to be complete.

20 *Did not obey.* If the preceding interpreta-

tion is correct, this could refer to the events of Gn. 6:1-4. Those who relate the spirits in prison to human beings suggest that Noah's contemporaries are singled out as being exceptionally wicked and therefore needing to be informed of Christ's victory or given a chance to repent: on this point commentators diverge who follow this interpretation. *Patience* was displayed by God as He gave them opportunity to repent while the ark was being built (*cf.* Gn. 6:3; 2 Pet. 3:5-9). *A few* is a biblical emphasis (*cf.* Mt. 7:14; 22:14; Lk. 13:23, 24). In the OT it is paralleled by the idea of the 'remnant' (*cf.* Rom. 9:27-29). Even so, Paul could write of the 'many' who will be made righteous (Rom. 5:19). *Through water* has a twofold reference: in the local sense the ark brought them safely through the water which was the means of inflicting God's judgment on others. The preposition also has an instrumental sense (as in AV 'by' or 'by means of'), and so the element which was the means of destruction for their contemporaries was for them the means of deliverance into a new life. Both ideas would appear to be involved.

21 *Corresponds.* The Greek word *antitypon* originally referred to the impression left on a surface by the *typos*, or seal, and so describes the kind of correspondence that a stamp has to its die. The picture strikes Peter as a parallel to baptism, for here the water symbolizes God's judgment on sin, and deliverance into a new life. Jesus spoke of His coming death, by which He underwent God's judgment on sin, as a baptism (*cf.* Mk. 10:38, 39; Lk. 12:50), and this association of ideas is preserved in Rom. 6:3ff., where baptism is seen as a mystical uniting of the believer with Christ in His death. So, paradoxically, the death which was the means of Christ's enduring God's judgment on sin is the means whereby the believer can enter into new life. Peter rids his readers of any false notions about baptism by stressing that the efficacy of baptism lies not in the outward symbolism of the *removal of dirt from the body*, but in the inner response of faith to God. *An appeal to God for a clear conscience* is a translation based on the use of the word *eperōtēma* (*appeal*) in the LXX and NT Greek. Reference to the papyri shows that contemporary usage employed this word for the solemnly attested pledge made by any party undertaking a contract: in that case the phrase could mean 'the pledge to God of a good conscience', and is closer to the AV 'answer'. In any case, the great fact which makes real and possible all that baptism typifies is *the resurrection of Jesus Christ*, and it is by this means ultimately that we are saved (*cf.* 1:3). **22** Reference to this great fact leads Peter to repeat the verb 'went' of v. 19, suggesting a triumphal procession on the part of Jesus, culminating in His session (in direct fulfilment of Ps. 110:1) and position of supreme power.

4:1 The RSV mg. readings are of little importance here, as neither adds anything to what has already been said in 3:18. *The same thought* appears from the context to refer to what has been said about Christ's death and the symbolism of baptism. Christ's sufferings led to the death of His flesh and enabled His spirit to enter a completely new mode of existence, and this should be seen also in the life of the believer. In this case *whoever has suffered* need not refer to those who undergo physical suffering, but includes all who in mystical union, symbolized in their baptism, share the sufferings of Christ. Such union should now be made effective by claiming cessation from sin and a new life of service to God. **2** *So as to live* can be taken either as the purpose of arming oneself with the same thought, or the consequence of ceasing from sin: probably both ideas are included. *Passions*. The plural stresses the diversity of desires and interests pulling a man in different directions (see the catalogue of them in v. 3): by contrast *the will* in the singular suggests that only in obedience to God can the human personality be properly integrated. **3** *Licentiousness* and all the following nouns are plural in the original, indicating a round of activities in which such behaviour is expressed. **5** *Living* is better than the old English 'quick', as in AV and the Creeds.

6 *The gospel was preached even to the dead* is taken above as referring to a possible source of attack on the Christians by their detractors. 'If you speak of the return of Christ, and possessing eternal life now, why do you die just like the rest of us?' the argument might run. 'Surely your people die no less than us: you are suffering just the same judgment as we do.' 'No,' says the apostle; 'those who have died (the dead) may be *judged in the flesh like men*, by suffering physical death, but, because *the gospel was preached* to them (while alive, when they responded), they are now living *in the spirit like God*.' The previous verse has emphasized the universality of judgment: men must either face it after death, or else anticipate it here on earth by responding to Christ and so having their sins dealt with in judgment by their union with Christ. In that case death will be merely the gateway to the fuller and freer life of the spirit: there will be no further judgment to bear. Others have interpreted *the dead* here as the spiritually dead, or as referring to all the dead, linking this preaching of the gospel with the proclamation of 3:19, and deducing therefrom a doctrine of the second chance of responding to the gospel being given after death; but this does not suit the context, and is not supported anywhere else in Scripture. *Like men . . . like God* can refer to judgment in the flesh as being the common lot of men, and life in the spirit the distinctive characteristic of God, or the preposition *kata* used here may mean 'in the sight of men' and 'in the sight of God'. Either rendering makes little difference to the meaning.

4:7-11 Use of opportunities

Mention of judgment prompts the reminder that the final judgment is no remote contingency, but that Christ's return to wind up this present order of things could happen at any time. For that reason it is urgent that Christians practise their calling, displaying self-control, mutual love, and a diligent stewardship of the gifts God has given them. This is the life which will bring glory to God (*cf.* Mt. 5:16).

Notes. 7 *End* is the Greek word *telos*, which also means 'goal'. The end of the present system is not only the climax but the purpose towards which God has been and is working. *Sane* means 'of safe mind': the Christian's aim in the midst of fears and uncertainty must be to keep in touch with God. Phillips's translation is helpful here: 'be calm, self-controlled men of prayer'. **8** *Unfailing*: see on 1:22. *Love covers a multitude of sins* is thought by some to be a reference to Pr. 10:12. It has been argued from this verse that love can earn forgiveness of sins, not only for the one who displays it, but for the recipient too. Most likely the meaning is that true love will overlook its neighbour's faults (*cf.* 1 Cor. 13:4–7 and Mt. 6:14, 15); it could just be taken to refer to God's love covering our sins, which is the motive for us to love one another. **9** *Hospitality* was an important factor in days of itinerant ministers and no church buildings (*cf.* Mt. 25:35; Rom. 12:13; 16:3–5a; 1 Tim. 3:2; Heb. 13:2). **10** *Each* implies that every Christian has some gift. Peter's remarks on stewardship are significant in view of the fact that Jesus spoke on this matter especially to Peter in Lk. 12:42ff. *Varied*: see on 1:6. **11** *Speaks . . . renders service* are taken as covering the two broad divisions of ministry within the Christian church—ministering the Word of God and 'serving tables' in various ways (see Acts 6:1ff.). Both ministries are equally God-given and can rely on God to make the necessary provision for their fulfilment. *Who utters* is not in the original, which could just as well be translated as AV, 'let him speak as the oracles of God'. *Oracles* is the Greek *logia*, which was used in classical times of divine utterances, and in Rom. 3:2 and Heb. 5:12 is applied to Scripture. *To him . . .* : for the significance of this ascription here see Introduction, under 'The unity of the letter' (p.1237).

4:12–19 Suffering for Christ

Peter now returns to his theme of suffering, and suggests further factors which will enable the Christian not merely to endure, but actually to rejoice in it. In the first place, it is a test to prove the reality of faith, and we should expect God to try (and thereby strengthen) this. It is also a sharing of Christ's sufferings, which were His pathway to glory, and so will they be for His follower. For that reason the Spirit of God will, even in persecution, be radiating the sufferer's life with glory; when persecution as a Christian is nobly borne by the innocent, his behaviour is a means of bringing glory to God. Such suffering is a reminder to His people that God is beginning His judgment with them, and they can at least look beyond the persecution to a glorious

future, in the light of which they can commit the issues of life in full confidence to the One who gave them life. By contrast the unrepentant sinner has nothing to look forward to here or hereafter once God begins to act in judgment.

Notes. 12 *Fiery ordeal* (Gk. 'exposure to fire with a view to testing'). This links with the argument of 1:6, 7. *Strange* is the adjective from the root of the verb used earlier in the verse and translated *do not be surprised*: 'surprising' would therefore be better, or else preserve *strange* in both places (as AV, RV). **13** *Be glad* is the verb used previously in 1:6, 8, and originally in Mt. 5:12. It has been argued from the usage in this verse of this verb in connection with the joy to be experienced at the unveiling of Christ that it should be a future tense and have the same reference in 1:8, but this is unnecessary in view of the other two references. See again 1:11; Rom. 8:17; 2 Tim. 2:12 for the association of suffering and glory. **14** *For the name* need not mean that it was already a criminal offence to be a Christian, for Jesus Himself suggested the possibility of suffering for His name's sake (*cf.* Mt. 10:22, and see Introduction, under 'Authorship', *b.*). *The spirit of glory . . .* : RV shows that *spirit* is missing from the first phrase in the original, and so it has been taken thus to refer to the Shekinah, the visible brightness which symbolized God's presence among His people (*cf.* Ex. 40:34, 35). This may be so, but the context and sentence structure make it more likely to be best taken as RSV: God's Spirit is the Spirit of glory as He manifests God's glory to His people by revealing Christ to them and transforming them into His image (*cf.* Jn. 16:14; 2 Cor. 3:18). The phrase may be coined from the LXX of Is. 11:2, though neither *glory* nor *power* (see RSV mg.) are mentioned there: *power* may have crept in from a marginal gloss. **15** *Mischief-maker* may seem out of place in this list of otherwise criminal characters, but there is a trace of grim humour in its conclusion. Christians are not likely to be guilty of the other more flagrant crimes, but are very often unable to resist the temptation to meddle in other people's affairs. **16** *Christian* occurs on only two other occasions in the NT, in Acts 11:26 and 26:28. In both cases it is generally assumed to have been used by others as a term of contempt, but there are two other possible derivations which may have significance. The Latin suffix *-ianus* may have been added to the Greek word *Christ* to indicate 'supporters of', in the same way that Herod's followers were called Herodians (Mk. 3:6, *etc.*). On the other hand, a Roman custom followed in adoption was that the person adopted into a Roman family took their name with this suffix and used it as his own. A person adopted into the family of Domitius would call himself Domitianus, and as Antioch was a very Roman city, the Christians there may well have applied the name to themselves as having been adopted into Christ's family (*cf.* Rom. 8:15–17; Eph. 1:5, *etc.*). *Under that name* is a better translation than AV 'on this behalf'. **17** *Judgment*: see Je. 25:29; Ezk. 9:6; Mal. 3:1–3 for this idea. *Household* is preferable to AV 'house'. **18** The quotation of Pr. 11:31 from the LXX underlines the argument of the previous verse, and is a reminder of Jesus' words in Lk. 23:31. **19** If such suffering is accepted in this light, then, far from giving up under it, the Christian will persevere in well-doing, and follow Christ's example by committing the outcome into God's hands. *Entrust* is the verb used by Jesus in Lk. 23:46 (citing the prayer of Ps. 31:5 used by the faithful Jew last thing at night) and this may be in mind here. Paul used the derivative noun in 2 Tim. 1:12 to express his confidence in God's safe keeping. *Creator* is used here probably as a reminder of God's power (see 1:5, and *cf.* the thought of Phil. 1:6).

5:1–4 Duties of the elders

The thought of the trial that is coming upon the people of God leads Peter to stress the need for leadership of the right kind. With his unique position and experience he urges the local church leaders to discharge their duties in a ready, enthusiastic and exemplary fashion, remembering to whom they are under-shepherds, and the reward He has promised for faithful service.

Notes. 1 *Elders* (Gk. *presbyteroi*) were appointed from earliest times to take spiritual charge of the infant churches which came into being with the spread of the gospel (*cf.* Acts 14:23; 20:17). Acts 15:2 shows that even the Jerusalem church had this order of ministry at an early date, and it probably derived from Jewish precedent (*cf.* Nu. 11:16–25 and see *NBD*, art. 'Elder'). Their task was primarily a pastoral one, and so in the early days of the church they were called not only by this title, which indicates their status, but also *episkopoi* ('bishops', 'overseers'), to describe their function. Hence the language of v. 2; Acts 20:28 shows the two words being used interchangeably. *Fellow elder* is not elsewhere found in the NT, but it is not an unusual word for Peter to use in this context, where he is anxious to emphasize his oneness with those he is exhorting. *Witness* has been objected to on the ground that Peter (according to Mt. 26:56; Lk. 23:49) was not present at the crucifixion. He was, however, present to see much of the Lord's sufferings, and such an objection cannot fairly be upheld (see Lk. 22:28, 54–62; Jn. 18:15–27). *Glory*: see on 4:13. **2** *Tend* is a pastoral metaphor (*i.e.* 'feed'; *cf.* Ps. 78:70–72) and a vivid reminder of the commission Peter had himself received from the Lord (Jn. 21:15ff.) and of Paul's charge to the Ephesian elders (Acts 20:28). *That is your charge* is an idiomatic phrase which could mean 'to the best of your ability': Erasmus and Calvin understood it thus, and so AV mg. suggests 'as much as in you is'. Either rendering suits the context: as translated by RSV it refers to that part of the flock which is each elder's particular responsibility. *Exercising the oversight* is left

in the margin as textual evidence is divided over its inclusion: nothing is lost by its omission. The verb used is the same root as that referred to in 2:25. *By constraint* can refer to a false sense of unworthiness, a reluctance for responsibility, or a desire to do no more than was morally required in the office: any one of these attitudes can lead to an unwillingness to take on the task or discharge it adequately. *As God would have you* (RSV mg.) is a possible translation of the Greek *kata theon*: it could also mean 'as God would do it', recalling the attitude of the Shepherd of souls in 2:25; Ps. 23; Jn. 10:11. *Shameful gain* suggests not that by this time the elders were receiving a stipend, but that there were opportunities for the unscrupulous man to make profit from illegitimate sources. This spirit need not be confined to the attitude to money: such self-seeking could also apply to the love of reputation or position. **3** *Domineering* is often the attitude of the worldly superior (*cf.* Mk. 10:42, where the same verb is used), but the Christian leader, rather than 'lording' it and getting what he can out of those in his charge, is to be an example, giving what he can contribute to them in the way of instruction, character-building, *etc*. *Those in your charge* (Gk. *klēroi*), *i.e.* 'your appointed portions'. *Klēros* was originally an allotment of land, then an office assigned by lot, and here refers to the flock assigned to a particular pastor. From this root comes our word 'cleric'. *Examples* is the word *typoi*, denoting a model or pattern to be copied (see on 3:21 for the derivative *antitypos*). **4** *Manifested*. Hitherto in the Epistle Peter has described the second advent in terms of an 'unveiling' or 'revelation' of Jesus Christ. The word used here (Gk. *phaneroō*) brings out the consequence of that revelation, that Jesus will be visible in His glory to all (*cf.* Rev. 1:7). *Unfading* is not the same word as in 1:4 (*amaranton*). Here it is *amarantinon*, 'of amaranth', a flower which gained its name from the former adjective because it was supposed to be unfading. This would contrast with the fading crowns of laurel leaves awarded to victors in the Greek games, which is the background of the allusion here (*cf.* 1 Cor. 9:25; 2 Tim. 4:8; Rev. 3:11; 4:4). *Of glory* probably refers to the share in glory also to be given to the wearer of the crown, as the 'crown of life' in Jas. 1:12; Rev. 2:10 speaks of the eternal life enjoyed by the wearer.

5:5–11 FINAL EXHORTATIONS AND ASSURANCE

As a consequence of his advice to the elders Peter urges younger men to show them a suitable respect and calls for a mutual attitude of humility. Anxieties should be committed into God's hands, since He is a caring Father, but the Christian is nonetheless called to be on his guard in view of the vigilance of the devil, who is always watching for an unwary victim. Victory will come from an unshakable faith, combined with the knowledge that those who suffer are not alone in doing so: fellow-Christians are also suffering, and suffering bravely and successfully. What is more, the Christian has the glorious assurance that since God is the Author of all these purposes in his life, such suffering will only be for a relatively brief while, after which this same God will restore and re-establish him. Such a God deserves every ascription of praise and power.

Notes. 5 *Likewise* could indicate the conduct required of others in the light of the instructions in the preceding verses, or it could be a reversion in thought to the thread of 2:13, 18; 3:1, 7. *Elders* could be in the ecclesiastical sense as v. 1, or could be extended to the general and primary sense, in which case this is a command to Christian young people to show due deference to age. *Clothe yourselves* is literally 'fasten on with a knot', 'bind unto yourselves', and Peter may well have had Jn. 13:4, 5, 15, 16 in mind. The quotation in this verse is from the LXX of Pr. 3:34, quoted also in Jas. 4:6; Jesus speaks of this principle in Mt. 23:12. 6 *The mighty hand of God* is a familiar phrase in the LXX, and is usually connected in thought with God's deliverance of His people from Egypt: here it would be a reminder that He can intervene in human affairs and bring blessing out of the acceptance of the lowly part, and even out of suffering rightly borne. 7 *Cast* is the vivid verb 'hurl', used in the LXX of Ps. 55:22/23. The reason given for the absence of anxiety is familiar from the words of Jesus in Mt. 6:25-34; 10:28-33, *etc.* 8 *Be sober*; *cf.* 1:13; 4:7. *Be watchful* is again a striking reference to the Lord's own words to Peter in Mt. 26:41; Mk. 14:38. *Adversary* is a legal term, but probably translates into Greek the Hebrew *śāṭān* used of the adversary of souls, as in Jb. 1:6, *etc.* Then here, as there, Satan could be seen as the instigator of persecution and suffering in order to test, and if possible destroy, the faith of God's children. Peter was familiar with this behaviour (*cf.* Mt. 16:23; Lk. 22:31). *Devil* is the Greek *diabolos* which means 'slanderer': in his role of undermining faith the devil slanders God to men (*cf.* Gn. 3:1, 4, 5) and men to God (*cf.* Jb. 1:9-11; 2:4, 5). *Prowls around*; *cf.* Jb. 1:7; 2:2. 9 *Resist* is the method recommended for dealing with the devil, as in Jas. 4:7 (*cf.* Eph. 6:11-17). It is the desires of the flesh one has to flee (*cf.* 1 Tim. 6:11; 2 Tim. 2:22). *Firm.* The word is used of material objects to denote solidity. No superficial faith will do here, since Peter probably has in mind the devil's desire to make apostates through persecution. Rev. 12:11 also suggests the way to victory in such trials. *Throughout the world*: in contrast to the group of churches in Asia Minor (*cf.* 1:1) to whom this letter is addressed. 10 *All grace.* The call to perseverance is matched by the doctrine of preservation. Since God has called us to share His eternal glory in Christ, we can ultimately rely on Him to bring us safely through to it (*cf.* 1:5; Phil. 1:6; 1 Thes. 5:24; Jude 24).

The verbs in this verse are best taken as future tenses (as RV, RSV) and not as optative mood (as AV): thus it is a promise, not a prayer. *Restore* is a verb often used of repairing ships after a battle or storm: in Mk. 1:19 it describes fishermen mending their nets. *Establish . . . strengthen*: the former word, used also in Lk. 22:32, and referring in its primary sense to physical objects, may denote fixity of position; the latter may be used for firmness of purpose. *Settle* (RSV mg.) means basically to 'give foundations', but is missing from several of the most ancient MSS. 11 *Dominion* is rightly ascribed to God here, as it is His over-ruling power which alone can bring the Christian through. This noun is formed from the same root as 'mighty' in v. 6.

5:12-14 CONCLUSION

Peter now sums up his twofold purpose of bringing encouragement and assurance, and mentions who has been his amanuensis. He set out to testify to them that the doctrine of salvation he has been expounding is truly God's grace at work, and in the light of that teaching to urge them to stand fast in it. Greetings are included, and the letter ends with the characteristic Hebrew blessing of *peace* being sent to all the Christian readers or hearers.

Notes. 12 *Silvanus* is probably the Silas of Acts 15:22 – 18:5 (*cf.* 2 Cor. 1:19; 1 Thes. 1:1; 2 Thes. 1:1). The exact part he played in the writing of the letter is discussed in the Introduction, under 'Authorship'. *A faithful brother* overlooks the definite article here, which led RV to translate 'our'. Its use may imply that Silvanus was known to the recipients of the letter, or may just stress his relationship to Peter. *This* could be taken more closely with v. 10 as referring to the possibility of growth in the Christian life, but is more likely to refer to the whole content of the letter. 13 *Babylon* has been taken to refer *a.* to the ancient city in Mesopotamia, *b.* to a Roman garrison town in Egypt, now Cairo, or *c.* to Rome. For reasons discussed in the Introduction (under 'Date and place of writing') it is probably best to understand the last reference. *She . . . likewise chosen* is usually referred to the local church, understanding an ellipse of the feminine word *ekklēsia*, 'church'. The suggestion by Alford that this refers to Peter's wife (*cf.* Mk. 1:30; 1 Cor. 9:5) is most unlikely, encouraged only by the following phrase. *My son Mark* most likely refers to the writer of the second Gospel, who may have alluded to himself in Mk. 14:51, and to whose home Peter came on his deliverance from prison (Acts 12:12). Mark accompanied Paul on missionary work (Acts 12:25 – 13:13), but subsequently left him and thus displeased the apostle, who preferred to take Silas as a companion (Acts 13:13; 15:36-40). However, Mark subsequently regained Paul's favour (2 Tim. 4:11) and was with him, probably at Rome, at the end of his life (Col. 4:10; Phm. 24). Eusebius quotes Papias as saying that Mark compiled a written record of Peter's recollections of the deeds and sayings of the Lord, and Mark's Gospel was from early times associated with the church at Rome. *Son* is used in the spiritual sense (*cf.* 1 Tim. 1:2, *etc.*). **14** *The kiss of love*, or 'holy kiss', is referred to on several occasions (*e.g.* Rom. 16:16; 1 Cor. 16:20; 2 Cor. 13:12; 1 Thes. 5:26) and appears to have been in common use when Christians met for fellowship: it may have been a common practice among the apostolic band (*cf.* Lk. 22:48). This was a practice which could be twisted to advantage by oppon-

ents who wished to slander the Christian faith. *Peace* is the wish with which the letter ends, as it began (1:2). But the reader has in the interval been made aware how this peace is made possible, even in the midst of suffering and in the difficult outworkings of personal relationships and the challenging onslaught of a pagan world. The source of this peace is to be found *in Christ*. Whatever his circumstances, the man who is *in Christ* (*cf.* Eph. 1:3ff.) can always know the peace of God, for it is freely available to *all* such.

2 Peter

INTRODUCTION

AUTHORSHIP

The evidence of the letter itself leaves no doubt on this question. The writer is 'Simon Peter, a servant and apostle of Jesus Christ' (1:1); he was on the Mount of Transfiguration with Jesus (1:16–18), where only Peter, James and John were with Him (see Mk. 9:2ff. and parallels); he had written earlier to the recipients of this letter (3:1), and is on familiar terms with them (3:1, 8, 14, 17); he could claim Paul as a 'beloved brother' (3:15), and at the time of writing he was expecting his own death to occur quite soon (1:14).

No MS evidence would suggest that any of these facts were later written into the letter to gain it acceptance, but a popular modern theory is that the letter is a pseudepigraph, *i.e.* a writing put out after the death of a great man, but published under his name as containing the kind of things he would say in that situation, and intended by such ascription to do him honour. Supporters of this view maintain it for various reasons, which may briefly be summarized as follows:

a. It is claimed that the language and style are not as closely akin to 1 Peter as would be expected. But in the former letter Peter had the assistance of Silvanus as his amanuensis (1 Pet. 5:12) and he was writing on different matters. In fact there are strong resemblances between the two Epistles: some words and phrases (*e.g.* 'excellence' used of God in 1 Pet. 2:9; 2 Pet. 1:3; 'removal' in 1 Pet. 3:21; 2 Pet. 1:14; '(un)ceasing from sin' in 1 Pet. 4:1; 2 Pet. 2:14) occur only in these letters and nowhere else in the NT. Other words not common elsewhere are 'love of the brethren' in 1 Pet. 1:22; 2 Pet. 1:7; the root of 'behold' used in 1 Pet. 2:12; 3:2; 2 Pet. 1:16; and 'supply' in 1 Pet. 4:11; 2 Pet. 1:5. Again there are similarities in the doctrines of prophecy

in 1 Pet. 1:10–12; 2 Pet. 1:20, 21; of Christian liberty in 1 Pet. 2:16; 2 Pet. 2:19; and of eschatology in 1 Pet. 1:5; 4:7; 2 Pet. 3:3, 10. In particular, traces of an authentic link with Peter can be seen in the linguistic connections between the letter and the apostle's speeches in the Acts: the peculiar use of 'godliness' in Acts 3:12; 2 Pet. 1:6; 'lawless' in Acts 2:23; 2 Pet. 2:8; 'obtained' in Acts 1:17; 2 Pet. 1:1; and the phrases 'reward of wickedness' in Acts 1:18; 2 Pet. 2:13, 15; and 'day of the Lord' in Acts 2:20; 2 Pet. 3:10. More recent research has shown that the objection on linguistic grounds has nothing like the evidence to support it that was once supposed (see further E. M. B. Green, *TNTC, 2 Peter and Jude*, pp. 16–19).

b. The other main objection to Petrine authorship of the Epistle comes from the apparent hesitancy of the early church to receive 2 Peter into the NT Canon. However, this is largely an argument based on silence, and the fact that the letter was finally included in the Canon, and that at a time when the church was rightly suspicious of pseudo-Petrine writings circulated by Gnostic circles, should not be underestimated.

c. The fact that this letter so strongly resembles that of Jude, especially in ch. 2, is felt to be further evidence against Petrine authorship. We shall have to consider the relationship between the two letters in greater detail later: suffice it to say here that the fact that most of Jude is included in 2 Peter has led many to conclude that therefore Jude was the earlier document: if Peter had written first there would be no reason for Jude to write. From this it is then argued that a leading apostle such as Peter would not have used material from one who, if he was the Lord's brother, did not believe until after the resurrection (see Mk. 6:3; Jn. 7:5). Here again the argument is far from conclusive. Jude could well have made a digest of 2 Peter to send to a church or churches to whom the latter had not written, and thus Peter could have written first. There is no reason why Peter should have refused to use another source for part of the letter: we have seen in introducing 1 Peter that he may possibly have used a sermon of his own or someone else's as the basis of that letter. Finally, it could be that both Peter and Jude used another common source.

d. Other arguments maintain that the teaching contained in the letter bears the marks of a late date. This is not necessarily true, as the false teaching attacked in this letter was germinally present in its doctrinal aspect in Colossae (Col. 2:18) and in its moral aspect at Corinth (1 Cor. 5; 6:12–20) at the time that Paul wrote his letters to these places. Moreover, the *parousia* teaching in this letter about Christ's return shows that the hope of His coming mentioned in 1 Peter is not missing from this letter. It is only the scoffers who are trying to dispose of it (3:4): the godly are still looking for it (3:12), and this doctrine provides the same motive for holy living as it does in the former letter (*cf.* 3:11–14 with 1 Pet. 1:7, 13, 17; 4:7, 13).

Recent conservative scholars have drawn attention to the fact that the pseudepigraphic theory raises an important moral problem. Later generations of the church condemned this device, and it had been attempted by the unorthodox in NT times, only to be denounced by Paul (2 Thes. 2:2; 3:17). It is almost unbelievable that a sincere writer could have included the false personal references of 1:1, 16–18; 3:1 in a letter in which he lays such stress on holiness and truth (1:3, 4, 12; 3:11, 17): such a deceit could not have been accepted in a church which called its members to such high standards in all other matters.

DATE

The language of 3:16 suggests that a number of Pauline letters had been written by the time Peter penned this letter. It is not necessary to conclude, as some do, from 1:12–17 that the Gospels were already widely circulating, or from 3:4 that at the time of writing the first generation of Christians had died. References to this letter in other works show that at the latest it must have been written early in the 2nd century; the undeveloped stage of the heresy attacked would argue for pushing the date back into the end of the 1st century; and if we are prepared to accept Petrine authorship, then a date shortly before the apostle's death (1:14), somewhere in the sixties, would seem most likely.

PLACE OF ORIGIN AND DESTINATION

The letter affords no clues about the place where it was written. If we accept its Petrine authorship and that 1 Peter was written in Rome, then it is likely that this letter was also from there. If 3:1 is a reference to 1 Peter, the addressees would

presumably be the same as in that letter: otherwise 1:1 could suggest that it was intended for a wider readership. The recipients are obviously Christian churches suffering from the beginnings of the Gnostic heresy, and this was known to have been spreading early in Asia Minor. They would probably have consisted both of Jews and Gentiles (see Introduction to 1 Peter): arguments based on odd phrases in the letter are as inconclusive here as in the former letter (*e.g.*, if 1:1 suggests Gentile readership, 3:2 can equally be pressed into suggesting Jewish).

SUBJECT-MATTER

The apostle writes as one who knows that his time on this earth is limited, and his letter has three main thoughts. *a.* Christians must match their Christian calling and resources with growth in practical holiness. *b.* Every attempt to delude them with false doctrine and its consequent licentiousness must be resisted and refuted. *c.* Finally, Christians must live their lives in the light of the coming day of God. The first and the last of these themes is familiar from the First Epistle: the second subject would appear to have been the main reason for the letter, but the writer prefers to set it in the right and positive perspective of Christian growth and destiny by placing it between the other two.

UNITY

In recent times various suggestions have been made that chs. 1 and 3 could have been the original letter, into which ch. 2 was later combined, or that each chapter at first circulated separately, ch. 1 being the earlier letter referred to in 3:1 and ch. 3 the sort of reminder promised in 1:13, again with 2 added in. A further analysis has attempted to isolate the so-called genuine Petrine sections of the letter, arguing that the rest is material added by a later editor. Two factors militate against these theories: there is no trace of MS evidence that any part of the letter at any time circulated on its own, and supporters of this theory are hard put to it to explain the marked unity of style throughout all three chapters.

THE LINK WITH JUDE

It is evident to the most casual reader that most of Jude 4–18 is found in 2 Peter, and this has given rise to three theories, which may be summarized as follows.

a. The priority of Jude. This is suggested by the fact that Peter adds so much other material: had Peter written first, then Jude would have added only a few verses to what was already in circulation. This is no objection if we consider the possibility that Jude abbreviated a document already in existence to meet the needs of churches to whom the earlier document had not been sent. Others suggest that Peter softened the harsh tones of Jude, telescoped his metaphors and excised his apocryphal references, *etc.*, each of which arguments could be turned in reverse to suggest that Jude rewrote the relevant portion of Peter, deliberately making the language more harsh, adjusting an inappropriate metaphor, and backing the argument with apocryphal references.

b. The priority of Peter. Arguments quoted above can be used either way, and so are used by advocates of this view. It has also been noted above that some feel that a man of Peter's standing would not have quoted from an obscure person like Jude. Further, it is argued that the dangers foreseen in the future by Peter (2:1) have been present for some time in Jude (v. 4). Here again, it can be pointed out on the other side that Peter is not consistent in his tenses, and frequently uses the present, speaking of

these dangerous teachers as already having begun their work (2:10b–19).

c. A common source behind both. The problems attached to either of the above views have led to the formulation of this hypothesis as a further alternative. While this does solve some of the problems mentioned above, it still leaves one largely unanswered, and that is why Jude bothered to write his letter if he merely repeated so much of the original source. It is far more reasonable to suppose that he made an abridgement of 2 Peter to meet his own particular needs.

In all fairness it must be admitted that there is no final answer to this problem of priority. There are marked resemblances also between 2 Peter and other parts of the NT, and these will be noted below in the Commentary.

OUTLINE OF CONTENTS

COMMENTARY

1:1, 2 OPENING ADDRESS

Following the pattern of the previous letter, the writer begins by introducing himself and his credentials, stating the identity of those to whom he is writing, and sending his Christian greetings to them.

Notes. 1 *Simon Peter*: see Introduction, under 'Authorship'. *Simon* is probably better read as 'Symeon' (as RV mg.) and is the straightforward transliteration of the Hebrew form of his name as used in Acts 15:14. This could well be a mark of authenticity: use of the two names together (as on the formal occasions of Mt. 16:16; Lk. 5:8; Jn. 21:15) could be a reminder of the change grace had wrought in the apostle's life. *Servant*

and apostle. The latter title is used alone in 1 Peter (the former by Jude). Together they doubly emphasize the authority by which he writes, as one who is only a servant, yet fully commissioned by his Master for His work. *Obtained* is the Greek *lachousin*, 'obtain by lot', which implies grace and not merit as the source of this gift. The *faith* referred to here appears to be the God-given ability to respond to His grace by personal commitment and trust, as in Eph. 2:8, 9. *Of equal standing* is used by contemporary writers to describe those who share the rights and privileges of citizenship. Some think that in this context it refers to the equality of Gentiles with Jews in the purposes of God, reflecting Peter's experience in Acts 10:34, 35, but it has been argued above that the letter is not necessarily addressed only to Gentiles. Alternatively, then, this could be a further touch of humility by the servant of Jesus Christ, showing that, though an apostle, he is still a sinner in need of the *righteousness of . . . Jesus Christ*, just as much as the newest convert among those to whom the letter is written. However, most commentators suggest that the *righteousness* refers not so much to the object of their faith, but that the word has an ethical rather than a forensic sense, referring to the sheer fairness of God. *Our God and Saviour Jesus Christ* is more close to the original Greek than the marginal *our God and the Saviour Jesus Christ*, and the analogous form of 1 Pet. 1:3 suggests that only one Person of the Trinity is referred to here (*cf.* 1:11; 2:20; 3:18; see also Tit. 2:13. These references could then be important biblical evidence for the deity of Christ). *Saviour* as a title for Jesus appears mainly in the later writings of the NT, but is a regular emphasis in the early preaching of Peter (*cf.* Acts 4:12; 5:31; and later references in this letter at 1:11; 2:20; 3:2,·18). **2** *May grace and peace be multiplied*: see on 1 Pet. 1:2. *Knowledge* is stressed here as the means by which grace and peace can be multiplied in the believer's life. The Gnostic deviationists exalted knowledge (Gk. *gnōsis*) as being superior to faith, and in reply orthodox writers stressed the importance for Christians to acquire *epignōsis*, 'full knowledge' (as here), in order to combat this heresy. Such knowledge is never merely speculative, as was the Gnostic variety, but springs from a personal relationship with and experience of *God* in *Jesus our Lord* (*cf.* Jn. 17:3; Phil. 3:10).

1:3-11 A CALL TO SPIRITUAL GROWTH

Just as attack is the best form of defence, so Peter stresses that the best answer to the false teaching he will later refute is for Christians to be progressing not only in their understanding but also in their practice of the faith. This is important for the further reasons that God has provided believers with all the resources necessary to make such growth possible, and that such progress is a factor in assuring the Christian of his standing before God.

1:3, 4 The means—provided by God

Peter explains that such progress in the Christian life is made possible and practical for the Christian by two factors—the power and the promises of God. God's calling is made known to the person who responds to Jesus Christ, and in knowing Him the believer has freely placed at his disposal all the resources of Christ necessary to enable him to work out the process of sanctification. These resources are assured to the believer by the very promises of God.

Notes. **3** *His* would appear, from what has preceded, to refer to Jesus. *Granted* here and in the next verse stresses the freeness of the gift. *Life* refers to all the abundance of eternal life which Christ gives the believer (*cf.* Jn. 10:10), while *godliness* is the Christlike character which such life should produce. *To* is probably better translated *by*, as RSV mg., RV. Then *his own glory and excellence* would refer to the divine character and high moral quality of the life and Person of Jesus, as witnessed by Peter and proclaimed by the apostolic testimony and proclamation to subsequent generations of Christians. Peter may be thinking of the transfiguration when he mentions the glory of Jesus, and his own call (Lk. 5:1-11) when he refers to His excellence, but it is more likely that he is referring to the total impact of the Person of Jesus on a believer (*cf.* Jn. 1:14). *Excellence* (Gk. *aretē*) is used in this sense in 1 Pet. 2:9. **4** *By which* refers to Christ's glory and excellence, and emphasizes that it is because of the quality of His life that the believer can receive the promise of sharing the very nature of God. This is the teaching of Rom. 6, that by virtue of who Christ is, and by means of faith-union with Him, here and now the Christian enjoys the possibility of a life free from sin and its defilement and constantly growing more like Jesus. *Promises*: such as Peter enumerated in 1 Pet. 1:3-5; 2:9. *Through these*; *i.e.* as you live by them. *Corruption* (Gk. *phthora*) is the steady process of dissolution to which all things mortal are subject. It was introduced into *the world* as a direct result of the Fall, which in turn arose through man's giving way to *passion*. The phrase may be understood in this way, or it may be a reference to the inevitable consequences of sin in each successive generation of mankind. In either case, God's way of escape lies in seizing hold of His promises and thereby obtaining a share in His own *nature*: the thoughts behind this phrase can be traced out in verses such as Jn. 1:12; 1 Jn. 3:2, 3.

1:5-8 The aim—fruitful discipleship

Since the Christian has these resources at his disposal, he is exhorted to utilize them in spiritual growth which will give practical expression to the relationship described as 'knowing' Jesus Christ. Faith must be seen at work in a life of moral excellence, and this must be backed by a steadily increasing knowledge of God. This in turn gives the ability to control oneself, and that is necessary if one is going to be able to cope with trying circumstances or people. Steadfastness keeps the eyes consistently on God and His purposes in spite of these difficulties, and so leads to godliness: in turn the right attitude to God produces the right attitude of brotherly affection to one's fellows. Beyond this, and as it were the coping-stone of the whole edifice of character, is Christian love, which reaches beyond the family of God to all men.

Notes. **5** *Supplement* has the idea of lavish provision, and is a verb used in classical Greek to describe the munificence of rich citizens who would finance a theatrical performance or fit out a warship for the state they were proud to belong to. The Christian response to sharing the life of God and being a citizen of heaven should be to aim at producing and being the finest and most attractive character for God. *Virtue* is the same noun as 'excellence' in v. 3, and may refer to the process of assimilation hinted at there. The connection between practical Christian living and developing *knowledge* is referred to again in v. 8 (*cf.* Jn. 7:17; Col. 1:10). **6** Since God alone can give us the power to control self, *self-control* will be acquired only as one's knowledge of Him increases (*cf.* 1 Pet. 4:2). *Steadfastness* (Gk. *hypomonē*) is the ability to hold fast to one's goal in spite of opposition and persecution (*cf.* the use in Heb. 12:1–3, where the same root is translated by 'perseverance' and 'endured'). *Godliness*: see on v. 3 above. **7** *Brotherly affection* is emphasized as a fruit of the new birth in 1 Pet. 1:22; 3:8, and is of course what Jesus enjoined as the mark of His disciples (Jn. 13:34, 35). *Love* is the crown of all the Christian virtues, as in 1 Cor. 13; Col. 3:14, *etc.*

1:9 The significance—awareness of one's status

To neglect this kind of progress suggests that the person who behaves in this way must have forgotten the depths from which he was rescued.

Notes. *Blind and shortsighted* seems a strangely mixed metaphor. Peter may mean that such a person is being blind to the glorious possibilities of spiritual development that are his in Christ, and shortsighted because he cannot see back far enough to remember the wonder of divine forgiveness and cleansing.

1:10, 11 The result—full and final salvation

By contrast the writer urges his fellow-Christians to pursue such a character and way of behaviour as shall not only bring them full assurance of their status here and now, but also enable them safely and certainly to reach the Christian's glorious destination.

Notes. **10** *Zealous* is the same root as 'effort' in v. 5, and may be a deliberate reference back. *Confirm your call and election* is the tension which runs right through the first letter. Christians are 'chosen and destined by God the Father' (1 Pet. 1:2), and yet must conduct themselves 'with fear and trembling' (1 Pet. 1:17; *cf.* Phil. 2:12, 13). So Peter even hints at the possibility that one can *fall* from grace (see also Jude 24, where the verb *ptaiō* is used in the same sense). It does not here refer to sinning (as in Jas. 3:2), and so there is no suggestion of sinlessness. **11** Instead of this gloomy prospect, the Christian's hope should be set on an *entrance* into Christ's *eternal kingdom*: this last phrase is used here in an eschatological sense. *Richly provided* is the same verb as in v. 5 ('supplement'): God's lavish reward is a spur to lavish living for Him.

1:12 – 2:22 REASONS FOR EMPHASIZING THESE THINGS

The writer now goes on to explain in detail why he finds it necessary to write in this vein. He is anxious to remind his Christian friends about the importance of spiritual progress, as he knows that he has not much longer to live. As an eyewitness he wishes to stress that the faith they share is founded on facts of history, and further, that these events are a confirmation of what was foretold by the prophets. Mention of this leads to a long warning about the false prophets who will arise in the church just as they did in the OT people of God. The danger of their teaching and the error of their ways are then fully exposed.

1:12–15 Personal—the writer's home-call is imminent

During his lifetime Peter knows that he must keep on reminding his friends of this subject, and now by writing to them about it he is ensuring that they will have a further reminder when he has died.

Notes. **12** *Remind*. Although Christian people *know* the truth, it is the preacher and teacher's task constantly to be setting it before them afresh. *Established*: see on 1 Pet. 5:10, where the same verb is used. **13** *Body* is the Greek *skēnōma*, 'tent', and is used to indicate the temporary nature of our time in this body (*cf.* 2 Cor. 5:1–8). **14** *Putting off*. The metaphor is that of doffing clothes, and is developed further in 2 Cor. 5:1–8. *Soon*. Paul expresses a similar premonition of approaching death in 2 Tim. 4:6. Note the RV rendering 'the putting off . . . cometh swiftly'. *Showed me* may refer to the Lord's words in Jn. 21:18, 19, or to a more recent revelation. **15** *Departure* is the Greek *exodos*, used of the Lord's impending death in Lk. 9:31. Its use here suggests that he may have had the transfiguration experience in mind. Death is the departure from this mode of existence and leads to the entrance (v. 11) into Christ's eternal kingdom. *At any time to recall* may refer to this letter, or to Peter's part in supplying Mark with the information on which his Gospel is based.

1:16–18 Historical—the faith is founded on facts

Peter reminds his readers that he was present at the transfiguration, an event which took place in time and space, and that here authentic witness to Him was borne by God the Father. Understanding of these verses will depend largely on the interpretation of *power and coming*. Both words could refer to the historic facts of the life of Jesus on earth, but the word *coming* is more customarily reserved in the NT for the second coming of Jesus (*cf.* Mt. 24:3, 27, *etc.*; 1 Thes. 3:13; and 3:12 of this letter). In this case both words could be used by hendiadys for the 'coming in power' of Jesus (*cf.* Mk. 13:26; 14:62). A third interpretation sees *power* as referring to the transfiguration and *coming* to the return of Christ, and notes a similar thought-connection in Mk. 9:1ff. The transfiguration was certainly an anticipation of the full glory of the divine Christ to be revealed at His return. Notes. **16** *Cleverly devised myths* were a feature of the theological systems of the Gnostic speculators. *Eyewitnesses*: a reminder of the claim in 1 Pet. 5:1; Lk. 1:2; Jn. 1:14; 1 Jn. 1:1–3. *Majesty* is used in the NT only to describe divine glory (*cf.* Lk. 9:43; Acts 19:27). **17** *This is . . .* This formula of the Voice from heaven, repeated at our Lord's baptism and the transfiguration, combines the prophecies of Ps. 2:7 (the coronation of the Son of God) and Is. 42:1 (the ordination of the suffering Servant). Peter omits the final clause, summoning men to listen to Jesus Christ. **18** *Holy* need not suggest a late date for the letter, when ecclesiastical traditions were crystallized: the *mountain* would naturally be thought of as holy, as the scene of a divine revelation (*cf.* Ex. 3:5; 19:23).

1:19–21 Confirmatory—these happenings fulfil prophecy

The events to which Peter has been referring were seen by the apostles as a remarkable fulfilment of the OT (*cf.* Mt. 1:22; 2:5, 6, *etc.*). Jesus Himself had pointed this out to them (Jn. 5:39; Lk. 22:37; 24:26, 27, 44), and the early preaching of the gospel emphasized it (Acts 2:25ff., 34ff.; 3:22–24, *etc.*). Since so much prophecy has been fulfilled in the first coming of Christ, Christians must pay all the more heed to what remains to be fulfilled at His second coming, especially as the prophecies are not the result of man's speculative thinking (as the myths of v. 16) but of God's revelation by His Spirit.

Notes. **19** *More sure.* Translations vary according to the interpretation of this phrase. Some think that the argument is that the word of prophecy is more certain than the Voice from the mount; others take it as above, that the events of the first coming of Jesus make belief in the prophecies of the second coming easier. *Lamp* is a well-known picture of Scripture (*cf.* Ps. 119:105). *Dark*: as this world must be without the true Light present (*cf.* Jn. 8:12). *The day*; *i.e.* of Christ's coming, as in 3:10; Rom. 13:12 (*cf.* Ct. 2:17). *Morning star* (Gk. *phōsphoros*): the star that brings the dawn, a word used in antiquity to refer to the planet Venus. Its use here accords with the Star-symbolism of Jesus in Nu. 24:17; Lk. 1:78; Rev. 22:16 (*cf.* Mal. 4:2; Eph. 5:14). *In your hearts* is felt by some to be difficult, as Christ's coming will be objective and visible, but the phrase may be elliptic: Christ's return will bring light and joy to the hearts of His own. It is possible, but less likely, that this phrase should be taken with the following clause: 'you must first of all understand this in your hearts.' **20** *You must . . .* is repeated in 3:3. *Prophecy of scripture* is distinct from the false prophecies to be alluded to in 2:1. *Interpretation* is a noun not used elsewhere in the NT; in Mk. 4:34 the verb is used of the explanation of parables. The statement is normally taken to assert that prophecy can be understood by the individual only as he is guided by the Spirit (some would say Spirit-filled church) who guided the writers. This strains the verb here into an unnatural

meaning, and it seems better to understand the reference to the origin rather than the understanding of Scripture: no prophecy of Scripture arises from a private explanation (*sc.* of events past, present or future) for the reasons following. **21** *Moved* (Gk. *pheromenoi*); *i.e.* borne along by the Spirit like a ship borne along by the wind. *Holy* (RSV mg.) is not in all the MSS, nor is the preposition *from*: hence the differences between the RSV and RSV mg. translations.

2:1–22 Admonitory—false prophets

Stress on the importance of looking forward to the fulfilment of Spirit-given prophecy leads Peter to issue a warning about the false prophecies that will be put forward. It is striking that this is a feature also of Jesus' teaching about the future (*cf.* Mk. 13:22, 23). This chapter should be compared carefully with Jude 4–18.

2:1–3 Their danger. This is threefold: they destroy themselves by their denial of Christ (*cf.* Mt. 10:33), they draw others to follow them and decry orthodox Christianity, and they will seek to make financial gain from genuine believers by their false teaching.

Notes. **1** *The people* seems, in the context, to refer to the OT people of God. The activities of *false prophets* are mentioned in Dt. 13:1–5; 1 Ki. 13:18; 22:5–23; Je. 5:13, 31; 6:13, *etc*. *False teachers*. The falsity may refer to the content of their teaching or to their claim to be teachers. Probably both are implied. *Secretly* is an undertone of the verb, which literally means 'to bring in in addition'. *Heresies* are the Greek *haireseis*, which simply means 'chosen beliefs'. In the Christian church it came to refer to a wrong belief deliberately chosen by a man (rather than a right one revealed to him by God). *Destructive* is a Hebraistic phrase referring to the consequence both for the holder of such views and any orthodox beliefs he might have. *The Master* (Gk. *despotēs*) is applied to Christ only here and in Jude 4, but is used of God ('Sovereign Lord') in Acts 4:24; Rev. 6:10 (*cf.* Lk. 2:29). *Bought* introduces the ransom aspect of the work of Christ (*cf.* Mk. 10:45), and produces the corollary that the Christian is therefore Christ's servant, and is not to please himself (see the argument of 1 Pet. 1:14–21 and 1 Cor. 6:19b, 20). **2** *Licentiousness* was one consequence of the tendency to make knowledge superior to practice: the false teachers of the day tended to argue that it did not matter how the Christian behaved, as grace could forgive every sin, no matter how great. The NT is unequivocal in contradicting this outlook, and Peter's arguments against it can be seen in 1 Pet. 1:15; 2:11, 12; 4:2; 2 Pet. 1:4; 3:11 (*cf.* Rom. 6:1, 2, 15, *etc.*). *The way* was an early name for the Christian faith (*cf.* Acts 9:2, *etc.*); *of truth* may be a reference to Ps. 119:30 or to Jn. 14:6. *Reviled*. Peter has earlier faced up to the fact that orthodox Christians will be reviled for their good behaviour (1 Pet. 3:16; 4:3–5), and now he sorrows that the immorality of pseudo-Christ-

ian sects will bring reproach upon the true faith.
3 *Exploit* has commercial connotations. *False*
means fabricated, made up to suit the ears of the
hearer (*cf.* 1 Thes. 2:5). *Not . . . idle* means that
judgment is impending; *cf.* Phillips 'hard on
their heels'. *Asleep* is a vivid metaphor (*cf.* NEB
'waits for them with unsleeping eyes'). Retribution is certain, though it may not be swift, for
the man who leads another astray.

2:4–10a Their condemnation. Peter now develops the theme of v. 3 more fully, drawing on
early incidents in the history of God's people
to show how His purposes both of salvation and
of condemnation are sure and will be completed.
Noah and Lot are cited as examples of how God
can deliver His own when their ungodly contemporaries are destroyed, while the fate of the
fallen angels is a pointer to the fact of a final
judgment, when man's rebellion, culminating
in the unbridled indulgence of self and rejection
of God's authority, will be duly punished.
Together the three examples show God's punishment of pride, disobedience and immorality.

Notes. **4** *Angels*: see Gn. 6:1–4 and Jude 6,
where the writer draws attention to pride as
being the cause of their downfall. *Hell* here is
a Greek concept (see RSV mg.) and refers in
Greek mythology to Tartarus, the lowest and
most terrible part of hell, reserved especially
for those superhuman beings who rebelled
against the supreme God. *Pits of nether gloom*
may fill out the picture with an allusion to the
underground granaries of the day: alteration
of one letter may give us another word meaning
'chains' (as AV, RV mg.) and this is then parallel
to Jude 6. The imagery appears to be drawn
from apocryphal writings. **5** *Noah*: see Gn.
6:8 – 9:28; 1 Pet. 3:20 where there is also mention of the eight being saved. *A herald*, together
with the reference in 1 Pet. 3:20 to the disobedient, suggests that Noah was commissioned to
call his contemporaries to repentance, but that
they chose to ignore or reject his message—as
the false teachers will do. Another apocryphal
work describes Noah's preaching. **6** *Sodom and
Gomorrah*: see Gn. 18:16 – 19:28. *An example*:
a fact to which Jesus alludes in Mt. 10:15; 11:23f.;
Lk. 17:29. **7** *Wicked* means 'lawless', *i.e.* the
consequence of having no fear of God and
therefore feeling completely free to live without
principles, indulging fallen nature. **8** *He was
vexed*. The verb means to be tortured (as NEB)
or tormented. It originally meant to test in order
to prove genuineness, and may suggest that the
godly man, living in an ungodly world, should be
prepared to prove the reality of his faith. **9**
Instead of making the second part of this sentence, dealing with punishment, the apodosis
of his conditional sentence (which logic would
require), Peter chooses to focus attention
on the positive aspect of God's mercy, that in
such a wicked world He can keep His own. The
switch in thought may have been prompted by
mention of the distress of Lot in v. 8: it is significant that this emphasis is absent from Jude.

Rescue . . . from trial: see 1 Pet. 1:6, 7; 5:10.
10a *Lust of defiling passion*: literally 'those who
go after flesh with a desire for pollution'.
Comparison with Jude 7 suggests that sodomy
is here referred to. *Authority* is Greek *kyriotēs*,
'lordship', and is most naturally taken as referring to the Lordship of Christ (*cf.* 1 Pet. 3:15).
On the other hand, it may anticipate the latter
part of the verse, if angels are there referred to,
and the word may refer to the authority of an
order of angels, as Jude 8; Eph. 1:21; Col. 1:16
are thought to do.

2:10b–22 Their character. The apostle now
proceeds to elaborate the danger these men
constitute by describing more fully their true
nature. They are insolent (vv. 10–12), licentious
(v. 13), immoral (v. 14) and greedy (vv. 14b–16).
By such behaviour they attract and enslave the
newly converted (vv. 17–19), and so Peter
concludes this section by uttering a warning of
the serious consequences of a Christian backsliding into immorality. In this passage the
language is complicated and unusual as the
writer piles word upon word to heighten the
enormity of their behaviour.

Notes. **10b** *Bold* suggests the spirit that has no
concern for others, or even for one's own danger;
wilful ('self-pleasing') describes the attitude of
being so obsessed with one's own wishes that
nothing else can be taken into consideration.
The glorious ones may refer to angels, in which
case they may *revile* them in the way in which
the men of Sodom reviled the angels who came
to the house of Lot (Gn. 19:1ff.), or it could be
that they used the behaviour of the fallen angels
in Gn. 6:1–4 as a justification for their own
immorality, and spoke evil of the unfallen
angels by holding that such behaviour was typical
of all angels. Alternatively, it could be argued
that the word is simply used for church leaders
('dignities', AV, RV). **11** *Angels*, by contrast,
have the right to complain to God of the behaviour of these arrogant mortals, but refuse to
do so: this may be a reference to the kind of
incident described in Jude 9. **12** As such behaviour is *irrational*, like that of *animals*, then the
destiny of these men will be similar too. *Cf.*
Jude 10. The *ignorance* of those who criticize the
Christian way of life is commented on by Peter
in 1 Pet. 2:15. *With them* could refer to the fate
of the animals (as NEB), or could describe the
final consequences of the corruption they have
allowed into their own lives (*cf.* Phillips 'will
most certainly be destroyed in their own corruption'). **13** *Suffering wrong*. This verb appears
to have here the connotation of the market-
place. RSV and NEB bring out the play on words,
but E. M. B. Green (*TNTC*, p. 109) suggests the
right metaphor with 'being defrauded of the
wages of fraud'. Sin attracts with its offer of
pleasure, but in the end he who indulges finds
that he has no pleasure at all. *Daytime* revelry
is a feature of extreme dissipation, and for the
Christian the day is the time for work (*cf.* Jn.
9:4; Rom. 13:13; 1 Thes. 5:7f.). *Blots* (Gk.

spiloi); *i.e.* 'spots', something disfiguring and painful. *Blemishes*. This and the preceding word occur in the NT with a negative prefix to describe what Christ was, and what His church should be (*cf.* Eph. 5:27; 1 Pet. 1:19; 2 Pet. 3:14; Jude 24). *Dissipation* could possibly be the alternative reading 'at their love feasts' (*cf.* RSV mg.), for some MSS read Greek *agapais* for *apatais*. This approximates to the text of Jude 12, and we know from 1 Cor. 11 that the love feast had early been the subject of abuse. *Carousing*. The Greek is a more neutral word, 'while they sit with you at table' (NEB). **14** *Eyes full of adultery* is a compressed phrase for 'always looking for a woman with whom to commit adultery' (Arndt): Phillips has 'their eyes cannot look at a woman without lust'. *Entice*. Such sinners are never content, but must lead others astray. *Accursed*, because they have rejected Christ (v. 2), who alone can deliver them from the curse (*cf.* Gal. 3:13); *children* is the Hebraism (as in 1 Pet. 1:14) 'children of', *i.e.* those who are subject to others. **15, 16** *Balaam* is cited as the classic example of the false teacher who leads people astray for his own personal gain. Nu. 22-24 show how Balaam tried time and again to prophesy against Israel in order to gain the reward Balak offered: in the end, after failing to destroy Israel verbally, he is shown as doing so morally (Nu. 31:16; *cf.* 25:1-9). Balaam is the prototype of the false teacher who seeks good rewards or popularity by persuading people that God's standards can be lowered. Peter here expands one example cited in Jude 11. *Madness*, because such behaviour is so contrary to all good sense.

17 *Waterless springs*. They do not give the satisfaction they claim to offer. *Mists* may refer to their instability: their teaching shifts with the least gust of wind (*cf.* Eph. 4:14). Or it may suggest failure to give the refreshing rain they promise. Others see in the phrase something which does no good, but only obscures the light. *Nether gloom*: see on v. 4. The Greek *zophos* was used from classical times to denote the darkness of the nether regions. **18** *Loud*. The Greek adjective conveys the idea of something larger than it has any right to be. *Entice*. One of the characteristics of sin is the way in which its adherents are always out to persuade others to share in their behaviour (*cf.* v. 14; Rom. 1:32). *Barely escaped*. False teachers frequently make for the newly converted, who are not yet rooted in orthodox Christian doctrine. **19** The *freedom* these teachers appear to offer is freedom from the obligation to serve Christ and grow in Him in the way set out in 1:3-11. In doing so they overlook that this kind of licence is only the old bondage of sin all over again (*cf.* Rom. 6 and Jn. 8:31-36). **20** *For . . . they . . .* seems to link in thought with the false teachers, and to explain why they are now in such total bondage to corruption. *Knowledge*: see on 1:2. *The last state*. Peter may have been recalling Jesus' words in Mt. 12:45; Lk. 11:26, though others see a link with Lk. 12:47, 48. **21** *It would have been better*:

because if they have rejected God's way in Christ there is no other way of salvation (*cf.* Heb. 6:4-8; 10:26-31). *Way*: see on v. 2. *Of righteousness* stresses the ethical consequences of following Christ. **22** *Proverb*. The first is found in Pr. 26:11, while the second appears to come from an extra-biblical source, the ancient *History of Ahikar*. Peter may be thinking also of Mt. 7:6.

3:1-16 A REMINDER OF THE COMING OF THE LORD

Peter has dealt at length with false teachers because he is so concerned about the damage they can do, but he now returns to the point from which he digressed in 2:1. He began the letter with an exhortation to growth in godliness, and is now going to adduce the second coming of Jesus as a further motive for godly living; but before doing so he pauses to stress the certainty of that coming, and to explain the reasons why God has delayed it.

3:1, 2 A call to remember the promise

Peter stresses the unity of this letter with his former one, and the consistency of his teaching with that both of prophets and of the other apostles.

Notes. **1** *The second letter* could be a reference to 1 Peter, or to chs. 1 and 2 of this letter (if the theory be accepted that they were written separately), or else to an earlier letter which has not been preserved to us. If the predictions and the commandment of v. 2 are to do with the second coming, they hardly describe Peter's first letter, and a lost letter is probably referred to here. Otherwise, taken as general terms, the words could describe the contents of 1 Peter. *Beloved*. The writer's heart warms as he turns from considering the false teachers to feed the flock of God. *Aroused*: see 1:13. *Sincere mind*, by contrast with the people described in ch. 2. The phrase can have a moral sense as well as meaning 'uncontaminated by prejudice'. **2** *Predictions . . . commandment . . .* : Peter's emphasis on the unity of the OT with the apostolic writings is reminiscent of 1 Pet. 1:10-12; 2 Pet. 1:19-21. *Commandment* appears to refer to Christ's teaching as a whole as set out by the apostles (*cf.* Jn. 14:26). *The Lord and Saviour* is the final authority behind both prophets and apostles (*cf.* Eph. 2:20). *Your apostles* is taken by some as a reference to 'those who brought you this message', but is more likely to emphasize their reliability than their function: 'those you trust and who have taught you the orthodox Christian faith' as distinguished from the false teachers who will arise. *Cf.* Jude 17.

3:3, 4 A warning to ignore scoffers

Every pastor knows how quickly despondency can spread in a fellowship, and so Peter takes care to warn his readers not to be put off by those who wrongly argue that God's inactivity means that He will not act. Jude 18 attributes this warning directly to the apostles themselves.

Notes. 3 *First of all*; *cf.* 1:20. *Scoffers*, together with the reference to their *passions*, makes it likely that the false teachers of ch. 2 are still in mind. Those who give way to their own lusts will always mock at any incentive to noble living. **4** *Where . . . ?* A similar complaint can be found in *1 Clement* 23:3f.; *2 Clement* 11:2–4, and rabbinic writings. *The fathers* could apply to early Christian leaders such as Stephen, James the son of Zebedee, *etc.*, or, indeed, to the older members of the first generation of Christians, who died between AD 30 and 60. Such reference is no argument for a late date, as the problem is the same as Paul faces in 1 Thes. 4:13ff. However, the reference to the Flood in vv. 5–7 makes it more likely that Peter has the OT patriarchs in mind.

3:5–7 A reason not to ignore this word

In actual fact, the argument used by the scoffers in v. 4 is phoney. They have conveniently forgotten that God did intervene in judgment at the time of the Flood, and this fact proves two things. It cannot be argued from the stability of the world that God will not interrupt its steady rhythm, and it is all the more certain that He will again carry out His promises in His own time.

Notes. 5 *By the word of God*; *cf.* Gn. 1:3, *etc.*; Ps. 33:6; Jn. 1:3; Heb. 11:3. *Out of water and by means of water* probably refers to water as one of the original elements created, out of which God formed the earth (*cf.* Gn. 1:2), and as one of the means by which He sustains it still. The present translation of the second preposition, giving it an instrumental rather than a local sense ('in the midst of'), is probably to be preferred. **6** *Through which* is a plural pronoun but probably refers to the doubly-mentioned water. The reference is obviously to the Flood (*cf.* Gn. 6–9). **7** *But* is probably meant to connect rather than contrast. *By the same word . . .* ; *cf.* Is. 66:15, 16; Zp. 1:18; Mal. 4:1–3; 1 Cor. 3:13; 2 Thes. 1:7f. *Now exist*, in contrast to the new heaven and new earth of the future (*cf.* Rev. 21:1). *Kept*; *cf.* 2:9, 10.

3:8, 9 Reasons why God is delaying

Having given reasons why God's promise of another intervention in the orderly courses of nature cannot be rejected, Peter goes on to state two factors which make it reasonable that He should delay such intervention as long as He likes. Time is of no consequence to God, and in His love for men He is keeping open for as long as possible the door of repentance.

Notes. 8 *Do not ignore* contrasts the wilful ignorance of the false teachers in vv. 5, 6. *With the Lord*. The following quotation from Ps. 90:4, with its corollary, stresses the fact that God is outside time, and so is in no hurry to work (*cf.* Hab. 2:3 on this point also). There is no warrant for building a doctrine of the millennium on this verse, as that is not the issue at stake here. **9** *Toward you*. Whether this or the marginal

reading ('on your account') is taken makes little difference to the sense. *Not wishing . . .* ; *cf.* Rom. 2:4; 1 Tim. 2:4. This verse has been cited as an argument for universalism: in fact it teaches the opposite. The plain thrust of it is that after the second coming, ushering in Christ's judgment, there will be no further opportunity for repentance, and so God in His mercy is giving men as long as possible to repent.

3:10–13 A reassertion of the fact and its consequences

The argument concerning the certainty of Christ's coming is rounded off with a further positive statement of the fact and its suddenness. Peter then goes on to state the consequences this coming will have for the physical world as we know it, and the consequences which the knowledge of this coming should produce in the life of the Christian believer, who should set his heart on this great happening.

Notes. 10 *Like a thief* stems from the Lord's words in Mt. 24:42, 43, which were well remembered in the early church (*cf.* 1 Thes. 5:2; Rev. 3:3; 16:15). *The heavens will pass away.* This also was mentioned by Jesus (Mk. 13:31, *etc.*). *Elements.* The Greek word could equally apply to the elemental substances of which the world is composed, or to the other heavenly bodies. *Works* could be either men's buildings and other material achievements, or their deeds in the moral sense: how this is interpreted depends on which of the three variant readings of the verb is taken. *Burned up* suggests a material sense, as does 'disappear', which is one possible alternative. 'Disclosed', the other alternative, suggests the moral sense, and is probably better on textual as well as contextual grounds. **11** *What sort of persons.* The second coming is used as an argument for godly living not only in the Lord's teaching (*e.g.* Lk. 12:35ff.), but also in Paul's letters (*cf.* Rom. 13:11ff.; 1 Thes. 5:3ff.) and earlier by Peter (1 Pet. 1:13; 4:7ff.). **12** *Hastening* is preferable to 'earnestly desiring' (RSV mg.), as it stresses the importance of human activity (in evangelism, *etc.*; *cf.* Acts 3:19–21) during the period of divine forbearance. *Because of which* is better than the purely temporal 'wherein' of AV: the advent of *the day* will cause these happenings. *Dissolved*; *cf.* v. 10 above and also Ps. 102:25–27; Heb. 1:10–12. **13** *Promise*: such as in Is. 65:17ff.; 66:22f.

3:14–16 An exhortation to right behaviour

The conclusion drawn from the present significance for Christians of the second coming is now repeated, and Peter urges his readers to holy living, not only in view of the fact that Christ could return at any moment, but also out of gratitude to God for His forbearance. This is a thought which Paul had expressed in his letters, and reference to them leads this writer to draw attention to the fact that his letters can be misunderstood, as certain people have done, perhaps deliberately.

Notes. 14 *Be zealous.* A reminder of the previous exhortation in 1:10. *To be found* at Christ's coming: the word may refer to v. 10 if the third alternative there is accepted. *Without spot or blemish* is in direct contrast to the teachers of 2:13 (*q.v.*; see also Jude 24). *Peace* is the content of a heart right with God. 15 *Count*; *i.e.* realize that, while God is waiting, He is both giving time for the unbeliever to be saved, and for the believer to be working out his salvation (*cf.* Phil. 2:12, 13) in terms of progress in sanctification. *So also* could refer either to the general teaching about the second coming, or to the last point about seeing God's delay as forbearance and not failure. Reference to 'this' (v. 16) being in all Paul's letters suggests that the former is the case, as there are in all of them frequent references to the second coming, but the other matter is hardly discussed outside Romans (*cf.* Rom. 2:4; 3:25; 9:22, 23; 11:22, 23). *Wisdom given* is a good reminder of the supernatural origin of Paul's Epistles (*cf.* 1 Cor. 2:13; 3:10). 16 *This*: see on v. 15. *All his letters* need not necessarily suggest that the corpus of Pauline letters had already been gathered, although no doubt collections of them were by now in circulation among the Christian communities. *Hard to understand* could mean 'ambiguous', 'obscure' (NEB), or capable of misinterpretation. Rom. 3:8 shows how Paul himself knew that the antinomians had twisted his teaching to suit their own purposes. Since *ignorant and unstable* men behave in this way, it is all the more important for the Christian to grow in knowledge and in building a firm foundation for the Christian life (*cf.* 1:3–11). *The other scriptures* can be argued, with equal success, as counting Paul's writings included in, or excluded from, Scripture. While we cannot form a conclusion from this text, Peter's previous arguments (1 Pet. 1:10–12; 2 Pet. 1:19–21; 3:2) show that Paul's letters possessed all the qualifications for acceptance as Scripture (the apostolic authority of the writer and the guidance of the Spirit as he wrote). Paul was of course conscious of this himself (*e.g.* 1 Cor. 2:13; 4:17; 2 Cor. 13:3–10; 1 Thes. 2:13).

3:17, 18 A CALL TO BE STEADFAST AND GROW; THE ASCRIPTION

The writer now draws to a conclusion by reverting to the great theme on which he began (*cf.* 1:3ff.). The best precaution against being infected by the false teachers and carried away by them is to be making spiritual progress. As those opening words reminded us, it is Christ alone who has done everything to make that possible, and so to Him we give all the glory now, as indeed we shall do throughout eternity when once He returns. So be it!

Notes. 17 *Knowing . . . beforehand* may suggest that this advice was given before the advent of the false teachers (*cf.* the future tense of 2:1), or more likely refers to the fact that Peter's readers are being alerted before this teaching has actually reached them. Antinomianism was certainly a live issue by the time Romans and 1 Corinthians were written. *Stability* is from the same root as the verb Peter used in 1 Pet. 5:10, and which Jesus used in Lk. 22:32; *i.e.* 'strengthen'. 18 *Grace and knowledge* are both regarded as divinely bestowed and are the gifts which enable growth along both moral and mental planes, along both of which, as this letter has shown, the Christian should be making parallel progress. *Jesus Christ* can help His followers to make this twofold progress, since He is both *Lord and Saviour*. *To him* is to Christ, and so the writer asserts unmistakably His deity. *The day of eternity* is literally 'the day of the age', the day which will usher in eternity, and so the day when Christ is coming. *Amen* is probably a later addition to the text: 'so be it' is certainly the response of a believing heart on reaching the end of this letter.

DAVID H. WHEATON

1 John

INTRODUCTION

This writing is usually called an 'Epistle', but it has neither address nor signature. Indeed, it lacks so many characteristics of a letter that some have thought that we must take 'Epistle' as no more than a courtesy title. They regard it as a homily rather than a letter. However, now and then there appear passages which justify us in thinking that this is a real letter (*e.g.* 2:1, 26), albeit one with some unusual characteristics. Perhaps the explanation is that it was originally meant for more than one community.

AUTHORSHIP

The traditional view is that the work is the product of John the apostle. No other author was suggested in antiquity. The marked tone of authority throughout the Epistle accords with this. Indeed, it has been suggested that only a person of such stature as the apostle could have sent out such a letter without giving his name. The writer was evidently an eyewitness of some, at any rate, of the things Jesus did (1:1–3; views that his 'we' refers generally to all Christians, or that it is simply an epistolary device seem untenable). The style and thought-forms resemble those of the Fourth Gospel, and all agree that there must be some connection. It is usual to think of the same author, in which case everything hinges on the authorship of that Gospel. A minority of critics, however, hold that the author of one of these writings was a disciple of the author of the other. These emphasize differences of style and theology. An example of the former is the contention that there are fewer compound words in the Epistle, and of the latter that there is a different view of the significance of the death of Jesus. Most scholars, however, agree that, while the differences should not be minimized, they are not great enough to demonstrate diversity of authorship. They are largely accounted for by the different purposes of the two writings and their different forms. J. R. W. Stott points out, 'The similarity between Gospel and Epistle is considerably greater than that between the Third Gospel and the Acts, which are known to have come from the same pen' (*The Epistles of John*, TNTC, 1964, p. 24).

Recent discussions make frequent mention of 'John the elder' (*cf.* 2 Jn. 1; 3 Jn. 1), and some see him as the author of the Gospel, some of the Epistle (or 2 and 3 John, or Revelation), some of both. This rather shadowy figure, however, is not a likely candidate. It cannot be demonstrated beyond doubt that a John the elder, distinct from John the apostle, ever existed. And if he did, the reasons for connecting him with this writing are not convincing, not nearly as convincing, *e.g.*, as the ancient tradition which ascribes it to the apostle.

We conclude that, while the Epistle makes no claim to any particular authorship, and while the case cannot be proved beyond doubt, the most reasonable hypothesis is that it, like the Fourth Gospel, came from the pen of the apostle John.

OCCASION

It is clear from the Epistle that its readers were confronted with a form of false teaching which denied the incarnation. In the 2nd century there appeared systems of thought which we call Gnosticism, and which took over both Christian and pagan ideas. They stressed knowledge (Gk. *gnōsis*), and thought of a way of salvation known only to the initiates. This consisted of the release of man from the material prison of the body, and his upward rise to God. There is dispute as to how early Gnosticism was. It is very probable that it was much later than the time of this Epistle, but it did not spring out of empty air. Many of the teachings which were later embodied in the fully-developed Gnostic systems were in circulation in the 1st century.

John is opposing some such system. The particular view relevant to our Epistle was that matter is inherently evil. God, being good, can have nothing to do with evil matter. Thus He could not have been incarnate in Jesus Christ. Some held that Christ only seemed to live in the flesh (they are called 'Docetists' from the Gk. *dokein*, 'to seem'). But it is probably affirming too much to say that John is confronting Docetists, for there is nothing in this Epistle about a phantom body or the like.

What he opposed seems to have been an early stage of the heresy that was to develop into Docetism. People were denying the incarnation and John regarded this as very serious. Its effect was to take the heart out of Christianity. For if Christ did not really become a man and did not really die for us, then no atonement has been made for our sins. So John emphasizes the reality of the incarnation. He also stresses the importance of upright living, for in their stress on knowledge some of the heretics evidently held that conduct did not matter much. John makes it clear that conduct is very important. Some of the false teachers had evidently been members of the church, but had now left it (2:19).

But it would be wrong to think that this Epistle is no more than a refutation of heresy. There is a very positive aim, as John tells us himself. He writes 'so that you may have fellowship with us . . . that our joy may be complete' (1:3f.). He makes this more specific by saying, 'I write this to you who believe in the name of the Son of God, that you may know that you have eternal life' (5:13). We may contrast this with the aim of the Gospel, which is 'that you may believe that Jesus is the Christ, the Son of God, and that believing you may have life in his name' (Jn. 20:31).

Whereas the Gospel has an evangelistic aim, the Epistle is thus directed rather at bringing its readers into a state of assurance and a true knowledge of what the faith implies. 'The Gospel contains "signs" to evoke faith (xx. 30, 31), and the Epistle tests by which to judge it' (Stott, *TNTC*, p. 23). John writes to take away his readers' anxieties as they come to realize their standing with God. He brings out what it means to be a Christian man. 'In the first Epistle, John sets forth three marks of a true knowledge of God and of fellowship with God. . . . These marks are, first, righteousness of life, second, brotherly love, and third, faith in Jesus as God

incarnate' (*Search the Scriptures*, 1967, p. 289). These three themes recur constantly.

The Epistle is dominated by two great thoughts: God is light (1:5), and God is love (4:8, 16). God is the source of light to the minds and warmth to the hearts of His children. These children should accordingly live up to the highest moral standard and this is stressed constantly (*e.g.* 2:1-6; 3:3, 6, 9; 5:1-3). But the Epistle contains no harsh admonition. Rather the writer addresses his readers with fatherly solicitude and tender concern: 'little children'; 'beloved'; 'little children, let no one deceive you'; 'little children, keep yourselves from idols'.

DATE

There is very little by which to date the writing. The relation to the Gospel is not definitive, for some hold that it was written before and some after that writing, and in any case the date of the Gospel is uncertain. It seems to me that the Epistle is better understood as following the Gospel than preceding it. Most accept this point of view and proceed to date it towards the end of the 1st century. That is about as close as we can get.

OUTLINE OF CONTENTS

COMMENTARY

1:1-4 Prologue

These verses, one highly compressed and complicated sentence in the Greek, form a prologue to the whole. John outlines some of the ideas he will develop as the Epistle unfolds.

1 The opening Greek word, rendered *that which*, is neuter. It thus appears to refer to the gospel message rather than to a person. But John goes on to speak of hearing, seeing, and

even touching, which makes it necessary for us to think of Jesus. This is the case also with *the word of life*. For while this term might well describe the gospel, we must also bear in mind that Jesus is called 'the Word', and that 'in him was life, and the life was the light of men' (Jn. 1:1, 4). This unusual opening, then, reminds us both of the gospel and of Him on whom the gospel centres.

From the beginning shows that the gospel is

no afterthought. It was always in God's plan. John moves on to the factuality of it all, which is his main point. The gospel is concerned not with some mythical figure like the shadowy forms in the Greek mysteries, but with a genuine historical Person. He had been *heard* and *seen* and *touched* (*cf.* Lk. 24:39; Jn. 20:20, 24ff.). There is a steadily-increasing emphasis on the reality of Jesus' manifestation. John is referring not to visions, but to something physical. So he says 'we have heard, we have seen with our eyes, we saw, and our hands handled'. RSV obscures the fact that there is a change of subject. The earlier verbs tell that *we* have done this or that. Now 'our hands' handled. The change may be stylistic only, or there may be an emphasis on the physical contact. It was what 'our hands' did.

2 John has the habit of emphasizing an idea by the simplest of devices, repetition. Here he begins a little aside by taking up *life*, the last word of v. 1, and repeating it three times in three lines. He is writing about life. But not life in general terms. It is the life that *was made manifest* that is his interest (the aorist tense in the Gk. may point to the decisive manifestation in one life). It is also the life that *we saw*. He has already spoken of seeing it (and will do so again in v. 3: he loves to hammer in an idea). Further, he and those with him who saw it *testify to it*, and they *proclaim* it. He has already spoken of it as 'from the beginning'. Now he puts the same thought another way when he speaks of *the eternal life*. And he carries on with his repetitions when he thinks of the life as *made manifest*. In the Gospel Jesus is called 'the life' (Jn. 14:6). We may deduce from this that it is Jesus to whom witness is borne and who is proclaimed. This might be our conclusion also from the expression *with the Father*, where the construction is the same as that used of 'the Word' in Jn. 1:1. *Father* is, of course, the characteristic Christian designation of God. It is found twelve times in this Epistle.

3 Once again John speaks of what *we have seen and heard*. This stress on eyewitness should not be overlooked, nor the fact that it is linked with *proclaim to you*. It is impossible to make good sense of this if we think of *we* as meaning 'we Christians'. It must mean only those believers who actually saw Jesus in the flesh. These *proclaim* what they saw to the rest of the church. Something of John's aim follows: *so that you may have fellowship with us*. We should not overlook the fact that he immediately goes on to speak of our fellowship as *with the Father and with his Son Jesus Christ*. The basic idea in fellowship (Gk. *koinōnia*) is that of possessing something in common, *i.e.* of partnership or sharing. It is often used of business affairs (*cf.* Lk. 5:10). Christian fellowship means sharing the common life in Christ through the Holy Spirit. It binds believers to one another, but the important thing is that it binds them also to God. It is *fellowship . . . with the Father and with his Son*

Jesus Christ. Notice the way Jesus Christ is linked with the Father thus early in the Epistle. One of John's strong emphases is on the place of Christ and he loses no time in bringing it forward.

4 There is some emphasis on both *we* and *are writing*. The message is in a precise and abiding form and it is written 'by those who had full authority to write' (B. F. Westcott, *Commentary on the Epistles of St. John*, 1883). There is some support for reading 'your' joy, but *our joy* is probably correct. It is only as John brings his friends into the kind of fellowship of which he has just written that his own joy is full, and, of course, the same is true of them. 'Your joy' and 'our joy' go together. As A. E. Brooke (*The Johannine Epistles*, ICC, 1912) reminds us, 'In the spiritual harvest, sower and reaper rejoice together.' For both, true joy comes only from fellowship with God.

1:5 – 2:6 Fellowship with God

John has made it clear that his purpose is to bring his readers into fellowship with God and with other believers. He proceeds to deduce from the nature of God the conditions of fellowship.

1:5 God is light. *This is the message* marks off the following as significant, and indeed as summing up the Christian message. This message is derivative (*we have heard from him*), and is not due to the originality of the apostles or others. Incidentally there is a problem centring on the meaning of *him*, a problem which will recur throughout this Epistle. There is no obvious antecedent. The Father and the Son were both mentioned two sentences back, and either could be in mind here. Perhaps it is a little more likely that the Son is meant, but the two are certainly in the closest connection.

The content of the message is summed up in the expression, *God is light* to which is attached (in a manner reminiscent of the Fourth Gospel where the conjunction of positive and negative is common) *and in him is no darkness at all* (*cf.* Ps. 27:1; Jn. 1:4–9). *Light* is mentioned often in the Gospel, but there it is linked rather with the Son than, as here, with the Father. It is found five times in this Epistle (1:5, 7; 2:8, 9, 10). To say that God is light is to draw attention to His uprightness, His righteousness. Light is a natural symbol for attractive righteousness, just as is darkness for the blackness of sin. There is an emphatic double negative with *darkness*. There is no darkness whatever in God. He is all *light*. There is probably also the thought that our lives are exposed to the illumination that streams from God. Nothing is hid from Him (*cf.* Ps. 90:8). Because He is light it is important that His people 'walk in the light' (v. 7).

1:6, 7 The first error. John is very fond of bringing out his point by making a supposition, and here he has a string of clauses beginning with *if* (vv. 6–10). He deals with three obstacles to fellowship. The first centres on the claim to have fellowship with God. John has already told us that his purpose is that his readers may enjoy this fellowship (v. 3). Now he makes it clear that more than words are necessary to back up a claim to enjoy fellowship with God. 6 If anyone says he has this fellowship but walks *in darkness* then, since God is light, he lies. 'Religion without morality is an illusion' (Stott). John drives this home with the negative. This does not read as RSV *we do not live according to the truth,* but 'we do not do the truth'. This is a very unusual expression found also in Jn. 3:21 and in the Qumran scrolls. Truth can be a quality of action as well as of speech.

7 Now comes the contrary supposition, namely that we really do *walk in the light.* Walking is a metaphor for the whole way of life. It is well adapted to bringing out the truth that the Christian should make steady, if unspectacular, progress. To walk in the light is to live day by day with a strict care for righteousness. Here it is reinforced in the strongest way possible with the addition *as he is in the light* (*cf.* Mt. 5:48). There is to be no trifling with a low standard, as though all that matters is to attain a decent human standard. The Christian is God's servant and he takes his standards from God. He is to live in a God-like way. After the previous verse with its denial of fellowship with God for those who walk in darkness we expect to hear that those who walk in the light really do enjoy fellowship with God. Instead we find that they *have fellowship with one another.* This of course includes fellowship with God (*cf.* v. 3). But that should not blind us to John's form of expression. The fellowship believers enjoy with one another is a thing of great worth.

To this John adds the further point that *the blood of Jesus his Son cleanses us from all sin.* The Saviour is called by the human name *Jesus,* but this is coupled with words which emphasize His uniqueness, *his Son.* We should miss the significance of neither. *Cleanses* is in a continuous tense. It refers not to a once-for-all cleansing, but to an activity which takes place day by day. A little later John recognizes the impossibility of the believer's being free from all sin (*cf.* vv. 8, 10). He is not accordingly speaking of sinless perfection. He is maintaining that when it is our habit to walk in the light, that is, to walk with God, the sins we commit are cleansed. John recognizes that we must live close to God, and that even those who so live need continuous cleansing. Some see in *the blood* (again in 5:6, 8) a symbol of life released from the flesh. But this does not accord with the facts. In the OT, as in the NT, the term points us to life yielded up in death. It is because Jesus has died for us that we have cleansing of sins. The singular, *sin,* sometimes denotes the principle of sin. But this cannot be the meaning here. *All sin* means 'every act of sin'.

1:8, 9 The second error. 8 John crystallizes the second error in the supposition that *we say we have no sin.* To 'have' sin is not a very usual expression (elsewhere Jn. 9:41; 15:22, 24; 19:11).

It means more than to 'commit' sin, and includes the thought of 'the principle of which sinful acts are the several manifestations' (Brooke). Sin is something that persists. It clings to the sinner. As in the case of the preceding and the following suppositions the positive statement is reinforced by a succeeding negative. When we say we have no sin *we deceive ourselves* (we certainly deceive no-one else!), *and the truth is not in us.* Truth is conceived dynamically. It can take up its abode in men of truth. But to say such an obviously false thing as that we have no sin excludes the possibility of the truth's dwelling in us. This has relevance for the modern man who says that sin is a disease or a weakness, and claims that it is due to heredity, environment, necessity or the like, so that he regards it as his fate, not his fault. Such a man deceives himself.

9 The contrasting position is that of those who confess their sins (the plural is significant: we confess specific sins, not simply that we sin). Because God is *faithful and just* He forgives. He can be thoroughly relied upon. Nothing is said as to the way in which He will *cleanse us from all unrighteousness.* But v. 7 is still in mind. It is the blood of Jesus that cleanses. Nothing else can remove our stains.

1:10 The third error. John next supposes that we say *we have not sinned.* All God's dealings with men rest on the basis that man is a sinner, and in need of salvation. To deny that one is a sinner is to *make him a liar.* Put negatively this means that *his word is not in us.* In many parts of the Bible the 'word' has a dynamic character. It effects God's purpose (*cf.* Is. 55:11). Anyone who denies that he is a sinner and who thus makes God out to be a liar shows by that fact that God's effectual word is not in him.

2:1, 2 The propitiation for sins. 1 John often calls his correspondents 'children'. Here he has the affectionate diminutive, *my little children* (Gk. *teknia*; found 7 times in 1 Jn. and once, perhaps twice, only in all the rest of the NT). He says that his reason for writing is *so that you may not sin.* He has already told us that he writes that his readers may enjoy fellowship (1:3), and that his joy might be filled full (1:4). This third statement accords with the others, for sin disrupts fellowship and destroys joy. Sin and vital Christianity are incompatible (*cf.* 3:6, 9; 5:18). But if the Christian does not live in sin it is also the case that he never in this life becomes completely sinless (*cf.* 1:8, 10). John now tells us that when *any one does sin, we have an advocate with the Father, Jesus Christ the righteous. Advocate* is a term with a legal ring about it, and it often indicates the counsel for the defence. It is the friend at court. The use of the term shows that the sinner is in no good case. He is in the wrong with the Father and needs help. It is not without its interest that Christ is called *the righteous.* We might have expected 'the merciful' or the like. But it is consistent NT teaching that God forgives in a way which accords with justice. Forgiveness does not abrogate the moral law but establishes it.

2 Christ is also called 'the propitiation (not *expiation*) for our sins'. RSV, by using a word which means simply the removal of the guilt of sin, obscures the fact that this term (Gk. *hilasmos*) signifies rather the removal of wrath. There is a divine wrath against every form of sin (*cf.* Rom. 1:18), and forgiveness does not mean ignoring this wrath. One way of looking at Christ's saving work is to see it as propitiation. This is not the whole story but it is part of it, a truth which much modern theology overlooks. John goes on to point out that Christ's saving work suffices for *the whole world*. Christ made ample provision.

2:3-6 Obedience. 3 Next comes a test by which men can know whether, in spite of their failures, they are in right relationship with God, and walking in fellowship with Him. The test is whether they *keep his commandments*. It is impossible for men who really know God to be unaffected in their daily living by this knowledge. Knowledge incidentally is an important theme in this Epistle. The verb 'to know' (Gk. *ginōskō*) occurs 25 times (and *oida* 15 times). For John the knowledge of God is not some mystic vision or intellectual insight. It is shown *if we keep his commandments*. Obedience is not a spectacular virtue, but it is at the basis of all true Christian service. **4** The man who claims to have this knowledge but *disobeys his commandments*, John says forthrightly, *is a liar*. He underlines this with the addition, *the truth is not in him*.

5 By contrast, *love for God is perfected* in the man who *keeps his word*. *Word* signifies God's commandments in general. John is not reducing Christianity to a form of legalism. But in Christ God has revealed Himself. Christ is His Word (1:1; Jn. 1:1). The coming of Christ is a challenge to our whole way of life. We are challenged to depart from self-seeking and to take up our cross. It is this that is involved in keeping His word. Now comes another of John's unexpected twists. Following on from v. 4 we expect something about the obedient man's being true, or having the truth of God in him. Instead we find that the love of God is in him, and not only in him but perfected. *Love* (Gk. *agapē*) is one of the leading concepts in 1 John. The word occurs 18 times, which is more than in any other book in the NT (next is 1 Corinthians, 14 times). As this book is so short this is very significant. John sees love primarily in the divine self-giving in Christ (4:10). But the term can also signify man's response to what God has done. This response is lived out in obedience. Love delights to do God's will.

At the end of the verse John speaks of knowing that we are *in him*. This is a new concept. He has spoken before of fellowship with Him (1:3), or walking in the light (1:7), and of knowing Him (2:3). But these are not so many different and unrelated ideas. If we are *in him* we enjoy fellowship with Him, we know Him, and we walk in the light. **6** We can be sure of all this if we *walk*

in the same way in which he walked. The earlier reference to being 'in him' (v. 5) looks like being 'in' God, but the reference to walking shows that *he* in this verse means Jesus Christ. In any case John regularly associates the two in the closest possible fashion, and it is often difficult to be quite sure which is meant.

2:7-17 The new commandment

2:7-11 Loving and hating. 7, 8 *Beloved*. Half a dozen times in this First Epistle John addresses his correspondents as *beloved*, which accords with his stress on love. He does not spell out the *commandment* which he speaks of as both *old* and *new*, but there is no doubt that he means the commandment to love (*cf.* 4:21; Jn. 15:12). This is not a novelty *but the word which you have heard*. It is fundamental to the Christian way and thus was inculcated from the first. But there is always a freshness about it and thus it is *a new commandment* (*cf.* Jn. 13:34). The old commandment has a new urgency for those for whom Christ died.

This command was first fulfilled by Christ (*is true in him*), who puts a like love into the hearts of His followers (*and in you*). Thus our attitude to our brother shows whether we are in *the darkness* that is *passing away* or in *the true light* which is *already shining*. If a man lives in love he walks with a sure foot, for love rids his heart of all that would make him stumble. Light is his atmosphere, his environment. But hatred and light are incompatible. **9-11** If a man *hates his brother*, let him say what he will, he is on the wrong track, a track which will lead him to ruin, for hatred blinds the eyes. Notice the threefold reference to *the darkness*. We must not miss the connection between hatred and darkness.

2:12-14 The family of faith. Two sequences, each with a threefold address, to *children*, *fathers*, and *young men* occur here. Considerable ingenuity has been expended on the definition of these classes, and on the change of tense from 'I write' to 'I wrote' (vv. 13c, 14, Gk.). It is true that there is a certain appropriateness in the allocation of qualities, for knowledge accords with fathers (those old in the faith), and strength with young men. But as all the qualities John mentions ought to be found in all believers it is probably best to regard the division as a stylistic device adding emphasis. As C. H. Dodd says (*The Johannine Epistles*, MNTC, 1946), 'All Christians are (by grace, not nature) children in innocence and dependence on the heavenly Father, young men in strength, and fathers in experience.' John is pointing out that his readers have the forgiveness of sins, the knowledge of God, the word of God abiding in them, and victory over the evil one. These are important attributes of the followers of Christ.

2:15-17 Love for the world. 15 We have noted John's little trick of emphasizing a word by simply repeating it. He now uses *world* three times in this verse and another three times in the two succeeding verses. It is an important concept. He draws attention to *the world* as something that could become of absorbing interest. But he says, *Do not love the world.* Some see a contradiction with 'God so loved the world' (Jn. 3:16). But that passage refers to God's saving love for all men, whereas this is concerned with setting one's heart on worldliness. John makes two points: *a.* love for the world in this sense is incompatible with love for the Father, and *b.* in any case the world and all that is in it are temporary. **16** *The lust of the flesh* points to the gratification of our fleshly desires. *The lust of the eyes* will refer to strong desire for what is seen, for the outward form of things. It is the lust after the superficial. *The pride of life* is the empty haughtiness of the worldly-minded. (With these three we might compare the three things which led Eve to disobey God, Gn. 3:6.) None of these things takes its origin in God (*not of the Father*). They are *of the world*, that world which is but a passing show on its way to ruin. **17** By contrast, *he who does the will of God abides for ever.*

2:18–27 The Christian and the antichrist

2:18, 19 Many antichrists. 18 There is no article with *hour*. John is not saying *it is the last hour*, but 'it is a last hour'. Human history proceeds by periods of slow unfolding until a crisis is reached, an age is ended, a new age begins, and men say, 'It can never be the same again.' John is affirming that such a last hour has come. He sees evidence in the appearance not simply of *antichrist*, but of *many antichrists*. The early church clearly expected at the end of time a mighty figure of evil it called *antichrist* (*cf.* 'the man of lawlessness', 2 Thes. 2:3). Though John uses the term four times (and once in 2 John) he is not interested in the future individual. His concern is for his readers, and he stresses that the spirit of antichrist is already abroad.

19 These many antichrists had been members of the church. They had belonged to the visible organization, but John is quick to say *but they were not of us.* He can go on, *they went out, that it might be plain that they all are not of us.* Though members of the organization, they had never really belonged. This is surely the doctrine of 'the church invisible' though that terminology is centuries later.

2:20, 21 Knowledge of the truth. 20 *You have been anointed by the Holy One* is another way of saying that all have received the gift of the Holy Spirit. *The Holy One* is an unusual expression but there can be no doubt but that it refers to the Holy Spirit. John proceeds *you all know* (this reading is is to be preferred to the RSV mg., 'you know everything'). The illumination afforded by the Spirit means that in Christianity there is no enlightened *élite* on whom all others depend. Every believer has knowledge. **21** John has this truth well in mind as he proceeds to the central tenet of the heresy he is opposing. The false teachers clearly denied the reality of the incarnation. We know that some false teachers in early

days held that there was a divine Christ who came down on the man Jesus at the baptism, but left him before the crucifixion. John was not necessarily opposed by men holding just this belief, but it was something like it.

2:22, 23 The lie. 22 They denied *that Jesus is the Christ.* John sees this as the fundamental lie. The man who goes wrong here is not to be depended upon anywhere. He is the *antichrist* who *denies the Father and Son.* The evidence that in Jesus of Nazareth God and man are indissolubly united is so strong in John's view that the man who will not accept it is fundamentally astray. He is guilty of the radical lie. **23** This denial of the Son has consequences. Without a right view of the Son one cannot have a right view of the Father. If Jesus is not the very Son of God and one with the Father, then it is not the love of God that we see revealed in His life and death. It is only as we receive Christ that we become sons of God (Jn. 1:12), so that if we reject Him we are not members of the heavenly family. We have no right to call God our Father.

2:24–27 Abiding in God. 24 *What you heard from the beginning* points back to the simple gospel message. If John's readers let that *abide* (this verb occurs 24 times in 1 John) in them then they *abide in the Son and in the Father.* **25** Thus is God's promise of *eternal life* fulfilled. **27** With this we must take *the anointing* of which John has already spoken (v. 20). It is owing to the enlightenment given by the Holy Spirit within them that they have the knowledge that matters and that they abide in God.

2:28 – 3:10 Children of God

2:28, 29 Confidence. John is anxious to establish the family relationship. So now he calls his readers *little children*, speaks of having *confidence* at the coming of Christ, and goes on to the way right conduct shows that one *is born of him.* *Born* (perhaps better, 'begotten') is important. Believers are not simply worldly men who are trying to live a little better. They are men who have been radically renewed. They have been born all over again. The habitual practice of righteousness is evidence of such divine activity.

3:1–3 What we shall be. 1 The wonder of it all arrests John. 'Look!' he says, 'Look at the love the Father has given us. We are called children of God. And we are!' The divine call in Scripture is often regarded as an effectual call, but John leaves no doubts. Not only are we *called* God's children, but we are such in reality. This has a consequence that *the world does not know us.* The incompatibility of the world and Christianity is a recurring theme in John's writings. The world's failure to know believers is not to be wondered at for *it did not know him.* Grammatically *him* should be the Father, but it is impossible to think that there is no reference to Christ. John's recognition of the reality of our sonship now does not blind him to the fact that the best is yet to be. **2** He puts this in the form of a reference to the beatific vision, *when he appears we shall be like him, for we shall see him as he is. He* and *him* grammatically ought to refer back to *God*, but it is more usual to speak of seeing Christ. But probably too much should not be made of this, for he that sees the Son sees also the Father (Jn. 12:45; 14:9). And to see God is to be transformed. **3** This prospect is a present stimulus, for *every one* who has this hope *purifies himself as he is pure*.

3:4 The necessity for right conduct. The false teachers seem to have held that knowledge is all-important, and that conduct does not matter. So John insists that sin is evidence of wrong relationship to God. *Sin*, he tells us, *is lawlessness*, the Greek construction implying that the two are interchangeable. The law in question is, of course, the law of God. The essence of sin, then, is disregard for God's law. It is the assertion of oneself against God's revealed way for man. It is the preference for selfishness over the service of God.

3:5–7 Christ and sin are incompatible. 5 Christ came *to take away sins*, which indicates complete hostility to evil. *In him there is no sin.* **6** This has effects in the Christian, for *no one who abides in him sins*. We must not water down statements like this. The Christian has no business with sin and he must never be complacent about it, even about occasional sin. But we must also notice the use of the Greek continuous present in both verbs. John is saying, 'No-one who continually abides in him makes a habit of sinning' and again, 'No-one who habitually sins has seen or known him.' He is not speaking about individual acts of sin (which would be better expressed by the Gk. aorist) but about habitual attitudes. The life a man lives reveals the source from which he draws his life. **7** To hold otherwise is to be deceived. It is not a matter of right thinking or of wide knowledge or of holding that the body is unimportant so that it does not matter what the body does as long as the soul is pure. John firmly sweeps aside all such specious arguments. *He who does right is righteous*. And the standard is Christ: *as he is righteous*.

3:8–10 Children of the devil. 8 The other side of this coin is that *he who commits sin is of the devil*. Both *does* and *commits* (actually the same word in the Gk.) point to the habitual practice. It is the habitual trend of the life of which John is writing. This opposition is underlined by the fact that *the reason* for Christ's coming was *to destroy the works of the devil*. The opposition is complete. *Destroy* is not specific; that is to say it tells us that Jesus came to do away with the devil, but it does not say how. **9** *Born of God* points to divine action. There is something supernatural about the life of the Christian. He has been regenerated by the very power of God. Once again we must give present tenses their full continuative force. The man *born of God* does not make a practice of sinning. Indeed, *he cannot sin*. John has already repudiated the doctrine of sinless perfection (1:8, 10),

and we must not interpret these words in such a way as to contradict those. He is saying that sin and the Christian are radically opposed. 'John is arguing rather the incongruity than the impossibility of sin in the Christian' (Stott). Should a Christian sin that would be an act completely out of character. On this occasion he gives a reason for the believer's inability to sin: *God's nature* (Gk. 'seed') *abides in him*. It is most unusual to have the metaphor pressed in this way (this is the one occurrence of 'seed' in John, but the verb rendered *born* is found ten times in this Epistle). It stresses the fact that there is a divine power at work within the believer. *Abides* shows that this is not occasional. It is God's continuing gift to His people. **10** John rounds off this section by contrasting *the children of God* and *the children of the devil*. The test is whether a man does right and loves his brother, or not.

3:11–18 Love one another

3:11–15 The antithesis of love. 11 Again John insists that love is the first command (*from the beginning*). It is not peripheral, but lies at the heart of the Christian *message*. **12** The point is brought out by referring to its antithesis. *Cain who was of the evil one* shows us the conduct we must avoid. Being of the evil one he *murdered his brother*. This is the logical outcome of a refusal to love (*cf.* Mt. 5:21f.). John's answer to the question *why did he murder him?* is a penetrating critique of human nature. It was no offence of Abel's, but simply his good life in the face of his brother's bad one. Evil men do not love the highest when they see it. It rebukes them and they crucify it. **13** This is made the basis of an injunction: *Do not wonder* ('stop wondering' is the force of it), *brethren, that the world hates you*. Christians usually find it difficult to understand this. They act from the best motives, with love in their hearts for their fellows. They seek nothing for themselves, but offer the priceless gift of the gospel. Yet the world does not respond with gratitude. It hates believers.

14 The love–hate antithesis continues here. Life and love go together. Notice once again John's use of *we know*. That all Christians have knowledge is important to him and he brings it out many times. *We have passed out of death into life* (*cf.* Jn. 5:24) is expressive and unusual. The unbeliever lives in a condition that can only be called *death*. Not so the believer. He has passed clean out of death and lives that life which really is life. The test whereby we may know this is that *we love the brethren*. John keeps coming back to that. He reinforces it here with the corresponding negative. *He who does not love remains* (this is the verb elsewhere translated 'abides'; it points to a continuing state) *in death*. **15** This is spelled out with an emphatic declaration about the meaning of hate. *Any one who hates his brother is a murderer*. Our Lord said that the lustful look is adultery and that the angry word breaks the command 'Thou shalt not kill' (Mt. 5:21f.). Following this example John goes to the deep roots of men's actions. Hatred is of the essence of murder. And *no murderer has eternal life abiding in him.* This does not mean that a murderer cannot repent and find forgiveness. It means that the man in whom is the attitude that brings murder is not the possessor of eternal life. The two are mutually exclusive.

3:16–18 Love is practical. 16 We can *know love* in the specifically Christian sense only because of what we see on Calvary, where *he laid down his life for us* (as often in this Epistle, *he* is not defined, but in this place there is no doubt but that Jesus is meant). Since the Christ to whom Christians owe their inspiration so died for men, Christians in their turn *ought to lay down* their *lives for the brethren.* This is the quality of *love* that is always demanded of the Christian.

17 The actual laying down of the life must have been rarely called for, even in the 1st century. But love has other outlets. It is constantly needed in daily life. The word rendered *goods* (Gk. *bion*, only here and 2:16 in this Epistle) is not common in such a connection. It more usually means 'life'. But the meaning is plain. *Sees* (Gk. *theōrē*) means more than a passing glance. The man sees his brother for long enough to be sure of the situation. But he *closes his heart.* The term *heart* yields an interesting example of the difference Christianity can make. The literal meaning of the word is 'the entrails', the part of the body which the Greeks held to be the special location of the emotions. The use of the word denoted accordingly that the man was emotionally involved. For the Greeks in general this commonly meant that he was angry (though other emotions were sometimes thought of). But for the Christians the same expression meant that he was moved with compassion. If a man fails to exercise compassion this shows that 'the love of God' (which might mean either our love for God or God's love for us) does not *abide* in him. **18** Again comes the familiar address, *little children,* as John exhorts to real love. Love is not simply a matter of profession. *Deed* and *truth* count for more than *word or speech.*

3:19–24 Confidence

Now comes a reassurance for sensitive consciences. We should live before God not in trembling anxiety but in calm confidence.

19 Another of John's tests; this is the way we know we are *of the truth* (the only place in the Epistle where men are said to be *of the truth,* though the expression is used of statements in 2:21). It draws attention to the importance of complete and utter honesty, and to the truth of the gospel. To know that we belong to truth is to receive assurance. **20** But sometimes believers lack assurance. *Our hearts condemn us.* This, however, is not the significant thing. It is God's condemnation or approval that matters

and *he knows everything.* He knows our motives and those deeds of love for which we may perhaps not dare to take credit (*cf.* Mt. 25:37–40). He knows that we are His and it is this that is important, not our misgivings. **21** But John does not wish to leave Christians accepting this kind of thing as the norm. Something better is the way for us. The promises of God are such that there is no reason for remaining in uncertainty. Thus we may *have confidence* before Him. Since we are His we have nothing to fear. **22** The connection with the preceding is not obvious. Receiving answers to prayer does not seem to follow on from the fact that our heart does not condemn us. But confidence is common to both, and answered prayer is bound to increase our confidence. This is connected with obedience. Both *keep* and *do* are in continuous tenses. Power in prayer is conditioned not by occasional bursts of obedience, but by lives characterized by obedience. Further we do *what pleases him.* This goes beyond the keeping of commandments. It is reminiscent of our Lord's attitude in the Sermon on the Mount. There is the same concern for the spirit, the same conviction that it is not sufficient to keep the letter of the law.

23 *The commandment* is now defined in terms of faith and love. The singular may be meant to indicate that 'but one thing is needful'. There is no great list of burdensome requirements. Further, faith and love are so intimately connected that they may be regarded as one. Faith is *in the name of his Son Jesus Christ.* The *name* stands for the whole person. It is faith in all that Jesus is and does. The second part of the commandment is that we must *love one another.* The place of love and our reciprocal responsibility are two of the great themes of this Epistle. We are to love *just as he has commanded us.* This addition to *his commandment* at the beginning of the verse emphasizes the fact that God is not indifferent to the way we live. **24** After the singular of v. 23 John returns to the plural, *commandments.* All who keep them *abide in him, and he in them.* This mutual indwelling is another characteristic theme of this Epistle. How do we know it has taken place? *By the Spirit which he has given us.* The Spirit is *given* (not earned), and the Spirit gives assurance.

4:1–6 The spirit of truth and the spirit of error

The reference to the Spirit raises the question of how to tell those who are truly inspired from those who claim falsely that the Spirit is in them. The problem was not new, for there were false prophets in OT times, and again, Paul had had to give a ruling on when a man is speaking 'by the Spirit of God' (1 Cor. 12:3).

1 *Many false prophets have gone out into the world.* The religions of antiquity commonly claimed to have spirit-possessed men. John warns that not every man who claims to speak under inspiration is to be regarded as uttering truth. His readers must not be ready to believe every one, but must *test the spirits.* That they had *gone out* may indicate that the people in mind were those already referred to as having left the church (2:19). **2** The test is the attitude to Jesus Christ. If *the spirit of God* is in a man he will confess *that Jesus Christ has come in the flesh*. More exactly he 'confesses Jesus Christ come in the flesh', *i.e.* the emphasis is on the Person not the proposition. The reference to *the flesh* puts emphasis on the incarnation. It is not simply that Jesus took human nature but *flesh* (*cf.* Jn. 1:14; 2 Jn. 7). The spirit which confesses that Jesus Christ has so come *is of God*. This is not a human discovery, but something God reveals. **3** But there is such a thing as a *spirit which does not confess Jesus*. To confess Jesus is the same as the confession 'that Jesus Christ has come in the flesh' of the previous verse. The spirit which refuses this confession is *not of God*, *i.e.* it is the antithesis of the spirit mentioned in the previous verse. In fact it is *the spirit of antichrist*. John has already said that there are many antichrists in the world (2:18), and has given a kind of definition of antichrist: 'This is the antichrist, he who denies the Father and the Son' (2:22). The thought here is similar. In both places the essential point about *antichrist* is the refusal to acknowledge that Jesus is the Christ, come in the flesh. In both John's readers had heard of the antichrist's coming as future, but he sees a present reality: there, many antichrists, here, *the spirit of antichrist*. His *now*, his *in the world*, and his *already* combine to stress the present reality.

4 But there is no need for Christians to be fearful. *You* is emphatic. Believers are in strong contrast. In the first instance they *are of God*, and in the second they *have overcome*. Apart from Revelation, which has it 17 times, this little Epistle employs the verb 'to overcome' more often than any other book (6 times). The note of victory is unusually prominent. In this case the verb is in the perfect tense which shows that the victory is more than a passing phase. It is decisive and continuous. The victory results because *he who is in you is greater than he who is in the world*. On neither occasion does John explain his *he*. The first could be any member of the Trinity and all that we can say is that it is a divine Person. The second cannot be other than the devil. John is saying that God is more powerful by far than the devil and that those in whom God dwells accordingly overcome evil.

5 Once again John uses the device of repeating a word for emphasis, for we have *world* three times in this verse as well as at the end of the preceding verse. It is with the *world* that these people are associated: they are *of* it, what they speak comes from it, and it is the world that forms their audience. **6** Christians should not be surprised if such people do not hear or understand them. They are of the wrong party. But Christians do have their hearers. *We* is emphatic and sets them in strong contrast with the preceding. Christians are *of God*. This enables John to lay down who it is who hears them and who

does not. The former class is described as *whoever knows God* and the latter as *he who is not of God*. Since this is the way *the spirit of truth and the spirit of error* are known it is a fair inference that these spirits dwell in the classes of men previously indicated.

4:7–21 God is love

Throughout this Epistle love is important. In this section John stresses this by drawing attention to the fact that love is rooted in God, who is, in fact, love.

4:7–12 Love one another. 7 The exhortation *let us love one another* is reinforced with the reminder that *love is of God*. The love of which John writes is not a human achievement. It is divine in origin. If a man loves in this sense it shows that he *is born of God and knows God*. **8** The negative helps bring the point out. The man *who does not love does not know God*. The reason for this is one of the greatest statements in the Bible: *God is love*. This means more than 'God is loving'. It means that God's essential nature is love. He loves, so to speak, not because He finds objects worthy of His love, but because it is His nature to love. His love for us depends not on what we are, but on what He is. He loves us because He is that kind of God. **9** The kind of love of which John is writing is not to be seen everywhere among men, or indeed anywhere among men. We know it because it *was made manifest* and this when *God sent his only Son into the world*. The purpose of this sending of the Son was to bring men life. Life in the full sense comes to men *through him* alone.

10 The real meaning of love and the real source of life are discerned only in the cross. We must not start with men if we are looking for specifically Christian love. It is *not that we loved God*. We will never find it out if we begin from the human side (*we* is emphatic; not that *we* loved). We find it when we see that *he loved us and sent his Son to be the expiation for our sins*. RSV's *expiation* is misleading here, for *hilasmos* means 'propitiation'. To see what love means we must see ourselves as sinners, as the objects of God's wrath, and yet as people for whom Christ died. 'So far from finding any kind of contrast between love and propitiation, the apostle can convey no idea of love to anyone except by pointing to the propitiation' (James Denney, *The Death of Christ*, 1951, p. 152). It is one of the NT's resounding paradoxes that it is God's love that averts God's wrath from us, and that indeed it is precisely in the averting of this wrath that we see what real love is. **11** This has consequences. When we see that God loves like that *we* (the word is emphatic) *also ought to love one another*. The mainspring for love of our fellow-man is the divine love shown in Christ's atoning work. **12** The importance of love for one another comes out in the fact that it is this love and not love toward God that John picks out as showing that *God abides in us*. When he tells us that *no man has ever seen God* (*cf.* Jn. 1:18) he is not discounting the visions related in the OT (*cf.*, *e.g.*, Ex. 24:11). But such visions were partial and incomplete. It is in Christ that we see God. And when we love, God dwells in us. Indeed, *his love is perfected* (*i.e.* reaches its aim) *in us*, a staggering statement.

4:13–16 Abiding in love. 13 John has already told us that it is 'by the Spirit' that we know that 'he abides in us' (3:24). He now adds the thought that *we abide in him*. Both are important and both receive stress in this Epistle. **14** In the spirit of the prologue he reverts to the apostolic testimony to what had been *seen*. The thought of witness looms larger as we approach the end of the Epistle. The verb 'to witness' occurs in 1:2, here, and four times in ch. 5, while the noun 'witness' is found six times in ch. 5. The content of the witness is that the Son is *the Saviour of the world* (an expression only here and in Jn. 4:42 in the NT). *Saviour* covers all aspects of Christ's work for men, and *world* the totality of mankind. It is a great salvation of which John writes. **15** But not all are saved. For that it is necessary to confess *that Jesus is the Son of God*. Then there follows a mutual indwelling of God and the believer.

16 We do not read elsewhere of 'knowing' and 'believing' love. We could fairly say that the thought of 'knowing' love is found, as in v. 10. But to *believe the love God has for us* is a most unusual expression. The love of God is never demonstrated in such a way that the worldly-minded cannot but see it. It is the man of faith and the man of faith only who discerns it. John repeats the great thought of v. 8, *God is love*, and draws the conclusion that to abide in love is to abide in God. The love exercised towards sinners is not a human achievement and where it is present it shows that God is present.

4:17–21 The perfecting of love. 17 This mutual abiding is the way love is *perfected with us*. This is with a view to *confidence for the day of judgment*, and confidence for that day is the ultimate in confidence. *As he is so are we in this world* points to the fact that the world did not welcome Christ and it does not welcome Christ's people. On the day of judgment the Judge will understand all. As He is so are we.

18 The thought of confidence is developed with the repudiation of *fear*. John uses this word three times in this verse (his way of emphasis), but nowhere else in the Epistle. The verb *fears* is also confined to this verse. Believers need not fear, for *fear* and *love* are incompatible. *Perfect love* throws it out. *Fear*, John proceeds, *has to do with punishment*. When we fear it is because we know we deserve punishment. But God's *perfect love* reassures us. His love makes provision so that we are saved, not punished. If we fear, that in itself shows we have not been *perfected in love* (John has already pointed out that the perfecting of love brings confidence even on the day of judgment, v. 17).

19 Some MSS read 'We love him (or God)', but this distorts the sense. It is true that our love

for God is an answering love, a response to His love. But John is saying not this, but rather that we love, in the sense of specifically Christian love, the love of the unworthy which proceeds from the nature of the lover not the worth of the loved one, only *because he first loved us*. **20** To say *I love God*, but to have hatred for one's *brother* (brother-Christian? brother-man?) is to show oneself to be a *liar*. Love to God is shown by love to man. If one is lacking so is the other. John goes so far as to say that if one does not love his brother he *cannot love God*. A distinction is made between the brother who is seen and God who is not. To affirm one's love for the unseen while failing to love the seen is to enter the realm of fantasy.

21 John rounds off the discussion by reminding his readers of the *commandment* that *we have from him*. John's *him* might be God or Christ. As often, he does not differentiate sharply. He has already spoken of the commandment to love (3:23) and now he reminds us again that love is not a suggested option. It is a positive command.

5:1–5 Faith's victory

The thought of love leads to that of relationship to God, and that in turn to victory. Love and faith are wrapped up in one another (*cf.* 4:16), and the believer overcomes the world.

1 Faith is inseparably connected with our view of Jesus, a truth insisted upon throughout this Epistle. It is necessary to believe *that Jesus is the Christ*. Then one becomes *a child of God* (Gk. 'has been begotten of God'). The confession that Jesus is the Christ is not the result of human insight. If a man makes it it shows that a divine work has taken place in him (*cf.* 1 Cor. 12:3). And he will love his fellow-believers for *every one who loves the parent loves the child*. **2** The love for God and for man are closely connected as John keeps insisting. Usually though he thinks of the love for God as shown in love for the brethren. Here he reverses the process. We know we *love the children of God, when we love God*. The love of God and man and the life lived in accordance with such love is a unity. John's practical turn of mind does not let him stop at the thought of love for God. He goes on, *and obey his commandments*. Real love is shown by a concern to do God's will. **3** Indeed he can define *the love of God* by saying *that we keep his commandments*. John is not a legalist. But he recognizes that love is busy. It finds its natural expression in doing the things that please the Beloved, and where will we find these things better than in *his commandments*? When John adds *his commandments are not burdensome* the thought is not that it is quite easy to discharge one's obligations to God. Rather John is saying that God's commandments are not an irksome burden. They may be difficult but they are a delight.

4 The thought moves to *victory*. The neuter *whatever* makes the statement quite general (*cf.* 1:1). *Our faith* (the noun here only in 1 John;

it is not in the Gospel or 2, 3 John) stands last with emphasis. It is worth noting that the preceding *overcomes* is rather 'overcame'. The decisive victory is in the past, when Christ died to overcome evil, and when believers came to trust in Him. **5** The rhetorical question stresses the place of faith. Victory comes to him *who believes that Jesus is the son of God*. Notice the emphasis, yet once more, on a right view of His Person. We see here also John's habit of emphasis by repetition, for in these two verses he has three references to overcoming the world. We cannot miss it.

5:6–12 The witness to the Son

Since a right view of Jesus matters so much it is important that He be attested. John cites now some of the testimony which establishes His position.

6 That He came *by water* must surely refer to His baptism, and *blood* to His death. At the baptism He heard the heavenly voice and He solemnly entered His life's work. Some heretics apparently held that the divine Christ came upon Jesus then but left Him before His death. John contests this with his emphasis on blood, *not with the water only but with the water and the blood*. There seem no doubts about *the water*, but John has to emphasize *the blood*. It was this that was the stumbling-block. But it was (and is) this that is the heart of the gospel. **7** John adds the information that *the Spirit is the witness* (the present participle 'the witnessing one' points to a continuing activity). He has an excellent qualification, for *the Spirit is the truth* (*cf.* the similar statement about Jesus, Jn. 14:6). (Notice that AV includes additional material at this point. But the words are clearly a gloss and are rightly excluded by RSV even from its margins.) **8** There are in fact *three witnesses*. The Spirit is mentioned first, perhaps because He has just been referred to, and perhaps because He is a Person and thus a more explicit witness than *the water, and the blood*. This witness is harmonious. The inner witness of the Spirit, and all that is involved in Christ's baptism and His death are not three unrelated items. The three point to one act of God in Christ for man's salvation.

9 John appeals to the well-known fact of human trust. We believe our fellow-men. We should accordingly accept the testimony of which he has been speaking, for *the testimony of God is greater*, and the testimony in question is His. God *has borne witness to his Son*. Now witness commits. And God has committed Himself in Christ. He has borne witness that this is what He Himself is like. **10** Whoever trusts God's Son *has the testimony in himself*, which seems to show that the witness of the Spirit (v. 7) is a witness to the man's own spirit. *He who believes in the Son of God* and *he who does not believe God* appear to be opposites. This will mean that John puts no great difference between believing and believing in, and between faith in the Son of God and faith in God. For him Jesus Christ

was God incarnate, so that to believe in Christ is to believe in God. But to disbelieve is to make Him *a liar* (*cf.* 1:10). The perfect tense in the verb *has made* views this as lasting. The unbeliever places himself in the position of permanently having a wrong view of God.

11 The content of the testimony is a little unexpected for it is what God has done, not what He has said. He *gave us eternal life*. Eternal life is God's own deed and God's own gift and as we contemplate it we see a revelation of God. The addition, *and this life is in his Son*, is important. We cannot think of eternal life apart from the Son nor can we think of *the testimony* apart from Him (*cf.* v. 9). Life eternal is life with Christ and in Christ. **12** This is emphasized in a crisp couplet. Life and the Son go together. It is impossible to have the one without the other.

5:13–21 The knowledge of eternal life

The Gospel according to John was written that its readers might believe and so have life (Jn. 20:31). By contrast this Epistle was written to give believers assurance, to let them know that they have life. John brings this out as his letter draws to a close.

5:13–15 Confidence. 13 The recipients are addressed as *you who believe*. This Epistle is not an evangelistic tract but a letter to Christians. John has said a good deal about knowledge and he comes back to the most important piece of knowledge, *that you may know that you have eternal life*. Incidentally this is the only place in this Epistle where he speaks of believing *in the name* of Jesus, *i.e.* in His full Person, all that the name stands for (in 3:23 the Gk. means 'believe the name').

14 Confidence is closely connected with assurance, and John moves suddenly into confidence in prayer. He gives it a very wide scope, for he thinks of asking anything, though he immediately qualifies this with *according to his will*. Prayer is not a device for inducing God to change His mind. It must be offered in accordance with His will if it is to be effective. When so offered He *hears us*. Elsewhere we learn that prayer must be in faith (Mk. 11:24), in the name of Jesus (Jn. 14:14), offered by those who abide in Christ (Jn. 15:7), and who have forgiven those who offend them (Mk. 11:25), and it must be accompanied by obedience (1 Jn. 3:22). It must not be for the gratification of one's passions (Jas. 4:3). **15** John now proceeds from the thought of God's hearing us to the consequence, namely that He grants our requests.

5:16, 17 Prayer for wrongdoers. 16 There is an abrupt change to the forgiveness of sin, which can be brought about by intercessory prayer. John distinguishes between *mortal* sin and sin which *is not mortal*, but he does not define either. He tells us that when we see a *brother* commit such a sin we should pray for him. God will hear the prayer and *give him life*. This may well indicate that he was not up till now a

Christian. He was not alive but 'dead through the trespasses and sins' (Eph. 2:1). In response to prayer *life* is given to him. We should regard *mortal sin* as a state rather than an act. There is no one specific sin men commit which we can call *mortal*, but there is a state of sin, of being in rebellion against God which John elsewhere characterizes as remaining in death (3:14). Our Lord warns that he who blasphemes against the Spirit 'will not be forgiven' (Lk. 12:10) and it is this kind of thing that is in mind here. John adds *I do not say that one is to pray* for mortal sin. This is not to introduce an element of calculation as to when we may and when we may not pray for others. It is a warning that sin damns men. **17** *All wrongdoing is sin.* We must not take sin lightly. But the believer may sin a sin which does not remove him from the category of the saved.

5:18–21 The believer's knowledge. 18 John has had a good deal to say about knowledge and now he introduces three statements in succession with *we know*. The first is that *any one born of God does not sin.* Again it is the habitual attitude that is meant. The reason is that he is kept safe by Him *who was born of God, i.e.* Jesus Christ. *The evil one* accordingly *does not touch him,* does not make effective contact with him. **19** The second statement concerns the origin of believers, that they *are of God.* By contrast *the whole world is in the power of the evil one*, literally 'lies in the evil one'. This is an unusual verb and

may point to the powerlessness of the world lying under Satan's sway, perhaps, too, to its inertness, its refusal to assert itself against its master.

20 The third of John's trilogy directs us to the incarnation. *The Son of God has come.* There is some emphasis on the actuality of the arrival (Gk. *hēkei*). Moreover He *has given us understanding.* The Christian faith is not a hindrance to thinking but a stimulus to right thinking. The understanding is so that we may *know him who is true.* Not only do we know Him, but we are *in him*, and this is further explained as *in his Son Jesus Christ.* As often in this Epistle the Father and the Son are seen in the closest possible relationship. To be 'in' the Father is the same as to be 'in' the Son. John goes on, *This is the true God and eternal life.* Once more it is not easy to see whether the Father or the Son is meant. But they are so close that there is little difference. For the men of the ancient world there were many gods. But John sees that they are all false gods. There is but one *true God*, and men have eternal life in Him.

21 For the last time John uses the affectionate diminutive, *little children.* In view of the whole preceding discussion it is unlikely that *idols* should be taken to mean images used in worship. The term means 'false gods'. John's readers have been given many gifts by God, including 'understanding' (v. 20). Let them keep themselves then from every false god.

2 and 3 John

INTRODUCTION

These short letters were not often quoted in the earliest times. This is not surprising, but it makes it difficult to solve problems concerning date and the like. Both claim to be written by 'the elder', but there is no further description. Considerations of style convince most scholars that they are by the same author as 1 John, but there is no unanimity. Donald Guthrie surveys the evidence and concludes:

'1. Authorship by the apostle John, which has such strong external support, is seen to be a quite reasonable deduction from the internal evidence.

'2. Authorship by the Elder John, proposed by most of those disputing apostolic authorship either of the Epistles or the Gospel, has far less ancient attestation but far more modern opinion behind it. It would have greater weight if the

Elder John (*i.e.* as distinct from the apostle) were known with certainty to have existed.

'3. Authorship by an unknown Elder has even less ancient testimony and cannot be considered as probable.

'The conclusion reached is that John, the Son of Zebedee, was the author of all three Epistles' (*New Testament Introduction: Hebrews to Revelation*, 1962, p. 212).

This seems to be a reasonable summary of the position. There can in the nature of the case be no certainty, but in the present state of our knowledge it seems best to accept the traditional view.

There is a problem as to the destination of 2 John. It is addressed to 'the elect lady and her children', but there is controversy as to whether this means an individual lady or whether it is a symbolic way of referring to a church. The 'children' would then be members of the congregation. The principal argument for the former view is that this is the most natural way of taking the words, while for the latter it is urged that the subject-matter is more appropriate for a church than for an individual, and that the letter lacks personal characteristics (in which it stands in contrast to 3 John). The problem seems insoluble with the information at our command, though perhaps it is slightly more likely that it is a letter to an individual. It seems a rather slight missive to be sent to a congregation.

2 John seems to reflect something of the same false teaching that lies behind 1 John. The letter then will be written to put its readers on their guard against it. Clearly there was some danger that the false teachers would be welcomed and thus their doctrines would spread. The Elder writes to forestall this. Some writers link 3 John with the same situation. It certainly is concerned with hospitality to visiting preachers. A certain Diotrephes was refusing to receive those the Elder commended, and it may be that he belonged to the opposite party accordingly. But this is very speculative. All that we can say is that Gaius is being reassured. The Elder will take action against Diotrephes in due course.

There is very little on which to estimate the dates of these writings. Most agree that they come from about the same period, and it is usual to see this as not too far from the time of 1 John, *i.e.* probably about the end of the 1st century.

2 John

COMMENTARY

1–3 Salutation. This is the normal type of opening to a 1st-century letter. **1, 2** The writer calls himself *the elder*, which may be an indication of age or possibly of an official position in the church. The letter is addressed to *the elect lady*, an expression which might also be rendered 'an elect lady'. Alternatively, one or both of the Greek terms may be taken as a proper name, 'Electa the Lady', 'the elect Kyria' or 'Electa Kyria'. RSV is probably correct. Whether an individual or a church is meant is disputed; see Introduction. The elder affirms that he loves the lady and her children *in the truth. Love* and *truth* are very prominent in this Epistle (*truth* occurs five times in the first four verses). Notice the sequence *whom I love . . . because of the truth. Truth* as John sees it leads to *love. The truth* can be known. It *abides* in believers and *will be with* them *for ever.* It is difficult to think that *the truth* thus described is altogether separate from our Lord Jesus Christ who could say 'I am . . . the truth' (Jn. 14:6).

3 The addition of *mercy* to *grace* and *peace* in the greeting is unusual (elsewhere only in 1, 2 Timothy). It strengthens the idea in *grace* which points us to the freeness of God's gift in Christ. It is also unusual to have it said that these things will be *with us.* In a salutation one expects 'with you'. This appears to be the only salutation in the NT which reads this way. It is an expression of solidarity linking writer and readers. All alike need *grace, mercy and peace.* Jesus is spoken of here as *the Father's Son,* and here only in the NT. He is not to be thought of as separate from the Father.

4–6 The command to love. 4 The writer *rejoiced greatly* when he found some of the *children* of the elect lady *following the truth.* This last expression is literally 'walking in truth' and must be very nearly equivalent to 'living the Christian life'. That it is put this way indicates the stress our writer places on the truth. To follow the truth is not an option selected by men but *we have been commanded by the Father.* In three verses here we have the verb 'command' or the noun 'commandment' four times. It is the repetition for emphasis we have already noticed in 1 John, and again in the opening verses. **5** The elder does not enjoin but says *I beg you, lady,* which is the language of polite request. He is not writing *a new commandment, but the one we have had from the beginning (cf.* 1 Jn. 2:7). The command to love, which our writer immediately spells out, is an old commandment. He does not speak of it as also new, as in 1 John. He is content to emphasize the obligation resting on Christians, namely *that we love one another.* This is the central thing, and it receives emphasis in all the Johannine writings.

6 *This is love* introduces something of a definition, and it is interesting that next comes *that we follow his commandments.* In modern times love and obedience are often contrasted, obedience being connected with a legalistic spirit. But this antithesis is a false one. True love delights to obey (*cf.* 1 Jn. 5:3). Those who know what love in the Christian sense really is are always eager to obey God's commandments. John repeats that he is not enunciating a novelty, but a commandment which had been heard *from the beginning.* Incidentally RSV's *follow* both times translates a verb which means 'walk'. The idea of steady progress should not be overlooked.

7–11 Sound doctrine. *For* gives the reason for

the preceding. *Many deceivers* (people who have taught erroneous views of the Christian way) *have gone out*. This implies that they had at one time been church members (*cf.* 1 Jn. 2:19). The essence of their error was their failure to *acknowledge the coming of Jesus Christ in the flesh* (*cf.* 1 Jn. 4:2f.). As in 1 John the importance of the incarnation is the point at issue. Jesus was indeed the very Christ of God come in the flesh. To fail to teach this is to fall into the most serious error. John calls the man who does this *the deceiver and the antichrist*. He has spoken of the teacher of this error as *antichrist* before (1 Jn. 4:3), but the epithet *deceiver* is new. Not only is such a man in error but he leads others astray.

8 *Look to yourselves* is a call to take stock of their position, for there was some danger that they would lose *what* they *have worked for*. The modern distaste for mentioning rewards and punishments is not shared by the NT writers. It is very true that it is never suggested that we serve simply to be rewarded. This is not a Christian attitude. The service we render God is that which springs naturally from the gratitude of redeemed hearts. But God will reward those who serve Him faithfully, and no NT writer appears to think this a thought for which he should apologize.

9 The false teachers evidently thought of themselves as 'advanced' thinkers. John thinks of him *who goes ahead* as having advanced right out of Christianity! Our aim should be not to be 'advanced' but to *abide in the doctrine of Christ*. Notice that it is necessary to be right about the Son if we are to be right with the Father (*cf.* 1 Jn. 2:23). **10** No countenance must be given to any other doctrine. John does not mean that common courtesy is not to be extended to a doctrinal opponent. But to receive a man into one's home at that time was to express appreciation of his message. And since the exercise of hospitality was what enabled preachers to move about with their message it was also to help him spread his teachings. So if a man *does not bring this doctrine* (*i.e.* the doctrine that Christ is God incarnate) he is not to be received. **11** John makes clear the reason. To greet such a man is to share *his wicked work*. The Christian is to avoid all evil.

12, 13 Conclusion. The elder explains that the reason for ending his letter at this point is not that he has run out of subject-matter. On the contrary, *I have much to write to you*. But he prefers talking to writing. So having said what is most important he lays down his pen and saves the rest of his news until he meets his friends. *I would rather not use paper and ink* is an unusual expression, but the meaning is not in doubt. *Face to face* is literally 'mouth to mouth'. The Greek is vivid. *Our joy* links the interests of writer and readers. **13** The letter ends with greetings in the normal fashion.

3 John

COMMENTARY

1 Salutation. As in 2 John, the writer calls himself simply *the elder*. The addressee is *the beloved Gaius*. Four times he calls Gaius *beloved*, and also says of him, *whom I love in the truth*. Clearly he had a deep affection for the man. *Truth* is found six times in this Epistle, so it is another important note. As in the earlier Epistles it probably is connected with the truth of the gospel, that truth that we see in Christ (*cf.* v. 8).

2–4 Following the truth. 2 It is customary in 1st-century letters to have a prayer at the beginning. Now John prays that Gaius's affairs may prosper in the same way as his soul does. RSV's *I know* is scarcely a translation. John simply says 'that you may prosper and be in health even as your soul prospers'. **3** The source of his immediate knowledge of his friend was the visit of *some of the brethren* who *testified to the truth of your life*. This is more literally 'testified to the truth of you' which may mean that Gaius knew and possessed the truth. *Follow the truth* is 'walk in truth' as in 2 Jn. 4. Gaius is progressing in the truth and John rejoices. **4** Indeed he has

no greater joy than *to hear that* his *children follow the truth* ('walk in the truth'). *My children* will mean 'my children in the faith', 'those converted through my ministry'. It is the greatest of joys to the elder to know that his converts make progress.

5–8 Hospitality. 5 The subject-matter proper of the letter (as opposed to the preliminaries) begins here. It reflects the custom of the early church whereby any Christian travelling in the interests of the gospel would look for hospitality from the local Christians. Probably there were few preachers wealthy enough to stand the expense of staying at inns, and in any case inns had a bad reputation. It must have meant a great deal for the spread of the faith that preachers could obtain a ready lodging. John commends Gaius for his hospitality. *It is a loyal thing* is rather 'a faithful thing'. It is an action in accordance with the faith that is commended. *When you render any service to the brethren* is not specific, but the following verse shows that hospitality is in mind. *Especially to strangers* is not quite right, for this implies that Gaius had helped non-strangers and also strangers. The Greek means 'and this to strangers', *i.e.* Gaius is commended because of hospitality to people who were all unknown to him.

6 These people have spoken of what Gaius has done *before the church*, so that his deeds were widely known. John commends his practice: *You will do well to send them on their journey.* *As befits God's service* is rather 'worthily of God'. It is God who is the standard, not His servants (*cf.* Jn. 13:20). **7** The wandering preachers *have accepted nothing from the heathen.* This might have compromised their message and they would not do it. It made them all the more dependent on men like Gaius. **8** There is an obligation (*we ought* is 'we owe it') resting on believers to *support such men. That* (Gk. *hina*) denotes purpose. The duty in question is not merely an exercise in hospitality, but is in order that we may set forward divine purposes in being *fellow workers in the truth.*

9–12 Diotrephes and Demetrius. 9 *Diotrephes* was clearly a man with authority, but exactly what his position was is not clear. He took the line opposite to that of Gaius and hindered both the elder and the preachers. John had *written something to the church*, but Diotrephes had apparently prevented the church from getting the letter. RSV's *does not acknowledge my authority* is not quite right. The Greek means 'does not receive us' (RSV translates the same verb by 'welcome' in v. 10). **10** Diotrephes had slandered the elder, *prating against me with evil words* (for *me* read 'us'). He had also used deeds as well as words: he himself refused *to welcome* (the tense denotes the continuing practice) *the brethren.* But he went further. He *stops those who want to welcome them and puts them out of the church.* Clearly he had an important position to be able to do this, and equally clearly his opposition to the preachers was implacable.

11 John uses this bad example to impress a lesson on Gaius, whom he calls *beloved* for the fourth time in this short letter. Gaius should not *imitate evil but . . . good.* The man who does good *is of God.* All good originates in Him. When a man does evil that is evidence that he *has not seen God.* **12** *Demetrius* is introduced without explanation, as one well known. He is well reported of in the church. But he also has testimony *from the truth itself.* This difficult expression perhaps means that Demetrius' conduct squares with the gospel, so that the truth of the gospel is declared in his life. *I testify* is really 'we testify'. The plural may be epistolary as RSV takes it, and refer to John alone. But it is also possible that he associates others with him. At any rate he makes it clear that Demetrius has his warm support.

13–15 Conclusion. John closes the Third Epistle as he did the Second by saying he has much to write but prefers to wait until he sees his friend. He uses the past tense, *I had much to write*, but the present in 2 Jn. 12, while he also replaces 'paper and ink' of the former passage with *pen and ink.* But there seems no difference in meaning. Similarly his hope to see his friend and talk with him is as in the previous Epistle. **15** *Peace* was a common greeting both on meeting and leaving friends. It is a little prayer that God's peace will surround them. Peace is not, as with us, a negative term meaning the absence of war, but rather the positive presence of blessing. John passes on greetings and asks Gaius to greet *the friends*, a description evidently precise enough for Gaius to know who were meant. *Every one of them* should really be 'by name'. Though he does not list the names he wants each friend to know that the greeting is personal. He is singled out by name.

LEON MORRIS

Jude

INTRODUCTION

AUTHORSHIP

The first verse tells us the bare facts about the writer: he claims to be by name Jude, by birth brother of James, and by calling a servant of Jesus Christ. Tradition has ascribed the letter to Jude, the brother of Jesus, mentioned in Mt. 13:55 and Mk. 6:3. This must have been a younger son of Mary, born to her and Joseph, together with James, Joseph and Simon, though it has been argued that he was an older brother by a former marriage. We know that the Lord's brothers refused to believe in Him during His lifetime (Jn. 7:5), but that James was converted, possibly as a result of a post-resurrection appearance of Jesus (1 Cor. 15:7), and subsequently became a leader in the Jerusalem church (Acts 12:17; 15:13; Gal. 1:19; 2:9, 12; Acts 21:18). This James has also traditionally been regarded as the author of the letter of that name (*q.v.*) and in view of his eminence it would be natural for Jude to refer to himself in this way as James's brother. The two may be referred to together in 1 Cor. 9:5.

It has been suggested that the writer could have been Jude the apostle, the 'Jude of James' as the Greek of Lk. 6:16 and Acts 1:13 describes him (the Thaddaeus (Lebbaeus) of Mt. 10:4 and Mk. 3:18). The difficulty here lies in the fact that an apostle would hardly have written v. 17 as Jude does, while normal Greek usage in Lk. 6:16 requires the word understood to be 'son' rather than 'brother'.

Again, the theory of a pseudepigrapher at work has been adduced for this Epistle, but it is difficult to see why, if the writer wished to publish his letter under a more distinguished name than his own, he should have chosen someone so obscure as Jude, the brother of James, and not fallen for the temptation to call himself the Lord's brother. The humility which prompted this description must in itself be regarded as a mark of genuineness, matched by his more eminent brother's similar behaviour (Jas. 1:1).

DATE

Some who question the traditional authorship do so on the grounds that the letter itself bears the marks of being a late composition. V. 3 suggests that the faith is already becoming a systematic body of doctrine, and vv. 17, 18 speak of the apostles as if their generation has already died out, though the recipients of this letter would appear to have been instructed by them. If we are prepared to accept Jude as author,

and that he was probably a younger brother of the Lord, then we can limit the latest date to within his lifetime. Eusebius relates a story from Hegesippus about this Jude's grandsons being brought before Domitian when the latter was Roman Emperor (AD 81–96). The same authority quotes them as being bishops in the time of Trajan (98–117), and this would make it reasonable for their grandfather to have been alive well into the latter part of the 1st century. If we accept the reasons quoted above why the letter suggests a fairly late date, and if we are at all convinced by the arguments for the priority of 2 Peter (see Introduction to that letter) it would have been perfectly possible for Jude to have written as he did in the late sixties of the 1st century. Some argue that the absence of a reference to the fall of Jerusalem in v. 5, where it could have been apposite, suggests a date before AD 70.

SUBJECT

There is nothing to indicate to whom the letter is written, or where the writer is situated, except that he is writing to Christian people (v. 1). He apparently intended to send them a more formal treatise on doctrine and Christian living (perhaps more on the lines of 1 Peter!), but the appearance and spread of heretical teachings has led him rather to send his readers a warning of the consequences of following those who propagate such false ideas, coupled with an exhortation to hold fast to the apostolic faith (v. 3).

A feature of the letter is that it makes use of Jewish apocryphal literature, and is unique among the canonical NT books in doing so. This has led some to argue that it must have been written for a Jewish readership, but that is not necessarily so: the quotations would spring from the writer's background, and not necessarily that of his readers. Jude quotes from the *Assumption of Moses* and the *Book of Enoch* in vv. 9, 15, and may also be referring to other apocryphal works in vv. 6 and 8. Subsequently, when the church was formulating her Canon, Jude came under suspicion because of his quotation of such works, but it should be remembered that a high doctrine of inspiration does not preclude the inspired writer's right to quote from non-canonical sources. Paul himself quoted from extra-biblical Jewish writings in 1 Cor. 10:7 and 2 Tim. 3:8, and even from heathen poets in a sermon at Athens (Acts 17:28) and his letter to Titus (1:12). While in some quarters the letter was therefore queried before being accepted into the Canon, quotations from early writers show that it was in use in the church at least from early in the 2nd century.

OUTLINE OF CONTENTS

COMMENTARY

1, 2 OPENING ADDRESS AND GREETING

The writer introduces himself in traditional fashion, describes those for whom the letter is intended, and prays for their spiritual growth.

1 *Jude.* See Introduction above on the authorship. *Servant* is the Greek *doulos*, 'a bond-slave': Jude is therefore a true 'brother' of Jesus (*cf.* Mk. 3:35). James (1:1) and Peter (2 Pet. 1:1) also use the title. *Brother of James.* This appears to·be best understood as James the brother of the Lord (Mt. 13:55) and leader of the Jerusalem church. Again see Introduction for fuller details. *Called, beloved . . . kept . . .* introduces a feature of this letter, *i.e.* groups of three words together. This description of the Christians to whom Jude writes emphasizes how much salvation is entirely of God. It is the result of His sovereignty, His love and His power, and its scope, suggested in these verbs, is from eternity, through time, and back to eternity (see Rom. 8:30; 1 Pet. 1:3–5). *In God* is an unusual phrase for 'by God' (Phillips), though it might be a parallel to the Pauline 'in Christ'; NEB 'who live in the love of God the Father' has this in mind. It would seem better to follow the suggestion that originally there was a space after the Greek *en* for the local place-name to be inserted, and then the dative *Theō(i)* would be instrumental: 'to those who are at *X*, loved by God . . .'. 'Sanctified' (AV) has less MSS authority than *loved. Kept for Jesus Christ* (*cf.* 1 Pet. 1:5) could be instrumental, 'kept by Jesus'. Some see a reference here to a Gentile destination, seeing in the phrase traces of 1 Pet. 2:9. **2** *Mercy, peace, and love* is a unique benediction for the NT, and more fulsome than most in other letters. Some would link them with the triad of v. 1: God's call bringing mercy, His love reaching out to them, and His keeping power leading to peace. Others would see a Trinitarian formula: God the Father bringing mercy, the Son peace, and the Spirit love. *Multiplied* is the prayer for abundance of blessings found in 1 Pet. 1:2 and 2 Pet. 1:2.

3, 4 CHALLENGE TO HOLD FIRM TO THE FAITH

The writer had intended writing on a different theme, but the appearance and activities of false teachers have led him rather to concentrate on exhorting them to strive in every way to uphold the orthodox faith.

3 *Beloved* stresses the affection Jude feels as a pastor for his addressees. *Our common salvation* is a reminder that he is on the same footing as they are in the sight of God. Tit. 1:4 speaks of the 'common faith'. The word also emphasizes that this salvation is open to all. *Contend* suggests the need of strenuous effort: the word is used of participants in athletic contests. Mental effort is needed in order to understand and teach the Word of God aright, and moral effort is needed to apply that understanding to everyday behaviour (*cf.* 1 Pet. 1:13ff.; 2 Pet. 1:5ff.). *The faith* here implies a recognized body of teaching, such as we know emerged from Peter's early sermons and began to crystallize in such expressions as 1 Cor. 15:3ff.; 11:23–26; 1 Tim. 1:15; 3:16, *etc. Once for all* emphasizes the finality of the revelation in Christ, and it is worth noting that many of the fundamental tenets set forth in the above verses are being called in question today. Jude's message still applies in the 20th century. **4** *Admission has been secretly gained* is all one Greek verb which means 'to sneak in stealthily' (for questionable purposes). *Designated* could have the idea of their names set out in heavenly books, as in Dn. 7:10; Lk. 10:20; Rev. 20:12. In that case *this condemnation* then must refer to what Jude is going to describe. It has been suggested that *long ago* could mean 'already', as in Mk. 15:44, and that the reference is then to 2 Pet. 2:3, from which Jude is hastily copying. Alternatively it could refer to the general denunciation of evil-doers in the OT. *Licentiousness.* Their teaching has the same end as that referred to in 2 Pet. 2; the arguments they would use would be those considered by Paul in Rom. 6 and 7. *Deny.* To claim to be a Christian and then to live a life of dissipation is a sheer contradiction in terms, and certainly shows no understanding of what it means to call Jesus *Master and Lord* (*cf.* 1 Cor. 6:19, 20). 'The only Master and our Lord Jesus Christ' (RSV mg.) may be the right reading, as normally the word Master (Gk. *despotēs*) refers to God the Father, though the one exception to this rule in 2 Pet. 2:1 may indicate a similar exception here. If the former is the case, then 1 Pet. 1:17 shows that belief in God the Father calls for holiness of life as its corollary.

5–7 REMINDER OF GOD'S PUNISHMENT OF DISOBEDIENCE IN THE PAST

The writer now points out that status by itself is no guarantee of salvation. All the people of Israel were delivered from Egypt, yet through unbelief they did not all enter the promised land. Even angels, once they behaved in a way inconsistent with their calling, met with swift punishment, while Sodom and Gomorrah, though cities of the promised land, and one of them numbering righteous Lot and his family among their inhabitants, were yet destroyed for their immoral conduct.

5 *Once for all fully informed* presumably in the catechetical instruction given prior to baptism. *He*. RSV mg. shows what a variety of readings there is. 'The Lord' (*cf.* NEB and Phillips) is probably best, as the same Person is seen as acting in judgment in v. 6, and so it could not be Joshua (Heb. form of Jesus) as some suggest. *Afterward* is literally 'the second time'. Ex. 6:9 has been suggested as the first occasion of unbelief, but the sense and order suggest that the adverb goes with 'destroyed'. In this case it is best either to take it generally, as RSV (though this is without parallel), or as a contrast with the Flood which 2 Peter mentions. 1 Cor. 10:1–11 is an instructive comment on this allusion. **6** *Angels* are also the subjects of God's purposes and are given privileges by Him. The allusion may be to the incident of Gn. 6:1–4, which was described more elaborately in certain apocryphal books of which Jude shows knowledge in the following verses (*cf.* also the parallel in 2 Pet. 2:4). Their *dwelling* was in heaven, except when dispatched to earth on divine business. It was sin which led them to try to settle on the earth (Gn. 6). *Keep . . . kept* is a play on words: those who do not keep what God entrusts to them are therefore not to be trusted and must be kept by Him. *Eternal chains . . . nether gloom*. See on 2 Pet. 2:4. **7** *Sodom and Gomorrah* are also cited in 2 Pet. 2:6ff. *Indulged in unnatural lust* is literally 'went after strange flesh' and may be linked with the reference in v. 6 to Gn. 6, because the sin of the men of Sodom (Gn. 18:20) reached its peak when they sought intercourse with the two angels sent to Lot (Gn. 19:5). *Punishment of eternal fire* is consistent with the teaching of Jesus; *cf.* Mt. 18:8; 25:41; Mk. 9:48, *etc.*

8–13 THE SINS OF THE FALSE BRETHREN

Jude now turns from examples from the past to the subjects of his present letter and shows that their behaviour is not only impure but also presumptuous. This contrasts with the behaviour of the archangel Michael, but follows in the unworthy succession of Cain, Balaam and Korah. As such they are a disgrace to any Christian fellowship, and Jude concludes by denouncing them in a flood of verbiage strongly reminiscent of Peter's outburst in 2 Pet. 2:10–17.

8 *Yet in like manner*. The words stress the surprise that, in spite of God's clear punishment of such behaviour in the past, these men have still dared to follow their ungodly example. *Dreamings* suggests that the false teachers may have claimed to receive some of their teaching by means of visions. *Defile . . . reject . . . revile* set out the three basic charges against them: they teach and practise immorality, they spurn the authority of God, and they speak evil of angels. *Authority* is Greek *kyriotēs*, which, in view of its affinity with *Kyrios*, 'Lord', seems best applied to God's authority. *Glorious ones*, as in 2 Pet. 2:10, is used for 'angels'. **9** *Archangel* is a word found only here and in 1 Thes. 4:16 in the NT. *Michael* is known from Rev. 12:7 and the book of Daniel (10:13, 21; 12:1) as a leader of the heavenly host. The incident referred to is described more fully in the apocryphal *Assumption of Moses*. Michael was sent to bury Moses, but the devil opposed him, claiming that the body, being material, belonged to him. Even in this context Michael did not revile, but answered in the words of Zc. 3:2, and in this his behaviour is a strong contrast to that of these men. **10** *Whatever they do not understand* is thought by some to refer to celestial beings (as in v. 8); it could more widely just mean 'spiritual things'. *By instinct*: in a natural or physical way. Having no time for spiritual things, they limit their knowledge to the physical world, and in this they find their downfall as they allow the physical side of their being to dominate, just like animals. **11** *Cain . . . Balaam . . . Korah*: *cf.* Gn. 4:1–16; Nu. 22–24; 16. These are classic examples of the disastrous effects of jealousy, greed and pride. The latter-day descendants of this trio are jealous of the Christian progress of others, and so seek to turn them aside to immorality (and so to murder them spiritually). They are so keen to gain money from teaching what certain people will pay to be told that they readily persuade them to immorality (*cf.* Nu. 25:1–9; 31:16 and see on 2 Pet. 2:15), and so great is their pride that they cannot bear to be told of any power (or knowledge) greater than their own. **12** *Blemishes* is an assimilation from 2 Pet. 2:13. The word is better interpreted as 'reefs' (see mg.), 'sunken rocks', *i.e.* a hidden danger (hence Phillips' 'menace'). *Love feasts* (*cf.* 2 Pet. 2:13) were regularly held with the Lord's Supper in the early church, and 1 Cor. 11:20ff. show that from the earliest times these could be an occasion for behaviour inconsistent with Christian love. *Boldly*; *i.e.* 'without fear' of the consequences. *Looking after themselves.* The Greek word for 'shepherding' is used here. The hallmark of a false pastor is that he uses his position to further his own ends, and not to feed the flock (*cf.* Ezk. 34:2ff.; Jn. 21:15ff.; 1 Pet. 5:2). *Waterless clouds. Cf.* 2 Pet. 2:17. Again the emphasis is on their failure to live up to appearances, and consequent instability. *Fruitless trees* which have no fruit at harvest time have failed to fulfil the function for which they exist (*cf.* Mt. 7:15–20; Mk. 11:12–14). *Twice dead*, because having tasted spiritual life they have now rejected that (*cf.* Heb. 6:4–8; 10:26–31; 2 Pet. 2:20–22). *Uprooted*: a picture of judgment (*cf.* Ps. 52:5; Je. 1:10; Mt. 3:10). 13 *Wild waves* suggests the restlessness of the tide, which, after all its noise and fuss, only leaves a deposit of scum and rubbish on the shore (*cf.* Is. 57:20). *Wandering stars* is a further reference to the *Book of Enoch*, where there are references to stars which have transgressed being bound together in prison. Some think this refers to the planets (*wandering* is Gk. *planētai*), whose movements were misunderstood by Jude and his contemporaries; others that they are the shooting stars which appear briefly to give light and then fall out into darkness. The thought seems to be that of Lk. 6:39; these teachers set themselves in a position where they claim to be guides, but are in fact themselves off course. *Nether gloom of darkness.* See on 2 Pet. 2:4, 17.

14–16 THE RELEVANCE OF ENOCH'S PROPHECY

Jude now draws his denunciation to a climax by quoting Enoch's prophecy in confirmation of their impending and certain punishment, and rounds it off with further well-chosen epithets.

14 *Enoch . . . Adam* (*cf.* Gn. 5:1–18). This description occurs in the *Book of Enoch*, as does the quotation which follows. The book was well known in NT days and so the reference is relevant (see Introduction above for a discussion of Jude's use of apocryphal literature). *The Lord*, for Enoch, is God and His *myriads* are the angels (*cf.* Dt. 33:2; Zc. 14:5). For the Christian the words refer to Christ coming with His angels (*cf.* Mt. 25:31; 2 Thes. 1:7). **15** *Ungodly* takes up and repeats the word used in v. 4 to describe these people; here it refers to them, their character and their behaviour. **16** *Grumblers*, against God and His ways (*cf.* Ex. 16:2, 9; 17:3; 1 Cor. 10:10, *etc.*); this behaviour was characteristic of Israel in the wilderness. *Malcontents*; lit. 'fault-finders'. *Following . . .* gives the reason for this behaviour: they are dissatisfied with God's ways of truth and justice because they want to fulfil their own lusts. *Loud-mouthed*; *i.e.* greater than they have any right to be. *Cf.* 2 Pet. 2:18 where the same word is used. *Flattering*; lit. 'admiring men's appearances': a

characteristic quite contrary to that of God (*cf.* Acts 10:34; Jas. 2:1ff.).

17–23 THE CHRISTIAN ANTIDOTE

By contrast Christians are exhorted to keep firm in their memories the apostolic warning, especially as these people lead to schisms. The positive way to avoid them and the effect they have is by Christian growth, prayer, abiding spiritually, waiting for the completion of the work Christ has begun in us, and reaching out to others in evangelistic zeal.

17 *But* contrasts Christian behaviour with that of the ungodly. *Remember* is also the theme of 2 Peter (1:12–14; 3:2), and see v. 5 above. *Predictions*: such as Acts 20:29, 30; 1 Tim. 4:1ff.; 2 Tim. 3:1ff.; *cf.* Mt. 24:23f. **18** *Said* can refer to writings and need not imply that these readers had actually heard the apostles. *In the last time* (*cf.* 1 Pet. 1:20). The period is that between the ascension and the return of Christ. *Scoffers*, as in 2 Pet. 3:3. There may be an otherwise unrecorded apostolic saying behind both these sources. The Petrine verse suggests the content of their mockery. **19** *Set up divisions*, by setting up themselves as superior to ordinary Christians, as the Gnostics did, dividing mankind into 'spiritual' and 'worldly' people. In actual fact, says Jude, they themselves are the *worldly* ones, since they do not possess the Spirit, as is evidenced by their lack of His fruit. On *worldly* (natural as opposed to spiritual man) see 1 Cor. 2:14–16. **20** *But you.* The opening words of v. 17 are repeated for emphasis. *Most holy faith* refers, as in v. 3, to the content of the Christian revelation, which is *most holy* as it is something given by God which, rightly interpreted and acted upon, leads to holy living. *In the Holy Spirit* refers to the Christian's experience of abiding in communion with God through Jesus Christ by the Holy Spirit (*cf.* Rom. 8:9, 16, 26; Eph. 6:18). **21** *Keep yourselves* complements what was earlier said in the address of v. 1. Once a person has realized that he is the unworthy object of the love of God in Jesus Christ, he is challenged to respond in love. That love must be shown in behaviour, and Jn. 15:9, 10 show that such response is the way to abide in the consciousness of God's love. Failure to respond will deaden the heart to God's love and will result finally in the loss of this consciousness. *Wait for the mercy.* Error is finally to be avoided by a keen sense of expectation of the return of the Lord, when His mercy, already experienced initially (v. 1) and daily (v. 2; *cf.* La. 3:22, 23) will be finally realized when the work of salvation is completed. Tit. 2:11–14; 1 Pet. 4:7 and 2 Pet. 3:11f. lay similar stress on the advent hope as a motive for godly living. **22, 23** *Some.* In case the reader should think from the last two verses that orthodoxy is simply quietism, nourishing one's own spiritual life, Jude now turns to the Christian's responsibility for others. The text here is in doubt, and there may be two or three groups in mind. RSV appears to offer the best solution to the problems; NEB and Phillips by contrast understand only two groups in mind. Following the RSV the first class are those who are in two minds about the false teaching, and one must set about convincing them by argument. Others are more deeply involved and their position is serious: no effort is to be spared to snatch them as from a fire (see Zc. 3:2, already quoted in v. 9; Am. 4:11). The third group is saddest of all, for one can only pity them (doing so in the right spirit of *fear* of God and the realization that 'There, but for the grace of God, go I'). *Garment* suggests the contaminating effect of their sin. Like the leper whose clothing was polluted by his disease (Lv. 13:47–52), they are to be seen as a source of pollution and therefore to be shunned.

24, 25 FINAL COMMENDATION AND ASCRIPTION OF PRAISE

After all these sad possibilities of error and apostasy Jude ends on the positive note of pointing his readers to the God who alone can keep them to the end of time and into eternity. With this glorious goal in view he ascribes all glory and might here and now to the God our Saviour whose praises His ransomed people will be singing through all eternity. So be it.

24 *Keep*: cf. 1 Pet. 1:5. *From falling*: the same root as the verb in 2 Pet. 1:10, which shows how this is to be achieved. *Present* is a formal word, suggesting introduction to a dignitary. *Without blemish* occurs in 1 Pet. 1:19; his sanctification completed, the Christian is now fully identified with the character of His glorious Saviour. *Rejoicing*: an intensive word, the verbal form of which was especially dear to Peter (cf. 1 Pet. 1:6, 8). **25** *Only* may suggest that false teachers were already urging a hierarchy of gods and demi-gods, as the later Gnostics did, or it may just emphasize again that our salvation is the work of God alone. *Through* could go closely with *Saviour*: through Jesus God has saved us (Acts 4:12). Or it could mean that our praises are to be through Jesus (cf. 1 Pet. 2:5; 4:11). Of the four qualities ascribed, *glory* stresses the splendour of God, as the radiance of light (cf. the description of heaven in Rev. 21:23; 22:5), *majesty* His position (cf. Heb. 1:3), *dominion* His ability to carry out His sovereign will, and *authority* the fact that He has the absolute right to do so. These qualities have always been His and always will be, for they are the qualities of eternity which in His love He has introduced into the world of space and time which He has created. To such a vision of the Almighty God the believing soul can only breathe in response a humble yet fervent *Amen*—so be it!

DAVID H. WHEATON

The Revelation

INTRODUCTION

AUTHORSHIP

The author of the Revelation designates himself simply as John. Though a resident of Asia Minor (or rather, proconsular Asia) he was clearly a Hebrew Christian, as the language and style of the book reveal, and held a position of influence among the churches of that area. It was natural, in view of the strong tradition that John the son of Zebedee migrated to Ephesus, for early Christian writers to identify John the apostle with the Seer who wrote the Revelation. The weightiest factor in support of such a conclusion is, perhaps, the manner in which the prophet simply calls himself 'John', as though there were no other Christian leader in that area with whom he could be confused. The many remarkable affinities of thought and diction between the Gospel and Apocalypse in matters of detail similarly demand the recognition of some sort of connection in the authorship of the two books.

On the other hand, the general presentation of thought and, still more, of style and diction in the Revelation differs so widely from the Gospel as to make a common authorship of the two books problematic. The matter would be considered settled from this consideration alone were it not complicated by the view, vigorously championed by C. C. Torrey, that the Revelation was written in Aramaic; on this assumption the extraordinary Greek of the book would be accounted for by its being translated with minute literalness. If another writer made this translation, the argument as to the difference of style in the Revelation and Gospel would fall to the ground, or at least lose its main force, for no-one can maintain that the fourth Evangelist wrote polished Greek.

Rather than make an arbitrary decision on so complicated a question, it is wiser to admit that at present we are not in a position to affirm or deny that the prophet was the apostle of the same name (see Leon Morris, *The Revelation of St. John*, TNTC, 1969, pp. 25–34). However, the authorship of this book is the least important question to be considered in regard to it; it does not in the least affect the interpretation of the text. In any case, the title in Greek, 'The Revelation of St John the Theologian' (AV, 'the Divine'; Gk. *Theologos*) is a misnomer; the book claims to be 'The revelation of Jesus Christ which God gave him . . . and he made it known by sending his angel to his servant John' (1:1). The book gains its value from its origin, not from the identity of its human author. The contents of the book are consistent with such an origin.

DATE

Recent writers on the Revelation have tended to support the earliest Christian tradition that it was written towards the close of Domitian's reign, *i.e.* *c.* AD 96. The book reflects the beginnings of a storm of persecution soon to burst in full fury on the Christians of Asia and ultimately on the church everywhere. John, a prominent Christian leader, has already been exiled, a fact which seems to point to official determination to eradicate the church, root and branch. Compulsion in respect of emperor-worship appears imminent. This accords perfectly with conditions existing in Asia Minor during the persecution instigated in Domitian's reign.

On the other hand, it should be mentioned that several notable scholars prefer an earlier date, either in Nero's reign (so Lightfoot, Westcott, Hort) or in Galba's short rule, AD 68 (so Torrey). The view is based on a literal interpretation of Rev. 11:1, 2 and 17:9–11. The balance of probability seems to favour the Domitianic date, but we cannot be certain.

INTERPRETATION

In the main the various types of exposition of the Revelation reduce themselves to four. The 'preterist' view regards the prophecies as wholly concerned with the circumstances of John's day, having no reference whatever to future ages. The 'historicist' interpretation construes the visions as a preview of history from the time of the writer to the end of the world. The 'futurist' explanation places the relevance of the visions entirely at the end of the age, largely divorcing them from the prophet's time. The 'poetic' view considers all hard and fast canons of interpretation to be illegitimate; the prophet simply describes, by means of his powers of artistry, the sure triumph of God over all evil powers.

Liberal scholars largely endorse the 'preterist' view and repudiate the predictive elements of the book; many, however, accept as valid the principles of God's moral government which lie at the root of the prophet's teaching. The Reformers generally adopted the 'historicist' view. They identified the persecuting power with papal Rome. Rigidly interpreted, however, this view seems to be contrary to the analogy of all other prophecy in the Bible. The 'futurist' view was that of the earliest centuries of the church and is widely held by evangelical Christians today. In its popular form, however, it is open to serious criticism, in that the historical setting of the book is almost wholly ignored. Indeed, it is often said that John wrote the Revelation not for his own age but for the church of the end-time. Hence the book is made to yield information and ideas such as the prophet had never dreamed of. Vagaries of this sort drive many readers to value the book solely from an aesthetic viewpoint, denying that it ever had a specific occasion in view.

The symbols, nevertheless, do mean something. John was more than a poet setting forth in vague images the triumph of God over all evil. He wrote for the churches under his care with a practical situation in view, viz. the prospect of the popular Caesar-worship of his day being enforced on all Christians. No man who said 'Jesus is Lord' could also confess 'Caesar is Lord'; the latter demand threatened the existence of the whole church of God. Grasping the principles involved, John was given to see the logical consummation of the tendencies at work, mankind divided to the obedience of Christ or antichrist. On the canvas of John's age, therefore, and in the colours of his environment, he pictured the last

great crisis of the world, not merely because, from a psychological viewpoint, he could do no other, but because of the real correspondence between his crisis and that of the last days. As the church was then faced with a devastating persecution by Rome, so will the church of the last days find itself violently opposed by the prevailing world power. The outcome of that great struggle will be the advent of Christ in glory, and with Him the establishment of the kingdom of God in power. John clearly regarded the end as at hand (1:1-3), but this 'foreshortened perspective' no more invalidates his utterances than it does those of the OT prophets and of our Lord Himself, for it is characteristic of all prophecy.

The following exposition, then, seeks to interpret the visions of this book as the readers must have done to whom they were first addressed, recognizing, nevertheless, that their proper fulfilment awaits the day known neither to man nor angel, but which is yet within the authority of God (Acts 1:6f.).

OUTLINE OF CONTENTS

1:1–8   Prologue

1:9–20   Vision of the Son of man

2:1 – 3:22   The letters to the seven churches

4:1 – 5:14   The vision of heaven

6:1 – 8:5   The seven seals

8:6 – 11:19 The seven trumpets

12:1 – 14:20 The background of the earthly conflict

15:1 – 16:21 The seven bowls

17:1 – 19:21 The fall of Babylon

20:1 – 22:5 The consummated kingdom

22:6–21   Epilogue

COMMENTARY

1:1-8 PROLOGUE

1:1-3 Superscription

Here are set forth the source of the book (v. 1), the nature of its contents (v. 2) and the blessed results of taking it to heart (v. 3).

1 A *revelation* is an uncovering of something hidden, used here in the sense of a 'vision and its interpretation' (Charles). The ultimate source of this revelation is God Himself; He gave it to Jesus Christ for the benefit of the church (*his servants*); it was therefore sent through the mediation of an angel to John who, in turn, passed it on to the 'seven churches' (v. 4), and so to the whole church of God. It tells of *what must soon take place*; 'soon' expresses the normal prophetic attitude and is emphasized throughout

the NT (see, *e.g.*, Lk. 18:8; Rom. 16:20; 1 Cor. 7:29–31; Jas. 5:8; 1 Pet. 4:7; Rev. 1:3; 22:20).

2, 3 The revelation is further defined as *the word of God . . . the testimony of* (borne by) *Jesus Christ, even to all that he* (the Seer) *saw.* In 1:9 and 20:4 the first two phrases are linked to stand for the whole truth of God; here it means the *words of the prophecy*.

The blessing is invoked on the one reading aloud to the assembled congregation and on those hearing and observing that which is enjoined. There are two classes here, not three; the last two participles are governed by one subject. *Cf.* Lk. 11:28.

1:4, 5a Greeting

4 *The seven churches that are in Asia, i.e.* the

Roman province of that name, are enumerated in v. 11. It is hardly to be doubted that they also represent the church in its completeness, as is seen in the conclusion to each of the seven letters, 'He who has an ear, let him hear what the Spirit says to the churches'. He *who is and who was and who is to come* is a title for God, stressing both His eternity and vital relation to history. The last clause (*who is to come,* instead of the expected 'who will be') is not only a conscious allusion to the second coming of Christ, but implies that the most important event of the future is that appearing which will also be the coming of God.

The seven spirits who are before his throne is probably a designation of the Holy Spirit. It may have originated in the Seer's mind through the popular interpretation of Is. 11:2, 3 as being a sevenfold spiritual endowment of the Messiah (the seven 'eyes of the Lord, which range through the whole earth' of Zc. 4:10; see Rev. 4:5 and 5:6) and his representation of the church by the seven churches to whom he particularly writes. Modern expositors (and some ancients, *e.g.* Andreas and Arethas) frequently interpret the seven spirits as angelic beings, perhaps the seven archangels of Jewish angelology, and regard the conception as going back, through the Persian religion, to the Babylonian worship of the sun, moon and five planets. Charles adheres to this view (though regarding their presence here as due to interpolation) because in 3:1 the seven spirits of God appear to be similar to the seven 'stars' (which represent the angels of the churches). But nowhere is it said that these spirits worship God, though all other classes of angelic beings are mentioned as so doing. Concerning 3:1 Kiddle writes, 'When we acknowledge that the seven in each instance conveys the idea of unity and completeness, rather than diversity, so that we are to think of the Spirit and the Church rather than seven Spirits and seven churches, then we are in sight of a possible solution. . . . The seven Spirits and the seven stars . . . are the prophetic Spirit and the celestial character of the Church, in whom the Spirit gives life' (*MNTC*, 1940, p. 87).

5a Jesus is *the faithful witness* not alone in respect of this revelation but as concerning the whole truth of God. *Cf.* Jn. 18:37. He is *the first-born of the dead* in the sense of being the first to rise from the dead, and so the 'first fruits of those who have fallen asleep' (see 1 Cor. 15:20; Col. 1:18). But John may also be quoting Ps. 89:27, 28. In this passage 'the first-born' was interpreted by the Jews of the Messiah in the sense of 'sovereign' (even God was sometimes called 'first begotten' or 'firstborn'). If this thought predominates in John's mind, then Jesus is here said to be 'sovereign of the dead', a fitting parallel to *ruler of kings on earth,* both titles being true of Him in virtue of His resurrection.

1:5b, 6 Benediction

The reading *lousanti* followed by the AV 'washed us' (instead of *lysanti,* 'loosed us') is almost certainly mistaken, being due perhaps to the influence of 7:14. The difference in tenses in the verbs of this doxology is significant, the love being constant, the redemption once for all. Loosing from sins by blood sets forth redemption in terms of ransom. The whole benediction harks back to the Exodus from Egypt, v. 6 being quoted from Ex. 19:6. Through the deliverance wrought by His death and resurrection, Christ has brought His people out of the bondage of sin and made them a *kingdom* in which all are priests. Some regard the *kingdom* as signifying a nation under a king, but in view of such passages as Rev. 5:10; 20:6; 22:5, it seems likely that it here means a nation of kings.

1:7, 8 The second advent

7 reproduces Mt. 24:30, except that the clauses are transposed: 'Then will appear the sign of the Son of man in heaven, and then all the tribes of the earth will mourn, and they will see the Son of man coming on the clouds of heaven with power and great glory.' The declaration links together two OT scriptures, Dn. 7:13 and Zc. 12:10. The corresponding point in the vision of this book is 19:11-21. As at the close of the book, so here, the prophet utters a hearty assent to this promise, 'It is so, Amen.'

8 *Alpha* and *Omega* are the first and last letters of the Greek alphabet. It is probable that the phrase translates for Greek readers the Hebrew idiom whereby the first and last letters of the Hebrew alphabet were used to express the entirety of a thing. It was said, *e.g.,* that Adam transgressed the law 'from aleph to tau'; Abraham, on the contrary, kept the law 'from aleph to tau'. Here the meaning is that God is the Lord of all history, its beginning, its end and the whole course between. Such an affirmation is needed by Christians in a day when the powers that be are opposed to the church. We may note that this saying is attributed to Christ in 22:13; older expositors sometimes thought that He is the speaker here also, but clearly the view is mistaken; it is spoken by *the Lord God . . . the Almighty,* a title which John frequently uses and which, in the LXX of Ho. 12:5 and Am. 9:5, translates the Hebrew 'Lord God of hosts'.

1:9-20 VISION OF THE SON OF MAN

The tribulation and kingdom in which John and his readers share as Christians are a present experience and possession, as also the patient endurance which Jesus supplies. All three elements are gained in union with Him, but the first and third lead to a fuller appropriation of the second at its consummation. *Cf.* Jn. 16:33; Rom. 5:3; 2 Tim. 2:12. **9** John's share of tribulation is alluded to in the mention of his being in Patmos *on account of the word of God and the testimony of Jesus;* He was there in consequence of his faithfulness to the gospel, not in voluntary exile to receive more revelations. *Cf.* Rev. 6:9. The fact that he says he *was* in Patmos may imply that he wrote the book after leaving the island.

10 *I was in the Spirit* means that John fell into a state of ecstasy (lit. 'became' in Spirit), so occasioning the vision that follows. It happened *on the Lord's day*, not, as some take it, 'on the day of the Lord', as though John was transported to live in that day, but 'on the day consecrated to the Lord', a phrase which became technical in the 2nd century for Sunday. The term 'the Lord's day', as Deissmann has shown, is probably the defiant Christian replacement of 'Emperor's day', which was celebrated at least monthly in Asia Minor, if not weekly. This originally indicated the day of the pharaoh's accession to the throne of Egypt, or his birthday (*EB*, III, p. 2815); the idea was taken over by the Roman emperors. As a memorial of the day of Christ's resurrection, and so of His exaltation to sovereignty, 'the Lord's day' is thus a peculiarly fitting title. The *loud voice like a trumpet* was presumably that of the Son of man.

11 It is difficult not to feel that *seven churches* are chosen because of the sacred nature of that number. The seven which were singled out, however, had a special claim to be recipients of these letters, as they lay on a route forming a sort of inner circle round the province of Asia. Moreover, according to Ramsay, these cities were centres of the seven postal districts of this area, and so would be the best centres for circulating the letters to the other churches in the province.

12 *The voice* here represents the speaker. The *seven golden lampstands* remind us of the seven-branched lampstand in the Holy Place of the Temple (Ex. 25:31; *cf.* Zc. 4:2). That Temple, however, had been destroyed and the lampstand transported to a heathen temple in Rome. Where the Jews had failed, the Christian churches were now called to succeed—to be lights in a dark world.

13 The phrase *one like a son of man* recalls Dn. 7:13; it implies that this Person is not just a man, and doubtless is used with the remembrance of our Lord's use of this title (it does not occur in the Epistles). The description that follows draws freely on Dn. 10:5, 6. The significance of this presence *in the midst of the lampstands, i.e.* the churches, scarcely requires mention. The word for the *robe* worn by Christ was used of the high priest's robe; but it is doubtful whether any such association is in mind here for this robe was worn also by men of high rank generally. **14** The description of the white hair is a deliberate reminiscence of Dn. 7:9, where it belongs to the 'Ancient of days'. The application to Christ of the attributes of God is a constant phenomenon in this book. **15** *Cf.* the feet *like burnished bronze* with Dn. 2:33–35. Swete thinks the *many waters* are the Aegean Sea roaring about Patmos.

16 A symbolic picture is given here that was never meant to be painted! The *stars* are in the power of Christ, the *sword* symbolizes His judicial authority and might. *The sun shining in full strength* goes back to Jdg. 5:31 but also recalls the transfiguration (Mt. 17:2).

17 *Cf.* Dn. 10:9; see also Jos. 5:14; Is. 6:5; Ezk. 1:28. *I am the first and the last* (also in 2:8 and 22:13) is spoken of Yahweh in Is. 44:6 and 48:12. Its meaning is the same as v. 8. **18** AV 'I am he that liveth, and was dead' is a better translation than RSV. It brings out more sharply the contrast between the eternal life inherent in the Son and the abject death that He suffered. That life triumphed over death, and so *I am alive for evermore*; this latter predicate is applied to the Father in 4:9, 10 and 10:6. The possession of *the keys of Death and Hades* was won by His resurrection and signifies the conquest of death.

19 RSV tends to obscure the rough division furnished by this verse of the Revelation given to John. AV and NEB are clearer. 'What you have seen' is the vision just given; 'what is now' relates to the existing state of the churches and the letters about to be given; 'what will be hereafter' is the subsequent visions of the book. This should not be pressed to imply that everything without exception in chs. 4–22 refers to the time future to John, let alone to the time of the end of all things.

20 The seven stars and seven lampstands of the vision are now interpreted for John. The latter represent the churches, but the former are more obscure. It seems strange to interpret the seven stars as being seven *angels* in the ordinary meaning of the term, even if they are guardian angels; for it would be superfluous to write to them by the agency of John (see, *e.g.,* 2:1) and, in any case, the contents of the letters are wholly concerned with the churches themselves. Many expositors, therefore, hold that the angels represent officials of some kind in the churches, whether delegates or overseers. This is possible, although it is wholly exceptional in apocalyptic for angels to symbolize men. It is perhaps better to regard them as personifying the heavenly or supernatural life of the churches as they are seen in Christ, and so the character which they are called to realize, just as the lampstands represent the earthly life of the churches as men see them outwardly.

2:1 – 3:22 THE LETTERS TO THE SEVEN CHURCHES

It has been suggested that these letters were written earlier than the main part of the book and were sent separately to the churches addressed; later they were amplified and joined together so that all the churches might benefit from them. The theory is not objectionable but it is doubtful, for the letters are closely connected with the beginning and the end of the book; excise the passages involved and what is left constitutes very abrupt messages. Each letter is addressed to the 'angel' of the church and opens with a description of Christ drawn from the introductory vision, the particulars mentioned having special relevance to the church in question. The designation of Christ in the letter to the Laodiceans forms an exception, being a reminiscence of the greeting with which the Revelation commences. Similarly a promise concerning rewards to be bestowed at the second advent concludes each letter; these promises usually have a special fitness for the individual churches and are given a visionary embodiment in the closing chapters of the book.

2:1-7 The letter to the church in Ephesus

Ephesus was the largest city of Asia and the centre of Roman administration in that province. It took the title of 'Temple Warden', originally in reference to the famous temple of Artemis, but later extending to the two or three temples devoted to the cult of the emperors. Here Paul founded the church which became the centre for evangelizing the rest of the province, and here resided the apostle John. The Ephesian church, accordingly, must have become by this time the foremost one in the East, with the possible exception of Antioch. Kiddle suggests that this letter was placed first, not so much because of the importance of the church as of the warning delivered to it. (For a similar reason the letter to the Laodiceans was placed last.)

1 The designation of Christ is both an encouragement and a warning. The seven stars are in His grasp (*i.e.* He maintains their spiritual life), and His presence is coextensive with all the churches. But the power that sustains is also capable of judicial removal; the title thus prepares the hearer for v. 5. 2, 3 *I know* is a truth of similar dual import. It heads every one of the seven letters, sometimes imparting comfort (*e.g.* 2:9, 13, *etc.*), sometimes causing shame (*e.g.* 3:1, 15). Here it precedes a commendation. The *works* of the Ephesians are *toil* and *patient endurance*; the former manifests itself in efforts to overcome false teachers, the latter in patient endurance in the face of opposition, whether from false prophets or from other sources. The *evil men* are those who call themselves prophets, but are not. *Cf.* Paul's predictions in Acts 20:29, 30; 1 Tim. 4:1-3. It is possible that the chief offenders are the Nicolaitans mentioned in v. 6.

4 The failure of the Ephesians is perhaps the perversion of their chief virtue; opposition to false brethren led to censoriousness and divisiveness in the church, so causing them to leave their first love. This would interpret the *love* referred to as brotherly love. It may, however, relate to love towards God; *cf.* Je. 2:2, 5. Since the one manifestation of love is impossible without the other, we may perhaps include both in our text (*cf.* Mk. 12:30, 31 with 1 Jn. 4:20). 5 *I will come to you* means that the Lord will 'come' in a special visitation of judgment. See also v. 16. An instance of His 'coming' in blessing is to

be found in 3:20. Such statements in no wise conflict with the truth of the final appearing, a fact which theologians have not always remembered when speaking of the 'coming' of Christ to the believer and of His 'advents' in history, as though the recognition of these lesser appearings in any way invalidated the truth of the great appearing.

6 The *Nicolaitans* were reputed from early times to have been the followers of Nicolaus of Antioch, one of the Seven (Acts 6:5). We gather from 2:14, 15 that they held the same error as the Balaamites, viz. teaching to eat things sacrificed to idols and to commit fornication. These were the chief matters condemned by the decree of the apostolic council (Acts 15:29). It is noteworthy that Balaam and Nicolaus have more or less the same etymology (Balaam—'he has consumed the people'; Nicolaus—'he overcomes the people'). If this is the teaching so strenuously resisted by the Ephesians (see v. 2) then it must have been widespread indeed.

7 The injunction *He who has an ear . . .* is repeated in connection with the promises to the overcomer in all the seven letters. It is frequently on the lips of our Lord in the Gospel records (Mt. 13:9, 43, *etc.*). *The Spirit* is the Holy Spirit, yet the speaker is Christ. For a similar phenomenon *cf.* Rom. 8:9-11 and 2 Cor. 3:17. The 'conqueror' depicts the Christian as a faithful warrior for Christ, 'the victorious member of the Church, as such, apart from all consideration of the circumstances' (Swete). There seems little justification for limiting the term, as some would wish, to the martyrs only, though it is true that the conqueror can finally demonstrate the completeness of his victory only by remaining faithful unto death. *Cf.* 2 Esdras 7:57, 58: 'This is the meaning of the contest which every man who is born on earth shall wage, that if he is defeated he shall suffer . . . , but if he is victorious he shall receive what you have said' (*i.e.* paradise).

To eat of the tree of life is to partake of the fullness of eternal life; the tree is situated *in the paradise of God*, the heavenly Jerusalem that is to be manifested on earth for redeemed man (see 21:10; 22:2). The blessings of the first creation, lost by man, are restored in yet fuller measure 'in the new world' (Mt. 19:28).

2:8-11 The letter to the church in Smyrna

This city was one of the most prosperous in Asia Minor and took the name of 'metropolis'. Here the Jews were unusually numerous and powerful; their bitter antagonism to the Christian church appears not only in this letter but in that of Ignatius to the Smyrnaeans.

8 This title of Christ appears in 1:17. This church, shortly to be severely tested, needed to be reminded that their Saviour was Lord of history and conqueror of death (*cf.* v. 10). Contrast the condition of the Christians in Smyrna with the material wealth and spiritual poverty of the Laodiceans (3:17). 9 The *slander* of the Jews would be against Jesus primarily,

but they were capable of slandering even the God they confessed. The Smyrnaean Christians later reported that the Jews joined the pagans in clamouring for the death of Polycarp, Bishop of Smyrna, on the ground of his opposition to the state religion! Hence, instead of their constituting an assembly of God, they had become *the synagogue of Satan* (see also 3:9). Since it is denied that the Jews had a right to retain their national name, it is evident that Christians are regarded as the true heirs of Abraham, as in Rom. 2:28. The things which the believers here are about to suffer may be connected with the opposition of the Jews.

10 Such distress is to extend for *ten days, i.e.* a short period. It is sometimes held to be identical with the 'great tribulation' of 7:14, but it seems more likely that a local persecution is in mind. The *devil* ('slanderer') will then be a means of testing the Christians; such testing by persecution is to be distinguished from that mentioned in 3:10, the hour of testing which is to come upon the whole world, for from the latter the Christians are to be preserved (*cf.* 7:2f., 12:6). The *crown of life* alludes to the wreath bestowed on the winner in the games, 'the crown which consists of life'. Swete points out that the crown is not a diadem, but an emblem of festivity. In this case the wreath is a fitting symbol of life, for the latter has to be understood in the light of the closing descriptions of the book, a life of holy privilege, enjoyment, and of distinctions of awards (*cf.* 1 Cor. 9:25, 27).

11 *The second death* is defined in 21:8 as 'the lake that burns with fire and brimstone'. It is a rabbinic phrase; *cf.* the oft-quoted Jerusalem Targum on Dt. 33:6, 'Let Reuben live in this age and not die the second death whereof the wicked die in the next world.' Charles aptly compares *1 Enoch* 99:11, 'woe to you who spread evil to your neighbours, for you shall be slain in Sheol', a concept which did not imply annihilation, as *1 Enoch* 109:3 makes clear.

2:12–17 The letter to the church in Pergamum

Pergamum (RV) was described by Arethas as 'given to idolatry more than all Asia'. Behind the city stood a hill, 1,000 feet high, covered with heathen temples. Foremost of all was the huge altar of Zeus on a platform cut out of the rock, dominating the city. Emperor-worship was established there earlier than at Ephesus or Smyrna so that in due course Pergamum became the recognized centre of the cult in Asia. Hence it was said of this church that it dwelt 'where Satan's throne is' (v. 13). Herein lay the cause of the peculiar difficulties of the Christians of Pergamum.

12 The title echoes 1:16 and anticipates 2:16. **13** *My faith* abbreviates 'faith in me'. **14** The information as to Balaam's teaching is gained through combining Nu. 25:1, 2 with 31:16. The Christian counterpart of Balaam probably despised the flesh, and so discounted the importance of physical purity, justifying his actions,

perhaps, by the perversion of Paul's teaching (repudiated by him in Rom. 3:8 and 6:1), 'Let us continue in sin, that grace may abound.' **15** The meaning is either, 'You also have in your midst Nicolaitans, who teach as Balaam taught Israel', or 'You also, as well as the Ephesians (v. 6), have the Nicolaitans with you', the comparison with Balaam being implicit. The former meaning seems preferable.

16 presents a preliminary 'second advent' to judgment if the Pergamenes do not repent. See note on 2:5. **17** The promise to the conqueror alludes to the current Jewish expectation that manna would descend from heaven again when Messiah is manifested. See *2 Baruch* 29:8. Here, of course, the manna typifies spiritual life, just as the 'water of life' (Rev. 22:17). The promise is particularly fitting for those tempted to join in festivities in which food sacrificed to idols was eaten. Denying themselves those dainties, the Christians were to look forward to richer fare in the kingdom of God.

The *white stone* is difficult to interpret owing to the many uses to which pebbles were put by the world of antiquity, each use yielding an excellent symbolic sense. A white stone given by a jury to one on trial signified acquittal, a black one guilt. The victor's pebble gave him entrance to all public festivals. The *tessera hospitalis* was in two parts, inscribed with two names and exchanged, so that each person had an open invitation to the house of the other. The high priest had twelve stones on his breastplate inscribed with the names of the twelve tribes. This by no means exhausts the possibilities.

Our interpretation will be partly conditioned by our understanding of the *new name* which is engraved on the stone. If the name is of Christ or of God (*cf.* 3:12 and 19:12), then there may be an allusion to the concept of the power inherent in the name of God; the Christian shares God's might and appropriates for himself, in a manner none other can, the character of God. If the name is a new one bestowed on the Christian, then the allusion is to the habit of bestowing new names on persons who have attained to a new status, as Abram and Jacob became Abraham and Israel; the white stone then signifies the overcomer's right to enter the kingdom of God in a character all of his own, moulded by the grace of God in him.

2:18–29 The letter to the church in Thyatira

Thyatira was the smallest of the seven cities. It had no temple devoted to the worship of the emperors, so that Christians here were not so troubled by the cult as those in the preceding churches. The problem of this church centred in the compromising situations created by commercial interests. Thyatira was an industrial city, renowned for its many trade guilds. To these societies it was as necessary to belong as it is for the modern artisan to be a member of his appropriate trade union; otherwise it involved an ostracism that would make business all but impossible. The difficulty in the path of the Christian linking up with such guilds was the necessity of joining in the periodical common meals when meat was eaten that had been dedicated to a pagan deity (perhaps the patron god of the guild). One can well see that certain broad-minded Christians would not hesitate to participate in such festivities, holding that 'an idol has no real existence' (1 Cor. 8:4). Excuse might soon be found for the licentiousness in which these meals so often culminated; and the next step would be to join in the general debauchery. This was openly advocated by the Nicolaitans, and one can understand how it found such a ready acceptance in Thyatira where 'business is business' would be the common sentiment.

18 The description of the eyes and feet is taken from 1:14, 15. *The eyes like a flame of fire* anticipate v. 23. **19** Charles holds that *your works* are defined by the qualities that follow, *love and faith and service and patient endurance.* If this is a correct reading, it is important for the interpretation of what the writer means by being 'judged by what they had done' (20:12–14).

20 The prophetess who imparts the teaching of the Nicolaitans is symbolically named *Jezebel,* for the queen of that name tried to establish an idolatrous cult in place of the worship of Yahweh and was herself accused of whoredom and witchcraft (2 Ki. 9:22). Note the curious insertion in some MSS of the possessive pronoun 'your' requiring the translation 'your wife Jezebel' instead of 'the woman Jezebel'. This would imply that the 'angel' of the church was its overseer.

21 From this verse we infer that 'Jezebel' had been earlier warned, without avail, either by John or by some other Christian leader. **22, 23** The bed into which Jezebel is to be cast is paralleled by *great tribulation,* so that it is a bed of suffering which is here meant. Hence RSV translates *sickbed* and NEB 'bed of pain'. The idiom is a Hebrew one and occurs in 1 Macc. 1:5 and Judith 8:3. It is possible that *those who commit adultery with her* are to be distinguished from *her children* in the sense that the former were sufficiently influenced by Jezebel as to compromise their Christian loyalties, the latter wholly embraced her doctrine; the former are to be chastised, the latter exterminated. By such judgments the churches will realize that Christ *searches mind* (lit. 'kidneys') *and heart.* In Hebrew usage, the kidneys are the seat of the emotions while the heart is the seat of the intellect.

24 *The deep things of Satan* may be a satirical allusion to the Gnostic claim exclusively to know the deep things of God; such wisdom is satanically inspired, not divine. Otherwise it reflects Nicolaitan teaching that the Christian should bodily participate in the excesses of heathenism and demonstrate that he is immune from their pollution. Christians who acted in this fashion boasted of their knowledge of the deep things of Satan and so scorned their more

scrupulous brethren. For *I do not lay upon you any other burden, cf.* Acts 15:28, 29; the two chief precepts of the apostolic council were abstention from food sacrificed to idols and from immorality. **25** This exhortation to perseverance occurs again at 3:11.

26, 27 The conqueror is here defined as he who *keeps my works until the end.* He is to receive a delegation of Christ's authority *over the nations* and share in His triumph over the rebellious peoples; the latter function is part of the former and anticipates the coming of Christ to judgment (19:11f.) rather than the millennial rule proper (20:4–6). The verb translated *rule* in v. 27 means 'shepherd'. But the reference to the *rod of iron* and 'smashing them to bits like earthenware' (NEB) shows that it is used here in the sense of 'destroy'. **28** *The morning star* appears to be Christ Himself (as in 22:16); greater than the privilege of ruling for Christ will be the unhindered enjoyment of His fellowship.

3:1–6 The letter to the church in Sardis

Sardis was a city of bygone glory. Once the capital of the ancient kingdom of Lydia, it sank into oblivion after the Persian conquest until Tiberius rebuilt it after an earthquake. The city was well known for two things: its dyeing and woollen industries, and its profligacy. The church in Sardis appears to reflect the history of the city; once it had a name for spiritual achievement, now it was lifeless (v. 1); licentiousness marked the Christians as well as the pagans, so that only a few had 'not soiled their garments' (v. 4), *i.e.* besmirched their Christian profession. Accordingly it was censured with a stringency surpassed only in the letter to the Laodiceans.

1 The title reflects 1:4 and 1:6. Christ is spoken of as the possessor of *the seven Spirits,* possibly to represent His complete knowledge of the deeds of the churches (see 5:6), though it may also hint at the spiritual gifts He is ready to impart in contrast to the lifelessness of the church. For *the seven stars,* see on 1:4, 20. Note that, although some Christians remain faithful to their Lord (*cf.* v. 4), the church as a whole is characterized as dead; for that condition all are held responsible. **2** For the first half, *cf.* Mt. 24:42; for the latter half *cf.* Dn. 5:27. **3** The tenses are unusually varied: 'Keep in mind (present) how you received and still hold on to the gift of God (perfect) and how you gave a hearing (aorist) to the gospel; continue to hold it fast (present) and bring yourself to repentance (aorist).' *If you will not awake* echoes Mt. 24:43, 44 and refers to the final advent. Some scholars consider that Rev. 16:15 has been displaced and should immediately precede this statement. Certainly 16:15 reads strangely in its present position and accords well here, but admittedly the suggestion is pure conjecture.

4 The Christians who *soiled* their garments presumably did so by accommodating themselves to the heathen customs of their neighbours. He who maintained in purity his character and testimony was to accompany the Christ in a robe of greater glory. For the walking with Christ Swete compares the companying of the Twelve with Him in the days of His ministry. The conqueror is doubly assured of this privilege. Contemporary apocalyptic literature viewed the resurrection body as a garment of glory. The idea is used by Paul (*e.g.* 2 Cor. 5:4), and seems to appear in this book also (*e.g.* 4:4). But 7:13, 14; 19:8 seem to have moral purity chiefly in mind in the use of this symbol, while, as Swete points out, the wearing of *white* sometimes expresses festivity (Ec. 9:8) and victory (2 Macc. 11:8). It would appear that a complexity of ideas attaches to this picture; it is wiser to accept the whole yet to recognize that the ethical element is especially in mind.

5 *His name.* Names, according to a contemporary usage, are synonymous with 'persons'. The blotting out from *the book of life* recalls Ex. 32:32, where the book is a register of the citizens of the theocratic kingdom; here it is the register of the eternal kingdom, as in Dn. 12:1 and many NT passages (see Lk. 10:20; Phil. 4:3; Heb. 12:23). See Rev. 20:12, 15 where this is explained. For the confession of the victor *cf.* Mt. 10:32.

3:7–13 The letter to the church in Philadelphia

Philadelphia, owing to its frequent earthquakes, had a small population; the church appears to have been correspondingly feeble (see v. 8, 'you have but little power'). There is no hint of persecution from pagan authorities, nor of heresies within the church; as at Smyrna, the Jews created the trouble here (v. 9). In impressive contrast to the letter that precedes and that which follows, there is neither rebuke nor warning from the Lord for this church, but simply commendation and exhortation.

7 The predicates *holy* and *true*, here applied to Christ, are in 6:10 referred to God, one of the many indications in this book that the attributes of God are shared by Christ. Jesus is *true* in the sense of 'true to His word', *i.e.* faithful. This is spoken in connection with His possessing *the key of David*, a phrase that recalls 1:18 but actually quotes Is. 22:22; it claims for Christ the power of admitting individuals or shutting them out from the city of David, the new Jerusalem, the Messianic kingdom.

8, 9 The relevance of this appears in the parenthesis of v. 8 and again in v. 9. The Jews of the city were no more worthy to be called Jews than their compatriots in Smyrna, and like them are designated a *synagogue of Satan*. V. 9 declares that one day, presumably at the establishment of the Messianic kingdom, they will be forced to recognize that these despised Christians are in truth the companions of the Son of man, the heirs of the kingdom of God. This latter claim the Jews had evidently so far denied. 'You Christians', said they, 'are excluded from the kingdom; it is for us Jews.' 'Not so', declares the Lord; 'I am true to my promise. I alone have the key of admission to the kingdom. I have set before my people a door of entrance into it which no-one can shut. They shall enter the kingdom, and the homage which you Jews expect the Gentiles to pay you (Is. 60:14) you will have to render to them.' This interpretation gives coherence to apparently disconnected statements and accords with the promise of v. 12. The faithfulness of this struggling community (v. 8) is to have its fitting compensation.

10 *The hour of trial* from which the Lord is to preserve these Christians is not the 'time' during which the judgments of God are on the earth, but the trials themselves. *Cf.* Mk. 14:35, where 'hour' represents the horrors of the cross and its attendant circumstances. The tribulation spoken of is directed towards *those who dwell upon the earth*, a phrase technical in this book for the unbelievers of the world (*cf.* 11:10). For a pictorial representation of this promise see 7:1–4.

11 *Cf.* 2:25. A note of urgency is now introduced. It appears again in the final chapter (see 22:7, 12, 20).

12 The conqueror is to be a *pillar in the temple* of the new age; 21:22 makes it clear that there is to be no Temple other than God and the Lamb in the heavenly Jerusalem. The promise here given is thus an assurance of inseparable unity with God in the eternity that is to be. I *I will write on him the name of my God* continues the metaphor of the pillar, so that the inscription is thought to be on the pillar and not on the victor's forehead, we may perhaps refer to 1 Macc. 14:26–48, which relates how the deeds of Simon Maccabaeus were inscribed on tablets of brass; these tablets were fixed 'upon pillars on Mount Zion', 'in a conspicuous place in the precincts of the sanctuary'. A permanent record of Simon's greatness was thus ensured. The boast of the conqueror, however, is not to be in his deeds but that he bears the name of God, and of the city of God, and Christ's new name; *i.e.* he belongs to God and to Christ manifested in glory (19:12), and is a citizen of the new Jerusalem, the eternal kingdom of God (21:2).

3:14–22 The letter to the church in Laodicea

Laodicea was situated on the bank of a river and stood at the junction of three great roads traversing Asia Minor. Naturally enough it became a large commercial and administrative centre. Three facts known about the city throw light on this letter: it was a banking centre and extremely wealthy; it manufactured clothing and woollen carpets; it had a medical school. The church was not accused of immorality, nor of idolatry, nor of open apostasy (persecution was unknown in Laodicea). The terrible condemnation pronounced over it was due to the pride and self-satisfaction of the pagan element within the church, so that it was all but entirely devoid of fellowship with Christ. The stern characterization of its spiritual condition (v. 17) and the admonition to repentance (v. 18) are both couched in terms of the three activities of the city.

14 As *the Amen* Jesus is the embodiment of the truthfulness and faithfulness of God (see Is. 65:16, RV mg.); the Christian use of 'Amen' adds the thought that He is also the Guarantor and Executor of the declared purposes of God. Such a designation stands in vivid contrast to the faithlessness of the Laodiceans. Similarly the title *the beginning of God's creation* (better translated 'the principle' or 'source' of creation) exalts Christ as Creator above the proud but puny creatures that boast in their self-sufficiency. **16** There is written a condemnation unequalled in the NT as an expression of the abhorrence of Christ. The reference is to the last judgment (*cf.* Lk. 13:25–28).

17, 18 form one statement: *For you say.* . . . *Therefore I counsel you to buy.* . . . The claim of the Laodiceans is not merely that they need nothing, but that their wealth, moral as well as material, is entirely due to their own efforts. Their real condition is shown to be one of poverty, in spite of their money; nakedness, despite their abundance of cloth; blindness, though they have many physicians. This church, therefore, alone of all the seven, is called 'the pitiable one'. Their only recourse is to 'buy' (*cf.* Is. 55:1) from Christ the tested gold of a regenerate spirit, purity of heart that may issue in resurrection glory (Rev. 7:13, 14) and grace to enable them to perceive spiritual realities (*cf.* 1 Cor. 3 and 2 Cor. 4). The nauseating condition of the Laodiceans has not quenched the love of Christ for them; His scathing judgments are but the expression of a deep affection that would lead them to repentance. The gracious invitation that follows is given, not to the church collectively (which would demand 'if *you* hear my voice . . .'), but to each individual within it, an offer of Christ to be a partner even in the commonest activities of life. Commensurate with the high privilege offered to these all but apostate Christians is a promise transcending the six that have preceded. Just as the believer asks Christ to share his domain in this transitory life, so the Lord will invite him, if he endures to the end, to share the throne given Him by the Father in the ages that are to be. The fulfilment of the promise is portrayed in Rev. 20:4–6, the millennial rule, and 22:5, the eternal reign in the new Jerusalem.

4:1 – 5:14 THE VISION OF HEAVEN

The scene of John's vision changes from earth to heaven and remains there until ch. 10, after which the point of view continually alternates. It is noticeable that, whereas the description of the throne of God in ch. 4 contains no reference to Christ, in the following chapter He dominates the picture as the slain Lamb of God. Concerning this Kiddle writes, 'In iv, the theme is that of the omnipotent Creator, reigning majestic and remote in a heaven from which

man is excluded. The God whom John sees is in the heaven of the old dispensation. In v, the focus of the seer's eyes changes, and with incomparable dramatic force he describes his vision of the Redeemer in whom lies every hope of man's salvation, every hope of a future kingdom of justice' (*MNTC*, p. 67).

4:1 *The first voice, which I heard speaking* is that of Christ. As the Lord revealed the true condition of His churches and His position in relation to them, so He now opens heaven to John's view, and His position in relation to that. The former was a revelation of 'what is'; this begins the unveiling of *what must take place after this* (*cf.* 1:19).

2 The fact that John saw a door opened in heaven implies that he was already in an ecstatic condition; the statement *at once I was in the spirit*, accordingly, may well indicate a yet higher degree of spiritual exaltation. The first object to catch John's eye was *a throne*. That is important; it hints that the first thing to be known about heaven is that the God who dwells therein possesses absolute authority over the universe. **3** The prophet does not describe God; he simply speaks of various colours seen through the light of a many-hued cloud, colours such as can emanate only from precious stones. Doubt attaches to the stones enumerated by John, but the most treasured type of *jasper* was green, the *carnelian* was red, while the word translated *emerald* is thought to be the rock crystal which shows a rainbow of prismatic colours. The object of the *rainbow* is primarily to conceal the form of God; yet it is significant that a rainbow and not an ordinary cloud performs this service, for the bow is a perpetual reminder of God's covenant to restrain His wrath from man on earth (Gn. 9:13); the memorial of the covenant in heaven is thus nothing less than the glory of God which hides Him from angelic view.

4 The *twenty-four elders*, though subordinate to the four living creatures (see v. 6), are mentioned before them, perhaps so as not to interrupt the description of the latter's activities. From the characteristics of the elders, as they appear in the subsequent visions, it is manifest that they are angelic beings; it is nevertheless not impossible to conceive of them as also the heavenly representatives of the people of God in their twofold aspect as priests and kings, in which case the number twenty-four, with its reminiscence of twelve tribes and twelve apostles, fittingly symbolizes the Messianic people of both dispensations, as the church has delighted to recognize. This view, however, is to be distinguished from that which regards the elders as a symbol for the people of God removed from earth and present in heaven.

5 For *the seven Spirits of God* see 5:6. **6** It is not said that the *sea of glass* is a literal sea but that it looks like one, *as it were a sea.* . . . It is an adaptation of the conception of waters above the firmament (Gn. 1:7; see *2 Enoch* 3:3), but is here introduced to emphasize the remoteness of the majesty of God. *Four living creatures* stand *round the throne*. Their description is drawn from Ezekiel's vision of the cherubim (Ezk. 1), but considerably modified. The chief differences are that the cherubim in Ezekiel each have four faces; here they have only one. The former possess 'wheels . . . full of eyes round about', but here the creatures themselves possess the eyes. **7, 8** The ceaseless worship rendered to God by them may well represent the subjection of all nature to God. The Jews themselves interpreted Ezekiel's vision in this way, regarding the *man* as chief representative of creatures, the *eagle* of birds, the *lion* of beasts, and the *ox* of cattle. The ancient symbolizing of the four winds and the four chief constellations of the Zodiac by these four figures, if known to John, would but serve to strengthen this view. The song of the cherubim implies that the certainty of the future triumph of God is rooted in His very nature; the Lord, who is holy and almighty, *is to come*.

9, 10 The thanksgiving of the living creatures, inspiring the renunciation by the twenty-four elders of their crowns, is not the continual worship of v. 8 but adoration given in special crises. See, *e.g.*, 5:8 and 14; 11:15–18; 19:4. **11** The elders recognize that only one is worthy to take preeminence in creation, and He the Creator. He willed the existence of all things. He has the right to deal with them in sovereign freedom. All creation should acknowledge its subjection to Him and ascribe the *glory* and the *honour* and the *power* to His name.

5:1 The Seer continues to describe what he saw. In the right hand of the Lord on the throne is a book, or scroll, *sealed with seven seals*. There has been much speculation as to the nature of the book so represented, but we shall not go far wrong in believing that it contains the record of God's judgments and redemption that issue in the kingdom of glory. It is a book of destiny, the Author of which is God. More precisely, it may well be that a testament is in mind. Zahn writes, 'The word *biblion* itself permits of many interpretations, but for the readers of that time it was designated by the seven seals on its back beyond possibility of a mistake. Just as in Germany before the introduction of money orders everyone knew that a letter sealed with five seals contained money, so the most simple member of the Asiatic churches knew that a *biblion* made fast with seven seals was a testament. When a testator died the testament was brought forward, and, when possible, opened in the presence of the seven witnesses who sealed it; *i.e.* it was unsealed, read aloud and executed. . . . The document with seven seals is a symbol of the promise of a future kingdom. The disposition long ago occurred and was documented and sealed, but it was not yet carried out . . .' (*Introduction to the New Testament*, 1909, Vol. III, pp. 393f.). It is an attractive interpretation, and is not to be set aside on the ground that the seals are opened singly and each direction carried out separately;

it was quite possible to construct a roll so sealed as to open in this manner. In any case the chief point in view is that the judgments and the kingdom are alike willed by God and subject to the authority of His Christ.

2 The angel needs to be *strong* since his voice has to carry throughout heaven, earth and the realm of the dead (v. 3). **3** *Under the earth* signifies Hades (*cf*. Eph. 4:9; Phil. 2:10). **5** *The Lion of the tribe of Judah* (Gn. 49:9), *the Root of David* (Is. 11:1, 10), won the victory for all time by virtue of His death and resurrection, so as *to open the scroll and its seven seals*. The redemption wrought by Christ had in view the establishment of God's kingdom in power. **6** The description of the *Lamb* combines two very different uses of this figure in Hebrew thought. It stands *as though it had been slain* and so reminds us of the slaughtered lamb of Is. 53:7; Jesus is the Servant of Yahweh, suffering in innocence for the sake of men. On the other hand, the lamb has *seven horns*. A horn in the OT symbolizes power (Ps. 75:4–7) and royal dignity (Zc. 1:18). Jesus has kingly power in a complete measure (the significance of *seven*); by His victory He fulfils the hope of Judaism that a Warrior-Lamb should arise and redeem Israel from her enemies (see, *e.g.*, *Testament of Simeon* 19:8). The nature of Christ's redemptive victory, however, was far removed from the current expectations of the Jews. Observe that the once-slain Lamb possesses *the seven Spirits of God sent out into all the earth*. *Cf*. Jn. 16:7f. In the OT the *seven eyes* (signifying omniscience) belong to Yahweh (*cf*. Zc. 4:10).

8 Though the four creatures fall down in worship with the twenty-four elders, it seems that only the latter have the harps and bowls of incense. The angelic nature of the elders is confirmed by the description of their offering up of the *prayers of the saints*; in Judaism this task is performed by the archangels (see Tobit 12:15; *Testament of Levi* 3:7). **9, 10** The creatures and the elders sing *a new song*, because Christ has opened a new era by His redemptive work and is shortly to consummate His victory in the triumphant kingdom of God. *Cf*. Is. 42:9, 10, which speaks of the new song in a similar context. The redemption is viewed as a purchase, at the price of Christ's life, a ransoming from the enslaving and hostile power of sin. The figure must not be pressed so as to answer, or even pose, the query 'To whom was the price paid?' That question was never meant to be asked. To be *a kingdom and priests* was Israel's vocation (Ex. 19:6), a privilege given also to the church (1 Pet. 2:9). The RV follows the harder, and therefore more likely, reading in the second half of v. 10, 'they reign (not *shall reign*) upon the earth'. Possibly this conveys the notion that Christians, not imperial dignitaries, are the true sovereigns of earth even in this dispensation. More probably it is a proleptic reference to the millennial rule of the saints (see 20:4–6), in which case it is erroneous to regard the millennium as the reign of the risen martyrs only, for this reference includes the whole church.

11-14 The angelic multitudes now take up the song of praise to the Lamb (*cf.* Dn. 7:10). The doxology has reference to the power and blessings received by Christ on the commencement of His Messianic reign (see 11:17). All creation in heaven earth, sea and Hades (v. 13) joins the host of angels and archangels. They sing the praise, not of the Lamb alone, not of God alone, but of God and the Lamb jointly. The exalted position of Christ in relation to God and the universe could not be more clearly set forth.

6:1 – 8:5 THE SEVEN SEALS

Many complex elements flow together to form the panorama which the prophet now describes. The division of the Messianic woes into seven may ultimately go back to the doom prophecy of Lv. 26 where four times it is stated 'I will chastise you . . . sevenfold for your sins' (vv. 18, 21, 24, 28). If that be so, the appropriateness of the testament with its seven seals to portray these judgments is a secondary factor and not the cause of the sevenfold division. Moreover, Charles has pointed out that our Lord's eschatological discourse contains the seven judgments enumerated by John; in Luke's Gospel (see ch. 21) they are in the same order, except that John places the earthquakes last, owing to his consistent portrayal of earthquakes as the immediate precursor of the consummation; see 8:5; 11:13; 16:18. Thus, in respect of the content of the seals, the prophet has apparently followed our Lord's discourse; but for the form of the opening four judgments he has used a vision of Zechariah (the vision of four chariots and horses that go to the four quarters of the earth, Zc. 6), adapting the symbolism to suit his purpose.

6:1, 2 The first seal

1 *Come!* The command is directed to the rider who appears on the opening of the seal. The same is true of vv. 3, 5, 7.

Many interpreters regard the conquering horseman as Christ and compare the vision of the returning Lord in 19:11f. It must be admitted, however, that the only thing in common with the two pictures is the *white horse*, which is a symbol of victory. Others hold that the ride represents the triumph of the gospel, and cite Mk. 13:10. This latter suggestion is more plausible, but in view of the similarity of the four riders it seems more natural to interpret all as portraying the last judgments. This horseman signifies invasion, or warfare generally.

6:3, 4 The second seal

4 The strife created by the rider on the *horse* that was *bright red* appears to denote both international and civil warfare. This doubling of the first woe has caused some to feel that the first rider represents a specific victorious empire

(especially the Parthian) while the second has a general reference. This is possible, but it should be noted that the same repetition occurs in each report of the eschatological discourse (Mt. 24:6, 7; Mk. 13:7, 8; Lk. 21:9, 10).

6:5, 6 The third seal

The rider on *a black horse* denotes famine. The balance in his hand suggests scarcity of food. The prices quoted are prohibitive. *A denarius* was a labourer's day wages (Mt. 20:1f.); *a quart of wheat* (Gk. *choinix*) would suffice for one man's daily ration, but not for his family. Wheat would therefore be unprocurable by the poor. *Three quarts of barley* would go further, but even so it would still remain a bare subsistence allowance with the possibility of starvation in some instances. On the other hand, *but do not harm oil and wine* presupposes ample supplies of less needed goods. A few years before the writing of this book (AD 92), an acute shortage of cereals, together with an abundance of wine in the Empire, caused Domitian to order the restriction of vine cultivation and an increase of corn growing; the order created such a furore it had to be abandoned. The text may have such a situation in mind.

6:7, 8 The fourth seal

Hades followed, accompanied by Death, a reminder that not even physical death would give respite to sinners; the nether world and the judgment awaited them. For the four plagues—sword, and famine, and pestilence (translated 'death' in the LXX), and beasts—see Ezk. 14:12-21.

6:9-11 The fifth seal

9 The souls of the martyrs were said to be *under the altar* because they had been 'sacrificed'; *cf.* Phil. 2:17; 2 Tim. 4:6. This position was one of honour, not humiliation. Charles quotes Aqiba as saying, 'Whoever was buried in the land of Israel was just as if he were buried under the altar, and whoever was buried under the altar was just as if he were buried under the throne of glory' (*Pirqe Aboth* R.M. 26). The martyrs were slain 'for the testimony (given by Jesus; see 12:17) which they held' (AV). This translation is to be preferred to RSV's *for the witness they had borne*; the testimony was that which they had received, not given. **10, 11** The *white robe* given to the martyrs signifies a pledge of the glorious immortality to be bestowed at the 'first resurrection' (20:4-6), with perhaps a hint that the victory was already theirs. Observe that this incident forms an integral part of the last judgments on earth, for the prayer for vengeance (v. 10) is answered and the end thereby hastened; see 8:1-5. For the thought that the coming of the day of God tarries for the last martyr, *cf.* 2 Esdras 4:33-36.

6:12-17 The sixth seal

The description of the effects of the sixth seal draws from numerous scriptures, including the

Gospels. The underlying thought of these cosmic disturbances is, perhaps, the impossibility that life should continue under such circumstances; the End is at hand, 'the great day of . . . wrath has come' (v. 17).

12 For the *earthquake* as a sign of the End, *cf.* Ezk. 38:19f.; for the *sun* and *moon*, Joel 2:31. **13, 14** For the falling of stars and the rolling up of heaven, *cf.* Is. 34:4. **15, 16** For the hiding in the rocks, *cf.* Is. 2:10; for the prayer to the mountains, Ho. 10:8. Note the sevenfold classification of mankind here. *Every one, slave and free* is included; but particular attention is drawn to the great and powerful. *The wrath of the Lamb* shows the Christ in the character hinted at in His possession of seven horns (5:6), *i.e.* complete power to establish righteousness and execute justice (*cf.* 6:10). **17** For the great and unbearable day of wrath, *cf.* Joel 2:11. These signs of the consummation are too regular in eschatological writings for them to be regarded as wholly figurative. Yet that they are not to be taken too literally appears from the picture of heaven being removed as a scroll at the close of the millennial age (20:11), and the imploring by men that the mountains, which have already moved out of their place, should fall on them.

7:1-17 An interlude between the sixth and seventh seals

An interlude in the progress of the visions is given in chapter 7. It explains the position of Christians during the execution of the judgments that have been described. First a backward look is taken, to show how the church is secured from the evils experienced by the godless world, then a forward look enables the Seer to relate the fulfilment of God's act of protection; he sees the triumphant people of God at the close of the great distress, arrayed in splendour and ascribing their salvation to the grace of God and the Lamb (v. 11). There seems little doubt that the two companies here in view are essentially the same. The 144,000 out of every tribe of the children of Israel (v. 4) symbolize the entire church of the end-time; this is implied by v. 3, for 'the servants of our God' in the Christian dispensation can only be the church. Further, since the distresses of the last days are world-wide the whole company of God's people need His protection, not simply one section of it (the Jews).

1 *After this* marks a new vision; it is not a note of time in relation to the events of the previous vision but introduces a fresh comprehension of truth by the prophet. For the purpose of this vision the earth is regarded as rectangular, an angel standing at each corner governing the destructive wind that blows from his quarter. **2–4** No further description is supplied to relate what happens when the four angels let loose their winds. Possibly John here recounts an earlier vision that portrayed the sealing of God's people against destruction caused by the four winds in the last days; the fury of winds would represent the whole manifestation of judgment symbolized by the seals, trumpets and bowls. For the thought of sealing the saints in a time of peril, *cf.* Ezk. 9. The 144,000 symbolizes 'fixedness and full completion, 12×12 taken a thousandfold' (Alford). Israel was often referred to as 'the twelve tribes' to denote the whole nation without any thought of its constituent parts (Acts 26:7).

5–8 The enumeration of the tribes one by one here serves to emphasize the completeness of the number of God's saints for whom He cares during the coming ordeal. For the church as the true Israel *cf.* Rom. 2:28, 29; Gal. 3:29; 6:16; Phil. 3:3; Jas. 1:1; 1 Pet. 1:1 with 2:9. The order of the tribes is curious in a number of ways. *Judah* heads the list, an unusual procedure amongst the Jews; here it is because it is the tribe of the Messiah. Dan is omitted whereas *Manasseh* appears, although the latter is included in *Joseph*. Irenaeus explained this as being due to the ancient belief that antichrist was to spring from Dan. The half-tribe of Manasseh was then inserted to make up the number twelve. Buchanan Gray discovered that if vv. 5c, 6 (*i.e.* Gad to Manasseh) were placed after v. 8, the list would conform to the usual enumeration of the Jewish tribes by which they are arranged according to descent from their mothers: the sons of Leah are Judah to Zebulun; the son of Rachel, Joseph and Benjamin; the sons of Leah's handmaid, Gad and Asher; the sons of Rachel's handmaid, Naphtali and Dan (here replaced by Manasseh). It is possible, therefore, that our text originally maintained this order but suffered a dislocation by a copyist in early days.

9 *After this* again marks a logical rather than a chronological sequence. The result of the sealing of Christ's faithful followers is their ultimate vindication in glory. *A great multitude*; the church is seen triumphant in heaven. *White robes* signify resurrection glory, and *palm branches* victory and gladness after war (*cf.* Mk. 11:8; 1 Macc. 13:51). **10** *Salvation belongs to our God . . . and to the Lamb* echoes Ps. 3:8; see also Rev. 19:1. The victors here ascribe their redemption to God and the Lamb. **12** The *Amen* of the angelic orders endorses the praise of the redeemed multitude, while they, too, add their thanksgiving.

13, 14 John's answer to the elder's question implies 'I also would like to know'. *The great tribulation* out of which the multitude has come is not intended as a general designation of tribulation, which is the Christian's normal lot, (the omission by AV of the definite article gives this impression), but has specific reference to the trial at the close of this age. On the other hand, there is no warrant for the common assumption that the multitude consists of martyrs only. The vision depicts the scene after the cessation of trials (the present tense 'come' (RV) is to be understood in the light of the statement 'they *have washed* their robes and *made* them white . . .'); it thus has in mind one generation only of Christians, the last. Yet the latter part of this section seems to refer to the whole church.

The difficulty is relieved if we remember that the Seer prophesies a day that to him is almost on the horizon; he has no thought of intervening ages. The last persecution may come at any moment. The church was still in its second generation and John had no reason to anticipate a third. The glorification of the bride with her Lord was at hand. To his mind, therefore, to speak of Christians who came through 'the great ordeal' (NEB) was to denominate the major part of the church. Those who had gone before, having witnessed a good confession, would doubtless be included in this throng, but it was superfluous to mention them. The church of the present was the subject in view and it fills John's canvas. For us, nearly two millennia later, the church is mainly the church triumphant in heaven; it is therefore possible to recognize that the AV rendering is spiritually true, 'These are they which came out of great tribulation . . .' and read therein our own names.

They *have washed their robes and made them white in the blood of the Lamb* is a symbolic expression, not to be taken literally, of the forgiveness of sins through faith in the Christ who died for men. It is possible to translate, as some do in 12:11, 'in the blood of the Lamb' as 'through the blood of the Lamb'; the washing and making white of robes then signifies the overcoming of sin in life by virtue of the power of Christ's atonement, a retrospect on the whole struggle of life rather than on the moment of conversion.

15 Charles translates the last part of the verse, 'He that sitteth upon the throne shall cause his Shekinah to abide upon them.' The phrase is unique. The Shekinah was the manifestation of God's presence amongst men, especially in the Tabernacle and the Temple at Jerusalem. After the pilgrimage through the wilderness it was of very rare occurrence in Israel; to the Christian it is promised as a constant privilege. 16, 17 are a statement drawn from Is. 49:10 and 29:8: Christ assuages the thirst of man by providing in Himself the antidote to his restlessness, the complete counterpart to man's unsatisfied desires.

8:1-5 The seventh seal

1 A *silence in heaven* occurred in order to hear the prayers of the saints. There is a Jewish tradition that 'in the fifth heaven are companies of angels of service who sing praises by night but are silent by day because of the glory of Israel', *i.e.* that Israel's praises may be heard. In our text, however, the thanksgiving of heaven is quieted to hear not praises but cries for deliverance from the suffering Christians on earth. 2 The appearance at this juncture of the seven archangels with seven trumpets interrupts the sequence of the vision and, in thought at least, is to be considered after v. 5. 3, 4 *Incense* offered with *the prayers of all the saints* serves to make them acceptable before God. If human prayers are to be effective they must be cleansed from all taint of selfishness. It is doubtful that two altars appear in v. 3. The one altar in heaven seems to partake of the character both of the altar for burnt-offerings and of the altar of incense that stood in the Holiest Place. 5 The prayers of the saints are answered. The fire that burned the incense is thrown to earth and becomes a means of judgment. There follow various phenomena which reveal that the End has come and the kingdom of God is established; see 11:19 (consequent on the seventh trumpet) and 16:18 (following the seventh bowl).

8:6 - 11:19 THE SEVEN TRUMPETS

As the seven seals fall into two groups of four and three, so the seven trumpets divide themselves, the first four having distinct reminiscences of the Egyptian plagues at the Exodus. In 15:3 the second coming is tacitly compared to the Exodus (the redeemed sing the song of Moses and of the Lamb); so here that redemption is heralded by like plagues on the ungodly. Note further that the eschatological use of the trumpet goes back to the sounding of a trumpet at the theophany of Sinai (Ex. 19:13-20). For examples of the use of the trumpet at the last day see Joel 2:1; 1 Cor. 15:52; 1 Thes. 4:16.

8:7 The first trumpet

The first trumpet affects one third of earth; *cf.* the plague of hail and fire in Ex. 9:24. *All green grass* was burned up, that is, in the third part of the earth which was affected; the locusts of 9:4 are forbidden to hurt the grass of the earth, which would not exist if this were a universal judgment.

8:8, 9 The second trumpet

The second trumpet affects one third of the sea. As the Nile was turned into blood in the first Egyptian plague (Ex. 7:20, 21), so does the third part of the sea here.

8:10, 11 The third trumpet

The third trumpet causes one third of fresh waters to become poisonous, and so continues the thought of the previous plague; *cf.* 16:3-7. Since the star that falls at the sounding of the fifth trumpet (9:1) is an angelic being, it is possible that *Wormwood* is also an angel. For the bitter waters *cf.* Je. 9:15; 23:15.

8:12, 13 The fourth trumpet

The fourth trumpet darkens a third part of the heavens. Instead of 'the day should not shine for the third part of it, and the night in like manner' (RV) read with the Bohairic version, 'the third part of them should not shine during the day and during the night in like manner'. This corresponds in a measure to the Egyptian plague of darkness (Ex. 10:21-23).

Woe is now thrice repeated by the angel because the three last plagues are particularly grievous and are entitled the first, second and third woes. They are directed to *those who dwell on the earth*, *i.e.* the non-Christian world in distinction from the church.

9:1–12 The fifth trumpet

1 The fifth trumpet introduces a plague of demonic locusts. The fact that the star seen by John lies *fallen from heaven to earth* does not necessitate its being a 'fallen' angel. The movement is narrated merely to show that the 'star' came down from heaven to earth to open the abyss, wherein dwelt the demonic hordes. **2, 3** This *bottomless pit* is the place into which Satan is thrown (20:1ff.). The reference to the *key* indicates that all its inhabitants are firmly under God's control. *Cf.* Lk. 8:31; Rom. 10:7. Clouds *like the smoke of a great furnace* is intended to convey the impression of an advancing cloud of locusts (see Joel 2:10). The comparison of these demon hosts to locusts goes back to the vision of Joel alluded to, where it is said that the locust armies look like war horses running to battle, rattle like chariots, charge like mighty men, darken the heavens (Joel 2:4–10) and have fangs like lions (Joel 1:6). In addition to these features, John declares the locusts have power to inflict pain like *scorpions*; see also 9:10. **4** indicates the reason for the scorpion sting; the locusts are sent not to harm vegetation but only such men as *have not the seal of God upon their foreheads*. **5, 6** *Five months* is the normal length of a locust's life (spring and summer). Scorpions inflict agony but rarely kill men. **7** The likeness between the head of a locust and that of a horse was often mentioned by ancient writers. The crowns of gold and human faces, however, emphasize that they are no ordinary locusts but demons. **8** The *hair like women's hair* refers to their long antennae; lion-like *teeth* to their destructiveness; **9** *iron breastplates* to their scales. **11** Hence their king is *Abaddon*, a name that in the OT denotes the depths of Sheol and means 'destruction' (*cf.* Jb. 28:22).

Whether this plague is intended to symbolize the pangs of men's stricken conscience (as Swete believes), or is intended to be taken more literally, it is hard to say. It is possible that both in this and the following woe John depicts the troubling of humanity by actual demonic powers; such a view would accord with the NT teaching on demons generally.

9:13–21 The sixth trumpet

The sixth trumpet brings a demonic army from the Euphrates. **13** A voice from *the . . . golden altar* initiates the plague, thus connecting it with the cries of the martyrs in heaven and the prayers of the saints on earth (*cf.* 8:4, 5). **14, 15** *The four angels* are ministers of wrath. The river Euphrates formed 'the ideal limit' of the land of Israel (Driver; see Gn. 15:18); beyond it used to lie the great Empires of Babylon and Assyria. As armies came from these unknown territories to ravage disobedient Israel of old,

so would more terrifying horses arise to punish the godless world. Nothing in the programme of God is accidental. The precise moment of this invasion is fixed 'in a definite hour of a definite day, in a definite month of a definite year' (Charles). **16–19** The unimaginable figure of two hundred million (see Ps. 68:17) hints that this whole description in these verses is not intended to be taken too literally. The horsemen seem to be of little account; it is the horses that terrify and destroy. Corresponding to the deadly *fire and smoke and sulphur* which proceed from the horses' mouths, the riders have breast-plates of fiery red, smoky blue and sulphurous yellow. Monsters of this sort were not unknown to heathen mythology; possibly John deliberately uses such terms to declare that the devices of this hellish multitude beggar the most terrifying imaginations of pagan superstition, even including the brutes of primaeval chaos. **20, 21** The plague fails to produce a salutary effect on the God-opposing world; men yet persist in idolatry, with its attendant evils, and find no place of repentance.

10:1 – 11:14 Interlude between the sixth and seventh trumpets

Just as John inserted a parenthesis between the sixth and seventh seals, so he does between the sixth and seventh trumpets. His purpose in this interlude is to emphasize the certain proximity of the End (10:1–7), the validity of his prophetic ministry (10:8–11), the security of the church (11:1, 2) and the power of its witness in the era of antichrist (11:3–13). Throughout this section the Seer lays prophetic writings much under contribution, both canonical and otherwise, and re-applies them with great freedom; particularly is it necessary to bear this in mind when interpreting ch. 11.

10:1–7 The proximity of the End. 1 The *mighty angel* is sometimes identified with Christ, but it is unlikely that He would be referred to as an angel; see Dn. 12:7. The *rainbow* about his head may be due to the radiance of his face gleaming through the cloud that surrounded him. **2** In view of v. 11, the *little scroll* seems to include the rest of the visions of this book. **3** *The seven thunders* were not uttered by the angel, for they followed his cry, but probably came from God or Christ (as also the command of v. 4). **4** For a reason not made known to us John is forbidden to reveal the message of the thunders. Some compare 2 Cor. 12:4, but not aptly, for the revelation could hardly be greater than that of chs. 4 and 5. Kiddle suggests it was a revelation given for John's own illumination but which he must not digress to record in view of the importance of the rest of this vision, a view which is as plausible as any yet propounded. **5–7** *Cf.* Dn. 12:7. The angel stands on earth and sea because his message is of world-wide importance. **6** The burden of his declaration is that there shall be *no more delay*. God's purpose for mankind, revealed to the prophets, is now to be accomplished; **7** the *seventh angel* is on the point of sounding his trumpet and then will the End come.

10:8–11 John's commission as a prophet reaffirmed. This part of the vision recalls Ezk. 2:9 – 3:3. As in Ezekiel's case, eating the book caused both sweetness and bitterness, a phenomenon due, however, to the mixture of blessings and woes to be announced rather than to the sweetness of obediently proclaiming what is bitter. The import of the passage seems to be a reaffirmation of John's prophetic commission.

11:1, 2 The security of the church. In this short oracle the Temple at Jerusalem is measured off, together with its worshippers, for protection in a period of trial (*cf.* Ezk. 40:3f.; Am. 7:7–9). The outer court of the Gentiles and the city itself are left to the domination of a heathen oppressor for three and a half years. Some expositors have interpreted this to mean that the prophecy was written before AD 70 while the Temple was still standing. But it is difficult to harmonize this standpoint with the book as a whole, which is concerned with the welfare of the Christian church, not the Jewish nation. John's vision is intended to portray the spiritual security of the church during the era of antichrist's sway. It follows that we should not expect to be able to allegorize every detail of the picture but be content with grasping its general meaning.

1 *The temple of God and the altar and those who worship there* convey one idea, the church (*cf.* 1 Cor. 3:16). **2** Similarly *the court outside the temple* and *the holy city* together represent the world outside the church. It is a bold transformation, but v. 8 implies that the one-time 'holy city' has now become one with sinful Sodom, Egypt the oppressor, and the tyrannous empire that wars against the Messiah. For the *forty-two months, cf.* 12:6 ('one thousand two hundred and sixty days') and 12:14 ('time, and times, and half a time'), all equivalent expressions for the three and a half years of antichrist's rule. The same reckoning appears in Dn. 7:25; 12:7, but its precise significance is still obscure.

11:3–14 The prophecy of the two witnesses. This involves similar principles as vv. 1, 2. The two witnesses originally were Moses and Elijah. For the latter's expected appearance before the Messiah's coming, see Mal. 4:5. Moses also was thought by some to have been translated to heaven and to be returning with Elijah; Johanan ben-Zakkai declared that God said to Moses, 'If I send the prophet Elijah, you must both come together.'

It could be argued that John intended the prophecy to be understood literally, but certain indications in the text suggest that the vision refers to the missionary activity of the whole church. The beast is said to 'make war' on the two witnesses (v. 7), a curious phrase in reference to two individuals, but it is applied to the church in 13:7; men from the whole world view their martyred forms and rejoice in their subjugation (v. 9), an impossible thought if two

individuals in Jerusalem were meant; and the witnesses are represented by lampstands (v. 4): a figure applied to the church in ch. 1. The passage, accordingly, illustrates the church's powerful witness in the era under review by means of a well-known Jewish expectation. V. 4 shows why there are two witnesses rather than only one (Elijah): John has in mind Zechariah's vision of the two olive-trees standing on either side of the golden lampstand (Zc. 4). There the two trees probably represented Joshua and Zerubbabel, the lampstand Israel. John makes the one lampstand become two to conform to the two trees, and declares that both the olive-trees and the lampstands mean the same thing, the church in its prophetic capacity. The lampstand had already become seven to represent the seven churches (1:12; 2:1); it is an easy transition to make them become two to correspond to the two prophets, though here the whole church is typified by the lampstands, not a part of it.

3 *Sackcloth* is worn by the witnesses because of the grave character of their message. **4** *Olive trees* and *lampstands*; see above. **5, 6** The extraordinary power of the church is set forth in terms reminiscent of Elijah and Moses. The destroying fire recalls 2 Ki. 1:10f.; the ability to prevent rain, 1 Ki. 17:1; the turning of waters to blood and the smiting of earth with plagues, Ex. 7-12. **7** We have the first mention of the *beast that ascends from the bottomless pit, i.e.,* as RV, 'that cometh up out of the abyss'. He is spoken of as if well known, but fuller descriptions of him occur in chs. 13 and 17. Note the similarity of words used in 13:7 to describe the warfare of the beast against the church. For *bottomless pit* see on 9:1.

8 *The great city* means what Bunyan represented as 'Vanity Fair' (Kiddle). Throughout the rest of the book the phrase is used of the harlot city Rome (16:19; 17:18; 18:10f.), so that in one remarkable stroke of the pen John identifies Jerusalem with Sodom, Egypt and Rome, and all together with the world that rejected and killed the Son of God. **9, 10** Jew and Gentile combine in seeking to crush the testimony of the faithful witnesses of Christ, just as they sought to destroy the Lord Himself. Refusal to allow a corpse to be buried signifies the greatest depth of ignominy to which a man could be subjected; see Ps. 79:3 and the book of Tobit. **11** The church is crushed by its enemies *for three and a half days* corresponding to the years of its testimony, 'a short triumph in point of fact, but long enough to bear the semblance of being complete and final' (Swete). At the conclusion of the three and a half days *a breath of life from God entered into them, and they stood upon their feet.* This is a quotation from Ezk. 37:10, which referred to the spiritual quickening of the nation Israel. Possibly, therefore, this resurrection is to be taken figuratively signifying a revival so tremendous as to awe the world; but it may describe the rapture of the saints (*cf.* 1 Thes. 4:16, 17) and so be equivalent to the first resurrection (20:4–6). *Cf.* the earthquake here (11:13) with that recorded in 6:12. **13** The number *seven thousand* would suitably indicate a tenth of the population of Jerusalem. In making the city represent the world-city of Vanity Fair, John had no need to alter the figure, for 7,000 could be interpreted to mean any considerable number. Note that these events at last evoked some sort of repentance from the hitherto unrepentant race.

11:15–19 The seventh trumpet

The seventh trumpet, as the seventh seal, is followed by the advent of the kingdom of God. Since the sounding of the seventh trumpet is intended to bring the third woe (v. 14) but no calamity is described, it is evident that we are to expect a further elucidation of the matter later on. Such an expansion is provided in 14:19, 20 and ch. 18. **15** Meanwhile, great voices proclaim, *The kingdom of the world has become the kingdom of our Lord and of his Christ*, a joint rule which is to know no end; it signifies the millennial reign merging into the eternal bliss of the new creation (20–22). **17, 18** The customary attribute of God is significantly shortened; no longer is it said that He 'is to come', for He 'has come'! *Thou hast taken thy great power, and begun to reign*; the eternal reign has 'begun' in that there has commenced a new exercise of the sovereignty of God over man, a sovereignty which at no time in history had been abandoned but which, in His wisdom, had been voluntarily limited. The song of thanksgiving marks an ordered progress of thought which is observed later in the book; God has begun His eternal rule, *i.e.* the millennial kingdom (20:4–6); the nations were angry, rising in rebellion (20:8, 9); God's wrath manifested itself in judgment (20:9); the dead were judged (20:11–15); the saints rewarded in the city of God (21) and the sinners destroyed in the lake of fire (20:15; 21:8).

19 The Temple in heaven is opened to reveal the ark of the covenant. The manifestation of the ark to men at this point implies that the goal of the covenant, which is the promise of the kingdom, is now in the act of coming to pass. Lightnings, earthquake and hail, *etc.* testify that the consummation has arrived (*cf.* 8:5; 16:17–21).

12:1 – 14:20 THE BACKGROUND OF THE EARTHLY CONFLICT

Since the seven trumpets followed on the seven seals, it is a natural expectation that the seven bowls will immediately be poured out, so that the story of the birth pangs of the kingdom may be completed. Instead, however, a lengthy parenthesis intervenes. It is necessary to reveal the true nature of the conflict which the Messiah ends at His appearing before the *débâcle* itself can be appreciated and understood. The struggle

in which the saints are involved is not simply the efforts of a minor religious community to resist the persecutions of an empire; this but forms the platform of a more terrifying contest wherein the age-old adversary of God and man strives by every subterfuge of politics and heathenism to thwart the purpose of God centred in His church. The 'parenthesis' is thus seen to be the core of the book. It covers the whole Messianic period, from the birth of Christ to the consummation.

12:1–17 The woman and her child

1ff. The Greeks told a story of the birth of Apollo remarkably parallel to that in vv. 1–6. The Egyptians similarly related the birth of Horus; in fact the story, in modified forms, seems to have been universally told. Clearly John has employed a well-known narrative (first adapted, apparently, by a Jew) both to illustrate his own theme and tacitly to exclude all heroes of other faiths from the position of world Redeemer. Such treatment of pagan sources is similar to his use of Jewish narratives, such as those in chs. 7 and 11; the message they are made to yield is in both cases neither pagan nor Jewish, but Christian through and through. To the heathen nations of the ancient world the travailing woman (12:1, 2) would have been a goddess crowned with the twelve stars of the Zodiac. The Jew would have seen in her his own people, headed by the twelve patriarchs. John shows that she represents neither of these, but the true believing people of God of both old and new dispensations, the Messianic community.

3 The *dragon* is identified in v. 9 with Satan. His *seven heads and ten horns* show him to be the antichrist of the spiritual world, just as his agent, 'the beast' (13:1), is the earthly antichrist sharing his characteristics. The figure was used in Daniel to describe the nature of the four successive world powers of history. In Daniel the seven heads were divided among the four beasts, while here they are retained in one horrible concentration of evil. The ten horns are similarly traditional and in the earthly anti-Christian power are applied to ten kings (Dn. 7:24; Rev. 17:12). **4** *His tail swept down a third of the stars of heaven* echoes a victory of the devil over angelic powers, but whether John intended by this feature anything more than an allusion to the dragon's great power is hard to say. **5** The statement of the child's destiny (see Ps. 2:9) explains the dragon's desire to devour him, for the nations he regarded as his legitimate prey. In its original reference the meaning would be that the child was snatched to the throne of God for safety while yet an infant; but the 'catching up' is sufficiently similar to the victorious ascension of Jesus to make plain its real meaning in this context.

6 The people of God are safe from the devil's wiles during the period of antichrist's reign of terror. This accords with the teaching of 7:1–8; 11:1, 2; it anticipates the downfall of Satan described in vv. 7–12 and is enlarged in 13–17. **7ff.** The *war . . . in heaven* may signify an attempt to storm the refuge of the Child-Redeemer. Hence the heavenly protagonist is an archangel leading the hosts of God; he it is who wins the victory over the devil and his demonic followers. His conquest brings in *the kingdom of our God* (v. 10; *cf.* Dn. 12:1–3). But the addition of v. 11 by our prophet transforms the whole scene. The real means of the dragon's overthrow was the atoning work of Christ; His people share that victory by their testimony to His saving power in their lives. The angelic conquest becomes a mere figure for the victory of Christ and His saints. The initiation of the kingdom of God through the redemption on the cross is a close parallel to the Johannine and Pauline teaching that our Lord's death and resurrection were the occasion of Satan's downfall and the establishment of the kingdom age with all its attendant blessings. The Revelation, accordingly, cannot be said to be wholly devoid of 'realized' eschatology. Charles has successfully solved a long-standing linguistic difficulty by translating v. 7 'Michael and his angels had to fight with the dragon'. See *ICC*, pp. 321, 322.

9 *That ancient serpent* is that which tempted Eve in Eden. *Devil* (Gk. *diabolos*) is the Greek equivalent of the Hebrew *Satan*, both meaning 'slanderer'. The text implies that Satan can no longer fulfil his function of falsely accusing the saints before God (see Jb. 1 and Zc. 3) for Christ has secured their acquittal and reconciled them to God through His atonement. Accordingly, the devil concentrates on his abilities as dragon, serpent and deceiver.

10 *Kingdom* is perhaps better rendered here 'sovereignty'; but *cf.* Col. 1:13, 14, where the thought is very similar; for the casting down of Satan *cf.* Jn. 12:31–33. **11** The redemption of Christ is the prime cause of the saints' victory; their testimony confirms its efficacy in their lives. **12** The expression *woe to you, O earth and sea* corresponds to John's frequent designation of the unbelieving world as 'those who dwell on the earth' (11:10; 13:8, *etc.*); it is here used in distinction from the heavenly sphere where Satan formerly dwelt. The extent of the *time* is defined in v. 14; the period of antichrist's reign is here seen to be an administration of the devil through him. **13** The dragon now turns his attention to the woman, *i.e.* the church, having failed in the case of its Lord: *cf.* Jn. 15:20. **14** See on v. 6 above. In the symbolism setting forth its attack on the woman the serpent is regarded as a water monster, indeed the personification of the sea. Hence the woman flees for refuge into *the wilderness*, where a sea monster can have no place. **15, 16** Not to be outdone, the serpent sends a flood of water after her, but the earth swallows it up, so that nothing more can be done by him. The picture well illustrates the spiritual security of believers against all that the devil can do in his attempts to destroy them.

17 *He stood*; AV reads 'I stood' and connects the sentence with 13:1. Both the MS evidence and the context favour the RSV reading.

13:1–18 Antichrist and his prophet

1–3 The dragon, having failed alone to crush the Christ and His people, calls to his aid a helper. The beast comes *out of the sea*, thereby showing its character as a sea monster (like the dragon; see notes on 12:3, 15, 16 and *cf.* Dn. 7:3) and as demonic (according to 11:7 the sea is equivalent to the abyss). The second beast, on the other hand, comes 'out of the earth'. This difference corresponds to that between Behemoth, the land monster (Jb. 40:15f.) and Leviathan, the sea monster (Jb. 41), creatures which, in the prophetic books, served to typify the God-opposing powers (see, *e.g.*, Is. 27:1; 51:9; Ezk. 32:2f., *etc.*).

The details of the sea monster are drawn from Dn. 7. We learn from Rev. 17:5, 9 that it represents the power of Rome, the *seven heads* being a succession of emperors and the *ten horns* ten allied kings (17:12); the *blasphemous names* are the divine titles claimed by Roman sovereigns. The characteristics of *leopard, bear* and *lion* in Dn. 7:4–6 were shared out among three prior empires. Here they combine in one terrifying unity of power and wickedness, the *leopard* signifying cruelty and cunning, the *bear* strength, the *lion* ferocity. One of the heads *seemed to have a wound, mortal but . . . was healed*. Clearly the reference is to the death of one of the emperors. But of whom is it said that the death-stroke was healed, the emperor in question or the Roman Empire of which he was a part? Gunkel believed the latter, for a monster suffering from the loss of one of its heads has received a mortal blow; the historical reference could then be to the murder of Julius Caesar, whose death endangered the security of the Empire (*one of its heads* in John's Hebraic Greek could mean 'the first of his heads'). Most expositors are inclined to interpret the healing of the death-stroke as of the head (emperor) in question, who is then identified with the beast itself (as in vv. 12, 14 and 17). That could only mean that one of the emperors was to rise from the dead and sum up in himself the character of the devil-inspired empire. Precisely that was being asserted of Nero at the time of the writing of this book; for though he committed suicide in AD 68, it was widely believed he would return to lead the eastern powers against Rome. See further on 17:8, 11, and the note on the anti-Christian empire (p. 1302).

4 The world worships both the devil and the false Christ who sums up in himself the characteristics of the Empire. **5** The *mouth speaking haughty and blasphemous words* is asserted of the anti-God power in Dn. 7:8, 20. For the *forty-two months cf.* 11:2, 3; 12:14. During this time the beast is said to be given authority *to continue, i.e.* to act wickedly; *cf.* Dn. 8:12; 11:36. Note that, although the dragon gave the beast his authority over the earth, the real permission for his blasphemous utterances and deeds, and even the duration of his reign, comes from God; see also vv. 7, 10, 14, 15. The sovereignty of God is never more apparent than during the rule of antichrist. **6** *Cf.* 2 Thes. 2:4. **7** *Cf.* Dn. 7:21. **8** The reference of the words *from the foundation of the world* is uncertain; they can be linked with the slaying of the Lamb, as in AV and RV, or with the writing of the saint's names in the book of life, as in RSV, RV mg. Both meanings are equally true; for the former *cf.* 1 Pet. 1:19, 20, for the latter Eph. 1:4. The difficulty is settled for most by an appeal to 17:8, where almost identical language is used, connecting the phrase with the writing in the book. Nevertheless the word order is decidedly against this interpretation, unless it were true that the book as we have it is a translation from John's original writing.

10 AV takes both parts of this couplet as referring to persecutors of the church ('He that leadeth into captivity shall go into captivity . . .'), and showing that justice will be meted out to them. RSV changes the sense by translating, *If anyone is to be taken captive . . .* , which expresses the resignation that Christians are to adopt in face of possible incarceration or martyrdom. This accords closely with Je. 15:2; 43:11, and is perhaps to be preferred. (If the AV is followed, the statement is made up by a combination of the utterances of Jeremiah referred to and Mt. 26:52.)

11 A second beast comes to the aid of the first as his prophet. *It had two horns like a lamb*, simulating the character of Christ, but its words were devilish; *cf.* Mt. 7:15. **12** That the second beast *makes the earth . . . worship the first beast* seems to indicate that this figure represents the priesthood of the cult of the emperor. It is later called 'the false prophet' (16:13; 19:20; 20:10). Yet as the seven-headed, ten-horned beast signifies the anti-Christian empire embodied in a personal antichrist, it is likely that this heathen priesthood is also represented in a supreme head that directs its devilish work. Such an interpretation agrees with the later statements that the false prophet and antichrist are thrown 'alive' into the lake of fire (19:20; 20:10), for it is doubtful that in such context one beast represents an individual and the other a corporate body. Those passages, in fact, may imply that the false prophet is a demonic being like the antichrist.

13–15 Heathen priests had little compunction in resorting to tricks, such as the production of fire, apparently from heaven, and by ventriloquism to make an idol talk. It is possible, however, that John means that the miracles wrought by the false prophet will be genuine. It is a recognized feature of Christian prophecy of the antichrist; *cf.* Mk. 13:22; 2 Thes. 2:9. **16** The mark of the beast on non-Christian people is a counterpart of the seal of God on Christians (7:1–8); they both serve to show

one's allegiance, whether to God or the devil. If the two designations are intended to denote spiritual qualities as well as a means of external identification, they hint that character tends to exclude influences not in accord with it—in the case of believers, Satanic influences, in the case of unbelievers, the gracious operations of the Holy Spirit. A man becomes increasingly in the image of his master. **17, 18** The immediate effect of receiving the mark of the beast consists in the social ostracism of those who refuse it. It involves nothing less than the proclamation by the state of economic warfare against the church.

The mark of the beast reproduced either his name or the number formed by adding together the numerical values represented by the letters of his name (in Greek and Hebrew there are no separate numerals, the letters of the alphabet have to serve this purpose also). *Its number is six hundred and sixty-six.* The solutions of this riddle amount to almost as many. Gunkel and many others insist that it does not represent the name of an individual; the phrase *it is a human number* simply means 'it is a human computation' in distinction from a supernatural reckoning (*cf.* 21:17). Such interpreters frequently regard the number as a symbol for the constant falling short of perfection by antichrist, since each digit is one less than seven; it is pointed out that the *Sibylline Oracles* (1:328) remarks that the number of the name of Jesus is 888, one better than perfection. Gunkel himself does not accept this suggestion, but thinks the number serves to identify the Roman Empire with the chaos monster, from which the portrait of the dragon and the beast is drawn in this book ('Primal Chaos' in Hebrew equals 666). The idea has been unduly minimized on the ground that John's readers could hardly have stumbled on such a remote solution, since they knew only Greek. Accordingly the modern exegete favours instead the solution 'Nero Caesar', written defectively in Hebrew! But if the former would be unintelligible to Greek-speaking people, so would the latter, even though 'Nero Caesar' transcribed in Hebrew from a Latin spelling gives the alternative number 616 which is found in some MSS. Clement's suggestion 'The Latin kingdom', written in Greek, is attractive; not only does it give the required 666, but 'The Italian kingdom' gives the alternative 616.

Strange as it may appear, it is not impossible that all the above solutions may be right. It is likely that since John used a Hebrew source in this chapter, the original name was a Hebrew one and the number was not invented by him. As he knew the chaos myth and was a Hebrew, the name *Tehom Qadmonah*, 'Primal Chaos', would not be beyond him. Further it is suggested in our interpretation of 17:8, 11 that the prophet fused the myths of the chaos monster and Nero *redivivus* to form his picture of the antichrist; the adversaries of the church so perfectly embodied the ancient power of evil that they could both be described under the same historical summary, viz. they were and are not, and are about to come up out of the abyss, and go into perdition. A number, therefore, which could denote that evil principle as well as the empire and individual in which it should be incarnated, was more than heart could wish for, a perfect representation of devilry.

14:1-5 The 144,000 on Mt. Zion

The purpose of this, and the following visions of this chapter, is to strengthen Christians for the trials implied in the preceding account of antichrist's reign. 1 The identity of the 144,000 seems determined by 7:1-8 and 5:9, 10. John would hardly represent two different groups by such an extraordinary and obviously symbolical number, especially when he adds that both companies bear the mark of God in their foreheads (7:3, 4; 14:1). The multitude is defined as those 'who had been redeemed from the earth' (v. 3), an echo of the description of the church in 5:9. Further, they are said to be standing on *Mount Zion, i.e.* the heavenly Jerusalem of the millennial age (21:9f.); this also conforms to the song of thanksgiving in 5:10, but it represents an advance on the previous picture of the 144,000 where this multitude is still on earth (7:1-8) and afterwards viewed in heaven, though not yet entered upon their kingly privileges (7:9-17). We therefore take this vision to portray the church possessing the advent glory of Christ in the millennial age.

The theme of the Lamb and the heavenly Jerusalem found in this chapter is expanded in 21:9f. The *name* written on the foreheads of the Christians explains the nature of the 'seal' spoken of in 7:1-8. 3 The angelic hosts sang *a new song* (*cf.* 5:9) but only the 144,000 could learn this one. Evidently it deals with the experience of redemption, which only saved sinners could know. Our interpretation of this verse is conditioned by our identification of this company with that in ch. 7; it is impossible, therefore, to regard it as numbering unmarried men only.

4 It seems best to interpret the language as symbolic, denoting the spiritual purity of men and women who form the bride of Christ (*cf.* 2 Cor. 11:2). Such terms are not inapt in a vision portraying the glorified church with her Lord in the heavenly Jerusalem; see 21:9f. If *aparchē* is to be rendered here *first fruits*, the latter part of the verse connects with such scriptures as Jas. 1:18; 2 Thes. 2:13, RV mg.; but it could be translated by its usual LXX meaning 'sacrifice', for such a thought is peculiarly apt in this prophecy of the testimony, suffering and martyrdom of Christ's chosen ones.

14:6-20 The day of wrath

The succession of short oracles in this section is unified by the use of six angels, who announce the judgment and carry it out. Equally with the former vision it is intended to strengthen the Christian's nerve, the one vision being a requital of good, the other a requital of evil works.

14:6, 7 The first angel. A last warning is given to unbelieving men. All the nations are summoned to repentance and the worship of God. The message is called an 'eternal gospel', for the eternal blessings of the good news still remain for those who will respond. This oracle seems to record the final fulfilment of Mk. 13:10.

14:8 The second angel. The fall of *Babylon* is recounted at greater length in ch. 18. This symbolic name for Rome appears in 1 Pet. 5:13, the *Sibylline Oracles* 5:143, 159 and *2 Baruch* 11:1.

14:9-13 The third angel. This is a warning that forms a complement to the preaching of the eternal gospel in vv. 6, 7. **10** For the *unmixed* cup (not 'watered down'), *cf.* Ps. 75:8. For the *fire and brimstone, cf.* Is. 34:8-10, which itself is reminiscent of Gn. 19:24, 25. **12** *The endurance of the saints* finds an additional spur in the contemplation of the awful doom of the worshippers of the beast, just as the knowledge that some of them will be called to suffer incarceration and death gives a like stimulus (13:10). **13** The benediction on *the dead which die in the Lord* serves the same purpose; Christians who face the prospect of suffering for the sake of the name know that they shall rest in the company of their Lord and receive a recompense for their faithfulness.

14:14-16 The fourth angel. It is common to regard these verses as depicting the gathering of the church by Christ at His coming and vv. 18-20 as the gathering of the unbelieving world for judgment; it is possible that this is the true reading of the passage, especially in view of the use of the phrase *one like a son of man* in v. 14 (*cf.* 1:13). Yet it seems strange that Christ should be commanded by an angel to perform His saving work. His description, too, lacks the splendour of the visions of the Lord in 1:12f. and 19:11f. It seems better, accordingly, to regard the humanlike form as an angel, sharing something of the glory of Christ like the 'mighty angel' of 10:1. The reaping of the wheat and gathering of grapes then represent one all-inclusive act of judgment as in Joel 3:13, on which these two visions are based. For the reaping of earth by angelic instrumentality *cf.* Mt. 13:41, 42.

14:17 The fifth angel. Observe that the angel here who also had a sharp sickle *came out of the temple* as did the fourth angel.

14:18-20 The sixth angel. 18 This angel who commands the vine-gatherer to reap the ripe grapes of the earth *came out from the altar*, and is specified: he who *has power over fire*. This links up with 6:9-11; 8:1-5; 9:13; 16:7, and exemplifies once more the connection between the sacrifice of God's saints and the advent of the kingdom. **19, 20** The symbolism of the Messianic judgment as a treading of grapes goes back to Is. 63:3. The city outside which the treading of the winepress takes place is presumably the world-city, 'Babylon the great' (see 11:8; 18:2).

15:1 – 16:21 THE SEVEN BOWLS

The bowls are said to initiate *plagues, which are the last, for with them the wrath of God is ended* (v. 1). This is often linked with the fact that no description was given of the seventh trumpet, although it brought the end (11:15); it is then suggested that the contents of the bowls consist of events consequent upon the sounding of the last trumpet. This is possible. It should be noticed, however, that the contents of the seven bowls are very similar to those of the seven trumpets; in most cases the difference appears to lie in the amplification of the earlier plagues by the later. The second and third bowls, for example, seem simply to reveal that the second and third trumpet plagues have increased in extent. The fourth trumpet affects the sun in one way, the fourth bowl in another (8:12; 16:8). The fifth and sixth trumpets have an extraordinary correspondence with the fifth and sixth bowls (9:1–21; 16:10–16). The earthquake after the seventh trumpet seems to be that consequent on the seventh bowl, only more fully described (11:19; 16:17f.). Thus the bowls give a fuller revelation of what had already been shown under the trumpet judgments, together with certain new features. As to the conquerors by the glassy sea (v. 2), their song celebrates the approaching conversion of the nations consequent on the completion of the 'righteous acts' of God (v. 4, RV); the vision therefore exults in the effects of the last plagues rather than heralds their coming; it is proleptic and serves to underline the statement of v. 1, *with them the wrath of God is ended*.

15:1–8 Visions introductory to the bowls

This chapter consists of two separate visions, the former portraying the Christian confessors who had emerged triumphantly from the great distress (vv. 2–4), the latter telling of the appearance from the heavenly temple of seven angels bearing the bowls of plagues (vv. 5–8). 1 serves as a superscription for chs. 15–16. It supplies a pictorial equivalent of the more formal prophetic utterance, 'The vision (or burden) of the last plagues'. The judgments are the *last* inasmuch as they are the culmination of what has gone before and include the final blows against the wickedness of a devil-inspired generation.

15:2–4 The first vision. 2 The glassy sea is *mingled with fire* because of impending judgment. The confessors have defied *the beast*, refused to adore *his image* and abjured the mark which is *the number of his name*. 3, 4 *The song of Moses . . . and the song of the Lamb* is one, recalling the triumph song of the Israelites on the shore of the Red Sea (Ex. 15). The name of Moses is conjoined with that of Christ because a similar, though greater, deliverance has been wrought from a similar, though greater, foe. The comparison of final redemption with the Exodus is common in the prophets (*cf.* Is. 51:9–11). Every line of the song is reminiscent of the prophets

and psalmists: *Great and wonderful are thy deeds*; *cf.* Pss. 98:1; 111:2; 139:14. *Just and true are thy ways*; *cf.* Ps. 145:17; Dt. 32:4. *King of the ages*; or 'of the nations'. *Who shall not fear . . . ?*; *cf.* Je. 10:7. *All nations shall come*; *cf.* Ps. 86:9. *Thy judgments have been revealed*; *cf.* Ps. 98:2; Is. 26:9.

15:5–8 The second vision. The tent of witness was the name given to the Tabernacle (see Nu. 9:15) because in it was kept the ark containing the tablets of the covenant. Since the ark was later housed in the Temple, the Temple itself was sometimes called a Tabernacle (Ps. 84:1, 2 AV; Ezk. 41:1 AV). Here, accordingly, the second clause is to be rendered 'the Temple, namely the Tabernacle (or tent) of the witness in heaven, was opened'. It emphasizes that the judgments about to be executed are the expression of God's righteousness. 6 RV says the angels were 'arrayed with precious stone, pure and bright', instead of *pure bright linen*. But the Greek words for 'stone' (*lithon*) and 'linen' (*linon*) are very similar, so that it is hard to tell which is right. See, however, Ezk. 28:13. 7 The *golden bowls*, as containers of the wrath of God, may have been prompted by the frequent OT use of 'cup' to denote God's measure of judgment on sinners (*cf.* Rev. 14:9, 10). 8 *The temple was filled with smoke from the glory of God*. For similar occasions of this phenomenon in the OT see Ex. 40:35; 2 Ch. 7:2, 3; Is. 6:4; Ezk. 10:4; 44:4.

16:1–21 The seven bowls described

16:2 The first bowl. The plague of the first bowl has no counterpart in those of the trumpets, but like several of the latter it recalls the Egyptian plagues (*cf.* Ex. 9:10, 11).

16:3 The second bowl. *Cf.* the first Egyptian plague (Ex. 7:17f.). Whereas the second trumpet affected a third of the sea (Rev. 8:8), this spreads through all seas.

16:4–7 The third bowl. The same Egyptian plague is in mind. *Cf.* the third trumpet (8:10, 11). 5 Note the divergence of texts followed by AV and RSV. The better MSS omit 'and shalt be'. The consummation has already arrived and there is therefore no need to speak of a future coming. 6 There may be a double thrust here. To be drunk with blood in the OT signifies slaughter by the sword; *cf.* Is. 49:26. The altar concurs in this judgment; *cf.* 6:10 and on 14:15–18.

16:8, 9 The fourth bowl. The fourth bowl stands in contrast to the fourth trumpet (8:12); but see vv. 10 and 11.

16:10, 11 The fifth bowl. The fifth bowl sends darkness on antichrist's empire; *cf.* Ex. 10:21 and the darkness over a third part of earth after the fourth trumpet. Charles suggests that the excessive pain of this plague is due to the demon locusts of the fifth trumpet, whose appearance, coinciding with smoke from the abyss, darkened the sky, and which caused torments to the adherents of the beast (9:1–6); such an interpretation would accord with the relation of the trumpets and bowls outlined in the introduction to chs. 15, 16.

16:12–16 The sixth bowl. 12 The sixth trumpet also affects the Euphrates (*cf.* 9:13f.), a matter that can hardly be coincident. But while the sixth trumpet brings forth demonic hosts, the sixth bowl prepares for the invasion of the empire by *the kings from the east*. These latter are further described in 17:12, 13; they put themselves at antichrist's behest (17:17), ravage the harlot city and war with the Lamb (17:14). **13, 14** For the identity of *the false prophet* see 13:11–18. *Like frogs*; these foul, demonic spirits are loathsome and offensive. Their task, like that of the lying Spirit in Ahab's story (1 Ki. 22:21ff.) is to persuade world rulers to join in the great final battle. **15** *Cf.* 3:3. If this is the original position of this verse, the warning is not without point (*cf.* Mt. 24:43f.; 1 Thes. 5:2, 4). There are seven benedictions in this book: *cf.* 1:3; 14:13; 19:9; 20:6; 22:7, 14. **16** The signification of *Armageddon* is unknown. The usual translation 'mountain of Megiddo' can hardly be correct for there is no mountain at Megiddo. Conjectural derivations from Hebrew (such as *har migdo*, 'his fruitful mountain', *i.e.* Jerusalem) are hardly to the point, since John's readers knew no Hebrew. It is possible that neither John nor his friends attempted any explanation of the name; it was used not so much to designate a place as an occasion, viz. the last well-known uprising of the wicked that issues in the establishment of the kingdom of God.

16:17–21 The seventh bowl. 17 The seventh bowl is poured *into the air*, conveying the notion of something even more portentous than the havoc wrought on the 'earth' (v. 2) or 'sea' (v. 3) or 'water' (v. 4) or 'sun' (v. 8); it signifies the final blow against the forces of evil, both human and satanic (Eph. 2:2). Hence the voice (of God?) proclaims *It is done! Cf.* 'It is finished' (Jn. 19:30) and see Rev. 21:6. **18, 19** At last the meaning is given of the lightnings, *etc.*, that followed the seventh trumpet (11:19) and seventh seal (8:5); they accomplish the destruction of the anti-Christian civilization. Through the earthquake (*cf.* 6:12) the great city was rent into three parts. **20** A hyperbolic description of the magnitude of the earthquake is given. **21** The size of the hailstones befits the terrifying proportions of this last shaking of the heavens and earth (Hg. 2:21). The Egyptians endured a plague of great hailstones (Ex. 9:24); an alliance of armies pursued by Joshua was routed by them in Beth-horon (Jos. 10:11), while the hosts of Gog were to expect a like fate (Ezk. 38:22). But the event eclipses all such descriptions. It subdues men, but it does not lead them to repentance. The ultimate issues of these happenings are given in greater detail in chs. 17–19.

17:1 – 19:21 THE FALL OF BABYLON

These three chapters expand the visions of the sixth and seventh bowls (16:12–21). 17:1–

19:10 are largely concerned with the fate of the empire (*i.e.* the seventh bowl); 19:11–21 recounts in fuller measure the destruction of antichrist and his followers (the sixth bowl). Ch. 17 explains the situation that leads up to the doom of God's enemies, with special reference to the anti-Christian kingdom (ch. 18) and at the same time sheds light on certain obscurities in ch. 13.

17:1–6 A vision of Babylon in her glory

1, 2 The angel's words to John could form a fitting title to chs. 17 and 18. *The judgment of the great harlot who is seated upon many waters.* As ch. 17 describes the circumstances of her downfall, the promise in the title is not actually fulfilled until ch. 18. The city of Tyre is called a harlot by Isaiah (23:16, 17), as also is Nineveh by Nahum (3:4f.), while the latter part of v. 2 quotes Jeremiah's description of Babylon (51:7), just as that latter city was addressed by the prophet as 'you who dwell on many waters' (Je. 51:13). From v. 9 it is clear that Rome is in John's mind. In this description, therefore, as in the apocalyptic figure of v. 3, he teaches that this Empire includes in itself the wickedness of all its predecessors. The beast that represents the Empire is similarly portrayed as the dragon (*cf.* 12:3), thereby showing its affinity with it. **3** The symbol of a woman sitting on *a scarlet beast* originally denoted a unity, the beast being an earlier, the woman a later, representation of one and the same chaos monster. For John, however, it forms a suitable picture to illustrate the relationship between the capital city and the Empire. At first sight it appears strange that in v. 1 the harlot is *seated upon many waters*, whereas in this verse she dwells in a *wilderness*. The explanation may be that John is recalling Isaiah's prophecy against Babylon, the title of which is 'the oracle concerning the wilderness of the sea' (Is. 21:1); it is noteworthy that the LXX omits the last three words. **4** The luxury and moral filth of the city are here vividly set forth, again with the aid of Jeremiah's characterization of Babylon. **5** The exhibition of the name on the harlot's forehead probably alludes to the custom of Roman harlots, who similarly displayed their names on their brows. The prefix *mystery* could be a part of the inscription; but it is more likely that it shows the name is not to be taken literally (*cf.* 11:8, 'the great city which is allegorically (or, spiritually) called Sodom and Egypt'). Moffatt translates 'by way of symbol'. The title serves to characterize the tyrant city as of the same nature as that against which the old prophets so vehemently prophesied; it is the *mother of harlots and of earth's abominations* (*i.e.* idolatries). Rome brought about the moral ruin of the whole Empire. **6** The allusion includes not only the Neronic persecution, but also the general custom of taking martyrs to Rome to die in the amphitheatre.

17:7-18 The vision explained: Babylon's doom

The interpretation of this section is rendered difficult by a fluctuation in the symbolism. In vv. 10 and 11 the beast is said to incarnate itself in a king who once lived and reappears as the last emperor of an unholy succession; *i.e.* he is an individual. Yet it is clear that vv. 1-6 speak of a city and empire, not an individual or even a line of rulers (emperors are only heads, not the whole beast). With this agree vv. 9, 10, the seven hills denoting the city of Rome, the headquarters of the anti-Christian empire. Since the use of the beast with seven heads and ten horns to represent the godless persecuting worldpower is traditional, it is almost certain that John is drawing on prior sources rather than composing something wholly original (*cf.* ch. 12); this may account for some of the ambiguity.

Most expositors interpret v. 8 with the aid of v. 11 and consider that the entire passage describes an individual antichrist; the expression 'was, and is not, and is to ascend' in v. 8 is felt to be wholly explicable by the myth of the resuscitated Nero, whose return from the dead to fight against Rome was widely expected when this book was written. With this expectation vv. 16 and 17 fit in admirably.

There is, however, another possible line of interpretation. It is admitted by all that vv. 1-6 portray the empire, not an individual. If John used an earlier writing in compiling vv. 7-18, that source also referred to the beast as the empire. It is thus not improbable that the Christian prophet also had the empire particularly in view. If so, v. 8a is to be explained primarily not of Nero resurrected but of the empire. From such scriptures as Is. 27:1; 30:7; 51:9, 10 it is clear that the OT prophets deliberately applied the symbol of the 'chaos monster' to the nations hostile to Israel, especially to Egypt, but not alone to that power. God had conquered that monster in the beginning. It is lying dormant for the time being (*cf.* Is. 30:7, RV), but it is about to strike again. At such a time God would destroy it once and for all. 'The beast that was, and is not, and is to ascend from the bottomless pit and go to perdition' (*cf.* Is. 27:1) thus describes this monster by outlining its history.

A reasonable solution appears to be that John here fused two symbols to convey his message, that of the chaos monster and that of Nero *redivivus*. The beast is the power of evil, manifesting itself throughout history in the godless empires, but now in the Roman Empire. Thus far it has lain more or less dormant; shortly it will rise from its recumbency and reveal itself in a fury of wickedness, incarnating itself in the resurrected Nero. With this key to the passage in mind, we may attend to its details.

7 The explanation given by the angel is a direct continuation of the preceding vision; it tells whom the woman and the beast represent. It is to be expected, therefore, that the interpretation will involve more than one member of the beast. **8** The beast *was, and is not*; *i.e.* it had an existence as an evil and anti-God power before, but has been silenced. Isaiah calls Egypt 'Rahab who sits still' (Is. 30:7), *i.e.* the chaos monster, rendered helpless by God. Rome is given a similar name here. It *was, and is not*, but *is to ascend from the bottomless pit* and achieve a work of horror like the pharaohs, the Assyrian kings and Antiochus Epiphanes of old. Nevertheless it is to *go to perdition*—the chaos monster cannot triumph over God, neither can Rome. As v. 11 relates this to Nero about to come again to earth, we may take it that the full possession by Rome of the characteristics of the chaos monster can be only when it incarnates itself in the returned Nero. This demonic king so fully shares the nature of the power of evil that their history can be delineated in the same terms. He is the beast incarnate. Such a fearful manifestation of supernatural power causes all on earth to wonder, except those whose names are written in the book of life.

9, 10 A dual interpretation of the *seven heads* is given so as to identify the beast beyond doubt. Rome was familiarly known as 'the city of the seven hills'. The beast is thus located in Rome. But the heads represent kings. Whatever the number *seven* may have meant to earlier writers, to John it was a symbol of completeness; *five . . . have fallen* means the majority have passed; the *one is* refers to the contemporary sovereign; another emperor will reign but *when he comes he must remain only a little while*; the short duration of his rule is enforced by the consideration that 'the time is near' (1:3).

11 After the last human emperor the beast will reveal itself in all its bestiality. The beast that 'was, and is not' is the age-long power of evil; he will show himself as the eighth king, yet not in reality an eighth, for he will manifest himself in the form of one of the seven, *i.e.* Nero. In the context of vv. 9 and 10 it seems that the statement *the beast . . . is an eighth* must mean that the whole empire, or rather the evil genius that characterizes the empire, incarnates itself in the eighth king. The emphasis is on the empire in its entirety. It must not be read as 'The beast Nero is an eighth king, as well as one of the seven'; the descriptive clause 'was, and is not' denotes the chaos monster Empire in the first instance, and only secondarily Nero. When, however, the beast is said to 'ascend from the bottomless pit', the emphasis is on the person who is its embodiment.

12, 13 The *ten kings* confederate with antichrist may be rulers of satellite states or governors of provinces. Bousset suggests, with less probability, they may be demonic powers of a like nature to their leader. **14** The ultimate fate of the ten kings is immediately recounted so as to complete their description. Logically this verse should follow v. 17 after the narration of their part in the destruction of the empire. Some commentators, accordingly, transfer it to that place. But apocalyptists do not always keep to a strictly logical sequence. This verse really anticipates 19:19f.; if from one point of view it is superfluous in this vision, from another its position here is fully intelligible. Its meaning is either that they that are with Him, *called and chosen and faithful*, will share in this conquest of antichrist and his helpers, or that they, as well as the Lamb, will conquer antichrist in their moral life (*cf.* 12:11).

15 While the waters of Babylon were literally meant in Jeremiah's prophecy (see note on v. 1) the prophet regards them as aptly symbolizing the peoples over which Rome rules. Antichrist, with his confederates, will help in the destruction of Rome, which is otherwise accomplished by the great earthquake (16:19). Both modes of destruction are due to the active providence of God. **16** The language is drawn from Ezekiel's description of the chastisement of Israel (Ezk. 23:25-29). No explanation is given why the anti-Christian ruler turns against the anti-Christian city. The popular Nero story expected him to arise solely to overwhelm the empire; yet this whole chapter, and 13:5 explicitly, assumes that he will first rule over the empire and with its aid rage against the works of God for three and a half years. This procedure well illustrates John's method of freely adapting his sources in order to convey the message God has given him for the instruction of His saints. **18** The *woman* is Rome, the mistress of the world of John's day.

18:1-24 A dirge upon Babylon

This chapter is modelled on the doom songs of the OT prophets over the hostile nations of their times. So reminiscent is it of these that it may be said to summarize all prophetic oracles on the doom of unrighteous peoples. The prophecies against Babylon (Is. 13, 21, 47; Je. 50, 51) and Tyre (Ezk. 26, 27) appear to have been especially in John's mind.

1 The glory of this angel is described in words used by Ezekiel of the Shekinah returning to the restored Temple (Ezk. 43:2). For similar portrayals of angelic splendour *cf.* 10:1f. and 14:14. **2** *Fallen, fallen is Babylon the great* is a quotation of Is. 21:9. For the rest of the verse *cf.* Is. 13:21, 22. Strictly speaking this picture is inconsistent with 19:3; it is not impossible that John deliberately mixes his symbolism, expecting his readers to exercise caution in interpreting it. *Cf.* vv. 1 and 2 with Is. 13:19-22. **3** Translate 'for she made all the nations to drink of the wine of the wrath of her fornication'. John lays to Rome's charge the responsibility for the corruption of the whole earth. RV follows an alternative reading *peptōkan* ('have fallen') instead of *pepōtiken* ('caused to drink').

4 *Cf.* Je. 51:6, 45; Is. 52:11. **5** *Cf.* Je. 51:9. **6** *Cf.* Je. 16:18; 50:29; Is. 40:2. Is the cry of v. 6 directed to the avenging armies of antichrist and his allies? See 17:12, 13, 16, 17. Rome's judgment is to be proportionate to her self-

glorification, wantonness and pride; *cf.* Is. 47:7-9. **8** RSV rightly translates *thanatos* (AV 'death') as *pestilence* (*cf.* 6:8). We may also translate *penthos* by 'calamity' instead of *mourning*, so making the three plagues 'pestilence and calamity and famine'. The destruction by fire is performed by the invading hosts under antichrist; *cf.* 17:16.

The lamentation over Babylon is uttered by the kings of the earth (vv. 9, 10), the merchants of the earth (vv. 11-17a) and the shipowners and sailors (vv. 17b-19). John is here particularly indebted to Ezekiel's doom song upon Tyre (Ezk. 26, 27). **9** Note that the *kings of the earth* are those mentioned in 17:18, not those in alliance with the beast (17:16, 17). *Cf.* Ezk. 26:16, 17. **10** The substance of each lamentation is the same, viz. *in one hour has thy judgment come* (see vv. 17, 19).

11 *Cf.* the list of merchant nations that traded with Tyre (Ezk. 27:12-24) and their astonishment and fear (Ezk. 27:35, 36). **12, 13** furnish a list of goods sold by the merchants to Rome. *Cf.* the imports of Tyre (Ezk. 27:12-24). *Scented wood* (AV 'thyine wood') was a sweet-scented, hard wood from N Africa and especially used for making expensive tables. *Ivory* was popular among Romans both for decorating furniture and ornaments. *Cinnamon* is an aromatic spice. *Spice* (*amōmon*) was a fragrant plant from India, used for making costly hair unguent. *Chariots* here are of a special kind (Gk. *rhedai*), having four wheels, often expensively decorated. Two words are used here for slaves: *sōmata*, 'bodies', and *psychai anthrōpōn, human souls*, the latter phrase occurring in Ezk. 27:13. Perhaps John employed both terms to express his abhorrence at so brutal a system that crushed men's bodies and souls alike.

14ff. Swete observes that while the kings lament over Babylon for the strength that has departed (v. 10), the merchants think mainly of the wealth that has vanished; so also the mariners in v. 19.

20 The appeal to heaven and the church to rejoice over the judgment of Babylon, forming a strong contrast to the foregoing lamentations, appears to come from the prophet himself. Whether it is meant as such or no, 19:1-7 forms a fitting response to the cry. **21ff.** The symbolic action of the angel is suggested by a like one performed over Babylon by Jeremiah (51:63, 64). **22** *Mousikōn*, translated *minstrels* (AV 'musicians'), should be rendered 'singers' as in *Testament of Judah* 23:2. The sentence recalls Ezk. 26:13. The clauses that follow, describing the cessation of crafts, industry, the joys of marriage, and all means of illumination, reproduce Je. 25:10, but in a different order. **23** *Thy merchants were the great men of the earth* was first spoken by Isaiah concerning Tyre (23:8). It is adduced as a reason for Rome's judgment because, to judge from v. 3, its merchants fostered the 'wantonness' of the city, and that out of sheer greed, and so were themselves bound up with the luxurious vice of Rome.

Isaiah had already commented on the sorceries of the original Babylon (47:12), and Nahum brought a similar charge against Nineveh (3:4). The *sorcery* here inveighed against may be taken in the literal sense of witchcraft, but more likely it represents 'the witchery of gay and luxurious vice and its attendant idolatries, by which the world was fascinated and led astray' (Swete).

24 *Cf.* Mt. 23:35, where our Lord so accuses Jerusalem. John's statement is justified not only by the ferocious persecutions which he anticipated to arise in the great distress but also by his conception of Rome as the incarnation of the spirit of evil that has ever assaulted God's people (see notes on 17:7–18).

Note on the anti-Christian empire

One main question calls for consideration from the reading of chs. 13, 17, 18. If Rome is the empire of John's visions, are they not discredited, seeing that Rome subsequently was not destroyed but became a world centre of Christianity? There is, of course, no doubt at all that Rome was indeed the harlot city of John's visions. The prophet all but names it in 17:9, 18 and by his use of the mystic name Babylon (see notes on 14:8). Rome was, to John, the quintessence of the anti-God spirit manifested in earlier ages but now come to the full. As such it was the last Empire over which the devil should hold sway. The impending appearance of a personal antichrist, who would embody its wickedness, was to be but a short-lived phenomenon. John seems to suggest that the Messianic judgments would soon fall and the sway of Rome give place to the millennial reign.

Before passing judgment on this matter, it is necessary to recall that John's viewpoint in no way differs from that of his predecessors in the prophetic office. All the prophets looked for the overthrow of the oppressor nation of their day, followed by the establishment of the kingdom of God. Isaiah looked for the Messianic deliverance to follow on God's judgment of Assyria (see, *e.g.*, Is. 10, 11), Habakkuk on the destruction of Babylon (Hab. 2:2, 3). Jeremiah, Isaiah and Ezekiel all prophesied of the setting up of the kingdom after the return of the Jews under Cyrus (*e.g.* Je. 29–31; Is. 49, 51; Ezk. 26). Haggai, writing after that return, foretold the advent of the kingdom following the completion of the Temple that was then in course of rebuilding (Hg. 2), while every vision of Daniel placed the end after the overthrow of Antiochus Epiphanes. Similarly in the NT the second coming of Christ appears to be expected in the not distant future (*e.g.* Rom. 13:11f.; 1 Cor. 7:29f.; Heb. 10:37; Jas. 5:8; 1 Pet. 4:7; 1 Jn. 2:18; Rev. 1:3). Even our Lord places His teaching regarding His second advent side by side with His prophecies concerning the fall of Jerusalem (see Mk. 13).

John was no exception to this rule. Revelations of the consummation of the age were given to him. They were not novel; they accorded with the faith of the rest of the church, though they formed an advance on it. The whole church looked for a last rebellion under an antichrist as the precursor of the End, and had no doubt as to the issue of the conflict. John saw that Rome was already playing the part of antichrist. As the outcome of these tendencies was precisely that which the former prophets had spoken of, he applied his visions to his situation. Rome was the harlot city, a demonic emperor was to be the personal antichrist, and the priesthood of the emperor's cult would supply the false prophet. The stage was set for the End and John described the drama. That the End did not come then does not invalidate the essence of his prophecy, any more than in the other prophets of whom we have spoken. The many antichrists since John's day have increasingly approximated to his portrait and will culminate in one who will suit it perfectly.

What of John's picture of antichrist himself? many expositors understand his apparent reproduction of the Nero legend in a literal sense. It should be noted, however, that John has not employed this idea in isolation but has fused it with the Tiamat saga. The latter is used in a purely allegorical sense, as is apparent from the fact that the monster represents the devil, the Empire and the personal antichrist in turn. That John gave the slightest credence to the original myth of the slaying of Tiamat by Marduk is out of the question, although he would almost certainly have known it. His ability to transform popular stories as a means for proclaiming the gospel is seen in his application of the World-Redeemer myth in ch. 12. In similar fashion he took over the legend of Nero's return from the dead as an excellent picture of antichrist, but with no thought of declaring his belief in it; he simply says that antichrist will be a devilish agent of a like order to the Nero of current expectation.

A consideration that clinches this point, for the present writer at least, is John's knowledge of a far earlier prophecy concerning one returning from death to take an active part in the end-time: Malachi had said that Elijah would come before the day of the Lord (Mal. 4:5). John must have known how our Lord applied this prophecy to John the Baptist; he himself put it to an even wider use in applying it to the church (ch. 11). It was therefore both simple and natural for him to represent antichrist as working 'in the spirit and power of Nero' (*cf.* Lk. 1:17) by employing the story of 'Nero *redivivus*' without further explanation; in view of the teaching about 'Elijah *redivivus*', none further was necessary.

19:1–10 Thanksgiving for the judgment of Babylon

The paeans of praise that thunder from heaven are inspired by the manifest justice of God in destroying the anti-Christian empire, but they may also incidentally form a response to the exultant cry of the prophet in 18:20. This finds confirmation if we may regard the first thanksgiving as coming from the angelic host (cf. 5:11, 12); the responsive 'Amen. Hallelujah' is then given by the twenty-four elders and four cherubim, followed by the pealing forth of the praises of the church (vv. 6, 7); this corresponds to the sequence in John's call for rejoicing: 'O heaven, O saints and apostles and prophets' (18:20). It is a constant phenomenon of this book to set over against the revelation of God's righteous judgments on the wicked the worship of heaven and redeemed humanity, the theme of such worship usually being the judgments referred to: see, e.g., 7:9f. after the seals; 11:15f. after the trumpets; 14:1f. after the ravaging of antichrist; 15:2ff. in anticipation of the bowls.

1 The statement that *salvation and glory and power* belong to our God coming at this point, implies that God has manifested these attributes. The song therefore expands 7:10 and has a similar meaning to 12:10. **2** *His judgments are true and just* was said by the altar after the outpouring of the third bowl (16:7); cf. also 15:3. The two great crimes of the harlot civilization were its corrupting of earth and murder of Christians. **3** If the new heaven and earth of 21:1f. is to be regarded as a completely new creation, the expression *for ever and ever* must here be limited to the 1,000 years of the millennium; the ashes of the ruined city presumably disappear with the old earth. The employment of this and kindred phrases in biblical literature is often very loose (cf. especially the Psalms), but in such passages as Rev. 4:9; 5:13; 11:15; 22:5 it clearly means eternity; presumably it has this meaning in 14:11. **4** The twenty-four elders and four living creatures endorse the thanksgiving of the angelic host (cf. 5:14). **5, 6** A voice *from the throne* calls on the church to join in this service of thanksgiving. As the four living creatures are closest to the throne, it is likely to be one of their number who so cries, certainly not Christ, who would never say *Praise our God* (cf. 3:12). The description of those called upon as *all you his servants, you who fear him, small and great* excludes the possibility that a select body from the church, such as the martyrs, is alone in view. The first line of the church's thanksgiving (v. 6) should be rendered 'Hallelujah: for the Lord God the Almighty has begun to reign' (cf. 11:17).

7 The Lamb's *Bride* is the whole church, not just a section of it. The marriage symbol applied to Christ and the church expresses the close and indissoluble union of Christ and His redeemed people. The marriage is said to have *come* at this point in the same sense in which Babylon was said to have 'fallen' in 14:8; *i.e.* it is on the point of coming to pass. The church is prepared. As soon as the beast and his armies are slain, the 'wedding' takes place and the bride begins her consummated life in the new age (20:4f.; 21:9ff.). For the symbol of the church as the bride of Christ, cf. Mt. 22:2f.; 25:1f.; 2 Cor. 11:2; Eph.

5:23f. **8** is probably a comment of John rather than a part of the song. Observe the delicate balance between the grace of God and human response: *it was granted her to be clothed with fine linen, bright and pure*; *i.e.* the raiment comes from God. But *the fine linen is the righteous deeds of the saints. Cf.* Phil. 2:12, 13. For the varying shades of meaning conveyed by the symbolism of the vesture of the saints, cf. 3:5; 6:11 and notes.

9 *Those who are invited* are conceived to have accepted the invitation, unlike those mentioned in Mt. 22:14. The guests and the bride are one; cf. 22:9, 10 where the bride is also the holy city. The angel's declaration *These are the true words of God* may relate particularly to the visions from 17:1 to this point, including the assurance of the coming of the marriage supper just alluded to. *Cf.* 21:6, which takes in the whole book. **10** The angel refuses John's worship by numbering himself with the rest of God's servants. See note on 22:8, 9. The angelic hosts and the church alike hold fast to *the testimony of* (i.e. borne by) *Jesus*. That testimony includes both the historic witness of the Lord, preserved by the Gospels, and that which He continues to impart by His Spirit, such as the revelations of this book. The explanatory clause that follows means either that the teaching of Christ made known in past and present is the *spirit* or essence (Moff. 'breath') of prophecy, or that the Holy Spirit who inspires prophecy interprets to the prophet Christ's testimony, both revealed and unrevealed. The former interpretation seems to fit the context better; the latter accords with Jn. 15:26, 27.

19:11-21 The Messianic judgment of Armageddon

11 The name *Faithful and True* recalls 3:14. The rest of the verse appears to have Is. 11:3-5 in view. **12** Christ has *many diadems* because He is King of kings and Lord of lords (v. 16); cf. 1 Macc. 11:13. His unknown name brings to mind the secret name He will bestow on His own after this event (2:17, and especially 3:12). In view of these last two references it is unlikely that all created beings are excluded from knowing His name (as Swete believes). Bousset suggests that the fact of its secrecy may be bound up with the popular belief that power attaches to the knowledge of a name. If Christ's name carries with it power over all creation, then at present He is sole possessor of that power, He alone knows His name; but when He has vanquished His enemies at His coming He will share His authority with His faithful ones and therefore His name too. The background of this conception is admittedly non-Christian, as John would fully recognize; but the spiritual meaning it is made to yield by this interpretation does find acknowledgment throughout the NT. It is possible, therefore, that this is the meaning intended. **13** The blood-spattered garment of the Lord is intended to remind the reader of

Is. 63:1–6. Christ is the heavenly vintager. If Bousset's interpretation of v. 12 is correct, the identification of the Messiah with *The Word of God* does not reveal the secret of the unknown name. Its mention here alludes, perhaps, to the creative power of the Lord, conjuring up for us the OT associations of 'the Word' (*cf.* also Wisdom 18:15).

14, 15 *The armies of heaven* certainly include angelic companies (*cf.* 12:7; 14:14–20) and probably risen saints too (see 17:14 and note on 2:27), though the saints' conquest referred to in 17:14 may only be their spiritual victory over the beast. On either view, the conquest is achieved primarily not by the following hosts but by the Lamb (*cf.* vv. 15, 21). In view of 15:4; 20:3, which imply the existence of nations at the beginning of the millennium, it seems that only those peoples hostile to Christ are in mind in vv. 15, 19–21. For the imagery employed, *cf.* 1:16; Is. 11:4; Ps. 2:9; Is. 63:1–6.

16 Swete thinks that Christ's third name is 'displayed on His habit where it falls over the thigh'. Since, however, some MSS omit the phrase *on his robe and*, while others simply omit *and*, it is possible that these words are a marginal note inserted to explain the text, and to show how the name could be observable on the Lord's thigh. Charles elucidates thus: 'The Seer sees in the vision the divine warrior and his heavenly horsemen—not halting but sweeping downwards from heaven and onwards against the serried armies of the beast, false prophet and the kings of the earth, and, as they thunder along, their garments stream behind them, and so on the thigh of the leader is disclosed the name: "King of Kings and Lord of Lords".'

17 The angel's summons to the birds of prey is drawn from Ezekiel's vision of the overthrow of Gog and Magog (39:17–20). It is to be observed, however, that the actual assault of Gog and Magog does not take place until the millennium has ended (Rev. 20:7–9); this accords with Ezekiel's vision, which places the last evil attack after the establishment of the Messianic kingdom. The picture of a feast for birds of prey at the dawn of the kingdom may be a satirical allusion to the well-known comparison of the kingdom of God with the spreading of a banquet; see Is. 25:6; Lk. 14:15f.; 22:30. **19ff.** No description in vv. 19–21 is given of the battle, only the array of the contending hosts. **20, 21** There is evidently no real struggle; the antichrist and his prophet are *thrown alive into the lake of fire that burns with brimstone* and their armies slain with a sword of Christ. The *lake of fire*, while having ultimately a similar meaning to Gehenna (Valley of Hinnom, see Je. 7:31), is a representation of hell developed from the conception of the abyss. In *1 Enoch* 18:4f. it is said, 'I saw there something like an invisible cloud; for by reason of its depth I could not look over, and I saw a flame of fire blazing brightly. . . . And I asked one of the holy angels who was with me and said to him, "What is this shining thing?

for it is not a heaven but only the flame of a blazing fire, and the voice of weeping and crying and lamentation and strong pain." And he said to me, "This place which you see, here are cast the spirits of sinners and blasphemers, and of those who work wickedness".' If John uses symbols drawn from this circle of ideas, it is clear that he cannot imply the annihilation of those cast into the lake; *cf.* also Rev. 20:10. The slaying of antichrist's armies by the sword that came out of Christ's mouth is to be interpreted by 14:14–20, *i.e.* it is wholly judicial; *cf.* Is. 11:4. Accordingly, such an interpretation as that of Swete, which makes the 'slaying' to be the annihilation of enmity against God in man (Eph. 2:16) and the 'sword' to be the word of God that saves man (*cf.* Heb. 4:12), so that Armageddon is in reality the conversion of the nations, is hardly to be received. The judgment here described appears to entail the physical destruction of those involved, their spirits presumably being despatched to Hades.

20:1 – 22:5 THE CONSUMMATED KINGDOM

Now that the judgments of God, described under the figures of seals, bowls and trumpets, have been completed (15:1) and the anti-Christian city, empire, ruler and false prophet have been destroyed (chs. 17–19), and God has begun His rule (19:6), and the marriage of the Lamb has come (19:7), we expect that at last the long-awaited and constantly heralded kingdom will be manifested. Our expectation is not disappointed: the establishment and nature of this kingdom form the theme of the closing chapters of the book.

We see that it is a kingdom in time (20:4–6) and eternity (21:1–5). Such was the usual interpretation of 20:1 – 22:5 by the early church and such is the generally accepted opinion of modern scholarship. It has been challenged afresh in recent years by expositors who prefer the line of interpretation popularized by Augustine, that the millennium is the present church age and the first resurrection the spiritual quickening of Christians by the Holy Spirit. Hendriksen, in his book *More Than Conquerors*, 1947, identifies the binding of Satan (20:1–3) with his ejection from heaven (12:9), the *thousand years* of the church's power (20:4–6) with its time of triumphant witness (11:2–6; 12:14f.), the onset of Gog and Magog (20:7–9) with the persecution of the church by antichrist (11:7f.; 13:7f.), the ensuing destruction of those armies (20:9) with Armageddon (16:14; 19:19–21), and the last judgment (20:11–15) with the Messianic judgment (14:14f.).

This is a possible and interesting reconstruction of John's visions, but the present writer feels that it can scarcely be maintained on close investigation. In 12:9 Satan is cast out from heaven, where he may no longer exercise his function of accusing the saints before God, to earth, which is thenceforward his permitted sphere of operations; 20:1-3 reveals an advance on this situation, for there he is taken from earth, which he may no longer corrupt, to the abyss, the abode of evil spirits and the penal section of Hades (9:1; 11:7); on no account is it permissible to confuse the earth with the abyss. Satan's expulsion from heaven to earth is followed by a more intense activity on his part among the nations (12:12f.; 13:1f.), but his imprisonment in the abyss renders him helpless with regard to them (20:3); while the former period is characterized as a short time (12:12) the latter lasts 1,000 years. The Messianic judgment of 14:14f., coming as it does at the close of the parenthesis of chs. 12–14, may have no specific counterpart among the other visions of the book, but may simply picture the fact of Christ's judgment of earth at the end of the age. If a corresponding vision be sought for it, we should probably identify it with Armageddon (*cf*. 14:19, 20 with 19:11–15, 21); in any case it is a judgment of the end-time, whereas 20:11f. describes the judgment of all generations of history. Furthermore, it appears to be overlooked that 20:1-3 is vitally linked with 19:20, 21; the latter tells of the fate of the antichrist and false prophet, the former continues without a break to narrate what happens to the one who inspires them; it is coincidence, and an unfortunate one, that the chapter division occurs at 19:21. For the unity of this evil trinity in the events described in 19:19 – 20:3 see 16:13–16. As 19:11f. expands the earlier account of Armageddon, so it completes the picture by outlining the fate of each instigator of the battle. It is our conclusion, therefore, that the reading of these verses compels the recognition of a doctrine of the millennium in ch. 20.

To decide what are the limits of the description of the millennium is a much more difficult task. With Kelly, Zahn and Charles (writers of very different modes of thought), the present writer inclines to add 21:9 – 22:5, 14, 15 to 20:1–10 as relating to the millennial kingdom, and that for the following reasons. First, 21:24–27 describes the heavenly Jerusalem in terms that presuppose a continuation of earthly existence; nations receive blessing from the city, kings bring their glory to it, the unclean are denied access to it. This may be an employment of earthly figures to describe heavenly realities, but it seems more natural to read it as portraying the earthly kingdom of God, particularly if it be granted that that kingdom is expounded in ch. 20. Secondly, the leaves of the tree of life heal the nations (22:2). This is comprehensible when applied to the millennium but strangely asserted of risen humanity existing in heavenly conditions. Thirdly, in connection with the imminence of Christ's return in glory (22:10–13), a blessing is pronounced on those who have the right to come to the tree of life and enter the city (22:14), and a warning given that evil-doers will be kept outside the city (22:15). Admittedly this could describe the good and evil in the eternal

state, but it seems more probable that the wicked have no part in the new heaven and earth but are confined to 'the lake of fire'; the statement is much more feasible if it represents conditions in the millennium, and the confusion of symbols created by the former view is thereby avoided.

On the whole, therefore, it seems best to regard 21:1–5 as descriptive of the city of God in the new heaven and earth, but 21:9 – 22:5 as portraying the city after its descent to earth in the millennial age. In that case, 20:1 – 22:5 forms a condensed and uninterrupted narrative of events from the coming of the Lord to the dawn of the timeless age, while 21:9ff. is a retrospect of the kingdom of God on earth. This view is not free from difficulties but it seems to do justice to the text better than the usual interpretation, which regards 21:1 – 22:5 as wholly relating to the eternal state.

20:1-3 The binding of Satan

1 For the *bottomless pit* (RV 'abyss'), *cf*. 9:1f.; 11:7. **2, 3** The conception of binding spirits and imprisoning them is adumbrated in Is. 24:21–23. The idea played a great part in later Jewish literature: see especially Tobit 8:3; *1 Enoch* 10:4, 11, 12; 88:1–3; *Jubilees* 23:29; *Testament of Levi* 18: 12. In these books there is no question of this figure being used to denote the restricting of one from certain activities in the world while leaving him free in other respects; it signifies a complete removal as to a prison, usually in the depths of the underworld. V. 7, accordingly, speaks of Satan's release at the end of the 1,000 years as a loosing 'from his prison'. The duration of the earthly kingdom of God of *a thousand years* appears elsewhere only in *2 Enoch* 33, a book of very uncertain date. There the history of the world is given as comprising 7,000 years, the first 6,000 corresponding to the six days of creation, the last 1,000 forming a counterpart to the sabbath. It is possible that John adopted the figure of 1,000 years for the kingdom of God on earth rather to show its character as God's 'rest' for mankind than as determining its duration in time (*cf*. 2 Thes. 1:7; Heb. 4:1f.; Acts 3:19–21). It is one of the many instances in this portion of the book of the 'last' things being made like the 'first' (*cf. Epistle of Barnabas* 6:13).

20:4-6 The millennium

It will be observed that no description is here given of the conditions of life in the millennium, only a bare statement as to what sort of persons exercise rule in it. A characterization of the life of this era is provided in 21:9 – 22:5. **4** The *thrones* seen by John recall Dn. 7:9. But who were those who were *seated on them*? Most exegetes interpret them as the company immediately named, viz. *the souls of those who had been beheaded*; it is then assumed that the further succeeding phrases also denominate this body, so that *who had not worshipped the beast or its image and had not received its mark on their* *foreheads or their hands* denotes the martyrs only. This exposition is only partly correct, for we have already seen that participation in the kingdom is promised to every Christian that overcomes (see 2:26–28; 3:12, 21), while 5:9, 10 declares that the whole church is to reign on earth, and 19:7 rejoices that 'the marriage of the Lamb has come, and his Bride has made herself ready'. It is curious exegesis that makes the bride of the Lamb in 19:5–9 the martyrs only but in 21:2f. the whole church. Accordingly, it seems best to interpret the clause *I saw thrones, and seated on them* . . . of 'Christ and His assessors, the apostles (Mt. 19:28) and saints (1 Cor. 6:3)'. The especial mention of the martyrs, in view of their place in this book, is only to be expected (*cf.* their position in 6:9–11; 8:3–5; *cf.* on 9:13; on 16:7) and is a deserved piece of encouragement. *They came to life again*; a figurative term for resurrection from the dead. It is likely that such as *had not worshipped the beast* . . . further denotes the martyrs. It is not impossible, however, that this latter half of the verse has in mind 'conquerors' who had escaped martyrdom and thus that the phrase *they came to life again* includes both a resurrection from the dead and the transformation of living saints (*cf.* 1 Cor. 15:51, 52).

5 The opening statement shows with all the clarity desired that *the first resurrection* is a literal resurrection from the dead, not a synonym for the new birth. An apocalyptist is at liberty to change his imagery freely so long as he makes his meaning clear, and in this John succeeds to a remarkable extent. It is a mistake to identify apocalyptic with chaotic thinking, as some writers imply; every line of this book refutes such a notion. One is reluctant, therefore, to believe that the prophet could speak so confusedly of two such different conceptions of resurrection without any indication of his change of reference.

6 Since *the second death has no power* over the participants in the first resurrection, we may infer that they have been finally acquitted and do not appear at the last judgment; *cf.* Jn. 5:24. It is to be admitted, however, that the last-named inference is by no means a necessary one. That Christians are to be *priests* as well as kings in the millennium hints that there is a ministry for them to perform in that age amongst earth's inhabitants, perhaps with especial reference to evangelism.

20:7-10 The last insurrection of evil

It has already been pointed out (in the note on 19:17, 19) that John is no innovator in placing the final assault of evil after the establishment of the kingdom of God on earth. In doing this he but follows faithfully Ezekiel's prophecy of the invasion of the Holy Land by Gog and Magog after the commencement of the Messianic kingdom (Ezk. 38, 39). (A similar sequence of events is given in the *Sibylline Oracles* (Bk. III, 663–674), *2 Baruch* 70:7 and the 3rd-century

Apocalypse of Elijah; 2 Esdras 13:30–36 should also be compared.)

7, 8 The loosing of Satan is according to God's command; the abyss is 'unlocked' by an angel (*cf.* v. 1). By this means the prophet parallels the divine oracle to Gog. 'I will bring you against my land, that the nations may know me, when through you, O Gog, I vindicate my holiness before their eyes' (Ezk. 38:16). In Ezekiel's prophecy Magog appears to be both the land from which Gog came (39:2) and a nation (39:6); it is therefore possible that Gog is to be viewed as the leader and Magog his people, with whom are associated the peoples of Meshech and Tubal (38:2). These nations were probably situated about the south-eastern parts of the Black Sea, a vague and unknown area as far as the knowledge of the Hebrews went. Other allies north of the Black Sea are enumerated in Ezk. 38:6, but Persians, Ethiopians and E Africans are mentioned in 38:5, so that John feels himself justified in using the terms *Gog and Magog* to denote all the members of the hostile alliance, coming from the four corners of the earth. Their number is said to be *like the sand of the sea*, but we may take it that John bore in mind the passage already quoted from Ezk. 38:16, which makes it clear that a strictly limited proportion of the earth's populace is involved in this last insurrection. 9 *The camp of the saints* presumably is the heavenly Jerusalem. An extraordinary parallel to this picture of the destruction by fire of Gog and Magog occurs in 2 Esdras 13:1–11. John, however, is still following Ezekiel (38:22). The devil shares the fate of the beast and false prophet. It suggests that the false prophet is regarded as truly an individual, and perhaps as demonic, as his two companions; see 13:11f.; 16:13f.; 19:20. But there is a contrary possibility; see 20:14.

20:11-15 The last judgment

If the departing of heaven and earth from the face of God is be to taken in any literal sense as a precursor of the new heavens and earth (*cf.* 2 Pet. 3:10–13), then the solitary spectacle of the great white throne as the one reality upon which men may gaze is indeed an awesome sight; *cf.* 2 Esdras 7:30–43. But the description may be purely poetic, to enhance the terrifying grandeur of the scene. The Judge is God Himself; but *cf.* 22:12. 12, 13 The second resurrection is taken for granted in v. 12 and only indirectly described in v. 13. The sea as a receptacle of the dead may be singled out for mention in view of the horror felt by the ancients at burial at sea. It is emphasized that all will be raised for judgment, whatever their mode of death and wherever their grave. The trial of men *by what they had done* as *written in the books* stresses the complete justice of the procedure. The picture is taken from Dn. 7:10, which may reflect both current court procedure and the habit of Persian kings to record every detail of their provinces through an elaborate spy system. It is to be noted that *the book of life* (*cf.* v. 15) has a testimony to give separate from that of the other books. Concerning this Alford writes: 'Those books and the book of life bore independent witness to the fact of men being or not being among the saved: the one by inference from the works recorded: the other in inscription or non-inscription of the name in the list. So the books could be as vouchers for the book of life.'

14, 15 *Death and Hades* represent the fact of dying and the condition entered upon after death, *i.e.* the unresurrected life. Both phenomena are symbolically represented as having ceased by their being cast into the lake of fire. For *the lake of fire* as the equivalent of Gehenna see note on 19:20. The thought is the same as 'the eternal fire' of Mt. 25:41, the complete reverse of 'eternal life' (Mt. 25:46). It may consequently be described as *the second death.* For an excellent parallel *cf.* *2 Baruch* 86:4: 'Go now . . . and instruct the people so far as you are able, that they may learn so as not to die at the last time, but may learn in order that they may live at the last times.'

21:1-8 The new creation

1 The creation of *a new heaven and a new earth* is taught in Is. 65:17; 66:22, and is implied in Ps. 102:25, 26; *cf.* Mt. 5:18; Mk. 13:31; Lk. 16:17; 2 Pet. 3:12. It finds frequent mention in the apocalyptists who, however, push to an extreme a thought undoubtedly latent in this doctrine, that the present creation (or at least its present form) is insufficient to be the scene of the perfected, eternal kingdom of God. (For an excellent statement of this view, see *2 Baruch* 44:8-12; 73:1 – 74:3.) The assertion that the sea is *no more* has in mind the current personification of the sea as the quintessence of evil; whatever else is meant here, therefore, the main sentiment is the exclusion of evil from the new order of life.

2 *The holy city* is further described in 21:9ff., though there its manifestation in the millennial age is probably in view, while here it is shown as the final goal of redeemed humanity in the eternal state. The city is in reality the church, *prepared as a bride adorned for her husband*; this aspect of the church's relation to Christ has already been set forth in 19:7-9 (see notes). **3** A voice from the throne proclaims God's unity with man henceforth. The dwelling of God (Gk. *skēnē*, 'tent'; AV 'tabernacle') may here relate not to the 'tabernacle in the wilderness' but to the Shekinah glory. The Greek word has a similar sound to the Hebrew Shekinah, and the latter came to be regularly used as one of the alternative terms for the name of God; *cf.* *Pirqe Aboth* 3:3, 'When two sit and there are between them words of Torah, the Shekinah rests between them.' Observe the textual variants in the last clause of this verse as seen in RSV mg. *Cf.* v. 4 and 7:17; 1 Cor. 15:54; Is. 35:10. **4, 5** The thought of both verses is applied in 2 Cor. 5:17 to the present experience of the Christian, who

has already been translated into the kingdom of God (Col. 1:13) and tastes the powers of the age to come (Heb. 6:5). **6** *It is done!* is preferable to RV 'they are come to pass'; see note on 16:17. Observe that God is *Omega* as well as *Alpha*, *the end* as well as *the beginning*; His character guarantees the truth of this revelation and the certainty of the consummation it heralds. The gracious promise added echoes Is. 55:1. **7** A final encouraging promise to the Christian who endures is given; the blessings of the holy city in the millennium and in the new creation, will be his inheritance.

8 In contrast to the conqueror who inherits the kingdom stand those who preclude themselves from it. Foremost are *the cowardly* who for fear of man deny Christ and worship antichrist (contrast 2 Tim. 1:7, 'God did not give us a spirit of timidity'). With these are conjoined the *faithless*, including both renegade Christians and pagans; *cf.* Tit. 1:15, 16. *The polluted* (AV 'abominable') have become so through their worship of the beast; see 17:4, 5. The sentiment of this verse echoes NT teaching as a whole; *cf.*, *e.g.*, Mt. 25:41-43; Lk. 13:28; Jn. 3:36; 1 Cor. 6:9, 10; Jas. 5:1f.; 1 Pet. 4:17, 18, *etc.*

21:9 – 22:5 The heavenly Jerusalem

For reasons that suggest that this section relates to the city of God in the millennial age, rather than in the eternal state, see introduction to chs. 20-22. The revelation of the bride has been anticipated in 19:7-9, where it is said that she has made herself ready for her Husband. Here the promise is fulfilled, not, however, in terms of the bridal metaphor but under the figure of a city. (For a strangely close parallel to this procedure, *cf.* 2 Esdras 10:25-27.) **21:10** is so similar to Ezk. 40:2 that we must suppose John had it in mind. It would seem, accordingly, that the prophet saw the city descend out of heaven on to the mountain whereon he stood. Heaven comes to earth in the kingdom of God. The city's light is compared to that of *a jasper, clear as crystal*; *i.e.* it has a glory like that of the Creator, whose appearance is also stated to be like a jasper (4:3).

12 The *great, high wall* serves the dual purpose of keeping out those who have no part in the blessings of the city (21:27; 22:14, 15) and of stressing the eternal security of its inhabitants. The *twelve gates* are inscribed with *the names of the twelve tribes of the sons of Israel, i.e.* the 'Israel of God', the church; see notes on 7:1-8; 11:1, 2. By this feature John claims that 'through the churches, in every part of the world (here twelvefold but one, as in chs. 1-3 they were sevenfold but one), lies the entrance to the city of God' (Kiddle). **14** The *twelve foundations* seem to be not superimposed on each other but to form a continuous chain of varied kinds of stone right round the city wall, divided up by its twelve gates. *The twelve apostles* correspond to 'the twelve tribes' of v. 12 and, like the latter, connote the collective whole of the body rather than the individual members; there is, therefore, no need to speculate as to whether or not Paul's name is included in the 'twelve' and if so whose name was omitted; the question does not arise.

16 *The city lies foursquare*; it is hardly to the point to cite that the Greeks regarded the square as a symbol for perfection; it is more likely that this shape is mentioned to recall the Holy of Holies in the ancient Temple, which also was a cube (1 Ki. 6:20); the whole city is a sanctuary for God and partakes of the holiness of the ancient inner shrine. *Twelve thousand stadia* represents 1,500 miles, though to translate it into modern mileage equivalents is to rob the measurement of its obvious symbolism —an infinite multiple of twelve (note the prominence of the number twelve in this vision of the church's glory). The meaning of this huge figure is illuminated by the rabbinical saying that Jerusalem would be enlarged till it reached the gates of Damascus and exalted 'till it reached the throne of God'. The heavenly Jerusalem stretches from earth to heaven and unites them into one. **17** *An hundred and forty and four cubits* (72 yds) again derives its significance from being a perfect multiple of twelve. If the preceding explanation of the great height of the city be acceptable, there is no need to stress the apparently absurd disparity between the height of the city and that of the wall; the wall is stout enough to serve its purpose, but the city has the extraordinary function of uniting earth and heaven.

18–21 There is little doubt that, as in the case of its measurements, so with the enumeration of the city's materials, John deliberately uses the language of symbol; he is not simply describing fantastic wealth. He has already said that the sheen of the city is like jasper, the appearance of God (see on v. 11); he now declares that the city wall is entirely built of it. The pure gold may allude to such a thought as that in 3:18. The twelve foundation stones of the wall, despite certain dissimilarities in our translations, appear to be identical with those of the high priest's breastplate (Ex. 28:17–20). From the testimony of Philo and Josephus we learn that each of these jewels represented one of the twelve signs of the Zodiac. On the basis of one correlation of the jewels and signs that has come down to us, it appears that John's list of jewels portrays the progress of the sun through the twelve signs of the Zodiac but in the reverse order. If this is a coincidence it is a remarkable one. It suggests that John thereby desired to dissociate his descriptions of the holy city from current pagan speculations about the city of the gods. That thought is accentuated by his mention of the names of the twelve tribes on the city gates and those of the apostles on the city's foundations.

22 In a city modelled on the Holy of Holies there is no need of a *temple*; all is holy and God is everywhere adored. *Cf.* Jn. 4:21. **23** *Cf.* on v. 11; see also Is. 60:19, 20. As in the latter pas-

sage, earthly conditions are clearly in view. The thought is enriched by recalling that the original readers would have been familiar with the heathen conception of the sun and moon as themselves deities; far from being gods, their native glory pales into dimness by reason of the splendour of the Lord God and the Lamb.

24–26 reproduce the substance of Is. 60:3–11. They depict the intercourse between the city of God and the nations of earth during the millennium. For all who will have it, fellowship between heaven and earth is unbroken in that age. **27** There still exist on earth, even when Satan no longer exercises his influence, the *unclean* and *any one who practises abomination or falsehood.* For such there is, as it were, 'a flaming sword which turned every way, to guard the way to the tree of life' (Gn. 3:24). With this and the following verses, *cf.* 22:14, 15.

22:1 The *river of the water of life*, in view of 7:17; 21:6; 22:17, denotes a purely spiritual conception, 'the fountains of the waters of life' perhaps being viewed, as it were, as the source of this pure river. We remember that the Garden of Eden had a river (Gn. 2:10) and in Ezekiel's vision a river flowed from the Temple, possessed of natural healing properties (Ezk. 47:8–11). The punctuation of RSV at the close of the verse is preferable to AV: the river proceeds from the throne through the middle of the street of the city. **2** *The tree of life*, unlike in Gn. 2:9; 3:22, is here treated collectively; there are trees on either side of the river, bearing a different fruit for every month of the year and leaves with healing properties. The picture is taken from Ezk. 47:7, 12 but, as in the case of the water of life, the healing powers of the leaves are taken in a purely spiritual sense. Through the church men will quench their spiritual thirst in the kingdom of God and receive spiritual sustenance, thus gaining healing for the wounds of sin. This supplies a pictorial counterpart to the prophetic song of 15:4.

3 *There shall no more be anything accursed* may simply mean that nothing unclean or abominable shall find entrance into the holy city (21:27). But it is more likely that we have here a deliberate contrast to the curse pronounced on the original paradise that brought woe on all creation (Gn. 3:14–19). The effects of that curse have been completely overcome in the new Jerusalem. **4** The goal of redeemed humanity is *they shall see his face.* Such a vision will involve the transformation of the beholders into the same likeness (1 Jn. 3:2). For the name on their foreheads see notes on 3:12; 19:12. **5** The absolute statement of the RSV is the better reading, *night shall be no more* (*cf.* RV). But the AV is essentially correct, 'there shall be no night there', for as in 21:23 the city of God is in mind (see note on 21:23). It is sometimes felt that the statement *they shall reign for ever and ever* is set over against 'they . . . reigned with Christ a thousand years' (20:4), the latter being temporal, the former eternal. This may be correct, but certainly not in the sense that the larger reference excludes the smaller, as though the millennium must have ended at this time; cf. the parallel assertion in regard to the rule of God in 11:15, where 'he shall reign for ever and ever' includes the millennial reign.

22:6–21 EPILOGUE

In this conclusion three themes find prominent expression: the authenticity of the visions narrated (vv. 6, 7, 16, 18, 19), the imminence of Christ's coming (vv. 6, 7, 10–12, 20), and the necessity for holiness in view of the impending consummation (vv. 10–15). It is impossible to be sure as to the identity of the speakers in the various paragraphs. Vv. 6, 7, 16 look like utterances of Christ, vv. 10–15 words of the angel, vv. 8, 9, 17–19, 20b, 21 additions of John. But a great deal of variation is possible, especially if, as some think, there have been dislocations in the text subsequent to its publication. In the last resort it matters little; the speaker is ultimately Christ, whose messenger the angel is (v. 9), and whose utterances John records as a prophet (v. 10).

6, 7 The speaker seems to be our Lord. His *words*, as His character, *are trustworthy and true* (*cf.* 3:14; 19:11). He comes *soon*: there is no warrant for translating the Greek *tachy* as 'suddenly'; such an interpretation would make strange sense of v. 6, 'things which must suddenly (*en tachei*) take place', an impossible rendering in view of the teaching of the book. See further the note on 1:1. **8, 9** The inclusion of these verses by John does not necessarily mean that some of his earliest readers engaged in angel-worship, though it is true that the practice had a place among the Jews (*e.g. Testament of Dan* 6:2; *Testament of Levi* 5:5) and even among Christians (Col. 2:18). John's experience is natural enough and its narration here needs no other explanation than its actual occurrence and intrinsic interest. It is not so much a polemic against angel-worship as a correction of the over-exaltation of all instruments of revelation; angels and prophets and ordinary Christians are all on one plane before God.

10 The injunction is the reverse of that in Dn. 8:26; 12:4, 9, and of what we see in Jewish apocalypses generally. Whereas the latter prophesied of (ostensibly) remote times, John's message was of immediate importance (*the time is near*) and was issued in his own name. **11** There is irony in the utterance of this verse in so far as it relates to the wicked. Daniel had said (Dn. 12:10) that in the last days many would be purified by their experience of trial, but the wicked would act wickedly; *i.e.* in the last crisis men will come out in their true colours and range themselves either on God's side or with the devil. That teaching is continually stressed in this book (7:1–8; 11:1, 2; 12:6; 13:1 – 14:5, etc.). Here it receives its final exposition. Since 'the time is near', let the man who insists on clinging to evil

continue therein; he shall soon meet his judgment. As for the righteous and holy, let them guard themselves, lest they fall away with the error of the wicked; their Lord will soon come for their redemption and reward. To make of this statement a doctrine of the irremediable fixity of men in the last times, which to John had all but dawned, is unwarrantable, both from the context and the general teaching of the book (*e.g.* 22:17; 14:6, 7; 15:4; 21:6–8). **12** *Cf.* 11:18; Is. 40:10; Rom. 2:6. See note on 1:8.

14 We have the last benediction of this kind in the book: *those who wash their robes* (AV 'they that do his commandments') virtually means 'those who conquer'; see on 6:11. The conjunction of v. 15 with this verse seems to demand that the *right* (to come) *to the tree of life* and to *enter the city by the gates* relate to privileges of the millennial kingdom; *cf.* 21:24 – 22:2.

15 almost repeats 21:8. See note on 21:27. Elsewhere in Scripture *dogs* denote adherents of heathenish worship; *cf.* Dt. 23:18 (where 'dog' means a male prostitute); Mt. 15:26; Phil. 3:2 (where 'dogs' means the mischievous Judaizers). Swete, accordingly, inclines to identify them here with the 'polluted' of 21:8 (see note).

16 is a further attestation by the Lord of the authenticity of the prophecy; *cf.* 1:1; 22:6. Christ as *the root and the offspring of David* fulfils Is. 11:1. As *the bright and morning star* He is Himself the fulfilment of His promise to the conqueror in 2:28 (see note).

17 Read naturally, this verse appears to teach that the Holy Spirit, especially as active in the prophets (19:10), joins the church in calling upon Christ to come to earth, according to His promise (vv. 7, 12). The hearer of the prophecy of this book, as it is read in the churches, is bidden to do likewise. The repentant sinner is invited to partake with the saints in the gift of eternal life from Christ. Some, however, interpret all the entreaties to *Come* as addressed to the sinner.

18, 19 John has been harshly judged by many for concluding his prophecy with the statement contained in these verses, which almost amounts to a curse. Certainly it was a customary precaution for ancient writers to protect their works against mutilation and interpolation by adding such an anathema (*cf. 1 Enoch* 104:10, 11; *2 Enoch* 48:7, 8; *Letter of Aristeas* 210–211). Swete, however, objects to such an interpretation of John's meaning: 'If the solemn warning of the present verse was intended in this sense, it has signally failed; for in no other book of the NT is the text so uncertain as in the Apocalypse. But, like its archetype in Deuteronomy (4:2; 12:32), it has a deeper reference; it is no mere *lapsus calami*, no error of judgment or merely intellectual fault which is condemned, but the deliberate falsification or misinterpretation of a divine message. It is not the letter of the Apocalypse, but its spirit which is thus jealously guarded.' We may thus not inaptly compare Paul's conclusion of 1 Cor. 16:22.

20 John's response to the promise of Christ

corresponds to the Aramaic watchword already referred to in 1 Cor. 16:22, RSV mg., 'Maranatha', 'Our Lord, come!' 21 The benediction reminds us that the prophecy is in reality a letter, its lessons to be personally appropriated. Only by the grace of the Lord Jesus can that victory be gained which shall receive the recompense portrayed in this book. Let us not receive it in vain.

G. R. BEASLEY-MURRAY